The African American Almanac

11TH EDITION

The African American Almanac

11TH EDITION

Formerly The Negro Almanac

Christopher A. Brooks
EDITOR

FOREWORD BY
Benjamin Jealous

GALE
CENGAGE Learning™

Australia • Brazil • Japan • Korea • Mexico • Singapore • Spain • United Kingdom • United States

GALE
CENGAGE Learning

The African American Almanac, Eleventh Edition
Christopher A. Brooks, Editor

Project Editor: Alan Hedblad

Contributing Editors: Angela Doolin, Paul Schummer, and Carol A. Schwartz

Rights Acquisition Management: Margaret Chamberlain-Gaston and Leitha Etheridge-Sims

Imaging: John Watkins

Product Design: Pamela A. E. Galbreath

Production Technology: Amanda Sams

Composition: Evi Seoud

Manufacturing: Rita Wimberley

Indexing: Katherine Jensen, Indexes etc.

Product Manager: Erin Podolsky Walker

Gale
27500 Drake Rd.
Farmington Hills, MI, 48331-3535

ISBN-13: 978-1-4144-4547-2
ISBN-10: 1-4144-4547-4
ISSN: 1071-9710

This title is also available as an e-book.
ISBN-13: 978-1-4144-5329-3
ISBN-10: 1-4144-5329-9
Contact your Gale sales representative for ordering information.

Printed in the United States of America
1 2 3 4 5 6 7 15 14 13 12 11

Contributors to the 11th Edition

Lean'tin L. Bracks
Associate Professor of African-American/English Literature, Fisk University
SIGNIFICANT DOCUMENTS IN AFRICAN AMERICAN HISTORY

Christopher A. Brooks
Professor of Anthropology, School of World Studies, Virginia Commonwealth University
AFRICA AND THE AFRICAN DIASPORA
BLUES AND JAZZ
ENTREPRENEURSHIP
MILITARY
SACRED MUSIC TRADITIONS

Myla Churchill
Professor, Tisch School of the Arts/ Gallatin School of Individualized Study, New York University
DRAMA, COMEDY, AND DANCE

Delano Greenidge-Copprue
Faculty Member, College of Humanities, Manhattan School of Music
EMPLOYMENT AND INCOME
MEDIA
POPULAR MUSIC
SPORTS

Morris G. Henderson
Senior Pastor, 31st Street Baptist Church
CHRONOLOGY
RELIGION

William A. Hobbs III
LITERATURE
POPULAR MUSIC

Robert D. Holsworth
President, Virginia Tomorrow, and Managing Principal, DecideSmart
POLITICS

Helen Houston
Professor, Department of Languages, Literature, and Philosophy, Tennessee State University
AFRICAN AMERICAN LANDMARKS
BIBLIOGRAPHY

Phyllis J. Jackson
Associate Professor of Art History, Department of Art and Art History, Pomona College
VISUAL AND APPLIED ARTS

Ticora V. Jones
Diplomacy Fellow, United States Agency for International Development (USAID)
SCIENCE AND TECHNOLOGY

Brenda M. Wood Kahari
Partner, B.W. Kahari Law Firm
LAW

Yvonnie Perrello
Education Management Professional
POPULATION

Gil V. Robertson IV
Co-founder, African American Film Critics Association (AAFCA), Editor, Robertson Treatment Syndicated Column
FILM AND TELEVISION

Robert L. Sims
Associate Professor, College of Visual & Performing Arts School of Music, Northern Illinois University
CLASSICAL MUSIC

Jessie Carney Smith
Dean of the Library and William and Camille Cosby Professor in the Humanities, Fisk University
AFRICAN AMERICAN FIRSTS
EDUCATION
NATIONAL ORGANIZATIONS

Doris Nearror Starks
Former Dean and Professor of Nursing, Coppin State University, Fellow, American Academy of Nursing
FAMILY AND HEALTH

Raymond A. Winbush
Director, Institute for Urban Research, Morgan State University
BLACK NATIONALISM

Linda T. Wynn
Instructor, Department of History, Fisk University, Assistant Director for State Programs, Tennessee Historical Commission
CIVIL RIGHTS

Contents

Foreword

In 2010, the NAACP celebrated its 101st year as one of this country's oldest civil rights organizations. As president and CEO of this pioneering organization, I am honored to speak on the importance of this historic edition of *The African American Almanac.* As I looked over the span of this landmark publication's history, I realized that the principal responsibility of each successive generation of African Americans is to tell its story based on the challenges confronting it and its aspirations for the future. The challenges of my predecessors in the quest for civil rights—great leaders such as James Johnson, Walter White, Roy Wilkins, and Kweisi Mfume—were different from those we face today, but I join them in accepting the responsibility of advancing human rights and human dignity. *The African American Almanac* has evolved in the same light, chronicling the history, culture, and consciousness of African Americans with renewed, updated perspectives that speak to the complexities of our times.

As African Americans, we have always immersed ourselves in history, recognizing it as something triumphant and ongoing. Our approach incorporates everything from folktales to the art of call and response, traditions that enhance history's instructive and interactive properties. Such an approach lifts history from individual facts to a shared experience.

The importance of this paradigm in assessing our history becomes clear when considering the early stages of the eighteenth, nineteenth, and twentieth centuries. The beginning of the eighteenth century marks the height of the cruel trans-Atlantic trade which brought enslaved Africans to the Americas. By the beginning of the nineteenth century, the descendants of those transplanted Africans were working plantations across the South, building the wealth of our nation. At the beginning of the twentieth century, those very descendants found themselves living in highly racially segregated settings. In Baltimore, for example, black people literally lived west of Charles Street, while white people lived east of it. Now that we have reached the twenty-first century, we are confronting yet another challenge. Although the United States has its first African American president, prison complexes pockmark our country like no other democracy in the world. The United States comprises only 5 percent of the world's population, yet it houses 25 percent of the world's prisoners.

My generation has been referred to as the "children of the dream," the kids who were born just as or just after the major civil rights victories were realized. We were told that "all the big victories have been won" and all that was left for us to do was "play hard by the rules, because the rules are now fair." Many articles in the almanac attest that this forecast proved true for many African Americans, and yet we came of age just in time to find ourselves the most murdered generation in the country and the most incarcerated generation on the planet. Therein lies the shadow or mandate, if you will, of the shining victories of the 1960s. The battle at any given moment is as multifaceted as it is multigenerational. Those who toil on the battlefield today recognize the complexities and urgency of the struggle.

My hope is that through a publication such as *The African American Almanac*, many will come to understand that there is no movement for education set apart from a movement for workers' rights or for reform of the justice system, and that the converse is also true. When the inextricable links and the dialectic of those issues are appreciated, it becomes easier to understand the pathway from schools to prison to the struggles of the poorest communities. I encourage all to read this eleventh edition of *The African American Almanac* in order to not only learn more about our glorious history but to assess what challenges us today and in the future. Two lines from brothers James Weldon and John Rosamund Johnson's inspiring anthem, "Lift Ev'ry Voice and Sing," provide us with marching orders for all times:

> Facing the rising sun of our new day begun,
> Let us march on 'til victory is won.

Benjamin Todd Jealous
President and CEO, NAACP

Introduction

My primary reason for accepting the invitation to serve as general editor of the eleventh edition of *The African American Almanac* was the historic election of Barack Obama as the forty-fourth president of the United States. In a small way, I thought my involvement in this premier and long-standing reference work of the African diasporan experience would serve as a contribution to his historic presidency. To that end, I made the request very early in the project that a picture of Barack Obama taking the presidential oath of office be featured on the cover. That request, along with several others, was honored as work began on this historic edition.

Although the almanac first appeared in 1967 as *The Negro Almanac*, edited by Harry A. Ploski and Roscoe C. Brown of New York University, works of this sort chronicling the growth, progress, and development of African Americans date back to the early twentieth century. The 1967 edition set out to "fill the need for a fingertip repository of vital information on the history and culture of the Negro—primarily in the United States, but throughout the rest of the world." That early volume attempted to realize an exhaustive yet comprehensible account of the progress made by African Americans up to that point, despite the fact that the country was in the throes of dramatic changes brought about by the civil rights movement of that period.

In subsequent editions, the almanac took on a decidedly more scholarly tone, while still maintaining its primary mission to keep the work accessible and user friendly. Instead of relying on a few editors and compilers of data (as was the case with Ploski and Brown), the almanac employed the expertise of professors from many historically African American colleges and universities, including Fisk University, Morgan State University, Alabama A&M University, and Tennessee State University, as participating contributors. We have continued that tradition in the current volume, and expanded the scholarly scope to include professors and consultants from Bowie State University, Coppin State University, Cornell University, New York University, Northern Illinois University, University of Iowa, Indiana University, Virginia Commonwealth University, and Virginia State University. This edition has also benefitted from contributors who are not currently affiliated with a college or university yet are experts in some aspect of the African American experience in regard to law, politics, and science and technology. The result is my unwavering confidence that this is the strongest edition of the almanac that has been produced to date.

NEW FEATURES IN THIS EDITION

This eleventh edition of *The African American Almanac* represents a major overhaul of the work, with updated text, pictures, captions, and tabular data, along with newly added sidebars and fact boxes, plus more than one hundred new biographical profiles. One of the significant changes that will be apparent to readers is a progressive move toward addressing dialogue in regard to slavery. Readers will notice an effort to avoid such words as *slave* and *slavery* in favor of *enslaved Africans* or simply *enslaved*. The condition that was imposed on those of African ancestry throughout the diaspora is associated with an inherent victimhood, which is reflected in the language traditionally used to discuss this history. But the time has come for serious scholarship to move beyond such dated terminology. Therefore, in this edition, we usher in the use of *enslaved Africans* or, in some instances, *forced African labor* to describe that unimaginable and cruel experience. Readers' adjustment to the different terminology will challenge how they view themselves as well as others. However, in the same way that our society (including earlier editions of this very almanac) made the transition from such terms as *colored*, *Negro*, and *black* to the vastly more appropriate and accurate *African American*, *The African American Almanac*, as the premier reference work for that experience, plays a significant role in moving in that direction.

There are several people for whom I wish to express my profound gratitude for their contributions in shaping the eleventh edition of the almanac into what it has become. At the top of that long list is Alan Hedblad, the project manager and a senior editor at Cengage/Gale. He walked me through this process with calmness, courtesy, and grace. I would also like to acknowledge Jessie Carney Smith at Fisk for her encouragement and support. She has already sat in the general editor's chair (for the eighth edition). I had the pleasure of marshalling the combined efforts of several current and former colleagues and advisors, including Robert Sims, Bob Daniels, Barbara A. Lynch-Freeman, Portia Maultsby, Venise Berry, Morris Henderson, Caroline Mbonu, William Hobbs III, and Thomas J. Brown. I would also like to express my appreciation for my students, Katherine Blanche and Christopher Yeamans. Katherine has worked with me on four other book projects and can now add this one to the list.

Without question, I salute the Cengage Learning staff members—especially senior editor Carol Schwartz (who directed the typesetting, proofreading, and indexing processes) and project editor Angela Doolin—for their professionalism and dedication to the production of this volume. I recognize that their efforts, together with the wonderful cast of contributing writers, form the heart of this important work. All of you have my profound gratitude.

Christopher A. Brooks
Virginia Commonwealth University

1

CHRONOLOGY

Morris G. Henderson

FIFTEENTH AND SIXTEENTH CENTURIES

1492. Africans are among the first explorers to the New World. Pedro Alonzo Niño, identified by some scholars as a black man, arrives with Christopher Columbus.

1501. The Spanish throne officially approves the use of enslaved Africans in the New World.

1502. Portugal brings its first shipload of enslaved Africans to the Western Hemisphere, selling them in what is now Latin America.

1513. Spain authorizes the use of enslaved Africans in Cuba. Thirty African men accompany Balboa when he discovers the Pacific Ocean.

1526. The first group of Africans to set foot on what is now the United States are brought by a Spanish explorer to South Carolina to erect a settlement. The African captives soon flee to the interior, however, and settle with Native Americans.

1538. Estevanico, a black explorer, leads an expedition from Mexico into what is now Arizona and New Mexico.

1562. Britain enters the slave trade when John Hawkins sells a large cargo of enslaved Africans to Spanish planters.

SEVENTEENTH CENTURY

1600. Historical records indicate that by the year 1600 over 900,000 slaves have been brought to Latin America. In the next century, 2,750,000 are added to that total. Slave revolts in the sixteenth century are reported in Hispaniola, Puerto Rico, Panama, Cuba, and Mexico.

1618. The Gambian government grants monopolies to a group of companies established for the purpose of slave trading.

1619, August. Twenty African indentured servants arrive in Jamestown, Virginia, aboard a Dutch vessel. Most indentured servants are released after serving one term, usually seven years in duration, and are allowed to own property and participate in political affairs. The arrival of these indentured servants is the precursor of active slave trade in the English colonies.

1624. The Dutch, who had entered the slave trade in 1621 with the formation of the Dutch West Indies Company, import enslaved Africans to serve on Hudson Valley farms.

1629. Enslaved Africans are imported into Connecticut. Five years later, the first African slaves in Maryland and Massachusetts arrive. New Amsterdam's first enslaved Africans come ashore in 1637.

1630. Massachusetts enacts a law protecting slaves from abusive owners.

1639. New England enters the slave trade when Captain William Pierce sails to the West Indies and purchases a group of enslaved Africans.

1640. The increasing use of sugar as a cash crop leads to a rapid rise in the number of enslaved Africans in the West Indies, although growth in mainland English colonies remains slow. The African slave population in Barbados, for example, grows from a few hundred in 1640 to 6,000 in 1645. In contrast, there are 300 enslaved Africans in Virginia in 1649 and 2,000 by 1671.

1640. Fugitive slave laws applying to both indentured servants and slaves are enacted in Connecticut, Maryland,

Elmina Castle. *At this Portuguese/Dutch fortress, founded in the fifteenth century in present-day Ghana, innumerable captured Africans were gathered for the European slave trade.* THE GRANGER COLLECTION, NEW YORK. REPRODUCED BY PERMISSION.

New Jersey, South Carolina, and Virginia. The Virginia law, passed in 1642, penalizes violators 20 pounds of tobacco for each night of refuge granted to a fugitive slave. Slaves are branded after a second escape attempt.

1641. Massachusetts becomes the first colony to legalize slavery, adding a modification that forbids capture by "unjust violence." This provision was subsequently adopted by all of the New England colonies.

1643. The groundwork is laid for eighteenth- and nineteenth-century fugitive slave laws in the United States when an intercolonial agreement of the New England Confederation declares that mere certification by a magistrate is sufficient evidence to convict a runaway slave.

1651. Anthony Johnson, a black man, imports five servants and qualifies to receive a 200-acre land grant along the Puwgoteague River in North Hampton, Virginia. Others soon join Johnson and attempt to launch an independent African community. At its height, the settlement has twelve African homesteads with sizable holdings.

1662. The Virginia colony passes a law providing that the slave or free status of children be determined by the lineage of the mother.

1663. Maryland settlers pass a law stipulating that all imported Africans are to be given the status of slaves. Free white women who marry enslaved Africans are also considered slaves during the lives of their spouses; children of such unions are also to be classified as slaves. In 1681, a law is passed stipulating that children born from a union of a white servant woman and an African are free citizens.

1670. Voting rights are denied to recently freed slaves and indentured servants in Virginia. All non-Christians imported to the territory "by shipping" are to be slaves for life. Slaves who enter Virginia by land route, however, are to serve until the age of thirty if they are children and

Enslaving Africans. *Some Africans participated in the slave trade by capturing and selling fellow Africans for goods and weapons.* THE GRANGER COLLECTION, NEW YORK. REPRODUCED BY PERMISSION.

for twelve years if they are adults when their period of servitude commences.

1672. A Virginia law is enacted providing for a bounty on the heads of Maroons—black fugitives who form communities in the mountains, swamps, and forests of southern colonies. Many members of Maroon communities attack towns and plantations.

1685. The French *code noir* is enacted in the French West Indies. The code requires religious instruction for enslaved Africans, permits intermarriage, outlaws working of slaves on Sundays and holidays, but forbids emancipation of mulatto children who have reached the age of twenty-one if their mothers are still enslaved. The code is largely ignored by the French settlers, however.

1688. Mennonites in Germantown, Pennsylvania, sign an antislavery resolution, the first formal protest against slavery in the Western Hemisphere. In 1696, Quakers importing slaves are threatened with expulsion from the society.

EIGHTEENTH CENTURY

1700. The population of enslaved Africans in the English colonies is estimated at 28,000. Approximately 23,000 of these Africans reside in the South.

1704. Elias Neau, a French immigrant, opens a "catechism school" for enslaved Africans in New York City.

1705. The Virginia assembly declares that "no Negro, mulatto, or Indian shall presume to take upon him, act in or exercise any office, ecclesiastic, civil or military." African Americans are forbidden to serve as witnesses in court cases and are condemned to lifelong servitude, unless they have been either Christians in their native land or free men in a Christian country.

1711. The colonial legislature, after receiving intense pressure from the Mennonite and Quaker communities, outlaws slavery in the Pennsylvania colony but is overruled by the British Crown.

1712, April 6. The Maiden Lane slave revolt in New York City claims the lives of nine whites and results in the execution of twenty-one slaves. Six others commit suicide.

1723. The colony of Virginia enacts laws to limit the rights of freed African Americans. Free African Americans are denied the right to vote and forbidden to carry weapons of any sort.

1739. Three South Carolina slave revolts occur, resulting in the deaths of fifty-one whites and many more enslaved Africans.

ABOLITION OF ENSLAVEMENT

1688. Mennonites in Germantown, Pennsylvania, sign an antislavery resolution, the first formal protest against slavery in the Western Hemisphere.

1711. The colonial legislature, after receiving intense pressure from the Mennonite and Quaker communities, outlaws slavery in the Pennsylvania colony but is overruled by the British Crown.

1774. Rhode Island enacts a law prohibiting slavery. However, this law does not apply to enslaved Africans brought into Rhode Island before 1774.

1777. Vermont becomes the first state to abolish slavery.

1787. Congress passes the Northwest Ordinance, which forbids the extension of slavery into new states to be created north and west of the Ohio River.

1804. New Jersey passes an emancipation law. All states north of the Mason-Dixon Line now have laws forbidding slavery or providing for its gradual elimination.

1808. Congress bars the importation of any new slaves into the territory of the United States (effective January 1, 1808). The law is widely ignored. There are one million enslaved Africans in the country.

1862. On September 22, Lincoln issues the Emancipation Proclamation, declaring freedom for all enslaved persons in Confederate states that did not return to the Union by January 1 of the following year.

1865. Abraham Lincoln is assassinated and dies on the morning of April 15. The Thirteenth Amendment, abolishing slavery and involuntary servitude in all of the United States, is ratified December 16.

1740. The South Carolina colony passes a slave code, which forbids enslaved Africans from raising livestock, provides that any animals owned by slaves be forfeited, and imposes severe penalties on slaves who make "false appeals" to the governor on the grounds that they have been placed in bondage illegally.

1744. The colony of Virginia amends its 1705 law declaring that African Americans cannot serve as witnesses in court cases; it decides, instead, to admit "any free Negro, mulatto, or Indian being a Christian," as a witness in a criminal or civil suit involving another African American, mulatto, or Indian.

1746. Enslaved African poet Lucy Terry writes "Bars Fight," a commemorative poem re-creating the Deerfield (Massachusetts) Massacre. Terry, generally considered the first African American poet in America, later tries unsuccessfully to convince the board of trustees at Williams College to admit her son to the school.

1747. The South Carolina assembly commends enslaved Africans for demonstrating "great faithfulness and courage in repelling attacks of His Majesty's enemies." It then makes provisions for the utilization of African American recruits in the event of danger or emergency.

1749. Prohibitions on the importation of enslaved Africans are approved in a Georgia law, which also attempts to protect slaves from cruel treatment and from being hired out.

1750. The slave population in the English colonies reaches 236,400, with over 206,000 of the total living south of Pennsylvania. Enslaved Africans comprise about 20 percent of the population in the colonies.

1752. George Washington acquires his estate at Mount Vernon, Virginia. Prior to Washington's arrival, there are eighteen slaves at Mount Vernon. This number eventually swells to 200. Records indicate that while Washington was concerned for the physical welfare of enslaved Africans, he did not advocate their freedom from servitude.

1754. A Quaker, John Woolman, publishes *Some Considerations on the Keeping of Negroes*, an exhortation to fellow members of the Society of Friends to consider emancipating their slaves on grounds of morality. Three years later, some Quakers take legal action against members who ignore this plea.

1760. Jupiter Hammon, an African American poet, publishes *Salvation By Christ With Penitential Cries*.

1767. Phillis Wheatley, a fourteen-year-old slave, writes *A Poem by Phillis, A Negro Girl, On the Death of Reverend Whitefield*. It is printed in 1770 by the University of Cambridge in New England.

1769. In the Virginia House of Burgesses, Thomas Jefferson unsuccessfully presses for a bill to emancipate enslaved Africans.

1770. **Philadelphia, Pennsylvania.** Led by Anthony Benezet, the Quakers open a school for African Americans.

1770, **March 5. Boston, Massachusetts.** African American Crispus Attucks is shot and killed during the Boston Massacre, becoming one of the first casualties of the American Revolution.

1773. **Savannah, Georgia.** George Liele and Andrew Bryan organize the first Baptist Church for African Americans in the state.

1774. The Continental Congress demands elimination of the transatlantic slave trade and calls for economic embargoes on exports to all countries participating in it. Rhode Island enacts a law prohibiting slavery. However, this law does not apply to enslaved Africans brought into Rhode Island before 1774.

1775. **Bunker Hill, Massachusetts.** Peter Salem, Salem Poor, and other African Americans fight heroically during the Battle of Bunker Hill.

1775. A German publisher prints Johann Friedrich Blumenbach's article refuting the theory that blacks are racially inferior; it is the first such theory ever in print. In *On the Natural Variety of Mankind*, Blumenbach asserts that the skulls and brains of African Americans are the same as those of Europeans. Blumenbach's paper serves as a counter to the views of French author Voltaire, Scottish philosopher David Hume, and Swedish botanist Carl von Linné (Carolus Linnaeus) that African Americans are akin to apes.

1775. **Philadelphia, Pennsylvania.** The Continental Congress bars African Americans from serving in the army during the American Revolution.

1775. **Philadelphia, Pennsylvania.** The first abolitionist society in the United States is organized.

1775. Lord Dunmore, British governor of Virginia, offers freedom to all male slaves who join the loyalist forces. General George Washington, originally opposed to the enlistment of African Americans, is alarmed by the response to the Dunmore proclamation and orders recruiting officers to accept free African Americans for service.

1776. **Philadelphia, Pennsylvania.** The amended form of the Declaration of Independence, which omits Thomas Jefferson's proposal denouncing slavery, is adopted.

1776. **Long Island, New York.** French general Marquis de Lafayette praises African American soldiers for successfully assisting Washington's retreat to Long Island. African Americans also help assist Washington's retreat at Trenton and Princeton.

1776. **Trenton, New Jersey.** Two African Americans, Prince Whipple and Oliver Cromwell, cross the Delaware with George Washington en route to an attack on the British and their Hessian mercenaries in Trenton, New Jersey.

1777. Vermont becomes the first state to abolish slavery.

1778. An African American battalion consisting of 300 former slaves is formed. They are compensated on a par with their white comrades-in-arms and promised freedom after the war. The battalion kills 1,000 Hessians and takes part in a battle at Ponts Bridge in New York.

1779. **New York.** Alexander Hamilton endorses the plan of South Carolina's Henry Laurens to use enslaved Africans as soldiers in the South. "I have not the least doubt that the Negroes will make very excellent soldiers" says Hamilton, "for their natural faculties are as good as ours." Hamilton reminds the Continental Congress that the British will make use of African Americans if the Americans do not. In Hamilton's

Lithograph of the Trading Settlement of Jean Baptiste Pointe du Sable. *Established by du Sable (*lower right*) in 1790, this was the first permanent settlement of the land that later became the city of Chicago. Du Sable's cabin and canoe are depicted at* lower left.

words: "The best way to counteract the temptations they will hold out, will be to offer them ourselves."

1780. The Pennsylvania assembly enacts a law providing for the gradual emancipation of slaves.

1782. Thomas Jefferson's *Notes on the State of Virginia* exhibits a curious mixture of perception and naiveté with regard to African Americans. On the one hand, Jefferson believes that "the whole commerce between master and slave is a perpetual exercise of the most boisterous passions." On the other hand, he invents the fantasy that African American "griefs are transient."

1783. Slavery in Massachusetts is abolished by the state's Supreme Court; tax-paying African Americans in the state are granted suffrage.

1783. At the end of the American Revolution, some 10,000 African Americans have served in the continental armies—5,000 as regular soldiers.

1787. New York City. The African Free School is opened by the New York Manumission Society.

1787. Congress passes the Northwest Ordinance, which forbids the extension of slavery into new states to be created north and west of the Ohio River.

1787. Philadelphia, Pennsylvania. African American preachers Richard Allen and Absalom Jones organize the Free African Society.

1787. The Constitution of the United States is adopted. In it, importation of slaves cannot be prohibited before 1808, and five slaves are considered the equivalent of three free men in congressional apportionment.

1790. According to the first census, there are 757,000 African Americans in the United States, comprising 1 percent of the total population. Nine percent of African Americans are free.

1790. Dominican Republic. African Americans comprise seven-eighths of the island's 529,000 inhabitants. Less than 3 percent are free. Mulattoes in French Santo Domingo own 10 percent of the slaves and land.

1790. Chicago, Illinois. Jean Baptiste Pointe du Sable, the son of a French mariner and an African slave mother,

Replica of Eli Whitney's Cotton Gin. *Whitney's 1793 invention strengthened the institution of slavery by vastly increasing the profits that could be made growing cotton.* BETTMANN/CORBIS. REPRODUCED BY PERMISSION.

establishes the first permanent settlement at what is to become the city of Chicago.

1791. Washington, D.C. On the recommendation of Thomas Jefferson, African American Benjamin Banneker—astronomer, inventor, mathematician, and gazetteer—is appointed to serve as a member of the commission charged with laying out plans for the city of Washington.

1791. Twenty-three enslaved Africans are hanged and three white sympathizers deported following suppression of a Louisiana slave revolt.

1791. Philadelphia, Pennsylvania. Congress excludes African Americans and Indians from serving in peacetime militias.

1793. Mulberry Grove, Georgia. Eli Whitney patents the cotton gin, which adds impetus to slavery by vastly increasing profits in cotton growing.

1793. Philadelphia, Pennsylvania. Congress passes the Fugitive Slave Act, which makes it a criminal offense to harbor a slave or prevent his or her arrest.

1793. The state of Virginia passes a law that forbids free African Americans from entering the state.

1794. Philadelphia, Pennsylvania. The First African Church of St. Thomas, the first African American Episcopal Congregation in the United States, is dedicated. This same year, Richard Allen organizes the Bethel Church, an African American Methodist Episcopal Church.

1795. Several slave uprisings are suppressed with some fifty African Americans killed and executed.

1796. Tennessee. Tennessee is admitted to the Union as a slave state. The state's constitution, however, does not deny suffrage to free African Americans.

1797. North Carolina. Congress refuses to accept the first recorded antislavery petition seeking redress against a North Carolina law which requires that enslaved Africans, although freed by their Quaker masters, be returned to the state and to their former condition.

1798. Washington, D.C. Secretary of the Navy Benjamin Stoddert forbids the deployment of African American sailors on man-of-war ships, in violation of a nonracial enlistment policy which had been operative in the U.S. Navy for many years. Nevertheless, a few African Americans slip past the ban, including William Brown, who serves as a "powder monkey" on the *Constellation*, and George Diggs, quartermaster of the schooner *Experiment*.

1799. Mount Vernon, Virginia. George Washington dies. His last will and testament declares: "It is my will and desire that all the slaves which I hold in my right, shall receive their freedom."

A Coromantyn Free Negro, or Ranger, Armed, etching by William Blake, 1806. *Drawings by John Gabriel Stedman, author of the book* Narrative, of a Five Years' Expedition, against the Revolted Negroes of Surinam *(2nd ed., 1806), were made into etchings by Blake for Stedman's book. In 1672, Virginia enacted a law providing a bounty on the heads of Maroons—black fugitives forming communities in the mountains, forests, and swamp regions of southern colonies.* **PRIVATE COLLECTION/© MICHAEL GRAHAM-STEWART/THE BRIDGEMAN ART LIBRARY**

NINETEENTH CENTURY

1800. Richmond, Virginia. Gabriel Prosser, a enslaved African insurrectionist, plans to lead thousands of slaves in an attack on Richmond. The plan fails and Prosser and fifteen of his followers are arrested, tried, and hanged.

1800. Washington, D.C. By a vote of 85–1, Congress rejects a petition by free African Americans in Philadelphia to gradually end slavery in the United States.

1803. South Carolina. The state legislature, which had been trying to limit importation of enslaved Africans, reopens the slave trade with Latin America and the West Indies.

1804. New Jersey. New Jersey passes an emancipation law. All states north of the Mason-Dixon Line now have laws forbidding slavery or providing for its gradual elimination.

1804. Ohio. The legislature enacts the first of a group of laws restricting the rights and movements of African Americans. Other western states soon follow suit. Illinois, Indiana, and Oregon later have anti-immigration clauses in their state constitutions.

1807. New Jersey. The state alters its 1776 constitution by limiting the vote to free white males.

1808, January 1. Congress bars the importation of any new slaves into the territory of the United States (effective January 1, 1808). The law is widely ignored. There are one million enslaved Africans in the country.

1810. Louisiana. Courts declare in *Adelle v. Beauregard* that an African American is free unless it is otherwise proven.

1811. Delaware. The state forbids the immigration of free African Americans and declares that any native-born free African American who has lived outside of Delaware for more than six months will be deemed a nonresident.

1811. Louisiana. U.S. troops suppress a slave uprising in two parishes (counties) of Louisiana, some 35 miles from New Orleans. The revolt is led by Charles Deslands. Some one hundred enslaved Africans are killed or executed.

1811. Westport, Connecticut. Paul Cuffe, son of African American and Indian parents and later a wealthy shipbuilder, sails with a small group of African Americans to Sierra Leone to underscore his advocacy of an African American return to Africa.

1812. Louisiana. Louisiana is admitted to the Union as a slave state. State law enables freed men to serve in the state militia.

1815. Fort Blount, Florida. African Americans and Creek Indians capture Fort Blount from Seminoles and use it as a haven for escaped slaves and as a base for attacks on slave owners. An American army detachment eventually recaptures the fort.

1816. Baltimore, Maryland. Bethel Charity School is founded by Daniel Coker, an African American.

1816. Louisiana. State laws are enacted that prohibit slaves from testifying against whites and free blacks, except in cases involving slave uprisings.

1816. New Orleans, Louisiana. James P. Beckwourth, an African American and one of the great explorers of the nineteenth century, signs on as a scout for General William Henry Ashley's Rocky Mountain expedition.

1816. Philadelphia, Pennsylvania. The African Methodist Episcopal Church is organized.

1816. Virginia. A slave rebellion led by George Boxley, a white man, fails.

1816. Washington, D.C. The American Colonization Society, which seeks to transport free African Americans to Africa, is organized. Protest meetings are subsequently held by many free African Americans in opposition to the society's efforts.

1817. Mississippi. Mississippi enters the union as a slave state. New York passes a gradual slavery abolition act.

1818. Connecticut. African Americans are denied the right to vote in Connecticut.

1818. Philadelphia, Pennsylvania. Free African Americans form the Pennsylvania Augustine Society "for the education of people of colour."

1819. Alabama. Alabama enters the Union as a slave state, although its constitution provides the legislature with the power to abolish slavery and compensate slave owners. Other measures include jury trials for slaves accused of crimes above petty larceny and penalties for malicious killing of slaves.

1820, February 6. New York. The *Mayflower of Liberia* sails for the West African nation of Sierra Leone with eighty-six African Americans aboard.

1820, March 3. The Missouri Compromise is enacted. It provides for Missouri's entry into the Union as a slave state and Maine's entry as a free state. There are thus twelve slave and twelve free states in the United States. All territory north of latitude 36°30′ is declared free; all territory south of that line is open to slavery.

1821. New York City. The African Methodist Episcopal Zion Church is founded with James Varick as its first bishop.

1821. New York. The state constitutional convention alters the voting requirements of 1777 by establishing higher property and longer residence requirements for African Americans.

1822. Charleston, South Carolina. The Denmark Vesey conspiracy, one of the most elaborate slave revolts on record, fails. Vesey, a sailor and carpenter, and thirty-six collaborators are hanged, an additional 130 blacks and four whites are arrested, and stricter controls are imposed on free African Americans and slaves. Following this insurrection, slave states adopt laws to further restrict the mobility of African Americans.

1822. Rhode Island. Free African Americans are denied the right to vote in Rhode Island.

1822. Liberia. Liberia is founded by African Americans with the aid of the American Colonization Society.

1823. Mississippi. A law is enacted in Mississippi that prohibits the teaching of reading and writing to African Americans and meetings of more than five slaves or free African Americans.

1824. As the United States moves toward universal male suffrage, more states in the North and West, as well as

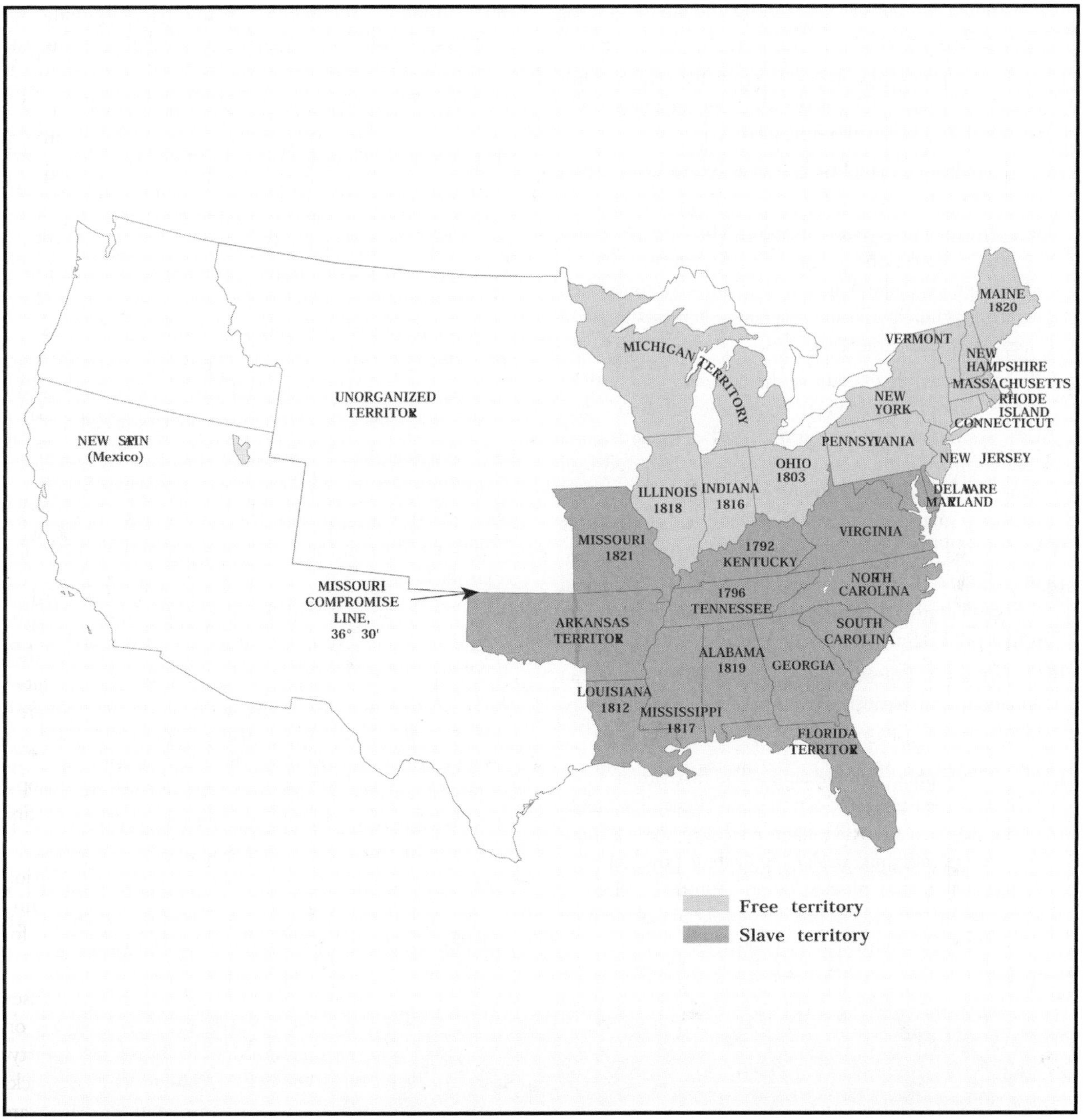

Map of the Expanding United States, pre–Civil War. *The map shows the status of states and territories following the 1820 enactment of the Missouri Compromise.* GALE

the South, move to deny the vote to African Americans. Illinois, Indiana, Iowa, and Michigan require African Americans to post bond in guarantee of good behavior.

1825. Maryland. Josiah Henson leads a group of slaves to freedom in Kentucky. Henson later crosses the border into Ontario and becomes leader of a community of former slaves.

1826. Virginia. Thomas Jefferson dies. His will stipulates that only five of his many slaves should be freed. The remainder are bequeathed to his heirs.

1827, March 16. New York City. *Freedom's Journal,* the first African American newspaper, begins publication.

1827, July 4. New York. Slavery is abolished in New York.

1828. Bennington, Vermont. William Lloyd Garrison, a journalist and reformer, writes his first antislavery article in the *National Philanthropist.*

1829. Boston, Massachusetts. David Walker, a free African American, publishes the antislavery pamphlet *An Appeal to the Colored People of the World,* which is distributed throughout the country and arouses a furor among slaveholders.

1829. Cincinnati, Ohio. After a riot in which whites attack black residents in Cincinnati and loot and burn their homes, 1,200 blacks flee to Canada.

1829. Philadelphia. The first National Negro Convention convenes.

1830. Philadelphia, Pennsylvania. The first National Negro Convention meets on September 20 at Philadelphia's Bethel Church. The four-day convention launches a church-affiliated program to improve the social status of African Americans.

1830. In an attempt to counter the increasing strength of the abolitionist movement, a number of states pass laws restricting the education, legal safeguards, and citizenship rights of slaves and free African Americans. Many states require the deportation of free African Americans; slave codes are enforced more strictly and the number of slave emancipations decline.

1830. The U.S. Census Bureau reports that 3,777 African American heads of families own slaves, mostly in Louisiana, Maryland, Virginia, North Carolina, and South Carolina.

1831, January 1. Boston, Massachusetts. *The Liberator*, an abolitionist newspaper, is founded by William Lloyd Garrison.

1831. Philadelphia, Pennsylvania. The first annual Convention of the People of Color meets at Wesleyan Church, where delegates from five states resolve to study African American conditions, explore settlement possibilities in Canada, and raise money for an industrial college in New Haven. Delegates oppose the American Colonization Society and recommend annual meetings.

1831, August. Southampton County, Virginia. Nat Turner leads the biggest slave rebellion in history. Some sixty whites are killed and the entire South is thrown into panic. Turner is captured on October 30 and hanged in Jerusalem, Virginia, twelve days later.

1831. Virginia. Thomas Dew, a legislator, proudly refers to Virginia as a "Negro-raising state" for the nation. Between 1830 and 1860, Virginia exports some 300,000 slaves, and South Carolina exports 179,000. The price of slaves increases sharply due to the expanding territory in which slaves are permitted and a booming economy in products harvested and processed by slave labor.

1832. Boston, Massachusetts. The New England Anti-Slavery Society is established by twelve whites at the African Baptist Church on Boston's Beacon Hill.

1833. Philadelphia, Pennsylvania. Black and white abolitionists organize the American Anti-Slavery Society.

1834. South Carolina. South Carolina enacts a law prohibiting the teaching of African American children, either free or slave.

1834. Great Britain. Parliament abolishes slavery in the British Empire; 700,000 slaves are liberated at a cost of twenty million British pounds sterling.

1835. North Carolina. North Carolina, the last Southern state to deny suffrage to African Americans, repeals a voting rights provision of the state constitution. The state also makes it illegal for whites to teach free blacks.

1835. Washington, D.C. President Andrew Jackson seeks to restrict the mailing of abolitionist literature to the South.

1836. Washington, D.C. The U.S. House of Representatives adopts the "gag rule" that prevents congressional action on antislavery resolutions or legislation.

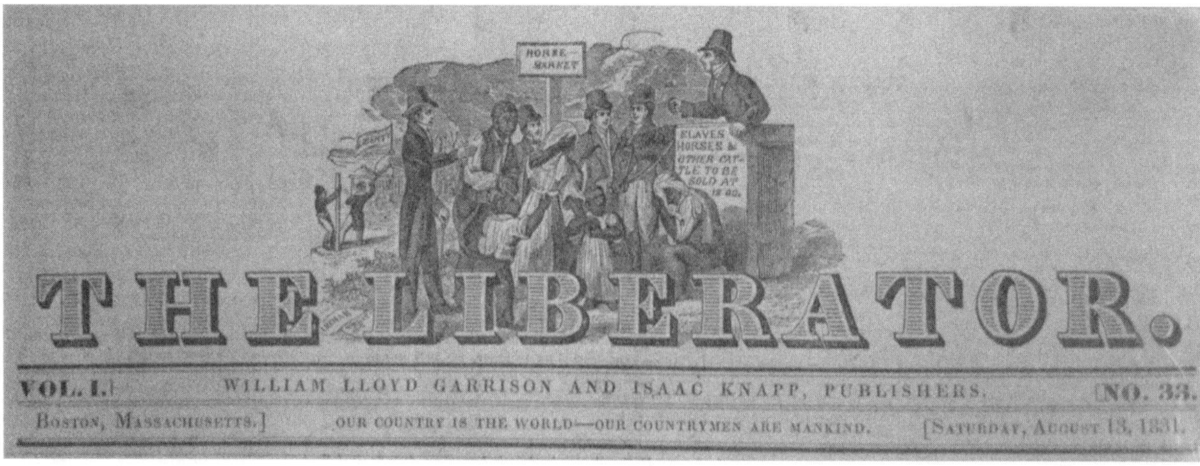

Masthead of the* Liberator *Newspaper, 1831. *William Lloyd Garrison founded this abolitionist newspaper in 1831 and published it through 1865. In the pages of the* Liberator, *Garrison worked to shift the sentiment of the nation away from the notion of gradual emancipation toward that of total abolition.* THE LIBRARY OF CONGRESS

1837. Alton, Illinois. Elijah P. Lovejoy, an abolitionist, is murdered by a mob in Alton after refusing to stop publishing antislavery material.

1837. Boston, Massachusetts. A series of abolitionist works are published including Reverend Hosea Eaton's *A Treatise on the Intellectual Character and Political Condition of the Colored People of the United States.*

1837. Canada. African Americans are given the right to vote in Canada.

1839. Montauk, New York. The slave ship *Amistad* is brought into Montauk by a group of Africans who have revolted against their captors. The young African leader, Joseph Cinque, and his followers are defended before the U.S. Supreme Court by former President John Quincy Adams and awarded their freedom.

1839. Warsaw, New York. The first antislavery political organization, the Liberty Party, is founded. African American abolitionists Samuel R. Ward and Henry Highland Garnet are among its leading supporters. The party urges boycotts of Southern crops and products.

1839. Washington, D.C. The U.S. State Department rejects an African American's application for a passport on the grounds that African Americans are not citizens.

1840. Massachusetts. Massachusetts repeals a law forbidding intermarriage between whites and blacks, mulattoes, or Indians.

1840. Vermont and New York institute a law advocating jury trials for fugitive slaves.

1840. Pope Gregory XVI declares the Roman Catholic Church's opposition to slavery and the slave trade.

1841. Massachusetts. Frederick Douglass begins his career as a lecturer with the Massachusetts Anti-Slavery Society.

1841. Throughout the country, increasingly restrictive segregation statutes are enacted. The New York state legislature grants school districts the right to segregate their educational facilities. South Carolina forbids white and black mill hands from looking out the same window. Whites and blacks in Atlanta are required to swear on different Bibles in court.

1841. Hampton, Virginia. Slaves aboard the vessel *Creole* revolt en route from Hampton, Virginia, to New Orleans. The slaves overpower the crew and sail the ship to the Bahamas, where they are granted asylum and freedom.

1842. Boston, Massachusetts. The capture of George Latimer, an escaped slave, precipitates the first of several famous fugitive slave cases straining North-South relations. Latimer is later purchased from his master by Boston abolitionists.

1842. Rhode Island. African Americans are granted the right to vote in Rhode Island.

1842. Washington, D.C. In the case *Prigg v. Pennsylvania*, the U.S. Supreme Court finds a Pennsylvania anti-kidnapping law unconstitutional, claiming that the authority to regulate the recapture of fugitive slaves was an exclusive power of Congress. The case arises when Edward Prigg is convicted of kidnapping for his recapture of an escaped slave.

LANDMARK CIVIL RIGHTS CASES

1839. The slave ship *Amistad* is brought into Montauk, New York by a group of enslaved Africans who have revolted against their captors. The young African leader, Joseph Cinque, and his followers are defended before the U.S. Supreme Court by former President John Quincy Adams and awarded their freedom.

1857. In the *Dred Scott v. Sandford* decision, the U.S. Supreme Court, by a six–three vote, opens federal territory to slavery, denies citizenship rights to African Americans, and decrees that enslaved persons do not become free when taken into free territory. The *Dred Scott* decision is followed by a ruling that African Americans are not entitled to land grants.

1896. The U.S. Supreme Court in the *Plessy v. Ferguson* decision upholds the doctrine of "separate but equal," paving the way for segregation of African Americans in all aspects of life.

1954. On May 17, by a unanimous vote, the U.S. Supreme Court in the case of *Brown v. Board of Education of Topeka, Kansas* declares that "separate but equal" educational facilities are "inherently unequal" and that segregation is therefore unconstitutional.

1961. On December 1, ruling on its first cases pertaining to student sit-ins, the U.S. Supreme Court decides unanimously to reverse the conviction of sixteen African American students. The cases *Briscoe v. Louisiana, Garner v. Louisiana,* and *Hoston v. Louisiana* result from a Baton Rouge lunch counter sit-in staged in March 1960.

1969. On October 29, ruling in the case of *Alexander v. Holmes County Board of Education,* the U.S. Supreme Court orders an end to all school segregation. The decision replaces the Warren Court's doctrine of "all deliberate speed," and is regarded as a setback for the Nixon administration.

1842. Washington, D.C. The Webster-Ashburton Treaty, in which Britain and the United States agree to prevent slave ships from reaching the African coast in order to suppress the slave trade there, is signed. No agreement is reached, however, to restrict the slave trade within the Western Hemisphere.

1843. Buffalo, New York. Henry Highland Garnet calls for a slave revolt and general strike while addressing the National Convention of Colored Men. Garnet, Samuel R. Ward, and Charles Ray participate in the Liberty Party convention, becoming the first African Americans to take part in a national political gathering.

1843. Massachusetts. The Massachusetts and Vermont state legislatures defy the Fugitive Slave Act and forbid state officials from assisting federal authorities in the recapture of escaped slaves.

1845. Washington, D.C. The U.S. Congress overturns the gag rule of 1836. Texas is admitted to the Union as a slave state.

1847. New York. The plan of abolitionist Gerrit Smith to parcel up thousands of acres of his land in New York to provide opportunities for free blacks to own property fails to attract prospective African American farmers. Lack of capital among African Americans and the infertility of the land doom the project.

1847. Rochester, New York. Frederick Douglass publishes the first issue of his abolitionist newspaper the *North Star.*

1847. St. Louis, Missouri. Dred Scott files suit for his freedom in the circuit court of St. Louis.

1848. Buffalo, New York. The convention of the Free Soil Party is attended by a number of African American abolitionists.

1848. Virginia. Postmasters are forced to inform police of the arrival of pro-abolition literature and turn it over to authorities for burning.

1849. Maryland. Harriet Tubman, soon to be a conductor on the Underground Railroad, escapes from slavery. Tubman later returns to the South no less than nineteen times to help transport more than 300 slaves to freedom. Also in 1849, the Maryland legislature enacts laws to override restrictions on the importation of slaves.

1849. Maryland. The Maryland Supreme Court establishes the "separate but equal" doctrine in response to a suit brought by Benjamin Roberts to have his daughter admitted to a white school.

1850. New York. Samuel R. Ward becomes president of the American League of Colored Laborers, a union of skilled African American workers who train African American craftsmen and encourage African American–owned business.

1850. Washington, D.C. The Compromise of 1850, also known as Clay's Compromise, is enacted, strengthening the 1793 Fugitive Slave Act. Federal officers are now offered a fee for the slaves they apprehend. California is admitted to the union as a free state.

1851. Virginia. New laws require freed slaves to leave Virginia within a year or be enslaved again.

1852. Akron, Ohio. Sojourner Truth addresses the National Woman's Suffrage Convention.

1852. Boston, Massachusetts. The first edition of Harriet Beecher Stowe's controversial *Uncle Tom's Cabin* is published.

1853. London. William Wells Brown publishes *Clotel, or, The President's Daughter: A Narrative of Slave Life in the United States*, the first published African American novel.

1853. Oxford, Pennsylvania. Lincoln University, the first African American college, is founded as Ashmun Institute.

1854. Boston, Massachusetts. Anthony Burns, a fugitive slave, is arrested and escorted through the streets of Boston by U.S. troops prior to being returned to his master. His master refuses an offer of $1,200 from Boston abolitionists attempting to purchase his freedom.

1854. The New England Emigration Society is founded to help settle former slaves in Kansas.

1854. Under the Kansas-Nebraska Act, the territories of Kansas and Nebraska are admitted to the Union without slavery restrictions, in direct contradiction to the provisions of the Missouri Compromise of 1820.

1855. The slavery issue is further polarized by enactment in Maine and Massachusetts of laws forbidding state officials from aiding the federal government in enforcement of the fugitive slave laws. The Massachusetts legislature abolishes school segregation and integration proceeds without incident.

1855. New York. The Liberty Party nominates Frederick Douglass for secretary of the U.S. State Department.

1856. Kansas. Proslavery forces sack the town of Lawrence, noted for its abolitionist, free-soil sentiment.

1857. Maine. Maine, in defiance of the fugitive slave laws, grants freedom and citizenship to people of African descent.

1857, March 6. Washington, D.C. In the *Dred Scott v. Sandford* decision, the U.S. Supreme Court, by a six-three vote, opens federal territory to slavery, denies citizenship rights to African Americans, and decrees that slaves do not become free when taken into free territory. The *Dred Scott* decision is followed by a ruling that African Americans are not entitled to land grants.

1858. Vicksburg, Mississippi. The Southern Commercial Convention calls for reestablishment of the slave trade, despite opposition from Tennessee and Florida delegations.

1859. Baltimore, Maryland. Businessmen attending a slaveholders convention complain that free African American laborers and entrepreneurs monopolize some service

Cover of the Book* The Boston Slave Riot and Trial of Anthony Burns *(1854). *A Boston mob attempted to rescue Burns, an escaped slave, from prison; later, federal troops escorted him onto a ship back to the South and slavery. Eventually, his freedom was bought by a Boston committee.* MPI/GETTY IMAGES

industries. However, a resolution to expel free African Americans from the state fails.

1859, October 16. Harpers Ferry, West Virginia. John Brown and his followers seize the U.S. Armory. Two African Americans are killed, two are captured, one escapes. Brown is captured and hanged at Charles Town, West Virginia.

1859. Washington, D.C. In the case of *Ableman v. Booth*, the U.S. Supreme Court upholds the Fugitive Slave Act of 1850. The case arises when Sherman Booth rescues a fugitive slave from a Wisconsin jail and is charged by federal marshals with violating federal law.

1860. As the Civil War approaches, the United States is sharply divided between proslavery and antislavery forces. In Virginia, a law stipulates that free African Americans can be sold into slavery for committing imprisonable offenses. Maryland forbids emancipation of slaves. President James Buchanan advocates a constitutional amendment confirming the Fugitive Slave Acts. The Democratic Party platform supports the *Dred Scott v. Sandford* decision. The Republican platform opposes the expansion of slavery into the western territories, and Abraham Lincoln, still a moderate on the subject of abolition, is elected president. On December 17, South Carolina secedes from the Union.

1861. Confederate forces attack Fort Sumter, South Carolina, marking the beginning of the U.S. Civil War. Jefferson Davis is elected president of the Confederate States of America and defends slavery as necessary to "self-preservation." The Confederates conscript slaves for military support jobs. Some Confederate states use free African Americans in their armed forces.

1861. Washington, D.C. The secretary of the U.S. Navy solicits enlistment of African Americans into the Union Army, but most African American offers to help militarily are rejected. Federal policy toward liberated slaves is erratic, depending mostly on the viewpoint of individual commanders. Lincoln moves warily, countermanding General Frémont's order that slaves of masters who fight against the Union are to be "declared free men."

1862. New York. The National Freedmen's Relief Association, one of many groups dedicated to assisting slaves in making the transition to freedom, is formed. Groups in Philadelphia, Cincinnati, and Chicago are eventually consolidated as the American Freedmen's Aid Commission.

1862. Washington, D.C. The U.S. Congress authorizes the enlistment of African Americans for military service in the Union Army.

1862. Washington, D.C. President Abraham Lincoln proposes a plan for the gradual, compensated emancipation of slaves. Included is a provision to subsidize emigration to Haiti or Liberia. Lincoln's cautious policies are clarified in a letter to Horace Greeley in which he states that his paramount objective is to save the Union, "not either to save or destroy slavery." However, Lincoln does sign bills abolishing slavery in the territories and freeing slaves of masters disloyal to the United States. Military commanders are forbidden from returning fugitive slaves to owners and, in September, Lincoln issues an ultimatum giving hostile areas until January 1 to cease fighting or lose their slaves.

1862, September 22. Washington, D.C. Lincoln issues the Emancipation Proclamation, declaring freedom for all slaves in Confederate states that did not return to the Union by January 1.

1863. Cow Island, Haiti. Lincoln sends a ship to bring back 500 African American settlers after a colonization attempt in Haiti fails.

1863. New York. In antidraft riots, 1,200 people, mostly African Americans, are killed. The riot is spurred in

MAJOR EVENTS IN AFRICAN AMERICAN HISTORY

1862. On September 22, Lincoln issues the Emancipation Proclamation, declaring freedom for all enslaved persons in Confederate states that did not return to the Union by January 1 of the following year.

1909. The NAACP is founded in New York. The signers of the original charter of incorporation include Jane Addams, John Dewey, W. E. B. Du Bois, William Dean Howells, and Lincoln Steffens. Ida Wells-Barnett is placed on the executive committee.

1955. On December 1, Rosa Parks refuses to surrender her seat on a city bus in Montgomery, Alabama to a white man, and is arrested. Four days later, the Reverend Martin Luther King Jr. urges the city's African American community to boycott the city buses. This marks the beginning of the Montgomery bus boycott, which leads to the desegregation of Montgomery's bus system the following year.

1957. On September 4, Nine African American students are turned away from Central High School in Little Rock, Arkansas by a white mob and the Arkansas National Guard when they arrive for classes. The National Guard, which was called to Little Rock by Governor Orval Faubus, is forced by court order to withdraw on September 20. On September 24, President Eisenhower issues Executive Order No. 10730 authorizing the use of federal troops to assist in the integration of Central High School.

1963. On August 28, Some 250,000 people gather at the Lincoln Memorial in Washington, D.C. to demonstrate on behalf of the civil rights bill pending in Congress. Martin Luther King Jr., one of many scheduled speakers, gives what will become his most famous speech, "I Have a Dream."

1968. On April 4, The world is shocked by the assassination of Martin Luther King Jr in Memphis, Tennessee. The killing triggers a wave of violence in over 100 cities including such urban centers as Baltimore, Chicago, Kansas City, Missouri, and Washington, D.C. Some 70,000 federal troops and National Guardsmen are dispatched to restore order.

2008. On November 4, Barack Obama is elected the forty-fourth president of the United States, beating Republican nominee John McCain. Obama received 365 electoral college votes to 173 for Senator McCain.

2009. In January, Barack Hussein Obama is inaugurated as U.S. president. He is the first African American president in the nation's history.

part by the provision that exemption from military service can be bought for $300, a provision bitterly resented by poor white immigrants who vent their frustrations on blacks.

1864. Louisiana. The Louisiana legislature, elected under the auspices of occupying Union forces, votes to abolish slavery. However, it denies suffrage to African Americans.

1864. Virginia. Fourteen African American soldiers are awarded the Medal of Honor by President Lincoln.

1865. Montgomery, Alabama. Jefferson Davis authorizes the enlistment of African Americans into the Confederate Army. However, Davis stipulates that the number of African American troops cannot exceed 25 percent of the able-bodied slave population.

1865, April. Appomattox, Virginia. The Confederacy surrenders. Of the 179,000 African Americans who served in the Union Army, 3,000 were killed in battle, 26,000 died from disease, and 14,700 deserted. African Americans represented 9 to 10 percent of the Union's armed forces.

1865. Tennessee. The Ku Klux Klan is formed with the purpose of reasserting white supremacy in the South.

1865. All-white legislatures in many states enact black codes. These codes impose heavy penalties for "vagrancy," "insulting gestures," "curfew violations," and "seditious speeches." South Carolina requires African Americans entering the state to post a $1,000 bond in guarantee of good behavior and entitles employers to whip African American employees.

1865. Wisconsin. Wisconsin, Connecticut, and Minnesota deny suffrage to African Americans.

1865. Washington, D.C. Abraham Lincoln is assassinated and dies on the morning of April 15. The new president, Andrew Johnson, calls for ratification of the Thirteenth Amendment, but opposes African American suffrage. The Thirteenth Amendment, abolishing slavery and involuntary servitude in all of the United States, is ratified December 16, 1865.

1865, December 6. Washington, D.C. Congress establishes the Freedmen's Bureau.

1866. In a race riot in Memphis, forty-eight blacks and two white sympathizers are killed. Also, thirty-five blacks are killed in a riot in New Orleans.

1866. Washington, D.C. Congress passes civil rights legislation despite President Johnson's veto. The act is intended to nullify the black codes. In the District of Columbia, a referendum is held on African American suffrage. Over 6,500 vote against extension of the franchise to African Americans; only thirty-five favor it. The Fourteenth Amendment passes the House and Senate despite opposition from Johnson.

1867. Iowa. Iowa and the Dakota Territory grant suffrage to African Americans.

CIVIL RIGHTS LEGISLATION

1866. Congress passes civil rights legislation (the Civil Rights Act of 1866) despite President Andrew Johnson's veto. The Fourteenth Amendment passes the House and Senate despite opposition from Johnson, and is formally ratified in 1868.

1875. Congress passes civil rights legislation prohibiting discrimination in such public accommodations as hotels, theaters, and amusement parks.

1941. The threat by African Americans to stage a massive protest march on the nation's capital results in the issuance of Executive Order No. 8802, prohibiting discrimination in the defense establishment.

1957. President Eisenhower signs a civil rights bill. The bill provides for the creation of a commission on civil rights to investigate allegations of civil rights and voting rights violations.

1960. On May 6, President Eisenhower signs the Civil Rights Act of 1960. This act authorizes judges to appoint referees who can help African Americans register to vote in federal elections. The act also prohibits intimidation of African American voters through bombing and mob violence.

1964. On June 2, A major civil rights bill, forbidding discrimination in public accommodations and employment, is signed into law by President Johnson.

1965. On August 6, President Lyndon B. Johnson signs the 1965 Voting Rights Act, providing for the registration by federal examiners of those black voters turned away by state officials.

1968. On April 10, the assassination of Martin Luther King Jr. moves the U.S. House of Representatives to submit to President Johnson a Senate-passed civil rights bill prohibiting racial discrimination in the sale or rental of 80 percent of the nation's housing. Johnson signs the measure on April 11 and counsels the nation to stay on the road to progress by recognizing "the process of law."

1868. Hampton, Virginia. Samuel Chapman Armstrong, a former Union officer, founds Hampton Institute.

1868. Nine states grant suffrage to African Americans, but two deny it. The Republican party platform omits demand for African American suffrage in Northern states.

1868. Many states are readmitted to the Union. The Alabama legislature votes to racially segregate all state schools.

1868. Louisiana. Oscar Dunn, a former slave and captain in the Union Army, is elected lieutenant governor of Louisiana.

1868. South Carolina. The South Carolina House is the first state legislature to have a majority of African Americans. Blacks outnumber whites eighty-seven to forty in the South Carolina legislature, but whites maintain a majority in the state Senate.

1868. Washington, D.C. The Fourteenth Amendment is ratified, establishing the concept of "equal protection" for all citizens under the U.S. Constitution.

1869. Washington, D.C. The Colored National Labor Union is organized and advocates purchase and distribution of land.

1870. Washington, D.C. Recruitment of African Americans for the U.S. Cavalry intensifies. By 1890, fourteen African American cavalrymen had received Medals of Honor for bravery in campaigns in the West.

1870. Washington, D.C. The Fifteenth Amendment to the Constitution, guaranteeing all citizens the right to vote, is ratified.

1871. Washington, D.C. Congress enacts the Ku Klux Klan Act to enforce the provisions of the Fourteenth Amendment.

1874. Washington, D.C. African American priest Patrick F. Healy is named president of Georgetown, the oldest Catholic university in the United States.

1875. Kentucky. Oliver Lewis, an African American jockey, rides the horse Aristides to victory in the first Kentucky Derby.

1875. Washington, D.C. Congress passes civil rights legislation prohibiting discrimination in such public accommodations as hotels, theaters, and amusement parks.

1876. Washington, D.C. In *United States v. Cruikshank*, the Supreme Court declares that the Fourteenth Amendment provides African Americans with equal protection under the law but does not add anything "to the rights which one citizen has under the Constitution against another." The Court rules that "the right of suffrage is not a necessary attribute of national citizenship."

1878. Washington, D.C. In the case *Hall v. DeCuir*, the U.S. Supreme Court rules that states cannot prohibit segregation on public transportation.

1878. Washington, D.C. The U.S. attorney general reveals widespread intimidation of African Americans attempting to vote and stuffing of ballot boxes in several Southern states.

1879. Frustrated by poverty and discrimination, large numbers of African Americans start to emigrate north and west. A leader of the emigration movement is Benjamin "Pap" Singleton, a former slave who had earlier escaped to Canada and favors separate African American communities. Emigration is vigorously opposed by many whites,

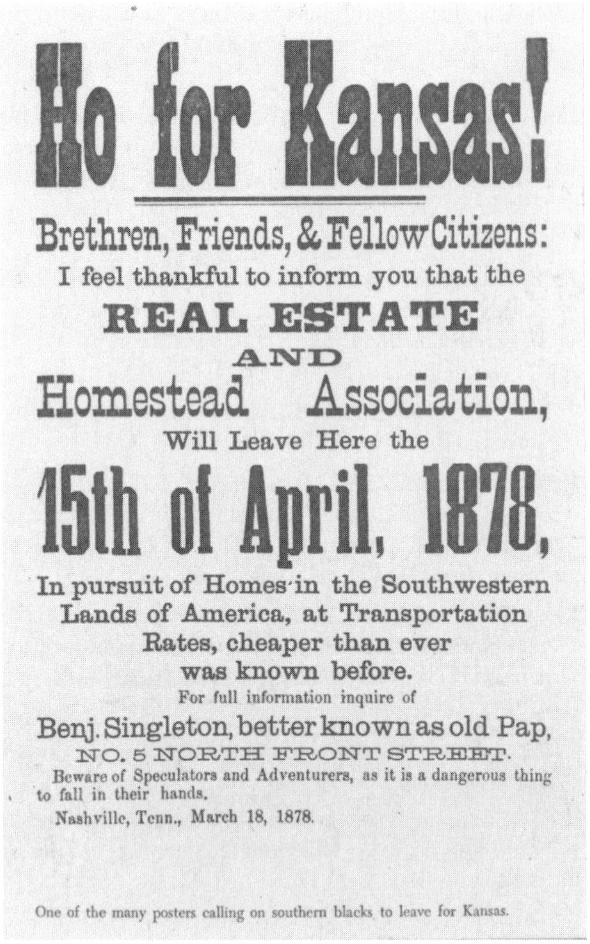

Ho for Kansas!
Brethren, Friends, & Fellow Citizens:
I feel thankful to inform you that the
REAL ESTATE
AND
Homestead Association,
Will Leave Here the
15th of April, 1878,
In pursuit of Homes in the Southwestern
Lands of America, at Transportation
Rates, cheaper than ever
was known before.
For full information inquire of
Benj. Singleton, better known as old Pap,
NO. 5 NORTH FRONT STREET.
Beware of Speculators and Adventurers, as it is a dangerous thing
to fall in their hands.
Nashville, Tenn., March 18, 1878.
One of the many posters calling on southern blacks to leave for Kansas.

Advertisement Encouraging African Americans to Migrate to Kansas, 1878. *A number of African American homesteaders migrated from the South to Kansas during the 1870s. A principal leader of this mass migration was Benjamin "Pap" Singleton (1809–1892), a former slave from Tennessee who established several colonies in Kansas, including the Nicodemus settlement.* **THE LIBRARY OF CONGRESS**

some of whom prevent ships from transporting blacks on the Mississippi River.

1879. Washington, D.C. Upon hearing the case of *Strauder v. West Virginia*, the U.S. Supreme Court rules that the Fourteenth Amendment ensures blacks all rights that, under law, are enjoyed by whites. In a separate case, the Court rules that one of the purposes of both the Thirteenth and Fourteenth Amendments is to raise the condition of blacks to one of perfect equality with whites.

1881. Tennessee passes a "Jim Crow" railroad law, which sets a trend soon taken up by Florida (1887), Mississippi (1888), Texas (1889), Louisiana (1890), and a host of other Southern and border states.

1881. Tuskegee, Alabama. Booker T. Washington opens the Tuskegee Institute with a $2,000 appropriation from the Alabama legislature.

1883. Washington, D.C. Upon hearing a set of cases challenging the Civil Rights Act of 1875, the U.S. Supreme Court declares the act unconstitutional.

1884. New York. The first issue of the *New York Freeman* is published by African American editor T. Thomas Fortune. The *Freeman* was reorganized and published as the *New York Age* in 1887.

1884. Washington, D.C. Former Reconstruction representative John Roy Lynch is elected temporary chairman of the Republican convention—the first African American to preside over a national political gathering.

1884. Memphis, Tennessee. Fiery journalist Ida Wells-Barnett is successful in her suit against the Chesapeake and Ohio Railroad Company for racial segregation on a trip from Memphis to Woodstock. The Tennessee Supreme Court reverses the decision on April 5, 1887.

1888. Richmond, Virginia. Two African American banks are founded—the Savings Bank of the Grand Fountain United Order of True Reformers in Virginia and the Capital Savings Bank in Washington, D.C.

1889. Washington, D.C. Frederick Douglass is appointed U.S. minister to Haiti.

1890. Mississippi. The Mississippi constitutional convention begins the systematic exclusion of African Americans from the political arena by adopting literacy and other complex "understanding" tests as prerequisites to voting. Seven other Southern states follow suit.

1890. Washington, D.C. In the *In re Green* decision, the U.S. Supreme Court sanctions control of elections by state officials, thus weakening federal protection for Southern black voters. In the case *Louisville, New Orleans and Texas Railway v. Mississippi*, the Court permits states to segregate public transportation facilities.

1891. Baffin Bay, Greenland. African American explorer Matthew Henson accompanies Admiral Robert E. Peary in his exploration of the Arctic.

1891. Chicago, Illinois. African American physician and surgeon Daniel Hale Williams founds Provident Hospital, the first nonsegregated hospital in the United States and the first with a training school for African American nurses.

1895. Atlanta, Georgia. Booker T. Washington delivers his famous "Atlanta Compromise" speech at the Cotton States International Exposition.

1896. Cambridge, Massachusetts. W. E. B. Du Bois publishes *Suppression of the African Slave Trade*, the first of some twenty annual sociological studies of African Americans in the United States.

1896. Washington, D.C. The National Association of Colored Women, a politically active self-help group, is formed.

1896. Washington, D.C. The U.S. Supreme Court in the *Plessy v. Ferguson* decision upholds the doctrine of

Photo of Tuskegee Institute Faculty with Andrew Carnegie, Tuskegee, AL (Frances Benjamin Johnston, 1906). *Opened in 1881, the Tuskegee Institute (now Tuskegee University) was one of the earliest schools for African Americans. Seated in front row* (left to right)*: R. C. Ogden, Margaret James Murray Washington, Booker T. Washington, Andrew Carnegie, and an unidentified person.* THE LIBRARY OF CONGRESS

"separate but equal," paving the way for segregation of African Americans in all aspects of life.

1898. Louisiana. The addition of a "grandfather clause" to the Louisiana state constitution enables poor whites to qualify for the franchise while curtailing black voter registration. In 1896, there were over 130,000 African American voters on the Louisiana rolls. Four years later, that number was reduced to roughly 5,000.

1898. Santiago, Cuba. Four African American regiments in the U.S. Army compile an outstanding combat record in and around Santiago during the Spanish-American War. Five African Americans receive Medals of Honor. At the close of the war, over 100 African Americans are promoted to officer status.

TWENTIETH CENTURY

1900. Boston, Massachusetts. Booker T. Washington organizes the National Negro Business League.

1900. London, England. W. E. B. Du Bois attends the conference of the African and New World Intellectuals, where he delivers an address incorporating his famous dictum: "The problem of the twentieth century is the problem of the color line." Du Bois also attends the first Pan-African Congress, an international body of concerned African nations protesting Western imperialism and promoting the concept of self-government among colonized peoples.

1902. Richmond, Virginia. Virginia joins other Southern states in adopting the "grandfather clause" as a means of denying African Americans access to the polls.

1903. Washington, D.C. Upon reviewing the case *Giles v. Harris*, the U.S. Supreme Court upheld the dismissal of the case by the U.S. district court, effectively upholding a state constitution's requirements for voter qualifications and registration.

1904. Atlanta, Georgia. Financier Andrew Carnegie brings together a group of prominent African American leaders, including Booker T. Washington and W. E. B. Du Bois, who discuss "the interests of the Negro race." The personal and ideological differences between Washington and Du Bois are evident at the meeting, though there is agreement that the group should press for "absolute civil, political, and public equality." The group shows little fire in advancing familiar proposals for African American self-help.

1905. Fort Erie, New York. Twenty-nine militant African American intellectuals from fourteen states organize the Niagara Movement, a forerunner of the National Association for the Advancement of Colored People (NAACP).

1906. Atlanta, Georgia. An extended riot, in which respected African American citizens are killed, brings the city to a standstill for several days. After the riot, interracial groups are formed and are charged with improving conditions for African Americans. Despite the efforts of these groups, many African Americans decide to leave Georgia.

1906. Brownsville, Texas. Several African American soldiers of the Twenty-fifth Infantry Division are involved in a riot with Brownsville police and merchants. Following the incident, President Theodore Roosevelt dishonorably discharges three companies of African American troops. These dishonorable discharges are finally reversed by the U.S. Army in 1972. The lone survivor from these companies is awarded $25,000 by the U.S. Army in 1973.

1907. Washington, D.C. The U.S. Supreme Court upholds the right of railroads to segregate passengers traveling between states, even when this runs counter to the laws of states in which the train is traveling.

1908. Washington, D.C. The U.S. Supreme Court, in the case *Berea College v. Kentucky*, upholds a state statute requiring segregation in private institutions.

1909. New York City. The NAACP is founded in New York. The signers of the original charter of incorporation include Jane Addams, John Dewey, W. E. B. Du Bois, William Dean Howells, and Lincoln Steffens. Ida Wells-Barnett is placed on the executive committee.

1909. African American explorer Matthew Henson places the flag of the United States at the North Pole. Henson was part of Admiral Robert E. Peary's expedition.

1910. On separate lecture tours of Great Britain, W. E. B. Du Bois and Booker T. Washington paint contrasting pictures of the African American condition in the United States. Washington tells the British that blacks are making progress; Du Bois underscores injustices and accuses Washington of acquiescing to powerful white interests.

1910. New York City. The first edition of *Crisis* magazine, edited by W. E. B. Du Bois, is published. Only 1,000 copies are in print, but before the end of the decade circulation of the magazine's circulation increases 100-fold.

1910. New York City. The National Urban League is founded. The new organization stresses employment and industrial opportunities for African Americans. Eugene Kinckle Jones serves as the first executive secretary.

ORGANIZATIONS

1833. Black and white abolitionists in Philadelphia, Pennsylvania, organize the American Anti-Slavery Society.

1839. The first antislavery political organization, the Liberty Party, is founded in Warsaw, New York. African American abolitionists Samuel R. Ward and Henry Highland Garnet are among its leading supporters. The party urges boycotts of Southern products.

1909. The NAACP is founded in New York. The signers of the original charter of incorporation include Jane Addams, John Dewey, W. E. B. Du Bois, William Dean Howells, and Lincoln Steffens. Ida Wells-Barnett is placed on the executive committee.

1914. Marcus Garvey forms the Universal Negro Improvement Association.

1930. W. D. Fard founds the Temple of Islam, later to become the Nation of Islam, in Detroit, Michigan.

1942. The Congress of Racial Equality (CORE), a civil rights group dedicated to a direct-action, nonviolent program, is founded in Chicago, Illinois. In 1943, CORE stages its first sit-in at a Chicago restaurant.

1957. The Southern Christian Leadership Conference (SCLC) is formed by Martin Luther King Jr. and others to coordinate the activities of nonviolent groups devoted to integration and full citizenship for African Americans.

1960. The Student Nonviolent Coordinating Committee (SNCC) is formed in Atlanta, Georgia, to organize student protest activities. Church "kneel-ins" and beach "wade-ins" soon join lunch counter and bus station sit-ins as effective means of protesting segregation.

1964. Malcolm X leaves the Black Muslim organization, Nation of Islam, to form the Organization for Afro-American Unity in New York City—an organization emphasizing black nationalism and social action.

1966. Huey P. Newton and Bobby Seale found the Black Panther Party in Oakland, California.

1912. New York City. James Weldon Johnson's *The Autobiography of an Ex-Colored Man* is published, spurring white recognition of African American culture and the advent of the Harlem Renaissance.

1913. Washington, D.C. President Woodrow Wilson refuses to appoint a National Race Commission to study the social and economic status of African Americans.

1914. Jamaica. Marcus Garvey forms the Universal Negro Improvement Association.

1915. Spurred by boll-weevil devastation of cotton crops, the great migration of African Americans to the North begins. Carter G. Woodson establishes the Association for the Study of Negro Life and History.

1915. New York City. The NAACP establishes the Spingarn Medal to recognize annually "the highest achievement of an American Negro."

1915. Washington, D.C. The U.S. Supreme Court in *Guinn v. United States* declares the Oklahoma "grandfather clause" unconstitutional.

1917. East St. Louis, Illinois. In an region unsettled by strikes and labor tensions, a riot erupts after African Americans are hired at a local factory. Forty African Americans are killed.

1917, July 28. New York City. Over 10,000 African Americans parade down Fifth Avenue in New York to protest lynchings and the East St. Louis riot. Marchers in the Silent Protest Parade include W. E. B. Du Bois and James Weldon Johnson. Women and children protesters dress in white and men wear black arm bands.

1917. The United States enters World War I. Joel Spingarn presses the War Department to establish an officer training camp for African Americans. Spingarn's proposal alienates many of his NAACP colleagues who feel that such a camp would only perpetuate segregation and validate theories of African American inferiority. Others concede that the move is prudent, since it is the only way for African American officers to be trained. The NAACP ultimately approves of separate training camps. In October, over 600 African Americans are commissioned officers, and 700,000 African Americans register for the draft.

1917. Washington, D.C. In the case of *Buchanan v. Warley*, the U.S. Supreme Court declares that a Louisville ordinance requiring segregation based on race is unconstitutional.

1918. France. Two African American infantry battalions are awarded the Croix de Guerre and two African American officers win the French Legion of Honor. African Americans are in the forefront of fighting from 1917 until the defeat of Germany in 1918.

1919. Membership in the NAACP approaches 100,000 despite attempts in some areas to make such membership illegal.

1919. Washington, D.C. The U.S. Supreme Court rules in the case *Strauder v. West Virginia* that African Americans should be admitted to juries.

1920. New York City. James Weldon Johnson becomes the first African American secretary of the NAACP and campaigns for the withdrawal of U.S. troops occupying Haiti.

1921. Tulsa, Oklahoma. Thousands of African Americans are left homeless when the prosperous black neighborhood of Greenwood is looted and burned during the Tulsa Riot of 1921, one of the worst race riots in U.S. history.

1922. Washington, D.C. Republicans in the Senate vote to abandon the Dyer Anti-Lynching Bill, which imposed severe penalties and fines on "any state or municipal officer convicted of negligence in affording protection to individuals in custody who are attacked by a mob bent on lynching, torture, or physical intimidation." The bill, which was approved by the House of Representatives, had also provided for compensation to the families of victims.

1923. New York City. Marcus Garvey is sentenced to a five-year term for mail fraud.

1924. Washington, D.C. Congress passes the Immigration Act, which excludes people of African descent from entering the country.

1924. Washington, D.C. New York representative Emanuel Cellar introduces legislation to provide for the formation of a blue-ribbon panel to study racial issues. The idea is met with disdain from the African American press, particularly the *Chicago Defender*, which editorializes: "We have been commissioned to death.... We have too many studies and reports already." The *Defender* asserts that African Americans need only to look after their own interests through the creation of a strong party vehicle and potent political leadership in the halls of Congress.

1925. A. Philip Randolph founds the Brotherhood of Sleeping Car Porters.

1926. New York City. Controversy rages among the African American intelligentsia after publication of *Nigger Heaven* by white writer Carl van Vechten. The book glamorizes the free-wheeling style of Harlem life amid the general contention that African Americans are less ashamed of sex and more morally honest than whites. W. E. B. Du Bois finds the assumptions deplorable; James Weldon Johnson, on the other hand, believes the book is neither scandalous nor insulting.

1926. New York City. Langston Hughes, writing in the *Nation* magazine, urges African American artists to write from their experience and to stop imitating white writers.

1926. Washington, D.C. Negro History Week is introduced by Carter G. Woodson and the Association for the Study of Negro Life and History.

1926. Washington, D.C. President Coolidge tells Congress that the country must provide "for the amelioration of race prejudice and the extension to all of the elements of equal opportunity and equal protection under the laws, which are guaranteed by the Constitution." Twenty-three African Americans are reported lynched during 1926.

1927. Atlanta, Georgia. Marcus Garvey is released from prison and deported to the British West Indies.

1927. Chicago, Illinois. The National Urban League organizes a boycott of stores that do not hire African Americans. In 1929, boycotts are started in several other Midwest cities.

1927. Washington, D.C. In the case of *Nixon v. Herndon*, the U.S. Supreme Court strikes down a Texas law that bars African Americans from voting in party primaries. Texas goes on to enact a law allowing local committees to determine voter qualifications.

1928. Illinois. Oscar DePriest, a Republican, is elected to Congress as the first African American representative from a Northern state.

1930. Detroit, Michigan. W. D. Fard founds the Temple of Islam, later to become the Nation of Islam.

1930. Washington, D.C. A campaign by the NAACP helps prevent confirmation of U.S. Supreme Court nominee John H. Parker, a onetime self-admitted opponent of the franchise for African Americans. The NAACP also helps unseat three of the senators who voted for him in later congressional elections.

1931. Alabama. The first trial of the Scottsboro Boys results in a battle between the NAACP and the International Labor Defense, a Communist-controlled group, for the right to represent the young defendants who are charged with rape. The case, which becomes a worldwide *cause célèbre* and important propaganda weapon for Communists, drags on for twenty years despite the recanting of a charge by one of the two plaintiffs and medical testimony that rape was not committed.

1932. Washington, D.C. Following the Supreme Court's 1927 ruling in *Nixon v. Herndon*, the state of Texas passes a statute authorizing the state Democratic Party to set up its own rules regarding primary elections. As a result, the state of Texas adopts a resolution that denies African Americans the right to vote in Democratic Party primaries. However, the Supreme Court rules that such legislation violates provisions of the Fourteenth Amendment.

1934. Chicago, Illinois. The headquarters of the Nation of Islam are established, with Elijah Muhammad as leader.

1934. Washington, D.C. A bill that prohibits lynching fails, as President Franklin D. Roosevelt refuses to support it.

1935. New York City. Mary McLeod Bethune founds the National Council of Negro Women.

1935. St. Louis, Missouri. The NAACP bitterly criticizes President Franklin Delano Roosevelt for his failure to present or support civil rights legislation.

W. D. Fard, Religious Leader, Detroit, MI, May 26, 1933. *The enigmatic Fard founded the Temple of Islam in 1930 in Detroit. The year after this photo was taken, Fard disappeared.* **AP PHOTO**

1935. Washington, D.C. In the case of *Grovey v. Townsend*, the U.S. Supreme Court upholds a Texas law that prevents African Americans from voting in the Texas Democratic primary. The decision is a setback to the NAACP, which has waged several effective legal battles to equalize the ballot potential of the African American voter.

1936. Berlin, Germany. Jesse Owens wins four gold medals in the 1936 Olympics, but is snubbed by the chancellor of Germany, Adolf Hitler.

1936. Washington, D.C. In the case of *Gibbs v. Montgomery County*, the U.S. Supreme Court requires Maryland University to admit an African American student, Donald Murray, to its graduate law school.

1937. New York City. Richard Wright becomes editor of *Challenge*, changes the title to *New Challenge*, and urges African Americans to write with greater "social realism."

1937. Pennsylvania. A new Pennsylvania state law denies many state services to unions discriminating against African Americans.

1937. Spain. As many as eighty of the 3,200 Americans who fight for the Republican side in the Spanish civil war are African Americans. Oliver Law, an African American from Chicago, commands the Lincoln Battalion.

1938, New York City. Boxer Joe Louis successfully defends his heavyweight title against German Max Schmeling.

1938. New York City. Adam Clayton Powell Jr. and other African American leaders convince white merchants in Harlem to hire African Americans and to promise equal promotion opportunities.

1938. Pennsylvania. Crystal Bird Fauset of Philadelphia, the first African American woman state legislator, is elected to the Pennsylvania House of Representatives.

1939. Miami, Florida. Intimidation and cross burning by the Ku Klux Klan in the black ghetto of Miami fail to discourage over 1,000 of the city's registered African American voters from appearing at the polls. The Klan parades with effigies of African Americans who will allegedly be slain for daring to vote.

1939. New York City. Jane Bolin is appointed judge of the Court of Domestic Relations in New York City by Mayor Fiorello LaGuardia, becoming the first African American woman judge in the United States.

1939. Washington, D.C. Marian Anderson, denied the use of Constitution Hall by the Daughters of the American Revolution, sings on Easter Sunday before 75,000 people assembled at the Lincoln Memorial.

Joe Louis vs. Max Schmeling, Yankee Stadium, New York City, June 22, 1938. *In a rematch of a fight from two years earlier, which had been won by Schmeling, Louis scored a first-round knockout to retain his heavyweight title.* AP IMAGES

1940. Eighty thousand African Americans vote in eight Southern states. Five percent of voting-age African Americans are registered.

1940. The 1940 census places life expectancy for African Americans at fifty-one years, compared with sixty-two years for whites. Nearly one-fourth of blacks live in the North and West.

1940. Virginia. The Virginia legislature chooses "Carry Me Back to Ole Virginia" (formerly "Virginny"), written by African American composer James A. Bland, as the official state song.

1940. Washington, D.C. Benjamin O. Davis Sr. is appointed as the first African American general in the history of the U.S. armed forces. Responding to NAACP pressure, President Franklin Roosevelt announces that African American strength in the armed forces will be proportionate to African American population totals. Several branches of the military service and several occupational specialties are to be opened to African Americans. However, Roosevelt rules out troop integration because it will be "destructive to morale and detrimental to ... preparation for national defense." At the start of Selective Service, less than 5,000 of 230,000 men in the U.S. Army are African American and there are only two African American combat officers. Approximately 888,000 African American men and 4,000 African American women are to serve in the armed forces during World War II. African Americans are mostly confined to service units.

1940. Washington, D.C. The U.S. Supreme Court rules that African American teachers cannot be denied wage parity with white teachers.

1941. Washington, D.C. Charles R. Drew, an African American physician, sets up the first blood bank.

1941. Washington, D.C. Robert Weaver is appointed director of the government office charged with integrating African Americans into the national defense program.

1941. Washington, D.C. The threat by African Americans to stage a massive protest march on the nation's capital results in the issuance of Executive Order No. 8802, prohibiting discrimination in the defense establishment.

1941. Washington, D.C. In the case of *Mitchell v. United States*, the U.S. Supreme Court rules that separate facilities in railroad travel must be substantially equal. The case is brought before the Supreme Court by African American congressman Arthur Mitchell.

1941, December 7. Pearl Harbor, Hawaii. African American Dorie Miller, messman aboard the USS *Arizona*, mans a machine gun during the Pearl Harbor attack, downs four enemy planes, and is awarded the Navy Cross.

1942. Chicago, Illinois. The Congress of Racial Equality (CORE), a civil rights group dedicated to a direct-action, nonviolent program, is founded. In 1943, CORE stages its first sit-in at a Chicago restaurant.

1942. Washington, D.C. The Justice Department threatens to file suit against a number of African American newspapers that it believes are guilty of sedition because of their strong criticism of the government's racial policies in the armed services. The NAACP steps in to suggest guidelines that will satisfy the Justice Department.

1944. The United Negro College Fund (UNCF) is founded.

1944. The NAACP secures the release of servicemen detained for protesting discrimination in the armed forces.

1944. The African American Ninety-ninth Pursuit Squadron flies its 500th mission in the Mediterranean Theater. Another African American unit, the Ninety-second Division, enters combat in Italy. On June 6, 500 African Americans land on Omaha Beach as part of the D-Day invasion of northern France. Among them is the 761st Tank Battalion, which spends 183 days in action and is cited for conspicuous courage. Also cited in January of 1945 is the 969th Field Artillery Battalion for their support in the defense of Bastogne.

1944. The restriction of African American seamen to shore duty ends, as does the exclusion of African Americans from the Coast Guard and Marine Corps. The War Department officially ends segregation in all army posts, but the order is widely ignored.

1944. Washington, D.C. In the case of *Smith v. Allwright*, the U.S. Supreme Court rules that "white primaries" violate the provisions of the Fifteenth Amendment.

1945. Italy. African American troops are at the forefront of victorious assaults in Germany and northern Italy. The use of African American troops in World War II, however, is more limited than in World War I or the Spanish-American War. Despite efforts by some enlightened naval officers, over 90 percent of African Americans in the U.S. Navy are still messmen when the war ends.

1945. New York. The first state Fair Employment Practices Commission is established in New York as a result of the Ives-Quinn Law penalizing discrimination against Jews and African Americans.

1945. Washington, D.C. Congress denies funds to the federal Fair Employment Practices Commission, which was established during the war to enforce fair employment policies.

1946. Washington, D.C. The U.S. Supreme Court rules in *Morgan v. Commonwealth of Virginia* that segregation on interstate buses is unconstitutional.

1947. Jackie Robinson becomes the first African American to play major league baseball, breaking the national pastime's color barrier.

1947. Atlanta, Georgia. The Southern Regional Council releases figures that demonstrate that only 12 percent of the African Americans in the Deep South (nearly 600,000) meet voting qualifications. In the states of Louisiana, Alabama, and Mississippi, the figure is approximately 3 percent. In Tennessee, more than 25 percent of adult African Americans meet the state voting requirements.

1947. CORE's first "freedom ride" travels through Southern states to press for the integration of transportation facilities.

1947. Tuskegee, Alabama. Statistics indicate that 3,426 African Americans have been lynched in the United States during the 1882–1947 period. Of these, 1,217 were lynched in the 1890–1900 decade. From 1947 to 1962, twelve African Americans were lynched.

1947. Washington, D.C. The Truman Committee on Civil Rights formally condemns racial injustice in America in the widely quoted report *To Secure these Rights.*

1948. California. The California Supreme Court declares the state statute banning racial intermarriage unconstitutional.

1948. New York City. Ralph Bunche is confirmed by the United Nations Security Council as acting UN mediator in Palestine.

1948. Washington, D.C. The U.S. Supreme Court in *Shelley v. Kraemer* rules that federal and state courts may not enforce restrictive covenants. However, the Court does not declare such covenants illegal. In a separate case, *Sipuel v. University of Oklahoma,* the Court holds that states are required to provide African Americans with the same educational opportunities as whites. President Truman issues Executive Order No. 9981 directing "equality of treatment and opportunity" in the armed forces and creates the Fair Practices Board of the Civil Service Commission to deal with complaints of discrimination in government employment.

1949. Connecticut. Connecticut becomes the first state in the Union to extend the jurisdiction of the Civil Rights Commission into the domain of public housing.

1949. Washington, D.C. Representative William L. Dawson becomes the first African American to head a congressional committee when he is named chairman of the House Committee on Government Operations.

1950. Yech'on, Republic of Korea. The African American Twenty-fourth Infantry Regiment recaptures the city of Yech'on, the first American victory in the Korean War.

1950. New York City. African American lawyer and judge Edith Sampson is appointed by President Truman as an alternate delegate to the United Nations, making her the first African American to officially represent the United States at the United Nations.

1950. Oslo, Norway. African American diplomat Ralph Bunche wins the Nobel Peace Prize for his 1940s efforts at diplomacy and mediation in Palestine.

1950. The 1950 census places the net ten-year African American emigration from the South at 1.6 million.

1950. Washington, D.C. Several U.S. Supreme Court decisions open university facilities to African Americans. In the case of *Henderson v. United States,* the Court rules that segregated tables on dining cars violate the provisions of the Interstate Commerce Act. A special committee reports to President Harry S. Truman that African American servicemen are still barred from many military specialties and training programs, but that the armed forces has largely been desegregated.

1952. In a series of legal maneuvers, the NAACP and other African American groups succeed in desegregating a number of colleges and high schools in Southern and border areas. In addition, public housing projects are opened to African Americans in some Northern and Midwestern cities and desegregation is achieved in several businesses and unions. A public swimming pool is integrated in Kansas City, a golf course in Louisville, and Ford's Theater in Baltimore.

1952. Tuskegee, Alabama. A Tuskegee report indicates that, for the first time in its seventy-one years of tabulation, no lynchings have occurred in the United States.

1953. Washington, D.C. District of Columbia Commissioners order the abolition of segregation in several district agencies. The fire department is among those which escape the mandate. The Defense Department orders an end to segregation in schools on military bases and in veterans hospitals.

1953. New York City. African American politician Hulan Jack is sworn in as borough president of Manhattan.

1953. Washington, D.C. The U.S. Supreme Court asks to rehear five school segregation cases first argued in 1942. Sensing a major opportunity, the NAACP puts 100 lawyers, scholars, and researchers to work in preparation. The NAACP also files a complaint with the Interstate Commerce Commission to execute earlier Supreme Court desegregation orders in transportation facilities.

1954, March 4. Washington, D.C. President Dwight D. Eisenhower appoints an African American, J. Ernest Wilkins, as undersecretary of labor.

1954, May 17. Washington, D.C. By a unanimous vote, the U.S. Supreme Court in the case of *Brown v. Board of Education of Topeka, Kansas* declares that "separate but equal" educational facilities are "inherently unequal" and that segregation is therefore unconstitutional. The decision overturns the "separate but equal" doctrine that has legalized segregation since 1896. In the case of *Hawkins v. Board of Control,* the Court rules that the University of Florida must admit African Americans regardless of any "public mischief" it might cause.

1954, September. In the autumn following the *Brown* decision, 150 formerly segregated school districts in eight states and the District of Columbia integrate. However, a

George E. C. Hayes, Thurgood Marshall, and James M. Nabrit, Washington, DC, 1954. *The three civil rights attorneys celebrate the U.S. Supreme Court's landmark decision in* Brown v. Board of Education, Topeka. **THE LIBRARY OF CONGRESS**

number of groups opposing integration emerge in the South. Most prominent among these are white citizens councils that soon claim 80,000 members and propose constitutional amendments reinstating segregation.

1954, October 1. Baltimore, Maryland. White parents and students protest the admission of African American students to Baltimore's Southern High School. Antidesegregation demonstrations are also staged in nearby Washington, D.C.

1954, October 1. Florida. State Attorney General Richard Ervin files a brief with the U.S. Supreme Court warning that violent resistance would result from any effort to force desegregation in Florida schools.

1954, October 30. Washington, D.C. The Department of Defense reports the end of "all-Negro" units in the U.S. Army. However, some bases still refuse to integrate. The Veterans Administration announces their hospitals have been desegregated, but the Department of Health, Education, and Welfare declares it will continue to give funds to segregated hospitals.

1954, November 13. Boca Raton, Florida. Governors attending the Southern Governors Conference pledge to uphold state control over schools and warn that forced school desegregation will create unrest which they claim does not currently exist in their states.

1955, January 7. New York City. Marian Anderson sings Ulrica in Giuseppe Verdi's *Un ballo in maschera,* making her the first African American to sing a solo role at the Metropolitan Opera House. Although opera arias had been a significant part of her singing career, this was the only role that she performed onstage.

1955, May 31. Washington, D.C. The U.S. Supreme Court orders school boards to draw up desegregation procedures. The Court asserts that school authorities have the responsibility of assessing and solving desegregation problems and must do so "with all deliberate speed." The decision reinforces the Court's ruling in *Brown v. Board of Education of Topeka, Kansas*. Reactions to this ruling in the South are mixed. Kansas, Missouri, Oklahoma, and Texas desegregate their school systems with minimal disruption. Georgia's Board of Education adopts a resolution revoking the license of any teacher who teaches integrated classes. Mississippi repeals its compulsory school-attendance law and establishes a branch of government for the sole purpose of maintaining segregation. White citizens councils in Mississippi initiate economic pressures against African Americans who try to register to vote, while more extreme groups resort to direct terror.

1955, July 14. Richmond, Virginia. The U.S. Circuit Court of Appeals rules that segregation on city buses is illegal. The Court claims that the same principle that outlawed segregation in public schools should be applied.

1955, August 31. Greenwood, Mississippi. Two white men are arrested in Greenwood on charges of kidnapping, beating, and shooting fifteen-year-old Emmett Till. Till, who allegedly whistled at and insulted a white woman, was found dead in the Tallahatchie River. Jurors acquit the defendants on grounds that the body could not be positively identified.

1955, November 25. Washington, D.C. In accordance with U.S. Supreme Court edicts, the Interstate Commerce Commission outlaws segregated buses and waiting rooms for interstate passengers. However, many communities ignore the order.

1955, December 1. Montgomery, Alabama. Rosa Parks takes a seat in the front of a city bus, refuses to surrender it to a white man, and is arrested. Four days later, the Reverend Martin Luther King Jr. urges the city's African American community to boycott the buses. This marks the beginning of the Montgomery bus boycott, which leads to the desegregation of Montgomery's city bus system the following year.

1956. Washington, D.C. In the case of *Flemming v. South Carolina Electric*, the U.S. Supreme Court strikes down a state statute requiring segregation on public transportation.

1956, February 3. Tuscaloosa, Alabama. African American student Autherine Lucy is admitted to the University of Alabama by court order, but riots ensue and she is expelled on a technicality.

1956, March 11. Washington, D.C. Southern members of the Senate, led by Harry Byrd of Virginia, launch a fight against school integration. Byrd obtains the signatures of 100 congressmen on a "Southern Manifesto," attacking the rulings of the U.S. Supreme Court.

1956, July 13. Washington, D.C. Southern members of the House of Representatives unite in opposition to an Eisenhower administration–sponsored civil rights bill. The bill would provide for the investigation of civil rights complaints and permit action by the U.S. attorney general in federal courts.

1956, September. By September of 1956, approximately 800 school districts containing 320,000 African American children are desegregated in compliance with the U.S. Supreme Court's 1954 decision. However, nearly 2.5 million African American children remain in segregated schools and there are still no desegregated districts in Virginia, North and South Carolina, Georgia, Florida, Mississippi, Alabama, and Louisiana.

1956, November 13. Washington, D.C. The U.S. Supreme Court rules that the segregation of city buses is unconstitutional.

1957. The Southern Christian Leadership Conference (SCLC) is formed by Martin Luther King Jr. and others to coordinate the activities of nonviolent groups devoted to integration and full citizenship for African Americans.

1957, February 26. Little Rock, Arkansas. Governor Orval Faubus signs four segregation bills enabling parents to

Rosa Parks, Montgomery, AL, December 5, 1955. *Four days after her arrest for refusing to surrender her seat on a Montgomery bus to a white man—and after being fined $1,000 plus court costs for violating the city's segregation ordinance for its buses—Parks (*left*) makes bond for an appeal to circuit court. On this same day, Martin Luther King Jr. launches the Montgomery bus boycott.* **AP IMAGES**

refuse to send their children to desegregated schools, authorizing the use of school district funds to pay legal expenses incurred in integration suits, creating a committee to make anti-integration studies, and requiring organizations such as the NAACP to publish membership rosters.

1957, April 9. Madison, Wisconsin. The state Supreme Court rules that African Americans can be refused membership in trade unions, since such organizations are voluntary associations.

1957, September 4. Little Rock, Arkansas. Nine African American students are turned away from Central High School by a white mob and the Arkansas National Guard when they arrive for classes. The National Guard, which was called to Little Rock by Governor Orval Faubus, is forced by court order to withdraw on September 20. As mobs of angry whites assemble outside of the school and the threat of mob violence escalates, President Dwight D. Eisenhower issues a proclamation on September 23 ordering an end to any obstruction to court-ordered integration. On September 24, the president issues Executive Order No. 10730 authorizing the use of federal troops to assist in the integration of Central High School.

1957, September 9. Washington, D.C. President Eisenhower signs a civil rights bill. The bill provides for the creation of a commission on civil rights to investigate allegations of civil rights and voting rights violations.

1958, February 19. New Orleans, Louisiana. The U.S. Court of Appeals rules that segregation on buses and streetcars in New Orleans is illegal. The Louisiana state assembly later passes a bill that stipulates that the first person seated in a bus's double seat can decide whether a rider of a different race may sit in the adjoining seat. The bill is vetoed by Governor Earl Long because it would require a white rider to request permission to sit next to an African American rider.

1958, April 14. Jackson, Mississippi. Governor J. P. Coleman asserts that African Americans in Mississippi are not ready to vote and vetoes a bill that would have given control of voter registration to a court-appointed registrar.

1958, July 16. Baton Rouge, Louisiana. Governor Earl Long signs a bill requiring that blood plasma be labeled according to the race of donor.

1960, February 1. Greensboro, North Carolina. Four African American students refuse to leave a segregated lunch counter, marking the beginning of sit-in protests throughout the South.

1960, April. Atlanta, Georgia. The Student Nonviolent Coordinating Committee (SNCC) is formed to organize student protest activities. Church "kneel-ins" and beach "wade-ins" soon join lunch counter and bus station sit-ins as effective means of protesting segregation.

1960, April 24. Biloxi, Mississippi. Rioting erupts when a group of African Americans attempts to swim at the city's 26-mile whites-only beach. A curfew is ordered by the mayor and riot police patrol the city. On April 27, the state legislature passes a law authorizing prison terms for anyone convicted of inciting a riot.

1960, May 6. Washington, D.C. President Eisenhower signs the Civil Rights Act of 1960. This act authorizes judges to appoint referees who can help African Americans register to vote in federal elections. The act also prohibits intimidation of African American voters through bombing and mob violence.

1960, July 31. New York City. Black Muslim leader Elijah Muhammad calls for the creation of a black state either in America or in Africa.

1960, August. As of August 1, sit-ins have led to the successful desegregation of lunch counters in fifteen American cities.

1960, September 8. New York City. New York governor Nelson Rockefeller, in an address at the National Urban League Conference, declares that the sit-ins are "an inspiration to the nation."

1960, October 3. The SCLC organizes voter "stand-ins" in several American cities to protest against the remaining barriers to African American voter registration.

1960, November 10. New Orleans, Louisiana. The city approves a plan to admit African American students to an all-white school. Meeting in a special session, the state legislature votes to take control of the city's school system and to have the schools closed on the day the African American students are scheduled to arrive. On November 14, U.S. marshals escort four African American students to the selected schools. On November 15, eleven whites are arrested in disturbances; on November 17 the city experiences severe rioting.

1960, November 14. Washington, D.C. In the case of *Gomillion v. Lightfoot*, the U.S. Supreme Court rules that a law designed to redraw the city boundaries of Tuskegee, Alabama, is unconstitutional. The case was brought before the Court after the city of Tuskegee redrew its borders, which excluded all but four or five of the city's 400 African American residents. The Court asserted that such legislation was in violation of the Fifteenth Amendment.

1960, November 23. Baton Rouge, Louisiana. At its annual convention, the Louisiana Teachers Association vows to resist all attempts to integrate the state's public schools.

1961, May 4. Washington, D.C. Several busloads of "freedom riders," organized by the Congress of Racial Equality (CORE), embark on a journey through the South to test the compliance of bus stations with the Interstate Commerce Commission's desegregation order. Many of the freedom riders are arrested or encounter angry mobs as they travel throughout the South.

1961, May 20. Montgomery, Alabama. A bus carrying "freedom riders" is attacked by a mob and set on fire. U.S. Attorney General Robert Kennedy orders federal marshals into Montgomery to maintain order. On May 21, a mob forms outside of the First Baptist Church, where Martin Luther King Jr. and Ralph Abernathy, pastor of the church, are conducting a meeting. The situation in Montgomery becomes so volatile that Governor John Patterson is forced to deploy the Alabama National Guard and declares martial law in the city.

1961, May 22. Washington, D.C. Upon hearing the case *Louisiana ex rel. Gremillion v. NAACP*, the U.S. Supreme Court unanimously rules that two Louisiana laws designed to harass the NAACP are unconstitutional. The laws required that organizations disclose members' names and attest that its officers are not affiliated with subversive activities.

1961, June 2. Montgomery, Alabama. Federal judge Frank Johnson Jr. issues a restraining order to prevent "freedom riders" from traveling through the state.

1961, September 29. Atlanta, Georgia. The Southern Regional Council reports that business establishments in more than 100 cities have been desegregated as a result of sit-ins.

1961, December 11. Washington, D.C. Ruling on its first cases pertaining to student sit-ins, the U.S. Supreme Court decides unanimously to reverse the conviction of sixteen African American students. The cases *Briscoe v. Louisiana*, *Garner v. Louisiana*, and *Hoston v. Louisiana* result from a Baton Rouge lunch counter sit-in staged in March 1960. The students, who had not been asked to leave by the proprietor, had refused a police order to leave and were charged with "disturbing the peace."

1962, February 26. Washington, D.C. The U.S. Supreme Court rules on a suit challenging Mississippi laws that require segregation in intrastate transportation. The case *Bailey v. Patterson* is remanded to district court since, as the Court contends, the issue is no longer litigable; no state may require racial segregation in either inter- or intrastate transportation.

1962, March 24. Columbia, South Carolina. The NAACP files suit in district court to prohibit the Orangeburg Regional Hospital from operating segregated facilities.

1962, May 2. Biloxi, Mississippi. A U.S. district court finds nine Mississippi laws requiring segregated travel accommodations unconstitutional.

1962, September 30. Jackson, Mississippi. Riots erupt on the campus of the University of Mississippi when James Meredith, a twenty-nine-year-old African American veteran, is admitted to the university by court order. Federal troops are sent to restore order.

The Reverends Martin Luther King Jr., Fred Shuttlesworth, and Ralph D. Abernathy, Birmingham, AL, 1963. *King, Shuttlesworth, and Abernathy* (left to right)*, early leaders of the Southern Christian Leadership Conference (SCLC), speak at a press conference in the midst of a major SCLC-led direct-action campaign targeting Birmingham's segregation system.* **AP IMAGES**

Bombing at Sixteenth Street Baptist Church, Birmingham, AL, 1963. *That year, on September 15, four African American children were killed in the bombing of the Sixteenth Street Baptist Church carried out by members of a Ku Klux Klan group.*
AP IMAGES. REPRODUCED BY PERMISSION.

1962, November 20. Washington, D.C. The Kennedy administration issues orders banning segregation in federally financed housing.

1963, April 3. Birmingham, Alabama. Martin Luther King Jr. targets Birmingham for a campaign against discrimination. The protesters are driven back by police armed with water hoses and attack dogs. The confrontation, which has been captured on film, awakens public opinion across the country.

1963, June 12. Jackson, Mississippi. Civil rights leader Medgar Evers is assassinated in the doorway of his home. Thousands attend a march mourning the death of Evers on June 15.

1963, August 28. Washington, D.C. Some 250,000 people gather at the Lincoln Memorial to demonstrate on behalf of the civil rights bill pending in Congress. The march has been organized by several civil rights organizations, including the NAACP, SCLC, CORE, the Urban League, and the Negro American Labor Council. Martin Luther King Jr., one of many scheduled speakers, gives what will become his most famous speech, "I Have a Dream."

1963, September. Less than 10 percent of African American public school students in the South attend integrated classes during the fall term. Governor George Wallace of Alabama declares: "I draw the line in the dust and toss the gauntlet before the feet of tyranny and I say, 'Segregation now, segregation tomorrow, segregation forever'."

1963, September 15. Birmingham, Alabama. Four African American children are killed in the bombing of the Sixteenth Street Baptist Church.

1963, November 22. Dallas, Texas. President John F. Kennedy, a major advocate of civil rights, is assassinated in Dallas, Texas. Kennedy's successor, Vice President Lyndon B. Johnson, promises to continue support for civil rights legislation.

1964, January 23. The Twenty-fourth Amendment to the Constitution is ratified, prohibiting the use of poll taxes in federal elections.

1964, March 8. New York City. Malcolm X leaves the Black Muslim organization, Nation of Islam, to form the Organization for Afro-American Unity—an organization emphasizing black nationalism and social action.

1964, June 2. Washington, D.C. A major civil rights bill, forbidding discrimination in public accommodations and employment, is signed into law by President Johnson.

1964, June 21. Philadelphia, Mississippi. Three young civil rights volunteers—James Chaney, Michael Schwerner, and Andrew Goodman—are murdered. A number of arrests on federal charges less severe than murder follow. Among the nineteen suspects are the sheriff and a deputy sheriff of Neshoba County. No convictions are obtained and charges are dismissed in December.

1964, June 25. St. Augustine, Florida. A mob attacks marchers protesting the city's prosegregation policies. State police watch as some fifty African Americans are prevented from using the city beach.

1964, July–August. New York and New Jersey. On July 18 riots erupt in Harlem. One person is killed, 140 injured, and 500 arrested. This is the first of many large riots to strike urban African American neighborhoods during the 1960s. Shortly after the Harlem disturbances, riots erupt in Brooklyn, Rochester, Jersey City, and Paterson, New Jersey.

1964, December 10. Oslo, Norway. Martin Luther King Jr. is awarded the Nobel Peace Prize.

1965, January 2. Selma, Alabama. Martin Luther King Jr. announces his intention to call for demonstrations if African Americans in Alabama are not permitted to register to vote in appropriate numbers. Twelve African Americans, including King himself, book rooms on January 18 at Selma's Hotel Albert, becoming the first African Americans accepted at this formerly all-white hotel. While signing the guest register, King is accosted by a white segregationist who is later fined $100 and given a sixty-day jail sentence. On January 19, Sheriff James G. Clark arrests sixty-two African Americans in Selma after they refuse to enter the Dallas County courthouse through an alley door. Clark and his deputies arrest 150 other African American voter registration applicants the next day. A federal district court order issued on January 23 bars law enforcement officials from interfering with voter registration and warns that violence against African American voters will not be tolerated.

1965, January 15. Philadelphia, Mississippi. A federal grand jury hands down indictments for the June 1964 slaying of three civil rights workers—James Chaney, Andrew Goodman, and Michael Schwerner—in Philadelphia, Mississippi. The following day, eighteen men, including two law enforcement officers, are arrested. On February 25, U.S. district court judge W. Harold Cox dismisses a federal indictment against seventeen of the accused.

1965, January 18. Washington, D.C. Ruling on the case *Cox v. Louisiana*, the U.S. Supreme Court reverses the conviction of protesters charged with disturbing the peace.

1965, February 1. Selma, Alabama. Reverend Martin Luther King Jr. and some 770 African Americans are arrested during protest demonstrations. King remains in jail for four days before posting bond. During this time, more than 3,000 persons are arrested. On February 4, a federal district court bars the county board of registrars from administering a literacy test to voter applicants or from rejecting their application on petty technicalities.

1965, February 21. New York City. Malcolm X (also known as El-Hajj Malik El-Shabazz), a thirty-nine-year-old black nationalist leader and former member of the Black Muslim sect, is shot to death in the Audubon Ballroom as he is about to deliver an address before a rally of several hundred followers. Following the murder, Black Muslim headquarters in New York and San Francisco are burned, and most Muslim leaders are placed under heavy police guard. Three African Americans—Talmadge Hayer, Norman 3X Butler, and Thomas 15X Johnson—are later taken into custody and charged with first-degree murder. The trio is convicted and sentenced to life imprisonment on March 10, 1966.

1965, March 26. Washington, D.C. President Lyndon B. Johnson announces the arrest of four Ku Klux Klan members in connection with the murder of Viola Gregg Liuzzo. Liuzzo, a thirty-nine-year-old white civil rights worker from Detroit, was slain on a Lowndes County highway during the Selma-to-Montgomery Freedom March. The president declares war on the Klan, calling it a "hooded society of bigots." Robert M. Shelton Jr., imperial wizard of the United Klans of America, Inc., answers the president's charges by branding him "a damn liar." On March 30, the House Un-American Activities Committee votes to open a full investigation of the activities of the Klan. The committee chairman, a Louisiana Democrat, asserts that the Klan is committing "shocking crimes."

1965, July 13. Washington, D.C. Thurgood Marshall is nominated as solicitor general of the United States, the first African American person to hold this office.

1965, August 6. Washington, D.C. President Johnson signs the 1965 Voting Rights Act, providing for the registration by federal examiners of those black voters turned away by state officials.

1965, August 11. Los Angeles, California. The arrest and alleged mistreatment of an African American youth by white policemen sparks an orgy of looting, burning, and rioting in the predominantly African American section ofWatts. Thousands of National Guardsmen and state police rush to quell the violence. The rioting, which lasts six days, claims the lives of thirty-five people and causes nearly $46 million in property damage. On August 20, President Johnson denounces the Los Angeles rioters, comparing them to Ku Klux Klan extremists. He declares that the existence of legitimate grievances in Watts is no justification for lawlessness. "We cannot ... in one breath demand laws to protect the rights of all our citizens, and then turn our back ... and ... allow laws to be broken that protect the safety of our citizens."

1966. Oakland, California. Huey P. Newton and Bobby Seale found the Black Panther Party.

1966, January 13. Washington, D.C. President Lyndon B. Johnson names Robert Weaver as head of the Department of Housing and Urban Development. Weaver is the first African American appointed to serve in a presidential cabinet in U.S. history. Lisle Carter, also African American, is named as an assistant secretary in the Department of Health, Education, and Welfare. Constance Baker Motley, former NAACP lawyer and borough president of Manhattan, becomes the first African American woman to be named to a federal judgeship.

1966, February 7. Lowndes County, Alabama. A federal court finds Lowndes County, Alabama, guilty of "gross, systematic exclusion of members of the African American race from jury duty." County officials are ordered to prepare a new jury list. Lowndes County is also ordered to desegregate its school system within two years, to close twenty-four "blacks-only" schools, and to introduce remedial programs designed to close the educational gap between white and African American students.

1966, February 23. Washington, D.C. In the case of *Brown v. Louisiana*, the U.S. Supreme Court reverses the convictions of five African Americans charged with disturbing the peace when they refused to leave a whites-only reading room in a public library.

1966, March 25. Washington, D.C. In the case of *Harper v. Virginia State Board of Elections*, the U.S. Supreme

Court outlaws the use of poll taxes in state elections. The ruling upholds the Twenty-Fourth Amendment, which bars the use of such taxes in federal elections.

1966, June 6. Tennessee. James Meredith is shot shortly after beginning a 220-mile voting rights pilgrimage from Memphis, Tennessee, to Jackson, Mississippi. Aubrey James Norvell is arrested at the scene and taken to jail where, according to authorities, he admits to the shooting. Meredith suffers multiple injuries, but recovers.

1966, June 26. Jackson, Mississippi. The march begun by James Meredith ends with a rally in front of the state capitol in Jackson. Addresses are delivered by Meredith, Martin Luther King Jr., and Stokely Carmichael, who urges the 15,000 African Americans in attendance to "build a power base ... so strong that we will bring them [whites] to their knees every time they mess with us." The march results in the registration of about 4,000 African American voters.

1966, July 10. Chicago, Illinois. Martin Luther King Jr. addresses a predominantly African American crowd of 30,000 to 45,000 at Soldier Field and launches a drive to make Chicago an "open city." The rally is sponsored by the Coordinating Council of Committee Organizations, a coalition consisting of some forty-five local civil rights groups. From July 12 to 15, violence erupts on Chicago's west side in protest of a decision by Chicago police to shut off a fire hydrant that had been opened illegally to give African American children relief from the stifling heat. Two African Americans are killed, scores of police and civilians wounded, and 372 persons are arrested.

1966, July 18. Cleveland, Ohio. Shootings, firebombings, and looting spread throughout Cleveland's east side. Four people are killed and fifty are injured. Most of the 164 persons arrested are charged with looting. The riot results in widespread property damage.

1966, September 16. Leontyne Price opens the new Metropolitan Opera House at Lincoln Center. She premieres Samuel Barber's newly commissioned opera, *Antony and Cleopatra.*

1967, January. Washington, D.C. Representative Adam Clayton Powell Jr. of New York is stripped of his chairmanship of the House Committee on Education and Labor and barred from assuming his seat in the Ninetieth Congress. A congressional committee investigating the case later proposes public censure, loss of seniority, and a $40,000 fine. Powell and his lawyers indicate their intention to challenge the constitutionality of this decision in federal court.

1967, February 15. Washington, D.C. President Lyndon B. Johnson asks Congress to pass new civil rights legislation pertaining to the sale and rental of housing. In a special address to Congress, Johnson outlines the scope of the proposed bill. The bill, Johnson states, is designed to end discrimination in jury selection, permit the Equal Employment Opportunity Commission to issue cease-and-desist orders, extend the life of the Commission on Civil Rights, and authorize appropriations for the Community Relations Service. The bill would enable individuals to file damage suits in housing discrimination cases. Violators of the bill would be subject to court orders and fines issued by the secretary of the Department of Housing and Urban Development.

1967, March 1. Washington, D.C. By a vote of 307–116, the U.S. House of Representatives bars Adam Clayton Powell Jr. from the Ninetieth Congress. Powell immediately files suit in U.S. district court to combat his ouster.

1967, March 29. The Fifth Circuit Court of Appeals upholds the legality of revised federal school-desegregation guidelines. The court, in an eight–four ruling, calls for the desegregation of all students, teachers, school transportation facilities, and school-related activities in six Southern states. The guidelines establish rough percentage goals to be used in determining compliance with the Civil Rights Act of 1964.

1967, May 3. Montgomery, Alabama. A federal district court overturns an Alabama statute designed to prevent school desegregation. The court rules that no state may nullify the action of "a federal department or agency without initiating Court action," which only the U.S. Supreme Court can review.

1967, May 10. Jackson, Mississippi. An African American delivery man, Benjamin Brown, is shot and killed during riots on the campus of Jackson State College. Within full view of police, Brown is left at the scene unattended until he is taken to the University Hospital by African American bystanders. The police, unable to contain the demonstrators, are reinforced by more than 1,000 National Guardsmen.

1967, June 2. Boston, Massachusetts. Rioting erupts in Boston's predominantly African American section of Roxbury. The disturbance occurs in the wake of an attempt by welfare mothers to barricade themselves inside a building as a protest against police brutality. The rioting results in the arrest of nearly 100 people, while scores of others are severely injured.

1967, June 12. Newark, New Jersey. The "long hot summer" begins in earnest in Newark, scene of the most devastating riot to sweep an urban center since the 1965 Watts uprising.

1967, June 13. Washington, D.C. Thurgood Marshall is appointed an associate justice of the U.S. Supreme Court, the first African American so designated.

1967, June 19. Washington, D.C. U.S. district court judge J. Skelly Wright rules that de facto segregation of African Americans in the District of Columbia is unconstitutional and orders the complete desegregation of the district's schools by the fall.

1967, June 27. Buffalo, New York. Three days of rioting result in more than eighty-five injuries, 205 arrests, and property damage estimated at $100,000.

1967, July 19. Washington, D.C. The U.S. House of Representatives passes legislation which states that it is a federal crime to cross state lines or to use interstate facilities for the purpose of inciting a riot. The bill is aimed at alleged professional agitators who travel from city to city to inflame the people. New York's Emanuel Celler finds the bill "neither preventive nor curative" and fears it will only arouse African American hostility even further.

1967, July 20. Newark, New Jersey. Despite objections by New Jersey governor Hughes, a four-day conclave of African American leaders, many of them Black Power advocates, convenes in Newark. Militancy and a call for separate nationhood dominate the meeting. One participant at the conference, Alfred Black of the Newark Human Relations Commission, states that "the black today is either a radical or an Uncle Tom. There is no middle ground."

1967, July 23. Detroit, Michigan. Rioting erupts in the early morning hours. By July 29, over 7,000 persons are arrested and forty-three persons killed in one of the worst urban riots in U.S. history.

1967, July 27. Washington, D.C. President Lyndon B. Johnson appoints a blue-ribbon panel to "investigate the origins of the recent disorders in our cities." The president instructs the commission to set aside political considerations and concern itself solely with the health and safety of American society and its citizens. On August 10, the National Advisory Commission on Civil Disorders urges President Johnson to increase the number of African Americans in the army and air national guard. The panel also recommends increased riot-control training for the guard, as well as a review of promotion procedures. The recommendations, delivered in a letter to President Johnson, are forwarded to U.S. Defense Secretary Robert McNamara.

1967, August 14. Dorchester County, Maryland. H. Rap Brown is indicted *in absentia* by a grand jury on charges of inciting to riot, arson, and other related actions which threaten the public peace. Brown is arrested in New York on August 19 and charged with carrying a gun across state lines while under indictment. After strenuous objections are voiced by his white lawyer, William Kunstler, Brown's bail is reduced to $15,000. On August 22, he is released from jail in time to address a crowd of 100 African Americans on the steps of the Foley Square courthouse. Pointing to whites nearby, Brown says: "That's your enemy out there. And you better not forget, because I ain't going to."

1967, August 19. New Haven, Connecticut. Nearly 450 persons are arrested during five days of looting, arson, and vandalism. No serious injuries are reported, and no shots are fired by police despite frequent curfew violations.

1967, October 20. Philadelphia, Mississippi. An all-white federal jury of five men and seven women returns a guilty verdict in a retrial for the 1964 murder of three civil rights workers near Philadelphia, Mississippi. Seven men are convicted of conspiracy. However, eight defendants are acquitted, and three are declared victims of a mistrial. Among the guilty are Chief Deputy Sheriff Cecil Price and Sam Bowers, imperial wizard of the Ku Klux Klan.

1968, February 5. Orangeburg, South Carolina. Three African American youths are shot to death and more than thirty people are wounded in a racial outburst involving police and students at South Carolina State College. The violence is the culmination of student protests against the segregation of a local bowling alley. On February 7, the campus is sealed off and classes are suspended in the wake of rock and bottle-throwing incidents. On February 8, three students are fired on by police who mistakenly believe one of their troopers has been shot. In reality, the trooper was knocked down by a piece of lumber thrown by a demonstrator. On February 9, Governor McNair orders a curfew and attributes the violence to "Black Power" advocates. On February 11, local African Americans call for the removal of the National Guard and announce plans for a boycott of white businesses. The city leaders counter by establishing a Human Relations Commission, which resolves to prevent further outbreaks of violence. On February 24, the Southern Regional Council issues a report analyzing the Orangeburg upheaval. The report blames the outbreak of violence on the emotional appeal of black power to young African Americans, overreaction by white citizens and police, feelings of hopelessness among African Americans, and the expectations by whites that police power and military force must be utilized to cope with all forms of public demonstrations.

1968, February 29. Washington, D.C. President Lyndon B. Johnson's National Advisory Commission on Civil Disorders issues an exhaustive report on the causes of the civil disorders that disrupted the nation in 1967. The commission identifies the major cause of the rioting as the existence of two separate bodies in America—"one black, one white, separate and unequal." It charges that white racism, more than anything else, was the chief catalyst in the already explosive mixture of discrimination, poverty, and frustration that ignited so many urban ghettos in the tragic summer of 1967. It reminds white America how deeply it is implicated in the existence of the ghetto. "White institutions created it, white institutions maintain it, and white society condones it." To overcome this terrible and crushing legacy, the commission implores the nation to initiate a massive and sustained commitment to action and reform, and it appeals for unprecedented levels of "funding and performance" in housing, education, employment, welfare, law enforcement, and the mass media.

1968, March 11. Washington, D.C. The U.S. Senate passes the Civil Rights Bill of 1968. Among its major provisions are sweeping housing and anti-riot measures which go far beyond the federal protection offered to civil rights workers in the 1967 House version of the bill.

1968, March 29. Memphis, Tennessee. A teenage African American youth is slain after a protest march led by Martin Luther King Jr. deteriorates into violence and looting. The march marks the culmination of six weeks of labor strike activity involving the sanitation workers of the city—90 percent of whom are African American. Civil rights leaders and African American ministers call for a boycott of downtown businesses and urge massive civil disobedience to express support for the strikers. Such action broadens the focus of the strike and transforms it into a general civil rights action. On the day of the march, disturbances begin almost immediately. Some African American students who have been refused the right to leave school and participate in the march begin pelting police with bricks; others smash department store windows along Beale Street. Most of the 6,000 to 20,000 marchers demonstrate peacefully. City and county police join the National Guard in quelling the disturbances. After King is spirited away to safety at the nearby Lorraine Motel, tear gas is fired at the crowds. More than 150 people are arrested, forty of them on looting charges.

1968, April 4. Memphis, Tennessee. The world is shocked by the assassination of Martin Luther King Jr. Felled by a single bullet, King is pronounced dead at St. Joseph's Hospital at 7:05 p.m. CST, barely one hour after the shooting. Attorney General Ramsey Clark, on hand to conduct the preliminary investigation in person, declares that the early evidence points to the crime as being the work of a single assassin. Witnesses report seeing a white man running from the doorway of a rooming house at 420 South Main Street minutes after the shooting. The killing triggers a wave of violence in over 100 cities including such urban centers as Baltimore, Chicago, Kansas City, Missouri, and Washington, D.C. Some 70,000 federal troops and National Guardsmen are dispatched to restore order. Official figures report forty-six dead: forty-one African Americans, five whites. Thousands are injured and

Funeral Procession for Martin Luther King Jr., Atlanta, GA, April 9, 1968. *After funeral services were held at Ebenezer Baptist Church, King's casket was carried in a mule-drawn wagon to Morehouse College, his alma mater, where a general memorial service was conducted. King was buried at South View Cemetery in Atlanta, though his body was later moved to a site next to Ebenezer Baptist Church.* AP IMAGES. REPRODUCED BY PERMISSION.

arrested. On April 5, Reverend Ralph Abernathy is named to succeed King and discloses that SCLC's first public gesture will be to lead the march King himself was planning. Three days later, Coretta Scott King takes her place in the front ranks of the marchers, locking arms with two of the 42,000 people on hand for the demonstration. King's body is put on public view at Ebenezer Baptist Church in Atlanta, Georgia, on April 6. He is buried at South View Cemetery on April 9 after funeral services are held at the church and a general memorial service is conducted at Morehouse College, his alma mater.

1968, April 10. Washington, D.C. The assassination of Martin Luther King Jr. moves the U.S. House of Representatives to submit to President Johnson a Senate-passed civil rights bill prohibiting racial discrimination in the sale or rental of 80 percent of the nation's housing. Johnson signs the measure on April 11 and counsels the nation to stay on the road to progress by recognizing "the process of law."

1968, May 11. Washington, D.C. Caravans of people representing the Poor People's Campaign begin arriving in Washington, D.C. The Defense Department alerts "selected troop units" to help District of Columbia police in the event of violence. On Mother's Day, May 12, Coretta Scott King leads a march of welfare mothers from twenty cities and declares at a subsequent rally that she will try to enlist the support of all the nation's women "in a campaign of conscience." The next day Ralph Abernathy, clad in blue denims and using carpenter's tools, presides at the christening of Resurrection City, the plywood shanty town erected within walking distance of the White House and the Capitol. Abernathy is able to report, as the campaign draws to a close, that certain gains have been recorded. The Department of Agriculture, for instance, agrees to "provide food to the neediest counties in this country." The U.S. Senate approves a bill to increase low-income housing construction and the Office of Economic Opportunity (OEO) allocates $25 million for expanded programs, including one encouraging participation from poor people.

1968, June 5. Los Angeles, California. Senator Robert Kennedy, a champion of civil rights, is shot and mortally wounded moments after leaving a rally celebrating

President Lyndon B. Johnson Signing the Civil Rights Act of 1968. *With various members of Congress and Supreme Court Justice Thurgood Marshall (*far right*) watching, Johnson signs what is commonly called the Fair Housing Act. The act was designed to end discrimination based on race, color, religion, or national origin in the sale or rental of 80 percent of the nation's housing.* AP IMAGES

his victory over Eugene McCarthy in the California Democratic primary. Kennedy dies the following day.

1968, June 8. London. James Earl Ray, alleged assassin of Martin Luther King Jr., is arrested.

1968, July 23. Cleveland, Ohio. Racial violence erupts in Cleveland's Glenville district, resulting in the deaths of eleven persons, eight of them African American, and three white policemen. Mayor Carl Stokes helps to restore order after a night of burning and looting which results in over $1 million worth of property damage. Over 3,000 National Guardsmen are on the scene, but they are not widely utilized. Ahmed (Fred) Evans, a thirty-seven-year-old antipoverty worker and head of the Black Nationalists of New Libya, is blamed for starting the disturbances. On June 26, Ahmed Evans is arraigned on three charges of first-degree murder.

1968, July 27. Washington, D.C. The Kerner Commission releases preliminary findings that indicate a sharp rise in the number of African Americans who accept urban riots as a justifiable or inevitable response to conditions prevailing in the nation's ghettos.

1968, August 7. Miami, Florida. Two days of looting, fire bombing, and shooting in the African American section of Miami culminate in Florida governor Claude Kirk's decision to summon the National Guard to quell the disorders. Despite Ralph Abernathy's plea for an end to the violence, crowds of African Americans battle police over an eight-block area. On August 8, three African Americans are killed in gun battles with law enforcement officials. Although Dade County mayor Chuck Hall accuses outsiders of instigating the trouble, the 10 percent unemployment rate among African Americans in the sixteen-to-twenty-two age bracket is cited as a major factor contributing to the violence.

1968, September 8. California. Black Panther Huey P. Newton is tried and convicted of manslaughter in the October 28, 1967, shooting death of a white policeman. Nearly three weeks later, Newton is sentenced to two to fifteen years imprisonment. The trial and the conviction introduce the nation at large to a new and formidable Black Panther Party.

1968, October 8. Washington, D.C. Some 250 African Americans protest the fatal shooting of an African American pedestrian by a policeman. Demonstrators set fires and block traffic until police reinforcements disperse them with tear gas. The policeman is eventually exonerated of all charges by a federal grand jury.

1968, December 1. New Jersey. Three members of the Black Panthers are arrested on charges of carrying out a machine gun attack on a Jersey City police station on November 29. A Black Panther spokesman claims that a December 1 bombing of party headquarters in Newark is in response to the Jersey City attack. A police sergeant cites the arrest of seven Newark Panthers on November 28 as the cause of the precinct attack.

1969, January 3. Washington, D.C. After a long and bitter debate concerning his qualifications and conduct, the House of Representatives votes to seat Adam Clayton Powell Jr. The House, however, fines him $25,000 for alleged misuse of payroll funds and travel allowances and demotes him to freshman status by stripping him of his seniority rank.

1969, February 6. Washington, D.C. President Nixon appoints James Farmer as an assistant secretary of the Department of Health, Education, and Welfare; Arthur Fletcher as an assistant secretary of the Department of Labor; and William Brown III, as chairman of the Equal Employment Opportunity Commission.

1969, June 6. Houston, Texas. Testimony released in a federal court indicates that the telephones of Martin Luther King Jr. and Elijah Muhammad were tapped by the FBI, despite the fact that President Lyndon B. Johnson had ordered a halt to all wiretaps in 1965.

1969, June 16. Washington, D.C. The U.S. Supreme Court rules that the suspension of Representative Adam Clayton Powell Jr. by the House of Representatives is unconstitutional.

1969, July 6. New York City. James Forman of the National Black Economic Development Conference receives a check for $15,000 from the Washington Square United Methodist Church. The church is the first predominantly white organization to support Forman's demand that American churches pay $500 million in reparations for helping to perpetuate slavery.

1969, August 1. Washington, D.C. The U.S. Justice Department files suit against the state of Georgia to end segregation in its schools. Governor Lester G. Maddox condemns the action as criminal and declares the state will "win the war against these tyrants."

1969, August 19. California. Black Panther leader Bobby Seale is arrested for the May 19 murder of alleged Panther informer Alex Rackley in New Haven, Connecticut. Bobby Seale's defense attorney accuses the Justice Department of initiating a national campaign to intimidate and harass the Black Panther Party. Seale is later extradited to Connecticut.

1969, August 25. Pittsburgh, Pennsylvania. Five construction sites are closed by several hundred African American construction workers and members of the Black Construction Coalition to protest "discriminatory hiring practices." Four hundred angry white workers stage counterdemonstrations on August 28 and 29 to protest the work stoppage.

1969, September 2. Hartford, Connecticut. After a relatively quiet summer, the nation is stunned when Hartford becomes the scene of widespread civil disorders, including fire bombings and sniping. Scores of people are placed under arrest, and a dusk-to-dawn curfew is imposed.

1969, September 23. Washington, D.C. Secretary of Labor George P. Schultz orders federally assisted construction projects in Philadelphia to follow the guidelines for minority hiring suggested in the so-called Philadelphia Plan.

1969, October 29. Washington, D.C. Ruling in the case of *Alexander v. Holmes County Board of Education*, the U.S. Supreme Court orders an end to all school segregation. The decision replaces the Warren Court's doctrine of "all deliberate speed," and is regarded as a setback for the Nixon administration.

1970, January 2. Washington, D.C. FBI director J. Edgar Hoover claims that, in 1969, there were over 100 attacks on police by "hate-type" African American groups, such as the Black Panthers.

1970, January 3. Mississippi. Governor John Bell Williams announces his intention to submit to the state legislature a proposal to authorize income tax credits of up to $500 a year for contributors to "private" educational institutions. The plan is designed to create a "workable alternative" to school desegregation. That same day, the Department of Health, Education, and Welfare reports that a comprehensive survey indicates that 61 percent of the nation's African American students and 65.6 percent of its white students attended segregated schools in 1968. On January 5, African American children are enrolled in three formerly all-white Mississippi districts under the watchful eyes of federal marshals and Justice Department officials. Scores of white parents picket the schools, while others keep their children home or send them to private schools.

1970, January 10. Georgia. Four Southern governors, Maddox of Georgia, Brewer of Alabama, McKeithen of Louisiana, and Kirk of Florida, promise to reject all busing plans designed for their states by the federal government or the courts. Maddox asks the state legislature to abolish compulsory attendance; McKeithen reveals no plan, but describes himself as "drawing the line in the dust"; Brewer denies that the courts have the constitutional authority to order busing as a device to achieve racial balance and promises to use his full executive powers to prevent it; Kirk vows to issue an executive order to block further desegregation of Florida schools.

1970, January 12. Washington, D.C. The U.S. Supreme Court refuses to review the ruling of an Ohio state court, which upholds an equal employment plan comparable to the Nixon administration's Philadelphia Plan. The plan requires state contractors to give assurances that they will employ a specified number of African American workers in projects constructed with federal funds or sponsored completely by the federal government. The Ohio contractor who brought suit in the case had refused to provide such assurances.

1970, January 15. Though it is not yet a federal holiday, the birthday of Martin Luther King Jr. is celebrated with impressive ceremonies, eulogies, and church services in many parts of the country. Public schools are closed in many cities; in others, they are kept open for formal study of King's life and work. In Atlanta, Coretta Scott King dedicates the Martin Luther King Jr. Memorial Center, which includes his home, the Ebenezer Baptist Church, and the crypt housing his remains.

1970, January 19. Washington, D.C. G. Harrold Carswell's nomination to the U.S. Supreme Court draws the immediate fire of civil rights advocates. On January 21, the NAACP condemns Carswell's "prosegregation record." Two days later, the SCLC's Ralph Abernathy sends a telegram to Senate leaders pleading for "reassurance to the black community that there is . . . understanding and support . . . for our needs." AFL-CIO President George Meany calls the appointment "a slap in the face to the nation's black citizens." Testifying before the Senate Judiciary Committee on January 27, Carswell states: "I am not a racist. I have no notions, secretive or otherwise, of racial superiority." This statement contrasts sharply with a 1948 remark that Carswell would yield to no man "in the firm, vigorous belief in the principles of white supremacy."

1970, February 6. Denver, Colorado. Approximately one-third of Denver school buses are destroyed by bombs in an attempt by segregationists to disrupt the city's school integration plans.

1970, February 16. Washington, D.C. President Richard M. Nixon establishes a cabinet-level task force to assist and counsel local school districts which have been ordered to desegregate their school immediately. The objective is to spare the public school system undue disruption while, at the same time, ensuring compliance with the law. On February 18 the Senate passes, by a fifty-six to thirty-six vote, an amendment to deny federal funds to school districts whose racial imbalance is the result of residential segregation. On February 19, Southerners in the House and Senate incorporate riders into two appropriation bills designed to restore "freedom-of-choice" school plans and to prevent the federal government from resorting to busing as a vehicle to promote racial balance.

1970, February 21. Texas. Texas governor Preston Smith recommends a statewide referendum to give voters the opportunity to approve or reject integrated public school busing. Governors Maddox of Georgia and McKeithen of Louisiana sign bills prohibiting busing and student/teacher transfers to achieve racial balance. Governor Brewer calls a special session of the legislature to sponsor a similar bill for Alabama.

1970, February 28. Washington, D.C. A memo written by Daniel Patrick Moynihan to President Richard M. Nixon is revealed. In the memo, Moynihan, domestic adviser to the president, counseled him that "the time may have come when the issue of race could benefit from a period of benign neglect." Moynihan later claims that the memo was intended to suggest ways that the "extraordinary black progress" in the last decade could be "consolidated." However, African American leaders, including Bayard Rustin and Representative John Conyers, charge that the memo is "symptomatic of a calculated, aggressive, systematic effort of the Nixon administration to wipe out civil rights progress of the past twenty years."

1970, March 6. Mississippi. The state Senate approves a tax relief bill designed to grant financial support to white parents who intend to enroll their children in private academies.

1970, March 9. Washington, D.C. The U.S. Supreme Court orders the Memphis school system to end racial segregation and remands the case to a lower court, where it issues instructions to develop an effective desegregation plan.

1970, April 7. Detroit, Michigan. The school board approves a busing plan for some 3,000 high school students and announces the initiation of a decentralization plan aimed at dispersing white students among the city's secondary schools. In Detroit, 63 percent of the system's 294,000 students are nonwhite, as are 42 percent of the teachers.

1970, May 12. Augusta, Georgia. Six African Americans are shot and twenty other people are wounded during a night of violence punctuated by looting, burning, and sniper activity. The immediate cause of the violence is said to be the killing of an African American youth in a county jail a few days earlier. Autopsies of African Americans slain during the protests indicate that they were shot in the back. The *New York Times* later reports that at least three of the dead were unarmed bystanders.

1970, May 14. Jackson, Mississippi. Two African American students are shot and killed after a night of violence outside a women's dormitory at Jackson State College. Witnesses charge that police simply moved in and indiscriminately blasted the residence hall with shotguns. President Richard M. Nixon dispatches Justice Department officials to search out the facts, but contradictory explanations make it impossible to assemble a wholly coherent story. On May 17, the Mississippi United Front vows to provide students and other groups with independent protection.

1970, May 23. Atlanta, Georgia. A five-day, 100-mile march against repression ends in downtown Atlanta with a rally by the SCLC and the NAACP. Speakers at the rally include Ralph Abernathy, Coretta Scott King, and Senator George McGovern. The speakers condemn racism, the Vietnam War, student killings at Kent State and Jackson State, and alleged police brutality in Augusta.

1970, July 10. Washington, D.C. The Internal Revenue Service announces its intention to tax private academies practicing racial discrimination in their admissions policies. The greatest impact of the policy is expected to be felt in the South. The new policy promises these schools sufficient flexibility to avoid immediate revocation of their tax-exempt status.

1970, August 7. San Rafael, California. A dramatic shootout results in the death of Superior Court Judge Harold Haley and three African Americans on trial. Later investigation traces the sale of the weapons used in the shootout to Angela Davis, controversial UCLA professor and self-admitted Communist. Davis flees the state following the trial and is placed on the FBI's ten most-wanted list.

1970, September. Some 300,000 African American children are integrated in over 200 Southern school districts. However, parental boycotts and delaying tactics by states and cities slow the pace of desegregation. Whites who are opposed to desegregation are encouraged by the Nixon administration's "Southern policy," which has delayed enforcement of integration orders. Nevertheless, the Internal Revenue Service continues to revoke the tax-exempt status of all-white private academies that refuse to admit African American students.

1970, October 13. New York City. Angela Davis is arrested and arraigned in federal court on charges of unlawful flight to avoid prosecution for her alleged role in the August 7 killing of superior court judge Harold Haley.

1970, November 5. Henderson, North Carolina. Violence erupts when African Americans protest the reopening of a segregated school. The National Guard is called out to restore order and over 100 arrests are made.

1970, December 30. Philadelphia, Pennsylvania. The U.S. Court of Appeals for the Third Circuit rules that the Department of Housing and Urban Development must promote fair housing when it considers applications for mortgage insurance and rent supplements.

1971, February 4. Washington, D.C. Eight African American federal employees file suit in federal court claiming that the Federal Service Entrance Examination, the principal test for qualifying college graduates for civil service posts, is "culturally and racially discriminatory."

1971, March 8. Media, Pennsylvania. Files stolen from a Federal Bureau of Investigation (FBI) office and released to the press reveal that in November 1970, J. Edgar Hoover ordered an investigation of all groups "organized to project the demands of black [college] students, because they posed a threat to the nation's stability and security."

1971, March 29. Washington, D.C. President Richard M. Nixon meets with the Congressional Black Caucus, which had been trying to schedule a meeting with him for several months. The African American members of Congress request increased attention to welfare services, desegregation, housing, and social justice programs.

President Nixon reportedly promises stronger enforcement of civil rights laws.

1971, May 5. Brooklyn. A riot erupts in Brooklyn's Brownsville section after thousands of residents take to the streets to protest cuts in state welfare, Medicaid, food stamps, and educational programs.

1971, May 17. Washington, D.C. Senator George McGovern of South Dakota urges the government to divert $31 billion of current federal spending to an effort to end racial discrimination by the end of the century. Milton Eisenhower, former chairman of President Lyndon B. Johnson's Commission on Causes and Preventions of Violence, warns that the United States faces a racial war if it does not remedy the social injustice, inequitable law enforcement, and the availability of firearms in American society.

1971, June 1. Washington, D.C. By a vote of five to four, the U.S. Supreme Court declares unconstitutional a Cincinnati city ordinance making it unlawful for small groups of people to loiter in an annoying manner in public places. Many African Americans claimed that such ordinances had been used by police to harass them.

1971, June 4. Washington, D.C. The Department of Labor announces that it is removing support from the voluntary "Chicago Plan," which was to hire 4,000 African Americans and Spanish-speaking Americans for construction jobs on federal projects. After eighteen months, fewer than 900 African Americans had been accepted in training programs and only a few had been admitted to Chicago construction unions.

1971, June 28. Washington, D.C. By an eight-to-zero vote, with Justice Thurgood Marshall abstaining, the U.S. Supreme Court overturns draft evasion charges against Muhammad Ali. In its decision, the Court agreed that Ali, a Muslim, was objecting to military service on religious grounds, rather than on a political basis, as the Department of Justice had charged.

1971, July 24. Columbus, Georgia. Fifteen African Americans are arrested and several hospitalized during racial disturbances following the dismissal of eight African American policemen. Fire bombings and sniping are reported. State troopers are summoned to maintain order.

1971, August 7. Georgia. State representative Julian Bond tours Georgia to spark the political interests of African Americans who remain unregistered six years after the passage of the Voting Rights Act. Bond notes that due to a blend of apathy and activism, many African Americans do not perceive the ballot as an effective political weapon that can be used to bring change in their lives. Bond cites as an example the failure of African Americans in 1970 to elect African American officials in a district where they represented a majority of the registered voters. Nevertheless, leaders of the SCLC announce that their goal of electing a Southern black to Congress is feasible in view of the redistricting in a number of Southern states.

1971, August 18. Jackson, Mississippi. Eleven members of the Republic of New Africa, a black separatist organization, are charged with murder and assault of federal officers after the death of Lieutenant I. Skinner, a Mississippi policeman. Skinner was shot when police and FBI agents raided the organization's headquarters in order to serve fugitive warrants on three members. The county district attorney requests that a special grand jury charge the separatists with treason and that the Justice Department allow these charges to take precedence over any federal prosecution.

1971, August 21. San Quentin, California. George Jackson, author of *Soledad Brothers* and a folk hero to many black and white radicals, is killed during a prison break. Some supporters of Jackson claim he was "set-up" for assassination, while others feel the official version of Jackson's death is essentially correct.

1971, October. Chicago, Illinois. "Black Expo," a four-day cultural and business exposition, attracts some 800,000 people. The exposition is conducted by Jesse Jackson and a number of African American businessmen.

1972, January 10. Richmond, Virginia. A federal judge orders the consolidation of Richmond's predominantly African American school system with two all-white suburban systems. Judge Robert R. Merhige Jr. bases his decision on the failure of state officials to take positive action to reverse de facto segregation.

1972, January 10. Baton Rouge, Louisiana. Two Black Muslims and two white police officers are killed in a shootout. Disturbances following the shootings injure thirty-one people and the National Guard is called in to restore order.

1972, March. Gary, Indiana. Some 8,000 African Americans representing a wide spectrum of political views attend the first National Black Political Convention. The convention is chaired by Imamu Amiri Baraka with Mayor Richard Hatcher of Gary, Indiana, as the keynote speaker. The group approves a political platform, the "Black Agenda" that demands reparations, proportional congressional representation for African Americans, an increase in federal spending to combat crime and drug trafficking, reduction of the military budget, and a guaranteed annual income of $6,500 for a family of four.

1972, March 16. Washington, D.C. President Nixon proposes a moratorium on all court-ordered busing until July of 1973. African American members of Congress charge that the president is suggesting a return to "separate but equal" schools.

1972, June 4. San Jose, California. After thirteen hours of deliberation, a jury of eleven whites and one Mexican

Mayor Richard Daley and the Reverend Jesse Jackson, Black Expo, Chicago, September 29, 1971. *Jackson, a major force behind the five-day exposition of black-owned businesses, was also one of Daley's most-outspoken critics. Daley's attendance speaks to the political and economic clout of the exposition, and he and Jackson exchange a soul-style handshake on opening day.* **BETTMANN/CORBIS**

American acquits Angela Davis of murder and other charges in connection with a 1970 courthouse shootout in San Rafael, California.

1972, June 6. Richmond, Virginia. A U.S. appeals court, by a five-to-one vote, overturns a plan which would have required the busing of school children between Richmond and two nearly all-white suburbs.

1972, July 12. Miami Beach, Florida. Senator George McGovern of South Dakota wins the presidential nomination at the Democratic Party's national convention. African American delegates make up approximately 15 percent of the total delegates in attendance. New York representative Shirley Chisholm, the first African American woman to seek a presidential nomination, receives 151 votes.

1972, August. Washington, D.C. Attorney General Richard Kleindienst files suit against the cities of Los Angeles, California, and Montgomery, Alabama, for discrimination in hiring for public-service jobs.

1972, November. Cincinnati, Ohio. The Association for the Study of Black Life History, meeting for its fifty-seventh annual convention, changes its name to the Association for the Study of African American History. The change is based on a mail ballot of the association's membership, some two-thirds of whom opt to substitute "African American" for "Black" in the title. Prominent speakers at the convention include: Andrew F. Brimmer, a governor of the Federal Reserve Board; Representative Louis Stokes of Cleveland; John Hope Franklin, professor of history at Duke University; and Rayford W. Logan, professor of history at Howard University.

1972, November. Richard M. Nixon is reelected president in a landslide victory over Senator George McGovern, despite the fact that some 86 percent of the African American vote went to McGovern. However, African Americans achieve a number of electoral successes as the number of African Americans in Congress increases from twelve to fifteen; Barbara Jordan of Houston, Texas, and Andrew Young of

Atlanta become the first Southern African Americans elected to Congress since Reconstruction. Senator Edward Brooke, an African American Republican from Massachusetts, wins reelection, and African American representation in state legislatures increases dramatically.

1972, November 16. Baton Rouge, Louisiana. Two young African American men, Denver A. Smith and Leonard Douglas Brown, are killed on the campus of Southern University during a confrontation between students and police. The students had been pressing for the resignation of the university's president, G. Leon Netterville, whom they charged with arbitrarily dismissing teachers he regarded as militant and for being unreceptive to student demands for better living and academic facilities. Following the shootings, Louisiana Governor Edwin W. Edwards closes the school and sends the National Guard to the Baton Rouge campus.

1972, December 14. Washington, D.C. In the case of *Banks v. Perks*, the U.S. Supreme Court rules unanimously that residents of racially segregated housing projects can sue to have them integrated. In its opinion, the Court states that white residents living in segregated housing projects suffer the same social and economic injuries as those denied access to these facilities.

1973, April 28. Washington, D.C. A government panel releases its final report determining whether the Tuskegee Syphilis Study, conducted between 1932 and 1972 by the Public Health Service, was justified. The study involved observing the effects of untreated syphilis on 430 African American men living in rural Macon County, Alabama. The panel found no evidence that participants in the study had been given any type of informed consent. The panel concluded that the study was unjustified on both scientific and humanitarian grounds and that all policies regarding research on humans be reformed.

1973, May 29. Los Angeles, California. Thomas Bradley is elected mayor of Los Angeles after defeating the incumbent Sam Yorty by 100,000 votes. Yorty had defeated Bradley in the 1969 mayoral election.

1973, June. Washington, D.C. The Joint Center for Political Studies reports that as of April 1973, 2,621 African Americans held elective offices in the United States at every level from school boards to the Congress. When the first list was compiled, in 1969, the total was only 1,185.

1974, March. Washington, D.C. The Department of Justice releases memos revealing that in the 1960s and early 1970s, the FBI had waged a campaign designed to disrupt, discredit, and neutralize black nationalist groups including the Black Panther Party. A major objective of the effort, according to the memo, was to prevent the emergence of an African American leader capable of uniting disparate factions and inspiring violence. Jesse Jackson remarks that the documents implicate the FBI in the deaths of Martin Luther King Jr., Malcolm X, and Fred Hampton.

1974, March 15. Little Rock, Arkansas. The second Black National Political Convention is held. Mayor Richard G. Hatcher of Gary, Indiana, and Imamu Amiri Baraka are among the speakers. Delegates to the convention approve several resolutions including the establishment of a fund to provide money for civil rights causes and a resolution voicing support for African liberation movements.

1974, April 8. Hank Aaron breaks Babe Ruth's long-standing major-league record for most career home runs, hitting his 715th.

1974, June. Washington, D.C. A draft report from the Senate committee investigating the Watergate scandal indicates that the Nixon administration tried to gain the support or neutrality of prominent African Americans during the 1972 presidential campaign by withholding federal funds for government programs. Among those contacted by the Nixon administration were Jesse Jackson, head of Operation PUSH, and James Farmer, an administration official during Nixon's first term.

1974, July 25. Washington, D.C. In the case of *Milliken v. Bradley*, the U.S. Supreme Court nullifies an attempt to implement the "metropolitan integration" of predominantly African American schools in Detroit with those of nearby white suburbs. Chief Justice Warren Burger, writing for the majority, declares that segregation in a city's schools does not justify its combination with schools in its suburbs. Justice Thurgood Marshall calls the Court's decision "an emasculation of the constitutional guarantee of equal opportunity."

1974, November. The number of African American elected officials increases at the federal, state, and local levels. African American members of Congress are reelected and one new member, Harold Ford of Memphis, Tennessee, is added. African Americans are also elected to the post of lieutenant governor in California and Colorado.

1974, December 11. Boston, Massachusetts. Violence erupts between supporters and opponents of public school integration.

1975, January 16. Washington, D.C. William T. Coleman is named secretary of transportation by President Ford, becoming the second African American in the nation's history to hold a cabinet post.

1975, May 3. Department of Labor figures report the national unemployment rate at 9 percent, the African American rate at 15 percent. Vernon L. Jordan Jr. of the National Urban League reports that the African American rate is actually 26 percent.

1975, August 18. Washington, D.C. District of Columbia Appellate Court Judge Julia Cooper is confirmed by the Senate, becoming the highest-ranking African American woman in the federal courts.

1975, August 20. Washington, D.C. Senator Edward Brooke calls for a $10 billion federal employment program to end the economic "depression" in black America by creating one million public-service jobs.

1975, August 29. Washington, D.C. General Daniel James Jr. becomes commander-in-chief of the North American Air Defense Command (NORAD). On the same day, he is promoted and becomes the first African American four-star general in U.S. history.

1975, September 27. Washington, D.C. The Congressional Black Caucus holds its fifth annual dinner. The major theme of the affair is "From Changing Structures to Using Structure—1879–1976." Panelists recommend the federal takeover of the welfare system and poverty assistance, that the states assume more fiscal responsibility for education, and that caucus-directed programs develop a national African American position on matters of policy.

1975, December. Washington, D.C. U.S. Attorney General Edward Levy opens an official review of the Martin Luther King Jr. assassination. Although James Earl Ray was convicted of the crime, many facts point to a conspiracy and suggest that those really responsible for the murder are still at large.

1976, April 26. New York City. The Metropolitan Applied Research Center, a major African American research organization founded to serve as an advocate for the urban poor, announces that it must close due to declining funds.

1976, August 31. Mississippi. A chancellery court orders the NAACP to pay the sum of $1,250,058 to twelve white Port Gibson merchants. The money is compensation for the financial hardships inflicted on the merchants due to the NAACP's successful boycott of white businesses in 1966.

1976, November 2. African American voters play a vital role in Jimmy Carter's victory over President Gerald Ford in the presidential election. Carter received about 94 percent of some 6.6 million African American votes.

1976, November 14. Plains, Georgia. The congregation of President-elect Jimmy Carter's Baptist church votes to drop its eleven-year ban on attendance by African Americans.

1976, December 16. Washington, D.C. President-elect Jimmy Carter appoints Andrew Young as chief delegate to the United Nations and Patricia Roberts Harris as secretary of the Department of Housing and Urban Development.

1977, January 20. Washington, D.C. Clifford Alexander Jr. is sworn in as the first African American secretary of the U.S. Army. President Carter appoints nineteen African Americans to his cabinet, while thirty-seven other African Americans obtain executive positions within the Carter administration.

1977, April 19. New York City. Author Alex Haley receives a Pulitzer Prize for his book *Roots*.

Author Alex Haley, London, April 11, 1977. *Haley's best-selling novel,* Roots, *was awarded the Pulitzer Prize on April 19 of that same year.* BETTMANN/CORBIS

1977, July 29. St. Louis, Missouri. Roy Wilkins, a forty-two-year veteran of the NAACP, announces his retirement during the organization's sixty-eighth annual convention.

1977, September 4. New York City. At a meeting of the National Urban League, fifteen African American members agree to form a loose coalition to combat perceived anti–African American sentiment within the nation and seek greater job opportunities for African Americans.

1978, January 17. Major Guion S. Bluford Jr., Major Frederick D. Gregory, and Ronald E. McNair join the space program and begin training as astronauts for future space missions.

1978, May 29. Washington, D.C. Files made public by the FBI reveal that an unidentified African American leader worked with the agency during the 1960s in an effort to remove Martin Luther King Jr. from national prominence in the civil rights movement. The information released is from the files of the late J. Edgar Hoover.

1978, June 28. Washington, D.C. Hearing the case *University of California v. Bakke*, the U.S. Supreme Court, in a 5–4 decision, orders that white student Allan P. Bakke be admitted to the medical school at the University of California, Davis. The Court rules that the refusal to admit Bakke is tantamount to reverse discrimination and that the use of racial or ethnic quotas is an improper means of achieving racial balance. The Court also holds that the college's affirmative action program is invalid since it had the effect of discriminating against qualified white applicants, although the Court perceived the goal of attaining a diverse student body as constitutional and permissible.

1978, December 3. The U.S. Census Bureau reports that from 1960 to 1977, the number of African Americans living in suburban areas increased from 2.4 million to 4.6 million, and that 55 percent of the 24.5 million African Americans in the United States live in central cities, indicating a decline from the 1970 figure of 59 percent.

1979, February 27. Washington, D.C. The Department of Housing and Urban Development announces that it will foreclose on the financially troubled Soul City, a new town in rural North Carolina that was to have been controlled by African Americans but open to members of all races. Since 1969, when Floyd B. McKissick announced the idea for the city, $27 million had been spent by federal, state, and local sources. McKissick vows to continue efforts to keep the project alive.

1979, May 2. Washington, D.C. The Congressional Black Caucus and delegates from eleven Southern states set up an "action alert communications network." This network is designed to exert pressure on at least 100 white congressional representatives from predominantly African American districts to vote with the caucus on important issues.

1979, June 19. The U.S. Census Bureau announces a study indicating that although African Americans have made enormous advances in employment, income, health, housing, political power, and other measures of social well-being, they remain far behind white Americans.

1979, June 25. Washington, D.C. Amalya L. Kearse becomes the first woman to receive an appointment to the U.S. Court of Appeals.

1979, June 29. Washington, D.C. In the case of *United States Steel v. Brian Weber*, the U.S. Supreme Court rules that private employers can legally give special preference to African American workers to eliminate "manifest racial imbalance" in traditionally white jobs.

1979, August 1. Washington, D.C. The U.S. House of Representatives votes 408–1 to place a bust of the late Martin Luther King Jr. in the Capitol. The bust is the first work of art in the Capitol honoring an African American.

1979, August 16. New York City. Andrew Young resigns as the chief U.S. delegate to the United Nations after being publicly criticized for conducting unauthorized talks with the Palestine Liberation Organization in New York. The resignation sets off a storm of controversy and animosity between segments of the Jewish and African American communities.

1979, December 22. Washington, D.C. The Joint Center for Political Studies reveals that between 1978 and 1979, the number of African Americans elected to public office increased by 104. This 2 percent increase is considered meager, especially because such officials were elected in states with substantial African American populations.

1980, February 6. Washington, D.C. The Congressional Black Caucus criticizes President Carter's fiscal 1981 budget proposals because they increase the amount of military spending while reducing the funding for social programs. Caucus members promise to initiate legislation to reduce military spending increases and pronounce the budget "an unmitigated disaster for the poor, the unemployed and minorities."

1980, April 22. Washington, D.C. Hearing the case *City of Mobile, Alabama v. Wiley L. Bolden*, the U.S. Supreme Court, in a six–three decision, overturns a lower court ruling that an at-large city electoral system is unconstitutional because it dilutes the voting strength of African Americans.

1980, May 11. Washington, D.C. Early primary results reveal that the African American community is supporting President Carter's second-term bid despite criticism of his record by national African American leaders. The "resounding" victories won by Carter in the Southern primaries are interpreted as African Americans lacking faith in their ability to enact a "Great Society–style social renewal" agenda as proposed by Senator Edward M. Kennedy.

1980, May 14. Birmingham, Alabama. J. B. Stoner, a white supremacist, is convicted for the 1958 bombing of an African American church in Birmingham, Alabama.

1980, May 18. Miami, Florida. The African American Liberty City area and predominantly African American Coconut Grove section of Miami erupt into riotous violence, ending with nine dead and 163 injured, following the acquittal of four white Dade County police officers in the beating death of a black man. In the nightlong unrest, stores are looted, property burned, and whites fatally beaten. During the violence, African Americans are heard screaming the name "McDuffie" (Arthur), the African American insurance executive beaten to death following a high-speed chase with Dade County police officers for a traffic violation. Dade County officials impose an 8 p.m. to 6 a.m. curfew; 350 National Guard troops set up headquarters in an armory with 450 more en route from Orlando.

1980, May 29. Fort Wayne, Indiana. Vernon E. Jordan Jr., president of the National Urban League, is shot and seriously wounded by an unknown assailant. Stating that the shooting evidenced "an element of premeditation," director of the FBI William H. Webster says, "the shooting was not accidental, and was in furtherance of an apparent conspiracy to deprive Vernon Jordan of his civil rights." The shooting occurred just outside Jordan's motel room.

1980, July 3. Washington, D.C. A ruling authorizing Congress to impose racial quotas to remedy past discrimination against minority contractors in federal jobs programs is upheld by the U.S. Supreme Court in a six–three vote. It validates the 10 percent minority set-aside of federal public works contracts, challenged by white contractors in *Fullilove v. Klutznick.*

1980, July 3. Cincinnati, Ohio. In a consent decree with the Justice Department, the city of Cincinnati agrees to hire and promote more African Americans and women within the police department. The decree permanently enjoins the city from engaging in any employment discrimination. Over a five-year period, 34 percent of new police officer vacancies will be filled by African Americans and 23 percent by women. The fire department of the city of Chicago, in a similar action (April 2, 1980), was permanently prohibited from discrimination against any candidate for promotion on the basis of race or national origin. The settlement of this discrimination action was filed in federal district court and resulted from a suit charging violations of the Civil Rights Act of 1964 and the Federal Sharing Act of 1972. In New York City, the U.S. Court of Appeals (August 1, 1980) overturned a lower court ruling that 50 percent of all new police officer hires be African American or Hispanic. The appeals court, however, ruled that the written test used for hiring had "significant disparate racial impact" in violation of the Civil Rights Act of 1964. It concluded that until a new test was implemented, one-third of all newly hired police must be African American or Hispanic.

1980, September 3. St. Louis, Missouri. St. Louis schools are desegregated peacefully after eight years of struggle. Over 16,000 students are bused on the first day of classes under court orders. No violence is reported.

1980, September 26. Detroit, Michigan. Federal district judge Horace W. Gilmore invalidates the 1980 census on the grounds that it undercounts African Americans and Hispanics, thus violating the one-person, one-vote principle. The action was precipitated by a suit initiated by the city of Detroit with support from dozens of other cities. The census was later upheld in higher courts.

1980, September 26. Washington, D.C. The Congressional Black Caucus marks its tenth anniversary with its annual legislative weekend. The group of bipartisan representatives cite as their major achievements the Humphrey-Hawkins Full Employment Bill and the 10 percent "minority-set-aside" law established to ensure minority firms a nearly representative share of federal contracts. The caucus identifies its current concern as the potential reapportionment of congressional districts affected by the outcome of the 1980 census.

1980, September 29. New York City. The Schomburg Center for Research in Black Culture opens a new $3.8 million building in Harlem.

1980, September 30. Washington, D.C. The first annual Black College Day is attended by 18,000 African American students. Speeches on the preservation of African American colleges and universities are given by African American officials and student leaders. The march is organized by African American journalist Tony Brown in an effort to draw public attention to the impact of integration and merging of African American private and public colleges and universities. Brown contends that seven out of ten African Americans attending predominantly white colleges do not graduate.

1980, November 23. Philadelphia, Pennsylvania. About 1,000 people from twenty-five states attend a convention and form the National Black Independent Party. The idea grows out of a National Black Political Assembly in Gary, Indiana, in 1972.

1980, December 12. Washington, D.C. African American leaders of the nation's major civil rights organizations meet with President-elect Ronald Reagan, who says he will defend the civil rights of minorities. The leaders urge him to appoint an African American to a cabinet position in his administration. Present at the meeting are Vernon E. Jordan Jr., president of the National Urban League; Benjamin Hooks, executive director, NAACP; and Dorothy I. Height, president of the National Council of Negro Women.

1980, December 18. San Antonio, Texas. A federal grand jury acquits Charles Veverka of four counts of violating the civil rights of Arthur McDuffie, an African American who was beaten to death while in police custody. The jury deliberates for sixteen hours, finally breaking an eleven-to-one deadlock that threatened a mistrial. Veverka was indicted following violent riots in Miami resulting from the acquittal of four white police officers accused of executing the fatal beating.

1980, December 23. Washington, D.C. Samuel R. Pierce Jr. is named by President-elect Ronald Reagan to the cabinet post of secretary of the Department of Housing and Urban Development. As such, Pierce is the highest-ranking African American appointee of the new administration. Pierce is a lifelong Republican, widely respected in legal, financial, and civil rights circles.

1981, February 7. Miami, Florida. Three black Miami youths are convicted of murder in connection with the beating deaths of three whites during the Liberty City riots in May of 1980. A fourth youth who was tried with the others is acquitted. Attorneys for the defendants announce plans to appeal the verdicts.

1981, May 7. Washington, D.C. Representative Robert S. Walker, a Republican from Pennsylvania, introduces a bill that prohibits the use of numerical quotas devised to increase the hiring or school enrollment of minorities and women. Titled the "Equal Employment Opportunity Act," it seeks to amend the Civil Rights Act of 1964 and to prevent the federal government from imposing rules on employers or schools to hire workers or to admit students on the basis of race, sex, or national origin. In effect, the proposal no longer requires companies and educational institutions to make up for past discrimination by taking on a set number of minorities and women within a specified time frame.

1981, May 13. Washington, D.C. The Labor Department proposes revisions of Executive Order No. 11246 (prohibiting employment discrimination by federal contractors based on race, sex, color, national origin, or religion) in its continuing effort to ease job-discrimination rules for federal contractors. The contents of an internal memorandum reveal the effort seems targeted toward reducing the record-keeping and affirmative action requirements for small contractors and eliminating "unnecessary confrontations" with all contractors.

1981, May 23. Washington, D.C. Attorney General William French Smith announces that the Justice Department will no longer continue its vigorous pursuit of mandatory busing and the use of racial quotas in employment-discrimination cases, calling these methods "ineffective" and unfair remedies to discrimination. The Justice Department also considers amendments which would make "reverse discrimination" illegal under the Civil Rights Act of 1964.

1981, June 10. Washington, D.C. The House once again approves an antibusing provision by a vote of 265 to 122, forbidding the Justice Department from taking any direct or indirect action to require the busing of students to schools other than those closest to where they live, with the exception of cases involving special education needs. The provision is known as an "antibusing rider" because of its attachment to the department's $2.3 billion authorized bill.

1981, June 16. Washington, D.C. The Reagan administration, in a letter to Attorney General William French Smith, requires the Justice Department to determine whether the political rights of minority Americans are best served by the Voting Rights Act of 1965. Stating that the act marks the nation's commitment to full equality for all Americans, the administration says that what must be answered is whether the act continues to be the most appropriate means of guaranteeing their rights. The completed report is due October 1.

1981, September 9. New York City. Roy Wilkins, former head of the NAACP and one of the key players in the civil rights movement of the 1960s, dies at New York University Medical Center at age eighty.

1981, September 10. New York City. Vernon Jordan announces his plans to resign as executive director of the National Urban League to join the Dallas-based law firm of Akin, Grump, Hauer, and Field. Jordan's office will be in Washington, D.C.

1981, November 28. Washington, D.C. The nomination of Clarence M. Pendleton, president of the Urban League of San Diego, to head the U.S. Commission on Civil Rights results in divided opinion over his suitability for the post. Pendleton's selection is controversial because of his promotion of private industry as a cure-all for African American economic problems and because of his opposition to other positions taken traditionally by the civil rights movement on issues such as busing and affirmative action.

1981, December 8. Washington, D.C. William Bradford Reynolds, assistant attorney general of the Justice Department's civil rights division, announces plans to seek a ruling by the Supreme Court that would find it unconstitutional to give minorities and women preference in hiring and promotion. Reynolds wants a reversal of the High Court's decision in *Weber v. Kaiser Aluminum and Chemical Corp.*, which upheld the legality of affirmative action hiring and promotion practices negotiated by the company and the United Steel Workers of America. Reynolds contends the *Weber* decision was "wrongly decided" and that different sets of rules for the public sector and the private sector should not exist. Under his direction, the Justice Department has ceased such hiring preferences; the action sought by Reynolds would prohibit individuals, the Labor Department, and the Equal Employment Opportunity Commission from seeking such preferences.

1982, January 2. Los Angeles, California. Los Angeles mayor Tom Bradley opens his campaign to become the first African American governor of California. The sixty-four-year-old former policeman has been elected as the city's mayor three times.

1982, January 20. Alabama. Two African American civil rights workers, Julia Wilder and Maggie Bozeman, are charged with vote fraud.

1982, February 1. New York City. Representative Shirley Chisholm, a Democrat from New York and the first African American woman to win a seat in Congress, announces that she will not seek another term. She has served the Brooklyn communities of Bedford-Stuyvesant and Bushwick since 1968.

1982, February 1. Washington, D.C. The Justice Department proposes that the city of Chicago be allowed to try to desegregate its schools following a plan that would rely mainly on voluntary student transfers rather than mandatory busing.

1982, February 6. Alabama. A small band of Southern civil rights workers, followed by 300 sympathizers, start a 140-mile march in support of the Federal Voting Rights Act and in protest against the vote fraud conviction of two African American political activists. The marchers travel from Carrollton, Alabama, through Selma to the state capital, Montgomery, a route made famous in early civil rights marches.

1982, April 4. Washington, D.C. The Bureau of Census reports that the 1980 census missed counting 1.3 million African Americans and that the undercount represented 4.8 percent of the nation's 28 million African Americans. The bureau says that in 1970 the census missed 1.9 million out of 24.4 million African Americans.

1983. Washington, D.C. A test case of the Justice Department to eliminate court-ordered busing to desegregate public schools is rejected by the U.S. Supreme Court. It was the contention of the Justice Department that a desegregation plan in Nashville, Tennessee, was contributing to "white flight" from the city.

1983. Louisiana. Louisiana repeals the United States' last racial classification law.

1983, January 12. Washington, D.C. A majority of the U.S. Civil Rights Commission charges that the Reagan administration's Justice Department has been moving in the direction of getting judicial approval to end affirmative action. The two-and-a-half-page text issued by the majority asserts that cases in several cities, given the current position of the Justice Department, could result in continued discrimination. The committee's assertion is opposed by the chairman of the committee, Clarence Pendleton, an African American Reagan appointee.

1983, April 13. Chicago, Illinois. Harold Washington becomes the first African American mayor of Chicago. Washington received 656,727 votes (51%), while his opponent, Bernard Epton, received 617,159 votes (48%). The voting followed racial lines with 90 percent of the votes in African American areas going to Washington, as well as some 44 percent of the vote in the city's white liberal areas.

1983, April 22. Greensboro, North Carolina. After 29 months of investigation, a federal grand jury indicts six Ku Klux Klansmen and three members of the American Nazi Party in the deaths of five members of the Communist Workers Party who participated in a "Death-to-the-Klan" rally in Greensboro, North Carolina, in 1979.

1983, May 18. New York City. Benjamin L. Hooks, executive director of the NAACP, is suspended indefinitely by the association's chairman, Margaret Bush Wilson. The controversy was said to have centered on a dispute over organization policy.

1983, May 25. Washington, D.C. In an 8–1 decision, the Supreme Court rules that private schools that discriminate on the basis of race are not eligible for tax exemptions. The ruling in *Bob Jones University v. IRS* rejects the Reagan administration's contention that because there is nothing in the Internal Revenue Service code banning such exemptions, they are permissible. The opinion, rendered by Chief Justice Warren E. Burger, stated that racial discrimination in education violates widely accepted views of elementary justice and that "to grant tax exempt status to racially discriminatory educational entities would be incompatible with the concepts of tax exemption."

1983, May 26. Washington, D.C. President Ronald Reagan presents three nominees to replace three current members of the U.S. Commission on Civil Rights. If confirmed, the administration would have a majority of its appointees on the six-member commission. A storm of protest and controversy arises from civil rights groups and members of Congress accusing the president of efforts to pack the commission. The three nominees are John H. Bunzel, Morris B. Abram, and Robert A. Destro. The commissioners to be replaced are Mary Frances Berry, Rabbi Murray Saltzman, and Blandina Cardenas Ramirez. However, lawyers from various private and governmental agencies indicate that the president probably does not have the legal authority to dismiss personnel who in effect are members of an independent bipartisan deliberative body with no powers. Jack Greenberg of the NAACP Legal Defense and Educational Fund states that it is illegal for the president to do what he proposes and that the fund would represent the commissioners if they decided to mount a challenge.

1983, May 28. New York City. The NAACP's executive director Benjamin L. Hooks is reinstated to his post after an eight-day suspension by board chairman Margaret Bush Wilson. Wilson states that the objective of the action has been achieved and its continuance no longer serves a useful purpose.

1983, August. Washington, D.C. Surveys in the state of Mississippi indicate a probability that enforcement of the Voting Rights Act will be extremely difficult in many counties. As a result, Assistant Attorney General William Bradford Reynolds announces that he will send 300 federal observers into the state to see that the act is enforced. Many civil rights leaders believe the response to be totally inadequate, and Jesse Jackson believes that the planned observers are untrained and will be unable to see or understand many violations.

1983, October 20. Washington, D.C. By a vote of seventy-eight to twenty-two, action is completed in the Senate and the president signs into law a bill making the third Monday of each January a day honoring the memory of slain civil rights leader Martin Luther King Jr. Initially opposed by President Ronald Reagan, many prominent Republican senators urged and got the president's support of the bill, thus ensuring passage in the Senate. The bill had previously passed in the house by a margin of 338–90. Senator Jesse Helms (R-NC) leads an effort to defeat the bill. Helms accuses King of "Marxist" ways. Helms also attempts to have controversial FBI tapes on King opened and made public in the hope that such disclosure would create public scandal. Senator Edward Kennedy (D-MA) is outraged by Helms and asks for a renunciation of the senator in the nation and in his home state.

1983, October 25. Washington, D.C. In a surprise move President Ronald Reagan fires three members from the U.S. Commission on Civil Rights because their views are critical of many aspects of the administration's policies in this area. Those fired were Mary Frances Berry, a professor of history and law at Howard University, Blandina Cardenas Ramirez of San Antonio, and Rabbi Murray Saltzman of Baltimore—all highly regarded as effective spokespersons for minorities.

1983, November 10. In general elections throughout the nation, African Americans make some significant gains. Wilson Goode is elected mayor of Philadelphia, becoming that city's first African American to serve in such capacity and making his city the fourth of the nation's six largest cities to have an African American as chief executive. Other African American winners are Democrat Harvey Gantt, who becomes the first African American elected mayor of Charlotte, North Carolina; James A. Sharp Jr., the first elected African American mayor of Flint, Michigan; Thirman Milner, who wins a second term in Hartford, Connecticut; and Richard Hatcher, who wins a fifth term in Gary, Indiana.

1983, December 1. Washington, D.C. In a supposed compromise bill, President Ronald Reagan signs into law a newly reorganized U.S. Commission on Civil Rights comprised of four presidential and four congressional appointees. As the first of his appointments, Reagan reappoints Clarence M. Pendleton Jr. as chairman of the new commission.

1984. The Centers for Disease Control releases figures on the homicide rate for young African American men. Between 1984 and 1988, the homicide rate among African American men ages fifteen to twenty-four rises 68 percent.

1984, June 6. Washington, D.C. Margaret Bush Wilson, former chairperson of the NAACP, loses the battle to get herself reinstated as a member of the association's governing board. Wilson was the first African American woman chairperson of the NAACP and had been a member of the national board of directors since 1963.

1984, June 13. Washington, D.C. In a six-to-three decision, the U.S. Supreme Court invalidated a U.S. district court decision that allowed the layoff of three white firefighters who had seniority over three African American firefighters. The Supreme Court decided that affirmative action employment gains are not preferential when jobs must be decreased and that "legitimate" seniority systems are protected from court intervention. However, a dissenting opinion by Justices Blackmun, Brennan, and Marshall argued that under Title 7 of the Civil Rights Act of 1964, race-related preferential practice was an acceptable application. As a result of the Court's decision, the Justice Department announces that it will reexamine all federal antidiscrimination settlements and will advise government agencies to not continue the practice of using racial employment quotas when negotiating affirmative action plans.

1984, July 6. Washington, D.C. Secret tapes of President John F. Kennedy are made public and demonstrate a sincere effort by Kennedy to get mayors, governors, and congressmen to accept integration and support his civil rights programs. The recordings made during the Kennedy presidency also reveal a dramatic conversation with Martin Luther King Jr. in which King, after a bombing in Birmingham, Alabama, that killed four children at an African American church, calls upon the president to send federal troops into the city to protect the African American community and to prevent riots. In a conversation with mayor Allen Thompson of Jackson, Mississippi, the president urges him to hire African American police officers. After the mayor assures the president that he will hire African Americans, he said to Kennedy, "don't get your feelings hurt" about public statements he may have to make about the president, to which Kennedy replies "well, listen I give you full permission to denounce me in public as long as you don't do it in private."

1984, November 12. Atlanta, Georgia. The Reverend Martin Luther King Sr. dies of a heart ailment at the age of eighty-two. For forty-four years, he had been pastor of the Ebenezer Baptist Church and was one of the South's most influential African American clergymen.

1984, November 14. Washington, D.C. The Supreme Court rules that redistricting plans and election laws that have discriminatory results are affirmed to be illegal under a provision of the 1982 Voting Rights Act. The ruling came as a result of a Mississippi redistricting plan.

1985, January 5. South Africa. Senator Edward Kennedy visits South Africa at the invitation of Nobel Peace Prize recipient Bishop Desmond Tutu. Kennedy also visits Winnie Mandela, the wife of jailed black nationalist Nelson Mandela, but his request to meet with the imprisoned leader is refused by the government.

1985, February 21. New York City. As a cost-savings measure, the NAACP will move from its headquarters in New York City to Baltimore, Maryland, by 1986. The association is negotiating the purchase of a suitable building for $2 million in Baltimore after being unable to find a suitable and economically viable location in New York City.

1985, February 26. Washington, D.C. The U.S. Commission on Civil Rights gives enthusiastic support to a Supreme

Court decision giving existing seniority systems preference over affirmative action programs, even though the African Americans were hired to remedy previously contended discriminatory hiring practices. U.S. Civil Rights Commissioners Mary Frances Berry and Blandina Cardenas Ramirez, in heated disagreement with the Supreme Court and the Civil Rights Commission's report, state that civil rights laws are designed to protect African Americans, minorities, and women, not white men. The statement creates new controversy as to the meaning of the existence of the Civil Rights Commission.

1985, March 7. Washington, D.C. Charging that the U.S. Commission on Civil Rights had already decided to oppose such measures as timetables and quotas, national civil rights groups boycott hearings on the use of such goals to achieve racial balance or to remedy discriminatory hiring practices.

1985, March 13. Washington, D.C. Clarence Pendleton, chairman of the U.S. Commission on Civil Rights, suggests that after the issue of preferential treatment is settled, the Civil Rights Commission should be abolished. Responsibility for civil rights, says Pendleton, should be in the hands of the Justice Department and the Equal Employment Opportunity Commission.

1985, May 1. Washington, D.C. A statue of Martin Luther King Jr. is dedicated at the Washington Cathedral as a memorial to his comprehensive contributions and celebrated leadership in the struggle for civil rights.

1985, May 6. Washington, D.C. The federal government and the state of Maryland reach tentative agreement on a plan to desegregate the state's public colleges and universities. White enrollment at traditionally black colleges will be increased to 19 percent and African American enrollment at predominantly white schools will reach 15 percent from 11 percent. The implementation of this plan is to take five years.

1985, August 2. Washington, D.C. Because of the policy of apartheid in South Africa, the U.S. House of Representatives gives final approval to a bill imposing economic sanctions against the South African government by a vote of 380–48. The Reagan administration remains opposed to the legislation.

1985, December 6. Yonkers, New York. Stating that "discriminatory housing practices" on the part of Yonkers, New York, were responsible for the segregation of blacks from whites in the city's schools, U.S. district court judge Leonard B. Sand indicated for the first time in school desegregation cases that a city's housing policies are inextricably linked to school segregation. Judge Sand held that since 1949 Yonkers public housing had been deliberately built in low-income neighborhoods, which had the effect of confining students to "inferior and racially unmixed schools." The Justice Department in 1980 charged the city of Yonkers with bias in housing and schools and received from the city a tentative plan in 1984 to build public housing in predominantly white East Yonkers.

1985, December 23. Birmingham, Alabama. Federal district judge Sam Pointer Jr. dismisses a reverse discrimination suit instituted on behalf of fourteen white firefighters in Birmingham, Alabama. It was claimed that the fourteen whites were denied advancement because of a city hiring and promotion plan favoring less-qualified African Americans. Judge Pointer ruled that the city accepted the consent decree along with the Justice Department in 1981, and therefore the decree is valid; he also ruled that the firefighters failed to prove that the plan violated that agreement.

1986, January 11. Richmond, Virginia. L. Douglas Wilder becomes the first African American lieutenant governor of the state of Virginia. Wilder, the grandson of a slave, was a Bronze Star recipient in the Korean War and a former member of the state senate.

1986, January 20. Martin Luther King Jr.'s birthday (January 15) is observed for the first time as a federal holiday on this date.

1986, March 19. Washington, D.C. The Supreme Court in *Wygant v. Jackson Board of Education*, the first of three major affirmative action decisions, rules five to four that broad affirmative action plans including hiring goals are permissible if they are carefully tailored to remedy past discrimination. In a ruling involving teachers laid off in Jackson, Michigan, the Court sends a mixed signal by deciding that public employers cannot give affirmative action plans as a substitute for seniority when reducing their workforces.

1986, June 16. Norfolk, Virginia. The U.S. Supreme Court denies an injunction sought by African American parents that would prevent the Norfolk, Virginia, school board from ending school busing to stem "white flight" from the city's public schools. According to the petition, the change would result in "a general resegregation of the public schools of the South."

1986, July 2. Cleveland, Ohio. The U.S. Supreme Court ruling on an action regarding Cleveland printers and New York sheet metal workers upholds the use of affirmative action plans designed to remedy past discrimination. The decision in *Sheet Metal Workers International v. EEOC* rejects the Reagan administration's argument that only specific victims of discrimination are entitled to such relief.

1986, August 5. Washington, D.C. African American leaders representing major African American organizations meet to urge the passage of legislation that would impose more stringent economic sanctions on South Africa.

1986, September 11. South Africa. Coretta Scott King visits South Africa, meets with Archbishop Desmond

Tutu, cancels a meeting with the prime minister, and later visits Winnie Mandela, wife of the imprisoned South African antiapartheid leader.

1986, October 3. Washington, D.C. In an effort to win Senate support for his veto of a sanctions bill against South Africa for their apartheid policies, Ronald Reagan appoints an African American career diplomat, Edward J. Perkins, to be the new American ambassador to that country. The bill had been overridden by a wide majority (313–83) in the House. The Senate, despite the appointment, votes with the House by a vote of 78–21 to override the veto.

1986, October 7. Washington, D.C. The thirty-two-year-old case of *Brown v. Board of Education of Topeka, Kansas* is reopened by the original plaintiff and others who maintain that the school district has failed to integrate fully its schools or to eradicate the remaining elements that permitted racial separation in the past. Richard Jones, the lawyer for the plaintiffs, says he will show that the school board approved boundaries that perpetuate racially separate schools and allowed white parents to avoid compliance with desegregation efforts by offering school attendance alternatives.

1986, October 20. Baltimore, Maryland. Four days of dedication ceremonies commence as the NAACP opens its new headquarters. The NAACP was founded in New York in 1909 and maintained its headquarters there until this move. There is official indication that the organization will begin new and diverse programs, including business development, in addition to its more fundamental activities, such as voter registration and protest demonstrations in its general goal of social and economic justice.

1986, November 4. Norfolk, Virginia. The Supreme Court declines to review two school desegregation cases, one which allows the city of Norfolk to end its busing plan, and another that attempts to sanction the authority of the Oklahoma City School Board to end busing for students in grades one through four. It is speculated that some High Court justices want to leave the lower courts with the means of interpreting law on a local and regional basis. In the Norfolk case, African American parents had claimed that the lower court ruling ending busing would have the effect of reinstating school segregation.

1986, December 21. Queens, New York. Michael Griffith, a twenty-three-year-old African American male, is struck by a car and killed while seeking safety from a white mob beating him with bats and fists. The incident occurred in the white community of Howard Beach, Queens. The whites were reported shouting, "Niggers, you don't belong here!" Griffith and two companions were in the neighborhood looking for a tow for their disabled car.

1987, January 7. Washington, D.C. New regulations are issued to strengthen the federal government's authority to reject changes in local election laws that have a discriminatory result. No longer does the legal process have to prove that the intent of the local law was to discriminate, it need only demonstrate that it could have a discriminatory result.

1987, February 11. Queens, New York. In Howard Beach, three white teenagers who participated in a racial attack against three African American youths are charged with murder as a result of the death of one of the black youths who was killed by a car along an adjacent parkway as he attempted to escape from his white attackers.

1987, April 5. Washington, D.C. Representative Charles Rangel (D-NY) introduces two measures in Congress to have the late revolutionary civil rights leader Marcus Garvey exonerated of the mail-fraud charges for which he was convicted in 1924. The move by Rangel came after Robert Hill, editor of the Marcus Garvey papers project at the University of California, Los Angeles, discovered new evidence that could indicate that Garvey's conviction may have been politically motivated. In 1927, Garvey's sentence was commuted by President Calvin Coolidge, after which Garvey was deported to Jamaica, his place of birth.

1987, April 7. Chicago, Illinois. Mayor Harold Washington wins reelection to a second four-year term, and his supporters win control of the city council for the first time. Voting was along strong racial lines, with Washington receiving 97 percent of the African American vote, and his white opponent Edward R. Vrdolyak receiving 74 percent of the white vote. Hispanics cast 57 percent of their vote for Washington.

1987, April 18. Los Angeles, California. Al Campanis, vice president of personnel for the Los Angeles Dodgers, is pressured to resign from his job after stating that African Americans might not be qualified to be managers or to hold executive positions in baseball. The remarks were made by Campanis on the ABC News program *Nightline.*

1987, April 25. Fort Smith, Arkansas. A federal grand jury indicts ten white supremacists on charges of conspiring to assassinate federal officials, including a judge, and to kill members of ethnic groups through bombings. Richard Girnt Butler, the leader of the Aryan Nations Church, was named in the indictment, along with nine others affiliated with the church and other white supremacist groups, such as the Order and the Ku Klux Klan.

1987, May 3. Washington, D.C. Japanese prime minister Yasuhiro Nakasone meets with the Congressional Black Caucus and other African American leaders after being accused of making racial slurs in a speech, angering African Americans and other ethnic groups. Following the meeting Nakasone agreed to pursue Japanese investments in minority-owned American banks, to set up exchange programs between Japanese colleges and African American colleges, and to locate Japanese companies in predominantly African American areas.

1987, July 1. Phoenix, Arizona. As a result of his decision to rescind the state observance of Martin Luther King Jr.'s birthday, Governor Evan Mecham (a Republican) faces a citizens' effort to recall him as the governor of the state. The plan has strong state support from both parties, and many Republicans wear "Recall Mecham" buttons.

1987, July 28. Montgomery, Alabama. After fifteen years a tentative settlement is reached between the Alabama State Police Department and the Justice Department. Accordingly, there will be an increase in the number of African Americans at various ranks on the force to as high as 25 percent over a three-year period. The department will promote fifteen African Americans to the rank of corporal in a month and will eventually have African Americans comprise 20 percent of its sergeants, 15 percent of its lieutenants, and 10 percent of its captains. Federal district judge Myron Thompson, who originally ordered the police department to hire one African American officer for every white officer hired, must approve the suggested settlement.

1988. Atlanta, Georgia. Jesse Jackson receives 1,218 delegate votes at the Democratic National Convention.

1988, August 15. Dallas, Texas. The predominantly African American Bishop College, at one time the largest African American college in the West, closes its doors, unable to pay creditors $20 million. Founded in 1881 in Marshall, Texas, Bishop moved to Dallas in 1961. In 1967, Bishop had an enrollment of 1,500; in 1987, its enrollment had dwindled to 300.

1988, August 26. Boston, Massachusetts. In an effort to prevent a housing settlement between the city of Boston and the U.S. Department of Housing from being implemented, the NAACP files suit to have the agreement blocked, stating that a housing settlement, among other things, should include monetary compensation for people previously denied public housing because of their race and therefore forced to pay higher rent. The Housing Authority of the city of Boston was the largest housing authority in the country to enter into a fair-housing voluntary compliance agreement with the federal government.

1988, October 4. Washington, D.C. The General Accounting Office of the federal government makes public a report charging that the Equal Employment Opportunity Commission failed to properly investigate as many as 82 percent of the claims made regarding job discrimination filed with the commission during a three-month period.

1988, November 26. Chicago, Illinois. As tensions increase between Jews and African Americans, the Reverend Jesse Jackson meets with Jewish leaders in an effort to reduce the anger and heal the wounds. The Congregation Hakafa turns out to overflow capacity to hear Jackson deliver the evening sermon and say, "The sons and daughters of the Holocaust, and the sons and daughters of slavery, must find common ground again." The tension between Jews and African Americans reached a zenith in May when Mayor Eugene Sawyer of Chicago was severely criticized for taking a week to condemn the anti-Semitic remarks made by Steve Cokley, an aide to the mayor. Underlying the problem is the political struggle for power in Chicago. In 1983, Jews gave Harold Washington almost 50 percent of their votes and helped give Chicago its first African American mayor; in that race, Washington defeated the white Republican candidate, Bernard Epton, who was Jewish.

1988, December 1. Washington, D.C. Lieutenant General Colin Powell, President Reagan's national security adviser and the top African American official in the administration, is nominated to become one of ten four-star generals in the U.S. Army. Along with the rank goes the assignment to command all U.S. troops in the continental borders of the country and to be responsible for mainland defense. Powell is credited with helping Reagan's summit meetings in Moscow and Washington, D.C., to become diplomatic successes.

1989, January 16. Miami, Florida. Rioting erupts on the evening of January 16 in the predominantly African American neighborhood of Overtown, following the killing of Anthony Lloyd, a twenty-three-year-old African American, by an Hispanic police officer. On January 18, Miami Mayor Xavier Suarez announces that an independent panel would be appointed to investigate the killing.

1989, January 23. Decatur, Alabama. Six members of the Ku Klux Klan receive jail sentences and fines for their part in harassing African Americans in a civil rights march conducted ten years earlier in Decatur, Alabama. The May 1979 march had been to protest the jailing of Tommy Lee Hines, a retarded African American man convicted of raping three white women. Hines's thirty-year jail sentence was overturned in 1980, and he was committed to a Montgomery mental hospital.

1989, January 23. Washington, D.C. Hearing the case *City of Richmond v. J. A. Croson Co.*, the Supreme Court strikes down a law in Richmond, Virginia, which required 30 percent of public works funds to be channeled to minority-owned construction companies. The landmark decision was decried by minority leaders, hailed by antiquota officials, and predicted to have national impact on affirmative action and set-aside programs. The "Richmond decision," which was written by Associate Justice Sandra Day O'Connor and carried by a six–three majority, said set-aside programs were only justified if they redressed "identified discrimination." O'Connor specifically suggested that "rigid numerical quotas" be avoided, in order to avoid racially motivated hirings of any kind. The ruling only pertains to the

Lieutenant General Colin Powell, U.S. Army, White House, Washington, DC, December 2, 1988. *On the previous day, Powell, President Ronald Reagan's national security adviser, was nominated for promotion to four-star general and commander-in-chief of the U.S. Forces Command.* AP PHOTO/MARCY NIGHSWANDER

disposition of federal, state, and local government contracts and does not affect affirmative action programs in private industry.

1989, February 7. The American Council on Education reports that the number of African American men attending college is declining. In 1976, 470,000 African American males were enrolled in college. Ten years later, that number dropped to 436,000. Meanwhile the number of African American female students grew during the same period, from 563,000 in 1976 to 645,000 in 1986. Reasons for the decline of African American male collegians were military enrollment, prohibitive college costs, "school phobia," and the seduction of crime or drugs.

1989, February 10. Washington, D.C. Washington lawyer Ronald H. Brown, who held high-level positions in the presidential campaigns of Senator Ted Kennedy and Reverend Jesse Jackson, is elected chairman of the Democratic National Committee. The election of Brown marks the first time an African American has been chosen to lead a major American political party.

1989, February 10. Washington, D.C. FBI director William Sessions orders sweeping changes in the bureau's affirmative action program after finding that the bureau had discriminated against minority employees. African American and Hispanic agents were immediately placed on lists for promotions. Sessions then ordered that FBI employees receive training in racial sensitivity and that the equal employment office budget be increased. Ironically, the FBI is the agency charged with enforcing the nation's civil rights laws.

1989, February 10. Washington, D.C. Louis W. Sullivan, on sabbatical leave as president of Morehouse School of Medicine in Georgia, becomes secretary of the Department of Health and Human Services. He is the only African American selected in the first round of cabinet posts by the Bush administration.

1989, March 6. Washington, D.C. The U.S. Supreme Court declares a second affirmative action plan unconstitutional in the case *Milliken v. Michigan Road Builders Association*. The Michigan law required that 7 percent of state contracts be awarded to minority-owned businesses.

1989, March 7. Washington, D.C. A student sit-in at Howard University results in the resignation of Republican National Committee chairman Lee Atwater from the university's board of trustees four days following his appointment. The students claim that Atwater's stand on civil rights is the cause for the protest.

1989, April. Los Angeles, California. Mayor Tom Bradley wins reelection to a fifth term by a total of 157,000 votes.

1989, April 21. New Orleans, Louisiana. The nation's first nonpartisan African American summit convenes April 21–23. Its purpose is to discuss "an African American agenda for the next four years and onto the year 2000," said general chairman and Democratic Party leader Richard Hatcher. More than 4,000 delegates from the United States, the District of Columbia, and the Virgin Islands were invited.

1989, June 5. Washington, D.C. In *Ward's Cove Packing Co. v. Atonio*, the U.S. Supreme Court toughens the requirements for proof of discriminatory impact in job-discrimination suits. The Court also declares in such cases that an employer might justify policies that have a discriminatory impact by providing a reasonable business explanation.

1989, June 12. Washington, D.C. In *Martin v. Wilks*, the Supreme Court rules by a five–four majority that white workers claiming unfair treatment due to affirmative action settlements can seek compensation under civil rights legislation. The case involved white firefighters in Birmingham, Alabama, who claimed that affirmative action had deprived them of promotions. Civil rights leaders call the decisions a civil rights setback.

1989, July 2. Washington, D.C. The Reverend George A. Stallings Jr. conducts the first Mass of the Imani Temple African American Catholic Congregation.

1989, August 6. Washington, D.C. The National Urban League holds its annual conference. Addressing the conference, President George H. W. Bush remarks that he will not strive for stronger affirmative action legislation. He claims that the 1990s will see a surplus of available jobs and a shrinking worker pool.

1989, August 23. Brooklyn, New York. Yusuf K. Hawkins, African American youth, is fatally shot by five white youths in Brooklyn's predominantly white Bensonhurst section, igniting racial tension throughout the New York City area. The attack is regarded as the most serious racial incident in the city since 1986. On August 31, marches are held protesting the killing. On September 2, blacks protesting in Bensonhurst are confronted by white residents. Of the five youths charged with the killing of Hawkins, only one is convicted.

1989, October 12. The publication of Ralph Abernathy's book *And the Walls Came Tumbling Down* is greeted with outrage. The book claims that Martin Luther King Jr. spent the night before his murder with two women. Twenty-seven African American leaders issue a statement denouncing Abernathy's book.

1989, November 5. Montgomery, Alabama. The first memorial dedicated to the civil rights movement is unveiled. The memorial is commissioned by the Southern Poverty Law Center and designed by Maya Lin, who also created the Vietnam War Memorial in Washington, D.C.

1989, November 7. African American candidates do well in elections. In Virginia, L. Douglas Wilder becomes the first elected African American governor in U.S. history. In New York City, David N. Dinkins is elected the city's first African American mayor. In Detroit, Coleman A. Young is reelected to a fifth consecutive term as mayor. Michael R. White is elected as mayor of Cleveland. African American mayors are also elected in Seattle, Washington; New Haven, Connecticut; and Durham, North Carolina, for the first time in history.

1990, January 9. The Quality Education for Minorities Project releases its report and recommendations aimed at making schools more responsive to the needs of minority students. The project concludes that minority students are taught in "separate and decidedly unequal" schools resulting in a "gap between minority and non-minority educational achievements."

1990, January 18. Washington, D.C. Mayor Marion S. Barry Jr. is arrested after being videotaped purchasing and smoking crack cocaine. Following a split verdict, Barry is sentenced to six months in prison. The arrest generates speculation that Jesse Jackson will enter the 1990 Washington, D.C., mayoral race.

1990, February 8. Selma, Alabama. African American students stage a sit-in following the firing of the city's first African American school superintendent, Norward Roussell, on February 5. The firing is viewed as a battle to control the city's school board—white school board members outnumber African American members six to five, while 70 percent of Selma's student population is African American. The conflict ends after six days of protest. The board amends its position to permit Roussell to stay on as superintendent until the end of his contract.

1990, February 23. Dallas, Texas. Bishop College, founded in 1881 by a group of freed slaves and once the largest African American college in the western United States, is sold at a bankruptcy auction.

1990, March 6. Washington, D.C. Clarence Thomas, chairman of the Equal Employment Opportunity Commission, is appointed judge on the U.S. Circuit Court of Appeals for the District of Columbia.

1990, April 18. Washington, D.C. By a five–four majority in the case *Missouri v. Jenkins*, the U.S. Supreme Court upholds the authority of federal judges to order local governments to increase taxes to finance school desegregation. The case arose when U.S. district court judge Russell G. Clark adopted a desegregation plan that would create magnet schools to lure whites back into the inner city. To support this plan, Clark ordered that 75 percent of the costs be paid by the state and 25 percent by the district.

1990, June 27. Washington, D.C. The U.S. Supreme Court, by a five–four majority in the case *Metro Broadcasting v. FCC*, upholds federal affirmative action policies created to increase the number of broadcast licenses held by minorities and women.

1990, August 9. Georgia. The state's runoff primary system is challenged by the Justice Department. The Justice Department claims that the system is biased against African American candidates who often win a plurality of the vote in multicandidate primaries, but lose when matched with a single white candidate in a runoff election. While seven Southern states have similar primary systems, Georgia is targeted in the lawsuit because, statistically, African Americans make up 26 percent of the population but hold only 10 percent of all elected positions.

1990, August 11. Chicago, Illinois. Operation PUSH (People United to Save Humanity) calls for a boycott of Nike products. The organization reveals that African American consumers purchase approximately 30 percent of all Nike products, but are not represented on Nike's board of directors or in upper management. Nike is one of the country's largest manufacturers of athletic gear.

1990, August 21. Washington, D.C. Paul R. Philip, the FBI's highest-ranking African American agent, is chosen to investigate racial discrimination within the bureau. The investigation centers around charges made by a black agent against several white agents in the Chicago and Omaha offices.

1990, September 26. The U.S. Census Bureau releases its annual report on household income. The bureau reports that the average household income of African Americans is $18,083; Hispanics, $21,921; whites, $30,406; and Asians, $36,102. Ten percent of whites live in poverty, while 26.2 percent of Hispanics and 30.7 percent of African Americans live in poverty. Fifty percent of African American children below age six are classified as poor.

1990, September 27. Washington, D.C. At its annual conference, members of the Congressional Black Caucus charge law enforcement officials with targeting African American politicians for harassment and investigation. The prosecution of Washington, D.C., mayor Marion Barry is cited as an example.

1990, October 12. Cook County, Illinois. The Illinois Supreme Court validates a lower court decision to bar the Harold Washington Party from the ballot. The court cited an inadequate number of nominating signatures as the reason for its decision. The party, a mostly African American third party slate of candidates, is named for the late mayor of Chicago. Cook County Democrats had expressed concern that the Harold Washington Party would take votes from their candidates and guarantee the election of Republicans.

1990, October 22. Washington, D.C. President George H. W. Bush vetoes the Civil Rights Act of 1990. On October 16, the Senate passed the bill by a vote of sixty-two to thirty-four; the House of Representatives passed the bill on October 17. The legislation was designed to reverse the Court's 1989 decision in the case *Ward's Cove Packing Co. v. Atonio*, which made it more difficult for minorities and women to prove job discrimination. Bush cites his fear of the introduction of quotas in the workplace as his reason for rejecting the act. On October 24, an attempt to override the veto in the Senate falls one vote short of the two-thirds majority needed.

1990, November 6. Arizona. Voters in Arizona defeat two initiatives to reestablish a Martin Luther King Jr. holiday. The holiday had been a source of conflict since the Democratic governor, Bruce Babbitt, marked the day in 1986 by an executive order only to see it rescinded in 1987 by his successor, Republican Evan Mecham.

1990, December 12. The Department of Education announces that it will bar colleges and universities that receive federal funds from awarding minority scholarships. The department claims that race-specific scholarships are discriminatory and violate federal civil rights laws. On December 18, the department revises the policy, allowing schools that receive federal funds to award minority scholarships if the money comes from private sources or federal programs designed to aid minority students. On March 20, 1991, the policy is reversed completely.

1990, December 18. Mississippi. Byron de la Beckwith is charged for the third time with the 1963 murder of civil rights leader Medgar Evers. Beckwith was tried twice in 1964 with both trials ending in a deadlock.

1991, January 8. Results from a nationwide survey sponsored by the National Science Foundation reveals that white Americans continue to hold negative stereotypes of African Americans and Hispanics. Three-quarters of the whites surveyed felt that blacks and Hispanics are more likely to prefer welfare to work. A Census Bureau report shows the household worth of whites with families to average eight times that of Hispanic households and ten times that of black households.

1991, January 15. Washington, D.C. In a five–three decision, the U.S. Supreme Court puts an end to court-ordered busing in the Oklahoma City school district. Ruling in the case *Oklahoma City Board of Education v. Dowell*, the Court declares that the reemergence of single-race schools, resulting from shifting housing patterns, does not justify continued court-ordered busing. The decision overturns an appeals court ruling refusing to turn the once-segregated school district over to local control.

1991, January 20. A *New York Times*/CBS poll of public support for military action in the Persian Gulf reveals that only 47 percent of blacks polled compared to 80 percent of whites favored intervention. One theory on the difference in support points to the disproportionate number of African Americans to whites serving in the armed forces. While accounting for only 12 percent of the total U.S. population, African Americans represent 24.6 percent of the U.S. troops in the Gulf. Many African Americans point to the problems of drugs and crime as better places to direct government resources.

1991, February 26. Detroit, Michigan. By a nine-to-one majority, the Detroit Board of Education approves the creation of an all-male school for kindergarten through grade eight. The school's goal would be to provide African American male students with an improved learning environment by focusing on the unique problems facing the African American male. Critics of the school label the program discriminatory. The American Civil Liberties Union and the National Organization for Women Legal Defense Fund both file suit in federal district court. On August 15, the court rules that such a school must also be open to girls.

1991, March 3. Los Angeles, California. Black motorist Rodney King is severely beaten by several white police officers after being stopped for a speeding violation. The incident is videotaped by a witness watching from his apartment balcony.

1991, May 6. Washington, D.C. The creation of a National African American Museum within the Smithsonian Institution is approved by the institution's board of regents. The museum will include print and broadcast images of African Americans, along with African American art and artifacts.

1991, May 12. Hampton, Virginia. Students at Hampton University hold a silent protest while President George H. W. Bush gives the commencement address. The students point to the administration's policies regarding civil rights as a reason for the demonstration.

1991, May 14. The Washington-based Urban Institute releases its study on job discrimination. The study, conducted in Washington, D.C., and Chicago, reveals that whites seeking entry-level positions were three times more likely to receive favorable treatment than equally qualified African Americans.

1991, June 3. Washington, D.C. In the case of *Edmonson v. Leesville Concrete Co.*, the U.S. Supreme Court rules that potential jurors cannot be excluded from civil cases on the basis of race. The Court had, in two earlier cases, ruled that jurors could not be excluded because of race in criminal cases.

1991, June 4. Washington, D.C. After defeating two other civil rights bills, the U.S. House of Representatives passes a civil rights bill designed to reverse the Supreme Court's 1989 ruling in *Ward's Cove Packing Co. v. Atonio* and make it easier for victims of job discrimination to sue for damages. President George H. W. Bush opposes such legislation, claiming that it will force employers to set quotas for hiring minorities in order to protect themselves from possible discrimination suits.

1991, June 20. Washington, D.C. The U.S. Supreme Court in two separate cases, *Chison v. Roemer* and *Houston Lawyers v. Texas*, rules that the Voting Rights Act of 1965 is applicable to judicial elections. The cases arose from lower court rulings in Louisiana and Texas that claimed that judges were not representatives and, therefore, the election of such was not covered by the act.

1991, June 27. Washington, D.C. U.S. Supreme Court Justice Thurgood Marshall, citing his poor health and advancing age, announces his plans to retire from the bench. Marshall, appointed to the Court by President Lyndon B. Johnson in 1967, was the first African American to serve on the nation's highest court.

1991, July. Washington, D.C. President George H. W. Bush nominates African American court of appeals judge Clarence Thomas to replace the retiring Justice Thurgood Marshall. Thomas, a conservative and former chairman of the Equal Employment Opportunity Commission, was appointed by Bush in 1990 to the federal appeals court. Stating that while chairman of the EEOC, Thomas failed to display sensitivity regarding affirmative action, major national organizations, including the NAACP, the NAACP Legal Defense and Educational Fund, the Leadership Conference on Civil Rights, and the Congressional Black Caucus, voice opposition to the Thomas nomination.

1991, July 4. Memphis, Tennessee. The National Civil Rights Museum, housed in the former Lorraine Motel, is dedicated. Martin Luther King Jr. was shot at the Lorraine Motel on April 4, 1968.

1991, August 19. Brooklyn, New York. Tensions between African Americans and Jews in Brooklyn's Crown Heights section increase, when seven-year-old Gavin Cato is struck and killed by a car driven by a Jewish driver. Rioting erupts, and a Jewish rabbinical student is stabbed to death.

1991, September 29. The Department of Justice releases its report on death-row inmates. The report reveals that 40 percent of the inmates awaiting execution in the United States are African American, whereas African Americans constitute only 12.1 percent of the general population.

1991, October 11. Los Angeles, California. Korean grocer Soon Ja Du is convicted of voluntary manslaughter for the death of Latasha Harlins. The shooting exacerbates racial tension between African Americans and Koreans.

1991, November 1. Washington, D.C. In a public ceremony, Judge Clarence Thomas is formally seated as the 106th associate justice of the U.S. Supreme Court.

1991, November 5. Washington, D.C. In the case *Hafer v. Melo*, the U.S. Supreme Court rules in a unanimous vote that state officials can be sued as individuals acting in an official status and be held personally liable in civil rights suits.

1991, November 7. Washington, D.C. The House of Representatives passes Senate Bill 1745, a new civil rights bill, which was passed by the Senate on October 30. President George H. W. Bush signs the bill into law on November 21. However, the signing ceremony for the long-anticipated law is dominated by controversy over a proposed presidential directive that tried to impose a conservative interpretation on the new legislation. Immediately after circulation of the draft, civil rights leaders, senators, and cabinet members condemn it as an attack on all civil rights progress.

1991, December 30. Alabama. U.S. district court judge Harold L. Murphy orders the Alabama state university system to rectify racial discrimination in its hiring, admissions, and financing practices. It is ruled that Alabama's

Dedication of National Civil Rights Museum, Memphis, TN, July 4, 1991. *With the Reverend Joseph Lowery holding her right arm and Judge D'Army Bailey holding her left, civil rights activist Rosa Parks attends the museum's dedication day. Other dignitaries attending include the Reverend Jesse Jackson* (second from left). **MICHAEL MCMULLAN/THE COMMERCIAL APPEAL/LANDOV**

higher education system, divided into predominantly white and predominantly African American schools, fosters inferior funding for the predominantly African American universities. Judge Murphy states he will retain jurisdiction over the case for ten years to ensure his orders are carried out.

1992, January 2. Washington, D.C. A lawsuit filed by the National Treasury Employees Union challenges the Equal Employment Opportunity Commission's policy which states that the 1991 Civil Rights Act does not apply to job discrimination lawsuits filed prior to the law's enactment in November of 1991.

1992, January 17. Atlanta, Georgia. President George H. W. Bush visits the Martin Luther King Jr. Center for Nonviolent Social Change to sign a proclamation officially declaring Martin Luther King Jr.'s birthday a federal holiday.

1992, January 19. The American Council on Education releases their tenth annual report confirming that the number of minority students attending college increased during the 1980s. The report shows 33 percent of black, 29 percent of Hispanic, and 39.4 percent of white high school graduates were attending college in 1990, up respectively from 21.6 percent, 26.1 percent, and 34.4 percent in 1985.

1992, January 20. Denver, Colorado. The seventh commemoration of Martin Luther King Jr.'s birthday as a federal holiday triggers violence in Denver between civil rights supporters and members of the Ku Klux Klan following a Klan rally. Civil rights supporters throw bricks and bottles at a bus carrying Klan members away from the rally.

1992, February 10. Seattle, Washington. Alex Haley, the Pulitzer Prize–winning author of *Roots* and *The Autobiography of Malcolm X*, dies of heart failure.

1992, February 15. Baltimore, Maryland. The NAACP's Benjamin L. Hooks announces his plans to resign from his position as the organization's director. The announcement is made after Hazel Dukes, the national president, and several other prominent board members are denied reelection.

1992, March 31. Washington, D.C. In the case of *Freeman v. Pitts*, the U.S. Supreme Court rules unanimously that school districts operating under court-supervised desegregation orders can slowly be released from court supervision to local control as they achieve racial equality. Reaction to the ruling by educators and civil rights experts is mixed, with general uncertainty as to how the decision will be applied by district courts reviewing individual desegregation orders.

1992, April 29. Los Angeles, California. Riots erupt in Los Angeles following the acquittal of four white police officers in the beating of black motorist Rodney King. The suburban Simi Valley jury that acquitted the police officers had no African American members. The videotaped beating was broadcast around the world and provoked outrage condemning police brutality. With the announcement of the verdict, looting and violence break out across the South Central section of Los Angeles. By the end of the first day, twelve people are dead and more than 100 arson fires engulf the area. Mayor Tom Bradley declares a local state of emergency and Governor Pete Wilson orders the National Guard to assist local police in controlling the increasing violence. President George H. W. Bush orders the deployment of 1,500 Marines and 3,000 U.S. Army troops to Los Angeles.

1992, June 26. Washington, D.C. In the case of *United States v. Fordice*, the U.S. Supreme Court rules eight–one that the state of Mississippi has not sufficiently desegregated its public universities. Despite "race-neutral" admissions standards, certain policies are targeted as causing informal segregation. Examples include wording of mission statements and higher admissions standards at the predominantly white colleges.

1992, July 23. Washington, D.C. The 1990 U.S. Census shows African American median household incomes at $19,758 compared to $31,435 for whites and $30,056 for the national median average. The statistics show that blacks earn 63 percent of the median white income, only slightly better than the 62 percent earned by blacks ten years prior.

1992, August 29. Washington, D.C. The FBI's Uniform Crime Reports gives the rate of violent offenses by juveniles (ages ten to seventeen) as 430 out of 100,000 in 1990. African American arrests are 1,429 out of 100,000, five times the amount of whites arrested.

1992, September 3. Washington, D.C. A 1991 U.S. Census Bureau report finds that the number of Americans below the poverty level is the highest number since 1964. In 1991, 14.2 percent of Americans were in poverty compared to 13.5 percent in 1990. In 1991, 32.7 percent of African Americans were in poverty compared to 31.9 percent in 1990.

1992, September 16. Washington, D.C. The U.S. Department of Education's report on high school dropout rates shows a 13.6 percent dropout of African American students (ages sixteen to twenty-four) in 1991 compared to 21.3 percent in 1972. The dropout rate of Hispanics rose from 34.3 percent to 35.3 percent, whereas the rate for whites dropped from 12.3 percent to 8.9 percent.

1992, September 28. Berkeley, California. The University of California, Berkeley, Law School is found in violation of federal civil rights laws by the U.S. Department of Education Office for Civil Rights. It is discovered that minority applicants to the school receive preferential treatment over other candidates. As a result of this ruling, the school's admission policies are revised.

1992, October 8. Boston, Massachusetts. A study conducted by the Federal Reserve's regional bank shows evidence of bank discrimination against minorities applying for mortgages. The study measures black, Hispanic, and white rejection rates when all applicants had similar application criteria. The findings show 17 percent rejection of minorities compared to 11 percent rejection of whites. This study is the first to investigate loan-application criteria.

1992, November 3. The presidential election brings sixteen new African American members to Congress for a total of thirty-eight. Senator Earl F. Hilliard is the first African American Alabaman elected to Congress. The District of Columbia's Marion Barry wins a seat on Washington's city council. Florida's first three African American representatives—Corrine Brown, Carrie Meek, and Alcee Hastings—benefit from court-ordered redistricting. In Georgia, three African Americans join Congress: Senator Nathan Deal, Representative Jackie Barrett, and Representative Cynthia McKinney. McKinney is the first African American woman voted into the Georgia House of Representatives.

1992, November. Detroit, Michigan. Two Detroit policemen are charged with murder and two policemen are charged with lesser criminal charges in the beating death of black motorist Malice Green. Larry Nevers and Walter Budzyn, two white police officers, pulled Green out of his car and beat him on the head with metal flashlights. Sergeant Freddie Douglas, a African American policeman, is charged with failing to stop the beating. White policeman Robert Lessnau is charged with participating in the beating and aggravated assault. Innocent pleas are entered for all four officers.

1992, November 6. Washington, D.C. U.S. Labor Department figures show a decrease in unemployment rates from 7.5 percent in September to 7.4 percent in October. In September, jobless rates drop from 6.7 percent to 6.5 percent for whites, from 11.9 percent to 11.8 percent for Hispanics, and rose to 13.9 percent from 13.7 percent for blacks.

1992, November 7. An outline for one of Martin Luther King Jr.'s speeches is purchased at an auction for $35,000 by New Jersey group Kaller and Associates. The King estate filed a lawsuit requesting the return of the document plus

$5 million in punitive damages from the dealer, Superior Galleries. King rarely made outlines or notes for his speeches, which explains the inflated worth.

1992, November 18. *Malcolm X*, Spike Lee's motion picture based on Alex Haley's biography of the slain civil rights leader, opens in theaters nationwide.

1992, December 12. Washington, D.C. President-elect Bill Clinton's cabinet and White House appointments include five African American men and one African American woman. They are: Clifton R. Wharton Jr. as deputy secretary of the Department of State; Hazel R. O'Leary as secretary of the Department of Energy; Mike Espy as head of the Agriculture Department; Ron Brown, the former Democratic National Committee chairman, as secretary of the Department of Commerce; Jesse Brown as Veterans Affairs secretary; and Joycelyn Elders as surgeon general.

1993, January 5. Washington, D.C. The House of Representatives passes by twenty-two votes a rules change that will allow an increase in voting rights to delegates from Washington, D.C., and the U.S. territories of American Samoa, Guam, Puerto Rico, and the U.S. Virgin Islands. (The District of Columbia and the Virgin Islands have large African American populations.) In the past, the delegates took part in committee actions and votes, but not votes on the House floor, which were restricted to representatives from "the states" because the Constitution stipulated that only "the states" should have legislative authority. Delegates may now participate in all but the final votes affecting legislation.

1993, January 7. Washington, D.C. Senator Carol Moseley Braun is one of two women elected to the Senate Judiciary Committee. Moseley Braun claimed she was inspired to run partly as a result of angry feelings over the Anita Hill–Clarence Thomas hearings in 1991. The all-male Judiciary Committee had been admonished by the public for its role in the handling of the hearings.

1993, January 18. New Hampshire renames its January holiday from Civil Rights Day to King Day. This is the first time that all fifty states have a holiday for Martin Luther King Jr.

1993, January 24. Bethesda, Maryland. Thurgood Marshall, the first African American Supreme Court justice and lifelong supporter of civil rights, dies of heart failure.

Denzel Washington as Malcolm X (1992). *Washington was nominated for an Academy Award for best actor for his performance in the title role.* © CONTENT MINE INTERNATIONAL/ALAMAY

1993, March 2. Washington, D.C. In the case of *Voinovich v. Quilter*, the U.S. Supreme Court rules that the authority to create voting districts dominated by ethnic minorities is held by individual states. The issue was brought before the Court because of concern over the reorganization practices of Ohio's state legislative voting districts in 1990.

1993, April 9. Baltimore, Maryland. Civil rights champion Benjamin F. Chavis Jr. is elected as executive director of the NAACP.

1993, April 17. Los Angeles, California. In a civil suit, two of the four Los Angeles police officers charged in the beating of African American motorist Rodney King are convicted, while the other two are acquitted. Officer Lawrence M. Powell is convicted of violating King's rights to an arrest without "unreasonable force." Powell delivered the majority of hits to King with his baton. Sergeant Stacey C. Koon is convicted of allowing the violation by Powell to occur. Officers Theodore J. Briseno and Timothy E. Wind are found not guilty on all charges. As a result of the riots in 1991, the people of Los Angeles were on edge awaiting the new verdict. Riot training for 7,000 Los Angeles police officers and advance notice of the verdict to the police prepared them for the possibility of further rioting.

1993, May 17. Washington, D.C. The U.S. Supreme Court sends the case of *American Family Mutual Insurance Co. v. National Association for the Advancement of Colored People* back to the lower courts. Until decisions by the lower courts, the federal Fair Housing Act may be interpreted to extend coverage toward homeowner's insurance. The NAACP charged that the insurance company refused to sell to African Americans or charged them exorbitant fees. The practice is also known as "redlining."

1993, May 23. Washington, D.C. The *Washington Post* begins publishing portions of the late Supreme Court justice Thurgood Marshall's papers. Immediately following Marshall's death, his papers are made available for use by "researchers or scholars engaged in serious research." These conditions were requested by Marshall when he turned his papers over to the Library of Congress after his retirement. Supreme Court chief justice Rehnquist wrote librarian James H. Billington a letter admonishing him for lack of judgment in releasing the papers so soon. Marshall's friends, family, and colleagues displayed similar feelings of anger at the papers' speedy release.

1993, June 3. Washington, D.C. President Bill Clinton retracts his nomination of Lani Guinier for the position of head of the civil rights division in the Justice Department. Guinier, an African American law professor, had expressed some controversial ideas relating to race and voting rights in previous professional writings. Clinton justifies his decision by explaining that the views expressed in the writings clashed with his own opinions on the same topics.

1993, June 7. Pop star Prince changes his name to a symbol that combines the signs for male and female.

1993, June 26. Woodland Hills, California. Hall of Fame catcher Roy Campanella, one of the first African Americans to play in the major leagues, dies of a heart attack.

1993, August 4. Los Angeles, California. A federal judge sentences Sergeant Stacey Koon and Officer Lawrence Powell to two and a half years in prison for violating the civil rights of motorist Rodney King during a 1991 beating.

1993, August 4. New York City. Leonard Jeffries Jr. is reinstated as chairman of City College's black studies department. A judge rules that the decision by college administrators to remove Jeffries following a controversial 1991 speech violated his constitutional right to free speech.

1993, August 23. Detroit, Michigan. Two white officers, Larry Nevers and Walter Budzyn, are convicted of second-degree murder in the beating death of motorist Malice Green.

1993, September 7. West Palm Beach, Florida. Two white men are convicted of kidnapping and setting afire an African American tourist on January 1, 1993. The men are also convicted of attempted murder and armed robbery. They are sentenced to life imprisonment on October 22.

1993, September 14. Philadelphia, Pennsylvania. The University of Pennsylvania decides not to suspend a group of African American students who seized 14,000 copies of the student newspaper, *Daily Pennsylvanian*. The students took the newspapers to protest what they viewed as the *Daily Pennsylvanian*'s conservative and racially biased views.

1993, October 8. New York City. Actor Ted Danson is chastised for appearing onstage in blackface and telling several racist and sexist jokes during a Friars Club roast for actress Whoopi Goldberg.

1993, October 18. Los Angeles, California. Two African American men are acquitted of attempted murder in the beating of truck driver Reginald Denny during the 1992 riot.

1993, October 20. Don Cornelius steps down as host of the syndicated television dance show *Soul Train* after twenty-two years.

1993, November 2. New York City. Mayor David Dinkins is defeated in a mayoral election by former U.S. attorney Rudolph Giuliani.

1993, November 2. Detroit, Michigan. Dennis Archer defeats Sharon McPhail to become mayor of Detroit, succeeding Coleman Young.

1994, February 3. Washington, D.C. Nation of Islam leader Louis Farrakhan censures aide Khalid Abdul Muhammad for anti-Semitic remarks made in a November 1993 speech.

1994, February 5. Jackson, Mississippi. Byron de la Beckwith, a white supremacist, is convicted of the 1963 murder of civil rights leader Medgar Evers. Beckwith is sentenced to life in prison.

1994, March 1. Berkeley, California. Former Black Panther leader Eldridge Cleaver is hospitalized after suffering a brain hemorrhage.

1994, March 23. Los Angeles, California. Earvin "Magic" Johnson is named coach of the Los Angeles Lakers.

1994, April 12. Washington, D.C. Randall Robinson, executive director of TransAfrica, a lobbying group for African and Caribbean issues, begins a liquid fast to protest the U.S. government's "discriminatory policy" on Haiti.

1994, May 24. Santa Ana, California. Denny's Restaurants agree to pay $54 million to settle lawsuits by African Americans who claim they were discriminated against by the restaurant chain.

1994, May 26. Dominican Republic. Pop star Michael Jackson and Lisa Marie Presley, daughter of Elvis Presley, are married.

1994, June 20. Los Angeles, California. Former football star O. J. Simpson is arrested and charged with the June 12 murder of his ex-wife, Nicole Brown Simpson, and her friend, Ron Goldman.

1994, August 20. Chicago, Illinois. Benjamin F. Chavis is ousted as executive director of the NAACP by the civil rights organization's board of directors. Earl T. Shinhoster is named interim director.

1994, October 3. Washington, D.C. Mike Espy, secretary of the U.S. Department of Agriculture, resigns following a federal ethics investigation in which Espy is accused of receiving gifts from businesses regulated by the U.S. Department of Agriculture.

1994, October 21. Atlanta, Georgia. Dexter Scott King, the youngest son of the late Reverend Martin Luther King Jr., is named chief executive and chairman of the Martin Luther King Jr. Center for Nonviolent Social Change.

1994, December 9. Washington, D.C. Joycelyn Elders resigns as U.S. surgeon general after making controversial statements regarding drug use and sex education.

1994, December 14. Washington, D.C. Representative Donald M. Payne, a Democrat from New Jersey, is elected to a two-year term as chairman of the Congressional Black Caucus.

1995, January 12. Minneapolis, Minnesota. Qubilah Bahiyah Shabazz, daughter of the late black nationalist leader Malcolm X, is arrested and charged with plotting to kill Nation of Islam leader Louis Farrakhan.

1995, June 21. Washington, D.C. The Senate rejects Dr. Henry Foster Jr.'s bid to become U.S. surgeon general. Foster, a gynecologist and obstetrician, is rejected due to pressure from antiabortion groups and Senate Republicans.

1995, June 29. Washington, D.C. The Supreme Court, by a five–four vote, rules that electoral districts drawn to ensure fair political representation of African Americans and other minorities are unconstitutional if race is used as the predominant factor in drawing district boundaries.

1995, July 20. Davis, California. The University of California votes to eliminate affirmative action policies in the admission of students.

1995, October 3. Los Angeles, California. O. J. Simpson is acquitted of the murder of his former wife Nicole Brown Simpson and her friend, Ron Goldman. The trial was televised daily throughout the United States and fueled extensive debate regarding race relations in America.

1995, October 3. Creve Coeur, Missouri. Eddie Robinson of Grambling State University in Louisiana reaches 400 wins in fifty-three seasons to become college football's winningest coach.

1995, October 16. Washington, D.C. The Million Man March, organized by Nation of Islam leader Louis Farrakhan, draws African American men to the nation's capital. The purpose of the march is to offer African American men an opportunity to meet for a day of atonement and to pledge their commitment to themselves, their families, and their communities.

1995, November 8. Alexandria, Virginia. Former chairman of the Joint Chiefs of Staff, Colin L. Powell, ends months of speculation by announcing that he will not run for the U.S. presidency in 1996.

1995, December 9. Chicago, Illinois. Kweisi Mfume is unanimously elected as president and chief executive officer of the NAACP.

1995, December 12. Washington, D.C. Jesse Jackson Jr., son of the famed civil rights activist, is elected as the representative of Illinois's Second Congressional District. He replaced Representative Mel Reynolds, who resigned from Congress after being sentenced to five years in prison for sexual misconduct.

1996, January 15. Five of the largest African American congregations in the United States announce the formulation of Revelation Corporation of America, a for-profit company designed to improve the buying power of African American consumers.

1996, January 17. Austin, Texas. Barbara Charline Jordan, scholar, educator, and politician, dies in a hospital of pneumonia and complications from leukemia. She had suffered from multiple sclerosis for several years. In 1966, Jordan became the first African American elected state senator in Texas. In 1972, she was elected to the U.S. Congress, becoming the state's first African American and first woman elected to the position. An excellent orator, Jordan gained national attention in 1974 when she called for the impeachment of President Richard M. Nixon for his involvement in the Watergate scandal. Two years later, she became the first African American woman to give a keynote address at the Democratic National Convention.

1996, January 30. Los Angeles, California. Los Angeles Lakers star Earvin "Magic" Johnson announces his return to the National Basketball Association (NBA) after retiring in 1991. He played in thirty-two of their forty games remaining. Later that year, he was named among the fifty Greatest NBA Players of all time. He retired again and purchased a minority share in the Lakers.

1996, March 11. Baltimore, Maryland. Political activist C. DeLores Tucker urges churches to boycott stores that sell "gangsta rap" on the grounds that it glorifies the use of violence and drugs and degrades women.

1996, April 3. Dubrovnik, Croatia. Commerce Secretary Ronald H. Brown and distinguished American business leaders are killed in a plane crash.

1996, April 8. Cleveland, Ohio. After seventeen years of busing, a federal judge lifts a school desegregation order, which district officials claim will save $10 million.

1996, May 28. Pensacola, Florida. Donnie Cochran, who in 1994 became the first African American commander of the U.S. Navy's Blue Angels flight demonstration team, resigns. He cites his own shortcomings in flying that could threaten the safety of his pilots and spectators.

1996, June 13. Washington, D.C. The U.S. Supreme Court declares unconstitutional two congressional districts in North Carolina and three in Texas because the districts—majority African American and majority Hispanic—were illegally drawn.

1996, June 22. Washington, D.C. The Senate approves Vice Admiral J. Paul Reason to become the U.S. Navy's first African American four-star admiral. President Bill Clinton nominated Reason for the promotion on May 13. Reason later assumes command of the U.S. Atlantic Fleet in Norfolk, Virginia.

1996, June 27. Washington, D.C. President Bill Clinton signs the Church Arson Bill, affecting racially motivated burnings. The bill authorizes $10 million to be used to help build churches that are underinsured and increases the sentence for such crimes.

1996, July 1. Washington, D.C. The U.S. Supreme Court confirms the ruling that race cannot be a factor in admitting students to the University of Texas Law School. Previously, separate and lower standards were used to admit African Americans and Hispanics.

1996, August 30. Tripoli, Libya. Louis Farrakhan receives the Gadhafi International Human Rights Award for organizing the Million Man March. However, U.S. law bars him from accepting gifts from terrorists.

1996, September 13. Las Vegas, Nevada. Rap artist Tupac Shakur, a victim of a drive-by shooting, dies. His career had been marked by violence and run-ins with law enforcement agents. Shakur was named after an Inca chief and raised by his mother, Afeni Shakur, a Black Panther Party member who was imprisoned while pregnant with her son. Tupac Shakur sold millions of records of "gangsta"-style rap music. In some of his works, he taunted the police and glorified violence and misogyny. He became a target for groups that aimed to clean up rap lyrics.

1996, September. Chicago, Illinois. Talk-show host Oprah Winfrey is the nation's highest-paid entertainer, earning $171 million during 1995–1996 season according to *Forbes* magazine.

1996, October 4. Washington, D.C. Congress passes a bill authorizing the creation of 500,000 black Revolutionary War Patriots commemorative coins. They are to depict the 275th anniversary of the birth of Revolutionary War hero Crispus Attucks.

1996, October 25. Tulsa, Oklahoma. J. B. Stradford, who died sixty years earlier, is cleared of charges that he was one of dozens of African Americans accused of inciting the Tulsa riot of May 31, 1921.

1996, November 5. Atlanta, Georgia. Cynthia McKinney, a Democrat from Georgia, is reelected to the U.S. House of Representatives after district lines are redrawn, making her district predominantly white.

1996, November 12. Washington, D.C. President Bill Clinton signs legislation creating the Selma-to-Montgomery National Historic Trail in Alabama, marking the route of the civil rights march that Martin Luther King Jr. led in 1965.

1996, November 15. White Plains, New York. Texaco Inc., a major oil company headquartered in White Plains, agrees to a $176.1 million settlement of a federal discrimination lawsuit filed in 1994 by African American Texaco employees—the largest race discrimination lawsuit ever filed. The company also agrees to help create an outside task force to oversee a Texaco diversity program. On November 4, the *New York Times* made public the existence of an audiotape containing Texaco executives' disparaging racial remarks including their reference to African American workers as "black jelly beans." The company has 27,000 employees, more than 1,400 of whom are African American.

1996, December 18. Oakland, California. The school board recognizes Black English, or Ebonics, as a separate language rather than slang or dialect. The board subsequently rescinds its decision to make Ebonics a second language.

1997, January 3. New York City. *Today Show* anchor Bryant Gumbel, the longest-serving host in the show's history, resigns after fifteen years.

1997, January 13. Washington, D.C. President Bill Clinton awards seven African American soldiers Medals of Honor.

Joseph Vernon Baker, seventy-seven, the only living recipient in the group, attended the awards ceremony. Baker was a second lieutenant in the U.S. Army's 92nd Infantry Division. None of the 433 Medals of Honor awarded to servicemen for acts of gallantry in World War II had been given to African Americans. African American veterans, however, petitioned the Department of the Army to honor African American servicemen as well.

1997, February 13. Washington, D.C. David Satcher is sworn in as U.S. surgeon general and assistant secretary for Health at the Department of Health and Human Services. A physician, educator, and former medical school president, he leaves the position he had held since 1993 as head of the Centers for Disease Control in Atlanta. He was the first African American to head the centers. President Bill Clinton nominated Satcher for the surgeon general's post on September 12, 1996.

1997, February 17. Richmond, Virginia. The Virginia House of Delegates retires the state song "Carry Me Back to Old Virginia" by unanimous vote. African American composer James A. Bland wrote the song in 1875; it was adopted by the state in 1940.

1997, February 26. Major League Baseball dedicates the season to Jackie Robinson, who on April 15, 1947—fifty years earlier—broke the league's color barrier.

1997, April 2. Nashville, Tennessee. Tennessee ratifies the Fifteenth Amendment 127 years after its ratification by Congress. The amendment guarantees the right to vote regardless of "race, color or previous condition of servitude."

1997, April 13. Augusta, Georgia. Eldrick "Tiger" Woods wins the sixty-first Masters with the lowest score in tournament history. He is the first African American and the youngest person to win the Masters.

1997, May 1. Washington, D.C. The U.S. Senate confirms Alexis M. Herman, assistant to President Bill Clinton, as U.S. secretary of labor.

1997, May 15. Washington, D.C. President Bill Clinton issues an apology to the few remaining survivors and relatives of the African American men who were involved in the federal government's "Tuskegee Experiment" that ended nearly a quarter of a century earlier.

1997, May 28. Chicago, Illinois. Eighty-four-year-old John H. Stengstacke, owner and publisher of the *Chicago Defender*, dies. He founded the Negro Newspaper Publishers Association.

1997, June 13. Baltimore, Maryland. After conducting a survey of the hotel industry as a part of its Economic Reciprocity Campaign, the NAACP gives failing grades to three major hotel chains for their hiring and promotion practices and relations with African American businesses. Receiving the grades were Holiday Inn, Westin, and Best Western.

1997, June 14. Washington, D.C. President Bill Clinton names seven people to the White House Initiative on Race and Reconciliation and appoints historian John Hope Franklin chair. The panel's charge is to lead a year-long national dialogue about race.

1997, June 14. San Diego, California. President Bill Clinton delivers a speech on race in the United States at the commencement exercises of the University of California, San Diego. He said, "Now we know what we will look like. But what will we be like? Can we be one America, respecting, even celebrating our differences, but embracing even more what we have in common?"

1997, June 23. New York City. Betty Shabazz, college educator and administrator and widow of slain black nationalist Malcolm X, dies after suffering from extensive burns on June 1. The fires causing her death were apparently set by her grandson, Malcolm Shabazz, a troubled twelve-year-old, in her Yonkers, New York, apartment. Betty Shabazz held numerous speaking engagements, often addressing such issues as health and education for disadvantaged youth and black self-determination.

1997, July 10. Birmingham, Alabama. The FBI reopens investigation into bombings of the Sixteenth Street Baptist Church where four young African American girls were killed on September 15, 1963, while attending Sunday school.

1997, July 24. Washington, D.C. The Army Corps of Engineers agrees to settle a race discrimination suit filed by African American deckhands on the dredge *Hurley*, based in Memphis, Tennessee. The Defense Department found that African American workers aboard the ship routinely endured racial epithets and jokes from whites and were denied promotions because they were African American. The sixteen deckhands each received $62,500 and were given the opportunity to move from part-time to full-time employment.

1997, August 4. Washington, D.C. Robert G. Stanton is sworn into office and becomes the first African American director of the Interior Department's National Park Service. He had worked with the park service from 1962 to January of 1967, then retired from the agency's national capital region.

1997, October. Oakland, California. The Black Panther Legacy Tour begins under the leadership of David Hilliard, former chief of staff for the Panthers. The bus tour winds through the Oakland neighborhood where the Panthers were founded in 1966 and other sites of significance to the history of the group.

1997, October 25. Philadelphia, Pennsylvania. Over 300,000 African American women arrive for the first Million Woman March. Among the speakers are Maxine Waters, Winnie Mandela, and rapper Sister Souljah.

1997, December 6. Houston, Texas. Lee P. Brown, Democrat, veteran law enforcement officer, and former "drug czar," is elected mayor, the first African American to hold the post. The city's population of 1.8 million reports a racial mix of one-third white, one-third black, and one-third Hispanic.

1998, January 15. Atlanta, Georgia. Martin Luther King III succeeds Joseph E. Lowery as head of the SCLC. Lowery held the post for twenty years.

1998, January 16. Maryland. A county school district in Maryland bans Toni Morrison's novel *Song of Solomon*.

1998, January 23. Cambridge, Massachusetts. Harvard University announces the appointment of Lani Guinier as a full tenured professor in the Harvard Law School. She is the first African American woman to receive tenure at the law school and is known for her outspoken stance on issues such as voting rights and affirmative action.

1998, February 2. Washington, D.C. Jane E. Smith becomes president of the National Council of Negro Women, succeeding Dorothy I. Height who held the post for forty years.

1998, February 5. Washington, D.C. Documents from Brown & Williamson Tobacco Company relating to marketing strategies aimed at teenagers and minorities are released during a House judiciary hearing. The documents date back to 1972 and had been used in state lawsuits against the tobacco industry. The Brown & Williamson papers document strategies to attract African Americans, suggesting that a Kool-brand basketball "could become an interesting symbol within the inner city."

1998, February 9. Baltimore, Maryland. Myrlie Evers-Williams announces that she will not seek a fourth term as chair of the NAACP's board of directors. She leaves the organization that she has headed since 1995 with what she calls a surplus of over $2 million and with restored credibility and financial integrity.

1998, February 21. Baltimore, Maryland. Civil rights activist and educator Julian Bond is elected chair of the NAACP's board of directors, succeeding Myrlie Evers-Williams. He announced his aim to continue the organization's progress "on our way to financial health and integrity."

1998, March 21. Jackson, Mississippi. The state of Mississippi releases documents relating to the now-defunct Mississippi State Sovereignty Commission that used spy tactics and intimidation to preserve racial segregation in the state during the civil rights era. Created in 1956, the commission promoted racial segregation in Mississippi and throughout the country. In 1989, U.S. District Judge William H. Barber ordered the files open. The documents show that previously secret files included information on individual civil rights workers, their religious beliefs, sexual behavior, and other details. License plate numbers were recorded outside civil rights meeting places. Many African American informers were used as spies. Some of the documents discuss the use of violence against the civil rights workers.

1998, March 22. Africa. President Bill Clinton begins an historic twelve-day tour of sub-Saharan Africa in the accompaniment of such notable African Americans as Jesse Jackson Sr., Congresswoman Maxine Waters, and Camille Cosby.

1998, April 14. Washington, D.C. Franklin D. Raines is named chief executive of the nation's largest mortgage financing company, Fannie Mae.

1998, April 23. Nashville, Tennessee. James Earl Ray, convicted killer of Martin Luther King Jr., dies of liver disease.

1998, May 1. In response to written objections concerning "the N word," *Merriam-Webster Dictionary* officials announce a plan to revise over 200 words regarded as offensive.

1998, May 2. Pomona, California. Eldridge Cleaver, writer, minister, and former leader of the Black Panther Party, dies of undisclosed causes.

1998, June 19. Boston, Massachusetts. Columnist Patricia Smith, on staff since 1990, resigns from the *Boston Globe* after admitting that she fabricated sections of her columns.

1998, July. Atlanta, Georgia. Myrlie Evers-Williams, who resigned as board chair of the NAACP, is named chairman emeritus at the organization's annual meeting.

1998, July 19. New York City. Historian and African history scholar John Henrik Clarke dies of a heart attack in Harlem at age eighty-three.

1998, July 22. Atlanta, Georgia. A federal judge rules that CBS News is not guilty of copyright infringement for airing film coverage of Martin Luther King Jr.'s famous "I Have a Dream" speech of 1963, and that the deceased leader's speech is in public domain. CBS used the footage in *The 20th Century with Mike Wallace*, shown in 1994. The King family sued CBS for its use of the film.

1998, July 24. Manning, South Carolina. In the largest award given to the victims of a hate crime, a jury orders the Ku Klux Klan and its grand dragon to pay $37.8 million for the 1995 burning of the Macedonia Baptist Church in Bloomville.

1998, September 7. Atlanta, Georgia. Hundreds of young people attend the Million Youth March supported by such organizations as the NAACP, the SCLC, and Operation PUSH (People United to Serve Humanity). A similar march was held earlier in New York City, but without the organizations' support.

1998, September 18. Washington, D.C. The White House Initiative on Race and Reconciliation, after fifteen months of examination, releases its report and confirms that racism is still a critical problem in the United States.

1998, September 21. Mission Viejo, California. Olympic star Florence Griffith Joyner, the first woman to win four Olympic medals, dies of an epileptic seizure while sleeping.

1998, November 1. Oxford, England. Genetic evidence, based on blood samples from living descendants of Thomas Jefferson and his slave, Sally Hemings, prove it is likely that Jefferson had fathered a son by Hemings. The DNA was analyzed by an Oxford University research team in England and the results published in the November 5 issue of *Nature*.

1998, November 9. Chicago, Illinois. U.S. Senator Carol Moseley Braun loses her bid for reelection to Republican Peter Fitzgerald.

1998, December 2. Washington, D.C. Mike Espy, former secretary of the U.S. Department of Agriculture, is acquitted of charges involving gifts received from businesses regulated by the department.

1999, February 2. Berkeley, California. Five civil rights advocacy groups file suit against the University of California, Berkeley, charging that the school discriminates against minorities in its admissions policies. The groups argue that the elimination of race-based admissions places too much importance on grade point averages (GPA), Scholastic Aptitude Test (SAT) scores, and advanced placement (AP) courses, which they already regard as inherently biased and discriminatory against minorities. The suit follows recent abolition of race-based admissions policies in California's state universities.

1999, February 4. Amadou Diallo, an unarmed African American immigrant from Guinea, is mistakenly shot and killed by four white policemen in New York City, raising a national outcry. Diallo was hit by nineteen shots in a volley of gunfire. Police said they thought the suspect was reaching for a gun when in fact he was attempting to pull out his wallet.

1999, February 19. Washington, D.C. President Bill Clinton pardons Henry O. Flipper, the first African American graduate of West Point who was court-martialed in 1881 and dishonorably discharged in 1882, fifty-nine years after Flipper's death. Clinton notes that "this good man now has completely recovered his good name." Flipper was ostracized by his white classmates. Although acquitted of apparently trumped-up charges of embezzling commissary funds, he was found guilty of "conduct unbecoming an officer" for lying to investigators. In 1976, the army formally exonerated Flipper, changed his discharge to honorable, and reburied him with full honors in his hometown, Thomasville, Georgia. An annual award is now given in his name to an outstanding West Point cadet.

1999, February 25. Jasper, Texas. White supremacist John William King is sentenced to die for his involvement in the murder of James Byrd Jr. on June 7, 1998. Byrd was tied to the rear of a truck and dragged to his death. Two other men accused in the murder, Lawrence Russell Brewer and Shawn Allen Berry, await trial.

1999, March 16. Miami, Florida. Henry Lyons, convicted of racketeering and grand theft, resigns as president of the National Baptist Convention USA—a position he had held since 1994. He had survived earlier attempts of his church denomination to oust him from the convention's presidency and retained the support of his parishioners at Bethel Metropolitan Baptist Church, the church he pastored in St. Petersburg, Florida. Lyons was convicted of pocketing $240,000 in donations earmarked to African American churches burned by arson and for swindling over $4 million from corporations seeking business transactions with the convention.

1999, April. Trenton, North Carolina. The Trenton Town Council unanimously selects its first African American and first woman mayor. Sylvia Willis succeeded white mayor Joffree Legett who resigned under pressure after denouncing African Americans as unfit to govern and claiming that blacks would rather be led by whites. Earlier, the town of about 200 residents—fifty of them African American—refused to annex three African American neighborhoods with about 100 residents. Intervention by the NAACP and an African American boycott of Trenton's white-owned businesses persuaded the town to annex the neighborhoods.

1999, April 12. Legendary band leader and composer Edward Kennedy "Duke" Ellington is awarded a posthumous Pulitzer Prize on the centennial of his birth. The special music citation was given "in recognition of his musical genius, which evoked aesthetically the principles of democracy through the medium of jazz and thus made an indelible contribution to art and culture."

1999, April 14. Washington, D.C. Federal district court judge Paul L. Friedman approves a settlement that could provide $2 billion for thousands of African American farmers who sued two years earlier because their access to government loans and subsidies had been denied. Over 18,000 farmers signed up for the settlement. Farmers with less documented evidence of discrimination in loan approvals may take a $50,000 settlement, $12,500 for taxes, and have their federal debts forgiven. Those with more evidence may appear before an independent arbitrator to petition for larger amounts in damages.

1999, April 20. San Francisco, California. U.S. District Judge William Orrick orders an end to sixteen years of race-based enrollment in the public schools of San Francisco and approves a lawsuit by Chinese Americans denied admission to preferred campuses in the city. Although African Americans and Hispanics protest his decision, Orrick rules that racial admissions violate Chinese Americans' constitutional rights to equal treatment in a school of their choice. The agreement repeals a limit of 45 percent of racial or ethnic enrollment in a single school and 40 percent in magnet schools.

1999, May 1. Belgrade, Yugoslavia. Jesse Jackson Sr. wins the release of the three U.S. soldiers—staff sergeants

William Carl King, President Bill Clinton, and Photograph of Henry Ossian Flipper, White House, Washington, DC, February 19, 1999. *King* (left)*, a descendant of Flipper, speaks at a ceremony held at the White House, in which Clinton* (center) *pardoned Flipper, West Point's first African American graduate, of charges of conduct unbecoming of an officer. The charges, leveled in 1881, were racially motivated.* CHRIS KLEPONIS/AFP/GETTY IMAGES

Andrew Ramirez and Christopher Stone and specialist Steven Gonzales—who Yugoslav authorities had held as prisoners of war since their capture on March 31 near the Yugoslavia-Macedonia border.

1999, June 15. Under legislation approved by the U.S. Congress on May 3, Rosa Parks receives the Congressional Gold Medal. Congressman John Lewis said that "one, simple, defining act" by Parks, who in 1955 stood up "for what is right and just," stoked the civil rights movement nationwide and led to the end of legalized segregation.

1999, June 15. Hattiesburg, Mississippi. A mistrial is declared in the reopened case against Mississippi businessman Charles Noble for the 1966 slaying of NAACP member Vernon Dahmer.

1999, July 10. Baltimore, Maryland. The U.S. Coast Guard posthumously honors Alex Haley, Pulitzer Prize–winning author of *Roots*, by commissioning a cutter in his name. Haley spent twenty years in the Coast Guard, rising from ship's steward to become the first head of the Guard's public affairs office.

1999, August 4. Former Detroit Pistons basketball player and NBC-TV basketball analyst Isiah Thomas announces that he has purchased majority ownership of the Continental Basketball Association (CBA). Thomas acquires the nine-team league for approximately $10 million.

1999, September 10. Judges in Charlotte, North Carolina, put an end to school busing, ruling that forced integration is no longer necessary. The program was originally put into place thirty years ago.

1999, September 11. New York City. Seventeen-year-old Serena Williams beats Martina Hingis of Switzerland 6–3, 7–6, to win the U.S. Open championship in tennis. She becomes only the second African American woman to take the title, after Althea Gibson in 1957 and 1958.

1999, September 20. Lawrence Brewer is found guilty of the June 7, 1998, murder of James Byrd Jr. Byrd died after being dragged by a chain behind a truck. Brewer is sentenced to death on September 23. A second man accused in the case, John King, was sentenced earlier in the year.

TWENTY-FIRST CENTURY

2000, January 14. Christopher Paul Curtis wins the Newbery Medal and the Coretta Scott King Author Award for his book, *Bud, Not Buddy*. Curtis is the first author to win both awards for one book. The awards are announced annually by the American Library Association (ALA): the Newbery is given for "distinguished contribution to American literature for children"; the Coretta Scott King Award honors African American authors and illustrators.

2000, January 19. Michael Jordan becomes a partial owner of the Washington Wizards. He will also serve as the new president of basketball operations for the team. Jordan's total stake is approximately 10 percent, which is valued between $20 million and $30 million. He joins the ranks of only five other African Americans who own portions of NBA teams: Former All-Star Earvin "Magic" Johnson has a small stake in the Los Angeles Lakers; Edward and Bettiann Gardner are part owners of Jordan's former team, the Chicago Bulls; and actor Bill Cosby owns a minority percentage of the New Jersey Nets.

2000, February 25. The four white plainclothes policemen charged in the February 1999 shooting of African American immigrant Amadou Diallo are acquitted on all charges. The defense for the officers asked that the trial take place in Albany, New York, instead of New York City to guarantee a fair hearing. The jury was composed of eight whites and four African Americans.

2000, April 18. Gustavas A. McLeod is the first man to pilot an open-cockpit plane to the North Pole. His 35,000-mile journey began in Maryland and was made in a former crop duster. There have been numerous flights to the North Pole since the first plane reached the area in 1937, but no one had successfully made the trip in an open cockpit because of the extreme temperatures.

2000, May 2. South Carolina governor Jim Hodges signs a bill to officially make Martin Luther King Jr.'s birthday a holiday for state workers. South Carolina is the last state to finally recognize the date as a state holiday.

2000, June 9. The U.S. Justice Department reports that after extensive investigation it has found no evidence that a conspiracy led to the 1968 assassination of Martin Luther King Jr. Some members of the King family called for the special investigation after a Memphis civil court concluded in 1999 that a federal conspiracy led to the shooting. In addition, James Earl Ray, the man convicted of the crime in 1969, claimed he did not work alone.

2000, July 1. Songwriter and producer Antonio "L.A." Reid takes over as president and chief executive officer (CEO) of Arista Records from founder Clive Davis, who has headed the company since its inception twenty-five years earlier.

2000, July 1. Columbia, South Carolina. After major protest rallies and an NAACP boycott of tourism, the governor of South Carolina removes the Confederate flag from the top of the state capitol dome in Columbia. The flag is considered by many to be a symbol of slavery.

2000, July 8. Twenty-year-old Venus Williams wins the singles title at Wimbledon, becoming the first African American woman to do so since Althea Gibson in 1957. She defeated defending champion Lindsay Davenport, 6–3, 7–6.

2000, July 10. Baltimore, Maryland. George W. Bush, Republican nominee for president, addresses the national convention of the NAACP in Baltimore, promising party support to African Americans. Republican presidential candidates from the two previous elections, Bob Dole in 1996 and George H. W. Bush in 1992, had both declined invitations from the group.

2000, July 11. Reverend Vashti Murphy McKenzie becomes the first woman bishop in the African Methodist Episcopal Church.

2000, July 23. St. Andrews, Scotland. Tiger Woods, age twenty-four, wins the British Open golf tournament, becoming the youngest golfer in history to have won all four Grand Slam events: the British Open, the U.S. Open, the Masters, and the PGA Championship. Only four golfers had previously won all four events: Gene Sarazan, Ben Hogan, Gary Player, and Jack Nicklaus.

2000, July 25. Joetta Clark-Diggs, her sister Hazel Clark, and sister-in-law Jearl Miles-Clark make history when all three win spots on the same U.S. Olympic team. It is also the first time that three members of the same family will compete in the same event. Hazel Clark won the top spot on the women's 800-meter track team, followed by Miles-Clark in second and Clark-Diggs in third.

2000, August 15. Stephanie Ready becomes the first woman to coach a men's professional basketball team when she is named assistant coach of the National Basketball Developmental League's Greenville (South Carolina) Groove.

2000, September 12. Selma, Alabama. James Perkins Jr., a former computer consultant, becomes the first African American mayor of Selma. He ousts Joseph T. Smitherman with 57 percent of the vote. Smitherman, age seventy, was running for his tenth consecutive term. He was mayor of Selma during the famous 1965 civil rights march.

2000, September 23. Los Angeles, California. The First Annual African American Women's Health Conference addresses the impact of breast cancer on the African American community. Workshops and speeches focus on education, risk assessment, early education, and alternative medical treatments. According to national statistics, breast cancer is the number one cause of death among African American women, and African American women who develop breast cancer are twice as likely to die as their white counterparts.

2000, September 23. Sydney, Australia. In the 2000 Summer Olympics, Marion Jones takes the 100-meter dash in 10.75 seconds, making her the fastest woman in the world. By the end of the games, Jones has won three gold and two bronze medals, the most medals won by a woman during a single Olympics.

2000, November 9. Providence, Rhode Island. When she takes the helm of Brown University, Ruth Simmons becomes the first African American president of an Ivy League college. She is also Brown's first woman president. Prior to being appointed, Simmons was on the faculty of Princeton University, where she served as vice provost in the early 1990s. Since 1995, she had been president of Smith College.

2000, December 16. General Colin L. Powell is appointed secretary of state by President George W. Bush. He is the first African American to hold the position.

2000, December 17. President George W. Bush announces the appointment of Condoleezza Rice as national security adviser. Rice, a Stanford University professor, becomes the first African American and the first woman to hold the post.

2001, January 30. The state of Georgia redesigns its state flag by replacing the large Confederate battle cross with the state seal. Although many Southerners see the Confederate flag as a symbol of Southern pride, others view it as a reminder of enslavement and segregation.

2001, February 2–4. Chicago, Illinois. The National Reparations Convention takes place in Chicago. Among those in attendance are Representative Bobby Rush of Illinois and Representative John Conyers of Michigan. The genesis of the convention can be traced back to April 26, 2000, when the issue of reparations for slavery was raised at a joint hearing of the Chicago City Council Finance and Human Relations committees. According to Rush, who spoke at the meeting, "the future of race relations will be determined by reparations for slavery."

2001, April 12. Cincinnati, Ohio. The mayor of Cincinnati declares a state of emergency after four days of racial rioting. The riots broke out after a white police officer fatally shot Timothy Thomas, an unarmed African American teenager. City officers have long been accused of racial profiling and using excessive force.

2001, April 17. In a controversial vote, Mississippi residents decide to retain the design of their state flag, which bears the Confederate battle cross. The state of Georgia redesigned its flag earlier in the year, leaving Mississippi as the only state that still prominently displays the "Southern Cross." Other states, including Arkansas and Alabama, incorporate only portions of the symbol in their state flags.

2001, May 1. Thomas E. Blanton Jr., one of four former Ku Klux Klan members charged with the 1963 bombing of the Sixteenth Street Baptist Church in Birmingham, Alabama, is convicted and sentenced to life in prison.

2001, May 25. The Eleventh U.S. Circuit Court of Appeals in Atlanta rules that author Alice Randall has every right to publish her book *The Wind Done Gone*. The book, which is a parody of Margaret Mitchell's *Gone with the Wind*, is surrounded by controversy. Representatives of Mitchell's estate try to stop it from being released, claiming Randall borrowed her plot and characters from Mitchell's 1939 novel, and thus violated copyright. According to the court, an attempt to stop Randall from publishing her book would be "a violation of the First Amendment." Randall's book is published by Houghton Mifflin in June. Approximately one year later, the two sides reach a confidential settlement under which Randall's novel must be subtitled "An Unauthorized Parody."

2001, May 29. In the largest settlement ever in a U.S. racial discrimination suit, the Coca-Cola Company agrees to pay out $192 million to approximately 2,000 African American employees. The suit was brought against the company by employees who worked for Coca-Cola between April 22, 1995, and June 14, 2000, and claimed that the company discriminated against African Americans in hiring and promoting.

2001, June 12–13. New York City. Russell Simmons, founder of Def Jam Records, holds the first two-day Hip-Hop Summit in New York City. The goal of the summit is to bring together a cross-section of America, including recording artists and label executives, in an effort to discuss issues that face rap music. Nation of Islam leader Louis Farrakhan gives the keynote speech.

2001, July 30. Harvard-educated Pamela Thomas-Graham is named president and chief executive officer of CNBC, making her the most powerful African American in the cable news industry.

2001, September 15. Representative Barbara Lee of California makes the news when she casts the lone dissenting vote allowing President George W. Bush "to use all necessary and appropriate force" against anyone associated with the September 11, 2001, terrorist attacks. The resolution passes unanimously in the Senate (98–0); the tally in the House is 420–1.

2001, September 24. At the Goodwill Games in Brisbane, Australia, Michael Johnson announces his retirement. Considered to be one of the greatest track-and-field athletes in history, Johnson has won five Olympic gold medals and nine World Championship gold medals during his career.

2001, September 26. Cincinnati police officer Steven Roach is found not guilty for the murder of Timothy Thomas, an unarmed nineteen-year-old African American who was shot to death in April 2001. Thomas's death touched off four days of rioting in the city. Following the verdict, there are some isolated incidents of violence, causing Cincinnati mayor Charlie Luken to impose a curfew.

2001, September 27. Robert L. Johnson, founder of Black Entertainment Television (BET), makes it on *Forbes* magazine's annual list of the top 400 richest people in America. He is number 172. Johnson earns the rank of "billionaire" after selling his 63 percent of BET stock, worth about $3 billion, to Viacom, Inc. He is the first African American billionaire in the United States.

2001, October 5. Barry Bonds of the San Francisco Giants hits seventy-three home runs, setting a new record for most homers in a single season.

2001, October 26. Dearborn, Michigan. Henry Ford Museum purchases the bus on which Rosa Parks took her famous "stand" in 1955. The bus had been lost for years, but finally came up on the auction block, along with certificates that document the bus's identification number and guarantee its authenticity. The bus is purchased for $492,000, and the museum announces plans for restoration and public viewing.

2001, November 13. Bishop Wilton Gregory of Belleville, Illinois, is elected the first African American president of the U.S. Conference of Catholic Bishops.

2002, February 25. Actor and comedian Bill Cosby announces that he will cancel a March 15 performance in Cincinnati, Ohio, to support a boycott of the city by African American groups. Groups such as the Coalition for a Just Cincinnati are targeting the city for its poor response to the riots that broke out as a result of the April 2001 shooting of African American teenager Timothy Thomas by a white police officer.

2002, March 25. Halle Berry becomes the first African American woman to win an Oscar for Best Actress, for her performance in *Monster's Ball.* Denzel Washington wins the best actor Oscar for his role in *Training Day.* He is only the second African American actor, following Sidney Poitier in 1963, to win the award.

2002, March 26. Law student Deadria Farmer-Paellmann files a federal lawsuit against FleetBoston Financial, the railroad firm CSX, and the Aetna insurance company. She files the suit on behalf of thirty-five million African Americans who are descendants of slaves, and who seek reparations for former injustices. According to the charges, all of the named defendants profited from the slave trade at some point in history. Claimants are asking for billions of dollars in compensation. Lawyers representing Farmer-Paellmann promise to bring charges against other corporations and institutions at a later date.

2002, May 22. Former Ku Klux Klan member Bobby Frank Cherry is convicted and sentenced to life in prison for the 1963 church bombing that killed four African American girls in Birmingham, Alabama. He is the last living member to face charges. Robert Chambliss was convicted in 1977, Thomas Blanton was convicted in 2001, and Frank Cash died in 1994 without being charged.

2002, June 19. Washington, D.C. The Juneteenth freedom march and rally begins at the historic home of abolitionist Frederick Douglass and ends on the steps of the U.S. Capitol. The goal of the gathering is to urge President George W. Bush to establish Juneteenth as a federal holiday. An official holiday in seven states, June 19 marks the date when word was officially brought to Texas by General Gordon Grander that the Civil War was over and enslaved Africans in the South were free. The year was 1865, and because of poor communication methods, slavery was still enforced in Texas at the time.

2003, January. Republican Michael Steele becomes Maryland's first African American lieutenant governor.

2003, January. Representative Elijah Cummings (D-MD) becomes the eighteenth head of the Congressional Black Caucus.

2003, January 10. Black Entertainment Television founder billionaire Robert L. Johnson became the first African American majority owner of a major professional sports team with the Charlotte Bobcats. Johnson also immediately assumed ownership of the WNBA's Charlotte Sting. In 2000, Johnson agreed to sell BET to Viacom, Inc., for about $3 billion. After the sale of BET, Johnson formed the RLJ Companies through which he owns or holds interest in companies operating in the hospitality, real estate, fast food, gaming, and media industries.

2003, January 14. The Cincinnati Bengals hire defensive coordinator Marvin Lewis as the football team's new head coach. Lewis, Tony Dungy, and Herman Edwards are the only African American coaches in the NFL.

2003, February. Carol Moseley Braun (D-IL), the nation's first African American woman senator, announces her candidacy for U.S. presidency. She drops out of the race in January 2004.

2003, February 1. The space shuttle *Columbia* disintegrates as it reenters the Earth's atmosphere after a sixteen-day space mission. All seven members of the crew are lost. The group included an African American and the first Indian American astronaut. The African American was U.S. Air Force Lieutenant Colonel Michael P. Anderson, payload commander.

2003, February 23. Maya Angelou wins a Grammy Award for best spoken-word album for *A Song Flung Up to Heaven.*

2003, March. *Forbes* magazine lists Oprah Winfrey as the first African American female billionaire. She is the only African American woman in film and television to own her own production company, Harpo Productions (which includes Harpo Studios, Harpo Films, Harpo Print and Harpo Video).

2003, March 19. The United States launches Operation Iraqi Freedom. Called a "decapitation attack," the pre-dawn air strike targets Saddam Hussein and other Iraqi leaders in Baghdad. Ground troops enter the country, crossing into southern Iraq from Kuwait. Coalition troops encounter fierce resistance. Over 25 percent of the troops serving in Iraq are African American.

2003, April 7. Colbert I. King, a *Washington Post* columnist, wins a Pulitzer Prize for Distinguished Commentary.

2003, May. Ann Fudge, former president of Kraft Foods, becomes chair and CEO of Young & Rubicam, a marketing and advertising firm.

2003, May 15. Marc Morial, former New Orleans mayor, is appointed to head the National Urban League.

2003, June 17. New regulation prohibits federal agents from using race or ethnicity in typical investigations, but does allow agents to consider the characteristics when information they receive about suspects includes race or ethnicity.

2003, June 23. The Supreme Court issues decisions in two cases, *Grutter v. Bollinger* and *Gratz v. Bollinger*, which challenged the use of race in admissions at the University of Michigan's Law School and the undergraduate College of Literature, Science, and the Arts. The Court upholds the concept of race as one of many factors in university admissions, but rejects approaches that fail to examine each student's record on an individual basis.

2003, July 7. Navy Rear Admiral Barry Black is the first African American chaplain of the U.S. Senate.

2003, July 17, Miami, Florida. The NAACP Board of Directors chairman Julian Bond names Constance Baker Motley, senior U.S. district judge for the Southern District of New York, the eighty-eighth Spingarn Award honoree. Judge Motley received the award during the ninety-fourth NAACP National Convention in Miami.

Barbara Grutter and Jennifer Gratz, July 8, 2003. *Grutter (left) and Gratz, leaving a news conference at the University of Michigan, were the lead plaintiffs in the landmark affirmative action cases decided by the U.S. Supreme Court on June 23, 2003.* **PHOTOGRAPH BY PAUL SANCYA. AP IMAGES. REPRODUCED BY PERMISSION.**

The Reverend Jesse Jackson, Michigan Union, Ann Arbor, MI, 2003. *With University of Michigan students holding signs in the background, Jackson* (center) *speaks in reaction to the U.S. Supreme Court's rulings on* Grutter v. Bollinger *and* Gratz v. Bollinger—*important affirmative action cases involving the admissions policies of the university's law school and undergraduate liberal arts school, respectively.* AP IMAGES

2003, October 3. New York City. The remains of more than 400 enslaved Africans arrive in New York and are taken in a procession up Broadway to their final resting place, the African Burial Ground, from which they had been removed twelve years earlier.

2004, January. Billionaire Oprah Winfrey celebrates her fiftieth birthday. Her annual salary is $210 million. Twenty-three million viewers a week in the United States and many more in over one hundred other countries watch her daily television show, which is the highest-rated talk show in television history.

2004, January. Heather McTeer Hudson is the first African American mayor of Greenville, Mississippi.

2004, February. Michael L. Lomax, former president of Dillard University, becomes head of the United Negro College Fund.

2004, February 8. Beyoncé Knowles ties Lauryn Hill, Norah Jones, and Alicia Keys, each with five Grammy Awards.

2004, February 10. Willie Adams Jr. is elected the first African American mayor of Albany, Georgia.

2004, April 5. Novelist Edward P. Jones wins the Pulitzer Prize for Fiction, and journalist Leonard Pitts of the *Miami Herald* wins the award for commentary.

2004, April 5. Phylicia Rashad wins the Tony Award for best leading actress in a Broadway show in the August Wilson play, *Gem of the Ocean.* Audra McDonald wins for best performance by a featured actress in a play. Anika Noni Rose wins for best performance by a featured actress in a musical.

2004, April 29. A memorial to sixteen million Americans who served in the U.S. armed forces opens in Washington, D.C. Of that number, 1.2 million were African Americans.

2004, May 31. Alphonso Jackson is confirmed as secretary of the U.S. Department of Housing and Urban Development.

2004, June 14. Washington, D.C. Official White House portraits of former president Bill Clinton and first lady Hillary Rodham Clinton are unveiled. The portraits were created by artist Simmie Knox, the first African American to be afforded this honor.

2004, June 23. President George W. Bush awards former U.S. senator Edward William Brooke III (R-MA) the

Presidential Medal of Freedom, the nation's top civilian honor.

2004, July 13. Hazel O'Leary, former U.S. secretary of energy, becomes president of Fisk University.

2004, November. Charles Steele Jr. becomes president of the SCLC.

2004, November 2. Barack Obama (D-IL) is the third African American elected to the U.S. Senate since Reconstruction and the second from Illinois. He becomes the fifth African American U.S. senator in history. Emanuel Cleaver (D-MO), former mayor of Kansas City, is elected to the U.S. Congress. Gwen Moore (D-WI) is the first African American elected to the U. S. Congress from Wisconsin.

2004, November. Jesse Jackson promises mass nonviolent protest over alleged voting irregularities in Florida. The NAACP plans to file lawsuits over the same issue.

2004, November 2. Former Virginia governor L. Douglas Wilder becomes the first elected African American mayor of Richmond, Virginia.

2005. Melvin Watts (D-NC) becomes head of the Congressional Black Caucus, with forty-three members, all Democrats.

2005. Edgar Ray Killen is convicted of killing civil rights workers James Chaney, Andrew Goodman, and Michael Schwerner in Philadelphia, Mississippi, in 1964.

2005. Former boxer Muhammad Ali is awarded the Presidential Medal of Freedom.

2005, January. Condoleezza Rice is appointed by President George W. Bush as U.S. secretary of state, the first African American woman to hold that position.

2005, February 12. Jamie Foxx receives the Academy Award for best actor for his performance in *Ray*, and Morgan

Actors Jamie Foxx and Morgan Freeman, February 2005. *Foxx (*left*) and Freeman sweep the male acting awards at the 77th Academy Awards—Foxx winning best actor for the film* Ray *and Freeman earning best supporting actor honors for* Million Dollar Baby.
AP IMAGES

Freeman wins the Academy Award for best supporting actor for his performance in *Million Dollar Baby*.

2005, June. Bruce Gordon is the fifteenth president of the NAACP.

2005, June 13. The U.S. Senate issues a formal apology for its decades-long failure to pass a law making lynching illegal. From 1882 to 1968, 4,742 people, 3,446 of them African American, were killed by lynch mobs.

2005, August 8. John H. Johnson dies at age eighty-seven. He was the founder of the Johnson Publishing Company, an international media and cosmetics empire headquartered in Chicago. *Ebony* and *Jet* magazines, along with Fashion Fair Cosmetics and *Ebony* Fashion Fair, were among the company's signature products. Johnson was the first African American to appear on the *Forbes* 400 list.

2005, August 29. Hurricane Katrina, one of the worst natural disasters in the nation's history, hits the Gulf Coast, taking an estimated 1,700 lives. The vast majority of the deaths are in Louisiana, including the heavily African American city of New Orleans.

2005, October 2. August Wilson dies at age sixty. A Pulitzer Prize–winning American playwright, he was celebrated for his major literary legacy, the *Pittsburgh Cycle*, a series of ten plays, each set in a different decade, depicting the comedy and tragedy of the African American experience in the twentieth century.

2005, October 24. Rosa Parks dies at age ninety-two.

2005, November 9. President George W. Bush presents the Presidential Medal of Freedom to baseball legend Frank Robinson.

2006, January. Secretary of State Condoleezza Rice joins First Lady Laura Bush in attending the inauguration of the president-elect of Liberia, Ellen Johnson Sirleaf, the first woman to be elected head of state on the continent of Africa.

2006, January 30. Coretta Scott King, wife of the late Dr. Martin Luther King Jr., dies. Congressional Black Caucus members called Mrs. King a symbol of strength and resolve during the life of her husband and an unflagging inspiration to millions of people around the world who sought justice and equality.

2006, May 16. Congressional Black Caucus members demonstrate in front of the Sudanese Embassy to dramatize the urgency of the crisis in Darfur. The protest results in the arrest of seven members of the caucus for disorderly conduct. Chairman Watts is joined by U.S. representatives Barbara Lee (D-CA), John Lewis (D-GA), Eddie Bernice Johnson (D-TX), Gwen Moore (D-WI), Al Green (D-TX), and D.C. delegate Eleanor Holmes Norton in calling for an end to the continuing genocide.

2006, July. President Bush signs a twenty-five-year extension of Voting Rights Act.

2006, October 23. Barack Obama's picture appears on the cover of *Time* magazine with the caption, "Why Barack Obama Could Be The Next President."

2006, November. Deval Patrick is elected governor of Massachusetts.

2006, November 9. Journalist Ed Bradley Jr., best known for his award-winning work on the long-running CBS News television magazine *60 Minutes*, dies at Mount Sinai Hospital in Manhattan of complications from chronic lymphocytic leukemia.

2006, December 15. President George W. Bush awards B. B. King the Presidential Medal of Freedom. B. B. King has sold more than forty million records, and has won fourteen Grammys. He has a place on the Hollywood Walk of Fame.

2007, February 4. Two African American NFL head coaches, Tony Dungy of the Indianapolis Colts and Lovie Smith of the Chicago Bears, meet for Super Bowl XLI at Dolphin Stadium in Miami Gardens, Florida. Dungy's Colts defeat the Bears, 29–17. The game

Cover of October 23, 2006, Issue of* Time *Magazine. *Joe Klein's prescient story discussed Barack Obama's chances in the 2008 presidential election.* LUCY NICHOLSON/REUTERS/LANDOV

marked the first time that African Americans served as head coaches for Super Bowl teams.

2007, February 10. Springfield, Illinois. Senator Barack Obama announces his candidacy for the office of president of the United States.

2007, March 9. Howard University, one of the foremost historically black colleges in the nation, celebrates its 140th anniversary.

2007, April 4. Radio personality Don Imus makes racist, sexist, and insensitive remarks about the African American women of the Rutgers basketball team. His remarks ignite national outrage, and Imus is fired. A brief national discussion about racial and gender-specific language in U.S. popular culture ensues.

2007, April 5. The *New York Times* reports that in the first three months of the year Barack Obama has raised $25 million for his 2008 presidential campaign, making him a frontrunner in the race along with Hillary Rodham Clinton.

2007, May. U.S. education secretary Margaret Spellings reports that the dropout rate for African American, Hispanic, and Native American students is close to 50 percent. Spellings called some schools "dropout factories" because of the terrible conditions students face in the classroom.

2007, August 5. Veteran civil rights attorney Oliver W. Hill Sr. dies at age 100. Hill was perhaps best known for his role in the landmark *Brown v. Board of Education* decision that significantly weakened official racial segregation that locked African Americans into second-class citizenship. In 1951, he and law partner Spottswood W. Robinson III filed a suit attacking segregation in the county schools that ultimately was wrapped into the *Brown* case that went before the Supreme Court.

2007, September. Virginia governor Timothy Kaine officially pardons Gabriel Prosser 207 years after his conviction and execution in 1800. This is apparently the first time the leader of a slave revolt has received a state pardon.

2008, March. Karen Bass becomes the first African American woman to serve as the speaker of the California State Assembly.

2008, May. Benjamin Todd Jealous is named the new national president of the NAACP.

2008, May. Zelma Henderson dies at age eighty-eight. She was the last surviving plaintiff from Topeka in the *Brown* case, which led to the U.S. Supreme Court decision in 1954 declaring segregated schools unconstitutional. In 1950, Mrs. Henderson and twelve other parents joined the lawsuit over Topeka's segregated schools. She had worked at Topeka State Hospital and had just opened a beauty shop in her home when she became involved in the lawsuit.

2008, July. Melvina Lathan becomes the first African American female chair of the New York State Athletic Commission that oversees boxing and wrestling in New York. She was formerly a longtime professional boxing judge who called 235 professional matches, including eighty-three world championship bouts. A Philadelphia native, she was also a member of the New Jersey Boxing Hall of Fame.

2008, August. Barack Obama accepts the Democratic Party nomination for presidency of the United States, making him the first African American to receive the endorsement of a major American party.

2008, November 4. Barack Obama is elected the forty-fourth president of the United States, beating Republican nominee John McCain. Obama received 365 electoral college votes to 173 for Senator McCain.

2008, November. Julian Bond steps down as chairman of the national NAACP.

2009, January 20. Barack Hussein Obama is inaugurated as U.S. president. He is the first African American president in the nation's history.

2009, January 30. Michael Steele becomes the first African American to lead the Republican Party as chairman of the Republican National Committee. He is only the second African American to lead either the Democratic or Republican parties, and was the first African American to chair any state party of the GOP.

2009, February 2. Eric Holder is sworn in as the first African American attorney general, the highest law enforcement officer in the United States.

2009, March. Circuit judge James Perry is appointed by Governor Charlie Crist as the second African American in Florida's seven-member Supreme Court.

2009, March. Barry Rand of Stamford, Connecticut, is named CEO by the American Association for Retired Persons (AARP), the organization's first African American CEO.

2009, March 25. Dr. John Hope Franklin dies at age ninety-four. Franklin was born January 2, 1915, in the all-black town of Rentiesville, Oklahoma, where he was often subjected to humiliating racism. He was instrumental in bringing down the legal and historical validations of such a world. His book *From Slavery to Freedom* was a landmark integration of African American history into American history and remains relevant more than sixty years after being published.

2009, April. First Lady Michelle Obama meets with Queen Elizabeth II. Commentators noted that the queen displayed uncharacteristic affection in her warm interactions with the first African American first lady.

2009, April. Bill Cosby receives the Mark Twain Prize for American Humor, which is the nation's top honor for humor. He was honored for a prolific career that focused on race relations and breaking down stereotypes.

2009, May. Thirteen African Americans were among the 210 new members elected to the American Academy of Arts and Sciences. Former Secretary of State Colin Powell and James Earl Jones, a two-time Tony Award–winning actor, were among the honorees.

2009, May. Judge Sonia Sotomayor becomes the nation's first Hispanic Supreme Court justice. She was appointed by President Barack Obama.

2009, June 25. Michael Jackson, fifty, also known as the King of Pop, dies from cardiac arrest. He was in the final stages of preparation for what he claimed was to be his final tour, called *This is It.* Three children, son Michael Joseph Jackson Jr., daughter Paris-Michael Katherine Jackson, and Prince Michael Jackson II, called Blanket, survived Michael Jackson.

2009, July. Ursula Burns becomes the first African American woman chief executive officer of Xerox, a *Fortune* 500 company. In 2007, she was named president of the company and was instrumental in helping revive the company's financial health.

2009, July. For the first time ever, the state of Florida holds the Miss Black Florida USA and Miss Black Florida Talented Teen USA Pageant. The event gives young women the opportunity to display their scholastic achievement and talent. The Miss Black USA Pageant has been an outstanding contribution to the African American landscape for twenty- two years in other states.

2009, August. Venus and Serena Williams, the tennis-playing sisters, become stakeholders in the Miami Dolphins. To date, the NFL has no African American majority team owner.

2009, August 1. Naomi Sims, the first African American supermodel, dies at age sixty-one. Sims started in the modeling business in the mid-1960s when she moved to New York City.

2009, September. Command Sergeant Major Teresa King becomes the first African American woman to take charge of the army's drill sergeants' school.

2009, October. Dr. Regina Benjamin is appointed by President Obama to the post of U.S. surgeon general, the nation's top doctor. She is a former recipient of the Nelson Mandela Award for Health and Human Rights and a MacArthur Foundation "genius" grant, and was the first African American woman to head a state medical society. Benjamin is the third African American woman to be U.S. surgeon general.

2009, October. Bernice King is the first woman in the fifty-two-year history of the SCLC to be named president. She is the daughter of Dr. Martin Luther King Jr., who was founder and president.

2009, December 10. Oslo, Norway. President Barack Obama receives the Nobel Peace Prize for his extraordinary efforts to strengthen international diplomacy and cooperation between peoples.

2

AFRICAN AMERICAN FIRSTS

Jessie Carney Smith

As history progresses, African Americans are making great strides, while at the same time those who preserve such events are taking greater care to record their accomplishments The following list describes African American men and women who were the first by race or gender to set a particular mark, thus giving a useful perspective to those who study history. The list covers a wide spectrum of pioneering events and people, encompassing such areas as the arts, education, law, media, medicine, politics, religion, science, business, the military, and sports. The most historically important event described here occurred in 2009: the inauguration of America's first African American president.

1619, August 20. At Jamestown Colony in modern-day Virginia, the first twenty Africans arrive in English North America from the Caribbean as indentured servants.

1623. The first African American child to be baptized a Christian in the colonies becomes a member of the Anglican Church in Jamestown. The child's name is William, son of Isabel and William.

1624. William Tucker, who is believed to have been the first African American child born in the American colonies, is born in Jamestown.

1746. Enslaved African poet Lucy Terry writes "Bars Fight," a commemorative poem about an Indian raid in Deerfield, Massachusetts. Terry is considered to be the first African American poet.

1752. Benjamin Banneker builds a striking clock, the first to be built in the American colonies.

1770. While leading fellow protesters in a confrontation with British soldiers, Crispus Attucks is shot and killed in Boston, thus becoming the first American to die during the Revolutionary period. The altercation later becomes known as the Boston Massacre.

1773. *Poems on Various Subjects, Religious and Moral* by seventeen-year-old Phillis Wheatley is published in London. It is the first book of poetry published by an African American.

1781. Harry Hosier (also spelled Hoosier, Hoshur, and Hossier), a circuit-riding preacher, delivers a sermon titled "Barren Fig Tree" at Adams Chapel in Fairfax County, Virginia, becoming the first African American to preach to a Methodist congregation. His dark complexion earns him the nickname Black Harry. In 1784, he preaches at Thomas Chapel in Chapeltown, Delaware, becoming the first of his race to preach to a white congregation.

1783. James Derham, born enslaved in Philadelphia in 1762, becomes the first African American physician in the United States. Having served as an assistant to his master (a doctor by profession), Derham purchases his freedom in 1783 and develops a thriving practice serving both black and white patients.

1785, May 15. John Morront of New York, the first African American missionary minister to work with Native Americans, is ordained a Methodist minister in London. Among his converts to Christianity are a Cherokee chieftain and his daughter.

1786. Lemuel Haynes, who served during the American Revolution as a minuteman in Connecticut, becomes the first African American minister to lead a white congregation.

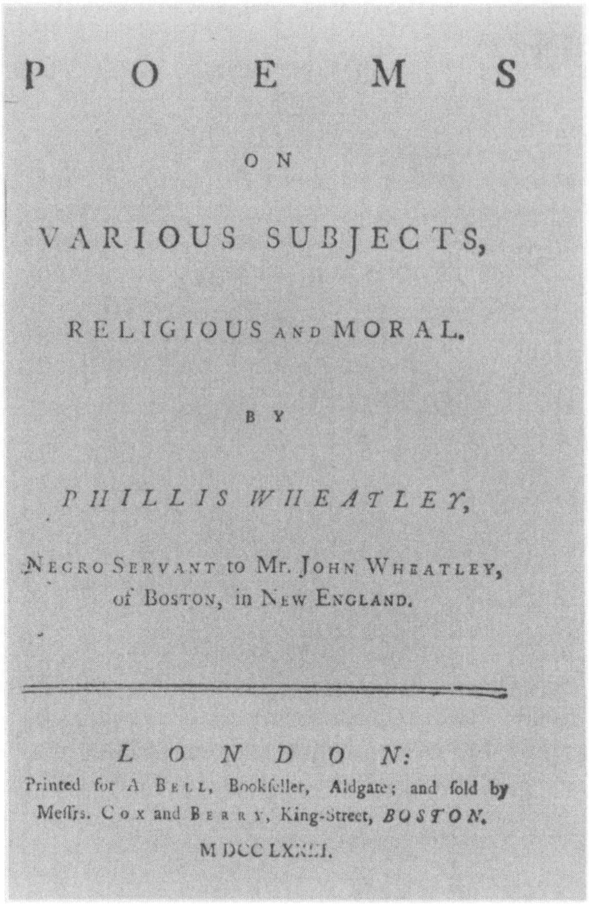
P O E M S

O N

VARIOUS SUBJECTS,

RELIGIOUS AND MORAL.

B Y

PHILLIS WHEATLEY,

NEGRO SERVANT to Mr. JOHN WHEATLEY,
of BOSTON, in NEW ENGLAND.

L O N D O N:
Printed for A. BELL, Bookſeller, Aldgate; and ſold by
Meſſrs. COX and BERRY, King-Street, BOSTON.
M DCC LXXIII.

Title Page, Phillis Wheatley's* Poems on Various Subjects, Religious and Moral *(1773). *Wheatley's book, published in London when she was just seventeen, is the first book of poetry published by an African American.* **SCHOMBURG CENTER FOR RESEARCH IN BLACK CULTURE; THE NEW YORK PUBLIC LIBRARY; ASTOR, LENOX AND TILDEN FOUNDATIONS**

1787, **April.** Richard Allen and Absalom Jones organize the Free African Society in Philadelphia. It is considered the first African American organization in the United States.

1787 Prince Hall organizes the first African American Masonic Lodge, African Lodge No. 459 in Boston.

1789. *The Interesting Narrative of the Life of Olaudah Equiano, or Gustavus Vassa, the African, Written by Himself* is published. It is considered the first autobiography written by an African American. The work becomes a best seller, with nine British editions and one American edition, including translations in Dutch, German, and Russian.

1794. The First African Church of St. Thomas, led by Absalom Jones, is dedicated in Philadelphia. It is the first African American Episcopal (AME) congregation in the United States.

1802. Pierre Bonza and his wife, who are African American, become the parents of the first non–Native American child to be born in what is today North Dakota. Bonza is known for riding wild buffaloes and in 1804 becomes an interpreter for the Northwest Fur Company.

1816. Richard Allen, founder of the African Methodist Episcopal Church, becomes the first African American bishop.

1817. The African Methodist Episcopal Church organizes the AME Book Concern in Philadelphia, the first African American–owned book-publishing enterprise in the United States. The Book Concern publishes its first title, *The Book of Discipline*, that same year.

1821. New York City's free African American community establishes the first African American theater, the African Grove Theatre, located at Mercer and Bleecker streets.

1823. The first play written and produced by an African American, Henry Brown's *The Drama of King Shotaway*, is presented by the African Grove Theatre in New York City.

1826. Ira Aldridge, one of the leading Shakespearean actors of the nineteenth century, becomes the first African American actor to attain international renown. The New York City native won acclaim for playing tragic, melodramatic, and comic roles, but he was most widely known for his portrayal of Othello.

1827. The first African American newspaper, *Freedom's Journal*, is published in New York City. Presbyterian minister Samuel E. Cornish and abolitionist and colonizationist John Brown Russwurm are the owners and editors.

1829. The first African American congregation of Catholic nuns, the Oblate Sisters of Providence, is founded by Mary Rosine Boegues, Mary Frances Balas, Mary Theresa Duchemin, and Elizabeth Lange.

1829. The first National Negro Convention meets in Philadelphia.

1831. The first Annual Convention of the People of Color meets at Wesleyan Church in Philadelphia. Delegates from five states resolve to study African American conditions, explore settlement possibilities in Canada, and raise money for an industrial college in New Haven, Connecticut.

1834. Henry Blair of Glenrose, Maryland, becomes the first African American believed to have been granted a patent, for a new type of seed planter, from the U.S. Patent Office.

1839. The first antislavery political organization, the Liberty Party, is founded in Warsaw, New York. Among its leading supporters are African American abolitionists Samuel R. Ward and Henry Highland Garnet.

1845. William Henry Lane, the first African American dance star, wins the title "King of All Dancers" after engaging in three competitions. Lane's stage name, Master Juba, was taken from an African dance known as the *juba.*

1845. Macon Allen becomes the first African American formally admitted to a state bar after he passes the bar examination in Worcester, Massachusetts.

1847. Frederick Douglass publishes the first issue of his abolitionist newspaper, the *North Star,* in Rochester, New York.

1847. David John Peck graduates from Rush Medical College, becoming the first African American to graduate from an American school of medicine.

1853. William Wells Brown's *Clotel, or, the President's Daughter* is published in London. It is the first novel published by an African American.

1854. Lincoln University, the first African American college that remains in its original location, is founded as Ashmun Institute in Oxford, Pennsylvania.

1854. John Mercer Langston is elected clerk of Brownhelm, Ohio, becoming the first African American elected to public office.

1854, June 10. James Augustine Healy is ordained at Notre Dame Cathedral in Paris, becoming the first African American ordained a priest in the Catholic Church. Later, his younger brothers Patrick and Alexander also became priests, and for a number of years they are the only black Catholic priests in the United States.

1855. Berea College is founded in Kentucky. It is the first college established in the United States for the specific purpose of educating black students and white students together.

1858. Abolitionist, author, and reformer William Wells Brown writes *The Escape, or, a Leap to Freedom,* the first play written by an African American. Although Brown's play was published in Boston, it was probably never formally produced.

1859. Harriet E. Adams Wilson becomes the first African American to publish a novel in the United States with the release of *Our Nig, or, Sketches from the Life of a Free Black, in a Two-Story White House, North, Showing that Slavery's Shadows Fall Even There.*

1860. The Brooklyn Excelsiors become the first African American baseball team to tour the United States.

1861. Nicholas Biddle becomes one of the first African Americans wounded during the Civil War. Biddle, who had been enslaved, attaches himself to a militia unit preparing to defend Washington, D.C., but the unit is stoned by an angry mob in Baltimore. Biddle manages to escape death only with the aid of his white comrades in arms.

ARTS AND LETTERS

1746. Enslaved African poet Lucy Terry writes "Bars Fight," a commemorative poem about an Indian raid in Deerfield, Massachusetts. Terry is considered to be the first African American poet.

1773. *Poems on Various Subjects, Religious and Moral* by seventeen-year-old Phillis Wheatley is published in London. It is the first book of poetry published by an African American.

1789. *The Interesting Narrative of the Life of Olaudah Equiano, or Gustavus Vassa, the African, Written by Himself* is published. It is considered the first autobiography written by an African American. The work becomes a best seller, with nine British editions and translations in Dutch, German, and Russian.

1823. The first play written and produced by an African American, Henry Brown's *The Drama of King Shotaway,* is presented by the African Grove Theatre in New York City.

1853. William Wells Brown's *Clotel, or, the President's Daughter* is published in London. It is the first novel published by an African American.

1935. *Mulatto* by Langston Hughes opens at the Vanderbilt Theatre in New York on October 24 and plays continuously until December 9, 1937, making it the first play by an African American author to become a long-run hit on Broadway.

1937. Self-taught sculptor William Edmondson becomes the first African American to have a solo exhibition at the Museum of Modern Art in New York City.

1950. Gwendolyn Brooks is awarded the Pulitzer Prize for her volume of poetry, *Annie Allen.* She is the first African American to win a Pulitzer and also the first African American woman elected to the National Institute of Arts and Letters.

1969. Moneta J. Sleet Jr. becomes the first African American man and the first African American photographer to win a Pulitzer Prize. His prize-winning photograph is a portrait of Coretta Scott King and her youngest child, Bernice, taken at the funeral of Martin Luther King Jr.

1976. Robert Hayden becomes the first African American poet laureate. He serves in that position at the Library of Congress until 1978.

EDUCATION

1847. David John Peck graduates from Rush Medical College, becoming the first African American to graduate from an American school of medicine.

1862. Mary Patterson becomes the first African American woman in the United States to earn a bachelor's degree, awarded by Oberlin College in Ohio.

1868. Howard University opens its College of Medicine, the first African American medical school in the United States.

1869. George Ruffin graduates from Harvard Law School and becomes the first African American to earn an LL.B. from Harvard and perhaps the first to graduate from a university law school in the United States.

1872. The first African American woman lawyer, Charlotte E. Ray, receives her degree from Howard University School of Law in Washington, D.C. She is admitted to practice law in any U.S. jurisdiction on March 2 and to practice at the bar of the U.S. Supreme Court on April 23.

1877. Henry O. Flipper becomes the first African American to graduate from the U.S. Military Academy at West Point.

1895. W. E. B. Du Bois becomes the first African American to be awarded a Ph.D. by Harvard University.

1906. The first African American collegiate fraternity, Alpha Phi Alpha, is organized at Cornell University.

1908. The first African American sorority, Alpha Kappa Alpha, is founded at Howard University in Washington, D.C.

1949. Wesley A. Brown becomes the first African American to graduate from the Naval Academy at Annapolis, Maryland.

1969. Federal judge A. Leon Higginbotham Jr. is elected a trustee of Yale University, the first African American to be so honored.

2001. On July 1, Ruth J. Simmons leaves the helm of Smith College to become the first African American and the first woman president of an Ivy League institution when she takes office as president of Brown University.

1861. William C. Nell is appointed postal clerk in Boston, becoming the first African American to hold a federal civilian post.

1862. Mary Patterson becomes the first African American woman in the United States to earn a bachelor's degree, awarded by Oberlin College in Ohio.

1863. Henry McNeal Turner becomes the first African American appointed a chaplain in the U.S. Army.

1863. Sergeant William H. Carney of the Fifty-fourth Massachusetts Infantry becomes the first African American to earn the Congressional Medal of Honor. He is recognized for combat valor during the Union charge on Fort Wagner, South Carolina, on July 18, 1863, although he was not issued his medal until 1900.

1864. Rebecca Davis Lee Crumpler, believed to be the first African American woman to become a physician, graduates from the New England Female Medical College.

1865. Henry Highland Garnet becomes the first African American to deliver a sermon in the chamber of the House of Representatives at the U.S. Capitol in Washington, D.C.

1865. Martin R. Delany becomes the first African American to attain the rank of major in the U.S. Army. A graduate of Howard University Medical School, Delany served in the Medical Corps. He was also a writer.

1865. Alexander T. Augusta becomes the first African American to hold a medical commission in the U.S. Army. A surgeon and physician with the rank of major, he becomes the highest-ranking African American officer during the Civil War when he is promoted on March 13 to brevet lieutenant colonel.

1865. John Rock becomes the first African American lawyer admitted to practice before the U.S. Supreme Court. His admittance is moved by Senator Charles Sumner of Massachusetts. Chief Justice Salmon P. Chase presides.

1865. The first African American newspaper in the South, the *Colored American*, begins publication in Augusta, Georgia.

1866. Edward G. Walker and Charles L. Mitchell are elected to the Massachusetts House of Representatives, becoming the first African Americans to serve in a state legislative assembly.

1867. Robert Tanner Freeman becomes the first African American to graduate from Harvard University's School of Dentistry.

1868. Howard University opens its College of Medicine, the first African American medical school in the United States.

POLITICS

1866. Edward G. Walker and Charles L. Mitchell are elected to the Massachusetts House of Representatives, becoming the first African Americans to serve in a state legislative assembly.

1870. Hiram R. Revels of Mississippi becomes the first African American elected to the U.S. Senate. Joseph H. Rainey of South Carolina and Jefferson F. Long of Georgia, elected later that year, were the first black elected members of the U.S. House of Representatives.

1872. Louisiana lieutenant governor P. B. S. Pinchback becomes the first African American state governor after the impeachment of the incumbent. He serves from December 9, 1872 to January 13, 1873, while the governor faces impeachment charges.

1872. The first African American delegates to the presidential nominating convention of a major party appear at the Republican National Convention in Philadelphia.

1950. United Nations undersecretary Ralph Bunche becomes the first African American to receive a Nobel Peace Prize.

1967. Thurgood Marshall is appointed an associate justice of the U.S. Supreme Court, becoming the first African American to serve on the nation's highest court. In 1965, he had become the first African American solicitor general, a position he held until he joined the Supreme Court.

1968. Shirley Chisholm of New York becomes the first African American woman elected to the U.S. Congress.

1977. Patricia Roberts Harris is appointed secretary of the Department of Housing and Urban Development, becoming the first African American woman to serve in a cabinet-level position.

2009. On January 20, Barack Obama is inaugurated as the forty-fourth U.S. president. He is the first African American ever to hold the nation's highest office.

1869. George Ruffin graduates from Harvard Law School and becomes the first African American to earn an LL.B. from Harvard and perhaps the first to graduate from a university law school in the United States.

1869. Ebenezer Don Carlos Bassett, believed to be the first African American to receive an appointment in the diplomatic service, becomes U.S. minister to Haiti.

1870. Richard Greener becomes the first African American to receive an undergraduate degree from Harvard. Active as a teacher and editor, Greener is admitted to the South Carolina bar in 1876 and becomes dean of Howard University Law School in 1879.

1870. Hiram R. Revels of Mississippi becomes the first African American elected to the U.S. Senate. Joseph H. Rainey of South Carolina and Jefferson F. Long, of Georgia, elected later that year, were the first black elected members of the U.S. House of Representatives.

1870. Jonathan Jasper Wright becomes the first African American elected to the State Supreme Court of South Carolina. He is also the first African American to be admitted to the bar in Pennsylvania.

1871. Alcorn College (now Alcorn State University) in Mississippi is founded as the first African American land-grant college.

1872. James Henry Conyers of South Carolina becomes the first African American midshipman at the U.S. Naval Academy. Conyers does not graduate, however, and leaves the academy the following year.

1872. Louisiana lieutenant governor P. B. S. Pinchback becomes the first African American state governor after the impeachment of the incumbent. He serves from December 9, 1872 to January 13, 1873, while the governor faces impeachment charges.

1872, February. The first African American woman lawyer, Charlotte E. Ray, receives her degree from Howard University School of Law in Washington, D.C. She is admitted to practice law in any U.S. jurisdiction on March 2 and to practice at the bar of the U.S. Supreme Court on April 23.

1872. The first African American delegates to the presidential nominating convention of a major party appear at the Republican National Convention in Philadelphia.

1873. The first African American municipal judge, Mifflin W. Gibbs, is elected in Little Rock, Arkansas.

1874. Republican Blanche K. Bruce is elected by the Mississippi state legislature to the U.S. Senate. He becomes the first African American to serve a full term in the Senate.

1875, May 17. Oliver Lewis, an African American jockey, becomes the winner of the first Kentucky Derby.

1875, June 10. Father James Augustine Healy becomes the second bishop of Portland, Maine, and the first African American Roman Catholic bishop in the

SPORTS

1875. On May 17, Oliver Lewis, an African American jockey, becomes the winner of the first Kentucky Derby.

1884. Moses Fleetwood Walker becomes the first African American major-league baseball player when the Toledo Bluestockings join the American Association.

1908. Jack Johnson wins a bout with Tommy Burns to become the first African American heavyweight champion.

1919. Fritz Pollard becomes the first African American to play professional football for a major team, the Akron Indians. In 1916, Pollard had been the first African American to play in the Rose Bowl, for Brown University.

1924. On July 8, William DeHart Hubbard becomes the first African American in Olympics history to win an individual gold medal when he takes the long jump at the Paris games.

1936. Jesse Owens becomes the first Olympian to win four gold medals, three of which were world record marks, at the Olympic Games in Berlin, with German chancellor Adolf Hitler in attendance. Hitler refuses to acknowledge the superiority of Owens and the other African American athletes.

1947. Jackie Robinson joins the National League's Brooklyn Dodgers and becomes the first African American to play major-league baseball in the twentieth century. He plays his first game as first baseman on April 15 in Brooklyn's Ebbets Field against the Boston Braves.

1950. On October 31, Basketball player Earl Lloyd of the Washington Capitals takes to the court, becoming the first African American to participate in a National Basketball Association (NBA) game. Chuck Cooper (Boston Celtics) and Nat Clifton (New York Knicks) join him as the NBA's first African American players in 1950.

1950. On November 15, Arthur Dorrington becomes the first African American to play organized hockey when he signs a contract to play with the Atlantic City Seagulls of the Eastern Amateur League.

1956. Tennis player Althea Gibson becomes the first African American to win a Grand Slam event (the French Open).

1997. Tiger Woods becomes the first African American to win a men's major golf championship (the Masters).

United States. He establishes more than sixty new churches in his diocese and becomes an advocate for Native Americans.

1876. Edward A. Bouchet becomes the first African American to earn a Ph.D. from an American university after receiving his doctorate in physics from Yale.

1877. George Washington Henderson is elected to Phi Beta Kappa, becoming the first African American to gain membership in the honor society.

1877. Henry O. Flipper becomes the first African American to graduate from the U.S. Military Academy at West Point.

1879, August 1. Mary E. Mahoney becomes the first African American woman to receive a diploma in nursing from New England Hospital for Women and Children in Boston.

1880, February 2. Samuel R. Lowery becomes the first African American lawyer to argue a case before the U.S. Supreme Court. Although John Rock was admitted to practice before the Court in 1865, Lowery is the first to actually appear before the Supreme Court to argue a case.

1882. The *Cairo Illinois Gazette*, published by W. S. Scott, becomes the first African American–owned daily newspaper.

1884. John Roy Lynch becomes the first African American to preside over a national political convention when he is nominated temporary chairman of the Republican Party's national convention.

1884. Moses Fleetwood Walker becomes the first African American professional baseball player when the Toledo Bluestockings join the American Association.

1885. The first African American professional baseball team, the Cuban Giants, is formed in New York City by Frank Thompson from a group of waiters working at a Long Island hotel.

1885. The first African American Protestant Episcopal bishop in the United States, the Reverend Samuel David Ferguson, is elected to the House of Bishops.

1886. Augustine Tolton, a formerly enslaved African American, is ordained a Roman Catholic priest in Rome. Because he is widely known and his work has been publicized, he is sometimes called the first African American to be ordained. However, the Healy brothers, whose racial identity is often not noted, predate him.

1890. Thomy Lafon, a real-estate speculator and money-lender in Louisiana, is believed to have become the first African American millionaire in the United States.

1891. Isaac Murphy (also known as Isaac Burns) wins the Kentucky Derby for the third time, becoming the first jockey to do so and the first to capture the Derby title for two consecutive years, having won his first Derby race in 1884 and his second in 1890. In 1884, Murphy became the only jockey to win the Kentucky Derby, the Kentucky Oaks, and the Clark Stakes at the same Churchill Downs meeting.

1891. Daniel Hale Williams, a physician and surgeon, founds Provident Hospital in Chicago, Illinois, which includes the first training school for African American nurses in the United States.

1891, December 19. When he is ordained a Catholic priest in Baltimore, Charles Randolph Uncles becomes the first African American ordained in the United States. Four other African Americans had been ordained before Uncles, but their ordinations all took place in Europe.

1892. The first African American college football game is played between Biddle College (now Johnson C. Smith University) and Livingstone College. Biddle wins 4 to 0.

1893. Dr. Daniel Hale Williams becomes the first surgeon to successfully enter the chest cavity and suture the heart of a living patient.

1893, September 19. E. R. Robinson patents the electric railway trolley.

1893. Nancy Green of Montgomery County, Kentucky, who had once been enslaved, becomes the first Aunt Jemima and the first living trademark in the world. She dresses in antebellum period costume and makes her debut at the Columbian Exposition in Chicago, where she makes and serves pancakes. For three decades, Green tours with the Aunt Jemima Mills Company and promotes its products. Her image helps to promote racial and gender stereotyping.

1895. W. E. B. Du Bois becomes the first African American to be awarded a Ph.D. by Harvard University.

1896. Marshall W. "Major" Taylor of Indianapolis, known as the "fastest bicycle rider in the world," becomes the first native-born African American to win a major bicycle race. His first professional start was a half-mile handicap held at Madison Square Garden, where he overcame racism and, according to some sources, became the first African American champion in any sport. After his race at Montreal's Queen Park on August 10, 1899, Taylor became the world champion bicycle rider and the second black world champion in any sport.

1903. Maggie Lena Walker becomes the first African American woman bank president when she founds the Saint Luke Penny Thrift Savings Bank in Richmond, Virginia.

1904, May 4. The first African American Greek letter organization, Sigma Pi Phi (or the Boulé), is founded in Philadelphia. Its mission is to meet the social needs of African American business leaders and professionals.

1905. The first African American–owned theater in the United States, the Pekin Theater in Chicago, opens. Founded by Robert Mott, it becomes known for stage productions, as well as concert series. The Pekin Stock Company is the first African American repertory company in the United States.

1905. The Louisville Free Public Library in Kentucky is established as the first public library in the nation built exclusively for African Americans.

1906. The first African American collegiate fraternity, Alpha Phi Alpha, is organized at Cornell University.

1907. John Hope is named president of Atlanta Baptist College, becoming the first African American to be appointed president at a Baptist school. As president, Hope expands the college with funds donated by John T. Rockefeller and Andrew Carnegie.

1907. Alain LeRoy Locke becomes the first African American to be awarded a Rhodes Scholarship.

1908. The first African American sorority, Alpha Kappa Alpha, is founded at Howard University in Washington, D.C.

1908. John Baxter Taylor Jr., collegiate champion, sets a world record in the 440-yard relay at the London Olympic Games, becoming the first African American to win an Olympic gold medal. The other members of his relay team are Nathaniel Cartmell, Melvin Sheppard, and William Hamilton.

1908. Jack Johnson wins a bout with Tommy Burns to become the first African American heavyweight champion.

1910. George Harriman becomes the first African American to achieve fame as a syndicated cartoonist with the launch of his strip *Krazy Kat.* Popular especially among intellectuals, the strip ran until July 25, 1944.

1911, January 5. Kappa Alpha Psi (originally named Kappa Alpha Nu) is founded on the campus of Indiana University in Bloomington.

1911, November 17. The Omega Psi Phi fraternity becomes the first Greek-letter fraternity formed by African Americans on an African American college campus when it is founded at Howard University in Washington, D.C.

1912. George Edmund Haynes becomes the first African American to receive a doctorate from Columbia University.

1914. Jesse Edward Moorland donates his private library of African American history to Howard University. Moorland's library was the first African American research collection at a major American university. It eventually became the core of the Moorland-Spingarn Research Center.

1915. Marine biologist Ernest Everett Just becomes the first recipient of a Spingarn Medal, the highest honor bestowed by the National Association for the Advancement of Colored People (NAACP).

1915. Frederick Douglass Patterson becomes the first African American car manufacturer. Between 1915 and 1919, he manufacturers more than thirty Greenfield-Patterson automobiles in Greenfield, Ohio. His company produces two models—a roadster and a large four-door touring car.

1915. Xavier University in New Orleans, founded by Katherine Drexel and the Sisters of the Blessed Sacrament, becomes the first (and remains the only) African American Catholic college.

1915. The Association for the Study of Negro Life and History (now the Association for the Study of African American Life and History) is established as the first learned society specifically devoted to the professional study of black history.

1917. Tenor Roland Hayes becomes the first African American to give a recital in Boston's Symphony Hall, one of the city's largest venues. Hayes self-promotes the sold-out concert, and hundreds of fans are unable to gain admittance.

1917. Eugene Jacques Bullard, flying for France, becomes the first African American aviator. A member of the French Air Service during World War I, he flies his first mission on September 8. Denied a commission three-quarters of a century earlier, Bullard is granted a posthumous commission by the U.S. Air Force in 1994.

1918. Starring on the Rutgers football team, Paul Robeson becomes the first African American to receive All-American honors.

1918. Hugh N. Mulzac becomes the first African American in the United States to earn a shipmaster's license, with the right to take command of a ship. However, Mulzac is unable to find employment as a shipmaster and instead must take jobs at sea as a cook and steward for the next twenty-four years. He finally takes command of a ship in 1942, a Liberty cargo vessel transporting troops and supplies into battle zones during World War II.

1919. Fritz Pollard becomes the first African American to play professional football for a major team, the Akron Indians. In 1916, Pollard had been the first African American to play in the Rose Bowl, for Brown University.

1920. Author, scholar, and activist James Weldon Johnson becomes the first African American secretary of the NAACP.

MUSIC

1917. Tenor Roland Hayes becomes the first African American to give a recital in Boston's Symphony Hall, one of the city's largest venues.

1933. Florence Price becomes the first African American woman composer to have a symphony performed by a major orchestra when her *Symphony in E Minor* is played by the Chicago Symphony Orchestra.

1936. William Grant Still becomes the first African American musician to conduct a major American symphony orchestra when he leads the Los Angeles Philharmonic at the Hollywood Bowl.

1941. David Roy "Little Jazz" Eldridge joins Gene Krupa's big band as a trumpeter and singer, becoming the first black musician to be a featured player in an integrated band. Before this, Teddy Wilson and Lionel Hampton were members of Benny Goodman's quartet, but not as featured performers.

1945. Operatic soprano Camilla Williams becomes the first African American to sign a full contract with a major U.S. opera company, the New York City Opera. She performs the title role in Puccini's *Madame Butterfly*.

1950. For her supporting performance as Bloody Mary in the musical *South Pacific*, Juanita Hall becomes the first African American to win a Tony Award.

1968. Henry Lewis becomes the first African American director of a major American orchestra, the New Jersey Symphony.

1972. Elayne Jones is invited to become the San Francisco Symphony's timpanist. Accepting the position, she becomes the first African American woman to hold a principal chair in a major American orchestra.

1988. The rap duo DJ Jazzy Jeff and the Fresh Prince (Jeffrey Townes and Will Smith) win a Grammy Award for the hit "Parents Just Don't Understand," making them the first African American rap group to win a Grammy.

1997. Wynton Marsalis becomes the first jazz musician to win a Pulitzer Prize, for his jazz opera *Blood on the Fields*.

1923. Charles Hamilton Houston becomes the first African American to receive a S.J.D. from Harvard University. While attending Harvard, Houston was the first African American editor of the *Harvard Law Review.*

1923. The first African American basketball team, known as the Renaissance (or Rens), is organized.

1923. Homer B. Roberts becomes the first African American to own a franchise for a new-car dealership when he opens his business in Kansas City, Missouri. By 1940, Roberts opens his fourth dealership, a Studebaker franchise.

1924, July 8. William DeHart Hubbard becomes the first African American in Olympics history to win an individual gold medal when he takes the long jump at the Paris games.

1926. Violette Anderson becomes the first African American woman lawyer to argue a case before the U.S. Supreme Court.

1926, February. Carter Goodwin Woodson, known as the father of black history, establishes Negro History Week; it is celebrated in February between the birthdays of Booker T. Washington, Abraham Lincoln, and Frederick Douglass. In 1976 it is replaced with Black History Month and celebrated throughout February.

1926, June 20. Mordecai Wyatt Johnson becomes the first African American president of Howard University. He retires in 1960.

1927. Artist Henry Ossawa Tanner becomes the first African American to be elected to the National Academy of Design.

1928. Oscar DePriest, a Republican from Illinois, is elected as the first African American representative to the U.S. Congress from a northern state.

1930. Nella Larsen, considered one of the most important writers of the Harlem Renaissance, becomes the first African American woman to be awarded a Guggenheim Fellowship.

1931. Estelle Massey Osborne becomes the first African American recipient in the United States of a master's degree in nursing education when she graduates from Columbia Teachers College.

1933. One of America's most popular social satirists, cartoonist Oliver Harrington, launches the first cartoon to focus on African American life. His comic strip *Boop* (later renamed *Scoop*) debuts in the *Pittsburgh Courier*, an African American newspaper, on March 11, 1933. The New York *Amsterdam News* begins running his panel *Dark Laughter* on May 25, 1935. Later that year, he introduces the character Bootsie to the panel, which continues to appear in African American newspapers for forty years.

Henry Ossawa Tanner, Painter, c. 1905. *In 1927 Tanner became the first African American elected to the National Academy of Design. Tanner's works are in the collections of numerous institutions, including the Art Institute of Chicago, Detroit Institute of Arts, and Pennsylvania Academy of the Fine of Arts.* HULTON ARCHIVE/GETTY IMAGES

1933. Hemsley Winfield becomes the first African American to dance at the Metropolitan Opera House when he performs the role of the Witch Doctor in *The Emperor Jones.*

1933. Florence Price becomes the first African American woman composer to have a symphony performed by a major orchestra when her *Symphony in E Minor* is played by the Chicago Symphony Orchestra.

1933. The first transcontinental flight by African American civilian pilots is made by Charles Alfred Anderson of Bryn Mawr, Pennsylvania, and Albert Ernest Forsythe of Atlantic City, New Jersey.

1934. Willa B. Brown becomes the first African American woman to hold a commercial pilot's license in the United States.

1935. *Mulatto* by Langston Hughes opens at the Vanderbilt Theatre in New York on October 24 and plays continuously until December 9, 1937, making it the first play by an African American author to become a long-run hit on Broadway.

1936. William Grant Still becomes the first African American musician to conduct a major American symphony orchestra when he leads the Los Angeles Philharmonic at the Hollywood Bowl.

1936. Jesse Owens becomes the first Olympian to win four gold medals, three of which were world record marks, at the Olympic Games in Berlin, with German chancellor Adolf Hitler in attendance. Hitler refuses to acknowledge the superiority of Owens and the other African American athletes.

1937. Self-taught sculptor William Edmondson becomes the first African American to have a solo exhibition at the Museum of Modern Art in New York City.

1937. William H. Hastie becomes the first African American federal judge when he is appointed to a federal district court in the Virgin Islands.

1938, November 8. Crystal Bird Fauset becomes the first African American woman representative in a state legislature when she is elected to the Pennsylvania House of Representatives.

1939. Jane Matilda Bolin becomes the country's first African American woman judge when she is appointed to the New York Court of Domestic Relations by Mayor Fiorello La Guardia.

1940. Kenneth Clark becomes the first African American to be awarded a Ph.D. in psychology from Columbia University.

1940. Benjamin O. Davis Sr. is promoted to the rank of brigadier general, becoming the first African American to hold this post in the U.S. Army.

1940. The first postage stamp honoring an African American, the ten-cent Booker T. Washington stamp, goes on sale at Tuskegee Institute. The stamp, which is part of the Famous Americans series, is the culmination of a seven-year campaign sponsored by Major R. R. Wright, president of the Citizens and Southern Bank and Trust Company of Philadelphia. (Seven years later, a three-cent postage stamp honoring George Washington Carver is issued on the fourth anniversary of the renowned scientist's death.)

1940, November 20. For her role as supporting actress in the movie *Gone with the Wind,* Hattie McDaniel becomes the first African American to win an Oscar from the Academy of Motion Picture Arts and Sciences.

1941. David Roy "Little Jazz" Eldridge joins Gene Krupa's big band as a trumpeter and singer, becoming the first black musician to be a featured player in an integrated band. Before this, Teddy Wilson and Lionel Hampton were members of Benny Goodman's quartet, but not as featured performers.

Booker T. Washington Stamp, April 7, 1940. *The ten-cent Booker T. Washington stamp was the first U.S. postage stamp issued to honor an African American.* SMITHSONIAN NATIONAL POSTAL MUSEUM

1941. Charles Richard Drew, an African American physician, sets up the nation's first blood bank in Washington, D.C. He became known as the father of blood plasma. Ironically, Drew died in a segregated hospital in North Carolina that had no blood plasma that might have saved his life.

1942. Bernard W. Robinson, a medical student at Harvard, becomes the first African American commissioned as an officer in the U.S. Naval Reserve.

1942. The first Liberty ship named for an African American, the S.S. *Booker T. Washington,* is christened by Marian Anderson and launched from a New Jersey shipyard to begin its career carrying war cargo to Europe during World War II.

1942. The U.S. Army lifts its color barrier and admits African American women into its women's branch, the Women's Army Corps (WACs).

1943. Pianist and composer Dorothy Donegan becomes the first woman, and the first African American, to play Chicago's Orchestra Hall, sharing the bill with pianist Vladimir Horowitz.

1943. The first warship with an African American crew, the USS *Mason,* sails into the North Atlantic. Among the crew is Thomas W. Young, who becomes the first African American war correspondent on a Navy warship.

Actress Hattie McDaniel, 1939. *McDaniel (*right*) appears with Vivien Leigh in a scene from the movie* Gone with the Wind. *For her portrayal of "Mammy," McDaniel won an Oscar for best supporting actress, becoming the first African American to earn an Academy Award.* MGM STUDIOS/HULTON ARCHIVE/GETTY IMAGES

1943. The USS *Harmon* becomes the first fighting ship to be named for an African American. Leonard Roy Harmon won the Navy Cross for his heroism aboard the USS *San Francisco* in a battle with the Japanese near the Solomon Islands. Harmon died of wounds suffered during the engagement.

1943. W. E. B. Du Bois becomes the first African American admitted to the National Institute of Arts and Letters. At the time of his admittance, Du Bois is head of the Department of Sociology at Atlanta University.

1943. Mary Thelma Washington Wylie becomes the first African American woman CPA (certified public accountant) in the United States. Later, she becomes the first African American woman member of the American Institute of Certified Public Accountants.

1944. Harry McAlpin of Atlanta's *Daily World* becomes the first accredited African American White House news correspondent.

1944, July. Irene Morgan (Kirkaldy) is jailed and fined after refusing to give up her seat to a white couple on an interstate bus in Gloucester, Virginia. Her case leads the courts to strike down segregation in interstate transportation.

1944, October 19. The U.S. Navy begins accepting African American women into the WAVES (Women Accepted for Volunteer Emergency Service).

1944, December. Charity Adams (later Charity Adams Earley) becomes the first African American WAC to be selected for overseas duty when she takes command of the newly formed 6888th Central Postal Battalion in Birmingham, England. The 850-woman unit was responsible for directing all incoming and outgoing mail for the seven million Americans serving in the European Theater.

1945. Phyllis Mae Daley becomes the first African American nurse commissioned in the U.S. Navy Reserve Corps. Daley, a registered nurse from New York City, is sworn in as an ensign.

1945, May 15. Operatic soprano Camilla Williams becomes the first African American to sign a full contract with a major U.S. opera company, the New York City Opera. She performs the title role in Puccini's *Madame Butterfly*.

1945, October 3. Irvin Charles Mollison becomes the first African American appointed to a judgeship in the contiguous United States when President Harry Truman names him to the U.S. Customs Court.

1946. Charles Spurgeon Johnson is appointed president of Fisk University, the first African American to hold the position. Before becoming president, Johnson served as chairman of Fisk University's Department of Social Sciences and established the Fisk Institute of Race Relations.

1946. Roy Campanella, a catcher for a Nashua, New Hampshire, team, becomes the first African American to manage an integrated professional baseball team when the regular manager, Walt Alston, is ejected from the field by the umpire. Nashua wins the game when an African American pitcher, Don Newcombe, hits a pinch-hit home run.

1946. The first coin honoring African Americans—a fifty-cent piece bearing a relief bust of Booker T. Washington, the founder of Tuskegee Institute—is issued.

1947. Jackie Robinson joins the National League's Brooklyn Dodgers and becomes the first African American to play major-league baseball in the twentieth century. He plays his first game as first baseman on April 15 in Brooklyn's Ebbets Field against the Boston Braves.

Jackie Robinson, Brooklyn Dodgers, April 15, 1947. *That year, future Hall-of-Famer Robinson becomes the first African American to officially integrate major league baseball. Infielder Robinson's teammates include:* (left to right) *Johnny "Spider" Jorgensen, Harold "Pee Wee" Reese, and Eddie Stanky.* NATIONAL BASEBALL HALL OF FAME LIBRARY/MAJOR LEAGUE BASEBALL PLATINUM/MLB PHOTOS VIA GETTY IMAGES

1947. Dan Bankhead of the National League's Brooklyn Dodgers becomes the first African American pitcher in the major leagues. The first African American pitcher in the American League, Leroy "Satchel" Paige, follows in 1948.

1947. Larry Doby becomes the first African American baseball player to play in the American League. He makes his debut with the Cleveland Indians on July 5.

1947. Louis Lautier, Washington Bureau chief of the Negro Newspaper Publishers Association, becomes the first African American issued credentials for both the Senate and the House press galleries. Lautier is admitted to the galleries on March 18 after a Senate Rules Committee overrides the refusal of the Standing Committee of Newspaper Correspondents to grant him the necessary credentials.

1947. John Lee of Indianapolis, Indiana, becomes the first African American commissioned officer in the U.S. Navy. His first assignment upon being commissioned is on the USS *Kearsarge*.

1948. Pianist and singer Hazel Scott becomes the first African American to host her own television show.

1948. William Thaddeus Coleman Jr. becomes the first appointed African American clerk of the U.S. Supreme Court when he is named to the post by Justice Felix Frankfurter.

1948. Alice Coachman wins the gold medal in high jump in the Olympic Games in London. She becomes the first African American woman to win gold and the only American woman to win a track event that year.

1948. Nancy Leftenant-Colon becomes the first African American member of the Regular Army Nurse Corps. She is commissioned in the Nurse Corps at Lockbourne Air Force Base, and gains experience as a flight nurse. In 1989, she becomes the only woman to hold the presidency of the Tuskegee Airmen.

1948. John Earl Rudder becomes the first African American commissioned officer in the U.S. Marine Corps.

1949. Representative William L. Dawson is named chairman of the U.S. House Committee on Government Operations, becoming the first African American to head a congressional committee.

1949. William A. Hinton becomes the first African American to be granted a professorship at Harvard Medical School.

1949. Jesse L. Brown becomes the first African American pilot in the U.S. Naval Reserve. On December 4, 1950, at Changjin Reservoir in Korea, Brown is the first African American naval pilot to be killed in action.

1949. Jazz trumpeter Louis Armstrong is the first African American to preside over the Mardi Gras parade in New Orleans. However, his appearance in blackface makeup in the parade results in negative opinions being expressed about him by other African American musicians who regard it as a demeaning gesture.

1949. Wesley A. Brown becomes the first African American to graduate from the Naval Academy at Annapolis, Maryland.

1949. The University of Oklahoma Law School admits its first African American student, Ada Lois Sipuel (Fisher). Her admission is ordered by the *Sipuel v. Board of Regents of the University of Oklahoma* case, reversing a lower court's decision to deny her entry into the school.

1949. William H. Hastie becomes the first African American judge appointed to the U.S. Circuit Court of Appeals. Hastie had previously been the first African American appointed governor of the U.S. Virgin Islands.

1949. Jackie Robinson becomes the first African American baseball player to win his league's Most Valuable Player award. The first African American to receive the award three times is Roy Campanella, who wins the title in 1951, 1953, and 1955.

1949. Lawyer and activist Truman K. Gibson becomes the first African American boxing promoter. Later, he cofounds National Boxing Enterprises, which helped broadcast popular Friday night fights on television.

1950. Tennis player Althea Gibson becomes the first African American to play in the U.S. Open at Forest Hills, New York.

1950. Gwendolyn Brooks is awarded the Pulitzer Prize for her volume of poetry, *Annie Allen*. She is the first African American to win a Pulitzer and also the first African American woman elected to the National Institute of Arts and Letters.

1950. United Nations undersecretary Ralph Bunche becomes the first African American to receive a Nobel Peace Prize.

1950. President Dwight D. Eisenhower appoints Archibald T. Carey Jr. as chair of the Committee on Government Employment Policy. Carey becomes the first African American to hold that position.

1950. For her supporting performance as Bloody Mary in the musical *South Pacific*, Juanita Hall becomes the first African American to win a Tony Award.

1950, April 15. Charles Cooper signs with the Boston Celtics, becoming the first African American to join a National Basketball Association (NBA) team.

1950, October 31. Basketball player Earl Lloyd of the Washington Capitals takes to the court, becoming the first African American to actually participate in an NBA game.

1950, November 15. Arthur Dorrington becomes the first African American to play organized hockey when he signs a contract to play with the Atlantic City Seagulls of the Eastern Amateur League.

1951. Janet Collins becomes the first African American woman to dance with the Metropolitan Opera in New York. Collins makes her debut in Verdi's *Aida*.

1951. William L. Rowe becomes the first African American deputy police commissioner when he is appointed to this position by New York mayor Vincent R. Impellitteri.

1952. Soprano Dorothy Leigh Maynor becomes the first African American artist to perform at Constitution Hall in Washington, D.C.

1952. Rookie of the Year Joe Black leads the Brooklyn Dodgers to a win over the New York Yankees and becomes the first African American pitcher to win a World Series game.

1952. Frank E. Petersen Jr. becomes the first African American Marine pilot. He becomes the first African American brigadier general in the U.S. Marines on February 23, 1979, and retires in 1988 with the rank of lieutenant general.

1953. Ralph Ellison, author of *The Invisible Man*, becomes the first African American to receive the National Book Award.

1953. The University of Virginia awards a doctoral degree to Walter Nathaniel Ridley, who becomes the first African American to earn a Ph.D. from a traditional southern white university. Ridley later becomes president of Elizabeth City State College (now Elizabeth City State University) in North Carolina.

1953. Second baseman Marcenia Lyle "Toni" Stone joins the Negro League's Indianapolis Clowns as the first African American woman to play on a regular big-league professional baseball team. She plays one season with the Clowns and another with the Kansas City Monarchs. The St. Paul, Minnesota, native was already an experienced player on men's teams, having played first with the San Francisco Sea Lions and next with the New Orleans Creoles.

1954. Norma Sklarek becomes the first African American woman to be licensed as an architect in the United States.

1954. Charles H. Mahoney becomes the first African American to be appointed a permanent delegate to the United Nations.

1954. Dr. James Joshua Thomas becomes the first African American pastor in the Reformed Dutch Church. He is installed as minister of the Mott Haven Reformed Church in the Bronx in New York City.

1954. Harry Belafonte's performance in *John Murray Anderson's Almanac* earns him a Tony Award, the first ever won by an African American man.

1954. Dorothy Dandridge becomes the first African American woman to receive an Oscar nomination for best actress when she is nominated for her performance in the all–African American musical *Carmen Jones*.

1954. The first African American radio network, the National Negro Network, begins programming. The New York outlet is station WOV. The network's first program, a weekday soap opera titled *The Story of Ruby Valentine*, starring Juanita Hall and sponsored by Philip Morris and Pet Milk, is carried on forty stations.

1954, October 27. Benjamin Oliver Davis Jr. becomes the first African American general in the U.S. Air Force.

1955, January 5. Marian Anderson becomes the first African American to perform in a solo role at the Metropolitan Opera when she appears as Ulrica in Verdi's *Un ballo in maschera*. Robert McFerrin Sr. follows two weeks later as Amonarso in Verdi's *Aida*, making him the first African American man to appear in a solo role with the company.

1955, April 17. Conductor and musician Everett Lee directs the New York Opera Company's performance of Verdi's *La traviata* and becomes the first African American to conduct an opera with a major company.

1956. Charles Dumas, a freshman at Compton College in California, becomes the first athlete to high jump over seven feet.

1956. Tennis professional Althea Gibson becomes the first African American to win the French Open after she captures both the women's singles and doubles titles.

1957. Perry H. Young becomes the first African American pilot for a scheduled passenger commercial airline, New York Airways.

1957. Althea Gibson wins both the mixed doubles and women's singles titles at Wimbledon, becoming the first African American tennis player to win a title there. Later that year, she wins the same two titles at the U.S. Open, also African American firsts.

1957. James Plinton Jr. becomes the first African American to fill an executive position at a major airline when Trans World Airlines names him executive assistant to the director of personnel and industrial relations.

1958. Ruth Carol Taylor becomes the first African American flight attendant when she is hired to work for Mohawk Airlines.

1958, January 18. Canadian Willie O'Ree breaks racial barriers in professional hockey when he plays his first of only two games during the 1957–1958 season for the Boston Bruins of the National Hockey League (NHL).

He then returns to the minor leagues for two seasons, making it back to the NHL for more than forty games during the 1961 season. Fellow Canadian Mike Marson, the second black man to play in the NHL, is drafted in 1974.

1959. Lorraine Hansberry's play *A Raisin in the Sun* becomes the first play by an African American to receive the New York Drama Critics' Circle Award for best American play.

1959. Hal DeWindt becomes the first male model in the *Ebony* Fashion Fair.

1959. John McLendon becomes the first African American to coach a racially integrated professional basketball team, the Cleveland Pipers of the National Industrial Basketball League.

1959. Harry Belafonte becomes the first African American to win an Emmy Award from the Academy of Television Arts and Sciences when he is deemed the best lead actor in a comedy, variety, or music series for *Tonight with Belafonte*.

1960. Charlie Sifford becomes the first African American to be issued a Professional Golf Association (PGA) card as an "approved player."

1960. Wilma Rudolph, who wore leg braces until she was nine years old, becomes the first African American woman to win three gold medals in track and field in a single Olympic year.

1960, May 10. Nashville, Tennessee, becomes the first major U.S. city to begin desegregating its public facilities.

1961. Wilma Rudolph becomes the first African American to receive the Sullivan Award as the country's top amateur athlete as selected by the Amateur Athletic Union.

1961. Ernie Davis becomes the first African American to be awarded college football's Heisman Memorial Trophy at the Downtown Athletic Club of New York City.

1961. At the age of twenty-four, opera singer Grace Bumbry becomes the first African American to appear in a leading role at the Bayreuth Festival in Germany when she sings the role of Venus in Wagner's *Tannhäuser*.

1961, August 10. President John F. Kennedy appoints James Benton Parsons judge of the U.S. District Court for the Northern District of Illinois. He is the first African American to hold this position and the first to receive a lifetime appointment in that post.

1962. A. Leon Higginbotham Jr. becomes the first African American and the youngest person ever to hold the post of commissioner on the Federal Trade Commission.

1962. Jackie Robinson becomes the first African American to be inducted into the National Baseball Hall of Fame.

1962. Mal Goode becomes the first African American television news correspondent when he begins working for ABC News as a United Nations correspondent.

1962. Harvey Russell Jr. is named vice president of the Pepsi-Cola Company and becomes the first African American man named vice president of a major American corporation.

1962. Lieutenant Commander Samuel L. Gravely Jr. becomes the first African American to command a U.S. warship when he assumes command of the USS *Falgout*, a destroyer escort.

1962. Former civil rights lawyer Thelton Henderson becomes the first African American to join the U.S. Justice Department's Civil Rights Division.

1963. Katherine Dunham becomes the first African American choreographer to work at the Metropolitan Opera House in New York.

1963. Sidney Poitier becomes the first African American man to win an Oscar, for his leading role in *Lilies of the Field*. Poitier is also the first African American to win an Oscar since Hattie McDaniel in 1939.

1963. Marian Anderson and Ralph Bunche become the first African Americans to receive a Presidential Medal of Freedom.

1963, December 1. In Jacksonville, Florida, Wendell Scott becomes the first African American to win a NASCAR race. The victory was initially granted to a white driver, Buck Baker, but a few days later Scott was declared the winner. In 1999, Scott becomes the first African American to be inducted into the International Motorsports Hall of Fame.

1964. Frederick O'Neal becomes the first African American president of Actors' Equity Association.

1965. The Freedom National Bank, the first commercial bank chartered and run by African Americans, is founded in Harlem.

1965. President Lyndon B. Johnson appoints Patricia Roberts Harris as U.S. ambassador to Luxembourg, making her the first African American woman to be named an American envoy.

1965. Vivian Malone Jones becomes the first African American graduate of the University of Alabama. Jones and James Hood were among the first African American students enrolled in the university in 1963.

1965. Pioneering print journalist and public relations expert Lillian Scott Calhoun becomes the first African American woman to work in the *Chicago Sun-Times* newsroom.

1966. The Texas Western University basketball team becomes the first college team to win the NCAA National Championship with an all–African American starting five. They beat the favored and all-white University of Kentucky.

1966. Norma Sklarek becomes the first African American woman to be named a fellow of the American Institute of Architects.

1966. Bill Cosby's work on *I Spy* earns him the first Emmy awarded to an African American for a leading role in a dramatic television series. He is only the second African American to win an Emmy of any kind.

1966. Toni Williams of Reading, Pennsylvania, becomes the first African American showgirl with Ringling Brothers Circus.

1966. Internationally known graphic artist George Olden becomes the first African American to design a U.S. postage stamp, the Emancipation Proclamation stamp.

1966. Emmett Ashford, the first African American umpire in the major leagues, makes his debut during the American League opening-day game between the Cleveland Indians and the Washington Senators. Ashford had umpired in the Southwestern International League in 1952 and in the Pacific Coast League, where he was umpire-in-chief, in 1965.

1966. Constance Baker Motley becomes the first African American woman to serve as a federal judge. She becomes judge on the U.S. District Court, the Southern District of New York.

1966. Robert C. Weaver is named secretary of the newly created Department of Housing and Urban Development, becoming the first African American appointed to serve in a presidential cabinet.

1966. Edward W. Brooke becomes the first African American elected to the U.S. Senate since Reconstruction. He is seated on January 10, 1967.

1966, April 18. Bill Russell, star center of the world champion Boston Celtics, becomes the first African American to direct a major-league sports team when he is named to succeed Red Auerbach as coach of the Boston basketball franchise.

1967. Renee Powell becomes the first African American woman to be issued a Ladies Professional Golf Association (LPGA) card.

1967. Emlen Tunnell becomes the first African American to be inducted into the Pro Football Hall of Fame.

1967. Cuban-born Sergio Oliva becomes the first African American to win the Mr. Olympia competition held by the International Federation of Bodybuilders. He successfully defends his title in 1968.

Thurgood Marshall, U.S. Supreme Court Justice, 1967. *Marshall, appointed by President Lyndon B. Johnson as the first African American to the Supreme Court, served as an associate justice from 1967 to 1991.* BACHRACH/ARCHIVE PHOTOS/GETTY IMAGES

1967. Thurgood Marshall is appointed an associate justice of the U.S. Supreme Court, becoming the first African American to serve on the nation's highest court. In 1965, he had become the first African American solicitor general, a position he held until he joined the Supreme Court.

1967, November 13. Carl B. Stokes becomes the first African American mayor of a major U.S. city when he is elected mayor of Cleveland. Stokes had become known in the 1960s as a symbol of minority voting strides. Richard G. Hatcher, mayor of Gary, Indiana, is elected in the same year, but is not sworn in until January 1, 1968, as the city's first African American mayor.

1968. Diahann Carroll begins playing the title role in the television show *Julia*, making her the first African American lead actress in a network television series.

1968. Arthur Ashe becomes the first African American to win the American Singles Tennis Championship. In 1963, Ashe had become the first African American to play on the U.S. Davis Cup team.

1968. Martin Briscoe joins the Denver Broncos, then in the American Football League, and becomes the first African American quarterback to play regularly.

1968. Henry Lewis becomes the first African American director of a major American orchestra, the New Jersey Symphony.

1968. Shirley Chisholm of New York becomes the first African American woman elected to the U.S. Congress.

1968. Miss Pennsylvania, Sandy Williams, wins the inaugural Miss Black America pageant, hosted by the J. Morris Anderson Production Company.

1968, August. Xernona Clayton becomes the first African American woman in the South to host a regular television program when her talk show debuts in Atlanta.

1969. James Earl Jones becomes the first African American to win a Tony Award for a lead role in a drama, for his performance as boxer Jack Jefferson—based on heavyweight champion Jack Johnson—in *The Great White Hope*.

1969. Federal judge A. Leon Higginbotham Jr. is elected a trustee of Yale University, the first African American to be so honored.

1969. Moneta J. Sleet Jr. becomes the first African American man and the first African American photographer to win a Pulitzer Prize. His prize-winning photograph is a portrait of Coretta Scott King and her youngest child, Bernice, taken at the funeral of Martin Luther King Jr.

1969, January. President Richard Nixon appoints Elizabeth Duncan Koontz director of the Women's Bureau of the U.S. Department of Labor, making her the first African American director of the department. Koontz later becomes deputy assistant secretary for Labor Employment Standards.

1970. Joseph L. Searles III becomes the first African American floor broker on the New York Stock Exchange. Searles, a former aide to New York City mayor John Lindsay, resigns from the administration to become a floor trader and a general partner for Newburger, Loeb and Company.

1970. Gail Fisher becomes the first African American to win an Emmy Award, for her supporting role in the series *Mannix*.

1970. Chris Dickerson becomes the first African American to win the title Mr. America, one of fifteen bodybuilding titles Dickerson will earn during his career. One of a set of triplets born in Montgomery, Alabama, on August 25, 1939, Dickerson proves to be an outstanding athlete throughout his school years. An early interest in singing and the desire to improve his voice quality and breath control led him to start bodybuilding in the mid-1960s.

1970. Renard Edwards becomes the first African American musician to perform for the Philadelphia Orchestra when he is hired as a violist for the 1970–1971 season. Edwards had formerly been with the Symphony of the New World, an integrated orchestra.

1971. Known as the father of black professional basketball for his contributions as coach and owner of the barnstorming New York Renaissance (the Rens), Robert L. Douglass becomes the first African American inducted into the Naismith Memorial Basketball Hall of Fame.

1971. Johnson Products, which sells items under the Ultra-Sheen label, becomes the first African American–owned company to trade on a major stock exchange.

1971. Samuel L. Gravely Jr. becomes the first African American admiral in the history of the U.S. Navy.

1971. C. DeLores Tucker becomes the first African American woman to serve as a state secretary of state and the first woman in Pennsylvania to serve in that role.

1972. U.S. congresswoman Shirley Chisholm seeks the Democratic nomination for the presidency, becoming the first African American woman to seek a major party nomination for the U.S. presidency.

1972. Approximately eight thousand African Americans attend the first National Black Political Convention in Gary, Indiana. The convention is chaired by Imamu Amiri Baraka, with Mayor Richard Hatcher of Gary featured as the keynote speaker.

1972. Elayne Jones is invited to become the San Francisco Symphony's timpanist. Accepting the position, she becomes the first African American woman to hold a principal chair in a major American orchestra.

1972, March 18. The U.S. Navy launches the destroyer escort USS *Jesse L. Brown*, marking the first time a Navy ship is named in honor of an African American naval officer. Brown was the first African American pilot in the U.S. Naval Reserve and the first African American naval pilot killed in action during the Korean conflict.

1972, November 17. Barbara Jordan wins a seat in the U.S. House of Representatives, becoming the first woman from Texas to be elected to Congress.

1973. Andrew Young wins the inaugural Martin Luther King Jr. Nonviolent Peace Prize.

1973. Coleman A. Young is elected mayor of Detroit, Michigan, the first African American to hold the post in the white-majority city. On the same evening, Maynard H. Jackson is elected mayor of Atlanta, Georgia.

1973. Physicist Shirley Ann Jackson becomes the first African American woman to earn a Ph.D. from Massachusetts Institute of Technology (MIT). Jackson had received her B.S. degree from MIT in 1968.

1973, May 29. Thomas Bradley of Los Angeles becomes the first African American to be elected mayor of a city with a population exceeding one million. He defeats the incumbent, Sam Yorty, by 100,000 votes. Yorty had defeated Bradley in the 1969 mayoral election.

1973, November. Attorney and former California state assemblywoman Yvonne Brathwaite Burke becomes the first African American woman from California ever elected to the U.S. House of Representatives.

1974. George L. Brown is elected in Colorado as the first African American lieutenant governor of the twentieth century. He is also the first African American to win statewide election in Colorado.

1974. The Athletics Congress of the USA inducts Ralph Boston, Lee Calhoun, Harrison Dillard, Rafer Johnson, Jesse Owens, Wilma Rudolph, and Malvin Whitfield into its National Track & Field Hall of Fame.

1974. The Mary McLeod Bethune Memorial is unveiled in Washington, D.C. It is the first monument to an African American, or a woman, to be erected on public land in the nation's capital.

Yvonne Brathwaite Burke, U.S. Representative from California, 1978. *In 1973, Burke became the first African American woman from California to be elected to the U.S. House of Representatives.* BETTMANN/CORBIS

1974. Representative Charles Rangel from New York becomes the first African American to serve on the House Ways and Means Committee.

1974. Barbara Hancock becomes the first African American woman to be named a White House Fellow.

1974. Cicely Tyson becomes the first African American woman to receive an Emmy Award for a leading role. Her performance in *The Autobiography of Miss Jane Pittman* earned her the honor in the category of comedy or drama special.

1974. *The River Niger* by Joseph A. Walker becomes the first play written by an African American to receive the Tony Award for best play.

1974. Leo Miles becomes the first African American to officiate at a Super Bowl game.

1974. Joe Gilliam Jr. becomes the first African American quarterback to start in an NFL game, making him a trailblazer for African American quarterbacks in modern times.

1974, November. The Thunderbirds, the U.S. Air Force Aerial Demonstration Squadron, gains its first African American pilot when Captain Lloyd W. "Fig" Newton joins the squad.

1975. The U.S. Navy commissions Donna P. Davis as a lieutenant in the Navy's medical corps, making her the first African American woman physician in the corps' history.

1975. General Daniel "Chappie" James Jr. becomes commander-in-chief of the North American Air Defense Command (NORAD). On the same day, the U.S. Air Force promotes him as the first African American four-star general in U.S. history.

1975. Frank Robinson becomes the first African American to manage a major-league baseball team and leads his Cleveland Indians to an opening-day victory over the New York Yankees.

1975. WGPR-TV in Detroit goes on the air, becoming the first television station in the United States that is owned and operated by African Americans.

1976. Congresswoman Barbara Jordan becomes the first African American to give a keynote address at the Democratic National Convention.

1976. Robert Hayden becomes the first African American poet laureate. He serves in that position at the Library of Congress until 1978.

1977. Drew S. Days becomes the first African American to head the Civil Rights Division of the U.S. Department of Justice.

1977. Pauli Murray, a distinguished lawyer and educator, becomes the first African American woman to be ordained a priest in the predominantly white Episcopal Church.

1977. Clifford Alexander Jr. becomes the first African American to be appointed secretary of the U.S. Army. He works to increase the number of African American officers within the ranks.

1977. Former basketball player Wayne Embry becomes the first African American general manager of an NBA team—the Milwaukee Bucks.

1977. Lionel J. Wilson becomes the first African American elected mayor of Oakland, California. In 1960, he had became the first African American judge in Alameda County, which encompasses Oakland.

1977. Karen Farmer becomes the first African American member of the Daughters of the American Revolution (DAR), an organization that had refused to allow Marian Anderson to perform at Constitution Hall in Washington, D.C., in 1939.

1977. Patricia Roberts Harris is appointed secretary of the Department of Housing and Urban Development, becoming the first African American woman to serve in a cabinet-level position.

1977. William B. Bryant becomes the first African American to serve as chief judge of the U.S. District Court for the District of Columbia. He held the post until 1981.

1978. Jack Tanner is assigned to the U.S. District Court for the Eastern and Western Districts of Washington, becoming the first African American federal judge in the Northwest.

1978. Faye Wattleton is elected president of Planned Parenthood, becoming the first African American woman and the youngest person to head the organization.

1978. Wendy Hilliard becomes the first African American member of the U.S. National Rhythmic Gymnastics Team.

1978. When he joins ABC-TV's *World News Tonight*, Max Robinson becomes the first African American network anchor.

1978. Retired singer Marian Anderson becomes the first African American to be awarded the Congressional Gold Medal, the highest honor that can be bestowed upon a civilian. The same year, she also becomes the first African American to receive a Kennedy Center Honor from the John F. Kennedy Center for the Performing Arts.

1978. Reverend Emerson Moore Jr. is named the first African American monsignor of the Catholic Church in the United States. Monsignor Moore is pastor of St. Charles Borromeo Church in New York City.

1979. Amalya L. Kearse becomes the first African American woman to receive an appointment to the U.S. Circuit Court of Appeals.

1979. U.S. Army Second Lieutenant Marcella A. Hayes, a graduate of the University of Wisconsin and the Army ROTC program, earns her aviator wings and becomes the first African American woman pilot in U.S. armed services history.

1979. Matthew Perry becomes the first African American federal judge for South Carolina.

1979. Audrey Neal becomes the first African American woman (or woman of any ethnic group) longshoreperson. Neal is employed at the Bayonne Military Ocean Terminal in New Jersey.

1979, October 30. City council member Richard Arrington Jr. becomes the first African American elected mayor of Birmingham, Alabama.

1980. Rosa Parks becomes the first woman to receive the Martin Luther King Jr. Nonviolent Peace Prize.

1980. Howard University launches WHMM-TV and becomes the first licensee of a public television station on an African American campus, with the only African American–owned public television station in the nation.

1980. Levi Watkins Jr., an African American surgeon, performs the first surgical implantation of an automatic implantable defibrillator in a human heart. The device corrects an ailment known as ventricular fibrillation or arrhythmia, which prevents the heart from pumping blood.

1980, September 30. The first annual Black College Day is held in Washington, D.C. Organized by African American journalist Tony Brown, the event draws public attention to the impact of integration and the merging of African American private and public colleges and universities.

1981. Charles P. Chapman becomes the first African American to swim across the English Channel.

1981. Isabel Sanford becomes the first African American woman to be awarded an Emmy Award for outstanding lead actress in a television comedy series for her performance in *The Jeffersons*.

1981. Pamela Johnson is named publisher of the *Ithaca Journal* and becomes the first African American woman to hold that position with a major U.S. newspaper.

1981. Ruth Love becomes the first African American to serve as superintendent of the Chicago school system. Prior to her appointment to this post, Love held a similar position in Oakland, California.

1982. Bryant Gumbel becomes the first African American to cohost *The Today Show* on NBC.

1982. Ralph Bradley becomes the first African American to complete the Iditarod Sled Dog Race. Though he finishes last in the 1,049-mile race, he wins the Red Lantern Prize with a time of 26:13:59:59.

1983. The nation's first African American quintuplets—Ashlee, Renee, Rhealyn, Brandon, and Joshua Gaither—are born at Indiana University Hospital. All weigh less than five pounds when they are born.

1983. Louis Gossett Jr. becomes the first African American man to be awarded an Academy Award for best supporting actor for his performance in *An Officer and a Gentleman.*

1983. Representing New York, Vanessa Williams becomes the first African American Miss America in the sixty-two-year history of the Atlantic City pageant. The first runner-up is Suzette Charles representing New Jersey, who is also African American and the first African American Miss New Jersey. When Williams is forced to surrender her title following the discovery of scandalous photos, Charles is crowned Miss America.

1983. Carla Dunlap becomes the first African American to win the Ms. Olympia competition held by the International Federation of Bodybuilders. Seven years later, Lenda Murray becomes the second African American to win the title and successfully defends it five times.

1983, April 19. Harold Washington is sworn in as mayor of Chicago, becoming the first African American to hold the position.

1983, August 30. Guion Bluford becomes the first African American to travel in space when he serves as a crew member on a six-day flight aboard the space shuttle *Challenger*.

1983, November. James A. Sharp Jr. is elected as the first African American mayor of Flint, Michigan.

1983, November 10. Democrat Harvey Gantt becomes the first African American elected mayor of Charlotte, North Carolina.

1984. Methodist Reverend Leontine Turpeau Current Kelly becomes the first African American woman bishop of a major religious denomination.

1984. W. Wilson Goode takes the oath of office as the first African American mayor of Philadelphia.

1984, April 2. Former Boston Celtics player John Thompson Jr. becomes the first African American coach to win an NCAA Division I basketball championship. He coaches the Georgetown University Hoyas, led by center Patrick Ewing, to victory.

1985. Prominent Oakland surgeon Clarence Avery Jr. becomes the first African American president of the California Medical Association. In 1976, he had become the first African American president of the Alameda–Contra Costa Medical Association.

1985. Author Ralph Ellison and singer Leontyne Price become the first African Americans to receive the National Medal of Arts from the National Endowment for the Arts.

1985. Gwendolyn Brooks assumes a one-year post as Poetry Consultant to the Library of Congress, thereby becoming the first African American woman to serve as U.S. poet laureate.

1986. Chuck Berry, James Brown, Ray Charles, Sam Cooke, Fats Domino, Robert Johnson, Little Richard, and Jimmy Yancey are among the first performers enshrined in the newly opened Rock and Roll Hall of Fame and Museum in Cleveland.

1986 A bust of Martin Luther King Jr., made by Boston artist John Woodrow Wilson, is unveiled in the Capitol Rotunda in Washington, D.C. This marks the first time that a work of art honoring an African American is displayed in the nation's Capitol.

Bronze Bust of Martin Luther King Jr. (John Wilson, 1986). *King's widow, Coretta Scott King, views the sculpture of the civil rights leader after it is installed in the U.S. Capitol, the first work of art to honor an African American in the Capitol building.* AP PHOTO/J. SCOTT APPLEWHITE

1986. Oprah Winfrey becomes the first African American woman to host a nationally syndicated, daily television talk show.

1986. Kay George Roberts earns a doctor of musical arts degree from Yale University, becoming the first woman and second African American to do so.

1986. Georg Stanford Brown becomes the first African American to win an Emmy Award for outstanding directing in a drama series. Brown wins for directing the episode "Parting Shots" for the acclaimed series *Cagney* & *Lacey*.

1986. Lieutenant Commander Donnie Cochran becomes the first African American pilot in the U.S. Navy to fly with the Blue Angels. Two years later, he becomes the first African American to head the squad. The precision flight team was formed in the 1940s and has performed its highly sophisticated aerobatics in air shows in the United States and Europe ever since.

1986. Debi Thomas becomes the first African American to win the U.S. Ladies Figure Skating Championship and the World Championship.

1986. Leslie B. Dunner takes third prize in 1986 at the Arturo Toscanini International Conducting Competition, becoming the first American to place at this prestigious event.

1986, January 11. L. Douglas Wilder becomes the first African American lieutenant governor of the Commonwealth of Virginia.

1986, January 20. The first Martin Luther King Jr. federal holiday is celebrated.

1986, November 22. By winning the Brunswick Memorial World Open in Chicago, George Branham III becomes the first African American bowler to win a Professional Bowling Association (PBA) title.

1987. Dain Blanton, in his third professional season, becomes the first African American to win a major tournament with the Association of Volleyball Professionals (AVP). He is the first and only African American on the AVP tour. Blanton and his partner, Canyon Ceman, won the $300,000 Miller Lite/AVP Hermosa Beach, California, Grand Slam.

1987. Former naval pilot Jill Brown becomes the first African American woman to work as a pilot for a major airline.

1987, December 8. Kurt L. Schmoke is inaugurated as the first elected African American mayor of Baltimore, Maryland.

1988. The rap duo DJ Jazzy Jeff and the Fresh Prince (Jeffrey Townes and Will Smith) win a Grammy Award for the hit "Parents Just Don't Understand," making them the first African American rap group to win a Grammy.

1988. America's Black Holocaust Museum, founded by James Cameron, opens in Milwaukee. It was the only museum chronicling the history of lynchings in the United States.

1988. Spelman College appoints its first African American woman president, Johnnetta B. Cole.

1988. Eugene Antonio Marino becomes the country's first African American Roman Catholic archbishop when he is named archbishop of the Atlanta archdiocese. Marino had been one of three auxiliary bishops in Washington, D.C.

1988. Doug Williams becomes the first African American to play quarterback with a Super Bowl team, the Washington Redskins. The Redskins defeat the Denver Broncos 42–10 in Super Bowl XXII.

1988. Florence Griffith Joyner ("Flo Jo") becomes the first American woman to win four gold medals in track and field at a single Olympics.

1988. Juanita Kidd Stoutt is appointed to the Supreme Court of Pennsylvania and becomes the first African American woman to serve on the highest court of any state.

1988. The first National Black Arts Festival in the United States, founded by educator and political leader Michael L. Lomax, is held in Atlanta, Georgia. It becomes the world's largest and most comprehensive showcase of African diasporan arts.

1989. Colonel Frederick Gregory, a Washington, D.C., native, becomes the first African American astronaut to command a space shuttle.

1989. Lawyer Ronald H. Brown is elected chairman of the Democratic National Committee, making him the first African American to head a major American political party.

1989. Norm Rice, who became known as "Mayor Nice," is elected mayor of Seattle, becoming the first African American to hold the position.

1989. Episcopal reverend Barbara C. Harris becomes the first woman bishop in the worldwide Anglican Communion. The Episcopal Church ruled in 1976 that women could be ordained priests.

1989. Rodney S. Patterson, an ordained Baptist minister, starts the first African American congregation in Vermont, a state with a small African American population. Patterson, who moved to Burlington to join the staff at the University of Vermont, names the church the New Alpha Missionary Baptist Church.

1989. U.S. Army general Colin Powell becomes the first African American to serve as chairman of the Joint Chiefs of Staff and principal military adviser to the president of the United States, the secretary of defense, and the National Security Council.

1989. Former St. Louis Cardinal first baseman Bill White assumes office as president of the National League, becoming the first African American to head a professional sports league.

1989. As a member of a consortium of seven investors that purchased the Texas Rangers, Comer Cottrell becomes the first African American to own a major-league baseball franchise. Cottrell uses his position to speak out about affirmative action in professional sports.

1989. Art Shell becomes the first African American head coach in the NFL modern era. He coaches the Oakland Raiders from 1989 to 1994 and in 1996.

1990. Lorna Simpson becomes the first African American woman to have her work featured in the Venice Biennale, an international art exhibition.

1990. The Wade H. McCree Jr. Professorship is established at the University of Michigan Law School. It is the first endowed chair at a major American law school to be named for an African American.

1990. David Dinkins becomes the first African American mayor of New York City.

1990. Carole Gist of Michigan becomes the first African American Miss USA.

1990. L. Douglas Wilder becomes the first African American elected governor of a state when he wins that role in Virginia.

1990. Sharon Pratt Dixon is elected mayor of Washington, D.C., making her the first African American woman to manage a major U.S. city.

1991. Robert L. Johnson's company, BET Holdings, becomes the first African American–owned business listed on the New York Stock Exchange.

1991. Corporal Freddie Stowers is posthumously awarded the Medal of Honor for serving in France during World War I. Stowers is the first African American to receive the medal for service in either world war. In 1988, the secretary of the army directed the U.S. Army to conduct a study to determine whether African American soldiers had been overlooked in the recognition process. Research found that Stowers had been recommended for the medal, but for reasons unknown, the recommendation had not been processed.

1991. Former Roman Catholic nun Rose Vernell is ordained a priest of the Imani Temple African American Catholic Congregation by Bishop George A. Stallings Jr. Vernell is the first woman priest in the church. The congregation was founded in 1989 when Stallings broke with the Roman Catholic Church in the first split from the church in the United States since 1904.

1991. Lee Haney wins an unprecedented eighth consecutive Mr. Olympia title, his last. In 1998, Ronnie Coleman wins his first of four consecutive Mr. Olympia crowns.

1991. Lynn Whitfield becomes the first African American woman to win an Emmy Award for outstanding lead actress in a miniseries or special for her performance in *The Josephine Baker Story.*

1991. John Singleton garners an Oscar nomination for best director for his film *Boyz N the Hood.* He is the first African American to be nominated for the award, and at twenty-three he is also the youngest director to be so honored.

1991, April. Reverend Leon H. Sullivan organizes and cochairs the first African and African American Summit, held at Abidjan in the Côte d'Ivoire.

1992. Carol Moseley Braun of Illinois is elected to the U.S. Senate, becoming the first African American woman senator.

1992. Mae C. Jemison, a physician and chemical engineer, becomes the first African American woman in space when she takes part in a mission onboard the U.S. space shuttle *Endeavour.* The crew studies the behavior of living organisms in a weightless atmosphere and looks for ways to cure space sickness.

1992. Captain William "Bill" Pinckney becomes the first African American to navigate a sailboat solo around the world. His journey on the *Commitment* began in Boston in 1990, covered 32,000 nautical miles, and included several stops.

1992. Awadagin Pratt becomes the first African American to win the Naumburg International Piano Competition.

1992. Bill Cosby becomes the first African American to win a Hall of Fame Emmy Award from the Academy of Television Arts and Sciences.

1992. Leah J. Sears becomes the first woman and the second African American to serve on the Georgia Supreme Court. After being appointed to that court, she is elected to a full judicial term.

1992, November 3. Jacquelyn H. Barrett is elected as the first African American woman sheriff of Fulton County, Georgia.

1992, November 3. Earl F. Hilliard becomes the first African American from Alabama elected to the U.S. Congress. Cynthia McKinney becomes the first African American woman voted into the Georgia House of Representatives.

1993. David Satcher, a physician, educator, and former medical-school president, is appointed head of the Centers for Disease Control in Atlanta. He is the first African American to hold the post.

1993. Mike Espy becomes the first African American secretary of agriculture when he is appointed by President Bill Clinton.

1993. Ronald "Ron" Dellums, who chaired the Defense Policy Panel, becomes the first African American to head the House Armed Services Committee.

1993. President Bill Clinton appoints Ronald H. Brown commerce secretary. He is subsequently confirmed by the U.S. Senate, and becomes the first African American secretary of commerce.

1993. Joycelyn Elders becomes the first African American and the second woman U.S. surgeon general. Formerly, Elders had been head of the Arkansas Health Department.

1993. Nima Warfield, an English major at Morehouse College, becomes the first African American student from a historically African American college to win a Rhodes Scholarship. He studied at Oxford's School of Modern History and English in 1994.

1993. Eleanor Holmes Norton becomes the first voting delegate in the U.S. House of Representatives for Washington, D.C. Previously, delegates representing the District of Columbia and the U.S. trust territories were not allowed to vote on the House floor because the U.S. Constitution restricts legislative authority to state representatives.

1993. African American candidates in Selma, Alabama, win a majority of seats on the city council for the first time, despite efforts by white council members to maintain a majority.

1993. South Carolina's Kimberly Clarice Aiken is crowned Miss America, becoming the first African American woman from a southern state to win the pageant.

1993. Sharon Sayles Belton becomes the first woman and first African American mayor of Minneapolis, Minnesota.

1993. In his thirteenth year as a National League umpire, Charlie Williams becomes the first African American to call balls and strikes in a World Series game.

1993, November 7. Toni Morrison becomes the first African American to receive a Nobel Prize for Literature.

1994. At the U.S. National Championships, Dominique Dawes becomes the first African American to win the all-around title as best gymnast.

1994. William G. Anderson becomes the first African American president of the American Osteopathic Association, a major medical organization.

1994. Whoopi Goldberg becomes the first African American to serve as sole host of the Academy Awards and the first African American Oscar winner to host the show.

1994. Working his way up the political ladder, John Stroger becomes the first African American president of Chicago's Cook County Board.

1994. Donnie Cochran, the only African American pilot in the Blue Angels, the U.S. Navy's precision flying squad, becomes the group's first African American commander.

1994. Louis Westerfield becomes the first African American academic dean at the University of Mississippi.

1994. Eighteen-year-old Tiger Woods becomes the youngest player and the first African American to win the U.S. Amateur Golf Championship.

1994. Forty-four-year-old Beverly Harvard becomes chief of police in Atlanta. She is the first African American woman to reach that position in a major U.S. city.

1994, February 3. Commander Charles Bolden leads NASA's first joint American-Russian mission aboard the space shuttle *Discovery.*

1995. Radio pioneer Herb Kent becomes the first African American disc jockey inducted into the Radio Hall of Fame.

1995. Atlanta Hawks coach Lenny Wilkens becomes the most successful coach in NBA history.

1995. Marcelite J. Harris, who became the U.S. Air Force's first African American general in 1990, becomes the first African American woman to earn the rank of major general.

1995. John Stanford, a retired U.S. Army major general, becomes the first African American school superintendent in Seattle, Washington.

1995. Ronald Kirk is elected Dallas's first African American mayor and becomes the first African American to lead a major Texas city.

1995. Gene C. McKinney becomes the first African American sergeant major, the highest noncommissioned officer in the U.S. Army.

1995. Willie L. Brown Jr., the former speaker and a thirty-one-year veteran of the California General Assembly, defeats incumbent Frank Jordan to become San Francisco's first African American mayor.

1995. Chelsi Smith of Texas becomes the first African American crowned Miss Universe.

1995. Orlando "Tubby" Smith becomes the first African American head basketball coach at the University of Georgia.

1995. Carolyn G. Morris becomes the first African American assistant director and the highest-ranking African American woman in the history of the FBI.

1995. Minnesota Vikings quarterback Warren Moon becomes the first quarterback to eclipse 60,000 yards in career passing.

1995. Bernard A. Harris Jr., a physician from Houston, Texas, becomes the first African American to walk in space during a mission on the space shuttle *Discovery.* In

1996, Winston E. Scott becomes the second African American to complete a spacewalk, from a bridge in the cargo bay of space shuttle *Endeavour.*

1995, March 26. Talk-show host Alan Keyes announces his candidacy for the U.S. presidency. In so doing, he becomes the first African American in the twentieth century to run for president as a Republican. He attracts little support, however, and does not win a primary.

1995, June. Dr. Lonnie Bristow becomes the first African American president of the 147-year-old American Medical Association.

1996. At the Summer Olympics in Atlanta, Georgia, Michael Johnson becomes the first man to win the 200-meter and 400-meter races in the same games.

1996. Franklin D. Raines becomes the first African American to head the U.S. Office of Management and Budget. This is the highest executive post ever held by an African American.

1996. Former U.S. secret serviceman Hubert T. Bell becomes the first African American inspector general of the Nuclear Regulatory Commission.

1996. BET Holdings, the parent company of the Black Entertainment Network, launches BET Movies/STARZ!, the nation's first African American–controlled premium cable movie channel.

1996. Adolpho A. Birch Jr. is sworn in as the first African American chief justice of the Tennessee Supreme Court. From 1987 until he joined the Tennessee Supreme Court in 1993, he had been the first African American to serve on the Tennessee Court of Appeals.

1996. Darlene Green becomes the first woman elected comptroller in St. Louis, Missouri.

1996. Richard N. Dixon, a member of the Maryland House of Delegates since 1983, is sworn in as Maryland's first African American state treasurer.

1996. Seventy-three-year-old composer George Walker wins the 1996 Pulitzer Prize for Music, becoming the first African American to win the prize in that category.

1996. Jacquelyn M. Belcher, the former president of Minneapolis Community College in Minnesota, is inaugurated president of Dekalb College in Georgia, making her the first African American woman president of a school in the University System of Georgia.

1996. The U.S. Navy appoints its first African American four-star admiral, Vice Admiral J. Paul Reason.

1996. Margaret A. Dixon becomes the first African American president of the American Association of Retired Persons (AARP).

1996. Sergeant Heather Lynn Johnson of the Third U.S. Infantry becomes the first woman to receive the U.S. Army's tomb-guard badge to become a sentinel at the Tomb of the Unknown Soldier in Arlington National Cemetery in Arlington, Virginia.

1996. The National Council of Negro Women dedicates its new headquarters building. The facility is the first African American–owned building on Pennsylvania Avenue between Capitol Hill and the White House.

1996. The White House unveils Henry Ossawa Tanner's painting *Sand Dunes at Sunset, Atlantic City,* an oil on canvas. The acquisition is the first work by an African American artist to become a part of the White House collection.

Painter Henry Ossawa Tanner. *Tanner's painting* Sand Dunes at Sunset, Atlantic City *(c. 1885) was hung at the White House in 1996, making it the first work by an African American artist to become part of the permanent White House collection.* SCHOMBURG CENTER FOR RESEARCH IN BLACK CULTURE. REPRODUCED BY PERMISSION.

1996. The University of Southern Mississippi names James Green head basketball coach, making him the first African American to hold the post.

1996. Barry Sanders of the Detroit Lions becomes the first running back in NFL history to rush for 1,000 yards in eight consecutive seasons, with 11,271 total yards.

1996. Marcus Allen becomes the NFL's all-time leader in rushing touchdowns, breaking the record held by former Chicago Bears star Walter Payton.

1996. Eighteen-year-old Chanté Griffin becomes the first African American to be crowned Miss Teen of America. She was elected Miss Teen of California in 1995.

1997. The *Sports Illustrated* swimsuit issue features supermodel Tyra Banks, who becomes the first African American model to be solely featured on the magazine's cover in its thirty-four-year history.

1997. Twenty-one-year-old Tiger Woods becomes the first African American and the youngest player to win the Masters golf tournament. He also records the largest victory margin and the lowest seventy-two-hole total in the tournament's history.

1997. Harvey Johnson is sworn in as the mayor of Jackson, Mississippi, becoming the first African American mayor in the state's capital. The ceremony is held on the steps of city hall, which was built by enslaved Africans before the Civil War. Johnson served a second and third term and later returned for a fourth.

1997. Wynton Marsalis becomes the first jazz musician to win a Pulitzer Prize, for his jazz opera *Blood on the Fields*.

1997. Moses Ector becomes the highest-ranking African American in the Georgia Bureau of Investigation. He is also the first African American to be named bureau chief of staff.

1997. Conrad L. Mallett Jr. becomes the first African American chief justice of the Michigan Supreme Court.

1997. Councilman Preston Daniels becomes the first African American elected mayor of Des Moines, Iowa.

1997. Massachusetts State Appeals Court justice Roderick Ireland is confirmed as the first African American justice on the state's Supreme Court.

1997. Robert Stanton is sworn in as director of the National Park Service, becoming the first African American to head the service in its eighty-year history.

1997. Proffitts Inc. elects Julius "Dr. J." Erving to its board of directors, making him the first African American on the thirteen-member board.

1997. The U.S. Army commissions West Point's first African American cadet, the formerly enslaved James Webster Smith, 123 years after he was expelled from the academy for failing an examination. The certificate is presented posthumously during a ceremony in Orangeburg, South Carolina.

1997. Alexis Herman is confirmed as U.S. secretary of labor, making her the first African American to head that department.

1997. Norma Holloway Johnson becomes the first African American woman to serve as chief judge of the U.S. District Court for the District of Columbia.

1997. Former Olympian Chris Campbell becomes the first African American executive director of U.S. Amateur Boxing, Inc.

1997. Thurgood Marshall Jr. is appointed an assistant to President Bill Clinton and secretary to the cabinet, making him the first African American to serve as secretary of a presidential cabinet.

1997. Earnest L. Tate becomes the first African American chief of police in Selma, Alabama, a city once known for its intolerance and brutality to civil rights protesters.

1997. Eric Holder becomes the highest-ranking African American law enforcement officer in the nation's history when he is sworn in as deputy U.S. attorney general, the second highest position in the U.S. Justice Department. He had become the first African American U.S. attorney for the District of Columbia in 1993.

1997. Dawn Peter becomes Chicago's first African American mounted police officer. Previously, she had served as a Chicago patrol and plainclothes officer.

1997. The nation's first known African American sextuplets (five girls and one boy) are born to Jacqueline and Linden Thompson at the Georgetown University Medical Center. One daughter is stillborn.

1997. Violet Palmer becomes the first African American NBA referee when she and Dee Kantner are named as the league's first two women officials.

1997. Charles Woodson, a defensive back for the University of Michigan, becomes the first predominantly defensive player to win football's Heisman Trophy.

1997. Fifty-seven-year-old Dorothy Walker becomes the first person in the country to undergo an experimental new laser heart-surgery procedure, thorascopic investigational heart surgery, at Northwestern Memorial Hospital in Chicago.

1997. The Association of Trial Lawyers of America elects its first African American president, Indianapolis attorney Richard D. Hailey.

1997. Dallas Mavericks forward A. C. Green breaks the NBA's consecutive game streak when he plays his 907th consecutive game.

1997. After coaching at the University of Georgia for two seasons, Orlando "Tubby" Smith becomes the first African American head basketball coach at the University of Kentucky. In 1998, he leads Kentucky to the national championship.

1997. Andrea Gardiner, a sixteen-year-old Bay City, Texas, native, becomes the first African American to win the junior women's title at the U.S. Figure Skating Championship.

1997. Vivian Fuller is named athletic director at Tennessee State University and becomes the country's first African American woman director of athletics at an NCAA Division I program.

1997. Ann Dibble Jordan, cochair of inaugural activities for President Bill Clinton's second term in office, becomes the first African American woman to serve in that role.

1997. Walter G. Sellers of Wilberforce, Ohio, is unanimously elected president of Kiwanis International and becomes the first African American to serve in that position.

1997, October 22. The first Kwanzaa stamp, designed by African American artist Synthia Saint James, is released by the U.S. Postal Service.

1997, October 29. The U.S. Senate confirms William E. Kennard as chairman of the Federal Communications Commission, making him the organization's first African American chairman. Previously, he had served the commission as general counsel.

1997, November 19. Drs. Paula Mahone and Karen Drake become the first African American physicians to assist in the delivery of septuplets—the McCaughey babies.

1997, December 6. Democrat Lee Patrick Brown becomes the first African American elected mayor of Houston, Texas. Police chief of the city from 1982 to 1990 and former "drug czar," Brown takes office on January 1, 1998.

1998. The first African American Male Empowerment Summit (AAMES) is held and attracts more than five hundred men.

1998. Chapman Holdings, Inc., of Baltimore becomes the first publicly traded African American–owned securities brokerage firm.

1998. Ben Ruffin, vice president of R. J. Reynolds Tobacco Company, is elected the first African American chair of the University of North Carolina's board, which approves policies for the sixteen campuses in the system.

1998. The U.S. Navy selects Captain James A. Johnson for promotion to rear admiral in the Navy Medical Corps, making him the first African American on active duty to hold that post in the corps' 127-year history.

1998. Glenn Ivey becomes the first African American to head Maryland's five-member Public Service Commission.

1998. J. C. Watts Jr., a U.S. congressman from Oklahoma's Fourth District, becomes the first African American Republican to fill a congressional leadership post in modern times when he is named chairman of the Republican Conference, the number-four position in the House. In 1990, Watts had become the first African American in Oklahoma to win statewide elective office when he captured a seat on the Oklahoma Corporate Commission, which regulates gas and oil utilities. In 1997, after President Bill Clinton delivered the State of the Union address, Watts became the first African American to present the opposing party's response.

1998. Seven of the more than two thousand African American soldiers who fought along with white soldiers in frontline battles in 1944 during World War II are awarded the Bronze Star. Vernon Baker, the lone surviving member of the group, is the only one to receive the award in person; the others are awarded posthumously. The white soldiers received their awards soon after the war.

1998. Three-time world champion calf roper Fred Whitfield becomes the first African American to earn more than $1 million in professional rodeo. He crosses the $1 million mark faster than any other cowboy in the history of the Professional Rodeo Cowboys Association.

1998. San Francisco Giants outfielder Barry Bonds becomes the only player in Major League Baseball to reach 400 home runs and 400 steals in a career.

1998. *Newsweek* magazine promotes Mark Whitaker to the position of editor, making him the first African American to helm a weekly news magazine. A Harvard graduate, Whitaker joined the magazine's staff in 1977.

1998. Twenty-two-year-old Jonathan Lee Iverson becomes the first African American and the youngest person ever to serve as ringmaster for Ringling Brothers and Barnum & Bailey Circus.

1998. Chamique Holdsclaw becomes the first African American woman basketball player to win the Sullivan Award, given to the top amateur athlete in the United States.

1998, January 23. Lani Guinier is named professor of law in the Harvard University School of Law, and becomes the first African American woman tenured in the law school.

1998, December 9. Lieutenant General Benjamin O. Davis Jr., former commander of the Tuskegee Airmen during World War II, receives his fourth star in a White House ceremony. Davis, a graduate of the U.S. Military Academy at West Point, is the son of the U.S. Army's first African American brigadier general, Benjamin O. Davis Sr.

1999. Ken Rudolph becomes the first African American on-air host for TVG, a popular wagering and horse-racing network.

1999. At the urging of the African American members of the House Agriculture Committee, the Republican chairman holds two full committee hearings to consider the plight of African American farmers, the first meetings on this issue in thirty years.

1999. Carolyn B. Lewis becomes the first African American to serve as chair of the American Hospital Association.

1999. Terry D. Bolton becomes the first African American chief of police of the Dallas Police Department and one of only a few African American police chiefs in the state of Texas.

1999. Major Shawna Kimbrell, an F16 pilot, becomes the first African American woman to complete fighter-pilot training in the U.S. Air Force. She received her pilot's wings in 1999 and flew her first combat sortie in 2001.

1999, January 20. During the impeachment hearing for President Bill Clinton, Cheryl Mills becomes the first African American to argue a case before the U.S. Senate.

1999, March. Rear Admiral Michelle J. Howard becomes the first African American woman to take command of a U.S. Navy ship, the USS *Rushmore.* In 2009, Howard leads the expeditionary strike group that frees the captain of the *Maersk Alabama* after Somali pirates take him hostage.

1999, March 15. Chess player Maurice Ashley, a Jamaican immigrant, becomes the first African American to earn grandmaster status in chess during a tournament sponsored by the Manhattan Chess Club.

1999, March 28. Purdue University coach Carolyn Peck leads the Lady Boilermakers to victory over Duke University, becoming the first African American woman coach to win a national championship in the history of women's college basketball.

2000. Florida governor Jeb Bush appoints three African American judges: Judge Marva L. Crenshaw of the Florida Thirteenth Judicial Circuit Court; Judge Sandra Edwards-Stephens of the Florida Fifth Judicial Circuit Court; and James E. C. Perry of the Florida Eighteenth Judicial Circuit Court. All are the first African Americans to serve on these circuit courts, and together they make up the most African American judges ever to be appointed in one state in a single year.

2000. James Perkins, a local businessman, defeats white incumbent Joseph Smitherman to become the first African American mayor of Selma, Alabama. Smitherman had been mayor in 1965, when civil rights marchers crossed the Edmund Pettus Bridge on what becomes known as Bloody Sunday. Perkins was reelected mayor in 2004.

2001. Colin Powell becomes the first African American secretary of state under President George W. Bush, marking the first time in U.S. history that an African American has held such a high governmental position. Bush calls Powell out of retirement to fill the post.

2001. Condoleezza Rice becomes the first woman of any race to serve as head of the National Security Council. She serves during the George W. Bush administration.

2001. Robert L. Johnson, founder and president of Black Entertainment Television (BET), is listed on the *Forbes* 400 as the first African American billionaire. Oprah Winfrey later becomes the first confirmed African American woman billionaire.

2001, January 24. Roderick Paige is sworn in as the first African American secretary of the U.S. Department of Education.

2001, April 23. Kenneth I. Chenault becomes the first African American head of a major financial company when he is elected chairman of the board and chief executive officer of American Express. He had served as the company's president since 1997 and as de facto CEO since January 1, 2001, when Harvey Golub stepped down.

2001, July 1. Ruth J. Simmons leaves the helm of Smith College to become the first African American and the first woman president of an Ivy League institution when she takes office as president of Brown University.

2001, July 2. Robert Tools becomes the first person to receive an implant of a self-contained heart, a breakthrough that leads to advances in transplant medicine.

2001, November 6. Shirley Clarke Franklin is elected mayor of Atlanta, becoming the first woman of any race to lead a major southern city. Franklin had served Atlanta for eight years as its top appointed official and had worked with Andrew Young and Maynard Jackson, both former mayors of Atlanta.

2001, November 13. Wilton D. Gregory becomes the first African American bishop to head the U.S. Conference of Catholic Bishops. Gregory had been elected vice president of the conference in 1998, which put him in line to become its next leader. The South Side Chicago native was ordained in 1973 and in 1983 became the first African American auxiliary bishop of the Archdiocese of Chicago.

2001, November 19. Thirty-seven-year-old Barry Bonds is named the National League's Most Valuable Player. He becomes the first baseball player to win the honor four times. Bonds won the award in 1990 and 1992 while playing for Pittsburgh. He was playing for the San Francisco Giants when he was honored in 1993.

2002. Venus Williams becomes the first African American tennis player to be ranked number one in the world. Her sister Serena Williams supplants her in July. They are the first sisters ever to be ranked first and second at the same time. After Serena wins the Wimbledon in 2010—her fourth as well as her second consecutive Wimbledon—she has a total of thirteen Grand Slam singles and is ranked alongside other women tennis greats.

2002. Suzan-Lori Parks becomes the first African American woman to win a Pulitzer Prize for Drama.

2002. The National Basketball Association awards an expansion franchise to Robert L. Johnson, founder of Black Entertainment Television. He becomes the first African American principal owner of a major professional sports team—a new franchise in Charlotte, North Carolina.

2002. The MG *Robert Smalls* is christened in Moss Point, Mississippi. The ship is the first U.S. Army vessel named for a Civil War hero and the first named for an African American. Born enslaved, Smalls became a deckhand and later pilot of a Confederate transport steamer known as the *Planter*.

2002, March 11. Vonetta Flowers becomes the first African American athlete to win a gold medal at a Winter Olympics when she wins the inaugural two-woman bobsled event. Garrett Hines and Randy Jones become the first African American men to win Winter Olympic medals, bringing home the silver as half of the U.S. four-man bobsled team.

2002, March 24. Halle Berry becomes the first African American woman to win an Academy Award for a leading role. The Oscar is awarded for her lead role in *Monster's Ball.*

2002, June. Brigadier General Sheila R. Baxter becomes the first woman general in the Army Medical Service. Earlier, she had served as assistant surgeon general for force sustainment for the U.S. Army.

2002, June 16. Tiger Woods wins the 102nd U.S. Open, becoming the first player since Jack Nicklaus in 1972 to win the first two majors of the year. Woods won the Masters on April 14. He is unsuccessful in the British Open, however, ending his quest for a true Grand Slam season.

2002, June 17. The Los Angeles Lakers beat the New Jersey Nets 113–107 to take the NBA championship. Laker Kobe Bryant becomes the first player to win three NBA championships by age twenty-three.

2003. Mississippi State University hires its first African American football coach, Sylvester Croom, who also becomes the first African American head football coach in the seventy-one-year history of the Southeastern Conference (SEC). Croom played one season in the NFL and then became graduate assistant for legendary coach Bear Bryant at the University of Alabama. Croom became assistant coach for the Tampa Bay Buccaneers in 1986 and subsequently served as assistant coach for five NFL teams.

2003. Ed Welburn becomes the first African American design chief for General Motors Corporation. A thirty-year GM veteran, he designs the Cadillac Escalade, the Hummer H2, and the Chevy SSR.

2003. William Burrus, president of the 380,000-member American Postal Workers union, becomes the first African American to head an AFL-CIO union.

2003. Media mogul Oprah Winfrey becomes the first African American woman and only the second black person (after BET founder Robert Johnson) on *Forbes*'s annual list of billionaires. Winfrey formed Oxygen Media LLC in 1998 and in 2002 launched *O: The Oprah Magazine.*

2003. Michael Copeland becomes the first African American inducted into the World Karate Union Hall of Fame. He also becomes the first person inducted under Kuden Jutsu, a new style of martial arts.

2003. Yvonne Scarlett-Golden is elected mayor of Daytona Beach, Florida, becoming the first African American to hold that position.

2003. Mike Hart, senior and tailback for Onondaga High School in New York City, scores more points (1,094) and more touchdowns (179) than any other player in high school football history. He plays for the University of Michigan Wolverines the following year, and is then drafted by the Indianapolis Colts.

2003. Kimberlydawn Wisdom becomes the state of Michigan's first surgeon general. She also served as an emergency medical physician at Henry Ford Health System in Detroit and as a medical educator at the University of Michigan Medical Center in Ann Arbor.

2003. For the first time in the fifty-year history of *Billboard*'s singles charts, all top-ten singles are by African American recording artists. Nine of them are rappers, demonstrating the popularity of hip-hop.

2003. Navy rear admiral Barry Black becomes the first African American and the first Seventh-day Adventist to be named U.S. Senate chaplain. Previously, he was chief of chaplains for the Navy and had been a leader in such high-profile events as the Pentagon 9/11 Memorial Service and the 1999 burial of John F. Kennedy Jr. at sea.

2003. Annetta W. Nunn becomes the first woman police chief of Birmingham, Alabama. She occupies the post that Bull Connor held during the cradle of the civil rights movement.

2003. Steve McNair of the Tennessee Titans becomes the first African American quarterback to win the Associated Press NFL Most Valuable Player Award. He shares the award with Payton Manning, the Indianapolis Colts quarterback.

2003, January. Jennette Bradley becomes the first African American woman to hold the position of lieutenant governor in Ohio.

2003, February 13. First Lieutenant Vernice Armour becomes the first African American female combat pilot in the U.S. Marine Corps.

2003, August 1. Adam W. Herbert becomes the first African American president of Indiana University in Bloomington. He had previously served as Regents Professor and executive director of the Florida Center for Public Policy and Leadership at the University of North Florida.

2004. Louisiana state representative Sharon Weston Broome, a Democrat from Baton Rouge, becomes the first woman to serve as House speaker pro tempore. She was elected to the state legislature in 1991 and became the first African American woman to represent East and West Baton Rouge parishes.

2004. Freelance writer Sheila Cherry becomes the first African American president of the National Press Club, the nation's best-known organization for journalists.

2004. Damon Evans becomes the first African American athletic director at the University of Georgia in Athens and in the Southeastern Conference (SEC). He played football for the university from 1988 to 1992.

2004. Kamala Harris becomes the first woman and first African American district attorney for San Francisco. With the appointment, she also becomes the first African American to hold the office statewide.

2004. Barry Bonds wins the National League MVP award for a record seventh time, and becomes the first player to win it four times in a row. In 2003, he became the third player to hit a career 700 home runs. Hank Aaron hit a record 765, and Babe Ruth 714.

2004. Harvard Law School professor Christopher Edley Jr. becomes the first African American to head a top-ranked U.S. law school when he is named dean of the Boalt Hall School of Law at the University of California, Berkeley.

2004. Earl Lewis becomes the first African American provost of Emory University in Atlanta and the highest-ranking African American administrator in the school's history. Previously, he had been dean of the Horace H. Rackham School of Graduate Studies and vice provost for academic studies/graduate affairs at the University of Michigan in Ann Arbor.

2004. Cortez Trotter, who headed Chicago's Office of Emergency Management and Communications, is appointed by Mayor Richard H. Daley as the city's first African American fire commissioner.

2004. Dennis Archer, former mayor of Detroit and justice on the Michigan Supreme Court, becomes the first African American president of the 125-year-old American Bar Association.

2004. Albany, Georgia, elects its first African American mayor, Willie Adams Jr., an obstetrician. Adams defeated the incumbent mayor by winning more than 60 percent of the vote in a city with a population that is two-thirds African American.

2004. Representative Percy Watson of Hattiesburg becomes the highest-ranking African American in the Mississippi State Legislature when he is appointed chair of the House Ways and Means Committee.

2004. Phillip West is sworn in as the first African American mayor of Natchez, Mississippi, since Reconstruction. The civil rights activist and former state representative wins by a narrow margin.

2004. Simmie Knox becomes the first African American artist to paint an official portrait of an American president when he completes a painting of President Bill Clinton. Knox also paints a portrait of Hillary Rodham Clinton. The paintings were commissioned in 2002 and unveiled in the White House two years later, where they hang along with those of other U.S. presidents. Other portraits by Knox include such luminaries as U.S. Supreme Court justices Thurgood Marshall and Ruth Bader Ginsburg, educator Mary McLeod Bethune, abolitionist Frederick Douglass, civil rights leader Martin Luther King Jr., and baseball legend Hank Aaron.

2004. Keeth Smart, the first U.S. fencer ranked No. 1 in the world, celebrates with the U.S. men's sabre team as they win the Grand Prix of Fencing World Cup sabre competition in New York City. This is his first gold-medal win in international competition.

2004. Phylicia Rashad becomes the first African American woman to win a Tony Award for best performance by a leading actress for her performance as Lena Younger in Lorraine Hansberry's *A Raisin in the Sun*.

Dennis Archer, Former Detroit Mayor and Michigan Supreme Court Justice, October 26, 2005. *Archer speaks at a news conference in Chattanooga, Tennessee, in support of an alliance between the medical and legal professions to create a pretrial assessment of expert witness testimony. In 2004, Archer became the first African American president of the 125-year-old American Bar Association.* AP PHOTO/MARK GILLILAND

2004. Pro Football Hall of Famer Art Shell becomes senior vice president for football operations with the NFL. In this post, he is responsible for supervising all of the league's regular season and postseason football operations and development.

2004. Wallace B. Jefferson becomes the first African American chief justice of the Texas Supreme Court. He had been the state Supreme Court's first African American member since 2001.

2004. Brigadier General Abraham Turner takes command of Fort Jackson, the U.S. Army's largest training base, in Columbia, South Carolina, becoming the first African American to hold that position.

2004. LeBron James, forward with the Cleveland Cavaliers, becomes the youngest NBA player to reach 2,000 career points. At nineteen years old and after only 272 days in the NBA, James was 277 days younger than Kobe Bryant was when he reached the 2,000-point mark on February 23, 1999, with the Los Angeles Lakers. After becoming a free agent in July 2010, James joins the Miami Heat.

2004. Democrat and Illinois state senator Barack Obama wins a landslide victory over Republican hopeful Alan Keyes to become the first African American man from Illinois elected to the U.S. Senate.

2004, January. Heather McTeer Hudson takes office as the first African American and first woman mayor of Greenville, Mississippi.

2004, September 14. Hip-hop performer Nelly becomes the first African American artist and rapper to release two separate CDs on the same day—*Sweat* and *Suit.* The three-time Grammy Award winner also hosts a hip-hop summit in his hometown, St. Louis.

2004, November 15. Legendary golfer Charlie Sifford becomes the first African American player elected to the World Golf Hall of Fame.

2005, January. Condoleezza Rice is appointed by President George W. Bush as U.S. secretary of state, becoming the first African American woman to hold that position.

2005. Navy Captain Bruce E. Grooms is appointed the eighty-first commandant of midshipmen at the U.S. Naval Academy in Annapolis, Maryland, becoming the first African American named to the number-two post at the academy. Grooms was also the first African American naval officer to command a submarine.

2005. John R. Batiste, a former deputy chief and a state trooper for twenty-six years, becomes the first African American chief of the Washington State Patrol.

2005. Pulitzer Prize–winning journalist Dean Baquet is appointed executive vice president and editor of the *Los Angeles Times*, making him the first African American named to the newspaper's top post. He had previously served in key positions at the *New York Times* and the *Chicago Tribune*.

2005. Iris Smith wins the World Wrestling Championship title in Budapest, becoming the first African American woman to hold that title.

2005. Ohio State University names Gene Smith athletic director, making him the first African American to hold that post. Smith had previously been athletic director at Arizona State University.

2005. Shonda Rhimes, who created the television series *Grey's Anatomy*, becomes the first African American woman to create and serve as executive producer of an hour-long series that remains on the air for more than one season.

2005. Jamie Foxx and Morgan Freeman win best-acting awards at the seventy-seventh annual Academy Awards and become the first African American men to be so honored in the same year. Foxx wins for his performance in *Ray*, a biographical film about Ray Charles, and Freeman wins for his supporting performance in *Million Dollar Baby*.

2005. Baltimore, Maryland, renames its airport the Baltimore/Washington International Thurgood Marshall Airport in honor of the Supreme Court justice and Baltimore native. This marks the first time that the airport has honored an African American. Marshall served on the nation's highest court from 1967 to 1991.

2005. Terry Bellamy becomes the first African American to win the mayoral race in Asheville, North Carolina.

2005. After winning his third Super Bowl title as New England's defensive coordinator, Romeo Crennel is named head coach of the Cleveland Browns, becoming the first African American to head the team.

2005. Laila Ali, daughter of boxing great Muhammad Ali, becomes the first African American woman to win a World Boxing Council title after she beats Erin Toughill at the MCI Center in Washington, D.C.

2005, July. Belle S. Wheelan is named president of the Commission on Colleges of the Southern Association of Colleges and Schools (SACS), becoming the first African American, the first woman, and the first community college president to hold this position.

2005, December. President George W. Bush signs a bill authorizing that a statue of civil rights leader Rosa Parks be placed in the U.S. Capitol's Statuary Hall. Parks is the first African American woman to be honored with a statue in the Capitol.

2005, December 11. Norries Wilson becomes the first African American coach at an Ivy League school when he is named head football coach at Columbia University.

2006, December 30. Gerald Washington, the first African American elected mayor in the history of Westlake, Louisiana, is shot to death before his swearing-in date, scheduled for January 2, 2007.

2006. NASA astronaut and mission specialist Robert L. Curbeam Jr. sets a new record for the most spacewalks completed during a shuttle mission by a single crew member. His exit from the Quest Airlock of the space shuttle *Discovery* at the International Space Station lasts six hours and thirty-eight minutes.

2006. Shani Davis wins the 1,000-meter speed-skating race in Turin, Italy, becoming the first African American to claim an individual gold medal in Winter Olympics history. In 2002, he became the first African American member of a U.S. Olympics speed-skating team. In 2005, he became the first African American speed skater to win the World Allround Speed-skating Championship.

2006. Jill Dunson is inaugurated as mayor of Portland, Maine, making her the city's first African American mayor.

2006. Sheila Johnson becomes the first African American woman to own a WNBA team when Lincoln Holdings LLC purchases the Washington Mystics.

2006. James Spencer is appointed chief judge of the U.S. District Court for the Eastern District of Virginia, becoming the first African American judge to hold the post in that district.

2006. North Carolina judge Patricia Timmons-Goodson is sworn into office on February 6, becoming the first African American to serve on the North Carolina Supreme Court. Previously, she had served on that state's Court of Appeals.

2006. Aetna, one of the largest health insurers in the United States, names Ronald A. Williams as its chief executive officer, making him the first African American to hold that position.

2006. Major General Lloyd J. Austin III becomes the first African American commanding general of the Eighteenth Airborne Corps at Fort Bragg in North Carolina. The Eighteenth Airborne Corps embraces the Eighty-second Airborne Division, the 101st Airborne Division, the Tenth Mountain Division, and the Third Infantry Division.

2006. Clifford W. Houston becomes the first black president-elect of the American Society for Microbiology in Washington, D.C.

2006. William E. McAnulty Jr., who had served on the Kentucky Court of Appeals, is appointed to the Kentucky Supreme Court, becoming the first African American to serve on that state's highest court.

2006. Jerome Holmes is confirmed as the first African American on the U.S. Court of Appeals for the Tenth Circuit based in Denver, becoming the first African American judge to serve on that court.

2006. Warren Moon becomes the first African American quarterback inducted into the Pro Football Hall of Fame. During seventeen seasons with the NFL, he passes for over 49,000 yards, throws 291 touchdowns, and plays in nine Pro Bowls.

2006. Cecelia "CiCi" Holloway, senior vice president for diversity, training, and development for Viacom Entertainment Group, becomes the first African American president of Women in Film.

2006. Israel L. Gaither becomes the first African American commander of the Salvation Army in the United States. He leads over sixty-thousand employees and 3.5 million volunteers who provide social services for the needy.

2006. Kimberly D. Walker becomes the first woman master gunnery sergeant to serve in the U.S. Marine Corps as a combat service support chief.

2006. Violet Palmer becomes the first African American woman to referee National Basketball Association playoff game. She officiates game two of the first-round series between the New Jersey Nets and the Indiana Pacers.

2006. Bessie L. Reggans becomes the first African American woman mastery gunnery sergeant to serve in the U.S. Marine Corps as a motor transport maintenance chief.

2006. The first African American sheriff in Newport News, Virginia, Gabriel A. Morgan Sr., is sworn into office.

2006. Candace Parker, freshman forward for the University of Tennessee, becomes the first woman basketball player to perform a dunk shot in an NCAA tournament game and the first to do it twice in any game.

2006. Larry R. Felix becomes the first African American director of the U.S. Bureau of Engraving and Printing, where he is responsible for the production of U.S. currency, government securities, and other documents.

2006. Memphis rap group Three 6 Mafia becomes the first hip-hop group to win an Academy Award when their song "It's Hard Out Here for a Pimp" is chosen as the best original song written for a motion picture.

2006. Reginald I. Lloyd becomes the first African American since Reconstruction to serve as U.S. attorney in South Carolina.

2006. Erroll B. Davis Jr. becomes the first African American chancellor of the University System of Georgia. As chancellor, he is responsible for the state's thirty-five public colleges and universities and the Georgia Public Library Service.

2006. Randal Pinkett becomes the first African American winner of Donald Trump's reality show *The Apprentice*. Pinkett is president and CEO of BCT Partners, a management, technology, and policy consulting firm in Newark, New Jersey.

2006. Minnesota state lawmaker and lawyer Keith Ellison becomes the first Muslim and the first nonwhite elected to the U.S. Congress from Minnesota. Ellison campaigns as a "peace first" candidate, calling for an end to the Iraq War and terrorism. When he takes the oath of office, he does so with his hand on the Koran.

2006, January 3. Carl Anthony Redus Jr. is sworn into office, becoming the first African American mayor of Pine Bluff, Arkansas.

2006, May 1. Georgetown University law professor Patricia A. King becomes the first African American woman member of the Harvard Corporation, Harvard University's governing board.

2006, July 16. Twenty-three-year-old J. R. Todd defeats legendary drag racer Tony Schumacher at the Bandimere Speedway in Morrison, Colorado, to become the first African American to win a National Hot Rod Association (NHRA) Top Fuel event. It is Todd's first appearance in a final and only the ninth professional event of his rookie season.

2007. Lorraine C. Miller becomes the first African American to serve as an official of the U.S. House of Representatives when she is named senior adviser to House Speaker Nancy Pelosi.

2007. Washington State University names Elson Floyd its tenth president, making her the first African American to hold that leadership post.

2007. Lucille Clifton becomes the first African American woman to win the $100,000 Ruth Lilly Poetry Prize honoring lifetime achievement by a U.S. poet.

2007. Seventy-five-year-old cancer survivor Barbara Hillary completes her trek to the North Pole and is believed to be the first African American woman to accomplish the feat.

2007. Naval officer Michelle Howard becomes the first African American woman to reach the rank of rear admiral.

2007. Hampton University chaplain Timothy Tee Boddie is elected president of the National Association of College and University chaplains, becoming the first African American to lead the organization in its fifty-nine-year history.

2007. Carl Brewer becomes the first elected African American mayor of Wichita, Kansas, after he wins 52 percent of the vote, defeating the incumbent mayor.

2007. Alvin V. Thomas Jr., professor of internal and pulmonary medicine at Howard University, becomes the first African American president of the American College of Chest Physicians at the organization's annual assembly in Chicago.

2007. Ivan T. Mosley Sr., a professor in the department of manufacturing systems at North Carolina A&T State University, is the first African American man to be elected vice chair of the executive board of the National Association of Industrial Technology, the premiere professional association for the promotion of industrial technology in business, industry, education, and government.

2007. Guinness World Records recognizes George Bell, a sheriff's deputy in Norfolk, Virginia, who is 7 feet, 8 inches tall, as the tallest man in the United States and the third tallest man in the world after record holders in Ukraine (8 feet, 5 inches) and China (7 feet, 8.95 inches).

2007. Patricia Hill Collins is elected the first African American woman president of the American Sociological Association.

2007. Gail P. Hardy becomes the first African American state's attorney in Connecticut's history.

2007. On winning her fourth Wimbledon title two years after winning her last Grand Slam title, Venus Williams becomes the first woman to receive the same prize money as the men's Wimbledon champion.

2007. After he lands at Opa-locka Executive Airport outside Miami, Barrington Irving sets two records in his single-engine piston plane *Inspiration*: the first African American and the youngest person to fly solo around the globe, a ninety-seven-day, 27,000-mile journey.

2007. Gregory M. Sleet becomes the first African American chief judge in Delaware. Sleet later heads the U.S. District Court in Wilmington.

2007. Traci Green becomes the first African American woman to head a sports team at Harvard University when she is named head coach of the women's tennis team.

2007, January 4. Deval Patrick is sworn into office as governor of Massachusetts, becoming the first African American head of that state and only the second African American elected governor in the United States. Patrick takes the oath of office with his hand on a Bible that enslaved Africans had given to John Quincy Adams after he helped to free them in what was known as the Amistad affair. Once a civil rights lawyer for the poor, Patrick led the Justice Department's civil rights division under President Bill Clinton.

2007, February. The first-ever video game featuring black college football is released, showcasing more than forty teams, bands and mascots, interactive half-time events, stadiums, and ten authentic black football classics. The game was created by Nerjyzed Entertainment, a digital entertainment company founded and run by Jacqueline Beauchamp, an alumna of Southern University at Baton Rouge.

2007, February 4. Anthony Kevin "Tony" Dungy of the Indianapolis Colts becomes the first African American head coach to win a Super Bowl when the Colts defeat the Chicago Bears in Super Bowl XLI. Dungy and Bears head coach Lovie Smith become the first two African American coaches to lead their teams to a Super Bowl.

2007, March. Rap pioneers Grandmaster Flash and the Furious Five become the first hip-hop artists inducted into the Rock and Roll Hall of Fame.

2008. Eight-year-old Naomi Mitchell of Norfolk, Virginia, becomes the youngest African American to win the U.S. Kids Golf World Championship, the largest golf tournament for four to twelve year olds. Cheyenne Woods (niece of Tiger Woods) and Austin DeGrate are the other two black winners.

2008. Retired NBA All-Star Kevin Johnson becomes the first African American elected mayor of Sacramento, California.

2008. LaShunda Rundles becomes the first African American woman to win the World Champion of Public Speaking competition after she delivers an address titled "Speak" at the Toastmasters International Speech Contest.

2008. Eugene T. Sutton is elected the fourteenth bishop of the Episcopal Diocese of Maryland, the first African American to hold that post. He is elected on the first ballot at a special diocesan convention and will lead 116 parishes and 50,000 members in Baltimore and surrounding counties.

2008. For the first time in NBA history, the top three draft (lottery) picks are black college freshmen: Derrick Rose, drafted by the Chicago Bulls; Michael Beasley, who joined the Miami Heat, and O.J. Mayo, drafted by the Minnesota Timberwolves.

2008. Byron V. Garrett takes the reins as the first African American and first male chief executive officer of the National Parent Teachers Association (PTA), the nation's largest volunteer child-advocacy organization.

2008. Cleveland native Phil Davis invents and patents the world's smallest personal-sized, portable microwave, the twelve-pound iWave Cube. Manufactured in China, it is FDA approved, super energy efficient, and quiet.

2008. Allyson Solomon becomes the first African American brigadier general and assistant adjunct general in the Maryland Air National Guard.

2008. Comedian Chris Rock performs a stand-up act to 15,900 fans at London's 02 arena, setting a record for the largest comedy audience in British history and breaking the previous record of 10,108 held by British comedian Lee Evans.

2008. Marshall Purnell, architect of record for the Martin Luther King Jr. National Memorial, is elected the first African American president of the American Institute of Architects (AIA). Based in Washington, D.C., the AIA represents more than eighty thousand licensed architects, emerging professionals, and affiliated partners.

2008. Jessica White becomes the only African American model ever featured in *Sports Illustrated*'s popular swimsuit issue for five consecutive years.

2008. Orthopaedic surgeon E. Anthony Rankin becomes the first African American president of the American Academy of Orthopaedic Surgeons at its seventy-fifth annual meeting in San Francisco.

2008. David A. Paterson, previously the first African American lieutenant governor of New York, is sworn in as the first African American governor of New York after Governor Eliot Spitzer resigns.

2008. Assemblywoman Karen Bass becomes the first African American woman elected speaker of the California State Assembly—the second most powerful post in state government behind the governor. Bass is also the first Democratic woman to hold the post in the state's history.

2008. Evelyn Hammonds becomes the first African American and the first woman dean of Harvard College, the undergraduate division of Harvard University.

2008, June. Jockey Sylvia Harris becomes the second African American woman to win a thoroughbred horse race in the United States and the first to win in Chicago horse-racing history.

2008, October 4. Tyler Perry, actor, playwright, and television and movie producer, opens Tyler Perry Studios in Atlanta, Georgia, becoming the first African American to own a major television and film studio.

2008, November. Democrat Donna Edwards becomes the first African American woman elected to represent Maryland in the U.S. Congress.

2008, November 4. After becoming the first African American U.S. presidential nominee for the Democratic Party, Barack Obama is elected president of the United States. Using the slogan "Yes, We Can," Obama changed the way campaigns are conducted and raised a record-breaking $745 million, much of it online, by tapping the potential of twenty-four-hour cable-television programming, online news outlets, blogs, YouTube, Facebook, and other nontraditional media. His win over Republican senator John McCain comes with 365 electoral votes.

2009. The Disney animated film *The Princess and the Frog* features Disney's first major African American female lead, Princess Tiana (voiced by actress Anika Noni Rose), and Disney's most extensive black cast. It is the studio's first hand-drawn, 2-D animated feature since 2004.

2009. During its meeting in Honolulu, the American Dental Association elects its first African American president, Raymond F. Fist, who practices general dentistry in Flint, Michigan. He assumes the presidency of the nation's largest dental association in October 2010.

2009. Command Sergeant Major Teresa King becomes the first woman to head the U.S. Army's Drill Sergeant School at Fort Jackson, South Carolina, the army's largest training installation.

2009. The Reverend Bernice King becomes the first woman to lead the Southern Christian Leadership Conference (SCLC) and the third in her family to serve as SCLC president. The group's first president was her father, Martin Luther King Jr., who held the post from 1957 until he was assassinated in 1968.

2009. For the first time in the U.S. Coast Guard's 133-year history, an African American woman leads the cadets when Jacqueline Fitch becomes regimental commander, the academy's highest-ranking cadet. As regimental commander, she serves as liaison between the commandant of the cadets and the cadet corps.

2009. Michael Steele, former lieutenant governor of Maryland and the state's first African American to serve in a statewide office, becomes the first African American elected to chair the Republican National Committee.

2009, January 20. Barack Obama is inaugurated as the forty-fourth U.S. president. He is the first African American ever to hold the nation's highest office.

2009, February. Following his confirmation, Eric Holder becomes the first African American U.S. attorney general, the country's chief law enforcer.

Barack Obama, President of the United States, January 2009. *The historic election of the forty-fourth (and first African American) president of the United States led to much media coverage and many honors for Obama.* PRNEWSFOTO/EBONY MAGAZINE/NEWSCOM

2009, **February** 1. Head Coach Mike Tomlin of the Pittsburgh Steelers becomes the youngest coach and the second African American to win a Super Bowl when the Steelers win the forty-third Super Bowl at Raymond James Stadium in Tampa, Florida.

2009, **June** 6. Alysa Stanton becomes the first African American woman rabbi and one of only 994 women ordained by the end of 2009. Stanton leads the predominantly white Congregation Bayt Shalom in Greenville, North Carolina, a synagogue affiliated with both the Reform and Conservative movements.

2009, **July**. Autumn Adkins becomes the first African American and the first woman to head Girard College, a boarding school in Philadelphia founded in the nineteenth century to educate poor, white, orphaned boys.

2009, **July**. Xerox corporation promotes Ursula Burns to chief executive, making the firm the largest U.S. company to be headed by an African American woman.

2009, **July** 15. Major General Charles Bolden becomes the first African American to head the National Aeronautics and Space Administration (NASA) after he is appointed by President Barack Obama and unanimously confirmed. Between 1986 and 1994, Bolden led two missions to space and orbited Earth four times. He was also a member of the first joint U.S.-Russian shuttle mission.

2009, **August**. Mignon L. Clyburn becomes the first African American woman commissioner of the Federal Communications Commission, the agency that regulates interstate and international communications made by radio, television, wire, satellite, and cable.

2009, **October**. Richard R. Buery Jr. becomes the first African American chief of the Children's Aid Society, a private charitable group that provides services to more than 150,000 children and their families in New York City.

2009, **November** 11. Country singer Darius Rucker, former front man with the group Hootie & the Blowfish, becomes the first African American performer to win the New Artist of the Year Award during the Country Music Association Awards ceremony in Nashville. His 2008 album, *Learn to Live*, sold more than one million copies.

2010 Katie Washington is the University of Notre Dame's first African American valedictorian. The twenty-one-year-old biology major is from Gary, Indiana.

2010, **February** 17. Chicago native Shani Davis wins his second straight Olympic title in 1,000-meter men's speed skating in Vancouver and becomes the first skater of any race to accomplish this feat twice at the Winter Games.

2010, **June**. The U.S. Senate unanimously confirms Tanya Walton Pratt as a federal judge for the Southern District of Indiana, making her the first African American federal judge in the state's history. In January, President Barack Obama nominated Pratt, who since 1997 has served as Marion Superior Court judge.

3

SIGNIFICANT DOCUMENTS IN AFRICAN AMERICAN HISTORY

Lean'tin L. Bracks

The text of proclamations and orders, legislative enactments, speeches, letters, and even poems and songs representing the course of American history display the presence of African Americans in the yesterday of this country and provide a picture of the changing place they have held in the national consciousness. The documents collected here separately capture for a moment in time the African American's role in American society. However, together these documents bear witness to the African American experience.

THE GERMANTOWN MENNONITE RESOLUTION AGAINST SLAVERY (1688)

The Mennonites, a group of Protestant Christians who settled mainly in Pennsylvania and the Northwest Territory, rejected the use of violence, refused to bear arms or take oaths, and advocated the separation of church and state and the separation of their community from society. The Germantown Mennonite resolution against slavery represents one of the earliest protests against slavery in colonial America. It was passed sixty-nine years after the introduction of the first African slaves in America, at a time when the number of slaves in the colonies was comparatively small. It was not until 1775, however, that the Quakers, a religious group similarly opposed to the institution, formed the first antislavery society in the colonies.

This is to the monthly meeting held at Richard Worrell's:

These are the reasons why we are against the traffic of men-body, as followeth: Is there any that would be done or handled at this manner? viz., to be sold or made a slave for all the time of his life? How fearful and faint-hearted are many at sea, when they see a strange vessel, being afraid it should be a Turk, and they should be taken, and sold for slaves into Turkey. Now, what is *this* better done, than Turks do? Yea, rather it is worse for them, which say they are Christians; for we hear that the most part of such negers are brought hither against their will and consent, and that many of them are stolen. Now, though they are black, we cannot conceive there is more liberty to have them slaves, as it is to have other white ones. There is a saying, that we should do to all men like as we will be done ourselves; making no difference of what generation, descent, or colour they are. And those who steal or rob men, and those who buy or purchase them, are they not all alike? Here is liberty of conscience, which is right and reasonable; here ought to be likewise liberty of the body, except of evil-doers, which is another case. But to bring men hither, or to rob and sell them against their will, we stand against. In Europe there are many oppressed for conscience-sake; and here there are those oppressed which are of a black colour. And we who know that men must not commit adultery—some do commit adultery *in* others, separating wives from their husbands, and giving them to others: and some sell the children of these poor creatures to other men. Ah! do consider well this thing, you who do it, if you would be done at this manner—and if it is done according to Christianity! You surpass Holland and Germany in this thing. This makes an ill report in all those countries of Europe, where they hear of [it], that the Quakers do here handel men as they handel there the cattle. And for that reason some have no mind or inclination to come hither. And who shall maintain this your cause, or plead for it? Truly, we cannot do so, except you shall inform us better hereof, viz.: that Christians have liberty to practice these things. Pray, what thing in the world can be done worse towards us, than if men should rob or steal us away, and sell us for slaves to strange countries; separating husbands from their wives and children. Being now this is not done in the manner we would be done at; therefore, we contradict, and are against this traffic of men-body. And we who profess that it is not lawful to steal, must, likewise, avoid to purchase such things as are stolen, but rather help to stop this robbing and stealing, if possible. And such men ought to be delivered out of the hands of the robbers, and set free as in Europe. Then is Pennsylvania to have a good report, instead, it hath now a bad one, for this sake, in other countries; especially whereas the Europeans are desirous to know in what manner *the Quaker* do rule in *their* province; and most of them do look upon us with an envious eye. But if this is done well, what shall we say is done evil?

If once these slaves (which they say are so wicked and stubborn men) should join themselves—fight for their freedom, and handel their masters and mistresses, as they did handel them before; will these masters and mistresses take the sword at hand and war against these poor slaves, like, as we are able to believe, some will not refuse to do? Or, have these poor negers not as much right to fight for their freedom, as you have to keep them slaves?

Now consider well this thing, if it is good or bad. And in case you find it to be good to handel these black in that manner, we desired and require you hereby lovingly, that you may inform us herein, which at this time never was done, viz., that Christians have such a liberty to do so. To the end we shall be satisfied on this point, and satisfy likewise our good friends and acquaintances in our native country, to whom it is a terror, or fearful thing, that men should be handled so in Pennsylvania.

This is from our meeting at Germantown, held ye 18th of the 2nd month, 1688, to be delivered to the monthly meeting at Richard Worrell's.

Garret Henderich,

Derick op de Graeff,

Francis Daniel Pastorius,

Abram op de Graeff.

THE DECLARATION OF INDEPENDENCE (1776)

A concept of particular interest to eighteenth-century men and women was the theory of natural rights, the idea that all individuals possess certain fundamental rights that no government can deny. Using this argument as a justification for revolt, the American colonists, on July 4, 1776, formally announced their intention to separate from Great Britain in a Declaration of Independence.

The responsibility of writing this document was given to Thomas Jefferson. In his original draft, Jefferson included among the colonists' grievances the denial of the "most sacred rights of life and liberty" to African slaves. However, the draft was revised, and the final version of the declaration was accepted by Congress without Jefferson's indictment against slavery.

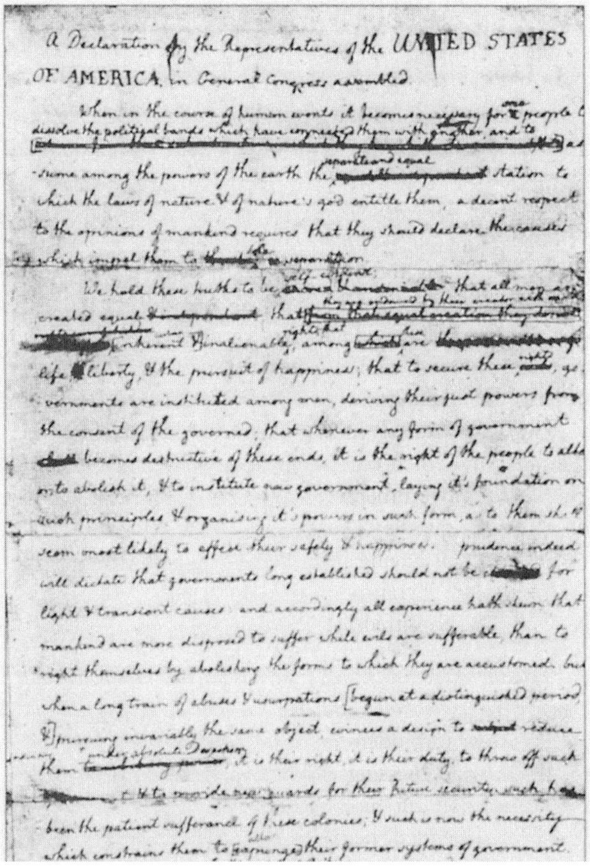
A Declaration by the Representatives of the UNITED STATES OF AMERICA, in General Congress assembled.

Rough Draft, Declaration of Independence, 1776. *In his original draft, Thomas Jefferson included among the colonists' grievances the denial of the "most sacred rights of life and liberty" to enslaved Africans. After the draft was revised, however, the final version of the declaration accepted by the Second Continental Congress excluded Jefferson's indictment against enslavement.* **THE LIBRARY OF CONGRESS**

In Congress, July 4, 1776. The unanimous Declaration of the thirteen United States of America,

When in the Course of human events, it becomes necessary for one people to dissolve the political bands which have connected them with another, and to assume among the Powers of the earth, the separate and equal station to which the Laws of Nature and of Nature's God entitle them, a decent respect to the opinions of mankind requires that they should declare the causes which impel them to the separation.

We hold these truths to be self-evident, that all men are created equal, that they are endowed by their Creator with certain unalienable Rights, that among these are Life, Liberty and the pursuit of Happiness. That to secure these rights, Governments are instituted among Men, deriving their just powers from the consent of the governed, That whenever any Form of Government becomes destructive of these ends, it is the Right of the People to alter or to abolish it, and to institute new Government, laying its foundation on such principles and organizing its powers in such form, as to them shall seem most likely to effect their Safety and Happiness. Prudence, indeed, will dictate that Governments long established should not be changed for light and transient causes; and accordingly all experience hath shown, that mankind are more disposed to suffer, while evils are sufferable, than to right themselves by abolishing the forms to which they are accustomed. But when a long train of abuses and usurpations, pursuing invariably the same Object evinces a design to reduce them under absolute Despotism, it is their right, it is their duty, to throw off such Government, and to provide new Guards for their future security.—Such has been the patient sufferance of these Colonies; and such is now the necessity which constrains them to alter their former Systems of Government. The history of the present King of Great Britain is a history of repeated injuries and usurpations, all having in direct object the establishment of an absolute Tyranny over these States. To prove this, let Facts be submitted to a candid world.

He has refused his Assent to Laws, the most wholesome and necessary for the public good.

He has forbidden his Governors to pass Laws of immediate and pressing importance, unless suspended in their operation till his Assent should be obtained; and when so suspended, he has utterly neglected to attend to them.

He has refused to pass other Laws for the accommodation of people, unless those people would relinquish the right of Representation in the Legislature, a right inestimable to them and formidable to tyrants only.

He has called together Legislative bodies at places unusual, uncomfortable, and distant from the depository of their Public Records, for the sole purpose of Fatiguing them into compliance with his measures.

He has dissolved Representative Houses repeatedly, for opposing with manly firmness his invasions on the rights of the people.

He has refused for a long time, after such dissolutions, to cause others to be elected; whereby the Legislative Powers, incapable of Annihilation, have returned to the People at large for their exercise; the state remaining in the meantime exposed to all the dangers of invasion from without, and convulsions within.

He has endeavoured to prevent the Population of these States; for that purpose obstructing the Laws of Naturalization of Foreigners; refusing to pass others to encourage their migration hither, and raising the conditions of new Appropriations of Lands.

He has obstructed the Administration of Justice, by refusing his Assent to Laws for establishing Judiciary Powers.

He has made Judges dependent on his Will alone, for the tenure of their offices, and the amount and payment of their salaries.

He has erected a multitude of New Offices, and sent hither swarms of Officers to harass our People, and eat out their substance.

He has kept among us, in times of peace, Standing Armies without the Consent of our legislature.

He has affected to render the Military independent of and superior to the Civil Power.

He has combined with others to subject us to a jurisdiction foreign to our constitution, and unacknowledged by our laws; giving his Assent to their acts of pretended legislation:

For quartering large bodies of armed troops among us:

For protecting them, by a mock Trial, from Punishment for any Murders which they should commit on the Inhabitants of these States:

For cutting off our Trade with all parts of the world:

For imposing taxes on us without our Consent:

For depriving us in many cases, of the benefits of Trial by Jury:

For transporting us beyond Seas to be tried for pretended offenses:

For abolishing the free System of English Laws in a neighboring Province, establishing therein in an Arbitrary government, and enlarging its Boundaries so as to render it at once an example and fit instrument for introducing the same absolute rule into these Colonies:

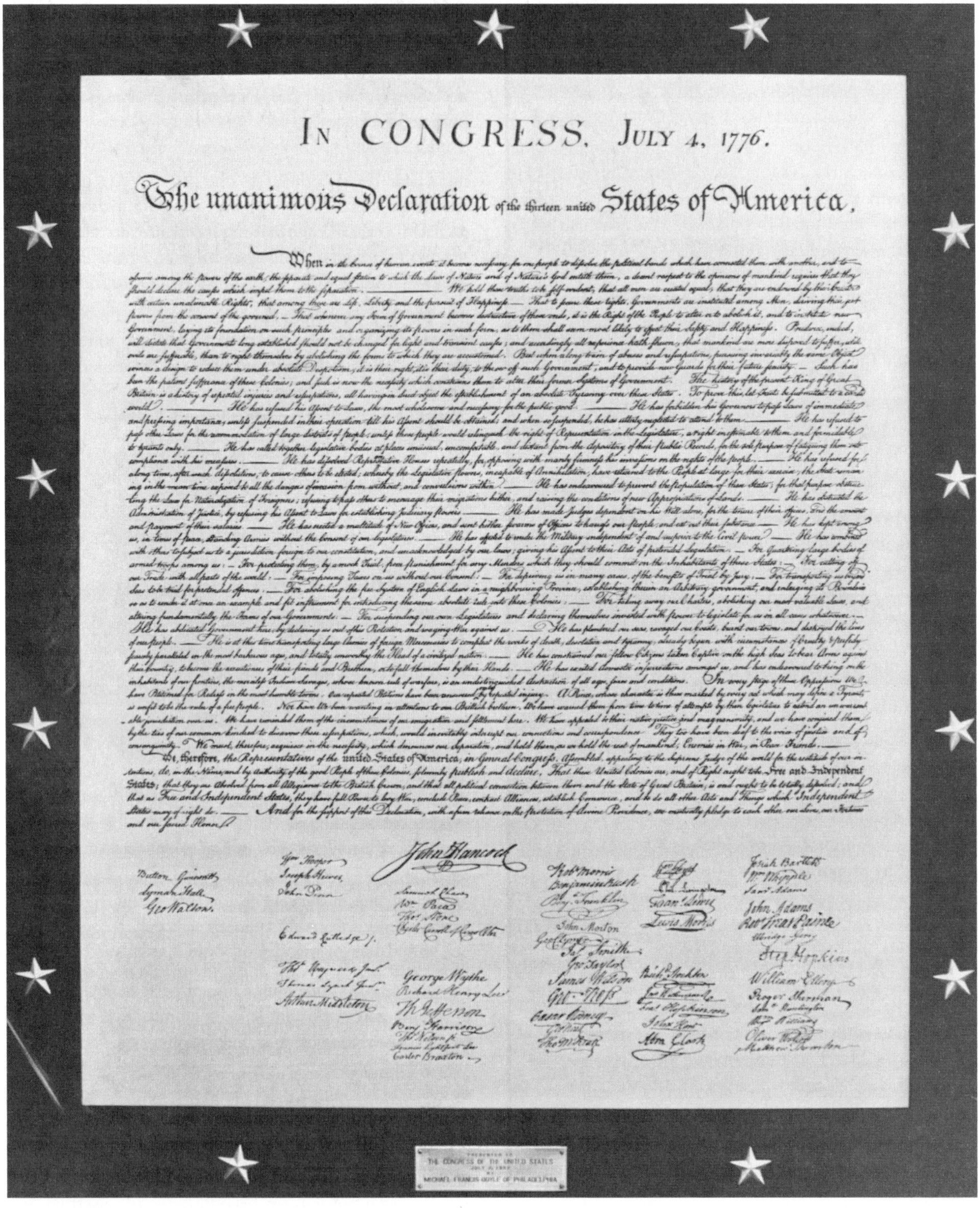

Declaration of Independence, Facsimile. *The document was signed on July 4, 1776—without Thomas Jefferson's indictment against slavery, which he had included in his original draft.* CORBIS

For taking away our Charters, abolishing our most valuable Laws, and altering fundamentally the Forms of our Governments:

For suspending our own Legislature, and declaring themselves invested with Power to legislate for us in all cases whatsoever.

He has abdicated Government here, by declaring us out of his Protection and waging War against us.

He has plundered our seas, ravaged our Coasts, burnt our towns, and destroyed the lives of our people.

He is at this time transporting large armies of foreign mercenaries to complete the works of death, desolation and tyranny, already begun with circumstances of Cruelty and perfidy scarcely paralleled in the most barbarous ages, and totally unworthy of the Head of a civilized nation.

He has constrained our fellow Citizens taken Captive on the high Seas to bear Arms against their Country, to become the executioners of their friends and Brethren, or to fall themselves by their Hands.

He has excited domestic insurrections amongst us, and has endeavoured to bring on the inhabitants of our frontiers, the merciless Indian Savages, whose known rule of warfare, is an undistinguished destruction of all ages, sexes and conditions.

In every stage of these Oppressions We have Petitioned for Redress in the most humble terms: Our repeated Petitions have been answered only by repeated injury. A Prince, whose character is thus marked by every act which may define a Tyrant, is unfit to be the ruler of a free People.

Nor We have been wanting in attention to our British brethren. We have warned them from time to time of attempts by their legislature to extend an unwarrantable jurisdiction over us. We have reminded them of the circumstances of our emigration and settlement here. We have appealed to their native justice and magnanimity, and we have conjured them by the ties of our common kindred to disavow these usurpations, which would inevitably interrupt our connections and correspondence. They too have been deaf to the voice of justice and of consanguinity. We must, therefore, acquiesce in the necessity, which denounces our Separation, and hold them, as we hold the rest of mankind, Enemies in War, in Peace, Friends.

We, therefore, the Representatives of the United States of America, in General Congress, Assembled, appealing to the Supreme Judge of the world for the rectitude of our intentions, do, in the Name, and by Authority of the good People of these Colonies, solemnly publish and declare, That these United Colonies are, and of Right ought to be Free and Independent States; that they are Absolved from all Allegiance to the British Crown, and that all political connection between them and the State of Great Britain, is and ought to be totally dissolved; and that as Free and Independent States, they have full Power to levy War, conclude Peace, contract Alliances, establish Commerce, and to do all other Acts and Things which Independent States may of right do. And for the support of this Declaration, with a firm reliance on the Protection of Divine Providence, we mutually pledge to each other our Lives, our Fortunes and our sacred Honor.

THE OMITTED ANTISLAVERY CLAUSE TO THE DECLARATION OF INDEPENDENCE (1776)

Thomas Jefferson's attitudes regarding enslaved Africans wavered during the course of his life. In his early years, Jefferson thought Africans to be biologically inferior. Later, spurred by his conviction that natural rights should be accrued to all men, he decided that slavery had a destructive conditioning effect that stamped Africans with "odious peculiarities."

When Jefferson was assigned the task of drafting a declaration calling for separation from Great Britain, he included a short, passionate attack on King George III's indulgence of the slave traffic. However, at the request of delegates from South Carolina and Georgia and of northern delegates whose ports sheltered and profited from slave ships, the clause was omitted from the final version. Many historians and critics have since argued that the elimination of this passage offers adequate proof that Africans in America were never meant to share in the fruits of independence and equality in their adopted homeland.

He [King George III] has waged cruel war against human nature itself, violating its most sacred rights of life and liberty in the persons of a distant people who never offended him, captivating and carrying them into slavery in another hemisphere, or to incur miserable death in their transportation thither. This piratical warfare, the opprobrium of *infidel* powers, is the warfare of the *Christian* king of Great Britain. Determined to keep open a market where MEN should be bought and sold, he has prostituted his negative for suppressing every legislative attempt to prohibit or restrain this execrable commerce.

THE CONSTITUTION OF THE UNITED STATES, ART.1, SECTIONS 2 AND 9, ART. 4, SECTION 2 (1787)

Drawn up in 1787 and ratified a year later, the Constitution of the United States outlines the fundamental principles upon which the American republic is built. In a historical context, the Constitution and its amendments are a manifestation of the issues that have faced Americans and their attempts at resolving these issues.

Among the concepts important to Americans living during the eighteenth century were the ideas that all people are created equal and are endowed with certain unalienable rights, and that a government derives its power from the consent of those it governs. However, despite the fact that almost 20 percent of the population was bound in slavery, the economic and social arguments of the time regarding the status of African slaves overrode the tenets of natural rights. In 1857, Chief Justice Roger Brook Taney, delivering the Court's opinion in the case Dred Scott v. Sandford, *summarized the attitude of the writers of the Constitution toward African slaves.*

> They are not included, and were not intended to be included, under the word "citizens" in the constitution, and can therefore claim none of the rights and privileges which that instrument provides and secures. ... On the contrary, they were at that time considered as a subordinate and inferior class of beings.

Specifically, Article I, Sections 2 and 9, and Article IV, Section 2, of the Constitution deal directly with the status of Africans in America.

PREAMBLE

We the People of the United States, in order to form a more perfect Union, establish Justice, insure domestic Tranquility, provide for the common defense, promote the general Welfare, and secure the Blessings of Liberty to ourselves and our Posterity, do ordain and establish this Constitution for the United States of America.

ARTICLE I

Section 2. ... Representatives and direct Taxes shall be apportioned among the several States which may be included within this Union, according to their respective Numbers, which shall be determined by adding to the whole Number of free Persons, including those bound to Service for a Term of Years, and excluding Indians not taxed, three-fifths of all other Persons. The actual Enumeration shall be made within three Years after the first Meeting of the Congress of the United States, and within every subsequent Term of Ten Years, in such manner as they shall by Law direct. ...

Section 9. The Migration or Importation of such Persons as any of the States now existing shall think proper to admit, shall not be prohibited by the Congress prior to the Year one thousand eight hundred and eight, but a Tax or duty may be imposed on such Importation, not exceeding ten dollars for each Person. ...

ARTICLE IV

Section 2. The Citizens of each State shall be entitled to all privileges and Immunities of Citizens in the several States.

A Person charged in any State with Treason, Felony, or other Crime, who shall flee from Justice, and be found in another State, shall on Demand of the executive authority of the State from which he fled, be delivered up, to be removed to the State having Jurisdiction of the Crime.

No Person held to Service or Labour in one State, under the Laws thereof, escaping into another, shall, in Consequence of any Law or Regulation therein, be discharged from such Service or Labour, but shall be delivered up on Claim of the Party to whom such Service or Labour may be due.

THE BILL OF RIGHTS (1791)

Ratified in 1791, the first ten amendments to the Constitution of the United States, commonly referred to as the Bill of Rights, further outline the fundamental rights and freedoms of citizens of the United States. This set of additions to the Constitution was a crucial part of the constitutional ratification process (several states had only ratified the Constitution on the condition that a bill of rights would be added), since eighteenth-century Americans held dearly to the concept of personal freedom. Despite these beliefs, it was not until after ratification of the Fourteenth Amendment to the Constitution and several civil rights laws that the freedoms protected in the Bill of Rights were extended to all U.S. citizens.

AMENDMENT 1

Congress shall make no law respecting an establishment of religion, or prohibiting the free exercise thereof; or abridging the freedom of speech, or of the press; or the right of the people peaceably to assemble, and to petition the government for a redress of grievances.

AMENDMENT 2

A well regulated Militia, being necessary to the security of a free State, the right of the people to keep and bear Arms, shall not be infringed.

AMENDMENT 3

No Soldier, shall, in time of peace be quartered in any house, without the consent of the Owner, nor in time of war, but in a manner to be prescribed by law.

AMENDMENT 4

The right of the people to be secure in their persons, houses, papers and effects, against unreasonable searches and seizures, shall not be violated and no Warrants shall issue, but upon probable cause, supported by Oath or affirmation, and particularly describing the place to be searched, and the persons or things to be seized.

AMENDMENT 5

No person shall be held to answer for a capital, or otherwise infamous crime, unless on a presentment or indictment of a Grand Jury, except in cases arising in the land or naval forces, or in the Militia, when in actual service in time of War or public danger; nor shall any person be subject for the same offense to be twice put in jeopardy of life or limb; nor shall be compelled in any criminal case to be a witness against himself, nor be deprived of life, liberty, or property, without due process of law; nor shall private property be taken for public use, without just compensation.

AMENDMENT 6

In all criminal prosecutions, the accused shall enjoy the right to a speedy and public trial, by an impartial jury of the State and district wherein the crime shall have been committed, which district shall have been previously ascertained by law, and to be informed of the nature and cause of the accusation; to be confronted with witnesses against him; to have compulsory process for obtaining witnesses in his favor, and to have the Assistance of Counsel for his defence.

AMENDMENT 7

In Suits at common law, where the value in controversy shall exceed twenty dollars, the right of trial by jury shall be preserved, and no fact tried by a jury, shall be otherwise re-examined in any Court of the United States, than according to the rules of the common law.

AMENDMENT 8

Excessive bail shall not be required, nor excessive fines imposed, nor cruel and unusual punishments inflicted.

AMENDMENT 9

The enumeration in the Constitution, of certain rights, shall not be construed to deny or disparage others retained by the people.

AMENDMENT 10

The powers not delegated to the United States by the Constitution, nor prohibited by it to the States, are reserved to the States respectively, or to the people.

FUGITIVE SLAVE ACT CH. 7, STAT. 302 (1793)

The Fugitive Slave Act of 1793 was designed to enforce Article IV, Section 2, of the Constitution and incur penalties against those who aided or abetted attempts of slaves to escape bondage.

Section 1. *Be it enacted by the Senate and House of Representatives of the United States of America in Congress assembled,* That whenever the executive authority of any state in the Union, or of either of the territories northwest or south of the river Ohio, shall demand any person as a fugitive from justice, of the executive authority of any such state or territory to which such person shall have fled, and shall moreover produce the copy of an indictment found, or an affidavit made before a magistrate of any state or territory as aforesaid, charging the person so demanded, with having committed treason, felony or other crime, certified as authentic by the governor or chief magistrate of the state or territory from whence the person so charged fled, it shall be the duty of the executive authority of the state or territory to which such person shall have fled, to cause him or her to be arrested and secured, and notice of the arrest to be given to the executive authority making such demand, or to the agent of such authority appointed to receive the fugitive, and to cause the fugitive to be delivered to such agent when he shall appear: But if no such agent shall appear within six months from the time of the arrest, the prisoner may be discharged. And all costs or expenses incurred to the state or territory making such demand, shall be paid by such state or territory.

Section 2. *And be it further enacted,* That any agent, appointed as aforesaid, who shall receive the fugitive into his custody, shall be empowered to transport him or her to the state or territory from which he or she shall have fled. And if any person or persons shall by force set at liberty, or rescue the fugitive from such agent while transporting, as aforesaid, the person or persons so offending shall, on conviction, be fined not exceeding five hundred dollars, and be imprisoned not exceeding one year.

Section 3. *And be it also enacted,* That when a person held to labour in any of the United States, or in either of the territories on the northwest or south of the river Ohio, under the laws thereof, shall escape into any other of the said states or territory, the person to whom such labour or service may be due, his agent or attorney, is hereby empowered to seize or arrest such fugitive from labour, and to take him or her before any judge of the circuit or district courts of the United States, residing or being within the state, or before any magistrate of a county, city or town corporate, wherein such seizure or arrest shall be made, and upon proof to the satisfaction of such judge or magistrate, either by oral testimony or affidavit taken before and certified by a magistrate of any such state or territory, that the person so seized or arrested, doth, under the laws of the state or territory from which he or she fled, owe service or labour to the person claiming him or her, it shall be the duty of such judge or magistrate to give a certificate thereof to such claimant, his agent or attorney, which shall be sufficient warrant for removing the said fugitive from labour, to the state or territory from which he or she fled.

Section 4. *And be it further enacted,* That any person who shall knowingly and willing obstruct or hinder such claimant, his agent or attorney in so seizing or arresting such fugitive from labour, or shall rescue such fugitive from such claimant, his agent or attorney when so arrested pursuant to the authority herein given or declared; or shall harbor or conceal such person after notice that he or she was a fugitive from labour, as aforesaid shall, for either of the said offenses, forfeit and pay the sum of five hundred dollars. Which penalty may be recovered by and for the benefit of such claimant, by action of debt, in any court proper to try the same; saving moreover to the person claiming such labour or service, his right of action for or on account of the said injuries or either of them.

BENJAMIN FRANKLIN'S ADDRESS TO THE PUBLIC (1789)

Despite the framers of the U.S. Constitution's handling of the slavery issue, influential opponents to slavery attempted to exert pressure on the Congress to enact an antislavery amendment to the Constitution. Among such groups was the Pennsylvania Society for Promoting the Abolition of Slavery and the Relief of Free Negroes Unlawfully Held in Bondage. Over the signature of the president of the society, Benjamin Franklin, the following "Address to the Public," urging abolition, was made on November 9, 1789.

It is with peculiar satisfaction we assure the friends of humanity that, in prosecuting the design of our association, our endeavors have proved successful, far beyond our most sanguine expectations.

Encouraged by this success, and by the daily progress of that luminous and benign spirit of liberty which is diffusing itself throughout the world, and humbly hoping for the continuance of the divine blessing on our labors, we have ventured to make an important addition to our original plan; and do therefore earnestly solicit the support and assistance of all who can feel the tender emotions of sympathy and compassion, or relish the exalted pleasure of beneficence.

Slavery is such an atrocious debasement of human nature, that its very extirpation, if not performed with solicitous care, may sometimes open a source of serious evils.

The unhappy man, who has long been treated as a brute animal, too frequently sinks beneath the common standard of the human species. The galling chains that bind his body do also fetter his intellectual faculties, and impair the social affections of his heart. Accustomed to move like a mere machine, by the will of a master, reflection is suspended; he has not the power of choice; and reason and conscience have but little influence over his conduct, because he is chiefly governed by the passion of fear. He is poor and friendless; perhaps worn out by extreme labor, age, and disease.

Under such circumstances, freedom may often prove a misfortune to himself, and prejudicial to society.

Attention to emancipated black people, it is therefore to be hoped, will become a branch of our national police; but, as far as we contribute to promote this emancipation, so far that attention is evidently a serious duty incumbent on us, and which we mean to discharge to the best of our judgment and abilities.

To instruct, to advise, to qualify those who have been restored to freedom, for the exercise and enjoyment of civil liberty; to promote in them habits of industry; to furnish them with employments suited to their age, sex, talents, and other circumstances; and to procure their children an education calculated for their future situation in life—these are the great outlines of the annexed plan, which we have adopted, and which we conceive will essentially promote the public good, and the happiness of these our hitherto too much neglected fellow-creatures.

A plan so extensive cannot be carried into execution without considerable pecuniary resources, beyond the present ordinary funds of the Society. We hope much from the generosity of enlightened and benevolent freemen, and will gratefully receive any donations of subscriptions for this purpose which may be made to our Treasurer, James Starr, or to James Pemberton, Chairman of our Committee of Correspondence.

Signed by order of the Society,

B. FRANKLIN, President

Philadelphia, 9th of November, 1789

GEORGE WASHINGTON'S LAST WILL AND TESTAMENT (1799)

By the eighteenth century, the slavery of Africans had become a firmly entrenched institution of American life, particularly in the South, where it was justified as an economic necessity. This argument notwithstanding, it was Washington's decision, at the writing of his last will and testament in 1799, to free all those slaves that he held in his "own right."

Life of George Washington—The Farmer *(Lithograph by Claude Regnier, after Painting by Junius Brutus Stearns, 1853).* *In his last will and testament, written in 1799, Washington arranged that all enslaved persons that he held in his "own right" be freed upon the death of his wife. He also left detailed instructions for the care of those newly freed from his estate.* THE LIBRARY OF CONGRESS

In the Name of God Amen

I, George Washington of Mount Vernon—a citizen of the United States,—and lately President of the same, do make, ordain and declare this Instrument; which is written with my own hand and every page thereof subscribed with my name, to be my last Will and Testament, revoking all other. ... Upon the decease of my wife, it is my Will and desire that all the Slaves which I hold in my *own right,* shall receive their freedom. ... And whereas among those who will receive freedom according to this devise, there may be some, who from old age or bodily infirmities, and others who on account of their infancy, that will be unable to support themselves; it is my Will and desire that all who come under the first and second description shall be comfortably clothed and fed by my heirs while they live;—and that such of the latter description as have no parents living, or if living are unable, or unwilling to provide for them, shall be bound by the Court until they shall arrive at the age of twenty-five year;—and in cases where no record can be produced, whereby their ages can be ascertained, the judgment of the Court upon its own view of the subject, shall be adequate and final.—The Negros thus bound, are (by their Masters or Mistresses) to be taught to read and write; and to be brought up to some useful occupation, agreeably to the Laws of the Commonwealth of Virginia, providing for the support of Orphan and other poor Children.—And I do hereby expressly forbid the Sale, or transportation out of the said Commonwealth of any Slave I may die possessed of, under any pretence whatsoever.—And I do moreover most pointedly, and most solemnly enjoin it upon my Executors hereafter named, or the Survivors of them, to see that this clause respecting Slaves, and every part thereof be religiously fulfilled at the Epoch at which it is directed to take place; without evasion, neglect or delay, after the Crops which may then be on the ground are harvested, particularly as it respects the aged and infirm;—Seeing that a regular and permanent fund be established for their Support so long as there are subjects requiring it; not trusting to the uncertain provision to be made by individuals.—And to my Mulatto man William (calling himself William Lee) I give immediate freedom; or if he should prefer it (on account of the accidents which have befallen him, and which have rendered him incapable of walking or of any active employment) to remain in the situation he now is, it shall be optional in him to do so: In either case however, I allow him an annuity of thirty dollars during his natural life, which shall be independent of the victuals and cloaths he has been accustomed to receive, if he chooses the last alternative; but in full, with his freedom, if he prefers the first;—and this I give him as a testimony of my sense of his attachment to me, and for his faithful services during the Revolutionary War.

ACT TO PROHIBIT THE IMPORTATION OF SLAVES CH. 22, 2 STAT. 426 (1807)

In adherence with the provisions of Article I, Section 9 of the U.S. Constitution, Congress passed and President Thomas Jefferson signed into law an act to end the slave trade. The act, however, which went into effect January 1, 1808, was not rigidly enforced. Evidence of this can be found in the fact that, between 1808 and 1860, some 250,000 slaves were illegally imported into the United States.

An Act to prohibit the importation of Slaves into any port or place within the jurisdiction of the United States, from and after the first day of January, in the year of our Lord one thousand eight hundred and eight.

Be it enacted, that from and after the first day of January, one thousand eight hundred and eight, it shall not be lawful to import or bring into the United States or the territories thereof from any foreign kingdom, place, or country, any negro, mulatto, or person of colour, as a slave, or to be held to service or labour.

Section 2. That no citizen of the United States, or any other person, shall, from and after the first day of January, in the year of our Lord one thousand eight hundred and eight, for himself, or themselves, or any other person whatsoever, either as master, factor, or owner, build, fit, equip, load or to otherwise prepare any ship or vessel, in any port or place within the jurisdiction of the United States, nor shall cause any ship or vessel to sail from any port or place within the same, for the purpose of procuring any negro, mulatto, or person of colour, from any foreign kingdom, place, or country, to be transported to any port or place whatsoever within the jurisdiction of the United States, to be held, sold, or disposed of as slaves, or to be held to service or labour: and if any ship or vessel shall be so fitted out for the purpose aforesaid, or shall be caused to sail so as aforesaid, every such ship or vessel, her tackle, apparel, and furniture, shall be forfeited to the United States, and shall be liable to be seized, prosecuted, and condemned in any of the circuit courts or district courts, for the district where the said ship or vessel may be found or seized. …

Section 4. If any citizen or citizens of the United States, or any person resident within the jurisdiction of the same, shall, from after the first day of January, one thousand eight hundred and eight, take on board, receive or transport from any of the coasts or kingdoms of Africa, or from any other foreign kingdom, place, or country, any negro, mulatto, or person of colour in any ship or vessel, for the purpose of selling them in any port or place within the jurisdiction of the United States as slaves, or be held to service or labour, or shall be in any ways aiding or abetting therein, such citizen or citizens, or person, shall severally forfeit and pay five thousand dollars, one moiety thereof to the use of any person or persons who shall sue for and prosecute the same to effect. …

Section 6. That if any person or persons whatsoever, shall, from and after the first day of January, one thousand eight hundred and eight, purchase or sell any negro, mulatto, or person, of colour, for a slave, or to be held to service or labour, who shall have been imported, or brought from any foreign kingdom, place, or country, or from the dominions of any foreign state, immediately adjoining to the United States, after the last day of December, one thousand eight hundred and seven, knowing at the time of such purchase or sale, such negro, mulatto, or person of colour, was so brought within the jurisdiction of the United States, as aforesaid, such purchaser and seller shall severally forfeit and pay for every negro, mulatto, or person of colour, so purchased, or sold as aforesaid, eight hundred dollars. …

Section 7. That if any ship or vessel shall be found, from and after the first day of January, one thousand eight hundred and eight, in any river, port, bay, or harbor, or on the high seas, within the jurisdictional limits of the United States, or hovering on the coast thereof, having on board any negro, mulatto, or person of colour, for the purpose of selling them as slaves, or with intent to land the same, in any port or place within the jurisdiction of the United States, contrary to the prohibition of the act, every such ship or vessel, together with her tackle, apparel, and furniture, and the goods or effects which shall be found on board the same, shall be forfeited to the use of the United States, and may be seized, prosecuted, and condemned, in any court of the United States, having jurisdiction thereof. And it shall be lawful for the President of the United States, and he is hereby authorized, should he deem it expedient, to cause any of the armed vessels of the United States to be manned and employed to cruise on any part of the coast of the

United States, or territories thereof, where he may judge attempts will be made to violate the provisions of this act, and to instruct and direct the commanders of armed vessels of the United States, to seize, take, and bring into any port of the United States all such ships or vessels, and moreover to seize, take, or bring into any port of the U.S. all ships or vessels of the U.S. wheresoever found on the high seas, contravening the provisions of this act, to be proceeded against according to law. . . .

EDITORIAL FROM THE FIRST EDITION OF *FREEDOM'S JOURNAL* (1827)

Published by Samuel Cornish and John B. Russwurm, Freedom's Journal *was the first African American owned and edited newspaper to be published in the United States. This editorial, printed here in its entirety, illustrates the* Journal*'s aim at bringing an end to slavery and discrimination.*

To Our Patrons

In presenting our first number to our Patrons, we feel all the diffidence of persons entering upon a new and untried line of business. But a moment's reflection upon the noble objects, which we have in view by the publication of this Journal; the expediency of its appearance at this time, when so many schemes are in action concerning our people—encourage us to come boldly before an enlightened public. For we believe, that a paper devoted to the dissemination of useful knowledge among our brethren, and to their moral and religious improvement, must meet with the cordial approbation of every friend to humanity.

The peculiarities of this Journal, renders it important that we should advertise to the world our motives by which we are actuated, and the objects which we contemplate.

We wish to plead our own cause. Too long have others spoken for us. Too long has the public been deceived by misrepresentations, in things which concern us dearly, though in the estimation of some mere trifles; for though there are many in society who exercise towards us benevolent feelings; still (with sorrow we confess it) there are others who make it their business to enlarge upon the least trifle, which tends to the discredit of any person of colour; and pronounce anathemas and denounce our whole body for the misconduct of this guilty one. We are aware that there are many instances of vice among us, but we avow that it is because no one has taught its subjects to be virtuous; many instances of poverty, because no sufficient efforts accommodated to minds contracted by slavery, and deprived of early education have been made, to teach them how to husband their hard earnings, and to secure to themselves comfort.

Education being an object of the highest importance to the welfare of society, we shall endeavor to present just and adequate views of it, and to urge upon our brethren the necessity and expediency of training their children, while young, to habits of industry, and thus forming them for becoming useful members of society. It is surely time that we should awake from this lethargy of years, and make a concentrated effort for the education of our youth. We form a spoke in the human wheel, and it is necessary that we should understand our pendency on the different parts, and theirs on us, in order to perform our part with propriety.

Though not desiring of dictating, we shall feel it our incumbent duty to dwell occasionally upon the general principles and rules of economy. The world has grown too enlightened, to estimate any man's character by his personal appearance. Though all men acknowledge the excellency of Franklin's maxims, yet comparatively few practice upon them. We may deplore when it is too late, the neglect of these self-evident truths, but it avails little to mourn. Ours will be the task of admonishing our brethren on these points.

The civil rights of a people being of the greatest value, it shall ever be our duty to vindicate our brethren, when oppressed; and to lay the case before the public. We shall also urge upon our brethren, (who are qualified by the laws of the different states) the expediency of using their elective franchise; and of making an independent use of the same. We wish them not to become the tools of party.

And as much time is frequently lost, and wrong principles instilled, by the perusal of works of trivial importance, we shall consider it a part of our duty to recommend to our young readers, such authors as will not only enlarge their stock of useful knowledge, but such as will also serve to stimulate them to higher attainments in science.

We trust also, that through the columns of the FREEDOM'S JOURNAL, many practical pieces, having for their bases, the improvement of our brethren, will be presented to them, from the pens of many of our respected friends, who have kindly promised their assistance.

It is our earnest wish to make our Journal a medium of intercourse between our brethren in the different states of this great confederacy: that through its columns an expression of our sentiments, on many interesting subjects which concern us, may be offered to the public: that plans which apparently are beneficial may be candidly discussed and properly weighed; if worth, receive our cordial approbation; if not, our marked disapprobation.

Useful knowledge of every kind, and everything that relates to Africa, shall find a ready admission into our columns; and as that vast continent becomes daily more known, we trust that many things will come to light, proving that the natives of it are neither so ignorant nor stupid as they have generally been supposed to be.

And while these important subjects shall occupy the columns of the FREEDOM'S JOURNAL, we would not be unmindful of our brethren who are still in the iron fetters of bondage. They are our kindred by all the ties of nature; and though but little can be effected to us, still let our sympathies be poured forth and our prayers in their behalf, ascend to Him who is able to succor them.

From the press and the pulpit we have suffered much by being incorrectly represented. Men whom we equally love and admire have not hesitated to represent us disadvantageously, without becoming personally acquainted with the true state of things, nor discerning between virtue and vice among us. The virtuous part of our people feel themselves sorely aggrieved under the existing state of things—they are not appreciated.

Our vices and our degradation are ever arrayed against us, but our virtues are passed by unnoticed. And what is still more lamentable, our friends, to whom we concede all the principles of humanity and religion, from these very causes seem to have fallen into the current of popular feeling and are imperceptibly floating on the stream—actually living in the practice of prejudice, while they abjure it in theory, and feel it not in their hearts. Is it not very desirable that such should know more of our actual condition; and of our efforts and feelings, that in forming or advocating plans for our amelioration, they may do it more understanding? In the spirit of candor and humility we intend by a simple representation of facts to lay our case before the public, with a view to arrest the progress of prejudice, and to shield ourselves against the consequent evils. We wish to conciliate all and to irritate none, yet we must be firm and unwavering in our principles, and persevering in our efforts.

If ignorance, poverty and degradation have hitherto been our unhappy lot; has the Eternal decree gone forth, that our race alone are to remain in this state, while knowledge and civilization are shedding their enlivening rays over the rest of the human family? The recent travels of Denham and Clapperton in the interior of Africa, and the interesting narrative which they have published; the establishment of the republic of Haiti after years of sanguinary warfare; its subsequent progress in all the arts of civilization; and the advancement of liberal ideas in South America, where despotism has given place to free governments, and where many of our brethren now fill important civil and military stations, prove the contrary.

The interesting fact that there are FIVE HUNDRED THOUSAND free persons of color, one half of whom might peruse, and the whole be benefitted by the publication of the Journal; that no publication, as yet, has been devoted exclusively to their improvement—that many selections from approved standard authors, which are within the reach of few, may occasionally be made—and more important still, that this large body of our citizens have no public channel—all serve to prove the real necessity, at present, for the appearance of the FREEDOM'S JOURNAL.

It shall ever be our desire so to conduct the editorial department of our paper as to give offence to none of our patrons; as nothing is farther from us than to make it the advocate of any partial views, either in politics or religion. What few days we can number, have been devoted to the improvement of our brethren; and it is our earnest wish that the remainder may be spent in the same delightful service.

In conclusion, whatever concerns us as a people, will ever find a ready admission into the FREEDOM'S JOURNAL, interwoven with all the principal news of the day.

And while every thing in our power shall be performed to support the character of our Journal, we would respectfully invite our numerous friends to assist by their communications, and our coloured brethren to strengthen our hands by their subscriptions, as our labour is one of common cause, and worthy of their consideration and support. And we most earnestly solicit the latter, that if at any time we should seem to be zealous, or too pointed in the inculcation of any important lesson, they will remember, that they are equally interested in the cause in which we are engaged, and attribute our zeal to the peculiarities of our situation; and our earnest engagedness in their well-being.

EDITORIAL FROM THE FIRST EDITION OF *THE LIBERATOR* (1831)

The Liberator, *one of the most well-known abolitionist newspapers in the nineteenth century, was published weekly out of Boston, Massachusetts, between 1831 and 1865. The paper's founder, William Lloyd Garrison, who was also the founder of the American Anti-Slavery Society, was white. However, most of* The Liberator*'s subscribers were black. During thirty-four years of publication, Garrison worked at shifting the sentiment of the nation away from the notion of gradual emancipation toward that of total abolition, as illustrated in this excerpt from the paper's first editorial.*

... During my recent tour for the purpose of exciting the minds of the people by a series of discourses on the subject of slavery, every place that I visited gave fresh evidence of the fact, that a greater revolution in public sentiment was to be effected in the free states—and particularly in New England—than at the south. I found contempt more bitter, opposition more active, detraction

THE LIBERATOR.

VOL. I.] WILLIAM LLOYD GARRISON AND ISAAC KNAPP, PUBLISHERS. [NO. 17.

BOSTON, MASSACHUSETTS.] OUR COUNTRY IS THE WORLD—OUR COUNTRYMEN ARE MANKIND. [SATURDAY, APRIL 23, 1831.

THE LIBERATOR IS PUBLISHED WEEKLY AT NO. 11, MERCHANTS' HALL.

WM. LLOYD GARRISON, EDITOR.

TERMS.

☞ Two Dollars per annum, payable in advance.
☞ Agents allowed every sixth copy.
☞ No subscription will be received for a shorter period than six months.
☞ All letters and communications must be POST PAID.

AGENTS.

CHARLES WHIPPLE, *Newburyport, Mass.*
JAMES E. ELLIS, *Providence, R. I.*
PHILIP A. BELL, *New-York City.*
JOSEPH CASSEY, *Philadelphia, Pa.*
HENRY OGDEN, *Newark, N. J.*
WILLIAM WATKINS, *Baltimore, Md.*

THE LIBERATOR.

'Is not the plea, that emancipation is impracticable, the most impudent hypocrisy and the most glaring absurdity ever propounded for contemplation?—Can any suppositious expediency, any dread of political disorder, or any private advantage, justify the prolongation of corruption, the enormity of which is unequalled, or repel the holy claim to its extinction? The system is so entirely corrupt, that it admits of no cure but by a TOTAL and IMMEDIATE abolition. For a gradual emancipation is a virtual recognition of the right, and establishes the rectitude of the practice. If it be just for one moment, it is hallowed for ever; and it be inequitable, not a day should it be tolerated.' BOURNE.

two committee men and a constable interfered, and would not permit him to take his seat! He was finally driven away, and the pew passed into other hands.

We purpose shortly to visit all our meeting-houses, and ascertain what places are provided for the accommodation of our colored people. A house dedicated to the worship of Almighty God, should be the last place for the exercise of despotic principles.—But here is the extract:

'With deep regret we have observed some articles in the columns of the "Liberator," of Boston, apparently from this city, in which its inhabitants are implicated; and which we believe the editor of that publication will deem very injudicious, as well as unkind, when knowing the truth in the case. So far from wishing to deprive the colored population of an opportunity to worship God, by the co-operation of the friends of religion with that part of the inhabitants, a good and convenient house was erected a few years since; clergymen of different denominations have often officiated, gratuitously, from Sabbath to Sabbath; and when disappointed in the labors of a Minister, lay brethren have attended at their request, and made exertions to promote the prosperity of their congregation; for many years a Sabbath School has been taught, composed entirely of colored children and adults; in addition to this, if we mistake not, at their request the public school money is given them in proportion to the number of their children, and they thus have a day school of their own.

After such interest had been shown for that class of people, was it to be expected that an attack should be made upon the very persons who have shown such liberality? This is indeed gratifying to the enemies of benevolent exertions: and were the

be elevated and improved in this country; unanimous in opposing their instruction; unanimous in exciting the prejudices of the people against them; unanimous in apologising for the crime of slavery; unanimous in conceding the right of the planters to hold their slaves in a limited bondage; unanimous in denying the expediency of emancipation, unless the liberated slaves are sent to Liberia; unanimous in their hollow pretence for colonizing, namely, to evangelize Africa; unanimous in their *true motive* for the measure—a terror lest the blacks should rise to avenge their accumulated wrongs. It is a conspiracy to send the free people of color to Africa under a benevolent pretence, but really that the slaves may be held more securely in bondage.* It is a conspiracy based upon fear, oppression and falsehood, which draws its aliment from the prejudices of the people, which is sustained by duplicity, which is impotent in its design, which really upholds the slave system, which fascinates while it destroys, which endangers the safety and happiness of the country, which no precept of the bible can justify, which is implacable in its spirit, which should be annihilated at a blow.

These are our accusations; and if we do not substantiate them, we are willing to be covered with reproach.

In attacking the principles, and exposing the evil tendency of the Society, we wish no one to understand us as saying, that all its friends are equally guilty, or actuated by the same motives. Nor let him suppose, that we exonerate any of them from

virtue. I doubt not this conviction will ultimately prevail in every community, where the obligations of religion and philanthropy are acknowledged; though the process may be slow; having to contend with much ignorance prejudice and error. This conviction, however, is but the first step towards a result so desirable as the total abolition of slavery. Every long established custom acquires a strong hold on the feelings of those who are habituated to its control; we know that its power in many cases is almost unconquerable; and this is especially the case, where a custom, however injurious in its tendencies, is a source of pecuniary emolument, or worldly aggrandizement to those interested in its continuance. It therefore becomes necessary for the attainment of this great and good object—the universal emancipation of our colored brethren—the complete overthrow of this abominable traffic in human flesh—to investigate the whole subject fairly and calmly; to discuss it fully and freely; to ascertain, as far as possible, what are the best means and methods for the accomplishment of this great end. On this point, I find there is great diversity of opinion. Men of equal talents, equal piety, and equal benevolence, take different and almost opposite views of the whole subject: my mind has been much perplexed, by hearing what seemed to me very strong arguments on both sides of the question.

With regard to the main subject, universal emancipation, as I before remarked, I have no doubt. I think it may, and it ought to be accomplished; but with regard to the means of its accomplishment, I do

Front Page of* The Liberator *Newspaper, April 23, 1831. The Liberator, *one of the best-known abolitionist newspapers in the nineteenth century, was founded in 1831 by William Lloyd Garrison and was published weekly through 1865. Although Garrison was white, most of the newspaper's subscribers were African American.* BETTMANN/CORBIS

more relentless, prejudice more stubborn, and apathy more frozen, than among slave owners themselves. Of course, there were individual exceptions to the contrary. This state of things afflicted, but did not dishearten me. I determined, at every hazard, to lift up the standard of emancipation in the eyes of the nation, within sight of Bunker Hill and in the birth place of liberty. That standard is now unfurled; and long may it float, unhurt by the spoliations of time or the missiles of a desperate foe—yea, till every chain be broken, and every bondman set free! Let Southern oppressors tremble—let their secret abettors tremble—let their Northern apologists tremble—let all the enemies of the persecuted blacks tremble.

I am aware that many object to the severity of my language; but is there not cause for severity? I will be as harsh as truth, and as uncompromising as justice. On this subject, I do not wish to think, or speak, or write, with moderation. No! No! Tell a man whose house is on fire to give a moderate alarm; tell the mother to gradually extricate her babe from the fire into which it has fallen;—but urge me not to use moderation in a cause like the present. I am in earnest—I will not equivocate—I will not excuse—I will not retreat a single inch—AND I WILL BE HEARD. . . .

William Lloyd Garrison

THE AMERICAN ANTI-SLAVERY SOCIETY'S *AMERICAN SLAVERY AS IT IS* (1839) (EXCERPT)

In 1839, the American Anti-Slavery Society compiled a massive portfolio of testimonies titled American Slavery as It Is, *which sought to document the inhumanities of slavery.*

The introduction, by Theodore D. Weld of New York, written in the style of a prosecutor addressing a court, stirred abolitionist sentiments in the North and was attacked by proslavery forces in the South.

READER, YOU are empanelled as a juror to try a plain case and bring in an honest verdict. The question at issue is not one of law, but of act—"What is the actual condition of slaves in the United States?"

A plainer case never went to jury. Look at it. TWENTY SEVEN HUNDRED THOUSAND PERSONS in this country, men, women, and children, are in SLAVERY. Is slavery, as a condition for human beings, good, bad, or indifferent?

We submit the question without argument. You have common sense, and conscience, and a human heart—pronounce upon it. You have a wife, or a husband, a child, a father, a mother, a brother or a sister—make the case your own, make it theirs, and bring in your verdict.

The case of Human Rights against Slavery has been adjudicated in the court of conscience times innumerable. The same verdict has always been rendered—"Guilty;" the same sentence has always been pronounced "Let it be accursed;" and human nature, with her million echoes, has rung it round the world in every language under heaven. "Let it be accursed. . . ."

As slaveholders and their apologists are volunteer witnesses in their own cause, and are flooding the world with testimony that their slaves are kindly treated; that they are well fed, well clothed, well housed, well lodged, moderately worked, and bountifully provided with all things needful for their comfort, we propose—first, to disprove their assertions by the testimony of a multitude of impartial witnesses, and then to put slaveholders themselves through a course of cross-questioning which will draw their condemnation out of their own mouths.

We will prove that the slaves in the United States are treated with barbarous inhumanity; that they are overworked, underfed, wretchedly clad and lodged, and have insufficient sleep; that they are often made to wear round their necks iron collars armed with prongs, to drag heavy chains and weights at their feet while working in the field, and to wear yokes and bells, and iron horns; that they are often kept confined in the stocks day and night for weeks together, made to wear gags in their mouths for hours or days, have some of their front teeth torn out or broken off, that they may be easily detected when they run away; that they are frequently flogged with terrible severity, have red pepper rubbed into their lacerated flesh, and hot brine, spirits of turpentine etc., poured over the gashes to increase the torture; that they are often stripped naked, their backs and limbs cut with knives, bruised and mangled by scores and hundreds of blows with the paddle, and terribly torn by the claws of cats, drawn over them by their tormentors; that they are often hunted with blood-hounds and shot down like beasts, or torn in pieces by dogs; that they are often suspended by the arms and whipped and beaten till they faint, and when revived by restoratives, beaten again till they faint, and sometimes till they die; that their ears are often cut off, their eyes knocked out, their bones broken, their flesh branded with red hot irons; that they are maimed, mutilated and burned to death, over slow fires. All these things, and more, and worse, we shall *prove*. . . .

We shall show, not merely that such deeds are committed, but that they are frequent; not done in corners, but before the sun; not in one of the slave states, but in all of them; not perpetrated by brutal overseers and drivers merely, but by magistrates, by legislators, by professors of religion, by preachers of the gospel, by governors of states, by "gentlemen of property and standing," and by delicate females moving in the "highest circles of society."

We know, full well, the outcry that will be made by multitudes, at these declarations; the multiform cavils, the flat denials, the charges of "exaggeration" and "falsehood" so often bandied, the sneers of affected contempt at the credulity that can believe such things, and the rage and imprecations against those who give them currency. We know, too, the threadbare sophistries by which slaveholders and their apologists seek to evade such testimony. If they admit that such deeds are committed, they tell us that they are exceedingly rare, and therefore furnish no grounds for judging of the general treatment of slaves; that occasionally a brutal wretch in the *free* states barbarously butchers his wife, but that no one thinks of inferring from that, the general treatment of wives at the North and West.

They tell us, also, that the slaveholders of the South are proverbially hospitable, kind, and generous, and it is incredible that they can perpetrate such enormities upon human beings; further, that it is absurd to suppose that they would thus injure their own property, that self-interest would prompt them to treat their slaves with kindness, as none but fools and madmen wantonly destroy their own property; further, that Northern visitors at the South come back testifying to the kind treatment of the slaves, and that slaves themselves corroborate such representations. All these pleas, and scores of others, are build in every corner of the free States; and who that hath eyes to see, has not sickened at the blindness that saw not, at the palsy of heart that felt not, or at the cowardice and sycophancy that dared not expose such shallow fallacies. We are not to be turned from our purpose by such vapid babblings. In their appropriate places, we proposed to consider these objections and various others, and to show their emptiness and folly.

HENRY HIGHLAND GARNET'S ADDRESS TO THE SLAVES OF THE UNITED STATES OF AMERICA (1843) (EXCERPT)

In 1843, Henry Highland Garnet attended the National Convention of Negro Citizens in Buffalo, New York, and on August 16 he delivered a militant oration calling for slave rebellions as the most assured means of ending slavery. It was perhaps the most radical speech by an African American during the period prior to the Civil War. The proposal moved the delegates, and its adoption failed by a single vote. After reading the speech, antislavery advocate John Brown had it published at his own expense in 1848.

Garnet's speech is, for all intents and purposes, addressed to an audience not present to receive it. Garnet speaks "to" the enslaved "on behalf of" the assembled conventioneers. Apologizing for the softness and ineffectiveness of abolitionist efforts, Garnet encourages slaves to "Arise! Strike for your lives and liberties." For Garnet's immediate audience, his message is one of anger, exasperation, and a summons for heightened militancy.

Brethren and fellow citizens: Your brethren of the North, East and West have been accustomed to meet together in national conventions, to sympathize with each other, and to weep over your unhappy condition. In these meetings we have addressed all classes of the free, but we have never, until this time, sent a word of consolation and advice to you. We have been contented in sitting still and mourning over your sorrows, earnestly hoping that before this day your sacred liberties would have been restored. But we have hoped in vain. Years have rolled on, and tens of thousands have been borne on streams of blood and tears to the shores of eternity. While you have been oppressed, we have also been partakers with you; nor can we be free while you are enslaved. We, therefore, write to you as being bound with you.

Many of you are bound to us, not only by the ties of a common humanity, but we are connected by the more tender relations of parents, wives, husbands and sisters and friends. As such we most affectionately address you.

Two hundred and twenty-seven years ago the first of our injured race were brought to the shores of America. They came not with glad spirits to select their homes in the New World. They came not with their own consent, to find an unmolested enjoyment of the blessings of this fruitful soil. … Neither did they come flying upon the wings of Liberty to a land of freedom. But they came with broken hearts from their beloved native land and were doomed to unrequited toil and deep degradation. Nor did the evil of their bondage end at their emancipation by death. Succeeding generations inherited their chains, and millions have come from eternity into time, and have returned again to the world of spirits, cursed and ruined by American Slavery.

[T]he time has come when you must act for yourselves. It is an old and true saying that, "if hereditary bondsmen would be free, they must themselves strike the blow." You can plead your own cause and do the work of emancipation better than any others. The nations of the Old World are moving in the great cause of universal freedom, and some of them at least will, ere long, do you justice. The combined powers of Europe have placed their broad seal of disapprobation upon the African slave trade. But in the slaveholding parts of the United States the trade is as brisk as ever. They buy and sell you as though you were brute beasts. The North has done much; her opinion of slavery in the abstract is known. But in regard to the South, we adopt the opinion of the *New York Evangelist*—"We have advanced so far, that the cause apparently waits for a more effectual door to be thrown open that has been yet." … [G]o to your lordly enslavers and tell them plainly that you are determined to be free. Appeal to their sense of justice and tell them that they have no more right to oppress you than you have to enslave them. Entreat them to remove the grievous burdens which they have imposed upon you, and to remunerate you for your labor. … Inform them that all you desire is freedom, and that nothing else will suffice. Do this, and forever after cease to toil for the heartless tyrants, who give you no other reward but stripes and abuse. If they then commence the work of death, they, and not you, will be responsible for the consequences. You had far better all die—die immediately—than live slaves and entail your wretchedness upon your posterity. If you would be free in this generation, here is your only hope. However much you and all of us may desire it, there is not much hope of redemption without the shedding of blood. If you must bleed, let it all come at once—rather die freemen than live to be slaves. It is impossible, like the children of Israel, to make a grand exodus from the land of bondage. The Pharaohs are on both sides of the blood-red waters!

Where is the blood of your fathers? Has it all run out of your veins? Awake, awake; millions of voices are calling you! Your dead fathers speak to you from their graves. Heaven, as with a voice of thunder, call on you to arise from the dust.

Let your motto be Resistance! Resistance! Resistance! No oppressed people have ever secured their liberty without resistance. What kind of resistance you had better make you must decide by the circumstances that surround you, and according to the suggestion of expediency. Brethren, adieu! Trust in the living God. Labor for the peace of the human race, and remember that you are three millions!

EDITORIAL FROM THE FIRST EDITION OF THE *NORTH STAR* (1847)

The first edition of Frederick Douglass's newspaper the North Star *was published on December 3, 1847, in Rochester, New York. Douglass, an escaped slave and leader in the abolitionist movement, dedicated his paper to the cause of blacks in America—as displayed in this, the paper's first editorial.*

To Our Oppressed Countrymen

We solemnly dedicate the *North Star* to your cause, our long oppressed and plundered fellow countrymen. May God bless the offering to your good! It shall fearlessly assert your rights, faithfully proclaim your wrongs, and earnestly demand for you instant and even-handed justice. Giving no quarter to slavery at the South, it will hold no truce with oppressors at the North. While it shall boldly advocate emancipation for our enslaved brethren, it will omit no opportunity to gain for the nominally free, complete enfranchisement. Every effort to injure or degrade you or your cause—originating wheresoever, or with whomsoever—shall find in it a constant, unswerving and inflexible foe.

THE NORTH STAR.

Front Page of an Edition of the North Star ***Newspaper*, 1848.** *Frederick Douglass, a leader in the abolitionist movement, first published this newspaper in December 1847, dedicating it to the cause of blacks in America. The paper's masthead proclaimed, "Right is of no Sex—Truth is of no Color—God is the Father of us all, and we are all Brethren."* THE LIBRARY OF CONGRESS

We shall energetically assail the ramparts of Slavery and Prejudice, be they composed of church or state, and seek the destruction of every refuge of lies, under which tyranny may aim to conceal and protect itself. . . .

While our paper shall be mainly Anti-Slavery, its columns shall be freely opened to the candid and decorous discussions of all measures and topics of a moral and humane character, which may serve to enlighten, improve, and elevate mankind. Temperance, Peace, Capital Punishment, Education,—all subjects claiming the attention of the public mind may be freely and fully discussed here.

While advocating your rights, the *North Star* will strive to throw light on your duties: while it will not fail to make known your virtues, it will not shun to discover your faults. To be faithful to our foes it must be faithful to ourselves, in all things.

Remember that we are one, that our cause is one, and that we must help each other, if we would succeed. We have drunk to the dregs the bitter cup of slavery; we have worn the heavy yoke; we have sighed beneath our bonds, and writhed beneath the bloody lash;—cruel mementoes of our oneness are indelibly marked in our living flesh. We are one with you under the ban of prejudice and proscription—one with you under the slander of inferior—one with you in social and political disfranchisement. What you suffer, we suffer; what you endure, we endure. We are indissolubly united, and must fall or flourish together. . . .

We shall be the advocates of learning, from the very want of it, and shall most readily yield the deference due to men of education among us; but shall always bear in mind to accord most merit to those who have labored hardest, and overcome most, in the praiseworthy pursuit of knowledge, remembering "that the whole need not a physician, but they that are sick," and that "the strong ought to bear the infirmities of the weak."

Brethren, the first number of the paper is before you. It is dedicated to your cause. Through the kindness of our friends in England, we are in possession of an excellent printing press, types, and all other materials necessary for printing a paper. Shall this gift be blest to our good, or shall it result in our injury? It is for you to say. With your aid, cooperation and assistance, our enterprise will be entirely successful. We pledge ourselves that no effort on our part shall be wanting, and that no subscriber shall lose his subscription—"*The North Star* Shall live."

FUGITIVE SLAVE ACT CH. 60, 9 STAT. 462 (1850)

For almost fifteen years, the provisions of the Missouri Compromise had quieted the debate over the expansion of slavery in the United States. However, following the annexation of Texas in 1845 and the ending of the war with Mexico in 1848, the question of expansion reignited tensions between proslavery forces and opponents to the institution.

With southern members of Congress threatening to withdraw, a compromise was reached in 1850 between advocates of expansion and their rivals. The compromise, a package of five statutes, attempted to address the major points of the conflict. One of the provisions of the compromise, which was supported by many southerners, was a strengthening of the existing federal fugitive slave law. On September 18, 1850, an act amending the 1793 fugitive slave statute was signed into law. Both the 1850 and the 1793 acts were finally repealed on June 28, 1864.

Section 5. That it shall be the duty of all marshals and deputy marshals to obey and execute all warrants and precepts issued under the provisions of this act, when to them directed; and should any marshal or deputy marshal refuse to receive such warrant, or other process, when tendered, or to use all proper means diligently to execute the same, he shall, on conviction thereof, be fined in the sum of one thousand dollars, to the use of such claimant, . . . and after arrest of such fugitive, by such marshal or his deputy, or whilst at any time in his custody under the provisions of this act, should such fugitive escape, whether with or without the assent of such marshal or his deputy, such marshal shall be liable, on his official bond, to be prosecuted for the benefit of such claimant, for the full value of the service or labor of said fugitive in the State, Territory, or District whence he escaped: and the better to enable the said commissioners, when thus appointed, to execute their duties faithfully and efficiently, in conformity with the requirements of the Constitution of the United States and of this act, they are hereby authorized and empowered, within their counties respectively, to appoint, . . . any one or more suitable persons, from time to time, to execute all such warrants and other processes as may be issued by them in the lawful performance of their respective duties. . . .

Section 6. That when a person held to service or labor in any State or Territory of the United States, has heretofore or shall hereafter escape into another State or Territory of the United States, the person or persons to whom such service or labor may be due, . . . may pursue and reclaim such fugitive person, either by procuring a warrant from some one of the courts, judges, or commissioners aforesaid, of the proper circuit, district, or county, for the apprehension of such fugitive from service or labor, or by seizing and arresting such fugitive, where the same can be done without process, and by taking, or causing such person to be taken, forthwith before such court, judge, or commissioner, whose duty it shall be to hear and determine the case of such claimant in a summary manner; and upon satisfactory proof being made, by deposition of affidavit, in writing, to be taken and certified by such court, judge, or commissioner, or by other satisfactory testimony, duly taken and certified by some court, . . . and with proof, also by affidavit, of the identity of the person whose service or labor is claimed to be due as aforesaid, that the person so arrested does in fact owe service or labor to the person or persons claiming him or her, in the State or Territory from which such fugitive may have escaped as aforesaid, and that said person escaped, to make out and deliver to such claimant, his or her agent or attorney, a certificate setting forth the substantial facts as to the service or labor due from such fugitive to the claimant, and of his or her escape from the State or Territory in which he or she was arrested, with authority to such claimant, . . . to use such reasonable force and restraint as may be necessary, under the circumstances of the case, to take and remove such fugitive person back to the State or Territory whence he or she may have escaped as aforesaid.

Section 7. That any persons who shall knowingly and willingly obstruct, hinder, or prevent such claimant, his agent or attorney, or any person or persons lawfully assisting him, her, or them, from arresting such a fugitive from service or labor, either with or without process as aforesaid, or shall rescue, or attempt to rescue, such fugitive from service or labor, from the custody of such claimant, . . . or other person or persons lawfully assisting as aforesaid, when so arrested, . . . or shall aid, abet, or assist such person so owing service or labor as aforesaid, directly or indirectly, to escape from such claimant, . . . or shall harbor or conceal such fugitive, so as to prevent the discovery and arrest of such person, after notice or knowledge of the fact that such person was a fugitive from service or labor . . . shall, for either of said offenses, be subject to a fine not exceeding one thousand dollars, and imprisonment not exceeding six months . . . ; and shall moreover forfeit and pay, by way of civil damages to the party injured by such illegal conduct, the sum of one thousand dollars, for each fugitive so lost as aforesaid. . . .

Section 9. That, upon affidavit made by the claimant of such fugitive . . . that he has reason to apprehend that such fugitive will be rescued by force from his or their possession before he can be taken beyond the limits of the State in which the arrest is made, it shall be the duty of the officer making the arrest to retain such fugitive in his custody, and to remove him to the State whence he fled, and there to deliver him to said claimant, his agent, or attorney. And to this end, the officer aforesaid is hereby authorized and required to employ so many persons as he may deem necessary to overcome such force, and to retain them in his service so long as circumstances may require.

ACT TO SUPPRESS THE SLAVE TRADE IN THE DISTRICT OF COLUMBIA CH. 63, 9 STAT. 467 (1850)

Although the importation of new slaves from Africa had been outlawed in 1808, the breeding and trading of slaves was still a big business. The Washington, Maryland, and Virginia area served as headquarters to some of the nation's largest traders.

The renewed debate in Congress over the expansion of slavery during the late 1840s led to what has been referred to as the Compromise of 1850—a package of five resolutions, one of which was the 1850 Fugitive Slave Act. Another of the provisions, a concession to the antislavery forces, was an act abolishing the slave trade in the District of Columbia.

Be it enacted, ... That from and after January 1, 1851, it shall not be lawful to bring into the District of Columbia any slave whatsoever, for the purpose of being sold, or for the purpose of being placed in depot, to be subsequently transferred to any other State or place to be sold as merchandise. And if any slave shall be brought into the said District by its owner, or by the authority or consent of its owner, contrary to the provisions of this act, such slave shall thereupon become liberated and free.

NARRATIVE OF SOJOURNER TRUTH, "BOOK OF LIFE" (1851) (EXCERPT)

In 1851, Sojourner Truth initiated a lecturing tour in western New York, accompanied by several distinguished abolitionists. To speak against slavery during this period was both unpopular and unsafe. Abolitionist meetings were frequently disrupted by proslavery forces, and the lives of speakers and attendees were threatened. During such times, Sojourner Truth was known to fearlessly maintain her ground, and, by her stately manner and well-timed remarks, she would disperse the mob and restore order.

After several months in western New York, she traveled to Akron, Ohio, in order to speak before a less-than-receptive audience at a woman's rights convention. Fearing negative publicity through an association with Sojourner Truth and the abolitionist movement, the conventioneers pleaded with Frances D. Gage, presiding member of the convention, not to allow Truth to lecture. On the second day, as the conventioneers struggled with the disruptive male clergy of various denominations, Truth slowly rose from her seat and moved toward the podium. Ignoring the requests of her fellow conventioneer, Gage introduced Truth to the audience. A profound hush fell across the audience as Sojourner Truth spoke these words:

Well, children, where there is so much racket there must be something out of kilter. I think that between the Negroes of the South and the women of the North all talking about rights, the white women will be in a fix pretty soon. But what's all this talk about? That man over there says that women need to be helped into carriages and lifted over ditches, and to have the best place everywhere. Nobody ever helps me into carriages, or over mud puddles, or gives me any best place [and raising herself to her full height and her voice to a pitch like rolling thunder, she asked], and ar'n't I a woman? Look at me! Look at my arm! [and she bared her right arm to the shoulder, showing her tremendous muscular power.] I have plowed, and planted, and gathered into barns, and no man could head me—and ar'n't I a woman? I could work as much and eat as much as a man (when I could get it), and bear de lash as well—and ar'n't I a woman? I have borne thirteen children and seen most all sold off into slavery, and when I cried out with a mother's grief, none but Jesus heard—and ar'n't I a woman? [The cheering was long and loud.]

FREDERICK DOUGLASS'S INDEPENDENCE DAY ADDRESS (1852)

In 1852, more than three million African Americans were being held as slaves in the United States. Knowing this and understanding the irony implicit in the notion of a holiday commemorating the independence of the United States, Frederick Douglass lost little time in laying bare the contradiction inherent in allowing slavery to exist within a society professedly dedicated to individual freedom.

Fellow Citizens

Pardon me, and allow me to ask, why am I called upon to speak here today? What have I or those I represent to do with your national independence? Are the great principles of political freedom and of natural justice, embodied in that Declaration of Independence, extended to us? And am I, therefore, called upon to bring our humble offering to the national altar, and to confess the benefits, and express devout gratitude for the blessings resulting from your independence to us?

Would to God, both for your sakes and ours, that an affirmative answer could be truthfully returned to these questions. Then would my task be light, and my burden easy and delightful. For who is there so cold that a nation's sympathy could not warm him? Who so obdurate and dead to the claims of gratitude, that would not thankfully acknowledge such priceless benefits? Who so stolid and selfish that would not give his voice to swell the hallelujahs of a nation's jubilee, when the chains of servitude had been torn from his limbs? I am not that man. . . .

I am not included within the pale of this glorious anniversary! Your high independence only reveals the immeasurable distance between us. The blessings in which you this day rejoice are not enjoyed in common. The rich inheritance of justice, liberty, prosperity, and independence bequeathed by your fathers is shared by you, not by me. The sunlight that brought life and healing to you has brought stripes and death to me. This Fourth of July is *yours,* not *mine.* You may rejoice, I must mourn. To drag a man in fetters into the grand illuminated temple of liberty, and call upon him to join you in joyous anthems, were inhuman mockery and sacrilegious irony. Do you mean, citizens, to mock me, by asking me to speak today? . . .

Fellow citizens, above your national, tumultuous joy, I hear the mournful wail of millions, whose chains, heavy and grievous yesterday, are today rendered more intolerable by the jubilant shouts that reach them. If I do forget, if I do not remember those bleeding children of sorrow this day, "may my right hand forget her cunning, and may my tongue cleave to the roof of my mouth!" To forget them, to pass lightly over their wrongs, and to chime in with the popular theme, would be treason most scandalous and shocking, and would make me a reproach before God and the world. My subject, then, fellow citizens, is "American Slavery." I shall see this day and its popular characteristics from the slave's point of view. Standing here, identified with the American bondman, making his wrongs mine, I do not hesitate to declare, with all my soul, that the character and conduct of this nation never looked blacker to me than on this Fourth of July. Whether we turn to the declarations of the past, or to the professions of the present, the conduct of the nation seems equally hideous and revolting. America is false to the past, false to the present, and solemnly binds herself to be false to the future. Standing with God and the crushed and bleeding slave on this occasion, I will, in the name of humanity, which is outraged, in the name of Liberty, which is fettered, in the name of the Constitution and the Bible, which are disregarded and trampled upon, dare to call in question and to denounce, with all the emphasis I can command, everything that serves to perpetuate slavery—the great sin and shame of America! "I will not equivocate; I will not excuse"; I will use the severest language I can command, and yet not one word shall escape me that any man, whose judgment is not blinded by prejudice, or who is not at heart a slave-holder, shall not confess to be right and just.

But I fancy I hear some of my audience say it is just in this circumstances that you and your brother Abolitionists fail to make a favorable impression on the public mind. Would you argue more and denounce less, would you persuade more and rebuke less, your cause would be much more likely to succeed. But, I submit, where all is plain there is nothing to be argued. What point in the anti-slavery creed would you have me argue? On what branch of the subject do the people of this country need light? Must I undertake to prove that the slave is a man? That point is conceded already. Nobody doubts it. The slave-holders themselves acknowledge it in the enactment of laws for their government. They acknowledge it when they punish disobedience on the part of the slave. There are seventy-two crimes in the State of Virginia, which, if committed by a black man (no matter how ignorant he be), subject him to the punishment of death, while only two of these same crimes will subject a white man to like punishment. What is this but the acknowledgment that the slave is a moral, intellectual, and responsible being? The manhood of the slave is conceded. It is admitted in the fact that the Southern statute-books are covered with enactments, forbidding, under severe fines and penalties, the teaching of the slave to read and write. When you can point to any such laws in reference to the beasts of the field, then I may consent to argue the manhood of the slave. When the dogs in your streets, when the fowls of the air, when the cattle on your hills, when the fish of the sea, and the reptiles that crawl, shall be unable to distinguish the slave from a brute, then I will argue with you that the slave is a man!

For the present it is enough to affirm the equal manhood of the Negro race. Is it not astonishing that, while we are plowing, planting, and reaping, using all kinds of mechanical tools, erecting houses, constructing bridges, building ships, working in metals of brass, iron, copper, silver, and gold; that while we are reading, writing, and ciphering, acting as clerks, merchants, and secretaries, having among us lawyers, doctors, ministers, poets, authors, editors, orators, and teachers; that while we are engaged in all the enterprises common to other men—digging gold in California, capturing the whale in the Pacific, feeding sheep and cattle on the hillside, living, moving, acting, thinking, planning, living in families as husbands, wives, and children, and above all, confessing and worshipping the Christian God, and looking hopefully for life and immortality beyond the grave—we are called upon to prove that we are men?

Would you have me argue that man is entitled to liberty? That he is the rightful owner of his own body? You have already declared it. Must I argue the wrongfulness of slavery? Is that a question for republicans? Is it to be settled by the rules of logic and argumentation, as a matter beset with great difficulty, involving a doubtful application of the principle of justice, hard to understand? How should I look today in the presence of Americans, dividing and subdividing a discourse, to show that men have a natural right to freedom, speaking of it relatively and positively, negatively and affirmatively? To do so would be to make myself ridiculous, and to offer an insult to your understanding. There is not a man beneath the canopy of heaven who does not know that slavery is wrong *for him.*

What! Am I to argue that it is wrong to make men brutes, to rob them of their liberty, to work them without wages, to keep them ignorant of their relations to their fellow men, to beat them with sticks, to flay their flesh with the lash, to load their limbs with irons, to hunt them with dogs, to sell them at auction, to sunder their families, to knock out their teeth, to burn their flesh, to starve them into obedience and submission to their masters? Must I argue that a system thus marked with blood and stained with pollution is wrong? No; I will not. I have better employment for my time and strength than such arguments would imply.

What, then, remains to be argued? Is it that slavery is not divine; that God did not establish it; that our doctors of divinity are mistaken? There is blasphemy in the thought. That which is inhuman cannot be divine. Who can reason on such a proposition? They that can, may; I cannot. The time for such argument is past.

At a time like this, scorching irony, not convincing argument, is needed. Oh! had I the ability, and could I reach the nation's ear, I would today pour out a fiery stream of biting ridicule, blasting reproach, withering sarcasm, and stern rebuke. For it is not light that is needed, but fire; it is not the gentle shower, but thunder. We need the storm, the whirlwind, and the earthquake. The feeling of the nation must be quickened; the conscience of the nation must be startled; the hypocrisy of the nation must be exposed; and its crimes against God and man must be denounced.

What to the American slave is your Fourth of July? I answer, a day that reveals to him more than all other days of the year, the gross injustice and cruelty to which he is the constant victim. To him your celebration is a sham; your boasted liberty an unholy license; your national greatness, swelling vanity; your sounds of rejoicing are empty and heartless; your denunciation of tyrants, brass-fronted impudence; your shouts of liberty and equality, hollow mockery; your prayers and hymns, your sermons and thanksgivings, with all your religious parade and solemnity, are to him mere bombast, fraud, deception, impiety, and hypocrisy—a thin veil to cover up crimes which would disgrace a nation of savages. There is not a nation of the earth guilty of practices more shocking and bloody than are the people of these United States at this very hour.

Go where you may, search where you will, roam through all the monarchies and despotisms of the Old World, travel through South America, search out every abuse and when you have found the last, lay your facts by the side of the every-day practices of this nation, and you will say with me that, for revolting barbarity and shameless hypocrisy, America reigns without a rival.

DRED SCOTT V. SANDFORD, 19 HOWARD 393 (1857)

In 1835, Dred Scott, born a slave in Virginia, became the property of John Emerson, an army doctor, in the slave state of Missouri. From there, he was taken into the free state of Illinois and later to the free territory of Minnesota. In 1847, Scott instituted suit in the circuit court of St. Louis County, Missouri, arguing that he should be given his freedom by virtue of his having resided on free soil. After nine years, his case was certified to the U.S. Supreme Court, where five of the nine justices were southerners.

Under the terms of the Missouri Compromise, Missouri was allowed to join the Union with a slave population of almost 10,000; Maine was admitted as a free state. However, the compromise also prohibited the expansion of slavery into any part of the Louisiana Territory north of latitude 36° 30′. It was here, into Illinois and the territory of Wisconsin, that Dred Scott's master brought him, and in 1846 Scott sued his master for his freedom.

After numerous delays, trials, and retrials, the case reached the U.S. Supreme Court in 1856. Hearing this case, the Court was not only faced with the question as to whether Scott was a free man, as a result of his sojourn in a free territory, but it also had to consider whether Congress had the authority under the Constitution to outlaw slavery in the territories. Although each of the nine justices delivered a separate opinion, the opinion of Chief Justice Roger Brooke Taney has been generally accepted as the Court's ruling on the matter.

In delivering his opinion, Chief Justice Taney declared that, by virtue of both the Declaration of Independence and the Constitution, African Americans could not be regarded as citizens of the United States. Moreover, the Court could not deprive slaveholders of their right to take slaves into any part of the Union, North or South. In effect, therefore, the Missouri Compromise, as well as other antislavery legislation, was declared to be unconstitutional.

The question is simply this: Can a negro, whose ancestors were imported into this country and sold as slaves, become a member of the political community formed and brought into existence by the constitution of the United States, and as such become entitled to all the rights, and privileges, and immunities, guaranteed by that instrument to the citizen? . . .

The words "people of the United States" and "citizens" are synonymous terms, and mean the same thing.

They both describe the political body who, according to our republican institutions, form the sovereignty, and who hold the power and conduct the government through their representatives. They are what we familiarly call the "sovereign people," and every citizen is one of this people, and a constituent member of this sovereignty. The question before us is, whether the class of persons described in the plea in abatement compose a portion of this people, and are constituent members of this sovereignty? We think they are not, and that they are not included, and were not intended to be included, under the word "citizens" in the constitution, and can therefore claim none of the rights and privileges which that instrument provides for and secures to citizens of the United States. On the contrary, they were at that time considered as a subordinate and inferior class of beings, who had been subjugated by the dominant race, and, whether emancipated or not, yet remained subject to their authority, and had no rights or privileges. . . .

It is not the province of the court to decide upon the justice or injustice, the policy or impolicy, of these laws. The decision of that question belonged to the political or law-making power; to those who formed the sovereignty and framed the constitution. The duty of the court is to interpret the instrument they have framed, with the best lights we can obtain on the subject, and to administer it as we find it, according to its true intent and meaning when it was adopted.

In discussing this question, we must not confound the rights of citizenship which a State may confer within its own limits, and the rights of citizenship as member of the Union. It does not by any means follow, because he has all the rights and privileges of a citizen of a State, that he must be a citizen of the United States. He may have all of the rights and privileges of the citizen of a State, and yet not be entitled to the rights and privileges of a citizen in any other State. For, previous to the adoption of the constitution of the United States, every State had the undoubted right to confer on whomsoever it pleased the character of citizen, and to endow him with all its rights. But this character of course was confined to the boundaries of the State, and gave him no rights or privileges in other States beyond those secured to him by the laws of nations and the comity of States. Nor have the several States surrendered the power of conferring these rights and privileges by adopting the constitution of United States. . . .

It is very clear, therefore, that no State can, by any act or law of its own, passed since the adoption of the constitution, introduce a new member into the political community created by the constitution of the United States. It cannot make him a member of this community by making him a member of its own. And for the same reason it cannot introduce any person, or description of persons, who were not intended to be embraced in this new political family, which the constitution brought into existence, but were intended to be excluded from it.

The question then arises, whether the provisions of the constitution, in relation to the personal rights and privileges to which the citizen of a State should be entitled, embraced the negro African race, at that time in this country, or who might afterwards be imported, who had then or should afterwards be made free in any State; and to put it in the power of a single State to make him a citizen of the United States, and endue him with the full rights of citizenship in every other State without consent? Does the constitution of the United States act upon him whenever he shall be made free under the laws of a State, and raised there to the rank of a citizen, and immediately clothe him with all the privileges of a citizen in every other State, and in its own courts?

The court thinks the affirmative of these propositions cannot be maintained. And if it cannot, the plaintiff in error could not be a citizen of the State of Missouri, within the meaning of the constitution of the United States, and, consequently, was not entitled to sue in its courts.

It is true, every person, and every class and description of persons, who were at the time of the adoption of the constitution recognized as citizens in the several States, became also citizens of this new political body; but none other; it was formed by them, and for them and their posterity, but for no one else. And the personal rights and privileges guaranteed to citizens of this new sovereignty were intended to embrace those only who were then members of the several State communities, or who should afterwards by birthright or otherwise become members, according to the provisions of the constitution and the principles on which it was founded. . . .

In the opinion of the court, the legislation and histories of the times, and the language used in the declaration of independence, show, that neither the class of persons who had been imported as slaves, nor their descendants, whether they had become free or not, were then acknowledged as a part of the people, nor intended to be included in the general words used in that memorable instrument. . . .

. . . The government of the United States had no right to interfere for any other purpose but that protecting the rights of the owner, leaving it altogether with the several States to deal with this race, whether emancipated or not, as each State may think justice, humanity, and the interests and safety of society, require. . . .

The act of Congress, upon which the plaintiff relies, declares that slavery and involuntary servitude, except as a punishment for crime, shall be forever prohibited in all that part of the territory ceded by France, under the name of Louisiana, which lies north of thirty-six degrees thirty minutes north latitude and not included within the limits of Missouri. And the difficulty which meets us at the threshold of this part of the inquiry is whether Congress was authorized to pass this law under any of the powers granted to it by the Constitution; for, if the authority is not given by that instrument, it is the duty of this Court to declare it void and inoperative and incapable of conferring freedom upon anyone who is held as a slave under the laws of any one of the states. . . .

We do not mean . . . to question the power of Congress in this respect. The power to expand the territory of the United States by the admission of new states is plainly given; and in the construction of this power by all the departments of the government, it has been held to authorize the acquisition of territory, not fit for admission at the time, but to be admitted as soon as its population and situation would entitle it to admission. It is acquired to become a state and not to be held as a colony and governed by Congress with absolute Authority; and, as the propriety of admitting a new state is committed to the sound discretion of Congress, the power to acquire territory for that purpose, to be held by the United States until it is in a suitable condition to become a state upon an equal footing with the other states, must rest upon the same discretion. . . .

But the power of Congress over the person or property of a citizen can never be a mere discretionary power under our Constitution and form of government. The powers of the government and the rights and privileges of the citizen are regulated and plainly defined by the Constitution itself. . . .

These powers, and others, in relation to rights of person, which it is not necessary here to enumerate, are, in express and positive terms, denied to the general government; and the rights of private property have been guarded with equal care. Thus the rights of property are united with the rights of person and placed on the same ground by the Fifth Amendment to the Constitution, which provides that no person shall be deprived of life, liberty, and property without due process of law. And an act of Congress which deprives a citizen of the United States of his liberty of property, without due process of law, merely because he came himself or brought his property into a particular territory of the United States, and who had committed no offense against the law, could hardly be dignified with the name of due process of law. . . .

It seems, however, to be supposed that there is a difference between property in a slave and other property and that different rules may be applied to it in expounding Constitution of the United States. And the laws and usages of nations, and the writings of eminent jurists upon the relation of master and slave and their mutual rights and duties, and the powers which governments may exercise over it, have been dwelt upon in the argument.

But, in considering the question before us, it must be borne in mind that there is no law of nations standing between the people of the United States and their government and interfering with their relation to each other. The powers of the government and the rights of the citizen under it are positive and practical regulations plainly written down. The people of the United States have delegated to it certain enumerated powers and forbidden it to exercise others. It has no power over the person of property of a citizen but what the citizens of the United States have granted. And no laws or usages of other nations, or reasoning of statesmen of jurists upon the relations of master and slave, can enlarge the powers of the government or take from the citizens the rights they have reserved. And if the Constitution recognizes the right of property of the master in a slave, and makes no distinction between that description of property and other property owned by a citizen, no tribunal, acting under the authority of the United States, whether it be legislative, executive, or judicial, has a right to draw such a distinction or deny to it the benefit of the provisions and guaranties which have been provided for the protection of private property against the encroachments of the government.

Now, as we have already said in an earlier part of this opinion, upon a different point, the right of property in a slave is distinctly and expressly affirmed in the Constitution. The right to traffic in it, like an ordinary article of merchandise and property, was guaranteed to the citizens of the United States, in every state that might desire it, for twenty years. And the government in express terms is pledged to protect it in all future time if the slave escapes from his owner. That is done in plain words—too plain to be misunderstood. And no word can be found in the Constitution which gives Congress a greater power over slave property or which entitles property of that kind to less protection than property of any other description. The only power conferred is the power coupled with the duty of guarding and protecting the owner in his rights.

Upon these considerations it is the opinion of the court that the act of Congress which prohibited a citizen from holding and owning property of this kind in the territory of the United States north of the line therein mentioned is not warranted by the Constitution and is therefore void; and that neither Dred Scott himself, nor any of his family, were made free by being carried into this territory; even if they had been carried there by the owner with the intention of becoming a permanent resident. . . .

THE EMANCIPATION PROCLAMATION NO. 17, 12 STAT. 1268 (1863)

In an attempt to bring an end to the Civil War, President Abraham Lincoln, acting on his authority as commander-in-chief, on September 22, 1862, issued a warning that slavery would be abolished in any state that continued to rebel. With the war still raging, Lincoln issued the Emancipation Proclamation on January 1, 1863, freeing slaves in those states that had seceded from the Union. The proclamation did not apply, however, to those areas occupied by Union forces—there remained some 800,000 slaves unaffected by the provisions of the document.

By the President of the United States of America: A Proclamation

Whereas on the 22d day of September, A.D. 1862, a proclamation was issued by the President of the United States, containing, among other things, the following, to wit:

"That on the 1st day of January, A.D. 1863, all persons held as slaves within any State or designated part of a State the people whereof shall then be in rebellion against the United States shall be then, henceforward, and forever free; and the executive government of the United States, including the military and naval authority thereof, will recognize and maintain the freedom of such persons and will do no act or acts to repress such persons, or any of them, in any efforts they may make for their actual freedom."

"That the executive will on the 1st day of January aforesaid, by proclamation, designated the States and parts of States, if any, which the people thereof, respectively, shall then be in rebellion against the United States; and the fact that any State or the people thereof shall on that day be in good faith represented in the Congress of the United States by members chosen thereto at elections wherein a majority of the qualified voters of such States shall have participated shall, in the absence of strong countervailing testimony, be deemed conclusive evidence that such State and the people thereof are not then in rebellion against the United States.":

Now, therefore, I, Abraham Lincoln, President of the United States, by virtue of the power in me vested as Commander-in-Chief of the Army and Navy of the United States in time of actual armed rebellion against the authority and government of the United States, and as a fit and necessary war measure for suppressing said rebellion, do, on this 1st day of January, A.D. 1863, and in accordance with my purpose so to do, publicly proclaimed for the full period of one hundred days from the first day above mentioned, order and designate as the States and parts of States wherein the people thereof, respectively, are this day in rebellion against the United States the following, to wit:

Arkansas, Texas, Louisiana (except the parishes of St. Bernard, Plaquemines, Jefferson, St. John, St. Charles, St. James, Ascension, Assumption, Terrebonne, Lafourche, St. Mary, St. Marti, and Orleans, including the city of New Orleans), Mississippi, Alabama, Florida, Georgia, South Carolina, North Carolina, and Virginia (except the forty-eight counties designated as West Virginia, and also the counties of Berkeley, Accomac, Northampton, Elizabeth City, York, Princess Anne, and Northfolk, including the cities of Norfolk and Portsmouth), and which excepted parts are for the present left precisely as if this proclamation were not issued.

And by virtue of the power and for the purpose aforesaid, I do order and declare that all persons held as slaves within said designated States and parts of States are, and henceforward shall be, free; and that the Executive Government of the United States, including the military and naval authorities thereof, will recognize and maintain the freedom of said persons.

And I hereby enjoin upon the people so declared to be free to abstain from all violence, unless in necessary self-defense; and I recommend to them that, in all cases when allowed, they labor faithfully for reasonable wages.

And I further declare and make known that such persons of suitable condition will be received into the armed service of the United States to garrison forts, positions, stations, and other places, and to man vessels of all sorts in said service.

And upon this act, sincerely believed to be an act of justice, warranted by the Constitution upon military necessity, I invoke the considerate judgment of mankind and the gracious favor of Almighty God.

FREEDMEN'S BUREAU ACT CH. 90, 13 STAT. 507 (1865)

On March 3, 1865, Congress passed legislation designed to provide basic health and educational services to former slaves and to administer abandoned land in the South. Under the act, the Bureau of Refugees, Freedmen, and Abandoned Lands, commonly referred to as the Freedmen's Bureau, was created.

An Act to Establish a Bureau for the Relief of Freedmen and Refugees

Be it enacted, That there is hereby established in the War Department, to continue during the present war of rebellion, and for one year thereafter, a bureau of refugees, freedmen, and abandoned lands, to which shall be committed, as hereinafter provided, the supervision and management of all abandoned lands and the control of all subjects relating to refugees and freedmen from rebel states, or from any district of country within the territory embraced in the operations of the army, under such rules and regulations as may be prescribed by the head of the bureau and approved by the President. The said bureau shall be under the management and control of a commissioner to be appointed by the President, by and with the advice and consent of the Senate.

Section 2. That the Secretary of War may direct such issue of provisions, clothing, and fuel, as he may deem needful for the immediate and temporary shelter and supply of destitute and suffering refugees and freedmen and their wives and children, under such rules and regulations as he may direct.

Section 3. That the President may, by and with the advice and consent of the Senate, appoint an assistant commissioner for each of the states declared to be in insurrection, not exceeding ten in number, who shall, under the direction of the commissioner, aid in the execution of the provisions of this act. ... And any military officer may be detailed and assigned to duty under this act without increase of pay of allowances. ...

Section 4. That the commissioner, under the direction of the President, shall have authority to set apart, for the use of loyal refugees and freedmen, such tracts of land within the insurrectionary states as shall have been abandoned, or to which the United States shall have acquired title by confiscation or sale, or otherwise, and to every male citizen, whether refugee or freedman, as aforesaid, there shall be assigned not more than forty acres of such land, and the person to whom it was so assigned shall be protected in the use and enjoyment of the land for the term of three years at an annual rent not exceeding six per centum upon the value of such land, as it was appraised by the state authorities in the year eighteen hundred and sixty, for the purpose of taxation, and in case no such appraisal can be found, then the rental shall be based upon the estimated value of the land in said year, to be ascertained in such manner as the commissioner may by regulation prescribe. At the end of said term, or at any time during said term, the occupants of any parcels so assigned may purchase the land and receive such title thereto as the United States can convey, upon paying therefor the value of the land, as ascertained and fixed for the purpose of determining the annual rent aforesaid. ...

AMENDMENT THIRTEEN TO THE UNITED STATES CONSTITUTION (1865)

Ratified December 18, 1865, the Thirteenth Amendment formally abolished slavery within the United States.

Section 1. Neither slavery nor involuntary servitude, except as a punishment for crime whereof the party shall have been duly convicted, shall exist within the United States, or any place subject to their jurisdiction.

Section 2. Congress shall have power to enforce this article by appropriate legislation.

BLACK CODES OF MISSISSIPPI (1865)

Following emancipation, many states sought to impose restrictions on African Americans to prevent them from enjoying equal social status with whites. These restrictions were designed to not only hold African Americans in a subordinate condition, but to impose restrictions upon them not unlike those which prevailed before the Civil War. Black codes imposed heavy penalties for "vagrancy," "insulting gestures," curfew violations, and "seditious speeches." In November 1865, Mississippi was the first state to enact such laws.

AN ACT TO CONFER CIVIL RIGHTS ON FREEDMEN, AND FOR OTHER PURPOSES

Section 1. All freedmen, free negroes and mulattoes may sue and be sued, implead and be impleaded, in all the courts of law and equity of this State, and may acquire personal property, and chooses in action, by descent or purchase, and may dispose of the same in the same manner and to the same extent that white persons may: Provided, That the provisions of this section shall not be so construed as to allow any freedman, free negro or mulatto to rent or lease any lands or tenements except in incorporated cities or towns, in which places the corporate authorities shall control the same.

Section 2. All freedmen, free negroes and mulattoes may intermarry with each other, in the same manner and under the same regulations that are provided by law for white persons: Provided, that the clerk of probate shall keep separate records of the same.

Section 3. All freedmen, free negroes or mulattoes who do now and have herebefore lived and cohabited together as husband and wife shall be taken and held in law as legally married, and the issue shall be taken and held as legitimate for all purposes; and it shall not be lawful for any freedman, free negro or mulatto to intermarry with any white person; nor for any person to intermarry with any freedman, free negro or mulatto; and any person who shall so intermarry shall be deemed guilty of felony, and on conviction thereof shall be confined in the State penitentiary for life; and those shall be deemed freedmen, free negroes and mulattoes who are of pure negro blood, and those descended from a negro to the third generation, inclusive, though one ancestor in each generation may have been a white person.

Section 4. In addition to cases in which freedmen, free negroes and mulattoes are now by law competent witnesses, freedmen, free negroes or mulattoes shall be competent in civil cases, when a party or parties to the suit, either plaintiff or plaintiffs, defendant or defendants; also in cases where freedmen, free negroes and mulattoes is or are either plaintiff or plaintiffs, defendant or defendants. They shall also be competent witnesses in all criminal prosecutions where the crime charged is alleged to have been committed by a white person upon or against the person or property of a freedman, free negro or mulatto: Provided, that in all cases said witnesses shall be examined in open court, on the stand; except, however, they may be examined before the grand jury, and shall in all cases be subject to the rules and tests of the common law as to competency and credibility.

Section 5. Every freedman, free negro and mulatto shall, on the second Monday of January, one thousand eight hundred and sixty-six, and annually thereafter, have a lawful home or employment, and shall have written evidence thereof as follows, to wit: if living in any incorporated city, town, or village, a license from the mayor thereof; and if living outside of an incorporated city, town, or village, from the member of the board of police of his beat, authorizing him or her to do irregular and job work; or a written contract, as provided in Section 6 in this act; which license may be revoked for cause at any time by the authority granting the same.

Section 6. All contracts for labor made with freedmen, free negroes and mulattoes for a longer period than one month shall be in writing, and a duplicate, attested and read to said freedman, free negro or mulatto by a beat, city or county officer, or two disinterested white persons of the county in which the labor is to be performed, of which each party shall have one: and said contracts shall be taken and held as entire contracts, and if the laborer shall quit the service of the employer before the expiration of his term of service, without good cause, he shall forfeit his wages for that year up to the time of quitting.

Section 7. Every civil officer shall, and every person may, arrest and carry back to his or her legal employer any freedman, free negro, or mulatto who shall have quit the service of his or her employer before the expiration of his or her term of service without good cause; and said officer and person shall be entitled to receive for arresting and carrying back every deserting employee aforesaid the sum of five dollars, and ten cents per mile from the place of arrest to the place of delivery; and the same shall be paid by the employer, and held as a set off for so much against the wages of said deserting employee: Provided, that said arrested party, after being so returned, may appeal to the justice of the peace or member of the board of police of the county, who, on notice to the alleged employer, shall try summarily whether said appellant is legally employed by the alleged employer, and has good cause to quit said employer. Either party shall have the right of appeal to the county court, pending which the alleged deserter shall be remanded to the alleged employer or otherwise disposed of, as shall be right and just; and the decision of the county court shall be final.

Section 8. Upon affidavit made by the employer of any freedman, free negro or mulatto, or other credible person, before any justice of the peace or member of the board of police, that any freedman, free negro or mulatto legally employed by said employer has illegally deserted said employment, such justice of the peace or member of the board of police issue his warrant or warrants, returnable before himself or other such officer, to any sheriff, constable or special deputy, commanding him to arrest said deserter, and return him or her to said employer, and the like proceedings shall be had as provided in the preceding section; and it shall be lawful for any officer to whom such warrant shall be directed to execute said warrant in any county in this State; and that said warrant may be transmitted without endorsement to any like officer of another county, to be executed and returned as aforesaid; and the said employer shall pay the costs of said warrants and arrest and return, which shall be set off for so much against the wages of said deserter.

Section 9. If any person shall persuade or attempt to persuade, entice, or cause any freedman, free negro or mulatto to desert from the legal employment of any person before the expiration of his or her term of service, or shall knowingly employ any such deserting freedman, free negro or mulatto, or shall knowingly give or sell to any such deserting freedman, free negro or mulatto, any food, raiment, or other thing, he or she shall be guilty of a misdemeanor, and, upon conviction, shall be fined not less than twenty-five dollars and not more than two hundred dollars and costs; and if the said fine and costs shall not be immediately paid, the court shall sentence said convict to not exceeding two months imprisonment in the county jail, and he or she shall moreover be liable to the party injured in damages: Provided, if any person shall, or shall attempt to, persuade, entice, or cause any freedman, free negro or mulatto to desert from any legal employment of any person, with the view to employ said freedman, free negro or mulatto without the limits of this State, such costs; and if said fine and costs shall not be immediately paid, the court shall sentence said convict to not exceeding six months imprisonment in the county jail.

Section 10. It shall be lawful for any freedman, free negro, or mulatto, to charge any white person, freedman, free negro or mulatto by affidavit, with any criminal offense against his or her person or property, and upon such affidavit the proper process shall be issued and executed as if said affidavit was made by a white person, and it shall be lawful for any freedman, free negro, or mulatto, in any action, suit or controversy pending, or about to be instituted in any court of law equity in this State, to make all needful and lawful affidavits as shall be necessary for the institution, prosecution or defense of such suit or controversy.

Section 11. The penal laws of this state, in all cases not otherwise specially provided for, shall apply and extend to all freedmen, free negroes and mulattoes. . . .

AN ACT TO REGULATE THE RELATION OF MASTER AND APPRENTICE, AS RELATES TO FREEDMEN, FREE NEGROES, AND MULATTOES

Section 1. It shall be the duty of all sheriffs, justices of the peace, and other civil officers of the several counties in this State, to report to the probate courts of their respective counties semiannually, at the January and July terms of said courts, all freedmen, free negroes, and mulattoes, under the age of eighteen, in their respective counties, beats, or districts, who are orphans, or whose parent or parents have not the means or who refuse to provide for and support said minors; and thereupon it shall be the duty of said probate court to order the clerk of said court to apprentice said minors to some competent and suitable person on such terms as the court may direct, having a particular care to the interest of said minor: Provided, that the former owner of said minors shall have the preference when, in the opinion of the court, he or she shall be a suitable person for that purpose.

Section 2. The said court shall be fully satisfied that the person or persons to whom said minor shall be apprenticed shall be a suitable person to have the charge and care of said minor, and fully to protect the interest of said minor. The said court shall require the said master or mistress to execute bond and security, payable to the State of Mississippi, conditioned that he or she shall furnish said minor with sufficient food and clothing; to treat said minor humanely; furnish medical attention in case of sickness; teach, or cause to be taught, him or her to read and write, if under fifteen years old, and will conform to any law that may be hereafter passed for the regulation of the duties and relation of master and apprentice: Provided, that said apprentice shall be bound by indenture, in case of males, until they are twenty-one years old, and in case of females until they are eighteen years old.

Section 3. In the management and control of said apprentices, said master or mistress shall have the power to inflict such moderate corporeal chastisement as a father or guardian is allowed to infliction on his or her child or ward at common law: Provided, that in no case shall cruel or inhuman punishment be inflicted.

Section 4. If any apprentice shall leave the employment of his or her master or mistress, without his or her consent, said master or mistress may pursue and recapture said apprentice, and bring him or her before any justice of the peace of the county, whose duty it shall be to remand said apprentice to the service of his or her master or mistress; and in the event of a refusal on the part of said apprentice so to return, then said justice shall commit said apprentice to the jail of said county, on failure to give bond, to the next term of the county court; and it shall be the duty of said court at the first term thereafter to investigate said case, and if the court shall be of opinion that said apprentice left the employment of his or her master or mistress without good cause, to order him or her to be punished, as provided for the punishment of hired freedmen, as may be from time to time provided for by law for desertion, until he or she shall agree to return to the service of his or her master or mistress: Provided, that the court may grant continuances as in other cases: And provided further, that if the court shall believe that said apprentice had good cause to quit his said master or mistress, the court shall discharge said apprentice from said indenture, and also enter a judgment against the master or mistress for not more than one hundred dollars, for the use and benefit of said apprentice, to be collected on execution as in other cases.

Section 5. If any person entice away any apprentice from his or her master or mistress, or shall knowingly employ an apprentice, or furnish him or her food or clothing without the written consent of his or her master or mistress, or shall sell or give said apprentice spirits without such consent, said person so offending shall be guilty of a misdemeanor, and shall, upon conviction there of before the county court, be punished as provided for the punishment of persons enticing from their employer hired freedmen, free negroes or mulattoes.

Section 6. It shall be the duty of all civil officers of their respective counties to report any minors within their respective counties to said probate court who are subject to be apprenticed under the provisions of this act, from time to time as the facts may come to their knowledge, and it shall be the duty of said court from time to time as said minors shall be reported to them, or otherwise come to their knowledge, to apprentice said minors as hereinbefore provided.

Section 9. It shall be lawful for any freedman, free negro, or mulatto, having a minor child or children, to apprentice the said minor child or children, as provided for by this act.

Section 10. In all cases where the age of the freedman, free negro, or mulatto cannot be ascertained by record testimony, the judge of the county court shall fix the age. . . .

AN ACT TO AMEND THE VAGRANT LAWS OF THE STATE

Section 1. All rogues and vagabonds, idle and dissipated persons, beggars, jugglers, or persons practicing unlawful games or plays, runaways, common drunkards, common night-walkers, pilferers, lewd, wanton, or lascivious persons, in speech or behavior, common railers and brawlers, persons who neglect their calling or employment, misspend what they earn, or do not provide for the support of themselves or their families, or dependents, and all other idle and disorderly persons, including all who neglect all lawful business, habitually misspend their time by frequenting houses of ill-fame, gaming-houses, or tippling shops, shall be deemed and considered vagrants, under the provisions of this act, and upon conviction thereof shall be fined not exceeding one hundred dollars, with all accruing costs, and be imprisoned, at the discretion of the court, not exceeding ten days.

Section 2. All freedmen, free negroes and mulattoes in this State, over the age of eighteen years, found on the second Monday in January, 1866, or thereafter, with no lawful employment or business, or found unlawfully assembling themselves together, either in the day or night time, and all white persons assembling themselves with freedmen, free negroes or mulattoes, or usually associating with freedmen, free negroes or mulattoes, on terms of equality, or living in adultery or fornication with a freed woman, freed negro or mulatto, shall be deemed vagrants, and on conviction thereof shall be fined in a sum not exceeding, in the case of a freedman, free negro or mulatto, fifty dollars, and a white man two hundred dollars, and imprisonment at the discretion of the court, the free negro not exceeding ten days, and the white man not exceeding six months.

Section 3. All justices of the peace, mayors, and aldermen of incorporated towns, counties, and cities of the several counties in this State shall have jurisdiction to try all questions of vagrancy in their respective towns, counties, and cities, and it is hereby made their duty, whenever they shall ascertain that any person or persons in their respective towns, and counties and cities are violating any of the provisions of this act, to have said party or parties arrested, and brought before them, and immediately investigate said charge, and, on conviction, punish said party or parties, as provided for herein. And it is hereby made the duty of all sheriffs, constables, town constables, and all such like officers, and city marshals, to report to some officer having jurisdiction all violations of any of the provisions of this act, and in case any officer shall fail or neglect any duty herein it shall be the duty of the county court to fine said officer, upon conviction, not exceeding one hundred dollars, to be paid into the county treasury for county purposes.

Section 4. Keepers of gaming houses, houses of prostitution, prostitutes, public or private, and all persons who derive their chief support in the employments that militate against good morals, or against law, shall be deemed and held to be vagrants.

Section 5. All fines and forfeitures collected by the provisions of this act shall be paid into the county treasury for general county purposes, and in case of any freedman, free negro or mulatto shall fail for five days after the imposition of any or forfeiture upon him or her for violation of any of the provisions of this act to pay the same, that it shall be, and is hereby, made the duty of the sheriff of the proper county to hire out said freedman, free negro or mulatto, to any person who will, for the shortest period of service, pay said fine and forfeiture and all costs: Provided, a preference shall be given to the employer, if there be one, in which case the employer shall be entitled to deduct and retain the amount so paid from the wages of such freedman, free negro or mulatto, then due or to become due; and in case freedman, free negro or mulatto cannot hire out, he or she may be dealt with as a pauper.

Section 6. The same duties and liabilities existing among white persons of this State shall attach to freedmen, free negroes or mulattoes, to support their indigent families and all colored paupers; and that in order to secure a support for such indigent freedmen, free negroes, or mulattoes, it shall be lawful, and is hereby made the duty of the county police of each county in this State, to levy a poll or capitation tax on each and every freedman, free negro, or mulatto, between the ages of eighteen and sixty years, not to exceed the sum of one dollar annually to each person so taxed, which tax, when collected, shall be paid into the county treasurer's hands, and constitute a fund to be called the Freedman's Pauper Fund, which shall be applied by the commissioners of the poor for the maintenance of the poor of the freedmen, free negroes and mulattoes of this State, under such regulations as may be established by the boards of county police in the respective counties of this State.

Section 7. If any freedman, free negro, or mulatto shall fail or refuse to pay any tax levied according to the provisions of the sixth section of this act, it shall be *prima facie* evidence of vagrancy, and it shall be the duty of the sheriff to arrest such freedman, free negro, or mulatto, or such person refusing or neglecting to pay such tax, and proceed at once to hire for the shortest time such delinquent taxpayer to any one who will pay the said tax, with accruing costs, giving preference to the employer, if there be one.

Section 8. Any person feeling himself or herself aggrieved by judgment of any justice of the peace, mayor, or alderman in cases arising under this act, may within five days appeal to the next term of the county court of the proper county, upon giving bond and security in a sum not less than twenty-five dollars nor more than one hundred and fifty dollars, conditioned to appear and prosecute said appeal, and abide by the judgment of the county court; and said appeal shall be tried *de novo* in the county court, and the decision of the said court shall be final. ...

CIVIL RIGHTS ACT CH. 31, 14 STAT. 27 (1866)

This act, enacted April 9, 1866, was designed to protect recently freed African Americans from black codes and other repressive state and local legislation. It was intended to provide all citizens with basic civil rights, including the right to make and enforce contracts, to bring suits in court, to purchase and sell real and personal property, and to enjoy security of person and property.

An Act to protect all Persons in the United States in their Civil Rights, and furnish the Means of their Vindication

Be it enacted ... That all persons born in the United States and not subject to any foreign power, excluding Indians not taxed, are hereby declared to be citizens of the United States; and such citizens, of every race and color, without regard to any previous condition of slavery or involuntary servitude, except as a punishment for crime whereof the party shall have been duly convicted, shall have the same right in every State and Territory in the United States, to make and enforce contracts, to sue, be parties, and give evidence, to inherit, purchase, lease, sell, hold, and convey real and personal property, and to full and equal benefit of all laws and proceedings for the security of person and property, as is enjoyed by white citizens, and shall be subject to like punishment, pains, and penalties, and to none other, any law, statute, ordinance, regulation, or custom, to the contrary notwithstanding.

Section 2. *And be it further enacted,* That any person who, under color or any law, statute, ordinance, regulation, or custom, shall subject, or cause to be subjected, any inhabitant of any State or Territory to the deprivation of any right secured or protected by this act, or to different punishment, pains, or penalties on account of such person having at any time been held in a condition of slavery or involuntary servitude, except as a punishment for crime whereof the party shall have been duly convicted, or by reason of his color or race, than is prescribed for the punishment of white persons, shall be deemed guilty of a misdemeanor, and, on conviction, shall be punished by fine not exceeding one thousand dollars, or imprisonment not exceeding one year, or both, in the discretion of the court. ...

AMENDMENT FOURTEEN TO THE UNITED STATES CONSTITUTION (1868)

This amendment, ratified July 23, 1868, provided a definition of both national and state citizenship. When the Supreme Court heard the case Dred Scott v. Sandford *in 1857, it ruled that Africans imported into this country as slaves, and their descendants, were not and could never become citizens of the United States. The passage of the Fourteenth Amendment resolved the question of African American citizenship.*

The amendment also reversed what had been the traditional federal-state relationship in the area of citizens' rights. The Fourteenth Amendment provides for the protection of the privileges of national citizenship and basic civil rights, and guarantees for all citizens equal protection under the law. It also provides the federal government with authority to intervene in cases where state governments have been accused of violating the constitutional rights of individuals.

Section 1. All persons born or naturalized in the United States, and subject to the jurisdiction thereof, are citizens of the United States and of the State wherein they reside. No state shall make or enforce any law which shall abridge the privileges or immunities of citizens of the United States; nor shall any State deprive any person of life, liberty, or property, without due process of law; nor deny to any person within its jurisdiction the equal protection of the laws.

Section 2. Representatives shall be apportioned among the several States according to their respective numbers, counting the whole number of persons in each State, excluding Indians not taxed. But when the right to vote at any election for the choice of electors for President and Vice President of the United States, Representatives in Congress, the Executive and Judicial officers of a State, or the members of the Legislature thereof, is denied to any of the male inhabitants of such State, being twenty-one years of age, and citizens of the United States, or in any way abridged, except for participation in rebellion, or other crime, the basis of representation therein shall be reduced in the proportion which the number of such male citizens shall bear to the whole number of male citizens twenty-one years of age in such State.

Section 3. No person shall be a Senator or Representative in Congress, or elector of President and Vice President, or hold any office, civil or military, under the United States, or under any State, who, having previously taken an oath, as a member of Congress, or as an office of the United States, or as a member of any State legislature, or as an executive or judicial officer of any State, to support the Constitution of the United States, shall have engaged in insurrection or rebellion against the same, or given aid or comfort to the enemies thereof. But Congress may by a vote of two-thirds of each House, remove such disability.

Section 4. The validity of the public debt of the United States, authorized by law, including debts incurred for payment of pensions and bounties for services in suppressing insurrection or rebellion, shall not be questioned. But neither the United States nor any State shall assume or pay any debt or obligation incurred in aid of insurrection or rebellion against the United States, or any claim for the loss or emancipation of any slave; but all such debts, obligations and claims shall be held illegal and void.

Section 5. The Congress shall have power to enforce, by appropriate legislation, the provisions of this article.

AMENDMENT FIFTEEN TO THE UNITED STATES CONSTITUTION (1870)

The Fifteenth Amendment, ratified March 30, 1870, was intended to protect the right of all citizens to vote. However, the amendment was not successful in ending techniques designed to prevent African Americans from voting; many state and local governments continued to employ such tactics

Lithograph Titled "The Fifteenth Amendment and Its Results" (c. 1870). *This lithograph depicts the supposedly foreseeable results of the passage of the Fifteenth Amendment, which was intended to protect the right of all citizens to vote. In spite of this amendment, however, many state and local governments continued to use a variety of tactics as prerequisites or deterrents to voting.* CORBIS

as grandfather clauses, literacy tests, "white primaries," and poll taxes as prerequisites or deterrents to voting.

Section 1. The right of citizens of the United States to vote shall not be denied or abridged by the United States or by any State on account of race, color, or previous conditions of servitude.

Section 2. The Congress shall have power to enforce this article by appropriate legislation.

KU KLUX KLAN ACT CH. 22, 17 STAT. 13 (1871)

Following the Civil War, white terrorist groups began to spring up throughout the South. These early organizations, consisting mainly of Confederate veterans still obsessed with the goals and aspirations of their southern heritage, terrorized blacks who sought increased participation in their communities and whites who aided them. Known as the Knights of the White Camelia, the Jayhawkers, or the Ku Klux Klan, by 1871 these groups had become well organized. The Ku Klux Klan Act of 1871 was an attempt by Congress to end intimidation and violence by such organizations. The law, however, failed to eradicate the Klan or to eliminate the continued use of terrorist tactics against blacks and those whites who gave support to black concerns.

Be it enacted ... that any person who, under color of any law, statute, ordinance, regulation, custom, or usage of any State, shall subject, or cause to be subjected, any person within the jurisdiction of the United States to the deprivation of any rights, privileges, or immunities secured by the Constitution of the United States; shall any such law, statute, ordinance, regulation, custom, or usage of the state to the contrary notwithstanding, be liable to the party injured in any action at law, suit in equity, or other proper proceeding for redress; such proceeding to be prosecuted in the several district or circuit courts of the United States, with and subject to the same rights of appeal, review upon error, and other remedies provided in like cases in such courts, under the provisions of the [Civil Rights Act of April 9, 1866] ... and the other remedial laws of the United States which are in their nature applicable in such cases.

Section 2. That if two or more persons within any State or Territory of the United States shall conspire together to overthrow, or to put down, or to destroy by force the government of the United States, or to levy war against the United States or to oppose by force the authority of the government of the United States, or by force, intimidation, or threat to prevent ... any person from accepting or holding any office or trust or place of confidence under the United States, or from discharging the duties thereof ... or to injure him in his person or property on account of his lawful discharge of the duties of his office, or to injure his person while engaged in the lawful discharge of the duties of his office, or ... to deter any party or witness in any court of the United States from attending such court, or from testifying in any matter pending in such court fully, freely, and truthfully, or to injure any party or witness in his person or property on account of his having so attended or testified, or by force, intimidation, or threat to influence the verdict, presentment, or indictment, of any juror or grand juror in any court of the United States, or to injure such juror in his person or property on account of any verdict, presentment, or indictment lawfully assented to by him, or on account of his being or having been such juror, or shall conspire together, or go in disguise upon the public highway or upon the premises of another for the purpose, either directly or indirectly, of depriving any person or any class of persons of the equal protection of the laws, or of equal privileges or immunities under the laws, or for the purpose of preventing or hindering the constituted authorities of any State from giving or securing to all persons within such State the equal protection of the laws, or shall conspire together for the purpose of in any manner impeding, hindering, obstructing, or defeating the due course of justice in any State or Territory, with the intent to deny to any citizen of the United States the due and equal protection of the laws, or to injure any person in his person or in his property for lawfully enforcing the right of any person or class of persons to the equal protection of the laws, or by force, intimidation, or threat to prevent any citizen of the United States lawfully entitled to vote from giving his support or advocacy in a lawful manner ... or to injure any such citizen in his person or property on account of such support or advocacy, each and every person so offending shall be deemed guilty of a high crime. ...

Section 3. That in all cases where insurrection, domestic violence, unlawful combinations, or conspiracies in any State shall so obstruct or hinder the execution of the laws thereof, and of the United States, as to deprive any portion or class of the people of such State of any of the rights, privileges, or immunities, or protection, named in the Constitution and secured by this act, and the constituted authorities of such State shall either be unable to protect, or shall from any cause fail in or refuse protection of the people in such rights, such facts will be deemed a denial by such State of the equal protection of the laws to which they are entitled under the Constitution of the United States; and in all such cases, or whenever any such insurrection, violence, unlawful combination, or conspiracy shall oppose or obstruct the laws of the United States or the due execution thereof, or impede or obstruct the due course of justice under the same, it shall be lawful for the President, and it shall be his duty to take such measures, by the employment of the militia or the land and naval forces of the United States, or either, or by other means, as he may deem necessary for the suppression of such insurrection, domestic violence, or combinations; and any person who shall be arrested under the provisions of this and the preceding section shall be delivered to the marshal of the proper district, to be dealt with according to law.

Section 4. That whenever in any State or part of a State the unlawful combinations named in the preceding section of this act shall be organized and armed, and so numerous and powerful as to be able, by violence, to either overthrow or set at defiance the constituted authorities of such State, and of the United States within such State, or when the constituted authorities are in complicity with, or shall connive at the unlawful purpose of, such powerful and armed combinations; and whenever, by reason of either or all of the causes aforesaid, the conviction of such offender and the preservation of the public safety shall become in such district impracticable, in every such case such combinations shall be deemed a rebellion against the government of the United States, and during the continuation of such rebellion, and within the limits of the district which shall be so under the sway thereof, such limits to be prescribed by proclamation, it shall be lawful for the President of the United States, when in his judgment the public safety shall require it, to suspend the privileges of the writ of habeas corpus, to the end that such rebellion may be overthrown. ...

Section 6. That any person, or persons, having knowledge that any of the wrongs conspired to be done and mentioned in the second section of this act are about to be committed, and having power to prevent or aid in preventing the same, shall neglect or refuse so to do, and such wrongful act shall be committed, such person or persons shall be liable to the person injured, or his legal representatives, for all damages caused by any such wrongful act which such first-named person or persons by reasonable diligence could have prevented; and such damages may be recovered in an action on the case in the proper circuit court of the United States, and any number of persons guilty of such wrongful neglect or refusal may be joined as defendants in such action. ...

CIVIL RIGHTS ACT OF 1875 CH. 114, 18 STAT. 335 (1875)

The Civil Rights Act of 1875 concerned itself primarily with the prohibition of racial discrimination in places of public accommodation. Eight years later, however, the U.S. Supreme Court addressed the issue. Ruling in a set of disputes that came to be known as the Civil Rights Cases, the Court declared the law unconstitutional, stating that Congress did not have the authority to regulate the prevalent social mores of any state.

An Act to Protect All Citizens in Their Civil and Legal Rights.

Whereas it is essential to just governments we recognize the equality of all men before the law, and hold that it is the duty of government in its dealings with the people to mete out equal and exact justice to all, of whatever nativity, race, color, or persuasion, religious or political; and it being the appropriate object of legislation to enact great fundamental principles into law: Therefore, *Be it enacted,* That all persons within the jurisdiction of the United States shall be entitled to the full and equal enjoyment of the accommodations, advantages, facilities, and privileges of inns, public conveyances on land or water, theaters, and other places of public amusement; subject only to the conditions and limitations established by law, and applicable alike to citizens of every race and color, regardless of any previous condition of servitude.

Section 2. That any person who shall violate the foregoing section by denying to any citizen, except for reasons by law applicable to citizens of every race and color, and regardless of any previous condition of servitude, the full enjoyment of any of the accommodations, advantages, facilities, or privileges in said section enumerated, or by aiding or inciting such denial, shall, for every such offense, forfeit and pay the sum of five hundred dollars to the person aggrieved thereby ... and shall also, for every such offense, be deemed guilty of a misdemeanor, and upon conviction thereof, shall be fined not less than five hundred nor more than one thousand dollars, or shall be imprisoned not less than thirty days nor more than one year. ...

Section 4. That no citizen possessing all other qualifications which are or may be prescribed by law shall be disqualified for service as grand or petit juror in any court of the United States, or of any State, on account of race, color, or previous condition of servitude; and any officer or other person charged with any duty in the selection or summoning of jurors who shall exclude or fail to summon any citizen for the cause aforesaid shall, on conviction thereof, be deemed guilty of a misdemeanor, and be fined not more than five thousand dollars.

Section 5. That all cases arising under the provisions of this act ... shall be renewable by the Supreme Court of the U.S., without regard to the sum in controversy. ...

FREDERICK DOUGLASS'S SPEECH ON WOMAN SUFFRAGE (1888) (EXCERPT)

In July 1848, Frederick Douglass was one of the few men present at the initial women's rights convention at Seneca Falls, New York, and it was he who encouraged outspoken feminist Elizabeth Cady Stanton to press for suffrage and who seconded the resolution proposed by Stanton that it was "the duty of the women of this country to secure to themselves their sacred right to the elective franchise." However, in later years, Douglass split ranks with Stanton and Anthony over philosophical differences regarding the Fifteenth Amendment and other matters. Yet, Douglass remained a staunch advocate for the right of women to vote.

In April 1888, Douglass gave a speech before the International Council of Women in Washington, D.C. In his message to the conventioneers, Douglass reflected on his role at the Seneca Falls convention and strongly endorsed woman suffrage. Douglass also insisted that it is women, not men, who should be the primary spokespersons for the suffrage cause. The text of Douglass's address appeared in the Woman's Journal *on April 14, 1888.*

Mrs. President, Ladies and Gentlemen:—I come to this platform with unusual diffidence. Although I have long been identified with the Woman's Suffrage movement, and have often spoken in its favor, I am somewhat at a loss to know what to say on this really great and uncommon occasion, where so much has been said.

When I look around on this assembly, and see the many able and eloquent women, full of the subject, ready to speak, and who only need the opportunity to impress this audience with their views and thrill them with "thoughts that berate and words that burn," I do not feel like taking up more than a very small space of your time and attention, and shall not. I would not, even now, presume to speak, but for the circumstances of my early connection with the cause, and of having been called upon to do so by one whose voice in this Council we all gladly obey. Men have very little business here as speakers, anyhow; and if they come here at all they should take back benches and wrap themselves in silence. For this is an International Council, not of men, but of women, and woman should have all the say in it. This is her day in court.

I do not mean to exalt the intellect of woman above man's; but I have heard many men speak on this subject; some of them the most eloquent to be found anywhere in the country; and I believe no man, however gifted with thought and speech, can voice the wrongs and present the demands of women with the skill and effect, with the power and authority of woman herself. The man struck is the man to cry out. Woman knows and feels her wrongs as man cannot know and feel them, and she also knows as well as he can know, what measures are needed to redress them. I grant all the claims at this point. She is her own best representative. We can neither speak for her, nor vote for her, nor act for her, nor be responsible for her; and the thing for men to do in the premises is just to get out of her way and give her the fullest opportunity to exercise all the powers inherent in her individual personality, and allow her to do it as she herself shall elect to exercise them. Her right to be and to do is as full, complete and perfect as the right of any man on earth. I say of her, as I say of the colored people, "Give her fair play, and hands off."

There is to-day, however, a special reason for omitting argument. This is the end of the fourth decade of the woman suffrage movement, a kind of jubilee which naturally turns our minds to the past.

The history of the world has given to us many sublime undertakings, but none more sublime than this. It was a great thing for the friends of peace to organize in opposition to war; it was a great thing for the friends of temperance to organize against intemperance; it was a great thing for humane people to organize in opposition to slavery; but it was a much greater thing, in view of all the circumstances, for woman to organize herself in opposition to her exclusion from participation in government. ... Men took for granted all that could be said against intemperance, war and slavery. But no such advantage was found in the beginning of the cause of suffrage for women. On the contrary, everything in her condition was supposed to be lovely, just as it should be. She had no rights denied, no wrongs to redress. She herself had no suspicion but that all was going well with her.

There are few facts in my humble history to which I look back with more satisfaction than to the fact, recorded in the history of the woman-suffrage movement, that I was sufficiently enlightened at that early day, and when only a few years from slavery, to support your resolution for woman suffrage. I have done very little in this world in which to glory except this one act—and I certainly glory in that. When I ran away from slavery, it was for myself; when I advocated emancipation, it was for my people, but when I stood up for the rights of woman, self was out of the question, and I found a little nobility in the act.

In estimating the forces with which this suffrage cause has had to contend during these forty years, the fact should be remembered that relations of long standing beget a character in the parties to them in the favor of the continuance.

The relation of man to woman has the advantage of all the ages behind it. Those who oppose a readjustment of this relation tell us that what is always was and always will be, world without end. But we have heard this old argument before, and if we live very long we shall hear it again. When any aged error shall be assailed, and any old abuse is to be removed, we shall meet this same old argument. Man has been so long the king and woman the subject—man has been so long accustomed to command and woman to obey—that both parties to the relation have been hardened into their respective places, and thus has been piled up a mountain of iron against woman's enfranchisement.

The universality of man's rule over woman is another factor in resistance to the woman-suffrage movement. We are pointed to the fact that men have not only always ruled over women, but that they do so rule everywhere, and they easily think that thing that is done everywhere must be right. Though the fallacy of this reasoning is too transparent to need refutation, it still exerts a powerful influence.

All good causes are mutually helpful. The benefits accruing from this movement for the equal rights of woman are not confined or limited to woman only. They will be shared by every effort to promote the progress and welfare of mankind everywhere and in all ages.

IDA B. WELLS-BARNETT'S SPEECH ON THE LYNCH LAW IN ALL ITS PHASES (1893) (EXCERPT)

Ida B. Wells-Barnett began organizing and lecturing in support of an international campaign against lynching after a mob destroyed the offices of her newspaper the Memphis Free Speech *on May 27, 1892. In both her speeches and writings, she used graphic, detailed descriptions of certain lynchings and scrutinized the media accounts through which her audiences were most likely to have heard of them. In her speech in Boston's Tremont Temple on February 13, 1893, Wells-Barnett again speaks out against lynchings and suggests a remedy for ending the heinous practice.*

The race problem or negro question, as it has been called, has been omnipresent and all-pervading since long before the Afro-American was raised from the degradation of the slave to the dignity of the citizen. It has never been settled because the right methods have not been employed in the solution.... The operations of law do not dispose of negroes fast enough, and lynching bees have become the favorite pastime of the South. As excuse for the same, a new cry, as false as it is foul, is raised in an effort to blast race character, a cry which has proclaimed to the world that virtue and innocence are violated by Afro-Americans who must be killed like wild beasts to protect womanhood and childhood.

In the past ten years over a thousand colored men, women and children have been butchered, murdered and burnt in all parts of the South. The details of these horrible outrages seldom reach beyond the narrow world where they occur. Those who commit the murders write the reports, and hence these lasting blots upon the honor of a nation cause but a faint ripple on the outside world. They arouse no great indignation and call forth no adequate demand for justice. The victims were black, and the reports are so written as to make it appear that the helpless creatures deserved the fate which overtook them.

Persons unfamiliar with the condition of affairs in the Southern States do not credit the truth when it is told to them. They cannot conceive how such a condition of affairs prevails so near them with steam power, telegraph wires and printing presses in daily and hourly touch with the localities where such disorder reigns.

The right of the Afro-American to vote and hold office remains in the Federal Constitution, but is destroyed in the constitution of the Southern states. Having destroyed the citizenship of the man, they are now trying to destroy the manhood of the citizen. All their laws are shaped to this end;—school laws, railroad car regulations, those governing labor liens on crops,—every device is adopted to make slaves of free men and rob them of their wages. Whenever a malicious law is violated in any of its parts, any farmer, any railroad conductor, or merchant can call together a posse of his neighbors and punish even with death the black man who resists and the legal authorities sanction what is done by failing to prosecute and punish the murders. The Repeal of the Civil Rights Law removed their last barrier and the black man's last bulwark and refuge. The rule of the mob is absolute.

Those who know this recital to be true, say there is nothing they can do—they cannot interfere and vainly hope by further concession to placate the imperious and dominating part of our country in which this lawlessness prevails. Because this country has been almost rent in twain by internal dissension, the other sections seem virtually to have agreed that the best way to heal the breach is to permit the taking away of civil, political, and even human rights, to stand by in silence and utter indifference while the South continues to wreak fiendish vengeance on the irresponsible cause. They pretend to believe that with all the machinery of law and government in its hands; with the jails and penitentiaries and convict farms filled with pretty race criminals; with the well-known fact that no negro has ever been known to escape conviction and punishment for any crime in the South—still there are those who try to justify and condone the lynching of over a thousand black men in less than ten years—an average of one hundred a year. The public sentiment of the country, by its silence in press, pulpit and in public meetings has encouraged this state of affairs, and public sentiment is stronger than law.

Do you ask the remedy? A public sentiment strong against lawlessness must be aroused. Every individual can contribute to this awakening. When a sentiment against lynch law as strong, deep and mighty as that roused against slavery prevails, I have no fear of the result. It should be already established as a fact and not as a theory, that every human being must have a fair trial for his life and liberty, no matter what the charge against him. When a demand goes up from fearless and persistent reformers from press and pulpit, from industrial and moral associations that this shall be so from Maine to Texas and from ocean to ocean, a way will be found to make it so.

BOOKER T. WASHINGTON'S "ATLANTA COMPROMISE" SPEECH (1895)

Booker T. Washington, a major voice in the movement for the advancement of African Americans, was often criticized for encouraging blacks to cultivate peaceful coexistence with whites. Washington advocated the use of technical and industrial self-help programs—even if such programs tended to discount the importance of the cultivation of intellectual and aesthetic values. In an address to the 1895 Atlanta Exposition, Washington outlined his philosophy.

Mr. President and Gentlemen of the Board of Directors and Citizens:

One-third of the population of the South is of the Negro race. No enterprise seeking the material, civil, or moral welfare of this section can disregard this element of our population and reach the highest success. I but convey to you, Mr. President and Directors, the sentiment of the masses of my race when I say that in no way have the value and manhood of the American Negro been more fittingly and generously recognized than by the managers of this magnificent Exposition at every stage of its progress. It is a recognition that will do more to cement the friendship of the two races than any occurrence since the dawn of our freedom.

Not only this, but the opportunity here afforded will awaken among us a new era of industrial progress. Ignorant and inexperienced, it is not strange that in the first years of our new life we began at the top instead of at the bottom; that a seat in Congress or the State Legislature was more sought than real estate or industrial skill; that the political convention or stump speaking had more attractions than starting a dairy farm or truck garden.

A ship lost at sea for many days suddenly sighted a friendly vessel. From the mast of the unfortunate vessel was seen a signal: "Water, water; we die of thirst!" The answer from the friendly vessel at once came back: "Cast down your bucket where you are." A second time the signal, "Water, water; send us water!" ran up from the distressed vessel, and was answered: "Cast down your bucket where you are." And a third and fourth signal for water was answered: "Cast down your bucket where you are." The captain of the distressed vessel, at last heeding the injunction, cast down his bucket, and it came up full of fresh, sparkling water from the mouth of the Amazon River. To those of my race who depend on bettering their condition in a foreign land, or who underestimate the importance of cultivating friendly relations with the Southern white man, who is their next door neighbor, I would say: "Cast down your bucket where you are"—cast it down in making friends in every manly way of the people of all races by whom we are surrounded.

Cast it down in agriculture, mechanics, in commerce, in domestic service, and in the professions. And in this connection it is well to bear in mind that whatever other sins the South may be called to bear, when it comes to business, pure and simple, it is in the South that the Negro is given a man's chance in the commercial world, and in nothing is this Exposition more eloquent than in emphasizing this chance. Our greatest danger is, that in the great leap from slavery to freedom we may overlook the fact that the masses of us are to live by the productions of our hands, and fail to keep in mind that we shall prosper in proportion as we learn to dignify and glorify common labor, and put brains and skill into the common occupations of life; shall prosper in proportion as we learn to draw the line between the superficial and the substantial, the ornamental gewgaws of life and the useful. No race can prosper till it learns that there is as much dignity in tilling a field as in writing a poem. It is at the bottom of life we must begin, and not at the top. Nor should we permit our grievances to overshadow our opportunities.

To those of the white race who look to the incoming of those of foreign birth and strange tongue and habits for the prosperity of the South, were I permitted, I would repeat what I say to my own race, "Cast down your bucket where you are." Cast it down among the 8,000,000 Negroes whose habits you know, whose fidelity and love you have tested in days when to have proved treacherous meant the ruin of your firesides. Cast down your bucket among those people who have, without strikes and labor wars, tilled your fields, cleared your forests, builded your railroads and cities, and brought forth treasures from the bowels of the earth, and helped make possible this magnificent representation of the progress of the South. Casting down your bucket among my people, helping and encouraging them as you are doing on these grounds, and, with education of head, hand and heart, you will find that they will buy your surplus land, make blossom the waste place in your fields, and run your factories. While doing this, you can be sure in the future, as in the past, that you and your families will be surrounded by the most patient, faithful, law-abiding, and unresentful people that the world has seen. As we have proved our loyalty to you in the past, in nursing your children, watching by the sick bed of your mothers and fathers, and often following them with tear-dimmed eyes to their graves, so in the future, in our humble way, we shall stand by you with a devotion that no foreigner can approach, ready to lay down our lives, if need be, in defense of yours, interlacing our industrial, commercial, civil, and religious life with yours in a way that shall make the interests of both races one. In all things that are purely social we can be as separate as the fingers, yet one as the hand in all things essential to mutual progress.

There is no defense or security for any of us except in the highest intelligence and development of all. If anywhere there are efforts tending to curtail the fullest growth of the Negro, let these efforts be turned into stimulating, encouraging, and making him the most useful and intelligent citizen. Effort or means so invested will pay a thousand percent interest. These efforts will be twice blessed—"blessing him that gives and him that takes."

There is no escape through law of man or God from the inevitable:

> The laws of changeless justice bind Oppressor with oppressed; And close as sin and suffering joined We march to fate abreast.

Nearly sixteen millions of hands will aid you in pulling the load upwards, or they will pull against you the load downwards. We shall constitute one-third and more of the ignorance and crime of the South, or one-third its intelligence and progress; we shall contribute one-third to the business and industrial prosperity of the South, or we shall prove a veritable body of death, stagnating, depressing, retarding every effort to advance the body politic.

Gentlemen of the Exposition, as we present to you humble effort at an exhibition of our progress, you must not expect over much. Starting thirty years ago with ownership here and there in a few quilts and pumpkins and chickens (gathered from miscellaneous sources), remember the path that has led from these to the invention and production of agricultural implements, buggies, steam engines, newspapers, books, statuary, carving, paintings, the management of drug stores and banks, has not been trodden without contact with thorns and thistles. While we take pride in what we exhibit as a result of our independent efforts, we do not for a moment forget that our part in this exhibition would fall far short of your expectations but for the constant help that has come to our educational life, not only from the Southern States, but especially from Northern philanthropists, who have made their gifts a constant stream of blessing and encouragement.

The wisest among my race understand that the agitation of questions of social equality is the extremist folly, and that progress in the enjoyment of all the privileges that will come to us must be the result of severe and constant struggle rather than of artificial forcing. No race that has anything to contribute to the markets of the world is long in any degree ostracized. It is important and right that all privileges of the law be ours, but it is vastly more important that we be prepared for the exercise of those privileges. The opportunity to earn a dollar in a factory just now is worth infinitely more than the opportunity to spend a dollar in an opera house.

In conclusion, may I repeat that nothing in thirty years has given us more hope and encouragement, and drawn us so near to you of the white race, as this opportunity offered by the Exposition; and here bending, as it were, over the altar that represents the results of the struggle of your race and mine, both starting practically empty-handed three decades ago, I pledge that, in your effort to work out the great and intricate problem which God has laid at the doors of the South, you shall have at all time the patient, sympathetic help of my race; only let this be constantly in mind that, while from representations in these buildings of the product of field, of forest, of mine, of factory, letters, and art, much good will come, yet far above and beyond material benefits will be that higher good, that let us pray God will come, in a blotting out of sectional differences and racial animosities and suspicions, in a determination to administer absolute justice, in a willing obedience among all classes to the mandates of law. This, coupled with our material prosperity, will bring into our beloved South a new heaven and a new earth.

PLESSY V. FERGUSON, 163 US 537 (1896)

On February 23, 1869, the Louisiana state legislature enacted a law prohibiting segregation on public transportation. In 1878, ruling in the case Hall v. DeCuir, *the U.S. Supreme Court declared that state governments could not prohibit segregation on common carriers. Twelve years later, the Court, hearing the case* Louisville, New Orleans, and Texas Railway v. Mississippi, *approved a state statute requiring segregation on intrastate carriers.*

In 1896, the Court once again faced the issue of segregation on public transportation. Homer Adolph Plessy, an African American traveling by train from New Orleans to Covington, Louisiana, was arrested when he refused to ride in the "colored" railway coach; Louisiana state law required that "separate but equal" accommodations be maintained in public facilities for blacks and whites. In its majority opinion, the Court declared that "separate but equal" accommodations constituted a "reasonable" use of state police power and that the Fourteenth Amendment "could not have been intended to abolish distinctions based on color, or to enforce social... equality, or a commingling of the two races upon terms unsatisfactory to either."

In effect, the Court's ruling had significantly reduced the authoritativeness of the Fourteenth and Fifteenth Amendments to the Constitution, which were designed to provide African Americans specific rights and protections. The "separate but equal" doctrine paved the way for

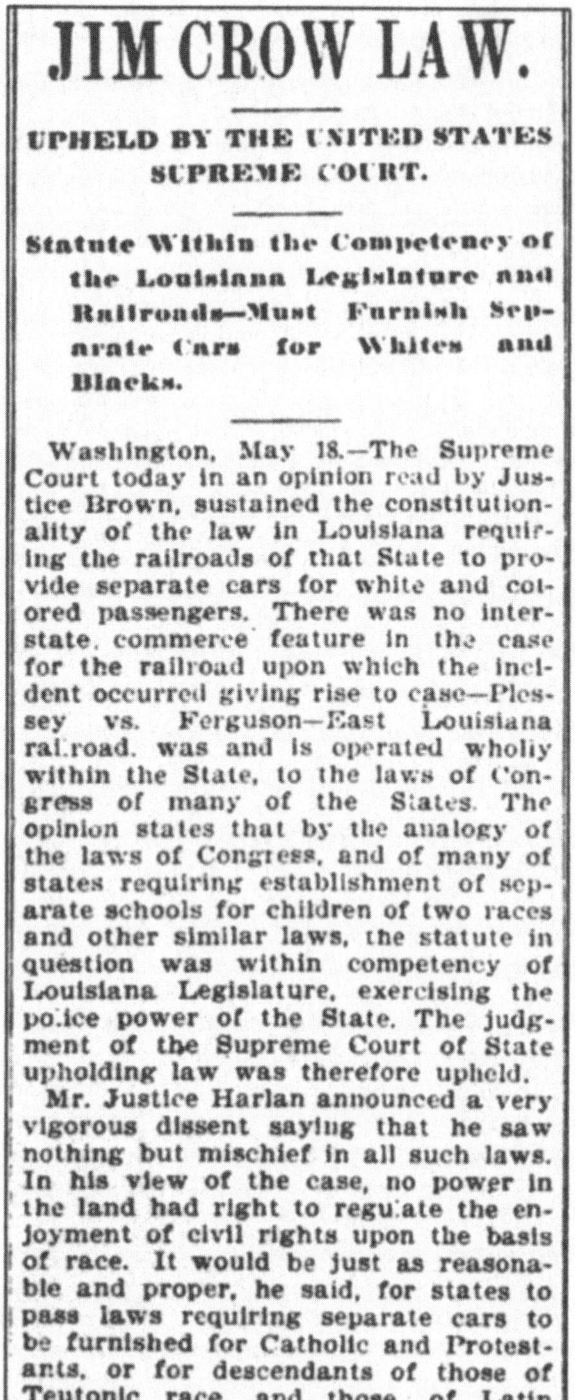

JIM CROW LAW.

UPHELD BY THE UNITED STATES SUPREME COURT.

Statute Within the Competency of the Louisiana Legislature and Railroads—Must Furnish Separate Cars for Whites and Blacks.

Washington, May 18.—The Supreme Court today in an opinion read by Justice Brown, sustained the constitutionality of the law in Louisiana requiring the railroads of that State to provide separate cars for white and colored passengers. There was no interstate commerce feature in the case for the railroad upon which the incident occurred giving rise to case—Plessey vs. Ferguson—East Louisiana railroad, was and is operated wholly within the State, to the laws of Congress of many of the States. The opinion states that by the analogy of the laws of Congress, and of many of states requiring establishment of separate schools for children of two races and other similar laws, the statute in question was within competency of Louisiana Legislature, exercising the police power of the State. The judgment of the Supreme Court of State upholding law was therefore upheld.

Mr. Justice Harlan announced a very vigorous dissent saying that he saw nothing but mischief in all such laws. In his view of the case, no power in the land had right to regulate the enjoyment of civil rights upon the basis of race. It would be just as reasonable and proper, he said, for states to pass laws requiring separate cars to be furnished for Catholic and Protestants, or for descendants of those of Teutonic race and those of Latin race.

0078068 PLESSY V. FERGUSON, 1896.
Credit: The Granger Collection, New York

Newspaper Article Announcing Verdict in* Plessy v. Ferguson *trial, 1896. *The U.S. Supreme Court's decision in this landmark case upheld the "separate but equal" doctrine and paved the way for segregation of African Americans in all walks of life. "Separate but equal" remained the standard doctrine in U.S. law until being repudiated in the* Brown v. Board of Education of Topeka, Kansas *decision of 1954.* THE GRANGER COLLECTION, NEW YORK. REPRODUCED BY PERMISSION.

Justice Henry Billings Brown delivered the opinion of the Court.

This case turns upon the constitutionality of an act of the General Assembly of the state of Louisiana, passed in 1890, providing for separate railway carriages for the white and colored races. . . .

The constitutionality of this act is attacked upon the ground that it conflicts both with the Thirteenth Amendment of the Constitution, abolishing slavery, and the Fourteenth Amendment, which prohibits certain restrictive legislation on the part of the states.

1. That it does not conflict with the Thirteenth Amendment, which abolished slavery and involuntary servitude, except as a punishment for crime, is too clear for argument. Slavery implies involuntary servitude—a state of bondage; the ownership of mankind as a chattel, or at least the control of the labor and services of one man for the benefit of another, and absence of a legal right to the disposal of his own person, property, and services. . . .

A statute which implies merely a legal distinction between the white and colored races—a distinction which is founded in the color of the two races, and which must always exist so long as white men are distinguished from the other race by color—has no tendency to destroy the legal equality of the two races, or reestablish a state of involuntary servitude. Indeed, we do not understand that the Thirteenth Amendment is strenuously relied upon by the plaintiff in error in this connection.

2. By the Fourteenth Amendment, all persons born or naturalized in the United States, and subject to the jurisdiction thereof, are made citizens of the United States and of the state wherein they reside; and the states are forbidden from making or enforcing any law which shall abridge the privileges or immunities of citizens of the United States, or shall deprive any person of life, liberty, or property without due process of law, or deny to any person within their jurisdiction the equal protection of the laws. . . .

The object of the amendment was undoubtedly to enforce the absolute equality of the two races before the law, but in the nature of things it could not have been intended to abolish distinctions based upon color, or to enforce social, as distinguished from political, equality, or a commingling of the two races upon terms unsatisfactory to either. Laws permitting, and even requiring, their separation in places where they are liable to be brought into contact do not necessarily imply the inferiority of either race to the other, and have been generally, if not universally, recognized as within the competency of the state legislatures in the exercise of their police power. The most common instance of this is connected with the establishment of separate schools for white and colored children, which has been held to be a valid exercise of the legislative power even by courts of states where the political rights of the colored race have been longest and most earnestly enforced. . . .

So far, then, as a conflict with the Fourteenth Amendment is concerned, the case reduces itself to the question whether the statute of Louisiana is a reasonable regulation, and with respect to this there must necessarily be a large discretion on the part of the legislature. In determining the question of reasonableness it is at liberty to act with reference to the established usages, customs, and traditions of the people, and with a view to the promotion of their comfort, and the preservation of the public peace and good order. Gauged by this standard, we cannot say that a law which authorizes or even requires the separation of the two races in public conveyances is unreasonable or more obnoxious to the Fourteenth Amendment than the acts of Congress requiring separate schools for colored children in the District of Columbia, the constitutionality of which does not seem to have been questioned, or the corresponding acts of state legislatures.

We consider the underlying fallacy of the plaintiff's argument to consist in the assumption that the enforced separation of the two races stamps the colored race with a badge of inferiority. If this be so, it is not by reason of anything found in the act, but solely the colored race chooses to put that construction upon it. The argument necessarily assumes that if, as has been more than once the case, and is not unlikely to be so again, the colored race should become the dominant power in the state legislature, and should enact a law in precisely similar terms, it would thereby relegate the white race to an inferior position. We imagine that the white race, at least, would not acquiesce in this assumption. The argument also assumes that social prejudices may be overcome by legislation and that equal rights cannot be secured to the Negro except by an enforced commingling of the two races. We cannot accept this proposition. If the two races are to meet upon terms of social equality, it must be the result of natural affinities, a mutual appreciation of each other's merits, and a voluntary consent of individuals. . . . Legislation is powerless to eradicate racial instincts or to abolish distinctions based upon physical differences, and the attempt to do so can only result in accentuating the difficulties of the present situation. If the civil and political rights of both races be equal, one cannot be inferior to the other civilly or politically. If one race be inferior to the other socially, the Constitution of the United States cannot put them upon the same plane.

It is true that the question of the proportion of colored blood necessary to constitute a colored person, as distinguished from a white person, is one upon with there is a difference of opinion in the different states, some holding that any visible admixture of black blood stamps the person as belonging to the colored race . . . others that it depends upon the preponderance of blood . . . and still others that the pre-dominance of white blood must only be in the proportion of three-fourths. . . . But these are questions to be determined under the laws of each state and are not properly put in issue in this case. Under the allegations of his petition it may undoubtedly become a question of importance whether, under the laws of Louisiana, the petitioner belongs to the white or colored race.

The judgment of the court below is therefore, *Affirmed.*

JUSTICE JOHN MARSHALL HARLAN DISSENTING

In respect of civil rights, common to all citizens, the Constitution of the United States does not, I think, permit any public authority to know the race of those entitled to be protected in the enjoyment of such rights. Every true man has pride of race, and under appropriate circumstances with the rights of others, his equals before the law, are not to be affected, it is his privilege to express such pride and to take such action based upon it as to him seems proper. But I deny that any legislative body or judicial tribunal may have regard to the race of citizens when the civil rights of those citizens are involved. Indeed, such legislation, as that here in question, is inconsistent not only with that equality of rights which pertains to citizenship, national and state, but with the personal liberty enjoyed by everyone within the United States.

The Thirteenth Amendment does not permit the withholding or the deprivation of any right necessarily inhering in freedom. It not only struck down the institution of slavery as previously existing in the United States, but it prevents the imposition of any burdens or disabilities that constitute badges of slavery or servitude. It decreed universal civil freedom in this country. This Court has so adjudged. But that amendment having been found inadequate to the protection of the rights of those who had been in slavery, it was followed by the Fourteenth Amendment, which added greatly to the dignity and glory of the American citizenship, and to the security of personal liberty, by declaring that "all persons born or naturalized in the United States, and subject to the jurisdiction thereof, are citizens of the United States and of the state wherein they reside," and that "no state shall make or enforce any law which shall abridge the privileges or immunities of citizens of the United States; nor shall any state deprive any person of life, liberty, or property without due process of law, nor deny to any person within its jurisdiction the equal protection of the laws." These two amendments, if enforced according to their true intent and meaning, will protect all the civil rights that pertains to freedom and citizenship. Finally, and to the end that no citizen should be denied, on account of his race, the privilege of participating in the political control of his country, it was declared by the Fifteenth Amendment that "the right of citizens of the United States to vote shall not be denied or abridged by the United States or by any state on account of race, color, or previous condition of servitude."

These notable additions to the fundamental law were welcomed by the friends of liberty throughout the world. They removed the race line from our governmental systems.

It was said in argument that the statute of Louisiana does not discriminate against either race but prescribes a rule applicable alike to white and colored citizens. But this argument does not meet the difficulty. Everyone knows that the statute in question had its origin in the purpose, not so much to exclude white persons from railroad cars occupied by blacks, as to exclude colored people from coaches occupied by or assigned to white persons. Railroad corporations of Louisiana did not make discrimination among whites in the matter of accommodation for travelers. The thing to accomplish was, under the guise of giving equal accommodation for whites and blacks, to compel the latter to keep to themselves while traveling in railroad passenger coaches. No one would be wanting in candor as to assert the contrary. The fundamental objections, therefore, to the statute is that it interferes with the personal freedom of citizens. If a white man and a black man choose to occupy the same public conveyance on a public highway, it is their right to do so, and no government, proceeding alone on grounds of race, can prevent it without infringing the personal liberty of each.

It is one thing for railroad carriers to furnish, or to be required by law to furnish, equal accommodations for all whom they are under a legal duty to carry. It is quite another thing for government to forbid citizens of the white and black races from traveling in the same public conveyance, and to punish officers of railroad companies for permitting persons of the two races to occupy the same passenger coach. If a state can prescribe, as a rule of civil conduct, that whites and blacks shall not travel as passengers in the same railroad coach, why may it not so regulate the use of the streets of its cities and towns as to compel white citizens to keep on one side of a street and black citizens to keep on the other? Why may it not, upon like grounds, punish whites and blacks who ride together in streetcars or in open vehicles on a public road or street? Why may it not require sheriffs to assign whites to one side of a courtroom and blacks to the other? And why may it not also prohibit the commingling of the two races in the galleries of legislative halls or in public assemblages convened for the consideration of the political questions of the day? Further, if this statute of Louisiana is consistent with the personal liberty of citizens, why may not the state require the separation in railroad coaches of native and naturalized citizens of the United States, or of Protestants and Roman Catholics?

The answer given as the argument to these questions was that regulations of the kind they suggest would be unreasonable and could not, therefore, stand before the law. Is it meant that the determination of questions of legislative power depends upon the inquiry whether the statute whose validity is questioned is, in the judgment of the courts, a reasonable one, taking all the circumstances into consideration? A statute may be unreasonable merely because a sound public forbade its enactment. But I do not understand that the courts have anything to do with the policy or expediency of legislation. The white race deems itself to be the dominant race in this country. And so it is, in prestige, in achievements, in education, in wealth, and in power. So, I doubt not, it will continue to be for all time, if it remains true to its great heritage and holds fast to the principles of constitutional liberty. But in view of the Constitution, in the eye of the law, there is in this country no superior, dominant, ruling class of citizens. There is no caste here. Our Constitution is color-blind and neither knows nor tolerates classes among citizens. In respect of civil rights all citizens are equal before the law. The humblest is the peer of the most powerful. The law regards man as a man and takes no account of his surroundings or of his color when his civil rights, as guaranteed by the supreme law of the land, are involved. It is, therefore, to be regretted that this high tribunal, the final expositor of the fundamental law of the land, has reached the conclusion that it is competent for a state to regulate the enjoyment by citizens of their civil rights solely upon the basis of race. . . .

The sure guarantee of the peace and security of each is the clear, distinct, unconditional recognition by our governments, national and state, of every right that inheres in civil freedom, and of the equality before the law of all citizens of the United States without regard to race. State enactments, regulating the enjoyment of civil rights, upon the basis of race, and cunningly devised legitimate results of the war, under the pretense of recognizing equality of rights, can have no other result than to render permanent peace impossible, and to keep alive a conflict of races, the continuance of which must do harm to all concerned. . . .

The arbitrary separation of citizens, on the basis of race, while they are on a public highway, is a badge of servitude wholly inconsistent with the civil freedom and the equality before the law established by the Constitution. It cannot be justified upon any legal grounds.

If evils will result from the commingling of the two races upon public highways established for the benefit of all, they will be infinitely less than those that will surely come from state legislation regulating the enjoyment of civil rights upon the basis of race. We boast of the freedom enjoyed by our people above all other peoples. But it is difficult to reconcile that boast with a state of the law which, practically, puts the brand of servitude and degradation upon a large class of our fellow-citizens, our equals before the law. The thin disguise of "equal" accommodations for passengers in railroad coaches will not mislead anyone, nor atone for the wrong this day has done. . . .

I am of opinion that the statute of Louisiana is inconsistent with the personal liberty of citizens, white and black, in that state, and hostile to both the spirit and letter of the Constitution of the United States. If laws of like character should be enacted in the several states of the Union, the effect would be in the highest degree mischievous. Slavery, as an institution tolerated by law, would, it is true, have disappeared from our country, but there would remain a power in the states, by sinister legislation, to interfere with the full enjoyment of the blessings of freedom; to regulate civil rights, common to all citizens, upon the basis of race, and to place in a condition of legal inferiority a large body of American citizens, now constituting a part of the political community called the People of the United States, for whom, and by whom through representatives, our government is administered. Such a system is inconsistent with the guarantee given by the Constitution to each state of a republican form of government, and may be stricken down by congressional action, constitutional or laws of any state to the contrary notwithstanding.

For the reasons stated, I am constrained to withhold my assent from the opinion and judgment of the majority. . . .

"LIFT EVERY VOICE AND SING" (1901)

Originally intended for use in a program given by a group of Jacksonville, Florida, schoolchildren to celebrate Abraham Lincoln's birthday, "Lift Every Voice and Sing" has become known as the "black national anthem." The song's words, written by poet and civil rights leader James Weldon Johnson, serve as a tribute to African American heritage. The song's music was composed by Johnson's brother and songwriting partner, J. Rosamond Johnson.

Lift every voice and sing, till earth and heaven ring,
Ring with the harmonies of liberty;
Let our rejoicing rise, high as the listening skies,
Let it resound loud as the rolling sea.
Sing a song full of the faith that the dark past has
taught us,
Sing a song full of the hope that the present has
brought us;
Facing the rising sun of our new day begun,
Let us march on till victory is won.

Stony the road we trod, bitter the chastening rod,
Felt in the days when hope unborn had died;
Yet with a steady beat, have not our weary feet,
Come to the place for which our fathers sighed?
We have come over a way that with tears has
been watered,
We have come, treading our path through the
blood of the slaughtered;
Out from the gloomy past, till now we stand at last
Where the white gleam of our bright star is cast.

God of our weary years, God of our silent tears,
Thou Who hast brought us thus far on the way;
Thou Who hast by Thy might, led us into the light,
Keep us forever in the path, we pray.
Lest our feet stray from the places, our God,
where we met Thee.
Lest our hearts, drunk with the wine of the
world, we forget Thee.
Shadowed beneath Thy hand, may we forever stand,
True to our God, true to our native land.

THE SOULS OF BLACK FOLK: ESSAYS AND SKETCHES, BY W. E. B. DU BOIS (1903) (EXCERPT)

Many scholars believe that among civil rights leader W. E. B. Du Bois's greatest achievements, his writings stand out. Throughout his lifetime, he penned many books and essays expressing his beliefs about racial assimilation, cooperation, and the use of education to end prejudice. Among these writings is The Souls of Black Folk, *an extremely popular analysis of the problem of race as it relates to African Americans throughout society.*

After the Egyptian and Indian, the Greek and Roman, the Teuton and Mongolian, the Negro is sort of seventh son, born with a veil, and gifted with second-sight in this American world,—a world which yields him no true self-consciousness, but only lets him see himself through the revelation of the other world. It is a peculiar sensation, this double-consciousness, this sense of always looking at one's self through the eyes of others, of measuring one's soul by the tape of a world that looks on in amused contempt and pity. One ever feels his two-ness,—an American, a Negro; two souls, two thoughts, two unreconciled strivings; two warring ideals in one dark body, whose dogged strength alone keeps it from being torn asunder.

The history of the American Negro is the history of this strife,—this longing to attain self-conscious manhood, to merge his double self into a better and truer self. In this merging he wishes neither of the older selves to be lost. He would not Africanize America, for America has too much to teach the world and Africa. He would not bleach his Negro soul in a flood of white Americanism, for he knows that Negro blood has a message for the world. He simply wishes to make it possible for a man to be both a Negro and an American, without being cursed and spit upon by his fellows, without having the doors of Opportunity closed roughly in his face.

MARCUS GARVEY'S SPEECH AT LIBERTY HALL, NEW YORK CITY (1922)

Marcus Garvey, black nationalist and founder of the Universal Negro Improvement Association (U.N.I.A.), dedicated his life to uplifting Africans throughout the world. In this 1922 address, Garvey outlined the goals of the Universal Negro Improvement Association.

Marcus Garvey, Black Nationalist, early 1920s. *Garvey, who founded the Universal Negro Improvement Association, supported Pan-Africanism. In annual conventions held at Liberty Hall in New York City in the 1920s, he advocated the establishment of an autonomous African nation-state.* THE LIBRARY OF CONGRESS

Over five years ago the Universal Negro Improvement Association placed itself before the world as the movement through which the new and rising Negro would give expression of his feelings. This Association adopts an attitude not of hostility to other races and peoples of the world, but an attitude of self-respect.

... Wheresoever human rights are denied to any group, wheresoever justice is denied to any group, there the U.N.I.A. finds a cause. And at this time among all the peoples of the world, the group that suffers most from injustice, the group that is denied most of those rights that belong to all humanity, is the black group ... even so under the leadership of the U.N.I.A., we are marshalling the 400,000,000 Negroes of the world to fight for the emancipation of the race and of the redemption of the country of our fathers.

We represent a new line of thought among Negroes. Whether you call it advanced thought or reactionary thought, I do not care. If it is reactionary for people to seek independence in government, then we are reactionary. If it is advanced thought for people to seek liberty and freedom, then we represent the advanced school of thought among the Negroes of this country. We of the U.N.I.A. believe that what is good for the other folks is good for us. If government is something that is worth while; if government is something that is appreciable and helpful and protective to others, then we also want to experiment in government. We do not mean a government that will make us citizens without rights or subjects without consideration. We mean a kind of government that will place our race in control, even as other races are in control of their own government.

... The U.N.I.A. is not advocating the cause of church building, because we have a sufficiently large number of churches among us to minister to the spiritual needs of the people, and we are not going to compete with those who are engaged in so splendid a work; we are not engaged in building any new social institutions, ... because there are enough social workers engaged in those praiseworthy efforts. We are not engaged in politics because we have enough local politicians, ... and the political situation is well taken care of. We are not engaged in domestic politics, in church building or in social uplift work, but we are engaged in nation building.

In advocating the principles of this Association we find we have been very much misunderstood and very much misrepresented by men from within our own race, as well as others from without. Any reform movement that seeks to bring about changes for the benefit of humanity is bound to be misrepresented by those who have always taken it upon themselves to administer to, and lead the unfortunate. . . .

. . . The Universal Negro Improvement Association stands for the Bigger Brotherhood; the Universal Negro Improvement Association stands for human rights, not only for Negroes, but for all races. The Universal Negro Improvement Association believes in the rights of not only the black race, the white race, the yellow race and the brown race. The Universal Negro Improvement Association believes that the white man has as much right to be considered, the yellow man has as much right to be considered, the brown man has as much right to be considered as the black man of Africa. In view of the fact that the black man of Africa has contributed as much to the world as the white man of Europe, and the brown man and yellow man of Asia, we of the Universal Negro Improvement Association demand that the white, yellow and brown races give to the black man his place in the civilization of the world. We ask for nothing more than the rights of 400,000,000 Negroes. We are not seeking, as I said before, to destroy or disrupt the society or the government of other races, but we are determined that 400,000,000 of us shall unite ourselves to free our motherland from the grasp of the invader. . . .

The Universal Negro Improvement Association is not seeking to build up another government within the bounds or borders of the United States of America. The Universal Negro Improvement Association is not seeking to disrupt any organized system of government, but the Association is determined to bring Negroes together for the building up of a nation of their own. And why? Because we have been forced to it. We have been forced to it throughout the world; not only in America, not only in Europe, not only in the British Empire, but wheresoever the black man happens to find himself, he has been forced to do for himself.

To talk about Government is a little more than some of our people can appreciate. . . . The average man . . . seems to say, "why should there be need for any other government?" We are French, English or American. But we of the U.N.I.A. have studied seriously this question of nationality among Negroes—this American nationality, this British nationality, this French, Italian or Spanish nationality, and have discovered that it counts for nought when that nationality comes in conflict with the racial idealism of the group that rules. When our interests clash with those of the ruling faction, then we find that we have absolutely no rights. In times of peace, when everything is all right, Negroes have a hard time, wherever we go, wheresoever we find ourselves, getting those rights that belong to us in common with others whom we claim as fellow citizens; getting that consideration that should be ours by right of the constitution, by right of the law, but in the time of trouble they make us all partners in the cause, as happened in the last war. . . .

We have saved many nations in this manner, and we have lost our lives doing that before. Hundreds of thousands—nay, millions of black men, lie buried under the ground due to that old-time camouflage of saving the nation. We saved the British Empire; we saved the French Empire; we saved this glorious country more than once; and all that we have received for our sacrifices, all that we have received for what we have done, even in giving up our lives, is just what you are receiving now, just what I am receiving now.

You and I fare no better in America, in the British Empire, or any other part of the white world; we fare no better than any black man wheresoever he shows his head. . . .

The U.N.I.A. is reversing the old-time order of things. We refuse to be followers anymore. We are leading ourselves. That means, if any saving is to be done . . . we are going to seek a method of saving Africa first. Why? And why Africa? Because Africa has become the grand prize of the nations. Africa has become the big game of the nation hunters. Today Africa looms as the greatest commercial, industrial and political prize in the world.

The difference between the Universal Negro Improvement Association and the other movements of this country, and probably the world, is that the Universal Negro Improvement Association seeks independence of government while the other organizations seek to make the Negro a secondary part of existing governments. We differ from the organizations in America because they seek to subordinate the Negro as a secondary consideration in a great civilization, knowing that in America the Negro will never reach his highest ambition, knowing that the Negro in America will never get his constitutional rights. All other organizations which are fostering the improvement of Negroes in the British Empire know that the Negro in the British Empire will never reach the height of his constitutional rights. What do I mean by constitutional rights in America? If the black man is to reach the height of his ambition in this country—if the black man is to get all of his constitutional rights in America—then the black man should have the same chance in the nation as any other man to become president of the nation, or a street cleaner in New York. If the black man in the British Empire is to have all his constitutional rights it means that the Negro in the British Empire should have at least the same right to become premier of Great Britain as he has to become a street cleaner in the city of London. Are they prepared to give us such political equality? You and I can live in the United States of America for 100 more years, and our generations may live for 200 years or for 5000 more years, and so long as there is a black and white population, when the majority is on the side of the white race, you and I will never get political justice or get political equality in this country. Then why should a black man with rising ambition, after preparing himself in every possible way to give expression to that highest ambition, allow himself to be kept down by racial prejudice within a country? If I am as educated as the next man, if I am as prepared as the next man, if I have passed through the best schools and colleges and universities as the other fellow, why should I not have a fair chance to compete with the other fellow for the biggest position in the nation? ...

We are not preaching a propaganda of hate against anybody. We love the white man; we love all humanity.... The white man is as necessary to the existence of the Negro as the Negro is necessary to his existence. There is a common relationship that we cannot escape. Africa has certain things that Europe wants, and Europe has certain things that Africa wants ... it is impossible for us to escape it. Africa has oil, diamonds, copper, gold and rubber and all the minerals that Europe wants, and there must be some kind of relationship between Africa and Europe for a fair exchange, so we cannot afford to hate anybody.

The question often asked is what does it require to redeem a race and free a country? If it takes man power, if it takes scientific intelligence, if it takes education of any kind, or if it takes blood, then the 400,000,000 Negroes of the world have it.

It took the combined power of the Allies to put down the mad determination of the Kaiser to impose German will upon humanity. Among those who suppressed his mad ambition were two million Negroes who have not yet forgotten how to drive men across the firing line ... when so many white men refused to answer to the call and dodged behind all kinds of excuses, 400,000 black men were ready without a question. It was because we were told it was a war of democracy; it was a war for the liberation of the weaker peoples of the world. We heard the cry of Woodrow Wilson, not because we liked him so, but because the things he said were of such a nature that they appealed to us as men. Wheresoever the cause of humanity stands in need of assistance, there you will find the Negro ever ready to serve.

He has done it from the time of Christ up to now. When the whole world turned its back upon the Christ, the man who was said to be the Son of God, when the world cried out "Crucify Him," when the world spurned Him and spat upon Him, it was a black man, Simon, the Cyrenian, who took up the cross. Why? Because the cause of humanity appealed to him. When the black man saw the suffering Jew, struggling under the heavy cross, he was willing to go to His assistance, and he bore that cross up to the heights of Calvary. In the spirit of Simon, the Cyrenian, 1900 years ago, we answered the call of Woodrow Wilson, the call to a larger humanity, and it was for that we willingly rushed into the war. ...

We shall march out, yes, as black American citizens, as black British subjects, as black French citizens, as black Italians or as black Spaniards, but we shall march out with a greater loyalty, the loyalty of race. We shall march out in answer to the cry of our fathers, who cry out to us for the redemption of our own country, our motherland, Africa.

We shall march out, not forgetting the blessings of America. We shall march out, not forgetting the blessings of civilization. We shall march out with a history of peace before and behind us, and surety that history shall be our breast-plate, for how can a man fight better than knowing that the cause for which he fights is righteous? ... Glorious shall be the battle when the time comes to fight for our people and our race.

We should say to the millions who are in Africa to hold the fort, for we are coming 400,000,000 strong.

EXECUTIVE ORDER NO. 8802, 3 C.F.R., 1938–1943 COMP. P. 957 (1941)

Issued by President Franklin D. Roosevelt on June 25, 1941, Executive Order 8802 was intended to eliminate discriminatory practices in the defense industry during World War II (1941–1945).

Whereas it is the policy of the United States to encourage full participation in the national defense program by all citizens of the United States, regardless of race, creed, color, or national origin, in the firm belief that the democratic way of life within the Nation can be defended successfully only with the help and support of all groups within its borders; and

Whereas there is evidence that available and needed workers have been barred from employment in industries engaged in defense production solely because of considerations of race, creed, color, or national origin, to the detriment of workers' morale and of national unity:

Now, Therefore, by virtue of the authority vested in me by the Constitution and the statues, and as a prerequisite to the successful conduct of our national defense production effort, I do hereby reaffirm the policy of the United States that there shall be no discrimination in the employment of workers in defense industries or Government because of race, creed, color, or national origin, and I do hereby declare that it is the duty of employers and of labor organizations, in furtherance of said policy and of this order, to provide for the full and equitable participation of all workers in defense industries, without discrimination because of race, creed, color, or national origin;

And it is hereby ordered as follows:

1. All departments and agencies of the Government of the United States concerned with vocational and training programs for defense production shall take special measures appropriate to assure that such programs are administered without discrimination because of race, creed, color, or national origin;

2. All contracting agencies of the Government of the United States shall include in all defense contracts hereafter negotiated by them a provision obligating the contractor not to discriminate against any worker because of race, creed, color, or national origin;

3. There is established in the Office of Production Management a Committee on Fair Employment Practice, which shall consist of a chairman and four other members to be appointed by the President. The Chairman and members of the Committee shall serve as such without compensation but shall be entitled to actual and necessary transportation, subsistence and other expenses incidental to performance of their duties. The Committee shall receive and investigate complaints of discrimination in violation of the provisions of this order and shall take appropriate steps to redress grievances which it finds to be valid. The Committee shall also recommend to the several departments and agencies of the Government of the United States and to the President all measures which may be deemed by it necessary or proper to effectuate the provisions of this order.

EXECUTIVE ORDER NO. 9981, 3 C.F.R. 1943–1948 COMP. P. 720 (1948)

Signed by President Harry S. Truman on July 26, 1948, Executive Order 9981 ended segregation in the Armed Forces of the United States.

Whereas it is essential that there be maintained in the armed services of the United States the highest standards of democracy, with equality of treatment and opportunity for all those who serve in our country's defense:

Now, therefore, by virtue of the authority vested in me as President of the United States, by the Constitution and the statutes of the United States, and as Commander-in-Chief of the armed services, it is hereby ordered as follows:

1. It is hereby declared to be the policy of the President that there shall be equality of treatment and opportunity for all persons in the armed services without regard to race, color, religion or national origin. This policy shall be put into effect as rapidly as possible, having due regard to the time required to effectuate any necessary changes without impairing efficiency or morals.

2. There shall be created in the National Military Establishment an advisory committee to be known as the President's Committee on Equality of Treatment and Opportunity in the Armed Services, which shall be composed of seven members to be designated by the President.

3. The Committee is authorized on behalf of the President to examine into the rules, procedures and practices of the armed services in order to determine in what respect such rules, procedure and practices may be altered or improved with a view to carrying out the policy of this order. The Committee shall confer and advise with the Secretary of the Army, the Secretary of the Air Force, and shall make such recommendations to the President and to said Secretaries as in the judgment of the Committee will effectuate the policy hereof.

4. All executive departments and agencies of the Federal Government are authorized and directed to cooperate with the Committee in its work, and to furnish the Committee such information or the services of such persons as the Committee may require in the performance of its duties.

5. When requested by the Committee to do so, persons in the armed services or in any of the executive departments and agencies of the Federal Government shall testify before the Committee and shall make available for the use of the Committee such documents and other information as the Committee may require.

6. The Committee shall continue to exist until such time as the President shall terminate its existence by Executive order.

BROWN V. BOARD OF EDUCATION OF TOPEKA, KANSAS, 347 U.S. 483 (1954)

Beginning in the late 1930s, the U.S. Supreme Court began to review numerous cases dealing with segregation in public education; by the 1950s, it had become evident that segregated educational facilities were not equal.

In 1938, in the case Missouri ex rel. Lloyd Gaines v. Canada, *the Court ruled that states were required to provide equal educational facilities for African Americans within their boundaries. (The state of Missouri at that time had maintained a practice of providing funds for African Americans to attend graduate and professional schools outside of the state, rather than provide facilities itself.) Taking an even greater step, in 1950 the Court in* Sweatt v. Painter *ruled that a separate law school for African Americans provided by the state of Texas violated the equal protection clause of the Fourteenth Amendment.*

In 1952, five different cases, all dealing with segregation in public schools but with different facts and from different places, reached the U.S. Supreme Court. Four of the cases— Brown v. Board of Education of Topeka, Kansas*;* Briggs v. Elliott *(out of South Carolina);* Davis v. Prince Edward

Protesters outside Convention Hall, Site of the Democratic National Convention, Philadelphia, PA, July 12, 1948. *A. Philip Randolph* (left), *president of the Board of Sleeping Car Porters and chairman of the League for Non-Violent Civil Disobedience against Military Segregation, worked tirelessly to combat Jim Crow policies, including the desegregation of the military.* BETTMANN/CORBIS

County School Board *(out of Virginia); and* Gebhart v. Belton *(out of Delaware)—were considered together. The fifth case,* Bolling v. Sharpe *coming out of the District of Columbia, was considered separately (since the district is not a state).*

After hearing initial arguments, the Court found itself unable to reach an agreement. In 1953, the Court heard reargument. Thurgood Marshall, legal counsel for the NAACP Legal Defense and Educational Fund, presented arguments on behalf of the African American students. On May 17, 1954, the Court unanimously ruled that segregation in all public education deprived minority children of equal protection under the Fourteenth Amendment. (In the Bolling *case, the Court determined that segregation violated provisions of the Fifth Amendment, since the Fourteenth Amendment is expressly directed to the states.)*

Chief Justice Earl Warren delivered the opinion of the Court.

These cases come to us from the States of Kansas, South Carolina, Virginia and Delaware. They are premised on different facts and different local conditions, but a common legal question justifies their consideration together in this consolidated opinion.

In each of these cases, minors of the Negro race, through their legal representatives, seek the aid of the courts in obtaining admission to the public schools of their community on a nonsegregated basis. In each instance, they had been denied admission to schools attended by white children under laws requiring or permitting segregation according to race. This segregation

African American Students for Whom the* Brown v. Board of Education of Topeka, Kansas *Case Was Brought, with Their Parents. *The U.S. Supreme Court's historic 1954 decision in* Brown *overturned the "separate but equal" doctrine that had prevailed since the Court's 1896 ruling in* Plessy v. Ferguson *and declared segregation in public education to be unconstitutional.* **CARL IWASAKI/ TIME LIFE PICTURES/GETTY IMAGES**

was alleged to deprive the plaintiffs of the equal protection of the laws under the Fourteenth Amendment. In each of the cases other than the Delaware case, a three-judge federal district court denied relief to the plaintiffs on the so-called "separate but equal" doctrine announced by this Court in *Plessy v. Ferguson*. Under that doctrine, equality of treatment is accorded when the races are provided substantially equal facilities, even though these facilities be separate. In the Delaware case, the Supreme Court of Delaware adhered to that doctrine, but ordered that the plaintiffs be admitted to the white schools because of their superiority to the Negro schools.

The plaintiffs contend that segregated public schools are not "equal" and cannot be made "equal," and that hence they are deprived of the equal protection of the laws. Because of the obvious importance of the question presented, the Court took jurisdiction. Argument was heard in the 1952 Term, and reargument was heard this Term on certain questions propounded by the Court.

Reargument was largely devoted to the circumstances surrounding the adoption of the Fourteenth Amendment in 1868. It covered exhaustively consideration of the Amendment in Congress, ratification by the states, then existing practices in racial segregation, and the views of proponents and opponents of the Amendment. This discussion and our own investigation convince us that, although these sources cast some light, it is not enough to resolve the problem with which we are faced. At best, they are inconclusive. The most avid proponents of the post-War Amendments undoubtedly intended them to remove all legal distinctive among "all persons born or naturalized in the United States." Their opponents, just as certainly, were antagonistic to both the letter and the spirit of the Amendments and wished them to have the most limited effect. What others in Congress and the state legislatures had in mind cannot be determined with any degree of certainty.

An additional reason for the inconclusive nature of the Amendment's history, with respect to segregated schools, is the status of public education at that time. In the South, the movement toward free common schools, supported by general taxation, had not yet taken hold. Education of white children was largely in the hands of private groups. Education of Negroes was almost non-existent, and practically all of the race were illiterate. In fact, any education of Negroes was forbidden by law in some states. Today, in contrast, many Negroes have achieved outstanding success in the arts and sciences as well as in the business and professional world. It is true that public school education at the time of the Amendment had advanced further in the North, but the effect of the Amendment on Northern States was generally ignored by the congressional debates. Even in the North, the conditions of public education did not approximate those existing today. The curriculum was usually rudimentary; ungraded schools were common in rural areas; the school term was but three months a year in many states; and compulsory school attendance was virtually unknown. As a consequence, it is not surprising that there should be so little in the history of the Fourteenth Amendment relating to its intended effect on public education.

In the first cases in this Court construing the Fourteenth Amendment, decided shortly after its adoption, the Court interpreted it as proscribing all state imposed discriminations against the Negro race. The doctrine of "separate but equal" did not make its appearance in this Court until 1896 in the case of *Plessy v. Ferguson* ... involving not education but transportation. American courts have since labored with the doctrine for over half a century. In this Court, there have been six cases involving the "separate but equal" doctrine in the field of public education. In *Cumming v. County Board of Education* ... and *Gong Lum v. Rice* ... the validity of the doctrine itself was not challenged. In more recent cases, all on the graduate school level, inequality was found in that specific benefits enjoyed by white students were denied to Negro students of the same educational qualifications. In none of these cases [*Missouri ex rel. Gaines v. Canada, Sipuel v. University of Oklahoma, Sweatt v. Painter,* and *McLaurin v. Oklahoma State Regents for Higher Education*] was it necessary to reexamine the doctrine to grant relief to the Negro plaintiff. And in *Sweatt v. Painter* ... the Court expressly reserved decision on the question whether *Plessy v. Ferguson* should be held inapplicable to public education.

In the instant cases, that question is directly presented. Here, unlike *Sweatt v. Painter,* there are findings below that the Negro and white schools involved have been equalized, or are being equalized, with respect to buildings, curricula, qualifications and salaries of teacher, and other "tangible" factors. Our decision, therefore, cannot turn on merely a comparison of these tangible factors in the Negro and white schools involved in each of the cases. We must look instead to the effect of segregation itself on public education.

In approaching this problem, we cannot turn the clock back to 1868 when the Amendment was adopted, or even to 1896 when *Plessy v. Ferguson* was written. We must consider public education in the light of its full development and its present place in American life throughout the Nation. Only in this way can it be determined if segregation in public schools deprives these plaintiffs of the equal protection of the laws.

Today, education is perhaps the most important function of state and local governments. Compulsory school attendance laws and the great expenditures for education both demonstrate our recognition of the importance of education to our democratic society. It is required in the performance of our most basic public responsibilities, even service in the armed forces. It is the very foundation of good citizenship. Today it is a principal instrument in awakening the child to cultural values, in preparing him for later professional training, and in helping him to adjust normally to his environment. In these days, it is doubtful that any child may reasonably be expected to succeed in life if he is denied the opportunity of an education. Such an opportunity, where the state has undertaken to provide it, is a right which must be made available to all on equal terms.

We come then to the question presented: Does segregation of children in public schools solely on the basis of race, even though the physical facilities and other "tangible" factors may be equal, deprive the children of the minority group of equal educational opportunities? We believe that it does.

In *Sweatt v. Painter* in finding that a segregated law school for Negroes could not provide them equal educational opportunities, this Court relied in large part on "those qualities which are incapable of objective measurement but which make for greatness in the law school." In *McLaurin v. Oklahoma State Regents for Higher Education* ... the Court, in requiring that a Negro admitted to a white graduate school be treated like all other students, again resorted to intangible considerations: " ... his ability to study, to engage in discussions and exchange views with other students, and, in general, to learn his profession." Such considerations apply with added force to children in grade and high schools. To separate them from others of similar age and qualifications solely because of their race generates a feeling of inferiority as to their status in the community that may affect their hearts and minds in a way unlikely ever to be undone. The effect of this separation on their educational opportunities was well stated by a finding in the Kansas case by a court which nevertheless felt compelled to rule against the Negro plaintiffs:

> Segregation of white and colored children in public school has a detrimental effect upon the colored children. The impact is greater when it has the sanction of the law; for the policy of separating the races is usually interpreted as denoting the inferiority of the negro group. A sense of inferiority affects the motivation of a child to learn. Segregation with the sanction of law, therefore, has a tendency to [retard] the educational and mental development of Negro children and to deprive them of some of the benefits they would receive in racial[ly] integrated school systems.

Whatever may have been the extent of psychological knowledge at the time of *Plessy v. Ferguson,* this finding is amply supported by modern authority. Any language in *Plessy v. Ferguson* contrary to this finding is rejected.

We conclude that in the field of public education the doctrine of "separate but equal" has no place. Separate educational facilities are inherently unequal. Therefore, we hold that the plaintiffs and others similarly situated for whom the actions have brought are, by reason of the segregation complained of, deprived of the equal protection of the laws guaranteed by the Fourteenth Amendment. This disposition makes unnecessary any discussion whether such segregation also violates the Due Process Clause of the Fourteenth Amendment.

Because these are class actions, because of the wide applicability of this decision, and because of the great variety of local conditions, the formulation of decrees in these presents problems of considerable complexity. On reargument, the consideration of appropriate relief was necessarily subordinated to the primary question—the constitutionality of segregation in public education. We have now announced that such segregation is a denial of the equal protection of the laws. In order that we may have the full assistance of the parties in formulating decrees, the cases will be restored to the docket, and the parties are requested to present further argument on Questions 4 and 5 previously propounded by the Court for the reargument this Term. The Attorney General of the United States is again invited to participate. The Attorneys General of the states requiring or permitting segregation in public education will also be permitted to appear as amici curiae upon request to do so by September 15, 1954, and submission of briefs by October 1, 1954.

It is so ordered.

CIVIL RIGHTS ACT OF 1957, PUB.L. NO. 85-315, 71 STAT. 634 (1957)

This act, signed by President Dwight D. Eisenhower on September 9, 1957, was the first piece of comprehensive legislation in the area of civil rights since the Civil Rights Act of 1875, which the Supreme Court in 1883 declared unconstitutional. The new act provided for the creation of a Commission on Civil Rights, extended the jurisdiction of the federal district courts to include civil action arising out of the act, and empowered the U.S. attorney general to take action in cases where rights secured by the act were believed to have been violated.

An Act to provide means of further securing and protecting the civil rights of persons within the jurisdiction of the United States.

PART I—ESTABLISHMENT OF THE COMMISSION ON CIVIL RIGHTS

Sec. 101. (a) There is created in the executive branch of the Government a Commission on Civil Rights (hereinafter called the "Commission").

(b) The Commission shall be composed of six members who shall be appointed by the President by and with the advice and consent of the Senate. Not more than three of the members shall at any one time be of the same political party.

(c) The President shall designate one of the members of the Commission as Chairman and one as Vice Chairman. The Vice Chairman shall act as Chairman in the absence or disability of the Chairman, or in the event of a vacancy in that office.

(d) Any vacancy in the Commission shall not affect its powers and shall be filled in the same manner, and subject to the same limitation with respect to party affiliations as the original appointment was made. . . .

PART IV—TO PROVIDE MEANS OF FURTHER SECURING AND PROTECTING THE RIGHT TO VOTE

Sec. 131. Section 2004 of the Revised Statutes (42 U.S.C. 1971), is amended as follows:

. . . No person, whether acting under cover of law or otherwise, shall intimidate, threaten, coerce, or attempt to intimidate, or coerce any other person for the purpose of interfering with the right of such other person to vote as he may choose, or of causing such other person to vote, for, or to vote as he may choose, or of causing such other person to vote for, or not to vote for, any candidate for the office of President, Vice President, presidential elector, Member of the Senate, or Member of the House of Representatives, Delegates or Commissioners from the Territories or possessions, at any general, special, or primary election held solely or in part for the purpose of selecting or electing any such candidate.

... Whenever any person has engaged or there are reasonable grounds to believe that any person is about to engage in any act or practice which would deprive any right or privilege secured by subsection (a) or (b), the Attorney General may institute for the United States, or in the name of the United States, a civil action or other proper proceeding for preventive relief, including an application for a permanent or temporary injunction, restraining order, or other order. In any proceeding hereunder the United States shall be liable for costs the same as a private person. ...

EXECUTIVE ORDER NO. 10730, 3 C.F.R. 1954-1958 COMP. P. 388 (1957)

In September 1957, Arkansas Governor Orval Faubus mobilized the Arkansas National Guard in an effort to prevent African American students from entering Little Rock's Central High School. As a result, on September 24, President Dwight D. Eisenhower issued an executive order authorizing the use of the National Guard and the Air National Guard of the United States to assist in desegregation in Little Rock.

Whereas on September 23, 1957, I issued Proclamation No. 3204 reading in part as follows:

Whereas certain persons in the State of Arkansas, individually and in unlawful assemblages, combinations, and conspiracies, have wilfully obstructed the enforcement of orders of the United States District Court for the Eastern District of Arkansas with respect to matters relating to enrollment and attendance at public schools, particularly at Central High School, located in Little Rock School District, Little Rock, Arkansas; and

Whereas such wilful obstruction of justice hinders the execution of the laws of that State and of the United States, and makes it impracticable to enforce such laws by the ordinary course of judicial proceedings; and

Whereas such obstruction of justice constitutes a denial of the equal protection of the laws secured by the Constitution of the United States and impedes the course of justice under those laws;

Court-Ordered Integration Proceeds at Central High School, Little Rock, AR, October 3, 1957. *Nine African American students, escorted by federal troops, were transported to and from the school in a U.S. Army station wagon each day. On this day, a demonstration began when thirty white students left the school building after the arrival of the black students.* **BETTMANN/CORBIS**

Now, therefore, I, Dwight D. Eisenhower, President of the United States, under and by virtue of the authority vested in me by the Constitution and Statutes of the United States, including Chapter 15 of Title 10 of the United States Code, particularly sections 332, 333 and 334 thereof, do command all persons engaged in such obstruction of justice to cease and desist therefrom, and to disperse forthwith, and

Whereas the command contained in that Proclamation has not been obeyed and wilful obstruction of enforcement of said court orders still exists and threatens to continue:

Now, therefore, by virtue of the authority vested in me by the Constitution and Statutes of the United States, including Chapter 15 of Title 10, particularly sections 332, 333 and 334 thereof, and section 301 of Title 3 of the United States Code, it is hereby ordered as follows:

Section 1. I hereby authorize and direct the Secretary of Defense to order into the active military service of the United States as he may deem appropriate to carry out the purposes of this Order, any or all of the units of the National Guard of the United States and of the Air National Guard of the United States within the State of Arkansas to serve in the active military service of the United States for an indefinite period and until relieved by appropriate orders.

Section 2. The Secretary of Defense is authorized and directed to take all appropriate steps to enforce any orders of the United States District Court for the Eastern District of Arkansas for the removal of obstruction of

Federal Troops Escorting African American Students into Central High School in Little Rock, AR, September 1957. *After the governor of Arkansas mobilized the state's National Guard to prevent the students from entering the high school, President Dwight D. Eisenhower issued an executive order authorizing the use of the U.S. National Guard and Air National Guard to assist in the court-ordered desegregation.* **AP IMAGES**

Racial Tension among Little Rock, AR, Students. *Johnny Gray, age fifteen, punches a white student during a scuffle in Little Rock. Gray and his sister, Mary (*standing behind him*), were en route to their segregated school when the two whites pictured here ordered them to get off the sidewalk. Racial tension plagued the Little Rock school system for years after court-ordered integration began in 1957. Governor Orval Faubus defied the courts by closing all the public schools in 1958; another court order reopened them in 1959.* BETTMANN/CORBIS

justice in the State of Arkansas with respect to matters relating to enrollment and attendance at public schools in the Little Rock School District, Little Rock, Arkansas. In carrying out the provisions of this section, the Secretary of Defense is authorized to use the units, and members thereof, ordered into the active military service of the United States pursuant to Section 1 of this Order.

Section 3. In furtherance of the enforcement of the aforementioned orders of the United States District Court for the Eastern District of Arkansas, the Secretary of Defense is authorized to use such of the armed forces of the United States as he may deem necessary.

Section 4. The Secretary of Defense is authorized to delegate to the Secretary of the Army or the Secretary of the Air Force, or both, any of the authority conferred upon him by this Order.

CIVIL RIGHTS ACT OF 1960, PUB.L. NO. 86-449, 74 STAT. 86 (1960)

This act, signed by President Dwight D. Eisenhower on May 6, 1960, further defined civil rights violations and outlined penalties connected with such violations. It guaranteed the provision of criminal penalties in the event a suspect crosses state lines to avoid legal process for the actual or attempted bombing or burning of any vehicle or building, and provided penalties for persons who obstructed or interfered with any order of a federal court.

An Act to enforce constitutional rights, and for other purposes.

TITLE II

Sec. 201. Chapter 49 of title 18, United States Code, is amended by adding at the end thereof a new section as follows:

Section 1074. Flight to avoid prosecution for damaging or destroying any building or other real or personal property.

... Whoever moves or travels in interstate or foreign commerce with intent either (1) to avoid prosecution, or custody, or confinement after conviction, under the laws of the place from which he flees, for willfully attempting to or damaging or destroying by fire or explosive any building, structure, facility, vehicle, dwelling house, synagogue, church, religious center or educational institution, public or private, or (2) to avoid giving testimony in any criminal proceeding relating to any such offense shall be fined not more than $5,000 or imprisoned not more than five years, or both.

... Violations of this section may be prosecuted in the Federal judicial district in which the original crime was alleged to have been committed or in which the person was held in custody or confinement. ...

Sec. 203. Chapter 39 of title 18 of the United States Code is amended by adding at the end thereof the following new section:

Section 837. Explosives; illegal use or possession; and, threats or false information concerning attempts to damage or destroy real or personal property by fire or explosives.

... Whoever transports or aids and abets another in transporting in interstate or foreign commerce any explosive, with the knowledge or intent that it will be used to damage or destroy any building or other real or personal property for the purpose of interfering with its use for educational, religious, charitable, residential, business, or civic objectives or of intimidating any person pursuing such objectives, shall be subject to imprisonment for not more than one year, or a fine of not more than $1,000 or both; and if personal injury results shall be subject to imprisonment for not more than ten years or a fine of not more than $10,000, or both; and if death results shall be subject to imprisonment for any term of years or for life, but the court may impose the death penalty if the jury so recommends.

... The possession of an explosive in such a manner as to evince an intent to use, or the use of, such explosive, to damage or destroy any building or other real or personal property used for educational, religious, charitable, residential, business, or civic objectives or to intimidate any person pursuing such objectives, creates rebuttable presumptions that the explosive was transported in interstate or foreign commerce or caused to be transported in interstate or foreign commerce by the person so possessing or using it, or by a person aiding or abetting the person so possessing or using it: Provided, however, that no person may be convicted under this section unless there is evidence independent of the presumptions that this section has been violated.

... Whoever, through the use of the mail, telephone, telegraph, or other instrument of commerce, willfully imparts or conveys, or causes to be imparted or conveyed, any threat, or false information knowing the same to be false, concerning an attempt or alleged attempt being made, or to be made, to damage or destroy any building or other real or personal property for the purpose of interfering with its use for educational, religious, charitable, residential, business, or civic objectives, or of intimidating any person pursuing such objectives, shall be subject to imprisonment for not more than one year or a fine of not more than $1,000, or both.

EXECUTIVE ORDER NO. 11053, 3 C.F.R. 1959–1963 COMP P.645 (1962)

On September 30, 1962, riots erupted on the campus of the University of Mississippi when Governor Ross Barnett attempted to block the court-ordered admission of African American student James H. Meredith. President John F. Kennedy quickly responded by authorizing the use of federal troops to restore order.

James Meredith, Civil Rights Activist, 1962. *That year, Meredith became the first African American student at the University of Mississippi. It took a U.S. Supreme Court decision and enforcement by federal marshals for Meredith to be able to attend the university.* HULTON ARCHIVE/ARCHIVE PHOTOS/ GETTY IMAGES

Whereas on September 30, 1962, I issued Proclamation No. 3497 reading in part as follows:

Whereas the Governor of the State of Mississippi and certain law enforcement officers and other officials of that State, and other persons, individually and in unlawful opposing and obstructing the enforcement of orders entered by the United States District Court for the Southern District of Mississippi and the United States Court of Appeals for the Fifth Circuit; and

Whereas such unlawful assemblies, combinations, and conspiracies oppose and obstruct the execution of the laws of the United States, impede the course of justice under those laws and make it impracticable to enforce those laws in the State of Mississippi by the ordinary course of judicial proceedings; and

Whereas I have expressly called the attention of the Governor of Mississippi to the perilous situation that exists and to his duties in the premises, and have requested but have not received from him adequate assurances that the orders of the courts of the United States will be obeyed and that law and order will be maintained:

Now, therefore, I, John F. Kennedy, President of the United States, under and by virtue of the authority vested in me by the Constitution and laws of the United States, including Chapter 15 of Title 10 of the United States Code, particularly sections 332, 333 and 334 thereof, do command all persons engaged in such obstructions of justice to cease and desist therefrom to disperse and retire peaceably forth-with; and

Whereas the commands contained in that proclamation have not been obeyed and obstruction of enforcement of those court orders still exists and threatens to continue:

Now, therefore, by virtue of the authority vested in me by the Constitution and laws of the United States, including Chapter 15 of Title 10, particularly Sections 332, 333 and 334 thereof, and Section 301 of Title 3 of the United States Code, it is hereby ordered as follows:

Section 1. The Secretary of Defense is authorized and directed to take all appropriate steps to enforce all orders of the United States District Court for the Southern District of Mississippi and the United States Court of Appeals for the Fifth Circuit and to remove all obstructions of justice in the State of Mississippi.

Section 2. In furtherance of the enforcement of the aforementioned orders of the United States District Court for the Southern District of Mississippi and the United States Court of Appeals for the Fifth Circuit, the Secretary of Defense is authorized to use such of the armed forces of the United States as he may deem necessary.

Section 3. I hereby authorize the Secretary of Defense to call into the active military service of the United States, as he may deem appropriate to carry out the purposes of this order, any or all of the units of the Army National Guard and of the Air National Guard of the State of Mississippi to serve in the active military service of the United States for an indefinite period and until relieved by appropriate orders. In carrying out the provisions of Section 1, the Secretary of Defense is authorized to use the units, and members thereof, ordered into the active military service of the United States pursuant to this section.

Section 4. The Secretary of Defense is authorized to delegate to the Secretary of the Army or the Secretary of the Air Force, or both, any of the authority conferred upon him by this order.

MARTIN LUTHER KING'S SPEECH AT THE LINCOLN MEMORIAL, WASHINGTON, D.C. (1963)

On August 28, 1963, some 250,000 people gathered at the Lincoln Memorial in Washington, D.C., in order to raise the nation's consciousness and to demonstrate on behalf of the civil rights legislation being debated in Congress. It was during this demonstration that Dr. Martin Luther King Jr. gave the "I Have a Dream" speech.

I am happy to join with you today in what will go down in history as the greatest demonstration for freedom in the history of our nation.

Five score years ago, a great American, in whose symbolic shadow we stand today, signed the Emancipation Proclamation. This momentous decree came as a great beacon of light of hope to millions of Negro slaves who had been seared in the flames of withering injustice. It came as a joyous daybreak to end the long night of their captivity.

But one hundred years later, the Negro is still not free. One hundred years later, the life of the Negro is still sadly crippled by the manacles of segregation and the chains of discrimination. One hundred years later, the Negro lives on a lonely island of poverty in the midst of a vast ocean of material prosperity. One hundred years later, the Negro is still languished in the corners of American society and finds himself an exile in his own land. So we have come here today to dramatize a shameful condition.

In a sense we have come to our nation's capitol to cash a check. When the architects of our republic wrote the magnificent words of the Constitution and the Declaration of Independence, they were signing a promissory note to which every American was to fall heir. This note was a promise that all men, yes black men as well as white men, would be guaranteed the unalienable rights of life, liberty, and the pursuit of happiness. It is obvious today that America has defaulted on this promissory note insofar as her citizens of color are concerned. Instead of honoring this sacred obligation, America has given the Negro people a bad check: a check which has come back marked "insufficient funds." But we refuse to believe that the bank of justice is bankrupt. We refuse to believe that there are insufficient funds in the great vaults of opportunity of this nation. So we have come to cash this check—a check that will give us upon demand the riches of freedom and the security of justice.

We have also come to this hallowed spot to remind America of the fierce urgency of now. This is not the time to engage in the luxury of cooling off or to take the tranquilizing drug of gradualism. Now is the time to make real the promises of democracy. Now is the time to rise from the dark and desolate valley of segregation to the sunlit path of racial justice. Now is the time to lift our nation from the quicksands of racial injustice to the solid rock of brotherhood. Now is the time to make justice a reality for all of God's children.

It would be fatal for the nation to overlook the urgency of the moment and to underestimate the determination of the Negro. This sweltering summer of the Negro's legitimate discontent will not pass until there is an invigorating autumn of freedom and equality. Nineteen hundred and sixty-three is not an end, but a beginning. Those who hope that the Negro needed to blow off steam, and will now be content will have a rude awakening if the Nation returns to business as usual. There will neither be rest nor tranquility in America until the Negro is granted his citizenship rights. The whirlwinds of revolt will continue to shake the foundations of our Nation until the bright day of justice emerges.

But there is something that I must say to my people who stand on the warm threshold which leads into the palace of justice. In the process of gaining our rightful place we must not be guilty of wrongful deeds. Let us not seek to satisfy our thirst for freedom by drinking from the cup of bitterness and hatred.

We must forever conduct our struggle on the high plane of dignity and discipline. We must not allow our

Martin Luther King Jr., "I Have a Dream" Speech, August 28, 1963. *On behalf of civil rights legislation being debated in Congress, King spoke from the steps of the Lincoln Memorial in 1963 as part of the March on Washington for Jobs and Freedom, a dramatic moment in the civil rights movement.* AFP/GETTY IMAGES

creative protest to degenerate into physical violence. Again and again we must rise to the majestic heights of meeting physical force with soul force. The marvelous new militancy which has engulfed the Negro community must not lead us to a distrust of all white people, for many of our white brothers, as evidenced by their presence here today, have come to realize that their destiny is tied up with our destiny and their freedom is inextricably bound to our freedom. We cannot walk alone.

And as we walk, we must make the pledge that we shall always march ahead. We cannot turn back. There are those who are asking the devotees of civil rights, "when will you be satisfied?" We can never be satisfied as long as the Negro is the victim of the unspeakable horrors of police brutality. We can never be satisfied as long as our bodies, heavy with the fatigue of travel, cannot gain lodging in the motels of the highways and the hotels of the cities. We cannot be satisfied as long as the Negro's basic mobility is from a smaller ghetto to a larger one. We can never be satisfied as long as our children are stripped of their self-hood and robbed of their dignity by signs reading "For Whites Only." We can never be satisfied as long as a Negro in Mississippi cannot vote and a Negro in New York believes he has nothing for which to vote. No. No, we are not satisfied, and we will not be satisfied until justice rolls down like waters, and righteousness like a mighty stream.

I am not unmindful that some of you have come here out of great trials and tribulations. Some of you have come fresh from narrow jail cells. Some of you have come from areas where your quest for freedom left you battered by the storms of persecution and staggered by the winds of police brutality. You have been the victims of creative suffering. Continue to work with the faith that unearned suffering is redemptive.

Go back to Mississippi, go back to Alabama, go back to South Carolina, go back to Georgia, go back to Louisiana, go back to the slums and ghettos of our northern cities, knowing that somehow this situation can and will be changed. Let us not wallow in the valley of despair.

I say to you today, my friends, that in spite of the difficulties and frustrations of the moment, I still have a dream. It is a dream deeply rooted in the American dream. I have a dream that one day this nation will rise up and live out the true meaning of its creed: "We hold these truths to be self-evident—that all men are created equal."

I have a dream that one day on the red hills of Georgia the sons of former slaves and the sons of former slave owners will be able to sit down together at the table of brotherhood. I have a dream that one day even the state of Mississippi, a desert state sweltering with the heat of injustice and oppression, will be transformed into an oasis of freedom and justice.

I have a dream that my four little children will one day live in a nation where they will not be judged by the color of their skin but by the content of their character.

I have a dream today.

I have a dream that one day the state of Alabama, whose governor's lips are presently dripping with the words of interposition and nullification, will be transformed into a situation where little black boys and black girls will be able to join hands with little white boys and white girls and walk together as sisters and brothers.

I have a dream today.

I have a dream that one day every valley shall be exalted, every hill and mountain shall be made low, the rough places will be made plain, and the crooked places will be made straight, and the glory of the Lord shall be revealed, and all flesh shall see it together.

This is our hope. This is the faith with which I return to the South. With this faith we will be able to transform the jangling discords of our nation into a beautiful symphony of brotherhood. With this faith we will be able to work together, to pray together, to struggle together, to go to jail together, to stand up for freedom together, knowing that we will be free one day.

This will be the day when all of God's children will be able to sing the new meaning "My country 'tis of thee, sweet land of liberty, of thee I sing. Land where my fathers died, land of the pilgrim's pride, from every mountainside, let freedom ring."

And if America is to be a great nation this must become true. So let freedom ring from the prodigious hilltops of New Hampshire! Let freedom ring from the mighty mountains of New York! Let freedom ring from the heightening Alleghenies of Pennsylvania!

Let freedom ring from the snowcapped Rockies of Colorado!

Let freedom ring from the curvaceous peaks of California!

But not only that; let freedom ring from Stone Mountain of Georgia!

Let freedom ring from Lookout Mountain of Tennessee.

Let freedom ring from every hill and mole hill of Mississippi. From every mountainside, let freedom ring.

When we let freedom ring, when we let it ring from every village and every hamlet, from every state and every city, we will be able to speed up that day when all God's children—black men and white men, Jews and Gentiles, Protestants and Catholics—will be able to join hands and sing in the words of that old Negro spiritual, Free at last! Free at last! Thank God almighty, we are free at last!

AMENDMENT TWENTY-FOUR TO THE UNITED STATES CONSTITUTION (1964)

By 1964, when the Twenty-fourth Amendment was ratified, most states had already discontinued the use of the poll tax, which had proved to be one of the most effective means of keeping African Americans from the polls—only the states of Alabama, Arkansas, Mississippi, Texas, and Virginia still implemented such a tax. The amendment, proposed in 1962, banned the use of poll taxes as a prerequisite to participating in federal elections. Ruling in the case of Harper v. Virginia Board of Elections, *the U.S. Supreme Court banned the use of poll taxes in state elections.*

Section 1. The right of citizens of the United States to vote in any primary or other election for President or Vice President, for electors for President or Vice President, or for Senator or Representative in Congress, shall not be denied or abridged by the United States or any State by reason of failure to pay any poll tax or other tax.

Section 2. The congress shall have power to enforce this article by appropriate legislation.

Martin Luther King Jr., Speaking at the Lincoln Memorial, August 28, 1963. *King addresses thousands gathered in Washington, D.C., for the March on Washington for Jobs and Freedom, along with millions of others, as his speech was carried live by network television stations.* **AP IMAGES. REPRODUCED BY PERMISSION.**

CIVIL RIGHTS ACT OF 1964, PUB.L. NO. 88–352, 78 STAT. 241 (1964)

This civil rights act was signed by President Lyndon B. Johnson on July 2, 1964, although it had been initiated by President John F. Kennedy in June 1963. More comprehensive than previous acts, the 1964 act contained eleven titles covering the areas of voting rights, access to public facilities, federal aid to schools engaged in the process of desegregation, discrimination in federally funded programs, and discrimination in employment. The act also strengthened earlier voter-registration protection; made racial discrimination in restaurants, hotels, and motels illegal; provided for equal access to public parks, pools, and other facilities; outlined unlawful employment practices; and mandated the creation of a federal Equal Employment Opportunity Commission.

An Act to enforce the constitutional right to vote, to confer jurisdiction upon the district courts of the United States to provide injunctive relief against discrimination in public accommodations, to authorize the Attorney General to institute suits to protect constitutional rights in public facilities and public education, to extend the Commission on Civil Rights, to prevent discrimination in federally assisted programs, to establish a Commission on Equal Employment Opportunity, and for other purposes.

TITLE I—VOTING RIGHTS

Sec. 101. Section 2004 of the Revised Statutes (42 U.S.C. 1971) . . . is further amended as follows: . . .

. . . "No Person acting under color of law shall—"

"(A) In determining whether any individual is qualified under State law or laws to vote in any Federal election, apply any standard, practice, or procedure different from the standards, practices, or procedures applied under such law or laws to other individuals within the same county, parish, or similar political subdivision who have been found by State officials to be qualified to vote;"

***Signing of Civil Rights Act of 1964, Washington, DC.** President Lyndon B. Johnson shakes hands with Martin Luther King Jr. after signing the Civil Rights Act on July 2, 1964. Initiated by President John F. Kennedy in June 1963, this act was more comprehensive than previous ones and included eleven titles covering such areas as voting rights, access to public facilities, and discrimination in employment.*
UPI/CORBIS-BETTMANN. REPRODUCED BY PERMISSION.

"(B) deny the right of any individual to vote in any Federal election because of an error or omission on any record or paper relating to any application, registration, or other act requisite to voting, if such error or omission is not material in determining whether such individual is qualified under State law to vote in such election; or"

"(C) employ any literacy test as a qualification for voting in any Federal election unless (I) such test is administered to each individual and is conducted wholly in writing, and (II) a certified copy of the test and of the answers given by the individual is furnished to him within twenty-five days of the submission of his request made within the period of time during which records and papers are required to be retained and preserved pursuant to title III of the Civil Rights Act of 1960 (42 U.S.C. 1974-74e; 74 Stat. 88). . . ."

Sec. 201. (a) All persons shall be entitled to the full and equal enjoyment of the goods, services, facilities, privileges, advantages, and accommodations of any place of public accommodation, as defined in this section, without discrimination or segregation on the ground of race, color, religion, or national origin.

(b) Each of the following establishments which serves the public is a place of public accommodation within the meaning of this title if its operations affect commerce, or if discrimination or segregation by it is supported by State action:

(1) any inn, hotel, motel, or other establishment which provides lodging to transient guests, other than an establishment located within a building which contains not more than five rooms for rent or hire and which is

actually occupied by the proprietor of such establishment as his residence;

(2) any restaurant, cafeteria, lunchroom, lunch counter, soda fountain, or other facility principally engaged in selling food for consumption on the premises, including, but not limited to, any such facility located on the premises of any retail establishment; or any gasoline station;

(3) any motion picture house, theater, concert hall, sports arena, stadium or other place of exhibition or entertainment; and

(4) any establishment (A)(I) which is physically located within the premises of any establishment otherwise covered by this subsection, or (II) within the premises of which is physically located any such covered establishment, and (B) which holds itself out as serving patrons of such covered establishment. . . .

(e) The provisions of this title shall not apply to a private club or other establishment not in fact open to the public, except to the extent that the facilities of such establishment are made available to the customers or patrons of an establishment within the scope of subsection (b).

Sec. 206. (a) Whenever the Attorney General has reasonable cause to believe that any person or group of persons is engaged in a pattern or practice of resistance to the full enjoyment of any of the rights secured by this title, and that the pattern or practice is of such a nature and is intended to deny the full exercise of the rights herein described, the Attorney General may bring a civil action in the appropriate district court of the United States. . . .

TITLE IV—DESEGREGATION OF PUBLIC EDUCATION

Sec. 407. (a) Whenever the Attorney General receives a complaint in writing—

(1) signed by a parent or group of parents to the effect that his or their minor children, as members of a class of persons similarly situated, are being deprived by a school board of the equal protection of the laws, or

(2) signed by an individual, or his parent, to the effect that he has been denied admission to or not permitted to continue in attendance at a public college by reason of race, color, religion, or national origin and the Attorney General believes the complaint is meritorious and certifies that the signer or signers of such complaint are unable, in his judgment, to initiate and maintain appropriate legal proceedings for relief and that the institution of an action will materially further the orderly achievement of desegregation in public education, the Attorney General is authorized, after giving notice of such complaint to the appropriate school board or college authority and after certifying that he is satisfied that such board or authority has had a reasonable time to adjust the conditions alleged in such complaint, to institute for or in the name of the United States a civil action in any appropriate district court of the United States against such parties and for such relief as may be appropriate. . . .

TITLE VI—NONDISCRIMINATION IN FEDERALLY-ASSISTED PROGRAMS

Sec. 601. No person in the United States shall, on the ground of race, color, or national origin, be excluded from participation in, be denied the benefits of, or be subjected to discrimination under any program or activity receiving Federal financial assistance. . . .

TITLE VII—EQUAL EMPLOYMENT OPPORTUNITY

Sec. 703. (a) It shall be an unlawful employment practice for an employer—

(1) to fail or refuse to hire or to discharge any individual, or otherwise to discriminate against any individual with respect to his compensation, terms, conditions, or privileges of employment, because of such individual's race, color, religion, sex, or national origin; or

(2) to limit, segregate, or classify his employees in any way which would deprive or tend to deprive any individual of employment opportunities or otherwise adversely affect his status as an employee, because of such individual's race, color, religion, sex, or national origin.

(b) It shall be an unlawful employment practice for an employment agency to fail or refuse to refer for employment, or otherwise to discriminate against, any individual because of his race, color, religion, sex, or national origin, or to classify or refer for employment any individual on the basis of his race, color, religion, sex, or national origin.

(c) It shall be an unlawful employment practice for a labor organization—

(1) to exclude or to expel from its membership, or otherwise to discriminate against, any individual because of his race, color, religion, sex, or national origin;

(2) to limit, segregate, or classify its membership, or to classify or fail or refuse to refer for employment any individual, in any way which would deprive or tend to deprive any individual of employment opportunities, or would limit such employment opportunities or otherwise adversely affect his status as an employee or as an applicant for employment, because of such individual's race, color, religion, sex, or national origin; or

(3) to cause or attempt to cause an employer to discriminate against an individual in violation of this section.

(d) It shall be an unlawful employment practice for any employer, labor organization, or joint labor-management committee controlling apprenticeship or other training or retraining, including on-the-job training programs to discriminate against any individual because of his race, color, religion, sex, or national origin in admission to, or employment in, any program established to provide apprenticeship or other training.

(e) Notwithstanding any other provision of this title, (1) it shall not be an unlawful employment practice for an employer to hire and employ employees, for an employment agency to classify, or refer for employment any individual, for a labor organization to classify its membership or to classify or refer for employment any individual, or for an employer, labor organization, or joint labor-management committee controlling apprenticeship or other training or retraining programs to admit or employ any individual in any such program, on the basis of his religion, sex, or national origin in those certain instances where religion, sex, or national origin is a bona fide occupational qualification reasonably necessary to the normal operation of that particular business or enterprise. . . .

Sec. 705. (1) There is hereby created a Commission to be known as the Equal Employment Opportunity Commission, which shall be composed of five members, not more than three of whom shall be members of the same political party, who shall be appointed by the President by and with the advice and consent of the Senate. . . .

EXECUTIVE ORDER NO. 11246, 3 C.F.R., 1964–1965 COMP. P.339–348 (1965)

On September 24, 1965, President Lyndon B. Johnson issued the following executive order, prohibiting discrimination in government employment and government contracting.

Under and by virtue of the authority vested in me as President of the United States by the Constitution and statutes of the United States, it is ordered as follows:

PART I—NONDISCRIMINATION IN GOVERNMENT EMPLOYMENT

Section 101. It is the policy of the Government of the United States to provide equal opportunity in Federal employment for all qualified persons, to prohibit discrimination in employment because of race, creed, color, or national origin, and to promote the full realization of equal employment opportunity through a positive, continuing program in each executive department and agency. The policy of equal opportunity applies to every aspect of Federal employment policy and practice.

Section 102. The head of each executive department and agency shall establish and maintain a positive program of equal employment opportunity for all civilian employees and applicants for employment within his jurisdiction in accordance with the policy set forth in Section 101.

Section 103. The Civil Service Commission shall supervise and provide leadership and guidance in the conduct of equal employment opportunity programs for the civilian employees of and applications for employment within the executive departments and agencies and shall review agency program accomplishments periodically. In order to facilitate the achievement of a model program for equal employment opportunity in the Federal service, the Commission may consult from time to time with such individuals, groups, or organizations as may be of assistance in improving the Federal program and realizing the objectives of this part.

Section 104. The Civil Service Commission shall provide for the prompt, fair, and impartial consideration of all complaints of discrimination in Federal employment on the basis of race, creed, color, or national origin. Procedures for the consideration complaints shall include at least one impartial review within the executive department or agency and shall provide for appeal to the Civil Service Commission.

Section 105. The Civil Service Commission shall issue such regulations, orders, and instructions as it deems necessary and appropriate to carry out its responsibilities under this Part, and the head of each executive department and agency shall comply with the regulations, orders, and instructions issued by the Commission under this Part.

PART II—NONDISCRIMINATION IN EMPLOYMENT BY GOVERNMENT CONTRACTORS AND SUBCONTRACTORS

Section 201. The Secretary of Labor shall be responsible for the administration of Parts II and III of this Order and shall adopt such rules and regulations and issue such orders as he deems necessary and appropriate to achieve the purposes thereof.

Section 202. Except in contracts exempted in accordance with Section 204 of this Order, all Government contracting agencies shall include in every Government contract hereafter entered into the following provisions:

"(1) The contractor will not discriminate against any employee or applicant for employment because of race, creed, color, or national origin. The contractor will take affirmative action to ensure that applicants are employed, and that employees are treated during employment, without regard to their race, creed, color, or national origin. Such action shall include, but not be limited to the following: employment, upgrading, demotion, or transfer; recruitment or recruitment advertising; layoff or termination; rates of pay or other forms of compensation; and selection for training, including apprenticeship. The contractor agrees to post in conspicuous places, available to employees and applicants for employment, notices to be provided by the contracting officer setting forth the provisions of this nondiscrimination clause."

"(2) The contractor will, in all solicitations or advertisements for employees placed by or on behalf of the contractor, state that all qualified applicants will receive consideration for employment without regard to race, creed, color, or national origin. ..."

PART III—NONDISCRIMINATION PROVISIONS IN FEDERALLY ASSISTED CONSTRUCTION CONTRACTS

Section 301. Each executive department and agency which administers a program involving Federal financial assistance shall require as a condition for approval of any grant, contract, loan, insurance, or guarantee thereunder, which may involve a construction contract, that the applicant for Federal assistance undertake and agree to incorporate, or cause to be incorporated, into all construction contracts paid for in whole or in part with funds obtained from the Federal Government or borrowed on the credit of the Federal Government pursuant to such grant, contract, loan, insurance, or guarantee, or undertaken pursuant to any Federal program involving such grant, contract, loan, insurance, or guarantee, the provisions prescribed for Government contracts by Section 202 of this Order or such modification thereof, preserving in substance the contractor's obligations thereunder, as may be approved by the Secretary of Labor, together with such additional provisions as the Secretary deems appropriate to establish and protect the interest of the United States in the enforcement of those obligations. ...

VOTING RIGHTS ACT OF 1965, PUB.L. NO. 89–110, 79 STAT. 437 (1965)

Signed by President Lyndon B. Johnson on August 6, 1965, the Voting Rights Act was an outgrowth of the protest demonstrations organized by African Americans to draw attention to discriminatory voter-registration practices in several southern states. The 1965 law abolished literacy, knowledge, and character tests as qualifications for voting; empowered federal registrars to register potential voters in any county where, in the judgments of the U.S. attorney general, registrars were indeed necessary to enforce the Fifteenth Amendment; and gave the U.S. attorney general the right to take whatever legal action he deemed necessary to eliminate any equivalent of the poll tax.

Although the single aim of the Voting Rights Act of 1965 was African American enfranchisement in the South, obstacles to registration and voting faced by all minorities were affected. Its potential as a tool for Hispanic Americans, however, was not fully realized for nearly a decade.

An Act to enforce the Fifteenth Amendment to the Constitution of the United States, and for other purposes.

Section 2. No voting qualification or prerequisite to voting, or standard, practice, or procedure shall be imposed or applied by any State or political subdivision to deny or abridge the right of any citizen of the United States to vote on account of race or color.

Section 4. (a) To assure that the right of citizens of the United States to vote is not denied or abridged on account of race or color, no citizen shall be denied the right to vote in any Federal, State, or local election because of his failure to comply with any test or device in any State with respect to which the determinations have been made under subsection (b) or in any political subdivision with respect to which such determinations have been made as a separate unit, unless the United States District Court for the District of Columbia in an action for a declaratory judgment brought by such State or subdivision against the United States has determined that no such test or device has been used during the five years preceding the filing of the action for the purpose or with the effect of denying or abridging the right to vote on account of race or color: *Provided,* That no such declaratory judgment shall issue with respect to any plaintiff for a period of five years after the entry of a final judgment of any court of the United States, other than the denial of a declaratory judgment under this section, whether entered prior to or after the enactment of this Act, determining that denials or abridgments of the right to vote on account of race or color through the use of such tests or devices have occurred anywhere in the territory of such plaintiff. ...

(d) For purposes of this section no State or political subdivision shall be determined to have engaged in the use of tests or devices for the purpose or with the effect of denying or abridging the right to vote on account of race or color if (1) incidents of such use have been few in number and have been promptly and

President Lyndon B. Johnson and Martin Luther King Jr., August 6, 1965. *Johnson (*left*) gives King (*right*) one of the pens used to sign the Voting Rights Act of 1965 into law. The act strikes down requirements such as literacy tests and poll tax payments that had been used to restrict African American participation in voting.* THE LIBRARY OF CONGRESS

effectively corrected by State or local action, (2) the continuing effect of such incidents has been eliminated, and (3) there is no reasonable probability of their recurrence in the future. . . .

Section 10. (a) The Congress finds that the requirement of the payment of a poll tax as a precondition to voting (I) precludes persons of limited means from voting or imposes unreasonable financial hardship upon such persons as a precondition to their exercise of the franchise, (II) does not bear a reasonable relationship to any legitimate State interest in the conduct of elections, and (III) in some areas has the purpose or effect of denying persons the right to vote because of race or color. Upon the basis of these findings, Congress declares that the constitutional right of citizens to vote is denied or abridged in some areas by the requirement of the payment of a poll tax as a precondition to voting. . . .

Section 11. (a) No person acting under color of law shall fail or refuse to permit any person to vote who is entitled to vote under any provision of this Act or is otherwise qualified to vote, or willfully fail or refuse to tabulate, count, and report such person's vote.

(b) No person, whether acting under color of law or otherwise, shall intimidate, threaten, or coerce, or attempt to intimidate, threaten or coerce any person for voting or attempting to vote, or intimidate, threaten, or coerce, or attempt to intimidate, threaten, or coerce any person for urging or aiding any person to vote or attempt to vote, or intimidate, threaten, or coerce any person for exercising any powers or duties under section 3 (a), 6, 8, 9, 10, or 12 (e). . . .

Section 14. (1) The terms "vote" or "voting" shall include all action necessary to make a vote effective in any primary, special, or general election, including, but not limited to, registration, listing pursuant to this Act, or other action required by law prerequisite to voting, casting a ballot, and having such ballot counted properly and included in the appropriate totals of votes cast with respect to candidates for public or party office and propositions for which votes are received in an election. ...

Sec. 17. Nothing in this Act shall be construed to deny, impair, or otherwise adversely affect the right to vote of any person registered to vote under the law of any state or political subdivision. ...

THE BLACK PANTHER MANIFESTO (1966)

The Black Panther Party relied on a strict and uncompromising regimen to mold its members into a unified and cohesive revolutionary force. Similar to the Nation of Islam, the party denounced all intoxicants, drugs, and artificial stimulants "while doing party work." The intellectual fare of every party member was the ten-point program, which every member was obliged to know, understand, and even commit to memory.

1. We want FREEDOM. We want power to determine the destiny of our Black Community.

We believe that black people will not be free until we are able to determine our destiny.

2. We want full employment for our people.

We believe that the federal government is responsible and obligated to give every man employment or a guaranteed income. We believe that if the white American businessman will not give full employment, then the means of production should be taken from the businessmen and placed in the community so that the people of the community can organize and employ all of its people and give a high standard of living.

3. We want an end to the robbery by the CAPITALIST of our Black Community.

We believe that this racist government has robbed us and now we are demanding the overdue debt of forty acres and two mules. Forty acres and two mules was promised 100 years ago as restitution for slave labor and mass murder of black people. We will accept the payment in currency which will be distributed to our many communities. The Germans are now aiding the Jews in Israel for the genocide of the Jewish people. The Germans murdered six million Jews. The American racist has taken

Black Panther Party Literature and Paraphernalia for Sale, New Haven, CT, 1970. *Founded in 1966, the Black Panther Party advocated black self-determination, militant resistance, and self-defense.* DAVID FENTON/GETTY IMAGES

part in the slaughter of over fifty million black people, therefore, we feel that this is a modest demand that we make.

4. We want decent housing, fit for shelter of human beings.

We believe that if the white landlords will not give decent housing to our black community, then the housing and the land should be made into cooperatives so that our community, with government aid, can build and make decent housing for its people.

5. We want education for our people that exposes the true nature of this decadent American society. We want education that teaches us our true history and our role in the present-day society.

We believe in an educational system that will give to our people a knowledge of self. If a man does not have knowledge of himself and his position in society and the world, then he has little chance to relate to anything else.

6. We want all black men to be exempt from military service.

We believe that Black people should not be forced to fight in the military service to defend a racist government that does not protect us. We will not fight and kill other people of color in the world who, like black people, are being victimized by the white racist government of America. We will protect ourselves from the force and violence of the racist police and the racist military, by whatever means necessary.

7. We want an immediate end to POLICE BRUTALITY and MURDER of black people.

We believe we can end police brutality in our black community by organizing black self-defense groups that are dedicated to defending our black community from racist police oppression and brutality. The Second Amendment to the Constitution of the United States gives a right to bear arms. We therefore believe that all black people should arm themselves for self-defense.

8. We want freedom for all black men held in federal, state, county and city prisons and jails.

We believe that all black people should be released from the many jails and prisons because they have not received a fair and impartial trial.

9. We want all black people when brought to trial to be tried in court by a jury of their peer group or people from their black communities, as defined by the constitution of the United States.

We believe that the courts should follow the United States Constitution so that black people will receive fair trials. The 14th Amendment of the U.S. Constitution gives a man a right to be tried by his peer group. A peer is a person from a similar economic, social, religious, geographical, environmental, historical and racial background. To do this the court will be forced to select a jury from the black community from which the black defendant came. We have been, and are being tried by all-white juries that have no understanding of the "average reasoning man" of the black community.

10. We want land, bread, housing, education, clothing, justice and peace. And as our major political objective, a United Nations-supervised plebiscite to be held throughout the black colony in which only black colonial subjects will be allowed to participate, for the purpose of determining the will of black people as to their national destiny.

When, in the course of human events, it becomes necessary for one people to dissolve the political bands which have connected them with another, and to assume, among the powers of the earth, the separate and equal station to which the laws of nature and nature's God entitle them, a decent respect to the opinions of mankind requires that they should declare the causes which impel them to the separation.

We hold these truths to be self-evident, that all men are created equal; that they are endowed by their Creator with certain inalienable rights; that among these are life, liberty, and the pursuit of happiness.

That, to secure these rights, governments are instituted among them, deriving their just powers from the consent of the governed; that, whenever any form of government becomes destructive of these ends, it is the right of the people to alter or to abolish it, and to institute a new government, laying its foundation on such principles, and organizing its powers in such form, as to them shall seem most likely to effect their safety and happiness.

Prudence, indeed, will dictate that governments long established should not be changed for light and transient causes; and, accordingly, all experience hath shown, that mankind are more disposed to suffer, while evils are sufferable, than to right themselves by abolishing the forms to which they are accustomed. But, when a long train of abuses and usurpations, pursuing invariably the same object, evinces a design to reduce them under absolute despotism, it is their right, it is their duty, to throw off such government, and to provide new guards for their future security.

CIVIL RIGHTS ACT OF 1968, PUB.L. NO. 90–284, TITLES VIII & IX, 82 STAT. 284 (1968)

Title VIII of Public Law 90-284, the Civil Rights Act of 1968, is better known as the Fair Housing Act. It was signed by President Lyndon B. Johnson on April 11, 1968, and created a national housing policy. The act made discrimination in the sale, rental, or financing of housing illegal, and empowered the U.S. attorney general to take action in such cases.

TITLE VIII—FAIR HOUSING

Sec. 801. It is the policy of the United States to provide, within constitutional limitations, for fair housing throughout the United States.

Section 804. As made applicable by section 803 and except as exempted by sections 803(b) and 807, it shall be unlawful—

(a) to refuse to sell or rent after the making of a bona fide offer, or to refuse to negotiate for the sale or rental of, or otherwise make unavailable or deny, a dwelling to any person because of race, color, religion, or national origin.

(b) to discriminate against any person in the terms, conditions, or privileges of sale or rental of a dwelling, or in the provision of services or facilities in connection there-with, because of race, color, religion, or national origin.

(c) to make, print, or publish or cause to be made, printed, or published any notice, statement, or advertisement, with respect to the sale or rental of a dwelling that indicates any preference, limitation, or discrimination based on race, color, religion, or national origin, or an intention to make any such preference, limitation, or discrimination.

(d) to represent to any person because of race, color, religion, or national origin that any dwelling is not available for inspection, sale, or rental when such dwelling is in fact so available.

(e) for profit, to induce or attempt to induce any person to sell or rent any dwelling by representations regarding the entry or prospective entry into the neighborhood of a person or persons of a particular race, color, religion, or national origin.

Sec. 805. After December 31, 1968, it shall be unlawful for any bank, building and loan association, insurance company or other corporation, association, firm or enterprise whose business consists in whole or in part in the making of commercial real estate loans, to deny a loan or other financial assistance to a person applying therefor for the purpose of purchasing, constructing, improving, repairing, or maintaining a dwelling, or to discriminate against him in the fixing of the amount, interest rate, duration, or other terms or conditions of such loan or other financial assistance, because of the race, color, religion, or national origin of such person or of any person associated with him in connection with such loan or other financial assistance or the purposes of such loan or other financial assistance, or of the present or prospective owners, leases, tenants, or occupants of the dwelling or dwellings in relation to which such loan or other financial assistance is to be made or given. . . .

TITLE IX—PREVENTION OF INTIMIDATION IN FAIR HOUSING CASES

Section 901. Whoever, whether or not acting under color of law, by force or threat of force willfully injures, intimidates or interferes with, or attempts to injure, intimidate or interfere with—

(a) any person because of his race, color, religion or national origin and because he is or has been selling, purchasing, renting, financing, occupying, or contracting or negotiating for the sale, purchase, rental, financing or occupation of any dwelling, or applying for or participating in any service, organization, or facility relating to the business of selling or renting dwellings; or

(b) any person because he is or has been, or in order to intimidate such person or any other person or any class of persons from—

(1) participating, without discrimination on account of race, color, religion or national origin, in any of the activities, services, organizations or facilities described in subsection 901(a). . . .

BARBARA JORDAN'S SPEECH ON PRESIDENTIAL IMPEACHMENT PROCEEDINGS (1974) (EXCERPT)

On July 25, 1974, Congresswoman Barbara Jordan appeared on television to offer her position on the impeachment of the president of the United States, Richard Nixon. Solemn and exhausted, she hunched over four annotated amended pages of her personal notes, as well as four pages of historical impeachment criteria set against the president's conduct. Her black-rimmed glasses reflected the glare of the lighting in the room as she examined her notes. At that moment, she improvised her speech while looking into the television cameras.

"We the people"—it is a very eloquent beginning. But when the Constitution of the United States was completed on the seventeenth of September in 1787, I was not included in that "We the people." I felt for many years that somehow George Washington and Alexander Hamilton just left me out by mistake. But through the process of amendment, interpretation, and court decision, I have finally been included in "We the people."

It is wrong, I suggest, it is a misreading of the Constitution for any member here to assert that for a member to vote for an Article of Impeachment means that the member must be convinced that the President should be removed from office. The Constitution doesn't say that. The powers relating to impeachment are an essential check in the hands of this body, the legislature, against and upon the encroachment of the Executive. In establishing the division between the two branches of the legislature, the House and the Senate, assigning to one the right to accuse and the other the right to judge, the framers of this Constitution were very astute. They did not make the accusers and the judges the same persons.

We know the nature of impeachment. We have been talking about it for a while now. "It is chiefly designed for the President and his high ministers" to somehow be called into account. It is designed to "bridle" the Executive if he engages in excesses. It is designed as a method of national "inquest into the conduct of public men. ..." The nature of impeachment is a narrowly channeled exception to the separation of powers maxim; the Federal Convention of 1787 said that. It limited impeachment to "high crimes and misdemeanors" and discounted and opposed the term "maladministration."

The drawing of political lines goes to the motivation behind impeachment; but impeachment must proceed within the confines of the constitutional term "high crimes and misdemeanors."

What the President did know on the twenty-third of June was the prior activities of E. Howard Hunt, which included his participation in the break-in of Daniel Ellsberg's psychiatrist, which included Howard Hunt's participation in the Dita Beard ITT affair, which included Howard Hunt's fabrication of cables, designed to discredit the Kennedy administration.

We have heard time and time again that the evidence reflects payment to the defendants of money. The President has knowledge that these funds were being paid and that these were funds collected for the 1972 presidential campaign.

Beginning shortly after the Watergate break-in and continuing to the present time, the President has engaged in a series of public statements and actions designed to thwart the lawful investigation by government prosecutors. Moreover, the President has made public announcements and assertions bearing on the Watergate case which the evidence will show he knows to be false. ...

James Madison said, again at the Constitutional Convention: "A president is impeachable if he attempts to subvert the Constitution."

The Constitution charges that President with the task of taking care that the laws be faithfully executed, and yet the President has counseled his aides to commit perjury, willfully disregarded the secrecy of grand jury proceedings, concealed surreptitious entry, attempted to compromise a federal judge while publicly displaying his cooperation with the processes of criminal justice. ...

If the impeachment provision in the Constitution of the United States will not reach the offenses charged here, then perhaps that eighteenth-century Constitution should be abandoned to a twentieth-century paper shredder. Has the President committed offenses and planned and directed and acquiesced in a course of conduct which the Constitution will not tolerate? That is the question. We know that. We know the question. We should now forthwith proceed to answer the question. It is reason and not passion which must guide our deliberations, guide our debate, and guide our decision.

PRESIDENT GEORGE H. W. BUSH'S MESSAGE TO THE SENATE RETURNING WITHOUT APPROVAL THE CIVIL RIGHTS ACT OF 1990, 26 WEEKLY COMP. PRES.DOC. 1632–34 (OCTOBER 22, 1990)

In June 1989, the U.S. Supreme Court delivered opinions in several cases dealing with seniority systems and racial discrimination in employment. Ruling in the cases Lorance v. AT&T Technologies Inc., Martin v. Wilks, Patterson v. McLean Credit Union, *and* Wards Cove Packing Co. v. Atonio, *the Court appeared to reverse earlier civil rights rulings. Civil rights organizations were quick to protest the rulings; opponents of the ruling, including the NAACP Legal Defense and Educational Fund, the Leadership Conference on Civil Rights, the American Civil Liberties Union, and the National Organization of Women, argued that the Court had undermined the protection granted by federal civil rights and equal employment legislation.*

On October 16 and 17, 1990, both houses of Congress approved a bill designed to reverse the Court's rulings. On October 22, President George H. W. Bush vetoed the bill, claiming that the bill's provisions would encourage employers to establish hiring quotas.

To the Senate of the United States.

I am today returning without my approval [Separate Bill] 2104, the "Civil Rights Act of 1990." I deeply regret having to take this action with respect to a bill bearing such a title, especially since it contains certain provisions that I strongly endorse.

Discrimination, whether on the basis of race, national origin, sex, religion, or disability, is worse than wrong. It is a fundamental evil that tears at the fabric of our society, and one that all Americans should and must oppose. That requires rigorous enforcement of existing antidiscrimination laws. . . .

. . . Despite the use of the term "civil rights" in the title of S. 2104, the bill actually employs a maze of highly legalistic language to introduce the destructive force of quotas into our Nation's employment system. Primarily through provisions governing cases in which employment practices are alleged to have unintentionally caused the disproportionate exclusion of members of certain groups, S. 2104 creates powerful incentives for employers to adopt hiring and promotion quotas. These incentives are created by the bill's new and very technical rules of litigation, which will make it difficult for employers to defend legitimate employment practices. In many cases, a defense against unfounded allegations will be impossible. Among other problems, the plaintiff often need not even show that any of the employer's practices caused a significant statistical disparity. In other cases, the employer's defense is confined to an unduly narrow definition of "business necessity" that is significantly more restrictive than that established by the Supreme Court in *Griggs v. Duke Power Co.* and in two decades of subsequent decisions. Thus, unable to defend legitimate practices in court, employers will be driven to adopt quotas in order to avoid liability.

Proponents of S. 2104 assert that it is needed to overturn the Supreme Court's *Wards Cove Packing Co. v. Atonio* decision and restore the law that had existed since the Griggs case in 1971. S. 2104, however, does not in fact codify Griggs or the Court's subsequent decisions prior to Wards Cove. Instead, S. 2104 engages in a sweeping rewrite of two decades of Supreme Court jurisprudence, using language that appears in no decision of the Court and that is contrary to principles acknowledged even by the Justice Stevens's dissent in Wards Cove: "The opinion in Griggs made it clear that a neutral practice that operates to exclude minorities is nevertheless lawful if it serves a valid business purpose."

I am aware of the dispute among lawyers about the proper interpretation of certain critical language used in this portion of S. 2104. The very fact of this dispute suggests that the bill is not codifying the law developed by the Supreme Court in Griggs and subsequent cases. This debate, moreover, is a sure sign that S. 2104 will lead to years—perhaps decades—of uncertainty and expensive litigation. It is neither fair nor sensible to give the employers of our country a difficult choice between using quotas and seeking a clarification of the law through costly and very risky litigation.

D. 3205 contains several other unacceptable provisions as well. One section unfairly closes the courts, in many instances, to individuals victimized by agreements, to which they were not a party, involving the use of quotas. Another section radically alters the remedial provisions in Title VII of the Civil Rights Act of 1964, replacing measures designed to foster conciliation and settlement with a new scheme modeled on a tort system widely acknowledged to be in a state of crisis. The bill also contains a number of provisions that will create unnecessary and inappropriate incentives for litigation. These include unfair retroactivity rules; attorneys fee provisions that will discourage settlements; unreasonable new statutes of limitation; and a "rule of construction" that will make it extremely difficult to know how courts can be expected to apply the law. In order to assist the Congress regarding legislation in this area, I enclose herewith a memorandum from the Attorney General explaining in detail the defects that make S. 2104 unacceptable.

Our goal and our promise has been equal opportunity and equal protection under the law. That is a bedrock principle from which we cannot retreat. The temptation to support a bill—any bill—simply because its title includes the words "civil rights" is very strong. This impulse is not entirely bad. Presumptions have too often run the other way, and our Nation's history on racial questions cautions against complacency. But when our efforts, however well intentioned, result in quotas, equal opportunity is not advanced but thwarted. The very commitment to justice and equality that is offered as the reason why this bill should be signed requires me to veto it. . . .

George Bush

The White House,

October 22, 1990

CIVIL RIGHTS ACT OF 1991, PUB.L. NO. 102–166, 105 STAT 1071 (1991)

After vetoing Congress's 1990 civil rights legislation, the Bush administration joined both houses of Congress in working on alternative bills. Following months of negotiation, the Senate passed Senate Bill 1745 on October 30; the House passed the bill on November 7. On November 21, President George H. W. Bush signed the Civil Rights Act of 1991.

This act is designed to provide additional remedies to deter harassment and intentional discrimination in the workplace, to provide guidelines for the adjudication of cases arising under Title VII ... and to expand the scope of civil rights legislation weakened by Supreme Court decisions, particularly the Court's ruling in *Wards Cove Packing Co. v. Atonio,* 490 US 642 (1989).

Sec. 2. Findings

The Congress finds that—

(1) additional remedies under Federal law are needed to deter unlawful harassment and intentional discrimination in the workplace;

(2) the decision of the Supreme Court in *Wards Cove Packing Co. v. Atonio,* 490 U.S. 642 (1989) has weakened the scope and effectiveness of Federal civil rights protections; and

(3) legislation is necessary to provide additional protections against unlawful discrimination in employment.

Sec. 3. Purposes.

The purposes of this Act are—

(1) to provide appropriate remedies for intentional discrimination and unlawful harassment in the workplace;

(2) to codify the concepts of "business necessity" and "job related" enunciated by the Supreme Court in *Griggs v. Duke Power Co.,* 401 U.S. 424 (1971), and in the other Supreme Court decisions prior to *Wards Cove Packing Co. v. Atonio,* 490 U.S. 642 (1989);

(3) to confirm statutory authority and provide statutory guidelines for the adjudication of disparate impact suits under title VII of the Civil Rights Act of 1964 (42 U.S.C. 2000e et seq.); and

(4) to respond to recent decisions of the Supreme Court by expanding the scope of relevant civil rights statutes in order to provide adequate protection to victims of discrimination.

TITLE I—FEDERAL CIVIL RIGHTS REMEDIES

Sec. 105. Burden of Proof in Disparate Impact Cases.

(a) Section 703 of the Civil Rights Act of 1964 (42 U.S.C. 2000e-2) is amended by adding at the end the following new subsection:

... An unlawful employment practice based on disparate impact is established under this title only if—

... A complaining party demonstrates that a respondent used a particular employment practice that causes a disparate impact on the basis of race, color, religion, sex, or national origin and the respondent fails to demonstrate that the challenged practice is job related for the position in question and consistent with business necessity. ...

... With respect to demonstrating that a particular employment practice causes a disparate impact as described in subparagraph (A)(i), the complaining party shall demonstrate that each particular challenged employment practice causes a disparate impact, except that if the complaining party can demonstrate to the court that the elements of a respondent's decisionmaking process are not capable of separation for analysis, the decisionmaking process may be analyzed as one employment practice.

... If the respondent demonstrates that a specific employment practice does not cause the disparate impact, the respondent shall not be required to demonstrate that such practice is required by business necessity. ...

Sec. 106. Prohibition Against Discriminatory Use of Test Scores.

Section 703 of the Civil Rights Act of 1964 (42 U.S.C. 2000e-2) (as amended by section 105) is further amended by adding at the end of the following new subsection:

... It shall be an unlawful employment practice for a respondent, in connection with the selection or referral of applicants or candidates for employment or promotion, to adjust the scores of, use different cutoff scores for, or otherwise alter the results of, employment related tests on the basis of race, color, religion, sex, or national origin. ...

TITLE II—GLASS CEILING

Sec. 202 Findings and Purpose.

(a) Findings—Congress finds that—

(1) despite a dramatically growing presence in the workplace, women and minorities remain underrepresented in management and decision-making positions in business;

(2) artificial barriers exist to the advancement of women and minorities in the workplace;

(3) United States corporations are increasingly relying on women and minorities to meet employment requirements and are increasingly aware of the advantages derived from a diverse work force;

(4) the "Glass Ceiling Initiative" undertaken by the Department of Labor, including the release of the report entitled "Report on the Glass Ceiling Initiative," has been instrumental in raising public awareness of—

(A) the underrepresentation of women and minorities at the management and decision-making levels in the United States work force;

(B) the underrepresentation of women and minorities in line functions in the United States work force;

(C) the lack of access for qualified women and minorities to credential-building developmental opportunities; and

(D) the desirability of eliminating artificial barriers to the advancement of women and minorities to such levels;

(f) the establishment of a commission to examine issues raised by the Glass Ceiling Initiative would help—

(A) focus greater attention on the importance of eliminating artificial barriers to the advancement of women and minorities to management and decision-making positions in business; and

(B) promote work force diversity. . . .

ORIGINAL OAKLAND RESOLUTION ON EBONICS (1996)

In order to improve the language skills of African American students, the Oakland, California, Board of Education adopted a language approach referred to as Ebonics, which was developed by an African American task force. Ebonics, which concerns what linguists identify as African American Vernacular English (AAVE), in part explores the linguistic development of African slaves who were brought to the United States; it has been argued that AAVE evolved from and was influenced by the various African languages spoken by the slaves. The introduction of this language approach initially brought a firestorm of controversy because its purpose was misunderstood. Critics bridled at its supposed political agenda, and it was feared that the program could limit the learning process and language acquisition of African American students. The purpose of the legislation was to instruct teachers in the structure and unique characteristics of AAVE so that they could better teach their students Standard English. The resolution was amended on January 15, 1997, to ensure that proficiency in Standard English be clearly specified in the document as the board of education's main goal.

RESOLUTION OF THE BOARD OF EDUCATION ADOPTING THE REPORT AND RECOMMENDATIONS OF THE AFRICAN-AMERICAN TASK FORCE; A POLICY STATEMENT AND DIRECTING THE SUPERINTENDENT OF SCHOOLS TO DEVISE A PROGRAM TO IMPROVE THE ENGLISH LANGUAGE ACQUISITION AND APPLICATION SKILLS OF AFRICAN-AMERICAN STUDENTS.

No. §597-0063

Whereas, numerous validated scholarly studies demonstrate that African American students as part of their culture and history as African people possess and utilize a language described in various scholarly approaches as "Ebonics" (literally Black sounds) or Pan African Communication Behaviors or African Language Systems; and

Whereas, these studies have also demonstrated that African Language Systems are genetically-based and not a dialect of English; and

Whereas, these studies demonstrate that such West and Niger-Congo African languages have been officially recognized and addressed in the mainstream public educational community as worth of study, understanding or application of its principles, laws and structures for the benefit of African American students both in terms of positive appreciation of the language and these students' acquisition and mastery of English language skills; and

Whereas, such recognition by scholars has given rise over the past 15 years to legislation passed by the State of California recognizing the unique language stature of descendants of slaves, with such legislation being prejudicially and unconstitutionally vetoed repeatedly by various California state governors; and

Whereas, judicial cases in states other than California have recognized the unique language stature of African American pupils, and such recognition by courts has resulted in court-mandated educational programs which have substantially benefitted African American children in the interest of vindicating their equal protection of the law rights under the 14th Amendment to the United States Constitution; and

Whereas, the Federal Bilingual Education Act (20 USC 1402 et seq.) mandates that local educational agencies "build their capacities to establish, implement and sustain programs of instruction for children and youth of limited English proficiency," and

Whereas, the interests of the Oakland Unified School District in providing equal opportunities for all of its students dictate limited English proficient educational programs recognizing the English language acquisition and improvement skills of African American students are as fundamental as is application of bilingual education principles for others whose primary languages are other than English; and

Whereas, the standardized tests and grade scores of African American students in reading and language art skills measuring their application of English skills are substantially below state and national norms and that such deficiencies will be remedied by application of a program featuring African Language Systems principles in instructing African American children both in their primary language and in English, and

Whereas, standardized tests and grade scores will be remedied by application of a program with teachers and aides who are certified in the methodology of featuring African Language Systems principles in instructing African American children both in their primary language and in English. The certified teachers of these students will be provided incentives including, but not limited to salary differentials,

Now, therefore, be it resolved that the Board of Education officially recognizes the existence and the cultural and historic bases of West and Niger-Congo African Language Systems, and each language as the predominantly primary language of African American students; and

Be it further resolved that the Board of Education hereby adopts the report recommendations and attached Policy Statement of the District's African American Task Force on language stature of African American speech; and

Be it further resolved that the Superintendent in conjunction with her staff shall immediately devise and implement the best possible academic program for imparting instruction to African American students in their primary language for the combined purposes of maintaining the legitimacy and richness of such language whether it is known as "Ebonics," "African Language Systems," "Pan African Communication Behaviors" or other description, and to facilitate their acquisition and mastery of English language skills; and

Be it further resolved that the Board of Education hereby commits to earmark District general and special funding as is reasonably necessary and appropriate to enable the Superintendent and her staff to accomplish the foregoing; and

Be it further resolved that the Superintendent and her staff shall utilize the input of the entire Oakland educational community as well as state and federal scholarly and educational input in devising such a program; and

Be it further resolved, that periodic reports on the progress of the creation and implementation of such an educational program shall be made to Board of Education at least once per month commencing at the Board meeting of December 18, 1996.

POLICY STATEMENT

There is persuasive empirical evidence that, predicated on analysis of the phonology, morphology and syntax that currently exists as systematic, rule governed and predictable patterns exist in the grammar of African-American speech. The validated and persuasive linguistic evidence is that African-Americans (1) have retained a West and Niger-Congo African linguistic structure in the substratum of their speech and (2) by this criteria are not native speakers of black dialect or any other dialect of English.

Moreover, there is persuasive empirical evidence that, owing to their history as United States slave descendants of West and Niger-Congo African origin, to the extent that African-Americans have been born into, reared in, and continue to live in linguistic environments that are different from the Euro-American English speaking population, African-American people and their children, are from home environments in which a language other than English language is dominant within the meaning of "environment where a Language other than English is dominant" as defined in Public Law 1-13-382 (20 U.S.C. 7402, et seq.).

The policy of the Oakland Unified School District (OUSD) is that all pupils are equal and are to be treated equally. Hence, all pupils who have difficulty speaking, reading, writing or understanding the English language and whose difficulties may deny to them the opportunity to learn successfully in classrooms where the language of instruction is English or to participate fully in classrooms where the language of instruction is English or to participate fully in our society are to be treated equally regardless of their race or national origin.

As in the case of Asian-American, Latino-American, Native American and all other pupils in this District who come from backgrounds or environments where a language other than English is dominant, African-American pupils shall not, because of their race, be subtly dehumanized, stigmatized, discriminated against or denied. Asian-American, Latino-American, Native American and all other language different children are provided general funds for bilingual education, English as Second Language (ESL) and State and Federal (Title VIII) Bilingual education programs to address their limited and non-English proficient (LEP/NEP) needs. African-American pupils are equally entitled to be tested and, where appropriate, shall be provided general funds and State and Federal (Title VIII) bilingual education and ESL programs to specifically address their LEP/NEP needs.

All classroom teachers and aids who are bilingual in Nigritian Ebonics (African-American Language) and English shall be given the same salary differentials and merit increases that are provided to teachers of the non-African American LEP pupils in the OUSD.

With a view toward assuring that parent of African-American pupils are given the knowledge base necessary to make informed choices, it shall be the policy of the Oakland Unified School District that all parents of LEP (Limited English Proficient) pupils are to be provided the opportunity to partake of any and all language and culture specific teacher education and training classes designed to address their child's LEP needs.

On all home language surveys given to parents of pupils requesting home language identification or designations, a description of the District's programmatic consequences of their choices will be contained.

Nothing in this Policy shall preclude or prevent African-American parents who view their child's limited English proficiency as being non-standard English, as opposed to being West and Niger-Congo African Language based, from exercising their right to choose and to have their child's speech disorders and English

Language deficits addressed by special education and/or other District programs.

THE PRESIDENT'S INITIATIVE ON RACE— THE ADVISORY BOARD'S REPORT TO THE PRESIDENT (1998) (EXCERPT)

On June 13, 1997, President Bill Clinton established the seven-member President's Advisory Board to the President's Initiative on Race. Headed by historian John Hope Franklin, the advisory board was given the responsibilities of promoting national dialogue on race issues, increasing the nation's understanding of the history and future of race relations, identifying and creating plans to calm racial tension and promote increased opportunity for all Americans, and addressing crime and the administration of justice.

On September 18, 1998, the advisory board concluded its work and presented its recommendations to President Clinton. Its report, One America in the 21st Century: Forging a New Future, *recommended that the president institute a standing advisory board to build upon its foundation and that a public education program be initiated to underscore the "common values" of a diverse multiracial nation.*

INTRODUCTION

America's greatest promise in the 21st century lies in our ability to harness the strength of racial diversity. Our greatest challenge is to work as one community to define ourselves with pride as a multi-racial democracy. At the end of the 20th century, America has emerged as the

Changing America, ***a Report by the Council of Economic Advisers for the President's Initiative on Race, September 18, 1998.*** *On this date two reports concerning race in the United States were presented to President Bill Clinton (*center*):* Changing America *and* One America in the 21st Century: Forging a New Future, *the latter issued by the Advisory Board to the President's Initiative on Race. John Hope Franklin (*bottom left*) served as chair of the Advisory Board.* AP PHOTO/RON EDMONDS

worldwide symbol of opportunity and freedom through leadership that constantly strives to give meaning to the fundamental principles of our Constitution. Those principals of justice, opportunity, equality, and inclusion must continue to guide the planning for our future.

THE ADVISORY BOARD AND ITS MANDATE

Members of the Advisory Board to the President's Initiative on Race have spent the past 15 months engaged in a process designed to examine race relations in America. Through study, dialogue, and action we have begun to engage the American people in a focused examination of how racial differences have affected our society and how to meet the racial challenges that face us. Our task was to take this necessary first step in the President's effort to articulate and realize a vision of a more just society.

In June 1997, through Executive Order No. 13050, President Clinton appointed Dr. John Hope Franklin (chairman), Linda Chavez-Thompson, Reverend Dr. Suzan D. Johnson Cook, Thomas H. Kean, Angela E. Oh, Bob Thomas, and William F. Winter to serve as members of the Advisory Board.

... [T]he Board forged ahead to meet the objectives set out by the President through his Executive Order. Those objectives included the following:

Promote a constructive national dialogue to confront and work through the challenging issues that surround race.

Increase the Nation's understanding of our recent history of race relations and the course our Nation is charting on issues of race relations and racial diversity.

Bridge racial divides by encouraging community leaders to develop and implement innovative approaches to calming racial tensions.

Identify, develop, and implement solutions to problems in areas in which race has a substantial impact, such as education, economic opportunity, housing, health care, and the administration of justice.

In addition, the Advisory Board examined issues related to race and immigration, the impact of the media on racial stereotyping, and enforcement of civil rights laws.

We wish to make it clear that this Report is not a definitive analysis of the state of race relations in America today. ... Rather, we were engaged in the task of assisting with the initial stages of this new America's journey toward building a more just society in the 21st century.

ACCOMPLISHMENTS, CHALLENGES, AND OPPORTUNITIES

... Many challenges lie ahead. As America's racial diversity grows, the complexity of giving meaning to the promise of America grows as well. It is these challenges that signal where opportunities may exist. This report attempts to frame the challenges, identify the opportunities, and recommended action. It provides an overview of information gathered from communities across the Nation, including diverse points of view about racial differences and controversial issues that are currently being debated and ideas for how strong leadership can continue to move our Nation closer to its highest aspirations.

REPORT OVERVIEW

... Although this Report concludes our year-long exploration of race and racism, our work is only the foundation for building one America. The work that lies ahead cannot be accomplished by a single group. Our experience has provided the Nation with the chance to identify leaders in many parts of this country, working in numerous fields, who will promote a vision of a unified, strong, and just society. The Race Initiative affirmed the efforts of Americans who have been, are, and will continue to give meaning to the words "justice," "equality," "dignity," "respect," and "inclusion." We urge bold and decisive action to further the movement toward "redeeming the promise of America."

BARACK OBAMA'S KEYNOTE ADDRESS AT THE DEMOCRATIC NATIONAL CONVENTION (2004)

On July 27, 2004, Barack Obama, the Democratic candidate for an Illinois U.S. Senate seat, delivered the keynote address at the Democratic National Convention in Boston. Obama was the third African American to deliver the keynote address for the convention. When Obama, a rising star in the Democratic Party, won the November Senate election, he became only the third black U.S. senator since Reconstruction.

On behalf of the great state of Illinois, crossroads of a nation, Land of Lincoln, let me express my deepest gratitude for the privilege of addressing this convention.

Tonight is a particular honor for me because—let's face it—my presence on this stage is pretty unlikely. My father was a foreign student, born and raised in a small

Barack Obama, Illinois State Senator and U.S. Senate Candidate, Democratic National Convention, Fleet Center, Boston, MA, July 27, 2004. *Obama catapulted himself to national prominence by delivering a powerful keynote address at the convention that nominated John Kerry as the Democratic presidential candidate. In the November election, Obama was victorious in his U.S. Senate contest, setting the stage for the historic presidential election of 2008.* SCOTT J. FERRELL/CONGRESSIONAL QUARTERLY/GETTY IMAGES

village in Kenya. He grew up herding goats, went to school in a tin-roof shack. His father—my grandfather—was a cook, a domestic servant to the British.

But my grandfather had larger dreams for his son. Through hard work and perseverance my father got a scholarship to study in a magical place, America, that shone as a beacon of freedom and opportunity to so many who had come before.

While studying here, my father met my mother. She was born in a town on the other side of the world, in Kansas. Her father worked on oil rigs and farms through most of the Depression. The day after Pearl Harbor my grandfather signed up for duty; joined Patton's army, marched across Europe. Back home, my grandmother raised their baby and went to work on a bomber assembly line. After the war, they studied on the G.I. Bill, bought a house through F.H.A., and later moved west all the way to Hawaii in search of opportunity.

And they, too, had big dreams for their daughter. A common dream, born of two continents.

My parents shared not only an improbable love, they shared an abiding faith in the possibilities of this nation. They would give me an African name, Barack, or "blessed," believing that in a tolerant America your name is no barrier to success. They imagined me going to the best schools in the land, even though they weren't rich, because in a generous America you don't have to be rich to achieve your potential.

They are both passed away now. And yet, I know that, on this night, they look down on me with great pride.

I stand here today, grateful for the diversity of my heritage, aware that my parents' dreams live on in my two precious daughters. I stand here knowing that my story is part of the larger American story, that I owe a debt to all of those who came before me, and that, in no other country on earth, is my story even possible.

Tonight, we gather to affirm the greatness of our nation—not because of the height of our skyscrapers, or the power of our military, or the size of our economy. Our pride is based on a very simple premise, summed up in a declaration made over two hundred years ago: 'We hold these truths to be self-evident, that all men are created equal. That they are endowed by their Creator with certain inalienable rights. That among these are life, liberty and the pursuit of happiness.'

That is the true genius of America—a faith in simple dreams,, an insistence on small miracles. That we can tuck in our children at night and know that they are fed and clothed and safe from harm. That we can say what we think, write what we think, without hearing a sudden knock on the door. That we can have an idea and start our own business without paying a bribe. That we can participate in the political process without fear of retribution, and that our votes will be counted at least, most of the time.

This year, in this election, we are called to reaffirm our values and our commitments, to hold them against a hard reality and see how we are measuring up, to the legacy of our forbearers, and the promise of future generations.

And fellow Americans, Democrats, Republicans, Independents—I say to you tonight: we have more work to do. More work to do for the workers I met in Galesburg, Ill., who are losing their union jobs at the Maytag plant that's moving to Mexico, and now are having to compete with their own children for jobs that pay seven bucks an hour. More to do for the father that I met who was losing his job and choking back the tears, wondering how he would pay $4,500 a month for the drugs his son needs without the health benefits that he counted on. More to do for the young woman in East St. Louis, and thousands more like her, who has the grades, has the drive, has the will, but doesn't have the money to go to college.

Now don't get me wrong. The people I meet—in small towns and big cities, in diners and office parks—they don't expect government to solve all their problems. They know they have to work hard to get ahead—and they want to.

Go into the collar counties around Chicago, and people will tell you they don't want their tax money wasted, by a welfare agency or by the Pentagon.

Go into any inner city neighborhood, and folks will tell you that government alone can't teach our kids to learn—they know that parents have to teach, that children can't achieve unless we raise their expectations and turn off the television sets and eradicate the slander that says a black youth with a book is acting white. They know those things.

People don't expect government to solve all their problems. But they sense, deep in their bones, that with just a slight change in priorities, we can make sure that every child in America has a decent shot at life, and that the doors of opportunity remain open to all.

They know we can do better. And they want that choice.

In this election, we offer that choice. Our Party has chosen a man to lead us who embodies the best this country has to offer. And that man is John Kerry. John Kerry understands the ideals of community, faith, and service because they've defined his life. From his heroic service to Vietnam, to his years as a prosecutor and lieutenant governor, through two decades in the United States Senate, he has devoted himself to this country. Again and again, we've seen him make tough choices when easier ones were available.

His values—and his record—affirm what is best in us. John Kerry believes in an America where hard work is rewarded; so instead of offering tax breaks to companies shipping jobs overseas, he offers them to companies creating jobs here at home.

John Kerry believes in an America where all Americans can afford the same health coverage our politicians in Washington have for themselves.

John Kerry believes in energy independence, so we aren't held hostage to the profits of oil companies, or the sabotage of foreign oil fields.

John Kerry believes in the Constitutional freedoms that have made our country the envy of the world, and he will never sacrifice our basic liberties, nor use faith as a wedge to divide us.

And John Kerry believes that in a dangerous world war must be an option sometimes, but it should never be the first option.

You know, a while back, I met a young man named Shamus [Seamus?] in a V.F.W. Hall in East Moline, Ill. He was a good-looking kid, six two, six three, clear eyed, with an easy smile. He told me he'd joined the Marines, and was heading to Iraq the following week. And as I listened to him explain why he'd enlisted, the absolute faith he had in our country and its leaders, his devotion to duty and service, I thought this young man was all that any of us might hope for in a child. But then I asked myself: Are we serving Shamus as well as he is serving us?

I thought of the 900 men and women—sons and daughters, husbands and wives, friends and neighbors, who won't be returning to their own hometowns. I thought of the families I've met who were struggling to get by without a loved one's full income, or whose loved ones had returned with a limb missing or nerves shattered, but who still lacked long-term health benefits because they were Reservists.

When we send our young men and women into harm's way, we have a solemn obligation not to fudge the numbers or shade the truth about why they're going, to care for their families while they're gone, to tend to the soldiers upon their return, and to never ever go to war without enough troops to win the war, secure the peace, and earn the respect of the world.

Now let me be clear. Let me be clear. We have real enemies in the world. These enemies must be found. They must be pursued—and they must be defeated. John Kerry knows this.

And just as Lieutenant Kerry did not hesitate to risk his life to protect the men who served with him in Vietnam, President Kerry will not hesitate one moment to use our military might to keep America safe and secure.

John Kerry believes in America. And he knows that it's not enough for just some of us to prosper. For alongside our famous individualism, there's another ingredient in the American saga. A belief that we're all connected as one people.

If there is a child on the south side of Chicago who can't read, that matters to me, even if it's not my child. If there's a senior citizen somewhere who can't pay for their prescription drugs, and has to choose between medicine and the rent, that makes my life poorer, even if it's not my grandparent. If there's an Arab American family being rounded up without benefit of an attorney or due process, that threatens my civil liberties.

It is that fundamental belief, it is that fundamental belief, I am my brother's keeper, I am my sister's keeper that makes this country work. It's what allows us to pursue our individual dreams and yet still come together as one American family.

E pluribus unum. Out of many, one.

Now even as we speak, there are those who are preparing to divide us, the spin masters, the negative ad peddlers who embrace the politics of anything goes. Well, I say to them tonight, there is not a liberal America and a conservative America—there is the United States of America. There is not a Black America and a White America and Latino America and Asian America—there's the United States of America.

The pundits, the pundits like to slice-and-dice our country into Red States and Blue States; Red States for Republicans, Blue States for Democrats. But I've got news for them, too. We worship an awesome God in the Blue States, and we don't like federal agents poking around in our libraries in the Red States. We coach Little League in the Blue States and yes, we've got some gay friends in the Red States. There are patriots who opposed the war in Iraq and there are patriots who supported the war in Iraq.

We are one people, all of us pledging allegiance to the stars and stripes, all of us defending the United States of America. In the end, that's what this election is about. Do we participate in a politics of cynicism or do we participate in a politics of hope?

John Kerry calls on us to hope. John Edwards calls on us to hope.

I'm not talking about blind optimism here—the almost willful ignorance that thinks unemployment will go away if we just don't think about it, or the health care crisis will solve itself if we just ignore it. That's not what I'm talking about. I'm talking about something more substantial. It's the hope of slaves sitting around a fire singing freedom songs. The hope of immigrants setting out for distant shores. The hope of a young naval lieutenant bravely patrolling the Mekong Delta. The hope of a millworker's son who dares to defy the odds. The hope of a skinny kid with a funny name who believes that America has a place for him, too.

Hope in the face of difficulty. Hope in the face of uncertainty. The audacity of hope! In the end, that is God's greatest gift to us, the bedrock of this nation. A belief in things not seen. A belief that there are better days ahead.

I believe that we can give our middle class relief and provide working families with a road to opportunity. I believe we can provide jobs to the jobless, homes to the homeless, and reclaim young people in cities across America from violence and despair. I believe that we have a righteous wind at our backs and that as we stand on the crossroads of history, we can make the right choices, and meet the challenges that face us.

America! Tonight, if you feel the same energy that I do, if you feel the same urgency that I do, if you feel the same passion I do, if you feel the same hopefulness that I do—if we do what we must do, then I have no doubts that all across the country, from Florida to Oregon, from Washington to Maine, the people will rise up in November, and John Kerry will be sworn in as president, and John Edwards will be sworn in as vice president, and this country will reclaim its promise, and out of this long political darkness a brighter day will come.

Thank you very much everybody. God bless you. Thank you.

U.S. SENATE, RESOLUTION 39, APOLOGIZING FOR LYNCHING (2005)

On February 7, 2005, members of the U.S. Senate presented a resolution of apology for the body's failure to enact antislavery legislation. Reflecting on the first antilynching bill submitted more than 105 years ago, the lack of Senate action resulted in the loss of many African American lives. The apology, known as Resolution 39, had eighty of the one hundred Senate members as cosigners of the bill. Missing from the list were the senators from the state that reported the most lynching incidents: Mississippi. The apology was signed on June 13, 2005.

Whereas the crime of lynching succeeded slavery as the ultimate expression of racism in the United States following Reconstruction; (Agreed to by Senate)

RES 39 ATS
109th CONGRESS
1st Session

S. RES. 39

Apologizing to the victims of lynching and the descendants of those victims for the failure of the Senate to enact anti-lynching legislation.

IN THE SENATE OF THE UNITED STATES

February 7, 2005

Ms. LANDRIEU (for herself, Mr. ALLEN, Mr. LEVIN, Mr. FRIST, Mr. REID, Mr. ALLARD, Mr. AKAKA, Mr. BROWNBACK, Mr. BAYH, Ms. COLLINS, Mr. BIDEN, Mr. ENSIGN, Mrs. BOXER, Mr. HAGEL, Mr. CORZINE, Mr. LUGAR, Mr. DAYTON, Mr. MCCAIN, Mr. DODD, Ms. SNOWE, Mr. DURBIN, Mr. SPECTER, Mr. FEINGOLD, Mr. STEVENS, Mrs. FEINSTEIN, Mr. TALENT, Mr. HARKIN, Mr. JEFFORDS, Mr. JOHNSON, Mr. KENNEDY, Mr. KOHL, Mr. LAUTENBERG, Mr. LEAHY, Mr. LIEBERMAN, Mr. NELSON of Florida, Mr. PRYOR, Mr. SCHUMER, Ms. STABENOW, Mr. SALAZAR, Mr. VITTER, Mr. OBAMA, Mrs. LINCOLN, Mr. SANTORUM, Mr. SARBANES, Mr. KERRY, Mr. BYRD, Mr. COBURN, Mr. COLEMAN, Mr. CRAIG, Ms. MIKULSKI, Mrs. MURRAY, Ms. CANTWELL, Mr. DEMINT, Mr. DOMENICI, Mr. DORGAN, Mr. INOUYE, Mrs. CLINTON, Mr. NELSON of Nebraska, Mr. CARPER, Mr. GRAHAM, Mr. BURR, Mr. MCCONNELL, Mr. BUNNING, Mr. MARTINEZ, Mr. BURNS, Mr. DEWINE, Mrs. DOLE, Mr. ROCKEFELLER, Mr. THUNE, Mr. WYDEN, Mr. WARNER, Mr. BAUCUS, Mr. ROBERTS, Mr. CHAFEE, Mr. SESSIONS, Mr. BOND, Mr. CHAMBLISS, Mr. ISAKSON, and Mr. INHOFE) submitted the following resolution; which was referred to the Committee on the Judiciary

June 13, 2005

Committee discharged; considered and agreed to

RESOLUTION

Apologizing to the victims of lynching and the descendants of those victims for the failure of the Senate to enact anti-lynching legislation.

Whereas the crime of lynching succeeded slavery as the ultimate expression of racism in the United States following Reconstruction;

Whereas lynching was a widely acknowledged practice in the United States until the middle of the 20th century;

Whereas lynching was a crime that occurred throughout the United States, with documented incidents in all but 4 States;

Whereas at least 4,742 people, predominantly African-Americans, were reported lynched in the United States between 1882 and 1968;

Whereas 99 percent of all perpetrators of lynching escaped from punishment by State or local officials;

Whereas lynching prompted African-Americans to form the National Association for the Advancement of Colored People (NAACP) and prompted members of B'nai B'rith to found the Anti-Defamation League;

Whereas nearly 200 anti-lynching bills were introduced in Congress during the first half of the 20th century;

Whereas, between 1890 and 1952, 7 Presidents petitioned Congress to end lynching;

Whereas, between 1920 and 1940, the House of Representatives passed 3 strong anti-lynching measures;

Whereas protection against lynching was the minimum and most basic of Federal responsibilities, and the Senate considered but failed to enact anti-lynching legislation despite repeated requests by civil rights groups, Presidents, and the House of Representatives to do so;

Whereas the recent publication of 'Without Sanctuary: Lynching Photography in America' helped bring greater awareness and proper recognition of the victims of lynching;

Whereas only by coming to terms with history can the United States effectively champion human rights abroad; and

Whereas an apology offered in the spirit of true repentance moves the United States toward reconciliation and may become central to a new understanding, on which improved racial relations can be forged: Now, therefore, be it

Resolved, That the Senate—

(1) apologizes to the victims of lynching for the failure of the Senate to enact anti-lynching legislation;

(2) expresses the deepest sympathies and most solemn regrets of the Senate to the descendants of victims of lynching, the ancestors of whom were deprived of life, human dignity, and the constitutional protections accorded all citizens of the United States; and

(3) remembers the history of lynching, to ensure that these tragedies will be neither forgotten nor repeated.

ALABAMA'S ROSA PARKS ACT (APRIL 21, 2006)

Governor Bob Riley of Alabama signed the Rosa Parks Act into law on April 21, 2006. The act, which received no official announcement and passed the House unanimously and the Senate with three dissenting votes, created a process to allow for a legal pardon for anyone arrested while disobeying Jim Crow laws, as civil rights activist Rosa Parks was in 1955. The law remains controversial because many activists see "no wrong," and therefore no need for a pardon, in challenging unjust laws. Jim Crow laws were created with the intent of promoting racial segregation and denying equal access and opportunity for African Americans. The Rosa Parks Act, which also admits the wrongdoing of the government, was amended to allow museums, such as the Rosa Parks Library and Museum in Montgomery, Alabama, to display arrest records of Parks and other protestors. Democratic Representative Thad McClammy, who sponsored the bill, presented it as a means to promote reconciliation among Alabamians whose freedom and rights as citizens were denied because of unjust laws.

CRIME BILLS THAT PASSED DURING THE 2006 REGULAR SESSION [ALABAMA SENTENCING COMMISSION BILLS]

Pardon of Persons—Rosa Parks Act

Act 2006-544

HB 592 McClammy

Effective July 1, 2006

This bill would provide a pardon to a person convicted of a state law or municipal ordinance the purpose of which was to maintain racial separation or racial discrimination. It requires that a pardon be granted within 42 days from submission of the application unless it is objected to by the state. A separate procedure is authorized for applying for a pardon by filing a sworn affidavit. In instances where the person to be pardoned is dead, the bill provides that an application may be filed by his or her relatives or any interested party. A specific provision for expungement of records of conviction is included for those granted a pardon. An expungement form is to be provided by the Administrative Office of Courts.

THE FANNIE LOU HAMER, ROSA PARKS, AND CORETTA SCOTT KING VOTING RIGHTS ACT REAUTHORIZATION AND ADMENDMENTS ACT, H.R. 9 (JULY 27, 2006)

[Extends the Voting Rights Act of 1965 and its amendments]

The Fannie Lou Hamer, Rosa Parks, and Coretta Scott King Voting Rights Act Reauthorization and Amendments Act was signed into legislation on July 27, 2006, by President George W. Bush. The reauthorization act extended the 1965 Voting Rights Act and its amendments for twenty-five years. The 1965 Voting Rights Act, which is considered one of the most important pieces of legislation ever passed by the U.S. Congress, banned discriminatory and racist voting practices by state, local, and federal agencies. To determine the continued need for the 1965 act and its amendments, Congress conducted twenty or more meetings where experts and individuals testified, thus creating more than 17,000 pages of data and testimony. The reauthorization act, which was named in honor of civil rights activists Fannie Lou Hamer, Rosa Parks, and Coretta Scott King, passed Congress by votes of 98–0 in the Senate and 390–33 in the House. Key provisions inclusive of Section 5, Section 203, and Sections 6–9 of the Voting Rights Act were not due to expire until 2007 but were extended as part of the reauthorization act. The Voting Rights Act of 1965 had been extended on four previous occasions: 1970, 1975, 1982, and 1992.

July 20, 2006

SUMMARY AND BACKGROUND

On July 17, 2006, H.R. 9, the *Fannie Lou Hamer, Rosa Parks, and Coretta Scott King Voting Rights Act Reauthorization and Amendments Act of 2006* was placed on the Senate calendar. H.R. 9 would amend provisions of the *Voting Rights Act of 1965* ("VRA") [42 U.S.C. § 19739(f)] relating to: the use of election examiners and observers; declaratory judgments on the issue of voting qualifications or standards intended to diminish the ability of U.S. citizens to elect preferred candidates; and the award of attorney fees in enforcement proceedings to include expert fees and other reasonable costs of litigation. The legislation also would amend the requirements for determining jurisdictions covered by the bilingual election section and order a study on the bilingual election requirement. Further, H.R. 9 would extend certain provisions for an additional 25 years, including the bilingual election requirement.

MAJOR PROVISIONS

Section 2: Congressional Purpose and Findings

The purpose of H.R. 9 is "to ensure that the right of all citizens to vote, including the right to register to vote and cast meaningful votes, is preserved and protected as guaranteed by the Constitution."

The bill includes the finding that despite the VRA's success "in eliminating first generation barriers experienced by minority voters," including increasing voter turnout and minority representation in federal, state and local elected bodies, voting discrimination still exists by way of second generation barriers. The bill also finds that the persistence of racially polarized voting in covered jurisdictions leaves racial and language minorities "politically vulnerable."

The legislation notes that *Reno v. Bossier Parrish II* and *Georgia v. Ashcroft* misconstrued Congress's original intent in enacting the VRA and narrowed the protections provided by section 5.

The bill provides evidence of continued voting discrimination and asserts that 40 years has not been enough time to rid the vested states of nearly 100 years of voting discrimination. The bill states that without the renewal of the temporary provisions of the VRA, racial and language minorities would be deprived of their opportunity to vote or would have their votes diluted.

Section 3: Changes Relating to Use of Examiners and Observers

Use of Observers

H.R. 9 would amend Section 8 of the VRA to require that the Director of Personnel Management assign the necessary number of observers to a jurisdiction whenever:

- a court has authorized appointment of observers to that jurisdiction;
- the Attorney General certifies that residents, elected officials, or civic organizations have submitted written meritorious complaints that a covered jurisdiction is likely to deny or abridge the right of voters covered by the VRA; or
- the Attorney General certifies that observers are needed in a covered jurisdiction to enforce the 14th or 15th Amendments.

Factors the Attorney General could consider include whether 1) the ratio of white to nonwhite registered voters is reasonably attributable to violations of the said of 14th or 15th Amendments; and 2) there is substantial evidence that the jurisdiction is making a bona fide effort to comply with the amendments.

The bill would authorize these observers to be at any place an election is being held to observe whether persons who are entitled to vote are allowed to do so. Similarly, it would authorize observers to be at any place where votes are being tabulated to observe whether votes cast by persons who are entitled to vote are being properly tabulated. The legislation would also require observers to investigate and report their findings to the Attorney General and, if necessary, to the authorizing court.

Modification of Section 13 (Termination of Election Observers)

H.R. 9 would amend Section 13 of the VRA to allow a jurisdiction to petition the Attorney General for the termination of election observers. Termination would occur if the Attorney General or District Court for the District of Columbia, in an action for declaratory judgment brought by the jurisdiction, determines that there is no longer reasonable cause to believe that persons covered under the VRA will be deprived or denied the right to vote; and upon the order of court which appointed the observers. The only jurisdictions covered under this section are ones in which more than 50 percent of nonwhite residents of voting age are registered to vote, as determined by the Director of the Census Bureau.

Repeal of Sections Relating to Examiners

H.R. 9 would repeal Sections 6, 7, and 9 of the VRA relating to examiners.

Substitution of References to "Observers" for References to "Examiners"

H.R. 9 would amend several sections of the VRA by substituting "observers" for "examiners."

Section 4: Reconsideration of Section 4 by Congress

H.R. 9 would amend paragraphs 7 and 8 of Section 4(a) of the VRA by striking the *Voting Rights Act Amendments of 1982* and inserting the name of this legislation, effectively extending the provisions in Sections 4 through 8 for an additional 25 years.

Section 5: Criteria for Declaratory Judgment

H.R. 9 would amend Section 5 by striking "does not have the purpose and will not have the effect" and inserting "neither has the purpose nor will have the effect." The bill would also add language that prohibits any voting qualification, prerequisite, standard, practice or procedure that has the purpose or effect of diminishing the ability of a citizen to elect their preferred candidates of choice or abridging a citizen's right to vote on account of race or color.

The legislation would deny preclearance of electoral changes which have "any discriminatory purpose." This provision would overturn *Bossier II.* The bill would also deny preclearance of electoral changes which have the purpose or effect of denying minority voters the ability to "elect their preferred candidates of choice. This provision would overturn *Georgia v. Ashcroft.*

Section 6: Expert Fees and Other Reasonable Costs of Litigation

H.R. 9 would amend Section 14(e) of the VRA by allowing, at the courts discretion, the prevailing party (other than the United States) to receive reasonable expert fees and other reasonable expenses associated with an action to enforce the voting guarantees of the 14th or 15th Amendment. Currently, the VRA provides for the recovery of reasonable attorneys' fees.

Section 7: Extension of Bilingual Election Requirements

H.R. 9 would amend Section 203 of the VRA to extend the bilingual election assistance requirements for limited-English speaking citizens for 25 years.

Section 8: Use of American Community Survey Census Data

H.R. 9 would amend Section 203 of the VRA to require the Director of the Census Bureau to use American Community Survey census data (starting in 2010 and in subsequent 5-year increments) or comparable census data when determining whether a jurisdiction will be covered under Section 203.

Section 9: Study and Report

H.R. 9 would require the Comptroller General to study the "implementation, effectiveness, and efficiency" of section 203 of the VRA, as well as any alternatives to its current implementation. The legislation would require that the results of the study be reported back to Congress in one year.

EMMETT TILL UNSOLVED CIVIL RIGHTS CRIME ACT OF 2007 (OCTOBER 7, 2008)

Introduced in 2007 and signed into law by President George W. Bush on October 7, 2008, the Emmett Till Unsolved Civil Rights Crime Act was named after an African American teenager from Chicago, Emmett Till, who was murdered in Mississippi in 1955 because he allegedly whistled at a white woman. Those responsible were never convicted. The "unsolved crimes" as noted in the act were primarily a result of lawlessness during the period of segregation and after the legal ending of segregation. The act directed that an annual allocation of $10 million over a ten-year period be provided to the Federal Bureau of Investigation and other agencies to revisit cold cases, primarily in the South. The legislation also provided for additional funding for local law enforcement agencies.

[The following summary was written by the Congressional Research Service, a well-respected nonpartisan arm of the Library of Congress.]

(This measure was not amended after it was passed by the House on June 20, 2007. The summary of that version is repeated here.)

Emmett Till Unsolved Civil Rights Crime Act of 2007—Directs the Attorney General to designate a Deputy Chief in the Criminal Section of the Civil Rights Division of the Department of Justice (DOJ). Makes the Deputy Chief responsible for investigating and prosecuting violations of criminal civil rights statutes in which the alleged violation occurred before January 1, 1970 and resulted in death.

Section 4

Directs the Attorney General to designate a Supervisory Special Agent in the Civil Rights Unit of the Federal Bureau of Investigation (FBI) of the DOJ to investigate violations of criminal civil rights statutes that occurred before January 1, 1970 and resulted in a death.

Section 5

Authorizes the Attorney General to award grants to state or local law enforcement agencies for the investigation and prosecution of such cases.

Section 6

Authorizes appropriations.

Section 8

Terminates the effectiveness of the above provisions at the end of FY2017.

Section 9

Amends the Crime Control Act of 1990 to authorize staff of an Inspector General to assist the National Center for Missing and Exploited Children by conducting reviews of inactive case files to develop recommendations for further investigations and engaging in similar activities.

DESIGNATION OF THE GREAT HALL OF THE CAPITOL VISITOR CENTER AS "EMANCIPATION HALL" (DECEMBER 18, 2007)

Congressman Jesse Jackson Jr. (D-IL) and Congressman Zach Wamp (R-TN) championed this bill, which renamed the

Signing of H.R. 3315, Renaming the Visitor Center of the U.S. Capitol Building as Emancipation Hall, December 18, 2007. *Sponsored by Congressman Zach Wamp (*left; *R-TN) and Congressman Jesse Jackson Jr. (*right; *D-IL), the bill is signed in the Oval Office by President George W. Bush (*center*).* JIM WATSON/AFP/GETTY IMAGES

great hall located in the Capitol Visitor Center as "Emancipation Hall." The name not only recognizes the nation's struggle to journey from slavery to freedom but also recognizes the slaves who built the U.S. Capitol building, their lives a testament to the enduring theme of emancipation. President George W. Bush signed the bill into law on December 18, 2007.

H.R. 3315

An Act

To provide that the great hall of the Capitol Visitor Center shall be known as Emancipation Hall.

Be it enacted by the Senate and House of Representatives of the United States of America in Congress assembled,

SECTION 1. DESIGNATION OF GREAT HALL OF THE CAPITOL VISITOR CENTER AS EMANCIPATION HALL.

(a) In General—The great hall of the Capitol Visitor Center shall be known and designated as "Emancipation Hall," and any reference to the great hall in any law, rule, or regulation shall be deemed to be a reference to Emancipation Hall.

(b) Effective Date—This section shall apply on and after the date of the enactment of this Act.

THE U.S. ARMY APOLOGIES TO TWENTY-EIGHT AFRICAN AMERICAN WORLD WAR II SOLDIERS (JULY 28, 2008)

The U.S. Army issued a formal apology to twenty-eight African American World War II soldiers wrongfully accused and convicted in 1944 in Seattle, Washington, of rioting and lynching an Italian prisoner of war. U.S. Representative Jim McDermott (D-WA) championed the decision to overturn the convictions and offer the apology based on the investigative information brought to light in the book On American Soil: How Justice Became a Casualty of World War II, *written by Jack Hamann in 2005. On the night of August 14, 1944, as a result of a scuffle between a black soldier from a segregated barracks and a white Italian prisoner of war housed near the barracks, a riot broke out. The following day, the Italian prisoner of war was found hanged. Forty-three black soldiers were charged with rioting and lynching, and twenty-eight were convicted.*

The apology, announced in Seattle near the Old Fort Lawton parade ground where the original events occurred, was given by Ronald James, assistant secretary of the army for manpower and reserve affairs. The army also set aside the convictions of the soldiers, their dishonorable discharges were changed to honorable discharges, and back pay was given to the two surviving soldiers and the surviving family members of the other soldiers. One of the two surviving soldiers, Samuel Snow, age eighty-three, died a few hours after the apology.

Secretary James stated:

We had not done right by these soldiers. The Army is genuinely sorry. I am genuinely sorry.

THE INAUGURAL ADDRESS OF BARACK HUSSEIN OBAMA, THE FORTY-FOURTH PRESIDENT OF THE UNITED STATES OF AMERICA (JANUARY 20, 2009)

On January 20, 2009, Baraka Obama was sworn in as the forty-fourth president of the United States and the first African American to be elected to this office. He won the 2008 election with 53 percent of the popular vote and an electoral margin of 365 votes to Republican candidate John McCain's 173 votes.

Obama's inauguration, which for many was considered an impossibility not long ago, occurred one day after the national celebration honoring the Reverend Dr. Martin Luther King Jr., a respected civil rights leader and humanitarian, and it marked the 200-year anniversary of the birth of Abraham Lincoln, the sixteenth president of the United States and Obama's political hero. For the swearing-in ceremony, Obama used the same Bible that Lincoln used in 1861 when he was sworn in as president. With more than two million people who had traveled to Washington, D.C. a city of 600,000, to share in the celebration, the National Mall was opened for the first time in U.S. history. Obama, who began writing his inaugural address in November 2008, brought his already proven oratorical skills and optimism to this historic moment. Among other historical benchmarks, Obama's inauguration was the most security-conscious and the most watched by the entire nation.

My fellow citizens: I stand here today humbled by the task before us, grateful for the trust you've bestowed, mindful of the sacrifices borne by our ancestors.

I thank President [George W.] Bush for his service to our nation as well as the generosity and cooperation he has shown throughout this transition.

Forty-four Americans have now taken the presidential oath. The words have been spoken during rising tides of prosperity and the still waters of peace. Yet, every so often, the oath is taken amidst gathering clouds and raging storms. At these moments, America has carried on not simply because of the skill or vision of those in high office, but because we, the people, have remained faithful to the ideals of our forebears and true to our founding documents.

So it has been; so it must be with this generation of Americans.

That we are in the midst of crisis is now well understood. Our nation is at war against a far-reaching network of violence and hatred. Our economy is badly weakened, a consequence of greed and irresponsibility on the part of some, but also our collective failure to make hard choices and prepare the nation for a new age. Homes have been lost, jobs shed, businesses shuttered. Our health care is too costly, our schools fail too many—and each day brings further evidence that the ways we use energy strengthen our adversaries and threaten our planet.

These are the indicators of crisis, subject to data and statistics. Less measurable, but no less profound, is a sapping of confidence across our land; a nagging fear that America's decline is inevitable, that the next generation must lower its sights.

Today I say to you that the challenges we face are real. They are serious and they are many. They will not be met easily or in a short span of time. But know this America: They will be met.

On this day, we gather because we have chosen hope over fear, unity of purpose over conflict and discord. On this day, we come to proclaim an end to the petty grievances and false promises, the recriminations and worn-out dogmas that for far too long have strangled our politics. We remain a young nation. But in the words of Scripture, the time has come to set aside childish things. The time has come to reaffirm our enduring spirit; to choose our better history; to carry forward that precious gift, that noble idea passed on from generation to generation: the God-given promise that all are equal, all are free, and all deserve a chance to pursue their full measure of happiness.

Barack Obama, President of the United States, January 20, 2009. *After being sworn in as president, Obama delivered his inaugural address to the nation from the west front of the U.S. Capitol.* NEW YORK DAILY NEWS ARCHIVE/GETTY IMAGES

In reaffirming the greatness of our nation we understand that greatness is never a given. It must be earned. Our journey has never been one of short-cuts or settling for less. It has not been the path for the faint-hearted, for those that prefer leisure over work, or seek only the pleasures of riches and fame. Rather, it has been the risk-takers, the doers, the makers of things—some celebrated, but more often men and women obscure in their labor—who have carried us up the long rugged path towards prosperity and freedom.

For us, they packed up their few worldly possessions and traveled across oceans in search of a new life. For us, they toiled in sweatshops, and settled the West, endured the lash of the whip, and plowed the hard earth. For us, they fought and died in places like Concord and Gettysburg, Normandy and Khe Sanh.

Time and again these men and women struggled and sacrificed and worked till their hands were raw so that we might live a better life. They saw America as bigger than the sum of our individual ambitions, greater than all the differences of birth or wealth or faction.

This is the journey we continue today. We remain the most prosperous, powerful nation on Earth. Our workers are no less productive than when this crisis began. Our minds are no less inventive, our goods and services no less needed than they were last week, or last month, or last year. Our capacity remains undiminished. But our time of standing pat, of protecting narrow interests and putting off unpleasant decisions—that time has surely passed. Starting today, we must pick ourselves up, dust ourselves off, and begin again the work of remaking America.

For everywhere we look, there is work to be done. The state of our economy calls for action, bold and swift. And we will act, not only to create new jobs, but to lay a new foundation for growth. We will build the roads and bridges, the electric grids and digital lines that feed our commerce and bind us together. We'll restore science to its rightful place, and wield technology's wonders to raise health care's quality and lower its cost. We will harness the sun and the winds and the soil to fuel our cars and run our factories. And we will transform our schools and colleges and universities to meet the demands of a new age. All this we can do. All this we will do.

Now, there are some who question the scale of our ambitions, who suggest that our system cannot tolerate too many big plans. Their memories are short, for they have forgotten what this country has already done, what free men and women can achieve when imagination is joined to common purpose, and necessity to courage. What the cynics fail to understand is that the ground has shifted beneath them, that the stale political arguments that have consumed us for so long no longer apply.

The question we ask today is not whether our government is too big or too small, but whether it works—whether it helps families find jobs at a decent wage, care they can afford, a retirement that is dignified. Where the answer is yes, we intend to move forward. Where the answer is no, programs will end. And those of us who manage the public's dollars will be held to account, to spend wisely, reform bad habits, and do our business in the light of day, because only then can we restore the vital trust between a people and their government.

Nor is the question before us whether the market is a force for good or ill. Its power to generate wealth and expand freedom is unmatched. But this crisis has reminded us that without a watchful eye, the market can spin out of control. The nation cannot prosper long when it favors only the prosperous. The success of our economy has always depended not just on the size of our gross domestic product, but on the reach of our prosperity, on the ability to extend opportunity to every willing heart—not out of charity, but because it is the surest route to our common good.

As for our common defense, we reject as false the choice between our safety and our ideals. Our Founding Fathers, faced with perils that we can scarcely imagine, drafted a charter to assure the rule of law and the rights of man—a charter expanded by the blood of generations. Those ideals still light the world, and we will not give them up for expedience sake.

And so, to all the other peoples and governments who are watching today, from the grandest capitals to the small village where my father was born, know that America is a friend of each nation, and every man, woman and child who seeks a future of peace and dignity. And we are ready to lead once more.

Recall that earlier generations faced down fascism and communism not just with missiles and tanks, but with the sturdy alliances and enduring convictions. They understood that our power alone cannot protect us, nor does it entitle us to do as we please. Instead they knew that our power grows through its prudent use; our security emanates from the justness of our cause, the force of our example, the tempering qualities of humility and restraint.

We are the keepers of this legacy. Guided by these principles once more we can meet those new threats that demand even greater effort, even greater cooperation and understanding between nations. We will begin to responsibly leave Iraq to its people and forge a hard-earned peace in Afghanistan. With old friends and former foes, we'll work tirelessly to lessen the nuclear threat, and roll back the specter of a warming planet.

We will not apologize for our way of life, nor will we waver in its defense. And for those who seek to advance their aims by inducing terror and slaughtering innocents, we say to you now that our spirit is stronger and cannot be broken—you cannot outlast us, and we will defeat you.

For we know that our patchwork heritage is a strength, not a weakness. We are a nation of Christians and Muslims, Jews and Hindus, and non-believers. We are shaped by every language and culture, drawn from every end of this Earth; and because we have tasted the bitter swill of civil war and segregation, and emerged from that dark chapter stronger and more united, we cannot help but believe that the old hatreds shall someday pass; that the lines of tribe shall soon dissolve; that as the world grows smaller, our common humanity shall reveal itself; and that America must play its role in ushering in a new era of peace.

To the Muslim world, we seek a new way forward, based on mutual interest and mutual respect. To those leaders around the globe who seek to sow conflict, or blame their society's ills on the West, know that your people will judge you on what you can build, not what you destroy.

To those who cling to power through corruption and deceit and the silencing of dissent, know that you are on the wrong side of history, but that we will extend a hand if you are willing to unclench your fist.

To the people of poor nations, we pledge to work alongside you to make your farms flourish and let clean waters flow; to nourish starved bodies and feed hungry minds. And to those nations like ours that enjoy relative plenty, we say we can no longer afford indifference to the suffering outside our borders, nor can we consume the world's resources without regard to effect. For the world has changed, and we must change with it.

As we consider the role that unfolds before us, we remember with humble gratitude those brave Americans who at this very hour patrol far-off deserts and distant mountains. They have something to tell us, just as the fallen heroes who lie in Arlington whisper through the ages.

We honor them not only because they are the guardians of our liberty, but because they embody the spirit of service—a willingness to find meaning in something greater than themselves.

And yet at this moment, a moment that will define a generation, it is precisely this spirit that must inhabit us all. For as much as government can do, and must do, it is ultimately the faith and determination of the American people upon which this nation relies. It is the kindness to take in a stranger when the levees break, the selflessness of workers who would rather cut their hours than see a friend lose their job which sees us through our darkest hours. It is the firefighter's courage to storm a stairway filled with smoke, but also a parent's willingness to nurture a child that finally decides our fate.

Our challenges may be new. The instruments with which we meet them may be new. But those values upon which our success depends—honesty and hard work, courage and fair play, tolerance and curiosity, loyalty and patriotism—these things are old. These things are true. They have been the quiet force of progress throughout our history.

What is demanded, then, is a return to these truths. What is required of us now is a new era of responsibility—a recognition on the part of every American that we have duties to ourselves, our nation and the world; duties that we do not grudgingly accept, but rather seize gladly, firm in the knowledge that there is nothing so satisfying to the spirit, so defining of our character than giving our all to a difficult task.

This is the price and the promise of citizenship. This is the source of our confidence—the knowledge that God calls on us to shape an uncertain destiny. This is the meaning of our liberty and our creed, why men and women and children of every race and every faith can join in celebration across this magnificent mall; and why a man whose father less than 60 years ago might not have been served in a local restaurant can now stand before you to take a most sacred oath.

So let us mark this day with remembrance of who we are and how far we have traveled. In the year of America's birth, in the coldest of months, a small band of patriots huddled by dying campfires on the shores of an icy river. The capital was abandoned. The enemy was advancing. The snow was stained with blood. At the moment when the outcome of our revolution was most in doubt, the father of our nation ordered these words to be read to the people:

> Let it be told to the future world ... that in the depth of winter, when nothing but hope and virtue could survive ... that the city and the country, alarmed at one common danger, came forth to meet [it].

America: In the face of our common dangers, in this winter of our hardship, let us remember these timeless words. With hope and virtue, let us brave once more the icy currents, and endure what storms may come. Let it be said by our children's children that when we were tested we refused to let this journey end, that we did not turn back nor did we falter; and with eyes fixed on the horizon and God's grace upon us, we carried forth that great gift of freedom and delivered it safely to future generations.

Thank you. God bless you. And God bless the United States of America.

THE U.S. SENATE'S FORMAL APOLOGY FOR SLAVERY (JUNE 18, 2009)

The U.S. Senate approved on June 18, 2009, a nonbinding resolution that apologized for the more than three centuries of slavery and segregation that had been legally imposed on African Americans. The Senate, which missed opportunities to pass laws that would have protected and saved the lives of many African Americans during the era of slavery and Jim Crow, unanimously voted for this resolution. This apology came five months after the election of the first African American president, Barack Obama. Although the House of Representatives had passed the resolution almost a year earlier on July 30, 2008, a disclaimer in the final resolution by the Senate, which denies its use for legal claims, caused some members of the Congressional Black Caucus to voice "serious concerns" regarding the resolution.

111th CONGRESS
1st Session

S. CON. RES. 26

Apologizing for the enslavement and racial segregation of African-Americans.

IN THE SENATE OF THE UNITED STATES

June 11, 2009

Mr. HARKIN (for himself, Mr. BROWNBACK, Mr. LEVIN, Mr. DURBIN, Mr. KENNEDY, Mr. LAUTENBERG, Ms. STABENOW, Mr. BOND, and Mr. COCHRAN) submitted the following concurrent resolution; which was ordered at the desk

CONCURRENT RESOLUTION

Apologizing for the enslavement and racial segregation of African-Americans.

Whereas, during the history of the Nation, the United States has grown into a symbol of democracy and freedom around the world;

Whereas the legacy of African-Americans is interwoven with the very fabric of the democracy and freedom of the United States;

Whereas millions of Africans and their descendants were enslaved in the United States and the 13 American colonies from 1619 through 1865;

Whereas Africans forced into slavery were brutalized, humiliated, dehumanized, and subjected to the indignity of being stripped of their names and heritage;

Whereas many enslaved families were torn apart after family members were sold separately;

Whereas the system of slavery and the visceral racism against people of African descent upon which it depended became enmeshed in the social fabric of the United States;

Whereas slavery was not officially abolished until the ratification of the 13th amendment to the Constitution of the United States in 1865, after the end of the Civil War;

Whereas after emancipation from 246 years of slavery, African-Americans soon saw the fleeting political, social, and economic gains they made during Reconstruction eviscerated by virulent racism, lynchings, disenfranchisement, Black Codes, and racial segregation laws that imposed a rigid system of officially sanctioned racial segregation in virtually all areas of life;

Whereas the system of de jure racial segregation known as "Jim Crow," which arose in certain parts of the United States after the Civil War to create separate and unequal societies for Whites and African-Americans, was a direct result of the racism against people of African descent that was engendered by slavery;

Whereas the system of Jim Crow laws officially existed until the 1960s —a century after the official end of slavery in the United States—until Congress took action to end it, but the vestiges of Jim Crow continue to this day;

Whereas African-Americans continue to suffer from the consequences of slavery and Jim Crow laws—long after both systems were formally abolished—through enormous damage and loss, both tangible and intangible, including the loss of human dignity and liberty;

Whereas the story of the enslavement and de jure segregation of African-Americans and the dehumanizing atrocities committed against them should not be purged from or minimized in the telling of the history of the United States;

Whereas those African-Americans who suffered under slavery and Jim Crow laws, and their descendants, exemplify the strength of the human character and provide a model of courage, commitment, and perseverance;

Whereas, on July 8, 2003, during a trip to Goree Island, Senegal, a former slave port, President George W. Bush acknowledged the continuing legacy of slavery in life in the United States and the need to confront that legacy, when he stated that slavery "was ... one of the greatest crimes of history. ... The racial bigotry fed by slavery did not end with slavery or with segregation. And many of the issues that still trouble America have roots in the bitter experience of other times. But however long the journey, our destiny is set: liberty and justice for all.";

Whereas President Bill Clinton also acknowledged the deep-seated problems caused by the continuing legacy of racism against African-Americans that began with slavery, when he initiated a national dialogue about race;

Whereas an apology for centuries of brutal dehumanization and injustices cannot erase the past, but confession of the wrongs committed and a formal apology to African-Americans will help bind the wounds of the Nation that are rooted in slavery and can speed racial healing and reconciliation and help the people of the United States understand the past and honor the history of all people.

Whereas the legislatures of the Commonwealth of Virginia and the States of Alabama, Florida, Maryland, and North Carolina have taken the lead in adopting resolutions officially expressing appropriate remorse for slavery, and other States legislatures are considering similar resolutions; and

Whereas it is important for the people of the United States, who legally recognized slavery through the Constitution and the laws of the United States, to make a formal apology for slavery and for its successor, Jim Crow, so they can move forward and seek reconciliation, justice, and harmony for all people of the United States: Now, therefore, be it

Resolved by the Senate (the House of Representatives concurring), That the sense of the Congress is the following:

(1) APOLOGY FOR THE ENSLAVEMENT AND SEGREGATION OF AFRICAN-AMERICANS.—The Congress—

(A) acknowledges the fundamental injustices, cruelty, brutality, and inhumanity of slavery and Jim Crows laws;

(B) apologizes to African-Americans on behalf of the people of the United States, for the wrongs committed them and their ancestors who suffered under slavery and Jim Crow laws; and

(C) expresses its recommitment to the principle that all people are created equal and endowed with inalienable rights to life, liberty, and the pursuit of happiness, and calls on all people of the United States to work toward eliminating racial prejudices, injustices, and discrimination from our society.

(2) DISCLAIMER.—Nothing in this resolution—

(A) authorizes or supports any claim against the United States; or

(B) serves as a settlement of any claim against the United States.

4

AFRICAN AMERICAN LANDMARKS

Helen Houston

Since the early days of exploration in America, people of African descent have played an integral role and made significant contributions in every facet of the nation's development: cultural, economic, educational, scientific, and social. The experiences and contributions of African Americans are commemorated throughout the United States by historical landmarks, including markers, plaques, statues, buildings, museums, and trails. Sites have been established to commemorate African American participation in the defense and building of the United States; the quest for knowledge; the trail from slavery to freedom by way of the many markers noting stations along the Underground Railroad; and the achievements of African Americans in the arts and sciences or in pursuit of equal rights. Landmarks, unlike most textual documents, stand through time as public testaments to the strength and courage of African Americans.

ALABAMA

BIRMINGHAM

Sixteenth Street Baptist Church

1530 6th Ave. N., at 16th St.
Telephone: (205) 251-9402
Web site: http://www.16thstreetbaptist.org

Wallace A. Rayfield, a local African American architect, designed the present sanctuary, and in 1911 Windham Brothers Construction Company, a local African American contractor, constructed the building. The church has continued to serve as a center for activities in the community. The church received national attention during the middle of the racial unrest of the 1960s, when four African American children—Addie Mae Collins, Denise McNair, Cynthia Wesley, and Carol Robertson—were killed in a bomb explosion near the sanctuary on September 15, 1963. The tragedy spurred Birmingham to address its racial problems and led to greater racial unity nationwide. The building was declared a national historic landmark on September 17, 1980.

FLORENCE

William Christopher Handy Birthplace, Museum, and Library

620 W. College St.
Telephone: (256) 760-6434

W. C. Handy, composer of "St. Louis Blues," was born in 1873. The cabin in which he was born was moved from its original site to its current location in Florence, Alabama. The restored cabin, constructed around 1845, contains his piano, trumpet, and other mementos.

MOBILE

Africatown

1959 Bay Bridge Cutoff Rd.
Telephone: (251) 300-8941

Africatown, also known as Africa Town, is located on a hill outside the city by the Alabama River where the last known slave ship bringing Africans for slavery landed. A community was formed here by some of the West Africans from the ship.

MONTGOMERY

Civil Rights Memorial

400 Washington Ave., corner of Hull St.
Web site: http://www.splcenter.org/civil-rights-memorial

This black granite monument includes a circular table on which the names of forty civil rights martyrs are inscribed. Water flows out of the center and across the top of the table. The memorial's design was inspired by Martin Luther King Jr.'s words: "Until justice rolls down like waters and righteousness like a mighty stream." These words appear on a curved wall behind the table. Commissioned by the Southern Poverty Law Center and designed by the architect Maya Lin, the memorial was dedicated in 1989.

Dexter Avenue King Memorial Baptist Church and Dexter Parsonage Museum

Church: 454 Dexter Ave.
Museum: 309 S. Jackson St.
Telephone: (334) 263-3970
Telephone: (334) 261-3270 (museum)
Web site: http://www.dexterkingmemorial.org

The Dexter Avenue King Memorial Baptist Church, erected in 1878, was the church where Martin Luther King Jr. organized the 1955 boycott of Montgomery's segregated bus system. Although the parsonage was damaged by a bomb on January 31, 1956, the boycott continued and spurred the 1956 Supreme Court ruling that bus segregation was illegal. It was this boycott that brought King into national prominence as a civil rights leader.

King pastored at the church from 1954 to 1959. The church houses a mural depicting scenes of the civil rights movement, as well as a library that includes personal mementos of King and his family. The church was declared a national historic landmark on June 3, 1974.

Rosa Parks Library and Museum

252 Montgomery St.
Web site: http://montgomery.troy.edu/rosaparks

The Rosa Parks Library & Museum, on the Montgomery Campus of Troy University, houses a

Rosa Parks, Posing with Mural, Dexter Avenue King Memorial Baptist Church, Montgomery, AL, 1985. *A seminal event in the civil rights movement was the Montgomery bus boycott, which Martin Luther King Jr. organized at this church. Parks began the boycott when she refused to give up her seat to a white man on December 1, 1955.* CAREY WOMACK/BETTMANN/CORBIS

Life-Size Bronze Sculpture of Rosa Parks, Rosa Parks Library and Museum, Montgomery, AL, 2000. *Following a ceremony dedicating the library and museum forty-five years after Parks famously refused to give up her bus seat, actress Cicely Tyson reacts upon seeing the museum's sculpture of Parks sitting on a bus bench. The building is located on the campus of Troy University on the corner where Parks had boarded the bus in 1955.* PHOTOGRAPH BY KEVIN GLACKMEYER. AP IMAGES. REPRODUCED BY PERMISSION.

wealth of materials related to the events and accomplishments of individuals associated with the Montgomery bus boycott. The museum includes a permanent exhibit, a time machine, temporary exhibit space, archives, classrooms, an auditorium, and conference room.

SELMA

Brown Chapel African Methodist Episcopal Church and King Monument

410 Martin Luther King Jr. St.
Telephone: (334) 874-7897

This church is housed in an imposing red-brick structure with twin towers. It was organized in 1866 and moved to its present site in 1908. Brown Chapel was closely allied with the civil rights movement of the 1960s; in 1965, it became the center for the voting rights campaign of the Southern Christian Leadership Conference (SCLC). Early in 1965, the church served as headquarters for the SCLC, housed rallies for Martin Luther King Jr. and other SCLC leaders, and was the site for the planning of demonstrations, including the ill-fated demonstration on March 7 known as Bloody Sunday. The voting campaign spurred the passage of the Voting Rights Act of 1965. A monument to King, which is located in front of the chapel, was dedicated in 1979. Brown Chapel was declared a national historic landmark on December 12, 1997.

Edmund Pettus Bridge

Broad St., U.S. Hwy. 80

On Sunday, March 7, 1965, three hundred civil rights demonstrators started out from Selma, Alabama, on what was to be a 54-mile march to Montgomery, Alabama, protesting the denial of voting rights to African Americans who had attempted to register in

Selma. Reaching the Edmund Pettus Bridge, the marchers were met by state troopers, who had been ordered to deploy by Governor George Wallace to enforce his executive order forbidding such demonstrations. The unarmed marchers were turned back by tear gas and nightsticks, resulting in numerous injuries.

On March 21, a second march, organized by the Reverend Martin Luther King Jr., started out. This march concluded four days later on the steps of the state capitol building in Montgomery. The two demonstrations aroused national concern and hastened Congress's efforts to pass a new voting-rights bill.

Built in 1940, the Pettus Bridge marks the site of an important era in African American history. It is part of the Selma to Montgomery National Historic Trail. A marker depicting the struggle at the bridge is located near Broad Street.

Selma to Montgomery National Historic Trail

State Hwy. 80
Telephone: (334) 877-1984
Web site: http://www.nps.gov/semo

This highway was the setting for the March 7, 1965, "Bloody Sunday" civil rights demonstration, during which nonviolent marchers were attacked by Alabama law enforcement officers. The violence received international media coverage. A second successful march with federal protection, held on March 21, led to the passage of the 1965 Voting Rights Act. The distance of 54 miles makes it the shortest historic route in the National Trails System.

TALLADEGA

Talladega College and Swayne Hall

627 W. Battle St.
Telephone: (256) 362-0206
Web site: http://www.talladega.edu

The first college for African Americans in Alabama, Talladega College was founded by the American Missionary Association in 1867 as a primary school. The school pursued a liberal arts program at a time when vocational education dominated African American institutions. Its Savery Library houses three fresco panels known as the celebrated *Amistad Murals* by Hale Woodruff, who studied in France under the renowned Henry Ossawa Tanner.

Swayne Hall, built in 1857, is the oldest building on the campus of Talladega College. The building was constructed by slave labor before the school was established and transferred to the college in 1867. It was declared a national historic landmark on December 2, 1974.

TUSKEGEE

Tuskegee University

1200 W. Montgomery Rd.
Telephone: (334) 727-8011
Web site: http://www.tuskegee.edu

Tuskegee Institute (now Tuskegee University), a world-renowned center for agricultural research and extension work, first opened on July 4, 1881, with a $2,000 appropriation from the Alabama state legislature. It consisted of a single shanty, a student body of thirty, and one teacher—Booker T. Washington. Tuskegee functioned originally as a normal school for the training of African American teachers, the first of its kind established in the United States. Eventually, it specialized in agricultural and manual training, areas that were to make both the school and Washington famous.

In 1882, Washington moved the school to a 100-acre plantation and began a self-help program that enabled students to finance their education. Most of the early buildings were built with the aid of student labor.

Next to Washington, the most notable person to be associated with the institute was George Washington Carver, who became its director of agricultural research in 1896. Carver persuaded many southern farmers to cultivate peanuts, sweet potatoes, and other crops instead of cotton, which was rapidly depleting the soil. Ultimately, Carver's research programs helped develop 300 derivative products from peanuts and 118 from sweet potatoes. At one point, he even succeeded in making synthetic marble from wood pulp.

Today, Tuskegee covers nearly 5,000 acres and has more than 150 buildings. There are more than twenty-seven landmarks associated with Washington and Carver. Places to visit include the Founder's Marker (site of Washington's original shanty), the Oaks (Washington's home), the Booker T. Washington Monument, grave sites for Washington (and two of his wives) and Carver, and the George Washington Carver Museum, which houses the scientist's plant, mineral, and bird collections and exhibits of various products that he developed. Tuskegee is also home to the George Washington Carver Foundation, a research center founded by Carver in 1940. Tuskegee was declared a national historic landmark on June 23, 1965.

The institute was also selected to host a "military experiment" in training African American pilots and aviation personnel during World War II. Beginning in 1941, nearly 16,000 pilots and support personnel participated in the "Tuskegee Airmen" project. A part of the campus, including Moton field and other training facilities, opened as the Tuskegee Airmen National Historic Site in 2008.

WHITEHALL

Lowndes County Interpretive Center

North of U.S. Hwy. 80
Telephone: (334) 877-1984

Opened in 2006, this center commemorates the 1965 Selma to Montgomery march to protest inequities in voting rights. The entrance has a curved ceiling that opens and reflects the Edmund Pettus Bridge, which leads to the state capitol.

ALASKA

FAIRBANKS

Mattie Crosby's Home

One of the few African American pioneers of Alaska, Mattie Crosby first came to the territory in 1900 with a Maine family that adopted her. During this period, some African Americans came into the territory as part of the gold rush, while others were occasionally seen onboard ships that brought in supplies. For nearly seventeen years, however, Crosby lived in Fairbanks, Alaska, without meeting another African American.

ARIZONA

TOMBSTONE

John Swain Grave Site

Boot Hill Cemetery
U.S. Hwy. 80
Telephone: (602) 457-3311

Born a slave in 1845, John Swain went to Tombstone, Arizona, in 1879 as a cowhand in the employ of John Slaughter. Swain was an expert rider and one of several African Americans to work for Slaughter.

In 1884, Swain is said to have fought and lost a one-round boxing match with John L. Sullivan, then heavyweight champion of the world. He died in 1945, just three months short of his 100th birthday, and was buried with honors by the citizens of Tombstone. A special tablet stands on the grave site, commemorating the close ties between Swain and Slaughter.

ARKANSAS

LITTLE ROCK

Central High School

1500 Park St., corner of 14th and Park Sts.
Telephone: (501) 374-1957
Web site: http://www.nps.gov/chsc

In the fall of 1957, the first major confrontation over implementation of the U.S. Supreme Court's 1954 ruling that outlawed racial segregation in public schools took place at Central High School in Little Rock, Arkansas. The school was built in 1927.

When they arrived for classes on September 23, 1957, African American students were turned away by the Arkansas National Guard on the order of Orval Faubus, the governor of Arkansas. President Dwight D. Eisenhower responded to the crisis by issuing an executive order on September 24 calling for the use of federal troops to enforce the Court's order to desegregate public schools.

As part of the Little Rock Central High School National Historic Site, the National Park Service runs a visitor center located at 2120 Daisy L. Gatson Bates Drive.

Ish House

1600 Scott St.

Private residence, exterior viewing only.

The home of Jefferson Ish was constructed in 1880. Ish worked to ensure high-quality education for African Americans in the area. After his death, the Ish School was established in the city to honor him. One of his sons, G. W. Ish, became an innovative physician and provided health care for both local residents and students at Philander Smith College. G. W. Ish also introduced isoniazid and streptomycin to treat pulmonary tuberculosis. The Ish house remained a private residence, but it was damaged by fire in 1996 and was damaged beyond repair by a tornado in 1999.

Philander Smith College

900 W. Daisy L. Gatson Bates Dr.
Telephone: (501) 375-9845
Web site: http://www.philander.edu

In 1877, this institution was opened in Little Rock, Arkansas, under the sponsorship of the African Methodist Episcopal Church as Walden Seminary. After receiving a large donation that enabled the school to construct a permanent brick edifice, the college was renamed.

Alphonso Trent House

1301 N. 9th St.

This is the childhood home of Alphonso Trent, a jazz musician of the 1920s and 1930s. His band was one of the first African American groups to use the front entrances to clubs and venues, rather than service entrances.

TEXARKANA

Orr School

831 Laurel St.

This is the school attended by Scott Joplin (1868–1917), known as the father of ragtime music. It is one of the few remaining buildings associated with Joplin and his hometown.

CALIFORNIA

ALLENSWORTH

Allensworth Colony

Star Rte. 1, Box 148
Telephone: (661) 849-3433
Web site: http://www.parks.ca.gov/?page_id=583

Established as an all–African American community, the town of Allensworth was founded by Allen Allensworth in 1910. Now a state park, this landmark serves as a memorial to its founder.

Allen Allensworth, a slave prior to the Civil War, was a well-known racing jockey in Louisville, Kentucky. With the beginning of the Civil War, Allensworth was allowed to enter the navy, where he advanced to the rank of chief petty officer. Following the war, Allensworth studied for the ministry and returned to the military service as chaplain of the famed Twenty-fourth U.S. Infantry. Around 1900, he migrated to California and dedicated himself to improving the status of African Americans.

BECKWOURTH

Beckwourth Pass

Web site: http://www.beckwourth.org

Beckwourth Pass, which runs through the Sierra Nevada in Beckwourth, California, was discovered by Jim Beckwourth (1798–1866), one of a number of African American traders and trappers dubbed "mountain men" by chroniclers of U.S. history. The log cabin that he built as his home in 1852 still stands near the Plumas County hamlet named for him.

HORNITOS

Gold Mining Camp

This ghost town was the home of Moses Rodgers (1835–1900), a successful and affluent African American mine owner who was one of the finest engineers and metallurgists in the state. Rodgers was one of several African American miners who struck it rich in gold and quartz.

JULIAN

Cemetery Markers

The Julian, California, cemetery in San Diego County commemorates the African American pioneers integral to the mining of goal and its discovery by A. E. (Frederick) Coleman, a rancher, miner, and entrepreneur. The site includes a plaque memorializing these pioneers' accomplishments, along with new headstones.

RED BLUFF

Oak Hill Cemetery

Cemetery Ln.
Telephone: (530) 527-4417
Web site: http://www.redbluffcemetery.com

This is the burial place of Aaron Coffey, the only black member of the Society of California Pioneers. Coffey, the descendant of an officer who fought under General Andrew Jackson at New Orleans, came to California as a slave in 1849. By day, he worked for his master; by night, he worked as a cobbler, accumulating money toward his $1,000 emancipation fee. Betrayed by his owner, he was forced to return to Missouri, where he was again sold. Coffey pleaded with his new master to allow him to return to California and earn the necessary money to free himself and his family, which he had left behind as collateral. When he completed that mission, Coffey returned to Red Bluff, took up farming, and settled down to a contented family life.

SACRAMENTO

St. Andrew's African Methodist Episcopal Church

2131 8th St.
Telephone: (916) 448-1428
Web site: http://www.standrewsame.org

St. Andrew's was the first African Methodist Episcopal congregation in California. Organized in a private residence in 1850, the congregation within four years had founded a school for African, Asian, and Native American children in the church's basement.

SAN FRANCISCO

African American Museum & Library

659 14th St.
Telephone: (510) 637-0200
Web site: http://www.oaklandlibrary.org/aamlo

This museum and library focus on the history of African Americans in California and the West, including their involvement with the Western Pacific Railroad and the Brotherhood of Sleeping Car Porters. A major force behind the labor organization was C. L. Dellums, the uncle of Bay Area politician Ron Dellums.

Leidesdorff St.

This street in San Francisco is named for William Alexander Leidesdorff (1810–1848), a wealthy and influential California pioneer of African and Danish ancestry and a native of the Danish West Indies. A merchant, Leidesdorff operated the first steamer to pass through the Golden Gate Strait and opened and operated the first hotel, City Hotel at Kearny and Clay streets. Leidesdorff was later appointed U.S. vice-consul and ultimately became a civic and educational leader in San Francisco.

Presidio

50 Moraga Ave.
Telephone: (415) 561-4323
Web site: http://www.presidio.gov

The "buffalo soldiers" were stationed here in 1902 and 1903.

COLORADO

BENT COUNTY

Fort Lyon

Founded in 1867, Fort Lyon served variously as an army fort, a navy hospital, and a Veterans Administration hospital. Several of the companies stationed here were African American, notable among them the buffalo soldiers.

CENTRAL CITY

"Aunt Clara" Brown's Chair

Central City Opera House
621 17th St.
Telephone: (303) 292-6500

"Aunt Clara" Brown, believed to have been the first African American resident of the Colorado Territory, was born a slave in Virginia. Brown moved to Missouri, where her husband and children were sold, before she gained freedom through her master's last will and testament. From Missouri, she headed for Kansas and then for the goldfields of Colorado, where she opened the territory's first laundry. She soon began putting aside money from her earnings toward the purchase of her family's freedom.

Even when the Emancipation Proclamation set her immediate family free in 1863, she returned to Missouri and brought a group of thirty-eight relatives back to Central City. She remained in the mining community for the rest of her life, nursing the sick and performing other charitable works.

Brown died in 1885 and was buried with honors by the Colorado Pioneer Association, of which she was a member. The Central City Opera House Association dedicated a chair to her in 1932.

DENVER

Barney L. Ford Building

1514 Blake St.

Barney L. Ford (1822–1902), a former Virginia slave, moved to Colorado and became a businessman, civic leader, and politician. His initial business ventures were housed in this building and included a restaurant, bar, barbershop, and hair salon. The building is privately owned and not open to the public.

Inter-Ocean Hotel

16th and Market Sts.

Built by Barney L. Ford, the Inter-Ocean Hotel in Denver was once a showplace for millionaires and presidents. Ford, an African American entrepreneur active during the gold rush days, joined the fight over the organization of the Colorado Territory and the question of statehood. Originally allowed to vote, Ford saw this privilege abrogated by the territorial constitution and, as a result, sought to delay statehood for the territory until African American voting rights were reinstated. Enlisting the aid of Charles Sumner, the famed Massachusetts abolitionist senator, Ford urged President Andrew Johnson to veto the bill for statehood.

After Ford retired, he spent the remainder of his life in Denver, where he died in 1902. He is buried alongside his wife, Julia, in Denver's Riverside Cemetery.

Justina Ford House/Black American West Museum

3091 California St.
Telephone: (303) 482-2242
Web site: http://www.blackamericanwestmuseum.com

Justina Ford was the first African American doctor in Denver. Between 1901 and 1952, she remained the city's only African American woman doctor. Unable to practice in the local hospital at first, her home, built in 1890, became her office as well. Ford, a family doctor and general practitioner, attracted patients from various races. During her career of over fifty years, she delivered more than seven thousand babies and became known as the "baby doctor." The Black American West Museum purchased the Ford home in 1986 to house the museum and to preserve the memory of Ford and her work. The museum includes photographs, memorabilia, and other documents on African American cowboys. The museum also shows how African Americans helped settle the West.

PUEBLO

El Pueblo History Museum

301 N. Union
Telephone: (719) 583-0453

Web site: http://www.coloradohistory.org/hist_sites/pueblo/pueblo.htm

El Pueblo History Museum houses a replica of the Gantt-Blackwell Fort, which Jim Beckwourth, African American explorer, scout, and trader, claimed to have founded in 1842. The validity of the claim has not been established, as Beckwourth had something of a reputation as a teller of tall tales.

CONNECTICUT

CANTERBURY

Prince Goodin Homestead

This parcel of land in Canterbury was once the home of Prince Goodin, a free African American who fought with the British against the French in the French and Indian War. Goodin enlisted in 1757, after hearing a fiery speech by Canterbury's Reverend James Cogswell that stressed the danger of encroachment against "properties, liberties, religion, and our lives." While serving at Fort William Henry, Goodin was captured during a French attack on the fort and taken to Montreal, where he was sold into slavery. After three years of captivity, Goodin was freed when the British took the city in 1760.

Prudence Crandall House

1 S. Canterbury Rd. (junction of Connecticut Rtes. 14 and 169)
Telephone: (860) 546-7800

The Crandall House, built in 1805, became a school for Canterbury residents in 1831. The admittance of Sarah Harris, a black woman, caused local resentment. Subsequently, Prudence Crandall dismissed her white students and converted the school into a training facility for prospective black teachers. Twenty such students were in residence in 1833. Still in protest, local shopkeepers refused to sell goods to Crandall. The Connecticut General Assembly passed a black law in May 1833 restricting African Americans from outside instruction in private schools without town approval. Crandall ignored the law, and, though she was jailed, her conviction was set aside because of technical errors. She closed the school in September 1834. The Crandall House was designated a national historic landmark on July 17, 1991. It is now home to the Prudence Crandall Museum.

ENFIELD

Paul Robeson Residence, "The Beeches"

1221 Enfield St., Rte. 5

Purchased by Paul Robeson and his wife in 1940, this residence served as their home until 1953. Robeson, a singer, actor, and civil rights activist, is best known for his roles in the film *The Emperor Jones* and the musical and film version of *Show Boat* (1936).

FARMINGTON

First Church of Christ

75 Main St.
Telephone: (860) 677-2601
Web site: http://www.firstchurch1652.org

When in 1839 the mutinied Cuban slave ship *Amistad* landed off the coast of Connecticut, abolitionists in the area demanded protection for the Africans. The First Church of Christ in Farmington, Connecticut, served as the center of community life for the *Amistad* insurrectionists while they awaited trial. The church was designated a national historic landmark on May 15, 1975.

WASHINGTON

Jeff Liberty Grave Site, Judea Cemetery

Judea Cemetery Rd.

Here lies the grave of Jeff Liberty, an African American soldier who served in the Continental Army during the American Revolution. His grave marker, erected by the Sons of the American Revolution, states simply "in remembrance of Jeff Liberty and his colored patriots." Liberty, a slave at the time of the rebellion, asked his owner to be allowed to serve in the struggle for independence. His request granted, he fought throughout the revolution with an all-black regiment and was granted freedman status at the end of the war.

DELAWARE

WILMINGTON

Old Asbury Methodist Episcopal Church

3rd and Walnut Sts.
Telephone: (302) 655-7060

The Old Asbury Methodist Episcopal Church was dedicated in 1789 by the distinguished orator Bishop Francis Asbury. Tradition has it that on one occasion a number of the town's leading citizens, many of whom were eager to hear Asbury preach but considered Methodism socially beneath them, stayed outside within hearing distance of the sermon, refusing to enter the church. The listeners were impressed by the eloquence of the man they heard—but, as it turned out, the voice they heard was not that of the bishop, but of his African American servant Harry Hosier (also known as "Black Harry"), whose compelling testimony reached their ears and inspired their admiration. In its early years, the church welcomed African American members. By 1805, however, African Americans had left this church, driven out by the decision of white worshippers to confine African American members to the gallery.

DISTRICT OF COLUMBIA

African American Civil War Memorial

Vermont Ave. and U St. NW
Web site: http://www.afroamcivilwar.org

The *Spirit of Freedom* statue was unveiled on July 18, 1998, in the Shaw neighborhood of northwest Washington, D.C. It is the centerpiece of the African American Civil War Memorial. Designed by sculptor Ed Hamilton of Louisville, Kentucky, who won a nationwide competition to do the work, the monument is the first to honor and salute African American soldiers and their white officers who fought and died in the Civil War. The memorial, designed by Paul S. Devrouax and landscape architect Edward D. Dunson, is located in a pie-shaped site nearly one block long. The *Spirit of Freedom* is a 9-foot-high, 3,000-pound bronze sculpture in a semicircular arc and high relief. The exterior consists of three infantrymen and a sailor working together to fight for family and freedom. The *Spirit of Freedom*, depicted as a woman with eyes closed and hands crossed over her chest, is positioned above the men to guide and protect them. In addition to the statue, the granite walls of the memorial are inscribed with the names of more than 209,000 Civil War veterans.

The Spirit of Freedom, *African American Civil War Memorial, Washington, DC. (Ed Hamilton, 1998).* *Hamilton won a nationwide competition to create this bronze monument, the first to honor African American soldiers who fought and died in the Civil War. It was dedicated on July 18, 1998.* PHOTOGRAPH BY LEITHA ETHERIDGE-SIMS. REPRODUCED BY PERMISSION.

The African American Civil War Memorial Freedom Foundation Museum and Visitors Center, which opened in January 1999, is located two blocks west of the memorial at 1200 U Street NW.

Ben's Chili Bowl

1213 U St. NW
Telephone: (202) 667-0909
Web site: http://www.benschilibowl.com

Located next to Lincoln Theatre and founded in 1958 by Ben Ali, this landmark restaurant is frequented by celebrities and politicians, such as Bill Cosby and Barack Obama.

Mary McLeod Bethune Council House

1318 Vermont Ave. NW
Telephone: (202) 673-2402
Web site: http://www.nps.gov/mamc

The Mary McLeod Bethune Council House was opened to the public in November 1979 as a museum and archives, and it was granted national historic-site status in October 1982. It is home to the Bethune Museum and Archives, which is dedicated to documenting the contributions made by African American women to society and to enriching the lives of American children through educational materials, programs, and other services. The Council House was built around 1885. It was Mary McLeod Bethune's last official Washington, D.C., residence and served as the first headquarters of the National Council of Negro Women.

Mary McLeod Bethune Memorial

Lincoln Park

The Mary McLeod Bethune Memorial, unveiled in 1974, is the first monument to an African American or a woman to be erected on public land in the nation's capital. Bethune, an educator, was concerned about the children of the laborers working on the Florida East Coast Railroad. In 1904, she established the Daytona Normal and Industrial Institute for Negro Girls. In 1926, she merged the institute with the Cookman Institute of Jacksonville to form what was later known as Bethune-Cookman University.

The monument, located in Lincoln Park, is inscribed with the following words:

> I leave you love, I leave you hope. I leave you the challenge of developing confidence in one another. I leave you a thirst for education. I leave you respect for the use of power. I leave you faith. I leave you racial dignity.

Blanche K. Bruce House

909 M St. NW

Blanche K. Bruce, from Mississippi, was the first African American to serve a full term in the U.S. Senate. Born in Farmville, Virginia, Bruce learned the printer's trade in Missouri. In 1861, prior to the Civil War, he escaped to Hannibal, Missouri, and set up a school for African Americans. He studied at Oberlin College in Ohio and, after moving to Mississippi, became a wealthy planter. A Republican, Bruce was elected by the Mississippi state legislature to the U.S. Senate in 1874. The Blanche K. Bruce House was designated a national historic landmark on May 15, 1975. It is a private residence.

Ralph Bunche House

1510 Jackson St. NE

Ralph Bunche had a long association with Howard University, where he served on the faculty and organized the political science department. While living in the District of Columbia, he commissioned local African American architect Hilyard Robinson to design his residence. Later, Bunche was appointed undersecretary general of the United Nations. He won the Nobel Peace Prize in 1950. The house was listed on the National Register of Historic Places on September 30, 1993. In 2001, the D.C. Preservation League placed the house on its list of "Most Endangered Places." It is a private residence.

Mary Ann Shadd Cary House

1421 W St. NW

Between 1881 and 1886, this three-story brick house, located in Washington, D.C., served as the residence of Mary Ann Shadd Cary, the first African American woman to coedit a newspaper, the *Provincial Freeman*. In 1883, she became one of the first African American women to earn a law degree. Cary, a lecturer, writer, educator, lawyer, and abolitionist, appeared before audiences throughout the country, usually speaking on the topics of slavery and woman's suffrage. The house was designated a national historic landmark on December 8, 1976. It is privately owned and not open to the public.

Frederick Douglass National Historic Site

1411 W St. SE
Telephone: (202) 426-5961
Web site: http://www.nps.gov/frdo

Cedar Hill, the twenty-room colonial mansion in which Frederick Douglass (1817–1895) lived for the last thirteen years of his life, has been preserved as a monument to the great nineteenth-century abolitionist. In 1988, it was declared a national historic site. Credit for the restoration and preservation of the home belongs largely to the National Association of Colored Women's Clubs, which worked hand-in-hand with the Douglass Association.

Edward Kennedy "Duke" Ellington Birthplace

2129 Ward Pl. NW

Born on April 29, 1899, Duke Ellington was one of the world's great jazz composers, pianists, and bandleaders. It has been said of him that "the man is the music, the music is the man." The house where Ellington was born has been razed, but a plaque to commemorate the spot was installed on April 29, 1989.

Emancipation Statue

Lincoln Park, E. Capitol St.

Former slaves were responsible for financing and erecting the oldest memorial to Abraham Lincoln in the Washington, D.C., area. Following Lincoln's assassination in 1865, the first five dollars for the statue were donated by a Mrs. Charlotte Scott of Marietta, Ohio. Contributions were soon pouring in. Congress finally set aside grounds for Thomas Ball's statue depicting Lincoln breaking slavery's chains. The memorial was dedicated on April 14, 1876—the eleventh anniversary of Lincoln's assassination.

Charlotte Forten Grimké House

1608 R St. NW

Charlotte Forten Grimké (1837–1914), born of wealthy free African American parents in Philadelphia, was among the first wave of northerners engaged in educating African Americans in the occupied Union territories of the South. Her activities as an activist, writer, poet, and educator forged a path for other African American women. The house, built around 1880, was designated a national historic landmark on May 11, 1976. It is a private residence.

General Oliver Otis Howard House (Howard Hall)

604 Howard Pl., Howard University

Howard University is named in honor of Oliver Otis Howard, a Union general and once head of the

Freedmen's Bureau. His residence is one of four original university buildings still standing. The restored house—a brick residence with a mansard roof, dormer windows, and a three-and-a-half-story tower—was privately built for Howard between 1867 and 1869. It was declared a national historic landmark on May 30, 1974.

Howard University

2400 6th St. NW
Telephone: (202) 806-6100
Web site: http://www.howard.edu

Howard University, founded in 1867, is the largest institution of higher learning established for African Americans immediately following the Civil War.

Covering more than 50 acres, the campus is situated on one of the highest elevations in the District of Columbia. Among the historic buildings are Andrew Rankin Memorial Chapel (1895), the Founders Library (1938), and Freedmen's Hospital (1909), which was renamed Howard University Hospital in 1967 and presently houses the university's colleges of nursing and allied health services. Founders Library contains more than 300,000 volumes and includes the Moorland-Spingarn Research Center, one of the finest collections of materials on African American life and history in the United States.

LeDroit Park Historic District

Boundary approximates Florida and Rhode Island Aves., 2nd and Elm Sts., and Howard University

A subdivision created in 1873, the land was part of that purchased as a site for Howard University. The excess was then sold to Amzi L. Barber, the school's acting president and son-in-law of real-estate brokers LeDroit Langdon and Andrew Langdon. Approximately sixty-five houses had been built in the park by 1887 and included various styles from Italianate villas to Gothic cottages. Originally an exclusive white community, the area became racially integrated in 1893. Afterward, many whites moved out, and it was almost totally occupied by African Americans. Among the African American residents were Judge Robert H. Terrell and his wife, Mary Church Terrell; Paul Laurence Dunbar; and much later, Mayor Walter Washington. The park was listed on the National Register of Historic Places on February 25, 1974.

Lincoln Memorial

Foot of 23rd St. NW, in West Potomac Park on the Mall
Web site: http://www.nps.gov/linc

The Lincoln Memorial, dedicated in 1922, has been the site of several important events underscoring African Americans' quest for dignity and struggle for equal opportunity. In 1939, when singer Marian Anderson was refused permission to appear at Constitution Hall by the Daughters of the American Revolution, she performed an Easter Sunday concert on the steps of the Lincoln Memorial before a crowd of 75,000. Her rendition of "Nobody Knows the Trouble I've Seen" prompted Walter White, executive secretary of the NAACP, to foresee the advent of "a new affirmation of democracy." Another such pivotal event involved the 1963 March on Washington, which was climaxed by the Reverend Martin Luther King Jr.'s "I have a dream" speech. The memorial was added to the National Register of Historic Places on October 15, 1966.

Metropolitan African Methodist Episcopal Church

1518 M St. NW
Telephone: (202) 331-1426
Web site: http://www.metropolitanamec.org

Completed in 1886, this Victorian, Gothic-style church was designed by architect George Dearing. The church had two forerunners: Israel Bethel A.M.E. (1821) and Union Bethel A.M.E. (1838). On July 6, 1838, Union Bethel was officially sanctioned by the Baltimore Conference, marking the founding of the Metropolitan AME Church. In 1872, the name was officially changed to Metropolitan African Methodist Episcopal Church. The new church building, which, according to the conference, had to be built "in close proximity" to the Capitol, was dedicated on May 30, 1886. Present at the ceremony were Bishop Daniel Payne, Frederick Douglass, and Francis Cardozo. The building has been the site of funeral services for many prominent African Americans, as well as the place for church services during the inauguration of President Bill Clinton. These services were an official part of the inaugural events, the first to be held at an African American church. It was listed on the National Register of Historic Places on July 26, 1973.

Miner Normal School

2565 Georgia Ave. NW

Myrtilla Miner's School for Colored Girls was established in 1851 as a model teaching facility for young African American women. It was the district's only school dedicated solely to teacher training. Although the Miner School, as it was known, operated for a time in different locations, in 1875 it was temporarily affiliated with Howard University's Normal Department. The District of Columbia built a new Miner School—a semipublic school—in 1877, and ten years later it was incorporated into the local public school system. In

1929, Congress expanded the school into a four-year degree-granting institution, known as Miner Teachers College. In 1955, the school merged with the local white teachers college to become the District of Columbia Teachers College. This operation ceased in 1977, when the college merged with two other institutions to become the University of the District of Columbia. The school was listed on the National Register of Historic Places on October 11, 1991.

M Street High School

128 M St. NW

The Fifteenth Street Presbyterian Church was the birthplace of M Street High School in 1870. The school was originally known as the Preparatory High School for Colored Youth. It moved to several locations until Congress saw a need for an elite school for its African American population and appropriated money to construct a facility for this purpose. The building was completed in 1891 and was one of the first high schools in the nation built with public funds to serve African Americans. The faculty was well educated, and the school offered business and college preparatory classes that were superior to lower-level programs in many U.S. colleges and universities. Graduates who became distinguished leaders included Carter G. Woodson and Rayford Logan. Among the early principals were Robert Terrell, Anna Julia Cooper, and Mary Church Terrell. The new Dunbar High School, built in 1916, became the new high school for African Americans, while M Street took junior high school status. School integration in 1954 eliminated the need for a separate facility for African Americans. The school was added to the National Register of Historic Places on October 23, 1986. The building is state owned and vacant as of 2010.

National Museum of African Art

950 Independence Ave. SW
Telephone: (202) 633-4600
Web site: http://www.nmafa.si.edu

A part of the Smithsonian Institution, the National Museum of African Art maintains exhibitions, research components, and public programs on the art and culture of sub-Saharan Africa. The museum was established in 1964 and incorporated as a bureau of the Smithsonian in 1979.

St. Luke's Episcopal Church

5th and Church Sts. NW
Telephone: (202) 667-4394
Web site: http://www.stlukesdc.org

From 1879 until 1894, the pulpit of St. Luke's Episcopal Church was filled by Alexander Crummell, an African American scholar who became a leading spokesman for African and African American liberation. He was the founder of the American Negro Academy, established with the intention of forming a cadre of African American intellectuals and scholars. The church, located in Washington, D.C., was designated a national historic landmark on May 11, 1976.

Mary Church Terrell House

326 T St. NW

Built in 1907, this house served as the residence of Mary Church Terrell (1863–1954), who achieved national prominence as an early educator, the first president of the National Association of Colored Women, and a civil rights and women's rights activist. She spoke at the sixtieth anniversary of the first women's rights convention in Seneca Falls, New York. Her lecture in German delivered in 1904 at the International Congress of Women led her to the nationwide lecture circuit. The Terrell House was designated a national historic landmark on May 15, 1975. The building, which is badly deteriorated, is owned by Howard University and is not in use.

Tidal Basin Bridge

Designed and constructed by the African American engineer Archie Alphonso Alexander, the Tidal Basin Bridge is one of Washington's major tourist attractions. Born in Ottumwa, Iowa, in 1888, Alexander later, in 1954, became the first Republican governor of the U.S. Virgin Islands.

Carter G. Woodson Home and the Association for the Study of Negro Life and History

1538 9th St. NW
Web site: http://www.nps.gov/cawo

Founded in 1915, the Association for the Study of Negro Life and History was formed to study and preserve the historical record of African American culture. The pioneer behind the association was Carter G. Woodson, who operated the organization out of his home until his death in 1950.

A scholar and lecturer, Woodson began publication of the *Journal of Negro History* in 1916. Ten years later, Woodson initiated the observance of "Negro History Week," to be celebrated in February as close as possible to the birthdays of both Frederick Douglass and Abraham Lincoln, during which African American leaders would be appropriately honored. Negro History Week has grown into what is now Black History Month.

The Woodson home, built around 1890, was designated a national historic landmark on May 11, 1976.

The organization Woodson founded is now known as the Association for the Study of African American Life and History, and it is headquartered at 525 Bryant Street NW. In 2001, the Woodson home was placed on the National Trust for Historic Preservation's list of the most endangered places in the United States. In 2005, the National Park Service purchased the home, which is now known as the Carter G. Woodson Home National Historic Site.

FLORIDA

AMELIA ISLAND

American Beach

American Beach is located on Amelia Island, just north of Jacksonville, Florida. It was founded in 1935 by Abraham Lincoln Lewis, president of Afro-American Life Insurance Company, the state's first insurance company. Lewis was Florida's first black millionaire and one of the wealthiest men in the southeast. Lewis bought the land so that the employees of the insurance company and other African Americans could enjoy the beach segregation free. It was placed on the National Register of Historic Places in January 2002.

DAYTONA BEACH

Bethune-Cookman University

640 Dr. Mary McLeod Bethune Blvd.
Telephone: (386) 481-2000
Web site: http://www.bethune.cookman.edu

One of the leading institutions in the South for the training of African American teachers, Bethune-Cookman University was founded in 1904 by Mary McLeod Bethune on "faith and a dollar-and-a-half." The school was first known as Daytona Normal and Industrial Institute for Negro Girls.

Bethune served as an adviser to Presidents Franklin D. Roosevelt and Harry S. Truman and directed the Division of Negro Affairs in Roosevelt's National Youth Administration. She was one of the most influential women in the United States between the two world wars.

Mary McLeod Bethune House

Bethune-Cookman University
Telephone: (904) 255-1401

The two-story frame house belonging to the African American activist and educator Mary McLeod Bethune was built around 1915 on the campus of the school that she established in 1904. The house was proclaimed a national historic landmark on December 2, 1974.

Mary McLeod Bethune, Educator and Civil Rights Activist, 1943. *Photographed in her office at Bethune-Cookman College in Daytona Beach, Florida, Bethune had founded the college in 1904 and developed it into one of the leading institutions in the South for the training of African American teachers.* **THE LIBRARY OF CONGRESS**

EATONVILLE

Eatonville, Zora Neale Hurston Memorial Park and Marker

11 People St.

Incorporated in 1887, Eatonville claims to be one of the oldest all–African American communities in the United States. The fourth mayor of the town, John Hurston, a former slave, was the father of the town's most celebrated resident, Zora Neale Hurston (1891–1960), a folklorist, anthropologist, and noted writer of the Harlem Renaissance. Still virtually all–African American, Eatonville is the site of the Zora Neale Hurston festival held each January to celebrate Hurston's life and work. In addition, a marker has been placed in the Zora Neale Hurston Memorial Park.

FORT GEORGE ISLAND

Kingsley Plantation

Telephone: (904) 251-3537
Web site: http://www.nps.gov/timu/historyculture/kp.htm

Zephaniah Kingsley, who traded extensively in slaves and married a slave (Anna Madgigine Jai, who was freed in 1811), operated the property from 1814 to 1837, and the headquarters for his operation was on this plantation on Fort George Island. His wife was active in plantation management and became a successful businesswoman. The oldest known plantation in Florida, the Kingsley Plantation was established in 1763. The plantation, which has been restored as a museum, displays exhibits and furnishings that depict the plantation and island life during the period from 1763 to 1783. The site was added to the National Park System on February 16, 1988, as part of the Timucuan Ecological and Historic Preserve. On September 29, 1970, it was added to the National Register of Historic Places.

FORT PIERCE

Zora Neale Hurston House

1734 School Court St.

Zora Neale Hurston lived and worked in this one-story concrete house in Fort Pierce. Her grave site in a segregated cemetery in Fort Pierce was unmarked until August 1973, when the writer Alice Walker placed a stone at the approximate site of her burial. The home in which she lived from 1957, when she worked as reporter and journalist for a local African American weekly newspaper and continued to write until she died in 1960, was designated a national historic landmark on December 4, 1991. It is a private residence.

FRANKLIN COUNTY

Fort Gadsden State Historic Site

Telephone: (904) 670-8988

In 1814, the British built the fort as a base for recruiting Seminole Indians and runaway slaves during the War of 1812. The British abandoned it to their allies in 1815, along with its artillery and military supplies. It became known as the Negro Fort and British Fort and served as a beacon for rebellious slaves and a threat to supply vessels on the river. On May 15, 1975, the British fort (only ruins remain) was named a national historic landmark.

KEY WEST

Fort Jefferson

Dry Tortugas National Park
Web site: http://www.nps.gov/drto

African American artisans and laborers worked on the construction of Fort Jefferson, a fort in Key West, Florida, that helped control the Straits of Florida. The largest all-masonry fortification in the Western world, Fort Jefferson served as a prison until 1873. Among the prisoners was Samuel A. Mudd, a physician who had set John Wilkes Booth's broken leg after the assassination of Abraham Lincoln.

MIAMI

Virginia Key Beach Park

Rickenbacker Causeway on the Island of Virginia Key
4020 Virginia Beach Dr.
Telephone: (305) 960-4600
Web site: http://www.virginiakeybeachpark.net

Virginia Key Beach Park, a "Colored Only" beach, was dedicated on August 1, 1945. It was the only beach in Miami-Dade County, Florida, that was open to the African American community. It was closed in 1982 and remained closed until its reopening in 2008. On June 28, 2002, the site was listed on the National Register of Historic Places, and it has also been designated a Florida Heritage Site.

OLUSTEE

Olustee Battlefield Historic Memorial

U.S. 90
Telephone: (904) 752-3866

This site commemorates the largest Civil War battle that took place in Florida. In the Battle of Olustee (1864), also known as the Battle of Ocean Pond, many African American troops fought bravely for the Union cause. The site was acquired by the state of Florida in 1909. The monument was built in 1912 and dedicated in 1913, just forty-nine years after the battle.

SAINT AUGUSTINE

Fort Mose Historic State Park

15 Fort Mose Tr.
Telephone: (904) 823-2232
Web site: http://www.floridastateparks.org/fortmose

Originally known as Gracia Real de Santa Teresa de Mose and located north of St. Augustine, this is the site of the first free black settlement legally sanctioned in what would become the United States. Chartered in 1738 by the Spanish governor of Florida, it became a haven for escaped slaves. The Fort Mose site was designated a national historic landmark on October 12, 1994.

GEORGIA

ANDERSONVILLE

Andersonville Prison

496 Cemetery Rd.
Telephone: (229) 924-0343
Web site: http://www.nps.gov/ande

Andersonville Prison, the infamous Confederate prison in Andersonville, Georgia, where thousands of Union soldiers perished as a result of the brutal manner in which they were confined, is now a national historic site. Corporal Henry Gooding of the all-black Fifty-fourth Massachusetts Volunteer Infantry regiment was imprisoned here, where he died on July 19, 1864. It was Corporal Gooding who had started a protest regarding the pay of African American soldiers, going over the heads of military brass to write President Abraham Lincoln. At that time, the pay of African Americans was a flat $7 per month. For whites, it ranged from $9 to $30. Encouraged by Colonel Robert Shaw, the African American soldiers of the Fifty-fourth refused to accept any remuneration unless it equaled that of their white comrades. This financial inequity was subsequently rectified, but Corporal Gooding died at Andersonville without ever having drawn a day's pay.

ATLANTA

Atlanta University Center District

Telephone: (404) 523-5148
Web site: http://www.aucenter.edu

Atlanta University was founded in 1865, holding its first classes for freed slaves in abandoned railway cars. Clark College was founded four years later. The two schools were consolidated as Clark Atlanta University in 1988. The Atlanta University Center is a consortium that includes Clark Atlanta and the other traditionally African American colleges located in the immediate vicinity: Morris Brown (1881), Morehouse (1867), and Spelman (1881), along with the Interdenominational Theological Center (1946).

Fountain Hall (formerly Stone Hall), built in 1882 and located on the Morris Brown campus, is the oldest building in the district. It was named a national historic landmark on December 2, 1974.

Ebenezer Baptist Church

407 Auburn Ave. NE
Telephone: (404) 688-7300

A Gothic-revival building constructed in 1922, Ebenezer Baptist Church had as its associate pastor the Reverend Martin Luther King Jr. It was from this church that King's movement radiated outward to the rest of the South, organizing chapters of the Southern Christian Leadership Conference (SCLC), the civil rights coalition of which he served as president.

When King was assassinated on April 4, 1968, funeral services were held in this church. As millions watched on television, mourners lined up for miles behind the mule-drawn wagon that carried King from Ebenezer to Morehouse College, his alma mater. There, the eulogies were delivered, and more than 150,000 mourners paid their last respects.

Ebenezer Baptist Church, Atlanta, GA. *Martin Luther King Jr. was the associate pastor at this church, built in 1922, and it was from this location that his civil rights movement radiated outward to the rest of the South.* **AP IMAGES. REPRODUCED BY PERMISSION.**

Birthplace of Civil Rights Leader Martin Luther King Jr., Atlanta, GA. *King was born in this house on January 15, 1929. The house, which was built in 1895, is part of the Martin Luther King Jr. National Historic District.* WILLIAM MANNING/ALAMY

Martin Luther King Jr. National Historic District

Auburn Ave.
Telephone: (404) 331-6922
Web site: http://www.nps.gov/malu

The district, which consists of several blocks of Atlanta's Auburn Avenue and Boulevard, includes Martin Luther King Jr.'s birthplace—a two-story Queen Anne–style house built in 1895—and his grave site, and the church where King served as assistant pastor. The environs of his childhood are largely intact. Private efforts to create a living monument to King and his beliefs have been carried on primarily through the Martin Luther King Jr. Center for Nonviolent Social Change, Inc. The Martin Luther King Historic District was designated a national historic landmark on May 5, 1977. The district was designated a National Historic Site and Preservation District in 1980 and eventually became a unit of the National Park System.

South View Cemetery

1990 Jonesboro Rd. SE
Telephone: (404) 622-5393
Web site: http://www.southviewcemetery.com

Martin Luther King Jr. was first laid to rest in South View Cemetery, where a marble crypt was inscribed with the words he used to conclude his famous speech delivered on the occasion of the 1963 March on Washington—"Free at last, free at last, thank God Almighty I'm free at last." In the early 1970s, Dr. King's body was moved from the South View Cemetery to a site next to the Ebenezer Baptist Church and the King Center in Atlanta. South View Cemetery was founded in 1886 by African Americans who balked at a prevailing policy requiring that they be buried in the rear of the municipal cemetery.

Sweet Auburn Historic District

Auburn Ave.

Although only a remnant of its original one-mile expanse has survived, the Sweet Auburn district typified the rapid growth of African American enterprise in the post–Civil War period. Forced to adjust to segregated residential and commercial patterns, wealthy African

Americans settled in the area once known as Wheat Street and the "richest Negro street in the world." The district survives as a center of African American business and social activity. The area was designated a national historic landmark district on December 8, 1976. It is now included in the Martin Luther King National Historic Site and Preservation District.

AUGUSTA

Laney-Walker North Historic District

Bounded by D'Antignac, 7th, Twiggs, Phillips, and Harrison Sts.; Walton Way; and Laney-Walker Blvd.

Developed during the nineteenth century as a self-sufficient, working-class community, the Laney-Walker district includes good examples of such houses as the plantation plain, shotgun, double pen, and Victorian cottage, as well as an indigenous Augusta house. Prominent African American residents of the area included the novelist Frank Yerby; Lucy C. Laney, an educator and the founder of the Haines Normal and Industrial Institute; Charles T. Walker, a minister and church founder; and numerous physicians, merchants, builders, and businesspeople. Businesses in the district are important landmarks in Augusta's African American community. Examples include the Pilgrim Health and Life Insurance Company (1898) and the Penny Savings Bank (1910). The area was listed on the National Register of Historic Places on September 5, 1985.

BRUNSWICK

Colored Memorial School and Risley High School

Albany St. near H St.

Risley High School opened in 1870 as the Freedmen's School and was later renamed in honor of Captain Douglas Gilbert Risley, who raised funds for the building; the Colored Memorial High School was built and named to honor the African American veterans of World War I. These schools are hailed as landmarks in Glynn County African American education.

COLUMBUS

"Blind Tom" Marker

Near intersection of Warm Springs and Grey Rock Rds.

This marks the grave site of the famous African American pianist "Blind Tom" Wiggins (1843–1908). Born Thomas Greene Bethune, son of a slave, he was a prodigy whose astonishing talent brought him into the salons of Europe, where royalty marveled at his virtuoso performances.

Gertrude Pridgett "Ma" Rainey House

805 5th Ave.

The Rainey House was the retirement residence of Ma Rainey (1886–1939), who was recognized as "Mother of the Blues." She made her singing debut when she was fourteen. In 1904, she married William "Pa" Rainey (who was about thirty years her senior) of the Rabbit Foot Minstrels and became known as "Ma." The team performed with various minstrels until they separated.

Ma Rainey worked out of Chicago during the 1920s and early 1930s and continued to tour the South. She had already won a national following as a gospel and blues performer long before she made her first recording in 1924. Rainey retired in 1934. She returned to Columbus in 1935 and lived in the house that she had earlier purchased for her mother. She died in 1939 and was buried in the local Porterdale Cemetery. The Rainey House was added to the National Register of Historic Places on November 18, 1992. The "Ma" Rainey House and Blues Museum is open for public tours Tuesdays through Saturdays.

Bragg Smith Grave Site and Memorial

Porterdale Cemetery
4th St. and 7th Ave.

This memorial, located in Porterdale Cemetery, was built in memory of Bragg Smith, who was killed in 1903 while attempting to rescue a city engineer trapped in a caved-in structure. The marble memorial is believed to have been the first civic memorial in the country dedicated to an African American.

MIDWAY

Dorchester Academy Boys' Dormitory

8787 E. Oglethorpe Hwy.
Web site: http://www.dorchesteracademy.com

Dorchester Academy, a primary school for African American boys, was founded by the American Missionary Association following the Civil War. The dormitory, which was declared a national historic landmark on September 20, 2006, is the only remaining structure. The academy was the primary training site of the Southern Christian Leadership Conference's Citizenship Education Program during the 1960s.

SAVANNAH

First Bryan Baptist Church

575 W. Bryan St.
Telephone: (912) 232-5526
Web site: http://www.firstbryanbaptistchurch.com

The land on which Bryan Church was built is considered the oldest real estate in the country continuously owned by African Americans. Deeds for the land are dated September 4, 1793. Andrew Bryan formed the First African Baptist Church in Savannah on January 20, 1788, and pastored the congregation that became

First Bryan Baptist Church in 1799. He remained there until his death in 1812.

Inside the First Bryan Baptist Church is a memorial dedicated to the Reverend George Leile (sometimes spelled Liele), a former slave and the first African American Baptist missionary. His work took him up and down the Savannah River, from Augusta to Savannah, several times a year, where he preached to slaves. One of the slaves that he converted and baptized was Andrew Bryan, for whom the church was named.

Ralph Mark Gilbert Civil Rights Museum

460 Martin Luther King Jr. Blvd.
Telephone: (912) 231-4800
Web site: http://www.savcivilrights.com

Named for a famous Savannah civil rights leader and a pastor of First African Baptist Church, this museum is dedicated to Savannah's African American and civil rights struggles. The museum, which features exhibits and photographs, is housed in what was the largest black bank in the United States.

WOODBURY

Red Oak Creek Covered Bridge

N. of Woodbury on Huel Brown Rd.

This 391-foot-long structure was built in the 1840s by the African American bridge builder Horace King, a former slave. King continued to work for his white master, John Goodwin, a contractor, after he was freed in 1848. One of the few extant in the state, the bridge is believed to be the oldest structure of its type in Georgia and the longest wooden bridge span in the state. King built other bridges in west Georgia, as well as the bridge across the Chattahoochee River in Columbus. The Red Oak Creek Covered Bridge was listed on the National Register of Historic Places on May 7, 1973.

HAWAII

HONOLULU

USS *Arizona* Memorial

This monument honors those who died in the 1941 Japanese attack on Pearl Harbor. African Americans played a major role in this war; among those commemorated is Dorie Miller. He was the first African American World War II hero, recognized by Franklin D. Roosevelt, and he received the Navy Cross in 1942 (the first African American to receive this honor).

ILLINOIS

CHICAGO

Robert S. Abbott House

4742 S. Martin Luther King Jr. Dr.

This house was occupied by Robert Sengstacke Abbott from 1926 until his death in 1940. Under Abbott, the *Chicago Defender*, a newspaper targeted to African American readers, encouraged African Americans in the South to migrate northward, particularly to Chicago. Probably more than any other publication, the *Defender* was responsible for the large northward migration of African Americans during the first half of the twentieth century. The house was named a national historic landmark on December 8, 1976. It is a private residence.

Black Metropolis—Bronzeville Historic District

39th St., State St., Pershing Rd., and King Dr.

Among the remaining structures of note in this historic district are the Eighth Regiment Armory (built 1914–1915), the first armory in the United States constructed for an African American military regiment; the Chicago Defender Building (1899), home of the *Chicago Defender* from 1920 to 1960; the Supreme Life Building (1921), the headquarters of the first insurance company in the northern United States owned and operated by African Americans; and the Victory Monument (1926), erected to honor the Eighth Regiment of the Illinois National Guard, an African American unit that served in France during World War I as part of the 370th U.S. Infantry.

Chicago Bee Building

3647–3655 S. State St.

The Chicago Bee Building was the last major structure built in Chicago's Black Metropolis, near State and 35th streets on the Near South Side. African American entrepreneur Anthony Overton (1865–1946) had the structure built to house his newspaper, the *Chicago Bee.* Opened in 1931, the building also housed his Overton Hygienic Manufacturing Company. It was the first building designed in the late 1920s Art Deco style and was one of the most picturesque structures in the metropolis. The building was listed on the National Register of Historic Places on April 30, 1986. It was purchased by the City of Chicago, and it now houses a Chicago Public Library branch.

Oscar Stanton DePriest House

4536–4538 S. Martin Luther King Jr. Dr.

This house served as the residence of the first African American elected to the House of Representatives from a northern state. Oscar Stanton DePriest was born in Florence, Alabama, but moved with his family to Kansas and later to Chicago. While in Chicago, he worked as a real-estate broker and, in 1928, was elected to the U.S. House of Representatives, where he served three terms. Following his tenure, he returned to the real-estate business but remained politically active in Chicago, including serving as vice chairman of the Cook County Republican Committee. The DePriest House was designated a national historic landmark on May 15, 1975. It is a private residence.

Jean Baptiste Point Du Sable Homesite

401 N. Michigan Ave.

Jean Baptiste Point Du Sable, born in Haiti around 1745 to a French mariner father and a black mother, immigrated to French Louisiana and became a fur trapper. He established trading posts on sites in the present-day cities of Michigan City, Indiana; Peoria, Illinois; and Port Huron, Michigan—but the most important post was in Chicago. This site, where he constructed a log home for his wife and family, is recognized as the first settlement in the Chicago area. In 1800, Du Sable sold his Chicago home and moved to Peoria. In 1813, he moved to St. Charles, Missouri, to live with his daughter. He remained in St. Charles until his death and burial there in 1818. He was buried in an unmarked grave; the grave was marked in 1968 by the Illinois Sesquicentennial Commission.

The homesite was designated a national historic landmark on May 11, 1976. The site of Du Sable's home is marked by a plaque on the northeast approach to the Michigan Avenue Bridge. Other plaques recognizing Du Sable can be found at the Chicago Historical Society and in the lobby of the Du Sable Leadership Academy at 4934 S. Wabash Avenue.

Milton L. Olive Park

Lake Shore Dr.

Milton L. Olive Park was dedicated by Chicago Mayor Richard Daley in honor of the first African American soldier to be awarded a Congressional Medal of Honor during the Vietnam War. Olive died in action after exhibiting extraordinary heroism, having saved the lives of several other soldiers exposed to a live grenade.

Provident Hospital and Training School

500 E. 51st St.

The original Provident Hospital and Training School was established in 1891 as the first school for African American nurses in the United States. It was founded by Daniel Hale Williams, the renowned surgeon who performed one of the first successful operations on the human heart in 1893. The current hospital was opened in 1933.

Quinn Chapel of the AME Church

2401 S. Wabash Ave.
Telephone: (312) 791-1847
Web site: http://www.quinnchicago.org

Quinn Chapel is the oldest African American congregation in Chicago. Its history dates to 1844, when several local African Americans organized a weekly, nonsectarian prayer group that met in a member's home. The group was organized in 1847 as a congregation of the African Methodist Episcopal Church and was named for William Paul Quinn (1788–1873), bishop, circuit rider, and key figure in the western advance of the church. The church served as a focal point for the social and humanitarian life of Chicago's elite African Americans. Erected in 1892, the church structure was added to the National Register of Historic Places on September 4, 1979.

Underground Railroad Marker

9955 S. Beverly Ave.

This marks one of many transit points used by slaves escaping from the South to Canada.

Victory Monument

35th St. and King Dr.

Sculpted by Leonard Crunelle, Victory Monument honors the African American soldiers of Illinois who served in World War I. The monument and tomb of Stephen A. Douglas, once the owner of much of the land in the area, is also located near 35th Street. The Victory Monument was designated a Chicago landmark on September 9, 1998.

Ida B. Wells-Barnett House

3624 S. Martin Luther King Jr. Dr.

This house was the home of the fiery 1890s journalist, civil rights advocate, and crusader for African American women, Ida B. Wells-Barnett. Wells-Barnett was exiled from the South after writing scathing articles about lynchings and race relations in Memphis, Tennessee, where her career in journalism began. She organized women's clubs in New England and Chicago and the Alpha Suffrage Club in Chicago. Wells-Barnett was a founder of the NAACP. The Wells-Barnett House was designated a national historic landmark on May 30, 1974. It is a private residence.

Daniel Hale Williams House

445 E. 42nd St.

This house was the home of one of America's first African American surgeons, whose accomplishments include performing one of the first successful heart operations in 1893 and establishing quality medical facilities for African Americans. Daniel Hale Williams was born in Hollidaysburg, Pennsylvania. He had managed a barbershop prior to apprenticing under Henry Palmer, who was surgeon-general of Wisconsin. Williams received his medical degree from Chicago Medical College in 1883 and later opened an office in Chicago; he was the first African American to win a fellowship from the American College of Surgeons. The Williams House was designated a national historic landmark on May 15, 1975. In 1993, the house was severely damaged by fire. It is a private residence.

QUINCY

Father Augustine Tolton Grave Site

St. Peter's Cemetery
Broadway and 32nd St.

The Father Augustine Tolton grave site marks the resting place of one of the first African Americans to be ordained as a Roman Catholic priest. Ordained in 1886, Father Tolton opened a school for African American children, was pastor at St. Joseph's Church in Quincy, and later served as pastor at St. Monica's Church in Chicago. He died in 1897.

INDIANA

BLOOMINGDALE

Underground Railroad Marker

U.S. Rte. 41

This marks one of several points once used to assist fugitive slaves seeking freedom and safety in Canada. One such slave, William Trail, liked Indiana so much he decided to stay and go into farming. His efforts were successful, and he became one of many prosperous farmers active in Union County, Indiana.

FOUNTAIN CITY

Levi Coffin House

113 U.S. 27 North
Telephone: (765) 847-2432
Web site: http://www.waynet.org/levicoffin

Born in North Carolina in 1798, Levi Coffin, a Quaker abolitionist who was also known as the "President of the Underground Railroad," used his own home in Fountain City (known at the time as Newport) as a way station for runaway slaves. Between 1827 and 1847, Coffin hid more than three hundred slaves heading for Illinois, Michigan, or Canada. The house was built in 1839, altered in 1910, and then restored to its former design. It was designated a national historic landmark on June 23, 1965, and purchased by the state of Indiana two years later.

Coffin left Fountain City for Ohio, where he continued his activities, eventually helping over 3,000 slaves escape from the South. He was still engaged in the resettlement of former slaves long after the Civil War had ended. Coffin died in Avondale, Ohio, in 1877.

HANOVER

St. Stephens American Methodist Episcopal Church

210 W. Main St.
Telephone: (812) 866-1435

This African American church, established in 1885, was added to the National Register of Historic Places on December 28, 2000. It is the oldest predominantly African American continuously functioning congregation in Jefferson County. Many of the early trustees were prominent members of the Underground Railroad.

INDIANAPOLIS

Madame C. J. Walker Building

617 Indiana Ave.
Telephone: (317) 236-2099
Web site: http://walkertheatre.com

The Madame C. J. Walker Building was constructed in 1927 to serve as the headquarters for the prosperous firm of Madame C. J. Walker (1867–1919). The Art Deco structure was architecturally significant and incorporated African, Egyptian, and Moorish motifs in its design. It housed a number of businesses, including a theater, pharmacy, ballroom, and the Walker Beauty College, where thousands of Walker's successful beauty agents were trained.

Walker's firm manufactured seventy-five beauty products, and its operations also included training programs, beauty schools, and shops nationwide. Her haircare business catapulted her into fame and wealth, and many called her the nation's first African American woman millionaire. She also gave generously to various charities. The Walker Building was designated a national historic landmark on July 17, 1991. It now houses the Madame Walker Theatre Center.

IOWA

CEDAR RAPIDS

African American Museum of Iowa

55 12th Ave. SE
Telephone: (319) 862-2101
Web site: http://www.blackiowa.org

The African American Museum of Iowa has as its mission to "preserve, publicize, and educate the public on the African American heritage and culture of Iowa." In addition to special exhibits and programs, the museum features the permanent exhibit *Endless Possibilities*, which uses a variety of materials to illuminate the journey of African Americans in Iowa.

CLINTON

Underground Railroad Marker

6th and S. 2nd Sts.

The small house that once stood at this location had been a point of shelter and sustenance for fugitive slaves escaping from Missouri (Iowa was a free territory by virtue of both the Northwest Ordinance of 1787 and the Missouri Compromise of 1820). Many Quakers, who had come to the state before the Civil War, took great pains to maintain an efficient and effective Underground Railroad network. The Lafayette Hotel was later built on the site.

DES MOINES

Fort Des Moines Provisional Army Officer Training School

SW 9th St.

Fort Des Moines Provisional Army Officer Camp was opened on June 15, 1917, for the purpose of training talented African American soldiers for officer's rank. On October 15, 1917, 639 African American soldiers were commissioned as second lieutenants and assigned to the American Expeditionary Forces being sent to France to fight in World War I. African American units, led by men trained at the school, were assembled in France as the Ninety-second Division. The camp was abandoned at the end of the war, and the site was designated a national historic landmark on May 30, 1974.

SIOUX CITY

Pearl St.

Sioux City was a refuge for many slaves escaping from Missouri. Pearl Street, once the city's main thoroughfare, was named for an African American who had arrived in the town by boat more than a century earlier and achieved widespread popularity as a cook.

KANSAS

BEELER

George Washington Carver Homestead Monument

County Rd. 312

Along Route K-96 in Ness County lies the plot of land once homesteaded by George Washington Carver, the famed African American agricultural scientist. He spent two years here (1886–1888) before attending college in Iowa. The homestead was listed on the National Register of Historic Places on November 23, 1977, and is indicated by a stone marker and bronze plaque.

NICODEMUS

Nicodemus National Historic Site

U.S. 24 (site approximates North St., E. Bend Rd., South St., and Seventh St.)
Telephone: (785) 839-4233
Web site: http://www.nps.gov/nico

Located 2 miles west of the Rooks-Graham county line, the Nicodemus National Historic Site is the last of three now virtually deserted colonies that were founded by the exodusters—a group of African American homesteaders that migrated from the South to Kansas during the 1870s. A principal leader of the mass migration was Benjamin "Pap" Singleton (1809–1892), a former slave from Tennessee who established eleven colonies in Kansas between 1873 and 1880. The name "Nicodemus" was derived from a slave who, according to legend, foretold the coming of the Civil War.

Arriving in 1877, the first settlers lived in dugouts and burrows during the cold weather. From the outset, they were plagued by crop failures. Although never more than five hundred in number, they managed nonetheless to establish a community with teachers, ministers, and civil servants. The state of Kansas has commemorated this site with a historical marker located in a roadside park in Nicodemus. The site was designated a national historic landmark district on January 7, 1976. The National Park Service designated Nicodemus a national historic site in 1996 and operates a temporary visitor center at the Nicodemus Township Hall.

OSAWATOMIE

John Brown Memorial State Park

10th and Main Sts.
Telephone: (913) 755-4384

This state park, named in honor of insurrectionist John Brown, contains the cabin in which he lived and engaged in abolitionist activities during his brief sojourn in Kansas. The cabin, built in 1854 on a site about 1 mile west of town, was dismantled, moved, and reconstructed in the park in 1912. In 1928, it was covered with a stone pergola. The cabin was listed on the National Register of Historic Places on March 24, 1971, and is now known as the John Brown Museum.

TOPEKA

Brown v. Board of Education National Historic Site

1515 SE Monroe St.
Telephone: (785) 354-4273
Web site: http://www.nps.gov/brvb

The historic area includes Sumner and Monroe elementary schools, both associated with the landmark Supreme Court case. In 1951, Linda Brown, who at first traveled a considerable distance to study at the all–African American Monroe Elementary School, was refused enrollment in Sumner Elementary School because she was African American. What followed was the landmark case *Brown v. Board of Education of Topeka, Kansas.* After hearing the case, the U.S. Supreme Court concluded that "separate education facilities are inherently unequal," striking down the 1896 *Plessy v. Ferguson* decision and giving the legal basis for desegregation in public schools. Sumner was designated a national historic landmark on May 4, 1987, and Monroe was included in 1991. The combined area was designated a national historic site on October 26, 1992, and subsequently became part of the National Park System.

KENTUCKY

BEREA

Lincoln Hall

Berea College
Telephone: (859) 985-3000
Web site: http://www.berea.edu/buildings/lincolnhall

Opened in 1855, Berea College was the first college established in the United States for the specific purpose of educating blacks and whites together. The school's Lincoln Hall, completed in 1887, was designated as a national historic landmark on December 2, 1974.

FRANKFORT

Monument to Kentucky's African American Civil War Soldiers

Old State Arsenal
E. Main St.

This monument is one of only four in the entire country dedicated to black soldiers who fought in the Civil War, and the only one in Kentucky.

LEXINGTON

Historic African American Health Center: Polk-Dalton Infirmary

148 Deweese

This office building housed prominent African American physicians. It was first occupied by Dr. John Polk, who opened his own medical practice. Polk was later joined by Dr. J. R. Dalton. This was also the location of the Polk-Dalton Pharmacy. Other physicians succeeded them. The structure is presently the headquarters of the Lexington-Fayette County Urban League, which opened in 1999.

LOUISVILLE

Kentucky Derby Museum

Churchill Downs
704 Central Ave.
Telephone: (502) 637-7097
Web site: http://www.derbymuseum.org

The Kentucky Derby Museum includes materials relating to early African American jockeys, who played an important part in racing history. Isaac Murphy, the first jockey to ride three Kentucky Derby horses to victory, is among those represented.

Louisville Free Public Library, Western Colored Branch

604 S. 10th St.
Telephone: (502) 574-1779
Web site: http://www.lfpl.org/branches/western.htm

This library, established in 1905, was the first public library in the nation built exclusively for African Americans. It was financed by Andrew Carnegie and played an important role in advancing African American culture in Louisville. Thomas F. Blue, the first librarian, opened a library education program at the facility in 1908 to prepare African Americans for positions in the library. The building was listed on the National Register of Historic Places on December 6, 1975.

Muhammad Ali Center

1 Muhammad Ali Plz.
144 N. 6th St.
Telephone: (502) 584-9254
Web site: http://www.alicenter.org

The Muhammad Ali Center, which opened in November 2005, is an interactive museum and educational center dedicated to the legacy and cultural impact of the boxing champion who was known as Cassius Clay in his early life and career. The museum displays memorabilia related to Ali, and it shares and teaches his six core values: respect, confidence, conviction, dedication, giving, and spirituality.

SIMPSONVILLE

Lincoln Institute Complex

Off U.S. Rte. 60
Telephone: (502) 722-8862

Lincoln Institute was Kentucky's leading center for the education of African American students in secondary school between 1908 and 1938. Whitney M. Young Sr. directed the school. When a state law in 1904 ordered Berea College to close its doors to biracial education, the college founded the Lincoln Institute. Kentucky's schools were integrated in the 1950s, and the institute became obsolete; it closed in 1965. On December 27, 1988, the complex was listed on the National Register of Historic Places. It is currently home to the Whitney M. Young Jr. Job Corps Center.

Whitney M. Young Jr. Birthplace

Off U.S. Rte. 60
Telephone: (502) 585-4733

Whitney M. Young Jr. was born in a simple, two-story frame building near Simpsonville. He grew up on the campus of the Lincoln Institute. Later, Young worked with the Urban League in Minnesota and Omaha before becoming dean of social work at Atlanta University (now Clark Atlanta). In 1961, Young was appointed executive director of the National Urban League, a position he held until 1971, when he died in Lagos, Nigeria. On April 27, 1984, the house in which he was born and lived was declared a national historic landmark.

LOUISIANA

ALEXANDRIA

Arna Bontemps African American Museum

1327 3rd St.
Telephone: (318) 473-4692
Web site: http://www.arnabontempsmuseum.com

Arna Wendell Bontemps was born in this modest Queen Anne Revival–style cottage in 1902 and remained there until his family relocated to California. Bontemps relocated to New York City in 1923 and became active as a Harlem Renaissance writer. Later, he taught in Huntsville, Alabama, and in Chicago. He moved to Nashville, Tennessee, in 1943 to become head librarian at Fisk University and remained there until he retired in 1965. He was then professor at the University of Illinois, Chicago Circle, as it was known then, and curator of the James Weldon Johnson Collection at Yale University. He returned to Fisk as writer-in-residence, the position that he held when he died on June 4, 1973. In his lifetime, he wrote numerous books, poems, and articles. His birthplace, now a museum, was listed on the National Register of Historic Places on September 13, 1993.

MELROSE

Melrose Plantation

Junction of Hwys. 119 and 493
Telephone: (318) 379-0055
Web site: http://http://www.caneriverheritage.org/main_file.php/melrose.php/

The Yucca Plantation, known after 1875 as Melrose Plantation, was established in the late eighteenth century by Marie Thérèse Coincoin, a former slave and wealthy businesswoman. The African House located on the plantation, a unique structure with an umbrella-like roof, is believed to be of direct African derivation. Melrose is also associated with Clementine Hunter (1880s), one of its African American workers, whose paintings of the plantation and its activities made her a famous folk painter. The site and its various buildings were designated a national historic landmark on May 30, 1984.

NEW ORLEANS

James H. Dillard House

571 Audubon St.

This house served as the home of James Dillard from 1894 to 1913. Dillard played an important role in African American education in the nineteenth century, strengthening vocational and teacher-training programs. Dillard's home was designated a national historic landmark on December 2, 1975. Dillard University, founded in 1869, was named for this educator.

Flint-Goodridge Hospital of Dillard University

Intersection of Louisiana Ave. and LaSalle St.

Flint-Goodridge Hospital was founded in 1911 and became the medical unit of Dillard University in 1932. In the 1930s, the hospital was the only institution in the state that offered internships to African American students preparing to become doctors. Flint-Goodrich was also the city's sole health-care facility that admitted African Americans. It was significant for its contributions to tuberculosis testing and treatment, infant and maternal care, and syphilis treatment. The hospital closed in 1983 and was added to the National Register of Historic Places on January 13, 1989.

PORT HUDSON

Port Hudson State Historic Site

Web site: http://www.crt.state.la.us/parks/ipthudson.aspx

Located near the Mississippi River some 25 miles north of Baton Rouge, Port Hudson was the scene of many heroic acts by African American soldiers during the Civil War, including Louisiana's celebrated regiment of African Americans, the Native Guards.

MAINE

PORTLAND

Abyssinian Meeting House

73–75 Newbury St.

This vernacular wood-frame building, constructed between 1828 and 1831, has a history of both social and religious action and serves as a significant source for the study of social practices in nineteenth-century Maine. The house was added to the National Register of Historic Places on February 3, 2006.

John B. Russwurm House

238 Ocean Ave.

John B. Russwurm, the second African American to receive a college degree, graduated from Bowdoin College in 1826. He coedited the nation's first African American newspaper, *Freedom's Journal*, then immigrated to Liberia. The historic house where he lived intermittently from 1812 to 1827, the only surviving structure closely tied to Russwurm, was listed on the National Register of Historic Places on July 21, 1983. It is a private residence.

MARYLAND

ANNAPOLIS

Banneker-Douglass Museum

84 Franklin St.
Telephone: (410) 216-6180
Web site: http://www.bdmuseum.com

This museum, located in Annapolis's historic district, is dedicated to the African American surveyor and inventor Benjamin Banneker and the abolitionist Frederick Douglass, both born in Maryland.

Matthew Henson Plaque

Maryland State House

The Matthew Henson Plaque, located inside the Maryland State House, honors the memory of the only man to accompany Admiral Robert E. Peary on all of his polar expeditions. On April 6, 1909, Henson became the first man actually to reach the North Pole. Peary himself, barely able to walk, arrived after Henson had taken a reading of his position and proudly planted the U.S. flag.

Thurgood Marshall Statue

North of Statehouse Cir.

A 7-foot bronze statue of U.S. Supreme Court Justice Thurgood Marshall was unveiled in Annapolis in November 1996. It is the state's first memorial dedicated to an African American.

BALTIMORE

Benjamin Banneker Marker

Westchester Ave. at Westchester School

This marker is a tribute to Benjamin Banneker, the black mathematician, astronomer, and inventor who, in 1792, produced an almanac regarded as among the most reliable. His scientific knowledge led to his assignment as a member of the surveying and planning team that helped lay out the nation's capital. Banneker's unmarked grave, located in a churchyard, is marked by a commemorative obelisk erected in 1977 by the Maryland Bicentennial Commission and the State Commission on African American History and Culture.

Beulah Myrtle Davis Special Collections Department

Soper Library, Morgan State University
1700 E. Cold Spring Ln.
Telephone: (443) 885-3458
Web site: http://library.morgan.edu/depart/spec/home1.htm

Morgan State University houses an interesting collection of artifacts on Benjamin Banneker, noted astronomer, compiler of almanacs, and—together with Pierre-Charles L'Enfant—surveyor of the District of Columbia. It also houses a number of artifacts on Frederick Douglass and Matthew Henson.

Frederick Douglass Monument

Morgan State University
1700 E. Cold Spring Ln.

On the campus of Morgan State University is the Frederick Douglass memorial statue created by the noted African American sculptor James Lewis. The work, completed in 1956, stands 12 feet tall (including the pedestal) and is located in front of Holmes Hall. Its simple inscription reads "Frederick Douglass 1817–1895 Humanitarian, Statesman."

CATONSVILLE

Oblate Sisters of Providence

701 Gun Rd.
Telephone: (410) 242-8500
Web site: http://www.oblatesisters.com

Mother Mary Elizabeth Lange was the founder and superior of the Oblate Sisters of Providence, the first religious order for African American women. She established the nation's first Catholic school for African American children.

ROCKVILLE

Uncle Tom's Cabin

11420 Old Georgetown Rd.

This is the site of the log cabin believed to have been the birthplace of Josiah Henson, the escaped slave immortalized as Uncle Tom in Harriet Beecher Stowe's famous abolitionist work of fiction.

Born in 1789, Henson was sold at auction at an early age and transferred among many masters until he managed to escape in 1830. After setting up a community for fugitive slaves in Dawn, Canada, Henson frequently returned to the South to liberate others. Meeting with Stowe, Henson outlined his slave experiences, which later formed the basis for her celebrated story. In the introduction to Henson's autobiography, published some years later, Stowe acknowledged his story as the source of her own tale.

MASSACHUSETTS

BOSTON

Abiel Smith School and Museum of African American History

46 Joy St.
Telephone: (617) 725-0022
Web site: http://www.afroammuseum.org/site13.htm

Now part of the Museum of African American History, this building, built in 1834, was the site of the city's first school for African American children. It is part of the Boston African American National Historic Site.

African Meeting House

8 Smith Ct.
Telephone: (617) 725-0022
Web site: http://www.afroammuseum.org/site14.htm

This is the site of the first black church in Boston and the oldest surviving black church building in the United States. The African Meeting House was designated a national historic site on May 30, 1974, and is a part of the Boston African American National Historic Site.

Boston African American National Historic Site

14 Beacon St.
Telephone: (617) 742-5415
Web site: http://www.nps.gov/boaf

This site includes the Black Heritage Trail and contains the largest concentration of pre–Civil War African American history sites anywhere in the United States. Among them are the African Meeting House (the oldest extant African American church building in the United States), the Smith Court residences (typical of African American families and built between 1799 and 1853), the Abiel Smith School (built in 1834), and the home of Lewis Hayden (the most documented of Boston's Underground Railroad stations). Hayden was an escaped slave from Kentucky who helped recruit the all-black Fifty-fourth Massachusetts Volunteer Infantry regiment. Congress authorized the African American National Historic Site on October 10, 1980. The site is federally owned and the National Park Service coordinates in components.

Bunker Hill Monument

Telephone: (617) 242-5642
Web site: http://www.nps.gov/bost/historyculture/bhm.htm

Standing in the Charlestown district of Boston, the Bunker Hill Monument commemorates the famous Revolutionary War battle that—contrary to popular belief—was actually fought on Breed's Hill on June 17, 1775. A number of African Americans fought alongside the colonists during the battle, including Peter Salem, Salem Poor, Titus Coburn, Cato Howe, Alexander Ames, Seymour Burr, Pomp Fiske, and Prince Hall, founder of the Negro Masonic order. The Battle of Bunker Hill Museum opened in 2007 across the street from the monument.

Crispus Attucks Monument

The Crispus Attucks Monument, located in the Boston Common, was dedicated in 1888 to the five victims of the Boston Massacre—Crispus Attucks, Samuel Maverick, James Caldwell, Samuel Gray, and Patrick Carr. The site of the massacre is marked by a plaque on State Street, near the Old State House.

Attucks is believed by many historians to have been the same man who, in 1750, was advertised as a runaway black slave from Framingham, Massachusetts. Although a stranger to Boston, he led a group that converged on a British garrison, which was quartered in King Street to help enforce the Townshend Acts. One of the soldiers of the garrison panicked and fired, and Attucks was the first to fall. Gray and Caldwell were also killed on the same spot; Maverick and Carr died later of wounds sustained during the clash. The British soldiers were later tried for murder but acquitted. The five men are buried a few blocks away in Granary Burying Ground, together with such famous Revolutionary figures as Samuel Adams, John Hancock, and Paul Revere.

William C. Nell House

3 Smith Ct.

From the 1830s to the end of the Civil War, William C. Nell was one of the leading African American abolitionists. Born in Boston, he studied law in the office of William I. Bowditch. Nell refused to take an oath to be admitted to the bar because he did not want to support the U.S. Constitution, which compromised on the issue of slavery. He then began organizing meetings and lecturing in support of the antislavery movement. The Nell house was designated a national historic landmark on May 11, 1976. It is a private residence.

Robert Gould Shaw and Fifty-fourth Regiment Memorial

Beacon and Park Sts.
Web site: http://www.nps.gov/boaf/historyculture/shaw.htm

Executed by the famed sculptor Augustus Saint-Gaudens and dedicated in 1897, this monument depicts Colonel Robert Gould Shaw and the Fifty-fourth Massachusetts Volunteer Infantry, an African American regiment that served in the Union Army during the Civil War. The regiment distinguished itself in the battle for Fort Wagner, on July 18, 1863, during which Colonel Shaw was killed. Sergeant William H. Carney's valiant exploits during this battle later earned him the Congressional Medal of Honor; Carney was the first African American to receive this award.

CAMBRIDGE

Maria Baldwin House

196 Prospect St.

This house was the permanent address of Maria Baldwin from 1892 until her death in 1922. Baldwin was the principal and later "master" of the Agassiz Grammar School in Cambridge, as well as a leader in such organizations as the League for Community Service, a gifted and popular speaker on the lecture circuit, and as a sponsor of charitable activities, such as establishing the first kindergarten in Atlanta, Georgia. Baldwin exemplified the achievements that were attainable by an African American in a predominantly white society. The house was designated a national historic landmark on May 11, 1976. It is a private residence.

Phillis Wheatley Folio

Harvard University

During her celebrated trip to England in 1773, Phillis Wheatley was presented with a folio edition of John Milton's *Paradise Lost*, which is now housed in the library of Harvard University in Cambridge.

Wheatley, who came to America in 1761 at the age of seven or eight, made rapid strides in mastering the English language and, by the time she was fourteen, had already completed her first poem. Always in delicate health, she died in Boston on December 5, 1784.

CENTRAL VILLAGE

Paul Cuffe Memorial

Paul Cuffe, son of a freedman, was born in 1759 and became a prosperous merchant seaman. Cuffe resolved to use his wealth and position to campaign for the extension of civil rights to African Americans. On one occasion, he refused to pay his personal property tax on the grounds that he was being denied full citizenship rights. A court of law eventually upheld his action, and he was granted the same privileges and immunities enjoyed by white citizens of the state. In 1815, Cuffe transported thirty-eight African Americans to Sierra Leone in what was intended to launch a systematic attempt to repatriate the African American inhabitants of the United States. With the growth of abolitionist sentiment, however, the repatriation movement lost favor.

DORCHESTER

William Monroe Trotter House

97 Sawyer Ave.

Built in the late 1880s or 1890s, this balloon-frame rectangular-plan house was the primary home of William Monroe Trotter (1872–1934), journalist, civil rights activist, insurance agent, and mortgage broker. He was a bitter opponent of Booker T. Washington and had a confrontation with Washington in Boston on July 3, 1903, that came to be known as the "Boston riot." Trotter formed the Boston Suffrage League and, in 1901, cofounded and became editor and publisher of the crusading newspaper the *Guardian*. His home was designated a national historic landmark on May 11, 1976. It is a private residence.

GREAT BARRINGTON

W. E. B. Du Bois Boyhood Homesite

Rte. 23

This location served as the boyhood home of the prominent African American sociologist and writer William Edward Burghardt Du Bois from 1868 to 1873. Du Bois was a major figure in the civil rights movement during the first half of the twentieth century. He fought discrimination against African Americans through his writing, as a college professor, and as a lecturer. On May 11, 1976, the Du Bois homesite was designated a national historic landmark. The ruins of the original house are located 2 miles west of Great Barrington on the north side of Route 23.

LYNN

Jan Ernst Matzeliger Statue

Downtown Lynn

This statue is one of the few extant memorials to the African American inventor Jan Ernst Matzeliger, whose shoelace machine revolutionized the industry and made mass-produced shoes a reality in the United States. A native of Dutch Guiana, Matzeliger came to the United States in 1876, learned the cobbler's trade, and set out to design a machine that would simplify shoe manufacturing. Always sickly, he died in 1889 at an early age, unable to capitalize on his successful patent, which was purchased by the United Shoe Machinery Company of Boston. After his death, Matzeliger was awarded a gold medal at the 1901 Pan-American Exposition.

NANTUCKET

Florence Higginbotham House

27 York St.
Telephone: (617) 725-0022
Web site: http://www.afroammuseum.org/bhtn_site10.htm

This is an eighteenth-century house built by Seneca Boston, father of Absalom Boston, whaling captain, which does not reflect the traditional perception of pre-Revolutionary African Americans. It was owned by the family from 1774 to 1919 and purchased by Florence Higginbotham, an African American, in 1920. The house is now owned by the Boston-based Museum of African American History.

NEW BEDFORD

New Bedford Whaling Museum

18 Johnny Cake Hill
Telephone: (508) 997-0046
Web site: http://www.whalingmuseum.org

This museum maintains a treasury of whaling artifacts and information, including the names and histories of African Americans who participated in the whaling industry. The museum also houses versions of the toggle harpoon, an invention of the African American metalsmith Lewis Temple that revolutionized the whaling industry.

WESTPORT

Paul Cuffe Farm and Memorial

1504 Drift Rd.

Paul Cuffe was a self-educated African American who became a prosperous merchant. He was a pioneer in the struggle for minority rights in the eighteenth and early nineteenth centuries and was active in the movement for black resettlement in Africa. The Paul Cuffe Farm was designated a national historic landmark on May 30, 1974. It is a private residence.

MICHIGAN

BATTLE CREEK

Sojourner Truth Grave Site

Oak Hill Cemetery

This site in the Oak Hill Cemetery marks the resting place of one of the most powerful abolitionists and lecturers of the nineteenth century, Sojourner Truth, who settled in Battle Creek after the Civil War but continued to travel on lecture tours until a few years before her death on November 26, 1883.

Sojourner Truth Institute

165 N. Washington Ave.
Telephone: (269) 965-2613
Web site: http://www.sojournertruth.org

This institute was established in 1998 to expand historical and biographical knowledge of the life of Sojourner Truth and to perpetuate her mission by teaching, demonstrating, and promoting projects that reflect the ideals and principles for which she stood. The institute was initially an affiliate of the Battle Creek Community Foundation; it merged with the foundation in 1999. The foundation has an extensive archive of artifacts and records related to Truth.

Sojourner Truth Monument

The Sojourner Truth Monument, designed by Tina Allen and completed in 1999, is a 12-foot bronze statue of Truth enveloped by a curved stone waterfall and flanked by two bronze plaques with quotations from Truth. The monument is located near the Sojourner Truth Downtown Parkway in the north corner of Monument Park at the corner of Main Street and Division.

CASSOPOLIS

Underground Railroad Marker

Rte. M-60

This marks one of many rest stops used by slaves escaping from the South to Canada. The Michigan historical marker is located approximately 2 miles east of Cassopolis in Cass County. In 1838, the first African American church was established in Calvin Township. The Michigan Antislavery Baptist Association (later the Chain Lake Baptist Association) was formed in 1856. Land donated the same year is now part of the Chain Lake Baptist Church and cemetery. The marker was erected in 1992.

DETROIT

Charles H. Wright Museum of African American History

315 E. Warren Ave.
Telephone: (313) 494-5800
Web site: http://www.maah-detroit.org

This museum is one of the largest facilities in the world dedicated to African American history. It includes more than thirty thousand artifacts; special archival collections related to the Underground Railroad, Harriet Tubman, Detroit mayor Coleman Young, and the Detroit labor movement; and areas for performances, interactive exhibits, library research, visual arts, and African American memorabilia.

Charles H. Wright Museum of African American History, Detroit, MI. *On its opening in April 1997, this 120,000-square-foot museum became the largest African American historical museum in the world.* ANDRE JENNY/ALAMY

Douglass-Brown Marker
William Webb House
E. Congress St.

The Douglass-Brown Marker indicates the site of the William Webb House, where fellow abolitionists Frederick Douglass and John Brown met in March 1859 to map out the strategy for the raid on the federal armory at Harpers Ferry, Virginia (now in West Virginia). Douglass was strongly opposed to this course of action. Nevertheless, on October 16, 1859, Brown's forces seized the fort, only to be overtaken by federal troops two days later.

Ralph Bunche Birthplace
5668 Anthon St.

A plaque once marked the site of the birthplace of Ralph Bunche, who was born in 1904 and went on to become the undersecretary general of the United Nations and to receive the Nobel Peace Prize. Bunche, the first African American to receive this honor, was awarded the prize in 1950 for his work as a United Nations mediator following the Arab-Israeli war of 1948.

Dunbar Hospital
580 Frederick St.
Web site: http://www.cr.nps.gov/nr/travel/detroit/d28.htm

Dunbar Hospital is a landmark in the East Ferry Historic District. In 1917, this townhouse structure became the city's first nonprofit hospital for African Americans, who had inadequate access to mainstream hospitals in Detroit. African American physicians established the Allied Medical Society (later known as the Detroit Medical Society) and raised funds to establish a medical facility, Dunbar Hospital. In 1928, the hospital moved to Brush and Illinois streets and operated as Parkside Hospital until it was lost to urban renewal in 1960. Built in 1892 as a private residence, the old Dunbar building served as the home of Charles C. Diggs Sr. starting in 1928 and housed his undertaking business. Later his son, Charles Jr., made the home his residence. The building was listed on the National Register of Historic Places on June 19, 1979. The Detroit Medical Society purchased the building in the late 1970s and subsequently converted it into a combined headquarters and museum, which is open to the public.

Elmwood Cemetery
1200 Elmwood Ave.
Telephone: (313) 567-3453
Web site: http://www.elmwoodhistoriccemetery.org

Elmwood Cemetery contains the grave sites of eighteen members of the 102nd U.S. Colored Infantry regiment, part of the Union Army during the Civil War.

Elijah McCoy Home Site
5720 Lincoln Ave.

A plaque marks the site of one of Elijah McCoy's residences. McCoy, born in Ontario, Canada, settled in the Detroit area, opening a manufacturing company in 1870. McCoy is best known for his self-lubricating device for locomotives and engines.

Motown Historical Museum
2648 W. Grand Blvd.
Telephone: (313) 875-2264
Web site: http://www.motownmuseum.com

This location served as the early headquarters of Motown Records, founded in 1959 by the songwriter and independent record producer Berry Gordy Jr. Performers including the Four Tops, Marvin Gaye, the Jackson Five, Martha and the Vandellas, Smokey Robinson, the Supremes, the Temptations, Mary Wells, and Stevie Wonder all played an important part in the early success of Motown. In 1972, the company moved its headquarters from Detroit to Los Angeles, but a museum containing restored sound studios and mementos is maintained at this site.

National Museum of the Tuskegee Airmen
Historic Fort Wayne
6325 W. Jefferson Ave.
Telephone: (313) 843-8849

This museum houses memorabilia of the Tuskegee Airmen, an all–African American unit of fighter pilots active during World War II. The airmen, who were trained at Alabama's Tuskegee Institute (as it was known then), played an important role in the fight against racial discrimination in the armed forces.

Virgil H. Carr Cultural Arts Center
Harmonie Bldg.
311 E. Grand River Ave.
Telephone: (313) 965-8430
Web site: http://www.artsleague.com/carr_center.htm

After years of neglect and decay, the venerable Harmonie Building has been restored to new beauty and purpose as the Virgil H. Carr Cultural Arts Center. It is the new home of the Arts League of Michigan, a learning advocate that fosters African American artistic enterprise in all its forms.

Motown Historical Museum, Detroit, MI, 2009. *Founded by Berry Gordy Jr. in 1959, Motown Records was the prime force behind the creation of the so-called Motown Sound through such noteworthy artists as the Four Tops, Marvin Gaye, the Jackson Five, and Martha and the Vandellas. This location served as the record company's early headquarters.* JIM WATSON/AFP/GETTY IMAGES

Underground Railroad Marker/Second Baptist Church

441 Monroe St.
Telephone: (313) 961-0920
Web site: http://secondbaptistdetroit.org

One of many stops along the Underground Railroad, the basement of the Second Baptist Church was used to hide runaway slaves. The church, founded in 1836, is one of the oldest African American congregations in the Midwest and the oldest in Michigan. It was added to the National Register of Historic Places on March 19, 1975. In an adjacent building, the church operates the Underground Railroad Reading Station Bookstore, which carries historical books and video materials.

MARSHALL

Crosswhite Boulder

Michigan Ave. and Mansion St.

The Crosswhite Boulder marks the site of two confrontations that occurred in 1846 in defense of Adam Crosswhite (1799–1878), a fugitive slave who had fled from Kentucky. The Crosswhite case is said to have been instrumental in the enactment of the Fugitive Slave Law of 1850.

MINNESOTA

DULUTH

Clayton Jackson McGhie Memorial

1st St. and 2nd Ave. East
Web site: http://www.claytonjacksonmcghie.org

This monument is in memory and honor of Elias Clayton, Elmer Jackson, and Isaac McGhie, three African American circus workers who, in 1920, were wrongfully accused, dragged by a mob to this spot, and lynched.

MINNEAPOLIS–ST. PAUL

Fort Snelling State Park

1 Post Rd.
Telephone: (612) 725-2389

Fort Snelling was the outpost in the Wisconsin Territory to which the slave later to become known as Dred Scott was transported from Illinois in 1836. Scott met and married his wife, Harriet, at the fort and saw his first child born there. Later taken to Missouri by his master, he filed suit for his freedom in 1846 and became a national figure as his case was tried before numerous tribunals en route to the U.S. Supreme Court in 1857. Scott argued that he should be considered free by virtue of his having previously resided in Illinois and at Fort Snelling.

MISSISSIPPI

GLENDORA

Emmett Till Historic Intrepid Center

33 Thomas St.

This museum, housed in a converted cotton gin, was named in memory of Emmett Till, who on August 27, 1955, was accused of whistling at a white shopkeeper and was brutally murdered at the age of fourteen. The museum also provides space for Sonny Boy Williamson, a native of Glendora and a legendary blues harmonica player.

JACKSON

Farish Street Neighborhood Historic District

Approximate boundary Amite, Mill, Fortification, and Lamar Sts.

This district, comprising 695 buildings on 125 acres in downtown Jackson, is the state's largest African American community. A segregated area for African American residents in the 1890s, it soon became known for professionals of local or national prominence. The district gives excellent examples of the vernacular buildings of the period from 1860 through the 1940s, although most of the buildings were erected between 1890 and 1930. The district was listed on the National Register of Historic Places on March 13, 1980. After that, the boundary increased to include Amite, Lamar, Mill, and Fortification streets and embraced structures built by local African American contractors. The expanded site was listed on the national register on September 18, 1980.

LORMAN

Alcorn State University Historic District

Alcorn State University campus
Telephone: (601) 877-6100
Web site: http://www.alcorn.edu

Alcorn State University, founded in 1871, is the oldest African American land-grant college in the United States. Land-grant status was designated in 1878, and the legislature changed the college's name to Alcorn Agricultural and Mechanical College. The state selected for its first president Hiram R. Revels, a distinguished leader during Reconstruction and the first African American to serve in the U.S. Congress. Buildings in the historic district include Lanier Hall, the Administration Building, and Harmon Hall. The Alcorn district was added to the National Register of Historic Places on May 20, 1983.

Oakland Memorial Chapel on the Alcorn University campus was built in 1838 as one of the first buildings of Oakland College, a white institution. In 1871, the state purchased the school to educate African Americans. The chapel was designated a national historic landmark on May 11, 1976.

MOUND BAYOU

Isaiah Thornton Montgomery House

W. Main St.

This location served as the home of Isaiah Thornton Montgomery, who in 1887 founded Mound Bayou—a place where African Americans could obtain social, political, and economic rights in a white supremacist South. The house, a two-story red brick structure built in 1910, was declared a national historic landmark on May 11, 1976. It is a private residence.

NATCHEZ

Natchez National Cemetery

41 Cemetery Rd.
Telephone: (601) 445-4981

This cemetery, established in 1840, is the final resting place of many African American war dead, including landsman Wilson Brown, a Congressional Medal of Honor recipient during the Civil War. Brown and seaman John Lawson received their medals for courage in action while serving aboard the USS *Hartford* in the Battle of Mobile Bay on August 5, 1864. The cemetery was added to the National Register of Historic Places on November 22, 1999.

Natchez National Historical Park

William Johnson House
210 State St.
Telephone: (601) 445-5345
Web site: http://www.nps.gov/natc

The Natchez National Historic Park District includes the home of William Johnson. After being freed from slavery as a child, Johnson became a successful barber who also maintained a diary of city activities between 1835 and 1851. The house is open to the public for tours conducted by the National Park Service.

Statue of James Meredith, University of Mississippi, Oxford, 2008. *In September 1962 Meredith became the first African American to enroll at the University of Mississippi, an important event in the civil rights movement.* DAVE DARNELL/THE COMMERCIAL APPEAL/LANDOV

OXFORD

Statue of James Meredith

University of Mississippi

This life-sized statue honoring James Meredith, the first African American to enroll at the University of Mississippi, is part of a larger civil rights monument at the university.

PINEY WOODS

Piney Woods Country Life School

5096 Hwy. 49, 20 miles south of Jackson
Telephone: (601) 845-2214
Web site: http://www.pineywoods.org

Laurence Clifton Jones established this school in 1909 to provide education for African Americans in Mississippi's backwoods. The curriculum combined industrial education and academics. In the early 1920s, the junior college program prepared future teachers. Jones gained nationwide attention in the 1950s as the "Little Professor of Piney Woods," when he was featured on the television program *This Is Your Life*. Today, enrolled students originate from both Mississippi and distant states.

MISSOURI

DIAMOND

George Washington Carver Birthplace and National Monument

5646 Carver Rd.
Telephone: (417) 325-4151
Web site: http://www.nps.gov/gwca

Located in a park in Diamond, Missouri, this national monument commemorates the place where the great African American scientist George Washington Carver (c. 1864–1943) was born and spent his early childhood. The cabin of his birth no longer exists.

Kidnapped when he was just six weeks old, Carver was eventually ransomed for a horse valued at $300. Raised in Missouri by the family of Moses Carver, his owner, he made his way through Minnesota, Kansas, and Iowa before being "discovered" by Booker T. Washington in 1896. That same year, Carver joined the faculty of Tuskegee Institute, where he conducted most of the research for which he is now famous.

The monument, one of the first created in honor of an African American, consists of a statue of Carver as a boy and encloses several trails leading to places of which he was particularly fond. The park also houses a visitors center and a museum displaying many of his discoveries and personal belongings. The monument was added to the National Park System on October 15, 1966.

JEFFERSON CITY

Lincoln University

820 Chestnut St.
Telephone: (573) 681-5000
Web site: http://www.lincolnu.edu

The more than $6,000 raised by the Sixty-second and Sixty-fifth U.S. Colored infantries constituted the initial endowment for a 22-square-foot room in which classes were held in 1866 at what is now Lincoln University. Known then as the Lincoln Institute, the school began receiving state aid to expand its teacher training program in 1870. It added college-level courses to its curriculum in 1877 and became a state institution in 1879. It has been known as Lincoln University since 1921 and has offered graduate programs since 1940.

KANSAS CITY

American Jazz Museum

1616 E. 18th St.
Telephone: (816) 474-8463
Web site: http://www.americanjazzmuseum.com

The American Jazz Museum opened in September 1997 as a monument to the music of the city that flourished between the 1920s and 1940s, as well as to spur redevelopment of the neighborhood where it is located, the historic 18th and Vine jazz district. The museum presents the sights and sounds of jazz through interactive exhibits and films, the Changing Gallery, the Blue Room jazz club, and the Gem Theater, a performing arts center.

Mutual Musicians Association Building

1823 Highland Ave.
Telephone: (816) 471-5212
Web site: http://www.thefoundationjamson.org

This building served as the home of the American Federation of Musicians Local 627 from the 1920s to the 1940s. Its African American members created the Kansas City style of jazz and included such greats as Count Basie, Herschel Evans, Lester Young, and Charlie Parker. The building was designated a national historic landmark on December 21, 1981, and remains in active use as a performance venue and headquarters of the Mutual Musicians Foundation in support of jazz and African American musicians.

Negro Leagues Baseball Museum

1618 E. 18th St.
Telephone: (816) 221-1920
Web site: http://www.nlbm.com

The Negro Leagues Baseball Museum is laid out as a timeline of the Negro Leagues and U.S. history. The museum aims to create "the look, sounds and feel of the game's storied past."

ST. LOUIS

Scott Joplin House

2685A Delmar Blvd.
Telephone: (314) 340-5790
Web site: http://www.mostateparks.com/scottjoplin.htm

A composer known as the "King of Ragtime," Scott Joplin (1868–1917) was born in Texarkana, Arkansas, but he left home to earn a living when he was fourteen years old. In his music he combined Midwestern folk and African American traditions with Western and European forms and provided an important foundation for modern American music. Joplin played piano in the St. Louis and Sedalia, Missouri, area, and this house built in the 1890s is the last surviving residence of Joplin. The house, a two-story row house separated into flats, was declared a national historic landmark on December 8, 1976.

Old Courthouse

11 N. 4th St.
Telephone: (314) 655-1600
Web site: http://www.nps.gov/jeff/planyourvisit/och.htm

It was in the Old Courthouse in 1846 that Dred Scott first filed suit to gain his freedom; for the next decade, the Dred Scott case was a burning political and social issue throughout America. In 1857, the case reached the U.S. Supreme Court, where Chief Justice Roger Taney handed down the decision that slaves could not become free by escaping or by being taken into free territory, nor could they be considered American citizens. Ironically, a few weeks after the decision was rendered, Scott was set free by his new owner. He died a year later. The courthouse is now part of the Jefferson National Expansion Memorial, a National Park Service national memorial.

Homer G. Phillips Hospital

26101 Whittier St.

Built between 1932 and 1936, the Homer G. Phillips Hospital provided for the health care of local African Americans. It was also one of the few well-equipped facilities for African Americans from across the country where medical technicians, doctors, and nurses could be trained. The hospital was named for the attorney who was successful in the fight to establish the facility. Inadequate municipal support resulting in budgetary problems forced the hospital to close as an acute-care facility on August 17, 1979. The building was listed on the National Register of Historic Places on September 23, 1982. It is now home to a 220-unit seniors residence, the Homer G. Phillips Dignity House/Senior Living Community.

MONTANA

BIG HORN COUNTY

Fort Manuel Marker

Captain William Clark and his party, which included a slave named York, camped at this site on July 26, 1806, a year before Manuel Lisa established Montana's first trading post. This site also was chosen by Major Andrew Henry as the Rocky Mountain Fur Company's first trading post; the leader of that expedition was Edward Rose, another of the famed African American mountain men and explorers active in the territory.

NEBRASKA

NEBRASKA CITY

Mayhew Cabin and Historic Village

2012 4th Corso
Telephone: (402) 873-3115
Web site: http://www.mayhewcabin.org

Formerly John Brown's cave, this is the only National Park Service Underground Railroad Network to Freedom site in Nebraska. The 1850s cabin still stands and was restored in 2005 to the original condition.

NEVADA

RENO

Beckwourth Trail

Web site: http://www.beckwourth.org/Trail

In the early days of pioneer settlement, the barren stretch of trail between Reno and the California line was the last obstacle before passing through to the West Coast. The original trail was laid out by an African American explorer, Jim Beckwourth (1798–1866), one of the legendary mountain men.

NEW HAMPSHIRE

JAFFREY

Amos Fortune Grave Site

This grave site marks the resting place of the eighteenth-century African slave Amos Fortune (c. 1710–1801), who purchased his freedom in 1770 when he was sixty years old. He became one of the leading citizens of Jaffrey, his adopted hometown. Nine years after purchasing his freedom, Fortune was able to buy freedom for his wife, Violet Baldwin, and his adopted daughter, Celyndia. In 1781, he moved to Jaffrey and worked as a tanner, employing both black and white apprentices. In 1795, six years before his death, Fortune founded the Jaffrey Social Library and, in his will, directed that money be left to the church and to the local school district. (The school fund begun by Fortune is still in existence.)

The Fortune house and barn still stand intact, and both Fortune and his wife lie in the meetinghouse burial ground. Fortune's freedom papers and several receipt slips for the sale of his leather are on file at the Jaffrey Public Library.

NEW JERSEY

BORDENTOWN

New Jersey Manual Training and Industrial School for Colored Youth

This state-supported boarding school for African Americans was called "Old Ironsides" and the "Tuskegee of the North." It was founded in 1886.

BURLINGTON

Bethlehem African Methodist Episcopal Church

213 E. Pearl St.
Telephone: (609) 386-6664

This is one of the oldest churches in New Jersey. In the cemetery beside it are a few of the graves of the state's soldiers who fought in the Civil War in the African American Union Army and Navy. In 1833, the Reverend Jeremiah H. Pierce legally challenged forced segregation of his four children into Burlington's all-black elementary schools and won.

Oliver Cromwell House
114 E. Union St.

The last home of Oliver Cromwell, an African American soldier in the Revolutionary War who crossed the Delaware and fought with George Washington. Washington personally signed his discharge papers and decorated him for his service.

LAWNSIDE

Site of Free Haven

Located just east of the city of Camden, New Jersey, is the town of Lawnside, originally known as Free Haven. The town served as a major stop on the Underground Railroad, and following the Civil War it attracted a large population of freed slaves from the South.

MEDFORD

Office of Dr. James Still
209 Church Rd.

This one-story frame building was once the office of Dr. James Still (1812–1882), one of the earliest medical doctors in New Jersey, and one who had a large biracial practice. Dr. Still consulted with Native Americans regarding medicinal plants and herbs, developed his own remedies and treatments, and included them in his autobiography, which became an early classic in African American nonfiction. The building, now a private residence, was added to the National Register of Historic Places on November 3, 1995.

RED BANK

T. Thomas Fortune House
94 W. Bergen Pl.

From 1901 to 1915, this location was the home of the African American journalist T. Thomas Fortune. Born a slave in Marianna, Florida, Fortune was freed by the Emancipation Proclamation in 1863. He received training as a printer and founded the *New York Age* newspaper. The Fortune House, built between 1860 and 1885, was designated a national historic landmark on December 8, 1976. It is a private residence.

WESTAMPTON TOWNSHIP

Timbuctoo
Church St., Blue Jay Hill Rd., and vicinity

Founded around 1820 and located between the townships of Willingboro and Mount Holly, Timbuctoo was a community of freed slaves and a safe place for fugitive slaves. It was named for the West African city of Timbuktu (or Tombouctou), famed as a commercial and intellectual center during the fourteenth to sixteenth centuries, when it was home to Sankore University (also known as the University of Timbuktu).

NEW MEXICO

LINCOLN

Old Court House
Lincoln State Monument
Telephone: (575) 653-4372

During the Lincoln County Cattle War of 1877 to 1881, Billy the Kid, the notorious outlaw, was held in custody at the Old Court House in Lincoln, New Mexico, now a frontier museum and part of Lincoln State Monument. African American cowhands were involved on both sides of this struggle, and, on one occasion, a group of African American cavalry men is said to have surrounded Billy the Kid during a particularly bloody battle.

PORTALES

Buffalo Soldier Hill
State Hwy. 114

In 1877, African American "buffalo soldiers" of the Tenth U.S. Cavalry pursued a band of Comanche warriors into this area. Lack of water and supplies resulted in the deaths of four soldiers during the unsuccessful mission.

RADIUM SPRINGS

Fort Selden State Monument
1280 Fort Selden Rd.
Telephone: (505) 526-8911
Web site: http://www.nmmonuments.org/inst.php?inst=10

Fort Selden was established in 1865. Buffalo soldiers were stationed here, and a young Douglas MacArthur lived here from 1884 to 1886.

ZUNI

Zuni Pueblo
Telephone: (505) 782-7000
Web site: http://www.ashiwi.org

In 1539, Estevanico, a Moorish slave, became the first European to encounter Zuni Pueblo. Estevanico had been one of the original party of Spanish explorers who landed in Tampa Bay in 1528.

Having heard of the legend of the Seven Cities of Gold, reputed to be located in the Southwest, Estevanico signed on as an advance scout for an expedition led by Friar Marcos de Niza. Often traveling ahead of the main party, Estevanico sent most of his messages back via friendly Indians. His last message—a giant cross emblematic of a major discovery—led the expedition to the Zuni Pueblo, which Estevanico apparently thought formed part of the legendary Seven Cities. By the time the expedition arrived, however, the suspicious Zuni had already put Estevanico to death. Today, Estevanico is credited with the European discovery of the territory comprising the states of Arizona and New Mexico.

NEW YORK

ALBANY

Preliminary Emancipation Proclamation

New York State Library
310 Madison Ave.
Telephone: (518) 474-5355
Web site: http://www.nysl.nysed.gov/library/features/ep

The New York State Library houses President Abraham Lincoln's preliminary draft of the Emancipation Proclamation, which was issued in September 1862. The draft was purchased by Gerrit Smith, a wealthy abolitionist and patron of the famed revolutionary John Brown. The January 1, 1863, version of the proclamation resides in the National Archives in Washington, D.C.

AUBURN

Harriet Tubman House

180–182 South St.
Telephone: (315) 252-2081
Web site: http://www.nyhistory.com/harriettubman

***Exterior View, Abyssinian Baptist Church, New York City.** The church building was completed in 1923, under the leadership of the Reverend Adam Clayton Powell Sr. Abyssinian is one of the oldest and largest African American Baptist congregations in the United States.* CORBIS.

Interior View, Abyssinian Baptist Church, New York City, 1949. *Abyssinian was the site of the funeral for the entertainer Bill "Bojangles" Robinson.* NATIONAL ARCHIVES

Born a slave in Maryland, Harriet Tubman (c. 1820–1913) escaped from enslavement when she was twenty-five, and she returned to the South at least nineteen times to lead others to freedom. Rewards of up to $40,000 were offered for her capture, but she was never arrested nor did she ever lose one of her "passengers" in transit.

During the Civil War, she served as a spy for Union forces. At the close of the war, Tubman settled in this house in Auburn, New York, years after it had outlived its original function as a major way station on the northbound freedom route of fugitive Africans. In 1953, the house was restored at a cost of $21,000. The house now stands as a monument to the woman believed to have led some three hundred slaves to freedom via the Underground Railroad. The house was designated a national historic landmark on May 30, 1974.

BUFFALO

The Reverend J. Edward Nash Sr. House

36 Nash St.
Telephone: (716) 856-4490
Web site: http://www.nashhousemuseum.org

GREATER NEW YORK CITY

Abyssinian Baptist Church

132 Odell Clark Pl.
Telephone: (212) 862-7474
Web site: http://www.abyssinian.org

The Abyssinian Baptist Church is one of the oldest and largest African American Baptist congregations in the United States. The church building was completed in 1923, under the leadership of the Reverend Adam Clayton Powell Sr. In 1937, Powell retired and was succeeded by his son Adam Clayton Powell Jr., who was elected to the U.S. Congress in 1944.

African Burial Ground National Monument

Corner of Duane St. and African Burial Ground Way (Elk St.)

Lower Manhattan
Telephone: (212) 637-2019
Web site: http://www.nps.gov/afbg

This property in Lower Manhattan had been lost to history until 1991, when it was rediscovered. The memorial honors the estimated fifteen thousand free and enslaved Africans who were interred in this location during the late 1600s and 1700s.

Amsterdam News Building

2293 7th Ave.

The *Amsterdam News* was founded on December 4, 1909, in the home of James H. Anderson on 132 West 65th Street in New York City. At that time one of only fifty African American "news sheets" in the country, the *Amsterdam News* had a staff of ten, consisted of six printed pages, and sold for two cents a copy. Since then, the paper has been printed at several Harlem addresses. This building, home of the paper from 1916 to 1938, was designated a national historic landmark on May 11, 1976.

Apollo Theater

253 W. 125th St.
Telephone: (212) 531-5300
Web site: http://www.apollotheater.org

The Apollo Theater in Harlem, once an entertainment mecca for all races, is one of the last great vaudeville houses in the United States. Erected in 1914, the building was listed on the National Register of Historic Places on November 17, 1983.

Fans of the Late Michael Jackson Gather outside the Apollo Theater, New York City, June 2009. *The Apollo, built in Harlem in 1914, was one of the most famous clubs to be associated almost exclusively with African American performers during the period of the Harlem Renaissance.* RICHARD H. COHEN/CORBIS

Louis Armstrong House

34-56 107th St.
Corona, Queens
Telephone: (718) 478-8274
Web site: http://www.louisarmstronghouse.org

For years this was the home of Louis Armstrong, the famous jazz musician whose talents entertained millions throughout the world. Whenever Armstrong was at his Corona home in Queens, New York, on a break from his concert dates, he was a favorite with neighborhood youngsters, often entertaining them in his home and on the street. The house, now the Louis Armstrong House Museum, was designated a national historic landmark on May 11, 1976.

Ralph Bunche House

115-125 Grosvenor Rd.
Kew Gardens, Queens

The house served as the home of Ralph Bunche, the distinguished African American diplomat and undersecretary general to the United Nations. In 1950, Bunche was awarded the Nobel Peace Prize for his contribution to peace in the Middle East. The house was designated a national historic landmark on May 11, 1976. It is a private residence.

Will Marion Cook Residence

221 W. 138th St.

This residence in New York City served as the home of the African American composer Will Marion Cook (1869–1944), whom Duke Ellington called "the master of all masters of our people." Cook was born in Washington, D.C. He began studying violin when he was thirteen years old, and, at fifteen, he won a scholarship to study with Joseph Joachim at the Berlin Conservatory. Syncopated ragtime music was introduced to theatergoers in New York City for the first time with

Cook's operetta *Clorindy*. The residence was designated a national historic landmark on May 11, 1976. It is a private residence.

Duke Ellington Statue

5th Ave. and 110th St.

A 25-foot-high cast-bronze monument featuring an 8-foot-high statue of Duke Ellington was unveiled on July 1, 1997, on the northeast corner of Central Park. Designed by the sculptor Robert Graham, it is the first public monument in the country honoring the jazz legend and composer. Bobby Short, a cabaret performer who led the drive to erect the memorial, said that the location is "a bridge between Duke Ellington's two worlds: The sophisticated world of the Upper East Side and the street world of Harlem."

Edward Kennedy "Duke" Ellington Residence

935 St. Nicholas Ave., Apt. 4A

When Duke Ellington recorded "Take the A Train" to Harlem, he meant just that, because the A train express stops on St. Nicholas Avenue and was the quickest way for Ellington to get home. This St. Nicholas Avenue address was the long-term residence of Ellington, who has been regarded by critics as the most creative African American composer of the twentieth century. The residence was designated a national historic landmark on May 11, 1976. It is a private residence.

Fraunces Tavern

Broad and Pearl Sts.
Telephone: (212) 425-1778
Web site: http://www.frauncestavernmuseum.org

One of the most famous landmarks in New York City, Fraunces Tavern was bought in 1762 from a wealthy Huguenot by Samuel Fraunces, a West Indian of black and French extraction. Known as the Queen's Head Tavern, it served as a meeting place for numerous patriots.

On April 22, 1774, the Sons of Liberty and the Vigilance Committee met at the tavern to map out much of the strategy later used during the war. George Washington himself was a frequenter of the tavern, as were many of his senior officers. Washington's association with Fraunces continued for a number of years, with Fraunces eventually coming to be known as Washington's "Steward of the Household" in New York City. It was at Fraunces Tavern, in fact, that Washington took leave of his trusted officers in 1783 before retiring to Mount Vernon.

Much of the tavern's original furnishings and decor are still intact. The third floor, now a museum, contains several Revolutionary War artifacts, while the fourth floor holds a historical library featuring paintings by John Ward Dunsmore. A restaurant is maintained on the ground floor.

Freedom National Bank

275 W. 125th St.

Freedom National Bank, Harlem's first African American–chartered and African American–run commercial bank, was founded in 1965. The bank is no longer in business, having closed in 1990.

Harlem Historic District

Approximating the northern tip of Manhattan

Once the political and cultural hub of black America in the twentieth century, Harlem is primarily known as the major site of the literary and artistic "renaissance" of the 1920s and 1930s. Following the migration of blacks from the South and Caribbean to Harlem in the initial decade of the twentieth century, the city became a nurturing ground for pioneering black intellectual (i.e., literature, art, and black nationalism) and popular (i.e., dance and jazz) movements, as well as a vibrant nightlife centered around such nightclubs as the Cotton Club, Small's Paradise, and the Savoy Ballroom.

Matthew Henson Residence

Dunbar Apartments
246 W. 150th St., Apt. 3F

This residence served as the home of Matthew Henson, the African American explorer who was an assistant to Robert E. Peary. Henson's best-known achievement came in 1909, when he became the first man to reach the North Pole. The residence was designated a national historic landmark on May 15, 1975. It is a private residence.

Hotel Theresa

2090 7th Ave. at 125th St.

Built in 1913, the Hotel Theresa was once a luxury hotel serving white clientele from lower Manhattan and accommodating "white only" dinner patrons in its luxurious Skyline Room. In 1936, Seidenberg Estates, a corporation headed by Love B. Woods, tried to take over the hotel and transform it into an African American business establishment. This move failed when the Seidenberg family, the owners of the property, set a price beyond the reach of the group. Woods, however, was eventually able to purchase the hotel, which now serves as an office building.

James Weldon Johnson Residence

187 W. 135th St.

From 1925 until his death in 1938, this was the New York City residence of James Weldon Johnson, the versatile African American composer of popular songs, as well as a poet, writer, and civil rights activist who served as general secretary of the NAACP. Johnson is best known for composing the song "Lift Every Voice and Sing," which has been called the "black national anthem." Johnson was born in Jacksonville, Florida, and studied at Columbia University. The residence was named a national historic landmark on May 11, 1976. It is a private residence.

Maiden Lane Slave Revolt

In 1712, on Maiden Lane and William Street, the first organized insurrection in New York City occurred. Approximately thirty enslaved Africans joined and attempted to fight their way to freedom. Many people were injured in the melee that ensued as the black captives escaped to the woods with the militia close behind. Surrounded in the woods, several of the escapees committed suicide. The rest were captured and subsequently executed.

Malcolm X Residence

23-11 97th St.
East Elmhurst, Queens

African American Muslim leader Malcolm X resided at this location with his family from 1954 until his death in 1965. The house, which was owned by the Nation of Islam while he and his family lived there, was the scene of a firebombing on February 13, 1965. Malcolm X and his family escaped without injury.

Claude McKay Residence

180 W. 135th St.
Telephone: (212) 912-2100

From 1941 to 1946, this residence in New York City was the home of the African American poet and writer Claude McKay, who has often been called the father of the Harlem Renaissance. McKay was born in Jamaica, British West Indies, and was in Kingston's constabulary prior to coming to the United States. His residence was named a national historic landmark on December 8, 1976. The building currently houses the Harlem YMCA.

Ronald McNair Monument

Ronald McNair Park
Brooklyn

A 9-foot granite monument of Ronald McNair, the African American astronaut who lost his life in the space shuttle *Challenger* accident in 1986, was unveiled in a dedication ceremony in Ronald McNair Park in 1994. Created by the Brooklyn artist Ogundipe Fayomi, the monument consists of three bronze plaques showing images from McNair's life and achievements. A quote from McNair is engraved on one side: "My wish is that we would allow this planet to be the beautiful oasis that she is, and allow ourselves to live more in the peace she generates."

Florence Mills Residence

220 W. 135th St.

This residence was the purported home of the popular African American singer Florence Mills, who in the 1920s achieved stardom both on Broadway and in Europe. The residence was designated a national historic landmark on December 8, 1976, though this designation was withdrawn in 2009 because of renovations at the property. It is a private residence.

Paul Robeson Residence

555 Edgecomb Ave.

This residence in New York City was the home of the famous African American actor and singer Paul Robeson. In the 1940s and the 1950s, Robeson suffered public condemnation for his socialist political sympathies, even while he was widely acclaimed for his artistic talents. The residence was named a national historic landmark on December 8, 1976. It is a private residence.

John Roosevelt "Jackie" Robinson House

5224 Tilden Ave.
Brooklyn

This house served as the home of Jackie Robinson, the baseball player who in 1947 became the first African American to play in the major leagues in the twentieth century. His baseball contract broke down the color barrier to African American participation in professional sports. While a Brooklyn Dodger, Robinson lived for many years in the same borough of New York City where he played baseball. The residence was designated a national historic landmark on May 11, 1976. It is a private residence.

St. George's Episcopal Church

3rd Ave. and E. 16th St.

Located in New York City, this was the church home of Harry Thacker Burleigh (1866–1949), the African American composer, arranger, and singer who helped establish the black spiritual as an integral part of

American culture. The church was designated a national historical landmark on December 8, 1976.

Schomburg Center for Research in Black Culture

515 Malcolm X Blvd.
Telephone: (212) 491-2200
Web site: http://www.nypl.org/locations/schomburg

Part of the New York Public Library System, the Schomburg Center for Research in Black Culture is devoted to documenting the black experience around the world. The collection is built around the private library of Arthur A. Schomburg, a Puerto Rican of African descent. It contains books, pamphlets, manuscripts, photographs, art objects, and recordings that cover virtually every aspect of black life—from ancient Africa to the present-day United States. The building was listed on the National Register of Historic Places on September 21, 1978.

Sugar Hill, Harlem

Sugar Hill is a handsome residential section in uptown Harlem. It is bordered on the west by Amsterdam Avenue, on the north by 160th Street, on the east by Colonial Park, and on the south by 145th Street. An area of tall apartment buildings and private homes, it is peopled largely by middle-class African Americans, sometimes referred to as the "black bourgeoisie." Its only counterparts in the area of central Harlem are Riverton and Lenox Terrace.

Hall of Fame for Great Americans

Bronx Community College
2183 University Ave.
Telephone: (718) 289-5161
Web site: http://www.bcc.cuny.edu/halloffame

Two African Americans are featured in this hall of fame: the educator Booker T. Washington, who founded Tuskegee Institute, and the botanist George Washington Carver, who served as Tuskegee's director of agricultural research.

Historic Weeksville

1698–1708 Bergen St.
Brooklyn
Telephone: (718) 756-5250
Web site: http://www.weeksvillesociety.org

Weeksville was once a thriving African American community in Brooklyn. On December 5, 1972, the four remaining buildings were added to the National Register of Historic Places. This site contains the four restored buildings and the Weeksville African American Museum.

Roy Wilkins House

147-15 Village Rd.
Jamaica, Queens

This location served as the home of the civil rights leader Roy Wilkins from 1952 until his death in 1981. Wilkins served as executive secretary of the NAACP for twenty-two years before retiring in 1977. The house is a private residence.

IRVINGTON

Villa Lewaro

N. Broadway

Designed by the noted African American architect Vertner Woodson Tandy for Madame C. J. Walker, the successful cosmetics manufacturer, Villa Lewaro illustrates the achievements of African Americans in both architecture and business. Built in 1918, Villa Lewaro was declared a national historic landmark on May 11, 1976. The building was sold in 1998 and will be used as a tourist attraction.

LAKE PLACID

John Brown Farm and Grave Site

115 John Brown Rd.
Telephone: (518) 523-3900
Web site: http://nysparks.state.ny.us/historic-sites/29/details.aspx

Just 6 miles south of Lake Placid on Route 86A is the farm John Brown purchased after he had left Ohio, now the location of his grave. The farm was part of 100,000 acres set aside by Gerrit Smith, a wealthy abolitionist, for both freedmen and those who had once been enslaved. Smith hoped to build an independent community that would serve those who had been formerly enslaved. He had envisioned that they would learn farming and other trades. Brown joined Smith in the venture, but the idea failed to take hold and was eventually abandoned. Brown lived there until he joined the free-soil fight in Kansas.

ROCHESTER

Frederick Douglass Monument

Central Ave. and St. Paul St.

New York governor Theodore Roosevelt dedicated the Frederick Douglass Monument in 1899, four years after Douglass's death. Douglass edited his newspaper, the *North Star*, in Rochester. He was buried in Mount Hope Cemetery, not far from the original location of the monument. In 1941, the statue of Douglass was moved to Highland Park in downtown Rochester.

SOUTH GRANVILLE

Lemuel Haynes House

Parker Hill Rd., off Rte. 149

Tragic Prelude ***(John Steuart Curry, c. 1940).*** *Curry's mural in the Kansas Statehouse in Topeka depicts the artist's interpretation of the abolitionist John Brown and the antislavery movement in Kansas. Brown engaged in abolitionist activities during his brief sojourn in Kansas.* PHOTOGRAPH FROM THE NATIONAL ARCHIVES. REPRODUCED BY PERMISSION.

This house, located in South Granville, Washington County, New York, was built in 1793. From 1822 to 1833, it served as the home of Lemuel Haynes, the first African American ordained minister in the United States. Haynes was also the first African American to minister to a white congregation. The South Granville home site was declared a national historic landmark on May 15, 1975.

NORTH CAROLINA

CHAPEL HILL

George Moses Horton Residence Hall

University of North Carolina

George Moses Horton (c. 1798–c. 1883), the first African American southern slave to publish a collection of poetry and the first African American professional poet, is remembered with a dormitory, three plaques summarizing his biography, and two of his poems in the lobby.

CHARLOTTE

Harvey B. Gantt Center for African-American Arts and Culture

551 S. Tryon St.
Telephone: (704) 547-3700
Web site: http://www.ganttcenter.org

Named for Charlotte's first black mayor, the Harvey B. Gantt Center for African-American Arts and Culture reopened in a new building in October 2009. Founded in 1974 by Mary Turner Harper and Bertha Maxwell Roddey, the center was originally known as the Afro-American Cultural Center and was first located in the former premises of the Little Rock A.M.E. Zion Church. The center continues to promote the contributions of Africans and African Americans to American culture.

DURHAM

North Carolina Mutual Life Insurance Company Building

114–116 W. Parish St.

This Parish Street address is the home office of North Carolina Mutual Life Insurance Company, an African

American–managed enterprise that was founded in 1898 and achieved financial success in an age of Jim Crow. The business was first located in the Mechanics and Farmers Bank, a six-story structure that symbolized the city's affluent African Americans. Among the outstanding leaders associated with the firm were John Merrick, Charles Clinton Spaulding, and Asa T. Spaulding. The site was declared a national historic landmark on May 15, 1975.

GREENSBORO

F. W. Woolworth Building

132 S. Elm St.
Web site: http://www.cr.nps.gov/nr/travel/civilrights/nc1.htm

A historical marker outside the building marks the sit-ins begun by four North Carolina A&T students (Ezell Blair Jr., Franklin McCain, Joseph McNeil, and David Richmond) at the Woolworth lunch counter in 1960. A section of the lunch counter is preserved at the Smithsonian Institution in Washington, D.C.

February One Monument

North Carolina A&T State University

This monument, located in front of the Dudley Building, is a bronze statue of the four A&T freshmen who carried out the lunch counter sit-ins in downtown Greensboro beginning on February 1, 1960.

International Civil Rights Center and Museum

132 S. Elm St.
Telephone: (336) 274-9199
Web site: http://www.sitinmovement.org

The International Civil Rights Center and Museum opened in 2010 in the former F. W. Woolworth building, the site of the 1960 Greensboro sit-ins. The museum commemorates the four North Carolina A&T students who led a nonviolent protest that was a key event of the civil rights movement.

MILTON

Yellow Tavern

Main St., bet. Lee St. and Farmer's Alley

For more than thirty years, the Yellow Tavern (also known as Union Tavern and the Thomas Day House) was the workshop of Thomas Day, one of the great African American artisans and furniture makers of the Deep South prior to the Civil War. Day began making hand-wrought mahogany furniture in 1818 and, within five years, accumulated enough money to convert the old Yellow Tavern into a miniature factory. Both white apprentices and black slaves were taught this skilled trade under his tutelage. Day's artistry was so revered by the citizens of Milton that they went to great pains to secure a special dispensation from a North Carolina law that made it illegal for any free black or mulatto to migrate into the state. The Yellow Tavern, built around 1910, was designated a national historic landmark on May 15, 1975. Examples of Day's furniture can be seen in the North Carolina Museum of History and at North Carolina A&T University in Greensboro.

RALEIGH

African American Cultural Complex

119 Sunnybrook Rd.
Telephone: (919) 250-9336
Web site: http://www.aaccmuseum.org

The African American Cultural Complex contains artifacts, documents, and exhibitions chronicling contributions made by African Americans to North Carolina and to the Americas. The collection is housed in several buildings located along a trail.

Chavis Community Center and Park

505 Martin Luther King Jr. Blvd.
Telephone: (919) 831-6989

This community center and park is named after John Chavis, an African American educator and preacher who founded an interracial school in Raleigh, which later numbered among its graduates several important public figures, including senators, congressmen, and governors. As a result of the abortive Nat Turner slave rebellion in 1831, however, African Americans were barred from preaching in North Carolina, obliging Chavis to retire from the pulpit. He died in 1838.

Dr. M. T. Pope House

511 S. Wilmington St.

This house was the home of surgeon and entrepreneur Manassa T. Pope, his wife, and his two daughters. Built in 1901 and representative of black middle-class living during segregation, the house was listed on the National Register of Historic Places on November 22, 1999.

SEDALIA

Palmer Memorial Institute Historic District

6136 Burlington Rd.
Telephone: (336) 449-4846
Web site: http://www.nchistoricsites.org/chb

Charlotte Hawkins Brown, a North Carolina native, founded the Palmer Memorial Institute at this site on October 10, 1902, naming it for her friend and benefactor, Alice Freeman Palmer. The school stressed academics and industrial and vocational education. The school was incorporated on November 23, 1907. By 1916, the school had four buildings and had begun to make its presence felt nationwide. By 1922, it was one of the nation's leading preparatory schools for African American students. The school changed its focus in the 1930s, after the public school system for African Americans improved and Palmer closed its elementary department, and functioned largely as a finishing and college-preparatory school. The school closed in 1971. In 1987, the state purchased the site and eventually developed it into the Charlotte Hawkins Brown Museum, which both memorializes the school and its founder and serves as a center for commemorating the educational and cultural history of African Americans in North Carolina. The site was added to the National Register of Historic Places on October 24, 1988, and includes several campus buildings, the Canary Cottage residence of Dr. Brown, and her grave site.

WINSTON-SALEM

George Black House and Brickyard

111 Dellabrook Rd.

George H. Black, son of a former slave, was a well-known African American bricklayer, sometimes called the "last bricklayer in America." He lived and worked in Winston-Salem from 1934 until his death in 1980 at age 101. He established his own business, built a brickyard near his home, and earned both national and international recognition for both the quality and durability of his work. When he was in his nineties, he was asked to go to Africa and share his knowledge. This property was listed on the National Register of Historic Places on January 28, 2000.

OHIO

AKRON

John Brown Monument

The John Brown Monument was built in honor of the abolitionist whose ill-fated Harpers Ferry revolt led to his conviction for treason and execution by hanging in 1859. The monument is located on property that is now part of the Akron Zoo.

BATAVIA

Clermont County Underground Railroad Freedom Trail

Web site: http://www.visitclermontohio.com/ugrrmain.htm

The trail contains thirty-three sites that are outlined in a brochure and Web site.

CINCINNATI

National Underground Railroad Freedom Center

50 E. Freedom Way
Telephone: (513) 333-7500
Web site: http://www.freedomcenter.org

This center commemorates the courage, cooperation, and perseverance of African Americans' flight and struggle for freedom. It also offers lessons and a shed that had served as a slave "pen" in Mason County, Kentucky.

Harriet Beecher Stowe House

2950 Gilbert Ave.
Telephone: (513) 751-0651
Web site: http://www.harrietbeecherstowehouse.org

The Harriet Beecher Stowe House has been preserved as a memorial to the internationally known author of *Uncle Tom's Cabin*. The house, which served as the Beecher family residence from 1832 to 1836, was added to the National Register of Historic Places on November 10, 1970.

CLEVELAND

African American Museum

1765 Crawford Rd.

This museum is housed in the original Hough branch of the Cleveland Public Library, built with support from Andrew Carnegie in 1907. The building remained in use from 1984 to 2006, when the museum was closed for renovations. As of 2010, the museum had not reopened.

DAYTON

Paul Laurence Dunbar House

219 N. Paul Laurence Dunbar St.
Telephone: (937) 313-2010
Web site: http://ohsweb.ohiohistory.org/places/sw03

Paul Laurence Dunbar (1872–1906), the first African American poet after Phillis Wheatley to gain anything approaching a national reputation in the United States, was also the first to concentrate on dialect poetry and exclusively African American themes. His first collection of poetry, *Oak and Ivy*, was published before he was twenty years old. By 1896, his book *Majors and Minors* had won critical favor in a *Harper's Weekly* review. The Dunbar House was built around 1890, but Dunbar bought it for his mother in 1903 and lived in it with her for the last three years of his life. Dunbar contracted tuberculosis in 1899, and his health continued to fail until his death on February 9, 1906. The house was designated a national historic landmark on December 29, 1962. It later became part

Slave "Pen," National Underground Railroad Freedom Center, Cincinnati, OH, 2004. A slave trader in Mason County, Kentucky, used this shed, which had been built in the early 1800s, as a holding "pen" to temporarily keep enslaved people before they were moved farther south for sale. MIKE SIMONS/GETTY IMAGES

of the Dayton Aviation Heritage National Historical Park, though it remained owned by the Ohio Historical Society.

MOUNT PLEASANT

Benjamin Lundy House

Union and 3rd Sts.

This residence was the home of the African American editor and abolitionist beginning in 1820, and the site where he published the antislavery newspaper, *Genius of Universal Emancipation.* The structure was in extreme disrepair by 2003, when the property was sold to an absentee landlord living in Hawaii. Local preservation societies have continued efforts to save the home.

OBERLIN

John Mercer Langston House

Wilder Hall, Rm. 402

Elected township clerk in 1855, John Mercer Langston is believed to have been the first African American to be elected to public office. Langston later served for the Freedmen's Bureau, became the first dean of the Howard University Law School, and served as a U.S. minister resident to Haiti. The Langston House, which served as his home from 1856 to 1871, was designated a national historic landmark on May 15, 1975.

Monument to the Followers of John Brown

Martin Luther King Park
E. Vine St.

Originally erected in Westwood Cemetery in 1805, this monument honors John Anthony Copeland Jr., Shields Green, and Lewis Sheridan Leary, antislavery activists and "colored citizens of Oberlin" who joined John Brown during the 1859 raid on the federal arsenal at Harpers Ferry, Virginia. Leary died at the scene, while

Copeland and Green were captured and executed on December 11, 1859. In 1999, the monument was moved to its present location.

Oberlin College

Telephone: (440) 775-8121
Web site: http://new.oberlin.edu

Before the Civil War, Oberlin was one of the centers of underground abolitionist planning. The college was one of the first institutions to graduate African Americans and women. Three of John Brown's raiding party at Harpers Ferry were identified as African Americans from Oberlin.

After the war, Oberlin was able to devote more time to its stated mission: providing quality education to all regardless of race. Among the distinguished alumni of Oberlin was Blanche K. Bruce, who was the first African American to be elected to and serve a full term in the U.S. Senate (1875–1881).

RIPLEY

John Rankin House and Museum

6152 Rankin Rd.
Telephone: (937) 392-1627
Web site: http://www.ripleyohio.net/htm/rankin.htm

An Underground Railroad station prior to the Civil War, the John Rankin House in Ripley, Ohio, is believed to have been the haven of the fugitive slave on whose story the novelist Harriet Beecher Stowe based the flight incident in *Uncle Tom's Cabin*. The house, which was built in 1828 and is now a museum, was designated a national historic landmark on February 18, 1997.

WILBERFORCE

Colonel Charles Young House

Rte. 42 bet. Clifton and Stevenson Rds.

This address was the residence of the highest-ranking African American officer in World War I and the first African American military attaché. Colonel Charles Young (1864–1922) was the son of former slaves and was born in Mays Lick, Kentucky. The army had declared Young unfit physically because of high blood pressure; to prove that he was physically fit, he rode horseback 500 miles from Wilberforce to Washington, D.C., in sixteen days. The army, however, still stuck by its ruling. The house was declared a national historic landmark on May 30, 1974. It is a private residence.

Wilberforce University

Telephone: (937) 376-2911
Web site: http://www.wilberforce.edu

Established by the Methodist Episcopal Church in 1856, Wilberforce University is named for William Wilberforce, an English abolitionist. In 1863, the school was purchased by the African Methodist Episcopal Church. Wilberforce is the site of the National Afro-American Museum and Cultural Center.

OKLAHOMA

BOLEY

Boley Historic District

Approximating Seward Ave., Walnut and Cedar Sts., and the southern city limits

This is the largest of the all–African American towns established in Oklahoma to provide African Americans with the opportunity for self-government in an era of white supremacy and segregation. The town was established in 1903 and named for a white official of the Fort Smith and Western Railway, who encouraged a development for the African American railway workers. Residents migrated from Georgia, Texas, Louisiana, Mississippi, Alabama, and Florida. The Boley Historic District was designated a national historic landmark on May 15, 1975.

PONCA CITY

101 Ranch

During the latter part of the nineteenth century, the 101 Ranch was one of the largest and most famous in the West. The ranch was established in 1879 and, in its prime, it employed several African American cowhands, the most celebrated of whom was Bill Pickett (1870–1932).

The originator of the art of bulldogging or steer wrestling, Pickett also perfected a unique style unlike any used by contemporary rodeo participants. In March 1932, though then in his seventies, Pickett was still active—the last of the original 101 hands. He died on April 21, 1932, after being kicked by a horse, and was buried on a knoll near the White Eagle Monument. The ranch was declared a national historic landmark on May 15, 1975.

PENNSYLVANIA

ERIE

Harry T. Burleigh Birthplace

A friend of the famous Bohemian composer Antonín Dvořák and a composer/arranger in his own right, Harry T. Burleigh was born in 1866 in Erie, Pennsylvania.

Burleigh set to music many of the stirring poems of Walt Whitman and arranged such unforgettable spirituals as "Deep River." He died in 1949.

LANCASTER

Thaddeus Stevens Grave Site

Shreiner's Cemetery
W. Chestnut and N. Mulberry Sts.

Senator Thaddeus Stevens of Pennsylvania, a white abolitionist and civil rights activist, was one of the chief architects of the Fourteenth Amendment to the U.S. Constitution. When Stevens died in 1868, five black and three white pallbearers escorted the body to Washington, D.C. Stevens's body lay in state on the same catafalque that had borne the body of Abraham Lincoln and was guarded by African American soldiers of the Fifty-fourth Massachusetts Volunteer Infantry regiment. Two days later the body was returned to Lancaster, where more than ten thousand African Americans attended the funeral. Stevens was buried in Shreiner's Cemetery (also known as Shreiner-Concord Cemetery), a cemetery for African Americans. In his will, he had rejected burial in a white cemetery because of segregationist policy.

MONTGOMERY COUNTY

James A. Bland Grave Site

Merion Cemetery
Bryn Mawr and Rockhill Rds.
Telephone: (610) 664-6699

In the Merion Cemetery (also known as Merion Memorial Park) in Montgomery County, Pennsylvania, lies the grave of the African American composer James A. Bland (1854–1911), who wrote "Carry Me Back to Old Virginny," now the emeritus state song of Virginia. Bland was one of the most popular African American minstrels of the nineteenth century.

PHILADELPHIA

African American Museum in Philadelphia

701 Arch St.
Telephone: (215) 574-0380
Web site: http://www.aampmuseum.org

The museum is "committed to telling the story of African Americans in all its permutations" in Philadelphia, the Delaware Valley, the Commonwealth of Pennsylvania, and the Americas.

Frances Ellen Watkins Harper House

1006 Bainbridge St.

This was the home of the African American writer and social activist Frances Ellen Watkins Harper, who participated in the nineteenth-century abolitionist, woman's suffrage, and temperance movements. Harper occupied the residence from 1870 to 1911. The house was named a national historic landmark on December 8, 1976.

Mother Bethel African Methodist Episcopal Church

419 S. 6th St.
Telephone: (215) 925-0616
Web site: http://www.motherbethel.org

The current building was erected in 1889; it is the fourth church to be erected on the site where Richard Allen and Absalom Jones founded the Free African Society in 1787. This organization later grew into the African Methodist Episcopal Church, one of the largest African American religious denominations in the United States.

Allen, the first African American bishop, was born a slave and became a minister and circuit rider after winning his freedom. In 1814, he and James Forten organized a force of 2,500 free African Americans to defend Philadelphia against the British. Sixteen years later, Allen organized the first African American convention in Philadelphia and was instrumental in getting the group to adopt a strong platform denouncing slavery and encouraging abolitionist activities. Allen died in 1831 and was buried in the church crypt.

Forten had been born free in 1766 and, despite his youth, served aboard a Philadelphia privateer during the Revolutionary War. In 1800, he was one of the signers of a petition requesting Congress to alter the Fugitive Slave Act of 1793. Opposed to the idea of resettling slaves in Africa, Forten chaired an 1817 meeting held at Bethel to protest existing colonization schemes. In 1831, he put up the funds that William Lloyd Garrison needed to found the *Liberator*. After his death, Forten's work was continued by his successors, who remained active in the abolitionist cause throughout the Civil War and fought for African American rights during Reconstruction. The Forten home served as a meeting place for many of the leading figures in the movement. The church was named a national historic landmark on May 30, 1974.

All Wars Memorial to Colored Soldiers and Sailors

Logan Square
20th St. and Benjamin Franklin Pkwy.

This monument was erected by the state of Pennsylvania in 1934 to pay tribute to its fallen African American soldiers. Originally located in a remote section of Fairmont Park, it was relocated to Logan Square on the Benjamin Franklin Parkway in 1994.

Bethel A.M.E. Church, Philadelphia, 1787. *In April 1787, Richard Allen and Absalom Jones founded the Free African Society. This organization would later grow into the African Methodist Episcopal Church.* SCHOMBURG CENTER/ART RESOURCE, NY

Bessie Smith Residence

7003 S. 12th St.

This location served as home to blues singer Bessie Smith from about 1926 until her death in 1937. It is a private residence.

Henry O. Tanner House

2903 W. Diamond St.

Born in Pittsburgh in 1859, Henry Ossawa Tanner, an internationally recognized painter, was the first African American to be elected to the National Academy of Design. The Diamond Street residence was the artist's boyhood home. The site also commemorates the work of Tanner's father, Benjamin Tucker Tanner, bishop in the African Methodist Episcopal Church and editor of the *A.M.E. Church Review*. The homesite, a three-story structure, became Tanner's residence about 1872. The house was designated a historical landmark on May 11, 1976. It is a private residence.

PITTSBURGH

August Wilson Center for African American Culture

980 Liberty Ave.

Telephone: (412) 258-2700

Web site: http://www.augustwilsoncenter.org

Formerly known as the African American Cultural Center of Greater Pittsburgh, this center is named in honor of the Pulitzer Prize–winning playwright August Wilson (1945–2005). Its mission involves documentation and celebration of African American culture. It serves as a multidisciplinary venue for visual and performing arts expression.

RHODE ISLAND

PORTSMOUTH

Battle of Rhode Island Historical Site

Junction of Rtes. 114 and 24

Portsmouth served as the site of the only American Revolutionary battle in which an all–African American unit participated. The Battle of Rhode Island took place on August 29, 1778. A monument at the site, which was designated a national historic landmark on May 30, 1974, commemorates the First Rhode Island Regiment.

SOUTH CAROLINA

BEAUFORT

Robert Smalls House

511 Prince St.

Robert Smalls (1839–1915), a former slave, served in both the state legislature and the U.S. Congress. While in office, Smalls was an advocate for the rights of African Americans. He had lived in Beaufort, South Carolina, both as a slave and as a free man. The Smalls house, a large-frame two-story structure built in 1843, was designated a national historic landmark on May 30, 1973. It is a private residence.

CHARLESTON

Avery Normal Institute

125 Bull St.
Telephone: (843) 953-7609
Web site: http://avery.cofc.edu

Founded by the American Missionary Association in 1865, the institute moved to Bull Street and provided college preparatory education and teacher training for Charleston's African American community. Francis Cardozo developed it into a prestigious private school. The school closed in 1954 because of financial difficulties. Today, the historic building houses the College of Charleston's Avery Research Center for African American History, founded in 1985.

DuBose Heyward House

76 Church St.

DuBose Heyward (1885–1940), the author of *Porgy*, the book on which George Gershwin's opera *Porgy and Bess* was based, lived here from 1919 to 1924. The house was designated a national historic landmark on November 11, 1971.

Old Slave Mart

6 Chalmers St.
Telephone: (843) 958-6467
Web site: http://www.charlestoncity.info/dept/content.aspx?nid=1469

The Old Slave Mart was built in 1859 to be used for the auction of slaves and other goods. Originally, the mart included two additional lots and three buildings. The buildings were holding points for slaves who were to be sold. The structure that remains is the only known extant facility used as a slave auction gallery in the state. It now houses the Old Slave Mart Museum, which reopened in 2007 after a lengthy renovation. The building was listed on the National Register of Historic Places on May 2, 1975.

COLUMBIA

African American History Monument

South Carolina State House Grounds

This monument is modeled on an African village in the round and "is designed to recapture the rich history of the African Americans (a map shows the original homelands of the slaves and their arrival in Charleston) and their contributions to the state of South Carolina."

Chapelle Administration Building

Allen University
1530 Harden St.
Telephone: (803) 376-5700

The Chapelle Administration Building is located at Allen University, a school founded in 1870. Originally known as Payne Institute and based in Cokesbury, the school moved to Columbia and changed its name in 1880 to Allen University after Bishop Richard Allen. The school was established primarily to educate clergy for the African Methodist Episcopal Church. The Chapelle building is one of the finest works of John Anderson Lankford (1874–1946), a pioneering African American architect who helped gain recognition for African American architects among the architectural community. The building was named a national historic landmark on December 8, 1976.

Modjeska Monteith Simkins House

2025 Marion St.
Telephone: (803) 252-7742

This was the home of Modjeska Monteith Simkins (1899–1992), the founding member and secretary of the South Carolina Conference of NAACP chapters and the state's only full-time African American public-health worker. A social activist, Simkins was a leader of African American public-health reform, social reform, and civil rights movements. The house, which is now managed by the Historic Columbia Foundation, was placed on the National Register of Historic Places on March 25, 1994.

Denmark Vesey House

56 Bull St.

This was the residence of Denmark Vesey, a free black Charleston carpenter whose hard work earned him substantial wealth and respect among Charleston's African American community. He planned a slave insurrection, carefully selecting leaders and participants who were believed to be his supporters. His plot for July 14, 1822, was uncovered and Vesey was executed twelve days before the scheduled coup. The Denmark Vesey House was declared a national historic landmark on May 11, 1976.

FOUNTAIN INN

Clayton "Peg Leg" Bates Statue

This statue recognizes Clayton "Peg Leg" Bates (1907–1998), who lost a leg but overcame it to become a famous dancer. His signature work was the imitation of a jet plane.

GEORGETOWN

Joseph H. Rainey House

909 Prince St.

Joseph Hayne Rainey (1832–1887), a former slave, was the first African American to serve in the U.S. House of Representatives. His election, along with the election of Hiram R. Revels, the first African American citizen to be elected to the U.S. Senate in 1870, marked the beginning of African American participation in the federal legislative process. The house, built around 1760, was designated a national historic landmark on April 20, 1984. Rainey lived most of his life at this location, and returned to it as a headquarters during his political career and recesses from Congress. He returned to the house in 1886 and died there the following year. The family lived in the house until it was sold in 1896. It is now a private residence.

RANTOWLES

Stono River Slave Rebellion Historic Site

Off U.S. 17 on west bank of Wallace River

This was the site of a 1739 slave insurrection, during which some one hundred slaves escaped. The site became a national historic landmark on May 30, 1974.

ST. HELENA ISLAND

Penn School Historic District

Rte. 45

Telephone: (843) 838-2432

Web site: http://www.penncenter.com

Penn School was founded in 1862 and was supported by northern missionaries and abolitionists. Ellen Murray of the Pennsylvania Freedmen's Relief Association and her friend, Laura Towne, opened the school in Murray's house. As enrollment expanded, the school relocated to Brick Church, then to a site adjacent to the church. The new school was named Penn School. The school provided exceptional education to local African American residents who were denied admission to the white schools. The school also addressed the health, agricultural, and financial needs of the African American residents of St. Helena. It collected and preserved the artifacts, musical recordings, oral history, and heritage of the residents. The school closed in 1948, but its buildings still serve the community. The traditions of the facilities are carried on by the nonprofit Penn Center, Inc. On December 2, 1974, the area was designated a national historic landmark district.

SULLIVAN'S ISLAND

Fort Moultrie National Monument

1214 Middle St.

Telephone: (843) 883-3123

Web site: http://www.nps.gov/fosu/historyculture/fort_moultrie.htm

This northeast corner of Charleston Harbor was the first reception location for slaves from West Africa and the West Indies brought to North America between 1700 and the American Revolution.

SOUTH DAKOTA

DEADWOOD

Adams Museum and House

54 Sherman St.

Telephone: (605) 578-1714

Web site: http://www.adamsmuseumandhouse.org

The Adams Museum was founded in 1930 by W. E. Adams to honor the pioneers who settled the Black Hills of South Dakota, including one of the claimants to the legendary title "Deadwood Dick." Nat Love (1854–1921), an African American, can back up his assertion, however, with a colorful autobiography that takes the reader through his childhood in slavery, his early bronco-busting efforts, and his fabled life as a range rider and fighter in the old West. Love claimed he won the title "Deadwood Dick" during a public competition held in Deadwood on July 4, 1876. The presence of other African American cowboys, gambling house operators, and escort soldiers in the area during those years, as well as the convincing style of Love's narrative, lend a high degree of credibility to his adventurous tales—although, like Jim

Beckwourth, he may have been given to moments of wanton exaggeration.

TENNESSEE

CLINTON

Green McAdoo Cultural Center

101 School St.
Telephone: (865) 463-6500
Web site: http://www.greenmcadoo.org

This museum, housed in a former all-black elementary school called Clinton Colored School, was opened in 2006 to honor the African American students known as the "Clinton 12." Clinton High School, the first public high school to desegregate in the Old South, graduated both the first African American from a state-supported public integrated high school in the South, in 1957, and the first African American female from a public integrated high school, a year later. The school was destroyed in a 1958 bombing but was later rebuilt.

HENNING

Alex Haley House and Museum

200 S. Church St.
Telephone: (731) 738-2240

Best known for the television adaptation of his Pulitzer Prize–winning book *Roots*, author Alex Haley (1921–1992) awakened both black and white Americans to the richness of African and African American history and culture. The house, built in 1919 by Haley's grandfather, served as his home from 1921 to 1929 and was where he heard many of the stories that inspired him to write *Roots*. The house, which now serves as a museum, was listed on the National Register of Historic Places on December 14, 1978.

JACKSON

Casey Jones Home and Railroad Museum

30 Casey Jones Ln.
Telephone: (731) 668-1222
Web site: http://www.caseyjones.com/caseyjones

The Casey Jones Home and Railroad Museum is filled with memorabilia of a bygone era. Jones (1863–1900) was immortalized through the song about his legendary train ride. The song, which became popularized in vaudeville and music halls, was written by Wallace Saunders, an African American fireman aboard Jones's locomotive. The museum serves as a reminder of the enormous unsung contributions of African Americans to the railroad industry in the United States.

MEMPHIS

Beale Street Historic District

Beale St. from 2nd to 4th Sts.
Web site: http://www.bealestreet.com

The "blues," a unique black contribution to American music, was born on a Beale Street lined with saloons, gambling halls, and theaters. The street was immortalized by William Christopher Handy (1873–1958), who composed "Beale Street Blues." Beale Street was designated a national historic landmark district on May 23, 1966.

William Christopher Handy Park

Beale St.

The city of Memphis, Tennessee, pays tribute to the famous blues composer William Christopher Handy in the form of a park and a heroic bronze statue overlooking the very same Beale Street that he immortalized in the tune "Beale Street Blues." The statue, showing Handy standing with horn poised, was executed by Leone Tommasi of Italy and was dedicated in 1960, at the close of a memorial campaign instituted by the city shortly after Handy's death in 1958.

Tom Lee Memorial and Sculpture

Riverside Dr., south of Beale St.

A 30-foot-high granite memorial was erected in 1954 to honor Tom Lee, an African American who, on May 8, 1925, saved the lives of thirty-two passengers aboard the *M. E. Norman*, an excursion boat that had capsized some 20 miles below Memphis near Cow Island. Alerted to the disaster, Lee pulled thirty-two people from the water onto his skiff. He was honored for his feat by the Memphis Engineers Club, which provided him with money for the duration of his life. A fund was also raised to purchase him a home. After his death in 1952, a committee raised the money needed to erect an obelisk memorial in Tom Lee Park. It was dedicated in 1954. In 2006, a sculpture depicting Lee rescuing a survivor was erected in the same park.

Lorraine Motel

450 Mulberry St.
Telephone: (901) 521-9699
Web site: http://www.civilrightsmuseum.org

Neon Sign, Beale Street, Memphis, TN. *Known as the "home of the blues," Beale Street was immortalized by William Christopher Handy in his 1916 song, "Beale Street Blues," and was designated a national historic landmark district fifty years later.* **VISIONS LLC/ PHOTOLIBRARY**

It was on the balcony of the Lorraine Motel that Martin Luther King Jr. was assassinated while emerging from a second-floor room in the presence of a pair of his trusted advisers, Ralph David Abernathy and Jesse Jackson. King died in the emergency room of St. Joseph's Hospital on April 4, 1968. The Lorraine closed for business in 1988. It is now operated as the National Civil Rights Museum.

NASHVILLE

Alpha Kappa Mu Honor Society

Tennessee State University

Alpha Kappa Mu was founded at Tennessee A&I State College in 1937 to recognize Negro scholars.

William Edmondson Park

17th Ave. North and Charlotte Ave.

This park was named in recognition of William Edmondson (1874–1951), a renowned primitive sculptor, who was the first African American to have a one-man show at the Museum of Modern Art in New York City.

Fisk University Historic District

Roughly bounded by 16th and 18th Aves. and Hermosa, Herman, and Jefferson Sts.
Telephone: (615) 329-8500
Web site: http://www.fisk.edu

Opened on January 9, 1866, and incorporated on August 22, 1867, Fisk University was founded in Nashville following the Civil War by the American Missionary Association to provide a liberal arts education for children of former slaves. Fisk School, as it was initially known, began operation in former Union Army barracks. In 1873, the campus was moved to a new site, the old Fort Gillem. On February 9, 1978, the 40-acre campus was added to the National Register of Historic Places. Among the historic buildings on campus are the residences once occupied by Arna Bontemps, Robert Hayden, Elmer S. Imes, and John W. Work. Several are of Victorian design.

A bronze statue of illustrious Fisk graduate W. E. B. Du Bois, standing with book in hand, is located on the campus. Jubilee Hall, a Victorian Gothic structure located on 17th Avenue North, is the South's first permanent structure built to educate African American students. The Fisk Jubilee Singers set out from Nashville in 1871 to raise money for their school, and in their concerts they introduced the Negro spiritual to the world. The singers raised enough money to save the school and to erect Jubilee Hall, which was dedicated on January 1, 1876. The hall was designated a national historic landmark on December 2, 1974.

James Weldon Johnson House

911 D. B. Todd Blvd.

The writer and civil rights leader James Weldon Johnson resided at this location from about 1931 until his death in 1938, teaching literature and writing at Fisk University. Johnson was born in 1871 in Jacksonville, Florida. In collaboration with his brother, J. Rosamond Johnson, he was responsible for creating the song "Lift Every Voice and Sing." Johnson's death mask is in the Fisk University Library's Special Collections. The house is a private residence.

Hadley Park

1032 28th Ave. N

This is the first public park in the United States set aside exclusively for the use of African Americans.

Ted Rhodes Golf Course

1901 Ed Temple Blvd.
Telephone: (615) 862-8463
Web site: http://www.nashville.gov/parks/golf/tedrhodes

This public golf course, owned by the city of Nashville, is named after Ted Rhodes (1913–1969), who is recognized as the first African American professional golfer. He was barred from competing on the PGA tour and most other professional venues because of a whites-only policy, but he received support from boxing champion Joe Louis in pursuing golf opportunities in Canada and California.

TEXAS

BASTROP

Ploeger-Kerr White House

806 Marion

Robert Kerr, a political and civic leader, was the first African American legislator from Bastrop and one of the first African Americans to hold office following Reconstruction.

DALLAS

African American Museum

Fair Park
3536 Grand Ave.
Telephone: (214) 565-9026
Web site: http://www.aamdallas.org

The African American Museum of Dallas began as a part of the Bishop College Special Collection before becoming an independent operation in 1979. According to its Web site, it is "the only museum in the Southwestern United States devoted to the preservation and display of African American cultural and historical materials."

HOUSTON

Freedmen's Town Historic District

Approximate boundaries: I-45, Dallas Ave., and Taft and W. Gray Sts.

This historic district, also known as the Fourth Ward, is the oldest existing post–Civil War African American community in the United States. Between 1910 and 1930, the area was the economic center for Houston's African American population. Many of the buildings in the district no longer exist, having fallen prey to developers and decay. In the interest of preserving some of the area's history, the Freedmen's Town home of Rutherford B. H. Yates, the first African American printer in Houston, was renovated and turned into the Rutherford B. H. Yates Museum. On January 17, 1985, the Freedmen's Town Historic District was added to the National Register of Historic Places. Another museum is planned for this district—the Pullum Health and Business Museum, which will highlight the history and achievements of African American doctors and health professional in the Houston area.

Buffalo Soldiers National Museum and Heritage Center

1834 Southmore Blvd.
Telephone: (713) 942-8920
Web site: http://www.buffalosoldiermuseum.com

This institution was founded in 2000 by African American veteran and military historian Paul J. Matthews. Its purpose is to present the military history and legacy of African American soldiers, with particular emphasis on the "buffalo soldiers" who served during the Indian Wars, the Spanish-American War, World War I, and World War II.

Buffalo Soldiers Motorcycle Club of Maryland Holds Tribute at the African American Civil War Memorial, Washington, DC, 2003. *The memorial's centerpiece is the* Spirit of Freedom *statue, named for the woman depicted watching over and guiding the African American infantrymen and sailors fighting for family and freedom.* MARVIN JOSEPH/THE WASHINGTON POST/GETTY IMAGES

UTAH

SALT LAKE CITY

Brigham Young Monument

Main and S. Temple Sts.

Brigham Young Monument contains the names of the three slaves who traveled with the first company of Mormon pioneers.

Mignon Richmond Park

450 East 600 South

This park is named for Mignon Richmond, who graduated from Utah State Agricultural College (later Utah State University) in 1921, becoming the first African American to graduate from a Utah college.

This Is the Place Monument

This Is the Place Heritage Park
2601 Sunnyside Ave.
Telephone: (801) 582-1847
Web site: http://www.thisistheplace.org

This Is the Place Monument, located at 2601 Sunnyside Avenue, lists the names of the three African Americans who traveled with the 1847 Mormon pioneers.

VIRGINIA

ALEXANDRIA

Bruin's Slave Jail

1707 Duke St.

This building, which is not open to the public, was used as a jail by Joseph Bruin, a slave dealer, to hold slaves awaiting sale.

Franklin and Armfield Office

1315 Duke St.

From 1828 to 1836, the office of the Franklin and Armfield slave-trading company in Alexandria, Virginia, was the South's largest slave-trading firm. (During the company's operation, Alexandria was part of the District of Columbia.) The building was designated a national historic landmark on June 2, 1978.

ARLINGTON

Benjamin Banneker SW-9 Intermediate Boundary Stone

18th and Van Buren Sts.

This boundary stone in Arlington, Virginia, commemorates the accomplishments of Benjamin Banneker (1731–1806), who helped survey the city of Washington, D.C., and who was perhaps the best-known African American in colonial America. Banneker, a mathematician and scientist, was born in Ellicott Mills, Maryland, and received his early schooling with the aid of a Quaker family. Banneker was a national hero for African Americans, and many schools have been named after him. The boundary stone was declared a national historic landmark on May 11, 1976.

Charles Richard Drew House

2505 1st St. S.

Located in Arlington, Virginia, this house served as the home of Charles Richard Drew from 1920 to 1939. Drew, a noted African American physician and teacher, is best remembered for his pioneer work in discovering means to preserve blood plasma. The house was named a national historic landmark on May 11, 1976. It is a private residence.

CHATHAM

Pittsylvania County Courthouse

U.S. Business Rte. 29

The Pittsylvania County Courthouse in Chatham, Virginia, was closely associated with the 1878 case *Ex parte Virginia.* This case took up the issue of African American participation on juries. It stemmed from a clear attempt by a state official to deny citizens the equal protection of law guaranteed by the Fourteenth Amendment to the U.S. Constitution. The courthouse was designated a national historic landmark on May 4, 1987.

GLEN ALLEN

Virginia Randolph Home Economics Cottage

2200 Mountain Rd.
Telephone: (804) 360-2071

As the first supervisor of the Jeanes Fund, set up by a wealthy Philadelphia Quaker to aid African American education, Virginia Randolph (1874–1958) worked to upgrade African American vocational training. The cottage in Glen Allen, Virginia, was named a national historic landmark on December 2, 1974. It houses a museum, which is open to the public.

GLOUCESTER

Holly Knoll House

6496 Allmondsville Rd.
Telephone: (804) 693-2645
Web site: http://www.gloucesterinstitute.org

From 1935 to 1940, this house served as the retirement home of Robert R. Moton. Moton, who succeeded Booker T. Washington as head of Tuskegee Institute in 1915, guided the school's growth for the next twenty years. He was an influential educator and active in many African American causes. The house, which was designated a national historic landmark on December 21, 1981, became the central building of the Moton Conference Center following Moton's death. In 2005, Holly Knoll was acquired by the Gloucester Institute, which continues Dr. Moton's support for African American educators, culture, and leadership development through conferences, institutes, and other activities designed to stimulate intellectual discussions and exchanges of ideas.

HAMPTON

Hampton University

Telephone: (757) 727-5000
Web site: http://www.hamptonu.edu

Founded in 1868 as Hampton Normal and Agricultural Institute, this was one of the earliest institutions of higher learning for African Americans in the United States. Samuel Chapman Armstrong, an agent of the Freedmen's Bureau, persuaded the American Missionary Association to purchase land for the school. Booker T. Washington, one of its graduates, later founded Tuskegee Institute in Alabama, modeling it after the Hampton tradition. Washington also taught for a time at Hampton. The Hampton area and several of its buildings were designated a national historic landmark district on May 30, 1974.

Hampton University Museum

11 Frissell Ave.
Telephone: (757) 727-5308
Web site: http://museum.hamptonu.edu

Located on the campus of Hampton University, this museum is the oldest African-American museum in the United States.

HANDY

Booker T. Washington National Monument

12130 Booker T. Washington Hwy.
Telephone: (540) 721-2094
Web site: http://www.nps.gov/bowa

The Burroughs plantation, on which the educator and scholar Booker T. Washington was born in 1856, can be found in a 200-acre park located 22 miles southeast of Roanoke, Virginia. Born a slave, Washington lived here until the end of the Civil War, when he and his mother moved to Malden, West Virginia.

JAMESTOWN ISLAND

Colonial National Historical Park

Telephone: (757) 898-2400
Web site: http://www.nps.gov/colo

Jamestown Island, located in Colonial National Historical Park, is where the first African American slaves arrived in the American colonies in 1619. In addition, the park also includes the site of the Battle of Yorktown, a 1781 struggle in which three African Americans held combat positions in patriot militia units and worked for the Hessian forces as musicians and servants.

LYNCHBURG

Anne Spencer House and Garden Museum

1313 Pierce St.
Telephone: (804) 845-1313
Web site: http://annespencermuseum.com

Anne Spencer (1882–1975), a poet and librarian, was a friend and confidante of many Harlem Renaissance luminaries. Her poetry was published largely in the 1920s, when the Harlem Renaissance was in full blossom. She maintained her relationship with the African American cultural leaders of Harlem, and they visited her in the garden that she provided for them. Now a museum, the Spencer home was listed on the National Register of Historic Places on December 6, 1976.

NORFOLK

West Point Monument

Elmwood Cemetery
238 E. Princess Anne Rd.
Telephone: (757) 441-2653

This granite monument honoring African American veterans of the Civil War marks a section of Norfolk's Elmwood Cemetery that includes the grave sites of nearly one hundred African American soldiers who served during either the Civil War or the Spanish-American War.

RICHMOND

Arthur Ashe Statue

Monument Ave. and Roseneath Rd.

A 12-foot bronze statue of tennis legend Arthur Ashe was unveiled in his hometown in July 1996. The statue depicts Ashe in a warm-up suit, holding books over his head in one hand and a tennis racket in the other. The inscription, taken from a Bible verse, is the opening passage of his autobiography, *Days of Grace*: "Since we are surrounded by so great a cloud of witnesses, let us lay aside every weight, and the sin which so easily ensnares us, and let us run with endurance the race that is set before us."

Jackson Ward Historic District

Bounded by Fourth, Marshall, and Smith Sts. and the Richmond-Petersburg Tpk.
Telephone: (804) 644-4305
Web site: http://www.hjwa.org

Jackson Ward was the foremost African American community of the nineteenth and early twentieth centuries and an early center for ethnic social organizations and protective banking institutions. The district was named a national historic landmark on June 2, 1978.

St. Luke Building

900 St. James St.

This Edwardian-style building, completed in 1902, served as the national headquarters for the Independent Order of St. Luke, an African American benevolent society founded in Baltimore in 1867 by Mary Prout, a former slave. The organization helped to ease the transition from slavery to freedom, providing financial aid and guidance to newly freed slaves. The oldest African American–affiliated office building in Richmond, it houses the Maggie Lena Walker office, now preserved as a memorial. The structure was remodeled and enlarged between 1915 and 1920. It was added to the National Register of Historic Places on September 16, 1982.

Sixth Mount Zion Baptist Church

14 W. Duval St.
Telephone: (804) 648-7511
Web site: http://www.smzbc.org

The renowned Reverend John Jasper founded the Sixth Mount Zion Baptist Church in 1867, while the current church building was constructed in 1887. The building contains the John Jasper Memorial Room, which has a collection of materials documenting the church's history. On December 16, 1996, the building was listed on the National Register of Historic Places.

Maggie Lena Walker National Historic Site

110 1/2 E. Leigh St.
Telephone: (804) 771-2017
Web site: http://www.nps.gov/mawa

In 1903, Maggie Lena Walker, an African American woman, founded the successful St. Luke Penny Savings Bank and became the first woman to establish and head a bank. In addition to being the first woman president of a bank, she was editor of a newspaper considered to be one of the best journals of its class in the United States. The house is located in the Jackson Ward Historic District of Richmond; it was declared a national historic landmark on May 15, 1975, and it became a part of the National Park System as a national historic site on November 10, 1978.

WASHINGTON

CENTRALIA

George Washington Park

Pearl and Main Sts.

This park is named after a liberated slave who escaped from slavery in Virginia when he was adopted by a white couple and taken to Missouri. He then left Missouri with a wagon train heading for the Pacific Northwest, settling on a homestead along the Chehalis River. After the location was reached by the Northern Pacific Railroad, Washington in 1875 laid out a town, setting aside acreage for parks, a cemetery, and churches. Soon more than two thousand lots were in the hands of a thriving population that formed the nucleus of Centerville, which was later renamed Centralia.

WEST VIRGINIA

HARPERS FERRY

Harpers Ferry National Historic Park

Telephone: (304) 535-6029
Web site: http://www.nps.gov/hafe

Harpers Ferry derives its historical fame from the much publicized antislavery raid conducted by John Brown and a party of eighteen men, including five African Americans, from October 16 to 18, 1859. Brown hoped to set up a fortress and refuge for slaves that he could transform into an important way station for black fugitives en route to Pennsylvania.

Brown lost two of his sons in the battle and was himself seriously wounded. He was later tried and convicted of treason, and hanged at Charles Town on December 2, 1859.

MALDEN

Booker T. Washington Monument

Booker T. Washington Park at West Virginia State University is situated on the site of the African Baptist Zion Church, the first black church in West Virginia.

WISCONSIN

MILTON

Milton House Museum

18 S. Janesville St.
Telephone: (608) 868-7772
Web site: http://www.miltonhouse.org

The Milton House, the first structure made of poured concrete in the United States, was once used as a hideaway for fugitive slaves escaping by means of the Underground Railroad. Built in 1844, the house was designated a national historic landmark on August 5, 1998.

PORTAGE

Ansel Clark Grave Site

Silver Lake Cemetery

Ansel Clark, "born a slave, died a respected citizen," settled in Wisconsin after the Civil War, in which he served as an impressed laborer in the Confederate cause before escaping. Brought to Portage by a man to whom he had tended in a Union hospital, Clark served as town constable and deputy sheriff. For thirty years, he worked in law enforcement, standing up to the town's rough characters and keeping them in line with his "firmness and dignity."

5

AFRICA AND THE AFRICAN DIASPORA

Christopher A. Brooks

The African continent has played a profound role in world history. Africa witnessed the evolution of the human species, sustaining its development through many long periods. Africa was home to many of the world's great ancient societies, but also experienced the greatest forced removal of population that the world has ever recorded. Like other parts of the globe, the African continent experienced occupation of external powers, but on a much greater scale. In more recent times, there have been collective triumphs, but there have also been numerous challenges and obstacles that the nations of Africa have been forced to confront. Civil wars, religious conflict, famine, and disease have been human realities that modern African nation states have had to address. Yet, Africa continues to make progress in spite of these major challenges.

AN ABRIDGED HISTORY OF AFRICA

For at least half a century, archaeological research has established lines of hominoid (an early manifestation in the human family tree) as far north as modern-day Ethiopia through Tanzania as well as South Africa. Early examples of *australopithecus* (a bipedal, apelike creature with a pelvis more similar to *Homo sapiens* than to an ape) have been located throughout the east African corridor. Later stages of australopithecine had an increasingly large brain capacity and had a strong presence in both regions of the continent. At some point (perhaps two million years ago), there was a split and the human forerunner, *Homo habilis*, developed into *Homo erectus*. In this form, there was movement to other parts of the African continent and beyond. Complex tool usage and cooperative activities such as hunting and living in groups was also a feature of this stage of hominid development. The most intact example of *Homo erectus* yet discovered was near Lake Turkana in Kenya in 1984; this discovery, known as the Nariokotome boy, is believed to be a twelve-year-old male. These levels of *Homo* (i.e., *habilis*, *erectus*, and eventually *Homo sapiens*) constructed tools to use for hunting, digging, and for cutting meat. Hominids began migrating to other parts of the globe, including Asia and southern Europe. Between 30,000 and 40,000 years ago, anatomically modern humans, now referred to as *Homo sapiens sapiens*, emerged, and the earlier forms of hominids seem to have interbred or died out because they lacked certain survival skills such as the ability to manipulate fire as well as the facility to identify rudimentary shelter such as caves. As the Stone Age developed, more sophisticated use of tools, such as employment of pointed projectile tips for bows and spears, were developed.

The genetic variation on the African continent manifested itself in later periods with the emergence of four distinctive physical types: the African Caucasoid, also referred to as "Mediterranean"; the Negroid; the Pygmoid, and the San (formerly referred to as Bushman, but also known as Bushmanoid or Capoid). All of these human variations can still be found on the continent, but the Negroid became the dominant group. Other evidence of more complex organizational structures can be gleaned from the rock art found in several parts of the continent, notably in the southern region.

While the use of tools represented a new level of accomplishment among early humans, greatly improving their ability to form small-scale communities throughout the continent, it was agricultural advancement and the

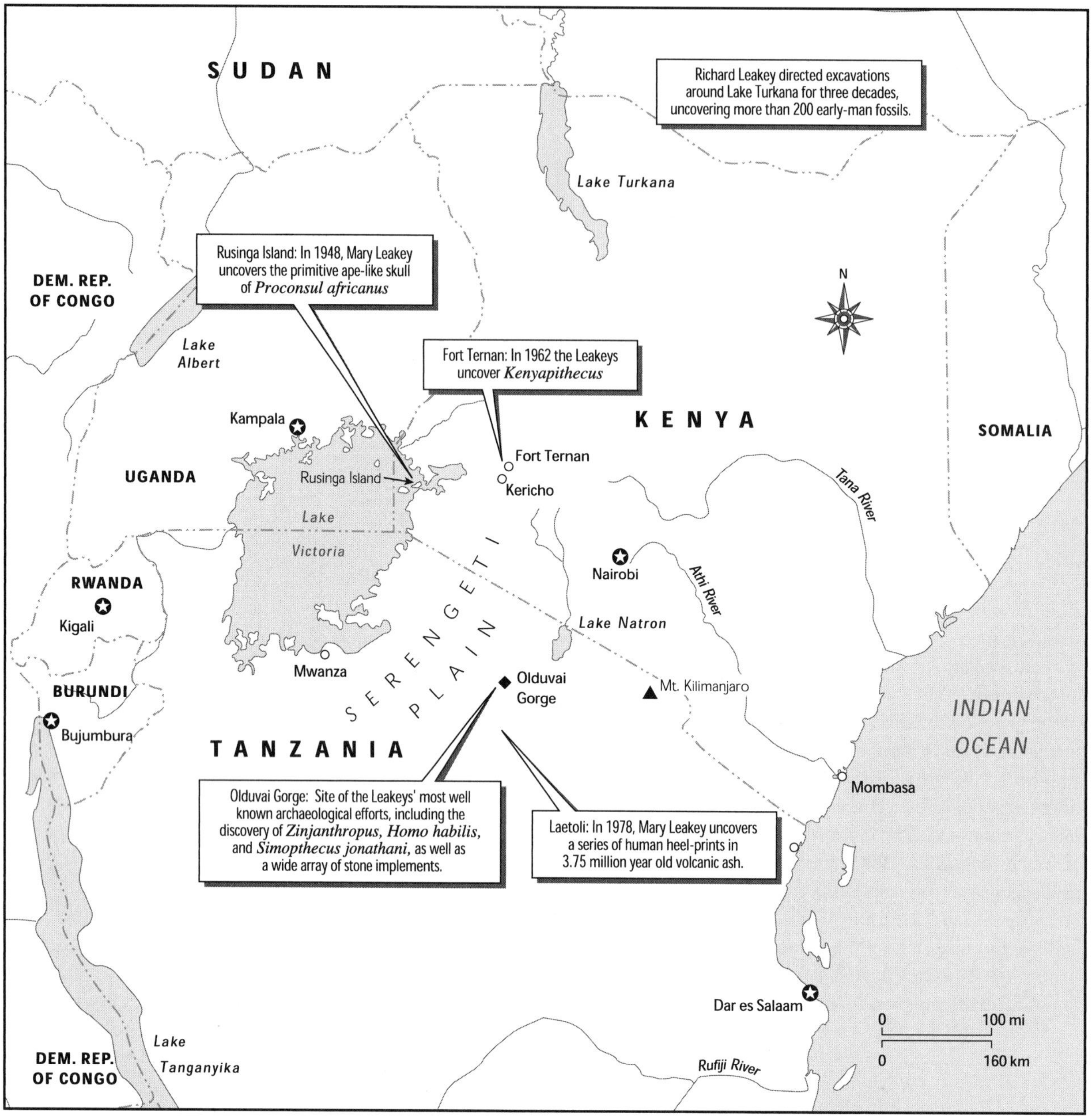

Map of Archaeological Discoveries of the Leakey Family in East Africa. *A series of major archaeological finds in eastern Africa has provided support for the theory that humans first evolved in Africa.* **MAP BY XNR PRODUCTIONS, INC. REPRODUCED BY PERMISSION OF GALE, A PART OF CENGAGE LEARNING.**

cultivation and mastery of irrigation methods in the Nile Valley region that laid the groundwork for the earliest known African states, circa 5000 BCE. The expansion of agriculture as an economic foundation facilitated population growth and the eventual emergence of the Egyptian state. Between 3200 and 2900 BCE, Upper Egypt (the southern part of the state) absorbed Lower Egypt (the northern part of the state) through conquest. The unified state produced many of the world's wonders (including the Great Pyramid of Giza), established complex religious beliefs (in which the Pharaoh or king was regarded as a god), and made dramatic advances in medicine and technology. Many practices of that society also became the foundation of many Western customs and traditions. Egypt eventually came under Roman control in 146 BCE.

Other early African states included Kush, which had a well-developed social structure and political history and lasted 1,500 years, into the fourth century CE. Within the

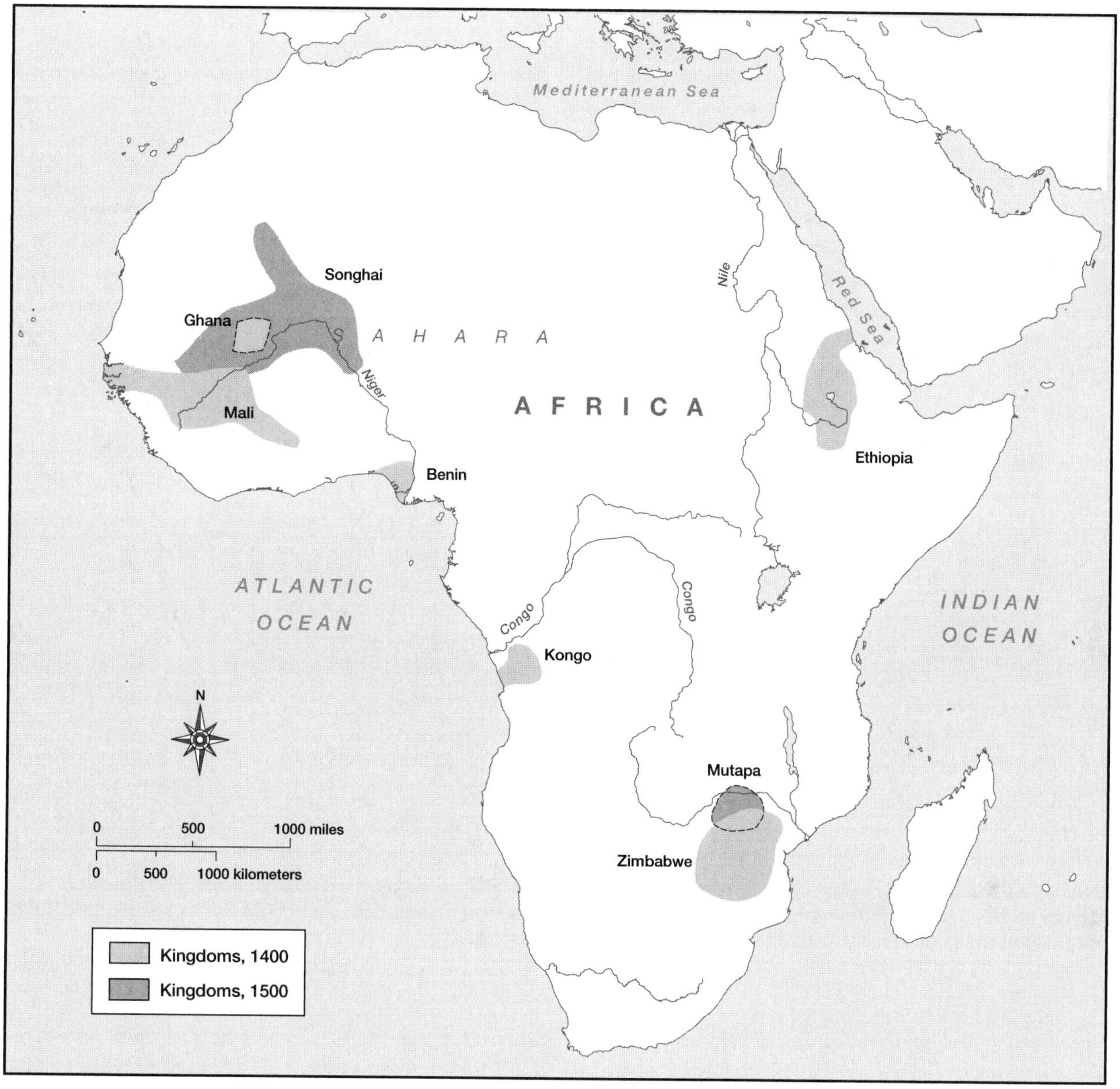

***African Kingdoms, fifteenth and sixteenth centuries* CE.** MAP BY XNR PRODUCTIONS, INC. REPRODUCED BY PERMISSION OF GALE, A PART OF CENGAGE LEARNING.

millennium, other African states emerged, including ancient Ghana (between 750 and 800 CE), well known for its abundance of gold and smelting techniques. Other West African states were Mali, Songhai, Djenne, and Gao. To the south, the state of Benin was established by the thirteenth century. It was followed by the founding of the Yoruba city of Oyo during the fifteenth century.

Islam's religious tenets began spreading throughout West Africa as a result of northern and eastern merchants engaging in commerce around the early eighth century. Those beliefs were eventually imposed through conquest. Several kingdoms in the region had an Islamic presence dating back to the eighth century, including Songhai (an empire in present-day Mali on the central portion of the Niger River), the Mali Empire (centered on the upper portion of the Niger River), and the ancient kingdom of Ghana. By the ninth century, Muslim merchants from North Africa began to trade regularly in gold and salt with the peoples of West Africa. The merchant class in West Africa was the first major group in the region to fall under the spell of Islam. Traditional leaders soon joined the West African merchants in their conversion to Islam.

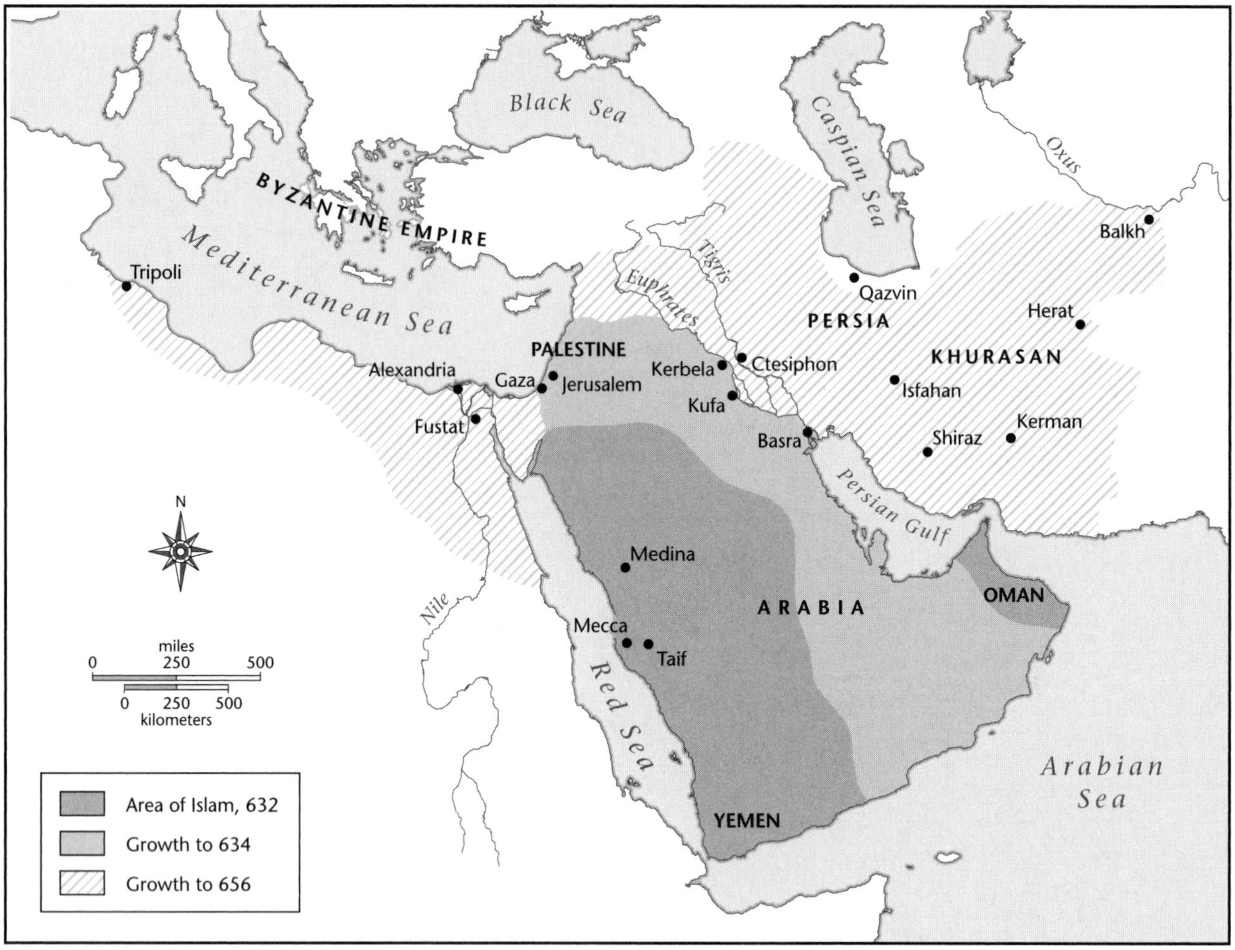

Map of the Middle East, middle 600s. *Muslim territories grew substantially in the years following the death of Muhammad, the founder of Islam, in 632. In less than three decades, Islam was being embraced by many in North Africa.* **MAP BY XNR PRODUCTIONS, INC. REPRODUCED BY PERMISSION OF GALE, A PART OF CENGAGE LEARNING.**

Arab traders first began to set up trading outposts along the East African coast in the twelfth century. Earlier, by the eleventh century, there was a movement to impose a more rigorous Islamic structure throughout the region by banishing certain customs and practices viewed as contrary to the belief. Even though stricter religious practices were observed with great vehemence, the unique character of Islam in West Africa (as well as where it is found in other parts of the continent) was its variation on local customs. By the sixteenth century, Islam was established in large sections of West Africa.

From the early sixteenth century through the first three to four decades of the nineteenth century, trade in human cargo profoundly changed the African continent as well as the Americas. Prior to the European desire for enslaved Africans, there were *jihads* (wars undertaken as a sacred duty by Muslims) in the western and eastern regions of Africa. When Muslim conquerors assumed control of a territory, the conquered peoples were typically sold into enslavement. While much scholarly attention has been devoted to the exportation of enslaved Africans, there was also internal enslavement throughout West Africa prior to any contact with Europeans.

The Christian (i.e., Catholic) presence in West Africa began as early as the fifteenth century. At that time, Portuguese traders sought to break the Muslim control of the maritime trade in the region. By the 1460s, the Cape Verde islands were colonized, and the Portuguese began building forts throughout the region, such as those on Goree Island (a part of modern-day Senegal) and in other coastal areas such as Elmina, in what became known as the Gold Coast (modern-day Ghana). This trading in gold provided a lucrative incentive for the Portuguese, and later other European powers, to establish contact with Africans who were in a position to mine gold and other precious commodities.

The sustained effort to convert Africans to Christianity did not begin until the 1840s, when the British, the French, and the Portuguese undertook missionary work in the western part of the continent. The French and Portuguese adopted a policy of assimilation, whereby the Africans in their colonies were equipped with the language, culture, and customs of the colonial power and afterward often considered themselves as French or Portuguese citizens. The French and Portuguese thus divided their colonial populations into those who had assimilated and those who had chosen to adhere to indigenous customs and practices. The indigenous were frequently Muslims, who had well-honed trading skills but did not have a Western-style education and were looked down upon by the colonial powers.

Although the British government declared the slave trade illegal in 1807, such commerce continued in varying degrees through most of the nineteenth century. Some African territories, stung by the British ban on African enslavement, turned to other European nations to continue such trading. When the British fleet deployed along the coast of West Africa to implement that country's ban on the forced exportation of Africans, human traders simply shifted their operations to areas not typically under surveillance. Africans were also captured and shipped from East African ports to the Americas.

Throughout the nineteenth century, the European presence on the African continent grew dramatically, but it was the period of the last two decades that would commonly become known as the "Scramble for Africa." That struggle, principally among Western European states, thereafter altered the continent and forged a precarious path for many African nation states well into the twenty-first century. To avoid armed conflict among the major European powers, Britain, France, Belgium, Germany, Italy, Spain, and Portugal met in Berlin (at the invitation of the German chancellor Otto von Bismarck) between 1884 and 1885 to determine how the continent should be divided and colonized. (The United States was invited, but ultimately declined to participate in the conference—its primary interest in West Africa was in Liberia.) Among the guidelines that the participants agreed upon were that a colonial power had to establish control of a territory, either through armed occupation, police presence, or through some form of indirect rule; it had to ensure access to trade routes; and it had to be committed to the abolition of enslavement in the claimed territory. In addition, a colonial power had to recognize all Christian denominations, primarily for missionary purposes. The collective African response to these events was pacifistic in some instances and violent resistance in others. In Dahomey (modern-day Benin), Chad, and the Gold Coast, Africans fought the French and British imposition of colonialism. Similar resistance movements took place in other parts of the continent, as when the Ethiopians defeated the Italians at Adowa in 1896. Indigenous African opposition emerged in the 1890s during the Shona/Ndebele Wars in Mashonaland and Matalbeleland (modern-day Zimbabwe, 1896–1897). By late in that decade, however, the "magnificent African cake" (a phrase coined by Belgium's King Leopold) had been carved up among the European powers.

The spread of the railroad system and the mining industry also played a major role in movement around the continent from the nineteenth into the twentieth centuries. The so-called Cape (i.e., Cape Town, South Africa) to Cairo (Egypt) Railway, while ultimately left unfinished, cost the lives of thousands of Africans in the development process.

Mining also transformed southern Africa. In parts of Southern Rhodesia (modern-day Zimbabwe), some 30,000 Africans died between 1900 and 1933 in what was known as *chibaro* (forced labor). Prisoners and child labor were used in railroad and mining industries throughout that region and other parts of the continent. The Portuguese colonizers in the territories of Angola and Mozambique were especially harsh in their use of forced labor to grow and harvest cotton, only to sell it at artificially low prices in Europe.

By the end of World War I, Germany's defeat dealt a blow to its colonial ambitions, but the remaining European colonizers were still well entrenched and thriving throughout the continent. Only Liberia (which was a protectorate of the United States) and Ethiopia escaped falling under the European colonial sphere.

In the 1920s, many African colonial governments were openly threatened by the Marcus Garvey movement in the United States. Garvey had preached from the other side of the Atlantic Ocean on the theme, "Africa for the Africans." This dictum resonated among many continental Africans, and chapters of Garvey's United Negro Improvement Association were established in South Africa, Kenya, Ghana, Nigeria, and other African colonies. Many of the chapters had to operate covertly. Those followers who paid the most attention to Garvey's speeches and writings were primarily educated professionals or civil servants who could appreciate the significance of an independent African continent.

North Africa saw most of the actual fighting on the continent during the World War II, although the European Allied forces drew heavily on their African colonists south of the Sahara to provide logistical support and labor in several crucial battles. After World War II, continental Africans and leaders of African descent from other nations met at the Fifth Pan-African Congress in Manchester, England, in 1945. One of the primary aims of this conference was to formulate strategies for ending colonialism on the African continent. The economic

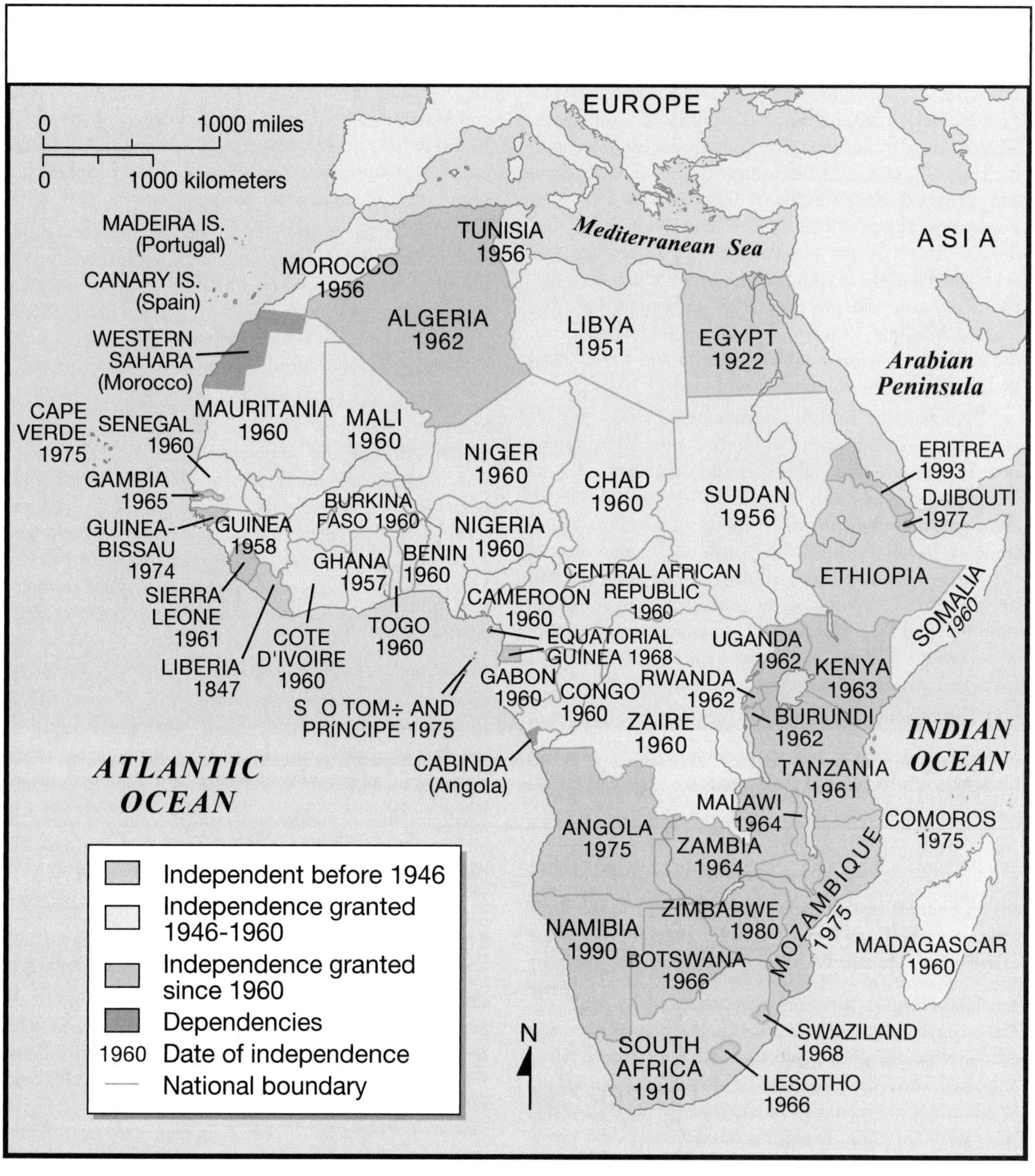

Modern African Countries and the Years They Become Independent Nations. MAP BY XNR PRODUCTIONS, INC. REPRODUCED BY PERMISSION OF GALE, A PART OF CENGAGE LEARNING.

impact of the war in Europe made it easier for independence movements around the African continent to gain new momentum with comparatively little resistance.

Colonialism's impact on the African continent was dramatic. While some scholars note the overall benefits of the colonial system, such as imposing a uniform language to facilitate communication among different language groups and providing a framework for other infrastructural improvements, colonialism fundamentally took away much more than it gave back, regardless of the advances.

Colonialism was autocratic and it set up artificial boundaries that gave privileges to certain regions (or ethnic groups within those regions). Colonial authorities exploited the territories they controlled for their mineral wealth, and agricultural potential was poorly developed. This troubling legacy was a huge challenge for the new governments that were established in the early postcolonial period.

Numerous African independence movements developed throughout the 1950s, but that which seemed to capture world attention took place in Kenya. Kenya's Land and Freedom Movement, called "Mau Mau" (a term of contempt used by the British colonizers), was a Kikuyu-inspired resistance struggle that lasted several years. Militarily, the movement was unsuccessful. Symbolically, however, it galvanized the country in its march toward independence like no other single occurrence.

The former Gold Coast was reborn during this period, taking the ancient name of Ghana as it became independent from the British in March 1957. By 1960, several African countries had freed themselves of their colonial masters or were actively engaged in struggles to achieve that goal. In the following decades, the African continent experienced many political, economic, and social challenges as well as moments of glory that have helped determine its current position in world history.

THE ORGANIZATION OF AFRICAN UNITY (OAU)

At the core of the idea of a united African continent was the Pan-Africanist Kwame Nkrumah (1909–1972), the first leader of an independent Ghana. His vision of a "United States of Africa" took a step forward with the formation of the Organization of African Unity (OAU) when the group's charter was signed on May 25, 1963, in Addis Ababa. Among the conditions for membership in the OAU were political independence and a majority-rule state on the continent. This organization consisted of thirty independent states, including Ghana, Morocco, Algeria, Libya, Nigeria, Liberia, Sierra Leone, Ethiopia, Senegal, and Chad, among others.

The OAU's general aims were to promote unity and solidarity among African states, respect and defend the sovereignty of their geographical and political borders, and promote intercontinental trade. However, there was no central authority that the OAU leadership could exercise over its member states or neighboring African countries. Many of the new African nations at that time could be classified as developing countries and as such chose socialist systems of governance. The Soviet Union, therefore, became their model for economic and political advancement. Embracing the notion of centrally planned economies, many of these countries developed into single-party states. Almost all African countries in the socialist sphere closely aligned themselves with the Soviet Union, which provided substantial military, political, and economic assistance. When the Soviet Union disintegrated in the early 1990s, many socialist-leaning African states were left without a major source of support. Socialism quickly fell into disfavor, with most countries in Africa turning to Western Europe and the United States for assistance. While the OAU used its influence to mediate or attempt to resolve various conflicts on the continent (e.g., the Somalia-Ethiopian War in 1977; civil conflicts in Chad in 1980–1981; Mozambique in the mid-1970s), as a unifying force similar to that which Nkrumah predicted, the OAU's record has been far less distinguished.

MILITARY GOVERNMENTS

The reality of military takeovers of civilian governments (*coup d'etats*) on the African continent has been a consistent hallmark of the postcolonial era. Between 1960 and 2005, there were more than 140 attempted coups throughout the continent, and close to half of that number were successful. The strong military presence in many African states is another legacy of colonialism (which also maintained a strong police presence to enforce law and order). By the turn of the twenty-first century, African countries were collectively spending more of their national budgets on military expenditures than on education and health systems combined.

Beginning in 1966, Kwame Nkrumah was ousted by the military, which stayed in power for a good deal of Ghana's independence. Similarly, Nigeria (Africa's most populous country) was the setting of a violent military overthrow in January 1967 in which the president, Abubakar Tafawa Balewa (1912–1966), and several other prominent politicians were assassinated. Subsequent events in that country led to the outbreak of a devastating civil war (1967–1970, also known as the Biafran War).

Such scenarios were recurrent on the continent, where military leaders assumed power to prevent the total breakdown of the government. In some cases, the political in-fighting, governmental corruption, and civil unrest would be so severe, military intervention was actually welcomed. This was the case with Nigeria in 1967 when its first coup took place. The reality, however, is that while they were able to enforce the rule of law, military governments were no better at addressing issues of poverty, health care, land reform for agricultural issues, and employment than the civilian governments that they toppled.

FORGING NATIONAL UNITY

The dilemma of nation building has been another major challenge facing most modern African nations. During the colonial era, it was common for the "divide and rule" strategy to manifest itself in one group being privileged over another because of its proximity to the seat of power or access to opportunities for commercial growth. The period before and after World War II (when nationalist sentiments began to thrive) was punctuated with the emergence of ethnic associations (sometimes referred to as "tribal" associations) and unions. In several cases, these associations became the basis of more formal political parties. While the various disparate factions had the common goal of independence from colonialism, ethnic sentiments frequently reemerged later with equal passion and became stumbling blocks in the construction of a national unity during the postcolonial era. With close to 1,000 different ethnic groups represented on the African continent, children are typically made aware of their ethnic identity as keenly (if not more) as they are made aware of their national identity.

Throughout the postcolonial era, conflicts surrounding the issue of ethnic and national identity have been routine. Whether it was Yoruba versus Hausa versus Igbo in Nigeria; Kikuyu versus Luo in Kenya; Shona versus Ndebele in Zimbabwe; Zulu versus Xhosa in South Africa; or Hutu versus Tutsi in Rwanda, these conflicts have continued to haunt many modern African states. In 1994, the outbreak of violence between Hutu and Tutsi led to a genocidal massacre in Rwanda, with close to 1 million lives lost. These events went largely unreported to the international community as they were taking place.

Ethnic-related conflicts in Africa have been the foundation of major internal skirmishes, and many modern political leaders have actively exploited such episodes for political gain. Such is typically the case when limited resources are available, and political leaders favor one group as a means of maintaining that group's loyalty and support.

Some countries have used creative strategies to combat ethnic polarization. After Nigeria's devastating civil war ended in 1970, it began a policy of mandatory national service for its youth. According to this program, after completing secondary school in their "home" territory, the participants are required to spend a year performing some service-related activity (such as tutoring younger students, or similar public service activities) in another part of the country. Ideally, they would be exposed to a different language and other cultural traditions.

Zimbabwe also adopted an innovative strategy in the early 1980s with its creation of Heroes Acres. These stylized cemeteries were established throughout the country to honor those who had died during the struggle for independence, known as "chimurenga." In honoring a deceased combatant or hero, the state sought to minimize the manifestation of ethnic polarization in funerary practices.

ONE-PARTY STATE (DE FACTO/DE JURE)

Another way in which a number of modern African leaders and countries attempted to combat the persistent problem of ethnic polarization was through the so-called single- or one-party state. In theory, by eliminating the opportunity for people to divide themselves politically along ethnic lines, more emphasis can be placed on nation building and tackling other social concerns such as economic development. Another argument in favor of the one-party state is that it offers individual talent, regardless of ethnicity, the opportunity to rise through the ranks of the party to offices of leadership. Yet another argument put forward in support of such governance is that democracy as it has been practiced in Western countries is a foreign concept to the African continent, which traditionally had chiefs, kingdoms, and top-down rule. Many prominent post-independence leaders have spoken in favor of this traditional form of government, including Julius Nyerere (1922–1999) of Tanzania and Kenneth Kaunda of Zambia.

In Africa, there has been the establishment of the one-party state by law, political statute, or referendum (de jure). The other form of a single-party state (de facto) exists where the ruling party has all major state apparatus (both social and developmental) at its disposal. Throughout much of the post-independence era, many African countries, which began as multi-party states, reformed constitutionally as single-party states. As of 2010, a majority of African states are effectively one-party ruled.

The reasons offered for adopting the one-party system, however, have not held up under scrutiny. Tanzania under Julius Nyerere performed very poorly economically because of his adherence to strict socialist ideology. One-party systems in Malawi, Zaire (now known as the Democratic Republic of Congo), and Uganda under the rules of Hastings Kamuzu Banda (c. 1900–1997), Mobutu Sese Seko (1930–1997), and Idi Amin (c. 1924–2003), respectively, were repressive, restrictive, and even brutal against those who differed in ideology or opposed their dictatorial rule. These were also examples in which ethnic loyalties were actively exploited. One-party states in Africa have also had a tradition of controlling the means of public communication, such as print and visual media as well as radio communications. This form of censorship has frequently made it difficult for dissenting views to be heard.

After years of political in-fighting and dramatic instances of violence in Zimbabwe, the two major political parties there, the Zimbabwe African People's Union (ZAPU) and the Zimbabwe African National Union (ZANU), emerged as a united single party, ZANU (PF), in 1987, thus forming a de facto single-party state. Other political parties were not outlawed, but the power apparatus clearly fell into the ZANU sphere of control. A viable opposition party did not emerge in Zimbabwe until early in the twenty-first century. At that time, the Movement for Democratic Change (MDC) seriously challenged ZANU rule. The ZANU government quickly passed laws and instituted restrictive practices (for instance, banning dissenting voices in the press and through other means) and engaged in alleged political intimidation to limit the access and opportunities of the rival party. Despite such repressive actions, the MDC pressed its agenda for free and open elections, which took place in March 2008. The Movement for Democrat Change won more votes than the ruling ZANU, requiring a run-off between the two parties. The results of the run-off (in which ZANU won a sizeable majority) were denounced internationally as fraudulent. South African President Thabo Mbeki (r. 1999–2008) was among a group of international dignitaries who brokered a power sharing agreement between ZANU and the MDC. The arrangement has been an uneasy one. In October, 2009, the MDC announced that it would stop cooperating with the ZANU government because of persecution of its members.

During the early 1990s, several autocratic African leaders fell from power as the forces of democratization swept across the continent. The socialist leadership of Benin was forced out. Similar changes took place in Mali, and Zambian President Kenneth Kaunda was defeated in 1991. Three years later, Malawi's Hastings Banda was also defeated at the polls.

One of the more positive developments took place in Kenya at the end of 2002. After years of de facto single-party rule by the Kenya Africa National Union, this party was defeated in free and fair national elections by the newly formed National Rainbow Coalition (NARC) with a minimum of disturbances.

Kenya's 2007 general elections, however, yielded very different and disturbing results. Held in December of that year, the general election was a contest between President Kibaki and his recently formed Party of National Unity (a spin-off party from his earlier NARC coalition) and rival Raila Odinga and his Orange Democratic Union. Although all of the pre-election polling indicated that Odinga would win the presidency, overnight it was announced that Kibaki had overtaken his rival and was subsequently declared the winner of the presidential contest. An already stunned country became even more upset when the president quickly had himself sworn into the office for a second term.

Protest around Kenya soon led to large-scale ethnic violence against Kikuyus (the group to which Kibaki belonged) who were living outside of their traditional home areas. This caused many Kikuyus to flee their homes and live in fields. More than 1,000 Kenyans died in the violence over the next two months and more than 200,000 were left homeless.

International intervention was required to settle the conflict. High-profile individuals like former United Nations Secretary General Kofi Annan led a blue ribbon delegation to mediate between the two parties, resulting in the formation of a grand coalition and the signing of the National Accord and Coalition Act in February, 2008. This Act stipulated that Mwai Kibaki would remain as president of Kenya and Raila Odinga would become prime minister.

ECONOMIC STRATEGIES

Throughout the postcolonial period, there have been many efforts to expand economic cooperation among African countries as a means of countering the unfair trade practices of nations outside of Africa. In 1967, the East Africa Community (EAC), which included Kenya, Tanganyika, Uganda, and Zanzibar, was established, but cooperation lasted only a decade until disputes between Kenya and Tanzania broke out. Also during this period, Tanzania invaded Uganda to oust dictator Idi Amin, further undermining the potential of the EAC. Another arrangement for economic cooperation, The Economic Community of West African States (ECOWAS), was established in 1975 to ease trade among its sixteen member states. Similarly, the Southern African Development Coordinating Conference (SADCC) was formed to combat South Africa's economic dominance of the region. These agreements, however, have come with difficulties. In the case of ECOWAS, for example, Nigeria, which has the largest population and economy in the region, has on more than one occasion forcibly exercised its will on the smaller states.

WOMEN

Until recently, the African story had been told exclusively from an elite male perspective. History recorded the Mau Mau conflict (formally known as the Land and Freedom Movement) in Kenya in the 1950s, but relatively little was said about the role of women in that struggle for independence. Many women took the Mau Mau oath of commitment to the movement. Women were also central to the struggle for independence in Zimbabwe, where they operated in traditional roles as nurses and caretakers, but with many also receiving formal military training in the Soviet Union, North Korea, Zambia, and Mozambique, among other places. When independence was won in that southern African country in 1980, women were rewarded with laws designed to expand and protect women's rights (including the right to vote).

In the realm of politics, African women have made significant gains, but there is still a long way to go. Most presidential cabinets on the continent will have a minister of state responsible for women's affairs. Women's numbers have swollen the ranks in cabinet positions as ministers of transportation, culture, and health, and they hold posts throughout the diplomatic corps. Several countries, including Zimbabwe and South Africa, have had women deputies or vice presidents. Burundi's second vice president, Alice Nzomukunda, resigned her position in 2006 after serving only one year in office. In November 2005, Liberia "broke" with African tradition and elected Ellen Johnson-Sirleaf as its head of state. That event marked the first time a woman was elected as a head of state on the African continent.

In many other areas, women have not experienced the same kinds of advances. Many countries have enacted laws banning the cutting of female genitalia (also referred to as female circumcision), but those laws have not been enforced strongly enough to make a significant impact. African women continue to struggle with other issues as well, including inheritance rights, reproductive rights, customary and traditional rights, and the need for equitable treatment in the courts regarding issues such as domestic violence.

The case of Wambui Otieno in Kenya is an example of the struggle that women continue to face. In the late 1980s, she had to fight in the courts for the right to bury her husband (S. M. Otieno, who was a well-known attorney) when his family insisted that as a member of the Luo clan they, by custom, had that responsibility and obligation. Although she lost the right to bury her husband, she retained their joint estate and finances. Wambui Otiono made national headlines in the country once more in 2003 when, at age sixty-seven, she married a twenty-eight-year-old man.

The impact of civil and military unrest on the continent has affected women more severely than men. Women who lose husbands, fathers, or brothers to conflict become more vulnerable and economically disadvantaged. In some cases, they may resort to commercial sex work as a means of economic survival.

Women's voices, however, are increasingly heard in areas of creative and expressive arts that, for a long time, were also dominated by men. The threat to this development appears to increase with the incidence of HIV cases, which, as of 2010, affected African women at a twelve-to-one ratio to men.

NEW DIRECTION AND CHALLENGES FOR A NEW CENTURY

In 2004, South Africa celebrated its tenth anniversary as an independent African state. Between 1948 to the early 1990s, the country suffered under state-organized racial segregation, oppression, and degradation, which privileged the country's whites over other racial groups.

After decades of political and often violent resistance, the African National Congress (ANC), under the leadership of Nelson Mandela, took control of the government in 1994. Four years earlier, Mandela had been released after twenty-seven years of imprisonment, and became an international symbol of resistance, perseverance, and reconciliation. Although he served only one term in office as South Africa's first president elected in a one-person, one-vote exercise, he has occupied a larger-than-life Nkrumah-like position throughout the African world.

As Africa's largest and most prosperous economy with impressive nuclear military credentials, South Africa is poised to lead the rest of the continent. In the early 2000s, then South African President Thabo Mbeki called for an African renaissance, which he envisioned as a regeneration of African pride, technology, innovativeness, and accomplishment. Sadly, that vision has not yet materialized. His administration also had to do worldwide damage control over his government's controversial stance on HIV/AIDS, which suggested that AIDS was not a viral disease caused by the HIV virus but instead was an immune system breakdown caused by the effects of poverty—poor nourishment and general ill-health. That position among others contributed to Mbeki's somewhat unceremonious departure from the presidency after a no-confidence vote in 2008.

The African renaissance, however, is in danger of being sidetracked by the HIV/AIDS pandemic. The numbers infected and those who have died from the disease have the potential to ravage the African continent in the same way the bubonic plague devastated sixteenth-century Europe. The occurrence of the disease also points out gender disparities and politics (for every one man infected, there are twelve women infected). How the African continent deals with this phenomena will determine in the success of its general social, political, and developmental objectives for the next generation.

The other social threat facing Africa is the repeated outbreak of religious violence in various countries. Nigeria has had several incidents of conflict between Christians and Muslims in recent years. Efforts to correct such tensions have been minimal and the root causes of these disputes have not really been addressed. In other parts of West Africa, there continue to be religious tensions, but they are not nearly as severe as in Nigeria. The Mano River Basin, comprising Guinea, Sierra Leone, and Liberia, has been economically devastated by civil conflict that has raged throughout much of the 1980s and 1990s. Religious institutions have played a significant role in helping to resettle refugees displaced by the fighting and have functioned as a vehicle for conflict resolution. The

World Conference of Religions for Peace (WCRP, founded in 1970), a coalition of representatives of the world's major religions, has encouraged Christian and Muslim leaders in the region to work together through the formation of organizations such as the Inter-religious Council of Sierra Leone (IRCSL, 1997), which in 1999 helped bring about the signing of the Lome Peace Accord in that nation. There are many African organizations that seek to address the delicate issue of religious intolerance on the continent. The Project for Christian-Muslim Relations in Africa (PROCMURA) has, among its primary aims, the facilitation of constructive engagement between Christians and Muslims and the reduction of worrying and negative relations. As part of the effort to improve relations, participants have shared gifts and sent greetings and goodwill messages on the occasion of major religious festivals. They have also formed joint committees of Christians and Muslims to address such issues as the implementation of Islamic law (*Shari'a*) in northern Nigeria and to encourage governments to stop making assistance programs and political appointments dependent on one's religious affiliation. They have spoken out against the polarization of society into Christian and Muslim; their efforts represent an African solution to an ongoing challenge in the region.

There are also Christian/Muslim tensions involved in the civil war in southern Sudan's Darfur region, but ethnic conflicts have been the primary source of strife in that area. Since 2003, there have been many documented cases of violence against the local population and more than two million people have lost their homes or have been forced into refuge in other countries. One of the major antagonists in the crisis has been the Sudanese government-supported militia (although such claims have been denied) known as the Janjaweed. They have carried out systematic violence against the non-Arab civilians in the region, and sexual assaults against women have been a routine occurrence. Opposing the Janjaweed have been two rebel groups, the Sudanese Liberation Army (SLM) and the Justice and Equality Movement (JEM). In 2006, the SLM signed a peace agreement, but there were dissenter affiliates of the organization who refused to sign. In 2007 the United Nations implemented a 25,000 troop peace-keeping force to minimize the atrocities. Earlier efforts to keep peace in the region have also been attempted by the African Union with a much smaller force. Also in 2007, the International Criminal Court (ICC) issued arrest warrants for several Janjaweed militiamen and other government leaders. The following year, the same court filed war crime warrants against Sudanese President Omar al-Bashir, accusing him of genocide and murder. The genocide charge has been the most controversial, as major governments including the United States, Britain, and China (which relies heavily upon Sudanese oil reserves) have been slower to embrace that charge.

THE MODERN DAY PEOPLE OF AFRICA

GEOGRAPHY

As the second-largest continent on the globe, Africa is divided by the equator and bordered to the west by the Atlantic Ocean and to the east by the Indian Ocean. Its more than 11.6 million square miles could contain North America, Argentina, Europe, India, and China. The continent is composed of fifty-three nation states and six islands. It also has 16,000 miles of coastline and eight time zones.

Africa is essentially a huge plateau divided naturally into two sections. Northern Africa, a culturally and historically Mediterranean region, includes the Sahara desert—the world's largest expanse of desert. Areas south of the Sahara also contain some desert land, but are primarily tropical, with rain forests clustered around the equator; vast savanna grasslands covering more than 30% of the continent and surrounding the rain forests on the north, east, and south; some mountainous regions; and rivers and lakes that formed from the natural uplifting of the plateau's surface.

There are many geographical wonders throughout the African continent, including Mounts Kenya and Kilimanjaro. Mount Kilimanjaro has the highest peak (over 19,000 feet) and is one of the tallest mountains in the world. Major bodies of waters include the rivers Niger, Senegal, Congo, Zambezi (home of the mile-wide Victoria Falls, one of the world's seven natural wonders), Orange, Limpopo, Malawi, and Nile (the longest river in the world); lakes Tanganyika, Albert, Rudolf, and Victoria (the second-largest freshwater body in the world). The Libyan, Nubian, and Kalahari are among the largest deserts on the continent.

ECONOMICS/NATURAL RESOURCES

A mineral-rich continent, Africa is a prime source of copper, diamonds, gold, manganese, oil, uranium, zinc, and several other deposits. The equatorial forests produce ebony, teak, and rosewood, while cash crops include bananas, cocoa, coffee, cloves, cotton, sisal, sugarcane, tobacco, yams, and all kinds of nuts, including cashews and groundnuts. Agriculture has formed the basis of most African economies for centuries, but the vast potential was not always developed during Africa's colonial period. Despite such resources, many African nations rank among the poorest in the world. The artificial boundaries set up by colonialism often facilitated one area or region being given preferential treatment. In turn, ethnic conflicts

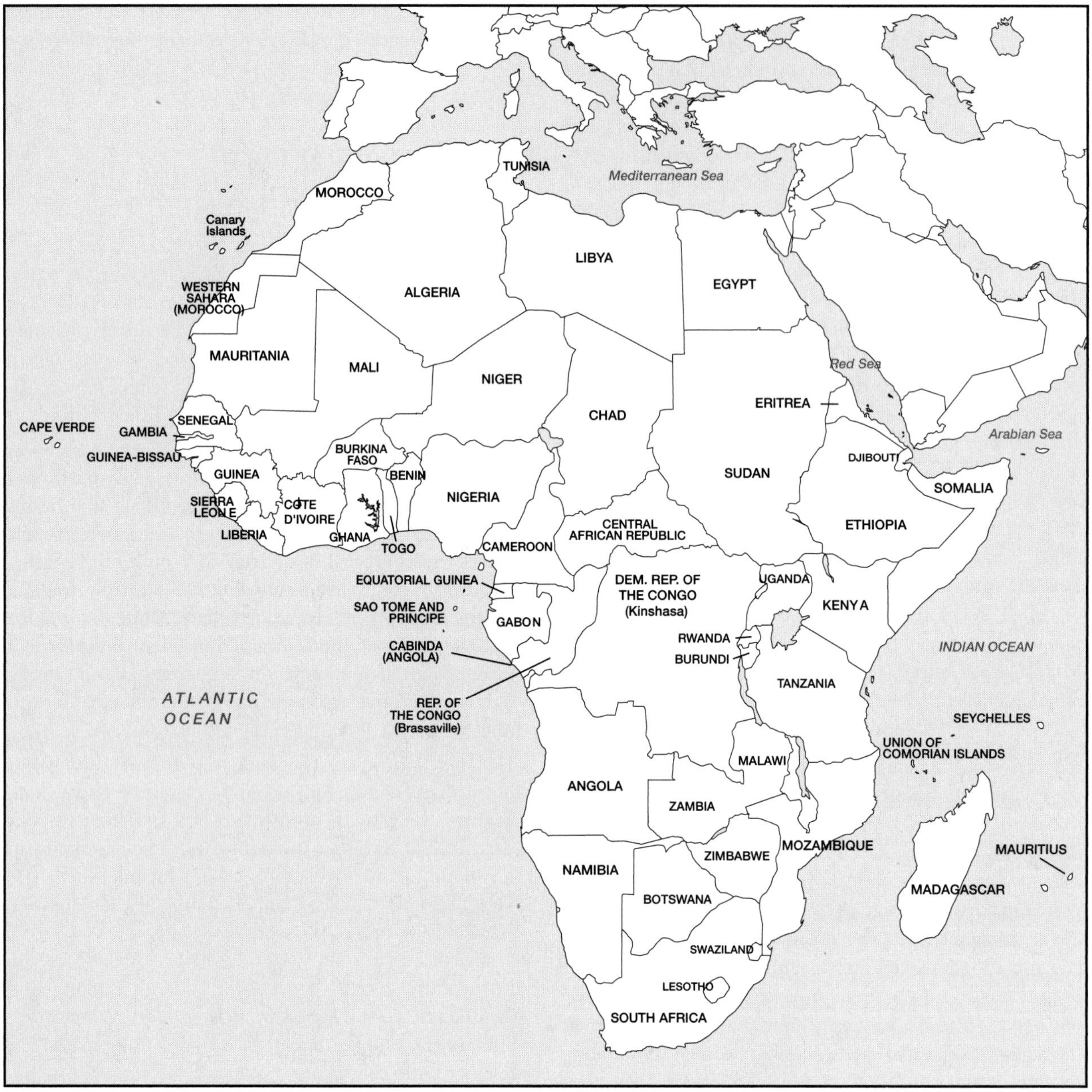

Map of Africa, early twenty-first century. GALE

broke out or were perpetuated. In addition, droughts, lack of technological skills, and at times, corrupt government have all contributed to the weak economies encountered in much of the continent.

Though Africa does have booming urban and industrial centers—for example, Durban, Cape Town, and Johannesburg, South Africa; Lagos, Nigeria; Dakar, Senegal; Harare, Zimbabwe; Accra, Ghana, and Cairo, Egypt—the continent is better known to visitors for the national parks and reserves of East and southern Africa. Wildlife concentrations in these locations vary, but include antelope, impala, Thompson's gazelles, and wildebeests; buffalo, hippos, and rhinos; elephants; giraffes; zebras; crocodiles; a variety of bird species; hyenas, jackals, and wild dogs; and cheetahs, leopards, and lions.

Kenya, located in East Africa, is one of the oldest and most popular game-viewing destinations for safari-seeking tourists. The Samburu National Reserve (at the banks of the Ewaso Nyiro River), Lake Nakuru (one of the soda lakes of the Rift Valley and home to many animals, including flamingos, warthogs, and rhinos), the Masai Mara National Reserve (established in 1961), and

Amboseli (which is northwest of Mount Kilimanjaro and borders Tanzania) attract regional and international visitors annually. In Tanzania itself, there is Lake Manyara National Park, Serengeti National Park (famous for it annual migration of zebras and wildebeests), and Ngorongoro Crater (a natural amphitheater that was formed by the collapse of a volcano). Uganda features Bwindi Forest, also known as the impenetrable forest, which is home of the Buhoma Gorilla Camp, and is also home to several species of monkeys and chimpanzees. In the southern region of Africa, South Africa contains ostrich farms; Kruger National Park, one of the continent's largest reserves; Cango Caves; and Kirstenbosch Botanical Gardens. In Zimbabwe, there is Lake Kariba (completed in 1960 and considered one of the greatest manmade achievements in the region), a permanent water source for monkeys, warthogs, waterbuck, and other species, including birds; Hwange, a game reserve filled with more than 107 species; and the Zambezi Nature Sanctuary and Crocodile Farm.

POPULATION

The African continent holds more than 1 billion people, which is approximately 15% of the world's population. Having a higher birthrate than any other continent, there are projections that Africa's population will exceed 2 billion by 2040. As of 2010, a majority of the population lives in rural areas, which poses challenges for tallying precise population numbers. Among those areas where there are heavy concentrations of population are Nigeria; southern Ghana; along the Gulf of Guinea; Benin and Togo; the Nile Valley; in northern Sudan; the East Africa highlands of Ethiopia, Kenya, and Tanzania; eastern Democratic Republic of the Congo; the eastern and southern coasts; and the inland High Veld of South Africa. The desert and mountain regions are largely uninhabited.

The collective emphasis that continental Africans place on childbirth makes the idea of population control foreign to most African countries. Because of limited resources, there is a fear that the continent's rapid population growth will cause later generations to struggle with severe food and water shortages. Unplanned urbanization is also a growing concern for several African governments. In the search for employment, many rural dwellers have moved to the cities, where there may not be appropriate resources and housing to support the growth. A growing number of African cities have populations in excess of 100,000, including Johannesburg, Ibadan, Lagos, Cairo, Nairobi, Harare, Lusaka, and Accra, among others. Zimbabwe began a controversial course of action in 2005 when it systematically destroyed informal housing and markets in high density areas throughout its capital. Called "Operation Murambatsvina," its stated objective was to remove the slums and associated inferior living conditions in Zimbabwe and replace them with decent, affordable housing. By 2009, however, the government had not replaced those destroyed homes with livable new dwellings. While the action was condemned internationally as a political ploy to weaken voter strength in urban areas, other African countries studied the Zimbabwean strategy in the event that they might have to implement similar plans.

LANGUAGE

There are an estimated 2,000–3,000 languages spoken on the African continent, with as many as 8,000 different dialects, including indigenized forms of English, French, and Portuguese. Hausa, followed by Swahili, are the most widely spoken languages on the African continent, but there are close to fifty languages that are spoken by groups of 1 million or more people. Among them are Afrikaans, Arabic (spoken mainly in North Africa), Ga, Fula, Igbo, Kikuyu, Lingala, Malinke, Nguni (which includes SiNdebele, Xhosa, and Zulu), SeTwana-SeSotho, Shona, and Yoruba.

The language is often found to be the name of the group that speaks it (i.e., Ashanti, Luo, and Wolof). Hausa and Swahili, however, would not fit that pattern neatly because many people use both languages across several borders for commercial purposes. It is common in many parts of the continent, especially in the south, for individuals to be fluent in several languages (as many as four or more). By and large, however, one can still move around the African continent with facility in English, French, and to a lesser extent, Portuguese.

Several African languages are tonal, which means for successful communication, the speaker must employ certain syllabic rises and descents. Speakers of languages that are not tonal (English, for example) find this concept difficult to understand. However, speakers of Chinese (a language that is also tonal) find it easier to learn an African tonal language.

Many African languages were never translated into written form before contact with European colonists in the nineteenth century. As a result, many cultures developed very long and rich oral traditions. In those scenarios, the oral tradition was the only method of conveying customs, practices, legacies, and history from generation to generation in ancient times. Specialists whose job it was to carry out this function were highly skilled professionals whose training typically began when they were children. Within many West African traditions, such a person was known as a *griot*, or oral historian. In many cases, the griots' knowledge and information is as factual as other sources because of their extensive preparation.

LITERATURE

African literature must be considered a composite of both written and oral tradition (which itself can be based on myths and legends), but because several dramatists had their written and oral works performed on the stage, the lines between oral tradition, written works, and stage portrayals become somewhat blurred. For example, the Nobel Prize-winning author Wole Soyinka's celebrated work *Death and the King's Horseman* became known to the world as a play, but it existed in oral tradition before that and was based on an actual incident from Nigeria's colonial past in the 1940s. To further blur the picture, the above-mentioned incident was adapted as a play by at least one other dramatist.

Much of the folklore of Africa is available only in the oral and dramatic form. One of the best examples of oral literature is the epic of Sundiata, founder of the West African kingdom of Mali in the thirteenth century. However, written literature is not without its own rich history in Africa. For centuries, written literature in Amharic, Arabic, Hausa, and Swahili has existed and, more recently, there has been a sharp increase in African literature written in the languages of the European colonial powers.

The West Coast of Africa, with its long tradition as a breeding ground for the arts, is (or was) home to some of the most important of today's African writers. Among these, Nigerian Chinua Achebe (now living in the United States, as of 2010), author of *Man of the People*, the story of a newly independent African state strangely reminiscent of Achebe's own country, rails against corruption and the cult of personality. All of his work, which includes *Things Fall Apart*, *Arrow of God*, *No Longer at Ease*, and *Home and Exile*, voice a concern for the loss of native culture in the flood of imported European values. This struggle between African traditions coming into conflict with modernization or Westernization is a recurring theme in several works. For example, in Nigerian writer Onuora Nzekwu's *Blade Among the Boys*, the clash between a sensitive young man's native Igbo religion and imported Christian ideals causes him a great deal of confusion. Other Nigerian writers who have or have had distinguished careers themselves include Cyprian Ekwensi (1921–2007), Tanure Ojaide, Funso Aiyejina, and Amos Tutuola (1920–1997).

Most of the best-known literature out of South Africa during the twentieth century has come from white authors uneasy about their country's racist policies. William Plomer's (1903–1973) *Turbott Wolfe*, published in 1925, well before the imposition of apartheid, argued for a mixing of white and black blood in South Africa to prevent a future in which the nation's whites dominated the country. Probably the best-known of the anti-apartheid novels is Alan Paton's (1903–1988) *Cry, the Beloved Country*. Other South African authors, such as Dan Jacobson, J. M. Coetzee, Andre Brink, and Nadine Gordimer, have elevated this literature of protest to a new level of excellence. Gordimer received the Nobel Prize for Literature in 1991 following fellow Africans Wole Soyinka of Nigeria in 1986 and Naguib Mahfouz (1911–2006) of Egypt in 1988. Among the better known black writers of South Africa are Sindiwe Magona, Zakes Mda, and Mandla Langa.

Other of Africa's best-known authors include Cameroon's Mongo Beti (1932–2001); Ghana's Ayi Kwei Armah and J. E. Casely-Hayford (1866–1930); Kenya's Ngugi wa Thiong'o; Lesotho's Thomas Mofolo (1876–1948); Nigeria's Buchi Emecheta, Flora Nwapa (1931–1993), and Ken Saro-Wiwa (1941–1995), who was executed by the Nigerian government for political activism; Senegal's Mariama Ba (1929–1981), Sembene Ousmane (1923–2007), and Leopold Sedar Senghor (1906–2001); Somalia's Nuruddin Farah; South Africa's Bessie Head (1937–1986), Ezekiel Mphahlele, and Lewis Nkosi; Uganda's Okot p'Bitek (1931–1982) and Moses Isegawa, and Dennis Brutus.

FILM

Film is a relatively new art form to Africa, but it has been embraced eagerly as yet another medium through which to tell the many stories of the continent. Perhaps more than any other section of the continent, West Africa (particularly the former French-speaking colonies) has been drawn to motion picture production. Among West Africa's leading filmmakers have been Senegal's Moussa Toure and the late Sembène Ousmane; Burkina Faso's Idrissa Ouedraogo, Drissa Toure, Gaston Kabore, and Dani Kouyate; and Mali's Cheik Oumar Sissoko and Abdoulaye Ascofare. From Cameroon have come the motion pictures of Jean-Marie Teno and Bassek Ba Kkobhio, while Cote d'Ivoire has also produced films.

The former English-speaking colonies of Africa have also managed to turn out a large number of well-received films. Among the more successful filmmakers in this group are Moses Adejumo (also known as Baba Sala) and Fred Chagu of Nigeria, John Akomfrah of Ghana, Simon Bright of Zimbabwe, and Barry Feinberg, Athol Fugard, and Peter Goldsmid of South Africa.

Over the last decade, African women have become more involved in motion pictures. Major political changes in South Africa have helped to open that market to a much wider range of "alternative" films and videos than was possible before.

In 1993, the films coming out of Africa were few in number but notable in quality. Among them, *Samba Traore*, directed by Idrissa Ouedraogo, employed an age-old plot line quite effectively: the flight of a young criminal to avoid punishment for his crime. Burundian director Leonce Ngabo cooperated with French and Swiss filmmakers in the production of *Gito the Ungrateful*, the tale of a youth searching for his identity. Director Roger Gneon M'Bala of the Cote d'Ivoire explored the subject of religion in his *In the Name of Christ*. One of the few notable African films of 1994 was *Le Ballon d'Or*, directed by Cheik Boukoure of Guinea, which related the story of a young boy's dream of becoming a world-class soccer player.

Some of the most impressive African films of 1995 came from the tiny West African country of Burkina Faso. These included Drissa Toure's *Haramuya*, Dani Kouyate's *Keita, Voice of the Griot*, and Idrissa Ouedraogo's *Africa, My Africa*. From Cameroon came *The Great White of Lambarene*, an African evaluation of the famous theologian, physician, philospher, and musician Albert Schweitzer. Also from Cameroon came one of the best African films of 1996: *Clando*, the story of a young foe of a repressive African regime, who immigrates illegally to Germany. Burkina Faso's film community produced some of the most notable motion pictures of 1997. Foremost among these were Idrissa Ouedraogo's *Kina and Adams*, which told the story of the relationship between two poor farmers, and Gaston Kabore's *Buud Yam*, the tale of a young man's quest to find medicine for his ailing foster sister. Stirring up controversy in 1997 was Guinea's *Dakan*, director Mohamed Camara's exploration of homosexuality, the first African motion picture to tackle the subject.

Significant African films of the late 1990s and the early years of the new millennium included South African music video director Akin Omotoso's *God Is African*, recounting the death of Nigerian writer Ken Saro-Wiwa, and Senegalese director Joseph Gai Ramaka's *Karmen Gei*. Zimbabwean Simon Bright's 1996 film *Flame* followed the different paths of two female combatants in that country's independence struggle. Also impressive were Guinea's *Temporary Registration*; Senegal's *L'Afrance* and *And So Angels Die*; Zimbabwe's *One Sunday Morning*; and Gabon's *Dollar*.

In 2005, the South African-produced film, *Tsotsi* (based on the Anthol Fugard novel) won the American Academy Award for the best foreign film. The year before another South African-produced film, *Yesterday*, dealt with the impact of the HIV/AIDS epidemic on a rural community.

MUSIC

To most Westerners, the mention of "African music" evokes the image of a drum. This, of course, is a mistaken impression that has been perpetuated by many stereotypes (several of which are negative) and fostered and reinforced, unfortunately, by a good deal of scholarship. However, there are a few generalizations that can correctly be made about African music. The first is that there are both group and solo instrumentalists to be found on the continent. The second and most important generalization is that accompanied song is far more universal on the African continent than any instrumental tradition. In fact, there are many stylized vocalities common on the African continent and among African-derived musical traditions, such as falsetto, ululation, yodels, glissandi, shouts, screams, and moans. These characteristics are often overlooked while traditional emphasis has been given to instrumental traditions, especially drumming.

Sustained interest in African music dates back to the 1930s, but there have been many who have collected and documented a variety of traditions that date much earlier. Late African scholars like Nicholas George Ballanta of Sierra Leone and Ephraim Amu of Ghana were active musicians and produced written works of historical importance. Among the eminent collectors/recordists was the late Hugh Tracey, who began documenting musical traditions in Southern and Central Africa in the 1920s and continued doing so into the 1970s. He founded the International Library of African Music in South Africa in the 1950s to preserved and study musical genres on the continent. The tradition was continued by his son, Andrew Tracey, and others.

By the early 1960s and into the 1970s, when many African countries were either independent or actively engaged in independence movements, several "African" voices (including Kwabena Nketia (b. 1921), Samuel Akpabot (1931–2000), Francis Bebey (1929–2001), and Kazadi wa Mukuna emerged as scholars, interpreters, and authorities on various African musical traditions. Since that time, there has been substantial interest in African popular musical styles. This interest has resulted in major radio programs dedicated to playing African music (such as Afro Pop worldwide), compact disk circulation, and videos being generated. In addition, many popular African musicians have now established international reputations.

Many popular musical styles have developed on the continent, several of which are hybrids or represent some blending with other sources. Kwela is a pennywhistle-based style that developed in townships of South Africa and was first noticed in the 1940s and 1950s. Highlife is one of the older twentieth-century African popular musical genres and appears to have been influenced by African American jazz bands as early as the 1920s. Ghana is the likely birthplace of the highlife style, which is characterized by the use of trumpets and saxophones. Juju, another older musical genre, is a drumming-derived style from the Yoruba that dates to the 1930s. Well-known early practitioners were I. K. Dairo (from the 1950s), Sunny Ade, Ebenezer Obey, and Twins Seven Seven.

Soukous, another well known popular musical genre, has its origins in Central Africa. The term is derived from the French word for "shake." A dance tradition, soukous has Afro-Cuban influences. Because the tradition has spread to other parts of the continent, soukous remains one of the most popular genres after more than fifty years. Apala is another popular Yoruba-derived drumming style. Apala has a very strong secular Muslim following in Nigeria, but has also spread to other parts of the region. In an earlier version, it was used to call worshippers to pray, but increasingly moved outside this sacred setting. Jit is a guitar-based style popularized in Zimbabwe in the late 1970s and 1980s. Also featuring drums, and influenced by highlife and soukous, Jit can be heard in dance halls throughout the region. Makossa is also a dance-related style found in the Cameroon. It seems to have appeared in the early 1950s. Morna, widely considered as the national music of Cape Verde, is a hybrid traditional music that incorporates several Portuguese influences and employs instruments such as violins, accordions, clarinets, and cavaquinho. Morna tends to be mournful and is frequently found in a minor key. Mbalax is a Senegalese (Wolof-derived) percussion tradition that has been popularized by Youssou N'Dour, one of the continent's most renowned popular musicians, who is also a gifted composer.

Musical Instruments, Mindelo, São Vicente, Cape Verde Islands, 1996. *The music of Cape Verde is often performed with instruments made in the town of Mindelo.* **ROBERT VAN DER HILST/CORBIS**

Some of Africa's biggest artists, "cross-over" or otherwise, include Angola's Kuenda Bonga (born Barcelo de Carvallo, he is a political-minded singer-songwriter) and Ruy Mingas (a famous Portuguese-African vocalist and, as of 2010, the current minister of culture for that country); Burkina Faso's Farafina (a group led by balafon virtuoso Mahama Konate); Cape Verde's Cesaria Evora ("The Barefoot Diva"); Congo-Kinshasa's Mbilia Bel (one of Africa's most successful female singers), 4 Etoiles (a group featuring soukous guitarist Syran Mbenza), and Ricardo Lemvo; Makina Loca (an Afro-Latino vocalist), Les Bantous (a rhumba band), Tabu Ley Rochereau (a soukous master), Sam Mangwana (known as "Le Pigeon," since his travels and music have produced mixtures of Cuban, Portuguese-African, and Caribbean rhythms), Tshala Muana ("Queen of Mutuashi," a dance form), Papa Wemba (one of the world's greatest singers), and Zap Mama (an all-female group led by poet Marie Daulne); Gabon's Pierre Akendengue (a blind singer, guitarist, poet, and playwright); Guinea's Bembeya Jazz National (featuring Sekou "Diamond Fingers" Diabate); Mali's Toumani Diabate (considered the world's greatest kora player), Oumou Sangare (the country's favorite female "praise singer"), and Ali Farka Toure (1939–2006, "The Bluesman of Mali"); Nigeria's King Sunny Ade ("The King of Juju") and Fela Anikulapo Kuti (1938–1997, an outspoken social critic, pianist, saxophonist, and singer); Senegal's Baaba Maal (known as "The Nightingale" because of his clear high-pitched voice), Youssou N'Dour (whose style includes a blend of mbalax, reggae, jazz, and calypso music), and Orchestre Baobab de Dakar; Sierra Leone's Abdul Tee-Jay (a London-based studio guitarist adept at several forms including highlife, soukous, makossa, and soca); South Africa's Ladysmith Black Mambazo (an a capella group led by tenor vocalist Joseph Shabalala), Simon "Mahlathini" Nkabinde (1937–1999, legendary, deep-voiced "King of the Groaners"), the Mahotella Queens (mbaqanga mavens), Miriam Makeba (1932–2008, universally proclaimed as "Mama Africa"), Hugh Masekela (trumpet and flugelhorn-playing jazz legend), West Nkosi (1940–1998), and The Soul Brothers (one of the nation's biggest-selling groups); Tanzania's Zuhura Swaleh (a female taarab singer); and Zimbabwe's Stella Chiweshe ("The Queen of Mbira").

Two of Zimbabwe's best-known popular musicians, Thomas Mapfumo and Oliver Mtukudzi, espouse different political viewpoints. Mapfumo, referred to as the "Lion of Zimbabwe," rose to fame during Zimbabwe's liberation struggle (*chimurenga*) and his music was explicitly linked to that movement. He was briefly jailed because of his political views. When independence was won in 1980, Mapfumo was hailed as a national figure. In the early 2000s, however, Mapfumo became critical of President Robert Mugabe's government (a government he had once supported) and composed songs alluding to its widespread corruption. He eventually left Zimbabwe and, as of 2010, lived in self-imposed exile in the United States. Oliver Mtukudzi, on the other hand, has not been as overtly political in his music as Mapfumo. His themes have dealt with social problems, such the spread of the HIV virus and the abuse of women. Mtukudzi's songs often suggest that people should seek God's intervention for their problems. While Mtukudzi continues to enjoy a celebrated and lucrative career in Zimbabwe, Mapfumo's songs have been banned from broadcast on state-run media.

While popular African musical styles have traditionally gained more attention, there is also a legacy of art music (more commonly referred to as classical music) on the African continent. The Nigerian-born Fela Sowande (1905–1987), a celebrated organist and composer, produced several orchestra suites, choral works, and art songs. The *Missa Luba*, a musical setting of the Catholic Mass produced in the 1950s, is a blend of Western art music and traditional Luba-style singing and drumming. More recent examples of this blend can be found in the performances of the Soweto String Quartet. Formed in the 1990s, the highly successful string ensemble has become popular around the world. Yet another South African-based singing group, Afrotenor, has successfully blended Western art music, traditional South African folk melodies, and popular songs. The group modeled itself after the African American performing group, Three Mo' Tenors.

South Africa is also leading in another musical genre—religious music (often referred to as gospel music). There are sacred music choirs found all over the country, and solo artist Rebecca Malope has become an international star, hailed as the country's "Queen of Gospel."

HEALTH

Although there is no continent on the planet that has not been affected by the HIV/AIDS pandemic, the spread of the virus on the African continent has been the most severe. As of 2010, more than 20,000,000 Africans had died of AIDS since the epidemic was first recognized in the early 1980s. Of that number, close to 4,000,000 have been children. There has also been a dramatic rise in the number of AIDS "orphans" who have lost one or both parents to the virus.

The statistics are staggering throughout the continent, but southern Africa has recorded the highest numbers of confirmed cases of HIV. By the beginning of the twenty-first century, South Africa had a 1-in-5 ratio of HIV-positive adults. Comparable statistics can be found in Zimbabwe, Swaziland, and other countries in the region. While there has been a sustained program to provide antiretroviral therapies for many affected, typically these medications will reach only about 20% of those in need. Even that effort, however, has been complicated by the presence of multiple strains of the virus in the different regions of the continent, which require ever-more sophisticated treatment regimens. Among other approaches that several clinics are employing to combat the virus is male circumcision, which reportedly can cut the risk of infection by as much as 60%. While several test vaccines were in the trial stage as of 2010, those solutions appear to be a few years away.

Several African countries took very aggressive steps in combating the virus early on and, as a result, leveled off the growing rates of infection among their populace. At the forefront was Uganda's head of state, Yoweri Museveni. In conjunction with grassroots organizations like The Aids Support Organization (TASO), founded by Noerine Kaleeba in 1987 (Kaleeba lost her husband to AIDS after he contracted the HIV virus from a blood transfusion), Museveni dealt frankly with how the virus is contracted (i.e., sexually) and how it can be avoided (i.e., abstinence, monogamy, or through condom use). TASO's slogan, ABC (Abstain, Be faithful, use Condoms), was touted throughout the country. Using traditional African means of disseminating information, such as impromptu skits, songs, and reenactments, TASO has proved to be an effective tool in the fight against the virus. After receiving funds in 2004 from the Bush administration's President's Emergency Plan for AIDS Relief (PEPFAR), however, TASO was encouraged to promote abstinence over condoms. Other countries on the continent have imitated the TASO model.

While HIV/AIDS has clearly been the most challenging health issue on the African continent, other long-term health problems continue to present themselves. Diseases such as malaria (which kills more people on the continent than HIV) and cholera have not been eradicated. Other conditions like hoof-and-mouth disease and rinderpest emerge periodically and can infect the livestock in certain regions. In 2006, a resistant strain of tuberculosis was detected in several South African townships. The general challenge of access to medicine and proper nutrition is also a barrier to improved overall health in areas that are troubled by civil conflict such as the Darfur region of Sudan.

In the mid-1990s, the highly contagious and deadly Ebola virus struck in the Democratic Republic of the Congo (formerly known as Zaire), Liberia, Gabon, and the Ivory Coast. After a mid-1996 outbreak in Gabon, there was a temporary lull on the Ebola front, until northern Uganda was struck by an outbreak in the fall of 2000. Uganda was struck again with the ebola virus in 2007 and the Democratic Republic of Congo the following year. Ebola is one of the most contagious and lethal viruses known to mankind, and the international scientific community has come together in trying to locate the sources of contamination in hopes of bringing an end to a virus whose newer strains have increased the fatality rate of the afflicted from 80% to 97% since earlier outbreaks dating back to the 1970s in the Sudan and the Democratic Republic of Congo.

Food shortages caused by drought and civil conflicts have caused mass starvation and malnutrition in Ethiopia, Somalia, Mozambique, as well as in parts of western Africa. In the late 1980s and into the 1990s, the international community has joined forces to try to alleviate the situation by sending food and aid to the needy and even resorting to peacekeeping military personnel in situations caused by ongoing civil disturbances. In fall 2009, more than fifteen West African countries were affected by heavy flooding, which caused a loss of life totaling more than 200 people.

The practice of female circumcision (sometimes referred to as genital mutilation) is one of many rites of passage performed in parts of Africa that have been denounced by Western society. Many argue that, apart from depriving a woman of an important part of her adult life, the practice often leads to medical problems for women later in life, including physical handicaps, chronic infections, and difficulty in childbirth. While an African and Western effort to stamp out the sometimes fatal ritual is growing, many others decry what they deem to be cultural interference. Tradition holds that the surgery preserves the chastity of those upon whom it is performed.

PEOPLE OF AFRICAN DESCENT IN THE WESTERN HEMISPHERE

Various scholars have demonstrated an African presence in the Americas long before the era of European exploration and settlement in the Western Hemisphere. For example, there has been a proposed link made between the huge Olmec heads found in the Mexican Gulf Coast and the African features they display. Yet another theory offers that Abu Bakari II, King of Mali, sent ships early in the fourteenth century across what is now the Atlantic Ocean and landed in modern-day Mexico as early as 1310. Voyages of exploration and trade between Africa and modern-day Central America seem to have been steady over the next 180 years.

Thus by the time Christopher Columbus arrived in the New World in the 1490s, an African presence had long preceded him in the region. Pedro Alonzo Niño, an African Spaniard, navigated Columbus's ship, the *Santa Maria*, in the explorer's initial voyage. At least thirty Africans accompanied Vasco Nunez de Balboa when he first reached the Pacific Ocean in 1513. What was recorded as one of the period's most daring exploration adventures was that of the African Portuguese, Estevan de Dorantes, who accompanied the explorer Panfilo de Narvaez on an expedition to modern-day Florida in 1527. Estevan and a surviving party of fellow explorers were captured by Native Americans, but eventually escaped. He was ultimately killed by Zuni Indians around 1540.

By the mid-sixteenth century, African arrivals to the New World had begun in earnest; however, unlike before, they did not come as explorers. An early sixteenth-century recommendation made by the activist priest, Bartolome de Las Casas (later Bishop of Chiapa), that "Africans" be used for labor purposes instead of the indigenous Indians fundamentally altered the course of human history. In response to the de las Casas request, Spain's King Charles I granted license in 1518 for the importation of thousands of captured Africans to Hispaniola, Puerto Rico, and Jamaica for the purpose of harvesting sugar and other types of spices. Many Spanish New World settlers took advantage of this opportunity and the infamous trans-Atlantic trade in Africans was under way. Although the Spanish had initial control of the enterprise, the Portuguese quickly joined along with other European powers. Over the next three centuries, between 20,000,000 and 30,000,000 Africans were transported forcibly to the Americas. The vast majority of the enslaved were taken to South America, enduring en route some of the most brutal and cruel treatment and living conditions ever recorded in human history.

The forced labor varied from territory to territory. Where large plantations developed, the labor was generally agricultural, but many enslaved Africans also worked in gold and silver mines to harvest precious minerals. Life for the enslaved Africans in the New World was generally harsh and unpleasant, and their frustration over the elusiveness of freedom sometimes boiled over into unrest and even outright revolt. In 1620, a group of escapees in Santo Domingo created a colony, which staged several uprisings. The island was also the setting of a well-known

Map of South America, Early Twenty-first Century. GALE

late-eighteenth-century rebellion, when close to 500,000 Africans led by Toussaint-Louverture took control of the territory from the British and Spanish. In 1801, Toussaint-Louverture conquered Santo Domingo, which had been ceded by Spain to France in 1795, and thus he governed the entire island. Following a hard-fought resistance to French colonial ambitions in the Western Hemisphere, Toussaint-Louverture struck a peace treaty with Napoleon in 1802.

Toussaint-Louverture's successful independence campaign in Haiti (as the island of Hispaniola later became known) inspired similar actions among enslaved Africans in North America. There are about four movements that have received extensive attention in U.S. history books (i.e., the Stono Rebellion in 1739 outside Charleston, South Carolina; the Gabriel Rebellion in 1800 in Richmond, Virginia; the Denmark Vesey Rebellion in 1822 also in Charleston, and the Nat Turner rebellion in 1831 in Southampton County, Virginia). However, between 1800 and 1850, close to 200 liberation movements were staged by enslaved Africans throughout the United States.

During and just after the American Revolutionary War, several newly created states formally abandoned African enslavement, but the southern states generally regarded the "peculiar institution" as part of their legacy and essential to their economic survival. By the 1820s, the foundation was laid for regional conflict.

There were several events that punctuated regional differences between northern and southern sentiments regarding African enslavement. For example, the 1839 *Amistad* incident in which enslaved Africans forcibly took control of a ship bound from Havana to Puerto Principe, Cuba and ordered the crew to steer the vessel back to the Africa. En route, the vessel was intercepted by the U.S. Navy and brought to shore in the northeastern United States. The Africans were charged with sedition, but ultimately found not guilty and allowed to return to Africa.

Active since the colonial period, the abolitionist movement dramatically increased its operation in the 1820s after the Missouri Compromise issue was settled. One of the results of the movement was the founding of the Underground Railroad, which gave secret aid to those seeking freedom. A variety of techniques were employed to assist in this process. "Alert" and "map" songs which secretly encoded information about escaping were among the vehicles used in the freedom quests. Quilts concealing escape routes in plain site were yet another means of communicating useful information to runaways. Escapees often used a strong-smelling liquid like turpentine to throw dogs off their scent.

Another example of the northern/southern divide on the issue of black enslavement was the passage of the Fugitive Slave Laws in the 1850s that allowed for a southern slaveholder to go anywhere throughout the country to reclaim his "property." This resulted in escapees having to seek safety outside U.S. borders in Canada or Mexico.

On the eve of the Civil War in 1860, blacks in the South numbered about 4 million, making up approximately one-third of the total population of the region. At the same time, there were about 500,000 free blacks living throughout the United States, slightly more than half of them in the South. Several defining events during this period further divided the country on the issue of African enslavement, including the Dred Scott decision, which ruled that even though an enslaved person lived in a "free" state, his or her enslaved status was not altered.

One of the immediate forerunners of the war was John Brown's raid on the Harpers Ferry Arsenal in northwestern Virginia (now a part of West Virginia). Brown recruited several black participants for his campaign. When he was subsequently captured and hanged, he became a martyr for the cruelty and inhumanity of black enslavement. After the Civil War broke out in 1861, few thought it would last long. Black troops eventually participated in the fighting, mostly for the Union, but by the end of the war, they were inducted to fight for the Confederacy as well. In the final analysis more than six hundred thousand lives were lost in the fighting, which lasted several years.

Constitutional amendments passed after the Civil War by the U.S. Congress gave statutory recognition to African Americans. For example, the Thirteenth, Fourteenth, and Fifteenth Amendments gave them freedom from enslavement, recognized African Americans as citizens of the country, and gave them the right to vote, respectively. Although these laws were on the books, they were often undermined, avoided, or simply not enforced in certain parts of the country, most notably in the South. It took another century for this group of Americans to begin to realize their basic rights as U.S. citizens, when the Civil Rights movement of the 1960s forced the country to begin to live up to its promises of justice for all.

Progress for African Americans (the term "African Americans" was not formally embraced in the U.S. until the late 1980s) continued through the 1970s, '80s, '90s, and into the twenty-first century. In 2008, however, U.S. voters took a historical step by electing Barack Obama as the nation's forty-fourth president. Of Kenyan ancestry, Obama embraced his African heritage, but held himself as an example of the American dream. His history-making election was heralded worldwide.

The system of African enslavement in the Caribbean was generally an extension of the European power that had governed the territory. However, unlike in the United States where African Americans represented a numerical minority, the African Caribbean population represented a clear majority on most of the islands throughout the region. There were rebellions and uprisings throughout the history of the Caribbean, but even more than forty years after independence in the 1960s, those of African ancestry still hold an inferior position to the smaller numbers of whites, Asians, and East Indian populations collectively. With regard to politics, entrepreneurial activity, and other sectors of the society, the African-derived population still lagged behind in terms of access to things such as education, health care, and other societal advancements. In places like Guyana, however, the East Indian population now outnumbers those of African descent.

In Jamaica, the Rastafarian movement has come to represent an anti-establishment symbol that has spread to other areas of the world, principally through reggae music. It represents one of several distinctive African-derived cultural developments to come out of the region. The collective economic situation in the West Indies continues to represent a challenge. For some time, Haiti has been the poorest country in the Western Hemisphere and has experienced continuous social, economic, and political upheaval well into the twenty-first century. Efforts by the United States to foster economic recovery in Haiti have largely been unsuccessful, and attempts to nurture the fledgling democracy, thus far, have yielded limited results.

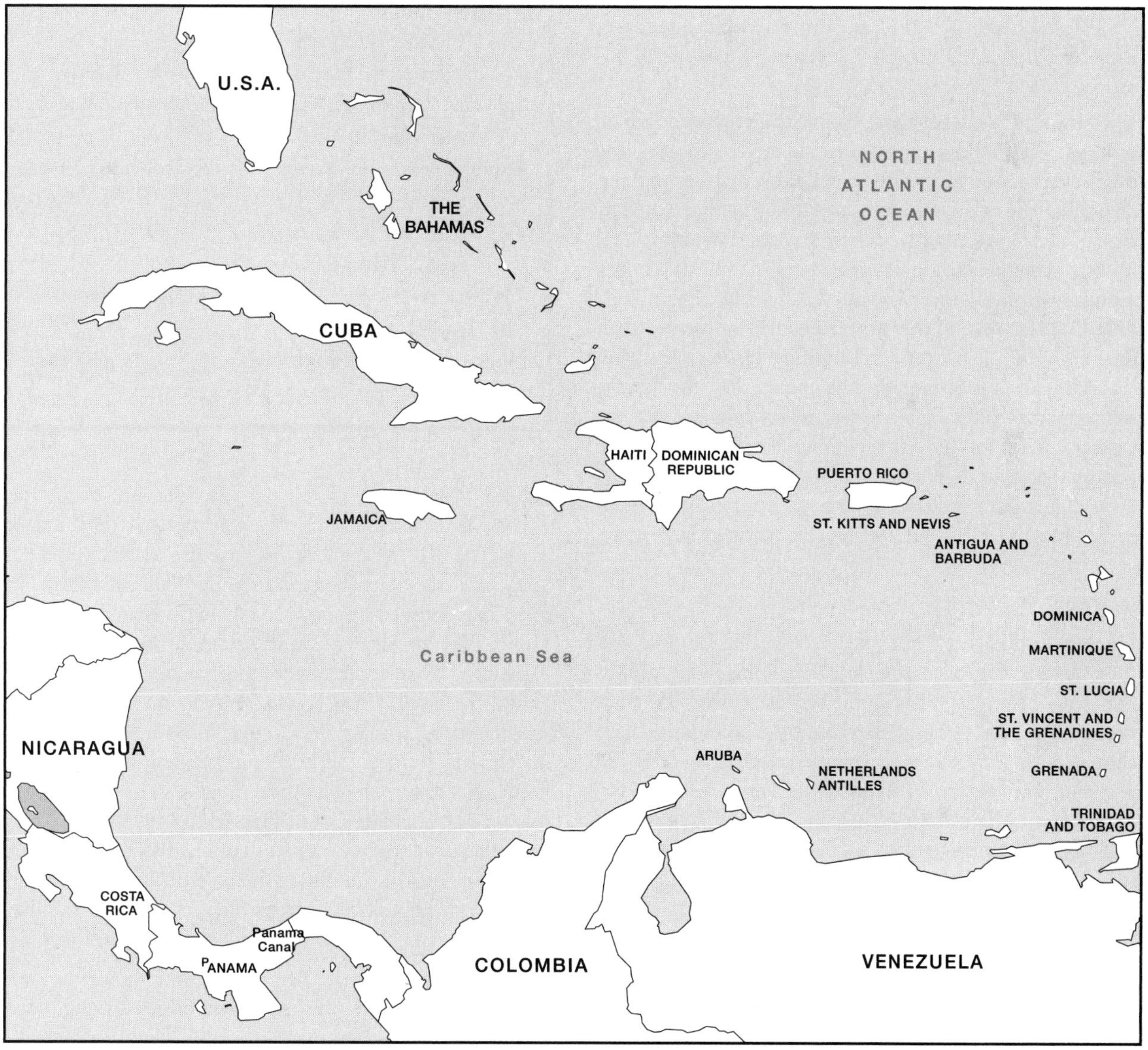

Map of the Caribbean, Early Twenty-first Century. GALE

The earthquake of January 2010 dealt another crippling blow to Haiti. By early February, the estimates of those who perished had reached more than 200,000, with close to 2 million left homeless. The Haitian devastation prompted an international response. All of the experts agree that it will take years for the country to recover from this latest calamity.

COUNTRY PROFILES: AFRICA

"Area" values are given in square kilometers as that is the unit of measurement most common to the countries covered. To figure the area in square miles, multiply the number by 0.3861.

Most of the statistical data in the country profiles come from the U.S. Central Intelligence Agency's publication, *World Factbook 2009*.

"Income" values for each nation are the gross domestic product (GDP) per capita figures as measured using the purchasing power parity (PPP) method, which attempts to determine the relative purchasing power of different currencies over equivalent goods and services. For example, if it costs someone in the United States US$300 to buy a month's worth of groceries, but it costs someone in Ghana only US$100 to buy the same amount of groceries, then the person in Ghana can purchase three times as much for the same amount of money. This means that, though the average citizen of Ghana may earn less money than the average citizen of the United States, money buys more because goods and services cost less in Ghana. Note that GDP figured at purchasing power parity may be three or more times as large as GDP figured at exchange rate parity.

ALGERIA

Since about the year 5 BCE, the area that makes up what is now Algeria has been populated by indigenous groups that have been progressively pushed back from the coast by invaders. As a result, the country's boundaries have shifted during various stages of the conquests. Nearly all Algerians are Muslim of Arab, Berber, or mixed stock.

French colonization of Algeria began in 1830 and continued until 1954, when the indigenous population staged a revolt. A small group of nationalists who called themselves the National Liberation Front (FLN, for the French name Front de Libération Nationale) launched the revolution. Negotiations led to a cease-fire signed by France and the FLN on March 18, 1962; France then declared Algeria independent on July 3 of that year.

Mohammed Ben Bella became Algeria's first post-independence president, but was ousted three years later by defense minister Houari Boumediènne. After Boumediènne died, Chadi Benjadid became the head of state. In 1991, Algeria held its first free election after 30 years of a one-party system, and the National Liberation Front was defeated by the fundamentalist Islamic Salvation Front (FIS) in the first round of voting for the National Assembly. When it appeared clear that the fundamentalist group would win a majority in the second round of voting scheduled for January 1992, the government and army intervened to cancel the elections. Mohammed Boudiaf, a former dissident in the FLN, was installed as president of the ruling State Supreme Council. In May 1992, Boudiaf was assassinated, allegedly by an FIS gunman while delivering a speech in Annaba, continuing the ongoing conflict between the government and the fundamentalist Muslims of the FIS. Algeria has since been in a declared state of emergency.

In 1994, Liamine Zeroual became president and greatly increased the power of that office through constitutional changes approved by voters. The conflict with religious extremists and the FIS continued as both groups boycotted the next round of elections in 1997. This move

ALGERIA

Official name: Democratic and Popular Republic of Algeria
Independence: 5 July 1962 (from France)
Area: 2,381,740 sq km
Form of government: republic
Capital: Algiers
Currency: Algerian dinar (DZD)
Income: US$6,900 (2008 est.)
Population: 34,178,000 (2009 est.)
Ethnic groups: Arab-Berber 99%, European less than 1%
Religious groups: Sunni Muslim (state religion) 99%, Christian and Jewish 1%
Languages: Arabic (official), French, Berber dialects
Literacy: 70% (fifteen years old and over who can read and write; 2006 est.)
Exports: petroleum, natural gas, and petroleum products 97%
Primary export partners: U.S. 23.9%, Italy 14.9%, Spain 11.1%, France 8.6% (2008)
Imports: capital goods, food and beverages, consumer goods
Primary import partners: France 19.8%, Italy 10.9%, China 9%, Germany 5.4% (2008)

allowed the military government to consolidate its hold on power as the level of violence increased in the country, as evidenced by the bloody Ramadan massacres and random killings of that same year. After a flawed election in April 1999, Abdelaziz Bouteflika became president. The new president struck a peace accord with rebels and won approval for an amnesty plan in a September 1999 referendum. Violence flared again in the spring of 2001, over the issue of Berber identity. Violent protests and boycotts of local elections caused the government to concede and recognize Berber as an official language in 2002. Abdelaziz Bouteflika was reelected in in 2004, and again to another five-year term in 2009, but the issue of the Berber autonomy campaign persists.

ANGOLA

Angola's boundaries were formally established by the Berlin West Africa Congress of 1884–1885. Following World War II, Portuguese interest in colonizing Angola increased, leading to the establishment of a strict and harsh colonial rule.

Discontent over Portuguese unwillingness to concede eventual independence led to the formation of the Popular Movement for the Liberation of Angola (MPLA), the National Front for the Liberation of Angola (FNLA), and the National Union for the Total Independence of Angola (UNITA). In January 1975, the Portuguese and leaders from the three liberation movements worked out a complicated agreement—the Alvor Accord—that provided for a transitional government composed of all three groups and for elections in preparation for independence in November of 1975.

Once the Portuguese departed in late 1975, Angola was left in the midst of a fierce struggle for power between the three divided liberation movements. Fueling the civil war was the involvement of such foreign powers as the United States, South Africa, the Soviet Union, and Cuba. South African troops, encouraged by the United States (the U.S. backed the FNLA-UNITA alliance), actually invaded Angola, but were repelled. The Marxist MPLA was finally able to establish control of the country under Augustinho Neto, who ruled as the newly independent country's first president until his death in 1979. José Eduardo Dos Santos succeeded Neto, but the MPLA government, weakened by continuing South African incursions into Angolan territory and by its own inflexible economic policies, had lost territory in the south of the country to UNITA by the early 1980s.

By the late 1980s, the embattled MPLA government was forced to abandon some of its most stridently Marxist economic policies, which opened the door to more cordial relations with Western countries. Hope for a lasting peace increased in 1991, when peace accords were signed between the MPLA and UNITA. However, war again erupted the following year, when UNITA refused to acknowledge its defeat in multiparty elections. The struggle between MPLA and UNITA for control of Angola continued into the late 1990s.

In 1997, a plan to install a government of national unity had to be abandoned when Jonas Savimbi, leader of UNITA, refused to come to Luanda because he feared for his life. Savimbi also balked at proposals that he surrender UNITA's control over most of the country's diamond business, arguing that the MPLA controlled all of Angola's lucrative oil trade. In 1998, escalating political and military tension between the Angolan government

ANGOLA

Official name: Republic of Angola
Independence: 11 November 1975 (from Portugal)
Area: 1,246,700 sq km
Form of government: transitional government, nominally a multiparty democracy with a strong presidential system
Capital: Luanda
Currency: kwanza (AOA)
Income: US$2,700 (2007 est. of purchasing power parity)
Population: 13,000,000 (July 2009 est.)
Ethnic groups: Ovimbundu 37%, Kimbundu 25%, Bakongo 13%, mestico (mixed European and native African) 2%, European 1%, other 22%
Religious groups: indigenous beliefs 47%, Roman Catholic 38%, Protestant 15%
Languages: Portuguese (official), Bantu, and other African languages
Literacy: 67% (fifteen years old and over who can read and write.)
Exports: crude oil 90%, diamonds, refined petroleum products, gas, coffee, sisal, fish and fish products, timber, cotton
Primary export partners: China 32.9%, U.S. 26%, South Africa 9.9%, France 5.5% (2008)
Imports: machinery and electrical equipment, vehicles and spare parts, medicines, food, textiles, military goods
Primary import partners: Portugal 19.1%, China 14.7%, U.S. 12.3%, South Africa 5.4%, France 4.4% (2008)

and UNITA led to a full-scale civil war. In August 1998, the Angolan government sent thousands of troops into neighboring Congo-Kinshasa (now known as the Democratic Republic of the Congo) in support of the regime of Laurent Kabila. As the civil war within Angola continued to rage, the United Nations in March 1999 withdrew its mission from the country. By 2001, the United Nations estimated that more than 1 million lives had been lost as a result of Angola's devastating civil war, and another 2.5 million had been left homeless. In February 2002, rebel leader Jonas Savimbi was killed during a conflict with government forces. His death resulted in a cease-fire. Following further negotiations, UNITA abandoned its military efforts and became the major opposition party in the country. The MPLA government of President Dos Santos announced its intention to hold elections in 2006 followed by a new multiparty constitution. The 2006 election did not take place. However, on September 5, 2008, parliamentary elections were held, the first such exercise in Angola since 1992. The MPLA government won with an 81% majority, with UNITA winning about 10%. Numerous voting irregularities were registered and Angola subsequently received a poor rating in the 2008 Ibrahim Index of African Governance, which monitors voting and human rights violations on the continent.

BENIN

During the pre-colonial era, Benin was a collection of small principalities, the most powerful of which was the Fon Kingdom of Dahomey. By the eighteenth century, the Portuguese and other Europeans established trading posts along the coast. From these posts, thousands of enslaved Africans were shipped to the New World, primarily to Brazil and the Caribbean. This part of West Africa became known as the Slave Coast.

In 1892, the King of Dahomey was subjugated, and the country organized as the French protectorate of Dahomey. It remained a French colony until independence in 1960, when the name was changed to the Republic of Dahomey, and Hubert Maga became president. Three years later, military commanders overthrew him. Mathieu Kérékou took over in 1975. In the same year, the name of the country was changed to the People's Republic of Benin. When the government reverted from military to civilian control in 1980, Kérékou was reelected president of the republic. Facing formidable internal dissent, Kérékou in 1989 abandoned his Marxist-Leninist ideology. A new constitution, adopted in 1990, laid the groundwork for the establishment of a multiparty republic. Nicéphore Soglo defeated Kérékou in presidential elections in 1991, Benin's first free ballot in 30 years. Although the country's economy improved, Soglo's personal popularity declined, and he was defeated by Kérékou in 1996 presidential elections. In his second term, Kérékou largely abandoned his socialist vision, instead pursuing policies of economic liberalization. Kérékou's policies apparently won favor with the country's electorate, leading to his reelection in a March 2001 run-off despite claims of voting irregularities. In 2006, general elections took place. President Kérékou and former President Soglo were banned from contesting because of their age and constitutional requirements (neither challenged the restriction). Yayi Boni won a run-off election in March 2006 and was sworn in as president the following

BENIN

Official name: Republic of Benin

Independence: 1 August 1960 (from France)

Area: 112,620 sq km

Form of government: republic under multiparty democratic rule; dropped Marxism-Leninism December 1989; democratic reforms adopted February 1990; transition to multiparty system completed 4 April 1991

Capital: Porto-Novo is the official capital; Cotonou is the seat of government

Currency: Communaute Financiere Africaine franc (CFAF)

Income: US$1,500 (2008 est. of purchasing power parity)

Population: 8,900,000 (2009 est.)

Ethnic groups: African 99% (42 ethnic groups, most important being Fon, Aja, Yoruba, Bariba)

Religious groups: indigenous beliefs 50%, Christian 30%, Muslim 20%

Languages: French (official), Fon and Yoruba (most common vernaculars in south), indigenous languages (at least six major ones in north)

Literacy: 35.6% (fifteen years old and over who can read and write; 2007 est.)

Exports: cotton, crude oil, palm products, cocoa

Primary export partners: China 19.7%, Japan 8.9%, India 6.3%, Niger 5.1%, U.S. 4.9%, Nigeria 4.5%, Togo 4.2% (2008)

Imports: foodstuffs, tobacco, petroleum products, capital goods

Primary import partners: China 39.8%, U.S. 14%, Thailand 6.9%, France 6.9%, Malaysia 4.2% (2008)

month. Benin's presidential succession was declared free and fair and the country was hailed as a model of African democracy.

The population of Benin comprises about twenty sociocultural groups. Four groups—the Fon, Aja (who are related), Bariba, and Yoruba—account for more than half of the population.

BOTSWANA

Europeans made first contact with the area around Botswana in the early nineteenth century. In the last quarter of that century, hostilities broke out between the Botswana and the Afrikaners from South Africa (Transvaal). Following appeals by the Botswana for assistance, the British government in 1885 proclaimed "Bechuanaland" to be under British protection. In 1909, despite South African pressure, inhabitants of Bechuanaland, Basutoland (now Lesotho), and Swaziland demanded and received British agreement that they not be included in the proposed Union of South Africa.

In June 1964, the British government accepted proposals for a form of self-government for Botswana that would lead to independence. Botswana became independent on September 30, 1966, and Seretse Khama was installed as the prime minister after the Bechuanaland Democratic Party (BDP) won majority votes. The country was later named Botswana, and upon Khama's death in 1980, Quett Ketumile Joni Masire assumed the presidency, an office to which he was reelected three times. Constitutional reforms in 1994–1995 allowed more political parties to participate in the government and greatly reduced the power of the central government. President Masire retired in 1998 and the road was paved for the orderly succession of his vice president, Festus Mogae, to the presidency in 1999. Mogae was reelected in 2004. In 2008, Ian Khama was elected as president after resigning from the Botswanan military.

Since winning independence, Botswana has maintained a nonaligned foreign policy. Although it opposed the former racist policies of neighboring South Africa, Botswana maintained close economic ties with that nation. Large deposits of diamonds have been discovered in Botswana in recent years, making the country one of the world's major producers of the valuable gemstone. Also contributing to the country's economic growth are cattle raising and the mining of copper and nickel. Botswana has one of the highest HIV/AIDS rates in the region, which, because of its relatively small population, has the potential to threaten its economic growth and development, which has consistently been one the strongest in that part of the continent. Because of its relative prosperity, Botswana has called on experts to assist the country as it combats the epidemic. It has some of the most progressive policies on the continent for caring for those with the virus, helping to diminish the stigma associated with it.

Some 75% of the country's population is made up of the Tswana (Botswana), which is divided into eight subgroups: Bamangwate, Bakwena, Batawana, Bangwaketse, Bakgatla, Bamalete, Barolong, and Batlokwa. The Kalanga, Herero, Basarwa, Yei, and Kgalagadi are minorities.

BOTSWANA

Official name: Republic of Botswana

Independence: 30 September 1966 (from United Kingdom)

Area: 600,370 sq km

Form of government: parliamentary republic

Capital: Gaborone

Currency: pula (BWP)

Income: US$9,200 (2004 est. of purchasing power parity)

Population: 1,940,115 (2009 est.)

Ethnic groups: Tswana (or Setswana) 79%, Kalanga 11%, Basarwa 3%, other, including Kgalagadi and white, 7%

Religious groups: Christian 72%, Badimo 6 %

Languages: English (official), Setswana

Literacy: 80% (fifteen years old and over who can read and write; 2003 est.)

Exports: diamonds 72%, vehicles, copper, nickel, meat, textiles

Primary export partners: European Free Trade Association (EFTA) 87%, Southern African Customs Union (SACU) 7%, Zimbabwe 4% (2000)

Imports: foodstuffs, machinery and transport equipment, textiles, petroleum products

Primary import partners: Southern African Customs Union (SACU) 74%, EFTA 17%, Zimbabwe 4% (2000)

BURKINA FASO (FORMERLY UPPER VOLTA)

Burkina Faso is one of the poorest nations in the world, with most inhabitants subsisting on agriculture and animal husbandry. The majority of the population belongs

BURKINA FASO

Official name: none
Independence: 5 August 1960 (from France)
Area: 274,200 sq km
Form of government: parliamentary
Capital: Ouagadougou
Currency: Communaute Financiere Africaine franc (CFA Franc)
Income: US$1,280 (2009 est. of purchasing power parity)
Population: 15,757,000 (July 2009 est.)
Ethnic groups: Mossi over 40%, Gurunsi, Senufo, Lobi, Bobo, Mande, Fulani
Religious groups: indigenous beliefs 40%, Muslim 50%, Christian (mainly Roman Catholic) 10%
Languages: French (official), native African languages belonging to Sudanic family spoken by 90% of the population
Literacy: 26.6% (fifteen years old and over who can read and write; 2003 est.)
Exports: cotton, animal products, gold
Primary export partners: Singapore 16.9%, China 16%, Belgium 12.9%, Thailand 9.1%, Ghana 7%, Niger 5.2%, Denmark 4.9% (2008)
Primary import partners: Cote d'Ivoire 26.4%, France 18.2%, Togo 7.3%, Libya 4.2% (2008)

to two major West African cultural groups, the Voltaic and the Mande. The Voltaic are far more numerous and include the Mossi, which make up about one-half of the population.

Until the end of the nineteenth century, the Mossi, who are believed to have come from central or eastern Africa in the eleventh century, dominated the history of Burkina Faso. When the French arrived and claimed the area in 1896, the Mossi resisted but were defeated when their capital at Ouagadougou was captured. After World War II, the Mossi renewed their pressure for separate territorial status, and the territory then called Upper Volta became an autonomous republic in the French Community on December 11, 1958. It achieved independence on August 5, 1960, under President Maurice Yaméogo. Austerity measures imposed by the Yaméogo government at the end of 1965 led to a confrontation between the nation's trade unions and the government. In the opening days of 1966, power was seized by General Sangoulé Lamizana, the army chief of staff. He named himself president and suspended the constitution. In 1980, Lamizana was ousted in a bloodless coup, which was followed by two more coups over the next three years. In August 1984, one year after the coup that brought Captain Thomas Sankara to power as head of the National Revolutionary Council, the country's name was changed from Upper Volta to Burkina Faso.

Sankara was overthrown and executed in an October 1987 coup led by Blaise Campaoré. In 1990, Campaoré introduced several democratic reforms and the following year was reelected. His party won a legislative majority in the May 1992 legislative elections. During the mid-1990s, Burkina Faso actively supported revolutionary movements in Gambia and Liberia, alienating it from its neighbors and most Western powers. However, in 1998, Burkina Faso hosted the African Cup of Nations soccer tournament, Africa's biggest sporting event. The nation received favorable international media coverage for its efforts.

Burkina Faso experienced extensive political and social unrest in the wake of the December 1998 deaths of journalist Norbert Zongo and three companions. At the time of his death, Zongo had been investigating the 1997 death in detention of the driver of the president's brother. In May 1999, President Campaoré promised a full investigation into Zongo's death. A month later, several presidential guards were arrested and charged with Zongo's murder. In August 2000, three of five soldiers on trial for Zongo's murder were convicted.

Burkina Faso continues to face challenges and international accusations regarding its human rights record and poorly run economy. Even by the region's standards, Burkina Faso's economy has consistently performed poorly. Large numbers of Burkina Faso's citizens have migrated to neighboring nations such as Ghana and Côte d'Ivoire in search of work, causing tensions and border conflicts in the region.

In 2005, Blaise Campaoré was reelected once again to a five-year term as President of Burkina Faso. He has served in this capacity continuously since 1987.

BURUNDI

Prior to the arrival of Europeans, Burundi was a kingdom with a highly stratified, feudal social structure. Rulers were drawn from princely dynastic families, or ganwa, from whom a king, or mwami, was chosen. A mwami continued to rule even after independence was granted.

European explorers and missionaries began making brief visits to the area as early as 1858. However, Burundi did not come under European administration until the 1890s, when it became part of German East Africa. In 1916, Belgian troops occupied the country, and the

BURUNDI

Official name: Republic of Burundi
Independence: 1 July 1962 (from U.N. trusteeship under Belgian administration)
Area: 27,830 sq km
Form of government: republic
Capital: Bujumbura
Currency: Burundi franc (BIF)
Income: US$400 (2006 est. purchasing power parity)
Population: 8,303,000 (July 2009 est.)
Ethnic groups: Hutu (Bantu) 85%, Tutsi (Hamitic) 14%, Twa (Pygmy) 1%, Europeans 3,000, South Asians 2,000
Religious groups: Christian 67% (Roman Catholic 62%, Protestant 5%), indigenous beliefs 23%, Muslim 10%
Languages: Kirundi (official), French (official), Swahili (along Lake Tanganyika and in the Bujumbura area)
Literacy: 51.6% (fifteen years old and over who can read and write; 2003 est.)
Exports: coffee, tea, sugar, cotton, hides
Primary export partners: Japan 22.3%, Germany 14.4%, Pakistan 7.5%, Rwanda 4.7%, Sudan 4.4% (2008)
Imports: capital goods, petroleum products, foodstuffs
Primary import partners: Saudi Arabia 18.3%, Kenya 10.7%, Belgium 7.9%, France 5.8%, Uganda 5.1%, China 4.9%, India 4.5%, Germany 4.3% (2008)

League of Nations mandated it to Belgium in 1923 as part of the Territory of Ruanda-Urundi, now the nations of Rwanda and Burundi. Burundi became independent on July 1, 1962. Just ten years after independence, an abortive coup d'état provoked brutal massacres, claiming the lives of more than 100,000 people.

Burundi's population is made up of three ethnic groups—Hutu, Tutsi, and Twa. Hutus, who make up 85% of the population, are primarily farmers whose Bantu-speaking ancestors first migrated into Burundi almost 1,000 years ago. The Tutsi, who make up 14% of the population, are a pastoral people who migrated from Ethiopia several hundred years later. Years of dispute with neighboring Rwanda escalated into more serious clashes in the 1990s. During this period, ethnic conflict between the Hutus and Tutsis led to many atrocities, most notably an explosion of violence in 1993 that claimed tens of thousands of lives and displaced nearly three-quarters of a million Burundians, both Tutsi and Hutu. A military coup in July 1996 increased ethnic strife within Burundi. In an effort to protect its borders, the country intervened in the civil conflicts of the Democratic Republic of the Congo in 1998. In December 1999, former South African President Nelson Mandela mediated peace talks that ultimately led to a provisional peace treaty, signed by most of the warring parties in August 2000 and witnessed by Mandela and U.S. President Bill Clinton. After attempted coups in April and July 2001, a transitional government in Burundi signed a power-sharing agreement in November of that year. Outbreaks of violence continued sporadically until a cease-fire was signed in 2003. Implementation of a provisional constitution in 2004 was abandoned when rebel factions refused to sign, making a lasting peace elusive. In 2005, Pierre Nkurunziza was elected president of Burundi. His former ties to Hutu rebels have been a cause for concern among the Tutsi and other ethnic groups. Nkurunziza has attempted to negotiate the Hutu/Tutsi conflicts, which continue to plague the region.

CAMEROON

Cameroon has about 200 ethnic groups, speaking at least as many languages and dialects. The earliest inhabitants of Cameroon were probably Mbuti (or Bambuti), who still inhabit the southern forests. However, Bantu-speaking people were among the first to invade Cameroon from equatorial Africa, settling in the south and later in the west. The Muslim Fulani from the Niger basin arrived in the eleventh and nineteenth centuries and settled in the north. Europeans first made contact with the area in the 1500s. For the next three centuries, Spanish, Dutch, and British traders visited the region.

In July of 1884, Germany, the United Kingdom, and France each attempted to annex Cameroon. A 1919 declaration divided the area between the United Kingdom and France, with the larger, eastern part under France. In December of 1958, the French trusteeship ended, and French Cameroon became the Republic of Cameroon on January 1, 1960.

The Republic of Cameroon consisted of a federal system integrating the French-controlled south and the British-controlled north under the leadership of Cameroon's first president, Ahmadou Ahidjo. The country depends heavily on foreign capital and has been faced with internal problems, both ethnic and social, under the leadership of Ahidjo's successor, Paul Biya. Despite sometimes violent confrontations between the nation's political parties, Biya was reelected in 1997 presidential elections,

CAMEROON

Official name: Republic of Cameroon

Independence: 1 January 1960 (from French-administered U.N. trusteeship)

Area: 475,440 sq km

Form of government: unitary republic; multiparty presidential regime (opposition parties legalized in 1990)

Capital: Yaoundé

Currency: Communaute Financiere Africaine franc (CFAF)

Income: US$2,130 (2009 est. of purchasing power parity)

Population: 19,522,000 (July 2009)

Ethnic groups: Cameroon Highlanders 31%, Equatorial Bantu 19%, Kirdi 11%, Fulani 10%, Northwestern Bantu 8%, Eastern Nigritic 7%, other African 13%, non-African less than 1%

Religious groups: indigenous beliefs 40%, Christian 40%, Muslim 20%

Languages: 24 major African language groups, English (official), French (official)

Literacy: 79% (fifteen years old and over who can read and write; 2003 est.)

Exports: crude oil and petroleum products, lumber, cocoa beans, aluminum, coffee, cotton

Primary export partners: Spain 18.7%, Italy 12.7%, U.S. 10%, South Korea 9.3%, France 7.7%, Netherlands 7.6%, China 5.3% (2008)

Primary import partners: France 21.6%, Nigeria 14.2%, China 9.2%, Belgium 6.2% (2008)

which were boycotted by the three main opposition parties. Despite health problems, relative economic prosperity and strong-arm tactics against opponents have enabled Biya to withstand both international and domestic opposition.

In 2001, President Biya moved to defuse reports of growing discontent within the country's military by ordering a total reorganization of the Cameroonian armed forces. He also disbanded the Operational Command (OC), a paramilitary crime-fighting unit he had created in 2000, in response to public anger at reports the OC had carried out hundreds of summary executions of suspected criminals. As of this writing, the most recent parliamentary elections were held in 2007, but President Biya's party, Cameroon People's Democratic Movement, remained in firm control at the executive and judicial level.

CAPE VERDE

Located in the North Atlantic Ocean, the Cape Verde archipelago remained uninhabited until the Portuguese visited there in 1456. Later, enslaved Africans were brought to the islands to work on Portuguese plantations. As a result, Cape Verdeans have mixed African and Portuguese origins.

In 1951, Portugal changed Cape Verde's status from a colony to an overseas province. In 1956, the African Party for the Independence of Guinea-Bissau and Cape Verde (PAIGC) was organized to bring about improvement in economic, social, and political conditions in Cape Verde and Portuguese Guinea. The PAIGC began an armed rebellion against Portugal in 1961. Acts of sabotage eventually grew into a war in Portuguese Guinea that pitted 10,000 Soviet

CAPE VERDE

Official name: Republic of Cape Verde

Independence: 5 July 1975 (from Portugal)

Area: 4,033 sq km

Form of government: republic

Capital: Praia

Currency: Cape Verdean escudo (CVE)

Income: US$3,470 (2009 est. of purchasing power parity)

Population: 506,000 (July 2009 est.)

Ethnic groups: Creole (mulatto) 71%, African 28%, European 1%

Religious groups: Roman Catholic (infused with indigenous beliefs); Protestant (mostly Church of the Nazarene)

Languages: Portuguese, Crioulo (a blend of Portuguese and West African words)

Literacy: 76.6% (fifteen years old and over who can read and write; 2003 est.)

Exports: fuel, shoes, garments, fish, bananas, hides

Primary export partners: Japan 37.8%, Spain 28.7%, Portugal 17.7% (2008)

Primary import partners: Portugal 39.5%, Netherlands 11.4%, Spain 6.5%, UK 6.3%, Cote d'Ivoire 4.4%, Brazil 4% (2008)

bloc-supported PAIGC soldiers against 35,000 Portuguese and African troops.

In December of 1974, the PAIGC and Portugal signed an agreement providing for a transitional government composed of Portuguese and Cape Verdeans. On June 30, 1975, Cape Verdeans elected a National Assembly, which received the instruments of independence from Portugal on July 5, 1975. After winning independence, the country voted for a union with Guinea-Bissau. In 1980, the link ended when João Vieira seized power in Guinea-Bissau. The PAIGC was dissolved and replaced by PAICV (African Party for the Independence of Cape Verde). Pedro Pires, a prominent nationalist, held office as prime minister of Cape Verde from 1975 to 1991. Under him, the nation followed a socialist path with programs of nationalization and agrarian reform. In the country's first free presidential elections made possible by political reforms, Antonio Mascarenhas Monteiro was elected in 1991. A new constitution, firmly establishing the country's new multiparty system, was adopted the following year. In 1996, Mascarenhas was reelected to another five-year term as president.

Cape Verde's privatization program, launched as part of the government's efforts to comply with World Bank/IMF recommendations for economic structural reform, came under fire in the year 2000 from the PAICV as well as certain members of the ruling Movement for Democracy. This rift within the ruling party eventually gave birth to a new party, the Democratic Renovation Party. The major issue in the 2001 legislative elections was the country's troubled economy. The PAICV captured the majority of the seats, winning for the party's leader, José Maria Neves, the office of prime minister. The PAICV prevailed again in the 2001 presidential elections, as its candidate, Pedro Pires, won the presidency. Pires also won a second term in 2006.

The official language of Cape Verde is Portuguese. However, most Cape Verdeans speak a Creole dialect, Crioulo, which consists of archaic Portuguese modified through contact with African and other European languages. Leading contemporary Afro-Cape Verdeans include Cesaria Evora, an internationally renowned singer.

CENTRAL AFRICAN REPUBLIC

Official name: Central African Republic
Independence: 13 August 1960 (from France)
Area: 622,984 sq km
Form of government: republic
Capital: Bangui
Currency: Communaute Financiere Africaine franc (CFAF)
Income: US$750 (2009 est. of purchasing power parity)
Population: 4,422,000 (July 2009 est.)
Ethnic groups: Baya 34%, Banda 27%, Sara 10%, Mandjia 21%, Mboum 4%, M'Baka 4%, Europeans (including French) < 1%
Religious groups: indigenous beliefs 24%, Protestant 25%, Roman Catholic 25%, Muslim 15%, other 11%
Languages: French (official), Sangho (lingua franca and national language), Arabic, Hunsa, Swahili
Literacy: 51% (fifteen years old and over who can read and write; 2003 est.)
Exports: diamonds, timber, cotton, coffee, tobacco
Primary export partners: Japan 43.2%, Belgium 10.4%, China 8.3%, Indonesia 6%, France 4.7%, Italy 4.3%, Democratic Republic of the Congo 4.3% (2008)
Primary import partners: France 17.3%, Cameroon 9.8%, Netherlands 7.3%, U.S. 6.7% (2008)

CENTRAL AFRICAN REPUBLIC

The first Europeans to settle in the area that is now the Central African Republic were the French, who established an outpost at Bangu. United with Chad in 1906, the outpost formed the Oubangui-Chari-Chad colony.

In 1910, the Central African Republic became one of the four territories of the Federation of French Equatorial Africa, along with Chad, Congo (Brazzaville), and Gabon. However, a constitutional referendum of September 1958 dissolved the federation. The nation became an autonomous republic within the newly established French Community on December 1, 1958, and acceded to complete independence as the Central African Republic on August 13, 1960. The first president and the founder of the Central African Republic was Bathelemy Boganda.

General Jean-Bédel Bokassa overthrew Boganda's successor, David Dacko, in 1966. The thirteen year reign of Bokassa marked one of the cruelest and most repressive periods in the country's history. He sanctioned terrible human rights abuses, and survived numerous assassination attempts and political coups. In response to these attempted overthrows, he ordered the executions of several military personnel for disloyalty (including some of his family members) and ultimately proclaimed himself emperor of the Central African Empire in 1977. During Bokassa's reign, the police were used to spy on citizens and foreign assistants (known as *cooperant*), maintained secret surveillance on dissidents (whether actual or perceived), and engaged in similar practices as directed by the dictator's repressive regime.

A 1979 *coup d'état* put Dacko back in power. General André Kolingba succeeded Dacko in 1981, and a multiparty state was established in 1991. The results of multiparty legislative and presidential elections, held in October 1992, were thrown out by the country's Supreme Court, which cited multiple irregularities. In September 1993 elections, Ange-Felix Patassé was elected president, succeeding Kolingba, who released Bokassa from prison as one of his last official acts. Patassé was at odds with the military for much of the 1990s, and French troops were needed to put down military mutinies in the late 1990s. In early 1998, the United Nations sent an all-African peacekeeping force to the Central African Republic to enforce the so-called Bangui Accords of 1997, which called for an armistice and new elections. Despite opposition party claims of election rigging, incumbent President Patassé was reelected to office in September 1999.

In February 2000, the remaining U.N. peacekeeping troops stationed in the Central African Republic withdrew. Political tensions in the capital, however, continued to run high. Although President Patassé promised to seek national reconciliation by bringing together representatives of all major political parties, a conference date was never set. A coup attempt in late May 2001 by army rebels loyal to former President Kolingba was successfully put down. The failed coup resulted in more than 1,000 members of the various armed branches (mostly within the army and national police who were loyal to Kolingba) fleeing across the river into the Democratic Republic of Congo. Kolingba and his family were abducted and presumed dead. The following year, the recently dismissed Army Chief of Staff, Francois Bozize, staged yet another coup attempt with the assistance of Chadian soldiers. This conflict, which lasted several months, resulted in the coup d'etat that removed President Ange-Felix Patasse from office in March 2003.

Since claiming the presidency in 2003, Francois Bozize continued to rely on Chadian soldiers for military support. This situation led to tense standoffs between the Chadians and the national police on several occasions throughout 2003 and 2004.

The Central African Republic is made up of more than eighty ethnic groups, each with its own language. About 70% of the population comprises Baya-Mandjia and Banda, with approximately 7% M'Baka. Sango, the language of a small group along the Oubangui River, is the national language spoken by the majority of Central Africans. The country is one of the poorest nations in Africa, with a high mortality rate and widespread malnutrition and illiteracy.

CHAD

The region that is now Chad was known to Middle Eastern traders and geographers as far back as the late Middle Ages. Since then, Chad has served as a crossroads for Muslims of the desert and savanna regions and the animist groups of the tropical forests.

The Sao people populated the Chari River basin for thousands of years, but the powerful chiefs of what were

CHAD

Official name: Republic of Chad

Independence: 11 August 1960 (from France)

Area: 1.284 million sq km

Form of government: republic

Capital: N'Djamena

Currency: Communaute Financiere Africaine franc (CFAF)

Income: US$1,600 (2008 est. of purchasing power parity)

Population: 11,206,000 (July 2009 est.)

Ethnic groups: 200 distinct groups; in the north and center: Arabs, Gorane (Toubou, Daza, Kreda), Zaghawa, Kanembou, Ouaddai, Baguirmi, Hadjerai, Fulbe, Kotoko, Hausa, Boulala, and Maba, most of whom are Muslim; in the south: Sara (Ngambaye, Mbaye, Goulaye), Moundang, Moussei, Massa, most of whom are Christian or animist; about 1,000 French citizens live in Chad

Religious groups: Muslim 51%, Christian 35%, animist 7%, other 7%

Languages: French (official), Arabic (official), Sara and Sango (in south), more than 100 different languages and dialects

Literacy: 47.5% (fifteen years old and over who can read and write French or Arabic; 2003 est.)

Exports: cotton, cattle, textiles

Primary export partners: U.S. 90.7%, China 3.3%, Japan 2.2% (2008)

Imports: machinery and transportation equipment, industrial goods, petroleum products, foodstuffs, textiles

Primary import partners: France 19.2%, Cameroon 16.2%, China 10.4%, U.S. 8.5%, Germany 6.1%, Saudi Arabia 5.1%, Netherlands 4.4% (2008)

to become the Kanem-Bornu and Baguirmi kingdoms overtook their relatively weak chiefdoms. At their peak, these two kingdoms and the kingdom of Ouaddai controlled a good part of what is now Chad, as well as parts of Nigeria and Sudan.

The French first made contact with the region in 1891. The first major colonial battle for Chad was fought in 1900 between the French major Lamy and the African leader Rabah. Although the French won that battle, they did not declare the territory for themselves until 1911, and thereafter armed clashes between colonial troops and local bands continued for many years. Although Chad joined the French colonies of Gabon, Oubangui-Charo, and Moyen Congo to form the Federation of French Equatorial Africa in 1910, Chad did not have colonial status until 1920.

In 1959, the territory of French Equatorial Africa was dissolved, and four states—Gabon, the Central African Republic, Congo (Brazzaville), and Chad—became autonomous members of the French Community. In 1960, Chad became an independent nation under its first president, François Tombalbaye. He was faced with the pressure of resolving the ongoing conflict between the Muslim north and the black south and responded by instituting authoritarian rule. Backed by Libya, FRONAT (Front de Libération Nationale) guerrillas of the north gained power, naming Goukouni Oueddei as head of state. In 1982, he was succeeded by Hisséne Habré, but civil war broke out one year later.

In 1990, Habré was ousted by a rebel group with Libyan support. Rebel leader Idriss Déby assumed the presidency. In January 1992, the Déby government claimed to have put down an uprising by forces loyal to Habré. An understanding was reached in 1994, ending the long-standing battle between the government and Habré forces. In mid-1996 elections under a newly adopted democratic constitution, Déby was elected president. After several postponements, Déby's party dominated legislative elections in 1997. Though Déby's defeated opponents claimed electoral fraud, international observers declared the elections free and fair.

Prospects for Chad's economy improved significantly in the year 2000 when the World Bank approved the country's proposed $3.4-billion oil-development project, designed to carry crude oil from the Doba Basin in the south of Chad to the sea through a pipeline passing through Cameroon. Oil production began in 2003. For its assistance in the project, the World Bank insisted that a substantial portion of the oil revenue be used for development throughout the country. President Déby handily won reelection in 2001. Charges from opposition parties that the election had been rigged were rejected by Chad's constitutional court. Déby's heavy-handed repression of subsequent protest demonstrations by the opposition cost him support both domestically and internationally. Deby won reelection again in 2006, but the election was basically regarded as a mere formality. There was an effort to overthrow him that year, but the coup was also repelled.

Chad is made up of more than 200 ethnic groups. Those in the north and east are generally Muslim, while most southerners are animists and Christians. Ethnic and religious divisions continue to run deep in Chad. The government continues to face armed resistance from rebels in the south demanding regional autonomy, and, in 1998, Amnesty International charged the government with arbitrarily killing civilians from the south.

COMOROS

Located in the Indian Ocean off the northwestern coast of Madagascar, the Comoros archipelago was visited by Portuguese explorers in 1505. In 1843, the sultan of Mayotte was persuaded to relinquish the island of Mayotte to the French. By 1912, France had established colonial rule over the additional islands of Grande Comore, Anjouan, and Mohéli and placed them under the administration of the governor general of Madagascar. After World War II, the islands became a French overseas territory and were represented in France's National Assembly. On July 6, 1975, the Comorian Parliament passed a resolution declaring unilateral independence. However, the deputies of Mayotte abstained; that island remains under French administration. As a result, the Comorian government has effective control over only Grande Comore, Anjouan, and Mohéli. This was followed by an extended period of political upheaval in Comoros including a series of political insurrections and coup d'états.

In 1996, Mohamed Taki Abdulkarim was elected president and unveiled a new constitution extending the powers of the president and making Islam the state religion. In 1997, the islands of Anjouan and Mohéli announced their intention to secede: in light of the relatively high standard of living enjoyed by Mayotte, they wished to return to French administration. After initially affirming its willingness to reincorporate the islands, France urged the Organization of African Unity (OAU) to find a peaceful settlement to the conflict. The OAU later worked out a framework agreement whereby the islands would have their own government within a new entity to be named the Union of Comorian Islands, which would have a separate administration. At an April 1999 peace conference in Madagascar, representatives of Grand Comore, Mohéli, and the Comoros government signed the agreement; the Anjouan delegation did not. Shortly afterward, army officers took over the Comoros

COMOROS

Official name: Federal Islamic Republic of the Comoros
Independence: 6 July 1975 (from France)
Area: 2,170 sq km
Form of government: independent republic
Capital: Moroni
Currency: Comoran franc (KMF)
Income: US$820 (2009 est. of purchasing power parity)
Population: 798,000 (July 2009 est.)
Ethnic groups: Antalote, Cafre, Makoa, Oimatsaha, Sakalava
Religious groups: Sunni Muslim 98%, Roman Catholic 2%
Languages: Arabic (official), French (official), Comoran (a blend of Swahili and Arabic)
Literacy: 56.5% (fifteen years old and over who can read and write; 2003 est.)
Exports: vanilla, ylang-ylang, cloves, perfume oil, copra
Primary export partners: U.S. 90.7%, China 3.3%, Japan 2.2% (2008)
Imports: rice and other foodstuffs, consumer goods; petroleum products, cement, transport equipment
Primary import partners: France 19.2%, Cameroon 16.2%, China 10.4%, U.S. 8.5%, Germany 6.1%, Saudi Arabia 5.1%, Netherlands 4.4% (2008)

Republic in an apparent coup, bringing to power Colonel Azali Assoumani.

The dominant issue in the first years of the new millennium continued to be the secession of Anjouan Island. In early 2000, after a referendum on Anjouan overwhelmingly supported the island's refusal to sign an OAU-brokered agreement, the OAU imposed sanctions on the island and later voted to support armed intervention to end the secession. In 2001, the OAU led talks between Anjouan and federal government officials that produced an agreement providing greater autonomy for Comoros's individual island governments but reserved foreign policy and defense for the national government. After an August 2001 coup unseated Anjouan's ruler, Lieutenant Colonel Said Abeid Abdermane, Colonel Mohamed Bacar took over as the island's head of state. In December 2001, Anjouan's voters overwhelmingly supported a new Comoros constitution formalizing the terms set forth in the OAU-brokered reconciliation agreement.

The Comorians inhabiting the islands of Grande Comore, Anjouan, and Mohéli (about 86% of the population) share African-Arab origins. Islam is the dominant religion, but substantial minorities of the citizens of Mayotte (the Mahorais) are Catholic and have been influenced strongly by French culture. The most common language is Shikomoro, a Swahili dialect. French and Malagasy are also spoken.

THE CONGO, DEMOCRATIC REPUBLIC OF

The area that is now the Democratic Republic of the Congo or Congo-Kinshasa is believed to have been populated as early as 10,000 years ago. An influx of peoples arrived in the seventh and eighth centuries, when Bantu people from the area now known as Nigeria settled in the region, bringing with them knowledge about the manufacture and use of metals. In 1482, the Portuguese arrived at the mouth of the Congo River. They found an organized society—the Bakongo Kingdom—that included parts of present-day Congo-Brazzaville, Congo-Kinshasa, and Angola. The Portuguese named the area Congo. At the Berlin Conference of 1885, Belgian King Leopold's claim to the greater part of the Zaire River basin was recognized. The Congo Free State remained his personal possession until he ceded it to the Belgian State in 1907, when it was renamed the Belgian Congo.

Following riots in Leopoldville in 1958, Belgian King Bedouin announced that the colony could look forward to independence. Roundtable conferences were convened at Brussels in January 1960, and Belgium granted independence on June 30, 1960. Parliamentary elections were held earlier, in April of that year. The Congolese National Movement (MNC) obtained a majority of the seats, and the populous leader, Patrice Lumumba, was named prime minister. After much maneuvering, the leader of the Alliance of the Bakongo (ABAKO) Party, Joseph Kasavubu, was named president.

Regional chaos began right after independence. Moise Tshombe, premier of Katanga Province, declared Katanga (rich with copper) independent. Belgian military intervened, and soon after, U.N. troops arrived to help normalize the situation. Meanwhile, Lumumba was assassinated. Tshombe served as prime minister until 1965, when Joseph Mobutu (who in 1972 renamed himself Mobutu Sese Seko) organized a coup d'état. While amassing great personal riches, Mobutu managed to bring resource-rich Congo-Kinshasa (between 1971 and 1997 the country was known as Zaire) to the brink of

DEMOCRATIC REPUBLIC OF THE CONGO

Independence: 30 June 1960 (from Belgium)
Area: 2,345,410 sq km
Form of government: dictatorship; presumably undergoing a transition to representative government
Capital: Kinshasa
Currency: Congolese franc (CDF)
Income: US$329 (2008 est. of purchasing power parity)
Population: 66,020,000 (2009)
Ethnic groups: over 200 African ethnic groups of which the majority are Bantu; the four largest cultural groups—Mongo, Luba, Kongo (all Bantu), and the Mangbetu-Azande (Hamitic)—make up about 45% of the population
Religious groups: Roman Catholic 50%, Protestant 20%, Kimbanguist 10%, Muslim 10%, other syncretic sects and indigenous beliefs 10%
Languages: French (official), Lingala (a lingua franca trade language), Kingwana (a dialect of Kiswahili or Swahili), Kikongo, Tshiluba
Literacy: 65.5% (fifteen years old and over who can read and write French, Lingala, Kingwana, or Tshiluba; 2003 est.)
Exports: diamonds, copper, coffee, cobalt, crude oil
Primary export partners: China 44.7%, Belgium 16.9%, Finland 10.5%, U.S. 8.9%, Zambia 4.8% (2008)
Imports: foodstuffs, mining and other machinery, transport equipment, fuels
Primary import partners: South Africa 22.1%, Belgium 11.5%, Zambia 8.3%, Zimbabwe 7%, Kenya 5.9%, China 5.6%, France 5.4% (2008)

bankruptcy during the more than thirty years that he held power. The country's increasingly fragile economy and pressures from a sharp influx in refugees all contributed to growing dissatisfaction with Mobutu's regime.

Anti-Mobutu guerrilla fighter Laurent-Désiré Kabila, leader of the Alliance of Democratic Forces for the Liberation of Congo, led rebel forces in seizing large portions of the country in the fall of 1996. In May 1997, as Kabila's forces neared Kinshasa, Mobutu stepped down and fled the capital. He died later that year in exile. The rebels took control of the country, which they renamed the Democratic Republic of the Congo. Kabila's regime faced heavy criticism from the international community, who suspected that his troops were responsible for the disappearance and assumed massacre of thousands of Hutu refugees. In addition, the political favoritism exhibited by Kabila led to serious civil strife that threatened to spark a broad regional conflict.

Attempts to quell the rebellion in the eastern provinces of the Congo in early 2000 were frustrated by President Kabila's demand that Uganda and Rwanda must unconditionally withdraw their troops from the region. Kabila was assassinated, reportedly by one of his bodyguards, in 2001. He was succeeded by his son, Joseph, who seemed more amenable than his father to dealing with eastern Congo rebel leaders in an effort to end the conflict. The younger Kabila also moved quickly to root out corruption at the higher levels of government. He met with leaders of three rebel groups and struck an agreement that created a framework for further dialogue. An October 2001 peace conference in Addis Ababa failed to make much progress, but delegates agreed to continue their efforts to resolve the crisis. Fighting in the eastern provinces was sharply reduced, and Uganda and Rwandan troops began withdrawing from the region. Later the Pretoria Accord was signed by the various warring parties and produced a level of peace in the region. A national unity government, which included several of Kabila's political opponents, was set up in 2003. In 2006, the country held its first multiparty elections since independence forty-five years earlier. Joseph Kabila won by a 25% margin, but the results were challenged by his closest competitor, Jean-Pierre Bemba. A run-off election yielded the same results. Although there was fighting by Bemba supporters, Bemba has accepted the results and is, as of this writing, the main opposition to the president.

As many as 250 ethnic groups in the Democratic Republic of the Congo have been distinguished and named. The largest group, the Kongo, may include as many as 2.5 million persons. Other socially and numerically important groups are the Luba, Lunda, Bashi, and Mongo. Some groups, including the aboriginal Pygmies, occupy isolated ecological niches and number only a few thousand.

Approximately 700 local languages and dialects are spoken; four serve as official languages. Lingala developed along the Congo River in the 1880s, in response to the need for a common commercial language. Swahili, introduced into the country by Arabs and especially the Zanzibari Swahilis during the nineteenth-century slaving operations, is spoken extensively in the eastern half of the country. Kikongo is used primarily in the area between Kinshasa and the Atlantic Ocean, as well as in parts of

Congo and Angola. Primarily, the ethnic groups of the south-central Democratic Republic of the Congo speak Tshiluba.

THE CONGO, REPUBLIC OF

The early history of the Congo is believed to have focused on three kingdoms—the Kongo, the Loango, and the Teke. Established in the fourth century, the Kongo was a highly centralized kingdom that later developed a close commercial relationship with the Portuguese, who were the first Europeans to explore the area.

With the development of African enslavement, the Portuguese turned their attention from the Kongo Kingdom to the Loango Kingdom. By the time the slave trade was abolished in the 1800s, the Loango Kingdom had been reduced to many small, independent groups. The Teke Kingdom of the interior, which had sold those enslaved to the Loango Kingdom, ended its independence in 1883, when the Teke king concluded a treaty with Pierre Savorgnan de Brazza, placing the Teke lands and people under French protection. The area then became known as Middle Congo.

In 1910, Middle Congo became part of French Equatorial Africa, which also included Gabon, the Central African Republic, and Chad. A constitutional referendum in September 1958 replaced the Federation of French Equatorial Africa with the French Community. Middle Congo, under the name Republic of the Congo, and the three other territories of French Equatorial Africa became fully autonomous members within the French Community. On April 15, 1960, Republic of the Congo became an independent nation but retained close, formal bonds with the community.

President Fulbert Youlou instituted a dictatorship for the first three years following independence and then was succeeded by a revolutionary government headed by Alphonse Massamba-Debat. In 1968, the military seized control of the nation under General Marien Ngouabi, who declared the Congo a republic to be governed under a one-party system. Assassinated in 1977, Ngouabi was succeeded as president by General Joachim Yhombi-Opango. Two years later, Yhombi-Opango was succeeded by Denis Sassou-Nguesso, who was reelected to the presidency in 1984 and 1989.

The 1990s brought increasing dissatisfaction with the Sassou-Nguesso regime, which was forced in 1992 to adopt a new constitution, making the country a multiparty democracy. Sassou-Nguesso lost in presidential elections that year to Pascal Lissouba, but Lissouba's government was soon plagued by accusations of ethnic favoritism. Clashes between various private militias exploded into civil war, killing between 6,000 and 10,000 people and largely destroying Brazzaville. Many of the country's citizens rallied behind opposition forces led by Sassou-Nguesso who, with considerable Angolan assistance, overthrew Lissouba in late 1997. Sassou-Nguesso promised national reconciliation, a return to civilian rule, and a professional military.

Civil war again broke out in January 1999 when rebel militias loyal to Lissouba began attacks in and around the capital city of Brazzaville. By the end of the year, army representatives signed a truce agreement with rebel leaders. In March 2001, President Sassou-Nguesso launched talks to draft a new constitution that would help restore peace in the country. Despite opposition charges that the new constitution placed too much power in the

REPUBLIC OF THE CONGO

Independence: 15 August 1960 (from France)
Area: 342,000 sq km
Form of government: republic
Capital: Brazzaville
Currency: Communaute Financiere Africaine franc (CFAF)
Income: US$2,950 (2008 est. of purchasing power parity)
Population: 3,686,000 (2009)
Ethnic groups: Kongo 48%, Sangha 20%, M'Bochi 12%, Teke 17%, Europeans NA%; *note:* Europeans estimated at 8,500, mostly French, before the 1997 civil war; may be half that of 1998, following the widespread destruction of foreign businesses in 1997
Religious groups: Christian 50%, animist 48%, Muslim 2%
Languages: French (official), Lingala and Monokutuba (lingua franca trade languages), many local languages and dialects (of which Kikongo has the most users)
Literacy: 83.8% (fifteen years old and over who can read and write; 2003 est.)
Exports: petroleum 50%, lumber, plywood, sugar, cocoa, coffee, diamonds
Primary export partners: U.S. 44.5%, China 32.8%, France 6% (2008)
Primary import partners: France 19.1%, China 15.6%, South Korea 15.2%, U.S. 4.8%, India 4.7%, Italy 4.5% (2008)

hands of the president, the document was adopted by the Congolese parliament in September 2001. The following year, President Sassou-Nguesso won a dramatic reelection after his main rival Lissouba and others were banned from contesting. The newly adopted constitution gave Sassou-Nguesso additional presidential powers. After years of continued political instability, yet another presidential election was held in 2009. To no one's surprise, Sassou-Nguesso was, again, announced as the victor.

CÔTE D'IVOIRE (IVORY COAST)

The French made their initial contact with Côte d'Ivoire in 1637, when missionaries landed at Assinie near the Gold Coast (now Ghana) border. In 1843 and 1844, France signed treaties with the kings of the Grand Bassam and Assinie regions, placing their territories under a French protectorate. French explorers, missionaries, trading companies, and soldiers gradually extended the area under French control until 1893, when Côte d'Ivoire was officially made a French colony.

In December of 1958, Côte d'Ivoire became an autonomous republic within the French Community. Côte d'Ivoire became independent on August 7, 1960. Félix Houphouët-Boigny led the country under a one-party system. He maintained strong ties with Europe, which helped bring about rapid development and economic stability. In October 1990, Houphouët-Boigny was elected to his seventh term as president in the country's first multiparty elections. He died in 1993 and was succeeded by Henri Konan Bédié, head of the National Assembly. Bédié was reelected to office in the 1995 but opposition parties protesting the government's political restrictions boycotted that contest. Continuing the policies of his predecessor, Bédié helped build a nation of political stability and limited economic prosperity. At the same time, he maintained a neocolonial dependence on France and blocked effective democratic reforms.

In 1999, a military coup ousted Bédié from power, replacing him with General Robert Gueï. In an attempt to broaden support for the new government, the military junta formed a coalition first with former Prime Minister Alassane Ouattara's Rally of Republicans, which was further strengthened in 2000 when four members of the Ivorian Popular Front party agreed to join the cabinet. Gueï lost to Ivorian Popular Front candidate Laurent Gbagbo in the 2000 presidential elections. At first, Gueï halted the vote count in a vain attempt to hold on to the presidency. He was soon forced from office by a popular revolt, and Gbagbo assumed office, despite strong opposition from some quarters. Political turmoil continued into 2001, and a coup was mounted against the Gbagbo regime. It was quickly put down. Later that year, Gbagbo proposed reconciliations talks that would bring together warring political leaders of the past and present. Such talks were held in November 2001. The following year, an assassination attempt on the life of Gbagbo, and the subsequent involvement of the French, resulted in fighting that further alienated the Muslim-dominated north. A unity government was formed at the urging of the U.N., but peace has been elusive. Fighting among government and rebel groups continues, as of this writing.

CÔTE D'IVOIRE (IVORY COAST)

Independence: 7 August 1960 (from France)

Area: 322,460 sq km

Form of government: republic; multiparty presidential regime established 1960

Capital: Yamoussoukro; *note*: although Yamoussoukro has been the official capital since 1983, Abidjan remains the administrative center; the United States, like other countries, maintains its Embassy in Abidjan

Currency: Communaute Financiere Africaine franc (CFAF)

Income: US$1,642 (2008 est. of purchasing power parity)

Population: 21,075,000 (2009)

Ethnic groups: Akan 42.1%, Voltaiques or Gur 17.6%, Northern Mandes 16.5%, Krous 11%, Southern Mandes 10%, other 2.8%

Religious groups: Christian 20–30%, Muslim 35–40%, indigenous 25–40% (2001); *note*: the majority of foreigners (migratory workers) are Muslim (70%) and Christian (20%)

Literacy: 50.9% (fifteen years old and over who can read and write, 2003 est.)

Exports: cocoa, coffee, tropical woods, petroleum, cotton, bananas, pineapples, palm oil, cotton, fish (2004)

Primary export partners: Germany 11.1%, U.S. 10.3%, Netherlands 9.9%, Nigeria 9.4%, France 6.5%, Burkina Faso 4.1% (2008)

Imports: food, consumer goods; capital goods, fuel, transport equipment

Primary import partners: Nigeria 32%, France 15.1%, China 7.8% (2008)

General elections which were scheduled for 2007, after having been postponed from the previous year, were rescheduled to take place in 2009.

Côte d'Ivoire's more than sixty ethnic groups usually are classified into seven principal divisions—Akan, Krou, Lagoon, Nuclear Mande, Peripheral Mande, Senoufo, and Lobi. The Baoule in the Akan division is probably the largest single subgroup, with perhaps 20% of the overall population. The Bete in the Krou division and the Senoufo in the north are the second- and third-largest groups, with roughly 18% and 15% of the national population, respectively.

DJIBOUTI

The French first settled the region now known as the Republic of Djibouti in 1862, as a result of growing French interest in British activity in Egypt. In 1884, France expanded its protectorate to include the shores of the Gulf of Tadjourah and the hinterland, designating the area French Somaliland. The boundaries of the protectorate, marked out in 1897 by France and Emperor Menelik II of Ethiopia, were affirmed by agreements with Emperor Haile Selassie I in 1945 and 1954.

In July 1967, a directive from Paris formally changed the name of the territory to the French Territory of Afars and Issas. In 1975, the French government began to accommodate increasingly insistent demands for independence. The following year, the territory's citizenship law, which had favored the Afar minority, was revised to reflect more closely the weight of the Issa Somali majority. In a May 1977 referendum, the electorate voted for independence, and the Republic of Djibouti was inaugurated on June 27, 1977. A republican form of government followed independence.

After independence, Hassan Gouled Aptidon, the republic's first president, led the country. Beginning in the 1980s, however, Gouled's tenure was marred by political repression, ethnic hostilities, and serious international debt. Opposition to the Gouled government sparked a sizeable Afar resistance movement in the 1990s; negotiations with the government led to a comprehensive treaty in December 1994. When Gouled had to leave the country from December 1995 until February 1996 to seek medical treatment in France, a destabilizing struggle for succession ensued. Upon his return, he suspended the civil rights of prominent opposition leaders and restated his intention to remain in office. Gouled retired in 1999, and his ruling party nominated Gouled's nephew, Ismail Omar Guelleh, to run for the president's post, which he won handily in a face-off with Moussa Ahmed Idriss, who represented a coalition of opposition parties. After his inauguration in 1999, Guelleh released a number of political prisoners but still came under fire from human rights organizations for the harassment of journalists, including Moussa Ahmed, who was arrested in September 1999.

In February 2000, Guelleh's government signed an agreement with rebel leaders of the Front for the Restoration of Unity and Dignity (FRUD) to end nearly a decade of fighting. The following month, Djibouti restored diplomatic relations with Eritrea and also sought to play peacemaker between warring factions in neighboring Somalia. In May 2001, the Guelleh government reached a peace accord with the radical wing of FRUD, following which FRUD fighters voluntarily disarmed. Guelleh was elected to his second six-year term as president of Djibouti in 2005.

The indigenous population of the Republic of Djibouti is divided between the majority Somalis (predominantly of the Issa with minority Ishaak and Gadaboursi representation) and the Afars and Danakils.

DJIBOUTI

Official name: Republic of Djibouti
Independence: 27 June 1977 (from France)
Area: 23,000 sq km
Form of government: republic
Capital: Djibouti
Currency: Djiboutian franc (DJF)
Income: US$2,300 (2008 est. of purchasing power parity)
Population: 864,000 (2009 est.)
Ethnic groups: Somali 60%, Afar 35%, French, Arab, Ethiopian, and Italian 5%
Religious groups: Muslim 94%, Christian 6%
Languages: French (official), Arabic (official), Somali, Afar
Literacy: 67.9% (fifteen years old and over who can read and write; 2003 est.)
Exports: reexports, hides and skins, coffee (in transit)
Primary export partners: Somalia 64.6%, Ethiopia 20.9%, UAE 3.3% (2008)
Imports: foods, beverages, transport equipment, chemicals, petroleum products
Primary import partners: Saudi Arabia 22.1%, India 16.6%, China 9.1%, U.S. 6.5%, Malaysia 4.5%, Ethiopia 4.3% (2008)

A Man with Two Kneeling Camels on the Dry Bed of Lake Abbe in Djibouti. *Located on the northeast coast of the Horn of Africa, Djibouti gained its independence from France in 1977. The nation's indigenous population is divided between the majority Somalis (predominantly of the Issa) and the Afars and Danakils.* TONY WALTHAM/ROBERT HARDING WORLD IMAGERY/CORBIS

EGYPT

Egypt has endured as a unified state for more than 5,000 years, and archaeological evidence indicates that a developed Egyptian society has existed much longer. In about 3100 BCE, Egypt was united under a ruler known as Mena, or Menes, who inaugurated the thirty pharaonic dynasties into which Egypt's ancient history is divided—the Old and Middle Kingdoms and the New Empire.

In 525 BCE, the Persians dethroned the last pharaoh of the twenty-sixth dynasty. The country remained a Persian province until the conquest of Alexander the Great in 332 BCE. After Alexander's death in 323 BCE, Macedonian commander Ptolemy established personal control over Egypt, assuming the title of pharaoh in 304 BCE. The Ptolemaic line ended in 30 BCE with the suicide of Queen Cleopatra. Roman Emperor Augustus then established direct Roman control over Egypt, initiating almost seven centuries of Roman and Byzantine rule.

Egypt was invaded and conquered by Arab forces in 642 CE and a process of Arabization and Islamization ensued. The French arrived in Egypt in 1798, remaining until an Anglo-Ottoman invasion force drove them out three years later. Following a period of chaos, the Albanian Muhammad Ali obtained control of Egypt.

In 1882, the British occupied Egypt and declared it a formal protectorate on December 18, 1914. In deference to growing nationalist feelings, Britain unilaterally declared Egyptian independence on February 28, 1922. King Faud I ruled after independence until 1952, when Gamal Abdel Nasser overthrew him. Upon Nasser's death, Anwar el-Sadat (1918–1981) took over the leadership until he was assassinated in 1981 and succeeded by Hosni Mubarak.

The Mubarak government came under increasing fire from Muslim fundamentalists who, in 1992, began launching violent attacks against Western tourists, Coptic Christians, and government officials. Shortly before parliamentary elections in 1995, Mubarak accused the opposition Muslim Brotherhood of aiding and abetting some of the Muslim fundamentalist groups.

EGYPT

Official name: Arab Republic of Egypt
Independence: 28 February 1922 (from United Kingdom)
Area: 1,001,450 sq km
Form of government: republic
Capital: Cairo
Currency: Egyptian pound (EGP)
Income: US$5,896 (2008 est. of purchasing power parity)
Population: 77,420,000 (2009 est.)
Ethnic groups: Eastern Hamitic stock (Egyptians, Bedouins, and Berbers) 99%, Greek, Nubian, Armenian, other European (primarily Italian and French) 1%
Religious groups: Muslim (mostly Sunni) 94%, Coptic Christian and other 6%
Languages: Arabic (official), English and French widely understood by educated classes
Literacy: 57.7% (fifteen years old and over who can read and write; 2003 est.)
Exports: crude oil and petroleum products, cotton, textiles, metal products, chemicals
Primary export partners: Italy 10.3%, U.S. 7.7%, Spain 6.7%, Syria 5.1%, Saudi Arabia 5%, Japan 4.9%, Germany 4.9%, France 4% (2008)
Imports: machinery and equipment, foodstuffs, chemicals, wood products, fuels
Primary import partners: U.S. 10.6%, China 10.2%, Italy 7.5%, Germany 7%, Saudi Arabia 5% (2008)

A number of members of the Muslim Brotherhood were arrested and imprisoned, and Mubarak's National Democratic Party won an overwhelming victory in the parliamentary balloting.

The Mubarak government vigorously prosecuted the country's militant Islamic organizations. In April 1999, the government sentenced more than eighty-five members of the al-Jihad organization to a variety of punishments, including lengthy prison terms and execution. The action seemed only to fuel the militants' determination to continue its jihad (war) against the government. In September of that year, an Islamic militant attempted to assassinate Mubarak but was unsuccessful. Mubarak was later reelected to his fourth six-year term as president.

Although he faced ongoing protest for his many years as the country's head of state, Mubarak won a fifth term in 2005 and later announced reforms in presidential election laws. His government has since had to address issues of human rights and religious repression. In 2007, Amnesty International released a report critical of the Egyptian government for its participation in illegal detainments and torture. The government maintained that such measures were in line with the war on terror being waged against religious extremists who used more severe methods in their campaigns.

The Egyptian population is fairly homogenous—Mediterranean and Arab influences appear in the north, as well as some mixing in the south with the Nubians of northern Sudan. Ethnic minorities include a small number of Bedouin Arab nomads dispersed in the eastern and western deserts and in the Sinai, as well as some 50,000–200,000 Nubians living along the Nile in Upper Egypt.

EQUATORIAL GUINEA

The first inhabitants of the region that is now Equatorial Guinea are believed to have been Baka, Aka, and Mbenga (often referred to as "pygmies," which is considered a pejorative term by many), of whom only isolated pockets remain in northern Rio Muni. Bantu migrations between the seventeenth and nineteenth centuries brought coastal ethnic groups and the Fang people to the area.

The Portuguese, seeking a route to India, landed on the island of Bioko in 1471. The Portuguese retained control there until 1778, when the island and adjacent islets were ceded to Spain. From 1827 to 1843, Britain established a base on the island to combat the trade in enslaved Africans. The Treaty of Paris settled conflicting claims to the mainland in 1900.

In 1959, the Spanish territory of the Gulf of Guinea was established. In 1963, the name of the country was changed to Equatorial Guinea. In March 1968, under pressure from Equatoguinean nationalists and the United Nations, Spain announced that it would grant independence to Equatorial Guinea. In September 1968, Francisco Macías Nguema was elected first president of Equatorial Guinea, and independence was granted in October. A military coup occurred in 1979 deposing Nguema, who was put to death for "crimes against humanity." Lieutenant Colonel Teodoro Obiang Nguema Mbasogo, leader of the coup that brought down Nguema, succeeded him as president.

Although Obiang Nguema's government made a show of various political reforms over the past few decades, outside observers remain harshly critical of the regime's repressive policies. In addition, Obiang Nguema's government has been sharply criticized for

EQUATORIAL GUINEA

Official name: Republic of Equatorial Guinea
Independence: 12 October 1968 (from Spain)
Area: 28,051 sq km
Form of government: republic
Capital: Malabo
Currency: Communaute Financiere Africaine franc (CFAF)
Income: US$18,600 (2008 est. of purchasing power parity)
Population: 676,000 (2009 est.)
Ethnic groups: Bioko (primarily Bubi, some Fernandinos), Rio Muni (primarily Fang), some Europeans, mostly Spanish
Religious groups: nominally Christian and predominantly Roman Catholic, pagan practices
Languages: Spanish (official), French (official), pidgin English, Fang, Bubi, Igbo
Literacy: 85.7% (fifteen years old and over who can read and write; 2003 est.)
Exports: petroleum, timber, cocoa
Primary export partners: U.S. 24%, Spain 19.3%, China 16.2%, France 8.4%, Italy 6.3% (2008)
Primary import partners: Spain 15.2%, U.S. 13.4%, France 12.4%, Cote d'Ivoire 11.9%, China 10.4%, Italy 6.3%, UK 5.8% (2008)

mishandling the national economy during the oil boom of the 1990s.

Although Equatorial Guinea's oil production increased sharply during the late 1990s and into the new millennium, making the country's economy the fastest growing in the world by 2001, the benefits of the wealth that had been generated reached relatively few of its citizens.

As the health of President Obiang Nguema deteriorated in 2001, many observers felt the scene was set for a power struggle between the president's two eldest sons, Teodorin Nguema Obiang Mangué and Gabriel Nguema Lima. In 2002, several prominent opposition groups withdrew from the presidential elections, citing accusations of fraud. Election observers generally condemned Teodorin Obiang's subsequent win as fraudulent. In 2004, Mark Thatcher (son of the former British prime minister) and British mercenary Simon Mann were implicated in an assassination attempt on President Obiang. However, Amnesty International reported the following year that it could not substantiate such claims. In 2008, President Obiang dismantled the parliament, in the face of increasing complaints against his government. As a concession, he announced that there would be presidential elections in 2010.

The majority of the Equatoguinean people are of Bantu origin. The largest ethnic group, the Fang, constitutes 80% of the population and is divided into about sixty-seven clans. Those to the north of Rio Benito on Rio Muni speak Fang-Ntumu, and those to the south speak Fang-Okak, two mutually intelligible dialects. The Bubi, who form about 15% of the population, are indigenous to Bioko Island. In addition, several coastal groups exist, who are sometimes referred to as "Playeros," and include the Ndowes, Bujebas, Balengues, and Bengas on the mainland and small islands, and Fernandinos, a Creole community, on Bioko. These groups comprise about 5% of the population.

ERITREA

As an integral part of the Aksum kingdom, Eritrea shared its destiny with Ethiopia. Islamic colonists became established in the coastal area and dominated the region until the latter half of the nineteenth century, when Egyptians settled in the area. Founded in 1890 by the Italians, the colony of Eritrea was annexed by Ethiopia after World War II. For years, the Eritrean People's Liberation Forum waged a struggle for independence that was eventually won on May 25, 1993.

Since independence, neighboring Sudan and Eritrea frequently swapped charges that one was helping opposition groups seeking the overthrow of the other's government. This growing enmity resulted in a severing of diplomatic relations between the two in December 1994. In 1996 Eritrea skirmished briefly with both Djibouti over a contested border and with Yemen over ownership of a collection of small Red Sea Islands. Perhaps most seriously, however, armed conflict with Ethiopia erupted again in June 1998. The immediate cause of the fighting was again a disputed border, but tensions over trade issues had been building for months. Despite efforts by the United States, the Organization of African Unity, and neighboring African countries to resolve the conflict diplomatically, the border war between Eritrea and Ethiopia continued throughout 1999, slowing Eritrea's economic performance significantly. In May 2000, Ethiopian forces occupied previously undisputed areas in central and western Eritrea while consolidating their control over such disputed areas as Badme and Zela Ambesa. In July 2000, the newly established United Nations Mission in Ethiopia and Eritrea (UNMEE) deployed 4,200 peacekeeping forces

ERITREA

Official name: State of Eritrea
Independence: 24 May 1993 (from Ethiopia)
Area: 117,600 sq km
Form of government: transitional government
Capital: Asmara (formerly Asmera)
Currency: nakfa (ERN)
Income: US$700 (2008 est. of purchasing power parity)
Population: 5,073,000 (2009 est.)
Ethnic groups: ethnic Tigrinya 50%, Tigre and Kunama 40%, Afar 4%, Saho (Red Sea coast dwellers) 3%
Religious groups: Muslim, Coptic Christian, Roman Catholic, Protestant
Languages: Afar, Amharic, Arabic, Tigre and Kunama, Tigrinya, other Cushitic languages
Literacy: 58.6% (2003 est.)
Exports: livestock, sorghum, textiles, food, small manufacturers
Primary export partners: India 31.7%, Italy 18.6%, Kenya 11.9%, China 11.5%, France 5.4% (2008)
Imports: machinery, petroleum products, food, manufactured goods
Primary import partners: Italy 16.9%, UAE 15.7%, China 13%, India 9.4%, U.S. 6.7%, Germany 6%, Turkey 5% (2008)

in the disputed region, and in December 2000, both countries signed a peace agreement in Algiers. The regime of President Isaias Afewerki came under increasing criticism, some of it from high-profile government officials. Afewerki cracked down viciously on one group of fifteen outspoken critics, known as G-15, which helped to increase the disaffection of average Eritreans with their government. In 2004, the U.S. State Department declared that Eritrea's worsening religious and human rights abuse situation required additional monitoring. In October 2008, the U.S. State Department's Africa specialist, Jendai Frazer, announced that Eritrea was a state sponsor of terrorism. The nation was subsequently added to the list of such countries. In 2009, under the Obama administration, Secretary of State Hillary Rodham Clinton claimed that Eritrea was supplying weapons to Somalian militant groups. With backing from the African Union, the U.S. planned to initiate economic sanctions against the country.

ETHIOPIA

Ethiopia is the oldest independent country in Africa and one of the oldest in the world. Herodotus, the Greek historian of the fifth century BCE, describes ancient Ethiopia in his writings, and the Old Testament of the Bible records the Queen of Sheba's visit to Jerusalem. Missionaries from Egypt and Syria introduced Christianity to Ethiopia in the fourth century CE. Europeans did not make contact with this nation, however, until the Portuguese arrived in 1493. In the nineteenth century, as several European nations annexed or

ETHIOPIA

Official name: Federal Democratic Republic of Ethiopia
Independence: oldest independent country in Africa and one of the oldest in the world—at least 2,000 years
Area: 1,104,300 sq km
Form of government: federal republic
Capital: Addis Ababa
Currency: birr (ETB)
Income: US$800 (2008 est. of purchasing power parity)
Population: 79,221,000 (2008 est.)
Ethnic groups: Oromo 34%, Amhara 26%, Tigre 6%, Sidamo 4%, Shankella 6%, Somali 6%, Afar 4%, Gurage 2%, other smaller ethnic groups numbering more than fifty, 1%
Religious groups: Muslim 45–50%, Ethiopian Orthodox 35–40%, animist 12%, other 3–8%
Languages: Amharic, Tigrinya, Oromigna, Guaragigna, Somali, Arabic, other local languages, English (major foreign language taught in schools)
Literacy: 42.7% (fifteen years old and over who can read and write; 2003 est.)
Exports: coffee, gold, leather products, oilseeds, qat
Primary export partners: U.S. 10.1%, Germany 10%, Saudi Arabia 7.6%, Netherlands 7.1%, Djibouti 6.5%, Italy 5.6%, China 4.9% (2008)
Imports: food and live animals, petroleum and petroleum products, chemicals, machinery, motor vehicles
Primary import partners: China 19.5%, Saudi Arabia 17.9%, India 7.2%, U.S. 5%, Italy 4.4% (2008)

colonialized various parts of Africa, Ethiopia, then led by Menelik II, repelled an Italian incursion into the country in the 1896 Battle of Adwa using inferior weaponry.

In 1930, Haile Selassie was crowned emperor of Ethiopia. His reign was interrupted in 1935, when Italian fascist forces invaded and occupied Ethiopia in revenge for the Battle of Adwa humiliation nearly forty years earlier. The emperor fled the country and lived in exile in England, despite his plea to the League of Nations for intervention. Diasporan Africans joined the call to boycott Italian goods in what became known as the "Abyssian Affair." Five years later, British and Ethiopian forces defeated the Italians, and the emperor returned to the throne. After a period of civil unrest, which began in February 1974, the aging Haile Selassie was deposed on September 13, 1974. After deposing Selassie, the military, led by Colonel Mengistu Haile Mariam, took over the government and nationalized nearly all the country's economic institutions.

Discontent had been spreading throughout Ethiopian urban elites, and an escalating series of mutinies, demonstrations, and strikes led to the seizure of state power by the armed forces coordinating committee, which later became the Provisional Military Administrative Council (PMAC). The PMAC formally declared its intent to remake Ethiopia into a socialist state. It finally destroyed its opposition in a program of mass arrests and executions known as the "red terror," which lasted from November 1977 to March 1978. Government forces killed an estimated 10,000 people, mostly in Addis Ababa. Mengistu's failure to respond to growing national problems—droughts, civil war with Eritrea and Tigray, and declining Soviet aid—ended his rule. Early in 1991, forces of the Ethiopian People's Revolutionary Democratic Front (EPRDF), led by Meles Zenawi, forced Mengistu into exile in Zimbabwe. In December 2006, Mengistu was convicted *in absentia* of genocide.

In 1994, Ethiopia was faced with a host of challenges: the economy stagnated, the government's heavy regulation of commerce discouraged agricultural production and food distribution, and famine threatened. International assistance saved many lives, however, and, in 1995, the government finally established a process for returning nationalized land to private control. This redistribution of land seemingly improved Ethiopia's agricultural fortunes: the country enjoyed good harvests in both 1996 and 1997.

In the mid-1990s, Ethiopia also witnessed significant political achievements: delegates to a new legislative body, the Council of People's Representatives, were elected and a new constitution giving special rights to several ethnic groups was also adopted. The name of the country was officially changed to the Federal Democratic Republic of Ethiopia in August 1995—the same month that Meles Zenawi was elected prime minister by the new legislature. However, the late 1990s were marked by ethnic strife and violent raids carried out by soldiers discharged at the end of Ethiopia's long civil war. In 1998, a border dispute with neighboring Eritrea threatened to end Ethiopia's peaceful recovery from years of warfare. The border conflict expanded in 1999, spreading into areas that were previously undisputed. Finally, in June 2000, a cease-fire agreement was reached between the two countries. In December of that same year, a comprehensive peace accord was signed in Algiers.

Political turbulence marked the early years of the new millennium in Ethiopia. In the spring of 2001, the ruling Ethiopian People's Revolutionary Democratic Front (EPRDF) coalition experienced a critical split within its Tigrayan People's Liberation Front (TPLF) faction. Twelve TPLF members opposing the pro-capitalist policies of the government were ousted from the party and held under house arrest. President Negasso Gidada, siding with the TPLF dissidents, was thrown out as party leader. In October 2001, the country's parliament elected Girma Wolde-Giorgis president, but the political infighting had left the EPRDF regime decidedly weakened. In May 2005, the country held general elections which the EPRDF won decisively, although international observers claimed that the voting exercise did not meet the standard of a free and fair contest. Subsequently, the government was involved in the suppression of uprisings in the Ogaden region of the country, but allowed many other political parties to register and exist in relative peace.

Ethiopia's population is highly diverse. Most of its people speak a Semitic or Cushitic language. The Amhara, Tigreans, and Oromo make up more than three-fourths of the population, but there are more than forty different ethnic groups within Ethiopia.

GABON

Gabon's first European visitors were Portuguese traders who arrived in the fifteenth century. The coast became a center of enslavement commerce. Dutch, British, and French traders later came in the sixteenth century. France assumed the status of protector by signing treaties with Gabonese coastal chiefs in 1839 and 1841. In 1910, Gabon became one of the four territories of French Equatorial Africa, a federation that survived until 1959. The territories became independent in 1960 as the Central African Republic, Chad, Congo (Brazzaville), and Gabon, which was led by Léon M'ba after independence. Upon M'ba's death in 1967, Albert (later known as Omar) Bongo Ondimba took over as head of state. Reelected in 1973, 1979, and 1986, Bongo Ondimba faced growing opposition inside Gabon as the 1990s

GABON

Official name: Gabonese Republic
Independence: 17 August 1960 (from France)
Area: 267,667 sq km
Form of government: republic; multiparty presidential regime (opposition parties legalized in 1990)
Capital: Libreville
Currency: Communaute Financiere Africaine franc (CFAF)
Income: US$9,900 (2008 est. of purchasing power parity)
Population: 1,475,000 (2009)
Ethnic groups: Fang, Eshira, Bapounou, Bateke.
Religious groups: Christian 55–75%, animist, Muslim less than 1%
Languages: French (official), Fang, Myene, Bateke, Bapounou/Eschira, Bandjabi
Literacy: 63.2% (fifteen years old and over who can read and write; 2003 est.)
Exports: crude oil, timber, manganese, uranium
Primary export partners: U.S. 25.4%, China 17.9%, Japan 10.2%, Malaysia 5.8%, France 5.4%, Spain 4% (2008)
Imports: machinery and equipment, foodstuffs, chemicals, petroleum products, construction materials
Primary import partners: France 32.1%, U.S. 11.1%, China 5.2%, Belgium 4.6%, Cameroon 4.4%, Netherlands 4.2% (2008)

began. The Bongo Ondimba administration moved toward establishment of a multiparty system, but opposition parties that charged Bongo's regime with fraud rejected early attempts in 1990. A constitution adopted in 1991 formalized the multiparty system, and in the first elections under the new system in December 1993, Bongo Ondimba received 51.5% of the presidential vote. Unrest soon broke out in reaction to these elections, which were widely regarded as fraudulent. The commotion led to mediation and all opposition parties being brought into the government. In 1996, voters approved a new constitution which added a senate to the legislature.

Reelected as president in December 1998, Bongo Ondimba named Jean-Francois Ntoutome-Emane prime minister in 1999. The rest of Bongo Ondimba's cabinet was dominated by ministers close to the president and included no members from opposition parties. Bongo Ondimba's appointments came at a time of violent student protests and was followed shortly thereafter by widespread labor strikes triggered by a drop in world oil prices. The government's announcement in late 1999 that it would privatize the postal and telecommunications sectors set off further labor unrest. Despite widespread criticism, the ruling Gabonese Democratic Party won 84 of 120 seats up for grabs in the December 2001 legislative elections. In November 2005, Bongo Ondimba was reelected by a wide margin to another presidential term, making him the longest-serving African head of state. In June 2009, Bongo Ondimba died in office. He was briefly replaced by Rose Francine Rogombe, but in October 2009, Bongo Ondimba's son, Ali Ben Bongo, was installed as president after winning an election the month before. Various opposition parties protested and boycotted the elections, arguing that they were fraught with governmental corruption.

GAMBIA, THE

Gambia was once part of the Empire of Ghana and the Kingdom of Songhai. When the Portuguese visited in the fifteenth century, it was part of the Kingdom of Mali. By the sixteenth century, Portuguese traders and gold seekers had settled and had sold exclusive trade rights on the Gambia River to English merchants. During the late seventeenth century and throughout the eighteenth century, England and France struggled continuously for political and commercial supremacy in the regions of the Senegal and Gambia Rivers.

In 1807, the trading of enslaved Africans was abolished throughout the British Empire, and the British tried unsuccessfully to end the enslavement traffic in Gambia. Later, an 1889 agreement with France established the present boundaries of the nation, and Gambia became a colony of the British Crown. Gambia achieved independence on February 18, 1965, as a constitutional monarchy within the British Commonwealth. In 1970, Gambia became a republic. Several attempts were made to establish a post-independence union with Senegal. A contingent of Senegalese soldiers was stationed in Gambia, but the arrangement soured. Coupled with mounting economic problems, the confederation collapsed in 1989, although a new friendship treaty between the two countries was signed in 1991. Sir Dawda K. Jawara, who had led the country since independence in 1965, was overthrown by the military in July 1994. The leaders of the coup set up a provisional ruling council headed by Yayeh Jammeh. Pressured to restore democracy, Jammeh adopted a new constitution in August 1996 that was widely criticized for the restrictions imposed on opposition parties. Jammeh retired from the military and ran successfully for president in September 1996.

THE GAMBIA

Official name: Republic of the Gambia
Independence: 18 February 1965 (from United Kingdom)
Area: 11,300 sq km
Form of government: republic under multiparty democratic rule
Capital: Banjul
Currency: dalasi (GMD)
Income: US$1,395 (2008 est. of purchasing power parity)
Population: 1,705,000 (2009 est.)
Ethnic groups: Mandinka 42%, Fula 18%, Wolof 16%, Jola 10%, Serahuli 9%, other 4%
Religious groups: Muslim 90%, Christian 9%, indigenous beliefs 1%
Languages: English (official), Mandinka, Wolof, Fula, other indigenous vernaculars
Literacy: 40.1% (fifteen years old and over who can read and write; 2003 est.)
Exports: peanuts and peanut products, fish, cotton lint, palm kernels
Primary export partners: India 32.4%, Japan 22.2%, China 10.7%, Belgium 5.5%, UK 4.7% (2008)
Imports: foodstuffs, manufactures, fuel, machinery and transport equipment
Primary import partners: China 22.7%, Senegal 11.7%, Cote d'Ivoire 8.4%, Brazil 7.4%, Netherlands 4.9% (2008)

Criticism of the Jammeh government in 1999 was led by Ousainou Darboe of the opposition United Democratic Party. Darboe charged that the Jammeh regime was not only dictatorial but also inefficient. In July 2000, Darboe and other members of his party were charged with murder after a supporter of the ruling party was killed during campaigning in the eastern portion of the country. Gambia's relations with neighboring Senegal deteriorated during that same year. In October 2001, Jammeh won reelection as president, defeating Darboe, who had since been cleared of the murder charge. Jammeh again won reelection five years later, vowing to provide development opportunities only for those areas that supported him. Although the elections were judged fair, there were still complaints of journalists being harassed in The Gambia. In 2009, Amnesty International issued a report critical of President Jammeh's administration, which had embarked on a campaign against those practicing withcraft and sorcery in the country.

GHANA

The first contact between Europe and the Gold Coast dates to 1470 when a party of Portuguese arrived. For the next three centuries, the English, Danes, Dutch, Germans, and Portuguese controlled various parts of the coastal areas. In 1821, the British government took control of the British trading forts on the Gold Coast. In 1844, Fanti chiefs in the area signed an agreement with the British. Between 1826 and 1900, the British fought a series of campaigns against the Ashantis, whose kingdom was located inland. By 1902, the British had succeeded in colonizing the Ashanti region.

On March 6, 1957, the United Kingdom relinquished its control over the Colony of the Gold Coast

GHANA

Official name: Republic of Ghana
Independence: 6 March 1957 (from United Kingdom)
Area: 238,540 sq km
Form of government: constitutional democracy
Capital: Accra
Currency: cedi (GHC)
Income: US$1,538 (2008 est. of purchasing power parity)
Population: 23,834,000 (2009)
Ethnic groups: Akan 44%, Moshi-Dagomba 16%, Ewe 13%, Ga 8%
Religious groups: indigenous beliefs 38%, Muslim 30%, Christian 24%, other 8%
Languages: English (official), African languages (including Akan, Moshi-Dagomba, Ewe, and Ga)
Literacy: 74.8% (fifteen years old and over who can read and write; 2003 est.)
Exports: gold, cocoa, timber, tuna, bauxite, aluminum, manganese ore, diamonds
Primary export partners: Netherlands 15.3%, UK 9.1%, France 6.5%, U.S. 5.8% (2008)
Imports: capital equipment, petroleum, foodstuffs
Primary import partners: China 15.9%, Nigeria 15.8%, U.S. 5.9%, France 4.7%, UK 4.7% (2008)

and Ashanti, the Northern Territories Protectorate, and British Togoland. The Gold Coast and the former British Togoland merged to form what is now Ghana. Focusing on an ideology of anti-imperialism and pan-Africanism, Ghana became a model for the whole continent. Kwame Nkrumah, who had led Ghana to independence, was idolized throughout the continent. However, in the years that followed, Nkrumah turned increasingly dictatorial. In 1966, he was overthrown and went into exile in nearby Guinea. When Jerry Rawlings, who had masterminded two successful coups in 1979 and 1981, became head of state in 1982, he promised to return the country to pluralism. In 1992, he was elected to the presidency of Ghana in a multiparty election, and he won reelection in 1996. With an improved economic and political climate, the appointment of Ghanaian diplomat Kofi Annan to head the United Nations in 1997, and U.S. President Clinton's historic 1998 visit, Ghana's prominence among African nations was restored.

President Rawlings announced early in 1999 that he would not run for reelection in 2000. He personally selected Vice President John Evans Atta Mills as his heir apparent, resulting in a split within the ruling National Democratic Congress and the formation of a new party, the National Reform Movement. Mills's leading opponent at the polls in 2000 was John Kufuor, leader of the New Patriotic Party. In the December 2000 presidential elections, neither Mills nor Kufuor received enough votes to score an outright victory, but, in a later runoff race, Kufuor won handily, with 57% of the vote. Kufuor assumed power in January 2001 and immediately turned his attention to the country's struggling economy. President Kufuor was elected to a second and final term as head of state in 2004. He oversaw the country's Golden Jubilee celebration when Ghana observed its 50th anniversary in March 2007. In 2009, John Evans Atta Mills was sworn in as president of Ghana. In July of that year, Ghana became the first African country to host U.S. President Barack Obama. The Obama administration made the two-day trip there as a gesture to "lift up" the country as an example of African democracy at work. Ghana has had years of stability including a peaceful transfer of power.

GUINEA

Official name: Republic of Guinea
Independence: 2 October 1958 (from France)
Area: 245,857 sq km
Form of government: military junta
Capital: Conakry
Currency: Guinean franc (GNF)
Income: US$1,400 (2008 est. of purchasing power parity)
Population: 10,069,000 (2009 est.)
Ethnic groups: Peuhl 40%, Malinke 30%, Soussou 20%, smaller ethnic groups 10%
Religious groups: Muslim 85%, Christian 8%, indigenous beliefs 7%
Languages: French (official), each ethnic group has its own language
Literacy: 43.9% (fifteen years old and over who can read and write; 2003 est.)
Exports: bauxite, alumina, gold, diamonds, coffee, fish, agricultural products
Primary export partners: Spain 11.6%, Russia 11%, Ukraine 9.7%, Germany 7.7%, South Korea 7.2%, U.S. 6.7%, China 5.6%, Ireland 4.8%, France 4.8% (2008)
Imports: petroleum products, metals, machinery, transport equipment, textiles, grain and other foodstuffs
Primary import partners: China 10.3%, France 7.8%, Netherlands 7.6% (2008)

GUINEA

The empires of Ghana, Mali, and Songhai were the dominant kingdoms on the African continent from about the tenth to the fifteenth centuries. French military penetration into Guinea began in the mid-nineteenth century. By signing treaties with the French in the 1880s, Guinea's Malinke leader, Samory Touré, secured a free hand to expand eastward. In 1890, he allied himself with the Toucouleur Empire and Kingdom of Sikasso and tried to expel the French from the area. However, he was defeated in 1898, and France gained control of Guinea and the Ivory Coast (now Côte d'Ivoire).

Guinea became an independent republic in 1958 and voted against entering the French community. Se'kou Touré was the first president until his death in 1984. Shortly after his death, the interim government was ousted in a military coup led by Colonel Lansana Conté, who became president and leader of the Military Committee for National Rectification. He took ambitious steps to democratize the nation and dismantle the existing socialist state. In 1993, Conté was elected president in the country's first multiparty elections. A military mutiny in 1996, however, took some sixty lives before the president was able to negotiate a truce with his troops. In an attempt to restore confidence in his ability to improve the financial situation of the country, Conté appointed an economist, Sidya Touré, to the office of prime minister that same year.

In mid-December 1998, Conté was elected to his second term as president. Shortly thereafter, he named Lamine Sadimé as the country's new prime minister. Border tensions escalated between Guinea and the neighboring countries of Liberia and Sierra Leone. In March 1999, Guinean forces attacked Sierra Leone rebels who were holding large sections of the Kambia district, prompting a retaliatory attack by the rebels on two Guinean border towns. Guinea responded to the border attacks by launching a counterattack into Sierra Leone. Liberian President Charles Taylor, meanwhile, accused Guinea of harboring Liberian rebels. These continuing conflicts eventually created a refugee problem in Guinea. Efforts by President Conté's party to modify the constitution to allow a president to serve more than two terms further exacerbated political tensions within the country. Conte remained in power until December 2008 when he was overthrown in yet another coup by the military. Moussa Dadis Camara, another military man, was installed as acting president. In 2009, Camara was wounded by an aid and was flown outside of the country for medical attention. In early 2010, Sekouba Konate, the defense minister and vice president, served as the acting president with Jean-Marie Dores as a transitional prime minister. A meeting was held among several leading officials including Konate and Dores, and they produced a statement of principles in which the country would be returned to civilian rule. Presidential elections are scheduled for late June and July 2010.

GUINEA-BISSAU

The rivers of Guinea and the islands of Cape Verde were one of the first areas in Africa to be explored by the Portuguese in the fifteenth century. Portugal claimed the region that came to be known as Portuguese Guinea in 1446. In 1630, a "captaincy-general" of Portuguese Guinea was established to administer the territory. With the assistance of the local people, the Portuguese entered the trade in enslaved Africans, exporting large numbers of them to the New World through Cape Verde. The trade declined in the nineteenth century, and Bissau, originally founded as a fort in 1765, became the major commercial center of Portuguese Guinea.

In 1956, Amilcar Cabral and Raphael Barbosa organized the African Party for the Independence of Guinea and Cape Verde (PAIGC). Despite the presence of more than 30,000 Portuguese troops, the PAIGC exercised influence over much of the country; the Portuguese were increasingly confined to their garrisons and larger towns. The PAIGC National Assembly declared the independence of Guinea-Bissau on December 24, 1973, the same year that PAIGC leader Amilcar Cabral was assassinated by the Portuguese secret police. Portugal granted de jure independence on September 19, 1974, when the United States recognized the new nation. Luís de Almeida Cabral, Amilcar's brother, became president of Guinea-Bissau and Cape Verde. In 1980, when João Bernardo Vieira overthrew Cabral to assume the presidency of Guinea-Bissau, Cape Verde broke away, ending the alliance between the two formerly Portuguese nations.

Vieira, who survived a coup attempt in November 1985, was elected to five-year terms as president in 1984, 1989, and 1994. However, his administration was

GUINEA-BISSAU

Official name: Republic of Guinea-Bissau

Independence: 24 September 1973 (unilaterally declared by Guinea-Bissau); 10 September 1974 (recognized by Portugal)

Area: 36,120 sq km

Form of government: republic, multiparty since mid-1991

Capital: Bissau

Currency: Communaute Financiere Africaine franc (CFAF); previously, the Guinea-Bissau peso (GWP) was used

Income: US$486 (2008 est. of purchasing power parity)

Population: 1,611,000 (2009 est.)

Ethnic groups: Balanta 30%, Fula 20%, Manjaca 14%, Mandinga 13%, Papel 7%

Religious groups: indigenous beliefs 50%, Muslim 45%, Christian 5%

Languages: Portuguese (official), Crioulo, African languages

Literacy: 42.4% (fifteen years old and over who can read and write; 2003 est.)

Exports: cashew nuts, shrimp, peanuts, palm kernels, lumber

Primary export partners: India 74.8%, Nigeria 20.5%, Pakistan 0.7% (2008)

Imports: foodstuffs, machinery and transport equipment, petroleum products

Primary import partners: Portugal 24.6%, Senegal 17.3%, Pakistan 4.8%, France 4.6%, Cuba 4% (2008)

criticized for entrenched corruption. During a five-month civil war in 1998, rebel forces seized most of the country and part of the capital city Bissau. In November 1998, Vieira agreed to a peace accord that called for new elections and the disarmament of the presidential guard. After the presidential guard refused to disarm, however, a breakaway army faction drove Vieira from office in May 1999. He first sought refuge in the Portuguese Embassy but was later allowed to leave the country.

After Vieira left office, he was replaced by interim President Malam Bacai Sanhá, president of the national assembly and leader of an anti-Vieira faction of the African Party for the Independence of Guinea-Bissau and Cape Verde (PAIGC). In a runoff presidential election in January 2000, however, Sanhá was defeated by Kumba Ialá of the Party for Social Renewal (PRS). In early 2001, a coalition between the PRS and the Guinea-Bissau Resistance-Bah Fatah Movement collapsed. In the wake of the coalition's breakup, the government's credibility was eroded, and calls mounted for the resignation of Ialá and his cabinet. Ialá also came under fire for his treatment of the Ahmadiyya Islamic group, the leaders of which he deported in 2001. In 2003, there was a bloodless coup that removed Ialá for not solving the country's worsening economic situation, and installed Henrique Rosa.

In 2005, former President Ialá attempted a political comeback, but was defeated by former president João Bernardo Vieira. On March 2, 2009, however, President Vieira was assassinated in what some believed to have been the military's revenge for the killing of a senior general the day before. PAIGC candidate Malam Bacai Sanhá subsequently won the presidency of the country, assuming office in September 2009.

KENYA

Official name: Republic of Kenya

Independence: 12 December 1963 (from United Kingdom)

Area: 582,650 sq km

Form of government: republic

Capital: Nairobi

Currency: Kenyan shilling (KES)

Income: US$1,711 (2008 est. of purchasing power parity)

Population: 39,802,000 (2009 est.)

Ethnic groups: Kikuyu 22%, Luhya 14%, Luo 13%, Kalenjin 12%, Kamba 11%, Kisii 6%, Meru 6%, other African 15%, non-African (Asian, European, and Arab) 1%

Religious groups: Protestant 38%, Roman Catholic 28%, indigenous beliefs 26%, Muslim 7%, other 1%

Languages: English (official), Kiswahili (official), numerous indigenous languages

Literacy: 85.1% (fifteen years old and over who can read and write; 2003 est.)

Exports: tea, coffee, horticultural products, petroleum products, fish, cement

Primary export partners: Uganda 16.4%, UK 9.1%, Netherlands 8.3%, Tanzania 7.9%, U.S. 5.8%, Pakistan 5.1% (2008)

Imports: machinery and transportation equipment, petroleum products, iron and steel

Primary import partners: UAE 12.5%, China 10.5%, Saudi Arabia 8.7%, India 8.3%, South Africa 6.6%, Japan 5.6%, U.S. 4.2% (2008)

KENYA

The Cushitic-speaking people, who occupied the area that is now Kenya around 1000 BCE, were known to have maintained contact with Arab traders during the first century CE. Arab and Persian settlements were founded along the coast as early as the eighth century CE. By then, Bantu and Nilotic peoples also had moved into the area. The Portuguese followed the Arabs in 1498, by Islamic control under the Imam of Oman in the 1600s, and by British influence in the nineteenth century. In 1885, European powers first partitioned East Africa into spheres of influence. In 1895, the British government established the East African Protectorate.

From October 1952 to December 1959, Kenya was under a state of emergency, arising from the Mau Mau rebellion against British colonial rule. While Mau Mau was not successful militarily, it galvanized the indigenous population against colonialism as never before. The first direct elections for Africans to the legislative council took place in 1957, and then Kenya became fully independent on December 12, 1963. Jomo Kenyatta, a Kikuyu, and head of the Kenya African National Union, became Kenya's first president. He adopted a moderate, pro-Western policy and pursued capitalism internally, allowing Kenya to achieve a higher level of economic prosperity than its neighbors. Kenyatta died in 1978 and was succeeded by Daniel arap Moi, who, in his first few years as president, pursued a populist course. However, in 1982, the constitution was modified to make the country a one-party state. Mounting opposition to his repressive rule through the 1980s put increasing pressure on Moi, who, in December 1991, agreed to legalize opposition parties. Moi was reelected in 1992, although he continued to be the target of criticism from opposition parties upset by cumbersome restrictions on their activities. In December 1997, Moi was again returned to office, leading to widespread violence and continual accusations of corruption, ethnic favoritism, and human rights abuses.

Criticism of Moi's leadership increased in 1999. His appointment of Francis Masakhalia as finance minister and his reinstatement of George Saitoti as vice president particularly incensed Moi's critics. Former Energy Minister Chris Okemo eventually replaced Masakhalia in August 1999. In January 2001, Moi joined with the leaders of Tanzania and Uganda to launch a new East African Economic Community. In March 2001, Richard Leakey resigned as head of the Kenyan Civil Service, giving rise to fears that it might signal an end to efforts to root out government corruption, which had been led by Leakey. Even more alarming to Moi's opponents was his engineering of a merger between his ruling Kenya African National Union and the National Development Party, the country's second-largest opposition party. The opposition fired back in June 2001 by forming a new party, the National Party of Kenya.

Constitutionally barred from running for the presidency, Moi stepped down and was replaced as president in 2002 by his former minister Mwai Kibaki, who headed the National Rainbow Coalition (NARC). The election and succession was relatively smooth and marked a triumph for democracy for the country and the continent.

The country's December 2007 general election was a contest between Kibaki and his recently formed Party of National Unity and rival Raila Odinga and his Orange Democratic Union. Although all of the pre-election polling indicated that Odinga would win the presidency, overnight Kibaki was declared the winner. Stunning the country even more, Kibaki quickly had himself sworn in for his second term. Protest around the nation soon led to large-scale ethnic violence against ethnic Kikuyus (the group to which Kibaki belongs) who were living outside of their traditional home areas. This caused many of them to flee their homes and live in fields. More than 1,000 people died in the violence over the next two months and more than 200,000 people were left homeless.

International intervention was required to settle the conflict. High-profile individuals like former United Nations Secretary General Kofi Anan led a delegation which helped to form a grand coalition and resulted in the signing of the National Accord and Coalition Act in February, 2008. That legislation stipulated that Mwai Kibaki would remain as president and Raila Odinga would become Prime Minister. In 2009, Kenyans made a bid for hosting U.S. President Barack Obama (who is of Kenyan ancestry) during his first trip to the continent as president, but were disappointed when the offer was declined.

LESOTHO

Until the end of the sixteenth century, the Qhuaique, pejoratively referred to as "bushmen," sparsely populated Basutoland, now Lesotho. Between the sixteenth and nineteenth centuries, refugees from surrounding areas gradually joined the Qhuaique to form the Basotho ethnic group. In 1818, Moshoeshoe I consolidated various Basotho groupings and became king. During his reign from 1823 to 1870, a series of wars with South Africa resulted in the loss of extensive lands, now known as the "Lost Territory." Moshoeshoe appealed to Queen Victoria for assistance,

LESOTHO

Official name: Kingdom of Lesotho

Independence: 4 October 1966 (from United Kingdom)

Area: 30,355 sq km

Form of government: parliamentary constitutional monarchy

Capital: Maseru

Currency: loti (LSL); South African rand (ZAR)

Income: US$1,304 (2008 est. of purchasing power parity)

Population: 2,067,000 (2009 est.)

Ethnic groups: Sotho 99.7%, Europeans, Asians, and other 0.3%

Religious groups: Christian 80%, indigenous beliefs 20%

Languages: Sesotho (southern Sotho), English (official), Zulu, Xhosa

Literacy: 84.8% (fifteen years old and over who can read and write; 2003 est.)

Exports: manufactures 75% (clothing, footwear, road vehicles), wool and mohair, food and live animals

Primary export partners: U.S. 93.6%, Madagascar 1.7%, Canada 1.5% (2008)

Imports: food, building materials, vehicles, machinery, medicines, petroleum products

Primary import partners: China 31.1%, Taiwan 23.5%, Hong Kong 19.4%, India 13.8%, Germany 5.2% (2008)

and, in 1868, the country was placed under British protection.

In 1955, the Basutoland Council asked that it be empowered to legislate on internal affairs and, in 1959, a new constitution gave Basutoland its first elected legislature. On October 4, 1966, the new Kingdom of Lesotho attained full independence. Leabua Jonathan soon became the head of state and embarked on a campaign to suppress internal opposition. When he appeared to have lost in the nation's first post-independence elections of 1970, he declared a state of emergency, jailed opposition leaders, and seized power. In 1986, Jonathan was overthrown by the Lesotho military. On an interim basis, executive and legislative powers were vested in King Moshoeshoe II, although a military council exercised most powers. Moshoeshoe II was exiled in March 1990 and replaced by his son, who was enthroned as Letsie III. After Letsie came under increasing criticism from leaders of neighboring states, he abdicated in 1995 and returned the crown to his father, Moshoeshoe II. The following year, Moshoeshoe was killed in an auto accident, and Letsie III returned to the throne.

Violent anti-government protests prompted South Africa and Botswana to send troops into Lesotho in September 1998. Although those troops were withdrawn by late spring 1999, the impact of their intervention continued to be felt long after their departure. The intervention left the Lesotho Congress for Democracy (LCD) government of Prime Minister Bathuel Pakalitha Mosisili in power, but it also set up the Interim Political Authority (IPA), made up of representatives from the country's twelve major political parties. This set up a conflict between the LCD government and the IPA over what form the country's future electoral system should take. This debate continued until February 2001 when all parties endorsed a plan drafted by the Independent Election Commission for the holding of elections. Elections were held in 2002 and the LCD won handily with 54% of the vote.

Lesotho has also been plagued by AIDS/HIV, having one of the highest rates of prevalance among adults (age fifteen to forty-nine) in the world. In 2006, the nation embarked on an ambitious program of testing everyone for HIV in a "know your status" campaign. Bill Clinton and Bill Gates have committed funds (from their charitable foundations) to help alleviate the severity of the pandemic in Lesotho.

LIBERIA

It is believed that the forebears of many present-day Liberians migrated into the area from the north and east between the twelfth and seventeenth centuries. Portuguese explorers visited Liberia's coast in 1461, and during the next 300 years European merchants and coastal Africans engaged in trade.

The history of modern Liberia dates from 1816, when the American Colonization Society, a private organization, was given a charter by the United States Congress to send formerly enslaved Africans to the west coast of Africa. The United States government, under President James Monroe, provided funds and assisted in negotiations with native chiefs for the ceding of land for this purpose. The first settlers landed at the site of Monrovia

LIBERIA

Official name: Republic of Liberia

Independence: 26 July 1847

Area: 111,370 sq km

Form of government: republic

Capital: Monrovia

Currency: Liberian dollar (LRD)

Income: US$373 (2008 est. of purchasing power parity)

Population: 3,955,000 (2009 est.)

Ethnic groups: indigenous African groups 95% (including Kpelle, Bassa, Gio, Kru, Grebo, Mano, Krahn, Gola, Gbandi, Loma, Kissi, Vai, and Bella), Americo-Liberians 2.5% (descendants of African American immigrants from the United States), Congo People 2.5% (descendants of Caribbean immigrants)

Religious groups: indigenous beliefs 40%, Christian 40%, Muslim 20%

Languages: English 20% (official), some twenty ethnic group languages, of which a few can be written and are used in correspondence

Literacy: 57.5% (fifteen years old and over who can read and write; 2003 est.)

Exports: diamonds, iron ore, rubber, timber, coffee, cocoa

Primary export partners: Malaysia 38.2%, U.S. 15.9%, Poland 12.3%, Germany 9%, Belgium 6% (2008)

Imports: fuels, chemicals, machinery, transportation equipment, manufactured goods, rice and other foodstuffs

Primary import partners: South Korea 27.5%, Singapore 25.2%, Japan 11.6%, China 11.2% (2008)

in 1822. In 1838, the settlers united to form the Commonwealth of Liberia, under a governor appointed by the American Colonization Society.

In 1847, Liberia became Africa's first independent republic. The republic's first 100 years have been described as a "century of survival" due to attempts by neighboring colonial powers, particularly France and Britain, to encroach on Liberia. Independence gave power to the so-called Americo-Liberians who formed an elite class. The excluded indigenous population lacked the access and the opportunities of the Americo-Liberians and this created social tension. In 1980, Sargent Samuel Doe and his Council of Popular Redemption came to power in a bloody coup and sustained power through planned and random violent acts. Doe leaned on the Soviet Union for support and established himself as a dictator. He was gruesomely executed, however, in a videotaped killing in 1990. The National Patriotic Front, a rebel group led by Charles Taylor, organized the insurrection that ousted Doe. Taylor's group pitted itself against the Liberian army, a monitoring group from the Economic Community of West African States (ECOWAS), and the United Liberation Movement of Liberia for Democracy (ULIMO), a group made up of former Doe allies. Several attempts at ending the civil war were unsuccessful, and the strife continued well into the 1990s. Finally, in 1997, a program to disarm warring factions was declared a success (with the backing of Libyan President Muammar Qaddafi). In July of that year, Taylor was elected president by a landslide. He worked to rebuild the nation's economy, which had been shattered by years of civil war.

Taylor's government came under fire in early 1999 from a number of its neighbors, who charged that Liberia was supporting Revolutionary United Front (RUF) rebels in Sierra Leone. Although Liberia's civil war officially ended in January 1999, the nation continued to experience extensive political instability. The unrest exploded in fighting in the northern part of the country, where government troops battled against rebels. Relations with Guinea deteriorated nearly to the point of war after Taylor charged Guinea with supporting the northern rebels. Similarly strained were relations with Western governments. The European Union in June 2000 suspended aid to Liberia, and, in October, the United States imposed diplomatic sanctions on Taylor and his associates. Foreign disapprobation grew in March 2001 when the UN Security Council voted to impose sanctions on Liberia unless it halted its support for RUF rebels in Sierra Leone.

By 2003, an estimated 200,000 people had died in Liberia's civil wars, but peace was still not at hand. Rebel activity reached Monrovia as Taylor's support diminished. That year he was forced to resign and accepted asylum in Nigeria after U.S. Naval ships positioned themselves off the shores of Liberia. In November 2005, Ellen Johnson-Sirleaf, a U.S.-educated former minister, won a runoff election and became the first woman elected as a head of state on the African continent. One of her early actions was to request the extradition of Charles Taylor from Nigeria, which was granted in 2006. Taylor was tried and found guilty of crimes against humanity in the Hague the following year.

LIBYA

In the seventh century CE, Arabs conquered the area that is now Libya. In the following centuries, most of the inhabitants of the region adopted Islam and the Arabic language and culture. The Ottoman Turks then conquered the

LIBYA

Official name: Great Socialist People's Libyan Arab Jamahiriya

Independence: 24 December 1951 (from U.N. Trusteeship)

Area: 1,759,540 sq km

Form of government: Jamahiriya (a state of the masses) in theory, governed by the populace through local councils; in fact, a military dictatorship

Capital: Tripoli

Currency: Libyan dinar (LYD)

Income: US$14,000 (2008 est. of purchasing power parity)

Population: 6,490,000 (2009 est.)

Ethnic groups: Berber and Arab 97%, Greeks, Maltese, Italians, Egyptians, Pakistanis, Turks, Indians, Tunisians

Religious groups: Sunni Muslim 97%

Languages: Arabic, Italian, English, all are widely understood in the major cities

Literacy: 82.6% (fifteen years old and over who can read and write; 2003 est.)

Exports: crude oil, refined petroleum products

Primary export partners: Italy 39.5%, Germany 12.5%, France 7.7%, Spain 7.1%, U.S. 6.7%, China 4.2% (2008)

Imports: machinery, transport equipment, food, manufactured goods

Primary import partners: Italy 22.8%, Germany 8.9%, China 8.5%, Turkey 6.3%, Tunisia 6%, U.S. 4.2%, France 4.2% (2008)

country in the sixteenth century. Libya remained part of their empire (although, at times, virtually autonomous) until Italy invaded in 1911 and, after years of resistance, incorporated Libya as its colony.

King Idris I, Emir of Cyrenaica, led a Libyan resistance to Italian occupation between the two world wars. Under the terms of the 1947 peace treaty with the Allies, Italy relinquished all claims to Libya. On November 21, 1949, the United Nations General Assembly passed a resolution stating that Libya should become independent before January 1, 1952. Libya declared its independence on December 24, 1951.

In a later military coup, King Idris was overthrown in 1969 by Muammar al-Qaddafi, who nationalized all the petroleum resources and embarked on a program of support for international terrorism against Western countries. Some of Qaddafi's activities also created friction with neighboring countries, and in 1986, the United States bombed Tripoli and Benghazi. Five years later, during the Persian Gulf War, Libya opposed Iraq's seizure of Kuwait as well as the use of force against Iraq by the United States and its allies. In 1992, the United Nations imposed sanctions against Libya for its refusal to extradite two suspects in the 1988 bombing of Pan Am Flight 103 over Scotland. Those sanctions were lifted in 1999 when Libya turned the suspects over to the U.N. for trial by a Scottish court. Despite five unsuccessful coup attempts and considerable international animosity, Qaddafi remained in office as leader of Libya.

Qaddafi in the late 1990s and early years of the new millennium seemed to moderate his harsh attitude toward the West and particularly toward the United States. Nowhere was this change in policy more evident than in Qaddafi's response to the September 11, 2001, terrorist attacks on the United States. The Libyan leader called the attacks "horrifying" and urged Muslim charitable agencies to provide aid to the United States. The Libyan regime also shared intelligence with U.S. officials about Libyan Islamist militants with ties to al-Qaeda.

Since 2003, Libya has abandoned its weapons of mass destruction, and paid compensation to the families killed in the Pan Am flightof 1988. In 2008, the United States took definitive steps to normalize diplomatic relations with Libya.

MADAGASCAR

Located east of the African mainland in the Indian Ocean, Madagascar is home to people who arrived from Africa and Asia during the first five centuries CE. Three major kingdoms ruled the island—Betsimisaraka, Merina, and Sakalava. In the seventh century CE, Arabs established trading posts in the coastal areas of what is now Madagascar. The Portuguese sighted the island in the sixteenth century and, in the late seventeenth century, the French established trading posts along the east coast.

In the 1790s, the Merina rulers succeeded in establishing hegemony over the major part of the island, including the coast. The Merina rulers and the British governor of Mauritius concluded a treaty abolishing the trade in enslaved Africans, which had been an important part of Madagascar's economy, and in return the island received British military assistance. British influence remained strong for several decades. The British accepted the imposition of a French protectorate over Madagascar in 1885. France established control by military force in 1895, and the Merina monarchy was abolished. The Malagasy Republic was proclaimed on October 14, 1958, as an autonomous state within the French

MADAGASCAR

Official name: Republic of Madagascar
Independence: 26 June 1960 (from France)
Area: 587,040 sq km
Form of government: republic
Capital: Antananarivo
Currency: Malagasy ariary (MGA)
Income: US$996 (2008 est. of purchasing power parity)
Population: 20,653,000 (2009 est.)
Ethnic groups: Malayo-Indonesian (Merina and related Betsileo), Cotiers (mixed African, Malayo-Indonesian, and Arab ancestry—Betsimisaraka, Tsimihety, Antaisaka, Sakalava), French, Indian, Creole, Comoran
Religious groups: indigenous beliefs 52%, Christian 41%, Muslim 7%
Languages: French (official), Malagasy (official)
Literacy: 68.9% (fifteen years old and over who can read and write; 2003 est.)
Exports: coffee, vanilla, shellfish, sugar, cotton cloth, chromite, petroleum products
Primary export partners: France 28.8%, U.S. 23.7%, Netherlands 7%, Germany 6.3%, China 4.8% (2008)
Imports: intermediate manufactures, capital goods, petroleum, consumer goods, food
Primary import partners: China 16.3%, France 12.1%, Iran 8.3%, South Africa 6%, Mauritius 4.3% (2008)

Community. A period of provisional government ended with the adoption of a constitution in 1959 and full independence in 1960.

Madagascar pursued a moderate policy after independence, and collaboration with France continued until 1972 when a military coup installed a socialist government headed by General Gabriel Ramanantsoa. Ramanantsoa, who aligned his government with the East Bloc, was ousted and replaced by Lieutenant Commander Didier Ratsiraka in 1975. Late that year, the country was renamed the Democratic Republic of Madagascar. Through the 1980s and into the early 1990s, Ratsiraka's government faced growing opposition. In August 1991, the government promised to make democratic reforms. A year later, a new constitution was approved by popular vote. Albert Zafy defeated Ratsiraka in a presidential runoff election in 1993. Zafy was impeached in 1996 for failure to reach agreement with the International Monetary Fund (IMF) on the Malagasy franc's exchange rate, stepped down in October 1996, and ran unsuccessfully against Ratsiraka for the presidency in December 1996.

In 1999, the country's ruling party, Vanguard of the Malagasy Revolution, faced a new challenger in the form of the Gó Alliance, a coalition of opposition parties. All parties to the new opposition coalition were united in their dissatisfaction with the policies of President Ratsiraka but remained divided on other key issues, including the economy. In the December 2001 presidential elections, Ratsiraka trailed opponent Marc Ravalomanana, mayor of the capital city, but since neither candidate had a majority, the outcome of the election remained in question. The result was a political struggle between Ratsiraka and Ravalomanana that split the country. In May 2002, a court declared Ravalomanana winner of the election. Ravalomanana initiated anti-corruption changes and was reelected handily in December 2006.

A little more than two years later, however, after months of protest from various segments of the country and pressure from the military, President Ravalomanana resigned from office in March, 2009. His successor, self-proclaimed president Andry Rajoelina, spoke of a new constitution and announced that general elections would be held within two years.

MALAWI

Official name: Republic of Malawi
Independence: 6 July 1964 (from United Kingdom)
Area: 118,480 sq km
Form of government: multiparty democracy
Capital: Lilongwe
Currency: Malawian kwacha (MWK)
Income: US$835 (2008 est. of purchasing power parity)
Population: 15,263,000 (2009)
Ethnic groups: Chewa, Nyanja, Tumbuko, Yao, Lomwe, Sena, Tonga, Ngoni, Ngonde, Asian, European
Religious groups: Protestant 55%, Roman Catholic 20%, Muslim 20%, indigenous beliefs
Languages: English (official), Chichewa (official), other languages important regionally
Literacy: 62.7% (fifteen years old and over who can read and write; 2003 est.)
Exports: tobacco, tea, sugar, cotton, coffee, peanuts, wood products
Primary export partners: South Africa 10.8%, Egypt 9.8%, Zimbabwe 8.7%, U.S. 7.4%, Netherlands 7%, Russia 5.8%, Germany 5.7% (2008)
Imports: food, petroleum products, semimanufactures, consumer goods, transportation equipment
Primary import partners: South Africa 35.7%, India 8.1%, China 7.2%, Tanzania 5.8%, U.S. 4.5% (2008)

MALAWI

Hominid remains and stone implements dating back more than 1 million years have been identified in Malawi. Early humans are believed to have inhabited the area surrounding Lake Malawi 50,000–60,000 years ago.

Malawi derives its name from the Maravi, the group that came from the southern Congo more than 600 years ago. By the sixteenth century, two divisions of the Maravi had established a kingdom stretching from north of today's city of Nkhotakota in central Malawi to the Zambezi River in the south and from Lake Malawi in the east to the Luangwa River in Zambia in the west.

The Portuguese first reached the area in the sixteenth century. British missionary and explorer David Livingstone reached the shore of Lake Malawi in 1859. By 1878, a number of traders, mostly from Scotland, formed the African Lakes Company to supply goods and services to missionaries in the region. In 1891, the British established the Nyasaland Protectorate, covering the region now known as Malawi. Nyasaland joined with northern and southern Rhodesia in 1953 to form the Federation of Rhodesia and Nyasaland.

Throughout the 1950s, Nyasaland experienced a growing sentiment for independence. In July 1958,

Dr. Hastings Kamazu Banda returned to the country after a long stay in the United States (where he had obtained his medical degree at Meharry Medical College in 1937), the United Kingdom, and Ghana. He assumed leadership of the Nyasaland African Congress, which later became the Malawi Congress Party (MCP). In 1959, Banda was sent to Gwele Prison for his political activities, but was released in 1960.

On April 15, 1961, the MCP won an overwhelming victory in elections for a new legislative council. During a second constitutional conference in London in November of 1962, the British government agreed to give Nyasaland self-governing status the following year. Dr. Banda became prime minister on February 1, 1963, although the British still controlled Malawi's finance and judicial systems. The Federation of Rhodesia and Nyasaland was dissolved on December 31, 1963, and Malawi became fully independent on July 6, 1964. Two years later, Malawi adopted a new constitution and became a republic with Dr. Banda as its first president. In 1994, in the country's first multiparty elections, Bakili Muluzi, leader of the United Democratic Front and a former cabinet minister, defeated Banda. Muluzi freed political prisoners and closed three prisons. In 1995, Banda and a top aide went on trial for the 1983 murders of four government officials: both were acquitted in December 1995. Banda died two years later in South Africa, reportedly at the age of 101.

President Muluzi managed to hold on to the presidency during elections in 1999, defeating his nearest opponent, Gwanda Chakuamba, by the narrowest of margins. In October 2000, the president dismissed his entire cabinet after a report implicated cabinet ministers in widespread corruption. The government continued to root out corruption in 2001, arresting a total of six government officials in February on charges of embezzlement from the Ministry of Education. In 2004, another multiparty election was held and Bingu wa Mutharika won the presidency in a largely free and fair contest. Mutharika was reelected in 2009, amid charges of election irregularities.

MALI

Official name: Republic of Mali
Independence: 22 September 1960 (from France)
Area: 1.24 million sq km
Form of government: republic
Capital: Bamako
Currency: Communaute Financiere Africaine franc (CFAF)
Income: US$1,200 (2008 est. of purchasing power parity)
Population: 13,010,000 (2009 est.)
Ethnic groups: Mande 50% (Bambara, Malinke, Soninke), Peul 17%, Voltaic 12%, Songhai 6%, Tuareg and Moor 10%, other 5%
Religious groups: Muslim 90%, indigenous beliefs 9%, Christian 1%
Languages: French (official), Bambara 80%, numerous African languages
Literacy: 46.4% (fifteen years old and over who can read and write; 2003 est.)
Exports: cotton 50%, gold, livestock
Primary export partners: China 29%, Thailand 9.9%, Denmark 6%, Pakistan 4.8%, Morocco 4% (2008)
Imports: machinery and equipment, construction materials, petroleum, foodstuffs, textiles
Primary import partners: Senegal 13%, France 11.3%, Cote d'Ivoire 11.1%, China 6% (2008)

MALI

Mali is the cultural heir to a succession of ancient African empires—Ghana, Malinke, and Songhai—that occupied the West African savanna. The Ghana Empire, dominated by the Soninke people and centered in the area along the Malian-Mauritanian frontier, was a powerful trading state from about 700 to 1075 CE. The Malinke kingdom of Mali, from which the republic takes its name, had its origins on the upper Niger River in the eleventh century. Expanding rapidly in the thirteenth century under the leadership of Soundiata Keita, it reached its height of power about the year 1325, when it conquered Timbuktu and Gao. The Songhai Empire expanded its authority from its center in Gao during the period of 1465 to 1530. At its peak under Askia Mohammad I, the Songhai encompassed the Hausa states as far as Kano (in present-day Nigeria) and much of the territory that had belonged to the Mali Empire in the west. It was destroyed by a Moroccan invasion in 1591.

French military penetration of the region around Mali began about 1880. A French civilian governor of Soudan (the French name for the area) was appointed in 1893, but resistance to French control persisted until 1898 when the Malinke warrior, Samory Touré, was defeated after seven years of war. In January 1959, Soudan joined Senegal to form the Mali Federation, which became fully independent within the French Community on June 20, 1960. The federation collapsed on August 20, 1960, when Senegal seceded. On September 22, Soudan proclaimed itself the Republic of Mali and withdrew from the French Community.

The first head of state, Modibo Keita, followed a socialist orientation and gradually increased his authoritarian leadership. In 1968, a coup by the Military Committee of National Liberation overthrew Keita's government and set up a ruling junta led by Lieutenant Moussa Traoré. Although the Traoré government did little to advance the country's economy, Traoré was returned to office in 1979 and 1985. However, a military coup in March 1991 deposed Traoré. In January 1992, a new constitution was adopted and Alpha Oumar Kounaré was elected president in multiparty elections in April of that year. He was reelected to office in May 1997.

Former President Traoré, his wife, and his brother-in-law were sentenced to death in January 1999 after being convicted of embezzlement of state funds, among other corruption charges. However, in September of that year, President Konaré commuted the death sentences to life imprisonment. The government also launched a drive at that time to root out government inefficiency and corruption. On May 7, 2001, Mali and Namibia became the first two OAU member states to join the Pan-African Parliament, a key component of the new organization scheduled to replace the OAU. President Konaré canceled a December 2001 referendum that would have given him immunity from prosecution after widespread criticism of the proposed economic and political reforms.

In 2002, Amadou Toure, a retired general, succeeded Konaré as president and the country. For most of the decade, Mali has been one of the more politically and economically stable countries on the continent.

MAURITANIA

Official name: Islamic Republic of Mauritania
Independence: 28 November 1960 (from France)
Area: 1,030,700 sq km
Form of government: republic
Capital: Nouakchott
Currency: ouguiya (MRO)
Income: US$2,055 (2008 est. of purchasing power parity)
Population: 3,291,000 (2009 est.)
Ethnic groups: mixed Maur/black 40%, Maur 30%, black 30%
Religious groups: Muslim 100%
Languages: Hasaniya Arabic (official), Pular, Soninke, Wolof (official), French
Literacy: 51.2% (fifteen years old and over who can read and write; 2003 est.)
Exports: iron ore, fish and fish products, gold
Primary export partners: China 39.9%, France 10.4%, Spain 7.1%, Italy 7%, Netherlands 5.5%, Belgium 4.8%, Cote d'Ivoire 4.1% (2008)
Imports: machinery and equipment, petroleum products, capital goods, foodstuffs, consumer goods
Primary import partners: France 16.3%, China 8.4%, Netherlands 6.2%, Spain 5.9%, Belgium 5.2%, U.S. 4.9%, Brazil 4.4% (2008)

MAURITANIA

Archaeological evidence suggests that Berber and Negroid Mauritanians lived beside one another in the territory now known as Mauritania, before the spread of the desert drove them southward. Migration of these people increased during the third and fourth centuries CE, when Berber groups arrived in the region seeking pastureland for their herds and safety from political unrest and war in the north. The Berbers established a loose confederation, called the Sanhadja, and trading towns to facilitate the trade of gold, ivory, and those enslaved.

In the tenth century, conquests by warriors from the Soudanese Kingdom of Ghana broke up the Berber confederation. By the eleventh century, the conquest of the Western Sahara regions by the Berbers firmly established Islam throughout Mauritania. The Berbers conquered the Ghanaian kingdom; however, Arab invaders defeated them in the sixteenth century.

French military penetration of Mauritania began early in the twentieth century. However, the area did not come under French control until about 1934. Until independence, the French governed the country largely by relying on the authority of the local chiefs, some of whom, such as the Emirs of Trarza and Adrar, had considerable authority. Under French occupation, enslavement was legally abolished.

Mauritania became a French colony in 1920. The Islamic Republic of Mauritania was proclaimed in November 1958. Mauritania became independent on November 28, 1960, and withdrew from the French Community in 1966.

Mokhtar Ould Daddah, leader of the Mauritian People's Party, was the first head of state, but a series of coups took place: the first, in 1978, replaced Daddah with Col. Moustabpha Ould Mohammed Salek, who was then replaced by Prime Minister Mohammed Khouma Ould

Haidalla. In 1984, another coup, this one led by Haidalla deputy Maawiya Ould Sid'Ahmed Taya, unseated Haidalla. Under increasing pressure to democratize, Taya in 1991 adopted a new constitution creating a multiparty state. In a disputed January 1992 election, Taya was chosen executive president. Even though important U.S. aid had been cut off due to a poor human rights record and allegations of slave trading, Taya was returned to office in 1996.

President Taya's ruling party and its allies easily won control of all local councils in two-stage local elections held in early 1999, largely because the balloting was boycotted by major opposition parties. In March of that year, prominent opposition leader Ahmed Ould Daddah, runner-up to Taya in the 1992 election, was charged with inciting intolerance and seeking to disrupt public order. In the 2001 legislative elections, the ruling Democratic and Social Republican Party won 64 of 81 seats in the National Assembly. Later that year, oil deposits were discovered in Mauritania. However, the country continues to suffer from a poor economy and a distressing human rights record. In August 2005, President Taya's twenty-one year rule came to an end when he was overthrown by Colonel Ely Ould Mohamed Vall. Colonel Vall was installed as president by a military council shortly afterward. Vall staged a national referendum the following year, during which Mauritanians approved of a new constitution limiting the duration of a president's stay in office. Vall abided by that decision, leaving office peacefully as his term expired.

In 2007 Sidi Ould Cheikh Abdallahi was elected president in a close race, but was overthrown the following year by several high-ranking generals. The political situation in the country was still tentative, as of 2010, in the face of the recent occurrences. In August 2008, the civilian government was overthrown in a military coup by General Mohammed Abdel Aziz. He resigned from that office in April 2009 to run for the office of president, which he formally won in July of that year.

MAURITIUS

Official name: Republic of Mauritius
Independence: 12 March 1968 (from United Kingdom)
Area: 2,040 sq km
Form of government: parliamentary democracy
Capital: Port Louis
Currency: Mauritian rupee (MUR)
Income: US$12,011 (2008 est. of purchasing power parity)
Population: 1,288,000 (2009 est.)
Ethnic groups: Indo-Mauritian 68%, Creole 27%, Sino-Mauritian 3%, Franco-Mauritian 2%
Religious groups: Hindu 52%, Christian 28.3% (Roman Catholic 26%, Protestant 2.3%), Muslim 16.6%, other 3.1%
Languages: English (official), Creole, French, Hindi, Urdu, Hakka, Bojpoori
Literacy: 85.6% (fifteen years old and over who can read and write; 2003 est.)
Exports: clothing and textiles, sugar, cut flowers, molasses
Primary export partners: UK 29.9%, France 14.7%, U.S. 8.3%, Madagascar 7%, Italy 6.4%, Belgium 5%, UAE 4.9% (2008)
Imports: manufactured goods, capital equipment, foodstuffs, petroleum products, chemicals
Primary import partners: India 21.3%, France 11.9%, China 9.4%, South Africa 7.6% (2008)

MAURITIUS

Portuguese sailors first visited Mauritius in the early sixteenth century, although Arabs and Malays knew the island much earlier. Dutch sailors, who named the island in honor of Prince Maurice of Nassau, established a small colony in 1638, but abandoned it in 1710. The French claimed Mauritius in 1715, renaming it Ile de France. In 1810, the British, whose possession of the island was confirmed four years later by the Treaty of Paris, captured Mauritius. After enslavement was abolished in 1835, indentured laborers from India brought an additional cultural influence to the island. Mauritius achieved independence on March 12, 1968. Sir Seewoosagur Ramgoolam, head of the Mauritius Labor Party (MLP), led the country for the first fourteen years of independence. The opposition Mauritian Military Movement (MMM), under the leadership of Aneerood Jugnauth, came to power in 1982. Pushed from power in an internal MMM struggle, Jugnauth formed a new opposition party, the Mauritian Socialist Movement (MSM). The MSM joined with the MLP in 1983 to win a parliamentary majority. The MSM-MLP coalition was again victorious in both 1987 and 1991. In 1992, the country became a republic, and the national assembly elected Cassam Uteem president. In December 1995, Navin Ramgoolam, son of Seewoosagur Ramgoolam, replaced Jugnauth as prime minister.

The island was rocked in early 1999 by three days of rioting by members of the Creole ethnic community, triggered by the death of a popular reggae singer in police custody. An opposition alliance of the Mauritian Militant Movement (MMM) and the Mauritian Socialist Movement (MSM) won a sweeping victory in the September 2000 legislative elections, capturing all but eight of the sixty-two legislative seats. The opposition's victory brought MSM leader Sir Anerood Jugnauth into the prime minister's office. Under the terms of the alliance between the MSM and MMM, Paul Berenger, leader of the MMM, was to take over the final two years as prime minister after Jugnauth had served the first three. Despite rumors of mounting tensions between Jugnauth and Berenger, their ruling coalition remained intact throughout 2001. Throughout this decade, Mayotte enjoyed tremendous political prosperity and stability. The elections held in May 2010 were smoothly run, and Mayotte continued to be a well-respected member of the Southern African Development Community, especially with regard to human and political rights.

MAYOTTE (MAHORÉ)

Part of the Comoros archipelago, Mayotte shares its history with the Comoros Federal Islamic Republic. When Comoros declared independence in 1975, Mayotte voted to remain an overseas territory of France. Although Comoros has since claimed Mayotte, the French have promised the islanders that they may remain French citizens for as long as they wish. Both the United Nations and the Organization of African Unity, however, have recognized Mayotte as part of the Comoros.

In March 2009, voters overwhelmingly approved a referendum that would change the island's status from French "overseas community" to become the 101st *département* of France, increasing its allegiance to the French legal and social system while receiving full benefits of the French welfare and health care systems (along with a proportionate increase in taxes). Mayotte's change in status becomes effective in 2011.

MAYOTTE

Official name: Territorial Collectivity of Mayotte
Independence: none (territorial collectivity of France)
Area: 374 sq km
Capital: Mamoudzou
Currency: French franc (FRF); euro (EUR)
Income: US$2,600 (2003 est. of purchasing power parity)
Population: 194,000 (2009 est.)
Religious groups: Muslim 97%, Christian (mostly Roman Catholic)
Languages: Mahorian (a Swahili dialect), French (official language)
Exports: ylang-ylang (perfume essence), vanilla, copra, coconuts, coffee, cinnamon
Imports: food, machinery and equipment, transportation equipment, metals, chemicals

MOROCCO

Arab forces began occupying Morocco in the seventh century CE, bringing with them Arab civilization and Islam. Morocco's location and resources led to early competition among Europeans in Africa, beginning with

MOROCCO

Official name: Kingdom of Morocco
Independence: 2 March 1956 (from France)
Area: 446,550 sq km
Form of government: constitutional monarchy
Capital: Rabat
Currency: Moroccan dirham (MAD)
Income: US$4,362 (2008 est. of purchasing power parity)
Population: 34,859,364 (2009 est.)
Ethnic groups: Arab-Berber 99.1%, other 0.7%, Jewish 0.2%
Religious groups: Muslim 98.7%, Christian 1.1%, Jewish 0.2%
Languages: Arabic (official), Berber dialects, French (often the language of business, government, and diplomacy)
Literacy: 51.7% (fifteen years old and over who can read and write; 2003 est.)
Exports: phosphates and fertilizers, food and beverages, minerals
Primary export partners: Spain 18.7%, France 17.1%, Brazil 6.9%, U.S. 4.4%, Belgium 4.3%, Italy 4.2% (2008)
Imports: semi-processed goods, machinery and equipment, food and beverages, consumer goods, fuel
Primary import partners: France 17%, Spain 14.2%, Italy 6.8%, Saudi Arabia 6.8%, China 6.3%, Germany 5.9%, U.S. 4.1% (2008)

successful Portuguese efforts to control the Atlantic coast in the fifteenth century. France showed a strong interest in Morocco as early as 1830. The Treaty of Fez (1912) made Morocco a protectorate of France. By the same treaty, Spain assumed the role of protecting power over the northern and southern (Saharan) zones. The Kingdom of Morocco recovered its political independence from France on March 2, 1956, and by agreements with Spain in 1956 and 1958.

Morocco's claim to sovereignty over the Western Sahara, also known as Spanish Sahara, is based largely on the historical argument of traditional loyalty of the Saharan traditional leaders to the Moroccan sultan as spiritual leader and ruler. The International Court of Justice, to which the issue was referred, delivered its opinion in 1975 that while historical ties exist between the inhabitants of the Western Sahara and Morocco, they are insufficient to establish Moroccan sovereignty.

Morocco, however, exerted pressure on Spain in 1974 and 1975 to relinquish the Western Sahara. When the Spanish left the territory in 1976, they ceded the northern two-thirds to Morocco and the southern one-third to Mauritania. However, the Polisario Front, a nationalist guerrilla organization, disputed the disposition of the territory. Polisario declared the territory an independent nation. All claimants skirmished over the territory for years, until a cease-fire was declared in 1991. The dispute, however, has not been fully resolved.

King Hassan II ruled Morocco from 1961 until his death in July 1999. Although he offered strong support for the Arab cause during the 1967 war with Israel, Arab extremists identified Hassan as soft on Israel, and several attempts were made on his life. In the late 1990s, Islamic extremists forced Hassan to create a new parliamentary body. Upon his death, Hassan's son, Mohamed VI, assumed the throne.

One of the first indications of the direction of Mohamed VI's rule came in 1999, when he began to strip power from Interior Minister Driss Basri, his father's closest adviser. By November of that year, the new king had dismissed Basri from office altogether. Mohamed VI's proposals in 2000 for a new family code met strong opposition from the country's Islamist movements. They were particularly outraged by plans to outlaw polygamy and give women greater equality with men. The progress of political liberalization slowed significantly during 2001, signaled by a crackdown on the press and the king's cancellation of a scheduled meeting with officials of the International Federation for Human Rights. In 2004, Morocco signed free trade agreements with the United States and the European Union. In 2006, the country celebrated its 50th anniversary as an independent state.

MOZAMBIQUE

Mozambique's first inhabitants were Bushmanoid hunters and gatherers, ancestors of the Khoisani peoples from southern Africa. During the first four centuries CE, waves of Bantu-speaking peoples migrated from the north through the Zambezi River Valley and then gradually into the plateau and coastal areas. When Portuguese explorers reached Mozambique in 1498, Arab trading settlements had existed along the coast for several centuries. Later, traders and prospectors penetrated the hinterland seeking gold and enslaved Africans.

After World War II, while many European nations were granting independence to their colonies, Portugal clung to the concept that Mozambique and other Portuguese possessions were "overseas provinces." In 1962, several Mozambican political groups formed the Front for Liberation of Mozambique (FRELIMO). Two

MOZAMBIQUE

Official name: Republic of Mozambique
Independence: 25 June 1975 (from Portugal)
Area: 801,590 sq km
Form of government: republic
Capital: Maputo
Currency: meticai (MZM)
Income: US$990 (2008 est. of purchasing power parity)
Population: 22,894,000 (2009)
Ethnic groups: indigenous 99.66% (Shangaan, Chokwe, Manyika, Sena, Makua, and others), Europeans 0.06%, Euro-Africans 0.2%, Indians 0.08%
Religious groups: indigenous beliefs 50%, Christian 30%, Muslim 20%
Languages: Portuguese (official), indigenous dialects
Literacy: 47.8% (fifteen years old and over who can read and write; 2003 est.)
Exports: prawns 40%, cashews, cotton, sugar, citrus, timber, bulk electricity
Primary export partners: South Africa 17.3%, Italy 14.9%, Spain 11.4%, Belgium 11.1%, UK 5.3%, China 4.9%, Zimbabwe 4.6% (2008)
Imports: machinery and equipment, mineral products, chemicals, metals, foodstuffs, textiles
Primary import partners: South Africa 34.3%, Australia 8.4%, China 6.1%, U.S. 5% (2008)

years later, FRELIMO initiated an armed campaign against Portuguese colonial rule. After ten years of sporadic warfare and major political changes in Portugal, Mozambique became independent on June 25, 1975.

Samora Machel led FRELIMO to independence in 1975 and immediately faced civil war with the Mozambique National Resistance (RENAMO). More than 600,000 people were killed in the civil war, while farms, roads, and railways were destroyed and half of the population was dislocated. After Samora was killed in an air crash in 1986, Joaquím Chissano became head of state. A cease-fire was reached with RENAMO in 1992, and the country's first multiparty elections were held in October 1994. Chissano was elected president, and FRELIMO, his party, won 129 of 250 assembly seats. A United Nations peacekeeping force, which had been deployed in December 1992, was withdrawn from Mozambique in early 1995. Privatization of industries there has led to significant foreign investment by international corporations and the World Bank.

President Chissano won reelection in the presidential elections held in late 1999. However, opposition leader Afonso Dhlakama, head of RENAMO, disputed the results. In 2000, RENAMO struck back at Chissano by charging that the president was responsible for the painfully slow arrival of foreign relief after massive flooding caused by Cyclone Eline earlier in the year. Widespread political unrest and sporadic fighting followed. Late in the year, Chissano and Dhlakama met in an effort to resolve the differences between the government and RENAMO. In 2004, the government of Mozambique approved new general election laws, which governed the presidential contest that year. Armando Guebuza of the FRELIMO party was inaugurated as president in 2005.

NAMIBIA

Official name: Republic of Namibia

Independence: 21 March 1990 (from South African mandate)

Area: 825,418 sq km

Form of government: republic

Capital: Windhoek

Currency: Namibian dollar (NAD); South African rand (ZAR)

Income: US$6,611 (2008 est. of purchasing power parity)

Population: 2,171,000 (2009)

Ethnic groups: black 87.5%, white 6%, mixed 6.5%

Religious groups: Christian 80% to 90% (Lutheran the majority), indigenous beliefs 10% to 20%

Languages: English 7% (official), Afrikaans (common language of most of the population and about 60% of the white population), German 32%, indigenous languages: Oshivambo, Herero, Nama

Literacy: 84% (fifteen years old and over who can read and write; 2003 est.)

Exports: diamonds, copper, gold, zinc, lead, uranium, cattle, processed fish, karakul skins

Imports: foodstuffs; petroleum products and fuel, machinery and equipment, chemicals

NAMIBIA

In 1878, the United Kingdom annexed Walvis Bay (a coastal city and region in what is now known as Namibia) on behalf of Cape Colony, and the area was incorporated into the Cape of Good Hope in 1884. In 1883, a German trader, Adolf Luderitz, claimed the remainder of the region after negotiations with a local chief. German administration ended during World War I, when South African forces occupied the territory in 1915.

On December 17, 1920, South Africa undertook the administration of South West Africa under the terms of Article 22 of the Covenant of the League of Nations and a mandate agreement confirmed by the League Council. The mandate agreement gave South Africa full power of administration and legislation over the territory as an integral part of South Africa. During the 1960s, as other African nations gained independence, pressure mounted on South Africa to liberate South West Africa.

In 1966, the United Nations General Assembly revoked South Africa's mandate. Also in 1966, the South West Africa People's Organization (SWAPO) began guerrilla attacks on Namibia, infiltrating the territory from bases in Zambia. In a 1971 advisory opinion, the International Court of Justice upheld United Nations authority over Namibia, determining that the South African presence in Namibia was illegal and that South Africa, therefore, was obligated to withdraw its administration from Namibia immediately. In 1977, the United Nations approved Security Council Resolution 435 that called for the holding of elections in Namibia under U.N. supervision and the cessation of hostile acts by all parties. South Africa agreed to cooperate in achieving implementation of Resolution 435. Nevertheless, in December 1978, in defiance of the U.N. proposal, South Africa unilaterally held elections in Namibia that were boycotted by SWAPO and other political parties.

Intense discussions between the concerned parties continued during the 1978–1988 period. In May 1988, a U.S. mediation team brought negotiators from Angola, Cuba, and South Africa and observers from the Soviet Union together in London. On April 1, the Republic of South Africa agreed to withdraw its troops. Implementation of Resolution 435 officially began on April 1, 1989. The elections held November 7–11, 1989, were certified as free and fair by the special representative, with SWAPO taking 57% of the vote; the Democratic Turnhalle Alliance, the principal opposition party, received 29% of the vote. By February 9, 1990, the constituent assembly had drafted and adopted a constitution. March 21 of that same year was set as the date for independence. SWAPO's Sam Nujoma won elections, and he became the first head of state in 1990.

For the next four years, until February 1994, South Africa continued to administer a small Namibian enclave containing the nation's major seaport, Walvis Bay. In 1994 elections, SWAPO won fifty-three of seventy-two seats in the National Assembly. However, dissatisfaction with SWAPO and Nujoma increased. The international community criticized Nujoma's plans to run for a third term as president (which the nation's constitution does not permit) as well as his government's lavish spending habits.

In the December 1999 presidential elections, Nujoma won reelection to a third term in a landslide, capturing more than 75% of the votes cast. His nearest rival in the election was Ben Ulenga, whose party, the Congress of Democrats, took over in early 2000 as the main opposition party. Nujoma's decision to allow Angolan armed forces to operate in the northern part of Namibia ensnared the country in the Angolan civil war. The resulting destabilization of northern Namibia continued through most of 2001. Nujoma backed his political ally, Hifikepunye Pohamba, in the country's next round of presidential elections and Pohamba was inaugurated as Namibia's second president in 2005. With a commanding 70% of the vote, Hifikepunye Pohamba was re-elected during the November 27–29th nationwide election. His nearest competitor polled a distant 10% of the vote.

Namibia is one of the least populated countries in Africa. Namibia's indigenous Africans are of diverse linguistic and ethnic origins. The principal groups are the Ovambo, Kavango, Herero/Himba, Damara, mixed race ("Colored" and Rehoboth Baster), white (Afrikaner, German, and Portuguese), Nama, Caprivian (Lozi), Bushman, and Tswana. The minority white population is primarily of South African, British, and German descent. Approximately 60% of the white population speaks Afrikaans (a variation of Dutch), 30% German, and 10% English.

NIGER

Considerable evidence indicates that, thousands of years ago, humans inhabited what has since become the desolate Sahara of northern Niger. Niger was an important ancient economic crossroads, and the empires of Songhai, Mali, Gao, Kanem, and Bornu, as well as a number of Hausa states, claimed control over portions of the area.

During recent centuries, the nomadic Taureg formed large confederations, pushed southward and, siding with various Hausa states, clashed with the Fulani empire of Sokoto, which had gained control of much of the Hausa territory in the late eighteenth century. In the nineteenth century, the first European explorers reached the area searching for the mouth of the Niger River.

Although French efforts at colonization began before 1900, dissident ethnic groups, especially the desert Taureg, were not defeated until 1922. On December 4,

NIGER

Official name: Republic of Niger
Independence: 3 August 1960 (from France)
Area:1,267,000 sq km
Form of government: republic
Capital: Niamey
Currency: Communaute Financiere Africaine franc (CFAF)
Income: US$739 (2008 est. of purchasing power parity)
Population: 15,299,000 (2009 est.)
Ethnic groups: Hausa 56%, Djerma 22%, Fula 8.5%, Tuareg 8%, Beri Beri (Kanouri) 4.3%, Arab, Toubou, and Gourmantche 1.2%, about 1,200 French expatriates
Religious groups: Muslim 80%, remainder indigenous beliefs and Christians
Languages: French (official), Hausa, Djerma
Literacy: 17.6% (fifteen years old and over who can read and write; 2003 est.)
Exports: uranium ore, livestock, cowpeas, onions
Primary export partners: Japan 80.4%, Nigeria 8.5%, France 2.9% (2008)
Imports: consumer goods, primary materials, machinery, vehicles and parts, petroleum, cereals
Primary import partners: France 19.4%, Nigeria 8.6%, China 8.5%, French Polynesia 7.6%, Belgium 5%, Cote d'Ivoire 4.9% (2008)

1958, after the establishment of the Fifth French Republic, Niger became an autonomous state within the French Community. Niger was granted full independence on August 3, 1960, and former Prime Minister Hamani Diori, one of the founders of the Nigerian Progressive Party (PPN), was appointed president of the new republic. Diori was overthrown in a military coup in 1974 and replaced by Col. Seyni Kountché as president. Thirteen years later, upon his death in 1987, Kountché was succeeded by his Chief of Staff Ali Saibou. More recently, Ibrahim Barré Mainassara was confirmed as president in elections held in July 1996. Mainassara had assumed the post as president earlier that year, after ousting Mahamane Ousmane, Niger's first democratically elected president.

President Mainassara was assassinated outside Niamey in early April 1999, after which the military assumed control of the country. Major Daouda Malam Wanké, commander of the presidential guard suspected of gunning down Mainassara, was named military ruler, and he promised an early return to civilian rule. In presidential elections later that year, retired army colonel Tandja Mamadou was elected the new civilian president. In early 2000, Mamadou installed a twenty-four member government and called for emergency action to revitalize the country's economy. The country experienced extensive civil unrest throughout 2001, much of it traceable to the continuing food crisis and the government's decision to reduce grants for university students. Mamadou was returned to the presidency for another term in 2004. He dissolved the country's parliamentary body in May 2009 after it refused to grant him a third term in office.

NIGERIA

Evidence shows that, more than 2,000 years ago, the Nok people, who lived in what is now the Plateau state (in the northeastern part of Nigeria), worked iron and produced sophisticated terra cotta sculpture. In the centuries that followed, the Hausa kingdom and the Bornu Empire near Lake Chad prospered as important terminals of north-south trade between North African Berbers and forest people who exchanged enslaved peoples, ivory, and kola nuts for salt, glass beads, coral, cloth, weapons, brass rods, and cowrie shells used as currency. In the southwest part of present-day Nigeria, the Uoruba kingdom of Oyo, which was founded about 1400 and reached its height between the seventeenth and nineteenth centuries, attained a high level of political organization and extended as far as modern Togo. In the south-central part of the area, as early as the fifteenth century, the kingdom of Benin had developed an efficient army, an elaborate ceremonial court, and artisans whose works in ivory, wood, bronze, and brass are prized throughout the world today.

NIGERIA

Official name: Federal Republic of Nigeria
Independence: 1 October 1960 (from United Kingdom)
Area: 923,768 sq km
Form of government: republic
Capital: Abuja
Currency: naira (NGN)
Income: US$2,100 (2008 est. of purchasing power parity)
Population: 154,729,000 (2009)
Ethnic groups: Nigeria, which is Africa's most populous country, is composed of more than 250 ethnic groups; the following are the most populous and politically influential: Hausa and Fulani 29%, Yoruba 21%, Igbo (Ibo) 18%, Ijaw 10%, Kanuri 4%, Ibibio 3.5%, Tiv 2.5%
Religious groups: Muslim 50%, Christian 40%, indigenous beliefs 10%
Languages: English (official), Hausa, Yoruba, Igbo (Ibo), Fulani
Literacy: 68% (fifteen years old and over who can read and write; 2003 est.)
Exports: petroleum and petroleum products 95%, cocoa, rubber
Primary export partners: U.S. 45.8%, Brazil 10.4%, Spain 8%, France 5% (2008)
Imports: machinery, chemicals, transport equipment, manufactured goods, food and live animals
Primary import partners: China 12.7%, Netherlands 10.5%, U.S. 8.2%, South Korea 5.6%, UK 5.2%, France 4.3% (2008)

Between the seventeenth and nineteenth centuries, European traders established coastal ports for the increasing traffic in captured Africans destined for enslavement in the Americas. In 1855, British claims to a sphere of influence in that area received international recognition, and in the following year, the Royal Niger Company was chartered. The company's territory came under the control of the British government in 1900. Fourteen years later, the area was formally united as the "Colony and Protectorate of Nigeria." Nigeria was granted full independence on October 1, 1960, as a federation of three regions.

Since independence, Nigeria has faced numerous coups and political turmoil. The Igbos (Ibos) tried to secede after the country's first coup d'etat in 1966. Yakubu Gowon (b. 1934) ascended to power as head of state at this time, ruling from 1966 to 1975. The coup led to tensions among various ethnic groups and ultimately to a tragic civil war (1967–1970). The presence of oil in the Southeastern region, however, allowed the country to recover economically from the war. Murtala Ramat Mohammed overthrew Yakubu Gowon and succeeded him as military head of state in 1975. Just seven months later, however, Mohammed was assassinated in a coup, and General Olusegun Obasanjo ruled Nigeria from 1976 to 1979. A return to civilian rule came in 1979 when Shehu Shagari was elected president of Nigeria. However, the military returned to power in 1984 when Mohammed Buhari seized the presidency in another coup, only to be ousted by Major General Ibrahim Babangida. Defense Minister Sani Abacha ascended to power on November 17, 1993. His government was internationally denounced for widespread human rights abuses including numerous executions. Under increasing domestic and international pressure, Abacha promised to implement a new constitution (drafted by a constitutional commission in 1995) following presidential elections in October 1998. However, Abacha died of a heart attack in June 1998. His successor, General Abdulsalam Abubakar, met with several opposition leaders and foreign diplomats, promised to respect the election timetable, and released many political prisoners. Following riots due to the death of famed political prisoner Moshood K. Abiola, Abubakar announced a new transition program that called for the military's withdrawal in May 1999.

In the country's first democratic elections in years, held in late May 1999, Olusegun Obasanjo, leader of the People's Democratic Party, was elected president. As his first order of business, Obasanjo focused on rooting out widespread government corruption. To help hasten Nigeria's transition to democracy, Obasanjo in 2000 continued his assault on government corruption and announced a major reform of the country's military. In April 2001, Obasanjo replaced the leaders of all of the branches of Nigeria's armed forces. Obasanjo also dismissed vice president Atiku Abubakar, who was among 135 politicians ruled as too corrupt to stand in the upcoming elections. Another social obstacle that Nigeria must contend with is the Christian-Muslim divide, which has resulted in violent riots on several occasions.

In 2007, general elections were held in Nigeria and Umaru Yar'Adua of the People's Democratic Party was elected. The election process, however, was condemned internationally as significantly flawed and fraught with corruption.

The most populous country in Africa, Nigeria accounts for one-quarter of sub-Saharan Africa's people. The dominant ethnic group in the northern two-thirds of the country is the Hausa-Fulani, most of whom are Muslims. Other major ethnic groups of the north are the Nupe, Tiv, and Kanuri. The Yoruba people are predominant in the southwest. About half of the Yorubas are Christian and half are Muslim. The predominantly Catholic Igbos (Ibos) are the largest ethnic group in the southeast, with the Efik, Ibibio, and Ijaw comprising a substantial segment of the population in that area as well. Nigeria also has a significant diasporan community that has immigrated to Europe and the United States.

RWANDA

Members of the Hutu tribe farmed the area that is now Rwanda alone until the fifteenth century, when Tutsi herders also settled in the area. In 1899, the court of Mwami (the Tutsi king) submitted to a German protectorate with resistance. Belgian troops from the Congo occupied Rwanda in 1916, and, after World War I, the League of Nations mandated Rwanda and its southern neighbor, Burundi, to Belgium as the Territory of Ruanda-Urundi. Following World War II, Ruanda-Urundi became a United Nations trust territory with Belgium as the administering authority. The Party of the Hutu Emancipation Movement (PARMEHUTU) won an overwhelming victory in a U.N. supervised referendum in 1961.

The PARMEHUTU government, formed as a result of the 1961 election, was granted internal autonomy by Belgium on January 1, 1962. A United Nations General Assembly resolution terminated the Belgian trusteeship and granted full independence to Rwanda (and Burundi) effective July 1, 1962. Gregiore Kayibanda, leader of the PARMEHUTU Party, became Rwanda's first elected president.

While ethnic clashes continued with neighboring Burundi, General Juvenal Habyarimana, who had been a military head of state, returned to power in the presidential elections of 1978 and 1983 (having been the only candidate in both elections). In 1994, shortly after ending peace talks with the Tutsi-backed Rwandan Patriotic Front (RPF), President Habyarimana and Burundian President Cyprien Ntaryamira were killed together when their plane was shot down near Kigali. Rwanda exploded in ethnic violence, and the Hutu-dominated Rwandan army went on a rampage, reportedly killing close to 1 million Rwandans, mostly Tutsis and Hutus sympathetic to the Tutsi cause. The murders were often arbitrary and brutal. Recruited hooligans carried out many of the killings. Even the accusation or rumor of someone being a Tutsi sympathizer was enough of a motive for that person to be attacked or eliminated. Various media outlets, especially Radio Rwanda, played a significant role in inciting the

RWANDA

Official name: Rwandese Republic
Independence: 1 July 1962 (from Belgium-administered U.N. trusteeship)
Area: 26,338 sq km
Form of government: republic; presidential, multiparty system
Capital: Kigali
Currency: Rwandan franc (RWF)
Income: US$1,043 (2008 est. of purchasing power parity)
Population: 10,473,282 (2009)
Ethnic groups: Hutu 84%, Tutsi 15%, Twa (Pygmoid) 1%
Religious groups: Roman Catholic 56.5%, Protestant 26%, Adventist 11.1%, Muslim 4.6%, indigenous beliefs 0.1%, none 1.7% (2006)
Languages: Kinyarwanda (official) universal Bantu vernacular, French (official), English (official), Kiswahili (Swahili) used in commercial centers
Literacy: 70.4% (fifteen years old and over who can read and write; 2003 est.)
Exports: coffee, tea, hides, tin ore
Primary export partners: China 9.1%, Thailand 8.8%, Germany 7.5%, U.S. 4.6%, Belgium 4.2% (2008)
Imports: foodstuffs, machinery and equipment, steel, petroleum products, cement and construction material
Primary import partners: Kenya 17.1%, China 6.2%, Uganda 6%, Belgium 5.9%, Germany 5.1% (2008)

violence. Forces of the RPF and the Rwandan army soon were in a full-blown civil war. A cease-fire was established in July 1994, and a government backed by the RPF was installed in Kigali. Promises of amnesty failed to convince many of the Hutus, who had fled into the former Zaire (now the Democratic Republic of the Congo), to return.

Regional instability continued to threaten Rwanda's recovery, as exhibited by renewed fighting along the Democratic Republic of the Congo border in 1998. Many Tutsi on both sides of the border aided Laurent-Désiré Kabila to oust then-Zaire's President Mobutu. But Kabila, facing pressure within his own country, purged his military of Rwandan and Congolese Tutsi in 1997. This breach of trust, combined with the continuing agitation of Hutu refugees in Congo, led Rwanda's government to support an armed rebellion against Kabila's government in the Democratic Republic of the Congo during 1998.

Rwanda remained caught up in the conflict with the Democratic Republic of the Congo throughout 1999. The Rwanda government, led by President Pasteur Bizimungu, repeatedly accused Congo President Laurent Kabila of sheltering and supporting Rwanda's extremist Hutu militia. Rwanda vowed to fight with anti-Kabila rebels to overthrow the Kabila regime. In March 2000, after conflicts with the predominantly Tutsi ruling party over cabinet appointments, President Bizimungu, himself a moderate Hutu, resigned and was replaced by Major General Paul Kagame. In May 2001, ethnic violence flared up again when Hutu rebels launched attacks in Rwanda's northwest. The government was successful in putting down the insurgency. Several prominent leaders of the genocide were tried through the International Criminal Tribunal for Rwanda. In 2003, a new constitution, which forbids discrimination based on ethnicity or religion, was put into place. Other reconciliation efforts continued long after the 1994 genocide. In 2006, French courts indicted several associates of Paul Kigame for war crime atrocities, but not Kigame himself as he is a head of state. In 2008, Théoneste Bagosora, one of the major figures in the genocide, was found guilty of crimes against humanity, including the death of Rwanda Prime Minister Agathe Uwilingiyamana and several Belgian peacekeepers.

SAINT HELENA

The islands of Saint Helena, Ascension, and Tristan da Cunha lie about one-third of the way from Africa to South America in the South Atlantic Ocean. The islands remained uninhabited until they were first explored by the Portuguese navigator, João de Nova, in 1502. In 1659, the British East India Company established a settlement on Saint Helena and, in 1673, was granted a charter to govern the island. Napoleon was exiled to Saint Helena from 1815 until his death in 1821.

SÃO TOMÉ AND PRÍNCIPE

Portuguese navigators first visited the uninhabited islands of São Tomé and Príncipe between 1469 and 1472. The first successful settlement of São Tomé was established in 1493. Príncipe was settled in 1500. By the mid-1500s, with the help of the labor of enslaved Africans, the Portuguese settlers had turned the two islands into Africa's foremost exporter of sugar. São Tomé and Príncipe were taken over and administered by the Portuguese crown in 1522 and 1573, respectively. By 1908, São Tomé had become the world's largest producer of cocoa, which is still the country's most important crop.

SAINT HELENA

Area: 308 sq km
Form of government: overseas territory of United Kingdom
Capital: Jamestown
Currency: Saint Helena pound (SHP)
Population: 7,637 (2009 est.)
Ethnic groups: African descent 50%, white 25%, Chinese 25%
Religious groups: Anglican (majority), Baptist, Seventh-Day Adventist, Roman Catholic, Jehovah's Witnesses
Languages: English
Literacy: 97% (twenty years old and over who can read and write; 2003 est.)
Exports: fish (frozen, canned, and salt-dried skipjack, tuna), coffee, handicrafts
Primary export partners: Tanzania 30.3%, U.S. 23.8%, Japan 10.4%, UK 7.1%, Spain 6.3% (2004)
Imports: food, beverages, tobacco, fuel oils, animal feed, building materials, motor vehicles and parts, machinery and parts
Primary import partners: UK 35.7%, U.S. 17.6%, South Africa 17.5%, Tanzania 10.4%, Australia 5.5%, Spain 4.1% (2004)

SÃO TOMÉ AND PRÍNCIPE

Official name: Democratic Republic of São Tomé and Príncipe
Independence: 12 July 1975 (from Portugal)
Area: 1,001 sq km
Form of government: republic
Capital: São Tomé
Currency: dobra (STD)
Income: US$1,711 (2008 est. of purchasing power parity)
Population: 212,679 (2009 est.)
Ethnic groups: Mestico, Angolares (descendants of enslaved Angolans), Forros (descendants of those who had been freed), Servicais (contract laborers from Angola, Mozambique, and Cape Verde), Tongas (children of Servicais born on the islands), Europeans (primarily Portuguese)
Religious groups: Christian 80% (Roman Catholic, Evangelical Protestant, Seventh-Day Adventist)
Languages: Portuguese (official)
Literacy: 79.3% (fifteen years old and over who can read and write; 2003 est.)
Exports: cocoa 90%, copra, coffee, palm oil
Primary export partners: Japan 75.5%, Belgium 7.5%, Netherlands 6.2% (2008)
Imports: machinery and electrical equipment, food products, petroleum products
Primary import partners: Portugal 55.9%, Belgium 9.6%, Japan 9.3% (2008)

The rocas system, which gave plantation managers a high degree of authority, led to abuses against the African farm workers. Although Portugal officially abolished enslavement in 1876, the practice of forced paid labor continued. Sporadic labor unrest and dissatisfaction continued well into the twentieth century, culminating in an outbreak of riots in 1953 in which several hundred African laborers were killed.

By the late 1950s, a small group of São Tomé residents had formed the Movement for the Liberation of São Tomé and Príncipe (MLSTP). In 1974, Portuguese representatives met with the MLSTP in Algiers and worked out an agreement for the transfer of sovereignty. After a period of transition, São Tomé and Príncipe achieved independence on July 12, 1975, choosing as its first president the MLSTP Secretary General Manuel Pinto da Costa. Four years after independence, da Costa consolidated his power by eliminating the position of prime minister and assuming those duties himself. He served until 1991, when Miguel Trovoada of the Independent Democratic Action (ADI) party was elected as president. A coup by military officers on August 15, 1995, removed Trovoada from office, but only briefly. He was reinstated as president seven days later after he agreed to amnesty for the officers engineering the coup. In 1996, he was reelected to a five-year term.

In March 1999, Prime Minister Guilherme Posser da Costa pledged the government to a renewed program of economic stability, aimed principally at reducing inflation, which was running at a rate of more than 20 percent at that time. The following year, da Costa reshuffled his cabinet after two ministers resigned. Although President Trovoada was unable to run for a third term in the country's 2001 presidential election, ADI candidate Fradique de Menezes won the race. Shortly after taking office, de Menezes called for a reshuffling of the cabinet. When da Costa balked at some of the new president's suggestions, Evaristo Carvalho replaced him as prime minister. In July 2003, the army occupied the government for a week in an attempted coup, but after negotiations, President de Menenzes stayed in office. In the 2006 presidential elections, de Menenzes won another term.

São Tomé and Príncipe's population consists of people descended from groups that have migrated to the islands since 1485. Six groups are identifiable: mestizo, of mixed-blood, descendants of enslaved Africans who were brought to the islands during the early years of settlement from Benin, Gabon, Congo, and Angola. There were also the Anglares, reputedly descendants of enslaved Angolans who survived a 1540 shipwreck and subsequently earned their livelihood fishing. There were the Forros, and the Servicais, who were contract laborers from Angola, Mozambique, and Cape Verde, living temporarily on the islands; Tongas, children of Servicais born on the islands; and Europeans, primarily Portuguese.

SENEGAL

Archaeological findings throughout the area indicate that Senegal was inhabited in prehistoric times. Islam was established in the Senegal River valley during the eleventh century. In the thirteenth and fourteenth centuries, the area came under the influence of the great Mandingo empires to the east, during which the Jolof Empire of Senegal was founded. The empire comprised the states of Cayor, Baol, Oualo, Sine, and Soloum until the sixteenth century, when they revolted for independence.

The Portuguese were the first Europeans to trade in Senegal, arriving in the fifteenth century. The Dutch and French soon followed. During the nineteenth century, the French gradually established control over the interior regions and administered them as a protectorate until 1920 and as a colony thereafter.

In January 1959, Senegal and the French Soudan merged to form the Mali Federation, which became fully independent on June 20, 1960. Due to internal political difficulties, the federation broke up on August 20, 1960; Senegal and Soudan (renamed the Republic of Mali) each proclaimed separate independence. Leopold Sedar Senghor, an internationally renowned poet, politician, and statesman, was elected Senegal's first president in August of 1960. Senghor instituted a multiparty system in 1976. He stepped down in 1980, naming Abdou Diouf, prime minister since 1970, as his successor. Senegal joined with Gambia in 1982 to form the confederation of Senegambia, headed by Diouf. The confederation collapsed at the end of the 1980s, although the two countries in 1991 signed a new treaty of cooperation.

SENEGAL

Official name: Republic of Senegal

Independence: 4 April 1960 (from France); complete independence was achieved upon dissolution of federation with Mali on 20 August 1960

Area: 196,190 sq km

Form of government: republic under multiparty democratic rule

Capital: Dakar

Currency: Communaute Financiere Africaine franc (CFAF)

Income: US$1,600 (2008 est. of purchasing power parity)

Population: 13,711,000 (2009 est.)

Ethnic groups: Wolof 43.3%, Pular 23.8%, Serer 14.7%, Jola 3.7%, Mandinka 3%, Soninke 1.1%, European and Lebanese 1%, other 9.4%

Religious groups: Muslim 92%, indigenous beliefs 6%, Christian 2% (mostly Roman Catholic)

Languages: French (official), Wolof, Pulaar, Jola, Mandinka

Literacy: 40.2% (fifteen years old and over who can read and write; 2003 est.)

Exports: fish, ground nuts (peanuts), petroleum products, phosphates, cotton

Primary export partners: Mali 19.5%, India 5.9%, France 5.5%, Gambia, The 5.4%, Italy 4.9% (2008)

Imports: foods and beverages, consumer goods, capital goods, petroleum products

Primary import partners: France 20%, UK 15.4%, China 7.5%, Belgium 4.6%, Thailand 4.5%, Netherlands 4.1% (2008)

Over time, the Senegalese public became increasingly disenchanted with Diouf and his Socialist Party's grip on power. In 1991, Diouf initiated electoral reforms, though the changes failed to satisfy opposition leaders. Diouf was again elected to a seven-year term as president in 1993. President Bill Clinton's 1998 visit to Senegal signaled a greater U.S. interest in the country.

Presidential elections in February 2000 produced no clear-cut victor, forcing a runoff election between incumbent Diouf and Abdoulaye Wade, a longtime opposition leader. Wade easily defeated Diouf and assumed the presidency on April 1, 2000. Just over a year later, on

April 29, 2001, Wade led a coalition of forty parties to victory in parliamentary elections, winning 89 of 120 seats in the National Assembly. Wade was reelected to the presidency in 2007.

Senegal is regarded regionally and internationally as the most stable democracy in Africa. The successive governments have addressed human rights issues, and often played a critical role in continental and international peacekeeping efforts.

SEYCHELLES

In 1742, the French governor of Mauritius sent an expedition to the Seychelles islands. A second expedition in 1756 reasserted formal possession by France. The Seychelles Islands were captured and freed several times during the French Revolution and the Napoleonic wars, then passed officially to the British under the Treaty of Paris in 1814. Negotiations with the United Kingdom resulted in an agreement by which Seychelles became a sovereign republic on June 29, 1976. The republic initially functioned as a multiparty government, but, one year after indepedence, Prime Minister France Albert René, founder of the People's United Party (later People's Progressive Front), was installed as president in a coup d'état. René instituted his People's Progressive Front as the nation's only party. Despite several attempted coups during the 1980s, René was able to hold onto power, and, in 1991, the government turned toward a multiparty state. René was elected to a fourth term in 1993, after which he implemented a number of free-market reforms, promoting the islands as a center for offshore banking. In addition, several national industries were privatized during this period.

Guy Morel, a former governor of the central bank, announced the formation of a new political party, the Social Democratic Party, in April 1999. Morel, previously a member of the ruling People's Progressive Front, said the government's failure to deal effectively with economic problems was the primary motivation for his actions. President René managed to hold on to his office in the September 2001 presidential elections in which the country's faltering economy was the key issue. René stepped down in 2004, and Vice President James Michel assumed the presidency. Michel was reelected to office in 2006.

The Seychelles ranked second on the Ibrahim Index of African Governance (out of forty-eight countries evaluated) in 2008, marking the nation as one of the most stable and well-governed countries on the continent.

Most Seychellois are descendants of early French settlers and the enslaved Africans brought to the Seychelles in the nineteenth century by the British, who freed them from slave ships on the East African coast. Indians and Chinese account for the other permanent inhabitants of the islands.

SEYCHELLES

Official name: Republic of Seychelles
Independence: 29 June 1976 (from United Kingdom)
Area: 455 sq km
Form of government: republic
Capital: Victoria
Currency: Seychelles rupee (SCR)
Income: US$9,640 (2008 est. of purchasing power parity)
Population: 87,000 (2009 est.)
Ethnic groups: Seychellois (mixture of Asians, Africans, Europeans)
Religious groups: Roman Catholic 82%, Anglican 6%, other 12%
Languages: English (official), French (official), Creole
Literacy: 91.9% (fifteen years old and over who can read and write; 2003 est.)
Exports: fish, cinnamon bark, copra, petroleum products (reexports)
Primary export partners: UK 22.1%, France 20%, Mauritius 10.5%, Japan 8.3%, Italy 8.1%, Netherlands 6.3%, Spain 4% (2008)
Imports: machinery and equipment, foodstuffs, petroleum products, chemicals
Primary import partners: Saudi Arabia 18.3%, Singapore 12.9%, France 10.8%, Spain 8.5%, Germany 7.4%, South Africa 5.7% (2008)

SIERRA LEONE

Sierra Leone was one of the first West African British colonies. In 1787, the territory that became known as Freetown received 400 freedmen from Great Britain, as the British initiated plans to make the area a refuge within the British Empire for formerly enslaved persons. Disease and hostility from the indigenous people almost eliminated this first group. Five years later, however, another group of settlers, 1,000 freed men and women who had fled from the United States to Nova Scotia, Canada during the American Revolution arrived under the auspices of the newly formed British Sierra Leone Company. In 1800, about 550 blacks arrived from Jamaica via Nova Scotia; these were the maroons and runaways who had maintained their independence in the mountains of Jamaica.

SIERRA LEONE

Official name: Republic of Sierra Leone
Independence: 27 April 1961 (from United Kingdom)
Area: 71,740 sq km
Form of government: constitutional democracy
Capital: Freetown
Income: US$724 (2008 est. of purchasing power parity)
Population: 6,440,053 (2009 est.)
Ethnic groups: 20 native African groups 90% (Temne 30%, Mende 30%, other 30%), Creole 10% (descendants of freed Jamaicans who were settled in the Freetown area in the late-eighteenth century), refugees from Liberia's civil war, small numbers of Europeans, Lebanese, Pakistanis, and Indians
Religious groups: Muslim 60%, indigenous beliefs 30%, Christian 10%
Languages: English (official, regular use limited to literate minority), Mende (principal vernacular in the south), Temne (principal vernacular in the north), Krio (English-based Creole, spoken by the descendants of freed Jamaicans who were settled in the Freetown area, a lingua franca and a first language for 10% of the population but understood by 95%)
Literacy: 35% (fifteen years old and over who can read and write English, Mende, Temne, or Arabic; 2004 est.)
Exports: diamonds, rutile, cocoa, coffee, fish
Primary export partners: Belgium 41%, U.S. 23.2%, France 5.7%, Netherlands 4.3% (2008)
Imports: foodstuffs, machinery and equipment, fuels and lubricants, chemicals
Primary import partners: China 10.5%, Cote d'Ivoire 8.9%, U.S. 7.9%, Belgium 6.7%, UK 6.7%, Thailand 5.2%, India 4.2% (2008)

A constitution in 1951 provided the framework for Sierra Leone's decolonization. Independence came in April 1961, when Sierra Leone became a parliamentary system within the British Commonwealth. In April 1971, it adopted a republican constitution, cutting the link to the British monarchy but remaining with the Commonwealth. Former Prime minister Siaka Stevens, who fought for government control of the country's major resources, namely iron and diamonds, led the nation as its first president until his retirement in November 1985. Major General Joseph Saidu Momoh succeeded him as president in January 1986. Guerrillas, spilling over into Sierra Leone from the Liberian civil war, captured some border towns in 1991. These border skirmishes eventually evolved into a civil war within Sierra Leone. Momoh was ousted by a military coup in April 1992 and was replaced by Captain Valentine Strasser. Strasser, criticized for the brutality of his regime, was removed from office in a 1996 bloodless coup. Ahmed Tehan Kabbah was elected president that year. A military junta deposed Kabbah in May 1997, but he was restored to office the following year. However, fighting between the government and rebel forces continued.

U.N. peacekeeping forces arrived in Sierra Leone late in 1999 to monitor implementation of a cease-fire agreement reached in Lomé, Togo, earlier in the year. However, the failure of Revolutionary United Front (RUF) rebels to disarm soon rendered the Lomé agreement effectively meaningless. The United Nations Mission in Sierra Leone (UNAMSIL) tried throughout 2001 to put into effect a peace accord based on the Lomé agreement and did manage to suppress fighting in several areas of the country.

In September 2007, Ernest Bai Koroma won a close runoff election with then Vice President Solomon Berewa to win the presidency of Sierra Leone. Bai Koroma was sworn in as president later that month.

SOMALIA

The British East India Company's desire for unrestricted harbor facilities led to the conclusion of treaties with the Sultan of Tajura as early as 1840. It was not until 1886, however, that the British gained control over northern Somalia through treaties with various Somali chiefs. The boundary between Ethiopia and British Somaliland was established in 1897 through treaty negotiations between British negotiators and Ethiopian Emperor Menelik II.

In 1855, Italy obtained commercial advantages in the area from the sultan of Zanzibar and, in 1889, concluded agreements with the sultans of Obbia and Caluula, who placed their territories under Italy's protection. Between 1897 and 1908, Italy made agreements with the Ethiopians and the British that marked out the boundaries of Italian Somaliland. In June 1940, Italian troops overran British Somaliland and drove out the British garrison. In 1941, British forces began operations against the Italian East African Empire and quickly brought the greater part of the Italian Somaliland under British control.

From 1941 to 1950, while Somalia was under British military administration, transition toward self-government

SOMALIA

Official name: Federal Republic of Somalia
Independence: 1 July 1960 (from a merger of British Somaliland, which became independent from the United Kingdom on 26 June 1960, and Italian Somaliland, which became independent from the Italian-administered U.N. trusteeship on 1 July 1960, to form the Somali Republic)
Area: 637,657 sq km
Form of government: parliamentary
Capital: Mogadishu
Currency: Somali shilling (SOS)
Income: US$795 (2008 est. of purchasing power parity)
Population: 9,832,000 (2009)
Ethnic groups: Somali 85%, Bantu and other (including Arabs) 15%
Religious groups: Sunni Muslim
Languages: Somali (official), Arabic, Italian, English
Literacy: 37.8% (fifteen years old and over who can read and write; 2001 est.)
Exports: livestock, bananas, hides, fish (2005)
Primary export partners: UAE 53.5%, Yemen 20%, Oman 6.4% (2008)
Imports: manufactures, petroleum products, foodstuffs, construction materials
Primary import partners: Djibouti 31.5%, India 8.3%, Kenya 8.2%, U.S. 6.4%, Oman 6.3%, UAE 5.9%, Yemen 5.1% (2008)

had begun. Elections for the Legislative Assembly were held in February 1960. The protectorate became independent on June 26, 1960; five days later, on July 1, it joined Italian Somaliland to form the Somali Republic. General Mohammed Siad Barre led a military coup in 1969 and established a Marxist political system. Years later, Barre concentrated power in his own family and clan. He was toppled in 1991, but opposing factions continued fighting for power. After years of civil war and severe drought, the United Nations, with U.S. leadership, introduced military forces into Somalia in late 1992 in an attempt to restore order and feed the country's many starving inhabitants. Attempts failed in the late 1990s to gather hundreds of warring clan leaders in an effort to hammer out some sort of truce. Pakistani forces took over the leadership of the U.N. mission, which finally retreated in March 1995.

Somalia remained without a functioning government until late in 2000. In May of that year, a reconciliation conference, meeting in nearby Djibouti, agreed on a plan for a three-year transitional government (TNG) and a transitional national assembly. The transitional government was finally seated in October with Abdiqassim Salad Hassan as president and Ali Khalif Galaid as prime minister. Although the country now had a nominal government, it seemed largely unable to deal with the continuing tensions between clans, some of which supported TNG, while others bitterly opposed it. In December 2001, an agreement between warring factions was signed in Nairobi, Kenya, but it too failed to bring to an end the country's long-simmering internal conflicts.

In 2002, several southwestern provinces sought to secede from the rest of the country. Although the announced secession was put down, it was one of several skirmishes that have hampered Somalia's progress. In December 2004, tsunamis struck the country and close to 160 lives were lost along with significant property damage. Two years later, Sheik Hassan Dahir Aweys of the Islamic Courts Union in Somalia declared that the nation was in a state of war. President Abdullahi Yusuf Ahmed resigned from office in 2008, citing that he had failed to stabilize the country politically or economically. Sharif Sheikh Ahmed was sworn in as president of Somalia in Djibouti in 2009, reflecting the lack of security in the country.

Since the early 1990s Somali pirates have interfered with international shipping activities, extracting more than $150 million from several countries by kidnapping crews and holding them for ransom. In April 2009, four Somali pirates took control of the United States vessel *Maersk Alabama* 300 miles off the Somali coast and took the captain, Richard Phillips, hostage. A few days later, United States Navy SEALs killed three of the pirates who held Phillips. The fourth pirate, who was aboard the *Maersk Alabama* negotiating terms for the captain's release, was taken into custody and brought to the United States to stand trial in New York City on piracy charges.

SOUTH AFRICA

The earliest inhabitants of South Africa, with ancestral ties to ethnic groups remaining there today, were Bushmen and Hottentots, who are members of the Khoisan language group. In 1488, the Portuguese were the first Europeans to reach the Cape of Good Hope on the Atlantic Coast of South Africa. Permanent white settlement began when the Dutch East India Company established a provisioning station in 1652. In subsequent decades, French Huguenot refugees, Dutch, and Germans

SOUTH AFRICA

Official name: Republic of South Africa
Independence: 31 May 1910 (from United Kingdom)
Area: 1,219,912 sq km
Form of government: republic
Capital: Pretoria; note: Cape Town is the legislative center and Bloemfontein the judicial center
Currency: rand (ZAR)
Income: US$10,130 (2008 est. of purchasing power parity)
Population: 49,052,489 (2009)
Ethnic groups: black African 79%, white 9.6%, colored 8.9%, Indian/Asian 2.5% (2001 census)
Religious groups: Christian 68% (includes most whites and coloreds, about 60% of blacks and about 40% of Indians), Muslim 2%, Hindu 1.5% (60% of Indians), indigenous beliefs and animist 28.5%
Languages: Eleven official languages, including Afrikaans, English, Ndebele, Pedi, Sotho, Swazi, Tsonga, Tswana, Venda, Xhosa, Zulu
Literacy: 86.4% (fifteen years old and over who can read and write; 2003 est.)
Exports: gold, diamonds, other metals and minerals, machinery and equipment
Primary export partners: U.S. 11.1%, Japan 9.8%, UK 9.6%, China 8.7%, Germany 6.8%, Netherlands 4.1% (2008)
Imports: machinery, foodstuffs and equipment, chemicals, petroleum products, scientific instruments
Primary import partners: Germany 10.8%, China 10.3%, U.S. 7%, Angola 6.8%, Saudi Arabia 5.7%, Japan 4.9%, UK 4.8%, Iran 4.4% (2008)

settled in the Cape area to form the Afrikaner segment of the modern population.

Britain seized the Cape of Good Hope at the end of the eighteenth century. Partly to escape British political rule and preserve cultural hegemony, many Afrikaner farmers (Boers) undertook a northern migration (the "Great Trek") beginning in 1836. This movement brought them into contact with several African groups, the most formidable of which were the Zulu. Under their powerful leader, Shaka (1787–1828), the Zulu conquered most of the territory between the Drakensberg Mountains and the sea (now Natal). The Zulu were defeated by the British at the Battle of Blood River in 1838.

The independent Boer republics of the Transvaal (the South African Republic) and the Orange Free State were created in 1852 and 1854. Following the two Boer wars from 1880 to 1881 and 1899 to 1902, British forces conquered the Boer republics and incorporated them into the British Empire. A strong resurgence of Afrikaner nationalism in the 1940s and 1950s led to a decision, through a 1960 referendum among whites, to give up dominion status and establish a republic. The republic was established on May 31, 1961. The National Party extended racial segregation, or the policy of apartheid, through passage of a number of legislative acts. In the 1960s and the 1970s, other laws were passed to further restrict every black African.

The African National Congress (ANC), a predominantly black South African political and eventually a paramilitary organization founded in 1912, is the oldest organization opposing legalized racism and white rule in South Africa. Between 1960 and 1990, the South African government banned the organization and forced it to operate underground.

In December 1988, under great international pressure, the government commuted the death sentences of the Sharpeville Six, who were convicted of murder for their presence in a crowd that killed a black township official. President F. W. de Klerk took several steps, beginning in 1989, to demonstrate his commitment to ending apartheid, including the release of ANC leader Nelson Mandela, imprisoned in 1962 and sentenced to life in 1964 for treason and sabotage, and other political prisoners and detainees; and removing the bans against the ANC and thirty-two other anti-apartheid organizations.

The tide of social and political changes instigated by de Klerk led to a new constitution and eventually multiparty elections in April 1994 that put Mandela in power as the first democratically elected president of the nation, with de Klerk and Thabo Mbeki serving as his two deputy presidents. In April 1996, the Truth and Reconciliation Commission (TRC), the body responsible for investigating crimes committed during the apartheid era in South Africa, began its hearings. Despite misgivings about both its impartiality and its effectiveness, most observers agree that the TRC helped reconcile the new South Africa with its past.

In late 1997, Mandela retired as head of the ANC and was replaced by Thabo Mbeki. Mandela had announced the year before that he would not seek a second term as president and Mbeki was his choice to succeed him. Mbeki won the 1999 election, and the ANC was able to form a coalition to give it a two-thirds majority, which is necessary to amend the constitution.

Early on, it became clear that Mbeki was very much his own man, putting his focus on "transformation" rather than the "reconciliation" that had been Mandela's major goal. However, it was also readily apparent that Mbeki lacked the incredible charisma of Mandela, as he came under fire from both domestic and international quarters by 2000. Mbeki's position on HIV was one example. Taking a cue from those in denial about AIDS, Mbeki maintained that the HIV virus was not the sole cause of the disease. This position brought Mbeki widespread criticism. The new president's push for privatization brought him and the ANC into increasing conflict with their traditional allies, the Congress of South African Trade Unions and the South African Communist Party. In 2001, in addition to his continuing privatization drive, Mbeki vowed to combat corruption within his government.

In 2004, Mbeki and the ANC won the elections with 69% of the vote. However, there was internal strife within his government which resulted in his premature departure from office. Mbeki dismissed his deputy president, Jacob Zuma, for involvement in corrupt activities, and then faced a no confidence vote at an ANC conference in Polokwane in September 2008. He resigned from the presidency several months prior to the end of his term of office. Kgalema Motlanthe served the remainder of Mbeki's term. Jacob Zuma, who had been dismissed by Mbeki three years earlier, ran in the general elections in behalf of the ANC ticket and won the presidency. In May 2009, he became the country's fourth president after independence. Two years earlier, the ANC celebrated its 95th anniversary, making it the oldest political organization on the African continent.

Apart from being the economic powerhouse on the continent, South Africa has increased its international profile in the arena of sports. In 2003 it hosted the Cricket World Cup and in 2007 the World Twenty Championship. In 2010 South Africa hosted the FIFA World Cup. The country underwent a dramatic building program to host these international soccer games, the first time an African country hosted them.

SUDAN

Until the nineteenth century, Sudan existed as a collection of small, independent states. In 1881, a religious leader named Mohammed Ahmed ibn Abdalla proclaimed himself the Mahdi, or "expected one," and began to unify groups in western and central Sudan. The Mahdi led a nationalist revolt culminating in the fall of Khartoum in 1885. He died shortly thereafter, but his state survived until overwhelmed by Anglo-Egyptian forces in 1898. In 1899, Sudan was proclaimed a condominium under Anglo-Egyptian administration. In February 1953, the United Kingdom and Egypt concluded an agreement providing for Sudanese self-government. Sudan achieved independence on January 1, 1956. In 1969, Col. Gaafar Muhammad al-Nimeiry, leading a group of army officers, seized power and set up government under a revolutionary council. Elected president in 1972, Nimeiry turned to the Soviet Union and Libya for support. However, after several coup attempts, allegedly backed by Libya and local communists, Nimeiry turned to Egypt and the West for assistance. Nimeiry was elected to a third term as president in 1983 but was removed from office two years later in a bloodless coup. After a year of military rule, Sadiq al-Mahdi was elected prime minister. Mahdi's regime was toppled in June 1989 by a military coup led by Omar Hassan al-Bashir. In 1993,

SUDAN

Official name: Republic of the Sudan

Independence: 1 January 1956 (from Egypt and United Kingdom)

Area: 2,505,810 sq km

Form of government: republic

Capital: Khartoum

Currency: Sudanese dinar (SDD)

Income: US$2,309 (2008 est. of purchasing power parity)

Population: 42,272,000 (2009 est.)

Ethnic groups: black 52%, Arab 39%, Beja 6%, foreigners 2%, other 1%

Religious groups: Sunni Muslim 70% (in north), indigenous beliefs 25%, Christian 5% (mostly in south and Khartoum)

Languages: Arabic (official), Nubian, Ta Bedawie, diverse dialects of Nilotic, Nilo-Hamitic, Sudanic languages, English

Literacy: 61.1% (fifteen years old and over who can read and write; 2003 est.)

Exports: oil and petroleum products, cotton, sesame, livestock, groundnuts, gum arabic, sugar

Primary export partners: China 56.3%, Japan 30%, Indonesia 4.9% (2008)

Imports: foodstuffs, manufactured goods, machinery and transport equipment, medicines and chemicals, textiles

Primary import partners: China 24.9%, Saudi Arabia 8%, UAE 5.9%, India 5.8%, Egypt 5.3% (2008)

Bashir took some steps toward establishment of a multiparty state, most of which were dismissed as cosmetic by the opposition. In 1996, Bashir and his party swept presidential and legislative elections. Meanwhile, a civil war continued to rage between the Arab peoples of the north and the black Africans in the south of Sudan.

Despite widespread skepticism, Sudan's introduction of multiparty politics at the beginning of 1999 showed early signs of success. A number of longtime opposition leaders were quick to form their own political parties. In December 1999, President Omar al-Bashir declared a state of emergency, fearing his authority was under threat from former ally Hassan al-Turaibi. The state of emergency continued in force through 2001, although al-Turaibi, the president's principal foe, was arrested in February of that year for allegedly signing a memorandum of understanding with rebels of the Sudanese People's Liberation Army.

In 2005, the government and rebel forces signed a Comprehensive Peace Agreement, which granted Southern Sudan six years of autonomy and would subsequently take up an independence referendum. In a major setback, the south's co-vice president, John Garang, died in a helicopter accident a few weeks after being sworn in, which set off a new round of rioting in the region.

In what has become one of the African continent's most dire conflicts, the genocide in Southern Sudan's Darfur region has attracted worldwide attention. Dating back to the 1970s, the central government in Khartoum ignored the Darfur region economically, leaving it vulnerable to attacks. Armed Arab militias known as Janjaweed routinely carry out attacks on the indigenous inhabitants. The fighting has displaced more than 1 million people and has caused severe refugee problems in neighboring countries. In 2004 the conflict was formally referred to as genocide. In 2006, the Sudanese government and the Sudan Liberation Movement (SLM) signed the Darfur Peace Agreement. The agreement called for the disarming of the notorious Janjaweed militia groups and the SLM and other rebel groups. However, reports of widespread violence by the government and the rebel forces continued.

In 2008 the International Criminal Court announced ten criminal charges against Sudanese President al-Bashir—including charges of war crimes and crimes against humanity. The indictment accused him of complicity in the violence against those in the Darfur region because of their ethnicity. Several major world powers (especially China, which relies on Sudanese oil reserves) have been slow to condemn al-Bashir and the events in the region.

SWAZILAND

Official name: Kingdom of Swaziland

Independence: 6 September 1968 (from United Kingdom)

Area: 17,363 sq km

Form of government: monarchy

Capital: Mbabane; note: Lobamba is the royal and legislative capital

Currency: lilangeni (SZL)

Income: US$5,749 (2008 est. of purchasing power parity)

Population: 1,185,000 (2009)

Ethnic groups: African 97%, European 3%

Religious groups: Christian (including Zionist religions blending Christianity with indigenous ancestral worship) 82%

Languages: English (official, government business conducted in English), siSwati (official)

Literacy: 81.6% (fifteen years old and over who can read and write; 2003 est.)

Exports: soft drink concentrates, sugar, wood pulp, cotton yarn, refrigerators, citrus and canned fruit

Imports: motor vehicles, machinery, transport equipment, foodstuffs, petroleum products, chemicals

SWAZILAND

Early ancestors of the people of the present Swazi nation migrated south before the sixteenth century to what is now Mozambique. After a series of conflicts with people living in the area that is now Maputo, the Swazi settled in northern Zululand in about 1750. Unable to match the growing Zulu strength there, the Swazi moved gradually northward in the early 1800s and established themselves in the area of modern Swaziland. The Swazi consolidated their hold in this area under several able leaders. The most important of these was Mswati, from whom the Swazi derive their name. Under his leadership in the 1840s, the Swazi expanded their territory to the northwest and stabilized the southern frontier with the Zulus.

The first Swazi contact with the British came early in Mswati's reign when he asked the British agent general in South Africa for assistance against Zulu raids into Swaziland. Agreements made between the British and the Transvaal (South Africa) governments in 1881 and 1884 provided that Swaziland should be independent. In 1903, Britain formally took over the administration of Swaziland.

Sobhuza II became head of the Swazi Nation in 1921. By the 1960s, political activity intensified, partly in response to events elsewhere in Africa. Several political parties were formed that agitated for independence. The traditional Swazi leaders, including King Sobhuza and his council, formed the Imbokodvo National Movement. In 1966, the British agreed to hold talks on a new constitution. The constitutional committee, consisting of representatives of the king and of the Swazi National Council, other political parties, and the British government agreed on a constitutional monarchy for Swaziland, with self-government to follow parliamentary elections in 1967. Swaziland became independent on September 6, 1968. In 1973, Sobhuza II repealed the constitution, dissolved the political parties, and assumed full power until his death in 1982. Mswati III became king in 1986.

In 1993, Mswati III called for Swaziland's first general election in twenty years, though he retained a great deal of political power; pro-democratic forces viewed the elections as inadequate. Swaziland was later affected by waves of general strikes, most of them organized by the Swazi Federation of Trade Unions (SFTU). A major strike in 1996 led to the formation of a Constitutional Review Commission, which Mswati promised would deliver several democratic reforms. But Mswati limited membership on the commission to his own appointees, prompting the SFTU and its allies to reject the commission and call for further strikes.

Political unrest increased in 1999 as opposition groups calling for the establishment of a multiparty democracy grew more militant. Bombings of a number of government facilities were charged to these opposition groups. In August 2001, after years of delay, the Constitutional Review Commission submitted its recommendations to the king. A constitution was approved in 2005, and became effective in 2006.

With a staggering 26.1% infection rate, Swaziland has the world's greatest HIV crisis. The problem was only recently acknowledged and the country has taken aggressive actions (such as offering men free circumcisions, which has proven to reduce the spread of the virus by up to 60%) to stem the spread of the disease. The high prevalence rate has also caused the life expectancy to fall from sixty years in 2000 to about thirty-three years in 2009.

TANZANIA

The area that is now Tanzania is believed to have been inhabited originally by ethnic groups using a click-tongue language similar to that of southern Africa's Bushmen and Hottentots. Although remnants of these early groups still exist, most were gradually displaced by Bantu farmers migrating from the west and south and by Nilotes and related Northern peoples.

The coastal area of present-day Tanzania first felt the impact of foreign influence as early as the eighth century. By the twelfth century, traders and immigrants had come

TANZANIA

Official name: United Republic of Tanzania

Independence: 26 April 1964; Tanganyika became independent 9 December 1961 (from United Kingdom-administered U.N. trusteeship); Zanzibar became independent 19 December 1963 (from United Kingdom); Tanganyika united with Zanzibar 26 April 1964 to form the United Republic of Tanganyika and Zanzibar; renamed United Republic of Tanzania 29 October 1964

Area: 945,087 sq km

Form of government: republic

Capital: Dodoma

Currency: Tanzanian shilling (TZS)

Income: US$1,353 (2008 est. of purchasing power parity)

Population: 43,739,000 (2009 est.)

Ethnic groups: mainland—native African 99% (of which 95% are Bantu consisting of more than 130 ethnicities), other 1% (consisting of Asian, European, and Arab); Zanzibar—Arab, native African

Religious groups: mainland—Christian 30%, Muslim 35%, indigenous beliefs 35%; Zanzibar—more than 99% Muslim

Languages: Kiswahili or Swahili (official), Kiunguju (name for Swahili in Zanzibar), English (official, primary language of commerce, administration, and higher education), Arabic (widely spoken in Zanzibar), many local languages

Literacy: 78.2% (fifteen years old and over who can read and write Kiswahili (Swahili), English, or Arabic; 2003 est.)

Exports: gold, coffee, cashew nuts, manufactures cotton

Primary export partners: India 10.1%, China 7.2%, Japan 6.4%, UAE 5.6%, Netherlands 5.4%, Germany 5% (2008)

Imports: consumer goods, machinery and transportation equipment, industrial raw materials, crude oil

Primary import partners: China 14.5%, South Africa 7.3%, Kenya 7.2%, India 6.3%, UAE 6.1% (2008)

from as far away as Persia (modern-day Iran) and India. The Portuguese navigator Vasco da Gama first visited the East African coast in 1498 on his voyage to India, and by 1506 the Portuguese claimed control over the entire coast. This control was nominal, however, for the Portuguese did not attempt to colonize the area or explore the interior. By the early eighteenth century, Arabs from Oman had assisted the indigenous coastal dwellers in driving out the Portuguese from the area north of the Ruvuma River. They established their own garrisons at Zanzibar, Pemba, and Kilwa and carried on a lucrative trade in enslaved Africans and ivory.

German colonial interests were first advanced in the region in 1884. Karl Peters, who formed the Society for German Colonization, concluded a series of treaties by which traditional chiefs in the interior accepted German protection. In 1886 and 1890, Anglo-German agreements were negotiated that delineated the British and German spheres of influence in the interior of East Africa. In 1891, the German government took over direct administration of the territory from the German East Africa Company and appointed a governor with headquarters at Dar es Salaam. German colonial administration sparked African resistance, culminating in the Maji Maji rebellion of 1905–1907. German colonial domination of Tanganyika ended with World War I. Control of most of the territory passed to the United Kingdom under a League of Nations mandate.

As the twentieth century progressed, Tanganyika moved gradually toward self-government and independence. In 1954, Julius K. Nyerere, a schoolteacher educated abroad, organized the Tanganyika African Union. In May 1961, Tanganyika became autonomous, and Nyerere became prime minister under a new constitution. Full independence was achieved on December 9, 1961. On April 26, 1964, Tanganyika united with Zanzibar to form the United Republic of Tanganyika and Zanzibar, renamed the United Republic of Tanzania on October 29, 1964. Nyerere in November 1985 became one of the few leaders on the continent to retire peacefully. Ali Hassan Mwinyi succeeded him as president. Opposition parties were legalized in 1992, paving the way for Tanzania's first multiparty elections in October 1995. The Revolutionary Party's Benjamin Mkapa was elected president and his party won the majority of the seats in the National Assembly. Continuing strife in countries bordering Tanzania fueled a surge in the flow of refugees into the country during the mid-1990s. In 1997, Tanzania began a repatriation plan to return the refugees to their homelands.

President Mkapa was reelected in a landslide in October 2000 elections. The Tanzanian islands of Pemba and Zanzibar experienced an explosion of civil unrest in late January 2001. Members of the opposition Civic United Front (CUF) party calling for new presidential elections led the protests. Tensions continued between CUF and the ruling Chama Cha Mapinduzi party throughout 2001, despite a peace accord signed by both parties in October.

Jakaya Kikwete, Minister of Foreign Affairs in Tanzania since 1995, was elected president in 2005. Two years later, Kikwete launched a national campaign for voluntary testing for HIV/AIDS. He was elected Chairman of the African Union in 2008, serving in that capacity for one year.

Tanzania's population consists of more than 120 ethnic groups, of which only the Sukuma has more than 1 million members. The majority of Tanzanians, including the Sukuma and the Nyamwezi, are of Bantu stock. Groups of Nilotic or related origin include the nomadic Masai and the Luo, both of which are found in greater numbers in neighboring Kenya. Two small groups speak languages of the Khoisan family peculiar to the Bushman and Hottentot peoples. Cushitic-speaking peoples, originally from the Ethiopian highlands, reside in a few areas of Tanzania.

TOGO

The Ewe people first moved into the area that is now Togo from the Niger River Valley beginning in the twelfth century. During the fifteenth and sixteenth centuries, Portuguese explorers and traders visited the coast. For the next 200 years, the coastal region was a major raiding center for Europeans in search of Africans to enslave, earning Togo and the surrounding region the name "the Slave Coast."

In an 1884 treaty signed at Togoville, Germany, declared a protectorate over the area. In 1914, Togoland was invaded by French and British forces and fell after a brief resistance. Following the war, Togoland became a League of Nations mandate divided for administrative purposes between France and the United Kingdom. By statute in 1955, French Togo became an autonomous republic within the French Union. In 1957, the residents of British Togoland voted to join the Gold Coast as part of the new independent nation of Ghana. On April 27, 1960, Togo severed its juridical ties with France, shed its United Nations trusteeship status, and became fully independent. Togo's first president, Sylvanus Olympia, was assassinated in a military coup three years after independence. Opposition leader Nicholas Grunitzky headed the government for a short period, until Colonel Gnassingbé Eyadéma seized power and instituted a one-party state in 1967. Reelected (in uncontested elections) in 1979 and 1986, Eyadéma in August 1991 agreed to share power with a transitional government until multiparty elections

TOGO

Official name: Togolese Republic
Independence: 27 April 1960 (from French-administered U.N. trusteeship)
Area: 56,785 sq km
Form of government: republic
Capital: Lomé
Currency: Communaute Financiere Africaine franc (CFAF)
Income: US$800 (2008 est. of purchasing power parity)
Population: 6,619,000 (2009)
Ethnic groups: native African (thirty-seven indigenous groups: largest and most important are Ewe, Mina, and Kabre) 99%, European and Syrian-Lebanese less than 1%
Religious groups: indigenous beliefs 51%, Christian 29%, Muslim 20%
Languages: French (official and the language of commerce), Ewe and Mina (the two major African languages in the south), Kabye (sometimes spelled Kabiye) and Dagomba (the two major African languages in the north)
Literacy: 60.9% (fifteen years old and over who can read and write; 2003 est.)
Exports: cotton, phosphates, coffee, cocoa
Primary export partners: Ghana 14.3%, Burkina Faso 12.4%, Germany 11%, Benin 7.8%, Brazil 5.6%, Belgium 5.4%, Mali 5%, Netherlands 4.8% (2008)
Imports: machinery and equipment, foodstuffs, petroleum products
Primary import partners: China 39.1%, Netherlands 7.9%, France 7.2%, Thailand 5.1% (2008)

could be scheduled. Though troops loyal to Eyadéma reportedly tried repeatedly to overthrow the interim regime, Eyadéma was reelected in multiparty elections in 1993, which were boycotted by the main opposition groups. Voting irregularities and human rights violations led to sanctions from the European Union that same year.

In 1997, Eyadéma's government blocked the creation of an independent electoral commission, and, after military harassment of opposition leaders marred the 1998 presidential campaign, Eyadéma's claim to have won reelection for another five years led to opposition protests and rioting. Political unrest stemming from the disputed 1998 presidential election intensified during 1999. Most opposition parties boycotted the March 1999 parliamentary elections, giving the ruling Rally of the Togolese People party all but two of the 81 seats in parliament.

With tensions rising between the government of President Eyadéma and major opposition parties, the government in early 2000 limited freedom of the press, subjecting any journalist found guilty of defaming the head of state to heavy fines and three months imprisonment. Shortly after Prime Minister Eugene Koffi Adoboli lost a vote of confidence in August 2000, he resigned and was replaced by Gabriel Agbéyomé Kodjo, speaker of the national assembly. In January 2001, the government announced that new parliamentary elections would be held later in the year, but the promised legislative vote was postponed at the last minute. In 2002, parliamentary elections were held and were again boycotted by the main opposition. That year, the country's constitution was amended to allow President Eyadéma to seek another term in office, which he easily won in 2003. Eyadéma died two years later, and the chief of the Togolese army placed Eyadéma's son, Faure Gnassingbé, in the office as president, contrary to constitutional mandate that the president be succeeded by the speaker of parliament in the event of such an occurrence. Parliament quickly adjusted the constitution to allow the action, but international protest caused Gnassingbé to step down, while an interim president was appointed. When elections were held, Gnassingbé was declared the winner, but that result sparked charges of mass voter fraud and riots. In 2006, there was an agreement to appoint Yawovi Agboyibo as prime minister with a mandate to bring about a national unity government. For the last several years there have been power struggles in the land. Togo is scheduled to have presidential elections in 2010 despite the political skirmishes.

TUNISIA

Tunisians are descended mainly from indigenous Berber and Arab groups that migrated to North Africa during the seventh century. Recorded history in Tunisia began with the arrival of Phoenicians, who founded Carthage and other North African settlements. In the seventh century, the Muslim conquest transformed North Africa, and Tunisia became a center of Arab culture until its assimilation into the Turkish Ottoman Empire in the sixteenth century. In 1881, France established a protectorate in Tunisia, where a twentieth-century rise in nationalism lead to Tunisia's independence in 1956.

One year after independence, Tunisian statesman and President Habib Bourguiba (1903–2000) instituted a socialist system, later declaring himself president for life.

TUNISIA

Official name: Republic of Tunisia
Independence: 20 March 1956 (from France)
Area: 163,610 sq km
Form of government: republic
Capital: Tunis
Currency: Tunisian dinar (TND)
Income: US$8,002 (2008 est. of purchasing power parity)
Population: 10,486,000 (2009 est.)
Ethnic groups: Arab 98%, European 1%, Jewish and other 1%
Religious groups: Muslim 98%, Christian 1%, Jewish and other 1%
Languages: Arabic (official and one of the languages of commerce), French (commerce)
Literacy: 74.3% (fifteen years old and over who can read and write; 2004 est.)
Exports: textiles, mechanical goods, phosphates and chemicals, agricultural products, hydrocarbons
Primary export partners: France 28.4%, Italy 18%, Germany 9.6%, Libya 5.8%, Spain 5% (2008)
Imports: machinery and equipment, hydrocarbons, chemicals, food
Primary import partners: France 22.4%, Italy 20.1%, Germany 9.4%, Libya 4.8%, Spain 4.6% (2008)

In late 1987, Bourguiba was declared senile, and he was replaced as president by Prime Minister Zine al-Abidine Ben Ali, who took steps to democratize the country. In April 1989 elections, Ben Ali was elected to a full term as president. In 1994, he ran unopposed for president and was reelected. Ben Ali worked to contain growing Muslim fundamentalism throughout the 1990s.

President Ben Ali won a resounding reelection victory in October 1999. Ben Ali's government in 2000 and 2001 came under increasing criticism for its record on human rights. Under growing pressure from within and outside the country, the president in 2001 promised to improve his record on human rights and, as a step in that direction, introduced a liberalized press law in August 2001. Nevertheless, public access to information was still restricted as of 2009, even as Internet use has grown dramatically in Tunisia, and various forms of censorship are common.

Presidential elections were held in October 2009. The results were never in question. President Ben Ali was the victor with 89% of the vote. His nearest competitor received a mere 5%.

UGANDA

Arab traders moving inland from Indian Ocean coastal enclaves reached the interior of Uganda in the 1830s and

UGANDA

Official name: Republic of Uganda
Independence: 9 October 1962 (from United Kingdom)
Area: 236,040 sq km
Form of government: republic
Capital: Kampala
Currency: Ugandan shilling (UGX)
Income: US$1,146 (2008 est. of purchasing power parity)
Population: 32,710,000 (2009)
Ethnic groups: Baganda 16.9%, Banyankole 9.5%, Basoga 8.4%, Bakiga 6.9%, Iteso 6.4%, Langi 6.1%, Acholi 4.7%, Bagisu 4.6%, Lugbara 4.2%, Bunyoro 2.7%, Other 29.6% (2002 census)
Religious groups: Roman Catholic 42%, Protestant 42%, Muslim 12%
Languages: English (official national language, taught in grade schools, used in courts of law, and by most newspapers and some radio broadcasts), Ganda or Luganda (most widely used of the Niger-Congo languages, preferred for native language publications in the capital and may be taught in school), other Niger-Congo languages, Nilo-Saharan languages, Swahili, Arabic
Literacy: 69.9% (fifteen years old and over who can read and write; 2003 est.)
Exports: coffee, fish and fish products, tea, electrical products, iron and steel
Primary export partners: Belgium 11.6%, Netherlands 9.8%, Germany 8.5%, Italy 6.6%, Rwanda 5.2%, France 4.9%, U.S. 4.7%, UAE 4% (2008)
Imports: vehicles, petroleum, medical supplies, cereals
Primary import partners: Kenya 31.1%, UAE 8.7%, China 7.6%, Japan 6.2%, South Africa 6%, India 5.1% (2008)

A Group of Berber Women in Festive Dress Attend a Sahara Festival, Douz, Tunisia. *Located in northern Africa on the Mediterranean Sea, Tunisia extends to the south into the Sahara. Tunisians are descended mainly from indigenous Berber and Arab groups that migrated to northern Africa during the seventh century CE.* PATRICK WARD/CORBIS

found several African kingdoms, including the Buganda kingdom, that had well-developed political institutions dating back several centuries.

In 1888, a royal charter assigned control of the emerging British sphere of interest in East Africa to the Imperial British East Africa Company, an arrangement strengthened in 1890 by an Anglo-German agreement confirming British dominance over Kenya and Uganda. In 1894, the Kingdom of Uganda was placed under a formal British protectorate. The period of British protectorate began drawing to a close formally in 1955 with the adoption of constitutional changes leading to Uganda's independence. The first general elections in Uganda were held in 1961, and the British government granted internal self-government to Uganda on March 1, 1962, with Benedicto Kiwanuka as the first prime minister. Full indepence for Uganda was recognized later that year.

In February of 1966, Prime Minister Milton Obote suspended the constitution, assumed all government powers, and removed the president and vice president. On January 25, 1971, Obote's government was ousted in a military coup led by armed forces commander Idi Amin Dada. Amin declared himself president, dissolved the parliament, and amended the constitution to place absolute power in his hands. Idi Amin's eight-year rule produced economic decline, social disintegration, and massive human rights violations. In 1978, Tanzanian forces pushed back an incursion by Amin's troops. Backed by Ugandan exiles, Tanzanian forces waged a war of liberation against Amin. On April 11, 1979, the Ugandan capital was captured, and Amin and his remaining forces fled. He eventually settled in Libya and remained there until his death in 2003. There followed a chaotic year or so in Uganda, during which three provisional presidents led the shattered country. In December 1980, Obote was once again elected to the presidency and then again overthrown by military coup in 1985. The military regime that followed was short-lived. In January 1986, National Resistance Army leader Yoweri Museveni seized power.

Within a year of Museveni's rise, the Holy Spirit Movement (HSM) emerged, under the self-proclaimed spirit medium, Alice Lakwena (born Alice Auma). Alice raised an army of more than 10,000,000 followers (mostly from the Acholi ethnic group in northern Uganda) with promises that if her followers remained pure they would repel the bullets of government soldiers. She also told them that she would be able to command the animals and insects to do her bidding and that the rocks would become hand grenades when used by her followers. The HSM came within thirty miles of Kampala before being repelled by government forces at the Jinja Bridge. Alice fled to Kenya and remained there until her death in early 2007. A successor rebel movement, the Lord's Resistance Army (LRA), was led by Joseph Kony, who has been linked to child kidnappings and other atrocities in Uganda over the last twenty years.

Museveni, elected president in 1996 in the country's first presidential elections in sixteen years, helped nurse Uganda's economy back to health.

Uganda's government, widely praised for its progress in revitalizing the economy, received pledges in 1999 of $2.2 billion in additional foreign aid over the following three years. Museveni won a resounding reelection victory in the 2001 presidential elections, despite a credible challenge mounted by Kiiza Besigye, a former associate of the incumbent president. General elections were again held in 2006. Although there were some charges of irregularities, Museveni again won out over his challenger Besigye.

Museveni has also received international praise for his handling of the HIV/AIDS crisis in Uganda. Through the assistance of grassroots organizations like The Aids Support Organization (TASO), the country has successfully reduced the spread of the disease.

ZAMBIA

About 2,000 years ago, the indigenous hunter-gatherer occupants of Zambia began to be displaced or absorbed by more advanced migrating groups. By the fifteenth century, major waves of Bantu-speaking immigrants arrived, with the greatest influx occurring between the late seventeenth and early nineteenth centuries. These groups came primarily from the Luba and Lunda of southern Zaire and northern Angola but were joined in the nineteenth century by Ngoni peoples from the south. By the latter part of that century, the various peoples of Zambia were largely established in the areas that their descendants occupy as of 2010.

Except for an occasional Portuguese explorer, the area now known as Zambia lay untouched by Europeans until the mid-nineteenth century, when European explorers, missionaries, and traders penetrated inland from coastal regions. In 1888, Northern and Southern Rhodesia were proclaimed British spheres of influence. In 1953, both Rhodesias were joined with Nyasaland to form the Federation of Rhodesia and Nyasaland.

ZAMBIA

Official name: Republic of Zambia

Independence: 24 October 1964 (from United Kingdom)

Area: 752,614 sq km

Form of government: republic

Capital: Lusaka

Currency: Zambian kwacha (ZMK)

Income: US$1,482 (2008 est. of purchasing power parity)

Population: 12,935,000 (July 2009)

Ethnic groups: African 99.5%, European and other 0.5%

Religious groups: Christian 50–75%, Muslim and Hindu 24–49%, indigenous beliefs 1%

Languages: English (official), major vernaculars include Bemba, Kaonda, Lozi, Lunda, Luvale, Nyanja, Tonga, and about 70 other indigenous languages

Literacy: 80.6% (fifteen years old and over who can read and write English; 2003 est.)

Exports: copper, cobalt, electricity, tobacco

Primary export partners: Switzerland 36.2%, South Africa 10.5%, China 8.1%, Democratic Republic of the Congo 5%, Saudi Arabia 4.9%, Egypt 4.7%, Italy 4.3% (2008)

Imports: machinery, transportation equipment, fuels, petroleum products, electricity, fertilizer, foodstuffs, clothing

Primary import partners: South Africa 49.3%, China 8.2%, UAE 7.9%, India 4.4% (2008)

Northern Rhodesia was the center of much of the turmoil and crises that characterized the federation in its last years. At the core of the controversy were insistent African demands for greater participation in government. A two-stage election held in October and December 1962 resulted in an African majority in the Legislative Council. The council passed resolutions calling for Northern Rhodesia's secession from the federation and demanding full internal self-government. On December 31, 1963, the federation was dissolved, and Northern Rhodesia became the Republic of Zambia on October 24, 1964. Led by first president Kenneth Kaunda (founder of the Zambian African National Congress and a leader of the United National Independence Party) for nearly thirty years, the country in 1991 held its first multiparty elections. Frederick Chiluba, leader of the Movement for Multiparty Democracy, defeated Kaunda by a wide margin. In 1996, a new constitution prevented Kaunda from running for president, as it introduced a provision that a candidate's parents had to be Zambian-born (Kaunda's parents were Malawian). Chiluba's party easily won elections that same year, amid widespread student riots and popular dissent.

In March 2000, former President Kaunda announced that he was retiring from politics and stepping down as leader of the United National Independence Party. Francis Nikhoma, a former governor of the central bank, succeeded Kaunda as party leader. President Chiluba's ruling party's regulations had forbidden a party member from seeking more than two terms as president, but in April 2001, the rules were changed to permit Chiluba to run for a third term in late 2001 elections. Only a month later, however, Chiluba reversed himself and said he would not run for reelection, largely in response to growing opposition within his own party. Lawyer Levy Mwanawasa was named the ruling party's candidate, and he handily won election to the presidency in late 2001. The elections were results were challenged, but they were sustained by the courts after consideration for over a year. Mwanawasa won reelection in 2006, but died in office two years later. His vice president, Rupiah Banda, succeeded him as president. Zambia has maintained a relatively stable economy during these years, although the country is plagued by a high rate of HIV prevalence.

ZIMBABWE

Archaeologists have found Stone Age implements and pebble tools in several areas of Zimbabwe, suggesting human habitation for many centuries before the common era. The ruins of stone buildings also provide evidence of early civilization.

In the sixteenth century, the Portuguese were the first Europeans to attempt colonization of south-central Africa, but the hinterland lay virtually untouched by Europeans until the arrival of explorers, missionaries, and traders some 300 years later. In 1888, the area that became Southern and Northern Rhodesia was proclaimed a British sphere of influence. The British South Africa Company was chartered in 1889, and the settlement of Salisbury (now Harare) was established in 1890.

In 1895, the territory was formally named Rhodesia. In 1923, Southern Rhodesia's white settlers were given the choice of being incorporated into the Union of South Africa or becoming a separate entity within the British Empire. The settlers rejected incorporation, and Southern Rhodesia was formally annexed by the United Kingdom. In September 1953, Southern Rhodesia was joined with the British protectorates of Northern Rhodesia and Nyasaland. The federation was dissolved at the end of 1963 after much crisis and turmoil with Northern Rhodesia, and Nyasaland became the independent states of Zambia and Malawi in 1964.

Although prepared to grant independence to Rhodesia, the United Kingdom insisted that the authorities at Salisbury first demonstrate their intention to move toward eventual majority rule. Desiring to keep their dominant position, the white Rhodesians refused to give

ZIMBABWE

Official name: Republic of Zimbabwe

Independence: 18 April 1980 (from United Kingdom)

Area: 390,580 sq km

Form of government: parliamentary democracy

Capital: Harare

Currency: Zimbabwean dollar (ZWD) until April 2009. Currencies such as the U.S. dollar and the South African rand are in wide circulation and are accepted by most merchants as a means of exchange.

Income: US$268 (2008 est. of purchasing power parity)

Population: 12,523,000 (2009)

Ethnic groups: African 98% (Shona 82%, Ndebele 14%, other 2%), mixed and Asian 1%, white less than 1%

Religious groups: syncretic (part Christian, part indigenous beliefs) 50%, Christian 25%, indigenous beliefs 24%, Muslim and other 1%

Languages: English (official), Shona, Sindebele (the language of the Ndebele), numerous but minor dialects

Literacy: 90.7% (fifteen years old and over who can read and write English; 2003 est.)

Exports: tobacco 29%, gold 7%, ferroalloys 7%, cotton 5%

Primary export partners: South Africa 36.1%, Democratic Republic of the Congo 8.9%, Botswana 8%, China 5.5%, Zambia 4.4%, Japan 4.1%, Italy 4.1% (2008)

Imports: machinery and transport equipment 35%, other manufactures 18%, chemicals 17%, fuels 14%

Primary import partners: South Africa 52.2%, China 7%, Botswana 4.5% (2008)

such assurance. On November 11, 1965, after lengthy and unsuccessful negotiations with the British government, Prime Minister Ian Smith issued a unilateral declaration of independence (UDI) from the United Kingdom. The British government considered the UDI unconstitutional and illegal, but made it clear that it would not use force to end the rebellion. The British government imposed unilateral economic sanctions on Rhodesia and requested other nations to do the same. On December 16, 1966, the United Nations Security Council, for the first time in its history, imposed mandatory economic sanctions on a state.

In the early 1970s, informal attempts at settlement were renewed between the United Kingdom and the administration in Rhodesia. In 1974, major African nationalist groups—the Zimbabwe African People's Union (ZAPU) and the Zimbabwe African National Union (ZANU), which split away from ZAPU in 1963—were united into the "Patriotic Front" and combined their military forces. In 1976, the Smith government agreed in principle to majority rule and to a meeting in Geneva with Black Nationalist leaders. Blacks represented at the Geneva meeting included ZAPU leader Joshua Nkomo, ZANU leader Robert Mugabe, United African National Council (UANC) chairman Bishop Abel Muzorewa, and former ZANU leader, the Reverend Ndabaningi Sithole. However, the meeting failed.

On March 3, 1978, the Smith administration signed an internal settlement agreement in Salisbury with Bishop Muzorewa, Rev. Sithole, and Chief Jeremiah Chirau. The agreement provided for qualified majority rule and elections with universal suffrage. Following elections in April 1979, in which his UANC party won a majority, Bishop Muzorewa assumed office on June 1, becoming Zimbabwe's first black prime minister. However, the installation of the new black majority government did not end a guerrilla conflict that had claimed more than 20,000 lives.

The British and the African parties began deliberations on a Rhodesian settlement in London on September 10, 1979. On December 21, the parties signed an agreement calling for a cease-fire, new elections, a transition period under British rule, and a new constitution implementing majority rule while protecting minority rights. The British government supervised the elections. Robert Mugabe's ZANU Party won an absolute majority and was asked to form Zimbabwe's first government. The British government formally granted independence to Zimbabwe on April 18, 1980. In 1985, Mugabe's party won by a landslide in the country's first general election since independence. Mugabe was reelected in 1990 and 1996.

President Mugabe came under fire in early 1999 for his aggressive land-reform and black-empowerment programs, particularly his threats to seize farms owned by absentee British owners and turn them over to black Zimbabweans. His Zimbabwe African National Union–Patriotic Front (ZANU-PF) government sought to institute a new constitution that would allow for major land reform, but the move was opposed by the newly created Movement for Democratic Change (MDC) party led by Morgan Tsvangirai.

When the constitutional amendment was rejected by the voters, Mugabe embarked on a radical land distribution that violently forced white farmers off of their land. These actions were supposedly carried out by "war veterans," but more likely were carried out by thugs acting on orders from the government. In 2000, legislative elections were held, and despite a very rigorous contest by ZANU-PF and MDC, the former party won. The elections were marred by extensive violence against MDC supporters.

In March 2002, during elections that many observers contended were conducted in an atmosphere of fear and intimidation, Mugabe claimed victory once again. Shortly thereafter, the Commonwealth of Nations suspended Zimbabwe for twelve months after the group's observers accused Mugabe of using his powers as incumbent to steal the election.

In 2005, the ZANU-PF government launched "Operation Murambatsvina" with the stated intention of clearing the capital of unauthorized housing and informal markets. The net effect, however, was to forcibly remove urban inhabitants who formed the basis of Mugabe's greatest opposition.

In March 2008, Zimbabwe held presidential and parliamentarian elections. The major presidential contenders were incumbent Mugabe (ZANU-PF) and Morgan Tsvangirai (MDC). Although the results were withheld for several weeks, Morgan Tsvangirai was the acknowledged victor, but did not take office because Zimbabwe law required him to win by a certain percentage margin. After additional international condemnation and threats of greater sanctions against the country, the two parties entered talks (led by then South African President Thabo Mbeki). In September 2008, the parties agreed to a power-sharing arrangement where Mugabe would retain the presidency and Tsvangirai would become prime minister. The new arrangement took effect in March 2009. In October 2009, Prime Minister Tsvangirai temporarily withdrew from the government after charging that ZANU-PF members in the government had continued to harass and intimidate members of his party.

As of 2010, Zimbabwe was experiencing an unprecedented food crisis resulting in significant insecurity for many of it people. This is especially ironic since the nation once had been the breadbasket of the region. In late 2008, a major cholera outbreak occurred in Zimbabwe, and there was insufficient medication to assist those in need. Life expectancy in Zimbabwe decreased dramatically during a fifteen-year span beginning in the mid-1990s, from sixty years to thirty-seven years for men and from sixty years to thirty-two years for women. The infant mortality rate has also increased during this period. To compound such problems, Zimbabwe's HIV/AIDS infection rate is among the world's worst.

COUNTRY PROFILES: WESTERN HEMISPHERE

ANGUILLA

According to legend, this slender island, named in Spanish for the eel its shape suggests, got the name Anguilla from no less a figure than Christopher Columbus, who is said to have sailed through this area of the Caribbean on one of his early voyages at the end of the fifteenth century. Some historians dismiss this story as fanciful and contend that the French were the first Europeans to visit the shores of Anguilla island. Whatever the story, it is certain that the British established the first colonial settlement there in 1650. Unlike many other islands in the region, Anguilla remained under the power of the British for the entire colonial period.

British settlers quickly established farms on the island, although these agricultural holdings were less expansive than the plantation-size holdings found on some of the other Caribbean islands held by the British. The difference in size was because the island itself was relatively small and its soil less fertile than that of other British-held islands. To work these farms, however, the British imported enslaved Africans. Because the island was small, the British decided in the early nineteenth century to link its colonial administration with that of Saint Christopher, better known as Saint Kitts, and Nevis, both of which lie to the south of Anguilla. The three-island colony's local administration was located on Saint Kitts, the largest of the islands.

Britain abolished enslavement in all of its colonial holdings in 1834, but most of those who had formerly been enslaved continued to work in farming or fishing for many years thereafter. In time, the harvesting of salt emerged as another major occupation for the freed people of the region. One of the enslavement traditions that lives on in contemporary celebrations is known as the "jollification." In this observance, Anguillans of both sexes, dressed as field workers, parade together to a location where a field is planted. Songs of Afro-Caribbean origins are sung as they proceed along their route and begin their field work.

In the late 1960s, as Saint Kitts and Nevis clamored for their independence from Britain, Anguillans decided their future would be brighter if they became a separate dependent territory tied to Britain. In 1967, the island issued a unilateral declaration of independence from Saint Kitts and Nevis, triggering a mini-invasion by British troops to quell the rebellion. In the early 1970s, the island was accorded the British crown colony status that it sought.

In March 1999, the ruling coalition of the Anguilla United Party and the Anguilla Democratic Party retained power, when each party won two of the seven seats in the National Assembly. The opposition Anguilla National Alliance party won the remaining three seats. By 2007, luxury tourism in the country had increased dramatically. Tourism and the services sector form the largest part of Anguilla's economy.

ANGUILLA

Area: 91 sq km
Form of government: Overseas territory of the United Kingdom
Capital: The Valley
Currency: East Caribbean dollar (XCD)
Income: US$8,800 (2008 est. of purchasing power parity)
Population: 13,770 (2009 est.)
Ethnic groups: black 90.1%, mixed, mulatto 4.6%, white 3.7%, other 1.6% (2001 census)
Religious groups: Anglican 29%, Methodist 24%, Pentecostal 7.7%, Seventh-Day Adventist 7.6%, Episcopalian 7.6%, Baptist 7.3%, Roman Catholic 5.7%
Languages: English (official)
Literacy: 95% (twelve years old and over who can read and write)
Exports: lobster, fish, livestock, salt
Imports: fuels, foodstuffs, manufactures, chemicals, trucks, textiles

ANTIGUA AND BARBUDA

Christopher Columbus first visited the islands of Antigua and Barbuda in 1493. Missionaries later attempted to settle on the island, but were hindered by the fierce Carib Indians, who inhabited the islands, and the absence of natural freshwater springs. In 1632, the British successfully

ANTIGUA AND BARBUDA

Independence: 1 November 1981 (from United Kingdom)
Area: 442 sq km (Antigua 281 sq km; Barbuda 161 sq km)
Form of government: constitutional monarchy with United Kingdom-style parliament
Capital: Saint John's
Currency: East Caribbean dollar (XCD)
Income: US$19,340 (2008 est. of purchasing power parity)
Population: 85,632 (2009 est.)
Ethnic groups: African-derived 90%, British, Portuguese, Lebanese, Syrian
Religious groups: Anglican (predominant), other Protestant, some Roman Catholic
Languages: English (official), local dialects
Literacy: 89% (fifteen years old and over who have completed five or more years of schooling)
Exports: petroleum products 48%, manufactures 23%, machinery and transport equipment 17%, food and live animals 4%, other 8%
Imports: food and live animals, machinery and transport equipment, manufactures, chemicals, oil

established a colony. Sir Christopher Codrington created the first large sugar estate in Antigua in 1674, bringing enslaved men and women from Africa's West Coast to work the plantations. Although the enslaved Antiguan Africans were emancipated in 1834, they remained bound to their plantation owners. Economic opportunities for the new freedmen were limited by a lack of surplus farming land, no access to credit, and an economy built on agriculture rather than manufacturing.

The majority of modern-day Antiguans are descended from the enslaved Africans imported by the British to work the island's sugar plantations. Although the sugar estates were extremely profitable for both their owners and Britain, generating more wealth in the 1780s than all of Britain's New England colonies combined, life for the island's enslaved population was very harsh. The harshness of life and work on the sugar plantations led to riots, including a noteworthy riot in 1831, just three years before the British ended enslavement on the island.

Led by Chief Minister Vere Cornwall Bird Sr., Antigua began to push for independence in the late 1960s. There was a separate push by Barbudans for their independence, but neither the Antiguan nor the British government supported this movement. Antigua and Barbuda became a single, fully independent nation in 1981. Antigua and Barbuda entered the twenty-first century ruled by its black majority.

ARGENTINA

Though traditionally known for its early Spanish and nineteenth-century Italian and German heritage, Argentina had a large black population during much of the colonial and independence periods. Today, the Afro-Argentine population is estimated at a few thousand.

The first enslaved Africans were brought into Argentina in the final two decades of the sixteenth century. By 1680, nearly 23,000 Africans had been imported legally, although those brought into the country illegally would certainly swell that figure considerably. Most of the

ARGENTINA

Official name: Argentine Republic
Independence: 9 July 1816 (from Spain)
Area: 2,766,890 sq km
Form of government: republic
Capital: Buenos Aires
Currency: Argentine peso (ARS)
Income: US$14,408 (2008 est. of purchasing power parity)
Population: 40,482,000 (2009 est.)
Ethnic groups: white (mostly Spanish and Italian) 97%, mestizo, Amerindian, or other nonwhite groups 3%
Religious groups: Christian 92%, Agnostic 3%, Muslim 2%, Jewish 1.3%, other 1%
Languages: Spanish (official), English, Italian, German, French
Literacy: 97.1% (fifteen years old and over who can read and write; 2003 est.)
Exports: edible oils, fuels and energy, cereals, feed, motor vehicles
Primary export partners: Brazil 22.3%, China 11.4%, U.S. 7.6%, Chile 6%, Spain 4.1% (2008)
Imports: machinery and equipment, motor vehicles, chemicals, metal manufactures, plastics
Primary import partners: Brazil 32.7%, U.S. 15.3%, China 11.5%, Germany 5.5% (2008)

enslaved persons brought into Argentina came from what is now the Congo and Angola. Although the local government in Argentina banned the importation of Africans in 1813, illegal activity continued for nearly thirty more years until a treaty with Britain in 1840 finally cut off this commerce in human cargo. As in most of the Americas, the enslaved Africans brought into Argentina were employed primarily as farm workers or domestic servants.

Until recent decades, Argentina's African heritage has received little attention, due perhaps in part to the scarcity of Afro-Argentines. The limited number of blacks in the country has allowed the country's historians and sociologists to indulge in a bit of revisionist history, insisting that blacks are of little historical relevance in Argentina. Regrettably, racist attitudes are not uncommon in modern-day Argentina. When the country's soccer team faced opposing teams made up largely of blacks, headlines in the sports pages referred to these opponents in a derogatory and decidedly racist manner.

Through most of the 1980s, Argentina's economy stagnated and was battered by high levels of inflation. The 1989 election of Carlos Menem, a member of the Partido Justicialista, better known as the Peronist party, was followed by a period of rapid economic growth for several years. However, the Menem administration's failure to deepen economic reforms eventually led to a period of decline and paved the way for the election in 1999 of Fernando de la Rua. The new president was unable to improve the economy, and his government collapsed after two years in a climate of growing civil unrest. In 2002, Peronist Eduardo Duhalde was appointed president. Nevertheless, Argentina defaulted on its international debt, leading to spiraling inflation. After a year of fluctuation, the economy began to stabilize and Nestor Kirchner was elected president in 2003. Kirchner helped to sustain the economic progress in Argentina, but forfeited his 2007 reelection campaign in favor of his wife, Cristina Fernandez de Kirchner, who was then a senator. Later that year, Cristina de Kirchner became the first elected female president of Argentina (Isabel Peron served between 1974–1975 but was not elected to the position). She maintained the economic reforms begun by her husband (for example, restructuring IMF loans) and increased a program of economic stimuli to re-ignite the economy.

ARUBA

Area: 193 sq km
Form of government: parliamentary democracy; part of the Kingdom of the Netherlands
Capital: Oranjestad
Currency: Aruban guilder/florin (AWG)
Income: US$21,400 (2004 est. of purchasing power parity)
Population: 103,065 (2009 est.)
Ethnic groups: mixed white/Caribbean Amerindian 80%
Religious groups: Roman Catholic 81%, Protestant 9%, Hindu, Muslim, Confucian, Jewish
Languages: Dutch (official), Papiamento (a Spanish, Portuguese, Dutch, English dialect), English (widely spoken), Spanish
Literacy: 97%
Exports: live animals and animal products, art and collectibles, machinery and electrical equipment, transport equipment
Primary export partners: U.S. 69.4%, Brazil 8.7%, France 6.4%, UK 4.5% (2008)
Imports: machinery and electrical equipment, crude oil for refining and reexport, chemicals; foodstuffs
Primary import partners: U.S. 57%, Netherlands 7.6%, Brazil 3.8% (2008)

ARUBA

Aruba is one of the few Caribbean islands whose people are still largely descended from an original indigenous population. More than 85% of Arubans are of mixed Arawak Indian and European ancestry. A majority of the remaining 15% are black immigrants from other Caribbean islands who have come to Aruba to fill some of the many available jobs in thriving tourist and oil industries.

The island's arid climate and relatively barren soil prevented the development of any major agricultural cultivation. This lack of large-scale farming helps to explain the absence of any significant African enslavement heritage on the island. When the first oil refineries began to spring up on Aruba in the 1930s, workers, many of them black, were imported from other islands in the Caribbean.

Though their numbers are relatively small, particularly when viewed against the backdrop of the Caribbean as a whole, the blacks of Aruba have made significant contributions to the island's culture in the relatively short time they have been present on the island. Papiamento, the local language, draws on elements of several European languages, the native Arawak tongue, and several African dialects.

In 1997, the legislature of Aruba was dissolved when a conflict broke out between the senior and junior members of the ruling coalition led by Prime Minister Henny Eman. However, in elections in December 1997, the coalition retained power in the legislature with a 12–9 majority over the opposition People's Electoral Movemement (MEP). Four years later, the opposition party wrested power from the coalition, taking twelve of the twenty-one seats in the legislature and bringing MEP leader Nelson Oduber to power as prime minister. Mike Eman, brother of former prime minister Henny Eman, was elected to serve in that capacity in 2009.

BAHAMAS, THE

Christopher Columbus first visited the islands of the Bahamas in 1492 when he landed in the Western Hemisphere, either at Long Bay, Samana Cay, San Salvador Island, or one of a number of other islands. In 1647, the first permanent European settlement was founded. In 1717, the islands became a British crown colony. Most of the British colonists in the islands were not large landowners, so African enslavement developed more slowly in the Bahamas than in several nearby islands. Nevertheless, over time, Africans came to dominate the islands, accounting for about 85% of the total population by the start of the twenty-first century.

Britain's abolition of enslavement in all its territories set free some 10,000 enslaved Africans scattered across the Bahamas. Under the terms of the British edict ending enslavement in 1834, the newly freed people were apprenticed to their former owners and required to remain with those owners as apprentices for a period of four years. Many of the emancipated men and women continued to pursue occupations in farming and fishing, even after their apprenticeships had ended. Eventually a black middle class developed on the islands as individual blacks managed to obtain a higher education and enter such professions as doctors, lawyers, and educators.

The twentieth-century boom in South Florida and the promise of better-paying jobs lured many black Bahamians to the United States, despite the racial discrimination they encountered upon their arrival. A psychological and cultural barrier developed between those Bahamians who left their homeland in an attempt to better themselves and those who chose to remain in the islands. A similar division was seen between those who were attracted to Nassau and the more rapidly developing islands and those who opted for the quiet life on the outer islands.

The Bahamas were granted self-government through a series of constitutional and political steps, culminating in independence on July 10, 1973. The Progressive Liberal Party led the Bahamas to independence and remained in power until the early 1990s. In August 1992, the Free National Movement (FNM) won parliamentary elections, and its leader, Hubert Ingraham, became prime minister. In March 1997 elections, Ingraham and the FNM were reelected.

The Ingraham government's economic policy of privatization hit a snag in the spring of 1999 when telecommunications workers rejected the government's retrenchment package. Also troublesome for the Bahamian economy during that period was the country's high crime rate, a potential threat to the country's critically important tourism industry. In 2000, the country's offshore banking business was rocked by charges that it

THE BAHAMAS

Official name: Commonwealth of the Bahamas
Independence: 10 July 1973 (from United Kingdom)
Area: 13,940 sq km
Form of government: constitutional parliamentary democracy
Capital: Nassau
Currency: Bahamian dollar (BSD)
Income: US$27,735 (2008 est. of purchasing power parity)
Population: 307,451 (2009)
Ethnic groups: black 85% (mostly of West African origin), white 12%, Asian and Hispanic 3%
Religious groups: Baptist 35%, Anglican 15%, Roman Catholic 14%, Pentecostal 8%, Methodist 4%, Church of God 5%, other Protestant 15%, none or unknown 3%, other 1%
Languages: English, Creole (among Haitian immigrants)
Literacy: 95.6% (fifteen years old and over who can read and write; 2003 est.)
Exports: pharmaceuticals, cement, rum, crawfish, refined petroleum products
Primary export partners: U.S. 20.8%, Singapore 18.2%, Poland 17.5%, Germany 7.3%, Japan 7.2%, Guatemala 5.5%, Switzerland 4.7% (2008)
Imports: foodstuffs, manufactured goods, crude oil, vehicles, electronics
Primary import partners: U.S. 27.1%, Japan 17.8%, South Korea 14.7%, Singapore 7.9%, Venezuela 5.4% (2008)

was not moving aggressively enough against money laundering, triggering a new government effort to step up its cooperation with other jurisdictions. In May 2002, the ruling Free National Movement, with former Parliamentary member and Minister of Public Works Tommy Turnquest now at its helm, replacing the retiring Ingraham, lost in parliamentary elections to the Progressive Liberal Party (PLP), which won twenty-nine of forty seats in the House of Assembly. The election brought PLP leader Perry Christie to power as prime minister.

Hubert Ingraham of the FNM assumed the prime minister's office again in 2007. He also began serving as Minister of Finance for the new government.

BARBADOS

It should hardly come as a surprise that Barbados is considered the most British of the Caribbean islands. For more than 300 years, the island was under the control of the British, whose institutions became firmly entrenched in the Barbadian culture and economy. The first British colonists arrived in 1627, bringing with them ten enslaved Africans. That enslaved population remained relatively small for the first few years, as most colonists were unable to afford to purchase slave labor and instead worked the land themselves or with the help of indentured servants from Europe. Although the number of those enslaved on the island was small, their role in the island's economy was pivotal. Enslaved Africans, along with some of the native Amerindian people who had been enslaved, were forced to handle the most challenging labor tasks.

With the rise of the sugar industry, beginning in the 1640s, Barbados became more heavily involved in the trade of Africans. Between 1645 and 1685, the number of Africans on the island skyrocketed from about 5,700 to nearly 60,000. By 1700, the enslaved population on Barbados was estimated at close to 135,000. Drawn mostly from West Africa, these bonded men and women spoke a variety of languages and represented a staggering number of ethnic groups, including the Fon, Fante, Ga, Asante, and Yoruba peoples. By the early eighteenth century, many of the European-born indentured servants who had carried much of the workload in the colony's early years began leaving Barbados in waves. This aggravated the problem of racial imbalance, worrying the white landowners and resulting in tough, new regulations to control the captive population.

Despite the imposition of strong regulations to discourage unrest among the huge enslaved population, Barbados experienced three major rebellions in 1649, 1675, and 1692. Colonial justice was harsh. Those who rebelled were tortured in an attempt to get them to name confederates. Of those captured and tried, most were sentenced to be executed, often by barbarous methods (some were even burned alive). Little resistance was recorded in the eighteenth century, but the British Parliament's 1807 ban on the international trade in humans, the Haitian Revolution that brought blacks to power, and the visits of abolitionists to the island culminated in the so-called Easter Rebellion in 1816. As many as 1,000 black men and women were killed in the fighting, nearly 150 were executed after the rebellion was put down, and others were deported from the island. The British government was so shaken by the uprising that it

BARBADOS

Independence: 30 November 1966 (from United Kingdom)
Area: 430 sq km
Form of government: parliamentary democracy; independent sovereign state within the Commonwealth of Nations
Capital: Bridgetown
Currency: Barbadian dollar (BBD)
Income: US$18,977 (2008 est. of purchasing power parity)
Population: 284,589 (2009 est.)
Ethnic groups: black 90%, white 4%, Asian and other 6%
Religious groups: Protestant 63% (Anglican 28%, Pentecostal 19%, Methodist 5%, other 11%), Roman Catholic 4%, none 21%, other 5%
Languages: English
Literacy: 99.7% (fifteen years old and over has ever attended school; 2003 est.)
Exports: sugar and molasses, rum, other foods and beverages, chemicals, electrical components, clothing
Primary export partners: Trinidad and Tobago 15.5%, Jamaica 13.6%, Brazil 9.9%, U.S. 8.6%, UK 7.8%, Saint Lucia 7.2%, Saint Vincent and the Grenadines 4.5% (2008)
Imports: consumer goods, machinery, foodstuffs, construction materials, chemicals, fuel, electrical components
Primary import partners: U.S. 27.8%, Trinidad and Tobago 26.3%, Russia 7.3%, Germany 4.2% (2008)

pressured Barbadian colonists to relax their hold on the enslaved population. In 1833, the British Parliament voted to end African enslavement in all British territories.

From 1958 to 1962, Barbados was one of ten members of the West Indies Federation, a group of Britain's Caribbean colonies that united with the intention to form a single, free Caribbean state. The Federation collapsed, but Barbados negotiated its own independence at a constitutional conference with the United Kingdom in June 1966. The country attained self-rule on November 30, 1966. Since that time, Barbados has been a member of the British Commonwealth of Nations and has assumed a leadership role in the Caribbean Community (CARICOM). Owen Arthur, a member of the Barbados Labour Party, assumed the prime ministership in 1994, after former Prime Minister Erskine Sandiford lost a vote of confidence in the National Assembly. Leading contemporary Afro-Barbadians include George Lamming, a novelist, critic, essayist, and educator.

The ruling Barbados Labour Party emerged victorious from January 1999 legislative elections, winning all but two of the twenty-eight seats in the National Assembly. A move was made in early 2000 to modernize the country's constitution, moving the government to a republican form of rulership.

Barbados has had a long history of political and economic stability. In October 2009 it ranked third after the United States and Canada in the Western Hemisphere's Human Development Index.

BELIZE

Belize, known until 1973 as British Honduras, is the only country in Central America in which blacks have made up

Women in Traditional French West Indies Dress, Bastille Day Celebrations, Marigot, St. Martin. *In the Caribbean, the system of African enslavement eventually led to an African Caribbean population that represented a clear majority on most of the region's islands. Into the early twenty-first century, however, those of African ancestry still held an inferior position to that of the smaller numbers of whites, Asians, and East Indians.* AP IMAGES/MARVIN HOKSTAM

BELIZE

Official name: none
Independence: 21 September 1981 (from United Kingdom)
Area: 22,966 sq km
Form of government: parliamentary democracy
Capital: Belmopan
Currency: Belizean dollar (BZD)
Income: US$7,953 (2008 est. of purchasing power parity)
Population: 322,000 (2009 est.)
Ethnic groups: mestizo 48.7%, Creole 24.9%, Maya 10.6%, Garifuna 6.1%, other 9.7%
Religious groups: Roman Catholic 50%, Protestant 27% (Pentecostal 7.4%, Anglican 5.3%, Seventh-Day Adventist 5.2%, Mennonite 4.1%, Methodist 3.5%, Jehovah's Witnesses 1.5%), other 14%, none 9%
Languages: English (official), Spanish, Mayan, Garifuna (Carib), Creole
Literacy: 77% (fifteen years old and over who can read and write; 2003 est. Note: sources vary widely, some listing as few as 40% of the population, others more than 90%)
Exports: sugar, bananas, citrus, clothing, fish products, molasses, wood
Primary export partners: U.S. 35%, UK 21.1%, Cote d'Ivoire 5.2%, Italy 4.4% (2008)
Imports: machinery and transportation equipment, manufactured goods, food, beverages, tobacco, fuels, chemicals, pharmaceuticals
Primary import partners: U.S. 37.7%, Mexico 12.5%, Cuba 7.8%, Guatemala 7.3%, Russia 5.1% (2008)

a majority of the population throughout the twentieth century. The country did not achieve full independence until September 21, 1981. Originally peopled largely by a succession of Native American peoples, including the Maya, Belize passed between British and Spanish control throughout the seventeenth century. A treaty between the two countries in 1765 maintained Spain's claim to the land, but recognized the British right to maintain coastal settlements for the harvesting of logwood, which was valued for its use in producing dyes. As the British log-harvesting efforts expanded, enslaved Africans were brought to the Caribbean to assist with the effort.

Once the presence of the British wood-harvesting enclave had been established by treaty, the woodcutters graduated from cutting logwood and began to go after mahogany. The nature of this work had a profound effect on Africans living in the colony. Those who were trusted roamed the forests of the land, often with little or no supervision, hunting for mahogany trees to be felled. Once found, they were reported to axmen, who came in to cut down the trees. Although the men employed in mahogany harvesting experienced greater freedom to range through the rain forest, the treatment of these individuals was not noticeably more humane than the treatment afforded enslaved persons involved in agriculture.

The British established the colony of British Honduras in 1840; it became a crown colony in 1862. Self-government was granted in January 1964. The official name of the territory was changed from British Honduras to Belize in June of 1973, and full independence was granted on September 21, 1981, with George C. Price of the People's United Party installed as head of government. In the December 1984 elections, voters elected Manuel Esquivel prime minister. Five years later, Price was again elected prime minister, a post that was recaptured by Esquivel in the 1993 elections.

In August 1998, the ruling United Democratic Party was soundly defeated by the People's United Party, bringing Said Musa to power as prime minister. Esquivel, who had served for fifteen years as prime minister, stepped down August 31, 1998. In his September 1999 state of the union message, Musa pointed to the progress made in building up Belize's economic infrastructure during his first year in office. In the March 2000 municipal elections, the governing People's United Party retained control of six of the country's seven municipalities. The country was hit hard in 2000 and 2001 by hurricanes Keith and Iris, respectively, both of which left thousands homeless. In 2005, the government's announcement of significant tax increases precipitated riots throughout the country with calls for Said Musa's resignation. In February 2008, Dean Barrow of the United Democratic Party became the country's first black prime minister

Leading contemporary Afro-Belizeans include Zee Edgell, a writer who has concentrated her writings on the Belizean independence movement, the nation's multiethnic traditions, and the lives of women in Belize.

BERMUDA

Located in the Atlantic Ocean about 650 miles east of North Carolina, Bermuda is relatively isolated. The first Europeans to visit the islands were Spanish explorers in 1503. In 1609, a group of British explorers became

BERMUDA

Area: 58.8 sq km
Form of government: parliamentary British overseas territory with internal self-government
Capital: Hamilton
Currency: Bermudian dollar (BMD)
Income: US$69,900 (2004 est.)
Population: 67,837 (July 2009 est.)
Ethnic groups: black 55%, white 34%, mixed 6%, other 5%
Religious groups: Anglican 23%, Roman Catholic 15%, African Methodist Episcopal 11%, other Protestant 18%, other 12%, none or unaffiliated 20%
Languages: English (official), Portuguese
Literacy: 98% (fifteen years old and over who can read and write; 1970 est.)
Exports: reexports of pharmaceuticals
Primary export partners: Brazil 22.4%, U.S. 14.6%, Germany 11%, South Africa 8.4%, Switzerland 6% (2008)
Imports: machinery and transport equipment, construction materials, chemicals, food, and live animals
Primary import partners: South Korea 31.7%, Italy 21.7%, U.S. 14.9%, UK 6.8%, Singapore 4.4%, France 4.2% (2008)

stranded in Bermuda and their reports aroused great interest about the islands in England. In 1612, British colonists arrived and founded the town of Saint George, the oldest continuously inhabited English-speaking settlement in the Western Hemisphere.

Enslaved Africans were brought to Bermuda soon after the colony was founded. Although the islands' soil and area were ill-suited for large-scale farming, the African laborers were put to work as fishermen, tradesmen, and, to a limited extent, as field hands. The enslaved Africans of Bermuda rose up against their masters on several occasions, most notably in 1730, after which the accused ringleader, Sarah Bassett, was burned at the stake. Thirty years later, between 600 and 700 slaves were accused of plotting a large-scale rebellion. A number of those accused were tried and subsequently executed. The trade in humans was outlawed in Bermuda in 1807, and those in bondage were freed in 1834.

Unfortunately for the newly freed Africans of the island nation, employment opportunities in the tobacco, shipbuilding, and salt mining industries, all of which had been mainstays of the Bermudian economy, began to shrink dramatically as those industries themselves started to decline. The island economy got a temporary boost during the U.S. Civil War, when Union ships blockaded the ports of the Confederacy. Southern importers arranged to have their incoming goods off-loaded in Bermuda and then smuggled through the blockade in smaller ships. However, with the end of the war, this temporary improvement in the local economy disappeared. Bermudians, with an area of less than twenty-one square miles on several small islands, turned to agricultural ventures to produce income. The cultivation of onions, potatoes, and Easter lilies eventually proved so successful and profitable that indentured servants had to be brought in from Portugal to help handle part of the workload.

For most of its first 300 years, the government of Bermuda was composed exclusively of wealthy white landowners or appointees of the British Crown. The protests of black Bermudians were not heeded until 1963, when universal adult suffrage was introduced. Landowners still had an edge, however, as the law provided them each with two votes. A new constitution in 1968 gave the locally elected government complete control over Bermuda's affairs. Bermuda remains an overseas territory of the United Kingdom in 2010, although debate continues on the issue of independence. A 1995 referendum on independence was easily defeated, with 73% voting against the measure.

Bermuda enjoyed the highest gross domestic product per capita in the world in 2007, and remains high on the list in 2010. Its economy is based on financial services for international business and luxury facilities for tourists.

BOLIVIA

Although those of African ancestry make up only about 2% of Bolivia's population, their history in the region dates back to the first half of the sixteenth century, when their ancestors arrived as enslaved persons. These blacks were imported from Peru to help supplement the labor of the indigenous Native American population, many of whom had succumbed to diseases introduced by European settlers. The African origins of those enslaved in Bolivia is the subject of debate, with some contending that they came from an area of the West African coast between the Senegal and Niger rivers, while others maintain they were brought from Angola. This question of the earliest Afro-Bolivians' origins is unlikely ever to be resolved, since Spain maintained no West African trading centers and thus drew African captives from a wide area,

BOLIVIA

Official name: Plurinational State of Bolivia
Independence: 6 August 1825 (from Spain)
Area: 1,098,580 sq km
Form of government: republic
Capital: La Paz (seat of government); Sucre (legal capital and seat of judiciary)
Currency: boliviano (BOB)
Income: US$4,345 (2008 est. of purchasing power parity)
Population: 9,775,246 (2009 est.)
Ethnic groups: Quechua 30%, Aymara 25%, mestizo (mixed white and Amerindian ancestry) 30%, white and other, 15%
Religious groups: Roman Catholic 95%, Protestant (Evangelical Methodist)
Languages: Spanish (official), Quechua (official), Aymara (official)
Literacy: 87.2% (fifteen years old and over who can read and write; 2003 est.)
Exports: soybeans, natural gas, zinc, gold, wood
Primary export partners: Brazil 60%, U.S. 8.3%, Japan 4.1% (2008)
Imports: capital goods, raw materials and semi-manufactures, chemicals, petroleum, food
Primary import partners: Brazil 27.8%, Argentina 14.8%, U.S. 10.9%, Chile 9.9%, Peru 7.4%, China 5.1% (2008)

and also because the record-keeping for these transactions was very poor. Frequently, there was an assumption that the captives came from an area close to their port of embarkation in Africa, but often this was not the case.

Those of African origin brought into Bolivia did not fare well at high elevations and under the stressful working conditions of the mineral mines in the area. By 1554, most of the enslaved Africans had been replaced in the country's silver mines by indigenous labor. The blacks were then put into other lines of work, some serving as domestic servants, others apprenticed to artisans skilled in the crafting of silver and other metals. The majority of the Africans, however, were moved to rural areas and pressed into service as cultivators of crops to feed the country's growing population. Within Bolivia, many of the blacks eventually mixed with other ethnic groups. Children of mixed African and European ancestry were sometimes classified as mulattos, while those of African and Native American descent were called zambos. Calculating the African or African-mixed population in Bolivia's past is difficult because of the haphazard manner in which records were kept.

Although their numbers were few, Afro-Bolivians joined the country's struggle to win its independence from Spain. Independence was achieved in 1825, and soon thereafter the nation's founding constitution called for the emancipation of all its African captives. However, not all blacks and Native Americans in bondage were set free. As of 1831, the country's constitution contained a "free-womb" statute that decreed that no one born after independence could be considered enslaved, but those previously in bondage continued to be recognized as slaves. Complete liberation of the Africans did not come until 1851.

Although not particularly active on the political front, Afro-Bolivians have had some impact on contemporary culture in Bolivia. In the early 1980s, a group of students from Coroico, Nor Yungas, formed a dance troupe to preserve some of the original Afro-Bolivian dance forms of the region. Called the Grupo Afroboliviano, the troupe performed throughout the country, helping to create awareness among their fellow citizens of the distinct Afro-Bolivian culture. This, in turn, has sparked a number of efforts to preserve this culture.

BRAZIL

Brazil was formally claimed in 1500 by the Portuguese and was ruled from Lisbon as a colony until 1808. Brazil successfully declared independence on September 7, 1822. Four major groups make up the Brazilian population: indigenous Indians of Tupi and Guarani language stock; the Portuguese; Africans brought to Brazil enslaved; and various European and Asian immigrant groups that have settled in Brazil since the mid-nineteenth century.

Slavery was introduced into Brazil in the 1530s and expanded greatly when sugar became important. The institution grew rapidly between 1580 and 1640, when Spain controlled the country. Estimates of the total number of enslaved Africans brought to Brazil varies from 6 million to 20 million. Enslavement did not finally end in Brazil until 1888. Though the practices in Brazil were often brutal, and the life expectancy of blacks on sugar, coffee, and cotton plantations was very low, large numbers of Africans achieved freedom. About 25 percent of Brazil's Africans were free before slavery was abolished.

In early-twentieth-century Brazil, a new African consciousness emerged in response to the appearance of a number of Afro-Brazilian publications. Also springing up during this period were a number of organizations that

BRAZIL

Official name: Federative Republic of Brazil
Independence: 7 September 1822 (from Portugal)
Area: 8,511,965 sq km
Form of government: federative republic
Capital: Brasilia
Currency: real (BRL)
Income: US$10,465 (2008 est. of purchasing power parity)
Population: 191,241,714 (2009)
Ethnic groups: white (includes Portuguese, German, Italian, Spanish, Polish) 49%, mixed white and black 42%, black 7%, other (includes Japanese, Arab, Amerindian) 1%
Religious groups: Roman Catholic (nominal) 73.6%, Protestant 15.4%
Languages: Portuguese (official), Spanish, English, French
Literacy: 88.6% (fifteen years old and over who can read and write; 2004 est.)
Exports: manufactures, iron ore, soybeans, footwear, coffee
Primary export partners: U.S. 14.6%, China 11.5%, Argentina 8.6%, Netherlands 4.9%, Germany 4.5% (2008)
Imports: machinery and equipment, chemical products, oil, electricity
Primary import partners: U.S. 14.9%, China 11.6%, Argentina 7.9%, Germany 7% (2008)

aspired to right some of the wrongs faced by the nation's black population. White Brazilians, in the years following the abolition of African enslavement, embarked on a policy of "whitening" (*branqueamento*) the country's population through intermixing with Afro-Brazilians. The Brazilian program of *branqueamento* was based on the notion that the presence of European blood in an individual was sufficient to make him or her white. Afro-Brazilian organizations fought against the discrimination and poverty stemming from this racist policy in the early twentieth century.

The black population of Brazil is the largest in the Americas. Only Nigeria in Africa has a larger population of blacks. The African influences on both the population and the culture of Brazil are all-pervasive. Perhaps no single event better illustrates the scope of the African contribution to Brazilian life than Carnival. However, behind the laughter and goodwill of this annual four-day celebration, the truth is somewhat less reassuring for those who would assume that racism is long dead in Brazil. In fact, Brazilians of African descent lack clout on both the political and the economic levels. Afro-Brazilians lag behind their fellow countrymen in quality of education, housing, employment, and health. Activists within the Afro-Brazilian community continue the struggle to achieve complete equality for everyone in the country, regardless of race. Leading contemporary Afro-Brazilians include: musicians Jorge Benjor, Carlinhos Brown, Gilberto Gil, husband and wife duo Airto Moreira and Flora Purim, and Milton Nascimento; literary figure Abdias do Nascimento; and internationally recognized sports figure Pelé.

After years of military rule, democracy returned to Brazil in 1985. Three years later, a new constitution was drafted. In the presidential elections of October 1998, Fernando Henrique Cardoso won a second term as president. One of Cardoso's first moves in his second term was to order a devaluation of the Brazilian *real* in January 1999 in an effort to link it more closely to the U.S. dollar. The country's economy showed signs of recovery in 1999 and 2000. However, a difficult external environment in 2001 limited growth and worsened public solvency indicators. In 2002, Luis Inácio Lula da Silva won the presidency after several attempts and was elected to a second term in 2006. However, the government continued to receive complaints of corruption. Brazil was also forced to confront its legacy of racial exclusion, in much the same way as the United States had been compelled to confront its own such legacy decades earlier.

In the year 2000, a disturbing survey was conducted by the Catholic-based Pastoral Land Commission documenting the presence of more than 25,000 forced workers in Brazil who were primarily living as modern day enslaved persons. The Brazilian government acknowledged (as a result of a U.N. investigation) that a segment of its citizen *were* essentially working under conditions "analogous to slavery." However, the government placed the number of those enslaved at twice that which appeared in the Pastoral Land Commission report. Many of these modern day enslaved Brazilians worked on sugar plantations. In 2007, the government embarked on a program to free the exploited workers. In some instances, raids were carried out to liberate the captive population. Close to 5,000 had been freed by 2008 in more than 200 locations throughout the country.

CANADA

People of African ancestry make up a tiny portion—only about 2%—of Canada's total population, but their contributions to the country's founding and its history are

CANADA

Independence: 1 July 1867 (from United Kingdom)
Area: 9,976,140 sq km
Form of government: parliamentary democracy and constitutional monarchy
Capital: Ottawa
Currency: Canadian dollar (CAD)
Income: US$39,098 (2008 est. of purchasing power parity)
Population: 33,843,000 (2009 est.)
Ethnic groups: British Isles origin 28%, French origin 23%, other European 15%, Amerindian 2%, other, mostly Asian, African, Arab 6%, mixed background 26%
Religious groups: Roman Catholic 43%, Protestant and other Christian 27%, none 16%, Muslim 2%, Jewish 1%, other 11%.
Languages: English 58.3% (official), French 21.6% (official), other 19.6% (2006)
Literacy: 99% (fifteen years old and over who can read and write; 2003 est.)
Exports: motor vehicles and parts, newsprint, wood pulp, timber, crude petroleum, machinery, natural gas, aluminum, telecommunications equipment, electricity
Primary export partners: U.S. 77.7%, UK 2.7%, Japan 2.3% (2008)
Imports: machinery and equipment, crude oil, chemicals, motor vehicles and parts, durable consumer goods, electricity
Primary import partners: U.S. 52.4%, China 9.8%, Mexico 4.1% (2008)

greatly disproportionate to their meager numbers. Africans are believed to have participated in several of the early exploratory missions to the region. Legend holds that one of the crew members on French explorer Jacques Cartier's initial expedition in 1534 was an African. However, Mathieu de Coste (d. 1623, sometimes rendered as da Costa), who served the governor of Acadia (in northeastern North America) as an interpreter to the local Micmac indigenous peoples, is generally regarded as the first black person in Canada. Early records indicate that the first African brought directly to Canada was a child, brought to Quebec in 1628 by Englishman David Kirke and sold to a local resident upon Kirke's departure the following year. The child was baptized Olivier Le Jeune in May 1633. According to records, he died in 1654.

Between 1628 and the British conquest of 1759, New France imported 1,132 enslaved Africans into the regions of Canada. Most of them came from the French West Indies or British colonies elsewhere in North America. One of the early governors of New France had petitioned Paris to permit a trade in Africans but was turned down, so there was no direct importation of Africans from the continent. The number of those enslaved living in the British-held colonies of Canada was relatively small until the time of the American Revolution. Loyalists fleeing the new American republic brought with them some 2,000 blacks. About 1,200 of that number went to the Maritimes, including New Brunswick, Nova Scotia, and Prince Edward Island. Of the remaining 800, about 300 went to Lower Canada, as Quebec was then known, and 500 went to Upper Canada (Ontario). Even more influential in Canada's development was the arrival of some 3,500 free black Loyalists, who fled to Canada following the American Revolution. Most of these black Loyalists settled in Nova Scotia and New Brunswick.

Slave codes were more severe in the British-held territories than in New France, where those enslaved could marry, own property, and maintain parental rights. However, the British did not sustain enslavement for long. London had divided Canada into two governments, Upper Canada and Lower Canada. The governor of Upper Canada, Colonel James Simcoe, an ardent abolitionist, induced the area's legislature to pass laws forbidding the importation of enslaved Africans and freeing every enslaved person born in the area by the age of twenty-five. As a result, black enslavement in Upper Canada soon collapsed.

Similar legislation was not enacted in Lower Canada. However, by 1800, the courts, through complex legal decisions, established the principle that an enslaved person could leave his owner whenever he wished. In the Maritime Provinces, courts also acted to eliminate African enslavement in fact if not in theory. African enslavement was formally abolished in Canada in 1833.

Meanwhile, starting slowly in the eighteenth century, Canada was becoming a haven for runaways fleeing across her southern borders. Those who had served with the British in the American War for Independence came to Halifax from New York in large numbers in 1782 and 1783. Though many were to migrate to Freetown on the West Coast of Africa, others stayed. In 1826, Canada defied the United States and formally refused to return fugitives. In 1829, the legislature of Lower Canada announced that every runaway that entered the province was immediately free, a declaration that gave impetus to the Underground Railroad and stimulated moves for resettlement by blacks in Canada.

The passage of the Fugitive Slave Act in the United States in 1850 meant that any escapee who remained in the United States was to be returned to his owner. Within a year after passage of the law, some 10,000 American runaways arrived in Canada, welcomed by a majority of Canadians who provided communities and services for them.

African Americans were accepted into the mainstream of Canadian life, were allowed to choose separate or integrated schools, and were elected to local office and served as officers in the Canadian Army. Black laborers contributed substantially to the expansion of the Canadian Pacific Railroad, as immigrants from Eastern and Southern Europe were to contribute to the development of railroads in the United States. Black skilled laborers were much in demand. By 1861, at the outbreak of the Civil War in the United States, there were 50,000 blacks in Canada. However, after the Civil War, feelings of fear among white Canadians led to discrimination in employment and schools. Many African Americans re-emigrated to the United States, feeling that, with enslavement outlawed there, a bright future awaited them. By 1871, the black population of Canada dipped to about 20,000.

Canada, the most sparsely populated country in the world with 1.5 persons per square mile, has become a haven for so many refugees that it has earned awards for outstanding achievement from human rights organizations. In fact, so many immigrants from Asia, Africa, the Caribbean, and elsewhere have moved to Canada, that the established British-Caucasian population has expressed fears it will become extinct (assimilated) within 100 years. Toronto alone has become one of the world's most cosmopolitan cities with more than 100 cultural or ethnic groups.

CAYMAN ISLANDS

During his fourth visit to the Caribbean in 1503, Christopher Columbus sighted the Cayman islands and dubbed them *Las Tortugas* for the large number of sea turtles he saw in the area. Later in the sixteenth century, Europeans passing through the area began calling the islands *Las Caymanas*, the Carib Amerindian term for crocodiles. However, many believe that the islands' many iguanas, rather than real crocodiles, inspired this new name. In any case, apart from brief visits to pick up fresh water and turtle meat, Europeans had little to do with these islands until the middle of the seventeenth century, when the first European settlement was made. The earliest settlements on the islands were established by a rather disreputable blend of characters including pirates, army deserters, debtors, and shipwrecked sailors. Under the Treaty of Madrid, the Caymans came under British control in 1670. More than sixty years later, the British established their first permanent settlement, made up largely of planters who had previously been located in Jamaica. Because of this relationship between Jamaica and the Caymans, the islands were considered dependencies of the former until 1962.

These earliest of British settlers began importing enslaved Africans into the islands, using them largely as domestic servants, fishermen, and subsistence farmers. The islands, not particularly fertile, were not considered an ideal setting for farming, so the large-scale agricultural undertakings the planters had enjoyed in Jamaica could not be duplicated in the Caymans. The absence of a plantation-type system and the relative proximity within which the planters and the newly imported Africans lived led, in time, to a good deal of intermarriage between the two groups. Nearly half of the population of the Caymans today is made up of islanders of mixed European and African descent.

When Jamaica won its independence in 1962, the Caymans became a directly held colony of Britain. Under the new arrangements with the United Kingdom, the islanders were given a new constitution and a larger measure

CAYMAN ISLANDS

Area: 259 sq km
Form of government: British crown colony
Capital: George Town
Currency: Cayman Islands dollar (KYD)
Income: US$43,800 (2004 est. of purchasing power parity)
Population: 49,035 (2009 est.)
Ethnic groups: mixed 40%, white 20%, black 20%, expatriates of various ethnic groups 20%
Religious groups: Christian 80% (United Church—Presbyterian and Congregational, Anglican, Baptist, Roman Catholic, Church of God in Christ, other Protestant)
Languages: English
Exports: turtle products, manufactured consumer goods
Primary export partners: mostly U.S.
Imports: foodstuffs, manufactured goods
Primary import partners: U.S., Trinidad and Tobago, UK, Netherlands Antilles, Japan

of control over their internal affairs. A tourist board launched in 1966 proved extremely successful in attracting tourists to the islands. By 1994, more than 1 million tourists, close to 70% of them from the United States, were visiting the islands annually. Another major source of income for the Caymans came from offshore banking. Shortly after its change in status with Jamaica, Cayman Islanders enacted new legislation to encourage company registration, offshore banking, and trust-company formation in the islands. Today, more than 500 banks do business in the Caymans, and the companies registered there number in the thousands. Prospering under existing conditions, islanders have made no major push for independence.

Long a major center for offshore banking, the Caymans came under increasing scrutiny in 1999 after accusations that the islands' government knowingly abetted tax evasion. Despite vehement denials by government officials, the intergovernmental Financial Action Task Force (FATF) blacklisted the Caymans as one of several countries around the world that had been determined to be uncooperative on matters of money laundering. In June 2001, the FATF eventually relented and removed the islands from its money laundering blacklist.

After taking office in 2009, U.S. President Barack Obama announced his intentions to pursue those American citizens who avoided paying taxes to the government by hiding their money in offshore accounts or engaging in other types of tax evasion, such as those allowed by Cayman Islands law. In response, the chairman of the Cayman Islands Financial Services Association wrote the president an open letter detailing how the island had assisted the United States in remaining competitive in the face of the global recession, and pledged the association's willingness to assist its powerful neighbor in any way possible.

CHILE

Official name: Republic of Chile
Independence: 18 September 1810 (from Spain)
Area: 756,950 sq km
Form of government: republic
Capital: Santiago
Currency: Chilean peso (CLP)
Income: US$14,529 (2008 est. of purchasing power parity)
Population: 16,928,873 (2009 est.)
Ethnic groups: white and white-Amerindian 95%, Mapuche 4%
Religious groups: Roman Catholic 70%, Evangelical 15%, Jehovah's Witnesses 1%, other Christian 1%, other 5%, none 8% (2002 census)
Languages: Spanish
Literacy: 96.2% (fifteen years old and over who can read and write; 2003 est.)
Exports: copper, fish, fruits, paper and pulp, chemicals
Primary export partners: China 14.2%, U.S. 11.3%, Japan 10.4%, Brazil 5.9%, South Korea 5.7%, Netherlands 5.2%, Italy 4.4% (2008)
Imports: consumer goods, chemicals, motor vehicles, fuels, electrical machinery, heavy industrial machinery, food
Primary import partners: U.S. 19.1%, China 11.9%, Brazil 9.3%, Argentina 8.8%, South Korea 5.6%, Japan 4.6% (2008)

CHILE

Africans first came to Chile with the expedition of Spanish explorer Diego de Almagro in 1536. Some served the expedition as enslaved crew members, while others served as soldiers. One such member of the expedition was Juan Valiente from Mexico, who was permitted to join Almagro as a soldier. He later distinguished himself in battle and in time rose to the rank of captain of the expedition's infantry. The earliest enslaved Africans brought into Chile were used to supplement the labors of indigenous workers in construction, farming, and the mining of gold. Relatively hard-strapped for money, Chile could not afford to import large numbers of captive Africans.

Despite the economic limits on the importation of slave labor, the country's black population, both free and enslaved, grew steadily during the final three decades of the sixteenth century. From a population of 7,000 among a total Chilean population of 624,000, the number of blacks surged by 1590 to a total of 20,000. Both in the rural countryside and in Chile's growing cities, free and enslaved blacks found livelihoods. In the cities, most Africans worked as domestic servants, while outside the cities, they toiled as miners, sheepherders, and cowboys. Free blacks drove coaches, made saddles, and reportedly even served as executioners. Even though the colonial Spanish law accorded blacks the lowest status possible, local authorities occasionally circumvented the Spanish Crown to give some enslaved Africans positions with supervisory responsibility. A select number of blacks had so distinguished themselves as soldiers that they received land grants. Juan Valiente from Mexico, who served the Almagro expedition as a soldier, became the first black in the Americas known to receive such a land grant.

At about the same time that Chileans first declared their independence from Spain in 1810, talk of abolition began to surface. It was not until 1823, however, that Chile became the first Spanish American republic to totally abolish slavery. Since the time of emancipation, the influence of the Afro-Chilean on the country's culture and development seems to have virtually disappeared. Unlike what has happened in many neighboring countries, there has been no Afro-Chilean cultural revival nor any organized involvement in politics by Afro-Chileans. The Chilean census of 1940 revealed a population of only 1,000 blacks and 3,000 mulattos. Some observers and scholars of the Chilean social scene suggest that continuing intermarriage and intermixing have combined to virtually wipe out the black population of the country.

COLOMBIA

The diversity of ethnic origins in Colombia results from the centuries-old intermixture of indigenous Indians, Spanish colonists, and enslaved Africans. In 1549, the area was established as a Spanish colony with the capital at Bogotá. In 1717, Bogotá became the capital of the viceroyalty of New Granada, an area which included what are now the nations of Venezuela, Ecuador, and Panama. On July 20, 1810, the citizens of Bogotá created the first representative council to defy Spanish authority. Total independence was proclaimed in 1813, and in 1819 the Republic of Greater Colombia was formed.

The African contributions to the population and culture of Colombia are many and varied. The high rate of intermarriage has resulted in a racially diverse population with more than half of its people classified as mestizos. The terminology used to refer to people of African ancestry or of mixed ancestry is somewhat complicated. The term black, or *negro* in Spanish, is common but avoided by many Colombians because of its sometimes disparaging connotations. More common are the terms *Moreno* (brown) and *gente de color* (people of color). In the rural area of the country near the Pacific coast, some of the people of African ancestry refer to themselves as *libres*, or free people, terminology that dates back to colonial times. Some people refer to blacks as *costenos* since many of the country's coastal residents are Afro-Colombians.

Enslaved Africans were first imported into communities along the northern coast of New Granada, a portion of which later became Colombia, in the 1520s. The port of Cartagena on the Caribbean coast developed into the principal trading port. The Africans brought into New Granada were used mostly in mining gold, although some saw service as domestic servants and farm workers. The supply of Native Americans, who had first been pressed into service in the mines, was rapidly being depleted, and the importation of Africans was deemed necessary to keep the mines operating.

Even during the years of African enslavement, there was a considerable amount of intermarriage and intermixing between the peoples of colonial New Granada. It is estimated that by the 1770s about 60% of the population was classified as "free people of color." As in most territories where Africans were held captive, masters sometimes decided to set some or all of their captives free, which often turned out to be a mixed blessing for those who could not find work on their own. Colombia won its independence in 1819, but slavery was not officially abolished there until 1851. In the late twentieth century, Colombia's black population was concentrated in three main areas of the country: the upper central portion of the Cauca Valley, which is heavily planted in sugarcane; the Pacific coast; and the Caribbean coastal region. In the 1990s, Pledad Corboda de Castro became the first black woman to be elected to the Colombian Senate. In 1993, she wrote a law instituting equal rights for

COLOMBIA

Official name: Republic of Colombia
Independence: 20 July 1810 (from Spain)
Area: 1,138,910 sq km
Form of government: republic
Capital: Bogotá
Currency: Colombian peso (COP)
Income: US$8,800 (2008 est. of purchasing power parity)
Population: 45,644,023 (2009 est.)
Ethnic groups: mestizo 58%, white 20%, mulatto 14%, black 4%, mixed black-Amerindian 3%, Amerindian 1%
Religious groups: Christian 95%, mainly Roman Catholic
Languages: Spanish
Literacy: 90.4% (fifteen years old and over who can read and write; 2005 census)
Exports: petroleum, coffee, coal, apparel, bananas, cut flowers
Primary export partners: U.S. 38%, Venezuela 16.2%, Ecuador 4% (2008)
Imports: industrial equipment, transportation equipment, consumer goods, chemicals, paper products, fuels, electricity
Primary import partners: U.S. 29.2%, China 11.5%, Mexico 7.9%, Brazil 5.9% (2008)

Afro-Colombians. Other leading contemporary Afro-Colombians include Totó la Momposina, a singer, dancer, and performer of traditional rhythms, and Manuel Zapata Olivella, a writer, physician, anthropologist, diplomat, and leading intellectual and artist of twentieth-century Latin America.

COSTA RICA

In 1502, on his fourth and last voyage to the New World, Christopher Columbus made the first European landfall in Costa Rica. Settlement of the area began in 1522. In 1821, Costa Rica joined other Central American provinces in a joint declaration of independence from Spain. Unlike most of their Central American neighbors, Costa Ricans are largely of European rather than mestizo descent, and Spain is the primary country of origin. The indigenous population today numbers less than 50,000. Blacks, descendants of nineteenth-century Jamaican immigrant workers, constitute a significant English-speaking minority, concentrated around the Caribbean port city of Limon.

The greatest influx of enslaved Africans into Costa Rica began during the late 1700s when Spanish colonists began importing slaves from neighboring colonies and directly from Africa to replace the dwindling labor force of indigenous Amerindian peoples, many of whom had contracted (and died from) diseases introduced by Europeans. The census of 1801, the first to provide figures on the black population, reported that 17% of the colony's population was made up of blacks or those of mixed-black descent, including mulattos, the result of black-white intermixing, and zambos of black and Amerindian descent.

More significant than the earlier importation of enslaved Africans was the immigration to Costa Rica by a substantial number of free black laborers from the islands of the Caribbean, particularly Jamaica. This wave of immigrants began arriving in the late nineteenth century, coming to help build the railroad designed to carry coffee from the country's interior to ports along its Atlantic Coast. When this construction project was completed, many West Indian laborers stayed in Costa Rica and found work in the banana plantations of the United Fruit Company. Since the majority of these workers had come from English-speaking islands in the Caribbean and continued to speak English among themselves after coming to Costa Rica, they were considered more valuable employees by United Fruit managers, most of whom were English-speaking as well. In the 1920s, when the banana plantations of eastern Costa Rica experienced problems, United Fruit began concentrating on production from western Costa Rica. Most West Indian blacks, whose population was concentrated along the Atlantic Coast, showed little interest in relocating westward. Additionally, the government of Costa Rica, feeling the effects of the worldwide Great Depression, enacted laws giving preferential treatment to Costa Rican nationals. Since most of the West Indian workers had never become citizens, they were left without the agricultural work to which they were accustomed. Many moved into cities to make a living. This gradual disintegration of the black coastal enclaves helped to speed black assimilation into the local culture.

Despite a small, elite group of black intellectuals, the average Afro-Costa Rican in the late twentieth century was poor and worked in subsistence farming or as a wage laborer. Although there was some organized effort by the elite to achieve equality for the country's blacks, few Afro-Costa Ricans ever have achieved political power.

COSTA RICA

Official name: Republic of Costa Rica
Independence: 15 September 1821 (from Spain)
Area: 51,100 sq km
Form of government: democratic republic
Capital: San José
Currency: Costa Rican colón (CRC)
Income: US$10,735 (2008 est. of purchasing power parity)
Population: 4,509,290 (2009 est.)
Ethnic groups: white (including mestizo) 94%, black 3%, Amerindian 1%, Chinese 1%, other 1%
Religious groups: Roman Catholic 76.3%, Evangelical 13.7%, other Protestant 0.7%, Jehovah's Witnesses 1.3%, other 4.8%, none 3.2%
Languages: Spanish (official)
Literacy: 96% (fifteen years old and over who can read and write; 2003 est.)
Exports: coffee, bananas, sugar, pineapples, textiles, electronic components, medical equipment
Primary export partners: U.S. 23.9%, Netherlands 13.3%, China 12.9%, UK 5%, Mexico 4.9% (2008)
Imports: raw materials, consumer goods, capital equipment, petroleum
Primary import partners: U.S. 42.9%, Mexico 6.9%, Venezuela 6.3%, Japan 5.4%, China 4.7%, Brazil 4.2% (2008)

Costa Rican Boruca Indians in Traditional Costumes and Masks. JUAN CARLOS ULATE/REUTERS/CORBIS.

CUBA

Cuba is a multiracial society with a population of mainly Spanish and African origins. When Columbus first visited the island in 1492, he found it inhabited by three Native American groups: the Ciboneys, Guanahuatabeys, and Taino Arawaks. As Spain developed its colonial empire in the Western Hemisphere, Havana became an important commercial seaport. Settlers eventually moved inland, devoting themselves mainly to sugarcane and tobacco farming. As the native Indian population died out, enslaved Africans were imported to work on the island's suger and coffee plantations, the first such group arriving in 1526. A 1774 census counted 96,000 whites, 31,000 free blacks, and 44,000 enslaved Africans in Cuba.

The trade in enslaved Africans grew rapidly in Cuba during the final third of the eighteenth century and the first quarter of the nineteenth century. Among the factors contributing to this dramatic growth was the collapse of the sugar trade out of Haiti following the revolution there, and Spain's decision to allow Cuba to trade with the outside world. By the early nineteenth century, the enslaved population of Cuba was estimated at more than a million individuals. Most of the indigenous population had fallen victim to disease or died in conflict with European settlers, leaving the Spaniards and those of African ancestry as the two main population groups within Cuba. Relations between the two groups were strained at times. In 1812, Jose Antonio Aponte, a free black working as a carpenter in Havana, plotted a conspiracy to overthrow colonial rule and abolish slavery in Cuba. A major factor working against the social advancement of blacks in Cuba was the fear of an uprising like the one that had occurred in Haiti. The impact of this phobia is best illustrated by the colonists' savage repression of the so-called Ladder Conspiracy in 1844. In its wake, colonial authorities, widely supported by the European population, executed thousands of blacks and mulattos.

CUBA

Official name: Republic of Cuba

Independence: 20 May 1902 (from United States)

Area: 110,860 sq km

Form of government: Communist state

Capital: Havana

Currency: Cuban peso (CUP)

Income: US$4,819 (2008 est. of purchasing power parity)

Population: 11,451,652 (2009 est.)

Ethnic groups: white 65%, mulatto and mestizo 25%, black 10% (2002 census)

Religious groups: nominally 85% Roman Catholic prior to Castro assuming power; many Protestant denominations, Jehovah's Witnesses, Jews, and Santeria are also represented

Languages: Spanish

Literacy: 97% (fifteen years old and over who can read and write; 2003 est.)

Exports: sugar, nickel, tobacco, fish, medical products, citrus, coffee

Primary export partners: Canada 27.8%, China 26.6%, Spain 6.2%, Netherlands 5.5% (2008)

Imports: petroleum, food, machinery, chemicals, semi-finished goods, transport equipment, consumer goods

Primary import partners: Venezuela 30%, China 11.9%, Spain 10.1%, Canada 6.4%, U.S. 6.3% (2008)

Blacks were allowed to form councils called *cabildos*. At first these groups were set up to correspond to the various sections of Africa from which blacks had originally come. In time, the councils evolved into all-African organizations, accepting members who had originated in all parts of the continent. Eventually, these *cabildos* developed into the twentieth-century clubs and mutual aid societies.

Afro-Cubans played a crucial role in the country's fight for independence from Spain, beginning with the Ten Years' War in 1868. The rebels' constitution declared that all residents of the republic who took up arms against the Spanish were to be considered free. Following that lead, the rebels' Central Assembly of Representatives proclaimed the abolition of those in bondage. However, the underlying fear of blacks felt by most white Cubans was exploited by Spanish forces to plant seeds of doubt in the minds of rebel leaders. Rebels were asked to consider the true intentions of blacks who rose through the ranks of the rebel military. Again, visions of a Haiti-type insurrection arose. The resulting divisions among rebel forces led eventually to the failure of their push for independence. The treaty with Spain ending the Ten Years' War provided for freedom only for the blacks who had fought in the revolution. A subsequent uprising, dubbed the Little War of 1879–1880, was discredited in the Spanish press as being racist in nature because many of its leaders were black. Although colonial authorities abolished slavery in 1880, they replaced it with a system called *patronato*, under which the freed Africans were apprenticed to their owners for a period of eight years. In 1886, the system of *patronato* was ended early, bringing freedom to all.

During the twentieth century, Fidel Castro, who seized power in 1959, transformed Cuba into a socialist nation with the aid of the Soviet Union. Castro became a champion of anti-colonialism, which made him popular in Third World countries struggling for independence. The collapse of the Soviet Union and the loss of its extensive aid to Cuba have exacerbated the island's economic difficulties. This, along with the politically repressive nature of the Castro regime, continues to prompt many Cubans to attempt to flee their country. Leading contemporary Afro-Cubans include: musical performers Alfredo "Chocolate" Armenteros, Rubén González, Pablo Milanés, Lázaro Ros, and Jesús (Chucho) Valdés; artists María Magdalena Campos-Pons and Manuel Mendive; film director Gloria Rolando; and literary figures Marcelino Arozarena, Nancy Morejón, and Excilia Saldaña.

Long-strained relations between Cuba and the United States eased somewhat in 1999. U.S. President Bill Clinton announced policy changes that allowed Americans to travel to Cuba and to explore the island's business opportunities. He also allowed U.S. citizens to sue foreign companies for conducting business on confiscated American properties in Cuba. In late July 1999, Fidel Castro urged the United States to cooperate with Cuba in the war on drugs. The first half of 2000 saw a deterioration in U.S.-Cuban relations as the two countries battled over the custody of six-year-old Elián Gonzalez, rescued off the coast of Florida in November 1999 after a disastrous crossing from Cuba in which his mother and several others had drowned. The child was eventually returned to the custody of his father, who took him back to Cuba. Relations with the United States took another hit when President George W. Bush appointed anti-Castro exiles to high-level government positions.

In February 2008, Fidel Castro formally resigned the presidency and his brother, Raúl Castro, assumed the office. Although the Bush administration maintained an adversarial posture with the Cuban government, in April 2009 the Obama administration indicated that it was time for a new beginning with the island nation, and was willing to ease some of the travel and remittance restrictions that had long been in place.

DOMINICA

Europeans first visited Dominica on Columbus's second voyage in 1493. Spanish ships frequently landed on Dominica during the sixteenth century, but failed to establish a stronghold on the island. In 1635, France claimed Dominica. As part of the 1763 Treaty of Paris that ended the Seven Years' War being fought in Europe, North America, and India, the island became a British possession.

In 1763, the British established a legislative assembly, representing only the white population. In 1831, reflecting a liberalization of official British racial attitudes, the "Brown Privilege Bill" conferred political and social rights on nonwhites. Three blacks were elected to the Legislative Assembly the following year, and, by 1838, the recently enfranchised blacks dominated that body. Most black legislators were smallholders or merchants, who held economic and social views diametrically opposed to the interests of the small, wealthy English planter class. Reacting to a perceived threat, the planters lobbied for more direct British rule. In 1865, after much agitation and tension, the colonial office replaced the elective assembly with one in which half of the members were appointed.

The power of the black population progressively eroded until all political rights for the vast majority of the population were effectively curtailed. On November 3, 1978, the Commonwealth of Dominica was granted independence by the United Kingdom. Almost all 81,000 Dominicans are descendants of enslaved Africans imported by planters in the eighteenth century.

DOMINICA

Official name: Commonwealth of Dominica

Independence: 3 November 1978 (from United Kingdom)

Area: 754 sq km

Form of government: parliamentary democracy; republic within the Commonwealth

Capital: Roseau

Currency: East Caribbean dollar (XCD)

Income: US$10,132 (2008 est. of purchasing power parity)

Population: 72,660 (2009 est.)

Ethnic groups: black 86.8%, mixed 8.9%, Carib Amerindian 2.9%, white 0.8%, other 0.7% (2001 census)

Religious groups: Roman Catholic 61.4%, Seventh-day Adventist 6%, Pentecostal 5.6%, Baptist 4.1%, Methodist 3.7%, Church of God 1.2%, Jehovah's Witnesses 1.2%, other Christian 7.7%, Rastafarian 1.3%, other 1.6%, none 6.1% (2001 census)

Languages: English (official), French patois

Literacy: 94% (fifteen years old and over who has ever attended school; 2003 est.)

Exports: bananas, soap, bay oil, vegetables, grapefruit, oranges

Primary export partners: Japan 33.5%, China 17.8%, Antigua and Barbuda 6.7%, Guyana 5.7%, Jamaica 4.7%, UK 4.7% (2008)

Imports: manufactured goods, machinery and equipment, food, chemicals

Primary import partners: Japan 43.2%, U.S. 17%, China 12.1%, Trinidad and Tobago 8.4% (2008)

DOMINICAN REPUBLIC

The island of Hispaniola, of which the Dominican Republic forms the eastern two-thirds and Haiti the remainder, was originally occupied by members of the Taíno tribe when Columbus and his companions landed there in 1492. Brutal colonial conditions reduced the Taíno population from an estimated 1 million to about 200 in only fifty years.

Santo Domingo, as the territory was known under Spanish rule, has long been considered the "cradle of blackness in the Americas" because it served as the port of entry for the first enslaved Africans traded to the Western Hemisphere. Beginning shortly after the first visit of Columbus, the trade in humans brought in waves of Christianized blacks, known as "Ladinos," and "bosales," as blacks imported directly from Africa were known. At first, these Africans were put to work in the country's gold mines. However, the mines were soon stripped, and efforts were undertaken to cultivate sugarcane on a large scale. Once the sugar business had been successfully established, after a period of fits and starts, more Africans were brought in to work the fields.

From early in the colony's history, blacks outnumbered whites by a significant margin. In 1542, only fifty years after the first visit of Columbus, the population was made up of 30,000 blacks, 6,000 whites, and only 200

DOMINICAN REPUBLIC

Official name: Dominican Republic
Independence: 27 February 1844 (from Haiti)
Area: 48,730 sq km
Form of government: representative democracy
Capital: Santo Domingo
Currency: Dominican peso (DOP)
Income: US$9,375 (2008 est. of purchasing power parity)
Population: 10,090,000 (2009 est.)
Ethnic groups: white 16%, black 11%, mixed 73%
Religious groups: Roman Catholic 95%
Languages: Spanish
Literacy: 84.7% (fifteen years old and over who can read and write; 2003 est.)
Exports: ferronickel, sugar, gold, silver, coffee, cocoa, tobacco, meats
Primary export partners: U.S. 58.1%, Haiti 9.3%, Netherlands 2.9% (2008)
Imports: foodstuffs, petroleum, cotton and fabrics, chemicals and pharmaceuticals
Primary import partners: U.S. 39.2%, Venezuela 7.7%, Mexico 5.4%, Colombia 4.9% (2008)

Taínos. By the close of the sixteenth century, blacks represented 61% of the total population. Eventually, the cultivation of sugar as the colony's main cash crop was superseded by the raising of livestock and the cultivation of ginger. These changes had a number of effects on the enslaved population; most importantly, fewer Africans were needed to raise livestock than were needed in the cultivation of sugarcane. The reduction in the need for such labor was ironically timely, because the late sixteenth and early seventeenth centuries saw the loss of a significant number of Africans to disease.

The colonial powers, worried by the possibility of a large-scale uprising by blacks, enacted a system of laws that closely regulated every aspect of their lives. These laws, however, failed to eliminate uprisings, of which several occurred in the early years of the colony. In the wake of the Haitian Revolution, Toussaint-Louverture, an enslaved Haitian who had become a military leader, seized control of Santo Domingo, bringing all of Hispaniola under his control. Toussaint-Louverture abolished enslavement throughout Santo Domingo. The following year, French soldiers invaded, taking control of Santo Domingo for France, which retained control until the War of Reconquest in 1809. Under French rule, slavery was reinstated. The War of Reconquest, plotted by creoles with the support of the Spanish governor of nearby Puerto Rico, returned Santo Domingo to Spanish control. In 1822, Haitian President Jean-Pierre Boyer seized the colony and maintained control for the next twenty-two years. Independence from Haiti was finally achieved in 1844.

One of the dominant figures in the Dominican Republic's twentieth-century history was dictator Rafael Trujillo, who ruled the country with an iron hand for more than thirty years. After Trujillo's dictatorship ended in a 1961 assassination, Joaquín Balaguer took over as president and instituted a police state. In 1962, former exile Juan Bosch was elected president in the country's first free elections in four decades. Criticized for being too soft on communism, Bosch was deposed in September 1963 and replaced by a three-man civilian junta. When pro-Bosch elements in the military rebelled against the government, U.S. forces intervened. Voters in 1966 returned Balaguer to the presidency. He won reelection easily in 1970 and 1974. However, in 1978 elections, Balaguer was unseated by Silvestre Antonio Guzmán. In July 1982, Salvador Jorge Blanco was elected to succeed him. Balaguer was returned to the presidency in 1986 elections. He was reelected in 1990 and 1994 but agreed to serve only two years of the last term to which he was elected after charges of election fraud. In 1996, Leonel Fernández Reyna was elected president.

Economic progress on the Dominican Republic was the big news locally in 1999. The country, with a growth rate of more than 6% for several years, was singled out as the best economic performer of the entire Latin American region. Much of its economic growth was credited to the aggressive campaign by President Fernández Reyna to attract foreign investment. The presidential elections of May 2000 brought to power Hipólito Mejía Dominguez, leader of the Dominican Republic Party, which had last been in power in 1986. The subsequent failure of the Mejía Dominguez administration to continue the robust economic growth of the recent past caused widespread disillusionment. In the 2004 elections, Leonel Fernandez Reyna reclaimed the presidency and won election again in 2008. He is credited with moving the country forward despite continued charges of corruption.

Because of their dark skin, Haitians in the Dominican Republic have persistently been discriminated against. These were the findings of a United Nations' investigation conducted in 2007. Although more than 90% of Dominicans have African ancestry, they hesitate to acknowledge this. Adjectives such as *canela* (cinnamon), *morena* (brown) *blanca oscura* (dark white), and *trigueno* (light brown) are among the terms local residents employ when describing their skin color. These racial stratifications were heightened during the Trujillo era, where discrimination against darker skinned Dominicans was tacitly allowed. Other South American countries (for example, Brazil) also employ a variety of descriptions to identify skin color.

Leading contemporary Afro-Dominicans include literary figures Manuel del Cabral and Blas Jiménez and musicians Juan Luis Guerra and Johnny Ventura.

ECUADOR

Together with Colombia, its neighbor to the north, and Panama, Ecuador shares a region that makes up the so-called Pacific Lowlands Black Culture. This region stretches from Panama's Darién province in the north through Colombia's Cauca Valley on to Esmeraldas province in Ecuador in the south. The Pacific coastal area stretching through the three countries developed its high concentration of Afro-Hispanics through the migration patterns of blacks and a tradition of racial intermixing that began in colonial times. In Ecuador, blacks historically settled in all three major geographical areas of the country: the Pacific coast, the Amazon lowlands in the eastern part of the country, and the highlands.

As in much of Latin America, Ecuador's Spanish colonial rulers followed a policy of racial and cultural whitening, encouraging widespread racial mixing as a logical avenue to reach that goal. Even in the early twenty-first century, remnants of that philosophy can be found in Ecuador. So deeply ingrained is the policy of whitening that even some black groups strongly advocate greater cultural and racial blending.

Enslaved Africans were first brought to Ecuador in the middle of the sixteenth century. Most were pressed into service as farm workers in portions of the colony where Indian labor was either scarce or nonexistent. An enclave of blacks grew in the northwest coastal province of Esmeraldas, after a small party of enslaved Africans being transported by ship between Panama and Peru escaped and settled in the area. The escapees mixed freely with the Indians of the region, and the resulting zambos of mixed black and Indian blood came to dominate this region. Although some blacks who joined in the fight for Ecuador's independence from Spain were freed in return for their military service, an official proclamation ending slavery in Ecuador did not come until 1851, nearly three decades after the nation was granted independence. Even then, an involuntary form of enslavement survived until 1894.

Leading contemporary Afro-Ecuadorians include literary figures Nelson Estupiñán Bass and Antonio Preciado Bedoya.

ECUADOR

Official name: Republic of Ecuador
Independence: 24 May 1822 (from Spain)
Area: 283,560 sq km
Form of government: republic
Capital: Quito
Currency: U.S. dollar (US$)
Income: US$7,785 (2008 est. of purchasing power parity)
Population: 14,573,101 (2009 est.)
Ethnic groups: mestizo (mixed Amerindian and white) 65%, Amerindian 25%, Spanish and others 7%, black 3%
Religious groups: Roman Catholic 95%
Languages: Spanish (official), Amerindian languages (especially Quechua)
Literacy: 92.5% (fifteen years old and over who can read and write; 2003 est.)
Exports: petroleum, bananas, shrimp, coffee, cocoa, cut flowers, fish
Primary export partners: U.S. 45.3%, Peru 9.2%, Chile 8.1%, Panama 4.8%, Colombia 4.2% (2008)
Imports: machinery and equipment, raw materials, fuels, consumer goods
Primary import partners: U.S. 19.1%, Venezuela 13.8%, Colombia 9.9%, China 8.4%, Brazil 4.8%, Japan 4.1% (2008)

EL SALVADOR

In the final days of the twentieth century, the black population of El Salvador was negligible, the lowest proportion of African-descended residents to be found anywhere in Central America. During the colonial period, some Africans were imported by El Salvador's Spanish rulers to help fill labor shortages created by the wholesale exportation of the indigenous Amerindian peoples to South America and Mexico. However, Central America's need for enslaved African labor was not as great as in other of Spain's New World colonies, largely because the mines in the region produced relatively modest yields and large-scale agriculture was virtually nonexistent. Without the profits from such enterprises, most landowners in El Salvador could ill afford the cost of importing Africans,

EL SALVADOR

Official name: Republic of El Salvador
Independence: 15 September 1821 (from Spain)
Area: 21,040 sq km
Form of government: republic
Capital: San Salvador
Currency: Salvadoran colon (SVC); U.S. dollar (US$)
Income: US$7,564 (2008 est. of purchasing power parity)
Population: 5,744,113 (July 2007 est.)
Ethnic groups: mestizo 90%, Amerindian 1%, white 9%
Religious groups: Roman Catholic 86%
Languages: Spanish, Nahua (among some Amerindians)
Literacy: 80.2% (ten years old and over who can read and write; 2003 est.)
Exports: offshore assembly exports, coffee, sugar, shrimp, textiles, chemicals, electricity
Primary export partners: U.S. 45.3%, Peru 9.2%, Chile 8.1%, Panama 4.8%, Colombia 4.2% (2008)
Imports: raw materials, consumer goods, capital goods, fuels, foodstuffs, petroleum, electricity
Primary import partners: U.S. 19.1%, Venezuela 13.8%, Colombia 9.9%, China 8.4%, Brazil 4.8%, Japan 4.1% (2008)

particularly since in most cases the available Amerindian laborers were sufficient to fill their needs.

By the early 1800s, the number of enslaved Africans was so low that it was difficult to find residents who identified themselves as having African roots. Between the low number of blacks and the high rate of intermixing between Europeans, indigenous people, and the few blacks in the colony, it had become virtually impossible to distinguish between those with African blood and the mestizos of mixed European and Indian ancestry. By 1824, the Central American Federation, from which the countries of Costa Rica, El Salvador, Guatemala, Honduras, and Nicaragua were eventually formed, had won its independence from Spain. Because the number of enslaved Africans throughout the area was small, particularly when compared with other territories in the New World, abolition of African enslavement was achieved without a great deal of trauma by all parties involved.

FRENCH GUIANA

The first European visitor to what is now French Guiana was Christopher Columbus, who stopped off there during the course of his third voyage to the New World. Struck by the beauty of the region, he wrote glowingly of its wonders. His writings later inspired other European explorers to visit the area, many of whom were convinced that the mythical El Dorado, the golden city, was to be found within the territory's interior. The French first visited the area in 1604, looking not only for gold but for territory that could be claimed for their country. The first enslaved Africans were brought into Guiana in 1652. Because the colony was sparsely settled, the African population grew very slowly. By 1765, Guiana's enslaved population totaled only about 5,700. Sixty-five years later, in 1830, it reached its peak of just over 19,000.

Although most of the Africans in French Guiana had come from tropical climates themselves, many died from tropical diseases in the area. Others fled from their masters in the more heavily settled coastal zone and escaped into the interior, where they reverted to a lifestyle as hunter-gatherers. Although French attempts to establish agricultural plantations in Guiana failed, the colonial powers were undaunted in their determination to develop the territory. The abolition of enslavement in 1848 sounded the death knell for Guiana's two main industries, lumber and sugar, which eventually collapsed. To give the colony a *raison d'être*, the French decided to transform Guiana into a penal colony. Between 1852 and 1939,

FRENCH GUIANA

Official name: Department of Guiana
Area: 91,000 sq km
Form of government: overseas department of France
Capital: Cayenne
Currency: euro (EUR)
Income: US$17,336 (2006 est. of purchasing power parity)
Population: 221,500 (2008 est.)
Ethnic groups: black or mulatto 66%, white 12%, East Indian, Chinese, Amerindian 12%, other 10%
Religious groups: Roman Catholic
Languages: French
Exports: shrimp, timber, gold, rum, rosewood essence, clothing
Imports: food (grains, processed meat), machinery and transport equipment, fuels and chemicals

France shipped more than 70,000 prisoners to the colony. Tropical diseases, including malaria and yellow fever, took an enormous toll on the prisoners, claiming the lives of nearly 90% of them.

Among the notable French Guianans of African descent, Félix Eboué stands out for his significant contributions as an adviser to General Charles de Gaulle during World War II. Born in 1884, Eboué was the descendant of Africans. He first distinguished himself through his reforms of the French colonial administration. Poet Léon-Gontran Damas is the country's most famous writer. In the early twenty-first century, a number of elements of the Afro-Guianan community were actively seeking to revive and preserve black culture in the country.

GRENADA

Similar to the rest of the West Indies, Grenada was originally settled to cultivate sugar, which was grown on estates using enslaved African labor. Most of Grenada's population is of African descent; very few of the early Arawak and Carib Indians remain.

Columbus first visited Grenada in 1498. Grenada remained uncolonized for more than 100 years after the first visit by Europeans, and British efforts to settle the island were unsuccessful. In 1650, a French company purchased Grenada from the British and established a small settlement. By 1753, the island's population was dominated by Africans, who numbered close to 12,000, against a total of 1,262 whites and 179 free blacks. Most of the free blacks were of mixed European-African descent, the result of intermixing between the island's French planters and the Africans. The island remained under French control for more than a century until captured by the British during the Seven Years' War. Slavery was outlawed in 1833, the same year Grenada was made part of the British Windward Islands Administration. In 1958, the Windward Islands Administration dissolved. Grenada became an associated state on March 3, 1967, but sought full independence, which the British government granted on February 7, 1974.

After several years of leadership by Grenada's first prime minister, Sir Eric Matthew Gairy, an opposition party called The New Jewel movement, led by Maurice Bishop, overthrew the government and assumed power in 1979. Bishop was subsequently overthrown and killed in 1983, when Communist Deputy Prime Minister Bernard Coard took over the country. The United States, along with forces from other English-speaking Caribbean countries, invaded Grenada to restore order. An interim advisory council then governed the nation until parliamentary elections in December 1984. Those elections established Herbert A. Blaize as Grenada's new prime minister. After Blaize's death, Nicholas Brathwaite was elected prime minister. Brathwaite's popularity plummeted in the wake of an economic slowdown in the early 1990s, and he announced he would resign as prime minister in 1995. George Brizan succeeded him in February of that year, followed quickly by Keith Mitchell, established as prime minister in parliamentary elections a few months later.

A new election was held in January 1999, two months after the ruling New National Party of Prime Minister Mitchell lost its parliamentary majority upon the resignation of Foreign Minister Raphael Fletcher. Mitchell and his party regained their majority. Despite aggressive action in 2001 to close down rogue offshore banks, Grenada was added that year to the blacklist of the

GRENADA

Independence: 7 February 1974 (from United Kingdom)

Area: 340 sq km

Form of government: constitutional monarchy and parliamentary democracy

Capital: Saint George's

Currency: East Caribbean dollar (XCD)

Income: US$11,464 (2008 est. of purchasing power parity)

Population: 90,739 (2009 est.)

Ethnic groups: black 82%, mixed black and European 12%, South Asian (East Indian) and European 6%, some Arawak/Carib Amerindian

Religious groups: Roman Catholic 53%, Anglican 13.8%, other Protestant 33%, Buddhist

Languages: English (official), French patois

Literacy: 96% (fifteen years old and over who can read and write; 2003 est.)

Exports: bananas, cocoa, nutmeg, fruit and vegetables, clothing, mace

Primary export partners: Saint Lucia 16.4%, U.S. 11.4%, UK 11.3%, Antigua and Barbuda 11.1%, Saint Kitts & Nevis 10%, Dominica 10%, France 6.4% (2008)

Imports: food, manufactured goods, machinery, chemicals, fuel (1989)

Primary import partners: Trinidad and Tobago 39.6%, U.S. 22.5%, Barbados 3.3% (2008)

Financial Action Task Force in its worldwide crackdown on money laundering.

One of the major success stories in Grenada during recent decades has been the growth experienced by the island's tourism industry. Grenada has proven particularly popular with divers, snorkelers, and sailors, and is known for its idyllic beaches and beautiful coastline. Also a major player in the island's economy is the spice industry. Grenada produces more spices per square mile than anywhere else on earth.

The island was hit heavily by Hurricane Ivan in 2004, which devastated the economy along with a majority of homes on the island. The following year, Hurricane Emily struck and caused another $100 million worth of damage. The country and the economy gradually recovered from the damage, but one of its premiere exports, nutmeg, is still struggling to regain its position. In July 2008 the National Democratic Congress (NDC) won the majority of seats in Grenada's Parliament, and NDC leader Tillman Thomas became Grenada's new prime minister.

GUADELOUPE

Official name: Department of Guadeloupe
Area: 1,780 sq km
Form of government: overseas department of France
Capital: Basse-Terre
Currency: euro (EUR)
Population: 405,500 (2008 est.)
Ethnic groups: black or mulatto 90%, white 5%, East Indian, Lebanese, Chinese less than 5%
Religious groups: Roman Catholic 95%, Hindu and pagan African 4%, Protestant 1%
Languages: French (official) 99%, Creole patois
Literacy: 90% (fifteen years old and over who can read and write)
Exports: bananas, sugar, rum
Primary export partners: France 60%, Martinique 18%, U.S. 4% (1999)
Imports: foodstuffs, fuels, vehicles, clothing and other consumer goods, construction materials
Primary import partners: France 63%, Germany 4%, U.S. 3%, Japan 2%, Netherlands Antilles 2% (1999)

GUADELOUPE

Columbus sighted Guadeloupe in 1493. The French permanently settled the area in the seventeenth century. The first enslaved Africans were brought to work plantations around 1650, and the first rebellion occurred in 1656. Guadeloupe was poorly administered in its early days and was a dependency of Martinique until 1775.

The enslaved Africans of Guadeloupe were slow to react to news of the French Revolution. The French abolition of slavery less than five years later was not preceded by any major uprisings on the island, although a handful of minor revolts did occur. Two members of the French Republican Convention, who brought the abolition decree to Guadeloupe, also recruited freed Africans to help drive out British invaders, who had occupied the island while France was preoccupied with its revolution at home. In the wake of the rout of British occupying forces, many white landowners and merchants sympathetic to the British cause were executed or exiled. As a result, the white ruling class was considerably weakened and depleted in numbers. In the years following the British occupation of the island, whites made up only about 10% of the population, compared to about 33% in 1735. As the white population was weakened, the black merchant class gained strength. Blacks and those of mixed African and European descent were welcomed into the colony's military.

A number of black soldiers in 1802 revolted against troops sent to the Caribbean by Napoleon Bonaparte to reinstitute slavery. Their resistance was quickly overcome, and France reimposed a particularly brutal brand of enslavement on its islands for the next forty-six years. By 1835, 13 years before abolition, free blacks on the island outnumbered whites by a margin of 19,000 to 12,000. In the wake of Britain's ban on African enslavement in its Caribbean colonies, attempts were made in the French island to make enslavement less dehumanizing. The hope was that by so doing the institution of slavery could be preserved. Despite legislated measures to give captive Africans some basic rights, the effort was a failure, since individual plantation owners were free to deal with their enslaved Africans as they wished.

The new millennium brought signs that Guadeloupe and other French overseas departments might soon win greater autonomy in the management of their local affairs. French President Chirac in March 2000 hinted strongly that the highly centralized relationship between Paris and its overseas department might be relaxed in favor of a less restrictive arrangement. Violent protests erupted on Guadeloupe in June 2001 after a number of island shopkeepers refused to observe the anniversary of the abolition on the island.

Most Guadeloupeans are of mixed Afro-European and Afro-Indian ancestry (descendants of laborers brought over from India during the nineteenth century). Several thousand metropolitan French reside there, including civil servants, business people, and their dependents. Leading contemporary Afro-Guadeloupeans include literary figures Jean Louis Baghio'o, Maryse Condé, and Simone Schwartz-Bart. May 27th is celebrated annually as Slavery Abolition Day, which was established in 1848. The holiday observance has ebbed and flowed over its long history.

GUATEMALA

Although blacks make up a very small percentage of Guatemala's population, there are traces of African influence to be found in the Central American country. Among these are a popular folk dance called the marimba, based on rhythms and steps brought to the country by Africans.

Beginning in the first half of the sixteenth century, measures were taken by Guatemalan whites to limit the number of blacks allowed into the colony. The heavy concentrations of Amerindian indigenous peoples provided an adequate labor supply for most of Guatemala, thus reducing the need for the importation of enslaved Africans. The Guatemalan town of Tianguey enacted an ordinance in 1537 prohibiting the entry of blacks or those of mixed-black ancestry without express permission from town officials. The aim was to prevent any intermixing with the indigenous peoples of the area. Even in the twentieth century, the country's government has attempted to legislate against immigration by blacks. Guatemala's 1945 constitution officially bans "immigration of individuals of the black race."

The late 1990s were marked by widespread violence and human rights abuses in Guatemala. A survey of Guatemalans taken in mid-1999 showed that 88% felt administration of justice in the country was inadequate. In November 1999 general elections, Alfonso Portillo Cabrera was elected president, and he assumed office in mid-January 2000, promising to revitalize the economy and reduce the power of the country's military. President Clinton had earlier admitted that the United States should not have provided military support to Guatemala. Scandals undermined support for the Portillo administration in 2001, and the president himself came under increasing fire for the continuing high crime rate and his frequent foreign journeys. More recently, Guatemala has enjoyed relative calm and has held successful elections. The country has signed the Central America Free Trade Agreement (CAFTA) in which the country will cooperate economically with the other participants.

GUATEMALA

Official name: Republic of Guatemala

Independence: 15 September 1821 (from Spain)

Area: 108,890 sq km

Form of government: constitutional democratic republic

Capital: Guatemala City

Currency: quetzal (GTQ), U.S. dollar (US$), others allowed

Income: US$4,907 (2008 est. of purchasing power parity)

Population: 14,000,000 (2009 est.)

Ethnic groups: mestizo (mixed Amerindian-Spanish or assimilated Amerindian, in local Spanish called Ladino) 55%, Amerindian or predominantly Amerindian 43%, whites and others 2%

Religious groups: Roman Catholic, Protestant, indigenous Mayan beliefs

Languages: Spanish 60%, Amerindian languages 40% (more than twenty Amerindian languages, including Quiche, Cakchiquel, Kekchi, Mam, Garifuna, and Xinca)

Literacy: 70.6% (fifteen years old and over who can read and write; 2003 est.)

Exports: coffee, sugar, bananas, fruits and vegetables, cardamom, meat, apparel, petroleum, electricity

Primary export partners: U.S. 39.4%, El Salvador 12.6%, Honduras 9.5%, Mexico 6.6%, Nicaragua 4.2%, Costa Rica 4.1% (2008)

Imports: fuels, machinery and transport equipment, construction materials, grain, fertilizers, electricity

Primary import partners: U.S. 36.7%, Mexico 9.7%, China 5.8%, El Salvador 4.8% (2008)

GUYANA

Guiana was the name given an area sighted by Columbus in 1498, comprising modern Guyana, Suriname, French Guiana, and parts of Brazil and Venezuela. The Dutch settled in Guyana in the late sixteenth century. Dutch control ended when the British became the de facto rulers in 1796. In 1815, the colonies of Essequibo, Demerara, and Berbice were officially ceded to the British by the Congress of Vienna and, in 1831, were consolidated as British Guiana.

Enslaved African uprisings, such as the one in 1763 led by Guyana's national hero, Cuffy, stressed the desire to obtain basic rights and were underscored by a willingness to compromise. Following the liberation of enslaved Africans in 1834, indentured workers were brought

GUYANA

Official name: Co-operative Republic of Guyana
Independence: 26 May 1966 (from United Kingdom)
Area: 214,970 sq km
Form of government: republic
Capital: Georgetown
Currency: Guyanese dollar (GYD)
Income: US$4,029 (2008 est. of purchasing power parity)
Population: 772,298 (2009)
Ethnic groups: East Indian 43.5%, black 30.2%, mixed 16.7%, Amerindian 9.1%, other 0.5% (2002 census)
Religious groups: Hindu 28.4%, Pentecostal 16.9%, Roman Catholic 8.1%, Anglican 6.9%, Seventh-day Adventist 5%, Methodist 1.7%, Jehovah's Witnesses 1.1%, other Christian 17.7%, Muslim 7.2%, other 4.3% (2002 census)
Languages: English, Amerindian dialects, Creole, Hindi, Urdu
Exports: sugar, gold, bauxite/alumina, rice, shrimp, molasses, rum, timber
Primary export partners: Canada 20.8%, U.S. 15.2%, UK 12.3%, Netherlands 7.2%, Portugal 4.7%, Trinidad and Tobago 4.7%, Jamaica 4.5%, Ukraine 4.3% (2008)
Imports: manufactures, machinery, petroleum, food
Primary import partners: U.S. 23.4%, Trinidad and Tobago 22.3%, Finland 7.7%, Cuba 6.1%, China 5.7% (2008)

primarily from India but also from Portugal and China. A scheme in 1862 to bring black workers from the United States was unsuccessful.

Independence was achieved in 1966, and Guyana became a republic on February 23, 1970, the anniversary of Cuffy's rebellion. During the rule of Prime Minister Forbes Burnham in 1978, Jim Jones, a fringe religious leader from the United States, gained the country unwanted international attention when his religious movement, the People's Temple, carried out a mass murder/suicide in Jonestown after murdering a U.S. congressional representative and critically injuring members of his staff.

Although the black population of Guyana trails that of the Indo-Guyanese, the African influences upon the country's culture are significant. Blacks played a major role in the development of modern-day Guyana, from the mid-seventeenth century when the first Africans were sold to Dutch planters through the early years after independence, when the country was ruled by authoritarian black governments. Forbes Burnham, an Afro-Guyanese leader of the PNC, led the country from 1968 until 1985. He ruled with a brutal and iron fist, resulting in mass defections to the United States and Canada. When Burnham died in office in 1985, Desmond Hoyte succeeded him, holding office until 1992. Then, in the country's first free elections since 1964, Cheddi Jagan of the People's Progressive Party (PPP), the first leader of the country after independence, was again voted into office. Jagan died suddenly in office in January 1997 and was succeeded by his widow, Janet, who won the presidency on her own in 1997. Other influential Afro-Guyanese include literary figures Martin Carter and Theodore Wilson Harris.

Citing failing health, President Janet Jagan stepped down in August 1999 and was replaced by Prime Minister Bharrat Jagdeo of the PPP. In early 2000, the country joined most of its neighbors in passing legislation that made money laundering a crime. In March 2001 general elections, Jagdeo won another five-year term as president. Jagdeo was reelected to serve another five-year term as President of Guyana in 2006.

HAITI

Columbus first visited the Island of Hispaniola in 1492, claiming the land for Spain. In 1697, Spain ceded the western third of Hispaniola (the area now known as Haiti) to France. During this period, Africans were enslaved and brought to the region to work the sugarcane and coffee plantations. Several decades later, a major revolt erupted—white French planters, enslaved Africans, and free mulattos clashed over issues of rights, land, and labor, as the forces of France, Britain, and Spain manipulated the conflict. At first, the slaves and mulattos shared the goals of the French revolution in opposition to the royalist French planters, but with time, a coalition of planters and mulattos arose in opposition to the interests of the enslaved Africans.

Toussaint-Louverture became the leader of the revolutionary forces, which by the mid-1790s consisted of a disciplined group of 4,000 formerly enslaved Africans. Toussaint-Louverture successfully waged a campaign against the British. At the height of Touissant-Louverture's power and influence in 1796, General Rigaud, who led the mulatto forces, sought to reimpose enslavement on the black islanders. Toussaint-Louverture quickly achieved victory, captured Santo Domingo, and by 1801 had virtual control of the Spanish part of the island. In 1802, a French expeditionary force was sent to reestablish French control

HAITI

Official name: Republic of Haiti
Independence: 1 January 1804 (from France)
Area: 27,750 sq km
Form of government: republic
Capital: Port-au-Prince
Currency: gourde (HTG)
Income: US$1,317 (2008 est. of purchasing power parity)
Population: 10,033,000 (2009)
Ethnic groups: black 95%, mulatto and white 5%
Religious groups: Roman Catholic 80%, Protestant 16%
Languages: French (official), Creole (official)
Literacy: 52.9% (fifteen years old and over who can read and write; 2003 est.)
Exports: manufactures, coffee, oils, mangoes
Primary export partners: U.S. 70.7%, Dominican Republic 8.9%, Canada 3.1% (2008)
Imports: food, machinery and transport equipment, fuels, raw materials
Primary import partners: U.S. 34%, Dominican Republic 23.1%, Netherlands Antilles 10.6%, China 4.5% (2008)

of the island. Following a hard-fought resistance to French colonial ambitions in the Western Hemisphere, Toussaint-Louverture struck a peace treaty with Napoleon. However, Toussaint-Louverture was tricked, captured, and sent to France where he died on April 7, 1803, in cruel conditions.

In the wake of its victorious struggle for independence, Haiti became a model for much of the black world. However, it was not long before the black-ruled country began to face enormous pressure, both from within the country and abroad. The country's new rulers were ill prepared for the responsibility of leading a nation, thus keeping the country in a state of instability. Haiti had no other country to which it could turn for either moral or financial support, because it was regarded as an outcast in a world that was largely controlled by whites. The very idea of the enslaved Africans overthrowing their masters to seize control of a country was frightening to most white-controlled governments. The country was in ruins in the wake of its battle to banish the French, and Jean-Jacque Dessalines, Toussaint-Louverture's trusted lieutenant and the first ruler of an independent Haiti, made a critical error when he pressed all Haitians who were not in the military into agricultural service on some of the surviving plantations. Further exacerbating problems for the new black republic was the growing enmity that developed between the country's black majority and the mulatto elite. After the death of Dessalines, control of the island was split between the blacks, who held the northern part of Haiti, and the mulattos, who were in control of the South.

In the twentieth century, the country languished under nearly thirty years of despotic rule by the Duvalier family. François Duvalier was elected president in 1957. In the 1960s, he declared himself president for life. When he died in 1971, his son, Jean-Claude, succeeded him. During this period, much of the Western world, including the United States, cut off foreign assistance to Haiti to express its collective outrage over the political situation there. In the 1980s, popular dissatisfaction with the Duvalier rule grew stronger, and, early in 1986, the young Duvalier was forced to flee the country. A politically tumultuous period followed, with one corrupt leader quickly succeeding another, until the election in December 1990 of former Catholic priest turned politician, Jean-Bertrand Aristide. Only eight months after his inauguration in February 1991, Aristide was ousted in a coup led by Brigadier General Raoul Cedras. Following Aristide's ouster, thousands of Haitians attempted to immigrate to the United States, with little success. In 1994, U.S. forces took control, and Aristide was returned to power. He handed power over to René Préval, his hand-picked successor, in December 1995. The country was in an economic and political shambles by the end of that decade.

President Préval effectively established one-man rule in early 1999 when he dissolved Parliament. Parliamentary elections originally scheduled for late 1999 were postponed until May 2000. Although the integrity of the voting process was widely questioned, the results showed an overwhelming majority for the Lavalas Family party of former president Jean-Bertrand Aristide. In the November 2000 presidential elections, Aristide won 91% of the vote. The former president returned to power in early 2001 against a backdrop of continuing economic decline and rapid deterioration of the country's economic infrastructure. In February 2004, Aristide was again overthrown and left the country under a U.S. Marine escort. In 2006, René Préval was formally elected and became Haiti's next president.

Haiti is one of poorest countries in the Western Hemisphere. The nation suffered a terrible blow when the densely populated area near its coastal capital, Port-au-Prince, experienced a catastrophic earthquake on January 12, 2010. More than 200,000 Haitians lost their lives as a result of the earthquake and its many aftershocks, and thousands more were seriously injured. Nearly 2 million people were subsequently left homeless as a result of the devastating natural disaster. Another 3 million Haitians were in need of food assistance and other emergency services. Many landmarks and building structures were severely damaged. In response to the devastation, close to $500,000 in donations were collected from international donor agencies including the World Food Program, UNICEF, and USAID. To combat several outbreaks of looting and other violence, international peace keepers were also deployed in the country within one month of the earthquake.

HONDURAS

The first shipment of enslaved Africans—a group of 165—arrived in Honduras in 1540. About five years later, the number of Africans within the colony had risen to 5,000, most of them brought in to replace Indian workers who had fallen victim to disease. Most of these enslaved Africans were employed as domestic servants or laborers on small farms that were cultivated solely to produce food for consumption within the colony. The absence of plantation-scale farming and mines kept the region's African population from growing dramatically. The black population grew more after Honduras won independence, when a large number of West Indian blacks of mixed African and Carib Indian ancestry arrived in the country. Up to 5,000 of these newly arrived immigrants known as Garifuna relocated from the Caribbean island of Saint Vincent to the island of Roatán, off the coast of Honduras, at the end of the eighteenth century. Over time, most of these Garifuna moved to the mainland.

Another influx of blacks arrived in Honduras in the 1830s when a group of white settlers from the Cayman Islands, fearful about their fate if Britain's plans to abolish black enslavement materialized, began settling in the Honduran Bay Islands. A number of these white Cayman Islanders brought their African captives with them. By the mid-nineteenth century, about 700 blacks from the Cayman Islands had moved to this island group, once again outnumbering the white population. When U.S. fruit companies established vast plantations in the eastern portion of the country, both the black Cayman Islanders and many of the Garifuna went to work for them. The new employment opportunities offered by the fruit estates eventually attracted further black immigration from throughout the Caribbean.

Honduras focused in 1999 on rebuilding from the catastrophic and widespread destruction caused by Hurricane Mitch in October 1998. In 2000, Honduras became the second Latin American country to qualify for debt relief under the Highly Indebted Poor Countries program, which cleared the way for the World Bank, IMF, and other international lenders to forgive portions of the country's debt and restructure other debts. In February, a border conflict with Nicaragua exploded into violence and later brought sanctions from both countries against one another. In November 2001, Ricardo Maduro of the National Party, who took office in January 2002, won a national election, the presidency. In 2006, Manuel Zelaya Rosales, known as Mel Zelaya, became the new president of Honduras. Two years later, the country experienced another devastating hurricane which severely impacted the annual harvest. In 2009, Honduras experienced a constitutional crisis and a coup d'etat. President Zelaya was removed from office and replaced by the head of the country's congress. By early 2010, no other country in the world, nor the United Nations, had recognized the new government.

HONDURAS

Official name: Republic of Honduras
Independence: 15 September 1821 (from Spain)
Area: 112,090 sq km
Form of government: democratic constitutional republic
Capital: Tegucigalpa
Currency: lempira (HNL)
Income: US$4,275 (2008 est. of purchasing power parity)
Population: 7,810,848 (2009 est.)
Ethnic groups: mestizo (mixed Amerindian and European) 90%, Amerindian 7%, black 2%, white 1%
Religious groups: Roman Catholic 47%, Evangelical Protestant 36%, other 17%
Languages: Spanish, Amerindian dialects
Literacy: 76.2% (fifteen years old and over who can read and write; 2003 est.)
Exports: coffee, bananas, shrimp, lobster, meat, zinc, lumber
Primary export partners: U.S. 62.1%, Guatemala 5.2%, El Salvador 5%, Mexico 4.1% (2008)
Imports: machinery and transport equipment, industrial raw materials, chemical products, fuels, foodstuffs
Primary import partners: U.S. 50%, Guatemala 7.6%, El Salvador 5.3%, Mexico 4.7%, Costa Rica 4.2% (2008)

JAMAICA

Jamaica was first visited in 1494 by Christopher Columbus and settled by the Spanish during the early sixteenth century. In the 1650s, British forces seized the island. Britain gained formal possession of Jamaica in 1670 under the Treaty of Madrid.

Sugar and enslaved Africans were important elements in Jamaica's history and development. By the early 1830s, the island's white minority dominated the social and economic affairs of the colony. As international pressure for an end to African enslavement began to build, events within Jamaica made clear that the days of the wicked system were numbered. In 1832, in a revolt known as the Baptist War, more than 20,000 participants rose up to destroy the brutal pratice. So expansive and violent was this insurrection that it caught the attention of the world outside Jamaica. Conjuring up images of the revolution that had occurred in Haiti about thirty years earlier, the Jamaican uprising hastened action in Britain's Parliament to end African enslavement. The vote that came in August 1833 freed more than 300,000 Africans in Jamaica. However, provisions of emancipation provided for a gradual transition from bondage to complete freedom. For most of the newly freed Africans, this meant a lengthy period of apprenticeship to their former masters. With the emancipation of the Africans, Jamaican settlers were forced to recruit other sources of cheap labor, and often resorted to the importation of Asian Indian and Chinese farm hands.

In the early twentieth century, Jamaica produced its first national hero, Marcus Garvey (1887–1940). His efforts helped to initiate one of the most important black nationalist movements of the century. Whether on the continent or throughout the diaspora, the Garvey movement had the overall impact of making those of African ancestry feel better about themselves.

In 1958, Jamaica joined nine other British territories in the West Indies Federation, but withdrew when, in a 1961 referendum, Jamaican voters rejected membership. Jamaica gained independence from the United Kingdom in 1962, but remained a member of the Commonwealth. In the country's first election following independence, Alexander Bustamante, a leader of the Labour Party, was elected prime minister. Bustamante retired five years later and passed power to Hugh Shearer. After a number of years under the Jamaican Labour party, the 1972 elections put Michael Norman Manley in power. Manley, who steered the country toward socialism, served until 1980, when voters selected Edward Seaga as prime minister. In 1989, voters returned Manley to the prime minister's office, but he stepped down in March 1992 because of ill health. His successor, Percival J. Patterson, handily won reelection in 1993.

Jamaica developed a debt crisis under the Manley and Patterson administrations that worsened in 1999 as loan repayments plus interest were estimated to account for more than 60% of the country's budget expenditures. In April 2000, Prime Minister Patterson announced that Jamaica would not borrow additional funds from the IMF but would ask the international agency to monitor its monetary and fiscal policies for the next two years. Throughout the period, the country's high crime rate remained a source of serious concern. In spring 2001, tourism suffered a blow when four cruise lines dropped Jamaica from their itineraries. In July 2001, at least

JAMAICA

Official name: none

Independence: 6 August 1962 (from United Kingdom)

Area: 10,990 sq km

Form of government: constitutional parliamentary democracy

Capital: Kingston

Currency: Jamaican dollar (JMD)

Income: US$8,967 (2008 est. of purchasing power parity)

Population: 2,825,928 (2009 est.)

Ethnic groups: black 91.2%, mixed 6.2%, other 2.6%

Religious groups: Church of God 24%, Seventh-day Adventist 11%, Pentecostal 10%, Baptist 7%, Anglican 4%, Roman Catholic 2%, United Church 2%, Methodist 2%, Jehovah's Witnesses 2%, Moravian 1%, Brethren 1%, unstated 3%, other 10% (includes Rastafarians, Muslims, Hindus, Jews, and Baha'is), none 21% (2001 census)

Languages: English, Creole

Literacy: 87.9% (fifteen years old and over has ever attended school; 2003 est.)

Exports: alumina, bauxite; sugar, bananas, rum

Primary export partners: U.S. 40.3%, Canada 10.6%, UK 9.2%, Netherlands 7.9%, France 5.4%, Russia 5.2% (2008)

Imports: machinery and transport equipment, construction materials, fuel, food, chemicals, fertilizers

Primary import partners: U.S. 39.4%, Trinidad and Tobago 17.5%, Venezuela 11.6% (2008)

twenty-five people were killed in gang violence in West Kingston. Jamaica installed new prime minister Portia Simpson-Miller, the country's first female head of state, in 2006.

MARTINIQUE

Christopher Columbus first visited Martinique in 1502 on his fourth voyage to the New World. The island's indigenous Carib Indian population was largely decimated by disease in the wake of Columbus's visit. The French permanently settled the area in the seventeenth century. Except for three short periods of British occupation, Martinique has been a French possession since 1635.

As sugar plantations sprang up on Martinique, the need for captive black labor grew quickly, particularly since the island's indigenous Carib Indians had been all but wiped out by disease introduced by the first European visitors. The island's population in 1789 was estimated at 12,000 whites, 65,000 enslaved Africans, and 5,000 free blacks. In 1848, less than sixty years later, the enslaved population had moved up by only about 12% to 73,000, while the total of free blacks had soared by almost 700%.

MARTINIQUE

Official name: Department of Martinique

Area: 1,100 sq km

Form of government: overseas department of France

Capital: Fort-de-France

Currency: euro (EUR)

Income: US$24,000 (2006 est. of purchasing power parity)

Population: 402,000 (2008 est.)

Ethnic groups: African and African-white-Indian mixture 90%, white 5%, East Indian, Chinese less than 5%

Religious groups: Roman Catholic 95%, Hindu and pagan African 5%

Languages: French, Creole patois

Literacy: 97.7% (fifteen years old and over who can read and write; 2003 est.)

Exports: refined petroleum products, bananas, rum, pineapples

Imports: petroleum products, crude oil, foodstuffs, construction materials, vehicles, clothing and other consumer goods

The white population, meanwhile, had shrunk to about 9,000. In the spring of 1848, the Africans of Martinique staged a large-scale revolt that precipitated abolition of enslavement in the French colonies one month later.

Martinique witnessed a number of dramatic changes during the twentieth century. The political realm, once largely restricted to the island's white minority, began to open up to those of African ancestry. In 1945, black poet and intellectual Aimé Césaire (1913–2008) was elected as a Martinician deputy to the French parliament. In addition to his continuing involvement in the politics of his country, Césaire was instrumental in jump-starting the country's cultural renewal with his book of poetry, *Cahier d'un retour au pays natal* (*Notebook of a Return to My Native Land*) published in 1947. A strong supporter of Martinique's status as an overseas department of France, Césaire fell out of favor with some of Martinique's young intellectuals for his failure to call for independence from France.

MEXICO

When Hernán Cortes stepped ashore in Mexico in 1519, he was accompanied by a free black named Juan Garrido, who later participated in the Spanish toppling of Tenochtitlán, the Aztec capital. By the middle of the sixteenth century, it is estimated that there were almost 150,000 enslaved Africans in the country. One of these black captives, Estevanico, is credited with opening up the northern interior lands—the area that is now New Mexico and Arizona—to Spanish conquest. During the sixteenth and seventeenth centuries, black Mexicans were believed to have outnumbered whites by a ratio of two to one. However, both groups were vastly outnumbered by the indigenous peoples of Mexico.

Beginning in the early part of the eighteenth century, the country's Afro-Mexican population started to decline, in part because of new Spanish restrictions on the slave trade. Although the enslaved Africans proved more resistant to many of the European-borne diseases than the indigenous peoples, many did succumb to foreign diseases including tuberculosis, yellow fever, and syphilis. Some of the enslaved blacks were simply worked to death. Furthermore, many of the Africans brought into the colony intermixed with indigenous peoples and whites. The reason for this large-scale intermixing was twofold: the Spaniards purposely limited the number of African women they brought into Mexico, and the prevailing caste system gave individuals with a lighter skin color a higher standing. In 1829, Mexico abolished enslavement in all its states except Texas, allowing it to remain there to pacify the United States. As enslavement in the United States moved westward into Texas, Mexico became a

MEXICO

Official name: United Mexican States
Independence: 16 September 1810 (from Spain)
Area: 1,972,550 sq km
Form of government: federal republic
Capital: Mexico City
Currency: Mexican peso (MXN)
Income: US$14,537 (2008 est. of purchasing power parity)
Population: 111,211,789 (2009 est.)
Ethnic groups: mestizo (Amerindian-Spanish) 60%, Amerindian or predominantly Amerindian 30%, white 9%, other 1%
Religious groups: Roman Catholic 76.5%, Protestant 6.3% (Pentecostal 1.4%, Jehovah's Witnesses 1.1%, other 3.8%), other 0.3%, unspecified 13.8%, none 3.1% (2000 census)
Languages: Spanish, various Mayan, Nahuatl, and other regional indigenous languages
Literacy: 97% (fifteen years old and over who can read and write; 2005 est.)
Exports: manufactured goods, oil and oil products, silver, fruits, vegetables, coffee, cotton
Primary export partners: U.S. 80.2%, Canada 2.4%, Germany 1.7% (2008)
Imports: metal-working machines, steel mill products, agricultural machinery, electrical equipment, car parts for assembly, repair parts for motor vehicles, aircraft, and aircraft parts
Primary import partners: U.S. 49%, China 11.2%, Japan 5.3%, South Korea 4.4%, Germany 4.1% (2008)

haven for escapees who slipped into the heart of the country and blended with the population.

Some 100,000 blacks, about 0.5% of the population, live in Mexico today, mostly in the coastal areas of the Costa Chica region (Pacific) and Veracruz (Gulf coast). Blacks in lesser numbers live in Mexico City and in border cities across the Rio Grande River from Texas.

MONTSERRAT

When Christopher Columbus first visited the Leeward Islands (Antigua, Anguilla, Barbuda, Montserrat, Nevis, and Saint Kitts) in 1493, the islands were inhabited by Carib Indians. English settlers who moved to Montserrat from nearby Saint Kitts and Nevis first colonized the island in 1632. Montserrat's first enslaved Africans were believed to have arrived in 1651. By the early 1670s, there were about 1,000 Africans on the island and by 1729 the number was 6,000. At that time, blacks outnumbered whites by about five to one.

The lives of enslaved Africans on Montserrat were closely regulated. Colonial laws prohibited slaves from becoming masons, shinglers, sawyers, tailors, coopers, or smiths. Furthermore, blacks were forbidden to plant indigo, ginger, cocoa, cotton, or coffee, the main cash crops of the region, although they could grow vegetables for their own use in small gardens. These restrictions ensured that few enslaved Africans would ever be able to make and set aside enough money to purchase their freedom.

Throughout the eighteenth century, the British and French warred for possession of Montserrat, which was finally confirmed as a British possession by the Treaty of Versailles (1783). By the early nineteenth century,

MONTSERRAT

Area: 100 sq km
Form of government: overseas territory of the United Kingdom
Capital: Plymouth (abandoned in 1997 because of volcanic activity; interim government buildings have been built at Brades, in the Carr's Bay/Little Bay vicinity at the northwest end of Montserrat)
Currency: East Caribbean dollar (XCD)
Income: US$3,400 (2002 est. of purchasing power parity)
Population: 5,097 (2009 est.)
Ethnic groups: black, white, mainly of mixed Irish and African descent
Religious groups: Anglican, Methodist, Roman Catholic, Pentecostal, Seventh-Day Adventist, other Christian denominations
Languages: English
Exports: electronic components, plastic bags, apparel, hot peppers, live plants, cattle
Primary export partners: U.S., Antigua and Barbuda
Imports: machinery and transportation equipment, foodstuffs, manufactured goods, fuels, lubricants, and related materials
Primary import partners: U.S., UK, Trinidad and Tobago, Japan, Canada

Montserrat had a plantation economy, but the abolition of enslavement in 1834, the elimination of the apprentice system, the declining market for sugar, and a series of natural disasters brought the downfall of the sugar estates.

Today, most of Montserrat's population is an intermixture of European settlers and the descendants of West Africans. In 1997, the 3,000-foot Soufriere Hills volcano erupted repeatedly, causing widespread devastation to property and crippling the island's economy. More than two-thirds of the country's residents sought shelter off the island in the wake of these disasters.

NETHERLANDS ANTILLES

The Spanish first landed on the island of Curaçao in 1499, and in 1527 they took possession of Curaçao, Bonaire, and Aruba. So poor was the soil on most of the islands that the Spanish called them *islas inutiles* (useless islands), capturing many of the native Arawak Indians and transporting them to nearby Spanish islands to work on plantations. In 1634, the three islands were passed to the Netherlands, where they have remained except for two short periods of British rule during the Napoleonic Wars.

The islands' rich salt deposits, particularly off the coasts of Saint Maarten, Bonaire, and Curaçao, were perhaps the main reason the Dutch had sought to gain their control. However, the mining of salt was both a difficult and labor-intensive job, and there were not nearly enough Dutch colonists willing to do it. The Dutch decided to import enslaved Africans to handle the workload. The first boatloads of Africans, mostly from the Congo and Angola, arrived in Curaçao in 1639. The Dutch West India Company, which handled the infamous slave trade for the Netherlands, increased dramatically in size during this period, becoming the second largest enslaver in the Atlantic by the 1640s. By 1700, the African population on Curaçao and Bonaire totaled 4,000 with another 1,000 blacks split between Saint Eustatius and Saint Maarten. A century later, between them, Saint Maarten and Saint Eustatius were home to some 9,000 Africans. Both Curaçao and Bonaire had experienced similar increases, although no exact figures from 1800 are available for those islands. African enslavement was abolished in this region in 1863.

Today, some forty nationalities are represented in the Netherlands Antilles and Aruba. The people of the Netherlands Antilles are primarily African or mixed African European descent.

NETHERLANDS ANTILLES

Area: 800 sq km

Form of government: part of the Kingdom of the Netherlands

Capital: Willemstad, Curaçao

Currency: Netherlands Antillean guilder (ANG)

Income: US$11,400 (2003 est. of purchasing power parity)

Population: 227,049 (2009 est.)

Ethnic groups: mixed black 85%, Carib Amerindian, white, East Asian

Religious groups: Roman Catholic 72%, Pentecostal 4.9%, Protestant 3.5%, Seventh-Day Adventist 3.1%, Methodist 2.9%, Jehovah's Witnesses 1.7%, other Christian 4.2%, Jewish 1.3%, other or unspecified 1.2%, none 5.2% (2001 census)

Languages: Dutch (official), Papiamento (a Spanish-Portuguese-Dutch-English dialect) predominates, English widely spoken, Spanish

Literacy: 96.7% (fifteen years old and over who can read and write; 2003 est.)

Exports: petroleum products

Primary export partners: U.S. 19%, Guatemala 10.6%, Dominican Republic 9.3%, Haiti 7.4%, Singapore 6.7%, Bahamas 5.9%, Italy 4.5%, Honduras 4.4%, Mexico 4.1% (2008)

Imports: crude petroleum, food, manufactures

Primary import partners: Venezuela 58.8%, U.S. 19%, Brazil 5.9% (2008)

NICARAGUA

In 1513, the explorer Balboa first landed in what is now Nicaragua and the Spanish began to develop the area. Because the economy could neither support nor did it require large-scale slave labor, early Spanish colonists brought relatively few enslaved Africans to what is now Nicaragua. However, the early 1600s saw the development of an English enclave along the territory's desolate Atlantic Coast, known as the Mosquito Coast. By the middle of the seventeenth century, these English settlers had begun to import enslaved Africans into their enclave to work the area's plantations and assist in harvesting coastal timber. A century later, when Britain was forced to abandon its Mosquito Coast protectorate, most of the blacks remained, creating black Creole villages, such as Pearl Lagoon and Bluefields. So far were these communities from the center of Spanish power in Managua that the blacks enjoyed considerable local autonomy. The abolition of African enslavement in the British colonies of the Caribbean in the early 1830s set off a new wave of immigration into the Mosquito Coast, as newly freed

NICARAGUA

Official name: Republic of Nicaragua
Independence: 15 September 1821 (from Spain)
Area: 129,494 sq km
Form of government: republic
Capital: Managua
Currency: cordoba (NIO)
Income: US$2,698 (2008 est. of purchasing power parity)
Population: 5,891,100 (2009 est.)
Ethnic groups: mestizo (mixed Amerindian and white) 69%, white 17%, black 9%, Amerindian 5%
Religious groups: Roman Catholic 58.5%, Evangelical 21.6%, Moravian 1.6%, Jehovah's Witnesses 0.9%, other 1.7%, none 15.7% (2005 census)
Languages: Spanish (official)
Literacy: 67.5% (fifteen years old and over who can read and write; 2003 est.)
Exports: coffee, shrimp and lobster, cotton, tobacco, beef, sugar, bananas, gold
Primary export partners: U.S. 32.3%, El Salvador 14.6%, Costa Rica 6.9%, Honduras 6.8%, Mexico 5.3%, Canada 5%, Guatemala 5% (2008)
Imports: machinery and equipment, raw materials, petroleum products, consumer goods
Primary import partners: U.S. 21%, Venezuela 14.3%, Mexico 8.4%, Costa Rica 8%, China 7.8%, Guatemala 6.1%, El Salvador 5.2% (2008)

PANAMA

Official name: Republic of Panama
Independence: 3 November 1903 (from Colombia; became independent from Spain 28 November 1821)
Area: 78,200 sq km
Form of government: constitutional democracy
Capital: Panama City
Currency: balboa (PAB); U.S. dollar
Income: US$11,361 (2008 est. of purchasing power parity)
Population: 3,360,474 (2009 est.)
Ethnic groups: mestizo (mixed Amerindian and white) 70%, Amerindian and mixed (West Indian) 14%, white 10%, Amerindian 6%
Religious groups: Roman Catholic 75–85%, Evangelical Christian 15–25% (2007 est.)
Languages: Spanish (official), English 14%
Literacy: 92.6% (fifteen years old and over who can read and write; 2003 est.)
Exports: bananas, shrimp, sugar, coffee, clothing
Primary export partners: U.S. 39.2%, Netherlands 10.7%, Costa Rica 5.8%, Sweden 5.4%, UK 5.4%, Spain 5%, China 4.1% (2008)
Imports: capital goods, crude oil, foodstuffs, consumer goods, chemicals
Primary import partners: U.S. 29.6%, Costa Rica 5%, China 5%, Japan 4.2% (2008)

Africans joined the free blacks there. Nicaragua won independence from Spain in 1838.

Today, Nicaragua is home to the largest African Diaspora population in Central America. Most of the Afro-Nicaraguans continue to live along the Atlantic coast.

PANAMA

Prior to the arrival of Europeans, Amerindian groups inhabited Panama. By 1519, the Spanish had established settlements, killing or enslaving much of the indigenous Indian population. Africans were brought in to replace the Indians who had been initially forced into servitude. Panama was a part of Colombia from the time of independence in 1821 until it broke away as a separate country in 1903.

One of the most dramatic changes in Panama was the construction of the Panama Canal connecting the Atlantic and the Pacific Oceans. Supported militarily by the United States, which desperately wanted to build the canal, Panama seceded from Colombia. Two weeks later, the United States and the newly independent Panama signed a treaty permitting the United States to build the canal and enjoy control over a five-mile stretch of Panamanian territory on either side of the waterway. Panama's existing black population was soon increased dramatically as black West Indian laborers arrived by the thousands to help in the massive construction project. Working and living conditions for blacks involved in the project were harsh, particularly since many of the American supervisors overseeing the project were natives of the U.S. South. Segregated living arrangements were put in place by these supervisors. Discrimination against blacks and other Panamanians working on the canal was blatant. They were paid less than Spaniards and Italians who had been imported into Panama to perform the same level of manual labor on the project. Of the 5,600 workers who died constructing the canal, more than 4,700 of them were of African ancestry.

Panama experienced decades of relative stability because of the commerce generated by the canal. But by the early 1970s, the country had experienced two coups by the military, and corruption was rampant. In 1977, the United States signed an agreement transferring control of the canal to Panama in 1999. After the mysterious death of President Omar Torrijos in 1981, General Manuel Noriega took control of the civilian government and the military. Although it was widely speculated that he covertly assisted the United States in its war against the Contras in Nicaragua, he was captured and indicted in the U.S. courts for drug smuggling after the Americans launched an attack on Panama in 1989. Noriega's prison sentence in the United States ended in 2007. However, pending extradition hearings in France and Panama (which Noriega is opposing in U.S. courts), he is still incarcerated as of 2009.

PARAGUAY

Since early colonial times, people of African descent (most of them brought into the territory enslaved) have played a significant role in the development of Paraguay and its culture. Because the colony lacked the wealth of natural resources of many of its neighbors in South America, the number of enslaved Africans imported was on a smaller scale than elsewhere. The nature of the work to which the early Africans (and Indians who were similarly pressed into service, in higher numbers than the Africans) were assigned was not much different in nature from in other Spanish colonies of the region: farm work, livestock raising, and domestic service. In later years, some blacks were employed for more specialized tasks including road construction and repair and the smelting of iron. As of 1650, surviving records indicate, the African population totaled 15,000 out of a total population of 250,000. However, unlike other Spanish-held territories where the African population continued to grow strongly into the nineteenth century, by 1782, Paraguay's enslaved Africans had dropped to less than 11,000 in number.

A system unique to Paraguay called *amparo* provided that any freed African who could not pay tribute to the Spanish Crown was turned over to the protective custody of the local government or religious orders. Under conditions similar to enslavement, many of these newly freed Africans were settled into all-black communities and compelled to work for their custodians. In Paraguay's battle for independence from Spain, it was unnecessary to draft the services of Afro-Paraguayans, free or enslaved. Thus when independence was achieved in 1811, colonial officials were under no obligation to begin freeing enslaved Africans in payment for their military services. In 1869, the government finally ordered the total abolition of slavery in Paraguay.

PARAGUAY

Official name: Republic of Paraguay
Independence: 14 May 1811 (from Spain)
Area: 406,750 sq km
Form of government: constitutional republic
Capital: Asunción
Currency: guaraní (PYG)
Income: US$4,786 (2008 est. of purchasing power parity)
Population: 6,349,000 (2009 est.)
Ethnic groups: mestizo (mixed Spanish and Amerindian) 95%
Religious groups: Roman Catholic 89.6%, Protestant 6.2%, other Christian 1.1%, other or unspecified 1.9%, none 1.1% (2002 census)
Languages: Spanish (official), Guarani (official)
Literacy: 94% (fifteen years old and over who can read and write; 2003 est.)
Exports: electricity, soybeans, feed, cotton, meat, edible oils
Primary export partners: Argentina 31.7%, Brazil 15.9%, Uruguay 11.7%, Chile 6.4%, Russia 5.7% (2008)
Imports: road vehicles, consumer goods, tobacco, petroleum products, electrical machinery
Primary import partners: Brazil 27.2%, U.S. 22.1%, Argentina 14.9%, China 10.4% (2008)

PERU

Peru is best known as the home of the Incas, whose rich culture was developed in the mountain strongholds of the Andes. Most students today are also familiar with the Spanish conquistadors who sought out the Incas' riches in gold and silver and toppled their sophisticated empire in the process. What few recognize is the very real contributions that enslaved Africans and their descendants made to the conquest and development of Peru. Among

PERU

Official name: Republic of Peru
Independence: 28 July 1821 (from Spain)
Area: 1,285,220 sq km
Form of government: constitutional republic
Capital: Lima
Currency: nuevo sol (PEN)
Income: US$8,594 (2008 est. of purchasing power parity)
Population: 29,132,013 (2009 est.)
Ethnic groups: Amerindian 45%, mestizo (mixed Amerindian and white) 37%, white 15%, black, Japanese, Chinese, and other 3%
Religious groups: Roman Catholic 81.3%, Evangelical 12.5%, other 3.3%, unspecified or none 2.9% (2007 Census)
Languages: Spanish (official), Quechua (official), Aymara
Literacy: 92.9% (fifteen years old and over who can read and write; 2007 census.)
Exports: fish and fish products, copper, zinc, gold, crude petroleum and by-products, lead, coffee, sugar, cotton
Primary export partners: U.S. 20%, China 15.2%, Canada 8.3%, Japan 7%, Chile 5.8%, Brazil 4.2% (2008)
Imports: machinery, transport equipment, foodstuffs, petroleum, iron and steel, chemicals, pharmaceuticals
Primary import partners: U.S. 23.7%, China 10.6%, Brazil 7.5%, Ecuador 6.5%, Chile 5.1%, Argentina 5%, Mexico 4.5% (2008)

the best known of the early blacks involved in the conquest of the Incan Empire was Juan Valiente, enslaved under Diego de Almagro, who himself accompanied Francisco Pizarro into Peru in 1524. For his services, Valiente was eventually rewarded with a land grant and a number of Indians who were required to pay tribute to him. Strangely, Valiente, despite his fortune, remained enslaved until his death. As his military superiors negotiated with his master for Valiente's freedom, he was killed in an engagement against local Araucanian Indians at Tucapel.

Peru's best-known religious icon was the Dominican, St. Martin de Porres. Born in 1579 of a Spanish nobleman and a formerly enslaved African woman, he is often referred to as the first black saint in the Americas. He dedicated his life to working for the poor and maintained a very austere life. Many miracles have been attributed to him, including the ability to levitate, as well as several unexplained dramatic healings. The patron saint of animals, Martin de Porres is said to have had the ability to communicate with them. He reportedly had a dog, a cat, a bird, and a mouse all eating together from the same dish. At the time of his death in 1639, those who viewed his remains took tiny pieces of his habit hoping for some miraculous event to befall them. It was said that his habit had to be replaced several times to accommodate so many.

During Peru's early colonial period, relatively few enslaved Africans were imported, since the bulk of the available work was in the mines high in the mountains, an environment for which the colonial authorities thought Africans ill-suited. Furthermore, there was plenty of Indian labor available for this work. As the country's arid coastal plain was gradually irrigated and put under cultivation, the need for forced African labor also grew. Obtaining enslaved Africans was a monumental challenge, as they had to be shipped from the west coast of Africa, across the Atlantic, around treacherous Cape Horn at the southern tip of South America, and north along the Pacific Coast to Panama, where they were unloaded. So arduous was the voyage that many did not survive. For those importing black captives, the cost of this trade was very high. However, well into the seventeenth century, Peru's demands for enslaved Africans remained strong. Argentine General José de San Martin, fighting for Peru's independence in the 1820s, tried to entice enslaved Africans into military service with promises of freedom for those who joined him. However, most blacks in Peru were not emancipated until 1854.

PUERTO RICO

Although Columbus visited Puerto Rico on his second voyage to the New World in 1493, the Spaniard Ponce de Leon conquered the island and was appointed governor there in 1509. Indigenous Carib Indians, almost all of whom were utilized by the Spaniards as plantation laborers, were eventually wiped out by diseases and harsh treatment and were replaced by enslaved Africans.

When Spain authorized Puerto Rico's trade in enslaved Africans in 1510, a number of free blacks from Seville immigrated to the island in search of broader opportunities. For the most part, these were Ladinos, or Christianized blacks, who sought jobs as domestic servants or mineworkers. Free blacks outnumbered enslaved Africans for most of the island's history. Puerto Rico's population, according to the 1845 census, included 216,083 whites, 175,000 free blacks, and 51,265

PUERTO RICO

Official name: Commonwealth of Puerto Rico
Area: 9,104 sq km
Form of government: commonwealth associated with the United States
Capital: San Juan
Currency: U.S. dollar
Income: US$19,600 (2007 est. of purchasing power parity)
Population: 3,966,213 (2009 est.)
Ethnic groups: white (mostly Spanish origin) 76.2%, black 6.9%, Asian 0.3%, Amerindian 0.2%, mixed 4.4%, other 12% (2007)
Religious groups: Roman Catholic 85%, Protestant and other 15%
Languages: Spanish, English
Literacy: 94.1% (fifteen years old and over who can read and write; 2002 est.)
Exports: pharmaceuticals, electronics, apparel, canned tuna, rum, beverage concentrates, medical equipment
Imports: chemicals, machinery and equipment, clothing, food, fish, petroleum products

enslaved Africans. Forced human bondage was formally abolished on the islands on March 22, 1873. Twenty-five years later, during the Spanish-American War, Puerto Rico gained its independence from Spain and became a protectorate of the United States.

Many Puerto Ricans today are of mixed black and Spanish ancestry. For the most part, the original Indian inhabitants of the island were exterminated in the sixteenth century. Leading contemporary Afro-Puerto Ricans include literary figures Isabelo Zenón Cruz, Angela María Dávila, and Ana Lydia Vega.

The legacy and contribution of African descendants to Puerto Rican history and culture is extensive. March 22 is celebrated on the island as "Abolition Day" to mark the anniversary of that occasion. The religion, language, sports, music, art, dance, and cuisine of Puerto Rico all reflect the African presence.

Santeria, an African religion older than Christianity, continues to be observed on the island. Because of the migration of Puerto Ricans to the United States, Santeria is also practiced in the U.S.

SAINT KITTS AND NEVIS

Christopher Columbus first visited the islands of Saint Kitts and Nevis in 1493 on his second voyage to the area. Although some historians have suggested that Columbus named the larger island San Cristobal (Saint Christopher) in his own honor or for his patron saint, Spanish sailors actually gave the name to the island. The island's nickname, Saint Kitts, comes from English sailors' slang for Saint Christopher. In 1624, Saint Christopher became England's first settlement in the West Indies, and from there colonists spread to other islands in the region. In 1624, the French colonized part of the island. However, the Treaty of Utrecht ceded it entirely to Britain in 1713.

By the 1660s, approximately one-half of the Saint Kitts' population of 6,000 was black. Over the next 100 years, the ratio changed dramatically, so that by the final quarter of the eighteenth century, the island had ten times as many blacks as whites. The only real industry on both Saint

ST. KITTS AND NEVIS

Official name: Federation of Saint Kitts and Nevis
Independence: 19 September 1983 (from United Kingdom)
Area: 261 sq km (Saint Kitts 168 sq km; Nevis 93 sq km)
Form of government: constitutional monarchy with Westminster-style parliament
Capital: Basseterre
Currency: East Caribbean dollar (XCD)
Income: US$13,826 (2008 est. of purchasing power parity)
Population: 42,696 (2009 est.)
Ethnic groups: predominantly black, some British, Portuguese, and Lebanese
Religious groups: Anglican, other Protestant, Roman Catholic
Languages: English
Literacy: 97.8% (fifteen years old and over has ever attended school; 2003 est.)
Exports: machinery, food, electronics, beverages, tobacco
Primary export partners: U.S. 65.7%, Azerbaijan 7.5%, Canada 6% (2008)
Imports: machinery, manufactures, food, fuels
Primary import partners: U.S. 46.8%, Trinidad and Tobago 14.8%, UK 4.1% (2008)

Kitts and Nevis was sugar. Sugar was also the primary reason for the high concentration of peoples of African descent, most of whom were brought to the islands in the sixteenth and seventeenth centuries as enslaved persons to work the sugarcane fields. In 1834, as in most English colonies, slavery was abolished in Saint Kitts and Nevis. There followed a mandatory four-year apprenticeship during which the newly freed Africans were obligated to continue to work for their former masters for a small salary. Consequently, not much changed for most blacks on the islands because they continued to toil in the sugar fields of their former masters, even after the end of their apprenticeships. However, they were now obligated to pay for housing and their food also. Thus many of the islands' blacks left in search of better work elsewhere.

The Federation of Saint Kitts and Nevis attained full independence on September 19, 1983. Today, blacks comprise the largest percentage of the population for Saint Kitts and Nevis.

SAINT LUCIA

The timing of the first European visit to the lush and beautiful island of Saint Lucia has long been the subject of debate. Many islanders believe the story, perhaps apocryphal, that Christopher Columbus discovered the island on December 13, 1502, the feast day of Saint Lucy. Whatever the truth about Saint Lucia's first European visitor and the timing of the visit, it is known that Europeans were unable to gain a foothold on the island until the middle of the seventeenth century because of the native Carib Indians' fierce resistance. Once European settlement began, the Spanish, British, and French squabbled over who had claimed the island first. The Spanish failed to press their claim, but the British and the French continued to fight over Saint Lucia until 1814, during which time the island changed hands seven times. This competition for control of Saint Lucia impeded large-scale development of plantations on the island.

French planters are believed to have imported the first enslaved Africans to Saint Lucia in about 1763, a relatively late start for the trade in Africans when compared to other French and British colonies in the region. The local patois language, a mixture of African dialects and French, developed during these years in Saint Lucia. French patois is still spoken throughout the island today. When Saint Lucia officially became a British territory in 1814, this already entrenched French-based patois made it difficult for the British colonists to communicate with the island's blacks. When enslavement was abolished throughout the British colonies in 1834, more than 13,000 enslaved Africans on Saint Lucia were freed. Most of the newly freed blacks fled their plantations and carved out tiny farms of their own.

SAINT LUCIA

Independence: 22 February 1979 (from United Kingdom)

Area: 620 sq km

Form of government: Westminster-style parliamentary democracy

Capital: Castries

Currency: East Caribbean dollar (XCD)

Income: US$10,750 (2008 est. of purchasing power parity)

Population: 160,267 (2009 est.)

Ethnic groups: black 82.5%, mixed 11.9%, East Indian 2.4%, other or unspecified 3.1% (2001 census)

Religious groups: Roman Catholic 67.5%, Seventh-day Adventist 8.5%, Pentecostal 5.7%, Rastafarian 2.1%, Anglican 2%, Evangelical 2%, other Christian 5.1%, other or unspecified 2.6%, none 4.5% (2001 census)

Languages: English (official), French patois

Literacy: 94.8% (fifteen years old and over has ever attended school; 2007 est.)

Exports: bananas 41%, clothing, cocoa, vegetables, fruits, coconut oil

Primary export partners: UK 23.6%, U.S. 19.3%, South Korea 16.6%, Antigua and Barbuda 5.9%, Dominica 5.8%, Barbados 5.2%, Trinidad and Tobago 4.8% (2008)

Imports: food 23%, manufactured goods 21%, machinery and transportation equipment 19%, chemicals, fuels

Primary import partners: Brazil 68%, U.S. 11.7%, Trinidad and Tobago 7.4% (2008)

Saint Lucia became an independent state within the British Commonwealth on February 22, 1979. Today, visitors from the United States, Canada, and Europe have been attracted by the island's multicultural heritage; Saint Lucia is now inhabited mainly by people of African and mixed African-European descent, with small Caucasian and Asian Indian minorities.

SAINT VINCENT AND THE GRENADINES

Similar to Saint Lucia, its neighbor to the north, Saint Vincent and the Grenadines, a chain of Caribbean

SAINT VINCENT AND THE GRENADINES

Independence: 27 October 1979 (from United Kingdom)
Area: 389 sq km (Saint Vincent 344 sq km)
Form of government: parliamentary democracy; independent sovereign state within the Commonwealth
Capital: Kingstown
Currency: East Caribbean dollar (XCD)
Income: US$10,163 (2008 est. of purchasing power parity)
Population: 120,000 (July 2008 est.)
Ethnic groups: black 66%, mixed 19%, East Indian 6%, Carib Amerindian 2%
Religious groups: Anglican 47%, Methodist 28%, Roman Catholic 13%, Seventh-Day Adventist, Hindu, other Protestant
Languages: English, French patois
Literacy: 88% (2004 est.)
Exports: bananas 39%, eddoes and dasheen (taro), arrowroot starch, tennis racquets
Primary export partners: Greece 31.8%, France 18.9%, India 9.9%, China 8.3%, Italy 7.5% (2008)
Imports: foodstuffs, machinery and equipment, chemicals and fertilizers, minerals and fuels
Primary import partners: Singapore 27.1%, Trinidad and Tobago 13.2%, U.S. 12.1%, China 8.5%, Italy 7.1%, Norway 5.1% (2008)

islands, saw no permanent European settlement until the seventeenth century. The Carib Indians, then occupying the islands, fiercely resisted European attempts to colonize. A group of Africans who survived the sinking of a Dutch slave ship on which they were being transported were the first outsiders allowed by the Caribs to settle on the islands. A treaty between the Caribs and Europeans in the early 1700s finally opened the way for European settlement. The first Europeans to gain a foothold on the islands were the French, who managed to coexist relatively peacefully with the Caribs. When the British moved into the islands and began competing with French planters to see who could carve out the larger plantations, friction with the Caribs was inevitable. After a Carib revolt late in the eighteenth century, British colonial authorities captured more than 5,000 Caribs and sent them into exile. Since most of the island's free blacks had lived among the Caribs, the blacks remaining in the islands were mostly enslaved.

In the early nineteenth century, a massive volcanic eruption caused widespread devastation on Saint Vincent, wiping out much of the island's coffee and cacao crops. When slavery was abolished in 1834, many of the newly freed blacks decided to try to carve out small farms for themselves. White plantation owners were forced to import Portuguese and Asian Indian indentured servants to work in the island's sugarcane fields. As the sugar industry began to slump in the final quarter of the nineteenth century, the government opted to turn over more land to small farmers. Well into the twenty-first century, the majority of the island's residents were engaged in small-scale agriculture, a prescription for a precarious economy given agriculture's vulnerability to the vagaries of nature.

SURINAME

Columbus first sighted the Suriname coast in 1498, and Spain claimed the area in 1593. Suriname became a Dutch colony in 1667. However, the new colony, Dutch Guiana, did not thrive. The colony experienced frequent uprisings by enslaved Africans, who were often treated with extraordinary cruelty. Many of them fled to the interior, where they resumed a West African culture and established the six major ethnic groups which are in existence today: the Ndjuka and the Saramaka, the two largest groups, and the Paramaka, Aluki, Swinti, and Matawai.

Well into the eighteenth century, the territory of Suriname was unique in its high percentage of African-born men and women—by the mid-1750s, about one-third of Dutch Guiana's slaves had arrived from Africa. Among the factors contributing to this phenomenon were a high mortality rate among the enslaved Africans and the need to keep importing them at a fast pace, in part to replace some who had escaped. Suriname experienced less in the way of violent slave revolts, such as those common throughout much of the New World—the most common form of protest among Suriname's enslaved blacks was escape.

The maroons, as the runaways were called, were not the only ones to take a stand against enslavement, however. Although Dutch Guiana saw less of the violence common to New World colonies where forced human bondage was practiced, there was a notable uprising in 1832, when enslaved Africans put much of the colony's capital to the torch. In 1860, virtually the entire enslaved population of the colony escaped to uninhabited parts of

SURINAME

Official name: Republic of Suriname
Independence: 25 November 1975 (from Netherlands)
Area: 163,270 sq km
Form of government: constitutional democracy
Capital: Paramaribo
Currency: Surinamese dollar (SRD)
Income: US$8,317 (2009 est. of purchasing power parity)
Population: 481,267 (2009 est.)
Ethnic groups: Hindustani (also known locally as East Indians; their ancestors emigrated from northern India in the latter part of the nineteenth century) 37%, Creole (mixed white and black) 31%, Javanese 15%, "Maroons" (their enslaved African ancestors were brought to the country in the seventeenth and eighteenth centuries and escaped to the interior) 10%, Amerindian 2%, Chinese 2%, white 1%, other 2%
Religious groups: Hindu 27.4%, Muslim 19.6%, Roman Catholic 22.8%, Protestant 25.2% (predominantly Moravian), indigenous beliefs 5%
Languages: Dutch (official), English (widely spoken), Sranang Tongo (Surinamese, sometimes called Taki-Taki, is native language of Creoles and much of the younger population and is lingua franca among others), Hindustani (a dialect of Hindi), Javanese
Literacy: 89.6% (fifteen years old and over who can read and write; 2004 est.)
Exports: alumina, crude oil, lumber, shrimp and fish, rice, bananas
Primary export partners: Canada 36.2%, Belgium 12.5%, Norway 12.4%, UAE 8.9%, U.S. 7.7% (2008)
Imports: capital equipment, petroleum, foodstuffs, cotton, consumer goods
Primary import partners: U.S. 31.2%, Netherlands 15.5%, Trinidad and Tobago 14.2%, China 7.7%, Japan 6.4% (2008)

the island. Bowing to these growing pressures, the Netherlands abolished the practice in 1863.

Starting in 1951, Suriname began to acquire an increasing measure of autonomy from the Netherlands. On December 15, 1954, Suriname became an autonomous part of the Kingdom of the Netherlands and gained independence on November 25, 1975. Désiré Bourtese led a military coup in 1980 and instituted a socialist state. A separate challenge to the government came from a guerrilla movement under the leadership of Ronny Brunswijk. The Surinamese Liberation Army (SLA), also known as the Maroon or Bush Negro insurgency, began operating in the northeast in July 1986. It struck against various economic targets including the Suriname Aluminum Company. The government responded with repression and the killing of civilians suspected of supporting the insurgency.

Political upheaval continued in spite of the elections held in 1987. International pressure eventually prevailed, and the military relinquished its control of the government. Ronald Venetiaan was elected president in 1991, followed by Jules Wijdenbosch in 1996. These elections marked the first time in independent Suriname's history that one democratically elected government passed peacefully to another.

The New Front party swept the May 2000 legislative elections, clearing the way for the election of its leader, Ronald Venetiaan, as the new president in August 2000. The new government under Venetiaan managed to improve the country's fiscal and economic stability. In 2005, President Venetiaan was sworn into office for a third term.

TRINIDAD AND TOBAGO

Columbus first visited the island of Trinidad in 1498 on his third voyage to the Western Hemisphere. The Spanish made the first successful attempt to colonize Trinidad in 1592. Trinidad continued under Spanish rule until the British captured it in 1797. Enslaved Africans were brought to the islands during the eighteenth century to provide labor on the sugarcane plantations. Following the abolition of African enslavement, Indian and Chinese labor was imported.

Trinidad was ceded formally to the United Kingdom in 1802, with the island of Tobago following in 1814. In 1888, Trinidad and Tobago merged to form a single colony. In 1958, the United Kingdom established the autonomous Federation of the West Indies. Jamaica withdrew in 1961, and, when Trinidad and Tobago followed, the federation collapsed. Trinidad and Tobago obtained full independence and joined the Commonwealth in 1962.

Eric Williams became prime minister at independence and held that position until he died in 1981. George Chambers, who had served as his agriculture minister, succeeded Williams. Arthur Napoleon Robinson succeeded Chambers in 1996. During an abortive coup attempt in July 1990, a group of more than 100 Muslim militants held Robinson and other government officials hostage. In December of that year, Patrick Manning was elected prime

TRINIDAD AND TOBAGO

Official name: Republic of Trinidad and Tobago
Independence: 31 August 1962 (from United Kingdom)
Area: 5,128 sq km
Form of government: parliamentary republic
Capital: Port-of-Spain
Currency: Trinidad and Tobago dollar (TTD)
Income: US$20,338 (2008 est. of purchasing power parity)
Population: 1,299,953 (2009 est.)
Ethnic groups: Indian (South Asian) 40%, African 37.5%, mixed 20.5%, other 1.2%, unspecified 0.8% (2000 census)
Religious groups: Roman Catholic 26%, Hindu 22.5%, Anglican 7.8%, Baptist 7.2%, Pentecostal 6.8%, Muslim 5.8%, Seventh-day Adventist 4%, other Christian 5.8%, other 10.8%, unspecified 1.4%, none 1.9% (2000 census)
Languages: English (official), Hindi, French, Spanish, Chinese
Literacy: 98.6% (fifteen years old and over who can read and write; 2003 est.)
Exports: petroleum and petroleum products, chemicals, steel products, fertilizer, sugar, cocoa, coffee, citrus, flowers
Primary export partners: U.S. 44.5%, Spain 7.8%, Jamaica 6.9%, Netherlands 6.9%, Mexico 4.9% (2008)
Imports: machinery, transportation equipment, manufactured goods, food, live animals
Primary import partners: U.S. 26.8%, Brazil 9.8%, Venezuela 7.9%, Colombia 6.2%, China 4.1%, Gabon 4% (2008)

minister. Black-led since 1956, the two-island nation elected its first Asian Indian prime minister, Basdeo Panday, in 1996. After the ruling United National Congress party lost its majority in the House of Representatives, tying with the opposition People's National Movement (PNM) in the number of seats won (twelve each), a period of political uncertainty followed. The two parties agreed to let President Robinson settle the matter. Robinson tapped PNM leader Patrick Manning to replace Basdeo Panday as prime minister.

A major center of African culture in the Caribbean, Trinidad and Tobago gave birth to calypso and steelpan, as the music of the steel drum is known locally. The country's annual Carnival festival is but one of the nation's many celebrations of music and dance. Leading contemporary Afro-Trinidadians include calypso singer Mighty Sparrow, visual artist/novelist Valerie Belgrave, and literary figures Rafael de Boissiere, Dionne Brand, Merle Hodge, and Earl Lovelace.

URUGUAY

The first Africans arrived in what is now Uruguay as early as 1534 in the company of Spanish explorers. These enslaved

URUGUAY

Official name: Oriental Republic of Uruguay
Independence: 25 August 1825 (from Brazil)
Area: 176,220 sq km
Form of government: constitutional republic
Capital: Montevideo
Currency: Uruguayan peso (UYU)
Income: US$12,784 (2008 est. of purchasing power parity)
Population: 3,494,382 (2009 est.)
Ethnic groups: white 88%, mestizo 8%, black 4%, Amerindian
Religious groups: Roman Catholic 47.1%, non-Catholic Christians 11.1%, nondenominational 23.2%, Jewish 0.3%, atheist or agnostic 17.2%, other 1.1% (2006)
Languages: Spanish, also Portuñol or Brazilero (Portuguese-Spanish mix on the Brazilian frontier)
Literacy: 98% (fifteen years old and over who can read and write; 2003 est.)
Exports: meat, rice, leather products, vehicles, dairy products, wool, electricity
Primary export partners: Brazil 18.7%, China 8.5%, Argentina 7.3%, Germany 6.5%, Mexico 4.9%, Netherlands 4.5%, Russia 4.3% (2008)
Imports: road vehicles, electrical machinery, metal manufactures, heavy industrial machinery, crude petroleum
Primary import partners: Argentina 19.9%, Brazil 16.5%, China 11.2%, U.S. 9.9%, Paraguay 6.6%, Nigeria 4.6% (2008)

men, most of whom were Ladinos, as Christianized Africans were known in Spain, joined their masters in the exploration of the Rio de la Plata. By the end of the sixteenth century, Spain was importing increasingly larger numbers of enslaved Africans from Angola in southwestern Africa. Most of those destined for labor in the New World were shipped to either Mexico or Cartagena, in what is now Colombia, for transshipment to other Spanish colonies throughout the region. The lengthy voyage of the ships from Angola to both Mexico and Cartagena took a tremendous toll on the enslaved Africans, and many died before reaching their destination. The Spanish began shipping some of their enslaved Africans to Buenos Aires on the Rio de la Plata in the southeast of South America. By the end of the seventeenth century, the Spanish discovered that Montevideo, also on the Rio de la Plata but 120 miles closer to the Atlantic, had a fine natural harbor. A settlement was begun there in 1724 and before long much of the slave trade in the region had moved from Buenos Aires to Montevideo, the future capital of Uruguay.

Although the numbers of enslaved Africans imported through Montevideo were impressively high, many of these slaves did not remain in Uruguay, but were shipped into other territories in the region where the demand for captive labor was strong. Within what is now Uruguay, there were little in the way of major mining or agricultural enterprises, and most Africans who remained there toiled as domestic servants. The bulk of the enslaved in Uruguay worked in the capital of Montevideo. Although freed in the 1840s, many continued to labor for their former enslavers under conditions not far removed from forced bondage. In 2010, about 4% of Uruguay's total population is of African descent. Most of these Afro-Uruguayans live in Montevideo.

VENEZUELA

Official name: Bolivarian Republic of Venezuela
Independence: 5 July 1811 (from Spain)
Area: 912,050 sq km
Form of government: federal republic
Capital: Caracas
Currency: bolivar (VEB)
Income: US$12,806 (2008 est. of purchasing power parity)
Population: 26,814,843 (2009 est.)
Ethnic groups: Spanish, Italian, Portuguese, Arab, German, African, indigenous people
Religious groups: nominally Roman Catholic 92%, Protestant, other, none 8%
Languages: Spanish (official), numerous indigenous dialects
Literacy: 95% (fifteen years old and over who can read and write; 2006 est.)
Exports: petroleum, bauxite and aluminum, steel, chemicals, agricultural products, basic manufactures
Primary export partners: U.S. 40.7%, Netherlands Antilles 7.8%, China 4.7% (2008)
Imports: raw materials, machinery and equipment, transport equipment, construction materials
Primary import partners: U.S. 26.3%, Colombia 12.7%, Brazil 10.3%, China 7%, Mexico 4.8% (2008)

VENEZUELA

In the sixteenth and seventeenth centuries, Caracas was a major center for the importation of enslaved Africans. In the early nineteenth century, blacks and mulattos composed more than half of the population of the Captaincy General of Caracas, as Venezuela was known at that time. In the latter stages of Venezuela's fight for independence from Spain, political and military leader Simón Bolivar made extensive use of blacks, mulattos, and zambos, admitting them to the ranks of his rebel army. These blacks played a critical role in the defeat of colonists loyal to Spain. By 1821, Venezuela had been largely wrested from Spain's control.

As early as 1819, Bolivar had called for the abolition of African enslavement, but he was overruled by a coalition of rebel leaders. Despite further attempts to loosen the bonds of forced servitude, the institution remained in force until it was abolished in Venezuela in 1854.

Today, possibly 20% of Venezuela's 27 million people are black or of mixed African and Indian descent. Blacks remain a significant element of the country's population, choosing to stay because of Venezuela's proximity to the Caribbean and employment opportunities that have been available in this oil-rich nation.

For about four decades, from 1958 until the mid-1990s, political power in Venezuela alternated between two political parties, Accion Democratica and the Comite de Organizacion Politica Electoral Independiente. Chronic economic weakness and recurrent scandals over government corruption helped to reduce support for both parties, particularly during the late 1980s and early 1990s. In 1998, Hugo Chavez of the Movimiento Quinta Republica was elected president on a platform pledged to radical political reform. The country's 1961 constitution was replaced with a left-leaning charter in a December 1999 referendum. In July 2000, Chavez was reelected with a comfortable majority. An unsuccessful coup was mounted against Chavez in April 2002. Of Afro-Latino heritage, President Chavez has openly embraced his African ancestry. He was especially critical of the policies of U.S. President George W. Bush. Since the 2008 election of Bush's successor, Barack Obama, President Chavez has signaled his interest in improving relations with the United States.

VIRGIN ISLANDS, BRITISH

Initially visited by Christopher Columbus in 1493, the Virgin Islands (an archipelago of seventy-four islands) is now divided into two distinct clusters—British Virgin Islands (six main islands, nearly forty islets) and the U.S. Virgin Islands (three main islands, sixty-five islets). Great Britain obtained title to the islands and islets in 1666 and, until 1960, administered them as part of the Leeward Islands. At present, a Crown-appointed administrator who is assisted by both executive and legislative councils heads the government.

During the latter half of the seventeenth century, British settlers discovered that the islands would support the cultivation of both cotton and sugar. However, to work the fields it was necessary to import forced labor from Africa. Life for the enslaved Africans in the British islands was particularly harsh, with inhumane penalties exacted for relatively minor infractions of the rules. A captive who refused his master's orders could have part of his body cut off or his nose split. In 1790, enslaved Africans in Tortola revolted after rumors spread that Britain had abolished slavery but local owners were withholding freedom. Although Britain abolished the trade in 1807, full emancipation did not come for Virgin Island Africans until 1834. A four-year apprenticeship program replaced enslavement, so that all enslaved Africans were initially required to remain in the custody of their former masters.

Today, almost the entire population of the British Virgin Islands is of African descent.

BRITISH VIRGIN ISLANDS

Official name: British Virgin Islands
Area: 150 sq km
Form of government: overseas territory of the United Kingdom
Capital: Road Town
Currency: U.S. dollar
Income: US$38,500 (2004 est. of purchasing power parity)
Population: 24,491 (2009 est.)
Ethnic groups: black 83.4%, white 7%, other (including Indian and mixed) 9.6% (2004 Census)
Religious groups: Protestant 86% (Methodist 33%, Anglican 17%, Church of God 9%, Seventh-Day Adventist 6%, Baptist 4%, Jehovah's Witnesses 2%, other 15%), Roman Catholic 10%, other 2%, none 2% (1991)
Languages: English (official)
Literacy: 97.8% (fifteen years old and over who can read and write; 1991 est.)
Exports: rum, fresh fish, fruits, animals, gravel, sand
Primary export partners: U.S. Virgin Islands, Puerto Rico, United States
Imports: building materials, automobiles, foodstuffs, machinery
Primary import partners: U.S. Virgin Islands, Puerto Rico, United States

VIRGIN ISLANDS, UNITED STATES

The Danish West India Company originally settled the U.S. Virgin Islands—the largest of which are the islands of Saint Croix, Saint John, and Saint Thomas. Saint

U.S. VIRGIN ISLANDS

Official name: United States Virgin Islands
Area: 352 sq km
Form of government: territory of the United States
Capital: Charlotte Amalie
Currency: U.S. dollar
Income: US$14,500 (2004 est. of purchasing power parity)
Population: 109,825 (2009 est.)
Ethnic groups: black 76.2%, white 13.1%, Asian 1.1%, other 6.1%, mixed 3.5% (2000 census)
Religious groups: Baptist 42%, Roman Catholic 34%, Episcopalian 17%, other 7%
Languages: English (official), Spanish, Creole
Literacy: 90-95% (2005 est.)
Exports: refined petroleum products
Primary export partners: United States, Puerto Rico
Imports: crude oil, foodstuffs, consumer goods, building materials
Primary import partners: United States, Puerto Rico

Thomas was the first to be colonized in 1672; in 1683, Saint John was colonized; and, by 1733, Saint Croix had been acquired from France. Twenty years later, the holdings of the company were taken over by the Danish Crown, which then reconstituted them as the Danish West Indies.

As in the neighboring British Virgin Islands, the Danish West Indies was found to be ideally suited for the cultivation of sugarcane and cotton. The first shipment of enslaved Africans, numbering 103, arrived in Saint Thomas in 1673. The island had some 160 plantations and more than 3,000 Africans by 1715, little more than four decades later. The island of Saint John witnessed a major uprising among the enslaved population in 1733. The life of enslaved Africans in the islands was harsh, but in the months preceding the Saint John revolt, their situation had been made even more difficult when the island was hit by a drought and two hurricanes. The actual revolt was set off by the passage in September 1733 of a set of harsh new regulations. Rebellion leaders captured the island's only fort and managed to hold it for six months. The Africans in the Danish islands finally won their freedom in 1848.

The United States bought the Virgin Islands territory from Denmark in 1917 for about $25 million and granted citizenship to its inhabitants ten years later. In 1931, administration of the U.S. Virgin Islands was transferred from the United States Navy to the Department of the Interior. The first black governor of the territory, William H. Hastie, was appointed in 1946. Melvin Evans was appointed governor in 1969, and two years later became the first black governor to be elected.

6

AFRICANS IN AMERICA: 1600–1900

Debra Newman Ham

THE PECULIAR INSTITUTION: AFRICAN ENSLAVEMENT IN AMERICA, 1619–1865

It is generally accepted that there was an African presence in the New World prior to the voyages of contact made by Christopher Columbus in the late fifteenth century. Historical accounts affirm that Africans sailed with the Europeans as they explored and began to conquer the peoples of the Americas in the late fifteenth and sixteenth centuries. Perhaps the most famous of the African explorers was Stephen Dorantes, known as Estevanico, who pioneered an expedition in 1539 from Mexico into what is now Arizona and New Mexico. Estevanico, a Muslim from Morocco, had also traveled with Álvar Núñez Cabeza de Vaca to Florida in 1528. The establishment of settlements that made use of enslaved African laborers in the Caribbean and Latin America predated North American communities by almost a century.

The resiliency of the people kidnapped from the African continent by Europeans is obvious even from the earliest historical documents. Ship logs and trading records from the sixteenth to the mid-nineteenth centuries show people of color not only as victims of a cruel system of enslavement and oppression, but also as actors who found effective ways to cope with the confines of human bondage. Even on board the vessels of their captivity, some of the millions of captured Africans mutinied against the European crews and took command of the ships that held them. Others unsuccessfully tried to regain their freedom by jumping ship or fighting their captors.

Unfortunately, the superior technology of the European enslavers, both in weaponry and transportation, subdued the African captives as effectively as it did the Native Americans in the New World. An eyewitness and victim of the trade, Olaudah Equiano, wrote in his 1789 autobiography that, when he was captured and sold at age eleven, some African men actually jumped off the ship on which they were captives to try to swim to shore, but members of the ship's crew jumped overboard to recapture and secure the captives for fear of losing their valuable cargo. The attempts of captive Africans to rebel or jump ship became so frequent that, during the centuries of the slave trade, many captains would not allow the Africans on deck even for exercise.

The slave-trading vessels had low decks, which allowed the chained captives to sit up but not stand. Some of the larger ships carried between five hundred and nine hundred Africans of all ages and both sexes. In 1862, President Abraham Lincoln had a notorious slave trader, Nathan Gordon, hanged because he was caught near the Congo River with a vessel holding 897 Africans. As a result of the cramped conditions, filth, and disease, many Africans lost their lives as they crossed the Atlantic. Many of the European crewmen also succumbed to disease.

The Atlantic Ocean route between Africa and the Americas was often referred to as the *Middle Passage* because it formed the middle leg of the triangular route from Europe, to the African continent, to the Americas, and back. And the "peculiar institution," also known as "slavery" in the Americas, became a reality. Scholars estimate that the number of Africans victimized by the trade ranges between nine million and twenty-five million. The trade in Africans continued for centuries because those who survived were usually strong and familiar with all aspects of tropical agriculture. They proved to be invaluable workers, and for some reason, Africans did not succumb to European diseases at the same rate as the indigenous population did. The trade in humans and the labor of African captives in the New World netted untold riches to their European and American captors for many generations.

BRITISH AMERICA

The first twenty Africans to arrive in British America were sold by a Dutch captain as indentured servants—people who served the one who purchased their passage for an agreed term, usually four to seven years—in Jamestown, Virginia, in 1619. The settlement, founded in 1607, was only twelve years old when the Africans came. Within a few decades, however, most of the Atlantic seaboard colonies were teeming with imported Africans forced to work as laborers. As the Atlantic coastal settlements increased in number and population in North America in the seventeenth century, European ships with Africans for sale appeared regularly. Planters who were looking for a cheap labor force proved ready customers. Africans were in great demand by the colonists, and British merchants continued to bring them in large numbers. Between 1675 and 1695, about three thousand Africans entered the Chesapeake region to be put to work, mostly on the tobacco plantations of Maryland and Virginia.

During the seventeenth century, soon after each colony was settled, ships carrying Africans as forced laborers would appear. Planters used Africans to plant and harvest their tobacco, rice, sugar, indigo, and wheat. Africans also constructed buildings, roads, and forts, and performed many household tasks. Africans were used in so many capacities in turning the American terrain into cities and plantations that the European settlers who could afford to do so continued to purchase and enslave them in large numbers. Most colonial historians acknowledge the vital role played by enslaved Africans in the planting of settlements in British America.

Geographically, the Africans came to the British colonies principally from various West African territories. They represented ethnic groups stretching from the region of the Gambia River and reaching around the coast to present-day Nigeria. Men and women, with complexions that ranged from brown to black, brought with them to America numerous languages and customs, including their own African religious beliefs. Occasionally, Muslims were among them, and sometimes Africans came from regions as far away as Madagascar.

Plantation owners often commented on the scarification—slave owners called them "country markings"—that the Africans had on their bodies. These markings appeared on their faces, arms, or torsos, and had a variety of distinctive designs. The markings sometimes indicated ethnic identity, but they also functioned as body ornamentation. African music, drums, and singing frightened whites, who soon outlawed many African practices—especially drumming. Africans wore little clothing when they came from the ships, sometimes only strings of beads. Many had filed teeth. Some had hair plaited in elaborate styles, while others had shaven heads. After a time, Africanized English became the language that the Africans and their owners all understood. The Africans received new names, and learned their work and the stringent boundaries within which they could operate.

By the eighteenth century, the American colonies were beginning to see a new generation of Africans who were born in America and did not know their parents' African homelands firsthand. Beginning in the 1700s, the enslaved population began to grow naturally and was consequently composed of both Africans and African Americans. In a few generations, Africa became a distant and often misunderstood land to most African Americans. The Constitution of the United States outlawed the African slave trade on January 1, 1808, but the law was generally ignored. Although African-born captives continued to arrive in the United States in smaller numbers until the Civil War (1861–1865), the American-born population dominated the cultural life of the enslaved.

With the invention of the cotton gin at the turn of the nineteenth century, cotton production began to climb and the value of enslaved people of color multiplied exponentially. Cotton production intersected with the growth of the textile industry in both Great Britain and the New England states, leading to revolutionary production rates. By the time the Civil War started, most slaveholders in the South had only a few black captives, but on large plantations, hundreds of enslaved Africans were producing more cotton than anywhere else in the world. As their "human" property became increasingly valuable, enslavers were more strongly determined to protect their right to hold their "property" in bondage.

In 1790, African Americans made up about one-fifth of the nation's population. By 1860 there were four and a half million people of color—enslaved and free—living in the United States. Although the new government of the United States was ambivalent about the rights of free people of color and unanimous in the denial of rights to this unique segment of the society, the Constitution of 1787 allowed southern states to count three-fifths of the enslaved population when determining how many legislators each state could send to the U.S. House of Representatives.

Early accounts provide glimpses of the lives of some captive Africans. Ayuba Suleiman Diallo was a well-educated Muslim merchant who was born about 1700 in an area

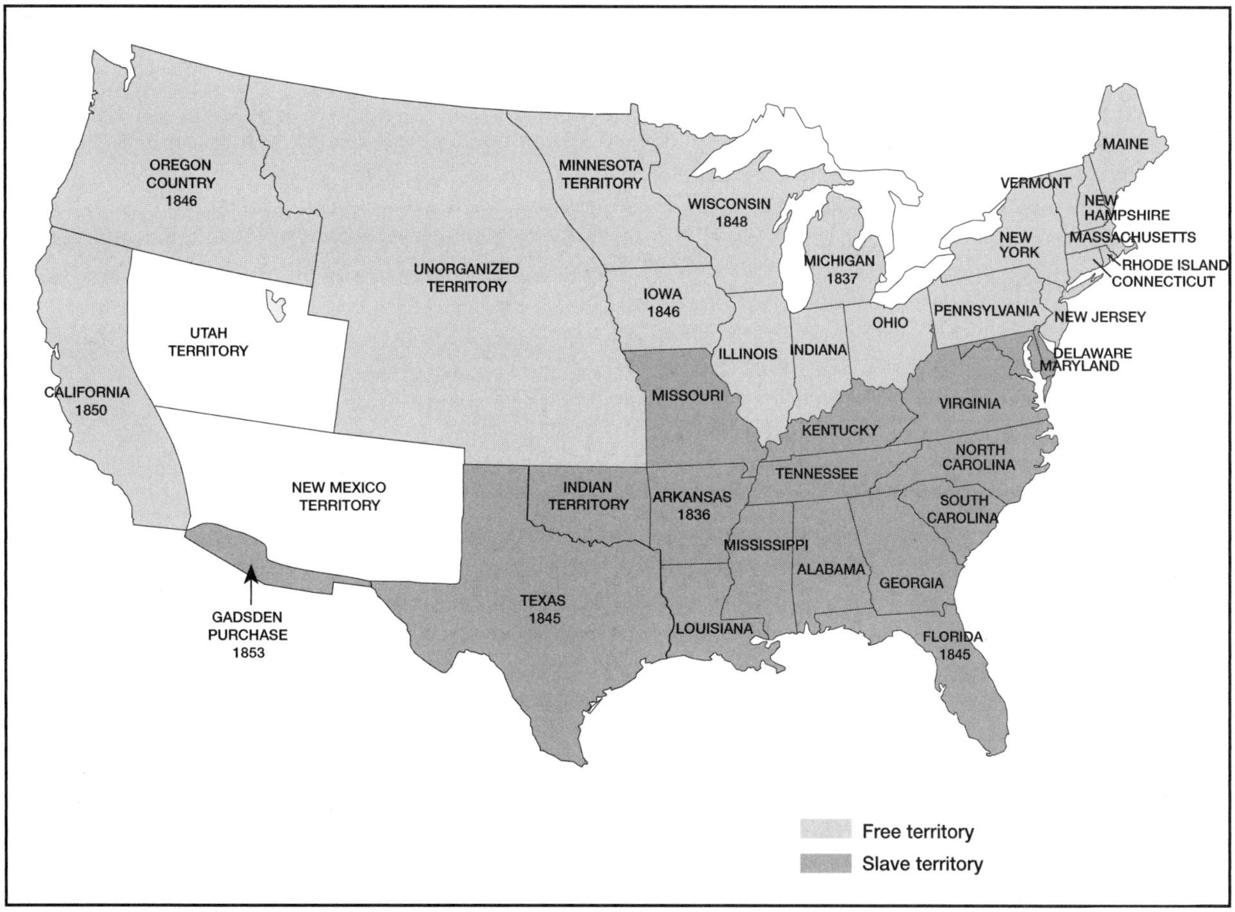

Map of the United States, Pre–Civil War. *Free territory, slave territory, and unorganized territory are shown, with the latter being free; Utah and New Mexico territories are unclaimed. Dates shown are the years states joined the Union, with the exception of the Gadsden Purchase and Oregon Country (the latter being the date when Oregon's northern boundary was settled).* GALE

located in what is now Mali. He was captured and enslaved after he traded two other Africans to a British merchant. He was taken to Annapolis, Maryland, where he was sold. He worked on a tobacco plantation for two years before being rescued and taken to England. Eventually, he was allowed to return to his home.

Charles Ball, who was enslaved and sold into the cotton kingdom from the state of Maryland, said in his 1859 autobiography that after the sale of his mother, his master also decided to sell his father to a southern enslaver. Ball claimed that his grandfather, a continental African who originally came to Charles County in 1730, secretly went to his son's cabin, gave him some cider and parched corn, prayed "to the god of his native country" to protect his son, and told him to run away. Ball never saw his father again.

In *Tobacco and Slaves* (1986), Allan Kulikoff used the records of several Chesapeake-area plantations to show the gradual changes that occurred in the growth of the enslaved population. On the Edmond Jennings plantation in Virginia in 1712, almost all the workers were Africans. By 1730, nine out of ten black men and almost all of the black women working on the Virginia plantation of Robert Carter were born in Africa. However, thereafter, the enslaved population began to grow naturally and was composed of both Africans and African Americans. In a few generations, Africa was a land most people of color in America had never seen. Presidents George Washington and Thomas Jefferson often instructed the overseers of their plantations not to drive the enslaved women so hard that they would miscarry or be unable to bear children. Every African American meant more wealth and an increased workforce for their owners.

The work of enslaved Africans varied by region. In the North, they generally worked as household servants, as laborers on small farms or in mines, or as craftspersons of various sorts, such as seamstresses, caulkers, coopers, smiths, and cooks. In the South, owners used enslaved individuals in a wide variety of roles for the maintenance of small farms and large plantations. Many of the records of the founding fathers of the United States clearly show their involvement with enslaved Africans and the trade that brought them to the country, particularly their dependence on that forced labor to make large landholdings maximally productive. Edwin Morris Betts, editor of *Thomas Jefferson's Farm Book* (1953), stated that Jefferson was never able to eliminate his enslaved Africans from his economy, "because to have done so would have destroyed the chief support of all of the activities of his plantation." The papers of both Jefferson—who was brilliant, but not frugal—and President James Monroe demonstrate that they often needed to sell or hire out captive blacks to meet their financial obligations.

Whether one looks at Virginia plantations such as Westover, Mount Vernon, or Monticello, or large estates in any other state in the South, it was largely African Americans who were responsible for the construction of the lovely plantation houses with their sturdy outbuildings, well-manicured gardens, and productive fields. In many areas of the North and South, people of color aided in the defense of their communities during Indian wars, unless they had escaped to Native American groups, in which case they fought against the settlers. The Papers of the Continental Congress included numerous letters about the Seminoles in Georgia and Florida who aided and abetted African runaways.

Although the vast majority of African Americans—male and female—did labor in the fields, W. E. B. Du Bois opined in *The Negro Artisan* (1902) that a small percentage of both enslaved and free blacks in the South also worked as artisans who toiled in tobacco factories, made barrels, ran steamboats, labored as masons, and specialized in many other areas. Colonial newspapers included many listings for the sale of bondspersons in which the skills of the enslaved persons are described. Although most who were trained as artisans utilized their skills on their owners' plantations, it was not uncommon for enslaved artisans to be hired out to other plantations. Men performed various services, such as blacksmithing, carpentry, hostelry, and coopering. Women were sometimes hired out as maids, cooks, hairdressers, milliners, and seamstresses.

Those who hired the bondsmen and bondswomen gave their owners payment for the slaves' service, but the artisan usually also received a small sum. Many industrious Africans scrupulously saved the small amount they received until they had earned enough to purchase their freedom at an amount stipulated by their owner. With any additional funds, they subsequently purchased their spouses and children. Sometimes, because the children followed the legal status of the mother, men would purchase their wives first, and then themselves and their enslaved children.

Slaves had no rights, a truth that U.S. Supreme Court Chief Justice Roger B. Taney—himself a Maryland enslaver—reinforced when he stated in the 1857 *Dred Scott* decision that blacks had no rights that whites were bound to respect. Therefore, an owner did not have to give enslaved laborers a percentage of their hired wages, although many did. Some owners bought enslaved laborers for the purpose of hiring them out. Bondspersons could not vote, testify against whites, bear arms, or claim any of the benefits of a U.S. citizen. However, some states, like Louisiana and South Carolina, afforded some privileges to those of mixed African and European ancestry, although they were not themselves allowed to enslave blacks.

The so-called slave narratives, gathered in the 1930s by the U.S. government's Works Progress Administration, document the experience of those held in bondage and how they coped with being treated as chattel, or human property. These records document how eagerly people of color embraced first the hope and then the reality of freedom.

By the end of the Revolutionary War, most northern states had provided for the emancipation of Africans within their boundaries. The few northern states that did not accomplish this by the end of the Revolution did so within a few decades afterward. So, as the number of enslaved Africans was diminishing in the North, by the time of the Civil War, more than half of the population of Virginia was made up of African Americans, the vast majority of whom were held in bondage. In South Carolina, that segment of the population was more than 400,000, while the white population was fewer than 300,000. The 1860 census indicates that the total number of African Americans in the United States was 4,441,830, of whom nearly four million were enslaved; there were 26,922,537 whites.

RESISTANCE TO AFRICAN ENSLAVEMENT

There were several well-documented so-called slave rebellions and mutinies that dispel the view that the enslaved Africans were docile or content with their fate. Fear of such revolts was common in the British American colonies from the earliest days of settlement. A perusal of any colonial newspaper indicates that runaways, acts of resistance, and fear of rebellions and insurrections were widespread. Especially after the successful rebellion of Afro-Haitians over the French colonials at the turn of the nineteenth century, white plantation owners experienced a widespread dread of reprisals from their enslaved Africans. A collection of reports about slave revolts dating

Map Showing Eighteenth-Century Revolts of Enslaved Africans, along with Maroon Communities, in the Americas. MAP BY XNR PRODUCTIONS, INC. REPRODUCED BY PERMISSION OF GALE, A PART OF CENGAGE LEARNING.

to the eighteenth century, titled *An Account of Some of the Principal Slave Insurrections,* by Joshua Coffin of the American Anti-Slavery Society, was published in 1860. It reports, for example, that in the spring of 1741, a series of fires broke out in Manhattan. Many believed that these fires were the work of rebellious Africans, and hysteria in the city led to the arrest of numerous enslaved persons. Between May 11 and August 29 of 1741, thirty black men and four whites were executed. About one hundred more black men were arrested and seventy-two were banished from the colony.

As the amount of cultivated land increased in acreage, the size of the black enslaved population grew to equal or exceed that of whites in some southern states. Enslavers realized that a unified revolt by those held in bondage could signal doom for their way of life. Fears increased in 1829 when a free black man in Boston, David Walker, published a pamphlet titled (in part) *Walker's Appeal, in*

Four Articles; Together with a Preamble to the Coloured Citizens of the World. The pamphlet called for blacks to rise up and overthrow their oppressors. Walker argued, "Look upon your mother, wife, children, and answer God Almighty; and believe this, that it is no more harm for you to kill a man, who is trying to kill you, than it is for you to take a drink of water when thirsty." The pamphlet caused much alarm in the South and was outlawed in various states. Walker subsequently had a price put on his head at the encouragement of several southern plantation owners. He died under mysterious circumstances shortly after the release of his *Appeal.* In 1830, the American Colonization Society's publication, *The African Repository,* reported that four free black men in New Orleans were arrested for circulating "the diabolical Boston pamphlet." The governor of Virginia, John Floyd, cited Walker's pamphlet as one of the causes of a major revolt in 1831.

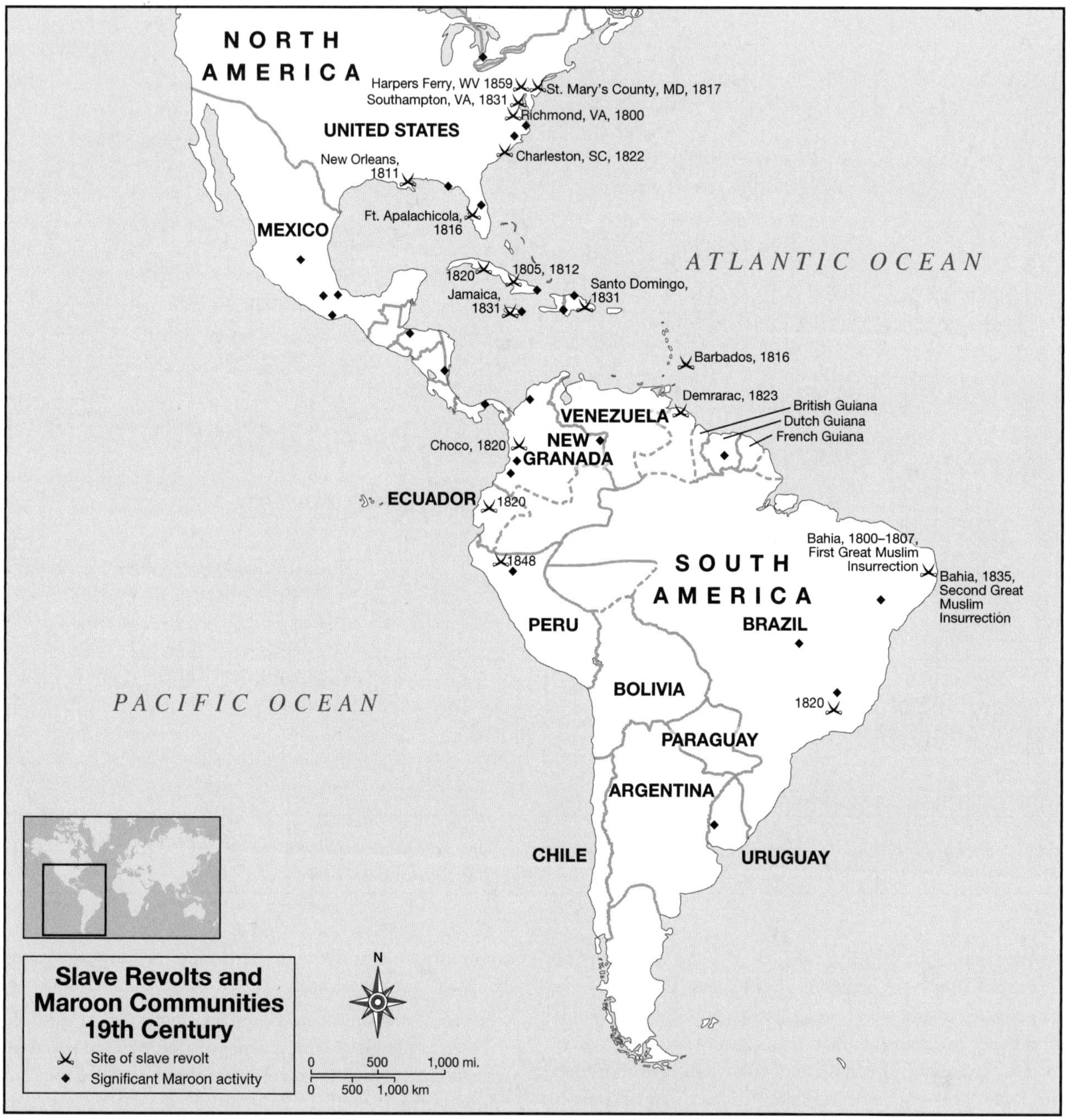

Map Showing Nineteenth-Century Revolts of Enslaved Africans, along with Maroon Communities, in the Americas. MAP BY XNR PRODUCTIONS, INC. REPRODUCED BY PERMISSION OF GALE, A PART OF CENGAGE LEARNING.

Small-scale slave revolts and plots were relatively common. Occasionally, however, revolts reached alarming proportions. This was particularly true with the Nat Turner insurrection in Southampton, Virginia, in 1831. Turner, who felt that God revealed to him the method of liberating his enslaved brethren, told only a few trusted companions about his plan because he understood that rebellions often failed because someone informed the authorities. Turner's strategy was to go to one household at a time, kill all the whites, free those enslaved there, and thereby add to the number of those who were in his rebel brigade. Before Turner and his followers were stopped, about sixty whites had lost their lives. The terrified Virginia government hanged Turner, but not before he dictated his confessions, which were subsequently published. Those who attended his trial later reported that Turner was poised, well spoken, and calm—like, they said, the devil incarnate—yet he was committed to his liberation movement.

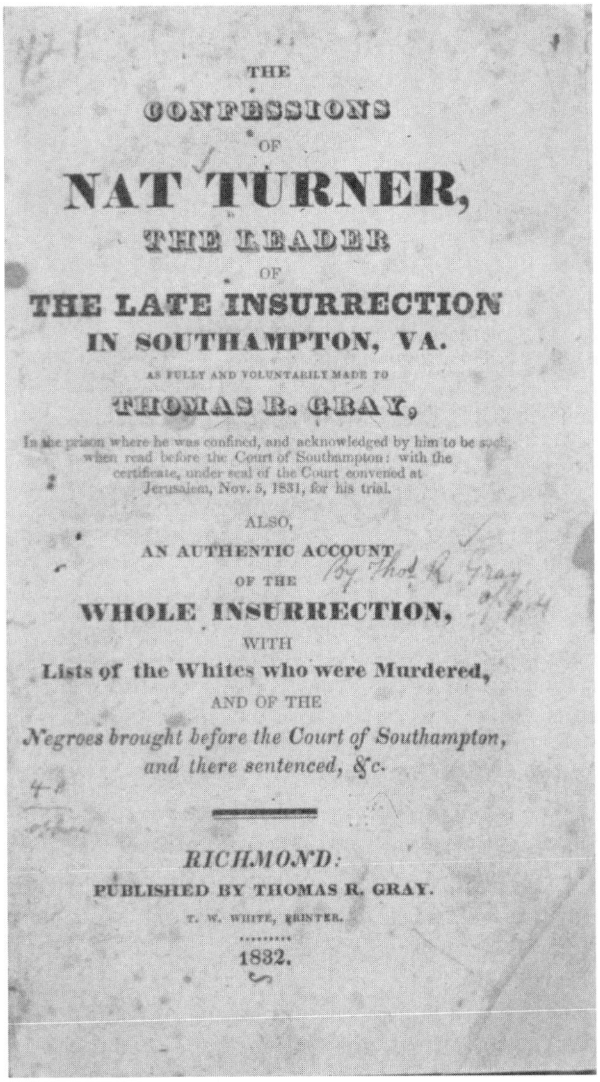
THE
CONFESSIONS
OF
NAT TURNER,
THE LEADER
OF
THE LATE INSURRECTION
IN SOUTHAMPTON, VA.
AS FULLY AND VOLUNTARILY MADE TO
THOMAS R. GRAY,
In the prison where he was confined, and acknowledged by him to be such, when read before the Court of Southampton: with the certificate, under seal of the Court convened at Jerusalem, Nov. 5, 1831, for his trial.
ALSO,
AN AUTHENTIC ACCOUNT
OF THE
WHOLE INSURRECTION,
WITH
Lists of the Whites who were Murdered,
AND OF THE
Negroes brought before the Court of Southampton, and there sentenced, &c.

RICHMOND:
PUBLISHED BY THOMAS R. GRAY.
T. W. WHITE, PRINTER.
1832.

Title Page of* The Confessions of Nat Turner *(1832).
Turner's Confessions *describes the slave rebellion that he led in Southampton, Virginia, in 1831. His insurrection was suppressed within two days, but not before about sixty whites had been killed. The Virginia state government subsequently executed Turner and dozens of other blacks accused of participating in the rebellion.*
THE LIBRARY OF CONGRESS

Many analyzed the reasons for the uprising and formulated methods that could be used to prevent similar bloody occurrences. Every state in the South that had not already done so passed laws forbidding anyone to teach African Americans to read and write. Hiram Revels, a free black North Carolinian who became a U.S. senator after the Civil War, wrote in a biographical sketch that, before the Turner insurrection, free people of color in North Carolina were allowed to vote, discuss political questions, have religious meetings, and pursue their education. After the revolt, however, the North Carolina legislature passed laws depriving free blacks of all political, religious, and educational rights and privileges.

Freedom movements, such as that staged by Turner, were curtailed all over the South. Free black people had to carry passes and could be interrogated by any white person. The manumission (emancipation) of enslaved Africans became illegal in many states, and blacks who were already free found it even more difficult to live in peace in certain regions of the country. It was from this period that all southern states forbade teaching enslaved persons to read and write.

The most famous mutiny of captured continental Africans occurred on board the Spanish vessel *Amistad*. After a group of continental Africans was sold in the Caribbean in 1839, they were loaded on a ship bound for a plantation. The captive Africans succeeded in murdering all but a few of the white crewmembers. Those remaining were ordered to steer the ship back to the African continent. About fifty Africans led by a Mende warrior named Cinque forced the crew to comply during the day, but at night the crew sailed the ship to the northwest, eventually landing off the coast of New York, where local authorities captured the ship and its occupants. The case caused great controversy, and several important and volatile issues presented themselves. Among the issues contested in court were: Should the U.S. government collaborate in the "slave" trade by returning the Africans to the owners of the vessel? Should the government hold the Africans and thereby become their enslaver? Should it sell the Africans and consequently become the equivalent of a slave merchant? Or, the most controversial alternative of all, should the United States free them and thereby become their emancipator?

Amistad, *Film, 1997.* *Starring Djimon Hounsou (*right*), the film was based on an actual revolt that took place on the slave ship* Amistad *in 1839 and the court case that followed.* ARCHIVES DU 7EME ART/PHOTOS 12/ALAMY

Southerners and northerners had debated the issue of slavery at great length during the Constitutional Convention in 1787. The case remained explosive during ensuing years in Congress as the controversy over human property led to passionate arguments on both sides of the issue. As new states joined the union, proslavery and antislavery advocates worked hard to keep the number of so-called slave states and free states equal. The *Amistad* case, which eventually made its way to the U.S. Supreme Court, added fuel to the controversy. John Quincy Adams, who had served as the sixth president of the United States, was then a member of the House of Representatives, where he tirelessly affirmed the rights of abolitionists to air their cause. Because of this, he was asked to defend the *Amistad* Africans. Adams presented a series of arguments so compelling that the High Court freed the Africans, and missionaries and well-wishers helped those who had survived the litigation process return to West Africa.

FUGITIVE AFRICANS

Although enslaved African Americans resisted their captivity in many ways, the most common method was to run away. Sometimes fugitives fled into areas unsettled by Europeans; other times they were able to ally with Native Americans. Occasionally, blacks were able to form communities of runaways, known as Maroons, in swamps or backwoods areas. Many blacks ran away during the Revolutionary War. Others fled to the British troops—during both the Revolution and the War of 1812—who hid them from their owners and took many blacks with them as they moved to their next battle or troop evacuation.

Pennsylvania began to abolish African enslavement through its Gradual Abolition Act in 1780. As a result, enslaved people in the upper South who lived close to Pennsylvania attempted escapes to areas where they could hide among the free black population. White and black abolitionists helped many enslaved people through the Underground Railroad, which was, in truth, neither underground nor a railroad. It was rather a network of secret travel routes and hiding places established for the purpose of guiding runaways from states where African enslavement was legal to the northern states or to Canada. Hundreds of runaways who were smuggled to the North attempted to blend into the large free black communities in New York, Baltimore, Washington, D.C., Philadelphia, and other cities.

Plantation owners invested a great deal of their resources to buy enslaved people and to serve their needs. They depended on this forced labor for their livelihood. For this reason, owners were very concerned when their human "property" ran away. There is little specific information about the number of runaways during the two and a half centuries of African enslavement. One census statistic shows that the number of runaways in Maryland for the year running from June 1849 to June 1850 was 279. In her book *Slavery and Freedom on the Middle Ground* (1985), Barbara Fields stated that this was probably a low figure because fugitives would, of course, be unwilling to admit their status to a census taker. Even using a low estimate of 300 runaways a year for 250 years meant that possibly 75,000 escaped from enslavement in Maryland. Underground Railroad conductor Harriet Tubman claimed to have led more than 300 Africans held in bondage out of Maryland. There

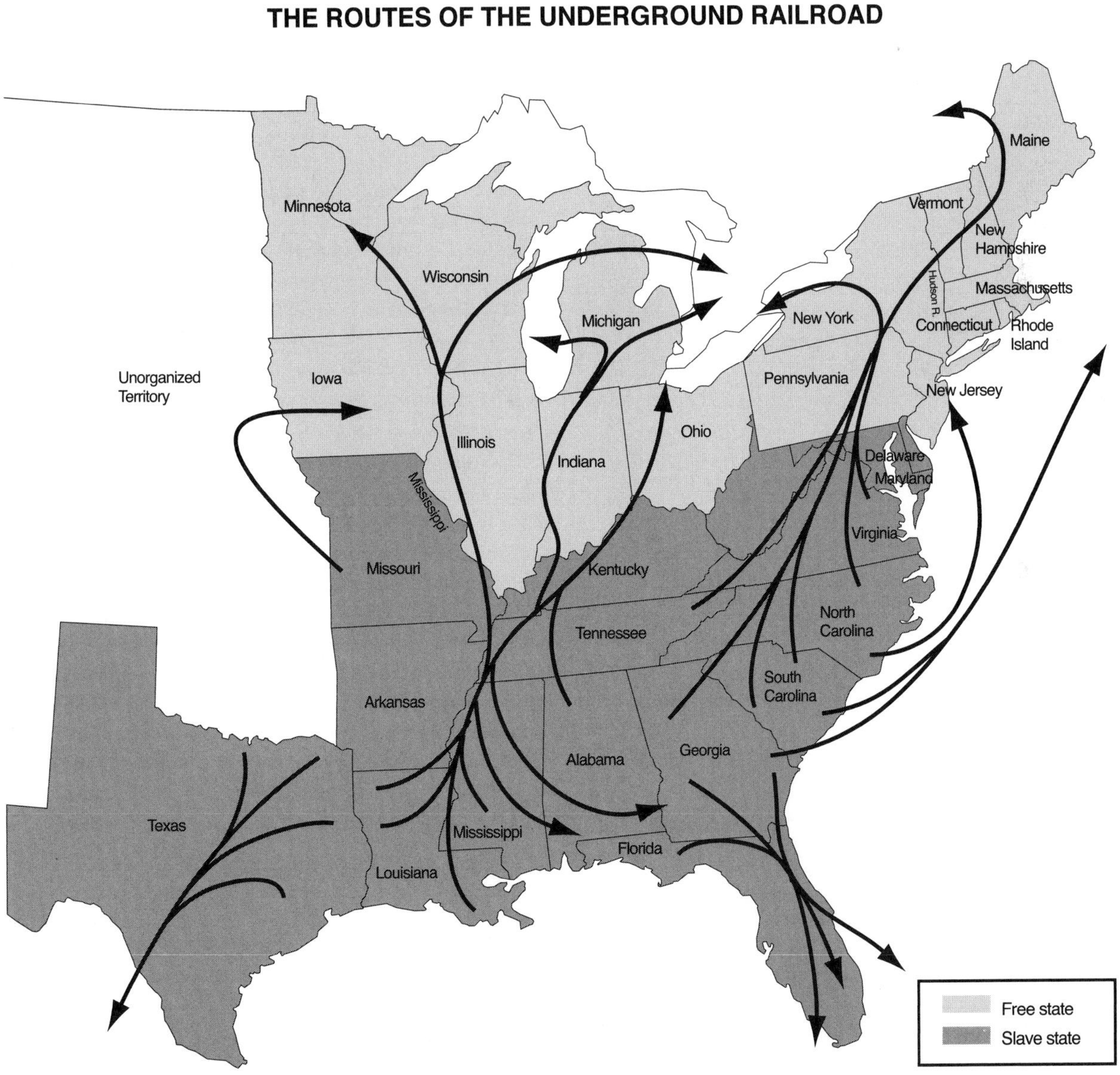

The Routes of the Underground Railroad. *White and black abolitionists helped many enslaved people through the Underground Railroad, guiding runaways from the slaveholding states to the northern states, Canada, Mexico, and the Caribbean. In the North, hundreds of runaways attempted to blend into the large free black communities in such cities as New York, Baltimore, Philadelphia, and Washington, D.C.* GALE

were thousands of runaways living in northern cities and in Canada.

Pre–Civil War newspapers listed hundreds of advertisements, which usually gave detailed descriptions of the runaways, including clothing and physical markings or defects such as scars. In case the runaways attempted to pass as free persons in order to find work, the owners listed the fugitives' skills, such as fiddling, cooking, sewing, or blacksmithing. Most of the runaways were men who traveled alone, but there were also women and families who fled to freedom. Many runaways, including Frederick Douglass, moved farther north than Pennsylvania. In 1850, when the U.S. Congress passed the Fugitive Slave Law, making the penalties more severe for those who aided runaways, many fugitives living in northern cities moved to Canada as a safe haven. In *Black Abolitionists* (1970), Benjamin Quarles stated that more than ten thousand fugitives fled into Canada in 1850 because of the new law. Yet, the exodus of runaways from the South did not cease. The number of fugitives in Maryland caused many white planters to abandon the use of enslaved African labor in the years before the Civil War.

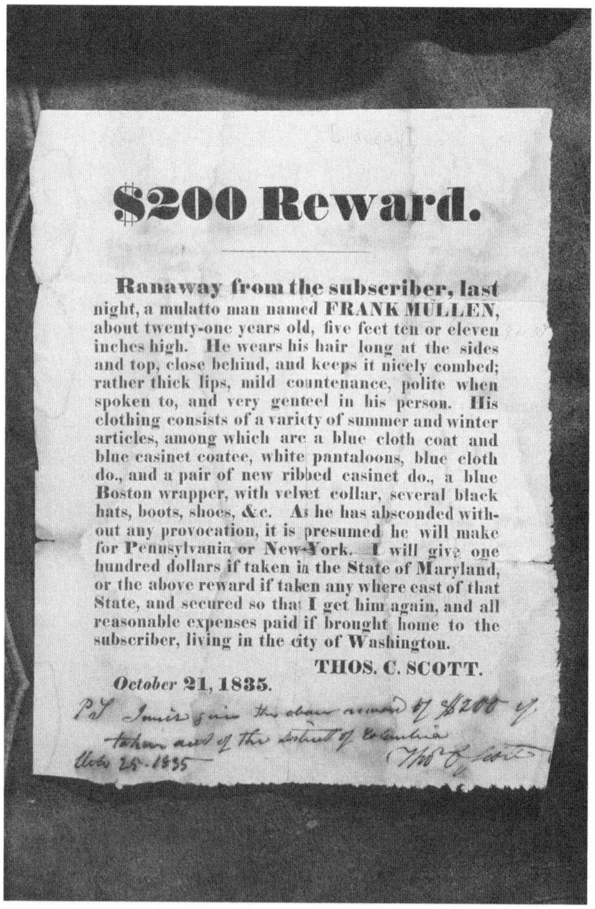

$200 Reward.

Ranaway from the subscriber, last night, a mulatto man named FRANK MULLEN, about twenty-one years old, five feet ten or eleven inches high. He wears his hair long at the sides and top, close behind, and keeps it nicely combed; rather thick lips, mild countenance, polite when spoken to, and very genteel in his person. His clothing consists of a variety of summer and winter articles, among which are a blue cloth coat and blue casinet coatee, white pantaloons, blue cloth do., and a pair of new ribbed casinet do., a blue Boston wrapper, with velvet collar, several black hats, boots, shoes, &c. As he has absconded without any provocation, it is presumed he will make for Pennsylvania or New-York. I will give one hundred dollars if taken in the State of Maryland, or the above reward if taken any where east of that State, and secured so that I get him again, and all reasonable expenses paid if brought home to the subscriber, living in the city of Washington.

THOS. C. SCOTT.

October 21, 1835.

Handbill Offering Reward for Return of Frank Mullen, October 21, 1835. *The most common way that African Americans resisted enslavement was to run away. Handbills and newspaper advertisements gave detailed descriptions of the runaways, including clothing and physical markings or defects such as scars. Fugitives' skills such as fiddling or sewing were often listed in case a runaway tried to pass as a free person and seek work.* LOUIE PSIHOYOS/CORBIS

As northern abolitionist sentiment began to grow, accounts of daring escape attempts were extremely popular. One of the most popular related to the escape of an enslaved tobacco factory worker named Henry Brown. Better known as Henry "Box" Brown, he escaped enslavement in Virginia when he mailed himself in a huge crate from Richmond to the Philadelphia Antislavery office in 1849. He had a friend build the crate, nail him inside with only some water to drink, and ship him by rail and boat to Philadelphia. His method of escape was so unique that his story became legendary and bolstered the abolitionist movement around the country. Brown, who was preliterate, had the abolitionist Charles Stearns assist him in producing his autobiography, *Narrative of Henry Box Brown, Who Escaped from Slavery, Enclosed in a Box 3 Feet Long and 2 Wide, Written from a Statement of Facts Made by Himself, with Remarks upon the Remedy for Slavery*. It was first published just several months after his escape, and was revised and republished in England in 1851.

A husband and wife team, William Craft and Ellen Craft, also gained great celebrity for their Christmas escape in 1848. Ellen, who was very light skinned, dressed as a man, and William, who had a brown complexion, pretended to be her slave. They took public conveyances to Philadelphia and appeared at the Underground Railroad office of William Still, safe and sound. In the book *Hidden in Plain View: A Secret Story of Quilts and the Underground Railroad* (1999), authors Jacqueline Tobin and Raymond Dobard document the many ingenious means of escape devised by runaways and those who assisted them, including the use of elaborate quilts that served as maps to guide those who had fled bondage.

Not all runaway attempts were successful or thrilling, but all were daring. Frederick Douglass's fiancée made him a sailor uniform. He then borrowed a black sailor's identification papers and simply boarded a train to Philadelphia, and to freedom.

FREE AFRICANS

From the seventeenth century on, there was a growing free black population in the British colonies. This population grew quickly in the antebellum years. African Americans were often emancipated for diligent work, good conduct, familial connections, or years of commendable service. The methods for manumission included court actions, instructions in owners' wills, self-purchase or purchase of one's family members' freedom with money earned when hired out, governmental decrees, or rewards for military service. Several thousand gained their freedom serving alongside their owners during the colonial wars. Thousands more fled to freedom behind the British lines during the Revolutionary War and the War of 1812.

Continental Army commander George Washington, who was himself a prosperous enslaver, mulled over the possibility of allowing blacks to serve as members of the regular troops. As he vacillated, the British invited enslaved blacks to join with his majesty's troops so that they could gain their freedom. Ultimately, many free and enslaved blacks fought on the side of the American patriots, but thousands more fled to and aided the British. Servicemen who were formerly enslaved gained their freedom as a result of their military service in the Continental Army. In addition to their freedom as payment for services rendered, the British took the formerly enslaved men with them to Canada, Jamaica, and England. In 1787, concerned British citizens repatriated hundreds of Africans from each of these regions to West Africa, where they established the colony named Sierra Leone.

Free blacks were rarely accorded the same privileges as their European American counterparts. States changed their laws relating to free blacks depending on the political climate and, more importantly, the size of the African American population. For a brief period, some free blacks had the right to vote in some areas, but several of those laws were later rescinded. Pennsylvania, for example, allowed free black men to vote until 1837, when that opportunity was denied to them. They were not allowed to vote again until after the passage of the Fifteenth Amendment in 1866. Free blacks usually could not carry firearms or testify against whites in court. Free blacks, especially children, lived under the constant threat of being beaten or kidnapped by whites who would sell them into enslavement. One of the reasons that European Americans formed abolition societies was to try to protect free blacks from kidnappers.

States passed and repealed laws prohibiting blacks from assembling as groups in public places without whites also being present. State governments often vacillated over the issue of whether free blacks could hold and bequeath property. Whites often sought to restrict the type of work blacks could do because they did not want to compete with them. In Pennsylvania, black men were barred from certain crafts. At various times, state legislatures attempted to pass laws prohibiting blacks from reading abolitionist literature, operating boats, obtaining licenses for peddling, participating in certain trades, or owning or driving vehicles such as hacks, carts, or drays. There was also an effort keep free blacks from owning dogs. Enslavers' motives for many of these restrictive laws (particularly those prohibiting free blacks from owning conveyances) was to prevent them from aiding runaways. There were also stringent laws to prevent blacks from marrying whites.

In spite of numerous restrictions, free blacks formed their own churches, schools, benevolent societies, fraternal organizations, and businesses. Many black churches were a part of larger denominations, which met periodically in various states to discuss both religious and political matters. Census records indicate that increasing numbers of free blacks could read and write. Free persons of color worked as domestics, small farmers, innkeepers, street vendors, ship caulkers, stevedores, sailors and boatmen, draymen, barbers, teamsters, blacksmiths, and liverymen. Blacks who had purchased their freedom were usually able to do so because they had earned money with their skilled labor. Some free blacks, like astronomer Benjamin Banneker and preacher Daniel Coker, recorded their experiences for posterity. Banneker was able to publish an almanac in the 1790s and aid in the planning of the District of Columbia, and Coker became one of the first emigrants to go back to Africa with the American Colonization Society.

African Americans, both free and enslaved, were successful at a variety of business ventures and were credited with numerous inventions. Harriet Beecher Stowe, author of the best-selling novel *Uncle Tom's Cabin* (1851–1853), even argued that it was not Eli Whitney but an enslaved black man who developed the cotton gin to separate the seed from the cotton. In addition to this disputed claim, there is documented evidence of a number of scientific inventions patented by blacks after emancipation. James Forten of Philadelphia, a Revolutionary War veteran, invented a sail hoist that made it easier to maneuver the huge sails on ships. He ran his own sail-making company, became quite wealthy, and eventually was a major supporter of the emancipation newspaper the *Liberator*, edited by militant abolitionist William Lloyd Garrison.

Paul Cuffee. In their quest for full political rights, free people of color were extremely articulate in their protests against the peculiar institution, but they also began to explore alternative solutions to racial problems. One example was Paul Cuffee, a Massachusetts-born free man of African and Native American ancestry, who learned to articulate the doctrines of freedom for oppressed African Americans. He eventually became an exponent of African colonization in general and of the British Sierra Leone scheme in particular. As a youth, he was able to obtain a limited education and then found work as a sailor and laborer. Eventually, he became a shipbuilder. By 1780, he had built a ship of his own, and by 1806 he owned a small fleet.

In spite of his accomplishments, Cuffee regularly confronted racial prejudice. Although his wealth continued to grow, as did his tax contributions to the Massachusetts government, he could not vote and his children could not attend public schools. Cuffee knew that the colonies had protested against Great Britain for taxation without representation during the Revolutionary War, and it seemed to him that the colonies were guilty of the same injustice by taxing free blacks without letting them reap the benefits that their tax dollars earned for other citizens. In defiance, Cuffee and his brother refused to pay their taxes. Subsequently, Cuffee financed a Quaker school, which he opened not only to black children but to all children in his community.

Even when the Massachusetts courts abolished the enslavement of Africans in 1783, the social, economic, and political problems that freed Africans encountered remained complex. Cuffee reasoned that the best avenue was for blacks to reestablish contact with West Africans for the purpose of colonization and trade. He argued that blacks would be able to make great commercial gains if they could work together to establish a shipping network of their own. Additionally, blacks who felt that the stigma attached to them was too severe could move to Sierra Leone, bringing both civilization and Christianity to their ancestral homeland. During Cuffee's 1811–1812 visit to Sierra Leone, he formed the Friendly Society with an African American emigrant named John Kizzell for the purpose of encouraging African American emigration and trade.

Cuffee was unable to interest anyone in financing his Sierra Leone colonization scheme. Consequently, he determined that he would finance it himself, but encountered one major problem. During the time he was formulating his plans, the United States and Great Britain were involved in the War of 1812, and Americans were not permitted to trade with England or its colonies. In 1814, Cuffee petitioned the U.S. Congress to lift the embargo against trade with Sierra Leone so that he could begin his venture. His petition passed the Senate, but was struck down by the House. Finally, after the cessation of hostilities in 1815, and at a personal expenditure of $4,000, Cuffee took nine free black families, totaling thirty-eight individuals, to settle in Sierra Leone. Although he had difficulty marketing his trade goods when he returned, Cuffee became even more determined that black Americans needed to emigrate if they were to achieve true independence and racial dignity. Many free blacks, as well as some whites, received Cuffee's emigration plan with enthusiasm, but few blacks were willing to give up their American citizenship.

AMERICAN COLONIZATION SOCIETY

Other emigrationists began to formulate ideas for the colonization of black Americans along the lines of what Paul Cuffee had envisioned. Some had ambitions to establish trade ventures, while others wanted to evangelize continental Africans. Many whites simply hoped to rid the United States of its free black population. Robert Finley, a New Jersey clergyman, was alarmed by the fact that the free black population in New Jersey quadrupled between 1790 and 1820. Disturbed by the extent of their poverty and political impotence, he feared that nothing would alter the inequality of the treatment of blacks in the state. Finley believed that "everything connected with their condition, including their colour," was against them. He felt that the "methodical colonization of free Negroes would both improve their condition and solve the larger problem of their future in America." Hence, he proposed a colony similar to Sierra Leone and advocated federal assistance for the colonization plan.

In December 1816, Finley visited Washington to see if he could get support. He met with a number of influential men, including Elias Caldwell, Bushrod Washington, Henry Clay, John Randolph, Daniel Webster, and about forty-five others. The response of those who met with Finley varied. Henry Clay, an enslaver who felt that free blacks were a threat to legal human bondage, proposed "to rid our country of a useless and pernicious, if not dangerous portion of its population." Some of the delegates proposed an African colony that would help in the suppression of the slave trade. Many of the organizers were primarily interested in the evangelization of Africa, and a few felt that a colony would give free blacks the opportunity to be truly free. Finally, on December 28, 1816, this group of delegates assumed the name American Society for Colonizing the Free People of Color in the United States. Soon, the organization was known simply as the American Colonization Society (ACS).

The newly formed society sought to recruit Paul Cuffee to lead their first emigrant expedition, but he died before the plans for the first group of settlers could be formulated. However, John Kizzell and the Friendly Society supervised many of the arrangements in Africa for the Colonization Society's first emigrants. Black leaders in Philadelphia, led by James Forten, Richard Allen, Absalom Jones, and Robert Douglas, immediately held a protest meeting. Cuffee, they contended, had been working to help black people, but the ACS was decidedly against the interests of black Americans. Finley assured the group that the society's motives were not sinister, and for a few months black protests were quieted. Nonetheless, because so many of the ACS organizers had made public their views against free blacks and emancipation, few African

Americans expressed any willingness to apply for colonization.

In addition to criticism by blacks, the ACS encountered considerable resistance from the federal government to pleas for funding their projects. Consequently, funds for the colonization scheme had to be solicited from the public. As a result, the ACS had to establish an African settlement largely at its own expense. Samuel J. Mills, a missionary, and Ebenezer Burgess, an ordained minister, raised funds to travel to West Africa to look for a settlement site. On November 5, 1817, they were appointed agents of the ACS and sailed for Africa. After stopping in England for a month to consult with organizers of the Sierra Leone colonization project, they sailed for Africa on February 2, 1818. They toured Sierra Leone and the surrounding villages for six weeks with Kizzell as their guide and interpreter. They decided on Sherbro Island as the site for the colony.

Mills died on the way home, but Burgess delivered their report on Sierra Leone to the ACS. With the aid of this report, the society began to plan for the voyage of the first group of emigrants. The African Americans who joined the first expedition as emigrants also worked for the U.S. government. A March 3, 1819, act of Congress authorized President Monroe to deliver African captives taken from slave ships to U.S. agents who would be stationed on the West African coast. The emigrants were hired to build shelters for the "recaptives." In southern Virginia, near the area of the Turner insurrection, hundreds of blacks were eager to move to Liberia because of the ferocity of the reaction of the white public. Yet, even in this region, more blacks preferred to stay or to move to another state than to emigrate outside of the country. During the entire nineteenth century, only a small minority of the free African American population chose to move to Liberia.

The African American Response to Colonization. Reverend Peter Williams, an African American Episcopal priest, gave the majority viewpoint at an oration on July 4, 1830: "Though delivered from the fetters of slavery, we are oppressed by an unreasonable, unrighteous, and cruel prejudice, which aims at nothing less than the forcing away of all the free coloured people of the United States to the distant shores of Africa." He said that he did not think that the motives of all of the members of ACS were impure. Some wanted, he believed, to abolish the trade in continental Africans, and others wanted to evangelize them. But other very influential members, he argued, simply wanted to rid the nation of free blacks. Williams continued his protest, stating that, ironically, the members of the ACS who felt that blacks were "vile" and "degraded" also felt that these same black people would have a beneficial and civilizing influence on continental Africans. This contradiction within the ACS's literature and fund-raising programs did not escape the notice of black Americans.

The issue of African colonization of African Americans arose frequently during the nineteenth century and was regularly a volatile issue at antebellum African American political meetings known as the Negro Convention movement. Frederick Douglass, who felt that the whole idea of colonization was rooted in racism and Negrophobia (fear and hatred of blacks) wrote and spoke out against it on many occasions. In a *North Star* editorial of January 1849, Douglass lambasted the U.S. Senate about "the wrinkled old 'red herring' of colonization." Douglass wrote:

> We are of the opinion that the free colored people generally mean to live in America, and not in Africa; and to appropriate a large sum for our removal, would merely be a waste of the public money. We do not mean to go to Liberia. Our minds are made up to live here if we can, or die here if we must; so every attempt to remove us will be, as it ought to be, labor lost. Here we are, and here we shall remain. While our brethren are in bondage on these shores; it is idle to think of inducing any considerable number of the free colored people to quit this for a foreign land.

The vast majority of black Americans were adamant about remaining in the United States. As such, the goals of the ACS and similar organizations that formed to repatriate African Americans were largely unfulfilled.

In spite of the doubt on the part of blacks and the suspect motives of some of the members of ACS, groups of black people left almost every year after 1820 to go to Liberia. Some chose to emigrate to Haiti in the 1820s, but many were dissatisfied there and returned to the United States. The idea of Haitian emigration was renewed in the mid-nineteenth century, but Liberian emigration, though limited, was relatively constant. Some of the Liberian emigrants returned to the United States disenchanted with the new colony. Because Liberia was thousands of miles away, however, it took money to return to the United States, and many of the settlers had no funds. One humorous Liberian saying at the time was "the love of liberty brought us here, the lack of money kept us here."

Indeed, it was the love of liberty that drew many free blacks to Liberia. It did not take long after the settlement of the colony for reports to begin coming to the United States about the life of the settlers. The reports described a small, struggling settlement. The Liberians fought against hostile indigenous people and various debilitating diseases. They suffered from homesickness. Somehow, however, there was some romance in the reports. It was clear that few whites could survive the climate and that, basically, it was black men who were building a nation. Despite the struggles of the settlers, many blacks believed that Liberia would one day be a great nation that would demonstrate to the world the prowess of the black race. In Liberia, black men could hold leadership positions, sit on juries, vote, and work for the fulfillment of their dreams. To a few black Americans, the promise of such a life, even amid the hardships and privations of the African continent, was enough to draw them away from everything familiar in their homeland. Some plantation owners wanted to emancipate their black captives, but the laws of their states tied their hands. Consequently, in order to free them, many indicated in their wills that their enslaved blacks had to emigrate to Liberia. Others gave them the option of going to Haiti, Liberia, or a free state. For years, some enslaved Africans felt that colonization was just a scheme to kidnap blacks and sell them farther south.

ABOLITION

During the period leading up to the 1860s, the country's small, free black population, aided by sympathetic whites, was outspoken—and creative—in their protest against African enslavement, an institution many of them knew from firsthand experience. Sermons called for liberty, while hundreds of newspaper articles, books, poems, speeches, and tracts echoed a call for freedom not unlike that of the American colonies from their perceived oppressor in the eighteenth century—Great Britain. In 1773, Phillis Wheatley published a poem to the Earl of Dartmouth that reasoned that some who perused her "song" would wonder where her "love of freedom sprung." She explained that she, "young in life," had been "snatch'd from Africa's fancied happy seat." Wheatley's position as a "pampered" enslaved Bostonian would have been enviable to many in bondage who endured physical and emotion abuse, but that did not squelch her longing for freedom. Beginning in 1776 with the promulgation of the Declaration of Independence, doctrines of equality and the inalienable rights of life, liberty, and the pursuit of happiness reached the ears of the free person of color and the enslaved African alike, and the oppressed longed to throw off the oppressor.

Hundreds of thousands of whites allied with free blacks to aid in the destruction of the peculiar institution. Quakers, for example, were speaking, writing, and petitioning in state legislatures against African enslavement from the eighteenth century until emancipation. In addition to formal methods of protest, grassroots networks emerged to fight against the system of enslavement. Members of both races acted as conductors on the Underground Railroad. There is a virtual mountain of records relating to antislavery efforts by great abolitionists, white and black, in the United States. These include the writings of people like Frederick Douglass, Susan B. Anthony, William Lloyd Garrison, Harriet Beecher Stowe, Henry Ward Beecher, Mary Ann Shadd Cary, Salmon P. Chase, Martin Delaney, Theodore Weld, Frances Ellen Watkins Harper, and William and Ellen Craft, to name only a few. Antislavery and proslavery political debates divided the nation, and led to violence and, ultimately, to the Civil War.

Uncle Tom's Cabin. Galvanized of by the passage of the Fugitive Slave Act of 1850, Harriet Beecher Stowe published *Uncle Tom's Cabin, or, Life among the Lowly* in forty installments from June 1851 to April of 1852 in *National Era*, a Washington, D.C., periodical. The novel riveted the attention of thousands of readers and engendered outrage in many about the institution of African enslavement. Although the story centers on the mistreatment of the pious and wise Uncle Tom, many other enslaved characters are featured in the story. The book targets even benign plantation owners as partners in the crime against humanity. Toward the end of Tom's life, his owner, Simon Legree, beats Tom severely because he knows that his humble servant has outwitted him in a matter relating to two runaway women. When Tom's former master finally rescues him, Tom survives only a few miles beyond the entrance of Legree's plantation.

In 1851, after Stowe finished the first five installments of *Uncle Tom's Cabin*, she consulted with Frederick Douglass about true stories relating to the American enslavement experience that she could weave into her story. When *Uncle Tom's Cabin* appeared in book form in March 1852, published in two volumes by J. P. Jewett, it sold 300,000 copies in one year. Stowe wrote *The Key to Uncle Tom's Cabin* the following year. In this work, she explained some of the incidents in the story and her motivations for writing them. An enthusiastic Douglass remarked: "Why Sir, look all over the North: look South, look at home, look abroad! Look at the whole civilized world! And what are all this vast multitude doing at this moment? Why, Sir, they are reading *Uncle Tom's Cabin*, and when they have read that, they will probably read *The Key to Uncle Tom's Cabin*." Before 1860, more than one million copies of *Uncle Tom's Cabin* had sold in the United States, and more than two million copies were sold abroad, authorized and unauthorized, principally in England, but also in France, Germany, and other nations.

Stowe's novel added measurably to the polarization of abolitionist and antiabolitionist sentiment in the United States and Europe. Douglass and other abolitionists, both white and black, had spent most of their lives exposing the horrors of African enslavement in the United States. Most of the abolitionists exulted that Stowe's books generated outrage against the peculiar institution, both nationally and internationally. Josiah Henson, who had been born and enslaved in Charles County, Maryland, in the late 1780s but escaped to Canada in the 1830s, claimed that he was the model for Uncle Tom, although some circumstances in his life differed greatly from those of Stowe's lead character.

Carl Sandburg reported in *Abraham Lincoln: The War Years* (1939) that during a White House visit, President Lincoln greeted Stowe with outstretched hands, saying, "So you're the little woman who wrote the book that made this great war." Historian Benjamin Quarles noted that at an 1863 abolitionist's celebration of Lincoln's Emancipation Proclamation, the crowd yelled for Stowe to come forward to receive an enthusiastic ovation for the service she had performed by writing *Uncle Tom's Cabin*.

THE CIVIL WAR

The furor over the Fugitive Slave Law of 1850, the controversy over the enslavement issue in Nebraska and Kansas, the *Dred Scott* decision of 1857, and John Brown's 1859 attack on Harpers Ferry all polarized the nation, but the election of President Abraham Lincoln in 1860 led southern politicians to finally do what they had been threatening for decades—secede from the Union. During the Civil War, black soldiers demonstrated that detractors who claimed they would flee in terror in the midst of battle were wrong. Black soldiers proved as able to wield guns as they did plows, hoes, or harnesses. They also worked behind the scenes, as well as on the front lines, with the Union troops. Thousands of enslaved blacks in the Confederacy emancipated themselves and fled to the Union encampments.

Moreover, African American civilians proved that they cared about their families and homes, in spite of claims that they were too negligent and immoral to do so. For example, Union chaplains and Freedmen's Bureau officials worked tirelessly to reunite families that had been sold and separated, and to help free people legitimize their marriage vows. A document in the Manuscript Division of the Library of Congress indicates that in 1863, a white

CAPTURE OF JOHN BROWN IN THE ENGINE-HOUSE.

Colored Engraving of John Brown, Abolitionist, 19th Century. *After Brown led a raid on the federal armory and arsenal in Harpers Ferry, West Virginia, on October 16, 1859, he was captured and later hanged.* PRIVATE COLLECTION/PETER NEWARK AMERICAN PICTURES/THE BRIDGEMAN ART LIBRARY

Union chaplain, Asa Fiske, once performed simultaneous wedding ceremonies for 119 African American couples who had fled to safety behind Union lines. For African Americans, the right to have a family, protect spouses and children, earn an honest living, and dwell in peace became one of the driving desires for freedom from enslavement. Herbert Gutman's book, *The Black Family in Slavery and Freedom, 1750–1925* (1977), documents the vitality of African American family ties, even during the era of enslavement.

As Union soldiers and northern teachers, preachers, businesspeople, and missionaries traveled into defeated areas of the Confederacy, they discovered aspects of African-derived culture hitherto unknown to them. African American spirituals, folk songs, churches, African folkways, and linguistic traits caused many northern observers to reassess their views about black creativity. Because plantation owners feared literate persons of color, every slaveholding state had passed laws forbidding African American education. This accentuated a longing for learning among the newly freed blacks that impressed almost every chronicler of the South in the period during and after the Civil War.

Newly freed African Americans, old and young, gathered in classrooms. The elderly often clutched their Bibles, longing to be able to read its pages for themselves. One-room schoolhouses, poorly paid teachers, and nascent institutions of higher education sprang up throughout the South. Freedmen's Bureau officials and thousands of white missionaries and teachers traveled throughout the former Confederacy to teach the education-starved blacks to read and write. Many historically black colleges and universities were founded within five years after the Appomattox surrender. The 1900 census indicated that in the period between the Civil War and the turn of the twentieth century, the majority of the African American population broke the bonds of illiteracy.

Although some black workers had joined the Union Army by 1862, blacks were not actively recruited until it became apparent that the war would be long and costly. As a war measure, Lincoln wrote the Emancipation Proclamation in September 1862, declaring that all enslaved people in the Confederacy should be "forever free" and providing for the use of African American soldiers in the Civil War. This document would go into effect January 1, 1863. Faced with a shortage of manpower among the rank and file, the War Department in 1863 finally established a policy encouraging the use of black men and, subsequently, thousands were actively recruited. By the end of the war, more than 186,000 black men had enlisted, resulting in a ratio of one black soldier for every eight white soldiers. White commissioned officers and both black and white noncommissioned officers led most units of black soldiers. Frederick Douglass and Martin Delaney were recruiters for the U.S. Colored Troops. Delaney, a Harvard-trained doctor, served as a major. Two of Douglass's sons joined the army. Although black troops were treated unfairly by both the Union and the Confederacy, they served faithfully and well.

RECONSTRUCTION AND ITS AFTERMATH

The immediate post–Civil War period saw the passage of the Thirteenth, Fourteenth, and Fifteenth Amendments to the Constitution, which abolished the enslavement of Africans, guaranteed equal protection under the law, and granted citizenship and male suffrage to all born in the United States, regardless of color or previous condition of servitude. Although these developments seemed to promise a new era of freedom for African Americans, troubles soon set in. Gains in civil rights legislation and political representation in the state and local legislatures and in the U.S. Congress were eroded within a few decades. Congressional reports chronicle the Ku Klux Klan's death threats to blacks who dared to participate actively in the political and economic arenas of the South. Tenancy, sharecropping, and peonage held many poor African Americans in a new kind of bondage from the 1870s through the turn of the century. Blacks had to begin anew to strive for social and political rights in their homeland.

Despite these setbacks, by the turn of the twentieth century, a race formerly barred from literacy by law was largely literate, had published thousands of books, and had produced scores of plays and musical compositions. Nevertheless, in 1896, the U.S. Supreme Court dealt a crushing blow to the struggle for freedom by declaring in the *Plessy v. Ferguson* case that it was legal to provide "separate but equal" accommodations for blacks on public conveyances. The concept of racial separation long predated *Plessy* and had crept through the fabric of American life, North and South. In *Betrayal of the Negro, from Rutherford B. Hayes to Woodrow Wilson* (originally published in 1954 as *The Negro in American Life and Thought: The Nadir, 1877–1901*), historian Rayford Logan described this period as the nadir of the historical experience of free blacks. Race riots and other types of racial violence ushered in a reign of terror in much of the South.

The voices of the nation's black citizens were not silenced by the onslaught of racial repression. Black journalists like Ida B. Wells-Barnett and T. Thomas Fortune, and up-and-coming scholars such as W. E. B. Du Bois and Carter G. Woodson, as well as educators such as Booker T. Washington, Kelly Miller, Mary

Church Terrell, and Fanny Jackson Coppin, spoke out against lynching and other forms of racial violence. Black leaders being trained at African American colleges and universities and a few integrated and mainstream universities formed the relentless vanguard for civil rights and equal opportunity for all in the twentieth century.

FIGURES OF THE PAST

(Some biographical profiles may appear in other chapters. To locate profiles more readily, please consult the index.)

JOHN QUINCY ADAMS (1767–1848)

President, Politician. John Quincy Adams, the sixth president of the United States, claimed he was not an abolitionist. Yet he respected the rights of all citizens to petition the American government. After his presidency, he was elected to the House of Representatives in 1830. During his tenure, the House banned the consideration of petitions of emancipation. This ban, called the "gag rule," was in force beginning in 1836. Adams tirelessly and successfully fought against the rule, which was rescinded in 1844. Although Adams did not consider himself to be an abolitionist, his views on human rights led abolitionists to recruit him as the lawyer for the *Amistad* Africans. This group of continental Africans staged a revolt at sea, but they were eventually captured and tried in a U.S. court. Adams successfully defended them, but the case reached the U.S. Supreme Court before it was resolved in favor of the captured Africans.

ALICE OF DUNK'S FERRY (c. 1686–1802)

Oral Historian. Alice was born around 1686 in Philadelphia to parents who had been enslaved in Barbados. When she was ten years old, she moved to Dunk's Ferry in Bucks County with her master, where she lived out the rest of what proved to be an incredibly long life, spending some forty of her 116 years collecting tolls at a bridge. Alice's long life, coupled with a remarkable memory, made her an ideal oral historian, recounting for listeners her vivid recollections of the early days of the colony. She could remember when the great city of Philadelphia was nothing more than a wilderness, populated by Native Americans and wild animals. Little is known about her life, although evidence suggests that she remained physically active well past the century mark of her life. She died enslaved just a few miles from Philadelphia in 1802.

RICHARD ALLEN

See chapter 17, Religion.

CRISPUS ATTUCKS (c. 1723–1770)

Revolutionary Patriot. A runaway who lived in Boston, Crispus Attucks was the first of five men killed on March 5, 1770, when British troops fired on a crowd of colonial protesters in the Boston Massacre. The most widely accepted account of the incident is that of John Adams, who said at the subsequent trial of the British soldiers that Attucks undertook "to be the hero of the night; and to lead this army with banners, to form them in the first place in Dock Square, and march them up to King Street with their clubs." When the crowd reached the soldiers, it was Attucks who "had hardiness enough to fall in upon them, and with one hand took hold of a bayonet, and with the other knocked the man down." At that point the panicked soldiers fired, and in the echoes of their volley, five men lay dying; the seeds of the Revolution were sown. Attucks is remembered as "the first to defy, the first to die."

CHARLES BALL (c. 1781–?)

Abolitionist, Author. Charles Ball, a formerly enslaved African, dictated his autobiography, *Fifty Years in Chains, or, The Life of an American Slave*, which was published in 1836. His narrative was very popular and was updated and reprinted several times. Born in Calvert County, Maryland, around 1781, Ball was the grandson of a continental African. His mother died when he was about four years old, and his father ran away when he learned that he was about to be sold. Ball himself was sold into bondage in Georgia when he was about thirty years old. He subsequently escaped and found his wife and children in Maryland. After living as a free man for a time, he was recaptured. After escaping again, he returned to find that his family members, who had been legally free, had been kidnapped and enslaved. Initially, *Fifty Years in Chains* was published anonymously. In the work, Ball discussed the wicked institution of enslavement, the kidnapping of African Americans, and the effect of the cotton gin on the lives of enslaved blacks.

BENJAMIN BANNEKER

See chapter 27, Science and Technology.

JIM BECKWOURTH

See chapter 14, Entrepreneurship.

HENRY "BOX" BROWN (B. 1815)

Abolitionist. Henry Brown got his nickname "Box" when he mailed himself from Richmond, Virginia, to the Philadelphia Antislavery office in Pennsylvania in 1849 to escape enslavement. Brown subsequently produced an autobiography, *Narrative of Henry Box Brown, Who Escaped from Slavery, Enclosed in a Box 3 Feet Long and 2 Wide, Written from a Statement of Facts Made by Himself, with Remarks upon the Remedy for Slavery,* with the assistance of Charles Stearns. It was first published several months after his escape and revised and republished in England in 1851. In his narrative, Brown explained that he was born in 1815 on the Barret plantation in Virginia. When Brown was fifteen years old, his master died, and Brown's family was divided among the owner's four sons. Taken to Richmond by William Barret, Brown began to work long hours in a tobacco factory. His new master regularly set aside small sums of money as a reward for Brown's work. Brown was no spendthrift so he was able to amass some savings.

Brown got permission to marry an enslaved woman named Nancy on the condition that he find a place for his family to live. After twelve years of marriage, Brown's wife and children were sold away and he had no idea where they had gone. To add to the calamity, some whites took everything Brown owned out of his house. Brown began formulating plans to flee from the terrible confines of enslavement. He wanted to find a way of escape that was unique. In 1849, with the help of two allies, Brown was shipped to Philadelphia in a crate. When Brown's Philadelphia contacts heard that the box had arrived, several witnesses, including the African American Underground Railroad conductor, William Still, were present for the opening of the crate. To their amazement, Brown was alive. After his escape, Brown began speaking on the antislavery circuit about the horrors of the system. He fled to England after the passage of the Fugitive Slave Act of 1850.

BLANCHE K. BRUCE

See chapter 11, Politics.

JOSEPH CINQUE (c. 1811–1879)

Mutineer, Insurrectionist. Joseph Cinque, a Mende warrior, was born Singbe-Piéh in Sierra Leone around 1811. When he was in his mid-twenties, he was captured and enslaved in his country and transported to the New World. He was eventually purchased by Spaniards in Havana, Cuba, in 1838. After he was sold, Joseph Cinque, as he was renamed by his enslavers, was placed, along with other captives, aboard the *Amistad,* a Spanish ship bound for Puerto Principe. The vessel set sail from Cuba on June 28, 1839. A few days later, Cinque led the other African captives in rebellion. They killed the captain and the cook, and ordered several other crewmembers to transport them back to Africa. During the day, the pilots steered the vessel eastward, but at night they headed north, ultimately arriving in August 1839 off Long Island, New York. There the ship was seized by U.S. government authorities, and the Africans were imprisoned after the white crewmen denounced them as rebellious pirates and murderers.

Portrait of Joseph Cinque ***(Nathaniel Jocelyn, c. 1840).*** *Cinque led the mutiny on the slave ship* Amistad. *While he awaited trial in New Haven, Connecticut, this portrait was painted.* AP IMAGES/NEW HAVEN COLONY HISTORICAL SOCIETY

Abolitionists took up the cause of the African captives and enabled Cinque to raise funds for judicial appeals by speaking on their lecture circuit. Almost overnight the incident became a cause célèbre. Led by the Mende warrior, Singbe-Piéh, the West Africans insisted that they be freed and returned to their continent. President Martin Van Buren and the Spanish administrators of Cuba maintained that they should be extradited to Cuba to stand trial for mutiny. The case ultimately went to the U.S. Supreme Court, where John Quincy Adams defended the *Amistad* Africans. Adams won the case, the Africans were declared free, and missionaries and wellwishers raised money for Cinque and the remaining Africans to return to West Africa.

JOSHUA COFFIN (1792–1864)

Abolitionist. Joshua Coffin was a white abolitionist and teacher who argued that the practice of African enslavement in the United States constituted a serious threat to public peace and security. His book, *An Account of Some of the Principal Slave Insurrections* (1860), explored how captive Africans rose up against their owners to demand their freedom. In the book, he described resistance through large and small-scale rebellions in the North and South, as well as work slowdowns, poisonings, arsons, and murders. He also discussed mutinies, including one that occurred on a Rhode Island ship when captives near Cape Coast Castle (in present-day Ghana) "murdered the captain and all the crew except the two mates, who swam ashore." Coffin was one of the founders of the New England Anti-Slavery Society.

DANIEL COKER (1780–1846)

Educator, Pastor, Missionary. Daniel Coker was an African American preacher, teacher, and missionary to Africa. He was born Isaac Wright in 1780 in Frederick County, Maryland, to an enslaved African father, Edward Wright, and a white mother, Susan Coker, who was an indentured servant. His mother also had an older white son named Daniel Coker. Isaac received a rudimentary education and ran away to New York, where he assumed his brother's name.

Coker was active in the Methodist movement under the traveling Bishop Francis Asbury. Coker became a minister in a Baltimore Methodist church that was modeled after Reverend Richard Allen's church in Philadelphia. Coker's church opened a school around 1800. In spite of the fact that early Methodists were encouraged to free their enslaved blacks, welcome African American members, and support abolition, many white preachers, trustees, and members did not agree to treat African American members of their congregation justly or courteously. Around 1810, Coker wrote a forty-three-page pamphlet containing a sermon protesting African enslavement, *A Dialog between a Virginian and an African Minister*. In it, he described himself as a "Minister of the African Methodist Episcopal Church in Baltimore," and in an appendix he lists the names of African ministers "who are in holy orders," as well as African local preachers, African churches, and the "names of the descendants of the African race, who have given proofs of talent."

In the introduction to the 1817 publication *The Doctrines and Discipline of the African Methodist Episcopal Church*, Daniel Coker, Richard Allen, and James Champion explained how they responded to their mistreatment by white Methodists after a number of years of dissatisfaction. They stated that the African American members of their church were "disposed to seek a place of worship for themselves" rather than legal redress against the white Methodist preachers and trustees who repeatedly tried to keep them from equality with whites.

In addition to pastoring, Coker established a church school, the Bethel Charity School. Several generations of blacks benefited from the teachers and preachers trained in this school. For unknown reasons, Coker was removed from the church in 1818, but he was restored a year later. During that year, it seems, Coker decided that he wanted to be a missionary in Africa.

Several years prior to the formation of the African Methodist Episcopal Church, Coker became interested in developments in Sierra Leone. Coker decided that he and his family would partner with the American Colonization Society (ACS) to return to Africa as missionaries. After their arrival, on an assignment from their white agents to govern the settlers, "African fever" struck the island off the coast of Sierra Leone. Many settlers got sick and some died, including the white ACS agent. Coker was appointed to lead the surviving settlers.

Some of the white settlers resented Coker's leadership, but he continued to serve until another white ACS agent arrived. The settlers moved to several locations before finally relocating in Freetown, the capital of Sierra Leone. When some of the settlers decided to move down the coast to found Liberia in 1822, Coker elected to remain in Sierra Leone, where he ministered until his death in 1846.

FANNY COPPIN

See chapter 16, Education.

WILLIAM CRAFT (1824–1900)

Abolitionist, Businessman.

ELLEN CRAFT (1826–1891)

Abolitionist, Educator. Ellen Smith's mother was enslaved in Georgia. Ellen's father was the plantation owner. As a youth, Ellen bore such a striking resemblance to her father, who was also her master, that she was sent away to live with his daughter in Macon, Georgia, where Ellen worked as a housemaid. In Macon, Ellen met and married William Craft, a carpenter.

After their marriage, the couple tried to devise escape plans. By Christmas of 1848 they came up with an idea by which Ellen would pose as a sickly young man. She dressed in men's clothing, wrapped her face with a scarf to hide the fact that she had no beard, and bandaged her right hand, pretending that she was wounded, so that no one would know that she could not read and write. Her husband, William, pretended that he was her slave accompanying her to Philadelphia. The two left at the beginning of the Christmas holidays with a pass from their owners. Because bondspersons were usually given some free time at Christmas, the young couple hoped that no one would look for them for several days. They bought fares with money that William had earned as a hired slave, and traveled by train and boat until they arrived in Philadelphia. Their escape was successful, with only a few frightening moments, particularly when Ellen was asked to produce papers showing the she was indeed William's owner.

The coupled traveled to various places in the North and spoke for the abolitionist cause. They settled in Boston until the arrival of slave catchers, and white abolitionists convinced them that they needed to go to England. In 1860, William published a book about their experiences, *Running a Thousand Miles for Freedom.* At the end of the Civil War, the Crafts returned to Georgia, where they opened a school for black children.

PAUL CUFFEE (1759–1817)

Shipbuilder, Ship Captain, Emigrationist. Paul Cuffee (or Cuffe) was a free African American man who learned to articulate the doctrines of freedom for oppressed African Americans. He eventually became an exponent of African colonization and of the British Sierra Leone settlement. Born in Massachusetts before the Revolutionary War, Cuffee was of mixed Native American and African parentage and the seventh of eleven children. As a youth, he was able to get some education and then found work as a sailor, as a laborer in shipyards, and as a shipbuilder. He saw opportunities in this line of work. By 1780, he had built a ship of his own, and by 1806 he owned one large ship, two brigs, and some smaller vessels and was able to engage very profitably in trade.

In spite of his accomplishments, Cuffee still regularly confronted racial prejudice. Although his wealth continued to grow, as did his tax contributions to the Massachusetts government, he could not vote and his children could not attend public schools. Cuffee knew that the American colonists had railed against Great Britain for taxation without representation during the Revolutionary War, and it seemed to him that the colonies were guilty of the same injustices by taxing free blacks without letting them reap the benefits of their tax dollars. In defiance, Cuffee and his brother refused to pay their taxes. Cuffee later financed a Quaker school, which he opened not only to black children but to all children in his community.

Even when the Massachusetts courts abolished African enslavement in 1783, Cuffee reasoned that the best avenue for blacks was to reestablish contact with West Africans for the purpose of colonization and trade. He thought that blacks could contribute both civilization and Christianity to their ancestral homeland. During a trip to Sierra Leone in 1811 to 1812, Cuffee formed the Friendly Society with an African American emigrant named John Kizzell for the purpose of encouraging emigration and trade.

Cuffee was unable to interest anyone in financing his Sierra Leone colonization plans, so he decided to finance it himself. He encountered one major problem, however. During the time he was formulating his plan, the United States and Great Britain became involved in the War of 1812, and Americans were not permitted to trade with England or its colonies. In 1814, Cuffee petitioned the U.S. Congress to lift the embargo against trade with Sierra Leone so that he could begin his venture. His petition passed the Senate but was struck down by the House. Finally, after the cessation of hostilities in 1815 and at a personal expenditure of $4,000, Cuffee took nine free black families totaling thirty-eight individuals to settle in Sierra Leone. The emigrant group consisted of nine men, ten women, six boys, and thirteen girls. Although he had difficulty marketing his trade goods when he returned, Cuffee became even more determined that black Americans needed to emigrate if they were to achieve true independence and racial dignity. Many free blacks, as well as some whites, received Cuffee's emigration plan with enthusiasm, but few African Americans were willing to give up their American citizenship. The United States was the only country they knew.

FREDERICK DOUGLASS (1818–1895)

Abolitionist, Editor, Diplomat, Government Official, Legislator. Born in Talbot County, Maryland, on February 14, 1818, Frederick Douglass was sent to Baltimore as a house servant when he was eight. There, his mistress taught him to read and write. After the death of his master, he was sent to the country to work as a field hand. During his time in the South, he was severely flogged for his resistance to his enslaved status. In his early teens, he began to teach in a Sunday school that was later forcibly shut down by hostile whites. After an unsuccessful escape attempt, he succeeded in making his way to New York disguised as a sailor in 1838. He found work as a day laborer in New Bedford, Massachusetts, and after an extemporaneous speech before the Massachusetts Anti-Slavery Society, he became one of its agents.

Douglass quickly became a nationally recognized figure among abolitionists. To prove to whites who refused to believe that such an articulate black man could never have been enslaved, Douglass wrote the first of several autobiographies, *Narrative of the Life of Frederick Douglass*, published in 1845. In it, he related his experiences as an enslaved child and young man, and he revealed his fugitive status and his current exposure to the danger of re-enslavement. In the same year, he traveled to England and Ireland, where he remained until 1847, speaking out against African enslavement and in support of women's rights. Ultimately, he raised sufficient funds to purchase his freedom. After returning to the United States, he founded the paper *North Star*. In the tense years before the Civil War, he was forced to flee to Canada when the governor of Virginia issued a warrant for his arrest.

Douglass returned to the United States before the beginning of the Civil War and, after meeting with President Abraham Lincoln, he assisted in the formation of the Fifty-fourth and Fifty-fifth Negro Regiments of Massachusetts. During Reconstruction, he became deeply involved in the civil rights movement, and in 1871 he was appointed to the territorial legislature of the District of Columbia. He served as one of the presidential electors-at-large for New York in 1872 and, shortly thereafter, became the secretary of the Santo Domingo Commission. After serving for a short time as the police commissioner of the District of Columbia, he was appointed marshal in 1871, and held the post until he was appointed the recorder of deeds in 1881. In 1890, his support of the presidential campaign of Benjamin Harrison won him his most important federal post: he became minister resident and consul general to the Republic of Haiti and, later, the chargé d'affaires of Santo Domingo. In 1891, he resigned the position in protest of the unscrupulous practices of U.S. businessmen. Douglass died at his home in Washington, D.C., on February 20, 1895.

Scholar and Activist W. E. B. Du Bois. *An educator and author of such works as* The Souls of Black Folks *(1903), Du Bois was a leader of the Niagara Movement, helped found the NAACP, and edited the* Crisis, *an NAACP magazine, from its inception in 1910 until 1934. He was also a pioneering advocate of Pan-Africanism.* **THE BETTMANN ARCHIVE. REPRODUCED BY PERMISSION.**

SARAH MAPPS DOUGLASS

See chapter 16, Education.

W. E. B. DU BOIS (1868–1963)

Scholar, Activist, Pan-Africanist. William Edward Burghardt Du Bois was born in Great Barrington, Massachusetts, the great-grandchild of Elizabeth Freeman, an eighteenth-century black woman who successfully sued for her freedom after she was hit with a hot shovel while protecting her daughter. Du Bois received a solid education, but he was not able to go to the college of his choice—Harvard—because of his African ancestry. He went instead to Fisk University in Tennessee, an institution of higher learning established for freed African Americans. After graduating from Fisk in 1888, Du Bois earned his doctorate degree from Harvard in 1895. His dissertation on the suppression of the African slave trade became the first in the series of Harvard Historical Studies.

In spite of his scholarly accomplishments, Du Bois faced continual discrimination. He nevertheless began to write about the history and culture of African Americans and to research a series of cultural-sociological essays and studies, including *The Philadelphia Negro* (1899) and *The Souls of Black Folks* (1903). He also taught at several historically black colleges.

In 1905, Du Bois met with a group of African American leaders in Niagara Falls, Canada, to articulate the political and social needs of blacks and to strategize ways of obtaining first-class citizenship. Some of the ideas of the Niagara Movement were incorporated by a group of activists—mostly whites—who wanted to form an organization to agitate for civil rights for people of color.

This group, the National Association for the Advancement of Colored People, formed in 1909, became popular largely because Du Bois became the editor of its monthly magazine, the *Crisis*, a position he filled from 1910 to 1934. Du Bois used the *Crisis* to showcase the accomplishments of Africans in the diaspora, while emphasizing the NAACP's platform for equal rights for all Americans. He also helped popularize the concept of Pan-Africanism, or the need for Africans worldwide to work together for political and social rights.

Du Bois was a tireless advocate for the rights of all. He edited four journals and wrote seventeen books, the most famous being *The Souls of Black Folks*. He took the United States to task on every national and international issue related to race relations. When he became disenchanted with the United States and the civil rights movement toward the end of his life, he joined the Communist Party and moved to Ghana in 1961, where he died two years later.

JEAN BAPTISTE POINTE DU SABLE

See chapter 14, Entrepreneurship.

OLAUDAH EQUIANO (c. 1750–1797)

Abolitionist, Writer. Olaudah Equiano was born around 1750 in an Ibo village in southern Nigeria. When he was eleven, he was kidnapped and enslaved in Africa before being shipped to the New World. His masters included a Virginia plantation owner, a British officer—who gave him the name Gustavus Vassa—and a Philadelphia merchant from whom he eventually purchased his freedom. Equiano then settled in England, where he worked diligently for the elimination of African enslavement. He even went so far as to present a petition to Parliament calling for its abolition.

Equiano's autobiography, *The Interesting Narrative of the Life of Olaudah Equiano, or Gustavus Vassa*, was published in London in 1789 and went through five editions in five years. It is regarded as a highly informative account of the evils of enslavement as it affected the master and the black captive, as well as the precursor to other important slave narratives, such as the *Narrative of the Life of Frederick Douglass*.

ESTEVANICO, STEPHEN DORANTES (c. 1503–1539)

Explorer. Born in Azamor, Morocco, young Estevanico's city was captured in a battle with the Portuguese when he was a baby. Eventually, Estevanico was sold into slavery in Spain to Andres de Dorantes (or Dorantz). Dorantes gave him the name Stephen; Estevanico is a nickname that means "Little Stephen."

Two decades later, Dorantes left Spain on an expedition to Florida, arriving in April 1528. After encountering hostile Indians, many of the six hundred colonists and soldiers with Estevanico were killed or enslaved. Those who escaped landed in Texas, but most of them lost their lives. Estevanico, Andres de Dorantes, Álvar Núñez Cabeza de Vaca, and Alonso Castillo managed to escape Indian captivity in 1534. Estevanico, who had a facility for languages, became a guide and scout for the Europeans. He was able to convince many Indians that he was a healer, and in that role he acted as a mediator between the Spaniards and the Indians. In his communication with the Indians he learned about seven cities of gold known as Cibola. Indians described these cities of wealth and gave him tokens they claimed were from the mysterious city.

The small group traveled with great difficulty through Texas and arrived in Mexico City in 1536. The viceroy there wanted Estevanico to lead an expedition to Arizona and New Mexico to find Cibola. Estevanico served as the scout for the expedition, which was led this time by Father Marcos de Niza. Estevanico sent back wooden crosses to mark the direction of his journey. Still introducing himself as a powerful healer, Estevanico attracted many Indians, who traveled with him. When he came to a Zuni pueblo with large stone structures, he sent back a cross much larger than the ones he had sent previously. Soon after that, communication with Estevanico ceased. Some believe he was killed by the Indians. Others speculate that he escaped his bondage.

JOHN FLOYD (1783–1837)

Governor of Virginia. John Floyd was the white governor of Virginia during the Nat Turner campaign in Southampton, Virginia, in 1831. He wrote an explanatory letter to the governor of South Carolina, James Hamilton Jr., detailing what he believed to be the causal factors of the rebellion. First, he blamed the restiveness of enslaved Africans to the presence of northerners traveling and doing business in the South. He especially noted that their teaching of Christianity caused enslaved blacks to feel that they were equal before God, and their participation in the Revolutionary War philosophies of liberty incited bondspersons' desire for freedom. Floyd also cited white women who, in their eagerness to evangelize blacks, taught them to read the Bible and religious tracts. He also said that owners allowed large religious meetings where African Americans were taught about equality before God and sang songs that expressed longings for freedom. In addition, Floyd mentioned the number of black preachers who spoke with the enslaved, insisting that they were probably all directly responsible for the revolt. Floyd was especially concerned about the infiltration of such publications as William Lloyd Garrison's newspaper, the *Liberator*, and David Walker's *Appeal.*

WILLIAM LLOYD GARRISON (1805–1879)

Abolitionist, Journalist. William Lloyd Garrison, a white abolitionist, was born in Newburyport, Massachusetts, in 1805. The Garrison family was abandoned by their father and had to find means for their own support. Young William was apprenticed several times as a youth, but in 1818 he began working as a writer and editor. In his twenties, Garrison began to actively support the movement for the abolition of slavery. He supported the American Colonization Society (ACS) for a while, but then decided that the ACS did not have the best interests of African Americans at heart. He was also concerned by the high mortality rate of African American settlers in Liberia.

In the late 1820s, Garrison met Benjamin Lundy, the editor of the antislavery newspaper, the *Genius of Universal Emancipation.* Garrison eventually founded his own newspaper, the *Liberator*, in 1831, and became a relentless opponent of the enslavement of Africans. Garrison argued for immediate, universal emancipation, and he believed that the U.S. Constitution was little more than a slavery document. He helped to organize the New England Anti-Slavery Society in 1832 and the American Anti-Slavery Society the following year. In 1839, Frederick Douglass began to read the *Liberator* and attend abolition meetings. By 1841, Douglass was traveling with Garrison and other abolitionists, speaking out against the enslavement of Africans. Many of the sponsors and subscribers to Garrison's newspaper were African Americans. After publishing almost two thousand issues of the *Liberator*, Garrison ceased publication during the Civil War.

ARCHIBALD H. GRIMKÉ

See chapter 10, Law.

LEMUEL HAYNES (1753–1833)

Religious Leader. Lemuel Haynes was born in West Hartford, Connecticut, in 1753, the son of a black father and white mother. He was abandoned as an infant, and brought up as an indentured servant by Deacon David Rose of Granville, Massachusetts. He was a precocious child and began writing mature sermons while still a boy. His preparation for the ministry was interrupted by the American Revolution. On April 19, 1775, he fought in the first battle of the war at Lexington, Massachusetts. He then joined the regular forces and served with Ethan Allen's Green Mountain Boys at the capture of Fort Ticonderoga. Haynes became qualified to preach in 1780 and accepted the pastorship of a new white congregation in Granville, where he remained for about five years. He was officially ordained in 1785. He later served as pastor of at least four other white congregations in New England.

JAMES AUGUSTINE HEALY

See chapter 17, Religion.

SALLY HEMINGS (1773–1835)

Enslaved African. Sally Hemings was born enslaved in Virginia in 1773. She was the daughter of a white man named John Wayles and a mulatto named Elizabeth Hemings. She became enslaved to (and most probably the concubine of) President Thomas Jefferson. While it is known that Hemings gave birth to several mulatto children, there is considerable scholarly debate over whether Thomas Jefferson was their father. Contemporaries claimed that Hemings's children bore a close resemblance to Jefferson, and scholars argue that all of Hemings's pregnancies correspond to a date that Jefferson was at home rather than on his extensive travels.

The Hemings offspring were among the few enslaved persons that Jefferson freed. One of the former president's contemporaries (albeit, a political enemy) accused him of miscegenation in 1802, but the furor over the exact nature of Jefferson's relationship with Sally Hemings did not pick up steam until the late twentieth century, when DNA tests on descendants of Sally Hemings concluded that either Jefferson or a close male relative had fathered Hemings's children. Those who maintain the existence of a sexual relationship between the two figures suggest that Jefferson first seduced Hemings in Paris when she was just fifteen, and that they maintained a thirty-eight-year relationship until his death in 1826.

JOSIAH HENSON (1789–1883)

Educator, Abolitionist, Religious Leader, Author. Born enslaved in Charles County near Rockville, Maryland, on June 15, 1789, Josiah Henson grew up with the experience of his family being cruelly treated by his owner. By the time he was eighteen years old, Henson was supervising his owner's farm. In 1825, he and his wife and children were moved to Kentucky, where conditions were greatly improved. In 1828, he became a preacher in a Methodist Episcopal Church. Under the threat of being sold, he and his family escaped to Ohio in 1830, and the following year entered Canada by way of Buffalo, New York. In Canada, he learned to read and write from one of his sons, and he soon began preaching in Dresden, Ontario.

While in Canada, Henson became active in the Underground Railroad, helping nearly two hundred slaves to escape to freedom. In 1842, he and several others attempted to start the British-American Manual Labor Institute, but the industrial school was unsuccessful. Henson related his story to Harriet Beecher Stowe (the author of *Uncle Tom's Cabin*), and it has been disputed whether or not her story is based on aspects of his life.

Henson traveled three times to England, where he met distinguished people, was honored for his abolitionist activities and personal escape from enslavement, and was offered a number of positions that he turned down in order to return to Canada. He published his autobiography, *The Life of Josiah Henson, Formerly a Slave, Now an Inhabitant of Canada, as Narrated by Himself*, in 1849 and rewrote and reissued it in 1858 and 1879. Henson died in Ontario in 1883.

HARRY HOSIER (c. 1750–1806)

Preacher. Most sources report that Harry Hosier (also spelled Hoosier, Hoshur, Hossier) was born enslaved near Fayetteville, North Carolina, around 1750. Although little is known about the circumstances, Hosier experienced a religious conversion to Methodism and gained his freedom. He is thought to have met Francis Asbury, the founder of Methodism and evangelist to those enslaved, sometime in 1780. Asbury described the meeting as "providentially arranged." The two men traveled together to spread the Gospel, with Hosier acting as Asbury's servant, guide, and circuit-riding partner.

Hosier was an eloquent speaker who, though uneducated, was intellectually alert and creative and possessed a remarkable memory. Those who heard him preach were instantly impressed. He preached with Asbury at the Fairfax Chapel in Falls Church, Virginia, as early as May 13, 1781. It is believed this made him the first black preacher to deliver a sermon to a white Methodist church in America. His fame as a preacher brought him into contact with several other major preachers, including Thomas Coke, who wrote of him, "I really believe he is one of the best Preachers in the world, there is such an amazing power attends his preaching, though he cannot read; and he is one of the humblest creatures I ever saw." Hosier actually resisted learning to read and write throughout his career, relying on his memory for biblical passages and hymns. He was present at the historic Christmas conference at the end of 1784, which saw the formal establishment of both the Methodist Episcopal Church and a permanent relationship between black and white Methodists. Although enormously popular, Hosier was never ordained in the Methodist church, possibly because of his rumored problems with alcohol.

ABSALOM JONES

See chapter 17, Religion.

JAMES ARMISTEAD LAFAYETTE (c. 1748–1830)

Continental Spy. Born enslaved, James Armistead risked his life behind enemy lines collecting information for the Continental Army. He furnished valuable information to the Marquis de Lafayette and enabled the French commander to check the troop advances of British general Charles Cornwallis. This action set the stage for General George Washington's victory at Yorktown in 1781 and for the end of the Revolutionary War. In recognition of his services, James was granted his freedom by the Virginia legislature in 1786, although it was not until 1819 that Virginia awarded him a pension of $40 a year and a grant of $100. He adopted the surname "Lafayette" in honor of his former commander, who visited him during a trip to the United States in 1824.

ISAAC LANE

See chapter 17, Religion.

LUCY C. LANEY

See chapter 16, Education.

JOHN MERCER LANGSTON

See chapter 11, Politics.

JARENA LEE

See chapter 17, Religion.

GEORGE LIELE

See chapter 17, Religion.

ONESIMUS (1700s)

Enslaved African, Scientific Discoverer. Onesimus was born and grew up in northern Africa, a member of the Garamantes people of the northern Sahara. He was captured in the early 1700s, and was enslaved in Boston. Beginning in 1706, he worked for religious leader Cotton Mather, who also was a contributor to scientific journals, such as *Philosophical Transactions of the Royal Society of London*. While reading an article in that magazine, Mather was struck by how closely the recounted practice of inoculation in Turkey resembled an African practice that Onesimus had described to him. Mather's description of Onesimus's account was printed in the *Yale Journal of Biology and Medicine* from a letter Mather wrote to the Royal Society. Nothing came of this information for another five years.

In 1721, Boston was hit with a smallpox epidemic, and Mather insisted that the medical community at least attempt his servant's method of disease prevention. A country doctor, Zabdiel Boylston, did so, and succeeded in saving his six-year-old son and two other enslaved individuals. Using this method, Boylston inoculated 286 more people, keeping careful records. Of those, 2.1 percent died, compared to 14.9 percent of those who acquired smallpox naturally. Boylston reported his findings to the Royal Society, and the medical community became convinced of the value of inoculation.

Through the accurate recounting of a procedure that had been carried out on him in Africa, Onesimus helped bring knowledge of inoculation to the Western world. This would remain the primary method for protecting people from the ravages of smallpox until the introduction of the Jennerian cowpox vaccination in 1798.

P. B. S. PINCHBACK

See chapter 11, Politics.

SALEM POOR (1747–?)

Revolutionary War Soldier. Salem Poor was born enslaved in 1747 in Andover, Massachusetts. He spent his childhood and the early years of his adult life on his owner's farm in Andover, before purchasing his freedom in 1769. In March 1774, after the Continental Congress directed certain units of the Massachusetts militia to serve as minutemen, the Massachusetts Committee of Safety permitted black volunteers to join town and village companies. A number of free black men promptly enlisted, including Poor, who joined the First Andover Company as a private. Like other minutemen, Poor was trained to respond at a minute's notice to British aggression.

When the American rebellion against the British turned into open warfare, Poor enlisted under Captain Samuel Johnson in the Fifth Massachusetts Regiment on April 24, 1775. He participated in the Battle of Bunker Hill, and fired the shot that killed British lieutenant colonel James Abercrombie. Poor was never far from active duty in the years between 1775 and 1780. Along with some five hundred other black sharpshooters in the Continental Army, he spent the legendary harsh winter of 1777 to 1778 with General George Washington in his Valley Forge encampment. Poor also served in the crucial battles of White Plains, New York, and Providence, Rhode Island. Only one instance is recorded of Salem Poor having been commended for his bravery, the submission of a petition of recommendation in December 1775. Two hundred years later, Poor's valor was publicly recognized. On March 25, 1975, as part of the U.S. Postal Service's Revolutionary War Bicentennial series of stamps titled *Contributors to the Cause*, a commemorative ten-cent stamp was issued in recognition of "Salem Poor—Gallant Soldier."

GABRIEL PROSSER (c. 1775–1800)

Insurrectionist. Gabriel Prosser was born around 1775. He became the coachman of Thomas Prosser of Henrico County, Virginia. Gabriel planned a large, highly organized revolt to take place on the last night of August 1800 around Richmond, Virginia. About 32,000 enslaved Africans but only 8,000 whites lived in the area at the time, and it was his intention to kill all of the whites except for the French, Quakers, elderly women, and children. His hope was that the remaining 300,000 people who were enslaved in Virginia would follow his lead and seize the entire state. The revolt was set to coincide with the harvest so that his followers would be spared any shortage of food, and it was decided that the conspirators would meet at the Old Brook Swamp outside of Richmond and marshal forces to attack the city.

The insurrection fell apart when a severe rainstorm made it impossible for many of the participants to assemble and a pair of house servants who did not wish their master killed revealed the plot. Panic swept through the city, martial law was declared, and those suspected of involvement were rounded up and hanged. When it became clear that the enslaved population would be decimated if all of those implicated were dealt with in similar fashion, the courts began to mete out less-severe sentences. Gabriel was apprehended in the hold of a schooner docked in Norfolk, Virginia. Brought back in chains, he was interrogated by the governor. When he refused to divulge details of the conspiracy, he was hanged.

JOSEPH H. RAINEY

See chapter 11, Politics.

HIRAM RHODES REVELS

See chapter 11, Politics.

GEORGE RUFFIN

See chapter 10, Law.

DRED SCOTT (c. 1795–1858)

Abolitionist. Born in Southampton County, Virginia, around 1795, Dred Scott's first name was simply Sam. He worked as a farmhand, handyman, and stevedore, and moved with his owner to Huntsville, Alabama, and later to St. Louis, Missouri. In 1831, his owner, Peter Blow, died, and Sam was bought by John Emerson, a surgeon in the U.S. Army. Sam accompanied his new master to Illinois (a free state) and Wisconsin (then a territory). Sometime after 1836, Sam received permission to marry, and by 1848 he had changed his name to Dred Scott. At various times, he attempted to buy his freedom or to escape, but was unsuccessful. In 1843, Emerson died and left his estate to his widow, Irene Emerson, who also

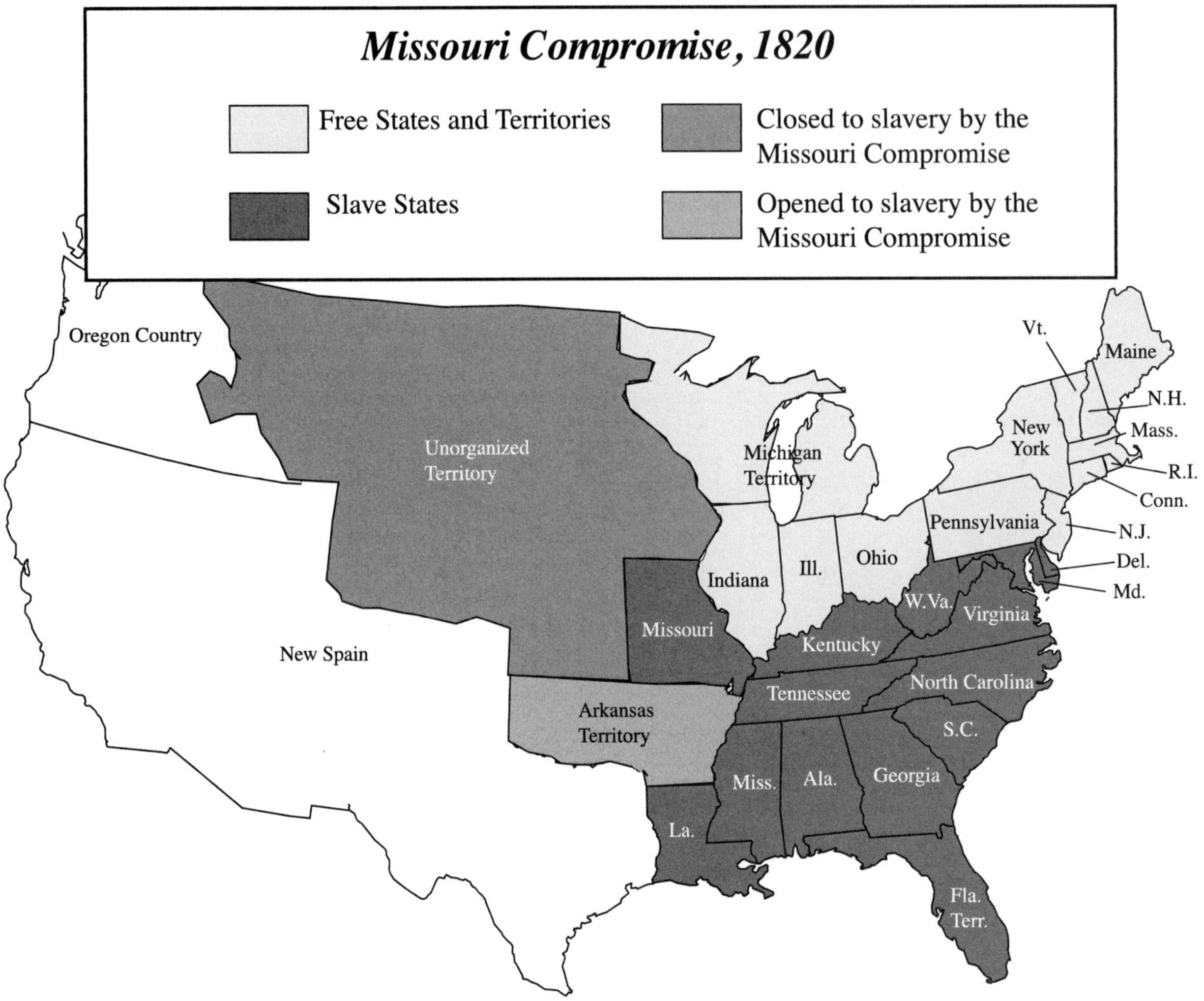

The Missouri Compromise attempted to settle the most serious crisis of the Monroe administration. From 1818 to 1820, Congress, the cabinet, and the public debated the admission of Missouri as a state and whether or not slavery would be permitted in the new state. The Missouri Compromise set the boundary for slavery at the 36°30' north parallel. But Missouri was admitted as a slave state, maintaining an equal number of slave states and free states.

Missouri Compromise of 1820. *Following contentious debate over the admission of Missouri as a state and whether or not slavery would be permitted there, a compromise was reached enabling Missouri to enter the Union as a slave state and Maine as a free state—thus maintaining an equal number of slave states and free states. In addition, all territory north of latitude 36° 30′ was declared free; all territory south of that line was open to slavery.* ILLUSTRATION BY ERIC WISNIEWSKI. REPRODUCED BY PERMISSION OF GALE.

refused to grant Scott his freedom. He then obtained the assistance of two attorneys, who helped him sue for his freedom in county court.

Scott lost this case, but the verdict was set aside, and in 1847 he won a second trial on the grounds that his enslaved status had been nullified once he entered a free state. Scott received financial backing and legal representation through the sons of Peter Blow, Irene Emerson's brother John Sanford, and her second husband, Dr. C. C. Chaffee, all of whom apparently saw the case as an important challenge to African enslavement. The case went all the way to the U.S. Supreme Court. In 1857, the Court ruled against Dred Scott, stating that those enslaved in the country were not legal citizens of the United States and, therefore, had no standing in the courts. Shortly after the decision was handed down, Mrs. Emerson freed Scott. The case led to the nullification of the Missouri Compromise of 1820, allowing the expansion of slavery into formerly free territories and strengthening the abolition movement.

WILLIAM STILL (1821–1902)

Underground Railroad Conductor, Author. In 1872, William Still published a 558-page book with the long title, *The Underground Rail Road: A Record of Facts, Authentic Narratives, Letters, &c., Narrating the Hardships, Hair-breadth escapes, and Death Struggles of the Slaves in their Efforts for Freedom as Related by Themselves and Others, or Witnessed by the Author, Together with Sketches of Some of the Largest Stockholders, and Most Liberal Aiders and Advisers, of the Road.* Born in New Jersey in 1821, William Still was the son of formerly enslaved Africans. As an employee of the Philadelphia-based Pennsylvania Society for the Abolition of Slavery, he began assisting large numbers of runaways, especially after the passage of the Fugitive Slave Act of 1850. At that time, the society made him chairperson of its Vigilance Committee, and Still listened to the accounts of many escapees and recorded their stories. In his book, he praises his friend and coconspirator Harriet Tubman for her bravery and tenacity as an Underground Railroad conductor. Even after slavery was abolished in the nation, Still continued to work for first-class citizenship for African Americans.

HARRIET BEECHER STOWE (1811–1896)

Abolitionist, Author. Harriet Beecher Stowe was a white teacher, abolitionist, and writer, but most people remember her only as the author of the novel *Uncle Tom's Cabin.* Harriet was born June 14, 1811, in Litchfield, Connecticut, to Lyman and Roxanna Foote Beecher. In 1836, Harriet married Calvin Stowe, who taught biblical literature at Lane Theological Institute in Cincinnati, where Harriet's father was president. The couple had seven children. Galvanized by the passage of the Fugitive Slave Act 1850, Stowe published *Uncle Tom's Cabin, or, Life among the Lowly,* in forty installments from June 1851 to April 1852 in *National Era,* a Washington, D.C., periodical. The story riveted the attention of thousands of readers, and engendered outrage in many about the institution of African enslavement.

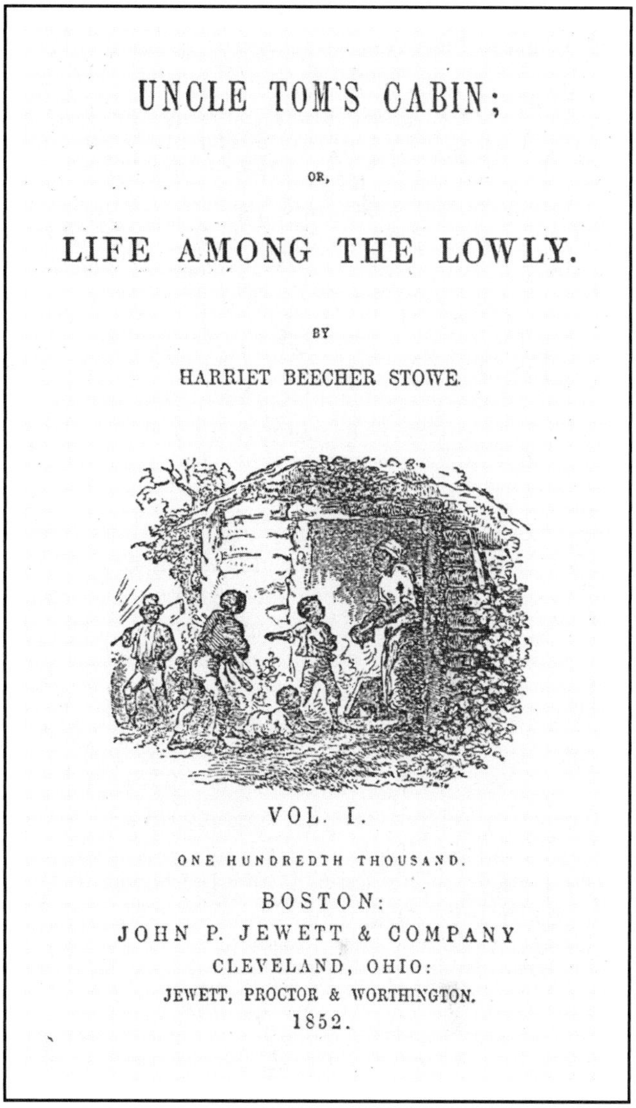
UNCLE TOM'S CABIN;

OR,

LIFE AMONG THE LOWLY.

BY

HARRIET BEECHER STOWE.

VOL. I.

ONE HUNDREDTH THOUSAND.

BOSTON:
JOHN P. JEWETT & COMPANY
CLEVELAND, OHIO:
JEWETT, PROCTOR & WORTHINGTON.
1852.

Title Page from First Edition of* Uncle Tom's Cabin *(by Harriet Beecher Stowe, 1852). *Stowe, a white abolitionist, wrote this novel after being galvanized by the Fugitive Slave Act of 1850. Originally published as a serial, the novel was an immediate best seller in book form and engendered outrage in many readers about the institution of slavery.* THE GRANGER COLLECTION, NEW YORK. REPRODUCED BY PERMISSION.

Although the story centers on the mistreatment of the pious Uncle Tom, many other enslaved characters are featured in the story. The book targets even benign plantation owners as partners in the crime against humanity. Toward the end of Tom's life, his owner, Simon Legree, who specializes in cruelty, beats Tom severely because he knows that Tom has outwitted him. When Tom's former owner rescues him, Tom survives only a short time after leaving Legree's plantation. When *Uncle Tom's Cabin* appeared as a book in March 1852, it sold 300,000 copies in one year. Before 1860, more than one million copies had sold in the United States and more than two million copies were sold in other countries. In 1853, 1856, and 1859, Stowe traveled abroad and was enthusiastically received by both common folks and nobility.

Stowe's novel added measurably to the polarization of abolitionist and antiabolitionist sentiment in the United States and Europe. Carl Sandburg reported in *Abraham Lincoln: The War Years* (1939), that during a White House visit, President Lincoln greeted Stowe with out stretched hands saying, "So you're the little woman who wrote the book that made this great war." Historian Benjamin Quarles noted that at an 1863 abolitionist's celebration of Lincoln's Emancipation Proclamation, the crowd yelled for Stowe to come forward to receive an enthusiastic ovation for the service she had performed by writing *Uncle Tom's Cabin.* Harriet Beecher Stowe died at age eighty-five in Hartford, Connecticut.

TOUSSAINT-LOUVERTURE (1743–1803)

Insurrectionist, Political Leader. François-Dominique Toussaint-Louverture (also spelled Toussaint L'Ouverture) was born enslaved on the island of Hispaniola (now Haiti and the Dominican Republic) in 1743. He learned to read and write under a benevolent owner. When he was fifty years old, a violent revolt erupted on the island. White French planters, enslaved Africans, and free mulattoes (some of whom enslaved Africans) clashed over issues of rights, land, and labor, as the forces of France, Britain, and Spain manipulated the conflict. Initially, the Africans and mulattoes shared the goals of the French Revolution in opposition to the royalist French planters, but with time a coalition of planters and mulattoes arose in opposition to the Africans.

Toussaint-Louverture became the leader of the revolutionary forces, which by mid-1790s consisted of a disciplined group of four thousand formerly enslaved Africans. He successfully waged a campaign against the British. At the height of Toussaint-Louverture's power and influence in 1796, General André Rigaud, who led the mulatto forces, sought to reimpose enslavement on the black islanders. Toussaint-Louverture quickly achieved victory, captured Santo Domingo, and by 1801 had virtual control of the Spanish part of the island. In 1802, a French expeditionary force was sent to reestablish French control of the island. Following a hard-fought resistance to French colonial ambitions in the Western Hemisphere, Toussaint-Louverture struck a peace treaty with Napoleon. However, Toussaint-Louverture was tricked, captured, and sent to France, where he died on April 7, 1803, under inhumane conditions.

SOJOURNER TRUTH (c. 1797–1883)

Lecturer, Abolitionist. Born Isabella Baumfree in Ulster County, New York, around 1797, she was freed by the New York State Emancipation Act of 1827 and lived in New York City for a time. After taking the name Sojourner Truth, which she felt God had given her, she assumed the "mission" of spreading "the Truth" across the country. She became famous as an itinerant preacher, drawing huge crowds with her oratory and, some said, with "mystical gifts." She became one of an active group of African American women abolitionists, lectured before numerous abolitionist audiences, and was friends with such leading white abolitionists as James and Lucretia Mott and Harriet Beecher Stowe. With the outbreak of the Civil War, Sojourner Truth raised money to purchase gifts for the soldiers, distributing them herself in the camps. She also helped African Americans who had escaped to the North find shelter. Age and ill health caused her to retire from the lecture circuit, and she spent her last days in a sanatorium in Battle Creek, Michigan.

HARRIET (ROSS) TUBMAN (c. 1821–1913)

Underground Railroad Conductor, Abolitionist, Nurse. Born around 1821 in Dorchester County, Maryland, Harriet Tubman experienced the hard childhood of an enslaved young girl. That meant much work, little schooling, and severe punishment. In 1848, she escaped, leaving behind her husband John Tubman, who threatened to report her to their master. As a free woman, she began to devise practical ways of helping others escape enslavement. During the next decade, she made about twenty trips from the North into the South and rescued more than three hundred black captives. Her reputation spread rapidly, and she won the admiration of leading abolitionists—some of whom sheltered her passengers. Eventually, a reward of $40,000 was posted for her capture.

Tubman met and aided John Brown in recruiting soldiers for his raid on Harpers Ferry. Brown referred to her as "General Tubman." One of her major disappointments was the failure of the raid, and she is said to have regarded Brown, not Lincoln, as the true emancipator of her people. In 1860, she began to canvass the nation, appearing at antislavery meetings and speaking on women's rights. Shortly before the outbreak of the Civil War, she was forced to leave for Canada, but she returned to the United States and served the Union as a nurse, soldier, and spy. She was particularly valuable to the army as a scout because of the knowledge of the terrain that she had gained as a conductor on the Underground Railroad.

Tubman's biography, from which she received the proceeds, was written by Sarah Bradford in 1868. Tubman's husband, John, died two years after the end of the war, and in 1869 she married the war veteran Nelson Davis. Despite receiving many honors and tributes, including a medal from Queen Victoria, she spent her last days in poverty, not receiving a pension until thirty years after the Civil War. With the $20 a month that she finally received, not for her own Civil War service but for her husband's, she helped to found a home for the aged and needy, which was later renamed the Harriet Tubman Home. She died on March 10, 1913, in Auburn, New York.

NAT TURNER (1800–1831)

Insurrectionist. Born enslaved in Southampton County, Virginia, on October 2, 1800, Nat Turner was an avid reader of the Bible who prayed, fasted, and experienced "voices," ultimately becoming a visionary mystic with a belief that God had given him the special destiny of overthrowing the American system of enslavement. On August 21, 1831, after recruiting a handful of conspirators, he struck at isolated homes in his immediate area, recruiting men at each home. Within forty-eight hours, the band of insurrectionists had reached sixty armed men. They killed fifty-five whites before deciding to attack the county seat in Jerusalem, but while en route they were overtaken by a posse and dispersed. Turner took refuge in the Dismal Swamp and remained there for six weeks before he was captured, brought to trial, and hanged along with sixteen other African Americans.

JAMES VARICK

See chapter 17, Religion.

DENMARK VESEY (1767–1822)

Religious Leader, Insurrectionist. Born in 1767, Vesey was sold by his owner at an early age and later bought back because of an epileptic condition. He sailed with his master, Captain Vesey, to and from the Virgin Islands and Haiti for twenty years. He enjoyed a considerable degree of mobility in his home port of Charleston, South Carolina, and eventually purchased his freedom using money he had won in a lottery. Denmark Vesey became a Methodist minister and used his church as a base to recruit supporters to take over Charleston. The revolt was planned for the second Sunday in July 1822.

Vesey's plans were betrayed when an enslaved house servant alerted the city's white authorities. Hundreds of African Americans were rounded up, though some of Vesey's collaborators most likely escaped to the Carolinas, where they fought as Maroons. After a twenty-two-day search, Vesey was apprehended and stood trial. During the trial, he adeptly cross-examined witnesses, but ultimately could not deny his intention to overthrow the city, and he was hanged along with several collaborators.

DAVID WALKER (1785–1830)

Abolitionist, Writer. David Walker was born free on September 28, 1785, in Wilmington, North Carolina, the offspring of a white mother and a black enslaved father. Walker acquired an education before moving to Boston in the late 1820s. After starting a used-clothing business, he became a member of the Massachusetts General Colored Association and an agent for the first African American newspaper, *Freedom's Journal.* In 1829, Walker published *Walker's Appeal, in Four Articles; Together with a Preamble to the Colored Citizens of the World,* a pamphlet that advocated the violent overthrow of the American system of African enslavement, the formation of African American civil rights and self-help organizations, racial equality in the United States, and independence for the peoples of Africa.

Walker's pamphlet alarmed southerners, who responded by enacting stricter laws against such "seditious" literature and against the education of free African Americans. In the North, Walker's pamphlet drew sharp criticism from such prominent abolitionists as William Lloyd Garrison and Benjamin Lundy. On June 28, 1830, nine months after publishing his pamphlet, Walker mysteriously died, leaving behind his wife, Eliza. Though never verified, rumor suggests that he was poisoned.

PHILLIS WHEATLEY

See chapter 18, Literature.

7

CIVIL RIGHTS

Linda T. Wynn

Throughout the history of the United States, African Americans have struggled to obtain basic civil rights. The struggle has spanned several centuries—from the mutinies by Africans during the Atlantic crossing to the insurrections organized by their enslaved ancestors in the New World. From the founding of the Free African Society and the abolition movement to the civil rights marches and demonstrations of the twentieth century, the struggle for human equality has been an ongoing saga.

EARLY RIGHTS MOVEMENTS

THE FREE AFRICAN SOCIETY

In 1787, as a result of segregation and discriminatory practices within the Methodist Church, the Reverends Richard Allen (1760–1831) and Absalom Jones (1746–1818) formed the Free African Society in Philadelphia. (Seven years later, Allen founded the Bethel African Methodist Church, the first African Methodist Episcopal [AME] Church in America; Jones later became the rector of a Protestant Episcopal church.) The society was an important model for political consciousness and economic organization for African Americans throughout the country. It provided spiritual guidance and religious instruction, medical and financial assistance to orphans, and economic aid, burial assistance, relief to widows. The society also advocated abolition and maintained channels of communication with African Americans in the South. Like the many other African American organizations that followed, the society was rooted in religious principles. Throughout the nineteenth century, a number of mutual-aid societies sprang up in African American communities in eastern cities, such as New York, Newport, and Boston, providing loans, insurance, and various other economic and social services to their members and the larger community. The societies also helped to facilitate communications between free African Americans throughout the country.

THE ABOLITION MOVEMENT

The press and the pulpit served as important tools in the antislavery movement. In 1827 Samuel Cornish (1795–1858) and John Russwurm (1799–1851) founded *Freedom's Journal* in New York, the first newspaper in the United States owned and operated by African Americans. *Freedom's Journal,* which ceased publication after only three years, was concerned not only with eradicating African enslavement but also with the growing discrimination and cruelty against free African Americans in both the South and North.

In 1847, abolitionist Frederick Douglass (1817–1895) published the first edition of the *North Star,* which eventually became one of the most successful African American newspapers prior to the outbreak of the Civil War (1861–1865). Douglass, who had escaped from enslavement in Maryland, became one of the best-known African American abolitionists in the country. He lectured extensively throughout the United States and England. In 1845, he published his autobiography, *Narrative of the Life of Frederick Douglass.*

Although the abolition movement was dominated by whites, numerous African American leaders played a major role in the movement, including such figures as Henry Highland Garnet (1815–1882), Harriet Tubman (c. 1821–1913), and Sojourner Truth (c. 1797–1883).

CIVIL RIGHTS DURING THE RECONSTRUCTION PERIOD

Following the Civil War, Republicans, who controlled the U.S. Congress, took up the cause of the newly freed African Americans. Between 1865 and 1875, Congress passed three amendments to the U.S. Constitution and a string of civil rights and Reconstructionist legislation. The Thirteenth Amendment, ratified December 18, 1865, abolished enslavement and involuntary servitude. The Fourteenth Amendment, ratified July 28, 1868, guaranteed citizenship and provided equal protection under the laws. The Fifteenth Amendment, ratified on March 30, 1870, protected the right of all citizens to vote. In 1866, 1870, 1871, and 1875, Congress passed civil rights legislation outlining and protecting basic rights, including access to public accommodations and the right to purchase and sell property. The Reconstruction Acts, passed between 1867 and 1869, called for new state constitutional conventions in those states that had seceded from the Union prior to the Civil War.

Reconstruction eventually produced a wave of anti–African American sentiment, though. White organizations, such as the Ku Klux Klan, which aimed at intimidating African Americans and preventing them from taking their place in society, sprang up throughout the North and the South. In 1871, Congress enacted the Ku Klux Klan Act as an effort to end intimidation and violence directed at African Americans. However, the act failed to eliminate the Klan and other terrorist organizations.

The civil rights and Reconstructionist legislation were difficult for many whites to accept, and they did little to change racist attitudes. The last of the civil rights acts, passed by Congress in 1875, prohibited discrimination in public accommodations. However, by the 1880s the debate as to the constitutionality of such legislation had reached the U.S. Supreme Court. Ruling in a group of five cases in 1883 that became known as the Civil Rights Cases, the U.S. Supreme Court concluded that the 1875 Civil Rights Act was unconstitutional on the grounds that the Fourteenth Amendment authorized Congress to legislate only against discriminatory state action and not discrimination by private individuals. The Court's ruling brought about an end to federal efforts to protect the civil rights of African Americans until the mid-twentieth century.

ANTILYNCHING EFFORTS

By the late nineteenth and early twentieth centuries, lynching had become a weapon used by whites against African Americans throughout the country. Between 1882 and 1990, approximately 1,750 African Americans were lynched in the United States. Victims included women who had been accused of a variety of "offenses," ranging from testifying in court against a white man to failing to use the word *mister* when addressing a white person. Ida B. Wells-Barnett (1862–1931), a journalist and social activist, became one of the leading voices in the antilynching crusade by writing and lecturing throughout the United States and England against its practice.

INSTITUTIONALIZED SEGREGATION

Prior to the case of *Plessy v. Ferguson* (1896), the U.S. Supreme Court had started to build the platform on which the doctrine of "separate but equal" would be based. In 1878, ruling in the case of *Hall v. DeCuir*, the Court declared that states could not prohibit segregation on common carriers, such as streetcars and railroads. Thereafter, segregation laws sprang up throughout the South. Three years after the *Hall v. DeCuir* ruling, Tennessee enacted the nation's first racial-segregation railways law.

In 1896, the U.S. Supreme Court faced the issue of segregation on public transportation. At the time, as was the case in many parts of the South, a Louisiana state law was enacted requiring that separate-but-equal accommodations for blacks and whites be maintained in all public facilities. When Homer Adolph Plessy (1862–1925), an African American man traveling by train from New Orleans to Covington, Louisiana, refused to ride in the "colored" railway coach, he was arrested.

With Justice Henry Billings Brown (1836–1913) delivering the majority opinion in the *Plessy* case, the Court declared that separate-but-equal accommodations constituted a reasonable use of state police power and that the Fourteenth Amendment could not be used to abolish social or racial distinctions or to force a comingling of the two races. The Supreme Court effectively reduced the significance of the Fourteenth Amendment, which was designed to give African Americans specific rights and protections. The ruling in the *Plessy* case, which was termed the *separate-but-equal doctrine*, paved the way for the segregation of African Americans in all walks of life.

CIVIL RIGHTS IN THE EARLY TWENTIETH CENTURY

BOOKER T. WASHINGTON AND W. E. B. DU BOIS

During the late nineteenth and early twentieth centuries, two figures—Booker T. Washington (1856–1915) and William Edward Burghardt Du Bois (1868–1963)—emerged as leaders in the struggle for African American political and civil rights. Washington, an educator and founder of the Tuskegee Normal and Industrial Institute in Alabama, was a strong advocate of practical, utilitarian education and manual training as a means for developing African Americans. (Founded in 1881, Tuskegee Normal and Industrial Institute was based on a program at Virginia's Hampton Institute that provided vocational training and prepared its students to survive economically in a segregated society.) In Washington's opinion, education should provide African Americans with the means to become economically self-supporting. Speaking at the Cotton States International Exposition in Atlanta in 1895, Washington outlined his philosophy of self-help and cooperation between African Americans and whites:

> To those of my race who depend on bettering their condition in a foreign land, or who underestimate the importance of cultivating friendly relations with the Southern white man, who is their next door neighbor, I would say: "Cast down your bucket where you are"—cast it down in making friends in every manly way of the people of all races by whom we are surrounded.

Later, W. E. B. Du Bois dubbed Washington's address the "Atlanta Compromise."

W. E. B. Du Bois, a young historian and Harvard graduate, challenged Washington's passive policies in a series of stinging essays and speeches. Du Bois advocated the uplifting of African Americans through an educated African American elite, which he referred to as the "Talented Tenth," or roughly a tenth of the African American population. He believed that these African Americans must become proficient in education and culture, which would eventually benefit all. In 1905, Du Bois, along with a group of other African American intellectuals, formed the Niagara Movement. The group drew up a platform that called for full citizenship rights for African Americans and public recognition of their contributions to America's stability and progress. The movement eventually evolved into what became known as the National Association for the Advancement of Colored People (NAACP).

A. PHILIP RANDOLPH

In 1941, A. Philip Randolph (1889–1979), organizer of an employment bureau for untrained African Americans and founder of the Brotherhood of Sleeping Car Porters, came up with the idea of leading a march of African Americans in Washington, D.C., to protest discrimination. On July 25, less than a week before the scheduled demonstration, President Franklin D. Roosevelt (1882–1945) issued Executive Order 8802, which banned discrimination in the defense industry and led to the creation of the Fair Employment Practices Committee.

CIVIL RIGHTS INTO THE TWENTY-FIRST CENTURY

The civil rights movement suffered many defeats in the first half of the twentieth century. Repeated efforts to obtain passage of federal antilynching bills failed. The all-white primary system, which effectively disenfranchised southern citizens of African descent, resisted numerous court challenges. The Great Depression worsened conditions in both rural and urban areas. On the positive side, the growing political power of African Americans in northern cities and an increasing liberal trend in the U.S. Supreme Court portended the legal and legislative victories of the 1950s and 1960s.

THE LITIGIOUS JOURNEY TO *BROWN V. BOARD OF EDUCATION OF TOPEKA*

After World War I (1914–1918), many African Americans sought graduate and professional training. However, such opportunities existed in only a few northern universities and at some privately supported African American institutions of higher learning, such as Howard, Fisk, and Atlanta universities. Concomitantly, it was believed that the public should offer graduate and professional training not only for whites but for African Americans as well. More than a few southern states took cognizance of this, and by 1935 their legislative bodies appropriated funds for out-of-state training for African Americans. African Americans were willing to seek redress from the judicial system to compel these states to carry out their obligations to their African American citizenry. As early as 1933, Thomas Hocutt of North Carolina sought admittance to the school of pharmacy at the University of North Carolina by filing a lawsuit against the university. When he neglected to establish his eligibility for admission, the court ruled against Hocutt on a legal technicality.

Beginning in the 1930s, the NAACP turned to the courts in an attempt to overcome legally sanctioned racial

SELECTED CIVIL RIGHTS FILMS

***Boycott* (2001)**
Clark Johnson, dir. With Jeffrey Wright, Terrence Howard, Iris Little-Thomas.

***A Child Shall Lead Them, Two Days in September 1957: The Desegregation of Nashville Public Schools* (2008)**
Rob McDonald, dir.

***Crisis at Central High* (1981)**
Lamont Johnson, dir. With Joanne Woodward, Charles Dunning, Henderson Forsythe, Calvin Levels, William Russ.

***The Ernest Green Story* (1993)**
Eric Laneuville, dir. With Morris Chestnut, Harry Wood II, Ossie Davis, Dennis Letts, Sean Serino.

***Eyes on the Prize* (1987)**
Henry Hampton, prod.

***4 Little Girls* (1997)**
Spike Lee, dir.

***Gandhi* (1982)**
Richard Attenborough, dir. With Ben Kingsley, Candice Bergen, Edward Fox, John Gielgud, Trevor Howard.

***Ghosts of Mississippi* (1996)**
Rob Reiner, dir. With Alec Baldwin, James Woods, Virginia Madsen, Whoopi Goldberg, Susanna Thompson.

***A Huey P. Newton Story* (2001)**
Spike Lee, dir. With Roger Guenveur Smith and H. Rap Brown.

***King* (1978)**
Abby Mann, dir. With Paul Winfield, Cicely Tyson, Tony Bennett, Roscoe Lee Brown, Lonny Chapman.

***Let Freedom Ring: Moments from the Civil Rights Movement, 1954–1965* (2009)**
Produced by NBC News. With Lester Holt.

***Little Rock Central: 50 Years Later* (2007)**
Brent Renaud and Craig Renaud, dirs.

***The Long Walk Home* (1990)**
Richard Pearce, dir. With Sissy Spacek, Whoopi Goldberg, Dwight Schultz, Ving Rhames, Dylan Baker.

***Malcolm X* (1992)**
Spike Lee, dir. With Denzel Washington, Angela Bassett, Delroy Lindo, Al Freeman Jr., Albert Hall.

***Miss Evers' Boys* (1997)**
Joseph Sargent, dir. With Alfre Woodard, Laurence Fishburne, Craig Sheffer, Joe Morton, Obba Babatundé.

***Mississippi Burning* (1988)**
Alan Parker, dir. With Gene Hackman, Willem Dafoe, Frances McDormand, Brad Dourif, R. Lee Ermey.

***The Murder of Fred Hampton* (1971)**
Mike Gray and Howard Alk, dirs.

***Passin' It On: The Black Panthers' Search for Justice* (1993)**
John Valadez, dir. With Dhoruba Bin Wahad.

***The Road to Freedom: The Vernon Johns Story* (1994)**
Kenneth Fink, dir. With James Earl Jones, Clifton James, Mary Alice, Cissy Houston.

***The Rosa Parks Story* (2002)**
Julie Nash, dir. With Angela Bassett, Peter Francis James, Tonea Steward, Von Coulter, Dexter King.

***Rosewood* (1997)**
John Singleton, dir. With Jon Voight, Ving Rhames, Paul Benjamin Jr., Mark Boone, Akosua Busia, Don Cheadle, Loren Dean.

***Ruby Bridges* (1998)**
Euzhan Palcy, dir. With Chaz Monet, Penelope Ann Miller, Kevin Pollak, Michael Beach, Lela Rochon.

***Scottsboro: An American Tragedy* (2000)**
Barak Goodman and Daniel Anker, dirs.

***Selma, Lord, Selma* (1999)**
Charles Burnett and Johnny Simmons, dirs. With Jurnee Smollett, Clifton Powell, Mackenzie Astin, Yolanda King, Stephanie Zandra Peyton.

***Separate But Equal* (1991)**
George Stevens, dir. With Sidney Poitier, Burt Lancaster, Richard Kiley, Cleavon Little, Gloria Foster.

***Understanding the Civil Rights Movement* (2000)**
Educational Video Network, prod.

***The Untold Story of Emmett Louis Till* (2004)**
Keith A. Beauchamp, dir.

***We Shall Not Be Moved: The Untold Chapter in the Struggle for American Civil Rights* (2001)**
Bernie Hargis, dir.

***When the Levees Broke: A Requiem in Four Acts* (2006)**
Spike Lee, dir.

***With All Deliberate Speed* (2004)**
Peter Gilbert, dir.

segregation. Headed by attorney Charles Hamilton Houston (1895–1950), the civil rights organization successfully litigated two cases between 1935 and 1938. He, along with his assistant, attorney Thurgood Marshall (1908–1993), devised a strategy to attack Jim Crow laws by striking at higher education. Four years after joining the NAACP, Marshall wrote the charter for the NAACP Legal Defense and Educational Fund (LDF), of which he became the first director. By 1950, the LDF had litigated three other important cases that chipped away at legally sanctioned segregation.

Murray v. Maryland was the first case. In 1935, Donald Gaines Murray (1914–1986), like Marshall before him, was denied entrance to the University of Maryland's School of Law because of it racial policies. Marshall argued that since there were no "black" law schools in the state with the same academic standing as the University of Maryland's law school, by denying Murray admittance, the university was violating the separate-but-equal principle as enunciated in the 1896 *Plessy v. Ferguson* case. He furthered argued that the disparities between the "white" and "black" law schools were so great that the only remedy would be to allow Murray to attend the university's law school. The Baltimore City Court agreed. Subsequently, the university appealed to the Maryland Court of Appeals. In 1936, the state Court of Appeals ruled in the plaintiff's favor and ordered the University of Maryland School of Law to admit the aspiring attorney. Murray graduated two years later.

The same year that the Maryland Court of Appeals heard the *Murray* case, the NAACP took on the case of Lloyd Gaines, a graduate student attending the all-black Lincoln University in Jefferson City, Missouri. Gaines, who applied to the University of Missouri Law School, was denied admittance because of his race. The state of Missouri offered Gaines a scholarship to a law school in a neighboring state. He refused the offer and filed suit against Missouri. When the *Missouri ex rel. Gaines v. Canada* case reached the U.S. Supreme Court in 1938, Houston defended his client on the grounds that offering him an out-of-state scholarship was no substitute for admission. Six members of the Court agreed, stating that since no black law school existed in the state of Missouri, it had to establish an equal facility or admit Gaines. Ten years later, Thurgood Marshall appeared before the Court arguing on behalf Ada Lois Sipuel (1924–1995).

Sipuel, an African American, had graduated summa cum laude with an undergraduate degree in political science from Langston University. In 1946, she applied to the University of Oklahoma Law School. Despite her excellent academic qualifications, Sipuel was denied admittance based on her race. Marshall and local attorney Amos T. Hall (1896–1971) argued her case before the Oklahoma district court, asking that the university be required to admit Sipuel. The court ruled in favor of the university. A year later, Oklahoma's State Supreme Court upheld the district court's decision. In 1948, Marshall and Amos took *Sipuel v. Board of Regents of the University of Oklahoma* to the U.S. Supreme Court. The country's highest tribunal reversed the lower courts and held that the state was required to provide African Americans with equal educational opportunities. Notwithstanding the Court's decision, George W. McLaurin (1887–1968) provided the case that damaged the separate-but-equal doctrine beyond repair.

McLaurin, a veteran educator with a master's degree from the University of Kansas, taught classes at Langston University until 1948, when he applied to the University of Oklahoma. In his sixties, the aspiring doctoral student wanted to pursue a degree in school administration. Although admitted to the university, he was relegated to separate niches in all areas of the educational process. McLaurin "was required to sit apart at a designated desk in an anteroom adjoining the classroom; to sit at a designated desk on the mezzanine floor of the library, but not to use the desks in the regular reading room; and to sit at a designated table and to eat at a different time from the other students in the school cafeteria." McLaurin felt that these conditions adversely affected his ability to learn, and he sought judicial relief. His case worked in conjunction with the *Sipuel* suit to desegregate higher education in Oklahoma. Marshall argued his case before the state courts and lost. However, he appealed the case to the U.S. Supreme Court, where he argued in *McLaurin v. Oklahoma State Regents* that the school's treatment of McLaurin violated the Fourteenth Amendment. On June 5, 1950, the Supreme Court ruled in favor of the appellant. Chief Justice Fred Vinson (1890–1953), writing for the Court, said that McLaurin "must receive the same treatment at the hands of the state as students of other races."

On the same day that the Supreme Court announced its ruling in *McLaurin*, it also handed down its opinion in *Sweatt v. Painter*. In 1946, Heman Marion Sweatt (1912–1982), an African American, applied to the University of Texas's white law school. To avoid integrating its classrooms, the state of Texas had established a law school for African Americans in 1947, but the school was severely underfunded. Marshall filed suit against the university, arguing that Sweatt could not receive the same level of academic quality at the school for African Americans that he could receive if he attended the state's law school for white students. The Supreme Court, in a unanimous decision, agreed with Sweatt. It was not possible, declared Chief Justice Vinson, for the black law school to provide the plaintiff with an education equal to that of the university law school, which had a strong faculty, experienced administrators, influential alumni, standing in the community, tradition, and prestige. The black law school and the white law school may have been separate, but they were not equal.

The legal system in the United States is set up on the standard of *stare decisis*—legal precedent establishes the law. The carefully planned stratagem of the LDF's attorneys was to get the U.S. Supreme Court to render a series of rulings that buttressed racial desegregation. Successful in its line of attack, these decisions became lawful paradigms and the underpinning for deconstructing segregation in public schools, thereby revealing the defectiveness of the Court-sanctioned public policy of separate but equal.

Numerous Supreme Court decisions between the 1930s and 1954 contain strong language condemning racial discrimination. On five separate occasions between 1938 and 1950, African Americans sought admittance to white graduate or professional schools, and five times the U.S. Supreme Court ordered their admission. While the decisions did not explicitly topple the doctrine of separate but equal, they did bring into focus the far-reaching inequality between schools for African Americans and those for whites. The Supreme Court's finding of ubiquitous inequality and its unremitting refusal to sustain racial classification paved the road for its 1954 decision in *Brown v. Board of Education of Topeka.*

Much of the civil rights struggle throughout this period was carried on by the NAACP, which began chipping away at the roots of legalized segregation in a series of successful lawsuits. A major breakthrough for the NAACP came in 1954, when the U.S. Supreme Court ruled in *Brown v. Board of Education of Topeka* that discrimination in education was unconstitutional. The *Brown* case involved the practice of denying African American children equal access to state public schools because of state laws requiring or permitting racial segregation. The U.S. Supreme Court unanimously held that such segregation deprived the children of equal protection under the Fourteenth Amendment to the U.S. Constitution, overturning the separate-but-equal doctrine established in *Plessy.*

ECONOMIC BOYCOTTS AND PROTESTS

The use by African Americans of economic boycotts and protests during their mid-twentieth-century struggle to secure their constitutional civil rights and liberties was not a new approach. In the 1800s, abolitionists in the North made use of boycotts when they refused to procure products from states that had legalized enslavement, not wanting to support the South's financial structure. Early African Americans themselves staged boycotts and protests to demonstrate against the unjust treatment they faced. After organizing several streetcar "ride-ins," abolitionist and feminist Sojourner Truth sued a driver who forced her off his streetcar, and won. Later, in the century's last decade, journalist Ida B. Wells-Barnett seized on the segregated transportation system with a demonstrated act of resistance.

At the dawn of the twentieth century, African Americans continued to employ the stratagems of economic boycotts and protests. From 1900 to 1906, African Americans in more than twenty-five southern cities organized boycotts of segregated streetcars. The principal leaders of these boycotts were clergy, businesspeople, newspaper editors, and others who followed Booker T. Washington's philosophy of accommodation, self-help, and uplift. These boycotts occurred during a period of disintegrating race relations, insidious racial violence, and white leaders' uncontrolled efforts to legally systematize the separation of African Americans and whites with de facto and de jure customs and laws. A half-century later, African Americans in Montgomery, Alabama, instituted a boycott and economic withdrawals against the city's public transportation system. Inspired by Mohandas K. Gandhi's philosophy of nonviolence and direct civil disobedience, this ideology not only sustained the Montgomery bus boycott for more than a year, it also permeated other phases of the modern struggle for civil rights.

There was an economic component to the campaigns for equal and just treatment of African Americans as consumers at such places as lunch counters, movie theaters, hotels, and amusement parks, which were the immediate targets in boycotts. Another element of economic pressure was the demand for employment opportunities long denied to African Americans. "Don't buy where you cannot be a salesman" became the slogan of such efforts.

After decades of struggle, an open crusade began in the 1950s against calcified racial intolerance and discrimination, a long-enduring undertaking that proved to be the century's most problematical. Although many whites played a role in the civil rights movement, pressure from African Americans was the elemental component in raising the question of race to prominence. The country's four major civil rights organizations—the NAACP, founded in 1909; the Congress of Racial Equality (CORE), founded 1942; the Southern Christian Leadership Conference (SCLC), founded in 1957; and the Student Nonviolent Coordinating Committee (SNCC), founded in 1966—all employed an assortment of boycott and protest methods to effectively wield economic pressure on the social and institutional forms of injustice and inequity carried out against American blacks.

Two years before the Montgomery movement seized the nation's attention and propelled Martin Luther King Jr. (1929–1968) into the modern civil rights movement, the Reverend T. J. Jemison initiated one of the first bus boycotts by American blacks in the South. In January 1953, in Baton Rouge, Louisiana, legislative members of Baton Rouge's parish council increased the bus fare from ten to fifteen cents. The fare increase angered African American patrons, who made up more than 80 percent of the system's clientele. As in other southern cities, while the front seats of the bus were reserved for whites, African Americans were forced to sit in the back and pay full fare. At the parish council meeting on February 11, Jemison, the pastor of the Mount Zion Baptist Church, condemned the fare increase and petitioned the council to terminate the codified system of reserved seating on city buses. Two weeks later, the council voted to amend Baton Rouge's seating code when it passed Ordinance 222.

The amended code, which became effective on March 19, 1953, permitted black riders to sit in the front seats of the buses if they did not occupy the same seat as or sit in front of a white passenger. While the ordinance abolished set-aside seating, it required blacks riders to board the buses from back to front and white passengers from front to back. For almost three months, city bus drivers ignored Ordinance 222. In early June, they were ordered to comply with the decree. On June 15, after two drivers were suspended for noncompliance, the city's bus drivers staged a four-day strike. The day before the bus drivers ended their strike, the city's black leaders established the United Defense League to organize a bus boycott. The black community of Baton Rouge conducted a seven-day boycott, which ended when city officials reaffirmed the ordinance. Although short-lived, the Baton Rouge bus boycott served as a paradigm for similar protests throughout the South, including the 1955 Montgomery bus boycott. Bus boycotts and their concomitant protests and economic withdrawals became effective nonviolent tactics used by movement leaders throughout the South.

African Americans also staged protests to secure fair wages and better working conditions, as demonstrated by the 1968 sanitation workers' strike in Memphis, Tennessee. The city's African American sanitation workers earned far less than did their white counterparts. While the primary impetus for the protest was economic, it brought into focus other societal maladies, including racial discrimination. Throughout the 1960s and into the twenty-first century, African Americans have protested with their wallets where they perceived covert remnants of racism. They have targeted such corporations as Texaco, Denny's, Coca-Cola, and Cracker Barrel, to name a few.

The efforts of African Americans to apply economic and political pressure reflected a concept put forth by theologian Reinhold Niebuhr in 1932: they "exert[ed] coercion upon the white man's life" and, more significantly, adversely influenced the profit and loss margins of his entrepreneurial enterprises. Through boycotts and protests, African American activists and others helped make America and its citizens more aware of and sensitive to all subjugated and oppressed groups singled out and discriminated against historically.

CIVIL RIGHTS IN THE 1960s

Rosa Parks (1913–2005), a Montgomery activist, was one of the major catalysts for the civil rights movement. On December 1, 1955, after she refused to give up her seat on a Montgomery bus to a white man—as the law required—she was arrested and sent to jail. As a result of Parks's arrest, African Americans throughout Montgomery refused to ride city buses. The Montgomery bus boycott, led by Martin Luther King Jr., was highly successful and ultimately led to the integration of all Montgomery city buses, when on November 13, 1956, the U.S. Supreme Court ruled in *Gayle v. Browder* that segregation on Montgomery buses was unconstitutional. Unlike the *Brown* case, *Gayle v. Browder* expressly overturned the Court's *Plessy v. Ferguson* decision because it—like *Plessy*—applied specifically to transportation.

The success of the Montgomery bus boycott encouraged a wave of demonstrations across the South. College students Ezell Blair Jr., Joseph McNeil, Franklin McCain, and David Richmond started the sit-in movement on February 1, 1960, after they were denied service at a Woolworth's lunch counter in Greensboro, North Carolina. Although these four students received the attention of the national media, a small cadre of Nashville students and adult leaders had begun testing the city's exclusionary racial policies in the final months of the preceding year. Twelve days after the sit-ins began in North Carolina, African American students in Nashville launched their first full-scale sit-ins. In response to white harassment, Nashville students formulated ten rules of conduct for demonstrators that later became the code of behavior for protest movements in the South. The Nashville student movement was described by Martin Luther King Jr. as among the "best organized and most disciplined movements in the South." On May 10, 1960, Nashville became the first major city to begin desegregating its public facilities. That same year, SNCC was created and included among its members Julian Bond, H. Rap Brown, Stokely Carmichael (1941–1998), and John Lewis.

The civil rights movement of the 1960s galvanized African Americans and sympathetic whites as nothing had ever done before, but was not without cost. Thousands of people were jailed because they defied Jim Crow laws. Others were murdered, and houses and churches were bombed. People lost their jobs and their homes because they supported the movement.

On August 28, 1963, nearly 250,000 people marched in Washington, D.C., to awaken the nation's conscience regarding civil rights and to encourage the passage of civil rights legislation that was pending in Congress. The march was a cooperative effort of several civil rights organizations, including SCLC, CORE, the NAACP, the Negro American Labor Council, and the National Urban League. It was during this demonstration that Martin Luther King Jr., in the shadow of the Lincoln Memorial, gave his well-known and oft-quoted "I Have a Dream" speech. More than an oration about a dream that America would at last practice the tenet expressed in the Declaration of Independence that all people are created equal, King told the nation that as far as African Americans were concerned, the country had failed to make payment on its promissory note—one that guaranteed the "unalienable rights of life, liberty and the pursuit of happiness" to all. He stated, "We have come to cash this check—a check that will give us upon demand the riches of freedom and the security of justice." Eighteen days after King's speech, white racists dynamited the Sixteenth Street Baptist Church in Birmingham, Alabama. Four young girls attending Sunday School—Denise McNair, who was eleven years old, and Addie Mae Collins, Carole Robertson, and Cynthia Wesley, all fourteen years old—were killed by the explosion. King later declared that "the innocent blood of these four little girls may well serve as the redemptive force that will bring new light to this dark city.... Indeed, this tragic event may cause the white South to come to terms with its conscience."

Black Power Advocates Stokely Carmichael and H. Rap Brown, Columbia University, New York City, April 26, 1968. *Carmichael (*left*) and Brown (*right*) talk to the news media outside Hamilton Hall, where black students took part in a sit-in protest against the war in Vietnam and concerning issues of racism at the university.* **BETTMANN/CORBIS. REPRODUCED BY PERMISSION.**

At its zenith, the civil rights movement was the most important event taking place in the United States. Through demonstrations, sit-ins, marches, boycotts, and soaring discourse, the movement aroused widespread public indignation. It also created an atmosphere in which it was possible to make positive changes in American society.

The Albany Movement, 1961–1962. In 1961, activists in southwest Georgia's largest city, Albany, launched a movement that became the first mass movement to have as its goal the desegregation of an entire community. It was in Albany that civil rights activists first used freedom songs as an integral part of demonstrations. In mid-November 1961, the city's major black-improvement organizations selected as their president Dr. William G. Anderson. With assistance from SNCC, SCLC, and the NAACP, organizers held mass meetings and protestors held marches. By December, law enforcement authorities had arrested and jailed more than seven hundred protestors, including Martin Luther King Jr., whom Albany's civil rights leaders summoned to bring national attention to their cause.

As the movement progressed, SNCC workers like Bernice Johnson Reagon tapped the power of community singing to encourage and bring together sizeable numbers of people. In choral demonstrations of harmony, black activists in Albany sang earnestly during meetings and protests, and even while sitting in jail. Activists adapted spirituals and church songs, such as "Ain't Gonna Let Nobody Turn Me Around," "This Little Light of Mine," and "We Shall Overcome." However, none of the civil rights advocates anticipated the nontraditional shift of Albany's police chief, Laurie G. Pritchett (1926–2000). He knew that they expected violent behavior from the police and that the press would capitalize on police viciousness as it had done in other cities across the South. Pritchett was also familiar with King's account of the Montgomery boycott in *Stride toward Freedom* (1958), had investigated Gandhian nonviolent philosophy, and understood the protesters' tactic of cramming the jails.

Even before King's arrival, Pritchett told reporters that Albany would not tolerate attempts by the NAACP, SNCC, or any other civil rights organization to overrun the city with demonstrations. In an attempt to circumvent the Albany movement, city officials gave Pritchett the power to act on behalf of the white community. Determined to short-circuit the protesters' efforts, Pritchett advised police officers to avoid violence, at least in front of the cameras. He also worked with law enforcement authorities in other counties to keep arrested demonstrators in their jails. In effect, Albany's police chief used the movement's strategy of nonviolence against the demonstrators, thereby denying them the opportunity to garner sympathetic publicity.

When arrests begun in Albany in December 1961, demonstrators, including King, were not arrested for noncompliance with Jim Crow laws but for such misdeeds as marching without permits, creating disturbances, loitering, trespassing, and contributing to the law-breaking behavior of minors by organizing young people to take part in demonstrations. Even the freedom riders were not exempt from Pritchett's tactics, which were highly nontraditional for southern law enforcement officials. On December 10, 1961, when SNCC conducted a ride from Atlanta to Albany, the police arrested all of the riders for "obstructing traffic." A series of marches took place in response to the arrest of the freedom riders, and hundreds of marchers were themselves arrested in the first week. Pritchett's tactics worked, insofar as the Kennedy administration never intervened in support of the Albany movement.

Although Albany's police chief manipulated the movement with his own strategy of nonviolence, there were other possible reasons that the Kennedy

Civil Rights March from Selma, AL, to the State Capital in Montgomery, March 1965. *Martin Luther King Jr. and his wife, Coretta Scott King, lead a voting rights march that becomes the political and emotional peak of the civil rights movement. Less than five months later, President Lyndon B. Johnson signs into law the Voting Rights Act of 1965.* WILLIAM LOVELACE/EXPRESS/GETTY IMAGES

administration never stepped in to assist the city's black community in its efforts to secure civil rights. James A. Gray, chairman of the state Democratic Party, was a staunch segregationist, as well as a friend of the president. Gray controlled the city's media outlets, including the only television station and a radio station, and had influence through family with the owner of the *Albany Herald*. His influence therefore kept the federal government out of Albany's concerns.

Some historians have asserted that the Albany movement failed because of Pritchett and his efforts to keep black protesters from filling the jails, as they had done in other cities. Other factors included the influence wielded by Gray, the Kennedy administration's nonintervention policy, fractured unity among civil rights organizations, and King's departure from Albany in August 1962. Disputes between SCLC and SNCC, and the SNCC leaders' criticism of King as "de Lawd," caused the NAACP to keep its distance from SNCC. However, rather than describing the Albany movement in terms of its position in the national context of the civil rights movement, it should be considered on its own terms, as a local movement. At the local level, the withdrawal of SCLC did not mark an end to black activism in Albany. Black activism continued in Albany long after August 1962, the date customarily considered to mark the end of the movement.

Civil rights leaders learned numerous lessons from their experiences in Albany that prepared them for the forthcoming battle in Birmingham, Alabama. The Albany movement underscored the importance of freedom songs and spiritual fortitude. Organizers also learned that an all-out campaign was not as effective as targeting specific discriminatory practices one at a time. The Albany movement also established the importance and influential role of the press in civil rights struggles.

JUSTICE BROUGHT TO CIVIL RIGHTS CRIMES OF THE 1960s

Four men believed to be members of the Ku Klux Klan were identified as suspects in the 1963 terror campaign against the Sixteenth Street Baptist Church in Birmingham, Alabama. The Federal Bureau of Investigation (FBI) led the original investigation. It was determined that Robert E. Chambliss, Bobby Frank Cherry, Herman Frank Cash, and Thomas E. Blanton Jr. planted the explosive device. To its credit, the Birmingham FBI office recommended that the suspects be prosecuted. FBI director J. Edgar Hoover (1895–1972) prevented prosecution and court proceedings, however, by refusing the recommendation that federal prosecutors be given testimony that identified the suspects. Five years after the Sixteenth Street Baptist Church bombing, no charges had been filed and the FBI closed the case.

In 1971, Alabama attorney general Bill Baxley reopened the case. Six years later, on November 18, Chambliss, also known as Dynamite Bob, was convicted of murder and sentenced to life in prison. He died in prison in 1985. The case was reopened again in 1988 and 1997 after informants tipped off the FBI. Cash died in 1994, before a case could be launched against him. On May 17, 2000, the remaining two suspects, Blanton and Cherry, were charged with the murders of the four girls. Almost a year later, Blanton was tried, convicted, and sentenced to life imprisonment.

Almost four decades after the Sixteenth Street Baptist Church bombing—one of the most heinous acts of terrorism perpetrated against the modern civil rights movement—the final terrorist was put on trial. Bobby Frank Cherry's trial was postponed, however, after Circuit Judge James Garrett initially ruled that he was mentally incompetent and unable to assist his attorney with his defense. In January 2002, Judge Garrett reversed his ruling after "experts" convinced him that Cherry was feigning the disability. Cherry was charged with four counts of murder and four counts of arson. On May 22, 2002, a jury of nine whites and three African Americans returned a guilty verdict against Cherry, who was later sentenced to life imprisonment. He died in prison in 2004.

Throughout the 1990s and into the first decade of the twenty-first century, civil rights cases from the 1960s and 1970s were reopened, despite the longing of some white southerners to conceal the region's racist past. In April 1998, officials in Natchez, Mississippi, reopened the investigation into the 1967 killing of Wharlest Jackson, treasurer of the Natchez NAACP. Jackson, who was killed when a bomb tore apart his pickup truck, had been promoted to a position—previously held only by whites—at a local tire plant. No one was ever arrested.

Sam Bowers, former imperial wizard for the Ku Klux Klan, was indicted and convicted in August 1998 for the 1966 murder of Vernon Dahmer Sr., president of the Hattiesburg, Mississippi, NAACP chapter. Dahmer was killed by an explosive device detonated at his home. Originally, fourteen Klansmen were tried for this murder, but only three were convicted. When authorities brought Charles Noble, another suspect in the Dahmer case, before the bar of justice in June 1999, the case ended in a mistrial. Sam Bowers died in prison in 2006.

In November 1999, Charles Caston, James Caston, and Hal Crimm were sentenced to twenty years in prison for the 1970 murder of Rainey Pool, a one-armed sharecropper from Midnight, Mississippi. Pool was beaten unconscious by a mob and thrown into the Sunflower River. Originally, seven white men were arrested, but the charges were dismissed. Two died, one was acquitted in June 1998, and another, Joe Oliver, pleaded guilty to manslaughter charges in 1999. Charles Caston later died in prison.

In February 2000, the FBI reopened the investigations in the 1964 murders of black teenagers Charles Eddie Moore and Henry Hezekiah Dee in Natchez, Mississippi. Two men were arrested, but the charges were later dismissed. In 2007, James Forde Seal was tried and convicted in a federal court for the deaths of Moore and Dee.

In 2000, Ernest H. Avants was indicted on federal charges for the June 10, 1966, murder of farmhand Ben Chester White. Avants was convicted and sentenced to life in prison in 2003. Authorities reported that White might have been killed in a plot designed to bring Dr. Martin Luther King to Mississippi in an attempt to assassinate the noted leader of the civil rights movement.

In early 2001, officers of the court reviewed the death of black truck driver Ben Brown, who was killed on May 11, 1967, during a civil rights protest in Jackson, Mississippi. The FBI also reopened its investigation of the 1965 murder of Oneal Moore, killed on a remote stretch of Louisiana's Route 21 in Varnado. Moore and his partner, Creed Rogers, were the first African Americans hired by the Washington Parish sheriff's office. A shotgun blast to the back of Moore's head killed him instantly, while Rogers lost an eye and sustained other serious gunshot wounds in the same incident. Shortly after the shooting, police arrested suspected Klansman Earnest Ray McElveen. Although he failed to give a confirmable alibi, McElveen was released and no further arrests were ever made in the case.

Two other reopened cases include the 1951 killings in Florida of NAACP members Harry T. Moore and his wife, who died when their home was bombed, and the 1957 murder of Willie Edwards Jr., a resident of Montgomery, Alabama, who jumped off a bridge when Klansmen threatened him with a gun. Prosecutors officially closed both cases.

In January 2001, the Mississippi attorney general stated that authorities were "vigorously pursuing" possible murder charges in the 1964 slayings of civil rights workers Michael Schwerner, Andrew Goodman, and James Chaney. In 2005, after evading justice for more than forty years, Mississippi authorities finally brought Edgar Ray "Preacher" Killen, a former Klan leader, to trial for the murders of Chaney, Goodman, and Schwerner. The 1964 "Freedom Summer" killings in Neshoba County, Mississippi, helped spur the modern civil rights movement that led to African Americans gaining access to voting rights, education, and public accommodations. On June 21, a jury composed of nine whites and three blacks took only five and one-half hours to find Killen guilty of manslaughter. The following day, the eighty-year-old Killen was sentenced by Judge Marcus Jordan to three consecutive terms of twenty years. Despite the threat of awakening specters of the Old South, a new generation of law enforcement officials and officers of the court have become prepared to reexamine civil rights crimes perpetrated against people of African descent during the 1960s and the 1970s.

In 2007, as part of its Civil Rights–Era Cold Case Initiative, the FBI began reassessing more than one hundred unsolved or inadequately solved racially motivated murders from the civil rights period. As of late 2009, the initiative had resulted in two successful federal prosecutions, with three additional cases referred to the states for prosecution.

CIVIL RIGHTS LEGISLATION IN THE 1990s

The civil rights movement of the 1950s and 1960s produced significant gains for African Americans. However, historic patterns of hiring and promotion left minorities vulnerable, especially during downward spirals in the national economy. In June 1989, the U.S. Supreme Court delivered opinions in four cases dealing with seniority systems and racial discrimination in employment. In its rulings in these cases—*Lorance v. AT&T Technologies Inc.*, *Martin v. Wilks*, *Patterson v. McLean Credit Union*, and *Ward's Cove Packing Co. v. Atonio*—the Court appeared to reverse earlier civil rights rulings.

Prior to the Court's ruling in *Ward's Cove*, the burden of proof in job discrimination suits had been placed on employers, requiring businesses to prove that there was a legitimate business reason for alleged discriminatory practices. With the *Ward's Cove* decision, the Court made it more difficult for groups to win such suits by requiring workers to prove that no clear business reason existed for an employer's use of practices that result in discrimination. Civil rights organizations were quick to protest the rulings; opponents of the ruling, including the NAACP Legal Defense and Educational Fund and the Leadership Conference on Civil Rights, argued that the Court had undermined the protections granted by federal civil rights and equal employment legislation.

On October 16 and 17, 1990, both houses of Congress approved a bill designed to reverse the Court's decision. The proposed legislation not only reversed the ruling in *Ward's Cove*, but it also strengthened provisions of the 1964 Civil Rights Act. On October 22, 1990, President George H. W. Bush vetoed the bill, claiming that its provisions would encourage employers to establish hiring quotas.

This was not the first time that Congress had moved to reverse a Court action in the area of civil rights. In 1988, Congress passed the Civil Rights Restoration Act, which reversed the Court's 1984 ruling in *Grove City College v. Bell.* In the *Grove City College* case, the Court ruled that not all of an institution's programs and activities were covered by Title IX of the Education Amendments of 1972, which prohibited discrimination in educational programs receiving federal financial assistance.

After vetoing Congress's 1990 civil rights legislation, the Bush administration joined both houses of Congress in working on alternative bills. Following months of negotiation, the Senate passed a bill designed to provide additional remedies for deterring harassment and intentional discrimination in the workplace, to provide guidelines for the adjudication of cases arising under Title VII of the Civil Rights Act of 1964, and to expand the scope of civil rights legislation weakened by Supreme Court decisions. The House of Representatives passed the bill on November 7, and on November 21, President George H. W. Bush signed the Civil Rights Act of 1991.

POLICE BRUTALITY IN THE 1990s AND EARLY 2000s

In the late 1960s, incidents of police abuse sparked civil unrest, costly and violent uprisings, and a lingering distrust between minority communities and the police. In an effort to understand the causes of these incidents, President Lyndon B. Johnson (1908–1973) created the National Advisory Commission on Civil Disorders, also known as the Kerner Commission after Illinois governor Otto Kerner (1908–1976), who chaired the commission. On July 27, 1968, the commission released its findings: among other things, twelve "deeply held grievances" had been identified in the communities that it studied, the most intense being police practices. Despite the commission's finding, major problems in police treatment of minority communities continued.

In late 1989, a pregnant white woman, Carol Stuart, was murdered in the racially divided city of Boston. Her husband told the police that her killer was an African American male. His allegations led police to conduct a manhunt in the predominantly black neighborhood of Roxbury. African Americans in the community were outraged when it was revealed that Charles Stuart had murdered his wife. Stuart, who was having an extramarital affair and financial problems, subsequently committed suicide. Roxbury residents charged the police department with applying a "double standard of justice." In response, Boston mayor Raymond Flynn appointed the St. Clair Commission to examine allegations of abuse of power by the police department.

In 1991, following a high-speed chase in Los Angeles, an African American motorist, Rodney King, was subdued with extreme force and arrested by officers of the Los Angeles Police Department (LAPD). Broadcasts of a videotape of King's beating galvanized international attention on police brutality in Los Angeles, and four LAPD officers were charged with assault and the use of excessive force. In April 1992, however, a predominantly white jury found the four officers not guilty of charges filed against them. The verdict ignited one of the worst race riots in the history of the United States. Later, the federal government indicted the officers on charges that they had violated King's civil rights. In 1993, two of the officers were convicted and sentenced to prison terms.

In response to this chain of events, Los Angeles mayor Tom Bradley (1917–1998) created an independent commission to investigate the LAPD. In July 1991, the Christopher Commission released its findings. The report noted that "within minority communities of Los Angeles, there is a widely held view that police misconduct is commonplace." The King beating had "refocused public attention" on "long-standing complaints by African-Americans, Latinos and Asians that LAPD officers frequently treat minorities differently from whites ... employing unnecessarily intrusive practices ... and engaging in use of excessive force." Documenting the systematic use of excessive force and racial harassment by the LAPD, the report called for structural reforms and the resignation of Los Angeles police chief Daryl Gates. He resigned in 1992.

Well into the 1990s, numerous other incidents of police brutality against blacks surfaced in cities across the nation. These included: the 1995 videotaped beating of Corey West in Providence, Rhode Island; the 1995 killing of motorist Jonny Gammage in Pittsburgh, Pennsylvania; the 1996 killing of TyRon Lewis in St. Petersburg, Florida; the fatal shooting in 1996 of the unarmed Nathaniel Gaines Jr. in New York City; the alleged beating of Jeremiah Mearday in 1997 in Chicago; and the 1998 fatal shooting of Tyisha Miller in Riverside, California.

Many of these incidents, which occurred under questionable circumstances, led to protests and investigations by the U.S. Commission on Civil Rights and prompted a national debate on police, race, and the use of deadly force. Civil rights organizations asserted that these incidents demonstrated a discriminatory use of deadly force and revealed critical problems, such as racially motivated police brutality and unprovoked stops and interrogation of minorities based on racial profiling.

Two of the most controversial and high-profile cases of police brutality occurred in New York within a two-year span. In 1997, law enforcement officers brutally assaulted Haitian immigrant Abner Louima, who worked as a security guard in Brooklyn, New York. In 1999, four officers from the New York City Street Crime Unit (SCU), working undercover and patrolling the Soundview neighborhood in the Bronx for a serial rapist, fired forty-one shots at Amadou Diallo, a twenty-two-year-old immigrant from Guinea.

In the Louima case, New York Police Department (NYPD) officers Justin Volpe, Charles Schwarz, Thomas Wiese, and Thomas Bruder from Brooklyn's Seventieth Precinct arrived at a brawl outside a nightclub at 4:00 a.m. on August 9, 1997. Louima was present, as was his cousin, who struck officer Volpe during the fracas. Volpe mistakenly believed that Louima had thrown the punch and arrested him. According to reports, the Haitian immigrant was beaten by the officers en route to the precinct. Once he arrived, Louima was taken to the restroom, where Volpe sodomized him with a wooden stick. Suffering serious internal injuries, he required numerous surgeries and was hospitalized for two months.

The four police officers were indicted for varying levels of involvement in the beating. On December 13, 1999, after pleading guilty, Volpe was sentenced to thirty years in prison, which he appealed. Schwarz was found guilty of holding Louima down while Volpe assaulted him, but Schwarz, Wiese, and Bruder were acquitted of beating Louima on the way to the precinct. On March 6, 2000, all three were found guilty of conspiracy to obstruct justice. Because of his role in the bathroom assault, Schwarz was convicted for violating Louima's civil rights. On June 27, 2000, Judge Eugene H. Nickerson of the U.S. District Court for the Eastern District of New York sentenced Schwarz to almost sixteen years imprisonment and ordered restitution to Louima in the amount of $277,495.

Retaining attorney Johnnie Cochran (1937–2005), Louima filed a $15.5 million civil rights violation suit against New York City, the Patrolmen's Benevolent Association, and individual officers. It was settled in July 2001 for $8.7 million, the highest settlement that New York has ever paid for a police brutality case.

On February 28, 2002, the Second Circuit Court of Appeals overturned the obstruction of justice convictions against Schwarz, Wiese, and Bruder, and ordered a new trial for Schwarz on the civil rights charge. Less than a month after the court overturned Schwarz's conviction, he was indicted on two counts of lying under oath. A new trial date for Schwarz was set on June 24, 2002. In July, a federal jury deadlocked on the civil rights charges but convicted Schwarz of perjury. Rather than face another trial on the civil rights charges, Schwarz agreed to a five-year sentence for the perjury charge and prosecutors dropped the other charges. Schwarz, his family, and his attorneys were barred from ever speaking publicly about the case. In March 2006, prosecutors contacted the Bureau of Prisons and recommended reducing Schwarz's sentence to forty-seven months. Prison official refused, stating that the law only allowed them to grant early freedom to terminally ill prisoners. Later in the month, a federal judge rejected Schwarz's plea for an early release.

In the Diallo case, which occurred on February 4, 1999, four officers from the New York City SCU (Edward McMellon, Sean Carroll, Kenneth Boss, and Richard Murphy) fired forty-one shots—with nineteen hits—at Amadou Diallo, an unarmed West African immigrant who was standing in the vestibule of his Bronx apartment. The officers contended that they suspected Diallo was a sought-after serial rapist and that he had reached for a gun. Some argued that the Diallo shooting was indicative of police brutality carried out by the NYPD toward people of color.

Incensed over the circumstances of the shooting, numerous persons and organizations, including the NAACP, staged a protest rally on March 18, 1999. On March 26, 1999, the officers were indicted on charges of second-degree murder. Five days later, all pleaded not guilty. They served a thirty-day suspension from police duties without pay and were assigned desk duty. The trial began on February 2, 2000. Judge Joseph Teresi ruled that the prosecution could not reveal that three of the four officers had fired their weapons at suspects in the past.

In addition to the second-degree murder charge, the jury was allowed to consider manslaughter and criminally negligent homicide. On February 23, 2000, after two days of deliberations, the jurors returned not-guilty verdicts for all the defendants. The next month, the U.S. Justice Department investigated whether a federal civil rights case was warranted. It issued a statement on January 31, 2001, that insufficient evidence existed to prove that the officers intended to use excessive force, which is a requirement to prove they violated Diallo's civil rights. Therefore, the federal civil rights charges against McMellon, Carroll, Boss, and Murphy were rescinded. On April 18, 2000, Diallo's family filed an $81 million civil suit against the city of New York. In 2004, Diallo's family agreed to accept a $3 million settlement. After the Diallo killing, the issues of police brutality and racial profiling became national concerns. Incidents of police brutality continued to occur however.

In July 2002, a videotape of sixteen-year-old African American Donovan Jackson being beaten and arrested at a gas station in Inglewood, California, captured national attention. Inglewood police officers were assisting two Los Angeles County sheriff's deputies, who were investigating a car with an expired vehicle registration. According to reports filed by the Associated Press, Jackson's father, Coby Chavis, was cited for driving with a suspended license and was booked for assault on a police officer. In a CNN interview, both father and son said they had no idea why the police questioned them and that they did nothing to provoke the officers. A tourist staying at a motel across the street captured video of officer Jeremy Morse picking up the prone, handcuffed Jackson, slamming him facedown onto the trunk of a squad car, and punching him. Morse put one hand on the back of Jackson's neck, punched him with his other hand, and then appeared to choke him. Two other officers attempted to intervene, with at least one trying to pull Morse away. Morse was suspended with pay, while the other officers involved were not suspended. Reminiscent of the 1991 beating of Rodney King, the incident elicited cries of racism and demands from civil rights groups for a federal investigation.

Donovan Jackson and Coby Chavis filed a federal civil rights lawsuit against the city of Inglewood, four of its police officers, Los Angeles County, and three of its sheriff's deputies on July 10, 2002. They sought unspecified damages and alleged negligence, misconduct, and violation of the constitutional rights of due process and against unreasonable search and seizure. The actions of the police were denounced publicly at all levels: the FBI opened an investigation; U.S. attorney general John Ashcroft expressed concern that the work of law enforcement had gone awry during the incident; and Inglewood mayor Roosevelt Dorn, an African American, promised that the conduct captured on tape would not be condoned "under any circumstances." In March 2005, three years after the federal civil rights lawsuit was filed, Jackson and his family settled for an undisclosed amount.

CIVIL RIGHTS IN THE TWENTY-FIRST CENTURY

Just as police brutality continued to be an issue in the twenty-first century, civil rights also remained a persistent concern.

AFFIRMATIVE ACTION

On May 15, 2002, President George W. Bush signed bipartisan civil rights legislation intended to crack down on discrimination and retaliation in the federal workplace. Known as the Notification and Federal Employee Antidiscrimination and Retaliation Act (No FEAR) of 2002, the law required federal agencies to pay for all court settlements or judgments for discrimination and retaliation cases, instead of allowing the agency to use a government-wide slush fund. The bill's notification requirement aimed to improve workforce relations by increasing managers' and employees' knowledge of their respective rights and responsibilities. In addition to the notification requisite, the No FEAR Act also mandated reporting requirements designed to assist in determining if a pattern of misconduct exists within an agency and whether the agency took appropriate action to address any problems.

While the No FEAR Act focused on the federal workplace, race-based affirmative action in college admissions policies remained on the national radar screen. In 1978, the U.S. Supreme Court endeavored to resolve the issue in *Regents of the University of California v. Bakke*. The Court considered the constitutionality of an affirmation action plan used by the University of California at Davis School of Medicine, which set aside sixteen of its one hundred openings for disadvantaged and minority applicants. Alan Bakke, a white male applicant, sued the university after it denied him admission. In 1976, the California Supreme Court ruled that Bakke should have been admitted, and the U.S. Supreme Court affirmed this decision on June 28, 1978, by a narrow margin of five to four. On a number of related legal issues, the Court was divided without a majority. Only one justice avowed that affirmative action cases should be judged on the same stringent level of scrutiny that applied to "invidious" discrimination. The eight remaining justices stated that race-conscious remedies could be used in some circumstances to correct past discrimination. In essence, the Court used two measurements to sustain affirmative action: (1) a compelling interest must exist before adopting an affirmation action plan; and (2) the plan must be narrowly tailored to suit that interest.

After the *Bakke* decision, institutions of higher education tailored their affirmative action plans by abolishing rigid quotas and set-asides. Implementing new plans, school officials began using a multifactored analysis that permitted admissions officers to consider their school's racial or ethnic diversity as they would consider such subjective factors as geographical diversity, life experience, interests and talents, and similar "plus factors." Almost twenty years later, with the majority of federal judges appointed by Republican presidents, conservative appellate courts began to strike down "plus factor" plans.

In *Cheryl J. Hopwood. v. Texas* (1996), the Fifth Circuit Court of Appeals—which covers Louisiana, Mississippi, and Texas—struck down the University of Texas Law School's "plus factor" affirmative action plan. Four years later, the Ninth Circuit Court of Appeals, in *Katuria Smith v. University of Washington Law School*, upheld the integrity of the admissions policy and allowed the consideration of race as one of the many factors in reviewing applications for admission. The Ninth Circuit stated, "educational diversity is a compelling governmental interest that meets demands of strict scrutiny of race-conscious measures."

On August 27, 2001, the Eleventh Circuit Court of Appeals—covering the states of Alabama, Florida, and Georgia—in *Jennifer L. Johnson v. Board of Regents of the University of Georgia*, declined to decide whether diversity in education could be a compelling interest. It did, however, strike down as unlawful a University of Georgia admissions policy that awarded "points" to applicants for qualities including minority status. According to Columbia Law School professor Michael C. Dorf, within days of the Eleventh Circuit's decision, the University of Florida said it would cease providing more than fifty minority scholarships. He surmised that further university policy changes would take place in states within the Eleventh Circuit. All of the lead plaintiffs in these cases were white females.

On May 14, 2002, the Sixth Circuit Court of Appeals—which includes Kentucky, Michigan, Ohio, and Tennessee—handed down a narrow decision upholding the affirmative action policies of the University of Michigan Law School. Barbara Grutter, the plaintiff, filed suit against the law school after being denied admission in 1997. Grutter, a white mother of two in her forties with a 3.8 grade point average and high scores on the Law School Admission Test (LSAT), alleged that had she been an African American or Hispanic, she would have been admitted. As a "nontraditional student," Grutter argued that she would have brought diversity to the student population. Using the characteristic rationale of reverse discrimination as a consequence of the school's purportedly narrow meaning of "diversity," the litigant challenged the law school's admissions policy that alleged a desire for diversity.

As noted in the case opinion, the University of Michigan Law School's policy explicitly expressed "a commitment to racial and ethnic diversity" with special reference to the inclusion of students from groups historically discriminated against, like African Americans, Hispanics, and Native Americans. The academy acknowledged that this guiding principle, in combination with other "soft" variables—such as letters of recommendation, the quality of the undergraduate institution, difficulty of undergraduate course selection, the quality of the applicant's essay, residency, leadership and work experience, and unique talents and interests—might result in the admittance of students with relatively low grade point averages and LSAT scores. As cited in the brief, while the University of Michigan Law School sought to enroll a meaningful number, or "critical mass," of underrepresented minorities, it denied that such "critical mass" represented any preset number or percentage of reserved seats being held for such students.

Upholding the use of race in admissions, the *Grutter v. Bollinger* ruling did little to end the discussion because it was a narrow five–four decision with strong dissenting opinions. Furthermore, it supported a ruling made by the Ninth Circuit but contradicted rulings by the Fifth and Eleventh Circuits that struck down the use of race in admissions. Still, the Sixth Circuit opinion stated, "We are satisfied that the law school's admissions policy sets appropriate limits on the competitive consideration of race and ethnicity."

Like the *Grutter* case, *Gratz v. Bollinger* was heard in the district court, was appealed to the Sixth Circuit Court of Appeals, and was then argued before the U.S. Supreme Court. Brought by Jennifer Gratz, an unsuccessful applicant to the University of Michigan in 1995, and Patrick Hamacher, an unsuccessful applicant in 1997, the case ended in a summary judgment—no trial was held—in the university's favor. On December 13, 2000, the judge ruled that the pursuit of diversity as an educational benefit is a compelling governmental interest, and the university's current admission policy was constitutional. The Center for Individual Rights, which consistently challenges affirmative action policies, appealed the judgment. The University of Michigan cross-appealed regarding its admission policy from 1995 to 1998, which the judge found unconstitutional. On June 23, 2003, the U.S. Supreme Court, by a six-to-three margin, ruled in favor of Gratz.

On November 7, 2006, Michigan voters approved a referendum, known as Proposition Two or the Michigan Civil Rights Initiative, calling for an end to race-sensitive admission at the University of Michigan. By a margin of 58 percent to 42 percent, voters approved the public referendum that banned the use of race or sex by any agency of state government, including the state's university system, in employment or contracting decisions. Jennifer Gratz, one of the plaintiffs who had challenged Michigan's affirmative action policies, campaigned vigorously for Proposition Two, along with Ward Connerly, an African American businessman and former University of California regent who pushed through California's Proposition 209 in 1996 and Washington State's Initiative 200 in 1998. According to the *New York Times*, although the initiative won by 58 percent of the vote, the divide between male and female voters, as well as African Americans and whites, was far greater. The Michigan initiative, which amended the state's constitution, came in response to the 2003 U.S. Supreme Court ruling that preserved affirmative action in admissions cases involving the University of Michigan and its law school. The Court upheld the law school's admissions process, but struck down the undergraduate admissions process that awarded minority students extra points toward admittance. While voters overwhelming approved the referendum, University of Michigan president Mary Sue Coleman pledged to "consider every legal option available" to continue the academy's fight for diversity.

In California, the number of black students in the state's public universities dropped after Proposition 209 was approved by voters in 1996. Proposition 209 amended the state constitution to prohibit preferential treatment "on the basis of race, sex, color, ethnicity, or national origin in the operation of public employment, public education, or public contracting." The proposition's immediate effects were apparent at the University of California at Berkeley, where 8,000 students were offered admission for the fall 1998 term. Only 191 were African American, compared to the 562 black students offered admission in 1997. According to the *Los Angeles Times* (April 17, 2003), the overall percentage of enrolled underrepresented minorities declined at both the University of California at Berkeley and University of California, Los Angeles (UCLA), the two largest universities in the University of California system. At UCLA, the number of black students admitted from California dropped from 3.3 percent to 2.8 percent in the fall of 2003. Three years later, in the fall of 2006, ninety-six of 4,800 UCLA freshmen, only 2 percent, were African American, which represented a thirty-year low. During the same semester, the freshman class at the Ann Arbor campus of the University of Michigan had 330 African American students, down from 499 in 2001 and 350 in the year after the Supreme Court case, when a new admissions process was adopted.

Two years after Connerly led the push for California's Proposition 209, he also led Washington State's Initiative 200, which ended affirmative action in that state. The year after Initiative 200 passed, the number of first-year minority students at the University of Washington dropped from 373 to 255. At Washington State University, the number of first-year minority students dropped from 396 to 284. The fall 2002 first-year class at the University of Washington included 138 black students, which represented just 3 percent of the class.

Opposition to affirmation action continued in numerous cities throughout the first decade of the twenty-first century. Connerly, in particular, continued his push to ban affirmative action. After his 1998 triumphant in Michigan, Connerly announced plans for similar ballot initiatives in numerous states. Initiatives were proposed in Arizona, Colorado, Missouri, Nebraska, and Oklahoma that gave voters the opportunity to decided if they wanted to do away with affirmative action in government-funded projects and public schools. Voters in Colorado chose to maintain affirmative action programs, while Nebraska voters eliminated affirmation action.

Jennifer Gratz, January 2004. *Gratz* (seated) *was the successful lead plaintiff in the U.S. Supreme Court's 2003 decision in* Gratz v. Bollinger, *which declared the University of Michigan's admission policy unconstitutional because of the way it used race as a factor in admissions.* AP IMAGES

The issue of the value of affirmation action again reached the U.S. Supreme Court in 2009 in *Ricci v. DeStefano*. This case involved firefighters in New Haven, Connecticut, who filed suit against the city because they felt they were denied promotion because of their race. The case resulted from New Haven's need to fill vacancies for lieutenants and captains in its fire department. An outside firm designed a test, which the city administered to seventy-seven candidates for lieutenant and forty-one candidates for captain. After the exams were scored, seventeen white firefighters and two Hispanic firefighters were eligible for promotion. However, because no black candidates and only two Hispanic candidates became eligible for promotion after taking the exam, New Haven officials feared that the city might be susceptible to claims that the test had a "disparate impact" on minorities, in violation of the 1964 Civil Rights Act. They therefore decided not to base promotion decisions on the exam results. White firefighters, led by Frank Ricci, felt that the decision violated the Civil Rights Act's ban on intentional discrimination. The case was argued before the U.S. Supreme Court on April 22, 2009.

Rally against Proposition 209, University of California at Berkeley, 1996. *Approved by California voters in November 1996, Proposition 209 prohibited the state's public institutions from using affirmative action programs. In the years following passage, the African American enrollment rate at California's public universities dropped significantly.* © ED KASHI/CORBIS. REPRODUCED BY PERMISSION.

On June 29, 2009, in a 5–4 decision, the Court ruled in favor of the nineteen firefighters in the *Ricci* case. The decision overturned a lower-court ruling supported by then federal appeals judge Sonia Sotomayor, now a Supreme Court justice and the first Hispanic appointed to the Court. Justice Anthony Kennedy wrote the Court's majority opinion. Chief Justice John Roberts and Justices Samuel Alito, Antonin Scalia, and Clarence Thomas joined Kennedy in the majority opinion. Kennedy wrote that an employer needs a "strong basis in evidence" to believe it will be held legally responsible in a disparate impact suit. In the majority's opinion, New Haven possessed so such proof. Justices John Paul Stevens, David Souter, and Stephen Breyer joined Justice Ruth Bader Ginsburg, who filed a dissenting opinion. In Ginsburg's dissent, she asserted that the Court should have evaluated "the starkly disparate results" of the exams against the backdrop of historical and ongoing inequality in New Haven's fire department. As of 2003, only one of its twenty-one fire captains was African American.

REAUTHORIZATION OF THE 1965 VOTING RIGHTS ACT

President Lyndon B. Johnson signed the Voting Rights Act into law on August 6, 1965. Enacted to provide protection to minority communities, the Voting Rights Act prohibited any practice that abridged a person's right to vote because of his or her race. The act effectively abolished any test or device, such as literacy tests or poll taxes, that might be used to prohibit persons from registering to vote or from voting. Since 1965, temporary provisions of the act have been renewed four times, in 1970, 1975, 1982, and 2006.

When the U.S. Congress amended the Voting Rights Act in 1982, some sections were made permanent. These included Section 2, which contained a general proscription on voting discrimination that could be enforced through federal district court litigation. The 1982 congressional action stipulated that proof of intentional discrimination is not required. Instead, the amendment focused on the electoral process and its accessibility to minority voters. Other sections of the act, such as Section 5, were extended for twenty-five years, or until July 1, 2007.

Although reauthorization had widespread bipartisan support, numerous Republican lawmakers in the House acted to amend, delay, or defeat the bill's renewal. Also known as the Fannie Lou Hamer, Rosa Parks, and Coretta Scott King Voting Rights Act Reauthorization and Amendments Act of 2006, the legislation passed in the House of Representatives by a vote of 390–33. On July 20, 2006, the Senate voted to pass the bill by a 98–0 vote, thereby permitting the federal government to continue its broad oversight of state voting procedures. Seven days later, President George W. Bush signed the bill into law, providing for a twenty-five-year reauthorization of the Voting Rights Act one year in advance of the 2007 expiration date.

HATE-CRIME TRENDS

Just as police brutality had become the center of national attention, so too did the proliferation of hate crimes against African Americans. Hate crimes are crimes against persons or property that are motivated in whole or in part by racial, ethnic, religious, gender, sexual orientation, and other prejudices. Based on the data collected under the Hate Crime Statistics Acts of 1990 and 1996, the number of hate crimes perpetrated against African Americans and reported to the FBI increased from 2,988 in 1995 to 3,838 in 1997. By 2008, the number of reported hate-crime incidents had risen to 7,783, more than half of them racially motivated. These malicious acts of violence, similar to lynchings of the past, were intended not only to be injurious to individuals but to intimidate and dispirit an entire group of people. Such crimes included the destruction of African American churches in the South.

Between 1995 and mid-1996, hundreds of churches were set ablaze in the South, many of them African American churches. These incidents of church arson invoked grievous memories of racist violence during the 1960s, particularly the 1963 bombing of Birmingham's Sixth Street Baptist Church, in which four girls were killed. In response, President Bill Clinton declared the "investigation and prevention of church arsons to be a national priority."

In June 1996, President Clinton established the National Church Arson Task Force and proposed a three-pronged strategy that called for prosecution of the arsonists, the rebuilding of church edifices, and the prevention of additional fires. In addition, on July 3, he signed the Church Arson Prevention Act of 1996, which passed both chambers of the Congress unanimously. On June 6, 1997, the National Church Arson Task Force released its report: Of the 429 incidents of church burnings, bombings, and attempted bombings investigated, 162 involved African American churches, 75 percent of which were located in the South. The majority of those convicted of destroying African American churches were white males.

Hate crimes were not restricted to the destruction of African American church buildings, though. Three of the more high-profile incidents included: the 1995 murder of two African American residents of Fayetteville, North Carolina, by three U.S. Army soldiers who identified themselves as "neo-Nazi skin heads"; the 1996 racial harassment of Bridget Ward and her two daughters who moved into a rented home in the virtually all-white Bridesburg neighborhood in Philadelphia; and the brutal murder in 1998 of James Byrd Jr. in Jasper, Texas, by three white males who chained him to the back of their pickup truck and dragged him to his death. Two of Byrd's assailants, self-proclaimed white supremacists John William King and Lawrence Russell Brewer, were convicted of capital murder and sentenced to death in 1999. The third assailant, Shawn Allen Berry, was sentenced to life in prison.

Hate crimes against African Americans increased throughout the 1990s. According to the FBI's 1999 hate-crime statistics, 7876 incidents of hate crimes were reported, involving 9,301 separate offenses, of which 4,295 were motivated by racial bias. Over 50 percent of the hate-crime victims were attacked because of their race, with the bias against African Americans accounting for 38 percent of all incidents.

The trend continued the following year. For 2000, the FBI report showed 8,063 incidents, involving 9,430 separate offenses, 9,924 victims, and 7,530 known offenders. At 53.7 percent, racial bias represented the largest percentage of single-bias offenses. African Americans accounted for 36 percent of all hate-crime victims, decreasing by only two percentage points between 1999 and 2000.

The first two years of the new millennium's decade saw a continued increase. The FBI's statistics showed that in 2001, 11,451 offenses were reported, 67.8 percent of which were crimes against persons. Of the 11,430 single-bias offenses, 46.3 percent were motivated by racial bias. Within those 5,290 offenses, it was determined that 66.7 percent, or 3,529, resulted from antiblack bias. The following year, the hate-crime statistics revealed a decrease in the number incidents reported, with only 7,462. However, the majority of these were single-bias incidents, and racial bias accounted for 48.8 percent of the single-bias incidents. Again, most offenses were perpetrated against blacks.

Data collected during 2003 showed that of the 7,489, hate-crime incidents reported, 7,485 were single-bias incidents, with 51.4 percent committed because of the offender's racial bias. That year, there were 2,548 antiblack incidents and 3,032 antiblack offenses. In 2004, FBI statistics showed that of the total 7,649 reported hate-crime incidents, involving 9,035 offenses, there were 7,642 single-bias incidents, with 9,021 offenses. Racial bias motivated more than half, or 53.9 percent, of these offenses. Once more, the number of incidents and offenses related to race illustrated that antiblack hate crimes far exceeded those perpetrated against any other racial group.

By mid-decade, the number of incidents and offenses reported was holding steady. The FBI's Uniform Crime Report on Hate Crime Statistics showed 7,163 hate-crime incidents and 8,380 offenses. Of the 7,160 single-bias incidents, 54.7 percent were racially motivated. As in the decade's previous years, antiblack incidents (2,630) and offenses (3,200) led those for all other racially classified groups.

In 2006, the FBI data showed 7,722 reported hate crimes involving 9,080 incidents. Among these were 7,720 single-bias incidents that involved 9,076 offenses, 51.8 percent of which were racially motivated. As in the preceding year, antiblack incidents (2,640), offenses (3,136), and victims (3,332) led the number of hate crimes against other racial groups. In the following year, there was a slight decrease in the number of hate crimes reported to the FBI, with 7,624 incidents involving 9,006 offenses. However, the number of incidents for racial bias increased slightly to 52.5 percent, from 51.8 percent the previous year. Antiblack incidents increased to 2,658.

The upward trend continued into 2008, with 7,783 reported hate-crime incidents involving 9,168 offenses. Of the 7,783 reported incidents, 7,780 were single-bias. The FBI reported that 4,704 offenses among single-bias, hate-crime incidents were racially motivated and that 72.6 percent, or 3,413, were antiblack. (The term *victim* as used by the FBI may refer to a person, business, institution, or society as a whole. Also, the term *known offender* does not imply that the identity of the suspect is known, only that an attribute of the suspect is identified that distinguishes her or him from an unknown offender.)

One notorious incident that was not included in the FBI's hate-crime report occurred at a high school in Jena, Louisiana, in 2006. Neither Jena nor LaSalle Parish was among the FBI's reporting agencies. The Jena case began in August 2006 after an African American student sat under a tree known as a gathering spot for white students. Three white students later hung nooses from the tree. Four months later, LaSalle Parish prosecutor Reed Walters charged six black students with attempted second-degree murder for beating Justin Baker, a white student, unconscious. The charges against the black students were later reduced, but no charges were brought against the white students who hung the nooses. The Jena Six case ignited protests by those who regarded the arrests and subsequent charges as excessive and racially discriminatory. On September 20, 2007, thousands of protesters marched on the Louisiana town. Considered the largest civil rights demonstration in years, protests were held in other cities across the country on the same day. Subsequent reaction included songs referencing the Jena Six, a plethora of editorials and opinion columns, and congressional hearings.

The Jena incident and a subsequent rash of similar nooses and other racially motivated occurrences across the nation led to civil rights protest marches that ended at the Justice Department in Washington, D.C., in November 2007. Earlier in the month, hundreds of protesters marched through Charleston, West Virginia, to pressure prosecutors to add hate-crime charges against six whites accused of beating, torturing, and sexually assaulting a twenty-year-old black woman discovered in September after several days of alleged captivity in a rural trailer.

Modern technology, especially the Internet, has created an opportunity for hate groups to spread their beliefs and increase their membership. Data compiled by the Southern Poverty Law Center, and reported in its Intelligence Report issued in spring 2006, showed that the number of hate groups operating in the United States rose from 762 in 2004 to 803 in 2005. This represented a 33 percent increase over the five-year period that began in 2000.

Hate-group activity in the United States was disturbing and widespread throughout 2008 as the number of hate groups operating in the nation continued to rise. That year, 926 hate groups were reported to be active, an increase from 888 in 2007, and more than a 50 percent increase since 2000, when there were 602 such groups. Some experts hypothesize that hate groups have been incited by the national immigration debate, but were likely fueled by two new forces that arose in 2008: the economic decline and Barack Obama's successful campaign to become America's first black president. Officials reported that Obama received more threats than any other presidential candidate. Several white supremacists were arrested for declaring that they would assassinate Obama or for purportedly conspiring to do so. The most active and terrifying white supremacist hate-group sectors during the first decade of the twenty-first century were Ku Klux Klan groups, neo-Nazis, and racist skinheads. The majority of the such groups are located in the South. The

Southern Poverty Law Center reported 932 hate groups active in the United States in 2009. The three states with the highest number of such groups in 2009 were: Texas, with sixty-six; California, with sixty; and Florida, with fifty-one.

Ten months after his inauguration, President Barack Obama signed a new hate-crime bill into law on October 28, 2009. The Matthew Shepard and James Byrd Jr. Hate Crime Prevention Act is part of newly expanded hate-crimes legislation and the first expansion of civil rights laws since the mid-1990s. It criminalizes violence or attempted violence against others because of their race, color, religion, or national origin, and adds four new categories to the list of biases—actual or perceived gender, gender identification, sexual orientation, and disability. In addition, the new law eliminates the provision that the crimes also be motivated by the victim's participation in one of several specific federally protected activities.

U.S. SENATE APOLOGY FOR LYNCHING

On February 7, 2005, the U.S. Senate passed Resolution 39, apologizing to the victims of lynching and the descendants of those victims for the failure of the Senate to enact antilynching legislation. The resolution acknowledged that the crime of lynching succeeded African enslavement as the ultimate expression of racism in the United States following the era of Reconstruction, and that it was a widely accepted practice in the nation until the middle of the twentieth century.

Lynchings occurred throughout the United States, with documented incidents in all but four states. Between 1882 and 1968, there were at least 4,742 people, principally African Americans, lynched in the United States. Almost all of the perpetrators escaped without penalty. Between 1920 and 1940, the U.S. House of Representatives passed three antilynching measures. Even after numerous requests from civil rights groups, presidents, and House members,

Table 7-1. Hate Crimes—Number of Incidents, Offenses, Victims, and Known Offenders by Bias Motivation: 2007

[The FBI collected statistics on hate crimes from 13,241 law enforcement agencies representing over 260 million inhabitants in 2007. Hate crime offenses cover incidents motivated by race, religion, sexual orientation, ethnicity/national origin, and disability]

Bias motivation	Incidents reported	Offenses	Victims[1]	Known offenders[2]
2007, Total	**7,624**	**9,006**	**9,535**	**6,965**
Race, total	**3,870**	**4,724**	**4,956**	**3,707**
Anti-White	749	871	908	828
Anti-Black	2,658	3,275	3,434	2,509
Anti-American Indian/Alaska native	61	75	76	63
Anti-Asian/Pacific Islander	188	219	234	165
Anti-multiracial group	214	284	304	142
Ethnicity/national origin, total	**1,007**	**1,256**	**1,347**	**1,155**
Anti-Hispanic	595	775	830	758
Anti-other ethnicity/national origin	412	481	517	397
Religion, total	**1,400**	**1,477**	**1,628**	**576**
Anti-Jewish	969	1,010	1,127	320
Anti-Catholic	61	65	70	31
Anti-Protestant	57	59	67	22
Anti-Islamic	115	133	142	104
Anti-other religious group	130	140	148	62
Anti-multi-religious group	62	64	66	32
Anti-atheism/agnosticism/etc	6	6	8	5
Sexual orientation, total	**1,265**	**1,460**	**1,512**	**1,454**
Anti-male homosexual	772	864	890	923
Anti-female homosexual	145	184	197	147
Anti-homosexual	304	362	375	349
Anti-heterosexual	22	27	27	19
Anti-bisexual	22	23	23	16
Disability, total	**79**	**82**	**84**	**70**
Anti-physical	20	20	20	27
Anti-mental	59	62	64	43

[1]The term "victim" may refer to a person, business, institution, or a society as a whole.
[2]The term "known offender" does not imply that the identity of the suspect is known, but only that an attribute of the suspect has been identified which distinguishes him/her from an unknown offender.

SOURCE: U.S. Department of Justice, Federal Bureau of Investigation, Uniform Crime Reports, "About Hate Crime Statistics, 2007."

Table 7-1. *Offenses directed against blacks continue to represent the largest proportion of hate crimes against various groups in the United States.*

however, the Senate considered but failed to passed any legislation dealing with antilynching.

EMMETT TILL UNSOLVED CIVIL RIGHTS CRIME ACT

Shortly after passing Resolution 39, the U.S. Senate moved toward enacting legislation that would create offices in both the U.S. Department of Justice and the FBI to investigate and prosecute unsolved civil rights–era murders. The bill was cosponsored by Senators Jim Talent and Christopher Dodd, and named the Emmett Till Unsolved Civil Rights Crime Act, or the Till Bill, after Emmett Louis Till, the fourteen-year-old Chicago boy murdered in Money, Mississippi, in 1955. In coordination with state and local law enforcement officials, these investigative units within the Justice Department and the FBI became responsible for investigating and prosecuting pre-1970 cases that resulted in death and remained unsolved. The bill passed the House in June 2007, but remained stalled in the Senate for more than a year. Finally, on September 24, 2008, the bill passed the Senate, and President George W. Bush signed it into law on October 8, 2008.

There are a number of pre-1970 civil rights murders that remain unsolved. They include, but are not limited to, the January 23, 1957, murder of Willie Edwards Jr., a truck driver for Winn-Dixie. Edwards was forced at gunpoint to jump from the Tyler-Goodwyn Bridge in Montgomery County, Alabama, by Ku Klux Klan members who had mistaken him for another African American man said to have dated a white woman. Edwards's decomposed body was found three months later. His killers never went to trial. On April 9, 1962, Corporal Roman Ducksworth Jr., a military police officer stationed at Fort Ritchie in Maryland and on emergency leave to visit his ailing wife, was awaken by police officer William Kelly and ordered off a bus that had just arrived in Taylorsville, Mississippi. Minutes later, Ducksworth was shot and killed. It was alleged that the officer may have thought Ducksworth was a freedom rider testing the state's compliance with interstate desegregation laws. In all of these cases, defenseless African Americans were brutally killed in cold blood. In each case, the perpetrator or perpetrators were racially prejudiced southern white men who were never brought to justice.

SONGS OF THE MOVEMENT

Freedom songs is an all-encompassing term for compositions associated with America's civil rights movement from about 1955 to 1966. Music and singing were integral to the methods of protest used by those involved in the struggle for freedom. The freedom songs were made known through word of mouth and through civil rights organizations. Many were adapted from earlier religious songs. Zilphia Horton (1910–1956), the wife of Myles Horton (1905–1990), for example, is credited by folk singer Pete Seeger with changing hymn "I Shall Overcome" to "We Shall Overcome" in 1946. Others credit Guy Carawan of the Highland Folk School in Monteagle, Tennessee, with adapting the song "I'll Be Alright" into "We Shall Overcome" and introducing it during the 1960 Nashville sit-in movement.

The use of spirituals in the struggle for freedom during the antebellum era had left a profound impression on the memory of American blacks. During the civil rights movement's modern era, foot soldiers in the social revolution's forces sang numerous songs of freedom. Many freedom songs were adaptations of spirituals, modified with contemporized lyrics, and as such they allowed participants to voice the demands of the movement. Songs such as "Oh Freedom," "I'm Gonna Sit at the Welcome Table," "Everybody Says Freedom," "If You Miss Me at the Back of the Bus," "Keep Your Eyes on the Prize," "Ain't Scared of Your Jails," "I Shall Not Be Moved," "This Little Light of Mine," and "We Shall Overcome" expressed the sentiments of those struggling to gain civil rights for blacks in America. Other popular freedom songs included "Ain't Gonna Let Nobody Turn Me Around," "Ain't Gonna Let Segregation Turn Me Around," "Which Side Are You On?" and "We'll Never Turn Back."

The Freedom Singers, an ensemble that included Charles Neblett, Bernice Reagon, Cordell Reagon, and Rutha M. Harris, became one of the best-known groups singing freedom songs. However, civil rights songs were recorded by many popular performers, both black and white, including Bob Dylan; Phil Ochs; Tom Paxton; Odetta; Joan Baez; Harry Belafonte; Pete Seeger; and Peter, Paul, and Mary.

Many black recording artists, including Nina Simone, Sam Cooke, the Impressions, and James Brown, shared their talents with the movement. In 1963, Simone recorded her first protest song, "Mississippi Goddam," in reaction to violence against black Americans that year, including the murder of Mississippi's civil rights activist Medgar Evers and the killing of four young girls in the bombing of the Sixteenth Street Baptist Church in Birmingham. Four years later, Simone recorded "I Wish I Knew How It Would Feel to Be Free." In 1964, Sam Cooke recorded the prophetic "A Change Is Gonna Come." Curtis Mayfield and the Impressions followed the next year with "People Get Ready," which was inspired by the 1963 March on Washington for Jobs and Freedom, the

Sixteenth Street Baptist Church bombing, and the assassination of President John F. Kennedy.

In August 1968, four months after King's assassination and two months after the assassination of presidential candidate Robert F. Kennedy, James Brown, known as the Godfather of Soul and Soul Brother Number One, among other monikers, recorded "Say It Loud, I'm Black and I'm Proud." He continued his social activism and worked with such organizations as Operation PUSH and the Black Panther Party's breakfast program. Brown expressed the attitude of most American blacks when in 1969 he released the socially conscious single, "I Don't Want Nobody to Give Me Nothing (Open Up the Door, I'll Get It Myself)."

While the traditional songs remained prevalent in the South, other musical renderings, such as "Burn, Baby, Burn" and the "Movement's Moving On," signaled a shift from the nonviolent movement for civil rights to the Black Power movement.

WOMEN AND THE CIVIL RIGHTS MOVEMENT

Historians have long agreed that women, particularly American black women, were pivotal in the critical battles for racial equality. However, in the consciousness of the public, men pervade the communal recollection of the civil rights movement. Although most of the more visible activists were men, women stood at the nucleus of the movement. Women were vital to every phase of the effort to halt America's legal system of racial segregation, from the 1954 *Brown v. Board of Education of Topeka* decision to the 1963 March on Washington, and even beyond the voting rights struggle.

Rosa Parks and the wives of the movement's three prominent male leaders—Coretta Scott King (1927–2006), Betty Shabazz (1936–1997), and Myrlie Evers-Williams—were among the most important women in the struggle. One of the most iconic occasions of the modern civil rights movement is the 1963 March on Washington for Jobs and Freedom, where King delivered his "I Have a Dream" speech. In spite of the vital role and leadership provided by Jo Ann Gibson Robinson (1911–1992), Daisy Bates (1914–1999), Ella Baker (1903–1986), Diane Nash, and others in planning and organizing the march, no woman was allowed to interject her voice into the activities of the day, with the exception of Mahalia Jackson (1911–1972), who sang "I Been 'Buked and I Been Scorned" before King took the podium. Although they, like Rosa Parks, Dorothy Height, Pauli Murray (1910–1985), and others, were invited to the march, the male leadership asked no woman to accompany them to the White House to meet with President Kennedy.

Many consider the 1954 *Brown v. Board of Education of Topeka* ruling and the murder of fourteen-year-old Emmett Till and the Montgomery bus boycott the following year as marking the beginning of the civil rights movement. While these events all played pivotal roles in launching the pursuit for full citizenship among African Americans, the Montgomery bus boycott signified a changed stratagem in the ongoing freedom struggle. The boycott marked a break from the litigious route taken by the NAACP, in that it used mass participation as a line of attack in the protest activities of the movement. Even though the Montgomery bus boycott was a peak in the numerous mountaintop and valley experiences that had for decades preceded the modern civil rights movement, these actions were, in fact, a mere link in the movement's chain of events. Historians and others who have analyzed the movement have documented the legal victories of the NAACP, the protest activities of black soldiers returning from World War II (1939–1945), and other similar activities, especially during the 1940s and the early 1950s. After these signal development, other direct-action protest events took place with rapidity. They included, but were not limited to, the school desegregation efforts of 1957, the early 1960s sit-ins, the 1961 freedom rides, the 1963 March on Washington, the Birmingham campaigns, the Freedom Summer campaigns of 1964, and the voting rights campaign. Throughout this period, the movement's leaders and participants devised new tactics, such as mass meetings, organizing, marches, boycotts, and other lines of attack, as they pursued their constitutional rights. From the opening salvo, women played an integral role in advancing the cause.

The participation of women in the civil rights movement did not begin with such activists as Irene Morgan (1917–2007), Margie Jumper (1914–2007), or even Rosa Parks. The roots of American black women's activism for racial equality dates back to their resistance activities in the antebellum South. Racial segregation, proscription, and antiblack mob violence increased with the empowerment of impoverished white men in the late 1820s and 1830s. Racial oppression solidified free black Americans' sense of themselves as a racial people and inspired anti-racist protest. Many black women, including Maria Stewart (1803–1879), Sarah Parker Remond (1826–1894), Sarah Mapps Douglass (1806–1882), Sojourner Truth (1797–1883), Frances Ellen Watkins Harper (1825–1911), and others, lent their voices to the movement for equality and justice. They organized and fought for the right to vote, access to educational opportunities, antilynching laws, and the abolishment of poll taxes and white primaries, all in an attempt to overturn Jim Crow laws. From the nineteenth century through the mid-twentieth century, black women maintained the practice of noncooperation with the de facto and de jure structure of Jim Crow.

After World War I, the search for connection and for significant associations became issues of discussion and demonstration in an ever-increasing black public domain. Although Jim Crow attempted to repress and contain American blacks, the 1830s minstrel character met a tough and resilient adversary in the "New Negro." Associated with uplift and resistance, the New Negro emerged in the first decade of the twentieth century. The arrival of a new generation of creative artists that congregated in Harlem were encouraged by black movement leaders to utilize their gifts to break down racial barriers. Through civil rights organizations and their publications, they were given avenues to assert their voices.

Ida B. Wells-Barnett and Mary Church Terrell (1863–1954) participated in the founding of the NAACP in 1909. The National Urban League, which was originally established as the Committee on Urban Conditions Among Negroes in 1910, merged in 1911 with the Committee for the Improvement of Industrial Conditions Among Negroes in New York and the National League for the Protection of Colored Women. The new organization presaged a transformation in the spirit of American blacks. Although from the 1890s to the 1950s it appeared that Jim Crow might defeat the era's New Negro, every impediment placed in their path brought forth a further commitment to their civil rights agenda.

The NAACP's *Crisis* magazine, edited by W. E. B. Du Bois, not only took on political issues but also published fiction and poetry, which symbolized the new race consciousness of American blacks. Serving as literary editor, Jessie Redmon Fauset (1882–1961) promoted such writers as Langston Hughes, Countee Cullen, Claude McKay, and Jean Toomer. Fauset's role in discovering, promoting, and giving a platform to African American writers helped to create an authentic "black voice" in American literature. A contributor to the *Crisis* magazine herself, Fauset, a novelist, wrote about people who adjusted to American race relations without internalizing the negative stereotypes and images that whites projected on them. Other women, like Hallie Q. Brown, Billie Holiday, Zora Neale Hurston, and Nella Larsen, among others, addressed issues of race and gender, barriers to economic and social participation in American society, and cultural issues of passing.

Musicians also lent their voices to the struggle for civil rights, as they had since the early days of the African presence in the New World, when such songs as "Follow the Drinking Gourd" were used as covert forms of communication. As Reconstruction gains slipped into Jim Crow deficits, American black music, such as jazz and blues, evolved. Delving into the emotional state of frustration, deprivation, and desolation that many in the black community experienced, the music also began to serve as a catalyst for social change. Before the 1960s, songs that promoted social activism were rare. However, in 1938, jazz singer Billie Holiday sang "Strange Fruit," one of the earliest songs of protest. "Strange Fruit" was a powerful story about the lynching of black Americans in the South. Holiday performed the song regularly. Because of the zeitgeist of the period and the song's perspective, she was deemed a race heroine. As the effects of the Great Depression took hold in the 1930s, the Harlem or Negro Renaissance wound down. Because of the economic downturn, the prominent contributors to the cultural birth of black America departed Harlem.

During the Great Depression, black protests against discrimination increased. The economic downturn hit black women the hardest. They protested the refusal of white-owned businesses in all-black neighborhoods to

Mary Church Terrell, Civil Rights Activist and Organization Executive, c. 1920–1930. *Terrell was elected the first president of the National Association of Colored Women when it was formed in 1896.* THE LIBRARY OF CONGRESS

hire and employ black salespersons. Because of such repudiations, the black Housewives' Leagues called for job creation and initiated "don't buy where you can't work" boycott campaigns in major cities.

As black women entered the 1940s and 1950s, they became even more involved in the movement for civil rights, with such women as Pauli Murray, Septima Clark (1898–1987), and Modjeska Simkins (1899–1992) taking an active role. In 1938, with assistance from the NAACP, Murray began a campaign to enter the University of North Carolina, an all-white educational institution. Although her case received national publicity, the university refused her admittance. Two years later, after refusing to sit at the back of a bus in Petersburg, Virginia, she was arrested, charged with disorderly conduct, jailed, and fined. While a student at Howard University's Law School, she and fellow law students conducted a series of sit-ins in Washington, D.C. NAACP lawyers used a paper Murray had written about *Plessy v. Ferguson* as it prepared for the *Brown v. Board of Education of Topeka* case.

Septima Clark, whom the Reverend Martin Luther King Jr. called the "mother of the civil rights movement," stood at the forefront of the struggle. She labored to put an end to the pay inequity between black teachers and white teachers in South Carolina. Working with the principal of Booker T. Washington High School in Columbia, NAACP attorney Thurgood Marshall, and South Carolina's civil rights attorney Harold R. Boulware to prepare the court case in 1945, their work came to fruition when federal district judge J. Waties Waring ruled in their favor. In 1952 Clark became affiliated with Highlander Folk School in Monteagle, Tennessee. After the student sit-in movement spread across the South, Clark hosted the first regional conference for students at Highlander. Like her fellow South Carolinian, Modjeska Simkins was active in the South Carolina Conference of the NAACP, especially in challenging segregation in public schools.

Black women fought to make the South and the nation adhere to U.S. Supreme Court rulings regarding race, as in the case of Irene Morgan, on whose behalf *Morgan v. Virginia* (1946) was litigated. The same year that the Court adjudicated *Morgan*, another Virginian, Margie Jumper, refused to yield to the proscriptions of Jim Crow public transportation. Eleven years after Morgan and nine years after Jumper, Rosa Parks, who refused to relinquish her seat on a Montgomery bus, provided the impetus for the Montgomery bus boycott and the *Gayle v. Browder* case.

In the 1940s, women such as Ada Sipuel went to court to gain access to higher education. The NAACP brought Sipuel's case to the U.S. Supreme Court, which decided in her favor in *Sipuel v. Board of Regents of the University of Oklahoma*. Modjeska Simkins, a plainspoken and forthright NAACP leader in South Carolina from the 1930s to the 1970s, assisted in drafting the petition for desegregated schools in the 1952 *Briggs v. Elliott* case, which was the first of five cases combined into *Brown v. Board of Education of Topeka*.

Constance Baker Motley (1921–2005), a member of the NAACP legal team, also had a major impact on the effort to end racial discrimination. Motley helped write briefs for the 1954 *Brown* case and was involved in the school desegregation case in Little Rock, Arkansas, which caused Governor Orval Faubus (1910–1994) to call out the Arkansas National Guard to prevent nine black students from entering Little Rock's Central High School. From 1961 to 1964, Motley litigated and won nine of ten civil rights cases she argued before the U.S. Supreme Court. When the movement transitioned from the courts to direct nonviolent resistance, women provided strong leadership and executed critical roles in organizing marches, leading protests, distributing leaflets, and expanding voter-registration drives.

Although the United States ostensibly entered World War II to make the world safe for democracy, at the end of the war, most of the racial restrictions enforced on African Americans remained sanctioned in the country by both custom and law. Unrepentant racialists dispossessed blacks of equal education, desegregated public accommodations, the right to vote, and other rights and privileges granted to white citizens across the South and, indeed, the country. Legally set apart from whites since 1896, racial segregation subjugated blacks from the beginning of life until the end. Yet, the civil rights activities of the 1940s and 1950s signaled a cyclonic change for the nation's race relations. Although the *Brown v. Board of Education of Topeka* decision held that the separate-but-[un]equal doctrine was unconstitutional, many Americans refused to recognize the mounting frustration of the country's black citizens with the highly formalized and codified structure of racism. The 1955 Montgomery bus boycott not only seized the nation's attention, it made the world aware of America's ill treatment of its black citizens and projected twenty-six-year-old Martin Luther King Jr. into the vanguard of the modern movement for civil rights.

Many identify the Montgomery bus boycott as a key episode for the civil rights movement because it established that well-coordinated and persistent economic pressure could produce a triumphant outcome. Two years before to the 1955–1956 boycott, black women were in the forefront of another bus boycott in Baton Rouge, Louisiana, which served as a model for Montgomery. Although the Rosa Parks incident incited tens of thousands of people in Montgomery to boycott the transit system, the Women's Political Council (WPC), started by Mary Fair Burks (1920s–1991) in 1946, also played a vital role. A year before Parks was arrested, black WPC members had begun concentrating their energies on the Jim Crow bus system. Because women often bore the brunt of mistreatment from white bus drivers, in March 1954 Jo Ann Gibson Robinson, president of the WPC, met with Montgomery's mayor, W. A. Gayle, and detailed desired changes to the Montgomery bus laws. In March and October of 1955, fifteen-year-old Claudette Colvin and Mary Louise Smith were arrested for refusing to relinquish their seats to white passengers.

Neither of these incidents, however, incited the black community like the imprisonment of Parks on December 1, 1955. When Montgomery's black community embarked on a long-term boycott, women played a critical role in sustaining it, especially the unidentified cooks, maids, and others who made long walks to and from their homes for a year to achieve the objective of desegregating the buses. In December 1956, after the U.S. Supreme Court ruling in *Gayle v. Browder*, Montgomery's blacks once again began using the now-desegregated public system of transportation.

Near the end of the 1950s, women remained steadfast in the cause for civil rights and full participation in American society. Daisy Bates was an adviser and counselor to the group of black students who became known as the Little Rock Nine as they stood in the forefront of efforts to desegregate Little Rock's Central High School in 1957. Bates and the students gained both national and international attention for their steadfastness and courage when Governor Orval Faubus called out the Arkansas National Guard to keep them from entering the school. As a civil rights activist and a leading member in the NAACP, Bates caught the attention of whites in Arkansas during the pretrial proceedings of the federal court case of *Aaron v. Cooper*, which set the stage for the desegregation of Central High School.

Two years after the Little Rock school desegregation crisis, the first major battle for voting rights in the rural South began in Tennessee's Fayette and Haywood counties. Viola McFerrin, Minnie Jamison, Wilola Mormon and their husbands, along with Gertrude Beasley and others, led blacks in an uprising against the racially restrictive voting system, causing white landowners to evict thousand of black sharecroppers from their homes. After being evicted, they were forced to live in an improvised community known as Tent City or Freedom Village. The Tennessee effort presaged the struggle that African Americans in other states would conduct to secure their constitutional right to vote. In 1959, black residents of Fayette County filed the first suit of its kind under the Civil Rights Act of 1957. Their actions sparked voter-registration drives throughout the South, especially in Mississippi and Alabama. As James Forman noted, if black participation in the electoral process could be achieved in west Tennessee, the same could happen in Mississippi.

In addition to Parks, who represents the beginning of the transformation from the litigious course to direct nonviolent protest, Ella Baker, the first staff person hired by the Southern Christian Leadership Conference (SCLC), blazed a trail for the organization's work. She helped organize the 1957 Prayer Pilgrimage that brought thousands of activists to Washington, D.C. Through her leadership, SCLC mobilized democratic coalitions in grassroots community associations across the country. She went to Highlander Folk School to help Septima Clark enable black southerners to exercise their voting rights. Baker also worked closely with southern civil rights activists in Georgia, Alabama, and Mississippi and was highly respected for her organizing abilities. One of her most important contributions to the movement was helping students establish the Student Nonviolent Coordinating Committee (SNCC) in 1960. A strong supporter of decentralized leadership, Baker encouraged the students to be their own leaders. Called the "godmother of SNCC," Baker was one of its most highly respected adult advisers. She influenced the thinking of many of the committee's important figures, including Diane Nash, one of SNCC's founders.

Diane Nash was an indomitable force in the Nashville student movement. In 1960, she convinced Nashville mayor Ben West to declare that lunch counters should be desegregated. The next year, she was in the forefront of reviving the freedom rides aborted by the Congress of Racial Equality because of violent retaliatory action by white mobs. Ruby Doris Smith-Robinson (1942–1967), another SNCC founder and the only woman to serve as the organization's executive secretary, became involved in the civil rights movement because of her exposure to racial discrimination in her native city of Atlanta. As a SNCC field representative, Robinson helped organize chapters in the South. In February 1961, she and other SNCC leaders, including Nash, traveled to Rock Hill, South Carolina, to participate in that city's sit-in movement. Because of their "jail, no bail" tactic, they were given a thirty-day jail sentence. After Robinson took part in the 1961 freedom rides, she served a forty-five-day jail term in Mississippi's Parchman Penitentiary, where she was violently maltreated by prison guards.

SNCC members also concentrated their efforts on voter-registration drives in the Deep South. One of the most important contributors to this phase of the movement was Fannie Lou Hamer (1917–1977), who became a SNCC member in 1962 and a registered voter and SNCC field secretary in 1963. Hamer risked her life and that of her family in her effort to register voters across the South. She also helped set up programs to that would be of economic benefit to underprivileged African Americans. Hamer was also a leader of the Mississippi Freedom Democratic Party (MFDP), founded in 1964 to challenge Mississippi's all-white delegation to the Democratic National Convention in Atlantic City. As a representative for the Democratic National Committee in August 1964, Hamer gained national recognition when she testified before the party's Credentials Committee. A year later Hamer, Victoria Gray (1926–2006), and Annie Devine (1912–2000) ran for Congress and contested the seating of the regular Mississippi representatives in the U.S. House of Representatives. Although this effort failed, Mississippi's 1965 elections results were later reversed. Hamer continued to be politically active and served as a member of the Democratic National Committee from Mississippi from 1968 to 1971.

Women's participation in the civil rights movement was not limited by age or education. Six-year-old Ruby Nell Bridges became the center of one of the most vividly recalled events of the civil rights era when she entered William Frantz Elementary School in New Orleans, Louisiana, in 1960, an event depicted in Norman Rockwell's 1964 painting, *The Problem We All Live With*. Bridges endured the jeers of the white racist crowd as she entered the building to begin the process of school desegregation. In school, she faced isolation from her classmates because she was not allowed to join them in the cafeteria or during recess.

As the civil rights movement transitioned toward the Black Power movement, women continued to be active participants and shared in leadership positions. Elaine Brown became the first woman to chair the Black Panther Party, founded by Huey Newton (1942–1989) and Bobby Seale in Oakland, California, in October 1966. Kathleen Cleaver, a former member of SNCC and a grassroots organizer for the Black Panther Party, became the communications secretary and the first female member of the party's decision-making apparatus. Angela Davis, another SNCC activist, also became affiliated with the Black Panthers.

THE ELECTION OF PRESIDENT OBAMA

Born in Honolulu, Hawaii, on August 4, 1961, Barack Hussein Obama was the son of Barack Obama Sr. (1936–1982), a native of Nyangoma-Kogelo in the Siaya District of Kenya, and Stanley Ann Dunham (1942–1995), a native of Wichita, Kansas, and a descendant of Jefferson Davis, the president of the Confederate States of America. Obama and his wife Michelle are the parents of two daughters, Malia Ann and Natasha (Sasha). Although he was not a neophyte to the political arena, Obama, the junior senator from Illinois, was relatively unknown when on February 10, 2007, he stood in front of the Illinois statehouse in Springfield and announced his candidacy for the presidency of the United States. The subsequent Democratic primaries yielded a historic first when two minorities, an African American and a woman, Senator Hillary Rodham Clinton, became the major candidates for their party's nomination.

Obama honed his political skills in the Illinois State Senate, where he represented the Thirteenth Legislative District. Elected in 1996, Obama worked with a coalition of Democrats and Republicans to pass bills that increased funding for AIDS prevention and care, expanded early childhood education, and attempted to curb racial profiling. After numerous death-row inmates in Illinois prisons were found to be innocent, Obama enlisted the support of law enforcement officials to draft legislation requiring the videotaping of interrogations and confessions in all capital cases.

Obama was elected to the U.S. Senate from the state of Illinois in November 2004 and was sworn into office on January 4, 2005. His election made him only the fifth African American (after Hiram Revels [1870–1871], Blanche K. Bruce [1875–1881], Edward Brooke [1967–1979], and Carol Moseley Braun [1993–1999]) elected to serve in the U.S. Senate and the only African American senator in the 110th U.S. Congress. Obama made his debut before the American public when he gave the keynote address at the Democratic National Convention in July 2004. While in the U.S. Senate, he served on the Foreign Relations Committee, the Veterans Affairs Committee, and the Health, Education, Labor, and Pension Committee.

As a candidate for president, Obama presented himself as a Washington outsider and a different kind of leader. He not only distanced himself from President George W. Bush's position on the Iraq War and domestic issues, but even from the positions of some in the Democratic Party. From the beginning, Obama opposed the Iraq War, which placed him on the opposing side of high-ranking black officials in the Bush administration, Colin Powell and Condoleezza Rice. Obama reiterated this position when he announced his candidacy. However, during the campaign, Obama emphasized his goals of building better schools, creating jobs, and fixing a broken health-care system. He also articulated his desire to make the United States more energy efficient and to protect the environment from global warming. His campaign for "change" voiced a theme of inclusivity across all social, economic, political, and racial lines. Obama was not the first African American to run for president. He was preceded by Shirley Chisholm (1924–2005), a seven-term U.S. congresswoman from New York, who ran in 1972; the Reverend Jesse Jackson, a civil rights activist who ran in 1984 and 1988; Alan Keyes, who ran in 1996 and 2000; and Senator Carol Moseley Braun and Reverend Al Sharpton, both of whom competed in the Democratic Party's primaries in 2000. Obama, however, was the first black candidate to capture the attention of both the media and the public.

Prior to entering the political arena, Obama, a graduate of Columbia University (1983) and Harvard Law School (1991), where he became the first African American president of the *Harvard Law Review*, worked with a church-based organization in Chicago, Illinois, that focused on the city's economically distressed environs. He later became a community organizer on Chicago's South Side. A civil rights attorney, Obama practiced law with the Miner, Barnhill and Galland firm, where he dealt with voting rights and employment rights cases. As an activist, he directed the Illinois Project Vote campaign, which registered more than 100,000 voters and facilitated the election of President Bill Clinton and Senator Moseley Braun, the first African American woman elected to the U.S. Senate. The same year that he graduated from Harvard Law School, Obama accepted the position of senior lecturer in constitutional law at the University of Chicago Law School.

As Illinois's junior senator, Barack Obama worked to promote civil rights and fairness in the criminal justice system, as he had done throughout his career. As a civil rights attorney, he litigated cases concerning employment discrimination, housing discrimination, and voting rights. As a leading advocate for protecting the right to vote, he helped to reauthorize the Voting Rights Act and led the opposition against discriminatory barriers to voting.

The core of the Obama campaign message was "change" that began at the grassroots level. To help that message resonate, he brought in young people, whose efforts became an essential element in his bid for the White House. To capitalize on his grassroots organizing experience, the campaign established "Camp Obama," which were three-to-four-day gatherings that trained approximately fifty volunteers on how to manage phone banks, knock on doors, and register voters. Young campaign workers also contributed to a precinct-by-precinct field operation. This line of attack changed standard methods of political field organizing and transformed thousand of communities across America. The Obama campaign adopted the "Yes, We Can" slogan used earlier by Deval Patrick, the first African American governor of Massachusetts. Patrick shared with Obama the lessons he had learned during his successful campaign for the governorship.

Obama's innovative use of new modes of communication and technology, such as social networking sites like MySpace and Facebook, aided in mobilizing support for his presidential bid. Students for Barack Obama, which began as a group on Facebook, became an official youth outreach program for his campaign that recruited students online and organized campaign events on university campuses. Obama and his team also used online videos and advertisements, e-mail, and text messaging to reach young adults and other voters. The campaign itself had an Internet social networking site that helped supporters create more than 35,000 local groups and host some 200,000 events in support of Obama's candidacy. This effective use of the Internet maximized opportunities for campaign volunteers to spread Obama's message of change.

As the Democratic primaries progressed, it became clear that the two front-runners were Obama and New York senator Hillary Rodham Clinton, the former first lady of the United States. On February 28, 2008, when twenty-three states held their primaries and caucuses, Obama outranked his opponent by three states and won 847 pledged delegates to Clinton's 834. Obama's supporters included black Americans, college-educated whites, and young voters. Clinton's voting demographic included women, Latinos, and non-college-educated whites. When the primaries were over and the Democrats held their national convention in Denver, Colorado, in August, Barack Obama and Delaware senator Joe Biden received their party's presidential and vice presidential nominations. On August 27, Senator Clinton interrupted the official roll call and moved that Obama be selected by acclamation. In the general election, Obama and Biden faced the Republican nominees, Arizona senator John McCain and Alaska governor Sarah Palin.

On November 4, 2008, Obama defeated McCain in both the Electoral College and the popular vote. He received 365 electoral votes to McCain's 173. In the popular vote, Obama carried sixty-three million votes, or 53 percent, to McCain's 55.8 million, or 46 percent. The election marked the first time since Lyndon B. Johnson won the presidency in 1964 that a Democrat had won more than 51 percent of the votes. On November 4, people from all social, economic, political, and racial backgrounds reaped the benefits of the civil rights struggle.

On January 20, 2009, Barack Obama was inaugurated as the forty-fourth president of the United States. Countless numbers of people of all races assembled in the nation's capital to witness history, as he was sworn in as the first black president of the United States. He and his family would occupy the White House on 1600 Pennsylvania Avenue.

Obama is the author of *Dreams from My Father: A Story of Race and Inheritance* (1995) and *The Audacity of*

Hope: Thoughts on Reclaiming the American Dream (2006), both of which became best sellers. In October 2009, the Norwegian Nobel Committee awarded President Obama the Nobel Peace Prize. The committee, led by chairman Thorbjørn Jagland, honored the president for his "extraordinary efforts to strengthen international diplomacy and cooperation between peoples." President Obama claimed to be "surprised and deeply humbled" by the prize. He said he "viewed the decision less as a recognition of his own accomplishments and more as call to action." On January 27, 2010, the president delivered his first State the Union address.

CIVIL RIGHTS ACTIVISTS

(Some biographical profiles may appear in other chapters. To locate profiles more readily, please consult the index.)

RALPH D. ABERNATHY (1926–1990)

Religious Leader, Civil Rights Activist, Organization Executive/Founder. Born March 11, 1926, in Linden, Alabama, the Reverend Ralph David Abernathy was ordained a minister in 1948. He received his bachelor's degree from Alabama State College (now Alabama State University) in 1950 and his master's degree from Atlanta University in 1951. The alliance between Abernathy and Martin Luther King Jr. stretched back to the mid-1950s. Earlier, while attending Atlanta University, Abernathy had the opportunity to hear King preach at Ebenezer Baptist Church.

After obtaining his master's degree, Abernathy returned to Alabama to serve as a part-time minister at the Eastern Star Baptist Church in Demopolis. In 1951, Abernathy moved to First Baptist Church in Montgomery. Around this time, King accepted a position at Montgomery's Dexter Avenue Baptist Church, and Abernathy and King became close friends.

In 1955, the two organized the Montgomery Improvement Association to coordinate a citywide bus boycott. The success of the Montgomery bus boycott led to the creation of the Southern Negro Leaders Conference; the organization's name was later changed to the Southern Leadership Conference and finally the Southern Christian Leadership Conference (SCLC). In January 1957, Dr. King was elected the organization's president.

From the time of Martin Luther King's death in 1968 until 1977, Abernathy served as president of the Southern Christian Leadership Conference. Abernathy continued as a leading figure in the movement until his resignation in 1977, when he made an unsuccessful bid for a U.S. congressional seat. In 1989, he published his autobiography, *And the Walls Came Tumbling Down*, which was criticized by some African American leaders for Abernathy's inclusion of details regarding King's extramarital affairs. Abernathy died of cardiac arrest on April 17, 1990.

ELLA BAKER (1903–1986)

Community Activist, Civil Rights Activist, Executive/General Manager. Ella Baker was born in 1903 in Norfolk, Virginia, to Blake and Georgianna Ross Baker, both educated people who worked hard to educate their children. The family and community in which Baker grew up instilled in her a sense of sharing and community cooperation. Baker's family imbued her with a sense of racial pride and resistance to any form of oppression. Her grandfather, a minister and community leader, was an ardent proponent of civil rights and universal suffrage, and passed his beliefs on to her.

When she was fifteen, Baker was sent to the Shaw Boarding School (now Shaw University) in Raleigh, North Carolina, where she graduated with a bachelor's degree as valedictorian in 1927. After graduation, she moved to New York City. Baker quickly became involved in progressive politics and attended as many meetings and discussions as she could. During the Depression, she was outraged at the poverty she saw in the African American areas of the city. Believing in the power of community and group action, she became one of the founders of the Young Negroes Cooperative League, a buying cooperative that bought food in bulk to distribute at low prices to members; in 1931, she became the national director of the league. When President Franklin Roosevelt's Works Progress Administration started, she became involved with its literacy program. Throughout these years, she worked closely with other politically aware and motivated people, discussing and evolving a political philosophy of cooperation, equality, and justice.

In the late 1930s, Baker began working for the NAACP. Between 1940 and 1943, she served as a field secretary, traveling all over the country setting up branch offices and teaching people to fight for their rights. During her travels, Baker developed a vast network of contacts in the South that she later relied on when working for the Southern Christian Leadership Conference (SCLC) and the Student Nonviolent Coordinating Committee (SNCC). In 1943, she became the director of branches for the NAACP. During the 1950s, she organized fund-raising activities in New York for the civil rights struggles in the South. In 1958, Baker moved to Atlanta to work with SCLC.

While working for SCLC, Baker became disillusioned with the male, clergy-dominated organizational structure of the group. In 1960, she quit SCLC and took a job with the Young Women's Christian Association (YWCA). When students began conducting sit-ins, Baker shifted her focus to the development of SNCC. She acted as an unofficial adviser for the group, counseling them to set up their own student-run organization rather than be subsumed under SCLC or the NAACP. Baker also helped launch the Mississippi Freedom Democratic Party that challenged the all-white Democratic delegation at the 1964 convention, and she acted as staff consultant for the interracial SCLC educational fund.

Baker returned to New York City in 1965, but kept working with national and international civil rights organizations. Among her other activities, she raised money to send to the freedom fighters in Rhodesia and South Africa. She remained an active organizer and speaker as long as her health allowed. Baker's belief in the power of communal action and her reliance on workers rather than leaders had an enormous impact. She worked for all of the major civil rights organizations at their time of greatest need. By the time SCLC and SNCC were formed, Baker had almost thirty years of civil rights and community organizing experience to offer. She continually strove to keep the movement people-oriented, and she succeeded in helping SNCC remain a student group. Through her philosophy and actions, Baker motivated hundreds to act and to help themselves and their neighbors.

DAISY BATES (1914–1999)

Publisher, Civil Rights Activist, Executive/General Manager. Daisy Lee Gatson Bates was born in Huttig, Arkansas, in 1914. After attending segregated schools in a district where all of the new equipment and up-to-date texts were reserved for whites, Bates spent much of her energy as an adult successfully integrating the schools of Little Rock, Arkansas.

Shortly after their marriage in 1942, Daisy and her husband Lucius Christopher Bates, a journalist, began publishing a newspaper, the *Arkansas State Press.* They made it a point in their paper to keep track and report incidents of police brutality and other racially motivated violence. Their paper became known throughout the state for its campaign to improve the social and economic circumstances of African Americans. Because of their work, the city of Little Rock began to hire African American police officers, and the number of race-related incidents decreased.

In 1952, Daisy Bates became the Arkansas president of the NAACP. After the 1954 Supreme Court decision in *Brown v. Board of Education of Topeka,* she became involved in school desegregation efforts, and began taking African American children to white schools to register. If the school refused to register the children, she would report it in her paper. In 1957, the superintendent of schools in Little Rock decided to try to integrate the schools and chose nine students, now called the "Little Rock Nine," to be the first African American children to attend Central High. Most white citizens of Little Rock objected. Bates organized the Little Rock Nine, accompanied them to Central High, and stood with them in the face of the state troopers that Governor Orval Faubus had sent to prevent the school's integration. For days she escorted the children to school, only to be turned away by an angry mob. On September 25, 1957, Bates and the nine students entered Central High in Little Rock escorted by one thousand troops sent by President Dwight Eisenhower. For the rest of their years at Central High, Bates kept track of the students and acted as their advocate when problems arose, frequently accompanying them and their parents to meetings with school officials.

In October 1957, Daisy Bates was arrested on charges of failing to provide NAACP membership information to city officials. The charges were later overturned. Two years later, the *Arkansas State Press* folded, but Bates kept active in the civil rights fight by touring and speaking. She also worked with SNCC to register voters. Her memoir of the Little Rock crisis, *The Long Shadow of Little Rock,* was published in 1962. Bates died on November 4, 1999.

JULIAN BOND

See chapter 11, Politics.

ELAINE BROWN (1943–)

Political Activist, Author. Elaine Brown became the first woman to chair the Black Panther Party, making her the highest-ranking woman in the organization, second only to Huey P. Newton. Newton and Bobby Seale founded the party in Oakland, California, in 1966, to protect local communities from police brutality and racism.

Brown was born on March 2, 1943, in Philadelphia to Dorothy Brown, a working-class mother. Her father, Dr. Horace Scott, never publicly acknowledged his daughter. Brown received her education from the Thaddeus Stevens School of Practice and the Philadelphia High School for Girls. She attended the Philadelphia Conservatory of Music and was enrolled at Temple University during the 1961–1962 school year. In 1965, she left Philadelphia for Los Angeles to pursue a career as a songwriter. Soon after arriving in Los Angeles, Brown was introduced to the Black Power movement.

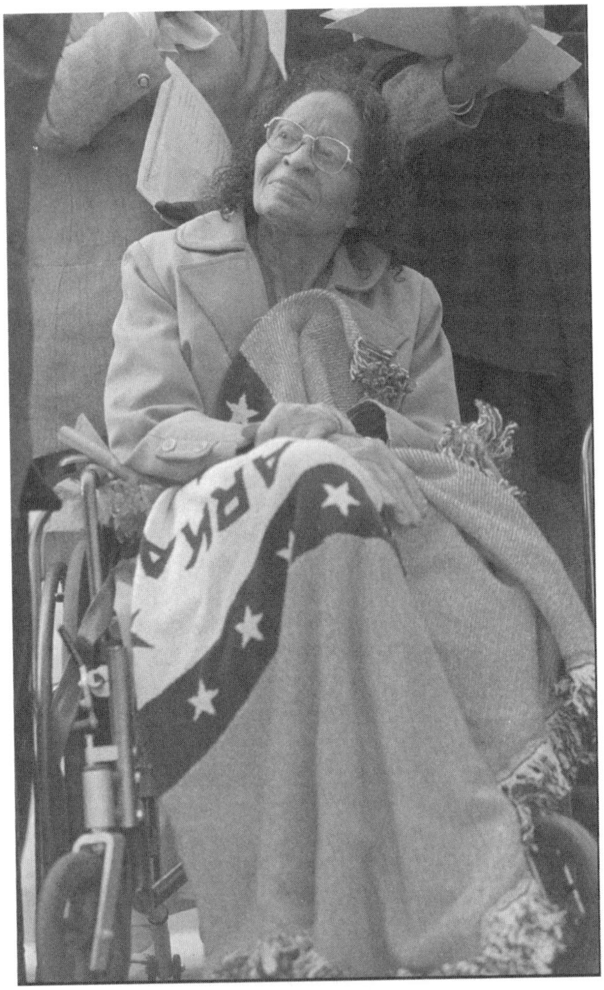

Newspaper Publisher and Civil Rights Activist Daisy Bates. *As the head of the NAACP in Arkansas, Bates played a critical role in the fight for school desegregation by leading the ultimately successful struggle to enable nine African American students (the "Little Rock Nine") to attend Central High in Little Rock, Arkansas.* **PHOTOGRAPH BY DANNY JOHNSTON. AP IMAGES. REPRODUCED BY PERMISSION.**

Later, she began writing for *Harambee* (Swahili for "pulling together"), the newspaper of the Los Angeles Black Congress, a group of black organizations whose objective was to serve the needs of the black community.

By 1967, Brown had become acquainted with the Black Panther Party, and in April 1968 she joined the party's southern California chapter. By the following year, Brown was the chapter's minister of information. In 1974, with the expulsion of Seale, Brown was named party chairperson, a position she held until 1977, when she left the party and moved to France with her daughter, Ericka Suzanne Brown. During Brown's tenure as chair, the Black Panther Party sought power through political channels. One of the party's objectives was to elect a black mayor in the city of Oakland. The party registered approximately 90,000 black Democrats, and Black Panther candidate Lionel Wilson was elected the first black mayor of Oakland in 1976.

Brown is also a singer and author. Her autobiography, *A Taste of Power: A Black Woman's Story*, was published in 1992. In 1998, Brown helped found Mothers Advocating Juvenile Justice, an Atlanta organization that advocates for juvenile offenders who are prosecuted as adults. In addition to her memoir, she is the author of *The Condemnation of Little B: New Age Racism in America* (2002). Her papers have been acquired by Emory University in Atlanta.

STOKELY CARMICHAEL (1941–1998)

Civil Rights Activist, Black Nationalist. Stokely Carmichael, who was responsible for popularizing the term *Black Power*, was one of the most influential leaders of the Student Nonviolent Coordinating Committee (SNCC). Carmichael was born in Trinidad on June 29, 1941, and moved to the United States with his family when he was eleven years old. As a teenager, Carmichael was jolted by ghetto life, and was not reassured when he entered Bronx High School of Science, where he encountered white liberals and felt he had been adopted by them as a mascot. Although he was offered scholarships to predominantly white universities, Carmichael opted to attend Howard University. In 1960, during his first year of college, he joined the Congress of Racial Equality (CORE) to assist in its efforts to desegregate public accommodations in the South. After graduation in 1964, he rejected scholarship opportunities for graduate school and went south to join SNCC. As one of its most effective organizers, he worked ceaselessly, registering and educating voters in the South. In 1966, he was elected chairperson of SNCC; however, as the organization's youngest chair, some members considered his views too radical.

Carmichael's cry for "black power" thrilled many disenfranchised young African Americans, but troubled others, who thought it sounded too militant. He was labeled as potentially violent by the media and by law enforcement authorities. Disagreement with SNCC members arose over the issues of self-defense versus nonviolence and the participation of whites in African American grassroots organizations. Carmichael resigned as chairperson in 1967, and was later expelled from SNCC.

Carmichael spent much of 1968 traveling around the world, speaking to many organizations, including some in communist countries. His travels included Ghana, where he joined the Pan-African movement. After returning to the United States, he went to work for the Black Panther Party. He was subject to almost constant harassment from the FBI because of his connection with the Panthers and because he had visited communist countries. In 1969, he resigned from the Black Panthers and moved to Guinea, where he was offered political asylum.

In Guinea, Carmichael turned his efforts to supporting Pan-Africanism. He organized many local chapters of the All-African People's Revolutionary Party. In 1978, to honor the two men who most influenced his Pan-African philosophical education, Guinean president Ahmed Sékou Touré and Ghanaian president Kwame Nkrumah, Carmichael changed his name to Kwame Toure. He died of prostate cancer on November 15, 1998, in Conakry, Guinea. Five years after his death, his autobiography, *Ready for Revolution: The Life and Struggles of Stokely Carmichael* was published by Scribner.

Stokely Carmichael, London, 1967. *Carmichael was at the forefront of the Black Power movement of the 1960s and was one of the most influential leaders of the Student Nonviolent Coordinating Committee.* BENTLEY ARCHIVE/POPPERFOTO/ CONTRIBUTOR/POPPERFOTO/GETTY IMAGES

MANDY CARTER (1948–)

Civil Rights Activist, Gay/Lesbian Rights Activist. Mandy Carter was born in Albany, New York, in 1948 and spent her childhood in orphanages. She attended community college for a time in Troy, New York, but moved to New York City in 1967 with a savings of $100. There she slept in Central Park before taking a job at drug guru Timothy Leary's League for Spiritual Discovery. Carter moved to San Francisco later that year and became active in protests against the war in Vietnam. For several years, Carter was involved with the War Resisters League, among whom she first admitted her sexual orientation. She worked for the group's San Francisco offices during the late 1970s, during which time she first became active in gay and lesbian politics.

In 1982, Carter moved to North Carolina, where she continued her work with the War Resisters League, in addition to becoming involved on a national level with gay and lesbian organizations. One of her accomplishments was helping coordinate the 1987 lesbian and gay march on the nation's capital, a role she reprised in 1993. In addition to coproducing an annual festival of women's music and art, Carter became instrumental—but ultimately unsuccessful—in campaigns to unseat North Carolina's right-wing Republican senator, Jesse Helms.

Carter was more successful with smaller tasks, such as lobbying Congress against antihomosexual legislation, often sponsored by Senator Helms or Robert Dornan, a Republican from California. She has also worked to combat the Christian Right's attempts to infiltrate African American churches in efforts to stymie support of gay and lesbian rights among the congregations. Carter has done this work first in her role as liaison and later as the director of the Human Rights Campaign Fund's National Black Gay and Lesbian Leadership Forum. Carter spoke of her political activism in the 1994 volume, *Uncommon Heroes: A Celebration of Heroes and Role Models for Gay and Lesbian Americans.* In the wake of the 2000 presidential election fiasco in Florida, Carter became a field organizer for the investigation by People for the American Way into minority voter intimidation. This work did not effect a change in the way that Florida conducts its elections, but it did raise awareness of the continued struggle African Americans and other minority groups face when attempting to exercise even their most basic civil rights.

SEPTIMA CLARK

See chapter 16, Education.

GEORGE CROCKETT JR.

See chapter 10, Law.

ANGELA Y. DAVIS (1944–)

Women's Rights Activist, Civil Rights Activist, Professor, Lecturer, Author, Organization Founder. Angela Yvonne Davis was born on January 26, 1944, in Birmingham, Alabama, to middle-class parents who stressed academic excellence, political awareness, and activism. Her mother had been politically active since her college days, and Angela participated in demonstrations with her from the time she was in elementary school. To ensure a better education than she would be able to receive in the segregated schools of the South, her parents sent her to Elizabeth Irwin High School, a private progressive school in New York. The school had many radical teachers and students, and Angela soon joined a Marxist study group.

After graduation, Davis majored in French at Brandeis University and studied at the Sorbonne in Paris during her junior year. After graduating in 1965, she pursued graduate studies in philosophy at the Johann Wolfgang von Goethe University in Frankfurt, West Germany. In 1967, Davis returned to the United States to study at the University of California at San Diego. When she had almost completed her doctorate, she took a teaching job at the University of California at Los Angeles (UCLA).

In 1969, Davis joined the Communist Party; the regents of UCLA tried to fire her, but she fought them in court. The following year, she became involved with the Black Panther Party. Guns registered in Davis's name were used by a member of the Black Panthers in a courtroom shooting in August 1970. Believing she was involved, the FBI sought her arrest. To evade federal authorities, Davis went underground. She was placed on the FBI's ten most-wanted list, and was arrested in October 1970. In 1972, she was acquitted of all charges, but was not reinstated by the university. California governor Ronald Reagan and the state's board of regents decreed that she would never teach in California schools again.

Following her trial, Davis founded the National Alliance against Racist and Political Repression, a legal group providing defense for minority prisoners. In 1980 and 1984, she ran for vice president of the United States on the Communist Party ticket. A writer and philosopher, Davis has published numerous books, including: *If They Come in the Morning* (1971); *Women, Race, and Class* (1983); *Violence against Women and the Ongoing Challenge to Racism* (1985); *Angela Davis: An Autobiography* (1988); *Women, Culture, and Politics* (1989); *Are Prisons Obsolete?* (2003); *Arbitrary Justice: The Power of the American Prosecutor* (2007); and *The Meaning of Freedom* (2010).

During the 1990s and early 2000s, Davis remained politically active and a popular yet controversial figure. Her 1995 appointment as presidential chair in charge of developing new ethnic studies courses at University of California at Santa Cruz was heavily opposed by state Republican legislators concerned with her Communist Party affiliation. Much sought after, though often protested against, Davis has lectured around the country about "envisioning a new movement" set apart from the radicalism of the 1960s. She continues to write and to support such causes as women's rights, workers' rights, health care, and nuclear disarmament.

W. E. B. DU BOIS (1868–1963)

Organization Executive/Founder, Civil Rights Activist, Professor, Author/Editor. An outstanding critic, editor, scholar, author, and civil rights leader, William Edward Burghardt Du Bois is among the most influential African Americans of the twentieth century. Born in Great Barrington, Massachusetts, on February 23, 1868, Du Bois received a bachelor's degree from Fisk University in 1888. Du Bois then entered Harvard University, where he earned a second bachelor's degree in 1890, a master of arts degree in 1891, and a Ph.D. degree in 1895, making him the first African American to earn a doctorate from Harvard. Du Bois later held teaching positions at Wilberforce University, University of Pennsylvania, and Atlanta University.

One of the founders of the NAACP in 1909, Du Bois served as that organization's director of publications and as the editor of *Crisis* magazine until 1934. In 1944, he returned from Atlanta University to become head of the NAACP's special research department, a post he held until 1948. Du Bois immigrated to Ghana in 1961 and became editor in chief of the *Encyclopaedia Africana*, an enormous Afrocentric publishing venture that was supported by Ghanaian president Kwame Nkrumah. Du Bois died in Ghana on August 27, 1963, at age ninety-five.

Du Bois's numerous books include: *The Suppression of the African Slave Trade to the United States of America, 1638–1870* (1896); *The Philadelphia Negro* (1899); *The Souls of Black Folk: Essays and Sketches* (1903); *John Brown* (1909); *The Quest of the Silver Fleece* (1911); *The Negro* (1915); *Darkwater* (1920); *The Gift of Black Folk* (1924); *Dark Princess* (1928); *Black Folk: Then and Now* (1939); *Dusk of Dawn* (1940); *Color and Democracy* (1945); *The World and Africa* (1947); *In Battle for Peace* (1952); and a trilogy, *The Black Flame* (1957–1961). It is this enormous literary output on such a wide variety of themes that offers the most convincing testimony in support of Du Bois's position that it was vital for African Americans to cultivate their own aesthetic and cultural values, even as they made valuable strides toward social emancipation. In this he was opposed by Booker T. Washington, who felt that African Americans should concentrate on developing technical and mechanical skills before all else.

Du Bois was one of the first male civil rights leaders to recognize the problem of gender discrimination. He was also among the first men to understand the unique problems of African American women and to value their contributions. Du Bois supported the woman's suffrage movement and strove to integrate this mostly white struggle. Additionally, Du Bois championed the reproductive freedom of women and women's economic independence from men. He encouraged many African American female writers, artists, poets, and novelists, featuring their works in *Crisis* and sometimes providing personal financial assistance to them. Several of his novels, most notably *The Quest of the Silver Fleece* and *Dark Princess*, feature women as prominently as men, an unusual approach for an author of his day. Du Bois spent his life working not just for the equality of all men, but for the equality of all people.

MEDGAR EVERS (1925–1963)

Civil Rights Activist. Medgar Evers was one of the first martyrs of the civil rights movement. He was born in 1925 in Decatur, Mississippi, to James and Jessie Evers. After serving in the U.S. Army during World War II, he enrolled in Alcorn Agricultural and Mechanical College in Mississippi, graduating in 1952. His first job out of college involved traveling around rural Mississippi and selling insurance. He soon grew enraged at the despicable conditions of poor African American families in his state and joined the Mound Bayou Chapter of the NAACP. In 1954, he was appointed Mississippi's first NAACP field secretary.

Evers was outspoken and his demands were radical for his rigidly segregated state. He fought, in particular, for the enforcement of the 1954 U.S. Supreme Court decision in *Brown v. Board of Education of Topeka*, which outlawed school segregation. Evers also fought for the right to vote, and he advocated boycotting merchants who discriminated against African Americans. He worked unceasingly, despite the threats of violence that his speeches engendered. Evers gave much of himself to this struggle, and in 1963 he gave his life. On June 12, 1963, he drove home from a meeting, stepped out of his car, and was shot in the back and killed.

Immediately after Evers's death, the shotgun that was used to kill him was found in nearby bushes, with the owner's fingerprints still fresh. Byron de la Beckwith, a vocal member of a local white-supremacist group, was arrested. Despite the evidence against him, which included an earlier statement that he wanted to kill Evers, two trials with all-white juries ended in deadlocked decisions, and Beckwith walked free. Twenty years later, in 1989, information surfaced that suggested jury tampering in both trials. The assistant district attorney, with the help of Evers's widow, Myrlie Evers-Williams, began putting together a new case. In 1990, Beckwith was arrested once again. On February 5, 1995, a multiracial jury found him guilty of Evers's assassination and sentenced him to life imprisonment. Beckwith died in 2001.

Evers did not die in vain. His death changed the tenor of the civil rights struggle. Anger replaced fear in the South, as hundreds of demonstrators marched in protest. His death prompted President John Kennedy to ask Congress for a comprehensive civil rights bill, which President Lyndon Johnson signed into law in July 1964. Evers's death, like his life, contributed much to the struggle for equality.

MYRLIE EVERS-WILLIAMS

See chapter 9, National Organizations.

JAMES L. FARMER JR. (1920–1999)

Civil Rights Activist, Educator, Organization Founder. James Leonard Farmer Jr., the founder of the Congress of Racial Equality (CORE), was born to James L. Farmer Sr. and Pearl Houston Farmer on January 12, 1920, in Marshall, Texas. After attending public schools throughout the South, he earned his B.S. in chemistry from Wiley College in Texas in 1938 and his B.D. in sacred theology from Howard University's School of Divinity in 1941. Active in the Christian Youth movement and onetime vice chairperson of the National Council of Methodist Youth and the Christian Youth Council of America, Farmer refused ordination when confronted with the realization that he would have to practice in a segregated ministry.

Farmer became a warrior in the struggle to dismantle America's all-encompassing system of racial segregation. In 1941, Farmer accepted a post as race relations secretary for the Fellowship of Reconciliation. Committed to direct, nonviolent protest, Farmer and a group of University of Chicago students became involved in efforts to desegregate Chicago housing. Later, in June 1942, he established CORE, the first protest organization in the United States to utilize the techniques of nonviolence and passive resistance advocated by the Indian nationalist leader Mohandas Gandhi. In June 1943, CORE staged the first successful sit-in demonstration at a restaurant in the Chicago Loop. The organization soon supplemented this maneuver with what came to be known as the standing-line, which involved the persistent waiting in line by CORE members at places of public accommodation where African Americans were denied admission.

During the early 1960s, under Farmer's leadership, CORE conducted freedom rides, voter-registration drives, and protest marches to eradicate racial segregation. In 1961, CORE introduced the freedom ride into the vocabulary and methodology of civil rights protest as the organization dispatched bus riders throughout the South for the purpose of testing the desegregation of terminal facilities. Attacked in Alabama and later arrested in Mississippi, the freedom riders eventually succeeded in securing the court-ordered desegregation of bus terminals in 1960, when the U.S. Supreme Court outlawed segregated interstate transportation.

In 1963, when President John F. Kennedy proposed legislation to enact a civil rights bill eliminating racial segregation in public accommodations, Farmer—along with Martin Luther King Jr., Whitney Young Jr., and Roy Wilkins—was one of the "big four" in the civil rights movement of the 1960s. As President Johnson shepherded the civil rights bill through Congress in 1964, three CORE workers—Andrew Goodman, Michael Schwerner, and James Chaney—disappeared while registering African American voters in Philadelphia, Mississippi. Outrage over their deaths and other atrocities suffered by southern citizens of African descent who attempted to register and exercise their right to vote led to the Voting Rights Act of 1965.

Farmer left CORE in 1966 after serving as national director for five years. Three years later, he joined the administration of President Richard Nixon as assistant secretary for administration in the Department of Health, Education, and Welfare. The appointment created a furor in some African American circles, where it was felt that it was inappropriate for a former civil rights leader to serve in the Nixon administration. In other circles, the appointment was praised by those who thought it necessary for African Americans to be represented in all areas. Farmer found that there was little substance to the position, however, and resigned at the end of 1970. During the 1970s, he developed a think tank, the Council on Minority Planning and Strategy (COMPAS), at Howard University, and the Fund for an Open Society, a nonprofit organization that granted low-interest mortgages to people planning to live in desegregated neighborhoods. His first book, *Freedom, When?*, was published in 1976, the same year that he broke all ties with CORE. After criticizing its leader, Roy Innis, for such actions as attempting to recruit African American Vietnam veterans as mercenaries in Angola's civil war, Farmer, along with Floyd McKissick, attempted to meet with Innis to reach an agreement on the future of the organization. These discussions failed. Disturbed over the course that the organization had taken, Farmer and a score of former CORE members attempted to create a new racially mixed civil rights organization in 1980.

Farmer entered the arena of higher education as a visiting professor at Mary Washington College in Fredericksburg, Virginia, in 1985. He also published *Lay Bare the Heart* in 1985. Farmer was celebrated for his civil rights achievements and was awarded nearly twenty honorary degrees. In January 1998, President Bill Clinton presented him with the country's highest civilian honor, the Presidential Medal of Freedom. Farmer, who had been in ill health, died at Mary Washington Hospital in Fredericksburg, Virginia, on July 9, 1999.

JAMES FORMAN (1928–2005)

Civil Rights Activist, Journalist, Author. James Forman was born on October 5, 1928, in Chicago, Illinois. For a brief period, he lived with his grandmother in Marshall, Mississippi. When he was six, Forman returned to Chicago, where he began his education in the city's Catholic schools. Later, he transferred to the Chicago public school system. In 1947, Forman graduated from Englewood High School with honors. After serving in the U.S. Air Force during the Korean War (1950–1953), he entered the University of South Carolina. Forman later transferred to Roosevelt University in Chicago, where he became a student political leader and chairman of Roosevelt's delegation to the National Student Association conference in 1956. He graduated from Roosevelt University the following year. He then entered Boston University, where he pursued a graduate degree. Later, he earned his M.A. in African and Afro-American history from Cornell University in 1980 and a Ph.D. from the Union of Experimental Colleges and Universities in 1982.

During the late 1950s, Forman became active in the civil rights struggle in the South. As a reporter for the *Chicago Defender*, he covered the Little Rock, Arkansas, school desegregation crisis. In 1960, under the auspices of the Congress of Racial Equality, Forman spent a year in Fayette County, Tennessee, assisting black sharecroppers who were evicted by white landowners because they sought to exercise their right to vote. Forman also traveled to Nashville, where he met Diane Nash, with whom he discussed the future of SNCC. In 1961, he joined other freedom riders protesting segregated facilities in Monroe, North Carolina. In Monroe, he was beaten, arrested, and jailed.

In October 1961, at the behest of Nash, James Bevel, and Paul Brooks, Forman became SNCC's executive secretary. Three years later, after participating in the failed effort of the Mississippi Freedom Democratic Party to remove the bloc of all-white delegates at the Democratic National Convention in Atlantic City, Forman and other SNCC members were invited to Guinea by that country's government. After his return from Africa, Forman became a critic of the federal government. He also promoted educational programs for civil rights workers to learn about Marxist and black nationalist views. As director of SNCC's international affairs, he worked to construct associations between African Americans and revolutionaries in the third world.

In the summer of 1964, under Forman's leadership, SNCC brought in almost a thousand young volunteers, black and white, to register voters, set up "freedom schools," establish community centers, and build the new Mississippi Freedom Democratic Party. Among those volunteers were Andrew Goodman, James Chaney, and Michael Schwerner, the three young men murdered along a muddy road near Philadelphia, Mississippi, in June 1964.

When Forman left SNCC in 1968, he joined the League of Revolutionary Black Workers. Forman become one of the first people to call for reparations to be paid to African Americans. He made reparations an issue in May 1969 when he interrupted a Sunday service at New York's Riverside Church to read his "Black Manifesto" and demand white churches pay $500 million in reparations for the injustices of African enslavement, racism, and capitalism.

Throughout his life, Forman remained active in the causes and struggles of blacks. He traveled to Africa and Europe on behalf of the Black Panther Party. In 1982, he planned a new March on Washington. Five years later, he lobbied against circuit court judge Robert Bork, President Ronald Regan's nominee to the U.S. Supreme Court. Six years later, Forman campaigned against the presidential bid of David Duke, the former Ku Klux Klan leader.

Forman was the author of *Sammy Younge, Jr.: The First Black College Student to Die in the Black Liberation Movement* (1968); *The Political Thought of James Forman* (1970); *The Making of Black Revolutionaries* (1972); and *Self-Determination: An Examination of the Question and Its Application to the African-American People* (1984). He died of colon cancer on January 10, 2005, in Washington, D.C., when he was seventy-six years old.

FRED D. GRAY (1930–)

Civil Rights Activist, Attorney, Minister, Politician, Author. Attorney Fred David Gray served as counsel for Rosa Parks and the Reverend Dr. Martin Luther King Jr., and for those involved in the Montgomery bus boycott, the Tuskegee syphilis study, the desegregation of Alabama schools, the freedom rides, and the Selma-to-Montgomery march. In 1954, when he opened his law office in Montgomery, Alabama, Gray was one of the few African American attorneys in the state. He began his law practice when he was twenty-four and moved to the legal forefront of the civil rights movement as one of America's leading civil rights attorneys. Gray played a pivotal role in dismantling legal segregation in Alabama.

The youngest of five children, Gray was born to Abraham and Nancy Jones Gray in Montgomery, Alabama. He went to school in Alabama until 1943, when his mother arranged for him to complete his education at the Nashville Christian Institute, an African American secondary school operated by the Church of Christ. The institute placed emphasis on teaching young men to become preachers. After completing his studies at the Church of Christ academy, Gray returned to his home state and entered Alabama State College for Negroes, from which he graduated in 1951. In September of the same year, he entered Case Western Reserve University Law School in Cleveland, Ohio.

Gray finished law school in 1954, the same year the U.S. Supreme Court handed down its *Brown v. Board of Education of Topeka* decision. Gray returned to Alabama, with the intention of methodically dismantling the state's segregation laws. He also defended Claudette Colvin and Rosa Parks against charges of disorderly conduct for refusing to give up their seats to white passengers. In addition, Gray served as a legal adviser to the Montgomery Improvement Association.

In 1956, Gray filed a petition that challenged the constitutionality of Alabama laws mandating racial segregation on buses, an effort that resulted in the *Gayle v. Browder* case. In November 1956, the U.S. Supreme Court ruled that racial segregation of public means of conveyances was unconstitutional. The same year, after state attorney general John Patterson outlawed the Alabama NAACP, Gray began providing legal counsel to the civil rights organization, a role he retained until 1964, when the NAACP was again allowed to operate in the state.

When the Reverend Martin Luther King Jr. was charged with tax evasion in 1960, Gray was a member of the defense team that won acquittal from an all-white jury. He also served as an attorney for students from Alabama State College who were expelled for their participation in sit-ins. Gray's other notable cases include *Gomillion v. Lightfoot* (1960), which challenged the Alabama legislature after it redrew the boundaries of the city of Tuskegee to exclude black neighborhoods, thereby denying African Americans the right to vote in municipal elections. Gray also aided in the representation of Vivian Malone and James Hood in their efforts to attend the University of Alabama, causing Governor George Wallace to "stand in the schoolhouse door." In addition, Gray served as the plaintiff's attorney in *Franklyn v. Auburn University* (1963), which resulted in the desegregation of the university.

Gray also participated in the 1965 *Williams v. Wallace* case, which resulted in the court ordering

Civil Rights Activist James Forman, Riverside Church, New York City, May 1969. *Forman interrupts a church service at New York's Riverside Church to read his "Black Manifesto" and demand that white churches pay $500 million in reparations for the injustices of slavery, racism, and capitalism.* UPI/CORBIS-BETTMANN. REPRODUCED BY PERMISSION.

Governor Wallace and the state of Alabama to protect protesters as they marched from Selma to Montgomery to present grievances for being denied the right to vote, a demonstration that led to the enactment of the Voting Rights Act of 1965. *Pollard v. United States of America* (1974) arose after it was revealed that the Tuskegee Syphilis Study (1932–1972) denied treatment to black men with syphilis. The U.S. government was ordered to continue its treatment program.

In 1970, citizens from Barbour, Bullock, and Macon counties elected Gray to the Alabama State Legislature (1971–1975) as a representative from Tuskegee. He became one of the first two African Americans to serve in the state legislature since Reconstruction. An ordained minister of the Church of Christ, Gray served as an assistant minister at several churches in Alabama, Kentucky, and Tennessee. In 1979, President Jimmy Carter nominated Gray for the position of U.S. district judge for the Middle District of Alabama. However, because there was opposition, Gray asked President Carter to withdraw his name from consideration. Gray is the author of two books: *Bus Ride to Justice, Changing the System by the System: The Life and Works of Fred Gray* (1995) and *The Tuskegee Syphilis Study: The Real Story and Beyond* (1998).

In July 2002, as senior partner in the law firm Gray, Langford, Sapp, McGowan, Gray & Nathanson, Gray became the first African American president of the Alabama Bar Association. The recipient of numerous awards, Grey kept his promise to destroy the bastions of racial segregation not only in his native state but also in America.

FANNIE LOU TOWNSEND HAMER (1917–1977)

Lecturer, Civil Rights Activist, Organization Executive/ Founder. As a poor sharecropper, Fannie Lou Hamer had only an elementary education, yet she became one of the most eloquent speakers for the civil rights movement in the South. She worked for political, social, and economic equality for herself and all African Americans. Hamer fought to integrate the national Democratic Party, and became one of its first African American delegates to a presidential convention.

The youngest of twenty siblings, Hamer was born on October 6, 1917, to Jim and Lou Ella Townsend in Montgomery County, Mississippi. She began picking cotton when she was six years old. Because she had to work full-time, Hamer dropped out of school in the sixth grade, and began working on a plantation as a sharecropper. In 1944, when the plantation's owner, W. D. Marlow, learned that she was literate, she was given a job as plantation time and record keeper. She continued in this position until 1962, when she lost her job after she tried to exercise her right to vote. Frightened by threats of violent reprisals, Hamer was forced to move away from her home and her family. Angered into action, she went to work for the Student Nonviolent Coordinating Committee helping other African Americans register to vote.

Because the Democratic Party refused to send African Americans as delegates to the national presidential convention in 1964, Hamer and others formed the Mississippi Freedom Democratic Party (MFDP). Arguing that the all-white delegation could not adequately represent their state, which had a large African American population, Hamer and the MFDP challenged the Democratic delegates from Mississippi for their seats at the convention in Atlantic City. Hamer's speech on their behalf so alarmed the incumbent President Lyndon Johnson that he tried to block the televised coverage of her efforts. The MFDP lost its bid that year, but their actions did result in a pledge from the national party not to exclude African Americans as delegates at the 1968 convention. In 1968, Fannie Lou Hamer was among the first African American delegates to the Democratic National Convention.

For the next decade, Hamer remained active in the struggle for civil and economic rights. In 1969, she founded the Freedom Farm Cooperative to help needy families raise food and livestock. The cooperative also provided basic social services, scholarships, and grants for education, and helped fund minority business opportunities. Hamer became a sought-after speaker, and in the 1970s, even as her health was failing from cancer, she toured the country speaking about civil rights. Hamer died on March 14, 1977.

MYLES FALLS HORTON (1905–1990)

Civil Rights Activist, Educator, Author. Myles Falls Horton was a trailblazer in the cause of social justice within America's southern region. Horton was an activist and a founder and director of the Highlander Folk School and the Highlander Research and Education Center in Tennessee. Concerned with developing new ideas about class and race, Horton's programs became a factor in the labor and civil rights movements. He was a controversial figure in Tennessee and throughout the South.

Horton, the oldest of four children, was born in Savannah, Tennessee, to socially active parents who imbued in him the core values of love, work, service, and education. As he matured, Horton held steadfastly to the outlook of his mother, Elsie Falls Horton, and sought to dedicate his life to serving others and building a humane society. It was through his experiences in the workplace and his educational journey that Horton advanced his personal and organizational values for social change.

Since education beyond the secondary level was not available in Savannah, Horton left home at fifteen to attend high school. He supported himself by working in a sawmill and later a box factory, where he gained an understanding of the strength of organizing and the power of collective action.

Horton received his undergraduate degree from Cumberland University in 1928. He later attended the University of Chicago and Union theological Seminary, where he studied under Reinhold Niebuhr, an outspoken advocate of socialist principles in social and economic matters. While he was a student at the University of Chicago, Horton toured the folk schools of Denmark, which were established as an experiment in populist education. While in Denmark, he decided to establish a school in the United States where students and teachers could dwell together, maintaining an unceremonious atmosphere in which they could propose and resolve problems. Horton believed that the experience itself would be the primary instructor.

In 1932, after he returned to Tennessee, Horton and Don West established the Highlander Folk School near Monteagle, Tennessee. Throughout the 1930s and 1940s, Highlander became a focal point for labor education in the American South. Through extension programs, Horton and his colleagues assisted striking coal miners, woodcutters, mill hands, government relief workers, and union members. Because of its activities, Highlander became the educational arm of the Congress of Industrial Organizations (CIO). In 1937, Horton joined the labor union's staff and organized one of the first CIO locals in the southern textile industry. Horton recognized the similarities between workers' rights and civil rights, and he understood that as long as the races remained segregated, labor would never be free. With that in mind, Horton designed workshops that would undermine the Jim Crow system. Horton parted ways with the CIO in the 1940s over his promotion of interracial unionism.

A year before the U.S. Supreme Court's 1954 decision in *Brown v. Board of Education of Topeka*, Horton began conducting workshops on school desegregation. Over the next two decades, he devoted his energy to creating programs to train and assist leaders and participants in the struggle for civil rights. The programs attracted hundreds of activists, both black and white, including Rosa Parks and Martin Luther King Jr. Under the leadership of Septima Clark, Highlander-sponsored Citizenship Schools, first held in 1957 on the South Carolina Sea Islands, taught thousands of blacks in Tennessee, Georgia, and Alabama the literacy skills they needed to secure the right to vote. In the early 1960s, as sit-in protests erupted across the South and at the urging of Ella Baker, college students gathered at Highlander to explore possible directions and goals for a new era of black protest. For many years, Highlander was the only place in the South where white and African American citizens lived and worked together, an arrangement that was illegal in that strictly segregated part of the country.

Highlander's involvement in the southern labor and civil rights movements earned it both praise and hostility. Although supported by such people as Eleanor Roosevelt and Reinhold Niebuhr, as well as educators, ministers, union leaders, philanthropists, and reform groups, Highlander's staff suffered condemnation from industrialists, politicians, so-called patriotic groups, and journalists for segregationist newspapers. As Highlander became more distinguished in the struggle for racial justice, outraged southern segregationists launched a sustained assault against what they described as a "Communist training school." Although the institution's members defended the school's dogma and teachings convincingly, their institutional practices made them susceptible in the 1950s. In 1962, following an investigation by the Tennessee General Assembly, a contrived police raid, and two sensational trials, the state of Tennessee rescinded Highlander's charter and confiscated its property.

Horton later extended the programs to Appalachia, hoping to build a multiracial alliance that would revolutionize America's economic, social, and political structure. In 1982, Horton and Highlander were nominated for the Nobel Peace Prize.

Myles Horton died on January 10, 1990. The same year, Doubleday published his autobiography, *Long Haul*, and Temple University Press published *We Make the Road by Walking: Conversations in Education and Social Change*, a dialogue between Horton and Paulo Freire.

JESSE L. JACKSON SR. (1941–)

Religious Leader, Civil Rights Activist, Organization Executive/Founder. Jesse Louis Jackson Sr. was born October 8, 1941, in Greenville, South Carolina. In 1959 Jackson left South Carolina to attend the University of Illinois. Dissatisfied with his treatment on campus, he decided to transfer to North Carolina Agricultural and Technical College. After receiving his B.A. in sociology, Jackson attended the Chicago Theological Seminary. In 1968, he was ordained a Baptist minister.

Jackson joined the Southern Christian Leadership Conference (SCLC) in 1965. The following year, he became involved with SCLC's Operation Breadbasket. From 1967 to 1971, Jackson served as the program's executive director. Resigning from SCLC in 1971, he formed his own organization, Operation PUSH (People United to Save Humanity). Through PUSH, Jackson continued to pursue the economic objectives of Operation Breadbasket and expanded into areas of social and political development.

Jackson soon became the most visible and sought-after civil rights leader in the country. While he described himself as a "country preacher," his magnetic personality had television appeal. Jackson's command of issues and his ability to reach to the heart of matters marked him as an individual of intellectual depth. Of all the civil rights leaders, Jackson was the one who could best relate to the young. In a phrase that became his trademark, "I am somebody," Jackson was able to bring out the best in them. Jackson's PUSH-Excel program sought to motivate schoolchildren to improve academically. In 1981, *Newsweek* credited Jackson with building a struggling community-improvement organization into a nationwide campaign to revive pride, discipline, and the work ethic in inner-city schools. With funding from the Carter administration, the PUSH-Excel program was placed in five other cities.

The Jesse Jackson of the 1980s will be best remembered for his two runs for the Democratic nomination for president of the United States. In 1983, many, but not all, African American political leaders endorsed the idea of an African American presidential candidate to create a "people's" platform, increase voter registration, and build a power base from which there could be greater input into the political process. Jackson's 1984 campaign was launched under the aegis of the National Rainbow Coalition, an umbrella organization of minority groups. African American support was divided, however, between Jackson and former vice president Walter Mondale. During the campaign, Jackson attracted considerable media coverage with controversial remarks and actions, demonstrating a lack of familiarity with national politics.

Jackson's 1988 campaign showed enormous personal and political growth. His candidacy was no longer a symbolic gesture but was a real and compelling demonstration of his effectiveness as a candidate. By the time the Democratic convention rolled around, media pundits were seriously discussing the likelihood of Jackson's nomination as the Democratic presidential candidate. "What to do about Jesse" became the focus of the entire Democratic leadership. At the end of the primary campaign, Jackson had finished a strong second to Massachusetts governor Michael Dukakis. He changed forever the notion that an African American president was inconceivable. Jackson took his defeat in stride and continued to campaign for the Democratic ticket until the November election.

Since the 1988 election, Jackson has worked less publicly, but no less energetically. In 1989, he moved with his Rainbow Coalition from Chicago to Washington, D.C., believing that the organization could be more effective in the nation's capital. Jackson continued to write, speak, and lead protests for social change. His primary concerns included crime, violence, drug use, and teenage pregnancy in inner-city neighborhoods, as well as voter registration, health care, affirmative action, and baseball hiring practices. In 1993, Jackson was awarded the Martin Luther King Jr. Nonviolent Peace Prize.

Jackson was active in foreign affairs as well. In 1991, he traveled to Iraq and convinced Saddam Hussein to begin releasing Americans held hostage after Hussein's invasion of Kuwait. In 1994, Jackson met with Fidel Castro in Cuba and, later during the year, President Bill Clinton sent him on a peace mission to Nigeria. Although many expected Jackson to run for the presidency again in 1992 or 1996, he decided against it, saying that he was too tired and the strain on his family was too severe. However, he did support his son, Jesse Jackson Jr., who was elected to the House of Representatives for Chicago's Second Congressional District on December 12, 1995. As the decade was coming to a close, Jesse Jackson Sr.

Jesse Jackson, Raleigh Civic Center, Raleigh, NC, 1987. *Jackson gives a speech announcing his candidacy for president. Jackson proved to be a serious candidate during his campaign for the 1988 Democratic presidential nomination.* UPI/CORBIS-BETTMANN. REPRODUCED BY PERMISSION.

continued to be a civil and human rights activist, as well as a political force in American society. As he had done since the mid-1980s in Syria, Cuba, and Iraq, in May 1999, Jackson successfully secured the release of three captive U.S. soldiers held as prisoners of war during the Kosovo crisis.

As the new millennium began, Jackson experienced many ups and downs. He received the nation's highest civilian honor, the Presidential Medal of Freedom, from President Bill Clinton on August 9, 2000. Just months later, in January 2001, it was revealed that Jackson had been involved in an extramarital affair, fathering a daughter with the former head of the Rainbow/PUSH Coalition office in Washington, D.C. The scandal threatened to end his public career, yet Jackson survived the turmoil. In August 2001, he celebrated the thirtieth anniversary of his Rainbow/PUSH Coalition with a five-day conference in Chicago.

The Reverend Jesse Jackson, March on Tallahassee, March 7, 2000. *Jackson speaks at a rally culminating from a march held to protest Florida governor Jeb Bush's "One Florida" plan to eliminate affirmative action in the state's public university system and in state contracts.* **AP IMAGES. REPRODUCED BY PERMISSION.**

VERNON N. JOHNS (1892–1965)

Minister, College President, Civil Rights Activist. Vernon Neapolitan Johns is considered by some to be the father of the modern civil rights movement. One of the movement's early trailblazers, Johns was noted, along with Mordecai Johnson and Howard Thurman, as one of the three great African American preachers.

Johns was born on April 22, 1892, in Darlington Heights, Virginia. He received a B.A. degree from Virginia Theological Seminary and College in 1915 and a B.D. degree from Oberlin College in 1918. The same year he graduated from Oberlin, Johns entered the University of Chicago, where he did graduate work in theology. Because the views of African American theologians were not included in discussion about biblical interpretation and social responsibility, and because their sermons were not being published, Johns submitted the sermons of Johnson and Thurman to publishing houses. When the manuscripts were rejected, he submitted his own sermon, "Transfigured Moments," which appeared in Joseph Fort Newton's anthology *Best Sermons* in 1926. The first African American to be published in the collection, Johns joined the ranks of such well-known theologians as Reinhold Niebuhr, Henry Sloan, and Willard L. Sperry.

In 1926, Johns delivered his first sermon at Howard University's Rankin Memorial Chapel and became director of the Baptist Educational Center in New York. A year later, he succeeded Mordecai Johnson as pastor of the First Baptist Church in Charleston, West Virginia. Two years later, he became president of Virginia Theological Seminary and College. Adhering to his rural roots and closeness to nature, and mindful of the needs of his people, he founded the Institute for Rural Preachers of Virginia and the Farm and City Club, which attempted to raise awareness about issues of economics among both rural and urban African Americans. Johns remained at the Virginia college until his retirement in 1934. After retiring, he spent ten years lecturing and preaching at colleges and mostly rural African American churches.

In 1947, Johns became the nineteenth pastor of Dexter Avenue Baptist Church in Montgomery, Alabama, where he served until 1952. Dexter's congregation consisted mostly of Montgomery's black middle class. In keeping with his social gospel position, Johns was a pioneering proponent of civil rights and he urged his congregation to challenged the city's Jim Crow practices. As one who practiced what he preached, Johns confronted Montgomery's segregated bus seating—long before Rosa Parks refused to move to the back of the bus—when he disembarked in protest and demanded a refund, which he received. After an African American motorist was brutally attacked by police while blacks stood watching, Johns responded with a sermon, "It's Safe to Murder Negroes in Montgomery," in which he criticized those present for not intervening.

Johns often found himself in conflict with church officials and his congregation. Because of his unorthodox views, country manner, and the tenor of his sermons, which denounced racial segregation, many became concerned that they would come under the scrutiny of Montgomery's white community and local authorities. Given the zeitgeist of the times, Johns advocated for Montgomery's blacks in dangerous ways. Twice he attempted to prosecute white men for raping African American girls. He protested both Jim Crow public transportation policies and segregated restaurants. In 1952, Johns resigned as pastor of the Dexter Avenue Baptist Church. However, his early activism and challenges to the power structure paved the way for Dexter's congregation to receive the Reverend Martin Luther King Jr.'s socially active ministry and for Johns to take a leading role in the Montgomery bus boycott. King later described Johns as "a brilliant preacher with a creative mind" and "a fearless man [who] never allowed an injustice to come to his attention without speaking out against it."

King and Malcolm X, who followed Johns as civil rights leaders, eclipsed his contributions to the movement. But Johns was a trailblazer who did not wait to begin the struggle for freedom and equality. He died on June 11, 1965, shortly after delivering a sermon titled "The Romance of Death" at Rankin Memorial Chapel. In 1994, a television film, *The Road to Freedom: The Vernon Johns Story*, lifted Johns from historical obscurity. The film was directed by Kenneth Fink and coproduced by Kareem Abdul Jabbar.

VIVIAN JUANITA MALONE JONES (1942–2005)

Civil Rights Activist. A pioneering activist during the modern civil rights era, Vivian Malone was one of two African American students whose 1963 enrollment in the University of Alabama was a decisive moment in the black American struggle for civil rights. She and James Hood attracted national attention when Alabama's governor, George Wallace, tried to keep an inauguration promise to maintain "segregation forever." Wanting to avoid violence, Robert F. Kennedy, the U.S. attorney general, negotiated what would take place when the two students enrolled. When they arrived to register for classes on June 11, 1963, Wallace blocked their entrance by standing in the doorway of Foster Auditorium. The governor read a statement citing states' right to organize education. Later that day, federalized National Guard troops escorted the two students to the school and through the halls to registration. They went to their respective dormitories, ate in the cafeteria, and experienced no further incidents that day.

The next day, Byron de la Beckwith, an outspoken opponent of equal rights for African Americans and a member of the Mississippi White Citizens Council, gunned down civil rights leader Medgar Evers in his driveway in Jackson, Mississippi. The death of Evers caused Malone, a transfer student from historically black Alabama Agricultural and Mechanical College, to become resolute in her determination not to surrender to the forces of violence. In mid-November, an explosion tore a hole in the street approximately 100 yards from Malone's dormitory. Despite bomb threats and other retaliatory acts, Jones remained at the university. However, the pressure proved too much for Hood, who transferred to Wayne State University in Detroit two months later. Two years after gaining admission, Malone became the first African American to graduate from the university, earning a degree in business management. Hood returned to the University of Alabama in 1995 and earned a Ph.D. in higher education.

After graduating, Malone had difficulty finding employment. She relocated to Washington, D.C., and was hired by the civil rights division of the U.S. Department of Justice. Malone later moved to Atlanta and became director of civil rights and urban affairs with the Environmental Protection Agency, in which position she helped pioneer the concept of environmental justice. While at the University of Alabama, Malone met Mack Jones, a student from Stillman College in Tuscaloosa, whom the university had hired to be her driver. They later married, and he became an obstetrician. Vivian Malone Jones remained active in civil rights and community organizations, including the NAACP, the Southern Christian Leadership Conference, and the National Council of Negro Women.

In October 1996, the George Wallace Family Foundation selected Jones as the first recipient of the Lurleen B. Wallace Award for Courage. The University of Alabama endowed a Vivian Malone Jones Scholarship Fund and hung her portrait in the College of Commerce building. In 2000, the university gave her an honorary doctorate. Jones died on October 13, 2005.

MARGIE JUMPER (1914–2007)

Civil Rights Activist. In 1946, Margie Jumper refused to surrender her seat to a white man on a streetcar in Roanoke, Virginia, nine years before Rosa Parks did the same on a Montgomery, Alabama, bus and two years after Irene Morgan did so on an interstate bus traveling from Virginia to Maryland. Like other cities in the South, Roanoke had invoked a Jim Crow ordinance that prohibited black and white passengers from sitting together. Roanoke's motormen and conductors could be cruel to blacks. They used racial slurs, and admonished young mothers riding with crying babies. The day that Jumper refused to adhere to Roanoke's expected code of behavior for blacks, the black section of the streetcar was nearly full, as was the white section, which was in the front; she sat in the middle of the streetcar, until a white passenger entered and asked the conductor to make her move. Refusing to do so, authorities pulled from her seat and arrested in front of Roanoke's Old City Hall. "It wasn't right, and I had the right to sit there," she said. Later, she pleaded guilty to violating the local ordinance, paid the fine, and became one of the many unsung actors in the freedom struggle narrative.

Margie Mitchell Jumper was born on July 13, 1914, to Burrell and Mary R. Mitchell, in Martinsville, Virginia. She moved to Roanoke as a young woman. Later, she married Clarence Jumper, a cook for Norfolk and Western Railroad. Because they had no car, the streetcar was her normal mode of transportation.

A lifetime member of the national and local NAACP, Jumper served as treasurer of the organization's Roanoke chapter. Known as the Rosa Parks of Roanoke Valley, she was featured in the *Roanoke Times* in 1986 for her spontaneous and courageous act of protest against Jim Crow laws in 1946. In 2003, the NAACP honored her with the Reverend R. R. Wilkinson Memorial Award for Social Justice. A year after her death in 2007, the state of Virginia commemorated the life of Margie Jumper with Senate Joint Resolution No. 33.

CORETTA SCOTT KING (1927–2006)

Organization Executive/Founder, Civil Rights Activist, Women's Rights Activist, Lecturer, Diplomat, Educator, Community Activist. As the wife of civil rights leader Martin Luther King Jr., Coretta Scott King was ready to continue his work and perpetuate his ideals after his 1968 assassination. While her primary role in the early years of marriage concerned the rearing of their four children, she became increasingly involved in the struggle for civil rights through her husband's activities. After his death, she quickly became a dynamic activist and peace crusader.

Born on April 27, 1927, to Obadiah Scott and Bernice McMurray Scott, King was a native of Marion, Alabama. During the Great Depression, she was forced to contribute to the family income by hoeing and picking cotton. Early in life, she resolved to overcome adversity, seek equal treatment, and achieve a sound education. In 1945, after graduating from the private Lincoln High School, she entered Antioch College in Yellow Springs, Ohio, on a scholarship, majoring in elementary education and music. A teaching career appealed to her, but she became disillusioned when she was not allowed to teach in the town's public schools.

Musical training in voice and piano absorbed much of her time. After receiving her undergraduate degree from Antioch College, she continued her studies at the New England Conservatory of Music in Boston, where she earned a degree in voice. She met Martin Luther King Jr. in Boston, and they married on June 18, 1953. An exceptional young minister, King's intense convictions and concern for humanity brought her a measure of rare self-realization early in life. Sensing his incredible dynamism, she suffered no regrets at the prospect of relinquishing her own possible career. The Kings had four children: Yolanda Denise (b. November 17, 1955; d. May 15, 2007); Martin III (b. October 23, 1957); Dexter (b. January 30, 1961); and Bernice (b. March 28, 1963).

After completing her studies in 1954, King moved back to the South with her husband, who became pastor of Dexter Avenue Baptist Church in Montgomery, Alabama. Within a year, Reverend King led the Montgomery bus boycott and brought forth a new era of civil rights agitation. Two years later, he helped to organize and was elected head of the Southern Christian Leadership Conference (SCLC).

Over the years, Coretta Scott King gradually became more involved in her husband's work. She occasionally performed at his lectures, raising her voice in song as he did in speech. She became involved in separate activities as well. In 1962, she served as a Woman's Strike for Peace delegate to the seventeen-nation Disarmament Conference in Geneva, Switzerland. In the mid-1960s, she sang in the freedom concerts that raised money for SCLC. When demands on her husband became too much, she filled the speaking engagements he could not keep. After his assassination, Coretta King kept many of his commitments. Soon, however, she became a much sought-after speaker in her own right.

Coretta Scott King's speech on Solidarity Day, June 19, 1968, is often identified as a prime example of her emergence from the shadow of her husband's memory. In it, she called on American women to "unite and form a solid block of women power" to fight the three great evils of racism, poverty, and war. Much of her subsequent activity revolved around plans for the creation of a Martin Luther King Jr. memorial in Atlanta, which she began to work on in 1969. Located in the Martin Luther King Jr. Historic District and designated a national historic landmark on May 5, 1977, the site became a unit of the National Park Service in 1980. In the same year that she began developing plans for the Martin Luther King Jr. Center for Nonviolent Social Change, King also published *My Life with Martin Luther King Jr.*, a book of reminiscences. On August 27, 1983, in celebration of the twentieth anniversary of the March on Washington, Coretta Scott King and the King Center summoned more than seven hundred organizations and convoked the New Coalition of Conscience, which represented one of the largest nonviolent and civil and human rights coalitions in the history of the United States. The number-one priority of the coalition was the establishment of the Martin Luther King Jr. holiday.

After years of lobbying to have Dr. King's birthday celebrated as a federal holiday, Coretta Scott King and others were rewarded for their efforts when in November of 1983, President Ronald Reagan signed the bill creating the King holiday. The following year, Coretta Scott King was elected chair of the Martin Luther King Jr. Federal Holiday Commission, established by Congress to formalize plans for the first legal celebration of the King holiday. On January 20, 1986, the country celebrated the first Martin Luther King Jr. federal holiday. Today, Dr. King's birthday is marked by annual celebrations in many countries.

Coretta Scott King's activism extended beyond the borders of the United States. In the mid-1980s, she and two of her children were arrested for demonstrating against apartheid outside of the South African embassy in Washington, D.C. In 1986, she visited South Africa for eight days, meeting with businessmen and antiapartheid leaders. King also condemned the human rights violations of the Haitian military regime. In 1993, she implored the United Nations to impose an embargo against the nation.

The Martin Luther King Jr. Center for Nonviolent Social Change became embattled in an ugly scuffle with the National Park Service over the issue of how best to utilize some of the historic Atlanta district in which the King memorial is located. As chief executive officer, Coretta Scott King was forced to mediate between the family's desire for an interactive museum with exhibitions and programs for children and the National Park Service's plan for a visitor's center on the same site. The dispute was not resolved until April 1995, a few months after King had officially stepped down as CEO, handing the reigns of leadership over to her son Dexter.

Controversy continued to brew. In 1964, Martin Luther King Jr. had given nearly 83,000 documents, including correspondence and other manuscripts, to Boston University. Coretta King had hoped to regain control of that legacy, but in April 1995, the Massachusetts Supreme Judicial Court ruled in favor of the university.

On a brighter note, Coretta Scott King remained an eloquent and respected spokesperson on behalf of African American and human rights causes and nonviolent philosophy. She was often recognized for keeping her husband's dream alive. In September 1995, King and two other famous civil rights widows, Myrlie Evers-Williams and Betty Shabazz, were honored for their influence by the National Political Congress of Black Women. King received numerous honorary degrees from colleges and universities, including Boston University, Morehouse College, Princeton University, and Bates College.

After many years of serving as a staunch freedom fighter for justice and equality for all, Coretta Scott King suffered a stroke and a mild heart attack in August 2005. Two weeks before her death, she made her last public appearance at a Salute to Greatness dinner as a part of the Martin Luther King Day Celebration in Atlanta, Georgia. As she received a standing ovation, supported by her children, she waved to the crowd.

Coretta Scott King, who was called the "matriarch of the civil rights movement" by the Reverend Fred Shuttlesworth, spoke out "on behalf of racial and economic justice, women's and children's rights, gay and lesbian dignity, religious freedom, the needs of the poor and homeless, full employment, health care, educational opportunities, nuclear disarmament and ecological sanity." She also devoted her time and energy to AIDS education and seeking ways to curb gun violence.

On January 30, 2006, at age seventy-eight, King died in her sleep at a holistic health center in Rosarito Beach, Mexico, where she had been undergoing treatment for advanced-stage ovarian cancer. The Reverend Joseph Lowery, former president of SCLC, remarked that "she bore her grief with dignity. She moved quietly but forcefully in the fray. She stood for peace in the midst of turmoil." King's body was interred in a temporary mausoleum on the grounds of the King Center until a permanent resting place, next to her husband, could be erected.

DEXTER KING (1961–)

Civil Rights Activist, Organization Executive. The younger son of Martin Luther King Jr. and Coretta Scott King, Dexter Scott King was born in Atlanta, Georgia, on January 30, 1961. Dexter's early days were filled with his parents' involvement in the civil rights movement. Not only did his father participate in the movement, but by the mid-1960s his mother was heavily involved as well.

King's early education occurred at both private and public academies. In 1979, he graduated from Atlanta's Frederick Douglass High School, where his interests included both music and athletics. Offered an athletic scholarship at the University of Southern California, Dexter opted to study at his father's alma mater, Morehouse College.

Dexter left Morehouse before graduating, and became involved in music video production. In collaboration with Phillip M. Jones, he produced a music video in observance of the first nationally celebrated Martin Luther King Jr. holiday. That endeavor led to an album in remembrance of Dr. King that included recordings by such performers as Prince, Whitney Houston, and Run-DMC. By 1989, Dexter King had returned to the civil rights arena when he was named president of the Jr. Center for Nonviolent Social Change, while his mother remained as CEO. He left the job after only four months because he was concerned that he only served as a titular head. However, with the retirement of Coretta Scott King in 1994, Dexter was reinstalled as CEO in 1995 by a unanimous vote of the board of directors.

In March of 1997, Dexter King confronted James Earl Ray, the man convicted of his father's assassination, at the Lois M. DeBerry Special Needs Facility in Nashville, Tennessee. Dexter King asked Ray if he had assassinated Martin Luther King Jr. Ray stated that he had not, and Dexter began working toward Ray's release from prison. However, James Earl Ray died of liver failure thirteen months after their meeting.

MARTIN LUTHER KING JR. (1929–1968)

Religious Leader, Civil Rights Activist, Author, Labor Activist, Organization Executive/Founder, Minister, Antiwar Activist. Martin Luther King Jr. and his policy of nonviolent protest was the dominant force in the civil rights movement during its decade of greatest achievement from 1957 to 1968. King was the prime mover of the Montgomery bus boycott (1955–1956), the keynote speaker at the March on Washington (1963), and the youngest Nobel Peace Prize laureate (1964).

King was born in Atlanta on January 15, 1929. He was one of the three children of Martin Luther King Sr., pastor of Ebenezer Baptist Church, and Alberta Williams King, a former schoolteacher. After attending grammar and high schools locally, King enrolled in Morehouse College in 1944 when he was fifteen years old. At this time, he was not inclined to enter the ministry, but he came under the influence of Dr. Benjamin Mays, a scholar whose manner and bearing convinced King that a religious career could bring intellectual satisfaction. After receiving his B.A. degree in 1948, King attended Crozer Theological Seminary in Chester, Pennsylvania. Graduating in 1951, King was the recipient of a J. Lewis Crozer Fellowship and the Plafker Award, given to the most outstanding student in the graduating class. In 1951, King entered Boston University to pursue a Ph.D. in theology. After completing the course work in two years and finishing his dissertation in 1955, King was granted a Ph.D.

Married by then to Coretta Scott, King returned to the South, accepting the pastorate of the Dexter Avenue Baptist Church in Montgomery, Alabama. He made his first mark on the civil rights movement by mobilizing Montgomery's African American community during a 382-day boycott of the city's bus lines beginning in December 1955. Working through the Montgomery Improvement Association, King endured arrest and violent harassment, including the bombing of his home. In 1956, the U.S. Supreme Court declared the Alabama laws requiring segregation on buses unconstitutional, thereby granting African Americans equal access on the buses of Montgomery.

A national hero and a civil rights figure of growing importance, King summoned together 115 African American leaders in 1957 and laid the groundwork for a new civil rights organization, now known as the Southern Christian Leadership Conference (SCLC). King was elected its president, and he soon sought to help other communities organize protest campaigns against discrimination and to promote voter-registration activities among African Americans.

After the 1958 publication of his first book, *Stride Toward Freedom: The Montgomery Story*, and a trip to India the following year, where he enhanced his understanding of the nonviolent strategies of Mohandas Gandhi, King returned to the United States and subsequently resigned as pastor of Dexter Avenue Baptist Church. In 1960, he returned to Atlanta where the headquarters of SCLC was located and became co-pastor with his father of Ebenezer Baptist Church.

A sympathizer with the African American southern student movement, King spoke at the organizational meeting of the Student Nonviolent Coordinating Committee (SNCC) in April 1960. He soon garnered criticism from the student activists, who were intent on maintaining their independence. King was arrested after participating in a student sit-in at Rich's Department Store in Atlanta on October 19, 1960. King refused to post bail and was incarcerated with the student protesters.

Three years later, in Birmingham, Alabama, where white officials were known for their anti–African American attitudes, King's nonviolent tactics were put to their most severe test. On April 16, King was arrested during a mass protest in support of fair hiring practices, the establishment of a biracial committee, and the desegregation of department store facilities. Police brutality (i.e., police dogs and fire hoses) used against the marchers dramatized the plight of African Americans to the nation and the world at large with enormous impact. Although arrested, King's voice was not silenced as he issued his classic "Letter from a Birmingham Jail" to refute the criticism of white clergy. In June 1963, President Kennedy agreed to send sweeping civil rights legislation to Congress.

Later that year, King was a principal speaker at the historic March on Washington, where he delivered the "I Have A Dream" speech, one of the most passionate addresses of his career. At the beginning of the next year, *Time* magazine designated him as its Man of the Year for 1963. He was also named recipient of the 1964 Nobel Peace Prize. After returning from Oslo, Norway, where he had gone to accept the award, King entered a new battle in Selma, Alabama, where he led a voter-registration campaign that culminated in the Selma-to-Montgomery freedom march. King next brought his crusade to Chicago, where he launched a slum rehabilitation and open housing program.

In the North, however, King soon discovered that young and angry African Americans cared little for his pulpit oratory and even less for his solemn pleas for peaceful protest. Their disenchantment was clearly one of the factors influencing his decision to rally behind a new cause and stake out a fresh battleground: the war in Vietnam. Although his aim was to fuse a new coalition of dissent based on equal support for the peace crusade and the civil rights movement, King antagonized many civil rights leaders by declaring the United States to be "the greatest purveyor of violence in the world."

The rift was immediate. The NAACP saw King's shift of emphasis as "a serious tactical mistake"; the Urban League warned that the "limited resources" of the civil rights movement would be spread too thin; Bayard Rustin claimed African American support of the peace movement would be negligible; and Ralph Bunche felt King was undertaking an impossible mission in trying to bring the campaign for peace in step with the goals of the civil rights movement.

From the vantage point of history, King's timing could only be regarded as superb. In announcing his opposition to the war and in characterizing it as a "tragic adventure" that was wreaking "havoc with the destiny of the entire world," King again forced the white middle class to concede that no movement could dramatically affect the course of government in the United States unless it involved deliberate and restrained aggressiveness, persistent dissent, and even militant confrontation. These were precisely the ingredients of the civil rights struggle in the South in the early 1960s.

As students, professors, intellectuals, clergymen, and reformers of every stripe rushed into the movement, King, in a sense, forced fiery black militants such as Stokely Carmichael and Floyd McKissick to surrender their control over antiwar polemics. King then turned his attention to a domestic issue that, in his view, was directly related to the Vietnam struggle: the war on poverty. At one point, he called for a guaranteed family income, threatened national boycotts, and spoke of disrupting entire cities by nonviolent "camp-ins." With this in mind, he began to draw up plans for a massive march of the poor on Washington, D.C., envisioning a popular demonstration of unsurpassed intensity and magnitude designed to force Congress and the political parties to recognize and deal with the unseen and ignored masses of desperate and downtrodden Americans.

King's decision to interrupt these plans to lend his support to the Memphis sanitation workers' strike was based in part on his desire to discourage violence, as well as to focus national attention on the plight of the poor, unorganized workers of the city. The men were bargaining for little else beyond basic union representation and long overdue salary considerations. Though he was unable to eliminate the violence that had resulted in the summoning and subsequent departure of the National Guard, King stayed in Memphis and was in the process of planning for a march that he vowed to carry out in defiance of a federal court injunction, if necessary. On April 3, 1968, King delivered his last and most foreboding speech, "I See the Promised Land," better known as "I've Been to the Mountaintop." Delivered at (the Bishop Charles H.) Mason Temple, King prophesied his demise.

Death came for King on the balcony of the African American–owned Lorraine Motel in Memphis on the evening of April 4. While standing outside with Jesse Jackson and Ralph Abernathy, a shot rang out. King fell over, struck in the neck by a rifle bullet. At 7:05 p.m. he was pronounced dead at St. Joseph's Hospital. His death caused a wave of violence in more than one hundred major cities across the country. However, King's legacy has lasted much longer than the memories of those post-assassination riots. In 1969, his widow, Coretta Scott King, organized the Martin Luther King Jr. Center for Nonviolent Social Change. Today, it stands next to his beloved Ebenezer Baptist Church in Atlanta and, with the surrounding buildings, is a national historic landmark under the administration of the National Park Service. Additionally, the Lorraine Motel, which is listed on the National Register of Historic Places, now serves as the National Civil Rights Museum.

On November 13, 2006, two U.S. presidents joined civil rights leaders, three of Dr. King's children, and thousands of others for the groundbreaking ceremony of the first monument to a black American on the National Mall. The four-acre monument will be built along the Tidal Basin between the Thomas Jefferson and Abraham Lincoln memorials. "It belongs here," said former president Bill Clinton. In 1996, Clinton signed the bill

Martin Luther King Jr. with his Family, October 27, 1960. *The King family celebrates the release of Dr. King from Reidsville State Prison in Georgia, after he had been arrested and jailed for participating in a student-led lunch-counter sit-in at Rich's Department Store in Atlanta.* PHOTOGRAPH BY HORACE CORT. AP IMAGES. REPRODUCED BY PERMISSION.

Stokely Carmichael, Student Nonviolent Coordinating Committee Leader, Rally on the Steps of the Mississippi State Capitol, June 1966. *Carmichael speaks at the rally held on the arrival in Jackson, Mississippi, of the March against Fear. At an earlier speech during the march, Carmichael began publicly articulating his "Black Power" philosophy, causing a rift between him and Martin Luther King Jr.* PHOTOGRAPH BY FLIP SCHULKE. CORBIS VIEW. REPRODUCED BY PERMISSION.

authorizing the creation of the monument on the site near the spot where, during the 1963 March on Washington, King delivered his "I Have a Dream" speech. The only twentieth-century American accorded a federal holiday, Dr. King's birthday is celebrated each year with educational programs, artistic displays, and concerts throughout the United States.

MARTIN LUTHER KING III (1957–)

Civil Rights Activist, Community Activist, Political Leader, Organization Executive/Founder. Martin Luther King III, the oldest son and second child of the Reverend Martin Luther King Jr. and Coretta Scott King, was born in Montgomery, Alabama, on October 23, 1957. Reared in Atlanta, Martin Luther King III received his primary and secondary education in the schools of Atlanta. After completing his secondary studies, King entered Morehouse College, majoring in political science and history.

King III was a child of the civil rights movement. After graduating from his father's alma mater, King devoted his energies to voter-registration campaigns, lobbying to make his father's birthday a federal holiday and pursuing political office. As a civil and human rights advocate, King has been involved in developing meaningful policy strategies to provide just and equal treatment to citizens throughout the world.

During the administration of President Jimmy Carter, King represented the president on two official delegations to promote peace in foreign countries. In 1984, as a member of the board of directors of the Martin Luther King Jr. Center for Nonviolent Social Change, he went to five poverty- and drought-stricken African nations on a fact-finding mission. This mission resulted in an initiative to end starvation in Africa. Later, he focused his energy on the injustices of South Africa's system of racial apartheid and joined in the struggle to gain the freedom of Nelson Mandela.

In 1986, King entered the political arena and was elected to office as an at-large representative on the Fulton County, Georgia, Board of Commissioners. Serving until 1993, his tenancy was characterized by enactments regulating minority business participation in public contracting, ethics, purification of the county's natural water resources, and strict hazardous-waste disposal provisions. After leaving office, King returned to public speaking, worked with Atlanta youth groups, and continued to be a community and human rights activist. Later, in response to California's Proposition 209, which outlawed policies of affirmative action, he organized Americans United for Affirmative Action (AUAA), a coalition of national groups. AUAA's purpose was to safeguard affirmative action programs and to maintain the principles of equal opportunity and diversity championed by the civil rights movement. On January 15, 1998, King was sworn into office as the fourth president of the Southern Christian Leadership Conference (SCLC), a position he retained until 2004. King was the first layperson in that role. He used the SCLC platform to speak out against injustices such as the racial profiling of minorities. In 2006, King founded Realizing the Dream, an international nonprofit organization devoted to continuing his parents' humanitarian work.

JAMES MORRIS LAWSON JR. (1928–)

Educator, Civil Rights Activist, Minister. A proponent of the Gandhian philosophy of direct nonviolent protest, the Reverend James M. Lawson Jr. was one of the leading theoreticians and tacticians in the African American struggle for freedom, equality, and justice. Lawson was born on September 22, 1928, in Uniontown, Pennsylvania, to the Reverend James Morris and Philane May Cover Lawson, who were politically active. Although born in Uniontown, he was reared with his nine siblings in predominately white Massillon, Ohio, where he received his primary and secondary education. While growing up, Lawson was exposed to the views of Mohandas Gandhi, who introduced the passive-resistance creed against injustice, through editorials in the *Cleveland Defender* and the *Pittsburgh-Courier*. Before he graduated from high school, he and a schoolmate, provoked by the unjust treatment that African Americans received in eating establishments, entered a Massillon restaurant and insisted that they be served. This was his first sit-in. Lawson continued his protest activity by testing white-only restaurants when he attended Methodist youth meetings in small midwestern cities. From his encounters with racially prejudiced whites, Lawson discerned that the midwestern mind-set was very much akin to that in the South.

In 1947, Lawson entered Baldwin-Wallace College in Berea, Ohio. His collegiate experience buttressed his belief in direct and vigorous activism. He became a member of the Fellowship of Reconciliation's local chapter, as well as a member of the Congress of Racial Equality (CORE), both of which were ardent advocates of direct nonviolent passive resistance to racism.

Firmly grounded the in guiding principles of nonviolence by 1949, Lawson became a "conscientious objector" as the United States immersed itself in the Cold War. Shortly after the Korean War began in 1950, Lawson's pacifism came under assault. Even though he could have taken a student or ministerial deferment, he remained unwaveringly committed to his principles as a pacifist and conscientious objector. After a warrant was issued for his arrest, Lawson turned himself in to the authorities, who charged him with violating U.S. draft laws. Found guilty in April 1951, he was sentenced to three years in federal prison. In May of the following year, Lawson was paroled from the maximum-security prison in Ashland, Kentucky. He returned to Baldwin-Wallace in the fall, and completed the requirements for a bachelor of arts degree.

After earning his degree, Lawson traveled to India to work with the Methodist Board of Missionaries. There until 1956, he studied the Gandhian philosophy of *Satyagraha*, or the strategy of nonviolence, which includes three basic principles: (1) the conviction that each person's opinions and beliefs represent part of the truth, and that individuals must share their truths cooperatively; (2) the refusal to inflict injury on others; and (3) commitment to communication and to the sharing of truth. According to this philosophy, violence shuts off channels of communication. The philosophy of *Satyagraha* also includes the willingness to shoulder any sacrifice that is occasioned by the struggle. Lawson's conviction that nonviolence is a form of power was solidified by his experience and studies in India. He asserted that nonviolent resistance is "a form of social political action. It's not an acquiescence." Lawson fully grasped these principles and later used them to combat racial segregation in the United States.

When Lawson returned to the United States in 1956, he entered Oberlin College's Graduate School of Theology. In February of the following year, he met and had a conversation with the Reverend Dr. Martin Luther King Jr. on campus. During the course of their conversation, Lawson gave King an abstract of his experiences. He said to King, "You know, one day I think I'll work in the South . . . I've had that on my mind for a long time." According to Lawson, King responded, "Come now. We need you," adding that, "We don't have any Negro ministers with your experience, your understanding." Lawson responded, "I'll come as soon as I can."

An old friend, A. J. Muste of the Fellowship of Reconciliation, arranged for Lawson to become the organization's southern secretary. Between 1958 and 1960, he served as a regional troubleshooter, moving in and out of southern cities. Headquartered in Nashville beginning in 1958, Lawson enrolled in Vanderbilt University's School of Divinity and became a member of the Nashville Christian Leadership Conference (NCLC), established in 1958 by the Reverend Kelly Miller Smith as a local affiliate of King's Southern Christian Leadership Conference (SCLC). As chair of the Action Committee, Lawson initiated a process to show that Montgomery's bus boycott victory could be replicated in Nashville. In the fall of 1958, with Lawson serving as organizer and teacher, NCLC convened an intensive weekly educational program on nonviolent activism that brought students, clergy, and laity together. During the training sessions, Lawson met, mentored, and cultivated a group of students who espoused the principles of *Satyagraha*. Members of this coterie of students later became many of the most widely respected student leaders in the freedom struggle across the South.

In November and December of 1959, the Reverends Lawson and Smith and students Diane Nash, Marion Berry, John Lewis, and James Bevel, among others, conducted "test sit-ins" at Nashville department stores, two months before the student sit-in in Greensboro, North Carolina, that launched the student protest known as the sit-in movement. On February 13, 1960, almost two weeks after the Greensboro sit-ins, Lawson and his group of students began full-scale sit-ins at Nashville stores. Because of its discipline and training, the Nashville student movement became the model for other movements across the South.

Lawson's involvement with Nashville's desegregation movement brought him into direct conflict with Vanderbilt University trustee James Geddes Stahlman, publisher of the *Nashville Banner*. On March 2, 1960, the Vanderbilt trustees gave Lawson the choice of withdrawing as a student or dismissal from the university. He refused to withdraw, and the following day, university officials expelled him.

In April 1960 at Shaw University in Raleigh, North Carolina, Lawson and the Nashville student delegation became leaders in the establishment of the Student Nonviolent Coordinating Committee (SNCC). The Nashville group's dedication to nonviolence and the Christian ideal of the "beloved community" helped establish SNCC's initial direction. SNCC's statement of purpose, written by Lawson and sanctioned by a student conference held in Atlanta in May, accentuated the religious and philosophical beliefs of nonviolent direct action.

After being expelled from Vanderbilt's School of Divinity, Lawson went to Boston University and earned his master of theology degree. In 1961, when the freedom riders were going through the Deep South assessing the region's compliance with the U.S. Supreme Court's decree in the *Boynton v. Virginia* case, Lawson participated in the ride's last leg. In 1962, officials of the Methodist Church appointed Lawson to the pastorate of the Centenary Methodist Church in Memphis, Tennessee. The following month, King asked Lawson to serve as director of nonviolent education for SCLC.

After moving to Memphis in 1962, Lawson continued in the struggle for equality and justice and became a moving force in the Bluff City movement and in helping to organize Community on the Move for Equality (COME). Lawson emboldened the city's sanitation workers to think of themselves as men, which led them to employ the well-known "I am a Man" signs. In 1968, Lawson asked Dr. King to come to Memphis to draw attention to the plight of striking sanitation workers. After King's assassination, Lawson pleaded for calmness and composure in the African American community of Memphis.

Although Lawson's contribution to the civil rights movement has been less celebrated than that of others, his impact and influence was substantial and enduring. He became noted in the struggle for African American civil rights for teaching Gandhi's nonviolent civil disobedience techniques and philosophy, which became the movement's most compelling and effective political weapon. Considered by King to be "the leading nonviolent theorist in the world," Lawson was awarded Vanderbilt University's 2005 Distinguished Alumni Award. Almost forty-six years after the university expelled him, Vanderbilt administrators appointed him as a distinguished visiting professor for the 2006–2007 academic year.

JOHN LEWIS

See chapter 11, Politics.

VIOLA FAUVER GREGG LIUZZO (1925–1965)

Civil Rights Activist. Civil rights activist and martyr Viola Liuzzo was the first woman and the only white woman murdered during the African American struggle for equality and justice. The shooting of Jimmie Lee Jackson by Alabama troopers on February 18, 1965, motivated civil rights leaders to stage a protest march from Selma, Alabama, to the capitol building in Montgomery, fifty miles away, to be led by Martin Luther King Jr., president of the Southern Christian Leadership Conference. Jackson's death on February 26, and the scheduled march from Selma to Montgomery impelled Liuzzo to become engaged in the civil rights movement. Although J. Edgar Hoover, the director of the FBI, depicted Liuzzo as a northerner, she was a product of the South.

Liuzzo was born to Eva Wilson and Heber Ernest Gregg, a coal miner, in California, Pennsylvania. She later lived in Georgia and Tennessee. Liuzzo was familiar with the southern code of Jim Crow and how it relegated African Americans to a rigid second-class status. A woman with a sense of fairness who was concerned about the rights of others, Liuzzo wanted to be part of a movement that transformed injustice into justice.

In 1965, when she drove from her home in Detroit to help with the voting rights march, Liuzzo was a thirty-nine-year-old wife, a mother of five children, and a student. As she drove other activists back to Selma after the march, members of the Ku Klux Klan fired through the driver's window of Liuzzo's car, instantly killing her with two shots to the head. The tragedy shocked the nation, and President Lyndon B. Johnson condemned her slaying on national television. Liuzzo's murder caused him to order a federal investigation of the KKK, and he petitioned Congress to expand the Federal Conspiracy Act of 1870 to make the murder of civil rights activists a federal crime. Liuzzo's death helped propel passage of the Voting Rights Act of 1965.

In 1979, the Liuzzo family filed a $2 million lawsuit against the FBI, which accused the agency of negligence in its hiring of informant Gary Thomas Rowe Jr., a member of the KKK. The suit alleged that Rowe actively participated in Liuzzo's murder. U.S. district court judge Charles Joiner presided over the trial without a jury, and on May 30, 1983, found that Rowe did not shoot her and that the U.S. government was not responsible for Liuzzo's death.

Memorials in Alabama and Detroit honor Liuzzo's memory. In 1991, the Women of SCLC placed a stone marker on Highway 80 in Alabama near the site where she was murdered. Because of the scandal surrounding her death, many consider her the most controversial of the civil rights martyrs.

ZEPHANIAH ALEXANDER LOOBY (1899–1972)

Attorney, Civil Rights Activist, Educator, Politician. Known in Nashville as the dean of African American attorneys and nationally for his work as a civil rights attorney for the NAACP, Z. Alexander Looby traversed the state of Tennessee in the company of other attorneys, arguing against Jim Crowism and racial discrimination. In 1951, he and fellow attorney Robert E. Lillard became the first African Americans elected to the Nashville City Council in forty years. When the World War II–era civil rights movement began, Looby became a local and state leader.

Looby was born in Antigua, British West Indies, on April 8, 1899. His mother died when he was six or seven years old, and his father passed away when he was fifteen. As a child, Looby spent time around the magistrate court, where he listened to white barristers argue their cases. After the death of his father, Looby signed on as a cabin boy on a whaling ship headed for the United States. In 1914, he arrived in New Bedford, Massachusetts. Eight years later, Looby earned a bachelor's degree from Howard University in Washington, D.C. In 1925, he received a bachelor of law degree from Columbia University. The following year, he earned a doctor of jurisprudence degree from New York University.

In 1937, Looby, along with Carl Cowan of Knoxville and Charles Houston of the NAACP, filed one of the first suits against segregation in Tennessee's higher educational system. This suit sought to secure the admission of William B. Redmond of Franklin, Tennessee, to the University of Tennessee's School of Pharmacy in Memphis. Redmond, a graduate of Tennessee A&I State College (now Tennessee State University), applied to the School of Pharmacy in 1936 and was denied admission. Because the state had recently enacted a statute providing a nominal tuition stipend for African American students to pursue postgraduate education outside of Tennessee, the court ruled against the plaintiff. Although Looby lost the case, his effort anticipated the litigious direction that African Americans would take in their struggle for equal access to public education. The following year, Looby, along with Cowan, Houston, Thurgood Marshall, and William H. Hastie, filed suit seeking the admission of Joseph M. Michael to the University of Tennessee School of Law. Despite the Supreme Court's 1938 ruling in the *Missouri ex rel. Gaines v. Canada* case, Tennessee steadfastly held to its earlier ruling.

In February 1946, a race riot broke out in Columbia, Tennessee, after an altercation occurred between a white man and a black man. In response, the State Highway Patrol and National Guard terrorized Columbia's African American community, beating and shooting several people. The press brought the racial disturbance in Columbia to the nation's attention, and the NAACP provided legal counsel for the thirty-one African Americans indicted on charges resulting from the melee. Twenty-five of those arrested were charged with attempted murder of four police officers. The NAACP hired Looby and Maurice Weaver, a white attorney from Chattanooga, to represent the accused. Weaver and Looby worked under the direction of Thurgood Marshall, the NAACP's lead attorney. The case was moved to Lawrenceburg in a change of venue, and on October 4, 1946, an all-white jury found twenty-three of the defendants not guilty.

Looby, Weaver, and Marshall returned to Columbia in mid-November to litigate the charges against the two remaining defendants. They won acquittal for one and a reduced sentence for the other. Their successful defense of the accused incensed white law enforcement officials. As the three attorneys drove out of Columbia on their way to Nashville, they were stopped by a group of law enforcement officers with a search warrant for their vehicle. After finding no incriminating evidence, the attorneys were allowed to continue their trip, with Looby driving. About a mile down the road, a group of eight police stopped them again. The police detained Marshall and ordered Looby and Weaver to go the other way. The officers proceeded with Marshall toward Duck River, but Looby refused to leave, and thwarted the men's plan to lynch Marshall. The police officers took Marshall back to Columbia and charged him with drunken driving, but he was released by a judge. After this close encounter, Marshall remarked, "Looby was one brave man."

In 1950, Looby, along with Carl Cowman and Avon N. Williams Jr., filed a school desegregation lawsuit in Anderson County. The attorneys successfully argued *McSwain v. Board of Anderson County, Tennessee* all the way to the U.S. Supreme Court. The case resulted in the court-ordered desegregation of Tennessee's public schools.

When Looby entered the race for a seat on the Nashville City Council in 1951, he pledged that if elected he would seek African American representation on the Board of Education, the Civil Service Commission, and other city boards; end segregation in terminal and restaurant facilities at the Nashville Municipal Airport and racial segregation on city buses; establish a nondiscriminatory merit system in public employment and civil service; require that no city contracts be granted to firms practicing discrimination against African Americans; enforce the city's ordinance against cross burning; and prompt the city to examine its health service so it could provide better-quality care, especially in facilities available to African Americans. On May 10, Looby and Lillard were elected to the council. They became the first African Americans on the Nashville City Council in almost forty years.

As a city council member and NAACP leader, Looby was in the vanguard of the civil rights movement in Nashville. He helped to desegregate public education in the city and county, as well as public golf courses and restaurants. Looby won equal pay for African American teachers, brought action that ended segregation in the courts, and successfully compelled city leaders to dismantle racially segregated visiting hours at Nashville's Parthenon.

In 1955, in the wake of the *Brown v. Board of Education of Topeka* ruling, Looby and his law partner, Avon Williams, in consultation with the NAACP and Thurgood Marshall, filed a class-action suit against the Nashville Board of Education. *Kelley v. Board of Education of Nashville* was filed on behalf of A. Z. Kelley, an African American barber. Kelley's son Robert was forced to take a bus across town to attend school, although he lived within a few blocks of an all-white school. The case was not heard until 1956, when a federal district judge ordered Nashville's board of education to prepare a plan for desegregation by January of the following year. In 1958, the board of education proposed the "grade-a-year-plan." Looby objected to the lenient student-transfer provisions of the plan and appealed the case to the Sixth Circuit Court of Appeals in Cincinnati, Ohio. Losing in the court of appeals, Looby and Williams appealed to the U.S. Supreme Court in 1959, but the Court refused to review the case. Looby and Williams never relinquished their resolve, and in 1971 a district judge ordered Nashville to implement a massive crosstown busing plan to desegregate its public schools.

In 1955, Looby ran for reelection and successfully retained his seat in the council. The following year, amidst the hysteria surrounding Senator Joseph McCarthy, Looby was one of seventy-eight NAACP members investigated by the House Un-American Activities Committee. In addition to investigating anyone with possible connections to the Communist Party, the committee also listed as subversive many who promoted racial equality. Looby welcomed the probe and was positive his good standing in the community would vindicate him.

On February 13, 1960, African American students from the city's predominately black colleges and universities conducted their first full-scale sit-in, leading to the arrests two weeks later of more than seventy-five students. As their cases reached the court dockets, Looby and twelve other African American attorneys defended the young demonstrators. In the predawn hours of April 19, 1960, Looby's home was bombed. Although he and his wife escaped with minor injuries, the blast proved a catalyst for Nashville's civil rights activists to confront the city's elected officials over the practice of segregated public-dining facilities. About three thousand people marched from Fisk University to the public square, protesting the bombing. During a spirited debate on the courthouse steps, Mayor Ben West recommended that Nashville's lunch counters be desegregated. When Martin Luther King Jr. addressed a crowd of four thousand at Fisk University the following day, the audience rose to its feet when Looby entered the hall. On May 10, 1960, Nashville became the first large city in the South to begin desegregating its lunch counters when six stores agreed to accommodate African Americans in their dining facilities.

The sit-ins resumed in November because segregation continued in most eating establishments, and institutionalized racism remained intact. In 1964, Looby lost his temper after a dispute with Judge Andrew Doyle during a hearing for thirty civil rights demonstrators. He and his law partner were held in contempt of court and fined. Refusing to pay the fines, Looby and Williams were taken into custody and incarcerated. Mayor Beverly Briley arranged to have the pair's fines paid, and they were released.

In 1971, Looby retired from public office after serving for more than two decades. He continued working as an attorney until he died on March 24, 1972. Nashville recognized Looby's distinguished contributions in 1976 when it named a library and community center in his honor.

AUTHERINE J. LUCY (1929–)

Civil Rights Activist. In 1952, Autherine Juanita Lucy became the first African American to enroll in the University of Alabama in Tuscaloosa. After university officials discovered her race, they denied her admittance.

However, after a three-year court battle waged by attorneys Arthur Shores and Thurgood Marshall of the NAACP Legal Defense and Educational Fund on her behalf, Lucy reenrolled in 1956. University officials expelled her after she attended only two full days of classes, claiming that they wished to protect her from mob violence. Thirty-two years later, the University of Alabama's board of trustees voted to overturn Lucy's expulsion, and she entered the university and earned her master's degree in education in 1992. The university also named an endowed scholarship after her and placed her portrait in Ferguson Center on campus.

Lucy was born and reared in Shiloh, Alabama. She was the last of Milton Cornelius and Minnie Hosea Lucy's ten children. After graduating from Linden Academy, Lucy entered Selma University, where she received a two-year teaching degree. In 1949 she entered Miles College in Birmingham, where she earned a bachelor's degree in English three years later.

While at Miles, Lucy met Hugh Lawrence Foster, her future husband, and Pollie Anne Myers, the woman who would thrust her into the vanguard of the civil rights movement. The two women became close friends, and shortly after graduating, Myers asked Lucy about applying to graduate school at the University of Alabama. Both women were accepted, but university admissions officials did not know that they were African American. When their race was discovered, the dean told Lucy and Myers that the admissions office had made a mistake, and he attempted to return their room deposits. He never mentioned that the decision was because of their race.

The two women retained Shores, who wrote to the university president requesting their admittance, to no avail. Shores and the NAACP took the matter to court, a battle that lasted three years. In 1955, the U.S. Supreme Court rendered its decision in *Brown v. Board of Education of Topeka (II)*, which outlawed segregation in schools. Shores and the NAACP knew that the efforts of Lucy and Myers to gain admittance to the University of Alabama would be the first test of the decision. Because of the *Brown II* decision and its impact on the University of Alabama, the school's administrators tried to discredit Lucy and Myers. They secured the services of a private investigator to investigate into their backgrounds. The investigation revealed that Myers had been pregnant and unmarried at the time of her application. On June 29, 1955, the case went before federal judge Harlan Grooms, who ruled for Myers and Lucy and later expanded the ruling to apply to all people of color seeking admission to the university. In January 1956, the university board of trustees voted to deny Myers admission based on its moral codes. However, it confirmed Lucy's admission with only one dissenting vote.

Lucy entered the University of Alabama on February 1, 1956, and attended her first class two days later. A group of students began marching and protesting her presence, and by February 6, she had to navigate her way through a hostile crowd. Because of the escalating violence, the university's board of trustees voted to exclude Lucy, allegedly for her own well-being. The NAACP filed a complaint against the university, accusing it of conspiring with the mob to prevent Lucy from attending classes. The university trustees then voted to permanently expel Lucy. Judge Grooms ordered Lucy's readmission, but he refused to reverse the trustees' expulsion. Attorneys for the NAACP conceded that the expulsion was legal, and Lucy left the campus. Seven years passed before another black student was allowed to enroll at the Tuscaloosa school.

MALCOLM X

See chapter 8, Black Nationalism.

HARRY T. MOORE (1905–1951)

Educator, Civil Rights Activist, Organization Founder. One of the unsung warriors who gave his life for the cause of civil rights and racial justice, Harry Tyson Moore was born on November 19, 1905, in Suwannee County, Florida, to Johnny and Rosa Tyson Moore. He received his education in the schools of Daytona Beach and Jacksonville, Florida. In 1925, Moore graduated from Florida Memorial College with a teaching degree. After graduation, he taught school in Cocoa for one year. In 1926, Moore began serving as principal of Titusville Colored School and later as principal of Mims Elementary School.

A member of the Florida State Teachers' Association, Moore organized the Brevard chapter of the NAACP in 1934. He investigated lynchings and mob brutality and launched a campaign against segregated schools and unequal compensation for African American teachers. In 1944, Moore cofounded and became executive secretary of the Progressive Voters' League. Under his leadership, the league successfully inaugurated a statewide voter-registration drive. Because of Moore's role in the struggle for civil rights among African Americans in the state of Florida, Brevard County officials relieved him of his duties as principal in 1946. In May of the same year, he became the first full-time, paid executive secretary of an NAACP state conference.

As the most visible and outspoken African American leader in Florida, Moore received numerous threats. The alleged rape of a Groveland white woman by four African American men in 1949 ignited four days of virulent rioting by unrestrained white mobs in African American neighborhoods. A month after the alleged incident,

Moore, to no avail, corresponded with President Harry S. Truman and Florida's congressional representatives, calling for a review of the Groveland riots and pressing for a special session of Congress to pass laws to protect the civil rights of African Americans. Because Moore sought justice for the accused individuals, he captured the ire of the Ku Klux Klan. His unrelenting campaign for racial equity also placed him at odds with local government officials. When the U.S. Supreme Court reversed the convictions and death sentences of the remaining two defendants in April of 1951, the hostilities over the Groveland case ignited once again.

In the summer of 1951, Moore earned his bachelor's degree from Bethune-Cookman College. Within months of completing his undergraduate studies, the death threats became reality when, on December 25, 1951, a bomb exploded beneath his bed. According to Ben Green's *Before His Time: The Untold Story of Harry T. Moore, America's First Civil Rights Martyr* (1999), Moore became the first person to lose his life for what became the modern civil rights movement. Recognizing his achievements and sacrifices, in 1952 the NAACP posthumously awarded Harry T. Moore the Spingarn Medal, the organization's highest honor.

In 1991, after new evidence surfaced, Florida governor Lawton Chiles ordered an investigation of the Moore murder, the same year that Byron de la Beckwith was reindicted for the 1965 murder of Medgar Evers. The investigation uncovered evidence implicating four members of the central Florida Ku Klux Klan, all of them deceased. By some accounts, Moore's death was as momentous as those of Evers, Malcolm X, and Martin Luther King Jr.

IRENE MORGAN KIRKALDY (1917–2007)

Civil Rights Activist. When she was twenty-seven years old, Irene Morgan Kirkaldy became the center of an important court case litigated by the NAACP after she refused to relinquish her seat to a white person on a Greyhound bus traveling from Virginia to Maryland. In 1946, *Morgan v. Virginia* reached the U.S. Supreme Court. By a seven–one margin, the justices outlawed racial segregation in interstate travel. The decision in this case caused the Congress of Racial Equality (CORE) to initiate its 1947 Journey of Reconciliation, a forerunner of the 1961 freedom rides. A trailblazer in the African American struggle, Morgan epitomized Gunnar Myrdal's contention in his classic 1944 study, *An American Dilemma: The Negro Problem and American Democracy*, "that the Jim Crow car [was] resented more bitterly among Negroes than most other forms of segregation."

Eleven years before Rosa Parks refused to surrender her seat on a Montgomery bus, Morgan similarly defied the laws of racial segregation. On July 16, 1944, she rebuffed southern racial etiquette by not relinquishing her seat on a Virginia bus to a white couple. Although the actions taken by Morgan and Parks were similar, there were important differences. Morgan was on an interstate bus traveling from Virginia to Maryland, whereas Parks was riding a city bus. Morgan was in her late twenties, while Parks was in her forties. Morgan was sitting at least three rows from the back of the bus, whereas Parks was seated near the middle of the Montgomery bus. Moreover, Morgan was not affiliated with any association committed to the struggle for equality and justice. Parks, in contrast, had been involved with the NAACP and had studied at Highlander Folk School, where she learned to be resolute in her activism. Morgan retaliated in self-defense, whereas Parks adhered to the principle of nonviolent protest. Notwithstanding these differences, both women were arrested and their cases were litigated through the judicial system, where, ultimately, the U.S. Supreme Court ruled in their favor.

While Morgan may not have been active in an organization fighting to secure the civil rights of African Americans, attitudinally, she possessed the spirit of Alain Locke's "New Negro," which primarily called for human dignity, civil liberties, and racial equality. By violating Virginia's 1930 statute, which proscribed racially mixed seating on public modes of transportation, Morgan courageously defied the southern code of behavior and remained seated in defense of her rights as an American.

After putting up a defense, Morgan, who was recovering from a miscarriage, was dragged from the bus by the sheriff and his deputy and arrested. After being taken into custody, she was charged with resisting arrest and breaching Virginia's transit laws. Three months later, Morgan pleaded guilty on the first charge and paid the assessed fine of $100. However, firmly believing that she was well within her rights and that Virginia's segregation law was not applicable to interstate travelers, she refused to pay the associated fine and court costs. Morgan was resolute that she had done nothing wrong. She had paid for her seat and sat in the designated Negro section. Morgan declared she would appeal her conviction, and, if necessary, take her case all the way to the Supreme Court.

Represented by attorneys from the NAACP, Morgan's case was taken to the Virginia Supreme Court, which on June 6, 1945, upheld the state's 1930 Jim Crow statute. Morgan's attorneys appealed the state supreme court's ruling to the country's highest tribunal. Almost a year later, on June 3, 1946, the U.S. Supreme Court sustained Morgan's appeal. *Morgan v. Virginia* represented a spirited attack on Jim Crow transportation.

However, as with most Supreme Court decisions that moved African Americans closer to equality and justice, most southern states disregarded the Court's edict.

Less than a year later, CORE and the Fellowship of Reconciliation organized and implemented the interracial Journey of Reconciliation throughout the upper South to test the Court's decision in the *Morgan v. Virginia* case. An interracial group of sixteen men, eight blacks and eight whites, prepared for a two-week bus trip through Virginia, North Carolina, Tennessee, and Kentucky. Organizers of this "freedom ride" understood that discriminatory social laws and patterns did not change because of decisions made by the U.S. Supreme Court and that progress would not come without struggle. The men employed a strategy of whites sitting in the back seats, blacks in front, and both side-by-side. Their purpose was to force southern states respect the *Morgan* decision. During the two-week journey, twelve of the men were arrested on six separate occasions. Morgan's act of refusal laid the foundation on which African Americans would construct other direct protest methods for civil liberties and equality.

Morgan faded into obscurity after the Court ruled in her favor. She became a widow when she was thirty-two. Later, she married Stanley Kirkaldy, and they reared her two children. A self-determined woman with an entrepreneurial spirit, Morgan Kirkaldy operated her own business providing maid and child-care services to families in New York. Her concern about matters of racial intolerance and social injustice continued.

After winning a scholarship in a radio contest during the 1980s, she entered St. John's University, where she majored in communications. She earned her degree in 1985, when she was sixty-eight years old. Morgan continued her education by pursuing an advance degree from Queen's College. In 1990, at age seventy-three, she was awarded a master of arts degree in urban studies.

Five years later, Irene Morgan Kirkaldy penetrated the public's consciousness when she made a brief appearance in *You Don't Have to Ride Jim Crow!* a documentary film about the 1947 Journey of Reconciliation. Six years later, on January 8, 2001, President Bill Clinton, who was born in the South the same year as the Supreme Court decision that bears her name, awarded Morgan Kirkaldy, along with twenty-seven others, including Fred Shuttlesworth and NAACP attorneys Jack Greenberg and Constance Baker Motley, the Presidential Citizens Medal. "When Irene Morgan boarded a bus for Baltimore in the summer of 1944," the award's approbation asserted, "she took for the first step on a journey that would change America forever."

DIANE J. NASH (1938–)

Civil Rights Activist. Diane Judith Nash stood in the vanguard of the national civil rights and antiwar movements from 1959 to 1967. She was born in Chicago on May 15, 1938, and reared in a Catholic middle-class home. Nash received her primary and secondary education in Chicago parochial and public schools. She began her collegiate career at Howard University, then transferred in 1959 to Fisk University in Nashville, where she was projected into the struggle for civil rights.

When Diana Nash arrived in Nashville, racial segregation permeated the city. Her personal encounters with the code of "separate but unequal" led her to seek rectification. Early in 1959, she attended workshops on nonviolence directed by Reverend James Lawson under the agency of the Nashville Christian Leadership Conference, an affiliate of SCLC. Nash became imbued with and an ardent supporter of the direct nonviolent protest philosophy.

In November and December of 1959, Nash was among those who "tested" the racial segregation policy of Nashville's downtown lunch counters. Elected chair of the Student Central Committee, she played a pivotal role in Nashville's student sit-in movement. Before the students could initiate their first full-scale sit-in, North Carolina A&T students staged a sit-in on February 1, 1960, in Greensboro.

When the Nashville students decided on the "jail, no bail" strategy, Nash stated to the judge, "We feel that if we pay these fines we would be contributing to and supporting the injustice and immoral practices that have been performed in the arrest and convictions of the defendants." Responding to her query about the immorality of segregation, Nashville mayor Ben West agreed that the city's lunch counters should be desegregated. On May 10, 1960, Nashville became the first southern city to begin desegregating its lunch counters.

In April 1960, Nash became one of the founding members of the Student Nonviolent Coordinating Committee (SNCC). In February 1961, she participated in the Rock Hill, South Carolina, protests for desegregation. After being arrested, Nash and the other students refused to pay bail. When CORE's original freedom riders were beaten in Alabama and aborted the last leg of the ride to New Orleans, John Lewis and Diane Nash decided that permitting the violence of the white mob to overwhelm the nonviolence of the demonstrators conveyed the wrong message to the movement's enemies. Nash accepted the responsibility of coordinating this monumental mission.

In May, Nash coordinated the freedom rides from Birmingham, Alabama, to Jackson, Mississippi. Three months later, Nash became the director of the direct-action wing of SNCC. Between 1961 and 1965, she worked for SCLC as a field organizer, strategist, and workshop instructor. After moving to Jackson, Nash was imprisoned for teaching African American children about the techniques of direct nonviolent protest. Holding steadfastly to the principles developed in Nashville, she chose jail rather than pay bail.

Nash's ideas were instrumental in initiating the 1963 March on Washington. She and James Bevel conceptualized and planned the initial strategy for the Selma right-to-vote movement that helped produce the Voting Rights Act of 1965. Nash's civil rights activities led her to the Vietnam peace movement. She continued working for political and social transformation through the 1970s and lectured nationally on the rights of women during the 1980s. Nash continues to lecture across the country. In October 2006, the faculty of Fisk University and the Fisk Board of Trustees voted to award Diane Nash an honorary doctorate at the university's 2007 commencement exercises.

EDGAR DANIEL NIXON SR. (1899–1987)

Labor Leader, Civil Rights Activist. Edgar Daniel Nixon Sr., the fifth of eight children, was born in Montgomery, Alabama, on July 12, 1899, to Wesley and Sue Ann (Chappel) Nixon. Edgar's mother died when he was eight

Diane J. Nash, Attending Republican Party Meeting, Chicago, July 20, 1960. *Questions about civil rights are discussed by members of the party's platform committee in advance of the 1960 Republican convention.* AP PHOTO

years old, and he went to live with his paternal Aunt Pinky in Autauga, Alabama. Because of segregation and the distance of the one-room school from his aunt's home, Nixon's school attendance was irregular. When he was fourteen, he became self-supporting and worked in Selma and Mobile, Alabama. Subsequent to working in the Union Station baggage room, Nixon was hired as a sleeping-car porter. Later influenced by A. Philip Randolph, he became a member of the Brotherhood of Sleeping Car Porters.

Randolph recognized and helped Nixon polish his organizational skills. When he first met Randolph, Nixon was already involved in local efforts to improve the quality of life for Montgomery's African American citizens. Earlier, he had waged an unsuccessful campaign to secure a swimming pool for African Americans after two children drowned while swimming in a drainage ditch.

In 1928, with Walter White and Roy Wilkins serving as counselors, Nixon helped establish state and local NAACP chapters in Alabama. During his tenure as state NAACP president, twenty-one branches were added to the Alabama NAACP, and the local membership increased from five to approximately three thousand. In the 1930s, Nixon organized the Montgomery Welfare League to help disadvantaged persons of color secure governmental assistance. When Randolph and Bayard Rustin began organizing the 1941 March on Washington to protest discrimination in the defense industries, Nixon was part of the process that ultimately caused President Franklin D. Roosevelt to issue Executive Order 8802, establishing the Fair Employment Practices Commission.

During the 1940s, Nixon organized the Montgomery Voters League, and served as president of the Progressive Democratic Association, which successfully addressed the issue of African Americans serving on the city's police force. He also threatened to file suit against city officials on behalf of Oak Park residents who were suffering from city neglect. As president of the state NAACP, he challenged the rule restricting African American seating on Montgomery's buses. However, Viola White, the plaintiff in the test case, died while appeals were adjudicated for ten years after the 1944 filing. In 1944, Nixon persuaded 750 African Americans to march on the courthouse and demand their right of the franchise. The following year, he became the first African American to run for a political office in Montgomery since Reconstruction when he campaigned for a county seat on the Montgomery Democratic Executive Committee. He was defeated in that election by only two hundred votes.

On December 1, 1955, when Rosa Parks was arrested for refusing to relinquish her bus seat to a white man, Nixon contacted Clifford Durr, a local white attorney, who found out the charges against Parks and the amount of bail money needed to secure her release. Nixon paid the $100 bail and had Parks's trial date set for December 5, 1955. He believed that the Parks case should be tested in the courts to nullify Montgomery's bus segregation laws and that African Americans should boycott the bus company. Although he and others made plans for a boycott, the Women's Political Council (WPC) set the wheels in motion. The day of Parks's trial, African American citizens staged a boycott of the city buses, The boycott was organized by Alabama State College English professor Jo Ann Gibson Robinson, president of the WPC, and others. The one-day boycott proved successful.

Nixon, along with Ralph Abernathy, H. H. Hubbard, and Edgar N. French, laid the groundwork for a long-term bus boycott and a new organization, which Abernathy named the Montgomery Improvement Association (MIA). At the organizational meeting of MIA, the Reverend Dr. Martin Luther King Jr. was elected as president and Nixon as treasurer. During his two-year tenure, Nixon personally raised approximately $100,000 and wrote checks amounting to almost $500,000 for the MIA and the boycott. He always recognized local whites who supported the movement. Nixon was the first MIA member to be indicted for boycott-related activities. Adhering to Rustin's instructions on how to throw law enforcement officials off guard, Nixon did not wait for them to come to his home and arrest him. He gave himself up, demonstrating to the other indicted individuals how to counter the offensive of the authorities.

For more than a year, thousands of African Americans in Montgomery, with "rested souls and weary feet," refused to ride the buses. Eventually, the loss of revenue and a ruling by the U.S. Supreme Court forced the Montgomery Bus Company to desegregate its buses. The boycott took 65 percent of the bus company's business, which caused it to cut schedules, lay off drivers, and increase fares. The city's merchants lost revenue as well. The Supreme Court's 1956 decision in *Gayle v. Browder* explicitly overturned the 1896 *Plessy v. Ferguson* decision, which also applied to transportation. The bus company not only consented to end segregation but also agreed to hire African American drivers and treat all customers with equal deference. On December 21, 1956, African Americans boarded buses in Montgomery and sat wherever they desired.

During his lifetime, Nixon received hundreds of commendations from state and local governments and national organizations. A self-educated person, he was awarded four honorary doctorates, including one from Alabama State University. In 1975, Nixon was appointed to the U.S. Commission on Civil Rights for the state of

Alabama, and served as vice president. He died on February 27, 1987.

ROSA PARKS (1913–2005)

Civil Rights Activist. Rosa Parks has been called "the patron saint" and the "mother" of the civil rights movement. Her courage to defy custom and law to uphold her personal rights and dignity inspired African Americans in Montgomery, Alabama, to stage one of the longest boycotts in American history.

Born Rosa Louise McCauley on February 4, 1913, in Tuskegee, Alabama, she was one of two children of James and Leona Edwards McCauley. Her mother, a schoolteacher, taught Parks until she was eleven, when she entered Montgomery Industrial School for Girls. Later, she attended Booker T. Washington High School. After attending segregated schools, she went to the all–African American Alabama State College.

In 1932, Rosa married Raymond Parks. Eleven years later, she and her husband joined the local NAACP chapter. One of the first women to join the NAACP, Parks served as the chapter's secretary from 1943 to 1956. Parks was also a member of the Montgomery Voters League, and during the summer of 1955, she attended workshops at Highlander Folk School in Monteagle, Tennessee, which had been active in the civil rights struggle since the 1930s.

On December 1, 1955, as Parks was riding Montgomery's Cleveland Avenue bus home from work, she was ordered by the driver to give her seat to a white man. When she refused to move, the driver threatened to call law enforcement officials. Parks was subsequently arrested and fined. Her case was the last straw for Montgomery's African American citizenry, who were as tired of being treated as underclass citizens as Parks. The Women's Political Council protested her arrest by organizing a boycott of the buses. A young, unknown minister named Martin Luther King Jr. soon became involved. Realizing the immensity of the opportunity to begin dismantling the code of southern segregation, he and other members of the community organized the Montgomery Improvement Association. African Americans and a few whites transported boycotters to and from work, and they continued, despite opposition from the city and state governments, for 382 days.

Following her trial, Park's attorneys advised her to refuse to pay the fine and court costs. Parks's case was appealed all the way to the U.S. Supreme Court. On December 20, 1956, the country's highest tribunal ruled Montgomery's segregated seating unconstitutional. When the boycott ended the following day, both Parks and King were national heroes. The mass movement of nonviolent social change that started in Montgomery lasted for more than a decade, and culminated in the Civil Rights Act of 1964, the Voting Rights Act of 1965, and the Fair Housing Act of 1968.

Because of the harassment that Rosa and Raymond Parks received during and after the boycott, in 1957 they and her mother moved to Detroit, Michigan. After working in various capacities, Parks became a staff assistant in Congressman John Conyers's Detroit office. Parks continued to be involved in the civil rights struggle, giving speeches and attending marches and demonstrations. She marched on Washington in 1963 and into Montgomery in 1965. Parks received numerous tributes for her dedication and inspiration: in 1979, she received the NAACP's Spingarn Medal; and in 1980, she became the first woman to receive the Martin Luther King Jr. Nonviolent Peace Prize. Three years later, Parks was inducted into the Michigan Women's Hall of Fame for her achievements in civil rights.

As she approached retirement, Parks became involved in other activities, such as the Rosa and Raymond Parks Institute for Self-development. In 1988, the same year that she retired from Conyers's office, Detroit's Museum of African-American History unveiled her portrait. Two years later, her birthday was celebrated in Washington's Kennedy Center. In addition to being a recipient of the Presidential Medal of Freedom in 1996 and the inaugural International Freedom Conductor Award in 1998, in April 1999 Congress passed legislation awarding her the Congressional Gold Medal. In 2000, the State of Alabama inducted Parks into the Alabama Academy of Honor. The same year, Alabama governor Don Siegelman awarded her the first Governor's Medal of Honor for Extraordinary Courage.

The honors continued in January 2001, when Parks attended the dedication of Troy University's Rosa Parks Library and Museum in Montgomery, Alabama, which features a statue in her likeness and an exhibit recounting her history-making encounter with the bus driver who told her to give up her seat in 1955. That same month, her former home in the South was added to the National Register of Historic Places. In 2002, her life story was retold in a made-for-television movie starring Angela Bassett. In 1999 Parks sued the hip-hop duo OutKast for using her name in a song without her permission. The case was settled in 2005.

In 2004, Parks was diagnosed with dementia, a disease that causes a progressive decline in cognitive function. Rosa Parks died at age ninety-two on October 24, 2005, in Detroit. Officials in both Detroit and Montgomery announced that the front seats of their respective city buses would be reserved with black ribbons in her honor until her funeral. On October 27, the U.S.

Senate passed a resolution to honor Parks by allowing her body to lie in honor in the U.S. Capitol Rotunda, a tribute reserved for the nation's most "revered leaders. Parks became the first woman, the first American who was not a governmental official, and the second African American (the first was Jacob Chestnut, a U.S. Capitol Police officer) to be so honored. Parks was interred between her husband, Raymond, and her mother, Leona McCauley, in Woodlawn Cemetery in Detroit. On December 1, 2005, the fiftieth anniversary of her arrest, President George W. Bush signed a house resolution directing that a statue of Parks be placed in the U.S. Capitol's National Statuary Hall, further immortalizing Parks's lifelong commitment to freedom, social justice, and equality.

A. PHILIP RANDOLPH

See chapter 9, National Organizations.

Rosa Parks, Capitol Hill, Washington, DC, 1999. *Parks, standing alongside Speaker of the House Dennis Hastert and President Bill Clinton, is honored for her achievements in civil rights with the Congressional Gold Medal, the highest civilian honor bestowed by the U.S. Congress.* AP PHOTO/KHUE BUI

JO ANN GIBSON ROBINSON (1912–1992)

Civil Rights Activist, Educator, Author. As president of the Women's Political Council (WPC) in Montgomery, Alabama, during the 1950s, Jo Ann Gibson Robinson was one of several significant originators of the 1955–1956 Montgomery bus boycott. The youngest of twelve children, she was born on April 17, 1912, to Owen Boston and Dollie Webb Gibson, near Culloden, Georgia. The first member of her family to obtain a college degree, Robinson graduated from Fort Valley State College and taught for five years in the Macon public schools. Moving to Atlanta, she earned a master's degree in English from Atlanta University.

In 1949, Robinson joined the faculty of Alabama State College as a professor of English. Later, she joined Montgomery's Dexter Avenue Baptist Church and the WPC. A young organization, the WPC was founded in the fall of 1946 by Mary Fair Burks, also a member of Alabama State's English Department. Burks was inspired to organize the WPC after hearing a sermon by the Reverend Vernon Johns, the pastor of Dexter Avenue Baptist Church. Organized to protest racial abuse, the WPC developed a four-point program of political action: voter registration; demonstrations protesting abuse on Montgomery city buses; the education of young people about democracy; and literacy.

Because she and others faced continuing abuse by Montgomery city bus drivers, Robinson and the WPC targeted the segregated seating practices. On several occasions, the WPC sought a remedy from city officials. In May 1954, a year and a half before Rosa Parks refused to give up her seat, and shortly after the unanimous Supreme Court decision in *Brown v. Board of Education of Topeka*, Robinson corresponded with Mayor W. A. Gayle and alluded to the possibility of a boycott by African Americans of the city's public transportation system if the abuses did not stop. After Parks's arrest on December 1, 1955, Robinson played a prominent role in the Montgomery bus boycott. As a member of the executive board of the Montgomery Improvement Association (MIA), Robinson wrote the organization's newsletter.

Martin Luther King Jr. described Robinson as "apparently indefatigable," remarking that "she perhaps more than any other person, was active on every level of the protest." Robinson's 1987 memoir, *The Montgomery Bus Boycott and the Women Who Started It*, elevated her and other middle-class women from their footnote status to the center of the civil rights narrative. Robinson died five years after the publication of her memoir.

RUBY DORIS SMITH ROBINSON (1942–1967)

Civil Rights Activist. Ruby Doris Smith, the second of seven children, was born to John Thomas and Alice Banks Smith in Atlanta, Georgia, on April 25, 1942. She was no stranger to racism, but the televised images of the courage of her fellow African Americans during the Montgomery bus boycott sharply focused her resolve, at a young age, to participate in overthrowing the vestiges of Jim Crow.

Her parents' commitment to racial justice became a guiding light as Smith matured into a socially conscious being. Under the tutelage of her parents, who stressed education, Smith completed secondary school and entered Spelman College in 1959. A year later, she became involved in Atlanta's student sit-in movement. Cognizant of her "blackness" during the years of segregation, Smith became motivated by the sit-in movement ignited by students at North Carolina A&T College in Greensboro. She protested with her older sister and other students from the Atlanta University Center in their attempt to desegregate Atlanta. In April 1960, she joined other students in Raleigh, North Carolina, as they, under the leadership of Ella Baker, established the Student Nonviolent Coordinating Committee (SNCC). A strong advocate of group-centered rather than leader-centered organizations, Baker encouraged the conference attendees to institute their own organization rather than become the student branch of the Southern Christian Leadership Conference (SCLC) or another existing civil rights group. Smith took to heart Baker's exhortation that the liberation movement was more than "the right to eat hamburgers at a lunch counter."

Smith, like other women supporters in the student sit-in movement, led in the transformation of SNCC from a coordinating office into a cadre of activists devoted to expanding civil rights for African Americans throughout the South. In February 1961, as students honored the first anniversary of the Greensboro sit-ins, Smith and Diane Nash were among the SNCC members who joined the protests in Rock Hill, South Carolina. The "jail, no bail" tactic used by the Rock Hill protesters served as an emotional leap forward for the civil rights movement. The Rock Hill approach was also a response to the group's lack of money for bail. Additionally, the national SNCC organization worked with local activists, underscoring a principle of grassroots organization that later influenced the broader civil rights movement.

Smith married Clifford Robinson in 1964. She died of leukemia on October 7, 1967, when she was twenty-five years old.

BAYARD RUSTIN

See chapter 9, National Organizations.

AL SHARPTON (1954–)

Religious Leader, Community Activist, Sports and Entertainment Promoter, Organization Executive/Founder, Author. Although he has been shunned by many middle-class African Americans, Al Sharpton draws support from the ranks of the youth and the disenfranchised. Alfred Charles Sharpton Jr. was born in 1954 in Brooklyn, New York. At the early age of four, Sharpton began delivering sermons, and by the time he was thirteen he was ordained a Pentecostal minister. During and after high school, Sharpton preached in neighborhood churches and went on national religious tours, often with prominent entertainers. Soon he was befriended by a number of well-known and influential African Americans, including Congressman Adam Clayton Powell Jr., Jesse Jackson Sr., and singer James Brown.

In 1969, Jackson appointed Sharpton youth director of Operation Breadbasket. Around this same time, James Brown hired Sharpton as one of his bodyguards and later as a promoter. In 1985, Sharpton married singer Kathy Jordan, and soon became involved with fight promoter Don King. Even though Sharpton promoted boxers and entertainers, he had long been a prominent social activist. In 1971, he founded the National Youth Movement (later called the United African Movement) ostensibly to combat drug use. Many criticized Sharpton, however, for using the organization to draw attention to himself. He urged children to forsake Christmas in favor of a Kwanzaa celebration and the elderly to protest New York City police tactics.

Sharpton positioned himself in the center of the publicity surrounding the Bernard Goetz murder trial in 1984, the Howard Beach racial killing in 1986, the Tawana Brawley debacle in 1987, and the Yusef Hawkins killing in Bensonhurst in 1989. In 1988, Sharpton was accused of being an FBI informant and of giving agents information about Don King, reputed organized crime figures, and various African American leaders. In 1989 and 1990, Sharpton was acquitted on charges of income-tax evasion and of embezzling National Youth Movement funds. In 1991, he was briefly hospitalized after being stabbed by a man wielding a pocket knife.

On August 2, 1994, Sharpton announced the formation of a new political party, the Freedom Party. He aimed to counter other liberal groups by reaching African American voters that traditional, mainstream parties had ignored. He unsuccessfully ran for the U.S. Senate in 1994 as a Freedom Party candidate, even participating in that year's New York Democratic primary.

Sharpton has stood at the forefront of the fight against police brutality and racial profiling. In 1999, Sharpton led a community effort to pursue the officer responsible for the 1997 arrest and sodomy of Haitian immigrant Abner Louima. That same year, he led a protest in the wrongful death of West African immigrant Amadou Diallo, who was shot to death by New York police in the vestibule of his apartment building. In 2003, Sharpton became involved in protests over the wrongful death of Ousmane Zongo, an African arts dealer from Burkina Faso who lived in New York. Like Diallo, Zongo was unarmed when a plainclothes policeman shot him in a Chelsea warehouse raid. Sharpton also organized protests after the death by police of Sean Bell in Queens in 2006. As with the earlier incidents, Sharpton claimed police brutality and racial profiling.

In the first decade of the 2000s, Sharpton continued to emerge as an outspoken national political figure. He made headlines with his protest of the U.S. Navy's use of the island of Vieques, Puerto Rico, for bombing operations. He was arrested on May 1, 2001, for trespassing on the island and was sentenced to a ninety-day jail term. While incarcerated, Sharpton went on a highly publicized hunger strike.

Shortly after his release, Sharpton announced that he would form an exploratory committee to evaluate a possible bid for the U.S. presidency in 2004. On January 5, 2003, he announced his candidacy for the presidential election, as a member of the Democratic Party. Sharpton insisted that he was running a broad-based campaign and sought to remind voters of the possibility that anyone, including Sharpton himself, could win with voter support. Sharpton's ten-point platform emphasized four goals: the right to vote, the right to high-quality public education, the right to high-quality health care, and equal rights for women. Despite the efforts of his detractors to use controversial episodes from his past against him, Sharpton made candid public addresses that helped to keep his issues at the forefront of the political race well beyond his March 2004 concession.

Sharpton's autobiography, *Go and Tell Pharaoh*, was published in 1996, followed by *Al on America*, published in 2002. Sharpton has also hosted radio programs and appears frequently on television talk shows. In 2009, Sharpton received international coverage when he delivered a eulogy at the public memorial service for pop star Michael Jackson.

FRED LEE SHUTTLESWORTH
(1922–)

Civil Rights Activist, Clergyman. Born March 18, 1922, in Mugler, Alabama, Fred L. Shuttlesworth was once referred to as "one of the nation's most courageous freedom fighters" by Dr. Martin Luther King Jr. Shuttlesworth earned an associate's degree from Selma University and a bachelor's degree from Alabama State College in 1955. From his 1956 founding of the Alabama Christian Movement for Human Rights through the historic Birmingham demonstrations of 1963, Shuttlesworth was driven by a sense of divine mission to end Jim Crow restrictions in Birmingham. His intensive civil rights campaign pitted him against the city's staunchly segregationist police commissioner, Eugene "Bull" Connor, and ultimately brought him to the side of Martin Luther King Jr. and to the White House during the Kennedy administration. Throughout these struggles, Shuttlesworth demonstrated courage and persistence in the face of peril.

When Shuttlesworth sustained only a bump on the head in the 1956 bombing of his home, members of his church called it a miracle. Shuttlesworth took it as a sign that he would be protected on the civil rights mission that had made him a target that night. Standing in front of his demolished home, Shuttlesworth vigorously renewed his commitment to integrate Birmingham's public facilities and police department. The incident transformed him, in the eyes of Birmingham's blacks, from an up-and-coming young minister to a virtual folk hero and, in the view of white Birmingham residents, from obscurity to shrewd agitator.

Shuttlesworth participated in lunch-counter sit-ins and took park in the 1961 freedom rides. When he developed Project Confrontation, Shuttlesworth invited King to Birmingham to lead the city's desegregation program through mass protest rallies and marches. Although Shuttlesworth was prepared to negotiate with white leaders for a diplomatic termination of racial segregation, he believed that they would not easily relinquish an entrenched system of apartheid that was maintained through violence. Shuttlesworth set about a course to force white authorities and business leaders to recalculate segregation's cost. Bull Connor unknowingly aided Shuttlesworth in his mission. The city's image was being destroyed as television viewers across the country saw Connor directing police to use vicious dogs to attack unarmed protesters and firefighters to use water hoses to blast protesters, including children, to the ground. The images had a profound impact on Americans' view of the civil rights struggle. Although on the national level, Shuttlesworth's efforts remained unsung, he was widely revered by both black and white Alabamians as one of the most unflinching warriors for social change.

Shuttlesworth founded the Greater New Light Baptist Church in Cincinnati, Ohio, in 1966. In 1969, he received a law degree from Birmingham Baptist College. He established the Shuttlesworth Housing

Foundation in 1988 to assist families who otherwise may not be able purchase their own homes.

Shuttlesworth has received a multitude of awards, including: the Rosa Parks Award from SCLC (1963); the Excellence Award from PUSH (1974); the Martin Luther King Jr. Civil Rights Award from the Progressive National Baptists (1975); the Founders Award from SCLC (1977); and President's Citizens Award (2001).

After serving as pastor of the Greater New Light Baptist Church for forty years, Shuttlesworth announced his retirement at the beginning of 2006 and preached his final sermon in March. In 2008, Birmingham honored him by changing the name of its airport to Birmingham-Shuttlesworth International Airport.

MODJESKA MONTEITH SIMKINS (1899–1992)

Civil Rights Activist, Educator. Modjeska Monteith Simkins was a key leader in the arena of African American public health and social reform and of the civil rights movement in South Carolina. Her association with progressive and vanguard movements on the state, regional, and national levels endowed her with a point of view that surpassed the confines of provincialism in the state of her birth. Simkins served in leadership positions that as a matter of course were unavailable to women in the civil rights movement.

Mary Modjeska Monteith, the oldest of eight children, was born on December 5, 1899, to Henry Clarence and Rachel Evelyn (Hull) Monteith in Columbia, South Carolina. Reared in a family with strong work ethics, a commitment to education, and a strong religious tradition, the Monteith children were also given a sense of racial pride and taught to be of assistance to those who were less fortunate. From her mother and aunts, she learned that community service was important. They helped organize medical care for tubercular patients through their involvement with the women's auxiliary of the Masons and were active members of the early NAACP. Simkins's mother was also involved in the Niagara Movement, which was organized by W. E. B. Du Bois, and often read to her children from its journal.

Simkins attended Benedict College in her native city, and earned an A.B. degree in 1921. She later attended Columbia University in New York and Morehouse College in Atlanta, and earned a graduate degree in public health at the University of Michigan at Ann Arbor. After earning her degree from Benedict College, Monteith taught for a year in the college's teacher-training department. The following year, she found employment teaching mathematics in the elementary education department at Booker T. Washington High School in Columbia, a job she held until 1929. It was here that her willingness to confront authority and steadfastly hold to her beliefs emerged. In 1929, she married Andrew Whitfield Simkins, an African American businessman who owned real estate and operated a service station in Columbia. Because Columbia's public school system did not allow married women to teach, Modjeska Monteith Simkins was forced to resign from her teaching position.

Simkins entered the field of public health in 1931 when she became the director of Negro work for the South Carolina Anti-Tuberculosis Association (SCATA), and she became the state's only full-time African American health-care worker. By raising funds and creating alliances with persons of both European and African descent, she had a substantial impact on the health of African Americans in South Carolina. Simkins traveled the state educating people about immunizations, maternity and child care, and sanitation. She published a newsletter and worked with African American teachers and physicians. It was during her eleven-year tenure with the Anti-Tuberculosis Association that she became a political activist, working with the NAACP and the Civil Welfare League.

In the 1930s, Simkins became active with and served as secretary of the Civil Welfare League, an organization that set about to improve municipal conditions for Columbia's African American population. The league protested against police brutality, the denial of the right to vote, substandard housing, and a multiplicity of other discriminatory practices. As one of only two women on the state NAACP board, Simkins worked with the Columbia branch of the NAACP as publicity director. In 1939, Simkins became one of the founders of the South Carolina Conference of Branches of the NAACP. Two years later, she was elected head of the publicity committee and a member of the speakers' bureau.

Because the conventional, tradition-bound administrators of SCATA considered Simkins's political activism to be seditious, they pressured her to discontinue working with the NAACP. When she refused, they discontinued funding for her position, and in effect fired Simkins in 1942. Released from employment, the independent-minded and outspoken Simkins came into her own as an agitator for civil rights. Simkins was elected state secretary of the NAACP, a position she held until 1957.

During this period, the South Carolina NAACP undertook lawsuits on behalf of the state's African American population. The first lawsuit concerned equalization of teachers' salaries across the state. When the movement for pay equity for African American teachers was launched in 1943, Simkins was the only woman on a committee of four appointed to raise funds to support the lawsuit. Once the NAACP's Teachers Defense Fund was established, she served as secretary of the project. In 1944, African American teachers won their case in Charleston. The following year, Columbia teachers won a similar case.

After the NAACP won the teachers' salary cases, it focused its attention on voting rights and on dismantling South Carolina's white primary. Simkins participated in planning in-court proceedings and attended courthouse sessions. She kept attorneys abreast of points they might have missed and financially supported George Elmore, the plaintiff in the first voting-rights case, *Elmore v. Rice*, which was won in 1947. However, the state's Democratic Party instituted strategies to get around the ruling. In an attempt to establish full voting rights for African Americans in South Carolina, the NAACP adjudicated a second case, *Brown v. Baskin*, which it won in 1948. The same year that the NAACP won the *Elmore v. Rice* case, it filed suit against Clarendon County in an attempt to force the state to provide bus transportation for both black and white students. The suit was thrown out on a technicality, but later became a demand to end racially segregated education.

The most significant civil rights case in which Simkins played a major role was the suit brought by the NAACP to end racial segregation in South Carolina's public schools and, ultimately, the country's public schools. As secretary, Simkins helped Clarendon County's NAACP chapter president, the Reverend Joseph A. Delaine, compose the statement for the school lawsuit that became *Briggs v. Elliott*. This case later became one of the five desegregation suits grouped together by the U.S. Supreme Court and decided as the historic 1954 *Brown v. Board of Education of Topeka* case. The *Brown* case overturned the Court's 1896 *Plessy v. Ferguson* decision, nullifying its separate-but-equal doctrine and terminating racial segregation in the nation's public schools.

Simkins was active in many organizations that fought against racial discrimination, injustice, and intolerance on the local, regional, and national levels. She worked with political actions groups, such as the Columbia Women's Council and the Richland County Citizens Committee. She also participated in regional organizations such as the Commission on Interracial Cooperation, the Southern Regional Council, the Southern Conference on Human Welfare, the Southern Organizing Committee for Economic and Social Justice, and the Southern Negro Youth Congress. On the national level, Simkins was a member of the Civil Rights Congress, the National Negro Congress, and the United Negro and Allied Veterans of America.

Considered the matriarch of South Carolina's civil rights movement, Simkins died on April 5, 1992. During her memorial service, Judge Matthew J. Perry noted that she "will be remembered as a woman who challenged everyone. She challenged the white leadership of the state to what was fair and equitable among all people and she challenged black citizens to stand up and demand their rightful place in the state and the nation."

ADA LOIS SIPUEL-FISHER (1924–1995)

Attorney, Civil Rights Activist, Educator. Ada L. Sipuel, the plaintiff in the U.S. Supreme Court case *Sipuel v. Board of Regents of the University of Oklahoma* (1948), was born on February 8, 1924, in Chikasha, Oklahoma. The daughter of a Baptist minister and a homemaker, she was reared with financial security and imbued with a strong sense of racial equality.

Sipuel attended segregated schools in Oklahoma. After completing her secondary education as valedictorian of her high school class, Sipuel entered Langston University, an African American school founded in 1897, a year after the *Plessy v. Ferguson* decision that enunciated the separate-but-equal doctrine. Sipuel married Warren Fisher on March 3, 1944, while she was a student at Langston. The following year, Sipuel-Fisher graduated with highest honors. The same year, Oklahoma NAACP officials asked her brother, Lemuel, to challenge the admissions policy of Oklahoma's white law school. He refused because he did not want to delay his entrance into law school with protracted litigation, having already put off his schooling because of military responsibilities during World War II. The Sipuels then suggested their daughter Ada, who accepted the challenge.

In 1946, Sipuel-Fisher applied for admission to University of Oklahoma Law School. University officials rejected her application. While the rejection notification acknowledged that the applicant was "scholastically qualified" to attend the university's law school, it stated that she could not be admitted because of Oklahoma's racial segregation laws. Her attorneys, Amos T. Hall and Thurgood Marshall, with written confirmation that her rejection was based on race, filed suit and alleged that the state failed to provide a law school for African Americans.

The arguments of Marshall and Hall were defeated in the Oklahoma court system. Consequently, they appealed *Sipuel v. Board of Regents of the University of Oklahoma* to the U.S. Supreme Court. In January 1948, the Court ordered the state to provide Sipuel-Fisher a legal education equal to that received by white students under the equal protection clause of the U.S. Constitution's Fourteenth Amendment. To comply with the Court's mandate, the State Board of Regents established a separate law school at Langston University, which Sipuel-Fisher refused to attend. Once again, she initiated litigation. Her attorneys filed a motion challenging the proposition that the Langston Law School facilities were equal to those at the University of Oklahoma. In mid-1949, Oklahoma's legislative body amended the state's statutes to allow qualified blacks to attend white professional and graduate schools, albeit on a segregated basis, and Sipuel-Fisher was admitted to the University of Oklahoma Law School. She completed her course of study and earned her law degree in 1951. She passed the bar examination the same year and practiced law in her native city until 1954, when she joined the firm of Bruce and Rowan in Oklahoma City.

Two years later, Sipuel-Fisher left the legal profession, where she had represented clients in segregation cases, to return to her alma mater to assume the position of public relations director. Later, she returned to the University of Oklahoma and earned a master's degree in history, subsequently becoming a member of Langston University's faculty. She retired in 1987. Following her retirement, Sipuel-Fisher became corporate counsel for Automation Research Systems in Alexandria, Virginia.

Sipuel-Fisher was the recipient of numerous awards. In 1981, the Smithsonian Institution named her one of the 150 African American women who had the most impact on the course of American history. In 1991, the University of Oklahoma awarded her an honorary doctorate. The following year, the governor of Oklahoma appointed her to the governing board of the state's higher education system. Shorty before her death on October 18, 1995, Sipuel completed her autobiography, *A Matter of Black and White*, which was published by the University of Oklahoma Press in 1996. The same year that her autobiography was published, Sipuel-Fisher was inducted into the Oklahoma Women's Hall of Fame. In 2002, she was inducted into the Oklahoma Higher Education Hall of Fame as well.

The struggle for African Americans to gain equal access to graduate and professional schools took on significant scope when Sipuel-Fisher applied to law school. The U.S. Supreme Court's ruling in the *Sipuel* case was an important link in the chain of legal precedents that resulted in the Court's unanimous ruling in 1954 in *Brown v. Board of Education of Topeka*, which led to the end of segregated schools across the United States.

MABEL K. STAUPERS

See chapter 27, Science and Technology.

CHARLES KENZIE STEELE (1914–1980)

Minister, Civil Rights Activist. Charles Kenzie (C.K.) Steele entered the movement for civil rights in 1956 when Wilhelmina Jakes and Carrie Paterson, two students from Florida Agricultural and Mechanic University (FAMU), refused to surrender their seats to a white woman on a Tallahassee bus. The only child of Henry L. and Lyde Bailor Steele, he became one of Tallahassee's most committed and prominent civil rights activists.

Ordained as a Baptist minister in 1935, Steele earned his undergraduate degree from Morehouse College Interdenominational Theological Seminary in Atlanta, Georgia, in 1938. While at Morehouse, Steele discerned that the struggle for social justice must be part of any African American cleric's mission, a deduction his more celebrated colleague and friend, Martin Luther King Jr., also came to while studying at Morehouse. In 1952, Steele moved to Tallahassee, Florida, where he became pastor of Bethel Baptist Church.

While serving as president of the Tallahassee chapter of the NAACP, Steele also became president of the Inter Civic Council (ICC), founded in May 1956 by Steele and other ministers from the Tallahassee Ministerial Alliance to direct the a bus boycott begun by black students at FAMU. The ICC's membership included people from all occupations within the community: laborers, domestic workers, ministers, professionals, businesspersons, and teachers. Like the Montgomery Improvement Association (MIA), the ICC held meetings and organized a carpool. However, it deviated from the MIA, which sought modified seating, by demanding the full integration of passengers on Tallahassee's city buses. As ICC president, Steele's fortitude and altruistic advocacy facilitated the boycott's success. Asserting that blacks in Tallahassee would "rather walk in dignity that ride in humiliation," he and other African Americans continued despite legal and financial impediments. Despite threats and destruction of property, little physical violence occurred in Tallahassee, due to Steele's impassioned urging of nonviolence.

Steele's activities in Tallahassee catapulted him to the forefront of the national civil rights movement. Steele adhered to the principle of nonviolence as a means for attaining civil rights for American blacks. In 1956, Steele joined King as a speaker at nonviolence workshops held at Tuskegee Institute, at the annual meeting of the National Baptist Convention, and at the MIA's Institute on Nonviolence for Social Change. A year later, he was among those who united with King in Atlanta, Georgia, for the founding of the Southern Christian Leadership Conference (SCLC). Steele was elected as the organization's first vice president.

Even though SCLC did not conduct a major campaign in Tallahassee, Steele backed the organization's efforts in other locations. In 1962, while King was imprisoned, Steele led demonstrations during the Albany movement. After King's assassination in 1968, Steele and the ICC organized a "Vigil for Poverty" in Tallahassee to recognize those who lacked the basic needs to sustain life.

Although not widely known outside of Tallahassee, the labors of the ICC gave hope to those engaged in the freedom struggle. Steele described this engagement as "the pain and the promise" of the civil rights movement. He fervently believed that the power of love and nonviolence would conquer violence and that the promise of the movement would be fulfilled. Diagnosed with cancer in 1977, Steele continued his ministry at Bethel Baptist Church and his activism for civil rights until his death in August 1980.

LEON H. SULLIVAN (1922–2001)

Civil Rights Activist, Organization Founder, Author. Leon Howard Sullivan was born October 16, 1922, in Charleston, West Virginia. Reared by his grandmother after his parents' divorce, Sullivan attended Charleston's segregated elementary and secondary schools. After being ordained a Baptist minister when he was seventeen years old, Sullivan earned a B.A. from West Virginia State College (1943) and an M.A. from Columbia University (1947). He also attended Union Theological Seminary (1945) and earned a doctor of divinity degree from Virginia Union University.

At age twenty-one, during the first March on Washington movement (1941–1942) organized by A. Philip Randolph, Sullivan was elected president of the South Orange Council of Churches. As president, Sullivan worked with civil rights leaders such as Bayard Rustin. From 1950 to 1988, Sullivan was the pastor of the Zion Baptist Church in Philadelphia. While there, he entered into a lifelong crusade to provide better job opportunities for African Americans. Using the method of direct nonviolent action taught him by Randolph, Sullivan fought racist hiring practices through protests and economic boycotts of Philadelphia businesses that employed too few African Americans.

Sullivan's campaign experienced some success, but businesses requested workers with technical skills that few African Americans possessed. A promoter of economic self-determination, Sullivan provided job training through the Opportunities Industrialization Center (OIC). Opening in 1964 with money from a Ford Foundation grant, the OIC offered training in electronics, cooking, power-sewing, and drafting. By 1980, the OIC operated programs in 160 cities. Sullivan also founded Zion Investment Associates, which made seed money available for new African American business ventures. His acceptance within the business community is well symbolized by his longtime membership on the boards of General Motors and Philadelphia's Girard Bank, as well as his association with Progress Aerospace Inc. and Mellon Bank.

Author of *Build, Brother, Build* (1969) and other works, Sullivan was the recipient of the Russwurm Award from the National Publisher's Association (1963); the Philadelphia Fellowship Communion Award (1964); the Philadelphia Book Award (1966); the American Exemplar Medal (1969); the NAACP's Spingarn Medal (1971); and the Franklin D. Roosevelt Four Freedom Medal (1987). In 1991, he received the Presidential Medal of Freedom and the Distinguished Service Award, Côte d'Ivoire's highest honor.

In the mid-1970s, Sullivan devised the "Sullivan Principles," which successfully encouraged American-owned companies in South Africa to hire more black workers and to treat them equitably in relation to promotions and working conditions. After retiring from the Zion Baptist Church in 1988, Sullivan was made pastor emeritus and concentrated his energies on concerns in Africa, especially South Africa's system of apartheid. He called on American corporations to sell their South African investments and petitioned the U.S. government to bring sanctions against the racially biased country. Sullivan parted company with President Ronald Reagan's "constructive engagement" policy toward South Africa and, in 1987, endorsed a policy of South African divestment.

Because of Sullivan's efforts, the departure of international businesses, and the sweeping institution of international sanctions, the shackles of South Africa's system of racial segregation were unchained. Sullivan subsequently founded the International Foundation for Education and Self-Help to combat illiteracy, famine, and joblessness in Africa and to advance the concept of African self-reliance. In April 1991, Sullivan organized and co-chaired the first African and African American Summit held at Abidjan, Côte d'Ivoire. Six months later, he officiated at the United Nations Day for Africa, a function he inaugurated to bring attention to the issue of debt relief for sub-Saharan African countries.

Sullivan died of leukemia on April 24, 2001, in Scottsdale, Arizona. A pathfinder, Sullivan made lasting contributions to the improvement of humankind throughout the world.

MARY E. CHURCH TERRELL (1863–1954)

Organization Executive/Founder, Civil Rights Activist. Mary Eliza Church Terrell, born on September 23, 1863, in Memphis, Tennessee, was the oldest child of Robert and Louisa Ayers Church. Because of the racial climate in her native city and its deficient educational facilities for African American children, Church's parents enrolled her in the Antioch College "Model School" in

Yellow Springs, Ohio. She attended the public schools in Yellow Springs and in 1879 completed her secondary education in Oberlin, Ohio. Church earned her bachelor's degree from Oberlin College in 1884. The following year, she accepted a faculty position at Wilberforce College in Xenia, Ohio. After two years at Wilberforce, Church joined the Colored High School faculty in Washington, D.C. She married Robert Heberton Terrell on October 18, 1891. Residing in Washington, the Terrells became the parents of two children, their daughter Phyllis, and Mary, an adopted daughter.

Terrell became active in the feminist movement and founded the Colored Women's League in 1892. Later, this organization merged with the Federation of Afro-American Women and became the National Association of Colored Women (NACW). Organized in 1896, she was elected its first president. In 1895, Terrell was appointed to the school board in the District of Columbia and served until 1901. She was the first woman of color to serve on such a board. Reappointed in 1906, she held the position for another five years.

By 1901, Terrell operated as a leader outside the sphere of women's organizations. She wrote numerous articles denouncing racial segregation. Writing under the pseudonym Euphemia Kirk, which she soon discarded, Terrell's treatises were covered in the national and international media. Terrell sought redress for the three companies of African American soldiers dismissed after the 1906 outbreak of racial violence in Brownsville, Texas. In 1909, she was one of two African American women who signed the "Call" for the organizational meeting of the NAACP. During the women's suffrage movement, Terrell worked with other women for the 1920 ratification of the U.S. Constitution's Nineteenth Amendment. In 1940, she published her autobiography, *A Colored Woman in a White World.*

After World War II, Terrell aggressively fought racial discrimination. In 1950, she filed suit against Thompson's Restaurant in Washington, D.C., for not adhering to the city's 1872 and 1873 public accommodation laws. As chair of the Coordinating Committee for the Enforcement of the District of Columbia Antidiscrimination Laws, Terrell focused on other segregated facilities. She led the picket lines when she was eighty-nine years old. On June 8, 1953, the Supreme Court ruled Washington's segregated eating facilities unconstitutional in *District of Columbia v. John R. Thompson*. Terrell fought for more than sixty-six years for gender and racial equality. She died on July 24, 1954, two months after the Supreme Court ruled school segregation unlawful in *Brown v. Board of Education of Topeka*.

WILLIAM M. TROTTER (1872–1934)

Organization Executive/Founder, Civil Rights Activist, Publisher. William Monroe Trotter was born to James Monroe and Virginia Isaacs Trotter on April 7, 1872, near Chillicothe, Ohio. Reared in predominantly white, suburban Hyde Park near Boston, he excelled academically at Hyde Park Grammar School and Hyde Park High School. In 1891, Trotter entered Harvard, where he became the university's first African American Phi Beta Kappa. He graduated magna cum laude in 1895 with a B.A. degree. In 1899, after working for various employers, Trotter started his business career as an insurance agent and mortgage negotiator. Two years later, he, along with William H. Scott and George W. Forbes, founded the *Guardian.* A militant newspaper, it addressed the needs and aspirations of African Americans and served as an organ against racial discrimination. The same year that he cofounded the newspaper, Trotter married Geraldine Louise Pindell, who assisted in publishing the *Guardian.*

An ideological opponent of the "Wizard of Tuskegee," in 1903 Trotter deliberately disrupted a meeting in Boston at which Booker T. Washington was advocating support of segregation. Subsequently, in 1905, Trotter joined W. E. B. Du Bois in founding the Niagara Movement. However, he refused to move with Du Bois into the NAACP because he felt it would be too moderate. Neither could he accept the financial and leadership role assumed by whites. Instead, Trotter formed the Negro Equal Rights League. In protest against the segregation policies of President Woodrow Wilson, Trotter led a delegation to the White House to meet with Wilson in 1914. After a heated debate between Trotter and the president, Wilson ordered the group to leave. The following year, he led demonstrations against the showing of D. W. Griffith's racist film *The Birth of a Nation*, which glorified the Ku Klux Klan. In 1919, Trotter appeared at the Paris Peace Conference in an unsuccessful effort to convince delegates to outlaw racial discrimination. Although the State Department had denied him a passport to attend the conference, he reached Paris by working as a cook on a ship.

Because of his strident unwillingness to work with established groups, chroniclers of the civil rights movement have been slow to recognize Trotter. However, many of his methods were adopted in the struggle for racial equality and justice in the late 1950s and 1960s, notably his use of nonviolent protest. Arrested numerous times, Trotter's purpose for consistent direct protest was to eradicate the virulent malevolence of racial segregation.

C. T. VIVIAN (1924–)

Minister, Civil Rights Activist, Author. The Reverend Cordy Tindell Vivian, a veteran of the civil rights movement, began his pilgrimage as a youth struggling to dismantle racial segregation. Cordy Tindell Vivian, better known as C. T., was born on July 28, 1924, in Boonville, Missouri, the only child of Robert and Euzetta Tindell Vivian. The Great Depression caused his mother and grandmother to lose everything, including their marriages. Because they wanted C. T. to have the best education possible, they moved to Macomb, Illinois. Macomb's school system was desegregated, and the city was home to Western Illinois University. Vivian received his primary education at Lincoln Grade School, where he first realized his leadership abilities and began to understand the power of nonviolence. Vivian then entered Edison Junior High School, and later Macomb High School, where he became a student leader. As a teenager, Vivian attended the Allen Chapel African Methodist Episcopal Church, where he taught in the Sunday School and served as president of the youth group. He graduated from Macomb High School in 1942, and entered Western Illinois University.

While Vivian was a student at Western Illinois University, he became disturbed by a number of issues, including racism. In the mid-1940s, he left the university and moved to Peoria, where he worked for the Carver Community Center as assistant boys' director. In 1947, Vivian participated in the first sit-ins in Peoria. The northern states practiced segregation by custom, in contrast to the South, where segregation was codified by law. In an effort to right Peoria's customs, Vivian became involved with an integrated group of individuals interested in opening the city's restaurants and lunch counters to all people, regardless of race.

In 1954, while working at Foster and Gallagher Mail Order Company, Vivian acknowledged his call to the ministry. Later that year, he gave his first sermon at Mount Zion Baptist Church. In 1955, Vivian moved to Nashville and entered American Baptist Theological Seminary, and later became the pastor of the First Community Church. In addition to his ministerial and academic responsibilities, Vivian worked as an editor for the National Baptist Sunday School Publishing Board of the National Baptist Convention, USA. As the civil rights movement dawned, Vivian found himself in a continuous tug-of-war with the more conventional editors of the publishing board, who wanted limited coverage of the new racial protests and the rise of the Reverend Dr. Martin Luther King Jr. The conflict led to a philosophical fissure between the board and Vivian, which caused him to leave.

In the late fall of 1956, Vivian boarded a Nashville Transit Authority bus and seated himself near the front of the half-filled vehicle. The driver ordered him to the rear. A heated debate ensued, and Vivian refused to comply with the driver's demands. The bus driver demanded that the other passengers vacate the bus, and he immediately drove Vivian to police headquarters. Earlier, the U.S. Supreme Court, in *Gayle v. Browder*, had ruled in favor of Montgomery, Alabama, plaintiffs in their efforts to desegregate intrastate transportation. Notwithstanding the ruling, Nashville's law enforcement officials did not know the city's policy on segregation in buses. After calling city hall, they learned that the city was in the process of ending segregated seating on public conveyances.

In the late 1950s, Vivian joined other ministers under the leadership of the Reverend Kelly Miller Smith Sr. and established the Nashville Christian Leadership Conference (NCLC). During NCLC's organizational meeting, Vivian was elected vice president. He met the Reverend James Lawson, who had arrived in Nashville in 1958, and others, who ultimately brought down Nashville's walls of racial segregation. As NCLC vice president, Vivian's responsibilities included overseeing the organization's direct-action component. Lawson became a member of and served as chair of NCLC's Action Committee. After formulating a plan to conduct workshops on the Gandhian method of protest, NCLC leaders and students tested Nashville's policy of racial segregation in November and December of 1959. Because the news media ignored Nashville's sit-in movement, it went largely unnoticed and was relegated to a footnote by the February 1, 1960, Greensboro, North Carolina, sit-in. Twelve days after the Greensboro sit-in, Nashville students began their movement in earnest. Two months later, NCLC and the Nashville Student Committee, with the help of Fisk University economics professor Vivian Henderson, initiated an economic withdrawal that all but paralyzed Nashville's retail district.

On April 19, with the economic boycott in full swing, someone tossed dynamite into the residence of Z. Alexander Looby, a well-known Nashville civil rights attorney. Although Looby and his wife escaped with minor injuries, leaders in Nashville's black community organized a mass protest march to Mayor Ben West's downtown office. Knowledgeable about New York's silent march against lynching in the early 1900s, Vivian demanded that the silent tactic be the march's modus operandi. As some four thousands persons of both races watched, the marchers walked in silence toward the mayor's office. When West came out to meet with them, Vivian read a prepared speech critical of the mayor's leadership. The mayor became angry, and the two men argued heatedly. When Vivian asked West "if he thought segregation was moral," the mayor answered, "No." At that point, the leaders of the march asked the mayor to use the standing of his office to stop racial segregation. Without delay, he appealed to all citizens to end discrimination and indicated that he believed the city's lunch counters should be desegregated. On May 10, 1960, the city of Nashville began desegregating its lunch counters.

In 1961, Vivian joined SNCC activists in the freedom rides. Earlier, because of threats of violence, CORE officials had halted its freedom ride from Washington, D.C., to Montgomery. Vivian later took part in a number of key civil rights struggles, including those in Albany, Georgia (1961); Birmingham, Alabama (1962); St. Augustine, Florida (1964); and Selma, Alabama (1965). In 1963, King assigned Vivian to SCLC's executive staff and named him national director of affiliates. He became the consultant to all SCLC organizations on issues relating to voter registration, consumer actions, nonviolent training, direct action, human relations, and community development. Two years later, on the courthouse steps in Selma, Alabama, Vivian challenged Sheriff Jim Clark during a voter-registration drive, and the sheriff assaulted him.

In 1970, Vivian published one of the first monographs on the civil rights movement: *Black Power and the American Myth.* Several television documentaries about the civil rights era focused on Vivian as an activist, analyst, and strategist. He was featured in *Eyes on the Prize* and *The Healing Ministry of Dr. C. T. Vivian*, both of which aired on the Public Broadcasting Service (PBS).

PERRY E. WALLACE JR. (1948–)

Attorney, Educator, Collegiate Basketball Player. Attorney, law professor, and Southeastern Conference (SEC) basketball pioneer Perry Eugene Wallace was the first African American to participate in varsity sports at Vanderbilt University and in SEC basketball. Wallace is a native of Nashville, Tennessee, and the youngest of six children born to Hattie Haynes Wallace and Perry E. Wallace Sr. A graduate of Pearl High School in Nashville, he played center on Pearl's basketball team, where he was known for his slam dunks and referred to as "king of the boards."

More than eighty colleges and universities recruited Wallace, who won All-Metro, All-State, and All-American

The Reverend C .T. Vivian, Traveling with Freedom Riders, 1961. *Among Vivian's numerous civil rights activities was his participation in Freedom Rides in the segregated South to assess compliance with the U.S. Supreme Court's 1960 ruling in* Boynton v. Virginia. **LEE LOCKWOOD/TIME LIFE PICTURES/GETTY IMAGES**

honors. The class valedictorian, he signed with Vanderbilt University in May 1966, which six years earlier, during the Nashville sit-in movement, had expelled the Reverend James Lawson, a student at Vanderbilt's Divinity School. Entering Vanderbilt on an athletic scholarship, Wallace played on the school's freshmen squad because the National Collegiate Athletic Association's regulations barred freshmen from participating on the varsity team. Fellow teammate Godfrey Dillard, an African American from Detroit, Michigan, joined Wallace.

During their first year, Wallace and Dillard encountered segregation at Mississippi State, the University of Tennessee, and Auburn University. Supporting each other, they remained silent about the threats they received. Later, Dillard suffered an injury that caused him to forgo varsity ball. On December 2, 1967, Wallace became the first African American student athlete to compete in the SEC. He experienced racism at its worst, particularly at SEC schools in Alabama and Mississippi. Cheerleaders led a barrage of harsh and insulting racist cheers. There were threats of beatings, castration, and lynching. He endured physical abuse on the court that referees refused to accept as fouls. Malevolent crowds abused him verbally and threatened Wallace physically throughout his SEC career. He never displayed antipathy against players who spitefully fouled him. He realized that any perceived transgression on his part could decelerate the advancement of desegregation in the SEC. He chose to play proficiently, with precision, passion, and adroitness, to beat his opponents, on and off the court.

Quietly taking the struggles of the civil rights movement to the basketball court, as Jackie Robinson did on the baseball field, Wallace played a crucial role in desegregating college basketball. In 1970, the first season after he graduated, the universities of Alabama, Florida, Georgia, and Kentucky desegregated their varsity teams; within the next decade, black athletes dominated SEC teams.

The first African American to complete four years in the SEC, Wallace ended his tenure as captain of the Vanderbilt varsity team and second-team All SEC. After graduating with a degree in electrical engineering and engineering mathematics from the Vanderbilt University School of Engineering in 1970, Wallace earned his law degree from Columbia University (1975), where he was awarded the Charles Evans Hughes Fellowship. During the administrations of Presidents Jimmy Carter and Ronald Reagan, Wallace served as an attorney in the U.S. Department of Justice.

Wallace has received numerous accolades, including induction into the Tennessee Sports Hall of Fame, and he has been honored as an SEC Living Legend. In 2004, Vanderbilt University retired Wallace's jersey, making him only the third athlete in the school's history to receive this honor. He was among the players and coaches featured in the documentary film *Black Magic* (aired on ESPN in 2008), which explored the collision of sports and America's racial turbulence during the modern civil rights era.

Wallace has been a professor of law at American University's Washington College of Law in Washington, D.C., since 1991. He is director of the JD/MBA Joint Degree Program, and specializes in environmental law, corporate law, and finance.

BOOKER T. WASHINGTON (1856–1915)

Lecturer, Civil Rights Activist, Educator, Organization Executive/Founder, Author. Booker Taliaferro Washington was born enslaved in Hale's Ford, Virginia, on April 5, 1856, to Jane Ferguson, a bonded woman. The first nine years of Washington's life were spent in bondage on the farm of James Burroughs, his place of his birth. After emancipation, his family was so poor that he worked in salt furnaces and coal mines from age nine. While attending school sporadically in Malden, West Virginia, Booker adopted the surname Washington. Always an intelligent and curious child, he yearned for an education and was frustrated when he could not receive one locally. When he was sixteen years old, he was allowed to quit work to go to school. His family had no money to help him, so he walked two hundred miles to attend the Hampton Institute in Virginia and paid his tuition and board there by working as a janitor.

Dedicating himself to the idea that education would raise his people to equality in the United States, Washington became a teacher. He first taught in his hometown, then at the Hampton Institute, and in 1881 he founded the Tuskegee Normal and Industrial Institute in Tuskegee, Alabama. As head of the institute, he traveled the country constantly to raise funds from both African Americans and whites. He soon became a well-known speaker.

In 1895, Washington was asked to speak at the opening of the Cotton States Exposition, an unprecedented honor for an African American man. His "Atlanta Compromise" speech explained his major thesis, that African Americans could secure their constitutional rights through their own economic and moral advancement rather than through legal and political changes. Although his conciliatory stand angered some African Americans who feared it would encourage the foes of equal rights, whites approved of his views. His major achievement, however, was to win over diverse elements among southern whites, without whose support the programs he envisioned and brought into being would have been impossible. Washington penned two autobiographies, *The Story of My Life and Work* (1900) and *Up from Slavery* (1901).

In addition to Tuskegee Institute (now Tuskegee University), which still educates many today, Washington instituted a variety of programs for rural extension work and helped to establish the National Negro Business League. Shortly after the election of President William McKinley in 1896, a movement was set in motion to name Washington to a cabinet post, but he withdrew his name from consideration, preferring to work outside the political arena. One of the most significant leaders among African Americans in the early twentieth century, Booker T. Washington died on November 14, 1915.

IDA B. WELLS-BARNETT (1862–1931)

Journalist, Lecturer, Civil Rights Activist, Feminist. The oldest of James and Elizabeth Warenton Wells's eight children, Wells-Barnett was born enslaved during the Civil War in Holly Springs, Mississippi, on July 16, 1862. After the yellow fever epidemic of 1878 claimed the lives of her parents and youngest brother, Wells-Barnett assumed responsibility for her siblings when she was sixteen years old. Leaving Shaw University (now Rust College) and passing a teachers' examination, she briefly taught in rural Mississippi to support her family. Wells-Barnett then moved to Memphis, Tennessee, and taught in the county and city public schools.

A train ride from Memphis to Woodstock was the beginning of Wells-Barnett's lifelong public campaign against the injustices faced by African Americans throughout the South. In 1884, after being forcibly removed from the first-class ladies' coach, she filed suit against the Chesapeake, Ohio, and Southwestern Railroad. Although she won in the Memphis Circuit Court, the state's supreme court reversed the lower court's decision in 1887 because the railroad company had satisfied Tennessee's 1881 statutory requirements to provide separate-but-equal accommodations.

Wells-Barnett published accounts of her experience in local African American newspapers and wrote for the African American press throughout the country. In 1889, she was elected secretary of the Afro-American Press Association. Wells-Barnett's editorials critical of the Memphis Board of Education led to her dismissal as teacher in 1891. Afterward, she became a full-time journalist and editor. The March 9, 1892, lynching of three African American male proprietors of the People's Grocery Store in Memphis caused Wells-Barnett to declare journalistic war on lynching. When her protest writings outraged white men in the South, a mob destroyed her newspaper office on May 27, 1892, and she was banished from the region.

Wells-Barnett moved to New York and continued her struggle against racial injustice and lynching as a columnist for the *New York Age*, edited by T. Thomas Fortune. On June 7, 1892, the *New York Age* published her detailed analysis of lynching, refuting the myth that, by killing African American men, white men intended to shield white women against rape. Her detailed statistics and findings formed the basis of two pamphlets, *Southern Horrors* (1892) and *A Red Record* (1895). Lecturing in Great Britain in 1893 and 1894, Wells-Barnett internationalized her antilynching campaign.

In 1893, Wells-Barnett focused her attention on the exclusion of African Americans from the World's Columbian Exposition in Chicago. Working with Frederick Douglass, Ferdinand Lee Barnett, and I. Garland Penn, Wells-Barnett co wrote an eighty-one-page pamphlet titled *The Reason Why the Colored*

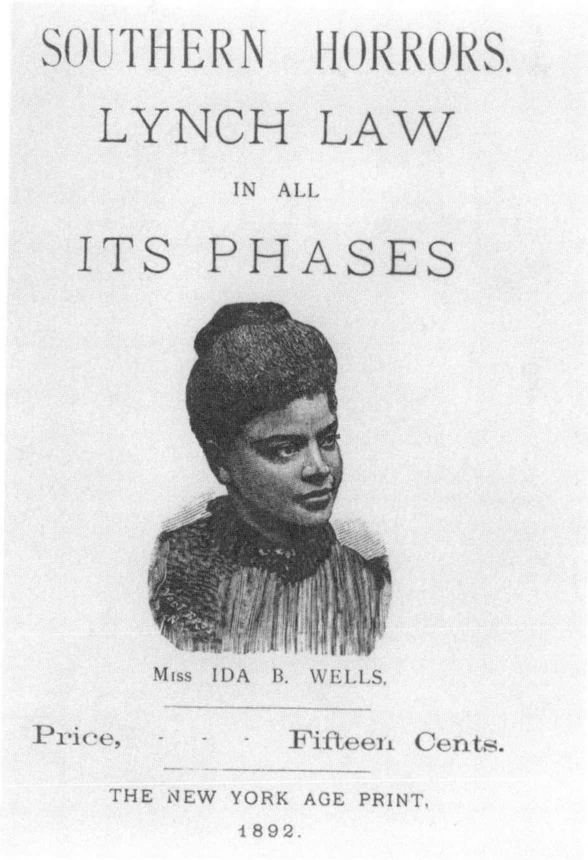

Cover Page,* Southern Horrors: Lynch Law in All Its Phases *(Ida B. Wells, 1892). *Based on her detailed analysis of lynching published in the* New York Age, *Wells's pamphlet refutes the myth that, by killing African American men, white men intended to shield white women against rape.* SCHOMBURG CENTER FOR RESEARCH IN BLACK CULTURE; THE NEW YORK PUBLIC LIBRARY; ASTOR, LENOX AND TILDEN FOUNDATIONS

American Is Not in the World's Columbian Exposition: The Afro-American's Contribution to Columbian Literature. Later in the year, she moved to Chicago and began working for the *Chicago Conservator,* the first African American newspaper in the city, founded by Ferdinand Barnett.

On June 27, 1895, Ida B. Wells-Barnett married Ferdinand Barnett, and they became the parents of four children. Domesticity did not distract Wells-Barnett from her crusade. Her militant views and support of Marcus Garvey caused her to be branded a radical by the U.S. Secret Service. Wells-Barnett continued to write articles and participate in local and national affairs. In 1898, she and others met with President William McKinley to seek redress for the lynching of an African American postmaster in South Carolina. They also urged passage of a federal antilynching bill.

Wells-Barnett was one of two African American women who signed the "Call" for a conference on the Negro. Convening on May 31, 1909, the conference led to the formation of the NAACP.

A champion of women's rights, Wells-Barnett was one of the founders of the National Association of Colored Women. Believing in the power of the ballot box, she founded the Alpha Suffrage Club of Chicago. As a delegate to the National American Woman Suffrage Association's parade in Washington, D.C., Wells-Barnett refused to march in the back of the procession. She desegregated the parade by joining the Illinois delegation. Wells-Barnett actively campaigned for Oscar DePriest, the first African American elected as an alderman in Chicago. In 1930, she made an unsuccessful bid for an Illinois State Senate seat.

With a passion for justice, Ida B. Wells-Barnett fought for civil and human rights. One of the most important persons of the late nineteenth and early twentieth centuries, she actively participated in the struggle from the 1890s until her death on March 25, 1931.

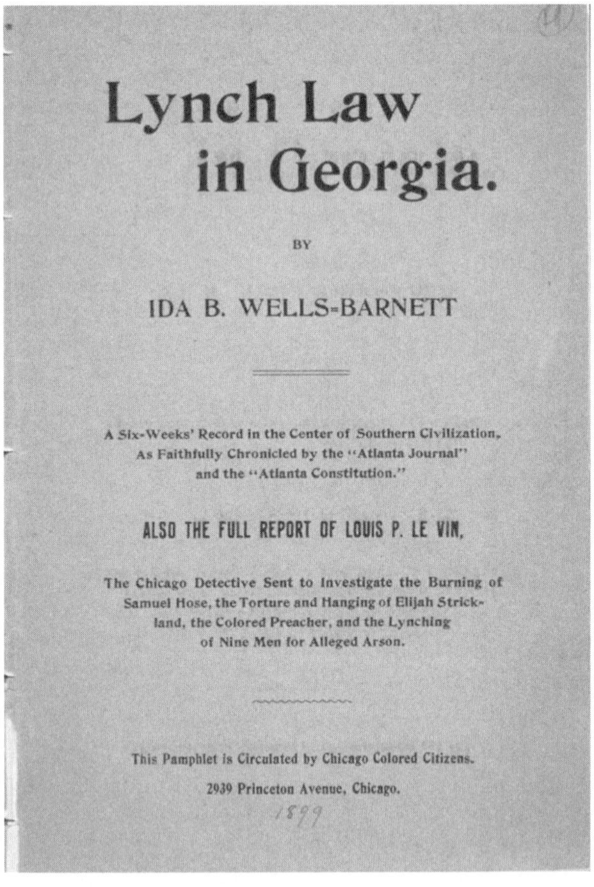

Lynch Law in Georgia.

BY

IDA B. WELLS-BARNETT

A Six-Weeks' Record in the Center of Southern Civilization, As Faithfully Chronicled by the "Atlanta Journal" and the "Atlanta Constitution."

ALSO THE FULL REPORT OF LOUIS P. LE VIN,

The Chicago Detective Sent to Investigate the Burning of Samuel Hose, the Torture and Hanging of Elijah Strickland, the Colored Preacher, and the Lynching of Nine Men for Alleged Arson.

This Pamphlet is Circulated by Chicago Colored Citizens.

2939 Princeton Avenue, Chicago.

1899

Cover of "Lynch Law in Georgia" (Ida B. Wells-Barnett, 1890). *Wells-Barnett, a journalist and social activist, became one of the leading voices in the antilynching crusade of the late nineteenth and early twentieth centuries through her writings and lectures.* THE LIBRARY OF CONGRESS

ANDREW YOUNG

See chapter 11, Politics.

FEDERAL AND STATE CIVIL RIGHTS AGENCIES

FEDERAL AGENCIES

U.S. Commission on Civil Rights
624 9th St. NW
Washington, DC 20425
Telephone: (202) 376-7700

U.S. Equal Employment Opportunity Commission
131 M St. NE
Washington, DC 20507
Telephone: (202) 663-4900

STATE AGENCIES

Alabama Attorney General's Office
500 Dexter Ave.
Montgomery, AL 36130
Telephone: (334) 242-7300

Alaska Human Rights Commission
800 A St., Ste. 204
Anchorage, AK 99501-3669
Telephone: (907) 274-4692

Arizona Attorney General's Office
1275 W. Washington St.
Phoenix, AZ 85007
Telephone: (602) 542-5025

Arkansas Attorney General's Office
323 Center St., Ste. 200
Little Rock, AR 72201
Telephone: (501) 682-2007

California Attorney General
1300 I St., Ste. 1101
PO Box 944255
Sacramento, CA 94244-2550
Telephone: (916) 322-3360

California Fair Employment and Housing Commission
455 Golden Gate Ave., Ste 10600
San Francisco, CA 94102
Telephone: (415) 557-2325

Colorado Attorney General's Office
1525 Sherman St., 7th Fl.
Denver, CO 80203
Telephone: (303) 866-4500

Connecticut Attorney General's Office
55 Elm St.
Hartford, CT 06106
Telephone: (860) 808-5318

Delaware Attorney General's Office
Carvel State Office Bldg., 820 N. French St.
Wilmington, DE 19801
Telephone: (302) 577-8400

Florida Attorney General's Office
The Capitol, PL-01
Tallahassee, FL 32399-1050
Telephone: (850) 414-3300

Georgia Commission on Equal Opportunity
2 Martin Luther King Jr. Dr. SE, Ste 1002,
West Tower
Atlanta, GA 30334
Telephone: (404) 656-1736

Hawaii Attorney General's Office
425 Queen St.
Honolulu, HI 96813
Telephone: (808) 586-1500

Idaho Commission on Human Rights
1109 Main St., Ste 450
Boise, ID 83720-0040
Telephone: (208) 334-2873

Illinois Department of Human Rights
James R. Thompson Ctr., 100 W. Randolph St., Ste.
10-100
Chicago, IL 60601
Telephone: (312) 814-6200

Indiana Civil Rights Commission
Indiana Government Center North, 100 N. Senate Ave.,
Rm. N-103
Indianapolis, IN 46204-2211
Telephone: (317) 232-2600

Iowa Department of Human Rights
Lucas State Office Bldg., 321 E. 12th St.
Des Moines, IA 50319
Telephone: (515) 242-5655

Kansas Human Rights Commission
Landon State Office Bldg., 900 SW Jackson St.,
Ste. 568-South
Topeka, KS 66612-2818
Telephone: (785) 296-3206

Kentucky Commission on Human Rights
332 W. Broadway, 7th Fl.
Louisville, KY 40202
Telephone: (502) 595-4024

Louisiana Attorney General's Office
1885 N. 3rd St.
Baton Rouge, LA 70802
Telephone: (225) 326-6079

Maine Human Rights Commission
51 State House Sta.
Augusta, ME 04330
Telephone: (207) 624-6050

Maryland Commission on Human Relations
6 Saint Paul St., Ste. 900
Baltimore, MD 21202
Telephone: (410) 767-8600

Massachusetts Attorney General's Office
One Ashburton Place, Rm. 2010
Boston, MA 02108-1698
Telephone: (617) 727-2200

Michigan Attorney General's Office
G. Mennen Williams Bldg., 7th Fl., 525 W. Ottawa St.
PO Box 30212
Lansing, MI 48909
Telephone: (517) 373-1110

Michigan Department of Civil Rights
Capitol Tower Bldg., 110 W. Michigan Avenue, Ste. 800
Lansing, MI 48933
Telephone: (517) 335-3165

Minnesota Department of Human Rights
190 E. 5th St., Ste. 700
St. Paul, MN 55101
Telephone: (651) 296-5663

Mississippi Attorney General's Office
Walter Sillers Bldg., 550 High St., Ste 1200
Jackson, MS 39201
Telephone: (601) 359-3680

Missouri Commission on Human Rights
3315 W. Truman Blvd., PO Box 1129
Jefferson City, MO 65102-1129
Telephone: (573) 751-3325

Montana Attorney General's Office
Justice Bldg., 215 N. Sanders, PO Box 201401
Helena, MT 59620-1401
Telephone: (406) 444-2026

Nebraska Equal Opportunity Commission
Nebraska State Office Bldg., 301 Centennial Mall S., 5th Fl.
PO Box 94934
Lincoln, NE 68509-4934
Telephone: (402) 471-2024

Nevada Equal Rights Commission
555 E. Washington Ave., Ste 4000
Las Vegas, NV 89101
Telephone: (702) 486-7161

New Hampshire Commission for Human Rights
2 Chenell Dr., No. 2
Concord, NH 03301-8501
Telephone: (603) 271-2767

New Jersey Attorney General's Office
Justice Complex, 25 Market St.
PO Box 080
Trenton, NJ 08625-0080
Telephone: (609) 292-4925

New Mexico Department of Work Force Solutions
Human Rights Division, 401 Broadway NE
Albuquerque, NM 87102
Telephone: (800) 841-4000

New York State Division of Human Rights
One Fordham Plz., 4th Fl.
Bronx, NY 10458
Telephone: (718) 741-8400

North Carolina Human Relations Commission
217 W. Jones St., Ste 2109
Raleigh, NC 27601
Telephone: (919) 807-4420

North Dakota Attorney General's Office
State Capitol, 600 E. Boulevard Ave., Dept. 125
Bismarck, ND 58505-0040
Telephone: (701) 328-2210

Ohio Civil Rights Commission
Rhodes State Office Twr., 30 E. Broad St., 5th Fl.
Columbus, OH 43215
Telephone: (614) 466-2785

Oklahoma Human Rights Commission
Jim Thorpe Bldg., 2101 N. Lincoln Blvd., Rm. 480
Oklahoma City, OK 73105-4904
Telephone: (405) 521-2360

Oregon Attorney General's Office
Justice Bldg., 1162 Court St. NE
Salem, OR 97310-4096
Telephone: (503) 378-4400

Pennsylvania Human Relations Commission
301 Chestnut St., Ste. 300
Harrisburg, PA 17101
Telephone: (717) 787-4410

Rhode Island Commission for Human Rights
180 Westminster St., 3rd Fl.
Providence, RI 02903
Telephone: (401) 222-2661

South Carolina Human Affairs Commission
2611 Forest Dr., Ste. 200
PO Box 4490
Columbia, SC 29204
Telephone: (803) 737-7800

South Dakota Attorney General's Office
1302 E. Highway 14, Ste. 1
Pierre, SD 57501-8501
Telephone: (605) 773-3215

Tennessee Human Rights Commission
710 James Robertson Pky., Ste. 100
Nashville, TN 37243-1219
Telephone: (615) 741-5825

Texas Attorney General's Office
300 W. 15th St.
Austin, TX 78701
Telephone: (512) 463-2100

Utah Attorney General's Office
Utah State Capitol Complex, 350 N. State St., Ste 230
Salt Lake City, UT 84114-2320
Telephone: (801) 366-0260

Vermont Attorney General's Office
Pavilion Office Bldg., 109 State St.
Montpelier, VT 05609-1001
Telephone: (802) 828-3171

Virginia Human Rights Council
1220 Bank St., Jefferson Bldg, 3rd Fl.
Richmond, VA 23219
Telephone: (804) 225-2292

Washington State Human Rights Commission
711 S. Capitol Way, Ste. 402
PO Box 42490
Olympia, WA 98504-2490
Telephone: (360) 753-6770

West Virginia Human Rights Commission
1321 Plaza E., Rm. 108A
Charleston, WV 25301-1400
Telephone: (304) 558-2616

Wisconsin Attorney General's Office
PO Box 7857
Madison, WI 53707-7857
Telephone: (608) 266-1221

Wyoming Attorney General's Office
123 Capitol Bldg., 200 W. 24th St.
Cheyenne, WY 82002
Telephone: (307) 777-7841

8

BLACK NATIONALISM

Raymond A. Winbush

THE IDEOLOGY OF BLACK NATIONALISM

Black nationalism is the ideology of creating a nation-state for Africans living in the *Maafa* (a Kiswahili term used to describe the continued suffering of Africans throughout the world). Black nationalism is expressed orally and in writing, with its core philosophy being the cultural and political return of African people to a place that would allow for complete self-determination in all aspects of their lives. The earliest protests against African enslavement in America had black nationalistic overtones, as evidenced by written narratives that emerged during the last half of the eighteenth century. The nineteenth century saw attempts to establish self-governing homelands for Africans in the Maafa that continue today in the United States and in Africa. At the core of all black nationalist philosophy is resistance to either cultural or political assimilation into Western culture. The expression of this resistance was seen in revolts of Africans during the Middle Passage and within certain countries where displaced Africans resided.

African nationalism is distinguished from Pan-Africanism, with the former describing political ideology focusing on Africa, and the latter describing its expression by Africans throughout the Maafa. Marcus Garvey (1887–1940), Kwame Nkrumah (1909–1972), Julius Nyerere (1922–1999), and Jomo Kenyatta (c. 1894–1978) advocated an "Africa for Africans" when they rebelled against colonialism during the twentieth century. Their ideological ancestors were Paul Cuffee (1759–1817), Martin Delany (1812–1885), Alexander Crummell (1819–1898), and other Pan-Africanists who linked black freedom with Africa.

Since their forced removal from Africa, Africans in the Maafa have created political and cultural representations of their yearning to return. These creations were often mythological, as in the folklore of captured Africans who felt that they could literally fly back to Africa. Beginning with the horrors of the Middle Passage, Africans created a folklore that emphasized joining forces with their ancestors to defeat their European captors. The often-repeated but mistaken notion that most of the Africans who jumped from ships during the Middle Passage were committing suicide ignores the fact that emerging from the folk traditions of many of the captives was the belief that they would reunite with their drowned ancestors and revolt against their enslavers. Similar resistance was demonstrated by the members of the Igbo who, after being removed from the hull of a slave ship bringing them to the Georgia Sea Islands in 1803, marched slowly but deliberately into the cold Atlantic Ocean and drowned themselves rather than undergo the humiliation of enslavement. The resistance aspect is often disconnected from the history of black nationalism, but it is fundamental to understanding how Africans responded to slavery and its aftermath. It explains how the Underground Railroad was a sophisticated resistance movement created by blacks to obtain their freedom, and that while whites participated at several levels, the movement was led by the notion of black self-determination—the cornerstone of black nationalism.

Nationalistic revolts took place frequently on the infamous slave ships, reaching their zenith in 1839 with the *Amistad* incident. Singbe-Piéh (renamed Joseph Cinque by his captors), a Mende farmer from Sierra Leone who mutinied aboard the Spanish ship, told its captain to return the ship and its human cargo to Africa. The incident, which garnered international attention, illustrated how black nationalism was more than a political ideology. It was a philosophy centered on resistance and self-determination. It was rooted in the desire for liberation and was reflected in movements as diverse as the Universal Negro Improvement Association of Marcus Garvey, the notion of a unified Africa in the writings of George Padmore (c. 1903–1959), and the Haitian revolution led by Toussaint-Louverture (1743–1803). In Europe, black nationalist thought appeared in the writings of several Africans captured during the Middle Passage. In Britain, African Olaudah Equiano's (c. 1750–1797) best-selling book, *The Interesting Narrative of the Life of Olaudah Equiano, or Gustavus Vassa* (1789), saw the return of Africans to that continent as critical to their future.

Drawing of Paul Cuffee, 1812. *Cuffee, considered by most historians to be the father of black nationalism in the United States, made an 1811–1812 voyage to Sierra Leone, where he founded the Friendly Society, which helped African Americans return to Africa.* **THE LIBRARY OF CONGRESS**

EARLY BLACK NATIONALISM IN THE UNITED STATES

Most historians consider Paul Cuffee to be the father of black nationalism in the United States. One of the wealthiest men in the American colonies, Cuffee believed that "commerce furnished to industry more ample rewards than agriculture," and he turned to shipbuilding as an expression of his belief. Cuffee acquired enormous wealth after the American Revolutionary War (1775–1783). The crews on his ships were always black, demonstrating Cuffee's belief that the best proof of black excellence was to show that they could manage, work exclusively with one another, and turn out quality products. In 1780, when he was twenty-one years old, Cuffee and his brother refused to pay taxes since blacks and Native Americans were excluded from voting in Massachusetts.

After his first voyage to Africa in 1811, Cuffee became convinced that economic and cultural exchange was possible between the continental Africans and those in the New World. James Forten (1766–1842), Absalom Jones (1746–1818), and Richard Allen (1760–1831) supported Cuffee's idea of providing African American workers to Sierra Leone to aid in the resettling of black Americans in Africa. Cuffee increasingly supported these efforts with his generous gifts to the American Colonization Society (ACS), a group dominated by whites who wanted free blacks to return to Africa. Several criticized Cuffee and accused him of being used by the ACS. This relationship marked the first time that black nationalists conferred with white supremacists in support of their philosophy of separatism. More than a century later, Marcus Garvey was the object of similar criticism from W. E. B. Du Bois (1868–1963) after he met secretly with the Ku Klux Klan to solicit their aid in financing an African resettlement program.

In the 1791 Haitian revolt, Toussaint-Louverture retained Boukman, a Jamaican, as his secretary because Toussaint-Louverture had heard of rebellious efforts in Jamaica. Discussions among enslaved Africans throughout the Maafa about insurrections were numerous and were influenced by persons such as Gabriel, more commonly known as Gabriel Prosser, of Virginia. In 1800, he organized six hundred people and nearly consummated what historians believe would have been a successful takeover of the town of Richmond, Virginia, by enslaved Africans. Only a last-minute thunderstorm and betrayal by nervous conspirators sabotaged the liberation movement. Denmark Vesey, though freed in 1800, later organized nine thousand people in 1822 to lead another nearly successful movement. Vesey saw both Prosser and Toussaint-Louverture as inspirations in his quest to free enslaved people in South Carolina.

Maria Stewart (1803–1879) of Boston, the first African American woman to record her speeches, spoke about slave rebellions and always referred to herself as an "African." She opposed the white-controlled American Colonization Society—a group that sought to repatriate free African Americans to Liberia—and helped to establish Boston as the seat of early black nationalism. Born in Connecticut in 1803, she remained outspoken about the need for African Americans to "build their own schools and stores." Her essays were published by the white abolitionist William Lloyd Garrison (1805–1879). Her book *Meditations from the Pen of Mrs. Maria Stewart* (1879) outlined her feelings about being an African in America.

The nineteenth century spawned other black nationalists who were vocal in their denunciation of African enslavement and their advocacy of an African homeland. In 1829, David Walker (1785–1830) published *Walker's Appeal in Four Articles: Together with a Preamble, to the Coloured Citizens of the World, but in Particular, and Very Expressly, to Those of the United States of America.* Widely known as Walker's *Appeal*, it asserted, "it is no more harm for you to kill the man who is trying to kill you than it is for you take a drink of water." The author saw violence as self-defense in the war against enslavement. Walker felt that peaceful means of eliminating this horrible system had failed and that violent retaliation was the only way to succeed. The *Appeal* was denounced by many abolitionists and supporters of repatriation, even by William Lloyd Garrison. The Georgia State Legislature placed a $10,000 reward on Walker's head if he were delivered alive and a $1,000 reward if he were delivered dead. In the South, it was illegal to distribute his powerful yet provocative missive. Walker died mysteriously nine months after the *Appeal* was published.

Walker's *Appeal* was well received by Pan-Africanist Martin Delany, the highest-ranking African American in the Union Army. Delaney's 1852 work, *The Condition, Elevation, Emigration, and Destiny of the Colored People of the United States*, was the first book that described the conditions of African Americans in the United States from a black nationalist perspective. Delany was strongly in favor of African Americans voluntarily immigrating to Africa, although he denounced the actions of the American Colonization Society as a form of forced emigration. In 1859, he signed a contract with the colonial territory known as the Slave Coast (modern-day Nigeria and adjacent territories) that allowed cotton production by free West Africans and the eventual repatriation of Africans in the Maafa.

Delany's ally, Alexander Crummell, shared similar emigrationist views. In 1861, he published *The Relations and Duties of Free Colored Men in America to Africa* and argued that because of the pervasiveness of white supremacist views in the United States, blacks should be motivated to return to Africa and support the continent's development. Crummell saw Christianity as a vehicle for achieving that development. In general, however, nineteenth-century black nationalists were ambivalent about the role that Christianity played in their liberation. Crummell adopted a traditional view of Christianity and molded it to fit his political views toward black nationalism. Although advocating self-help, which took the form of establishing the American Negro Academy while he taught at Howard University, Crummell was highly critical of Booker T. Washington's (1856–1915) obsequious attitude toward whites. Crummell's Christianity informed his 1882 book *The Greatness of Christ*, which argued for a social gospel that fused religion and works into the liberation of Africans from slavery.

In 1787, Richard Allen and Absalom Jones founded the Free African Society, and Allen's subsequent establishment of the African Methodist Episcopal (AME) Church reflected the "spiritual nationalism" advocated by late eighteenth- and nineteenth-century black nationalists, showing their firm commitment to Christianity. Remnants of African religious rites were already part of this modified Christianity in the form of music, worship, and scriptural interpretation. They formed the basis for what would be known in the twentieth century as *black theology*. Henry McNeal Turner (1834–1915) expanded the membership of Allen's AME Church during the latter half of the nineteenth century and advocated emigration to Haiti as he grew more disgruntled with the treatment of African Americans after the Civil War (1861–1865). His views were echoed by Henry Highland Garnet (1815–1882), who, like David Walker, called for violence in the fight to end slavery. Garnet ended a 1843 speech in Buffalo, New York, by declaring to the audience at the National Negro Convention:

> Let your motto be Resistance! Resistance! Resistance! No oppressed people have ever secured their Liberty without resistance. What kind of resistance you had better make, you must decide by the circumstances that surround you, and according to the suggestion of expediency. Brethren, adieu. Trust in the living God. Labor for the peace of the human race, and remember that you are three millions.

In the speech, Garnet cited the movements of Vesey, Turner, and Cinque as examples of the type of resistance that would eventually lead to the freedom of Africans in America. The use of violence as an alternative was a common thread through many of the writings of early black nationalists.

The century came to a close with the writings of one of the greatest Pan-Africanist theorists, Edward Wilmot Blyden (1832–1912). Born in the Virgin Islands, Blyden's unwavering devotion to Africa led him to attend

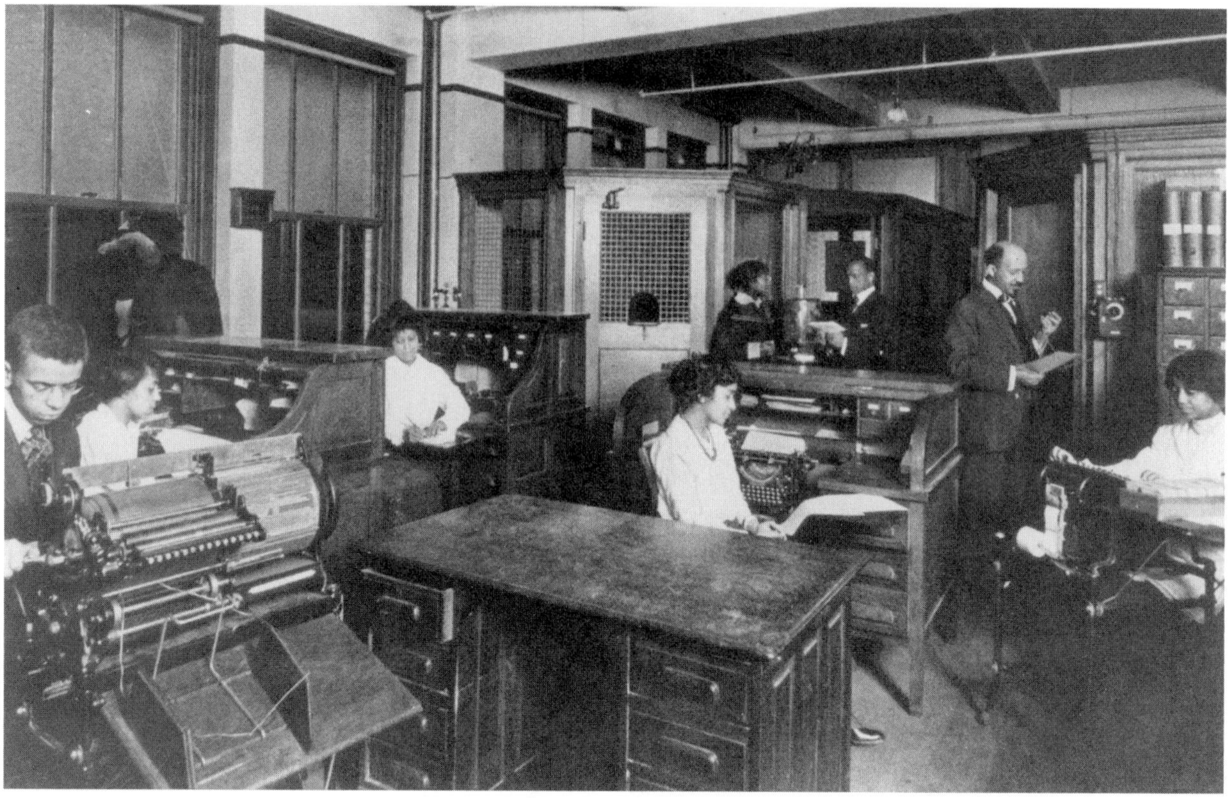

W. E. B. Du Bois, c. 1932. One of the leading figures of the black nationalist movement during the first quarter of the twentieth century, Du Bois (right) *is shown here with his production staff for the* Crisis, *an NAACP publication.* HULTON ARCHIVE/ARCHIVE PHOTOS/GETTY IMAGES

school in 1850 in the American Colonization Society's Liberian colony. Blyden's *A Vindication of the African Race* (1857) was one of the earlier treatises that challenged the notion of black intellectual inferiority. Blyden became a Liberian citizen, and his devout Christian beliefs resembled those of many nineteenth-century black nationalists. Blyden, like Crummell and Walker, considered a love for capitalism, Christianity, and Western education as key to the liberation of Africans in the Maafa. The contradictions in this view became the focus of contemporary black scholars, such as Wilson Jeremiah Moses and Frances Cress Welsing, who saw Christianity as part of the system of white supremacy that had historically oppressed Africans in the Maafa.

There was an elitism about nineteenth-century black nationalism that became even more apparent during the colonial struggle against the European powers during the second half of the twentieth century. This elitism emerged as one of the major deterrents to a "United States of Africa," as advocated by Kwame Nkrumah and Julius Nyerere.

The differences that emerged among the various factions of Pan-Africanism during the late nineteenth century were set aside in 1884 when German chancellor Otto von Bismarck (1815–1898) convened a meeting in Berlin of fourteen European nations regarding the partitioning of Africa. No Africans were invited, and what became known as the "scramble for Africa" began. The conference gave the European nations the opportunity to expand their political and economic powers without resorting to military conflict in Europe or Africa. From a Pan-African viewpoint, the conference was the most destructive action toward the African continent since the advent of enslavement. The economic dependency that the Berlin Conference spawned among African nations is still being felt on the continent in the twenty-first century.

BLACK NATIONALISM IN THE TWENTIETH CENTURY

Sixteen years after the Berlin summit, Henry Sylvester Williams (1869–1911) called the first Pan-African Conference in London as a reaction to what Europeans were doing in Africa. Thirty delegates attended the meeting, including a recent graduate of Fisk University named W. E. B. Du Bois (who at that time was working on a graduate degree at Harvard University), later to be dubbed the father of Pan-Africanism. There were discussions about bringing African persons together through better communication, but what united the delegation was the anxiety over how the European powers were shaping the destiny of Africans in the Maafa. It was in London that Du Bois first uttered his famous and prophetic phrase that the "problem of the twentieth century [would be] the problem of the color line—the relation of the darker to the lighter races of men in Africa, in America, and the islands of the sea."

Du Bois, along with Marcus Garvey of Jamaica and George Padmore of Trinidad, dominated the black nationalist movement during the first half of the twentieth century. Du Bois drew deeply from the influence of Crummell and Delany, but rejected their amalgam of Christianity in his Pan-Africanism. Garvey and Du Bois would clash despite the similarity of their views. The issue of skin color ran through the early writings of Du Bois, who referred to Garvey as a "fat black monkey." Garvey, in turn, called Du Bois, who claimed to be part Dutch and part French, a "mongrel." The dislike that the two leaders had for each other was personal and intense. Du Bois sought links with whites and other progressives interested in the future of Africa, while Garvey generally saw whites as destroying black self-determination. Garvey therefore wanted to exclude their participation in the Universal Negro Improvement Association (UNIA).

Du Bois's founding of the National Association for the Advancement of Colored People (NAACP) in 1909 became an anathema to Garvey. The First Black Parliament held in New York by Garvey in 1916 rivaled the 1900 London Pan-African Conference in size. Du Bois countered these large meetings by convening the First Pan-African Conference in Paris in 1919 and several others in following years. It was clear that Du Bois's meetings were more elitist and drew from the European-educated leaders of Pan-Africanism. No amount of editorializing by Du Bois against Garvey during his editorship of the NAACP's *Crisis* magazine affected Garvey's influence over the masses of black people throughout the African diaspora. What was even more frustrating to Du Bois was the tangible manifestation of Garvey's Pan-Africanism. Ships, businesses, and newspapers flourished under his leadership, whereas Du Bois's vision of Pan-Africanism remained primarily theoretical. Even during Garvey's imprisonment, his wife, Amy Jacques Garvey (1896–1973), ran the UNIA, while Henrietta Davis (1860–1941) directed the Black Star Line, a UNIA shipping company. Du Bois gloated when Garvey was convicted in 1922 by the government and deported in 1926, although their black nationalist goals were nearly identical. Garvey had been successful in mobilizing the largest mass movement ever among African Americans, but the visceral contempt that he and Du Bois had for one another hindered the realization of their dream of an "Africa for Africans."

In 1909, Du Bois proposed the publication of an "Encyclopedia Africana," a Pan-African treatise that would examine the world from an African-centered point of view—an important perspective not found in European-centered encyclopedias. Lacking the funds in the United States for its completion, Du Bois later revived the project at Kwame Nkrumah's invitation during his self-imposed exile in Ghana, but he never saw the project realized. The project was later resurrected by a publishing team in Accra, Ghana, under the title *Encyclopaedia Africana*.

The 1920s saw the emergence of black nationalistic expression throughout the Maafa. In the United States, it was called the Harlem Renaissance and was led by the poetry and writing of persons such as Claude McKay, Zora Neale Hurston, Countee Cullen, Langston Hughes, Jessie Fauset, and Alain Locke. In Africa and in other parts of the diaspora, Aimé Césaire, Léon Damas, and Léopold Senghor created a movement known as *Négritude*. A reaction against colonialism in general and Francophone colonialism specifically, the movement had inherent contradictions. While describing an "African personality" common to all black people in the world, it was heavily influenced by a love for the colonial powers and sought to merge the two together in what was really an "African-European" personality. The effects of nearly a half-century of colonialism were evident in the psychological attachment that many Africans still felt toward their European colonizers, and while Négritude reacted to the colonized mentality, many felt it did not go far enough in its denunciation of European domination and its support of the nascent freedom struggles beginning in Africa.

Garvey's influence on black nationalism lasted for the remainder of the twentieth century and was dynamically linked to several movements. Jamaicans were attracted to his reference to the rise of kings in Africa. In 1928, when Lij Ras Tafari Makonnen (1892–1975) was crowned Haile Selassie I of Ethiopia, another black nationalist religion, Rastafarianism, was born. Rastafarianism established its roots in Jamaica, but its influence has been global with musicians such as Bob Marley and Peter Tosh teaching others about the white supremacist world known as "Babylon." It emphasized pride in appearance, and the religion's "dreadlocks" hairstyle has become famous around the world.

Garvey's death in 1940 did not subdue his influence on black nationalism. Elijah Poole (1897–1975), a Georgia farmer who had come under the influence of Islam in 1931, began to carve out an urban religion known as the

Nation of Islam. The new religion included a mystical theology that described the white man as the "devil" and characterized African Americans as a "lost people" in a strange land. C. L. R. James (1901–1989) fused Marxism with black nationalism in England. In 1938, James published *The Black Jacobins*, a book that provided a Marxist critique of the Haitian Revolution under Toussaint-Louverture. With Duse Mohamed Ali (1866–1945) and Adelaide Hayford (1868–1960), England became the center of black nationalism in Europe by the 1920s. George Padmore befriended Du Bois and Nkrumah as the Gold Coast (modern-day Ghana) began its struggle for independence from the United Kingdom. Padmore rejected Marxism when it took a soft approach to the colonization of Africa, and his vocal opposition to its indifference toward the Third World led to his break from the philosophy. His criticism of the Communist Party eventually led to his ouster in 1934, and he spent his final years in England and the Gold Coast.

The aftermath of World War II (1939–1945) forced the end of the colonial system. The colonized nations of Africa with their allies in the United States and Great Britain took notice of this and called for a Fifth Pan-African Congress in 1945. This conference, held in Manchester, England, included T. R. Makonnen of Ethiopia, George Padmore of Trinidad, Kwame Nkrumah of the Gold Coast, Jomo Kenyatta of Kenya, and Chairman Peter Millard of British Guiana. Its honorary chair was W. E. B. Du Bois. Padmore advised the politically minded Nkrumah to return to the Gold Coast and become involved with the rapidly evolving anticolonial waves sweeping the country. Nkrumah's subsequent rise to power in the Gold Coast was heavily influenced by the ideas of Padmore.

Nkrumah made several attempts at uniting Africa's newly independent nations. The Gold Coast attended and was inspired by the final declaration of the 1955 Bandung Conference, where twenty-four nations called for increased economic, political, and educational cooperation among their countries. The conference also featured a forceful condemnation of colonialism on the continent. In 1958, just one year after becoming prime minister of the newly independent Ghana, Nkrumah called for the first Conference of Independent African States. The eight states in attendance included members above and below the Sahara, whose delegates discussed the challenges ahead of them as independent states. That same year, Guinea became independent of France under the leadership of Ahmed Sékou Touré (1922–1984) and rejected France's offer to become part of what was referred to as the "New French Community." France's anger led it to order its colonial bureaucrats home, which caused the collapse of the infrastructure of the country. Touré turned to several nations to aid the newly freed Guinea. Nkrumah answered Touré's call and formed a union between the two nations outlined in the Conakry Declaration of 1959. The Central Intelligence Agency (CIA) added to the chaos of independence by participating in the destabilization of the Congo and the assassination of Patrice Lumumba in 1964. Nkrumah was ousted from Ghana in a coup d'état in 1966.

In the United States, black nationalism took a back seat to integration when the nation began a long period of national introspection over treatment of its African American citizens after the *Brown v. Board of Education of Topeka* decision in 1954 declared segregated schools unconstitutional. Rosa Parks (1913–2005) and Martin Luther King Jr. (1929–1968) became household names as the struggle for liberation in the form of desegregation engulfed the nation. The most significant group espousing black nationalism during this time was the Nation of Islam. Elijah Poole had become the Honorable Elijah Muhammad and had built a religious group that rejected

Detail of a Mural Showing an Imprisoned Martin Luther King Jr. *The mural also depicts other key figures and events related to black nationalism.* FLIP SCHULKE/HISTORICAL/CORBIS

Christianity as a tool of the white man and encouraged its followers to change their last name to "X."

Before his release from prison in 1952, Malcolm Little (1925–1965) discovered the urban prophet's writings and converted to Islam, changing his name to Malcolm X. Marcus Garvey's legacy influenced Malcolm indirectly because his father had been an active member of the Universal Negro Improvement Association in Michigan. Despite his early career as a criminal, Malcolm had been transformed by the ideology in the teachings of those who told black people in the Maafa to look inward for self-determination. Malcolm's attraction to the Nation of Islam and his outspoken critique of white America soon became the subject of newspaper articles and television documentaries. The religion flourished with the attention toward civil rights and through Malcolm's fiery oratory.

Television aided the personalization of the civil rights movement, and Malcolm provided a counterpoint to Martin Luther King Jr.'s racial inclusiveness in a way similar to that of Du Bois, who had castigated Booker T. Washington. A speech that Malcolm delivered shortly after the 1963 March on Washington criticized the entire civil rights establishment, and his story about the "field Negro" and the "house Negro" captured the black nationalist philosophy of separation. His break with the Nation of Islam and his trips to Africa led him to increase his more-inclusive Pan-African views. He was assassinated in 1965 before these views could be fully articulated in a theory of Pan-Africanism. After the death of Elijah Muhammad in 1975, the Nation of Islam struggled with internal division, but would be revitalized by Louis Farrakhan. His Million Man March in 1995 attracted global attention.

The political assassinations of the 1960s brought a renewed interest in black nationalism as a result of the cynicism that African Americans felt toward the civil rights movement. Stokely Carmichael (1941–1998, later known as Kwame Ture), H. Rap Brown (now known as Jamil Abdullah Al-Amin), and others forced integrationists to deal with the issue of black pride and self-determination. The Black Pride movement begun by Malcolm X and exemplified in South Africa by Steven Biko (1946–1977) led to the Black Arts movement of the 1960s, which saw the most creative expression of black artists since the Harlem Renaissance. Nikki Giovanni, Don Lee (now known as Haki Madhubuti), and Gwendolyn Brooks (1917–2000) wrote poetry that was uncompromising in its call for black introspection into white supremacy. Plays, books, films, and festivals celebrated the African roots of the black struggle and created meetings that discussed black self-determination. In 1966, Maulana Karenga introduced Kwanzaa, an African American holiday that would be celebrated by many African Americans by the end of the century.

A 1972 meeting in Gary, Indiana, established a black political agenda similar to the Negro conventions of the nineteenth and early twentieth centuries. There were tensions that had always existed between those who wanted a Marxist approach to political empowerment and those who wanted nothing to do with any white philosophy. There had always been a close relationship between blacks and Marxists dating back to the early 1920s. Du Bois, Padmore, A. Philip Randolph (1889–1979), and later Amiri Baraka believed that a coalition of labor, progressive whites, and committed blacks could eliminate racial injustice. The most organized, though short-lived, movement of black Marxism was the Black Panther Party of the 1960s. Though it is popular to portray the organization as being all black, the Black Panther Party allowed for white membership from its very beginning. Haki Madhubuti, offering a stinging rebuke of Marxism as a viable alternative to black suffering, argued in his 1978 book *Enemies: The Clash of Races*:

Poet Gwendolyn Brooks, at her desk in her Chicago home. *Black nationalism was a key theme in the poetry of Brooks, who was the first African American writer awarded a Pulitzer Prize.* **AP PHOTO**

Father and Son Lighting Kwanzaa Candles. *The renewed interest in black nationalism in the 1960s prompted the author and political activist Maulana Karenga to introduce Kwanzaa, an African American holiday that by the early twenty-first century was celebrated by many African Americans.* CORBIS

The conflict between black nationalists and Marxists continued with the formation of the Black Radical Congress, which convened its first annual meeting in June 1998. Formed immediately after the Million Man March, part of its aim was to regain influence over young black people, whom the organization's leaders believed had deserted Marxism in favor of the Afrocentric analysis espoused by Marimba Ani, Molefi Asante, John Henrik Clarke, and Théophile Obenga. The Black Radical Congress held its first meeting in Chicago and pointedly denounced Louis Farrakhan as being sexist, homophobic, and exclusionary. Attendees included socialists such as Angela Davis, Amiri Baraka, Manning Marable, Cornel West, and Barbara Smith. It was noted by many in attendance that "exclusionary ideologues," such as the Afrocentrists and the Nation of Islam's leaders, were absent as main program participants. Black nationalists argue that the absence of spirituality in Marxist ideology is antithetical to religious expression, which is an ever-present factor in most black nationalist ideology. Most black nationalists see spirituality as necessary in a world replete with white supremacy, and they struggle with a religious expression that will fit their aims. The rise of "urban religions" among young African Americans, such as the Ausar Auset Society, the Five Percent Nation, and the Nation of Islam, reflects the need of a younger generation to embrace faiths that speak to their condition. Contemporary hip-hop artists openly mention Louis Farrakhan and the "Mother" (Africa) in their lyrics. Their rhymes reflect the black nationalist tradition of making all things black, including religion.

> Our major problem is not with the white communists, but with their trained Black ones who are trying to co-opt Black nationalism and Pan Afrikanism to make these ideologies and movements something they ain't. There is in our midst the subtle presence of "Black Marxists" pushing a European socialist analysis of Black nationalism and Pan Afrikanism. The Marxist position is that white racism—which to us is the only functional system of racism in the world—is a result of the profit motive brought on by the European slave trade and that white racism or anti-Black feelings didn't exist before such time. The left (generally described as Marxist-Leninist) whether white or black has always been anti–Black nationalism and this can be documented. Yet, one of the major facts of history is that white racism preceded and advanced itself thousands of years before European capitalism and imperialism was even systematically conceived. It is important to understand that the ideology of white supremacy precedes the economic structure of capitalism and imperialism, the latter of which are falsely stated as the cause of racism.

REPARATIONS

Toward the end of the twentieth century, it became clear that the most significant contribution of black nationalism was its effort to build global support for reparations for Africans and people of African descent living in other places. With leaders such as Queen Mother (Audley) Moore (1898–1997), the reparations movement, long thought to be a marginalized black nationalist issue, entered mainstream dialogue when Randall Robinson's *The Debt: What America Owes to Blacks* (2000) hit best-seller lists. Robinson had been instrumental in focusing public attention during the 1980s on the antiapartheid movement. In *The Debt*, he eloquently expressed the enormous obligation that the United States owed the descendants of enslaved Africans. Groups that had strongly advocated reparations for many years, such as the National Coalition of Blacks for Reparations in America (N'COBRA), the National Black United Front (NBUF), and the December 12th Movement (D12), forged ties among their organizations and with traditional civil rights groups.

Randall Robinson, Executive Director of TransAfrica, 1984. *Robinson, who helped focus public attention during the antiapartheid movement of the 1980s, later pushed the issue of reparations into mainstream consciousness with his 2000 book,* The Debt: What America Owes to Blacks. TERRY ASHE/TIME & LIFE PICTURES/GETTY IMAGES

The first formal call for reparations occurred in Massachusetts in 1782 when an ex-slave known only as Belinda petitioned the Massachusetts legislature for reparations from her former master, Isaac Royall, whom she claimed had denied her "the enjoyment of one morsel of [his] immense wealth, a part whereof hath been accumulated by her own industry." The petition of an enslaved African to the legislature of Massachusetts is an eloquent statement and captured the essence of the reparations struggle by Africans in America. The poignancy of the appeal is reflected in the first sentences:

> To the honourable the senate and house of representatives, in general court assembled:
>
> The Petition of Belinda, an African
>
> THAT seventy years have rolled away; since she, on the banks of the Rio de Valta [Volta River in Ghana] received her existence. The mountains, covered with spicy forests—vallies, loaded with the richest fruits spontaneously produced—joined to that happy temperature of air, which excludes excess, would have yielded her the most complete felicity, had not her mind received early impressions of the cruelty of men, whose faces were like the moon, and whose bows and arrows were like the thunder and lightning of the clouds.

These opening sentences reveal Belinda's sense of dislocation, wrought by her enslavement. Belinda called herself an African and spoke longingly of her homeland and the mental anguish of being kidnapped at twelve and placed in bondage.

The "posttraumatic slave syndrome" is a recurring theme in the black redress movement and has been documented by several writers. Black social scientists have not been alone in discussing the lingering effects of enslavement on contemporary Africans and the need for addressing posttraumatic slave syndrome. White psychiatrists have long discussed this so-called mark of oppression, as have black psychiatrists and psychologists. The reparations struggle has been characterized by literature pointing to the need for "internal healing" and "self-repair" as a necessary condition for reparations. In fact, the two and a half centuries of enslavement saw a narrowing, but continual, stream of consciousness about things African—a river (to use Vincent Harding's metaphor) between newly stolen Africans conversing and already enslaved Africans who wanted to know about the lost homelands where they or their ancestors had been born.

Belinda knew that her petition for reparations was based on the damage done by her being stolen from Ghana. Her words reveal her awareness of being traumatized in her separation from her homeland, her parents, her friends, and her sense of self.

Belinda's petition argues that her labor had enriched her former master and that she had a right to lay claim on the accumulated wealth. Her appeal was successful for her freedom and the freedom of her daughter. She was also granted a small pension ($15 per month) from the wealth that had been accumulated by the Royall family on the Ten Hills Plantation operations as restitution for her forty years of enslavement. As a footnote, scholars speculate that the actual petition could not have been written by Belinda since she was illiterate, but was probably written by the black poet Phillis Wheatley or Primus Hall, the son of Prince Hall, who founded the first black Masonic lodge in the United States.

Belinda's petition was a milestone in reparations history. First, it showed how deeply embedded the black redress movement has always been in the lives of Africans in America. There are those who wish to mark the beginning of the reparations movement with the practice of giving freed African Americans "forty acres and a mule" during the Civil War, more than eighty-three years after Belinda's petition. Second, the petition showed how even during the period of enslavement, an American legal body recognized the justice of reparations for unpaid labor, unjust enrichment, and crimes against humanity. This position would be affirmed sixty years later when President John Tyler (1790–1862), on December 6, 1842, in his second State of the Union address, quoted from the Tenth Article of the Treaty of Ghent, signed in 1814 by the United States and Great Britain, which ended the War of 1812. It plainly and unequivocally stated that "the traffic in slaves is irreconcilable with the principles of humanity and justice." Third, the Massachusetts legislature did not view Belinda's petition as a "handout," but rather a compensatory act for an injustice perpetrated on her and her family. It affirmed Belinda's efforts to secure reparations from those who committed crimes against humanity in the form of enslavement.

The most common thread running through the black nationalist movement in the United States is reparations. Its largest modern expression occurred during the United Nations World Conference against Racism (WCAR), held in Durban, South Africa, in august and September 2001. At the conference, black nationalists from all over the world persuaded the United Nations to declare the transatlantic slave trade a crime against humanity and made reparations one of the gathering's top three issues. Even though the tragic events of September 11, 2001, occurred within one week of the close of the UN conference, the issue of reparations became part of the global dialogue on race. In October 2002, nearly 1,200 delegates from thirty countries met in Bridgetown, Barbados, and formed the Global Afrikan Congress (GAC). The GAC was a direct outgrowth of the African and African Descendants Caucus formed at the WCAR. GAC members represent more than thirty-five nations, and the congress is arguably the largest Pan-African/black nationalist group in the world, since organizations and not individuals seek membership, a model based on the work of Marcus Garvey.

Though in existence prior to the WCAR, the Reparations Coordinating Committee—chaired by Harvard law professor Charles Ogletree and consisting of other high-profile attorneys, such as Johnnie Cochran (1937–2005), Willie Gary, and Alexander Pires—began to seek legal redress for the impact of enslavement on African Americans. Deadria Farmer-Paellmann, a longtime reparations advocate, filed suit in New York in March 2002 against three corporations, Aetna Life Insurance, CSX Railroad, and Fleet Bank, for their active roles in perpetuating African American enslavement. Another suit quickly followed, with the expectation that several more would come to challenge the complicity of

Demonstration for Reparations, National Mall, Washington, DC, 2002. *One of the hundreds of people demonstrating for reparations was Borneti Phillips, whose ancestor, Robson, had been enslaved in Uganda and brought to the United States in 1786.*
MANNY CENETA/GETTY IMAGES

Demonstration for Reparations for Racial Injustices, New Haven, CT, June 2002. *Reparations activism, anchored firmly in the black nationalist tradition, became the most significant social justice movement in the United States since the civil rights era.* **AP IMAGES**

private corporations and the U.S. government in the enslavement of Africans. During the first half of 2005, JPMorgan Chase and Wachovia Bank not only apologized for their slave-trading pasts, but "made restitution" for them by establishing scholarships for African American high school graduates in Louisiana and donating to traditional civil rights organizations in North Carolina. These funds totaled nearly $16 million dollars and were cynically referred to by some black nationalists as "reparations down payments."

On December 13, 2006, Farmer-Paellmann won a historic victory for the reparations movement. In the U.S. Court of Appeals in Chicago, the three-judge panel ruled that corporations concealing their slave-trading past from consumers were guilty of consumer fraud. This was the first legal victory in the long struggle for reparations and will, no doubt, form the basis of many lawsuits in the future.

Reparations activism, anchored firmly in the black nationalist tradition, became the most significant social justice movement in the United States since the civil rights era and caught many mainstream human rights groups off guard. Many were forced to balance advocacy for reparations with white board members who saw reparations as an "extremist" movement devoid of civil rights implications. The leaders of these groups, however, knew that at the grassroots level—where black nationalism historically has its strongest following—it had grown into an issue that mainstream civil rights groups could not ignore. Furthermore, the international conversation on reparations forged strong bonds between black nationalist groups and traditional civil rights organizations, with dialogues that would have been impossible in the late 1990s. The dialogues continue into the twenty-first century, with major civil rights organizations (e.g., the NAACP) holding major forums on reparations during their conventions.

With the 2008 election of Barack Obama as president of the United States, there was mounting concern among many black nationalists that Obama's presidency would somehow hinder the struggle for reparations and lull Africans into a dreamlike state of acceptance of a world that assaulted them physically, psychologically, culturally, economically, and educationally. History belies this concern, since the black nationalist struggle has always been independent of the tenure of elected officials and not dependent on any administration in office in any nation. This is not only true in the United States but internationally as well. Nigerian M. K. O. Abiola's (1937–1998) strong advocacy of reparations took place under the repressive regimes of Ibrahim Babangida and Sani Abacha (1943–1998), resulting in Abiola's mysterious death, rumored to have been orchestrated by the CIA. Similarly, the work of Queen Mother Moore, Marcus Garvey, and James Forman (1928–2005) took place during periods when reparations for enslaved American Africans were unthinkable. The anxious and conspiratorial reaction to the Obama presidency by some black nationalists failed to consider the legacy of Africans' struggle for justice, regardless of *who* is in office.

A somewhat paternalistic view about the euphoria surrounding Obama's rise to power and those who supported him was voiced by some black nationalists immediately after his election, as if the thinking of Africans had been put on hold and their brains downloaded with "Obamania." Others saw Obama's election as an *achievement* rather than a *victory*, since the struggle for racial justice would continue. Most black nationalists viewed his election as an opportunity to consolidate the drive for reparations and expand the efforts of greater political education among Africans. They argued that black political organizing and the exposure of young people to the philosophy of black nationalism would be much easier given Obama's popularity in black communities both nationally and internationally.

The reaction to his election should be understood not only *politically*, but *psychologically* as well. Some reasoned that the tears Africans shed on the night of November 4, 2008, were similar to the ones cried in 1967 when Carl Stokes became the mayor of Cleveland, Ohio, and ushered in the modern era of black elected officials holding high offices. Nationalists openly discussed the psychological impact among Africans of seeing an intact black family occupying the most powerful political residence in the world. Local, state, and national political action has always been a hallmark of black nationalism and continues to be in what has been dubbed the "age of Obama."

BLACK NATIONALISTS AND PAN-AFRICAN THEORISTS

(Some biographical profiles may appear in other chapters. To locate profiles more readily, please consult the index.)

RICHARD ALLEN

See chapter 17, Religion.

MARIMBA ANI (1943–)

Pan-Africanist Scholar, Civil Rights Activist, Author. Marimba Ani was brought to the Department of Africana and Puerto Rican Studies by Dr. John Henrik Clarke in 1974 as she was completing her Ph.D. dissertation at the Graduate Faculty of the New School in New York City. She had worked as a field organizer for the Student Nonviolent Coordinating Committee (SNCC) in Mississippi from 1963 to 1966, and had acted as director of freedom registration for the Mississippi Freedom Democratic Party in 1964, which challenged the all-white Mississippi delegation to the Democratic National Convention in Atlantic City that summer. Dr. Clarke became Marimba Ani's *Jegna* (warrior-teacher, intellectual father, ideological influence) as she moved back to New York and into graduate school. It was through his influence that she became committed to Pan-African liberation.

After having traveled in Africa, Marimba Ani (born Dona Richards) began formal study of the nature of African civilization, focusing on the "deep thought" that underlies its fundamental common cultural themes and the varying constructs of African social organization. She has done extensive work on African spiritual conceptions and systems. She is using her articulation of the African worldview as a frame of reference from which to critique European cultural thought, and to construct paradigms for Pan-African reconstruction.

Marimba Ani has developed the concepts of *Maafa*, *Asili*, *Utamawazo*, and *Utamaroho* as part of an ongoing process of African-centered reconceptualization that involves several Pan-African scholars. She has helped to initiate an intellectual and ideological movement, the purpose of which is to construct a theoretical framework that will allow people of African descent to explain the universe as it reflects their collective interests, values, and vision.

Dr. Ani's most recent work has been the development of the Maat/Maafa/Sankofa paradigm as an analytical tool for understanding and explaining the African experience in the diaspora and to suggest modalities for cultural reconstruction. Dr. Ani lectures throughout the United States, the Caribbean, Europe, and Africa on this new theoretical construct, which is part of her endeavor to develop a pragmatic African cultural science that can become the basis for the creation of African institutions and nation-building in the diaspora.

EDWARD WILMOT BLYDEN (1832–1912)

Black Nationalist, Educator, Repatriationist. Although he was not American, Edward Blyden had a great influence on American Pan-African philosophy. He wrote about blacks in Africa and America and about Christianity and Islam. Later, he held many different political and diplomatic offices in Liberia.

Blyden was born in 1832 in St. Thomas, Virgin Islands. When he was twelve, a white pastor undertook his education and encouraged him to become a minister. When he was eighteen, he went to the United States, but was unable to find a seminary that would accept a black student. Instead, under the sponsorship of the New York Colonization Society, he traveled to Liberia to study at the new Alexander High School in Monrovia. Seven years later, he became the principal of the school.

As a writer and editor, Blyden constantly defended his race, championed the achievements of other blacks, attacked slavery, and advocated the repatriation of blacks in Africa. As a teacher, he held many prominent posts at Liberia College. He was a professor of classics from 1862 to 1871 and the school's president from 1880 to 1884. At the same time, Blyden was also a politician and diplomat in Liberia, holding many different offices. He was secretary of state from 1864 to 1866, minister of the interior from 1880 to 1882, minister to Britain from 1877 to 1878, as well as in 1892, and minister plenipotentiary to London and Paris in 1905.

Blyden traveled to the United States eight times. In 1861, he was commissioned by the Liberian government to interest Americans in a Liberian education. He returned the following year to recruit African American immigrants to Africa. His last visit in 1895 was in hope of furthering racial accommodation in the South so that racial problems in the United States would not travel to Africa with new emigrants.

Because of his own religious training, Blyden was interested in Islam as a religion for Africans. Between 1901 and 1906, he was director of education in Sierra Leone. He studied both Christianity and Islam extensively and summed up his views in an influential book, *Christianity, Islam, and the Negro Race* (1887).

STOKELY CARMICHAEL

See chapter 7, Civil Rights.

JACOB H. CARRUTHERS (1930–2004)

Black Nationalist, Educator, Author. Born on February 15, 1930, in Dallas, Texas, Jacob Hudson Carruthers received his B.A. from Sam Houston College, his M.A. from Texas Southern University, and his Ph.D. in political science from the University of Colorado. In 1950, he was among the first African Americans to integrate the University of Texas Law School. After teaching at Kansas State University from 1966 to 1968, he moved to Chicago and joined the faculty of the Center for Inner City Studies at Northeastern Illinois University. The center is considered one of the foremost institutions in the world in studying the impact of African culture, politics, and history on the world.

Carruthers was the author of several books, including *Essays in Ancient Egyptian Studies* (1984), and *The Irritated Genie: An Essay on the Haitian Revolution* (1985), and *Intellectual Warfare* (1999). He was also one of the founders of the Association for the Study of Classical African Civilizations. He lectured at universities around the world and was well-known for his study tours of ancient Egypt. It is estimated that the study tours included nearly two thousand students, teachers, artists, and scholars from across the world.

Carruthers died on January 4, 2004, in Chicago. In honor of his work, the Center for Inner City Studies at Northeastern Illinois University was renamed the Jacob Carruthers Center for Inner City Studies.

JOHN HENRIK CLARKE (1915–1998)

Black Nationalist, Educator, Author. John Henrik Clarke was born on January 1, 1915, in Alabama. His family moved to Georgia when he was four, and he was raised in the South. Despite an aptitude for reading, he was forced from school after the eighth grade by poverty. In 1933, he left Georgia to go to Harlem and begin a new life.

In Harlem, Clarke discovered new reading materials on African American history. He studied at New York and Columbia universities, and found a mentor in the historian Arthur Schomburg. After serving in the U.S. Army during World War II, he began to teach African American history at community centers in Harlem. From 1956 to 1958, he taught at the New School for Social Research in New York. He then traveled to West Africa and taught at universities in Ghana and Nigeria.

In 1964, Clarke was licensed to teach at People's College on Long Island and began a career in academia. Clarke was a leading exponent of Afrocentric scholarship and the Black Power movement. In 1969, he began teaching at Hunter College, City University of New York, and in 1970 was appointed a professor in the Department of Black and Puerto Rican Studies. Clarke retired in 1985.

On July 16, 1998, Clarke died of a heart attack. He made contributions to African and African American studies for more than six decades. He wrote six books and edited or contributed to seventeen others, in addition to helping found several important black periodicals. Besides his academic work, Clarke published more than fifty short stories.

ALEXANDER CRUMMELL (1819–1898)

Black Nationalist, Repatriationist, Minister, Author. Alexander Crummell was born in New York City on March 3, 1819. Crummell began his education at the Mulberry Street School in New York City. In 1831, he began attending high school but transferred in 1835 to a school founded by abolitionists in Canaan, New Hampshire. The school was destroyed by a mob of angry townspeople, and Crummell began attending the Oneida Institute in Whitesboro, New York. He later studied in Boston and was ordained in the Episcopal Church in 1844. In 1847, he traveled to England, where he studied at Queens College, Cambridge, from 1851 to 1853 and was awarded an A.B. degree.

Crummell then spent several years in Liberia as professor of mental and moral science at the College of Liberia and in Sierra Leone. In 1873, he returned to St. Mary's Mission in Washington, D.C., and founded the St. Luke's Protestant Episcopal Church. In 1897, he was instrumental in the founding of the American Negro Academy.

Crummell published three collections of his essays and sermons, titled *The Future of Africa* (1862), *The Greatness of Christ* (1882), and *Africa and America* (1892). Crummell died on September 10, 1898, at Point Pleasant, New York.

PAUL CUFFEE (1759–1817)

Black Nationalist, Repatriationist, Entrepreneur. Paul Cuffee was born January 17, 1759, on Cuttyhunk Island near New Bedford, Massachusetts. He was the son of Cuffee Slocum and Ruth Moses, a Wampanoag Indian.

When Cuffee was sixteen, he became a sailor on a whaling vessel. After making numerous voyages, he was captured by the British and later released. He then studied arithmetic and navigation, but soon returned to the sea. By 1795, he had his own ship, the *Ranger*, and in eleven years he had become a landholder and owner of numerous other sailing vessels. He employed only African Americans on all of his ships because he believed in creating wealth within African American communities and showing whites that blacks were competent in the business of merchant seamanship.

Besides being a merchant seaman, Cuffee was also a black nationalist activist. He discarded his father's slave surname and took his father's Christian first name in its place. He filed suffrage complaints in Massachusetts court and, although unsuccessful, his legal action laid the groundwork for later civil rights legislation.

Cuffee was also a believer in free blacks repatriating to Africa. In 1811, he sailed to Sierra Leone, where he founded the Friendly Society, which helped African Americans return to Africa. In 1815, he sailed with thirty-eight colonists for Africa. It was to be his last voyage. He died on September 9, 1817.

ANGELA Y. DAVIS

See chapter 7, Civil Rights.

MARTIN ROBINSON DELANY (1812–1885)

Black Nationalist, Repatriationist, Military Officer, Physician, Author. Born in Charles Town, Virginia, in 1812, Martin Delany received his early education from a book peddler who also served as an itinerant teacher. Since African Americans in the South were forbidden to learn to read, his family was forced to flee north to Pennsylvania so that their children could continue to study. When Delany was nineteen years old, he left home to seek further education. He then studied with a divinity student and a white doctor for a time.

Martin Robinson Delany, c. 1865. *A physician who served in the Civil War as a surgeon with the 54th Massachusetts Volunteer Infantry, Delany was an ardent black nationalist who advocated emigration to establish an independent colony for African Americans in South America or Africa.* **HULTON ARCHIVE/ ARCHIVE PHOTOS/GETTY IMAGES**

As an adult, Delany became involved in the antislavery and literacy movements. He also began to publish the *Mystery*, a weekly newspaper devoted to news of the antislavery movement. When it folded after only a year, Delany became coeditor of the *North Star*, a newspaper started by Frederick Douglass.

In 1848, Delany quit the *North Star* to pursue his medical studies. After being rejected because of his race by several prominent Pennsylvania medical schools, he was able to attend Harvard Medical School. However, after a year, he was expelled because of his race. Although he did not receive his degree, he did learn enough to practice medicine for the rest of his life. In the 1850s, he saved many lives during a fierce cholera epidemic in Pittsburgh.

Delany became an ardent black nationalist and recommended emigration to establish an independent colony for African Americans in South America or Africa. He wrote on the subject, held several national conventions, and set out on an exploratory expedition to Africa.

After the Emancipation Proclamation of 1863, Delany met with President Abraham Lincoln to discuss the establishment of African American regiments in the army. Lincoln commissioned him as the first African American major and highest-ranking person of color in the U.S. Army.

After the Civil War, Delany worked with reconstructionists to get fair treatment for newly freed slaves, and he continued to advocate emigration to Africa. He also continued to pursue his scholarship and published *Principia of Ethnology: The Origin of Races and Color* in 1879, in which he discussed the role of black people in the world's civilization. He died in 1885, before he was able to move to Africa.

WALLACE D. FARD

See chapter 17, Religion.

LOUIS FARRAKHAN (1933–)

Black Nationalist, Nation of Islam Leader. Born in New York City in 1933, Louis Farrakhan (then known as Louis Eugene Walcott) was an honor student at Boston English High School. After high school, he attended Winston-Salem Teacher's College, but left before graduating. Farrakhan then made a living as a violinist and calypso singer. While working as a singer in the 1950s, Farrakhan converted to Elijah Muhammad's Nation of Islam. He quickly worked his way up to a leadership position, becoming the minister of the Boston mosque.

In 1963, Farrakhan denounced Malcolm X after Malcolm's split with Elijah Muhammad, and Farrakhan assumed leadership of Malcolm's Harlem mosque. After Elijah Muhammad's death in 1975, Farrakhan briefly supported Muhammad's son and designated successor, Warith Muhammad, as leader of the Nation of Islam. Shortly after Warith Muhammad began accepting whites as members of the Nation of Islam, now renamed the World Community of Al-Islam in the West, Farrakhan split from the group and established a rival organization with about ten thousand members.

Farrakhan's vigorous support for Jesse Jackson's presidential candidacy in 1984 quickly became an issue after Farrakhan made several controversial statements, most notably, calling Judaism a "gutter religion." Overshadowed in the controversy was the involvement of Nation of Islam leaders in American electoral politics for the first time. Previously, Muslims had generally followed Elijah Muhammad's counsel not to vote or take part in political campaigns.

In January 1995, Qubilah Bahiyah Shabazz, the daughter of Malcolm X, was arrested and charged with trying to hire a Federal Bureau of Investigation (FBI) informant, Michael Fitzpatrick, to kill Farrakhan, whom some believe was involved in the 1965 assassination of her father. Farrakhan publicly defended Shabazz and claimed that the charges were an FBI attempt to entrap her.

On October 16, 1995, African American men from across the United States convened in Washington, D.C., for the Million Man March, organized by Farrakhan. Marchers were urged to make a commitment to improve themselves, their families, and their communities. The U.S. Park Service and organizers of the march have disagreed as to how many people actually attended the rally, in which Farrakhan challenged the marchers to return home and work to make their communities "safe and decent places to live."

Farrakhan embarked on an eighteen-nation tour of Africa and the Middle East in early 1996. During the tour, he visited Iran and Libya, nations that the United States believes support international terrorism. Farrakhan, always a lightning rod for controversy, was criticized for the trip.

In 1999, Farrakhan became gravely ill with prostate cancer and sought medical treatment in Phoenix, Arizona. He rebounded in 2000 and continued to be politically active. In June 2001, Farrakhan met with nationally prominent rabbi Marc Schneier as a first step toward repairing his relationship with American Jews.

Later that same year, the British High Court overturned a fifteen-year ban on Farrakhan's entering the country. After the September 11, 2001, terrorist attacks on the United States, however, the British Parliament began deliberating whether it was safe to have Farrakhan in the country because of his very public views concerning America's retaliation against Osama bin Laden and the U.S. bombing of Afghanistan. In 2002, the British ban against Farrakhan was reinstated. In a U.S. court battle, Farrakhan was vindicated in early 2002 when the highest court in Massachusetts ruled that he had a legal right to bar women from a speech he gave there in 1994.

JAMES FORTEN (1766–1842)

Black Nationalist, Entrepreneur. James Forten was born to free African American parents in Philadelphia in September 1766. He studied at a Quaker school, but quit when he was fifteen to serve as a powder boy aboard the privateer *Royal Louis* during the American Revolution. He was captured by the British and held prisoner for seven months. Forten eventually spent a year in England, where he was introduced to abolitionist philosophy.

After returning to America, Forten became an apprentice to a sailmaker. In 1786, he became foreman, and by 1798 he was owner of the company. The business prospered and employed forty workers in 1832. By the 1830s, Forten had become active in the abolitionist movement and was a strong opponent of African colonization. He became a noted pamphleteer, a nineteenth-century form of social activism, and was an early fund-raiser for William Lloyd Garrison's abolitionist newspaper, the *Liberator.*

Forten was president and founder of the American Moral Reform Society and was active in the American Antislavery Society. He was a vigorous opponent of northern implementation of the Fugitive Slave Act of 1793. Forten died in Philadelphia on March 4, 1842.

HENRY HIGHLAND GARNET (1815–1882)

Black Nationalist, Religious Leader. Henry Highland Garnet was born a slave in Maryland on December 23, 1815. His family escaped to Pennsylvania and later moved to New York. In 1826, Garnet began attending the African Free School, where he was first exposed to abolitionism. In 1829, he made several voyages on schooners, working as a steward. After returning from one of these voyages, he discovered his family was in hiding from slave catchers and all their possessions had been taken.

In 1835, Garnet and his friend Alexander Crummell attended the Noyes Academy in Canaan, New Hampshire, until hostile residents destroyed the school. They then attended the Oneida Institute in Whitesboro, New York. Garnet graduated with honors in 1840 from Oneida.

Garnet worked as a Presbyterian minister and abolitionist after his graduation. He was also active in the temperance movement. By this time, Garnet had become dissatisfied with the moral suasion used by abolitionists, and he urged direct action by slaves against the institution of slavery. He also became active in the American Colonization Society.

Garnet supported the employment of African American soldiers by the Union Army during the Civil War, and, in 1865, he became the first African American to deliver a sermon in the chamber of the U.S. House of Representatives. Garnet was appointed minister to Liberia in 1881. He died there the following year.

MARCUS GARVEY (1887–1940)

Black Nationalist, Pan-African Theorist. Marcus Garvey was born in St. Ann's Bay, Jamaica, on August 17, 1887. He moved to Kingston when he was fourteen years old and found work in a print shop. Garvey became acquainted with the living conditions of the laboring class in Kingston, and he quickly involved himself in social reform, participating in the first Printers' Union strike in Jamaica in 1907 and setting up a newspaper, the *Watchman.* He left Jamaica to earn money, and found similar living conditions for blacks in Central and South America.

Black Nationalist Marcus Garvey Boarding Ship Bound for Jamaica from New Orleans, 1927. *Hundreds of supporters bid farewell to Garvey when he was deported following his jailing on mail-fraud charges.* **EVERETT COLLECTION/SUPERSTOCK**

Universal Negro Improvement Association (UNIA) Hand Card Bearing Portrait of Marcus Garvey and the UNIA Flag and Star. *Garvey founded the UNIA in 1914 to support his plan to build an African nation-state. Thousands eventually joined the organization, and more than thirty branches were soon created.* SCHOMBURG CENTER FOR RESEARCH IN BLACK CULTURE; THE NEW YORK PUBLIC LIBRARY; ASTOR, LENOX AND TILDEN FOUNDATIONS

Garvey returned to Jamaica in 1911 and began to lay the groundwork for the Universal Negro Improvement Association (UNIA). He left for England in 1912 to find additional financial backing. While there, he met a Sudanese-Egyptian journalist, Duse Mohamed Ali. While working for Ali's publication, *African Times and Oriental Review*, Garvey began to study history, particularly of Africa. He also read Booker T. Washington's *Up from Slavery* (1901), which advocated black self-help. After corresponding with Washington, Garvey traveled to the United States, arriving on March 23, 1916. In the United States, he conducted a lecture tour and visited Washington in Tuskegee.

In 1914, Garvey organized the UNIA and its coordinating body, the African Communities League. In 1920, the organization held its first convention in New York. The convention opened with a parade down Harlem's Lenox Avenue. That evening, before a crowd of 25,000, Garvey outlined his plan to build an African nation-state. In New York City, his ideas attracted support, and thousands enrolled in the UNIA. He began publishing the newspaper the *Negro World*, and toured the United States preaching black nationalism. In a matter of months, he had founded more than thirty UNIA branches and launched various business ventures, including the Black Star Shipping Line.

In the years following the organization's first convention, the UNIA began to decline in popularity. With the Black Star Line facing serious financial difficulties, Garvey promoted two new business organizations, the African Communities League and the Negro Factories Corporation. He also tried to salvage his colonization scheme by sending a delegation to persuade the League of Nations to transfer the African colonies taken from Germany during World War I (1914–1918) to the UNIA.

Mail-fraud charges led to Garvey's imprisonment in 1925 in the Atlanta Federal Penitentiary for a five-year term. In 1927, his sentence was commuted and he was deported to Jamaica by order of President Calvin Coolidge. Garvey then became involved in Jamaican politics, but electoral defeats ended his career. He died on June 10, 1940, in London.

ASA HILLIARD III (1933–2007)

Psychologist, Educator, Author. A professor of educational psychology, Asa Grant Hilliard III was born in Galveston, Texas, on August 22, 1933. After completing high school, Hilliard attended the University of Denver, earning his B.A. in 1955, his M.A. in counseling in 1961, and an Ed.D. in educational psychology in 1963.

After earning his bachelor's degree in psychology, Hilliard began teaching in the Denver public school system, where he remained until 1960. That year, he began as a teaching fellow at the University of Denver, where he remained until he earned his doctorate. Joining the faculty at San Francisco State University in 1963, Hilliard spent the next eighteen years there. While at San Francisco State, Hilliard first became department chairman and spent his final eight years as dean of education. He also served as a consultant to the Peace Corps and as superintendent of schools in Monrovia, Liberia, for two years. Departing from San Francisco State in 1980, Hilliard became the Fuller E. Callaway Professor of Urban Education at Georgia State University, serving in both the Department of Educational Policy Studies and the Department of Educational Psychology and Special Education.

Hilliard was a founding member of the Association for the Study of Classical African Civilizations and served as vice president. He also served as an expert witness in several federal court cases regarding test validity and bias, and was the developer with Listervelt Middleton of a 1986 educational television series, *Free Your Mind, Return to the Source: African Origins.* Hilliard wrote, cowrote, and edited numerous books and published many articles on a wide variety of topics, including ancient African history, teaching strategies, and public policy. Hilliard was the recipient of the Outstanding Scholarship Award from the Association of Black Psychologists (1984) and the Distinguished Leadership Award from the Association of Teachers of Education (1983), and in 1972 he was named a knight commander of the Liberian Humane Order of the African Redemption.

After contracting malaria in Ghana, Hilliard died on August 13, 2007, in Cairo Egypt. He was survived by his four children and his wife, Patsy Jo, the former mayor of East Point, Georgia, and a former school board member for the South San Francisco Unified School District.

ABSALOM JONES

See chapter 17, Religion.

CHARSHEE MCINTYRE (1932–1999)

Educator, Black Nationalist, Author. Charshee Charlotte Lawrence McIntyre was born in Andover, Massachusetts, on May 14, 1932, and was raised in Roxbury, Massachusetts. She married jazz instrumentalist Makanda Ken McIntyre in 1958, and helped George Wein, founder of the Newport Jazz Festival, to bring key jazz figures to the event. In her early thirties, McIntyre entered Central State University in Ohio to pursue her education. She transferred to Wesleyan University in Connecticut, majored in African history, and was inducted into Phi Beta Kappa after graduating summa cum laude in 1971. She earned an M.A. in philosophy (1975), an M.A. in African history (1978), and a Ph.D. in history (1984) from the State University of New York (SUNY) at Stony Brook. She taught at various universities in New York and New Jersey, including SUNY Old Westbury, Rutgers, and City College.

McIntyre was the first woman president of the African Heritage Studies Association. She also was active in the National Council for Black Studies, the Association for the Study of Classical African Civilizations (whose membership included John Henrik Clarke), First World, and the African American Heritage Association of Long Island.

In 1993, McIntyre published *Criminalizing a Race: Free Blacks during Slavery*, about the impact of African, Native American, and European worldviews on people of African descent. She believed that the struggle of Africans in the Maafa was primarily based on the ancient and sacred relationship between African men and women—a critical bond that had been severely damaged during the period of slavery and its aftermath. Her belief in the male-female bond in Africa influenced many black nationalists to reconsider and, in most cases, abandon their belief in the primacy of males at the expense of women.

When the 1999 African–African American Conference convened in Ghana on May 15, 1999, its proceedings paused when the news of her death reached the delegates.

AUDLEY MOORE (1898–1997)

Black Nationalist, Pan-African Theorist, Community Organizer. Audley Moore was born in New Iberia, Louisiana, on July 27, 1898. Her parents were both dead by the time she was fourteen, and she became the primary supporter for her two sisters. She worked as a nurse during World War I, and after moving to Anniston,

Audley "Queen Mother" Moore, during Tribute in New York, 1996. *Moore was a renowned African American community organizer and is widely considered one the leading black nationalist figures of the twentieth century. She is pictured with Winnie Madikizela-Mandela,* right, *and Kwame Ture (the former Stokely Carmichael),* center. AP PHOTO/KATHY WILLENS

Alabama, organized the first United Service Organizations (USO) for African American soldiers who had been denied entrance by the official USO. She also assisted them in receiving medical care and food.

Moving with her husband and sisters to New York City in the 1920s, Moore became an active member of the Communist Party and helped organize support for the 1932 Scottsboro Boys case in Alabama. She was considered the best African American community organizer in the country and helped local groups protest racist policies in housing discrimination, political prosecutions, and unfair employment practices. She created the model for organizing legal redress for political prisoners in the United States.

Moore became increasingly disenchanted with the Communist Party and resigned her membership in the 1950s. Her roots in Marcus Garvey's teachings could be heard in speeches that encouraged "denegroization" and a demand for reparations for Africans living in the Maafa. During the last twenty years of her life, she traveled internationally and continued to exhort others to pay attention to the "little people" who needed help against racism in the community. She traveled to Ghana, where she was officially installed in an Ashanti ceremony as a "queen mother." Nelson Mandela met with her during his visit to New York in 1990. She, Rosa Parks, and Dorothy Height were featured prominently by Louis Farrakhan at the Million Man March. Many believe that Queen Mother Moore, Marcus Garvey, and Elijah Muhammad are the greatest organizers of black nationalism of the twentieth century. She died on May 2, 1997.

Religious Leader Elijah Muhammad, 1960. *Nation of Islam leader Muhammad is considered one of the most important twentieth-century organizers of black nationalism.* HULTON ARCHIVE/GETTY IMAGES

ELIJAH MUHAMMAD (1897–1975)

Black Nationalist, Nation of Islam Leader. Elijah Muhammad was born Elijah Poole in Sandersville, Georgia, on October 10, 1897. His father was a Baptist preacher and former slave. As a boy, Elijah worked as a manual laborer. When he was twenty-six years old, he moved with his wife and two children to Detroit. In 1930, he met Fard Muhammad, also known as W. D. Fard, who had founded the Lost-Found Nation of Islam. Poole soon became Fard's chief assistant, and in 1932 Poole moved to Chicago, where he established the Nation of Islam's Temple Number Two. In 1934, he returned to Detroit. When Fard disappeared later that year, political and theological rivals accused Poole of foul play. He returned to Chicago where he organized his own movement's followers. In the resultant organization, which came to be known as the "Black Muslims," Fard was deified as Allah, and Elijah (Poole) Muhammad became known as "Allah's Messenger."

During World War II, Elijah Muhammad expressed support for Japan, on the basis of its being a nonwhite country, and was jailed for sedition. The time Muhammad served in prison was significant in his later, successful attempts to convert large numbers of black prison inmates, including Malcolm X, to the Nation of Islam. During the 1950s and 1960s, the Nation grew under Muhammad's leadership. Internal differences between Muhammad and Malcolm X, followed by a break between the two men and Malcolm's assassination, yielded a great deal of unfavorable media coverage but did not slow the movement's growth. In the late 1960s and early 1970s, Elijah Muhammad moderated the Nation's criticism of whites. When Muhammad died on February 25, 1975, the Nation was an important religious, political, and economic force among African Americans, especially in major cities.

Elijah Muhammad was not original in his rejection of Christianity as the religion of the oppressor. Noble Drew Ali and the Black Jews had arrived at this conclusion well before him. However, Muhammad was the most successful salesman for this brand of African American religion. He was able to build the first strong, African

National Convention of "Black Muslims," Chicago, February 1963. *In the 1950s and early 1960s, the Nation of Islam grew into an influential black nationalist organization under the leadership of Elijah Muhammad.* BETTMANN/CORBIS

American religious group in the United States that appealed primarily to unemployed and underemployed city dwellers. In addition, his message on the virtues of being black was explicit and uncompromising. He also sought to bolster the economic independence of African Americans by establishing schools and businesses under the auspices of the Nation of Islam.

KHALLID ABDUL MUHAMMAD (1948–2001)

Black Nationalist, Nation of Islam Leader. Khallid Abdul Muhammad was born Harold Moore Vann in January 1948 in Houston, Texas. He excelled in academics and athletics as a youth and graduated from high school in 1966. He then spent four years at Dillard University, where his attendance at a 1967 speech given by Nation of Islam figure Louis Farrakhan changed his life. He became one of Farrakhan's original security personnel and soon changed his name to Khallid Abdul Muhammad.

After the death of longtime Nation of Islam leader Elijah Muhammad in 1975, Khallid Muhammad relocated to Uganda to work with black nationalist leader Idi Amin. He returned to the United States after learning that Farrakhan was reviving the Nation of Islam. By the late 1970s, Muhammad was a minister of the group's Los Angeles mosque. Farrakhan depended heavily on him to help resurrect the Nation of Islam. Beginning in 1978, he and Farrakhan traveled by car throughout the United States establishing study groups and making speeches that eventually led to Farrakhan announcing the rebirth of the

Nation in 1981. Muhammad led the Nation's fund-raising, spoke on Farrakhan's behalf, and organized mosques that had deteriorated since the death of Elijah Muhammad. He later headed congregations in New York City and Atlanta. He continued to play a role in the Fruit of Islam, the security team assigned to protect the outspoken Farrakhan. In 1988, Khallid Muhammad was charged with the fraudulent use of a Social Security number to obtain a mortgage, and spent nine months in prison.

After his release, Muhammad became supreme captain of the Fruit of Islam, and in 1991 he became Farrakhan's national assistant, a position once held by Farrakhan and Malcolm X under Elijah Muhammad. Khallid Muhammad's speeches soon attracted renewed interest in the Nation of Islam, especially among prominent figures in rap music. His discourses often promoted an independent nation for people of African descent. In a 1993 oration in Union, New Jersey, Khallid Muhammad uttered fiery pronouncements about black-white relations, as well as anti-Semitic remarks, causing a controversy inside and outside the Nation of Islam. Farrakhan demoted Muhammad soon afterward. Despite the demotion, Khallid Muhammad continued to be popular on the lecture circuit, and he maintained ties with the Nation. He organized the Million Youth March in New York in October 1998.

From 1998 until his death from a brain aneurysm on February 17, 2001, Muhammad served as national chairman of the New Black Panther Party for Self-Defense, an organization dedicated to the self-help and defense of Africans in America. Rooted politically in Huey P. Newton's Black Panther Party of the 1960s, the group is active in the reparations movement. Attorney Malik Zulu Shabazz was elected to replace Muhammad, his close friend, as the group's chairman after Muhammad's death.

HUEY P. NEWTON

See chapter 9, National Organizations.

BOBBY SEALE

See chapter 9, National Organizations.

HENRY MCNEAL TURNER (1834–1915)

Black Nationalist, Repatriationist, Minister. Henry McNeal Turner was born on February 1, 1834, near Abbeville, South Carolina. He was ordained a minister in the African Methodist Episcopal (AME) Church in 1853 and became a bishop in 1880. In 1863, Turner became the first African American Army chaplain. He was also president of Morris Brown College in Atlanta for twelve years.

Turner was a leading advocate of repatriation. In 1876, he was elected vice president of the American Colonization Society. Turner was convinced that African Americans had no future in the United States. Instead, he felt that God had brought Africans to the New World as a means of spreading Christianity and preparing them to redeem Africa. Turner made several trips to Africa and lectured throughout the world. He edited and published several papers, including *Voice of Missions* and *Voice of the People*, in which he advocated African American repatriation to Africa. Turner died on May 8, 1915.

ROBERT F. WILLIAMS (1925–1996)

Civil Rights Activist. Robert Franklin Williams was born in Monroe, North Carolina, on February 26, 1925. In 1956, he was elected president of the Monroe NAACP. The chapter's membership had dwindled to six, so Williams went out and recruited working-class people and the unemployed to become members. This approach stood in contrast to the NAACP's usual practice of enlisting middle- and upper-class professionals.

Williams then targeted institutions in Monroe for desegregation. He first tried the county library, which was desegregated without protest. Williams then worked to desegregate Monroe's municipal swimming pool, which failed. In response, Williams led groups of African American youths on sit-ins and other organized protests.

In 1959, responding to the acquittal in Monroe of a white man for the attempted rape of a pregnant African American woman, Williams pronounced: "Since the federal government will not bring a halt to lynching in the South, and since the so-called courts lynch our people legally, if it's necessary to stop lynching with lynching, then we must be willing to resort to that method. We must meet violence with violence." The next day the national office of the NAACP suspended Williams for six months. Despite his suspension, he was reelected president of Monroe's NAACP in 1960.

After Williams was indicted for kidnapping, a charge he denied, he became a fugitive and fled to Cuba. While in Cuba during the early 1960s, Williams produced a revolutionary radio program, *Radio Free Dixie*, as well as a Cuban edition of the *Crusader*. In 1966, Williams sought refuge in the People's Republic of China. He published a pamphlet, *Listen Brother!* (1968), hoping to persuade African American servicemen to refuse to fight in Vietnam.

In 1968, a group of African Americans, dedicated to establishing a separate African American nation within the United States, formed the revolutionary Marxist-Leninist Republic of New Africa (RNA). The RNA elected Williams as its president-in-exile. In 1969, the U.S. embassy granted Williams a passport to return to the United States. Disillusioned with the RNA's internal struggles, he resigned as its president in December 1969.

Williams won a Black Image Award from a Michigan chapter of the NAACP in 1992. He died from Hodgkin's disease in Grand Rapids, Michigan, on October 15, 1996.

CONRAD W. WORRILL (1941–)

Civil Rights Activist. Conrad Walter Worrill was born August 15, 1941, in Pasadena, California. His mother, Anna, was the first African American to sing with the Pasadena Philharmonic Orchestra, and his father, Walter, managed a local YMCA. When Conrad was nine, the Worrill family moved to Chicago. He was interested in sports, and his early encounters with racism occurred when he was harassed by competitors during swim meets. Worrill was drafted into the U.S. Army in 1962, and was stationed in Okinawa, Japan. During this time, he became a voracious reader of African history and African American history, politics, education, and culture. Worrill entered college after his discharge from the army in 1964. He received a bachelor's degree in behavioral sciences from George Williams College in 1968 and a doctorate in 1973 from the University of Wisconsin. He also became an activist in the Black Power movement.

Worrill was instrumental in organizing for the election of Chicago's first black mayor, Harold Washington, in 1983. He was also one of the primary field organizers of the 1995 Million Man March in Washington, D.C., and was elected economic commissioner for the National Coalition of Blacks for Reparations in America (N'COBRA). In 1997, he led a delegation to Geneva, Switzerland, and presented to the United Nations a petition with more than 150,000 signatures charging the United States with genocide. Considered one of the most effective community organizers in the nation, Worrill was also involved with organizing the Durban 400, the largest delegation of Africans at the UN World Conference against Racism in Durban, South Africa, in 2001. Worrill also served as national chair of the National Black United Front, one of the oldest black nationalist organizing groups in the United States.

BOBBY E. WRIGHT (1934–1982)

Civil Rights Activist, Author. Bobby Eugene Wright was born March 1, 1934, in Hobson City, Alabama, one of six children of Myrtle and Bennie Wright. After high school, Wright moved to Chicago, where he showed an early interest in mathematics and science. During the 1960s and 1970s, he became one of the first African Americans to predict the future ubiquity of computers; though scorned for this predication, he encouraged others to learn the technology at a time when computer access was only available to a few. Wright received his doctorate in clinical psychology in 1972 from the University of Chicago, the first conferred upon an African American in twenty-two years. He was a special guest on the Committee of Science and Technology at the Sixth Pan-African Congress held at Tanzania in 1974, and he became very active in the "Chicago school" of black nationalism, which emphasized organizing, political involvement at all levels of the community, and coalition building with groups dedicated to Pan-Africanism.

Wright coined the term *mentacide*, which he defined as the "deliberate and systematic destruction of a group's mind with the ultimate objective being the extirpation of the group." In 1974, he published his seminal paper, "The Psychopathic Racist Personality," in the fall issue of *Black Books Bulletin*. He argued that racism and white supremacy are mental disorders and should be classified as such by the American Psychiatric Association. In the article, Wright notes:

> In a bullfight, after being brutalized while making innumerable charges at the movement of a cape, there comes a time when the bull finally turns and faces his adversary with the only movement being his heaving bloody sides. It is believed that for the first time he really sees the matador. This final confrontation is known as "the moment of truth." For the bull, this moment comes too late.

According to Dr. Wright, the experience of black people all over the world presents an analogous situation. For hundreds of years, European (white) matadors have been holding up the capes of democracy, capitalism, Marxism, religion, and education, and for hundreds of years, black people have been charging at the movement of these "capes." Like the bull, they are suffering from near fatal wounds and "indeed have arrived at our 'moment of truth.'"

Wright's organizational ties included the Association of Black Psychologists, the National Black United Front, and the Temple of the African Community of Chicago. The latter was founded by Dr. Jacob Carruthers, and Wright's association with the temple refutes the assertion by some groups that Wright was an "atheist." Instead, he rejected white expressions of religious thought among African people.

In the mid-1970s, Wright became director of the Garfield Park Comprehensive Mental Health Center on

Chicago's West Side, the largest mental health center in the United States. It was renamed the Bobby E. Wright Comprehensive Behavioral Center after his untimely death from cancer at age forty-eight on April 6, 1982.

MALCOLM X (EL-HAJJ MALIK EL-SHABAZZ) (1925–1965)

Black Nationalist. Born Malcolm Little in Omaha, Nebraska, on May 19, 1925, Malcolm was the son of a Baptist minister who was a supporter of Marcus Garvey's Universal Negro Improvement Association. In 1929, the family moved to Lansing, Michigan. While in Michigan, Malcolm's father was killed. In his autobiography, written with Alex Haley, Malcolm asserted that his father might have been killed by members of the Ku Klux Klan. His mother, stricken by the death of her husband and the demands of providing for the family, was committed to a mental institution.

Malcolm left school after the eighth grade and made his way to New York, where he worked as a waiter at Small's Paradise, a nightclub in Harlem. Malcolm eventually began selling and using drugs, then turned to burglary and was sentenced to a ten-year prison term on burglary charges in 1946. While in prison, Malcolm converted to the Nation of Islam, headed by Elijah Muhammad. Following his parole in 1952, Malcolm soon became an outspoken defender of Muslim doctrines, accepting the basic argument that evil was an inherent characteristic of the "white man's Christian world."

Unlike Elijah Muhammad, Malcolm sought publicity by making provocative statements on white supremacy to both black and white audiences. Based on the theology taught by Elijah Muhammad, he branded white people "devils," and spoke of a philosophy of self-defense and "an eye for an eye" when white supremacists attacked African Americans. When, in 1963, he characterized the Kennedy assassination as a case of "chickens coming home to roost," he was suspended from the Nation of Islam by Elijah Muhammad.

Disillusioned with Elijah Muhammad's teachings, Malcolm formed his own organizations, the Organization of Afro-American Unity and the Muslim Mosque, Inc. In 1964, he made a pilgrimage to Islam's holy city, Mecca, and adopted the name El-Hajj Malik El-Shabazz. The pilgrimage gave birth to the views that not all whites were evil and that African Americans could make gains by working through established channels.

Malcolm X, Nation of Islam National Minister, May 14, 1963. *Malcolm X addresses a rally in Harlem in support of desegregation in Birmingham, Alabama. He was assassinated in Harlem less than two years later.* BETTMANN/CORBIS

Malcolm's new view brought him death threats. On February 14, 1965, his home was firebombed. A week later, Malcolm was shot and killed at the Audubon Ballroom in Harlem. Although three men were arrested for the crime, there remains a controversy to the present day over who conspired to kill Malcolm.

Malcolm X had a profound influence on both blacks and whites. Many African Americans responded to a feeling that he was a man of the people, experienced in the ways of the street rather than the pulpit or the college campus, which traditionally had provided the preponderance of African American leaders. His emphasis on black pride and doing for oneself was in the tradition of black nationalism and was similar to the philosophy of Steven Biko of South Africa. Malcolm X provided a contrast to Martin Luther King Jr. and his idea of integration.

9

NATIONAL ORGANIZATIONS

Jessie Carney Smith

Organizations are one of the largest and most influential societal forces in the United States. Organizations emerged as the result of a recognized need in the African American community and have played an important part in the economic, social, cultural, and educational development of the targeted groups that they served. An important stimulus was the church, which early on encouraged literary societies among youth and also organized welfare leagues in cities where African American women migrated. In addition, important African American leaders such as Booker T. Washington called for group organization to promote black economic development, as seen, for example, in the formation of the National Negro Business League. Therefore, to study the history and culture of these organizations is to study important aspects of the life and culture of African American people and their social and cultural strivings. In *From Slavery to Freedom,* the historian John Hope Franklin acknowledges the various ways in which "African Americans were attempting to take their fate into their own hands and solve the problems as best they could" (8th ed., 2000, p. 318). Associations serve as the voice of their members and have been crucial in developing and disseminating information, ensuring representation for private interests, and promoting social and policy objectives.

A BRIEF HISTORY

EARLY AFRICAN AMERICAN ORGANIZATIONS

Because of restrictive ordinances and limited tolerance by whites, prior to the eighteenth century only the most informal and limited assembling of African Americans was permitted. Often meeting as religious assemblies, African Americans were forced to meet secretly and in small numbers. Thus, the very first African American organizations to exist in the United States cannot definitively be identified.

The Free African Society, organized in Philadelphia in 1787, has been generally accepted as the first African American organization in the United States. Founded by two ministers, Richard Allen and Absalom Jones, the Free African Society served as an important source of political consciousness and welfare for African Americans throughout the country by combining economic and medical aid for poor African Americans with support of abolition and communications with African Americans in the South.

The abolitionist movement of the nineteenth century produced numerous organizations concerned with issues of importance to African Americans, including the American Colonization Society (founded in 1816), the New England Anti-Slavery Society (founded in 1832), and the American Anti-Slavery Society (founded in 1833). Although most of these organizations were dominated by whites, African American leaders, including Paul Cuffee and Frederick Douglass, played an active role in the movement and in antislavery organizations of the time.

During the late nineteenth and early twentieth centuries, many African American organizations came into existence. The primary concern of most of these groups was education, improvement of the race as a whole, and religious training. In 1895, the National Medical Association was founded to further the interests of African American physicians, pharmacists, and nurses.

Original Leaders of the Niagara Movement, Posing in Front of Niagara Falls, NY, 1905. *Founded by a group of African American intellectuals headed by W. E. B. Du Bois* (second from right, center row)*, the Niagara Movement from its creation called for full equality for African Americans in American life.* SCHOMBURG CENTER FOR RESEARCH IN BLACK CULTURE; THE NEW YORK PUBLIC LIBRARY; ASTOR, LENOX AND TILDEN FOUNDATIONS

African American women also sought a national network to bring about reform for women and for the race. In 1896, the National Federation of Afro-American Women and the Colored Women's League fused to create the National Association of Colored Women. Mary Church Terrell was its first president. In 1900, Booker T. Washington organized the National Negro Business League to promote commercial development. The success of these organizations stimulated an increase in new African American organizations, such as the National Negro Bankers Association, the National Negro Press Association, and the National Negro Funeral Directors Association.

THE MOVEMENT

The Niagara Movement of 1905 marked a turning point in African American history. This new organization was founded by a group of African American intellectuals from across the nation—headed by W. E. B. Du Bois—and approved a "Declaration of Principles," or resolutions calling for full equality for African Americans in American life.

The Niagara Movement, however, suffered from weak finances and its initial policy that restricted membership to African American intellectuals. In 1909, the Niagara Movement was succeeded by a new organization that was later known as the National Association for the Advancement of Colored People (NAACP).

National Association for the Advancement of Colored People. The new organization was largely the brainchild of three people: William English Walling, a white southerner who feared that racists would soon carry "the race war to the North"; Mary White Ovington, a wealthy young white woman who had attended the 1905 meeting of the Niagara group as a reporter for the *New York Evening Post* and had experience with conditions in the African American ghettos of New York City; and Henry Moskowitz, a New York social worker. The trio proposed that a conference be called "for the discussion of present evils, the voicing of protests, and the renewal of the struggle for civil and political liberty." The three-day conference was followed by four meetings, the results of which were an increase in membership and the selection of an official name—the National Negro Committee. The organization adopted its current name in 1910 and was incorporated in New York State the following year. By 1914, the association had established some fifty branches throughout the country.

Over the years, the NAACP has attempted to improve the condition of African Americans through litigation, legislation, and education. The *Crisis* magazine, edited by Du Bois, became its chief vehicle for the dissemination of information. Perhaps its most significant legal victory was won in 1954 when the historic *Brown v. Board of Education of Topeka, Kansas* case threw out the "separate but equal" doctrine established by the Supreme Court in 1896 in *Plessy v. Ferguson* and eliminated legal segregation in public education.

NAACP Legal Defense and Educational Fund, Inc. Established in 1940 by the NAACP, the NAACP Legal Defense and Educational Fund (LDF) maintained its own board, program, staff, office, and budget for some twenty years. It has served at the forefront of legal assaults against discrimination and segregation and has an outstanding record of victories. In addition to its litigation, the LDF provides scholarships and training for young lawyers, advises lawyers on legal trends and decisions, and monitors federal programs.

Originally for tax purposes, the LDF had been maintained as a separate arm of the NAACP, until it officially was divorced from its parent organization in 1957. Following the separation of the organizations, a dispute over identity and the use of the parent organization's name erupted. The NAACP sued the LDF for name infringement. After several months of legal wrangling, however, a federal court ruled that the LDF could keep NAACP in its name because the NAACP was its parent organization.

ORGANIZATIONS CONCERNED WITH URBAN PROBLEMS

During the early part of the twentieth century, several organizations concerned with the plight of urban African Americans emerged. In 1906, a group of African Americans and whites met for the purpose of studying the employment needs of African Americans. This group, known as the Committee for the Improvement of Industrial Conditions among Negroes in New York, studied the racial aspects of the labor market—particularly the attitudes and policies of employers and unions—and sought to find openings for qualified African Americans.

At the same time, the National League for the Protection of Colored Women was established to provide similar services for African American women in New York and Philadelphia arriving from various parts of the South. These women, who often had no friends or relatives in the North, often fell prey to unscrupulous employment agencies, which led them into low-wage jobs.

A third organization, the Committee on Urban Conditions among Negroes, appeared in 1910. It was organized by Ruth Standish Baldwin, the widow of the former Long Island Railroad president, and George Edmund Haynes, one of only three trained African American social workers in the country and the first African American to receive a doctorate from Columbia University. Haynes was named the first executive secretary of the new agency. A year later, the organization

***Regional Headquarters of the National Association for the Advancement of Colored People (NAACP), Detroit, c. 1950s.** The NAACP gained what many consider its most significant legal victory in 1954 when the historic* Brown v. Board of Education of Topeka, Kansas *case eliminated legal segregation in public education.* CORBIS

merged with the Committee for the Improvement of Industrial Conditions among Negroes in New York and the National League for the Protection of Colored Women to form the National League on Urban Conditions among Negroes. That name was later shortened to the National Urban League.

From the outset, the organization focused on the social and economic needs of African Americans, seeking training, job assistance, and improved housing, health, and recreation for African Americans. The organizational model that the league had established in New York City attracted attention, and affiliates were formed in various cities across the United States.

A major goal of the National Urban League was to broaden economic opportunities for African Americans. It was not until the 1960s when Whitney M. Young Jr. became its new leader that the league began to emerge as a force in the civil rights struggle.

LEADERSHIP CONFERENCE ON CIVIL AND HUMAN RIGHTS

The Leadership Conference on Civil and Human Rights (formerly the Leadership Conference on Civil Rights) was organized in 1950 by A. Philip Randolph, Roy Wilkins, and Arnold Aronson to implement the historic report of President Harry S. Truman's Committee on Civil Rights, *To Secure These Rights*. Beginning with only thirty organizations, the conference has grown in numbers, scope, and effectiveness and was responsible for coordinating the campaigns that resulted in the passage of the civil rights legislation of the 1950s and 1960s, including the Civil Rights Act of 1957, the Civil Rights Act of 1960, the

Civil Rights Act of 1964, the Voting Rights Act of 1965, and the Fair Housing Act of 1968 (also known as the Civil Rights Act of 1968).

The Leadership Conference consists of nearly two hundred national organizations representing minorities, women, major religious groups, persons with disabilities, older Americans, labor, and minority businesses and professions. These organizations speak for a substantial portion of the population and together constitute one of the most broad-based coalitions in the nation. The Leadership Conference continues as the nation's premiere civil and human rights coalition.

SOUTHERN CHRISTIAN LEADERSHIP CONFERENCE AND THE ARREST OF ROSA PARKS

Just days after the arrest of Rosa Parks, who had refused to give up her seat on a public bus in Montgomery, Alabama, on December 1, 1955, Martin Luther King Jr. and Ralph David Abernathy organized the Montgomery Improvement Association to coordinate a citywide bus boycott. The success of the boycott led to the creation of a new organization.

This new organization, consisting mainly of African American ministers, met at the Ebenezer Baptist Church in January 1957 and elected King as its first president. Initially called the Southern Negro Leaders Conference and later the Southern Leadership Conference, the Southern Christian Leadership Conference grew to become one of the most influential and effective of all the civil rights organizations.

ORGANIZATIONS AND THE COURT

Although public and private associations of all kinds have traditionally flourished in the United States, this has not always been true for African American organizations. The freedom of association—the freedom to assemble, without state scrutiny—similar to the First Amendment freedoms of speech and press, has from time to time been questioned and challenged.

Since the founding of the NAACP and similar organizations, state and local governments have attempted to prevent the operation of such groups. During the late 1950s, the state of Alabama set out to ban the NAACP from conducting activities within the state, claiming that the association had failed to comply with statutes governing corporations operating within the state. The dispute of *NAACP v. Alabama* was finally resolved by the U.S. Supreme Court in 1958 in favor of the association. The NAACP, however, met with other interferences—resulting in a number of notable court cases, including *Bates v. Little Rock* (1960), *Louisiana ex rel. Gremillion v. NAACP* (1961), and *Gibson v. Florida Legislative Investigation Committee* (1963).

CONGRESS OF RACIAL EQUALITY

The Congress of Racial Equality (CORE), an interracial organization organized to confront racism and discrimination, was founded in 1942 by James Farmer as the result of a campaign protesting discrimination at a Chicago restaurant. From Chicago, the organization spread to other cities and other causes, organizing sit-ins and freedom rides throughout the South.

By the mid-1960s, CORE had changed directions, and Farmer turned leadership of the organization over to Floyd McKissick, a North Carolina lawyer. With McKissick as national director, the organization moved toward an exclusively African American membership and staff. At its 1967 convention, CORE eliminated the word *multiracial* from its constitution. McKissick left the organization in 1968 and was replaced by the current national director, Roy Innis, the former chairperson of the Harlem chapter.

STUDENT NONVIOLENT COORDINATING COMMITTEE

In 1960, a group of African American college students founded the Student Nonviolent Coordinating Committee (SNCC) to coordinate the activities of students engaged in direct action protest. The SNCC achieved enormous results in the desegregation of public facilities and earned respect for its determination to act peacefully, no matter how violent or demeaning the provocation.

By 1964, the organization's leader, Stokely Carmichael, had become convinced that the United States could not be turned around without the threat of wholesale violence. In 1967, Carmichael left the organization to join the more militant Black Panther Party. H. Rap Brown, the former minister of justice in the old organization, took over leadership, renaming the organization the Student National Coordinating Committee and promoting violent retaliation in some situations. The organization gradually declined in membership and is now essentially defunct

BLACK PANTHER PARTY

From its founding by Huey P. Newton and Bobby Seale in 1966, the Black Panther Party was a departure from the platform and tactics of other civil rights organizations. It rejected the institutional structure that, in its view, made American society corrupt; rejected established channels of authority that oppressed the African American community; and rejected middle-class values, which it felt

Four Members of the Black Panther Party, New Brunswick, NJ, February 20, 1969. *The party imposed strict discipline on its members, who were obliged to know and understand the party's ten-point program. By 1970 most of the organization's leadership was either jailed, in exile, or dead.* AP IMAGES

contributed to indifference toward, and contempt for, African American urban youth.

The party imposed strict discipline on its members, denouncing the use of intoxicants, drugs, and artificial stimulants "while doing party work." The intellectual fare of every party member was the ten-point program (supplemented by daily reading of political developments), which every member was obliged to know and understand.

By 1969, most of the organization's leadership was either jailed, in exile, or dead. Newton was jailed in 1968 on manslaughter changes; Seale had been jailed on charges stemming from the 1968 Chicago convention riot; Eldridge Cleaver, the minister of information, fled to Algeria in 1969 to avoid a prison sentence; and Mark Clark and Fred Hampton were killed during a police raid in 1969.

In June 1997, former Black Panther leader Geronimo Pratt made headlines when he was released from prison after being wrongfully convicted of the 1968 murder of a woman in Santa Monica, California. Throughout his twenty-seven years in prison, Pratt (also known as Geronimo ji Jaga) maintained his innocence. In his decision, Superior Court Judge Everett W. Dickey held that the prosecution denied Pratt a fair trial in violation of his constitutional rights. The prosecution had suppressed material evidence relating to the question of guilt and to the credibility of a material witness, in violation of the 1963 U.S. Supreme Court ruling in *Brady v. Maryland.*

ORGANIZATIONS PROVIDING COMMUNITY SUPPORT

In 1967, the National Urban Coalition was founded to improve the quality of life for the disadvantaged in urban areas through the combined efforts of business, labor, government, and community leaders. Another organization, the National Black United Fund, which provides financial and technical support to projects serving the critical needs of African American communities nationwide, was founded in 1972.

The Reverend Jesse L. Jackson Sr. organized Operation PUSH (People United to Save Humanity, later changed to People United to Serve Humanity) in 1971. The organization worked to motivate young people through its PUSH Excel program, which is designed to instill pride and build confidence in young people. Jackson left Operation PUSH to organize another group, the National Rainbow Coalition, Inc., in 1984. The two organizations merged in 1996 to form the Rainbow PUSH Coalition.

ORGANIZATIONS RESPONDING TO AFRICA AND THE CARIBBEAN

During the nineteenth and early part of the twentieth centuries, a number of individuals and organizations arose to unite Africans throughout the world. Most notable was the Universal Negro Improvement Association, founded in 1914 by the black nationalist Marcus Garvey. The organization's goals were to instill pride in African Americans by gaining economic and political power for African Americans in the United States, establishing an independent black colony in Africa, and promoting African nationalism. In February 1919, under the leadership of W. E. B. Du Bois, the first Pan-African Congress was held in Paris. The meeting was attended by blacks from around the world and focused on the problems facing blacks worldwide.

More recently, new organizations have formed to address the concerns of blacks around the world. TransAfrica, founded in 1977 by Randall Robinson, has worked to influence U.S. foreign policy regarding political and human rights in Africa and the Caribbean by informing the public of violations of social, political, and civil

Eldridge Cleaver, Minister of Information, Black Panther Party, September 11, 1968. *Cleaver stands outside the group's headquarters in Oakland, California, after two of the city's police officers fired shots into the building. The following year Cleaver fled to Algeria to avoid a prison sentence.* AP IMAGES

rights. Other organizations have also taken a stand on policies affecting blacks around the world.

GREEK LETTER ORGANIZATIONS

The first Greek letter fraternity established in the United States was Phi Beta Kappa, organized on December 5, 1776, at the College of William and Mary in Williamsburg, Virginia. At first a secret social club with scholastic, inspirational, and fraternal aims, it later abandoned its secrecy and became an honorary fraternity based on scholarship. It was not until 1877, however, that Phi Beta Kappa accepted its first African American into membership—George Washington Henderson at the University of Vermont. The undergraduate fraternity movement began to spread throughout colleges in New England and the mid-Atlantic states. Women's sororities also emerged in the mid-nineteenth century. Although many colleges were racially integrated during this period, their fraternities and sororities were not.

The first decade of the twentieth century was a period of great organizational activity for African Americans, with the founding of organizations dealing with business, education, social, and economic conditions, as well as other issues. African American colleges and schools of this period also enjoyed the spirit of brotherhood, and their students found social outlets in clubs, literary societies, and other groups. But both on and outside campus, African Americans were confronted by the pressures of racism and sexism and sought relief in a number of ways. African Americans explored ways to form strong social bonds through the founding of their own Greek letter organizations. In time, these organizations became a dominant force in undergraduate college life, as well as in the African American community.

HISTORICAL AFRICAN AMERICAN FRATERNITIES

Sigma Pi Phi Fraternity, also known as the Boulé, was founded by six African American men in Philadelphia in 1904. It serves as the forerunner of the Greek letter organizations existing in the African American community today. It focuses on the postcollege years and historically has comprised an elite group of college graduates who have "like attributes, education, skills, and attainments," or who have "made places for themselves in their communities through useful service."

Two other well-established Greek letter fraternities were actually founded on white college campuses. Initially organized as a social study club, Alpha Phi Alpha was founded on December 4, 1906, by a small group of men at Cornell University. Kappa Alpha Psi was founded in 1911 at Indiana University. Most of the African American Greek letter fraternities and sororities, however, were founded at Howard University in Washington, D.C. Other historically prominent African American fraternities include Omega Psi Phi, founded in 1911, and Phi Beta Sigma, established in 1914.

HISTORICAL AFRICAN AMERICAN SORORITIES

African American Greek letter sororities date back to 1910, when nine students founded Alpha Kappa Alpha Sorority. Those organizations that followed included Delta Sigma Theta in 1913, organized by twenty-two young women, and Zeta Phi Beta, established in 1920. Sigma Gamma Rho was founded in 1922 at Butler University in Indianapolis, the only African American sorority founded on a white college campus. The mutual interests of both sororities and fraternities have been promoted by the National Pan-Hellenic Council, established in 1930.

In addition to these organizations, other African American Greek letter organizations were founded as early as 1906 with specialized professional interests in mind. Examples of such groups are Phi Delta Kappa Sorority (education) and Alpha Pi Chi Sorority (business and other professions).

PRESENT-DAY AFRICAN AMERICAN FRATERNITIES AND SORORITIES

Present-day chapters of Greek letter fraternities and sororities for African Americans have been founded on many traditional white college campuses. Chapters also extend beyond campus grounds into the community, where graduate chapters—sometimes more than one in a city—have been established. Members of both undergraduate and graduate chapters include many well-known individuals who have left their mark on Greek letter organizations as well. For example, in 1914 Mary Church Terrell wrote the "Delta Oath" for Delta Sigma Theta Sorority—an oath that is still recited at formal meetings. The poet and journalist Alice Dunbar-Nelson wrote the lyrics and the internationally known singer Florence Cole Talbert wrote the music for the official "Delta Hymn." The historian Charles Wesley wrote the history of Sigma Pi Phi, as well as the history of Alpha Phi Alpha fraternity.

African American Greek letter organizations continue to focus on various areas of need in the African American community, such as health, education, literacy, housing, juvenile delinquency, teenage pregnancy, and family issues, and on generally improving the human condition for African Americans. Some have even established nonprofit educational foundations to provide for scholarships, research, and foreign travel.

NATIONAL ORGANIZATION LEADERS

(Some biographical profiles may appear in other chapters. To locate profiles more readily, please consult the index.)

RALPH D. ABERNATHY

See chapter 7, Civil Rights.

H. RAP BROWN (1943–)

Former SNCC Chairperson. Hubert Rap Brown was born on October 4, 1943, in Baton Rouge, Louisiana. In 1967, he took over leadership of the Student Nonviolent Coordinating Committee, renaming the organization the Student National Coordinating Committee. During his leadership of the committee, Brown was an advocate of violence against the white establishment and used fiery rhetoric in many of his speeches, often saying that "violence is as American as cherry pie." Since the late 1960s, the organization has gradually declined in membership and is now essentially defunct.

In 1968, Brown was charged with inciting a riot in Cambridge, Maryland, and was convicted in New Orleans on a federal charge of carrying a gun between states. A year later, Brown published the book *Die Nigger Die*. He disappeared in 1970 after being slated for trial in Maryland, and, in 1972, he was shot, arrested, and eventually convicted for a bar holdup in New York City.

While in prison, Brown converted to the Islamic faith and took the name of Jamil Abdullah Al-Amin.

After his release, he founded a community grocery store in Atlanta and led the Community Mosque in Atlanta.

In August 1994, Al-Amin was arraigned on weapons possession and assault charges stemming from a shooting in an Atlanta city park. Al-Amin claimed that the charges were the result of harassment by federal agents who targeted him because of his radical past and Muslim beliefs.

In March 2000, Al-Amin was arrested in Alabama and charged with murdering a sheriff's deputy. The incident in question occurred in Atlanta on March 16, 2000. Two years later, Al-Amin was convicted of this crime and sentenced to life in prison without parole. At sentencing, the jury rejected the prosecution's request for the death penalty.

BENJAMIN F. CHAVIS (MUHAMMAD) JR. (1948–)

Former NAACP Executive Director. Benjamin Franklin Chavis Jr. was born on January 22, 1948, in Oxford, North Carolina. He received a B.A. from the University of North Carolina in 1969, an M.A. from the Duke University Divinity School, and a Ph.D. in theology from Howard University in Washington, D.C.

He came to national attention in 1971 when, as a civil rights organizer for the United Church of Christ, he was indicted along with nine other people for the fire bombing of a grocery store in Wilmington, North Carolina, during a period of racial unrest. In the controversial trial that followed, all of the "Wilmington 10" were found guilty. Chavis was sentenced to a prison term of twenty-nine to thirty-four years. Chavis was later granted parole, and in 1980 his conviction was reversed amid conflicting testimony by various witnesses.

Prior to becoming active in the civil rights movement, Chavis taught chemistry at the high school level. He also worked as an AFSCME labor organizer (1969), a civil rights organizer for the Southern Christian Leadership Conference (1967–1969), as a minister for the United Church of Christ, and as director of their Commission for Racial Justice in Washington, D.C. (1972). In 1985, he was appointed executive director of the Commission for Racial Justice. Chavis has also served as cochairperson of the National Alliance against Racism and Political Repression and as cochairperson of the Southern Organizing Committee for Economic and Social Justice. Since 2001, he has been CEO and cochair of the Hip-Hop Summit Action Network.

In 1977, Chavis wrote *Let My People Go: Psalms from Prison*. That same year, he received the George Collins Community Service Award given by the Congressional Black Caucus, the William L. Patterson Award given by the Patterson Foundation, and the Shalom Award presented by the Eden Theological Seminary. He is also a recipient of the Gertrude E. Rush Distinguished Service Award, J. E. Walker Humanitarian Award, and the Martin Luther King Jr. Freedom Award. Chavis was also active in the South African civil rights struggle.

On April 9, 1993, the NAACP's board of directors elected Chavis to succeed retiring executive director Benjamin Hooks. Chavis assumed leadership of the NAACP with an agenda designed to increase the membership of young African Americans and revitalize an organization that some people viewed as stagnant. However, Chavis's early initiatives, which included defending "gangsta rap" music, meeting with street gang leaders, and seeking closer ties with the Reverend Louis Farrakhan, the controversial leader of the Nation of Islam, angered many of the NAACP's more traditional members. By the time the NAACP met for its eighty-fifth annual convention in July 1994, the NAACP had been split into two factions, one supporting Chavis and the other that believed the organization was being overrun by radical and extremist elements.

In August 1994, it was disclosed that Chavis committed hundreds of thousands of dollars of NAACP money during the preceding autumn to settle a sexual harassment suit against him. On the weekend of August 20, 1994, the NAACP board of directors met and voted to oust Chavis as executive director. Chavis sued the NAACP, claiming that he had been wrongfully terminated. The NAACP settled out of court with Chavis, but he was not reinstated as executive director.

Following his dismissal from the NAACP, Chavis formed a new civil rights organization, the National African American Leadership Summit. He continued his close association with Farrakhan, and together they organized the Million Man March, which convened on October 16, 1995, in Washington, D.C. Chavis also served as a talk show host on Washington, D.C., radio station WOL-AM. In 1997, he converted to Islam, took the name Benjamin Chavis Muhammad, and joined the Nation of Islam headed by Farrakhan. Chavis has continued to speak on the benefits of the Nation of Islam and has spoken out against those who look to silence those of color in the United States. In 2001, he cofounded the Education Online Services Corporation.

W. E. B. DU BOIS

See chapter 7, Civil Rights.

RAMONA HOAGE EDELIN (1945–)

National Urban Coalition President and Chief Executive. Born in Los Angeles on September 4, 1945, Ramona Hoage Edelin received her B.A. (magna cum laude) from Fisk University, her M.A. from the University of East

Anglia in Norwich, England, and her Ph.D. from Boston University. She has been a lecturer at the University of Maryland and a visiting professor at Brandeis University, and has served as chair of Afro-American studies at Emerson College.

In 1977, Edelin joined the National Urban Coalition as an executive assistant to the president. This organization, dedicated to improving the quality of life for the disadvantaged in urban areas, has been active in advocating initiatives designed to encourage youth and promote leadership. Between 1979 and 1982, Edelin progressed from director of operations to vice president of operations to senior vice president of program and policy directing programs in housing, health, education, and advocacy. In 1988, Edelin became the organization's chief executive.

In 1992, Edelin chaired a National Political Congress of Black Women commission in an effort to place black women in prominent positions within the administration of President Bill Clinton. Clinton was so impressed by her that he appointed her to the Presidential Board on Historically Black Colleges and Universities. She joined Clinton as a member of the 1998 U.S. delegation to South Africa.

Edelin has served as treasurer of the Black Leadership Forum; chair of the Commission on Appointments of African American Women of the National Political Congress of Black Women; and in various capacities with the Center for Policy Alternatives, the Network for Instructional Television, Inc., the Federal Advisory Committee for the Black Community Crusade for Children, the advisory board of the Civic Network Television, Inc., and the National Civic League's Alliance for National Renewal. She chaired the District of Columbia Educational Goals 2000 Panel; served on the District of Columbia Committee on Public Education; and chaired the board of the D.C. Community Humanities Council and the Public Education and Prevention Strategy Team, as well as the District of Columbia Drug Control Policy. She has also served on the D.C. Commission on Budget and Financial Priorities. Edelin has been recognized as a leader in *Ebony* magazine's listings of the 100 Most Influential Black Americans and Organizations, and she received the IBM Community Executive Program Award. She is also a noted national lecturer, moderating for the Civic Network Television's Building Community Series.

MARIAN WRIGHT EDELMAN (1939–)

Children's Defense Fund President. Born in Bennettsville, South Carolina, on June 6, 1939, Marian Wright Edelman received her undergraduate degree from Spelman College in 1960, where she was class valedictorian. That fall, she entered Yale University Law School as a John Hay Whitney Fellow and received her law degree in 1963. Later that year, she joined the NAACP Legal Defense and Educational Fund (LDF) as staff attorney. One year later, she organized the Jackson, Mississippi, branch of the LDF, serving as its director until 1968, when she founded the Washington Research Project of the Southern Center for Public Policy, which later developed into the Children's Defense Fund (CDF).

Wright has served as director of the Harvard University Center for Law and Education, as chairperson of the Spelman College board of trustees, as a member of the Yale University Corporation and the National Commission on Children, and on the boards of the Center on Budget and Policy Priorities, the U.S. Committee for UNICEF, and the Joint Center for Political and Economic Studies.

As president of the CDF, Edelman has become the nation's most effective lobbyist on behalf of children. Even while social spending was being cut she managed to score some victories. In 1986, nine federal programs known as "the Children's Initiative" received a $500 million increase in their $36 billion budget for families and children's health care, nutrition, and early education.

The most visible focus of the CDF is its teen pregnancy prevention program. Through Edelman's efforts, Medicaid coverage for expectant mothers and children was boosted in 1984. The following year, Edelman began holding an annual teen-pregnancy prevention conference, bringing thousands of religious leaders, social and health workers, and community organizations to Washington to discuss ways of dealing with the problem.

In her 1987 book *Families in Peril: An Agenda for Social Change*, Edelman wrote, "As adults we are responsible for meeting the needs of children. It is our moral obligation. We brought about their births and their lives, and they cannot fend for themselves." Her other books include *Portrait of Inequality: Black and White Children in America*, *The Measure of Our Success: A Letter to My Children*, *Guide My Feet: Prayers and Meditations on Loving and Working for Children*, and *The Sea Is So Wide and My Boat Is So Small: Charting a Course for the Next Generation.*

In 2000 President Bill Clinton awarded the Presidential Medal of Freedom to Edelman for her work at the CDF. Since then, she has continued to speak out on health-care reform, race in the media, threats to school diversity, and the fight against childhood obesity.

MYRLIE EVERS-WILLIAMS (1933–)

Former NAACP Chair, Civil Rights Activist, Civic Worker. Known for many years as the widow of civil rights worker Medgar Evers, Myrlie Evers-Williams has become prominent in her own right as a civil rights activist, speaker, and the second African American woman to chair the NAACP's board of directors. As board chair, she rekindled the spirit of the organization, led it to greater fiscal integrity, and increased national membership.

Evers-Williams was born Myrlie Louise Beasley on March 17, 1933, in Vicksburg, Mississippi. In 1950, she enrolled at Alcorn Agricultural and Mechanical College (later Alcorn State University) in Lorman, Mississippi, where she met Medgar Evers on her first day. They married on Christmas Eve of the following year.

The couple lived in the historic, all–African American town of Mound Bayou, Mississippi. During the 1950s and early 1960s, Medgar Evers became active with the NAACP as field secretary. The racially charged atmosphere in Mississippi, as well as the death threats that they received, led the family to take extreme precautions. Their home was firebombed in the spring of 1963. On June 12 of that same year, the death threats became a reality when Medgar Evers was shot in the driveway of his home and died soon afterward at the University of Mississippi Hospital. Eventually, the home was donated to Tougaloo College. After thirty years of Evers-Williams's dogged determination for justice, on February 5, 1994, Byron De La Beckwith was convicted for the murder of her husband and sentenced to life in prison.

Evers-Williams and her three children moved to Claremont, California, in July 1964. She became highly visible in the NAACP and lectured to branches around the country about her life and the work of her husband. She also continued her education and graduated from Pomona College in 1968 with a bachelor's degree in sociology. Later, she received a certificate from the Simmons College's School of Management in Boston, and then became director of planning at Claremont College's Center for Educational Opportunity.

From 1973 to 1975, she was vice president for advertising and publicity with the New York–based firm of Seligman & Latz. In 1975, Evers-Williams moved to Los Angeles and became national director for community affairs at Atlantic Richfield Company (ARCO). She unsuccessfully ran for a seat in California's Twenty-fourth Congressional District, as well as a seat on the Los Angeles City Council. Also in 1975, she married Walter Edward Williams.

A longtime member of the NAACP, Evers-Williams's work with the organization was acknowledged among its leadership. In 1995, she was elected chairperson of the NAACP's board of directors. Immediately upon taking office, Evers-Williams faced unpaid organization debts and a cloud of uncertainty among the national membership over the organization's future. Evers-Williams led a successful campaign to restore the NAACP's posture as a viable civil rights organization, strengthen its financial base, and increase membership. After turning around the NAACP, Evers-Williams resigned from the office in 1998 and was succeeded by Julian Bond.

Evers-Williams has been active in other arenas as well. In 1967, she recounted Evers's family life in Mississippi in her book *For Us, the Living.* She followed this book up in 1999 with *Watch Me Fly: What I Learned on the Way to Becoming the Woman I Was Meant to Be,* Evers-Williams's adult-life story of single motherhood and civil rights battles. She was also a contributing editor to the *Ladies' Home Journal.* Among the many honors that have been bestowed on her is the Spingarn Medal, which the NAACP awarded her in 1998. She continues to lecture widely and appear on radio and television programs. In 2005, she published her husband's autobiography, *Medgar Evers: A Hero's Life and Legacy Revealed through His Writings, Letters, and Speeches.*

JAMES FARMER

See chapter 7, Civil Rights.

FIZZELL GRAY

See Kweisi Mfume bio in chapter 11, Politics.

PRINCE HALL (C. 1735–1807)

Founder of Black Freemasonry in the United States. Prince Hall is believed to have been born in Bridgetown, Barbados, around 1735. Historians contend that he migrated to the United States in 1765, while others claim that during the late 1740s he had been a slave to William Hall of Boston, Massachusetts, and was freed on April 9, 1770.

In March 1775, Hall, along with fifteen other African Americans, were initiated into a lodge of British army freemasons stationed in Boston. The group of African American masons was issued a permit to meet at a lodge on March 17, 1775, and on July 3, 1775, they organized the African Lodge No. 1, with Hall as master of the lodge. The lodge received official recognition from England as a regular Lodge of Free and Accepted Masons in 1784 and was designated the African Lodge No. 459.

In addition to leading the organization of African American Freemasonry, Hall was active as an abolitionist. In January 1777, he was the prime force behind an African American petition sent to the Massachusetts state legislature requesting the abolition of slavery in the state. Another important petition drawn up under his leadership in 1788 called for an end to the kidnapping and sale of free African Americans into slavery. He also actively lobbied for the organization of schools for African American children in Boston. Hall died on December 4, 1807, in Boston.

GEORGE EDMUND HAYNES (1880–1960)

NUL Cofounder, Sociologist, Educator. A pioneer in the area of social work and an advocate for the urban African American worker, George Edmund Haynes helped found the National Urban League (NUL) in 1910 and became its first executive director. He also led NUL into its role as advocate for the needs of the African American urban poor.

Born in Pine Bluff, Arkansas, on May 11, 1880, Haynes moved to Hot Springs in search of better educational, social, and vocational opportunities. He was encouraged during a visit to Chicago where he saw a close-knit African American community engaged in discussions about contemporary issues involving their status. After one year of study at the Agricultural and Mechanical College in Normal, Alabama, and a college preparatory course at Fisk University in Nashville, he enrolled in the latter institution in 1899 and received his B.S. in 1903. Haynes received a master's degree in sociology from Yale University in 1904 and then entered the Yale Divinity School. He also enrolled in summer courses at the University of Chicago in 1906 and 1907. In 1912, he became the first African American to receive a doctorate from Columbia University. The research for his dissertation was on the working life of African Americans in New York City, culminating in the dissertation topic "The Negro at Work in New York City."

After college, Haynes worked with the Colored Department of the International Committee of the YMCA, but he left in 1908 to continue graduate study. In 1911, Haynes founded the Association of Colleges and Secondary Schools and was its first secretary. He was a member of the Fisk University faculty from 1910 to 1921, although he was on leave between 1918 and 1921. At Fisk, he chaired the social science department, developed a pioneer program in social work education, and led the university to become a preeminent institution for social work education. He also established affiliate programs in social work education with other African American colleges. In turn, the National Urban League gave fellowships to promising students in the field to pursue advanced degrees in social work.

Haynes had been active in several organizations, including three that were the precursors of the NUL: the National League for the Protection of Colored Women, the Committee on Urban Conditions among Negroes, and the Committee for Improving Industrial Conditions of Negroes. These organizations merged in 1910 and became the National Urban League. Haynes was the NUL's executive director until 1918.

Haynes served as director of Negro economics for the U.S. Department of Labor between 1918 and 1921. From 1921 to 1947, he was executive secretary of the Department of Race Relations of the Federal Council of Churches. Under his leadership, the department established Race Relations Sunday, which is observed nationwide on a Sunday in January or February. From 1942 to 1955, he was a YMCA regional consultant in South Africa, where he collected and disseminated data on the organization's work in these countries. From 1950 to 1959, he was lecturer at the City College of New York.

Throughout his life, Haynes was active in numerous organizations, and he served on the boards of trustees at Fisk and Dillard universities and the State University of New York. His publications included: *The Negro at Work during the World War and during Reconstruction* (1921); *The Trend of the Races* (1922); *Africa: Continent of the Future* (1950); articles for the *Social Work Yearbook*; and entries on African Americans in the *Encyclopedia Britannica.*

Because of Haynes's efforts, the NUL continues its focus on social work initiatives at local and national levels. After a brief illness, Haynes died in King County Hospital in Brooklyn on January 8, 1960.

DOROTHY I. HEIGHT (1912–2010)

National Council of Negro Women President, Civil Rights Activist. Born on March 24, 1912, in Richmond, Virginia, Dorothy Irene Height earned a master's degree from New York University and also studied at the New York School of Social Work. In the fall of 1952, she served as a visiting professor at the Delhi School of Social Work in New Delhi, India. Six years later, she began a ten-year stint as a member of the state of New York's Social Welfare Board. In 1957, she was named president of the National Council of Negro Women (NCNW), an organization founded by Mary McLeod Bethune in 1935.

Before becoming the NCNW's fourth president, Height had served on the organization's board of directors. Her career also included positions at a number of other organizations, including associate director for leadership training services for the Young Women's Christian Association, member of the Defense Advisory Committee on Women in the Services, president of Delta Sigma Theta Sorority, vice president of the National Council of Women, and president of Women in Community Services, Inc. Height also founded the Black Family Reunion in the 1980s to combat negative media stereotypes of African Americans.

In 1994, President Bill Clinton presented Height and nine other distinguished Americans with the Medal of Freedom, the nation's highest civilian honor. She was also awarded the Salute to Greatness Award. Height retired

Dorothy I. Height and President Bill Clinton, White House, Washington, DC, 1994. *Clinton applauds Height, president of the National Council of Negro Women, after presenting her with the Presidential Medal of Freedom.* AP PHOTO/DOUG MILLS

from the presidency of NCNW in February 1998 and was named chair and president emeritus of the organization. Jane E. Smith then became NCNW's president and CEO. Height published her autobiography, *Open Wide the Freedom Gates,* in 2003. In 2004, President George W. Bush presented Height with the Congressional Gold Medal. Following her retirement, Height continued to make appearances on the behalf of the NCNW, including lending her voice to a 2001 audiobook focusing on the speeches of Martin Luther King Jr. After her death in Washington, D.C., on April 20, 2010, at age ninety-eight, President Barack Obama called her "the godmother of the civil rights movement."

BENJAMIN L. HOOKS (1925–2010)

Former NAACP Executive Director, Minister. Benjamin Lawson Hooks was born in Memphis, Tennessee, on January 31, 1925, and attended Le Moyne College and Howard University. He received his J.D. from DePaul University in 1948. During World War II, he served in the Ninety-second Infantry Division in Italy.

From 1949 to 1965, and again from 1968 to 1972, Hooks worked as a lawyer in Memphis. In 1965, Hooks became the first African American judge to serve in the Shelby County (Tennessee) criminal court. As an ordained minister, he preached at Middle Baptist Church in Memphis and the Greater New Mount Moriah Baptist Church in Detroit. As a prominent local businessman, he was the cofounder and vice president of the Mutual Federal Savings and Loan Association in Memphis.

On November 6, 1976, Hooks was unanimously elected executive director of the NAACP by the board of directors, succeeding the retiring Roy Wilkins. Under Hooks's progressive leadership, the association took an aggressive posture on U.S. policy toward African nations. Among his many battles on Capitol Hill, Hooks led the historic prayer vigil in Washington, D.C., in 1979 against the Mott antibusing amendment, which was eventually defeated in Congress; led in the fight for passage of the District of Columbia Home Rule Act; and was instrumental in gathering important Senate and House votes on the Humphrey-Hawkins Full Employment Act of 1978.

At the NAACP's national convention in 1986, Hooks was awarded the association's highest honor, the Spingarn Medal. In April 1993, Hooks retired as executive director of the NAACP and was replaced by Benjamin F. Chavis.

Following his retirement, Hooks became senior vice president of Chapman Company, a minority-controlled brokerage firm, and returned to the pulpit as minister of Greater Middle Baptist Church in Memphis. He was also installed as professor of social justice at Fisk University with a distinguished chair named in his honor. In 1998, Hooks was selected as one of five judges to sit on a special supreme court to rule on the election of appellate judges in Tennessee. When not running special events for the NAACP, Hooks continued to teach and preach the values of equality and fairness. He died in Memphis on April 15, 2010.

ROY INNIS (1934–)

CORE Chairperson. Born June 6, 1934, in St. Croix, Virgin Islands, Roy Emile Alfredo Innis has lived in the United States since the age of twelve. He attended Stuyvesant High School in New York City and majored in chemistry at the City College of New York.

In 1963, Innis joined the Congress of Racial Equality (CORE). He was elected chairperson of the Harlem branch in 1965 and went on to become associate national director two years later. In 1968, Innis became national director of the organization. Innis founded the Harlem Commonwealth Council, an agency designed to promote the development of African American–owned businesses and economic institutions in Harlem. He also worked in journalism, serving with William Haddad as coeditor of the *Manhattan Tribune*, a weekly featuring news from Harlem and the Upper West Side.

Innis's leadership of CORE, however, has been marked with controversy. Numerous members have left the organization, charging that Innis has run CORE as a

Roy Innis, National Chairman, Congress of Racial Equality. *Speaking at a news conference in New York City in February, 2000, Innis uses a copy of the* New York Times *to illustrate what he called media censorship of Republican presidential candidate Alan Keyes (*left*).* AP PHOTO/ROBERT F. BUKATY

one-man show. CORE was also the target of a three-year investigation by the attorney general's office of the state of New York into allegations that it had misused charitable contributions. An agreement was reached in 1981 that relieved CORE from admitting to any wrongdoing in its handling of funds but stipulated that Innis would have to contribute $35,000 to the organization over the next three years. Innis was challenged by a group of former CORE members, headed by James Farmer, the founder and former chairperson of organization, but the effort was unsuccessful and Innis continued as head of the organization. In 1981, Innis became national chairperson of the organization.

While remaining chairperson of the largely inactive CORE, Innis has sought to build a political base in Brooklyn and run for public office on several occasions. In 1986, Innis was a Democratic candidate for Brooklyn's Twelfth Congressional District, but lost the election. He also ran unsuccessfully for the Democratic mayoral nomination in New York City in 1993 against David Dinkins. In 1994, Innis unsuccessfully challenged Mario Cuomo for the governorship of New York. In 2000, Innis was one of the main backers of Alan Keyes's presidential campaign. He was able to work closely with his son, Niger Innis, who was the state chair of the Keyes campaign in New York and a Keyes delegate for New York's Seventeenth Congressional District. After Keyes's campaign folded, Innis continued to push for African Americans in governmental positions.

JESSE L. JACKSON SR.

See chapter 7, Civil Rights.

JOHN E. JACOB (1934–)

NUL President. Born in Trout, Louisiana, on December 16, 1934, John Edward Jacob grew up in Houston, Texas. He received his B.S. and M.S. in social work from Howard University. During the early 1960s, Jacob worked for the Baltimore Department of Public Welfare, first as a caseworker, then later as a child welfare supervisor. In 1965, he joined the Washington Urban League as director of education and youth incentives.

During his early career with the organization, he held a number of increasingly important positions: director of its northern Virginia branch in 1966, associate director for administration of the affiliate in 1967, and acting executive director from 1968 until 1970. He also spent several months as director of community organizing and training in the eastern regional office of the National Urban League (NUL).

Jacob left the Washington Urban League in 1970 to serve as executive director for the San Diego Urban League, a post he held until his return to the Washington Urban League in 1975 as that organization's president. In 1982, Jacob replaced Vernon E. Jordan Jr. as president of the NUL, following Jordan's retirement after ten years at the helm.

In 1994, Jacob retired as NUL president and was succeeded by Hugh B. Price. Jacob then became an executive vice president for Anheuser-Busch Inc. He was responsible for a broad range of worldwide communications activities including public relations, employee communications, and the company's efforts to promote responsible alcohol consumption. He was also a close adviser to August A. Busch III, the company's chairman and president, and, more importantly, one of a handful of senior officers responsible for developing strategic directions and strategies for the company. He retired from Anheuser-Busch late in 2006. Among other positions, Jacob also served on the Howard University board of trustees, the board of the Local Initiatives Support Corporation, the board of A Better Chance, Inc., the Community Advisory Board of New York Hospital, and the National Advertising Review Board.

BENJAMIN T. JEALOUS (1973–)

NAACP President and Chief Executive Officer. Born in Pacific Grove, California, on January 18, 1973, Benjamin Todd Jealous grew up on the Monterey Peninsula. Early in life he believed that there was no higher calling than to promote the cause of freedom in America and worldwide. He was deeply committed to social justice, public service, and activism in the area of human rights. When he was fourteen years old, he helped organize voter registration for Jesse Jackson's presidential bid. He took his human rights commitment with him when he enrolled in Columbia University to pursue a bachelor's degree.

While a student at Columbia, he was a community organizer in Harlem for the NAACP Legal Defense and Educational Fund. He also led campuswide protests at Columbia, including boycotts and pickets to support the rights of the homeless, and engaged in an environmental justice battle with the university. His actions led to his suspension, along with three other student leaders. While off campus, Jealous was a field organizer in Mississippi and helped to lead a campaign that kept the state of Mississippi from closing two of its public historically black universities and making one of them a prison. He also worked to secure equitable funding for these colleges. His activism in Mississippi in the mid-1990s continued, and he became a reporter for the *Jackson Advocate*, an African American newspaper. Jealous exposed corruption among high-ranking officials at the state prison in Parchman, which had gained national attention earlier when students in the civil rights movement of the 1960s

Benjamin Jealous, President and CEO of the NAACP, 2009. *At the 100th annual NAACP convention in New York, Jealous helped announce a "rapid response system" that lets people use their cell phones to report incidents of police misconduct.* AP PHOTO/SETH WENIG

were jailed there. Later he was promoted to managing editor of the *Advocate*.

Jealous returned to Columbia University in 1997 and completed his bachelor's degree in political science. He was accepted to Oxford University as a Rhodes Scholar and completed a master's degree in social policy. He served as executive director of the National Newspaper Publishers Association, a federation of more than two hundred African American community newspapers, and rebuilt its ninety-year-old news service. He was director of the U.S. Human Rights Program at Amnesty International from 2002 to 2005, where he focused on federal legislation against prison rape and racial profiling, and exposed the sentencing of child offenders to life without the possibility of parole. In 2005, Jealous became president of the Rosenberg Foundation, a private, nonprofit venture-capital organization that funds civil and human rights projects that benefit California's working families, especially immigrants and the historically disadvantaged.

In 2005, the NAACP began its search for a leader to replace Bruce Gordon, who left the post after twenty months. Their search led to Jealous, who in 2008 was elected the seventeenth president and chief executive officer of the NAACP, and at age thirty-five was the youngest person to become its national leader. Jealous was the only finalist that the search committee presented to the board. He was elected by a thirty-four to twenty-one vote, and took office on September 1, 2008. His challenge was to lead an organization that needed money, an increase in membership, and more visibility. His first action was to reach out to other civil rights advocates, consultants, and church leaders to help create a plan to strengthen the organization. During his first weeks in office, Jealous launched Upload to Lift, the NAACP's online voter-registration drive. He also focused the NAACP's resources on legislative issues, such as educational disparities, criminal justice, racial profiling, health care, and the home-mortgage crisis.

VERNON E. JORDAN JR. (1935–)

Former NUL President, Presidential Adviser. Vernon Eulion Jordan Jr. was born in Atlanta on August 15,

1935. After graduating from DePauw University in 1957 and from Howard University School of Law in 1960, he returned to Georgia.

From 1962 to 1964, Jordan served as field secretary for the Georgia branch of the NAACP. Between 1964 and 1968, Jordan served as director of the Voter Education Project of the Southern Regional Council and led successful drives that registered nearly two million African Americans in the South. In 1970, Jordan moved to New York to become executive director of the United Negro College Fund, helping to raise record sums for its member colleges, until he was selected by the National Urban League (NUL) to succeed Whitney M. Young Jr. as the organization's president.

Taking over leadership of the NUL in January 1972, Jordan moved the organization into new areas, including voter registration in northern and western cities, while continuing and strengthening the league's traditional social service programs. An outspoken advocate of the cause of African Americans and the poor, Jordan took strong stands in favor of busing, an income-maintenance system that ends poverty, scatter-site housing, and a federally financed and administered national health-care system. Maintaining that the "issues have changed" since the 1960s, Jordan called for "equal access and employment up to and including top policy-making jobs."

The nation was stunned on May 29, 1980, when Jordan, who had just delivered an address to the Fort Wayne Urban League, was shot by a sniper as he returned to his motel. Jordan was confined to the hospital, first in Fort Wayne and later in New York City, for ninety days.

On September 9, 1981, Jordan announced his retirement, after ten years as head of the NUL. During Jordan's tenure, the league increased its number of affiliates from 99 to 118, its staff from 2,100 to 4,200, and its overall annual budget from $40 million to $150 million. Following his departure from the NUL, Jordan became a senior partner at the Washington, D.C., law firm of Akin, Gump, Strauss, Hauer and Feld, a position he held until 2000.

In January 1993, Jordan served as a member of President Bill Clinton's transition team. President Clinton appointed Jordan to his Foreign Intelligence Advisory Board in April 1993. Many of his achievements during this period were overshadowed by his role in getting intern Monica Lewinsky a job in the White House in 1995.

In 2000, Jordan stepped down from his government position and returned to the private sector, becoming a senior managing director of Lazard Freres and Company, a New York investment firm, while also serving on several boards of directors. In 2001, he was awarded the NAACP's Spingarn Medal. In the same year, Jordan was the speaker at Albany State University's commencement in Georgia. Jordan said he had mixed feelings about returning to Albany, where marches and protests in the early 1960s were aimed at ending segregation in that city. He also wrote a memoir, published in 2001, called *Vernon Can Read!*

JOSEPH E. LOWERY (1921–)

Former SCLC President, Minister. Joseph Echols Lowery was born in Huntsville, Alabama, on October 6, 1921. He holds a Ph.D. in divinity and has attended numerous educational institutions including Clark College, the Chicago Ecumenical Institute, Garrett Theological Seminary, Payne College and Theological Seminary, and Morehouse College. Lowery's ministry began in 1952 at the Warren Street Church in Mobile, Alabama, where he served until 1961. From there he moved on to become pastor of St. Paul Church in Birmingham, Alabama, from 1964 to 1968.

Lowery was one of the cofounders of the Southern Negro Leaders Conference (which later became the Southern Christian Leadership Conference [SCLC]), serving as vice president. In 1977, Lowery succeeded Ralph David Abernathy as president of the SCLC. Under his leadership, the SCLC broadened its activities to include reinstituting its Operation Breadbasket; encouraging businesses that earn substantial profits in the African American community to reinvest equitably and employ African Americans in equitable numbers; becoming involved in the plight of Haitian refugees jailed by the U.S. government; and organizing a march from Selma to Washington, D.C., in coordination with the renewal of the Voting Rights Act of 1982. From 1986 until he retired in 1992, Lowery served as pastor of Cascades United Methodist Church in Atlanta. Lowery stepped down from the SCLC post in 1997 and was succeeded by Martin Luther King III.

In late 2001, Clark Atlanta University established the Joseph E. Lowery Institute for Justice and Human Rights, a think tank for issues related to civil and human rights. This coincided with Atlanta's Ashby Street being renamed Joseph E. Lowery Boulevard. Both of these events took place in honor of Lowery's eightieth birthday that year.

JEWELL JACKSON MCCABE (1945–)

Former President of the National Coalition of 100 Black Women. Jewell Jackson was born in Washington, D.C., on August 2, 1945. McCabe studied at New York City's High School of the Performing Arts as a teen and studied dance at Bard College from 1963 to 1966. While at Bard, she married Frederick Ward, who worked in advertising, whom she later divorced. Her marriage to Eugene McCabe, president of North General Hospital in New York City, also ended in divorce, but she chose to keep his name.

In 1970, several years after studying at Bard, McCabe took a job as director of public affairs for the New York Urban Coalition and, concurrently, joined the New York Coalition of 100 Black Women, an organization founded by her mother, businessperson Julia Jackson. At the time, the group was about seventy-five women shy of the one hundred mark; the group reached this goal by the mid-1970s. McCabe left the Urban Coalition in 1973 to become the public relations officer for New York City's Special Services for Children. She took a post two years later as associate director of public information in the Women's Division of the Office of the Governor in New York City and then became director of government and community affairs at WNET-TV in 1977.

From 1975 to 1977, she published the monthly newsletter *Women in New York* and also donated her time to the United Way, the NAACP, the United Hospital Fund, and the Association for a Better New York. In 1977, because of her good work, she was named president of the National Coalition of 100 Black Women, a post she held until 1991, when she became chair of the board of directors. By 1981, McCabe had established the organization nationally with chapters in twenty-two states, attracting some of the most well-known African American women in the United States.

Within two years of taking charge of the coalition, McCabe received several prestigious awards, including an Eastern Region Urban League Guild Award in 1979 and a

Jewell Jackson McCabe* (left), *Deborah C. Wright, and Senator Hillary Rodham Clinton, New York City, 2001. *McCabe's career has included positions with a number of organizations, including president of the New York Coalition of 100 Black Women.*
SUSAN WATTS/NEW YORK DAILY NEWS/GETTY IMAGES

Seagrams Civic Award, a Links Civic Award, and an outstanding community leadership award from Malcolm/King College, all in 1980. Also in 1980, she served as deputy grand marshal of the annual Martin Luther King Jr. Parade in New York City. In addition to her chair duties for the coalition, McCabe is president of her own Jewell Jackson McCabe Associates, a firm that does consulting work on government relations, marketing, and events dealing with minority issues. Her client list includes Panasonic, American Express, the NAACP Legal Defense and Educational Fund, the Federation of Protestant Welfare Agencies, and the Associated Black Charities.

In 1993, McCabe was a finalist for the position of executive director of the NAACP. McCabe was interviewed by the NAACP's board of directors but was not chosen for the job. Later, to quote *Philadelphia Inquirer* columnist Claude Lewis, McCabe "asserted ... that the NAACP's male-dominated board was unwilling to consider seriously a female applicant to head the powerful organization." Her outspokenness on the issue was one of a series of complaints of discrimination based on sex leveled at the NAACP around this time. McCabe's weighing in on this issue undoubtedly played a part in the 1995 election of Myrlie Evers-Williams as chairwoman of the group's board of directors.

Over the years, McCabe has held several gubernatorial appointments for the state of New York. Perhaps the most important of these was chairmanship of the $205 million, forty-six-member Jobs Training Partnership Council, a program that providing education and skills training to some 50,000 people in New York every year. McCabe has also served on the New York State Council on Fiscal and Economic Priorities, the Tax Reform Committee, and the New York State Council on Families, where she was assigned to the Committee on Teen Pregnancy Prevention. In addition to these state affiliations, she has served on the advisory boards of a number of private nonprofit and for-profit corporations, including the Economic Club of New York and the National Alliance of Business.

FLOYD B. MCKISSICK (1922–1981)

Former CORE National Director. Born in Asheville, North Carolina, on March 9, 1922, Floyd Bixler McKissick did his undergraduate work at Morehouse and North Carolina Colleges. Having determined that he wanted to become a lawyer, McKissick applied to the Law School at the University of North Carolina at Chapel Hill. Because the school was racially segregated at that time, he was denied admission. With the help of NAACP lawyer Thurgood Marshall, McKissick sued the university and won, and he went on to become the first African American to earn an LL.B. degree at that institution.

While still in school, McKissick had become an active member of the Congress of Racial Equality (CORE). When McKissick replaced James Farmer as head of CORE on January 3, 1966, he quickly made a name for himself. Under McKissick's direction, the organization moved more firmly into the Black Power movement, refusing to support Martin Luther King Jr.'s call for massive nonviolent civil disobedience in northern cities, concentrating instead on programs aimed at increasing the political power and improving the economic position of African Americans. In 1967, the organization moved to eliminate the word *multiracial* from its constitution.

McKissick resigned as national director of CORE in 1968. He then launched a plan to establish a new community, Soul City, in Warren County, North Carolina. McKissick envisioned Soul City as a community with sufficient industry to support a population of 50,000. For his venture, he received a $14 million bond issue guarantee from the Department of Housing and Urban Development and a loan of $500,000 from the First Pennsylvania Bank.

Soul City ran into difficulties, however, and despite the best efforts of McKissick the project never developed as planned. In June 1980, the Soul City Corporation and the federal government reached an agreement allowing the government to assume control of the project. Under the agreement, the company retained eighty-eight acres of the project, including the site of a mobile-home park and a 60,000-square-foot building that had served as the project's headquarters.

McKissick died on April 28, 1981, of lung cancer and was buried at Soul City.

KWEISI MFUME

See chapter 11, Politics.

HUEY P. NEWTON (1942–1989)

Black Panther Party Cofounder. The youngest of seven children, Huey P. Newton was born in Monroe, Louisiana, on February 17, 1942. He attended Oakland City College in Oakland, California, where he founded the Afro-American Association, and later studied at San Francisco Law School. In 1966, Newton joined forces with Bobby Seale and established the Black Panther Party for Self-Defense.

Newton and his partner almost immediately became targets of police resentment and uneasiness. The hostility came to a climax in 1967, when Newton allegedly killed an Oakland police officer. His eight-week trial was a cause

Huey P. Newton, Cofounder, Black Panther Party, Oakland, CA, 1966. *Shortly after founding the Black Panther Party in 1966, Newton and Bobby Seale became targets of police resentment and uneasiness.* AP IMAGES. REPRODUCED BY PERMISSION.

célèbre in which more than 2,500 demonstrators surrounded the courthouse chanting Panther slogans and demanding his release. Newton was convicted of voluntary manslaughter and sent to the California Men's Colony. His conviction was later overturned by a California appellate court.

By the 1970s, the Black Panther Party had become a potent political force in California. Coleader Seale made an almost successful bid for the mayorship of Oakland in 1973. In 1977, the Panthers helped elect the city's first African American mayor, Lionel Wilson. Meanwhile, Newton continued to have problems with the law. He was charged with shooting a prostitute, but after two hung juries, the charges were dropped. He was retried and convicted for the 1967 death of the police officer and again the conviction was reversed.

In 1980, he earned his Ph.D. in philosophy from the University of California; his doctoral thesis was "War against the Panthers: Study of Repression in America." This achievement, however, was followed by further problems. He was charged with embezzling state and federal funds from an educational and nutritional program that he headed in 1985. Two years later, he was convicted of illegal possession of guns. On August 22, 1989, in Oakland, he was fatally shot by a small-time drug dealer.

FREDERICK D. PATTERSON (1901–1988)

UNCF Founder, Former College President. Frederick Douglass Patterson was the force behind the first collective fund-raising efforts among African American colleges—the United Negro College Fund. He was also influential in the development of African American higher education through his presidency of the Tuskegee Institute. It was during his administration that the internationally known Tuskegee Airmen was formed.

Patterson was born in the Anacostia neighborhood of Washington, D.C., on October 10, 1901. His parents died before young Patterson was two years old, forcing him to live with various family members while attending school. He worked his way through veterinary school, receiving B.S. (1923) and M.S. (1927) degrees in veterinary medicine from Iowa State University. Before and after receiving his master's degree, Patterson taught at Virginia State College (now University) in Petersburg. In 1928, he moved to Tuskegee Normal and Industrial Institute (now University) in Alabama, where he was a teacher and the head of the Veterinary Department. He obtained a Ph.D. in bacteriology from Cornell University in 1932 and returned to Tuskegee as head of the Agriculture Department. A year later, he was named president of Tuskegee. He also chaired the Robert R. Moton Memorial Institute and served as director of education for the Phelps-Stokes Fund.

Among Patterson's accomplishments at Tuskegee was the establishment of an accredited school of veterinary medicine. It remains the only such school ever established on an African American college campus. Patterson began a program in commercial aviation in 1939 to train

Tuskegee's students as pilots. He was lobbied successfully to have a training program for military pilots at Tuskegee and train commercial aviators as well. His military trainees became the celebrated Tuskegee Airmen, an African American pilots group that fought in World War II. In 1940, Patterson founded the George Washington Carver Foundation to encourage and financially support scientific research by African Americans. In 1948, he started the School of Engineering at Tuskegee.

In 1943, Patterson proposed the creation of an African American college consortium to raise money for their mutual benefit. In 1944, twenty-seven schools came together to form the United Negro College Fund (UNCF). Some view Patterson's efforts as the most important act of his career. He served as UNCF president from 1964 to 1966. UNCF continues as an important national fund-raising effort for its member colleges. Its annual telethons, which featured Lou Rawls as host until the singer's death in 2006, raise millions of dollars and promote financial support for member colleges both locally and nationally.

Frederick D. Patterson, President of Tuskegee Institute, and Botanist George Washington Carver, 1940. *Patterson and Carver discuss the upcoming celebration honoring Booker T. Washington, founder of the Tuskegee Institute.* **BETTMANN/ CORBIS**

In 1953, Patterson retired from Tuskegee and became president of the Phelps-Stokes Fund, an organization established in 1911 to support the education of African, African American, and Native American students in the United States. He left the fund in 1970 to head the Robert R. Moton Memorial Institute, another effort to boost the endowments of African American colleges.

President Ronald Reagan honored Patterson in 1987 with the Presidential Medal of Freedom. Patterson's autobiography, *Chronicles of Faith,* was published after his death on April 26, 1988. In recognition of his work, he received the Spingarn Medal from the NAACP posthumously in 1988. Later, in 1996, the UNCF named its new institute the Frederick D. Patterson Research Institute.

HUGH B. PRICE (1941–)

Former NUL President and CEO. When Hugh B. Price was named president and CEO of the National Urban League in 1994, he inherited an organization with financial problems and a lack of visibility. He proved to be the right person to address and eradicate those problems. Born on November 22, 1941, in Washington, D.C., Price graduated from Amherst College in 1963 and then received his LL.B. from Yale University in 1966. Immediately going to work in the inner city, Price worked as an attorney for the New Haven Legal Assistance Association and later as executive director of the Black Coalition of New Haven.

In 1970, Price continued to focus on inner-city issues by joining the urban affairs consulting firm of Cogen, Holt and Associates in New Haven, specializing in the analysis of municipal government. After serving as human-resources administration director for the city of New Haven, Price was offered the opportunity to express his opinions to a much larger audience on the editorial board of the *New York Times.* Price primarily concentrated on writing about domestic policy issues.

After spending six years at WNET-TV, New York City's public television station, Price became vice president of the Rockefeller Foundation, helping minorities obtain more opportunities from groups served by the organization. With his extensive background, Price caught the attention of the NUL board of directors and was named president in 1994.

Price continued to focus on poorly funded schools, inner-city youth, and unemployment. He vowed that the NUL would not be race-specific in its help—it would be need-specific. During his tenure, the NUL changed its focus by helping entire urban neighborhoods, instead of singling out a particular race in that neighborhood. This approach gained Price much deserved attention in the media. Price left the NUL in the spring of 2003. He joined the Brookings Institution in 2006 as a senior fellow. He also wrote a weekly newspaper column that appeared in a number of major newspapers across the country.

A. PHILIP RANDOLPH (1889–1979)

Brotherhood of Sleeping Car Porters, A. Philip Randolph Institute Founder. Asa Philip Randolph was born in Crescent City, Florida, on April 15, 1889. He attended Cookman Institute in Jacksonville, Florida, before moving to New York City.

In New York, Randolph worked as a porter, a railroad waiter, and an elevator operator. While attending the College of the City of New York, he was exposed to the socialist movement, and in 1917 he organized the *Messenger*, a socialist newspaper. In 1925, Randolph founded the Brotherhood of Sleeping Car Porters to help African American railway car attendants working for the Pullman Palace Car Company. After a ten-year struggle, Randolph and the union negotiated a contract with Pullman in 1935.

Randolph served as a member of New York City's Commission on Race and as president of the National Negro Congress. In 1941, Randolph organized a march on Washington, D.C., to bring attention to discrimination in employment. He was appointed to the New York Housing Authority in 1942 and to the AFL-CIO executive council in 1955.

In 1960, Randolph organized the Negro American Labor Council. He was also one of the organizers of the 1963 March on Washington. In 1965, he cofounded the A. Philip Randolph Institute in New York City, an organization dedicated to eradicating discrimination and defending human and civil rights. Randolph died on May 16, 1979.

RANDALL ROBINSON (1941–)

TransAfrica Founder and Director. Randall Robinson, the brother of television news anchor Max Robinson (1939–1988), was born in Richmond, Virginia, on July 6, 1941, and is a graduate of Virginia Union University and Harvard Law School. In 1977, Robinson founded TransAfrica to lobby Congress and the White House on foreign policy matters involving Africa and the Caribbean. Since its creation, the organization has grown from two to over 15,000 members.

In 1984 and 1985, in protest to the policy of apartheid in South Africa, TransAfrica organized demonstrations in front of the South African embassy in Washington, D.C.; Robinson, along with other protesters, including the singer Stevie Wonder, were arrested. In addition, the organization has advocated for the cessation of aid to countries with human rights problems. In 1981, TransAfrica Forum, an educational and research arm of TransAfrica, was organized to collect and disseminate information on foreign policy affecting Africa and the Caribbean and to encourage public participation in policy debates.

In 1994, the United States was besieged by scores of refugees seeking to escape Haiti's brutal military dictatorship. Many of these refugees, upon reaching the United States or the U.S. military base in Guantánamo, Cuba, were often sent back to Haiti without receiving asylum hearings. On April 12, 1994, Robinson began a liquid-fast diet in an attempt to increase awareness of the plight of Haitian refugees and to pressure the administration of President Bill Clinton to change its refugee policy. On May 8, Robinson ended his fast after the Clinton administration announced that it would grant Haitian refugees asylum hearings.

On March 16, 1995, Robinson announced that TransAfrica would lead a group of prominent African Americans to pressure Nigeria's brutal military leaders to step down from power. Along with other demonstrators, Robinson was arrested during protests in front of the Nigerian Embassy in Washington, D.C. On November 10, 1995, Robinson, along with South African archbishop Desmond Tutu, announced that they would seek economic sanctions or an oil embargo against Nigeria after its military regime executed a prominent Nigerian writer and eight other minority rights activists.

In 1998, Robinson published his memoirs, *Defending the Spirit: A Black Life in America*, which follows Robinson through his triumphs and his hopes for the future. He followed this book up in 2000 with *The Debt: What America Owes to Blacks*, which focuses more on the responsibilities the U.S. government has to the African American community, as well as to people of color around the world. *The Reckoning: What Blacks Owe to Each Other* hit bookstores in 2002. In this companion piece to *The Debt*, Robinson talks directly to the African American community and discusses how the community overall needs to improve if it is to be taken seriously by the nation. His later books include *Quitting America* (2004) and *An Unbroken Agony: Haiti from Revolution to the Kidnapping of a President* (2008).

BAYARD RUSTIN (1910–1987)

Former A. Philip Randolph Institute Executive Director, Civil Rights Organizer. Bayard Rustin was born in West Chester, Pennsylvania, on March 17, 1910. While in school, he was an honor student and star athlete, experiencing his first act of discrimination when he was refused restaurant service in Pennsylvania while on tour with the football team. He attended Wilberforce University,

Cheyney State Normal School (now Cheyney University of Pennsylvania), and the City College of New York.

Rustin was active in various peace organizations, efforts to restrict nuclear armaments, and movements toward African independence. Between 1936 and 1941, Rustin worked as an organizer of the Young Communist League. In 1941, he joined the Fellowship of Reconciliation, a nonviolent antiwar group, and later served as its director of race relations. In 1942, Rustin, along with James Farmer, became active in the Chicago Committee of Racial Equality, out of which the Congress of Racial Equality was formed.

Rustin was one of the founding members of the Southern Christian Leadership Conference. In 1963, he was named chief logistics expert and organizational coordinator of the March on Washington. From 1965 to 1979, Rustin served as executive director of the A. Philip Randolph Institute in New York City. In 1975, he founded the Organization for Black Americans to Support Israel.

Throughout the 1960s, Rustin maintained support for the nonviolent philosophy to which he had dedicated his life. Nonviolence, he argued, was not outdated; it was a necessary and inexorable plan called for by the African American's condition in the United States. Rustin continued to be active in the civil rights movement until his death on August 24, 1987, at the age of seventy-seven.

BOBBY SEALE (1936–)

Black Panther Party Cofounder. Born Robert George Seale in Dallas, Texas, on October 22, 1936, Bobby Seale, along with Huey P. Newton and Bobby Hutton, was one of the founding members of the Black Panther Party for Self-Defense. His family moved from Dallas to Port Arthur, Texas, before settling in Oakland, California.

After leaving high school, Seale joined the U.S. Air Force and trained as a sheet-metal mechanic. He was discharged, however, for disobeying an officer. Returning home, he found sporadic work as a sheet-metal mechanic. In 1959, Seale enrolled at Merritt College in Oakland and studied engineering drafting. While attending Merritt, Seale joined the Afro-American Association, a campus organization that stressed African American separatism and self-improvement. It was through this organization that Seale met Panther cofounder Newton.

Seale and Newton soon became disenchanted with the association. In 1966, Seale and Newton formed the Black Panther Party for Self-Defense. One of their objectives was to form armed patrols to protect citizens from what they considered racist police abuse. When the 1968 Democratic Convention was held in Chicago, it was marked by violent protests and rioting. Eight men—Abbie Hoffman, Jerry Rubin, Tom Hayden, David Dellinger, Lee Weiner, John Froines, Rennie Davis, and Bobby Seale—were held responsible and scheduled for trial in September that year; they became known as the "Chicago Eight." Seale was so contemptuous that he was severed from the trial and sentenced to five years in prison for contempt of court. After that, the remaining defendants were known as the Chicago Seven.

In March 1971, Seale was charged with kidnapping and killing Panther Alex Rackley, a suspected police informant. A mistrial was declared, however, and the charges were dismissed. Seale began to steer the Panthers away from their revolutionary agenda and toward the creation of community-action programs. In 1974, Seale left the party to form Advocates Scene, an organization aimed at helping the underprivileged through grassroots political coalitions.

More recently, Seale has served as a community liaison for Temple University's African American Studies Department. He has lectured throughout the country and has written several books, including *Seize the Time: The Story of the Black Panther Party* (1970), *A Lonely Rage: The Autobiography of Bobby Seale* (1978), and *Barbeque'n with Bobby* (1988).

LEON H. SULLIVAN

See chapter 7, Civil Rights.

MARY E. CHURCH TERRELL

See chapter 7, Civil Rights.

WILLIAM M. TROTTER

See chapter 7, Civil Rights.

FAYE WATTLETON (1943–)

Former Planned Parenthood Executive Director, Women's Rights Activist. One of the most influential African American women in the area of reproductive rights, Faye Wattleton propelled the Planned Parenthood Federation of America into a high-profile, aggressive, and vocal public-health organization.

Born Alyce Faye Wattleton on July 8, 1943, in St. Louis, Missouri, her family, although poor, stressed the importance of helping others who were less fortunate. She graduated from Ohio State University Nursing School in 1964 and then spent two years as a maternity nursing instructor for the Miami Valley Hospital School of Nursing in Dayton. In 1967, Wattleton received an M.S. degree in maternal and infant health care from Columbia University, as well as a certification as a nurse-midwife, after studying on a full scholarship. While at Columbia, she interned at Harlem Hospital and saw firsthand the risks involved in induced abortions by the untrained. The death of a young woman taught Wattleton the importance of safe abortions.

Wattleton returned to Dayton in 1967 as assistant director of Public Health Nursing Services. She also joined the local Planned Parenthood board and became its executive director two years later. In 1975, she chaired a council representing executive directors of Planned Parenthood affiliates around the country, increasing her visibility nationally. Three years later, she was elected president of the Planned Parenthood Federation of America, becoming the first African American woman and the youngest person to head the organization.

Immediately after her appointment, Wattleton insisted that the organization become a strong advocate for women's rights and reproductive freedom. She worked to unite the mostly white, middle- and upper-class women who belonged to the organization and the mostly poor women who were clients in its clinics. Wattleton also argued for equal access to the full range of health services by the rich and poor. In recognition of her work, she received an impressive list of awards and honors, including the American Humanist Award (1986), Women's Honors in Public Service from the American Nursing Association (1986), Congressional Black Caucus Foundation Humanitarian Award (1989), and the American Public Health Association's Award of Excellence (1989).

In January 1992, Wattleton retired from her position with Planned Parenthood and became host of a syndicated talk show that originated in Chicago. Later, in 1995, she helped found the Center for the Advancement of Women and served as the organization's president. Wattleton's autobiography, *Life on the Line*, published in 1996, focuses on her political background as well as the rights of women. Wattleton continues to tour and speak on the issues of abortion and contraceptives.

WALTER WHITE (1893–1955)

Former NAACP Executive Secretary. Walter Francis White was born on July 1, 1893, into a middle-class family that lived on the boundary between African American and white neighborhoods in Atlanta. His family was modestly successful, allowing him to attend Atlanta University. He eventually came to the attention of the NAACP and began to work for the organization in 1918.

White's light completion and hair color allowed him to conduct several undercover investigations of lynching in the South during the 1920s. This later provided him with material for his novel *The Fire in the Flint*, a brutal depiction of the lynching of an innocent African American doctor. Along with his national efforts to end lynching, the book aroused controversy and brought White greater recognition.

In 1931, White became executive secretary of the NAACP, helping to lift the organization from obscurity to a position of influence in which its support was sought even by U.S. presidents. Under his leadership, the NAACP fought for the right to vote, the right of African Americans to be admitted to professional and graduate schools in state universities, and for equal pay for African American teachers in public schools.

Walter White did not live to see the flowering of the civil rights movement in the second half of the 1950s. He died of a heart attack on March 21, 1955. More than three thousand people attended his funeral, and President Dwight D. Eisenhower praised him as "a vigorous champion of justice and equality."

ROY WILKINS (1901–1981)

Former NAACP Executive Director. Born in St. Louis, Missouri, on August 30, 1901, Roy Wilkins was reared in St. Paul, Minnesota. He attended the University of Minnesota, where he majored in sociology and minored in journalism. He served as night editor of the *Minnesota Daily* (the school paper) and edited an African American weekly, the *St. Paul Appeal*. After receiving his B.A. in 1923, he joined the staff of the *Kansas City Call*, a leading African American weekly.

In 1931, Wilkins left the *Call* to serve under Walter White as assistant executive secretary of the NAACP. In 1934, he succeeded W. E. B. Du Bois as editor of the *Crisis* magazine. Wilkins was named acting executive secretary of the NAACP in 1949, when White took a year's leave of absence from the organization. Wilkins assumed the position of executive secretary of the NAACP in 1955. He quickly established himself as one of the most articulate spokesmen in the civil rights movement. He testified before innumerable congressional hearings, conferred with U.S. presidents, and wrote extensively.

For several years, Wilkins served as chairperson of the Leadership Conference on Civil Rights, an organization of more than one hundred national civic, labor, fraternal, and religious organizations. He was a trustee of the Eleanor Roosevelt Memorial Foundation, the Kennedy Memorial Library Foundation, and the Estes Kefauver Memorial Foundation. He was also a member of the board of directors of the Riverdale Children's Association, the John LaFarge Institute, and the Stockbridge School, as well as the international organization Peace with Freedom. Wilkins died on September 8, 1981.

CARTER G. WOODSON

See chapter 16, Education.

Walter White with Roy Wilkins **(left)** ***and Thurgood Marshall*** **(right)*****, c. 1940s.*** *As executive secretary of the NAACP from 1931 until 1955, White significantly increased the organization's influence while fighting for the right to vote, equal pay for African American teachers in public schools, and other causes. Wilkins assumed White's position in 1955, quickly establishing himself as one of the most articulate spokesmen in the civil rights movement.* CORBIS

WHITNEY M. YOUNG JR. (1922–1971)

Former NUL Director. Whitney Moore Young Jr. was born in Lincoln Ridge, Kentucky, on July 31, 1922. He received his B.A. degree from Kentucky State College (now University) in 1941. He went on to attend the Massachusetts Institute of Technology, and, in 1947, he earned an M.A. degree in social work from the University of Minnesota.

In 1947, Young was made director of industrial relations and vocational guidance for the St. Paul, Minnesota, Urban League. In 1950, he moved on to become executive secretary of the St. Paul chapter. Young served as dean of the Atlanta University School of Social Work from 1954 to 1961. He also was a visiting scholar at Harvard University through a Rockefeller Foundation grant.

In 1961, the board of directors of the NUL elected Young as president of the organization. Young instituted new programs such as the National Skills Bank, the Broadcast Skills Bank, the Secretarial Training Project, and an on-the-job training program with the U.S. Department of Labor. Between 1961 and 1971, the organization grew from sixty-three to ninety-eight affiliates.

In addition to his work with the NUL, Young served as president of the National Association of Social Workers and the National Conference on Social Welfare; on the boards and advisory committees of the Rockefeller Foundation, Urban Coalition, and Urban Institute; and on seven presidential commissions. In 1969, Young was selected by President Lyndon B. Johnson to receive the Presidential Medal of Freedom, the nation's highest civilian award. Young wrote two books, *To Be Equal* (1964) and *Beyond Racism: Building an Open Society* (1969). He was also coauthor of *A Second Look: The Negro Citizen in Atlanta* (1958).

Young died on March 11, 1971, while attending a conference in Africa.

NATIONAL ORGANIZATIONS

100 Black Men of America, Inc.
141 Auburn Ave.
Atlanta, GA 30303-2503
Telephone: (404) 688-5100
Web site: http://www.100blackmen.org
Founded: 1963

100 Black Men of America, Inc., is a national alliance of leading African American men of business, industry, public affairs, and government, devoting their combined skills and resources to confronting the challenges facing African America youth. Its mission is to "improve the quality of life within our communities and enhance educational and economic opportunities for all African Americans." A total of 106 national chapters and six international chapters are responsible for mentoring, educational, antiviolence, and economic-development programs. These programs nurture creativity, emphasize academic achievement, and reinforce social responsibility. In 1997, the organization purchased its world headquarters building on Atlanta's historic Auburn Avenue.

A. Philip Randolph Institute
815 16th St. NW, 4th Fl.
Washington, DC 20006-4101
Telephone: (202) 508-3710
Web site: http://www.apri.org
Founded: 1965

This organization promotes cooperation between the African American community and the labor force. The institute's primary interest is political action through coalition building and the organization of affiliate groups. It also conducts research, runs specialized education programs, and maintains a speaker's bureau. It is responsible for administering the A. Philip Randolph Educational Fund.

Africa Action
1634 Eye St. NW, Ste. 810
Washington, DC 20006-4013
Telephone: (202) 546-7961
Web site: http://www.africaaction.org
Founded: 2001

Africa Action works for political, economic, and social justice in Africa. Through predecessors dating as far back as 1953, it is the oldest organization that works on African affairs. Its mission is to change relations between the United States and Africa.

Africa-America Institute
420 Lexington Ave., Ste. 1706
New York, NY 10170-0002
Telephone: (212) 949-5666
Web site: http://www.aaionline.org
Founded: 1953

This institute works to further development in Africa, improve African American understanding, and enlighten and inform Americans about Africa. In addition, it engages in training, development assistance, and informational activities. It sponsors African American conferences, media and congressional workshops, and regional seminars. A multiracial, multiethnic nonprofit organization with headquarters in New York City and offices in South Africa and Mozambique, it has a presence in more than fifty African countries through its alumni network.

Africa Faith and Justice Network
125 Michigan Ave. NE, Ste. 480
Washington, DC 20017-1004
Telephone: (202) 884-9780
Web site: http://www.afjn.org
Founded: 1983

The Africa Faith and Justice Network is a network of Catholic groups and individuals focused on Africa and the experience of its people. The organization is committed in faith to collaborate in the task of transforming U.S. mentality and policy on Africa. It stresses peace-building and human rights and seeks to be an instrument of education and advocacy on behalf of social justice for Africa.

Africa Inland Mission International
PO Box 178
Pearl River, NY 10965-0178
Telephone: (845) 735-4014
Web site: http://www.aimint.org/usa/
Founded: 1895

Africa Inland Mission International's 850 missionaries conduct Bible teaching, community development, education, medical work, and evangelization in Angola, Central African Republic, Chad, Democratic Republic of Congo, Kenya, Lesotho, Madagascar, Mozambique, Namibia, Rwanda, Sudan, Tanzania, Uganda, the islands of the Indian Ocean, and urban centers in the United States, Canada, and the United Kingdom. The group's activities include theological education, radio and television ministries, youth work, technical assistance services, agricultural and community development, relief work, and special, industrial, and secondary education.

Africa Network
3567 Benton St.
Santa Clara, CA 95051-4404
Telephone: (510) 685-4435
Web site: http://www.theafricannetwork.org
Founded: 1981

This nonprofit consortium of liberal arts colleges is centered on a commitment to literacy and a concern for Africa in U.S. higher education. Its mission is "to develop and enhance a lasting presence for Africa in the academic programs and campus life of the nation's liberal arts institutions." Its members work to defend just law, freedom, and human rights. It also offers educational-outreach programs, in addition to sponsoring programs commemorating important historical events of South Africa, including Sharpeville Memorial Day and Soweto Anniversary Commemoration. The group was originally named for Dennis Brutus, a former political prisoner, South African poet, scholar, and antiapartheid activist who was granted political asylum in the United States in 1983.

Africa Travel Association
166 Madison Ave., 5th Fl.
New York, NY 10016-5432
Telephone: (212) 447-1357
Web site: http://www.africatravelassociation.org
Founded: 1975

This organization is an international, nonprofit, nonpolitical, professional travel industry association that conducts regional seminars and trade show exhibitions and sponsors the Africa Guild to help develop a general interest in Africa.

AfricaLink
c/o USAID/AFR/SD/ANRE
1325 G St. NW, Ste. 400
Washington, DC 20005-3121
Telephone: (703) 235-5415
Web site: http://www.usaid.gov/alnk/

AfricaLink is comprised of individuals and organizations with an interest in the economic and community development of Africa. It promotes sustainable development suitable to local needs and capacities. It identifies and distributes appropriate technologies, facilitates the establishment of improved communications networks, and sponsors research and educational programs.

African American Breast Cancer Alliance
PO Box 8981
Minneapolis, MN 55408-0981
Telephone: (612) 825-3675
Web site: http://www.aabcainc.org
Founded: 1990

This organization is committed to helping black women, people of color, families, and communities cope with breast cancer. It sponsors a breast-cancer support group for patients and survivors at various stages of their experiences, and addresses the specific needs of black women diagnosed with breast cancer. In addition to this work, the alliance also sponsors celebrations and health events for survivors, families, friends, and communities.

African American Cultural Alliance
PO Box 22173
Nashville, TN 37202-2173
Telephone: (615) 251-0007
Web site: http://www.aacanashville.org
Founded: 1983

The African American Cultural Alliance seeks to promote African culture and increase public awareness of the cultural and historical heritage of people of African descent by offering educational programs for children through theater, music, dance, history, and poetry. The organization conducts research and maintains a speaker's bureau. It also sponsors the annual African Street Festival held the third weekend in September on the main campus of Tennessee State University in Nashville.

African American Life Alliance
PO Box 3722
Capitol Heights, MD 20791-3722
Founded: 1991

A small, religious, antichoice organization that works to educate the African American community about how "sexual promiscuity and illicit moral activities have invaded the communities and are eroding the families, organizations, schools, and churches."

African-American Women Business Owners Association
3363 Alden Pl. NE
Washington, DC 20019-1314
Telephone: (202) 399-3645
Web site: http://www.blackpgs.com/aawboa.html
Founded: 1982

Made up of small business owners in all industries, particularly business services, this organization seeks to assist in developing a greater number of successful self-employed black women through business and personal development programs, networking, and legislative action.

African Cradle, Inc.
4043 El Camino Wy.
Palo Alto, CA 94306-4009
Telephone: (650) 461-9192
Web site: http://www.africancradle.org

African Cradle is a full-service, nonprofit adoption agency that works with the Ethiopian government to find homes for children in need of adoption, and provides necessary care to infants and children in Ethiopia. Its mission is to provide effective programs that address the problems of orphaned, abandoned, abused, and neglected children in the United States and abroad.

African Development Institute Inc.
PO Box 1644
New York, NY 10185-1621
Toll Free: (888) 619-7535
Web site: http://www.africainstitute.com
Founded: 1995

This institute seeks to find practical solutions to Africa's developmental crisis through nonpartisan policy research. It conducts study and discussion forums, special events, and educational-outreach programs.

Africare
Africare House
440 R St. NW
Washington, DC 20001-1961
Telephone: (202) 462-3614
Web site: http://www.africare.org
Founded: 1970

Africare seeks to improve the quality of life in rural Africa. It provides health and environmental-protection services in rural areas of Africa, works to improve African water and agricultural resources, and conducts public-education programs in the United States on African development.

Afro-American Historical and Genealogical Society, Inc.
PO Box 73067
Washington, DC 20056-3067
Telephone: (202) 234-5350
Web site: http://www.aahgs.org
Founded: 1977

This society encourages scholarly research in African American history and genealogy as it relates to American history and culture. The group collects, maintains, and preserves materials related to its purpose, which the society makes available for research and publication. It also conducts seminars and workshops.

All-African People's Revolutionary Party
PO Box 863
New York, NY 10116-0861
Web site: http://www.panafricanperspective.com/aaprp/
Founded: 1971

Founded by Africans and persons of African descent who support Pan-Africanism, "the total liberation and unification of Africa under Scientific Socialism." In 1980, the organization established the All-American Women's Revolutionary Union, its internal women's wing.

Alpha Kappa Alpha Sorority, Inc.
5656 S. Stony Island Ave.
Chicago, IL 60637-1906
Telephone: (773) 684-1282
Web site: http://www.aka1908.com
Founded: 1908

Alpha Kappa Alpha is a service sorority founded on the campus of Howard University in 1908. It is the oldest Greek letter organization established for African American women who are college educated.

Alpha Phi Alpha Fraternity, Inc.
2313 Saint Paul St.
Baltimore, MD 21218-5211
Telephone: (410) 554-0040
Web site: http://www.alpha-phi-alpha.com
Founded: 1906

Alpha Phi Alpha is a service fraternity founded at Cornell University in 1906.

Alpha Pi Chi National Sorority, Inc.
PO Box 26
Kensington, MD 20895-0026
Web site: http://www.alphapichi.org
Founded: 1963

Alpha Pi Chi is a service sorority founded in 1963.

American Association of Blacks in Energy
1625 K St. NW, Ste. 405
Washington, DC 20006-1678
Telephone: (202) 371-9530
Web site: http://www.aabe.org
Founded: 1977

This association was founded by African Americans in energy-related professions, including engineers, scientists, consultants, academicians, and entrepreneurs; government officials and public policy makers; and interested students. The organization represents African Americans and other minorities in matters involving energy use and research, the formulation of energy policy, the ownership of energy resources, and the development of energy technologies. It seeks to increase the knowledge, understanding, and awareness of the minority community in energy issues by serving as an energy information source for policy makers, recommending African Americans and other minorities to appropriate energy officials and executives, encouraging students to pursue professional careers in the energy industry, and advocating for the participation of African Americans and other minorities in energy programs and policy making activities. It also updates members on key legislation and regulations being developed by the Department of Energy, the Department of the Interior, the Department of Commerce, the Small Business Administration, and other federal and state agencies.

American Black Book Writers Association
PO Box 10458
Venice Beach, CA 90295
Telephone: (323) 822-5195
Founded: 1980

This association represents African Americans in the U.S. publishing industry. It encourages the development of African American authors and works to preserve and advance African American literature. Its activities include promoting and providing market support to member's works, holding mutual promotions and tours, sponsoring cooperative advertising in African American–oriented media, and conducting research on problems affecting African American authors and their works in the United States.

American Tennis Association, Inc.
1100 Mercantile Ln., Ste. 115A
Largo, MD 20774-5380
Telephone: (301) 583-4631
Web site: http://www.atanational.com
Founded: 1916

Founded by persons interested in tennis, this organization promotes and develops tennis among African Americans. It supports training programs for coaches, and sponsors tournaments and training programs for young players.

Association for the Preservation and Presentation of the Arts
2011 Benning Rd. NE
Washington, DC 20002-4725
Telephone: (202) 396-4661
Founded: 1964

This organization was founded by individuals representing the visual and performing arts and interested others. It serves as a vehicle for the promotion of blacks in the arts, while also seeking to increase public awareness and appreciation of the arts and its representation of African American culture. Other areas of focus include developing musical and dance productions, producing children's shows, and sponsoring lectures. The association offers scholarships to children and young people interested in the arts.

Association for the Study of African American Life and History
C.B. Powell Bldg., Ste. C-142
525 Bryant St. NW
Washington, DC 20059-1005
Telephone: (202) 865-0053
Web site: http://www.asalh.org
Founded: 1915

A sponsor of Black History Month, the Association for the Study of African American Life and History (ASALH) is comprised of historians, scholars, and students interested in the research and study of black people as a contributing factor in civilization. ASALH works to promote historical research and writings, collects historical manuscripts and materials relating to black people throughout the world, and brings about harmony among the races by interpreting one to the other. In addition, it encourages the study of black history and training in the social sciences, history, and other disciplines. ASALH cooperates with governmental agencies, foundations, and peoples and nations in projects designed to advance the study of ethnic history, with an emphasis on black heritage and programs for the future.

Association of African American Museums
PO Box 427
Wilberforce, OH 45384-0427
Telephone: (937) 376-4944, ext. 123
Web site: http://www.blackmuseums.org
Founded: 1978

This association represents museums, scholars, and museum professionals concerned with preserving, restoring, displaying, researching, and collecting African American culture and history. The group also provides technical assistance to African American museums, conducting professional training workshops, surveys, and evaluations.

Association of African Women Scholars
c/o Department of World Languages & Cultures
Cavanaugh Hall 543A, Indiana University
425 University Blvd.
Indianapolis, IN 46202-5148
Telephone: (317) 278-2038
Web site: http://www.africanwomenstudies.org
Founded: 1995

This association promotes scholarship among women of African descent worldwide and seeks to form intellectual links among scholars studying Africa, colonialism, and related topics. It serves as a clearinghouse on African history, culture, economics, and development, particularly as these issues impact women. Additional activities include providing information and advice to policy makers, participating in advocacy work, and promoting research and educational programs.

Association of Black Admissions and Financial Aid Officers of the Ivy League and Sister Schools
PO Box 381402
Cambridge, MA 02238-1402
Web site: http://www.abaschools.org
Founded: 1970

This association was founded by present and former minority admissions and financial aid officers employed at Ivy League or sister schools. These schools include Barnard College, Brown University, Bryn Mawr College, Columbia University, Cornell University, Dartmouth College, Harvard University, Massachusetts Institute of Technology, Mount Holyoke College, University of Pennsylvania, Princeton University, Smith College, Stanford University, Vassar College, Wellesley College, and Yale University. The organization aids minority students who wish to pursue a college education and seeks to improve methods of recruitment, admittance, and financial services that support the growth and maintenance of the minority student population at these institutions. It encourages Ivy League and sister schools to respond to the needs of minority students and admissions and financial aid officers.

Association of Black Anthropologists
c/o American Anthropological Association
2200 Wilson Blvd., Ste. 600
Arlington, VA 22201-3357
Telephone: (703) 528-1902
Web site: http://www.aaanet.org/sections/aba/htdocs/
Founded: 1970

This association works to formulate conceptual and methodological frameworks to advance understanding of all forms of human diversity and commonality; advance theoretical efforts to explain the conditions that produce social inequalities based on race, ethnicity, class, or gender; and develop research methods that involve the peoples studied and local scholars in all stages of investigation and in the dissemination of findings.

Association of Black Cardiologists, Inc.
2400 N St. NW, Ste. 604
Washington, DC 20037
Toll Free: (800) 753-9222
Web site: http://www.abcardio.org
Founded: 1974

This association seeks to improve prevention and treatment of cardiovascular diseases.

Association of Black Foundation Executives
333 7th Ave.
New York, NY 10001
Telephone: (646) 230-0306
Web site: http://www.abfe.org
Founded: 1971

This organization encourages increased recognition of economic, educational, and social issues facing African Americans in the grant-making field. It seeks to promote support of African Americans and their status as grant-making professionals, increase the number of African Americans entering the grant-making field, and help members improve their job effectiveness. Though involved with grant-making organizations, the association itself does not award grants.

Association of Black Nursing Faculty, Inc.
PO Box 580
Lisle, IL 60532-0580
Telephone: (630) 969-0221
Web site: http://www.abnf.net
Founded: 1987

This association works to promote health-related issues and educational concerns of interest to the African American community and the association's members. It serves as a forum for communication and the exchange of information among members, and it also develops strategies for expressing concerns to other individuals, institutions, and communities. Among its aims are assisting members in professional development, developing and sponsoring continuing education activities, fostering networking and guidance in employment and recruitment activities, and promoting health-related issues in legislation, government programs, and community activities.

Association of Black Psychologists
PO Box 55999
Washington, DC 20040-5999
Telephone: (202) 722-0808
Web site: http://www.abpsi.org
Founded: 1968

The Association of Black Psychologists aims to do the following: enhance the psychological well-being of African American people; define mental health in consonance with newly established psychological concepts and standards; develop policies for local, state, and national decision-making that affects the mental health of the African American community; support established African American sister organizations; and aid in the development of new, independent African American institutions to enhance the psychological, educational, cultural, and economic situation.

Association of Black Sociologists
4200 Wisconsin Ave. NW, PMB 106-257
Washington, DC 20016-2143
Telephone: (202) 365-1759
Web site: http://www.blacksociologists.org
Founded: 1968

The purposes of this organization are to promote the professional interests of African American sociologists; promote an increase in the number of professionally trained sociologists; help stimulate and improve the quality of research and the teaching of sociology; provide perspectives regarding African American experiences, as well as expertise for understanding and dealing with problems confronting African American people; and protect the professional rights and safeguard the civil rights stemming from executing the above objectives.

Association of Black Sporting Goods Professionals
PO Box 772074
Coral Springs, FL 33077-2074
Toll Free: (888) 294-7020
Founded: 1990

This association promotes the benefits of diversity and seeks to facilitate access to career opportunities for its members. It serves as a clearinghouse on the sporting goods industry and conducts industry research. Additional services and programs include the Job Information Services and Career Awareness Program to encourage increased participation by African Americans in the sporting goods industry; and the Partners in Progress Program to enhance the understanding of culturally diverse markets among sporting goods executives.

Association of Black Women Attorneys
255 W. 36th St., Ste. 800
New York, NY 10018
Telephone: (212) 300-2193
Web site: http://www.abwanewyork.org
Founded: 1976

An affiliate of the National Bar Association, the ABWA is an organization for African American women lawyers. Its mission is "to encourage and enhance the professional development of women of color." It provides information and opportunities for networking and mentoring.

Association of Black Women in Higher Education
PO Box 210
Princeton, NJ 08542-0210
Telephone: (609) 258-7801
Web site: http://www.abwhe.org
Founded: 1978

Comprised of faculty members, education administrators, students, retirees, consultants, managers, and affirmative action officers, this organization's objectives are to nurture the role of black women in higher education and to provide support for the professional development goals of black women. Association members conduct workshops and seminars.

Association of Concerned African Scholars
c/o Kristin Peterson
University of California, Anthropology Department
3151 Social Sciences Plz.
Irvine, CA 92697-5100
Telephone: (949) 824-9652
Web site: http://www.concernedafricascholars.org
Founded: 1977

This association facilitates scholarly analysis and opinion in order to impact U.S. policy toward Africa, formulates alternative government policy toward Africa and disseminates it to the public, and works to develop a communication and action network among African scholars. It mobilizes support on current issues, participates in local public education programs, stimulates research on policy-oriented issues and disseminates findings, and informs and updates members on international policy developments.

Association of Public and Land-Grant Universities
1307 New York Ave. NW, Ste. 400
Washington, DC 20005-4722
Telephone: (202) 478-6040
Web site: http://www.aplu.org
Founded: 1968

This organization was founded to collect, organize, interpret, and disseminate data on thirty-five predominantly African American public colleges. The colleges, located in eighteen states, enroll over 135,000 students.

The Balm in Gilead, Inc.
701 E. Franklin St., Ste. 1000
Richmond, VA 23219-2503
Telephone: (804) 644-2256
Web site: http://www.balmingilead.org
Founded: 1989

The mission of this private organization is to improve the health status of people of the African diaspora by building the capacity of faith communities to address life-threatening diseases, especially HIV/AIDS. It develops educational and training programs to meet the needs of black churches and faith communities that aim to become centers for HIV/AIDS ministries. The organization partners with faith communities in Côte d'Ivoire, Kenya, Nigeria, Tanzania, and Zimbabwe to address their HIV/AIDS challenges.

A Better Chance
240 W. 35th St., 9th Fl.
New York, NY 10001-2506
Telephone: (646) 346-1310
Web site: http://www.abetterchance.org
Founded: 1963

A Better Chance identifies, recruits, and places talented minority students into leading secondary and public schools. Member schools provide financial aid for needy students. The group also conducts research and offers technical assistance on expanded opportunities for minority students in secondary and higher education.

Black, Indian, Hispanic, and Asian Women in Action
1830 James Ave. N
Minneapolis, MN 55411-3164
Telephone: (612) 521-2986
Founded: 1983

This organization strives to empower black, Indian, Hispanic, and Asian women through the implementation of educational projects. It acts as an advocate for women of color in the areas of racism, ageism, family violence, chemical dependence, education, and physical and mental health. BIHA, as the group is known, also works for social change, the health of the family, and the advancement of socioeconomic status.

Black Affairs Center for Training and Organizational Development
c/o Margaret V. Wright
10918 Jarboe Ct.
Silver Spring, MD 20901-1419
Telephone: (301) 681-9822
Founded: 1970

This center is a multidisciplinary management research organization that promotes social change, educational improvement, organization renewal and goal achievement, systematic problem solving, and multicultural skills development through custom-designed training programs and consultation services. The organization offers individuals, groups, educational systems, and governmental and community agencies programs such as equal employment opportunity training; employee motivation, productivity and improvement training; and career education and development training. Programs are continually being developed in such areas as women's concerns, single parenthood, youth and sex, drugs and alcoholism, the aging, day care, sexual harassment, and stress management.

Black American Cinema Society
3617 Montclair St.
Los Angeles, CA 90018-2442
Telephone: (213) 737-3292
Founded: 1975

Made up of faculty members, students, senior citizens, and film and jazz enthusiasts, this society works to bring about an awareness of the contributions made by African Americans to the motion picture industry in silent films, early talkies, and short and feature films. The group maintains a collection of early black films owned by the Western States Black Research and Educational Center. It conducts research projects, film shows, and Black History Month seminars. Other activities include providing financial support to independent black filmmakers, compiling statistics, maintaining a speakers bureau, and sponsoring a traveling film festival.

Black American Response to the African Community
127 N. Madison Ave., Ste. 400
Pasadena, CA 91101-1717
Telephone: (818) 584-0303
Founded: 1984

This grassroots organization of entertainers, journalists, clergy, and business, health, and community leaders works to assist the victims of drought and famine in Africa. The group focuses on emergency efforts involving medical needs, water irrigation, housing, and food supplies. In addition, it provides relief for orphans through its Family Network Program and disseminates current information on drought-stricken areas in Africa. Other activities include assisting in the development of regeneration projects in affected areas, maintaining a national education task force to educate Americans on the African crisis, and sponsoring media updates. The group raises funds through television documentaries, benefit movie premieres, art exhibits, and collection boxes.

Black Americans for Life
9504 E. 63rd St.
Raytown, MO 64133
Telephone: (816) 353-4113
Web site: http://kcblacksforlife.org
Founded: 1984

Black Americans for Life provides outreach programs to the black community to help save black babies and to educate, identify, and mobilize people within the community to build pro-life grassroots groups. It works through a variety of groups to achieve its goals.

Black Americans in Publishing
c/o Phelps-Stokes Fund Affiliate
PO Box 6275, FDR Sta.
10 E. 87th St.
New York, NY 10128
Telephone: (212) 427-8100
Web site: http://www.baip.org
Founded: 1979

This organization is a networking and support group whose purpose is to encourage minorities interested in all sectors of the print industry, including book, newspaper, and magazine publishing. It promotes the image of minorities working in all sectors of the industry and recognizes achievements of minorities in the media. It works for a free and responsible press and facilitates the exchange of ideas and information among members, especially regarding career planning and job security. Members are kept informed about the publishing industry and their impact on it. The group encourages and works to maintain high professional standards in publishing and collaborates with other organizations in striving to improve the status of women and minorities.

Black and Indian Mission Office
2021 H St. NW
Washington, DC 20006-4207
Telephone: (202) 331-8542
Web site: http://www.blackandindianmission.org/
Founded: 1884

This office supports dioceses with their evangelization programs from the inner cities to the outlands. It supports Catholic evangelization efforts among blacks, Indians, and indigenous communities across the United States.

Black Broadcasters Alliance
3474 William Penn Hwy.
Pittsburgh, PA 15235-5410
Telephone: (412) 829-9788
Founded: 1997

This organization is comprised of African American broadcasters working to better educate and assist those who seek career opportunities in the industry. It places emphasis on increasing African American representation in ownership, management, engineering, and sales. It also exercises the right to inform, lobby, and influence the public, as well as local and national governmental bodies, as to equal participation in the industry.

Black Career Women
PO Box 19332
Cincinnati, OH 45219-0332
Telephone: (513) 531-1932
Web site: http://www.bcw.org
Founded: 1977

Black Career Women is a national organization made up of African American professional women that is dedicated to promoting the professional advancement of its members. The organization also seeks to establish and support "formal black women's networks." In addition, it provides career development resources and educational courses to members, develops information and research on black women workers, and serves as a "supportive forum for the black woman dealing with the complexities of personal and professional development."

Black Caucus of the American Library Association, Inc.
PO Box 1738
Hampton, VA 23669-0738
Telephone: (757) 727-5190
Web site: http://www.bcala.org
Founded: 1970

This organization promotes librarianship and encourages the active participation of African Americans in library associations and boards at all levels of the profession. It monitors the activities of the American Library Association (ALA) with regard to its policies and programs and how they affect African American librarians and library users. In addition, it reviews, analyzes, evaluates, and recommends to the ALA actions that influence the recruitment, development, advancement, and general working conditions of African American librarians. It facilitates library services that meet the informational needs of African American people, including increased availability of materials related to social and economic concerns, and encourages the development of authoritative information resources concerning African American people and the dissemination of this information to the public.

Black Coaches & Administrators
Pan American Plz.
201 S. Capitol Ave., Ste. 495
Indianapolis, IN 46225-1089
Telephone: (317) 829-5600
Web site: http://bcasports.cstv.com
Founded: 1988

This organization promotes the creation of a positive environment in which issues such as stereotyping, lack of significant media coverage, and discrimination can be exposed, discussed, and resolved. It provides member services and petitions the National Collegiate Athletic Association legislative bodies to design, enact, and enforce diligent guidelines and policies to improve professional mobility for minorities.

Black Community Crusade for Children
25 E St. NW
Washington, DC 20001
Telephone: (202) 628-8787
Web site: http://www.childrensdefense.org/

This organization is composed of African American clergy, educators, policy makers, and community leaders who seek to ensure "no child is left behind, and that every child has a Healthy Start, a Head Start, a Fair Start, a Safe Start, and a Moral Start in life, with the support of caring parents and nurturing communities." The group works to mobilize the black community on behalf of children. It conducts programs in such areas as community building; spiritual, character, and leadership development; intergenerational mentoring; interracial and interethnic communication; interdisciplinary networking; and training. The group organizes Freedom Schools, which provide meals and education and cultural enrichment programs in local communities; operates Student Leadership Network for Children (SLNC); and maintains a farm once owned by the African American author Alex Haley.

Black Data Processing Associates
9500 Arena Dr., Ste. 350
Largo, MD 20774-3715
Telephone: (301) 322-3434
Web site: http://www.bdpa.org
Founded: 1975

This organization seeks to accumulate and share information-processing knowledge and business expertise in order to increase the career and business potential of minorities in the information-processing field.

Black Entertainment and Sports Lawyers Association
PO Box 441485
Fort Washington, MD 20749-1485
Telephone: (301) 248-1818
Web site: http://www.besla.org
Founded: 1980

This association provides efficient and effective legal representation to African American entertainers and athletes. It offers a referral system for legal representation and a resource bank for providing information to students, groups, and nonprofit and civic organizations involved in the entertainment industry. It also serves as an industry watchdog in protecting the rights of African Americans within the entertainment community.

Black Farmers and Agriculturalists Association
PO Box 61
Tillery, NC 27887-0061
Telephone: (252) 826-2800
Web site: http://www.bfaa-us.org
Founded: 1997

This association is a grassroots organization united in direct response to the decline in African American farmers and landowners.

Black Filmmaker Foundation
133 Varick St., Ste. 937
New York, NY 10013-1443
Telephone: (212) 253-1690
Web site: http://www.dvrepublic.com
Founded: 1978

This group assists emerging filmmakers and fosters audience development by programming local, national, and international film festivals. It maintains a video library and conducts seminars and workshops.

Black Filmmakers Hall of Fame, Inc.
405 14th St.
Oakland, CA 94612
Telephone: (510) 465-0804
Founded: 1973

This organization studies, teaches, and preserves the contributions of African American filmmakers to American cinema. It fosters cultural awareness through educational, research, and public service programs in the film arts. It also holds film lecture series, the Black Filmworks Festival, and an annual international film competition.

Black Flight Attendants of America, Inc.
1060 Crenshaw Blvd., Ste. 202
Los Angeles, CA 90019-1900
Toll Free: (888) 682-2322
Web site: http://www.bfaoa.com
Founded: 1974

This organization of aviation professionals seeks to expand educational opportunities through travel for at-risk communities, supports and mentors aviation professionals, promotes civic and charitable endeavors in African American communities, and assists corporations in identifying qualified minorities for management and professional positions. The group also sponsors career days in inner-city schools.

Black Mental Health Alliance for Education and Consultation, Inc.
733 West 40th St., Ste. 10
Baltimore, MD 21211-2107
Telephone: (410) 338-2642
Web site: http://blackmentalhealth.com
Founded: 1984

This organization seeks to increase awareness among clinicians, clergy, educators, and social service professionals of the mental health needs and concerns of African Americans on such issues as stress, violence, racism, substance abuse, and parenting. It provides consultation, public information, and resource referrals. It conducts a public awareness campaign, educates the community about available resources, and develops programs that benefit African American children and families. It offers training to human service workers, teachers, police officers, and other service providers who work with culturally diverse populations. It also maintains a speakers bureau. The support group provides emotional support, education, and interaction for family members experiencing the stresses of caring for or living with a mentally ill relative. It provides a resource referral service and maintains an extensive list of African American mental health professionals who are sensitive to and appreciate cultural differences.

Black Methodists for Church Renewal, Inc.
201 8th Ave. S
Nashville, TN 37203-3919
Telephone: (615) 749-6351
Web site: http://www.bmcrumc.org
Founded: 1968

This group serves as platform from which African Americans can express concerns to the general church on such issues as revival and survival of the African American church; involvement of African Americans within the structure of the church; the conduct of the church as it relates to investment policies and social issues; economic support in the African American community; and the support of the twelve African American colleges. It encourages African American Methodists to work for economic and social justice and works to expose racism in agencies and institutions of the United Methodist Church. The group also seeks improvement of educational opportunities for African Americans, the strengthening of African American churches, and an increase in the number of African American persons in Christian-related vocations. It advocates liberation, peace, justice, and freedom for all people and supports programs that alleviate suffering in developing countries.

Black Military History Institute of America
PO Box 1134
Fort Meade, MD 20755-3134
Telephone: (410) 757-4250
Founded: 1987

This institute is made up of individuals interested in promoting the military achievements of African Americans and publicizing other aspects of black history. The organization seeks to provide archival facilities to collect, preserve, and exhibit materials pertaining to military history; motivate and support underprivileged youths by using military role models as a source of inspiration; and foster a spirit of camaraderie and goodwill among all persons sharing an interest in community involvement programs for the underprivileged. The organization also sponsors slide lectures and photographic exhibits, in addition to maintaining a speakers bureau.

Black Pilots of America, Inc.
PO Box 7463
Pine Bluff, AR 71611-7463
Telephone: (870) 879-6612
Web site: http://www.bpapilots.org
Founded: 1997

This organization trains African Americans to participate and advance in various areas within the field of aviation. It also encourages youth to enter the field of aviation, promotes opportunities in the field of aviation by lecturing in schools, and encourages recognition of the contributions of blacks in aviation.

Black Psychiatrists of America
2020 Pennsylvania Ave. NW, No. 725
Washington, DC 20006-1811
Toll Free: (877) 272-1967
Web site: http://www.blackpsych.org
Founded: 1969

This organization is composed of African American psychiatrists, either in practice or training, united to promote African American behavioral science and foster high-quality psychiatric care for African Americans and minority group members. The group also sponsors a public-information service.

Black Retail Action Group, Inc.
PO Box 1192
Rockefeller Center Station
New York, NY 10185
Telephone: (212) 319-7751
Web site: http://www.bragusa.org
Founded: 1970

This organization is composed of minorities dedicated to the inclusion of all groups in the mainstream of the U.S. economy. It promotes leadership skills of its members and assists major retailers in selecting, developing, and advancing diverse people of color.

Black Revolutionary War Patriots Foundation
729 15th St. NW, Ste. 500
Washington, DC 20005-2105
Telephone: (202) 452-1776
Founded: 1985

This foundation aims to present an accurate depiction of African Americans' involvement in the American Revolution and the founding of the United States. It raises private funds for the establishment of a memorial in Washington, D.C., to commemorate African American patriots of the American Revolutionary War.

Black Rock Coalition
PO Box 1054, Cooper Sta.
New York, NY 10276
Telephone: (212) 713-5097
Web site: http://www.blackrockcoalition.org
Founded: 1985

This group promotes, produces, and distributes alternative African American music and provides information, technical expertise, and performance and recording opportunities for "musically and politically progressive musicians." It also works to increase the visibility of African American rock artists in music media and on college radio stations.

Black Stuntmen's Association
8949 W. 24th St.
Los Angeles, CA 90034-2009
Telephone: (310) 202-9191
Founded: 1966

This association is composed of men and women ages eighteen to fifty who are members of the Screen Actors Guild and the American Federation of Television and Radio Artists. The organization serves as an agency for stunt persons in motion pictures and television, conducts stunt performances at local schools, and offers placement services.

Black Theatre Network
763 Belmont Pl. E, No. 105
Seattle, WA 98102-4453
Telephone: (352) 495-2116
Web site: http://www.blacktheatrenetwork.org
Founded: 1986

The network is made up of individuals involved in higher education and professionals in black theater. It serves as a networking organization for those with interests in black theater—either in academia or at the professional level—and also organizes workshops.

Black Veterans for Social Justice, Inc.
665 Willoughby Ave.
Brooklyn, NY 11206-6903
Telephone: (718) 852-6004
Web site: http://www.bvsj.org
Founded: 1979

This group seeks to aid African American veterans in obtaining information concerning their rights, ways to upgrade a less-than-honorable discharge, and Veterans Administration benefits due them and their families. It seeks to prohibit discrimination against African American veterans, provides educational programs, and facilitates veterans' sharing of skills acquired while in service. The group's activities include counseling and community workshops on veteran issues and a program to provide services to veterans in local prisons. It also assists veterans who have suffered from the effects of Agent Orange, an herbicide containing dioxin and used as a defoliant in Vietnam until 1969.

Black Women in Church and Society
700 Martin Luther King Jr. Dr.
Atlanta, GA 30314-4143
Telephone: (404) 527-5713
Web site: http://www.itc.edu/pages/wsp/WSPHome.htm
Founded: 1981

This group was founded to provide structured activities and support systems for African American women whose goals include participating in leadership roles in church and society, and a platform for communication between laywomen and clergywomen. It conducts research into questions and issues pivotal to African American women in church and society and maintains a research library and resource center with subject matter pertaining to liberation and African American theology, feminism, and feminist movements.

Black Women in Sisterhood for Action
PO Box 1592
Washington, DC 20013-1592
Telephone: (301) 460-1565
Web site: http://www.feminist.com/bisas1.htm
Founded: 1980

A national nonprofit organization, Black Women in Sisterhood for Action promotes alternative strategies for educational and career development for black women;

provides support and social assistance to senior black women in the community; and furnishes role models and mentors to young people, as well as management and leadership skills training, networking, team building, communication techniques, and image building. It also provides scholarships to deserving young people.

Black Women Organized for Educational Development, Black Women's Resource Center
449 15th St., 3rd Fl.
Oakland, CA 94612
Telephone: (510) 763-9523
Founded: 1984

This organization fosters self-sufficiency in and encourages empowerment of low-income and socially disadvantaged women by establishing and maintaining programs that improve their social and economic well-being. The group sponsors a mentor program for young women in low-income urban areas and offers support groups, workshops, and seminars. In addition, it maintains the Black Women's Resource Center, an information and referral service for African American women and youth.

Black Women Organized for Political Action
920 Peralta St., Ste. 2A
Oakland, CA 94607-1926
Telephone: (510) 763-9523
Web site: http://www.bwopa.org
Founded: 1968

This organization is an outgrowth of the Bay Area Women for Dellums, an initial group of twelve women who worked to elect Ron V. Dellums to Congress. It was strengthened in 1971, when over 350 women who were interested in political activities came together; it is now the oldest such organization in California. The group reorganized in 1999 and began to focus on special leadership needs of African American women. The organization also established a second nonprofit agency, the Training Institute for Leadership Enrichment. BWOPA builds meaningful coalitions and recognizes the changing political landscape in the Bay Area.

Black Women's Health Imperative
1726 M St. NW, Ste. 300
Washington, DC 20036-4520
Telephone: (202) 548-4000
Web site: http://www.blackwomenshealth.org
Founded: 1981

This organization encourages mutual and self-help advocacy among women to bring about a reduction in health-care problems prevalent among African American women. It urges women to communicate with health-care providers, seek out available health-care resources, become aware of self-help approaches, and communicate with other African American women to minimize feelings of powerlessness and isolation, and thus realize they have some control over their physical and mental health. The organization points out that higher incidence of high blood pressure, obesity, breast and cervical cancers, diabetes, kidney disease, arteriosclerosis, and teenage pregnancy occur among African American women than among other racial or socioeconomic groups. It also notes that African American infant mortality is twice that of whites and that African American women are often victims of family violence. The organization offers seminars outlining demographic information, chronic conditions, the need for health information and access to services, and possible methods of improving the health status of African American women.

Black Women's Roundtable
c/o National Coalition on Black Civic Participation
1900 L St. NW, Ste. 700
Washington, DC 20036-5061
Telephone: (202) 659-4929
Web site: http://ncbcp.org/programs/bwr/
Founded: 1983

A program of the National Coalition on Black Civic Participation, the Black Women's Roundtable (BWR) consists of African American women's organizations committed to social justice and economic equity through increased participation in the political process. The BWR organizes voter-registration, education, and empowerment programs in the African American community, emphasizing the importance of the women's vote. It seeks to develop women's leadership skills through nonpartisan political participation and encourage African American women's involvement in discussions concerning the influence of the women's vote in elections. It supports volunteer coalitions that work on voter registration, voter education, and get-out-the-vote efforts.

Black World Foundation
PO Box 22869
Oakland, CA 94609-5869
Telephone: (510) 547-6633
Web site: http://www.theblackscholar.org
Founded: 1969

This foundation is composed of African Americans united to develop and distribute African American educational materials and to develop African American cultural and political thought. It offers books in the areas of African American literature, history, fiction, essays, political analysis, social science, poetry, and art. The foundation also publishes a journal titled the *Black Scholar*. In addition, it maintains a library.

Blacks in Government
3005 Georgia Ave. NW
Washington, DC 20001-3807
Telephone: (202) 667-3280
Web site: http://www.bignet.org
Founded: 1975

This group was founded by federal, state, and local government employees and retirees concerned with the present and future status of African Americans in government. It develops training and other programs to enhance the liberty and sense of well-being of African Americans in government.

Blacks in Law Enforcement
256 E. McLemore Ave.
Memphis, TN 38106-2833
Telephone: (901) 774-1118
Founded: 1986

This organization seeks to educate the public concerning the contributions made by African Americans in the field of law enforcement. It documents the lives and achievements of the first African Americans to participate in law enforcement in the United States. It also develops programs to improve the public image of law enforcement officers and has established a short-term training program for law enforcement officers.

Books for Africa
253 East 4th St., Ste. 200
St. Paul, MN 55101-1643
Telephone: (651) 602-9844
Web site: http://www.booksforafrica.org
Founded: 1988

This organization seeks to end the book famine in Africa by ensuring the availability of books and educational materials throughout the continent.

Center for Constitutional Rights
666 Broadway, 7th Fl.
New York, NY 10012-2399
Telephone: (212) 614-6464
Web site: http://www.ccrjustice.org
Founded: 1966

Through litigation, this organization works "to advance the law in a positive direction, to guarantee the rights of those with the fewest protections and least access to legal resources." It works in such areas as abuse of the grand jury process, women's rights, civil rights, freedom of the press, racism, electronic surveillance, criminal trials, and affirmative action. It conducts the Ella Baker Summer Internship Program, the Movement Support Network, and, in Mississippi, the Voting Rights Project.

Chi Eta Phi Sorority, Inc.
3029 13th St. NW
Washington, DC 20009-5303
Telephone: (202) 232-3858
Web site: http://www.chietaphi.com
Founded: 1932

This sorority was founded by registered and student nurses. Among its objectives are encouraging continuing education, stimulating friendships among members, and developing working relationships with other professional groups for the improvement and delivery of health care services. It sponsors leadership training seminars and conducts educational programs for entrance into nursing and allied health fields. It offers scholarships and other financial awards to assist students, sponsors recruitment and retention programs for minority students, operates a speakers bureau on health education, and maintains biographical archives on African American nurses.

Citizens for a Better America
PO Box 7647
Van Nuys, CA 91409-7647
Telephone: (818) 574-8911
Web site: http://www.cfaba.org
Founded: 1975

The churches and individuals who are members of this organization aim to create a better America by strengthening individual rights in the United States. The group serves as a public advocacy organization that lobbies for civil rights and environmental legislation. It conducts legal research in civil rights cases and provides research services to communities investigating such issues as fair housing and toxic-waste disposal.

Coalition of Black Trade Unionists
1625 L St. NW
Washington, DC 20036-5665
Telephone: (202) 429-1203
Web site: http://www.cbtu.org
Founded: 1972

This organization aims to maximize the strength and influence of African American and minority workers in organized labor. Among its members are African American workers from more than fifty national and international unions. Activities include voter registration and education, improvement of economic development, employment opportunities for minority and poor workers, and the sponsorship of regional seminars.

College Language Association
c/o Dr. Yakini B. Kemp, CLA Treasurer
PO Box 38515
Tallahassee, FL 32315-8515
Telephone: (850) 599-3737
Web site: http://www.clascholars.org
Founded: 1937

This association was founded by teachers of English and several foreign languages at historically African American colleges and universities. The association maintains placement services and a speakers bureau.

Conference of Minority Public Administrators
1301 Pennsylvania Ave. NW, Ste. 840
Washington, DC 20004-1735
Telephone: (202) 393-7878
Web site: http://www.compaonline.org
Founded: 1971

This group is composed of members of the American Society for Public Administration who belong to a minority group or are interested in the promotion of minorities within public administration. The group's mission is "to advance the science, processes, technology, art, and image of public administration" by helping those in the public sector to eliminate discrimination based on race, gender, religion, or sexual preference.

Congress of National Black Churches
1225 Eye St. NW, Ste. 750
Washington, DC 20005
Telephone: (202) 371-1091
Founded: 1978

This organization is a coalition of eight major historically African American denominations. It was founded to find answers to problems that confront blacks in the United States and Africa, including economic development, family and social support, housing, unemployment, education, and foreign relations. The focus is on religious education and evangelism.

Congress of Racial Equality (CORE)
817 Broadway, 3rd Fl.
New York, NY 10003-4709
Telephone: (212) 598-4000
Web site: http://www.core-online.org
Founded: 1942

CORE is the third-oldest civil rights groups in the United States and champions equality for all people regardless of race, creed, sex, age, disability, religion, or ethnic background. The organization seeks to establish, in practice, the inalienable right for all people to determine their own destiny, to decide for themselves what social and political organizations can operate in their best interest, and to do so without gratuitous and inhibiting influence from those whose interest is diametrically opposed. CORE administers several major programs including: Project Independence, which is designed to address the lack of skills among inner-city young adults by providing intensive training in office skills and helping them to find meaningful employment; Project Internet Watch; Civil Rights Boot Camp; a legal defense fund; and an immigration program.

Congressional Black Caucus
1720 Massachusetts Ave. NW
Washington, DC 20036-1903
Telephone: (202) 263-2800
Web site: http://www.cbcfinc.org
Founded: 1969

This Congressional Black Caucus (CBC) was founded by the thirteen African American members of the U.S. House of Representatives. The CBC seeks to address the legislative concerns of African American and other underrepresented citizens and to formalize and strengthen the efforts of its members. It establishes a yearly legislative agenda setting forth the key issues that it supports, including full employment, national health care, education, minority business assistance, urban revitalization, rural development, welfare reform, and international affairs. It works to implement these objectives through personal contact with other House members, through the dissemination of information to individual African American constituents, and by working closely with African American elected officials in other levels of government. The CBC also operates the Congressional Black Caucus Foundation.

Delta Sigma Theta Sorority, Inc.
1707 New Hampshire Ave. NW
Washington, DC 20009-2501
Telephone: (202) 986-2400
Web site: http://www.deltasigmatheta.org
Founded: 1913

This service sorority was founded by twenty-two women at Howard University.

Diversity Information Resources
2105 Central Ave. NE
Minneapolis, MN 55418-3767
Telephone: (612) 781-6819
Web site: http://www.diversityinforesources.com
Founded: 1968

This group compiles and publishes minority business directories and sponsors minority purchasing seminars.

Educational Equity Center
Academy for Educational Development
1825 Connecticut Ave. NW
Washington, DC 20009
Telephone: (202) 884-8000
Web site: http://www.aed.org/About/index.cfm
Founded: 1982

This center, part of the Academy for Educational Development (AED), was organized to create educational programs and materials that are free of sex, race, and disability bias. It offers training programs for parents, teachers, and students, and conducts seminars, symposia, and workshops. It also provides conference planning, consulting, and materials development services. It conducts the Women and Disability Awareness Project, which discusses and writes on matters concerning disabled women, feminism, and the links between the disability rights and women's movements. A nonprofit organization, AED works globally to create lasting solutions to critical problems in health, education, and social and economic development. It works collaboratively with groups worldwide. AED is engaged in more than three hundred programs in all fifty states and more than 150 countries.

Episcopal Commission for Black Ministries
815 2nd Ave.
New York, NY 10017
Telephone: (212) 922-5343
Founded: 1973

This commission works to strengthen the witness of African American Episcopalians in the church through programs that include parish and clergy development, scholarships and grants, and international relations. It provides financial assistance and consultations to parishes and church organizations.

Eta Phi Beta Sorority, Inc.
19983 Livernois Ave.
Detroit, MI 48221-1299
Telephone: (313) 862-0600
Web site: http://www.etaphibetanational.com
Founded: 1942

Eta Phi Beta is a national business and professional women's sorority founded by eleven women in Detroit.

Executive Leadership Council
1001 N. Fairfax St.
Alexandria, VA 22314
Telephone: (703) 706-5200
Web site: http://www.elcinfo.com
Founded: 1986

This is an independent, nonprofit national organization comprised of African American executive officers of large corporations who provide a network for black businesspeople. Members also work to improve opportunities for African American executives and conduct charitable activities. The council's activities are supported by contributions to its affiliate, the Executive Leadership Foundation.

Frontiers International Inc.
6301 Crittenden St.
Philadelphia, PA 19138-1031
Telephone: (215) 549-4550
Web site: http://www.frontiersinternational.com
Founded: 1936

This multinational group focuses on social justice. The group works through member services to help individual communities focus on constructive action by their members.

Global Alliance for Africa
703 W. Monroe St.
Chicago, IL 60661-3515
Telephone: (312) 382-0607
Web site: http://www.globalallianceafrica.org

This organization promotes community-based healthcare development programs for impoverished people living in remote rural areas and urban slums throughout Africa.

Global Coalition for Africa
1818 H St. NW
Washington, DC 20433-0001
Telephone: (202) 473-1000
Web site: http://go.worldbank.org/9Y1AGE7PV0
Founded: 1990

The Global Coalition for Africa is an innovative, intergovernmental policy forum whose participants include international development and finance organizations. The coalition seeks to "forge policy consensus on development priorities among African governments and their northern partners," serves as a catalyst for development action, and works to improve cooperation between African and overseas development programs and agencies. It assists African governments in the formulation of public development programs and policies, in addition to conducting outreach activities.

HBCU Library Alliance
1438 West Peachtree St., Ste. 200
Atlanta, GA 30309-2955
Telephone: (404) 592-4820
Web site: http://www.hbculibraries.org
Founded: 2002

The HBCU Library Alliance is a consortium that supports the collaboration of information professionals dedicated to providing a variety of resources that aim to strengthen historically black colleges and universities, as well as their constituents. Among its initiatives is the development of a digital collection of African American resources located in the member libraries.

Institute for the Advanced Study of Black Family Life and Culture, Inc.
1012 Linden St.
Oakland, CA 94607-2728
Telephone: (510) 836-3245
Web site: http://www.iasbflc.org
Founded: 1980

This institute seeks to reunify African American families and to revitalize the African American community. It advocates the reclamation of what the group considers traditional African American culture. In addition, it conducts research on issues affecting the African American community, such as teen pregnancy, child-rearing practices, mental-health support systems, and the effects of alcohol and drugs. It also maintains the HAWK Federation ("HAWK" standing for high achievement, wisdom, and knowledge), a training program employed in school systems to aid in the character development of young African American males. The institute sponsors in-service training for agencies, school systems, and the juvenile justice system, and develops training curricula for teen parents.

International Association of Black Professional Fire Fighters
1020 N. Taylor Ave.
St. Louis, MO 63113-2800
Telephone: (513) 763-9312
Web site: http://www.iabpff.org
Founded: 1970

This association strives to promote interracial communication and understanding; recruit African Americans for the fire services; improve working conditions for African Americans in the fire services; assist African Americans in career advancement; promote professionalism; and represent African American firefighters before the community.

International Black Women's Congress
645 Church St., Ste. 200
Norfolk, VA 23510-1772
Telephone: (757) 625-0500
Founded: 1983

The objective of this organization is to unite members for mutual support and socioeconomic development by conducting annual networking tours to Africa; establishing support groups; assisting women in starting their own businesses; assisting members in developing résumés and other educational needs; and offering to answer or discuss individual questions and concerns. It encourages membership by women from all walks of life.

International Black Writers and Artists
PO Box 43576
Los Angeles, CA 90043-0576
Telephone: (323) 964-3721
Web site: http://www.ibwala.com
Founded: 1974

This group was founded by African American writers and artists in the United States and West Indies. It provides encouragement and support to its members.

Jack and Jill of America, Inc.
1930 17th St. NW
Washington, DC 20009-6207
Telephone: (202) 667-7010
Web site: http://national.jackandjillonline.org
Founded: 1938

This parental group is designed to help African American parents learn more about their children. The group seeks to increase community awareness, ensure equal opportunity and advancement for all children, and improve the quality of life of African American children.

Kappa Alpha Psi Fraternity, Inc.
2322–24 N. Broad St.
Philadelphia, PA 19132-4590
Telephone: (215) 228-7184
Web site: http://www.kappaalphapsi1911.com
Founded: 1911

This social fraternity was founded on the campus of Indiana University as Kappa Alpha Nu and then was renamed Kappa Alpha Psi in 1915.

Leadership Conference on Civil and Human Rights
1629 K St. NW, 10th Fl.
Washington, DC 20006
Telephone: (202) 466-3311
Web site: http://www.civilrights.org
Founded: 1950

This organization is a coalition of national organizations working to promote passage of civil rights, social, and economic legislation, and the enforcement of laws already on the books. It has released studies examining tax and budget programs in such areas as housing, elementary and secondary education, social welfare, Native American affairs, and tax cuts. It has also evaluated the civil rights enforcement activities of the U.S. Department of Justice and reviewed the civil rights activities of the U.S. Department of Education. In 2010, St. Jude Children's Research Hospital in Memphis, Tennessee, recognized the fraternity for working through its Sunday of Hope national fund-raising program and raising $1 million in five years for the hospital.

Links, Incorporated
1200 Massachusetts Ave. NW
Washington, DC 20005-4501
Telephone: (202) 842-8686
Web site: http://www.linksinc.org
Founded: 1946

A nonprofit organization for women of color, the Links, Incorporated, was founded in Philadelphia. It is committed to enhancing the quality of life in the African American community. The organization focuses on community service through four main facets: national trends and services, services to youth, international trends and services, and the arts.

Minority Business Enterprise Legal Defense and Education Fund
419 New Jersey Ave. SE
Washington, DC 20003-4007
Telephone: (202) 289-1700
Founded: 1980

This fund was organized in the public interest and serves as an advocate and legal representative for the minority business community nationwide. It encourages the promotion and growth of minority businesses.

NAACP Legal Defense and Educational Fund, Inc.
99 Hudson St., Ste. 1600
New York, NY 10013
Telephone: (212) 965-2200
Web site: http://www.naacpldf.org
Founded: 1940

The NAACP Legal Defense and Educational Fund (LDF) is the legal arm of the civil rights movement, functioning independently of the National Association for the Advancement of Colored People since 1957. The LDF works to provide and support litigation on behalf of African Americans, other racial minorities, and women, defending their legal and constitutional rights against discrimination in employment, education, housing, and other areas. In addition, the LDF represents civil rights groups and individual citizens who have bona fide civil rights claims. Contributed funds are used to finance court actions for equality in schools, jobs, voting, housing, municipal services, land use, and delivery of health-care services. It has organized litigation campaign for prison reform and the abolition of capital punishment and hosts an annual institute to develop public awareness of new problems being faced by minorities. The LDF also maintains the Herbert Lehman Education Fund, through which scholarships are awarded to African American students attending state universities, and sponsors the Earl Warren Legal Training Program, which provides scholarships to African American law students.

National Action Council for Minorities in Engineering
440 Hamilton Ave., Ste. 302
White Plains, NY 10601-1813
Telephone: (914) 539-4010
Web site: http://www.nacme.org
Founded: 1974

This organization's mission is "to provide leadership and support for the national effort to increase the representation of successful African American, American Indian, and Latino women and men in engineering and technology, math- and science-based careers." The council works with support organizations to motivate and encourage precollege students to engage in engineering careers. It operates a project to assist engineering schools in improving the retention and graduation rates of minority students.

National African American Speakers Association
c/o Dr. Michael V. Wilkins Sr.
3033 Western Ave.
Park Forest, IL 60466-1834
Telephone: (708) 785-7371
Founded: 1994

This association is made up of professional and in-training speakers learning to inspire, challenge, and educate. It offers training programs specifically designed to develop interpersonal, communication, and presentation skills, while enhancing marketable skills.

National Alliance of Black Interpreters, Inc.
PO Box 77372
Washington, DC 20013-7372
Toll Free: (877) 626-2487
Web site: http://www.naobi.org
Founded: 1987

The mission of this alliance is "to promote excellence and empowerment among African Americans/Blacks in the profession of sign language interpreting in the context of a multicultural, multilingual environment."

National Alliance of Black School Educators
310 Pennsylvania Ave. SE
Washington, DC 20003-1147
Telephone: (202) 608-6310
Web site: http://www.nabse.org
Founded: 1970

The purpose of this organization is to promote awareness, professional expertise, and commitment among African American educators. Its goals are to eliminate and rectify the results of racism in education; work with state, local, and national leaders to raise the academic achievement level of all African American students; increase members' involvement in legislative activities; facilitate the introduction of a curriculum that more completely embraces African America; improve the ability of African American educators to promote problem resolution; and create a meaningful and effective network of strength, talent, and professional support.

National Alumni Council of the United Negro College Fund
8260 Willow Oaks Corporate Dr.
PO Box 10444
Fairfax, VA 22031-8044
Toll Free: (800) 331-2244
Web site: http://www.uncf.org/alumni/NAC.asp
Founded: 1946

The National Alumni Council provides a structure for cooperation among African American college alumni groups and friends of African American colleges and works to acquaint the public with the value of African American colleges and higher education. It informs students and the public about contributions of African American college alumni to civic betterment and community progress and recruits students for United Negro College Fund member colleges.

National Association for Black Veterans, Inc.
PO Box 11432
Milwaukee, WI 53211-0432
Toll Free: (877) NABVETS
Web site: http://www.nabvets.com
Founded: 1970

This association is open to African American and other minority veterans, primarily those who fought in Vietnam. It represents the interests of minority veterans before the Veterans Administration and operates the Metropolitan Veterans Service to obtain honorable discharges for minority and low-income veterans who, in the organization's opinion, unjustly received a less-than-honorable discharge. In addition to these services, it defends incarcerated veterans through its Readjustment Counseling Program, operates a job-creation program, and offers services to geriatric and homeless veterans. The association also conducts workshops to acquaint lawyers and clinicians with problems associated with post-traumatic stress disorder, sponsors geriatric seminar and training program, operates library of military regulations, compiles statistics, and maintains a speakers bureau.

National Association for Equal Opportunity in Higher Education
209 3rd St. SE
Washington, DC 20003-1904
Telephone: (202) 552-3300
Web site: http://www.nafeo.org
Founded: 1969

This association represents public and private historically African American community and four-year colleges and universities in their attempt to continue as a viable force in the education community. It seeks to increase funding for member schools through federal and private sources. In addition, it compiles biographical data on schools and individuals, provides placement services, and collects statistics.

National Association for the Advancement of Colored People
4805 Mt. Hope Dr.
Baltimore, MD 21215-3206
Telephone: (410) 580-5777
Web site: http://www.naacp.org/
Founded: 1909

The NAACP was founded by persons "of all races and religions" who believe in the association's objectives and methods, which are to achieve equal rights through the democratic process and eliminate racial prejudice by removing racial discrimination in housing, employment, voting, schools, the courts, transportation, recreation, prisons, and business enterprises. It offers referral services, tutorials, and day care; sponsors seminars; maintains a law library; and awards the Spingarn Medal annually to an African American for distinguished achievement.

National Association for the Study and Performance of African-American Music
c/o William Smiley
PO Box 20191
Greensboro, NC 27420-0191
Telephone: (336) 889-2527
Web site: http://www.naspaam.org
Founded: 1972

This association's purpose is to foster the creation, study, and promotion of African American–derived music in education. It seeks to heighten public awareness of the problems faced by African American music educators and students and to increase public understanding of these problems. Other services include providing a forum for the discussion of concerns; coordinating and disseminating materials concerning African American–derived music in order to assist music teachers in teaching African American music and students; encouraging African Americans to aspire to leadership positions and demand inclusion in the development and presentation of activities organized by MENC: The National Association for Music Education, including participation in MENC's regional conferences; sponsoring collegiate and high school gospel choir competitions; and bestowing annual national achievement awards to educators successful in demonstrating values inherent in music education. The association also compiles lists of music, books, and related music materials by African Americans.

National Association of African American Catholic Deacons
10125 Fabled Waters Ct.
Spring Valley, CA 91977-3458
Telephone: (619) 670-8339
Web site: http://www.afacd.org
Founded: 1993

This association was established for ordained African American Roman Catholic deacons. It provides a national forum for its members and helps them to promote diaconal unity and address common issues and concerns about their work. Through its programs and activities, the association works to promote the well-being of African American families.

National Association of African American Chambers of Commerce
750 North St. Paul Pl., Ste. 1920
Dallas, TX 75201-3280
Telephone: (214) 871-3060
Founded: 1996

Successor to the U.S. African American Chambers of Commerce, this association was organized to promote the growth and development of African American–owned enterprises. The organization nurtures working relationships among minority businesses, corporations, and trade association members nationwide. It promotes investment, trade, travel, and tourism throughout the country and, on behalf of its members, lobbies governments at the local, state, and federal levels.

National Association of African American Studies
PO Box 6670
Scarborough, ME 04070-6670
Telephone: (207) 839-8004
Web site: http://www.naaas.org
Founded: 1992

This association seeks to further the cause of research in African American studies and promote acquaintanceship among those interested in the field. It provides information and support for researchers, serves as a forum for research and artistic endeavors, and conducts educational programs.

National Association of African Americans in Human Resources
PO Box 311395
Atlanta, GA 31131-1395
Telephone: (404) 346-1542
Web site: http://www.naaahr.org
Founded: 1999

Founded by human-resource professionals, this association is dedicated to providing a national forum where African Americans can share and gain information, while also providing leadership on issues affecting individual careers and the quality of the work life for other African Americans.

National Association of Black Accountants, Inc.
7474 Greenway Center Dr., Ste. 1120
Greenbelt, MD 20770-3559
Telephone: (301) 474-6222
Web site: http://www.nabainc.org
Founded: 1969

This association was founded to unite accountants and accounting students who have similar interests and ideals, who are committed to professional and academic excellence, who possess a sense of professional and civic responsibility, and who are concerned with enhancing opportunities for minorities in the accounting profession.

National Association of Black Catholic Administrators
204 Douthit St., Ste. A1
Greenville, SC 29601-1701
Telephone: (864) 242-2233
Web site: http://www.nabcaonline.org
Founded: 1976

This association was founded to assist the church in its role of evangelization and in defining its mission to the African American community and to provide an inner resource for the social and spiritual needs and concerns of Catholics of African ancestry.

National Association of Black Consulting Engineers
2705 Bladensburg Rd. NE
Washington, DC 20018-1424
Telephone: (202) 339-9100
Founded: 1975

The purpose of this association is to gain recognition and increase professional opportunities for African American consulting engineers by lobbying the federal government.

National Association of Black County Officials
1090 Vermont Ave. NW, Ste. 1290
Washington, DC 20005-4963
Telephone: (202) 350-6696
Web site: http://www.blackcountyofficials.com
Founded: 1975

Black county officials organized this association to provide program planning and management assistance to counties in the United States. The association acts as a clearinghouse for the exchange of technical information to develop resolutions to problems on the local and national levels. It also promotes the sharing of knowledge about and methods of improving resource utilization and government operations, and conducts seminars and training sessions.

National Association of Black Geologists and Geophysicists
4212 San Felipe St., Ste. 420
Houston, TX 77027-2902
Web site: http://www.nabgg.org
Founded: 1981

This association was founded to assist minority geologists and geophysicists in establishing professional and business relationships. It informs minority students of career opportunities in geology and geophysics and seeks to motivate minority students to utilize existing programs, grants, and loans. The association provides scholarships and oversees the educational careers of scholarship recipients.

National Association of Black Journalists
1100 Knight Hall, Ste. 3100
College Park, MD 20742
Telephone: (301) 405-0248
Web site: http://www.nabj.org
Founded: 1975

The aims of this association are to strengthen the ties between African Americans in the African American media and African Americans in the white media; sensitize the white media to the "institutional racism in its coverage"; expand the white media's coverage and "balanced reporting" of the African American community; and become an exemplary group of professionals that honors excellence and outstanding achievement among African American journalists. The association works with high schools to identify potential journalists and awards scholarships to journalism programs that are particularly supportive of minorities.

National Association of Black Owned Broadcasters
1201 Connecticut Ave. NW, Ste. 200
Washington, DC 20036-2636
Telephone: (202) 463-8970
Web site: http://www.nabob.org
Founded: 1976

This association represents the interests of existing and potential African American radio and television stations. It works with the Office of Federal Procurement Policy to determine which government-contracting major advertisers and advertising agencies are complying with government initiatives to increase the amount of advertising dollars received by minority-owned firms. It conducts lobbying activities and provides legal representation for the protection of minority ownership policies.

National Association of Black Professors
PO Box 526
Crisfield, MD 21817-0526
Telephone: (410) 968-2393
Founded: 1974

The goals of this association are to provide a forum for the exchange of information among college professors, enhance education for African American people and enrich the educational process in general, and support and promote the intellectual interests of African American students.

National Association of Black Social Workers, Inc.
2305 Martin Luther King Ave. SE
Washington, DC 20020-5813
Telephone: (202) 678-4570
Web site: http://www.nabsw.org
Founded: 1968

This association was founded to support, develop, and sponsor community welfare projects and programs that serve the interest of the African American community and aid it in controlling its social institutions. It also assists with adoption referrals.

National Association of Black Storytellers
PO Box 67722
Baltimore, MD 21215-0018
Telephone: (410) 947-1117
Web site: http://www.nabsinc.org
Founded: 1984

National Association of Blacks in Criminal Justice
North Carolina Central University
PO Box 19788

Durham, NC 27707-0024
Telephone: (919) 683-1801
Web site: http://www.nabcj.org
Founded: 1974

This association was founded by criminal justice professionals concerned with the impact of criminal justice policies and practices on the minority community. It advocates with local, state, and federal criminal justice agencies for the improvement of minority recruitment practices and for the advancement of minority career mobility within those agencies. It also sponsors regional conferences, career development seminars, and annual training institutes; maintains a speakers bureau; and provides financial and in-kind services to community groups.

National Association of Colored Women's Clubs, Inc.
1601 R St. NW
Washington, DC 20009-6420
Telephone: (202) 667-4080
Web site: http://www.nacwc.org
Founded: 1896

This association is a federation of African American women's clubs. It carries on civic service, education, social service, and philanthropy programs and is particularly concerned with programs that benefit women and children.

National Association of Health Services Executives
1050 Connecticut Ave. NW, 10th Fl.
Washington, DC 20036
Telephone: (202) 772-1030
Web site: http://www.nahse.org
Founded: 1968

This association aims to promote the advancement and development of health-care leaders who are African American and to elevate the quality of health-care services provided to poor and disadvantaged communities. The organization also awards scholarships to students enrolled in health-services administration programs in academic institutions.

National Association of Investment Companies
1300 Pennsylvania Ave. NW, Ste. 700
Washington, DC 20004-3024
Telephone: (202) 204-3001
Web site: http://www.naicvc.com
Founded: 1971

This association represents the minority small business investment company industry by monitoring regulatory action and collecting and disseminating trade and business information.

National Association of Minority Contractors
Ronald Reagan Bldg.
1300 Pennsylvania Ave. NW, Ste. 700
Washington, DC 20004-3024
Telephone: (202) 204-3093
Web site: http://www.namcnational.org
Founded: 1969

This association was founded by minority construction contractors and companies interested in doing business with minority contractors. It identifies procurement opportunities, provides specialized training, and serves as a national advocate for minority construction contractors.

National Association of Minority Media Executives
7950 Jones Branch Dr.
McLean, VA 22102-3302
Toll Free: (888) 968-7658
Web site: http://www.namme.org
Founded: 1990

This is an organization for media managers and executives of color who work in newspapers, magazines, broadcasting, and new media. It encourages diversity in the management ranks of the media industry and is the leading resource for multicultural talent in the industry. It also has alliances with media companies and organizations who come together to review multicultural issues.

National Association of Negro Business and Professional Women's Clubs, Inc.
1806 New Hampshire Ave. NW
Washington, DC 20009-3206
Telephone: (202) 483-4206
Web site: http://www.nanbpwc.org
Founded: 1935

This association was founded by women actively engaged in a business or a profession and who are committed to rendering service through club programs and activities. A community-based social service organization, it is committed to volunteerism and focuses on programs that impact the African American community, including education, health, economic development, employment, and housing. It also offers youth leadership and educational development programs.

National Association of Negro Musicians, Inc.
11551 S. Laflin St.
PO Box 43053
Chicago, IL 60643-0053
Telephone: (773) 568-3818
Web site: http://www.nanm.org
Founded: 1919

This association was founded to promote the advancement of all types of music, especially among young African American musicians. It sponsors annual competitions in which winners compete for scholarships.

National Bankers Association
1513 P St. NW
Washington, DC 20005-1909
Telephone: (202) 588-5432
Web site: http://www.nationalbankers.org
Founded: 1927

This association was founded by minority banking institutions. It serves as an advocate for the minority banking industry, monitors legislative issues, and maintains relationships with federal supervisory agencies.

National Bar Association
1225 11th St. NW
Washington, DC 20001-4217
Telephone: (202) 842-3900
Web site: http://www.nationalbar.org
Founded: 1925

This association was founded by minority attorneys, members of the judiciary, law students, and law faculty. It sponsors educational and research programs.

National Beauty Culturists' League, Inc.
25 Logan Cir. NW
Washington, DC 20005-3725
Telephone: (202) 332-2695
Web site: http://www.nbcl.org
Founded: 1919

This organization is dedicated to upgrading professional standards in cosmetology and to ensuring equal opportunity for African Americans through licensing and practices in state regulations.

National Black Alcoholism and Addictions Council, Inc.
5104 N. Orange Blossom Trl., Ste. 111
Orlando, FL 32810-1013
Telephone: (407) 523-2747
Web site: http://www.nbacinc.org
Founded: 1978

This organization works to support and initiate activities that will improve alcoholism treatment services and lead to the prevention of alcoholism in the African American community. It provides training on how to treat African American alcoholics from a cultural perspective and compiles statistics concerning alcoholism among African Americans.

National Black Association for Speech-Language and Hearing
700 McKnight Park Dr.
Pittsburgh, PA 15237
Telephone: (412) 366-8804
Web site: http://www.nbaslh.org
Founded: 1978

Comprised of professionals and other individuals concerned with blacks with communication disorders, the association strongly encourages the recruitment and training of African American professionals to work with individuals suffering from speech, language, and hearing problems. It maintains that conditions such as race, socioeconomic class, and cultural differences must be taken into account in order to understand and sensitively study the communicative process and to treat communicative disorders. The association supports related research, solicits and provides financial support for the training of black students in speech-language pathology and audiology, and disseminates information.

National Black Catholic Clergy Caucus
Resurrection Catholic Church
2815 Forbes Dr.
Montgomery, AL 36110-1307
Telephone: (404) 226-8170
Web site: http://www.nbccc-us.com
Founded: 1968

This organization was founded by African American priests, brothers, seminarians, and deacons. Its purpose is to support the spiritual, theological, educational, and ministerial growth of the African American Catholic community within the Catholic Church and to serve as a vehicle to bring contributions of the African American community to the Catholic Church. It also advances the fight against racism within the Catholic Church and society.

National Black Catholic Congress
320 Cathedral St.
Baltimore, MD 21201-4421
Telephone: (410) 547-8496
Web site: http://www.nbccongress.org
Founded: 1985

Comprised of Catholic dioceses, this organization works to devise ways and means of improving the condition of African American Catholics both religiously and socially. It conducts an annual pastoral ministry workshop for clergy and others who minister in African American communities and parishes, and sponsors an intensive training program for clergy and lay leaders in the African American apostolate.

National Black Caucus of Local Elected Officials
1301 Pennsylvania Ave. NW, Ste. 550
Washington, DC 20004-1747
Telephone: (202) 626-3191
Web site: http://www.nbc-leo.org
Founded: 1970

An affiliate of the National League of Cities (NLC), this caucus was founded by elected African American municipal and county officials united to recognize and deal with problems of members. The caucus attempts to provide the organizational structure required to better present and respond to issues affecting constituents. It seeks to influence the NLC in the development of policies affecting African Americans and promotes legislative and economic development initiatives directed toward the needs of the African American community.

National Black Caucus of State Legislators
444 N. Capitol St. NW, Ste. 622
Washington, DC 20001-1581
Telephone: (202) 624-5457
Web site: http://www.nbcsl.org
Founded: 1977

This group was organized to provide more political networking opportunities to African American legislators at the federal and state levels. Its goals are to provide a network through which state legislators can exchange information and ideas on state and national legislation, provide a unified front or platform, and serve as a focal point for the involvement of African American legislators in the "new federalism." Its activities include arranging meetings between all governmental groups representing African American elected officials, analyzing and forming a position on the new federalism, conducting seminars, maintaining a speakers bureau and biographical archives, and compiling statistics.

National Black Chamber of Commerce
1350 Connecticut Ave. NW, Ste. 405
Washington, DC 20036-1721
Telephone: (202) 466-6888
Web site: http://www.nationalbcc.org
Founded: 1993

This organization was founded by African American chambers of commerce organized to create a strategy for members of local chambers to share in the collective buying power of African American minority communities. Its primary focus is on the tourism industry because, according to the association, African Americans spend approximately $25 billion in the tourism market each year, but African American–owned businesses net very little from this industry. The organization conducts training sessions to acquaint African American businesspeople with the tourism market and marketing strategies.

National Black Child Development Institute, Inc.
1313 L St. NW, Ste. 110
Washington, DC 20005-4110
Telephone: (202) 833-2220
Web site: http://www.nbcdi.org
Founded: 1970

This institute conducts direct services and advocacy campaigns aimed at both national and local public policies focusing on issues of health, child welfare, education, and child care. It organizes and trains networks of members in a volunteer grassroots affiliate system to voice concerns regarding policies that affect African American children and their families. It stimulates communication between African American community groups, through conferences and seminars, to discuss and make recommendations that will be advantageous to the development of African American children. In addition, it analyzes selected policy decisions and legislative and administrative regulations to determine their impact on African American children and youth. Finally, it informs national policy makers of issues critical to African American children.

National Black Church Initiative
PO Box 65177
Washington, DC 20035
Telephone: (202) 744-0184
Web site: http://www.naltblackchurch.com
Founded: 1991

This is a coalition of 34,000 African American and Latino churches that work to eradicate racial disparities in health care, education, housing, and the environment. Its mission is "to provide critical information to all of its members, congregants, churches, and the public." The NBCI partners with major organizations and officials to achieve its goals.

National Black Coalition for Media Justice
920 Dodge Ave.
Evanston, IL 60202
Telephone: (847) 328-4849
E-mail: karenbond@nbcmj.org
Founded: 2005

This coalition addresses media justice from the perspective of people of color and demands accountability from media outlets that aim to attract African American audiences. Its objectives include setting an agenda for people of color and structuring a national network to address their needs.

National Black Coalition of Federal Aviation Employees
PO Box 845
Hampton, GA 30228-0901
Web site: http://www.nbcfae.org
Founded: 1976

This organization promotes professionalism and equal opportunity in the workplace; locates and trains qualified minorities for Federal Aviation Administration (FAA) positions; helps the FAA meet its affirmative action goals; monitors African American, female, and minority trainees; educates members and the public about their rights, and FAA personnel about promotion qualifications; and develops a voice for African American, female, and minority FAA employees.

National Black College Alumni Hall of Fame Foundation, Inc.
230 Peachtree St. NW, Ste. 530
Atlanta, GA 30303-1521
Telephone: (404) 524-1106
Web site: http://www.nbcahof.org
Founded: 1984

Founded by alumni of historically black colleges and universities, this foundation seeks to increase awareness of the importance of these colleges. It also encourages graduates of black colleges and universities to donate funds to their alma maters and conducts fund-raising activities.

National Black Deaf Advocates, Inc.
PO Box 32
Frankfort, KY 40602-0032
Web site: http://www.nbda.org
Founded: 1982

This organization advocates for the rights of African Americans who are deaf or hearing impaired, while also seeking to promote these individuals' well-being, culture, and empowerment. It conducts educational outreach programs, offers leadership training and training for interpreters and transliterators of color, and sponsors the Miss NBDA Pageant.

National Black Farmers Association
PO Box 74433
Richmond, VA 23236-0008
Telephone: (434) 848-1592
Web site: http://www.blackfarmers.org
Founded: 1995

This community-based organization provides leadership in areas that promote the rights of African American farmers and landowners. Its mission is to "encourage the participation of small and disadvantaged farmers in gaining access to resources of state and federal programs administered by the United States Department of Agriculture." The association also works to improve the quality of life in rural communities and advocates credit for small farmers, family farm enterprise development, distribution of food, and rural economic development. Association-led protests from 1996 to 1998 resulted in the establishment of a federal advisory committee on civil rights that monitors such federal legislation.

National Black Law Students Association
1225 11th St. NW
Washington, DC 20001-4217
Toll Free: (866) 518-6863
Web site: http://www.nblsa.org
Founded: 1968

This association was founded by African American law students united to meet the needs of African American people within the legal profession and to work for the benefit of the African American community. The objectives of the association are to articulate and promote professional competence, needs, and goals of African American law students; focus on the relationship between African American students and attorneys and the American legal system; instill in African American law students and attorneys a greater commitment to the African American community; and encourage the legal community to bring about change to meet the needs of the African American community.

National Black Leadership Initiative on Cancer
720 Westview Dr. SW
Atlanta, GA 30310-1458
Telephone: (404) 756-5205
Web site: http://www.nblic.org
Founded: 1989

This initiative is made up of African Americans and health-care professionals concerned with the prevention, diagnosis, and treatment of people with cancer, particularly those of African American descent. It seeks to facilitate "closing the gap in cancer incidence and mortality and increasing survival from cancer" by increasing awareness among African Americans of cancer and its prevention and treatment. It also conducts educational programs to develop volunteer leaders in African American communities, with an emphasis on increasing understanding of breast, colorectal, and prostate cancer and the role played by diet in their prevention.

National Black Leadership Roundtable
1025 Connecticut Ave. NW
Washington, DC 20036
Telephone: (202) 331-2030
Founded: 1983

The goals of this organization are to provide a forum for leaders of national African American organizations to discuss and exchange ideas on issues critical to African Americans; aid in the development of political, economic, and networking strategies that are advantageous to the needs of the African American community; and ensure that elected and appointed officials represent and are accountable to the African American community.

National Black MBA Association, Inc.
180 N. Michigan Ave., Ste. 1400
Chicago, IL 60601-7478
Telephone: (312) 236-2622
Web site: http://www.nbmbaa.org
Founded: 1970

This association was founded by business professionals, lawyers, accountants, and engineers concerned with the role of African Americans who hold master of business administration degrees. It encourages African Americans to pursue continuing business education; assists students preparing to enter the business world; provides programs for minority youths, students, and professionals including workshops, panel discussions, and the Destination MBA seminar; works with graduate schools; and grants scholarships to graduate business students.

National Black McDonald's Operators Association
PO Box 820668
South Florida, FL 33082-0668
Telephone: (954) 389-4487
Web site: http://www.nbmoa.org
Founded: 1972

This association was founded to provide a forum for the exchange of ideas on the improvement of community relations and on the operation and management of restaurants. It seeks to build and improve the McDonald's restaurant image throughout the community and sponsors training seminars on marketing, better sales practices, labor relations, and profit sharing.

National Black Nurses Association, Inc.
8630 Fenton St., Ste. 330
Silver Spring, MD 20910-3803
Telephone: (301) 589-3200
Web site: http://www.nbna.org
Founded: 1971

This association was founded to function as a professional support group and as an advocacy group for the African American community and its health-care needs. It recruits and assists African Americans interested in pursuing nursing as a career.

National Black Police Association
30 Kennedy St. NW, Ste. 101
Washington, DC 20011-5219
Telephone: (202) 986-2070
Web site: http://www.blackpolice.org
Founded: 1972

This association seeks to improve relationships between police departments and the African American community, recruit minority police officers on a national scale, and eliminate police corruption, brutality, and racial discrimination.

National Black Programming Coalition
68 E. 131st St., 7th Fl.
New York, NY 10037-2904
Telephone: (212) 234-8200
Web site: http://www.nbpc.tv
Founded: 1979

This consortium is comprised of public telecommunications systems and television stations, academic institutions, and interested individuals. Its objectives include assisting the public broadcasting system in supplying programming that serves the needs of all population segments of the United States; serving as a collection, distribution, and archival center for black-oriented television programming; coproducing black programming; serving as a liaison between the black community and telecommunications systems with regard to black programming; and providing funds for and encouraging more and better black productions. The consortium also participates in the acquisition and distribution of programs for the cable and international markets and sponsors children's programs.

National Black Public Relations Society, Inc.
9107 Wilshire Blvd., Ste. 450
Beverly Hills, CA 90210-5535
Toll Free: (888) 976-0005
Web site: http://www.nbprs.org
Founded: 1987

This organization was founded by African American public relations professionals who are either self-employed or employed by advertising agencies, radio and television stations, businesses, or nonprofit organizations. It provides a forum for discussion of topics related to public relations; holds professional development workshops; conducts seminars; and maintains a speakers bureau to promote the image of African Americans in business.

National Black Sisters' Conference
101 Q St. NE
Washington, DC 20002

Telephone: (202) 529-9250
Founded: 1968

This organization seeks to develop the personal resources of African American women and challenges society, especially the church, to address issues of racism in the United States. Its activities include retreats; consulting, leadership, and cultural understanding; and formation workshops for personnel. It maintains educational programs for facilitating change and community involvement in inner-city parochial schools and parishes and operates Sojourner House to provide spiritual affirmation for African American religious and laywomen.

National Black State Troopers Coalition
c/o Charron Leachman
PO Box 66464
Baton Rouge, LA 70896-6464
Telephone: (337) 247-5361
Web site: http://www.nbstc85.org
Founded: 1985

This coalition promotes communication among minority state troopers, while also encouraging members to participate in self-improvement programs, prepare and compete for promotions, and request assignments to specialized units to advance their careers and better serve their communities.

National Black United Federation of Charities
40 Clinton St., 5th Fl.
Newark, NJ 07102
Telephone: (973) 643-3767
Web site: http://www.nbufcharities.org

Comprised of African American charities, this federation works to help national and local organizations gain resources in order to provide for the needs of African American communities. The group also conducts fundraisers.

National Black United Front
1809 E. 71st St. Ste. 211
Chicago, IL 60649
Telephone: (773) 493-0900
Web site: http://www.nbufront.org
Founded: 1980

The purpose of this organization is to unite African American people of diverse political ideologies, age groups, socioeconomic backgrounds, and religious beliefs in order to build "a viable force for social transformation." Its goals include the elimination of racism, sexism, bigotry, and racial violence; the redistribution of the resources and wealth of the nation to provide abundantly for all citizens; and the elimination of the "genocidal miseducation system," police brutality, and denial of human rights nationally and internationally. The group believes that current conditions in the United States threaten the survival of African American people as a whole and urges African Americans to overlook individual differences by working together for common goals. It also addresses such issues as unemployment, budget cuts harmful to African American communities, and the resurgence of the Ku Klux Klan. The group conducts seminars and forums, maintains a speakers bureau, offers charitable programs, and sponsors competitions. Other activities include organizing boycotts, holding demonstrations, engaging in electoral politics, and seeking new vehicles for change.

National Black United Fund, Inc.
40 Clinton St.
Newark, NJ 07102
Telephone: (973) 643-5122
Web site: http://www.nbuf.org
Founded: 1972

The National Black United Fund (NBUF) provides financial and technical support to projects serving the critical needs of African American communities nationwide. Local affiliates solicit funds through payroll deduction to support projects in the areas of education, health and human services, economic development, social justice, arts and culture, and emergency needs. Programs supported by the NBUF emphasize self-help, volunteerism, and mutual aid.

National Black Women's Consciousness Raising Association
1906 N. Charles St.
Baltimore, MD 21218-6029
Telephone: (410) 727-8900
Founded: 1975

This association is open to African American women interested in women's rights and women's issues. It acts as a support group for women and provides educational and informational workshops and seminars on subjects of concern to black women and women in general. The group annually recognizes individuals, especially for academic achievement.

National Bowling Association, Inc.
9944 Reading Rd.
Cincinnati, OH 45241-3106
Telephone: (513) 769-1985
Web site: http://www.tnbainc.org
Founded: 1939

The nation's largest and oldest sports organization founded by African Americans, the National Bowling Association was formed to provide its members and other nonwhites an opportunity to participate in and enjoy tenpin bowling as an organized sport. Membership is encouraged regardless of race, religion, or gender. It encourages youth membership through its Junior Program and Scholarship Program.

National Brotherhood of Skiers, Inc.
1525 East 53rd St., Ste. 418
Chicago, IL 60615-4530
Telephone: (773) 955-4100
Web site: http://www.nbs.org
Founded: 1974

The National Brotherhood of Skiers promotes recreational and competitive skiing among minorities. Its mission is to "to identify, develop, and support athletes of color who will win international and Olympic winter sports competitions representing the United States."

National Catholic Conference for Interracial Justice
3033 4th St. NE
Washington, DC 20017-1102
Telephone: (202) 529-6480
Founded: 1960

This Catholic organization working for interracial justice and social concerns in the United States initiates programs within and outside the Catholic Church to end discrimination in community development, education, and employment.

National Caucus and Center on Black Aged, Inc.
1220 L St. NW, Ste. 800
Washington, DC 20005-4023
Telephone: (202) 637-8400
Web site: http://www.ncba-aged.org
Founded: 1970

This organization was founded to improve living conditions for low-income elderly Americans, particularly African Americans. It advocates changes in federal and state laws to improve the economic, health, and social status of low-income senior citizens. Other activities include the following: promoting community awareness of problems and issues affecting the low-income aging population; operating an employment program involving two thousand older persons in fourteen states; sponsoring, owning, and managing rental housing for the elderly; and conducting training and intern programs in nursing home administration, long-term care, housing management, and commercial property maintenance.

National Center of Afro-American Artists
300 Walnut Ave.
Boston, MA 02119-1324
Telephone: (617) 442-8614
Web site: http://www.ncaaa.org
Founded: 1968

This center is open to African American artists, institutions, and interested others. Its goals are to promote cultural activities in African American history and culture, encourage the development of artistic and cultural expression within black communities, and increase awareness and appreciation of the achievements of black artists. The center organizes and conducts cultural events, theatrical productions, and concerts. It sponsors workshops on topics such as nineteenth-century black America, Africa, and the Caribbean.

National Coalition of 100 Black Women, Inc.
1925 Adam C. Powell Jr. Blvd., Ste. 1L
New York, NY 10026
Telephone: (212) 222-5660
Web site: http://www.ncbw.org
Founded: 1981

This organization was founded by African American women actively involved with such issues as economic development, health, employment, education, voting, housing, criminal justice, the status of African American families, and the arts. It seeks to provide networking and career opportunities for African American women in the process of establishing links between the organization and the corporate and political arenas. It encourages leadership development and sponsors role-model and mentor programs to provide guidance to teenage mothers and young women who are in high school or who have graduated from college and are striving for career advancement.

National Coalition of Black Meeting Planners
8630 Fenton St., Ste. 126
Silver Spring, MD 20910
Telephone: (202) 628-3952
Web site: http://www.ncbmp.com
Founded: 1983

This organization acts as a liaison with hotels, airlines, convention centers, and bureaus in an effort to assess the impact of minorities working in these industries; assesses the needs of the convention industry and how best to meet these needs; enhances members' sophistication in planning meetings; and maximizes the employment of minorities in the convention industry.

National Coalition of Blacks for Reparations in America
PO Box 90604
Washington, DC 20090-0604
Telephone: (202) 291-8400

Web site: http://www.ncobra.org
Founded: 1989

This organization seeks to obtain reparations from the U.S. government, other governments, and corporations that profited from the labor of African people who were treated as slaves. It also compiles statistics, offers educational and research programs, and maintains a speakers bureau.

National Coalition on Black Civic Participation
1050 Connecticut Ave. NW, Ste. 1000
Washington, DC 20036-5334
Telephone: (202) 659-4929
Web site: http://www.ncbcp.org
Founded: 1976

Originally organized as the National Coalition on Black Voter Participation, this group is dedicated to increasing African American participation in civil society. Its programs include Operation Big Vote, the Black Women's Roundtable, Voices of the Electorate, the Unity Civic Engagement and Voter Empowerment Campaign, and Black Youth Vote! The organization is dedicated to training and engaging African American leaders and community activists in overcoming institutional barriers that have hindered the growth of African American communities politically, socially, and economically.

National Conference of Black Lawyers
PO Box 998
New York, NY 10024
Toll Free: (866) 266-5091
Web site: http://www.ncbl.org
Founded: 1968

This organization maintains projects in legal services to community organizations, voting rights, and international affairs; provides public education on legal issues affecting African Americans and poor people; researches racism in law schools and bar admissions; conducts programs of continuing legal education for member attorneys; maintains a general law library; compiles statistics; and maintains lawyer referral and placement services.

National Conference of Black Mayors
101 Marietta St., Ste. 3410
Atlanta, GA 30303-2711
Telephone: (404) 765-6444
Web site: http://www.ncbm.org
Founded: 1974

The National Conference of Black Mayors was founded to improve the executive management capacity and efficiency of member municipalities in the delivery of municipal services; create viable communities within which normal government functions can be performed efficiently; provide the basis upon which new social overhead investments in the infrastructure of municipalities can use federal, state, local, and private resources to encourage new industry and increase employment; and assist municipalities in stabilizing their population through improvements of the quality of life for residents and, concurrently, create alternatives to outward migration. The organization also facilitates small-town growth and development through energy conservation.

National Conference of Black Political Scientists
3695-F Cascade Rd. SW, Ste. 212
Atlanta, GA 30031
Web site: http://www.ncobps.org
Founded: 1969

This organization was founded by political and social science faculty, lawyers, and related professionals interested in African American politics and related fields. It seeks to encourage research, publication, and scholarship by African Americans in political science and to improve the political life of African Americans.

National Congress of Black Women, Inc.
1251 4th St. SW
Washington, DC 20024-2307
Telephone: (202) 678-6788
Web site: http://www.nationalcongressbw.org
Founded: 1984

The National Congress of Black Women works to encourage African American women to engage in political activities. It offers training in understanding and operating within the political process; strives to develop, educate, and encourage African American women to seek office; and encourages the appointment of these women at all levels of government.

National Council for Black Studies
Georgia State University, Dept. of African American Studies
PO Box 4109
Atlanta, GA 30302-4109
Telephone: (404) 413-5131
Web site: http://www.ncbsonline.org
Founded: 1975

This organization strives to bring members, students, and institutions together to promote and strengthen academic and community programs in black and/or African American studies. The council sponsors undergraduate and graduate student essay contests. It offers a professional opportunities referral service and compiles statistics on black studies activities, including information on students, faculty, research, and curricula.

National Council of Negro Women, Inc.
633 Pennsylvania Ave. NW
Washington, DC 20004
Telephone: (202) 737-0120
Web site: http://www.ncnw.org
Founded: 1935

This organization was founded by Mary McLeod Bethune to assist in the development and utilization of the leadership of women in community, national, and international life. It maintains the Women's Center for Education and Career Advancement, which offers programs designed to aid minority women in pursuing nontraditional careers, and the Bethune Museum and Archives for Black Women's History.

National Dental Association
3517 16th St. NW
Washington, DC 20010-3041
Telephone: (202) 588-1697
Web site: http://www.ndaonline.org
Founded: 1913

The National Dental Association (NDA) was formed by minority health professionals who had been denied access to national associations formed by whites. The NDA champions the interests and concerns of poor and minority patients and their doctors. It has several auxiliary chapters and sponsors symposia and student organizations.

National Forum for Black Public Administrators
777 N. Capitol St. NE, Ste. 807
Washington, DC 20002-4291
Telephone: (202) 408-9300
Web site: http://www.nfbpa.org
Founded: 1983

This organization was founded to promote, strengthen, and expand the role of African Americans in public administration. It seeks to focus the influence of African American administrators toward building and maintaining viable communities; develop specialized training programs for managers and executives; provide a national public administrative leadership resource and skills bank; work to further communication among African American public, private, and academic institutions; and address issues that affect the administrative capacity of African American managers. The organization maintains an Executive Leadership Institute, which grooms midlevel executives for higher positions in government; the Mentor Program, which matches aspiring African American managers with seasoned executives over an eight-month period; and the Leadership Institute for Small Municipalities, which provides intensive training for elected and appointed officials from small communities. It offers training programs for black South Africans intent on achieving public administrative positions in the postapartheid era. It also sponsors the National Minority Business Development Forum to increase the participation of small and minority businesses in local government procurement and contracting programs.

National Funeral Directors and Morticians Association, Inc.
3951 Snapfinger Pkwy., Ste. 570
Decatur, GA 30035-3298
Toll Free: (800) 434-0958
Web site: http://www.nfdma.com
Founded: 1924

This association of state and local embalmers and funeral directors seeks to promote ethical standards and laws for the profession. It was initially organized as the Independent National Funeral Directors Association.

National Hook-Up of Black Women, Inc.
1809 E. 71st St., Ste. 205
Chicago, IL 60649-2000
Telephone: (773) 667-7061
Web site: http://www.nhbwinc.com
Founded: 1974

This membership organization includes women from business, professional, and community-oriented disciplines representing all economic, educational, and social levels. The group's purpose is to provide a communications network in support of black women who serve in organizational leadership positions, especially those elected or appointed to office and those wishing to elevate their status through educational and career ventures. The group works to form and implement a black women's agenda to provide representation for women, families, and communities and to help surmount economic, educational, and social barriers. It supports efforts of the Congressional Black Caucus to use the legislative process to work toward total equality of opportunity in society. The organization seeks to highlight the achievements and contributions of black women and also operates a speakers bureau.

National Medical Association
1012 10th St. NW
Washington, DC 20001-4402
Telephone: (202) 347-1895
Web site: http://www.nmanet.org
Founded: 1895

This is a professional society formed by African American physicians. It maintains twenty-four separate scientific sections representing major specialties of medicine. The association also hosts a symposium and conducts workshops.

National Minority Health Association
10 E. Baltimore St., Ste. 1404
Baltimore, MD 21202-1609
Founded: 1987

This association was founded by health-care providers and associations, consumers, executives and administrators, educators, pharmaceutical and health insurance companies, and other organizations with an interest in health. It seeks to focus attention on the health needs of minorities.

National Minority Supplier Development Council, Inc.
1359 Broadway, 10th Fl.
New York, NY 10018
Telephone: (212) 944-2430
Web site: http://www.nmsdc.org
Founded: 1972

The primary objective of this organization is to provide a direct link between corporate America and minority-owned enterprises. It aims to increase procurement and business opportunities for minorities regardless of the size of the business.

National Newspaper Publishers Association
3200 13th St. NW
Washington, DC 20010-2410
Telephone: (202) 319-1291
Web site: http://www.nnpa.org
Founded: 1940

This association promotes the interests of the African American press in governmental and corporate areas, while also encouraging its members to participate in cooperative efforts.

National Optometric Association
PO Box 198959
Chicago, IN 60619-8959
Toll Free: (877) 394-2020
Web site: http://www.natoptassoc.org
Founded: 1969

The National Optometric Association was founded by predominantly minority optometrists who aimed to update and enhance knowledge in the field and to develop the professional skills of its members. Its primary aim is "the delivery of effective and efficient eye and vision care services to the minority community." The organization recruits African American youth into the profession.

National Organization for the Professional Advancement of Black Chemists and Chemical Engineers
PO Box 77040
Washington, DC 20013-8040
Toll Free: (800) 776-1419
Web site: http://www.nobcche.org
Founded: 1972

This organization was founded to aid African American scientists and chemists in reaching their full professional potential. It encourages African American students to pursue scientific studies and employment and promotes the participation of African Americans in scientific research. The group provides volunteers to teach science courses in selected elementary schools, sponsors scientific field trips for students, maintains a speakers bureau for schools, and provides summer school for students of the U.S. Naval Academy. It also conducts technical seminars in Africa.

National Organization of Black County Officials
1090 Vermont Ave. NW, Ste. 1290
Washington, DC 20005-4963
Telephone: (202) 350-6696
Web site: http://www.nobcoinc.org
Founded: 1982

This organization was founded by African American county officials to provide program planning and management assistance to selected counties in the United States. The group acts as a technical information exchange to develop resolutions to problems on the local and national levels, promotes the sharing of knowledge about and methods of improving resource utilization and government operations, and conducts seminars and training sessions.

National Organization of Black Law Enforcement Executives
4609-F Pinecrest Office Park Dr.
Alexandria, VA 22312-1442
Telephone: (703) 658-1529
Web site: http://www.noblenatl.org
Founded: 1976

This organization was founded to provide a platform from which the concerns and opinions of minority law enforcement executives and command-level officers can be expressed, to facilitate the exchange of programmatic information among minority law enforcement executives, to increase minority participation at all levels of law enforcement, to eliminate racism in the field of criminal justice, to secure increased cooperation from criminal justice agencies, and to reduce urban crime and violence. It seeks to develop and maintain channels of communication between law enforcement agencies and the community, and it encourages coordinated community efforts to prevent and abate crime and its causes.

National Pan-Hellenic Council, Inc.
3951 Snapfinger Pkwy., Ste. 218
Decatur, GA 30035-3200
Telephone: (404) 592-6145
Web site: http://www.nphchq.org
Founded: 1930

This coalition of the nine largest African American Greek letter fraternities and sororities was incorporated in 1937. Its mission and purpose are to advance and strengthen the fraternity and sorority movement and to empower the African American community for economic and social development. The council promotes interaction among member organizations through meetings, forums, and other mediums.

National Pharmaceutical Association
The Courtyards Office Complex
107 Kilmayne Dr., Ste. C
Cary, NC 27511-4434
Toll Free: (877) 215-2091
Web site: http://www.npha.net
Founded: 1947

This organization provides minority pharmacists an outlet to contribute to their common improvement and to public concerns.

National Society of Black Engineers
205 Dangerfield Rd.
Alexandria, VA 22314-2833
Telephone: (703) 549-2207
Web site: http://national.nsbe.org
Founded: 1975

This society was founded to increase the number of minority graduates in engineering and technology. It develops programs to increase the participation of African American and other minorities in engineering and engineering technologies. Membership includes students and professionals.

National Society of Black Physicists
1100 N. Glebe Rd., Ste. 1010
Arlington, VA 22201-5786
Telephone: (703) 536-4207
Web site: http://www.nsbp.org
Founded: 1977

This organization addresses the needs of African American physicists, works to create opportunities for minorities in the field, and sponsors mentor programs and lectures on research findings.

National Sorority of Phi Delta Kappa, Inc.
8233 S. King Dr.
Chicago, IL 60619
Telephone: (773) 783-7379
Web site: http://www.sororitynpdk.org
Founded: 1923

Phi Delta Kappa is an international organization for professional educators. It works with adults and young people who are in or out of school, promotes literacy, and aims to improve the quality of education nationally.

National Trust for the Development of African-American Men
c/o Dr. Garry Mendez Jr.
672 13th St.
Oakland, CA 94612
Founded: 1989

This organization was founded by individuals interested in improving the self-esteem of African American men. It promotes increased understanding of and appreciation for traditional African value systems, and works to "create and diffuse a new consciousness in the African rooted people in America." The group also conducts research and educational programs, with an emphasis on issues facing incarcerated men and their families.

National Urban Coalition
2120 L St. NW, Ste. 510
Washington, DC 20037-1534
Telephone: (202) 986-1460
Founded: 1967

The National Urban Coalition seeks to improve the quality of life for the disadvantaged in urban areas through the combined efforts of business, labor, government, and community leaders. It operates programs that work to increase participation by minority students in science, math, and computer education. It also runs the Say Yes to a Youngster's Future program.

National Urban League
120 Wall St.
New York, NY 10005
Telephone: (212) 558-5300
Web site: http://www.nul.org
Founded: 1910

The National Urban League (NUL) was founded to eliminate racial segregation and discrimination in the

United States and to achieve parity for African Americans and other minorities in every phase of American life. The NUL works to eliminate institutional racism and to provide direct service to minorities in the areas of employment, housing, education, social welfare, health, family planning, developmental disabilities, law and consumer affairs, youth and student affairs, labor affairs, veterans' affairs, and community and minority business development.

Negro Airmen International, Inc.
PO Box 23911
Savannah, GA 31403-3911
Telephone: (912) 232-7524
Web site: http://www.blackwingsonline.com
Founded: 1967

This organization works to increase African Americans' personal and professional mobility through participation in all fields of aviation, especially piloting. It is dedicated to educating the public and improving international service in support of its goals.

NIH Black Scientists Association
PO Box 2262
Kensington, MD 20891-2262
Telephone: (301) 435-4568
Web site: http://www.nih.gov/science/blacksci/bsaabout.html

Made up of scientists, physicians, technologists, and science administrators at the National Institutes of Health (NIH), this association provides communication and dissemination of information about issues of common interest, the development of important personal and professional contacts, career support and enhancement, and group advocacy on issues of importance to underrepresented minorities at NIH and beyond. The group maintains a membership database and a speakers bureau.

Office of Black Ministries/Episcopal Church Center
c/o Episcopal Church
815 2nd Ave.
New York, NY 10017
Telephone: (212) 922-5343
Founded: 1973

This organization, a commission of the Episcopal Church, is comprised of black members of the Episcopal Church representing geographically diverse dioceses, including one diocese outside of the United States. It works to strengthen the witness of black Episcopalians in the church through programs that include parish and clergy development and international relations. It also compiles statistics and provides financial assistance and consultations to parishes and church organizations.

Omega Psi Phi Fraternity, Inc.
3951 Snapfinger Pky.
Decatur, GA 30035
Telephone: (404) 284-5533
Web site: http://www.omegapsiphifraternity.org
Founded: 1911

Omega Psi Phi is a social fraternity founded at Howard University.

Operation Crossroads Africa
PO Box 5570
New York, NY 10027-5588
Telephone: (212) 289-1949
Web site: http://www.operationcrossroadsafrica.org
Founded: 1958

Operations Crossroads Africa was founded to enable students and professionals, mostly from the United States, to live with African counterparts and work with them on self-help community-development projects in Africa during the months of July and August. Opportunities are provided for interaction with village elders, educators, and political and other community leaders. The group emphasizes community growth from within a Third World structure. Before departure, participants make an intensive study of Africa; after their return, they give speeches about their experiences. Participants pay part of the cost of the project. The group also organizes work-camp projects in the Caribbean for U.S. high school students and handles the visits of African and Caribbean leaders to the United States. It also sponsors training and exchange programs.

Organization of Black Aerospace Professionals
1 Westbrook Corporate Ctr., Ste. 300
Westchester, IL 60154-5709
Toll Free: (800) 538-6227
Web site: http://www.obap.org
Founded: 1976

This organization was founded to enhance minority participation in the aerospace industry. It maintains liaison with airline presidents and minority and pilot associations; conducts lobbying efforts, including congressional examinations into airline recruitment practices; and provides scholarships.

Organization of Black Designers
300 M St. SW, Ste. N-110
Washington, DC 20024-4004
Telephone: (202) 659-3918
Web site: http://www.obd.org
Founded: 1990

The Organization of Black Designers is comprised of African American designers holding college degrees who are practicing graphic, industrial, fashion, textile, and interior design. The organization provides a forum for discussion, offers educational programs, and promotes business, career, and economic development. It also sponsors competitions and maintains a speakers bureau.

Phi Beta Sigma Fraternity, Inc.
145 Kennedy St. NW
Washington, DC 20011-5294
Telephone: (202) 726-5434
Web site: http://www.pbs1914.org
Founded: 1914

Phi Beta Sigma is a service fraternity that sponsors the Sigma Beta Club for high school–age males.

Phylaxis Society
PO Box 2212
Tacoma, WA 98401-2212
Web site: http://www.thephylaxis.org
Founded: 1973

The Phylaxis Society was founded by Prince Hall Masonic writers and editors of Masonic publications.

Program for Research on Black Americans
University of Michigan, 5062 Institute for Social Research
PO Box 1248
Ann Arbor, MI 48106-1248
Telephone: (734) 763-0045
Web site: http://rcgd.isr.umich.edu/prba
Founded: 1976

This organization collects, analyzes, and interprets empirical data and disseminates findings based on national and international studies of people of African American and African descent. The group provides research and training opportunities for black social scientists and students. It also fosters high-quality research on factors related to mental health and mental disorders among Americans of African descent.

Project BAIT: Black Awareness in Television
30 Josephine, 3rd Fl.
Detroit, MI 48202-1810
Telephone: (313) 871-3333
Web site: http://projectbait.blakgold.net
Founded: 1970

Project BAIT produces black media programs for television, video, radio, film, and theater. It trains individuals in the media and conducts research projects, including surveys. In addition, the organization produces public affairs, cultural arts, soap opera, and exercise programs; sponsors theater companies; seeks television exposure for black-produced products and black performing artists; and promotes the September Is Black Reading Month program.

Project Equality
6301 Rockhill Rd., Ste. 315
Kansas City, MO 64131
Telephone: (816) 361-9222
Founded: 1965

Project Equality is a nationwide interfaith program enabling religious organizations, institutions, and others to support equal opportunity employers with their purchasing power. Services include validation of hotels for conventions and meetings of organizations, validations of suppliers to member organizations and institutions, and consulting and educational services to assist employers in affirmative action and equal employment opportunity programs.

Quality Education for Minorities Network
1818 N St. NW, Ste. 350
Washington, DC 20036-2493
Telephone: (202) 659-1818
Web site: http://www.qem.org
Founded: 1990

This organization was founded to implement the plan developed by the Quality Education for Minorities Project. The network believes that minorities are underserved by the educational system and thus disproportionately lack the skills needed to participate effectively in a society increasingly based on high technology. It plans to work with school systems, communities, universities, and public and private-sector institutions to ensure that minority students have equal access to educational opportunities.

Rainbow PUSH Coalition
930 E. 50th St.
Chicago, IL 60615-2702
Telephone: (773) 373-3366
Founded: 1996

This organization was founded by the Reverend Jesse L. Jackson Sr. to build a consensus in the area of civil rights, government, politics, labor, education, and business. It provides a platform for debate and encourages the development of a new political leadership committed to progressive domestic and international policies and programs. The Rainbow PUSH Coalition is the result of the merger of Operation PUSH, which Jackson founded in 1971, and the National Rainbow Coalition, founded in 1984.

Sigma Gamma Rho Sorority, Inc.
1000 Southhill Dr., Ste. 200
Cary, NC 27513-8630
Telephone: (919) 678-9720
Web site: http://www.sgrho1922.org

Sigma Gamma Rho promotes unity among women with a legacy that bonds members in the United States and the Caribbean. Its national programs include Habitat for Humanity, seminars for children, an essay contest, and other projects to address the needs of school-age children.

Sigma Pi Phi Fraternity
225 Broadway
New York, NY 10010
Telephone: (212) 964-3235
Web site: http://www.sigmapiphi.org
Founded: 1904

Sigma Pi Phi was founded as a social fraternity and is the oldest African American Greek letter society in the United States. It maintains the Boulé Foundation.

Southern Christian Leadership Conference
320 Auburn Ave. NE
Atlanta, GA 30303-2604
Telephone: (404) 522-1420
Web site: http://www.sclcnational.org
Founded: 1957

The Southern Christian Leadership Conference (SCLC) is a nonsectarian coordinating and service agency for local organizations seeking full citizenship rights, equality, and the integration of African Americans in all aspects of life in the United States. The SCLC subscribes to the Gandhian philosophy of nonviolence. It works primarily in sixteen southern and border states to improve civic, religious, economic, and cultural conditions. The SCLC also fosters nonviolent resistance to all forms of racial injustice, including state and local laws and practices; conducts leadership training programs embracing such subjects as registration and voting, social protest, the use of the boycott, picketing, the nature of prejudice, and understanding politics; sponsors citizenship education to teach reading and writing; helps people pass literacy tests for voting; provides information about income-tax forms, tax-supported resources, aid to handicapped children, public health facilities, how government is run, and social security; and conducts Crusade for the Ballot, which aims to double the African American vote in the South through increased voter registration.

Southern Poverty Law Center
400 Washington Ave.
Montgomery, AL 36104-4344
Telephone: (334) 956-8200
Web site: http://www.splcenter.org
Founded: 1971

The Southern Poverty Law Center (SPLC) was founded to protect and advance the legal and civil rights of poor people, regardless of race, through education and litigation. The SPLC does not accept fees from clients. It is currently involved in several lawsuits representing individuals injured or threatened by activities of the Ku Klux Klan and related groups and attempts to develop techniques and strategies that can be used by private attorneys. It also operates Klanwatch.

Southern Regional Council
1201 W. Peachtree St. NE, Ste. 2000
Atlanta, GA 30309-3453
Telephone: (404) 522-8764
Web site: http://www.southerncouncil.org
Founded: 1944

The Southern Regional Council (SRC) was founded by leaders in education, religion, business, labor, the community, and the professions interested in improving race relations and combating poverty in the South. The SRC comprises an interracial research and technical assistance center that addresses issues of social justice and political and economic democracy. It seeks to engage public policy as well as personal conscience in pursuit of equality. It develops educational programs; provides community-relations consultation and field services when requested by official and private agencies; distributes pamphlets pertaining to desegregation of various public facilities; fosters elimination of barriers to African American voting and registration; and acts as an official sponsor of overseas government officials, leaders, and other visitors who wish to learn about race relations in the South.

Thurgood Marshall College Fund
80 Maiden Ln., Ste. 2204
New York, NY 10038-4815
Telephone: (212) 573-8888
Web site: http://www.thurgoodmarshallfund.org
Founded: 1987

This fund provides scholarships to students attending the nation's historically black public colleges and universities.

Top Ladies of Distinction, Inc.
2914 Southmore Blvd.
Houston, TX 77004-7710

Telephone: (512) 291-0847
Web site: http://www.tlodinc.org
Founded: 1964

This organization encourages professional women to guide and assist youth. It also addresses the moral and social problems of youth, enhances the status of women, and enriches the lives of senior citizens.

TransAfrica
1629 K St. NW, Ste. 1100
Washington, DC 20006
Telephone: (202) 223-1960
Web site: http://www.transafricaforum.org
Founded: 1977

This group is concerned with the political and human rights of people in Africa and the Caribbean, as well as those of African descent throughout the world. It attempts to influence U.S. foreign policy in these areas by informing the public of violations of social, political, and civil rights and by advocating a more progressive attitude in the U.S. policy stance. It supports the work of the United Nations in Africa and sponsors TransAfrica Action Alert to mobilize African American opinion nationally on foreign policy issues by contacting influential policy makers.

TransAfrica Forum
1629 K St. NW, Ste. 1100
Washington, DC 20006
Telephone: (202) 223-1960
Web site: http://www.transafricaforum.org
Founded: 1981

TransAfrica Forum is the research and education arm of its parent organization, TransAfrica. Through its publications, TransAfrica Forum seeks to provide an independent review of differing perspectives on political, economic, and cultural issues affecting African American communities globally. It also conducts seminars with scholars and government officials.

Tuskegee Airmen, Inc.
PO Box 830060
Tuskegee, AL 36083-0060
Web site: http://tuskegeeairmen.org
Founded: 1972

This organization was founded by members of the all-black World War II Army Corps veterans who were trained at Tuskegee Airfield in Tuskegee, Alabama. Membership is now open to all supporters. Its mission is "to inspire young people to seek aviation-related careers." It provides scholarships to high school graduates.

Union of Black Episcopalians
1550 Magnolia Dr.
Cincinnati, OH 45215-1914
Toll Free: (800) 806-5837
Web site: http://www.ube.org
Founded: 1968

The Union of Black Episcopalians is dedicated to involving Christians in every facet of church life. It encourages mission, stewardship, education, evangelism, and involvement in church governance and politics.

Unitarian Universalist Association, Black Concerns Working Group
25 Beacon St.
Boston, MA 02108
Telephone: (617) 742-2100
Founded: 1985

The Black Concerns Working Group was founded to raise denominational public awareness of racism as a current justice issue. It works to implement recommendations regarding racial justice that were adopted by the Unitarian Universalist General Assembly in 1985 and conducts local and regional workshops in an effort to coordinate racial justice work among Unitarian Universalist congregations.

United Black Church Appeal
c/o Christ Church
860 Forest Ave.
Bronx, NY 10456-7829
Telephone: (718) 588-7500
Founded: 1980

This organization was founded to awaken the power of the African American clergy and the African American church in order to provide leadership for the liberation of the African American community. It is concerned with African American economic development and political power and the strengthening of African American families and churches. It believes pastors in African American churches should reestablish legitimate leadership roles within the African American community. The group works with troubled African American youths in the community and rallies against drugs in urban areas. It also supports community betterment projects, including surplus food programs and the distribution of food to needy families.

United Black Fund, Inc.
2500 Martin Luther King Jr. Ave. SE
Washington, DC 20020-5210
Telephone: (202) 783-9300
Web site: http://www.ubfinc.org
Founded: 1969

This fund is comprised of nonprofit agencies that provide human care services to low-income or disabled blacks and other minorities. It assists disadvantaged African Americans and other minorities in becoming self-sufficient by providing funding to member agencies for the establishment of health and welfare programs. It sponsors fund-raising activities to support day-care service, education, senior citizens, and drug and alcohol rehabilitation programs, and monitors the establishment and development of such programs.

United Church of Christ Commission for Racial Justice
c/o United Church of Christ
700 Prospect Ave. E
Cleveland, OH 44115-1110
Telephone: (216) 736-2161
Founded: 1965

This organization was founded to ensure racial justice and social equality for ethnic and racial minorities worldwide. It maintains higher-education programs to provide scholarships to minority college students.

United Negro College Fund
8260 Willow Oaks Corporate Dr.
PO Box 10444
Fairfax, VA 22031-8044
Toll Free: (800) 331-2244
Web site: http://www.uncf.org
Founded: 1944

The United Negro College Fund was founded as a fund-raising agency for historically African American colleges and universities that are private and fully accredited. It provides information on educational programs, sponsors college fairs for high school and community college students, and administers scholarship awards and corporate and foundation programs.

Urban Financial Services Coalition
1200 G St. NW, Ste. 800
Washington, DC 20005-6705
Telephone: (202) 289-8335
Web site: http://www.ufscnet.org
Founded: 1974

The Urban Financial Services Coalition was founded by minority professionals in the financial services industry. It is the only trade association that represents the interests of minority- and women-owned banks.

Visions Foundation
14802 Debenham Way
Bowie, MD 20721-3242
Telephone: (301) 385-1916
Founded: 1983

The Visions Foundation promotes understanding of African American culture. It conducts media-related and educational programs to teach the public about the contributions of blacks to society and culture in the United States.

Washington Office on Africa
212 E. Capitol St.
Washington, DC 20003-1036
Telephone: (202) 547-7503
Founded: 1972

This organization was founded to monitor and analyze developments in U.S. policy toward southern Africa and work with national and local groups that support the attainment of majority rule. It also lobbies on congressional legislation affecting southern Africa.

Zeta Phi Beta Sorority, Inc.
1734 New Hampshire Ave. NW
Washington, DC 20009-2526
Telephone: (202) 387-3103
Web site: http://www.zphib1920.org
Founded: 1920

This organization was founded as a service and social sorority. It maintains the Zeta Phi Beta Sorority Educational Foundation. Its programs focus on a variety of concerns, such as on youth, senior citizens, substance abuse, illiteracy, child care, and voter registration.

10

LAW

Brenda M. Wood Kahari

This chapter will highlight key aspects of U.S. law and the American legal system as they relate to the status and rights of African Americans. The essay will also explore the accomplishments of African Americans who worked within the legal and justice system despite the obstacles they had to overcome.

THE LEGAL STATUS OF AFRICAN AMERICANS

SLAVERY

With the exception of indentured servants and prisoners, the majority of Europeans ventured to America voluntarily during the seventeenth century seeking a better way of life. In contrast, the Africans who arrived in America had been captured in their homeland and forced into enslavement. Indentured servants and prisoners, after satisfying certain legal requirements, had a right to and expectation of freedom and equality. This was not the case for enslaved Africans, who were dependent on their owner's authorization and the various laws that applied to the enslaved. From 1619 to 1865, people of African descent were by law defined as chattel—that is, goods or movable property—and the laws of property ownership applied to them (see Massachusetts Body of Liberties [1641], *Belt v. Dalby* [1786], the Fugitive Slave Act [1850], and the *Dred Scott* decision [1857]). Their rights, if they had any, were based on this legal status. This unequal treatment under the law was to have a profound and lasting effect not only on the economic, social, and cultural aspects of African American life, but on the way of life of all Americans.

THE U.S. CONSTITUTION

The euphoria of creating a new government based on equality and democracy after the victory achieved in the American Revolution (1775–1783) did not bring with it any commitment to abolish African enslavement or even a recognition that the institution was inconsistent with such principles. The declaration of universal equality expressed in the U.S. Constitution as adopted in 1787 did not include people of color. In short, the United States began with a contradiction that centered on race, and from its beginning, the country was mired in a debate over the question of slavery.

The constitutional debates of the 1780s highlighted the nation's contradictory, confusing positions on race questions. The country was founded on the principle of individual liberty, but that liberty did not extend to the enslaved Africans and their progeny. The leading questions of the era were: Should those enslaved be counted for purposes of representation? Should Congress be empowered to prohibit slavery and the trade in humans? Should the person who escaped enslavement be "free" to live among the rest of society? Delegates from southern states, whose population included a large number of enslaved Africans, wanted them counted toward representation in the U.S. House of Representatives, while still insisting that the black captives were property. This contradiction led to a compromise in which slaves counted as three-fifths of a person for representational purposes. However, this compromise indicated that the issue of American enslavement would not easily recede.

Although the institution of human slavery vexed members of the Constitutional Convention, the words *slavery* and *slave* do not appear in the document that was submitted for ratification. The contradiction between the equality espoused by the Constitution and the reality of African enslavement that the Constitution tolerated would tear the country apart less than a century later.

The original Constitution forbade the new federal government from abolishing the slave trade or otherwise addressing matters of race before the year 1808. Runaways were referred to as "person[s] held to service or labour in one state ... escaping into another." This fugitive-slave clause (Article 4, section 2) sought to ensure that the plantation owners' escaped "property" would be returned when found. The purpose of these provisions was to ensure the political superiority of white Americans over the enslaved Africans and their progeny. At the time of the Constitution's framing, the enslaved and their descendants were treated as politically inferior to white people.

The framers of the Constitution recognized the peculiar dilemma of racial discrimination, yet they decided that they could postpone a decision on the "race question." The idea that matters of racial justice and racial equality could be put off was established. After the Civil War (1861–1865) and the deaths of many, the Constitution was eventually amended to include the Thirteenth, Fourteenth, and Fifteenth Amendments, which prohibit discrimination and inequality.

COURT DECISIONS

Because of these conflicting constitutional antecedents, the U.S. Supreme Court has been enormously conflicted on racial matters. The Court takes its cases as it finds them, and cases on race have never been easily or calmly settled.

***Prigg v. Pennsylvania*, 41 U.S. (16 Peters) 539 (1842).** Before the 1800s, the Court had few opportunities to render a decision directly on the question of black enslavement because slavery was an accepted institution and a feature of American life. The law clearly recognized this captive population as property and therefore subject to regulation like other chattel, goods, or movable property. This view was often justified by citing the fugitive-slave clause of the Constitution. One of the few pre–Civil War cases to address the slavery question and state regulatory powers was *Prigg v. Pennsylvania.*

Pennsylvania had enacted a statute prohibiting any person from removing blacks from the state by force or violence with the intention of detaining them as enslaved persons. The Court explained that the fugitive-slave clause "contemplates the existence of a positive, unqualified right on the part of the owner of the slave, which no state law or regulation can in any way qualify, regulate, control, or restrain." The statute was declared invalid with respect to escaped Africans because, in the words of the Court, "any state law which interrupts, limits, delays, or postpones the right of the owner to the immediate possession of the slave, and the immediate command of his service and labor, operates *pro tanto* a discharge of the slave there from." The Court further held that the clause implicitly vested Congress with the power to assist owners in securing the return of those who had escaped, that Congress had exercised that power by enacting the Fugitive Slave Act of 1793, that this national power was exclusive, and that any state laws regulating the means by which those enslaved were to be delivered up were unconstitutional.

Prigg announced no landmark policy. It simply affirmed the social and political realities of its time. During the 1790–1883 period, however, two major cases involving African Americans and the issues of race did reach the Supreme Court: *Dred Scott v. Sandford*, 60 U.S. (19 Howard) 393 (1857), and the *Civil Rights Cases*, 109 U.S. 3 (1883), along with the relatively minor case, *Strauder v. West Virginia*, 100 U.S. (10 Otto) 303 (1880). As a whole, they revealed the abiding ambivalence that has consistently characterized American race relations.

Dred Scott v. Sandford. The 1800s were consumed with sectional strife, primarily strife about race. In 1856, *Dred Scott* was decided. The case would generate an impetus toward civil war. Few cases in American judicial history have achieved as much notoriety as *Dred Scott.* The case continues to symbolize the marginal status that African Americans have often held in the nation's social and political order.

Dred Scott was an African enslaved by John Emerson, a U.S. Army surgeon from Missouri. In 1834, Scott traveled with Emerson to live in Illinois, where African enslavement was prohibited. They later lived in the Wisconsin Territory, where African enslavement was prohibited by the Missouri Compromise. In 1838, Scott returned to Missouri with Emerson. Emerson died there in 1843, and three years later Scott sued Emerson's widow for his freedom.

Scott's claim was based on the argument that his former residence in a free state and a free territory made him a free man. A Missouri state circuit court ruled in Scott's favor, but the Missouri Supreme Court later reversed that decision. Meanwhile, Scott had become the legal property of John F. A. Sandford of New York. Because Sandford did not live in Missouri, Scott's lawyers were able to transfer the case to a federal court. The lower federal court ruled against Scott, and his lawyers appealed to the U.S. Supreme Court.

By a seven-to-two vote, the Supreme Court ruled that Scott could not bring a suit in federal court. The decision was announced on March 6, 1857, two days after the inauguration of President James Buchanan. The *Dred Scott* decision declared that no African American, whether free or enslaved, could claim U.S. citizenship. It also held that Congress could not prohibit enslavement in the U.S. territories. In his opinion, Chief Justice Roger Brooke Taney (1777–1864) wrote that African Americans had "no rights which any white man was bound to respect."

This decision—only the second in the nation's history in which the Supreme Court declared an act of Congress unconstitutional—was a clear victory for the political interests that supported the enslavement of Africans. Southerners had long argued that neither Congress nor the territorial legislature had the power to exclude African enslavement from a territory. Only a state could do so, they maintained.

The *Dred Scott* ruling also aroused anger and resentment in the North and in other parts of the country, and launched the nation further along the course toward civil war. In addition, the ruling influenced the introduction and the adoption of the Fourteenth Amendment to the Constitution in 1868, which explicitly overruled *Dred Scott*, extended citizenship to former slaves, and sought to give them full civil rights.

Each justice in the majority wrote a separate opinion. Chief Justice Taney's opinion, however, is most often cited because of its far-reaching implications for sectional crisis and for the view of the rights of African Americans that it announced. Speaking for the majority, Taney declared that Scott was not entitled to such rights as the right to vote or to sue in a federal court because, as an African American, he was not a citizen of the United States. The Court did not dismiss the case after ruling on Scott's citizenship. Because there was a growing national desire for a ruling on the constitutionality of such laws as the Missouri Compromise of 1820, the Taney Court seized the opportunity to express its views on both congressional power and the legal status of African Americans.

The Missouri Compromise had forbidden African enslavement in the Louisiana Territory north of the latitude 36° 30′, except for Missouri. Instead of dismissing the suit, the Court discussed this issue as a part of its decision in *Dred Scott*. By the same seven-to-two margin, it ruled that the Missouri Compromise, which had been repealed in 1854, was unconstitutional. Taney argued that because the black captives were property, Congress could not forbid slavery in territories without violating a plantation owner's right to own property under the Fifth Amendment. As for Scott's temporary residence in the free state of Illinois, the majority ruled that Scott then had still been subject to Missouri law. Dred Scott was sold shortly afterward, and his new owner gave him his freedom two months after the decision.

The *Dred Scott* decision energized the newly created Republican Party, which had been formed to curb the expansion of African enslavement into the western territories. The decision forced Democrat Stephen A. Douglas (1813–1861), an advocate of popular sovereignty, to devise a system that would enable settlers to ban black enslavement in their jurisdictions. President Buchanan and a majority of the Supreme Court justices, along with many in the South, had hoped that the decision would end the antislavery agitation that consumed the country. Instead, the decision increased antislavery sentiment in the North, strengthened the Republican Party, and fed the sectional antagonisms that finally exploded into war in 1861.

***Strauder v. West Virginia* and the *Civil Rights Cases*.** Between the time of the Civil War and the *Civil Rights Cases*, the only case to protect the rights of African Americans was *Strauder v. West Virginia* (1880). West Virginia permitted only "white male persons who are 21 years of age" to serve on juries in the state. This, of course, meant that it was impossible for African Americans to serve on a jury. The Supreme Court invalidated this provision as a violation of the Fourteenth Amendment's guarantee of equal protection.

The Civil War, caused in part by Chief Justice Taney's decision in *Dred Scott* that Congress could not bar African enslavement in the territories, actually resulted in the destruction of slavery. Moreover, the war created a completely new balance of power between the national and the state governments. Federalism, unlike how it had been understood prior to the Civil War, now would function with a totally new calculus in which the federal government was the dominant power.

The Thirteenth, Fourteenth, and Fifteenth Amendments to the Constitution were enacted following the Civil War to emancipate and empower former enslaved Africans. These three amendments are compelling evidence of the relationship between the federal and state governments. The text of the Fourteenth Amendment, overturning *Dred Scott*, emphasized the significance of this new relationship and the new power realignments.

U.S. citizenship was redefined as being protected by the national Constitution, not as a byproduct of state citizenship. State citizenship was subordinate to national citizenship. Augmented by Congress's enforcement powers, these amendments were the constitutional foundations that supported Reconstruction. A principal legislative result of this period was the passage of the Civil Rights Act of 1875. According to the statute, its purpose was "to protect all citizens in their civil and legal rights."

Even though couched in general terms, the statute was designed to aid recently emancipated men and women.

The 1870s became unique years for testing race relations in the United States. During this period, there were no state laws requiring the separation of the races in places of public accommodation. Practices in particular establishments or jurisdictions were matters of local custom, individual choice, or personal preference. An earlier statute, the Civil Rights Act of 1866, and the ratification of the Fourteenth Amendment in 1868 had spawned cases throughout the country, including suits for denying sleeper accommodations to African Americans on trains traveling between Washington and New York, for refusing to sell theater tickets to African Americans in Boston, for restricting African Americans to front platforms in Baltimore streetcars, and for barring African American women from the waiting rooms and parlor cars on railroads in Virginia, Illinois, and California. There also had been massive resistance on the part of whites to the social integration of the races.

Faced with these challenges, the Republican-controlled Congress enacted the Civil Rights Act of 1875. It invalidated all racially motivated interference with individuals' use of "the accommodations, advantages, facilities, and privileges of inns, public conveyances and theatres" (109 U.S. 9–10). In short, the statute sought to provide legislative specificity to the constitutional norms embodied in the Fourteenth Amendment.

The decision in the *Civil Rights Cases* resulted from the consolidation of several cases, including *United States v. Singleton, United States v. Stanley, United States v. Nichols, United States v. Ryan, United States v. Hamilton,* and *Robinson v. Memphis & Charleston Railroad.* Five of the cases were criminal prosecutions that directly challenged the constitutionality of the 1875 statute.

United States v. Singleton involved the refusal of Samuel Singleton, doorkeeper of New York's Grand Opera House, to honor the tickets of William R. Davis Jr. and his fiancée. On November 22, 1879, the pair had attempted to see a matinee performance of Victor Hugo's *Ruy Blas.* Davis, the business agent of the African American newspaper the *Progressive-American,* was obviously African American. His fiancée, who had purchased the tickets earlier, had a light complexion. When the couple returned for the performance, they were denied entrance because of Davis's race.

Stanley involved the refusal of hotelier Murray Stanley to serve a meal to Bird Gee, an African American, in his Kansas hotel. *Nichols* involved the refusal of the Nichols House in Jefferson City, Missouri, to accept an African American as a guest. In *Ryan,* the doorkeeper at Maguire's Theater in San Francisco had denied an African American man entry to the dress circle at the theater. In *Hamilton,* the conductor of the Nashville, Chattanooga, and St. Louis Railroad denied an African American access to the ladies' car. Instead, she was relegated to a smoking car.

The sixth case, *Robinson v. Memphis & Charleston Railroad,* was not a criminal case. It involved travel on the Memphis & Charleston Railroad by a young African American woman, Sallie Robinson, and her nephew, Joseph C. Robinson. Mr. Robinson was described as a young African American "of light complexion, light hair, and light blue eyes." The train's conductor attempted forcibly to refuse the two passengers entry to the first-class parlor car for which they had purchased tickets. The conductor mistook the pair for a white man and his paramour. The railroad conceded the constitutionality of the 1875 statute, but argued that it did not apply to the conductor's actions. The trial judge ruled that motive was dispositive under the act. Thus, if the conductor believed Sallie Robinson to be a prostitute, whether reasonable or not in that assumption, the exclusion was not based on race and the railroad was not liable. The jury found for the railroad, and the Robinsons appealed.

The United States, represented before the Supreme Court by Solicitor General Samuel F. Phillips (1824–1903), argued that the act should be upheld in every case. In addition, the government's brief discussed the history of American race relations and the genesis of the Civil War amendments and their statutory descendants. The government stressed particularly the importance of equal access to public accommodations. The solicitor general emphasized that this act was one of several enacted by "a Congress led by men who had fought in the Civil War and had framed the war amendments." Implicit in the solicitor general's position was the idea that Congress understood, as clearly as anyone could, that it was not sufficient to outlaw African enslavement and to declare equal protection to be the law of the land. Specific statutory protection was necessary to ensure that every vestige of slavery and every reminder of its stigma were eliminated from public life.

The government's arguments, however, did not persuade the Supreme Court. It announced its decision on October 15, 1883. The Court ruled eight to one against the United States. Justice Joseph Bradley (1813–1892) wrote the opinion of the Court, which asserted two conclusions: the Fourteenth Amendment is prohibitory on the states only, and the Thirteenth Amendment relates only to enslavement and involuntary servitude.

Bradley maintained that the Fourteenth Amendment operated only as a prohibition and restriction against the states. Because the Civil Rights Act of 1875 sought to outlaw the actions of private individuals, shopkeepers, and other businesses, it violated the Constitution. This "state action" doctrine holds that because the government was not the actor in these cases, the Fourteenth Amendment did not empower Congress to outlaw these practices. Also, Bradley's opinion held that, while Congress was empowered by the Thirteenth Amendment to eliminate slavery and all its vestiges, the denial of access to accommodations in commercial establishments, public conveyances, and public amusements was not a "badge or incident of slavery." The opinion halted the progress of civil rights and limited the ability of the federal government, acting through Congress, to eliminate and eradicate racial discrimination for almost ninety years.

Justice John Marshall Harlan (1833–1911) dissented. At the time, Harlan was the Court's only southerner and a former enslaver. Although he had been a bitter critic of the Civil War amendments during the 1860s, he had undergone a transformation. His dissent was not announced on the day of the majority's decision and may not have been written until November. In it, he said that the grounds for the majority's assertions were "too narrow and artificial" and that the majority refused to embrace both "the substance and the spirit" of the Civil Rights Act: "It is not the words of the law but the internal sense of it that makes the law. The letter of the law is the body; the sense and reason of the law is the soul." And, in Justice Harlan's view, the purpose of the act "was to prevent *race* [emphasis in original] discrimination." The majority, as Harlan developed the dissent, betrayed this purpose "by a subtle and ingenious verbal criticism."

Neither the majority of the U.S. Supreme Court nor the nation it represented cared to do much else to promote the civil rights of its new African American citizens. Harlan's dissent in the *Civil Rights Cases* forecasted his more famous one in *Plessy v. Ferguson*, in that the decision in the *Civil Rights Cases* led to the black codes, Jim Crow laws, and other examples of *de jure* (by law) segregation that came to define American race relations. The *Plessy* decision's "separate-but-equal doctrine" was interpreted as approval for laws requiring the separation of races. These laws became known as *Jim Crow*, referring to the negative stereotypic characterization of African Americans performed in popular minstrel shows around the time of the Civil War. Jim Crow or black-code laws were set up to ensure segregation on the basis of race for every aspect of life, denying equal rights and creating a second-class citizenry for African Americans in the South such that rights acquired by legislation following the Civil War were virtually nullified.

The *Civil Rights Cases* revealed the nation's ambivalence on the questions of race. On one hand, Congress had sought to guarantee the rights of the recently freed men, women, and children by proposing constitutional amendments that were ultimately ratified. Congress went further and augmented the constitutional guarantees with additional legislative protections and safeguards. The Supreme Court, however, frustrated these constitutional and legislative initiatives with a constricted reading of the Thirteenth and Fourteenth Amendments.

John Marshall Harlan. *As an associate justice of the U.S. Supreme Court from 1877 to 1911, Harlan consistently championed racial and other civil liberties. He was the lone dissenter in two infamous Court cases—the* Civil Rights Cases *(1883) and* Plessy v. Ferguson *(1896).* **THE LIBRARY OF CONGRESS**

FEDERAL LEGISLATIVE INITIATIVES

Emancipation Act (1862) (ch. 54, 12 state. 376). This law, enacted on April 16, 1862, abolished enslavement in the District of Columbia.

Emancipation Act (1862) (ch. 111, 12 Stat. 432). This act, abolishing enslavement in all other territories of the United States, was enacted on June 19, 1862.

Amendment Thirteen to the U.S. Constitution (1865). This amendment, abolishing slavery and involuntary servitude in all of the United States, was ratified on December 16, 1865.

Civil Rights Act (1866) (ch. 31, 14 Stat. 27). This law was enacted on April 9, 1866, to provide all citizens, especially recently freed men and women, with basic civil rights, including the right to make and enforce contracts, to bring suits in court, to purchase and sell real and personal property, and to enjoy security of person and property.

Amendment Fourteen to the U.S. Constitution (1868). This amendment defined U.S. and state citizenship and provided all citizens with the privileges and immunities of citizenship, equal protection under the law, and the right to life, liberty, and property. It was ratified July 20, 1868.

Amendment Fifteen to the U.S. Constitution (1870). This amendment prohibited the use of race, color, or previous condition of servitude to deny anyone the right to vote. It was ratified March 30, 1870.

Civil Rights Act (1870) (ch. 114, 16 Stat. 140). This statute was enacted on May 31, 1870, to carry out the provisions of the Fifteenth Amendment. It established penalties for violations of the provisions of the amendment.

Civil Rights Act (1871) (ch. 99, 16 Stat. 433). This law was enacted on February 28, 1871, to further define the protections established in the Fifteenth Amendment.

Civil Rights Act (1871) (ch. 22, 17 Stat. 13). This law was enacted on April 20, 1871, to further outline the protections established by the Fourteenth Amendment. It provided for the vindication of crimes committed under the act in federal court.

Civil Rights Act (1875) (ch. 114, 18 Stat. 335). This act was designed to provide all citizens with equal access to public places. Ruling in 1883 in a set of cases known as the *Civil Rights Cases*, the U.S. Supreme Court invalidated the act.

Civil Rights Act of 1957 (Pub.L. No. 85–315, 71 Stat. 634). This act created the Commission on Civil Rights and empowered it to investigate allegations of deprivation of a U.S. citizen's right to vote, to appraise laws and policies of the federal government with respect to equal protection of the law, and to submit a report to the president and to Congress within two years.

Civil Rights Act of 1960 (Pub.L. No. 86–449, 74 Stat. 86). This law guaranteed the provision of criminal penalties in the event a suspect crosses state lines to avoid legal process for the actual or attempted bombing or burning of any vehicle or building. It also provided penalties for persons who obstructed or interfered with any order of a federal court.

Civil Rights Act of 1964 (Pub.L. No. 88–352, 78 Stat. 241). This act prohibited discrimination in the use of public accommodations whose operations involve interstate commerce and provided enforcement measures to ensure equal access to public facilities. It also prohibited racial discrimination in any program receiving federal aid and discrimination on the basis of race, color, religion, sex, or national origin in most areas of employment. It authorized the U.S. attorney general to use lawsuits to desegregate schools and public facilities.

Amendment Twenty-four to the U.S. Constitution (1964). This amendment prohibited the use of a poll tax or any other tax—a common method to keep poorer people, especially African Americans, from voting—as a requirement for voting. It was ratified January 23, 1964.

Voting Rights Act of 1965 (Pub.L. No. 89–110, 79 Stat. 437). This act struck down such requirements as literacy and knowledge tests and poll-tax payments, which had been used to restrict African American participation in voting. The legislation also provided for federal registrars to register voters should state registrars refuse to do so. It further stipulated that registered voters cannot be prohibited from voting.

Civil Rights Act of 1968 (Pub.L. No. 90–284, 82 Stat. 73). This act provided for open housing by prohibiting discrimination based on race, color, religion, or national origin.

Equal Employment Opportunity Act of 1972 (Pub.L. No. 92–261, 86 Stat. 103). This act provided the Equal Employment Opportunity Commission (established by the Civil Rights Act of 1964) with the authority to issue judicially enforceable cease-and-desist orders in cases involving discriminatory employment practices.

Public Works Employment Act of 1977 (Pub.L. No. 95–28, 91 Stat. 116, Title I). This statute provided that 10 percent of funds expended as a result of federal grants be earmarked for minority business enterprises.

Voting Rights Act of 1965 Amendment (Pub.L. No. 97–205, 96 Stat. 131 [1982]). This amendment was a congressional response to the Supreme Court's ruling in *City of Mobile, Alabama v. Wiley L. Bolden*, 446 U.S. 55 (1980), which required proof of discriminatory intent in voting-rights cases. Section 2 of the Voting Rights Act prohibited any voting practice or procedure "imposed or applied by any state or political subdivision in a manner which results in a denial or abridgement of the right of any citizen of the United States to vote on account of race or color."

Civil Rights Commission Act of 1983 (Pub.L. No. 98–183, 87 Stat. 1301). This act created an eight-member bipartisan commission with four members appointed by the president, and two by the Senate and House respectively. The commissioners are appointed to four- or six-year terms and can be fired only for neglect of duty or malfeasance in office. The statute was enacted after President Ronald Reagan attempted to fire commissioners who did not express his views on civil rights. The act extended the life of the Civil Rights Commission Authorization Act of 1978, which had been scheduled to expire in 1983.

Civil Rights Restoration Act of 1988 (Pub.L. No. 100–259, 102 Stat. 31). The U.S. Supreme Court ruled in 1984 in *Grove City College v. Bell* that not all programs and activities of an institution were covered by Title IX of the education amendments of 1972 (Public Law 89–10, 79 Stat. 27) and that discrimination can be barred only in programs that directly receive federal funds. The act amended portions of the Civil Rights Act of 1964 and refined the definition of programs and activities that were covered by the Civil Rights Act and other legislation. Specifically, the amendment addressed Title IX of the education amendments of 1972, which prohibits discrimination in educational programs receiving federal financial assistance.

Fair Housing Amendments Act of 1988 (Pub.L. No. 100–430, 102 Stat 1619). This act strengthened laws that resulted from the passage of the Fair Housing Act of 1968. The 1988 act gave the Department of Housing and Urban Development (HUD) the authority to issue discrimination charges, allowed administrative-law justices the ability to review housing-discrimination cases, and removed the $1,000 limit on punitive damages that a victim of discrimination may receive.

Civil Rights Act of 1991 (Pub.L. 102–166, 105 Stat. 1071). This act was designed to provide additional remedies to deter harassment and intentional discrimination in the workplace, provide guidelines for the adjudication of cases arising under Title VII of the Civil Rights Act of 1964, and expand the scope of civil rights legislation weakened by Supreme Court decisions, particularly the Court's ruling in *Ward's Cove Packing Co. v. Atonio*, 490 U.S. 642 (1989).

Glass Ceiling Act of 1991 (Pub.L. 102–166, 105 Stat. 1081). This law was designed to establish a means for studying and addressing the underrepresentation of women and minorities at management and decision-making levels in the workforce. The Glass Ceiling Commission, set up in 1992, published its final report with recommendations in November 1995.

U.S. SUPREME COURT DECISIONS—SYNOPSIS

VOTING AND ELECTIONS—ACCESS TO POLLS

United States v. Reese, 92 U.S. 214 (1876). Prior to the ratification of the Fifteenth Amendment, states regulated all details of state and local elections—they prescribed the qualifications of voters and the manner in which those desiring to vote at an election should make their qualifications known to the election officers. The Fifteenth Amendment changed the past practice and provided rules not prescribed by state law. However, the Court restricted the scope of the Fifteenth Amendment and the ability of Congress to enforce it by not punishing election officials who unlawfully interfered with, and prevented the free exercise of, the right to vote. In the *Reese* case, the federal government had indicted two Kentucky election inspectors for refusing to receive and count the vote of an African American citizen. The Supreme Court held that Congress had not yet provided "appropriate legislation" for the punishment of the offense charged under any sections of the Fifteenth Amendment.

Guinn v. United States, 238 U.S. 347 (1915). In 1910, an amendment to the constitution of Oklahoma restricted voting rights by providing that no illiterate person could be registered. A "grandfather clause," however, granted an exemption for persons who resided in a foreign country prior to January 1, 1866, and had been eligible to register prior to that date, or had a lineal ancestor who was eligible to vote at that time. Since no African Americans were eligible to vote in Oklahoma prior to 1866, the law disenfranchised all African Americans. The U.S. Supreme Court ruled that the grandfather clause was invalid in Oklahoma or in any other state.

Nixon v. Herndon, 273 U.S. 536 (1927). Dr. L. A. Nixon, an African American, was refused the right to vote in a primary election because of a state statute that prohibited African Americans from participating in Democratic Party primaries in Texas. Nixon filed suit against the election officials, and his case ultimately reached the U.S. Supreme Court. Justice Oliver Wendell Holmes (1841–1935) wrote: "It is too clear for extended argument that color cannot be made the basis of a statutory classification affecting the right set up in this case." As a result, the Texas statute was declared unconstitutional.

Nixon v. Condon, 286 U.S. 73 (1932). As a result of the U.S. Supreme Court ruling in *Nixon v. Herndon*, the Texas legislature passed a new statute. This statute empowered the state Democratic executive committee to set up its own rules regarding primary elections. The party promptly adopted a resolution stipulating that only white Democrats be allowed to participate in primaries. Dr. Nixon again filed suit, and his right to vote was again upheld by the U.S. Supreme Court.

Lane v. Wilson, 307 U.S. 268 (1939). In an attempt to restrict voter registration, the Oklahoma legislature stated that all Oklahomans who were already registered would remain qualified voters and that all others would have to register within twelve days (from April 30 to May 11, 1916) or be forever barred from the polls. In 1934, I. W. Lane, an African American, was refused registration on the basis of this statute. The U.S. Supreme Court declared that the statute was in conflict with the Fifteenth Amendment to the U.S. Constitution and was unconstitutional.

Smith v. Allwright, 321 U.S. 649 (1944). The Texas State Democratic Party, during its convention in 1932, limited the right of membership to white electors. As a result, nonwhites were unable to participate in the state's Democratic Party primary. In *Grovey v. Townsend,* 295 U.S. 45 (1935), the Supreme Court had upheld this limitation because it was made by the party in convention, not by a party executive committee. In *Smith v. Allwright,* the Court overruled *Grovey,* stating: "The United States is a constitutional democracy. Its organic law grants to all citizens a right to participate in the choice of elected officials without restriction by any state because of race." The Court noted that a political party makes its selection of candidates as an agency of the state. Therefore, it cannot exclude participation based on race and remain consistent with the Fifteenth Amendment.

Gomillion v. Lightfoot, 364 U.S. 339 (1960). African American citizens challenged an Alabama statute that redefined the boundaries of the city of Tuskegee. The statute altered the shape of Tuskegee and placed all but four of Tuskegee's four hundred African American voters outside of the city limits, while not displacing a single white voter. The Court struck down the statute as a violation of the Fifteenth Amendment.

Baker v. Carr, 369 U.S. 186 (1962). The *Baker* case was brought to the Supreme Court by electors in several counties of Tennessee. The electors asserted that the 1901 legislative reapportionment statute was unconstitutional because the numbers of voters in the various districts had changed substantially since 1901. The plaintiffs requested that the Supreme Court either direct a reapportionment by mathematical application of the same formula to the 1960 census, or instruct the state to hold direct at-large elections. The state district court had dismissed the case

Voting Rights Act of 1965. *African American voters, able to vote for the first time in rural Wilcox County, Alabama, line up in front of the Sugar Shack, a local general store serving as a polling station, on May 3, 1966. The Voting Rights Act had struck down requirements such as literacy tests and poll tax payments that had been used to restrict African American participation in voting.* BETTMANN/CORBIS

on the grounds that it was a political question and did not fall within the protection of the Fourteenth Amendment. The U.S. Supreme Court ruled that the case involved a basic constitutional right rather than a political question and thereby was in the jurisdiction of the U.S. district court and federal courts in general. In later cases, such as *Gray v. Sanders*, 372 U.S. 368 (1963), and *Reynolds v. Sims*, 377 U.S. 533 (1964), the U.S. Supreme Court explained that the standards to be applied to voting districts in each state give reasonably equal representation, resulting in a principle popularly referred to as "one man, one vote."

South Carolina v. Katzenbach, 383 U.S. 301 (1966). The Voting Rights Act of 1965 was designed to eliminate racial discrimination in voting, which had influenced the electoral process for nearly a century. The act abolished literacy tests, waived accumulated poll taxes, and allotted the U.S. attorney general vast discretionary powers over regions suspected of discriminatory legislation and practices against African American voters. South Carolina's petition asserted that the Voting Rights Act encroached on state sovereignty, thus violating the U.S. Constitution. The Supreme Court dismissed the petition because section 1 of the Fifteenth Amendment to the Constitution says, "The right of citizens of the United States to vote shall not be denied or abridged by the United States or by any state on account of race, color, or previous condition of servitude."

Allen v. State Board of Elections, 393 U.S. 544 (1969). The Supreme Court emphasized that subtle as well as obvious state regulations "which have the effect of denying citizens their right to vote because of their race" are prohibited. The Court confirmed that section 5 of the Voting Rights Act covered a variety of practices other than voter registration.

Georgia v. United States, 411 U.S. 526 (1973). This case confirmed the propriety of the Voting Rights Act of 1965, which forbids states with a history of racial discrimination (e.g., Alabama, Georgia, Louisiana, Mississippi, North Carolina, South Carolina, and Virginia) from implementing any change in voting practices and procedures without first submitting the proposed plan to the U.S. attorney general for approval.

White v. Regester, 412 U.S. 755 (1973). The Supreme Court struck down a Texas multimember districting scheme that was used to prevent African Americans from being elected to public office. The Court upheld a finding that even though there was no evidence that African Americans faced official obstacles to registration, voting, or running for office, they had been excluded from effective participation in the political process in violation of the equal protection clause of the U.S. Constitution.

City of Mobile, Alabama v. Wiley L. Bolden, 446 U.S. 55 (1980). A class-action suit was filed in the U.S. District Court for the Southern District of Alabama on behalf of African American citizens in Mobile. The suit alleged that the city's practice of electing commissioners at large by a majority vote unfairly diluted the voting strength of African Americans in violation of the Fourteenth Amendment and the Fifteenth Amendment. The district court ruled that the constitutional rights of Mobile's African American citizens had been violated and entered a judgment in their favor. The court also ruled that Mobile's city commissioners be replaced by a municipal government consisting of a mayor and a city council composed of persons selected from single-member districts. The lower court decision was upheld by the Supreme Court.

Thornburg v. Gingles, 478 U.S. 30 (1986). *Thornburg* was the Supreme Court's first decision interpreting the provisions of the 1982 amendments to section 2 of the Voting Rights Act. The amendments prohibited voting schemes that result in a denial or abridgment of the right to vote because of race or color. In this decision, the Court ruled that the redistricting plan adopted by the North Carolina legislature—which unintentionally led to racially polarized voting by whites and diluted African Americans' voting strength—was in violation of the Voting Rights Act. The Voting Rights Act prohibits neutral voting requirements that have a discriminatory effect, as well as those that are intentionally discriminatory.

Shaw v. Reno, 509 U.S. 630 (1993). The Court ruled that using race as a principle for drawing the boundaries of a voting district solely to increase the number of minority voters is a violation of the equal protection clause.

Miller v. Johnson, 515 U.S. 900 (1995). The Court ruled that a congressional district purposely drawn to contain a majority of African American voters is a violation of the equal protection clause.

Hunt v. Cromartie, 532 U.S. 234 (2001). The Supreme Court ruled that evidence that race was a conscious factor in drawing the boundaries of a congressional district does not automatically make the results unconstitutional if other permissible political reasons were dominant motivating factors. Evidence as to motivation must be presented in court to make a determination of permissibility.

EDUCATION

Missouri ex rel. Lloyd Gaines v. Canada, 305 U.S. 337 (1938). *Gaines v. Canada* was brought before the Supreme Court by Lloyd Lionel Gaines, an African American who had been refused admission to the

Lloyd Gaines, 1938. Denied admission to the University of Missouri's law school because he was African American, Gaines took the matter to court. His suit was eventually settled in his favor by the U.S. Supreme Court in Gaines v. Canada *(1938).* AP PHOTO

School of Law of the State University of Missouri. Gaines contended that the University of Missouri's actions were a violation of his rights under the Fourteenth Amendment of the U.S. Constitution.

The University of Missouri defended its action by maintaining that Lincoln University, a predominantly African American institution, would eventually establish its own law school. The Supreme Court of Missouri dismissed Gaines's petition and upheld the university's decision to reject his application. The U.S. Supreme Court, however, reversed this decision, maintaining that the state of Missouri was obliged to provide equal facilities for African Americans or, in the absence of such facilities, to admit them to the existing facility.

Sipuel v. Board of Regents of the University of Oklahoma, 332 U.S. 631 (1948). Ada Lois Sipuel, an African American, was denied admission to the law school of the University of Oklahoma in 1948. Sipuel and the NAACP filed a petition in Oklahoma requesting an order directing her admission. The petition was denied on the grounds that the *Gaines* decision did not require a state with segregation laws to admit an African American student to its white schools. In addition, the Oklahoma court maintained that the state itself was not obligated to set up a separate school unless first requested to do so by African Americans desiring a legal education. The court's decision was affirmed by the Supreme Court of Oklahoma. The U.S. Supreme Court, however, reversed this decision, and held that the state was required to provide African Americans with equal educational opportunities.

Sweatt v. Painter, 339 U.S. 629 (1950). Heman Marion Sweatt was refused admission to the University of Texas Law School on the grounds that substantially equivalent facilities were already available in another Texas state law school open only to African American

Heman Marion Sweatt, 1950. *In its 1950 decision in* Sweatt v. Painter, *the U.S. Supreme Court ruled that Sweatt, shown here with Ronnie Dugger (*left*), had been unconstitutionally refused admission to the University of Texas Law School.* JOSEPH SCHERSCHEL/TIME & LIFE PICTURES/GETTY IMAGES

students. The U.S. Supreme Court ruled that Sweatt be admitted to the University of Texas Law School. Chief Justice Fred M. Vinson (1890–1953) wrote that "in terms of number of the faculty, variety of courses and opportunity for specialization, size of the student body, scope of the library, availability of law review and similar activities, the University of Texas Law School is superior" to those in the state law school for African Americans. Therefore, the refusal to admit Sweatt to the University of Texas Law School was unconstitutional.

McLaurin v. Oklahoma State Regents for Higher Education, 339 U.S. 637 (1950). After having been admitted to the University of Oklahoma, G. W. McLaurin, an African American, was required by school officials to occupy a special seat in each classroom and a segregated table in both the library and the cafeteria because of his race. The U.S. Supreme Court declared unanimously that African American students must receive the same treatment at the hands of the state as other students and could not be segregated.

Gray v. University of Tennessee, 342 U.S. 517 (1952). This case resulted from the refusal of a U.S. district court to force the University of Tennessee to admit African American students. The lone judge to whom the matter was then referred ruled that the African American students were entitled to admission, but the judge did not order the university to enforce this ruling. The Supreme Court was asked to refer the case back to the district court for further proceedings. Pending this appeal, however, one of the students seeking admission was enrolled at the University of Tennessee. Since the Court found no suggestion that persons "similarly situated would not be afforded similar treatment," the case was dismissed as moot.

Brown v. Board of Education of Topeka, Kansas, 347 U.S. 483 (1954). This case involved the practice of denying African American children equal access to state public schools because of state laws requiring or permitting racial segregation. The U.S. Supreme Court unanimously held that segregation deprived the children of equal protection under the Fourteenth Amendment to the U.S. Constitution. The separate-but-equal doctrine of *Plessy v. Ferguson* was overturned. After reargument a year later, the case was remanded (along with its four companion cases) to the district court, which was instructed to enter the necessary orders to ensure the admission of all parties to public schools on a racially nondiscriminatory basis.

Hawkins v. Board of Control, 347 U.S. 971 (1956). This case resulted from a ruling of the Florida Supreme Court that denied an African American the right to enter the University of Florida Law School on the grounds that he had failed to show that a separate law school for African Americans was not substantively equal to the University of Florida Law School. The U.S. Supreme Court vacated the judgment and remanded the case to the Florida Supreme Court for a decision in light of the ruling in *Brown v. Board of Education of Topeka, Kansas* which overruled the separate-but-equal doctrine. After two years, the Florida Supreme Court continued to deny Hawkins the right to enter the University of Florida. In addition, it had appointed a commissioner to determine if there was a time in the future that Hawkins could be admitted "without causing public mischief." However, the Supreme Court ruled that Hawkins should be admitted to the school promptly, since there was no palpable reason for further delay.

Tureaud v. Board of Supervisors, 347 U.S. 971 (1954). This case was the result of a provisional injunction requiring the admittance of African Americans to Louisiana State University. The state court of appeals reversed this action, declaring that it required the decision of a district court of three judges. The U.S. Supreme Court vacated this judgment and remanded the case for consideration in light of *Brown v. Board of Education of Topeka, Kansas.*

Frazier v. University of North Carolina, 350 U.S. 979 (1956). The U.S. Supreme Court affirmed a district court judgment that African Americans may not be excluded from institutions of higher learning because of their race or color.

Cooper v. Aaron, 358 U.S. 1 (1958). The impact of *Brown v. Board of Education of Topeka, Kansas* was very slight until the Justice Department began to initiate its own desegregation lawsuits. Arkansas state officials passed state laws contrary to the Fourteenth Amendment holdings in *Brown I* and *Brown II* that forbid states to use their governmental powers to bar children on racial grounds from attending schools where there is state participation through any arrangement, management, funds, or property. The cases also ordered the states to immediately cease and desist from desegregation practices. In *Cooper*, the U.S. attorney general filed a petition on behalf of the U.S. government to enjoin the governor of Arkansas and officers of the National Guard from preventing the admittance of nine African American children into Central High School in Little Rock in September 1957. A law was passed relieving schoolchildren from compulsory attendance at racially mixed schools. The Supreme Court declared that the Fourteenth Amendment outlined in the *Brown* case was the supreme law of the land and could not be nullified by state legislators, executive or judicial officers, or evasive schemes for segregation.

Lee v. Macon County Board of Education, 389 U.S. 25 (1967). The U.S. Supreme Court affirmed a lower court decision ordering the desegregation of Alabama's school districts and declared state school grants to white students attending segregated private schools unconstitutional.

Alexander v. Holmes County Board of Education, 396 U.S. 19 (1969). The U.S. Supreme Court ordered all thirty-three school districts in Mississippi to desegregate. The Department of Health, Education, and Welfare (HEW) had asked that the districts be granted more time to desegregate. This was the first time HEW had sought a delay in integration, but the Court ordered that integration proceed immediately.

North Carolina State Board of Education v. Swann, 402 U.S. 43 (1971), and Swann v. Charlotte Mecklenburg Board of Education, 402 U.S. 1 (1971). In these two cases, the U.S. Supreme Court affirmed the use of busing and faculty transfers to overcome the effects of dual school systems—segregated school systems resulting from residential patterns. Writing the decision, Chief Justice Warren E. Burger (1907–1995) noted that "bus transportation has long been a part of all public educational systems and it is unlikely that a truly effective remedy could be devised without continued reliance upon it." The Court declared that segregation resulted from past misconduct and affirmed the lower court's order that the school board transfer students by bus to achieve a racial mix at each school. The ruling, however, left local district judges the authority to decide whether a desegregation plan was constitutionally adequate.

Wright v. City of Emporia, 407 U.S. 451 (1972), and Cotton v. Scotland Neck Board of Education, 407 U.S. 485 (1972). The Supreme Court held that two towns with heavy concentrations of white students could not secede from a largely African American county school system and form its own school district in an attempt to frustrate integration.

Richmond, Virginia, School Board v. State Board of Education, 412 U.S. 92 (1973). In a four–four vote, the Supreme Court declined to reinstate an order to integrate the predominantly African American schools in Richmond with those of two white suburbs. Integrationists expressed concern that permitting de facto segregation to stand in this manner would hinder corrective action in other metropolitan areas, perpetuate "neighborhood" one-race schools, and lessen the extent of integration in unitary school systems.

Milliken v. Bradley, 418 U.S. 717 (1974). After failing to reach a decision in *Richmond, Virginia, School Board*, the full Court reached a decision outlawing inter-district remedies to end segregation in schools. The school system of Detroit had become heavily African American as a result of white flight to the suburbs. Fearing that *Brown v. Board of Education of Topeka, Kansas* would be crippled, the district court ordered busing between the districts of Detroit and its white suburbs. However, the Court overturned this decision because there was no evidence that the suburbs had contributed to the segregation. Integrationists attacked this decision as the end of *Brown*.

Runyon v. McCrary, 427 U.S. 160 (1976). In a unanimous decision, the Court held that the Constitution places no value on discrimination, and that even though private discrimination was not socially desired by the members of the Court, it may be characterized legally as a form of freedom of association protected by the First Amendment. However, the families of two African American children who were denied admission to private schools in Virginia argued that the Civil Rights Act of 1866 prohibited racial discrimination in the making and enforcing of contracts. The children's parents sought to enter into a contractual relationship with the private schools on an equal basis to white and nonwhite students.

Regents of the University of California v. Bakke, 438 U.S. 265 (1978). Allan Bakke, a white male who had been denied admission to the University of California Medical School at Davis for two consecutive years, charged that the university's minority quota system—

Allan Bakke, 1982. *In its 1978 decision in* University of California Regents v. Bakke, *the U.S. Supreme Court ruled that Bakke had been unconstitutionally excluded from the University of California's medical school at Davis because of affirmative action quotas. Bakke was admitted to the school and is shown here at his graduation ceremony.* ROGER RESSMEYER/STARLIGHT/CORBIS

under which only disadvantaged members of certain minority races were considered for sixteen of the one hundred places in each year's class—denied him equal protection.

The trial court declared that the school could not take race into account in making the admissions decision and held that the challenged admissions program violated the federal and state constitutions and Title VI of the 1964 Civil Rights Act. The university appealed. The Supreme Court ruled that Bakke had been illegally discriminated against and that numerical quotas based on race were unconstitutional, but held that "the State has a substantial interest that legitimately may be served by a properly devised admission program involving the competitive consideration of race and ethnic origin."

Bob Jones University v. IRS, 461 U.S. 574 (1983). Contrary to long-standing Internal Revenue Service (IRS) policy, the Reagan administration sought to extend tax-exempt status to schools that discriminate on the basis of race. The U.S. Supreme Court recognized the inability of the Justice Department to argue the case fairly, and requested that former secretary of transportation William T. Coleman present the argument. The Supreme Court rebuffed the Justice Department's arguments and unanimously agreed with Coleman's position that the IRS could deny tax-exempt status to racially discriminatory schools.

Allen v. Wright, 468 U.S. 737 (1984). Parents of African American children instituted a nationwide lawsuit claiming that the IRS's failure to deny tax-exempt status to racially discriminatory private schools constituted federal financial aid to racially segregated institutions and diminished the ability of their children to receive an adequate education. The U.S. Supreme Court refused to hear the case on the grounds that the plaintiffs did not have "standing" because they failed to show that the injury suffered was "fairly traceable" or caused by the conduct of the IRS. In addition, the Court maintained that the remedy was "speculative" since there was no evidence that the withdrawal of tax-exempt status would cause schools to end their racially discriminatory practices.

Oklahoma City Board of Education v. Dowell, 498 U.S. 237 (1991). The Court ruled that when a school district petitioned to end a desegregation order, the petition could be approved if the district has been in good faith compliance with the order from the beginning and if remnants of past discrimination have been eliminated to the degree possible in the situation.

United States v. Fordice, 505 U.S. 717 (1992). The Court ruled that when a state higher-education system continues to use educational practices that were started to keep the races segregated and that perpetuate segregation, the practices violate the equal protection guarantee if they can be ended without significantly changing the quality of the education offered.

Jenkins v. Missouri, 515 U.S. 70 (1995). The Court ruled that a federal district court erred in ordering increased salaries for school-system employees as part of a program to motivate attendance by nonminority students living outside the district in an effort to increase desegregation.

EMPLOYMENT

Griggs v. Duke Power Co., 401 U.S. 424 (1971). African American employees challenged their employer's requirement that they possess a high school diploma or pass intelligence tests as a condition of employment. African Americans were employed only in the labor department, where the highest-paying jobs paid less than the lowest-paying jobs in other departments. When the company abandoned its policy restricting blacks to labor in 1965, completion of high school and median scores on two aptitude tests were required to transfer from labor to another department.

The Supreme Court found that the objective of Congress in Title III was to achieve equality of employment opportunities and remove barriers that have operated in the past. Under the act, practices, procedures, or tests neutral on their face and even neutral in their intent cannot be maintained if they operate to "freeze" the status quo of prior discrimination. The employment practice must be related to job performance.

It was determined that neither the high school diploma nor the intelligence tests were demonstrably related to successful job performance. Good intent or absence of discriminatory intent does not redeem employment procedures and practices. The employment policies had a discriminatory effect toward African American employees and were struck down.

Albemarle Paper Co. v. Moody, 422 U.S. 405 (1975). African American employees of a paper mill in Roanoke Rapids, North Carolina, successfully challenged the company's use of written tests that allegedly measured numerical and verbal intelligence. Based on the standards enunciated in 1971 in *Griggs v. Duke Power Co.*, the U.S. Supreme Court determined that the tests were discriminatory because they were not job-related and did not predict success on the job. The Court held that the plaintiffs were entitled to "complete justice" and necessary relief that would "make them whole." The Court awarded the African American employees back pay and made it clear that back pay should rarely be denied once there has been a showing of discrimination. The Court also stated that back pay cannot be denied simply because the employer acted in good faith or did not intend to discriminate.

Hazelwood School District v. United States, 433 U.S. 299 (1977). Several African American teachers seeking jobs in suburban St. Louis, Missouri, offered statistical data indicating that they had been denied employment opportunities. The plaintiffs attempted to prove their case by showing that the percentage of African American students was greater than the percentage of African American teachers in the school district. Although the U.S. Supreme Court affirmed that "statistics can be an important source of proof in employment discrimination cases," it rejected the plaintiffs' statistical evidence and called it irrelevant. The Court concluded that relevant statistical data would be the percentage of qualified African American teachers in the relevant geographical area compared with the percentage of African Americans in Hazelwood's teaching staff.

Teamsters v. United States, 431 U.S. 324 (1977). In enforcing the Civil Rights Act of 1964, the Supreme Court held that victims of past discrimination from unions were entitled to retroactive seniority benefits. The Supreme Court required proof of "intent to discriminate," however, in order to establish that a given seniority system is illegal. Subsequent cases in lower federal courts during the late 1970s entitled discrimination victims to retroactive back pay in addition to retroactive seniority benefits.

Louis Swint and Willie Johnson v. Pullman Standard and the United Steelworkers of America, 72 L.Ed. 66 (1982). African American employees of Pullman Standard brought a lawsuit against Pullman Standard and the United Steelworkers of America. The lawsuit alleged that Title VII of the Civil Rights Act of 1964 was violated by a seniority system. In its decision, the district court ruled "that the difference in terms, conditions or privileges of employment resulting from the seniority system are not the result of an intention to discriminate because of race or color" and held that the system satisfied the requirements of section 703(h) of the Civil Rights Act. This decision was later reversed by the Fifth Circuit Court of Appeals, which stated: "Because we find the differences in the terms, conditions and standards of employment for black workers and white workers at Pullman Standard resulted from an intent to discriminate because of race, we hold that the system is not legally valid under Section 703(h) of Title VII U.S.C. 2000e-2(h)."

Watson v. Fort Worth Bank and Trust, 487 U.S. 977 (1988). Clara Watson, an African American woman, alleged that she was repeatedly denied promotion to supervisory positions that were awarded to white employees with equivalent or lesser experience. The bank contended that its promotion decisions were based on various subjective criteria, including experience, previous supervisory experience, and the ability to get along with others. The U.S. Supreme Court held that Watson did not have to prove intentional discrimination. The Court concluded that subjective, facially neutral selection devices that disadvantage African Americans in much the same way as objective criteria (e.g., written tests) are unlawful.

Patterson v. McLean Credit Union, 491 U.S. 164 (1989). An African American female was employed as a teller and file coordinator for ten years until she was laid off. She alleged that she had been harassed, denied promotion to accounting clerk, and later discharged because of her race. She filed suit asserting violations of section 1981 of the Civil Rights Act. The Court ruled that racial harassment relating to conditions of employment is not actionable under section 1981—which provides that "all persons . . . shall have the same right to make and enforce contracts . . . as any white citizen"—because that provision does not apply to conduct that occurs after the formation of a contract, including the breach of the contract's terms and enforcement thereof. Rather, the harassment asserted by the petitioner is past formation conduct of the employer and, therefore, actionable only under Title VII of the Civil Rights Act of 1964.

Ward's Cove Packing Co. v. Atonio, 490 U.S. 642 (1989). This case was brought by a class of nonwhite salmon cannery workers who alleged that their employer's hiring and promotion practices were responsible for the workforce's racial stratification. There were two types of jobs: unskilled cannery jobs, which were filled predominately by nonwhites; and noncannery jobs, mostly classified as skilled positions, which paid more and were held by whites. Statistics were used to show a high percentage of nonwhites in cannery jobs and a low percentage in noncannery positions.

The Supreme Court found that the cannery workforce did not reflect the pool of qualified job applicants or the qualified labor-force population. An employer's selection methods or employment practices cannot be said to have a disparate impact on nonwhites if the absence of minorities holding such skilled jobs reflects a dearth of qualified nonwhite applicants. A mere showing that nonwhites are underrepresented in the noncannery jobs will not suffice for a Title VII violation.

Martin v. Wilks, 490 U.S. 755 (1989). In an attempt to remedy past racial discrimination in hiring and promotion practices, the city of Birmingham and its fire department consented to hiring African Americans as firefighters as part of a settlement. White firefighters subsequently challenged the city, alleging that because of their race they were denied promotions in favor of less-qualified African Americans in violation of Title VII. Promotion decisions were made on the basis of race, in reliance on the consent decree. The Court held that a voluntary settlement between one group of employees and their employer cannot possibly settle the conflicting claims of another group of employees who do not join in the agreement. This settlement would result in persons being deprived of their legal rights in a proceeding to which they were not a party.

JURY SELECTION AND SERVICE

Neal v. Delaware, 103 U.S. 370 (1880). In this case, the Court found that a jury commissioner's conduct was in violation of the U.S. Constitution when an African American criminal defendant proved that African Americans were excluded from the jury based on their race. Every citizen is afforded the right to equal protection of the laws, including that of juror selection, when jurors will pass judgment on a defendant's life, liberty, or property. The exclusion of members of the defendant's race is unconstitutional.

Strauder v. West Virginia, 100 U.S. 303 (1880). The Supreme Court overturned the conviction of an African American criminal defendant because of racial discrimination in the selection of jurors. West Virginia passed a state law that prohibited African American men from eligibility to serve as members of a grand jury or a petit jury in the state. According to the Court, this law denied equal protection of the laws to a citizen.

Virginia v. Rives, 100 U.S. 313 (1880). The petitioners asserted that African Americans had never been allowed to serve as jurors in their county in any case where an African American man was involved, even though Virginia had no formalized or specific statute restricting African American jurors from certain trials. The Supreme Court held that a mixed jury in a particular case is not essential to the equal protection of the laws and that the right is not given by any state or federal statute.

Hollins v. Oklahoma, 295 U.S. 394 (1935). Hollins, an African American, was charged with rape and convicted at a trial held in the basement of the jail. Three days before his scheduled execution, the NAACP secured a stay of execution. Later the Supreme Court of Oklahoma reversed his conviction. The U.S. Supreme Court—in a memorandum opinion—affirmed the principle that the conviction of an African American by a jury from which all African Americans had been excluded was a denial of the equal protection clause of the Fourteenth Amendment to the U.S. Constitution.

Hale v. Commonwealth of Kentucky, 303 U.S. 613 (1938). In 1936, Joe Hale, an African American, was charged with murder in McCracken County, Kentucky. Hale moved to set aside the indictment on the grounds that the jury commissioners had systematically excluded African Americans from jury lists. Hale established that one out of every six residents of the county was African American, and that at least seventy African Americans out of a total of 6,700 persons were qualified for jury duty. Still, there had not been an African American on jury duty between 1906 and 1936. Hale's conviction and death sentence were upheld by the Court of Appeals of Kentucky, but both were struck down by the U.S. Supreme Court on the grounds that Hale had been denied equal protection of the law.

Patton v. Mississippi, 332 U.S. 463 (1947). This case involved Eddie Patton, an African American who was convicted of the murder of a white man in Mississippi. At his trial and as part of his appeal, Patton alleged that all qualified African Americans had been systematically excluded from jury service solely because of race. The state maintained that since jury service was limited by statute to qualified voters and since few African Americans were qualified to vote, such a procedure was valid in the eyes of the law. The Supreme Court, however, reversed Patton's conviction on the grounds that such a jury plan, resulting in the almost automatic elimination of African Americans from jury service, constituted an infringement on Patton's rights under the Fourteenth Amendment.

Shepherd v. Florida, 341 U.S. 50 (1951). In a case involving African American defendants, the Supreme Court reversed the convictions of a Florida state court solely on the grounds that the method of selecting the grand jury discriminated against African Americans.

Turner v. Fouche, 396 U.S. 346 (1970). The Supreme Court affirmed the right of defendants to bring an action in federal court to end discrimination in jury selection.

Castaneda v. Partida, 430 U.S. 482 (1977). The Supreme Court upheld the use of statistical evidence demonstrating that Mexican Americans had been systematically excluded from jury selection. The Court also ruled that such discrimination on the basis of race or color violated the equal protection clause of the Fourteenth Amendment. The principle established in this case—that statistical evidence can be used to prove intentional discrimination—has been applied in later cases involving employment, housing, voting, and education.

Batson v. Kentucky, 476 U.S. 79 (1986). Justice Lewis F. Powell (1907–1998), writing for the majority, held that the prosecution in a criminal case may not use its peremptory challenges—challenges to an individual juror for which no cause need be stated—to exclude African American jurors in a case involving an African American defendant.

Turner v. Murray, 476 U.S. 28 (1986). The Supreme Court expanded the right of African American defendants in capital cases to question potential white jurors to uncover their racial prejudices and biases.

PUBLIC ACCOMMODATIONS

Hall v. DeCuir, 95 U.S. 485 (1878). This case involved an unsuccessful attempt of the Louisiana legislature to prohibit segregation in any form of transportation in the state. The statute was attacked as an interference with interstate commerce because it imposed a direct burden and control over common carriers when entering the state. The statute was declared unconstitutional because it required common carriers to transport African American passengers in Louisiana in the same cabin with white passengers.

Civil Rights Cases, 109 U.S. 3 (1883). This group of civil rights cases was heard before the Supreme Court in an effort to determine the constitutionality of the Civil Rights Act of 1875, the first piece of national legislation that attempted to guarantee people of all races "full and equal enjoyment" of all public accommodations, including inns, public conveyances, theaters, and other places of amusement. The Court ruled, however, that the act was unconstitutional inasmuch as it did not spring directly from the Thirteenth and Fourteenth Amendments to the Constitution. In the view of the Court, the Thirteenth Amendment was concerned exclusively with the narrow confines of slavery and involuntary servitude. The Fourteenth Amendment did not empower Congress to enact direct legislation to counteract the effect of state laws or policies. The ruling essentially deprived African Americans of the very protections that the three postwar "freedom amendments" were designed to provide.

Plessy v. Ferguson, 163 U.S. 537 (1896). Homer Plessy, an African American, was assigned to the wrong coach on a train traveling within Louisiana and was arrested for being there. He challenged the 1890 state statute that provided for separate-but-equal railway carriages for whites and blacks. In the majority opinion of the Supreme Court, separate-but-equal accommodations for African Americans constituted a "reasonable" use of state police power. Furthermore, the Court said that the Fourteenth Amendment "could not have been intended to abolish distinctions based on color, or to enforce social

... equality or a co-mingling of the two races on terms unsatisfactory to either."

Morgan v. Commonwealth of Virginia, 328 U.S. 373 (1946). Irene Morgan, an African American, refused to move to the rear seat of a Greyhound bus in which she was traveling from Virginia to Washington, D.C. She was convicted in Virginia for violating a state statute requiring segregation of the races on all public vehicles. NAACP attorneys carried the case through the Virginia courts and on to the U.S. Supreme Court, where it was decided that the Virginia statute could not apply to interstate passengers or motor vehicles engaged in such traffic.

Bob-Lo v. Michigan, 333 U.S. 28 (1948). The operator of a line of passenger ships that were used to transport patrons from Detroit to an island amusement park was convicted of violating the Michigan Civil Rights Act for refusing passage to an African American. The Supreme Court upheld the application of the Michigan Civil Rights Act.

Rice v. Arnold, 340 U.S. 848 (1950). This case involved the successful attempt to abolish segregation on a Miami, Florida, golf course owned and operated by the city. The U.S. Supreme Court overturned the judgment of the Florida Supreme Court, which had authorized the segregated use of the course.

District of Columbia v. John R. Thompson, 346 U.S. 100 (1952). The Supreme Court unanimously held that a restaurant owner had violated federal law by discriminating against and refusing service to patrons on the basis of race.

Muir v. Louisville Park Theatrical Association, 347 U.S. 971 (1954). In 1954, several African Americans were refused admission to an amphitheater located in a city park in Louisville, Kentucky. The park was leased and operated by a private group not affiliated in any way with the city. The Kentucky Court of Appeals found no evidence of unlawful discrimination, but the U.S. Supreme Court overturned this judgment and remanded the case for consideration in the light of the prevailing legal climate as articulated in *Brown v. Board of Education of Topeka, Kansas.*

Mayor and City Council of Baltimore v. Dawson, 350 U.S. 877 (1955). The Supreme Court affirmed a judgment that the enforcement of racial segregation in public beaches and bathhouses that are maintained by public authorities is unconstitutional.

Holmes v. Atlanta, 350 U.S. 879 (1955). This case involved a suit brought by African Americans to integrate a golf course that was owned and operated by the city of Atlanta, Georgia. The segregated arrangements were deemed constitutionally acceptable by a lower court, but that order was overturned by the U.S. Supreme Court and the case was remanded to the district court with directions to enter a decree for the plaintiffs in conformity with *Mayor and City Council of Baltimore v. Dawson.*

Flemming v. South Carolina Electric, 351 U.S. 901 (1956). This case involved a suit brought by an African American passenger against a bus company after the bus driver required her to change seats in accordance with South Carolina's segregation law. The trial judge dismissed the case on the grounds that the statute in question was valid, but the court of appeals reversed this decision, holding that the separate-but-equal doctrine was no longer valid. The Supreme Court upheld the court of appeals decision.

Gayle v. Browder, 352 U.S. 903 (1956). This case challenged the constitutionality of state statutes and ordinances in Montgomery, Alabama, that required the segregation of whites and blacks on public buses. These statutes were declared unconstitutional by the decision of a three-judge federal district court. The Supreme Court affirmed.

Katzenbach v. McClung, 379 U.S. 294 (1964), and Heart of Atlanta Motel v. United States, 379 U.S. 241 (1964). The U.S. attorney general sued Ollie's Barbecue Restaurant in Birmingham, Alabama, for its refusal to serve African Americans in its dining accommodations, a direct violation of the antidiscriminatory public accommodations clause of the 1964 Civil Rights Act. The U.S. District Court for the Northern District of Alabama held that the Civil Rights Act could not be applied under the Fourteenth Amendment because there was no "demonstrable connection" between food purchased in interstate commerce and sold in a restaurant that would affect commerce. The U.S. Supreme Court, however, held that "the Civil Rights Act of 1964, as here applied, [is] plainly appropriate in the resolution of what [Congress has] found to be a national commercial problem of the first magnitude."

The *Heart of Atlanta* case dealt with a Georgia motel that solicited patronage in national advertising and had out-of-state residents as guests from time to time. The motel had already instituted the practice of refusing to rent rooms to African Americans prior to the passage of the 1964 Civil Rights Act and continued this practice afterward. The motel owner filed suit, maintaining that the act violated his rights under both the Fifth Amendment and the Thirteenth Amendment. The United States countered with the argument that the refusal to accept African Americans interfered with interstate travel, and that Congress, in voting to apply nondiscriminatory standards to interstate commerce, was not violating either amendment. The Supreme Court upheld the right of congressional regulation, stating that the power of Congress was not confined to the regulation of commerce among the states: "It extends to those activities intrastate which so affect interstate commerce, or the exercise of the power of Congress over it, as to make regulation of them appropriate means to the attainment of a legitimate end."

Bell v. Maryland, 378 U.S. 226 (1964). The Supreme Court ordered a Maryland district court to reconsider its affirmation of a state court conviction of twelve African Americans for trespassing when they declined to leave a restaurant that refused to serve them entirely on the basis of their color.

Evans v. Newton, 382 U.S. 296 (1966). The Supreme Court ruled that the transfer of a city park in Macon, Georgia, from municipal ownership to a board of private trustees did not remove Macon's obligations under the Fourteenth Amendment to guarantee equal rights to all citizens to use the park.

Shuttlesworth v. Birmingham, 394 U.S. 147 (1969). The Supreme Court invalidated Birmingham's parade permit law, which had been used in 1963 to harass participants in an Easter march organized by Dr. Martin Luther King Jr.

New York State Club Association v. City of New York, 487 U.S. 1 (1988). In a unanimous decision, the Supreme Court upheld the constitutionality of a New York City ordinance that forbids private clubs from discriminating against women and minorities.

INTERRACIAL MARRIAGE

Loving v. Virginia, 388 U.S. 1 (1967). This case nullified antimiscegenation laws. It concerned a white man and an African American woman, residents of Virginia, who married in Washington, D.C. Virginia indicted and convicted them of violating its laws against interracial marriage when the couple returned to Virginia and attempted to reside there, but released them when the couple agreed not to live in the state for twenty-five years. The Lovings, however, decided to challenge the agreement and the law. Their appeal was rejected by the Virginia courts but upheld by the U.S. Supreme Court, which ruled the Virginia law unconstitutional. Soon thereafter, federal district courts in other states that forbade interracial marriage ordered local officials to issue marriage licenses to interracial couples applying for them.

Mildred and Richard Loving, 1967. *The Lovings, an interracial married couple, hold a press conference after the U.S. Supreme Court unanimously rules in their favor in* Loving v. Virginia. *This landmark decision overturned Virginia's antimiscegenation statute and led federal district courts to declare similar statutes in other states unconstitutional as well.* FRANCIS MILLER/TIME & LIFE PICTURES/GETTY IMAGES

REQUIREMENTS FOR LEGISLATIVE MEMBERSHIP

Powell v. McCormack, 395 U.S. 486 (1969). According to the Constitution, only three basic factors govern eligibility to serve as a legislator in the U.S. House of Representatives: a minimum-age requirement, the possession of U.S. citizenship, and the fulfillment of the state's residency requirement. When U.S. Representative Adam Clayton Powell Jr. (1908–1972) was excluded from the Ninetieth Congress on the grounds that he had misused public funds and defied the courts of his home state, he filed suit in federal court in an attempt to force the House of Representatives to review only the necessary credentials for membership.

The district court dismissed the first petition on the grounds that it lacked jurisdiction. By the time the case was heard before the U.S. Supreme Court, the Ninetieth Congress had adjourned. Powell, however, was reelected and finally seated in the Ninety-first Congress, a gesture that did not settle the case or render it moot. The legal point on which the case hinged involved the distinction between "expulsion" and "exclusion." Despite the more than two-thirds majority required for expulsion, the Court ruled that the intent of the House was to "exclude," not to "expel." The Court summation stated flatly that "the House was without power to exclude him from its membership."

RESTRICTIVE COVENANTS—PROPERTY OWNERSHIP

Buchanan v. Warley, 245 U.S. 60 (1917). The plaintiff in this case brought an action for the performance of a sale of real estate in Louisville, Kentucky. The purchaser, Warley, an African American, maintained that he would be unable to occupy the land since it was located within what was defined by a Louisville ordinance as a white block. The ordinance prohibited whites from living in black districts, and vice versa. Buchanan alleged that the ordinance was in conflict with the Fourteenth Amendment to the U.S. Constitution. The U.S. Supreme

Court maintained that the ordinance was unconstitutional.

Shelley v. Kraemer, 334 U.S. 1 (1948), and Hurd v. Hodge, 334 U.S. 24 (1948). In 1945, an African American family, the Shelleys, received a warranty deed to a parcel of land that was subject to a restrictive covenant barring its sale to African Americans. A lawsuit was subsequently brought in the Circuit Court of St. Louis seeking to divest the Shelleys of the title to the land. The Supreme Court of Missouri directed the trial court to strip the petitioners of their warranty deed. The U.S. Supreme Court reversed this decision, maintaining that restrictive covenants, though valid contracts, could not be enforced by state courts. In *Hurd v. Hodge*, involving a similar set of circumstances, federal courts were similarly prohibited from enforcing racially restrictive covenants.

Reitman v. Mulkey, 387 U.S. 369 (1967). In 1964, California voters passed a referendum granting "absolute discretion" to real-estate owners in the sale and rental of real property. Lincoln Mulkey filed suit against property owners in Orange County to challenge the validity of the referendum. Mulkey's arguments failed in the lower courts but were accepted by the California Supreme Court on the grounds that the California referendum violated the Fourteenth Amendment of the U.S. Constitution. The U.S. Supreme Court upheld the decision.

Jones v. Alfred H. Mayer, Co., 392 U.S. 409 (1968). Joseph Lee Jones, an African American, alleged that his race was the sole reason that a real-estate agent refused to sell him a home. The Supreme Court held that 42 U.S.C. 1982, a federal statute created during the Reconstruction era to eliminate the vestiges of slavery, prohibits all racial discrimination, public and private, in the sale or rental of property.

Trafficante v. Metropolitan Life Insurance, 409 U.S. 205 (1972). The U.S. Supreme Court ruled that a complaint of racial discrimination in housing may be brought by parties who have not themselves been refused accommodation but who, as members of the same

Barbara Jo and Joseph Lee Jones, 1967. *When the Joneses accused a private construction firm of refusing to sell them a house because of race, their case made its way to the U.S. Supreme Court. In its 1968 decision in* Jones v. Alfred H. Mayer Co., *the Court ruled in their favor, stating that the U.S. Congress could regulate the sale or rental of private property to prevent racial discrimination.*
BETTMANN/CORBIS

housing unit, allege injury by discriminatory housing practices. The suit had been filed by a black resident and a white resident of a housing development in San Francisco who contended that the owner of the development was depriving plaintiffs of the right to live in a racially integrated community.

SENTENCING AND INCARCERATION

McKleskey v. Kemp, 481 U.S. 279 (1987). Warren McKleskey, a thirty-eight-year-old African American man accused of killing a police officer while robbing a furniture store, was sentenced to death by the state of Georgia. In support of his claim that the sentence violated his constitutional rights, McKleskey introduced a sophisticated statistical study that analyzed more than two thousand murder cases in Georgia. The study demonstrated that there was a disparity in the imposition of capital punishment based on the race of the victim, as well as the race of the defendant.

Defendants charged with killing white persons received the death penalty in 11 percent of the cases, but defendants charged with killing African Americans received the death penalty in only 1 percent of the cases. The study further showed that prosecutors asked for the death penalty in 70 percent of the cases involving black defendants and white victims, and only 19 percent of the cases involving white defendants and African American victims. In sum, the analysis revealed that African Americans who killed whites were 4.3 times more likely to receive a death sentence.

The Supreme Court acknowledged that it had accepted statistics as proof of intent to discriminate in employment, housing, and voting cases. The Court rejected, however, McKleskey's claim that the death penalty in Georgia was applied in a racially discriminatory manner. The Court's reasoning was that although McKleskey showed the existence of racial discrimination in sentencing, he failed to prove that "racial considerations played a part in his sentence." Finally, Justice Powell expressed concern that acceptance of McKleskey's argument would open the floodgates of litigation by African American defendants seeking to introduce statistical evidence to demonstrate that race affected the outcome of their case.

AFRICAN ENSLAVEMENT

Prigg v. Pennsylvania, 41 U.S. (16 Peters) 539 (1842). After Edward Prigg, a professional slave catcher, captured Margaret Morgan, an escapee residing in Pennsylvania, Prigg was tried and convicted under an 1826 Pennsylvania antikidnapping statute. Hearing the case, the Supreme Court ruled that the Pennsylvania law was unconstitutional on the grounds that the statute

Table 10-1. Jail Inmates by Sex, Race, and Hispanic Origin: 1990 to 2008

[Data based on the Annual Survey of Jails, a sample survey and subject to sampling variability]

Characteristic	1990	1995	2000	2004	2005	2006	2007	2008
Total inmates[1, 2]	**405,320**	**507,044**	**621,149**	**713,990**	**747,529**	**765,819**	**780,174**	**785,556**
Incarceration rate per 100,000 residents	163	193	220	243	252	256	259	259
Rated capacity[3, 4]	389,171	545,763	677,787	755,603	789,001	794,984	810,543	828,413
Adult	403,019	499,300	613,534	706,907	740,770	759,717	773,341	777,852
Male	365,821	448,000	543,120	619,908	646,807	661,164	673,346	678,677
Female	37,198	51,300	70,414	86,999	93,963	98,552	99,995	99,175
Juveniles[5]	2,301	7,800	7,615	7,083	6,759	6,102	6,833	7,703
White, non-Hispanic	169,600	203,300	260,500	317,400	331,000	336,500	338,200	333,300
Black, non-Hispanic	172,300	220,600	256,300	275,400	290,500	295,900	301,700	308,000
Hispanic/Latino	58,100	74,400	94,100	108,300	111,900	119,200	125,500	128,500
Other[6]	5,400	8,800	10,200	12,900	13,000	13,500	13,900	14,000

[1]Total does not include offenders who were supervised outside of jail facilities.
[2]Race/Hispanic origin data do not include the two or more race data.
[3]Beginning 1995, rated capacity subject to sampling error.
[4]Rated capacity is the number of beds or inmates assigned by a rating official to facilities within each jurisdiction.
[5]Juveniles are persons held under the age of 18. Includes juveniles who were tried or awaiting trial as adults.
[6]Excludes persons of Hispanic or Latino origin. Includes American Indians, Alaska Natives, Asians, and Pacific Islanders.

SOURCE: U.S. Department of Justice, Office of Justice Programs, Bureau of Justice Statistics, Jail Inmates at Midyear, Series NCJ 2221945 and NCJ 225709 annual.

Table 10-1. *While the number of individual African Americans incarcerated for various crimes has risen steadily over the past two decades, their collective percentage of the total inmate population has declined during this period.*

Table 10-2. Prisoners Under Sentence of Death by Characteristic: 1980 to 2007

[Excludes prisoners under sentence of death who remained within local correctional systems pending exhaustion of appellate process or who had not been committed to prison]

Characteristic	1980	1990	1995	1999	2000	2001	2002	2003	2004	2005	2006	2007
Total[1, 2]	**688**	**2,346**	**3,064**	**3,540**	**3,601**	**3,577**	**3,562**	**3,377**	**3,320**	**3,245**	**3,233**	**3,220**
White	418	1,368	1,732	1,960	1,989	1,968	1,939	1,882	1,856	1,802	1,806	1,804
Black and other	270	978	1,332	1,580	1,612	1,609	1,623	1,495	1,464	1,443	1,427	1,416
Under 20 years old	11	8	20	16	11	4	4	1	1	—	—	1
20 to 24 years old	173	168	264	251	237	192	153	133	95	61	51	42
25 to 34 years old	334	1,110	1,068	1,108	1,103	1,099	1,058	965	896	816	735	680
35 to 54 years old	186	1,006	1,583	1,958	2,019	2,043	2,069	1,969	1,977	2,012	2,043	2,060
55 years old and over	10	64	119	194	223	243	273	306	345	365	399	437
Years of school completed:												
7 years or less	68	178	191	201	214	212	215	213	207	192	186	183
8 years	74	186	195	221	233	236	234	227	221	206	195	189
9 to 11 years	204	775	979	1,142	1,157	1,145	1,130	1,073	1,053	1,030	1,015	989
12 years	162	729	995	1,157	1,184	1,183	1,173	1,108	1,091	1,105	1,098	1,089
More than 12 years	43	209	272	307	315	304	294	270	262	256	248	248
Unknown	163	279	422	499	490	501	511	483	480	465	486	522
Marital status:												
Never married	268	998	1,412	1,689	1,749	1,763	1,746	1,641	1,622	1,586	1,577	1,558
Married	229	632	718	731	739	716	709	684	658	649	626	635
Divorced[3]	217	726	924	1,107	1,105	1,102	1,102	1,049	1,034	1,019	1,025	1,027
Time elapsed since sentencing:												
Less than 12 months	185	231	287	259	208	151	147	137	117	122	105	110
12 to 47 months	389	753	784	800	786	734	609	495	421	399	382	352
48 to 71 months	102	438	423	499	507	476	468	451	388	299	262	262
72 months and over	38	934	1,560	1,969	2,092	2,220	2,333	2,291	2,388	2,434	2,479	2,496
Legal status at arrest:												
Not under sentence	384	1,345	1,764	2,088	2,202	2,189	2,165	2,048	2,026	1,979	1,952	1,963
Parole or probation[4]	115	578	866	886	921	918	909	845	809	792	778	760
Prison or escaped	45	128	110	125	126	135	141	137	145	144	142	143
Unknown	170	305	314	428	344	339	342	344	334	339	356	354

—Represents zero.
[1]Revisions to the total number of prisoners were not carried to the characteristics except for race.
[2]Includes races not shown separately.
[3]Includes persons married but separated, widows, widowers, and unknown.
[4]Includes prisoners on mandatory conditional release, work release, other leave, AWOL or bail. Covers 28 prisoners in 1990; 33 in 1995; 26 in 1998; 21 in 1999 and 2000; 17 in 2001, 2002, and 2003; 15 in 2004; and 14 in 2005, 2006 and 2007.

SOURCE: U.S. Department of Justice, Office of Justice Programs, Bureau of Justice Statistics, *Capital Punishment*, Series NCJ 224528, annual.

Table 10-2. *The percentage of African Americans and other minorities among incarcerated individuals under sentence of death has risen since 1980, and remains disproportionately high.*

interfered with Congress's power under Article IV, section 2 of the U.S. Constitution.

Strader v. Graham, 51 U.S. (10 Howard) 82 (1850). In 1841, three enslaved Africans owned by Christopher Graham of Kentucky, boarded a steamboat owned by Jacob Strader and traveled to Cincinnati. They ultimately escaped to freedom in Canada. Graham sued Strader for the value of the enslaved Africans and the expenses incurred while trying to recover them. Graham won the case. Strader appealed, though, claiming that those enslaved had become free under Ohio law and provisions of the Northwest Ordinance. The Supreme Court ruled unanimously that each state had the right to determine the status of an enslaved person within its jurisdiction, that their status was to be determined by the state of Kentucky, and that the Northwest Ordinance was no longer in force, since those territories had become states.

Dred Scott v. Sandford, 60 U.S. (19 Howard) 393 (1857). In 1835, Dred Scott became the property of John Emerson, a U.S. Army doctor, in the slave state of Missouri. From there, he was taken into the free state of Illinois, and later to the free territory of Wisconsin. In 1847, Scott initiated suit in the circuit court of St. Louis County, arguing that he should be given his freedom by virtue of having resided on free soil. After nine years, his case came before the U.S. Supreme Court.

In delivering his opinion, Chief Justice Roger Brooke Taney declared that, by virtue of both the Declaration of Independence and the U.S. Constitution, African Americans could not be regarded as citizens of the United States. Moreover, the Court could not deprive enslavers of their right to take those whom they held into any part of the Union. In effect, therefore, the Missouri Compromise, as well as other antislavery legislation, was declared to be unconstitutional.

Ableman v. Booth, 62 U.S. (21 Howard) 506 (1859). Abolitionist Sherman Booth was held in a state jail for violating the federal fugitive slave laws by helping an escapee to freedom. Booth secured a writ of habeas corpus from a state judge, who declared the federal laws unconstitutional; the Wisconsin Supreme Court affirmed. The U.S. Supreme Court unanimously upheld Congress's fugitive slave law and all its provisions, ruling that the state court had stepped beyond its sphere of authority. Although the Wisconsin government was deemed sovereign within its territorial limits, it was limited and restricted by the U.S. Constitution. Booth's conviction was upheld.

STATE AND LOCAL AFFIRMATIVE ACTION REQUIREMENTS

United Steelworkers of America v. Brian Weber, 433 U.S. 193 (1979). The United Steelworkers of America and Kaiser Aluminum Company entered into a collective-bargaining agreement that included a voluntary affirmative action plan designed to eliminate conspicuous racial imbalances in Kaiser's skilled workforce, which was almost exclusively white. The plant in Gramercy, Louisiana, agreed to reserve 50 percent of the openings in the skilled job-training programs for African Americans until the percentage of black skilled workers was equal to the percentage of blacks in the local labor force. Brian Weber, a white production worker, who was turned down for the training program although he had more seniority than many accepted blacks, sued the United Steelworkers of America, claiming that the affirmative action program discriminated against whites.

The Supreme Court limited the issue to the narrow question of whether Title VII prohibited private employers and unions from establishing voluntary affirmative action plans. In a five–two decision, the Court upheld the affirmative action plan and established three factors to determine the validity of racial preference. The Court approved the plan because it was designed to break down Kaiser's historic patterns of racial segregation, it did not unnecessarily diminish the rights of white employees since it did not require the firing of white employees, and it was a temporary measure not intended to maintain racial balance but simply to eliminate an imbalance.

Fullilove v. Klutznick, 448 U.S. 448 (1980). The Supreme Court upheld a provision of the Public Works Employment Act of 1977 that required a 10 percent set-aside of federal funds for minority business enterprises on local public-works projects. The provision had been challenged as a violation of the equal protection clause of the Fourteenth Amendment.

Firefighters Local Union No. 1784 v. Stotts, 467 U.S. 561 (1984). In May 1981, for the first time in its history, the city of Memphis announced layoffs of city employees because of a projected budget deficit. The layoffs, which also affected the fire department, were to be made based on a citywide seniority system that had been adopted in 1973. Carl Stotts, an African American firefighter, sued to stop the layoffs, claiming that since blacks had been hired pursuant to the affirmative action provisions of a 1980 court decree, they would be laid off in far greater numbers than their white coworkers. In a six–three decision, the Court held that since the 1980 court decree did not say that African Americans had special protection during a layoff, the layoffs had to be made according to the 1973 seniority system.

Wygant v. Jackson Board of Education, 476 U.S. 267 (1986). The U.S. Supreme Court dealt a blow to affirmative action in this case involving a public school system's affirmative action plan. The record reflected that the first African American schoolteacher was not hired in Jackson, Michigan, until 1953. By 1969, only 3.9 percent of the teachers were African American, although 15.2 percent of the students were African American. In response, the school board developed an affirmative action plan that protected African American faculty members during layoffs. Although the U.S. Supreme Court had approved affirmative action plans in prior cases, it rejected the Jackson plan. The Court found that the goal of the plan—to remedy societal discrimination and afford positive role models to African American students—was nebulous and not sufficiently compelling.

Local No. 93, International Association of Firefighters v. City of Cleveland, 478 U.S. 501 (1986). The city of Cleveland, Ohio, which had a long history of racial discrimination, negotiated a consent decree with black firefighters who had filed a lawsuit alleging that they had been unlawfully denied jobs and promotions. The decree included an affirmative action plan with numerical goals for promotion of blacks to the position of supervisor. In response to the union's challenge on behalf of white firefighters, the Supreme Court ruled that the lower courts had broad discretion to approve decrees in which employers settle discrimination suits by agreeing to preferential promotions of blacks, in spite of the objections of white employees.

Local 28, Sheet Metal Workers International Association v. EEOC, 478 U.S. 421 (1986). After finding that the all-white union had discriminated against African Americans and Hispanics seeking to enter the sheet-metal trades for more than a decade, the trial court ordered the union to establish a 29 percent nonwhite membership goal. The court also ruled that the union would have to pay substantial fines if it failed to meet the goals. After the union failed to reach the goal, the court found the union in contempt and established a new goal of 29.3 percent. The union challenged the court's order. The Supreme Court upheld the affirmative action goal in light of the union's "persistent or egregious discrimination" and in the interest of eliminating "lingering effects of pervasive discrimination." This was the first time the Court expressly approved the use of race-conscious relief to African Americans and Hispanics who were not identified victims of discrimination.

United States v. Paradise, 480 U.S. 149 (1987). This case originated in 1972 when the NAACP sued the Alabama Department of Highways because of its long-standing history of racially discriminatory employment practices. More than eleven years later, after the department had failed to hire or promote African Americans, the trial court ordered the promotion of one black trooper for every white trooper who was promoted. The U.S. attorney general challenged the constitutionality of the plan. The U.S. Supreme Court upheld the use of strict racial quotas and found that the plan was "narrowly tailored to serve the compelling government interest" of remedying "egregious" past discrimination against African Americans.

Johnson v. Transportation Agency, Santa Clara County, California, 480 U.S. 616 (1987). The U.S. Supreme Court held that the state transportation agency's voluntary affirmative action plan, under which a female had been promoted to the position of road dispatcher over a male, was consistent with Title VII of the Civil Rights Act of 1964. The Court held that an employer does not have to admit or prove that it has discriminated in order to justify efforts designed to achieve a more racially balanced workforce. The employer only needs to demonstrate that there is a "conspicuous ... imbalance in traditionally segregated job categories."

City of Richmond v. J. A. Croson Co., 488 U.S. 469 (1989). The Supreme Court upheld a court of appeals decision that Richmond's Minority Business Utilization Plan was not sufficiently narrowly tailored to remedy past discrimination in the construction industry. The plan allowed minorities a fixed 30 percent quota of the public contracts based solely on their race.

Adarand Constructors, Inc. v. Pena, 515 U.S. 200 (1995). The Court ruled that the federal government's affirmative action programs for construction contracts can only be acceptable if they show a compelling interest for the program and if the program is narrowly tailored to accomplish this interest.

THE CRIMINAL JUSTICE SYSTEM

Criminal justice in the United States consists of three major components: law enforcement, judicial and legal services, and corrections. Like all other aspects of the American way of life, African Americans were not accorded equality under the law and in many instances were victims of the judicial system established to protect them.

In *Strauder v. West Virginia,* 100 U.S. 303 (1880), the Supreme Court held that it was unlawful for African Americans to be excluded from juries. However, under the Jim Crow laws, African Americans were not allowed to vote in the South. Since jurors were selected from the voter rolls, the effect was that African Americans were barred from jury service. This meant that African Americans were tried, convicted, and sentenced by a justice system of all white Americans. In some states, particularly Alabama, the criminal justice system was nothing more than another system of African American enslavement. This system was maintained through the state's "convict-lease system," whereby the state sentenced African American males to imprisonment, which they spent working without pay for private companies while the state was paid for the prisoner's labor. The state, under such a system, had a direct pecuniary interest in the imprisonment of men who were mostly African Americans. An example was the Tennessee Coal, Iron, and Railroad Company, a subsidiary of the U.S. Steel Corporation, which paid the state for the labor of prisoners.

Since the 1970s, African Americans have assumed significant leadership roles in both law enforcement and correctional services as evidenced by the rising number of African American judges, prosecutors, and defense attorneys. However, since 1970, the employment of African Americans as judges and prosecutors has not increased at a rate that gives African Americans working in the system a formidable presence.

LAW ENFORCEMENT

As the largest arm of the criminal justice system, police are the most visible criminal justice servants. As the first point of contact for persons entering the system, officers make discretionary, often quasi-judicial decisions as to whether an arrest should be made when an offense is alleged to have occurred. Law enforcers have been organized and empowered to support the interest of those with means to shape law, a factor that had significant bearing on the prior relationship African Americans had with the police.

Like any other community, African Americans look to law enforcement for protection from criminal elements in their midst. However, until the recent integration of many urban police departments, law enforcement officers were used as agents of segregation and fear in many areas. This legacy still causes problems in African American relations with the police.

JUDICIAL AND LEGAL SERVICES AND THE CORRECTIONAL SYSTEM

In the 1990s, a serious debate on the merits of sentencing and capital punishment arose. Statistics showed that African Americans are likely to receive stiffer penalties for killing whites than whites receive for killing African Americans. This is also true in the administration of the death penalty, which disproportionately is used against African Americans who kill whites. In 1987, the Supreme Court took up the issue in *McKleskey v. Kemp*, and ruled that statistics could not be used to prove that the death penalty was being administered in a discriminatory manner. The Court required more evidence and evinced a fear that if the justices had ruled the other way, all African Americans on death row would come forward with claims. The issue did not die, however; in 1999, Illinois announced a moratorium on executions to study the issue. The moratorium remained in place as of 2010.

"THE TRIAL OF THE CENTURY"

On June 12, 1994, a brutal, double murder led to one of the most sensational criminal trials of the twentieth century. Nicole Brown Simpson, the former wife of African American football legend O. J. Simpson, was brutally slain outside her house, along with her friend, Ron Goldman. Almost immediately, evidence pointed to O. J. Simpson as the primary suspect. The subsequent, year-long trial was aired on television, allowing viewers to witness the entire spectacle almost as if it were a soap opera.

Prosecutors Marcia Clark (a white American) and Christopher Darden (an African American) portrayed Simpson as a jealous husband who had been locked in a

O. J. Simpson trial, Criminal Courts Building, Los Angeles, October 3, 1995. *Simpson, flanked by defense attorneys F. Lee Bailey (*left*) and Johnnie Cochran (*right*) reacts as he is found not guilty of murdering his ex-wife Nicole Brown Simpson and her friend Ron Goldman.* AP IMAGES

pattern of domestic violence and abuse. The murder of a spouse by a habitual abuser is common, they argued, and the prosecutors used this as the motive. Simpson's "Dream Team" of defense attorneys focused on an alleged police conspiracy based on race. Simpson was found not guilty by a predominately African American jury in October 1995. Ultimately, the case had little to do with the actual murders. *Broadcasting & Cable* magazine reported that "the verdict ... broke all previous TV viewing records, with over 150 million people tuning in."

Rather than addressing the crime, the proceedings brought the ugly underbelly of the country's prejudices, fears, and values to light. Polls showed that most whites thought Simpson was guilty, while blacks were divided on the verdict. Many African Americans viewed Simpson as another African American man caught in a discriminatory judicial system enforced by the Los Angeles Police Department, which had a history of racial prejudice and violence against African Americans. The trial was the first in which DNA evidence did not persuade the jury of the defendant's guilt. The defense attorneys alleged it had been rendered useless by the errors and omissions of police who were racist and determined to have the defendant incarcerated for a crime he did not commit because the victims were white.

Following the verdict, the Brown and Goldman families won a wrongful death civil suit against Simpson, forcing him to sell most of his assets. Simpson was innocent in the eyes of the court, but guilty in the eyes of many, and he became a recluse until he brazenly authored a book titled *If I Did It* in 2006. His book sparked anger in the parents of the victims and others who considered him guilty. A court order was obtained to remit the profits from the book as compensation to the families of his victims. Simpson was arrested and convicted in 2008 on other charges, and is now in prison.

THE CASE OF MUMIA ABU-JAMAL

Though not as big a newsmaker as the O.J. Simpson spectacle, the case of outspoken journalist and former Black Panther Mumia Abu-Jamal caused quite a ripple in the legal system during the mid-1990s. During an altercation between a Philadelphia police officer and Jamal's brother, Jamal claims to have interceded in order to keep his brother from being beaten. Though details are sketchy and contested, the aftermath of the fray left the officer dead and Jamal wounded by a bullet from the officer's gun. Arrested and convicted of murder, Jamal was sentenced to death in 1982.

Groups of national and international supporters advocated for Jamal's release, alleging that aspects of Jamal's case were improperly handled in regard to the U.S. Constitution and correct legal procedure. Many believe Jamal was framed by the Philadelphia police, who wanted to keep the blunt and forthright reporter from exposing evidence of corruption within the law enforcement agency. In 2008, the U.S. Third Circuit Court of Appeals invalidated Jamal's death sentence, citing several problems, including improper jury instructions. The appeals court denied Jamal's request for a new trial but indicated that he was entitled to a new sentencing hearing. In January 2010, the U.S. Supreme Court refused to set aside Jamal's conviction or death sentence. Instead, it reversed the decision granting a new sentencing hearing and remanded the case back to the appeals court to reconsider its ruling.

THE FEDERAL COURTS

Less than 4 percent of all federal judges are African American. Nonetheless, despite a complete lack of legal rights as enslaved persons, African Americans made their first inroads toward civil rights via the court system. In separate incidents, escapee Elizabeth Freeman, New Englander Lucy Prince, and the better known Dred Scott all battled racial barriers through the courts.

African Americans did not enter the courts just as parties to actions; they also participated in the system in professional capacities. In 1844, Macon Allen (1816–1894) became the first African American admitted to a state bar. Charlotte E. Ray (1850–1911) later became the first African American woman to gain the same distinction. Other pioneering women followed, including Ellen Craft (c. 1826–1891), Frances Ellen Watkins Harper (1825–1911), Laetitia Rowley, Maria Stewart (1803–1879), Mary Church Terrell (1863–1954), and Ida B. Wells-Barnett (1862–1931). In 1865, John S. Rock (1825–1866) became the first African American lawyer admitted to practice before the Supreme Court. In 1873, Mifflin Gibbs (1823–1915) became the first African American municipal judge. Though he only served a single term, his reputation for fairness was legendary, and he was named U.S. consul to Madagascar in 1897. Jonathan Jasper Wright (1840–1885) was elected to the South Carolina State Supreme Court in 1870. In 1937, President Franklin D. Roosevelt appointed William H. Hastie (1904–1976) to the Territorial Court of the Virgin Islands, making him the first African American federal district court judge. In 1939, Hastie was succeeded by Herman E. Moore, another African American. Jane Matilda Bolin (1908–2007) became the first African American female judge when she was appointed judge of domestic relations for the City of New York. In 1945, President Harry Truman appointed Irvin C. Mollison (1898–1962) to the U.S. Customs Court (now the U.S. Court of International Trade), which made him the first African American lifetime appointee to a federal court.

Nominated by the U.S. president and confirmed through Senate hearings, federal judgeships are lifetime appointments. Of the roughly one thousand active federal judges—including U.S. district courts, U.S. circuit courts, U.S. courts of appeals, and the Supreme Court—about eighty were African American in 2002. According to the Just the Beginning Foundation, the number had risen by 2008. At that time, there were eighty-nine active and twenty-four senior African American judges in the federal court system, one being on the Supreme Court. Still, African Americans have received appointments since the early 1960s, beginning with James B. Parsons (1911–1993), who was nominated by President John F. Kennedy to sit on the bench of the U.S. District Court for the Northern District of Illinois in 1961. At that time, the lack of federal African American judges was noticeable. Kennedy appointed Wade Hampton McCree Jr. (1920–1987) to the U.S. District Court for the Eastern District of Michigan in 1961, and Thurgood Marshall (1908–1993) to the Second Circuit Court of Appeals in 1962. In five years, Marshall would go on to become the first African American appointed to the U.S. Supreme Court.

President Lyndon B. Johnson followed Kennedy's lead, nominating eleven African Americans to federal benches. Among them were A. Leon Higginbotham Jr. (1928–1998), Johnson's first appointee, and Constance Baker Motley (1921–2005). As a member of the U.S. District Court for the Southern District of New York, Motley became the first African American woman to hold a federal judgeship in 1966. The next female appointee did not come for twelve years, when Mary Johnson Lowe (1924–1999) was appointed by President Jimmy Carter to the same district court. Carter also chose Amalya Lyle Kearse, in 1979, to become the first African American woman on the U.S. Court of Appeals. She was seated in the same venue in which Thurgood Marshall began his judicial career. Overall, Carter appointed thirty-seven African Americans in four years.

Republican presidents have had the poorest record of nominating African Americans to the federal courts. Richard Nixon nominated only six and Gerald Ford three over the combined eight years of their presidential terms. Lyndon Johnson nominated more in half the time. Ronald Reagan appointed only seven African Americans to federal courts in eight years. His successor, President George H. W. Bush, appointed thirteen in four years, including U.S. Supreme Court Justice Clarence Thomas. In contrast, Democrat Bill Clinton appointed sixty-three African Americans to federal courts by August 2000. He tried to appoint more, but the Republican-controlled Senate would not hold hearings or approve many of his judicial nominations, creating numerous vacancies. However, Clinton did help integrate the U.S. Court of Appeals for the Fourth Circuit. After the Senate refused to consider four nominations he made to this court, Clinton nominated an African American lawyer, Roger Gregory, as a "recess appointment" in December 2000. Since the Senate had ended its business for the year, Gregory served through most of 2001 without Senate approval. The maneuver pressured the administration of President George W. Bush to renominate Gregory in May 2001. When Democrats took control of the Senate that spring, the Senate approved Gregory, who became the first African American lifetime federal judge on the Fourth Circuit Court of Appeals.

THE NATIONAL BAR ASSOCIATION

In 1925, twelve African American lawyers (George H. Woodson, S. Joe Brown, Gertrude E. Rush, James B. Morris, Charles P. Howard Sr., Wendell E. Green, C. Francis Stradford, Jesse N. Baker, William H. Haynes, George C. Adams, Charles H. Calloway, and L. Amasa Knox) with a mutual interest in and dedication to justice and civil rights, established the National Bar Association (NBA) in Des Moines, Iowa, to represent the interest of African American attorneys. The stated objectives of the NBA are, among other things:

> To improve the administration of justice; ... promote legislation that will improve the economic condition of all American citizens, regardless of race, sex or creed in their efforts to secure a free and untrammeled use of the franchise guaranteed by the Constitution of the United States; and to protect the civil and political rights of the citizens and residents of the United States.

From its beginnings with only a few members, the association has grown in size and influence. Today, it represents a network of more than twenty thousand African American lawyers, judges, law professors, and law students, with eighty-four chapters in the United States, and affiliates in several African nations, the Caribbean, the United Kingdom, and Canada.

Since its inception, members of the NBA have been at the forefront of the fight for the rights of African Americans, rendering their professional services and expertise on a variety of legal issues, including criminal law, voting rights, and property covenant restrictions. In the 1940s, long before the federal government began providing legal aid to the indigent in the 1960s, the NBA offered free legal clinics to the poor. In 1986, for example, the NBA set up a free legal service to provide information and legal representation to elderly African American homeowners victimized by fraud scams and facing the loss of their home.

Through resolutions and other activities, the NBA has participated in the legal fight for social, economic, and political development around the world. In the late 1970s, seeing parallels in the struggle for equality in the United States and the liberation struggle against apartheid, the NBA urged President Carter and his administration to impose sanctions on the apartheid government in Rhodesia (now Zimbabwe). The NBA's other notable international achievements, as listed on its Web site, include:

- In 1983, the NBA issued a joint report with twenty-four other organizations, *Namibia: The Crisis in United States Policy toward Southern Africa*, which called for an end to South Africa's intransigence in independent Namibia and to the U.S. policy of "constructive engagement" in South Africa. The report received worldwide acclaim and unanimous acceptance by the Organization of African Unity.
- In 1991, the NBA held its first international affiliate chapter meetings in Dakar, Senegal, and Abidjan, Côte d' Ivoire. Since then, similar meetings have been held in London (1992 and 2000), South Africa (1993 and 1995), Toronto (1994); Accra, Ghana (1996), Bahia, Brazil (1997), Tanzania and Kenya (1998), Israel and Jordan (1999), and Paris (2000).
- In 1992, the NBA took a delegation of American lawyers and judges on a study tour of South Africa. The tour lasted approximately fourteen days and included joint meetings and seminars on democratic principles and other areas of law relevant to preparing black African lawyers for leadership and participation in a new government.
- In April 1994, as the only bar group sanctioned by the International Elections Committee, nine representatives of the NBA participated in a U.S. delegation that served as official observers for the first all-race democratic election conducted in South Africa.
- In April 1995, the NBA brought a delegation of twelve lawyers and other legal experts from Ghana, Kenya, Tanzania, and Uganda on a thirty-day study tour of the United States.
- In June 1995, the NBA sent delegations of attorneys on economic development and democratic tours of Ghana, Kenya, Tanzania, Uganda, and South Africa.
- The NBA issued a comprehensive report to the U.S. Senate, Nations Africa Group, and the U.S. Anti-Apartheid Committee on the illegality of the Zimbabwe-Rhodesian constitution.

In 1982, the NBA established the National Bar Institute to, among other things, assist law students and enhance the quality of legal education, provide financial assistance for litigation, support public forums related to debates on legal issues, and promote administration of justice and high ethical standards for judges and lawyers. In 1984, the association purchased a building for its headquarters in Washington, D.C.

In 2001, the NBA held the first Crump Law Camp at Howard University. The camp is a two-week summer program for high school students to learn about the American legal and judicial system. The program is named after the association's director emeritus, John Crump, who was saluted, along with the NBA, at a meeting of the American Bar Association in February 2010.

THE HOWARD UNIVERSITY SCHOOL OF LAW

Howard University was established in 1867 by a Charter from the U.S. Congress as a private institution. In 1869 the university started a law department that would later become the Howard University School of Law. During this period following the Civil War, the law school was established with just six students studying part time at night in the homes of faculty. Its primary focus was to train lawyers who were committed to safeguarding the newly acquired rights of African Americans. From 1887 until 1936 the law school occupied a house at Fifth Street in northwest Washington, D.C., and then merged with the other schools and departments at Howard University's main campus on Georgia Avenue NW. In 1974, the Dunbarton College at 2900 Upton Avenue, NW, Washington, D.C., was acquired for use exclusively by the Howard School of Law.

Graduates of Howard School of Law have been known not only as lawyers who safeguard the rights of African Americans and the less privileged but also as catalysts for social change and beacons for justice. Many of the pioneers for social change and the civil rights movement were graduates of Howard University School of Law. Howard has a full complement of faculty members and diversified curriculum and is fully accredited by the American Bar Association (ABA) and Association of American Law Schools (AALS). It has an average of 185 graduates per year for its juris doctorate and master's in law degrees. Its student body is predominately African American; however, there are also students from South America, the Caribbean, Africa, and Asia. The law school's focus remains to train lawyers who are "social engineers" and "capable of achieving positions of leadership in law, business, government, education, and public service."

ATTORNEYS, JUDGES, AND LEGAL SCHOLARS

(Some biographical profiles may appear in other chapters. To locate profiles more readily, please consult the index.)

CLIFFORD L. ALEXANDER JR. (1933–)

Attorney, Educator, Federal Government Official. Clifford Leopold Alexander Jr. was born in New York City on September 21, 1933. Alexander went to Harvard and earned his B.A. in 1955, graduating cum laude. He attended Yale Law School and, in 1958, earned his LL.B. He served as the assistant district attorney of New York County from 1959 to 1961, and as executive director of the Hamilton Grange Neighborhood Conservation district in Manhattanville from 1961 to 1962. In 1963, he became a staff member of the National Security Council.

Alexander was hired by President Lyndon Johnson as his deputy special assistant in 1964, and he quickly rose to become the president's deputy special counsel. In 1967, Alexander became chairman of the Equal Employment Opportunity Commission, where he was accused of bullying reluctant employers into complying with federal guidelines for minority employment. He left the position in 1969.

From 1969 to 1976, Alexander worked for several different law firms. He also became an overseer at Harvard, where he was involved in working with craft unions to improve minority employment opportunities.

In 1977, President Jimmy Carter appointed Alexander secretary of the Department of the Army. He was the first African American to serve in that position. Alexander won the Outstanding Civilian Service Award from the Department of the Army in 1980. In 1981, he became president of Alexander Associates, Inc., and served as a consultant on minority hiring practices to Major League Baseball. In the early 1990s, Alexander served as the District of Columbia's chief negotiator in the city's efforts to hammer out a deal to build a new stadium for the National Football League's Washington Redskins.

During the 1970s, Alexander produced and hosted his own television program, *Black on White*. He was also director of several money funds, served on the board of directors for the Mexican American Legal Defense and Educational Fund, and taught at Howard University.

JOYCE LONDON ALEXANDER (1949–)

Judge, Educator. Joyce London Alexander was born in Cambridge, Massachusetts, in 1949. She graduated in 1969 from Howard University after studying there on a scholarship from the NAACP. Alexander worked briefly for U.S. Representative and Speaker of the House Tip O'Neill, and then graduated in 1972 from the New England School of Law. She practiced law for several public foundations and worked as an assistant professor at Tufts University before being appointed to a U.S. district court as a magistrate. In 1996, she was named chief judge, becoming the first African American so honored.

Alexander is known for her activities in the legal community. She has held various positions for the National Bar Association and has founded several educational programs for her peers and for children. In 2002, she became general counsel for the Massachusetts Board of Higher Education and a legal editor for WBZ-TV, in addition to serving as an assistant professor at Tufts. She retired from the bench in 2009.

VIOLETTE ANDERSON (1882–1937)

Judge, Attorney. Violette Neatley Anderson was born on July 16, 1882, in London. When Anderson was a child, her family moved to the United States and settled in Chicago, where she attended North Division High School from 1895 to 1899. She attended the Chicago Athenaeum in 1903 and the Chicago Seminar of Sciences from 1912 to 1915.

From 1905 to 1920, Anderson worked as a court reporter, which sparked her interest in law. In 1917, she enrolled in the Chicago Law School, where she earned her LL.B. in 1920. She began a private practice that year, becoming the first African American woman to practice law in the U.S. District Court, Eastern Division. From 1922 to 1923, she served as the first female city prosecutor in Chicago. After five years of practice before the high court of Illinois, Anderson was admitted to practice for the U.S. Supreme Court, becoming the first African American woman to obtain this privilege. Her admission became a precedent for other African American women.

Anderson also belonged to the Federal Colored Women's Clubs, and was the first vice president of the Cook County Bar Association. In addition, she served as president of the Friendly Big Sisters League of Chicago and secretary of the Idlewild Lot Owners Association. She was a member of the executive board of the Chicago Council of Social Agencies. She died on December 24, 1937.

DEBORAH A. BATTS (1947–)

Judge. Deborah A. Batts, the first openly lesbian federal judge, was confirmed in 1994 to the U.S. District Court for the Southern District of New York. Batts was born in Philadelphia, and graduated from Radcliffe College (1969) and Harvard Law School (1972). She clerked for a federal judge before joining Cravath, Swaine and Moore in New York, where she worked as a litigator for six years.

She left the firm in 1979 to serve as assistant U.S. attorney in New York, before accepting a teaching post at Fordham University in 1984.

A supporter of equal rights for gays and lesbians, Batts is known to be an independent thinker, unafraid to speak her mind. She was drawn to the legal field after experiencing the political turmoil of the 1960s. She was initially recommended for a federal judgeship during the George H. W. Bush administration, but did not receive a nomination. U.S. Senator Daniel Moynihan recommended her a second time when President Bill Clinton assumed office. Clinton's nomination of Batts was confirmed by the Senate with no challenges on May 6, 1994.

DERRICK ALBERT BELL JR. (1930–)

Attorney, Educator. Derrick Albert Bell Jr. was born in Pittsburgh, Pennsylvania, on November 6, 1930. He attended Duquesne University, graduating in 1952, and received his LL.B. from the University of Pittsburgh Law School in 1957. He married Jewel A. Hairston in 1960, and the couple has three children. Bell is a member of the bar in Washington, D.C., Pennsylvania, New York, and California; the U.S. Supreme Court; the U.S. Courts of Appeals for the Fourth, Fifth, Sixth, Eighth, and Tenth Circuits; and several federal district courts.

After graduating from law school, Bell worked for the U.S. Department of Justice from 1957 to 1959, the Pittsburgh Branch of the NAACP as executive secretary from 1959 to 1960, and the NAACP Legal Defense and Educational Fund as staff attorney from 1960 to 1966. In 1966, he was made deputy assistant to the secretary for civil rights for the Department of Health, Education, and Welfare. He also served for a year as the director of the Western Center on Law and Poverty in Los Angeles.

Bell began as a lecturer on law at Harvard Law School in 1969, became a professor in 1971, and left in 1980 to become dean of the University of Oregon Law School for five years. After spending one year teaching at Stanford University, he returned to Harvard Law School in 1986. Four years later, Bell took an unpaid extended leave from his teaching duties at Harvard in protest over

Attorney and Educator Derrick Albert Bell Jr., Harvard Law School Campus, 1990. *The first African American tenured professor in the history of Harvard Law School, Bell took a voluntary unpaid leave of absence to protest the law school's practice of not granting tenure to minority women professors. Later, he was formally removed from the Harvard faculty.* STEVE LISS//TIME LIFE PICTURES/GETTY IMAGES

the institution's lack of a tenured black woman professor. Bell was formally removed from his position in 1992. He became a visiting professor of law at New York University in 1991.

Bell's many books include: *Race, Racism, and American Law* (1973; 6th ed., 2008); *And We Are Not Saved: The Elusive Quest for Racial Justice* (1987); *Faces at the Bottom of the Well: The Permanence of Racism* (1992); *Confronting Authority: Reflections of an Ardent Protester* (1994); *Gospel Choirs: Psalms of Survival in an Alien Land Called Home* (1996); *Afrolantica Legacies* (1998); *Ethical Ambition: Living for a Life of Meaning and Worth* (2002); and *Silent Covenants:* Brown v. Board of Education *and the Unfulfilled Hopes for Racial Reform* (2004). In 2005, New York University Press published *The Derrick Bell Reader*, edited by Richard Delgado and Jean Stefancic.

JANE MATILDA BOLIN (1908–2007)

Judge, Attorney. In 1939, when she was thirty-one years old, Jane Matilda Bolin was chosen by New York mayor Fiorello La Guardia to be the first African American female judge in the United States. Her appointment was renewed three times by Mayors William O'Dwyer, Robert F. Wagner Jr., and John Lindsay, and Bolin presided over the Domestic Relations Court of the City of New York (later called the Family Court of the State of New York) for forty years. By the end of her fourth term, she had reached the mandatory retirement age.

Bolin was born on April 11, 1908, in Poughkeepsie, New York. Her father was the first African American graduate of Williams College. Bolin attended Wellesley College and Yale Law School, where she received her LL.B. in 1931. She worked with her father until she passed the New York State bar examination in 1932, and then practiced law in Poughkeepsie before moving to New York City with her husband, Ralph E. Mizelle, also a lawyer.

In 1937, Bolin was named assistant corporation counsel for New York City, a post that she held until she was appointed to the Domestic Relations Court. Despite the demands of her career, Bolin became active in the Wiltwyck School for Boys, the Child Welfare League of America, the Neighborhood Children's Center, and the local and national NAACP. She also traveled extensively and met several African heads of state. Her friends included Eleanor Roosevelt, educator Mary McLeod Bethune, and Judge Julius Waties Waring, who ruled in the first public school desegregation case. Bolin received honorary degrees from Morgan State University, Western College for Women, Tuskegee Institute, Hampton University, and Williams College.

After her retirement, Bolin became a volunteer reading teacher for the New York City public schools. She also joined the Regents Review Committee of the New York State Board of Regents, where she reviewed cases involving professional discipline. Bolin was honored for her distinguished service by the corporation counsel's office on May 17, 1993. She died in New York City in early 2007.

YVONNE BRATHWAITE BURKE

See chapter 11, Politics.

JOHNNIE COCHRAN (1937–2005)

Attorney. Born in Shreveport, Louisiana, on October 2, 1937, Johnnie L. Cochran Jr. grew up in Los Angeles. He received a B.A. in 1959 from the University of California, and passed the California bar exam after finishing his law studies at the Loyola Marymount University School of

Attorney Johnnie Cochran, 2002. *Cochran became one of the best-known attorneys in the country thanks to his role as one of the lead defense lawyers in O. J. Simpson's 1995 murder trial.* **ROBERT MORA/GETTY IMAGES**

Law in 1963. Cochran began his law career as prosecutor in the criminal division of the deputy city attorney's office in Los Angeles. He left that post to join criminal lawyer Gerald Lenoir in private practice. In 1965, Cochran opened his own law firm in Los Angeles—Cochran, Atkins and Evans.

Cochran quickly established himself by defending high-profile African American clients, such as the family of Leonard Deadwyler, a young man shot to death by police while driving his pregnant wife to the hospital, and Geronimo Pratt, a former Black Panther charged with murder. Cochran lost both cases, but he demonstrated how such cases could garner media attention and foment action among the African American community.

Cochran returned to the Los Angeles County district attorney's office in 1978. After two years as a prosecutor, he returned to private practice. Shortly thereafter, Cochran won a settlement for the family of Ron Settles, a college student who had been strangled by a police choke hold, though his death was originally ruled a suicide by hanging.

As Cochran become more prominent, he began representing celebrities, such as pop singer Michael Jackson, actor Todd Bridges, and Sean "Diddy" Combs. Beginning in the summer of 1994, Cochran served on the team of defense lawyers for O. J. Simpson, who was accused of murdering his ex-wife Nicole Brown Simpson and her friend, Ronald Goldman. Cochran wore down the prosecution by challenging evidence and concentrating on racially prejudiced officers. Cochran's closing arguments alleged that the police had framed Simpson. The jury acquitted Simpson on all counts in October 1995.

Following the Simpson case—described in the media as the "trial of the century"—Cochran became one of the best-known lawyers in the country and was offered a million-dollar advance for his memoirs. He later served as an adjunct professor at both the Los Angeles School of Law and the Loyola University School of Law. He also served as chairman of the Rules Committee of the Democratic National Convention in 1984. In 1995, he was awarded the Trumpet Award by Turner Broadcasting System.

Beginning in 1997, Cochran took part in a daily show for Court TV. He left the show in 1999 to create the "Cochran Firm," one of the largest personal-injury law firms in the United States. In 2002, he announced that he was organizing yet another firm to look into the possibility of reparations for the descendants of formerly enslaved blacks. Cochran died on March 29, 2005, from a brain tumor.

WILLIAM T. COLEMAN (1920–)

Civil Rights Activist, Attorney, Government Official. William Thaddeus Coleman was born in Philadelphia on July 7, 1920. Coleman graduated summa cum laude in 1941 from the University of Pennsylvania. His law studies at Harvard University were interrupted by World War II, but he returned to Harvard after the war and, in 1946, received his LL.B., graduating first in his class. He was the first African American to serve on the editorial board of the *Harvard Law Review*.

In 1948, Coleman became the first African American to clerk for a Supreme Court justice when Justice Felix Frankfurter hired him. In the mid-1950s, Coleman joined the Philadelphia firm of Dilworth, Paxon, Kalish, Levy and Green. By the mid-1960s, he had become a partner in the firm. In 1959, Coleman served on an employment commission for President Dwight D. Eisenhower, and he later worked in various capacities for Presidents John F. Kennedy, Lyndon B. Johnson, and Richard M. Nixon.

Coleman played an important role in many landmark civil rights cases. He coauthored the brief presented to the Supreme Court in the 1954 case of *Brown v. Board of Education of Topeka, Kansas*, and he served as co-counsel on *McLaughlin v. Florida* (1964), which established the constitutionality of interracial marriages. In 1971, he was elected President of the NAACP Legal Defense and Educational Fund.

In 1975, President Gerald Ford appointed Coleman as the secretary of transportation. Coleman reorganized the department and issued a statement of the department's goals. President Ford's defeat in the 1976 election ended his tenure at the department, and Coleman returned to private practice in Washington, D.C. In 1995, president Bill Clinton presented him with the Presidential Medal of Freedom.

GEORGE CROCKETT JR. (1909–1997)

Attorney, Legislator, Civil Rights Activist. Born in Jacksonville, Florida, on August 10, 1909, George William Crockett Jr. got his first job delivering groceries when he was twelve. He graduated from Morehouse College in 1931. After receiving a law degree from the University of Michigan in 1934, Crockett returned to his hometown and opened a law practice. In 1939, his accomplishments as a lawyer and community activist led him to be chosen as the first African American attorney in the U.S. Department of Justice.

Crockett distinguished himself in Washington as counsel for cases concerning the Fair Labor Standards Act. In 1943, his work led to his appointment by President Franklin D. Roosevelt as an examiner with the Fair Employment Practices Committee. That same year, he was hired by the United Auto Workers in Detroit to serve as director of their Fair Employment Practices Office during a time of increased racial tensions in the city. In 1946, Crockett entered private practice in Detroit with a firm that took on major civil rights cases. Crockett once argued a case on behalf of accused Communists, which landed him in prison for four months for contempt of court.

Crockett became intensely involved in the civil rights struggle in the South during the 1960s, leaving Michigan for a time to direct the National Lawyers Guild's civil rights effort, Project Mississippi. In 1966, he was elected to the Detroit Recorder's Court, which handled the city's criminal docket. In 1969, members of a leftist group who were meeting at an African American church were brought en masse into police custody after a shooting outside the church. Crockett went down to the station in the middle of the night and set up his own impromptu court, releasing most of the people for constitutional reasons. He was vilified by Detroit's white establishment for his application of the Bill of Rights.

In 1980, two years after he had left the Recorder's Court bench, Crockett was elected as a Democratic congressional representative for a Michigan district that included part of Detroit. He served in Washington for the next decade, continuing to speak out on civil rights issues and even serving another stint in jail for participating in a demonstration against apartheid in South Africa. Crockett was also a vocal opponent of the Reagan administration's policies in Central America, especially during his tenure as chair of the Foreign Affairs Subcommittee on the Western Hemisphere. Crockett retired from politics in 1990. He died in 1997.

DREW S. DAYS III (1941–)

Attorney, Educator. Drew Saunders Days III was born in Atlanta, Georgia, on August 29, 1941. He received his B.A. from Hamilton College in 1963 and continued his studies at the Yale Law School. During his free summer months, Days returned to Georgia to champion civil rights causes and represent the poor as an intern. In 1966, after graduating from law school near the top of his class, Days moved to Chicago to represent minorities in cases of housing discrimination. Later, Days quit practicing law to work in Honduras for the U.S. Peace Corps.

After returning to the United States, Days worked for the NAACP's Legal Defense and Educational Fund. At the same time, he served as an associate professor at Temple University in Philadelphia. In 1977, Days accepted a post as the first African American to head of the Civil Rights Division of the U.S. Department of Justice. He left the government in 1980 to join the law faculty at Yale University.

In 1992, President Bill Clinton nominated Days to the position of solicitor general of the United States, the second-highest post at the Justice Department. As solicitor general, Days criticized poorly conceived or poorly managed minority-assistance programs. In 1995, he argued before the Supreme Court to keep in place minority voting districts in the Deep South. Days resigned from the Justice Department in 1996 and returned to Yale Law School, where he is the Alfred M. Rankin Professor of Law. Since 1997, he has also been counsel for the law firm Morrison & Foerster.

JOSEPH JEROME FARRIS (1930–)

Attorney, Judge. Judge Joseph Jerome Farris was born on March 4, 1930, in Birmingham, Alabama. He earned his B.S. degree from Morehouse College in 1951, and in 1952 he joined the U.S. Army Signal Corps. He received an M.S.W. from Atlanta University in 1955 and a J.D. from the University of Washington in 1958. Farris is married to Jean Shy and has two children.

Farris began his legal career in 1958 with the firm of Weyer, Schroeter, and Sterne. In 1959, he became a partner. He remained in private practice until 1969, when he became a Washington State Court of Appeals judge. Farris served as the chairman of the State Federal Judicial Council of Washington from 1983 to 1987. In addition, he served as president on the Washington State Jr. Chamber of Commerce from 1965 to 1966, as a trustee with the Pacific Northwest Ballet from 1978 to 1983, and from 1985 to 1997 as a regent of the University of Washington.

President Jimmy Carter nominated Farris to the Ninth Circuit Court of Appeals in July 1979. The nomination was confirmed by the Senate on September 26, 1979, and in March 1995, Farris assumed senior status.

Farris was honored with the Clayton Frost Award from the Jaycees in 1966. He received an honorary LL.D. from Morehouse College in 1978, as well as the Order of the Coif from the University of Washington Law School.

ARCHIBALD H. GRIMKÉ (1849–1930)

Attorney, Writer, Activist, Diplomat. Archibald Henry Grimké was born on a plantation near Charleston, South Carolina, on August 17, 1849. His father, a white enslaver, was a successful lawyer. His mother had been an enslaved servant who worked as a nurse for Henry Grimké's first wife, Selena. Archibald was considered enslaved at the time. He and his mother and siblings were passed on to relatives after his father's death. Grimké attended a special school during his youth. He later enrolled in a school directed by Frances Pillsbury and impressed the instructors there with his superior academic abilities. He completed undergraduate studies in only three years and obtained his master's degree in 1872 from Lincoln University.

Grimké practiced law in Boston from 1875 to 1883. Beginning in 1885, he presided over the Massachusetts Woman Suffrage Association. In the early 1890s, Grimké wrote for Boston-area publications, before receiving a four-year appointment as American consul for the Dominican Republic in 1894. Grimké was head of the American Negro Academy from 1903 to 1919. In 1913, he also became president of the Washington, D.C., chapter of the NAACP. Grimké wrote several books, including biographies of William Lloyd Garrison (1891) and Charles Sumner (1892), as well as numerous essays and speeches. He died on February 25, 1930.

WILLIAM H. HASTIE (1904–1976)

Attorney, Judge, State Government Official. From 1949 to 1971, William Henry Hastie served as a U.S. Court of Appeals judge for the Third Circuit. He was the first African American man to hold a federal appellate court position. Hastie was born in Knoxville, Tennessee, on November 17, 1904, the son of William Henry and Roberta Child Hastie. He received his A.B. from Amherst College in 1925, an LL.B. in 1930, and an S.J.D. in 1933 from Harvard University. He received honorary LL.D.s from many institutions, including Rutgers University, Howard University, and Temple University. In 1943, he married Beryl Lockhart. The couple had three children.

William H. Hastie, 1949. *After a three-year stint as governor of the Virgin Islands, Hastie became the first African American to hold a federal appellate court position, serving on the Third Circuit Court of Appeals from 1949 to 1971.* BETTMANN/CORBIS

Hastie was admitted to the bar in 1930 and was in private practice from 1930 to 1933. In 1933, he became assistant solicitor of the U.S. Department of the Interior, where he served until 1937. In 1937, he became a judge for the District Court of the Virgin Islands, leaving in 1939 to become dean of the Howard University School of Law. In 1942, he became the first civilian aide to the secretary of war. He was governor of the Virgin Islands between 1946 and 1949, before becoming a U.S. circuit court judge. Hastie was also a trustee of Amherst College and a fellow of the American Academy of Arts and Sciences. He died on April 14, 1976, in Philadelphia.

JOSEPH W. HATCHETT (1932–)

Attorney, Judge, Author. Judge Joseph Woodrow Hatchett was the first African American to be appointed to the highest court of a state since Reconstruction, the first African American to be elected to public office in a statewide election in the South, and the first African American to serve on a federal appellate court in the South.

Born in Clearwater, Florida, on September 17, 1932, Hatchett received his A.B. from Florida A&M University in 1954 and his J.D. from Howard University in 1959. He also earned certifications from the Naval Justice School in 1973, an appellate judge course in 1977, and an American Academy of Judicial Education appellate judge course in 1978.

From 1959 to 1966, Hatchett was in private practice in Florida, where he also served as the contract consultant for the city of Daytona Beach. He became an assistant U.S. attorney in Jacksonville in 1966, then served as the first assistant of the U.S. attorney for the Middle District of Florida. In 1971, he became the U.S. magistrate for the Middle District of Florida, and was a justice on the Florida State Supreme Court from 1975 to 1979. A nominee of President Jimmy Carter, Hatchett was a circuit judge for the Fifth Circuit U.S. Court of Appeals from 1979 until his transfer to the Eleventh Circuit on October 1, 1981. In 1996, he became chief judge of the court, serving in that capacity until his retirement on May 14, 1999. Later that year, he joined Akerman Senterfitt, Florida's largest law firm, where he serves as chair of appellate practice.

Hatchett was honored with a Howard University Postgraduation Achievement Award in 1977. He was also named Most Outstanding Citizen by the Broward County National Bar Association in 1976. In addition, he received a Medallion for Human Relations from Bethune-Cookman College in 1975, and has been awarded several honorary doctorates. Hatchett was inducted into the National Bar Association Hall of Fame in 2005. In 2007, he was given the Spirit of Excellence Award from the American Bar Association Commission on Racial and Ethnic Diversity in the Profession.

A. LEON HIGGINBOTHAM JR. (1928–1998)

Judge, Author. Aloysius Leon Higginbotham Jr. was appointed in 1977 by President Jimmy Carter as a judge of the Third Circuit U.S. Court of Appeals. He became the circuit's chief judge before his retirement in 1993. Higginbotham was also the first African American and the youngest person ever to hold the post of commissioner with the Federal Trade Commission. Born in Trenton, New Jersey, on February 25, 1928, Higginbotham began as an engineering student at Purdue University, but later went to Antioch College to study liberal arts. He received his LL.B. in 1952 from Yale Law School.

After graduation, Higginbotham became an assistant district attorney in Philadelphia and later moved into private practice. He was sought out by Pennsylvania governor David Lawrence to become a member of the Pennsylvania Human Rights Commission. Elected president of the Philadelphia chapter of the NAACP, Higginbotham later earned the honor of "One of the 10 Outstanding Young Men in America" by the U.S. Junior Chamber of Commerce. He was appointed a federal district judge in 1964, and served until he became a federal appellate judge in 1977. Higginbotham was also a lecturer at Harvard Law School and an adjunct professor at the University of Pennsylvania. In 1993, he was nominated for a position on the New York Times Company board of directors.

In 1995, a retired Higginbotham leveled criticism at Supreme Court Justice Clarence Thomas, whose judicial philosophy differed greatly from his own. While Higginbotham advocated social engineering through legislation, Thomas vigorously held that law should be colorblind. Higginbotham was criticized for what some saw as an unprovoked attack on a colleague.

Higginbotham was known for his writing, and was praised for his logic and language. He authored more than one hundred articles, as well as an acclaimed book, *In the Matter of Color: Race and the American Legal Process: The Colonial Period* (1978). In his esteemed career, he was awarded numerous honorary degrees. Higginbotham was also awarded the nation's highest civilian honor in 1995 when the Presidential Medal of Freedom was bestowed on him by President Bill Clinton He died on December 14, 1998.

ANITA HILL (1956–)

Educator, Author, Lecturer. Born on July 30, 1956, in Morns, Oklahoma, Anita Faye Hill was a relatively unknown law professor at the University of Oklahoma until 1991. It was during the Senate confirmation hearings for eventual U.S. Supreme Court justice Clarence Thomas that Hill became famous after she came forward with sexual harassment charges against Thomas that shocked the nation. Television cameras and viewers watched as she poured out details of Thomas's alleged wrongdoings, purportedly committed when both had worked for the Equal Employment Opportunity Commission. Hill claimed that Thomas repeatedly pressured her to date him, told her plots of pornographic movies, and bragged about his sexual exploits. When asked why she did not quit her job or report Thomas when the incidents occurred during the early 1980s, Hill answered that she feared she would not be able to get another job. Thomas told a conflicting story, and without corroborative evidence for either side, was confirmed by the Senate.

Following the hearings, Hill continued to be hounded by the press. Several books were written, and a seventy-six-minute documentary composed of testimony clips titled *Sex and Justice: The Highlights of the Anita Hill/ Clarence Thomas Hearings* was released in 1993. The experience changed Hill's life. She decided to take a yearlong sabbatical in order to look at the possibility of founding an institute with the purpose of researching racism and sexism. Hill also made many speeches around the country.

Controversy did not escape her on campus. Several lawmakers made news when they requested that Hill be fired. However, the University of Oklahoma dean and other members of the faculty supported her. In 1993, a university professorship to be established in Hill's name was proposed. Though the suggestion met much opposition, the endowed chair was approved two years later. The Anita Faye Hill Professorship, which was dropped in 1999 under renewed political pressure, provided a salary and money for research and travel expenses incurred in the study of women's rights in the workplace.

On March 9, 1995, Hill announced her resignation from the university, but after taking an unpaid leave during which she intended to write, she resumed her teaching post in September of the same year. In 1997, Hill joined the faculty of Brandeis University as a professor of social policy, law, and women's studies in the Heller School for Social Policy and Management. *Race, Gender, and Power in America*, coedited by Hill and Emma Coleman Jordan, was published in 1995. Hill's second book, *Speaking Truth to Power*, came out in 1997. In 2007, Hill was a visiting scholar at Wellesley College's Newhouse Center for the Humanities and Wellesley Centers for Women. She won the First Amendment Award from the Ford Hall Forum in 2008.

ERIC HOLDER (1951–)

Lawyer, Government Official. Eric Himpton Holder Jr. became the eighty-second attorney general of the United States in 2009. Appointed by President Barack Obama, he is the first African American to hold the position.

Holder was born January 21, 1951, in Queens, New York. He earned a bachelor of arts degree in American history from Columbia University in 1973, and a law degree (juris doctor) from Columbia Law School in 1976. From 1977 to 1988, Holder worked as a trial lawyer for the Public Integrity Section of the Department of Justice. He later served as a judge on the Superior Court of the District of Columbia (1988–1993), U.S. attorney of the District of Columbia (1993–1997), and deputy attorney general of the United States (1997–2001). He also worked as a litigation partner at the law firm of Covington & Burling in Washington, D.C. (2001–2009). In addition, he served as senior legal adviser to then-Senator Barack Obama during Obama's campaign for the presidency and was one of three members of Obama's Vice Presidential Selection Committee.

CHARLES HAMILTON HOUSTON (1895–1950)

Attorney, Educational Administrator. Charles Hamilton Houston was born in Washington, D.C., on September 3, 1895. After he finished high school at fifteen, he attended Amherst College and earned his A.B. in 1915 as one of six valedictorians. He briefly taught English, then enlisted in the U.S. Army in 1917 and served in France and Germany. He attended Harvard Law School and became the first African American editor of the *Harvard Law Review*. Houston received his LL.B. in 1922, and was in the top 5 percent of his class. In 1923, he became the first African American to receive an S.J.D. from Harvard University. Later that year, he received a Sheldon Fellowship and studied civil law at the University of Madrid. He was admitted to the Washington, D.C., bar in 1924.

Houston was in private practice with his father from 1924 to 1950. Between 1929 and 1935, he was vice dean of the school of law at Howard University. He also served as special counsel to the NAACP from 1935 to 1940 and as a member of the National Legal Aid Committee from 1940 to 1950. From 1944 to 1950, Houston was the vice president of the American Council on Race Relations. He became a member of the President's Commission on Fair Employment Practices in 1944.

While with the NAACP, Houston teamed with the American Fund for Public Service to direct a program of legal action and education aimed at the elimination of segregation. Former student Thurgood Marshall served under Houston for several years. While in this position, Houston argued several cases before the U.S. Supreme Court, including *Missouri ex rel. Lloyd Gaines v. Canada*. The Court ruled that Missouri could not keep an African American from attending the white state law school because no such school existed for African Americans.

Historically, Houston's major impact was in his strengthening of Howard University's Law School, as well as his work in civil rights litigation. Many of the cases he argued were instrumental in setting precedents that were to be used in the historic cases *Brown v. Board of Education of Topeka, Kansas* and *Bolling v. Sharpe*, which outlawed racial segregation. In addition, he was a columnist for the *Afro-American*.

Houston died April 22, 1950, of a heart ailment and was buried in Lincoln Memorial Cemetery. Five Supreme Court justices attended his funeral. He received a great deal of recognition after his death, including a posthumous Spingarn Medal, awarded by the NAACP.

NORMA HOLLOWAY JOHNSON (1932–)

Judge. Born in Lake Charles, Louisiana, Norma Holloway Johnson left Louisiana when she was fourteen to attend high school in Baltimore, Maryland. She was the valedictorian in 1955 at Miner Teacher's College, and graduated in 1962 from the Georgetown Law Center while working as a teacher.

Johnson worked in the Justice Department until 1967, when she became chief of the juvenile division for the District of Columbia. In 1970, President Richard M. Nixon appointed her associate judge for the district's superior court. In 1980, President Jimmy Carter nominated Johnson to fill a vacant seat on the U.S. Circuit Court for the District of Columbia. She was confirmed by the Senate on May 9, 1980. Johnson served as chief judge of the court from 1997 to 2001, and on June 18, 2001, she assumed senior status. During her tenure, she rendered many high-profile decisions involving corruption and civil rights. Johnson retired in 2003.

ELAINE R. JONES (1944–)

Attorney, Organization Executive, Civil Rights Activist. Elaine Jones was born on March 2, 1944, in Norfolk, Virginia. She earned a B.A. with honors in 1965 from Howard University, and became the first African American female law student admitted to the University of Virginia School of Law. Jones received her law degree in 1970 and was offered a job with a prestigious Wall Street firm. She turned down the job on Wall Street and went to work instead for the NAACP Legal Defense and Educational Fund (LDF). The LDF had argued more cases before the Supreme Court than any other organization except the U.S. Department of Justice.

In 1973, Jones became the managing attorney in the LDF's New York City office. In the late 1970s, she helped set up and run the LDF's new Washington, D.C., office. In 1988, Jones was promoted to deputy director-counsel of the LDF, making her second-in-command to the director, Julius Chambers. Jones used this higher-profile position to challenge the administrations of Ronald Reagan and George H. W. Bush on their federal judicial appointments. She was an outspoken opponent of both Robert Bork in 1987 and Clarence Thomas in 1991.

Julius Chambers resigned from the LDF directorship in 1993, and the organization's board unanimously chose Jones to succeed him. As president and director-counsel, Jones broadened the organization's agenda to include more cases of environmental and health-care discrimination. In addition to litigation, she was concerned with the group's fund-raising efforts. She resigned as head of the LDF in 2004.

NATHANIEL R. JONES (1926–)

Judge, Civil Rights Activist. Born on May 13, 1926, in Youngstown, Ohio, Nathaniel Raphael Jones has been a judge, an attorney, and an administrator. On October 5, 1979, President Jimmy Carter appointed him to the Sixth Circuit Court of Appeals in Cincinnati, Ohio, where he served until his retirement on March 30, 2002. Prior to that, he was general counsel for the NAACP from 1969 to 1979; executive director of the Fair Employment Practices Commission of the city of Youngstown, Ohio, from 1966 to 1969; in private practice; and a U.S. attorney for the Northern District of Ohio.

While with the NAACP, Judge Jones organized the attack against northern school segregation and also argued in the Supreme Court case *Milliken v. Bradley*. The Dayton and Columbus, Ohio, school-desegregation cases heard before the Supreme Court were also organized by Jones. He headed a three-man team that investigated grievances of African American servicemen in Germany and responded to the attacks against affirmative action. He was made deputy general counsel to the President's Commission on Civil Disorders in 1967 and cochairman of the Civilian Military Task Force on Military Justice in 1972.

Jones received a B.A. from Youngstown University in 1951, and an LL.B. in 1956. He has honorary degrees from Youngstown University and Syracuse University. In April 2002, Jones joined the law firm of Blank Rome as senior counsel.

STAR JONES (1962–)

Attorney. Star Jones was born Starlet Marie Jones in 1962 and grew up in Trenton, New Jersey. She shortened her name in 1979 after entering American University. In college, Jones served as a national officer of Alpha Kappa Alpha. After earning a law degree from the University of Houston, she went to work for the Kings County district attorney's office, whose jurisdiction included the crime-plagued New York City borough of Brooklyn. She served as a member of its prosecuting staff from 1986 until her promotion to senior assistant district attorney in 1991.

In 1991, Jones landed an invitation to appear on Court TV, a cable television network that broadcast high-profile trials interjected with commentary from experts on the judicial system. The channel soon hired her to appear regularly in conjunction with the William Kennedy Smith rape trial in Florida. Jones's performance earned her network attention.

NBC lured Jones away from her tough job at the Brooklyn district attorney's office by offering her its legal correspondent slot. During her two years at NBC, Jones covered several notable trials, attracting the attention of the American viewing public. She provided commentary as well as explanation of some of the more complex legal points on both the *Today* show and *NBC Nightly News*. The cases she covered included the criminal trial of the Los Angeles police officers charged with beating motorist Rodney King and the rape trial of boxer Mike Tyson.

In 1994, Group W Communications offered Jones her own syndicated television show. Debuting that fall, *Jones & Jury* gave parties to pending small-claims lawsuits a chance to resolve their disputes on television before a studio audience. Jones would then render the verdict. The show was canceled in 1995.

Jones was a cohost for the ABC daytime talk show *The View* from 1997 to 2006. She was nominated for an Emmy Award for outstanding talk show host for her

Star Jones, 1992. *A lawyer and television personality, Jones has served as a legal correspondent for Court TV and NBC and spent nearly ten years as cohost of the daytime talk show* The View.
KIMBERLY BUTLER/TIME & LIFE IMAGES/GETTY IMAGES

continuing analysis and clarification of social and legal events. On November 13, 2004, Jones married banker Al Reynolds following considerable sustained publicity. They were divorced four years later.

Jones has published two books, *You Have to Stand for Something, or You'll Fall for Anything* (1998) and *Shine: A Physical, Emotional, and Spiritual Journey to Finding Love* (2006). In 2002, she launched a nonprofit foundation, the Starlet Fund, aimed at benefiting women and girls around the world. In 2007, Jones agreed to take a position with Court TV (now truTV) as executive editor of daytime programming and host of her own talk show. The show was canceled in 2008, but Jones remained with the network as a legal commentator.

AMALYA LYLE KEARSE (1937–)

Judge. Amalya Lyle Kearse was born June 11, 1937, in Vauxhall, New Jersey. She received her B.A. in 1959 from Wellesley College and her J.D. in 1962 from the University of Michigan. Kearse was in private practice from 1962 to 1969 with the Wall Street firm of Hughes, Hubbard, and Reed. She also worked as an adjunct lecturer for the New York University Law School from 1968 to 1969. On June 21, 1979, President Jimmy Carter appointed her to a judgeship in the U.S. Court of Appeals for the Second Circuit. She was the first black woman and the second African American (after Thurgood Marshall) to sit on that court.

Kearse has won the Jason L. Honigman Award for outstanding contributions to the *Michigan Law Review.* She has also served on the board of directors for the NAACP Legal Defense and Educational Fund, as well as the National Urban League. She was appointed to the President's Commission for the Selection of Judges and served between 1977 and 1978. She served on the executive committee for Civil Rights under Law for nine years, has been a member of the American Law Institute since 1977, and has been a fellow in the American College of Trial Lawyers since 1979. Kearse is also an expert bridge player and is a member of the Laws Committee of the World Bridge Federation. During the 1970s, she published two books on bridge, *Bridge Conventions Complete* (1975; 3rd ed., 1990) and *Bridge at Your Fingertips* (1979).

DAMON J. KEITH (1922–)

Judge, Attorney. Damon Jerome Keith was appointed to the U.S. district court by President Lyndon B. Johnson and served from 1967 to 1977. In 1977, he began service as a judge for the Sixth Circuit U.S. Court of Appeals in Cincinnati, Ohio. He assumed senior status in the court on May 1, 1995.

Born on July 4, 1922, in Detroit, Keith attended West Virginia State College and received his A.B. in 1943. Following graduation, he served in the U.S. Army for three years. After his discharge, he returned to school and earned his LL.B. in 1949 from Howard University. In 1951, Keith took a job as an attorney for the Office of the Friend of the Court in Detroit, a position he held until 1955. He received an LL.M. from Wayne State University in 1956.

Keith worked for the Wayne County Board of Supervisors from 1958 to 1963. He was in private practice from 1964 to 1967, before being appointed a judge. He also became active in the Michigan Civil Rights Commission, and was involved in the Medical Corporation of Detroit, the Citizens Advisory Committee on Equal Educational Opportunity, the Detroit chapter of the NAACP, the management committee of the Detroit YMCA, the Detroit council of the Boy Scouts of America, the Detroit Arts Commission, and the United Negro College Fund of Detroit. Keith was also a trustee of the Interlochen Arts Academy and the Cranbrook School.

Judge Keith was named one of the 100 Most Influential Black Americans by *Ebony* magazine in 1971 and 1977. He also received a citizen award from Michigan State University and was a Spingarn medalist in 1974. In 1997, he won the Edward J. Devitt Distinguished Service to Justice Award from the American Judicature Society. In addition, Keith has received honorary degrees from the University of Michigan, Howard University, Wayne State University, Michigan State University, New York Law School, and Harvard University.

CARMEL CARRINGTON MARR (1921–)

Attorney, Diplomat, Government Official. Carmel Carrington Marr was born in Brooklyn on June 23, 1921, and received her B.A. in 1945 from Hunter College. She earned her J.D. from Columbia University Law School in 1948. As an expert in international law, she was appointed by President Harry Truman to the position of legal adviser to the U.S. mission to the United Nations in 1953. She remained in that post until 1967, keeping in constant contact with missions from other parts of the world and serving on a number of key committees in the UN General Assembly.

Marr worked in private practice in 1949 to 1953. In 1967, after serving as legal adviser to the United Nations for fourteen years, she became the senior legal officer of the UN Secretariat. She left that post after one year to become a member of the New York State Human Rights Appeals Board, a job she held until 1971. Between 1971 and 1986, she served as commissioner of the New York State Public Service Commission as a regulator of utilities. From 1987 to 1990, she worked as a consultant on issues relating to energy.

Marr was also the chairperson of the advisory council of the Gas Research Institute between 1979 and 1986, the U.S. Department of Transportation Technology Pipeline Safety Standards Commission from 1979 to 1985, and the National Association of Regulatory Utility Commissioners (NARUC) Gas Commission from 1984 to 1986. She became president of NARUC's Great Lakes Conference of Public Utility Commission and was on the board of the National Arts Stabilization Fund. Marr was honored for outstanding community service by the Brooklyn Urban League and received accolades from the Gas Research Institute, the New York State Public Service Commission, the American Red Cross, the National Council of Churches, and *Mademoiselle* magazine.

THURGOOD MARSHALL (1908–1993)

Supreme Court Justice, Federal Government Official, Attorney, Civil Rights Activist. Thurgood Marshall's long and illustrious career was capped by his 1967 nomination to the U.S. Supreme Court. He was the first African American to hold the position of Supreme Court justice. Born in Baltimore, Maryland, on July 2, 1908, Marshall earned a B.A. from Lincoln University and hoped to become a dentist. He changed his mind, and instead went to Howard University Law School, where he graduated in 1933 at the top of his class. He immediately entered private practice in Baltimore. In 1936, Marshall began what was to be a long and fruitful career with the NAACP, starting as an assistant special counsel, and eventually becoming director-counsel of the Legal Defense and Educational Fund (LDF), where he remained until 1961. In 1938, as NAACP national special counsel, he handled all cases involving the constitutional rights of African Americans. In 1950, he was named director-counsel of the LDF.

In 1954, Marshall was the lead lawyer for the NAACP before the U.S. Supreme Court in *Brown v. Board of Education of Topeka, Kansas.* He also figured prominently in such important cases as *Sweatt v. Painter* and *Smith v. Allwright.* Of the thirty-two cases that Marshall argued before the Supreme Court, he won twenty-nine.

Marshall was also known for his lifelong support of rights for women. Constance Baker Motley commented that Marshall hired her for an NAACP counsel position when virtually every other employer had turned her down. He also encouraged her when she argued cases before the Supreme Court, and made certain he pointed out other African American women role models.

In 1961, Marshall became a federal judge for the Second Circuit. In 1946, he was awarded the prestigious Spingarn Medal for his many achievements. He had over twenty honorary degrees to his credit, including LL.D. honors in 1960 from the University of Liberia, in 1964 from the University of Michigan, and in 1968 from the University of Otago in Dunedin, New Zealand. In addition, Marshall was a representative for the White House Conference on Youth and Children, as well as a member of the National Bar Association. He was sent by President John F. Kennedy to represent the United States at the independence ceremonies of Sierra Leone.

Marshall retired on June 27, 1991. He died at age eighty-four on January 24, 1993, and was laid in state in the Great Hall of the Supreme Court on the same bier where Abraham Lincoln once rested. More than twenty thousand mourners paid their respects.

WADE HAMPTON McCREE JR. (1920–1987)

Judge, Attorney. Wade Hampton McCree Jr. was solicitor general under President Jimmy Carter from 1977 to 1981. McCree had already led a distinguished career as a judge and lawyer by the time he reached that position. He was born in Des Moines, Iowa, on July 3, 1920, and graduated from Fisk University, earning his A.B. in 1941. In 1944, he received his LL.B. from Harvard University. He was admitted to the bar in Michigan in 1948.

McCree ran a private law practice from 1948 to 1952. From 1952 to 1954, he was commissioner of the Michigan Workmen's Compensation Commission. He served as a circuit judge for Wayne County in Michigan from 1954 until 1961, as well as judge for the U.S. District Court, Eastern District, in Michigan from 1961 to 1966. McCree had the honor of being the first African American federal judge in the state of Michigan. From 1966 to 1977, he served as a Sixth Circuit U.S. Court of Appeals judge. From 1981 until his death in 1987, he was a member of the faculty at the University of Michigan Law School. In 1984, the Wade H. McCree Jr. Professorship was established at the University of Michigan Law School, making it the first endowed chair at a major American law school to be named after an African American. McCree was awarded more than thirty honorary degrees in his lifetime, including LL.D.s from Howard University, Harvard University, Boston University, Brandeis University, and Tuskegee Institute.

GABRIELLE KIRK McDONALD (1942–)

Judge. Gabrielle Anne Kirk McDonald was born on April 12, 1942, in St. Paul, Minnesota. She attended Boston University and Hunter College before graduating cum laude from the Howard University School of Law in 1966. McDonald worked as a staff attorney for the NAACP Legal Defense and Educational Fund until 1969, when she went into private practice in Houston, Texas, with her husband.

McDonald earned a reputation as one of the top litigators in Texas and won several large settlements for her clients in civil rights cases. Her record attracted national attention, and in 1979 President Jimmy Carter appointed her a federal district court judge. In 1988, she resigned from her position and went back into private practice. She also taught at several law schools, including St. Mary's University School of Law in San Antonio and Texas Southern University's Thurgood Marshall School of Law in Houston.

In 1993, McDonald became the only U.S. citizen elected to the United Nations International War Crimes Tribunal for the former Yugoslavia at the Hague, Netherlands. She was reelected in 1997 and became the presiding judge of the tribunal, a position she held until her resignation on November 17, 1999. In 2001, McDonald was honored by the American Bar Association Commission on Women in the Profession with its Margaret Brent Women Lawyers of Achievement Award.

***Gabrielle Kirk McDonald, 1998.** A judge on the United Nations' International Criminal Tribunal for the former Yugoslavia from 1993 to 1999, McDonald served as the tribunal's president from 1997 to 1999.* AP PHOTO/PETER DEJONG

THEODORE McMILLIAN (1919–2006)

Judge, Educator. Born on January 28, 1919, in St. Louis, Missouri, Theodore McMillian received his B.S. in 1941 from Lincoln University and his LL.B. from St. Louis University Law School in 1949. He served in the U.S. Signal Corps from 1942 to 1946.

McMillian became a circuit judge for the state of Missouri and served as an assistant circuit attorney for St. Louis from 1953 to 1956. In 1972, he became the first African American judge on the Missouri Court of Appeals. He was named a U.S. Circuit Court of Appeals judge for the Eighth Circuit on September 23, 1978. Judge McMillian also served on the faculties of a number of colleges and universities, including St. Louis University Law School, the University of Missouri at St. Louis, and Webster College.

Judge McMillian was a member of the board of trustees for Blue Cross. He also served on the Danforth Foundation Advisory Council, on the Presidential Council of St. Louis University, as board chairman for Human Development Corporation between 1964 and 1977, and on the National Legal Aid Advisory Board. He was honored with an Alumni Merit Award from St. Louis University, an Award of Honor from the Lawyers Association in 1970, and a Man of the Year Award in 1970. On his eightieth birthday in 1999, McMillian donated $250,000 to St. Louis University's School of Law to establish the Theodore McMillian Endowed Scholarship. He died on January 18, 2006, in St. Louis.

CONSTANCE BAKER MOTLEY (1921–2005)

Government Official, Judge, Civil Rights Activist, Attorney. Born on September 14, 1921, in New Haven,

Connecticut, Constance Baker Motley was the first African American woman to become a federal judge when she was appointed in 1966 by President Lyndon B. Johnson to the U.S. District Court for Southern New York. While still a law student at Columbia University, Motley began working with the NAACP Legal Defense and Educational Fund. In 1946, she was awarded her LL.B. and began to work fulltime with the NAACP, eventually becoming an associate counsel. During her twenty-year career with the organization, Motley argued nine successful NAACP cases before the U.S. Supreme Court, and participated in almost every important civil rights case that passed through the courts.

In 1964, Motley made a successful run for the New York State Senate. She became the first African American woman elected to that position. After only a year in the Senate, Motley ran for the position of Manhattan Borough president, emerging the victor by the unanimous final vote of the city council. In winning this position, she became the first woman to serve as a borough president and also the first woman on the New York City Board of Estimate.

Motley was appointed to the U.S. District Court in 1966. In 1982, she was named chief judge of the federal district court that covers Manhattan, the Bronx, and six counties north of New York City. In 1986, she became senior U.S. district judge.

Motley received numerous awards for her contributions to the legal profession and for her role in the advancement of civil rights. She held more than twenty honorary degrees from prestigious universities, including Princeton and Howard. In 1993, Motley was inducted into the National Women's Hall of Fame. She died on September 28, 2005.

ELEANOR HOLMES NORTON

See chapter 11, Politics.

BARACK OBAMA

See chapter 11, Politics.

CHARLES J. OGLETREE JR. (1952–)

Lawyer, Educator. Charles J. Ogletree Jr. was born on December 31, 1952, in Merced, California, and attended Stanford University. In 1974, he received his B.A., followed by an M.A. in 1975. While at Stanford, he edited a Black Panther newspaper and traveled to Africa and Cuba with student groups. His attendance at Angela Davis's trial first attracted him to a career in the law.

Ogletree graduated in 1978 from Harvard Law School and went to work as a public defender in Washington, D.C. He established a reputation as a top trial lawyer and taught at American University and Antioch Law School. In 1985, while in private practice, Ogletree became a visiting professor at Harvard Law School and helped the school develop its trial advocacy workshops.

Ogletree served as Anita Hill's attorney during her testimony before the U.S. Senate concerning the nomination of Clarence Thomas to the Supreme Court. In 1989, he became a full professor at Harvard, where he was named the Jesse Climenko Professor of Law in 1998. Since 2005, he has been executive director of the Charles Hamilton Houston Institute for Race and Justice at Harvard Law School. In 2009, he was awarded the Spirit of Excellence Award from the American Bar Association. Ogletree is the author of numerous articles and several books, including: *All Deliberate Speed: Reflections on the First Half-Century of* Brown v. Board of Education (2004); *From Lynch Mobs to the Killing State: Race and the Death Penalty in America* (2006) and *When Law Fails: Making Sense of Miscarriages of Justice* (2009), both edited with Austin Sarat; and *The Presumption of Guilt: The Arrest of Henry Louis Gates and Race, Class, and Crime in America* (2010).

BERNARD PARKS (1943–)

Police Chief. Bernard C. Parks was born in Beaumont, Texas, on December 7, 1943, but was raised in Los Angeles. After bouncing between jobs, Parks became a police officer in Los Angeles in 1965. Parks received his B.A. in 1973 from Pepperdine University and his M.A. in public administration in 1976 from the University of Southern California.

Parks steadily moved up the ladder at the Los Angeles Police Department (LAPD). By 1988, he was the assistant police chief. The Los Angeles riots of 1992 forced incumbent police chief Daryl Gates from his position after Gates was accused by many of racism during his tenure as chief. An African American chief was picked to replace Gates. The new chief, Willie Williams, clashed frequently with Parks. In 1994, Williams demoted Parks from assistant chief back to deputy chief, with a cut in pay. However, the city council later restored Parks's salary. In 1997, Parks became head of the LAPD after Williams was removed as chief. Parks held the post until June 2002, retiring after he was denied a second five-year term by the Los Angeles Police Commission.

During his tenure as chief, Parks attempted to reform the department with the institution of a new officer-accountability policy. He also streamlined procedures for the citizen complaint system, by which citizens can file complaints against officers. During Parks's term, though, the department was wracked by the widely publicized

Rampart scandal. The chief also suffered the loss of his granddaughter, Lori Gonzalez, in a gang-related shooting in June 2000.

Parks was elected to the Los Angeles City Council in 2003. His campaign for the position of mayor ended with a fourth-place finish in the 2005 primary election.

JAMES B. PARSONS (1911–1993)

Judge. James Benton Parsons was born August 13, 1911, in Kansas City, Missouri. He graduated in 1934 from the James Milliken University and Conservatory of Music and began to teach at Lincoln University. He later taught in Greensboro, North Carolina, until he joined the U.S. Navy in 1942. After World War II, he received an M.A. in political science and a J.D. from the University of Chicago.

Parsons went into private practice and taught constitutional law at the John Marshall Law School. He served as assistant U.S. district attorney for nine years, until he became a judge for the Cook County Superior Court. He was appointed a U.S. district court judge in 1961 by President John F. Kennedy. Parsons was the first African American to sit as a federal judge in the contiguous United States. In 1975, he was named chief judge of the court.

Parsons retired in 1992, after many tributes from other African American judges. He died on June 19, 1993, in Chicago.

SPOTTSWOOD ROBINSON (1916–1998)

Attorney, Judge. Spottswood William Robinson III was born July 26, 1916, in Richmond, Virginia. He received his B.A. in 1936 from Virginia Union University and his LL.B. in 1939 magna cum laude from Howard University Law School.

Robinson has had a long career in private and public practice. He was an attorney in Richmond until 1960. He also taught at the Howard University Law School from 1945 until 1964, serving as dean of the school of law from 1960 to 1964. Robinson gained notoriety during this period for his work alongside Thurgood Marshall for the NAACP's Legal Defense and Educational Fund (1948–1950). From 1951 to 1960, Robinson was the regional counsel for the NAACP in the southeast.

In 1964, President Lyndon B. Johnson appointed Robinson as a federal circuit court judge in Washington, D.C. In 1966, Robinson was promoted to the U.S. Court of Appeals for the District of Columbia Circuit. He also served on the U.S. Civil Rights Commission from 1961 to 1963. Robinson died on October 11, 1998, in Richmond.

GEORGE RUFFIN (1834–1886)

Judge, Attorney, Civil Rights Activist. George Lewis Ruffin was born in Richmond, Virginia, in 1834, the first son of free African Americans. In 1853, the family moved to Boston. Ruffin graduated from Chapman Hall school and joined the Republican Party. He moved for a short while to Liverpool, England, after becoming disillusioned by the 1857 *Dred Scott* decision. Returning to Boston, Ruffin worked as a barber. He wrote a review for the *Anglo-African* newspaper in 1863 and attended the National Negro Convention in 1864.

Ruffin also began to read law with a local firm. He graduated in 1869 from Harvard Law School, becoming the first African American to earn an LL.B. from Harvard and perhaps the first to graduate from a university law school in the United States. He joined the firm of Harvey Jewell, and then won a seat on the Massachusetts legislature in 1869, becoming the second African American to serve in that body.

Ruffin became known as an exceptional speaker and debater as he focused his attention on the problems of the South. In 1876 and 1877, he won election to the Boston Common Council, and he presided over the Negro Convention of New Orleans in 1872. He was a friend of Frederick Douglass, who asked Ruffin to contribute an introduction to the 1881 revision of *The Life and Times of Frederick Douglass*. When Ruffin was appointed in November 1883 as judge of a municipal court in Charlestown, Massachusetts, he became the first African American judge in the state. In 1883, he was named consul resident for the Dominican Republic in Boston. In addition, he served as president of the Wendell Phillips Club of Boston, president of the Banneker Literary Club of Boston, and superintendent of the Twelfth Baptist Church of Boston. Ruffin died of Bright's disease on November 20, 1886.

KURT L. SCHMOKE

See chapter 11, Politics.

DRED SCOTT

See chapter 6, Africans in America.

ROBERT H. TERRELL (1857–1925)

Educator, Judge, Attorney. Robert Heberton Terrell was born in Charlottesville, Virginia, on November 27, 1857. He worked in a dining hall to pay for his classes at Harvard, where he graduated magna cum laude in 1884. He worked in the public schools in Washington, D.C., while he attended Howard University Law School. Terrell earned his LL.B. in 1889 and his LL.M. in 1893. In 1889, he became chief clerk in the office of the auditor of the U.S. Treasury Department. He married Mary Church, a civil rights and women's rights activist, on October 28, 1891.

Terrell was involved in the private practice of law from 1892 to 1898, until he became a teacher, and later became principal, at the M Street High School. He was elected to the Board of Trade in the 1890s. In 1901, he was appointed as a justice of the peace in Washington, D.C. Like many African Americans of his day, Terrell was torn between his strongly held civil rights beliefs and Booker T. Washington's conservative ideas. Through Washington's influence, Terrell was nominated by President William H. Taft for the position of judge of the Municipal Court of the District of Columbia in 1910. Despite racial protests in the Senate, Terrell signed the appointment and held the position until his death on December 20, 1925. Terrell suffered two strokes and battled asthma while on the court.

CLARENCE THOMAS (1948–)

Attorney, Government Official, Supreme Court Justice. Clarence Thomas was born June 23, 1948, in Pin Point, Georgia. As a youth, Thomas lived with his maternal grandparents in Savannah. Although his grandfather had little education, he was determined that young Clarence would go to school and make something of himself. Thomas attended various Catholic schools and intended to enter the priesthood, but left the seminary when he encountered racist classmates.

Thomas earned his B.A. from Holy Cross College. He was accepted into Yale Law School in 1971 after Yale adopted an affirmative action program. In 1974, he earned his J.D. After graduating, Thomas became an assistant attorney general for the state of Missouri. He worked briefly at Monsanto Company in St. Louis, specializing in pesticide, fungicide, and rodenticide law. He also worked as a legal assistant for Senator John C. Danforth.

From 1981 to 1982, Thomas was an assistant secretary for civil rights with the Department of Education. In 1982, he became chair of the Equal Employment Opportunity Commission (EEOC), where he remained until 1990. His tenure there was controversial in that he was not allied with liberals or civil rights leaders but did not feel comfortable with the white conservative hierarchy either.

In 1990, after Robert H. Bork resigned his circuit court position, Thomas was appointed to the post. He served there until he became an associate justice on the U.S. Supreme Court in 1991. Thomas's nomination hearings were marred by accusations of sexual harassment leveled against him by former EEOC employee Anita Hill. Hill became a household name when she came forward with her allegations. The Senate was divided by her testimony. Though Thomas denied the charges and many of his former coworkers testified for him, the case became highly politicized. Thomas was nominated by a vote of fifty-two to forty-eight, one of the closest margins in Supreme Court history.

Clarence Thomas, South Lawn, White House, Washington, DC, 1991. *Thomas, pictured with U.S. President George H. W. Bush and Thomas's wife, Virginia Lamp Thomas, takes the constitutional oath to become an associate justice of the U.S. Supreme Court.* AP PHOTO/MARCY NIGHSWANDER

Thomas has gone on to carve out a prominent role as one of the most conservative justices on the Court. Together with Justice Antonin Scalia, Thomas forms the right-wing backbone of the Court. In his tenure, Thomas has presented strong opinions against affirmative action and desegregation. He also supports limiting the powers of the federal government. He has consistently been criticized by African American lawyers and judges for his conservative stances. In 1998, he rebuffed his critics at a speech before the National Bar Association. In 1992, Thomas was one of ten people to receive the Horatio Alger Award. He published a memoir, *My Grandfather's Son*, in 2007.

EVELYN WILLIAMS (c. 1922–)

Attorney, Activist. Williams was born in North Carolina but grew up in a close-knit family in Queens, New York.

After graduating from Brooklyn College, she became a social worker for New York City. Shaken by the poverty she encountered and hoping to help her community, Williams became a juvenile probation officer, but that also offered little satisfaction.

In the late 1950s, Williams graduated from St. John's University Law School as one of two African Americans in her class. By 1960, she was defending those accused of crimes who had little means for expensive legal representation. She also helped raise a niece, Assata Shakur, who became involved with the Black Liberation Army in the early 1970s.

For several years, Williams—then working with the New York University Urban Affairs and Poverty Law Program—served as the attorney for her niece and her codefendants against a series of legal charges involving a shootout with police. The case, which included the mysterious death of one of Williams's fellow attorneys, was chronicled in her 1993 autobiography, *Inadmissible Evidence: The Story of the African-American Trial Lawyer Who Defended the Black Liberation Army.*

Williams's high-profile defense of Shakur would cost her in more ways than she had imagined. During the 1980s, Williams again entered private practice, but she lost business after she became the target of an unsuccessful Federal Bureau of Investigation sting operation. From 1987 to 1989, Williams taught at City College of New York. By 1989, she had joined the firm of Stevens, Hinds & White in New York City.

11

POLITICS

Paulette Coleman
Robert D. Holsworth

RACE, POLITICS, AND GOVERNMENT

The history of African American participation in the political process is complex and includes multiple responses to the deliberate and systematic exclusion of African Americans from American life. In colonial times, most African Americans were enslaved and as such were denied the basic rights of citizenship. Legally, they were prohibited from voting and other means of political expression. Though they could not participate formally in the political process, enslaved Africans found other avenues for political expression, including various forms of resistance.

A small number of free African Americans were occasionally allowed to vote in certain places. There is evidence that some free African Americans voted in South Carolina's 1701 gubernatorial election. In the early eighteenth century, African Americans petitioned the courts and political leaders for legal protection but with limited success.

Prior to the Revolutionary War (1775–1783), political participation by African Americans was rare. Though so-called slave revolts were an exception, the revolutionary fervor of the times did not go unnoticed by African Americans. The revolutionary rhetoric resonated with the enslaved population and served as a catalyst for the filing of petitions with state legislatures and even with Congress to protest African enslavement. During the Revolutionary War, some freedmen saw military service as a way to be included as citizens in the new nation.

The American Colonization Society, founded by African Americans in 1816, promoted immigration to Africa. Members of this immigration movement eventually established the African nation of Liberia. Meanwhile, others immigrated to Canada, Central and South America, and island nations such as Haiti.

In 1830, free African Americans in Philadelphia convened the National Negro Convention. For two decades, the national convention movement continued its development as a mass self-help movement involving African American churches, fraternal organizations, and mutual-aid societies. The more militant participants became dominant in the convention by the 1850s. As a result, there was a growing dual determination to build African American institutions while demanding the rights of full participation as citizens of the United States.

The abolitionist movement of the 1830s was part of a multiracial quest for African American emancipation and equality. In addition to campaigning for civil rights through traditional legal means, the abolitionists took a daring step by operating the Underground Railroad system, a covert network of safe havens that assisted fugitive slaves in their flight to freedom in the North. Approximately fifty thousand enslaved Africans are believed to have escaped to the northern United States and Canada through the Underground Railroad prior to the Civil War (1861–1865).

In the 1850s, new efforts were made to exclude African Americans from citizenship with the passage of the Fugitive Slave Act (1850). Similarly, the Kansas-Nebraska Act (1854) attempted to extend black enslavement into new territories. The U.S. Supreme Court's decision in the *Dred Scott* (1857) case held that African Americans had no rights as U.S. citizens and that a state could not forbid black enslavement. These legal decisions convinced large numbers of African Americans and others that radical action was necessary. Among them were Martin Delany and Henry

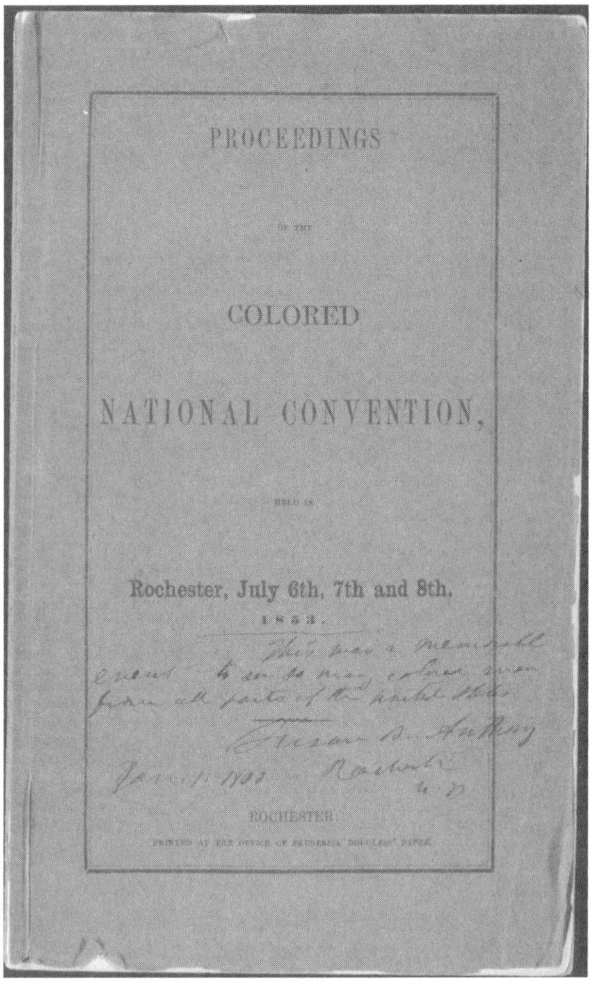

Proceedings of the Colored National Convention Held in Rochester July 6th, 7th, and 8th, 1853. *In a compromise between two factions of the African American community in the pre–Civil War era, the attendees of this convention advanced the idea of a separate African American society on U.S. soil.* THE LIBRARY OF CONGRESS

McNeal Turner, who advocated separation from the white race, and John Brown, who believed nothing short of a violent overthrow of African enslavement would yield any meaningful results. Frederick Douglass, who opposed efforts like those suggested by Brown, pushed for African Americans to seek rights through assimilation. The ultimate compromise between the two factions was proposed in 1853 when the Colored National Convention in Rochester, New York, advanced the idea of a separate African American society on American soil.

RECONSTRUCTION-ERA GAINS

The Union victory in the Civil War and the abolition of black enslavement under President Abraham Lincoln consolidated African American political support in the Republican Party. This affiliation lasted through the end of the nineteenth century and into the early decades of the twentieth century, even after the Republicans began to loosen the reins on the Democratic South in 1876 after the last federal troops were removed.

During the Reconstruction era, from 1865 to 1877, African Americans made significant gains toward increased participation in the political process. The Civil Rights Acts of 1866 and 1870 and the Fourteenth Amendment—ratified by the states in 1868—to the U.S. Constitution were intended to provide full citizenship with all its rights and privileges to all African Americans. For the first time, black males could participate legally in the electoral system. Among the rights that had been denied prior to these acts were the right to sue and be sued, the right to own real and personal property, and the right to testify and present evidence in legal proceedings.

The Fifteenth Amendment, ratified in 1870, granted African American men the right to vote. The voting-rights amendment failed, however, in its attempts to guarantee African Americans the real freedom to choose at the ballot box. Poll taxes, literacy tests, gerrymandered districts, and grandfather clauses were established by some state and local governments to deny African Americans their right to vote. The poll tax, for example, would not be declared unconstitutional until 1964, with the passage of the Twenty-fourth Amendment. Black codes also restricted the newly won freedom of African Americans by controlling their ability to move about the country, in spite of the fact that the Civil Rights Act of 1875 outlawed racial discrimination in hotels, inns, theaters, and other places of entertainment and public transportation.

Even though these legalized forms of exclusion presented obstacles to African American advancement in the politics of the United States, African Americans were able to achieve a degree of political participation during the Reconstruction era shortly after the end of the Civil War. Between 1879 and 1901, more than one thousand African Americans served in local and state elected offices, including a governor and six lieutenant governors. For example, Richmond, Virginia, had thirty-three black city council members between 1871 and 1896. In Atlanta, William Finch was elected to the city council. Likewise, Holland Thompson was elected to the city council of Montgomery, Alabama.

During that same time, there were twenty African American U.S. representatives and two U.S. senators. In 1869, Ebenezer Don Carlos Bassett became the first African American diplomat when he was appointed consul general to Haiti. In 1870, the Mississippi legislature elected Hiram R. Revels to represent the state in the U.S. Senate after that state was readmitted to the Union. Serving just over a year, Revels was the first African American U.S. senator. Blanche K. Bruce became the first African American elected to the U.S. Senate for a full six-year term in 1874.

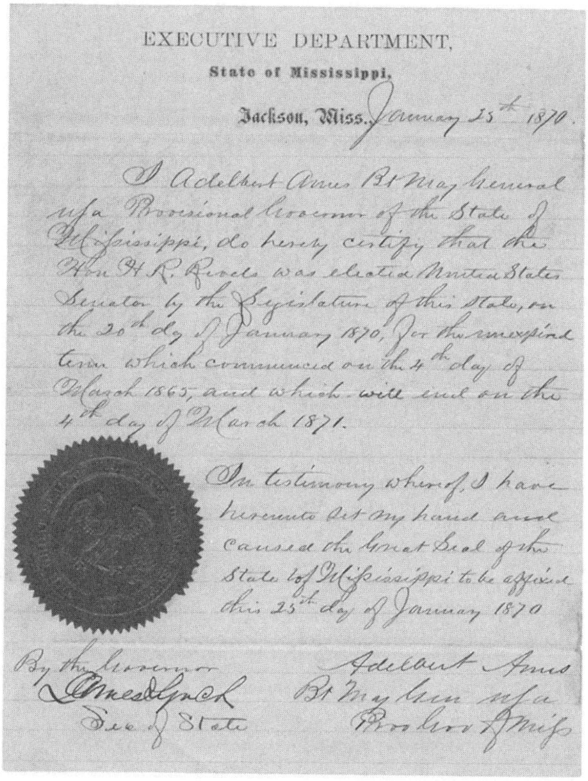
EXECUTIVE DEPARTMENT,
State of Mississippi,
Jackson, Miss. January 25th 1870.

I Adelbert Ames Bt Maj General U.S.A. Provisional Governor of the State of Mississippi, do hereby certify that the Hon H. R. Revels was elected United States Senator by the Legislature of this State, on the 20th day of January 1870, for the unexpired term which commenced on the 4th day of March 1865, and which will end on the 4th day of March 1871.

In testimony whereof, I have hereunto set my hand and caused the Great Seal of the State of Mississippi to be affixed this 25th day of January 1870

By the Governor
Jas Lynch
Sec of State

Adelbert Ames
Bt Maj Gen U.S.A.
Prov Gov of Miss

Credentials of Hiram Rhodes Revels, 1869. *Elected in 1870 by the Mississippi legislature to represent the state in the U.S. Senate, Revels was the first African American U.S. senator.* NATIONAL ARCHIVES

P. B. S. Pinchback won a U.S. Senate seat in 1873, but a vote by the other senators ousted him in 1876. The same thing happened one year earlier when, in 1875, Pinchback was removed from a House seat to which he had been elected in 1872. A colorful individual, Pinchback made enemies because his strong support of equal rights for African Americans and because of his gambling habit. Pinchback was the nation's first African American governor. Named lieutenant governor of Louisiana in 1871, Pinchback became acting governor after the impeachment of Governor Henry Clay Warmoth on bribery charges. Pinchback served forty-three days, but was defeated when an election was held for a new governor.

POST-RECONSTRUCTION DISENFRANCHISEMENT

In the mid-1870s, when the northern political and military presence withdrew from the South, black political participation diminished considerably. Voting fraud, voter intimidation, redistricting, and the transition from ward to at-large elections were among the factors that all but eliminated black participation in electoral politics. There were some exceptions, however, and among them was the 1896 election of George Henry White of North Carolina to Congress. White was in office from 1897 to 1901. Charles L. Mitchell and Edward G. Walker of Boston were elected to the state legislature in 1866. This was significant because they were the first African Americans elected to office from an urban area. In 1883, George L. Ruffin, a member of Boston's Common Council, became the first African American appointed to the Massachusetts judiciary.

Reconstruction came to an end in 1877 after considerable controversy about the 1876 presidential election. Rutherford B. Hayes, the Republican, claimed victory based on the electoral college vote, while Democratic candidate Samuel Tilden made a claim to the presidency as a result of the popular vote. Furthermore, the election results from Florida, South Carolina, and Louisiana were disputed. Hayes was declared the winner, but the controversy weakened the federal government's role in southern politics and the civil rights process.

As the government in Washington, D.C., withdrew support for the progressive policies on race instituted during the era of Reconstruction, African Americans witnessed a swift decline in their political power and an increased infringement on their civil rights. This assault was expressed in various ways, such as the Jim Crow laws, voting-rights abuses, and physical violence, including nearly 3,500 lynchings between 1889 and 1922. The lynchings occurred primarily in the southern states of Alabama, Georgia, Louisiana, and Mississippi, but also in some northern cities. After Reconstruction and with the elimination of African Americans from most southern electoral politics by 1889, most blacks were fighting against disenfranchisement in the South and seeking congressional support to prevent violations of their hard-won constitutional rights. In the post-Reconstruction period, there were more African Americans appointed to government or political posts than were elected.

During the nineteenth century, most African Americans were supporters of the Republican Party, but as the century drew to a close, a backlash occurred. In the 1890s, a group of white Republicans calling themselves the "Lily Whites" were heavily opposed to rights for African Americans and resented the presence of the so-called Black and Tan Republicans in their party. African Americans migrating from the South to the North were becoming increasingly disenchanted with the Republican Party and its efforts to gain support from conservative white voters. Further, there was no support from the Republican Party when issues of race arose in northern cities. African Americans began to question the benefits of supporting Republican Party candidates, although they remained locked into a pattern of almost automatic support for Republicans until the late 1920s.

By 1900, southern blacks were disenfranchised and northern blacks were not able to wield any significant political influence. During this period, black political power was almost nonexistent, with the exception of business and political leaders such as Robert Church Jr. in Memphis, Charles Anderson in New York City, and educator Booker T. Washington of Tuskegee, Alabama. By the turn of the twentieth century, Booker T. Washington had gained prominence as the chief spokesperson on behalf of African Americans and had considerable influence over Republican Party patronage. Recognized throughout the United States as a prominent African American leader and mediator, he advocated for accommodation as the preferred method of attaining civil rights. His leading opponents included journalist T. Thomas Fortune, an African American historian, and scholar W. E. B. Du Bois.

Fortune, who had founded the New York *Freeman* newspaper in 1884, attempted to create a national political organization for African Americans. His short-lived, Chicago-based National Afro-American League was aimed at remedying the disenfranchisement of African Americans. Du Bois, on the other hand, felt it was necessary to take more aggressive measures in the fight for equality. In addition to participating in the first Pan-African Conference in London in 1900, in 1905 he spearheaded the Niagara Movement, a radical African American intellectual forum. Members of the group merged with white progressives four years later to form the National Association for the Advancement of Colored People (NAACP). After Booker T. Washington's death in 1915, the NAACP became a greater force in the struggle for racial reform.

Women played a significant role at the turn of the century as well, coming together as the National Association of Colored Women (NACW) in 1896. The female activists met with success in their agitation for rights. Standouts included NACW founder Mary Church Terrell and NACW presidents Ida B. Wells-Barnett and Mary McLeod Bethune. Chief among their causes were speaking out against lynching and the promotion of women's rights. Arguably, ratification of the Nineteenth Amendment, which gave women of all races the right to vote in 1920, did not make that much of a practical difference in the lives of African American women.

THE IMPACT OF THE GREAT MIGRATION AND GREAT DEPRESSION

The migration of large numbers of blacks from the South to cities in the North and Midwest, coupled with their residential concentration, meant potential political power for African Americans. For example, Oscar DePriest, an African American Republican, was elected to Chicago's Board of Aldermen when a predominantly black district was created there. Later, in 1928, DePriest was elected the first northern black congressman.

Racist attitudes, combined with the desperate economic pressures of the Great Depression, exerted a profound effect on politics nationwide during the 1930s. Democrat Franklin D. Roosevelt won the presidency in 1932 with his reform agenda. He attracted African American voters with his "New Deal" relief and recovery programs. In addition to benefits from the socioeconomic programs of the New Deal, the growing activism of labor unions, and the consolidation of machine politics in big cities caused many African Americans to become aligned with the Democratic Party. For seventy years, African Americans had been faithful to the Republican Party, but their belief in Roosevelt and his New Deal led many to switch to the Democratic Party. African Americans, as well as others, benefited from the housing and employment opportunities that came about as a result of Roosevelt's programs. As beneficiaries of these new programs, African Americans saw a direct link between their votes for the Democratic Party and jobs, housing, and other benefits to their community. By 1936, most African Americans had switched to the Democratic Party. Democrats did not fully embrace a civil rights agenda, but offered more symbolic support for African Americans' demands for greater equality.

The Communist Party of the United States of America offered an alternative for African Americans alienated by the Republicans and the Democrats. White Communists actively recruited African Americans to their ranks, supporting civil rights through demonstrations and boycotts. They even selected an African American, James Ford, as their vice presidential candidate during the U.S. presidential campaigns of 1932, 1936, and 1940.

WORLD WAR II

World War II (1939–1945) ushered in an era of unswerving commitment to the fight for civil rights. As African Americans migrated to the North in search of jobs, several urban entities gained new concentrations of African Americans. In cities such as Detroit, New York, Philadelphia, and Cleveland, African Americans had such a presence that they swayed the course of local politics by the strength of their vote. At times, the African American vote affected the balance of power on the national front as well.

Adam Clayton Powell Jr. was elected the first African American member of the New York City Council in 1941. By 1944, Powell had gained a seat in the U.S. House of Representatives. As a House member, he challenged a white racist representative who refused to sit next to him. During his tenure, he also initiated legislation against lynching, poll taxes, and discriminatory job-hiring practices. The term *Powell amendment* referred to his attempts to tack antidiscriminatory measures onto each and every measure that came before the House.

THE POSTWAR MOVEMENT FOR AFRICAN AMERICAN RIGHTS

African Americans were advancing in all areas—national associations, political organizations, unions, the federal branch of the U.S. government, and the nation's court system. Civil rights became a national political issue when the Democratic National Convention adopted a strong civil rights platform that prompted protests by the white party faithful from the South. After Harry S. Truman was elected president, he contributed much to African American advancement by desegregating the military, establishing fair employment practices in the federal service, and beginning the trend toward integration in public accommodations and housing. In 1949, Representative William L. Dawson became the first African American to head a standing committee of Congress when he was elected chairman of House Committee on Expenditures. Meanwhile, the civil rights proposals of the late 1940s came to fruition a decade later during President Dwight D. Eisenhower's administration. Eisenhower's administrative aide, E. Frederic Morrow, was the first African American granted an executive position among White House staff.

After World War II, the African American populations in urban northern communities continued to grow as the white population moved from urban centers to the suburbs. In 1953, Hulan Jack, a New York state assemblyman, was elected Manhattan borough president. When the U.S. Supreme Court struck down the "white primary," which denied many African Americans the right to vote, more blacks registered, and they applied increased pressure for full voting rights. As black political power grew, efforts to neutralize it included at-large elections, annexation of suburbs with urban centers, the merging of black districts with white areas, and various forms of gerrymandering to dilute black voting strength.

The Civil Rights Act of 1957, also known as the Voting Rights Act of 1957, was the first major piece of civil rights legislation passed by Congress in more than eight decades. It expanded the role of the federal government in civil rights matters and established the U.S. Commission on Civil Rights to monitor the protection of African Americans' civil rights. The commission determined that unfair voting practices persisted in the South, with African Americans still being denied the right to vote in certain southern districts. Because of these abuses, a second act was passed in 1960 that offered more protection to African Americans at the polls. In 1965, the third Voting Rights Act was passed to eliminate literacy tests and safeguard African Americans' rights during the voter-registration process.

The postwar movement for African American rights yielded slow but significant advances in school desegregation and suffrage, despite bold opposition from some whites. By the mid- to late 1950s, as the African American fight for equality and progress gained momentum, white resistance continued to mount. The Reverend Martin Luther King Jr. took the helm of the fledgling civil rights movement and launched a multiracial effort to eliminate segregation and achieve equality for blacks through nonviolent resistance. The movement began with the boycott of city buses in Montgomery, Alabama, and by 1960, became a national crusade for black rights. During the course of the next decade, civil rights workers organized economic boycotts of racist businesses and attracted front-page news coverage with African American voter-registration drives and antisegregationist demonstrations, marches, and sit-ins. Bolstered by the new era of independence that was sweeping through sub-Saharan Africa, the movement for African American equality gained international attention, exposing glaring discrepancies between American ideals of freedom and its actual practice.

Racial tensions in the South reached violent levels with the emergence of new white supremacist organizations and an increase in Ku Klux Klan activity. Racially motivated discrimination in all arenas—from housing to employment—rose as southern resistance to the civil rights movement intensified. By the late 1950s, racist hatred had once again degenerated into brutality and bloodshed, with African Americans being murdered for the cause, and their white killers escaping punishment.

THE MODERN CIVIL RIGHTS MOVEMENT

Democrat John F. Kennedy gained the African American vote in the 1960 presidential elections. His domestic agenda espoused an expansion of federal action in civil rights cases, especially through the empowerment of the U.S. Department of Justice on voting-rights issues and the establishment of the Committee on Equal Employment Opportunity. Civil rights organizations continued their peaceful assaults against barriers to integration, but African American resistance to racial injustice was escalating. The protest movement heated up in 1961 when groups such as the Congress of Racial Equality (CORE), the Student Nonviolent Coordinating Committee (SNCC), and the Southern Christian Leadership Conference (SCLC) organized "freedom rides" that defied segregationist policies on public transportation systems.

Major demonstrations were staged in Birmingham, Alabama, under the leadership of King. Cries for equality met with harsh police action against the African American crowds. In 1963, Mississippi's NAACP leader, Medgar Evers, was assassinated. Meanwhile, on August 28, 1963, more than 200,000 black demonstrators and white demonstrators convened at the Lincoln Memorial to push for the passage of a new civil rights bill. This historic March on Washington, highlighted by King's legendary "I Have a Dream" speech, brought the promise of stronger legislation from the president. Leaders of the civil rights movement had been frustrated by the relatively slow pace of activity in the Kennedy administration, and political protest and direct action were crucial in prodding Kennedy to act.

After Kennedy's assassination that November, President Lyndon Baines Johnson initiated an aggressive civil rights program. The passage of the Civil Rights Act of 1964 sparked

Attack on Freedom Ride, 1961. *Freedom riders sit next to their bus after the vehicle was set on fire by a mob that had followed it out of Anniston, Alabama. In the early 1960s, several civil rights groups organized freedom rides that defied segregationist policies on public transportation systems.* **BETTMANN/CORBIS**

violence throughout the country, including turmoil in the cities of New York, New Jersey, Pennsylvania, and Illinois. The Ku Klux Klan stepped up its practice of intimidation with venomous racial slurs, cross burnings, firebombings, and acts of murder.

The call for racial reform in the South became louder early in 1965. King, who had been honored with the Nobel Peace Prize for his commitment to race relations, commanded the spotlight for his key role in the 1965 Freedom March from Selma to Montgomery, Alabama. African Americans were disheartened, however, by the lack of true progress in securing civil rights. Despite the legislative gains made over two decades, economic prospects for African Americans were bleak.

Black Power. African American discontent over economic, employment, and housing discrimination reached frightening proportions in the summer of 1965, with rioting in the Watts section of Los Angeles. This event marked a major change in the temper of the civil rights movement. Nearly a decade of nonviolent resistance had failed to remedy the racial crisis in the United States, and a more militant reformist element began to emerge. "Black Power" became the rallying cry of the middle and late 1960s, and more and more civil rights groups adopted all-black leadership. Groups such as the Black Panther Party emerged on the scene, promoting black self-determination, militant resistance, and self-defense. The Black Panther Party operated free breakfast and educational programs in their communities, with a special emphasis on children and youth. King's assassination in 1968 only compounded the nation's explosive racial situation. The new generation of African American leaders seemed to champion independence and separatism for African Americans, rather than integration into white American society.

THE FORMATION OF THE CONGRESSIONAL BLACK CAUCUS AND OTHER ELECTORAL ADVANCES

Although many African Americans despaired of winning justice within the American political system during this time of turmoil, there were many others who continued to work within the system on behalf of their brethren. Through the 1960s, some prominent African Americans served as members of Congress. Shirley Chisholm was elected to the U.S. House of Representatives in 1968, making her the first African American woman to serve in Congress. The next year, Charles Diggs Jr., a

Martin Luther King Jr. Displaying His Nobel Peace Prize Medal, Oslo, Norway, December 10, 1964. *During the following year, King, honored with the Nobel Prize for his commitment to race relations, commanded the spotlight for his key role in the 1965 Freedom March from Selma to Montgomery.* **AP IMAGES. REPRODUCED BY PERMISSION.**

member of the U.S. House of Representatives, founded the Democratic Select Committee, a group comprised of the eight other African American members of Congress. Two years later, they renamed themselves the Congressional Black Caucus (CBC). Small gains were also made with the elections of Carl Stokes in 1967 and Richard Hatcher in 1972 as the first African American mayors of Cleveland, Ohio, and Gary, Indiana, respectively. Andrew Young of Georgia and Barbara Jordan of Texas became the first African Americans elected to Congress from the South in the twentieth century. Also in 1972, more than five thousand African American activists and elected officials gathered in Gary, Indiana, for the First National Black Political Assembly. An important result of the meeting was a national strategy for black political empowerment.

In 1970, the creation of the Joint Center for Political Studies, geared toward monitoring political developments in the African American community, became one the CBC's most important contributions. Data provided by the Joint Center assisted the Reverend Jesse Jackson during his 1984 presidential campaign. After its founding, the center expanded to include economic studies and currently operates as the Joint Center for Political and Economic Studies.

The CBC also laid the groundwork for TransAfrica, a 40,000-person organization dedicated to African American foreign affairs. Founded by Randall Robinson in 1977, TransAfrica came about after the CBC protested against U.S. governmental policy toward minority white rule in such African nations as Rhodesia. Meeting with 130 leaders in September 1976, the CBC helped Robinson's initiative gain credibility.

In the 1990s, the CBC produced such leaders as Kweisi Mfume, who would later head the NAACP. In 2006, Mfume lost the Maryland Democratic primary in his bid for the U.S. Senate. In that same year, another former CBC member, Harold Ford Jr., ran a very competitive senatorial campaign, losing the senatorial race by less than three percentage points.

In the late 1970s, President Jimmy Carter moved assertively to help African Americans. During his tenure, he appointed African Americans to key cabinet positions. For

Black Panther "Black Power" Poster, on Display in Miami, FL, April 1968. *The Black Panther Party was among the political groups that emerged on the scene in the late 1960s, promoting black self-determination, militant resistance, and self-defense.* **AP IMAGES**

example, Andrew Young was named U.S. ambassador to the United Nations, and Patricia Roberts Harris became first the African American secretary of Housing and Urban Development and then secretary of Health, Education, and Welfare. Fear of black advancement led many whites to shift their allegiance to the Republican Party in the late 1960s. With the exception of Carter's term in office from 1977 to 1981, Republicans remained in the White House for the rest of the 1970s and 1980s. The rise of conservatism gave birth to such important figures as African American conservatives Thomas Sowell, Anne Wortham, and Shelby Steele. A new era of African American liberal activity began with the institution of Reverend Jesse Jackson's Rainbow Coalition. Despite two unsuccessful campaigns for the presidency in the 1980s, Jackson worked to ensure that the Democratic Party recognized the essential contribution made to it by African American voters.

In 1989, L. Douglas Wilder became the nation's first African American elected governor with his victory in Virginia. The Old Dominion was, to many observers, one of the most unlikely places for such an achievement to occur. Richmond had served for a time as the capital of the Confederacy. Virginia had been the home of "Massive Resistance" policy to the civil rights movement and to the *Brown v. Board of Education* decision in the 1950s. And Wilder had found that his first decision to seek statewide office—an ultimately successful run for lieutenant governor in 1985—was initially seen by many of his fellow Democrats as an act of supreme selfishness that would not only result in his defeat but the downfall of the entire party ticket. But campaigning as the moderate representative of the "New Mainstream" in Virginia, Wilder put together a coalition that included strong support from African Americans, and he obtained more than 42 percent of the white vote to achieve a historic victory. Many commentators thought that Wilder's success would lead to an immediate round of new electoral advances for African Americans, but it was seventeen years later in 2006 when Deval Patrick of Massachusetts became the country's second African American elected governor.

Jesse Jackson, Democratic National Convention, Atlanta, GA, 1988. *Jackson addresses the convention after finishing a strong second to Massachusetts Governor Michael Dukakis in the campaign for the Democratic presidential nomination.* PHOTOGRAPH BY DONN DUGHI. UPI/CORBIS-BETTMANN. REPRODUCED BY PERMISSION.

GROWTH IN AFRICAN AMERICAN PARTICIPATION IN POLITICS IN THE 1990s.

After a dozen years of conservatism under presidents Ronald Reagan and George H. W. Bush, Bill Clinton was elected in 1992 by projecting a moderate image, as Wilder had done in Virginia. Clinton espoused policies that would cut across the lines of gender, race, and economics and offered a vision of social reform, urban renewal, and domestic harmony for the United States. Once in office, Clinton appointed African Americans to key posts in his cabinet, and the African American population began wielding unprecedented influence in government.

In the 1990s, African American participation in government and politics was significant. Gary Franks became the only black Republican in Congress in 1990 when he was elected from Connecticut. He was joined four years later by another African American Republican, J. C. Watts Jr., an ordained Baptist minister, who had left the Democratic Party in 1989. Watts declined membership in the liberal CBC.

The year 1992 saw the election of the first black woman, Carol Moseley Braun, to the U.S. Senate. She shocked political observers by scoring a stunning upset over incumbent Senator Alan Dixon in the Democratic primary on March 17, 1992. In the November election, she was elected senator. Her term was marred by scandal, however, and she was defeated in 1998 in her bid for reelection. She served two years as ambassador to New Zealand and Samoa and ran unsuccessfully in the Democratic primary for president in 2004.

President Bill Clinton's cabinet included a record number of African Americans. Jesse Brown became the first African American to head the Veterans Affairs Department. In the second term, Togo West was named secretary of veterans affairs. In addition, Lee P. Brown was selected as head of the Office of National Drug Control Policy; Ron Brown was chosen as secretary of commerce; Dr. Joycelyn Elders was named U.S. surgeon general; Michael Espy was awarded the position of secretary of agriculture; Hazel O'Leary was chosen as secretary of energy; Rodney Slater was appointed secretary of transportation; and Clifton Wharton Jr. became the deputy secretary of the State Department. Clinton also nominated a number of African Americans to major positions in federal government agencies, including Jacqueline L. Williams-Bridgers to the State Department as inspector general and Shirley A. Jackson to the Nuclear Regulatory Commission as chairperson. As director of the White House Office of Public Liaison, African American Alexis Herman was one of the president's most trusted advisers and became secretary of labor during Clinton's second term. Also during Clinton's administration, the Justice Department's Civil Rights Division was headed by Deval Patrick, an African American who was elected governor of Massachusetts in 2006.

In 1996, Alan Keyes became the first African American Republican in modern times to seek the nomination of the party for the presidency. Keyes attracted little notice, however, and faded from the spotlight. After the reelection of President Clinton, the Supreme Court dealt African Americans a blow in a series of cases that invalidated "black majority" congressional districts. These gerrymandered districts were created to ensure African Americans were elected to the U.S. House of Representatives. The Court ruled in several cases—including *Reno, U.S. Attorney General, v. Bossier Parish School Board* (1999)—that race could not be the only factor in creating a district.

The Democratic Party has relied on African American voters to sustain Democratic candidates in tough elections. In the 1998 congressional elections, the Democrats, crippled by the personal, ethical, and legal scandals surrounding President Clinton, relied on the African American vote to prevent any losses in either chamber of Congress. Republican leaders acknowledged after the election that they needed to reach out to the African American community.

THE GEORGE W. BUSH ADMINISTRATION

In large part, the presidential election in 2000 confirmed the importance of the African American vote to the Democratic Party and to presidential candidate and then vice president Al Gore. Though the election took place on November 7, 2000, the outcome of the election was not official until December 12, when the U.S. Supreme Court decided that hand recounts of votes should be suspended immediately because the recount was unconstitutional. With that decision, the Supreme Court ended the controversy over chads, dimpled and pregnant ballots, and premature calls of the winner of the presidential election by the major networks. Many voters continue to argue that Al Gore won the popular vote and that the manual recounts of Miami-Dade, Broward, Palm Beach, and Volusia counties in Florida would have determined his victory. What is known is that many African Americans and some new immigrant voters experienced unprecedented scrutiny and some harassment in their efforts to vote. Whether there was a conspiracy to deny African Americans and others the right to vote remained hotly debated into 2002. As a result of this election debacle, reforms were discussed not only in Florida, but nationally.

George W. Bush, a Republican, became the forty-third president of the United States as a result of the hotly contested election. President Bush did not appoint as many African Americans as did President Clinton, but the appointments he did make were in very significant and nontraditional departments. Colin L. Powell, a retired four-star general, became the first African American head of the U.S. Department of State, making him the top diplomat in the country. Rodney Paige also was the first African American to hold his post when President Bush named him secretary of the Education

Department. President Bush also appointed Alphonso Jackson as secretary of the Department of Housing and Urban Development. Another significant appointment of a high-ranking African American by the Bush administration was the president's selection of Condoleezza Rice, former provost of Stanford University and a scholar of the Soviet Union, as his national security adviser. During President Bush's second term, Rice became the first African American and only the second woman secretary of state. As a result of these major appointments and the growing number of young, conservative African Americans, there is a reexamining of the African American community's relationship with the Democratic Party. For the foreseeable future, however, African Americans will continue to be closely allied with the Democratic Party, while pursuing options to maximize their political interests.

Barack Obama, an African American Democrat from Illinois, won his 2004 Senate race comfortably, becoming the fifth African American to serve in the U.S. Senate. Obama delivered the keynote address at the 2004 Democratic National Convention in Boston, Massachusetts. Echoes of voting irregularities surfaced around the country in the 2004 election. There were allegations of extremely long voting lines, malfunctioning voting machines, dissemination of incorrect information about location and hours of operation at voting sites, and other forms of voter suppression, especially in African American and other communities of color. Florida, Ohio, and Georgia were notable among the states in which there were numerous complaints during the 2004 elections.

In the 2006 midterm elections, national voter turnout rose less than 1 percent compared to 2002. Black voter turnout increased slightly and represented about 10 percent of the vote. In some of the larger states, such as California, New York, and Illinois, turnout increased modestly because there were no hotly contested races. In other states, where there was a significant increase in African American voter turnout, black voters were important in electing a Democratic governor in Ohio, reelecting Democratic governors in Michigan and Pennsylvania, and reelecting Democratic U.S. senators in Florida and Michigan. Large turnouts by blacks in Missouri, Ohio, Pennsylvania, and Virginia were critical in electing four new U.S. senators in those states. According to an analysis by the Joint Center for Political and Economic Studies, the black vote was somewhat more female than male in 2006. Young African American voters, independents, and African Americans in the Midwest gave 95 percent of their votes to Democratic congressional candidates.

In statewide elections in 2006, African American Democrats achieved victories in Massachusetts, where Deval Patrick was elected governor, becoming the second black since Reconstruction to hold a state's highest office. In addition, David Paterson succeeded in becoming New York's first black lieutenant governor. Paterson ascended to the governorship after a sex scandal led to the resignation of Governor Eliot Spitzer in 2008. Other African Americans who won statewide positions in 2006 were Anthony Brown, who became Maryland's lieutenant governor; Thurbert Baker, elected Georgia attorney general; Michael Thurmond, elected Georgia commissioner of labor; Jesse White, who became Illinois secretary of state; and Denise Nappier, who was elected Connecticut treasurer.

During the 2006 midterm elections, all black Democratic congressional incumbents won reelection except the beleaguered U.S. representative William Jefferson of Louisiana, who won later in a runoff. Three black Democratic candidates became newcomers to the U.S. House of Representatives: Hank Johnson of Georgia, Keith Ellison of Minnesota, and Yvette Clark of New York. Ellison became the first black U.S. representative from Minnesota and the first Muslim ever elected to the U.S. House. With the new Democratic majority in Congress after the 2006 elections, three Congressional Black Caucus members became chairs of full standing committees in the 110th Congress: John Conyers of Michigan chaired the House Judiciary Committee; Bennie Thompson of Mississippi chaired the House Homeland Security Committee; and Charles Rangel of New York chaired the powerful House Ways and Means Committee.

BARACK OBAMA AND THE 2008 ELECTIONS

In 2007, Senator Barack Obama announced his decision to seek the 2008 Democratic nomination for the presidency, hoping to capitalize on the accolades he had received for his 2004 convention speech and his extraordinary popularity with Democratic activists across the country. Senator Hillary Rodham Clinton of New York, the former first lady, had been anointed by the media as the frontrunner for the nomination and was widely perceived as the prohibitive favorite. But the Obama campaign became a force that far exceeded conventional expectations. Obama himself was an extraordinary candidate, drawing enthusiastic crowds that amazed even seasoned observers of presidential races. The organization of the campaign quickly became a likely model for political candidates in both parties. Obama's strategy was perfectly tailored to the mix of caucus and primary states that made up the Democratic Party's nominating process. The campaign raised far more money than any candidate ever had in a presidential election. And it utilized new technologies, especially social networking tools, to interact directly with voters, particularly young voters, with whom Obama developed very strong ties.

Obama's message in the nomination phase was also pitch perfect. He repeatedly criticized Clinton for her vote in support of the Iraq War, a sore point among the activist base of the party. At the same time, he promised a new form of politics that transcended party divisions and appealed to independent voters, who were allowed to participate in

Democratic Party primaries in a number of states. The Clinton campaign was put off stride by Obama's early successes, and, despite significant wins in a number of highly unionized Midwest and mid-Atlantic states, Clinton was never successful in blunting Obama's overall momentum and appeal.

The primary surge carried over into the general election. The Republican nominee, John McCain, attempted to distance himself from the unpopularity of the Bush administration. Yet despite his background as a Vietnam War hero and his reputation as a so-called maverick in the Senate, he was never able to convince Americans that he represented a real break from business as usual in Washington or that he was an individual who had a genuine vision for the future of America. By contrast, Obama continued to emphasize his primary themes about the need for a new form of politics that would change the culture of Washington and a renewed focus on the economy and jobs that would address the economic anxieties that were pervasive in the country.

Obama not only won the election with more than 52 percent of the vote, he transformed the electoral map, which had become relatively static in the previous eight years. Obama won states such as Virginia, which the Democrats had not carried in forty-four years. He also carried such states as Colorado and Nevada, which were undergoing major demographic transitions as the result of growing Latino populations. The size and scope of his victory worried Republican strategists, who feared that the GOP was becoming a regional party of the South and losing its national appeal.

Yet the realities of governing in a time of economic distress posed significant challenges for the Obama presidency in its first two years. Working with large Democratic majorities in both chambers of Congress, Obama was able to pass major legislation. A stimulus package designed to preserve jobs and maintain the capacities of state and local governments to provide citizen services was a major accomplishment in 2009. In 2010, Obama supported and signed a history-making reform of the American health-care system, one that promised to extend coverage to more than thirty million uninsured Americans and to require insurance companies not to deny coverage to individuals on the basis of preexisting conditions. But these accomplishments came with a significant political cost. Republicans maintained that the administration was too intrusive in the economy and was moving America far to the left. Obama's approval ratings through the first half of 2010 remained in positive territory, though a number of his policy initiatives polled less than majority support.

By the middle of 2010, it had become difficult to predict the trajectory of the Obama administration in terms of public support. Would an economic recovery revitalize his ratings, as had occurred for Ronald Reagan after the 1982 elections? Or had the public become so disenchanted with what had been described as "federal overreach" that Obama's reelection in 2012 was in jeopardy?

President Barack Obama, Joint News Conference with Hamid Karzai, President of Afghanistan, White House, Washington, DC, 2010. *One of the many challenges faced by Obama in the first years of his presidency was the ongoing war in Afghanistan.* CHIP SOMODEVILLA/GETTY IMAGES

CONGRESSIONAL BLACK CAUCUS MEMBERS (111th U.S. CONGRESS)

Chair, Rep. Barbara Lee
2444 Rayburn
(202) 225-2261
California

First Vice Chair, Rep. Emanuel Cleaver
1641 Longworth
(202) 225-4535
Missouri

Second Vice Chair, Rep. Donna Christensen
1510 Longworth

(202) 225-1790
Virgin Islands

Secretary, Rep. G. K. Butterfield
413 Cannon
(202) 225-3101
North Carolina

Whip, Rep. Yvette Clark
1029 Longworth
(202) 225-6231
New York

Rep. Sanford D. Bishop Jr.
2429 Rayburn
(202) 225-3631
Georgia

Rep. Corrine Brown
2336 Rayburn
(202) 225-0123
Florida

Sen. Roland Burris
523 Dirksen
(202) 224-2854
Illinois

Rep. André Carson
2455 Rayburn
(202) 225-4011
Indiana

Rep. William Lacy Clay Jr.
434 Cannon
(202) 225-2406
Missouri

Rep. James E. Clyburn
2135 Rayburn
(202) 225-3315
South Carolina

Rep. John Conyers Jr. (founding member)
2426 Rayburn
(202) 225-5126
Michigan

Rep. Elijah E. Cummings
2235 Rayburn
(202) 225-4741
Maryland

Rep. Artur Davis
208 Cannon
(202) 225-2665
Alabama

Rep. Danny Davis
2159 Rayburn
(202) 225-5006
Illinois

Rep. Donna Edwards
2470 Rayburn
(202) 225-8699
Maryland

Rep. Keith Ellison
1130 Longworth
(202) 225-4755
Minnesota

Rep. Chaka Fattah
2301 Rayburn
(202) 225-4001
Pennsylvania

Rep. Marcia Fudge
1009 Longworth
(202) 225-7032
Ohio

Rep. Al Green
425 Cannon
(202) 225-7508
Texas

Rep. Alcee L. Hastings
2353 Rayburn
(202) 225-1313
Florida

Rep. Jesse L. Jackson Jr.
2419 Rayburn
(202) 225-0773
Illinois

Rep. Sheila Jackson Lee
2160 Rayburn
(202) 225-3816
Texas

Rep. Eddie Bernice Johnson
1511 Longworth

(202) 225-8885
Texas

Rep. Hank Johnson
1133 Longworth
(202) 225-1605
Georgia

Rep. Carolyn Cheeks Kilpatrick
2264 Rayburn
(202) 225-2261
Michigan

Rep. John Lewis
343 Cannon
(202) 225-3801
Georgia

Rep. Kendrick Meek
1039 Longworth
(202) 225-4506
Florida

Rep. Gregory W. Meeks
2342 Rayburn
(202) 225-3461
New York

Rep. Gwen Moore
1239 Longworth
(202) 225-4572
Wisconsin

Rep. Eleanor Holmes Norton
2136 Rayburn
(202) 225-8050
Washington, D.C.

Rep. Donald M. Payne
2209 Rayburn
(202) 225-3436
New Jersey

Rep. Charles B. Rangel (founding member)
2354 Rayburn
(202) 225-4365
New York

Rep. Laura Richardson
2233 Rayburn
(202) 225-7924
California

Rep. Bobby L. Rush
2416 Rayburn
(202) 225-4372
Illinois

Rep. David Scott
417 Cannon
(202) 225-2939
Georgia

Rep. Robert C. Scott
1201 Longworth
(202) 225-8351
Virginia

Rep. Bennie G. Thompson
2432 Rayburn
(202) 225-5876
Mississippi

Rep. Edolphus Towns
2232 Rayburn
(202) 225-5936
New York

Rep. Maxine Waters
2344 Rayburn
(202) 225-2201
California

Rep. Diane E. Watson
125 Cannon
(202) 225-7084
California

Rep. Melvin L. Watt
2236 Rayburn
(202) 225-1510
North Carolina

GOVERNMENT OFFICIALS

(Some biographical profiles may appear in other chapters. To locate profiles more readily, please consult the index.)

DENNIS ARCHER (1942–)

Municipal Government Official, Attorney. Former Michigan State Supreme Court justice Dennis Archer became mayor of Detroit on January 3, 1994. During his campaign, he promised better city services, a tougher stance on crime, and increased incentives for businesses choosing to locate in the city. Following Coleman Young's combative reign, Archer represented a distinct change.

Born on January 1, 1942, in Detroit, Archer's family moved to Cassopolis, Michigan, when he was an infant. After graduating from Cassopolis High School in 1959, Archer worked his way through college. Following studies at Wayne State University and the Detroit Institute of Technology, Archer received his B.S. from Western Michigan University in 1965.

While working as a teacher of emotionally disturbed children he met Trudy DunCombe, who became his wife in 1967. Archer earned a J.D. from the Detroit College of Law in 1970. He practiced law for several years as a partner with Hall, Stone, Allen, Archer and Glenn, and later with Charfoos, Christensen and Archer, until he was appointed to the Michigan Supreme Court in 1985 by Governor James Blanchard.

Active in Democratic politics during the late 1970s and early 1980s, Archer directed campaigns for Mayor Coleman Young and Congressman George Crockett Jr. Archer's decision to run against Coleman Young in 1993 was a daunting proposition. Young, however, decided not to run for a sixth term, but backed Sharon McPhail, a former city council member and Archer's rival for the position.

Archer was considered the candidate of the white business establishment and was charged with being an upper-class elitist. He balanced these assessments by recalling the hard times of his early life and by going on record in support of the city's children, homeless, and disenfranchised. Though Archer did not receive the majority of the African American vote, he won the election with 57 percent of the overall vote.

High-profile economic-development projects, such as hosting the 1994 G-7 International Jobs Conference and building a downtown casino and a new stadium for the Detroit Tigers were among Archer's efforts to heal racial breaches and bring all of Detroit together with common goals. His first term was characterized by a robust economy, a balanced budget, a low unemployment rate, and downtown revitalization. Perhaps the most important legacy of Archer's first term in office was the restoration of civic pride and confidence in the city's future. Following his successful first term in office, Archer handily won a second term in 1997 with over 83 percent of the vote.

After his reelection, school reform became Archer's priority. His plan required new legislation at the state level that would wrest power and control of the schools from the locally elected school board. Under the reform scheme, the mayor would have the authority to appoint a new school board and the top administrators. Other aspects of the proposal for educational reform included reduced class size, the hiring of 1,200 new certified teachers, legislative benchmarks for assessing the school system's success or failure, mandatory summer school in particular cases, a substantial array of after-school programs, technical training for teachers, and site-based decision making.

In the spring of 1999, a group called the Black Slate spearheaded the effort to collect enough signatures to recall Archer. Backers of the recall cited such factors as the mayor's handling of a riverfront housing-development project, problems with snow removal in January 1999, damage done to Detroit's People Mover from the implosion of the J. L. Hudson building, and Archer's failure to grant one of Detroit's casino licenses to an African American. The recall effort failed.

Archer announced on April 16, 2001, that he would not seek a third term as mayor of Detroit. He did serve as president of the National League of Cities during his last year as mayor. Following his tenure, Archer returned to the law firm of Dickinson Wright PLLC as chairman. He became chairman emeritus in 2009. In 2002, Archer became the first African American president-elect of the American Bar Association; he served as president of that body from 2003 to 2004.

MARION BARRY (1936–)

Municipal Government Official. Marion Shepilov Barry was born in Itta Bena, Mississippi, on March 6, 1936, and grew up in Memphis, Tennessee. He earned a B.S. and M.S. in chemistry by 1960, and while a graduate student at Fisk University became active in NAACP politics and the civil rights movement. He eventually participated in founding the famous Student Nonviolent Coordinating Committee (SNCC), a civil rights protest group that made significant gains in erasing the last institutional vestiges of racism in the South. Barry was SNCC's first national chairperson.

After he moved to Washington, D.C., in the mid-1960s, Barry became active in local politics through efforts to move the capital city toward self-government free from congressional interference. Among other achievements, he was instrumental in obtaining federal funding for a citywide youth employment and community-service program and was elected to the local school board in 1970. When the "Free D.C." political movement succeeded in loosening congressional rule over the city, Barry ran for a seat on its first council, which he held for three years.

In 1977, Barry was wounded in an altercation involving the seizure of Washington's District Building by radical Muslims. Elected mayor in 1978, over the next few years his administration was marked by both controversy and achievement. His former wife was charged with embezzling federal funds, but Barry himself was never under any suspicion. As mayor, he initiated programs to improve employment opportunities and housing conditions for Washington's more disadvantaged neighborhoods. During Barry's administration, access to contracting opportunities increased for women- and minority-owned businesses. One of the hallmarks of Barry's tenure as mayor was the launching of large numbers of youth development and summer-employment programs. He was reelected in 1982 and again in 1986. Near the end of his third term, Barry was indicted by a federal grand jury for drug possession. He was convicted of a misdemeanor for usage after being filmed snorting crack cocaine. He served the maximum six months.

Despite the setback, Barry's support among his Washington, D.C., constituency did not diminish. In 1992, he again won a city council seat, and he ran successfully for mayor in 1994. His fourth term was sullied when Congress established a control board in 1995 to oversee the district's financial recovery. The city faced a growing debt in excess of $722 million. In 1997, Congress and the president extended the control board's power to nearly every facet of the D.C. government, thus stripping Barry of most of his executive power. He did not seek reelection.

In 2004, Barry ran in the Democratic primary for the Ward Eight council seat he had held prior to becoming mayor. He won the general election with more than 95 percent of the vote. Barry pleaded guilty to misdemeanor charges of failing to pay local and federal taxes and was sentenced to three years probation. Throughout his legal problems and struggle with addiction, Barry continued to serve on the council and to work as an investment-banking consultant.

SIDNEY JOHN BARTHELEMY (1942–)

Sociologist, Municipal Government Official, State Legislator. Sidney Barthelemy was born in New Orleans on March 17, 1942. He attended Epiphany Apostolic Junior College in Newburgh, New York, from 1960 to 1963 with the intent of entering the priesthood. In 1967, Barthelemy received a B.A. from St. Joseph Seminary in Washington, D.C. Two years later, he earned an M.S.W. from Tulane University. After graduation, Barthelemy worked in administrative and professional positions in various organizations, including Total Community Action, the Parent-Child Development Center, Family Health Inc., and the Urban League of New Orleans. From 1972 to 1974, Barthelemy was the director of the Welfare Department of the City of New Orleans. In 1974, he was elected to the Louisiana State Senate. Barthelemy left the state legislature in 1978 after winning a seat on the New Orleans City Council, where he stayed until his 1986 election as mayor.

Barthelemy was mayor for eight years during the economic slump and oil-bust period of high unemployment. New Orleans faced a $30 million deficit, which he gradually eliminated. During his tenure, riverboat gambling and land-based casinos were legalized. He recognized tourism as a major economic engine for his city and was successful in New Orleans' selection as the host city for the 1988 Republican Convention and the National Collegiate Athletic Association (NCAA) Final Four tournament in 1993. He also oversaw the opening of the Aquarium of the Americas and other projects, as well as the historic visit of Pope John Paul II in 1987.

Barthelemy taught at Xavier University as an associate professor of sociology from 1974 to 1986. He also taught at Tulane University and the University of New Orleans. In addition, he was vice chairman for voter registration for the Democratic National Party, second vice president for the National League of Cities, and president of the Louisiana Conference of Mayors. Barthelemy belongs to the NAACP, the National Association of Black Mayors, the Democratic National Committee, the National Institute of Education, the National League of Cities, and the New Orleans Association of Black Social Workers. He has won numerous awards, including Outstanding Alumnus of Tulane University and the 1987 Louisiana Chapter of the National Association of Social Workers' Social Worker of the Year Award. He has also received the American Freedom Award presented by the Third Baptist Church of Chicago (1987), the American Spirit Award given by the U.S. Air Force Recruiting Service (1989), and the NAACP's New Orleans Chapter Daniel E. Byrd Award (1990).

In 1993, Barthelemy decided not to seek another term as mayor of New Orleans and returned to teaching. He also began working in governmental affairs for a real-estate development company in New Orleans, and joined other city and state officials in formulating flood-protection plans after Hurricane Katrina hit the region in 2005.

SHARON SAYLES BELTON (1951–)

Municipal Government Official. Sharon Sayles Belton was born in St. Paul, Minnesota, in 1951. She attended Macalester College, but dropped out before graduating when she became pregnant. Belton worked in the Twin Cities as a volunteer, eventually establishing a series of rape shelters in the area. Her community involvement led her to pursue a city council seat in Minneapolis. She was elected to the city council in 1984, representing the Eighth Ward. In 1993, Belton made the decision to run for mayor. She was endorsed by incumbent mayor Don Fraser and won nearly 60 percent of the vote, despite the fact that less than a quarter of the voters were African American.

Belton served as mayor of Minneapolis from 1994 to 2001. As mayor, she sought to build coalitions to solve the city's problems, as she had done while serving as a member of the city council. She reduced crime rates by redirecting resources to public safety and by deploying more police officers to high-crime areas. She also appointed many women and minorities to positions of power within the city government, changing the political culture in Minneapolis. Belton was reelected to a second term in 1997, but lost a bid for a third in 2000. In May 2002, Belton joined the University of Minnesota's Humphrey Institute of Public Affairs as a senior fellow in the Roy Wilkins Center for Human Relations and Social Justice, where she works on antiracism initiatives, information sharing between community organizations and academic institutions, and leadership development among people of color and new immigrants.

MARY FRANCES BERRY (1938–)

Educator, Federal Government Official, Civil Rights Activist, Attorney. Mary Frances Berry was born in 1938 in Nashville, Tennessee. She received her B.A. from Howard University in 1961 and her M.A. in 1962. In 1966, she received a Ph.D. from the University of Michigan. She earned her J.D. from the University of Michigan Law School in 1970. Berry worked for several years as a professor of history and law at various universities throughout the United States. She was appointed assistant secretary of education in the U.S. Department of Health, Education, and Welfare (HEW) by President Jimmy Carter in 1977. Prior to her stint at HEW, Berry was provost at the University of Maryland, College Park, and chancellor at the University of Colorado at Boulder.

In 1980, Berry was appointed by President Carter and confirmed by the Senate as a commissioner and vice chairman of the U.S. Commission on Civil Rights. She was fired from the commission by President Ronald Reagan in 1983 for criticizing his civil rights policies. Berry sued the president and won reinstatement in federal court. On November 19, 1993, President Bill Clinton named her chair of the Commission on Civil Rights. He reappointed her to the commission for another six-year term in 1999. In her role as chair, Berry led the investigation that examined minority voter disenfranchisement in Florida during the 2000 presidential election. During her tenure, the commission also issued major reports on police practices in New York, environmental justice, percentage plans and affirmative action, and church burnings. Berry left office in 2004 before her term expired. She was succeeded by Gerald A. Reynolds, an African American Republican. Since 1987, Berry has been the Geraldine R. Segal Professor of American Social Thought at the University of Pennsylvania, where she teaches law and history.

Berry was once again in the public eye when she was unanimously selected in 1997 to become chair of the Pacifica Radio Board. The board initiated new policies and changes in the station's programming and format, which led to protests, litigation, and widespread opposition. Berry left the board at the end of her term.

Berry has published numerous articles and essays. Her books include: *Black Resistance, White Law: A History of Constitutional Racism in America* (1971); *Military Necessity and Civil Rights Policy: Black Citizenship and the Constitution, 1861–1868* (1977); *Long Memory: The Black Experience in America*, written with John Blassingame (1982); *Why ERA Failed: Politics, Women's Rights, and the Amending Process of the Constitution* (1986); *The Politics of Parenthood: Child Care, Women's Rights, and the Myth of the Good Mother* (1993); *The Pig Farmer's Daughter and Other Tales of American Justice: Episodes of Racism and Sexism in the Courts from 1865 to the Present* (1999); *My Face Is Black Is True: Callie House and the Struggle for Ex-Slave Reparations* (2005); *And Justice for All: The United States Commission on Civil Rights and the Continuing Struggle for Freedom in America* (2009); and *Power in Words: The Stories behind Barack Obama's Speeches, from the State House to the White House* (2010), written with Josh Gottheimer.

UNITA BLACKWELL (1933–)

Municipal Government Official, Civil Rights Activist. Unita Blackwell was born on March 18, 1933, in the small Delta town of Lula, Mississippi. The daughter of sharecroppers, Blackwell's family constantly migrated between Arkansas, Mississippi, and Tennessee in search of work. This transitory lifestyle lasted well into her early adulthood. Blackwell worked throughout the South at such jobs as chopping cotton and peeling tomatoes, until she finally settled in Mayersville, Mississippi, in 1962.

Initially, Blackwell's lack of an education beyond eighth grade kept her in the fields, but she also became involved with the Student Nonviolent Coordinating Committee's (SNCC) activities in Mississippi. Blackwell began canvassing the state on behalf of SNCC, organizing and registering African American voters. In 1964, Blackwell joined fellow activist Fannie Lou Hamer in the formation of the Mississippi Democratic Freedom Party. The party challenged the white-controlled Democratic political machine in the state, pushing for laws preventing black children's employment as sharecroppers and establishing African American schools that would teach mathematics and science. In 1967, Blackwell cofounded Mississippi Action Community Education, an organization that promoted the incorporation of rural districts into towns, enabling them to get government aid for the installation of streetlights and electricity. Her work as a community-development specialist with the National Council of Negro Women in the early 1970s led to the building of low-income housing units throughout the South and in Puerto Rico.

When Blackwell was elected mayor of Mayersville in 1976, she became the first African American woman mayor in Mississippi. During her tenure, the city paved the roads and acquired streetlights, a fire truck, and a sewer system. She also instituted an effective food-assistance program and sponsored the construction of housing for the elderly and disabled. In 1982, Blackwell earned a master's degree in regional planning from the University of Massachusetts at Amherst. She was elected president of the National Conference of Black Mayors in 1990, a position she held until 1992. Blackwell remained mayor of Mayersville until 2001.

Blackwell was a fellow at Harvard University's John F. Kennedy School of Government in 1991. In 1992, she received a MacArthur Foundation "Genius Award." She also received a Southern Christian Leadership Award (1992) and the American Planning Association's Leadership Award for elected officials (1994). She published her autobiography, *Barefootin': Life Lessons from the Road to Freedom*, written with JoAnne Pritchard Morris, in 2006.

JULIAN BOND (1940–)

State Legislator, Civil Rights Activist, Organization Executive, Educator, Media Personality and Executive. Horace Julian Bond was born on January 14, 1940, in Nashville, Tennessee. His father, Dr. Horace Mann Bond, was an eminent scholar and the first African American president of Lincoln University in Pennsylvania, where the family lived until Dr. Bond became dean of the School of Education at Atlanta University. After graduating from a Quaker school in 1957, Julian Bond entered Morehouse College. He was not an exceptional student, but he won a varsity letter in swimming and was one of the founders of the *Pegasus*, a literary magazine.

While at Morehouse, Bond developed an interest in civil rights activism. He and several other students formed the Atlanta Committee on Appeal for Human Rights (COAHR). COAHR held nonviolent direct-action anti-segregation protests for three years, winning integration of Atlanta's movie theaters, lunch counters, and parks. These activities attracted the attention of Dr. Martin Luther King Jr. and other civil rights leaders, who invited the students, among them Bond, to Shaw University in North Carolina to help devise new civil rights strategies. At this conference, the Student Nonviolent Coordinating Committee (SNCC) was created as an autonomous organization. SNCC eventually absorbed COAHR, and Bond accepted a position as the SNCC director of communications. In this position, he edited the SNCC newsletter, *Student Voice*, and organized voter-registration drives in the rural South.

In 1965, Bond campaigned for a seat in the Georgia House of Representatives, and won a one-year term in a special election following court-ordered reapportionment of the state legislature. As he prepared to take his seat he became embroiled in controversy when he announced his opposition to U.S. involvement in Vietnam. This stance outraged many conservative members of the Georgia House of Representatives, and on January 10, 1966, they voted to prevent Bond's admission to the legislature. Bond sought legal recourse to overturn this vote, and the case eventually went to the U.S. Supreme Court. On December 5, 1966, the Court ruled that the Georgia House vote was a violation of Bond's First Amendment right of free speech and ordered that he be admitted to the legislature. The members of the Georgia House of Representatives reluctantly allowed Bond to take his seat, but they treated him as an outcast.

In 1968, Bond and several other members of the Georgia Loyal National Delegation to the Democratic Convention protested Governor Lester Maddox's decision to send only six African American delegates out of 107 to the Democratic National Convention. Bond and his supporters arrived at the convention and set up a rival delegation. After several bitter arguments with Georgia's official delegation, Bond's delegation captured nearly half of Georgia's delegate votes. He became the Democratic Party's first African American candidate for the U.S. vice presidency, but withdrew his name because he did not meet the minimum age requirement.

From 1978 to 1989, Bond was president of the Atlanta branch of the NAACP. He was elected to the Georgia Senate in 1975 and remained a member until 1987. In 1976, he declined an invitation to become a part of President Jimmy Carter's administration. Bond ran for a seat in the U.S. Congress in 1986 but lost the election to John Lewis. In 1989, he divorced his wife after twenty-eight years of marriage. During the bitter divorce proceedings, allegations of drug use surfaced. Shortly thereafter, Bond became embroiled in a paternity suit. He initially denied the allegations, but admitted in May 1990 to fathering the child and was ordered to pay child support.

Bond has served as a visiting professor at Drexel and Harvard universities. He is a lecturer and writer and is often called upon to comment on political and social issues. Bond hosted the long-running television program *America's Black Forum* and served as narrator for the highly acclaimed public television series *Eyes on the Prize*, as well as a film on the life of artist Henry O. Tanner, the documentary *The American Experience: Duke Ellington—Reminiscing in Tempo*, and the Academy Award–winning documentary, *A Time for Justice*. Bond also wrote a nationally syndicated newspaper column.

In 1994, Bond became involved in a power struggle with NAACP board chairman William Gibson, which cost Bond his position on the board. In 1998, Bond was elected chair of the NAACP board of directors and chair of the board of the NAACP's magazine, the *Crisis*. He is currently a distinguished scholar-in-residence at American University and a professor of history at the University of Virginia, where he is also codirector of Explorations in Black Leadership.

Bond has written and edited a number of books, including *Black Candidates: Southern Campaign Experiences* (1968); *Mose T's Slapout Family Album* (1996), with Robert Ely; and *Lift Every Voice and Sing: A Celebration of the Negro National Anthem* (2000), edited with Sondra Kathryn Wilson. A collection of Bond's essays, *A Time to Speak, a Time to Act*, was published in 1972.

CORY BOOKER (1969–)

Attorney, Municipal Government Official. Cory Anthony Booker represents a new breed of African American politicians who reached adulthood in the post–civil rights era. They are often populists or social justice activists with Ivy League educations and corporate experience. Some veteran politicians are critical of newcomers like Booker and their crossover appeal.

Cory Booker, Mayor of Newark, NJ, 2007. *The son of civil rights activists, Booker was elected mayor of Newark in 2006 and was reelected four years later. Among the areas of focus for his administration were reducing crime, improving housing, and creating high-achieving schools.* JOHN O'BOYLE/STAR LEDGER/CORBIS

Born on April 27, 1969, in Washington, D.C., to civil rights activists, Booker's parents were among the first African American managers at IBM. He grew up in Harrington Park, New Jersey, an affluent, predominantly white community. Booker earned his B.A. in political science in 1991 from Stanford University, where he was a scholar, athlete, and leader. He was elected to Stanford's Council of Presidents, played varsity football, and ran a student-run crisis hotline. Following the completion of his master's degree in sociology at Stanford in 1992, Booker won a Rhodes Scholarship. He studied at Oxford University for two years and was awarded a degree in modern history with honors in 1994.

Upon returning to the United States, Booker entered Yale Law School and earned his J.D. in 1997. While in law school, he started and operated free legal clinics for poor people in New Haven, mentored young boys through the Big Brother program, and was active in the Black Law Students Association.

After graduation, Booker moved back to New Jersey, where he worked as a staff attorney for the Urban Justice Center in New York and program coordinator of the Newark Youth Project. Booker attracted public attention when he moved into the Brick Towers, an infamous public housing project, and began organizing the tenants.

Booker's first political race was in 1998, when he successfully unseated a four-term incumbent to get elected to the Newark City Council. As a council member, he was principled and outside the conventional political mode. He went on a hunger strike, protested open-air drug dealing, and lived in a motor home for five months on various street corners to bring attention and police action to known drug-trafficking locations. In spite of his energy and penchant for drawing media attention to important social issues, such as housing, drug abuse, and education, in Newark, many of his council bills were overwhelmingly defeated by a seven-vote bloc of his council colleagues.

When Booker decided to run for the Newark mayor's office in 2002, his opponent, Sharpe James, was a five-term veteran of the mayor's office and a local political powerhouse. The hotly contested and brutal mayoral race received national media attention and was the subject of the 2005 documentary *Street Fight*, which received an Academy Award nomination. James won the race with 53 percent of the vote to Booker's 47 percent.

In 2003, Booker founded Newark Now, a nonprofit organization. He also became a partner in a New Jersey law firm and a fellow in public policy and planning at Rutgers University. Booker announced his second candidacy for mayor of Newark in 2006. Ron Rice, a veteran state senator and council member, who was serving as deputy mayor, also announced his intention to run for mayor, provided Mayor James did not seek reelection. James did not seek reelection as mayor, but continued to serve in the New Jersey Senate.

Booker had at least a $6 million campaign fund, which enabled him to run a very professional and effective campaign. With 72 percent of the vote, he won a resounding victory over Rice. The entire slate of victorious council candidates had allied themselves with Booker.

On July 1, 2006, Booker was sworn in as mayor. For almost four decades, only two other people had held that position, Kenneth Gibson and Sharpe James. Reducing crime, especially drug trafficking, improving housing and other quality-of-life indicators for all Newark residents, working for high-achieving schools while improving educational options for students, and being accessible to city residents were among the areas of focus for Mayor Booker's administration. He was reelected to a second term as mayor in May 2010.

THOMAS BRADLEY (1917–1998)

Civil Rights Activist, Municipal Government Official, Organization Executive, Attorney. Thomas Bradley was born December 29, 1917, in Calvert, Texas, the son of a sharecropper. In 1924, he moved with his family to Los Angeles, where he graduated from Polytechnic High School in 1937 and attended the University of California, Los Angeles, on an athletic scholarship. He excelled at track before quitting college in 1940 and joining the Los Angeles Police Department (LAPD). While a member of the police force, Bradley worked as a detective and a community-relations officer and in the department's juvenile division. In the early 1950s, Bradley began studying law at two Los Angeles universities, Loyola University and later Southwestern University. He was awarded an LL.B. from Southwestern University in 1956. Bradley stayed with the LAPD until 1961, when he entered private law practice.

In 1963, Bradley became the first African American elected to the Los Angeles City Council. He was reelected in 1967 and 1971. In the 1973 election, Bradley became mayor of Los Angeles, winning 56 percent of the vote. During his time as mayor, Bradley was both lauded and criticized. His defenders credited him with opening city government to minorities and women, expanding social services to the urban poor, and spurring growth. While Bradley was mayor, Los Angeles overtook San Francisco as the West Coast's financial center and gained international prominence. Though Bradley is credited with turning Los Angeles into a modern metropolis, his detractors accused him of not keeping up with the city's problems.

One of the toughest situations Bradley faced was the 1992 riots that followed the announcement of not-guilty verdicts for the LAPD officers who were charged with beating African American motorist Rodney King. Bradley was vilified for what some considered to be his lack of response to the incident. Many demanded the firing of Police Chief Daryl Gates. Under the limits of the law, however, Bradley could do no more than ask Gates to resign. Though Gates eventually did leave his post, many considered the situation a serious challenge to Bradley's authority.

Bradley did attempt to heal the community in other ways. Even before the rioting had ended, he set up the nonprofit organization Rebuild LA. That organization was criticized for creating unreal expectations, but Bradley's Neighbor to Neighbor group was viewed in a positive light. Comprised of nearly eight hundred volunteers, the outreach group regularly canvassed neighborhoods to give residents an outlet for discussing problems and to help citizens organize in order to solve their own difficulties. In a second trial, two of the four police officers charged with violating Rodney's King's civil rights were found guilty.

One of Bradley's final acts as a city official was to sign a bill that banned smoking in all restaurants. He was honored for his years of service by the U.S. Conference of Mayors in June 1993. He officially left the mayoral post on July 1, 1993, ending a thirty-year public career. After his last term, Bradley returned to the private practice of law. He was then ensnared in a political-finance scandal that also caught other California lawmakers, including Governor Pete Wilson and Senator Dianne Feinstein. Laundered campaign funds were traced to Evergreen America Corp., the world's largest container-shipping company. The Los Angeles Ethics Commission ordered Bradley and others to repay a total of $15,000, but Bradley refused, claiming he did not know the money had been improperly donated.

Bradley served as president of the National League of Cities and the Southern California Association of Governments. He also belonged to the Urban League of Los Angeles and was a founding member of the NAACP's Black Achievers Committee. On the national level, he served on President Gerald Ford's National Committee on Productivity and Work Quality and on the National Energy Advisory Council. Bradley won numerous awards and honors, including the 1974 University of California's Alumnus of the Year, the 1974 Thurgood Marshall Award, the 1978 Award of Merit given by the National Council of Negro Women, and the NAACP's 1985 Spingarn Medal.

EDWARD W. BROOKE (1919–)

Attorney, Federal Legislator. Edward William Brooke III was born on October 26, 1919, in Washington, D.C. He moved to Massachusetts and, in a state that was overwhelmingly Democratic and in which African Americans constituted only 3 percent of the population, became a popular Republican figure. He first achieved statewide office in 1962 when he defeated Elliot Richardson to become attorney general. His record in that post led to his 1966 election to the U.S. Senate over former Massachusetts governor Endicott Peabody.

Born into a middle-class environment, Brooke attended public schools and went on to graduate from Howard University in 1941. Inducted into an all–African American infantry unit during World War II, Brooke rose to the rank of captain and was ultimately given a Bronze Star for his work in intelligence. Returning to Massachusetts after the war, Brooke attended the Boston University Law School, compiling a top academic record and editing the school's law review. After completing law school in 1948, he established himself as an attorney and also served as chairman of the Boston Finance Commission from 1961 to 1962.

In 1962, Brooke was nominated for the attorney general's office. He encountered stiff opposition within his own party, but won both the Republican primary and the general election against his Democratic opponent. Brooke was elected to the U.S. Senate in November 1966, becoming the first popularly elected African American U.S. Senator. In the Senate, Brooke espoused the notion that the Great Society could not become a reality until it was preceded by the "Responsible Society," which he described as a society in which "it's more profitable to work than not to work. You don't help a man by constantly giving him more handouts." Initially, he strongly supported U.S. participation in the Vietnam War, though most African American leaders were increasingly opposing it. However, in 1971, Brooke supported the McGovern-Hatfield Amendment that called for withdrawal of the United States from Vietnam.

Matters of race, rather than foreign affairs, were to become Brooke's area of expertise in the Senate. Brooke was a cautious legislator, but as pressure mounted from civil rights groups and African American militants he decided to attack President Richard Nixon's policies. Brooke was roused into a more active role by the administration's vacillating school-desegregation guidelines, its firing of Department of Health, Education, and Welfare (HEW) official Leon Panetta, and the nominations to the U.S. Supreme Court of judicial conservatives Clement Haynsworth and G. Harrold Carswell.

Brooke was reelected to the Senate overwhelmingly in 1972, even though Massachusetts was the only state not carried by his party in the presidential election. Although Brooke seconded the nomination of President Nixon at the 1972 Republican Convention, he became increasingly critical of the Nixon administration. He also began appearing publicly at meetings of the Congressional Black Caucus, a group he had earlier avoided. Brooke was considered a member of the moderate wing of the Republican Party. In 1978, his bid for a third term in the Senate was denied by Democrat Paul Tsongas. He returned to private law practice following his Senate career.

Brooke was the recipient of more than thirty honorary degrees and various awards, including the NAACP Spingarn Medal and the National Conference of Christians and Jews' Charles Evans Hughes Award. In 1996, Brooke became the first chairman of Alpha Phi Alpha's World Policy Council, a think tank established to broaden the fraternity's involvement in international affairs.

In 2002, Brooke was diagnosed with breast cancer and became involved in raising national awareness of the disease among men. In 2004, he was awarded the Presidential Medal of Freedom for his "especially meritorious contribution to the security or national interests of the United States, world peace, cultural or other significant public or private endeavors." He was awarded the Congressional Gold Medal in 2008. Brooke published a memoir, *Bridging the Divide: My Life*, in 2007.

LEE P. BROWN (1937–)

Municipal Government Official. Lee Patrick Brown was born in Wewoka, Oklahoma, on October 4, 1937. He began his professional career in law enforcement in 1960 as a police officer in San Jose, California. He earned his bachelor's degree in criminology that same year from Fresno State University. In 1964, Brown received his master's degree in sociology from San Jose State University. He earned a second master's degree in 1968 and his Ph.D. in criminology in 1970 from the University of California, Berkeley.

Brown embarked on a university teaching career with an appointment as assistant professor at San Jose State in 1968. After earning his second master's, he established the Department of Administration of Justice at Portland State University in Oregon, becoming chairman at the rank of professor. In 1972, Brown joined the faculty at Howard University as associate director of the Institute of Urban Affairs and Research, professor of public administration, and director of criminal justice programs.

In 1974, Brown returned to law enforcement as sheriff of Multnomah County in Oregon, a position he held until 1976, when he became director of the state's Department of Justice Services. After an extensive national search, Brown was selected as public safety commissioner of Atlanta, a position he held from 1978 to 1982. As safety commissioner, he was responsible for Atlanta's police, fire, corrections, and civil defense departments. During his tenure, the police department solved the Atlanta child murders cases.

From 1982 to 1990, Brown served as chief of police of Houston, Texas. His appointment by Mayor Kathy Whitmire marked the first time an African American had been named Houston's police chief. Brown was an innovative and transformative leader. He reformed the troubled Houston Police Department and pioneered the concept of community policing. The Houston Police Department became a model agency, and Brown became known as the "father of community policing." During this period, Brown returned to teaching when he became a professor at Texas Southern University and director of the university's Black Male Initiative Program. Following his success in Houston, he was selected to serve as police commissioner of New York City, where he implemented community policing citywide and oversaw a dramatic reduction in crime in the city.

In 1993, President Bill Clinton nominated Brown for the post of director of the Office of National Drug Control Policy. He was unanimously confirmed by the U.S. Senate and sworn in as a member of the president's cabinet on June 21, 1993. As "drug czar," Brown shifted the nation's drug-control strategy to place more emphasis on reducing the demand for drugs.

Brown was elected mayor of Houston, America's fourth largest city, in 1997. He presided over one of the most prosperous periods in the history of that city. During Brown's administration, Houston revitalized the downtown area; started its first light-rail system; expanded public transportation with increased bus service, park and ride, and high-occupancy vehicle lanes; built and opened new state-of-the-art sports venues (football, baseball, and basketball); built and renovated libraries and police and fire stations; constructed the Hobby Center for the Performing Arts; doubled the size of the city's convention center; and increased the number of foreign consulates.

Brown was reelected in 1999. In 2001, he was narrowly reelected to a third term as mayor in a hotly contested race against city council member Orlando Sanchez. Brown won by a margin of three percentage points, with heavy voter turnout in predominantly black precincts. Houston's term-limit statute prevented him from seeking a fourth term, and he stopped down as mayor in early 2004.

After leaving office, Brown became chairman and CEO of Brown Group International, a consulting firm specializing in public safety, homeland security, crisis management, government relations, and international trade. He was also one of the founders of the National Organization of Black Law Enforcement Executives.

RON BROWN (1941–1996)

Attorney, Federal Government Official, Organization Executive. Ronald Harmon Brown was born in Washington, D.C., on August 1, 1941, and raised in Harlem in New York City. He attended White Plains High School and Rhodes and Walden Preparatory Schools. Brown graduated from

Middlebury College in Vermont with a B.A. in political science in 1962. Upon graduating, he enlisted in the U.S. Army, where he achieved the rank of captain while serving in West Germany and Korea. In 1970, Brown graduated from St. John's University School of Law in New York City.

While attending law school, Brown began working in 1988 for the National Urban League's job-training center in the Bronx. He continued with them until 1979, working as general counsel, Washington spokesperson, deputy executive director, vice president of Washington operations, and lobbyist. In 1980, he resigned to become chief counsel of the U.S. Senate Judiciary Committee. Largely because of his effectiveness in this position, he became the general counsel and staff coordinator for Senator Edward Kennedy. Brown also became chief counsel for the Democratic National Committee (DNC) and subsequently the DNC deputy chairman. After his term as deputy chairman expired, Brown joined the law firm of Patton, Boggs and Blow.

In 1989, Brown became chairman of the DNC, making him the first African American to head a major American political party. As head of the DNC, Brown proved to be a successful fund-raiser and an effective team-builder. During Brown's tenure, Democrats elected an African American governor in Virginia and an African American mayor in New York City. Brown was also considered one of the architects of President Bill Clinton's 1992 election victory. In 1993, President Clinton appointed Brown commerce secretary. He was subsequently confirmed by the U.S. Senate, thus becoming the first African American secretary of commerce.

As commerce secretary, Brown took the lead in developing trade and economic policies that were sometimes controversial. In addition, he opened doors that allowed women and minorities to become more involved and aware of business opportunities through the Commerce Department. Brown's service as a cabinet member was marred by charges of financial impropriety and influence peddling, leading to the appointment of an independent counsel to investigate the allegations. Brown's last official act was leading a group of American businesspeople to war-torn Croatia so that they might assist in rebuilding the country. Brown died in a plane crash on April 3, 1996, near the Croatian coast.

BLANCHE K. BRUCE (1841–1898)

Federal Government Official and Legislator, Civil Rights Activist. Blanche Kelso Bruce was born enslaved in Farmville, Prince Edward County, Virginia. He received his early formal education in Missouri, where his parents had moved while he was young, and may have studied at Oberlin College in Ohio. In 1868, Bruce settled in Floreyville, Mississippi, where he became a successful educator. He later worked as a planter and eventually built up a considerable fortune in property.

In 1870, Bruce entered politics and was elected sergeant-at-arms of the Mississippi Senate. A year later, he was named assessor of taxes in Bolivar County. In 1872, he began serving as county sheriff and as a member of the Board of Levee Commissioners of Mississippi. Bruce was nominated to run for the U.S. Senate from Mississippi in February 1874. He was elected, becoming the first African American person to serve a full term in the Senate. Bruce became an outspoken defender of the rights of minority groups, including the Chinese and Native Americans. In 1879, he became the first African American to preside over the Senate during a debate. He chaired the investigation into the failure of the Freedmen's Savings and Trust and worked for the improvement of navigation on the Mississippi River in the hope of increasing interstate and foreign commerce. Bruce also supported legislation aimed at eliminating reprisals against those who had opposed African American emancipation.

After Bruce completed his term in the Senate in 1881, he failed to win a second term due to a loss of power and influence among Radical Republicans in the South. He rejected an offer for a diplomatic post to Brazil because slavery was still practiced there. In 1881, Bruce was named register of the U.S. Treasury Department by President James A. Garfield. Bruce held this position until 1885, when the Democrats regained power. He wrote articles and lectured until 1889, when President Benjamin Harrison appointed him recorder of deeds for the District of Columbia. Bruce served in this post until 1893, when he became a trustee for the District of Columbia public schools. In 1897, President William McKinley reappointed him to his former post as register of the treasury. Bruce died on March 17, 1898, in Washington, D.C.

RALPH J. BUNCHE (1904–1971)

Federal Government Official, Diplomat, Educator. The first African American to win the Nobel Peace Prize, Ralph Johnson Bunche was an internationally acclaimed statesman whose record of achievement places him among the most significant American diplomats of the twentieth century. Bunche received the Peace Prize in 1950 for his role in effecting a cease-fire in the Arab-Israeli dispute.

Born in Detroit on August 7, 1904, Bunche graduated summa cum laude in 1927 with Phi Beta Kappa honors from the University of California, Los Angeles. A year later, he received his M.A. in government from Harvard. Soon thereafter, he was named head of the Department of Political Science at Howard University, where he remained until 1932, when he resumed work toward his doctorate at Harvard. He later studied at Northwestern University, the London School of Economics, and the University of Cape Town in South African. Before World War II broke out in 1939, Bunche did fieldwork with the Swedish sociologist

Gunnar Myrdal, author of the widely acclaimed *An American Dilemma: The Negro Problem and Modern Democracy* (1944). During the war, Bunche served initially as a senior social analyst for the Office of the Coordinator of Information in African and Far Eastern Affairs. He was later reassigned to the African Section of the Office of Strategic Services. In 1942, he helped draw up the territories and trusteeships sections ultimately earmarked for inclusion in the United Nations charter.

The event that brought Bunche into the international spotlight occurred soon after his appointment in 1948 as chief assistant to Count Folke Bernadotte, the United Nations' mediator in the Palestine crisis. When Bernadotte was assassinated, Bunche continued cease-fire talks between Egypt and Israel. After six weeks of intensive negotiations, Bunche worked out the Four Armistice Agreements, which brokered an immediate cessation of hostilities between the two combatants. Once the actual cease-fire was signed, Bunche received numerous congratulatory letters and telegrams from many heads of state and was given a hero's welcome upon his return to the United States.

Bunche served as undersecretary of special political affairs from 1957 to 1967. By 1968, Bunche had attained the rank of undersecretary-general, the highest position ever held by an American at the United Nations. Bunche retired in October 1971 and died on December 9, 1971. The library of the Department of State was renamed the Ralph J. Bunche Library in May 1997 in recognition of his political and humanitarian contributions.

YVONNE BRATHWAITE BURKE (1932–)

Attorney, State Legislator. In November 1972, attorney and former California state assemblywoman Yvonne Brathwaite Burke became the first African American woman from California ever elected to the U.S. House of Representatives. More than twenty years later, she became the first woman and the first African American to chair the Los Angeles County Board of Supervisors. Prior to her governmental career, Burke was a practicing attorney, during which time she served as a deputy corporation commissioner, a hearing officer for the Los Angeles police commissioner, and an attorney for the McCone Commission that investigated the Watts riots.

Born on October 5, 1932, in Los Angeles, Burke received a bachelor of arts degree in political science from the University of California, Los Angeles, in 1953, and a juris doctor degree from the University of Southern California in 1956. She served in the State Assembly for six years prior to her election to Congress. During her final two years, she was chairperson of the Committee on Urban Development and Housing and a member of the Health, Finance, and Insurance committees. As a state legislator, Burke was responsible for the enactment of bills that provided for needy children, for the relocation of tenants, and for the owners of homes taken by governmental action. She also sponsored legislation that required major medical insurance programs to grant immediate coverage to newborn infants of the insured.

Burke's district, created in 1971 by the California legislature, was about 50 percent African American. In 1972, the district gave 64 percent of its vote to Burke. During Burke's first term in the House, she proved to be an ardent spokesperson for the downtrodden. She became a member of the Committee on Appropriations in December 1974, and used her position on this committee to advocate an increase in funding for senior-citizen services and community nutrition and food programs. Although her proposal for increased spending was defeated by the House of Representatives, Burke's efforts earned the respect of the African American community. In January 1977, Burke worked diligently for the passage of the Displaced Homemakers Act, which proposed the creation of counseling programs and job-training centers for women entering the workforce for the first time.

In 1978, Burke resigned from the House to run for the office of attorney general in California. She lost the race but was appointed to the Los Angeles County Board of Supervisors. She resigned from the board in December 1980 and returned to private law practice. Burke remained a prominent figure in California politics, taking on a number of civic responsibilities, including serving as a member of the University of California Board of Regents. In 1992, Burke was elected to the Los Angeles County Board of Supervisors. She was reelected to the board of supervisors in 1996, 2000, and 2004. Burke retired from the board in 2008.

CHUCK BURRIS (1951–2009)

Municipal Government Official. Charles Burris was born in New Orleans in 1951 and was raised in Atlanta. He received his B.A. in 1971 from Morehouse College. In 1975, he received an LL.B. from John Marshall Law School. Burris worked on several of the campaigns of Maynard Jackson and Andrew Young. He worked for the city of Atlanta as a member of the Crime Analyst Team and as a budget officer. He was also affiliated with the city's housing department.

While working for the state of Georgia, Burris first discovered the town of Stone Mountain. The city is the birthplace of the modern Ku Klux Klan and is known for its large carved monument to the Confederacy. Burris moved to the town and, in 1991, won election to the city council. Burris was determined to change the town's image from intolerance to inclusiveness. In 1997, he was elected as the mayor of Stone Mountain, a symbolic achievement that attracted national attention. After leaving office in

2001, he moved to Maryland to work for Lockheed Martin. Burris died in 2009 from complications related to amyloidosis.

BILL CAMPBELL (1953 –)

Municipal Government Official. Bill Campbell was born in 1953 in Raleigh, North Carolina. Campbell became mayor of Atlanta in 1994 when he was forty-one years old. He was the third African American to hold that position. His election signaled the advent of a new generation of leadership for the people of Atlanta.

In 1974, Campbell graduated cum laude from Vanderbilt University, completing a triple major (history, political science, and sociology) in just three years. He received his J.D. from Duke University in 1977 and went to work for an Atlanta law firm. Campbell worked from 1980 to 1981 for the U.S. Justice Department in Atlanta.

Campbell began his political career in 1981 when he was elected to the Atlanta City Council. He served three consecutive terms through 1993, cosponsoring more than three hundred pieces of legislation. By 1993, he had become a partner in an Atlanta law firm, along with serving as floor leader of the city council under Atlanta mayor Maynard Jackson. When Jackson's health began to wane, Campbell was mentioned as a mayoral candidate. The importance of the mayoral election was heightened by the city's preparations for the 1996 Olympics.

The 1993 election for mayor featured a large contingent of candidates, including other city council members, former mayoral candidates, and twelve nonpartisan candidates. Campbell won 49 percent of the vote, shy of the 50 percent needed to win the office outright. He won the runoff election with 73 percent of the vote.

Campbell appointed Beverly J. Harvard to be the first female police chief of a major American city. He installed mini-police precincts in Atlanta's housing projects, planned alliances between the city and historically African American colleges, and encouraged young people to become active in community services. In 1996, Campbell hosted many dignitaries, including President Bill Clinton, in celebration of the tenth official celebration of Martin Luther King Jr. Day. Campbell proposed a $150 million plan to repair Atlanta's infrastructure before the Olympics. Following the Olympics, Campbell's major efforts focused on downtown redevelopment, privatization of the Water Department, and reform of Atlanta's housing authority, which was one of the worst in the nation.

Campbell won reelection as Atlanta's mayor in 1997. During his second term, he was attacked for the city's affirmative action program, which he vigorously defended. He won praise, however, for his handling of a widely publicized shooting rampage that occurred in the city in 1999. In 2000, it was revealed that Campbell was under federal investigation in a corruption probe. Campbell could not seek a third term due to term limits. Following the inauguration of Mayor-elect Shirley Franklin, Campbell moved to Palm Beach Gardens, Florida, where he practiced law.

In August 2004, Campbell was indicted by a federal grand jury on racketeering, bribery, and wire-fraud charges after a five-year federal investigation of corruption in his administration during his tenure as mayor. The investigation led to the conviction of more than a dozen city contractors and several senior city officials, including three of Campbell's top aides, on corruption-related charges. Mayor Campbell was found guilty of three counts of tax fraud relating to false tax returns for the three years from 1997 to 2000 and was sentenced to two years and six months in federal prison. He reported to prison in Miami in August 2006. He was released from custody in 2008.

SHIRLEY CHISHOLM (1924–2005)

Educator, Federal Legislator, Organization Executive, Civil Rights Activist. Shirley Chisholm was born November 30, 1924, in New York City but spent much of her early life in Barbados with her extended family. She graduated cum laude from Brooklyn College in 1946 with a B.A. in sociology and in 1952 from Columbia University with an M.A. in elementary education. She had an early career in child care and preschool education, culminating in her directorship of the Hamilton-Madison Child Care Center in New York. From 1959 to 1964, she was a consultant to the Day Care Division of New York City's Bureau of Child Welfare.

In 1964, Chisholm was elected New York state assemblywoman, representing the fifty-fifth district in New York City. In 1968, she became the first African American woman elected to the U.S. House of Representatives after defeating Republican James Farmer. When she was assigned to the House Forestry Committee, she protested and demanded reassignment, and was placed on the Veterans' Affairs Committee. She supported Hale Boggs as House majority leader over John Conyers. Subsequently, Boggs assigned her to the powerful Education and Labor Committee. In 1969, Chisholm became one of the founding members of Congressional Black Caucus. When she retired from Congress in 1982, she was the third-highest-ranking member of the caucus.

In 1972, Chisholm announced her candidacy for the Democratic presidential nomination. She campaigned and entered primaries in twelve states, winning twenty-eight delegates and 152 first-ballot votes. Chisholm served as a delegate to the Democratic National Midterm Conference in 1974 and as a Democratic National Committee member. After retiring from politics, she was named to the Purington Chair at Mount Holyoke College, where she taught political science for four years. In 1984, Chisholm cofounded the National Political Congress of Black Women. She spent the next year as a visiting scholar at Spelman College. In 1993, President Bill Clinton nominated Chisholm as ambassador to Jamaica, but due to declining health, she withdrew her name from consideration. A member of Delta Sigma Theta sorority, Chisholm was inducted into the National Women's Hall of Fame in 1993. She retired to Florida and died there on January 1, 2005.

Chisholm was the author of *Unbossed & Unbought* (1970) and *The Good Fight* (1973). She was a member of the NAACP, the National Association of Colored Women, and the League of Women Voters. She won numerous awards, including the 1965 Woman of Achievement Award, presented by Key Women Inc., and the 1969 Sojourner Truth Award, given by the Association for the Study of Negro Life and History.

WILLIAM CLAY SR. (1931–)

Civil Rights Activist, Federal Legislator. William Lacy Clay Sr., the first African American to represent the state of Missouri in the U.S. Congress, was born on April 30, 1931, in the lower end of what is now St. Louis's first district. Clay received a degree in political science at St. Louis University, where he was one of four African Americans in a class of 1,100. After serving in the U.S. Army until 1955, Clay became active in a host of civil rights organizations, including the NAACP Youth Council and the Congress of Racial Equality (CORE). During this time, he worked as a cardiographic aide, bus driver, and insurance agent.

In 1959 and 1963, Clay was elected alderman of the predominantly African American Twenty-sixth Ward. During his first term, he served nearly four months of a nine-month jail sentence for demonstrations at a local bank. In 1964, Clay stepped down from his alderman's post to run for ward committeeman; he won and was reelected in 1968.

Clay's election platform in 1969 included a number of progressive, even radical, ideas. He argued that all penal institutions should make provisions for the creation of facilities in which married prisoners could set up house with their spouses for the duration of their sentences. He branded most testing procedures and diploma requirements, as well as references to arrest records and periods of unemployment, unnecessary obstacles, complicating the path of a prospective employee. In his view, a demonstrated willingness to work and an acceptance of responsibility should be the criteria determining one's selection for a job.

Clay's last job before his election to Congress was as race relations coordinator for Steamfitters Union Local 562. Subjected to considerable criticism from other St. Louis African Americans who labeled the union racist, Clay pointed out that dramatic changes in the hiring practices of the union since he had joined it in 1966 were responsible for the employment of thirty African American steamfitters in St. Louis. Still, Clay conceded that the high-paying job had led him to reduce his active involvement with the civil rights struggle to some degree.

As a congressman, Clay sponsored many pieces of legislation, including the Hatch Act Reform Bill, the City Earnings Tax Bill, the IRS Reform Bill, and the Family and Medical Leave Bill, which was the first bill that President Bill Clinton signed into law. Clay served as chairman of the Subcommittee on Postal Operations and Civil Service, the House Education and Labor Committee, and the House Administration Committee. He was also a member of the board of directors for Benedict College, Tougaloo College, and the Congressional Black Caucus Foundation. In 1990, Clay's first book, *To Kill or Not to Kill: Thoughts on Capital Punishment*, was published. In 1993, Clay published *Just Permanent Interests: Black Americans in Congress, 1870–1991*. He published *Bill Clay: A Political Voice at the Grass Roots* in 2004. Clay served thirty-two years in Congress, from 1969 to 2001, and was succeeded in that position by his son, William Lacy (Bill) Clay Jr.

EVA CLAYTON (1934–)

Federal Legislator. Eva McPherson Clayton was born in Savannah, Georgia. She earned a B.S. in 1955 from Johnson C. Smith University in Charlotte, North Carolina, and an M.S. in 1963 from North Carolina Central University. She later attended the University of North Carolina Law School.

Clayton first ran for a congressional seat in 1968 without success. In the 1970s, she was one of the founders of Soul City, a federally funded project to build a model planned community. She later worked for the campaign of Jim Hunt, who was elected governor of North Carolina. Clayton was rewarded with the post of assistant secretary for the Department of Natural Resources. She became active in politics, serving as a Warren County Commissioner for ten years and as chair of that commission for eight years.

When the first district congressman died in office, Clayton was named to fill his unexpired term and was elected to a full term in 1992. However, her district and others came under fire for being racially gerrymandered. Though the district is no longer an African American–majority district, Clayton held her seat until she retired in 2002. She was the first woman to serve in Congress from North Carolina and the first African American elected to Congress from that state since 1898. In 2003, she was named assistant director-general of the UN Food and Agriculture Organization, a post she held until 2006. She also established Eva Clayton Associates International, Inc., a consultancy firm.

JAMES E. CLYBURN (1940–)

Federal Legislator. James Enos Clyburn was born July 21, 1940, in Sumter, South Carolina. He was the eldest son of a fundamentalist preacher and a civic-minded beautician. From his family he learned the importance of religious faith and community service. He was active in the NAACP from his youth, serving as president of his youth council when he was twelve years old. As a student at South Carolina State College in Orangeburg, he became a leader and activist. He participated in marches and demonstrations that sometimes led to arrests, including the infamous 1960 Orangeburg rebellion in which 388 college students, including Clyburn, were arrested. He was also jailed during a 1961 march on the South Carolina State Capitol.

During one of his incarcerations, Clyburn met Emily England, whom he married on June 24, 1961. He began his career in Charleston as a teacher of history in the public schools. Later, he worked as an employment counselor, a director of youth and community-development programs, and the executive of a program serving migrant and seasonal farmworkers.

In 1970, Clyburn ran unsuccessfully for the South Carolina House of Representatives and later joined the staff of the newly elected governor. As an adviser to the governor, he was the first African American to hold such a position since Reconstruction. After four years on the governor's staff, Clyburn was appointed the human affairs commissioner of South Carolina, a position he held for almost two decades. Clyburn ran twice for the office of secretary of state, in 1978 and again in 1986, but without success.

Clyburn resigned his position as human affairs commissioner in 1992 and vigorously pursued his lifelong dream of serving in the U.S. Congress. With five Democratic primary hopefuls, Clyburn won handily with 56 percent of the vote, and avoided a runoff. When he easily won the general election, Clyburn became the first African American to serve in the U.S. Congress from South Carolina since 1897.

In January 1993, Clyburn was sworn in as a member of the U.S. House of Representatives from South Carolina's Sixth Congressional District. His leadership skills were evident from the outset, when he was elected copresident of his freshman class. In 1999, he was unanimously elected chair of the Congressional Black Caucus. He also won a seat on the Appropriations Committee. In 2002, he became vice chair of the House Democratic Caucus. Four years later, Clyburn was unanimously elected chair of the caucus.

On November 16, 2006, Clyburn became the first South Carolinian and the second African American to be elected majority whip, the third-ranking position in the House of Representatives. In addition to serving as House majority whip, Clyburn is the leader of the House Democrat's Faith Working Group.

CARDISS COLLINS (1931–)

Federal Legislator, Civil Rights Activist. Collins was born Cardiss Robertson on September 24, 1931, in St. Louis, Missouri. Her family moved to Detroit when she was a child, and she graduated from Commerce High School. After high school, she moved to Chicago, where she worked as a secretary for the state's Department of Revenue. She began studying accounting at Northwestern University and was promoted to accountant and then auditor. She married George Washington Collins, a local politician, in 1958.

In 1973, Collins was elected U.S. representative from Illinois' seventh district, filling the seat vacated by her husband, who was killed in an airplane crash. She became the first African American and the first woman to hold the position of Democratic whip-at-large. Collins served on congressional subcommittees dealing with consumer protection, national security, hazardous materials, narcotic abuse and control, and energy concerns. At various points, she also served as active secretary, vice chair, and chair of the Congressional Black Caucus (CBC).

Collins was a proponent of civil rights, airline safety, women's rights, affirmative action, and antiapartheid legislation. She served as chair of the Government Activities and Transportation Subcommittee from 1989 to 1991. In that position, she worked for legislation to control the transport of toxic materials and the location of landfills and incinerators in minority communities. Collins introduced the Nondiscrimination in Advertising Act, which sought to correct systematic discrimination against minority-owned ad agencies and broadcast stations. Her investigations into Title IX led to legislation that required institutions of higher education to disclose gender participation rates and program expenditures. Collins was a persistent advocate for universal health insurance and fought successfully for the establishment of a federal office on minority health.

In 1994, the CBC Foundation elected her the group's chair. Early in 1995, Collins became the top Democrat on the Government Reform and Oversight Committee. Following her reelection on November 8, 1995, Collins announced her decision to retire after twenty-four years in the House. Her twelve terms in Congress, from 1973 to 1997, made her the longest-serving African American female member of Congress. Collins belongs to the NAACP, the Chicago Urban League, the Northern Virginia Urban League, the National Women's Political Caucus, Alpha Kappa Alpha, the Congressional Women's Caucus, Alpha Kappa Psi, Black Women's Agenda, and the National Council of Negro Women. She has honorary degrees from Barber-Scotia College, Winston-Salem State University, and Spelman College. The Black Coaches Association named Collins Sportsperson of the Year in 1994, after she supported the group's contention that standardized college-entrance examinations are racially and culturally biased and, therefore, should not be used by the National Collegiate Athletic Association to establish athletic eligibility.

JOHN CONYERS (1929–)

Attorney, Federal Legislator and Government Official, Civil Rights Activist, Organization Executive. John Conyers was born in Detroit on May 16, 1929. In 1950, three years after graduating from high school, he enlisted in the U.S. Army as a private and served in Korea before being honorably discharged in 1957 as a second lieutenant. He attended Wayne State University in Detroit, and, after studying in a dual program, he received a B.A. in 1957 and a J.D. in 1958.

Conyers served as a legislative assistant to Congressman John Dingell Jr. from 1958 to 1961 and was a senior partner in the law firm of Conyers, Bell and Townsend from 1959 to 1961. In 1961, he took a referee position with the Michigan Workman's Compensation Department. In 1964, he won election as a Democrat to the U.S. House of Representatives. He has represented the fourteenth district (it was the first district until 1993) since 1965. Conyers's longevity in Congress is legendary. In the 111th Congress, he is the second-longest-serving member of the House, after John Dingell. Conyers is a founding member of the Congressional Black Caucus (CBC) and is considered the dean of the CBC. He has the longest tenure in Congress of any African American and is considered one of the most liberal members of Congress.

Conyers became active in the Democratic Party at a young age, belonging to the Young Democrats and the University Democrats, and serving as a precinct delegate to the Democratic Party. After his election, Conyers was assigned to the powerful House Judiciary Committee. In January 2007, when the Democrats became the majority in the 110th Congress, Conyers became chairman of the House Judiciary Committee. As a member of the Judiciary Committee, Conyers has worked on legislation dealing with civil rights, Medicare, immigration reform, and truth-in-packaging laws. Earlier in his legislative career, he was an opponent of U.S. involvement in Vietnam and an early proponent of the Voting Rights Act of 1965. Following Martin Luther King Jr.'s assassination in 1968, Conyers introduced the bill to make King's birthday a federal holiday.

More recently, Conyers has supported efforts to regulate online gambling. Concerned about possible voter-repression activities in the 2004 presidential election, Conyers issued *What Went Wrong in Ohio: The Conyers Report on the 2004 Presidential Election*, which details reports of faulty electronic-voting machines, statistical differences in exit-poll results and actual votes registered, and the inability to validate the totals on machines used to tally votes. Since the September 11, 2001, terrorist attacks, Conyers has been vigilant in providing the necessary law enforcement and intelligence authority to the administration to prevent terrorism without sacrificing the civil liberties and civil rights of citizens. An advocate for working families, Conyers has a history of fighting for equal pay for women and minorities, raising the minimum wage, full employment for all Americans, and universal health care

In 1994, Conyers supported a grassroots movement comprised of nearly one thousand individuals seeking reparations from the federal government on behalf of their enslaved ancestors. The participants held their fifth annual Conference on Reparations in Conyers's hometown of Detroit. Other prominent African Americans lending support included Reverend Jesse Jackson. In 1998 and 1999, Conyers served as the ranking Democrat on the House Committee of Impeachment.

Conyers has been vice chairman of the National Board of Americans for Democratic Action and the American Civil Liberties Union. He is on the executive board of the Detroit chapter of the NAACP and belongs to the Wolverine Bar Association. He is the recipient of the 1967 Rosa Parks Award and in 1969 received an honorary law degree from Wilberforce University. He was reelected in November 2008 to his twenty-third term in the House.

RONALD V. DELLUMS (1935–)

Social Worker, Federal Legislator, Organization Executive, Lecturer. Ronald Vernie Dellums was born in Oakland, California, on November 24, 1935. After attending McClymonds and Oakland Technical High Schools, Dellums joined the U.S. Marine Corps in 1954 and was discharged after two years of service. He returned to school, receiving an A.A. degree from Oakland City College in 1958, a B.A. from San Francisco State College in 1960, and an M.S.W. from the University of California, Berkeley, in 1962.

For the next eight years, Dellums engaged in a variety of social-work positions. He was a psychiatric social worker with the Berkeley Department of Mental Hygiene starting in 1962, and two years later became the Bayview Community Center's program director. Dellums spent one year as director of the Hunters Point Youth Opportunity Center and one year as a consultant to the Bay Area Social Planning Council. In 1967, Dellums worked as a program director for the San Francisco Economic Opportunity Council. From 1968 to 1970, Dellums lectured at San Francisco State College and the University of California's School of Social Work. He also served as a consultant to Social Dynamics Inc.

Dellums was elected to the Berkeley City Council in 1967, and served until his election as a Democrat to the U.S. House of Representatives in 1971. As a representative, he chaired the House Committee on the District of Columbia and served on the House Armed Services Subcommittee on Military Facilities and Installations, as well as the Subcommittee on Military Research and Development. In 1983, Dellums published *Defense Sense: The Search for a Rational Military Policy*.

Dellums, who chaired the Defense Policy Panel, became the first African American to head the House Armed Services Committee on January 27, 1993. Once a militant pacifist, he was recognized as one of the most highly regarded members of Congress to extensively work toward U.S. demilitarization. Dellums chastised President Bill Clinton for giving in to fear and ignorance when the president did not follow through on his promise to lift the ban on homosexuals in the military. Dellums retired in 1998 after twenty-seven years in Congress and became president of Healthcare International Management Company. He was elected mayor of Oakland, California, in November 2006.

OSCAR STANTON DEPRIEST (1871–1951)

County Commissioner, Federal Legislator. Oscar DePriest was the first African American to win a seat in the U.S. House of Representatives in the twentieth century. Born in Florence, Alabama, in 1871, DePriest moved to Kansas with his family when he was six years old. His formal education consisted of business and bookkeeping classes that he completed before running away to Dayton, Ohio, with two white friends. By 1889, he had reached Chicago and become a painter and master decorator.

In Chicago, DePriest amassed a fortune in real estate and the stock market, and in 1904, he entered politics successfully when he was elected Cook County commissioner. In 1908, he was appointed an alternate delegate to the Republican National Convention and in 1915 became Chicago's first African American alderman. He served on the Chicago City Council from 1915 to 1917 and became Third Ward committeeman in 1924. In 1928, DePriest became the Republican nominee for the congressional seat vacated by fellow Republican Martin Madden. DePriest won the November election over his Democratic rival and an independent candidate to become the first African American from outside of the South to be elected to Congress.

Following his election to Congress, DePriest became the unofficial spokesman for the eleven million African Americans in the United States during the 1920s and 1930s. He proposed that states that discriminated against African Americans should receive fewer congressional seats. Also, he proposed that a monthly pension be given to ex-slaves over the age of seventy-five. During the early 1930s, with the United States mired in the Great Depression, DePriest was faced with a difficult dilemma. Although he empathized with the plight of poor Americans, both black and white, he did not support the emergency federal relief programs proposed by President Franklin Roosevelt. Rather, DePriest and his fellow Republicans believed that aid programs should be created and implemented by individual states or local communities. DePriest's stance on the issue of federal relief programs dismayed many of his constituents. In 1934, he was defeated by Arthur Mitchell, the first African American Democrat elected to serve in Congress.

DePriest remained active in public life, serving from 1943 to 1947 as alderman of the Third Ward in Chicago. His final withdrawal from politics came about after a dispute with the Republican Party. DePriest returned to his real-estate business, and he died on May 12, 1951.

CHARLES C. DIGGS JR. (1922–1998)

Federal Legislator. Charles Coles Diggs Jr. was born in Detroit on December 2, 1922. His father, an undertaker and funeral-home owner, was elected to the Michigan State Legislature in the 1940s. Diggs attended the University of Michigan and Fisk University in Nashville. After serving in the U.S. Air Force during World War II, he earned a B.S. in mortuary science from Wayne State University in 1946.

Upon receiving his degree, Diggs joined his father in the family mortuary business and soon followed him into politics. Diggs was elected to his father's seat in the state senate in 1951, and was elected to the U.S. Congress in 1954 as a representative of Michigan's thirteenth district.

Diggs was Michigan's first African American representative. During his early years in Congress, he emerged as a strong voice for the civil rights movement, attending the Emmett Till murder trial in Mississippi as an observer, calling for the desegregation of public transportation, and traveling to the flashpoint of Selma, Alabama, in the 1960s. In 1969, Diggs was a key player in organizing the Congressional Black Caucus.

In the 1970s, Diggs chaired the African Affairs Subcommittee of the House Committee on Foreign Relations. During this period, he pressed for the elimination of apartheid segregation in South Africa, and advocated U.S. aid to newly independent African nations. TransAfrica, a "think tank" devoted to African affairs, was founded in Diggs's office in 1978. From 1973 to 1978, he held the chairmanship of the House District Committee, which was charged with overseeing the affairs of Washington, D.C. His work on the committee played a major role in the establishment of a home-rule government for the District of Columbia.

In 1978, Diggs was charged with illegally diverting $60,000 in office operating funds to pay his own personal expenses. He easily won reelection that year, but was soon convicted of the charges. Diggs was censured by the House and stripped of his committee memberships. He resigned his seat in 1980 after twenty-five years in Congress.

Following appeals of his conviction, Diggs served seven months in prison. He returned to the mortuary business following his release. During the 1980s, he earned a political science degree from Howard University, and also launched a brief comeback attempt with an unsuccessful run for a Maryland state legislative seat. Diggs died of a stroke in Washington, D.C., on August 24, 1998.

DAVID DINKINS (1927–)

Attorney, Municipal Government Official, State Legislator. In September 1989, David Dinkins surprised political observers by defeating incumbent mayor Edward I. Koch in New York City's Democratic mayoral primary. Two months later, in the November election, he defeated Republican contender Rudolph Giuliani. Dinkins's victory marked the first time an African American was elected mayor of New York City. Dinkins faced the difficult task of leading a racially polarized and financially troubled city. While many supporters cited Dinkins's calm, professional demeanor as having a soothing effect upon New York's festering racial problems, others chided him for not responding forcefully enough to the many fiscal and social challenges facing the city.

David Dinkins was born in Trenton, New Jersey, in 1927. His parents separated when he was young, and he moved to Harlem with his mother and sister. He returned to Trenton to attend high school. Following a stint in the U.S. Marines during World War II, he attended Howard University in Washington, D.C., and graduated in 1950 with a B.S. In 1956, Dinkins graduated from the Brooklyn Law School. He became an attorney and eventually a partner in the law firm of Dyett, Alexander, Dinkins, Patterson, Michael, Dinkins and Jones.

Dinkins's first foray into the world of politics occurred in 1965, when he won an election to the New York State Assembly. He served until 1967, but did not seek reelection after his district was redrawn. In 1972, Dinkins was appointed president of elections for the city of New York and served for one year. Two years later, in 1975, he was appointed as city clerk and served until 1985. Dinkins ran for the office of Manhattan borough president in 1977 and 1981. He lost both elections by a wide margin. Dinkins ran again in 1985 and was elected. As Manhattan borough president, he was viewed as a mediator who tried to address a myriad of community concerns, such as school decentralization, AIDS treatment and prevention services, and pedestrian safety.

As mayor, Dinkins remained true to the issues he had addressed as Manhattan borough president. Other causes he championed included tolerance and acceptance of gays and lesbians, economic parity for women and minorities, and affirmative action. Dinkins set up a program to provide government contracts to businesses owned by women and minorities. Though the program was blemished by faulty bookkeeping and by the complexity of determining which companies were truly eligible, Dinkins's successor kept it in place.

In 1991, when riots erupted between African Americans and Jews in the Crown Heights neighborhood, Dinkins entreated both sides to think about their actions and possible consequences rather than react to the emotional volatility surrounding an incident in which a Jewish man's automobile accidentally struck and killed an African American youth. When riots seized Los Angeles in 1992, most of the nation feared that the violence would spread to other large urban areas with mixed or predominately African American populations. But Dinkins was able to assuage his constituents and prevent the terror and destruction that incapacitated Los Angeles.

In November 1993, Dinkins's bid for reelection fell short when he was narrowly defeated by Rudolph Giuliani. Dinkins left office on December 31, 1993. Poor management had been an Achilles' heel of the Dinkins administration. In 1994, the New York Court of Appeals fined the city more than $3.5 million to compensate five thousand homeless families forced to live in inadequate shelters. In 1994, Dinkins began hosting a radio talk show. Later in the year, he became a member of the AMREP Corp. board of directors and began teaching at Columbia University. Dinkins successfully underwent triple bypass heart surgery in 1995. He continues his professorship in the practice of public affairs at the Columbia School of International and Public Affairs.

JULIAN C. DIXON (1934–2000)

Attorney, Federal Legislator, Women's Rights Activist. Julian Carey Dixon was born August 8, 1934, in Washington, D.C. He served in the U.S. Army from 1957 to 1960, and received a B.S. in political science from California State University in 1962 and an LL.B. from Southwestern University Law School in 1967. In 1972, Dixon was elected on the Democratic ticket to the California State Assembly. In 1978, he was elected to the U.S. House of Representatives.

While in the House of Representatives, Dixon served on the House Committee on Standards of Official Conduct, the West Point Board of Supervisors, and the Appropriations Subcommittee on Foreign Operations. He also chaired the Appropriations Subcommittee on the District of Columbia. This latter appointment made Dixon the first African American to chair an appropriations subcommittee. Dixon was an original cosponsor of the equal rights amendment and was active in the Congressional Black Caucus. He died on December 8, 2000, in Los Angeles after suffering a heart attack. He was sixty-six.

SHEILA DIXON (1953–)

Municipal Government Official. Sheila Dixon became the forty-eighth mayor of Baltimore on January 17, 2006,

Sheila Dixon, Former Mayor of Baltimore, 2007. The city's first female mayor, Dixon resigned from office in early 2010 after a jury found her guilty of misdemeanor embezzlement stemming from her use of more than $600 in retail store gift cards intended for the city's needy families. MARK L. DENNIS/REUTERS/LANDOV

when her predecessor, Mayor Martin O'Malley, was elected governor of Maryland. She ascended to the position of mayor from her seat as city council president. Dixon was Baltimore's first woman mayor, as well as the first African American women to serve as city council president. She was first elected to the Baltimore City Council in 1987, and became city council president in 1999. Prior to her involvement in politics, Dixon was a community activist and initiated a number of programs for inner-city residents, including community food cooperatives.

A native of Baltimore, Dixon was educated in the Baltimore public school system and received a bachelor's degree from Towson University and a master's degree from Johns Hopkins University. She later worked as an elementary school and Head Start teacher. For seventeen years, Dixon was an international trade specialist with the Maryland Department of Business and Economic Development. An avid athlete, Dixon has been a strong advocate for health issues, such as HIV/AIDS, breast cancer, and lead poisoning in children. She champions programs that improve children's health through a more nutritious diet and exercise routine.

In December 2009, Dixon was convicted of embezzling more than $600 worth of gift cards that had been donated to the city for charity use. She resigned from office in February 2010.

KEITH ELLISON (1963–)

Attorney, State Legislator, Federal Government Official. A native of Detroit, Michigan, Keith Ellison earned a B.A. in economics from Wayne State University in 1987. He moved to Minnesota in 1987 when he entered the University of Minnesota Law School. Ellison graduated from law school in 1990, and joined the firm of Lindquist and Vennum. Three years later, he became executive director of the Legal Rights Center, a nonprofit organization that represents low-income people facing legal problems. He later returned to private practice as a litigator with the law firm of Hassan and Reed, Ltd.

A longtime community advocate, Ellison promoted an increase in the state's minimum wage and improved police-community relations. For eight years, he hosted a public affairs program on community radio and frequently testified before state legislative committees on such issues as privacy, welfare reform, indigent defense, and environmental justice.

In 2002, Ellison was elected to the Minnesota State House of Representatives. He was reelected in 2004. As a state representative, he promoted efforts to protect Minnesota's children from environmental pollutants and toxins. He also sponsored legislation to restore the voting rights of ex-offenders, and successfully advocated for an increase in the state's minimum wage.

In 2006, Ellison ran successfully for the U.S. Congress with a message of "generosity and inclusiveness." He represents Minnesota's Fifth Congressional District, which includes Minneapolis and the surrounding suburbs. It is one of the state's most ethnically diverse districts. With his election, Ellison made history as the first African American representative from Minnesota and the first Muslim ever elected to the U.S. Congress. A controversy arose when Ellison used a Qur'an belonging to Thomas Jefferson for his swearing-in ceremony.

MICHAEL ESPY (1953–)

Federal Government Official, Attorney. Michael Espy was born November 30, 1953. He received a B.A. from

Keith Ellison, 2006. *Ellison thanks voters in Minneapolis, Minnesota, for their support during a Democratic primary. He later won the general election, becoming the first African American from Minnesota and the first Muslim ever elected to the U.S. Congress.* MELANIE STETSON FREEMAN/THE CHRISTIAN SCIENCE MONITOR/GETTY IMAGES

Howard University in 1975, and a J.D. from the Santa Clara School of Law in 1978. After graduating, Espy practiced law in Yazoo City, Mississippi, and managed Central Mississippi Legal Services from 1978 to 1980. Espy also worked for the state of Mississippi as assistant secretary of state for public lands, and from 1984 to 1985 he was assistant attorney general for consumer protection.

Espy was elected to the U.S. House of Representatives in 1986, where he served on numerous committees, including the House Budget Committee; the House Agricultural Committee; the Select Committee on Hunger; the Subcommittee on Cotton, Rice, and Sugar; the Subcommittee on Conservation, Credit, and Rural Development; and the Consumer Relations and Nutrition Committee. In addition, he chaired the Domestic Task Force on Hunger. In 1993, Espy was appointed secretary of agriculture by President Bill Clinton, becoming the first African American to hold this post. However, Espy quickly became the subject of a federal ethics investigation into charges that he accepted gifts from companies that were regulated by the agency he headed. Although he denied any wrongdoing, Espy resigned his post on December 31, 1994. Nearly one year later, allegations surfaced that Espy, while still a cabinet member, had improperly approached an agribusiness lobbyist for money, asking him to help pay off a debt incurred by his brother, who had unsuccessfully run for a House seat.

Espy was the object of a four-year investigation by an independent counsel, who charged him with thirty counts of political corruption. The investigation was based on allegations that he had accepted $33,000 in free gifts, sports tickets, and expensive meals from companies that sought to benefit from good relations with Espy in their dealings with the Department of Agriculture. Espy was exonerated in December 1998 when the jury returned not-guilty verdicts on all the counts.

Espy practices law in Mississippi. He is affiliated with the American Bar Association, the Mississippi Trial Lawyers

Association, and the National Conference of Black Leaders, and is on the board of directors of the Jackson Urban League.

CHAKA FATTAH (1956–)

State Legislator, Civil Rights Activist. Born as Arthur Davenport in Philadelphia, Pennsylvania, on November 21, 1956, Fattah was renamed after the legendary Zulu warrior Chaka by his mother, who with her husband, took new Swahili root names to represent their African heritage. Fattah's mother, Falaka Fattah, started the nationally known youth program House of Umoja as a means of combating and controlling gangs. At age fourteen, in an effort to assist his mother, Fattah received twenty abandoned houses in the neighborhood after giving a slide presentation and written proposal to the First Pennsylvania Bank. Falaka Fattah used the structures to expand the growing House of Umoja youth program.

Fattah continued to work with the youth program while in high school. With the help of Congressman Bill Gray, Fattah won a federal grant to renovate the houses. Meanwhile, at Overbrook High School, Fattah organized the Youth Movement to Clean Up Politics. In 1974, Fattah and his family launched No Gang War in '74 to end gang violence that had resulted in forty deaths the previous year. He was so immersed in his mission of saving young African American men and preventing violence that Fattah quit school. After receiving his GED, Fattah took classes at the Community College of Philadelphia in 1974 and 1975. Even though he became a single father at eighteen, he made caring for his infant daughter and completing his education his top priorities. He continued his education through the Wharton Community Education Program at the University of Pennsylvania, and he was later able to transfer those credits toward a degree.

In 1978, Fattah ran for the office of city commissioner, his first political race, but he came in fourth among twenty-two contenders. Because of his advocacy for the poor and his knowledge of housing, he was hired by the director of the Department of Housing. He advanced rapidly and soon became a special assistant to the managing director.

In 1982, Fattah decided to run for the Pennsylvania House of Representatives. His campaign was unique in that he enlisted and trained hundreds of students from his old high school as campaign workers. He successfully challenged a powerful political machine and, at age twenty-five, became the youngest person ever elected to the Pennsylvania General Assembly. While serving as a representative, Fattah was selected for the highly competitive Senior Executive Program for State Officials at Harvard University's Kennedy School of Government. Harvard officials were so impressed with Fattah's exemplary performance that they invited him to return and pursue the M.P.A. He declined the offer in order to keep his new seat in the Pennsylvania legislature. In 1986, he completed a master's degree in government administration at the Fels Institute of Government at the University of Pennsylvania.

In 1988, Fattah won an election for state senator in the seventh district. As a state senator, Fattah raised money for the city of Philadelphia and pioneered programs to rebuild one hundred of the country's deteriorating cities. In 1994, Fattah won a seat in the U.S. House of Representatives. He received an "outstanding contribution award" from the Pennsylvania House of Representatives and the Simpson Fletcher Award for religion and race.

In 1994, Fattah was a strong advocate for GEAR UP, the country's largest college-awareness initiative. By 2006, the program had spent $2 billion putting more than six million students on the path to college. In 2003, Fattah, in conjunction with municipal and public school officials, started the CORE Philly program, which has provided college scholarships to almost seven thousand Philadelphians.

Fattah announced plans to run for Philadelphia mayor in 2006, but he did not win the Democratic primary. In 2008, he was reelected to his ninth term in Congress.

WALTER E. FAUNTROY (1933–)

Federal Legislator, Religious Leader, Civil Rights Activist. Born February 6, 1933, Walter Edward Fauntroy represented the District of Columbia in the House of Representatives from 1971 until 1990. Fauntroy is a 1955 graduate of Virginia Union University and a 1958 graduate of Yale University Divinity School. He became pastor of New Bethel Baptist Church in Washington, D.C. in 1959, and has held that position for more than half a century.

Fauntroy was the Washington, D.C., coordinator for the March on Washington for Jobs and Freedom in 1963, as well as the coordinator for the Selma to Montgomery march in 1965, the D.C. coordinator of the Meredith Mississippi Freedom March in 1966, and the national coordinator for the Poor People's Campaign in 1969. Fauntroy served as chairman of the caucus task force for the 1972 Democratic National Committee and of the platform committee of the National Black Political Convention. In addition, he was the chief architect of legislation in 1973 that permitted the District of Columbia to elect its own mayor and city council, and he engineered the passage by both the House and Senate of a constitutional amendment calling for full congressional representation for District of Columbia residents in the U.S. Congress.

During his tenure in the House of Representatives, Fauntroy built a record of achievement by playing key roles in the mobilization of African American political power from the National Black Political Convention in 1972 to the presidential elections of 1972 and 1976. For fifteen years, Fauntroy chaired a bipartisan congressional task force on Haiti. In November 1984, Fauntroy and two prominent national leaders launched the Free South Africa Movement (FSAM) with their arrest at the South African Embassy. He served as cochair of the steering committee of the FSAM. He was also a member of the House Select Committee on Narcotics Abuse and Control and cosponsored the $2.7 billion antidrug bill in 1988.

In the Ninety-fifth Congress, Fauntroy was a member of the House Select Committee on Assassinations and chairman of its Subcommittee on the Assassination of Martin Luther King Jr. He was a ranking member of the House Banking, Finance, and Urban Affairs Committee and chairman of its Subcommittee on Government Affairs and Budget. He was also the first ranking member of the House District Committee.

Fauntroy was the recipient of several awards during his political career. In 1984, he was presented with the Hubert H. Humphrey Humanitarian Award by the National Urban Coalition. He also received honorary degrees from Georgetown University Law School, Yale University, and Virginia Union University. After leaving public service, Fauntroy founded Project We Care, a social service located in the Washington, D.C., area. The project was comprised of teams of ministers and church members who canvassed neighborhoods in order to serve as conduits between residents and the city. Fauntroy also began his own company.

Fauntroy contracted tuberculosis in the mid-1990s. Through a diligent regimen, he remained healthy and became an unofficial spokesperson for the disease, urging the public to get tested. A discovery was made that he had incorrectly listed a church donation on a disclosure form presented to the Congress. In 1995, Fauntroy was sentenced to two years of probation, a $1,000 fine, and three hundred hours of community service after pleading guilty to a misdemeanor charge of falsifying a financial report to Congress. Continuing his fight for human rights, Fauntroy, a leader of the Free Sudan Movement, was arrested on April 13, 2001, for chaining himself to the gates of the Sudanese Embassy in Washington, D.C., in a protest against Sudan's black slave trade.

ADRIAN FENTY (1970–)

Municipal Government Official. Adrian Fenty is the youngest mayor ever elected in the District of Columbia. In one of the most expensive mayoral races ever conducted, each candidate raised almost $2 million. Fenty defeated longtime council chair Linda Cropp in a victory that was unprecedented because he carried every precinct in both the primary and the general elections. Fenty won the general election with 89 percent of the vote. Fenty and his team campaigned in every precinct and are said to have worked every block in the district.

A native of Washington, D.C., Fenty graduated from Oberlin College in Ohio with a bachelor's degree in 1992 and received his J.D. from Howard University School of Law in 1996. In 2001, Fenty won his first electoral position by defeating four-term incumbent Charlene Drew Jarvis to become the District of Columbia's Ward Four council member. His performance regarding constituent services set a new standard. He attracted new jobs, businesses, and housing to his ward, and addressed nuisance-property violations. He also expanded community policing and improved police response times. During his first term, twelve schools and a recreation center were constructed or renovated in Ward Four. In 2003, Fenty and another

Adrian Fenty, Mayor of Washington, DC, April 2010. *Fenty became the youngest-ever mayor of the District of Columbia following his victory in the 2006 election. He was age thirty-six when he assumed office in January 2007.* KEVIN DIETSCH/UPI/LANDOV

council member sponsored legislation to ban smoking in nearly all indoor workplaces, including bars and restaurants. The ban took full effect in January 2007.

In 2004, Fenty easily won reelection and provided leadership for the passage of the School Modernization Act. The bill is important because it requires the Board of Education and the superintendent to develop a comprehensive Facilities Master Plan for the public school system. The legislation also provides stable long-term funding to rebuild and modernize school facilities, and it establishes an advisory committee to oversee the construction effort.

FLOYD FLAKE

See chapter 17, Religion.

HAROLD E. FORD JR. (1970–)

Federal Legislator. Harold Eugene Ford Jr. was born May 11, 1970, in Memphis, Tennessee. His father, Harold Ford Sr., was a congressman and a member of the prominent Ford family of Memphis. In addition to the Ford family's involvement in public service and Democratic politics, members of the family were successful in the mortuary business.

Harold Ford Jr. attended public school in Memphis, but when his father was elected to Congress in 1972, the family moved to Washington, D.C. He graduated from St. Albans School for Boys and received his B.A. in American history from the University of Pennsylvania in 1992. After graduation, he worked on the staff of the Senate Budget Committee and as a special assistant to the U.S. Department of Commerce. He later entered the University of Michigan Law School, graduating in 1996.

In 1996, Ford's father did not seek reelection to a twelfth term in Congress, paving the way for the candidacy of his son. Harold Ford Jr. campaigned vigorously while completing his last semester in law school. Typically, he left Michigan on Thursday afternoon or evening for Memphis and returned to school on Monday evening for classes the next day. His family's name recognition, connections, and political organization, along with Ford's campaign skills, made his Democratic primary victory predictable. He won the November election handily and was reelected four times with an average of 80 percent of the vote.

Ford gained national prominence when he was featured as a keynote speaker at the 2000 Democratic National Convention in support of then–Vice President Al Gore's nomination as the Democratic Party's presidential candidate. Following the Democratic losses in 2002, Ford challenged Nancy Pelosi, then–House minority whip, for the position of House Democratic leader. He made a good showing, but was unsuccessful

While in Congress, Ford was considered a moderate, but was self-described as a "pro-life" candidate who voted to ban same-sex marriage and benefits for same-sex couples. He was one of the few Democrats who voted for the bankruptcy bill. He also opposed the president's energy legislation, which would have allowed oil drilling in the Arctic National Wildlife Refuge.

After a decade in Congress and with the retirement of Tennessee's senior senator, William Frist, Ford launched his campaign for the Senate on May 25, 2005. He was successful in raising funds nationally and within the state. He assembled an effective campaign staff with numerous volunteers throughout the state and won the Democratic primary overwhelmingly. For much of the campaign, the race was too close to call, though Ford had a slight lead at various times; however, he lost the Senate race by three percentage points.

In 2007, Ford was named chairman of the Democratic Leadership Council. He also became a visiting professor of public policy at Vanderbilt University in Nashville, where he taught a class on American political leadership. In February 2007, Ford was named a vice chairman and senior policy adviser at Merrill Lynch. The following month, he joined the Fox News Channel as a political commentator and analyst on international affairs. In 2008, he left Fox and became a political analyst for rival MSNBC. In 2009, Ford joined the faculty of New York University's Wagner School of Public Service.

SHIRLEY C. FRANKLIN (1945–)

Municipal Government Official. A native of Philadelphia, Shirley Clarke Franklin became the fifty-eighth mayor of Atlanta in 2002. She was the first woman to hold this position, and the first African American woman to preside over any major city in the South. Franklin graduated from Howard University in 1968 with a B.A. in sociology. In 1969, she earned an M.A. in the same field from the University of Pennsylvania. Franklin worked as a contract officer with the U.S. Department of Labor and as an instructor at Talladega College before marrying and relocating to Atlanta in 1972.

In 1978, Franklin began her career with the city of Atlanta as the director and commissioner of cultural affairs during Maynard Jackson's tenure as mayor. From 1982 to 1990, Franklin was the chief administrative officer for Mayor Andrew Young. During those eight years, Franklin was responsible for many successful large-scale public-works projects, including the construction of a new city hall and municipal court building, completion of 14,000 units of new housing, and expansion of Hartsfield International Airport. When Maynard Jackson was elected to a third term, Franklin became executive officer for operations.

Franklin left city government from 1991 to 1996 to serve as senior vice president for external relations of the Atlanta Committee for the Olympic Games. She was responsible for the development of Centennial Olympic Park and worked with various labor unions, civil rights organizations, and other community groups to insure their participation in all aspects of hosting the Olympic Games.

Before running for mayor in 2000, Franklin worked with several development companies and headed her own company, Shirley Clarke Franklin and Associates, a community-affairs management and consulting firm. In 1998, Franklin served as head of Roy Barnes's transition team when he was elected governor of Georgia.

In a very close mayoral race, Franklin defeated two opponents, who were both council veterans, without a runoff. Succeeding Bill Campbell, whose administration was under federal investigation for corruption, Franklin emphasized integrity and accountability in city government. Her administration was characterized by efficiency, transparency, and effectiveness. A results-oriented administrator, Franklin made tough fiscal decisions that resulted in balanced budgets and generated a healthy reserve for the city. Franklin also led the initiative to secure the Martin Luther King Jr. papers for the city of Atlanta with corporate and community partnerships that guaranteed a loan for $32 million to accomplish this. During her inauguration in 2002, Franklin vowed to make Atlanta a cleaner and better place for families by making city government more open and responsive.

Franklin easily won reelection in 2005. She left office in 2010, after completing her second term. In 2010, she began a one-year post at Spelman College as a Cosby endowed professor of social science.

GARY A. FRANKS (1953–)

Federal Legislator, Organization Executive. Gary Alvin Franks was born February 9, 1953, in Waterbury, Connecticut. He received a B.A. from Yale University in 1975. Before being elected to the U.S. House of Representatives, Franks was active in local politics and business, and president of GAF Realty in Waterbury. Franks also served on the Waterbury Board of Aldermen, and was vice chairman of the Zoning Board, a member of the Environmental Control Commission, director of the Naugatuck (Connecticut) chapter of the American Red Cross, president of the Greater Waterbury Chamber of Commerce, and a member of the Waterbury Foundation.

In 1991, Franks was elected to the U.S. House of Representatives, becoming the only African American Republican in the House until J. C. Watts was elected in 1995. Franks served on the Armed Services Committee, the Small Business Committee, and the Select Committee on Aging. In 1993, he was appointed to the House Energy and Commerce Committee, a highly prized position.

Franks fulfilled a controversial role as an African American who is opposed to affirmative action and other programs based on preference for women and minorities. With such views, Franks experienced his share of congressional ruckuses. Formerly the only Republican member of the Congressional Black Caucus, he was voted out of the organization in 1993 by members who did not consider Franks a legitimate African American spokesperson. In 1994, Franks testified in support of a lawsuit to dismantle the African American–majority Eleventh Congressional District of Cynthia McKinney, an African American Democrat from Georgia. Franks and his political cohorts felt that the district had been improperly designed to increase African American voting strength in the area at the expense of the white electorate.

Franks was known as one of the Republican Party's most prominent African American lawmakers. He entered the political landscape at a time when African American Republicans were nonexistent as members of the Senate and absent at municipal and state levels as mayors of major American cities or governors of any states. Franks was defeated in 1997 after serving three terms. He was named an Outstanding Young Man by the Boys Club in 1980 and Man of the Year by the Negro Professional Women's Club.

LENORA FULANI (1950–)

Political Party Leader, Psychologist, Social Therapist. Born Lenora Branch on April 25, 1950, in Chester, Pennsylvania, she adopted the name Fulani in 1973. Fulani earned a bachelor's degree from Hofstra University, a master's degree from Columbia University Teachers College, and a Ph.D. from the New York Institute for Social Therapy and Research. She worked as a guest researcher at Rockefeller University from 1973 to 1977. Fulani opened her own therapy practice in Harlem in the 1970s, the Eastside Center for Short Term Psychotherapy. She also founded the National Alliance Party (NAP), a political party that worked for social change.

Fulani made bids for election as lieutenant governor of New York in 1982 and governor in 1986 and 1990. She also campaigned for election as mayor of New York City in 1985. In 1988 and 1992, she campaigned for election as president of the United States. She made history in 1988 when she became the first woman and the first African American to be included on the presidential ballot in all fifty states. In 1992, she became the first woman to qualify for federal primary matching funds to run her campaign. In 1994, she made a run again for governor of New York, garnering 21 percent of the votes in the primary.

Following her gubernatorial defeat, Fulani contributed to the formation of the Patriot Party. The Patriot Party planned to gain wide-range support by appealing to voters independent of the two main political parties in the 1996 elections. The formation of this party was followed by Fulani's creation of the Committee for a Unified Independent Party. In the 2000 presidential election, Fulani made news by backing the Reform Party candidate, Pat Buchanan. In 2004, Fulani was a key supporter of Ralph Nader's candidacy for president as an independent. In 2005, Fulani assembled a network of black and Latino community leaders to organize African American voters to support Republican Michael Bloomberg's bid for reelection as mayor of New York City.

Fulani has written widely on the subject of politics. Her books include *Independent Black Leadership in America* (1990), written with Louis Farrakhan and Al Sharpton, and a memoir, *The Making of a Fringe Candidate, 1992* (1993). In the mid-1990s, her column, *This Way for Black Empowerment,* was carried in more than 140 newspapers nationwide. She is the founder and executive producer of the All-Stars Talent Show, the largest antiviolence program for inner-city youth in the country. She also hosted her own cable television show, *Fulani!*, which aired weekly in more than twenty cities. Fulani remains a leading advocate for the Reform Party and chairs the Committee for a Unified Independent Party. Fulani combines her career as a psychologist and social activist to crusade for structural political reforms, such as term limits, ballot-access reform, and same-day voter registration.

W. WILSON GOODE (1938–)

Municipal Government Official. Willie Wilson Goode was born on August 19, 1938, in Seaboard, North Carolina. He received a B.A. in 1961 from Morgan State University. Goode served in the U.S. Army from 1961 to 1963, earning a commendation medal for meritorious service and rising to the rank of captain with the military police. In 1968, he earned a master's degree in public administration from the University of Pennsylvania's Wharton School.

Between 1966 and 1978, Goode held a wide variety of positions, including probation officer, building maintenance supervisor, insurance claims adjuster, and president of the Philadelphia Council for Community Advancement. From 1978 to 1980, Goode was chairman of the Pennsylvania Public Utilities Commission. He served as managing director of the City of Philadelphia from 1980 to 1982. In 1983, Goode was elected the first African American mayor of Philadelphia.

Goode's tenure as mayor of Philadelphia was marred by charges that he was a weak and ineffective leader who was unable to handle the traditionally rough and tumble politics of Philadelphia city government. In May 1985, during a violent confrontation between the city of Philadelphia and members of MOVE, a radical "back-to-nature" cult that took over a row house in West Philadelphia, Goode ordered police to drop a bomb on the roof of the house to evict MOVE members. The massive explosion and fire that resulted killed eleven people, destroyed sixty-one homes, and caused $8 million in damage.

Goode barely won reelection in 1987 and was faced with mounting problems. Decades of corruption, racial tension, and urban decay had dampened Philadelphia's civic spirit and created a sense of apathy. Acute tensions between Goode and the city council resulted in a huge budget deficit. In September 1990, Goode announced that the city was on the verge of bankruptcy. Although a consortium of banks helped to avert disaster, Philadelphia reported a massive $200 million deficit in June 1991.

Barred by law from seeking a third term, Goode was succeeded as mayor by Edward Rendell in January 1992. That same year, he published his autobiography, *In Goode Faith.* After leaving office, Goode started his own company and worked for several years as deputy assistant secretary for the Department of Education.

In 2000, when he was sixty-two years old, Goode earned a doctorate of ministry from Eastern Baptist Theological Seminary. His dissertation was about moving congregations from looking inward to looking outward toward their community. Goode's research showed that a congregation would become involved in the problems of a community if asked by their faith leader to do so. In 2000, he became the organizer and director of Amachi, a nonprofit mentoring and youth-development program for children of incarcerated parents. Using a faith-based recruitment strategy, Goode called upon pastors to enlist and train their members as mentors. With Goode at the helm, this program established more than 240 programs across the country. In 2006, Good won the Civic Ventures Purpose Prize for his work with Amachi.

WILLIAM H. GRAY III (1941–)

Federal Legislator, Organization Executive, Diplomat. Born to a minister and a high school teacher in Baton Rouge, Louisiana, on August 20, 1941, William Herbert Gray III earned a B.A. from Franklin and Marshall College in 1963. During his senior year, he served as an intern for Pennsylvania congressman Robert N. C. Nix. Gray received a master of divinity degree from Drew Theological School in 1966 and a master of theology degree from Princeton Theological Seminary in 1970. He also attended the University of Pennsylvania, Temple University, and Oxford University.

Gray served as assistant pastor at Union Baptist Church in Montclair, New Jersey, from 1964 until 1966. He was promoted to senior pastor in 1966 and served in this capacity until 1972. Gray moved to Philadelphia in 1972 to become pastor of Bright Hope Baptist Church, a 5,000-member congregation for which he served as senior pastor until 2007.

In 1976, Gray decided to become involved in politics, challenging Nix for his congressional seat. Gray's first attempt to unseat Nix was unsuccessful. However, in 1978, Gray defeated Nix and was elected to Congress. Gray became a vocal and influential member of the House, challenging the administration of Ronald Reagan on such issues as social spending and U.S. support for the government of South Africa. He served on the House Budget Committee, becoming chair in 1985, and earned the admiration and respect of even his most implacable political foes. Gray was a member of the House Foreign Affairs Committee for twelve years. For ten of those twelve years, he served on the Appropriations Subcommittee on Foreign Operations. He was also vice chair of the Congressional Black Caucus.

Gray left the House of Representatives in 1991 to head the United Negro College Fund, where he remained until 2004. He also worked for the government-relations firm of Buchanan Ingersoll and Rooney in Washington, D.C. On May 8, 1994, President Bill Clinton appointed Gray as his special envoy to Haiti. In this capacity, Gray played an instrumental role in the eventual removal of Haiti's brutal military government in October 1994.

Gray was honored in 1997 as one of four recipients of the Four Freedoms Award. He has also served on the boards of numerous companies, including Chase Manhattan Bank, EDS, Visteon, Dell, and Pfizer. He serves as cochair of GrayLoeffler, LLC, a consulting firm specializing in government relations, education, and diversity. He is also vice chair of the Pew Commission on Children in Foster Care.

Patricia Roberts Harris Stamp, 2000. *Harris was honored with a 33-cent stamp as part of the Black Heritage series. She was the first African American woman to serve in a presidential cabinet (Jimmy Carter's) and the first African American woman to be a U.S. ambassador (Luxembourg).* AP IMAGES/USPS

PATRICIA ROBERTS HARRIS (1924–1985)

Organization Executive, Diplomat, Civil Rights Activist, Federal Government Official, Attorney, Educator. Born in Mattoon, Illinois, on May 31, 1924, Patricia Harris received her undergraduate degree in 1945 from Howard University. While at Howard, Harris also served as vice chairman of a student branch of the NAACP and was involved in early nonviolent demonstrations against racial discrimination. Harris worked for the YWCA in Chicago and served as executive director of Delta Sigma Theta, an African American sorority, from 1953 to 1959. After completing postgraduate work at the University of Chicago and at American University, she earned her Ph.D. in jurisprudence from George Washington University Law School in 1960.

An attorney and professor before she entered politics, Harris was appointed cochair of the National Women's Committee on Civil Rights by President John F. Kennedy. She was later named to the Commission on the Status of Puerto Rico. In 1965, Harris was chosen by President Lyndon B. Johnson to become U.S. ambassador to Luxembourg, the first African American woman ever to be named an American envoy. In 1969, Harris was appointed dean of the Howard University Law School and served in that role until 1970, when she joined a major Washington, D.C., law firm.

Harris served as secretary of the Department of Health and Human Services and as secretary of Housing and Urban Development under President Jimmy Carter. Harris was the first African American woman to serve in a cabinet post. In 1982, she ran an unsuccessful campaign for mayor of Washington, D.C. She became a law professor at George Washington University in 1983 and remained there until her death from cancer on March 23, 1985.

WILLIE W. HERENTON (1940–)

Municipal Government Official. A native of Memphis, Tennessee, Willie Wilbert Herenton became the first African American mayor of Memphis in 1991. He was reelected to his fifth term as mayor in 2007. He resigned from office in July 2009, before completing his term, and announced his plan to run for a seat in the U.S. Congress. He was defeated, however, in the 2010 primary.

Herenton graduated from LeMoyne Owen College in 1963, and earned a master's degree from the University of Memphis in 1966. He completed his doctorate at Southern Illinois University in 1971. From 1979 to 1991, Herenton served as superintendent of the Memphis City Schools. Herenton's administration posted balanced budgets throughout his tenure as mayor, though there were two property-tax increases during the twelve-year period.

Herenton has served on several corporate boards, including First Tennessee National Corporation and Promus Companies Incorporated. In 2002, Herenton was named Municipal Leader of the Year by *American City and County Magazine.*

ALEXIS HERMAN (1947–)

Federal Government Official. Alexis Margaret Herman was born in Mobile, Alabama, on July 16, 1947. She attended Edgewood College and Spring Hill College before earning her B.A. from Xavier University in 1969. She later did graduate work at the University of South Alabama.

After graduation from Xavier, she worked for a short time with Interfaith Mobile. She began her professional career in 1969 as a social worker with Catholic Charities, developing employment-training opportunities for unemployed youth and directing programs for training and employing black women in rural areas of the southeast. In 1976, President Jimmy Carter appointed the twenty-nine-year-old Herman as director of the Women's Bureau of the Department of Labor. She was the youngest person to ever hold that position and the highest-ranking African American in the Labor Department.

In 1981, after the election of President Ronald Reagan, Herman left government and founded A. M. Herman and Associates, a marketing and management company. She remained active in Democratic politics. In 1989, Herman was selected by her longtime friend Ron Brown, chair of the Democratic National Committee, to become chief of staff. By 1992, Herman was chief executive officer in charge of the successful Democratic National Convention held at Madison Square Garden, where Bill Clinton was selected as the Democrats' candidate for the presidency.

After Clinton's election as president, Herman was named deputy director of the Clinton-Gore presidential transition team. In this capacity, she facilitated the shift from twelve years of Republican control of government to the Democrats. Herman was one of five assistants to President Clinton when she became director of the Office of Public Liaison, where her responsibilities primarily entailed managing interaction between the Clinton administration and the public.

After Clinton won his second term, he appointed Herman as secretary of labor. She was the first African American to be named to the cabinet post. Her appointment was initially opposed by Republicans in Congress and by labor unions, but she won confirmation. During her tenure at the Department of Labor, Herman instituted a global child-labor standard, moved people from welfare to work with dignity, and launched an aggressive work initiative directed at unemployed youth. Her efforts focused on bringing minorities and women into the economic mainstream.

Despite her stellar reputation and success as a businesswoman, Herman was investigated after allegations surfaced that she had taken kickbacks and been involved in improper fund-raisers held at the White House. She was completely exonerated and the inquiry ended.

After leaving government, Herman became the chair and chief executive officer of New Ventures, Inc. She also chaired the Coca-Cola Company Task Force and the Toyota Advisory Board on Diversity. She has served on the boards of several major corporations, including Cummins, MGM Mirage, Entergy, and Prudential.

JESSE L. JACKSON JR. (1965–)

Federal Legislator, Civil Rights Activist, Organization Executive. U.S. Representative Jesse Louis Jackson Jr. was born to the Reverend Jesse Jackson Sr. and Jacqueline (Davis) Jackson on March 11, 1965, in Greenville, South Carolina. He attended Le Mans Academy and St. Albans Episcopal Prep School. After completing his secondary education, Jackson entered North Carolina Agricultural and Technical University in Greensboro, where he graduated magna cum laude in 1987 with a bachelor of science degree in business management. Three years later, he earned a master of arts degree in theology from Chicago Theological Seminary. Jackson continued his education and received a juris doctorate from the University of Illinois College of Law in 1993. Two years before completing law school, Jackson married Sandra Lee Stevens.

In 1986, Jackson was arrested for taking part in a demonstration against apartheid at the South African Embassy in Washington, D.C. He also participated in protests held in front of the South African consulate in Chicago. Jackson's longtime stance against South Africa's system of racial discrimination provided him the unique opportunity of being the only American to share a platform with Nelson Mandela, the major symbol of the struggle for human rights in South Africa, following Mandela's February 1990 release from prison.

During the Democratic National Convention in 1988, Jackson was the last of his siblings to introduce his father, the Reverend Jesse Jackson Sr. The younger Jackson's introduction of his father catapulted him to a successful public-speaking career. While pursuing his law degree, Jackson frequently campaigned for Democratic candidates. After graduating from the University of Illinois College of Law, he became the national field director for the Rainbow Coalition, a political action organization founded by his father. While serving in this position, Jackson established a nationwide nonaligned program that successfully registered thousands of new voters. He also inaugurated a program to educate citizens about the importance of participating in the political system, including how to utilize technology to win at the polls and to more effectively participate in the political arena. Additionally, he established new local chapters of Operation PUSH (People United to Save Humanity).

Jackson resigned his position at the Rainbow Coalition in 1995. A Democrat, he entered the world of politics as a candidate for Chicago's Second Congressional District, a seat previously held by Mel Reynolds. After winning the primary and general elections, Representative Jackson became a member of the 104th Congress in the U.S. House of Representatives on December 12, 1995. In 1996, Jackson published the book *Legal Lynching: Racism, Injustice, and the Death Penalty*, written with his father.

Self-described as "a public servant—not a politician—with a progressive agenda," Representative Jackson is part of a new generation of African American leaders who see their work as an extension of their parents' struggle to eradicate the remaining covert vestiges of discrimination. Jackson was reelected to his seventh term in Congress in 2008.

JESSE L. JACKSON SR.

See chapter 7, Civil Rights.

MAYNARD JACKSON (1938–2003)

Attorney, Municipal Government Official, Organization Executive. Maynard Holbrook Jackson was born on March 23, 1938, in Dallas, Texas, the son of a minister, Maynard Jackson Sr., and a college professor, Irene Dobbs Jackson. Though born in Texas, he spent much of his youth in Atlanta. When he was fourteen years old, he was admitted to Morehouse College as a Ford Foundation Early Admissions Scholar. He graduated with a B.A. in 1956, with a concentration in history and political science. After graduation, he worked for the Ohio State Bureau of Unemployment Compensation as a claims examiner from 1957 to 1958 and as a sales manager for P.F. Collier Inc. from 1958 to 1961.

In 1964, Jackson received a J.D. from the North Carolina Central University School of Law and then worked as a lawyer for the National Labor Relations Board. From 1968 to 1969, Jackson was managing attorney and director of community relations for the Emory Community Legal Service Center in Atlanta. He served as a senior partner in the law firm of Jackson, Patterson and Parks from 1970 to 1973.

Jackson had been active in Democratic politics and was the vice mayor of Atlanta from 1970 to 1974. In 1974, he was elected mayor, becoming the first African American mayor of a major city in the Deep South. At the time of his election to Atlanta's highest office, Jackson was also the youngest mayor of a major U.S. city. He remained mayor of Atlanta until 1982. After leaving office, Jackson returned to private life and worked as a bond lawyer before being reelected mayor of Atlanta in 1989. The selection of Atlanta as host of the 1994 Super Bowl and the site of the 1996 Summer Olympic Games were two of the greatest achievements of Jackson's second term.

In 1993, Jackson vetoed domestic partnership legislation, claiming that the city council did not provide details on funding benefits for partners of city employees. The response of the gay and lesbian community was fervent, as leaders of forty Atlanta-based lesbian and gay organizations coordinated a barrage of protests during the 1993 Fourth of July holiday. Jackson was also deluged with complaints from angry city taxpayers who felt that his decision to order more than $45,000 worth of furniture for the mayor's office was wasteful. Jackson admitted that city purchasing guidelines had not been followed.

Even after leaving office, Jackson fell into controversy. Accusations were leveled against him that while he was in office he improperly influenced the manner in which a $1.3 billion financial portfolio was invested. A city audit revealed that nearly 80 percent of the city's 1993 investments were turned over to a firm whose principal was Jackson's 1989 campaign treasurer. Jackson emphatically denied the allegations that he swayed any investment decisions.

Despite the alleged improprieties, Jackson earned a reputation as an aggressive and outspoken mayor. He led Atlanta through the difficult transition years from predominantly white leadership to a mixed power structure. Under Jackson, Atlanta made major gains as a financial center and distribution hub. In addition, an expansion of the city's international convention facilities turned Atlanta into a major convention center. In 1981, the *Almanac of Places* rated Atlanta as the best major city in which to live and work. Jackson had taken advantage of affirmative action programs to improve city housing and social conditions. He also transformed the mass-transit system into one of the most modern in the country.

Shortly after his last term, Jackson became chairman of the board and a majority stockholder in Jackson Securities Inc., a banking firm. He also held an interest in Jackmont Hospitality, a group of real-estate companies that hoped to stimulate the economy of some of Atlanta's depressed areas. In 1995, Jackson became the principal owner of a joint venture to operate a TGI Friday's restaurant at the city's Hartsfield International Airport. Many complained that Jackson's use of Atlanta's affirmative action program to land the premier location was an abuse of a system designed to aid the disadvantaged.

Jackson served as vice chairman of the White House Committee on Balanced Growth and Economic Development and the White House Committee on the Windfall Profits Tax. He also served as the national chairman of the Democratic National Committee's Voting Rights Institute from 2001 to 2002. He was founding chairman of the Atlanta Economic Development Corporation, as well as the chairman of the Atlanta Urban Residential Finance Authority. Jackson belonged to the Georgia and New York bar associations, the National League of Cities, and the National Black Caucus of Local Elected Officials.

Jackson died on June 23, 2003, in Arlington, Virginia, after suffering a heart attack. He was survived by his second wife, Valerie Richardson, an Atlanta public radio personality, and five children.

Sheila Jackson Lee, U.S. Representative from Texas, December 2006. *The first vice-chairwoman of the Congressional Black Caucus, Jackson Lee has used her position on the House Judiciary Committee to direct attention to civil rights and abortion rights.* AP PHOTO/HARAZ N. GHANBARI

SHEILA JACKSON LEE (1950–)

Federal Legislator, Attorney. Sheila Jackson Lee was born in Queens in 1950 and was raised in New York City. She graduated in 1972 from Yale University with a B.A. In 1975, she graduated from the University of Virginia Law School with a J.D. Her husband was an official at the University of Houston, and Jackson Lee began her practice in Texas.

After three unsuccessful attempts to become a local judge, Jackson Lee was appointed an associate judge in the Houston municipal court system in 1987. Three years later, she was elected to an at-large position on the city council. In 1994, she defeated an incumbent Democrat in the congressional primary and was then elected to the seat once held by Barbara Jordan, who had been her mentor.

Jackson Lee has been a member of the U.S. House of Representatives since 1995. She serves on the House Judiciary committee and has used this position to direct attention to civil rights and abortion rights. Jackson Lee has spoken out against racism in South Africa and has advocated for sanctions against Sudan. She was arrested in 2006 along with other members of Congress and activists outside the Sudanese Embassy in Washington for disorderly conduct while protesting ethnic cleansing in Darfur.

Jackson Lee is a member of the Congressional Black Caucus, for which she has served as the first vice chair. In 1997, she was named the caucus's whip. Jackson Lee served on the House Judiciary Committee that impeached President Bill Clinton and made a name for herself as one of the president's staunchest defenders. She is also chair of the Congressional Children's Caucus, a senior member of the Homeland Security Committee, and the ranking member on the Judiciary Subcommittee on Immigration, Border Security, and Claims. She was reelected to her eighth term in Congress in 2008.

BARBARA JORDAN (1936–1996)

Educator, Federal and State Legislator, Civil Rights Activist, Attorney. Barbara Jordan was born on February 21, 1936, in Houston, Texas. Afflicted with multiple sclerosis, she died of viral pneumonia, a complication of leukemia, on January 17, 1996.

Jordan attended Phillis Wheatley High School, and in 1952, graduated as a member of the honor society. In 1956, Jordan received a B.A. from Texas Southern University in history and political science. She earned a J.D. from Boston University in 1959. After teaching at Tuskegee Institute for one year, Jordan returned to Houston, where she practiced law and was appointed administrative assistant to a Harris County judge.

In 1966, Jordan was elected to the Texas Senate. She was the first African American to serve as president pro tem of that

Barbara Jordan, Legislator and Educator. *Known as a champion of civil rights for all, Jordan was elected to the U.S. House of Representatives in 1972, thus becoming the first African American woman from a southern state, Texas, elected to Congress.* CORBIS

body and to chair the important Labor and Management Relations Committee.

In 1972, Jordan was elected to the U.S. House of Representatives, becoming the first African American woman from a southern state elected to Congress. As a member of Congress, she served on the Judiciary Committee, which heard the impeachment proceedings of President Richard M. Nixon. She also served on the House Judiciary and Government Operations committees. During her terms in both the Texas Senate and U.S. House, Jordan was known as a champion of civil rights for all and especially minorities and the poor. In 1976, she became the first African American to deliver the keynote address at the Democratic National Convention.

From 1979 to 1982, Jordan taught at the Lyndon Baines Johnson School of Public Affairs at the University of Texas. In 1982, she was appointed to the Lyndon Baines Johnson Centennial Chair of National Policy, a post she held until her death. In 1993, Jordan was appointed chair of the U.S. Commission on Immigration Reform by U.S. president Bill Clinton. She was lauded for her efforts to address the burgeoning U.S. hostility toward immigrants. She also served on the Democratic Caucus Steering and Policy Committee.

Jordan published two books, *Barbara Jordan: A Self-Portrait* (1979), written with Shelby Hearon, and *The Great Society: A Twenty Year Critique* (1986), which she edited with Elspeth D. Rostow. Jordan belonged to the American Bar Association as well as the Texas, Massachusetts, and District of Columbia bars. She was a member of the Character Counts Coalition, a group whose aim is to address the values of American society, emphasizing youth. She served on the boards of directors of the Mead Corporation and the Henry J. Kaiser Family Foundation.

Jordan received numerous awards, including the 1984 Eleanor Roosevelt Humanities Award and membership in the Texas Women's Hall of Fame (1984). She also appeared on the *Ladies Home Journal*'s "100 Most Influential Women in America" and *Time* magazine's 1976 "Ten Women of the Year" lists. In 1994, President Clinton gave her the Presidential Medal of Freedom, the nation's highest civilian honor, for her distinguished career in public service. Jordan also received twenty-seven honorary doctorate degrees. The Lyndon Baines Johnson School of Public Affairs named an endowed chair in her honor and holds the Barbara Jordan Forum each year in February around the time of her birthday. In 2007, the University of Texas Press published a collection of her speeches, *Barbara Jordan: Speaking the Truth with Eloquent Thunder*, edited by Max Sherman.

SHARON PRATT KELLY (1944–)

Attorney, Municipal Government Official, Media Executive, Educator. Sharon Pratt Kelly was born Sharon Pratt in Washington, D.C., on January 30, 1944. For a time, she worked under the name Sharon Pratt Dixon, assuming the surname of her former husband. She graduated from Howard University with a B.A. in political science in 1965 and received a J.D. in 1968. In 1967, she edited the Howard University law school journal.

From 1970 through 1971, Kelly was the house counsel for the Joint Center for Political Studies in Washington, D.C. Between 1971 and 1976, she was an associate in the law firm of Pratt and Queen, her father's firm. During this time, she also taught at Antioch Law School. In 1976, Kelly began a fourteen-year association with the Potomac Electric Power Company, where she gained a reputation as a decisive, hardworking, and effective utilities executive. While there, she held increasingly important positions, including associate general counsel, director of consumer affairs, and vice president of public policy.

In 1976 and 1977, Kelly was general counsel to the Washington, D.C., Democratic Committee. Between 1985 and 1989, she was treasurer of the Democratic Party and also sat on the Washington, D.C., Democratic State Committee.

In 1990, Kelly was elected mayor of Washington, D.C. When she won the election, she became the first African American woman mayor of a major American city. She was not able to deliver on campaign promises to reform city government and to fire two thousand middle managers in the D.C. bureaucracy. Her relations with the Democratic Congress were strained and Kelly's administration was perceived as ineffective, which helped pave the way for her 1994 defeat and the comeback of former mayor Marion Barry.

Kelly belongs to the American Bar Association and the Washington, D.C., Women's Bar Association. She is affiliated with the Legal Aid Society, the American Civil Liberties Union, and the United Negro College Fund. Kelly was a Falk Fellow at Howard University and has received numerous awards, including the 1983 NAACP Presidential Award, the 1985 United Negro College Fund's Distinguished Leadership Award, and the 1986 Distinguished Service Award presented by the Federation of Women's Clubs. In 2002, Kelly opened Pratt Consulting, LLC, a firm specializing in energy policy, homeland security, financial management, and technology.

ALAN L. KEYES (1950–)

Federal Government Official, Diplomat, Lecturer. Alan Lee Keyes was born on August 7, 1950, in New York City. Keyes lived in both the United States and Italy during his childhood. He began his political career by serving as president of his high school's student council and as the first African American president of the American Legion Boys Nation. Keyes entered Cornell University after completing high school, but left the school after his life was threatened when he refused to participate in a demonstration. Keyes earned a B.A. from Harvard in 1972. He received his Ph.D. in political science from Harvard in 1979.

In 1978, Keyes took a position at the U.S. State Department, where he worked for eleven years. He recruited Jeane Kirkpatrick as a mentor by defending her from verbal attack while serving as U.S. vice consul in India. At the State Department, Keyes served in the South African Affairs Division and on the Policy Planning Council. Keyes was appointed ambassador to UNESCO (the United Nations Educational, Scientific, and Cultural Organization) by President Ronald Reagan in 1983 and remained as UN ambassador until 1985, when he was appointed assistant secretary of state for international organizations. Keyes was one of the youngest ever to serve in these posts. He was also the highest-ranking African American at the State Department in 1988, but he resigned in response to a dispute over the allocation of U.S. funds to the United Nations. During his tenure at the State Department, Keyes adamantly supported President Reagan's policy opposing economic sanctions against South Africa and its system of apartheid. After leaving government service, Keyes formed Citizens against Government Waste (CAGW) and established the organization's National Taxpayers' Action Day. He served as president of CAGW until 1991. He also served as interim president in 1991 for Alabama A&M University.

In 1988 and 1992, Keyes lost senatorial elections in Maryland. In 1992, following his second defeat, Keyes started his own talk-radio show in Baltimore, *America's Wake-up Call: The Alan Keyes Show.* Bolstered by the response to his radio show, Keyes announced his candidacy for the U.S. presidency on March 26, 1995. In so doing, he became the first Republican African American in the twentieth century to run for president. He attracted little support, however, and did not win a primary. Despite the showing, Keyes made another unsuccessful run for the GOP nomination in 2000. In 2002, he briefly hosted a televised talk show, *Alan Keyes Is Making Sense.*

In 2004, Keyes was drafted by the Illinois Republican Party to run against Democrat Barack Obama for the U.S. Senate after the Republican nominee withdrew because of a sex scandal. Some viewed Keyes as a carpetbagger because he moved to Illinois from Maryland just before the election.

A devout Catholic, Keyes is pro-life, raising the standard of the unalienable rights of the unborn. He is also antihomosexual and is said to have severed relations with his only daughter, who describes herself as a lesbian. Keyes is the author of *Masters of the Dream: The Strength and Betrayal of Black America* (1995) and *Our Character, Our Future: Reclaiming America's Moral Destiny* (1996). Keyes's political priorities are best summarized in this quote from his Web site:

> I aim to strengthen the foundations of political liberty in America. I believe that it remains the destiny of the American people to uphold the right of all humankind to practice responsible self-government.
>
> Dedication to this Providential purpose is the heart and soul of what it means to be an American. I will labor to: abolish the income tax; liberate entrepreneurial and charitable initiative; honor marriage and the family; respect the equal dignity of all human beings, born, and unborn; reclaim American sovereignty from global bureaucracy; and show, by word and deed, the role of statesmanship in a free republic.

RON KIRK (1954–)

Attorney, Municipal and Federal Government Official. Ronald Kirk was born on June 27, 1954, in Austin, Texas. He received a B.A. in political science and sociology from Austin College in 1976. In 1974, while he was in college, Kirk served as a legislative aide to the Texas Constitutional Convention. This experience prompted an interest in politics and drove him to complete his law degree in 1979 at the University of Texas School of Law.

After two years, Kirk became unsatisfied as a private practice attorney. He moved to Washington, D.C., where he worked for U.S. Senator Lloyd Bentsen from 1981 to 1983. He returned to Dallas in 1983 to work for the Dallas City Attorney's Office and became the chief lobbyist of Dallas. In 1989, he began working for the firm of Johnson and Gibbs and volunteered for Big Brothers/Big Sisters of America, the Dallas Zoological Society, Dallas Helps, and the North Texas Food Bank, among other organizations.

In 1994, then Texas governor Ann Richards named Kirk secretary of state. The following year, Kirk ran a very successful campaign and was elected the mayor of Dallas with 62 percent of the vote. In 1999, Kirk was reelected mayor of Dallas with 74 percent of the vote. In 2001, Kirk announced that he was resigning as the city's mayor in order to seek the nomination as the Democratic candidate for the U.S. Senate seat vacated by retiring Republican Phil Gramm. Kirk lost with 43 percent of the vote to his Republican opponent's 55 percent.

After his defeat, Kirk returned to the law firm of Gardere Wynne Sewell in Dallas and remained active in Democratic politics. He is a partner with the Houston-based law firm of Vinson and Elkins, where his principal area of practice is public finance and public policy. He was honored in 1992 with a Volunteer of the Year Award from Big Brothers/Big Sisters and a Distinguished Alumni Award from the Austin College Alumni Association. He was named Citizen of the Year by Omega Psi Phi in 1994, the same year that he earned the C. B. Bunkley Community Service Award from the Turner Legal Association.

In 2004, the Anti-Defamation League presented Kirk with the coveted Jurisprudence Award. In 2006, Kirk's alma mater, Austin College, gave him an honorary doctorate. In 2007, Kirk was listed among the best lawyers in America in government relations law. In March 2009, the U.S. Senate confirmed Kirk's nomination as U.S. trade representative. In this role, he serves as the president's principal adviser and negotiator on trade issues.

JOHN MERCER LANGSTON (1829–1897)

Educational Administrator, Federal Legislator, Diplomat, Attorney, Lecturer. Congressman John Mercer Langston was born in Virginia in 1829. Upon the death of his father, Langston was emancipated and sent to Ohio, where he was given over to the care of a friend of his father. Langston spent his childhood there, attending private school in Cincinnati before graduating in 1849 from Oberlin College. Four years later, after getting his degree from the theological department of Oberlin, he studied law and was admitted to the Ohio bar.

Langston began his practice in Brownhelm, Ohio. He was chosen in 1855 to serve as clerk of the township by the Liberty Party. During the Civil War, he was a recruiting agent for African American servicemen, helping to organize such regiments as the Fifty-fourth and Fifty-fifth Massachusetts and the Fifth Ohio. In 1867, Langston served as inspector-general of the Freedmen's Bureau. He was dean and vice president of Howard University from 1868 to 1875. In 1877, he was named minister resident to Haiti and chargé d'affaires to Santo Domingo, remaining in diplomatic service until 1885.

Soon after returning to his law practice in the United States, Langston was named president of the Virginia Normal and Collegiate Institute. In 1888, he was elected to Congress from Virginia, but was not seated for two years until vote-counting irregularities had been investigated. He was defeated in his bid for a second term. In 1894, Langston published an autobiography, *From the Virginia Plantation to the National Capital.* He died in 1897.

GEORGE THOMAS "MICKEY" LELAND (1944–1989)

Civil Rights Activist, Federal Legislator, Educator. Mickey Leland was born on November 27, 1944, in Lubbock, Texas. He graduated from Texas Southern University in 1970 with a B.S. in pharmacy. Leland had been active in the civil rights movement during his student years. He was elected to the Texas state legislature in 1973. In 1978, he was elected to the U.S. House of Representatives to fill Barbara Jordan's vacated seat. While a representative, Leland served on various committees, including Interstate and Foreign Commerce, Post Office and Civil Service, and the committee on the District of Columbia.

Leland was devoted to easing the hunger of starving persons in the United States and in other countries, especially African countries. He chaired the House Select Committee on World Hunger and visited starving peoples throughout Africa. In 1989, while traveling to a United Nations refugee camp in Ethiopia, the plane on which Leland was traveling crashed near Gambela, Ethiopia, killing all on board.

JOHN ROBERT LEWIS (1940–)

Civil Rights Activist, Federal Legislator, Organization Executive. John Lewis was born in Troy, Alabama, on

John Robert Lewis, 2006. *Civil rights leader the Reverend Jesse Jackson (left) watches as Rep. John Lewis tells Jackson's wife, Jacqueline Lavinia Brown, that the U.S. Senate has passed the Voting Rights Reauthorization Act 98–0, July 2006.* **CHIP SOMODEVILLA/GETTY IMAGES**

February 21, 1940, into a sharecropping family. He received a B.S. in 1961 from the American Baptist Theological Seminary and a B.A. from Fisk University in 1967. While attending these two schools in Nashville, he became involved in the sit-in movement, the freedom rides, and other efforts to desegregate the South. He was arrested more than forty times, attacked by angry mobs, and severely beaten by police and other law enforcement personnel. During this time, Lewis became committed to nonviolence and the advancement of African Americans. He was a leader in the peaceful and orderly march across the Edmund Pettus Bridge in Selma toward Montgomery that came to be known as Bloody Sunday because of the vicious and savage attack by police on the more than six hundred nonviolent protestors. Before entering politics, Lewis was associated with numerous social justice organizations, including the Student Nonviolent Coordinating Committee, for which he served as president. He also served as associate director of the Field Foundation, project director of the Southern Regional Council, and executive director of the Voter Education Project Inc., beginning in 1970.

Lewis first ran for elective office in 1977 to fill a vacancy created when incumbent Georgia congressman Andrew Young was appointed U.S. ambassador to the United Nations. Lewis lost that race to Wyche Fowler, but was subsequently elected Atlanta city councilman-at-large. When Fowler ran for the U.S. Senate, voters sent Lewis to the U.S. House of Representatives as a Democrat in 1987, representing Georgia's Fifth Congressional District, which includes Atlanta. While in the House, Lewis has served on the Public Works, Interior, and Insular Affairs committees, as well as the powerful House Ways and Means Committee. He has also been a member of the Select Committee on Aging. Lewis's pet project over the years was a bill to establish a museum of African American history at the Smithsonian Institution in Washington, D.C. In 2003, President George W. Bush signed legislation creating the National Museum of African American History and Culture.

Lewis denounced the rhetoric of his homophobic colleagues during a House debate that ultimately led to the adoption of legislation to discourage the enlistment of homosexual men and women in the military. He considered the Republican Contract with America as the genesis of a wave of intolerance in American society that arose in the early to mid-1990s. In 1995, Lewis headed a group of nearly one hundred trade unionists that interrupted a speech on proposed Medicare changes by House Speaker Newt Gingrich during a conference sponsored by the Congressional Institute. Many of Lewis's critics suggested that the demonstration did little but gain media attention, but Lewis countered that saving Medicare benefits for the elderly was his priority, and he was willing to seize any opportunity to stir up a public debate.

Although Lewis was well known for his involvement with the U.S. civil rights movement, he abstained from the 1995 Million Man March because he felt that he could not participate in an effort led by Louis Farrakhan. Lewis worked steadfastly in the mid-1990s to help produce a spirit of racial harmony in Atlanta as the city prepared for the 1996 Olympics.

Lewis is a 1975 recipient of the Martin Luther King Jr. Nonviolent Peace Prize and was named by *Ebony* magazine as "One of the Nation's Most Influential Blacks" (1991–1992) and *Time* magazine as "One of America's Rising Leaders" (1974). He belongs to the Martin Luther King Jr. Center for Social Change, the National Democratic Institute for International Affairs, Friends of Vista, and the African-American Institute.

Lewis received a special honor in 2001, the fortieth anniversary of the 1961 freedom rides in which he participated, when he was named the winner of a John F. Kennedy Profile in Courage Award for lifetime achievement. He has received numerous honorary degrees and other awards from colleges and universities throughout the United States. Lewis has been honored by many imminent national and international institutions. He is the author of an autobiography titled *Walking with the Wind: A Memoir of the Movement* (1998), written with Michael D'Orso.

KWEISI MFUME (1948–)

Federal Legislator, Educator, Civil Rights Activist, Organization Executive. Kweisi Mfume was born Frizzell Gerald Gray in Baltimore on October 24, 1948. He dropped out of school, got in trouble with the law, and fathered five children out of wedlock before turning to education and obtaining his GED in his early twenties. He continued his studies at the Community College of Baltimore, where he was president of the Black Student Union and editor of the school newspaper. He later attended Morgan State University and graduated magna cum laude with a B.S. in 1976. In 1984, he completed a master's degree in liberal arts from Johns Hopkins University with a concentration in international studies.

In 1979, Mfume was elected to the Baltimore City Council by a margin of three votes. He worked hard to diversify city government, improve public safety, enhance minority business development, and divest city funds from South Africa. Active in Democratic politics, Mfume was a member of the Maryland Democratic State Central Committee and a delegate to the Democratic national conventions in 1980, 1984, and 1988.

Mfume was elected to the U.S. House of Representatives in 1987. During his tenure, he served on the Small Business Committee, the Education and Labor Committee, the Narcotics Abuse and Control Subcommittee, and the Banking, Finance, and Urban Affairs Committee. The House Speaker chose Mfume to serve on the Ethics Committee and on the Joint Economic Committee of the House and Senate. He also was vice chair, and later chairperson, of the Congressional Black Caucus. In addition, Mfume was a member of the Caucus for Women's Issues, the Congressional Arts Caucus, and the Federal Government Service Task Force.

In February 1996, Mfume became president and CEO of the NAACP after the organization's board of directors unanimously elected him to that post. His priorities were to restore the confidence of members and supporters in this seminal organization, to ensure greater fiscal accountability, and to secure private-sector funding. Within weeks of Mfume's appointment, Nissan Motor Corporation USA donated $100,000 to the NAACP. Among Mfume's accomplishments were eliminating the association's debt, setting new standards and expectations for NAACP branches nationwide, and working to engage seasoned local volunteers and a new generation of younger civil rights activists in the mission of the NAACP. In 2000, Mfume led calls for more minority representation on network television. Under his leadership, the NAACP threatened a boycott against NBC, but relented when the network agreed to hire more minorities to write, produce, and direct its television shows. Mfume served as NAACP president until 2004.

Mfume announced his candidacy for the U.S. Senate seat held by Paul Sarbanes in March 2005. He ran a vigorous campaign but was defeated by U.S. Congressman Ben Cardin. There were speculations that Mfume would run for mayor of Baltimore, but he expressed his belief that everyone should give the current mayor, Sheila Dixon, the opportunity to lead.

Mfume published his inspiring autobiography, *No Free Ride: From the Mean Streets to the Mainstream*, in 1996. He is a trustee of the Baltimore Museum of Art and the Morgan State University Board of Regents, where he previously taught political science and communications. He is also a member of the senior advisory committee of Harvard's John F. Kennedy School of Government and the board of trustees for the Enterprise Foundation. In 2010, Mfume became executive director of the National Medical Association.

ARTHUR W. MITCHELL (1883–1968)

Civil Rights Activist, Federal Legislator, Lecturer, Attorney, Organization Executive. Born to enslaved parents in 1883 in Chambers County, Alabama, Arthur Wergs Mitchell was educated at Tuskegee Institute and at Columbia and Harvard universities. By 1929, he had founded Armstrong Agricultural School in West Butler, Alabama, and become a wealthy landowner and a lawyer with a thriving practice in Washington, D.C. When he left the nation's capital that year, it was with the purpose of entering politics and becoming a representative from Illinois.

Mitchell won Democratic approval only after Harry Baker died suddenly. Aided by the overwhelming national sentiment for the Democratic Party during this period, he unseated Oscar DePriest by the slender margin of three thousand votes. Mitchell's most significant victory on behalf of civil rights came not in the legislative chamber but in the courts. In 1937, Mitchell brought suit against the Chicago and Rock Island Railroad after having been forced to leave his first-class accommodations en route to Hot Springs, Arkansas, and sit in a "Jim Crow" car. He argued his own case before the Supreme Court in 1941 and won a decision that declared Jim Crow practices illegal.

Mitchell proposed that states that discriminated against African Americans should receive fewer congressional seats and advocated strong sanctions against states where lynchings took place. In addition, he worked for the elimination of poll taxes to make it easier for African Americans to vote. Following the end of World War II, Mitchell argued that because African Americans fought bravely for the United States, they should be able to vote for their government representatives.

Mitchell retired from Congress in 1942 and continued his civil rights activism as a private citizen. He also lectured occasionally and pursued farming on his estate near Petersburg, Virginia, where he died in 1968 at age eighty-five.

MARC MORIAL (1958–)

Municipal Official. Morial was born in January 3, 1958, to a prominent African American family in New Orleans. His father, Ernest "Dutch" Morial, was New Orleans' first African American mayor. Marc Morial received his B.A. in 1980 from the University of Pennsylvania and his J.D. three years later from the Georgetown University Law School.

Morial became a supporter of the Reverend Jesse Jackson Sr. and worked for Jackson's 1988 campaign for president. In 1991, Morial was elected to the state senate in Louisiana. Two years later, he announced his candidacy for mayor of New Orleans. The election was marred by racial questions and a runoff was needed before Morial could be declared the winner.

Morial battled crime in his first term as mayor, introducing several innovative and controversial reforms within the police department. In 1998, he began his second term as mayor, grabbing national headlines as the city filed a lawsuit against gun manufacturers. From 1994 to 2002, Morial maintained a 70 percent approval rating. As mayor, he reduced crime by 60 percent, reformed the beleaguered police department, oversaw massive improvements to the city's infrastructure, built fifteen thousand new homes, and brought professional sports to the city when the National Basketball Association's Hornets moved to New Orleans. In 2001, Morial served as president of the U.S. Conference of Mayors, a position his father had held sixteen years earlier. Morial stepped down as mayor after completing his second term in 2002. In 2003, he became the eighth president and CEO of the nation's largest direct-services organization, the National Urban League, which empowers African Americans and other ethnic communities through effective economic strategies.

CAROL MOSELEY BRAUN (1947–)

Attorney, Federal Legislator. Born Carol Moseley in Chicago on August 16, 1947, Moseley Braun received her B.A. from the University of Illinois in 1969 and her J.D. in 1972 from the University of Chicago Law School. While attending law school, Moseley Braun worked as a legal intern and an associate attorney for a number of law firms. After finishing law school, Moseley Braun served as an assistant U.S. attorney for the Northern District of Illinois from 1973 until 1977. In 1979, she was elected an Illinois state representative from the twenty-fifth district, where she became known as an ardent supporter of civil rights legislation. After her bid for the lieutenant governorship was thwarted, Moseley Braun was elected in 1986 as the Cook County recorder of deeds.

In 1992, Moseley Braun became the nation's first African American woman elected to the U.S. Senate, making her an icon of the "Year of the Woman." The following year, Moseley Braun, along with Senator Dianne Feinstein, was selected for the formerly all-male Senate Judiciary Committee. Her first major legislative proposal—an amendment to an omnibus crime bill that would try young offenders implicated in serious crime from the age of thirteen and up as adults—was overwhelmingly approved by the Senate.

A recipient of many honors, Moseley Braun won the 1981 and 1982 Best Legislation Award presented by the Independent Voters of Illinois. She has also won the 1981 National Association of Negro Business and Professional Women's Clubs' Community Recognition Award, the 1981 Chicago Alliance of Black School Educators' Recognition of Excellence in Education Award, the 1982 Afro-American Voters Alliance Community Recognition Award, and a

Carol Moseley Braun, Democratic Convention, New York City, 1992. *Moseley Braun won election to the U.S. Senate from the state of Illinois later in 1992, becoming the first black female senator.* PHOTOGRAPH BY BARRY THUMMA. AP IMAGES. REPRODUCED BY PERMISSION.

1993 Essence Award for African American women of achievement. In 1993, she was chosen as the keynote speaker for the annual National Urban League dinner. Moseley Braun belongs to the League of Black Women, Operation PUSH, and the Women's Political Caucus. She is a member of the federal, Illinois, and Chicago bar associations.

In spite of her national prominence, her celebrity status, and the numerous honors, Moseley Braun's senate career was dogged by ethical questions that often overshadowed her legislative record. The Federal Elections Commission investigated $249,000 in unaccounted campaign expenditures. The investigation, which lasted nearly five years, found the allegations to be without merit, and no fines or sanctions were levied against Moseley Braun or her campaign. In spite of the findings, Moseley Braun was defeated in her bid for a second term in 1998.

In 1999, Bill Clinton named her a special consultant to the Department of Education and later nominated Moseley Braun as ambassador to New Zealand and Samoa. In the fall of 2001, following her term as ambassador, she became a visiting professor of politics at Morris Brown College in Atlanta. In February 2003, Moseley Braun announced her candidacy for the Democratic presidential nomination. Four days before the Iowa caucus, Moseley Braun withdrew from the race and endorsed Howard Dean. After the campaign, Moseley Braun began practicing law as a private attorney in Chicago.

C. RAY NAGIN (1956–)

Municipal Government Official. Clarence Ray Nagin was born in New Orleans, Louisiana, in 1956 and lived there until he went to college at Tuskegee University to study accounting. He graduated in 1978 with a B.S. In 1994, he completed his M.B.A. at Tulane University.

Much of Nagin's early career was in the private sector. Prior to his entry into politics, Nagin was the vice president and general manager for Cox Communications in Southeast Louisiana. In this position, Nagin produced remarkable results for the cable company by transforming one of Cox's poorest-performing markets into one of its most profitable assets. To achieve this, Nagin utilized the best technology

New Orleans Mayor Ray Nagin, Inauguration Parade, June 1, 2006. *Nagin began his second four-year term as mayor less than a year after Hurricane Katrina devastated New Orleans.* MARIO TAMA/GETTY IMAGES

available, hired and developed an efficient staff, and emphasized customer service to turn things around.

With no political experience, Nagin entered the 2002 New Orleans mayoral race as a long shot. He promised to reform the city's image, fight political corruption, and restore confidence in New Orleans as a well-run city. In the crowded primary, Nagin received 29 percent of the vote, which placed him in a runoff with Police Chief Richard Pennington. Nagin's victory in the runoff with 59 percent of the vote was impressive given that he received 85 percent of the white vote and 40 percent of the African American vote.

During his first term, Nagin launched a far-reaching anticorruption campaign targeting the Taxicab Bureau and the Utilities Department. Among the results of this effort were the arrests of eighty-four city workers and a reorganization of the Utilities Department. When investigations revealed rampant corruption among city vehicle-inspection certification workers, Nagin fired all of the workers in that department. Nagin's unorthodox methods and commitment to changing the culture of government for the better were met with surprise and disbelief. His relationship with the city council was rocky, and the council did not support much of the legislation he favored.

The real test for his administration came on August 28, 2005, when Katrina approached New Orleans as a category 4 hurricane. Nagin declared a mandatory evacuation of the city, with the Superdome serving as a shelter of last resort for those who could not leave. On August 29, 2005, when Hurricane Katrina hit, 80 percent of the city was flooded. There was much criticism of the slow handling of relief and evacuation efforts by federal, state, and local government officials. Recovery efforts in New Orleans continued at what many considered a snail's pace.

Because of post-Katrina devastation and the fact that the majority of New Orleans' citizens were still living elsewhere, the mayoral elections were postponed by the state until April 2006. There were twenty-three challengers for the mayor's post, and most of them were white. Among the most prominent was Lieutenant Governor Mitch Landrieu, scion of a powerful political family. Nagin received much criticism during this period because of several ill-considered statements about New Orleans as a chocolate city and Katrina as a result of God's anger with America and African Americans in particular. Nagin was the top vote-getter in the election of April 22, 2006, with 38 percent to Landrieu's 29 percent. In the May runoff, Nagin beat Landrieu with 52 percent of the vote to 48 percent. This time, Nagin received 80 percent of the African American vote and 20 percent of the white vote.

Nagin's second term was not without controversy. His 100-day plan to rebuild New Orleans produced few results. He was criticized for rarely being seen in New Orleans while traveling extensively on a national speaking tour. He also continued to make public statements that were considered controversial. In early 2007, Nagin hired Edward Blakely, an internationally renowned city planner, to lead New Orleans' rebuilding effort. Because of term limits, he could not seek a third term, and left office in May 2010.

ELEANOR HOLMES NORTON (1938–)

Attorney, Federal Legislator, Civil Rights Activist, Organization Executive, Educator. Eleanor Holmes Norton was born on April 8, 1938, in Washington, D.C. She attended Antioch College in Ohio but transferred to Yale University and received an M.A. in American studies in 1963 and a J.D. in 1964 from Yale Law School.

After finishing law school, Norton clerked for a federal judge in Philadelphia before joining the American Civil Liberties Union (ACLU) in 1965 as a litigator specializing in free speech issues. She stayed with the ACLU until 1970, reaching the position of assistant legal director and successfully arguing a First Amendment case before the U.S. Supreme Court. In 1970, she became chairwoman of the New York City Commission on Human Rights, a post she held until 1977, when President Jimmy Carter chose her to become the first woman to chair the Equal Employment Opportunity Commission. In 1981, she was a senior fellow at the Urban Institute. In 1982, she became a professor of law at Georgetown University. Norton had previously taught African American history at Pratt Institute in Brooklyn and law at New York University Law School.

In 1990, Norton was elected as the nonvoting congressional delegate to the U.S. House of Representatives for the District of Columbia. Though elected by the citizens of the District of Columbia, Norton does not have all the rights and privileges of a full representative. She cannot vote on the House floor, though she may vote in committee. Norton came to Congress as a national figure who had been active in civil rights and feminist issues. She had also previously served on the boards of three *Fortune* 500 companies.

In 1993, Norton sponsored legislation that would make Washington, D.C., the fifty-first state. She was also allowed to cast a vote in the full house, thus becoming the first resident of the district to vote on the floor of Congress. In 1995, however, the House voted to strip Washington, D.C., of its floor-voting privileges. Norton protested that she was elected by federal tax-paying citizens who are entitled to full representation. She continues her fight for full congressional voting representation and full democracy for the citizens of the District of Columbia.

Norton was named to the *Ladies' Home Journal* 1988 "One Hundred Most Important Women" list and the 1989 "One Hundred Most Powerful Women in Washington" list by *Washington* magazine. She is a recipient of the 1985 Distinguished Public Service Award presented by the Center for National Policy. She has received more than fifty honorary degrees.

BARACK OBAMA (1961–)

President of the United States. Barack Obama was born August 4, 1961, in Oahu, Hawaii. He is the son of a Kenyan economist and white American mother. His parents divorced when he was only two years old. His father went on to Harvard to pursue doctoral studies. His mother married an Indonesian, and the family moved to Jakarta in 1967. Obama returned to Hawaii and was raised by his maternal grandparents in Honolulu. After graduation from high school in 1979, he studied at Occidental College in Los Angeles, and then transferred to Columbia University in New York, where he majored in political science. He graduated in 1983 with a bachelor's degree and worked briefly in corporate America.

In 1985, Obama relocated to Chicago to do community organizing and to help local churches organize job-training programs for low-income people. In 1988, Obama enrolled in Harvard Law School, where he had a stellar career. He was elected the first African American president in the 104-year history of the *Harvard Law Review*. After graduating magna cum laude from Harvard in 1991, he directed a voter-registration drive and became an associate with the law firm of Miner, Barnhill and Galland, specializing in civil rights. Obama also taught constitutional law at the University of Chicago.

In 1996, Obama was elected to the Illinois State Senate and became chairman of the Senate Health and Human Services Committee when the Democrats regained control. In 2000, Obama ran unsuccessfully in the Democratic primary against four-term incumbent congressman Bobby Rush. Obama was defeated by a two-to-one vote margin.

The year 2004 was pivotal for Obama. He ran for the U.S. Senate seat vacated by Peter Fitzgerald, and he was

President-Elect Barack Obama and Family, Grant Park, Chicago, November 4, 2008. *After his historic election to the U.S. presidency, Obama gave his victory speech before a huge crowd gathered in Chicago's Grant Park.* DOUG MILLIS/THE NEW YORK TIMES/REDUX PICTURES

catapulted into national celebrity status by his powerful keynote address at the Democratic National Convention. For a brief period leading up to the general election, Obama was unopposed because the Republican primary winner withdrew after damaging allegations of sexual misconduct were revealed in divorce proceedings involving child custody. In August 2004, less than three months before the election, the Republican Party recruited Alan Keyes, a resident of Maryland, to become the replacement nominee. Obama won the general election with 70 percent of the popular vote to Keyes's 27 percent.

On January 4, 2005, Obama was sworn in as the junior senator from Illinois in the 109th Congress. Obama served as a member of the Senate Foreign Relations Committee, the Homeland Security and Governmental Affairs Committee, the Veterans' Affairs Committee, and the Health, Education, Labor, and Pensions Committee.

After much speculation, Obama announced his candidacy for the 2008 U.S. presidential election. He was elected as the forty-fourth president of the United States in November 2008. When he was sworn in as president in January 2009, he became the country's first African American president.

HAZEL O'LEARY (1937–)

Attorney, Federal Government Official, Financial Planner, University President. Hazel O'Leary was born Hazel Reid on May 17, 1937, in Newport News, Virginia. She graduated Phi Beta Kappa in 1959 from Fisk University with a B.A. She received her J.D. in 1966 from Rutgers University School of Law. O'Leary was a utilities regulator under Presidents Gerald Ford and Jimmy Carter, an executive vice president of the Northern States Power Co., and a Washington lobbyist. A proponent of energy conservation and alternative energy sources, she was secretary of energy in President Bill Clinton's administration from 1993 to 1997.

In addition to formulating energy policy, O'Leary worked to dismantle the nation's nuclear weaponry complex and to help energy producers finance nuclear-waste storage programs. Reorganizing the Department of Energy at the end of the Cold War was one of the first accountabilities assigned to O'Leary. She campaigned to unveil the expansive network of secret atomic laboratories and weapons plants harbored in the nation. Results of Cold War nuclear tests, radiation releases, and experiments on civilians were also revealed. O'Leary also encouraged domestic resource development.

In the mid-1990s, O'Leary came under heavy scrutiny. First, she was criticized for having spent thousands of government dollars to pay a consultant firm to rank reporters according to which had given her the most favorable coverage. Then it was disclosed that she had spent much more than other cabinet members on overseas travel. Vice President Al Gore came to O'Leary's defense by noting that her trips had helped create new job opportunities in the United States. For example, O'Leary led a delegation of nearly one hundred aides, energy experts, and business leaders to South Africa to uncover possibilities in the newly democratic country.

O'Leary is a certified financial planner and a member of the New Jersey and Washington bars. She has been vice president and general counsel of O'Leary Associates in Washington, D.C. In 1993, the Congressional Black Caucus honored O'Leary for her achievements. After completing her term as secretary of energy, O'Leary resigned and returned to the private sector, where she became president and CEO of Blaylock and Partners. In 2004, O'Leary became president of her alma mater, Fisk University.

DEVAL PATRICK (1956–)

Governor, Attorney. Deval Patrick was born on the South Side of Chicago on July 31, 1956. His father was a musician who left the family when Patrick and his sister were young. Patrick was a bright student and one of his teachers encouraged him to apply to A Better Chance, a nonprofit program that identifies, recruits, and develops leaders among academically talented students of color. He was accepted and received a scholarship to Milton Academy, graduating in 1974.

Patrick graduated with honors from Harvard University in 1978. After receiving his bachelor's degree, he spent a year working on a United Nations youth training program in the Darfur region of Sudan. Returning to Cambridge in 1979, he entered Harvard Law School. While he was in law school, Patrick was elected president of the Harvard Legal Aid Bureau, a student-run organization that provides legal services to the poor.

After finishing law school, Patrick served as a clerk to a federal appellate judge before joining the NAACP Legal Defense and Educational Fund. In 1986, Patrick joined the Boston law firm of Hill and Barlow, where he became a partner when he was thirty-four years old.

President Bill Clinton nominated Patrick as assistant attorney general for civil rights in 1994, and upon confirmation he became the nation's top civil rights lawyer. At the Justice Department, Patrick and his staff worked on a wide range of issues, including racial profiling, police misconduct, employment discrimination, enforcement of fair lending laws, and prosecution of such hate crimes as church burnings and abortion clinic violence.

In 1997, Patrick returned to private practice and joined the Boston firm of Day, Berry and Howard. Later in 1997, he was appointed by a federal district court to serve as the first chairperson of Texaco's Equality and Fairness Task Force following lawsuits from employees alleging discrimination. The task force reformed Texaco's corporate employment culture and developed a more equitable workplace.

In 2001, Patrick was hired as executive vice president and general counsel at the Coca-Cola Company following turmoil within the country after minority workers filed discrimination suits. The next year, Patrick was elected as corporate secretary and served as a member of the company's executive committee.

When Patrick announced his candidacy in 2005 for Massachusetts governor, he was considered a long shot. Patrick won the primary with 49 percent of the vote, carrying every county. Winning the general election handily in November 2006, Patrick became the state's first African American governor and only the second African American ever elected governor in the history of the nation.

CLARENCE McCLANE PENDLETON JR. (1930–1988)

Federal Government Official, Organization Executive. Clarence Pendleton Jr. was born in Louisville, Kentucky, on November 10, 1930. Raised in Washington, D.C., he attended Dunbar High School and received a B.S. in 1954 from Howard University. Pendleton served three years in the U.S. Army and was assigned to a medical unit. After his discharge in 1957, Pendleton returned to Howard University, where he received a master's degree in 1961 and coached swimming, football, rowing, and baseball.

In 1968, Pendleton became the recreation coordinator of the Baltimore Model Cities Program. Two years later, he became the director of the Urban Affairs Department of the National Recreation and Parks Association. Pendleton soon began attracting national attention, and in 1972 he headed San Diego's Model Cities Program. In 1975, he became the director of the San Diego Urban League.

By 1980, a change took place in Pendleton's political philosophy. He began to feel that African Americans' reliance on government programs was trapping them in a cycle of dependence and welfare handouts. Pendleton believed that it was in the best interest of African Americans to build ties with a strong, expanding private sector and to eschew the more traditional ties with liberal bureaucrats and liberal philosophies.

To this end, he supported the election of Ronald Reagan to the presidency and was appointed chairman of the Civil Rights Commission by President Reagan in 1981. Pendleton's chairmanship was controversial, mostly because of his opposition to affirmative action and to forced busing as a means of desegregating schools. Pendleton retained a more liberal philosophy on other matters, however, by supporting the equal rights amendment and the Voting Rights Act. Pendleton died unexpectedly of a heart attack on June 5, 1988, in San Diego.

P. B. S. PINCHBACK (1837–1921)

Attorney, Federal Legislator, State and Municipal Government Official. Pinckney Benton Stewart Pinchback was born in Macon, Georgia, on May 10, 1837. Although his mother had been enslaved, she was emancipated at Pinchback's birth by Pinchback's father. Moving to Ohio with his mother, Pinchback attended high school in Cincinnati in 1847, and he began working on riverboats as a cabin boy and then as a steward in 1848.

At the outbreak of the Civil War, Pinchback went to Louisiana and in 1862 enlisted in the Union Army. He soon began recruiting soldiers for an African American unit known as the Louisiana Native Guards or the Corps d'Afrique. Racial problems soon arose with the military hierarchy, and Pinchback resigned his commission in protest. After the war, Pinchback became active in Louisiana politics. He organized a Republican club in 1867 and was a delegate to the state constitutional convention in 1868. In that year, he was also elected to the state senate. He became president pro tempore of that body in 1871. Pinchback became lieutenant governor of Louisiana through the line of political succession. In late 1872 and early 1873, Pinchback served as governor of Louisiana while the elected governor underwent impeachment proceedings. Pinchback was elected to the U.S. House of Representatives in 1872 and the U.S. Senate in 1873, but was denied seating both times when the elections were contested, and his Democratic opponent was named to Congress.

In 1877, Pinchback switched his allegiance to the Democratic Party, and in 1882 he was appointed surveyor of customs for New Orleans. In 1887, he began attending law school at Straight University in New Orleans and was later admitted to the bar. In 1890, Pinchback moved to Washington, D.C., where he died December 21, 1921.

ADAM CLAYTON POWELL JR. (1908–1972)

Federal Legislator. Born on November 29, 1908, in New Haven, Connecticut, Adam Clayton Powell Jr. was raised in New York City and graduated in 1930 from Colgate University. In 1931, Powell graduated from Columbia University with a master's degree in religious education. Powell launched his career as a crusader for reform during the Great Depression. He forced several large corporations to drop their unofficial bans on employing African Americans and directed a kitchen and relief operation that fed, clothed, and provided fuel for thousands of Harlem's needy and destitute. He was instrumental in persuading officials of Harlem Hospital to integrate their medical and nursing staffs. He also helped many African Americans find employment along 125th Street, and campaigned against the city's bus lines, which were discriminating against Negro drivers and mechanics.

When his father retired from the leadership of Abyssinian Baptist Church in 1936, Adam Clayton Powell Jr., who had already served as manager and assistant pastor there, was named his successor. In 1939, Powell became chairman of the Coordinating Committee on Employment, which organized a picket line before the executive offices of the World's Fair in the Empire State Building and eventually succeeded in securing employment at the fair for hundreds of African Americans.

Powell won a seat on the New York City Council in 1941 with the third-highest number of votes ever cast for a candidate in municipal elections. In 1942, he turned to journalism and published and edited the weekly *People's Voice*, which he called "the largest Negro tabloid in the world." He became a member of the New York State Office of Price Administration in 1942 and served until 1944.

In 1944, Powell was elected to the U.S. Congress, representing a constituency of 300,000, 89 percent of whom were African American. Identified at once as Mr. Civil Rights, he encountered a host of discriminatory procedures upon his arrival in the nation's capital. He could not rent a room or attend a movie in downtown Washington. Within Congress itself, he was not allowed to use such communal facilities as dining rooms, steam baths, showers, and barber shops. Powell met these rebuffs head on by making use of all such facilities and insisting that his entire staff follow his lead.

As a first-year legislator, Powell engaged in fiery debates with segregationists, fought for the abolition of discriminatory practices at U.S. military installations, and sought to deny federal funds to any project where discrimination existed. The latter effort was called the Powell amendment and eventually became part of the Flanagan School Lunch Bill, making Powell the first African American congressman since Reconstruction to have legislation passed by both houses.

Powell also sponsored legislation advocating federal aid for education, a minimum-wage scale, and greater benefits for the chronically unemployed. He drew attention to certain discriminatory practices on Capitol Hill and worked toward their elimination. It was Powell who first demanded that an African American journalist be allowed to sit in the Senate and House press galleries. He also introduced the first anti–Jim Crow transportation legislation and the first bill to prohibit segregation in the armed forces. At one point in his career, the Congressional Record reported that the House Committee on Education and Labor had processed more important legislation than any other major committee. In 1960, Powell, as senior member of this committee, became its chairman. He had a hand in the development and passage of such significant legislation as the Minimum Wage Bill of 1961, the Manpower Development and Training Act, the Anti-Poverty Bill, the Juvenile Delinquency Act, the Vocational Educational Act, and the National Defense Education Act. The Powell committee helped pass forty-eight laws involving a total outlay of $14 billion. Powell, however, was accused of putting an excessive number of friends on the congressional payroll. He was also accused of a high rate of absenteeism from congressional votes and of living a permissive lifestyle.

In 1967, the controversies and irregularities surrounding him led to censure in the House and a vote to exclude him from his seat in the Ninetieth Congress. The House based its decision on the allegation that he had misused public funds and was in contempt of the New York courts due to a lengthy and involved defamation case that had resulted in a trial for civil and criminal contempt. Despite his exclusion, Powell was readmitted to the Ninety-first Congress in 1968. In mid-1969, the

Supreme Court ruled that the House had violated the Constitution by excluding him from membership.

Rather than return to Congress, Powell spent most of his time on the West Indian island of Bimini, where process servers could not reach him. But photographers reached him, and the ensuing photos of Powell vacationing on his boat while crucial votes were taken in Congress had an impact in his home district. In 1970, he lost the Democratic congressional primary to Charles Rangel by 150 votes. Powell retired from public office but continued working as a minister at the Abyssinian Baptist Church. On April 4, 1972, he died in Miami.

COLIN L. POWELL

See chapter 28, Military.

JOSEPH H. RAINEY (1832–1887)

Civil Rights Activist, Federal Legislator and Government Official. Joseph Hayne Rainey, the first African American member of the House of Representatives, was born on June 21, 1832, in Georgetown, South Carolina. Rainey's father purchased his family's freedom and moved them to Charleston. During the Civil War, Rainey was drafted to work on Confederate fortifications in Charleston harbor and serve passengers on a Confederate ship. However, Rainey escaped with his wife to the West Indies and remained there until the end of the Civil War in 1865.

Rainey and his wife returned to South Carolina in 1866. In 1868, Rainey was elected as a delegate to the state constitutional convention. He was elected to the state senate in 1870. A year later, he was elected to the U.S. House of Representatives. As a member of Congress, Rainey presented some ten petitions for a civil rights bill that would have guaranteed African Americans full constitutional rights and equal access to public accommodations. On one occasion, Rainey dramatized the latter issue by refusing to leave the dining room of a hotel in Suffolk, Virginia, until he was forcibly ejected from the premises. Rainey was a staunch supporter of legislation that prevented racial discrimination in schools, on public transportation, and in the composition of juries. He supported legislation that protected the civil rights of the Chinese minority in California and advocated the use of federal troops to protect African American voters from intimidation by the Ku Klux Klan. Rainey was reelected in 1872 and, during a debate on Indian rights in 1874, became the first African American representative to preside over a session of Congress. Rainey gained reelection to Congress in 1874 and 1876.

Rainey retired from Congress in 1879. He was appointed as a special agent for the U.S. Treasury Department in Washington, D.C. He served there until 1881, after which he worked for a banking and brokerage firm. After the firm failed, Rainey took a job at a wood and coal factory. In 1886, he returned to Georgetown, where he died on August 2, 1887.

CHARLES RANGEL (1930–)

Federal Legislator. Harlem-born Charles Rangel entered the national spotlight in 1970, when he defeated Adam Clayton Powell Jr. for the Democratic nomination in New York's Eighteenth Congressional District. Born June 11, 1930, Rangel attended Harlem elementary and secondary schools before volunteering to serve in the U.S. Army during the Korean War. While stationed in Korea with the Second Infantry, he saw heavy combat and received the Purple Heart and the Bronze Star Medal for valor, as well as U.S. and Korean presidential citations. Discharged honorably as a staff sergeant, Rangel returned to finish high school and to study at New York University's School of Commerce, from which he graduated in 1957. In 1960, Rangel received his J.D. while on scholarship at St. John's University.

After being admitted to the bar, Rangel was appointed in 1961 as assistant U.S. attorney in the Southern District of New York. For the next five years, he worked as legal counsel to the New York City Housing and Redevelopment Board, as legal assistant to Judge James L. Watson, as associate counsel to the speaker of the New York State Assembly, and as general counsel to the National Advisory Commission on Selective Service. In 1966, Rangel was chosen to represent the seventy-second district, central Harlem, in the New York State Assembly. He also served as a member of, and secretary to, the New York State Commission on Revision of the Penal Law and Criminal Code.

Rangel was elected to the U.S. Congress in 1970. In his first term, he was appointed to the Select Committee on Crime and was influential in passing the 1971 amendment to the drug laws that authorized the president to cut off all military and economic aid to any country that refused to cooperate with the United States in stopping the international traffic in drugs. In 1976, Rangel, a leading congressional expert on the subject, was appointed to the Select Committee on Narcotics Abuse and Control.

Rangel served as chairperson of the Congressional Black Caucus from 1974 to 1975 and was a member of the Judiciary Committee when it voted to impeach U.S. president Richard M. Nixon. In 1975, he moved to the Ways and Means Committee, becoming the first African American to serve on that committee. Two years later, his colleagues in the New York congressional delegation voted him the majority whip for New York State. Rangel, who has served as deputy whip for the House Democratic leadership, was a speaker at the 1995

Charles Rangel, U.S. Representative from New York, 2007. *Longtime House member Rangel is a founding member of the Congressional Black Caucus and in 2007 became the first African American chairman of the powerful House Ways and Means Committee. He later relinquished this chairmanship because of an ethics controversy.* ALEX WONG/STAFF/GETTY IMAGES NEWS/GETTY IMAGES

Million Man March. With the new Democratic majority, Rangel became chairman of the powerful House Ways and Means Committee in 2007; he later relinquished this chairmanship because of an ethics controversy. He also served as chair of the board of the Democratic Congressional Campaign Committee.

Rangel has consistently called for reinstatement of the draft in large part due to the disproportionate representation of poor and minority group members in the enlisted ranks of the military. He is considered a liberal, but is also known as a pragmatic deal maker.

In his capacity as chairman of the Apollo Foundation, Rangel came under fire in the late 1990s for the foundation's management of the historic Harlem theater. In particular, allegations focused on dealings between Rangel and his longtime friend, businessman Percy Sutton. In 1999, both men were cleared of any wrongdoing by New York attorney general Eliot Spitzer. Following the attorney general's announcement, Rangel left the board in September 1999. Rangel published an autobiography, *And I Haven't Had a Bad Day Since: From the Streets of Harlem to the Halls of Congress*, in 2007.

KENNETH REEVES (1951–)

Municipal Government Official, Attorney. Elected mayor of the city of Cambridge, Massachusetts, in 1992, Kenneth Reeves was the first openly gay mayor and the first African American mayor in the state. Reeves was popular enough to be elected to a second term in 1994, running on the promise to break down the barriers between city government and local political groups. He was elected to a third term as mayor in 2006.

Born to Jamaican parents, Reeves grew up in a middle-class Detroit neighborhood. After high school, he attended Harvard College. While there, he was active in community service, working at a housing development in Dorchester, Massachusetts. After graduation, Reeves traveled to the African nation of Benin, studying there for one year before returning to the United States. In 1976, he graduated from the University of Michigan Law School.

Seeking a position in Cambridge, Massachusetts, he was hired by the National Consumer Law Center. He ran for public office in a grassroots effort but lost. He opted to run for city council a second time and was elected in 1989. During that time, he also founded the W. E. B. Du Bois Academy, a mentor program pairing established African American professional men with young African American males for intense tutoring sessions.

Reeves was reelected to his ninth term on the Cambridge City Council in 2009. He served as chairman of the Cambridge School Committee for four years. His political career is characterized by his efforts to bring together diverse groups of people to work collaboratively.

HIRAM RHODES REVELS (1822–1901)

Federal Legislator. Hiram Rhodes Revels, a native of North Carolina, was the first African American to serve in the U.S. Senate. Revels was elected from his adopted state of Mississippi, and served for approximately one year, from February 1870 to March 1871.

Born in 1827, in Fayetteville, North Carolina, Revels was educated in Indiana and attended Knox College in Illinois. Ordained a minister in the African Methodist Church, he worked among African American settlers in Kansas, Maryland, Illinois, Indiana, Tennessee, Kentucky, and Missouri before settling in 1860 in Baltimore. There he served as a church pastor and school principal.

During the Civil War, Revels helped organize a pair of Negro regiments in Maryland, and went to St. Louis in 1863 to establish a freedmen's school and to carry on his work as a recruiter. For a year, he served as chaplain of a Mississippi regiment before becoming provost marshal of Vicksburg. Revels settled in Natchez, Mississippi, in 1866 and was appointed alderman by the Union military governor of the state. In 1870, Revels was elected to the U.S. Senate to replace Jefferson Davis, the former president of the Confederacy. Revels's appointment caused a storm of protest from white southerners. However, Revels was allowed to take his seat in the Senate.

As a U.S. senator, Revels quickly won the respect of many of his constituents for his alert grasp of state issues and for his courageous support of legislation that would have restored voting and office-holding privileges to disenfranchised southerners. He believed that the best way for African Americans to gain their rightful place in American society was not through violent means, but by obtaining an education and leading an exemplary life of courage and moral fortitude. He spoke out against the segregation of Washington, D.C.'s public school system and defended the rights of African Americans who were denied work at the Washington Navy Yard because of their race.

After Revels left the Senate, he was named president of Alcorn University near Lorman, Mississippi. He left Alcorn in 1873 to serve as Mississippi's secretary of state on an interim basis. He returned to Alcorn in 1876. That year, he became editor of the *South-Western Christian Advocate*, a religious journal. In 1882, he retired from Alcorn University. Revels lived in Holly Springs, Mississippi, during his later years and taught theology at Shaw University. He died on January 16, 1901.

CONDOLEEZZA RICE (1954–)

Federal Government Official, Educator. Condoleezza Rice was born on November 14, 1954, in Birmingham, Alabama. She completed her bachelor's degree in political science in 1974, graduating cum laude and Phi Beta Kappa from the University of Denver. In 1974, she received her master's degree from the University of Notre Dame, and earned a Ph.D. from the Graduate School of International Studies at the University of Denver in 1981.

Rice joined the faculty of Stanford University in 1981 as a professor of political science. At Stanford, Rice's research and teaching interests included the politics of the Soviet Union and Eastern Europe. In 1984, Rice was awarded the Walter J. Gores Award for Excellence in Teaching, and the following year, she became a fellow at the prestigious Hoover Institution. In 1993, she received the School of Humanities and Sciences Dean's Award for Distinguished Teaching.

Rice served as an adviser to the Joint Chiefs of Staff on strategic nuclear policy in 1987. In 1989, she was named director of Soviet and East European affairs on the National Security Council, a position in which she advised President George H. W. Bush during the collapse of the Soviet Union. Following her tenure with the first Bush administration, Rice returned to Stanford. She served as the university's provost from 1993 to 1999, earning accolades for her handling of the school's finances and her implementation of new academic programs. Rice left Stanford in 2000 to serve as a foreign policy adviser during the George W. Bush presidential campaign. When Bush was elected, he appointed Rice as his national security adviser. She became the first woman and the first African American to hold the position. In 2005, during President Bush's second term, Rice was named secretary of state. She returned to Stanford University and the Hoover Institution after President Bush left office in 2009.

Rice's publications include: *The Soviet Union and the Czechoslovak Army, 1948–1983: Uncertain Allegiance* (1984); *The Gorbachev Era* (1986), edited with Alexander Dallin; and *Germany Unified and Europe Transformed: A Study in Statecraft* (1995), written with Phillip Zelikow. She has also published numerous articles in prominent foreign

Condoleezza Rice, White House, Washington, DC, November 2008. *For President George W. Bush (left), Rice served as national security adviser during his first term and as secretary of state during his second.* MARK WILSON/GETTY IMAGES NEWS/GETTY IMAGES

policy journals and news magazines, including *Journal of International Affairs*, *Studies in Comparative Communism*, *Time*, *World Politics*, and *Current History*. In addition to her posts in academia and government, Rice has served on the boards of many companies and institutions, including Chevron, Charles Schwab, the William and Flora Hewlett Foundation, the University of Notre Dame, the San Francisco Symphony, Hewlett-Packard, and San Francisco's public broadcasting network, KQED.

NORM RICE (1943–)

Municipal Government Official. Norman B. Rice was born on May 4, 1943, in Denver, Colorado, and attended the University of Colorado. He was disappointed by the university's segregated housing and labor practices, and dropped out in his second year. Moving to Seattle in 1969, Rice went back to college in the Economic Opportunity Program at the University of Washington, earning a B.A. in communications and an M.P.A. in 1974.

In 1978, when he was thirty-five years old, he ran for a seat on the Seattle City Council and beat the incumbent. In 1983, Rice was named president of the council and was encouraged to run for mayor. He was defeated in 1985 but regrouped and ran again in 1989. He won, and served two terms from 1990 to 1997, becoming Seattle's forty-ninth mayor and the first African American to hold the office. Rice began his first term by convening an education summit to include all those interested in discussing ways to improve Seattle's public schools. An outgrowth of that summit was the Families and Education Levy, which raised $69 million for student health services, drug and alcohol counseling, and after-school activities. Because African Americans constituted only 10 percent of Seattle's population, Rice forged a broad-based coalition to win an overwhelming victory in 1993 for reelection. During his second term, he led the rejuvenation of downtown Seattle. Along with his many duties as mayor of Seattle, Rice also served as president of the U.S. Conference of Mayors from 1995 to 1996.

In March 1996, Rice announced his candidacy for the governorship of Washington, but he lost the election. Rice did not seek a third term as mayor in 1997. In 1998, after nineteen years in public service, Rice became president of the Federal Home Loan Bank of Seattle, a post he held until 2004. He also became vice president of Capital Access LLC, an investment-banking firm specializing in municipal, energy, and philanthropic enterprises. In 2006, Rice was appointed distinguished practitioner-in-residence at the Evans School of Public Affairs at the University of Washington. In 2009, he became president and CEO of the Seattle Foundation.

EDITH SAMPSON (1901–1979)

Attorney, Diplomat, Judge, Lecturer. Edith Sampson was born on October 13, 1901, in Pittsburgh, Pennsylvania. The first African American woman to be named an official representative to the United Nations, Sampson served in that post from 1950 until 1953, first as an appointee of President Harry S. Truman and later during a portion of the Eisenhower administration. Sampson acquired an LL.B. from the John Marshall Law School in Chicago in 1925 and two years later became the first woman to receive an LL.M. from Loyola University.

A member of the Illinois bar since 1927, she argued in front of the Supreme Court in 1934. During the 1930s, she maintained her own private practice, specializing in domestic relations and criminal law. After her UN appointment, Sampson traveled around the world as a lecturer. She was elected associate judge of the Municipal Court of Chicago in 1962, becoming the first African American woman ever to sit as a circuit court judge. Sampson presided over divorce courts, traffic courts, and landlord-tenant relations courts. She retired from the Cook County Circuit Court in 1978.

Former First Lady Eleanor Roosevelt and Edith Sampson, United Nations, New York, September 1950. *Sampson (right) in 1950 became the first African American woman to be named an official representative to the United Nations.* FRANKLIN D. ROOSEVELT PRESIDENTIAL LIBRARY AND MUSEUM

Sampson died on October 7, 1979, at Northwestern Hospital in Chicago.

KURT L. SCHMOKE (1949–)

Attorney, Municipal Government Official, Federal Government Official, Educator. Born on December 1, 1949, Kurt L. Schmoke was inaugurated as the first elected African American mayor of Baltimore on December 8, 1987. Schmoke graduated with honors from Baltimore City College High School. In 1967, he won the award as the top scholar-athlete in the city. Schmoke received his bachelor of arts degree from Yale University in 1971 and studied at Oxford University as a Rhodes scholar. He earned his law degree from Harvard University Law School in 1976.

After graduating from Harvard, Schmoke began his law practice with the prestigious Baltimore firm of Piper and Marbury. Shortly thereafter, he was appointed by President Jimmy Carter to the White House domestic policy staff. After Carter left office, Schmoke returned to Baltimore as an assistant U.S. attorney, where he prosecuted narcotics and white-collar crime cases. He then returned to private practice and was involved in various civic activities.

In November 1982, Schmoke was elected state's attorney for Baltimore, the chief prosecuting office of the city. He created a full-time narcotics unit to prosecute all drug cases and underscored the criminal nature of domestic violence and child abuse by setting up separate units to handle those cases. Schmoke also hired a community-liaison officer to make sure that his office was responsive to neighborhood questions and concerns.

In his inaugural address as mayor, Schmoke set the tone and future direction for his administration when he said that he wanted Baltimore to combat illiteracy and reduce its high school dropout and teenage pregnancy rates. He oversaw the passage of the largest-ever increase in the city's education budget, and, in partnership with Baltimore businesses and community-based organizations, Schmoke developed the Commonwealth Agreement and the College Bound Foundation with the goal of guaranteeing opportunities for jobs or college entrance to qualifying high school graduates. Schmoke also launched major initiatives in housing, economic development, and public health. Schmoke proposed educational programs to prepare Baltimore's citizens for high-tech jobs, and he pushed growth at Baltimore's Inner Harbor.

Schmoke came under fire in the early 1990s because of Baltimore's persistent crime problems and his failed attempt to privatize nine Baltimore public schools. In 1992, President George H. W. Bush awarded Schmoke the National Literacy Award for his efforts to promote adult literacy. In 1994, President Bill Clinton praised Schmoke's efforts to improve public housing and enhance community economic development. The Clinton administration also designated Baltimore one of six cities with an empowerment zone.

Despite being considered a leading contender for the office of Maryland governor, Schmoke decided to run for a third term as Baltimore mayor. Interested in drug reform, Schmoke ran on a platform of decriminalizing drugs to stop related crime. An unexpectedly high turnout of close to 52 percent of registered Democrats gave Schmoke a racially polarized election win in 1995. In December 1998, Schmoke announced he would not seek a fourth term as mayor. Following his final term in office, Schmoke joined the international law firm of Wilmer, Cutler and Pickering as a partner. On January 1, 2003, Schmoke was appointed dean of the Howard University School of Law.

Throughout his career, Schmoke has been active in the civic and cultural life of the Baltimore community by serving as a member of numerous boards of trustees. In recognition of his commitment to excellence in education and his service to the community, Schmoke has received honorary degrees from several colleges and universities.

ROBERT SMALLS (1839–1916)

Federal Legislator. Robert Smalls served a longer period in the U.S. Congress than any other African American Reconstruction congressman. Born enslaved in Beaufort, South Carolina, in 1839, Smalls received a limited education before moving to Charleston with the family of his enslaver. While in Charleston, Smalls worked at a number of odd jobs and eventually became adept at piloting boats along the Georgia and South Carolina coasts.

At the outbreak of the Civil War, Smalls was forced to become a crew member on the Confederate ship *Planter*. On the morning of May 13, 1862, Smalls smuggled his wife and three children on board, assumed command of the vessel, and sailed it into the hands of the Union squadron blockading Charleston harbor. His daring exploit led President Abraham Lincoln to name him a pilot in the Union Navy. He was also awarded a large sum of money for what constituted the delivery of war booty. In December 1863, during the siege of Charleston, Smalls again took command of the *Planter* and was promoted to captain, the only African American to hold such a rank during the Civil War.

After the war, Smalls was elected to the South Carolina House of Representatives and served from 1868 to 1870. In 1870, Smalls became a member of South Carolina's state senate and served until 1874. Smalls campaigned for a U.S. congressional seat in 1874 against an independent candidate and won the election. He took his seat in Congress on March 4, 1875. During his tenure in Congress, Smalls supported a wide variety of progressive legislation, including a bill to provide equal accommodations for African Americans in interstate travel and an amendment designed to safeguard the rights of children born to interracial couples. He also sought to protect the rights of African Americans serving in the armed forces.

Smalls won reelection in 1876, an election that was bitterly contested by Smalls's Democratic challenger, George Tillman. Tillman tried unsuccessfully to have Smalls's election overturned. However, Tillman's supporters were undeterred. In 1877, Smalls was accused of taking a $5,000 bribe while serving as a senator. Although Smalls was exonerated by Governor William D. Simpson, his popularity plummeted. Smalls lost his reelection bid in 1878. In 1880, Smalls ran again for Congress. He lost the election, but maintained that the results were invalid due to vote-counting irregularities. Smalls's charges were substantiated, and he was allowed to take his seat in Congress in July 1882. Two months later, another congressional election was held, and Smalls lost his seat to fellow Republican Edward W. M. Mackey. When Mackey died in January 1884, Smalls was designated to serve the remainder of Mackey's term. In 1886, Smalls lost an election to Democratic challenger William Elliott. After leaving office, Smalls remained involved in political activities. From 1889 to 1913, he served as collector of the port of Beaufort. He died on February 22, 1916.

Carl B. Stokes, 1967. *After serving in the Ohio General Assembly, Stokes in 1967 was elected mayor of Cleveland, Ohio, becoming the first African American mayor of a major U.S. city.* **BETTMANN/CORBIS**

CARL B. STOKES (1927–1996)

Municipal Official. Carl Burton Stokes was born in Cleveland, Ohio, on June 21, 1927. Stokes and his older brother, Louis, were raised by their mother following the death of their father in 1929. Stokes joined the U.S. Army when he was eighteen, and served in Europe near the end of World War II. Following the war, Stokes studied at West Virginia State and Western Reserve universities. He served as a liquor enforcement agent from 1950 to 1953. He returned to school at the University of Minnesota, earning a B.S. in law in 1954. Stokes then completed his J.D. degree at the Cleveland-Marshall College of Law.

Along with his brother, Stokes started a law practice in Cleveland in 1957. A year later, he was appointed assistant city prosecutor by Cleveland mayor Anthony Celebrezze. During this period, Stokes became involved in the civil rights movement. He joined the Urban League and served on the executive board of the Cleveland chapter of the NAACP. In 1962, he won a seat in the Ohio General Assembly, becoming the first black Democrat to hold that office. He twice won reelection and served in the assembly until his election as mayor of Cleveland in 1967.

Stokes's victory made him the first African American mayor of a major U.S. city. In the election, Stokes won 50 percent of the vote in a city with a 37 percent black population. The Stokes administration was defined by its attempt to increase city services to underserved communities. Stokes also opened city-hall jobs to African Americans. His term was marked by a deadly shootout in the city during urban riots in July 1968. Further damage was done when it was later revealed that money from the mayor's program, Cleveland Now!, had been paid to the black nationalist group implicated in the shootout.

Although Stokes won reelection in 1969, the shootout weakened the people's goodwill toward his administration and created a lasting friction among the administration, the police department, and the city council. Stokes, who enjoyed wide national recognition and was elected to the presidency of the National League of Cities in 1970, announced in 1971 that he would not seek a third term as mayor.

In 1972, Stokes left Cleveland and became the first African American news anchor in the New York City area. He worked for WNBC television for eight years, serving as urban affairs editor and foreign correspondent in Africa. In 1973, Simon and Schuster published Stokes's *Promises of Power: A Political Autobiography.* Stokes returned to law practice in Cleveland in 1981. He reentered the political arena in 1983 and was elected as a municipal court judge, a seat he held until 1994, when President Bill Clinton appointed him ambassador to the Seychelles. Stokes left the Seychelles after he was diagnosed with cancer of the esophagus in 1995. He died in Cleveland on April 3, 1996.

LOUIS STOKES (1925–)

Civil Rights Activist, Federal Legislator, Attorney. Louis Stokes was born in Cleveland, Ohio, on February 23, 1925. He served in the U.S. Army from 1943 until 1946. After leaving the service, he attended Case Western Reserve University (1946–1948). He was awarded a J.D. in 1953 from Cleveland-Marshall College of Law. After fourteen years in private practice with the law firm of Stokes, Character, Terry and Perry, he was elected as a Democrat to the U.S. House of Representatives in 1969.

As Ohio's first African American representative, Stokes served on a number of committees, including the Committee on Education and Labor, the House Internal Security Committee, and the Appropriations Committee. He also chaired the House Ethics Committee. As part of the House Assassination Committee, Stokes investigated the deaths of Martin Luther King Jr. and President John F. Kennedy. In 1972 and 1973, Stokes chaired the Congressional Black Caucus, and he was a delegate to the Democratic National Convention in 1972, 1976, and 1980. Stokes was the first African American to chair the House Intelligence Committee and the only African American to serve on the Iran-Contra Committee. When he retired in 1999, Stokes became the first African American in the history of the U.S. Congress to retire having completed thirty years of service. After leaving Congress, Stokes became senior counsel at the global law firm Squire, Sanders, and Dempsey, LLP. He also became a distinguished visiting professor at the Mandel School of Applied Social Sciences at Case Western Reserve University.

Stokes belongs to the Urban League, the American Civil Liberties Union, the American Legion, and the African American Institute. He served on the board of trustees of the Martin Luther King Jr. Center for Social Change and was vice president of the Cleveland chapter of the NAACP in 1965 and 1966. He is a recipient of the Distinguished Service Award, the William C. Dawson Award, and a Certificate of Appreciation from the U.S. Commission on Civil Rights, of which he was vice chairman of the Cleveland subcommittee in 1966. In addition, a number of landmarks throughout the city of Cleveland bear his name, including the Louis Stokes Cleveland Veterans Administration Hospital and the Louis Stokes Annex of the Cleveland Public Library. He has received numerous honorary doctorates and was awarded the Congressional Distinguished Service Award. In 2007, the Cuyahoga Metropolitan Housing Authority in Cleveland opened the Louis Stokes Museum in honor of Stokes's efforts to improve the quality of life for public-housing residents. The museum is housed in Cleveland's Outhwaite Homes, where Stokes was raised.

JOHN F. STREET (1943–)

Municipal Government Official. John Franklin Street was born in Norristown, Pennsylvania, on October 15, 1943. He attended Oakwood College, a Seventh-day Adventist school in Huntsville, Alabama, majoring in English. His professional career began as an elementary school and Opportunities Industrialization Center English teacher. Street obtained his law degree from Temple University in 1975. After law school, he became a clerk at Common Pleas Court and the U.S. Department of Justice. He practiced law before being elected to the Philadelphia City Council in 1975.

Street represented the North Philadelphia and Center City districts and became known for his advocacy for fair housing, increased spending for public education, and neighborhood improvements. In 1992 and 1996, Street was unanimously chosen by his colleagues to serve as council president. With his detailed knowledge of the city's budget process and in collaboration with his predecessor, Mayor Edward Rendell, Street was instrumental in reducing Philadelphia's $250 million deficit and turning it into a large surplus.

Street worked to revitalize Philadelphia's declining neighborhoods by investing in them and tearing down abandoned buildings. In spite of initial opposition, his emphasis on neighborhoods resulted in an appreciation in property values, as well as a 14 percent growth in the Center City population between 1990 and 2000 and the creation of nearly four thousand market-rate apartments and condominiums

In addition to forming the Philadelphia Children's Commission, Street privatized Philadelphia's public schools. Edison Schools and area universities were allowed to operate some of the city's worst-performing schools. Health and wellness was another important focus of the Street administration. In 1999, when *Men's Fitness* magazine rated Philadelphia as the fattest city in the nation, Street created the Office of Health and Fitness and initiated a citywide walking campaign. Street also worked to make Philadelphia a wireless city, with plans to construct a citywide wireless network. However, crime, including a rising murder rate and youth violence, remained a significant problem.

Members of Street's administration became the subject of a Federal Bureau of Investigation (FBI) investigation in which wiretaps and other listening devices were placed in the mayor's office. The former city treasurer and one of Street's fund-raisers were involved in a corruption scheme that led to a ten-year jail term for the treasurer. The fund-raiser died before going to trial. Street himself was never the subject of the federal investigation and was never charged with criminal wrongdoing. After leaving office in 2008, Street joined the political science faculty at Temple University.

LOUIS W. SULLIVAN (1933–)

Educational Administrator, Federal Government Official. Louis Wade Sullivan was born on November 3, 1933, in Atlanta, Georgia. On March 1, 1989, the U.S. Senate confirmed Dr. Sullivan as secretary of health and human services by a vote of ninety-eight to one, making him the first African American appointed to a cabinet position during the administration of President George H. W. Bush.

Sullivan graduated from Morehouse College magna cum laude with a B.S. in 1954, and received his M.D. in 1958 from Boston University. He completed his internship at New York Hospital–Cornell Medical Center and his medical and general pathology residencies at Cornell Medical Center and Massachusetts General Hospital. He then fulfilled two fellowships and served in a variety of positions with Harvard Medical School, Boston City Hospital, New Jersey College of Medicine, Boston University Medical Center, the Boston Sickle Cell Center, and other medical institutions. Sullivan was instrumental in the development of the Morehouse School of Medicine, which he founded in 1975 as a separate entity from Morehouse College. Sullivan also served as professor of biology and medicine. In 1981, he became Morehouse School of Medicine's first dean and president.

Sullivan has been involved in numerous educational, medical, scientific, professional, and civic organizations, and has received many professional and public-service awards. Sullivan's research has focused on hematology, a branch of biology that deals with the formation of blood and blood-forming organs. He has authored or coauthored more than sixty publications on this and other subjects. In addition, Sullivan was the founding president of the Association of Minority Health Professions Schools.

As secretary of health and human services, Sullivan was responsible for promoting health education and ensuring the safety of food, drugs, and medical research. Upon the expiration of his term in January 1993, he returned to Atlanta to resume his presidency of the Morehouse School of Medicine. Sullivan served in that capacity until his retirement on May 31, 2002. He continues to serve on the Morehouse School of Medicine Board of Trustees, teaching and assisting in national fund-raising activities. Sullivan also serves on the boards of Bristol-Myers Squibb and 3M.

HAROLD WASHINGTON (1922–1987)

Federal Legislator, Municipal Government Official, Attorney. Harold Washington was born in Chicago on April 15, 1922. After serving with the U.S. Army Air Corps in the Pacific theater during World War II, he received a B.A. from Roosevelt University in 1949. Washington earned a J.D. in 1952 from Northwestern University Law School. He worked as an assistant city prosecutor in Chicago from 1954 to 1958, and as an arbitrator with the Illinois Industrial Commission from 1960 to 1964.

Running on the Democratic ticket, Washington was elected to the Illinois House of Representatives in 1965 and served until 1976, when he was elected to the Illinois Senate. He served in the state senate until 1980. While a state legislator, Washington helped establish Illinois's Fair Employment Practices Commission, secured passage of consumer-protection legislation, and worked to designate Martin Luther King Jr.'s birthday as a state holiday. After the death of longtime Chicago mayor Richard J. Daley in 1976, Washington finished third in the four-man contest for the Democratic nomination for mayor. In 1980, Washington was elected to the U.S. House of Representatives and became a member of the Ninety-seventh Congress. He served on the Education and Labor, Government Operations, and Judiciary committees. Shortly after his reelection to the House, Washington won the Democratic nomination for Chicago mayor. In 1983, he won the election to become the city's first African American mayor.

Although Washington's mayoralty was marked by political infighting, he did manage to institute reforms, including increased city hiring of minorities, deficit reduction, the appointment of an African American police commissioner, and reduction of patronage influence. Washington died while in office on November 25, 1987.

MAXINE WATERS (1938–)

Federal and State Legislator. Maxine Waters was born in St. Louis on August 15, 1938. After graduating from high school, she moved to Los Angeles, where she worked at a garment factory and for a telephone company. She earned a B.A. in sociology from California State University in 1970. Waters became interested in politics after teaching in a Head Start program and serving as a delegate to the Democratic National Convention in 1972.

In 1976, Waters was elected to the California State Assembly, where she served on numerous committees, including the Ways and Means Subcommittee on State Administration, the Joint Committee of Public Pension Fund Investments, the Joint Legislative Budget Committee, the Judiciary Committee, the Joint Committee on Legislative

Ethics, the Select Committee on Assistance to Victims of Sexual Assault, the California Committee on the Status of Women, the Natural Resources Committee, and the Elections, Reapportionment, and Constitutional Amendment Committee. As a member of the California Assembly, she created the nation's first statewide child-abuse prevention training program, gained passage of a law prohibiting strip searches for nonviolent misdemeanors, and promoted legislation to prevent toxic chemical catastrophes.

In 1990, Waters was elected to the U.S. House of Representatives, where she has become an outspoken figure. In 2008, she was reelected to her tenth term in the House with 80 percent of the votes in California's thirty-fifth district, which encompasses much of South Central Los Angeles, as well as the communities of Westchester, Playa del Rey, Gardena, Hawthorne, Inglewood, and Lawndale. In addition to holding the position of chair of the Congressional Black Caucus from 1997 to 1998, Waters has served on the Banking, Finance, and Urban Affairs Committee, the Judiciary Committee, and the Veterans' Affairs Committee. She has served in the influential position of chief deputy whip for the Democratic Party since the 106th Congress. Following the 2000 presidential election, Waters was named chair of the Democratic Caucus Special Committee on Election Reform. She has fought for legislation promoting aid to poor and minority neighborhoods in American cities and combating apartheid in South Africa.

Waters opposed the Iraq War and voted against the 2002 Iraq War Resolution. In 2005, she became the founding member and chair of the "Out of Iraq" Congressional Caucus, which encourages debate in Congress about the war in Iraq and advocates the departure of U.S. military forces there. She is also a member of the Congressional Progressive Caucus. During the 111th Congress, Waters served on the Judiciary Committee and the Financial Services Committee, for which she chaired the Subcommittee on Housing and Community Opportunity.

Waters has served on the board of directors of *Essence* magazine, and has been involved with the National Women's Political Caucus, the National Steering Committee on Education of Black Youth, and the National Steering Committee of the Center for the Study of Youth Policy.

J. C. WATTS JR. (1957–)

Federal Legislator, Religious Leader. Julius Caesar Watts was born on November 18, 1957, in Eufaula, Oklahoma. His father was a minister and Eufaula city councilman, and his uncle once headed Oklahoma's NAACP chapter. Educated at the University of Oklahoma, Watts was a star quarterback and was named Most Valuable Player of the 1980 and 1981 Orange Bowls. He graduated with a journalism degree but chose to continue in athletics, joining the Canadian Football League's Ottawa Rough Riders. He played five years with the Rough Riders and one with the Toronto Argonauts. An ordained minister and motivational speaker for youth and church groups, Watts served as youth director at the Sunnylane Baptist Church at Del City, Oklahoma, and presided over the Watts Energy Corp.

Though he had long considered himself a Democrat, Watts became disenchanted with the direction the party was taking and decided to become a Republican in 1989. He was also approached by prominent Oklahoma Republicans to run in the state Republican primary. The following year, he was elected chairperson of Oklahoma's Corporation Commission. The win made him the first African American Oklahoman to win a statewide election. Strongly in favor of welfare reform, defense spending cuts, and a balanced budget, the charismatic Watts built a rapport with his home state that led to his 1994 election victory over the Democratic incumbent to the U.S. House of Representatives. In doing so, Watts became the first African American Republican from a southern state to win a seat in Congress since Reconstruction, and only the second African American Republican to win a seat in the House in sixty years. Watts received national publicity when he declined membership in the Congressional Black Caucus because, in his opinion, many of the members were Democratic liberals who betray black Americans.

Watts was reelected to Congress in 1996, 1998, and 2000. In a 1996 speech before the Republican National Convention, Watts spoke eloquently about character. In 1997, he delivered the Republican response to President Bill Clinton's State of the Union address. Shortly after the 1998 elections, Watts was elected to become GOP conference chair, the party's fourth-highest position. On July 1, 2002, Watts announced that he would not seek a fifth term in Congress in order to spend more time with his family. He became chairman of GOPAC, which was formed in 1978 to build a cadre of Republican officeholders to run for higher state and national office. He served in that capacity until February 2007. After leaving politics, Watts became founder and chairman of JC Watts Companies, a multi-industry firm that provides business development, communications, public affairs, diversity training, and other services to clients.

ROBERT C. WEAVER (1907–1997)

Lecturer, Federal Government Official, Educator. Robert Clifton Weaver became the first African American appointed to a presidential cabinet post when President Lyndon B. Johnson named him head of the newly created Department of Housing and Urban Development on January 13, 1966. Previously, Weaver had served as head of the Housing and Home Finance Agency from 1961 to 1966.

Robert Weaver was born on December 29, 1907, in Washington, D.C., where he attended Dunbar High School and worked during his teens as an electrician. Encountering discrimination when he attempted to join a union, Weaver decided to go to college and concentrated on economics. Weaver attended Harvard University, where he received a B.S., an M.S., and a Ph.D. Weaver's grandfather, Dr. Robert Tanner Freeman, was the first African American to earn a degree in dentistry at Harvard.

Weaver was a professor of economics at the Agricultural and Technical College of North Carolina in Greensboro from 1931 to 1932. He was one of the academics brought to Washington during the New Deal. From 1934 to 1938, he served in the Department of the Interior in various roles. He was also a part of President Franklin D. Roosevelt's "Black Cabinet." After leaving the Interior Department, Weaver served as a special assistant to the head of the National Housing Authority from 1938 to 1940. From 1940 to 1944, Weaver continued his work with the federal government through the War Production Board and the Negro Manpower Commission.

Weaver left the federal government because he felt implementation of antidiscriminatory measures was moving too slowly. He moved in 1944 to Chicago, where he divided his time between teaching and government service. He directed the Mayor's Committee on Race Relations, and in 1947 he became a lecturer at Northwestern University. He later joined the faculties at Teachers College (Columbia University) and the New York University School of Education. He also became a professor of economics at the New School for Social Research. From 1949 to 1955, he was director of the Opportunity Fellowships Program of the John Hay Whitney Foundation. Weaver also served as a member of the National Selection Committee for Fulbright Fellowships from 1952 to 1954, chairman of the Fellowship Committee of the Julius Rosenwald Fund, and a consultant to the Ford Foundation from 1959 to 1960.

In 1955, Weaver was named deputy state rent commissioner by New York's governor W. Averell Harriman. By the end of the year, he had become state rent commissioner and the first African American to hold state cabinet rank in New York. From 1960 to 1961, he served as vice chairman of the New York City Housing and Redevelopment Board, a three-man body that supervised New York's urban renewal and middle-income housing programs. Weaver headed the Department of Housing and Urban Development until 1968. From 1969 to 1970, he served as president of Baruch College. Weaver accepted a teaching position at the Department of Urban Affairs at Hunter College in New York in 1971. After he retired from Hunter College in 1978, Weaver continued to serve on the boards of corporations, as well as educational and public institutions. He wrote four books and 185 articles. In 1985, he was inducted into the American Academy of Arts and Sciences. Weaver died in his New York City home on July 17, 1997.

WELLINGTON WEBB (1941–)

Municipal Government Official. Born February 17, 1941, Wellington Webb had to leave his South Side Chicago home as a child to live with his grandmother in Denver, Colorado, because of his asthma. After graduating from Colorado State College in 1964 with a B.A. in education, Webb worked in various public-service jobs, including forklift operator, welfare caseworker, and special-education teacher, while obtaining a master's degree. In 1971, Webb received his M.A. in sociology from the University of Northern Colorado at Greeley.

In 1972, Webb was elected to the Colorado State Legislature as a representative from the northeast section of Denver. He served there for four years and rose to prominence within the Democratic Party in 1976 when Democratic presidential hopeful Jimmy Carter chose Webb to head the state's national election committee. Upon Carter's election as president, Webb was named a regional director of the U.S. Department of Health, Education, and Welfare. After leaving federal government service in 1981, Webb received an appointment from Colorado's governor as executive director of the Colorado Department of Regulatory Agencies. During his tenure in the early 1980s, Webb was the only African American in the state cabinet.

Webb ran for mayor of Denver in 1983, but lost. In 1987, he ran successfully for the city auditor post. As city auditor, he was credited with restoring professionalism to the office. In 1991, he faced his city hall colleague, a popular African American district attorney, in another mayoral race. Webb won with 58 percent of the vote, despite being outspent by his well-financed opponent. He was reelected for a second term in 1995. Counted among Webb's accomplishments as mayor are a 40 percent decrease in crime, an unemployment rate below 2 percent, completion of the new Denver International Airport and a new sports stadium, expansion of the Denver Art Museum, development of a new African American Research Library, and creation of some fifty thousand jobs. Webb won a third term in 1999 with a platform promising the revitalization of Denver's poorer neighborhoods, the creation of more affordable housing, and the improved management of traffic congestion. Webb also served as president of the U.S. Conference of Mayors, as well as head of the National Conference of Black Mayors.

After his twelve-year tenure as mayor of Denver, Webb briefly campaigned for the office of chairman of the Democratic National Committee in late 2004. He withdrew from consideration, however, and endorsed

Howard Dean. In 2003, Webb established Webb Group International, a consulting firm offering economic development and public-relations expertise to cities and businesses. Webb frequently lectures on civic issues at such places as Harvard University's Kennedy School of Government. He published an autobiography, *Wellington Webb: The Man, the Mayor, and the Making of Modern Denver*, in 2007.

MICHAEL R. WHITE (1951–)

Municipal Government Official. Born and raised on the east side of Cleveland, Ohio, Michael Reed White was elected mayor of Cleveland in 1989. At the time, 40 percent of the city's population was living at or below the poverty line.

An alumnus of Ohio State University, White received a bachelor's degree in education in 1973 and a master's degree in public administration in 1974. His political career started in 1974 when he became a special assistant for the mayor's office in Columbus, Ohio. In 1978, White began six years on Cleveland's city council, followed by four years in Columbus as a state senator. In 1989, White entered Cleveland's mayoral race, running against three white candidates and city council president George Forbes. White won the election.

The central issue for White's administration was the future of Cleveland's young people. Two focal points White worked toward were an upgrade of public education and the development of new jobs programs. White also supported the development of the Lake Erie waterfront, and the completion of the Rock and Roll Hall of Fame and Museum.

When Bill Clinton became president in 1992, White was invigorated by the potential changes in the federal government's relationship to U.S. cities. He was an outspoken supporter of Clinton's plans to get rid of the old welfare system. In 1995, White met with the National Football League commissioner Paul Tagliabue to try and keep the Browns from moving to Baltimore. White secured a new team, which began play in 1999, the same year a new football stadium opened.

In 1999, White launched a major investigation of Cleveland's police department. The inquiry focused on allegations of racism within the force. Despite the appearance of racist graffiti in a number of station locker rooms and accusations that some of the city's officers had worn white supremacist symbols on their uniforms, the investigation ended in March 2000 with White announcing no evidence had been found indicating the operation of hate groups in the department.

White did not seek a fourth term as mayor. He finished serving his third term on December 31, 2001. White retired to an alpaca farm in Ohio after the new mayor assumed office.

L. DOUGLAS WILDER (1931–)

Attorney, State Government Official. Lawrence Douglas Wilder was born on January 17, 1931, in Richmond, Virginia. He graduated from Virginia Union University in 1951 with a B.S. in chemistry. After graduation, he was drafted into the U.S. Army and assigned to a combat infantry unit in Korea. During the Korean War, he was awarded a Bronze Star for bravery and valor in combat. After being discharged in 1953, Wilder worked as a chemist in the Virginia state medical examiner's office. Later, he studied law under the G.I. Bill, graduating in 1959 with a J.D. from Howard University Law School.

After cofounding the firm of Wilder, Gregory, and Associates, Wilder practiced law in Richmond until 1969, when he became the first African American elected to the Virginia State Senate since Reconstruction. Wilder chaired the important Privileges and Elections Committee and worked on legislation supporting fair housing, union rights for public employees, and minority hiring. He also voted against capital punishment (a position he has since rescinded). In 1985, Wilder was elected lieutenant governor, becoming the first African American elected to a statewide executive position in the South in the twentieth century. In 1989, he became Virginia's first African American governor, winning the election by one-third of 1 percent of the vote. In recognition of this extraordinary achievement, the NAACP awarded Wilder the Spingarn Medal, its highest honor, in 1990.

As governor, Wilder streamlined the state's budget, eliminated Virginia's $2.2 billion deficit, and worked to get civil rights legislation passed. Virginia law does not allow its governor to serve consecutive terms. After his term as governor, Wilder remained active in Virginia politics. From 1995 to 2001, Wilder hosted a popular weekly radio program, *The Doug Wilder Show*. In 1998, he was selected as president of his alma mater, Virginia Union University, but rescinded his acceptance of the position shortly before he was to be inaugurated as president. In 2004, Wilder ran successfully for the office of mayor of Richmond, garnering 79 percent of the vote. Wilder was the first directly elected mayor of Richmond in years.

In 1979, Wilder won the Distinguished Alumni Award presented by Virginia Union University. In succeeding years, he received the President's Citation from Norfolk State University (1982), was named Alumnus of the Year from the Howard Law School Alumni Association (1993),

Douglas Wilder, with Crowd in Boston, MA, January 2007. *Wilder served as governor of Virginia from 1990 to 1994, in the process becoming the first African American to be elected as a governor of a U.S. state. Wilder later served as mayor of Richmond, Virginia, from 2005 to 2009.* AP PHOTO/STEVEN SENNE

and earned the Distinguished Postgraduate Achievement in Law and Politics Award (1985). Wilder belongs to the Richmond Urban League, the Richmond Bar Association, the American Judicature Society, the American Trial Lawyers Association, the Virginia Trial Lawyers Association, the National Association of Criminal Defense Lawyers, and the NAACP. He has also served as vice president of the Virginia Human Relations Council.

Wilder continues to work toward the selection of a site and the construction of a slavery museum in Virginia. In February 2002, he was appointed by Governor Mark Warner as chairman of a thirteen-member commission to study the effectiveness and efficiency of Virginia's state government. In 2004, Virginia Commonwealth University named its School of Government and Public Affairs in his honor. The Virginia Union University library is also named in honor of Wilder.

ANDREW YOUNG (1932–)

Diplomat, Municipal Government Official, Federal Legislator, Civil Rights Activist. Andrew Young was born in New Orleans on March 12, 1932, and received a bachelor of science degree from Howard University in 1951 and a bachelor of divinity degree in 1955 from the Hartford Theological Seminary. He was ordained a minister in the United Church of Christ and then served in churches in Alabama and Georgia before joining the staff of the National Council of Churches in 1957.

The turning point of Young's life came in 1961, when he became a trusted aide and close confidant of Reverend Martin Luther King Jr. He became executive vice president of the Southern Christian Leadership Conference (SCLC) in 1967, and remained with King until King's 1968 assassination. During his years with SCLC, Young organized antiwar protests, voter-registration drives, and other civil rights projects.

In 1970, Young lost a bid for a seat in the U.S. House of Representatives. In the aftermath of the election, Young was appointed chair of Atlanta's Community Relations Committee (CRC). Though the CRC was an advisory group with no enforcement powers, Young took an activist role, pressing the city government on many issues, from sanitation and open housing to mass transit, consumer affairs, and Atlanta's drug problem. Young's leadership in the CRC led to a higher public profile and answered critics' charges that he was inexperienced in government.

Young launched another bid for a congressional seat in 1972. African Americans comprised only 44 percent of the voters in Young's congressional district. However, Young captured 23 percent of the white vote and 54 percent of the total vote to win by a margin of eight thousand votes. Young was the first African American representative to be elected from Georgia since Jefferson Long in 1870. One year later, Young was named the recipient of the Martin Luther King Jr. Nonviolent Peace Prize.

Young was one of the most vocal supporters of his fellow Georgian Jimmy Carter's campaign for the U.S. presidency in 1976. Following President Carter's inauguration, Young left Congress in 1977 to become America's ambassador to the United Nations. Young's tenure there was marked by controversy, and his outspoken manner sometimes ruffled diplomatic feathers. Among his most important contributions were helping to bring peace and a new constitution to Zimbabwe, improving relations with Nigeria, and fostering improved relations between the United States and developing countries.

Young's career as a diplomat came to an end in 1979 when he met secretly with a representative of the Palestine Liberation Organization (PLO) to discuss an upcoming vote in the United Nations. The United States had a policy that none of its representatives would meet with the PLO as long as it refused to recognize the right of Israel to exist as a state. When news of Young's meeting leaked out, an uproar followed. Young tendered his resignation, which President Carter accepted. The incident badly strained relations between African Americans and Jewish Americans because many African Americans felt that Jewish leaders were instrumental in Young's removal from office.

When Maynard Jackson was prevented by law from running for his third term of office as mayor of Atlanta in 1981, Young entered the race. During the campaign, Jackson charged African Americans who supported the white candidate, state legislator Sidney Marcus, with "selling out" the civil rights movement. Jackson's remarks were widely criticized, and it was feared that they would create a backlash against Young. However, Young ended up with 55 percent of the vote. He won 10.6 percent of the white vote, compared to the 12 percent he had won in the primary, and 88.4 percent of the black vote, up from 61 percent earlier.

Young took office at a time when Atlanta was facing a number of economic and social problems, including a shrinking population and a stagnating tax base. In addition, almost a quarter of the city's residents were living below the poverty line, and the city was still shaken by the recent murders of twenty-eight African American youths and the disappearance of another. Some critics doubted Young's ability to deal with Atlanta's problems. He was seen as a weak antibusiness administrator. But, by 1984, the city had become so successful in attracting new businesses that it was experiencing a major growth spurt. In addition, the crime rate dropped sharply and racial harmony prevailed. Young was decisively reelected.

Limited by law to two terms as mayor, Young ran unsuccessfully for the governorship of Georgia in 1990. His wife died of cancer four years later. In 1994, Young published his autobiography, *A Way Out of No Way: The Spiritual Memoirs of Andrew Young.* He was cochair of the Atlanta Committee for the 1996 Olympic Games and a member of various boards of directors, including those of Delta Airlines and Host Marriott Corp. He was also president of Young Ideas, a consulting firm he founded. In 1995, Young became head of the Southern Africa Enterprise Development Fund, which offered low-interest loans to small businesses in South Africa and other countries in the region. In 2001, he met with Zimbabwe's president, Robert Mugabe, in an attempt to resolve the issue of forcible land seizures from white landowners by black war veterans.

In 1996, Young became founder and cochair of Good Works International, a consulting firm that offers market- and political-risk analysis on key emerging markets in Africa and the Caribbean. In February 2006, Young became chair of Working Families for Wal-Mart, an organization sponsored by the retail giant in response to public criticism that the company exploits its workers and discriminates against women and African American employees and that many of Wal-Mart's employees and their children are on public assistance. Six months later, following comments in an interview that were interpreted as controversial and racist, Young ended his involvement with Wal-Mart.

COLEMAN A. YOUNG (1918–1997)

Municipal Government Official. Longtime Detroit icon Coleman Alexander Young announced on June 22, 1993, that he would not seek reelection for the mayoralty of the city that fall. Young had won each of his mayoral elections by a wide margin. He was the only mayor in the history of Detroit to serve five consecutive terms, leading the media to dub him "mayor for life." Once recognized as an urban savior, Detroit's highly publicized problems—crime, declining population, and poor economic standing—finally instilled doubts in the voters regarding Young's abilities.

Young was born in Tuscaloosa, Alabama, on May 24, 1918. His family moved to Detroit in 1926, after the Ku Klux Klan ransacked a Huntsville neighborhood where his father was learning to be a tailor. In Detroit, Young attended Catholic Central and then Eastern High School, graduating from the latter with honors. He had to reject a scholarship to the University of Michigan when the Eastern High School Alumni Association, in contrast to policies followed with poor white students, declined to assist him with costs other than tuition.

Young entered an electrician's apprentice school at the Ford Motor Company. He finished first in the program but was passed over for the only available electrician job in favor of a white candidate. Working on the assembly line, he soon became engaged in underground union activities. After being attacked one day by a company man, Young defended himself by hitting his assailant on the head with a steel bar, leading to Young's dismissal.

During World War II, Young was a navigator in the U.S. Army Air Force and was commissioned a second lieutenant. Stationed at Freeman Field, Indiana, he demonstrated against the exclusion of African Americans from segregated officers' clubs and was arrested along with one hundred other African American airmen, including Thurgood Marshall and Percy Sutton, former president of New York's borough of Manhattan. Young spent three days in jail. Shortly thereafter, the clubs were opened to African American officers.

After the war, Young returned to his union organizing activities and was named director of organization for the Wayne County AFL-CIO in 1947. However, the union fired him in 1948 when he supported Henry Wallace, candidate of the Progressive Party, in the presidential election. The union suspected Wallace of being an agent of the Communist Party and supported Harry Truman instead. Young managed a dry-cleaning plant for a few years, then founded and directed the National Negro Labor Council in 1951. The council successfully prevailed on Sears Roebuck and Co. and the San Francisco Transit System to hire African Americans. However, they also aroused the interest of the House Un-American Activities Committee, which was in the midst of hunting for alleged communists. When brought before the committee, Young, who denied he was ever a communist, refused to name anyone. Though he emerged from the hearing with his self-respect intact, his council was placed on the attorney general's subversive list. In 1956, the council was disbanded, and charges of Young's communist involvement were used against him, albeit unsuccessfully, during his first mayoral campaign.

After working at a variety of jobs, Young won a seat on the Michigan Constitutional Convention in 1961. The following year, he lost a race for state representative but became director of campaign organization for the Democratic gubernatorial candidate in Wayne County, which includes Detroit. Young sold life insurance until 1964, when, with union support, he was elected to the state senate. In the senate, he was a leader of the civil rights forces fighting for low-income housing for people dislocated by urban renewal. He also fought for an end to discrimination in the hiring practices of the Detroit police force.

Young declared his candidacy for mayor of Detroit in 1973, and mounted a vigorous campaign for the office. He won after a racially divisive campaign. Among his early successes in office were the integration of the Detroit police department and promotion of African American officers into administrative positions. The new mayor also created a coalition of business and labor to preserve the industries remaining in Detroit and attract new ones. Young's outspoken and opinionated nature and his fondness for using expletives earned him both passionate supporters and bitter enemies. A Democrat and one of the first big-city mayors to support Jimmy Carter's presidential campaign in 1976, Young had a close relationship with the Carter administration. He turned down a federal cabinet position, but his relationship with the president proved helpful in securing funds for Detroit.

In the 1980s, Young was intensely critical of the administrations of presidents Ronald Reagan and George H. W. Bush, with their cutbacks in federal aid to urban areas. The federal government seized several opportunities to scrutinize Young as well. Over the years, Young's administration was investigated on several charges, including improprieties in the awarding of city contracts and illegal personal use of city funds by the police department; however, Young himself was never personally implicated in the scandals.

Young's popularity was bolstered by a number of citywide improvements credited to him, such as the expansion of riverfront attractions, which brought increased convention and tourist traffic to the city, and favorable tax abatements that attracted new businesses, including two major automobile plants. Middle-class and white flight to the suburbs, which had begun at the end of the 1960s, continued to rob the city's coffers of essential tax revenue. Some critics argued that Young's attitude toward suburbanites contributed to the phenomenon. Near the end of his tenure, Young endured a barrage of disapproval for his autocratic style and his emphasis on cosmetic improvements rather than true remedies for the decay of the city.

In 1989, Coleman Young won his fifth term as mayor. Despite a high unemployment rate, a shortage of cash, and a high crime rate, the voters returned the popular Young to office. In 1990, both Detroit and its mayor were targets of highly critical feature stories in the *New York Times* and on CBS. Commentary revolved around Detroit's sagging economy, brutal crime statistics, racial stratification, and a supposed general air of despair. Young countered that under his administration, the city had managed to balance its budget despite a dramatic cutback in federal and state aid. He also noted that many neighborhoods had undergone extensive renovation and that a new automobile-manufacturing plant had opened within the city limits.

In 1993, when Young felt that he no longer had the necessary vitality to run a big city, a major chapter in Detroit politics came to a close. Young turned his attention toward writing, publishing *Hard Stuff: The Autobiography of Coleman Young*, written with Lonnie Wheeler, in 1994. After he left politics, Young became a professor of urban affairs at Detroit's Wayne State University, where he continued to raise dialogue about race and class issues. Young was in poor health during his last years and suffered from heart trouble, chronic emphysema, and other respiratory problems. He died on November 29, 1997.

12

POPULATION

Audrey Y. Williams
Yvonnie Perrello

The study of population involves the systematic analysis of data derived from periodic censuses and other sources. Such analyses help statisticians predict changes in population growth patterns. In the United States, an ccurate analysis of population trends among African Americans is critical in shaping public policies in such areas as employment and education, and in determining how to allocate resources.

THE AFRICAN AMERICAN POPULATION FROM 1619 TO THE CIVIL WAR

Although there is evidence that blacks were living in South America before Christopher Columbus arrived in the Caribbean in 1492, the earliest record of blacks in what is now the United States dates from 1619 when a group of African and European indentured servants landed in Jamestown, Virginia, with a small number of British colonists. Historians differ on the exact number, but between fourteen and twenty African indentured servants were part of this early settlement. The practice of enslaving Africans began within a short time, and soon spread throughout the colonies. In 1630, there were sixty enslaved Africans in the American colonies; by 1660, the number had increased to 2,920, almost fifty times as many.

By 1680, the colonies were growing and prospering. The thriving agrarian society needed strong workers to till the fertile fields. And thus was born the commerce of human flesh known as the "slave trade." Within seventy years after the first Africans were brought to the colonies, the enslaved black population in the American colonies had grown to 16,729. By 1740, the slave population had reached 150,000; the number had increased to 575,000 by 1780. Although a free black population did exist in early America, it grew at a slower rate than the enslaved population; in 1780, there was only one free black for every nine slaves.

Fewer than 8 percent of African Americans lived in the Northeast or Midwest by the time the Emancipation Proclamation was signed in 1863. After the Civil War (1861–1865), the percentage of blacks living in the Northeast declined slightly, while the percentage in the Midwest rose.

The first official American census, taken in 1790, listed 757,000 blacks. At that time, African descendants constituted 19.3 percent of the nation's population, of which 9 percent, or 59,527, were not enslaved. By 1790, Pennsylvania, Massachusetts, Connecticut, Rhode Island, New York, New Jersey, and the Northwest Territory had enacted legislation providing for the gradual emancipation of slaves. By 1860, there were almost four million persons of African descent in the United States, more than 90 percent of them in the South. The free population, most of whom lived in the North, numbered less than half a million.

POPULATION GROWTH AFTER 1865

The decline and eventual cessation of the slave trade, coupled with increased European migration, resulted in demographic changes. In 1900, there were 8.8 million African Americans in the United States, representing 11.6 percent of the total population. Between 1910 and 1930, the percentage of African Americans in the U.S. population declined, reaching a low point in 1930, when African Americans accounted for only 9.7 percent of the total.

Since 1930, the African American population has grown at a rate faster than the national average. The percentage of blacks living in the South continued to decrease until 1970. At that time, about 39 percent of African Americans were northerners, 53 percent were southerners, and the majority of the others lived in the West.

Thirty years later, the regional distribution of African Americans had changed. According to the 2000 census, the overall American population numbered approximately 281.4 million, with 19 percent of all Americans living in the South and 22 percent living in the West. Corresponding figures for the African American population in 2000 indicate a different settling pattern from that of the total population: 17.6 percent lived in the Northeast, 18.75 percent in the Midwest, 54.8 percent in the South, and 8.85 percent in the West.

The 2000 census data indicated a strong growth trend for the African American population. According to the 1990 census, the African American population constituted 12.1 percent of the American population, up from 11.7 percent in 1980. By 1997, the African American population in the United States had grown to 32.3 million, or 12 percent of the nation's total resident population. By 2000, the African American population had increased to 34.7 million, or 12.3 percent of the total population.

The growth of the African American population since the 1980 census is largely due to high birth rates and increased immigration from countries with black populations. The increase in the number of births over deaths since 1980 was due mainly to two factors: a larger percentage of African Americans of childbearing age and a reduction in infant mortality.

The African American population has also grown as a result of legal and illegal immigration. Although the streams of Asian and Hispanic immigrants to the United States have been more highly publicized, black immigration has also increased. The Caribbean, primarily Haiti and Jamaica, is one source of black immigrants, who enter the United States to find work. The 1980 Mariel boatlift also brought some blacks from Cuba. In addition, harsh political and economic conditions in Africa have provided many Africans with the incentive to immigrate to the United States. African American population figures have also been augmented by African students who overstay their student visas and begin working in the United States. Estimates of the size and effects of some of these sources of new population growth are speculative, but according to the U.S. Census Bureau, legal immigration in 1996 from several Caribbean countries (with the exception of Jamaica, Haiti, Dominican Republic, Trinidad and Tobago, and Cuba and African nations) amounted to approximately 170,000.

REGIONAL DISTRIBUTION FROM 1790 TO 1900

From 1790 until 1900, approximately 90 percent of the African American population lived mostly in rural areas of the South. The abolition of black enslavement after the Civil War had little impact on the southern rural character of the African American population. The newly freed Africans were mostly illiterate with agrarian skills. Sharecropping became a way of life for many who agreed to work for very low wages in return for shelter and a portion of the crop. Sharecropping was not much different from enslavement for uneducated African Americans, who were easily taken advantage of by dishonest landowners. Once the Reconstruction period ended, some African American leaders urged blacks to migrate from the South, particularly since former Confederates were still in control in the post–Civil War era.

AFRICAN AMERICAN TOWNS AND SETTLEMENTS

The Cherokee, Choctaw, Chickasaw, Creek, and Seminole peoples, often called the Five Civilized Nations, were driven from their lands in the South into what is today known as Oklahoma, when former Confederates and white supremacists regained control of most of the southern states and local governments after Reconstruction. Between 1830 and 1840, this area was called Indian Territory. These Native American groups brought their slaves with them as they set up an agricultural way of life. Some black runaways were befriended by the Native Americans, and others were personal property. In some instances, Native Americans and African Americans intermarried and had families. After the Civil War, in which both African Americans and Native Americans participated, most of the Native American nations freed their enslaved blacks.

The freedmen and approximately ten thousand African American settlers migrated west to Kansas and Oklahoma, establishing between twenty-five and twenty-seven towns and settlements in the Indian and Oklahoma territories. Today, there are no traces of most of those communities, although a few key towns and settlements survive in Oklahoma, Kansas, and the South.

NICODEMUS, KANSAS

By 1879, thousands of African Americans from the Deep South had moved to the North and West to seek a livelihood free from the sharecropping form of slavery.

Two African American men, Henry Adams of Louisiana and Pap Singleton of Tennessee, encouraged migration to Kansas. Fifty thousand African Americans moved to Kansas from southern Louisiana during this period. Nicodemus is the last survivor of the African American communities founded in Kansas after the Civil War.

The founding settlers were called *exodusters*. Although the Nicodemus exodusters were poor and lacked sufficient tools and seed money, they managed to survive the first winter, some by selling buffalo bones, others by working for the Kansas Pacific Railroad at Ellis, thirty-five miles away. In 1800, the town had an African American population of more than four hundred. Hopes that the railroad would come their way and add to the town's fortune never materialized. In 1974, Nicodemus was designated a National Historic Landmark District.

On November 12, 1996, Nicodemus was named a National Historical Site. As such, the National Park Service is responsible for aiding the community in the preservation of historic structures and in the interpretation of the town's history for the benefit of present and future generations. The Nicodemus Historical Society is the town's only remaining business. In 2000, the population numbered about twenty.

LANGSTON, OKLAHOMA

In 1890, Edwin P. McCabe (1850–1920) and his wife Sarah helped establish Langston, Oklahoma, one of the many towns founded by blacks who migrated from the South to northern and western communities. Edwin McCabe was an African American state auditor in Kansas who wanted to make Oklahoma an all–African American state as a refuge for black Americans who wished to escape the discrimination that prevailed elsewhere. McCabe named the town Langston in honor of John Mercer Langston (1829–1897), a black member of the Fifty-first U.S. Congress from Virginia.

Although McCabe was unsuccessful in his efforts to make Oklahoma an African American state, Langston flourished. By 1897, Langston had a population of more than two thousand residents, and the Oklahoma territorial legislature granted the settlement enough land to establish the Colored Agricultural and Normal University, the first African American agricultural and mechanical college. The institution, now known as Langston University, is the most western of the historically black colleges and universities. Langston is also home to the Beulah Land Cemetery, which boasts markers and graves of former slaves and city founders, and the Melvin B. Tolson Black Heritage Center, which holds African and African American history and heritage exhibits, an art collection, and multimedia resources. The current population in Langston is less than two thousand, the majority of whom are black.

BOLEY, OKLAHOMA

Boley, Oklahoma, was founded in 1903 and incorporated in 1905 as Boley, Creek Nation, Indian Territory. The name was changed to Boley, Oklahoma, when the State of Oklahoma was formed in 1907, without any federal guarantees that African Americans would have full citizenship and not be harassed. Boley consisted of 160 acres that belonged to Abigail Barnett McCormick, who had inherited the land from the government as the daughter of James Barnett, a Creek freedman. Booker T. Washington (1856–1915), the most prominent African American leader of that period, encouraged African Americans to migrate to Boley to develop an all–African American town. Washington believed that it was important for African Americans to be self-sufficient and learn crafts and skills to take care of their communities. By 1911, Boley had a population of about four thousand, with five grocery stores, five hotels, seven restaurants, four cotton gins, three drug stores, one jewelry store, four department stores, two livery stables, two insurance agencies, one funeral home, one lumber yard, two photographers, and an ice plant. Boley also had the first black-owned electric company and one of the first black-owned banks.

Migration to Boley slowed during the late 1920s and came to a halt during the Great Depression in the early 1930s. Many residents left at this time. The current population is less than one thousand, with black residents making up approximately 60 percent.

EATONVILLE, FLORIDA

Eatonville, Florida, is located approximately ten miles northeast of downtown Orlando. Eatonville was incorporated in 1887 and is the oldest African American municipality in the United States. Zora Neale Hurston (1891–1960), the Harlem Renaissance writer and anthropologist, spent part of her childhood in Eatonville, and described the town in several of her books. Her father served three terms as mayor of Eatonville. Hurston later studied at Howard University and was the first African American woman to graduate from Barnard College. Many years later, a combination of community pride and the support of literary artists such as Alice Walker and Maya Angelou prevented the construction of a major highway through the center of the town. In the late 1980s, a civic group called Preserve the Eatonville Community was formed to protect and maintain the historic town. Eatonville now has historic landmark status and holds an annual Zora Neale Hurston Festival. Eatonville has a population of more than two thousand black residents and about two hundred white residents.

AMERICAN BEACH, FLORIDA

American Beach, about twenty acres of land on Amelia Island, Florida, was given its name by Abraham Lincoln Lewis (1865–1947), who purchased the land in 1935. At the time that Lewis bought the land, Jim Crow laws were prevalent in the South. The area's beaches and resorts were open to whites only and did not allow blacks, even millionaires such as Lewis, to use the facilities. Lewis planned to encourage other well-to-do African Americans to follow his example and eventually build an area for African Americans to enjoy. There were 2,432 people living in American Beach according to the 2000 census, of which about 90 percent were African American. The residents of American Beach have had to fend off aggressive developers who want to buy up land for malls and franchises, erasing the town's original character.

BEYOND CENSUS 2000

According to the 2002 census supplement, African Americans made up 13 percent of the U.S. population. That percentage represents thirty-six million people. By 2004, the black population was estimated to be 39.2 million, or 13.4 percent. In 2004, the percentages of blacks living in specific regions remained similar to the 2002 figures, which show that the majority of African Americans (55%) lived in the South. Figures from the U.S. Census Bureau (2003) show 37.1 million African Americans living in the United States (12.9% of the total population). At the time of the 2000 Census, 54.8 percent of African Americans lived in the South, 17.6 percent lived in the Northeast, and 18.7 percent in the Midwest. Only 8.9 percent lived in the West. In comparison, 69 percent (194.8 million) of the U.S. population was non-Hispanic white in 2002. Of that number, 33 percent lived in the South, 27 percent in the Midwest, 21 percent in the Northeast, and 19 percent in the West.

New York (3.5 million), Florida (2.9 million), and Texas (2.7 million) were the states with the largest black populations in 2002. Black Americans are concentrated primarily in the cities. In 2002, more than half (52 %) of all blacks lived in a central city within a metropolitan area, compared to 21 percent of non-Hispanic whites. Approximately 57 percent of American whites lived outside a central city, but within a metropolitan area, compared with 36 percent of blacks.

A significant portion of the black population is represented by young people. In 2002, 33 percent of all blacks were less than eighteen years old, compared with 23 percent of whites. In addition, a larger proportion of black males than white males was younger than eighteen (35% compared with 24%). In contrast, 7 percent of black males and 12 percent of white males were sixty-five or older. Only 8 percent of all African Americans were sixty-five and older, compared with 14 percent of white Americans. A higher percentage of black females (30%) were under eighteen, compared to 21 percent of white females. The black female population also had a lower percentage of women sixty-five years old or older, 9 percent, compared to 22 percent for white females.

In the 2008 general election, an estimated 131.1 million African Americans voted. That was 5.4 million more than had voted in the 2004 election. While the majority of the black voters (55%) were between eighteen and twenty-four years old, the turnout rate for all African American voters was 49 percent. This translated into an increase of approximately 5 percent since the 2004 elections.

In the months leading up to the 2008 presidential election, and for a period following the swearing in of the first African American president, Barack Obama, politicians and journalists discussed predictions that, by 2050, there would be a shift in the population, such that the white population would become a minority, while the former minority populations (consisting of Hispanics, African Americans, Asian Americans, and those of mixed heritage) would become the majority. While Hispanics are projected to have the largest representation, the projected estimate for the African American population in 2050 (barring unexpected variables) is 65.7 million.

THE AFRICAN AMERICAN POPULATION FROM 2006 TO 2008

According to Census Bureau data, there has not been a substantial increase in the number of African Americans in the United States since 2004. At that time, there were an estimated 39.2 million blacks living in the United States, or 13.4 percent of the population. By July 2008, the total number of African Americans had reached 41.1 million, which placed the percentage at approximately 13.5 percent. While the factors that contributed to this minimal population increase among African Americans are unclear, the nation is and continues to be more diverse than it was decades earlier.

In 2008, 30.5 percent of the black population was younger than eighteen, and 8 percent was older than sixty-five. African Americans make up the largest minority group among military veterans, approximately 2.3 million in 2008.

The Census Bureau's population projections indicate an increase in the total number of African Americans, from 41.1 million (13.5%) in 2008 to 65.7 million (15%) in 2050. However, these estimates predict an increase of less than 2 percent in forty years. It is important

Table 12-1. Resident Population (U.S.) by Race, Hispanic Origin, and State: 2008

[**In thousands (304,060 represents 304,060,000). As of July**. Persons of Hispanic origin may be any race. Due to the complexities associated with the production of detailed characteristics' estimates at the state level, the values of the estimates at lower levels of geography may not necessarily sum to estimates at higher levels of geography]

State	Total population	One race					Two or more races	Hispanic origin	Non-Hispanic White alone
		White alone	Black or African American alone	American Indian/ Alaska Native alone	Asian alone	Native Hawaiian and Other Pacific Islander alone			
U.S.	**304,060**	**242,639**	**39,059**	**3,083**	**13,549**	**562**	**5,167**	**46,944**	**199,491**
AL	4,662	3,311	1,230	25	45	2	50	135	3,191
AK	686	485	29	105	31	4	32	42	451
AZ	6,500	5,623	270	316	162	13	116	1,956	3,796
AR	2,855	2,307	450	24	31	3	41	160	2,160
CA	36,757	28,170	2,451	444	4,582	157	952	13,457	15,538
CO	4,939	4,432	211	60	131	7	97	997	3,507
CT	3,501	2,951	362	13	121	3	51	419	2,584
DE	873	648	183	4	25	1	12	59	597
DC	592	237	322	2	20	1	10	51	196
FL	18,328	14,628	2,916	91	416	18	259	3,845	11,059
GA	9,686	6,333	2,908	36	277	8	124	777	5,629
HI	1,288	382	40	8	506	117	236	112	321
ID	1,524	1,442	14	23	17	2	25	156	1,297
IL	12,902	10,209	1,920	45	559	9	159	1,967	8,348
IN	6,377	5,612	578	20	87	3	77	332	5,305
IA	3,003	2,828	81	13	47	2	33	126	2,711
KS	2,802	2,486	172	29	62	2	51	255	2,250
KY	4,269	3,838	329	11	42	2	46	102	3,748
LA	4,411	2,860	1,410	28	64	2	47	148	2,731
ME	1,316	1,269	14	8	12	(Z)	14	17	1,254
MD	5,634	3,572	1,658	20	286	4	93	376	3,252
MA	6,498	5,601	456	20	321	6	94	557	5,147
MI	10,003	8,121	1,425	62	237	4	155	414	7,751
MN	5,220	4,649	239	65	185	3	80	217	4,458
MS	2,939	1,781	1,093	15	24	1	26	66	1,724
MO	5,912	5,027	679	30	86	5	85	190	4,856
MT	967	875	7	62	6	1	17	29	851
NE	1,783	1,630	80	19	30	1	23	140	1,500
NV	2,600	2,103	211	39	161	14	72	669	1,486
NH	1,316	1,256	16	4	25	1	14	35	1,225
NJ	8,683	6,602	1,256	30	664	8	123	1,419	5,354
NM	1,984	1,667	59	192	28	3	36	891	828
NY	19,490	14,310	3,363	111	1,369	21	317	3,250	11,697
NC	9,222	6,819	1,992	116	177	7	112	685	6,198
ND	641	586	7	36	5	(Z)	7	13	575
OH	11,486	9,736	1,382	29	181	4	153	302	9,474
OK	3,642	2,846	290	291	63	4	148	279	2,600
OR	3,790	3,416	76	54	138	11	94	416	3,033
PA	12,448	10,634	1,343	27	304	6	134	594	10,134
RI	1,051	930	67	7	29	1	17	122	828
SC	4,480	3,080	1,276	19	55	3	48	184	2,921
SD	804	709	9	68	6	(Z)	11	21	692
TN	6,215	4,995	1,043	21	83	3	70	231	4,791
TX	24,327	20,046	2,898	185	841	31	326	8,870	11,526
UT	2,736	2,543	35	38	54	21	46	329	2,236
VT	621	599	5	2	7	(Z)	7	9	591
VA	7,769	5,674	1,546	29	378	7	135	531	5,201
WA	6,549	5,520	245	113	438	32	201	644	4,944
WV	1,814	1,715	65	4	12	1	18	21	1,696
WI	5,628	5,047	342	56	115	2	67	286	4,787
WY	533	500	7	14	4	1	8	41	463

Z = Less than 500.

SOURCE: U.S. Census Bureau, "Annual State Resident Population Estimates for 6 Race Groups (5 Race Alone Groups and One Group with Two or more Race Groups) by Age, Sex, and Hispanic Origin: April 1, 2000 to July 1, 2008" (released May 14, 2009).

***Table 12-1.** The data compares the numbers of African Americans (and other groups) to the total population for each state.*

Table 12-2. People Below Poverty Level and Below 125 Percent of Poverty Level by Race and Hispanic Origin: 1980 to 2007

[Based on Current Population Survey, Annual Social and Economic Supplement (ASEC).]

	Percent below poverty level					Below 125 percent of poverty level
Year	All races[1]	White[2]	Black[3]	Asian and Pacific Islander[4]	Hispanic[5]	Percent of total population
1980	13.0	10.2	32.5	(NA)	25.7	18.1
1985	14.0	11.4	31.3	(NA)	29.0	18.7
1986	13.6	11.0	31.1	(NA)	27.3	18.2
1987[6]	13.4	10.4	32.4	16.1	28.0	17.9
1988	13.0	10.1	31.3	17.3	26.7	17.5
1989	12.8	10.0	30.7	14.1	26.2	17.3
1990	13.5	10.7	31.9	12.2	28.1	18.0
1991	14.2	11.3	32.7	13.8	28.7	18.9
1992[7]	14.8	11.9	33.4	12.7	29.6	19.7
1993[8]	15.1	12.2	33.1	15.3	30.6	20.0
1994	14.5	11.7	30.6	14.6	30.7	19.3
1995	13.8	11.2	29.3	14.6	30.3	18.5
1996	13.7	11.2	28.4	14.5	29.4	18.5
1997	13.3	11.0	26.5	14.0	27.1	17.8
1998	12.7	10.5	26.1	12.5	25.6	17.0
1999[9]	11.9	9.8	23.6	10.7	22.7	16.3
2000[10]	11.3	9.5	22.5	9.9	21.5	15.6
2001	11.7	9.9	22.7	10.2	21.4	16.1
2002[11]	12.1	10.2	24.1	10.1	21.8	16.5
2003	12.5	10.5	24.4	11.8	22.5	16.9
2004[12]	12.7	10.8	24.7	9.8	21.9	17.1
2005	12.6	10.6	24.9	11.1	21.8	16.8
2006	12.3	10.3	24.3	10.3	20.6	16.8
2007	12.5	10.5	24.5	10.2	21.5	17.0

NA Not available.
[1]Includes other races not shown separately.
[2]Beginning 2002, data represent White alone, which refers to people who reported White and did not report any other race category.
[3]Beginning 2002, data represent Black alone, which refers to people who reported Black and did not report any other race category.
[4]Beginning 2002, data represent Asian alone, which refers to people who reported Asian and did not report any other race category.
[5]People of Hispanic origin may be any race.
[6]Implementation of a new March CPS processing system.
[7]Implementation of 1990 census population controls.
[8]The March 1994 income supplement was revised to allow for the coding of different income amounts on selected questionnaire items. Limits either increased or
decreased in the following categories: earnings increased to $999,999; social security increased to $49,999; supplemental security income and public assistance
increased to $24,999; veterans benefits increased to $99,999; child support and alimony decreased to $49,999.
[9]Implementation of Census-2000-based population controls.
[10]Implementation of sample expansion by 28,000 households.
[11]Beginning with the 2003 Current Population Survey (CPS), the questionnaire allowed respondents to choose more than one race. For 2002 and later, data
represent persons who selected this race group only and exclude persons reporting more than one race. The CPS in prior years allowed respondents to report only one race group.
[12]Data have been revised to reflect a correction to the weights in the 2005 ASEC.

SOURCE: U.S. Census Bureau, *Current Population Reports*, P60–235 (published August 2008).

Table 12-2. *The number of African Americans living below the poverty level declined significantly between 1980 and 2007, before the start of a recessionary period in December of that year.*

to note, however, that these projections were of persons classified as single-race blacks. The 2010 census may call for a slight adjustment to the 2050 population projections.

INCOME, POVERTY, AND HEALTH INSURANCE

According to Census Bureau data for 2007, the annual median income of black households in the United States was approximately $33,916. In the previous year, this figure was $32,876. Among full-time workers fifteen years old and older, the median income for black males was $36,068, while black women earned only $31,009. The percentage of African Americans living in poverty was 24.5, which had not changed from the previous year. Although the economic and political climate brought the health-care debate to the forefront in 2010, the reality is that approximately 19.5 percent of single African Americans reportedly lacked health-insurance coverage in 2007. In 2006, this number was 20.5 percent.

Andrew A. Beveridge, a demographer at Queens College of the State University of New York, analyzed 2005 Census Bureau data and reported that in one of New York City's boroughs, Queens, the median income for blacks was almost $52,000, surpassing the median income of whites in the borough. No other county in the nation with a population of more than 65,000 has a black median income that is higher than that of whites. The household income of African Americans is higher than that of white residents in Mount Vernon, New York; Westchester, New York; Pembroke Pines, Florida; Brocton, Massachusetts; and Rialto, California—all of which have populations smaller than Queens. Beveridge's analysis notes that Queens has a high number of two-parent African American families, many of whom are immigrants from the Caribbean. Further analysis showed that foreign-born black heads of household earned more than native-born black heads of household.

REGIONAL DISTRIBUTION BY STATE IN 2008

By 2008, there were eighteen states where the total population of African Americans exceeded one million. New York had the highest number of African Americans, with more than three million, although African Americans made up only 17 percent of the state's total population. California, Florida, Georgia, and Texas also had high numbers of African American residents in 2008. The southern states continue to have the highest percentages of African Americans, however, with Mississippi (37.2%), Louisiana (32%), and Georgia (30%) heading the list.

From 2006 to 2007, the population of the state of Georgia saw a substantial growth of 83,000 African Americans. Other states also saw large increases in their African American population, including Texas, Florida, and North Carolina. In 2007, Cook County in Illinois, which includes Chicago, had the largest black population of all counties in the United States, 1.4 million. Orleans Parish in Louisiana, which encompasses New Orleans, had the largest increase in the number of black residents in the country between 2007 and 2008. Louisiana's St. Bernard Parish recorded a 97 percent increase in its black population over the same period. Much of this increase resulted from the return of the black population to the area after Hurricane Katrina, although it is statistically impossible to determine how many were returning and how many were new residents (U.S. Census Bureau, mid-2007 estimate).

Mississippi's total African American population was more than one million in 2008. The state of Mississippi also had the largest percentage of African Americans, with approximately 37.2 percent. In 2007, Mississippi also had the highest rate of home-ownership among African Americans, at 59 percent, which was higher than the national home-ownership rate of 46 percent.

The northern states have the smallest African American populations. Vermont had the smallest black population in 2008, with approximately 5,378 African American residents, which was less than 1 percent of the state's total population. Montana had the lowest percentage of African Americans, with 0.7 percent, or 6,504 black residents among a total population of 967,440 in 2008. Other states with low numbers of African American residents included Wyoming (6,884), North Dakota (6,956), and South Dakota (9,185).

13

EMPLOYMENT AND INCOME

Verna J. Henson
Michael D. Woodard
Delano Greenidge-Copprue

The last quarter of the twentieth century brought about significant changes in the social and economic status of African Americans. Educated and skilled African Americans experienced considerable upward mobility. Analysts pointed to the passage of equal opportunity legislation during the civil rights era as the primary reason why African Americans with education and skills were able to take advantage of once-denied opportunities in employment and income growth. On the other hand, downsizing, job restructuring, and job dislocation were widespread in the government and private sector. Companies eliminated many blue-collar jobs—some by relocating them to countries with cheaper labor—that once provided upward mobility for the less skilled. As a result, African Americans with less education and less skill have experienced decreased income, higher rates of unemployment, or removal from the labor force altogether.

EMPLOYMENT TRENDS

The most significant change in twentieth-century American race relations was that African Americans began participating in all areas of employment. Historically, including much of the twentieth century, African Americans were restricted to service jobs in all industry sectors. For example, in the corporate arena, the idea of an African American leading a major corporation was not considered. In the entertainment industry, African Americans were severely underutilized, and the roles available to them were limited to buffoonery. African Americans were locked out of professional sports and restricted to segregated leagues, ignored in the arts, and not considered seriously as politicians.

By 2010, while still underrepresented, African Americans headed major corporations and sat on corporate boards. African Americans were well represented in both Democratic and Republican administrations, heading important federal departments, influencing the policy by which this and other countries operate, and culminating in the 2008 election of Barack Obama as president of the United States. There was a plethora of African American stars in the music, television, and film industries. In addition, African Americans were increasingly making strides in production and executive positions. Once admitted, African Americans dominated in professional sports, including golf and tennis. Indeed, for the first time in history, both football teams competing for the 2007 Super Bowl were coached by African Americans, Lovie Smith of the Chicago Bears and Tony Dungy of the Indianapolis Colts. In 2009, Jim Caldwell, head coach of the Colts following the retirement of Dungy, became the third African American to lead his team to the Super Bowl. To say that the racial caste system in employment opportunities did not improve for African Americans would certainly be inconsistent with the facts.

Despite the recent dramatic changes in employment opportunities, not every segment of the African American population benefited. The growing African American middle class experienced a greater range of occupational and economic opportunities than ever before, but an increasing number of African Americans who are disadvantaged were, in effect, locked out of the mainstream of American life. This growing schism in the social and economic conditions among African Americans has serious implications for the way African Americans should be

Table 13-1. Employed Civilians by Occupation, Sex, Race, and Hispanic Origin: 2008

[**145,362 represents 145,362,000**. Civilian noninstitutional population 16 years old and over. Annual average of monthly figures. Based on Current Population Survey. Occupational classifications are those used in the 2000 census]

Occupation	Total employed (1,000)	Percent of total			
		Female	Black[1]	Asian[1]	Hispanic[2]
Total, 16 years and over	**145,362**	**46.7**	**11.0**	**4.8**	**14.0**
Management, professional and related occupations	**52,761**	**50.8**	**8.3**	**6.3**	**7.1**
Management, business, and financial operations occupations	22,059	42.7	7.2	5.2	7.5
Management occupations[3]	15,852	37.4	6.4	4.6	7.3
Chief executives	1,655	23.4	3.9	4.0	4.8
General and operations managers	985	30.1	5.4	4.3	6.2
Advertising and promotions managers	77	62.1	7.6	5.8	9.7
Marketing and sales managers	922	42.0	4.9	4.1	6.2
Administrative services managers	100	32.6	8.9	2.3	5.7
Computer and information systems managers	475	27.2	7.7	10.2	5.3
Financial managers	1,168	54.8	7.9	5.7	8.6
Human resources managers	293	66.3	8.2	4.0	7.3
Industrial production managers	243	14.5	4.9	3.8	9.6
Purchasing managers	193	40.4	12.9	2.5	3.7
Transportation, storage, and distribution managers	239	17.0	7.7	1.7	12.7
Farm, ranch, and other agricultural managers	217	23.9	0.9	1.7	4.6
Farmers and ranchers	751	24.4	1.0	0.7	2.4
Construction managers	1,244	8.2	3.7	1.4	9.1
Education administrators	829	65.1	12.2	2.6	7.6
Engineering managers	109	6.3	1.1	8.0	4.9
Food service managers	1,039	44.8	7.3	11.8	12.9
Lodging managers	177	46.7	5.5	12.2	9.1
Medical and health services managers	561	69.4	10.1	4.2	7.3
Property, real estate, and community association managers	558	49.6	7.7	3.1	8.2
Social and community service managers	338	68.1	10.1	2.2	7.7
Business and financial operations occupations[3]	6,207	56.2	9.4	6.5	7.9
Wholesale and retail buyers, except farm products	191	47.6	7.6	6.1	12.2
Purchasing agents, except wholesale, retail, and farm products	264	56.5	6.7	4.8	11.2
Claims adjusters, appraisers, examiners, and investigators	312	65.7	14.6	3.6	7.6
Compliance officers, except agriculture, construction, health and safety, and transportation	179	52.3	7.9	3.1	6.4
Cost estimators	100	10.0	0.7	1.2	5.3
Human resources, training, and labor relations specialists	803	70.7	14.0	3.5	7.9
Management analysts	731	43.5	6.2	5.8	4.6
Accountants and auditors	1,762	61.1	8.3	10.2	7.6
Appraisers and assessors of real estate	102	33.4	5.2	2.0	7.2
Financial analysts	110	38.8	6.0	12.9	9.8
Personal financial advisors	430	34.3	5.9	5.9	6.1
Insurance underwriters	82	80.3	13.3	5.5	7.1
Loan counselors and officers	392	58.0	10.6	4.4	11.5
Tax preparers	105	66.6	9.1	5.7	12.6
Professional and related occupations	30,702	56.7	9.0	7.1	6.7
Computer and mathematical occupations[3]	3,676	24.8	7.2	16.7	5.1
Computer scientists and systems analysts	837	27.5	9.7	13.7	5.3
Computer programmers	534	22.4	5.7	14.1	4.0
Computer software engineers	1,034	20.9	4.7	29.0	3.7
Computer support specialists	382	27.7	11.1	8.2	7.9
Database administrators	93	29.2	6.3	13.5	3.8
Network and computer systems administrators	227	21.4	8.0	9.8	7.4
Network systems and data communications analysts	422	23.7	7.1	9.2	6.4
Operations research analysts	75	47.6	8.6	4.1	8.3
Architecture and engineering occupations[3]	2,931	13.5	5.1	9.6	6.7
Architects, except naval	233	24.8	3.3	6.1	8.2
Aerospace engineers	137	10.3	6.1	11.1	5.0
Civil engineers	346	10.4	3.2	11.2	9.2
Electrical and electronics engineers	350	7.7	3.0	13.4	5.3
Industrial engineers, including health and safety	177	14.9	5.9	7.6	5.2
Mechanical engineers	318	6.7	4.5	10.6	4.1
Drafters	162	23.4	3.0	7.2	9.0
Engineering technicians, except drafters	416	18.5	10.9	5.4	10.3
Surveying and mapping technicians	105	4.9	1.5	1.2	8.0

Table 13-1. Employed Civilians by Occupation, Sex, Race, and Hispanic Origin: 2008 [CONTINUED]

[**145,362 represents 145,362,000**. Civilian noninstitutional population 16 years old and over. Annual average of monthly figures. Based on Current Population Survey. Occupational classifications are those used in the 2000 census]

Occupation	Total employed (1,000)	Percent of total			
		Female	Black[1]	Asian[1]	Hispanic[2]
Life, physical, and social science occupations[3]	1,307	46.1	7.1	12.0	4.7
Biological scientists	101	52.9	4.2	13.3	3.9
Medical scientists	132	52.3	8.1	24.8	2.7
Chemists and materials scientists	118	33.1	4.7	22.3	6.9
Environmental scientists and geoscientists	85	29.3	4.0	2.7	4.1
Market and survey researchers	134	57.0	5.7	3.3	5.8
Psychologists	176	66.9	7.2	3.1	6.6
Community and social services occupations[3]	2,293	60.3	19.0	2.5	8.9
Counselors	674	68.0	20.5	2.2	8.9
Social workers	729	79.4	24.5	2.9	10.0
Miscellaneous community and social service specialists	303	61.4	20.9	2.6	14.5
Clergy	441	14.8	10.2	2.7	3.6
Legal occupations	1,671	51.9	7.0	2.8	6.6
Lawyers	1,014	34.4	4.6	2.9	3.8
Paralegals and legal assistants	346	87.7	11.6	2.2	10.3
Miscellaneous legal support workers	257	74.5	10.0	3.9	13.3
Education, training, and library occupations[3]	8,605	74.0	9.2	3.8	7.5
Postsecondary teachers	1,218	46.1	5.2	11.9	4.0
Preschool and kindergarten teachers	685	97.6	11.7	3.5	9.8
Elementary and middle school teachers	2,958	81.2	9.9	2.2	6.8
Secondary school teachers	1,210	56.0	7.2	1.8	6.5
Special education teachers	387	84.9	8.0	1.3	3.7
Other teachers and instructors	751	66.9	9.3	3.8	8.2
Librarians	197	83.5	6.7	3.5	3.7
Teacher assistants	1,020	91.7	13.9	2.8	15.0
Arts, design, entertainment, sports, and media occupations[3]	2,820	47.8	6.1	4.1	8.3
Artists and related workers	213	48.6	2.0	3.7	5.4
Designers	834	57.5	5.6	6.1	8.2
Producers and directors	154	38.5	8.9	4.0	7.3
Athletes, coaches, umpires, and related workers	252	32.5	10.3	2.3	8.3
Musicians, singers, and related workers	186	29.3	9.7	1.6	10.8
News analysts, reporters and correspondents	94	45.4	2.1	3.9	2.9
Public relations specialists	135	61.6	5.1	1.7	7.3
Editors	171	54.8	3.5	2.5	2.2
Writers and authors	186	57.3	4.1	1.1	3.3
Miscellaneous media and communication workers	83	72.2	6.1	12.1	27.4
Broadcast and sound engineering technicians and radio operators	98	16.1	11.0	5.9	12.9
Photographers	181	44.1	4.3	3.9	10.1
Healthcare practitioner and technical occupations[3]	7,399	74.6	10.2	8.0	5.9
Dentists	152	27.2	3.3	12.0	5.2
Dietitians and nutritionists	100	90.0	20.3	3.7	7.1
Pharmacists	243	51.8	8.7	12.6	2.5
Physicians and surgeons	877	30.5	6.2	16.6	5.8
Physician assistants	99	66.9	6.6	5.2	9.3
Registered nurses	2,778	91.7	10.0	7.8	4.7
Occupational therapists	87	95.9	1.2	6.3	5.5
Physical therapists	197	69.0	3.9	13.0	3.5
Respiratory therapists	109	68.3	10.4	4.6	7.4
Speech-language pathologists	133	98.1	2.3	4.8	6.2
Clinical laboratory technologists and technicians	351	75.7	14.6	8.8	9.0
Dental hygienists	143	97.7	4.1	2.0	5.3
Diagnostic-related technologists and technicians	298	72.0	8.8	5.3	5.0
Emergency medical technicians and paramedics	138	30.2	4.7	0.1	6.6
Health diagnosing and treating practitioner support technicians	447	76.7	10.8	5.2	10.8
Licensed practical and licensed vocational nurses	566	93.3	22.1	3.6	7.1
Medical records and health information technicians	98	95.0	13.9	4.0	9.9
Service occupations	**24,451**	**57.2**	**15.9**	**4.6**	**20.2**
Healthcare support occupations[3]	3,212	88.8	25.8	4.2	13.6
Nursing, psychiatric, and home health aides	1,889	88.7	34.5	4.3	13.1
Massage therapists	147	84.5	7.0	8.0	7.4
Dental assistants	263	96.3	6.9	2.0	17.3
Medical assistants and other healthcare support occupations	831	88.8	16.9	4.2	15.3

Table 13-1. Employed Civilians by Occupation, Sex, Race, and Hispanic Origin: 2008 [CONTINUED]

[**145,362 represents 145,362,000**. Civilian noninstitutional population 16 years old and over. Annual average of monthly figures. Based on Current Population Survey. Occupational classifications are those used in the 2000 census]

Occupation	Total employed (1,000)	Percent of total			
		Female	Black[1]	Asian[1]	Hispanic[2]
Protective service occupations[3]	3,047	22.8	19.1	1.8	10.9
First-line supervisors/managers of police and detectives	117	14.7	12.5	2.9	6.1
Fire-fighters	293	4.8	8.2	0.3	9.4
Bailiffs, correctional officers, and jailers	403	30.0	22.0	0.6	10.4
Detectives and criminal investigators	139	19.2	10.6	2.3	9.5
Police and sheriff's patrol officers	674	14.7	13.6	1.8	11.6
Private detectives and investigators	89	39.4	13.8	0.8	6.5
Security guards and gaming surveillance officers	867	23.6	31.0	3.0	12.4
Lifeguards and other protective service workers	148	52.3	5.7	0.8	9.6
Food preparation and serving related occupations	7,824	56.0	12.1	5.4	21.0
Chefs and head cooks	351	17.0	10.3	14.1	22.7
First-line supervisors/managers of food preparation and serving workers	635	57.8	14.4	3.8	14.1
Cooks	1,997	40.1	18.1	5.0	30.2
Food-preparation workers	724	60.7	9.8	6.6	24.6
Bartenders	365	58.3	3.5	2.3	9.6
Combined food preparation and serving workers, including fast food	323	68.5	15.6	2.0	17.2
Counter attendants, cafeteria, food concession, and coffee shop	323	64.1	12.2	4.5	15.4
Waiters and waitresses	2,010	73.2	7.3	6.2	14.6
Food servers, nonrestaurant	187	70.5	20.5	6.5	18.0
Dining room and cafeteria attendants and bartender helpers	349	47.8	13.1	5.6	26.9
Dishwashers	289	22.7	12.0	3.4	35.7
Hosts and hostesses, restaurant, lounge, and coffee shop	263	88.7	6.2	3.0	11.6
Building and grounds cleaning and maintenance occupations	5,445	40.2	15.0	2.8	33.4
First-line supervisors/managers of housekeeping and janitorial workers	296	39.9	18.6	1.1	23.7
First-line supervisors/managers of landscaping, lawn service, and groundskeeping workers	258	7.5	4.5	0.6	16.8
Janitors and building cleaners	2,125	32.2	18.4	3.4	28.2
Maids and housekeeping cleaners	1,434	89.8	18.1	3.7	40.5
Grounds maintenance workers	1,262	6.1	7.7	1.6	41.0
Personal care and service occupations[3]	4,923	78.4	14.7	7.4	14.2
First-line supervisors/managers of gaming workers	155	38.6	7.2	3.2	10.3
First-line supervisors/managers of personal service workers	174	73.2	11.1	13.8	7.5
Nonfarm animal caretakers	157	73.5	2.9	1.9	12.3
Gaming services workers	111	51.5	13.1	21.8	3.5
Barbers	87	20.8	33.3	4.1	20.2
Hairdressers, hairstylists, and cosmetologists	773	90.6	11.3	6.5	11.0
Miscellaneous personal appearance workers	229	82.3	4.4	55.0	6.3
Baggage porters, bellhops, and concierges	72	17.3	23.9	8.1	19.9
Transportation attendants	139	71.0	16.8	3.3	13.1
Child care workers	1,314	95.6	17.4	2.7	20.0
Personal and home care aides	871	85.4	21.8	6.7	17.4
Recreation and fitness workers	353	68.1	9.6	3.3	9.5
Residential advisors	70	65.8	28.1	0.1	4.7
Sales and office occupations	**35,544**	**63.2**	**11.5**	**4.2**	**12.3**
Sales and related occupations[3]	16,295	49.5	9.7	4.7	11.7
First-line supervisors/managers of retail sales workers	3,471	43.3	7.3	5.2	10.4
First-line supervisors/managers of non retail sales workers	1,287	26.1	6.9	4.9	11.0
Cashiers	3,031	75.5	16.3	6.4	16.6
Counter and rental clerks	161	50.4	14.8	7.9	13.7
Parts salespersons	119	10.8	7.5	1.7	14.7
Retail salespersons	3,416	52.2	10.7	4.1	12.3
Advertising sales agents	216	54.7	10.3	2.2	8.4
Insurance sales agents	573	46.9	7.6	2.7	9.4
Securities, commodities, and financial services sales agents	388	27.9	7.2	5.1	9.2
Travel agents	98	71.6	9.8	10.3	6.4
Sales representatives, services, all other	521	34.4	8.9	4.5	8.8
Sales representatives, wholesale and manufacturing	1,343	27.3	3.9	3.8	8.6
Models, demonstrators, and product promoters	74	79.0	8.0	6.7	6.6
Real estate brokers and sales agents	962	54.4	7.2	3.5	8.6

Table 13-1. Employed Civilians by Occupation, Sex, Race, and Hispanic Origin: 2008 [CONTINUED]

[**145,362 represents 145,362,000**. Civilian noninstitutional population 16 years old and over. Annual average of monthly figures. Based on Current Population Survey. Occupational classifications are those used in the 2000 census]

Occupation	Total employed (1,000)	Percent of total			
		Female	Black[1]	Asian[1]	Hispanic[2]
Telemarketers	139	66.3	23.6	0.7	16.6
Door-to-door sales workers, news and street vendors, and related workers	243	62.2	9.5	3.7	14.4
Office and administrative support occupations[3]	19,249	74.8	13.0	3.7	12.8
First-line supervisors/managers of office and administrative support workers	1,641	71.2	10.4	3.4	10.5
Bill and account collectors	232	68.0	20.0	2.2	18.2
Billing and posting clerks and machine operators	516	90.9	13.5	3.6	12.6
Bookkeeping, accounting, and auditing clerks	1,434	91.5	6.9	4.4	8.0
Payroll and timekeeping clerks	158	90.1	11.8	4.1	10.8
Tellers	466	84.8	12.3	6.1	15.8
Court, municipal, and license clerks	100	75.6	11.1	3.7	10.5
Customer service representatives	1,908	68.3	18.3	3.7	14.5
File clerks	364	83.8	15.5	4.4	12.0
Hotel, motel, and resort desk clerks	120	71.9	19.1	3.9	9.6
Interviewers, except eligibility and loan	146	82.2	18.4	1.9	17.7
Library assistants, clerical	107	83.8	8.9	4.5	5.7
Loan interviewers and clerks	122	84.7	7.1	2.4	18.3
Order clerks	112	58.8	11.8	1.5	18.0
Receptionists and information clerks	1,413	93.6	9.8	3.8	15.2
Reservation and transportation ticket agents and travel clerks	136	60.9	14.3	6.5	14.8
Couriers and messengers	261	17.4	13.9	1.7	21.1
Dispatchers	286	57.4	15.9	1.9	11.8
Postal service clerks	167	53.7	27.0	8.5	10.5
Postal service mail carriers	373	33.0	14.5	6.4	9.8
Postal service mail sorters, processors, and processing machine operators	90	42.7	34.1	10.9	11.4
Production, planning, and expediting clerks	269	58.2	8.9	3.7	7.3
Shipping, receiving, and traffic clerks	543	32.8	11.6	2.8	20.2
Stock clerks and order fillers	1,481	35.4	16.8	3.6	18.6
Secretaries and administrative assistants	3,296	96.1	8.1	2.3	9.6
Computer operators	134	51.4	19.9	4.3	5.1
Data entry keyers	415	77.3	17.6	5.2	12.9
Word processors and typists	149	92.9	17.3	3.6	13.1
Insurance claims and policy processing clerks	275	83.4	19.4	2.8	12.2
Mail clerks and mail machine operators, except postal service	123	49.0	20.8	7.1	12.9
Office clerks, general	1,176	84.4	15.4	4.7	14.1
Natural resources, construction, and maintenance occupations	**14,806**	**4.2**	**6.9**	**1.9**	**25.0**
Farming, fishing, and forestry occupations[3]	988	21.1	4.5	1.7	39.3
Logging workers	73	1.0	5.9	—	12.3
Construction and extraction occupations[3]	8,667	2.5	6.3	1.4	29.6
First-line supervisors/managers of construction trades and extraction workers	844	2.7	3.0	1.2	16.1
Brickmasons, blockmasons, and stonemasons	230	0.4	7.4	1.2	39.9
Carpenters	1,562	1.5	6.0	1.3	25.7
Carpet, floor, and tile installers and finishers	224	2.3	1.9	1.0	42.7
Cement masons, concrete finishers, and terrazzo workers	90	(–)	7.4	0.1	57.7
Construction laborers	1,651	3.1	7.7	1.9	44.1
Operating engineers and other construction equipment operators	398	1.5	5.1	0.5	17.4
Drywall installers, ceiling tile installers, and tapers	209	2.1	3.6	0.4	56.9
Electricians	874	1.0	5.9	2.7	16.2
Painters, construction and maintenance	647	6.3	7.3	2.2	40.1
Pipelayers, plumbers, pipefitters, and steamfitters	606	1.4	6.4	0.6	19.5
Roofers	234	1.3	8.4	0.4	42.9
Sheet metal workers	136	4.8	6.2	1.2	11.8
Structural iron and steel workers	77	0.9	2.2	0.3	14.4
Helpers, construction trades	113	4.1	18.1	0.3	41.3
Construction and building inspectors	93	9.5	9.2	1.6	5.4
Highway maintenance workers	103	1.9	17.2	(–)	10.2
Installation, maintenance, and repair occupations[3]	5,152	3.9	8.5	2.8	14.5
First-line supervisors/managers of mechanics, installers, and repairers	300	8.0	6.7	1.0	8.7
Computer, automated teller, and office machine repairers	335	10.5	10.8	7.5	13.0
Radio and telecommunications equipment installers and repairers	200	11.4	13.7	4.4	11.8

Table 13-1. Employed Civilians by Occupation, Sex, Race, and Hispanic Origin: 2008 [CONTINUED]

[**145,362 represents 145,362,000**. Civilian noninstitutional population 16 years old and over. Annual average of monthly figures. Based on Current Population Survey. Occupational classifications are those used in the 2000 census]

Occupation	Total employed (1,000)	Percent of total: Female	Black[1]	Asian[1]	Hispanic[2]
Electronic home entertainment equipment installers and repairers	75	1.6	13.5	8.0	16.2
Aircraft mechanics and service technicians	153	1.7	5.5	6.4	13.8
Automotive body and related repairers	157	2.1	5.2	0.7	27.2
Automotive service technicians and mechanics	852	1.6	6.5	2.9	19.7
Bus and truck mechanics and diesel engine specialists	358	0.9	7.5	1.7	11.6
Heavy vehicle and mobile equipment service technicians and mechanics	217	1.1	5.0	0.4	10.5
Heating, air conditioning, and refrigeration mechanics and installers	397	2.0	8.6	2.2	13.2
Industrial and refractory machinery mechanics	439	2.6	8.8	3.0	13.0
Maintenance and repair workers, general	461	3.5	10.2	2.4	13.7
Electrical power-line installers and repairers	109	1.4	8.7	0.3	8.9
Telecommunications line installers and repairers	204	3.3	16.2	1.1	15.0
Production, transportation, and material occupations	**17,800**	**22.4**	**14.5**	**3.8**	**20.4**
Production occupations[3]	8,973	29.7	12.2	5.2	21.1
First-line supervisors/managers of production and operating workers	874	18.1	9.5	5.0	14.9
Electrical, electronics, and electromechanical assemblers	203	57.8	12.2	17.5	19.4
Bakers	194	55.7	12.1	5.0	28.9
Butchers and other meat, poultry, and fish processing workers	309	26.8	14.6	6.7	38.4
Food batchmakers	73	53.5	11.7	6.2	29.0
Cutting, punching, and press machine setters, operators, and tenders, metal and plastic	105	20.2	9.1	4.0	22.0
Machinists	409	6.9	7.0	4.2	12.1
Tool and die makers	71	1.0	0.9	1.2	5.9
Welding, soldering, and brazing workers	598	4.7	8.7	3.7	21.0
Printing machine operators	213	19.8	9.1	2.9	20.5
Laundry and dry-cleaning workers	239	60.8	22.4	7.7	29.3
Sewing machine operators	226	78.2	9.4	14.1	36.8
Tailors, dressmakers, and sewers	71	84.2	6.1	12.2	24.4
Cabinetmakers and bench carpenters	85	6.5	2.8	5.7	13.0
Stationary engineers and boiler operators	101	1.7	13.1	2.4	7.2
Water and liquid waste treatment plant and system operators	71	8.6	12.3	(–)	7.0
Crushing, grinding, polishing, mixing, and blending workers	108	13.3	14.5	1.4	20.6
Cutting workers	80	26.7	8.0	5.1	27.4
Inspectors, testers, sorters, samplers, and weighers	751	41.3	13.4	5.8	14.2
Medical, dental, and ophthalmic laboratory technicians	95	56.9	6.2	6.9	13.8
Packaging and filling machine operators and tenders	261	51.5	15.0	5.0	42.5
Painting workers	183	13.6	13.2	1.1	26.2
Transportation and material-moving occupations[3]	8,827	14.9	16.9	2.5	19.7
Supervisors, transportation and material-moving workers	208	20.5	14.4	5.5	12.0
Aircraft pilots and flight engineers	141	2.6	1.8	2.4	2.5
Bus drivers	651	49.0	30.4	1.8	12.2
Driver/sales workers and truck drivers	3,388	4.9	14.3	1.5	17.8
Taxi drivers and chauffeurs	373	13.3	26.3	10.5	18.9
Parking lot attendants	83	12.6	15.7	8.7	27.3
Service station attendants	87	14.8	10.3	4.4	12.4
Industrial truck and tractor operators	568	8.9	23.4	1.5	26.7
Cleaners of vehicles and equipment	317	9.5	17.4	0.9	28.8
Laborers and freight, stock, and material movers, hand	1,889	17.1	15.9	2.4	21.2
Packers and packagers, hand	391	58.1	15.3	4.6	43.7
Refuse and recyclable material collectors	98	14.0	16.4	2.4	31.1

—Represents or rounds to zero.
[1]The Current Population Survey (CPS) allowes respondents to choose more than one race. Data represent persons who selected this race group only and exclude persons reporting more than one race.
[2]Persons of Hispanic or Latino ethnicity may be any race.
[3]Includes other occupations not shown separately.

SOURCE: U.S. Bureau of Labor Statistics, "Employment and Earnings Online," January 2009.

Data show the number of African Americans and other minority groups as a percentage of the total workforce employed in various occupations.

viewed as a group, as well as for public policy that focuses on African Americans in the twenty-first century.

LABOR FORCE PARTICIPATION AND UNEMPLOYMENT

In March 2000, there were approximately sixteen million African Americans in the civilian labor force, constituting 12 percent of the total. The labor-force participation rate for black men was 68.1 percent, compared to 63.9 percent for black women. The labor-force participation rate for white men was 74.3 percent, compared to 60.8 percent for white women. Thus, black men were less likely to be in the job market than white men. In 2008, overall black participation in the civilian labor force stood at 63.7 percent, compared to 66.3 percent for white Americans and 67 percent for Asian Americans.

Unemployment remained a major problem among African Americans in the labor force, and high levels of unemployment have persisted for several decades. Data from the U.S. Bureau of the Census showed that this pattern continued. For example, during the early 1990s, the unemployment rate for African Americans fluctuated but remained above 11 percent. It was not until 1995 that the unemployment rate for African Americans dropped below 11 percent. In 1997, the African American unemployment rate was 10 percent, and by 1999 the figure had declined to 9 percent. The steady decline in unemployment was attributed to the overall health of the economy. Even with this decline, since the 1950s, the unemployment rate for African Americans was consistently twice as high as the rate for whites, which stood at 4 percent for white men and 3 percent for white women in 1999.

As a result of the global recession that began in 2008, the United States experienced record highs in unemployment rates, moving from 3.8 percent in April 2000 to 10.1 percent in October 2009. By February 2010, the national unemployment rate had dipped to 9.7 percent, with the unemployment rate among whites right at the national average; during this same period, the unemployment rate for Asians stood at 8.4 percent, while the unemployment rate for African Americans reached 16.2 percent.

THE EFFECTS OF OCCUPATIONAL DISCRIMINATION

Much of the variance in unemployment rates between blacks and whites is a direct result of discrimination in the job market, past and present. In fact, for a long time, there were many occupations that African Americans

Table 13-2. Per Capita Money Income in Current and Constant (2007) Dollars by Race and Hispanic Origin: 1990 to 2007

[**In dollars.** Constant dollars based on CPI-U-RS deflator. People as of March of following year. Based on the Current Population Survey, Annual Social and Economic Supplement (ASEC).]

	Current dollars					Constant (2007) dollars				
Year	All races[1]	White[2]	Black[3]	Asian, Pacific Islander[4]	Hispanic[5]	All races[1]	White[2]	Black[3]	Asian, Pacific Islander[4]	Hispanic[5]
1990	14,387	15,265	9,017	(NA)	8,424	22,125	23,476	13,867	(NA)	12,955
1995[6]	17,227	18,304	10,982	16,567	9,300	23,273	24,727	14,836	22,381	12,564
2000[7, 8]	22,346	23,582	14,796	23,350	12,651	26,905	28,394	17,815	28,114	15,232
2002	22,794	24,142	15,441	24,131	13,487	26,271	27,825	17,796	27,812	15,544
2003	23,276	24,626	15,775	24,604	13,492	26,240	27,762	17,784	27,738	15,210
2004[9]	23,857	25,223	16,025	26,165	14,105	26,188	27,687	17,591	28,721	15,483
2005	25,036	26,496	16,874	27,331	14,483	26,590	28,141	17,922	29,028	15,382
2006	26,352	27,821	17,902	30,474	15,421	27,100	28,610	18,410	31,339	15,858
2007	26,804	28,325	18,428	29,901	15,603	26,804	28,325	18,428	29,901	15,603

NA Not available.
[1]Includes other races not shown separately.
[2]Beginning with 2002, data represents White alone, which refers to people who reported White and did not report any other race category.
[3]Beginning with 2002, data represents Black alone, which refers to people who reported Black and did not report any other race category.
[4]Beginning with 2002, data represents Asian alone, which refers to people who reported Asian and did not report any other race category.
[5]People of Hispanic origin may be any race.
[6]Data reflect full implementation of the1990 census-based sample design and metropolitan definitions, 7,000 household sample reduction, and revised race edits.
[7]Implementation of Census 2000-based population controls.
[8]Implementation of a 28,000 household sample expansion.
[9]Data have been revised to reflect a correction to the weights in the 2005 ASEC.

SOURCE: U.S. Census Bureau, *Current Population Reports*, P60–235.

Table 13-2. *Per capita income for African Americans collectively continues to be less than that of whites in the United States, although the income gap has narrowed a bit since 1990.*

could not hold, regardless of their education level. This resulted in an occupational structure for blacks substantially different from that for whites, remaining in place despite the passage of civil rights legislation.

According to the 2000 U.S. census, in 1997, 7.3 percent of all employed African Americans held managerial and professional specialty positions; 15.1 percent were employed as operators, fabricators, or laborers; and 17.6 percent worked in service occupations; with most of the remainder working in the realms of media, education, and sales. African American males were more likely than any other group to be in the most vulnerable blue-collar occupational category: operators, fabricators, and laborers. Furthermore, the occupational marginalization of African American men seemed to be worsening. In 1999, 31 percent of all employed black males held these types of jobs, compared to 17 percent of all white males. In addition, 17 percent of employed black males maintained jobs in the lower-paying service sector, compared to 8 percent of white males. In contrast, only 17 percent of employed black males held managerial and professional jobs, compared to 32 percent for white males. Whereas the operators, fabricators, and laborers category was the largest occupation group for black men, the managerial and professional category was the largest single category for white men. For females, the greatest disparity was in service jobs and managerial and professional jobs: white women had greater representation in managerial and professional jobs (35%); black women had greater representation in service jobs (27%).

Racial discrimination continued to exacerbate African American employment problems. A single-minded focus on racial discrimination in the workplace, however, would neglect and discount the impact of economic changes in the global economy on a skewed occupational distribution, increased joblessness, and lowered real wages among many African Americans since the mid-1980s. These economic changes included the shift from mass production in a manufacturing-based economy to highly computerized data management in an information-based economy; the decrease in the number, quality, and variety of blue-collar jobs; and shifting patterns and location of business and industry.

These economic changes have had an adverse effect on demand for blue-collar labor. Coupled with the cumulative experiences of racial restrictions, the higher number of less-skilled African American workers suffered the most. This circumstance was further compounded for the less-skilled, inner-city African Americans who were geographically isolated from the growing number of jobs that shifted to the suburbs and socially isolated from informal job networks that have become a major source of job placement.

Structural changes in labor demand did not just benefit the more educated and highly trained African Americans and white Americans, though. The impact of these structural changes on African Americans was first noted by William J. Wilson in his pathbreaking book, *The Declining Significance of Race: Blacks and Changing American Institutions* (1978), and was further elaborated in his later books *The Truly Disadvantaged: The Inner City, the Underclass, and Public Policy* (1987) and *When Work Disappears: The World of the New Urban Poor* (1996). Nevertheless, one cannot ignore the persistent impact of racial discrimination in maintaining disparity between blacks and whites even when education levels are the same.

THE FEDERAL GOVERNMENT RESPONSE TO EMPLOYMENT DISCRIMINATION

DISCRIMINATION LAWSUITS

Although job discrimination does still occur, African Americans found recourse in the court system in the late 1990s as several high-profile lawsuits forced companies to treat their employees equally, regardless of race. In 1996, African American workers won a case against Circuit City after charging that the retailer had systematically discriminated against them in promotions at the company's headquarters. That same year, Texaco agreed to pay $176 million in the largest race-discrimination settlement ever, after 1,350 African American employees filed a class-action suit to protest the oil company's discriminatory work environment. In addition to the settlement, the company set up diversity workshops for all twenty thousand of its employees and boosted its minority hiring from 23 percent to 26 percent.

The federal government has not been exempt from discrimination lawsuits. In 1999, Secretary of Agriculture Dan Glickman settled a class-action lawsuit against his department that was filed by African American farmers in 1997. The settlement attempted to make amends to the thousands of minority farmers who were denied government loans over the years because of their race. According to the terms of the settlement, each farmer would receive $50,000, and any government loans would be forgiven. Many farmers pointed out that their commercial loans, which would not be forgiven and which generally carry a higher interest rate than government loans, far exceeded the amount of money being granted, leaving them with significant debts they might not have accrued had they been granted government loans in the first place. In addition, none of the agents who applied discriminatory practices was punished for his past actions. However, upon taking office, the George W. Bush administration set aside the black farmers' hard-won settlement. In February 2010, the Justice Department and the U.S. Department of Agriculture announced a settlement of $1.25 billion to be awarded to black farmers in an attempt to close, as Secretary of Agriculture Tom Vilsack noted, "this sad chapter."

INCOME TRENDS

The median income for African American families has increased since the early 1990s. In 1993, the median income for African American families was $22,974; by 1999, it had increased to $27,900, and by 2005 it had increased to $30,858, a 34.5 percent increase since 1993. In comparison, the median income for white families was $40,195 in 1993; $44,400 by 1999; and $50,784 by 2005, a 26.3 percent increase. In contrast, the median income for Hispanic households was $35,967, and Asian households had the greatest median income at $61,094 in 2005. Although black families experienced a greater percentage income increase from 1993 to 2005 than white families, black families had the lowest median income among race groups.

The income disparity was even more troubling when factoring in educational attainment. Sociological studies have consistently shown that blacks with comparable levels of education, occupation, and experience tend to earn less than their white counterparts. Data on household income from the U.S. Census Bureau confirm those findings. Table 13-5, "Mean Earnings by Highest Degree Earned: 2007," presents average income by educational level and reveals that greater education translates into greater income for both blacks and whites. However, the income benefit that white males derive from education far outstrips that for black men and black women, as well as white women. According to the Census Bureau, in 2007, the average income for blacks with doctorates was $96,092, compared to $97,254 for whites. Although this figure may suggest a closing of the overall earnings gap, the economic divide between blacks and whites continues to prove alarming. For example, the median income for a white American with a master's degree was $71,321 in 2007, whereas the median for a black American with a master's degree was only $56,398.

Another troubling pattern is that the degree of disparity between blacks and whites increases as the

Table 13-3. Money Income of Households—Median Income by Race and Hispanic Origin in Current and Constant (2007) Dollars: 1980 to 2007

	Median income in current dollars					Median income in constant (2007) dollars				
Year	All households[1]	White[2]	Black[3]	Asian, Pacific Islander[4]	Hispanic[5]	All households[1]	White[2]	Black[3]	Asian, Pacific Islander[4]	Hispanic[5]
1980	17,710	18,684	10,764	(NA)	13,651	42,429	44,762	25,788	(NA)	32,704
1990	29,943	31,231	18,676	38,450	22,330	46,049	48,029	28,721	59,131	34,341
1995[6]	34,076	35,766	22,393	40,614	22,860	46,034	48,317	30,251	54,867	30,882
1999[7]	40,696	42,325	27,910	50,960	30,746	50,641	52,668	34,731	63,414	38,260
2000[8]	41,990	43,916	29,667	55,757	33,168	50,557	52,876	35,720	67,133	39,935
2001	42,228	44,517	29,470	53,635	33,565	49,455	52,136	34,514	62,815	39,310
2002	42,409	45,086	29,026	52,626	33,103	48,878	51,963	33,454	60,653	38,152
2003	43,318	45,631	29,645	55,699	32,997	48,835	51,443	33,421	62,793	37,200
2004[9]	44,334	46,658	30,095	57,504	34,271	48,665	51,216	33,035	63,122	37,619
2005	46,326	48,554	30,858	61,094	35,967	49,202	51,569	32,774	64,887	38,200
2006	48,201	50,673	31,969	64,238	37,781	49,568	52,111	32,876	66,060	38,853
2007	50,233	52,115	33,916	66,103	38,679	50,233	52,115	33,916	66,103	38,679

NA Not available.
[1]Includes other races not shown separately.
[2]Beginning with 2002, data represents White alone, which refers to people who reported White and did not report any other race category.
[3]Beginning with 2002, data represents Black alone, which refers to people who reported Black and did not report any other race category.
[4]Beginning with 2002, data represents Asian alone, which refers to people who reported Asian and did not report any other race category.
[5]People of Hispanic origin may be any race.
[6]Data reflect full implementation of the1990 census-based sample design and metropolitan definitions, 7,000 household sample reduction, and revised race edits.
[7]Implementation of Census 2000-based population controls.
[8]Implementation of a 28,000 household sample expansion.
[9]Data have been revised to reflect a correction to the weights in the 2005 ASEC.

SOURCE: U.S. Census Bureau, *Current Population Reports*, P60–235 (published August 2008).

Table 13-3. *Median household income for African Americans in the U.S. lags far behind the median income for white, Asian, and Hispanic households.*

Table 13-4. Unemployed and Unemployment Rates by Educational Attainment, Sex, Race, and Hispanic Origin: 2000 to 2008

[3,589 represents 3,589,000. Annual averages of monthly figures. Civilian noninstitutional population 25 years old and over. Based on Current Population Survey.]

Year, sex, and race	Unemployed (1,000)					Unemployment rate[1]				
	Total	Less than high school diploma	High school graduates, no college	Some college or-associate's degree	Bachelor's degree or more	Total	Less than high school diploma	High school graduates, no college	Some college or-associate's degree	Bachelor's degree or more
Total:[2]										
2000	3,589	791	1,298	890	610	3.0	6.3	3.4	2.7	1.7
2005	5,070	967	1,798	1,349	955	4.0	7.6	4.7	3.9	2.3
2008	6,094	1,092	2,166	1,678	1,158	4.6	9.0	5.7	4.6	2.6
Male:										
2000	1,829	411	682	427	309	2.8	5.4	3.4	2.6	1.5
2005	2,617	514	973	636	494	3.8	6.4	4.6	3.7	2.3
2008	3,377	682	1,270	839	585	4.8	8.8	5.9	4.6	2.5
Female:										
2000	1,760	380	616	463	301	3.2	7.8	3.5	2.8	1.8
2005	2,453	453	826	713	461	4.2	9.7	4.8	4.0	2.4
2008	2,717	410	896	838	573	4.4	9.4	5.3	4.5	2.7
White:[3]										
2000	2,644	564	924	667	489	2.6	5.6	2.9	2.4	1.6
2005	3,627	669	1,257	973	729	3.5	6.5	4.0	3.4	2.1
2008	4,475	807	1,570	1,211	888	4.1	8.2	5.1	4.1	2.4
Black:[3]										
2000	731	179	315	169	68	5.4	10.7	6.4	4.0	2.5
2005	1,075	231	440	295	110	7.5	14.4	8.5	6.9	3.5
2008	1,187	209	482	355	141	7.9	14.5	9.3	7.4	4.0
Asian:[3, 4]										
2000	146	28	34	35	49	2.7	5.7	3.0	3.2	1.8
2005	203	26	47	32	99	3.5	5.5	4.6	3.2	3.0
2008	229	30	51	42	106	3.5	6.4	4.3	3.8	2.8
Hispanic:[5]										
2000	569	297	150	85	38	4.4	6.2	3.9	3.2	2.2
2005	773	354	216	138	66	4.8	6.2	4.5	4.1	2.9
2008	1,120	485	344	195	97	6.1	8.2	6.2	5.0	3.4

[1]Percent unemployed of the civilian labor force.
[2]Includes other races not shown separately.
[3]Beginning 2005 data are for persons in this race group only.
[4]2000 data include Pacific Islanders.
[5]Persons of Hispanic or Latino origin may be any race.

SOURCE: U.S. Bureau of Labor Statistics, "Employment and Earnings Online," January 2009.

***Table 13-4.** As the data from the U.S. Bureau of Labor Statistics clearly show, the unemployment rate for African Americans in the United States remains disproportionately high, even among those holding a bachelor's degree.*

educational level increases. At the high school graduation level, black men earn an average of $22,698 annually, while white male high school graduates earn an average of $29,782. In other words, black men with a high school diploma earn 76 percent of the income that high school–educated white men earn. Black men with a bachelor's degree earn 75 percent of the amount of their white counterparts. Those with professional degrees earn 61 percent. At the doctorate level, black men earn only 54 percent as much as white men with the same education. To make the point another way, in 1999, black men with doctorates averaged less income than white men with bachelor's degrees. Table 13-5 also makes clear that, regardless of race, men derive greater income benefit from their educational accomplishments than women. Therefore, black women receive the smallest financial increase at each level of educational attainment. In 2008, it was reported that 44 percent of U.S. low-income students attended college, adding to the employment and income gap.

Table 13-5. Mean Earnings by Highest Degree Earned: 2007

[In dollars. For persons 18 years old and over with earnings. Persons as of March the following year. Based on Current Population Survey.]

Characteristic	Total persons	Mean earnings by level of highest degree (dol.) Not a high school graduate	High school graduate only	Some college, no degree	Associate's	Bachelor's	Master's	Professional	Doctorate
All persons[1]	**42,064**	**21,484**	**31,286**	**33,009**	**39,746**	**57,181**	**70,186**	**120,978**	**95,565**
Age:									
25 to 34 years old	37,352	21,678	28,982	31,843	36,741	48,256	55,401	81,458	74,489
35 to 44 years old	48,851	24,383	36,060	41,542	42,489	63,124	75,739	134,240	94,631
45 to 54 years old	51,058	25,801	36,562	44,201	45,145	68,131	81,419	127,818	110,410
55 to 64 years old	49,214	24,842	34,161	40,838	42,344	61,862	71,063	138,844	102,956
65 years old and over	36,497	24,703	25,678	31,938	32,021	48,245	51,519	93,672	73,417
Sex:									
Male	50,110	24,985	36,839	39,375	47,190	70,898	86,966	142,282	108,941
Female	32,899	15,315	24,234	26,527	33,276	43,127	54,772	83,031	69,251
White[2]	43,139	22,289	32,223	33,465	40,373	58,652	71,321	122,885	97,254
Male	51,781	25,886	38,214	40,508	48,444	73,477	89,678	144,371	110,480
Female	32,899	15,278	24,276	26,007	33,223	42,846	54,532	82,758	69,778
Black[2]	33,333	17,439	27,179	31,318	36,445	46,502	56,398	94,049	96,092
Male	35,668	19,705	29,640	32,236	38,921	53,029	63,801	(B)	(B)
Female	31,317	14,869	24,724	30,599	34,774	41,560	51,695	(B)	(B)
Hispanic[3]	29,910	21,303	27,604	29,384	35,348	44,696	68,040	84,512	(B)
Male	33,040	23,923	30,932	33,643	42,140	50,805	81,069	95,907	(B)
Female	25,262	15,574	22,283	24,884	29,279	38,584	54,263	(B)	(B)

B Base figure too small to meet statistical standards for reliability of a derived figure.
[1]Includes other races not shown separately.
[2]For persons who selected this race group only.
[3]Persons of Hispanic origin may be any race.

SOURCE: U.S. Census Bureau, Current Population Survey.

Table 13-5. *The census data show mean earnings by African Americans according to highest level of educational attainment, in comparison with other groups categorized by age, gender, race, and ethnicity.*

THE IMPACT OF FAMILY STRUCTURE ON THE INCOME OF AFRICAN AMERICAN FAMILIES

Family structure also has an impact on the income potential of African American families. In 1998, 28 percent of all African Americans had incomes of $50,000 or more, with married couples more likely than other family types to be in this group. Forty-eight percent of African American married couples earned $50,000 or more, and 23 percent reported incomes that exceeded $75,000. For white married-couple families, 58 percent had incomes that exceeded $50,000, with 33 percent in excess of $75,000.

Single parent, female-headed families were concentrated more in the lower-income groups. Sixty-seven percent of black female-headed families had incomes of less than $25,000. Forty-six percent of white female-headed families earned less than $25,000. For male-headed families, 43 percent of black families had incomes of less that $25,000, while 26 percent of white families earned less than $25,000. Among racial comparisons based on family structure types, black female-headed households fared the worst.

AGE OF HOUSEHOLDER AND AFRICAN AMERICAN FAMILY INCOME

Age is a reasonably accurate measure of work experience and therefore one of the most important factors to consider when assessing income. One fact that is often overlooked when considering the income differences between blacks and whites is the significant variation in the age distributions of the two groups—variation in itself reflecting sociological factors. In other words, it is necessary to compare blacks and whites in the same age categories to obtain a complete picture of the African American income situation.

Family income data for the 2005 *Current Population Survey* confirm the relationship between income and age. Generally speaking, family income increases for African

Americans as the age of the householder increases. African American householders in the fifteen- to twenty-four-year-old age category had a median family income of $17,986. For those between twenty-five and thirty-four, the median family income was $27,530. Family income gradually rises for African Americans until it peaks at $49,842 for householders between forty-five and fifty-four years old. Beyond that age, there is a gradual and expected decline in income as individuals withdraw from the labor force. Nonetheless, in no age category do blacks equal whites in median family income. The figures range from 50 percent as much in the twenty-four to thirty-five age group to 66 percent as much in the forty-five to fifty-four age group. Overall, black householders under age sixty-five earn only 58 percent as much as their white counterparts. According to the 2006 median annual earnings, the wage ratio between whites and blacks stood at 78 percent, while the wage ratio between whites and Hispanics stood at 62 percent.

REGIONAL DIFFERENCES IN BLACK FAMILY INCOME

Income for African American families is likely to vary among different regions of the country. The South continued to have the lowest median household income of any region. At $38,410, the South's average represented about 86 percent of the median household income of the remaining regions. Notably, about half of the African American population resides in this region. The 2000 median household incomes in the other regions were $44,744 in the West, $44,646 in the Midwest, and $45,106 in the Northeast. These differences reflect variations in regional economies and occupational opportunities for blacks and whites.

POVERTY AND THE AFRICAN AMERICAN COMMUNITY

Employment, unemployment, and income all have an impact on the level of poverty that exists in the African American community. Government statistics on poverty showed a 20 percent decrease in the number of African Americans living in poverty since 1960. In 1959, there were 9.9 million blacks living below the poverty line. By 2000, the number had declined to 7.9 million. The major difference was the poverty rates in the two periods. In 1959, the poverty rate was 55.2 percent. The poverty rate for African Americans had declined to 22.1 percent by 2000, a historical low. The economic recovery after the 1990–1991 recession accounted for the decline in the poverty rate for blacks.

Perhaps a more telling number is the percentage of children under eighteen who live in poverty. According to the U.S. Bureau of the Census, in 2007, 19 percent of all children under eighteen lived in poverty; of that population, 10.6 percent were white, 33.9 percent were black, 30.6 percent were Hispanic, and 13.3 percent were Asian.

The difference between the African American poverty rate and the white poverty rate narrowed between 1996 and 2005. In 1996, the poverty rate for whites was 9.6 percent, while the poverty rate for blacks was 26.1 percent. By 2005, the poverty rate for whites had fallen to 8.6 percent, while the poverty rate for blacks had declined to 22.1 percent. The reality remained, however, that the proportion of blacks living at or below the poverty line was nearly three times as great as for whites.

An even more troubling picture of economic hardship can be seen when examining the depth of poverty. Slightly less than half (3.4 million) of the black poor in 2000 were "severely poor"—that is, they had incomes less than 50.7 percent of the poverty threshold. These are the families William J. Wilson described in *The Truly Disadvantaged.* They suffer from the relocation of jobs and are disproportionately locked in the central city, thus outside of the job-information network. In total, some 10.1 million African Americans were near poor in 2000—that is, they had incomes above the poverty threshold, but by only 25 percent or less. Taken together, the severely poor, the poor, and the near poor constituted 33 percent of the African American population.

POVERTY AND AFRICAN AMERICAN TEENAGE PREGNANCY

One problem associated with poverty in the African American community is that of single-parent families. Those headed by teenage mothers are the most challenged. Rates of pregnancy and nonmarital childbirth are higher for black teenagers than whites, though the gap closed at the end of the twentieth century. Studies indicate that the differences between the two groups can be explained by differences in sexual activity, rates of abortion, the use of contraceptives, and rates of marriage before the child's birth.

Irrespective of the causes of African American teenage pregnancy, the consequences are dramatic for the African American community. Generally speaking, teenage mothers are more likely to be poor and are less likely to finish high school. In more cases than not, the fathers are absent or nonsupportive. Thus, it is not unusual for teenage mothers to be dependent on public assistance as a means of support. In large part, this accounts for 38.7 percent of female-headed (spouse absent) households falling below the poverty line in 2000. Teenage mothers tend to be unprepared for the adult responsibilities of parenting. Their children are more likely to be the victims of child abuse and to suffer physical, emotional, and educational problems later in life.

African American community organizations have attempted to tackle the problem of teenage pregnancy. Such groups as the Children's Defense Fund, the National Urban League, Delta Sigma Theta, and a host of others have developed teenage-pregnancy prevention programs. Often, these efforts focus on teenage males as well as females.

FEDERAL AND STATE PROGRAMS THAT ADDRESS POVERTY

African American teenage pregnancy is only one dimension of the overall problem of poverty within the African American community. Many of the programs that address the needs of the poor, such as Head Start, Medicaid, Medicare, the Food Stamp Program (now the Supplemental Nutrition Assistance Program), and several other forms of assistance, were part of a comprehensive effort referred to as the War on Poverty. Critics argue that these programs are expensive, wasteful, and ineffective. Supporters claim that the programs have not failed but that Americans are ambivalent in their determination to provide equal opportunity in employment and the political arena.

WELFARE REFORM

The most abrupt shift in public policy regarding poverty occurred in 1996 when President Bill Clinton signed sweeping welfare-reform legislation into law, replacing the traditional Aid to Families with Dependent Children (AFDC) program with a new program called Temporary Assistance to Needy Families (TANF). Welfare reform, for the first time, required many welfare recipients either to obtain jobs or to prepare for work.

Welfare reform appeared to accomplish its goals. After its implementation, child poverty began to drop at an unprecedented rate for black children, Hispanic children, and children in female-headed families. Between 1995 and 2001, poverty in each of these three groups dropped by at least 11 percentage points. Among the nation's poor, the impact of this legislation was swift, especially in the African American community. In early 1997, African Americans accounted for 37 percent of the nation's welfare caseload, even though they only constituted 13 percent of the general population. After reform, child poverty declined twice as rapidly among African Americans and Hispanics as it did among whites. For example, Hispanic child poverty fell by nearly one-third, from 40 percent in 1995 to 28 percent in 2001. According to the Department of Health and Human Services, welfare reform helped to move 4.7 million Americans from welfare dependency to self-sufficiency within three years of enactment, and the number of welfare caseloads has declined by 54 percent since 1996. Most studies demonstrated that approximately 50 percent of those who left welfare had jobs, though many of them paid only minimum wage. According to the Census Bureau, African Americans and Hispanics constituted less than 50 percent of welfare cases in the United States by 2002.

CRITICISM OF AFFIRMATIVE ACTION PROGRAMS

The social intervention created the greatest backlash against affirmative action. Affirmative action was initiated in the 1960s during the Kennedy and Johnson era. As such, it provided guidelines and required the establishment of goals and timetables in the hiring of underutilized groups, specifically racial/ethnic minorities, the disabled, and women. The guidelines do not require, however, the hiring of unqualified individuals, despite what opponents argue. Rather, the rules of affirmative action require the documentation of a good-faith effort to hire qualified persons from underutilized groups. Affirmative action has been effective in changing hiring practices because it has the weight of federal government enforcement. As a direct result, a broader range of opportunities became available for African Americans in government, the corporate world, and colleges and universities.

Affirmative action programs came under particularly heavy attack in the 1990s, with several programs being restricted or dismantled altogether. For instance, the landmark U.S. Supreme Court ruling in *City of Richmond v. J. A. Croson Co.* (1989) struck down as unconstitutional under the Fourteenth Amendment a city ordinance of Richmond, Virginia, requiring that 30 percent of each public construction contract be set aside for minority businesses. In June 1995, Adarand Constructors Inc. filed suit against the U.S. Department of Transportation claiming that consideration of "disadvantaged" status—assumed to include women and minorities—in awarding subcontracts violated the equal protection component of the Fifth Amendment's due process clause. The U.S. Supreme Court, in *Adarand Constructors, Inc. v. Pena* remanded the case for further consideration at the appellate level using the "strict scrutiny" criteria established in *Croson*. The *Adarand* and *Croson* rulings greatly limited the access of disadvantaged entrepreneurs to procurement opportunities in the private and government sectors.

Studies have documented that while white Americans support the general principle of equality for all, most do not support the idea of programs and social intervention specifically designed to improve the conditions of African Americans and other minorities. The American belief in rugged individualism leads white Americans to the opinion that social and economic differences between blacks and whites are due to individual factors, not systemic factors.

Affirmative action programs have their share of African American critics as well. Many African American conservatives argue that affirmative action programs do not help the disadvantaged. They claim that these programs primarily benefit the African American middle class—a group, they say, that needs no assistance in achieving its economic goals. In addition, critics of affirmative action argue that it unfairly stigmatizes all African Americans, whereby the success of African Americans in any field is often dismissed as being due to affirmative action. In other words, many whites perceive the need for affirmative action as confirming their belief in the inferiority of blacks.

SOCIAL AND ECONOMIC STATUS

The social and economic status of African Americans is complex. It is clear that major improvements have occurred as a result of the civil rights movement, civil rights legislation, and affirmative action policies. Many African Americans are holding more high-status jobs and earn higher incomes than ever before. While the percentage of poor African Americans is declining slightly, the number of African Americans who are impoverished remains extremely high. In other words, when one speaks of the future of the African American community, one has to be clear that it is a community that consists of many segments. The lifestyles and opportunities for African Americans in one segment may be vastly different than the conditions experienced by those in another.

Despite the dramatic changes that have occurred within the African American community as a whole, one thing has remained the same: Blacks have yet to achieve equality with whites on any measure of social and economic standing. African Americans have consistently had rates of unemployment at least twice as high as those for whites. Blacks who are employed are more likely than whites to hold blue-collar jobs—the type of jobs most likely to be eliminated during the restructuring of the American economy. African Americans are more likely than whites to be among the severely poor. The future will continue to be filled with obstacles for African American workers, families, and businesses.

The disparity in economic indicators also leads to disparity in access to health care. In 2005, 247.3 million Americans had health insurance coverage, while 46.6 million were without such coverage. The uninsured rate for whites was 11.3 percent and accounted for 22.1 million persons, whereas the uninsured rate for blacks stood at 19.6 percent and accounted for 7.2 million persons.

TOWARD GREATER SELF-SUFFICIENCY

At the beginning of the twenty-first century, resistance and resentment has increasingly emerged toward programs that address poverty and racial discrimination in employment. Such programs that secure economic opportunities for African Americans and other minorities have had some success. As opportunities decline for whites, the competition for good jobs is expected to increase. Blacks and other minority populations are growing at rates that far exceed that of whites. As these populations become better educated, the struggle for desirable jobs will intensify.

The political climate in the new millennium is such that major social-intervention programs are not likely to be initiated by the federal government within the near future. Because of the social and political climate in the United States, many African Americans are advocating a greater emphasis on self-help and internal community development. One sociological model of African American community development is the *black organizational autonomy model*. This model maintains that viable African American communities possess community-based organizations with five basic components: (1) economic autonomy; (2) internally developed and controlled data sources; (3) programs to develop and promote African American female leadership; (4) programs that emphasize African American history and culture; and (5) programs that are socially inclusive in leadership. The model proved successful in Little Rock, Arkansas, in a church-based African American community organization, and has considerable potential for meeting the needs of African American communities nationwide.

However, community action may be hampered by a growing schism within the African American community itself. Following on the work of William J. Wilson, Henry Louis Gates Jr. commented on "the two nations of Black America." Gates sees a troubling divide between African American professionals and the African American underclass in the inner cities. According to Gates, the African American middle and upper classes have more in common with their white colleagues than with the poor of their own race. This disassociation could hinder the upward mobility of the black underclass and cause community efforts to improve the conditions of the poor to stagnate if those African Americans with the resources to help feel less inclined to invest in a community of which they are not a part.

AFRICAN AMERICANS AND THE STOCK MARKET

African Americans have traditionally steered clear of the investment arena—both in terms of employment and of participation in the buying and selling of stocks. Growing up without an understanding of the benefits of long-term investing, most African American children become adults who are leery of putting money into a system they do not understand. A 1998 survey showed that 64 percent of black noninvestors attributed their lack of participation to a "lack of knowledge," compared with 55 percent of whites. When African Americans did choose to invest, they typically selected avenues with low-yield returns such as insurance funds, savings accounts, or real estate—the result being that their money grew at a much slower rate than white Americans with a substantially greater number of stock portfolios.

The effect of this cautious investment strategy was a gross economic disparity between blacks and whites, particularly in the retirement years. A study of wealth distribution by the Rand Corporation revealed that, among people over seventy, blacks have less than 10 percent of the average financial assets available to whites. Many elderly African Americans become overly dependent on Social Security and fall into poverty. The African American community is already financially handicapped by lower wages and over-representation in blue-collar jobs with few benefits programs such as 401(k) plans. The reluctance to become involved in the stock market has a further crippling effect on African American economic growth.

Toward the end of the 1990s, however, African American distrust of the stock market began to dissolve. Buoyed by a strong market, many African Americans sought out information on how to invest wisely, and investment companies started active minority-recruitment programs to entice these new investors. Investment seminars specifically geared toward African American women have been particularly effective in recruiting a group that has typically been too burdened with family concerns to set aside money for investing. In addition, African American groups, such as the Coalition of Black Investors, have formed to promote financial literacy among African Americans and to connect black investors and investment clubs in order to exchange ideas and investment strategies.

Even as blacks close the investment gap, though, they continue to be far outnumbered by whites in investment jobs. Of the country's ninety thousand brokers, only six hundred were African American in 1998. The percentage of African American employees in the securities industry actually fell from 10.6 percent in 1990 to 8.4 percent in 1996. In 1998, the Reverend Jesse Jackson held a three-day conference with some of the top names on Wall Street to discuss ways to improve minority participation in the financial arena. The result was a rise in the number of black financial bankers and investment firms. Despite this development, obstacles remain. According to the Bureau of Labor and Statistics, the jobless rate for black male college graduates in 2010 was 8.4 percent, compared with 4.4 percent for white male college graduates. A study by the *American Economic Review* showed that job seekers with "black sounding" names were less likely to receive callbacks for jobs in the economic sector. White, Asian, and Hispanic managers are more likely to hire white over black candidates, a trend that has influenced the number of black investors and finance professionals.

MORTGAGE LENDING

African Americans have also experienced racism in the mortgage market. A 1993 study conducted by the Federal Reserve Bank of Boston posited that lending bias against minorities has been rampant. In their much-debated findings, the researchers concluded that Boston-area banks rejected 11 percent of mortgage applications by whites and 29 percent of applications by minorities. Such numbers, they argued, proved that discrimination in lending still existed. However, other analysts claim that the study was flawed in its interpretation of the data, and discrepancies that appear to point to discrimination actually clear up under careful analysis.

Apart from the debate, it is undisputed that there are far more white homeowners than African American homeowners. In spite of the fact that the overall rate of home ownership reached a record 65.7 percent in 1997, a study found that while 71.3 percent of whites were homeowners, only 43.6 percent of blacks could boast the same. According to a report by the Federal Reserve Board and the Joint Center for Housing Studies at Harvard University, the main reason for this disparity was *red-lining*—the practice by banks of refusing mortgage loans to low-income buyers, usually minorities. Unable to buy homes, African Americans have frequently been forced to rent in city neighborhoods, which are often destabilized by the lack of homeowners.

Some court decisions and corporate initiatives have addressed incidents of lending bias. In 1998, three Texas mortgage lenders agreed to make nearly $1.4 billion available to low-income and minority home buyers through 2001 after the lenders were found to have applied discriminatory practices against minority applicants. These civil rights violations were discovered when white federal government housing officials who posed as applicants received better treatment and larger loans than minority applicants of similar financial standing. In the aftermath of the bursting of the housing bubble, many black homeowners who took out mortgages at subprime rates lost their homes, leading to a further increase in the racial wealth gap detailed in 2010 by the Brandeis University Institute on Assets and Social Policy.

14

ENTREPRENEURSHIP

Michael D. Woodard
Christopher A. Brooks

African Americans have a unique history of entrepreneurship in the United States. They have been in business since before the Civil War (1861–1865), and their entrepreneurial tradition has continued over time. Well into the twenty-first century, there continues to be an entrepreneurial spirit among African Americans, even as their businesses and sales have suffered the impact of the economic downturn that began in 2007. Some of the significant developments since the 1970s have occurred because of the positive impact of affirmative action programs, which have given African American businesspeople the opportunity to compete for local, state, and federal contracts, among other opportunities once denied to them.

This chapter will present an analysis of the impact of affirmative action on black entrepreneurship. The discussion draws heavily from sociologist Michael D. Woodard's *Black Entrepreneurs in America: Stories of Struggle and Success* (1997) and economist Thomas Boston's seminal *Affirmative Action and Black Entrepreneurship* (1999). The idea common to these books is that opportunity matters.

AMERICAN LAW AND BLACK ENTREPRENEURSHIP

Throughout its history, America has taken in various immigrant groups attempting to escape religious intolerance, find political freedom, and enjoy greater economic opportunity. Continental Africans, however, are the only group that was forcibly transported to the American shore, not to enjoy increased freedom, but to serve as forced labor to advance the economic interest of the American plantation class. Prior to the Civil War, African enslavement defined the existence of most blacks in America. The antebellum period denied enslaved Africans economic rights in the truest sense of the term and excluded them from private enterprise altogether. Free Africans who could accumulate the capital to generate business activity developed and sustained enterprises in almost every area of business, including merchandising, real estate, manufacturing, construction, transportation, and extractive industries.

As impossible as it was for the enslaved class to engage in private enterprise, it was also hazardous for free Africans to do so. Free blacks lived under constant fear of being labeled as "runaway slaves" and sold into slavery. The major problem confronting African American entrepreneurs during the antebellum era stemmed from the inability of whites to tolerate the economic success of any person of African origin. Whites feared that even isolated instances of economic success would undermine the system of racial oppression. As a consequence, the full force of the law and many acts of violence were imposed to extinguish the entrepreneurial spirit among African Americans. For instance, in areas where free African Americans lived, laws called *code noir* (black code) were passed to restrict their movement and their economic freedom.

In the aftermath of the Revolutionary War (1775–1783), African American benevolent societies and fraternal organizations began emerging. They offered systematic aid to the formerly enslaved Africans who were freed as a result of their support of the Continental forces. Such organizations as the African Union Society (Newport, Rhode Island, 1780), the African Society of Boston (1796), the Free African Society (Philadelphia, 1787), the Brown Fellowship (Charleston, South Carolina 1793), and the Society of Free Africans (Baltimore, c. 1790s) were founded under religious auspices, but they also had a mission to teach their members how to save and build wealth. The Philadelphia-based Free African Society also had a burial program, which guaranteed its members an appropriate funeral if they contributed dues (i.e., an early insurance policy).

By 1835, Virginia, Maryland, and North Carolina had passed laws forbidding free African Americans to carry arms without a license. The right of assembly was also denied African Americans throughout the South, making it illegal for African American civic, business, or benevolent organizations to convene. In 1865, many southern states passed regulations declaring that any black man who did not have an employer was subject to arrest as a vagrant, including any black man working independently. Black codes reflected white slave owners' fears of an African American uprising, and these legal restrictions had the purpose and effect of making it difficult for free African Americans to earn a living.

President Lincoln's Emancipation Proclamation of 1863 offered the promise of freedom and political enfranchisement for African Americans, but that promise was soon undermined by judicial rulings. In 1878, the U.S. Supreme Court ruled in *Hall v. DeCuir* that a state could not prohibit segregation on a common carrier. In 1896, with the *Plessy v. Ferguson* ruling, "separate but equal" became the law of the land. Following these decisions, a pattern of rigid segregation of the races was established that remained the norm throughout the nation until the civil rights movement in the 1960s.

Even in the face of such oppressive practices by federal, state, and local governments to suppress African American entrepreneurship, several major leaders of the late nineteenth and early twentieth centuries continued to promote business activity among black entrepreneurs. In 1899, W. E. B. Du Bois (1868–1963) edited a report called *The Negro in Business* after attending an annual meeting of African American experts on the subject in Atlanta. The work dealt frankly with the inherent obstacles facing African American businesspersons, including systematic racism, state and local barriers that impeded their ability to compete fairly, unfair competition from newly arrived European and Asian immigrants, and the threat of violence directed against African American businesses, primarily from disenfranchised whites in the South. Henry M. Minton's *Early History of Negroes in Business* (1913) followed the tradition of Du Bois's work.

Booker T. Washington (1856–1915) of the Tuskegee Institute in Alabama offered African Americans another collective entrepreneurial approach. In his celebrated 1895 Atlanta Exposition speech, Washington urged African Americans to put aside their appeals for civil rights and political power in favor of achieving technical skills. This, in Washington's view, would secure African Americans a firm economic basis from which they could then make certain social and political claims. He was attacked by the likes of Du Bois and William Monroe Trotter (1872–1934), but secretly Washington funded court cases challenging Jim Crow practices that placed obstacles before African Americans who sought economic and social rights throughout the South.

The most widespread collective grassroots movement to encourage African Americans to demonstrate their economic power came from the Jamaican-born civil rights leader Marcus Garvey (1887–1940). Garveyism spelled out a program of black nationalism that was articulated in the charter of his Universal Negro Improvement Association (UNIA). It advocated the establishment of many black-owned businesses, including an ill-fated shipping line. Garvey's entrepreneurial ambitions reached well beyond the aspirations of African Americans to the entire African world. His program of self-help and African repatriation encouraged African Americans to start businesses and support them. Garvey's celebrated dictum of "Be Black, buy Black, and think Black, and all else will take care of itself" had the effect of selling African Americans to themselves. Because his movement promoted African American economic independence at a time when the race was still being oppressed, Garvey was targeted and neutralized by federal forces.

What is unique about twentieth-century American race relations is that segregation laws applied almost exclusively to African Americans. In the economic arena, segregation laws restricted blacks from competing against any other entrepreneur in an open market. In contrast, Chinese, Mexican, Jewish, and Native American entrepreneurs could operate businesses in the open market. They could also compete against black businesses in black neighborhoods. In addition, every ethnic group but African Americans had access to public accommodations and could drink at public fountains, eat in restaurants, and sleep in hotels. The intent of this rigid caste system was to deny African Americans social and political rights and privileges, strangling their economic rights and opportunities. This virulent system of caste segregation shaped African American business development for a century before the civil rights movement.

Segregation restricted black businesses to seven categories: (1) personal services, such as cleaning and pressing shops; (2) eating and drinking establishments; (3) shoe repair; (4) funeral parlors; (5) barber shops and beauty salons; (6) miscellaneous retail gas stations; and (7) grocery stores. These businesses tended to be small, served a black clientele, and operated with few or no employees, and their owners tended not to be college graduates. In his

Staff of the Dunbar National Bank, Harlem, NY, c. 1920. *The Dunbar National Bank was the first in Harlem to be managed and staffed by African Americans.* SCHOMBURG CENTER FOR RESEARCH IN BLACK CULTURE; THE NEW YORK PUBLIC LIBRARY; ASTOR, LENOX AND TILDEN FOUNDATIONS

1947 book *Negro Business and Business Education*, sociologist Joseph Pierce coined the term *traditional businesses* to refer to this first generation of black-owned businesses that characterized most of the twentieth century. The civil rights movement brought about change in the traditional black business pattern.

THE CIVIL RIGHTS MOVEMENT AND BLACK BUSINESSES

The civil rights movement was the greatest effort at social reform in the history of the United States because it significantly improved opportunities available to African Americans. It was a reformist movement that focused on changing the laws that denied African Americans the rights guaranteed to other citizens by the U.S. Constitution. Indeed, the civil rights movement changed the way in which laws were promulgated.

Prior to the movement, laws such as those sanctioning African enslavement, black codes, and Jim Crow segregation were designed to subordinate African Americans. Beginning with Executive Order 8802 in 1942, which prohibited government contractors from engaging in employment discrimination based on race, color, or national origin, laws were designed to protect the rights of African Americans, as well as promote access to public accommodations, jobs, public education, and business opportunities. Other important legislative acts, court decisions, and executive orders that serve as indicators of the success of the civil rights movement include: *Brown v. Board of Education of Topeka* (1954), in which the Supreme Court ruled that racial segregation in public education is unconstitutional; the *Gayle v. Browder* (1956) decision, which ruled that segregated seating on public buses is unconstitutional; the Civil Rights Act of 1964; the Voting Rights Act of 1965; and Executive Order 11246 (1965), which barred any contractor or subcontractor who does business with the federal government from discriminating against anyone on the basis of race or creed.

Perhaps the greatest boost to African American entrepreneurship came in 1967 with the Equal Opportunity Act that created the U.S. Department of Commerce's Small Business Administration 8(a) program. Section 8(a) of the Small Business Act Amendments (Pub.L. 90-104) directed that a portion of all federal government procurement contracts be reserved for competition only among disadvantaged businesspersons. The 8(a) provision became one of the primary means by which minorities gained access to federal procurement through what became known as *set-asides*. Participation in the 8(a) program is restricted to small and disadvantaged businesses, including nonminority small businesses but excluding larger African American–owned businesses. Participation in the 8(a) program for small and disadvantaged businesses is contingent upon Small Business Administration approval of the business plan prepared by the prospective firms.

The total dollar value of contracts processed through Section 8(a) grew from $8.9 million in 1969 to $2.7 billion in 2000. Through this program, many small and African American–owned businesses were able to stabilize and grow. During the early 1980s, however, the Section 8(a) program was criticized because less than 5 percent of the participating firms had achieved open-market competitiveness, implying that the program was assisting marginal entrepreneurs more than it was helping promising, self-employed, minority businesspersons.

The 1977 Public Works Employment Act (Pub.L. 95-28) and the Omnibus Small Business Act of 1978 established percentage goals in procurement for minority firms for the first time. These acts required that at least 10 percent of all federal procurement contracts for local public-works projects be expended with minority businesses. The Small Business Administration 8(a) program, the 1977 Public Works Employment Act, and the Omnibus Small Business Act constituted the first attempts at establishing set-asides to provide access to contracts for small, disadvantaged, and minority businesses. As a result of these laws, the amount of federal procurement funds expended with minority-owned firms increased from 3.4 percent in 1981 to 8.3 percent in 1994, or $14.4 billion.

ATLANTA, GEORGIA—A CASE STUDY IN AFFIRMATIVE ACTION PROCUREMENT

In *Affirmative Action and Black Entrepreneurship* (1999), Thomas Boston analyzed the way in which Atlanta, Georgia, implemented its affirmative action procurement program. According to Boston, black entrepreneurs got their first opportunity to participate in city contracting in a significant way in 1974 after Maynard Jackson became the first African American mayor of Atlanta. Jackson demanded the immediate implementation of affirmative action policies in employment and business contracting. The minority business program created by Jackson opened new markets and generated new opportunities for black entrepreneurs. The 1973 *Annual Report of the Atlanta Office of Contract Compliance* indicated that blacks did not receive their first contracts from the city until 1973, the year that Jackson was elected mayor. The total dollar amount of contracts awarded to black businesses was just $41,800 of the $33.1 million awarded in contracts that year. A study of the city's contracting history with blacks and other minorities revealed that insidious forms of discrimination were practiced until the 1970s. The city once maintained separate job-qualification registers for blacks and whites, as well as separate water fountains, and did not provide blacks with knowledge of bid opportunities.

To ensure more equitable access to public-works projects, Mayor Jackson targeted the newly planned $1 billion Hartsfield International Airport project. His goal was to direct 25 percent of the awards for construction toward minority-owned businesses. That meant, for the first time, that black contractors could move out of small-scale commercial and residential construction and repairs. These large-scale projects also required architectural and engineering services, construction management, and public relations and related expertise. Atlanta's affirmative action procurement program brought about a significant change in the city's black-owned businesses.

Indeed, the ability of minority businesses to diversify away from traditional personal service and retail activities into nontraditional industries is the most important legacy of affirmative action policies. New market opportunities meant faster growth possibilities, greater profitability, and increased employment capacity. Black-owned firms that did not receive city contracts directly benefited nonetheless because affirmative action hastened the decline in racial stereotypes, improved networks between black and white entrepreneurs, and encouraged private-sector companies to emulate public-sector affirmative action initiatives.

Maynard Jackson, Mayor-Elect of Atlanta, GA, 1973. *With his wife, Bunnie, Maynard Jackson celebrates his election as mayor of Atlanta. As mayor, Jackson implemented affirmative action programs, creating new business and employment opportunities for black entrepreneurs.* BETTMANN/CORBIS

The opportunities created by Atlanta's affirmative action program attracted blacks out of corporate management, administrative, and executive positions and into entrepreneurial careers. These opportunities also encouraged black entrepreneurs in other parts of the country to migrate to the city, such that Atlanta soon became known as the "Black Mecca." More than one hundred cities across the nation followed Atlanta's lead in affirmative action procurement, and for ten years the Atlanta plan was the model for other cities to follow. Between 1987 and 1992, the number of black-owned businesses in Atlanta more than doubled, from 11,804 to 23,488. The Atlanta experience demonstrates that opportunity matters in black business development.

SECOND-GENERATION ENTREPRENEURS

As racial barriers began to fall in Atlanta and across the nation as a result of the civil rights movement, a second generation of black-owned businesses emerged. Firms established between 1970 and 1990 were not mere replicas of earlier traditional black-owned businesses. Many black entrepreneurs were now graduates of the nation's leading business schools, and had acquired years of managerial experience in corporations and public-sector employment. The new business opportunities made available through affirmative action public- and private-sector procurement programs converged with the enhanced educational and business experience of blacks, and the outcome changed the character of black-owned businesses.

By 2002, black business owners were more likely to hold graduate degrees when they started or acquired ownership in their business (about 25%) than the national average (19%). Second-generation businesses operate in nontraditional, skill-intensive industries such as finance, business and professional services, information technology, wholesaling, and manufacturing. They also serve a more diverse and national client base. In addition, the number of paid employees has increased significantly. Civil rights–era laws created a more-level playing field in public procurement and private enterprise and stimulated the fastest growth in the skill- and capital-intensive lines of business with black ownership. Although there remains a concentration of small traditional businesses, a coinciding trend exists toward establishing highly skilled and capital-intensive firms, referred to as *emerging* or *second-generation* firms.

BACKLASH TO EMERGING FIRMS

Because of the success of affirmative action programs at the local and federal levels, a strong backlash emerged among white entrepreneurs who were threatened by competition from African American and other disadvantaged groups. In Atlanta, opposition to the affirmative action procurement plan was powerful. For instance, the Hartsfield International Airport project was one of the largest construction projects in the South. Not only was there strong resistance to the 25 percent minority participation requirement, but race relations grew even more intense when, in addition to the airport mandate, Mayor Jackson threatened to withdraw city funds from local banks unless they took steps to elevate minorities to executive positions. In response to an earlier suit, the Georgia Supreme Court issued a ruling in November 1987 that affirmed the constitutionality of Atlanta's minority business program.

THE *CROSON* AND *ADARAND* DECISIONS

The white backlash to the advancement of black businesses resulting from affirmative action procurement programs reached a crescendo with the *Croson* decision. The fundamental concept of affirmative action and set-aside minority-assistance programs was called into question during the Reagan-Bush era. In 1989, the landmark U.S. Supreme Court ruling in *City of Richmond v. J. A. Croson Co.* struck down as unconstitutional under the Fourteenth Amendment a city ordinance of Richmond, Virginia, requiring that 30 percent of each public construction contract be set aside for minority businesses. In ruling against the Richmond ordinance, the Supreme Court made the distinction between local- and state-mandated business-development programs and federally enacted business-development programs, holding that the U.S. Congress has far more authority than the states in formulating remedial legislation.

The *Croson* decision had a devastating impact on minority businesses. In July 1987, when a lower court first ruled against Richmond's set-aside program, 40 percent of the city's total construction dollars were allocated for products and services provided by minority-owned construction firms. Immediately following the court's decision, the share of contracts going to minority businesses fell to 15 percent, later dropping to less than 3 percent. In Tampa, Florida, the number of contracts awarded to African American–owned companies decreased 99 percent, and contracts with Latino-owned firms fell 50 percent after *Croson*. Such dramatic decreases in the number of contracts awarded to minority businesses occurred throughout the country. More than thirty-three states and political subdivisions began taking steps to dismantle their racial/ethnic set-aside programs, and more than seventy jurisdictions began conducting studies or holding hearings to review and evaluate their programs in light of *Croson*.

The *Croson* decision legitimated the idea of reverse discrimination in government procurement, just as the decision in *Regents of the University of California v. Bakke* (1978) had done in higher education. This issue would surface again in *Adarand Constructors, Inc. v. Pena* (1995). Adarand filed suit against the U.S. Department of Transportation, claiming that consideration of social and disadvantaged status, which was assumed to include women and minority groups, in awarding subcontracts violated the equal protection component of the Fifth Amendment's due process clause. The court of appeals rejected Adarand's claims, but in June 1995, the Supreme Court remanded the case for further consideration using the "strict scrutiny" criteria established in *Croson*. Together, the two decisions had the effect of greatly limiting the access of disadvantaged entrepreneurs to procurement opportunities in the private and government sectors.

The government's ambivalence in supporting economic opportunities for African Americans and other minority groups should be viewed as a reflection of society's ambivalence regarding the extent to which African Americans are entitled to economic rights. Nevertheless, the civil rights movement helped African American entrepreneurs gain greater access to capital and to government and private-sector procurement opportunities for the first time in history. And as a result, many small African American–owned businesses were able to grow and stabilize. However, the continued growth of second-generation black-owned firms is threatened by the demise of affirmative action procurement. Affirmative action procurement is declining, black businesses still do not have equal access to private markets, and, in the face of these adversities, a third generation of black entrepreneurs appears to be emerging.

ECONOMIC TRENDS: THIRD-GENERATION BLACK ENTREPRENEURS

The number of African American–owned firms grew steadily as the country moved into the twenty-first century. In 1972, 187,602 firms were enumerated. By 2002, the number of black-owned firms had increased 638.4 percent to nearly 1.2 million. Gross receipts of African American businesses increased more than fourfold, from less than $20 billion in 1977 to $88.9 billion in 2002. In 2002, there were 10,727 black-owned firms with receipts of $1 million or more, an increase of 30 percent since 1997. Revenue for these firms was about $49 billion, compared to $40 billion in 1997, up 22 percent. Businesses that grossed more than $1 million annually accounted for 1 percent of the total number of black-owned firms in 2002 and 55 percent of the total receipts of all black-owned businesses.

This significant growth of black-owned businesses is evidence of the strong entrepreneurial tradition among African Americans and the emergence of a third generation of black entrepreneurs. Third-generation entrepreneurs have more private-sector networks, a greater reliance on equity as a source of growth, and more strategic alliances with nonminority-owned companies. The companies that master these attributes are more likely to succeed going forward. Today, more black-owned businesses are going public, merging, or acquiring other companies. In addition, more venture capital and equity funds are being established with the express purpose of investing in fast-growing black-owned businesses, which would never have occurred in the past. The quintessential example of a third-generation entrepreneur is Reginald Lewis of Beatrice Foods. In 1987, Lewis amassed sufficient capital and business acumen to become the principal shareholder of Beatrice Foods, until his premature death in 1993. While the number of third-generation businesses remains small, businesses that rely on strategic alliances will extend the next frontier of black entrepreneurship.

Indeed, the robust growth rate in the number and the sales and receipts of black-owned businesses for 2002 confirms that these firms are among the fastest-growing segments of the American economy. Over time, segments of the African American population have exhibited the same entrepreneurial spirit as other ethnic groups that migrated to this country. The entrepreneurial tradition continues as a fundamental element of African American culture, even in the face of strong institutional adversity.

Black-owned firms continue to exhibit a geographic concentration matching the African American population concentration. In 2002, six states were home to 55 percent of African American–owned businesses, whereas in 1997, these same states claimed 49 percent of African American–owned firms. New York had the greatest number with 129,324 black-owned businesses, followed by California (112,874), Florida (102,053), Georgia (90,461), Texas (88,768), and Maryland (69,410). While New York had the greatest number of African American–owned firms, California firms had the greatest sales and receipts. In 2002, the total sales and receipts of California's black-owned firms reached $9.7 billion, while the total for firms in New York was $7.5 billion. For Texas, the total sales and receipts of black-owned firms reached $6.4 billion; Georgia, $5.7 billion; Florida, $5.7 billion; and Maryland, $4.7 billion. Other states with high numbers of black-owned businesses include Illinois with 68,699 firms and $5 billion in sales and receipts; North Carolina with 52,122 firms and $3.6 billion; Michigan with 44,366 and $4.3 billion; Virginia with 41,165 and $3.7 billion; and Louisiana with 40,243 and $1.9 billion.

African American–owned firms tend to be concentrated in urban areas. In 2002, New York City had more black-owned firms than any other city in the country at 98,076. Chicago had the second-largest number of black-owned businesses (39,424), followed by Los Angeles (25,958), Houston (21,226), and Detroit (19,530). Washington, D.C., which had historically ranked in the top five, fell to sixth in the number of black-owned firms, with 12,198.

The location of corporate headquarters in urban areas has provided increased business opportunities for African American business-service enterprises. Administrative and service functions have become the dominant economic activities in the country's large cities. The growth in corporate and government administration in central business districts has created a need for complementary advertising, accounting, information technology, computer, legal, temporary human resources, and maintenance business services. In addition, the aging demographics of the American population have created a need for a variety of health-care services. Health care and social service was the industry sector with the greatest number of black-owned businesses in 2002 (a full census study on black-owned businesses was scheduled to be published early in 2011).

By 2002, African Americans tended to concentrate in skill-intensive service-producing industries. Health care and social services; other services; administrative support, waste management, and remediation services; and professional, scientific, and technical services account for 57.9 percent of black-owned businesses.

CONTINUED DEVELOPMENT OF THE AFRICAN AMERICAN BUSINESS COMMUNITY

The development of African American–owned businesses in the new millennium likely will continue to reflect their emphasis on services. However, services of the twenty-first century are not personal services but high-skill and capital-intensive services, and an increasing number of African American entrepreneurs are focused on the unique challenges posed by what is called professional services. By 2002, two-thirds of African American–owned businesses were concentrated in health and social services, scientific and technical services, and administrative and waste-management and waste-remediation services. Success stories are numerous, and continued educational advances, especially in technology and business education, have translated into an increasing number of business successes among aspiring entrepreneurs.

The relative well-being of the African American community is directly linked to the vitality of its business segment. African American communities must continue to give birth to and nurture successful businesses. Indeed, African Americans must strive to increase the rate at which they found and develop businesses. Even in the face of persistent institutional adversity, the responsibility for greater entrepreneurial growth rests with African Americans. The research clearly shows that black-owned firms are more likely to hire African Americans, whether these firms are located in low-income neighborhoods or in the suburbs. In contrast, black workers are a distinct minority in white-owned firms, even if such firms are located in distressed urban areas that are predominantly black. In 2002, an estimated 94,862 black-owned firms had paid employees and receipts of $69.8 billion, or about $735,586 per firm. In addition, 973 of these firms had one hundred or more employees, representing an increase of 9 percent compared to 1997, when there were 889 such firms. African Americans must continue to establish and work for the growth of firms with employees to ensure the well-being of the African American community.

Thomas Boston argued for a strategy of Twenty by Ten to encourage the growth of black-owned businesses and provide employment in the black community. The Twenty by Ten strategy called for the government and the private sector to pursue policies that were designed to create a sufficient number of black-owned firms, such that their combined employment capacity would be equal to 20 percent of the black labor force by 2010: hence, Twenty by Ten. Because of the economic slowdown that began in 2007, this goal has not been met, and the unemployment rate among African Americans has increased.

Boston estimated that, between 1982 and 1992, the number of black-owned businesses grew at a rate of 7.25 percent annually, and their employment capacity grew at a rate of 11.02 percent annually. In 1992, 620,912 black-owned firms were enumerated, and they had an employment capacity that was equal to 2.3 percent of the African American workforce. Boston suggested that by 2010, given a sustained estimated 7.5 percent growth rate for African American firms from 1992 to 2010, there would be 2.2 million black-owned firms employing between 2.3 million and 3 million African American workers, equivalent to approximately 16.6 percent of the projected workforce. With this calculation, Boston argued that, "If the current trends hold, 80 percent or 2.5 million of the new jobs that these firms create will go to blacks. And if we can improve our efforts just slightly, we can easily reach Twenty by Ten." As stated, however, the goals had not been met as of 2010.

In 2002, the U.S. census enumerated 1,191,567 black-owned firms for a growth rate of 4.8 percent annually since 1992. At a sustained 4.8 percent annual growth rate, approximately 1.74 million black-owned firms would have been created by 2010. Differing calculations aside, Boston's strategy and challenge to the African American community and to the American society at large is laudable. Black-owned businesses are more likely than white-owned businesses to locate in low-income neighborhoods and hire low-income persons. But whether a black-owned firm locates in a low-income neighborhood or in a suburban industrial park, black-owned firms are more likely to hire black workers, reduce black unemployment, and sustain the economic development of the African American community.

To increase the number of black-owned businesses and provide more employment opportunities for blacks, African Americans must continue to strive to eliminate internal barriers. Successful entrepreneurship must come to be viewed as an honorable career path, like that of teachers, lawyers, physicians, social workers, and ministers. Increasingly, entrepreneurship has become part of the curriculum or an extracurricular activity at many high schools and community organizations. Moreover, parents must explicitly include entrepreneurship in the mix of career options presented to their children.

The second internal barrier is commitment. The sacrifice necessary to achieve a business goal is considerable. Success in business is difficult to achieve regardless of race. Success in business is enhanced by acquiring the necessary educational background and work experience to be technically competent, and by saving sufficient start-up capital.

In terms of external barriers, the community and government must take responsibility for eliminating artificial barriers to the products, credit markets, and public-sector procurement that have impeded the investment possibilities and profit potential of African American–owned businesses. Analysis conducted by the National Bureau of Economic Research to determine the extent to which minority-owned businesses encountered discrimination in applying for loans concluded that African American–owned businesses faced significant and persistent constraints in the credit market. Furthermore, the study revealed that these constraints extended beyond the availability of credit to also include the cost of credit. In other words, African American–owned businesses paid higher interest rates on their loans than did their majority counterparts.

In addition, many successful black-owned businesses are dependent on government contracting. Gaining access to government procurement opportunities and subcontracting opportunities is critical if growth of black-owned businesses is to be sustained. The perpetual assault on affirmative action procurement is troubling. Therefore, an immediate concern is to find creative ways to support and extend government contracting programs to address racial disparities in public-sector contracting. The accomplishments of African American entrepreneurs over time provides evidence that the entrepreneurial spirit among African Americans burns bright as the United States moves into the second decade of the new millennium.

ENTREPRENEURS AND BUSINESS EXECUTIVES

(To locate biographical profiles more readily, please consult the index at the back of the book. For example, media executives appear in the Media chapter.)

WALLY AMOS JR. (1936–)

Entrepreneur. Wallace Amos Jr. was born in Tallahassee, Florida, on July 1, 1936, and grew up there until his parents' divorced when he was twelve years old. Following

Wally "Famous" Amos, Tallahassee, FL. *Amos is best known as the founder, in 1975, of Famous Amos Chocolate Chip Cookies. Based on his Aunt Della's recipe, the cookies quickly became a nationwide success.* PHOTO BY MARK T. FOLEY. AP IMAGES. REPRODUCED BY PERMISSION.

his parents' divorce, he moved to New York City to live with his Aunt Della. She loved to cook and often made Amos her special chocolate chip cookies. After spending several years in New York City, he dropped out of high school to join the U.S. Air Force, where he earned his high school equivalency degree.

After being discharged from the Air Force, Amos achieved success as the first African American talent agent for the William Morris Agency. Starting there as a mail clerk, he worked his way up to executive vice president. Among his celebrated "discoveries" for the agency was Simon & Garfunkel. He served as agent for such well-known acts and entertainers as the Supremes, the Temptations, Marvin Gaye, Dionne Warwick, and Patti LaBelle.

In 1975, Amos founded Famous Amos Chocolate Chip Cookies. Based on his Aunt Della's recipe, the cookies became a nationwide success as they spread across the country from his original store on Sunset Boulevard in Los Angeles. By 1980, Amos was selling $5 million worth of cookies each year, and his operation had expanded to include a large production facility in Nutley, New Jersey. Amos's success and expansion were enhanced by the backing of such well-known personalities as Bill Cosby and Helen Reddy. In 1985, Amos became vice chairman of the company.

Amos left the Famous Amos Cookie Corporation in 1989 following financial difficulties and a dispute with a group of investors. He began a new business, Wally Amos Presents ... Chip & Cookie, in 1990. In 1993, Amos started yet another company, Uncle Noname Cookie Company, and serves as its president. Uncle Noname Cookie Company, based in Honolulu, Hawaii, specializes in five varieties of gourmet cookies. Proceeds from the sale of its cookies are donated to the support of Cities in Schools, a national dropout-prevention program. Amos has been a member of the Cities in Schools board.

Amos has donated personal items to the Business Americana Collection at the Smithsonian's Collection of Advertising History. He received the Presidential Award for Entrepreneurial Excellence from President Ronald Reagan in 1986. In 1987, Amos received a citation from the Horatio Alger Association. Since the late 1970s, Amos has devoted a considerable amount of time and resources to various literacy projects around the country; he served as the national spokesperson for Literacy Volunteers of America from 1979 to 2002.

JIM BECKWOURTH (1798–1866)

Author, Trapper, Entrepreneur. James Pierson Beckwourth was born on April 26, 1798, near Fredericksburg, Virginia. His father, Jennings Beckwith, was a white landowner and a member of a prominent Virginia family. His mother was an African American woman who had probably been enslaved. The family moved to a farm near St. Charles, Missouri, in 1806, and Jim attended school in St. Louis from 1810 to 1814. He was apprenticed to a St. Louis blacksmith but soon headed west. Like many other events in Beckwourth's life, there are conflicting stories concerning the dissolution of the apprenticeship. Evidently at this time, Beckwourth also changed the spelling of his last name.

In 1824, Beckwourth joined a westward-bound fur-trapping and trading expedition under the leadership of William Henry Ashley. Beckwourth soon became known as a man of many adventures and exploits. Although the basis of these stories are factual, many, with Beckwourth's approval, have been greatly exaggerated. Nevertheless, he undoubtedly embodied the spirit of the legendary mountain men of the American West. In 1827, while still engaged in the fur trade, he married a Blackfoot woman.

ETTLING.
A.B.
Jim Beckwith, mulâtre americain, d'abord prisonnier, puis chef d'une bande de Sioux, mort au fort Laramie en 1867. — Dessin de Janet-Lange, d'après une photographie.

Jim Beckwourth (Beckwith), Explorer. *Beckwourth's travels took him from the Everglades of Florida to the Pacific Ocean and from southern Canada to northern Mexico.* **BIBLIOTHEQUE DES ARTS DECORATIFS, PARIS, FRANCE/ARCHIVES CHARMET/THE BRIDGEMAN ART LIBRARY**

In 1829, he took refuge from a debt collector by hiding with the Crow, where he married again. Marriage on the western frontier was a much less formal arrangement at the time. Beckwourth claimed he was made a Crow chief in recognition of his fighting prowess against the Blackfeet.

By 1837, Beckwourth was serving with the U.S. Army in Florida as a scout during the Seminole wars. He soon returned to the Rocky Mountains, married a woman in New Mexico, and, in 1842, opened a trading post near what is now Pueblo, Colorado. Between 1844 and 1850, he fought in the California uprising against Mexico and in the Mexican-American War. In 1850, Beckwourth joined the California gold rush, and, while in the Sierra Nevada, he discovered a mountain pass that bears his name today. He increased the access to the gap, opened an inn, and, by 1851, was guiding wagon trains through the pass.

Beckwourth's memoir, *The Life and Adventures of James P. Beckwourth, Mountaineer, Scout, and Pioneer,* ghostwritten in part by Thomas D. Bonner, was published in 1856. Beckwourth traveled to St. Louis and Kansas City, where the popularity of his book enhanced his reputation and he was regarded as a celebrity. He returned to Denver, married again, opened a trading post, and was acquitted on a charge of manslaughter. Tiring of city life, he signed on with the U.S. Army as a scout and fought the Cheyenne Indians. Beckwourth probably died of food poisoning on or around September 25, 1866, while riding to a Crow encampment. Accounts of his purposely being poisoned by the Crow are largely discounted today.

DAVE BING (1943–)

Politician, Business Executive, Professional Basketball Player. Dave Bing was born November 29, 1943, in Washington, D.C. He sustained an eye injury as a child that, because it was untreated at the time, left him with compromised vision in that eye. Bing played basketball at Spingarn High School in Washington, D.C., and was named to play on a national all-star team. As a result of his performance, he was voted most valuable player on the tour. Bing attended Syracuse University on a basketball scholarship, graduating in 1966 with a B.A. in economics. He was chosen by the Detroit Pistons as the second overall pick in the 1966 National Basketball Association (NBA) draft.

During his first season, Bing was the league's top rookie. He was the league's high scorer during his second year. In the 1974–1975 season, Bing played for the Washington, D.C., Bullets. He played with the Boston Celtics during the 1977–1978 season. Bing played in seven NBA All-Star games and was voted the league's most valuable player in 1976. The Professional Basketball Writers Association of America gave him their Citizenship Award in 1977. In 1989, he was elected to the Naismith Memorial Basketball Hall of Fame.

After retiring from basketball, Bing worked in a steel mill. He founded Bing Steel in 1980 in Detroit. After sustaining setbacks in his early business career, he became associated with management programs at the National Bank of Detroit, Chrysler Corporation, and Paragon Steel. Bing Steel Inc., later known as the Bing Group, grew into a successful steel supplier to the automobile industry. In its first five years, the company doubled its revenues. In 1984, Bing was named National Minority Small Businessperson of the Year. Among his major clients were General Motors and the U.S. government. In 2000, a disgruntled employee burned down the company's main offices and warehouse, but Bing managed to rebuild.

During the heat of the 2008 presidential election that brought Barack Obama to the highest office in the country, Dave Bing announced his candidacy for the Detroit mayor's office. He won in a special election held in May 2009. Bing served the balance of disgraced mayor Kwame Kilpatrick's term. Bing won his first full term as mayor in November 2009. Bing has served on the boards of directors of Children's Hospital of Detroit, the Michigan Association of Retarded Children and Adults, the Black United Fund, the Detroit Urban League, and the March of Dimes.

MARIE DUTTON BROWN (1940–)

Literary Agent, Entrepreneur. Marie Dutton Brown was born in Philadelphia in 1940. She received a degree in psychology in 1962 from Pennsylvania State University, where only 1 percent of the student body was African American. After graduating, she went to work as a social studies teacher in the Philadelphia public school system. Two years later, when a salesperson from Doubleday, a publishing firm in New York, visited her school, Brown was offered a position with Doubleday.

Brown stayed at Doubleday for two years and then moved to Los Angeles with her new husband, Kenneth Brown. She moved back to New York in 1972 and returned to Doubleday as an associate editor. During the 1970s, as interest in African American literary titles grew, Brown became established in the publishing world. She brought many ethnic titles to print.

In 1980, Brown quit Doubleday to become founding editor of *Elan* magazine, which focused on the cultural life of the international black community. After only three issues, Brown's financial backers pulled out, leaving her jobless. She went to work at a bookstore, which gave her firsthand retail experience.

In the fall of 1984, Brown started her own business, Marie Brown Associates, a literary agency that she ran from her Harlem apartment. Although, like any new business venture, times were lean for the first several years, things started to turn around as Brown began signing more and more writers. As the 1990s began, larger publishing houses began courting African American writers, but Brown was far ahead of them as one of only five African American literary agents in the country. Brown still contributes her time to the community, and has sat on several boards, including that of the Studio Museum of Harlem.

MALCOLM CASSELLE (1970–)

Computer Entrepreneur. Born on March 22, 1970, in Allentown, Pennsylvania, Malcolm CasSelle accomplished a great deal at a young age. Growing up in Allentown, CasSelle developed a passion for writing computer programs in high school. He later graduated from Massachusetts Institute of Technology (MIT).

CasSelle left for Japan three days after finishing his undergraduate degree in order to enter MIT's Japan program. While overseas, he worked for Schroders Securities and NTT Software Labs. After returning to the United States, he took a job with Apple Computers. After earning a master's degree at Stanford University, he worked as director of digital publishing and marketing for Blast Publishing. CasSelle would later introduce E. David Ellington, his partner, to the wonders of cyberspace.

Along with Ellington, CasSelle founded NetNoir Inc., an African American–oriented Web site. Based in San Francisco and available through America Online, NetNoir offered a wide range of news and information. *VIBE* magazine, along with Motown Records and the clothing company Blue Marlin, channeled their services and goods through CasSelle's site. In 2008, International Finance Capital Limited appointed Malcolm CasSelle as an executive vice president.

Malcolm CasSelle, Computer Company Executive, 1999. *On October 28, 1999, Senior Vice President CasSelle visits the new Hong Kong offices of Pacific Century, with employees Violet Huang* (top)*, and Grace Lo* (center)*. In 2008 CasSelle was appointed an executive vice president of International Finance Capital Ltd.* NEWSCOM

EMMA CHAPPELL (1941–)

Banking Executive. Emma Carolyn Chappell was born in Philadelphia on February 18, 1941. As a member of the Zion Baptist Church, she began to work for the Continental Bank. She took classes at both Temple and Rutgers universities and slowly moved up the bank's hierarchy. By 1977, she was its first African American female vice president.

Chappell was active in the community during her assent to Continental's top tier. She worked for a variety of community-action groups that were concerned with redeveloping the inner city. In 1984, she took time off from Continental to serve as treasurer for the Reverend Jesse Jackson's presidential campaign.

In 1987, Chappell and a group of community business leaders founded the United Bank of Philadelphia, the only African American–owned bank in the city. The bank struggled to find funding in the late 1980s. By March 1992, however, it opened for business with sufficient backing. United struggled after its opening and, in 1995 and 1996, neared insolvency, but only one year later the bank had reached $106 million in assets. *Black Enterprise* chose it as the financial company of the year in 1995. It also began issuing credit cards and embarked on a partnership with American Express to offer investment advice and financial services to its depositors.

In June 2000, Chappell stepped down from her duties as chairman of the board and chief executive officer, but United continued its campaign to improve banking services in historically poor neighborhoods of Philadelphia and the surrounding cities. In addition to serving on the boards of Philadelphia-area organizations, she took over directorship of the Rainbow/PUSH Coalition's Wall Street Project, which aims to make the business world equitable toward African Americans.

KEN CHENAULT (1951–)

Corporate Executive. Born on June 2, 1951, in Mineola, New York, Kenneth Irvine Chenault grew up in the town of Hempstead on Long Island. He attended the upscale, private, untraditional Waldorf School. Following high school, he attended Springfield College on an athletic scholarship. After one year there, he decided to concentrate more on academics and transferred to Bowdoin College, where he received a B.A. in history in 1973, graduating magna cum laude. In 1976, Chenault graduated from Harvard Law School with a juris doctorate.

After finishing law school, Chenault spent two years working for a corporate law firm before transferring to a firm that specialized in business consultancy. In 1981, he joined American Express as director of strategic planning for the Travel Related Services division. He moved up to become vice president of the Merchandise Services Division in 1983, and from 1984 to 1986 he served as senior vice president and general manager of marketing for the division. Under his direction, the division saw its annual sales jump from $150 million to $500 million. In the second half of the 1980s, Chenault served as executive vice president and general manager for American Express Platinum/Gold Division, executive vice president of the Personal Card Division, and president of American Express Consumer Card Group, USA, a post he held until 1991.

That year, Chenault was promoted to president of the American Express Card. Two years later, became president of American Express Travel Related Services, USA. With the business on an upswing, Chenault became vice chairman of the company in 1995, making him the highest-ranking African American executive in corporate America. Two years later, he made waves when he was named president and chief operating officer. In 2001, Chenault took over as CEO of American Express. Named as the second most powerful African American executive by *Fortune* magazine, Chenault faces the challenge of leading American Express through the country's economic slump.

COMER COTTRELL (1931–)

Entrepreneur. Comer Cottrell was born in Mobile, Alabama, on December 7, 1931. He began his sales career when he was eight years old, joining his father, an insurance salesman, on visits to clients. Cottrell continued his sales career at Sears Roebuck after graduating from the University of Detroit in 1952. Years later, while managing a post exchange at a military base, Cottrell observed that there were no hair products for the African American soldiers. He resolved to form a company that would sell products specifically for hairstyles worn by African Americans.

In 1970, Cottrell began his company in an empty Los Angeles warehouse with $600 and a typewriter. Initially, he sold hairspray to African American beauticians and barbers. With the moderate success of this product, the Pro-Line company was born. Five years later, Pro-Line opened a distribution center in Birmingham, Alabama. By 1980, Pro-Line had moved to Dallas, coinciding with the release of the Curly Kit Home Permanent product. Soon Pro-Line enjoyed sales in excess of $11 million and began to expand into overseas markets. By 1989, with sales of $36 million annually, Pro-Line was ranked nineteenth on *Black Enterprise*'s list of the top 100 African American businesses. Pro-Line expanded its sales to $104 million by 2000.

In 1989, Cottrell joined a fourteen-member consortium of investors that purchased the Texas Rangers, making him the first African American to own a Major League Baseball franchise. Cottrell used his position to speak out about affirmative action in professional sports. In 1990, he purchased the bankrupt Bishop College, a Dallas school founded in 1881 by newly freed Africans and Baptist missionaries, and he convinced Paul Quinn College to relocate from Waco, Texas, to the Bishop College campus. In 1994, Cottrell visited South Africa as part of a group of African American business leaders sponsored by Langston University's National Institute for the Study of Minority Enterprise to establish links with black-owned businesses there.

JEAN BAPTISTE POINT DU SABLE (c. 1750–1818)

Entrepreneur, City Founder. Jean Baptiste Point du Sable was born in Haiti around 1750 to a French mariner and an enslaved African-born woman. It is believed that he may have been educated in Paris, and that he worked as a sailor during his young adult years. Du Sable entered North America through either Louisiana or French Canada.

In the early 1770s, du Sable established the first settlement in the area later called Chicago. Having impressed the British as a well-educated man and capable frontiersman, he was sent to the St. Clair region to manage trade and act as a liaison between Native Americans and the British. Later returning to his original settlement, du Sable built a bakery, dairy, smokehouse, horse mill and stable, workshop, and poultry house. He also traded, trapped, and served as the local cooper and miller. Through du Sable's efforts, Chicago became a major center for frontier commerce.

In 1788, du Sable wedded a Potawatomi woman named Kittihawa, or Catherine, with whom he raised two children. Once married, du Sable became increasingly involved in the community. His bid in 1800 for tribal chieftaincy failed, and soon thereafter he sold his holdings and moved from the Chicago area. Real-estate records suggest that he moved to St. Charles, Missouri, and that he probably died there in poverty on August 28, 1818.

E. DAVID ELLINGTON (1960–)

Computer Entrepreneur. E. David Ellington was born in New York City on July 10, 1960. Growing up in Harlem, he was raised primarily by his mother. While attending Adelphi University, where he received a bachelor's degree in history in 1981, Ellington worked in the office of a U.S. congressman. In 1983, he received his master's degree in political science from Howard University, then spent some time traveling in Europe and Asia. In 1989, he completed a juris doctorate, specializing in international tax law, at Georgetown University Law Center. In 1990, he founded the Law Offices of E. David Ellington in Los Angeles. During this period, he also chaired the International Law Section of the Beverly Hills Bar Association.

In 1995, Ellington and computer entrepreneur Malcolm CasSelle cofounded NetNoir, an African American–oriented Web site. Billing itself as "the Cybergateway to Afrocentric Culture," NetNoir offered a wide range of news and information. Contributors included journalist Charlayne Hunter-Gault and athlete Carl Lewis. Extremely innovative, NetNoir was named one of the "25 Cool Companies of the Year" by *Fortune* magazine. With minority investors, NetNoir News Media Services ventured into CD-ROMs and Web design in 1996. Ellington served as chairman and chief executive officer of NetNoir Inc. until 2001.

In 2002, San Francisco mayor Willie Brown named Ellington trustee and commissioner of the San Francisco Employees' Retirement System Board, a post he held until early 2008. For the next two years, he was a managing partner with Emory Capital Group, LLC. In 2009, Ellington became cofounder and president of GridSpeak Corporation.

ANN MARIE FUDGE (1951–)

Corporate Executive. Ann Marie Fudge was born April 23, 1951, in Washington, D.C. She received a B.A. with honors from Simmons College in 1973 and an M.B.A. from Harvard Business School in 1977. Fudge began her business career at General Electric (GE) in 1973 as a manpower specialist. She worked at GE until 1975, when she took a job at General Mills in Minneapolis. There she worked as a marketing assistant until she was promoted to assistant product manager in 1977, product manager in 1980, and marketing director in 1983. She remained the General Mills marketing director until she joined Kraft General Foods in 1986.

Fudge started at Kraft as the associate director of strategic planning, but by 1989 her worth to the company earned her a vice presidency in charge of marketing and development of the Dinners and Enhancers Division, where she worked on such products as Log Cabin Syrup, Minute Rice, and Stove Top Stuffing. She managed to reposition the products and increase sales in the overburdened food market. In 1991, she was promoted to general manager of the division. She became executive vice president in 1994. The same year, she became president of the Coffee and Cereals Division. Fudge served in a variety of senior executive positions at Kraft before retiring in 2001. In 2003, she became chairman and CEO of Young & Rubicam Brands, a job she held until 2007.

Fudge has served as president and vice president of the Executive Leadership Council and holds memberships with the National Black MBA Association and the Junior League. She has also served on the boards of directors for the Federal Reserve Bank of New York, Allied Signal, General Electric, Liz Claiborne, Unilever, Novartis, and Catalyst. In addition, Fudge served on the Harvard Board of Overseers and the Gates Foundation's U.S. Programs Advisory Board. She has also been a trustee of the Rockefeller Foundation, the Brookings Institution, and Morehouse College. In 2010, President Obama appointed Fudge to the bipartisan National Commission on Fiscal Responsibility and Reform.

S. B. FULLER (1905–1988)

Entrepreneur. Samuel B. Fuller was born on June 4, 1905, in Monroe, Louisiana. He moved with his family to Memphis, Tennessee, where he dropped out of school after the sixth grade and worked at various jobs. In 1928, he moved to Chicago and began selling products door-to-door. By the mid-1930s, he had established a successful business on the South Side of Chicago.

In 1947, Fuller acquired Boyer International Laboratories, a white-owned cosmetics company, and greatly expanded his business. His company grew in size, and he became famous for his motivational techniques. However, when whites in the South learned that Boyer was owned by an African American, they boycotted Boyer's products. In 1969, Fuller Products was forced to declare bankruptcy.

Fuller reorganized the company, and it reemerged from bankruptcy in the early 1970s. The company reestablished its sales techniques and grew into a large company again. Fuller died on October 24, 1988, after receiving numerous honors.

ARTHUR G. GASTON (1892–1996)

Entrepreneur. Arthur George Gaston stated many times in interviews that one of his primary rules for business success was "find a need and fill it." Gaston's business accomplishments are a testimony to his lifelong adherence to this rule.

Gaston was born on July 4, 1892, in Demopolis, Georgia, a small rural town. He started his business career in 1923 by founding the Booker T. Washington Burial Society, which guaranteed African Americans a decent burial. In 1932, it had grown large enough to be incorporated. In 1930, Smith and Gaston Funeral Directors was formed to complement the services of the burial society. The "Smith" was A. L. Smith, Gaston's father-in-law, who had helped him financially when he first started in business.

Finding it hard to staff his growing company with skilled clerical workers, Gaston started the Booker T. Washington Business College in 1939. The college trained African American students in stenography, the operation of business machines, and other clerical skills.

In 1946, Gaston started the Brown Belle Bottling Company, which produced Joe Louis Punch. He also acquired a cemetery in 1947, a motel in 1954, an investment firm in 1955, a savings and loan association in 1957, a senior citizens home in 1963, and two radio stations in 1975. In 1986, at age ninety-four, Gaston opened the A. G. Gaston Construction Company. His companies brought in more than $24 million in revenues in 1991. Gaston died on January 19, 1996, in Birmingham, Alabama.

ARCHIBALD H. GRIMKÉ

See chapter 10, Law.

LA-VAN HAWKINS (1960–)

Fast-Food Restaurant Entrepreneur. La-Van Hawkins was born and raised in Chicago. As a youth, he became involved in drugs and gangs. He turned around his life after he started working at a McDonald's in Chicago. He quickly rose through the ranks at McDonald's, becoming director of operations before leaving the company to work for Kentucky Fried Chicken (now KFC) in the late 1970s.

Hawkins managed inner-city projects for KFC and eventually became a district manager. In 1986, he joined T. Boone Pickens in various investment schemes that earned him large amounts of money. In 1990, Hawkins began franchising Checkers restaurants. By 1995, the success of this chain had made him a multimillionaire.

In 1995, officials for Burger King approached Hawkins about fronting several of their restaurants in urban areas. Hawkins accepted the offer and eventually owned more than two dozen Burger King restaurants in various cities and several federal empowerment zones. He broke with Burger King in 2001 and began investing in Pizza Hut franchises in the Detroit area. He also launched a southern-themed restaurant chain known as Sweet Georgia Brown.

Hawkins fell from grace quickly when in 2002 he was fined for failing to pay taxes. Two years later, he was indicted on fraud and perjury charges. In 2007, Hawkins was sentenced to a thirty-three month sentence for wire fraud. In 2009, he received a ten-month concurrent sentence for federal tax evasion.

ROBERT HOLLAND JR. (1940–)

Business Executive. Robert Holland Jr. was born in April 1940, in Albion, Michigan. Holland earned a bachelor of science degree in mechanical engineering from Union College in Schenectady, New York, in 1962. In 1969, he completed a master's degree in business administration with an emphasis on international marketing at Baruch College in New York City. In 1968, Holland left his job as an engineer and sales manager at the Mobil Oil Company to join McKinsey and Company, a consulting firm, where he worked as an associate and eventually a partner. During that time, he worked in the Netherlands, England, Mexico, and Brazil. He returned to Michigan in 1981 and became CEO of City Marketing, a beverage distributor. In 1987, he became chair at Gilreath Manufacturing in Howell, Michigan, a manufacturer of plastic injection molds.

In 1991, Holland started Rohker-J Inc. in White Plains, New York. The company bought struggling companies, turned them around, and sold them. In 1994, Holland's business savvy and his whimsy with poetic verse won him a position as president and CEO of Ben & Jerry's Homemade Ice Cream. After accomplishing his goals of stabilizing Ben & Jerry's manufacturing operations and bringing more professional management to the company, he resigned in October 1996. In 1997, he founded WorkPlace Integrators, a leading dealer of office furniture, in Bingham Farms, Michigan. In addition to his business, Holland has served on the board of directors for the Harlem Junior Tennis Program, UNC Ventures, Yum Brands, and Atlanta University Center. He has also served as chairman of the board at Spelman College.

GEORGE E. JOHNSON (1927–)

Business Executive. George Ellis Johnson was born in Richton, Mississippi, on June 16, 1927. He attended Wendell Phillips High School in Chicago, then went to work as a chemist for Fuller Products, which produced cosmetics for African Americans. While there, he developed a hair straightener for men and began marketing it himself in 1954. By 1957, he had formed Johnson Products, which sold hair-care products under the Ultra-Sheen label. The company prospered and, by 1971, its stock was traded on the American Stock Exchange. Johnson Products was the first African American–owned company to trade on a major stock exchange. In June 1993, Joan Johnson, chair and CEO of Johnson Products and George Johnson's ex-wife, announced the sale of the company to Ivax Corporation, a white-owned pharmaceutical firm.

Johnson served as a director of the Independence Bank of Chicago, the U.S. Postal Service, and the Commonwealth Edison Company. He also founded the George E. Johnson Foundation, which funds charitable and educational programs for African Americans. Johnson has received the Abraham Lincoln Center's Humanitarian Service Award (1972), *Ebony* magazine's Black Achievement Award (1978), a public-service award presented by the Harvard Club of Chicago, the Horatio Alger Award (1980), and the Babson Medal (1983). Johnson has also received honorary degrees from Chicago State University (1977), Fisk University (1977), the Tuskegee Institute (1978), and other educational institutions.

KARL KANI

See chapter 26, Visual and Applied Arts.

DENNIS KIMBRO (1950–)

Author, Educator, Motivational Speaker. Dennis Paul Kimbro was born on December 29, 1950, in Jersey City, New Jersey. He graduated from Oklahoma University with a bachelor's degree in 1972. He earned a Ph.D. in political economics at Northwestern University while working as a salesperson at SmithKline Beckman, a pharmaceutical corporation. In 1987, Kimbro left SmithKline when he was hired by ABC Management Consultants, where he worked until 1991. Meanwhile, Kimbro also worked at revising a manuscript written by Napoleon Hill, the author of *Think and Grow Rich*, a best-selling self-help book first published in 1937. Hill had been working on a version for an African American audience when he died, and the manuscript was turned over to the publisher W. Clement Stone, who gave the manuscript to Kimbro. Kimbro interviewed many successful African Americans to chart how they managed to maximize potential and channel positive thinking to build their success.

In 1991, Kimbro's *Think and Grow Rich: A Black Choice*, coauthored by Hill, was published by Ballantine Books and became the first major African American self-help book. Over the next two years, it became a best seller among African American readers, selling more than 250,000 copies and earning Kimbro an Award of Excellence from the Texas Association of Black Personnel in Higher Education in 1992. The same year, Kimbro became an associate professor and director of the Center for Entrepreneurship at the Clark Atlanta University School of Business Administration. Kimbro's second book, *Daily Motivations for African-American*

Success, was published by Ballantine in 1993. In 1997, Kimbro published *What Makes the Great Great: Strategies for Extraordinary Achievement*, which outlined nine "stones of greatness" that underlay true success. In 2003, Kimbro published *What Keeps Me Standing: Letters from Black Grandmothers on Peace, Hope, and Inspiration.*

REGINALD F. LEWIS (1942–1993)

Business Executive. Reginald Francis Lewis was born December 7, 1942, in Baltimore, Maryland. He received an A.B. from Virginia State College in 1965 and a law degree from Harvard Law School in 1968. Lewis worked with the firm of Paul, Weiss, Rifkind, Wharton, and Garrison until 1970. He then became a partner in Murphy, Thorpe, and Lewis, the first African American law firm on Wall Street, where he worked until 1973. Between 1973 and 1989, Lewis was in private practice as a corporate lawyer.

In 1983, Lewis formed a holding company known as the TLC Group. In 1987, he became president and CEO of TLC Beatrice International Holdings after TLC's leveraged acquisition of the Beatrice International Food Company. Lewis thus became head of the largest African American–owned business in the United States. TLC Beatrice had revenues of $1.54 billion in 1992.

Reginald F. Lewis, Business Executive, 1992. *Under Lewis's leadership, TLC Beatrice International became the largest African American–owned company in the United States.* **AP PHOTO/IRA BLOCK**

Lewis was a member of the American and National Bar Associations and the National Conference of Black Lawyers. He also served on the boards of directors of the New York City Off-Track Betting Corporation, the Central Park Conservancy, the NAACP Legal Defense and Educational Fund, and WNET-Channel 13, the public television station in New York. He was the recipient of the Distinguished Service Award presented by the American Association of MESBIC (1974) and the Black Enterprise Achievement Award (1979). Lewis died from brain cancer on January 19, 1993, in New York.

J. BRUCE LLEWELLYN (1927–2010)

Business Executive. James Bruce Llewellyn was born July 16, 1927, in New York City. He served in the U.S. Army Corps of Engineers from 1944 to 1948. After his discharge, he attended City College of New York, graduating in 1955. Llewellyn later attended Columbia University's Graduate School of Business and New York University's School of Public Administration, before receiving a law degree in 1960 from New York Law School.

Before law school, Llewellyn was the proprietor of a retail liquor store. From 1958 to 1960, while attending law school, he was a student assistant in the District Attorney's Office for New York County. After graduating, he practiced law with the firm of Evans, Berger, and Llewellyn. Between 1964 and 1969, he worked in a variety of professional positions for various governmental agencies, including the Housing Division of the Housing and Re-Development Board (1964–1965), the Small Business Development Corporation (1965), and the Small Business Administration (1965–1969).

In 1969, as part of a syndicate buyout, he became president of Fedco Food Stores of New York. By 1975, the company had grown from eleven to fourteen stores and had annual revenues of $30 million and 450 employees. In 1985, Llewellyn became chairman of the Philadelphia Coca-Cola Bottling Company, the second-largest firm on the *Black Enterprise* Industrial/Service 100 list.

Llewellyn served on the boards of the City College of New York, the American Can Company, American Capital Management Research, and the Freedom National Bank. He also belonged to the Harlem Lawyers Association, the New York Interracial Council for Business Opportunity, and the New York Urban Coalition and its Venture Capital Corporation. Llewellyn held honorary doctorates from Wagner College, City University of New York, and Atlanta University. He died on April 7, 2010, of renal failure in New York at eighty-two years old. His personal wealth at the time was estimated to have been more than $150,000,000.

SAMUEL METTERS (1934–)

Entrepreneur. Samuel Metters, a native of Austin, Texas, received his B.S. in architectural engineering from Prairie View A&M University, a B.A. in architecture and urban planning from the University of California–Berkeley, and an M.S. in systems management and public administration and a Ph.D. in public administration from the University of Southern California.

Metters founded Metters Industries in 1981 after a career that included a stint in the U.S. Army. The firm, which has over 350 employees, is a strategic planning and analysis company that works in conjunction with various governmental entities and private businesses. Metters's customers have included the Internal Revenue Service, the U.S. Patent and Trade Office, the U.S. Army, the U.S. Navy, the Department of Homeland Security, and the Department of Veterans Affairs, as well as Northwest Airlines, Howard University, Federal Express, and Fox Studios. Metters has also worked in Saudi Arabia, building new cities and handling the logistical problems that go along with new development. In 2001, Metters began work on a $4.5 million development project in Prairie View, Texas, near the campus of his alma mater. In 2000, with sales of $34 million, Metters Industries ranked among the *Black Enterprise* Industrial/Service 100 leading African American–owned businesses.

In 1987, Metters joined the board of directors of U.S. Black Engineers Publications. He has also been active in the USC Alumni Association, the Boy Scouts, and Prairie View A&M University.

ROSE META MORGAN (c. 1912–)

Entrepreneur. Rose Meta Morgan was born around 1912 in Shelby, Mississippi, but spent most of her childhood in Chicago. She started her own business at the early age of ten, making and selling artificial flowers door-to-door with the assistance of other neighborhood children. By the time Morgan was fourteen, she was earning money styling hair. Morgan claims she was a high school dropout, even though she may have actually finished. Either way, she attended Morris School of Beauty in Chicago, and after graduating, she rented space in a salon and began styling, grooming, and cutting hair full time. In 1938, Morgan met Ethel Waters, a popular actress and singer, during a run of performances in Chicago. Waters invited Morgan to New York because of the stylist's prowess in hair design.

Within six months of moving to New York, Morgan opened her own beauty shop. Later, running out of room, she signed a ten-year lease for a dilapidated mansion and began to renovate it. Three years later, Morgan's salon—the Rose Meta Morgan House of Beauty—was the most prestigious and most successful African American beauty salon in the world. By 1946, she was drawing nearly one thousand customers a week and had increased her staff to twenty-nine people, including a nurse and masseurs. Morgan also began producing and selling a line of cosmetics and hosting fashion shows that matured into major social events at the Renaissance Casino and Rockford Plaza in Harlem. Soon, she was one of the richest businesswomen in New York. Customers came from all over the country to visit the House of Beauty, and Morgan traveled abroad with her cosmetics, fashion designs, and ideas about beauty and women of color.

In the mid-1950s, Morgan bought and refurbished a new building for the House of Beauty. Thousands of people attended the grand opening, and the building was dedicated by the wife of the mayor of New York. The new salon offered more features, such as a dressmaking department, a charm school, a fitness department, and later a wig salon to cash in on the renewed popularity of hair pieces. In 1965, Morgan established the Freedom National Bank, New York's only commercial bank run by and for African Americans. In 1972, she created the Trim-Away Figure Contouring business. She retired in the 1980s.

Morgan's marriages were less successful than her businesses. In 1955, she married heavyweight boxing champion Joe Louis, but their marriage was annulled in 1958. Later, Morgan married lawyer Louis Saunders, and though they separated in the early 1960s, Saunders died before they were divorced.

STANLEY O'NEAL (1951–)

Corporate Executive. Born in Roanoke, Alabama, on October 7, 1951, Stanley O'Neal's family later moved from rural Alabama to Atlanta, Georgia, where O'Neal attended high school. He worked in a General Motors (GM) plant while studying for his undergraduate degree, which he received from the General Motors Institute (now Kettering University) in Flint, Michigan, in 1974. O'Neal earned an M.B.A. in finance from Harvard Business School in 1978. As an executive for GM from 1978 to 1986, O'Neal held a series of financial-management jobs in the company's Madrid and New York offices. He later served as general assistant treasurer, a position giving him responsibility for GM's mergers and acquisitions.

O'Neal left GM to join the investment firm of Merrill Lynch in 1986. As an investment banker, he made a name for himself in the early 1990s with his resuscitation of the company's junk-bond business. O'Neal held a variety of positions at Merrill Lynch, including managing director and head of global capital markets, managing director in investment banking and head of the Financial Services Group, codirector of the Corporate and Institutional Client Group, and CEO of the Private Client Group. In 2001, he was named president and chief operating officer of Merrill Lynch. In its July 22, 2002, issue, *Fortune* magazine named O'Neal the most powerful black executive in the United States. O'Neal became the CEO of Merrill Lynch in 2003, but as the subprime-mortgage crisis plunged the country into a deep economic recession at the end of 2007 and into 2008, he bore the responsibility for losing the company $8 billion in revenue. He was ousted from Merrill Lynch in 2008, but was subsequently named to the board of directors of Alcoa.

Stanley O'Neal, Business Executive, 2006. *Beginning his professional career as an analyst with General Motors, O'Neal eventually rose to become the chairman, chief executive officer, and president of Merrill Lynch.* AP PHOTO/LOUIS LANZANO

HENRY G. PARKS (1916–1989)

Entrepreneur, Business Executive. Henry Green Parks Jr. was born on September 29, 1916, in Atlanta, Georgia. He received a B.S. in 1939 from Ohio State University and did graduate work there in marketing. After graduating, Parks worked at the Resident War Production Training Center in Wilberforce, Ohio, where he was associated with the educator Mary McLeod Bethune. In 1939, he became a national sales representative for the Pabst Brewing Company. He also became involved in a variety of other enterprises, mostly in Baltimore, including real estate, drug-store operations, cement-block production, theatrical bookings, and a failed attempt at marketing a beverage with former heavyweight boxing champion Joe Louis.

In 1949, Parks bought a part interest in Crayton's Southern Sausage Company of Cleveland, Ohio. After becoming familiar with the meat-packing industry, he sold his interest in the company for a profit. In 1951, he launched H. G. Parks Inc., a sausage packer and distributor, with the aid of a group of investors. By 1971, the company had annual revenues of $10.4 million and was distributing its products to more than twelve thousand stores on the East Coast.

Parks served as vice president of the Chamber of Commerce of Metropolitan Baltimore, was on the board of directors of Magnavox, held a seat on the Baltimore City Council, and purchased an interest in Leonard Evans's Tuesday Publications. He died on April 24, 1989, in Towson, Maryland.

RICHARD DEAN PARSONS (1948–)

Corporate Executive. Born in the Bedford-Stuyvesant neighborhood of Brooklyn, New York, on April 4, 1948, Richard Dean Parsons grew up in the borough of Queens. He graduated from high school when he was sixteen and attended the University of Hawaii, where he played varsity basketball. He earned a bachelor's degree from the university in 1968, and continued his education at Union University's Albany Law School in New York. He graduated at the top of his class and received the highest score on the state bar exam in 1971.

Parsons started his law career as a member of New York governor Nelson Rockefeller's legal staff. He continued in this capacity when Rockefeller became vice president of the United States under Gerald Ford in 1974. Later, Parsons provided legal counsel for President Ford as deputy counsel and then as associate director of the domestic council. He left government service in 1977 to join the New York City law firm Patterson, Belknap, Webb and Tyler, where he became a partner in 1979 and represented such clients as Happy Rockefeller and Estée Lauder.

Parsons was appointed chief operating officer of the Dime Savings Bank of New York in 1988, becoming the first African American male to manage a financial institution of Dime's size. Parsons led the bank back from severe debt. In 1993, newly elected mayor Rudolph Giuliani chose Parsons to head his transition council and later to be the deputy mayor for economic development. Parsons instead chose to act as chairman of the Economic Development Corporation for the city. In December 2001, Parsons was named to replace Gerald Levin as the CEO of the AOL Time Warner Corporation, which in 2003 was renamed Time Warner. He stepped down as CEO of Time Warner in 2007.

Parsons has served on boards for Time Warner, Philip Morris, TriStar Pictures, Howard University, and the Metropolitan Museum of Art. He has also served as a member of the Presidential Drug Task Force, as chairperson of Wildcat Service Organization, and as a member of the board of the New York Zoological Society. In 2009, Parsons was named chairman of Citigroup. He has also advised President Barack Obama and was under consideration for a cabinet position.

HERMAN J. RUSSELL (1930–)

Housing Construction Entrepreneur. Herman Jerome Russell was born December 23, 1930, in Atlanta, Georgia. When he was sixteen, he and his father bought a small piece of land and built a duplex on it. Russell used the money he accrued from rent to pay for his education at Tuskegee Institute. In 1953, he went to work for his father as a plastering subcontractor. After his father's death in 1957, he took over the family home-improvement business.

In 1962, Russell launched H.J. Russell & Company, a construction contractor. He built a reputation for high-quality work that allowed him to overcome many racial barriers to success. He began to bid on large construction jobs and has worked on many of the biggest projects built in Atlanta since the 1960s, including Hartsfield International Airport, the Coca-Cola Company World Headquarters, and the Georgia Dome. He also continued to build affordable housing, despite the high-profile success of his company.

In 1997, Russell retired from the direct management of the company, passing it down to his children, although he remained chairman. He is well known in the Atlanta area for his philanthropy and for his work in the inner city.

RUSSELL SIMMONS (1957–)

Music Company Executive, Producer, Music Promoter. Russell Simmons was born on October 4, 1957, in the Hollis district of the borough of Queens in New York City. Although he grew up in a middle-class neighborhood, Simmons got involved with gangs in his teens. The 1970s brought change to Simmons's life, however, as he enrolled in classes at the Harlem branch of the City College of New York. While studying sociology, Simmons began noticing the influence rap music had on young inner-city African Americans. The boasting and storytelling skills of various rappers drew crowds on street corners and in neighborhood parks. Simmons found himself in the middle of a movement that would shape the sound of popular music.

Simmons left college to promote local rap artists. Hard work and perseverance led to the formation of Def Jam Records in 1984. Simmons and his partner, Rick Ruben, signed a deal with CBS Records to distribute their material. Simmons was primarily interested in promoting rap images that displayed the life and style of tough urban streets. Acts such as the Beastie Boys, LL Cool J, and Run-DMC propelled Def Jam Records to early success. Other groups, such as Public Enemy, enjoyed Simmons's input as their careers developed. Simmons was married to hip-hop clothing designer and model Kimora Lee from 1998 to 2009.

The music Simmons promoted not only revolutionized hip-hop but helped bring fashion to the forefront as well. High-top Adidas tennis shoes, black leather jackets, and T-shirts displaying the Def Jam logo flooded the streets. These influences laid a foundation for Simmons's own line of clothing called Phat Farm. Simmons furthered his professional growth by getting involved in film production. He contributed to *Krush Groove* (1985) and *Tougher than Leather* (1988). Simmons is CEO of Rush Communications, which by 1992 was the nation's second-largest African American–owned entertainment company. Rush is comprised of record labels, management companies, and clothing, radio, film, and television divisions. In 1998, Simmons launched an hour-long syndicated series *Oneworld's Music Beat with Russell Simmons.*

Music Company Executive Russell Simmons, New York City, April 13, 2005. *Simmons (*holding microphone*) sits with (*from left*) Antonio "L.A." Reid, Jay Z, and Tony Austin at a press conference announcing the launch of the Russell Simmons Music Group.* SCOTT GRIES/GETTY IMAGES

In 2001, Simmons went to Washington, D.C., to speak out on the behalf of rap artists, promoting the fact that they have brought to the forefront many social issues and that they should not be blamed for the violence that many have associated with their songs. That same year, Simmons published his autobiography *Life and Def: Sex, Drugs, Money, and God*, written with George Nelson. In 2001, with sales of $192 million—sixteenth on the BE Industrial/Service 100—*Black Enterprise* magazine named Rush Communications its Industrial/Service Company of the Year. Simmons was also named a trustee of the National Urban League. In addition, he heads a number of philanthropic organizations, including the Hip-Hop Summit Action Network and the Rush Philanthropic Arts Foundation. He is believed to have a net worth in excess of $300 million.

NAOMI R. SIMS (1948–2009)

Business Executive, Model. Naomi Ruth Sims was born March 30, 1948, in Oxford, Mississippi. She attended New York University, where she studied psychology, and the Fashion Institute of Technology, where she graduated in 1967. Sims was a fashion model with the Ford Agency in New York from 1970 to 1973. She was the first African American woman to become a high fashion model and the first to appear in a television commercial. She also appeared on the cover of *Life* magazine.

In 1970, Sims started lecturing and writing fashion and beauty articles on a freelance basis. In 1973, she helped develop a new fiber for her line of wigs and founded the Naomi Sims Collection, which by 1977 had annual revenues of $4 million. Sims also wrote a number of self-help books, including *All about Health and Beauty for the Black Woman* (1975), *How to Be a Top Model* (1979), *All about Hair Care for the Black Woman* (1982), and *All about Success for the Black Woman* (1982).

In 1969 and 1970, Sims was voted Model of the Year by International Mannequins and won the *Ladies' Home Journal* Women of Achievement Award. For her work with underprivileged children in Bedford-Stuyvesant, she won an award from the New York City Board of

Naomi Sims. *Sims's appearances in the 1970s on the covers of major U.S. magazines helped promote the "black is beautiful" cultural movement. Sims also went on to write several books, such as* How to Be a Top Model *(1979).* THE WASHINGTON POST/GETTY IMAGES

Education. In 1977, Sims was voted into the Modeling Hall of Fame. She made the International Best-Dressed List several times during the 1970s. She also received recognition for her fund-raising efforts for sickle-cell anemia and cancer research. She was a life member of the NAACP and worked closely with drug-rehabilitation programs.

In 1984, Sims founded Naomi Sims Beauty Products Ltd. in New York City. She died of breast cancer on August 3, 2009, in Newark, New Jersey.

PERCY E. SUTTON (1920–2009)

Business Executive, Attorney. Percy Ellis Sutton was born November 24, 1920, in San Antonio, Texas. He graduated from Phillis Wheatley High School and attended a number of colleges, including Prairie View A&M University, Tuskegee Institute, and Hampton Institute. His education was interrupted by World War II, when Sutton enlisted in the U.S. Army Air Corps. He was promoted to captain and served as a combat intelligence officer in the Italian and Mediterranean theaters. Sutton was decorated with combat stars for his service.

After his discharge, Sutton attended law school on the GI Bill, first at Columbia University in New York and then Brooklyn Law School, where he received an LL.B. in 1950. During the Korean conflict, Sutton served as an intelligence officer and a trial judge advocate with the U.S. Air Force.

Returning to civilian life, Sutton opened a law office in Harlem with his brother and another attorney. In 1964, he was elected to the New York State Assembly, where he served until 1966. In 1966, he was appointed and later elected to the office of president of the borough of Manhattan, a post he held until 1977.

With his brother Oliver and Clarence B. Jones, Sutton cofounded the Inner City Broadcasting Corporation in 1971. The company purchased radio station WLIB-AM, making it the first black-owned station in New York City. Inner City Broadcasting also produced television programs and videos for entertainment companies around the country, including *Showtime at the Apollo.* Sutton retired from the company in 1990, but continued to serve as chairman emeritus.

Sutton was a civil rights advocate both as an attorney and a politician. He was a national director of the Urban League and a past president of the New York branch of the NAACP. He was voted Assemblyman of the Year by the Intercollegiate Legislative Assembly in 1966. Sutton also served as a director of the Museum of the City of New York and the American Museum of Natural History. He died when he was eighty-nine years old on December 26, 2009.

JOHN W. THOMPSON (1949–)

Business Executive. John W. Thompson was born April 24, 1949, in Fort Dix, New Jersey. He graduated from Florida A&M University in 1971 with a bachelor's degree in business administration. Thompson earned a master's degree in management sciences from the Massachusetts Institute of Technology's Sloan School of Management in 1982.

Thompson spent twenty-eight years with industry giant IBM, working his way up from an entry-level sales position to occupy one of the company's senior executive posts—general manager of IBM's Americas unit. Though his name was mentioned in some print sources as a possible candidate for IBM's top position, he left the company on April 14, 1999, to become president and chief executive officer of Symantec Corporation, a software company in Cupertino, California.

The Silicon Valley company, though long-established and financially viable, was sluggish in its performance. A well-known manufacturer of antivirus and utility software, Symantec was facing stiff competition. Thompson focused the company's objectives on one area, Internet security. Well-publicized technology issues, such as the looming Y2K system failures, global e-mail viruses, and the activities of hackers, helped Symantec's focus on corporate security solutions pay off. During Thompson's first years as CEO, Symantec's revenues picked up substantially, growing from $632 million to $944 million in two years. According to company information, under Thompson's leadership, Symantec served ninety-eight of the *Fortune* 100 companies and more than 100 million customers.

Thompson has served on the boards of a number of companies and organizations, including UPS, NiSource, Seagate and Crystal Decisions, Florida A&M Industry Cluster, Teach for America, and the Illinois Governor's Human Resource Advisory Council. He was named one of *Fortune* magazine's fifty most powerful African American executives in its July 22, 2002, issue. During the administration of President George W. Bush, Thompson was a member of the National Infrastructure Advisory Committee, which made recommendations to the Department of Homeland Security regarding the security of the country's infrastructure and information systems. In 2009, Thompson retired as CEO of Symantec but retained his position as board chairman. The following year, he became CEO of Virtual Instruments, an information technology company specializing in network storage and communications. In 2009, he was appointed to the Financial Crisis Inquiry Committee, a U.S. congressional panel investigating the causes of the global financial crisis

MADAME C. J. WALKER (1867–1919)

Entrepreneur. Madame C. J. Walker was born Sarah Breedlove near Delta, Louisiana, in 1867. She was orphaned as a child, raised by a sister in Vicksburg, Mississippi, married at age fourteen, and widowed in 1887 when she was twenty.

After her husband died, Walker moved with her daughter to St. Louis, where she earned a living by taking in laundry and sewing. By 1905, she had become interested in hair-care products for women and began developing a hot comb and a product known as Wonderful Hair Grower. In 1906, she moved to Denver, where, with $1.50 in her pocket, she started a hair-preparations company. She soon married C. J. Walker, a newspaperman who taught her the fundamentals of advertising and mail-order promotion. They divorced in 1912.

In 1908, she moved with her daughter to Pittsburgh, where she founded a beauty school, the Walker College of Hair Culture, which trained cosmetologists in the use of her products. In 1910, with a more central location in mind, Walker moved to Indianapolis, Indiana, where she established a laboratory and factory and developed a nationwide network of five thousand sales agents, mostly African American women, known as the Madame C. J. Walker Hair Culturists Union of America. Her business prospered, and Walker became the first African American female millionaire. She owned a town house in Harlem and a mansion on the Hudson River near Irvington, New York. She died in New York on May 25, 1919.

Walker was a strong believer in self-reliance and education. She was proud of her accomplishments, especially of providing employment for thousands of African Americans who might otherwise have had less-meaningful jobs. Walker was also a genius at marketing, promotion, and mail-order sales. Beneficiaries of her estate included Mary McLeod Bethune's school in Daytona, Florida, and other African American schools, the NAACP, and the Frederick Douglass home-restoration project in Florida.

MAGGIE LENA WALKER (1867–1934)

Banker. Maggie Lena Walker was born on or around July 15, 1867, in Richmond, Virginia. She was the daughter of Elizabeth Draper, who had formerly been enslaved, and Eccles Cuthbert, a New York journalist of Irish descent. Walker attended Richmond public schools, including Armstrong Normal School, which functioned as a high school. After graduating in 1883, she taught in the Richmond schools for three years before marrying building contractor Armstead Walker in 1886.

While she was in school, Walker joined the Grand United Order of Saint Luke, a mutual-aid society that served as an insurance underwriter for African Americans. Walker became active in the organization and held a number of lesser positions before becoming the "right worthy grand secretary" in 1899. She soon changed the name of the organization to the Independent Order of Saint Luke and moved its headquarters to Richmond.

In 1903, Walker became head of the Saint Luke Penny Bank and the first woman in the United States to hold such a position. Although legally separate, the bank had a close financial association with the Independent Order of Saint Luke. The bank later became the Saint Luke Bank and Trust Company and, finally, the Consolidated Bank and Trust Company. By 1924, under Walker's guidance, the order had a membership of 100,000, a new headquarters building, more than two hundred employees, and its own newspaper—the *Saint Luke Herald*.

Walker was active in many other organizations, including the National Association of Colored Women, the Virginia Federation of Colored Women's Clubs, and its Industrial School for Colored Girls. In 1912, she founded the Richmond Council of Colored Women and was a founding member of the Negro Organization Society, a blanket association for African American clubs and organizations. Walker was a board member of the NAACP from 1923 to 1934 and the recipient of an honorary degree from Virginia Union University. In 1927, she received the Harmon Award for Distinguished Achievement. Walker died on December 15, 1934.

TERRIE M. WILLIAMS (1954–)

Business executive. Terrie Michelle Williams was born on May 12, 1954, in Mount Vernon, New York. She attended Brandeis University, where she graduated cum laude with a bachelor's degree in 1975. Williams earned a master's degree from Columbia University in 1977. Her first job after graduate school was as a medical social worker at New York Hospital. She held this job until 1980, when she became the program administrator of the Black Filmmaker Foundation. In 1982, Williams became vice president and director of corporate communications at Essence Communications, a position she held until 1987, when she formed her own company, the Terrie Williams Agency, a communications and public relations firm.

The multifaceted Terrie Williams Agency offers marketing and communications consulting and executive-skills training to individuals and corporate clients. Among the agency's first clients were giants of the entertainment world, such as Miles Davis and Eddie Murphy. The agency has also worked with such clients as the National Basketball Association, the National Hockey League, Revlon, and the Nickelodeon television network. In addition, Williams works with organizations and programs that provide services for at-risk and underprivileged youth.

Williams is the author of four books: *Personal Touch: What You Really Need to Succeed in Today's Fast-Paced Business World* (1994), written with Joe Cooney; *Stay Strong: Simple Life Lessons for Teens* (2001); *Plentiful Harvest: Creating Balance and Harmony through the Seven Living Virtues* (2002); and *Black Pain: It Just Looks Like We're Not Hurting* (2008). She is the recipient of the Public Relations Society of America Philip Dorf Mentoring Award, the New York Women in Communications Matrix Award in Public Relations, and the Citizens Committee for the New York Marietta Tree Award for Public Service.

15

FAMILY AND HEALTH

Doris Nearror Starks

The normative, nuclear family is usually regarded as a husband and wife living together in the same household. The U.S. Census Bureau defines a family as two or more persons, one of whom is the householder, who reside together and are related by birth, marriage, or adoption. This is the definition used most often when shaping public policy. However, due to the rise of single-parent households, same-sex marriages, cohabitation, and trends in divorce and remarriage that result in "blended families," American families are taking alternative forms. Whether traditionally or alternatively structured, families are dynamic units in which individuals interact with each other and respond to internal and external forces. Ideally, whatever their structure or origin, families support their members throughout their lives. Family units are the building blocks of communities.

Major factors affecting the quality of life for families include income, housing, education, and access to high-quality, affordable health care. When there are unmet needs in these areas, the family's stability is threatened and family members cannot reach their maximum potential.

FAMILY STRUCTURE AND STABILITY

It is undeniable that the brutal system of enslavement had an adverse affect on African American families. Although there were family strengths that Africans brought with them from the African continent, slavery was a system that weakened African families in America. Little regard was given to family ties, with slaveholders selling slaves on the basis of economic considerations.

To illustrate this point, Bushrod Washington (1762–1829), the nephew of George Washington (1732–1799) and a slave owner in Virginia, inherited the Mount Vernon plantation from his uncle. When Bushrod Washington became suspicious that some of his male slaves were plotting against him, he decided to sell them on the grounds that the farm at Mount Vernon was losing money and could no longer support so many slaves. In 1821 Washington sold fifty-four of his eighty-three slaves to two men from Louisiana. The slaves spent two days in the slave jail in Alexandria, Virginia, before they were taken to Louisiana.

Although Washington claimed that he tried to keep families together, he gave no consideration to the African tradition of the extended family. The slaves who remained at Mount Vernon considered themselves kin to those who had been sold. Both groups were deeply grieved and bereft, with relatives separated from one another. Later, in November 1829, when Washington and his wife died within two days of each other, the executors of Washington's estate divided his slaves among his nephews and his niece. This division was also made on the basis of dollar value, rather than kinship ties.

Under the threat of constant selling and reselling, the family relationship that endured the most among enslaved Africans was that of mother and child. Although many children were sold, others remained with their mothers. During the Reconstruction era, former slaves went to great lengths to find their family members, on their own or with the help of the Freedmen's Bureau. Those who could not locate their families were taken into other families, remarried, or formed other family-like units.

Until about 1900, the African American family resembled the family of the Reconstruction era. Households

Table 15-1. Family Groups With Children Under 18 Years Old by Race and Hispanic Origin: 1990 to 2008

[**In thousands. As of March (34,670 represents 34,670,000).** Family groups comprise family households, related subfamilies, and unrelated subfamilies. Excludes members of Armed Forces except those living off post or with their families on post. Beginning 2005, population controls based on Census 2000 and an expanded sample of households. Based on Current Population Survey.]

Race and Hispanic origin of householder or reference person	Number (1,000)					Percent distribution		
	1990	2000	2005	2007	2008	1990	2000	2008
All races, total[1]	**34,670**	**37,496**	**39,317**	**39,983**	**38,938**	**100**	**100**	**100**
Two-parent family groups[2]	24,921	25,771	26,482	28,276	27,344	72	69	70
One-parent family groups	9,749	11,725	12,835	11,707	11,594	28	31	30
Maintained by mother	8,398	9,681	10,366	9,965	9,753	24	26	25
Maintained by father	1,351	2,044	2,469	1,742	1,841	4	5	4
White, total[3]	**28,294**	**30,079**	**30,960**	**31,357**	**30,451**	**100**	**100**	**100**
Two-parent family groups[2]	21,905	22,241	22,319	23,646	22,857	77	74	75
One-parent family groups	6,389	7,838	8,641	7,711	7,594	23	26	25
Maintained by mother	5,310	6,216	6,747	6,359	6,138	19	21	20
Maintained by father	1,079	1,622	1,894	1,353	1,456	4	5	5
Black, total[3]	**5,087**	**5,530**	**5,495**	**5,761**	**5,603**	**100**	**100**	**100**
Two-parent family groups[2]	2,006	2,135	2,065	2,404	2,256	39	39	40
One-parent family groups	3,081	3,396	3,430	3,357	3,347	61	61	59
Maintained by mother	2,860	3,060	3,037	3,067	3,080	56	55	55
Maintained by father	221	335	393	289	267	4	6	5
Asian, total[3]	**(NA)**	**1,469**	**1,757**	**1,794**	**1,789**	**100**	**100**	**100**
Two-parent family groups[2]	(NA)	1,184	1,472	1,568	1,513	(NA)	81	84
One-parent family groups	(NA)	285	285	226	276	(NA)	19	15
Maintained by mother	(NA)	236	222	185	225	(NA)	16	12
Maintained by father	(NA)	49	63	42	51	(NA)	3	3
Hispanic, total[4]	**3,429**	**5,503**	**6,752**	**7,193**	**7,213**	**100**	**100**	**100**
Two-parent family groups[2]	2,289	3,625	4,346	4,984	5,072	67	66	70
One-parent family groups	1,140	1,877	2,406	2,209	2,141	33	34	30
Maintained by mother	1,003	1,565	1,964	1,987	1,903	29	28	26
Maintained by father	138	313	442	221	238	4	6	3
Non-Hispanic White, total[3, 4]	**(NA)**	**24,847**	**24,730**	**24,697**	**23,765**	**100**	**100**	**100**
Two-parent family groups[2]	(NA)	18,750	18,253	18,956	18,099	(NA)	75	76
One-parent family groups	(NA)	6,096	6,476	5,741	5,666	(NA)	25	24
Maintained by mother	(NA)	4,766	4,984	4,585	4,423	(NA)	19	18
Maintained by father	(NA)	1,331	1,492	1,155	1,243	(NA)	5	5

NA Not available.
[1]Includes other races and non-Hispanic groups not shown separately.
[2]Beginning 2007, includes children living both with married and unmarried parents.
[3]Beginning with the 2003 Current Population Survey (CPS), respondents could choose more than one race. Beginning 2005, data represent persons who selected this race group only and exclude persons reporting more than one race. The CPS prior to 2003 allowed respondents to report only one race group. See also comments on race in the text for this section.
[4]Hispanic persons may be any race.

SOURCE: U.S. Census Bureau, Current Population Reports, P20–537, and earlier reports; and "Families and Living Arrangements."

Table 15-1. *The census data show the high percentage of single-parent families among African American households in 2008.*

were kin-related, had not changed in size, and included long-married couples. However, the number of households headed by females more than forty years of age had started to increase. In some cases, this was attributable to the death of the husband, or because the male head of the household had gone away to work. From about 1910 to the late 1960s, during the Great Migration of African Americans from the rural South to the North, the African American family remained largely intact, and most families continued to be headed by two parents.

According to a 1983 study published by the Joint Center for Political Studies, until 1960, 75 percent of black families included both a husband and a wife. Beginning in the 1960s, however, rapid urbanization and the conditions of life in the inner city adversely affected many black families. Black males often could not find work, which weakened family stability. Furthermore, there was a continuing failure to prevent and address the problems caused by these external social influences on black families.

The structure and stability of the African American family sustained damage because of continuing racism, injustice, lack of adequate education, and poverty. In 1965 Daniel P. Moynihan (1927–2003), then an assistant secretary in the Office of Policy Planning and Research of the U.S. Department of

Labor, released *The Negro Family: The Case for National Action*, which became known as the *Moynihan Report*. The report pointed out that although there was an emerging black middle class, conditions for lower income black families were worsening. Moynihan attributed this situation to: (1) the legacy of African enslavement; (2) growing urbanization; (3) the traditional black family structure; and (4) discrimination in employment and education. Moynihan felt that problems within the black family were contributing to a breakdown in the social fabric of the black community, and causing rising rates of school dropouts, crime, illegitimacy, and welfare dependency. He proposed that a concerted national effort was needed to strengthen black families and help them take advantage of opportunities to advance themselves. The *Moynihan Report* was often used to characterize the black family as a pathological unit, an assumption that shaped public policy.

Some social scientists countered that the black family had its own strengths and had demonstrated its worth and viability. Sociologist Andrew Billingsley, for example, challenged Moynihan's findings by arguing that, in the 1960s, two-thirds of African American families living in metropolitan areas were headed by husbands with wives. In addition, half of them were socioeconomically middle class.

According to the U.S. Census Bureau, the real median household income for black families was $34,218 in 2008, the lowest of any racial group. The highest real median household income was $65,637 for Asian families, followed by $55,530 for white, non-Hispanic families, and $37,913 for Hispanics of any race. Since black families have historically received less income than other racial groups in the United States, it has been harder for them to meet their housing, education, and health-care needs.

In part because of the recession that started in December 2007, the real median household income for black families declined 2.8 percent the following year. However, the change in the number of black families living below the poverty level from 2007 to 2008 was essentially unchanged; in 2007, the poverty rate was 24.5 percent, and in 2008 it was 24.7 percent. To help determine the number of families with incomes at the poverty level, the U.S. Census Bureau issues annual guidelines based on the number of persons in a family. For example, for 2009, in the forty-eight contiguous states, a family of four earning $22,050 or less had an income at the poverty level. In Hawaii and Alaska, the income levels were slightly higher.

The U.S. Bureau of Labor Statistics reported in September 2009 that the seasonally adjusted unemployment rate for white men twenty years old or older was 9.6 percent; for African American men in the same category, it was 16.5 percent. The unemployment rate for white women twenty years of age or older was 7 percent in September 2009, whereas the unemployment rate for black women in this age group was 12.5 percent. This was a clear disparity in earnings, which meant that there were more African American families living in poverty.

During the "economic meltdown" of 2007 to 2008, African American families were disproportionately affected by the loss of jobs and the loss of homes through foreclosure. Many subprime loans were made to African American families, and some were made under fraudulent circumstances. Consequently, thousands lost their homes and became homeless. Entire neighborhoods were affected by the downturn in the real-estate market, further destabilizing African American families and communities.

African American families that generally manage better economically tend to be two-parent families with both parents employed and college-educated. These families are more likely to have resources to meet their needs.

Since economic well-being is vital to the maintenance of a stable family, *Black Enterprise* magazine set forth what it has identified as the "Ten Wealth for Life Principles." They are:

1. I will live within my means.
2. I will maximize my income potential through education and training.
3. I will effectively manage my budget, credit, debt, and tax obligations.
4. I will save at least 10 percent of my income.
5. I will use home ownership as a foundation for building wealth.
6. I will devise an investment plan for my retirement needs and children's education.
7. I will ensure that my entire family adheres to sensible money-management principles.
8. I will support the creation and growth of minority-owned businesses.
9. I will guarantee that my wealth is passed on to future generations through proper insurance and estate planning.
10. I will strengthen my community through philanthropy.

The purpose of the "Ten Wealth for Life Principles" is to strengthen families and communities by creating generational wealth. A decrease in the poverty rate would positively enhance family stability.

Substance abuse continues to present a problem for the African American family. Addiction is associated with crime, incarceration, and loss of self-respect, and it can lead to child neglect and abuse, spousal abuse, and health problems, particularly HIV/AIDS. Addiction is costly to families and communities.

The Pew Charitable Trusts reported in 2009 that an examination of U.S. Department of Justice data from 2006 found that while one in thirty white men between the ages of twenty and thirty-four is behind bars, the figure is one in nine for African American males in that age group. For African American women in their mid- to late thirties, the incarceration rate is one in one hundred. The reasons for higher incarceration rates for African Americans than for whites require further investigation, but it is clear that incarceration contributes to family instability.

Table 15-2. Marital Status of the U.S. Population by Sex, Race, and Hispanic Origin: 1990 to 2008

[**In millions, except percent (181.8 represents 181,800,000).** As of **March. Persons 18 years old and over.** Excludes members of Armed Forces except those living off post or with their families on post. Beginning 2005, population controls based on Census 2000 and an expanded sample of households. Based on Current Population Survey.]

Marital status, race, and Hispanic origin	Total				Male				Female			
	1990	2000	2005	2008	1990	2000	2005	2008	1990	2000	2005	2008
Total[1]	**181.8**	**201.8**	**217.2**	**224.5**	**86.9**	**96.9**	**104.8**	**108.8**	**95.0**	**104.9**	**112.3**	**115.8**
Never married	40.4	48.2	53.9	58.3	22.4	26.1	29.6	32.0	17.9	22.1	24.3	26.3
Married[2]	112.6	120.1	127.4	128.7	55.8	59.6	63.3	64.1	56.7	60.4	64.0	64.5
Widowed	13.8	13.7	13.8	14.3	2.3	2.6	2.7	2.9	11.5	11.1	11.1	11.4
Divorced	15.1	19.8	22.1	23.3	6.3	8.5	9.2	9.8	8.8	11.3	12.9	13.6
Percent of total	**100.0**	**100.0**	**100.0**	**100.0**	**100.0**	**100.0**	**100.0**	**100.0**	**100.0**	**100.0**	**100.0**	**100.0**
Never married	22.2	23.9	24.8	25.9	25.8	27.0	28.2	29.4	18.9	21.1	21.6	22.7
Married[2]	61.9	59.5	58.6	57.3	64.3	61.5	60.4	58.9	59.7	57.6	56.9	55.7
Widowed	7.6	6.8	6.4	6.4	2.7	2.7	2.6	2.7	12.1	10.5	9.9	9.8
Divorced	8.3	9.8	10.2	10.4	7.2	8.8	8.8	9.0	9.3	10.8	11.5	11.7
White, total[3]	**155.5**	**168.1**	**177.5**	**182.6**	**74.8**	**81.6**	**86.6**	**89.5**	**80.6**	**86.6**	**90.9**	**93.1**
Never married	31.6	36.0	39.7	42.8	18.0	20.3	22.6	24.4	13.6	15.7	17.0	18.5
Married[2]	99.5	104.1	108.3	108.8	49.5	51.8	54.0	54.5	49.9	52.2	54.2	54.3
Widowed	11.7	11.5	11.5	11.9	1.9	2.2	2.3	2.4	9.8	9.3	9.2	9.4
Divorced	12.6	16.5	18.1	19.1	5.4	7.2	7.6	8.2	7.3	9.3	10.4	10.9
Percent of total	**100.0**	**100.0**	**100.0**	**100.0**	**100.0**	**100.0**	**100.0**	**100.0**	**100.0**	**100.0**	**100.0**	**100.0**
Never married	20.3	21.4	22.3	23.5	24.1	24.9	26.1	27.2	16.9	18.1	18.7	19.8
Married[2]	64.0	62.0	61.0	59.6	66.2	63.5	62.4	60.9	61.9	60.3	59.7	58.3
Widowed	7.5	6.8	6.5	6.5	2.6	2.7	2.6	2.7	12.2	10.8	10.2	10.1
Divorced	8.1	9.8	10.2	10.5	7.2	8.8	8.8	9.1	9.0	10.7	11.5	11.7
Black, total[3]	**20.3**	**24.0**	**25.2**	**26.4**	**9.1**	**10.7**	**11.2**	**11.8**	**11.2**	**13.3**	**13.9**	**14.6**
Never married	7.1	9.5	10.2	10.9	3.5	4.3	4.7	5.1	3.6	5.1	5.5	5.8
Married[2]	9.3	10.1	10.3	10.6	4.5	5.0	5.0	5.2	4.8	5.1	5.2	5.4
Widowed	1.7	1.7	1.7	1.7	0.3	0.3	0.3	0.3	1.4	1.4	1.4	1.4
Divorced	2.1	2.8	2.9	3.2	0.8	1.1	1.1	1.2	1.3	1.7	1.8	2.0
Percent of total	**100.0**	**100.0**	**100.0**	**100.0**	**100.0**	**100.0**	**100.0**	**100.0**	**100.0**	**100.0**	**100.0**	**100.0**
Never married	35.1	39.4	40.6	41.3	38.4	40.2	42.0	42.9	32.5	38.3	39.5	39.7
Married[2]	45.8	42.1	41.0	40.1	49.2	46.7	45.5	44.2	43.0	38.3	37.4	37.0
Widowed	8.5	7.0	6.6	6.5	3.7	2.8	2.7	2.8	12.4	10.5	10.0	9.6
Divorced	10.6	11.5	11.7	12.1	8.8	10.3	9.8	10.1	12.0	12.8	13.3	13.7
Asian, total[3]	**(NA)**	**(NA)**	**9.4**	**10.3**	**(NA)**	**(NA)**	**4.5**	**4.8**	**(NA)**	**(NA)**	**4.9**	**5.4**
Never married	(NA)	(NA)	2.3	2.6	(NA)	(NA)	1.3	1.5	(NA)	(NA)	1.0	1.2
Married[2]	(NA)	(NA)	6.2	6.7	(NA)	(NA)	2.9	3.1	(NA)	(NA)	3.3	3.5
Widowed	(NA)	(NA)	0.4	0.5	(NA)	(NA)	0.1	0.1	(NA)	(NA)	0.3	0.4
Divorced	(NA)	(NA)	0.5	0.4	(NA)	(NA)	0.2	0.1	(NA)	(NA)	0.3	0.3
Percent of total	**100.0**	**100.0**	**100.0**	**100.0**	**100.0**	**100.0**	**100.0**	**100.0**	**100.0**	**100.0**	**100.0**	**100.0**
Never married	(NA)	(NA)	24.8	25.8	(NA)	(NA)	29.7	30.9	(NA)	(NA)	20.3	21.2
Married[2]	(NA)	(NA)	65.6	65.1	(NA)	(NA)	64.7	64.7	(NA)	(NA)	66.5	65.4
Widowed	(NA)	(NA)	4.3	4.9	(NA)	(NA)	1.3	1.6	(NA)	(NA)	6.7	7.7
Divorced	(NA)	(NA)	5.3	4.3	(NA)	(NA)	4.1	2.8	(NA)	(NA)	6.4	5.6
Hispanic, total[4]	**13.6**	**21.1**	**27.5**	**30.3**	**6.7**	**10.4**	**14.1**	**15.6**	**6.8**	**10.7**	**13.4**	**14.6**
Never married	3.7	5.9	8.6	9.7	2.2	3.4	5.2	5.8	1.5	2.5	3.4	3.9
Married[2]	8.4	12.7	15.6	17.2	4.1	6.2	7.8	8.7	4.3	6.5	7.8	8.5
Widowed	0.5	0.9	1.0	1.1	0.1	0.2	0.2	0.2	0.4	0.7	0.8	0.8
Divorced	1.0	1.6	2.2	2.3	0.4	0.7	0.9	0.9	0.6	1.0	1.3	1.4
Percent of total	**100.0**	**100.0**	**100.0**	**100.0**	**100.0**	**100.0**	**100.0**	**100.0**	**100.0**	**100.0**	**100.0**	**100.0**
Never married	27.2	28.0	31.3	32.0	32.1	32.3	36.7	37.2	22.5	23.4	25.6	26.7
Married[2]	61.7	60.2	57.0	56.8	60.9	59.7	55.6	55.8	62.4	60.7	58.7	58.2
Widowed	4.0	4.2	3.7	3.6	1.5	1.6	1.5	1.3	6.5	6.5	6.1	5.5
Divorced	7.0	7.6	7.9	7.6	5.5	6.4	6.3	5.8	8.5	9.3	9.7	9.6

Table 15-2. Marital Status of the U.S. Population by Sex, Race, and Hispanic Origin: 1990 to 2008 [CONTINUED]

[**In millions, except percent (181.8 represents 181,800,000).** As of **March. Persons 18 years old and over.** Excludes members of Armed Forces except those living off post or with their families on post. Beginning 2005, population controls based on Census 2000 and an expanded sample of households. Based on Current Population Survey.]

Marital status, race, and Hispanic origin	Total				Male				Female			
	1990	2000	2005	2008	1990	2000	2005	2008	1990	2000	2005	2008
Non-Hispanic White, total[3, 4]	**(NA)**	**(NA)**	**151.9**	**154.5**	**(NA)**	**(NA)**	**73.4**	**74.9**	**(NA)**	**(NA)**	**78.5**	**79.6**
Never married	(NA)	(NA)	31.8	34.0	(NA)	(NA)	17.8	19.1	(NA)	(NA)	13.9	14.9
Married[2]	(NA)	(NA)	93.5	92.7	(NA)	(NA)	46.6	46.3	(NA)	(NA)	47.0	46.3
Widowed	(NA)	(NA)	10.6	10.9	(NA)	(NA)	2.1	2.2	(NA)	(NA)	8.5	8.6
Divorced	(NA)	(NA)	16.0	16.9	(NA)	(NA)	6.8	7.3	(NA)	(NA)	9.2	9.6
Percent of total	**100.0**	**100.0**	**100.0**	**100.0**	**100.0**	**100.0**	**100.0**	**100.0**	**100.0**	**100.0**	**100.0**	**100.0**
Never married	(NA)	(NA)	20.9	22.0	(NA)	(NA)	24.3	25.5	(NA)	(NA)	17.7	18.8
Married[2]	(NA)	(NA)	61.5	60.0	(NA)	(NA)	63.5	61.8	(NA)	(NA)	59.7	58.2
Widowed	(NA)	(NA)	6.9	7.1	(NA)	(NA)	2.8	3.0	(NA)	(NA)	10.8	10.8
Divorced	(NA)	(NA)	10.6	10.9	(NA)	(NA)	9.3	9.7	(NA)	(NA)	11.7	12.1

NA Not available.
[1]Includes persons of other races not shown separately.
[2]Includes persons who are married with spouse present, married with spouse absent, and separated.
[3]Beginning 2005, data represent persons who selected this race group only and exclude persons reporting more than one race. The CPS in 1990 and 2000 only allowed respondents to report one race group.
[4]Hispanic persons may be any race.

SOURCE: U.S. Census Bureau, *Current Population Reports*, P20–537 and earlier reports; and "Families and Living Arrangements."

Table 15-2. *The percentage of African Americans who are married is far less than that of the U.S. population collectively.*

In 2009 the Family and Youth Services Bureau awarded $9.3 million to 209 mentoring programs nationwide. In keeping with the bureau's New Service Delivery Demonstration Program, participants may receive vouchers to take part in mentoring services. The goal is to help youngsters who have an incarcerated parent develop trusting relationships, receive healthy messages about life and social behavior, obtain appropriate guidance from a positive adult role model, and participate in educational, civic, and community activities. Many churches, sororities and fraternities, and other groups in the African American community offer mentoring services to help at-risk families and minimize the likelihood that children of incarcerated parents will turn to crime as a way of life.

Social scientists and others are examining the continuing prevalence of violence and crime by teenagers in some distressed African American communities. In Chicago, for example, a teenager was beaten to death by a group of other young people in a mob-like scene while returning home from school in September 2009. After photographs and cell phone videos of the incident were circulated widely, the issue of youth violence in Chicago received international attention. Questions were raised about how such unprovoked rage could arise, and how some persons could witness such a crime and not notify the authorities. Did this reflect the problems of a troubled and disturbed community that the children lived in every day?

The "stop snitchin'" code among some African American teenagers further complicates efforts to maintain safe communities. Persons who have knowledge of crimes are afraid to report them because they think that they, in turn, might be harmed by the perpetrators. This code is a source of great frustration for teenagers and also for law enforcement.

On the other hand, the election of Barack Obama as president of the United States in 2008 offered a clear, positive example of a successful African American family. The president's wife and daughters, along with his mother-in-law, present a beautiful representation of an intact, supportive African American family.

Many African American families try to maintain stability through family reunions. Families use these occasions to renew their ties and remember their kin through the generations. They inculcate their culture by passing along family traditions and sharing their love and respect for one another.

PROBLEMS OF CHILDREN AND YOUTH

The Southern Poverty Law Center (SPLC) highlighted problems juveniles in Mississippi were having with the criminal justice system.

The SPLC filed a lawsuit in the U.S. District Court on April 20, 2009, against Harrison County, Mississippi (*D. W., et al. v. Harrison County, Miss.*). The suit alleged that youths held in the Harrison County Detention Center were confined to unsanitary jail cells and subjected to physical

Barack and Michelle Obama, Washington, DC, 2009. *President Obama dances with the first lady at the Western Inaugural Ball.* CHIP SOMODEVILLA/UPI/LANDOV

and emotional abuse that violated their civil rights. Some cells were said to be overcrowded, which required some juveniles to sleep on thin mattresses on the floor. Most of those being held at the facility had not been found guilty of any crime and were awaiting court hearings. Further, children were forced to endure shackling and physical assaults by staff. Medical and mental health services were deemed inadequate for the young people. As a result of the conditions in which they were held, many contracted scabies and staphylococcal infections.

The plaintiff in the SPLC case was a seventeen-year-old boy who was forced to sleep on a concrete floor with a thin mat that smelled of urine. Even though the boy attempted suicide in his cell, detention center personnel did not provide mental health treatment or counseling for him. He was also harassed and assaulted by guards.

A settlement and agreement reached with Harrison County officials on September 30, 2009, provided guidelines for the use of restraints and force, and enhanced suicide prevention policies and practices. The agreement also included strategies for preventing overcrowding and outlined arrangements for proper supervision of detained youth.

The SPLC claims that juvenile justice and education reform are among the most pressing civil rights issues of the twenty-first century, noting that in Mississippi:

- The incarceration rate for African American children is double the rate for white children;
- The overwhelming majority of incarcerated juveniles are low-level, nonviolent offenders; and
- Almost 40 percent of public school children drop out, frequently because of ineffective discipline practices, the lack of appropriate special-education services and alternative education programs that do little more than warehouse children.

Many African American young people are thriving and doing well in stable, supportive homes. Their parents or guardians involve them in organizations that promote their growth and socialization, and they manage to steer clear of the criminal justice system and succeed in school. Some children, however, live in households that do not support their development and success in life. Even their day-to-day existence is a challenge. One of the most commonly cited factors causing childhood needs to remain unmet is poverty.

The U.S. Bureau of Labor Statistics reported that the rate of unemployment in September 2009 was 9.8 percent, which meant that overall the country was experiencing its highest rate of unemployment since 1983. The unemployment rate for African Americans was 15.4 percent, compared to 9 percent for whites. The largest job losses were in construction, manufacturing, retail trade, and government. A downturn in these areas has a major impact on the earning power of African American families and, therefore, affects the quality of life for African American children. The unemployment rate for African Americans continued to trend higher in December 2009, when it reached 16.2 percent, even as the overall unemployment rate reached 10.2 percent.

More and more children are living in impoverished households headed by single women. This situation is further complicated by the high rate of incarceration for African American males. The children of these imprisoned men are usually left in the care of their mother or another female relative. Grandparents also sometimes care for their grandchildren when their adult children are unable to do so. Reasons for this form of kinship care, other than incarceration, include illness, substance abuse, divorce, or the loss of a home.

Another issue is the need for adequate health care and nutrition for children. On February 4, 2009, President Obama signed into law the Children's Health Insurance Program Reauthorization Act, which took effect on April 1, 2009. The program is jointly financed by the federal and state governments and serves millions of children who otherwise would not be covered by health insurance.

Table 15-3: Key benefits available to children in poor and low-income families.

Category	Benefit
Income	Temporary Aid to Needy Families (TANF) Earned Income Tax Credit (EITC) State EITC Child Tax Credit Supplemental Security Income (SSI)
Health	Medicaid State Children's Insurance Program
Nutrition	Supplemental Nutrition Program for Women, Infants, and Children (WIC) Supplemental Nutrition Assistance Program (Food stamps) National school lunch and school breakfast programs
Early care and education	Child-care subsidies Head Start and Early Head Start
Housing	Housing subsidies Housing mobility programs

SOURCE: Rima Shore and Barbara Shore. *KIDS COUNT Indicator Brief: Reducing the Child Poverty Rate* (Baltimore, MD: Annie E. Casey Foundation, 2009).

Table 15-3. *A number of government programs are targeted specifically to assist children of low-income families.*

Women and children whose family incomes are at the poverty level and who have been determined by a health professional to be at nutritional risk may receive assistance from the Special Supplemental Nutrition Program for Women, Infants, and Children (WIC). This program is administered by the Food and Nutrition Service of the U.S. Department of Agriculture. Two major types of nutritional risk are recognized for WIC eligibility: (1) medical risks, such as anemia, underweight, overweight, history of pregnancy complications, or poor pregnancy outcomes; and (2) dietary risks, such as failure to meet dietary guidelines or inappropriate nutritional practices. Nutritional risk is determined by a health professional, such as a physician, nutritionist, or nurse, and is based on federal guidelines.

Foods covered by the WIC program include iron-fortified formula and cereal for infants, iron-fortified cereal for adults, fruit or vegetable juice that is rich in vitamin C, eggs, milk, cheese, peanut butter, dried beans and peas, and canned fish. Special therapeutic infant formulas and medical foods may be covered when prescribed by a physician. Soy-based beverages, tofu, fruits and vegetables, baby foods, whole-wheat bread, and other whole-grain foods are also included.

INFANT MORTALITY

In the United States, the rate of infant mortality for non-Hispanic blacks is more than double that for non-Hispanic whites, as shown in Table 15-4. Several factors may contribute to this disparity. Black women are more likely to receive no (or inadequate) prenatal care. In addition, the mother's lifestyle choices, such as alcohol consumption, other drug use, or smoking, may contribute to the likelihood that she will have a baby with a low birth weight.

LIFE EXPECTANCY

The term *life expectancy* refers to the number of years a person is expected to live based on statistical data that may include such considerations as age, race, and sex. In *Deaths: Preliminary Data for 2007* (2009), the Centers for Disease Control and Prevention (CDC) reported that the life expectancy for all groups in the United States, in the aggregate, had reached nearly seventy-eight years (77.9). The CDC also noted that the increase in life expectancy—up from 77.7 in 2006—represented a trend. Over a decade, life expectancy had increased 1.4 years from 76.5 years in 1997 to 77.9 in 2007. The CDC report further noted that for the first time, life expectancy for black American males reached seventy years.

ELDERLY AFRICAN AMERICANS

Although many African American families have limited resources, they are more likely to keep elderly relatives at home than place them in an institution. However, when it is necessary to place an elderly relative in an extended-care facility, the

Table 15-4. Infant Mortality Rates by Race—U.S. States: 1980 to 2006

[**Deaths per 1,000 live births, by place of residence**. Represents deaths of infants under 1 year old, exclusive of fetal deaths. Excludes deaths of nonresidents of the United States.]

	Total[1]				White				Black			
State	**1980**	**1990**	**2000**	**2006**	**1980**	**1990**	**2000**	**2006**	**1980**	**1990**	**2000**	**2006**
United States	**12.6**	**9.2**	**6.9**	**6.7**	**10.9**	**7.6**	**5.7**	**5.6**	**22.2**	**18.0**	**14.1**	**13.3**
Alabama	15.1	10.8	9.4	9.0	11.6	8.1	6.6	6.7	21.6	16.0	15.4	14.2
Alaska	12.3	10.5	6.8	6.9	9.4	7.6	5.8	4.5	19.5	(B)	(B)	(B)
Arizona	12.4	8.8	6.7	6.4	11.8	7.8	6.2	6.0	18.4	20.6	17.6	16.9
Arkansas	12.7	9.2	8.4	8.5	10.3	8.4	7.0	6.9	20.0	13.9	13.7	15.7
California	11.1	7.9	5.4	5.0	10.6	7.0	5.1	4.8	18.0	16.8	12.9	12.1
Colorado	10.1	8.8	6.2	5.7	9.8	7.8	5.6	5.5	19.1	19.4	19.5	12.4
Connecticut	11.2	7.9	6.6	6.2	10.2	6.3	5.6	4.9	19.1	17.6	14.4	14.8
Delaware	13.9	10.1	9.2	8.3	9.8	9.7	7.9	6.2	27.9	20.1	14.8	14.3
District of Columbia	25.0	20.7	12.0	11.3	17.8	(B)	(B)	(B)	26.7	24.6	16.1	14.5
Florida	14.6	9.6	7.0	7.3	11.8	6.7	5.4	5.9	22.8	16.8	12.6	11.9
Georgia	14.5	12.4	8.5	8.1	10.8	7.4	5.9	5.8	21.0	18.3	13.9	12.9
Hawaii	10.3	6.7	8.1	5.6	11.6	6.1	6.5	(B)	(B)	(B)	(B)	(B)
Idaho	10.7	8.7	7.5	6.8	10.7	8.6	7.5	6.7	(NA)	(B)	(B)	(B)
Illinois	14.8	10.7	8.5	7.3	11.7	7.9	6.6	6.0	26.3	22.4	17.1	13.7
Indiana	11.9	9.6	7.8	8.0	10.5	7.9	6.9	6.7	23.4	17.4	15.8	18.7
Iowa	11.8	8.1	6.5	5.1	11.5	7.9	6.0	4.9	27.2	21.9	21.1	(B)
Kansas	10.4	8.4	6.8	7.1	9.5	8.0	6.4	6.1	20.6	17.7	12.2	19.3
Kentucky	12.9	8.5	7.2	7.5	12.0	8.2	6.7	6.8	22.0	14.3	12.7	15.0
Louisiana	14.3	11.1	9.0	9.9	10.5	8.1	5.9	6.2	20.6	16.7	13.3	15.8
Maine	9.2	6.2	4.9	6.3	9.4	6.7	4.8	6.2	(B)	(B)	(B)	(B)
Maryland	14.0	9.5	7.6	8.0	11.6	6.8	4.8	6.0	20.4	17.1	13.2	11.8
Massachusetts	10.5	7.0	4.6	4.8	10.1	6.1	4.0	4.6	16.8	11.9	9.9	8.0
Michigan	12.8	10.7	8.2	7.4	10.6	7.4	6.0	5.8	24.2	21.6	18.2	14.9
Minnesota	10.0	7.3	5.6	5.2	9.6	6.7	4.8	4.7	20.0	23.7	14.6	8.3
Mississippi	17.0	12.1	10.7	10.6	11.1	7.4	6.8	7.1	23.7	16.2	15.3	14.6
Missouri	12.4	9.4	7.2	7.4	11.1	7.9	5.9	6.1	20.7	18.2	14.7	14.9
Montana	12.4	9.0	6.1	5.8	11.8	6.0	5.5	5.0	(NA)	(B)	(B)	(B)
Nebraska	11.5	8.3	7.3	5.6	10.7	6.9	6.4	5.2	25.2	18.9	20.3	10.6
Nevada	10.7	8.4	6.5	6.4	10.0	8.2	6.0	5.8	20.6	14.2	12.7	15.7
New Hampshire	9.9	7.1	5.7	6.1	9.9	6.0	5.5	5.7	22.5	(B)	(B)	(B)
New Jersey	12.5	9.0	6.3	5.5	10.3	6.4	5.0	4.4	21.9	18.4	13.6	11.5
New Mexico	11.5	9.0	6.6	5.8	11.3	7.6	6.3	5.7	23.1	(B)	(B)	(B)
New York	12.5	9.6	6.4	5.6	10.8	7.4	5.4	4.9	20.0	18.1	10.9	9.2
North Carolina	14.5	10.6	8.6	8.1	12.1	8.0	6.3	6.0	20.0	16.5	15.7	15.1
North Dakota	12.1	8.0	8.1	5.8	11.7	7.2	7.5	4.9	27.5	(B)	(B)	(B)
Ohio	12.8	9.8	7.6	7.8	11.2	7.8	6.3	6.1	23.0	19.5	15.4	16.9
Oklahoma	12.7	9.2	8.5	8.0	12.1	9.1	7.9	6.8	21.8	14.3	16.9	15.4
Oregon	12.2	8.3	5.6	5.5	12.2	7.0	5.5	5.3	15.9	(B)	(B)	(B)
Pennsylvania	13.2	9.6	7.1	7.6	11.9	7.4	5.8	6.2	23.1	20.5	15.7	15.2
Rhode Island	11.0	8.1	6.3	6.1	10.9	7.0	5.9	5.7	(B)	(B)	(B)	(B)
South Carolina	15.6	11.7	8.7	8.4	10.8	8.1	5.4	5.7	22.9	17.3	14.8	13.8
South Dakota	10.9	10.1	5.5	6.9	9.0	8.0	4.3	5.3	(NA)	(B)	(B)	(B)
Tennessee	13.5	10.3	9.1	8.7	11.9	7.3	6.8	6.8	19.3	17.9	18.0	16.0
Texas	12.2	8.1	5.7	6.2	11.2	6.7	5.1	5.5	18.8	14.7	11.4	12.0
Utah	10.4	7.5	5.2	5.1	10.5	6.0	5.1	5.1	27.3	(B)	(B)	(B)
Vermont	10.7	6.4	6.0	5.5	10.7	5.9	6.1	5.6	(B)	(B)	(B)	(B)
Virginia	13.6	10.2	6.9	7.1	11.9	7.4	5.4	5.4	19.8	19.5	12.4	13.3
Washington	11.8	7.8	5.2	4.7	11.5	7.3	4.9	4.4	16.4	20.6	9.4	7.4
West Virginia	11.8	9.9	7.6	7.4	11.4	8.1	7.4	6.7	21.5	(B)	(B)	28.6
Wisconsin	10.3	8.2	6.6	6.4	9.7	7.7	5.5	5.0	18.5	19.0	17.2	18.3
Wyoming	9.8	8.6	6.7	7.0	9.3	7.5	6.5	6.6	25.9	(B)	(B)	(B)
Puerto Rico	(NA)	(NA)	9.7	8.8	(NA)	(NA)	10.2	9.5	(NA)	(NA)	(B)	(B)
Virgin Islands	(NA)	(NA)	13.4	(B)	(NA)	(NA)	(B)	(B)	(B)	(B)	(B)	(B)
Guam	(NA)	(NA)	5.8	13.3	(NA)	(NA)	(B)	(B)	(B)	(B)	(B)	(B)
American Samoa	(NA)	(NA)	(B)	(B)	(B)	(B)	(B)	(B)	(B)	(B)	(B)	(B)
Northern Marianas	(NA)	(NA)	(B)	(B)	(B)	(B)	(B)	(B)	(B)	(B)	(B)	(B)

B Base figure too small to meet statistical standards for reliability.
NA Not available.
[1]Includes other races, not shown separately.

SOURCE: U.S. National Center for Health Statistics, National Vital Statistics Reports (NVSR), *Deaths: Final Data for 2006*, Vol. 57. No. 14, April 17, 2009 and earlier reports.

Table 15-4. *U.S. mortality rates for African American infants are more than double those for white babies.*

Table 15-5. Expectation of Life at Birth, 1970 to 2006, and Projections, 2010 to 2020

[**In years.** Excludes deaths of nonresidents of the United States.]

Year	Total			White			Black		
	Total	Male	Female	Total	Male	Female	Total	Male	Female
1970	70.8	67.1	74.7	71.7	68.0	75.6	64.1	60.0	68.3
1975	72.6	68.8	76.6	73.4	69.5	77.3	66.8	62.4	71.3
1980	73.7	70.0	77.4	74.4	70.7	78.1	68.1	63.8	72.5
1981	74.1	70.4	77.8	74.8	71.1	78.4	68.9	64.5	73.2
1982	74.5	70.8	78.1	75.1	71.5	78.7	69.4	65.1	73.6
1983	74.6	71.0	78.1	75.2	71.6	78.7	69.4	65.2	73.5
1984	74.7	71.1	78.2	75.3	71.8	78.7	69.5	65.3	73.6
1985	74.7	71.1	78.2	75.3	71.8	78.7	69.3	65.0	73.4
1986	74.7	71.2	78.2	75.4	71.9	78.8	69.1	64.8	73.4
1987	74.9	71.4	78.3	75.6	72.1	78.9	69.1	64.7	73.4
1988	74.9	71.4	78.3	75.6	72.2	78.9	68.9	64.4	73.2
1989	75.1	71.7	78.5	75.9	72.5	79.2	68.8	64.3	73.3
1990	75.4	71.8	78.8	76.1	72.7	79.4	69.1	64.5	73.6
1991	75.5	72.0	78.9	76.3	72.9	79.6	69.3	64.6	73.8
1992	75.8	72.3	79.1	76.5	73.2	79.8	69.6	65.0	73.9
1993	75.5	72.2	78.8	76.3	73.1	79.5	69.2	64.6	73.7
1994	75.7	72.4	79.0	76.5	73.3	79.6	69.5	64.9	73.9
1995	75.8	72.5	78.9	76.5	73.4	79.6	69.6	65.2	73.9
1996	76.1	73.1	79.1	76.8	73.9	79.7	70.2	66.1	74.2
1997	76.5	73.6	79.4	77.2	74.3	79.9	71.1	67.2	74.7
1998	76.7	73.8	79.5	77.3	74.5	80.0	71.3	67.6	74.8
1999	76.7	73.9	79.4	77.3	74.6	79.9	71.4	67.8	74.7
2000[1]	76.8	74.1	79.3	77.3	74.7	79.9	71.8	68.2	75.1
2001[1]	76.9	74.2	79.4	77.4	74.8	79.9	72.0	68.4	75.2
2002[1]	76.9	74.3	79.5	77.4	74.9	79.9	72.1	68.6	75.4
2003[1, 2]	77.1	74.5	79.6	77.6	75.0	80.0	72.3	68.8	75.6
2004[1, 2]	77.5	74.9	79.9	77.9	75.4	80.4	72.8	69.3	76.0
2005[1, 2]	77.4	74.9	79.9	77.9	75.4	80.4	72.8	69.3	76.1
2006[1, 2]	77.7	75.1	80.2	78.2	75.7	80.6	73.2	69.7	76.5
Projections:[3]									
2010	78.3	75.7	80.8	78.9	76.5	81.3	73.8	70.2	77.2
2015	78.9	76.4	81.4	79.5	77.1	81.8	75.0	71.4	78.2
2020	79.5	77.1	81.9	80.0	77.7	82.4	76.1	72.6	79.2

[1] Life expectancies for 2000–2006 were calculated using a revised methodology and may differ from those previously published.
[2] Multiple-race data were reported by 25 states and the District of Columbia in 2006, by 21 states and the District of Columbia in 2005, by 15 states in 2004, and by 7 states in 2003. The multiple-race data for these reporting areas were bridged to the single-race categories of the 1977 OMB standards for comparability with other reporting areas.
[3] Based on middle mortality assumptions; for details, see source. Source: U.S Census Bureau, 2008 National Population Projections, released August, 2008.

SOURCE: Except as noted, U.S. National Center for Health Statistics, National Vital Statistics Reports (NVSR), *Deaths: Final Data for 2006*, Vol. 57, No. 14, April 17, 2009.

Table 15-5. *Life expectancy has risen dramatically for African Americans since 1970.*

care they receive is often substandard. Whereas 40 percent of those in substandard nursing homes are African American, 9 percent of residents in those particular homes are white (Carol Forsloff, "Racial Disparities in Senior Care Might Mean Separate and Unequal," *Digital Journal* [March 11, 2009]).

Before accepting placement at a facility for the elderly, it is especially important to ensure that the nursing home is licensed by the state and will be monitored by state inspectors. Relatives should also check the appearance of other residents. Are they engaged in activities? Are there opportunities for privacy? What are the visiting hours? Is the facility near enough so that family can visit? Is there an ombudsman for solving client problems? What are the arrangements for any kind of therapy the relative requires? Are the meals and menus acceptable? Relatives should also check with the state health department for information on problems that inspectors may have noted with the facility.

It is possible to live an enjoyable, fulfilling life in one's later years with the assistance of family and community. Staying engaged with religious and social groups seems to enhance the quality of life and delay the loss of cognition. Taking good care of oneself during one's younger years helps to ensure a high quality of life as one ages.

ENVIRONMENTAL HEALTH

There is a high correlation between pollution—air, water, and soil pollution—and health status. Health problems often associated with environmental hazards include asthma, lead poisoning, cancer, and infections. In addition, infertility, birth defects, miscarriages, and neurological deficits may be linked to environmental pollution. Unfortunately, many toxic dumps and hazardous-waste sites are located in or near African American communities. The "not in my back yard" mantra of influential residents in high- and middle-income neighborhoods often leads to the placement of hazardous-waste sites in areas where impoverished African Americans live. It is postulated that persons residing in such polluted neighborhoods are politically powerless and, therefore, vulnerable to exploitation. The practice of locating hazardous-waste sites or discarded pollutants in vulnerable neighborhoods is referred to as *environmental racism*.

In *Toxic Wastes and Race at Twenty* (2007), Clark Atlanta University professor of sociology Robert Bullard and his colleagues noted that people of color made up the majority (56%) of those living in neighborhoods within 1.8 miles of commercial hazardous waste facilities in the United States. Bullard's study concluded that: (1) racial and socioeconomic disparities in the location of the nation's hazardous waste facilities are geographically widespread throughout the country; (2) people of color are concentrated in neighborhoods and communities with the greatest number of hazardous waste facilities, and by 2007 were more concentrated in areas with commercial hazardous waste sites than in 1987; and (3) race continues to be a significant independent predictor of the locations of commercial hazardous waste facilities when socioeconomic and other nonracial factors are taken into account.

The U.S. Environmental Protection Agency (EPA) defines *environmental justice* as "the fair treatment and meaningful involvement of all people regardless of race, color, culture, national origin, income, and educational levels with respect to the development, implementation, and enforcement of protective environmental laws, regulations and policies." In 1992, in response to public concern, the Office of Environmental Justice was established within the EPA. This office is responsible for the integration of environmental justice into policies, programs, and activities throughout the EPA. It also serves as the lead on the federal interagency working group that endeavors to incorporate environmental justice into all federal programs.

On February 11, 1994, President Bill Clinton issued Executive Order 12898, which was intended to focus federal attention on the environmental and human health conditions of minority and low-income citizens, with the goal of achieving environmental protection for all communities. The order directed federal agencies to develop environmental justice strategies to identify and correct adverse human health or environmental effects resulting from government programs, policies, and activities, especially those with a disproportionate impact on minority and low-income populations.

The Deep South Center for Environmental Justice at Dillard University in New Orleans was founded in 1992. Under the guidance of its director, Beverly H. Wright, a sociologist and environmentalist, the center provides opportunities for researchers and community decision makers to work together to achieve environmental justice, particularly in New Orleans's at-risk neighborhoods. Even before Hurricane Katrina hit the Gulf Coast in 2005, the 85-mile petrochemical corridor between Baton Rouge and New Orleans was known as Cancer Alley because of the area's high level of industrial pollutants and the high incidence of cancer among its residents. Wright strongly advocated for environmental justice in Cancer Alley, using collaboration strategies, publications, and speeches to unite people in their struggle for a safe, toxin-free environment.

Hurricane Katrina left New Orleans with broken levees, destroyed sewage systems, and polluted water. Wright and Bullard noted in "Cleaning Up Toxic 'Time Bombs' Left Behind by Katrina" (*FOCUS Magazine* 34, no. 10 [2006]: 15–16) that "Katrina caused six major oil spills that released a total of 7.4 million gallons of oil.... The storm hit 60 underground storage tanks, five Superfund sites, and 466 industrial facilities that stored highly dangerous chemicals." Responsibility for cleaning up the storm's "toxic soup" rested primarily with the U.S. Army Corps of Engineers, but citizen groups also became involved in making New Orleans a safer, more habitable place to which displaced persons could return. The Deep South Center for Environmental Justice played a key role in the effort.

In 2009 President Obama appointed Lisa P. Jackson as EPA administrator. Jackson, who grew up in New Orleans and earned a master's degree in chemical engineering from Princeton University, is the first African American to hold that position. According to the EPA, Jackson made it "a priority to focus on vulnerable groups including children, the elderly, and low-income communities that are particularly susceptible to environmental and health threats. In addressing these and other issues, she has promised all stakeholders a place at the decision making table." The catastrophic crude oil spill in the Gulf of Mexico, which began in April 2010 as a result of an explosion on an oil-drilling rig, presented major challenges for Jackson and the EPA. The agency conducted continual testing of the area's water, air, and soil. It collaborated with other governmental organizations and nongovernmental interests to protect human health as well as the environment from the oil and also from the chemicals used to clean up the record-breaking spill.

In October 2009, environmental activists met in Atlanta with Region Four EPA officials (Region Four is composed of Alabama, Florida, Georgia, Kentucky, Mississippi, North and South Carolina, Tennessee, and Indian tribes from this area) to demand that the agency be revamped to better meet the needs of vulnerable communities. The primarily African American group, under the leadership of Robert Bullard, represented six southern states (Alabama, Florida, Georgia, Mississippi, South Carolina, and Tennessee). It included community activists, environmental attorneys, and families affected by chemical waste. On leaving the meeting, however, some attendees stated that little had been accomplished.

Lead poisoning is common among children who have lived in older buildings with lead-based paint, which children can inhale or ingest. Such buildings are often located in inner-city neighborhoods. Children may also encounter lead-based paint on toys, especially cheaper toys made in countries with guidelines that are not as strict as those in the United States. Both children and adults can also be exposed to lead in the atmosphere, water, and soil.

Lead is not easily removed from the body because it is a heavy metal. In children, it can cause weight loss, abdominal pain, learning difficulties, anemia, irritability, and vomiting. In some cases, lead poisoning can cause death. The symptoms in adults are muscular weakness, abdominal pain, memory loss, mood disorders, reduced sperm count for men, and miscarriages for women. Lead poisoning is classified as mild, moderate, or severe, based on the level of lead in the bloodstream.

HEALTH DISPARITIES

The phrase *health disparities* refers to differences in incidence and outcomes related to health problems among particular groups of people. According to *Health Disparities: A Case for Closing the Gap* (2009), a report issued by the Office of Health Reform of the U.S. Department of Health and Human Services (HHS), 48 percent of African American adults suffer from a chronic disease, compared to 39 percent of the general population.

A federal program known as Healthy People 2010 outlined a set of health objectives for the United States to achieve between 2000 to 2010. It built on earlier reports and goals, including a 1979 surgeon general's report titled *Healthy People*, as well as *Healthy People 2000: National Health Promotion and Disease Prevention Objectives*, released in 1990 by the Public Health Service. Both of these publications served as the basis for state- and community-level plans for the improvement of health indicators. Healthy People 2010 incorporated input from many experts in disease treatment and prevention. The program was managed by the HHS Office of Disease Prevention and Health Promotion and was designed to have measurable outcomes. The two overarching goals for Healthy People 2010 were: (1) increase quality and years of healthy life; and (2) eliminate health disparities.

The Healthy People 2010 goals were used by states and other health-focused organizations as a basis for their own projects, goals, and objectives. The extent to which those goals and objectives were met was evaluated throughout the ten-year time frame. Summary data might not be available until final data are collected and analyzed after 2010.

The initial framework and objectives for healthy people 2020 have been developed. They reflect assessments of major determinants of health and wellness. Input was solicited from citizens and professional groups and from experts for science-based ideas to improve the nation's health. The objectives cover a wide range of health needs and problems. They can be viewed online at http://www.healthypeople.gov/healthypeople2020.

In an effort to enhance the health of the overall population and address the continuing problem of health disparities, President Obama nominated Dr. Regina Benjamin for the position of surgeon general of the United States. Dr. Benjamin is a family practice physician who has spent most of her career attending to the needs of poor clients at the Bayou La Batre Rural Health Clinic, which she founded in 1987. Because Benjamin's clinic is on the Gulf Coast of Alabama, it was heavily damaged by Hurricane George in 1998 and Hurricane Katrina in 2005. The clinic also suffered fire damage in 2006, but Benjamin rebuilt it after each catastrophe. Her dedication to the community and to her clients is well respected.

According to the Office of Minority Health and Health Disparities at the CDC, the ten leading causes of death among African Americans in 2006 were:

1. heart disease
2. cancer
3. stroke
4. unintentional [accidents]
5. diabetes
6. homicide
7. nephritis, nephrotic syndrome, nephrosis (kidney disease)
8. chronic lower respiratory disease
9. HIV/AIDS
10. septicemia (bacteria in the blood)

The mortality rate is linked to many factors, but especially to the availability of health-care coverage. According to

Table 15-6. U.S. Health Insurance Coverage Status by Selected Characteristics: 2006 and 2007

[(296,824 represents 296,824,000). Persons as of following year for coverage in the year shown. Government health insurance includes Medicare, Medicaid, and military plans. Based on Current Population Survey, Annual Social and Economic Supplement (ASES). As of March.]

	Number (1,000)							Percent			
		Covered by private or government health insurance						Covered by private or government health insurance			
			Private		Government						
Characteristic	Total persons	Total[1]	Total	Group health[2]	Medicare	Medicaid	Not covered by health insurance	Total[1]	Private	Medicaid	Not covered by health insurance
2006[3]	**296,824**	**249,829**	**201,690**	**177,152**	**40,343**	**38,281**	**46,995**	**84.2**	**67.9**	**12.9**	**15.8**
2007	**299,106**	**253,449**	**201,991**	**177,446**	**41,375**	**39,554**	**45,657**	**84.7**	**67.5**	**13.2**	**15.3**
Age:											
Under 18 years	74,403	66,254	47,750	44,252	518	20,899	8,149	89.0	64.2	28.1	11.0
Under 6 years	24,944	22,326	14,793	13,971	235	8,364	2,618	89.5	59.3	33.5	10.5
6 to 11 years	23,820	21,355	15,567	14,621	138	6,604	2,465	89.7	65.4	27.7	10.3
12 to 17 years	25,639	22,573	17,391	15,661	145	5,932	3,066	88.0	67.8	23.1	12.0
18 to 24 years	28,398	20,407	17,074	13,747	180	3,563	7,991	71.9	60.1	12.5	28.1
25 to 34 years	40,146	29,817	26,430	24,505	501	3,237	10,329	74.3	65.8	8.1	25.7
35 to 44 years	42,132	34,415	31,067	29,009	924	3,027	7,717	81.7	73.7	7.2	18.3
45 to 54 years	43,935	37,161	33,350	30,805	1,795	3,103	6,774	84.6	75.9	7.1	15.4
55 to 64 years	33,302	29,291	25,114	22,569	3,179	2,462	4,011	88.0	75.4	7.4	12.0
65 years and over	36,790	36,103	21,206	12,558	34,278	3,263	686	98.1	57.6	8.9	1.9
Sex:											
Male	146,855	122,309	99,180	88,077	17,943	17,976	24,546	83.3	67.5	12.2	16.7
Female	152,250	131,140	102,811	89,369	23,431	21,578	21,111	86.1	67.5	14.2	13.9
Race:											
White alone[4]	239,399	205,099	167,905	146,398	35,117	27,172	34,300	85.7	70.1	11.4	14.3
Black alone[4]	37,775	30,403	20,169	18,525	4,303	8,986	7,372	80.5	53.4	23.8	19.5
Asian alone[4]	13,268	11,034	9,067	8,107	1,195	1,528	2,234	83.2	68.3	11.5	16.8
Hispanic origin[5]	46,026	31,256	20,194	18,551	2,887	10,348	14,770	67.9	43.9	22.5	32.1
Household income:											
Less than $25,000	55,267	41,728	16,650	10,325	15,822	18,976	13,539	75.5	30.1	34.3	24.5
$25,000–$49,999	68,915	54,400	39,742	33,099	12,567	11,436	14,515	78.9	57.7	16.6	21.1
$50,000–$74,999	58,355	49,867	43,967	39,782	5,779	4,730	8,488	85.5	75.3	8.1	14.5
$75,000 or more	116,568	107,453	101,633	94,240	7,207	4,412	9,115	92.2	87.2	3.8	7.8
Persons below poverty	37,276	25,741	7,893	5,076	5,106	16,247	11,535	69.1	21.2	43.6	30.9

[1]Includes other government insurance not shown separately. Persons with coverage counted only once in total, even though they may have been covered by more than one type of policy.
[2]Related to employment of self or other family members.
[3]The estimates are revised from the originally published data.
[4]Refers to people who reported specified race and did not report any other race category.
[5]Persons of Hispanic origin may be any race.

SOURCE: U.S. Census Bureau, Current Population Reports; Income, Poverty, and Health Insurance Coverage in the United States: 2007, P60–235; issued August 2008. Table HI01 Health Insurance Data, Health Insurance Coverage Status and Type of Coverage by Selected Characteristics: 2007. Table HI02. Health Insurance Coverage Status and Type of Coverage by Selected Characteristics for People in the Poverty Universe: 2007.

Table 15-6. *According to U.S. census data, the percentage of African Americans not covered by any form of health insurance exceeds the national average.*

the U.S. Census Bureau, the uninsured rate for African Americans in 2008 was 19.1 percent, compared to 10.8 percent for non-Hispanic whites. With the economic downturn, more African Americans were living in poverty in 2009, and even fewer families had access to health care because of lost jobs. Therefore, the effect of denied health care was felt even more acutely.

A 2009 study conducted by researchers at Harvard Medical School and the Cambridge Health Alliance determined that an estimated 45,000 deaths each year are associated with a lack of health insurance (Andrew Wilper et al., "Health Insurance and Mortality in US Adults," *American Journal of Public Health* 99, no. 12 [December 2009]: 2289–2295). The study controlled for such factors as exercise, smoking, and drinking, making its findings more credible, especially in light of the fact that 7.3 million African Americans lived without health-care coverage in 2008. Many of these deaths could have been prevented if the individuals had been insured. This fact helped to generate public demand for a government-sponsored health-care plan that is available to all U.S. citizens and permanent residents.

Because health-care reform was a central part of the platform on which Barack Obama ran for president, the discussion on the need for a change in the health-care system continued during his first year in office. Some of the points for discussion were:

1. Is health care a right or a privilege?
2. How much can the government afford to pay for health care?
3. What is the role of insurance and pharmaceutical companies in health care?

The highly partisan debate continued in the Congress, where some legislators made efforts to craft a more equitable health-care system. Polls indicated that many respondents preferred a "public option" that would serve as a competitor to plans provided by commercial insurance companies, thereby encouraging them to lower their fees. This structure would also allow far more African Americans to be covered by health insurance than are currently covered.

COMMON HEALTH PROBLEMS AMONG AFRICAN AMERICANS

ASTHMA

Low-income groups, minorities, and children who live in inner cities are more likely to visit hospital emergency rooms, to be hospitalized, or to die from asthma than the general population. This breathing problem, which is not clearly understood, seems to result from a reaction to specific allergens. It can also occur without an identifiable reason. Causes that can be identified include tobacco smoke, furry or feathered animals, dust mites, certain molds, and chemicals.

CDC data from 2005 through 2007 indicate that non-Hispanic African American and Puerto Rican children had higher incidences of asthma than non-Hispanic white children. Nine percent of non-Hispanic African American children and 15.6 percent of Puerto Rican children suffered from asthma, whereas only 7.7 percent of non-Hispanic white children had the disease.

CANCER

Cancer refers to a large group of potentially life-threatening disorders characterized by abnormal cell growth and spread. Cancer has a multiplicity of causes, and more treatment options have become available in recent years.

According to the CDC, African Americans are 50 percent more likely to develop and die of cancer than any other racial group. In 2004 the incidence of cancer in African American men was 607.3 per 100,000, compared to 527.2 per 100,000 in the white male population, which is a significant disparity. For most types of cancer, African Americans have the highest death rate and shortest survival of any racial and ethnic group in the United States. According to the American Cancer Society's *Cancer Facts & Figures for African Americans, 2007–2008*, the most common form of cancer in African American men is prostate cancer (see Table 15-7), while the most common form of cancer in African American women is breast cancer (see Table 15-8).

Research led by Edith Mitchell and Gloria Morris at Jefferson Medical College of Thomas Jefferson University in Philadelphia revealed that African American women are more likely to have later-stage and higher-grade breast tumors at diagnosis. This means that African American women's breast

Table 15-7: New cancer cases per 100,000 men (2005).

Cancer	All Men	African American Men	Non-Hispanic White Men
All Sites	510.1	587.6	538.0
Stomach	11.0	16.6	8.5
Lung	68.7	93.6	72.2
Prostate	147.1	220.3	145.3
Pancreas	13.0	16.8	13.0
Colon and Rectum	52.8	62.7	53.7

SOURCE: CDC.

Table 15-7. *As these 2005 data from the Centers for Disease Control and Prevention indicate, African American men have a higher incidence of all forms of cancer than white men in the United States.*

Table 15-8: New cancer cases per 100,000 women (2005).

Cancer	All Women	African American Women	Non-Hispanic White Women
All Sites	396.7	394.9	430.1
Stomach	5.5	7.7	3.6
Cervical	7.7	8.7	6.2
Pancreas	10.3	15.3	10.1
Colon and Rectum	40.3	51.4	40.6
Breast	121.5	113.9	133.6

SOURCE: CDC.

Table 15-8. *African American women have a lower rate of cancer generally, and breast cancer more specifically, than white women in the United States, according to these 2005 data from the Centers for Disease Control and Prevention.*

tumors are more aggressive and invasive than those of white women. In addition, the researchers found that breast tumors in African American women had characteristics that predicted worse prognoses and poorer outcomes.

According to the National Cancer Institute, whites have a higher survival rate for all types of cancer. This disparity is thought to be reflective of differences in socioeconomic status, education, workplace and environmental factors, and access to health care, as well as overall living standards. Because of a lack of timely access to health care, many cancers are diagnosed too late for treatment and management for optimum survival. Cancer screening continues to be recommended by most caregivers as the best way to prevent cancer from occurring and spreading to other parts of the body.

DIABETES

Diabetes mellitus is a chronic metabolic disorder that affects several physiologic systems, the most critical of which is glucose metabolism, with altered fat and protein metabolism.

Type 1 Diabetes Mellitus. Genetic, autoimmune, and environmental factors are involved in the development of this type of diabetes. This form of the disease is sometimes referred to as juvenile-onset diabetes. It requires insulin injections for management.

Type 2 Diabetes Mellitus. This type of diabetes is sometimes referred to as maturity-onset diabetes or non-insulin-dependent diabetes. It can occur at any age, but usually becomes apparent after age forty. There is a strong causal relationship between type 2 diabetes and obesity. Other risk factors include physical inactivity and a family history of diabetes.

Gestational Diabetes. Gestational diabetes occurs in some women during pregnancy. It is common among African American women, and must be managed during pregnancy to prevent harm to the baby.

H1N1 OR SWINE FLU

When outbreaks of H1N1 influenza, also known as swine flu, arose in the United States in 2009, experts observed that in some cities more African Americans and Hispanics acquired the disease than did other groups. For example, in fall 2009, the Boston Public Health Commission reported that 37 percent of all swine flu cases in Boston occurred among African Americans, although the African American population accounted for only 25 percent of Boston's total population. Similarly, Hispanics, who constituted 14 percent of Boston's population, accounted for 33 percent of all confirmed swine flu cases in the city. The hardest-hit areas of Boston were largely populated by minorities.

In addition, by the time children arrived at the hospitals for care, they were usually in a crisis stage because they had not been seen earlier when intervention would have been most effective. The *Boston Globe* reported on August 18, 2009, that the children's lack of earlier care was probably due to their lack of health insurance. This factor led to a higher mortality rate for children from swine flu in Boston. Health experts postulated that such swine flu disparities might also result from parents' inability to stay home from work to care for their children, so that sick children went to school and spread the disease. Other experts attributed the disparity to crowded living conditions. Boston and CDC health authorities promised to monitor the situation and study it for further implications for the nation's health.

HIV/AIDS

The presence in the body of the human immunodeficiency virus (HIV) is a chronic disease that is associated with progressive deterioration of the immune system. The first stage after exposure to the virus is described as HIV infection. It is manifested by the appearance of HIV antibodies in the blood, usually within six to twelve weeks after exposure. The stage from the initial HIV infection, usually without symptoms, to a diagnosis of acquired immunodeficiency syndrome (AIDS) is referred to as HIV/AIDS. Because of their immunodeficiency, those with HIV/AIDS are susceptible to several severe opportunistic infections.

According to the CDC, while African Americans constituted only 12 percent of the U.S. population by the end of 2006, they represented a higher proportion of cases at all stages of HIV/AIDS—from initial infection to death—compared to members of other races and ethnicities. In 2007 African Americans accounted for 51 percent of the 42,655 newly diagnosed HIV/AIDS cases (including children) in the thirty-four states that collected such data. African Americans accounted for 48 percent of the 551,932 persons (including children) living with HIV/AIDS in these states. For African American women with HIV/AIDS, the most common methods of transmission were high-risk heterosexual contact and injectable-drug use. For African American men, the most common methods of HIV transmission were sexual contact with other men, followed by injectable-drug use and high-risk heterosexual contact.

Although HIV/AIDS was initially identified in 1981 among white homosexual males, it is now occurring more frequently among African Americans. In 2007 the rates of AIDS diagnoses decreased among African Americans, but they were still higher than those of any other ethnic group in the country. Risk factors that make HIV/AIDS more prevalent within the African American community are interrelated and multifaceted, but include the use of intravenous drugs and needle sharing.

African American women who have unprotected sex with men who have had sex with other men (whether situationally, as with a formerly incarcerated man, or with a man who has sex with men and women routinely) are causing an increase in the incidence of HIV/AIDS among black women.

This situation is complicated by the fact that men who are in the latter category often do not wish to disclose their sexual practices to their heterosexual partners (in some cases their wives), which puts the women at greater risk. In addition, because of the large number of incarcerated African American men, the number of black males available for sexual relationships has declined. This poses a problem for African American women who seek intimate relationships with African American men.

HYPERTENSION AND STROKE

Blood pressure is the force of blood flow in the blood vessels as it moves throughout the body. When blood pressure rises above normal limits, it is referred to as *hypertension*, and the heart has to work harder to supply all parts of the body with blood and oxygen and to help other organs perform their metabolic functions. A person with hypertension is at risk for associated problems, such as heart attack, stroke, kidney disease, and impaired vision. Hypertension is known as the "silent killer" because it can occur with few warning signs.

According to the National Stroke Association, one in three African Americans suffers from hypertension, which means a predisposition to strokes and other diseases. African Americans are also twice as likely to die of strokes as whites. Further, first strokes tend to occur earlier in life for African Americans than for whites. The numbers are devastating when one considers that half of all African American women will die of stroke or heart disease.

SICKLE-CELL ANEMIA

Sickle-cell anemia occurs predominately in African Americans. It is an inherited form of anemia; about one in every ten black Americans has the sickle-cell trait, and approximately one out of every five hundred has sickle-cell anemia. People with sickle-cell anemia do not have enough healthy red blood cells to carry sufficient oxygen throughout the body to help it perform other metabolic functions.

Red blood cells are normally round and move easily through the blood vessels. But people with sickle-cell anemia have sickle- or crescent-shaped red blood cells, which cannot move readily through the blood vessels. Sickle-shaped cells can block the flow of blood in some vessels and interfere with the distribution of oxygen throughout the body. People with sickle-cell anemia are prone to episodes of pain, jaundice, infection, and impaired vision. The first symptom is often swollen hands and feet. There is no cure for sickle-cell anemia but symptoms can be managed with appropriate treatment.

In 2004, the Sickle Cell Disease Association of America named Willarda V. Edwards as its president and chief operating officer. The organization aims to find a universal cure for the disease and to improve the quality of life for those who live with the condition. Five years later, Edwards was selected to be the 110th president of the National Medical Association, an organization that promotes the health interests of African American physicians and their patients. In her installation speech, she pledged to reduce health-care disparities, increase the pipeline for minority physicians, and promote cultural competence.

Willarda V. Edwards, 2004. *On January 21, 2004, as president of the Maryland State Medical Society (MedChi), Edwards participated in a rally by Maryland doctors calling for tort reform. In 2009 she became president of the National Medical Association.* AP PHOTO/DON WRIGHT

PROMOTING HEALTHY LIFESTYLES

Unnecessary and preventable deaths can be decreased through the promotion and adoption of healthy lifestyles. This approach involves community health education and collaboration with community groups and individuals. Resources such as media, organizations, and community leaders cooperate to encourage citizens to incorporate into their daily lives strategies to help them live more healthfully. The central components of healthier living include nutrition, exercise, smoking cessation, stress management, and avoidance of addictive substances, such as alcohol and other drugs.

NUTRITION

Obesity is a significant problem among African Americans, for whom obesity has reached epidemic levels. In 2009 the CDC reported that African American women were more obese than any other gender or racial group. Among African American adults overall, 78 percent of women and 60 percent of men were obese. "Overweight" is usually described as body mass index (BMI) at or above the sex-and-age-specific ninety-fifth percentile cutoff as calculated by the CDC's National Health Examination Survey.

Only a small percentage of the human population can eat whatever they like without much change in their body weight. However, because of their genes, some people have a very difficult time losing weight. The traditional African American diet is high in calories from fat, usually animal fat from such foods as pork. The typical African American diet is also high in sodium, since foods like ham and sausages are preserved with salt. However, traditional African American recipes can be altered to make them more in keeping with a healthy lifestyle. For example, substituting smoked turkey for smoked pork can help lower one's saturated fat intake. A nutritionist can help modify recipes so that they retain their cultural appeal but are more healthfully prepared.

People living in inner-city neighborhoods often do not have access to fresh fruits and vegetables, which form the cornerstone of a nutritious diet. In light of this challenge, some urban communities have started their own gardening projects that can produce enough vegetables for the gardeners and sometimes enough to share with others. One notable urban garden was planted in 2009 at the White House by First Lady Michelle Obama with the help of Washington, D.C., schoolchildren. The project cost less than $200, but it yielded more than 740 pounds of produce. Most of the food was sent to Miriam's Kitchen, a nearby facility that serves meals to the homeless, but some was used in the White House kitchen.

First Lady Michelle Obama with Students, White House Vegetable Garden, Washington, DC, 2009. *As part of her campaign to reduce childhood obesity, Obama began the first vegetable garden at the White House since Eleanor Roosevelt's Victory Garden in World War II.* TIM SLOAN/AFP/GETTY IMAGES

Table 15-9. Age-Adjusted Percentage of Persons Engaging in Physical Activity and Fitness by Selected Characteristic: 2006

[**In percent.** Covers persons 18 years old and over. Based on the National Health Interview Survey, a sample survey of the civilian noninstitutionalized population. Leisure-time physical activity is assessed by asking respondents a series of questions about participation in moderate and vigorous-intensity physical activities. To assess muscle-strengthening activities, respondents were asked about leisure-time physical activities specifically designed to strengthen their muscles.]

Characteristic	No leisure-time physical activity[1]	Regular Physical activity-moderate or vigorous[2]	Muscular strength and endurance[3]
Total	**39.2**	**30.9**	**19.4**
Sex			
Male	38.1	33.1	22.0
Female	40.1	28.9	17.0
Age[4]			
18 to 24 years old	34.4	38.1	26.5
25 to 44 years old	34.7	33.4	22.5
45 to 64 years old	39.4	29.5	17.3
65 to 74 years old	47.6	26.2	12.1
75 years old and over	59.3	17.3	9.4
Race			
Race alone			
White	38.0	31.8	19.7
Black or African American	48.1	24.9	17.8
American Indian or Alaska Native	33.6	29.0	16.5
Asian or Pacific Islander	(NA)	(NA)	(NA)
Two or more races	34.7	29.9	25.7
Hispanic Origin and Race			
Hispanic or Latino	53.0	22.6	13.1
Not Hispanic or Latino	37.0	32.3	20.5
White, non-Hispanic	48.2	33.7	18.0
Black, non-Hispanic	35.1	24.8	21.1
Education level (persons aged 25 years and over):			
Less than 9th grade	66.6	15.0	5.3
Grades 9 thru 11	59.5	17.3	7.2
High School graduate	47.2	23.5	13.3
Some college or AA degree	34.7	31.7	20.7
College graduate or above	23.1	43.4	28.6

[1]Persons with no moderate- or vigorous-intensity activity for at least 10 minutes at a time.
[2]Regular physical activity is moderate-intensity physical activity at least 5 times a week for 30 minutes/time or vigorous-intensity physical activity for at least 3 times/week for 20 minutes/time.
[3]Persons who participated in muscle strengthening activities at least 2 times/week.
[4]Age data are not age-adjusted.

SOURCE: U.S. National Center for Chronic Disease Prevention and Health Promotion,"Nutrition and Physical Activity"and unpublished data.

Table 15-9. *According to these 2006 data from the National Center for Chronic Disease Prevention and Health Promotion, only about half of all African Americans reported having a regular share in physical fitness activities.*

In February 2010, Michelle Obama also introduced her signature initiative to combat childhood obesity. Called "Let's Move!," the ten-year project has four core principles, promoting:

- easier access to healthful foods
- increased physical activity
- more nutrition information
- personal responsibility

On the same day that the initiative was announced, President Obama signed a memorandum that will provide $1 billion per year in federal funds for ten years to support the program. The memorandum also established a national task force on childhood obesity, with members drawn from the Departments of Health and Human Services, the Interior, Agriculture, and Education.

Fast food, which is usually high in calories, fat, salt, and sugar, is detrimental to a prudent diet. Fast food contributes to many of the illnesses that plague African Americans, such as obesity, heart disease, stroke, and diabetes. Fast-food portions are typically too large for the average person. A single fast-food meal might contain enough calories for an entire day and, in most cases, will be deficient in fiber. A sweetened drink that accompanies a fast-food entree may contain one hundred additional empty calories.

EXERCISE

Regular exercise has proven to be an effective strategy in maintaining normal weight and preventing diseases related to obesity. Experts recommend twenty to thirty minutes of regular exercise per day. Regular exercise, under the guidance of a physician, can enhance heart health, strengthen bones, and decrease the probability of developing breast or colon cancer.

A 2007 study by Dena Bravata in the *Journal of the American Medical Association* demonstrated that the use of a pedometer, an inexpensive pocket-sized device that counts the number of steps a person takes each day, can help a person become more physically active, lose weight, and reduce blood pressure. Organizations such as Shape Up America! encourage adults to walk at least ten thousand steps each day. Bravata's research demonstrated that pedometer users increased their physical activity by 2,100 steps daily. In addition, Bravata noted that systolic blood pressure fell by an average of 3.8 millimeters of mercury—noteworthy because just 2 millimeters of mercury reduction in blood pressure was linked to a 10 percent reduced risk of death by stroke and a 7 percent reduced risk of death from cardiovascular disease.

STRESS MANAGEMENT

Stress occurs when a person is trying to cope with the demands of everyday living. Stress is the body's emotional and physical response to conditions that it perceives to be beyond its control. The first step in stress management is to identify the problems or concerns that are causing it. Although there are many things in one's life that cannot be changed, there are others that one can control and change. Self-help strategies for stress management include: (1) adopting a healthy lifestyle that includes a good diet and adequate exercise, recreation, and rest; and (2) avoiding smoking and addictive substances, as well as people and circumstances that cause stress.

SMOKING

Smoking significantly elevates the risk for stroke resulting from cerebrovascular disease. According to the CDC's 1998 *Surgeon General's Report*, the rate of cerebrovascular disease was more than twice as high among African American men (53.1 per 100,000) as white men (26.2 per 100,000). It was also almost twice as high among African American women (40.6 per 100,000) as white women (22.6 per 100,000).

COMMUNITY HEALTH CLINICS

During the economic downturn that began in 2007, many people lost their access to basic health care. In some cities and neighborhoods, community health clinics attempted to meet the needs of those who would not otherwise receive care. According to the National Association of Community Health Centers, community health clinics served more than twenty million clients in 2009, two million more than were seen at such clinics a decade earlier. Fees at these facilities are usually based on income.

One such clinic, the Coppin State University Nursing Center, opened across the street from the campus of Coppin State University in Baltimore in 1995, with Doris Nearror Starks as its first director and dean of the school of nursing. The clinic's mission is to provide readily accessible, high-quality health care at a low cost. The reason for basing a community health clinic at an educational institution was to address the issue of health disparities in a medically underserved area, while at the same time educating nurses to care for an urban population. The clinic meshes education with community service, with the expectation that student caregivers who came from the community to learn are more likely to return to their community to care for residents. Services at the Coppin clinic are provided by nurse practitioners, as well as nurse practitioner faculty and nursing students under supervision. The staff also includes a physician. Clinic staff refer clients to other facilities when they require a higher level of care than that provided by the clinic.

Some clients at the Coppin State University Nursing Center have insurance and can pay for their care. Members of the nursing faculty also receive grants that help fund the clinic, and the clinic has contracts for some services. Community health clinics ideally maintain multiple streams of revenue to keep them fiscally viable, since many patients cannot pay for their services.

Many community health clinics also offer a variety of programs based on the needs of the community, including support groups for clients with specific problems, seminars for people who are newly released from prison, and classes in parenting skills. One notable project at the Coppin State University Nursing Center involved collaboration with the insurance company BlueCross BlueShield (CareFirst of Maryland) and the Baltimore chapter of the National Coalition of 100 Black Women to provide free HIV/AIDS testing, education, and counseling. Such projects demonstrate how agencies can work together for the good of the community.

MEDICAID

Medicaid is a government-sponsored health-care program for low-income individuals and families. Eligibility for participation in the program is determined by federal and state laws. Money for care is not paid to the individual but to the state in which the care is given. In some states, the client is asked to pay a small portion of the cost for care, or a co-payment.

Participants in the Medicaid program are screened for many factors, such as age, disability, income, and citizenship. The rules for determining income vary from state to state, and eligibility for children is based on the children's status, not the parents'.

C. Virginia Fields, 2005. *As president and chief executive officer, National Black Leadership Commission on AIDS, Fields is responsible for leading the organization in its mission to inform, coordinate and organize the volunteer efforts of the African American community's leaders, including clergy, elected officials, medical practitioners, business professionals, social policy experts, and media, to meet the challenge of fighting HIV/AIDS in their local communities.* **AP PHOTO/MICHAEL NAGLE**

SELECTED FAMILY AND HEALTH ADVOCATES

(Some biographical profiles may appear in other chapters. To locate profiles more readily, please consult the index.)

ROBERT D. BULLARD (1942–)

Educator, Activist. Robert D. Bullard is the Ware Professor of Sociology and director of the Environmental Justice Resource Center at Clark Atlanta University in Georgia. He is widely known as the father of environmental justice. Since the 1980s, Bullard has worked on behalf of communities of color that have been affected by environmental racism.

In 1987 Bullard's work gained national attention when he published a study documenting that the selection of sites for hazardous-waste facilities is likely to be based on the race and class of people living in the area. In 2007 Bullard published a follow-up study, *Toxic Wastes and Race at Twenty: 1987–2007*, which demonstrated that communities of color were still heavily burdened by the presence of toxic-waste dumps and other hazardous-waste sites in their areas.

BENJAMIN S. CARSON (1951–)

Physician, Educator, Activist. Benjamin S. Carson is a neurosurgeon and professor of neurosurgery at Johns Hopkins University in Baltimore. He is also a noted advocate for children and youth. In 1994 Carson and his wife Candy established the Carson Scholars Fund, which gives scholarships to students who strive for academic excellence and have a strong commitment to their communities. Since its inception, the Carson Scholars Fund has awarded almost four thousand scholarships to students in thirty-four states.

In discussions and speeches, Carson often talks about the difficult circumstances of his own upbringing. He describes his mother's encouragement in helping him learn to read and the new world that reading opened up for him and his brother. In light of that experience, Carson has encouraged a love of reading through the Ben Carson Reading Project, which has established reading rooms across the country, so that students, educators, and the community can come together to enjoy reading.

(See Carson's profile in chapter 27, Science and Technology, for additional details about his life and career.)

MARIAN WRIGHT EDELMAN

See chapter 9, National Organizations.

C. VIRGINIA FIELDS (1946–)

Social Worker, Politician, Activist. C. Virginia Fields is president and chief executive officer of the National Black Leadership Commission on AIDS (NBLCA). After many years as a social worker and service as president of the borough of Manhattan in New York City, Fields became keenly aware of the needs of the community and the threat that HIV/AIDS poses to the country's health and to the health of African Americans.

As head of NBLCA, Fields is responsible for leading the organization in its mission to inform, coordinate, and organize the volunteer efforts of the black community. The organization focuses on community leaders such as clergy, health practitioners, elected officials, and social policy experts. Under Fields's leadership, NBLCA also conducts research on HIV/AIDS policy and tries to influence decision making at the local, state, and national levels. In addition, Fields and the NBLCA have assisted community organizations in collaborating with the CDC to develop more culturally sensitive programs for HIV/AIDS prevention.

FRED GRAY (1930–)

Attorney, Activist. Fred Gray, a prominent Alabama civil rights attorney, began his career by serving as an attorney for the Montgomery Improvement Association (MIA). The MIA was the organization that supported Rosa Parks following her arrest for refusing to give up her seat for a white male passenger on a bus in Montgomery, Alabama, December 1, 1955. The arrest of Parks on that occasion was the event that precipitated the Montgomery bus boycott by African American citizens. On February 1, 1956, Gray, then twenty-five years old, filed a suit in the Federal District Court titled *Gayle v. Browder*, which challenged the legality of segregated seating on buses. The case eventually reached the U.S. Supreme Court, where on November 13, 1956, the Court outlawed racial segregation on all buses in all states, finding it unconstitutional.

Gray also represented victims of the notorious Tuskegee syphilis study. In 1932 the U.S. Public Health Service began a study of the affects of untreated syphilis on more than six hundred African American males in Macon County, Alabama. Participants were never told that they were part of a study, but were led to believe that they were receiving appropriate treatment. After the study became public in 1972, Gray filed a lawsuit against Alabama and the U.S. Public Health Service. It was settled in 1974 for $10 million. The settlement also included medical treatment for the participants who were still alive.

When Gray was a child, it was his mother's dream that he become a minister in the Church of Christ. In 1957 he agreed to serve as full-time minister for Montgomery's Newton Church of Christ. He served in that capacity until he moved to Tuskegee in 1973, where he continues to perform ministerial duties from time to time while maintaining a law practice.

CLARA (1905–1992) AND LORRAINE (1926–) HALE

Humanitarians, Educators, Hale House Cofounders. Following Clara's retirement as a foster parent, her daughter Lorraine directed infants of drug-addicted mothers to her own mother for care. Lorraine had worked in positions of schoolteacher, guidance counselor, and psychologist. During that phase of Mother Hale's service, she had 22 children in her care who were born addicted to drugs. Because of her involvement with the babies, her home became known as Hale House. In 1971, Hale House received a city grant and a federal grant, which helped the child-care facility move to its own five-story building in Harlem. Later, in 1976, Hale House received permission from New York to manage an official "boarding home."

Mother Hale received numerous awards for public service. She was invited by President Ronald Reagan to attend his State of the Union address in 1985. Hale died December 18, 1992.

After her mother's death, Lorraine Hale expanded the foundation's services to assist mothers and children diagnosed with AIDS. This aspect of the foundation's work was the focus of Hale's 1992 book, *Hale House: Alive with Love*.

In 2001, amid financial investigation by the New York Attorney General's Office, Lorraine Hale resigned her leadership position with the foundation. She and her husband were indicted in 2002 on charges related to the improper use of donations intended for the use of the Hale House foundation.

The Mother Hale Learning Center in central Harlem continues to serve children. It is guided by Mother Hale's principles and provides early childhood education to infants, younger toddlers, older toddlers, and preschool children.

ALICIA KEYS (1981–)

Singer, Songwriter, Musician, Activist. Singer and songwriter Alicia Keys considers herself a "citizen of the world." She answered the call of her African and Indian sisters and brothers for help in obtaining medicines to treat HIV/AIDS when she was moved by mothers, with babies in their arms, who pleaded with her for medicines. She responded by establishing the Keep a Child Alive foundation, to which Keys herself donates and through which she encourages others to give one dollar a day toward the purchase of medicines for those who would otherwise be unable to receive them.

SHIRLEY NATHAN-PULLIAM (1939–)

Politician, Registered Nurse. Shirley Nathan-Pulliam, a registered nurse, was elected in 1994 to the Maryland House of Delegates, where she made health care, especially closing the gap in health-care disparities, her primary focus. As a Maryland delegate, she sponsored the Healthcare Disparities Prevention Act (HB883) that was enacted in 2003. She also sponsored legislation to establish the Office of Minority Health and Health Care Disparities (HB 86) that was enacted in 2004. Nathan-Pulliam's key legislative initiatives also included funding for breast-cancer diagnosis and treatment programs, an oral-cancer mortality-reduction program, and treatment for disorders related to substance abuse and mental illness. Nathan-Pulliam has received numerous awards and citations, including the 2005 Distinguished Legislator of the Year Award from the American Public Health Association.

Shirley Nathan-Pulliam. *A registered nurse who is a member of the Maryland House of Delegates, Nathan-Pulliam has been instrumental in getting laws passed which help the poor and uninsured to receive higher-quality health care. She is also an advocate for many family-centered policies.* COURTESY OF SHIRLEY NATHAN-PULLIAM.

Victoria Rowell, Actress, Clifton, NJ, 2007. *Holding a copy of her memoir,* The Women Who Raised Me, *television actress Rowell attends a book signing. The book relates Rowell's life in the Maine foster-care system and the women who loved and mentored her.* AP PHOTO/JENNIFER GRAYLOCK

VICTORIA ROWELL (1959–)

Actress, Activist. Victoria Rowell is an actress who starred briefly on the daytime drama *As the World Turns* before obtaining a role on *The Young and the Restless*, where she starred for seventeen years as Drucilla Winters. She was reared under difficult circumstances, however, and spent her youth in the foster-child care system. Because of her upbringing, Rowell has a continuing interest in foster children, and has often addressed the plight of these children in her performances. In 1990 she founded the Rowell Foster Children's Positive Plan, an organization dedicated to providing arts and sports opportunities for children in the foster-care system.

Rowell strongly supported President Obama's efforts in 2009 to improve the health-care system for children in foster care. She often spoke of her experiences as a child and how she was not always able to obtain the health care she needed while in foster care.

IAN K. SMITH (1969–)

Physician, Activist, Reporter. Ian K. Smith is a physician who specializes in helping individuals and groups lose weight and maintain optimum health. Since obesity is a precursor to many chronic diseases, Smith initiated the "50 Million Pound Challenge." Through this program and others, he has worked with thousands of people in their efforts to enhance their health through weight loss. Smith often collaborates with community-based groups to reach participants who can help implement his goal of achieving optimum health for as many people as possible.

Ian K. Smith with Daunte Culpepper during the 50 Million Pound Challenge Tour in Miami, FL, 2007. *Smith (*right*), a judge on VH1's* Celebrity Fit Club, *created the national challenge to encourage Americans to adopt healthy lifestyles. On this date he is joined by Miami Dolphins quarterback Culpepper.* AP PHOTO/J. PAT CARTER

Smith hosts a nationally syndicated radio show, *HealthWatch*, and is a frequent guest and reporter on television shows covering issues related to health and obesity. He has written numerous articles on health issues, and has authored several books, including the best-selling *Fat Smash Diet* (2006).

BLAIR UNDERWOOD (1964–)

Actor, Activist. Actor Blair Underwood is active in the fight against HIV/AIDS and serves as spokesperson for the AIDS Healthcare Foundation (AHF), a global treatment, prevention, and advocacy organization. Underwood supports the organization's efforts to reduce the incidence of HIV/AIDS through education, testing, and counseling. In September 2009, AHF opened the AHF Blair Underwood Healthcare Center, a free HIV/AIDS clinic in Washington, D.C. This new facility is sorely needed in Washington, D.C., because of the city's high incidence of HIV/AIDS.

CHARLESZETTA "MOTHER" WADDLES (1912–2001)

Community Activist, Spiritual Leader. Mother Waddles, as she was commonly known, was born Charleszetta Lena Campbell in St. Louis, Missouri, in 1912, and married at age fourteen. She worked as a domestic and was widowed before she was twenty years old. Waddles remarried but left her second husband after they had relocated to Detroit. In Detroit, she married her third husband, Payton Waddles, and eventually had a total of ten children.

During her childhood, Mother Waddles was greatly influenced by an experience involving her father, whom she felt was treated unfairly by his fellow church members after his business failed. She sought to live her life in a way that demonstrated what she considered true Christian principles.

Payton Waddles was very supportive of his wife's efforts to reach out to poor, struggling individuals and families in Detroit. She often collected food and money to help families

Blair Underwood, Actor and AIDS Activist, Washington, DC, 2009. *Underwood speaks at the opening of the nonprofit AIDS Healthcare Foundation's first AIDS treatment center in Washington. He advocates personal responsibility to be tested for HIV and to stop the spread of the disease.* TIM SLOAN/AFP/GETTY IMAGES

feed their children and stay in their homes. Mother Waddles also took a Bible study course and became an ordained Pentecostal minister. She blended her religious principles and activities with charitable work. In 1950, Waddles opened the Helping Hand restaurant, where poor people could enjoy a sit-down, home-cooked meal for thirty-five cents.

In 1956, Waddles expanded the mission and goals of the restaurant when she founded the Perpetual Mission for Saving Souls of All Nations. That entity later received the more simplified name of The Mother Waddles Perpetual Mission. Over the years the center has been home to numerous community outreach programs, including a medical clinic, job placement service, and a tutoring program. The programs are staffed entirely by volunteers and financed with donations. Mother Waddles received numerous awards and commendations, including the Urban League's Humanitarian Award. Although Waddles died July 12, 2001, at age eighty-eight, work at the center continues in her name, through the efforts of her children and other volunteers.

BEVERLY H. WRIGHT (1947–)

Sociologist, Activist, Writer. Beverly H. Wright has worked tirelessly to improve the lives of people in Louisiana's at-risk communities, especially those who live in the area known as Cancer Alley between Baton Rouge and New Orleans. She has labored to call the nation's attention to the dangers to human health caused by petrochemical pollutants in Louisiana. As executive director of the Deep South Center for Environmental Justice at Dillard University in New Orleans, Wright collaborates with others to help protect the health of vulnerable populations.

In 2005 Wright lost her own home to Hurricane Katrina, but she has continued to work to make New

Beverly H. Wright. *Wright, professor of sociology and director of the Deep South Center for Environmental Justice at Dillard University in New Orleans, is a leading advocate for environmental justice. In 2009, she received the Heinz Award in Environmental Studies from the Heinz Family Philanthropies.* **COURTESY OF BEVERLY WRIGHT.**

Orleans a safe place to live. She developed a neighborhood clean-up project called "A Safe Way Back Home" that trains small businesses and contractors in hazardous-waste removal, mold remediation, and health and safety methods. Project leaders also enlisted and trained volunteers from around the country to help Louisiana residents clean up their devastated homes so they could return. In 2009 Wright received the Heinz Award for her efforts to correct environmental racism and raise the profile of environmental issues in poor and minority communities nationwide.

16

EDUCATION

Jessie Carney Smith

EDUCATIONAL OPPORTUNITIES IN COLONIAL AMERICA

Historically, the attainment of education for African Americans has been a struggle. There is some evidence of sporadic, systematic instruction of Africans in colonial America as far back as the late 1600s to the mid-1700s. Prior to 1830, some were even taught to read, write, and, in some instances, perform simple arithmetic. However, between 1830 and 1835, stringent laws were passed prohibiting whites from teaching African Americans to read and write. In spite of these laws, many individuals struggled to provide informal and formal education to African Americans. In addition, churches and charitable organizations also played an important role in the creation of educational institutions for African Americans.

EARLY CHRISTIAN MISSIONARY ENDEAVORS

Early attempts to educate African Americans can be traced back to the missionary efforts of Christian churches in the early 1600s. French Catholics in Louisiana were probably the earliest group to provide instruction to African American laborers. Although the primary goal was to convert them to Christianity, the process often involved general education. In addition, the French system of laws known as the *code noir* (black code) made it incumbent upon masters to educate those who had been enslaved.

Pennsylvania Quakers, who were opposed to the institution of African enslavement, organized monthly educational meetings for African Americans during the early 1700s so that they might have the opportunity for improvement. One such Quaker, Anthony Benezet (1713–1784), established an evening school in his home in 1750 that was successful until 1760. In 1774, Quakers in Philadelphia joined together to open a school for African Americans.

The Society for the Propagation of the Gospel in Foreign Parts, organized by the Church of England in 1701 for the purpose of converting enslaved Africans to Christianity, was another organization that provided educational opportunities to African Americans. In 1751, the society sent Joseph Ottolenghi to convert and educate African Americans in Georgia. Ottolenghi "promised to spare no pains to improve the young children."

AFRICAN AMERICAN EDUCATIONAL INSTITUTIONS IN THE NINETEENTH CENTURY

AFRICAN FREE SCHOOLS IN NEW YORK AND PHILADELPHIA

Like the churches, the antislavery movement played an important part in the creation of schools. In 1787, the Manumission Society founded the New York African Free School; by 1820, more than five hundred African American children were enrolled. Support increased as other African Free Schools were established in New York until 1834, when the New York Common Council took over control of the schools.

In the North, there were opportunities for elementary education for African Americans in mostly segregated schools or in schools run in conjunction with African American churches. For example, in 1804, African Episcopalians in Philadelphia organized a school for African American children.

In 1848, an African American industrial training school opened in Philadelphia at the House of Industry. Other schools in operation in Philadelphia included the Corn Street Unclassified School (1849), the Holmesburg Unclassified School (1854), and the Home for Colored Children (1859). By the mid-1860s, there were 1,031 pupils in the African American public schools of Philadelphia, as well as 748 in the charity schools, 211 in the benevolent schools, and 331 in private schools. However, high schools in the North were largely inaccessible to African Americans for most of the nineteenth century.

FREEDMEN'S ORGANIZATIONS AND AGENCIES

At the close of the Civil War (1861–1865), hundreds of thousands of newly freed African Americans were left without homes and adequate resources. As a means for providing temporary assistance to those formerly enslaved, numerous organizations were formed. The American Missionary Association (AMA), established on September 3, 1846, had maintained an interest in African American education before and after the war. The AMA opened its first school for those who were newly freed on September 17, 1861, at Fortress Monroe, Virginia. Mary S. Peake (1823–1862) became the first teacher in an AMA school. The AMA also established a network of elementary schools, normal schools, and colleges throughout the South. In time, however, most of these schools were absorbed into local and state systems of education. Following the AMA's early efforts, other voluntary and denominational groups responded to the need for freedmen's aid and sent teachers into the southern and border states to establish elementary schools on plantations, in small towns, and in larger cities in the South. Although most of the schools were to be racially integrated, few whites attended.

The New England Freedmen's Aid Society, organized in Boston on February 7, 1862, was founded to promote education among free African Americans. Supporters of the organization included Edward Everett Hale, Samuel Cabot, Charles Bernard, William Lloyd Garrison, and William Cullen Bryant. In New York, a similar organization was founded on February 20, 1862: the National Freedmen's Relief Association. The Port Royal Relief Committee, later known as the Pennsylvania Freedmen's Relief Association, founded in Philadelphia on March 3, 1862, followed this trend. In 1863, several of these organizations merged to form the United States Commission for the Relief of the National Freedmen, which, in 1865, became the American Freedmen's Aid Union.

The federal government also responded to the needs of African Americans in the South. During the 1860s, Congress passed several Freedmen's Bureau Acts, creating and financing an agency designed to provide temporary assistance to newly freed blacks. Under the acts, the bureau's chief functions were to provide food, clothing, and medical supplies. Working in conjunction with various benevolent organizations, bureau commissioner General Oliver Otis Howard (1830–1909) established and maintained schools and managed to provide for teachers. By 1870, the Freedmen's Bureau operated more than 2,600 schools in the South, with 3,300 teachers educating 150,000 students; almost 4,000 schools were in operation prior to the abolition of the agency in 1872.

INDEPENDENT SCHOOLS IN THE LATE NINETEENTH CENTURY

The education of African Americans has been largely a function of independent schools, private institutions founded to meet the educational and employment needs of African Americans. In the second half of the century, these schools filled the gap until 1890, when African American land-grant colleges were founded after the passage of the second Morrill Act. Independent schools also supplied many of the African American teachers in the South.

One of the earliest surviving African American independent schools, Tuskegee Normal and Industrial Institute (now Tuskegee University), was established in 1881 by an act of the Alabama General Assembly. Booker T. Washington (1856–1915), the school's organizer and first principal, established a curriculum that provided African American students with the means to become economically self-supporting.

Similarly, other independent schools developed around the country. In 1883, in a lecture room at the Christ Presbyterian Church in Savannah, Georgia, Lucy Craft Laney (1854–1933) opened what would become the Haines Normal and Industrial Institute. In 1901, Nannie Helen Burroughs (1879–1961) founded the National Training School for Women and Girls in Washington, D.C. By the end of the first year, the school had enrolled thirty-one students. Twenty-five years later, more than two thousand women had trained at the school. In Sedalia, North Carolina, Charlotte Hawkins Brown (c. 1883–1961) founded the Palmer Memorial Institute in 1901.

With only $1.50 and five students, Mary McLeod Bethune (1875–1955) founded Daytona Educational and Industrial Training School for Negro Girls (now Bethune-Cookman University) in 1904 in Daytona Beach, Florida. Nineteen years later, the institute merged with the Cookman Institute of Jacksonville, Florida, founded in 1872 by D. S. B. Darnell. More than three thousand students now study at Bethune-Cookman University.

EARLY AFRICAN AMERICAN INSTITUTIONS OF HIGHER EDUCATION

Lincoln University in Pennsylvania (founded in 1854 as Ashmun Institute) and Wilberforce University (founded in 1856) are often regarded as the oldest of the historically

Mary McLeod Bethune, Educator and Civil Rights Activist, 1943. *Bethune, founder of the institution that became Bethune-Cookman University, also served as an adviser on minority affairs to President Franklin D. Roosevelt.* GORDON PARKS/ HISTORICAL/CORBIS

African American institutions of higher education. Wilberforce College, as the latter school was first known, was founded by the African Methodist Episcopal (AME) Church and named for the English abolitionist William Wilberforce (1759–1833). The school awarded its first degree in 1857. Wilberforce and Lincoln were the first African American colleges to remain in their original location and to develop into degree-granting institutions. The oldest institution in operation today, however, is Cheyney University of Pennsylvania (earlier known as the Institute for Colored Youth and, eventually, Cheyney State College), which was founded in 1837. The primary purpose of these institutions was to train African American youth for service as teachers and ministers.

Between 1865 and 1871, several predominantly African American institutions of higher learning were founded, including: Atlanta University (now Clark Atlanta University), Shaw University, and Virginia Union University (1865); Fisk University and Lincoln Institute in Missouri (now Lincoln University; 1866); Talladega College, Augusta Institute (now Morehouse College), Biddle University (now Johnson C. Smith University), Howard University, and Scotia Seminary (now Barber-Scotia College; 1867); Hampton Institute (now Hampton University; 1868); Tougaloo College (1869); and Alcorn College (now Alcorn State University) and Benedict College (1871). Religious organizations were instrumental in the founding and supporting of these early African American institutions. The Freedmen's Bureau either founded or aided in the development of Howard University, St. Augustine's College, Lincoln Institute in Missouri, and Storer College (now merged with Virginia Union University). The American Missionary Association founded seven African American colleges; the first of these was Hampton. Other AMA-founded institutions were Atlanta, Fisk, LeMoyne (now LeMoyne-Owen College), Straight (now merged with New Orleans University to become Dillard University), Talladega, Tillotson (now Huston-Tillotson University), and Tougaloo. Benedict College, Shaw University, and Virginia Union University were founded and supported by the American Baptist Home Mission Society.

Alcorn College, founded in 1871, was the first African American land-grant college. This was made possible under the Morrill Act of 1862, which provided federal land-grant funds for higher education. In 1890, Congress passed the second Morrill Act, also known as the Land Grant Act of 1890. The second act stipulated that no federal aid was to be provided for the creation or maintenance of any white agricultural and mechanical school unless that state also provided for a similar school for African Americans. As a result, a system of separate, African American land-grant institutions developed and became the basis of publicly supported higher education of African Americans in the South.

African American colleges offered diversity in history, purpose, and curriculums. For example, early in their history, some African American colleges prepared their students for careers in medicine and medical-related fields. Those that prepared students for degrees in dentistry and medicine included Howard University, Meharry Medical College, Shaw University, and New Orleans Medical School. The nation's only degree program in veterinary medicine among historically African American colleges and universities is still offered at Tuskegee University. Bennett College (founded 1873 and later renamed Bennett College for Women) and Spelman College (founded 1881) are the only two African American women's colleges. At first coeducational, Bennett became a women's two-year college in 1926. Xavier (founded in 1925) is the nation's only Catholic-supported college for African Americans. By 1900, there were some thirty-four African American institutions in the United States for higher education and more than two thousand African Americans with earned degrees.

PHILANTHROPY AND EDUCATION

Pre–Civil War efforts did not fully address the educational needs and desires of African Americans, especially those who had been enslaved. Northern philanthropy took up some of the burden of improving African American education. Agencies of the antebellum period aided in educating African Americans through their support of private and sectarian schools before and after the Civil War. By the end of the war, however, the South—the region where African Americans were concentrated—still had not addressed the educational needs of African Americans. Neither the newly freed Africans nor their children had access to free public education.

In 1867, a new type of support for education began when Massachusetts merchant George Peabody (1795–1869) established the first educational philanthropy in the country. In his concern for the desolate South, he created the Peabody Education Fund to provide "elementary education to children of the common people." The fund later was credited with stimulating states to develop systems of free schools for the races, "creating favorable public opinion to levy tax to support the schools, and stimulating the development of state teachers associations and normal schools."

So successful was the Peabody effort that in 1882 Connecticut manufacturer John Fox Slater (1815–1884), impressed with the developments, created the Slater Fund to uplift the "lately emancipated people of the South." It was the first philanthropy devoted to the education of African Americans. Through the fund's efforts, private African American colleges and four-year high schools for African Americans were developed. The Slater Fund stimulated vocational and industrial training and established the idea of county training schools. The Daniel Hand Fund, established in 1888 and entrusted to the American Missionary Association, provided for the education of "needy and indigent" African Americans in the South. By 1914, the Peabody and Slater funds were working in similar areas, and Peabody transferred its assets to Slater.

In 1907, Anna T. Jeanes (1822–1907) further advanced the education of African Americans by giving $1 million to Booker T. Washington of the Tuskegee Institute and Hollis B. Frissell (1851–1917) of the Hampton Institute to strengthen rural schools for African Americans in the South. The gift established the Fund for Rudimentary Schools for Southern Negroes, known as the Jeanes Fund. Initially, the fund supported teachers who moved from school to school in the South teaching industrial and utilitarian subjects. The concept was expanded to provide master teachers, known as "Jeanes teachers," to supervise the African American schools. Later, the program added new teaching methods, organized in-service training for teachers, and generally improved instruction. The program lasted from 1908 until 1968, when counties took over the Jeanes teachers' work and paid their salaries. Much of the credit for the program was due to the efforts of Virginia E. Randolph (1870–1958), the first Jeanes teacher. In recognition of her work, the Jeanes teachers established the Virginia Randolph Fund to supplement the Jeanes Fund in 1936.

The Julius Rosenwald Fund was incorporated in Chicago in 1917 as a nonprofit corporation. For a number of years its founder, businessman and philanthropist Julius Rosenwald (1862–1932) controlled the fund and initiated a program of personal beneficence. After Rosenwald met Booker T. Washington in 1911, the interests of black Americans realized the foremost benefits of Rosenwald's philanthropy through support of programs in education and other areas. The Rosenwald-Washington relationship spurred Rosenwald to build rural schoolhouses for southern blacks that were constructed on a matching basis. Washington and the Tuskegee Institute handled the schoolhouse project at first. When the project became too extensive for Tuskegee, the Rosenwald Fund's Chicago office established a branch in Nashville in 1920 and oversaw the project from 1909 to 1928. Between 1909 and 1932, the Rosenwald Fund built more than five thousand schools, teachers' homes, shops, and other buildings in sixteen southern and border states. Many Jeanes teachers taught in the Rosenwald schools. These schools uplifted immeasurably the education of black youth in the South. In some villages and counties, both blacks and whites raised additional funds to support these schools.

The Jeanes Fund and the Slater Fund, then working in similar areas, merged in 1937 to form the Southern Education Foundation (SEF). Later that year, the Virginia Randolph Fund was incorporated into the SEF. The SEF extended the work of the predecessor funds and ensured that innovative approaches to the education of African Americans continued. From 1937 to 1950, the SEF concentrated on supporting the Jeanes teachers. It also worked with such agencies as the General Education Board, the Julius Rosenwald Fund, the Carnegie Corporation, and State Agents for Negro Schools. The General Education Board was a source of support for African American colleges, library collections, and sometimes library buildings. It also supported African American teachers and other aspects of education and welfare for African Americans.

Early on, the Carnegie Corporation had provided grants to the Slater and Jeanes programs. Later, the corporation built African American branches of public libraries in various cities in the South. During the first quarter of the twentieth century, several African American colleges received funds from the Carnegie Corporation and from Andrew Carnegie (1835–1919) himself to support the construction of library buildings. They included the institutions of Atlanta, Cheyney, Fisk, Howard, Tuskegee, and Wilberforce.

In addition, the SEF worked to prepare the South to resolve racial problems. When the U.S. Supreme Court's *Brown v. Board of Education of Topeka* decision was rendered in 1954, bringing about desegregation of public education, the SEF contributed to the decision by conducting studies of African American education in the South, largely through support of the Ford Foundation. Its efforts to desegregate public education continued after Brown, when southern states that failed to desegregate higher education were challenged by the lawsuit originally known as *Adams v. Richardson*. The SEF supported the Legal Defense and Educational Fund in litigation and helped dismantle the dual system of public education. It also supported conferences, studies, and publications dealing with desegregation of higher education. Its report *Miles to Go*, published in 1998, is an example of the SEF's efforts. The study found that more than two decades of efforts to desegregate higher education had left blacks in the South and elsewhere out of pace with whites in undergraduate and graduate school enrollment, rates of graduation, and faculty diversity, among other areas.

Located in Atlanta since 1948, the SEF is now a public charity that has several interests, including programs to increase the supply of minority teachers in the South and to strengthen African American colleges. The SEF, its predecessor agencies, and other private and public agencies, figure prominently in the history and progress of African American education.

AFRICAN AMERICAN EDUCATION IN THE TWENTIETH CENTURY

EARLY PROMOTERS OF AFRICAN AMERICAN STUDIES

From its beginnings, the purpose of African American studies has been to disseminate knowledge about the social, cultural, political, and historical experiences of Africans. One of the forerunners in the field, theologian and educator Reverend Alexander Crummell (1819–1898), along with a group of African American intellectuals, founded the American Negro Academy in Washington, D.C., in 1897. The purpose of the organization was to foster scholarship and promote literature, science, and art among African Americans. The organization's members hoped that through the academy, an educated African American elite would shape and direct society. Crummell first conceived the idea of an American Negro Academy while a student at Cambridge University in England. The organization's founding members included Paul Laurence Dunbar (1872–1906), William Sanders Scarborough (1852–1926), and W. E. B. Du Bois (1868–1963), among other noted educators. Following Crummell's death in 1898, Du Bois was elected president of the academy.

In September 1915, Carter G. Woodson (1875–1950), a Harvard Ph.D. graduate, helped to organize the Association for the Study of Negro Life and History (now the Association for the Study of African American Life and History). The association's primary purpose was to promote research, encourage the study of, and publish material on African American history. In 1916, the organization began publishing the *Journal of Negro History*, for which Woodson served as editor until his death in 1950.

Other early scholars of African American studies include: sociologist E. Franklin Frazier (1894–1962); John Edward Bruce (1856–1924); Arthur Schomburg (1874–1938), founder of the Negro Society for Historical Research (1911); and Alain Locke (1885–1954), founder of the Associates in Negro Folk Education (1934).

THE END OF LEGAL SEGREGATION IN PUBLIC EDUCATION

In the years that followed the U.S. Supreme Court's 1896 ruling in *Plessy v. Ferguson*, segregation in public education became the general practice. Prior to the Court's decision in *Brown v. Board of Education of Topeka*, African American children were often subjected to inferior educational facilities. However, by the 1930s, a string of school-desegregation cases reached the Court.

When Lloyd Lionel Gaines, an African American, was refused admission to the law school of the State University of Missouri in 1936, he applied to the state court for an order to compel admission on the grounds that refusal constituted a denial of his rights under the Fourteenth Amendment to the U.S. Constitution. At that time, the state of Missouri maintained a practice of providing funds for African Americans to attend graduate and professional schools outside of the state, rather than provide facilities itself. The university defended its action by maintaining that Lincoln University, a predominantly African American institution, would eventually establish its own law school, which Gaines could then attend. Until then, the state would allow him to exercise the option of pursuing his studies outside the state on a scholarship. Ruling in the case *Missouri ex rel. Lloyd Gaines v. Canada* in 1938, the U.S. Supreme Court decided that states were required to provide equal educational facilities for African Americans within state borders.

Taking an even greater step, the U.S. Supreme Court ruled in 1850 that a separate law school for African Americans provided by the state of Texas violated the equal protection clause of the Fourteenth Amendment. According to the Court, the rights of Heman Marion Sweatt (1912–1982) were violated when he was refused admission to the law school of the University of Texas on the grounds that substantially equivalent facilities were already available to African Americans at another Texas school. Ruling in the case *Sweatt v. Painter*, the Court decided that the petitioner must be admitted to the University of Texas Law School since: "in terms of number of the faculty, variety of courses and opportunity for specialization, size of the student body, scope of the library, availability of law review and similar activities, the University of Texas Law School is superior."

In 1952, five different cases, all dealing with segregation in public schools, reached the U.S. Supreme Court. Four of the cases—*Brown v. Board of Education* (out of Kansas), *Briggs v. Elliott* (out of South Carolina), *Davis v. Prince Edward County School Board* (out of Virginia), and *Gebhart v. Belton* (out of Delaware)—were considered together. The fifth case, *Bolling v. Sharpe*, coming out of the District of Columbia, was considered separately since the District of Columbia is not a state.

After hearing initial arguments, the Court found itself unable to reach a decision. In 1953, the Court heard reargument. Thurgood Marshall (1908–1993), legal counsel for the NAACP Legal Defense and Educational Fund, presented arguments on behalf of the African American students. On May 17, 1954, the Court unanimously ruled that segregation in all public education deprived minority children of equal protection under the Fourteenth Amendment. In the *Bolling* case, the Court determined that segregation violated provisions of the Fifth Amendment, since the Fourteenth Amendment is expressly directed to the states.

More than fifty years after the Supreme Court's decision and a nationwide effort to dismantle racially separate schools, the United States faces an emerging problem of resegregation in public schools. This is the result of white students enrolling in private schools or transferring from predominantly black schools to schools with a predominantly white enrollment. Resegregation has also emerged because of moves to promote neighborhood schools in racially segregated communities, as occurred in Nashville, Tennessee, in 2009. In 2010, the U.S. Department of Justice had 201 open desegregation cases, most dating to the 1950s and 1960s. Of that number, 160 are in the Deep South, particularly in Alabama, Georgia, Mississippi, and Louisiana.

AFRICAN AMERICAN COLLEGES AND UNIVERSITIES

Many African American students choose to attend *historically black colleges and universities* (HBCUs), and these schools continue to account for a significant number of

Table 16-1. Children With Parental Involvement in Home Literacy Activities: 1993 to 2007

[**In percent.** For children 3 to 5 years old not yet enrolled in kindergarten who participated in activities with a family member. Based on the School Readiness Early Childhood Program Participation Surveys of the National Household Education Surveys Program.]

Characteristic	Read to[1]		Told a story[1]		Taught letters, words, or numbers[1]		Visited a library[2]	
	1993	2007	1993	2005	1993	2005	1993	2007
Total	**78**	**83**	**43**	**54**	**58**	**77**	**38**	**36**
Age:								
3 years old	79	84	46	54	57	75	34	36
4 years old	78	83	41	53	58	77	41	35
5 years old	76	83	36	55	58	80	38	39
Race/ethnicity:								
White, non-Hispanic	85	91	44	53	58	76	42	41
Black, non-Hispanic	66	78	39	54	63	81	29	25
Hispanic[3]	58	68	38	50	54	74	26	27
Other	73	87	50	64	59	82	43	46
Mother's home language:[4]								
English	81	88	44	55	58	78	39	38
Not English	42	57	36	45	52	69	26	24
Mother's highest education:[4]								
Less than high school	60	56	37	39	56	70	22	20
High school	76	74	41	51	56	78	31	29
Vocational ed or some college	83	86	45	57	60	79	44	33
College degree	90	95	48	56	56	75	55	43
Graduate/professional training or degree	90	95	50	64	60	76	59	53

[1]Three or more times in the past week.
[2]At least once in the past month.
[3]Persons of Hispanic origin may be any race.
[4]Excludes children with no mother in the household and no female guardian.

SOURCE: U.S. National Center for Education Statistics, Statistical Brief, NCES 2000–026, November 1999; the Early Childhood Program Participation Survey, National Household Education Surveys Program, 2005, unpublished data; and the School Readiness Survey, 2007, unpublished data.

Table 16-1. *This 2007 data from the National Center for Education Statistics shows a significant improvement among African American parents in providing home literacy activities for their children.*

African American graduates. In 1980, the total enrollment in these colleges was 233,557, of which 190,989 were black. By 1990, the total enrollment had reached 257,152, of which 208,682 were black. In 2000, there were 275,680 students enrolled in the HBCUs; 227,239 of these students were black. According to reports from the U.S. Department of Education, fall enrollment at two-year and four-year HBCUs stood at 306,515 in 2007. This figure includes students of other racial or ethnic backgrounds—for example, Africans, Asians, Hispanics, and whites. The total number of African American students enrolled in HBCUs for the same period is 253,415. Thus, the overall number of students enrolled in HBCUs, as well the number of black students, has continued to increase.

In 2000, Florida A&M University was the leading producer of African Americans receiving baccalaureate degrees. Between 1991 and 1995, Fisk University was grouped with such large institutions as the University of Michigan, Harvard University, and University of California, Berkeley, in the number of African American undergraduates who earned doctorates from the thirteen most productive schools. Xavier University in New Orleans has led all colleges and universities in the number of African American students accepted into medical school each year since 1995. The academic and historical significance of HBCUs was honored in 2001 as President George W. Bush proclaimed September 24–30, 2001, National Historically Black Colleges and Universities Week.

The racial composition of some African American colleges has changed dramatically; some of these colleges now have a predominantly white student body. Mandated by court order to raise its white population to 50 percent, the enrollment at Tennessee State University in 1998 was about

Table 16-2. Educational Attainment by Race, Hispanic Origin, and Sex: 1970 to 2008

[In percent.]

Year	All races[1]		White[2]		Black[2]		Asian and Pacific Islander[2]		Hispanic[3]	
	Male	Female	Male	Female	Male	Female	Male	Female	Male	Female
High School Graduate or More[4]										
1970	51.9	52.8	54.0	55.0	30.1	32.5	61.3	63.1	37.9	34.2
1980	67.3	65.8	69.6	68.1	50.8	51.5	78.8	71.4	45.4	42.7
1990	77.7	77.5	79.1	79.0	65.8	66.5	84.0	77.2	50.3	51.3
1995	81.7	81.6	83.0	83.0	73.4	74.1	(NA)	(NA)	52.9	53.8
2000	84.2	84.0	84.8	85.0	78.7	78.3	88.2	83.4	56.6	57.5
2004	84.8	85.4	85.3	86.3	80.4	80.8	88.7[5]	85.0[5]	57.3	59.5
2005	84.9	85.5	85.2	86.2	81.0	81.2	90.4	85.2	57.9	59.1
2006	85.0	85.9	85.5	86.7	80.1	81.2	89.6	85.5	58.5	60.1
2007	85.0	86.4	85.3	87.1	81.9	82.6	89.8	85.9	58.2	62.5
2008	85.9	87.2	86.3	87.8	81.8	84.0	90.8	86.9	60.9	63.7
College Graduate or More[4]										
1970	13.5	8.1	14.4	8.4	4.2	4.6	23.5	17.3	7.8	4.3
1980	20.1	12.8	21.3	13.3	8.4	8.3	39.8	27.0	9.4	6.0
1990	24.4	18.4	25.3	19.0	11.9	10.8	44.9	35.4	9.8	8.7
1995	26.0	20.2	27.2	21.0	13.6	12.9	(NA)	(NA)	10.1	8.4
2000	27.8	23.6	28.5	23.9	16.3	16.7	47.6	40.7	10.7	10.6
2004	29.4	26.1	30.0	26.4	16.6	18.5	53.7[5]	45.6[5]	11.8	12.3
2005	28.9	26.5	29.4	26.8	16.0	18.8	54.0	46.8	11.8	12.1
2006	29.2	26.9	29.7	27.1	17.2	19.4	52.5	47.1	11.9	12.9
2007	29.5	28.0	29.9	28.3	18.0	19.0	55.2	49.3	11.8	13.7
2008	30.1	28.8	30.5	29.1	18.7	20.4	55.8	49.8	12.6	14.1

NA Not available.
[1]Includes other races not shown separately.
[2]Beginning 2004, for persons who selected this race group only.
[3]Persons of Hispanic origin may be any race.
[4]Through 1990, completed 4 years of high school or more and 4 years of college or more.
[5]Starting in 2004, data are for Asians only, excludes Pacific Islanders.

SOURCE: U.S. Census Bureau, U.S. Census of Population, 1970 and 1980, Vol. 1; and Current Population Reports, P20–550, and earlier reports; and data published on the Internet.

***Table 16-2.** As the census data clearly shows, African Americans have made great progress in educational attainment (both high school and college degrees) since 1970.*

30 percent white. Those historically African American institutions with predominantly white enrollments by 1998 are Lincoln University in Missouri (72 percent white), Bluefield State College in West Virginia (89 percent white), and West Virginia State University (85 percent white).

INDEPENDENT SCHOOLS

For years, independent schools have been established in order to exert greater control, ensure quality in education, and meet the needs of African American children. In 1932, in order to promote religious growth in the African American Muslim community, the Nation of Islam founded the University of Islam, an elementary and secondary school to educate African American Muslim children in Detroit. Clara Muhammad (1899–1972), the wife of Elijah Muhammad (1897–1975), served as the school's first instructor. In 1934, a second school was opened in Chicago; by 1965, schools were operating in Atlanta and Washington, D.C. The current system of African American Muslim schools, named for Clara Muhammad, is an outgrowth of the earlier University of Islam.

Gertrude Wilks and other African American community leaders in East Palo Alto, California, organized the Nairobi Day School, a Saturday school, in 1966. In 1969, the school became a full-time school. It closed in 1984. The

Table 16-3. Educational Attainment by Selected Characteristics: 2008

[For persons 25 years old and over. As of March. Based on the Current Population Survey.]

	Percent of population—highest level					
Characteristic	Not a high school graduate	High school graduate	Some college, but no degree	Associate's degree[1]	Bachelor's degree	Advanced degree
Total persons	13.4	31.2	17.2	8.8	19.1	10.3
Age:						
25 to 34 years old	11.9	28.1	18.4	9.3	23.5	8.8
35 to 44 years old	11.4	28.6	17.1	9.9	21.8	11.2
45 to 54 years old	10.8	32.0	17.5	10.2	19.2	10.4
55 to 64 years old	11.2	30.7	18.1	8.9	18.3	12.8
65 to 74 years old	19.0	35.7	15.9	6.0	13.4	10.0
75 years old or over	26.7	38.1	14.1	4.1	10.3	6.7
Sex:						
Male	14.1	31.2	16.7	7.9	19.1	11.0
Female	12.8	31.1	17.7	9.6	19.2	9.7
Race:						
White[2]	12.9	31.3	17.2	8.9	19.3	10.4
Black[2]	17.0	35.1	19.5	8.8	13.6	6.1
Other	13.8	23.0	13.9	7.5	25.8	16.1
Hispanic origin:						
Hispanic	37.7	29.6	13.3	6.1	9.4	4.0
Non-Hispanic	9.8	31.4	17.8	9.1	20.6	11.2
Region:						
Northeast	11.9	33.9	12.8	8.2	20.5	12.8
Midwest	10.2	34.2	18.3	9.5	18.5	9.3
South	15.3	31.5	17.2	8.4	18.0	9.6
West	14.6	25.6	19.8	9.1	20.5	10.4
Marital status:						
Never married	14.2	30.3	17.4	7.8	20.9	9.4
Married, spouse present	11.1	29.9	16.5	9.1	21.1	12.1
Married, spouse absent[3]	28.2	28.4	14.6	6.9	13.2	8.7
Separated	23.4	34.3	18.7	7.2	12.4	4.0
Widowed	26.9	39.1	14.9	5.5	9.0	4.5
Divorced	11.4	33.7	21.8	10.7	14.9	7.5
Civilian labor force status:						
Employed	8.6	28.5	17.7	10.1	22.6	12.5
Unemployed	20.1	37.2	17.8	8.1	12.2	4.5
Not in the labor force	22.1	35.8	16.2	6.3	13.0	6.6

[1]Includes vocational degrees.
[2]For persons who selected this race group only.
[3]Excludes those separated.

SOURCE: U.S. Census Bureau, Current Population Survey.

Table 16-3. Slightly less than half of all African Americans continue their formal education after graduating from high school, according to 2008 census data.

New Concept Development Center in Chicago, founded as a Saturday school program in 1972, set out to create an educational institution that promoted self-respect, cooperation, and an awareness of African American history and culture. In 1975, Marva Collins, a public school teacher and nurse, founded the Westside Preparatory School in Chicago. The school remained in operation until 2008.

In recent years, the educational and social needs of urban youth, particularly African American males, have been given increased attention. Studies show that nearly 40 percent of adult African American males are functionally illiterate, and that the number of African American males incarcerated far outnumbers the number of African American males in college. Addressing these issues, large urban school systems, including those in Baltimore, Detroit, and Milwaukee, have attempted to create programs that focus on the needs of African American males.

Although African American students have shown improved performance on achievement tests, gaps between black students and white students still exist. Progress has been made in the quality of education for African American children, yet inadequacies remain in the provision of resources for their education. Efforts at creating alternative schools designed to meet the needs of African American children and to reflect the cultural and social experiences of African Americans have received increased attention. In 1999, the Institute for Independent Education, an organization providing technical assistance to independent neighborhood schools, reported that an estimated sixty thousand African American children attended independent community-based schools in the United States.

EDUCATIONAL TRENDS

AFROCENTRISM

An educational methodology that has sparked both widespread praise and criticism is *Afrocentrism.* Afrocentrism is based, in part, on the belief that the ancient Greeks stole most of their great philosophical and mathematical thought from the Egyptians, an African people. Afrocentrists argue that the Greek philosopher Aristotle gleaned much of his philosophy from books plundered from the Egyptian city of Alexandria, and that the famous Greek philosopher Socrates was black. Afrocentrists further claim that the current educational system in the United States is deeply flawed and promotes white supremacy. It teaches history, arts, science, and other disciplines from a purely traditional European point of view, while African contributions to these fields of endeavor are ignored entirely or given inadequate consideration. Proponents of Afrocentrism theorize that teaching African American children from an African-centered perspective through the championing of black culture, history, and achievement will increase their feelings of self-worth and give them a greater sense of identity and ethnic pride.

The doctrine of Afrocentrism is not new. A number of prominent early twentieth-century African Americans, such as Marcus Garvey (1887–1940) and Carter G. Woodson, were among its most ardent supporters. Afrocentrism was later championed by many African American scholars, including most prominently Molefi K. Asante, Leonard Jeffries, Asa Hilliard (1933–2007), and John Henrik Clarke (1915–1998). Some public school systems with predominantly African American enrollment, such as those in Atlanta, New Orleans, Cleveland, Indianapolis, New York, Oakland, and Philadelphia, have introduced African-centered principles into their curriculums.

Afrocentrism is not without its critics, however. Among them is Mary Lefkowitz, a professor of humanities at Wellesley College. In her book *Not Out of Africa: How Afrocentrism Became an Excuse to Teach Myth as History* (1996), Lefkowitz disagrees with the assertions of Afrocentrists that the Greeks stole their philosophical and mathematical thought from the Egyptians or that Socrates was black. She argues that Afrocentrist beliefs are based on myth and conjecture, not historical fact, and are designed to promote a political agenda. This criticism is echoed by Arthur Schlesinger (1917–2007), author of *The Disuniting of America* (1991). Schlesinger remarks that African-centered education is divisive and un-American and promotes the teaching of inaccuracy and distorted history. Whether one is a supporter or critic, it is clear that Afrocentrism will continue to inspire heated debate for many years to come.

EBONICS VERSUS STANDARD ENGLISH

Black English, considered by most linguists to be a dialectal form of English (that is, a dialect such as, to pick one example, Appalachian English), came to the forefront of discussion in 1996. The languages that the enslaved Africans brought to the United States influenced their learning and use of English. While Black English has been studied since the first half of the twentieth century, in 1996 some scholars renamed it *Ebonics*—a combination of the words *ebony* and *phonics*. In the 1960s and 1970s, Black English was called Black Vernacular English (BVE); in the 1980s and 1990s, it was known as African American Vernacular English (AAVE). It shares many basic characteristics with other dialects, the most important being distinct grammar and syntax patterns (dialects are learnable precisely because they are "rule based" in this sense).

When the Oakland, California, school board passed a resolution in 1996 to make Ebonics "a second language" and declared that all of the teachers in the system should be trained in its grammar (and should respect it as the native form of speech spoken by many of their African American students), a storm of criticism followed nationally. Opponents contended that Black English was simply substandard grammar and, if regarded as a legitimate language, would be detrimental to African American students. As national attention spotlighted the controversy, in May 1997 the school board reaffirmed what it called its original intention: "to improve the English language acquisition and application skills of African-American students" and, as much as possible, to help students master Standard English.

According to John Rickford and Russell Rickford in *The Spoken Soul: The Story of Black English* (2000), the board never intended to replace Standard or mainstream English with Ebonics or any other "language" or dialect peculiar to any racial or ethnic group. In 1997, the U.S. Congress supported Oakland's efforts by awarding the district $1 million to continue research on the linguistic and cultural resources of African American students. *The Spoken Soul* embraces the perspective that Black English is not only "the language of jazz, funk, hip-hop, and rap," all currently popular in American culture, but it is also the home dialect of many African Americans. Before teaching their students additional, standard forms, educators need to be aware of how and what their students actually speak. By 2010, Black English continued to be a topic for research in higher education. Extensive bibliographies have been compiled on the subject, and the trends seen in the 1990s are under review.

ABANDONING AFFIRMATIVE ACTION

National debate, lawsuits, and voter reaction over the issue of affirmative action have had an impact on the education of African American students. Since the U.S. Supreme Court's validation of the use of race as a factor in college and university admissions programs in the case of *Regents of the University of California v. Bakke* (1978), many race-conscious admissions policies have come under attack in courts of law. Recent decisions in federal courts cloud the issue, and may lead to another Supreme Court review of affirmative action policies at institutions of higher learning. In 2001, a decision by the Eleventh Circuit Court of Appeals in *Johnson v. Board of Regents of the University of Georgia* struck down the race-conscious admissions policy for freshmen at the University of Georgia. The decision mirrored a 1996 Fifth Circuit Court of Appeals ruling that invalidated a similar policy at the University of Texas Law School. On the other hand, the affirmative action admissions policy at the University of Michigan Law School was upheld by a Sixth Circuit Court of Appeals ruling in May 2002. On June 23, 2003, the U.S. Supreme Court ruled five to four in favor of the law school's use of race in considering enrollment.

In a number of states, voter initiatives and executive action have dealt race-conscious admissions policies more setbacks. Voters in California passed Proposition 209 in 1996. The law banned the use of race as a consideration for acceptance to the state's universities. Washington State voters passed a similar measure, Initiative 200, in 1998, and Jeb Bush, then governor of Florida, instituted the One Florida Initiative in 2000. The effects of such measures can be severe, resulting in a drop in the enrollment of African American students at state institutions of higher learning. A 2002 NAACP Education Department report, *NAACP Call for Action in Education*, points out that following the passage of California's Proposition 209, only one African American student enrolled in a class of more than three hundred at the University of California, Berkeley's school of law in 1999. The same year, only two black students were among the entering law-school class at the University of California, Los Angeles.

Derek Bok and William G. Bowen, advocates of race-conscious admission policies, completed a major study that challenges much of the conservative thinking about affirmative action. In their findings, published in *The Shape of the River: Long-Term Consequences of Considering Race in College and University Admissions* (1998), the two scholars studied race-conscious admissions in elite higher education and confirmed that such practices "create the backbone of the black middle class."

Some mainstream institutions have seen a decrease in the number of black students enrolled and have responded by developing plans to rebuild that enrollment. This occurred, for example, in Kentucky, where over a third of college-bound African American students chose the University of Louisville over the University of Kentucky. This caused some state lawmakers and faculty at the University of Kentucky to question the university's commitment to diversity. The university responded by adding a scholarship program to increase diversity on campus. The City University of New York (CUNY) launched a systemwide African American Male Initiative aimed at improving "the success and retention of the Black men on its 11 senior-college campuses." Similar initiatives followed in the University System of Georgia and elsewhere. Although affirmative action opponents stifle such programs, the initiatives are viewed by many leaders as well-intentioned.

VOUCHER SYSTEMS AND CHARTER SCHOOLS

Some educators regard voucher programs and charter schools as logical parts of a broad educational mix. The voucher idea originated in the 1960s; it aimed to permit students to transfer from failing public schools to successful private schools. Critics feared, however, that the brightest students, both black and white, would be drawn away, leaving the inner-city schools, in terms of characteristics, African American and poor. Critics also raised questions about the use of public funds in private institutions, particularly those maintained and operated by churches or religious organizations. Voucher systems have been initiated in a handful of cities, including Cleveland, Milwaukee, and

Detroit, and are being considered in about half of the fifty states. The voucher programs that are operational serve low-income, largely African American and Hispanic American children. In July 2002, the U.S. Supreme Court validated the constitutionality of Ohio's voucher program, opening the door for the wider use of school-voucher programs throughout the nation.

Charter schools, or independent public schools, may be established by parents, community groups, local or state school boards, colleges and universities, or other individuals or groups. They are becoming increasingly popular throughout the country. In 2009, there were more than five thousand charter schools serving more than 1.5 million children across the United States. For the 2009–2010 school year, 419 new charter schools opened. Some charter schools were once private schools, others were converted from existing public schools, and still others are newly established educational institutions. Generally, the schools report directly to the state and bypass local unions or other traditional bureaucracy. They are schools of choice for students and teachers; therefore, they must operate with the highest regard for equity and academic excellence or they may be closed. Since Tennessee's law creating charter schools was passed in 2002, three such schools—including one in Nashville in 2010—were closed for failing to meet specific guidelines. Supporters of charter schools have little faith in traditional education systems and look to the charter schools as a viable solution to the problems of public school education. They see charter schools as a means of providing inner-city children the kind of education that students receive in the affluent suburbs. Some educators and parents see the charter-school movement as another threat to public school education. By 2009, however, thirty-nine states and the District of Columbia had passed charter-school laws.

Charter schools have been established in African American communities or for African Americans and others who are underserved in such cities as Chicago, Oakland, and Atlanta, and in the Harlem section of New York. In Atlanta, for example, the first such school, the Charles R. Drew Charter School (named for the African American who pioneered in the preservation of blood plasma and established blood banks), was created by the East Lake Foundation in August 2000.

Table 16-4. High School Dropouts by Race and Hispanic Origin: 1980 to 2007

[In percent.]

Item	1980	1985	1990[1]	1995	2000	2001	2002	2003	2004	2005	2006	2007
Event dropouts[2]												
Total[3]	**6.0**	**5.2**	**4.5**	**5.4**	**4.5**	**4.7**	**3.3**	**3.8**	**4.4**	**3.6**	**3.5**	**3.3**
White[4]	5.6	4.8	3.9	5.1	4.3	4.6	3.0	3.7	4.2	3.1	3.5	2.8
Male	6.4	4.9	4.1	5.4	4.7	5.3	3.0	3.9	4.9	3.4	3.9	2.8
Female	4.9	4.7	3.8	4.8	4.0	3.8	3.0	3.4	3.5	2.7	3.1	2.7
Black[4]	8.3	7.7	7.7	6.1	5.6	5.7	4.4	4.5	5.2	6.9	3.7	4.3
Male	8.0	8.3	6.9	7.9	7.6	6.1	5.1	4.1	4.8	7.5	3.2	4.9
Female	8.5	7.2	8.6	4.4	3.8	5.4	3.8	4.9	5.7	6.2	4.3	3.6
Hispanic[5]	11.5	9.7	7.7	11.6	6.8	8.1	5.3	6.5	8.0	4.7	6.4	5.5
Male	16.9	9.3	7.6	10.9	7.1	7.6	6.2	7.7	11.5	5.6	6.3	5.5
Female	6.9	9.8	7.7	12.5	6.5	8.7	4.4	5.4	4.6	3.9	6.6	5.6
Status dropouts[6]												
Total[3]	**15.6**	**13.9**	**14.4**	**13.9**	**12.4**	**13.0**	**12.3**	**11.8**	**12.1**	**11.3**	**11.0**	**10.2**
White[4]	14.4	13.5	14.1	13.6	12.2	13.4	12.2	11.6	11.9	11.3	10.8	10.0
Male	15.7	14.7	15.4	14.3	13.5	15.3	13.7	13.3	13.7	13.2	12.4	11.7
Female	13.2	12.3	12.8	13.0	10.9	11.4	10.6	9.8	10.0	9.4	9.2	8.3
Black[4]	23.5	17.6	16.4	14.4	15.3	13.8	14.6	14.2	15.1	12.9	13.0	10.2
Male	26.0	18.8	18.6	14.2	17.4	16.9	16.9	16.7	17.9	14.8	11.2	10.0
Female	21.5	16.6	14.5	14.6	13.5	11.0	12.5	12.0	12.7	11.2	14.7	10.3
Hispanic[5]	40.3	31.5	37.7	34.7	32.3	31.7	30.1	28.4	28.0	27.3	26.2	25.3
Male	42.6	35.8	40.3	34.2	36.8	37.1	33.8	31.7	33.5	32.1	31.0	29.2
Female	38.1	27.0	35.0	35.4	27.3	25.5	25.6	24.7	21.7	21.8	21.0	21.1

[1]Beginning 1990, reflects new editing procedures for cases with missing data on school enrollment.
[2]Percent of students who drop out in a single year without completing high school. For grades 10 to 12.
[3]Includes other races, not shown separately.
[4]Beginning 2003, for persons who selected this race group only.
[5]Persons of Hispanic origin may be any race.
[6]Percent of the population who have not completed high school and are not enrolled, regardless of when they dropped out. For persons 18 to 24 years old.

SOURCE: U.S. Census Bureau, Current Population Reports, PPL-148; and earlier PPL and P-20 reports; and data published on the Internet.

Table 16-4. *The percentage of African American students completing their high school education has risen dramatically since 1980.*

It opened with 240 children in kindergarten through fifth grade and now serves more than 820 students in preschool through eighth grade. With its rich and academically challenging curriculum, the Drew Charter School achieved one of the highest rates of improvement for students in Atlanta and in Georgia, and competes with some of the state's best private schools.

Harlem's Promise Academy Charter Schools operate free of charge. They began in September 2004 with the opening of Promise Academy 1 elementary and middle schools. They were created in partnership with Harlem Children's Zone, Inc. (HCZ), as a way to impact the centerpiece of a child's educational experience. The mission is "to give children in Harlem high-quality, well-rounded education." The schools operate on an extended school day and year to give students time to master basic skills and to explore the arts and sciences as well. College graduation for every child in the program is the ultimate goal. A study commissioned by the school's founder, Geoffrey Canada, affirms with scientific evidence that Promise Academy is one of the nation's gap-closing schools for disadvantaged children. The Harlem Children's Zone is a high-profile initiative that combines charter schools with wrap-around community services for minority students and their low-income families. Canada's experiment with HCZ, which has turned around neighborhoods in New York, caught the attention of President Barack Obama, who called the program a model and in 2009 set in motion plans to replicate what he calls the Promise Neighborhoods in twenty cities across the nation.

Urban Prep Academy, founded in Chicago in 2006, is another example of a successful charter school for black students in urban areas. The only public, all-male, all-black high school in Chicago, Urban Prep opened in a troubled neighborhood; most of its freshman class read below grade level. In 2010, however, the entire 107-member senior class was accepted to four-year colleges.

SINGLE-GENDER SCHOOLS AND RACE-BASED ENROLLMENT

The United States has seen a number of single-gender schools opened since the 1990s. One such school opened in the fall of 1996, when the Young Women's Leadership

Harlem Children's Zone Promise Academy, New York, 2009. *Children play during a lunch break at the academy. A charter school, the academy offers an extended school day and year, as well as after-school programs, as it strives to give the children an exceptional, well-rounded education. President Obama highlighted the success of these programs in 2009.* E. JASON WAMBSGANS/MCT/LANDOV

School, an experimental public school for girls, opened in East Harlem. It emphasizes mathematics and science, subjects in which girls often lag behind boys in performance. The school originally provided for fifty-six seventh-grade girls, and had expanded to 360 students in grades seven through twelve by 2000. By 2010, more than 420 students were enrolled in grades six through twelve. Advocates of the Young Women's Leadership School cited studies that showed that girls, particularly those from poor communities, performed better when boys were not present. Some groups, such as the New York Civil Liberties Union, have challenged the Young Women's Leadership School, arguing that single-gender schools violate the U.S. Constitution, as well as federal statutory law. The group has challenged plans for other single-gender, single-race schools for young African American men in New York, Detroit, and Milwaukee.

More than half a century after *Brown v. Board of Education of Topeka*, segregated public schools continue to operate. Evidence of racial isolation in urban schools, as seen in Hartford, Connecticut, in 1997, led the state's highest court to issue a mandate to desegregate the schools. Under the order, racially isolated students in urban schools are able to enroll in predominantly white suburban schools on a space-available plan. The Connecticut decision seems to be running counter to the current trend to abandon racial "quotas" in schools, where predominance of one race is not necessarily grounds for legal relief unless the cause lies in segregation patterns of the past. The concern over affirmative action, however, is shifting from colleges and universities to public school districts. Districts that have adopted voluntary desegregation plans, such as Montgomery County, Maryland, and Arlington, Virginia, wonder if they can continue race-conscious policies.

Desegregation orders imposed by the courts decades earlier are being lifted. In such cities as Nashville, Oklahoma City, Denver, Wilmington, Cleveland, and Little Rock, courts have declared that past segregation practices have been remedied and judicial monitoring is no longer needed. A U.S. Supreme Court decision on June 28, 2007, struck down school-integration plans in Louisville and Seattle, halting the practice of determining enrollment in public schools on the basis on race.

AFRICAN AMERICAN LEADERSHIP INITIATIVES

A growing trend in education is a focus on leadership programs, whether or not they are gender-based. In 2006, the North Carolina Community College System held a Conference on African American Males in Education as the community's response to the success of African American males in postsecondary education. HBCUs have become more concerned about leadership training for their administrators. One HBCU, Hampton University, sponsors an executive leadership summit called "On the Road to the Presidency." The program is designed for newly appointed college presidents and chancellors, provosts, vice presidents, deans, and others in executive posts. Other leadership training programs have been held or are operational at such HBCUs as Bennett College for Women, Fisk University, and Morehouse College.

ADMINISTRATORS, EDUCATORS, AND SCHOLARS

(Some biographical profiles may appear in other chapters. To locate profiles more readily, please consult the index.)

MOLEFI K. ASANTE (1942–)

Scholar. Molefi Kete Asante was born Arthur Lee Smith Jr. on August 14, 1942, in Valdosta, Georgia. His name was legally changed in 1973. In 1962, Asante graduated with an associate's degree from Southwestern Christian College. He graduated cum laude with a B.A. from Oklahoma Christian College in 1964, then received an M.A. from Pepperdine University in 1965 and a Ph.D. from the University of California, Los Angeles (UCLA), in 1968.

Asante has taught speech and communications at many universities in the United States. He was an instructor at California State Polytechnic University at Pomona (1966–1967) and California State University, Northridge (1967). In 1968, he accepted an assistant professorship at Purdue University in Lafayette, Indiana, where he remained until 1969, when he began teaching at UCLA. There he advanced from assistant to associate professor of speech and also served as the director of the Center for Afro-American Studies (1970–1973). In 1973, Asante accepted the position of professor of communications at the State University of New York at Buffalo. He soon became department chairman, a position he held until 1979, when he became a visiting professor at Howard University in Washington, D.C. (1979–1980). In 1981 and 1982, he was a Fulbright professor at the Zimbabwe Institute of Mass Communications. In 1984, he became a professor at Temple University in Philadelphia in the Department of African American Studies.

Asante is a prolific author, with dozens of books dealing with both communication theory and the African American experience. His titles include: *Afrocentricity: The Theory of Social Change* (1980); *African Culture: The Rhythms of Unity* (1985), edited with Kariamu Welsh Asante; *The Afrocentric Idea* (1987); *Kemet, Afrocentricity, and Knowledge* (1990); *Historical and Cultural Atlas of African-Americans* (1991), written with Mark Mattson; *African American History: A Journey of Liberation* (1995); *African Intellectual Heritage: A Book of Sources* (1996), edited with Abu Abarry; *The Painful Demise of Eurocentrism: An Afrocentric Response to Critics* (2000); *The Egyptian Philosophers: Ancient African Voices from Imhotep to Akhenaten* (2000); *Socio-Cultural Conflict between African American and Korean American* (2000), edited with Eungjun Min; *Erasing Racism: The Social Survival of the American Nation* (2003, 2nd ed. 2009); *Race, Rhetoric, & Identity: The Architecton of Soul* (2005); *The History of Africa: The Quest for Eternal Harmony* (2007); and *Maulana Karenga: An Intellectual Portrait* (2009).

Asante is also a founding editor of the *Journal of Black Studies* and was a member of the advisory board of the *Black Law Journal* (1971–1973) and *Race Relations Abstract* (1973–1977). In addition, Asante has served as the vice president for the National Council of Black Studies and the African Heritage Studies Association.

HOUSTON A. BAKER JR.

See chapter 18, Literature

MARIA LOUISE BALDWIN (1856–1922)

Educator. Born on September 13, 1856, in Cambridge, Massachusetts, Maria Louise Baldwin was one of the most distinguished educators in the United States at the turn of the twentieth century. She was the principal of the Agassiz School in Cambridge, which children of affluent and established white families attended—a rarity for a woman and an African American.

Educated in Cambridge, Baldwin taught first in Chestertown, Maryland, and then was appointed teacher in Agassiz Grammar School. Eventually, she taught all grades in the school—from first to seventh—and in 1889 was promoted to school principal. In 1916, a new school was erected and more grades were added, with Baldwin's position changing to master. She strengthened her credentials by enrolling in courses at nearby Harvard University. She remained at Agassiz until 1922.

Baldwin lectured throughout the country on such luminaries as Paul Laurence Dunbar, Abraham Lincoln, and Thomas Jefferson and on women's suffrage, poetry, and history. On January 9, 1922, she collapsed and died at Boston's Copley Plaza Hotel during a lecture. The entire nation mourned her death. About a year later, Agassiz School recognized her by unveiling a tablet created in her memory. Other memorials followed, including the naming in her honor of the Agassiz School auditorium and a women's residence center at Howard University in Washington, D.C.

LERONE BENNETT JR. (1928–)

Historian, Journalist, Editor. Born on October 17, 1928, in Clarksdale, Mississippi, Lerone Bennett Jr. was educated at Morehouse College, receiving an A.B. in 1949. Bennett worked as a journalist and editor for the *Atlanta Daily World* and *Jet* magazine before joining *Ebony* magazine in 1954. He was named executive editor in 1987. Beyond these positions though, Bennett has achieved fame for his essays and other writings.

Bennett's 1962 book, *Before the Mayflower: A History of the Negro in America, 1619–1962*, made him one of the best-known and most influential African American historians of the twentieth century. *Before the Mayflower* was revised and reprinted several times (later editions were subtitled *A History of Black America*). Bennett's 1964 biography of Morehouse College classmate Martin Luther King Jr., *What Manner of Man*, was welcomed as an evenhanded analysis of the African American leader's life and his role in fundamentally changing the nature of racial dynamics in the United States.

Also in 1964, Bennett published *The Negro Mood and Other Essays*, a collection that demonstrated a sharper editorial bite than his previous works. Probing such issues as the failed integration of African Americans into American life and the ways in which African Americans are denied the fruits of society, Bennett takes aim at the white liberal establishment for ignoring the accomplishments of African Americans and for mouthing the words of racial justice rather acting on them. Bennett has written a number of other works, including *Pioneers in Protest* (1968), *The Shaping of Black America* (1974), *Wade in the Water: Great Moments in Black History* (1979), and *Forced into Glory: Abraham Lincoln's White Dream* (2000).

Bennett served as a visiting professor at Northwestern University during the 1968–1969 school year. In addition, he was a senior fellow of the Institute of the Black World in 1969. In 2002, Bennett won an American Book Award for lifetime achievement from the American Book Association.

MARY MCLEOD BETHUNE (1875–1955)

School Founder and Administrator, Educator. Born on July 10, 1875, near Mayesville, South Carolina, Mary McLeod received a sporadic education in local schools. She eventually won a scholarship and studied for seven years at the Scotia Seminary in Concord, North Carolina. In 1893, she enrolled at the Moody Bible Institute in Chicago in hopes of securing a missionary position in Africa. In 1895, after the Presbyterian Mission Board declined to send her to Africa, she began teaching at the Haines Institute in Augusta, Georgia, and then at the Kendall Institute in Sumter, South Carolina. She married Albertus Bethune in Sumter in 1898. Between 1900 and 1904, she taught in Palatka, Florida.

In 1904, Bethune founded her own school in Daytona Beach, Florida—the Daytona Educational and Industrial Training School for Negro Girls. John D. Rockefeller became an early admirer and supporter of the school after hearing a performance by its choir. Bethune also founded the Tomoka Missions and, in 1911, the McLeod Hospital. In 1922, her school merged with the Cookman Institute to become Bethune-Cookman College (later Bethune-Cookman University).

Bethune's work received national attention, and she served on two conferences under President Herbert Hoover.

Educator and Civil Rights Activist Mary McLeod Bethune, Bethune-Cookman College, Daytona Beach, FL, January 1943. *In a photograph taken by Gordon Parks, Bethune says goodbye to a group of students after resigning as president of the college. Nearly forty years earlier, she had founded a school for training African American teachers, which eventually evolved into Bethune-Cookman University.* THE LIBRARY OF CONGRESS

In 1936, President Franklin Roosevelt appointed her director of the Division of Negro Affairs of the National Youth Administration. During World War II, she served as special assistant to the secretary of war, responsible for selecting Women's Army Corps officer candidates of African American descent.

Bethune also served on the executive board of the National Urban League and was a vice president of the NAACP. She received the Spingarn Award in 1935, the Frances A. Drexel Award in 1936, and the Thomas Jefferson Medal in 1942. Bethune was also instrumental in the founding of the National Council of Negro Women. She retired from public life in 1950 on her seventy-fifth birthday and died five years later on May 18, 1955.

Much of Bethune's philosophy concerned ennobling labor and empowering African Americans to achieve economic independence. Although a tireless fighter for equality, she eschewed rhetorical militancy in favor of a doctrine of universal love.

CHARLOTTE HAWKINS BROWN (1883–1961)

School Founder, Educator, Civic Leader. Charlotte Hawkins Brown was a pioneer in quality preparatory education for African American youth. She set her ideas and experiments in place at the Palmer Memorial Institute, which she founded in Sedalia, North Carolina, and headed for more than half a century.

Lottie Hawkins was born on June 11, 1883, in Henderson, North Carolina. She and eighteen members of her family moved to Cambridge, Massachusetts, in 1888 in search of better social and educational opportunities. By the time of her graduation from Cambridge English School, she had changed her name to Charlotte Eugenia Hawkins. In 1900, she enrolled in the State Normal School in Salem, Massachusetts. She left the school in October 1901 to teach at the American Missionary Association's Bethany Institute near McLeansville, North Carolina. The school closed at the end of the year.

Hawkins returned to Cambridge in 1902 and discussed with benefactor Alice Freeman Palmer, whom she had met at the end of her high school studies, her plan to start a school in Sedalia, North Carolina. Palmer and other northern philanthropists provided Hawkins funds for the school, and on October 10, 1902, Hawkins founded the Alice Freeman Palmer Institute, named in honor of her friend. After Palmer died that fall, the school was renamed Palmer Memorial Institute. It was incorporated on November 23, 1907. By then, Hawkins had a diploma from the Salem Normal School, had studied at Harvard University and Wellesley and Simmons colleges, and had married Edward Sumner Brown.

By 1916, the school was housed in four buildings. Fires in 1917 and 1922 destroyed two buildings; one of these, Memorial Hall, was replaced in 1922 with the Alice Freeman Palmer Building. By 1922, the school had built a fine reputation as one of the country's leading preparatory schools for African Americans. A junior college academic program that focused on agricultural and vocational training, which Brown had introduced in the mid-1920s, gave way to secondary and postsecondary education. Later on, the school also emphasized good manners and social graces as it prepared young African Americans to assume positions in society. The school's presence, already felt strongly in the South, was now known across the country, and students responded by enrolling in greater numbers. In 1922, Palmer graduated its first high school class.

Brown emerged as a national leader, and she was recognized for her work in directing the institute, as well as her strong resolve in advancing the life of African Americans and African American women in particular. She was a staunch public opponent of lynching. She also helped organize the North Carolina State Federation of Negro Women's Clubs and was active in the national African American women's club movement. In addition, she persuaded the state to establish homes for young African American women who were in legal difficulty, such as the Efland Home for Wayward Girls. As president of the North Carolina Teachers Association from 1935 to 1937, she helped effect change in the education of the state's African American residents. She was a key figure in the southern interracial women's movement and became the first African American member in the Twentieth Century Club of Boston.

Brown became known for her writings as well. Her works included *Mammy: An Appeal to the Heart of the South* (1919) and *The Correct Thing to Do, to Say, and to Wear* (1940). The latter work, originally used as a guide for Palmer students, attracted the attention of young people across the country and was reprinted five times.

After fifty years of service, Brown retired as president of Palmer on October 5, 1952, but she remained on campus until 1955 as vice chairman of the board of trustees and director of finances. Wilhelmina Marguerite Crosson replaced Brown as president. By the end of the decade, the school enrolled annually about two hundred junior and senior students who came from across the country, the Caribbean, and Africa.

Brown died in Greensboro on January 11, 1961, and was buried on the Palmer campus. Although Brown's spirit and ideals continued for a while, the school began to suffer from declining enrollment, the rising cost of maintenance, and reduced support from benefactors. Another fire in 1971 destroyed the Alice Freeman Palmer Building. In November of that year, Bennett College for Women in nearby Greensboro assumed the institute's debts and took over the site. The home that Brown had built on campus, Canary Cottage, has been preserved and, in 1983, was declared a state historic site. It was declared a national historic landmark in 1988. The institute's entire campus was designated a state historic site in the previous year.

NANNIE HELEN BURROUGHS (1879–1961)

Educator, School Founder and Administrator. Born in Orange Springs, Virginia, on May 2, 1879, Nannie Helen Burroughs was one of the most significant Baptist lay leaders of the twentieth century, a lifelong booster of women's education, and a tireless civic organizer. She addressed the National Baptist Convention in Virginia in 1900 on the subject "How the Sisters Are Hindered from Helping," and, from that time until her death more than sixty years later, she exercised pivotal leadership. She was elected corresponding secretary for the Woman's Convention, Auxiliary to the National Baptist Convention, U.S.A., Inc., and in 1948 she became president of the Woman's Convention.

In 1901, Burroughs founded and presided over the National Training School for Women and Girls, which emphasized industrial arts and proficiency in African American history. After only one year, she had recruited thirty-one students. In honor of her efforts, the school's curriculum was changed to accommodate elementary education, and its name was changed to the Nannie Helen Burroughs School.

Burroughs was active in the antilynching campaign and a longtime member of the Association for the Study of Negro Life and History. She helped organize the Women's Industrial Club of Louisville and was responsible for organizing Washington, D.C.'s first African American self-help program. She also edited such periodicals as the *Christian Banner* and was the author of *Roll Call of Bible Women*. She died on May 20, 1961.

JOE CLARK (1939–)

Educator, Lecturer, Executive Director. Joe Clark is best known as the feisty, dedicated, baseball bat–wielding school principal portrayed by actor Morgan Freeman in the 1989 film *Lean on Me*. Clark has served as an exemplar of school discipline and boasts a distinguished record of achievements and laurels. A fourteen-year member of the New Jersey Board of Education and an elementary and secondary school principal until 1989, he has been honored by the White House, the NAACP, his alma mater Seton Hall University, and various newspapers and magazines.

Born in Rochelle, Georgia, in 1939, Clark served in the U.S. Army Reserve from 1958 to 1966. He received a B.A. from New Jersey's William Paterson College in 1960 and his master's degree from Seton Hall in 1974. From 1960 to 1974, Clark served on the board of education in Paterson, New Jersey. He was a coordinator of language arts from 1976 until 1979. Clark became a school principal for the first time in 1979 and quickly earned the admiration and respect of educators for his somewhat controversial, no-nonsense managerial style.

In 1983, Clark received the NAACP Community Service Award and was named New Jerseyan of the Year by the *Newark Star Ledger*. The following year, *New Jersey Monthly* honored Clark as outstanding educator. In 1985, Clark appeared in Washington, D.C., to receive honors at a presidential conference on academic and disciplinary excellence. Seton Hall and Fairleigh Dickinson University also honored him. The National School Safety Center gave Clark the Principal of Leadership Award in 1986, and the National Black Policemen's Association bestowed their Humanitarian Award on him in 1988.

In 1989, Clark ended his tenure as principal of Eastside High School in Paterson, New Jersey, and traveled the country as a lecturer. He also published *Laying Down the Law: Joe Clark's Strategy for Saving Our Schools* (1989). Clark accepted a job as the director of the Essex County, New Jersey, Youth House, a juvenile detention center in Newark, in August 1995.

KENNETH CLARK (1914–2005)

Psychologist, Educator, Writer. Born on July 24, 1914, in the Panama Canal Zone, Clark was brought to the United States as a youth by his mother so that he could be educated. He attended school in Harlem and then entered Howard University. He was awarded a B.A. in 1935 and an M.S. in 1936 in psychology. In 1940, he became the first African American awarded a Ph.D. in psychology from Columbia University. He then taught at the Hampton Institute, but left because of the school's conservative views. In 1942, he joined the faculty of the City College of New York (CCNY), and remained there for the rest of his academic career.

Clark was deeply troubled by school segregation and studied its effects with his wife, the psychologist Mamie Phipps Clark. The Clarks' research came to the attention of the NAACP during its postwar campaign to overturn legalized segregation. Kenneth Clark was intimately involved in the long legal struggle that culminated in 1954 with *Brown v. Board of Education of Topeka*. He testified as an expert witness at three of the four cases leading up to the Supreme Court's review of *Brown*, and his report on the psychology of segregation was read carefully by the justices. The *Brown* case was not only a milestone in the modern civil rights movement, it made Kenneth Clark into an academic superstar. He eventually became the most influential African American social scientist of his generation.

In the 1960s, Clark founded the HARYOU (Harlem Youth Opportunities Unlimited) program in New York and the MARC Corp. (Metropolitan Applied Research Center) in Washington, D.C. Both were efforts to move integration forward in public schools and to set test score–based standards for schools and teachers. Both projects, however, were terminated for political reasons.

Clark retired from CCNY in 1975 and formed his own consultancy to counsel companies on integrating their workforces. Clark continued to write vehemently on the subject of integration. He died on May 1, 2005.

SEPTIMA CLARK (1898–1987)

Educator, Civil Rights Activist. Septima Poinsette Clark had a major impact on the voting rights of thousands of African American southerners. Clark dedicated her life to education because she believed that before one could persuade people to register and vote, one had to teach them to read and write.

Clark was born in Charleston, South Carolina, in 1898. She received a teaching certificate in 1916 from Avery Normal Institute, a school run by the American Missionary Association in Charleston. African Americans were not allowed to teach in Charleston's public schools at the time, so Clark secured a job at an African American school on St. John's Island, where she taught until 1919. Thereafter, Clark became active in the NAACP and other civic organizations fighting for reform in public schools. She also continued her education. She briefly studied under W. E. B. Du Bois at Atlanta University in 1937. She received a B.A. from Benedict College in 1942, and an M.A. from Hampton Institute four years later.

In 1956, after teaching for nearly a decade in Charleston, the school board fired her because of her association with the NAACP. Clark was then hired by the progressive Highlander Folk School in Monteagle, Tennessee, where she began the "citizenship schools" program. Students in Highlander's citizenship schools were taught how to write their names, balance checkbooks, fill out a voting ballot, and understand their rights and duties as U.S. citizens. The program was a success, and by 1961 had grown too big for Highlander to handle. The Southern Christian Leadership Conference (SCLC) expressed an interest in taking over, so Clark went to work for the SCLC as director of education.

After retiring from the SCLC in 1970, Clark stayed active in civil rights struggles. In 1974, when she was seventy-six years old, she was elected to serve on the Charleston school board—the same school board that had fired her eighteen years earlier for her involvement with the NAACP. She died in Charleston on December 15, 1987.

JOHNNETTA B. COLE (1936–)

Educator, Anthropologist, College President, Museum Director. Distinguished scholar Johnnetta Betsch Cole has served on the faculties of Washington State University, the University of Massachusetts at Amherst, Hunter College, Spelman College, and Emory University. Born in Jacksonville, Florida, on October 19, 1936, Cole attended Oberlin College in Ohio, which awarded her a B.A. in 1957. She later earned master's and doctorate degrees in anthropology at Northwestern University in 1959 and 1967, respectively.

In 1967, Cole began her first teaching assignment at Washington State University, where she taught anthropology and served as director of black studies. The university honored her as Outstanding Faculty Member of the Year in 1970. From 1970 until 1983, Cole was professor of anthropology and African American studies at the University of Massachusetts at Amherst. She left Amherst in 1983 for a position as professor of anthropology at Hunter College in New York. Cole also served as director of Latin American and Caribbean studies at Hunter College from 1984 until 1987. In 1987, Cole was named president of Spelman College and became known as "America's sister president." She resigned in 1997 and took a professorship at Emory University in Atlanta. In 2002, she again became president of a historically black college, Bennett College for Women in Greensboro, North Carolina. Cole retired from the presidency of Bennett effective June 2007, and later became director of the Smithsonian Institution's National Museum of African Art in Washington, D.C.

As an anthropologist, Cole has done fieldwork in Liberia and Cuba, as well as in the African American community. A prolific writer, she has published in many mainstream periodicals and scholarly journals. Since 1979, she has been a contributor and advising editor to the *Black Scholar*. She is the author of *Conversations: Straight Talk with America's Sister President* (1993), *Dream the Boldest Dreams and Other Lessons of Life* (1997), and *Who Should Be First? Feminists Speak Out on the 2008 Presidential Campaign* (2010), edited with Beverly Guy-Sheftall. Cole is a member of the National Council of Negro Women and a fellow of the American Anthropological Association.

Cole has received numerous awards and more than forty honorary degrees. She was presented with the Elizabeth Boyer Award in 1988 and the *Essence* Award in Education in 1989. In 1990, Cole won the American Women Award and the Jessie Bernard Wise Woman Award, and she was inducted into the Working Woman Hall of Fame. She also received the Jewish National Fund's highest honor, the Tree of Life Award (1994), the Smithsonian's McGovern Behavioral Science Award (1999), the Alex de Tocqueville Award for community service from United Way of America (2001), and the Independent Sector's John W. Gardner Leadership Award (2006) for her long commitment to advancing social justice nationally and globally.

MARVA COLLINS (1936–)

Educator, School Founder and Director. Marva Delores Nettles Collins was born in Monroeville, Alabama, on August 31, 1936. She received a bachelor's degree from Clark College in 1957 and pursued graduate studies at Chicago Teachers College and Columbia University from 1965 until 1967.

Collins's teaching career began in 1958 at the Monroe County Training School in her hometown. She taught at Chicago's Delano Elementary School from 1960 until 1975. In 1975, Collins founded the Westside Preparatory School in Chicago. She served as its director until the school closed in 2008 for financial reasons.

Collins has conducted educational workshops throughout the United States and Europe, and has appeared on several television programs, including *60 Minutes*, *Good Morning America*, and *The Phil Donahue Show*. She has served as director of the Right to Read Foundation and became a member of the President's Commission on White House Fellowships in 1981. That same year, Hallmark Hall of Fame presented *The Marva Collins Story* on CBS. The show chronicled the life of Collins as a dedicated teacher in an inner-city school in the Midwest. Collins has also been a consultant to the National Department of Children, Youth, and Family Services and a council member of the National Institutes of Health.

A number of organizations have honored Collins for her distinguished career, including the NAACP, the Reading

Reform Foundation, the Fred Hampton Foundation, the Chicago Urban League, the United Negro College Fund, Phi Delta Kappa, and the American Institute for Public Service. Among the institutions that have given her honorary degrees are Washington University, Amherst College, Dartmouth University, Chicago State University, Howard University, and Central State University. Collins received the National Humanities Medal in 2004.

ANNA JULIA COOPER (c. 1858/9–1964)

Author, Educator, Scholar. Anna Julia Cooper was a strong proponent of justice, equality for women, and racial uplift. She was born on August 10, 1858 or 1859, in Raleigh, North Carolina, to an enslaved mother. Her father was possibly her mother's enslaver. Cooper attended Saint Augustine's Normal School and Collegiate Institute (now Saint Augustine's College) in Raleigh and became a teacher at the school when she graduated. She was married briefly to George A. C. Cooper, who died in 1879.

Anna Cooper graduated from Oberlin College in Ohio in 1884, then taught modern languages at Wilberforce University from 1884 to 1885. The next year, she returned to Saint Augustine's and taught mathematics, Latin, and German. In 1888, she received an M.A. degree in mathematics from Oberlin and moved to Washington, D.C., where she taught at the Preparatory High School for Colored Youth and was school principal from 1902 to 1906. The school later became the M Street High School, then the Paul Laurence Dunbar High School. She was removed from the principalship after she protested the board of education's plan to dilute the school's curriculum. From 1906 to 1910, Cooper chaired the languages department at Lincoln University in Missouri. She then returned to the M Street School as a Latin teacher. On March 23, 1925, when she was sixty-six years old, she successfully defended her doctoral dissertation at the Sorbonne and became the fourth African American woman to earn a doctorate and the first woman to do so in France.

Cooper also became established as a lecturer and writer. As early as 1890, while teaching full time, she lectured to educators and African American women's groups. In 1900, she delivered a lecture on "The Negro Problem in America" at the first Pan-African Conference, then toured Europe. As a writer, she is best known for *A Voice from the South* (1892); the work marked her as a dedicated feminist and advocate for the African American race. Anna Cooper died on February 27, 1964, when she was 104 or 105 years old.

FANNY COPPIN (1837–1913)

Educator, Activist. Fanny Jackson Coppin was born enslaved in 1837 in Washington, D.C. After her aunt purchased her freedom, Coppin became the second African American woman to receive a degree from Oberlin College in Ohio.

In 1865, Coppin was appointed principal of the women's department of the Institute for Colored Youth in Philadelphia, a high school established by Quakers in 1837. She became principal of the entire school in 1869. In 1894, Coppin founded the Women's Exchange and Girls' Home in Philadelphia. She served as president of the local Women's Mite Missionary Society and the Women's Home and Foreign Missionary Society and as a vice president of the National Association of Colored Women. Coppin was also an active member of the African Methodist Episcopal (AME) Church, and served as president of the AME Home Missionary Society. In 1902, she accompanied her husband, Levi J. Coppin, on a missionary venture to South Africa. Shortly before her death at her Philadelphia home on January 21, 1913, Coppin completed an autobiography, *Reminiscences of School Life and Hints on Teaching.*

HOWARD DODSON JR. (1939–)

Historian, Educator, Curator. Born in Chester, Pennsylvania, on June 1, 1939, Howard Dodson Jr. was near the top of his class throughout junior high and high school. Out of eighty-nine students at Chester High School, Dodson was one of nine who later graduated from college. In 1961, he received a bachelor of science degree from West Chester State College, and in 1964 he received a master's degree in history and political science from Villanova University. In 1964, driven by an interest in African people transplanted in the Western Hemisphere, Dodson went to Ecuador as a member of the U.S. Peace Corps.

In 1969, after spending a year in Puerto Rico, Dodson entered the doctoral program in black history and race relations at the University of California, Berkeley. During that time, Dodson studied the sociopolitical factors behind the civil rights and Black Power movements. As part of his doctoral studies, Dodson earned a position at the Institute of the Black World, a research branch of the Martin Luther King Jr. Center for Nonviolent Social Change in Atlanta. Dodson served as director of the institute from 1974 to 1979.

Dodson's doctoral dissertation, "The Political Economy in South Carolina: 1780–1830," demonstrated that African American slave workers were not simply victims of their circumstances, but rather contributors to a complex socioeconomic system. In addition to his dissertation, Dodson has written widely on the subject of African American history. He served as editor in chief of *Black World View* magazine in 1977, and he has published a number of books, including: *Thinking and Rethinking U.S. History* (1988), a book for children written with Madelon Bedell; *Black Photographers Bear Witness: 100 Years of Social Protest* (1989), published by Williams College Museum of Art and written with Deborah

Willis; *Ideology, Identity, and Assumptions* (2007), *Cultural Life* (2007), *Origins* (2008), and *The Black Condition* (2009), four volumes in the Schomburg Studies on the Black Experience series, edited with Colin Palmer; and *Becoming American: The African-American Journey* (2009).

In 1984, Dodson took a post as the head of the Schomburg Center for Research in Black Culture, a branch of the New York Public Library in Harlem. As a result of his ministrations and fund-raising efforts, the Schomburg Center was able to open an expanded complex in 1991. In 2010, he announced his plan to retire as director of the center in 2011. Dodson has served as consultant to the National Endowment for the Humanities, the African American Museums Association, the Library of Congress, the U.S. Department of Education, the Congressional Black Caucus, and the National Council of Churches. He won the Association for the Study of Afro-American Life and History Service Award in 1976 and a Governor's Award for African Americans of Distinction in 1982.

SARAH MAPPS DOUGLASS (1806–1882)

Educator, Abolitionist. The free-born Sarah Mapps Douglass was an outspoken antislavery activist and accomplished educator. She attended the Ladies Institute of the Pennsylvania Medical University. In the 1820s, she organized a school for African American children in Philadelphia.

Douglass was an active member of the Philadelphia Female Anti-Slavery Society, which provided support to her school. She also belonged to the New York Anti-Slavery Women and served as vice chairman of the Freedmen's Aid Society. In 1853, Douglass was appointed head of the girls' department at the Institute of Colored Youth (the forerunner of Cheyney State College). She remained there until her retirement in 1877. Douglass died in Philadelphia on September 8, 1882.

MICHAEL ERIC DYSON (1958–)

Educator, Writer. Michael Eric Dyson was born into a middle-class family in Detroit, Michigan, in 1958. He was ordained as a Baptist minister and attended divinity school at Tennessee's Knoxville College, ultimately earning a bachelor's degree in 1982 from Carson-Newman College. Three years later, he accepted a graduate fellowship at Princeton University, obtaining his master's degree and doctorate by 1993. Dyson became an assistant professor at Brown University. A nontraditional scholar, he chose to target his interests to a larger audience. Dyson reviewed books and films for newspapers, contributed record reviews to *Rolling Stone*, and became a columnist for *Christian Century* and the *Nation*. *Reflecting Black: African-American Cultural Criticism* (1993), Dyson's first book-length collection of essays, examined African American pop culture icons.

In 1995, Dyson published *Making Malcolm: The Myth and Meaning of Malcolm X*. The book was written in response to a confrontation with some of Dyson's African American male students at Brown University who objected to the presence of whites in his course on the radical Muslim leader. True to his goal of reaching beyond the scholarly community, Dyson's book was deliberately marketed to a wide, youthful readership. In his third book, *Between God and Gangsta Rap* (1996), Dyson analyzed rap music from a cultural and social perspective, and established himself as an authority. As a result, he was asked to testify on the genre before a congressional subcommittee, gained popularity as a lecturer, and became a sought-after guest on talk shows.

His later works include: *Race Rules: Navigating the Color Line* (1996); *I May Not Get There with You: The True Martin Luther King Jr.* (2000); *Holler if You Hear Me: Searching for Tupac Shakur* (2001); *Is Bill Cosby Right, or Has the Black Middle Class Lost Its Mind?* (2005); *Come Hell or High Water: Hurricane Katrina and the Color of Disaster* (2006); *Debating Race* (2007); *April 4, 1968: Martin Luther King, Jr.'s Death and How It Changed America* (2008); and *Can You Hear Me Now? The Inspiration, Wisdom, and Insight of Michael Eric Dyson* (2009).

Dyson is considered one of a group of "new intellectuals." From 1995 to 1997, he headed the Institute of African American Research at the University of North Carolina in Chapel Hill and continued to address issues of race and culture in both scholarly and popular publications. He served as a visiting professor at Columbia University from 1997 to 1999, before taking a position with DePaul University in Chicago. In 2002, he joined the faculty at Pennsylvania State University as the Avalon Foundation Professor in the Humanities and African American Studies. In 2007, Dyson was named University Professor of Sociology at Georgetown University. Dyson often appears as a guest on television and radio talk shows, and in 2006 he became host of his own syndicated radio program, *The Michael Eric Dyson Show*.

JOHN HOPE FRANKLIN (1915–2009)

Historian. John Hope Franklin was born in Rentiesville, Oklahoma, in 1915. He received his bachelor's degree from Fisk University in 1935 and then enrolled at Harvard University, which awarded him a master's degree in 1936 and a Ph.D. in 1941. He taught history at Fisk University and St. Augustine's College while completing his doctorate. He later taught at North Carolina College at Durham, Howard University, Brooklyn College (where he chaired the history department), Cambridge University, and the University of Chicago. He joined the history faculty of Duke University in 1982.

Franklin's many publications include: *From Slavery to Freedom: A History of Negro Americans* (first published in

1947 and now in its ninth edition); *The Militant South: 1800–1861* (1956); *Reconstruction after the Civil War* (1962); *The Emancipation Proclamation* (1963); *A Southern Odyssey* (1976); *Race and History: Selected Essays, 1938–1988* (1989); *The Color Line: Legacy for the Twenty-first Century* (1993); and *Runaway Slaves: Rebels on the Plantation, 1790–1860* (1999) and *In Search of the Promised Land: A Black Family and the Old South* (2006), both written with Loren Schweninger. He published his autobiography, *Mirror to America*, in 2005.

Twice a Guggenheim fellow, Franklin received honors from the Fellowship of Southern Writers, *Encyclopedia Britannica*, and many other organizations. The American Studies Association established the John Hope Franklin Publication Prize in his name in 1986. Franklin received numerous honorary degrees. In 1995, he received both the Spingarn Medal from the NAACP and the Presidential Medal of Freedom, America's highest civilian honor, from President Bill Clinton. Franklin was honored with a Harold Washington Literary Award in 2000 for his impressive body of work, and that same year he won a Lincoln Prize for his distinguished contribution to the study of the Civil War. In 2006, he received the Kluge Prize for lifetime achievement in the study of humanity.

John Hope Franklin, Historian and Scholar, Kluge Center, Washington, DC, 2003. *The Kluge Center, founded to bring scholars and political leaders together for greater understanding, awarded its lifetime achievement in the study of humanity prize to Franklin in 2006.* NEWSCOM

In 1997, President Clinton named Franklin as chair of the White House Initiative on Race and Reconciliation, a position that enabled him to lead a yearlong dialogue on race in cities across the nation. He was the James B. Duke Professor Emeritus of History at Duke University until his death on March 25, 2009.

E. FRANKLIN FRAZIER (1894–1962)

Educator, Sociologist, Activist. Edward Franklin Frazier left a thirty-year legacy of research and writings on the African American family, youth, the church, and the middle class. He combined theory with practice, and his work remains an authoritative source for later generations of scholars.

Born on September 24, 1894, in Baltimore, Maryland, Frazier attended the segregated schools of Baltimore and graduated from the Colored High School. On scholarship, he entered Howard University in Washington, D.C., and used income from odd jobs to support his college career. He graduated cum laude in 1915 and a few months later began teaching mathematics at Tuskegee Institute (now Tuskegee University) in Alabama. He left two years later and taught at various African American schools and colleges. After spending some time in military service, he enrolled in Clark University in Worcester, Massachusetts, and graduated in 1920 with a master's degree in sociology.

Frazier was a fellow of the American Scandinavian Foundation from 1921 to 1922. In the fall of 1922, he moved to Atlanta, where he held a dual position as director of the School of Social Work and professor of sociology at Morehouse College. He remained productive in research and writing during his Atlanta years. He moved to Chicago and studied full time for his doctorate at the University of Chicago. In 1929, he moved to Fisk University in Nashville, Tennessee, and in 1931 completed his Ph.D. dissertation, "The Negro Family in Chicago," which was regarded as a landmark study. Frazier left Fisk in 1934 and moved to Howard University in Washington, D.C., where he remained for twenty-eight years as head of the Department of Sociology. Prominent among his publications were *The Negro in the United States* (1949) and his most controversial book, *Black Bourgeoise* (1957).

Frazier later headed UNESCO's Division of Applied Sciences for two years and traveled and lectured abroad. He retired from Howard University as professor emeritus in 1959, but continued to teach there and at Johns Hopkins School of Advanced International Studies. Frazier died on May 17, 1962. His book *The Negro Church in America* was published posthumously in 1963.

HENRY LOUIS GATES JR. (1950–)

Literary Scholar, Educator, Critic. Henry Louis Gates Jr. was born on September 16, 1950, in Keyser, West Virginia. He graduated summa cum laude in 1973 from Yale University, where he earned a bachelor's in history. He received a master's in 1974 and a Ph.D. in 1979 from Clare College at Cambridge University in England, where he studied with Nobel laureate and playwright Wole Soyinka of Nigeria. Gates's postgraduate studies examined African American literature as it has derived from the traditions of Africa and the Caribbean. Gates also served as a staff correspondent for *Time* magazine in London until 1975. He returned to the United States as a guest lecturer for Yale periodically from 1976 to 1979.

In 1979, Gates accepted an assistant professorship in the English Department at Yale, where he also served as director of the undergraduate Afro-American Studies Department until 1985. In 1981, the MacArthur Foundation awarded him $150,000 for his critical essays about African American literature. When he republished Harriet E. Wilson's *Our Nig, or, Sketches from the Life of a Free Black, in a Two-Story White House, North, Showing that Slavery's Shadows Fall Even There* in 1983, he vaulted to the top of the world of African American scholarship. He has also been a Rockefeller Foundation fellow and has enjoyed grants from the National Endowment for the Humanities. During this time, he created the PBS television series *The Image of the Black in the Western Imagination*, which aired in 1982.

From 1985 to 1990, he served as a professor of English and African Studies at Cornell University and from 1988 to 1990 as W. E. B. Du Bois Professor of Literature at Duke University. He moved to Harvard in 1990, where he was named W. E. B. Du Bois Professor in the Humanities, and in 1991 became chair of the Department of African American Studies. Gates earned prestige for the department by attracting some of the country's leading scholars to Harvard. In addition to his chairmanship, he is now Alphonse Fletcher Jr. University Professor at Harvard.

In 1989, Gates won the American Book Award for *The Signifying Monkey: A Theory of Afro-American Literary Criticism.* In 1994, Gates's memoir, *Colored People*, was published; the work encompasses his experiences growing up in rural West Virginia. In addition, Gates and Kwame Appiah edited *Encarta Africana*, a multimedia encyclopedia on compact disc, released in January 1999.

Other works that Gates has written, edited, or contributed to include: *Facing History: The Black Image in American Art, 1710–1940* (1990), edited by Guy C. McElroy; *Josephine Baker and La Revue Negre: Paul Colin's Lithographs of Le Tumulte Noir in Paris, 1927* (1998, introduction); *Pioneers of the Black Atlantic: Five Slave Narratives from the Enlightenment, 1772–1815* (1998), edited with William L. Andrews; *Black Imagination and the Middle Passage* (1999), edited with Maria Diedrich and Carl Pedersen; *The Civitas Anthology of African American Slave Narratives* (1999), edited with William L. Andrews; *Wonders of the African World* (1999); *The Bondswoman's Narrative by Hannah Crafts, a Fugitive Slave, Recently Escaped from North Carolina* (2002), edited by Gates; *African American National Biography* (2008), edited with Evelyn Brooks Higginbotham; and *In Search of Our Roots: How 19 Extraordinary African Americans Reclaimed Their Past* (2009).

Henry Louis Gates Jr., Educator, 2005. *A distinguished scholar of African American literature and culture, Gates has won numerous awards, including a MacArthur grant, a Rockefeller Foundation fellowship, and an American Book Award.* WPN/PHOTOSHOT

Gates became embroiled in controversy after he was arrested at his Cambridge, Massachusetts, home in 2009 for what local law enforcement officers called "disorderly conduct." The incident received widespread attention, sparking a national debate on race and prompting President Barack Obama to invite Gates and the arresting officer to the White House for a friendly dialogue.

WILLIAM L. HANSBERRY (1894–1965)

Historian, Educator. William Leo Hansberry was born on February 25, 1894, in Gloster, Mississippi. He earned a bachelor's degree in anthropology from Harvard University in 1921. Determined to eliminate American ethnocentrism regarding Africa, he issued a manifesto to African American schools and colleges titled *Announcing an Effort to Promote the Study and Facilitate the Teaching of the Fundamentals of Negro Life and History*. The flier brought Hansberry three job offers from schools, and he accepted a post at Howard University in Washington, D.C. Beginning in 1922, he began designing courses on African and African American history.

Although Hansberry could verify the material taught in his courses, the board of Howard University pulled his financial backing after spurious accusations by colleagues. The university agreed to retain the African studies program, but the scuffle cost Hansberry funds and promotions. In 1932, Hansberry returned to Harvard to complete his master's degree in anthropology and history. He continued his studies in the mid-1930s at the University of Chicago's Oriental Institute. His research won him a Rockefeller Foundation grant that allowed him to study at Oxford University in England from 1937 to 1938, when Howard University finally recognized his achievements with an assistant professorship. Entrenched racial prejudice kept Hansberry from earning more grants and fellowships to continue his work.

Howard University made little effort to compensate him, and after more than twenty years of service, he remained only an associate professor. But the university climate gradually changed, and Hansberry was named adviser to African students in 1946. In 1950, he was appointed to Howard's Emergency Aid to the African Students' Committee, in addition to his teaching responsibilities. Because of an increased interest in African studies, Hansberry won a Fulbright Scholarship to lecture at Cairo University and to study in Egypt, Ethiopia, and the Sudan in 1953. He also visited Kenya, Uganda, and Zimbabwe. Hansberry died in Chicago on November 3, 1965.

BELL HOOKS (1952–)

Social Activist, Educator, Writer. Feminist educator bell hooks (it is her preference that her name appear in lowercase letters) has done her most important work as a teacher in programs that allow a critique of racism that was absent during her own undergraduate years. She contributes essays to a variety of scholarly journals and also publishes fiction and poetry. She has gained notoriety as a writer of critical essays on systems of domination, making herself a prominent name in feminist debate.

Born Gloria Jean Watkins in 1952, hooks grew up with five siblings in Hopkinsville, a small town in rural Kentucky. Despite her family's poverty and hardship, hooks reveled in lessons of diligence and community. She attended segregated public schools, where her role models were single African American female teachers. Orally and through poetry, hooks began defiantly resisting the sexism she perceived within her neighborhood. Rejecting her expected role as an obedient southern girl, she eventually adopted a pseudonym to represent a new sense of self—a woman who spoke her mind and was not afraid to talk back.

When hooks won a scholarship to Stanford University, she sought out intellectual and political affirmation from the campus feminist movement. Disillusioned and alienated by the absence of material by or discussion about African American women, hooks began criticizing the persistent racism within feminism. Having gained her bachelor's degree in 1973 from Stanford University, hooks faced obstacles at the University of Wisconsin–Madison, where she completed a master's degree (1976), and the University of California, Santa Cruz, where she pursued doctoral studies. She felt that male faculty members were determined to prevent her from becoming a university professor. In 1981, hooks published *Ain't I a Woman: Black Women and Feminism*, which was sharply criticized for its defiance of academic convention. Nonetheless, the work became central to discussions of racism and sexism. She persisted with her studies, earned her Ph.D. in 1983, and taught African American and women's studies at Yale University, Oberlin College, and City College of New York. In 2004, hooks became distinguished professor in residence in Appalachian studies at Berea College in Kentucky.

Her numerous works include: *Talking Back: Thinking Feminist, Thinking Black* (1989); *Black Looks: Race and Representation* (1992); *Killing Rage: Ending Racism* (1995); *Black Is a Woman's Color* (1996); *Bone Black: Memories of Girlhood* (1996); *Feminism Is for Everybody: Passionate Politics* (2000); *The Will to Change: Men, Masculinity, and Love* (2004); and *Belonging: A Culture of Place* (2009).

JOHN HOPE (1868–1936)

Educator, Civil Rights Activist, College President. John Hope's life was committed to improving the U.S. system of education to afford more minority access. Hope was one of the most influential leaders of his time in the field of higher education.

Hope was born in 1868 in Augusta, Georgia. He graduated from Worcester Academy in Massachusetts in 1890. In 1894, Hope graduated from Brown University in Providence, Rhode Island, and was elected class orator for the commencement service. In later years, Hope would receive an honorary degree from Brown, along with admittance into the Phi Beta Kappa Society. After graduating, Hope accepted a teaching job at Roger Williams University in Nashville, Tennessee. Four years later, he accepted a teaching position at Atlanta Baptist College in Georgia, where he began a longtime friendship with the educator W. E. B. Du Bois. They both attended the 1895 Macon Convention, which turned into the Georgia Equal Rights Convention.

bell hooks, Author and Educator, New York, 2003. *Berea College professor hooks has published numerous books on many subjects, from* Ain't I a Woman: Black Women and Feminism, *to the children's book* Happy to Be Nappy, *to* The Will to Change: Men, Masculinity, and Love. LIBRADO ROMERO/THE NEW YORK TIMES/REDUX PICTURES

In 1906, Hope became acting president of Atlanta Baptist College, and the next year he was named president. He was the first African American to be appointed president at a Baptist school. As president, Hope expanded the college with funds donated by John T. Rockefeller and Andrew Carnegie. In 1913, the school was renamed Morehouse College. During the 1920s, the college continued to expand as Hope developed the Atlanta School of Social Work.

In 1929, Hope fulfilled an ambition to establish a formal relationship among Atlanta's African American schools when the presidents of Spelman College and Morehouse College agreed to an affiliation with Atlanta University. Hope was appointed president of the new institution, now known as Atlanta University Center, while continuing as president of Morehouse College. Hope received the Harmon Award in 1930 for distinguished achievement in education. He died in Atlanta on February 20, 1936.

FREDERICK HUMPHRIES (1935–)

College President, Educator. Frederick Humphries was born in Apalachicola, Florida, on December 26, 1935. He graduated magna cum laude with a bachelor's degree in chemistry from Florida A&M University in 1957. Following two years as a second lieutenant in the U.S. Army Security Agency, Humphries spent the next five years working on his Ph.D. at the University of Pittsburgh, while earning a living as an academic tutor. He received his doctorate in 1964, and took an associate professorship at his alma mater.

In 1967, Humphries became a full professor at Florida A&M after spending two years at the University of Minnesota. Along with the professorship, Humphries also became a program director of the Thirteen-Colleges Curriculum Program, which initially involved thirteen historically African American colleges. As director, Humphries advocated new methods of looking at the particular problems facing African American students with the intent of improving students' overall educational progress. Humphries and his colleagues instituted successful experimental curriculum changes that made classrooms "student-centered academic environment(s)." A scientist himself, Humphries also strove to increase African American students' accessibility to math and science.

Tennessee State University hired Humphries as its president in 1974. He served in the post until 1985, when he returned, once again, to his alma mater—this time as its president. Under Humphries, Florida A&M's status as an institute of higher learning was greatly elevated. In 1992, 1995, and 1997, the school attracted more National Achievement Scholars, the nation's top African American students, than any other institution. Florida A&M's enrollment more than doubled under the leadership of Humphries; innovative programs that increased the number of African American students going on to pursue graduate studies were also implemented. Humphries retired on June 30, 2001.

CHARLES S. JOHNSON (1893–1956)

Scholar, Educator, College President. Charles Spurgeon Johnson was born in Bristol, Virginia, in 1893. He earned a B.A. from Virginia Union University and worked on a Ph.D. at the University of Chicago. Johnson occupied a number of diverse positions, from editor to administrator. He served as the assistant executive secretary of the Chicago Commission on Race Relations and as research director of the National Urban League, where he founded the organization's journal *Opportunity*.

In 1928, Johnson was made chairman of Fisk University's Department of Social Sciences. While at Fisk, he established the Fisk Institute of Race Relations. In 1933, he was appointed director of Swarthmore College's Institute of Race Relations. In 1946, Johnson was appointed president of Fisk University—the first African American to hold the position. He died on October 27, 1956 in Louisville, Kentucky, while on his way to a meeting of the Fisk Board of Trustees in New York.

Johnson wrote several books, including *The Negro in American Civilization* (1930), *The Economic Status of Negroes* (1933), *The Negro College Graduate* (1938), and *Educational and Cultural Crisis* (1951).

MORDECAI W. JOHNSON (1890–1976)

College President, Minister, Educator, Orator. As president of Howard University in Washington, D.C., for thirty-four years, Mordecai Wyatt Johnson became a highly respected minister, educator, and orator. He built the university into a visible academic institution that became known as the "capstone of Negro education."

Johnson's parents had been enslaved. He was born in Paris, Tennessee, on December 12, 1890, and attended Roger Williams University in Nashville and the Howe Institute in Memphis. He transferred to Atlanta Baptist College, now known as Morehouse College, where he graduated with a B.A. in 1911. Johnson taught at the college for a year, then continued his studies at the University of Chicago, where he received a second undergraduate degree in 1913. In 1916, Johnson received a bachelor of divinity degree from Rochester Theological Seminary in New York.

Johnson was pastor of the First Baptist Church in Charleston, West Virginia, for nine years. He took a leave of absence to study at Harvard University Divinity School, graduating in June 1922. In 1926, Johnson was elected eleventh president and the first African American president of Howard University. In this role, he concentrated first on providing financial stability for the school. Starting with the medical school, he received solid support from the Julius Rosenwald Fund and the General Education Board. Then he moved to strengthen the law school, appointing Charles Hamilton Houston as dean of the school. He also approached the country's top law schools for recommendations for Howard's law-school faculty. One of Howard's most notable law-school graduates was Thurgood Marshall. The law school also engaged in research and analysis involving important civil rights issues that went before the court. Johnson was awarded the Spingarn Medal, the NAACP's highest award, in 1928.

During the first half of his tenure, Johnson faced sharp criticism because he lacked a terminal academic degree and because some faculty and staff opposed his administrative style. He survived the controversy, maintained the support of the board of trustees, and continued fruitful contacts with foundations for financial support. He attracted outstanding scholars to the Howard faculty, including philosopher Alain Locke, cell biologist Ernest E. Just, chemist Percy Julian, political scientist Ralph Bunche, historian Rayford Logan, and Charles Drew, who became known for his research with blood plasma. Johnson also erected new buildings and established several honor societies on campus, including a chapter of Phi Beta Kappa.

Johnson traveled widely; his lectures, given without notes, often lasted forty-five minutes and held audiences spellbound. His themes focused on racism, segregation, and discrimination. He retired from the presidency of Howard in 1960 and died on September 10, 1976, when he was eighty-five years old.

LAURENCE CLIFTON JONES (1884–1975)

Educator, School Founder and Administrator. Laurence Clifton Jones founded a school in the deep woods of Mississippi's Black Belt and made it possible for thousands of African American youths to receive elementary and high school education. He uplifted the community as well by helping uneducated men and women to enhance their lives. He became known as the "Little Professor of Piney Woods."

Jones was born on November 21, 1884, in St. Joseph, Missouri, and worked his way to a degree from Iowa State University. Booker T. Washington inspired Jones, first through his writings and later when he offered Jones a position at Tuskegee Institute (now Tuskegee University), which, Jones declined. Instead, in 1910, Jones founded what he called a "country life school" in Piney Woods, Mississippi. When the students lacked money for school expenses, he accepted payments in produce.

On June 29, 1912, Jones married Grace M. Allen, whom he had met while he was in college. Together the Joneses engaged in fund-raising activities and enabled the Piney Woods School to grow. Grace became a member of the school's faculty and taught useful skills to community residents. With the help of a school ensemble known as the Cotton Blossom Singers, the Joneses traveled around the United States staging fund-raising concerts. In the late 1930s, Laurence Jones organized the International Sweethearts of Rhythm, a music group that also appeared in fund-raising concerts for the school until striking out on its own in 1941.

The Piney Woods School added a department for blind children in the late 1920s. Jones and the school drew national attention after they were featured on the television program *This Is Your Life* in December 1954. An appeal for support made during the program resulted in substantial funding for Piney Woods. Jones retired from the presidency in 1974, but continued to travel on official school business until he died in 1975. Today, the Piney Woods School has approximately two hundred students in grades nine through twelve.

E. J. JOSEY (1924–2009)

Librarian, Activist, Author. Elonnie Junius Josey was born in Norfolk, Virginia, on January 20, 1924. He studied music and played the church organ until 1943, when he was drafted into the U.S. Army, serving for three years. Josey, known simply as E. J., completed his education at Howard University's School of Music. He then entered Columbia University's master's program in history and the State University of New York's Library School. In 1953, Josey began his library career, and he rapidly became a leader in confronting segregation in libraries.

After the Georgia Library Association denied him membership in 1960, Josey ushered a resolution through the American Library Association, forbidding segregation in state and regional chapters. Josey persevered in a diverse public and academic library career and gained a reputation as a wise, impassioned speaker on social issues. His *Black Librarian in America* (1970) was a pioneering look into conditions for African American librarians. Its 1994 sequel, *The Black Librarian in America Revisited*, was an appraisal of changes that had been made in the intervening years. Josey helped organize the Black Caucus of the American Library Association, which fought institutional racism and widespread discrimination, both within the profession and in conjunction with library services.

As president of the American Library Association from 1984 to 1985, Josey fostered awareness of the value of libraries as an integral part of the nation's infrastructure. Fighting against severe budget cuts imposed by the Reagan administration, Josey rallied library advocates in Washington, D.C., to march with him in protest. In addition to his professional achievements, Josey led community advocacy for civil and human rights as a leading member of the NAACP, was a contributor to intellectual development in emerging African countries, and was awarded four honorary doctorates. In the late 1980s, Josey joined the faculty of the School of Library and Information Science at the University of Pittsburgh and devoted himself to achieving a racial balance in library education. He retired in 1995. For his long service to promoting reading and diverse library selections, Josey was presented with an honorary doctorate of humane letters from Clarion University of Pennsylvania in 2001. He died in Washington, North Carolina, on July 3, 2009.

MAULANA KARENGA (1941–)

Activist-scholar, Educator, Ethicist. Maulana Karenga is a professor in the Department of Africana Studies at California State University, Long Beach. He became known in the mid-1960s for creating and popularizing the Kwanzaa holiday, now celebrated through the United States. Karenga earned a B.A. (1963) and M.A. (1964) in political science from the University of California, Los Angeles. In 1976, he was awarded a Ph.D. in political and social science from United States International University in San Diego. He earned a second Ph.D. in 1994 from the University of Southern California, with a focus on the classical African ethics of ancient Egypt. He has also been awarded an honorary doctorate from the University of Durban-Westville in South Africa for his "intellectual and practical work on behalf of African people."

Karenga was born Ronald McKinley Everett in Parsonburg, Maryland, in 1941. He came to prominence in the 1960s as founder of Organization Us, a cultural and social-change group whose name, he explains, "simply means us Black people and stresses the communitarian focus of the organization and its philosophy Kawaida, which is an ongoing synthesis of the best of African thought and practice in constant exchange with the world." Karenga and Us have greatly influenced the development of black studies, the black arts, black student movements, Afrocentricity, and ancient Egyptian studies. They have also advanced the independent school and rites-of-passage movements through the Nguzo Saba (the Seven Principles of Kawaida).

Karenga and Us played important roles in the founding of the initial Black Power conferences in the 1960s and the National Black United Front in the 1980s. More recently, they were in the forefront of organizing the National African American Leadership Summit and the 1995 Million Man March and Day of Absence. Karenga was a member of the executive council for the landmark gathering in Washington, D.C., and authored its mission statement, coediting the subsequent volume, *The Million Man March/Day of Absence: A*

Commemorative Anthology (1996). Organization Us continues its declared commitment to "to provide a philosophy, a set of principles and a program which inspires a personal and social practice that not only satisfies human need but transforms people in the process, making them self-conscious agents of their own life and liberation."

An internationally recognized activist-scholar, Karenga has published numerous articles and books, among them the widely used *Introduction to Black Studies* (1982, 3rd ed. 2002); *Selections from the Husia: Sacred Wisdom of Ancient Egypt* (1984), a retranslation and commentary on ancient Egyptian texts; the influential *Kwanzaa: A Celebration of Family, Community, and Culture* (1997, 2nd ed. 2008); *Maat, the Moral Ideal in Ancient Egypt: A Study in Classical African Ethics* (2003); and *Kawaida and Questions of Life and Struggle: African American, Pan-African, and Global Issues* (2007). He has lectured throughout the United States and the world and has earned numerous scholarships and leadership and community service awards.

ELIZABETH DUNCAN KOONTZ (1919–1989)

Educator, Administrator. Elizabeth Duncan Koontz was a teacher, an assistant state school superintendent, a leader in state and national teachers' associations, and the first African American president of the National Education Association (NEA). Born on June 3, 1919, in Salisbury, North Carolina, she was the youngest of seven children. She graduated from Livingstone College with honors in 1938 and received a master's degree in elementary education from Atlanta University in 1941.

After serving as an elementary school teacher in Dunn, North Carolina, she spent the 1940–1941 school year at Aggrey Memorial School in Landis. She then moved to the Fourteenth Street School in Winston-Salem, where she stayed until 1945. From then until 1949, she taught special education classes at Price High School in Salisbury.

Koontz's participation in the NEA began in 1952, when she became a member of the North Carolina Negro Teachers Association, which was later admitted to the state NEA chapter. She served two terms as secretary, one as vice president, and one as president-elect of the NEA's Department of Class room Teachers. In 1965, she became the department's first African American president. On July 6, 1968, Koontz was installed as the first African American president of the NEA. During her tenure, she brought about a shift in the association, from traditionally conservative to liberal. She supported agitation and, if necessary, strikes to bring about necessary change. She also endorsed militant teachers and strongly supported teacher commitment and responsibility.

In January 1969, President Richard Nixon appointed Koontz director of the Women's Bureau of the U.S. Department of Labor, making her the agency's first African American director. Later, she became deputy assistant secretary for labor employment standards. In the latter capacity, she became in 1975 the U.S. delegate to the United Nation's Commission on the Status of Women. She was active in numerous civic, religious, and educational organizations, and received honorary degrees from various colleges and universities. Koontz held a variety of other positions before she retired in April 1982. She suffered a heart attack at her home in Salisbury and died on January 6, 1989.

LUCY C. LANEY (1854–1933)

Educator, School Founder. Lucy Craft Laney spent her life assuring African Americans, particularly women, that they deserved to be educated and had the freedom to educate others. She was born on April 11, 1854, in Macon, Georgia, to parents who had been enslaved. When she was fifteen, Laney entered Atlanta University. She graduated in 1873 in the first class of the university's normal school. Laney pursued graduate studies at the University of Chicago during the summer months.

Although she was virtually penniless, Laney opened a school in 1883 for African American youth in Augusta, Georgia. Classes were held in Christ Presbyterian Church. The school was chartered in 1886 under Georgia law as a normal and industrial school. Haines Normal and Industrial Institute established the city's first kindergarten and nurse-training department in the early 1890s. Later, the nursing department became the school of nursing at Augusta's University Hospital. By the 1930s, Haines had dropped elementary education and offered a four-year high school program and some college-level courses. The Presbyterian Board of Missions, the schools' primary source of funds, withdrew support during the Great Depression. The Haines school declined as a result, then closed its doors in 1949. Later, a new public structure, the Lucy C. Laney High School, was built on the site. Laney died on October 23, 1933, in Augusta. She was later recognized as a leading African American educator in the South.

SARA LAWRENCE-LIGHTFOOT (1944–)

Educator, Sociologist, Writer. Harvard professor Sara Lawrence-Lightfoot earned a bachelor's degree in psychology from Swarthmore University in 1966. She received a Ph.D. in the sociology of education from Harvard University in 1972. She has spent most of her academic career on the Harvard faculty, where she has been the Emily Hargroves Fisher Professor of Education since 1998. In her scholarly writings, she has attempted to draw a clearer picture of the reality of African Americans lives to correct earlier writings that she believes give a distorted view of African Americans.

Lawrence-Lightfoot's first book, *Worlds Apart: Relationships between Families and Schools* (1978), promoted cooperation between parents and teachers in the education of children. Her third book, *The Good High School: Portraits of Character and Culture* (1983), chronicled the methods of six successful schools in the United States, which Lawrence-Lightfoot believes can serve as models for institutional change. Her 1994 book, *I've Known Rivers: Lives of Loss and Liberation*, details life in the African American middle class through interviews with six African American professionals. Her other writings include: *Respect: An Exploration* (1999); *The Essential Conversation: What Parents and Teachers Can Learn from Each Other* (2003); and *The Third Chapter: Passion, Risk, and Adventure in the 25 Years after 50* (2009).

After she was named a MacArthur Fellow in 1984, Lawrence-Lightfoot departed from sociology to write *Balm in Gilead: Journey of a Healer* (1988), an account of the life of her mother, Margaret Morgan Lawrence, a pioneering child psychologist. Lawrence-Lightfoot has also written numerous scholarly articles, and has served on many committees and national boards, among them the advisory board of the W.E.B. Du Bois Institute at Harvard, the Peer Panel Review and other committees for the National Academy of Education, and the board of directors of the John D. and Catherine T. MacArthur Foundation, for which she became chair in 2002. She has been a fellow of the National Academy of Education since 1989. In 2008, she received the Margaret Mead Award from the American Academy of Political and Social Science.

David Levering Lewis, Historian and Educator, New York, 2001. *Lewis's two biographical volumes on W. E. B. Du Bois have each won a Pulitzer Prize; he has also received numerous other awards, including a MacArthur grant, a Guggenheim Fellowship, and an American Book Award.* AP PHOTO/ED BAILEY

DAVID LEVERING LEWIS (1936–)

Educator, Writer. David Levering Lewis was born May 25, 1936, in Little Rock, Arkansas. He earned a bachelor's degree in history from Fisk University in 1956 and continued his studies at Columbia University, where he earned a master's degree in 1958. He received his Ph.D. from the London School of Economics and Political Science in 1962. Lewis published his first paper as an undergraduate: "History of the Negro Upper Class in Atlanta, Georgia 1890–1958."

Lewis began studying African American history after spending a number of years teaching French history at such schools as the University of Ghana, Notre Dame University, and Howard University. In 1971, he published a scholarly biography of Martin Luther King Jr., *Martin Luther King: A Critical Biography*. Lewis followed this work with one on anti-Semitism called *Prisoners of Honor: The Dreyfus Affair* (1973), after which he accepted a teaching post at Federal City College in Washington, D.C. In 1974, he became a full professor of history at the University of the District of Columbia.

Throughout the 1970s, Lewis studied the Harlem Renaissance of the 1920s and 1930s, writing a work of definitive scholarship on the subject, *When Harlem Was in Vogue: The Politics of the Arts in the Twenties and Thirties*, published in 1981. Next, Lewis examined the life of W. E. B. Du Bois, the great scholar and writer, in *W. E. B. Du Bois: Biography of a Race, 1868–1919*, which won a Pulitzer Prize for Biography and a National Book Award in 1994. In 1999, Lewis received a MacArthur Foundation "genius grant" to continue his research. In 2000, he published *W. E. B. Du Bois: The Fight for Equality and the American Century, 1919–1963*, which also won a Pulitzer Prize.

Lewis took a position as the chair of the history department of Rutgers University in 1993. He became Julius Silver University Professor and professor of history at New York University in 2003. He contributes regularly to scholarly journals and the *Washington Post*. He published *God's Crucible: Islam and the Making of Europe, 570 to 1215* in 2008. Lewis was awarded the National Humanities Medal in 2009.

ALAIN LOCKE (1885–1954)

Scholar, Educator. Born on September 3, 1885, in Philadelphia, Alain LeRoy Locke graduated Phi Beta Kappa with a B.A. degree from Harvard University in 1907. He was then awarded a Rhodes Scholarship for two years of study at Oxford University in England and did further graduate study at the University of Berlin (1910–1911). After returning to the United States, Locke took an assistant professorship in English and philosophy at Howard University in Washington, D.C. He received his Ph.D. from Harvard in 1918 and the same year was made chairman of the philosophy department at Howard, where he stayed until his retirement in 1953.

In 1934, Locke founded the Associates in Negro Folk Education. In 1942, he was named to the Honor Roll of Race Relations. A prolific author, Locke's first book was titled *Race Contacts and Inter-Racial Relations* (1916). His best-known works include *The New Negro: An Interpretation* (1925), a book that introduced America to the Harlem Renaissance, and *The Negro in Art: A Pictorial Record of the Negro Artist and of the Negro Theme in Art* (1940). Locke died in New York City on June 9, 1954.

BENJAMIN E. MAYS (1894–1984)

Educator, College President. In addition to occupying the president's office at Morehouse, Benjamin Elijah Mays wrote, taught mathematics, worked for the Office of Education, served as chairman of the Atlanta Board of Education, preached in a Baptist church, acted as an adviser to the Southern Christian Leadership Council, and was a church historian.

Born in Epworth, South Carolina, in 1894, Mays attended Bates College and later received his master's degree and Ph.D. from the University of Chicago. He served as a pastor at Georgia's Shiloh Baptist Church from 1921 to 1924, and later taught at Morehouse College and South Carolina's State College at Orangeburg. After a stint at the Tampa Urban League, he worked for the YMCA as national student secretary and then directed a study of African American churches for the Institute of Social and Religious Research. From 1934 to 1940, he was dean of Howard University's School of Religion, before taking up the presidency of Morehouse from 1940 to 1967. He served in several other distinguished posts, including the Atlanta Board of Education chairmanship and positions at the Ford Foundation and the Department of Health, Education, and Welfare. May's numerous awards include forty-three honorary degrees, the Dorie Miller Medal of Honor, and the 1971 Outstanding Older Citizen Award. He died at his Atlanta home on March 21, 1984.

JESSE EDWARD MOORLAND (1863–1940)

Archivist, Clergyman. Jesse Moorland was born on September 10, 1863, in Coldwater, Ohio. Following the untimely death of his parents, Moorland was reared by his grandparents. His early education consisted of sporadic attendance at a small rural schoolhouse and being read to by his grandfather. Moorland eventually attended Normal University in Ada, Ohio, married, and taught school in Urbana, Ohio. He attended Howard University in Washington and graduated with a degree in theology in 1891.

Moorland was ordained a congregational minister and, between 1891 and 1896, he served at churches in South Boston, Virginia, Nashville, and Cleveland. In 1891, he also became active in the YMCA, an association he would maintain for much of his life.

In 1909, Moorland's well-known essay "Demand and the Supply of Increased Efficiency in the Negro Ministry" was published by the American Negro Academy. In it, Moorland called for a more pragmatic ministry, both in terms of the education of its members and its approach to social issues.

By 1910, Moorland had become quite active in the YMCA and was appointed secretary of the Colored Men's Department. In this position, Moorland raised millions of dollars for the YMCA's construction and building fund. After reaching the mandatory retirement age in 1923, Moorland resigned from the YMCA and began devoting his time and considerable energy to other pursuits. He became involved with the Association for the Study of Negro Life and History, the National Health Circle for Colored People, and the Frederick Douglass Home Association.

From 1907 onward, Moorland served as a trustee of Howard University. In 1914, he donated his private library of books and materials related to African American history to the university. Out of this gift grew the Moorland Foundation. The collection was renamed the Moorland-Spingarn Collection and later became the core of the Moorland-Spingarn Research Center. This collection of documents on African American history and culture was the first African American research collection at a major American university. Moorland died in New York on April 30, 1940.

ROD PAIGE (1933–)

Athletic Director, Educator, Government Official. Roderick Raynor Paige was born on June 17, 1933, in Monticello, Mississippi. He attended Lawrence County Training School, where he was both a solid student and a standout football player. His athletic skills earned him a scholarship to Jackson State University, where Paige earned a bachelor of science degree in 1955, graduating with honors. Following graduation, Paige became a head football coach, first at Utica Junior College and then at Jackson State from 1962 to 1969. During this period, he also earned a master of science degree in 1964 and a doctorate in physical education in 1969, both from Indiana University.

In 1971, Paige took a coaching job at Texas Southern University. With it came the position of athletic director and a faculty appointment. By 1984, he had risen to the post of dean of the school of education. He served in that capacity through 1990. Paige was elected to the Houston Independent School District Board of Education in 1989. He was named district superintendent in 1994. During his tenure, Paige helped to turn around the state's largest school district by giving more responsibility to effective principals, addressing the issue of unqualified teachers, and making Houston's schools safe for students and faculty. Within five years, the district's test scores had risen substantially, and the dropout and violent crime rates had fallen.

Paige was honored in 1999 by the Council of the Great City Schools, who named him one of the top educators in the nation. The next year, he was named as the first African American secretary of education by President George W. Bush. In his first two years in the post, Paige helped to create and promote the administration's vision for education reform, which focused on the issues of national assessment testing and school vouchers. He also helped to implement the 2001 No Child Left Behind Act. In 2001, the American Association of School Administrators named Paige the National Superintendent of the Year.

Paige resigned his government post in 2005 and became chair of the Chartwell Educational Group, an international consulting firm. He also became a public policy scholar at the Woodrow Wilson International Center for Scholars in Washington, D.C. In addition, Paige published two books: *The War against Hope: How Teachers' Unions Hurt Children, Hinder Teachers, and Endanger Public Education* (2006); and *The Black-White Achievement Gap: Why Closing It Is the Greatest Civil Rights Issue of Our Time* (2010), written with Elaine Witty.

FREDERICK D. PATTERSON

See chapter 9, National Organizations

BENJAMIN F. PAYTON (1932–)

Educator, University President. Born in Orangeburg, South Carolina, in 1932, Benjamin Franklin Payton received a bachelor's degree with honors from South Carolina State College in 1955. He earned a bachelor of divinity degree from Howard University in 1958, a master's degree from Columbia University in 1960, and a Ph.D. from Yale University in 1963. He took a position as assistant professor at Howard University before working for the National Council of Churches as the executive director of social justice for the Commission on Religion and Race—a position that he retained even as he took over the presidency of Benedict College in 1967. He left Benedict in 1972 for a job at the Ford Foundation, where he remained until he became the president of Tuskegee University in 1981. Payton sought to increase the visibility of the university, and in 1999 he was instrumental in establishing the nation's first African American bioethics center on the campus.

Payton holds honorary degrees from Eastern Michigan University, Morris Brown College, Benedict College, and Morgan State University. A recipient of the Napoleon Hill Foundation Gold Medal Award and the Benjamin E. Mays Award, he served as educational adviser to Vice President George H. W. Bush on Bush's seven-nation tour of Africa in 1982. Payton is a member of several professional and social organizations, including the National Association for Equal Opportunity in Higher Education, the Alabama Industrial Relations Council, the National Association of Independent Colleges and Universities, and the National Consortium for Educational Access. In May 2001, the Alabama House of Representatives presented Payton with a resolution of commendation for "outstanding achievement and dedicated service." Payton retired from the presidency of Tuskegee on July 31, 2010.

ARTHUR A. SCHOMBURG (1874–1938)

Archivist, Organization Founder and President. Born in Puerto Rico in 1874, Arturo Alfonso Schomburg led a richly varied public life. He worked as a law clerk and was a businessman, journalist, editor, lecturer, curator at the New York Public Library, and teacher of Spanish.

In 1911, Schomburg cofounded the Negro Society for Historical Research. He also became a lecturer for the Universal Negro Improvement Association. Schomburg was a member of the New York Puerto Rico Revolutionary Party and served as secretary of the Cuban Revolutionary Party. In 1922, he headed the American Negro Academy, an organization founded by Alexander Crummell in 1879 to promote African American art, literature, and science.

Schomburg collected thousands of books, manuscripts, and artworks on African American culture over his lifetime. In 1926, his personal collection was purchased by the Carnegie Corporation and given to the New York Public Library. He became curator of Fisk University's Negro Collection in 1929, where he built a distinguished collection similar to his own. He left in 1932 and became curator of the Division of Negro Literature, History, and Prints at the New York Public Library, renamed as the Schomburg Collection of Negro Literature and History. In 1973, the name was changed again to the Schomburg Center for Research in Black Culture. The center is located in Harlem.

SHELBY STEELE (1946–)

Scholar, Author. Shelby Steele was born January 1, 1946, in Chicago. He grew up in Phoenix, Illinois, a blue-collar suburb of Chicago, and attended high school in Harvey, Illinois, where he was student council president his senior year, prior to graduating in 1964. Steele then attended Coe College in Cedar Rapids, Iowa, where he was active in SCOPE—an organization associated with Martin Luther King Jr.'s Southern Christian Leadership Conference. Steele graduated in 1968, and in 1971 he received an M.S. degree in sociology from Southern Illinois University. He received a Ph.D. in English literature from the University of Utah in 1974. While at Southern Illinois University, he taught African American literature to impoverished children in East St. Louis. In 1994, Steele became a research fellow at the Hoover Institution at Stanford University, where he concentrates on race relations, American social culture, and identity politics.

In 1990, Steele published *The Content of Our Character: A New Vision of Race in America,* which won the National Book Critics Circle Award. In this controversial book, Steele argued that African American self-doubt and its exploitation by the white and black liberal establishment cause as many problems for African Americans as more traditional forms of racism. Steele's other books include: *A Dream Deferred: The Second Betrayal of Black Freedom in America* (1998); *White Guilt: How Blacks and Whites Together Destroyed the Promise of the Civil Rights Era* (2006); and *A Bound Man: Why We Are Excited about Obama and Why He Can't Win* (2007). Steele has also written numerous articles on this theme for such respected publications as *Harper's*, the *New Republic*, *American Scholar*, *Commentary*, the *New York Times*, and the *Wall Street Journal.*

Because of his beliefs, Steele has been identified as part of an emerging African American neoconservative movement. However, in an interview appearing in the August 12, 1991, issue of *Time* magazine, he categorized himself as a classic liberal focusing on the freedom and sacredness of the individual. He was awarded the National Humanities Medal in 2004.

H. PATRICK SWYGERT (1943–)

University President, Lawyer, Educator. H. Patrick Swygert was president of Howard University in Washington, D.C., from 1995 to 2008. After taking office as Howard's fifteenth president, Swygert worked to move the institution into the twenty-first century. He saw Howard's role as one of shaping and implementing an academic and research agenda for African Americans, and he aimed to place the university on a firmer financial footing.

Born on March 11, 1943, in Philadelphia, Swygert graduated from Howard University in 1965 with an A.B. degree and received his J.D. from the Howard University School of Law in 1968. After graduation, Swygert was law clerk to Chief Justice William H. Hastie of the U.S. Court of Appeals, Third Circuit, in Philadelphia. Swygert later served as administrative assistant to Congressman Charles B. Rangel of New York. He held various positions at Temple University, first as vice president for university administration, then special counsel to the president. He later became acting dean of the law school. He was also a full professor on the law-school faculty. After serving as visiting professor at both the University of Ghana and Tel Aviv University, he worked as a visiting lecturer in Cairo, Rome, and Athens.

Swygert has also held several positions with the U.S. government, including general counsel to the U.S. Service Commission. He was president of the State University of New York at Albany for five years, until he became president of Howard University on August 1, 1995. He remained committed to sustaining Howard's stature among higher education institutions that serve African Americans. Swygert retired from Howard on June 30, 2008.

IVAN VAN SERTIMA (1935–2009)

Scholar. Born in British Guyana in 1935, anthropologist, linguist, and literary critic Ivan Van Sertima was a longtime professor of African studies at Rutgers University. In 1976, Van Sertima published *They Came before Columbus: The African Presence in Ancient America.* Drawing from various disciplines, Van Sertima presented evidence of pre-Columbian contact with the New World by Africans. The book earned him the Clarence L. Holte Prize in 1981, although it also drew criticism from anthropologists who argued that he ignored critical evidence that would disprove his theory.

In 1979, Van Sertima founded the *Journal of African Civilizations*, which presents a revisionist approach to world history. He was also the author of *Caribbean Writers* (1968), a collection of essays, and *Early America Revisited* (1998), among other works.

CORNEL WEST

See chapter 17, Religion

CLIFTON R. WHARTON JR. (1926–)

University President, Government Official. Clifton Reginald Wharton Jr., born on September 13, 1926, was the first African American to head the largest university system in the United States—the State University of New York (SUNY). He was also president of Michigan State University and served as chairman and CEO of the Teachers Insurance and Annuity Association (TIAA) and the College Retirement Equities Fund. He also served briefly as President Bill Clinton's deputy secretary of state.

A native Bostonian, Wharton took a bachelor's degree cum laude from Harvard University in 1947. He received a master's degree in international affairs at Johns Hopkins the following year as the first African American admitted into the university's School for Advanced International Studies. In 1956, he earned a second M.A. from the University of Chicago, which awarded him a Ph.D. in economics in 1958. Between degrees, Wharton worked as a research associate for the University of Chicago. He then proceeded to the Agricultural Development Council, where he worked for twelve years. He also held a post as visiting professor at the University of Malaya and served as director and eventually vice president of the American Universities Research Program.

Wharton took over the presidency of Michigan State in 1970 and stayed there for eight years. He became chancellor of the SUNY system in 1978, and held the position until he resigned in 1986. He then became chief executive of the

TIAA, the largest pension fund in the world, and later the first African American to chair the Rockefeller Foundation.

Wharton achieved yet another first in 1993 when President Clinton selected him as his deputy secretary of state, the first African American to fill that post. He was only at the job eight months before he resigned in frustration over political struggles within the administration. He then returned to the TIAA as an overseer, and also became a director of the New York Stock Exchange and Harcourt General. He later worked as an economist and vice president of the Agricultural Development Council. Wharton won the President's Award on World Hunger in 1983 and has earned honorary degrees from numerous colleges and universities.

CARTER G. WOODSON (1875–1950)

Educator, Writer, Publisher, Organization Founder. Often called the father of black history, Carter Godwin Woodson was a tireless advocate for the inclusion of African American history in school curriculums. He also promoted African American achievements and heritage through the Association for the Study of Negro Life and History (now the Association for the Study of African American Life and History, or ASALH), an organization he cofounded, and through the observation of Negro History Week (now Black History Month).

Woodson was born to formerly enslaved parents in 1875 in New Canton, Virginia. In 1898, he enrolled at Berea College in Kentucky, then taught school in Fayette County, West Virginia. In 1900, he was appointed principal of his alma mater, Douglass High School, then returned to Berea until the school, racially integrated at first, was forced to close its doors to African American students because of the state's segregation laws. Woodson then studied at the University of Chicago and returned to Berea after it readmitted African Americans. He received a B.A. in literature from Berea in 1903.

Woodson then taught school and later served as a school supervisor in the Philippines. He spent a semester at the Sorbonne, where he improved his French speaking skills. He then returned to the University of Chicago, where he received a second B.A. in 1907 and an M.A. degree in history, romance languages, and literature in 1908. Woodson began studying for his doctorate at Harvard University in 1908 and later taught at several schools in the District of Columbia; his longest tenure was at the M Street High School, where he remained from 1911 to 1917. He completed his dissertation and received his Ph.D. from Harvard in 1912, becoming the second African American man to earn a Harvard doctorate (the first was W. E. B. Du Bois).

Deeply devoted to the study and promotion of African American history and to the preservation of the culture of his race, Woodson joined several other men in founding the Association for the Study of Negro Life and History in 1915. Woodson's interest in the history of African Americans remained foremost throughout his life's work. In 1916, the association began publishing the widely respected *Journal of Negro History* (now the *Journal of African American History*).

Woodson held several positions in academia in the District of Columbia: principal of Armstrong Manual Training School (1918–1919); faculty member, dean, and head of the graduate faculty at Howard University (1919–1920); and dean at West Virginia Collegiate Institute (1920–1922). Thereafter, he concentrated on the work of the ASALH. In 1921, he organized Associated Publishers, the publishing arm of ASALH. Among his own works issued by the press were *The History of the Negro Church* (1921) and *The Mis-education of the Negro* (1933).

Woodson remained determined that young people, teachers, and others should know about African American history. As a partial solution, beginning in February 1926, he promoted a special commemoration, known as Negro History Week, to incorporate the birthdays of Booker T. Washington, Abraham Lincoln, and Frederick Douglass. The celebration had national appeal, and in 1976 Negro History Week became Black History Month. To further promote African American history in schools, Woodson founded the *Negro History Bulletin* in 1937. On April 3, 1950, Woodson died in Washington, D.C.

HISTORICALLY AND PREDOMINANTLY AFRICAN AMERICAN COLLEGES AND UNIVERSITIES

Alabama A&M University
Established 1875
4900 Meridian St.
Normal, AL 35762
Telephone: (256) 372-5000
Website: www.aamu.edu

Alabama State University
Established 1867
915 S. Jackson St.
Montgomery, AL 36101
Telephone: (334) 229-4100
Website: www.alasu.edu

Albany State University
Established 1903
504 College Dr.
Albany, GA 31705
Telephone: (229) 430-4600
Website: www.potentialrealized.org

Alcorn State University
Established 1871
1000 ASU Dr.
Alcorn State, MS 39096
Telephone: (601) 877-6100
Website: www.alcorn.edu

Allen University
Established 1870
1530 Harden St.
Columbia, SC 29204
Telephone: (803) 376-5700
Website: www.allenuniversity.edu

Arkansas Baptist College
Established 1884
1621 Dr. Martin Luther King Dr.
Little Rock, AR 72202
Telephone: (501) 244-5168
Website: www.arkansasbaptist.edu

Atlanta Metropolitan College
Established 1974
1630 Metropolitan Pky. SW
Atlanta, GA 30310
Telephone: (404) 756-4000
Website: www.atlm.edu

Barber-Scotia College
Established 1867
145 Cabarrus Ave. W
Concord, NC 28025
Telephone: (704) 789-2900
Website: www.b-sc.edu

Benedict College
Established 1870
1600 Haren St.
Columbia, SC 29204
Telephone: (803) 253-5000
Website: www.benedict.edu

Bennett College for Women
Established 1873
900 E. Washington St.
Greensboro, NC 27401
Telephone: (336) 517-2100
Website: www.bennett.edu

Bethune-Cookman University
Established 1904
640 Dr. Mary McLeod Bethune Blvd.
Daytona Beach, FL 32114
Telephone: (386) 481-2000
Website: www.bethune.cookman.edu

Bishop State Community College
Established 1965
351 N. Broad St.
Mobile, AL 36603-5898
Telephone: (251) 405-7000
Website: www.bscc.cc.al.us

Bluefield State College
Established 1895
219 Rock St.
Bluefield, WV 24701-2198
Telephone: (304) 327-4000
Website: www.bluefieldstate.edu

Bowie State University
Established 1865
14000 Jericho Park Rd.
Bowie, MD 20715-9465
Telephone: (301) 860-4000
Website: www.bowiestate.edu

Central State University
Established 1887
1400 Brush Row Rd.
Wilberforce, OH 45384
Telephone: (800) 388-2781
Website: www.centralstate.edu

Charles Drew University of Medicine and Science
Established 1966
1731 E. 120th St.
Los Angeles, CA 90059-3025
Telephone: (323) 563-4800
Website: www.cdrewu.edu

Cheyney University of Pennsylvania
Established 1837
1837 University Cir., PO Box 200
Cheyney, PA 19319-0200
Telephone: (610) 399-2275
Website: www.cheyney.edu

Chicago State University
Established 1867
9501 S. King Dr.
Chicago, IL 60628-1598
Telephone: (773) 995-2000
Website: www.csu.edu

Claflin University
Established 1869
400 Magnolia St.
Orangeburg, SC 29115
Telephone: (803) 535-5000
Website: www.claflin.edu

Clark Atlanta University
Established 1988
223 James P. Brawley Dr. SW
Atlanta, GA 30314
Telephone: (404) 880-8000
Website: www.cau.edu

Clinton Junior College
Established 1894
1029 Crawford Rd.
Rock Hill, SC 29730
Telephone: (803) 327-7402

Coahoma Community College
Established 1949
3240 Friars Point Rd.
Clarksdale, MS 38614
Telephone: (662) 627-2571
Website: www.ccc.cc.ms.us/

Concordia College
Established 1922
1804 Green St.
Selma, AL 36701
Telephone: (334) 874-5700
Website: www.concordiaselma.edu

Coppin State University
Established 1900
2500 W. North Ave.
Baltimore, MD 21216-3698
Telephone: (410) 951-3000
Website: www.coppin.edu

Cuyahoga Community College, Metropolitan Campus
Established 1963
2900 Community College Ave.
Cleveland, OH 44115
Telephone: (800) 954-8742
Website: www.tri-c.cc.oh.us

Delaware State University
Established 1891
1200 N. DuPont Hwy.
Dover, DE 19901
Telephone: (302) 857-6060
Website: www.desu.edu

Denmark Technical College
Established 1947
1126 Solomon Blatt Blvd.
Denmark, SC 29042
Telephone: (803) 793-5149
Website: www.den.tec.sc.us/

Dillard University
Established 1869
2601 Gentilly Blvd.
New Orleans, LA 70122
Telephone: (504) 283-8822
Website: www.dillard.edu

J. F. Drake State Technical College
Established 1961
3421 Meridian St.
North Huntsville, AL 35811
Telephone: (256) 539-8161
Website: www.dstc.cc.al.us

Edward Waters College
Established 1866
1658 Kings Rd.
Jacksonville, FL 32209
Telephone: (904) 470-8000
Website: www.ewc.edu

Elizabeth City State University
Established 1891
1704 Weeksville Rd.
Elizabeth City, NC 27909
Telephone: (252) 335-3400
Website: www.ecsu.edu

Fayetteville State University
Established 1867
1200 Murchison Rd.
Fayetteville, NC 28301
Telephone: (910) 672-1111
Website: www.uncfsu.edu

Fisk University
Established 1866
1000 17th Ave. N
Nashville, TN 37208-3051
Telephone: (615) 329-8500
Website: www.fisk.edu

Florida A&M University
Established 1887
1700 Lee Hall Dr.,
304 Foote-Hilyer
Tallahassee, FL 32307
Telephone: (850) 599-3000
Website: www.famu.edu

Florida Memorial University
Established 1879
15800 NW 42nd Ave.
Miami Gardens, FL 33054
Telephone: (305) 626-3600
Website: www.fmuniv.edu

Fort Valley State University
Established 1895
1005 State University Dr.
Fort Valley, GA 31030
Telephone: (478) 825-6211
Website: www.fvsu.edu

Grambling State University
Established 1901
403 Main St.
Grambling, LA 71245
Telephone: (800) 569-4714
Website: www.gram.edu

Hampton University
Established 1868
Hampton, VA 23668
Telephone: (757) 727-5000
Website: www.hamptonu.edu/

Harris-Stowe State University
Established 1857
3026 Laclede Ave.
St. Louis, MO 63103
Telephone: (314) 340-3366
Website: www.hssu.edu/

Hinds Community College, Utica Campus
Established 1917
34175 Miss. 18 West
Utica, MS 39175-9599
Telephone: (601) 354-2327
Website: www.hindscc.edu

Howard University
Established 1867
2400 6th St. NW
Washington, DC 20059
Telephone: (202) 806-6100
Website: www.howard.edu

Howard University School of Law
Established 1869
2900 Van Ness St. NW
Washington, DC 20008
Telephone: (202) 806-8000
Website: www.law.howard.edu

Huston-Tillotson University
Established 1876
900 Chicon St.
Austin, TX 78702-2795
Telephone: (512) 505-3000
Website: www.htu.edu

Interdenominational Theological Center
Established 1958
700 Martin Luther King Jr. Dr.
Atlanta, GA 30314-4143
Telephone: (404) 527-7700
Website: www.itc.edu

Jackson State University
Established 1877
1400 Lynch St.
Jackson, MS 39217
Telephone: (800) 848-6817
Website: www.jsums.edu

Jarvis Christian College
Established 1912
PO Box 1470
Hawkins, TX 75765
Telephone: (903) 769-5700
Website: www.jarvis.edu

Johnson C. Smith University
Established 1867
100 Beatties Ford Rd.
Charlotte, NC 28216
Telephone: (704) 378-1000
Website: www.jcsu.edu

Kennedy-King College
Established 1966
6301 S. Halsted St.
Chicago, IL 60621
Telephone: (773) 602-5000
Website: www. kennedyking.ccc.edu

Kentucky State University
Established 1886
400 E. Main St.
Frankfort, KY 40601
Telephone: (502) 597-6000
Website: www.kysu.edu

Knoxville College
Established 1875
901 Knoxville College Dr.
Knoxville, TN 37921
Telephone: (865) 524-6525
Website: www.knoxvillecollege.edu/

LaGuardia Community College
Established 1971
31-10 Thomson Ave.
Long Island City, NY 11101
Telephone: (718) 482-7200
Website: www.lagcc.cuny.edu

Lane College
Established 1882
545 Lane Ave.
Jackson, TN 38301
Telephone: (731) 426-7500
Website: www.lanecollege.edu/

Langston University
Established 1897
PO Box 1500
Langston, OK 73050
Telephone: (877) 466-2231
Website: www.lunet.edu

Lawson State Community College
Established 1965
3060 Wilson Rd. SW
Birmingham, AL 35221
Telephone: (205) 925-2515
Website: www.ls.cc.al.us/

LeMoyne-Owen College
Established 1862
807 Walker Ave.
Memphis, TN 38126
Telephone: (901) 435-1701
Website: www.loc.edu/

Lewis College of Business
Established 1928
17370 Meyers Rd.
Detroit, MI 48235
Telephone: (313) 862-6300
Website: www.lewiscollege.edu

Lincoln University (Missouri)
Established 1866
820 Chestnut St.
Jefferson City, MO 65101
Telephone: (573) 681-5000
Website: www.lincolnu.edu

Lincoln University (Pennsylvania)
Established 1854
1570 Baltimore Pike, PO Box 179
Lincoln University, PA 19352
Telephone: (484) 365-8000
Website: www.lincoln.edu

Livingstone College
Established 1879
701 W. Monroe St.
Salisbury, NC 28144
Telephone: (800) 835-3435
Website: www.livingstone.edu

Medgar Evers College, City University of New York
Established 1969
1650 Bedford Ave.
Brooklyn, NY 11225
Telephone: (718) 270-6021
Website: www.greatcollegetown.com/medgar.html

Meharry Medical College
Established 1876
1005 Dr. D. B. Todd Jr. Blvd.
Nashville, TN 37208
Telephone: (615) 327-6000
Website: www.mmc.edu

Miles College
Established 1905
5500 Myron Massey Blvd.
Fairfield, AL 35064
Telephone: (205) 929-1000
Website: www.miles.edu

Mississippi Valley State University
Established 1946
14000 Hwy. 82 W.
Itta Bena, MS 38941
Telephone: (662) 254-9041
Website: www.mvsu.edu

Morehouse College
Established 1867
830 Westview Dr. SW
Atlanta, GA 30314
Telephone: (404) 681-2800
Website: www.morehouse.edu

Morehouse School of Medicine
Established 1975
720 Westview Dr. SW
Atlanta, GA 30310-1495
Telephone: (404) 752-1500
Website: www.msm.edu

Morgan State University
Established 1867
1700 E. Cold Spring Ln.
Baltimore, MD 21251
Telephone: (443) 885-3333
Website: www.morgan.edu

Morris Brown College
Established 1881
643 Martin Luther King Jr. Dr.
Atlanta, GA 30314
Telephone: (404) 739-1010
Website: www.morrisbrown.edu

Morris College
Established 1908
100 W. College St.
Sumter, SC 29150-3599
Telephone: (803) 934-3200
Website: www.morris.edu

New York City Technical College
Established 1946
300 Jay St.
Brooklyn, NY 11201
Telephone: (718) 260-5500
Website: www.citytech.suny.edu

Norfolk State University
Established 1935
700 Park Ave.
Norfolk, VA 23504
Telephone: (757) 823-8600
Website: www.nsu.ed

North Carolina A&T State University
Established 1891
1601 E. Market St.
Greensboro, NC 27411
Telephone: (336) 334-7500
Website: www.ncat.edu

North Carolina Central University
Established 1910
1801 Fayetteville St.
Durham, NC 27707
Telephone: (919) 530-6100
Website: www.nccu.edu

Oakwood University
Established 1896
7000 Adventist Blvd. NW
Huntsville, AL 35896
Telephone: (256) 726-7000
Website: www.oakwood.edu

Paine College
Established 1882
1235 15th St.
Augusta, GA 30901
Telephone: (706) 821-8200
Website: www.paine.edu

Paul Quinn College
Established 1872
3837 Simpson Stuart Rd.
Dallas, TX 75241-4398
Telephone: (214) 376-1000
Website: www.pqc.edu

Philander Smith College
Established 1877
900 Daisy L. Gatson Bates Dr.
Little Rock, AR 72202
Telephone: (501) 375-9845
Website: www.philander.edu

Prairie View A&M University
Established 1876
PO Box 519
Prairie View, TX 77446-0519
Telephone: (936) 261-3311
Website: www.pvamu.edu

Roxbury Community College
Established 1973
1234 Columbus Ave.
Roxbury Crossing, MA 02120
Telephone: (617) 427-0060
Website: www.rcc.mass.edu

Rust College
Established 1866
150 Rust Ave.
Holly Spring, MS 38635
Telephone: (662) 252-8000
Website: www.rustcollege.edu

Saint Augustine's College
Established 1867
1315 Oakwood Ave.
Raleigh, NC 27610-2298
Telephone: (919) 516-4000
Website: www.st-aug.edu/

Saint Paul's College
Established 1888
115 College Dr.
Lawrenceville, VA 23868-9988
Telephone: (434) 848-3111
Website: www.saintpauls.edu

Savannah State University
Established 1890
3219 College St.
Savannah, GA 31404
Telephone: (912) 356-2181
Website: www.savannahstate.edu

Selma University
Established 1878
1501 Lapsley St.
Selma, AL 36701
Telephone: (334) 872-2533
Website: www.selmauniversity.org

Shaw University
Established 1865
118 E. South St.
Raleigh, NC 27601
Telephone: (919) 546-8275
Website: www.shawuniversity.edu/

Simmons College of Kentucky
Established 1879
1018 S. 7th St.
Louisville, KY 40203
Telephone: (502) 776-1443
Website: www.simmonscollegeky.edu/

Sojourner-Douglass College
Established 1972
200 N. Central Ave.
Baltimore, MD 21202
Telephone: (410) 276-0306
Website: www.sdc.edu/

South Carolina State University
Established 1896
300 College St. NE
Orangeburg, SC 29117
Telephone: (803) 536-7000
Website: www.scsu.edu

Southern University and A&M College at Baton Rouge
Established 1880
PO Box 9901
Baton Rouge, LA 70813
Telephone: (225) 771-4500
Website: www.subr.edu

Southern University at New Orleans
Established 1956
6400 Press Dr.
New Orleans, LA 70126
Telephone: (504) 286-5000
Website: www.suno.edu

Southern University at Shreveport
Established 1964
Martin Luther King Jr. Dr.
Shreveport, LA 71107
Telephone: (318) 670-6000
Website: www.susla.edu

Southwestern Christian College
Established 1949
PO Box 10
Terrell, TX 75160
Telephone: (972) 524-3341
Website: www.swcc.edu/

Spelman College
Established 1881
350 Spelman Ln. SW
Atlanta, GA 30314-4399
Telephone: (404) 681-3643
Website: www.spelman.edu

Stillman College
Established 1876
PO Box 1430
Tuscaloosa, AL 35403
Telephone: (800) 841-5722
Website: www.stillman.edu

Talladega College
Established 1867
627 W. Battle St.
Talladega, AL 35160
Telephone: (256) 362-0206
Website: www.talladega.edu

Tennessee State University
Established 1912
3500 John A Merritt Blvd.
Nashville, TN 37209
Telephone: (615) 963-5000
Website: www.tnstate.edu

Texas College
Established 1894
2404 Grand Ave.
Tyler, TX 75702
Telephone: (800) 306-6299
Website: www.texascollegeonline.edu

Texas Southern University
Established 1947
3100 Cleburne Ave.
Houston, TX 77004
Telephone: (713) 313-7011
Website: www.tsu.edu

Tougaloo College
Established 1869
500 W. County Line Rd.
Tougaloo, MS 39174
Telephone: (601) 977-7700
Website: www.tougaloo.edu

Trenholm State Technical College
Established 1963
PO Box 10048
Montgomery, AL 36108
Telephone: (334) 420-4200
Website: www.trenholmtech.cc.al.us

Tuskegee University
Established 1881
1200 W. Montgomery Rd.
Tuskegee Inst, AL 36088
Telephone: (334) 727-8011
Website: www.tuskegee.edu

University of Arkansas at Pine Bluff
Established 1873
1200 University Dr.
Pine Bluff, AR 71611
Telephone: (870) 575-8000
Website: www.uapb.edu

University of Maryland–Eastern Shore
Established 1886
2800 University of Maryland Eastern Shore
Princess Anne, MD 21853
Telephone: (410) 651-2200
Website: www.umes.edu

University of the District of Columbia
Established 1976
4200 Connecticut Ave. NW
Washington, DC 20008
Telephone: (202) 274-5000
Website: www.udc.edu

University of the Virgin Islands
Established 1962
2 John Brewers Bay
St. Thomas, Virgin Islands, 00802-9990
Telephone: (340) 693-1160
Website: www.uvi.edu

Virginia State University
Established 1882
1 Hayden Dr.
Petersburg, VA 23806
Telephone: (804) 524-5000
Website: www.vsu.edu

Virginia Union University
Established 1865
1500 N. Lombardy St.
Richmond, VA 23220
Telephone: (804) 257-5600
Website: www.vuu.edu

Virginia University of Lynchburg
Established 1886
2058 Garfield Ave.
Lynchburg, VA 24501
Telephone: (434) 528-5276
Website: www.vsu.edu

Voorhees College
Established 1897
PO Box 678
Denmark, SC 29042
Telephone: (803) 780-1234
Website: www.voorhees.edu

Wayne County Community College District
Established 1967
801 W. Fort St.
Detroit, MI 48226
Telephone: (313) 496-2600
Website: www.wcccd.edu

West Virginia State Community and Technical College
Established 1891
PO Box 1000
Institute, WV 25112-1000
Telephone: (304) 766-3118
Website: www.wvsctc.edu

Wilberforce University
Established 1856
1055 N. Bickett Rd.
Wilberforce, OH 45384-1001
Telephone: (937) 376-2911
Website: www.wilberforce.edu

Wiley College
Established 1873
711 Wiley Ave.
Marshall, TX 75670
Telephone: (903) 927-3300
Website: www.wileyc.edu

Winston-Salem State University
Established 1892
601 S. Martin Luther King Jr. Dr.
Winston-Salem, NC 27110
Telephone: (336) 750-2000
Website: www.wssu.edu

Xavier University of Louisiana
Established 1925
1 Drexel Dr.
New Orleans, LA 70125
Telephone: (504) 486-7411
Website: www.xula.edu

RESEARCH INSTITUTIONS

Anacostia Community Museum
1901 Fort Pl. SE
Washington, DC 20020
Telephone: (202) 633-4820
Website: www.anacostia.si.edu

Association for the Study of African American Life and History
C.B. Powell Bldg., 525 Bryant St. NW, Ste. C142
Washington, DC 20059
Telephone: (202) 865-0053
Website: www.asalh.org

Bennett College for Women, Johnnetta B. Cole Global Diversity & Inclusion Institute
Sebastian House, 1402 W. Washington St.
Greensboro, NC 27401
Telephone: (336) 517-2272
Website: www.jbcinstitute.org

Black Arts Research Center
30 Marion St.
Nyack, NY 10960
Website: www.barc0.tripod.com/

Boston University, African American Studies Program
138 Mountfort St.
Brookline, MA 02446
Telephone: (617) 353-2795
Website: www.bu.edu/afam

Bowie State University, Center for Excellence in Teaching and Learning (CETL)
14000 Jericho Park Rd.
Bowie, MD 20715-9465
Telephone: (301) 860-4000
Website: www.bowiestate.edu/about/cabinet/AcademicAffairs/cetl/

Brooklyn College, City University of New York, Africana Studies Department
2900 Bedford Ave., 3105 James Hall
Brooklyn, NY 11210
Telephone: (718) 951-5597
Website: www.depthome.brooklyn.cuny.edu/africana/

Brown University, Center for the Study of Ethnicity and Race in America
Dyer House, 150 Power St.
Providence, RI 02912
Telephone: (401) 863-3080
Website: www.brown.edu/Departments/Race_Ethnicity

Brown University, Department of Africana Studies
155 Angell St., PO Box 1904

Providence, RI 02912
Telephone: (401) 863-3137
Website: www.brown.edu/Departments/Africana_Studies/

Brown University, Watson Institute for International Studies
111 Thayer St., PO Box 1970
Providence, RI 02912-1970
Telephone: (401) 863-2809
Website: www.watsoninstitute.org/

Center for Third World Organizing
1218 E. 21st St.
Oakland, CA 94606
Telephone: (510) 533-7583
Website: www.ctwo.org

Charles Drew University of Medicine and Science
1731 E. 120th St.
Los Angeles, CA 90059
Telephone: (310) 668-3177
Website: www.cdrewu.edu

City University of New York, Institute for Research on the African Diaspora in the Americas and the Caribbean (IRADAC)
365 5th Ave., Rm. 7114
New York, NY 10016
Telephone: (212) 817-2076
Website: www.ccny.cuny.edu/iradac

Claflin University, Center for Excellence in Teaching
400 Magnolia St.
Orangeburg, SC 29115
Telephone: (803) 535-5000

Claflin University, Jonathan Jasper Wright Institute for the Study of Southern African History, Culture, and Policy
400 Magnolia St.
Orangeburg, SC 29115
Telephone: (803) 535-5092
Website: www.claflin.edu/Academic/J.J.WrightInstitute.html

Claflin University, South Carolina Center for Biotechnology
400 Magnolia St.
Orangeburg, SC 29115
Telephone: (803) 535-5253
Website: www.claflin.edu/Academic/SC_Biotechnology.html

Clark Atlanta University, Center for Cancer Research and Therapeutic Development
James P. Brawley Dr. at Fair St. SW
Atlanta, GA 30314-4385
Telephone: (404) 880-6763
Website: www.ccrtd.cau.edu

Clark Atlanta University, Environmental Justice Resource Center
223 James P. Brawley Dr.
Atlanta, GA 30314
Telephone: (404) 880-6911
Website: www.ejrc.cau.edu

Clark Atlanta University, Research Center for Science and Technology
223 James P. Brawley Dr.
Atlanta, GA 30314-4385
Telephone: (404) 880-6990
Website: www.cau.edu/Research_Programs.aspx

Clemson University, Charles H. Houston Center for the Study of Black Experience in Education
201 Sikes Hall
Clemson, SC 29634
Telephone: (864) 656-3311
Website: www.clemson.edu/centers-institutes/houston/

College of Staten Island, City University of New York, History Department
2800 Victory Blvd.
Staten Island, NY 10314
Telephone: (718) 982-2000

Colorado State University, Ethnic Studies Department
357 SE Aylesworth
Fort Collins, CO 80523-1790
Telephone: (970) 491-2418
Website: ethnicstudies.colostate.edu

Columbia College Chicago, Center for Black Music Research
600 S. Michigan Ave.
Chicago, IL 60605
Telephone: (312) 369-7559
Website: www.colum.edu/cbmr/

Columbia University, Institute for Research in African-American Studies
758 Schermerhorn Ext., MC 5512, 1200 Amsterdam Ave.
New York, NY 10027
Telephone: (212) 854-7080
Website: www.iraas.com

Cornell University, Africana Studies and Research Center
310 Triphammer Rd.
Ithaca, NY 14850
Telephone: (607) 255-4625
Website: www.asrc.cornell.edu

Delaware State University, College of Agriculture and Related Sciences
1200 N. DuPont Hwy.
Dover, DE 19901
Telephone: (302) 857-6060
Website: www.desu.edu/Agriculture_and_Related_Sciences

Duke University, Center for Documentary Studies (CDS)
1317 W. Pettigrew St.
Durham, NC 27705
Telephone: (919) 660-3663
Website: www-cds.aas.duke.edu

Duke University, Mary Lou Williams Center for Black Culture
201 W. Union Bldg., Box 90880
Durham, NC 27708-0880
Telephone: (919) 684-3814
Website: www.studentaffairs.duke.edu/mlw/about-us

Fisk University, Center for Photonic Materials and Devices
1000 17th Ave. N
Nashville, TN 37208
Telephone: (615) 329-8654
Website: www.fisk.edu/Academics/NaturalSciencesAndMathematics/Physics/PhysicsResearch/CPMD.aspx

Florida A&M University, Center for Environmental Equity and Justice
Tallahassee, FL 32307
Telephone: (850) 599-3550
Website: www.famu.edu

Florida A&M University, Center for Environmental Technology Transfer
Tallahassee, FL 32307
Telephone: (850) 599-3550

Florida A&M University, Center for Viticultural Sciences & Small Fruit Research
Tallahassee, FL 32307
Telephone: (850) 599-3996

Florida A&M University, Center for Water Quality
Tallahassee, FL 32307
Telephone: (850) 599-3770

Florida A&M University, Environmental Sciences Institute
Tallahassee, FL 32307
Telephone: (850) 599-8183

Florida A&M University, Florida Advanced Center for Composite Technologies
Tallahassee, FL 32307
Telephone: (850) 410-6339

Florida A&M University, Institute of Building Sciences
Tallahassee, FL 32307
Telephone: (850) 599-3007

Florida A&M University, Institute of Public Health
Tallahassee, FL 32307
Telephone: (850) 599-3354

Florida A&M University, Small Business Development Center
Tallahassee, FL 32307
Telephone: (850) 599-3407

Florida International University, African and African Diaspora Studies
1120 SW 8th St.
Miami, FL 33199
Telephone: (305) 348-6860
Website: casgroup.fiu.edu/africana/

Florida State University, African American Studies Program
106 Bellamy Bldg.
Tallahassee, FL 32306-2151
Website: www.fsu.edu/-blkstudy/

Frederick D. Patterson Research Institute
8260 Willow Oaks Corporate Dr., PO Box 10444
Fairfax, VA 22031-4511

Telephone: (703) 205-3400
Website: www.pattersonresearchinstitute.org

Hampton University, Aeropropulsion Center
Hampton, VA 23668-0199
Telephone: (757) 727-5000
Website: set.hamptonu.edu/research/aeropropulsion.cfm

Hampton University, Behavior Sciences Research Center
114 Phoenix Hall
Hampton, VA 23668-0199
Telephone: (757) 727-5000
Website: www.hamptonu.edu/bsrc/contact.htm

Hampton University, Center for Advanced Medical Instrumentation
Hampton, VA 23668-0199
Telephone: (757) 727-5277
Website: www.hamptonu.edu/academics/schools/science/physics/research.htm

Hampton University, Center for Atmospheric Sciences
Hampton, VA 23668
Telephone: (757) 727-5277
Website: cas.hamptonu.edu/

Hampton University, Center for Laser Sciences and Spectroscopy
School of Science
Hampton, VA 23668-0199
Telephone: (757) 727-5277
Website: www.hamptonu.edu/academics/schools/science/physics/research.htm

Hampton University, Center for the Study of the Origin and Structure of Matter
GPRC Bldg.
Hampton, VA 23668
Telephone: (757) 728-6497
Website: www.hamptonu.edu/academics/schools/science/cosm.htm

Hampton University, Cloud Aerosol Lidar and Infrared Pathfinder Satellite Observations (CALIPSO) Quid Pro Quo (QPQ) Validation
Hampton, VA 23668-0199
Telephone: (757) 728-728-6745
Website: www.hamptonu.edu/

Hampton University, Data Conversion and Management Laboratory
Hampton, VA 23668-0199
Telephone: (757) 727-5000
Website: hudcml.hamptonu.edu/

Hampton University, Eastern Seaboard Intermodal Transportation Application Center
Hampton, VA 23668-0199
Telephone: (757) 727-5000
Website: www.hamptonu.edu/

Hampton University, International Coordination Group for Laser Atmospheric Studies
Hampton, VA 23668-0199
Telephone: (757) 727-5000
Website: www.hamptonu.edu/

Hampton University, National Center for African American Marriages and Parenting
Hampton, VA 23668-0199
Telephone: (757) 727-5000
Website: www.hamptonu.edu/

Hampton University, Penn Center to Reduce Health Disparities
Hampton, VA 23668-0199
Telephone: (757) 727-5000-
Website: www.hamptonu.edu/

Hampton University, Proton Therapy Institute
PO Box 6043
Hampton, VA 23668-0199
Telephone: (877) 251-6838
E-mail: info@hamptonproton.org
Website: www.hamptonu.edu/

Hampton University, Skin of Color Research Institute
Hampton, VA 23668-0199
Telephone: (757) 727-5000
Website: huscri.hamptonu.edu/

Hampton University, Virtual Parts Engineering Research Center
School of Engineering and Technology
Hampton, VA 23668-0199
Telephone: (757) 727-5000
Website: set.hamptonu.edu/research/vperc/

Hampton University, Virtual Parts Engineering/Modeling and Simulation
School of Engineering and Technology
Hampton, VA 23668-0199
Telephone: (757) 727-5000
Website: set.hampton.edu/research/

Harvard University, W.E.B. Du Bois Institute for African and African American Research
104 Mount Auburn St. 3R
Cambridge, MA 02138
Telephone: (617) 495-8508
Website: www.dubois.fas.harvard.edu

Howard University, Center for Drug Abuse Research
Holy Cross Hall, Rm. 400
Washington, DC 20008
Telephone: (292) 806-8600
Website: www.howard.edu/cdar/default.htm

Howard University, Center for Urban Progress
HU Research Bldg. 1, 1840 7th St. NW, 3rd Fl.
Washington, DC 20001-3108
Telephone: (202) 865-8572
Website: www.coas.howard.edu/hucup/

Howard University, Moorland-Spingarn Research Center
500 Howard Pl. NW
Washington, DC 20059
Telephone: (202) 806-7240
Website: www.founders.howard.edu/moorland-spingarn/

Howard University, National Human Genome Center, College of Medicine
2041 Georgia Ave. NW, Cancer Center Bldg., Rm. 615
Washington, DC 20060
Telephone: (202) 806-9438
Website: www.genomecenter.howard.edu/

Howard University, Ralph J. Bunche International Affairs Center
2218 6th St. NW
Washington, DC 20059
Telephone: (202) 806-4363
Website: www.howard.edu/RJB/

Indiana State University
200 N. 7th St.
Terre Haute, IN 47809
Telephone: (800) 468-6478
Website: www.indstate.edu

Indiana University, Archives of African American Music and Culture
2805 E. 10th St., Ste. 180–181
Bloomington, IN 47408-2601
Telephone: (812) 855-8547
Website: www.indiana.edu/~aaamc/

Indiana University, Neal-Marshall Black Culture Center
275 N. Jordan Ave.
Bloomington, IN 47405
Telephone: (812) 855-9271
Website: www.indiana.edu/~nmbcc

Jackson State University, Center for Business Development & Economic Research
1400 John R. Lynch St.
Jackson, MS 39217
Telephone: (601) 979-2121
Website: www.jsums.edu/business/cbder/

Jackson State University, Center for Environmental Health
1400 John R. Lynch St.
Jackson, MS 39217
Telephone: (601) 979-2121
Website: www.jsums.edu/cset/or/centers/centceh.htm

Jackson State University, Center for Excellence for Natural Disasters, Coastal Infrastructure, and Emergency Management
1400 John R. Lynch St.
Jackson, MS 39217
Telephone: (601) 979-2121

Jackson State University, Center for Minority Health Disparities
1400 John R. Lynch St.
Jackson, MS 39217
Telephone: (601) 979-2121

Jackson State University, Fannie Lou Hamer Institute on Citizenship and Democracy
Box 17081, 1400 John R. Lynch St.
Jackson, MS 39217
Telephone: (601) 979-2121
E-mail: hamer.institute@jsums.edu
Website: www.jsums.edu//hamer.institute/

Jackson State University, Institute for Epidemiology and Health Services Research
1400 John R. Lynch St.
Jackson, MS 39217
Telephone: (601) 979-2121

Jackson State University, Interdisciplinary Alcohol/ Drug Studies Center
1400 John R. Lynch St.
Jackson, MS 39217
Telephone: (601) 979-2121

Jackson State University, Margaret Walker Alexander Research Center
1400 John R. Lynch St.
Jackson, MS 39217
Telephone: (601) 979-2121
Website: www.jsums.edu/margaretwalker/

Jackson State University, Mississippi Center for Technology Transfer
1400 John R. Lynch St.
Jackson, MS 39217
Telephone: (601) 979-2121

Jackson State University, Mississippi e-Center
1400 John R. Lynch St.
Jackson, MS 39217
Telephone: (601) 979-2121

Jackson State University, Mississippi Learning Institute
1400 John R. Lynch St.
Jackson, MS 39217
Telephone: (601) 979-2121

Jackson State University, Mississippi Urban Research Center
1400 John R. Lynch St.
Jackson, MS 39217
Telephone: (601) 979-2121

Jackson State University, National Center for Biodefense Communications
1400 John R. Lynch St.
Jackson, MS 39217
Telephone: (601) 979-2121
Website: ncbc.jsums.edu/

Jackson State University, Southern Institute for Mental Health Advocacy, Research, and Training
1400 John R. Lynch St.
Jackson, MS 39217
Telephone: (601) 979-2121
Website: www.jsums.edu/smhart/

Jackson State University, Trent Lott Geospatial and Visualization Research Center
1400 John R. Lynch St.
Jackson, MS 39217
Telephone: (601) 979-2121
Website: www.jsums.edu/cset/or/centers/centtlgsdr.htm

Johns Hopkins University, Institute for Global Studies in Culture, Power, and History
3400 N. Charles St.
Baltimore, MD 21218
Telephone: (410) 516-7515
Website: sites.jhu.edu/igs/

Joint Center for Political and Economic Studies
1090 Vermont Ave. NW, Ste. 1100
Washington, DC 20005-4928
Telephone: (202) 789-3500
Website: www.jointcenter.org

Kent State University, Department of Pan-African Studies
101 Oscar Ritchie Hall
Kent, OH 44242
Telephone: (330) 672-3000
Website: www.kent.edu/CAS/PAS/

Kentucky State University, Center of Excellence for the Study of Kentucky African Americans
400 E. Main St.
Frankfort, KY 40601
Telephone: (502) 597-6000
Website: www.kysu.edu/about/heritage/ceskaa/

King Center
449 Auburn Ave. NE
Atlanta, GA 30312
Telephone: (404) 526-8900
Website: www.thekingcenter.org

Meharry Medical College, Center for AIDS Health Disparities Research
1105 Dr. D. B. Todd Blvd.
Nashville, TN 39208
Telephone: (615) 327-6000
Website: www.mmc.edu/research/centers/chd/chd_mission.html

Meharry Medical College, Center for Optimal Health
1105 Dr. D. B. Todd Blvd.
Nashville, TN 39208
Telephone: (615) 327-6000
Website: www.mmc.edu/research/centers/coh/coh_mission.html

Meharry Medical College, Center for Molecular and Behavioral Neuroscience
1105 Dr. D. B. Todd Blvd.
Nashville, TN 39208
Telephone: (615) 327-6000
Website: www.mmc.edu/research/centers/cmbn/cmbn_mission.html

Meharry Medical College, Center for Women's Health Research
1105 Dr. D. B. Todd Blvd.
Nashville, TN 39208
Telephone: (615) 327-6000
Website: www.mmc.edu/research/centers/cwhr/index.html

Meharry Medical College, Clinical Research Center
1105 Dr. D. B. Todd Blvd.
Nashville, TN 39208
Telephone: (615) 327-6000
Website: www.mmc.edu/research/clinical_research_center/index/html

Meharry Medical College, Sickle Cell Center
1105 Dr. D. B. Todd Blvd.
Nashville, TN 39208
Telephone: (615) 327-6000
Website: www.mmc.edu/research/centers/sicklecell/index.html

Mississippi Valley State University, Delta Research and Cultural Institute
14000 Hwy. 82 W
Itta Bena, MS 38941-1400
Telephone: (662) 254-3856
Website: www.mvsu.edu/university/delta_research.php

Mississippi Valley State University, Institute for Effective Teaching Practices
14000 Hwy. 82 W
Itta Bena, MS 38941
Telephone: (662) 254-3718
Website: www.mvsu.edu/academics/colleges/education/support_service/institute_for_effective_teaching_practices.php

Morehouse College, Andrew Young Center for International Affairs
830 Westview Dr. SW
Atlanta, GA 30314-3773
Telephone: (404) 614-8565
Website: www.morehouse.edu/centers/andrewyoungctr/index.html

Morehouse College, Bonner Office of Community Service
830 Westview Dr. SW
Atlanta, GA 30314-3773
Telephone: (404) 681-7575
Website: www.morehouse.edu/OCS/

Morehouse College, Brisbane Institute
830 Westview Dr. SW
Atlanta, GA 30314
Website: www.morehouse.edu/centers/brisbane/index.html

Morehouse College, Center for Teacher Preparation
830 Westview Dr. SW
Atlanta, GA 30314-3773
Telephone: (404) 614-8552
Website: www.morehouse.edu/centers/teacherprep/index.html

Morehouse College, Entrepreneurship Center
830 Westview Dr. SW
Atlanta, GA 30314
Telephone: (404) 681-2800, ext. 2555
Website: www.morehousecenter.org/centers/entrepreneuship/index.html

Morehouse College, Leadership Center at Morehouse College
830 Westview Dr. SW
Atlanta, GA 30314
Telephone: (404) 614-8565
Website: www.morehouse.edu/centers/leadershipcenter/index.html

Morehouse College, Morehouse Research Institute
830 Westview Dr. SW
Atlanta, GA 30314
Telephone: (404) 215-2676
Website: www.morehouse.edu/centers/mri/index.html

Morehouse College, Public Health Sciences Institute
830 Westview Dr. SW
Atlanta, GA 30314
Website: www.morehouse.edu/centers/phsi/

Morgan State University, Biomedical Research Center
101 Jenkins Bldg., Cold Spring Ln. and Hillen Rd.
Baltimore, MD 21251
Telephone: (443) 885-3134

Morgan State University, Center for Advanced Microwave Research and Applications
101 Jenkins Bldg., Cold Spring Ln. and Hillen Rd.
Baltimore, MD 21251
Telephone: (443) 885-3134
Website: www.camracenter.org/

Morgan State University, Center for Civil Rights Education
101 Jenkins Bldg., Cold Spring Ln. and Hillen Rd.
Baltimore, MD 21251
Telephone: (443) 885-3134

Morgan State University, Center for Excellence in Mathematics and Science Education
Banneker Rm. 101, 1700 East Cold Spring Ln.
Baltimore, MD 21251
Telephone: (443) 885-3134
Website: www.morgan.edu/Academics/Special_ProgramsCenters/Center_for_Excellence_in_Mathematics_and_Science.html

Morgan State University, Center for Excellence in Systems Engineering for Space
101 Jenkins Bldg., Cold Spring Ln. and Hillen Rd.
Baltimore, MD 21251
Telephone: (443) 885-3134

Morgan State University, Center for Health Disparities Solutions
Montebello Complex, D Wing, Rm. 102
Baltimore, MD 21251
Telephone: (443) 885-4030
Website: www.morgan.edu/Academics/Special_ProgramsCenters/Center_for_Health_Disparities_Solutions.html

Morgan State University, Center for Microwave, Satellite, and RF Engineering
101 Jenkins Bldg., Cold Spring Ln. and Hillen Rd.
Baltimore, MD 21251
Telephone: (443) 885-3134
Website: comsare.eng.morgan.edu/

Morgan State University, Estuarine Research Center
10545 Mackall Rd.
St. Leonard, MD 20685
Telephone: (410) 586-9700
Website: www.morgan.edu/Estuarine_Research_Center.html

Morgan State University, Institute for Urban Research
Montebello Complex, D216, 1700 E. Cold Spring Ln.
Baltimore, MD 21251
Telephone: (443) 885-4800
Website: www.morgan.edu/Academics/Special_ProgramsCenters/Institute_for_Urban_Research.html

Morgan State University, National Transportation Center
Montebello Complex, D206, 1700 E. Cold Spring Ln.
Baltimore, MD 21251
Telephone: (443) 885-3666
Website: www.morgan.edu/School_of_Engineering/Research_Centers/National_Transportation_Center.html

National Afro-American Museum and Cultural Center
1350 Brush Row Rd., PO Box 578
Wilberforce, OH 45384
Telephone: (937) 376-4944

National Black Child Development Institute, Inc.
1313 L St. NW, Ste. 110
Washington, DC 20005
Telephone: (202) 833-2220
Website: www.nbcdi.org

National Caucus and Center on Black Aged
1220 L St. NW, Ste. 800
Washington, DC 20005
Telephone: (202) 637-8400
Website: www.ncba-aged.org

National Council for Black Studies
PO Box 4109
Atlanta, GA 30302-4109
Telephone: (404) 413-5131
Website: www.ncbsonline.org

National Urban League, Policy Institute
120 Wall St.
New York, NY 10005
Telephone: (212) 558-5300
Website: www.nul.org/content/national-urban-league-policy-institute

New York University, Institute of African-American Affairs
41 E. 11th St., 7th Fl.
New York, NY 10003-6687
Telephone: (212) 998-2130
Website: www.africanastudies.as.nyu.edu/page/IAAA

North Carolina A&T State University, Center for Advanced Materials and Smart Structures
1601 E. Market St.
Greensboro, NC 27411-0001
Telephone: (336) 256-0858
Website: camss.ncat.edu/

North Carolina A&T State University, Center for Autonomous Control and Information Technology
1601 E. Market St.
Greensboro, NC 27411-0001
(336) 256-0858

North Carolina A&T State University, Center for Composite Material Research
1601 E. Market St.
Greensboro, NC 27411-0001
Telephone: (336) 256-0858

North Carolina A&T State University, Center for Cooperative Systems
1601 E. Market St.
Greensboro, NC 27411-0001
Telephone: (336) 256-0858
Website: abner.ncat.edu/cooperativeresearchcenter/

North Carolina A&T State University, Center for Energy Research and Technology
1601 E. Market St.
Greensboro, NC 27411-0001
Telephone: (336) 256-0858
Website: cert.ncat.edu/

North Carolina A&T State University, Center for Human-Machine Studies
1601 E. Market St.
Greensboro, NC 27411-0001
Telephone: (336) 256-0858

North Carolina A&T State University, Institute for Advanced Journalism Studies
1601 E. Market St.
Greensboro, NC 27411-0001
Telephone: (336) 256-2261
Website: www.ifajs.org

North Carolina A&T State University, Institute for Public Health
1601 E. Market St.
Greensboro, NC 27411-0001
Telephone: (336) 256-0858
Website: www.ncat.edu/~iph/

North Carolina A&T State University, Interdisciplinary Center for Entrepreneurship and E-Business
1601 E. Market St.
Greensboro, NC 27411-0001
Telephone: (336) 256-0858

North Carolina A&T State University, Interdisciplinary Scientific Environmental Technology Cooperative Science Center
1601 E. Market St.
Greensboro, NC 27411-0001
Telephone: (336) 256-0858

North Carolina A&T State University, International Trade Center
1601 E. Market St.
Greensboro, NC 27411-0001
Telephone: (336) 256-0858

North Carolina Central University, Alternative Resolution Institute
1801 Fayetteville St.
Durham, NC 27707
Telephone: (919) 530-6100
Website: www.nccu.edu/academics/institutesandcenters/ari.cfm

North Carolina Central University, Biomanufacturing Research Institute and Technology Enterprise
1801 Fayetteville St.
Durham, NC 27707
Telephone: (919) 530-6100
Website: brite.nccu.edu/

North Carolina Central University, Biomedical Biotechnical Research Institute
1801 Fayetteville St.
Durham, NC 27707
Telephone: (919) 530-6100
Website: www.nccu.edu

North Carolina Central University, Biotechnology and Pharmaceutical Law
1801 Fayetteville St.
Durham, NC 27707
Telephone: (919) 530-6100
Website: www.nccu.edu/academics/institutesandcenters/bpl.cfm

North Carolina Central University, Center for Human Development and Family Studies
1801 Fayetteville St.
Durham, NC 27707
Telephone: (919) 530-6100
Website: www.nccu.edu

North Carolina Central University, Center for Innovation in Health Disparities Research
1801 Fayetteville St.

Durham, NC 27707
Telephone: (919) 530-6100
Website: www.nccu.edu/academics/institutesandcenters/cihdr.cfm

North Carolina Central University, Center for University Teaching and Learning
1801 Fayetteville St.
Durham, NC 27707
Telephone: (919) 530-6100
Website: www.nccu.edu

North Carolina Central University, Institute for Civic Engagement and Social Change
1801 Fayetteville St.
Durham, NC 27707
Telephone: (919) 530-6100
Website: www.nccu.edu

North Carolina Central University, Institute for Homeland Security Research and Workforce Development
1801 Fayetteville St.
Durham, NC 27707
Telephone: (919) 530-6100
Website: www.nccu.edu/academics/institutesandcenters/hls/index.cfm

North Carolina Central University, Institute for the Study of Children, Youth, and Family
1801 Fayetteville St.
Durham, NC 27707
Telephone: (919) 530-6100
Website: www.nccu.edu

North Carolina Central University, Juvenile Justice Institute
1801 Fayetteville St.
Durham, NC 27707
Telephone: (919) 530-6100
Website: www.nccu.edu/academics/institutesandcenters/jji.cfm

Northern Illinois University, Center for Black Studies
DeKalb, IL 60115
Telephone: (815) 753-1709
Website: www.cbs.niu.edu/blackstudies/index.shtml

Ohio University, African American Studies Department
Lindley Hall 302
Athens, OH 45701
Telephone: (740) 593-4546
Website: www.ohio.edu/aas/

Prairie View A&M University, Cooperative Agricultural Research Center
PO Box 519, MS 2008
Prairie View, TX 77446
Telephone: (936) 261-3311
Website: www.pvamu.edu/

Prairie View A&M University, International Goat Research Center
PO Box 519, MS 2008
Prairie View, TX 77446
Telephone: (936) 261-3311
Website: www.pvamu.edu/

Princeton University, Center for African American Studies
Stanhope Hall
Princeton, NJ 08544
Telephone: (609) 258-4270
Website: www.princeton.edu/africanamericanstudies/

Purdue University, African American Studies and Research Center
Beering Hall of Liberal Arts and Education, Rm. 6182, 100 N. University St.
West Lafayette, IN 47907-2098
Telephone: (765) 494-5680
Website: www.cla.purdue.edu/african-american/

Queens College, Africana Studies Program
65-30 Kissena Blvd.
Flushing, NY 11367
Telephone: (718) 997-2845

Rutgers University, Institute of Jazz Studies
John Cotton Dana Library, 185 University Ave.
Newark, NJ 07102
Telephone: (973) 353-5595
Website: www.libraries.rutgers.edu/rul/libs/jazz/jazz.shtml

Savannah State University, Center of Excellence in Marine Sciences
3219 College St.
Savannah, GA 31404
Telephone: (912) 356-2186
Website: www.savannahstate.edu/cost/nat-science/marine-sci.shtml

Savannah State University, Center of Excellence in Mass Communications
3219 College St.
Savannah, GA 31404
Telephone: (912) 356-2186

Website: www.savannahstate.edu/class/departments-mass-comm.shtml

Savannah State University, Center of Excellence in Social Work
3219 College St.
Savannah, GA 31404
Telephone: (912) 356-2186
Website: www.savannahstate.edu/class/departments-social-work.shtml

Schomburg Center for Research in Black Culture
515 Malcolm X Blvd.
New York, NY 10037-1801
Telephone: (212) 491-2200
Website: www.nypl.org/locations/schomburg

South Carolina State University, Center for Excellence in Transportation
300 College St. NE
Orangeburg, SC 29117
Telephone: (803) 536-8863
Website: www.utc.scsu.edu/

South Carolina State University, Environmental Policy Institute
300 College St. NE
Orangeburg, SC 29117-0001
Telephone: (803) 536-8863
Website: www.utc.scsu.edu/

Southern University and A&M College, Agricultural Research and Extension Center
PO Box 10010
Baton Rouge, LA 70813
Website: www.suagcenter.com/

Southern University and A&M College, Capital Small Business Development Center
1933 Wooddale Blvd., Ste. E
Baton Rouge, LA 70806
Telephone: (225) 922-0998
Website: www.subr.edu/research/orsi/researchcenters.htm

Southern University and A&M College, Center for Energy and Environmental Studies
PO Box 9764
Baton Rouge, LA 70813
Telephone: (225) 771-4724
Website: www.subr.edu/research/orsi/research/researchcenters.htm

Southern University and A&M College, Center for International Development Programs
PO Box 10604
Baton Rouge, LA 70813
Telephone: (225) 771-2008
Website: www.subr.edu/research/orsi/research/researchcenters.htm

Southern University and A&M College, Center for Rural Small Development
PO Box 9938
Baton Rouge, LA 70813
Telephone: (225) 771-3785
Website: www.subr.edu/research/orsi/research/researchcenters.htm

Southern University and A&M College, Center for Social Research
PO Box 9503
Baton Rouge, LA 70813
Telephone: (225) 771-4249
Website: www.subr.edu/research/orsi/research/researchcenters.htm

Southern University and A&M College, Center for Wellness
PO Box 11491
Baton Rouge, LA 70813
Telephone: (225) 771-5802
Website: www.subr.edu/research/orsi/research/researchcenters.htm

Southern University and A&M College, Health Research Center
PO Box 9921
Baton Rouge, LA 70813
Telephone: (225) 771-4240
Website: www.subr.edu/research/orsi/research/researchcenters.htm

Southern University and A&M College, National Plant Data Center
PO Box 74490
Baton Rouge, LA 70874
Telephone: (225) 775-6280
Website: www.subr.edu/research/orsi/research/researchcenters.htm

Southern University and A&M College, Research Institute of Pure and Applied Sciences
PO Box 11220
Baton Rouge, LA 70813
Telephone: (225) 771-4130

Website: www.subr.edu/research/orsi/research/researchcenters.htm

Southern University and A&M College, Small Farm Family Development Center
PO Box 9508
Baton Rouge, LA 70813
Telephone: (225) 771-3660
Website: www.subr.edu/research/orsi/research/researchcenters.htm

Southern University and A&M College, Urban Recreation Research Center
PO Box 9656
Baton Rouge, LA 70813
Telephone: (225) 771-4182
Website: www.subr.edu/research/orsi/research/researchcenters.htm

Spelman College, Center for Biomedical and Behavioral Research
350 Spelman Ln. SW
Atlanta, GA 30314

Spelman College, Center for Energy and Environmental Studies
350 Spelman Ln. SW
Atlanta, GA 30314

Spelman College, Center for Molecular Biology
350 Spelman Ln. SW
Atlanta, GA 30314

Spelman College, MacVicar Health Center for Education and Research
350 Spelman Ln. SW
Atlanta, GA 30314
Telephone: (404) 270-5249
Website: www.spelman.edu/students/current/services/health/

Spelman College, Minority Access to Research Careers/Undergraduate Student Training in Academic Research
350 Spelman Ln. SW
Atlanta, GA 30314
Website: www.spelman.edu/academics/research/marc/

Spelman College, Model Institutions for Excellence Program
350 Spelman Ln. SW
Atlanta, GA 30314

Spelman College, Research Infrastructure in Minority Institutions
350 Spelman Ln. SW
Atlanta, GA 30314
Telephone: (404) 270-5781
Website: www.spelman.edu/academics/research/rimi/

Spelman College, Research Initiative for Scientific Enhancement
350 Spelman Ln., PO Box 1475
Atlanta, GA 30314-4399
Telephone: (404) 270-5713
Website: www.spelman.edu/academics/research/rise/

Spelman College, Women in Science and Engineering
350 Spelman Ln. SW
Atlanta, GA 30314
Telephone: (404) 270-5859
Website: www.spelman.edu/academics/research/wise/

Spelman College, Women's Research & Resource Center
350 Spelman Ln. SW, Box 115, Cosby 2nd Fl.
Atlanta, GA 30314
Telephone: (404) 270-5625
Website: www.spelman.edu/womenscenter/

Temple University, Center for African American Research and Public Policy
1115 W. Berks St., Ste. 663, Gladfelter Hall
Philadelphia, PA 19122
Telephone: (215) 204-0097
Website: www.temple.edu/caarpp

Tennessee State University, Center for Health Research
3500 John A. Merritt Blvd.
Nashville, TN 37209-1561
Telephone: (615) 320-3005
Website: www.tnstate.edu/interior.asp?mid=3243

Tennessee State University, Center of Excellence for Battlefield Sensor Fusion
3500 John A. Merritt Blvd.
Nashville, TN 37209
Telephone: (615) 963-5396
Website: www.tnstate.edu/ce-bsf/

Tennessee State University, Center of Excellence in Information Systems
3500 John A. Merritt Blvd.
Nashville, TN 37209
Telephone: (615) 277-1600
Website: coe.tsuniv.edu/index.htm

Tennessee State University, Center of Excellence for Research and Policy in Basic Skills
3500 John A. Merritt Blvd.
Nashville, TN 37209-1561
Telephone: (615) 963-7231

Tennessee State University, Small Business Development Center
330 10th Ave. N
Nashville, TN 37203-3401
Telephone: (615) 963-7179
Website: www.tsbdc.org/center.aspx?center=47060&subloc=0

Tulane University, Amistad Research Center
6823 St. Charles Ave.
New Orleans, LA 70118
Telephone: (504) 862-3222
Website: www.amistadresearchcenter.org

University at Albany, State University of New York, Department of Africana Studies
1400 Washington Ave. BA 115
Albany, NY 12222
Telephone: (518) 442-4730
Website: www.albany.edu/africana/

University of Alabama, Frances S. Summersell Center for the Study of the South
Dept. of History, PO Box 870212
Tuscaloosa, AL 35487
Telephone: (205) 348-1862
Website: scss.ua.edu/

University of California, Berkeley, Department of African American Studies
660 Barrows Hall 2572
Berkeley, CA 94720
Telephone: (510) 642-7084
Website: africam.berkeley.edu/

University of California, Los Angeles, Department of Sociology
264 Haines Hall, 375 Portola Plz.
Los Angeles, CA 90095-1551
Telephone: (310) 825-1313
Website: www.soc.ucla.edu/

University of California, Los Angeles, Ralph J. Bunche Center for African American Studies
160 Haines Hall, Box 951545
Los Angeles, CA 90095-1545
Telephone: (310) 825-7403
Website: www.bunche.ucla.edu

University of California, San Francisco, Center for Aging in Diverse Communities
3333 California St., Ste. 335
San Francisco, CA 94118
Telephone: (415) 502-4088
Website: dgim.ucsf.edu/cadc/

University of California, Santa Barbara, Center for Black Studies Research
4603 South Hall
Santa Barbara, CA 93106-3140
Telephone: (805) 893-3914
Website: www.research.ucsb.edu/cbs/

University of Charleston, Avery Research Center for African American History and Culture
66 George St.
Charleston, SC 29424
Telephone: (843) 953-7609
Website: avery.cofc.edu/

University of Chicago, Committee on African and African-American Studies
5828 S. University
Chicago, IL 60637
Telephone: (773) 702-8344

University of Cincinnati, Department of African American Studies
609 Old Chemistry Bldg., PO Box 210370
Cincinnati, OH 45221-0370
Telephone: (513) 556-0350
Website: www.artsci.uc.edu/afamstudies/

University of Connecticut, Institute for African American Studies
241 Glenbrook Rd., Unit 2162
Storrs, CT 06269-2162
Telephone: (860) 486-3630
Website: www.iaas.uconn.edu/

University of Florida, African American Studies Program
103 Walker Hall, PO Box 118120
Gainesville, FL 32611
Telephone: (352) 392-5724
Website: www.clas.ufl.edu/afam/

University of Georgia, Institute for African American Studies
312 Holmes/Hunter Academic Bldg.
Athens, GA 30602
Telephone: (706) 542-5197
Website: www.uga.edu/iaas

University of Houston, African American Studies Program
629 Agnes Arnold Halls
Houston, TX 77204-3047
Telephone: (713) 743-2811
Website: www.class.uh.edu/aas

University of Illinois at Chicago, Institute for Research on Race and Public Policy
CUPPA Hall (MC 347), 412 South Peoria St., Ste. 322
Chicago, IL 60607
Telephone: (312) 996-6339
Website: www.uic.edu/cuppa/irrpp/

University of Illinois at Urbana-Champaign, Department of African American Studies
1201 W. Nevada
Urbana, IL 61801
Telephone: (217) 333-7781
Website: www.afro.illinois.edu

University of Kansas, Schiefelbusch Institute for Life Span Studies
Dole Human Development Center, Center Rm. 1052, 1000 Sunnyside Ave.
Lawrence, KS 66045
Telephone: (785) 864-4295
Website: www.ku.edu/~lsi/

University of Maryland at College Park, David C. Driskell Center for the Study of Visual Arts and Culture of African Americans and the African Diaspora
1214 Cole Student Activities Bldg.
College Park, MD 20742
Telephone: (301) 314-2615
Website: www.driskellcenter.umd.edu/

University of Maryland at College Park, Nyumburu Cultural Center
Bldg. 232, Ste. 1120, Office of the VP for Academic Affairs
College Park, MD 20742
Telephone: (301) 314-7758
Website: www.nyumburu.umd.edu/

University of Massachusetts at Boston, William Monroe Trotter Institute
100 Morrissey Blvd.
Boston, MA 02125-3393
Telephone: (617) 287-5880
Website: www.trotter.umb.edu

University of Michigan, Center for Afroamerican and African Studies
505 S. State St., 4700 Haven Hall
Ann Arbor, MI 48109-1045
Telephone: (734) 764-5513
Website: www.lsa.umich.edu/caas

University of Michigan, Program for Research on Black Americans
5062 Institute for Social Research, PO Box 1248
Ann Arbor, MI 48106-1248
Telephone: (734) 763-0045
Website: www.rcgd.isr.umich.edu/prba/

University of Mississippi, Center for the Study of Southern Culture
Barnard Observatory, PO Box 1848, Sorority Row and Grove Loop
University, MS 38677
Telephone: (662) 915-5993
Website: www.olemiss.edu/depts/south/

University of Pennsylvania, Center for Africana Studies
Ste. 331A, 3401 Walnut St.
Philadelphia, PA 19104-6228
Telephone: (215) 898-4965
Website: www.sas.upenn.edu/africana/home.html

University of Rochester, Frederick Douglass Institute for African and African-American Studies
Morey 302
Rochester, NY 14627
Telephone: (585) 275-7235
Website: www.rochester.edu/College/aas/

University of Texas at Austin, John L. Warfield Center for African and African American Studies
JES A232A, MC D7200
Austin, TX 78712
Telephone: (512) 471-1784
Website: www.utexas.edu/cola/centers/caaas

University of Virginia, Carter G. Woodson Institute for African-American and African Studies
108 Minor Hall, PO Box 400162
Charlottesville, VA 22904-4162
Telephone: (434) 924-3109
Website: www.artsandsciences.virginia.edu/woodson/

University of Virginia, Center for the Study of Race and Law
580 Massie Rd.

Charlottesville, VA 22903
Telephone: (434) 924-3299
Website: www.law.virginia.edu/html/academics/race/mission.htm

University of Wisconsin–Madison, African Studies Program
205 Ingraham Hall, 1155 Observatory Dr.
Madison, WI 53706
Telephone: (608) 262-2380
Website: www.africa.wisc.edu/

Vanderbilt University, Kelly Miller Smith Institute on Black Church Studies
411 21st Ave. S
Nashville, TN 37240
Telephone: (615) 936-8453
Website: www.vanderbilt.edu/divinity/kmsi.php

Virginia State University, Dr. George H. Bennett Office for International Education
Rm. 203 Foster Hall, PO Box 9086
Petersburg, VA 23806
Telephone: (804) 524-5986

Virginia State University, Institute for the Study of Race Relations
Petersburg, VA 23806
Telephone: (804) 524-6999
Website: www.vsu.edu/pages/3409.asp

Wayne State University, Walter P. Reuther Library
5401 Cass Ave.
Detroit, MI 48202
Telephone: (313) 577-4024
Website: www.reuther.wayne.edu/

Wesleyan University, Center for African American Studies
343 High St.
Middletown, CT 06459
Telephone: (860) 685-2190
Website: www.wesleyan.edu/afam/

Western Michigan University, Africana Studies
3061 Moore Hall
Kalamazoo, MI 49008-5311
Telephone: (269) 387-2665
Website: www.wmich.edu/afs/

Xavier University of Louisiana, Center for Intercultural and International Programs
1 Drexel Dr.
New Orleans, LA 70125
Telephone: (504) 520-5490
Website: www.xula.edu/ciip/

Xavier University of Louisiana, Center for the Advancement of Teaching
1 Drexel Dr., Box 78
New Orleans, LA 70125
Telephone: (504) 520-7512
Website: cat.xula.edu/

Xavier University of Louisiana, Center for Undergraduate Research
1 Drexel Dr., Box 78
New Orleans, LA 70125
Telephone: (504) 520-7633

Xavier University of Louisiana, Institute for Black Catholic Studies
1 Drexel Dr.
New Orleans, LA 70125
Telephone: (504) 520-7691
Website: www.xula.edu/ibcs/index.php

Yale University, Gilder Lehrman Center for the Study of Slavery, Resistance, and Abolition
PO Box 208206
New Haven, CT 06520-8206
Telephone: (203) 432-3339
Website: www.yale.edu/glc/index.htm

AFRICAN AMERICANS HOLDING ENDOWED UNIVERSITY CHAIRS, CHAIRS OF EXCELLENCE, OR CHAIRED PROFESSORSHIPS (2010)

Endowed university chairs are an honor—both for the person for whom the chair is named and the person who is named to the chair. Endowments are bestowed on academicians of great talent who have distinguished themselves in their careers. Usually an organization separate from a collegiate institution will approach a university in hopes of setting up a chair and endowment fund. The reverse may also occur, as universities seek funds to attract, support, and recognize distinguished faculty by having a chair endowed for them. Such chairs may also bring a level of prestige to the institution. For example, in 2009, the University of South Carolina began to solicit funds to establish an endowed chair named for noted

African American educator and school founder Mary McLeod Bethune. The first endowed chair named for an African American woman and the first endowed chair in African America studies in the United States is the Grace Towns Hamilton Chair at Emory University, held by Delores P. Aldridge. Some universities appoint scholars to endowed or distinguished chairs for one semester or for one or two years, while others continue the appointment for the duration of the professor's tenure. Professors may retire with the title and with the added honor of emeritus professor. A number of African Americans have held endowed chairs at several universities. John Hope Franklin was such an example.

In 2001, 136 African American professors were known to hold endowed chairs, including at least ten of those named for African Americans. Many such professors have either retired from endowed chairs, are professors emeriti, or are deceased, including T. J. Anderson (Tufts University); David C. Driskell (University of Maryland); Edgar G. Epps (University of Chicago); John Hope Franklin (three: Cambridge University, Duke University, and University of Chicago); James Lowell Gibbs Jr. (Stanford University); Edmund Gordon (Columbia Teachers College); Harry E. Groves (University of North Carolina at Chapel Hill); James E. Jones Jr. (University of Wisconsin); Barbara C. Jordan (University of Texas at Austin); C. Eric Lincoln (Duke University and Clark University); Bertha Maxwell-Roddy (University of North Carolina, Charlotte); William H. Peterson (Campbell University); Samuel DeWitt Proctor (Rutgers University); Charlotte H. Scott (University of Virginia); Nathan A. Scott (University of Virginia); John B. Turner (University of North Carolina at Chapel Hill); and Marilyn V. Yarborough (University of North Carolina at Chapel Hill).

By 2010, twenty-three chairs have been identified as endowed and/or named for African American men and women, including Sterling A. Brown, Ray Charles, Constance E. Clayton, William and Camille Cosby, Charles R. Drew, W. E. B. Du Bois, Grace Towns Hamilton, Benjamin L. Hooks, John E. Jacob, James Earl Jones, Quincy Jones, Ernest Everett Just, Martin Luther King Jr., James M. Lawson, LaSalle D. Leffall Jr., Benjamin E. Mays, Wade H. McCree Jr., Ronald E. McNair, Ernest N. Morial, Willa B. Player, Samuel DeWitt Proctor, Paul Robeson, and Roy Wilkins. At least 172 African American scholars scattered throughout the country now hold endowed chairs.

Delores P. Aldridge, Grace Towns Hamilton Professor of Sociology and African-American Studies, Emory University.

Gloria Long Anderson, Fuller E. Callaway Professor of Chemistry, Morris Brown College.

Maya Angelou, Reynolds Professor of American Studies, Wake Forest University.

Regina Austin, William A. Schnader Professor of Law, University of Pennsylvania.

Randall Bailey, Andrew W. Mellon Professor of Hebrew Bible, Interdenominational Theological Center, Atlanta.

Houston A. Baker Jr., Distinguished University Professor, Vanderbilt University.

Oscar A. Barbarin, L. Richardson and Emily Preyer Bicentennial Distinguished Professor for Strengthening Families, University of North Carolina at Chapel Hill.

Xylina Bean, W. K. Kellogg Professorship in Pediatrics, Meharry Medical College.

Mary Frances Berry, Geraldine R. Segal Professor of American Social Thought and Professor of History, University of Pennsylvania.

Vladimir Berthaud, Endowed Professor in Infectious Diseases, Meharry Medical College.

Richard J. M. Blackett, Andrew Jackson Chair of History, Vanderbilt University.

Lawrence D. Bobo, W. E. B. Du Bois Professor of the Social Sciences, Harvard University.

Kofi Bota, K. A. Huggins Professor of Chemistry, Clark Atlanta University.

Joanne M. Braxton, Frances L. and Edwin L. Cummings Professor of English and the Humanities, College of William and Mary.

Violet Harrington Bryan, Andrew W. Mellon Foundation Professor in the Humanities, Xavier University of Louisiana.

Frank Brown, Cary C. Boshamer Distinguished Professor of Educational Leadership, University of North Carolina at Chapel Hill.

Herrington J. Bryce, Life of Virginia Professor of Business Administration, College of William and Mary.

Robert Bullard, Edmund Asa Ware Professor of Sociology, Clark Atlanta University.

Walter G. Bumphus, A. M. Aiken Jr. Regents Chair in Leadership, University of Texas at Austin.

John S. Butler, Herb Kelleher Chair for Entrepreneurship and Small Business, and Gale Chair in Entrepreneurship, University of Texas at Austin.

Clive O. Callender, LaSalle D. Leffall Professor of Surgery, Howard University College of Medicine.

J. W. Carmichael, Xavier University State of Louisiana Chair in Sciences, Xavier University of Louisiana.

Loftus C. Carson II, Ronald D. Krist Professor in Law, University of Texas at Austin.

Norvella Carter, Houston Endowment Inc. Endowed Chair in Urban Education, Texas A&M University.

Stephen L. Carter, William Nelson Cromwell Professor of Law, Yale University Law School.

Robert G. Clark, Distinguished Visiting Professor, Delta Cultural Research Institute, Mississippi Valley State University.

Pearl Cleage, Cosby Endowed Chair, Humanities, Spelman College.

'Niyi Coker Jr., E. Desmond Lee Endowed Professor of African/African American Theater and Cinema, University of Missouri, St. Louis.

James P. Comer, Maurice K. Falk Professor of Child Psychiatry, Yale University.

William W. Cook, Israel Evans Professor of Oratory and Belles Lettres, Dartmouth College.

Xavier Creary, Charles L. Huisking Professor of Chemistry, University of Notre Dame.

William A. Darity Jr., Arts and Sciences Professor of Public Policy, Duke University.

Leon Dash, Swanlund Professor of Journalism, University of Illinois at Urbana-Champaign.

N. Gregson G. Davis, Andrew W. Mellon Professor of Classical Studies, Duke University.

Thadious M. Davis, Geraldine R. Segal Professor of American Thought and Professor of English, University of Pennsylvania.

Addie Dawson-Euba, Community Coffee/Frank Hayden Professor of Visual Arts, Southern University A&M College, Baton Rouge.

Charles Edward Daye, Henry P. Brandis Professor of Law and Deputy Director of the Center for Civil Rights, University of North Carolina at Chapel Hill.

Dennis C. Dickerson. James M. Lawson Chair of History, Vanderbilt University.

Katherine Dobie, Endowed Professor, Economics and Transportation/Logistics Institute, North Carolina A&T State University.

Gary Donaldson, John LaFarge Professor of Social Justice, Xavier University of Louisiana.

Ronald Dorris, Class of '58 Professor of Liberal Arts, Xavier University of Louisiana.

Rita Dove, Commonwealth Professor of English, University of Virginia.

Michael Eric Dyson, University Professor of Sociology, Georgetown University, Washington, D.C.

Gerald Early, Merle S. Kling Professor of Modern Letters, Washington University in St. Louis.

Harry J. Elam Jr., Olive H. Palmer Professor in the Humanities, Stanford University.

Marquetta Faulkner, Joy McCann Professor for Women in Medicine, Meharry Medical College.

Edward Fort, Endowed Professor, School of Education, North Carolina A&T State University.

Frances Smith Foster, Charles Howard Candler Professor of English and Women's Studies, Emory University.

Joseph S. Francisco, William E. Moore Distinguished Professor of Physical Chemistry, Purdue University.

Shirley Clarke Franklin, Cosby Professor of Social Science, Spelman College.

Henry Frye, Distinguished Professor, College of Arts and Sciences, North Carolina A&T State University.

Vivian Gadsden, William T. Carter Professor in Child Development in Education, University of Pennsylvania.

Steven H. Gale, Endowed Professor of Humanities, Whitney M. Young Jr. College of Leadership Studies, Kentucky State University.

Fannie Gaston-Johansson, Elsie M. Lawler Professor, Department of Acute and Chronic Care, Johns Hopkins University.

Henry Louis Gates Jr., Alphonse Fletcher University Professor, Harvard University.

Sylvester James Gates Jr., John S. Toll Professor of Physics, University of Maryland.

Jewelle Taylor Gibbs, Zellerbach Family Fund Chair in Social Policy, Community Change and Practice, University of California, Berkeley.

Cheryl Townsend Gilkes, John D. and Catherine T. MacArthur Professor of African-American Studies and Sociology, Colby College.

Nikki Giovanni, University Distinguished Professor, Virginia Tech University.

Richard A. Goldsby, John Woodruff Simpson Lecturer and Professor of Biology, Amherst College.

Peter J. Gomes, Plummer Professor of Christian Morals, Harvard University.

Jacquelyn Grant, Fuller E. Calloway Professor of Systematic Theology, Interdenominational Theological Center, Atlanta.

Beverly Guy-Sheftall, Anna Julia Cooper Professor of Women's Studies, Spelman College.

John H. Hall Jr., Bruce Rauner Professor of Chemistry, Morehouse College.

Michael Steven Harper, University Professor, Brown University.

Jessica B. Harris, Ray Charles Endowed Chair in African American Material Culture, Dillard University.

Trudier Harris, J. Carlyle Sitterson Professor of English, University of North Carolina at Chapel Hill.

Winfred Harris, Howard Hughes Professor of Biology, Clark Atlanta University.

J. K. Haynes, David E. Packard Professor in Science, Morehouse College.

James K. Hildreth, HCA Endowed Professorship in Health Disparities Research, Meharry Medical College.

Darlene Clark Hine, Board of Trustees Professor of African American Studies and History, Northwestern University.

Matthew Holden Jr., Wepner Distinguished Professor in Political Science, University of Illinois, Springfield.

Karla F. C. Holloway, James B. Duke Professor of English, Duke University.

Robert Holmes, Distinguished Professor of Political Science, Clark Atlanta University.

Thomas Holt, James Westfall Thompson Distinguished Service Professor, Department of History, University of Chicago.

Gerald Horne, John and Rebecca Moores Professor of History and African American Studies, University of Houston.

Alton E. Hornsby, Fuller E. Calloway Professor of History, Morehouse College.

James O. Horton, Benjamin Banneker Professor of American Studies and History, George Washington University.

Tasha R. Inniss, Clare Booth Luce Professor of Mathematics, Trinity College, Washington, D.C.

Shubha Kale Ireland, W. K. Kellogg Professor of Liberal Arts, Xavier University of Louisiana.

Edward Irons, Distinguished Professor of Finance, Clark Atlanta University.

Jacqueline Jordan Irvine, Charles Howard Candler Professor of Urban Education, Emory University.

Francesina R. Jackson, Evelyn Berry Chair of Education, Paine College.

James Sidney Jackson, Daniel Katz Distinguished University Professor of Psychology, University of Michigan.

Charles Johnson, S. Wilson and Grace Pollock Professorship for Excellence in English, University of Washington.

James H. Johnson Jr., William Rand Kenan Jr. Distinguished Professor of Strategy and Entrepreneurship, University of North Carolina at Chapel Hill.

Richard A. Joseph, Asa G. Candler Professor of Politics, Department of Political Science, Emory University.

Kathleen B. Kennedy, Malcolm Ellington Endowed Professor of Health Disparities, Xavier University of Louisiana.

Preston King, Woodruff Professor of Political Philosophy, Emory University; Distinguished Professor of Political Philosophy, Morehouse College.

Paul Kwame, Curb/Beaman Chair for the Fisk Jubilee Singers, Fisk University.

Sonja Lanehart, Brackenridge Endowed Chair in Literature and the Humanities, University of Texas at San Antonio.

David G. Lanoue, RoseMary Professor of English, Xavier University of Louisiana.

Sara Lawrence-Lightfoot, Emily Hargroves Fisher Professor of Education, Harvard University.

LaSalle D. Leffall Jr., Charles R. Drew Professor of Surgery, Howard University College of Medicine.

Chance Lewis, Houston Endowment Inc. Endowed Chair in Urban Education, Texas A&M University.

David Levering Lewis, Julius Silver University Professor and Professor of History, New York University.

Richard A. Long, Atticus Haygood Professor Emeritus, Emory University.

Kenneth R. Manning, Thomas Meloy Professor of Rhetoric and of the History of Science, Massachusetts Institute of Technology.

Ali A. Mazrui, Albert Schweitzer Professor of Political Science, State University of New York at Binghamton.

Reuben R. McDonald Jr., Charles and Elizabeth Prothro Regents Chair in Health Care Management, University of Texas at Austin.

Patricia McFadden, Cosby Endowed Chair, Social Sciences, Spelman College.

John McFaddon, Distinguished Professor Emeritus, Benjamin Elijah Mays Distinguished Professor Emeritus, University of South Carolina.

Donald F. McHenry, Distinguished Professor in Practice of Diplomacy, Georgetown University.

Ruth G. McRoy, Ruby Lee Piester Centennial Professor Emerita, University of Texas at Austin.

Ronald E. Mickens, Fuller E. Callaway Professor of Physics, Clark Atlanta University.

Ivor Mitchell, Christine McEachern Smith Professor of Marketing, Clark Atlanta University.

Joseph Monroe, Jefferson Pilot/Ronald McNair Professor of Computer Science and Dean of the College of Engineering, North Carolina A&T State University.

Brian Moore, John D. and Catherine T. McArthur Chair in History and Africana and Latin American Studies, Colgate University.

Kathleen M. Morgan, Keller Foundation Professor of Science, Xavier University of Louisiana.

Toni Morrison, Robert F. Goheen Professor, Council of the Humanities, Princeton University.

John Howard Morrow Jr., Franklin Professor of History, University of Georgia.

Valentin Y. Mudimbe, Newman Ivey White Professor of Literature, Duke University.

Samuel L. Myers Jr., Roy Wilkins Professor of Human Relations and Social Justice, Hubert H. Humphrey Institute of Public Affairs, University of Minnesota, Minneapolis.

Celestine A. Ntuen, Distinguished Professor, Cognitive Engineering Simulation, Human-Machine Systems Engineering, North Carolina A&T State University.

Tumani Nyajeka, Cornelius and Dorothye Henderson Chair and E. Stanley Jones Professor of Evangelism, Interdenominational Theological Seminary, Atlanta.

Olufunmilayo I. Olopade, Walter L. Palmer Distinguished Service Professor of Medicine, University of Chicago.

Robert G. O'Meally, Zora Neale Hurston Professor of English, Columbia University.

Reginald Owens, F. Jay Taylor Endowed Chair of Journalism, Louisiana Tech University.

Nell Irvin Painter, Edwards Professor of American History Emerita, Princeton University.

Colin Palmer, Dodge Professor of History, Princeton University.

Peter J. Paris, Elmer G. Homrighausen Professor of Christian Social Ethics, Princeton Theological Seminary.

Nell A. Parker, Herbert G. Kayser Professor of Civil Engineering, City University of New York, City College.

Orlando H. L. Patterson, John Cowles Professor of Sociology, Harvard University.

Arlie O. Petters, Benjamin Powell Professor, Duke University.

Leslie Pollard, Callaway Professor of History, Paine College.

Richard J. Powell, John Spencer Bassett Professor of Art History, Duke University.

Albert Jordy Raboteau, Henry W. Putnam Professor of Religion, Princeton University.

Arnold Rampersad, Sara Hart Kimball Professor in the Humanities, Stanford University.

Rosalie Richards, Kaolin Endowed Chair in Science, Georgia College and State University.

John R. Rickford, Martin Luther King Jr. Centennial Professor of Linguistics, Stanford University.

Joe Ritchie, Knight Professor of Journalism Student Enhancement, School of Journalism, Media and Graphic Arts, Florida A&M University.

Kay George Roberts, Nancy Donahue Endowed Professorship in the Arts, University of Massachusetts, Lowell.

Lemma W. Senbet, William E. Mayer Professor of Finance, University of Maryland at College Park.

William Serban, Ernest N. Morial Professor of Public Affairs and Public Policy, Xavier University of Louisiana.

Lonnie Sharpe Jr., Massie Chair of Excellence, Professorship of Engineering in the Environmental Disciplines, Tennessee State University.

George Shirley, Joseph Edgar Maddy Distinguished University Emeritus Professor of Voice, University of Michigan.

Diana T. Slaughter-Defoe, Constance E. Clayton Professor in Urban Education, University of Pennsylvania.

Earl Smith, Ernest Rubin Distinguished Professor of American Ethnic Studies, Wake Forest University.

Edwin M. Smith, Leon Benwell Professor of Law, International Relations, and Political Science, University of Southern California.

Jessie Carney Smith, William and Camille Cosby Professor in the Humanities and Dean of the Library, Fisk University.

Hortense Spillers, Gertrude Conaway Vanderbilt Professor, Vanderbilt University.

Susan F. Spillman, William Arcenaux Professor of French, Xavier University of Louisiana.

Claude M. Steele, Lucie Sterns Professor in the Social Sciences, Stanford University.

Chuck Stone, Walter Spearman Professor Emeritus, School of Journalism and Mass Communication, University of North Carolina at Chapel Hill.

Dorothy S. Strickland, Samuel DeWitt Proctor Professor of Education, State of New Jersey Professor of Reading, Rutgers University.

Quintard Taylor Jr., Scott and Dorothy Bullitt Professor of American History, University of Washington.

Stephen B. Thomas, Philip Hallen Chair in Community Health and Social Justice, School of Social Work, University of Pittsburgh.

Gerald E. Thomson, Lambert and Sonneborn Professor of Medicine Emeritus, Columbia University.

Susanne Tropez-Sims, Joy McCann Endowed Professor for Women in Medicine, Meharry Medical College.

William L. Turner, Betts Chair of Education and Human Development, Vanderbilt University.

Shirley Verrett, James Earl Jones Distinguished Professor of Voice, University of Michigan.

Gloria Wade-Gayles, Eminent Scholar Endowed Chair, Spelman College.

Sheila S. Walker, Annabel Irion Worsham Centennial Professor and Director, Center for African and Afro-American Studies, University of Texas at Austin.

Jerry W. Ward Jr., Distinguished Professor of English, Dillard University.

John Ware, Keller Foundation Professor of Arts and Humanities, Xavier University of Louisiana.

Leland Ware, Louis L. Redding Professor for the Study of Law and Public Policy, University of Delaware.

Isiah M. Warner, Boyd Professor and Philip W. West Professor of Analytical and Environmental Chemistry, Louisiana State University.

Cornel West, Class of 1943 Professor, Princeton University.

Michael White, Rosa and Charles Keller Jr. Chair in the Arts and Humanities, Xavier University of Louisiana.

Kevin Eric Whitfield, Research Professor, Psychology and Neuroscience, Duke University.

DeWayne Wickham, Distinguished Professor, Institute for Advanced Journalism Studies, North Carolina A&T State University.

James H. Williams Jr., School of Engineering Professor of Teaching Excellence Emeritus, Massachusetts Institute of Technology.

John E. Williams, Mills Bee Lane Professor of Banking and Finance, Morehouse College.

Preston Noah Williams, Houghton Research Professor of Theology and Contemporary Change, Harvard University.

Walter E. Williams, John M. Olin Professor of Economics, George Mason University.

Scott C. Williamson, Robert H. Walkup Professor of Theological Ethics, Louisville Presbyterian Theological Seminary.

William Julius Wilson, Lewis P. and Linda L. Geyser University Professor, Harvard University.

Herbert Graves Winful, Arthur F. Thurnau Professor of Electrical Engineering and Computer Science, University of Michigan.

May L. Wykle, Marvin E. and Ruth Durr Denekas Professor and Dean of Nursing, Florence Payne Bolton School of Nursing, Case Western Reserve University.

17

RELIGION

Stephen W. Angell
Genevieve Slomski
Morris G. Henderson

The first people to imagine and conceive of a transcendent reality (which was also called God) were the Africans of antiquity. The first Africans who arrived in the New World may have arrived empty-handed, but they were not devoid of spirituality. While some were Muslim or Christian prior to being kidnapped by their enslavers, many adhered to and struggled to maintain their indigenous belief systems. Those captive Africans believed there was a present but invisible God who was the creator of the world and was actively involved in the affairs of the world.

ORIGINS AND HISTORY OF AFRICAN AMERICAN RELIGIOUS TRADITIONS

The peoples of ancient Ethiopia and Egypt were firm believers in the afterlife and the idea of salvation. Consequently, the earliest theory of salvation is the Egyptian theory. The ancient Egyptians developed a complex system of religious thought called the *Mysteries*, which was the very first system of salvation. They developed secret systems of writing and teaching, and forbade initiates from repeating what they had learned. The Nile Valley was the home of the most profound religious knowledge of the ancient world.

For nearly 5,000 years, foreigners were prohibited from studying the Egyptian Mystery system for the purposes of religious education. After the invasion of Alexander the Great in 332 B.C.E. and the death of Aristotle in 322 B.C.E., the Greeks were able to make inroads into Egyptian culture and religion. In the aftermath of Alexander's invasion, Egypt's royal temples and libraries were plundered. Aristotle converted the library at Alexandria into a research center, from which he was able to produce the unusually large number of books ascribed to him.

With the rise of the Roman Empire, Emperors Theodosius (fourth century C.E.) and Justinian (sixth century C.E.) abolished the temples in Egypt, and the Greeks were able to claim the Egyptian Mystery system as their own. Eventually, Western history would conclude that the African continent was backward, and that its people, culture, and religion were unenlightened.

Prior to the edicts of the Roman emperors, the Egyptian religion spread not only to Italy, but also throughout the Roman Empire. The Egyptian religion was found to be an obstacle standing in the way of the rising new religion, Christianity. The edicts of Theodosius and Justinian paved the way for Christianity to overtake African traditional religions in the early Christian era.

THE MYSTICAL QUALITIES OF AFRICAN AMERICAN FAITH

Though knowledge of African traditional religions has faded, remnants of them still linger in the practices and rituals of many African American faith traditions, including Christianity. Wyatt Tee Walker stated that without the mystical quality of Christianity, the contemporary African American church could never have withstood the inexpressible emotional and psychological cruelties of America's racism. He pointed to the biblical Job's statement as epitomizing the mystical quality of the Jesus faith: "Though He slay me, yet will I trust Him" (Job 13:15).

Unlike Western culture, the African tradition draws few sharp distinctions between the sacred and the secular in actual practice. In all aspects of daily living, the presence of God is acknowledged. Therefore, the African American church takes a "holistic" view of religion and life, meaning that every dimension of life—socioeconomic, political, and psycho-spiritual (mind, body, and soul)—has some connection. Even as Western Christianity and its missionaries sought to Christianize the African, the mystical qualities of the African American faith led to an Africanization of Christianity.

In the Western model of Christian dispensation, the African has been exposed to capitalism, racism, and militarism. The mystical nature of the traditional African religion has often allowed the African American faith to counteract this unholy trinity. Among the many forms of counterposition are the exploration of the world of faith healing and ecstatic joy in religion, while being tolerant of such practices as speaking in tongues and holy dancing in worship.

A rich diversity of faith traditions emerged from the various peoples of the African continent. The Yoruba people, for example, believed in a pantheon of deities called *orisha*. These orisha operated under the supreme creator Olorun, who is the source of Ashe (ah-shay), the life force that exists in every thing and being in the cosmos. Elements of the Yoruba traditional belief system can be found today in some modern African-derived religions, such as Santeria (in which spirit possession plays a prominent role) and the "holy rollers" of Pentecostalism. In other parts of the Western hemisphere where people of African descent have settled, the practice of magic, commonly known as *vaudou* (also voodoo, vodou, or vodun) or *conjure*, is found. This practice, designed to help friends (*myalism*) or hurt enemies (*obeah*), is magic as viewed from an Afrocentric perspective.

That which could rightfully be called *African spirituality* is at the root of many of the religions practiced by Africans in the Americas. African spirituality merges many African cultural rites and religious traditions. While much debate surrounds the degree to which African traditional religions have been retained in African-derived religions, scholars have made persuasive arguments for the presence of African spirituality in many African American funeral rites, as well as in African American family structure and religious organizations.

EARLY AFRICAN AMERICAN BELIEF SYSTEMS

Because the African family was seen as the primary social and economic unit of the community, the family was responsible for the socialization of young people and the shaping of behaviors that gave order to society. The expression of reverence for ancestors was a means of securing blessings and prosperity for the family unit specifically and the community as a whole, but it was not an act of worship. It is therefore wrong to describe African religion as ""ancestor worship," because Africans do not worship dead family members. Though many families build shrines for the departed and mention them in prayers, these acts of remembrance should not be mistaken for worship. Such practices do show, however, a people's belief that a deceased family member reaching back four to five generations should not be forgotten. In many African-derived religious practices, it is believed that as long as a departed family member's name is spoken, they are not truly dead.

THE SEVENTEENTH CENTURY: MISSIONARY EFFORTS BY CHRISTIANS

Beginning in the sixteenth century, Spanish Catholics made a sustained efforts to convert Africans to Christianity. The Spanish Christianized Africans on the west coast of Africa by giving Western names to their black captives before loading them aboard ships destined for the Americas. The first efforts at converting African Americans by were made by the Anglican Society for the Propagation of the Gospel in Foreign Parts, an organization founded in 1701. These initial missionary drives to organize and proselytize met with great resistance when those who attempted to imitate white missionaries too closely were mocked. In the early seventeenth century, there was no enslavement in any of the colonies, but indentured servitude of both blacks and whites was legal and statutory. Slavery did not become institutionalized until 1639 when Massachusetts became the first colony to legalize the enslavement of Africans.

Once Africans reached the shores of North America, there was occasional opposition to efforts to convert them, because white slave masters feared that their captives would lay claim to freedom on the basis of their Christianity. Nevertheless, New World Africans maintained a spiritual connection to traditional African religious through the continued practice of rituals in the basements and "root cellars" of their living quarters. However, when laws made it clear that the acceptance of baptism and the Christian faith would not result in freedom for the enslaved, opposition to Christianization efforts began to diminish. Some enslavers even pointed to the need for Christianization as justification for the enslavement of Africans.

Slavery was formally legalized in Virginia in 1670. The law written in the Jamestown general assembly said any "Negro, mulatto, or Indian" coming by land or sea from a non-Christian country would be enslaved for the rest of his or her natural life. At the time the law was written, there were about six hundred free Africans living in Virginia who were never enslaved. But after the passage of the 1670 law, the transatlantic slave trade began in earnest.

EARLY CHRISTIAN CONGREGATIONS

The first African American Baptist church in America was most likely the Silver Bluff Baptist Church, founded sometime between 1773 and 1775 in South Carolina, across the river from Augusta, Georgia. The church was organized, under the watchful eye of a white preacher, by David George (c. 1743–1810), an enslaved Christian who often preached there before immigrating to Nova Scotia 1782 during the Revolutionary War (1775–1783). David George was associated with black Baptist preacher George Liele (c. 1752–1820), who left South Carolina for Jamaica around 1782. Andrew Bryan (1737–1812), who also preached at the Silver Bluff Baptist Church, eventually founded the First African Baptist Church in Savannah, Georgia, in 1788.

In the 1760s, an enslaved man named Gowan Pamphlet (c. 1750–1807) began preaching in Williamsburg, Virginia. His owner was a widow named Jane Vobe, who also owned King's Arms Tavern, an establishment frequented by George Washington, Thomas Jefferson, George Wythe, Patrick Henry, and other early American political leaders. Vobe sent several of her enslaved Africans to the local Bray School for tutoring in reading, writing, and numbers ciphering. This is probably how Gowan Pamphlet became literate. A free African American named Moses had started preaching earlier to his enslaved brethren in secret gatherings in the Williamsburg area. Local slave owners, fearing the nature of these meetings, arrested Moses, and he was publicly flogged for preaching. When Moses left the area, Reverend Pamphlet became the leading preacher.

At first, Pamphlet preached to his flock in secret, meeting in "brush arbors" outside city limits. By 1781, however, his congregation had grown to around two hundred members, and his preaching fell under the scrutiny of the white Baptist leadership. By 1791, Pamphlet's congregation had grown to over five hundred members, and later that year he petitioned the Dover Baptist Association for admission of the Williamsburg Baptist Church.

A turning point in Pamplet's life occurred in September 1793 when his then owner, David Miller, deeded manumission to the enslaved preacher, and he became a free man. The next month, Pamphlet attended the Dover Baptist Association meeting, and by the time he left, he was the official pastor of the Williamsburg Baptist Church and the church had been granted membership in the association. In some quarters, Pamplet's Williamsburg Baptist Church holds the distinction of being the first African American church organized for blacks by blacks in the history of the United States.

In 1776, Prince Hall (c. 1748–1807) and other blacks founded Boston's African Lodge No. 1, which was connected with a British army lodge. The newly formed organization received its official warrant in 1787 as African Lodge No. 459. Prince Hall and Chaplain John Marrant (1755–1791) regularly preached and conducted Masonic rites for public funerals of lodge members. In 1787, Prince Hall and seventy-five other blacks from Boston petitioned the city's general court for permission to immigrate to Africa. Their plan was to form a religious society or Christian church on the continent to be pastored by blacks.

In some cities, black preachers led white congregations. Lemuel Hayes pastored an all-white congregation in Vermont, while William Lemon pastored an all-white congregation in Gloucester, Virginia, in 1801.

THE EIGHTEENTH CENTURY

As the religious revival known as the Great Awakening began in America in the 1740s, the Presbyterians, the Baptists, and later the Methodists were successful in attracting enslaved Africans. However, African Americans did not begin to join these denominations in large numbers until after the American Revolution. The Methodists and Baptists did not require their ministers to be well educated, thereby leaving the door open to African American ministers. This was important because many aspiring African American ministers lived in states where they were forbidden by statute to learn to read or write.

THE NINETEENTH CENTURY

In the nineteenth century, Baptist and Methodist churches were the most successful in attracting African American members. Furthermore, the Baptists and Methodists were not as unreceptive to the emotionalism of African American preachers and congregations as were the more staid denominations, such as the Episcopalians. Finally, the antislavery stance of some Methodist and Baptist leaders, such as John Wesley, Francis Asbury, and John Leland, and the greater degree of equality nurtured within many Baptist and Methodist congregations were attractive to African Americans.

Francis Asbury (1745–1816), the founding bishop of American Methodism, established the precedent for circuit riding, having traveled 270,000 miles and preaching 16,000 sermons as he made his way throughout early frontier America supervising clergy. Bishop Asbury traveled with a trusted servant known as Black Harry (Hoosier), and churches were crowded with people who would come to shake hands with Bishop Asbury and hear Black Harry preach.

John Jasper (1812–1901) was born enslaved in Fluvanna County, Virginia, the youngest of twenty-four children. His father, Phillip Jasper, was a slave preacher. John was raised in the "big house" that provided him the opportunity to learn the ways and manners of his master. He learned to read and write with the help of another slave named William Jackson. When he was thirteen years old, Jasper was sent to Richmond, Virginia, to work as an industrial slave. On July 4, 1839, his twenty-seventh birthday, "the light broke through," and John Jasper converted to Christianity. In 1842, he was baptized in the First African Baptist Church in Savannah. Jasper developed great oratory skills and became known as a master of painting pictures with words. He began his career as a funeral preacher and could speak both colloquially and using the King's English with equal facility. He preached to both black and white congregations; however, as a slave preacher he could only speak with the permission of his slave owner, Samuel Hargrove. When Jasper preached outside of Richmond, those requiring his services were expected to pay Hargrove one dollar for each day Jasper was away.

On September 3, 1867, Jasper and some close associates founded the Sixth Mount Zion Baptist Church in Richmond. Of his many sermons, Jasper is most noted for "De Sun Do Move," first delivered in 1878, about the rotation of the sun. In this sermon, Jasper argued that Earth was the center of the solar system and the sun and heavenly bodies revolved around it. He held to the Bible and was driven to believe, contrary of existing scientific knowledge, that the sun moved around Earth. The sermon was very popular and was preached by Jasper more than 250 times, once before the Virginia General Assembly.

EMANCIPATION EFFORTS OF AFRICAN AMERICAN CHURCH LEADERS

The emancipation of the Africans in America and the religious transformation of those once enslaved provided the fuel for change in both church and country. The antislavery efforts of the mid-nineteenth century would lead to the independent church movement for African American religion.

The cause of racial separation in American religion can be traced to incidents of white discrimination and the moral failure of white American Christianity. In November 1787, for example, the trustees of the St. George's Methodist Church in Philadelphia pulled several black members and local preachers from their knees during prayer at a public service and ushered them out for not sitting in the gallery where blacks were suppose to be seated. This event would be the impetus in 1794 for the formation by Richard Allen (1760–1831) and Absalom Jones (1746–1818) of the first two African Methodist Episcopal Church congregations with their own buildings in the city. Moreover, there were white proscriptions (e.g., the deliberate exclusion of African Americans from positions of power) to biracial congregations and denominations. Whites were, by and large, unwilling to share authority with and extend modes of participation to African Americans. Such practices were potentially the motivation behind the separatist movements that initiated the African Methodist Episcopal Church. This church was the first major religious denomination in the Western world that originated because of sociological rather than theological differences. The African Methodist Episcopal Church stands as the first African American denomination organized and incorporated in the United States.

Some African American churchmen were led to support emancipation programs sponsored by the American Colonization Society, which promoted the idea of black emigration back to Africa. Such notable black clergymen as Virginia Baptist pastor Lott Carey (1780–1828) and Maryland Methodist minister Daniel Coker (1780–1846) were prominent among the religious leaders who immigrated to Africa in the 1820s. There was such a concentration of African American Methodists in Liberia by the 1850s that the Methodist Episcopal Church consecrated an African American bishop, Francis Burns (1809–1863), to serve the Liberian churches.

As the nineteenth century came to an end, the African American church was firmly established in the cultural and religious landscape of American society, and was poised to become the driving force of the civil rights movement in the twentieth century.

DISCRIMINATION IN WHITE CHURCHES

While European American preachers urged African Americans to convert, and many predominately white congregations welcomed African Americans into membership, racial prejudice was never entirely absent from the country's religious history. Although the level of discrimination varied from region to region and congregation to congregation, some factors were relatively constant.

One of the major factors was the relative paucity of ordained African American clergy. Some African American ministers, for example, were ordained as deacons within the Methodist Episcopal Church prior to 1820, but none was ordained in the following decades. No African American

Methodist minister was ordained by the Methodist Episcopal Church to the higher office of elder and none was consecrated as a bishop prior to the Civil War (1861–1865), unless he was willing to immigrate to Liberia.

Other discriminatory practices also formed part of the religious landscape. The Methodists and many other denominations tried to reserve the administration of sacraments as the exclusive province of white clergy. Segregated seating in churches was pervasive in both the North and the South. In addition, church discipline was often unevenly applied. Of course, racial discrimination in the churches was only a small part of the much larger political and moral controversy over African enslavement.

Resistance to racial discrimination took many forms. In the North, Richard Allen in Philadelphia, James Varick (1750–1827) in New York, and Peter Spencer (1782–1843) in Wilmington, Delaware, led their African American followers out of white Methodist churches and set up independent African American congregations. Each of these men then used his congregation as the nucleus of a new African American Methodist denomination. Spencer formed the African Union Church in 1807, and the African Methodist Episcopal Zion Church (AME Zion) was formed in 1821 with Varick as its first bishop.

Meanwhile, in South Carolina, a more explosive situation was taking shape. Morris Brown (1770–1849), an African American Methodist minister from Charleston who had helped Richard Allen organize the African Methodist Episcopal Church, established an independent African American Methodist church in his home city. Although local authorities harassed the members of Brown's church, and sometimes arrested its leaders, more than three-quarters of Charleston's African American Methodists had joined within a year. The oppression of African Americans in Charleston was so severe that many members of Brown's congregation, including prominent lay leaders, joined the insurrection planned by Denmark Vesey in 1822 to take over the Charleston armory and eventually the city of Charleston. The conspirators were apprehended before they could carry out their plans, and they testified that Brown had not known of the movement. Brown was allowed to move to Philadelphia, where Richard Allen made him the second bishop of the African Methodist Episcopal Church.

A few African Americans became acquiescent because of Christianity. One such example was Pierre Toussaint (1766–1853), a black Haitian slave who fled to New York with his white Catholic owners, the Bérards, in 1787, just prior to the Haitian Revolution. On her deathbed in 1811, Mrs. Bérard manumitted Toussaint. Over the next forty years, he became a notable philanthropist, contributing funds to the building of St. Patrick's Cathedral in Manhattan. When the cathedral opened, Toussaint did not protest when a white usher refused to seat him for services. Some American Catholics recently revived the controversy over Toussaint by campaigning for his canonization. Many African American Catholics, however, have strongly objected, seeing Toussaint as passive and servile and thus a poor candidate for sainthood.

EMANCIPATION EFFORTS OF AFRICAN AMERICAN CHURCH LEADERS

The mid-nineteenth century saw increased antislavery activity among many African American church leaders and members. Some gave qualified support to the gradual emancipation program sponsored by the American Colonization Society, which sought to encourage free African Americans to immigrate to Africa in order to Westernize and Christianize the Africans. Virginia Baptist pastor Lott Carey and Maryland Methodist minister Daniel Coker were the two most prominent African American religious leaders to immigrate to Africa in the 1820s. By the 1850s, enough African American Methodists were in Liberia for the Methodist Episcopal Church to consecrate an African American bishop, Francis Burns, to serve the Liberian churches. While some African Americans were immigrating to Africa, others immigrated to the West Indies. Episcopal bishop James T. Holly (1829–1911), for example, settled in Haiti to undertake missionary work.

Because they faced extreme repression in the slave states, African Americans were unable to openly express their views on political issues. However, they often made their views clear through indirect means. For example, a white minister who dwelled too long on the biblical text describing how servants should obey their masters was apt to find his African American listeners deserting him. In addition, African American Christians often held secret meetings in "brush arbors," rude structures made of pine boughs, or in the middle of the woods. There they could sing spirituals and pray openly for freedom.

Slave revolts, on the other hand, were violent outbreaks of dissent much feared by whites. The 1831 movement of Nat Turner (1800–1831), a Baptist preacher, in Northampton County, Virginia, was suppressed only after much blood, both white and black, had been shed. Frightened whites in the South intensified their surveillance of African American churches in the aftermath of the Turner revolt. Even conservative African American preachers, such as Presbyterian John Chavis (1763–1838) in North Carolina and the Baptist "Uncle Jack" (d. 1843) in Virginia, were prohibited from preaching.

African American resistance across 150 years of U.S. history was inspired by the words of Henry Highland

Garnet (1815–1882), an abolitionist and clergyman. On August 16, 1843, Garnet spoke to a group of northern free blacks gathered to discuss the future prospects of black America. Frustrated at the lack of progress, he advocated action: "Strike for your lives and liberties.... Let your motto be Resistance! Resistance! Resistance!" Other prominent religious leaders, including African Methodist Episcopal bishop Daniel Payne (1811–1893) and African Methodist Episcopal Zion bishop Christopher Rush (1777–1873), both emigrants from the Carolinas to the North, also became outspoken abolitionists.

Frederick Douglass (1818–1895) was one of the few leading African American abolitionists who did not pursue a ministerial career, although he briefly served as an African Methodist Episcopal Zion preacher in New Bedford, Massachusetts. African American clergy were extraordinarily active in recruiting African American men to join the Union Army during the Civil War, after the Emancipation Proclamation (1863) opened up the possibility of military service to them. During the Civil War, nearly a dozen African American ministers, including the African Methodist Episcopal Church's Henry McNeal Turner (1834–1915), served as chaplains to African American army regiments.

AFRICAN AMERICAN FEMALE RELIGIOUS LEADERSHIP

Early African American women ministers sometimes served as traveling evangelists, especially within African American denominations. While the oratory of Sojourner Truth (c. 1797–1883) has become appropriately famous, Maria Stewart (1803–1879), Jarena Lee (1783), Zilpha Elaw (1790), and other early nineteenth-century women also spoke eloquently. Lee and Elaw traveled widely and labored diligently. None of these women were formally ordained, but Elizabeth (no last name known), a former enslaved African from Maryland whose ministry began in 1796, spoke for many female preachers when, after she was accused of preaching without a license, she protested, "If the Lord has ordained me, I need nothing better." Rebecca Cox Jackson (1795–1871) left the African Methodist Episcopal Church in the 1830s when she felt that the denomination's men denied her the chance to exercise her ministry, and she eventually became head elder of a predominantly African American Shaker community in Philadelphia.

After the Civil War, some African American women sought and obtained formal ordination from their denominations. Sarah Ann Hughes, a successful North Carolina evangelist and pastor in the African Methodist Episcopal Church, was ordained by Bishop Henry McNeal Turner in 1885, but complaints from male pastors caused her ordination to be revoked two years later. The AME Church would not ordain another woman until 1948, when Rebecca Glover was elevated to that position.

Two women were ordained by African Methodist Episcopal Zion bishops not long after the Hughes controversy: Mary J. Small (1850–1945) in 1895 as a deacon and in 1898 as an elder, and Julia A. J. Foote (1823–1901) in 1894 as a deacon and 1900 as an elder. Pauli Murray (1910–1985), a distinguished lawyer and educator, in 1977 became the first African American woman to be ordained a priest in the predominately white Episcopal Church. Throughout American history, many African American women exercised their ministry through para-ecclesiastical structures, such as women's temperance and missionary societies. Some, such as Anna Cooper (1858–1964) and the African Methodist Episcopal Church's Fanny Jackson Coppin (1837–1913), became renowned educators.

AFRICAN AMERICAN CHURCHES DURING RECONSTRUCTION

African American church membership grew explosively after the Civil War, especially in the South, where the African American clergy played a prominent part in the Reconstruction governments. African Methodist Episcopal minister Hiram Revels (1827–1901) became the first African American to serve as a U.S. senator when the Mississippi legislature sent him to Washington, D.C., in 1870. Many other African American ministers served in Congress or in their state governments during this period. African American participation in Reconstruction politics was effective in large part because ministers in the AME and AME Zion churches, as well as many Baptist ministers, carefully and patiently educated their congregations on civic and political issues. The exception to this rule was the Colored Methodist Episcopal Church, a newly established African American denomination that generally avoided politics during the Reconstruction period.

By the end of the Reconstruction era in the 1880s, African Americans had mostly been expelled from southern state governments by statute. Nevertheless, many African American ministers and church members continued to play an active role in such issues as temperance, often campaigning on behalf of prohibition referenda. Still, the southern white campaign of terror, lynching, and disfranchisement steadily reduced African American political power and participation. This scenario remained in place until the mid-twentieth century, when the civil rights movement challenged these social contracts.

As the system of racial segregation imposed in the 1880s and 1890s manifested itself, African American

Senator Hiram Rhodes Revels, c. 1870–1871. *Revels, the first African American senator, was a minister in the African Methodist Episcopal Church; he served as a chaplain in the Civil War. Upon leaving the Senate he became a university president.* THE LIBRARY OF CONGRESS

ministers coordinated a wide-ranging response. First, they forthrightly challenged new segregation laws, engaging in civil disobedience and boycotts. For example, when the city of Nashville, Tennessee, segregated its streetcars in 1906, influential Baptist minister R. H. Boyd (1843–1922) led an African American streetcar boycott, even operating his own streetcar line for a time. No defeat was ever seen as final.

Secondly, African American ministers helped to nurture a separate set of institutions to serve African Americans excluded from white establishments. Congregationalists, Baptists, and northern Methodists established schools in the South for African Americans during Reconstruction. The African Methodist Episcopal, African Methodist Episcopal Zion, and Christian Methodist Episcopal bishops forged ahead with the establishment of their own networks of schools. African American denominations also built up their publishing houses and produced books and periodicals that were vital to the black community. Virtually every institution with ties to African American communities received some support from African American churches.

Thirdly, some African American ministers believed that the civil rights retreats of the late nineteenth century should have spurred African Americans to leave the United States for a destination where their full civil rights would be respected. A "Back to Africa" movement grew to enable African Americans to find a home where they could run governments, banks, and businesses without interference from whites. To that end, Bishop Turner helped to organize a steamship line to carry African Americans to Africa, and two shiploads of African American immigrants sailed to Liberia in 1895 and 1896. Some African American church leaders, such as Christian Methodist Episcopal bishop Lucius Holsey (1842–1920) and AME bishop Richard H. Cain (1825–1887), held views similar to those advocated by Turner, but a larger majority of church leaders opposed Turner's immigration plan vigorously. Simultaneously, African American missionary work continued to occupy the attention of many African Americans at the end of the nineteenth century. Under the guidance of Bishops Payne and Turner, for example, the African Methodist Episcopal Church had an active missionary presence in Sierra Leone, Liberia, and South Africa.

AFRICAN AMERICAN CHURCHES IN THE TWENTIETH CENTURY

In the twentieth century, African American religious life was characterized by a far greater degree of diversity and pluralism. At the same time, traditional African American concerns, including the continuing quest for freedom and justice, were not only maintained but also strengthened. Pentecostalism, which burst onto the American scene in 1906, became a major religious force within the African American experience. William Joseph Seymour (1870–1922), a preacher from Louisiana, led an extraordinary interracial revival in Los Angeles between 1906 and 1909 that enabled Pentecostalism to spread worldwide. The claim that all heavenly gifts that were available to early Christians, including faith healing and speaking in tongues, were available to modern Christians gave great impetus to the movement. The Pentecostal-oriented Church of God in Christ, founded by Charles H. Mason (1866–1961), who attended Seymour's revival, became the second-largest African American denomination in the United States. In the latter part of the century, the charismatic or neo-Pentecostal movement revitalized many congregations within mainline African American denominations.

The liturgy of the African American churches was transformed with the introduction of sacred music and organizations that promoted it in the early twentieth century. Influenced by the work of such composers as Charles Albert Tindley (1851–1933), Charles Price Jones (1865–1949), Lucie Campbell Williams (1885–1963), and Thomas A. Dorsey (1899–1993), the new music

Thomas A. Dorsey at the Piano with His Band, the Wandering Syncopators Orchestra, in 1923. *The liturgy of the African American churches was transformed with the introduction of sacred music and organizations that promoted it in the early twentieth century. Influenced by the work of composers such as Dorsey, the new music enabled worshippers to praise God with rhythms and harmonies imported from more secular musical genres, such as the blues.* AP IMAGES.

enabled worshippers to praise God with rhythms and harmonies imported from more secular musical genres, such as the blues.

This new fusion sparked the creation of compositions that expressed the deep religious feelings of ordinary worshippers more appropriately than any previous music. New instruments were brought into the churches for the performance of these compositions, including guitars, drums, and later synthesizers and electronic instruments. The newer musical styles initially met with strong resistance in many African American congregations. As time passed, however, the popularity of such performers as Mahalia Jackson (1912–1972) enabled the genre to win wide acceptability. Church choirs and ensembles, such as the Dixie Hummingbirds, helped to gain for gospel music an ever-increasing audience. While both Methodists and Baptists played a part in the spread of gospel music, the Holiness-Pentecostalist churches that stemmed from the 1906 revivals in Los Angeles played an especially important role in its increasing popularity.

The black nationalism of Bishop Turner came full circle in the work of such men as Marcus Garvey (1887–1940) and his chaplain general, George A. McGuire (1866–1934), as well as Elijah Muhammad (1897–1975) and Malcolm X (1925–1965). This black nationalism aided the growth of non-Christian religions, such as the Nation of Islam and Black Judaism, among African Americans. Black nationalists often rejected Christianity as too complicit with slaveholding and racial oppression. A spectacular rise of storefront churches occurred, some of which were led by flamboyant showmen, such as Father Divine (1879–1965) and "Sweet Daddy" Grace (1881–1960). Each of these religious movements was aided by African American migrations after 1915 from southern states to the North, which greatly strengthened northern African American communities.

A somewhat later migration from the Caribbean provided support for the growth of a diverse range of religions within African American society, including the Episcopal Church, Seventh-day Adventism, Roman Catholicism, Rastafarianism, and Santeria and other African-derived religious practices. An early Caribbean migrant was Sarah Mae Manning, who brought up her son, Louis Eugene Walcott, in Boston within the Episcopal Church. He later achieved

Dixie Hummingbirds, c. 1970. *The long-lived Dixie Hummingbirds, with varying members over the years, are an ensemble with great influence in gospel music. In 1973 the group won a Grammy for Best Soul Gospel Performance.* MICHAEL OCHS ARCHIVES/GETTY IMAGES

fame as a Nation of Islam leader by the name Louis Farrakhan.

Many black ministers became advocates of a social gospel movement as well. One of the most famous was Reverdy Ransom (1861–1959) of the African Methodist Episcopal Church, who came into prominence between 1901 and 1904 as pastor of an institutional church in Chicago. (Institutional churches provided a range of social services to needy members and neighbors, in addition to regular worship.) The social gospel movement highlighted the reality of collective, societal sin, such as the starvation of children and denial of human rights, and maintained that Christian repentance for these sins must be followed by concrete actions to rectify injustice and to assist the poor. The Reverend Dr. Martin Luther King Jr. (1929–1968) was profoundly influenced by this social gospel movement.

Many ministers and congregations maintained a style of political involvement that built on a long tradition among African Americans, often with social gospel concerns in mind. Chicago AME minister Archibald Carey Jr. (1908–1981), a behind-the-scenes political organizer, effectively represented the interests of his African American congregation. New York's Adam Clayton Powell Jr. (1908–1972) and Floyd Flake and Atlanta's Andrew Young and John Lewis were ministers who achieved election to the U.S. House of Representatives, with Powell rising to the chairmanship of the influential Education and Labor Committee during the 1960s.

Other African American ministers, including Malcolm X, Al Sharpton, and Calvin Butts, have played important roles as community organizers without serving in elective office. Jesse Jackson's attempt to gain the Democratic nomination for president in 1984 and 1988 brought the electoral clout of the African American church into the spotlight. The church's strong involvement in political, economic, and social affairs helps to point out its continuing and central relevance—even indispensability—within the national context.

The civil rights movement was deeply influenced by the African American church, from which several of its most prominent organizers, most notably Martin Luther King Jr., sprang. Its demonstrations, speeches, and movement songs were suffused with biblical imagery drawn from the book of Exodus and other parts of the Bible. It was their religious faith that made it possible for activists to keep progressing along a nonviolent path, even when, in 1956, King's home in Montgomery was firebombed, and even after the Sixteenth Street Baptist Church in Birmingham was bombed in 1963, killing four young girls. In a significant sense, King inherited his activism from his father, Martin Luther King Sr. (1899–1984), also a Baptist pastor, who had led rallies and staged economic boycotts against racial discrimination as far back as the 1930s.

Many African American religious leaders in the 1960s thought that King's brand of social activism was too extreme. One of King's most determined critics during the 1960s was the theologically conservative president of the National Baptist Convention, Joseph H. Jackson (c. 1904–1990). An attempt by King's ministerial allies to unseat Jackson as president of the convention in 1960 and 1961 led to a schism, with King and his supporters forming a new body, the Progressive National Baptist Convention. King came under further criticism when, in 1967 and 1968, he made it clear that his advocacy of pacifism extended to opposition to U.S. military involvement in Vietnam.

BLACK LIBERATION THEOLOGY

The black liberation theology movement attempted to fashion a critique of the prevalent Christian theology out of the materials that Malcolm X, James H. Cone, and the Black Power movement provided. Black liberation theology maintains that African Americans must be liberated from multiple forms of bondage—social, political, economic, and religious. This formulation views Christian theology as a theology of liberation that involves empowerment and seeks the rights of self-definition, self-affirmation, and self-determination.

Some African American theologians were skeptical of the integrationist and nonviolent thrusts of the civil rights movement. Many called on African Americans to cultivate greater pride in and reliance on their own cultural resources. An advocate of this position was the theologian Albert Cleage (Jaramogi Abebe Agyeman, 1911–2000), pastor of the Shrine of the Black Madonna in Detroit. He argued that Jesus was a black messiah and that his congregation should follow the teachings of Jehovah, a black god. "Almost everything you have heard about Christianity is essentially a lie," he stated. Cleage was representative of many black theologians in arguing that black liberation should be seen as situated at the core of the Christian gospels. Beginning in the 1980s, a number of African American women, including Jacquelyn Grant, Delores Williams, and Katie Cannon, formulated "womanist" theologies, which seek to redress the triple oppression of race, class, and gender that most African American women face.

The Reverend Dr. James A. Forbes Jr., Senior Minister Emeritus, Riverside Church, New York City, 2010. *Forbes speaks at the funeral of Percy Sutton, who was a Tuskegee Airman, Malcolm X's attorney, and the man who saved the Apollo Theater. Forbes was the first African American to serve as senior minister at Riverside.* AP PHOTO/RICHARD DREW

THE FOLK ART OF PREACHING

In most congregations, sermonizing is an interpersonal skill that African Americans have elevated to the level of art, with such notable elements as call and response and repetition of phrases. The art and science of African American proclamation can be defined as a statement of faith drawn from the biblical tradition and expressing itself through the authentic being of the preacher. The exuberance of all participants is highly dependent upon the tradition within which one worships. For example, in the more highly liturgical traditions, such as Roman Catholicism and Eastern Orthodoxy, sermons tend to be instructional. By contrast, nonliturgical Protestant denominations, including Baptist and Pentecostal churches, tend to view sermons as verbal sacraments.

In the 1990s, nondenominational churches reached new heights of popularity. Such churches usually centered around a solitary, charismatic figure. Because the medium is the message, performance was as important as the words themselves. Among the most highly regarded preachers are Gardner C. Taylor, pastor emeritus of Brooklyn's Concord Baptist Church of Christ; Barbara L. King, founder and minister of Atlanta's nondenominational Hillside International Chapel and Truth Center; James A. Forbes, senior minister of New York City's Riverside Church; and Miles Jerome Jones, professor of homiletics at the Samuel DeWitt Proctor School of Theology at Virginia Union University, who was known as the "preachers' preacher." In 1996, both Forbes and Taylor were deemed two of the country's twelve most effective preachers by a Baylor University survey. President Bill Clinton named Taylor as one of his favorite evangelists.

EVOLVING TRENDS AMONG AFRICAN AMERICAN CHURCHES

In the twenty-first century, African American religions are undergoing substantial changes. The religious search of prosperous middle-class African Americans has brought about surging enrollment at African American megachurches in many of the nation's metropolitan areas, such as Atlanta, Chicago, Dallas, Memphis, and Washington, D.C. The growing interest in do-it-yourself spirituality has greatly enlarged the readership of inspirational writers, such as Iyanla Vanzant and T. D. Jakes. There has also been unprecedented interest in racial reconciliation among conservative Christian churches. Several have joined liberal Christians who have pioneered in this area since the 1960s, even while an upsurge in African American church burnings, especially in the rural South, demonstrated that the nation still has much work to do in addressing racism at the religion level. Nation of Islam leader Louis Farrakhan achieved spectacular success with his Million Man March in October 1995, stressing such spiritual themes as atonement, but he has yet to fashion an effective follow-up to this headline-grabbing event. Meanwhile, the urban poor, especially young African American men, seem to be staying away from churches in ever-increasing numbers.

The diverse offerings of large African American churches, such as the Ebenezer African Methodist Episcopal Church in Maryland with 12,000 members, have attracted African American middle-class worshippers in unprecedented numbers. Ebenezer African Methodist Episcopal Church, for example, offers marriage counseling, workshops on financial planning, a program for lawyers, and a socially involved, intellectually informed ministry. Many African American megachurch congregations reach out to poor young men, even though the churches are often located in the suburbs, miles away from inner-city problems. Some African American churches have traditionally had large memberships, but the new megachurches boast younger pastors, often in their thirties to fifties, many with doctorates. Unlike their white counterparts, African American megachurches often promote uplift and social involvement with the poor.

Increasingly, African American ministerial leadership is passing from those who were on the front lines of civil rights struggles in the 1960s to their children's generation. Perhaps this reality is best symbolized by events in Atlanta in the late 1990s. In July 1997, then seventy-five-year-old Joseph Lowery, who had helped to found the Southern Christian Leadership Conference (SCLC) with his colleagues Martin Luther King Jr. and Ralph Abernathy, stepped down from the presidency of that organization. By 2009, Dr. King's daughter, Bernice King, who was five years old when her father was assassinated, was elected the first woman president of the organization founded by her father. Like her father, King preaches a message of forgiveness and reconciliation, and she calls on churches to build fellowship across racial and ethnic lines. Meanwhile, Atlanta's Ebenezer Baptist Church, where Martin Luther King Jr. preached, opened a new sanctuary seating 1,600 worshippers in March 1999. The old church building, only half as large, was taken over by the National Park Service and is maintained as part of the Martin Luther King Jr. National Historic Site.

AFRICAN AMERICAN CHURCHES AND SOCIAL ISSUES

Overall, African American churches continue to address a wide variety of social problems affecting African Americans. For example, many churches have strong antidrug programs, and some have undertaken vigorous action against crack houses. Parochial schools, feeding centers, and housing for senior citizens are also part of the African American churches' outreach to the community.

Many African American ministers have noted, however, the growing division of African Americans along social-class lines, and they have exhorted middle-class African Americans to give more generously to programs that aid the disadvantaged. James Cone, a leading African American theologian, has stated that African American churches need to devote less time and attention to institutional survival and more to finding ways of dealing with such issues as poverty, gang violence, and HIV/AIDS. In 1997, five historically African American denominations formed Revelation Corporation of America, a partnership between corporations, charities, and churches. The income from the corporation was used to subsidize home ownership among moderate-income residents in big cities, such as Philadelphia and Memphis.

African American churches have also been involved in a wide variety of interdenominational efforts with white churches. While mainstream Christian organizations, such as the National Council of Churches of Christ, have been involved in interracial reconciliation efforts and have worked to promote human rights for all since the 1960s, it has only been since the 1990s that evangelical Christian organizations have joined in similar movements.

In 1994, African American and white Pentecostal churches formed an interracial umbrella organization for the first time. The Promise Keepers, a Christian men's movement designed to motivate men to become better husbands and fathers, fully included African Americans in the staff and leadership of the organization. In June 1995, the Southern Baptist Convention adopted a resolution apologizing for its previous defense of African enslavement and "unwaveringly" denouncing "racism, in all its forms, as deplorable sin."

In 1997, the predominately white National Association of Evangelicals and the National Black Evangelical Association agreed to hold their future meetings jointly. Still, some racial discontent continued to surface among evangelical Christians. The National Baptist Convention withheld its support from one of the Reverend Billy Graham's crusades because of Graham's refusal to support affirmative action. In addition, E. Edward Jones, former president of the National Baptist Convention of America, refused to accept the Southern Baptist Convention's apology for enslavement and racism, charging that the resolution was simply a cover for aggressive evangelism in the African American community that would draw members away from historically African American churches.

Dialogue among individual denominations continues to nurture the spirit of cooperation between them, with the result of establishing closer working relationships on the national and community levels. In June 1997, leaders of eight historically African American denominations met in Hampton, Virginia, in a weeklong conference. The church leaders evinced a remarkable spirit of unity, but agreed to disagree on such issues as whether it was the church's responsibility to help redeem society by pursuing social and economic change, or whether the church was only responsible for the salvation of individual souls.

African American men from four Methodist denominations met in Atlanta in October 1998 to address issues relating to families, male mentoring, and reconciliation between their various traditions. Bishops from these four denominations—the predominately white United Methodist Church and three African American Methodist denominations (the African Methodist Episcopal, the African Methodist Episcopal Zion, and the Christian Methodist Episcopal churches)—continue to explore the possibility of a merger in the twenty-first century.

In the era of the megachurch, storefront churches continue to offer Bible study and a sense of community in an intimate setting. An urban phenomenon, storefront churches are usually created by nonordained ministers and are independent of denominational hierarchies. These churches are often the lifeblood of urban communities plagued by violence and poverty. The social services and community outreach they offer, in some cases to populations considered beyond help, pick up where government leaves off.

African American churches also have found themselves compelled to address issues related to ethnic tensions. In the aftermath of the devastating arson attacks on black churches in 1996, white churches and African American churches joined together in some cities to offer workshops against racism. Leading African American pastors in Los Angeles denounced both the police violence revealed in the 1991 beating of Rodney King and the subsequent violence of rioters, while advocating urgent attention to the problems of inner-city residents. For example, James Lawson of the Holman United Methodist Church stated that those who burned buildings during the 1992 Los Angeles riots were "responding to a society of violence, not simply a society of racism," and issued "a call to repent." In 1991 in New York City, an African American Baptist congregation in Queens warmly welcomed the opportunity to perform an ordination service for a Korean American minister, Chong S. Lee.

Black ministers and congregations have increasingly opened themselves to frank discussions of human sexuality, demanded, in part, by the public health threat posed by the HIV crisis, which has hit African American communities especially hard. In 1999, 5,000 churches participated in the annual Black Church Week of Prayer for the Healing of AIDS, a 100 percent increase in only ten years. (In 2010, the Black Church Week of Prayer expanded into the National Week of Prayer for the Healing of AIDS.) W. Franklyn Richardson, senior pastor of Grace Baptist Church in Mount Vernon, New York, has openly discussed AIDS with his congregation since his brother died of AIDS in 1993. Some African American congregations remain uncomfortable about encouraging sexually active individuals to use condoms to protect themselves from sexually transmitted diseases, and favor their traditional advocacy of monogamy and premarital abstinence. Often, African American ministers from conservative religious traditions (e.g., many Roman Catholics, Muslims, and Pentecostals) are able to discuss this matter with their congregations only in an informal manner, if at all.

African American churches continue to make progress in the area of gender equality. While two predominately white denominations, the United Methodist and Protestant Episcopal churches, elevated African American women to the episcopacy in the 1980s, historically African American denominations have only done so since the 1990s. Nevertheless, women in some African American churches are achieving more prestigious ministerial assignments. Vashti McKenzie, a former model, disc jockey, and radio program director, served as pastor of the Payne Memorial AME Church, an "old-line" church in Baltimore, in the 1990s. In 2000, McKenzie was elected and consecrated bishop of the AME Church, becoming the first woman to hold that position. From 2000 to 2004, she served as bishop of the Eighteenth Episcopal District of the AME Church, a post that comprises Botswana, Lesotho, Mozambique, and Swaziland in southeast Africa. In 2005, she became the head of the AME Church's Council of Bishops. She also became prelate for the Thirteenth Episcopal District, which includes Tennessee and Kentucky. By 2010, more than 600 female pastors were ensconced in the African Methodist Episcopal Church.

Preaching the gospel in a faithful but relevant fashion remains the most important objective of African American church leaders. Ministerial training and financial support are other areas needing improvement in many African American churches. African American churches are not in danger of losing sight of their many vital and extremely significant functions, within both African American and American society. It is safe to predict that African American churches will continue to sustain and develop their important and prophetic function.

MEMBERSHIP GROWTH WITHIN AFRICAN AMERICAN CHURCHES

While many African American Methodist and Baptist denominations have shown only limited membership growth, other African American denominations are showing marked membership increases. Foremost among these are the Pentecostal churches, whose lively worship and extensive social ministries are attracting members from all classes within the African American community. The largest of these denominations, the Church of God in Christ, had an estimated membership of more than five million in the early 2000s. Charismatic congregations, also known as neo-Pentecostal churches, within such mainline African American churches as the African Methodist Episcopal Church, are thriving for similar reasons.

Other groups that have made substantial membership gains among African Americans include the Roman Catholic and Episcopal churches and Islam. While estimates differ, more than 1.5 million African Americans probably belong to the Roman Catholic Church, which has worked hard to be sensitive to their needs. In many inner cities, the Catholic Church has maintained churches and schools in predominately African American neighborhoods, although some have closed in the early 2000s, primarily for financial reasons. Yet certain Catholic dioceses, such as Detroit, are increasing in membership. Moreover, the Roman Catholic Church has been receptive to some liturgical variation, allowing gospel choirs and African vestments for priests in African American churches. Nevertheless, Roman Catholics confront serious problems in serving African American parishioners. Fewer than three hundred of the 54,000 priests in the United States are African American, meaning that some African American congregations must be served by white priests. In 1989, George A. Stallings Jr., a priest in Washington, D.C., broke away from Roman Catholicism, arguing that the Catholic Church was still racist and did not do enough for its African American members. He subsequently formed the Imani Temple of the African American Catholic Congregation, and was eventually excommunicated from the Roman Catholic Church.

Theologian George A. Stallings Jr., Howard University Law School, Washington, DC, July 2, 1989. *Stallings, a priest, broke with the Roman Catholic Church over what he considered the church's racial insensitivity. He founded the Imani Temple African-American Catholic Congregation and on this date the first Mass was celebrated in its temporary location.* **UPI/CORBIS-BETTMANN. REPRODUCED BY PERMISSION.**

In such large cities as New York, Afro-Caribbean immigrants are swelling the ranks of the Episcopal Church. For example, a substantial number of the members of St. Paul's Episcopal Church in Brooklyn are Caribbean immigrants. At least three Episcopal churches in New York have escaped closing by church authorities because of the influx of members from the Caribbean. The Episcopal Church is not the only predominately white denomination seeking to attract new immigrants of African descent. Officials of the Presbyterian Church (USA) hoped to increase their denomination's ethnic-minority membership, in part by targeting their outreach to new immigrants of African descent.

Mainstream Islam, despite raising its own complexities, has also made large gains in the United States. Of the estimated six million Muslims in this country, one million are believed to be African American. Most African American Muslims do not distinguish between people of different races, and they worship cordially alongside recent Muslim immigrants from Asia and Africa. In contrast, Louis Farrakhan's Nation of Islam retains Elijah Muhammad's black separatist teachings, and continues to maintain a devoted following. Farrakhan has become embroiled in much controversy over the years because of his negative statements about Jews, Palestinian Arabs, and Asians.

Because of its conservative stance on gender issues, Islam has been more popular among African American men than African American women. Following his successful Million Man March in 1995, Farrakhan was able to fill the house, even in smaller cities such as Tallahassee, Florida, and hold his audiences spellbound for hours with a mixture of religious prophecy, candid social commentary, and moral exhortation for youth. The chief organizer of the Million Man March, Benjamin Chavis, eventually converted to the Nation of Islam, and then suffered the termination of his ministerial standing in his former denomination, the United Church of Christ.

Farrakhan, along with other prominent African Americans, including then Senator Barack Obama, marked the tenth anniversary of the Million Man March by staging a second march, the Millions More Movement, in Washington, D.C, in October 2005. African and Afro-Caribbean religions, such as the Yoruba worship of the deities (orisha), Cuban Santeria, and Haitian vodun, have also been gaining ground in African American communities and on some African American college campuses. Caribbean immigrants to the United States have helped to stimulate the growth of these African-derived traditions. A typical Haitian American vodun congregation in Brooklyn, New York, was the subject of Karen McCarthy Brown's groundbreaking work *Mama Lola: A Vodou Priestess in Brooklyn* (1991). Some African Americans in the United States are also attracted by the honor shown to ancestors in these African traditions. Iyanla Vanzant was raised as a Christian, but later identified herself as a Yoruba priestess. Vanzant has provided low-key advocacy of these traditions in her best-selling works.

SUCCESS AND FAILURE WITHIN AFRICAN AMERICAN CHURCHES

The most successful African American ministers today employ as many forms of media as possible in order to find and keep their audiences. T. D. Jakes, for example, might appear to be a typical pastor of a megachurch, the Potter's House in Dallas, with over 35,000 members. What sets him above the crowd, however, is his television cable network and an active revival schedule that finds him packing venues like Atlanta's Georgia Dome. His popular Web site also makes his ministry widely available. Some former Potter's House members have been critical of the church, claiming that its leadership exercises excessive control and legalism.

Johnnie Colemon, founder of Christ Universal Temple in Chicago, runs a seminary for pastors and also has an influential radio ministry. Her fellow Chicagoan, Louis Farrakhan of the Nation of Islam, also gets his message out through radio broadcasts and an active publishing program, including a weekly newspaper, the *Final Call*, sold on street corners nationwide and available online. While pastors continue to spread their ideas through sermons on CDs, DVDs, online, and in print, the most successful find many more ways to reach out.

One prominent African American religious leader who encountered failure was Henry J. Lyons, a Baptist minister in St. Petersburg, Florida, who in 1994 became president of the National Baptist Convention, U.S.A. On July 9, 1997, Lyons's wife, Deborah, was arrested and charged with arson at a Florida home that her husband owned with Bernice Edwards, Henry Lyons's alleged mistress and director of public relations for his denomination. This incident eventually led to a criminal investigation and indictments against Henry Lyons. Florida authorities charged Lyons with racketeering and grand theft in February 1998. They alleged that he had misappropriated denominational funds and swindled millions of dollars from large corporations by selling bogus membership lists. Five months later, Lyons was indicted by the federal government on fifty-six counts of extortion, fraud, and tax evasion. Lyons requested forgiveness from his congregation and denomination. On February 27, 1999, he was convicted of three counts brought against him by the state of Florida. On March 16, 1999, he resigned as president of the National Baptist Convention, and S. C. Cureton (1930–2008) assumed the post until new elections were held. Lyons then pleaded guilty to five charges brought by the federal government. He was sentenced to sixty months in a federal penitentiary and had to return $214,500 in donations that he had not distributed.

CHURCH BURNINGS IN THE SOUTH

African American churches in the South came literally under fire in the 1990s and the early 2000s. These arson incidents invoked grievous memories of the racist violence of the 1960s, particularly the tragic bombing of Birmingham's Sixteenth Street Baptist Church in 1963. In 1996, the peak year for church arsons, 119 of 297 churches set fire nationwide were predominately African American. Although African American churches constituted about 6 percent of the nation's churches, more than 40 percent of church arsonists that year targeted African American churches.

In response, President Bill Clinton declared the "investigation and prevention of church arsons to be a national priority." In June 1996, the president established the National Church Arson Task Force and proposed a three-pronged strategy that called for prosecution of the arsonists, the rebuilding of church edifices, and the prevention of additional fires. On July 3, he signed the Church Arson Prevention Act of 1996, which passed both chambers of Congress unanimously.

Independently, Mac Charles Jones (1950–1997), associate general secretary for racial justice at the National Council of Churches of Christ, met in 1996 with pastors of more than thirty burned churches and heard numerous stories of racist graffiti and threats issued against the pastors. To that end, the National Association for the Advancement of Colored People (NAACP) urged the Justice Department to investigate; in response, a full-scale civil rights investigation was initiated. The Southern Christian Leadership Conference also instituted a fund for the affected congregations.

Despite federal government involvement, only about one-third of the cases was solved by the end of the 1990s, and some investigations continue. Although the Federal Bureau of Investigation (FBI) and the Bureau of Alcohol, Tobacco, Firearms and Explosives (ATF) had more than two hundred agents investigating the church burnings, they were not able to find a common link among these crimes.

In 2006, three white university students at Birmingham-Southern College, a Methodist-affiliated liberal arts college, gained national attention after they were arrested for setting fire to nine rural Alabama churches. Allegedly, the first five fires were set as a "joke"; the next four were meant to lead the police astray. Five of the churches were white, and four were African American.

VISION OF THE AFRICAN AMERICAN CHURCH FOR THE TWENTY-FIRST CENTURY

In the twenty-first century, church leaders and laity will need tools for empowerment that will allow the African American Church to address pressing issues of the day. To that end, social justice, church administration, and church and community relations are important areas of discussion and study. Distinguished scholars and theologians, as well as community leaders, must be willing and able to research and reflect on these issues. The contemporary African American church must also function as a think tank, where clergy and theologians can come together to analyze and discuss the issues confronting the African American church and community.

Furthermore, the leaders of the twenty-first-century African American church must understand its function as dialectic between the priestly (ceremonial and ritual) and the prophetic (social, economic, and political) responsibilities of ministry. Ministry is more than just intellectual categories to be analyzed and discussed; it constitutes one of the burning issues of social justice in an African American institution in a white racist society. African American pastors must realize their priestly responsibilities and attempt to fulfill them with sensitivity to the condition of oppression experienced by people of African descent on a daily basis. On the other hand, it is this very condition of oppression that serves as the cause for a prophetic ministry designed to mitigate the oppression and lead to liberation. This is not an either/or question, but rather a question of the legitimate synthesis of the two (prophetic and priestly) functions into a ministry that can be described as holistic. Some pastors may not bother to agonize over this subject because they realize that their survival requires no more than the faithful fulfillment of the priestly expectations of their churches. The challenge for African American churches of the twenty-first century centers on the need for the proper balance between priestly functions and prophetic functions.

A holistic approach to ministry must begin with a holistic view of life: that is, there is to be no false dichotomy between what is sacred and what is secular—all of life is sacred. The political, economic, social, and educational realities that affect people's lives must be addressed by any ministry that seeks to be relevant. The need of African American people to have their pastors visit them during times of sickness and bereavement must be balanced by their need to have their pastors engage the political and corporate rulers of this society in ways that will result in their liberation from oppression. The need for rituals and celebration of the faith within the sanctuary must be balanced by the need to confront the principalities, powers, and rulers of darkness in the streets and inside the chambers and boardrooms where decisions are made that profoundly affect the quality of African Americans' lives.

Every African American pastor of the twenty-first century should have a holistic approach to ministry that seeks to combine relevance with reverence. The tension from the dialectic between the priestly and prophetic roles of the pastor should be constant if a holistic ministry is to be achieved.

THE AFRICAN AMERICAN CHURCH IN THE AGE OF PRESIDENT BARACK OBAMA

The African American church in the age of President Barack Obama is responsible for providing a vision of a new society. In this regard, the church can act as a hospital for healing the diseases (poverty, social issues of discrimination, etc.) of the African American community. The African American church's responsibility is to extend grace, not only to its membership, but also to the outcast segments of the African American community.

The twenty-first-century African American church should be able to present God to the African American churched and unchurched as a friend. Many African American religious leaders argue that the church must change its negative attitude toward the outcast members of the African American community in order to become a transforming agent in their lives. Some forty years after Martin L. King Jr.'s observation that eleven o'clock Sunday morning is the most racially segregated hour in America, the African American church in the era of the Obama presidency should be about unity. The church should be about the business of trying to break down barriers of separation and segregation based on racial, cultural, and religious differences. By doing so, the African American church of the twenty-first century can began to participate in a significant way to the formation of a new society. Many houses of worship have begun to use alternative names. Increasingly, the terms *non-denominational faith centers* and *ministries* are used to replace the term *church*. These alternative approaches to ministry allow faith-based organizations to widen the scope and breath of their ministries. Such approaches allow for a broad cross-section of racial, cultural, and religious ideologies to find common ground. They will play an important role in the legacy of the African American church in the era of the Obama presidency.

AFRICAN AMERICAN FAITH COMMUNITIES

AFRICAN AMERICAN CATHOLIC CONGREGATION

Before the Civil War, African American Catholics were confined largely to Maryland and Louisiana. However, Catholics made greater efforts to convert African Americans after the Civil War. By the end of the nineteenth century, nearly 200,000 African American Catholics were worshipping in the United States. However, there were still more African American Protestant ministers than African American Catholic priests.

Black Catholic reaction to the 1989 departure and excommunication of George Stallings and the establishment of the Imani Temple were mixed. Many African American Catholics expressed sympathy for Stallings's concerns but were unwilling to leave the Roman Catholic Church. Stallings assumed the title of archbishop of Imani Temple in 1991 and, at the same time, ordained a woman to the priesthood of the African American Catholic Congregation. Stallings also relaxed the Catholic teaching on abortion for his congregation members and declared Martin Luther King Jr. to be a saint.

In forming his denomination, Stallings experienced some setbacks. Several formerly close associates split with Stallings in 1991, alleging a lack of fiscal accountability in the church and accusing him of taking his liturgical innovations too far. In 1994, Stallings dedicated a new cathedral for his denomination in Washington, D.C. As of 2010, there were seven Imani temples under Stallings's leadership, six in the United States and one in Lagos, Nigeria.

AFRICAN METHODIST EPISCOPAL CHURCH

The African Methodist Episcopal (AME) Church was founded in 1816 at a conference convened in Philadelphia by Richard Allen, who was elected as its first bishop. In the following years, it grew throughout the North and Midwest and, after the Civil War, expanded quickly throughout the South and West. By 2006, the church claimed about 3.5 million members, about one million of whom are found in churches in Africa, South America, and the Caribbean as a result of successful missionary efforts. The AME Church oversees about 8,000 churches, and sponsors several colleges, seminaries, and education centers in the United States, Liberia, and South Africa.

Payne Theological Seminary is located in Wilberforce, Ohio, at the site of the church's oldest school, Wilberforce University, which was founded in 1856. Turner Theological Seminary is one of six schools that joined to form the Interdenominational Theological Center in Atlanta. About one-third of local AME congregations sponsor low-income housing, schools, Job Corps programs, or care for senior citizens. The AME Church's chief governing bodies are the General Conference, the Council of Bishops, and the General Board. It publishes the following periodicals: *Christian Recorder*, *Voice of Missions*, and *AME Church Review*. In 2000, Reverend Vashti McKenzie was elected the church's first woman bishop.

AFRICAN METHODIST EPISCOPAL ZION CHURCH

Originally known as the African Methodist Episcopal Church, the African Methodist Episcopal Zion Church was founded in 1821 in New York City. James Varick was elected its first "superintendent"; the title of the presiding officer was later changed to bishop. In 1848, the word *Zion* was added to the name of this church in order to avoid confusion with the church founded by Richard Allen. It grew slowly prior to 1860 but expanded quickly in southern states such as North Carolina and Alabama after the Civil War.

In 2003, the church reported more than 1.4 million members and over 3,800 ministers. The African Methodist Episcopal Zion Church oversees more than 3,000 churches worldwide, with thousands of church members in Africa, England, India, South America, and the Caribbean. The church supports three colleges, two of which are junior colleges, and one seminary. The four-year college and the seminary are Livingstone College and Hood Theological Seminary, both located in Salisbury, North Carolina. The denomination is governed by a general conference, a board of bishops, and a correctional council. Its publications include the weekly *Star of Zion*, the *Quarterly Review*, the monthly *Missionary Seer*, and the quarterly *Church School Herald*.

AFRICAN ORTHODOX CHURCH

The African Orthodox Church was founded in 1921 by Archbishop George A. McGuire, once a priest in the Protestant Episcopal Church. McGuire was the chaplain for Marcus Garvey's Universal Negro Improvement Association, but Garvey disavowed his chaplain's efforts to establish a new denomination. This church is today an autonomous and independent body adhering to an "orthodox" confession of faith. Its nearly 5,000 members worship in about seventeen churches.

AFRICAN THEOLOGICAL ARCHMINISTRY

In 1973, a group of African Americans founded a Yoruba-derived kingdom in South Carolina called Oyotunji. This kingdom was run by the leader of the African Theological Archministry, King Efuntola (1928–2005), formerly Walter King. The king and his followers relocated to South Carolina from Harlem, moving their Shango Temple to Beaufort County. King Efuntola received his religious training in Nigeria, and his followers worship various gods and deities from the Yoruba pantheon. The affiliated membership of the group in 2002 was estimated at 10,000.

AFRICAN UNION FIRST COLORED METHODIST PROTESTANT CHURCH, INC.

This denomination, the first independent African American denomination in the United States, was formed in 1866 by a merger of the African Union Church and the First Colored Methodist Protestant Church. The African Union Church traced its roots to a Union Church of Africans founded in 1813 by Peter Spencer in Wilmington, Delaware. This denomination includes forty congregations in several states and has a membership of over 8,000.

APOSTOLIC OVERCOMING HOLY CHURCH OF GOD, INC.

This Pentecostal denomination, originally known as the Ethiopian Overcoming Holy Church, was incorporated in Alabama in 1920. Evangelistic in purpose, it emphasizes sanctification, holiness, and the power of divine healing. In 2008, the Apostolic Overcoming Holy Church of God reported some 13,000 members led by thirteen bishops and thirty-three overseers. About half of its 130 congregations were in Alabama.

BIBLE WAY CHURCH OF OUR LORD JESUS CHRIST WORLD-WIDE, INC.

Founded in 1957, this Pentecostal tradition claimed 300 churches and 250,000 members as of 2006, with twenty-eight bishops in 2008. It publishes the *Bible Way News Voice* biweekly.

BLACK JEWS

Nearly 100,000 African Americans identify themselves as Jewish. Included among these are the Commandment Keepers, founded in Harlem in 1919 by a Nigerian man known as Rabbi Wentworth Arthur Matthew

(1892–1973). This category also includes the Church of God and Saints in Christ, founded in 1896 in Lawrence, Kansas, by William Crowdy (1847–1908), and the Church of God, founded in Philadelphia by Prophet F. S. Cherry. In terms of doctrine, these groups share little more than a dislike of Christianity and affection for the Old Testament. Some Black Jews claim to be descended from the Falasha Jews of Ethiopia, who now reside in Israel. However, few Black Jews are recognized as Jewish by orthodox rabbis.

The Church of God and Saints of Christ is probably the largest of these groups, with a membership of around 38,000 and more than forty tabernacles in the United States in 2008, as well as one in Jamaica and about seventy in Africa. The World African Hebrew Israelite Community, a religious sect that believes blacks in the Western Hemisphere are the descendants of the original Hebrews and as such are the rightful heirs to the Holy Land of Israel, has about 3,000 members throughout the United States and an additional 1,500 living in Israel. Since the late 1960s, they have been led by Ben Ami Ben-Israel, formerly a Chicago bus driver named Ben Carter.

CHRISTIAN METHODIST EPISCOPAL CHURCH

The Christian Methodist Episcopal (CME) Church, known until 1954 as the Colored Methodist Episcopal Church, is the third-largest African American Methodist body in the United States. It was founded after the Civil War, when some African American Methodist churches decided not to join the African Methodist Episcopal or African Methodist Episcopal Zion churches, and successfully petitioned the Methodist Episcopal Church, South, for the right to form their own denomination. The first CME General Conference was held at Jackson, Tennessee, in 1870. The church's first two bishops were William H. Miles (1828–1892) and Richard Vanderhorst (1813–1872).

In 2002, the CME Church reported 850,000 members served by 3,300 clergy in the United States, with approximately 75,000 members overseas. It oversees about 3,400 churches and maintains five church-affiliated colleges, as well as the Phillips School of Theology, a seminary that is part of the consortium known as the Interdenominational Theological Center in Atlanta. The church's periodicals include the bimonthly *Christian Index* and the monthly *Missionary Messenger.*

CHURCH OF CHRIST (HOLINESS) U.S.A

This denomination was organized in 1907 by Bishop Charles Price Jones, a renowned and prolific gospel song and hymn writer. The organization traces its roots to an 1897 church established by Jones and Charles H. Mason. Jones and Mason parted company thirteen years later after the two men disagreed about whether speaking in tongues was a requirement for baptism into the Holy Spirit. (Jones insisted that it was not.) Some 160 churches and more than 9,000 members belong to this denomination, which upholds the possibility of sanctification and Christian perfection. The church operates Christ Missionary and Industrial College in Jackson, Mississippi.

CHURCH OF GOD BY FAITH

This Pentecostal denomination was founded in Florida in 1914. Its membership is concentrated in the Southeast.

CHURCH OF GOD IN CHRIST

The Church of God in Christ (COGIC) was organized by two former Baptist preachers, Charles H. Mason and Charles Price Jones, and was initially strongest in Alabama, Mississippi, and Tennessee. Mason reorganized COGIC in 1907, when he and Jones parted over the issue of speaking in tongues. At that time, Mason was appointed "general overseer and chief apostle" of the church, as well as its first bishop. It subsequently expanded rapidly throughout the United States, especially in inner-city African American neighborhoods.

By the early 1990s, COGIC claimed more than five million members and 15,300 churches. It operates the All Saints Bible College in Memphis and a junior college. Its Charles H. Mason Theological Seminary is part of the Interdenominational Theological Center in Atlanta. COGIC is governed by a general assembly, a general council of elders, a board of bishops, and a general board made up of twelve bishops elected by the general assembly to four-year terms. By the first decade of the twenty-first century, COGIC had become the fastest-growing Christian group in the United States. Charles E. Blake became COGIC's presiding bishop in 2007.

CHURCHES OF GOD, HOLINESS

This denomination was organized by K. H. Burruss in Georgia in 1914. It split off from the Church of Christ (Holiness) U.S.A. The total membership in the group's approximately forty churches totals around 25,000.

FIRE BAPTIZED HOLINESS CHURCH

This church was organized on an interracial basis as the Fire Baptized Holiness Association in Atlanta, Georgia, in 1898. Its African American members formed the Fire Baptized Holiness Church in 1908. The church subscribes to standard Pentecostal doctrine on divine healing, speaking in tongues, and sanctification. In 2006, the church included about 160 congregations throughout the United States.

NATION OF ISLAM

After the death of Elijah Muhammad in 1975, his son, Warith D. Mohammed (1933–2008), assumed leadership of the movement. Mohammed shifted dramatically away from his father's teachings of black nationalism, and he stated that whites could become Nation of Islam members. Mohammed sought to bring his movement in accord with Orthodox Islam, and eventually succeeded. In 1976, he changed the organization's name to World Community of Al-Islam in the West, and two years later to the American Muslim Mission.

Three other splinter groups formed, the largest headed by Louis Farrakhan, who split from Mohammed to reestablish the Nation of Islam on the basis of Elijah Muhammad's original black separatist teachings. The remaining two traditions are led by John Farrakhan and Caliph Emmanuel A. Muhammad.

NATIONAL BAPTIST CONVENTION OF AMERICA, INC

The National Baptist Convention of America was formed in 1915 as a result of a schism with the National Baptist Convention, U.S.A. over control of the denominational publishing house. The supporters of Richard Henry Boyd, chairman of the board of the publishing house, established this convention when Boyd's opponents attempted unsuccessfully to bring the publishing house more firmly under denominational control. In 2008, the National Baptist Convention of America claimed about three million members and 5,000 churches. A number of congregations split off in 1988 to form the National Missionary Baptist Association after the new denomination also tried to assert control over its publishing house. The National Baptist Convention of America has missions in Jamaica, Panama, Haiti, the Virgin Islands, and Africa, and supports a number of colleges and seminaries.

NATIONAL BAPTIST CONVENTION OF THE U.S.A., INC

The National Baptist Convention of the U.S.A. was formed in 1895, through the union of three smaller church organizations, the oldest of which had been founded only fifteen years earlier: the Baptist Foreign

Thomas A. Dorsey, Chicago, c. 1959. *Composer and pianist Dorsey, whose father was a minister and whose mother was an organist, composed more than 400 gospel songs, including "Take My Hand, Precious Lord." Dorsey performed at the National Baptist convention in 1930.* TED WILLIAMS/HISTORICAL/CORBIS

Mission Convention of the U.S.A., the American National Baptist Convention, and the National Baptist Educational Convention of the U.S.A. The National Baptist Convention incorporated itself after a dispute over the publishing house led to a schism in 1915.

The National Baptist Convention of the U.S.A. is governed by a fifteen-member board of directors and a nine-member executive board. It is a supporter of the American Baptist Theological Seminary in Nashville, Tennessee, and six other colleges. Its publications include the semimonthly *National Baptist Voice*. The convention dedicated its World Center Headquarters in Nashville, Tennessee, in 1989. In 1994, Reverend Dr. Henry J. Lyons was elected as the sixth president of the National Baptists, the largest African American religious order in the United States. On March 16, 1999, Lyons resigned his office amidst serious state and federal charges against him. S. C. Cureton assumed the post of president until new elections could be held. William J. Shaw was elected president of the organization in 1999. He held the post for ten years, and was succeeded in 2009 by Julius R. Scruggs. As of 2009, the convention included more than 41,000 churches and over 8,300,000 members, making it the second-largest Baptist organization in the world.

NATIONAL MISSIONARY BAPTIST CONVENTION OF AMERICA

The National Missionary Baptist Convention of America was founded in 1988. As of 2007, it had more than five hundred churches, and its membership was an estimated one million. In 2006, Reverend C. C. Robertson was elected president of the convention.

NATIONAL PRIMITIVE BAPTIST CONVENTION OF AMERICA

African American and white Primitive Baptists separated after the Civil War. Having long avowed opposition to church organization above the congregational level, it was not until 1907 that African American Primitive Baptists formed the National Primitive Baptist Convention. Each congregation is independent, and a decision by officials of a local church is final. Belief in "the particular election of a definite number of the human race" is included within its creed. Elder Thomas W. Samuels was elected president in 1995. He was succeeded by Elder Ernest Ferrell in 2005.

PENTECOSTAL ASSEMBLIES OF THE WORLD, INC

An estimated one million members belong to about 1,760 churches of the Pentecostal Assemblies of the World, an organization founded in 1906 and headquartered in Indianapolis, Indiana. The church holds that speaking in tongues is vital to spiritual rebirth and that believers should be baptized only in the name of Jesus. Since its origins, it has accepted the ordination of women in the ministry. In 2004, Bishop E. Horace Smith became presiding bishop of the Pentecostal Assemblies of the World.

PROGRESSIVE NATIONAL BAPTIST CONVENTION, INC

The Progressive National Baptist Convention was formed in 1961 as a result of a schism in the National Baptist Convention of the U.S.A. The schism resulted from a dispute over tactical strategies employed in the civil rights movement of the era. Those committed to nonviolent tactics and civil disobedience, including aligning themselves with Martin Luther King Jr., left to form the new organization. The convention's motto is "Unity, Service, Fellowship, and Peace." The Progressive National Baptist Convention is a financial supporter of six colleges and has active missions in Haiti and Africa. The convention claims 2.5 million members and more than 2,000 churches, and is governed by a sixty-member executive board. In 2006, the church elected Reverend T. DeWitt Smith as president. Although it has no publishing house of its own, it does publish a quarterly periodical titled *Baptist Progress*.

RASTAFARIANS

Rastafarians regard the Ethiopian emperor Haile Selassie (1892–1975) as a supreme being. Marcus Garvey, a Jamaican-born nationalist who advocated a back-to-Africa movement in the United States in the early 1920s, is considered to be a John the Baptist–like figure in the faith. Jamaican reggae musician Bob Marley (1945–1981), a Rastafarian, helped to increase the religion's popularity in the United States, mostly through his music.

Today, "Rastas" differ on specific dogma, but they believe that they descended from black Hebrews exiled in Babylon and, therefore, view themselves as the true Israelites. They also believe that Haile Selassie, whose name before ascending the throne was Lij Ras Tafari Makonnen, is the direct descendant of Solomon and Sheba, and that God is an African. Most white men, they believe, have been worshipping a dead god and have attempted to teach blacks to do likewise. Rastafarians also hold that the Bible was distorted by King James, and that the black race sinned and was punished by God through enslavement. Rastafarians view Ethiopia as Zion and the Western world as Babylon, and they believe that one day they will return to Zion. They preach love, peace, and reconciliation among all races, but warn that Armageddon is imminent.

Rastafarians do not vote, tend to be vegetarians, abhor alcohol, and wear their hair in long, uncombed plaits called dreadlocks. The hair is never cut, since it is part of the spirit, nor is it ever combed. Estimates of their numbers in the United States and around the world vary widely.

TRIUMPH THE CHURCH AND KINGDOM OF GOD IN CHRIST

Founded in 1902, this denomination is identified by its belief in the Pentecostal forms of baptism, in addition to its rejection of speaking in tongues. The baptism ceremony in this church is called "fire-baptism."

UNITED CHURCH OF JESUS CHRIST

The United Church of Jesus Christ split from the Church of God in Christ in 1945 over the issue of the Holy Trinity versus a theory of the "Oneness in Godhead," which it follows. This splinter group was established by Bishop Randolph Carr and originally named the Church of God in Christ (Apostolic). In 1965, disputes over the lifestyle of Bishop Carr led Monroe Saunders and most of the church's members to leave and found the present-day United Church of Jesus Christ. As of 2006, the general minister and president was Reverend John H. Thomas.

RELIGIOUS LEADERS

(Some biographical profiles may appear in other chapters. To locate profiles more readily, please consult the index.)

JARAMOGI ABEBE AGYEMAN (1911–2000)

Religious Leader, Civil Rights Activist. Jaramogi Abebe Agyeman was born Albert Cleage Jr. in 1911 in Indianapolis, Indiana. His father was a physician who relocated the family to Detroit a short time later. Cleage was employed as a social worker before earning a degree in divinity from Oberlin College in 1943. After his ordination, he headed congregational churches in Kentucky and Massachusetts. Cleage's congregational work was notable for its community outreach and economic programs. Returning to Detroit, Cleage became head of a Presbyterian congregation that split off into its own church in 1953.

This fellowship, known as the Central United Church of Christ (CUCC), soon became a political powerhouse in Detroit's increasingly important African American community during the 1950s. Cleage's growing interest in the Black Power movement of the 1960s, especially the teachings of Nation of Islam leader Malcolm X, led the pastor to create a separate denomination in 1967 based on historical theories that Jesus was of African descent. The focal point of the church and the symbolic gesture that attracted many to it was a powerful 18-foot mural of the Black Madonna. The black Christian nationalist movement and its cornerstone congregation, the Shrine of the Black Madonna, became an influential religious, social, political, and economic force in the city.

The Reverend Albert B. Cleage Jr. (Jaramogi Abebe Agyeman), National Chairman, Black Christian Nationalist Church Headquarters, Detroit, MI, 1973. *Cleage, founder of the Shrine of the Black Madonna in Detroit, changed his name to Jaramogi Abebe Agyeman.* AP PHOTO/JMC

Basing the church's teachings on visionaries such as Malcolm X, Elijah Muhammad, and Marcus Garvey, Cleage preached economic self-sufficiency to his flock. He put his words into action by creating several social service programs, including a community grocery outlet, in response to the inflated prices then common among white-owned stores in African American neighborhoods. He also established a bookstore stocked with African nationalist literature. The Shrine of the Black Madonna expanded to other American cities over the next several years, but the imprint it left on Detroit was perhaps his most significant achievement.

In the late 1960s and early 1970s, after the contentious 1967 race riots put aside any hope of smooth integration between a diminishing white population and an increasingly frustrated African American citizenry, Cleage and the church's active membership were credited with helping elect a number of African American political leaders, judges, and school-board members who remained a vital force in Detroit well into the 1990s. Cleage authored two books, *The Black Messiah* (1968) and *Black Christian Nationalism: New Directions for the Black Church* (1972), before taking the name Jaramogi Abebe Agyeman in the 1970s. He died of heart disease on February 20, 2000, in Calhoun Falls, South Carolina, at age eighty-eight.

NOBLE DREW ALI (1886–1929)

Moorish Science Temple Founder. Noble Drew Ali was born Timothy Drew in North Carolina in 1886. His principal contribution was his role in establishing a North American religious movement combining black nationalism and Islam. He rejected Christianity as the religion of whites. In 1913, he established the first Moorish Science Temple in Newark, New Jersey. He taught that African Americans were "Asiatics" who had originally lived in Morocco before enslavement. Every people, including African Americans, needed land, he proclaimed, and North America, which he termed an "extension of the African continent," was the proper home for African Americans. The holy book for the Moorish Science Temple was a "Holy Koran" that was "divinely prepared by the Noble Prophet Drew Ali." (This book should not be confused with the Qur'an of Islam.) Every member of the temple carried a card stating that "We honor all the Divine Prophets, Jesus, Mohammed, Buddha and Confucius" and that "I am a citizen of the U.S.A."

RICHARD ALLEN (1760–1831)

Civil Rights Activist, African Methodist Episcopal Bishop. Born enslaved in Philadelphia on February 14, 1760, Richard Allen converted to Christianity in 1777 and soon thereafter bought his freedom. He then traveled widely through the mid-Atlantic states as an exporter. Francis Asbury, the first bishop of the Methodist Episcopal Church, asked Allen to join him as a traveling companion, stipulating that Allen would not be allowed to fraternize with enslaved people and would sometimes have to sleep in his carriage. Allen refused to accept such an offer, instead settling in Philadelphia, where he and fellow religious leader Absalom Jones founded the Free African Society, an African American society for religious fellowship and mutual aid.

In 1787, Allen was praying in Philadelphia's St. George's Methodist Church when he and Absalom Jones were pulled off their knees by white deacons who insisted that Allen and Jones were worshipping outside the area reserved for African Americans. Allen left the church, establishing his own church for Philadelphia's African Americans in a converted blacksmith shop in 1794. White Methodists tried to exert their control over his church in various ways, which Allen resisted successfully. In 1816, after the Pennsylvania Supreme Court settled a suit over this church in Allen's favor, Allen called for a conference of African American Methodists. The African Methodist Episcopal Church was founded at this conference, and Allen was consecrated as its first bishop. Allen remained both religiously and politically active in his later years, and he was especially active in opposing schemes to colonize African Americans in Africa.

CARL BEAN (1946–)

Unity Fellowship Bishop, Civil Rights Activist. Since the mid-1980s, Bishop Carl Bean has been running two projects: the Minority AIDS Project (MAP) and the Unity Fellowship Church for African American gays and lesbians. Starting as a Bible study group, the church quickly took root, with chapters spreading to New York City, Detroit, Washington, D.C., Philadelphia, Atlanta, and other cities. Meanwhile, MAP has become the largest AIDS agency serving African Americans in the United States.

Born and raised as a Baptist in Baltimore, Bean was an avid churchgoer in his youth. He grew up singing gospel music. In the early 1960s, he lived and performed in Harlem and appeared at the Apollo Theater. He also performed on Broadway in a gospel revue, and became a recording artist before turning to a vocation in the ministry. Ordained a minister in 1982, Bean first chose to work in South Central Los Angeles.

Openly gay, Bean wanted to help liberate ostracized people of color—gay or straight—because he himself had once felt shunned by the church. Reaching out to the disenfranchised, Bean's followers believe that "Love is for everyone." In 1991, the fellowship embarked on a campaign to work with gangs. Often getting referrals from social workers, Bean's congregation earned a reputation for doing whatever is required to get people's lives on track. From distributing cash grants for food and bills to paying for funerals, Unity Fellowship members give back to the community.

Bean has received numerous awards for his community work, including an NAACP Image Award in 1987; a Prophetic Witness Award in 1993 from the Southern Christian Leadership Conference; and a Lambda Legal Defense and Education Fund Liberty Award in 1994.

He was a strong opponent of California's Proposition Eight, a constitutional amendment approved by voters in 2008 that defined marriage as a union between a man and woman, overturning a California Supreme Court decision giving gay couples the right to marry.

SISTER THEA BOWMAN (1937–1990)

Roman Catholic Writer and Educator. Born Bertha Bowman in Canton, Mississippi, in 1937, the daughter of a physician, Thea joined the Roman Catholic Church at age twelve because of the Catholic education she had received. Three years later, she joined the Franciscan Sisters of Perpetual Adoration. She eventually earned a Ph.D. in literature and linguistics and was a distinguished teacher who taught at elementary and high schools, and lectured at several universities. She helped found the Institute for Black Catholic Studies at Xavier University in New Orleans, and was a distinguished scholar, known especially for her writings on Thomas More. However, she will be best remembered for the spiritual inspiration that she provided in numerous lectures, workshops, and concerts. She claimed that she brought to her church "myself, my black self, all that I am, all that I have, all that I hope to become, my history, my culture, my experience, my African American song and dance and gesture and movement and teaching and preaching and healing." Thea Bowman died of cancer in 1990. Many schools around the country have been named in her honor.

CALVIN O. BUTTS III (1949–)

Baptist Minister, Community Activist. Calvin Butts spent the first eight years of his life on the Lower East Side of New York City, where he was born in 1949. In 1957, the family moved to Queens. During summer breaks from school, Butts's parents sent him to stay with his grandmothers, who lived near one another in rural Georgia. It was in these early formative years that Butts first became acquainted with the church.

After graduating from Flushing High School in 1967, where he was class president his senior year, Butts was accepted to Morehouse College in Atlanta. It was an explosive time in the American civil rights struggle. At Morehouse, Butts attended lectures, rallies, and speeches by Martin Luther King Jr. and other African American leaders.

The Reverend Dr. Calvin O. Butts III, Abyssinian Baptist Church, Harlem, NY, c. 2006. *In addition to serving as pastor of the Abyssinian Baptist Church, Butts is president of the State University of New York, College at Old Westbury* NEWSCOM

Following one of these emotional events, Butts found himself immersed in a riot and participated in the firebombing of a local store. Shortly thereafter, he renounced violence.

Just before graduating in 1972 with a bachelor's degree in philosophy, Butts was approached by two young seminarians from Union Theological Seminary in New York who were recruiting students for their school. Butts attended the seminary and received a master of divinity degree. He later earned a doctor of ministry degree in church and public policy from Drew University in New Jersey. While attending the seminary, Butts raised eyebrows by advocating civil rights for gays, a group he had once denounced. He has continued to defend this position.

Butts was recruited as a junior minister in 1972 by William Epps, an assistant minister at Abyssinian Baptist Church in Harlem. During this time, Butts's responsibilities included making hospital visits and conducting funeral services. From the beginning, Butts's realized that the Abyssinian pulpit provided a great foundation from which to preach, and he became vocal in his opposition to police brutality, along with any other form of violence.

Since assuming the pastoral role at Abyssinian Baptist Church, which boasts more than 5,000 parishioners, Butts has remained involved in the community. He cofounded the Abyssinian Development Corporation, a community-based organization that has donated $300 million to housing and commercial development projects in Harlem. He also assisted in establishing Harlem's Thurgood Marshall Academy for Learning and Social Change, a public school. Butts is also president of the State University of New York College at Old Westbury, served as president of the Council of Churches of the City of New York, and sat on the board of the Harlem YMCA.

Butts has received numerous honors and awards for his service to the community, including the Louise Fisher Morris Humanitarian Award. His campaign to eliminate negative billboard advertising in central Harlem and throughout New York City garnered national attention and sparked similar efforts throughout the country.

KATIE CANNON (1950–)

Presbyterian Minister, Educator, Feminist. Katie Geneva Cannon was born January 3, 1950, in Kannapolis, North Carolina. At age twelve, she began working as a domestic alongside her aunt, and later realized that her only way out of a life of menial labor was through education. As she approached adulthood, Cannon found that only two roads were available to most African American women in her community: they could either work in the local mill or become schoolteachers. Given the role that teachers had played in her personal growth and development, she found the academic environment more appealing, and it also offered her a modicum of protection against the racial biases of the day. African Americans were prohibited from public places in Kannapolis, such as the library and the local pool, and Cannon was determined to escape.

Cannon enrolled in Barber-Scotia College in Concord, North Carolina, and participated in workshops and classes offered at a nearby Presbyterian Church. She graduated with a B.S. degree in 1971, after rising to the top of her senior class. The following fall, Cannon enrolled at Johnson C. Smith Seminary of the Interdenominational Theological Center (ITC) in Atlanta, which was one of the two accredited African American seminaries at the time. During her time there, Cannon was exposed to every aspect of the ministry. Majoring in Old Testament studies, she was one of only four women in her class. Cannon received a master's degree in divinity in 1974.

Cannon served as pastor at the Ascension Presbyterian Church in New York City for three years. Her work there was followed by an administrative position at the New York Theological Seminary. In New York City, she discovered feminism, studied Christian ethics, and began writing about black women. She resumed her scholarly endeavors and attended Union Theological Seminary in Richmond, Virginia, where she received a master's degree in philosophy, followed by a Ph.D. in 1983.

Cannon served as an associate professor of Christian ethics at Philadelphia's Temple University and also taught at the Episcopal Divinity School and New York Theological Seminary. She is the Annie Scales Rogers Professor of Christian Ethics at Union Theological Seminary in Richmond, Virginia. Cannon has written numerous articles and has published or edited a number of books, including *Black Womanist Ethics* (1988); a compilation of essays called *Katie's Canon: Womanism and the Soul of the Black Community* (1995); and *Teaching Preaching: Isaac Rufus Clark and Black Sacred Rhetoric* (2002).

ALBERT CLEAGE JR.

See Jaramogi Abebe Agyeman.

JOHNNIE COLEMON (1920s–)

Educator, Religious Leader. The only child of John Haley and Lula Haley Parker, Johnnie Colemon was named after her father, who wanted a boy. Colemon grew up in Mississippi during the 1920s. A graduate of Union Academy in Mississippi and then Wiley College in Texas, Colemon became a schoolteacher in Mississippi and later moved to Chicago to teach. Colemon was diagnosed in 1953 with an incurable disease and told she had only six months to live. However, all of her symptoms had disappeared by 1956 after she moved to Kansas City to study at the Unity School of

Christianity. Colemon faced racial discrimination at the Unity School. Just before graduating, she threatened to leave the school to protest the overt racism she had experienced. As a concession, she was allowed to live on campus and eat in the campus cafeteria. Her South Side Chicago church began as a study group in 1956 with only five members. In 1958, she named her group the Christ Universal Temple, and in 1963 she moved to the Chatham section of South Chicago.

In the early 1970s, Colemon served as the first African American president of the Association of Unity Churches. She continued to encounter pronounced racism within the predominately white denomination. Consequently, in 1974, she formed the Universal Foundation for Better Living (UFBL), an association of churches devoted to the "positive thinking" derived from the New Thought movement. The UFBL sponsors the Johnnie Colemon Institute and the Johnnie Colemon Theological Seminary in Carol City, Florida, devoted to teaching Colemon's New Thought doctrines. Colemon also began a broadcast ministry in the 1980s. Teaching her congregation to discover the power of God within them, she has been a longtime advocate of holy materialism and practical Christianity. Colemon published *Open Your Mind and Be Healed* in 1997.

JAMES H. CONE (1938–)

Writer, Theologian, Educator. James Hall Cone was born in Fordyce, Arkansas, in 1938 and was raised in the small town of Bearden, Arkansas. The segregation and racism Cone experienced as a child led him to question how the whites in town could consider themselves good Christians. At sixteen years old, James Cone was called to the ministry and became a pastor a year later. He received a B.A. from Philander Smith College in 1958, a B.D. from Garrett Evangelical Seminary in 1961, and an M.A. in 1963 and Ph.D. in 1965 from Northwestern University. After teaching at Philander Smith College and Adrian College during the 1960s, Cone moved in 1969 to Union Theological Seminary in New York, where he became the Charles A. Briggs Professor of Systematic Theology in 1977.

Cone is the author of numerous books, including *Black Theology and Black Power* (1969); *The Spirituals and the Blues* (1972); *God of the Oppressed* (1975); *My Soul Looks Black* (1982); *For My People: Black Theology and the Black Church* (1984); *Martin and Malcolm and America: A Dream or a Nightmare* (1991); and *Risks of Faith: The Emergence of a Black Theology of Liberation, 1968–1998* (1999). He has also contributed to numerous journals, magazines, and anthologies.

Perhaps more than any other African American theologian, Cone has provided a systematic exposition of the argument that since God, according to the Bible, is on the side of the poor and oppressed, then in the American context, God sides with the black liberation struggle. Cone has made this argument using diverse sources, including the writings of modern European theologians such as Karl Barth and the writings and speeches of Malcolm X and Martin Luther King Jr. Cone has worked painstakingly for decades to build ties between black, feminist, and third-world liberation theologians.

SUZAN JOHNSON COOK (1957–)

Writer, Baptist Minister. Reverend Suzan Denise Johnson Cook was born on January 28, 1957, in New York City. She was raised in the Bronx, and was a mass communications studies major at Emerson College in Boston when she traveled to Ghana as an exchange student. While she was in Africa, she entertained notions of joining the ministry. After receiving her bachelor's degree in 1976, she enrolled at the United Theological Seminary, where she received a doctor of ministry degree in 1991. Just as her role model, Presbyterian minister Katie Cannon, had earlier found, entering the pastorship was difficult for a woman, but Cook persevered. Eager to assist other women in pursuing the ministry, she later directed Black Women in the Ministry, a program sponsored by the New York City Mission Society, designed to encourage other African American women to pursue the ministry.

In 1983, Cook began eleven years of preaching at Mariner's Temple, the oldest Baptist facility in Manhattan. Her rapport with the small congregation led her to become the first African American women elected as senior pastor of a Baptist church in the United States. Her preaching skills won her recognition as one of the "15 Greatest Black Women Preachers" by *Ebony* magazine in November 1997.

During her years with the church, membership swelled from sixty to more than 1,000. Cook became the first woman to be appointed chaplain of the New York City Police Department in 1990 when then Mayor David Dinkins selected her. Three years later, President Bill Clinton chose her for a White House fellowship, the first female minister to be so recognized. She subsequently served on President Clinton's National Advisory Board on Race.

Cook is the cofounder and chief operating officer of JONCO Productions, a sales, management, and diversity firm with a speakers bureau and media and book distribution. She is also an advocate for children and youth and served as the executive director of the Multiethnic Center for Children and Families. Cook lives in New York City with her husband and two sons.

Cook has authored a number of books, including *Too Blessed to Be Stressed* (1998); *Praying for the Men in Your Life* (2003); *Live Like You're Blessed* (2006), and *Moving*

Up: Ten Steps to Turning Your Life Around and Getting to the Top! (2008). She also edited *Wise Women Bearing Gifts: Joys and Struggles of Their Faith* (1988), and *Sister to Sister: Devotions for and from African American Women* (Vol. 1: 1995, Vol. 2: 1999), which was released as an audio book in 2003.

ALEXANDER CRUMMELL
See chapter 8, Black Nationalism.

WALLACE D. FARD (c. 1877–c. 1934)

Religious Leader. W. D. Fard's background is fiercely contested. According to the Nation of Islam, Fard was born in Mecca in 1877 to a black man named Alfonso and a Caucasian woman. Members of the Nation believed that Fard had been educated in England and at the University of Southern California, and that he had been trained as an Arabian diplomat. The Federal Bureau of Investigation, however, contended that Fard was born in New Zealand or Oregon to either Hawaiian or Polynesian parents (possibly one parent was British), and that he was convicted as a bootlegger during the Prohibition period. In 1926 he received a sentence of six months to six years for selling drugs in California.

Muhammad Speaks *Newspaper, Chicago, February 26, 1964.* *The man who became the Nation of Islam's spirtual leader, Elijah Muhammad, began the publication of this newspaper in 1961. This edition's headline story marks the anniversary of the birth of Wallace D. Fard, the movement's founder.* **BETTMANN/ CORBIS**

After his release from prison in 1929, Fard moved to Detroit, where he sold silk and raincoats as a door-to-door salesman. He also began advising his customers on diet and health and teaching them about the religion of black people in Africa and Asia, which he said was their true religion. Fard had clearly been influenced by the teachings of the Moorish Science Temple and the Ahmadiyya Muslim movement, an Islamic splinter group that preached the imminent arrival of the *mahdi* or messiah. Fard told his listeners of the one true God, Allah, and presented himself as the intermediary between God and humanity. He claimed that Allah was soon to destroy the wicked white world and establish a heaven on earth for his followers. Fard taught his followers that they were not American, that they owed no allegiance to the American flag, and that they should discard their "slave names." His mission, however, was to achieve "freedom, justice, and equality" for African Americans. He established a University of Islam to teach African Americans the truth about their past, and a paramilitary organization, the Fruit of Islam. Fard attracted numerous followers, perhaps as many as 8,000 within the African American community in Detroit. His most capable follower was a Georgia-born man named Elijah Poole, later known as Elijah Muhammad. In 1931, Fard designated Elijah Muhammad as his supreme minister.

The already considerable interest of the Detroit police in Fard's activities increased further in November 1932 when one of his followers killed a white neighbor as a sacrifice to Allah. Fard strongly denied that he had ordered the killing, asserting that his teachings had been misunderstood. Still, the police, fearing the growing strength of Fard's movement, put pressure on him to leave Detroit. Lowering his profile, Fard was able to remain in Detroit for several months, transferring control of the movement to Elijah Muhammad during that time. In May 1933, Fard was arrested for disturbing the peace, and he finally consented to demands from the police that he leave the city.

Fard's later life is as mysterious as his early years. It is said that he moved to Chicago and that Elijah Muhammad kept in contact with him for about one year, but his whereabouts after June 1934 are unknown. Following Elijah Muhammad's guidance, most members of the Nation of Islam continue to regard Fard as Allah, who appeared in person to lead African Americans.

LOUIS FARRAKHAN

See chapter 8, Black Nationalism.

FATHER DIVINE (1879–1965)

Religious Leader, Organization Founder. Father Divine was born George Baker in 1879 in Rockville, Maryland. In 1902, he moved to Baltimore. Baker visited California in 1906 and attended the Azusa Street Revival, which marked the beginning of Pentecostalism. After returning to Baltimore the following year, he adopted a new moniker, The Messenger. He also became associated with Sam Morris, an African American from Pennsylvania who called himself Father Jehovia, and John Hickerson, also known as "Reverend Bishop St. John the Divine," in a house church. All three men had been influenced by the New Thought movement of the Unity Church, and considered themselves to be inwardly divine. After a series of personal and theological quarrels, the three men parted company in 1912.

In 1914, Father Divine moved to Valdosta, Georgia. Threatened by local authorities, he left Georgia the same year. After travels in the South, he settled in Brooklyn in 1917, where he worked as an "employment agent" for the few followers still loyal to him. His first marriage was to an African American woman named Peninniah, whom he apparently met while living in Brooklyn. Calling his meeting place "Heaven," he soon attracted a larger following and moved to Sayville on Long Island in 1919. It was at this time that Father Divine began to provide shelter and food to the poor and homeless.

Spiritually, Father Divine fostered what amounted to a massive cooperative, based on the communal spirit of the Last Supper. His movement practiced complete racial equality. Services included songs and impromptu sermons and were conducted without Scripture readings or use of clergy. Once, he was sentenced to six months in jail as a public nuisance, but the ensuing publicity only enhanced his popularity.

The Divine movement, a nonritualistic group whose followers worshipped their leader as God incarnate on earth, grew rapidly in the 1930s and 1940s, with Father Divine speaking around the country and publicizing his views in *New Day*, a weekly magazine published by his organization. He set up Peace Mission Kingdom (a program through which members were able to obtain food, shelter, a job, and a reformed life with the mission's assistance) in the United States and throughout the world. After Peninniah's death in 1946, Father Divine married his "Sweet Angel," a twenty-one-year-old Canadian stenographer, known thereafter as Mother Divine.

Father Divine died peacefully at Woodmont, an estate that he had acquired in the Philadelphia suburbs in 1965. His wife pledged to continue the work of the movement.

ELIJAH JOHN FISHER (1858–1915)

Community Activist, Baptist Minister. Elijah Fisher was an example of the great charismatic African American preachers of the nineteenth and early twentieth centuries. With very little formal education, he built large religious institutions, promoted racial pride, and espoused the cause of African Americans as a people.

Born in LaGrange, Georgia, in 1858, the youngest of eight boys in a family of seventeen children, Fisher's father was a nonordained preacher for a Baptist congregation that met in a white church. Fisher worked in a Baptist parsonage as a boy, and was taught to read by a former houseworker and a white missionary. In his teens, he worked in mines in Alabama and then as a butler, while studying theology on his own time. Though he lost a leg in a mining accident, Fisher became pastor of several small country churches in his early twenties, and in 1889 he became head of the Mount Olive Baptist Church in Atlanta. He enrolled in the Atlanta Baptist Seminary, passed his examinations, and went to preach in Nashville. Fisher eventually moved to Chicago, where he led the Olivet Baptist Church from 1902 until his death in 1915.

Throughout his life, Fisher continued his studies, preached from coast to coast, and involved churches in youth work, food programs for poor people, and African American businesses. An active member of the Republican Party, Fisher strongly criticized African Americans who advised their brethren to rely solely on the goodwill of whites and publicly criticized Booker T. Washington for not speaking out against lynching.

FLOYD FLAKE (1945–)

African Methodist Episcopal Leader, Member of Congress. Born on January 30, 1945, in Los Angeles, Floyd Flake came from humble beginnings. He was one of thirteen children, born to a father who worked as a janitor. Flake graduated with a B.A. degree from Wilberforce University in 1967 and an M.A. from Payne Theological Seminary in 1970. He was subsequently employed as a social worker, as a marketing analyst, and as a student dean before being called to pastor Allen AME Church in Queens in 1976. The church prospered under his leadership, and by 1986 Allen AME had a membership of 6,000.

Flake also founded a Christian school at Allen and headed the Allen Home Care Agency for the Elderly. In the latter role, he supervised the construction of a $12 million facility. In 1986, Flake ran as a Democrat and won a seat in the U.S. House of Representatives from the Sixth New York Congressional District. He served in Congress for eleven years, while remaining pastor of Allen AME Church. He was particularly interested in small business and affirmative action issues, and was influential in securing federal set-aside funding for minority-owned small businesses. In November 1997, Flake resigned his seat in Congress so that he could devote his energies again to his church, now the Greater Allen AME Cathedral of New York.

Flake is a fellow at the Manhattan Institute for Policy Research and is president of Wilberforce University in Wilberforce, Ohio. He has published several books, including *Practical Virtues: Everyday Values and Devotions for African American Families* (2003), written with his wife, M. Elaine McCollins Flake, and *African American Church Management Handbook* (2005), written with his wife and Edwin C. Reed. In 2006, Flake co-chaired Republican Ken Blackwell's unsuccessful bid for the governorship of Ohio.

HENRY HIGHLAND GARNET

See chapter 8, Black Nationalism.

"SWEET DADDY" GRACE (1881–1960)

Religious Leader. Grace was born in 1881 in the Cape Verde Islands as Marceline Manoël de Graça. He was later known as Charles Manuel "Sweet Daddy" Grace. He immigrated to New Bedford, Massachusetts, around 1908, and probably opened his first church there in 1921. Five years later, he opened a church in Charlotte, North Carolina. Grace's church, the United House of Prayer for All People, had an ecstatic worship style, and speaking in tongues was encouraged. Grace claimed great powers, including the power of faith healing. He claimed that "Grace has given God a vacation, and since God is on His vacation don't worry Him. ... If you sin against God, Grace can save you, but if you sin against Grace, God cannot save you." Even the numerous products that he sold, such as "Daddy Grace" coffee, tea, soaps, and hand creams, were reputed to have healing powers. At the time of his death in 1960, the church had 375 branches and about 25,000 members nationwide.

BARBARA C. HARRIS (1930–)

Episcopal Bishop. Barbara Clementine Harris was born in Philadelphia in 1930. She graduated from Philadelphia High School for girls in 1948 and enrolled in college, but did not graduate. She was hired by Joseph Baker Associates, a public relations firm, in 1958. In 1960, Harris married, but the marriage ended in divorce three years later. She actively participated in the struggle for civil rights and marched with Martin Luther King Jr.

Harris, who felt a strong connection with the church she attended as a child—St. Barnabas Episcopal Church, where her mother was choir director—was a strong advocate for women's rights in the church. She was ordained a deacon in the Protestant Episcopal Church in 1979, and became a priest one year later. Harris served as the priest-in-charge of an Episcopalian church in Norristown, Pennsylvania, as interim pastor of a church in Philadelphia, and as executive director of the publishing company associated with the Episcopal Church. In February 1989, she was consecrated as suffragan, or assistant bishop, for the diocese of Massachusetts. Harris thus became the first woman bishop in the history of the Episcopal Church. Although her appointment stirred controversy among conservative members of the clergy, she received a considerable amount of support. Her supporters argued that, despite her lack of a college degree or seminary training, she would broaden the outreach of the church. She remained a strong spokesperson for women in the clergy throughout her tenure as bishop. Harris retired in November 2002, shortly before she reached the mandatory retirement age of seventy-two. The following year, Harris began serving as assistant bishop for the diocese of Washington, D.C.

LEMUEL HAYNES

See chapter 6, Africans in America.

JAMES AUGUSTINE HEALY (1830–1900)

Roman Catholic Bishop. Born in 1830 in Macon, Georgia, James Augustine Healy was the son of an Irish planter, Michael Morris Healy, and an enslaved woman. Although born enslaved, Healy later became the first African American Roman Catholic bishop in the United States. (Healy's brother, Patrick Francis Healy, was a Jesuit priest who served as president of Georgetown University from 1873 to 1882.) For twenty-five years, James Healy presided over a diocese covering the states of Maine and New Hampshire.

Healy received his education in the North, first at Franklin Park Quaker School in Burlington, New York, and later at College of the Holy Cross in Worcester, Massachusetts, from which he graduated in 1949 with honors. Healy continued his studies abroad and was ordained in Paris at Notre Dame Cathedral in 1854 before returning to the United States.

Healy became the pastor of a predominantly Irish congregation in Boston that was at first reluctant to accept him. Fr. Healy performed his priestly duties with devotion and eventually won the respect and admiration of his parishioners, particularly after they witnessed his commitment during a typhoid epidemic. Thereafter, he was named assistant to Bishop John Fitzpatrick of Boston, who appointed him chancellor and entrusted him with a wide variety of additional responsibilities. In 1875, Healy became bishop of Portland, Maine, and, in this capacity, he founded sixty parishes, as well as eighteen schools. He died in Portland on August 15, 1900.

JOSEPH HARRISON JACKSON (c. 1904–1990)

Baptist Leader. From 1953 to 1982, Joseph H. Jackson was the president of the National Baptist Convention, U.S.A., the third largest Protestant denomination in the United States and the largest of the predominantly African American churches. Born in Rudyard, Mississippi, around 1904, Jackson received a B.A. from Jackson College, an M.A. from Creighton University, and a B.D. from Colgate Rochester Divinity School. After serving as pastor of several churches in Mississippi, Jackson accepted a call to pastor the historic Olivet Baptist Church in Chicago in 1941. He maintained a conservative stance during the civil rights movement. He was supportive of the efforts of Martin Luther King Jr. during the Montgomery bus boycott of 1955, but criticized the massive nonviolent civil disobedience campaigns of the early 1960s.

Jackson emphasized the need for African Americans to build a viable economic base. His favorite slogan was "From Protest to Production." He was supportive of Baptist missions in Africa and attempted to finance them by developing farmland in Liberia.

T. D. JAKES (1957–)

Writer, Pentecostal Minister. Thomas Dexter Jakes, a West Virginia native, was born June 9, 1957, in South Charleston, West Virginia, and came from a United Pentecostal background. He began preaching when he was a student at West Virginia State University. After the chemical plant that employed him closed, and his father died of kidney disease, Jakes devoted himself to the ministry full time. Initially, he ministered in Morgantown, West Virginia, and then in Dallas, Texas, where the Potter's House, his nondenominational megachurch congregation, was founded in 1996. His church has approximately 35,000 members. Jakes's services and sermons are broadcast on several television networks, including Black Entertainment Television (BET).

As one of the most famous Pentecostal ministers in the United States, Jakes travels widely to lead revival services that draw thousands of attendees. In 2005, *Time* magazine named him one of America's twenty-five most influential evangelicals. His books are aimed at encouraging and uplifting African American men and women. His two most popular books, which are filled with extensive passages from and interpretation of the Bible, are *Women, Thou Art Loosed* (1996), which was made into a movie in 2004, and *The Lady, Her Lover, and Her Lord* (1998). Jakes's other works include a self-empowerment book, *He-Motions: Even Strong Men Struggle* (2004), which became a best seller; *Ten Commandments of Working in a Hostile Environment* (2005); *Promises from God for Single Women* (2005); the novel *Not Easily Broken* (2006); *Before You Do: Making Great Decisions that You Won't Regret* (2008); and *Memory Quilt: A Christmas Story for Our Times* (2009). Jakes's record label, Dexterity Sounds/EMI Gospel, won a Grammy Award in 2004 for Best Gospel Choir or Chorus Album for *A Wing and a Prayer*, recorded by Jakes and the Potter's House Mass Choir.

ABSALOM JONES (1746–1818)

Episcopal Priest. Absalom Jones rose from slavery to become the first African American Episcopal priest and the principal founder of the African Church of St. Thomas, the first African American Episcopal church. Jones was born enslaved in Sussex, Delaware, on November 6, 1746. In 1762, his mother, five brothers, and sisters were sold, and Jones was taken to Philadelphia, where he worked in a store and learned to read and write. In 1778, he began to purchase his freedom, but he was not formally manumitted until 1784.

Jones became a licensed Methodist lay preacher in 1787 at Philadelphia's St. George's Methodist Church along with his colleague Richard Allen. He and Allen focused on teaching and pastoral work for the congregation's black population. In May 1787, Jones joined Allen and others in forming the Free African Society. The African Church of St. Thomas was dedicated in 1794. As the official leader of the church, Jones seemed an obvious choice to become a lay reader. He was ordained a deacon on August 6, 1795. Jones became the first African American Episcopal priest in 1804. He died in 1818.

LEONTINE T. C. KELLY (1920–)

United Methodist Bishop. In 1984, the Western Jurisdictional Conference of the United Methodist Church elected Leontine Turpeau Current Kelly as the first African American woman bishop in any large U.S. denomination. Kelly was born in Washington, D.C., in 1920. She received a master of divinity degree from

Union Theological Seminary in Richmond, Virginia, in 1969. She served as a schoolteacher, pastor of Virginia churches, and staff member of the Virginia Conference of Churches before being elected a bishop in the United Methodist Church. Kelly presided over the California-Nevada conference, and served there until she retired in 1989. Kelly has been a civil and human rights activist and has taught at the Pacific School of Religion in Berkeley, California. In 2000, Kelly was inducted into the National Women's Hall of Fame in Seneca Falls, New York.

ISAAC LANE (1834–1937)

Educational Administrator, Colored Methodist Episcopal Bishop Isaac Lane was born enslaved in Jackson, Tennessee, in 1834. Primarily self-educated, in 1856 Lane was granted a license to exhort (a lesser category assigned to African Americans, who were forbidden to preach) in the Methodist Episcopal Church South. Lane was ordained a minister in 1865.

In 1873, he was made a bishop of the Colored Methodist Episcopal (CME) Church (now known as the Christian Methodist Episcopal Church) at a salary so low that he had to raise cotton to supplement his income and support his wife and eleven children. His missionary work was instrumental in establishing the CME Church in Louisiana and Texas. In the 1880s, he established Lane College in Jackson, Tennessee, with $9,000 that he had raised. He died in 1937.

JARENA LEE (1783–1849)

Women's Rights Activist, African Methodist Episcopal Minister. Born in 1783 in Cape May, New Jersey, Jarena Lee worked as a servant for a family that lived near Philadelphia. She had a conversion experience in 1804, but was unable to find a church with which to unite until she heard Richard Allen, founder of the African Methodist Episcopal Church, preach in Philadelphia. Lee experienced a call to preach in 1808, and she sought permission to do so from Allen on two occasions. On her first attempt in 1809 to seek Allen's sanction, he refused her request. Eight years later, however, he granted it and licensed her as a preacher.

Subsequently, Lee traveled throughout the North and Midwest, and many of her listeners, especially women, were moved by her eloquent preaching. After Allen's death in 1831, male African Methodist Episcopal preachers in Philadelphia attempted to deny her permission to preach from their pulpits, but she continued her ministry, despite such harassment.

In 1848, Jarena Lee attempted to form a link among female African Methodist Episcopal preachers for mutual support, but her organizational efforts soon fell apart. Many African American women, especially within the African Methodist Episcopal Church, view Jarena Lee as a courageous foremother and a model for church activism.

GEORGE LIELE (c. 1750–1820)

Baptist Leader. Born enslaved in Virginia around 1750, George Liele was sold to a Georgian plantation owner as a young child. He experienced a Christian conversion after hearing a sermon by Matthew Moore, a white preacher, in 1773. Liele began conducting worship services on nearby plantations and, with Moore's sponsorship, soon became the first ordained African American Baptist preacher in the American colonies. Liele preached at the Silver Bluff Church in Silver Bluff, South Carolina, probably the first independent African American congregation formed in North America, as well as at locations outside Savannah. One of his notable converts was Andrew Bryan, who founded the First African Baptist Church in Savannah.

Some whites attempted to re-enslave Liele, but a British officer in Savannah ensured that Liele would remain free. Liele immigrated to Jamaica in 1784, accompanied by a woman he had converted and married in Savannah. He started a school and preached to a small Baptist congregation in Kingston.

EUGENE A. MARINO (1934–2000)

Roman Catholic Archbishop. Born May 29, 1934, in Biloxi, Mississippi, Eugene Antonio Marino received his Catholic training at Epiphany Apostolic College and St. Joseph Seminary. He was ordained to the priesthood in 1962. The next year, Marino was made director of St. Joseph Seminary. He also continued his studies at Catholic University of America, Loyola University in New Orleans, and Fordham University, where he earned a master of arts degree in 1967. In 1971, Marino was named vicar general of the Josephites. He served as an auxiliary bishop in Washington, D.C., after his ordination to the episcopate in 1974. Marino became the first African American Roman Catholic archbishop in 1988, when he was appointed to preside over the Atlanta archdiocese. He retired in 1990 in the midst of a sex scandal, when an affair he was having with a woman was exposed. Marino died of an apparent heart attack on November 12, 2000, in Manhasset, New York. He was sixty-six years old.

CHARLES H. MASON (1866–1961)

Holiness Leader. Born in 1866 to formerly enslaved parents on a farm outside Memphis, Tennessee, Charles

H. Mason was converted to Christianity at fourteen years old and joined a Missionary Baptist church. Mason obtained a preaching license from the Missionary Baptists in 1893 and, in the same year, he claimed to have had the experience of entire sanctification, and aligned himself with the Holiness movement. He had little formal education beyond a brief period of study at the Arkansas Bible College.

In 1895, the Baptists expelled him because of his beliefs on sanctification. Mason then held Holiness revivals in Mississippi with the help of Charles Price Jones, a prolific writer of hymns and gospel songs, and others. His meetings were held in an abandoned cotton-gin house in Lexington, Mississippi. Despite an armed attack, probably by hostile African Americans, he won many new converts with his revivalist preaching. In 1897, Mason and Jones founded a new Holiness church and called it the Church of God in Christ. They worked together harmoniously over the next decade.

In 1907, Mason attended the Azusa Street Revival conducted by William Seymour in Los Angeles, and he received the gift of speaking in tongues. He believed that the ability to speak in tongues was a necessary precondition for baptism of the spirit. He and Jones disagreed on this issue and parted company. Mason reformed the Church of God in Christ along the lines of his new spiritual insights. Over the next four decades, Mason, as bishop, general overseer, and "chief apostle," shepherded his denomination through a period of tremendous growth. He traveled extensively, preaching at revivals throughout the United States and around the world. He was imprisoned for making pacifist statements during World War I. Mason died in 1961.

VASHTI MURPHY McKENZIE (1947–)

African Methodist Episcopal Bishop. Vashti Murphy was born on May 28, 1947, and raised in Baltimore, Maryland. She attended Morgan State University until her junior year, when she married professional basketball player Stan McKenzie. Following a brief period in Phoenix, the couple returned to the Baltimore area. McKenzie completed her bachelor's degree at the University of Maryland. After graduation, she worked as a fashion model and a newspaper, radio, and television journalist. In her late thirties, McKenzie realized that she was called to preach. With the support of her husband and three children, she enrolled in the Howard University School of Divinity, eventually earning a master of divinity degree. McKenzie later earned a doctor of ministry degree from United Theological Seminary in Dayton, Ohio.

After graduating from Howard, McKenzie was assigned to a small church in Chesapeake City, Maryland. In 1990, she became the first female pastor of Baltimore's Payne Memorial African Methodist Episcopal (AME) Church. One of the few female senior pastors in the AME Church at the time, McKenzie had to overcome the obstacle of sexism in her first years at the church. During her tenure, the church grew from around three hundred members to nearly 1,700, and established fifteen new ministries. McKenzie worked to help the church erase a long-standing division between itself and the community. The congregation's nonprofit community service agency, Payne Memorial Outreach, built many successful community programs, including summer youth camps, a food pantry, and a job service that supported more than 1,000 clients.

On July 11, 2000, McKenzie was elected as the first female bishop in the 213-year history of the AME Church. As bishop, McKenzie was assigned to lead the Eighteenth Episcopal District in southeast Africa, which encompasses Lesotho, Botswana, Mozambique, and Swaziland. In 2005, she became the head of the AME Church's Council of Bishops. She also became prelate for the Thirteenth Episcopal District, which comprises Tennessee and Kentucky. In her capacity as bishop, McKenzie has addressed the African and African American HIV/AIDS crisis, economic development, church membership, and educational development.

McKenzie is the author of *Not without a Struggle: Leadership Development for African American Women in Ministry* (1996); *Strength in the Struggle: Leadership Development for Women* (2001); *Journey to the Well* (2002); and *Swapping Housewives: Rachel and Jacob and Leah* (2007). McKenzie is also the recipient of numerous awards and honors from a number of civic, educational, business, and governmental organizations. *Ebony* magazine cited her in its "Year of the Black Woman" issue in 1992 and named her one of the "15 Greatest Black Women Preachers" in 1997. She received a letter of commendation from the United Nations High Commissioner for Refugees for Payne Memorial AME Church's support of the Love Baton Project in 1996. McKenzie delivered the closing day invocation at the 2000 Democratic National Convention.

WILLIAM HENRY MILES (1828–1892)

Colored Methodist Episcopal Bishop. Born enslaved in Kentucky in 1828, William Miles was manumitted by his owner in her will. He joined the Methodist Episcopal Church, South, and soon felt a call to preach. He was ordained a deacon in 1959. Uncertain about his church affiliation after the Civil War, he investigated the possibility of joining the African Methodist Episcopal Zion Church, but eventually abandoned that idea. He remained a preacher in the Methodist Episcopal Church, South, until its African American members who had decided not to join the African Methodist Episcopal or African Methodist Episcopal Zion churches were allowed to form a separate denomination, the Colored Methodist Episcopal (CME) Church.

At the initial General Conference of the Colored Methodist Episcopal Church in 1870, Miles was elected as one of the denomination's two bishops. He was an active advocate for African American colleges, especially those affiliated with the CME Church, such as Lane College in Jackson, Tennessee, and Paine Seminary in Atlanta, Georgia. He died in 1892.

PAUL SYLVESTER MORTON (1950–)

Baptist Bishop, Recording Artist. Paul Sylvester Morton was born in Windsor, Ontario, Canada. He moved to New Orleans in 1972, and in 1975 became pastor of the Greater St. Stephen Missionary Baptist Church. Under his leadership, the ministry grew from 647 to more than 20,000 members. In 1992, Morton founded the Full Gospel Baptist Church Fellowship, and his church thereafter became Greater St. Stephen Full Gospel Baptist Church. In 1997, Morton's ministry purchased a former military base and renamed it St. Stephen City. The development provides affordable housing to more than seventy-five families, and includes an apartment complex, St. Stephen Manor, which provides housing to over fifty families.

Morton is host of *Changing a Generation*, a radio and TV show. His books include *Why Kingdoms Fall: The Journey from Breakdown to Restoration* (1999) and *The Enemy inside Your Mind* (2005). Morton is also an accomplished musician. His recordings include *Crescent City Fire* (1999), *Still Standing* (2006), and *Cry Your Last Tear* (2008), recorded with the Full Gospel Baptist Church Fellowship Mass Choir.

AVA MUHAMMAD (1951–)

Nation of Islam Leader, Lawyer. Born in 1951, Ava Muhammad grew up in a middle-class Methodist home in Columbus, Ohio. After graduating from the Georgetown University Law Center in 1975, she became a criminal defense attorney. In 1979, Muhammad was diagnosed with cancer. She began searching for spiritual support, looking first to the church of her youth, but ultimately converting to Islam after hearing Louis Farrakhan speak in New York City. After joining the Nation of Islam in 1981, Ava Muhammad began to work as Farrakhan's attorney. She defended him in 1986 when he was arrested following his return from Libya, on which President Ronald Reagan had placed a travel ban. In another high-profile case, she won a defamation lawsuit against the *New York Post*, which in a 1994 story implicated Farrakhan in the assassination of Malcolm X.

In addition to her legal work, Ava Muhammad gained prominence and recognition in the Nation of Islam, despite the limitations the organization had historically placed on women. She published *The Myths and Misconceptions of the Role of Women in Islam* in 1996. The following year she delivered a speech at the Million Woman March, speaking on the topic, "The Further Development of Black Women Who Are or Wish to Become Professionals, Entrepreneurs, and/or Politicians." On July 28, 1998, Muhammad was appointed by Louis Farrakhan as southern regional minister with the Nation of Islam. In this role, Muhammad became the first woman in Islam's 1,400-year history to be appointed to a leadership position of the cloth. She has published a number of other books, including *The Force and Power of Being* (1997) and *Real Love* (1999). She serves as the national spokesperson for the Nation of Islam.

ELIJAH MUHAMMAD

See chapter 8, Black Nationalism.

KHALLID ABDUL MUHAMMAD

See chapter 8, Black Nationalism.

HAROLD ROBERT PERRY (1916–1991)

Educator, Roman Catholic Religious Leader. When Harold Robert Perry was consecrated a bishop of New Orleans on January 16, 1966, he became the first African American Roman Catholic bishop in the United States in the twentieth century. One of six children, Perry was born the son of a rice-mill worker and a domestic cook in Lake Charles, Louisiana, in 1916. He entered the Divine Word Seminary in Mississippi when he was thirteen and was ordained a priest in 1944. He spent the next fourteen years in parish work.

In 1958, Perry was appointed rector of the seminary. Louisiana has the largest concentration of African American Catholics in the South. In 1989, Perry was one of thirteen African American bishops serving Catholic parishes around the nation. He died on July 17, 1991.

ADAM CLAYTON POWELL SR. (1865–1953)

Baptist Minister, Community Activist. Adam Clayton Powell Sr., father of the U.S. representative from Harlem, was largely responsible for building the Abyssinian Baptist Church into one of the most celebrated African American congregations in the world. Born in Franklin County, Virginia, in 1865, Powell attended a local school and, between sessions, worked in the coal mines of West Virginia. After deciding to enter the ministry, he began his studies at Wayland Academy (now Virginia Union University), working his way through school as a janitor and waiter. He later attended the Yale University School of Divinity and served as pastor of the Immanuel Baptist Church in New Haven, Connecticut, between 1893 and 1908.

In 1908, Powell became pastor of Abyssinian Baptist Church in Harlem. He was a charismatic preacher, and managed to increase the congregation substantially. In 1920, Powell bought land in Harlem for the church at West 138th Street, and by 1923 a new church building had been constructed. Powell was responsible for building one of the first community recreation centers in Harlem. He also established a social/religious education program, and by the mid-1930s Abyssinian Baptist Church, with a membership of more than 14,000, had become one of the largest Protestant congregations in the United States.

During the Great Depression, Powell opened soup kitchens for Harlem residents and served thousands of meals. Later, he and his son campaigned vigorously to expand job opportunities and city services in Harlem. Powell retired as Abyssinian's pastor in 1937. He died in 1953.

FREDERICK K. C. PRICE (1932–)

Pentecostal Leader, Writer. Born on January 3, 1932, in Santa Monica, California, Frederick Kenneth Cercie Price began preaching in a Baptist church in 1955 while also working as a paper cutter. He then pastored African American Methodist Episcopal (AME) and Presbyterian churches before finally joining the Christian and Missionary Alliance at West Washington Community Church in 1965. In 1970, he experienced a "baptism of the Holy Spirit," and finally felt satisfied with the direction of his ministry.

In 1973, Price and three hundred parishioners moved from West Washington to establish the Crenshaw Christian Center in Inglewood, California. Membership at the church began to grow exponentially as more and more people became interested in Price's neo-Pentecostal message, which was defined, in part, by speaking in tongues, healing, and prosperity teachings. In the 1970s, Price began broadcasting a radio program, *Ever Increasing Faith*, which eventually became a television show. By the early 1980s, the program was broadcast to five major U.S. cities. In 1981, the church purchased the former campus of Pepperdine University and began construction of the 10,146-seat Faith Dome, which was dedicated in 1990. By the early 2000s, *Ever Increasing Faith* aired weekly in fifteen of the country's largest markets, reaching more than fifteen million American households. The Crenshaw Center's congregation had grown to include an estimated 22,000 members by 2002. In addition to its television program, Price's ministry also operates an online network and releases regular podcasts and a quarterly magazine. Price's wife Betty and their son Frederick Jr. also hold leadership positions at the Crenshaw Christian Center.

Price, who had completed two years of study at Los Angeles City College, returned to school at the Friends International Christian University in Merced, California, earning a bachelor's degree in 1978, a doctor of ministry degree in 1988, and a Ph.D. in religious studies in 1992. He has authored more than fifty books, including the

Dr. Frederick K. C. Price, Pastor, Crenshaw Christian Center East, New York City, 2005. *Price founded the Crenshaw Christian Center (CCC) in 1973 in Inglewood, California. The New York CCC was established in 2001.* NEWSCOM

popular *How Faith Works* (1996); *Integrity: The Guarantee for Success* (2000); *Answered Prayer Guaranteed!* (2006); and *Prosperity: Good News for God's People* (2008). Price received an honorary diploma from Rhema Bible Training Center in 1976 and an honorary doctorate of divinity from Oral Roberts University in 1982. In 1998, Price received the Horatio Alger Award and the Kelly Miller Smith Interfaith Award from the Southern Christian Leadership Conference.

JOSEPH CHARLES PRICE (1854–1893)

Civil Rights Activist, African Methodist Episcopal Zion Minister. Born in Elizabeth City, North Carolina, in 1854 to a free mother, Price was educated in a school established for freed African Americans, and later at Shaw and Lincoln universities, graduating from the latter in 1879. At twenty-one years old, he was licensed to preach in the African Methodist Episcopal Zion Church, and he received the ordination of elder six years later. Price was renowned for the eloquence of his public addresses.

Price was most responsible for the African Methodist Episcopal Zion Church's success in establishing a church college—Livingstone College in North Carolina, opened in 1882—after ministers in that denomination had failed in several previous attempts. As president of Livingstone College, he quickly gave his school a solid grounding, both academically and financially. For example, he raised $10,000 for his school during a lecture tour of England. He was an active participant in politics, campaigned for civil rights and prohibition, and assumed such offices as chairman of the Citizens' Equal Rights Association of Washington, D.C. He died from kidney failure in 1893.

WILLIAM JOSEPH SEYMOUR (1870–1922)

Civil Rights Activist, Pentecostal Leader. Born in Centerville, Louisiana, in 1870 to parents who had been enslaved, William Joseph Seymour taught himself to read and write. In 1900, he encountered Martin Knapp, a prominent promoter of Holiness doctrine, and began studying under him. Seymour then suffered a bout of smallpox that left him blind in one eye. He was ordained as an evangelist by the Evening Light Saints, a group that eventually became known as the Church of God (Anderson, Indiana). After moving to Houston, Seymour sat outside the door of white evangelist Charles Parham's segregated classroom while Parham lectured on Christian doctrine and, especially, the importance of speaking in tongues.

In 1906, Seymour moved to Los Angeles to pastor a small African American Holiness church, but his new congregation opposed Seymour's contention that speaking in tongues was an important part of the Christian experience, and dismissed him after one week. Seymour continued to hold religious meetings, attracting an interracial audience. A widely publicized outburst of speaking in tongues brought him an even larger audience, so he moved his Apostolic Faith Gospel Mission to a former African Methodist Episcopal Church building on Azusa Street.

The extremely successful meetings that he held before ecstatic, interracial audiences over the next three years have been acknowledged as the beginning of modern Pentecostalism, both in the United States and around the world. Seymour was greatly saddened when the racial unity displayed in the early stages of Pentecostalism began to break down under the pressures exerted by racial discrimination in the nation at large. He continued to hold services at the Azusa Street mission until his death in 1922.

AL SHARPTON

See chapter 7, Civil Rights.

FRED LEE SHUTTLESWORTH

See chapter 7, Civil Rights.

AMANDA BERRY SMITH (1837–1915)

Evangelist, Missionary. Born in Long Green, Maryland, in 1837, Amanda Berry Smith was manumitted during her childhood after her father paid for her freedom. Smith experienced a spiritual conversion in 1856 and began attending religious meetings faithfully. She resisted identification with any single denomination, and her religious practice was most strongly influenced by Quakers and Methodists. Attendance at the religious meetings of white evangelists Phoebe Palmer and John Inskip introduced her to Holiness doctrine, and she experienced entire sanctification in 1868. Her husband died the following year, and Smith soon became a full-time traveling evangelist. She never sought to breach the barriers against women's ordination erected by male preachers, stating that the calling she had received came directly from God, which was justification enough for her ministry.

From 1878 to 1890, Smith worked as a missionary in England, Ireland, Scotland, India, and Liberia. A Methodist bishop who heard her preach in India stated that he "had never known anyone who could draw and hold so large an audience as Mrs. Smith." After she returned to the United States in 1890, she preached widely and wrote *An Autobiography: The Story of the Lord's Dealings with Amanda Smith, the Colored Evangelist*, published in 1893, an extremely detailed work now regarded as a classic. Her last twenty years were devoted to the construction and management of the Amanda Smith Orphans' Home for African-American Children in Illinois. She died in 1915.

STEPHEN GILL SPOTTSWOOD (1897–1974)

African Methodist Episcopal Zion Bishop, Civil Rights Activist. Bishop of the African Methodist Episcopal Zion Church from 1952 to 1972, and board chairman of the NAACP from 1961 until his death in 1974, Bishop Stephen Gill Spottswood embodied the religious faith and intellectual incisiveness that has produced so many effective African American religious activists.

Spottswood was born in Boston on July 18, 1897. He attended Albright College and Gordon Divinity School, and then received a Ph.D. in divinity from Yale University. Spottswood was president of the Ohio Council of Churches and served on the boards of numerous interfaith conferences, as well as heading the African Methodist Episcopal Zion Church.

His involvement with the NAACP began in 1919, when he joined the organization. He was appointed to the national board in 1955. In 1971, he was at the center of a political storm when he chastised the Nixon administration for its politics toward African Americans. Spottswood refused, under strong pressure from the administration, to retract his comments. He died on December 1, 1974.

GEORGE AUGUSTUS STALLINGS JR. (1948–)

Founder and Leader of Imani Temple African American Catholic Congregation. Born on March 17, 1948, in New Bern, North Carolina, George Stallings is the eldest of six children. He received a B.A. from St. Pius X Seminary in 1970, a B.S. in theology from the University of St. Thomas Aquinas in 1973, and an M.A. in pastoral theology the following year. In 1975, he was granted a licentiate in sacred theology by the University of St. Thomas Aquinas. In 1974, Stallings was ordained a priest and named pastor of St. Teresa of Avila Catholic Church, located in one of Washington, D.C.'s poorest African American neighborhoods. In 1976, while pastor at St. Teresa, Stallings stressed that the contributions of African Americans to Christianity should be recognized and that the Catholic Church must address the needs of African Americans. In an effort to confront what he considered the Catholic Church's racial insensitivity, he made use of what is known as the Rite of Zaire, incorporated jazz and gospel music into the Mass, and added readings by celebrated African American writers to the liturgy. For these actions, Stallings received much criticism from church authorities. In 1988, he was removed from St. Teresa of Avila and named head of evangelism for Washington, D.C.

In 1989, with Stallings still convinced that the Catholic Church was not meeting the cultural, spiritual, and social needs of African American Catholics, he announced that he would leave the diocese to found a new congregation, the Imani Temple African American Catholic Congregation, headquartered in Washington, D.C. Stallings not only advocated that priests be allowed to marry but also believed that women should be able to serve as priests. In 1990, Stallings was excommunicated from the Roman Catholic Church. In 1991, he ordained former Roman Catholic nun Rose Vernell as a priest in his church. Since his 1989 departure from standard Roman Catholicism, Stallings has established six Imani Temples in the United States and one in Nigeria.

Stallings is the author of *I Am ... Living in the Rhythm of God Within: In the Key of G Minor* (2003) and was reportedly working on his autobiography, *Confessions of a Renegade Priest.* He is in demand as a speaker both nationally and internationally.

LEON H. SULLIVAN

See chapter 7, Civil Rights.

GARDNER C. TAYLOR (1918–)

Civil Rights Activist, Baptist Preacher. Reverend Gardner Calvin Taylor is widely revered as the dean of the nation's African American preachers. Taylor received a B.A. degree from Leland College in 1937 and a B.D. degree from the Oberlin Graduate School of Theology in 1940. He has long been a community activist. He demonstrated for civil rights and suffered arrest for civil disobedience with Martin Luther King Jr. in the 1960s, and he introduced Nelson Mandela to a New York audience in 1990.

Taylor was a trusted counselor to former New York mayor David Dinkins. Taylor served on the New York City Board of Education, is the past president of the New York Council of Churches, and the past vice president of the Urban League in New York City. After forty-two years as pastor of the Concord Baptist Church in Brooklyn, which became the most prestigious African American church in the United States, Taylor resigned his post in 1990. In 2000, President Bill Clinton awarded Taylor the Presidential Medal of Freedom, the nation's highest civilian award.

Taylor is considered by some to be the greatest living African American preacher. After retiring, Taylor remained in demand throughout the United States as a lecturer. He has been the recipient of more than one hundred honorary degrees and is the author of the six-volume series, *The Words of Gardner Taylor.*

HOWARD THURMAN (1899–1981)

Writer, Theologian, Civil Rights Activist, Educator. Born in Daytona Beach, Florida, on November 18, 1899, Howard Thurman studied at Morehouse College, Rochester Theological Center, and Haverford College. Thurman, named by *Life* magazine as one of the twelve greatest preachers of the twentieth century, served as a pastor to a Baptist church in Ohio, and, from 1944 to 1953, he pastored an interracial and interdenominational Fellowship church that he founded in San Francisco. He also served as dean of the chapel at Howard University from 1932 to 1944, as well as on the faculty of Boston University from 1953 until his retirement.

Thurman was one of the leading theologians of his time. His books include *The Negro Spiritual Speaks of Life*

The Reverend Gardner C. Taylor, Brooklyn, NY, April 1962. *Taylor (*right*), shown with parishioners after an Easter service, is considered one of the greatest African American preachers. A longtime community activist who was also involved in the civil rights movement, Taylor served as pastor of Brooklyn's Concord Baptist Church for forty-two years until his retirement in 1990.* **AP IMAGES**

and Death (1947) and *This Luminous Darkness: A Personal Interpretation of the Anatomy of Segregation and the Ground of Hope* (1965), about his opposition to segregation and support of the civil rights movement. His autobiography, *With Head and Heart*, was published in 1979. He died on April 10, 1981.

SOJOURNER TRUTH (c. 1797–1883)

Orator, Women's Rights Activist. Sojourner Truth was born Isabella Baumfree (or Bomefree) around 1797 on the estate of Colonel Johannes Hardenburgh (or Hardenbergh) in Swartekill, a Dutch settlement in New York State. Isabella was owned by Hardenburgh, as were her parents, Elizabeth and James Baumfree. Her mother was thought to have pure Guinea Coast ancestry. Until she was nine years old, Isabella spoke only Dutch. After her mother died, she was sold to Colonel Hardenburgh's son, Charles, who mistreated her. She was an intelligent child and learned English quickly.

After Charles Hardenburgh died in 1808, Isabella was sold to John Neely, who whipped her mercilessly. It was during this time that Isabella turned to religion to ease her suffering. She was sold, yet again, to Martinus Schryver, a tavern owner, then in 1810 to John Dumont of New Paltz, New York. At the Dumont estate, she fell in love with an enslaved man named Robert, but he was not owned by Dumont and was eventually driven off the estate. Still, she gave birth to Robert's daughter a short time later. She was married off to an older man, a fisherman named Thomas, about 1817, and had four more children with him. She remained with the Dumont family until about 1827, when she escaped after she was not freed as promised by Dumont. After praying for guidance, she found a home with Isaac Van Wagenen (or Wagener) and his wife, a kind couple for whom she worked.

It was when Isabella was working in this household that she had a life-altering religious experience and was inspired to preach. She attended the local Methodist church until 1829, when she left town with a white evangelical teacher. Isabella's reputation as an inspirational preacher spread, and she began working as a housekeeper for a fundamentalist religious reformer named Elijah Pierson and his group of followers. Pierson died in 1834, and Isabella was implicated in his death but was later acquitted.

Isabella then moved to New York City, but wanted to make her way as a traveling preacher. She changed her name to Sojourner Truth in 1843 and traveled to Massachusetts, where she met many famous abolitionists, including Frederick Douglass. She dictated her memoirs to a member of the Northampton Association of Education and Industry, and her book, *The Narrative of Sojourner Truth*, was published in 1850. After the release of her book, she was in demand as a speaker. She later moved to a small town near Battle Creek, Michigan, to live among a community of Spiritualists, who shared her values and beliefs.

Orator and Human Rights Activist Sojourner Truth, c. 1864. *One of the most powerful abolitionist and women's rights speakers of the nineteenth century, Sojourner Truth preached in both white and black churches. In 1864 she addressed an audience at the White House, with President Abraham Lincoln in attendance.* THE LIBRARY OF CONGRESS

Both intelligent and fiercely dedicated to the cause of freedom, Sojourner Truth was one of the most famous antislavery speakers of her time and preached in both white and black churches. There were many attempts to silence her, however, and she was occasionally physically attacked for her beliefs. The news of her speeches spread throughout the North as well as the South, and, in 1864, she addressed an audience at the White House, with President Abraham Lincoln in attendance. Sojourner

Truth died on November 26, 1883, at her home in Battle Creek, Michigan.

IYANLA VANZANT (1953–)

Writer, Yoruba Priestess, Lawyer. Iyanla Vanzant is the author of numerous books on spirituality, including *Tapping the Power Within* (1992); *Acts of Faith: Daily Meditations for People of Color* (1993); *Interiors: A Black Woman's Healing* (1995); *Value in the Valley: A Black Woman's Guide through Life's Dilemmas* (1995); *The Spirit of a Man: A Vision of Transformation for Black Men and the Women Who Love Them* (1996); *In the Meantime: Finding Yourself and the Love That You Want* (1998); *One Day My Soul Just Opened Up: 40 Days and 40 Nights toward Spiritual Strength and Personal Growth* (1998); *Yesterday, I Cried: Celebrating the Lessons of Living and Loving* (1999); *Until Today: Daily Devotions for Spiritual Growth and Peace of Mind* (2000); *Living through the Meantime: Learning to Break the Patterns of the Past and Begin the Healing Process* (2001); and *Up from Here: Reclaiming the Male Spirit* (2002). Her own life has furnished rich material for her books and has served as an inspiration for many of her readers.

Vanzant was born in Brooklyn in 1953. Her mother died when she was two years old, and as she grew older, she experienced sexual assault, spousal abuse, and nervous breakdowns. Yet she managed to turn her life around. Her years of dependence on welfare ended in 1978 when she matriculated at Medgar Evers College in Brooklyn, from which she graduated with honors in 1982. She subsequently completed law school, and she served as a public defender in Philadelphia for several years before becoming a public speaker and a writer of self-help books.

In 1998, Vanzant founded the Inner Visions Institute for Spiritual Development, headquartered in Silver Spring, Maryland. She is director of the institute and conducts workshops and classes dedicated to spiritual empowerment. She is in great demand as a public speaker, and frequently appears on television. Brought up in the Baptist and Pentecostal faiths, she has been initiated as a Yoruba priestess. Her writings and teachings draw widely from such diverse sources as African spirituality, Christianity, and New Thought, as well as Eastern religions, such as Buddhism.

JAMES VARICK (c. 1750–1827)

Abolitionist, African Methodist Episcopal Zion Bishop. Born near Newburgh, New York, around 1750, to an enslaved mother, James Varick was a leader in the movement among African American Methodists in New York to set up a separate congregation. This was accomplished with the formation of the Zion Church in 1796. Ten years later, Bishop Francis Asbury ordained Varick as a deacon. Varick sought to obtain full ordination as elder for himself and other African American ministers and would have preferred to have received such an ordination within the Methodist Episcopal Church, but this did not prove possible. He did not favor joining Richard Allen's African Methodist Episcopal Church, especially since Allen had been attempting to set up a New York congregation considered by Varick as in competition with the Zion Church.

Eventually, Varick participated in setting up the African Methodist Episcopal Zion Church in 1821, and he was elected the first superintendent or bishop. He was also deeply involved in issues relating to freedom and human rights, preaching against the slave trade in 1808 and subscribing to the first newspaper in the United States owned by African Americans, *Freedom's Journal.* He died on July 22, 1827.

While many African American churches continued to be served by white ministers until 1865, African American pastors, licensed ministers, and exhorters ministering to African American Baptist and Methodist congregations were not at all unusual at this time, in neither the South nor the North.

CORNEL WEST (1953–)

Writer, Educator, Social Critic. The grandson of Reverend Clifton L. West Sr., pastor of the Tulsa Metropolitan Baptist Church, Cornel West was born on June 2, 1953, in Tulsa, Oklahoma. West began developing his skills of critical thinking and political action as a child. He enrolled as an undergraduate student at Harvard at age seventeen. Taking eight courses per semester during his junior year, he was able to graduate magna cum laude one year early, with a degree in Near Eastern languages and literature in 1973. He then completed his M.A. (1975) and Ph.D. (1980) at Princeton University.

As a professor in Princeton's Department of Religion and Center for African American Studies, West's analytical speeches and writings on issues of morality, race relations, cultural diversity, and progressive politics have made him a keeper of the prophetic African American religious tradition. West taught the philosophy of religion at both Union Theological Seminary (1977–1983, 1988) and Yale Divinity School (1984–1987). In 1994, he joined Harvard's faculty, but returned permanently to Princeton in 2002 after a public rift with Harvard president Lawrence Summers. A complex individual, West juggles his theological concerns with his political convictions. He serves dual roles as prophet and intellectual within and beyond the African American community. His writings combine castigation for moral failure with an optimism that insists on the possibility—through struggle—of making a world of stricter morality real.

West's first books were published in the early 1980s, but he wrote many of them in the late 1970s. In the early 1980s, he encountered the Democratic Socialists of America, an organization that shaped the version of democratic socialism that he would subsequently adopt and promote in his works. Those include *Black Theology and Marxist Thought* (1979); *Prophesy Deliverance! An Afro-American Revolutionary Christianity* (1982); and *The Ethical Dimensions of Marxist Thought* (1991). West's impassioned and insightful writings also make a resounding appeal for cross-cultural tolerance and unity, while urging individuals to recognize the power of diversity within a society. Following those lines are such works as *Breaking Bread: Insurgent Black Intellectual Life* (1991), written with bell hooks; *Beyond Eurocentrism and Multiculturalism* (1993); *Race Matters* (1993), perhaps his best-known book; and *Jews & Blacks: A Dialogue on Race, Religion, and Culture in America* (1996), written with Michael Lerner.

West has teamed up with other well-known scholars and public figures to produce such writings as *The Future of the Race* (with Henry Louis Gates Jr., 1996); *The Future of American Progressivism: An Initiative for Political and Economic Reform* (with Roberto Mangabeira Unger, 1998); *The War against Parents: What We Can Do for America's Beleaguered Moms and Dads* (with Sylvia Ann Hewlett, 1998); and *The African-American Century: How Black Americans Have Shaped Our Country* (with Gates, 2000). West's other books include *Democracy Matters: Winning the Fight against Imperialism* (2004); *Hope on a Tightrope: Words and Wisdom* (2008); and *Brother West: Living and Loving Out Loud* (2009). During his career, West has been the recipient of numerous honors and awards, including the American Book Award (1993).

18

LITERATURE

Linda M. Carter
Genevieve Slomski
William A. Hobbs III

African American literature has as storied a history as the people, philosophies and cultures it challenges, champions and treasures. The foundation established during crucial periods such as the literature of Slavery and Freedom, Harlem Renaissance, and Black Arts Movement, allows modern African American writers more critical acclaim, artistic and thematic freedom, and commercial success than their predecessors.

The literature of Slavery and Freedom was invaluable in the fight to end the enslavement of Africans in North America by helping to debunk theories of the enslaved being too ignorant to be worthy of freedom and full citizenship. The literature of the Reconstruction of the New Negro Renaissance established the philosophies of self-determination that African Americans subscribed to as newly emancipated members of society. The Harlem Renaissance of the 1920s proved to be an exceptional decade of creativity and afforded insight into the importance of the black community's artistic cache as a vehicle for social change. The Realism, Naturalism and Modernism period featured Pulitzer Prize–winning literature, commercial success that was unheard of for African American writers at that time, and solidified urban realism as a means to convey the plight of blacks nationwide. The Black Arts movement of the 1960s and 1970s proved to be one of the most controversial artistic movements, with its politically charged call for a black cultural aesthetic in stark contrast to the mainstream. The movement fostered the growth of African American studies at numerous universities around the country. In the 1980s and 1990s, African American writers produced more distinguished writing than at any earlier period, in genres as diverse as scriptwriting to poetry. During the first decade of the twenty-first century, African American literature maintained the high level of visibility and commercial success established in the 1980s and 1990s. Black writers continue to explore a diversity of genres and African American identities as well as inspire new scholarship.

AFRICAN AMERICAN LITERATURE OF COLONIAL AMERICA

The African American literary tradition is believed to have begun in 1746 when Lucy Terry, at sixteen, composed the poem "Bars Fight." The tradition was sustained during the colonial era by such writers as Jupiter Hammon, Phillis Wheatley, Briton Hammon, James Gronniosaw, and Olaudah Equiano. Although Terry's poem was composed in 1746, it was preserved only in song until its publication in 1855. Thus, Jupiter Hammon's "An Evening Thought, Salvation, by Christ, with Penitential Cries," published as a broadside in 1760, was the first poem published by an African American. Thirteen years later, Phillis Wheatley became the first African American—and the second woman—to publish a book in the colonies. *Poems on Various Subjects, Religious and Moral, by Phillis Wheatley, Negro Servant to Mr. John Wheatley, of Boston, in New England,* published in 1773, had a tremendous impact on white colonial America, since many felt that African Americans were not capable of the depth of feeling required to write poetry. Soon after its publication, Wheatley gained such international recognition that she was granted her freedom.

While Terry, Jupiter Hammon, and Wheatley composed poetry, Briton Hammon, Gronniosaw, and

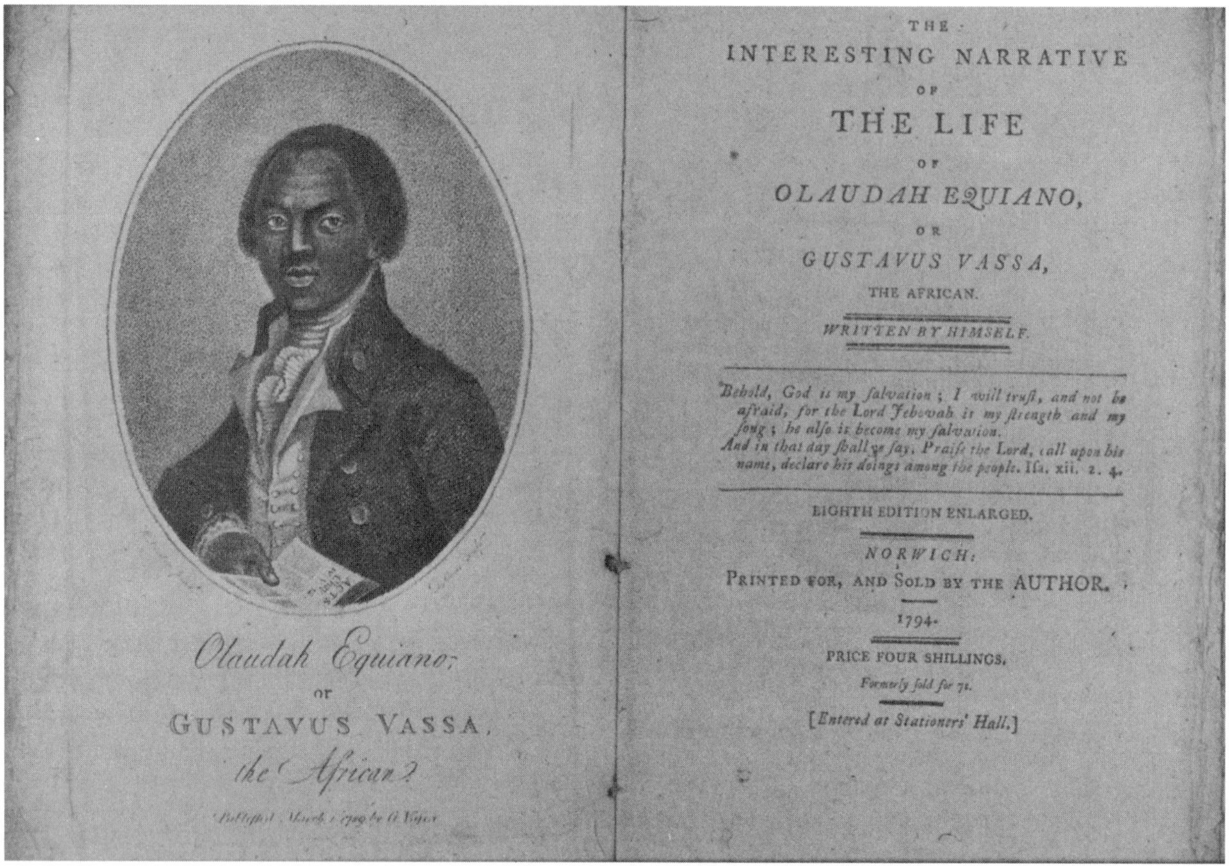

Front Matter of* The Interesting Narrative of the Life of Olaudah Equiano, or, Gustavus Vassa, the African *(1789). *Olaudah Equiano's autobiography was the first American slave narrative.* THE LIBRARY OF CONGRESS

Equiano wrote autobiographies. In 1760 *The Narrative of the Uncommon Sufferings and Surprizing Deliverance of Briton Hammon, a Negro Man* was published. Hammon's *Narrative* only contains fourteen pages, but it is considered the first African American autobiography. A more developed autobiography, *A Narrative of the Most Remarkable Particulars in the Life of James Albert Ukawsaw Gronniosaw* was printed in 1770 and reprinted in later editions.

Gronniosaw is mentioned in Equiano's two-volume work, *The Interesting Narrative of the Life of Olaudah Equiano, or, Gustavus Vassa, the African, Written by Himself* (1789). The autobiographies of Gronniosaw and Equiano provided a dual perspective—about life in Africa and life in America—that subsequent narratives of enslaved Africans lacked. Equiano's autobiography became a best seller during his lifetime, with nine English editions and one American edition, as well as translations in Dutch, German, and Russian. Equiano died in 1797, yet his autobiography influenced many nineteenth-century black autobiographers. These African American authors clearly demonstrated that they could eloquently express themselves in English—a second language for most blacks during the colonial era—and represent themselves effectively in a variety of literary genres.

AFRICAN AMERICAN LITERATURE DURING THE ANTEBELLUM PERIOD

Perhaps the greatest satisfaction for African American writers during the period prior to the Civil War (1861–1865) was having the freedom to write. Even knowing how to read and write was a tremendous accomplishment for many African Americans. Only sporadic attempts at systematic instruction of Africans had been made in colonial America, and stringent laws were later passed in the nineteenth century that prohibited whites from teaching African Americans to read and write.

NARRATIVES OF ENSLAVED AFRICANS

The narratives of the victims of the North American slave trade are literary milestones. The eighteenth-century autobiographies of Briton Hammon, James Gronniosaw, and Olaudah Equiano, along with their nineteenth-century counterparts, are the progenitors of full-length African American prose. These first-person narratives represented more than their individual authors; they provided a literary voice for the silent, enslaved masses without the opportunity to document the stories of their lives. In doing so, the autobiographers utilized the language of their captors as a method of rebellion.

During the nineteenth century, narratives by those bound to servitude established themes and structural considerations that had been previously overlooked. Literary critic Frances Smith Foster, in *Witnessing Slavery: The Development of Ante-Bellum Slave Narratives* (1979), has identified four chronological phases prevalent in such narratives: (1) the loss of freedom, (2) the cognizance of options to enslavement and a determination to gain freedom, (3) escape, and (4) freedom realized. Although readers may consider the narratives by such figures as Frederick Douglass, William Wells Brown, or Harriet Jacobs more political than artistic, their ability to adapt and utilize language in a manner that showed the glaring inconsistencies and inhumanity of enslaved Africans was an accomplishment of letters. The full extent of these writers' revolutionary thoughts was channeled through the traditional themes of the Bible and neoclassicism. However, the restructuring and inclusion of the African American perspective created a viable means of resistance and expression.

The three most prominent authors of such narratives were Frederick Douglass, William Wells Brown, and Harriet Jacobs. Douglass wrote three autobiographies: *Narrative of the Life of Frederick Douglass, An American Slave* (1845), which is considered the preeminent slave narrative; *My Bondage and My Freedom* (1855); and *The Life and Times of Frederick Douglass* (1881). Douglass's fellow abolitionist William Wells Brown also authored three autobiographies: *Narrative of William W. Brown, a Fugitive Slave* (1847), his most popular autobiography; *Three Years in Europe, or, Places I Have Seen and People I Have Met* (1852); and *My Southern Home* (1880).

Jacobs's *Incidents in the Life of a Slave Girl* (1861) is an important work in that it is the most comprehensive narrative by a woman. The autobiographies of Douglass, Brown, and Jacobs remain in print, and they, along with other slave narratives, are available in various collections, such as Yuval Taylor's two-volume *I Was Born a Slave: An Anthology of Classic Slave Narratives* (1999) and the Library of America's one-volume *Slave Narratives* (2000), edited by William L. Andrews and Henry Louis Gates Jr. The nineteenth-century slave narratives continued the tradition of black self-definition and self-assertion that had been established in the eighteenth century. The narratives of both centuries served as a preface and a foundation for subsequent expression through fiction, poetry, autobiography, essays, and other genres.

NOVELS AND OTHER GENRES

Although the majority of African American works published during the antebellum period were narratives, African Americans made significant contributions to other literary genres. Antebellum African American writers, following in the footsteps of their colonial predecessors, continued to write poetry. George Moses Horton, for example, published three volumes of verse: *The Hope of Liberty* (1829); *The Poetical Works of George M. Horton, The Colored Bard of North Carolina* (1845); and *Naked Genius* (1865).

Poetry and narratives were genres that African Americans, free and enslaved, employed during the eighteenth century. In the nineteenth century, African Americans demonstrated their ability to compose fiction as well. Victor Sejour's short story "The Mulatto" (1837) is the earliest extant work of African American fiction. In 1859 Frances E. W. Harper's "The Two Offers," the earliest known short story by an African American woman, was published.

The first African American novels were published during the antebellum period. The most well-known are William Wells Brown's *Clotel, or, The President's Daughter* (1853), the first African American novel; Frank Webb's *The Garies and Their Friends* (1857); Harriet Wilson's *Our Nig, or, Sketches from the Life of a Free Black, in a Two-Story White House, North, Showing that Slavery's Shadows Fall Even There* (1859), the first published novel by an African American woman; and Martin Delany's *Blake, or, The Huts of America* (1859). In 2002 Hannah Crafts's *The Bondwoman's Narrative* was published. Crafts's handwritten manuscript, dating from the 1850s, was recovered by Henry Louis Gates Jr. and authenticated in 2001. Crafts's work appears to be the first novel written by a formerly enslaved female, and it may be the first novel by an African American woman.

The first African American drama, *The Escape, or, A Leap for Freedom*, was published in 1858. Its author is William Wells Brown, the same individual who wrote one of the most influential slave narratives and the first African American novel. He is considered the first African American author of belles lettres.

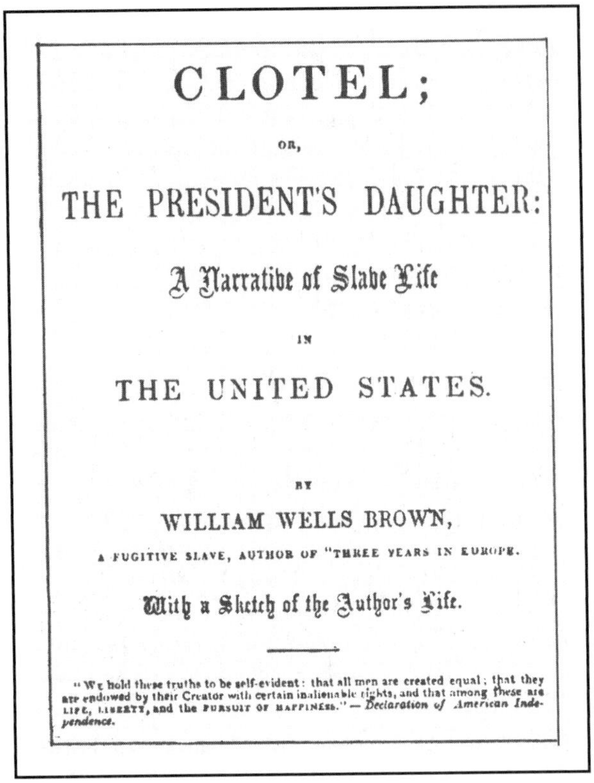

CLOTEL;

OR,

THE PRESIDENT'S DAUGHTER:

A Narrative of Slave Life

IN

THE UNITED STATES.

BY

WILLIAM WELLS BROWN,

A FUGITIVE SLAVE, AUTHOR OF "THREE YEARS IN EUROPE."

With a Sketch of the Author's Life.

"We hold these truths to be self-evident: that all men are created equal; that they are endowed by their Creator with certain inalienable rights, and that among these are LIFE, LIBERTY, and the PURSUIT OF HAPPINESS." — *Declaration of American Independence.*

Title Page of **Clotel, or The President's Daughter: A Narrative of Slave Life in the United States** ***(1853).*** *Considered to be the first African American novel, this melodramatic book about miscegenation was written by novelist and playwright William Wells Brown and first published in London.*

AFRICAN AMERICAN LITERATURE FROM RECONSTRUCTION TO THE HARLEM RENAISSANCE

With the end of the Civil War and the beginning of the era of Reconstruction, African American writers were eager to address subjects of personal and individual freedom. However, prevalent attitudes forced black writers to continue to address the "master mentality" and "plantation politics." Few writers could support themselves by their writing, and many remained unknown.

As the United States moved toward the close of the nineteenth century and the first decade of the twentieth century, some African American writers, including Frances E. W. Harper, Paul Laurence Dunbar, Pauline Hopkins, and Charles Waddell Chesnutt, found an audience that appreciated their works. Works published during this period include: Harper's novel, *Iola Leroy, or, Shadows Uplifted* (1892); Dunbar's volume of verse, *Lyrics of a Lowly Life* (1896), which was his third of eleven volumes; Hopkins's novel, *Contending Forces: A Romance Illustrative of Negro Life North and South* (1900); and Chesnutt's short stories, "The Conjure Woman" (1899) and "The Wife of His Youth and Other Stories of the Color Line" (1899), as well as his three novels, *The House Behind the Cedars* (1900), *The Marrow of Tradition* (1901), and *The Colonel's Dream* (1905). The most widely known African American work of this period, Booker T. Washington's *Up from Slavery* (1901), was the best-selling narrative of its kind for the period of the late nineteenth and the early twentieth centuries.

Because white society still controlled much of the American publishing industry, African American work was often filtered and distorted through the publishers' lens. As a result, much of the work published by African Americans attempted to prove that they could fit into middle-class American society. In fact, much of the literature of this era portrayed African Americans as happy with their assigned lot. Yet some writers—Harper, Dunbar, Hopkins, and Chesnutt, for example—tried to break the chains of this imposed expression. They presented a view of African American life as it really was, not as white America wanted it to be.

The accomplishments of African American writers during the time prior to the Harlem Renaissance attest to both their use of literary forms and their purpose in finding their own voices. Although themes were often muted and subjected to continuous scrutiny, the use of imagery, language, and a new perspective opened the way for African American writers to focus more on the wealth of their culture and the African American experience in a truthful and honest fashion.

THE HARLEM RENAISSANCE

The Harlem Renaissance was an era of prolific African American creativity in literature, art, and music. Resistant to the easy categorization of a timeline, the Harlem Renaissance began around the onset of World War I in 1914 and extended through the 1930s. It began with the movement of African American artists and writers into Harlem from practically every state in the country.

By the 1920s, Harlem was the largest community of black individuals in the United States, encompassing Africans from the West Indies, the Caribbean, and the Americas. This community, similar to many urban communities in the North, saw the collective energies of persons joining together to celebrate the artistic talents of African Americans. While Harlem served as the hub of artistic activity, Washington, D.C., also became a place where many artists congregated to explore the new perspectives and ideas of the time. The largest group of women participants in the Harlem Renaissance found their literary identities not so much in Harlem but in Washington in the company of poet Georgia Douglas Johnson and other artists.

As African American journals, such as *Opportunity*, edited by Charles S. Johnson, and W. E. B. Du Bois's *Crisis*, began to flourish, it became possible for African American writers to publish in a style that suited their tastes. Du Bois and Johnson were among the older established authors, critics, and editors who encouraged younger writers. Jessie Redmon Fauset, who was an author of four novels and the editor of *Crisis* magazine, did much to support the work of younger authors and women writers. In fact, Langston Hughes and others contended that the Harlem Renaissance came about because of this nurturing of younger writers by older writers like Fauset and Alain Locke, a Howard University professor and literary critic. In addition, African American writers discovered that some white patrons in the publishing field were interested in promoting their works, and, as a result, books by black authors came to be published with unprecedented frequency.

In addition to Du Bois and Fauset, important writers of this era include Langston Hughes, Zora Neale Hurston, Wallace Thurman, Countee Cullen, Claude McKay, Nella Larsen, Eric Walrond, Rudolph Fisher, Jean Toomer, and Arna Bontemps. Among the most significant works of the era are Locke's *The New Negro* (1925), an anthology of Harlem Renaissance works; Thurman's *Infants of the Spring* (1932), a novel that satirizes the Harlem Renaissance; and Hughes's *The Big Sea* (1940), his first autobiography, which provides the best account of the Harlem Renaissance by one of its participants.

Although free expression was essential to artists of the Harlem Renaissance, the stereotypes that permeated American culture made their writings appear rebellious. The conscious agenda of these mostly young, African American artists concerned the definition and celebration of African American art and culture, coupled with a desire to change the preconceived and erroneous notions most Americans had of African American life. Such views are eloquently expressed in Hughes's essay "The Negro Artist and the Racial Mountain" (1926), which was a manifesto for his contemporaries and has served as inspiration for subsequent generations of African Americans. The essay ends with this bold declaration:

> We younger Negro artists who create now intend to express our individual dark-skinned selves without fear or shame. If white people are pleased we are glad. If they are not, it doesn't matter. We know we are beautiful. And ugly too. The tom-tom cries and the tom-tom laughs. If colored people are pleased we are glad. If they are not, their displeasure doesn't matter either. We build our temples for tomorrow, strong as we know how, and we stand on top of the mountain, free within ourselves.

Langston Hughes, Writer, New York, 1958. *A multitalented writer, Hughes wrote novels, short stories, poetry, newspaper columns, and opera lyrics. One of his most well-known poems is "Harlem" (1951), and its first line: "What happens to a dream deferred?"* ROBERT W. KELLEY/TIME & LIFE PICTURES/GETTY IMAGES

The Harlem Renaissance shifted away from the moralizing that had been characteristic of much post-Reconstruction writing that decried racism. Du Bois and Locke, along with many emerging young writers, realized that literary efforts that catered to changing the American conscience were no longer useful, nor should such efforts be a primary consideration for artists. These writers felt that communicating the African American experience through every facet of many artistic mediums would, of itself, expound upon the ills of a racist world. Issues then could be expressed through the lives of working-class and middle-class characters as the text sought to paint a realistic picture.

In this time of discovery for African Americans of the view from within, many also saw the changing relationship between blacks and whites. Literature reintroduced white America to a people who needed, wanted, and would eventually demand full participation in the society for which they had lived, labored, and died. Rather than attempt to convince white Americans of African American entitlement, this literature focused on self-education and exploration of the quality of the African American experience. It paved the way for power through art to inspire the masses and the writers of the 1960s.

AFRICAN AMERICAN LITERATURE OF THE MID-TWENTIETH CENTURY

As the Great Depression of the 1930s deepened, the Harlem Renaissance slowly faded. Richard Wright's publication in 1940 of his classic novel *Native Son* marked the beginning of a transition period in African American literature that would last until 1955. Writers during this period bridged the richly creative era of the Renaissance with the more intense creativity and sociopolitical activity that was to define the work produced during the civil rights movement.

With the publication of *Native Son*, Wright maintained that the Harlem Renaissance—with its motto of "art for art's sake"—must end and be replaced with works directly aimed at ending racism. He also believed that African Americans were an essential part of American society. These tenets became the foundation for the ideology of the civil rights movement.

During this period, other African American writers, notably poets, were taking a different road in their quest to be heard. Such poets as Gwendolyn Brooks, Melvin B. Tolson, Margaret Walker, and Robert Hayden employed classical and mythical themes. Brooks won a Pulitzer Prize in 1950 for her book *Annie Allen* (1949) and was the first African American to receive the award. These poets blended extreme eclecticism with realistic, African American issues. The blend was successful, and their writing was met with acceptance in the university community.

Other literary works that brought serious African American issues to mainstream culture were Ann Petry's novel *The Street* (1946); Ralph Ellison's *Invisible Man* (1952), arguably one of the best novels published in the United States during the twentieth century; and James Baldwin's novel *Go Tell It on the Mountain* (1953), as well as his collections of essays, such as *Notes of a Native Son* (1955), *Nobody Knows My Name: More Notes of a Native Son* (1961), and *The Fire Next Time* (1963). In addition, many African American works were gaining acceptance with the mainstream literary establishment.

In 1959, on the "eve" of the Black Arts movement, Lorraine Hansberry's play *A Raisin in the Sun* opened in New York. Hansberry was the first African American woman to have a play produced on Broadway, and the first African American to win the New York Drama Critics' Circle Award. The play's title was inspired by a line in Langston Hughes's poem "Harlem: A Dream Deferred." Hansberry's play centers around the Younger family's desire to move from Chicago's South Side to a white neighborhood. Thus, art imitated reality as *A Raisin in the Sun* mirrored the many efforts to integrate neighborhoods across America during the 1950s.

THE BLACK ARTS MOVEMENT

The Black Arts movement, sometimes called the Black Aesthetic movement, was the first major African American artistic movement since the Harlem Renaissance. Beginning in the early 1960s and lasting through the mid-1970s, this movement was fueled by the anger of Richard Wright, James Baldwin, Ralph Ellison, Ann Petry, and other notable African American writers.

The artistic movement flourished alongside the civil rights marches and the call for the independence of the African American community. As phrases such as "black is beautiful" were popularized, African American writers of the Black Arts movement consciously set out to define what it meant to be a black writer in a white culture. While writers of the Harlem Renaissance seemed to investigate their identity within, writers of the Black Arts movement desired to define themselves and their era before being defined by others.

For the most part, participants in the Black Arts movement were supportive of separatist politics and a black nationalist ideology. Larry Neal wrote in the essay "The Black Arts Movement" (1968) that the movement was the "aesthetic and spiritual sister of the Black Power concept." Rebelling against the mainstream society by being essentially anti-white, anti-American, and anti–middle class, these artists moved from the Harlem Renaissance view of art for art's sake into a philosophy of art for the sake of politics.

Artists of the Black Arts movement attempted to produce works of art that would be meaningful to the

Photo of Sidney Poitier in* A Raisin in the Sun *(Gordon Parks, March 17, 1959). *Lorraine Hansberry's play debuted on Broadway that year, starring Poitier and Ruby Dee* (right)*. The play was named the best American play of 1959 by New York Drama Critics' Circle.* GORDON PARKS/TIME LIFE PICTURES/GETTY IMAGES

African American masses. Toward this end, popular African American music of the day, including John Coltrane's jazz and James Brown's soul, along with street talk, became inspirational forces for the movement. In fact, much of the language used in these works was aggressive, profane, and shocking—this was often a conscious attempt to show the vitality and power of African American activists. These writers tended to be revolutionaries, supporting both radical and peaceful protests for change as promoted by Malcolm X and Martin Luther King Jr. In addition, they believed that artists were required to do more than create: artists also had to be political activists in order to achieve nationalist goals.

Leading writers in this movement included Amiri Baraka (LeRoi Jones), whose poetry and plays were as well known as his political prowess, and Haki Madhubuti (Don L. Lee), a poet and essayist who sold thousands of copies of his books without a national distributor. On the other hand, Ishmael Reed—an early organizer of the Black Arts movement—later dissented with some of the movement's doctrines and became inspired more by the black magic and spiritual practices of the West Indies (in what he called the HooDoo Aesthetic). Other organizers and essayists include Larry Neal, Etheridge Knight, Addison Gale Jr., and Maulana Karenga.

Nikki Giovanni was one of the first poets of the Black Arts movement to receive recognition. In her works, she advocated militant replies to white oppression, and she demonstrated through her performances that music is an inextricable part of the African American tradition in all aspects of life. Poet Sonia Sanchez was another leading voice of the movement. She managed to combine feminism with her commitment to nurturing children and men in the fight for black nationalism. Sanchez was a member of the Nation of Islam from

1972 to 1975, and through her association with the Black Arts movement, she managed to instill stronger support for the role of women in that religion.

Two major Black Arts presses were run by poets: Dudley Randall's Broadside Press in Detroit and Haki Madhubuti's Third World Press in Chicago. From 1961 to 1976, the most important African American magazine was *Negro Digest* (renamed *Black World* in 1970); its editor, Hoyt Fuller, published the works of Black Arts poets and prose writers. Landmark publications of the movement include: *Black Fire* (1968), an anthology of Black Arts writing edited by Amiri Baraka and Larry Neal; *The New Black Poetry* (1969), edited by Clarence Major; *The Black Woman* (1970), the first major African American feminist anthology, edited by Toni Cade Bambara; *The Black Poets* (1971), edited by Dudley Randall; and *Understanding the New Black Poetry* (1972), an anthology edited by Stephen Henderson.

AFRICAN AMERICAN LITERATURE OF THE LATE TWENTIETH CENTURY AND EARLY TWENTY-FIRST CENTURY

Before the Black Arts movement ended in the mid-1970s, Marvin Gaye's album *What's Going On* (1971) was released. On the album's title track, Gaye sings about the social problems of the late 1960s and early 1970s: the Vietnam War (1957–1975), protest demonstrations, and police brutality. The title of his classic album was not only a popular greeting but also testimony to the African American literary tradition. Since the end of the Black Arts movement, African Americans have written about "what's going on" in greater numbers and to greater recognition than at any other time in literary history.

Important developments in African American literature during the last three decades of the twentieth century include the success of many African American women writers, as well as a growth in the number of authors who found that they could work in more than one genre. The works of black writers appear more frequently on best-seller lists, and, at times, works of several African American authors have appeared concurrently on such lists. In addition, African American writing has become more legitimate in the United States, and African American studies departments have emerged in many universities around the country.

One of the first books of the contemporary renaissance of African American literature was Alex Haley's *Roots* (1976), one of the greatest African American writing coups of the late twentieth century. Haley's book, as well as the highly popular television miniseries based on it, encouraged many black Americans to discover their own African roots. Since then, other books that explore the history of African Americans in the American West, South, and North have been published and eagerly received by African Americans readers.

A multitude of themes are explored in the large number of African American literary works that have been published since the 1980s. Many writers have shifted their attention away from the lack of equality between blacks and whites and toward themes of self-reflection, self-definition, and healing. Numerous African American women write in response to the Black Arts movement, protesting the role that they feel women played in the male-oriented black nationalist movement.

Zora Neale Hurston's novel *Their Eyes Were Watching God* (1937) and her other works were resurrected and served as inspiration. The women's liberation movement also supported these writers by allowing their works to reach a wider audience. In this way, the female-repressive politics of the Black Arts movement provoked women writers to express their own unique voices. Maya Angelou, Alice Walker, Gayl Jones, Toni Morrison, Terry McMillan, and Gloria Naylor are among the successful women writers who became prominent figures.

Since the 1980s, African American women writers have been at the leading edge of the publishing industry—in quality as well as quantity of work. In addition to Walker, Jones, Morrison, McMillan, and Naylor, other prominent women working primarily as novelists include Edwidge Danticat, Gwendolyn Parker, Jamaica Kincaid, Lucinda Roy, Marita Golden, Bernice McFadden, Toni Cade Bambara, Diane McKinney-Whetstone, Helen Lee, Yolanda Joe, Dawn Turner Trice, Pearl Cleage, and Barbara Chase-Riboud. African American men writers are outnumbered by black women writers; African American male novelists of the period include Ernest Gaines, Ishmael Reed, Walter Mosley, John Edgar Wideman, Albert French, and E. Lynn Harris. In the late 1980s, Trey Ellis's landmark essay "The New Black Aesthetic" spoke of an emerging sensibility that explored the complexities of racial identity. The movement came to be known as the Post Soul Aesthetic and includes writers such as Colson Whitehead, Darryl Pinckney, Brian Keith Jackson, Brent Wade, and Kevin Powell. The Post Soul Aesthetic's interests runs deep in African American literature; African American novelists often confront issues of identity, offering interpretations of womanhood and manhood. Challenged by W. E. B. Du Bois's statement about dual identity as an American and as a black person, they collectively provide panoramic insight into African American life.

Author Alex Haley with Clifford Alexander Jr., Secretary of the Army, at the Pentagon, Washington, DC, 1977. *Haley* (right*), author of the novel* Roots, *presents Alexander with a recording of his book. The publication awakened interest in many African Americans about their own genealogy.* **AP PHOTO**

The decade of the 1990s and the first decade of the twenty-first century benefited from works that explored a broad spectrum of the African American experience. Themes centered on the lives of enslaved ancestry are prevalent in the works of writers who focused on the African American past. In a number of coming-of-age novels by African American writers, the protagonists are portrayed as maturing during the civil rights era. Other important themes in contemporary African American literature relate to family and coming-of-age issues. Many writers chose to focus on the dynamics of modern-day romantic relationships.

Barriers have been dismantled in various genres. Rivaling their European American contemporaries, Octavia Butler and Samuel Delany created works of science fiction; Tananarive Due crafts supernatural novels; Walter Mosley, Barbara Neely, Valerie Wilson Wesley, and Eleanor Taylor Bland write detective fiction; and the plays of August Wilson and Suzan-Lori Parks have been staged on Broadway. Clearly, variety exists in contemporary African American writing. Novels of folk history, such as Colson Whitehead's *John Henry Days* (2001), and novels of the urban experience, such as Richard Wright's posthumous *Rite of Passage* (1994), are equally well received. Many artists work in more than one genre—Walter Mosley, Alice Walker, Gayl Jones, J. California Cooper, and Andrea Lee are good examples.

With the exception of the novel, the most dynamic form of African American writing during the late twentieth and early twenty-first centuries is the autobiography. Memoirs and autobiographies have become a popular mode of expression for writers ranging from entertainers and educators to civil rights leaders and motivational speakers.

A memoir worthy of distinction is Arthur Ashe's *Days of Grace* (1993), a work he coauthored with professor and literary critic Arnold Rampersad. In it, the tennis legend reveals that living with AIDS was not his life's greatest burden; living as a black person in America was.

One of the most popular autobiographies at the end of the twentieth century was *Having Our Say: The Delany Sisters' First 100 Years* (1993), by Sarah (Sadie) L. Delany and A. Elizabeth (Bessie) Delany (with Amy Hill Hearth). Their autobiography was published when Sadie, a former educator, was 104 years old, and Bessie, a former dentist and civil rights activist, was 102. Philanthropist, entrepreneur, and foundation executive Camille Cosby acquired the stage, film, and television rights to the autobiography. Consequently, a dramatic adaptation of *Having Our Say* opened on Broadway in 1995, and was later made into a television film. During the summer of 2002, *Having Our Say* was recommended reading for a new District of Columbia program designed to encourage individuals to read.

"Amateur" writers are not the only individuals publishing their memoirs, however. Maya Angelou's first autobiography, *I Know Why the Caged Bird Sings* (1970), is greatly responsible for the revitalization of African American autobiography. Angelou has written five additional autobiographies, including *A Song Flung Up to Heaven* (2002). In 1977, seventeen years after Richard Wright's death, his second autobiography, *American Hunger*, was published. It is comprised of the section that Wright's publisher deleted from *Black Boy* (1945).

In 1995, political aspirant Barack Obama published his memoir, *Dreams from My Father*, which was generally seen as a launch of his now celebrated political rise. After Obama's Illinois Senate primary victory and his subsequent appearance at the 2004 Democratic National Convention, the book was republished as interest in the young politician began to increase. As a result of the public interest, the book was featured on several best-selling lists. The story is a narrative of Obama's early life, his Kenyan father and European-American mother and her family in Hawaii where Obama grew up. The work received positive reviews from scholars/authors such as Toni Morrison, among other well regarded writers. *Dreams from My Father* played a significant role in Obama's subsequent rise to the presidency in 2008 and continues to be widely read.

Thanks to hip hop and the spoken word movement, poetry remains a popular vehicle for black expression. A number of poets who began publishing in the 1960s, such as Mari Evans, Amiri Baraka, Sonia Sanchez, Jayne Cortez, Haki Madhubuti, and Nikki Giovanni, continued to publish in the 1990s and beyond, as did poets who were first published in the 1970s, such as Maya Angelou, Lucille Clifton, Ai, Toi Derricotte, and Yusef Komunyakaa. Joining them are poets who began publishing in the 1980s, such as Rita Dove and Cornelius Eady, as well as poets who began publishing in the 1990s, including Kevin Powell, Elizabeth Alexander, and Kevin Young.

Important anthologies and collections that include poetry published since the 1990s include: *On the Verge: Emerging Poets and Artists* (1993), edited by Thomas Sayers Ellis and Joseph Lease; *The Furious Flowering of African American Poetry* (1999), edited by Joanne Gabbin; and *Words with Wings: A Treasury of African-American, Poetry and Art* (2000), edited by Belinda Rochelle. In 1994, James Madison University in Harrisburg, Virginia, hosted the Furious Flower Conference, dedicated to the then seventy-seven-year-old Gwendolyn Brooks. The conference, which featured three generations of poets, was the largest gathering of African American poets and critics in more than two decades. A second Furious Flower Conference was held in Harrisburg in 2004, with more than sixty distinguished poets and scholars in attendance.

Whether writing in traditional forms, such as the sonnet, or under the influence of rap or hip-hop, African American poets tackle the same issues as their counterparts in prose: identity, racism, sexism, classism, relationships, politics, and urban life. Since the 1980s, poetry has become more popular and more accessible in the United States. Bookstores, universities, and literary groups continue to host established poets who read their verse before audiences. In addition, bookstores and cafés hold poetry slams and open-mike nights, where amateur poets can present their works. There is also a variety of Internet sites that encourage novices to submit their verse.

African American writers and their works continue to be heralded on the national and international stage. Many African American writers have won National Book Awards since the 1980s, including Alice Walker, Charles Johnson, Ai, and Lucille Clifton. Pulitzer Prize winners include Alex Haley, August Wilson, and Rita Dove. Two African American women writers recorded landmark achievements in 1993: Rita Dove was named U.S. poet laureate, and Toni Morrison won the Nobel Prize in Literature.

In the twenty-first century, African American writers continue to look into their own world for answers, rather than letting others define their past, present, or future. Contemporary black authors are the beneficiaries of the vast legacy established by writers of the colonial period, the antebellum period, the Reconstruction era, the Harlem Renaissance, and the Black Arts movement. Twenty-first-century writers, empowered by their talents and their literary ancestors, are expanding and enhancing the African American literary tradition.

AFRICAN AMERICAN AUTHORS AND LITERARY CRITICS

(Some biographical profiles may appear in other chapters. To locate profiles more readily, please consult the index.)

RAYMOND ANDREWS (1934–1991)

Novelist. Born in 1934 in Madison, Georgia, the fourth of ten children, Raymond Andrews left his sharecropper home for Atlanta at age fifteen. He attended Booker T. Washington High School at night, and later joined the U.S. Air Force. After four years with the Air Force, he attended Michigan State University, then moved to New York City, where he held a variety of jobs—airline reservations clerk, hamburger cook, photo librarian, proofreader, inventory taker, mailroom clerk, messenger, air-courier dispatcher, and bookkeeper—at the same time that he pursued his passion for writing.

His first publication was an article about baseball for *Sports Illustrated* in 1975. A first novel, *Appalachee Red*, was published in 1978 to critical acclaim, and won the first annual James Baldwin Prize. Employing a narrative style influenced by the oral tradition of his childhood, Andrews confronts his readers with an impassioned intermingling of race, sex, status, and revenge in the lives of characters in an African American society in Appalachee, a fictional town in rural Georgia. *Appalachee Red* began the Muskhogean County trilogy, which Andrews uses to shed light on the African American rural life from before World War I to the beginning of the civil rights era in the 1960s.

Rosiebelle Lee Wildcat Tennessee: A Novel, published in 1980, chronicled the forty-year reign, beginning in 1906, of the spiritual and temporal leader of Appalachee. Andrews published *Baby Sweets* in 1983, a novel that takes its name from the brothel operated by the eccentric son of the town's leading citizen. This half-ugly, half-benign exposition of a brothel that provides mostly African American prostitutes to the town's white elite completes the Muskhogean trilogy. All of the books in the trilogy were published by Dial Press and illustrated by Andrews's brother, Benny.

In 1990 Andrews published *The Last Radio Boy*, a memoir about growing up talented yet impoverished in Georgia. The following year, he published *Jessie and Jesus and Cousin Claire*. He died of a self-inflicted gunshot wound on November 25, 1991, in Athens, Georgia.

MAYA ANGELOU (1928–)

Novelist, Poet, Actress. Maya Angelou was born Marguerite Johnson on April 4, 1928, in St. Louis, Missouri. A writer, journalist, poet, actress, singer, dancer, playwright, director, and producer, Angelou spent her formative years shuttling between her native St. Louis; Stamps, Arkansas, a tiny segregated town where her grandmother lived; and San Francisco, where she realized her ambition of becoming that city's first African American streetcar conductor. She made her true mark later in life, as her words became a symbol of hope that touched the soul of the people of the United States. Perhaps the ultimate recognition of her talent came when President-Elect Bill Clinton asked Angelou to compose and recite a poem for his inauguration in 1993.

During the 1950s, Angelou studied dance with Pearl Primus in New York City, and later appeared as a nightclub singer there, as well as in San Francisco and Hawaii. She toured with the U.S. State Department's production of *Porgy and Bess* in the mid-1950s, and the following decade became northern coordinator of the Southern Christian Leadership Conference. She married South African activist and lawyer Vusumzi L. Make in 1960, and the couple lived in Cairo, Egypt, for three years, during which time Angelou edited the *Arab Observer*, an English-language weekly published in Cairo. The couple divorced in 1963. While living in Accra, Ghana, under the black nationalist regime of Kwame Nkrumah, she taught music and drama and wrote for the *Ghanian Times*. Angelou later went to Sweden to study cinematography.

Angelou became a national celebrity in 1970 with the publication of *I Know Why the Caged Bird Sings*, the first volume of her autobiography, which detailed her encounters with racism in the South and a prepubescent rape by her mother's lover. The work was nominated for that year's National Book Award. Four additional volumes of Angelou's autobiography followed: *Gather Together in My Name* (1974); *Singin' and Swingin' and Gettin' Merry Like Christmas* (1976); *The Heart of a Woman* (1981); and *A Song Flung Up to Heaven* (2002).

Angelou's other published works include: *Just Give Me a Cool Drink of Water 'fore I Diiie: The Poetry of Maya Angelou* (1971); *Oh Pray My Wings Are Gonna Fit Me Well* (1975); *And Still I Rise* (1978); *Shaker, Why Don't You Sing?* (1983); *All God's Children Need Traveling Shoes* (1986); *Mrs. Flowers: A Moment of Friendship* (1986); *Now Sheba Sings the Song* (1987); *Wouldn't Take Nothing for My Journey Now* (1993); *Phenomenal Woman: Four Poems Celebrating Women* (1994); *Even the Stars Look Lonesome* (1997); *Mother: A Cradle to Hold Me* (2006); *Celebrations: Rituals of Peace and Prayer* (2006); *Letter to My Daughter* (2008).

Angelou also dabbled in film, both in front of and behind the camera. In 1977 she was nominated for an Emmy Award for her portrayal of Nyo Boto in the

Maya Angelou, Writer, Paramount Theater, Austin, TX, April 25, 2009. *The first volume of Angelou's autobiography,* I Know Why the Caged Bird Sings, *came out in 1970 to critical acclaim. Angelou has since written four more volumes, in addition to numerous other published works.* GARY MILLER/FILMMAGIC/GETTY IMAGES

television adaptation of Alex Haley's best-selling novel *Roots*. She also appeared in the 1993 made-for-television movie *There Are No Children Here*, which costarred Oprah Winfrey. That same year, Angelou wrote poetry for John Singleton's *Poetic Justice* and played a small role in the film. The following year, she appeared in a television commercial, reading a version of her poem "Still I Rise" for the United Negro College Fund's fiftieth anniversary. She costarred with Winona Ryder, Anne Bancroft, and Ellen Burstyn in *How to Make an American Quilt* (1995). Also active behind the scenes, she became the first African American woman to have a movie produced with *Georgia, Georgia* (1972), based on one of her books. She also directed the films *All Day Long* (1974) and *Down in the Delta* (1998). In 2004 Angelou published a cookbook with essays, *Hallelujah! The Welcome Table: A Lifetime of Memories with Recipes*.

The 1990s held many highlights for the sought-after poet, who remained as active as she had been earlier in her career. On January 20, 1993, Angelou read her new poem "On the Pulse of Morning" during Clinton's inauguration. This event occurred just a few days after her one-act musical *And Still I Rise* (based on her poetry) was performed in Washington, D.C. In 1994 Angelou narrated a World Choir concert held at the Georgia Dome. The festival featured ten thousand singers from ten different countries. She also gave a reading at the National Black Arts Festival that year. In 1995 Angelou recited her poem "A Brave and Startling Truth" at the United Nation's fiftieth anniversary ceremony in San Francisco. She also read Sterling Brown's "Strong Men" at the inauguration of Washington, D.C., mayor Marion Barry, and was a keynote speaker, along with First Lady Hillary Rodham Clinton, at the twenty-fifth anniversary of the Joint Center for Political and Economic Studies.

Angelou has been the recipient of many honorary degrees and awards, including a Golden Eagle Award for the 1977 television documentary *Afro-American in the Arts*; a Matrix Award from Women in Communications, Inc., in 1983; a North Carolina Award in literature in 1987; a "best-mannered" citation from the National League of Junior Cotillions in 1993; a Medal of

Distinction from the University of Hawaii's Board of Regents in 1994; and a Spingarn Medal from the NAACP in 1994. In 1981 Wake Forest University gave Angelou a lifetime appointment as Reynolds Professor of American Studies. In 2000 she was awarded the National Medal of Arts by President Bill Clinton. A year later, she was honored with the Aaron Davis Hall Harlem Renaissance Award. In 2006 Angelou received the Mother Teresa Award for her devotion and service to humanity. That same year, Angelou began hosting a weekly radio show on the Oprah Radio channel of XM Satellite Radio. She was honored with the Ford's Theatre Society's Lincoln Medal in 2008, and the Marian Anderson Award (honoring artists whose leadership benefits humanity) that same year.

Angelou's *Letter to My Daughter*, released in 2008, is a collection of twenty-eight short essays and poems focusing on motherhood, life, humanity and faith. It is a deeply personal reflective work that represents Angelou's and other's philosophies on a variety of life experiences.

HOUSTON A. BAKER JR. (1943–)

Writer, Literary Critic, Scholar, Educator. Houston Alfred Baker Jr. was born in Louisville, Kentucky, on March 22, 1943. Surmounting the racist attitudes that permeated his childhood environment, he attended Howard University and received a bachelor's degree in English. He later earned master's and doctoral degrees in Victorian literature from the University of California, Los Angeles. Early in his career, Baker switched from the study of British Victorian literature to African American literature and culture. He also became an advocate for the Black Power movement of the late 1960s and 1970s. Baker's critical perspective called for an African American aesthetic in literature. He considered art an instrument of cultural expression in the liberation of black people—an instrument that he believed should be recognized in the study of African American works.

As editor of *Black Literature in America* (1971), an anthology of African American writing, Baker began to promote the artistic and literary experiences found in the study of African American literature. Baker's works include: *Twentieth-Century Interpretations of* Native Son (1972); *A Many-Colored Coat of Dreams: The Poetry of Countee Cullen* (1974); *No Matter Where You Travel, You Still Be Black* (1979); *The Journey Back: Issues in Black Literature and Criticism* (1980); *Narrative of the Life of Frederick Douglass, an American Slave* (1982); *Blues, Ideology, and Afro-American Literature: A Vernacular Theory* (1984); *Modernism and the Harlem Renaissance* (1987); *Afro-American Poetics: Revisions of Harlem and the Black Aesthetic* (1988); *Black Feminist Criticism and Critical Theory* (1988); *Afro-American Literary Study in the 1990s* (1989, edited with Patricia Redmond); *Black Studies, Rap, and the Academy* (1993); *Passing Over* (2000); *Critical Memory: Public Spheres, African American Writing, and Black Fathers and Sons in America* (2001); *Turning South Again: Re-Thinking Modernism/Re-Reading Booker T.* (2001); *I Don't Hate the South: Reflections on Faulkner, Family, and the South* (2007); and *Betrayal: How Black Intellectuals Have Abandoned the Ideals of the Civil Rights Era (2008).*

A prolific contributor to numerous scholarly journals and publications, Baker is considered one of the leading African American intellectuals of his time. He has taught at Yale, the University of Virginia, Duke University, and the University of Pennsylvania, where he was director of the Center for the Study of Black Literature and Culture. He also served as president of the Modern Language Association in 1992. In 2006 Baker became Distinguished University Professor and professor of English at Vanderbilt University in Nashville, Tennessee. Among his many honors and awards is the 2003 Hubbell Medal for lifetime achievement in American literary studies.

JAMES BALDWIN (1924–1987)

Novelist, Essayist, Playwright. The work of James Baldwin is best known for exploring the themes of personal and sexual identity and for providing vivid depictions of the civil rights struggle in the United States. Born in Harlem on August 2, 1924, Baldwin was raised in poverty. He never knew his biological father; his mother, a domestic worker, married a factory worker who was also a storefront preacher and a violent and cruel man. Baldwin assumed the surname of his stepfather, who died in a mental institution in 1943.

A voracious reader as a child, Baldwin turned to writing after an early career as a boy preacher in Harlem's storefront Pentecostal churches. Baldwin's first story appeared in a church newspaper when he was about twelve years old. He attended Frederick Douglass Junior High School in Harlem and later graduated from DeWitt Clinton High School, where he was editor of the school magazine. Three years later, he won a Eugene Saxton Fellowship, which enabled him to write full time. Baldwin's issues with his stepfather, his own sexual identity, the suicide of a friend, and racism drove him away from the United States in 1948. He spent a good part of his adult life in Paris, London, and Istanbul.

Baldwin's first novel, *Go Tell It on the Mountain*, was published in 1953 to critical acclaim. Two years later, his first collection of essays, *Notes of a Native Son*, was also favorably received. This work was followed in

1956 by the publication of his second novel, *Giovanni's Room.* His second collection of essays, *Nobody Knows My Name,* established him as a major voice in American literature.

In 1962 *Another Country,* Baldwin's third novel, was a critical and commercial success. A year later, he published *The Fire Next Time,* an immediate best seller that is regarded as one of the most important essays about the history of African American protest. In the mid-1960s, two of Baldwin's plays—*Blues for Mister Charlie* (1964) and *The Amen Corner* (1954)—were produced in New York, where they achieved modest success. In 1968 he published *Tell Me How Long the Train's Been Gone,* which he regarded as his first "grown-up novel." It generated little enthusiasm among critics.

Notes of a Native Son *Book Cover (1955).* *Modern Library ranks author James Baldwin's collection of essays as number nineteen on its list of 100 Best Nonfiction books. Baldwin's works brought serious African American issues to the mainstream.* ILLUSTRATION BY BURT GLINN/MAGNUM PHOTOS, DESIGN BY MARC J. COHEN. BEACON PRESS. REPRODUCED BY PERMISSION.

After a silence of several years, the question of whether Baldwin had stopped writing was widely debated. In 1974 he published another novel, *If Beale Street Could Talk,* which portrays the problems besetting a ghetto family with sensitivity and humor. Baldwin's skill as a novelist is evident as he conveys his own sophisticated analyses through the mind of the protagonist, a young woman. To many critics, however, the novel lacked the relevance and power of his early polemical essays.

Baldwin's other works during this time include: *Going to Meet the Man* (1965, short stories); *No Name in the Street* (1972); *One Day When I Was Lost* (1973), a scenario based on Alex Haley's *The Autobiography of Malcolm X* (1965); *A Rap on Race*; (1971), written with Margaret Mead; and *A Dialogue* (1973), written with Nikki Giovanni. He was one of the rare authors who worked well alone or in collaboration. Other books by Baldwin include: *Nothing Personal* (1964), with photographs by Richard Avedon; *The Devil Finds Work* (1976), about the movies; *Just above My Head* (1979), his sixth novel; and *Little Man, Little Man: A Story of Childhood* (1977), a book for children. Baldwin's *Just above My Head* dealt with the intertwined lives of a gospel singer, his brother, and a young girl who is a child preacher. Meanwhile, in his lectures, Baldwin remained pessimistic about the future of race relations.

Baldwin's last three books were *The Evidence of Things Not Seen* (1985), about the killing of twenty-eight African American youths in Atlanta, Georgia, in the early 1980s; *The Price of the Ticket: Collected Nonfiction, 1948–1985* (1985); and *Harlem Quartet* (1987).

Baldwin spent most of the remainder of his life in France. In 1986 the French government named him a commander of the Legion of Honor, France's highest civilian award. He died of stomach cancer at his home in France on November 30, 1987, at the age of sixty-three.

TONI CADE BAMBARA (1939–1995)

Writer. Toni Cade Bambara was born Miltona Mirkin Cade in New York City in 1939. She took the name Toni about the time she entered kindergarten, and assumed the name Bambara after finding the signature "Bambara" on a sketchbook in her great-grandmother's trunk. Bambara's mother, who was influenced by the Harlem Renaissance and who profoundly influenced her daughter, encouraged her to explore her creative side and the influences of culture.

Coming of age in the 1960s and 1970s allowed Bambara to participate in both the nationalist and the women's liberation movements. In 1970 she edited *The Black Woman: An Anthology,* which, being the first of its kind, was recognized as inaugurating a renaissance of African American women's literature.

While working in community-focused positions and pursuing her writing, Bambara received her B.A. degree from Queens College in New York in 1959 and an M.A. degree from City College of New York in 1964. Bambara's career in academia and her numerous awards have exemplified her desire to use art to promote the social and political welfare of the African American community, but not at the expense of African American women. Her works, which are infused with both laughter and rage, include: *Gorilla, My Love* (1972); *The Sea Birds Are Still Alive* (1977); and *The Salt Eaters* (1980), which received the American Book Award.

On December 9, 1995, Bambara died of colon cancer in Philadelphia. Her last novel, *Those Bones Are Not My Child*, edited by Toni Morrison, was published posthumously in 1999.

Cover of the Book* The Salt Eaters *(1980). *In addition to this novel, author Toni Cade Bambara published many short stories and edited an anthology of women's literature. Her last novel,* Those Bones Are Not My Child, *was published posthumously in 1999.* ILLUSTRATION BY RICHARD TADDEI. REPRODUCED BY PERMISSION OF VINTAGE BOOKS, A DIVISION OF RANDOM HOUSE, INC.

AMIRI BARAKA (LEROI JONES) (1934–)

Poet, Playwright, Essayist. Amiri Baraka was born Everett LeRoi Jones in Newark, New Jersey, on October 7, 1934. He attended Rutgers University in Newark and Howard University in Washington, D.C., and lived in Greenwich Village in New York City in the 1950s. In 1958 Baraka founded *Yugen* magazine, which he coedited with his wife, Hattie Cohen, and Totem Press. From 1961 to 1964, Baraka worked as an instructor at New York's New School for Social Research. In 1964 he founded the Black Arts Repertory Theater/School, which dissolved in only a few months. He later taught at the State University of New York at Stony Brook, the University of Buffalo, Columbia University, George Washington University, and San Francisco State University, and has served as director of the community theater, Spirit House, in Newark.

In 1961 Baraka published his first book of poetry, *Preface to a Twenty Volume Suicide Note*. His second book, *The Dead Lecturer*, was published in 1964. Fame eluded him, however, until the publication in 1964 of his play *Dutchman*, which received the Obie Award for the best off-Broadway play of the season. The shocking honesty in Baraka's treatment of racial conflict in this and later plays became the hallmark of his work.

After El-Hajj Malik El-Shabazz (more commonly known as Malcolm X) was assassinated in 1965 and following the close of the theater school, LeRoi Jones moved to Harlem, divorced his white Jewish wife, changed his name to Amiri Baraka, and became an advocate for the black nationalist movement. In 1967 Baraka married African American poet Sylvia Robinson, who changed her name to Amina Baraka. He became a Black Muslim the next year, and added the title *imamu* (spiritual leader) to his name. He thereafter led his own Black Muslim organization, called the Temple of Kawaida, in Newark. Baraka described this organization as an "African religious institution—to increase black consciousness." It soon became a focal point of African American political activism in the racially polarized city of Newark. In 1972 Baraka achieved prominence in his role as chairman of the National Black Political Convention.

In 1974, after Baraka began to espouse Marxist-Leninist philosophy and dedicated himself to the working class, he dropped the title imamu. In 1966 Baraka's play *The Slave* won second prize in the drama category at the First World Festival of Dramatic Arts in Dakar, Senegal. Baraka's other published dramatic works include: *The Toilet* (1964); *The Baptism* (1966); *Four Black Revolutionary Plays*

(1969); *J-E-L-L-O* (1970); and *The Motion of History and Other Plays* (1978). He edited, with Larry Neal, *Black Fire: An Anthology of Afro-American Writing* (1968) and *African Congress: A Documentary of the First Modern Pan-African Congress* (1972).

Baraka's works of fiction include the novel *The System of Dante's Hell* (1965) and the story collection *Tales* (1967). He also published: *Black Music* (1967); *Blues People: Negro Music in White America* (1963); *Home: Social Essays* (1966); *In Our Terribleness: Some Elements and Meanings in Black Style* (1970), written with Billy Abernathy (Fundi); *Raise, Race, Rays, Raze: Essays since 1965* (1971); *It's Nation Time* (1970); *Kawaida Studies: The New Nationalism* (1972); *Funk Lore: New Poems (1984–1995)* (1996); *Somebody Blew Up America, and Other Poems* (2004); and *Tales of the Out and the Gone* (2006). In addition to the Obie Award, Baraka's many literary prizes and honors include Guggenheim Foundation and National Endowment for the Arts fellowships.

ARNA W. BONTEMPS (1902–1973)

Poet, Novelist, Dramatist. Arna Wendell Bontemps was one of the most productive African American writers of the twentieth century and a major figure in the Harlem Renaissance. Born in Alexandria, Louisiana, on October 13, 1902, and raised in California, Bontemps received his B.A. degree from Pacific Union College in Angwin, California, in 1923 and his M.A. degree from the University of Chicago in 1943. In 1924 his first poetry appeared in *Crisis* magazine, the NAACP periodical edited by W. E. B. Du Bois. Two years later, "Golgotha Is a Mountain" won the Alexander Pushkin Poetry Prize, and in 1927 "Nocturne at Bethesda" achieved first honors in the *Crisis* poetry contest. *Personals*, Bontemps's collected poems, was published in 1963.

In the late 1920s, Bontemps decided to try his hand at prose, and over the next decade he produced such novels as *God Sends Sunday* (1931); *Black Thunder* (1936); and *Drums at Dusk* (1939). His books for young people include: *We Have Tomorrow* (1945); *Story of the Negro* (1948); *Sad-Faced Boy* (1937); and *Slappy Hooper* (1946). He also edited *American Negro Poetry* (1963) and two anthologies with Langston Hughes, among other works, including a volume of children's poetry. Other publications included: *One Hundred Years of Negro Freedom* (1961); *Anyplace but Here* (published in 1966 in collaboration with Jack Conroy); *Great Slave Narratives* (1969); *The Harlem Renaissance Remembered: Essays* (1972); and *The Old South.* In 1997 *The Pasteboard Bandit*, a children's book written in the 1930s with Langston Hughes, was published posthumously. Bontemps died in Nashville on June 4, 1973, of a heart attack.

GWENDOLYN BROOKS (1917–2000)

Poet. Gwendolyn Brooks was the first African American to win a Pulitzer Prize. Brooks received this prestigious award in 1950 for *Annie Allen*, a volume of poetry that had been published one year earlier. Brooks has been associated with the Black Aesthetic and Black Arts movement of the late 1960s and early 1970s. The trailblazer became the first African American woman to be appointed poetry consultant by the Library of Congress in 1985.

Brooks was born on June 7, 1917, in Topeka, Kansas, but moved to Chicago at an early age. She graduated from Wilson Junior College in 1936 and identified herself with the South Side of Chicago throughout her life. In 1945 she completed a book of poems, *A Street in Bronzeville*, and was selected by *Mademoiselle* magazine as one of the year's ten most outstanding American women. She became a fellow of the American Academy of Arts and Letters in 1946, and received Guggenheim Fellowships for 1946 and 1947. In 1949 she won the Eunice Tietjen Prize for Poetry, an annual competition sponsored by *Poetry* magazine, for the same work that won her the 1950 Pulitzer. She was named poet laureate of the state of Illinois in 1968.

Brooks's insights into the potential alienation in African American life have been represented in her work, which includes a collection of children's poems, *Bronzeville Boys and Girls* (1956); a novel, *Maud Martha* (1953); and the poetry collections *The Bean Eaters* (1960) and *Selected Poems* (1963). She also wrote *In the Mecca* (1968), winner of the 1968 Anisfield-Wolf Award; *Riot* (1969); *The World of Gwendolyn Brooks* (1971); *Report from Part One* (1972), an autobiography; *Family Pictures* (1970); *Beckonings* (1975); *Aloneness* (1971); *Primer for Blacks* (1980); *To Disembark* (1981); *Report from Part Two* (1996); and *In Montgomery: and Other Poems* (2003). Her poems and stories have also been published in magazines and anthologies, including *Soon, One Morning: New Writing by American Negroes, 1940–1962* (1963) and *Beyond the Angry Black* (1966). The publication of *Selected Poems* in 1963 earned her the Robert F. Ferguson Memorial Award. She edited *A Broadside Treasury* (1971) and *Jump Bad: A New Chicago Anthology* (1971).

In 1970 Western Illinois University established the Gwendolyn Brooks Cultural Center. In 1988 Brooks was inducted into the National Women's Hall of Fame. She won an Essence Award that year, and a Frost Medal from the Poetry Society of America in 1990. The Gwendolyn Brooks Center for Black Literature and Creative Writing was founded at Chicago State University in 1990. In 1994 Brooks was asked by the National Endowment for the Humanities to give the Jefferson Lecture in the Humanities. The lectureship is the highest honor bestowed by the U.S. government for intellectual achievement in the humanities. The same year, Chicago's Harold Washington Library Center unveiled a bronze bust of Brooks, and the National Book Foundation awarded her the Medal for Distinguished Contribution to American Letters and $10,000 for her lifetime of achievement. In 1995 Brooks received the National Medal of Arts from President Bill Clinton.

Brooks died of complications from cancer in 2000. Survivors include her daughter, Nora Brooks Blakely; a son, Henry Blakely III; and a grandson. Her husband, poet and writer Henry Blakely Jr., died in 1996.

CLAUDE BROWN (1937–2002)

Novelist. Claude Brown was born on February 23, 1937, in New York City. His claim to literary fame rests largely in his best-selling autobiography, *Manchild in the Promised Land*, published in 1965 when he was twenty-eight years old. The book is the story of Brown's life in Harlem and gives a highly realistic documentary of life in the ghetto. It tells of Brown's escapades with the Harlem Buccaneers, a "bopping gang," and of his later involvement with the Forty Thieves, an elite stealing division of this same gang.

After attending the Wiltwyck School for emotionally disturbed and deprived boys, Brown returned to New York City. He was later sent to Warwick Reform School three times, and eventually made his way downtown to a small loft apartment near Greenwich Village. There, Brown changed his lifestyle, finished high school, and went on to graduate from Howard University in 1965.

Brown began work on his autobiography in 1963, submitting a manuscript of some 1,500 pages that was eventually cut and reworked over a two-year period into the published volume. Brown completed law school in the late 1960s and began practicing in California. In 1976 he published *The Children of Ham*, a story about a group of young African Americans living as a family in a condemned Harlem tenement, begging, stealing, and doing whatever was necessary to survive.

Brown died on February 2, 2002, in New York City, of a lung condition. He was sixty-four.

WILLIAM WELLS BROWN (c. 1815–1884)

Novelist, Playwright. William Wells Brown was the first African American to publish a novel, the first to publish a drama, and the first to publish a travel book. Born enslaved in Lexington, Kentucky, around 1815, and taken to St. Louis as a young boy, Brown worked for a time in the offices of the *St. Louis Times* and then took a job on a riverboat on the Mississippi. In 1834 Brown fled to Canada, taking his name from a friendly Quaker he met there. While working as a steward on Lake Erie ships, he educated himself and became well known as a public speaker. In 1849 he went to England and Paris to attend the Peace Congress, remaining abroad for five years.

Brown's first published work, *The Narrative of William W. Brown* (1847), went into three editions within eight months. A year later, a collection of his poems was published—*The Anti-Slavery Harp*—and in 1852 his travel book, *Three Years in Europe*, appeared in London. Brown's *Clotel, or, The President's Daughter*, a melodramatic novel about miscegenation, was first published in London in 1853. As the first novel by an African American (it subsequently went through two revisions), its historical importance transcends its aesthetic shortcomings.

Brown's other books include: the first African American drama, *The Escape, or, A Leap for Freedom* (1858); *The Black Man: His Antecedents, His Genius, and His Achievements* (1863); *The Negro in the American Rebellion: His Heroism and Fidelity* (1867); and *The Rising Son* (1874).

ED BULLINS (1935–)

Playwright, Essayist, Poet. Ed Bullins was born in Philadelphia on July 2, 1935, and grew up in Los Angeles. Bullins is a writer of drama, and one of the founders of Black Arts/West in the Fillmore District of San Francisco. He patterned this experiment after the Black Arts Repertory Theater/School in Harlem, which was founded and directed by Amiri Baraka. In 1977, when *Daddy*, the sixth play in his Twentieth-Century Cycle, opened at the New Federal Theatre in New York's Henry Street Settlement, Bullins, in an interview with the *New York Times*, foresaw African American theatrical producers taking plays to cities with large African American populations. A leader of the African American theater movement and creator of more than fifty plays, he has yet to have a play produced on Broadway.

Bullins's main themes are the violence and tragedy of drug abuse and the oppressive lifestyle of the ghetto. He presents his material in a realistic and natural style. Between 1965 and 1971, he wrote *Dialect Determinism (or The Rally)*; *How Do You Do*; *Goin' a Buffalo*; *Clara's Ole Man*; *The Electronic Nigger*; *In the Wine Time*; and *The Fabulous Miss Marie*.

Bullins has been a member of Black Arts Alliance, working with Baraka in producing films on the West

Coast. Bullins has also been connected with the New Lafayette Theatre in Harlem, where he was a resident playwright. His books include: *Five Plays* (1970); *New Plays from the Black Theatre* (editor, 1969); *The Reluctant Rapist* (1973); *The New Lafayette Theatre Presents* (editor, 1974); *The Theme Is Blackness* (1972); *Four Dynamite Plays* (1971); *The Duplex: A Black Love Fable in Four Movements* (1971); *The Hungered One: Early Writings* (1971); and *How Do You Do: A Nonsense Drama* (1965).

In 1995 Bullins took up the position of professor of theater and distinguished artist in residence at Northeastern University in Boston. He held this position until 2000. He is artistic director of the Roxbury Crossroads Theatre in Massachusetts. Bullins is the recipient of a number of honors, awards, and fellowships, including three Obie Awards for distinguished playwriting.

OCTAVIA E. BUTLER (1947–2006)

Novelist. Born in Pasadena, California, on June 22, 1947, Octavia Estelle Butler was a graduate of Pasadena City College. She attended science fiction workshops, including the Clarion Science Fiction Writers' Workshop, and was a member of Science Fiction Writers of America. Her writing focused on the impact of race and gender on future society. In 1985 Butler won three of science fiction's highest honors for her novella *Bloodchild and Other Stories*: the Nebula, Hugo, and Locus awards. She also won a Hugo in 1984 for her short story "Speech Sounds." The 1987 novella *The Evening and the Morning and the Night* was nominated for a Nebula Award. In 1995 Butler won a MacArthur Foundation fellowship.

Butler's other works include: the Patternmaster series, consisting of the novels *Patternmaster* (1976), *Mind of My Mind* (1977), *Survivor* (1978), *Wild Seed* (1980), and *Clay's Ark* (1984); the historical fantasy *Kindred* (1979); the Xenogenesis trilogy, consisting of *Dawn: Xenogenesis* (1987), *Adulthood Rites* (1988), and *Imago* (1989); the dystopian *Parable of the Sower* (1993); and a sequel, *Parable of the Talents* (1998). She has also served as a contributor to such science fiction publications as *Clarion*, *Future Life*, and Isaac Asimov's *Science Fiction Magazine*.

Butler died after hitting her head during a fall at her home in Lake Forest Park, Washington, in 2006.

BARBARA CHASE-RIBOUD

See chapter 26, Visual and Applied Arts.

CHARLES W. CHESNUTT (1858–1932)

Novelist. Called the first major African American fiction writer and the first of his race to balance African American and white characters in an African American novel, Charles Waddell Chesnutt holds a prominent place in American literary history. His best fiction dealt with the themes of prejudice, social injustice, and segregation. He handled satire entertainingly, and he was direct and insightful in his nonfiction works and speeches.

Born in Cleveland, Ohio, on June 20, 1858, Chesnutt moved to North Carolina with his family at the age of eight. Largely self-educated, he was admitted to the Ohio bar in 1887, the same year in which his first story, "The Goophered Grapevine," was published in the *Atlantic Monthly*. This was followed in 1899 by two collections of stories: *The Conjure Woman* and *The Wife of His Youth*.

Chesnutt's first novel, *The House behind the Cedars* (1900), dealt with a young girl's attempt to "pass" for

Charles W. Chesnutt Stamp. *The Chesnutt stamp is part of the Black Heritage series, which began in 1978 and honors one African American each year. Chesnutt (1858–1932) wrote novels and short stories, as well as a biography of Frederick Douglass.* **AP PHOTO/USPS**

white. A year later, *The Marrow of Tradition* examined the violence of the post-Reconstruction period. His final novel, *The Colonel's Dream*, was published in 1905 and typified Chesnutt's ingratiating approach to his art—an approach that the writers of the Harlem school were later to reject. Chesnutt also wrote a biography, *Frederick Douglass* (1899). He died on November 15, 1932.

ALICE CHILDRESS (1920–1994)

Playwright, Novelist. Alice Childress was born to a working-class family in Charleston, South Carolina, on October 12, 1920, but moved to and attended public school in Harlem. Childress studied acting at the American Negro Theatre and attended Radcliffe Institute from 1966 to 1968 through a Harvard University appointment as a scholar-writer. During this time, she became involved in a number of social causes. Her plays include: *Florence* (1949, one act); *Gold through the Trees* (1952); *Just a Little Simple* (1950, based on Langston Hughes's *Simple Speaks His Mind*); *Trouble in Mind* (1955); *Wedding Band* (1966); *Wine in the Wilderness* (1970); and *When the Rattlesnake Sounds* (1975), a play about Harriet Tubman.

Childress also edited *Black Scenes* (1971), which included excerpts from plays in the Zenith series for children. Her other works include: *Like One of the Family: Conversations from a Domestic's Life* (1956); *A Hero Ain't Nothing but a Sandwich* (1973), one of her most influential and controversial works; *A Short Walk* (1979); *Rainbow Jordan* (1981); and *Many Closets* (1987). Childress's play *Trouble in Mind* won the Obie Award in 1956 as the best original off-Broadway production. In the 1980s, she wrote a play based on the life of African American comedienne Jackie (Moms) Mabley. The play was produced in New York City. Childress's work was noted for its frank treatment of racial issues, its compassionate yet discerning characterizations, and its universal appeal. Her books and plays often dealt with such controversial subjects as miscegenation and teenage drug addiction. Childress died of cancer complications on August 14, 1994.

***Book Cover of* A Hero Ain't Nothin' but a Sandwich (1973).** *Novelist and playwright Alice Childress's controversial book portrays the viewpoint of a thirteen-year-old Harlem resident on his way to becoming a heroin addict.* REPRODUCED BY PERMISSION OF AVON BOOKS, INC.

J. CALIFORNIA COOPER

Short Story Writer, Novelist, Playwright. Joan California Cooper was born to Joseph and Maxine Cooper in Berkeley, California. She attended a technical high school and studied at San Francisco State College and the University of California. After living for a time in Texas and Alaska, she returned to northern California. Cooper adopted the name "California" after someone compared her writing to that of Tennessee Williams. Cooper believes that age is unimportant, and refuses to reveal the year of her birth. Although little is known about Cooper's private life, her writing has brought her to the attention of the literary world.

Cooper once stated that she could tell stories before she could write. During her childhood, she created plays and performed them for family and friends. Her plays, some of which have not been published, include: *Everytime It Rains*; *System, Suckers, and Success*; *How Now?*; *The Unintended*; *The Mother*; *Ahhh*; *Strangers*, for which Cooper was named San Francisco's Best Black Playwright in 1978; and *Loners*, which is included in Eileen J. Ostrow's *Center Stage* (1981). Cooper's plays have been performed in several Bay Area theaters and venues, including Berkeley's Black Repertory Theatre and the San Francisco Palace of Fine Arts, as well as on college campuses, public television, and the radio. After Alice Walker read Cooper's work, she encouraged Cooper to write short stories.

Walker's publishing company, Wild Trees Press, published Cooper's first collection of short stories, *A Piece of Mine* (1984). In a foreword to Cooper's collection, Walker wrote that "in its strong folk flavor, Cooper's work reminds us of Langston Hughes and Zora Neale Hurston. Like theirs, her style is deceptively simple and direct, and the vale of tears in which some of her characters reside is never so deep that a rich chuckle at a foolish person's foolishness cannot be heard." Cooper's second collection of stories, *Homemade Love* (1986), won an American Book Award in 1989. Her subsequent short story collections are *Some Soul to Keep* (1987); *The Matter Is Life* (1991); *Some Love, Some Pain, Sometime* (1995); and *The Future Has a Past* (2000). She has also published a collection of stories titled *Wild Stars Seeking Midnight Suns* (2006). Her short stories have been reprinted in various publications, such as *Daughters of Africa: An International Anthology of Words and Writings by Women of African Descent from the Ancient Egyptian to the Present* (1992), edited by Margaret Busby, and *Cornerstones: An Anthology of African American Literature* (1996), edited by Melvin Donaldson. Cooper has published novels, including: *Family* (1991); *In Search of Satisfaction* (1994); *The Wake of the Wind* (1998); *Some People, Some Other Place* (2004); and *Life Is Short but Wide* (2009).

Cooper's additional awards include the Literary Lion Award and the James Baldwin Award, both from the American Library Association. In addition, she was named Woman of the Year by the University of Massachusetts and Best Female Writer in Texas. J. California Cooper is one of today's most popular African American authors.

COUNTEE CULLEN (1903–1946)

Poet. Born Countee LeRoy Porter on May 30, 1903, in Baltimore, the details of Cullen's early life are sketchy. He was orphaned at an early age and adopted at age fifteen by the Reverend Frederick Cullen, pastor of New York's Salem Methodist Church. At New York University, Cullen won Phi Beta Kappa honors and was awarded the Witter Bynner Poetry Prize. In 1925, while still a student at New York University, Cullen completed *Color*, a volume of poetry that received the Harmon Foundation's first gold medal for literature two years later.

In 1926 Cullen earned his M.A. at Harvard, and a year later finished both *The Ballad of the Brown Girl* and *Copper Sun*. This was Followed in 1929 by *The Black Christ*, written during a two-year sojourn in France on a Guggenheim Fellowship. In 1927 he edited *Caroling Dusk: An Anthology of Verse by Negro Poets*. The book was reprinted in 1972.

Upon his return to New York City, Cullen began a teaching career in the public school system. During this period, he also published a novel, *One Way to Heaven* (1932), as well as *The Medea and Other Poems* (1935), *The Lost Zoo* (1940), and *My Lives and How I Lost Them* (1942). Throughout his life, Cullen promoted the works of other African American writers and was a leading figure in the Harlem Renaissance. In 1947, a year after his death, Cullen's own selection of his best work was collected in a volume published under the title *On These I Stand*. Cullen died of uremic poisoning on January 9, 1946, in New York City.

SAMUEL R. DELANY (1942–)

Novelist, Literary Critic. Born in Harlem on April 1, 1942, Samuel Ray Delany was a published writer by the age of nineteen. He became an award-winning and prolific writer of science fiction, novelettes, and novels. His first book was *The Jewels of Aptor* (1962), followed by *Captives of the Flame* (1963); *The Towers of Toron* (1964); *City of a Thousand Suns* (1965); *The Ballad of Beta-2* (1965); *Babel-17* (1966); *Empire Star* (1966); *The Einstein Intersection* (1967); *Out of the Dead City* (1968); and *Nova* (1968). *Babel-17* and *The Einstein Intersection* both won Nebula Awards from the Science Fiction Writers of America, as did his short stories "Aye, and Gomorrah" and "Time Considered as a Helix of Semi-Precious Stones," which also won a Hugo Award at the World Science Fiction Convention in Heidelberg. Delany coedited the speculative fiction quarterly *Quark* (nos. 1, 2, 3, 4) with his former wife, award-winning poet Marilyn Hacker. He also wrote, directed, and edited the half-hour film *The Orchid*. In 1975 Delany was Visiting Butler Chair Professor of English at the State University of New York at Buffalo. During the 1990s, he taught at the University of Massachusetts–Amherst. In 2001 he became professor of English and creative writing at Temple University in Philadelphia.

Delany's other books include: *Distant Stars* (1981); *Stars in My Pocket Like Grains of Sand* (1984); *Flight from Nevèrÿon* (1985); *Neveryóna* (1986); *The Bridge of Lost Desire* (1988); the controversial *Hogg* (1996); the novella *Phallos* (2004); and the novel *Dark Reflections* (2007). His nonfiction works include: *The Jewel-Hinged Jaw: Notes on the Language of Science Fiction* (1977; rev. ed. 2009); *The American Shore* (1978); *Starboard Wine: More Notes on the Language of Science Fiction* (1984); *The Straits of Messina* (1989); *The Motion of Light in Water* (autobiography, 1988); *The Mad Man* (1994); *They Fly at Ciron* (1995);

Memorial to Countee Cullen ***(Meredith Bergmann, 1995).*** *This sculpture of Cullen, a poet of the Harlem Renaissance, was commissioned by the Bronx Council on the Arts for exhibition in Woodlawn Cemetery, New York, where Cullen is buried. It is now at the Countee Cullen Branch of the New York Public Library.* CLARENCE DAVIS/NEW YORK DAILY NEWS ARCHIVE/GETTY IMAGES

Atlantis: Three Tales (1995); *Times Square Red, Times Square Blue* (1999); and *Shorter Views: Queer Thoughts & the Politics of the Paraliterary* (1999).

RITA DOVE (1952–)

Poet, Educator. Rita Dove was born on August 28, 1952, in Akron, Ohio. She received a B.A. from Miami University in Oxford, Ohio, in 1973, and an M.F.A. from the University of Iowa in 1977. Dove also attended the University of Tübingen in Germany in 1974 and 1975.

Dove began her teaching career at Arizona State University in 1981 as an assistant professor. She spent 1982 as a writer-in-residence at Tuskegee Institute (now Tuskegee University). By 1984, she was an associate professor, and by 1987, a full professor. Dove, who has served on the editorial boards of the literary journals *Callaloo*, *Gettysburg Review*, and *TriQuarterly*, joined the University of Virginia's English Department in 1989. She teaches creative writing.

Dove won the 1987 Pulitzer Prize for Poetry for a collection titled *Thomas and Beulah*. Her themes are universal, encompassing much of the human condition and occasionally commenting on racial issues. She also published *Yellow House on the Corner* (1980); *Museum* (1983); *Fifth Sunday* (short stories, 1985); *Grace Notes* (1989); *Selected Poems* (1993); *Through the Ivory Gate* (novel, 1993); *Mother Love* (1995); *The Darker Face of the Earth: A Verse Play in Fourteen Scenes* (1995); *On the*

Rita Dove, Poet, 2009. *Dove, who won the Pulitzer Prize for* Thomas and Beulah *(1986), was appointed poet laureate of the United States in 1993. In 2009 she published* Sonata Mulattica: A Life in Five Movements and a Short Play: Poems, *about the violinist George Bridgetower.* DAMON WINTER/THE NEW YORK TIMES/REDUX PICTURES

Bus with Rosa Parks (1999); *American Smooth* (2004); and *Sonata Mulattica* (2009).

In addition to the Pulitzer Prize, Dove has won many honors, including a Presidential scholarship (1970); a Fulbright scholarship (1974, 1975); grants from the National Endowment for the Humanities (1978, 1989); a Guggenheim Fellowship (1983–1984); the General Electric Foundation Award for Younger Poets (1987); the Ohio Governor's Award (1988); an Andrew W. Mellon fellowship (1988–1989); a University of Virginia Center for Advanced Studies fellowship (1989–1992); the Walt Whitman Award (1990); the Kennedy Center Fund for New American Plays Award for *The Darker Face of the Earth*; and the National Humanities Medal (1996). Dove served as poet laureate of the Commonwealth of Virginia from 2004 to 2006, and she became a fellow of the American Academy of Arts and Sciences in 2006. So also became a chancellor of Academy of American Poets in 2006.

Dove was named U.S. poet laureate, a one-year Library of Congress post, in 1993. She was the first African American and the youngest person ever to earn the appointment. On April 22, 1994, PBS aired a piece titled "Poet Laureate Rita Dove" on *Bill Moyers' Journal,* in which Dove said she hoped to use the position to revive public interest in serious literature.

PAUL LAURENCE DUNBAR (1872–1906)

Poet, Novelist, Short Story Writer, Essayist. The first African American poet to gain a national reputation in the United States and precursor to the Harlem Renaissance, Paul Laurence Dunbar was also the first to use African American dialect within the formal structure of his work. Born of formerly enslaved parents in Dayton, Ohio, on June 27, 1872, Dunbar worked as an elevator operator after graduating from high school. His first book of poetry, *Oak and Ivy,* was privately printed in 1893. It was followed two years later by *Majors and Minors.* Neither book was an immediate sensation, but there were enough favorable reviews in such magazines as *Harper's* to encourage Dunbar in the pursuit of a full-fledged literary career. In 1896 Dunbar completed *Lyrics of a Lowly Life,* the single work upon which his subsequent reputation was irrevocably established.

Before his untimely death of tuberculosis in 1906, Dunbar had become the dominant presence in the world of African American poetry. His later works included: *Lyrics of Sunshine and Shadow* (1905); *Li'l Gal* (1904); *Howdy, Honey, Howdy* (1905); *A Plantation Portrait* (1905); *Joggin' Erlong* (1906); and *Complete Poems,* published posthumously in 1913. This last work contains not only the dialect poems that were his trademark, but many poems in conventional English as well. The book enjoyed such enormous popularity that it has never gone out of print. Dunbar also published four volumes of short stories and four novels, including *The Sport of Gods* (1902), considered his best; *The Love of Landry* (1900); and *The Uncalled* (1898). Dunbar, whose work was rediscovered in the second half of the twentieth century, is sometimes referred to as the African American Alexander Pushkin or Alexandre Dumas, fils.

RALPH ELLISON (1914–1994)

Novelist, Essayist. Ralph Ellison's critical and artistic reputation rests largely on a single masterpiece, his first and only novel, *Invisible Man* (1952), a story about an unnamed black man's search for identity in 1940s New York. An instant classic, the novel was given the National Book Award for fiction in 1952 and the Russwurm Award in 1953. Years in the making, the novel's success heralded the emergence of a major writing talent. Ellison worked on a second novel for more than forty years, but at the time of his death, the untitled work was still incomplete.

Ellison was born in Oklahoma City, Oklahoma, on March 1, 1914, and came to New York City in the late 1930s, after having studied music at Tuskegee Institute for three years. Initially interested in sculpture, he turned to writing after coming under the influence of T. S. Eliot's poetry and as a direct consequence of his friendship with novelist Richard Wright. Ellison worked for the Federal Writers' Project and wrote for a variety of publications during the late 1930s to early 1940s. In 1942 he became the managing editor of the *Negro Quarterly*. He began writing *Invisible Man* in 1945. During World War II, Ellison worked as a cook in the U.S. Merchant Marines.

In addition to the National Book Award, Ellison won a Rockefeller Foundation Award in 1954, was elected to the National Institute of Arts and Letters, received a Medal of Freedom from President Lyndon Johnson in 1969, was named chevalier de l'Ordre des Arts et Lettres by France in 1969, and was given a National Medal of Arts in 1985. Ellison was also the recipient of more than a dozen honorary degrees, including doctor of letters degrees from Harvard University (1974) and Wesleyan University (1980). Three years after the publication of *Invisible Man*, the American Academy of Arts and Letters awarded Ellison the Prix de Rome, which enabled him to live and write in Italy until 1957.

Back in the United States, Ellison began an academic career. He taught Russian and American literature courses at Bard College in Annandale-on-Hudson, New York, for three years and spent the early 1960s as a visiting professor at the University of Chicago, Yale, and Rutgers, where he was a writer-in-residence. From 1970 to 1980, Ellison was the Albert Schweitzer Professor of Humanities at New York University.

Ellison's second work was a book of essays titled *Shadow and Act*. Published in 1964, excerpts from the book were printed in several literary journals. Ellison began writing his second novel in 1954 and continued to revise it until he died. A 1967 fire destroyed 350 pages of his manuscript. A condensed version of the novel's manuscript was edited by John F. Callahan and published in 1999 with the title *Juneteenth*. A longer version of Ellison's manuscript was prepared by Callahan and Adam Bradley for publication in 2010.

Invisible Man: A Memorial to Ralph Ellison, *New York City (Elizabeth Catlett, 2003)*. *Dedicated on May 1, 2003, the bronze sculpture is located in Manhattan's Riverside Park, a place Ellison, author of the novel* Invisible Man *(1952), often visited.* **NANCY SIESEL/THE NEW YORK TIMES/REDUX PICTURES**

In 1982, the thirtieth anniversary edition of *Invisible Man*, with a new introduction by Ellison, was published. In 1986, a second collection of essays and talks was published as *Going to the Territory*. *The Collected Essays of Ralph Ellison*, edited by Callahan, was published posthumously in 1995.

Ellison died of pancreatic cancer in New York City on April 16, 1994. On May 26, 1994, a memorial tribute to him was held at the American Academy of Arts and Letters in New York.

MARI EVANS (1923–)

Poet. Mari Evans was born in Toledo, Ohio, in 1923, and studied at the University of Toledo. She is best known as a poet and social critic, but has also published plays, songs, and children's books. In 1963 her poetry was published in *Phylon*, *Negro Digest*, and *Dialog*. Two years later, she was awarded a John Hay Whitney Fellowship. One of her better-known poems is "The Alarm Clock," which deals with the rude awakening of the African American to the white "establishment." This work captures and summarizes the civil rights scene of the 1960s in the United States.

Evans's books include: *I Am a Black Woman* (1970); *Where Is All the Music?* (1968); *Black Women Writers (1950–1980): A Critical Evaluation* (1984), edited by Evans, covering fifteen African American women poets, novelists, and playwrights; *Nightstar: 1973–1978* (1980); *J. D.* (1973); *I Look at Me* (1974); *Jim Flying High* (1979); *Singing Black: Alternative Nursery Rhymes for Children* (1998); *Dear Corinne, Tell Somebody! Love, Annie: A Book about Secrets* (1999); and *Clarity as Concept: A Poet's Perspective* (critical essays, 2006).

Evans has taught at Cornell University and Indiana University.

JESSIE REDMON FAUSET (1882–1961)

Writer, Editor, Educator. Jessie Redmon Fauset, born April 27, 1882, was a central figure during the Harlem Renaissance—she was sometimes called the "Mother of the Harlem Renaissance"—not only for encouraging the careers of many of the major writers of the era, but also through her own literary contributions. In 1919 Fauset became literary editor of *Crisis* magazine, founded by W. E. B. Du Bois. She held that position until 1927. Fauset excelled as an editor, and under her leadership, *Crisis* outsold its rival magazine, *Opportunity*, started by Charles S. Johnson. She also realized Du Bois's plan for a periodical for children aged six to sixteen called the *Brownies Book* and was its functional editor.

Fauset's editorial experiences and travel heightened her own sensibilities about the images of African Americans. Her writings professed an awareness of the racism and sexism that existed during the 1920s and 1930s. She contributed numerous short stories, essays, critiques, poetry, and reviews to the magazine. She published her first novel, *There Is Confusion*, in 1924. The book was her response to an unrealistic portrayal of African Americans by white novelist T. S. Stribling. After Fauset's break from *Crisis* in 1927, she established her place as an author and published *Plum Bun: A Novel without a Moral* (1929), *The Chinaberry Tree* (1931), and *Comedy, American Style* (1933).

Fauset was the first black woman to matriculate at Cornell University. She received her B.A. (Phi Beta Kappa) from Cornell in 1905 and her M.A. from the University of Pennsylvania in 1919. She later taught at Fisk University in the summer and in various high school and college settings. In her later years, she returned to teaching, in part because the publishing world was still not ready for an African American, let alone a woman.

Fauset died in Philadelphia on April 30, 1961, of hypertensive heart disease. Fauset's contributions to the dialogue about race, class, and gender were more fully recognized after her death. She challenged the world of publishing with her own work, and assisted other artists, making it possible for unrealistic and negative perceptions of African Americans to be confronted.

RUDOLPH FISHER (1897–1934)

Writer, Physician, Community Leader. Although he was a radiologist, Rudolph Fisher is best known as a leading writer of the Harlem Renaissance. Fisher wrote short stories and novels that depicted real life in the Harlem community. He also became the first African American to write detective fiction.

Fisher was born on May 9, 1897, in Washington, D.C. He grew up in a middle-class family who saw that he was rigorously educated at primary and secondary schools in Providence, Rhode Island, and New York City. He graduated Phi Beta Kappa from Brown University with B.A. and M.A. degrees. In 1924 Fisher graduated summa cum laude from Howard University Medical School in Washington. During his medical internship at Freedmen's Hospital in the same city, he published his first short story, "The City of Refuge," in the *Atlantic Monthly*.

Continuing his medical education, Fisher trained at Columbia University's College of Physicians and Surgeons from 1925 to 1927, after which he entered private practice. During this time, Fisher continued writing, publishing five short stories in *Atlantic Monthly* and *McClure's*, an essay in *American Mercury*, and an article in the *Journal of Infectious Diseases*.

Fisher published his first novel, *The Walls of Jericho*, in 1928. In the novel, Fisher blends all of Harlem life into one story and bridges the gap between the classes. *The Conjure-Man Dies: A Mystery Tale of Dark Harlem* (1932) was his second novel and the first full-length detective novel with all African American characters published by an African American author. Fisher published two children's stories in 1932 and 1933, "Ezekiel" and "Ezekiel Learns," and in 1933 he published the short stories "Guardians of the Law" and "Miss Cynthie." The latter story appeared in *Best Short Stories of 1934*.

In addition to his writing career, Fisher was superintendent of the International Hospital in Manhattan from 1929 to 1932 and was also a gifted musician. Between 1930 and 1934, he was a roentgenologist (radiologist) for the New York City Health Department and served in the 369th Infantry. He died of cancer on December 16, 1934, in New York City.

CHARLES FULLER (1939–)

Playwright. Charles Fuller was born on March 5, 1939, in Philadelphia, Pennsylvania. He became stage struck in his high school days when he went to the Old Walnut Street Theater in his native Philadelphia and saw a Yiddish play starring Molly Picon and Menasha Skulnik. He did not understand a word of it, but, he said, "it was live theater, and I felt myself responding to it."

In 1959 Fuller entered the army and served in Japan and South Korea, after which he attended Villanova University and La Salle College. While Fuller was working as a housing inspector in Philadelphia, the McCarter Theater in Princeton, New Jersey, produced his first play, *The Village: A Party* (1968), also known as *The Perfect Party*. The theme concerned interracial marriage, and Fuller later described it as "one of the world's worst interracial plays." However, during this time he met members of the Negro Ensemble Company (NEC) and, in 1974, he wrote *In the Deepest Part of Sleep* for them. For the NEC's tenth anniversary, Fuller wrote *The Brownsville Raid* about African American soldiers who were dishonorably discharged on President Theodore Roosevelt's orders in 1906 after a shootout in Brownsville, Texas. The play was a hit, and Fuller followed it a few seasons later with *Zooman and the Sign*, a melodrama that won two Obie Awards.

A Soldier's Play, which won the Pulitzer Prize for Drama in 1982, was his fourth play for the NEC. This drama, dealing with a murder set in a backwater New Orleans army camp in 1944, opened the NEC's fifteenth anniversary season in 1981 with a long run and was hailed by the *New York Times* as "tough, taut and fully realized." *A Soldier's Play* was retitled *A Soldier's Story* when it was produced as a film in 1984 by Columbia Pictures. Fuller wrote the screenplay, and Howard E. Rollins Jr. was the film's star. In 1999 Fuller wrote and produced a three-part interlocking script called *Love Songs* for Showtime. The three different sections featured Louis Gossett Jr., Robert Townsend, and Andre Braugher. The recipient of fellowships from the Guggenheim Foundation, the Rockefeller Foundation, and the National Endowment for the Arts, Fuller describes himself as a playwright who happens to be African American, rather than an African American playwright.

ERNEST J. GAINES (1933–)

Novelist, Short Story Writer. Ernest James Gaines was born on January 15, 1933, on a plantation in Oscar, Louisiana. The rural folk culture of this area has played an important role in his fiction. He moved to California in 1949, where he did his undergraduate study at San Francisco State College. In 1959 he received the Wallace Stegner Fellowship in creative writing. The following year, he was awarded the Joseph Henry Jackson Literary Award.

Gaines's first novel was *Catherine Carmier* (1964). Others followed, including *Of Love and Dust* (1967); *Barren Summer* (completed in 1963, but never published); *The Autobiography of Miss Jane Pittman* (1971); *A Long Day in November* (1971, for young people); and *In My Father's House* (1978). Ironically, *The Autobiography of Miss Jane Pittman* was banned in a Conroe, Texas, seventh-grade racial tolerance course in 1995 because of what the school considered a liberal use of racial slurs. A 1974 television adaptation starring Cicely Tyson boosted Gaines's reputation. His *A Gathering of Old Men*, published in 1983, was also made into a film.

In 1994 Gaines's novel *A Lesson before Dying* won the National Book Critics Circle Award for fiction and became the October 1997 selection of the Oprah Book Club. *A Lesson before Dying* was adapted for the small screen by HBO in 1999, and won an Emmy Award for Outstanding Made-for-Television Movie. Gaines's *Mozart and Leadbelly: Stories and Essays* was published in 2005.

HENRY LOUIS GATES JR. (1950–)

Literary critic, Scholar, Educator. Henry Louis Gates Jr. was born in Keyser, West Virginia, on September 16, 1950. His father, Henry Louis Gates Sr., a gifted storyteller, worked at the local paper mill; his mother cleaned houses in addition to raising her two children, in whose education she was actively involved.

Initially enrolling at Potomac State College, Gates later transferred to Yale, where he graduated with a B.A. in history. At Yale, Gates volunteered to work at a mission hospital in Tanzania and traveled throughout Africa in fulfillment of the nonacademic portion of his degree requirement. Gates then attended Cambridge University, where he studied English literature, and, with the aid of a Ford Foundation Fellowship, worked toward his M.A. and Ph.D. in English. At Cambridge, he met the Nigerian playwright Wole Soyinka, who was denied an appointment at the school because, at the time, African literature was not considered "real literature." Soyinka, who later went on to win the Nobel Prize in Literature, became Gates's mentor.

In 1976, after dropping out of the Yale Law School and working as a secretary in the Afro-American Studies Department, Gates became a lecturer and then an assistant professor in the department. Denied tenure at Yale, Gates moved to Cornell University, Duke University, then Harvard, where he was appointed professor of the humanities and English. He is also chair of the African and African American Studies Department at Harvard and directs Harvard's W. E. B. Du Bois Institute for African and African American Research. In 2002 Gates was selected to give the Jefferson Lecture for the National Endowment for the Humanities. He was named Alphonse Fletcher Jr. University Professor at Harvard in 2006, and the following year was honored as one of *Time* magazine's twenty-five most influential Americans.

In addition to Gates's many honors and awards, he was named a MacArthur Foundation Fellow in 1981. Gates, a literary theorist, cultural critic, and historian dedicated to preserving the texts of African and African American writers and artists, published *The Signifying Monkey* in 1988. This seminal work, which attempted to define a black cultural aesthetic, won the 1989 American Book Award. Gates's position between separatist and traditionalist perspectives in his approach to integrating African American literature into the canon of Western literature has stirred controversy on both sides of the cultural spectrum. His works also include: *Loose Canons: Notes on the Culture Wars* (1992); *Colored People: A Memoir* (1994); *Thirteen Ways of Looking at a Black Man* (1997); *The African-American Century: How Black Americans Have Shaped Our Century* (2000), with Cornel West; *America behind the Color Line: Dialogues with African Americans* (2004); and *Finding Oprah's Roots: Finding Your Own* (2007). He has also edited numerous books, including *Africana: The Encyclopedia of the African and African Experience* (1999), with K. Anthony Appiah; *African American Lives* (2004), with Evelyn Brooks Higginbotham; and the eight-volume *African American National Biography* (2008), also with Higginbotham.

Gates serves as editor in chief for the online Oxford African American Studies Center, as well as the *Root*, an online magazine that covers African American news and culture. In addition, Gates has been involved in a number of educational projects for public television, including *Wonders of the African World* (2000), *America beyond the Color Line* (2004), and the documentary series *African American Lives* (2006) and *African American Lives 2*, which explored African American history through genealogy and science.

NIKKI GIOVANNI (1943–)

Poet, Educator, Activist. Nikki Giovanni was born Yolande Cornelia Giovanni in Knoxville, Tennessee, on June 7, 1943, but she was raised in Cincinnati, Ohio. She studied at the University of Cincinnati from 1961 to 1963 and received her B.A. from Fisk University in 1967. She also attended the University of Pennsylvania School of Social Work for one year and Columbia University School of the Arts for one year in the late 1960s.

In 1969 Giovanni taught at Queens College of the City University New York (CUNY) and Rutgers University before founding a communications and publishing company called NikTom, Ltd. In the mid- to late 1980s, she resumed teaching, spending 1984 as a visiting professor at Ohio State University and the subsequent three years at the College of Mount Saint Joseph on the Ohio as a creative writing professor. Since 1987, Giovanni has taught at Virginia Polytechnic Institute and State University, first as a visiting professor and then as a full professor of English beginning in 1989. That year, she also directed the Warm Hearth Writer's Workshop. From 1990 to 1993, Giovanni served on the board of directors for the Virginia Foundation for the Humanities and Public Policy.

Giovanni's first book of poetry, *Black Feeling, Black Talk*, published in the mid-1960s, was followed by *Black Judgment* in 1968. These two works were combined as *Black Feeling, Black Talk, Black Judgment* in 1970. By 1974, Giovanni's poems could be found in many African American literature anthologies, and she also became a media personality through her television appearances, during which she read her poetry. Many of her poems were put to soul or gospel music accompaniment. Such recordings include *Truth Is on Its Way*, winner of the National Association of Radio and Television Announcers Award in 1972, and *Spirit to Spirit*, a video produced by PBS, winner of the Oakland Museum Film Festival Silver Apple Award in 1988.

Giovanni's first poetry collections filtered experience through a black perspective, and were considered revolutionary. Later in her career, her experience as a mother became a major driving force in her poetry.

A prolific author, Giovanni's many books include: *Re: Creation* (poetry, 1970); *Spin a Soft Black Song: Poems for Children* (1971); *Night Comes Softly: Anthology of Black Female Voices* (editor, 1970); *My House* (poetry, 1972); *Gemini: An Extended Autobiographical Statement on My First Twenty-five Years of Being a Black Poet* (nonfiction, 1971); *Ego Tripping and Other Poems for Young People* (1973); *A Dialogue* (nonfiction, written with James Baldwin, 1973); and *A Poetic Equation: Conversations between Nikki Giovanni and Margaret Walker* (nonfiction, 1974).

Other works include: *The Women and the Men: Poems* (1975); *Cotton Candy on a Rainy Day* (poetry, 1978); *Vacation Time: Poems for Children* (1980), dedicated to her son, Tommy, and winner of the Children's Reading Roundtable of Chicago Award; *Those Who Ride the Night Winds* (poetry, 1984); *Sacred Cows ... and Other Edibles* (nonfiction, 1988), winner of the Ohioana Library Award in 1988; *Grand Mothers: Poems, Reminiscences, and Short Stories about the Keepers of Our Traditions* (1994); *Racism 101* (nonfiction, 1994); *Knoxville, Tennessee* (coauthored with Larry Johnson, 1994); *The Selected Poems of Nikki Giovanni* (1995); *Blues for all the Changes* (poems, 1999); *Grand Fathers: Reminiscences, Poems, Recipes, and Photos of the Keepers of Our Traditions* (1999); *Quilting the Black-Eyed Pea* (poems, 2002), a book for children; *Jimmy Grasshopper versus the Ants* (2007); *Rosa* (2005), a picture book about Rosa Parks, the civil rights pioneer; *Acolytes* (2007), her latest collection of poems; and *On My Journey Now: Looking at African-American History through the Spirituals* (2007).

Giovanni has won numerous awards, including the Highest Achievement Award in 1971 from *Mademoiselle*; life membership to the National Council of Negro Women in 1973; the Outstanding Woman of Tennessee Award in 1985; the Post-Corbett Award in 1986; the Langston Hughes Award for Distinguished Contribution to Arts and Letters in 1996; the NAACP Image Award for Literature in 1998; and a Governor's Award in the Arts from the Tennessee Arts Commission in 1999. In addition, Giovanni has received honorary degrees from numerous institutions.

ELOISE GREENFIELD (1929–)

Children's Author. Born Eloise Little on May 17, 1929, in Parmele, North Carolina, Greenfield's family moved to Washington, D.C., when she was still a baby, and she grew up happily in a close-knit, public housing development in an urban neighborhood. After attending Miner Teachers College, she worked in various clerical and secretarial positions. By 1950, she had begun experimenting with creative writing. After years of studying and persevering, Greenfield met fellow writers and made valuable contacts when she joined the District of Columbia Black Writers Workshop in the early 1970s. Soon thereafter, her first picture book, *Bubbles*, was published.

With that initial success, Greenfield established her own niche within the arena of children's books and has published, on average, one book each year. With the goal of encouraging children to develop positive attitudes about themselves, Greenfield's stories capture both the unique and universal experiences of growing up African American. Much of her fiction, as in the novel *Sister* (1974), is concerned with bonding within African American families. Greenfield's biographies of distinguished African Americans, as well as her poetic picture books, have appeared on numerous lists of notable book and have placed the author in demand as a speaker at writers' conferences and in classrooms.

Greenfield has also published *Honey, I Love, and Other Love Poems* (1978); *William and the Good Old Days* (1993); *Sweet Baby Coming* (1994); *On My Horse* (1995); *For the Love of the Game: Michael Jordan and Me* (1996); *Angels* (1998); *Water, Water* (1999); *I Can Draw a Weeposaur and Other Dinosaurs* (2001); *How They Got Over: African Americans and the Call of the Sea* (2002); *In the Land of Words: New and Selected Poems* (2003); *The Friendly Four* (2006); *When the Horses Ride By: Children in the Times of War* (2006); and *Brothers & Sisters: Family Poems* (2009).

Greenfield's many honors and awards include the 1990 Recognition of Merit Award from the George G. Stone Center for Children's Books, and the 1997 Award for Excellence in Poetry for Children, given by the National Council of Teachers of English. In 1999 she became a member of the National Literary Hall of Fame for Writers of African Descent.

ALEX HALEY (1921–1992)

Journalist, Novelist. The author of the widely acclaimed novel *Roots* was born Alexander Palmer Haley in Ithaca, New York, on August 11, 1921, and reared in Henning, Tennessee. The oldest of three sons of a college professor father and a mother who taught grade school, Haley graduated from high school at fifteen and attended college for two years before enlisting in the U.S. Coast Guard as a mess boy in 1939.

A voracious reader, Haley began writing short stories while at sea, but it took eight years before small magazines began accepting his stories. By 1952, the Coast Guard had created a new rating for Haley—chief journalist—and he began handling Coast Guard public relations. In 1959 after twenty years of military service, he retired from the Coast Guard and launched a new career as a freelance writer. He eventually became an assignment writer for *Reader's Digest* and moved on to *Playboy*, where he initiated the "Playboy Interviews" feature.

One of the personalities Haley interviewed was Malcolm X—an interview that inspired Haley's first book, *The Autobiography of Malcolm X* (1965). Translated into eight languages, the book has sold more than six million copies. Pursuing the few slender clues of oral family history told to him by his maternal grandmother in Tennessee, Haley spent the next twelve years traveling three continents tracking his mother's family back to a Mandingo youth named Kunta Kinte, who was kidnapped from the small village of Juffure in the Gambia in West Africa and sold into enslavement. During this period, Haley lectured extensively in the United States and Great Britain on his discoveries about his family in Africa, and he wrote many magazine articles on his research in the 1960s and the 1970s. He received several honorary doctor of letters degrees for his work.

The book *Roots*, excerpted to acclaim in *Reader's Digest* in 1974, was finally published in the fall of 1976 with wide publicity and many reviews. In January 1977, ABC produced a twelve-hour miniseries based on the book, which set records for the number of viewers. With cover stories, book reviews, and interviews with Haley in scores of magazines and newspapers, the book became the number-one national best seller and sold millions of copies. It was published as a paperback in 1977. *Roots* truly became a phenomenon. It was serialized in the *New York Post* and the *Long Island Press*. Haley made instructional packages, lesson plans, records, and tapes based on *Roots*, and other books about *Roots* were published for schools.

Haley's book stimulated interest in Africa and in African American genealogy. The U.S. Senate passed a resolution paying tribute to Haley and comparing *Roots* to the influential antislavery novel *Uncle Tom's Cabin* (1852), by Harriet Beecher Stowe. Haley's book received many awards, including a special citation of merit from the National Book Award history panel, and a special Pulitzer Prize for making an important contribution to the literature of African enslavement, both in 1977.

Roots was not without its critics, however. A 1977 lawsuit brought by Margaret Walker charged that *Roots* plagiarized her 1966 novel *Jubilee*. Another author, Harold Courlander, also filed a suit, charging that *Roots* plagiarized his 1967 novel, *The African*. Courlander received a settlement after several passages in *Roots* were found to match text in *The African*. Haley claimed that researchers helping him had given him this material without citing the source.

Haley received the NAACP's Spingarn Medal in 1977. In a survey conducted by *Scholastic Magazine*, four thousand deans and department heads of colleges and universities throughout the country selected Haley as America's foremost achiever in the literature category. The ABC network presented another series, *Roots: The Next Generation*, in 1979 (also written by Haley).

In 1988 Haley conducted a promotional tour for a novella titled *A Different Kind of Christmas*, about black escapees in the 1850s. He also promoted a drama, *Roots: The Gift*, a two-hour television program shown in December 1988. This story revolved around two principal characters from *Roots* who are involved in an escape attempt on Christmas Eve. Haley's drama *Queen*, which he had begun writing before his death, was completed by David Stevens. *Queen* was adapted for television, and aired on CBS in 1993, with Halle Berry starring. Stevens also completed Haley's novel *Mama Flora's Family*, published in 1998; it was also made into a film.

Haley died on February 10, 1992, of a heart attack.

VIRGINIA HAMILTON (1936–2002)

Children's and Young Adult Author. Virginia Hamilton was born on March 12, 1936, into a large extended family in rural Yellow Springs, Ohio. Her career as an author was directly influenced by her parents, who were avid storytellers themselves. She attended nearby Antioch College from 1952 to 1955, ultimately graduating from Ohio State University in 1958. Determined to be a writer, Hamilton settled in New York City and studied the craft at the New School for Social Research. She worked at a variety of jobs and moved back to Yellow Springs before publishing her first book, *Zeely*, in 1967. Issued during an era of racial strife, *Zeely* was one of the first books for young readers in which African American characters were portrayed as people living with average, universal circumstances, as opposed to constantly dealing with politically and racially related problems, such as integration.

After her second novel, *The House of Dies Drear* (1968), received the Edgar Allan Poe Award for best juvenile mystery of the year, Hamilton went on to write and edit more than thirty children's and young adult books within various genres, including the award-winning *M. C. Higgins, the Great* (1974). Her canon includes well-researched historical fiction, contemporary urban novels about teenagers, science fiction and supernatural tales, biographies of the historical figures Paul Robeson and

W. E. B. Du Bois, and collections of African American folklore and antebellum "liberation" stories.

Hamilton was repeatedly honored for her work. Her awards include the Hans Christian Andersen Medal, a Newbery Honor Book citation, a National Book Award, a Coretta Scott King Award, and a 1995 MacArthur Foundation Fellowship. Many of her works have appeared on notable best-books lists, and she has inspired an annual Virginia Hamilton Conference at Kent State University. Hamilton stands as one of the predominant creative forces behind multicultural works for young readers.

On February 19, 2002, Hamilton died in Dayton, Ohio, of breast cancer. She was sixty-five.

JUPITER HAMMON (1711–c. 1790/1806)

Poet, Tract Writer. Jupiter Hammon was born October 17, 1711, probably near Oyster Bay on Long Island, New York. He was one of the first African American poets to have his work published in the United States. *An Evening Thought, Salvation by Christ, with Penitential Cries* appeared in 1761, when Hammon was enslaved by a Mr. Lloyd of Long Island.

Most of Hammon's poetry is religious and is usually dismissed by critics as being of little aesthetic value because of its pious platitudes, faulty syntax, and forced rhymes. Hammon's best-known work is a prose piece, "An Address to the Negroes of the State of New York," which he delivered before the African Society of New York City on September 24, 1786. This famous speech, which draws on Christian themes to promote gradual emancipation, was published the following year, went into three editions, and continues to appear in anthologies.

Hammon died between 1790 and 1806.

LORRAINE HANSBERRY (1930–1965)

Playwright. Born in Chicago on May 19, 1930, Hansberry studied art at the Art Institute of Chicago, the University of Wisconsin, and, finally, in Guadalajara, Mexico. She wrote the award-winning play *A Raisin in the Sun* while living in New York's Greenwich Village, having conceived the play after reacting negatively to what she called "a whole body of material about Negroes. Cardboard characters. Cute dialect bits. Or hip-swinging musicals from exotic scores." The play opened on Broadway on March 11, 1959, at a time when it was generally held that all plays dealing with African Americans were "death" at the box office. Produced, directed, and performed by African Americans, it was later made into a successful movie starring Sidney Poitier. It was later adapted into *Raisin*, a musical that won a Tony Award in 1974.

Hansberry's second Broadway play, *The Sign in Sidney Brustein's Window*, dealt with "the western intellectual poised in hesitation before the flames of involvement." Hansberry succumbed to cancer on January 12, 1965, in New York City, shortly after her second play opened on Broadway.

In addition to the two plays, other works by Hansberry include: *The Movement: Documentary of a Struggle for Equality* (1964); *To Be Young, Gifted and Black*, an autobiographical work adapted by Robert Nemiroff and published in 1969; and *Les Blancs: The Collected Last Plays of Lorraine Hansberry* (1972).

FRANCES E. W. HARPER (1825–1911)

Writer, Poet, Activist. Frances Ellen Watkins Harper, the first African American woman to publish a short story, was one of the most prolific African American women writers of the nineteenth century. She was known also for essays, poetry, and her single novel, *Iola Leroy*. Beyond her writings, Harper was an effective traveling lecturer and a supporter of emancipation, the temperance movement, and the African American women's movement.

Harper was born to free parents in Baltimore, Maryland, on September 24, 1825. She was never able to reconcile the death of her mother, a traumatic experience that occurred when Harper was only three years old. She was raised by relatives and attended William Watkins Academy for Negro Youth—a prestigious school in Baltimore that her uncle founded. Uncomfortable in Baltimore because of its tolerance of African enslavement, Harper moved to Ohio in 1850 and became the first woman teacher at the newly founded Union Seminary, later a part of Wilberforce University. In 1854 she became a permanent lecturer for the Maine Anti-Slavery Society and spoke throughout New England, Ohio, New York, and elsewhere. The "bronze muse," as she became known, gave fiery speeches and often incorporated her poetry into her lectures. So successful and stirring were her presentations that the Pennsylvania Anti-Slavery Society hired her as a lecturer as well. She held her audiences spellbound and spoke with dignity and composure. Although she wrote and lectured on other topics, her attention to the antislavery theme caused scholars to refer to her as an abolitionist poet.

Harper's first volume of poems and prose was published in 1851 as *Forest Leaves*, also printed as *Autumn Leaves*. Her literary career was actually launched in 1854 when she published *Poems on Miscellaneous Subjects*; the work was printed in Boston and Philadelphia and reissued in 1857, 1858, 1864, and 1871. Included in the work were several antislavery poems, such as "The Slave Mother" and "The Slave Auction," yet most of the poems dealt with women's rights, temperance, religion, and other issues of the day.

Her writings in the *Christian Recorder* promoted her work as a journalist. Harper's writings in the journal included the serialized novel *Minnie's Sacrifice*, the dramatic poem "Moses: A Story of the Nile," a series of poems by "Aunt Chloe," and the fictionalized essays "Fancy Etchings." She wrote other serials, but it was not until 1892 that she published in book form her first and best-known work, *Iola Leroy, or, Shadows Uplifted.* The novel aims to present a true picture of African enslavement and the Reconstruction, to promote humanity, and to foster a sense of racial pride in African Americans. Her collections of poems that followed included works previously issued but supplemented with other examples of her writings: *The Sparrow's Fall and Other Poems* (c. 1894); *Light beyond Darkness: The Martyr of Alabama* (c. 1895); and *Atlanta Offering: Poems* (1895). In 1900 she published *Poems* and, the following year, *Idylls of the Bible.*

Harper's activities also included work with the YMCA, for which she helped develop Sunday schools; the Colored Section of the Philadelphia and Pennsylvania Women's Christian Temperance Union; and the American Woman Suffrage Association. She helped organize the National Association of Colored Women. Harper died in Philadelphia on February 20, 1911.

E. LYNN HARRIS (1955–2009)

Novelist. Everette Lynn Harris was born in Flint, Michigan, on June 20, 1955. He grew up in Little Rock, Arkansas. He attended the University of Arkansas, where he became the first African American male cheerleader. After completing a degree in journalism, he worked for several years as a computer salesman for IBM. He self-published his first book, *Invisible Life*, a novel about African American men who were publicly heterosexual, but secretly having sex with other men. Harris sold the book out of his car at beauty salons and similar venues, but eventually located a New York agent who sold the book to Anchor Books. Harris subsequently produced several best-selling books in a similar tradition, highlighting African American gay and bisexual men as the main characters, including *Just as I am*, *If This World Were Mine*, and *A Love of My Own.* Several of his books were featured on *New York Times* best-seller lists. They were especially popular among African American women. In his memoir, *What Becomes of the Brokenhearted*, Harris revealed his past abuse by his stepfather, Odis Harris, his first male-to-male sexual experience while in junior high school, and his attempted suicide in 1990. Although he was in apparent denial about his homosexuality for years, Harris eventually became public about it. However, he steadfastly resisted aligning himself with gay rights issues. Harris died of an apparent cardiac episode on July 23, 2009, in Los Angeles. His most recent book, *Mama Dearest*, went on sale later in the year with book signings being hosted by his friends and former colleagues.

ROBERT E. HAYDEN (1913–1980)

Poet. Robert Earl Hayden was born Asa Bundy Sheffey on August 4, 1913, in Detroit, Michigan, to a poor family. His parents left him to be raised by foster parents. Extremely nearsighted, he turned to books rather than sports activities in his childhood.

A graduate of Detroit City College, now Wayne State University, Hayden was chief researcher on African American history and folklore for the Federal Writers' Project in 1936. He went on to do advanced work in English, play production, and creative writing at the University of Michigan. While there, he twice won the Jule and Avery Hopwood Prize for poetry. Hayden also completed radio scripts and a finished version of a play about the Underground Railroad, *Go Down Moses.*

Hayden's first book of poems, *Heart-Shape in the Dust*, was published in 1940, shortly before he became a music and drama critic for the *Michigan Chronicle.* He taught at Fisk University from 1946 to the early 1970s and later at the University of Michigan.

His works include: *The Lion and the Archer* (1948, with Myron O'Higgins); *A Ballad of Remembrance* (1962); *Selected Poems* (1966); *Words in the Mourning Time* (1970); and *The Night-Blooming Cereus* (1972). He edited *Kaleidoscope: Poems by American Negro Poets* (1967) and *Afro American Literature: An Introduction* (1971, with David J. Burrows and Frederick R. Lapsides). His other books include: *Figure of Time* (1955); *Angle of Ascent: New and Selected Poems* (1975); and *American Journal* (1978).

In 1975 the Academy of American Poets elected Hayden its fellow of the year, and in 1976 he was awarded the Grand Prize for Poetry at the First World Festival of Negro Arts in Dakar, Senegal. From 1976 to 1978, he was consultant in poetry—later known as poet laureate—at the Library of Congress. He was the first African American to receive this appointment. Hayden was a professor of English at the University of Michigan at the time of his death on February 25, 1980. Hayden's *Collected Prose*, edited by Frederick Glaysher, was published in 1984. His *Collected Poems*, also edited by Glaysher, was published a year later.

ESSEX HEMPHILL (1957–1995)

Poet, Essayist, Editor, Gay Rights Activist. Essex Hemphill was born in 1957 in Chicago, but spent parts of his childhood in Indiana, South Carolina, and Washington, D.C. He began writing at fourteen. After attending the University of Maryland and the University of the District of Columbia, Hemphill began to explore through poetry the inner conflicts—loneliness, isolation, denial—as well as the homophobia he experienced as a gay African American male. For several years, Hemphill was a contributor of verse to such journals as *Essence, Black Scholar,* and *Obsidian.* In the late 1980s, he became involved with a project begun by Joseph Beam, an anthology of gay African American poetry called *In the Life.* Hemphill was a contributor to the 1986 volume and took the editorship of its sequel after Beam died of AIDS-related illnesses in 1988. The work was published as *Brother to Brother: New Writings by Black Gay Men* in 1991.

Hemphill became involved in several film projects around this time as well, nearly all of them controversial in some way, which coincided with his aim to make the two communities, the African American and the gay American, enter into a new, more contemporary dialogue with one another. He wrote verse for *Looking for Langston,* a 1989 British film that addressed the sexuality of Harlem Renaissance poet Langston Hughes and brought down the ire of the executor of the Hughes estate. Hemphill also contributed to and appeared in the 1989 film *Tongues Untied.* This last project, Marlon Riggs's celebratory look at gay African American male culture, was initially deemed too spicy even for public television.

In 1992 Hemphill saw another book of his own verse published, *Ceremonies: Prose and Poetry.* During the early part of the decade, he became involved in a project interviewing elderly members of the African American gay community in order to provide a glimpse into a period before either gay or civil rights were mentioned. He also contributed to the book *Life Sentences: Writers, Artists, and AIDS* (1994). Hemphill died of AIDS complications on November 4, 1995, at the age of thirty-eight.

CHESTER HIMES (1909–1984)

Novelist. Born to a middle-class family in Jefferson City, Missouri, on June 29, 1909, Chester Himes was educated at Ohio State University and later lived in France and Spain. In 1945 he completed his first novel, *If He Hollers Let Him Go,* the story of an African American working in a defense plant. His second book, *The Lonely Crusade* (1947), was set in similar surroundings. His other books include: *The Third Generation* (1954); *Cotton Comes to Harlem* (1965); *Pinktoes* (1961); *The Quality of Hurt: The Autobiography of Chester Himes* (1972); and *Black on Black: Baby Sister and Selected Writings* (1973).

Although his talent went relatively unnoticed in the United States, Himes's series of detective novels was later compared with those of Dashiell Hammett, Raymond Chandler, and the African American writer Walter Mosley. Following a stroke that confined him to a wheelchair, Himes and his wife lived in Alicante, Spain. In 1977 they returned to New York City for the publication of the concluding volume of his autobiography, *My Life of Absurdity.* Himes died of Parkinson's disease in Spain on November 12, 1984, at the age of seventy-five. Himes was a prolific author of almost twenty books, and several of his popular novels have been reprinted posthumously in hardcover and paperback editions.

PAULINE E. HOPKINS (1859–1930)

Writer, Editor, Playwright, Singer, Actress. Although her contemporaries gave her less recognition than modern scholars do, Pauline Elizabeth Hopkins became known for promoting racial issues in her short stories and novels and in her work as editor of the journal *The Colored American.* She is sometimes referred to as the "dean of African American women writers."

Born in Portland, Maine, in 1859, Hopkins moved to Boston when she was still a child and graduated from Girls High School. At age fifteen, she entered a writing contest supported by writer William Wells Brown and sponsored by the Congregational Publishing Society in Boston. She won a ten-dollar prize for her essay, "The Evils of Intemperance and Their Remedies."

Hopkins established a theater troupe, the Colored Troubadours, and performed with the group for twelve years. On July 5, 1880, in Boston, the Troubadours performed her first play, *Slaves' Escape, or, The Underground Railroad,* also known as *Peculiar Sam,* which Hopkins had completed a year earlier. During her tenure with the group, she also wrote the play *One Scene from the Drama of Early Days.*

Hopkins helped to establish the magazine the *Colored American*; its first issue in May 1900 published her short story "The Mystery within Us." Later, the magazine published Hopkins's series of biographical sketches "Famous Women of the Negro Race" and "Famous Men of the Negro Race." About this time, the magazine published serialized versions of three of her novels: *Hagar's Daughter: A Story of Southern Caste Prejudice* (1901–1902); *Winona: A Tale of Negro Life in the South and Southwest* (1902); and *Of One Blood, or, The Hidden Self* (1902–1903). Her first novel, however, *Contending Forces: A Romance Illustrative of Negro Life North and*

South, was published by a Boston firm in 1900. She resigned from the *Colored American* in 1904.

In 1905 Hopkins wrote briefly for *Voice of the Negro*; after that, her literary career began to decline. She founded her own publishing company, P. E. Hopkins and Company, and in February and March 1916 contributed two articles to *New Era Magazine*. She lived in obscurity after 1916 and died on August 13, 1930.

GEORGE MOSES HORTON (c. 1797–c. 1883)

Poet. George Moses Horton was the first African American professional man of letters in the United States and one of the first professional writers of any race in the South. He was also the first African American southerner to have a volume of poetry published.

Horton was born enslaved in North Carolina around 1797. While growing up on a farm, he cultivated a love of learning. Horton's mother taught him to read using her Wesleyan hymnal, although he did not learn to write until years later. While working as a janitor at the University of North Carolina, Horton wrote light verses for some students in exchange for spending money.

Some of Horton's early poems were printed in the newspapers of Raleigh and Boston. When Horton published his first book of poems in 1829, he titled it *The Hope of Liberty*, in the belief that profits from its sales would be sufficient to pay for his freedom. His hopes did not materialize, however, and he remained enslaved until the Emancipation Proclamation (the book was reprinted in 1837 under the title *Poems by a Slave*). In 1865 he published "Naked Genius," a poem containing many bitter lines about his former condition that were in sharp contrast to the conformist verse of earlier African American poets. Although he lived in Philadelphia for a while, it appears that he returned to the South, where he died around 1883. Richard Walser's *The Black Poet* (1967) was written about Horton.

LANGSTON HUGHES (1902–1967)

Poet, Novelist, Playwright. Born in Joplin, Missouri, on February 1, 1902, James Mercer Langston Hughes moved to Cleveland at the age of fourteen, and graduated from Central High School. His love of books developed at a young age. After his parents separated, then divorced, he was raised primarily by his grandmother, Mary Langston, who instilled in him a feeling of racial pride. Langston's unstable childhood was to have a major impact on the poetry he later wrote.

Hughes spent a year in Mexico before studying engineering—at his father's request—at Columbia University. After roaming the world as a seaman and writing some poetry as well, Hughes returned to the United States. While attending Lincoln University in Pennsylvania, he won the Witter Bynner Prize for undergraduate poetry. In 1930 he received the Harmon Award, and in 1935, with the help of a Guggenheim Fellowship, he traveled to Russia and Spain.

The long and distinguished list of Hughes's works includes: *Not without Laughter* (1930); *The Big Sea* (1940); *I Wonder as I Wander* (1956), his autobiography; *The Weary Blues* (1926); *The Dream Keeper* (1932); *Shakespeare in Harlem* (1942); *Fields of Wonder* (1947); *One Way Ticket* (1949); *Selected Poems* (1959); and the posthumously published *The Panther and the Lash: Poems of Our Times* (1969).

Although Hughes had a great influence on the Harlem Renaissance, he criticized those writers who embraced Eurocentric values and culture. Hughes was also an accomplished song lyricist, librettist, and newspaper columnist. Through his newspaper columns, he created Jesse B. Semple, a Harlem character known as Simple. Simple is the quintessential "wise fool" whose experiences and insights capture the frustrations felt by African Americans. Hughes's Simple sketches have been collected in several volumes and were adapted for the 1957 musical *Simply Heavenly*.

Through much of the 1960s, Hughes edited several anthologies in an attempt to popularize African American authors and their works. Some of these works are *An African Treasury* (1960); *Poems from Black Africa* (1963); *New Negro Poets: U.S.A.* (1964); and *The Best Short Stories by Negro Writers* (1967). *Good Morning Revolution: Uncollected Social Protest Writings* was published posthumously in 1973. Hughes also wrote many plays, including *Emperor of Haiti* (1936) and *Mulatto* (1935). He also wrote gospel music plays, such as *Tambourines to Glory* (1963); *Black Nativity* (1961); and *Jericho—Jim Crow* (1963). Hughes gained an international reputation in the 1950s and 1960s. He died of complications related to abdominal surgery for prostate cancer on May 22, 1967.

ZORA NEALE HURSTON (1891–1960)

Novelist, Folklorist. Zora Neale Hurston was born on January 7, 1891, in Notasulga, Alabama. After traveling north as a maid with a Gilbert and Sullivan company, Hurston acquired her education at Morgan State College, Howard University, and Columbia University. While studying at Howard under Alain Locke's influence, she became a figure in the Harlem Renaissance, publishing short stories in *Opportunity* and serving with Langston Hughes and Wallace Thurman on the editorial board of the magazine *Fire!*

Zora Neale Hurston, Novelist, New York Times Book Fair, 1937. *Hurston studied anthropology and used it to great advantage in her published works, which included novels, short stories, and folklore.* THE LIBRARY OF CONGRESS

In 1934, after her return to Florida, the novel *Jonah's Gourd Vine* was published. Her most important novel, *Their Eyes Were Watching God* appeared three years later. In 2005 it was adapted into a film starring Halle Berry and produced by Oprah Winfrey. *Moses, Man of the Mountain* (1939) was followed in 1948 by *Seraph on the Suwanee.* Her other works include two books of folklore, *Mules and Men* (1935) and *Tell My Horse* (1938), and the memoir *Dust Tracks on a Road* (1942).

Toward the end of her life, Hurston became a drama instructor at the North Carolina College for Negroes in Durham (now North Carolina Central University). She died in obscurity and poverty on January 28, 1960. In 1973 Alice Walker, the African American novelist and scholar, found and marked Hurston's grave and rekindled interest in her life and work. Since then, six of her works, including her autobiography with several chapters restored, have been reprinted with new introductions. Hurston is celebrated each year in Eatonville, Florida, where the Zora Neale Hurston Festival is held.

CHARLES R. JOHNSON (1948–)

Novelist, Essayist, Cartoonist. Charles Richard Johnson, only the second African American man to win the National Book Award for fiction (Ralph Ellison was the first), was born on April 23, 1948, in Evanston, Illinois. He began his career as a political cartoonist in the early 1970s; his work led to a television series on cartooning on PBS. During the same period, he was heavily involved in organizations that supported the formation of African American studies as a discipline.

Johnson's development as a novelist took shape while he pursued his B.A. (1971) from Southern Illinois University at Carbondale and, subsequently, his M.A. in philosophy (1973). Out of these experiences, Johnson developed situations in his books that dealt with philosophical discussions about race, identity, and culture.

Johnson's literary works include both novels and short stories, beginning with *Faith and the Good Thing* (1974), which was followed by *Oxherding Tale* (1982); *The Sorcerer's Apprentice* (short stories, 1986); *Middle Passage* (1990), which received the National Book Award; and *Dreamer* (1998); *Africans in America: America's Journey through Slavery* (1998, written with Patricia Smith to accompany a PBS series with the same title); and its companion, *Soulcatcher and Other Stories.* In 2003 he published a collection of essays, *Turning the Wheel,* on his experiences as an African American Buddhist. Johnson's *Dr. King's Refrigerator and Other Bedtime Stories* was published in 2005.

Johnson is the S. Wilson and Grace M. Pollock Endowed Professor of English at the University of Washington. Among other honors, he is the recipient of fellowships from the MacArthur Foundation (1998) and the Guggenheim Foundation (1987).

GEORGIA DOUGLAS JOHNSON (c. 1880–1966)

Poet, Playwright. As one of the first modern African American women poets to gain recognition, and sometimes referred to as the most famous woman poet of the Harlem Renaissance, Georgia Douglas Johnson, whose collections of verse were published between 1918 and 1930, is an important link in the chain of African American women lyric poets. Johnson's life spanned most of the literary movements of the twentieth century, and her Washington, D.C., home was a popular gathering place for early Harlem Renaissance writers.

Johnson was born in Atlanta, Georgia, on September 10, c. 1880 (her birth year varies widely among published sources, from 1877 to 1887). She was educated in the public schools of the city and at Atlanta University, and she went on to attend Howard University in Washington, D.C., and Oberlin Conservatory of Music in Ohio. Initially, she was interested in musical composition, but gradually Johnson turned to lyric poetry. After teaching school in Alabama, she moved to Washington, D.C., with her husband, who had been appointed as recorder of deeds by President William Howard Taft. While in the nation's capital, she too engaged in government work while completing such books as *The Heart of a Woman* (1918) and *Bronze* (1922).

After her husband's death in 1925, Johnson supported herself and her two sons with a series of temporary jobs and created her own supportive environment by hosting Saturday night open houses that became among the greatest literary salons of the period. Johnson was a prolific writer; more than two hundred of her poems were published in her four literary works; other poems and several dramas appeared in journals and books, primarily edited by African Americans. Her poetry collections include *An Autumn Love Cycle* (1928) and *Share My World* (1962). She also wrote many plays in the 1920s, but most of the manuscripts did not survive. She died of a stroke on May 14, 1966.

James Weldon Johnson. *In addition to his career as an author, Johnson was a lawyer and an educator. He also wrote the lyrics for "Lift Every Voice and Sing," which his brother, John Rosamond Johnson, set to music in 1900.* THE LIBRARY OF CONGRESS

JAMES WELDON JOHNSON (1871–1938)

Poet, Lyricist, Civil Rights Leader. Like W. E. B. Du Bois, African American intellectual James Weldon Johnson played a vital role in the civil rights movement of the twentieth century as poet, teacher, critic, diplomat, and NAACP official. He was also an important figure in the Harlem Renaissance. Johnson is perhaps best remembered as the lyricist for "Lift Every Voice and Sing," the song that is often referred to as the African American national anthem.

Born on June 17, 1871, in Jacksonville, Florida, Johnson was educated at Atlanta and Columbia universities. His career included service as a school principal, a lawyer, and a diplomat (as the U.S. consul at Puerto Cabello, Venezuela, and later in Nicaragua). Johnson published a novel about a black man passing for white called *The Autobiography of an Ex-Colored Man* anonymously in 1912. From 1916 to 1930, he was a key policy maker for the NAACP, eventually serving as the organization's executive secretary. From 1932 until his death, he was professor of creative writing at Fisk University in Nashville, Tennessee.

In his early days, Johnson's fame rested largely on his lyrics for popular songs, but in 1917 he completed his first book of poetry, *Fifty Years and Other Poems*. Five years later, he followed this work with *The Book of American Negro Poetry*, which he edited, and in 1927 he established his literary reputation with *God's Trombones*, a collection of seven folk sermons in verse. Over the years, this work has been performed countless times on stage and television.

In 1930 Johnson finished *St. Peter Relates an Incident of the Resurrection*, and three years later, his lengthy autobiography, *Along This Way* appeared. Johnson died on June 26, 1938, following an automobile accident in Maine.

GAYL JONES (1949–)

Novelist, Poet, Short Story Writer, Educator. Born in Lexington, Kentucky, in 1949, Gayl Jones received a bachelor's degree in English from Connecticut College in 1971, a master's degree in creative writing from Brown University in 1973, and a doctorate in creative writing from Brown in 1975. From 1975 to 1981, she was a professor of English at the University of Michigan. Jones's work includes four novels: *Corregidora* (1975); *Eva's Man* (1976); *Healing* (1998), which was a finalist for the National Book Award; and *Mosquito* (1999). She has also written short stories, nonfiction, and poetry, including *Song for Anninho* (1981); *The Hermit Woman* (1983); *Xarque and Other Poems* (1985); and *Liberating Voices: Oral Tradition in African American Literature* (1991), her first book of literary criticism. Although sometimes considered controversial in its subject matter—particularly *Eva's Man*, which deals with the sexual molestation and violence inflicted on African American girls by African American men—Jones's work is both multilayered and complex.

After the release of *Healing* in 1998, Jones's husband Bob Jones had an encounter with the police in Kentucky that resulted in his suicide. This traumatic event caused Jones to step out of the spotlight of the literary world and to seek professional therapy for depression.

JUNE JORDAN (1936–2002)

Poet, Novelist. Born in Harlem on July 9, 1936, poet, novelist, essayist, educator, and activist June Jordan attended Barnard College and the University of Chicago. Throughout the 1960s and 1970s, she taught Afro-American literature, English, and writing at several colleges and universities, including the City University of New York, Connecticut College, Sarah Lawrence College, Yale University, and State University of New York at Stony Brook, where she spent most of her career as director of the poetry center and creative writing program. She left Stony Brook in 1989 to teach Afro-American studies and women's studies at the University of California at Berkeley. In Berkeley, Jordan cofounded and codirected Voice of the Children, Inc., a creative workshop for young people.

A prolific writer, Jordan's poems have been published in many magazines, newspapers, and anthologies, and she received a Rockefeller grant for creative writing in 1969. Her poetry collections include: *Who Look at Me* (1969); *Some Changes* (1971); *New Days: Poems of Exile and Return* (1974); *Passion: New Poems, 1977–1980* (1980); *Living Room: New Poems* (1985); *Lyrical Campaigns: Selected Poems* (1989); and *Naming Our Destiny: New and Selected Poems* (1989). Jordan's books for children and young people include: *His Own Where* (1971), nominated for the National Book Award; *Fannie Lou Hamer* (1972); *Dry Victories* (1972); and *Kimako's Story* (1981). Basic Books published her memoir, *Soldier: A Poet's Childhood*, in 2000.

The author of two plays, Jordan also published essays, including: "Civil Wars" (1981); "On Call: Political Essays" (1985); "Moving towards Home: Political Essays" (1989); and "Technical Difficulties: African American Notes on the State of the Union" (1992). In addition, she edited several anthologies, including *Soulscript: Afro-American Poetry* (1970, reissued in 2004).

In 2001 Jordan received a Barnes & Noble Writers for Writers Award from the Poets & Writers organization. The award recognized Jordan's Poetry for the People project, which offers poetry workshops to underserved communities. Jordon passed away, on June 14, 2002, at her home in Berkeley, California, of breast cancer. She was sixty-five. *Some of Us Did Not Die: New and Selected Essays of June Jordan*, was published in 2002, shortly after her death.

ADRIENNE KENNEDY (1931–)

Writer, Playwright. Born in Pittsburgh, Pennsylvania, on September 13, 1931, Adrienne Lita Hawkins grew up in Cleveland, Ohio. She received a B.A. in education from Ohio State in 1953, and married Joseph C. Kennedy one month later. In 1955 they moved to New York, where she studied writing at the American Theatre Wing and at Columbia University. She completed her first play, *Pale Blue Flowers*, during this period, but it was never produced or published.

In 1960 Kennedy and her husband traveled to Europe and then Ghana on a grant from the Africa Research Foundation. Her writing became more focused, and she published a story in *Black Orpheus* magazine. At the age of twenty-nine, Kennedy wrote *Funnyhouse of a Negro*, a one-act play. Edward Albee selected the play for production and codirected it at New York's Circle in the Square. It ran from January 14 to February 9, 1964, at the East End Theatre in New York.

Kennedy's next play, *The Owl Answers*, produced in 1965, won her a second Stanley Award from Wagner College of Staten Island, New York. Since the mid-1960s, she has written many full-length and one-act plays, including *Sun: A Poem for Malcolm X Inspired by His Murder* (1968); *A Movie Star Has to Star in Black and White* (1976); *Black Children's Day* (1980); and *Diary of Lights* (1987). Later, the University of Minnesota Press published collections of her work, including *The Alexander Plays* (1992). In 1996 two of her plays, *Sleep Deprivation Chamber* and *June and Jean in Concert*, were produced at the Joseph Papp Public Theater in New York City and the Susan Stein Shiva Theater at Vassar College in Poughkeepsie, respectively. Kennedy also wrote an autobiography, *People Who Led to My Plays*, published in 1987.

Kennedy's plays are hallmarks of the American experimental theater, avant-garde and nontraditional in the extreme. She has won many awards for her bold and clear vision, including several Obie Awards and a Lecomte du Novy Award from the Lincoln Center in 1994. In addition to winning many fellowships and grants, Kennedy has been a lecturer at several universities, including Yale, Princeton, Brown, Harvard, and the University of California at Berkeley. She also served as an International Theatre Institute representative in Budapest in 1978.

More recently, Kennedy adapted the Greek tragedy *Oedipus the King* for the Hartford Stage Company in

Connecticut. The University of Minnesota Press published a comprehensive collection of her work, appropriately called *The Adrienne Kennedy Reader*, in 2001. And Kennedy's play *Mom, How Did You Meet the Beatles?* written with her son Adam, was staged at New York's Public Theater in February 2008.

JOHN O. KILLENS (1916–1987)

Novelist, Essayist, Screenwriter. John Oliver Killens was born in Macon, Georgia, on January 14, 1916. He attended several colleges, including Edward Waters College, Morris Brown College, Atlanta University, Howard University, Robert H. Terrell Law School, Columbia University, and New York University. From 1942 to 1945, he was a member of the U.S. Army's South Pacific Amphibian Forces.

Killens attributed his writing career to his paternal great-grandmother, who was seven years old when the Emancipation Proclamation was signed. During his childhood, she told Killens stories about the past. Sometimes, when she finished talking about days gone by, she would tell him, "The half ain't never been told!" Although his original plan to become a doctor was abandoned when he decided to study law, Killens ultimately accepted his ancestor's challenge to tell the untold half and became a writer.

In 1950 Killens became one of the founders and the first chairperson of the Harlem Writers Guild, which provided a forum for writers of the African diaspora to develop, write, and publish their works. Killens's first novel, *Youngblood* (1954), about an African American family's struggle to survive in the South, was the first book published by a member of the guild. Four more novels followed: *And Then We Heard the Thunder* (1962), based on Killens's encounters with racism in the military during World War II; *'Sippi* (1967), which focuses on struggles over voting rights in the 1960s; and *The Cotillion, or, One Good Bull Is Half the Herd* (1971), a satirical interpretation of the black bourgeoisie. *Great Black Russian: A Novel on the Life and Times of Alexander Pushkin* (1989), published posthumously, was the result of more than twelve years of research.

In the late 1960s, Killens traveled to the Soviet Union, where he met with other Pushkin scholars and visited sites associated with the Russian poet. While researching and writing *Great Black Russian*, Killens lectured on Pushkin to students and literary groups throughout the United States. The novel was one of the first works to consider Pushkin's African ancestry. Killens completed *Great Black Russian* shortly before his death.

Among Killens's additional works are: *Black Man's Burden* (1965), a collection of essays; *Great Gittin' Up Morning: Biography of Denmark Vesey* (juvenile literature, 1972); *A Man Ain't Nothin' but a Man: The Adventures of John Henry* (juvenile literature, 1975); and *Black Southern Voices: An Anthology of Fiction, Poetry, Drama, Nonfiction, and Critical Essays* (1992), coedited with Jerry W. Ward Jr. and published after Killens's death. Killens also wrote screenplays.

Killens taught at a number of institutions, including Fisk University, Columbia University, Howard University, Bronx Community College, and Medgar Evers College (CUNY). Both *And Then We Heard the Thunder* and *The Cotillion* were nominated for Pulitzer Prizes. On October 27, 1987, Killens died of cancer in Brooklyn.

JAMAICA KINCAID (1949–)

Writer. Jamaica Kincaid was born Elaine Potter Richardson on May 25, 1949, in St. Johns, Antigua. After leaving Antigua at sixteen years of age, she entered the United States as Jamaica Kincaid and moved to New York. Kincaid held several positions while seeking her niche in the United States. Her writing career began as a contributor to the *New Yorker* magazine. Once a staff member, Kincaid's collection of stories and other short pieces, most of which ran in the magazine from 1974 to 1976, was published under the title *At the Bottom of the River* (1983). The collection was nominated for the PEN/Faulkner Award.

Kincaid published her first novel, *Annie John*, in 1985. This work was followed by *A Small Place* (1988), *Annie, Gwenn, Lilly, Pam, & Tulip* (1989), *Lucy* (1990), *The Autobiography of My Mother* (1996), *My Brother* (1997), *Talk Stories* (2000), *My Garden* (2001), *Mr. Potter* (2002); and *Among Flowers: A Walk in the Himalaya* (2005).

With her lyrical style and semiautobiographical focus, Kincaid addresses themes about lasting scars from childhood experiences, ambivalence toward parents, the mother-daughter relationship, and the search for identity.

YUSEF KOMUNYAKAA (1947–)

Poet, Educator. Yusef Komunyakaa was born James Willie Brown Jr. in 1947 in the segregated, culturally desolate mill town of Bogalusa, Louisiana. He came to love reading and poetry as a child, and at age sixteen began pursuing his own talents. After high school graduation, Komunyakaa joined the U.S. Army and was sent to Vietnam to act as a reporter and editor for a military newspaper in 1969.

Although he felt estranged from American society upon his return from Vietnam, Komunyakaa enrolled at

Yusef Komunyakaa, Poet and Educator, c. 1998. *Komunyakaa received the Pulitzer Prize for his poetry collection,* Neon Vernacular: New & Selected Poems 1977–1989 *(1993).* JAMES KEYSER//TIME LIFE PICTURES/GETTY IMAGES

the University of Colorado and later attended graduate school at Colorado State University. He later received a second master's degree from the University of California at Irvine. A creative writing workshop proved inspirational, and his first book of poetry, *Dedications and Other Darkhorses*, was published in 1977. With the release of his second volume two years later, Komunyakaa accepted a series of fellowships and teaching positions, enabling him to pursue a career as a poet. For personal and religious reasons, the poet changed his name from James Willie Brown Jr. to Yusef Komunyakaa.

While working in New Orleans in 1983, Komunyakaa began to come to terms with his experiences in Vietnam through his writing. This challenge resulted in several sophisticated books filled with cultural influences that portray basic elements of humanity. In 1985 the poet left New Orleans to accept a position as a visiting professor at Indiana University in Bloomington. By 1987, having published two more books of poetry, Komunyakaa became an associate professor in the Afro-American Studies and English departments. After a decade at Bloomington, he began teaching creative writing at Princeton University. He later moved to New York University, where he became senior distinguished poet in the Graduate Writing Program. Komunyakaa was elected a chancellor of the Academy of American Poets in 1999.

With the publication of *Neon Vernacular* (1993), he was awarded the 1994 Pulitzer Prize in poetry, along with the $50,000 Kingsley Tufts Poetry Award given by Claremont Graduate School. Komunyakaa's themes of memory and self-definition—as an African American man and a veteran of the Vietnam War—lend his works a sense of strength and spiritual tenacity.

Komunyakaa's collections of poetry include: *Talking Dirty to the Gods* (2000), *Pleasure Dome: New and Collected Poems* (2001), *Taboo* (2004); and *Warhorses: Poems* (2008). He also published *Gilgamesh: A Verse Play* (2006), a dramatic adaptation of the *Epic of Gilgamesh*. In 2001 Komunyakaa was awarded the Ruth Lilly Poetry Prize. This award, which includes a cash prize of $100,000, is for lifetime achievement by a U.S. poet.

NELLA LARSEN (1891–1964)

Novelist, Librarian, Nurse. Nella Larsen was born in 1891 in Chicago to a Danish mother and a West Indian father. She attended Fisk University in Nashville, Tennessee, from 1909 to 1910, and continued her education from 1910 to 1912 at the University of Copenhagen in Denmark. She also attended the Lincoln School for Nurses in New York City from 1912 to 1915. In addition to her writing, she worked alternately as a nurse and a librarian, having attended the New York Public Library training school from 1921 to 1923. After one year as head nurse at Tuskegee Institute, she became supervising nurse at the Lincoln Hospital in New York City until 1918, when she joined the city's department of health. During the next forty years, she worked at the New York Public Library as a children's librarian (1924–1926), at Gouverneur Hospital (1944–1961), and at the Metropolitan Hospital (1961–1964), all in New York City. Writing, however, is what made her famous.

In the 1920s, Larsen began contributing to children's magazines. At the same time, she found herself immersed in the literary and political activities of the Harlem Renaissance. Larsen's first novel, *Quicksand* (1928), received a bronze medal from the Harmon Foundation. The groundbreaking novel developed themes around African American women's sexuality and about mixed racial identity. Her second major work, *Passing* (1929), led to her becoming the first African American woman to be awarded a Guggenheim Fellowship in creative writing (1930). More than thirty years after her death on March 20, 1964, Larsen's novels were reissued, and she finally achieved recognition as one of the most important writers of the Harlem Renaissance.

JULIUS LESTER (1939–)

Writer, Educator. Julius Lester was born in St. Louis, Missouri, in 1939. He grew up in Kansas City, Kansas, and Nashville, Tennessee, where his father led congregations as a Methodist minister. Lester spent the summers of his youth in rural Arkansas, experiencing racism and segregation firsthand. A gifted student, he was an avid musician and aspired to become a writer.

Lester obtained a B.A. in English from Fisk University in 1960. He became politically active in the civil rights struggle as a folksinger and photographer of southern rallies. As a member of the Student Nonviolent Coordinating Committee (SNCC) in the mid-1960s, Lester became head of its photo department and visited North Vietnam to document the effects of U.S. bombing missions. He began publishing ideological books that defended African American militancy, including *The Angry Children of Malcolm X* (1966) and *Revolutionary Notes* (1969). From 1966 to 1968, Lester served as director of the prestigious Newport Folk Festival and released two record albums himself.

Having achieved fame for his artistic pursuits, Lester was hired to host live radio shows at the public broadcasting station WBAI-FM in New York City. Around the same time, he published two books for children that saw immediate success. *Black Folktales* (1969) compiled African legends and slave narratives, and *To Be a Slave* (1968), a collection of stories based on oral history accounts, received a Newbery Honor Book citation. In 1971 Lester began hosting the New York public television program *Free Time*. His career as an award-winning academician began that same year, when he was hired as professor of Afro-American studies at the University of Massachusetts–Amherst. He settled there in 1975 and became a full-time professor and author.

Author and Educator Julius Lester. *Lester, who writes both for children and adults, in 2006 won the Coretta Scott King Award for his children's book* Day of Tears: A Novel in Dialogue. © JERRY BAUER. REPRODUCED BY PERMISSION.

Lester flourished as an author by releasing novels and storybooks (with illustrator Jerry Pinkney) that reflected his interests in African American history, folklore, and politics. *Long Journey Home: Stories from Black History* (1972), a finalist for the National Book Award, explores the everyday lives of African Americans during the Reconstruction period. Lester's *Tales of Uncle Remus: The Adventures of Brer Rabbit* (1987), traditional stories retold in a contemporary southern African American voice, were well received by teachers and librarians, who granted it the Coretta Scott King Award. His 1994 adult novel, *And All Our Wounds Forgiven*, tracks dramatic events in the 1960s. Lester's individualism and resistance to racial and religious categorization is evident in two autobiographies: *All Is Well* (1976), and *Lovesong: Becoming a Jew* (1988).

In the second half of the 1990s, Lester alternated between tales for children and adult works. His younger audience enjoyed titles such as: *Black Cowboy, Wild Horses: A True Story* (1998); *Albidaro and the Mischievous Dream* (2000); and *Ackmarackus: Julius Lester's Sumptuously Silly Fantastically Funny Fables* (2001). More mature audiences were treated to a historical view of African enslavement with *From Slave Ship to Freedom Road* (1997) and a dark trip into the psychosis of two young children in *When Dad Killed Mom* (2001). Lester published a racially repositioned novelization of *Othello* for young adults in 1995 called *Othello: A Novel.*

Lester subsequently published: *The Autobiography of God* (2004); *Day of Tears* (2005); *On Writers for Children and Other People* (2005), a literary memoir; *Time's Memory* (2006); and *Cupid* (2007). In 2006 he won the Coretta Scott King Award for his 2005 novel *Day of Tears.*

In 1988, after he converted to Judaism in midlife, Lester was ousted from Amherst's renamed African American Studies Department. Persevering through yet another career change, he moved to the university's Near Eastern and Judaic Studies Department and also taught in the history and English departments. He retired from the University of Massachusetts in 2003.

AUDRE LORDE (1934–1992)

Poet, Novelist, Essayist. Audre Lorde was born in New York City's Harlem on February 18, 1934. Her parents were emigrants from Granada. Lorde began writing poetry at the age of twelve. She received a bachelor's degree in literature and philosophy from Hunter College in 1959 and a master's degree in library science from Columbia University in 1960. In 1962 she married Edward Rollins, an attorney, and had two children. The couple divorced in 1970.

In 1968 Lorde became poet-in-residence at Tougaloo College in Mississippi. She also taught at Lehman College in the Bronx, John Jay College, and City College of New York. She received a National Endowment for the Arts grant in 1968. Lorde attempted to join the Harlem Writers Guild, but was disappointed by what she perceived as the group's overt homophobia and left.

Her books of poetry included: *The First Cities* (1968); *Cables to Rage* (1970); *From a Land Where Other People Live* (1973), which was nominated for a National Book Award; *The New York Head Shop and Museum* (1974); *Between Ourselves* (1976); *The Black Unicorn* (1978); *Chosen Poems: Old and New* (1982); *Zami: A New Spelling of My Name* (1982); and *Sister/ Outsider: Essays and Speeches* (1984). Lorde's poetry has been published in many anthologies, magazines, and lesbian books and periodicals, including *Lesbian Poetry: An Anthology* (1982).

Six months after undergoing a mastectomy in 1978 for breast cancer, Lorde began documenting her battle with the disease in journal entries that later became *The Cancer Journal* (1980). Lorde gained critical and popular acclaim for her moving and honest portrayal of life with the disease. Lorde lived for fourteen years after her diagnosis, but succumbed to cancer on November 17, 1992.

HAKI MADHUBUTI (DON L. LEE) (1942–)

Poet, Essayist, Publisher. Haki Madhubuti was born Don L. Lee on February 23, 1942, in Little Rock, Arkansas. His family moved to Detroit a year later. He moved to Chicago at age sixteen to live with an aunt after his father left home and his mother died. He graduated from Chicago City College with an A.A. degree and later received an M.F.A. degree from the University of Iowa.

From 1961 to 1966, Madhubuti prepared to become a writer. He read a book daily and wrote a two-hundred review of each book. He published his first volume of poetry, *Think Black*, in 1966. In 1967 he joined Johari Amini (Jewel Latimore) and Carolyn Rogers in launching the Third World Press, which grew into the country's largest independent publisher of African American literature. Madhubuti's other works of poetry include *Black Pride* (1968) and *Don't Cry, Scream* (1969). He also taught and served as a writer-in-residence at numerous universities, including Chicago State, Cornell, Howard, Morgan State, and the University of Illinois.

In 1971 Madhubuti published *Directionscore: Selected and New Poems* and contributed to *To Gwen with Love: An Anthology Dedicated to Gwendolyn Brooks.* His *Dynamite Voices*, published in 1971 by Broadside Press, provided a critical context for writers of the Black Arts movement. Here the writer defined the role of the African American literary critic and set standards for fellow critics. The next year, Madhubuti founded *Black Books Bulletin.*

In 1973 Madhubuti changed his name from Don L. Lee to Haki Madhubuti, which means "justice," "awakening," and "strong" in Swahili. That year, he also moved to Howard University as poet-in-residence. During the 1980s, he began teaching at Chicago State, where he remained as professor of English until 2010. His works from the 1970s into the 1990s include: *Enemies: The Clash of Races* (1978); *Say That the River Turns: The Impact of Gwendolyn Brooks* (1987); *Killing Memory, Seeking Ancestors* (1987); *Black Men: Obsolete, Single, Dangerous?* (1990); and *Claiming Earth: Race, Rage, Rape, Redemption: Blacks Seeking a Culture of Enlightened Empowerment* (1994). He also edited *Why L.A. Happened: Implications of the '92 Los Angeles Rebellion* (1993).

Among his honors, Madhubuti has received the DuSable Museum Award for Excellence in Poetry, the National Council of Teachers of English Award, the Sidney R. Yates Advocate Award, and the African Heritage Studies Association citation. He was also honored with the Distinguished Writers Award from the Middle Atlantic Writers Association in 1984 and the American Book Award in 1991. In 1984 he was the only poet selected to represent the United States at the International Valmiki World Poetry Festival held in New Delhi, India.

Madhubuti continues to serve as publisher and editor of Third World Press. The press published Madhubuti's *Heartlove: Wedding and Love Poems* (1998); *Tough Notes: A Healing Call for Creating Exceptional Black Men* (2001); and *Yellow Black: The First Twenty-one Years of a Poet's Life* (2005).

PAULE MARSHALL (1929–)

Writer. Paule Marshall was born Valenza Pauline Burke on April 9, 1929, in Brooklyn, New York. Marshall's parents were emigrants from Barbados, and she grew up in a community with strong West Indian influences. She grew to love poetry from an early age and was inspired by the women's conversations that often took place around her mother's kitchen table. Although Marshall did some writing in her childhood years, her serious devotion to writing began in 1954 as exercise at the end of her work day. The result was her first short story, "The Valley Between" (1954).

Marshall's work, which centers on people of African descent, sets out to create images that celebrate the human spirit and put asunder all forms of political and social oppression. Her major themes include the search for identity (both personal and cultural), alienation, and cultural conflict.

Marshall has received numerous awards and fellowships, including a Guggenheim Fellowship in 1960. Her novels include: *Brown Girl, Brownstones* (1959); *Soul Clap Hands and Sing* (1961); *The Chosen Place, the Timeless People* (1969); *Praisesong for the Widow* (1983); *Daughters* (1991); *The Fisher King* (2000); and *Triangular Road: A Memoir* (2009). Short stories and essays are also a part of Marshall's contributions to an African-centered literary experience.

Claude McKay, Poet and Novelist. *Born in Jamaica, McKay immigrated to the United States in 1912. One of the earliest writers of the Harlem Renaissance, he wrote some of his works in Jamaican dialect.* THE LIBRARY OF CONGRESS

CLAUDE McKAY (1889–1948)

Poet, Novelist. Born the son of a farmer in Jamaica (then British West Indies) on September 15, 1889, Festus Claudius McKay was the youngest of eleven children. He began writing early in life. Two books of his poems, *Songs of Jamaica* and *Constab Ballads*, were published just after he turned twenty. In both, he made extensive use of the Jamaican dialect.

In 1913 McKay came to the United States to study agriculture at Tuskegee Institute and at Kansas State University, but his interest in poetry induced him to move to New York City, where he published his works in small literary magazines. McKay then made a trip to England. While there, he completed a collection of lyrics titled *Spring in New Hampshire* (1920). When he returned to the United States, he became associate editor of the *Liberator* under Max Eastman. In 1922 he completed *Harlem Shadows*, a landmark work of the Harlem Renaissance period.

McKay then turned to the writing of such novels as *Home to Harlem* (1928) and *Banjo* (1929), and four other books, including an autobiography and a study of Harlem. *The Passion of Claude McKay: Selected Prose and Poetry 1912–1948*, edited by Wayne Cooper, was published in 1973. McKay traveled abroad before returning to the United States, where he died on May 22, 1948. His final work, *Selected Poems*, was published posthumously in 1953.

During World War II, when Winston Churchill addressed a joint session of the U.S. Congress in an effort to enlist American aid in the battle against Nazism, the climax of his oration was his reading of the famous poem "If We Must Die," originally written by McKay in the 1920s to assail lynchings and mob violence in the South. While in Moscow during the 1920s, McKay published *Trial by Lynching* and *The Negroes in America*, which were not released in English-language editions until the 1970s. Many of his works have been reprinted since his death, including: *Home to Harlem*; *Banana Bottom* (1933); *Banjo*; *A Long Way from Home* (1937); *Harlem: Negro Metropolis* (1940); and *Selected Poems of Claude McKay* (1953). McKay's early collections *Songs of Jamaica* and *Constab Ballads* were bound together in 1972 as *The Dialect Poetry of Claude McKay*. Wayne F. Cooper's *Claude McKay: Rebel Sojourner in the Harlem Renaissance* (1987) is an important book detailing McKay's life and work.

NELLIE Y. McKAY (c. 1940s–2006)

Literary Critic. Nellie Yvonne McKay, the daughter of West Jamaican parents Harry and Nellie McKay, was born in Harlem in the 1940s. She received three degrees in English and American literature: a B.A. (cum laude with honors) from Queens College (CUNY) in 1969; an M.A. from Harvard University in 1971; and a Ph.D. from Harvard in 1977.

McKay knew how to read before she began her formal education. During her childhood, she decided she wanted to teach. Until two college professors encouraged McKay to teach on the college level, she had planned to become a kindergarten teacher. McKay taught at Simmons College in the 1970s before joining the faculty of the University of Wisconsin–Madison in 1978. Her joint appointment to teach in the African American Studies and English departments was expanded to allow McKay to teach in the Women's Studies Department as well. Wisconsin's departments of African American Studies and Women's Studies were floundering until McKay's arrival. McKay, who was one of the most pre-eminent scholars and literary critics in the United States, made significant contributions to the departments. Consequently, the University of Wisconsin–Madison enjoyed national attention in both areas. McKay declined numerous offers to leave Madison, including an offer from Harvard, her alma mater.

McKay specialized in nineteenth- and twentieth-century African American literature with an emphasis on fiction, autobiography, and black women's writings. Her first book was her doctoral thesis, *Jean Toomer, Artist: A Study of His Literary Life and Work, 1894–1936* (1984). McKay's other books include: *Critical Essays on Toni Morrison* (1988); *The Norton Anthology of African American Literature* (1997, 2nd ed. 2003), coedited with Henry Louis Gates Jr.; *Approaches to Teaching the Novels of Toni Morrison* (1997), coedited with Kathryn Earl; *Beloved: A Casebook* (1998), coedited with William L. Andrews; and the *Norton Critical Edition of Harriet Jacobs's "Incidents in the Life of a Slave Girl"* (2000), coedited with Frances Smith Foster.

The Norton Anthology of African American Literature is McKay's most prominent publication. McKay and Gates were the general editors, and along with nine other African American literary scholars, they created the definitive anthology of African American literature. The first edition presented the works of 120 authors, including fifty-two women, from 1746 to 1997, and thirteen major works were reprinted in their entirety. Cornel West hailed *The Norton Anthology of African American Literature* as "a classic of splendid proportions," while Letty Cottin Pogrebin pointed out, "With the publication of this extraordinary collection, no one can ever again claim ignorance of the rich, rewarding legacy of the African-American literary tradition—and especially of Black women's pre-eminent contribution to this heritage." In addition to her full-length publications, McKay wrote essays for literary journals and other books. She also wrote various introductions and afterwords to new and recently reprinted books on African American and women's writing.

McKay received a variety of honors and awards during her career, including the Vilas Associate Award (1987–1989) and the Chancellor's Distinguished Teaching Award (1992) from the University of Wisconsin–Madison; the MELUS Award for Distinguished Contribution to Ethnic Studies (1996); and honorary membership in the University of Wisconsin's chapter of Phi Beta Kappa (1999). McKay died of colon cancer on January 22, 2006.

TERRY McMILLAN (1951–)

Novelist. Terry McMillan was born on October 18, 1951, and raised in Port Huron, Michigan. She attended Los Angeles City College, but transferred to the University of California, Berkeley, and then to Columbia University in New York City to study film. She later enrolled in a writing workshop at the Harlem Writers Guild and was accepted at the MacDowell Colony in New Hampshire in 1983. She has taught at the University of Wyoming and the University of Arizona.

McMillan published her first short story when she was twenty-five years old. Her subsequent novels include: *Mama* (1987); *Disappearing Acts* (1989); and *Waiting to Exhale* (1992). She also edited *Breaking Ice: An Anthology of Contemporary African-American Fiction* (1990). In 1997 she published *How Stella Got Her Groove Back*, and in 2001, *A Day Late and a Dollar Short* was released. In 2005 she published the novel *The Interruption of Everything*.

Waiting to Exhale hit the *New York Times* best-seller list within one week of being in print and remained there for several months. Hardcover publisher Viking printed 700,000 copies and Pocket Books, which published the paperback version, paid $2.64 million for the rights to the work. In 1995 the novel was adapted into one of the most highly touted films of the year. Directed by Forest Whitaker, the film version starred Angela Bassett, Whitney Houston, Lela Rochon, and Loretta Devine. Wesley Snipes and Gregory Hines had smaller roles. *How Stella Got Her Groove Back* was also made into a popular film in 1998, and *Disappearing Acts* was brought to the small screen in 2000.

In 1993 New York Women in Communication gave McMillan a Matrix Award. McMillan was also honored by the NAACP Legal Defense and Educational Fund at a luncheon in 1994. McMillan received publicity in 2005 during her acrimonious divorce from Jonathan Plummer, a Jamaican twenty-four years her junior—and the model for one of the characters in her fictionalized best seller, *How Stella Got Her Groove Back.*

JAMES ALAN McPHERSON (1943–)

Short Story Writer. James McPherson, born in Savannah, Georgia, on October 16, 1943, received his B.A. degree in 1965 from Morris Brown College in Atlanta, a law degree from Harvard University in 1968, and an M.F.A. degree from the University of Iowa in 1969.

McPherson has taught writing at several universities, including the University of Virginia in Charlottesville, where he taught fiction writing. He has taught writing at the University of Iowa since 1981, and is also a contributing editor for *Atlantic Monthly.*

McPherson's short stories have appeared in numerous magazines. *Hue and Cry,* a collection of short stories published in 1969, was highly praised by Ralph Ellison. McPherson was named a Guggenheim fellow in 1972 (for fiction). His second book of short stories, *Elbow Room,* was published in 1977 and received the Pulitzer Prize for Fiction the following year. McPherson was one of the three African American writers who were awarded five-year grants by the MacArthur Foundation in 1981. For twenty years, McPherson taught and put no new literature on the market. Then, in 1997, he published the memoir *Crabcakes.* He followed this up in 2000 with a collection of personal essays and reviews in *A Region Not Home: Reflections from Exile.*

LOFTEN MITCHELL (1919–2001)

Playwright. Born on April 15, 1919, in Columbus, North Carolina, and raised in Harlem in the 1920s, Loften Mitchell began to write as a child, creating scripts for backyard shows that he and his brother performed. After completing junior high school, he decided to enroll at New York Textile High because he had been promised a job on the school newspaper. But Mitchell soon realized that he needed the training of an academic high school, and, with the help of one of his teachers, he transferred to DeWitt Clinton.

Mitchell graduated high school with honors, and found a job as an elevator operator and a delivery boy to support himself while he studied playwriting at night at the City College of New York. He met a professor from Talladega College in Alabama who helped him win a scholarship to study there. He graduated with honors in 1943, having won an award for the best play written by a student.

After two years of service in the U.S. Navy, Mitchell enrolled as a graduate student at Columbia University in New York. A year later, he accepted a job with the city's department of welfare as a social investigator and continued to attend school at night. During this time, he wrote one of his first successful plays, *Blood in the Night,* and in 1957 he wrote *A Land beyond the River,* which had a long run at an off-Broadway theater and was also published as a book.

The following year Mitchell won a Guggenheim award, which enabled him to return to Columbia University and write for a year. Later, he wrote a play called *Star of the Morning,* the story of Bert Williams (1874–1922), an African American entertainer.

Mitchell was an early leader of the Black Theatre movement, and in 1967 Mitchell published a study of African American theater titled *Black Drama.* His other books include: *Tell Pharaoh* (1987), a play; *The Stubborn Old Lady Who Resisted Change* (1973), a novel; and *Voices of the Black Theatre* (1976). Mitchell also wrote the books for various Broadway musicals, including *Ballads for Bimshire* (1963); *Bubbling Brown Sugar* (1975); *Cartoons for a Lunch Hour* (1978); *A Gypsy Girl* (1982); and *Miss Ethel Waters* (1983).

Mitchell died on May 14, 2001, in Queens, New York. He was eighty-two.

TONI MORRISON (1931–)

Novelist, Editor. Born Chloe Anthony Wofford in Lorain, Ohio, on February 18, 1931, Toni Morrison received a B.A. degree from Howard University in 1953, and an M.A. from Cornell in 1955. After working as an instructor in English and the humanities at Texas Southern University and Howard University, Morrison eventually became a senior editor at Random House in New York City, where, for more than twenty years, she was responsible for the publication of many books by African Americans, including Middleton Harris's *The Black Book* (1974), which Morrison edited, and books by Toni Cade Bambara. From 1971 to 1972, Morrison was also an associate professor at the State University of New York at Purchase. Throughout the 1970s and 1980s, she wrote and published her novels, in addition to holding visiting professorships at Yale University and Bard College. From 1984 to 1989, she served as Albert Schweitzer Professor of the Humanities at the State University of New York at Albany. In 1989 Morrison became the Robert F. Goheen Professor of the Humanities at Princeton University.

Morrison's first novel, *The Bluest Eye,* was published in 1969, followed by *Sula,* which won the 1975 Ohioana Book Award and also gained the honor in 2002 of being selected for Oprah Winfrey's book club. Morrison's third novel, *Song of Solomon* (1977), received the 1977

Author Toni Morrison. *Morrison, shown here with an enlargement of the cover of the January 19, 1998, issue of* Time *magazine on which she appeared, became in 1993 the first African American recipient of the Nobel Prize for Literature.* © ROBERT MAASS/CORBIS

National Book Critics Circle Award and the 1978 American Academy and Institute of Arts and Letters Award. *Tar Baby* was published in 1981, followed by the play *Dreaming Emmett*, first produced in Albany in 1986.

Beloved, published in 1987, is regarded by some as her most significant work. The historical novel won both the Pulitzer Prize for Fiction and the Robert F. Kennedy Award. *Beloved* was also a finalist for the 1988 National Book Critics Circle Award and was one of the three contenders for the Ritz Hemingway Prize in Paris, from which no winner emerged. In addition, *Beloved* was a National Book Award finalist. *Beloved* was also adapted for the silver screen by television talk-show host and actress Oprah Winfrey. In the 1990s, Morrison wrote a collection of essays and two novels—*Jazz* (1992) and *Paradise* (1997). She published a novel, *Love*, in 2003; a nonfiction work titled *Remember: The Journey to School Integration* in 2004; and another novel, *A Mercy*, in 2008.

Morrison was elected to the American Institute of Arts and Letters in 1981 and gave the keynote address at the American Writers' Congress in New York City in the fall of that year. She won the New York State Governor's Art Award in 1986. In 1993 the American Literature Association's Coalition of Author Societies founded the Toni Morrison Society, an education group, in Atlanta. Later in the year, Morrison received her highest honor and made history when she became the first African American recipient of the Nobel Prize in Literature, an award that included an $825,000 prize. In 1995 her alma mater, Howard University, awarded her an honorary doctorate.

In 2001 Morrison was honored by Alfred A. Knopf and the Toni Morrison Society at a seventieth birthday celebration. In 2006 the Toni Morrison Society launched the Bench by the Road Project, a community outreach initiative aimed at marking significant sites of African American history with steel benches.

In 1999 Morrison published the first of a series of illustrated children's books written with her son, Slade Morrison. In 2006 Morrison announced that she was retiring from her post at Princeton. That same year, the *New York Times Book Review* named *Beloved* the best novel of the past twenty-five years.

WALTER MOSLEY (1952–)

Novelist and Short Story Writer. Walter Mosley achieved national publicity when, during the 1992 U.S. presidential campaign, Bill Clinton called him his favorite mystery writer. Born on January 12, 1952, and raised in the Watts and Pico-Fairfax districts of Los Angeles, Mosley's unique heritage is attributed to an African American father from the Deep South and a white Jewish mother whose family emigrated from Eastern Europe.

After drifting through a variety of jobs, including potter, caterer, and computer programmer, Mosley settled in New York City and attended the writing program at City College. By 1987, he had become a full-time writer. Although Mosley's first book, a short psychological novel titled *Gone Fishin'* was turned down by numerous agents (it was finally released in 1997), he achieved success in 1990 with *Devil in a Blue Dress*. In the next several years, *A Red Death* (1991), *White Butterfly* (1992), and *Black Betty* (1994) were also greeted with critical acclaim.

Mosley incorporates social and racial issues into gripping novels that authentically portray inner-city life in the African American neighborhoods of post–World War II Los Angeles. His multidimensional depiction of the private investigator and World War II veteran Ezekiel (Easy) Rawlins was heavily influenced by the experiences of Mosley's own father as an African American soldier in World War II and later a southern immigrant in California. With his African American viewpoint and confrontation of shifting societal and moral issues, Mosley has been praised for breaking new ground within the mystery and detective genre and inspiring a new brand of African American fiction.

Mosley has received numerous honors, including the John Creasey Memorial Award and the Shamus Award for outstanding mystery writing. In 1990 the Mystery Writers of America nominated *Devil in a Blue Dress* for an Edgar Award. The film version of *Devil in a Blue Dress*, with a screenplay by the author, was released in 1996. Directed by Carl Franklin, the film starred Denzel Washington as Rawlins. In 1995 Mosley published *R. L.'s Dream*, a fictional meditation on the blues. The following year, he released *A Little Yellow Dog*. In 1997 he published the book *Always Outnumbered, Always Outgunned*, introducing his most compelling new character since the debut of Easy Rawlins: Socrates Fortlow, a tough, brooding ex-convict determined to challenge and understand the violence and anarchy in his world and in himself. Mosley continued with the character of Socrates Fortlow in his 1998 offering *Walkin' the Dog*.

Tackling the e-market, Mosley published *Whispers in the Dark* and *The Greatest* in 2000, available solely on the Internet. In 2001 Mosley shifted gears once again, this time introducing Paris Minton, a seller of secondhand books, in *Fearless Jones*. Mosley went back to the short story for his 2002 book, *Futureland: Nine Stories of an Imminent World*, about a grim cyber-filled future. He also won a Grammy Award in 2002 for best album liner notes for *Richard Pryor ... And It's Deep Too! The Complete Warner Bros. Recordings (1968–1992)*. Mosley published five books in the Rawlins series from 2002 to 2010, along with several more volumes in his Fearless Jones and Socrates Fortlow series. Other works include: *The Wave* (2006); a science fiction novel; *47* (2005), a historical novel for young adults; *Fortunate Son* (2006); and *The Tempest Tales* (2008). In 2009 Mosley introduced a new series with *The Long Fall*, featuring detective Leonid McGill.

WALTER DEAN MYERS (1937–)

Young Adult Writer and Poet. Walter Milton Myers was born in Martinsburg, West Virginia, in 1937. Upon the death of his mother when he was three years old, Myers was raised by foster parents, Herbert and Florence Dean, in Harlem. Myers began writing as a child and was praised in grade school for his academic achievements. Determined to further his education, he joined the U.S. Army at age seventeen, enabling him to pay part of his college tuition with money from the GI Bill. In 1969, upon the publication of his first picture book for children, Myers was determined to become a professional writer. *Where Does the Day Go?* was honored by the Council on Interracial Books for Children and established Myers as an author who addressed the needs of minority children.

In the 1970s, while Myers worked as a senior editor for the Bobbs-Merrill publishing house, he released more picture books and began writing young adult stories. Since then, he has published numerous novels in which he tackles urban social issues, such as teen pregnancy, crime, drug abuse, and gang violence. Myers's authentic dialogue and ability to capture the universal ties and strengthening powers of family and friendship within African American communities prompted an enthusiastic response from teenage readers.

Committed to producing quality literature for African American children, Myers branched into fairy tales, ghost stories, science fiction, and adventure sagas. He also published a popular biography, *Malcolm X: By Any Means Necessary*, in 1993. Myers has won a variety of awards, including the Coretta Scott King Award and a

Walter Dean Myers, 2004. *Myers is a critically acclaimed author of many books for children and young adults, including* The Cruisers *(2010). A number of his children's books have been illustrated by his son, Christopher Myers.* HOWARD EARL SIMMONS/NEW YORK DAILY NEWS ARCHIVE VIA GETTY IMAGES

Newbery Honor Book citation for *Scorpions* (1988). Myers's novels, particularly *Hoops* (1981), *Fallen Angels* (1988), and *Motown and Didi: A Love Story* (1984), are an enduring presence on both high school and young adult recommended-reading lists. A prolific author, Myers published numerous books in the first decade of the twenty-first century, including: *Antarctica: Journeys to the South Pole* (2004); *Here Is Harlem: Poems in Many Voices* (2004); *Shooter* (2004); *Autobiography of My Dead Brother* (2005); *The Hellfighters: When Pride Met Courage* (2006); *Street Love* (2006); *Harlem Summer* (2007); *What They Found* (2007); *Sunrise over Fallujah* (2008); *Ida B. Wells, Let the Truth Be Told* (2008); *Amiri & Odette* (2009); and *Dope Sick* (2009).

GLORIA NAYLOR (1950–)

Novelist. Gloria Naylor was born in New York City on January 25, 1950, and still lives there. She received a B.A. in English from Brooklyn College in 1981 and an M.A. in Afro-American Studies from Yale University in 1983. She has taught writing and literature at George Washington University, New York University, Brandeis University, Cornell University, and Boston University. In 1983 she won the American Book Award for first fiction for her novel *The Women of Brewster Place* (1982), which was adapted for television in 1988. Her second novel was *Linden Hills*, published in 1985. Her third novel, *Mama Day* (1988), was written with the aid of a grant from the National Endowment for the Arts. In 1988 Naylor was awarded a Guggenheim Fellowship. In 1992 she published a new novel, *Bailey's Café*.

In 1998 Naylor returned to familiar ground with *The Men of Brewster Place*. This novel offered a different spin on the gritty but secure community that had brought Naylor into the public spotlight, and much like *The Women of Brewster Place*, this book was hailed by critics for its characterization and positive messages.

In 2005 Naylor published a semiautobiographical work titled *1996*, about government surveillance and mind control. She was also reportedly working on a sequel to *Mama Day*—called *Sapphira Wade*.

ANN LANE PETRY (c. 1912–1997)

Novelist, Short Story Writer. Ann Petry was born in Old Saybrook, Connecticut, where her father was a pharmacist. After graduating from the College of Pharmacy at the University of Connecticut, she went to New York where she worked as a social worker and newspaper reporter while studying creative writing at night.

Her early short stories appeared in *Crisis* and *Phylon*. In 1946, after receiving a Houghton Mifflin Fellowship, she completed and published her first novel, *The Street*, about the lives of African American women in a crowded tenement. Through her exploration of this subject, Petry became the first African American woman writer to address the problems of poor African American women living in the inner city.

Petry also wrote: *Country Place* (1947); *The Narrows* (1953); and *Miss Muriel and Other Stories* (1971). Her works for children and young people include: *The Drugstore Cat* (1949); *Harriet Tubman: Conductor on the Underground Railroad* (1955); *Tituba of Salem Village* (1964); and *Legends of Saints* (1970). Many of her earlier novels were reprinted in the 1980s and 1990s. Petry died on April 28, 1997.

ARNOLD RAMPERSAD (1941–)

Literary Critic. Arnold Rampersad was born on November 13, 1941, in Trinidad. He received a B.A. and M.A. from Bowling Green State University in Ohio, as well as an M.A. and Ph.D. from Harvard University. Rampersad, who was named a MacArthur Foundation fellow in 1991, has taught at Stanford University (1974–1983), Rutgers University (1983–1988), Columbia University (1988–1990), and Princeton University (1990–1998). In 1998 Rampersad returned to Stanford University as the Sara Hart Kimball Professor (now emeritus) in the Humanities.

Rampersad's first book is *Melville's Israel Potter: A Pilgrimage and Progress* (1969). Starting with Rampersad's next book, *The Art and Imagination of W. E. B. Du Bois* (1976), he began chronicling the lives and works of the most prominent African American men of the twentieth century. Rampersad is the coauthor of tennis player Arthur Ashe's *Days of Grace: A Memoir* (1993) and the author of *Jackie Robinson: A Biography* (1997). Rampersad also edited new Library of American editions of the works of Richard Wright and four volumes of the works of Langston Hughes. His *Ralph Ellison: A Biography* (2007) was a National Book Award finalist.

Rampersad is best known for his two-volume *The Life of Langston Hughes*, Volume 1: *1902–1941: I, Too, Sing America* (1986), which won the 1987 Anisfield-Wolf Book Award in Race Relations and the 1988 Clarence L. Holte Prize. The second volume, *1941–1967: I Dream a World* (1988), was a 1989 Pulitzer Prize finalist in biography and winner of a 1990 American Book Award. Rampersad's work is considered the definitive biography of Hughes. Rita Dove, in the *New York Times Book Review*, wrote: "In his superlative study of . . . the most prominent Afro-American poet of our century, Arnold Rampersad has performed that most difficult of feats: illuminating a man who, despite all his public visibility, was quite elusive." John A. Williams commented in the *Los Angeles Times Book Review*: "No other biography of Hughes can match the grace and richness of Rampersad's writing, or his investigative and interpretive abilities." And David Nicholson opined in the *Washington Post Book World*: "This may be the best biography of a black writer we have had."

Rampersad coedited *Slavery and the Literary Imagination* (1989) with Deborah McDowell. He also served on the editorial board for *The Norton Anthology of African American Literature* (1997), the benchmark compilation of the African American literary tradition, a project led by general editors Henry Louis Gates Jr. and Nellie McKay. Rampersad is also coeditor of the Race and American Culture book series published by Oxford University Press.

ISHMAEL REED (1938–)

Novelist, Poet, Playwright. Born in Chattanooga, Tennessee, on February 22, 1938, Ishmael Reed grew up in Buffalo, New York. He attended the State University of New York at Buffalo from 1956 to 1960. Reed worked as a reporter and later as an editor for the *Newark Advance* in New Jersey before cofounding the *East Village Other* in 1965. Reed spent the next few years teaching prose and guest lecturing at different institutions, including the University of California at Berkeley. In 1971 he cofounded Yardbird Publishing Company. After four years as the editorial director, he cofounded Reed, Cannon & Johnson Communications Company, a publisher and producer of videos. The following year Reed established the Before Columbus Foundation, which produced and distributed works by ethnic writers.

One of the most controversial figures in African American letters, Reed has published poetry, novels, plays, and prose satirizing American political, religious, and literary repression. Considered by some to be misogynistic and cynical, others find his work innovative. He is committed to creating an alternative African American aesthetic, which he calls "Neo-HooDooism." One hallmark of the aesthetic is a reliance on satire and social criticism.

Reed's works of poetry include: *catechism of d neoamerican hoodoo church* (1971); *Conjure* (1972), which was nominated for the National Book Award; *Chattanooga* (1973); *A Secretary to the Spirits* (1978); and *New and Collected Poetry* (1988). He edited *From Totems to Hip-Hop: A Multicultural Anthology of Poetry across the Americas, 1900–2002*, published in 2003. Reed's own poetry has appeared in numerous anthologies, including *The Poetry of the Negro, 1746–1970* (1970); *The New Black Poetry* (1969); and *The Norton Anthology of African American Literature* (1997); and in the magazines *Cricket* and *Scholastic*.

Reed's novels include: *The Free-Lance Pallbearers* (1967); *Yellow Back Radio Broke Down* (1969); *Mumbo Jumbo* (1972), which received a National Book Award nomination; *The Last Days of Louisiana Red* (1974); *Flight to Canada* (1976); *The Terrible Twos* (1982); *Reckless Eyeballing* (1986); *The Terrible Threes* (1989); and *Japanese by Spring* (1992). Reed has also written plays, including: *The Lost State of Franklin* (1976); *Savage Wilds* (1988); and its sequel *Savage Wilds II* (1990).

Prose works by Reed include: *Shrovetide in Old New Orleans* (1978); *God Made Alaska for the Indians: Selected Essays* (1982); *Writin' Is Fightin': Thirty-seven Years of Boxing on Paper* (1988); *Airing Dirty Laundry* (1993); *Blues City: A Walk in Oakland* (2003); *Another Day at the Front: Dispatches from the Race War* (2003); and *Mixing It Up: Taking on the Media Bullies and Other Reflections* (2008). He was also the editor of *Multi-America: Essays on Cultural Wars and Cultural Peace* (1997).

In 1974 Reed won the Guggenheim Memorial Foundation Award for fiction. The next year he received a Rosenthal Foundation Award and an honor from the National Institute of Arts and Letters. In 1978 Reed was given the Lewis Michaux and American Civil Liberties awards. The following year he won the Pushcart Prize. He has received fellowships from the Wisconsin Board, Yale University's Calhoun College, and the MacArthur Foundation, as well as grants from New York State, the National Endowment for the Arts, and the California Arts Council.

SONIA SANCHEZ (1934–)

Poet, Playwright. Sonia Sanchez was born Wilsonia Driver on September 9, 1934, in Birmingham, Alabama. Her mother died in Sanchez's infancy, and she was sent to live with her grandmother and other relatives. She joined her father and siblings in Harlem at the age of nine. Sanchez completed her B.A. at New York's Hunter College in 1955, and began postgraduate work at New York University. She married and divorced Albert Sanchez, and was later briefly married to Etheridge Knight, an African American writer of poetry and fiction. She taught at San Francisco State College during the 1960s. Sanchez began teaching in the Black Studies Department of Temple University in Philadelphia in 1977 and held the Laura Carnell Chair in English until her retirement in 1999. She remains poet-in-residence at Temple.

Sanchez's plays were published in *The Drama Review* (summer 1968) and in *New Plays from the Black Theatre*

(1969), edited by Ed Bullins. Her poems have been published in many other magazines and anthologies. Her volumes of poetry include: *Homecoming* (1969); *We a Bad People* (1970); *It's a New Day* (1971); *A Blues Book for Blue Black Magical Women* (1973); *Love Poems* (1975); *I've Been a Woman* (1978); *Under a Soprano Sky* (1987); *Wounded in the House of a Friend* (1994); *Like the Singing Coming off the Drums* (1997); *Shake Loose My Skin: New and Selected Poems* (2000); and *Morning Haiku* (2010). Sanchez has edited two anthologies: *Three Hundred and Sixty Degrees of Blackness Coming at You: An Anthology of the Sonia Sanchez Writers Workshop at Countee Cullen Library in Harlem* (1971), and *We Be Word Sorcerers: Twenty-five Stories by Black Americans* (1973). She has also written *A Sound Investment* (1979), a collection of short stories, and *Homegirls and Handgrenades* (1984), which won an American Book Award.

NTOZAKE SHANGE (1948–)

Playwright, Poet, Novelist. Playwright and poet Paulette Linda Williams was born in Trenton, New Jersey, on October 18, 1948; she changed her name to Ntozake Shange in 1971. Shange graduated from Barnard College and received her master's degree from the University of Southern California, where she did further graduate work. She studied Afro-American dance while in California and performed with the Third World Collective, Raymond Sawyer's Afro-American Dance Company, Sounds in Motion, and West Coast Dance Works.

Shange taught at Sonoma Mills College in California from 1972 to 1975. She went on to teach at the City College of New York and Douglass College before becoming the Mellon Distinguished Professor of Literature at Rice University in Houston, Texas, in 1983. For three years, she also worked as an associate professor of drama at the University of Houston.

Shange's play *For Colored Girls Who Have Considered Suicide/When the Rainbow Is Enuf*, a "choreopoem" (poetry and dance), was first produced in Berkeley, California, in 1975. The following year, the play opened at an off-Broadway theater in New York City, where it ran for several months before moving to Broadway and later to other cities. It earned Tony and Grammy Award nominations in 1977, and was later adapted for television. Shange's other plays include: *Spell #7* (1979); *A Photograph: Lovers in Motion* (1979); *Boogie Woogie Landscapes* (1979); and *From Okra to Greens* (1984). *For Colored Girls* was published as a book, and Shange's collection *Three Pieces* (1981) contains her plays *Spell #7, A Photograph: Lovers in Motion*, and *Boogie Woogie Landscapes.*

Other books by Shange include: *Nappy Edges* (poetry, 1978); *Sassafrass, Cypress & Indigo* (novel, 1982); *A Daughter's Geography* (poetry, 1983); *See No Evil: Prefaces & Accounts, 1976–1983* (1984); *Betsey Brown* (novel, 1985); *Liliane: Resurrection of the Daughter* (novel, 1994); *I Live in Music* (poetry, 1994); *Whitewash* (children's novel, 1997); a history of food called *If I Can Cook You Know God Can Cook* (1998); *Daddy Says* (children's novel, 2002); *Floodlight and Butterfly* (children's novel, 2002); *The Sweet Breath of Life: A Poetic Narrative of the African-American Family* (2004, with photographer Frank Stewart); *Coretta Scott* (poetry, 2009); and *We Troubled the Waters* (poetry, 2009).

A stage version of *Betsey Brown*, with music by the jazz trumpeter and composer Baikida Carroll, opened the American Music Theater Festival in Philadelphia on March 25, 1989. Shange directed Ina Césaire's *Fire's Daughters* in 1993. Shange received an Obie Award in 1981 for *Mother Courage and Her Children*, and a Los Angeles Times Book Prize for poetry that year for *Three Pieces.* A Guggenheim fellow, Shange has been given awards by the Outer Critics Circle and the National Black Theater Festival. She also won the Pushcart Prize.

LUCY TERRY (c. 1730–1821)

Poet. Lucy Terry is generally considered one of the first African American poets in the United States. In a ballad that she called "Bars Fight," she re-created an Indian massacre that occurred in Deerfield, Massachusetts, in 1746 during King George's War. "Bars Fight" has been hailed by some historians as the most authentic account of the massacre.

Terry was semiliterate but enslaved. She was sold in Rhode Island and purchased, it is believed, by the Terry family in Enfield, Connecticut. At the age of five, she was sold again and lived in the household of Ensign Ebenezer Wells of Deerfield, Massachusetts. She learned to read and may have been taught while in the Wells household, where she remained until 1756, when she married a freed African named Abijah Prince. Terry won her freedom with the assistance of either her husband or Wells. The Prince house served as a center for young people who gathered to listen to their hostess's storytelling in the oral tradition of the period. Only "Bars Fight" was ever published because Harriet Hitchcock, a Deerfield resident, wrote it down from memory after Terry's death. Lucy Terry was a strong woman who argued eloquently for her family's rights in several cases.

WALLACE H. THURMAN (1902–1934)

Novelist, Playwright, Journalist. A caustic critic of African American writing, Wallace Henry Thurman was a participant in the New Negro movement known as the Harlem

Renaissance. Thurman, called Wally by his friends, was born on August 16, 1902, in Salt Lake City. He graduated from the University of Utah in 1922, having studied premedicine, and did postgraduate work in 1923 at the University of Southern California. Thurman read widely and became aware of the Harlem Renaissance then taking place in New York. He tried to establish a West Coast counterpart of the Harlem Renaissance and launched his own short-lived literary magazine, *Outlet*. He moved to New York City the following year.

Thurman was managing editor of the *Messenger* from spring to fall 1926, then moved to the *World Tomorrow*, a white-owned monthly. By now, Thurman and Langston Hughes had become good friends. Their group of writers and artists included Arna Bontemps (whom Thurman had known in Los Angeles), Nella Larsen, Dorothy West, Countee Cullen, Jessie Fauset, Aaron Douglas, Zora Neale Hurston, and Gwendolyn Bennett. In the summer of 1926, Thurman and the group established *Fire!*, a short-lived literary magazine that was both obscene and revolutionary. The magazine was intended to provide another outlet beyond the *Crisis* and *Opportunity* magazines for young African American writers to have their works published. Thurman financed the magazine himself and spent four years paying its debt.

In 1927 a number of Thurman's articles were published in prestigious magazines, such as *New Republic* and *Dance Magazine*, further helping to establish him as a critic. The next year, McFadden Publications added Thurman to its editorial staff, and he continued to write. In 1929 he published the work for which he is best known, *The Blacker the Berry the Sweeter the Juice*, an autobiographical novel that embraced intra-race color prejudice and self-hatred. Thurman also served as a ghostwriter for several magazines and books. He wrote plays as well; one of them, based on his story "Cordelia the Crude," premiered on Broadway in 1929 to mixed reviews. The production later toured Chicago and Los Angeles.

In 1932 Thurman published two novels: *Infants of the Spring* and *The Interne*. An alcoholic homosexual, Thurman was often depressed and suicidal. He became ill with tuberculosis and died in New York on December 22, 1934.

JEAN TOOMER (1894–1967)

Novelist, Poet. Jean Toomer's *Cane*, published in 1923, has been called one of the three best novels ever written by an African American—the others being Richard Wright's *Native Son* and Ralph Ellison's *Invisible Man*. According to critic Robert Bone, "*Cane* is by far the most impressive product of the Negro Renaissance."

A mixture of poems and sketches, *Cane* was written during that period in which most African American writers were reacting against earlier "polite" forms by creating works marked by literary realism. Toomer even went beyond this realm to the threshold of symbol and myth, using a "mystical" approach, which is more akin to the contemporary mood than it was to the prevailing spirit of his own day. *Cane* sold only five hundred copies on publication, and it remained little known until it was reprinted decades later in several editions with new introductions. Much was written about Toomer and *Cane* thereafter, and a critical edition of Toomer's novel, edited by Darwin Turner, was published in 1988.

Nathan Pinchback Toomer was born in Washington, D.C., in 1894. He was one of eight children of sharecroppers. His father left shortly after his son's birth, and his mother, Nina Toomer, named the boy Nathan Eugene, a name he later shorted to Jean. Toomer was educated in law at the University of Wisconsin and City College of New York before he turned to writing. The transcendental nature of his writings is said to have stemmed in part from his early study under G. I. Gurdjieff, the Russian mystic.

Toomer had a reputation for scandalous affairs with married women. In 1931 he married Margery Latimer, the daughter of a wealthy New York Stock Exchange member, a friend of his former lover, Georgia O'Keeffe, and a well-known author. Like Toomer, she was a follower of Gurdjieff.

Toomer published a great deal of poetry in his lifetime. Darwin Turner edited *The Wayward and the Seeking: A Collection of Writings by Jean Toomer* (1980), a book of his poetry, short stories, dramas, and autobiography. Important books about Toomer and his writings include: Therman O'Daniel's *Jean Toomer: A Critical Evaluation* (1988), which includes more than forty scholarly essays on Toomer; Robert B. Jones and Margery Toomer Latimer's *The Collected Poems of Jean Toomer* (1988); and Nellie Y. McKay's *Jean Toomer, Artist: A Study of His Literary Life and Work, 1894–1936* (1984). Toomer died of cancer on March 10, 1967.

ALICE WALKER (1944–)

Poet, Novelist. Alice Walker was born in Eatonton, Georgia, on February 9, 1944. She was educated at Spelman College (1961–1963) and Sarah Lawrence College (1964–1965), from which she received her B.A. After college, she worked as a voter registrar in Georgia and for the welfare department in New York City. In 1967 she moved to Mississippi, where she was an African American literature consultant for Friends of the Children of Mississippi. From 1968 to 1971, she was a writer-in-residence at Jackson State and Tougaloo colleges. Moving to Boston, she lectured at Wellesley College and the University of Massachusetts until 1973. While teaching in the early 1970s, she was a Radcliffe Institute fellow.

Walker's work began to be published in the late 1960s, starting with *Once: Poems* in 1968. Two years later, she published the novel, *The Third Life of Grange Copeland.* These were followed by a succession of works, including: *Revolutionary Petunias and Other Poems* (1973), which earned a National Book Award nomination and the Lillian Smith Award; *In Love and Trouble: Stories of Black Women* (1974), recipient of a Richard and Hinda Rosenthal Foundation Award from the American Academy and Institute of Arts and Letters; and *Langston Hughes: American Poet* (1974, for children).

Community Activist Al Sharpton with Novelist Alice Walker, Broadway Theatre, New York City, 2005. *Walker's 1983 novel* The Color Purple *opened on Broadway as a musical production in December 2005. Walker and Sharpton attend the opening.* **BRAD BARKET/GETTY IMAGES ENTERTAINMENT/GETTY IMAGES**

The novel *Meridian* (1976) was followed in 1979 by a book of poetry titled *Good Night, Willie Lee, I'll See You in the Morning* and an edited work titled *I Love Myself When I Am Laughing . . . and Then Again When I Am Looking Mean and Impressive: A Zora Neale Hurston Reader.* The book on Hurston brought about a resurgence of interest in a Harlem Renaissance writer who had been overshadowed by better-known authors.

In the 1980s, Walker formally resumed her teaching career, spending 1982 as the Fannie Hurst Professor of Literature at Brandeis University, while also serving as a distinguished writer as the University of California at Berkeley. In 1984 she co-founded Wild Trees Press. During this decade, Walker published the short story collection *You Can't Keep a Good Woman Down* (1981); two collections of essays and journal entries, *In Search of Our Mothers' Gardens: Womanist Prose* (1983) and *Living by the Word: Selected Writings, 1973–1987* (1988); a book of poetry titled *Horses Make a Landscape Look More Beautiful* (1984); *To Hell With Dying* (a juvenile story, 1988); and the novel *The Temple of My Familiar* (1989). In 1986 she received the O. Henry Award for her short story "Kindred Spirits."

Walker's most well-received work, however, was the 1982 novel *The Color Purple.* Written in the form of a series of letters, the novel was nominated for the National Book Critics Circle Award and won an American Book Award and the Pulitzer Prize in 1983. Walker was the first African American woman to win the Pulitzer Prize. In 1985 Walker's best-selling book was adapted into an award-winning film directed by Steven Spielberg and featuring Whoopi Goldberg, Danny Glover, Oprah Winfrey, and Margaret Avery. The novel was also adapted into a successful stage musical that opened on Broadway in 2005.

In the 1990s, Walker published *Possessing the Secret of Joy* (1992), a loose sequel to *The Color Purple. The Same River Twice: Honoring the Difficult* came out four years later. *By the Light of My Father's Smile* was published in 1998, and *Now Is the Time to Open Your Heart* was published in 2005. Walker also published a book of short stories in 2000 titled *The Way Forward Is with a Broken Heart.* In 2006 Walker published a book for children titled *There Is a Flower at the Tip of My Nose Smelling Me.* The holder of numerous honorary degrees, Walker has received a Merrill Fellowship for writing, a National Endowment for the Arts grant, a Radcliffe Institute Fellowship, and other honors.

MARGARET A. WALKER (1915–1998)

Poet, Novelist. Margaret Abigail Walker was born on July 7, 1915, in Birmingham, Alabama. She received her early education in Alabama, Louisiana, and Mississippi. Walker earned her B.A. from Northwestern University and both her M.A. (1940) and Ph.D. (1966) from the University of Iowa.

In 1942 Walker published *For My People* and, two years later, she was awarded a Rosenwald Fellowship for creative writing. She taught English and literature at Livingston College in North Carolina, West Virginia State College, and Jackson State College in Mississippi. Her novel *Jubilee* appeared in 1966. *For My People* was reprinted in 1969. Her other works include: *Prophets for a New Day* (1970); *How I Wrote Jubilee* (1972); *October Journey* (1973); *A Poetic Equation: Conversations between Nikki Giovanni and Margaret Walker* (1974); and *Richard Wright: Daemonic Genius* (1988).

A second edition of *A Poetic Equation: Conversations between Nikki Giovanni and Margaret Walker* was published in 1983. Walker's poetry, which became increasingly political, had a major impact on African American poets of the 1960s and 1970s. She died of breast cancer on November 30, 1998, in Chicago.

DOROTHY WEST (1907–1998)

Novelist, Short Story Writer, Journalist. Dorothy West was the last surviving member of the Harlem Renaissance, the period of the late 1920s and early 1930s when an outpouring of writing and poetry exuded from the pens and typewriters of African American writers based in Harlem. West was known as "The Kid" by such luminaries as Countee Cullen, Langston Hughes, Richard Wright, and Zora Neale Hurston. West wrote short stories for the *New York Daily News* in the 1930s, and twice, during the Great Depression, founded African American literary journals, most notably the *New Challenge*.

West was born on June 2, 1907, in Boston. She later moved to New York City, but eventually returned home, moving into her family's summer home in Oak Bluffs on Martha's Vineyard in 1943. Five years later, she wrote her first novel, *The Living Is Easy*, the work for which she is best known, about the affluent world of African American achievers. West continued to write short stories for the *Daily News* from her Oak Bluffs home for the next twenty-five years.

In the 1950s, West began a second novel, *The Wedding*, but could not find a publisher interested in handling it. With its theme of interracial marriage, it may have been too hot a topic for the times and was put aside by West in an unfinished state. Instead, West started contributing short pieces to the Vineyard's daily newspaper in the 1970s.

In 1992 West's stories caught the eye of former First Lady Jacqueline Onassis, an editor at Doubleday and a summer resident of Martha's Vineyard. Onassis encouraged West to finish *The Wedding*, and the two of them began meeting weekly. With Onassis acting as West's editor, the novel finally was published in 1995. West dedicated the novel to Onassis. The story was made into a television movie, produced by Oprah Winfrey, and aired in 1998. In 1995 West published *The Richer, the Poorer: Stories, Sketches, and Reminiscences*. She died on August 16, 1998.

In 2005 the University of Massachusetts Press published *Where the Wild Grape Grows: Selected Writings, 1930–1950*, a collection of West's out-of-print or previously unpublished writings. *The Last Leaf of Harlem: Selected and Newly Discovered Fiction by the Author of "The Wedding,"* edited by Lionel Bascom, was published in 2008.

PHILLIS WHEATLEY (c. 1753–1784)

Poet. Born in Senegal around 1753, Phillis Wheatley was brought to the United States enslaved and received her name from Susannah Wheatley, the wife of the Boston tailor who bought Phillis. Wheatley received her early education in the household of her master. Her interest in writing stemmed from her reading of the Bible and the classics under the guidance of the Wheatleys' daughter Mary.

In 1770 Phillis's first poem was printed under the title "A Poem by Phillis, a Negro Girl, on the Death of Reverend George Whitefield." Her book, *Poems on Various Subjects: Religious and Moral*, was published in London in 1773, the first book of poetry published by an African American. She took a trip to England for health reasons, but later returned to the United States and was married. She published the poem "Liberty and Peace" in 1784, shortly before her death. Most of the old books of her poems, letters, and memories about her life were reprinted in the late 1960s and early 1970s. Two notable books about Wheatley are Julian D. Mason Jr.'s *The Poems of Phillis Wheatley* (1966) and William H. Robinson's *Phillis Wheatley: A Biography* (1981). Robinson also compiled and published *Phillis Wheatley: A Bio-bibliography* (1981).

Although George Washington was among Wheatley's admirers (she once sent him a tributary poem, which he graciously acknowledged), her poetry is considered important today largely because of its historical role in the growth of African American literature. Wheatley's poetry reflects Anglo-Saxon models rather than her African heritage. It is, nevertheless, a typical example of the verse manufactured in a territory—the British colonies—not yet divorced from its maternal origins. Wheatley died on December 5, 1784.

JOHN EDGAR WIDEMAN (1941–)

Writer, Educator. John Edgar Wideman has been one of the leading chroniclers of life in urban black America. He depicts the widening chasm between the urban poor and the white power structure in the United States, and is known for intertwining ghetto experiences with experimental fiction techniques, personal history, and social events to highlight deep cultural conflicts. A prolific writer, Wideman is the only two-time winner of the prestigious PEN/Faulkner Award for literature—for *Sent for You Yesterday* (1983) and *Philadelphia Fire* (1990). He also published the novels *The Cattle Killing* (1996), *Two Cities* (1998), and *Fanon* (2008), among other works.

In addition to novels, Wideman has written short stories and nonfiction, including *Brothers and Keepers* (1984), a juxtaposition of his life and that of his younger brother, who was incarcerated for larceny and murder. Wideman's examination of the two brothers' different lives was nominated for the National Book Critics Circle Award. Wideman's short story collections include: *Damballah* (1981); *Fever* (1989); *All Stories Are True* (1993); and *God's Gym* (2005).

Born on June 14, 1941, in Washington, D.C., Wideman was the first of five children. Growing up in Pittsburgh, where the family moved, Wideman attended the highly regarded Peabody High School. A top student, he was also class president and captain of the basketball team. Enrolling at the University of Pittsburgh on a scholarship, he earned a B.A. in 1963. During his undergraduate career, Wideman made the Big Five Basketball Hall of Fame, won the university's creative writing prize, and was elected to Phi Beta Kappa. In 1963 he was awarded a Rhodes Scholarship to study in England, becoming the first African American to receive such recognition in more than fifty years. With a B.A. in philosophy obtained from Oxford's New College in 1966, Wideman began writing and teaching at such institutions as the universities of Pennsylvania, Wyoming, Massachusetts at Amherst, and Brown.

AUGUST WILSON (1945–2005)

Playwright. One of the most important voices in the American theater, playwright August Wilson became a spokesperson for the black experience in America. Since his first stage success, *Ma Rainey's Black Bottom* in 1984, he celebrated people of color in several plays, all set in a different decade in the twentieth century. In 1997 he elicited a public debate involving many prominent theater critics on the use of theater as a vehicle for cultural nationalism.

Wilson was born Frederick August Kittel in Pittsburgh, Pennsylvania, in 1945, the oldest of six children. His mother was a house cleaner; his absent father was a baker. He left school at fifteen due to the racist abuse he endured there. But he continued his education in the local library, reading all the literature by African American writers, such as Ralph Ellison, Langston Hughes, and Richard Wright. He published a few poems in *Black World and Black Lines* in the early 1970s after absorbing the works of Robert Frost, Dylan Thomas, and Amiri Baraka.

It was when Wilson discovered the writings of Malcolm X that he decided to use cultural nationalism, African American people working toward cultural self-determination, as a basis for playwriting. In 1969 he helped found the African American activist theater company Black Horizon Theatre on the Hill in Pittsburgh, which focused on politicizing the community and raising African American consciousness. He staged some early plays through this association, but moved to St. Paul, Minnesota, in 1978, where he says he gained clarity and became less radicalized. He wrote *Jitney* (1979) for the Minneapolis Playwrights' Center and won a fellowship prize.

Wilson moved the location of *Jitney* and his next work, *Fullerton Street*, back to Pittsburgh and produced them at the Allegheny Repertory Theater in 1982. After two years of work at the National Playwrights Conference at the Eugene O'Neill Theater Center in Waterford, Connecticut, his first major work, *Ma Rainey's Black Bottom*, caught the eye of Yale Repertory Theatre's artistic director Lloyd Richards. Together, they staged almost all of Wilson's works, Richards directing them himself.

Each of Wilson's plays tells the story of a different segment of the African American experience. *Ma Rainey's Black Bottom* concerns how African American entertainers were exploited by whites in the 1920s. His next play, *Joe Turner's Come and Gone* (1988), explored the migration of African Americans from rural southern areas to the industrial cities of the North. *Fences* became an immediate hit when it opened on Broadway in 1987. Actor James Earl Jones played the main character, Troy Maxson, who dreams of playing professional baseball in the 1950s, only to be victimized by white racism. This play won the Pulitzer Prize and other awards for Wilson.

In 1990 Wilson won his second Pulitzer Prize for *The Piano Lesson*, a play that focuses on a family conflict over the selling of an heirloom piano once traded for enslaved ancestors whose portraits are carved into it. Wilson's next play, *Two Trains Running* (1992) is set in the late 1960s, when racial strife and the Vietnam War divided the nation.

Wilson moved to Seattle in the early 1990s. His next play, *Seven Guitars*, opened in 1996. Set in Pittsburgh in 1948, the unseen main character's death is being mourned at a wake. The seven characters reminisce with music, and dream about the future. This was another successful production by Wilson and Lloyd Richards. Other plays in the cycle include: *King Hedley II* (1999); *Gem of the Ocean* (2003); and *Radio Golf* (2005).

A debate began in 1997 when Wilson gave a keynote speech to the Theater Communications Group Conference titled "The Ground on which I Stand." In the speech, Wilson celebrated the achievements of African American theater and insisted that such theater could only be understood and appreciated by those living the African American experience. He castigated the New York mainstream theater and its critics for lack of support for African American theater. In response, many New York critics, including Robert Brustein, Frank Rich, and John Simon, published editorial columns analyzing Wilson's speech. Ultimately, a face-to-face debate between Wilson and Brustein was held in January 1998 to discuss the cultural intentions of theater. At the end of the evening, the issues remained unresolved. Wilson had revisited his earlier black nationalist beliefs and continued to evoke questions about the African American experience.

In 2001 Wilson was presented with the prestigious Washington Literary Award, and in 2002 he became the first American playwright to be honored with an Olivier Award. Wilson died of liver cancer in Seattle on October 2, 2005. Fourteen days after his death, the Virginia Theatre on Broadway was renamed the August Wilson Theatre in his honor. Wilson's greatest legacy is not only his cycle of ten plays depicting the effects of racism on the African American community during each decade of the twentieth century, but also his impact on a new generation of African American writers.

RICHARD WRIGHT (1908–1960)

Novelist. Born on September 4, 1908, on a plantation near Natchez, Mississippi, Wright drew on his personal experience to dramatize racial injustice and its brutalizing effects. In 1938, under the auspices of the Works Progress Administration's (WPA) Illinois Writers' Project, Wright published *Uncle Tom's Children*, a collection of four novellas based on his Mississippi boyhood memories. The book won an award for the best work of fiction by a WPA writer, and Wright received a Guggenheim Fellowship.

Richard Wright Commemorative Stamp, 2009. *Novelist Richard Wright was honored with a 61-cent U.S. postage stamp (with artwork by Kadir Nelson) for the Literary Arts series. Wright, a onetime postal worker, set his novel* Native Son *in the African American ghetto of Chicago.* CHICAGO TRIBUNE/MCT/LANDOV

Two years later, *Native Son*, a novel of Chicago's African American ghetto, further enhanced Wright's reputation. A Book-of-the-Month Club choice, it later became a successful Broadway production under Orson Welles's direction and was filmed in South America with Wright himself in the role of Bigger Thomas. Wright published *Twelve Million Black Voices* in 1941.

In 1945 Wright's largely autobiographical *Black Boy* was selected by the Book-of-the-Month Club and went on to become his second best seller. Wright later moved to Paris where he continued to write fiction and nonfiction, including: *The Outsider* (1953); *Black Power* (1954); *Savage Holiday* (1954); *The Color Curtain* (1956); *White Man Listen* (1957); *The Long Dream* (1958); *Lawd Today* (1963); *Eight Men* (1961); and *American Hunger* (1977), a continuation of Wright's autobiographical work, *Black Boy*.

Wright died of a heart attack on November 28, 1960. Numerous books have been written about Wright and his work, including two casebooks on *Native Son*, a children's book, and a critical pamphlet in a writer's series.

19

MEDIA

Debra Newman Ham
Delano Greenidge-Copprue

BOOK PUBLISHERS

By the early nineteenth century, African Americans had begun to publish their own books, pamphlets, tracts, and newspapers. Educated African Americans wanted to speak for themselves and meet the social and intellectual needs of their own communities. Many African Americans felt that biased writers gave such an inaccurate portrayal of their experience that it was essential to write and publish their own materials. There have been more than one hundred publishing houses started by African American churches, individuals, organizations, universities, and cultural institutions dating back to this period. The publishing industry in the African American community managed to prosper despite obstacles. Since the inception of African American book publishing, three types of publishers have emerged: religious, institutional, and commercial (trade).

RELIGIOUS PUBLISHERS

African American religious denominations established religious publishing enterprises to publish works that would provide religious instruction and would assist the clergy and laity in recording denominational history. Some religious publishers also released books on secular subjects that celebrated some aspect of African American culture or documented African American history.

Prior to the Civil War (1861–1865), two African American religious publishing enterprises existed. The African Methodist Episcopal (AME) Church organized the AME Book Concern in Philadelphia in 1817. It was the first African American–owned book-publishing enterprise in the United States. After publishing its first book, *The Book of Discipline*, in the same year, the AME Book Concern published a host of classic religious and secular books until its operations were suspended in 1952 by the church's General Conference. In 1841, the African Methodist Episcopal Zion Church formed the AME Zion Publishing House in New York City. Both of these denominations published devotionals, biblical studies and commentaries, church histories and biographies, Sunday school materials, and hymnals. The AME Sunday School Union and Publishing House—established in Bloomington, Indiana, in 1882, and moved to Nashville in 1886—published literature for Sunday school students.

The Colored Methodist Episcopal (CME) Church—also known as the Christian Methodist Episcopal Church—started the CME Publishing House in 1870 in Memphis, Tennessee. The CME Publishing House only publishes books on religious subjects. Its stated purpose is to disseminate official CME proclamations, publish and distribute denominational literature, record the church's history, safeguard CME doctrine, and increase loyalty to the church through a fuller appreciation of CME history. The CME Publishing House considers itself the "literary mind of the church."

One of the most successful African American religious publishers to arise during the nineteenth century was the National Baptist Publishing Board (NBPB). The NBPB was organized in Nashville in 1896 under the leadership of Dr. Richard Henry Boyd and the auspices of the National Baptist Convention, USA. By 1913, this well-managed firm, which published both religious and secular books, had grown into one of the largest African American–owned businesses in the country. In 1915, however, a dispute arose between Boyd and the National Baptist Convention over the ownership of the NBPB. In a legal battle, the Tennessee Supreme Court decided in favor of Boyd. The NBPB—now named R.H. Boyd Publishing Corporation in honor of its founder—is owned by the Boyd family. With more than a century of publishing experience, R.H. Boyd Publishing continues to thrive as a religious enterprise by publishing hymnals, Bibles, and Sunday school materials, as well as books about family, education, and history.

Faced with the loss of the NBPB in 1916, the National Baptist Convention, USA, established the Sunday School Publishing Board of the National Baptist Convention in Nashville. Over the years, this firm developed into one of the largest African American–owned publishing enterprises, publishing religious and secular books and pamphlets.

In 1907, the Church of God in Christ established the Church of God in Christ Publishing House in Memphis. Restricting its publications to religious books and pamphlets, this publisher met the ever-expanding need for religious literature for one of the fastest-growing African American religious denominations.

INSTITUTIONAL PUBLISHERS

During the post–Civil War decades of the nineteenth century and the early decades of the twentieth century, educational, cultural, social, and political institutions published a variety of materials to meet the specific needs of African Americans.

Colleges and Universities. Hampton Institute (now Hampton University) in Virginia became the first African American educational institution to publish books

Pressmen at Work, Printing Shop, Hampton Institute, Hampton, VA, c. 1899. *Hampton Institute became the first African American educational institution to publish books by establishing the Hampton Institute Press in 1871. The press remained active until 1940, publishing travel books, poetry, textbooks, songbooks, conference proceedings, and the* Southern Workman, *a leading African American periodical.* **BUYENLARGE/GETTY IMAGES**

when the Hampton Institute Press was established in 1871. An active publisher until 1940, the Hampton Institute Press published travel books, poetry, textbooks, songbooks, conference proceedings, and the *Southern Workman*, one of the leading national African American periodicals, published between the press's inception in 1871 and its demise in 1939. Institutions like Hampton played a vital role in preserving primary and secondary resources related to the history of African Americans in general and these institutions in particular. For example, in 1927, the Hampton Institute Press published a volume edited by R. Nathaniel Dett titled *Religious Folk-Songs of the Negro as Sung at Hampton Institute.*

In 1896, the Atlanta University Press entered the book-publishing market with the release of the Atlanta University Publication Series, which consisted of monographs reporting on the findings of studies conducted by the university's department of sociology under the direction of W. E. B. Du Bois, a pioneer not only in African American studies but also in the development of sociological methodology. These works represented some of the earliest studies in urban sociology conducted in the South. The Atlanta University Press remained in operation until 1936.

Industrial Work of Tuskegee Graduates and Former Students during the Year 1910 (1911), compiled by Monroe N. Work, a sociology professor, was the first book released by the Tuskegee Institute Press. With the publication of this book and other works, Booker T. Washington sought to publicize Tuskegee's success to white philanthropists in the North and to celebrate the achievements of the school's alumni. The Tuskegee Institute Press, which was active until 1958, published several other important works, including John A. Kenney's *The Negro in Medicine* (1912).

In 1910, another book-publishing enterprise was launched on the campus of Tuskegee Institute: the Negro Yearbook Publishing Company. The company was a partnership consisting of Robert E. Park, Monroe Work, and the famed white sociologist Emmett J. Scott, secretary to Booker T. Washington. This firm published the first edition of *The Negro Yearbook* in 1912, which to that date was the most comprehensive reference book on African Americans. *The Negro Yearbook* was highly regarded as the definitive work on statistics and facts on blacks worldwide. The Negro Yearbook Publishing Company experienced financial trouble in 1929, but the Tuskegee Institute continued to finance its operation until 1952. Between 1912 and 1952, *The Negro Yearbook* stood as a model for most general reference works on blacks.

John W. Work's *Folk Songs of the American Negro* (1915) was the first book issued by the Fisk University Press. During the 1930s and 1940s, when Charles Spurgeon Johnson chaired the university's department of sociology, Fisk University Press issued several important studies, including *The Free Negro Family* (1932) by E. Franklin Frazier, *The Economic Status of Negroes* (1933) by Charles Spurgeon Johnson, and *People vs. Property* (1947) by Herman Long and Charles Spurgeon Johnson. The last publication released by the Fisk University Press was *Build the Future: Addresses Marking the Inauguration of Charles Spurgeon Johnson* (1949).

Although the board of trustees of Howard University approved the establishment of a university press in 1919, the university did not officially organize the press until 1974. Nonetheless, between 1919 and 1974, several books bearing the "Howard University Press" imprint were published, including *Founding the School of Medicine of Howard University, 1868–1873* (1929) by Walter Dyson, and *The Housing of Negroes in Washington, D.C.: A Study in Human Ecology* (1929) by William H. Jones.

When the press was officially organized as a separate administrative unit within Howard University in 1974, it had a staff of twelve professionals experienced in book publishing. Its mission was to support the university by "providing leadership for America and the global community through the publication of noteworthy new scholarship that addresses the contributions, conditions, and concerns of African Americans, other people of African descent, and people of color around the world." The press published works with a variety of perspectives and in a number of disciplines, including politics, economics, the social sciences, history, health, education, communications, the fine arts, science and technology, literature, and drama.

The Howard University Press's inaugural list of thirteen books included *A Poetic Equation: Conversations between Nikki Giovanni and Margaret Walker* and *Saw the House in Half*, a novel by Oliver Jackman, both published in 1974. Another of the press's first titles was *How Europe Underdeveloped Africa* by Walter Rodney, originally published in London in 1972 and reprinted by the Howard University Press in 1974 and 1981. Later releases include *Genocide in Rwanda: A Collective Memory* (1999) by Carol Pott Berry and John A. Berry, *Mordecai: The Man and His Message: The Story of Mordecai Wyatt Johnson* (1997) by Richard I. McKinney, *Black Writers and Latin America Cross Cultural Affinities* (1998) by Richard Jackson, and *The Black Seminole Legacy and North American Politics, 1693–1845* (1999) by Bruce Edward Twyman. Two of the press's popular works were the direct result of scholarly conferences: *Black Bibliophiles and Collectors: Preservers of Black History* (1990), edited by Elinor Des Verney Sinnette, W. Paul Coates, and Thomas C. Battle; and *Global Dimensions of the African Diaspora*, edited by

Joseph E. Harris, first published in 1982, with a second edition released in 1992.

During the twentieth century, Howard University Press was one of the leading publishers of African American scholarship. The press published foundational critical studies of such authors as Ralph Ellison and Jean Toomer, as well as works the explored the African American experience in the global context. One popular volume was *First Freed: Washington, D.C., in the Emancipation Era*, edited by Elizabeth Clark-Lewis, first published in 1998 by the Foundation Press in Washington, D.C., and reprinted by the Howard University Press in 2002. More recent works include *A Right Worthy Grand Mission: Maggie Lena Walker and the Quest for Black Economic Empowerment* (2003) by Gertrude Woodruff Marlowe, and *No Boundaries: A Cancer Surgeon's Odyssey* (2005) by LeSalle D. Leffall Jr.

Cultural and Professional Organizations and Institutions. African American cultural and professional organizations and institutions have also developed publishing programs that include book publishing. The works published by these organizations generally document African American history and various aspects of African American culture.

The need to demonstrate that blacks could excel in literature, arts, and sciences led to the formation of the American Negro Academy on March 5, 1897, by Reverend Alexander Crummell, the eminent African American scholar, clergyman, and missionary. The major purpose of the American Negro Academy was the production of scholarly works and the "vindication of the Negro" through raising the level of intellectual pursuits. The academy, whose membership included many of the foremost African American intellectuals of the day, quickly organized a publishing program and released twenty-one occasional papers as pamphlets and monographs. These include Crummell's *Civilization: The Primal Need of the Race* (1897), Charles C. Cook's *A Comparative Study of the Negro Problem* (1899), and Archibald Grimké's *The Ballotless Victim of One-Party Governments* (1913). The American Negro Academy ceased to exist in 1928, but many of the papers were reprinted by Arno Press in 1969.

The Association for the Study of African American Life and History (ASALH), formerly known as the Association for the Study of Afro-American Life and History and originally founded by Carter G. Woodson in 1915 as the Association for the Study of Negro Life and History, began publishing the *Journal of African American History* (originally the *Journal of Negro History*) in 1916. The ASALH started its book-publishing program two years later. By 1940, the association had published twenty-eight books. The association's book-publishing activities thereafter declined, until Woodson died in 1950 and provided in his will for the transfer of the Associated Publishers Inc. to the ASALH. The press's most enduring work is Woodson's *The Mis-education of the Negro*, published in 1933. Woodson famously remarked in this work:

> When you control a man's thinking you do not have to worry about his actions. You do not have to tell him not to stand here or go yonder. He will find his "proper place" and will stay in it. You do not need to send him to the back door. He will go without being told. In fact, if there is no back door, he will cut one for his special benefit. His education makes it necessary.

Howard University philosophy professor Alain Locke organized the Associates in Negro Folk Education in the mid-1930s in Washington, D.C., with a grant from the American Adult Education Association. From 1935 to 1940, the associates published a series of seven books known as Bronze Booklets. Written by black scholars on various aspects of African American life and edited by Locke, titles in the series included *A World View of Race* (1936) by Ralph J. Bunche, *The Negro and Economic Reconstruction* (1937) by Timothy Arnold Hill, and *Negro Poetry and Drama* (1937) by Sterling A. Brown.

Civil Rights, Social Welfare, and Political Organizations. In 1913, five years after its founding, the National Association for the Advancement of Colored People (NAACP) launched its publishing program with three books: *A Child's Story of Dunbar* by Julia L. Henderson, *Norris Wright Cuney: A Tribune of the Black People* by Maud Cuney-Hare, and *Hazel* by Mary White Ovington. George Williamson Crawford's *Prince Hall and His Followers* was published in 1914, followed in 1919 by *Thirty Years of Lynching in the United States, 1889–1918.* After 1919, the NAACP published few books, with the organization limiting its publishing operation to pamphlets, annual reports, and the *Crisis*, a bimonthly magazine.

The *Crisis*, edited by W. E. B. Du Bois from its inception in 1910 until 1934, gained phenomenal popularity. Circulation rose from several thousand each month to nearly fifty thousand by 1917, reaching more than 100,000 in 1919. Many credit the early popularity of the NAACP to Du Bois and his editorship of the *Crisis.* Now published quarterly, the magazine remains dedicated to discussing critical issues confronting people of color, American society, and the world. In addition, it highlights the historical and cultural achievements of diverse peoples. Through essays, interviews, and in-depth reporting, writers explore past and present issues concerning race and its impact on educational, economic, political, social, moral, and ethical issues. Each issue includes a special section, "The NAACP Today," which reports on the

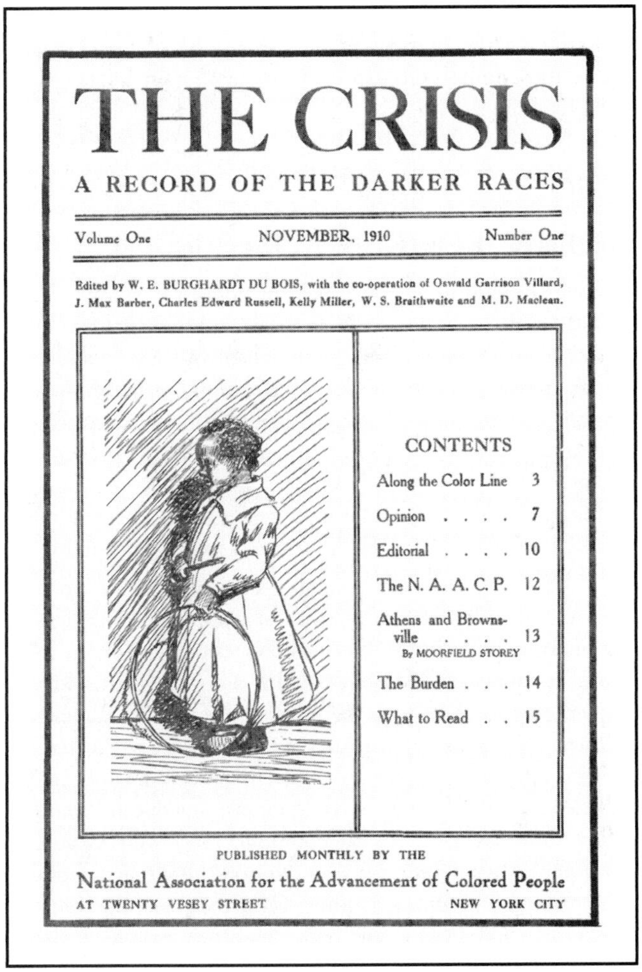
THE CRISIS

A RECORD OF THE DARKER RACES

Volume One NOVEMBER, 1910 Number One

Edited by W. E. BURGHARDT DU BOIS, with the co-operation of Oswald Garrison Villard, J. Max Barber, Charles Edward Russell, Kelly Miller, W. S. Braithwaite and M. D. Maclean.

CONTENTS

PUBLISHED MONTHLY BY THE

National Association for the Advancement of Colored People

AT TWENTY VESEY STREET NEW YORK CITY

Cover of the* Crisis, *Volume 1, Number 1, November 1910. *This magazine, edited by W. E. B. Du Bois from its inception in 1910 to 1934, became the NAACP's chief vehicle for the dissemination of information.*

news and events of the organization on a local and national level.

In contrast, the National Urban League (NUL) has been a very active book publisher. The league first embarked on book publishing in 1927 when it published *Ebony and Topaz*, an anthology of Harlem Renaissance writers, poets, and artists, edited by Charles Spurgeon Johnson. Through the years, NUL released numerous sociological and economic studies on the plight of African Americans, including *Negro Membership in American Labor Unions* (1930), *Race, Fear, and Housing in a Typical American Community* (1946) by William L. Evans, and *Power of the Ballot: A Handbook for Black Political Participation* (1973).

In addition to these monographs, the NUL began publishing *The State of Black America* in 1976. *The State of Black America* is an annual NUL report that addresses the issues central to African Americans in the current year, such as progress in education, home ownership, entrepreneurship, health, and other areas. The series has served as a barometer of the conditions, experiences, and opinions of American Americans. Each year, the publication forecasts certain social and political trends and proposes solutions to the most pressing challenges facing the black community and the country as a whole. *The State of Black America 2006*, for example, examined these issues against the backdrop Hurricanes Katrina and Rita, noting that black Americans continued to hover at 0.73 of the status of white Americans. The 2009 volume focused on the challenges facing the new administration of President Barack Obama. The 2010 report examined levels of unemployment among black Americans.

Other reports and studies issued by the NUL include *Crime and Justice in Black America* (1999) by Christopher E. Stone, *The Impact of Social Security on Child Poverty* (2000) by Valerie A. Rawlston, and *The Urban League's Assessment of the President's Education Plan* (2001) by Hugh B. Price. The Urban League also publishes the periodicals *Urban Influence* and *Opportunity Journal.*

The publishing program of Marcus Garvey's Universal Negro Improvement Association (UNIA) and African Communities League focused on the publication of the *Negro World*, a weekly newspaper founded in 1918. It was published in French and Spanish, as well as English. The *Negro World*, which glorified African history and heroes, ceased publication during the 1930s. The UNIA also published *The Philosophy and Opinions of Marcus Garvey*, which was compiled and edited by Amy Jacques-Garvey in two volumes released from 1923 to 1925.

COMMERCIAL PUBLISHERS

Before the 1960s, most African American commercial book-publishing enterprises were short-lived. Two publishing houses founded in the 1960s changed this trend: Broadside Press, established in 1965 in Detroit by Dudley Randall, and Third World Press, founded in 1967 in Chicago by Haki Madhubuti (Don L. Lee). Broadside Press published poetry by African American authors, many of whom became icons, including Gwendolyn Brooks, Margaret Danner, Robert Hayden, Langston Hughes, LeRoi Jones (Amiri Baraka), Sonia Sanchez, Melvin Tolson, Margaret Walker, and Madhubuti.

An additional African American press, the Urban Research Press, was founded in 1969 by Dempsey Travis, a Chicago businessman and author. Over the years, publishers learned that a sizable African American readership exists, and several major African American publishers have emerged since 1970. Black Classic Press, for example, was founded in 1978 by librarian Paul Coates to publish obscure but significant works by and about people of African descent, and Open Hand Publishing was founded by Anna Johnson in 1981.

Inspired by the dearth of books for his courses, former Rutgers University African studies instructor Kassahun Checole founded the Africa World Press in 1983 to publish material on the economic, political, and social development of Africa. By the end of the twentieth century, Africa World Press, which published nearly sixty titles annually, was the premier publisher of books on African, African American, Caribbean, and Latin American issues. Its sister company, Red Sea Press, established in 1985, was one of the largest distributors of material by and about people of African descent throughout the world.

Just Us Books, Inc., founded by Wade Hudson and Cheryl Willis Hudson, publishes books and educational material for children that focus on the African American experience. The idea to start the company first came to Cheryl Hudson in 1976 when she was unable to find African American images to decorate her daughter's nursery. Just Us Books published its first book in 1988—an alphabet book featuring African American children posed to create the letters. Diaspora Press of America, established in 1995, publishes African American diasporic folktales, fiction, nonfiction, poetry, and children's stories. Amber Books, which publishes self-help and career-guide books for African Americans, was founded in 1998 by Tony Rose.

Independent African American–owned bookstores have benefited from a resurgence of African American authors and an abundance of titles, but major bookstore chains and Internet booksellers make competition stiff. With the decline in hardcover sales, publishers were more cautious about placing books with specialty stores for fear that a book would lose mainstream appeal.

With the increasing demand for African American–oriented books, especially those written by African Americans, two diverging opinions arose from the African American literary community. Some believed that the creation by large publishers of imprints for African American books, such Strivers Row (Villard/Random House), Amistad (HarperCollins), Harlem Moon (Random House), and Dafina Books (Kensington), diminished the opportunity to showcase different genres. Furthermore, this faction insisted that African American books released by major publishers were often too formulaic. Others believed that the abundance of African American books allowed for all kinds of literature, ultimately increasing the number of African American authors published each year. Although the two groups disagreed on the quality of African American literature being published, both agreed that the proliferation of African American writers and the subsequent successful sales of their titles were most important, especially if they retain long-term marketability.

COMIC BOOK PUBLISHERS

African American comics peaked in popularity during the 1990s. Once relegated to a form of children's entertainment, comic books found an audience with young adults in their twenties and thirties. One reason for the growth among the African American adult readership is collectability; since most African American series are short-lived, each issue has the potential to become a rarity. In addition, African American comics began to better reflect the cultural and artistic interests of the African American community.

African American comic-book characters of yore, often grotesquely drawn by whites, were either sidekicks or afterthoughts—never the stars. For example, Ebony, an African American character, paraded around with a white superhero, the Spirit, in the 1940s. Meanwhile, Captain America had Falcon, his black version of the Lone Ranger's Native American sidekick, Tonto. Other African American characters were portrayed as ignorant, uneducated, and inept at worst. Blatantly stereotypical, most were created and drawn by white males who did not know much about the reality of African Americans. Over the years, the status of African American comic-book characters evolved in the same negative ways that whites' perceptions of blacks did. By the 1960s and 1970s, African Americans were depicted either as drug addicts or Uncle Toms.

True change did not occur until a few enterprising African Americans took matters into their own hands. By 1993, Africa Rising Comics, Afrocentric Books, Dark Zulu Lies, Omega 7 Comics, and UP Comics had created ANIA (the Swahili word for "serve and protect") Comics under the leadership of Eric Griffin. The group's goal was to become a major publishing force by pooling their talents. The mainstream comic-book publishers responded by producing comic books that featured black characters to capitalize on the market that ANIA's creators started. Disbanding soon thereafter, ANIA's existence highlighted the growing line of nonwhite superheroes. Their titles included *Brotherman, Malcolm 10, Heru, Zwanna, Purge,* and *Ebony Warrior.*

In the mid-1990s, Big City Comics produced *Brotherman,* which revolved around a public defender who also fought crime as "the dictator of discipline." Omega 7, based in Kansas City, was founded by Alonzo Washington, a former member of ANIA. Omega 7 introduced fans to the Original Man, a champion of morality and the supporter and protector of African American women; the Mighty Ace, who brought an antidrug, antigang, antiviolence message; and Darkforce, a revolutionary African American hero. Other characters included Omega Man, Original Boy, Original Woman, and the Omega 7. Washington developed each comic and wrote the storylines.

UP Comics offered Purge, which detailed the trials of a man whose sole goal was to rid his city of evil. Lionheart, from Prophesy Comics, also emphasized morality. In a unique twist, Castel Publications came up with the Grammar Patrol, multiethnic heroes with a penchant for the rules of speech and writing. Geared toward children, it showed that the medium could be educational as well as entertaining.

Most of these companies were completely African American, from the owners and artists to the storywriters and marketers. Mainstream publishers entered the fray when industry giant DC Comics began distributing Milestone Comics in 1991 as part of their new imprint, Milestone Media, formerly an African American–owned independent publishing house run by Derek T. Dingle. With a broad, full-process color system at hand, the company made history as the first major publisher to support African American creators. Their titles included *Hardware, Blood Syndicate, Icon, Kobalt, Shadow Cabinet, Xombi,* and *Static,* the latter featuring a teen hero who also became the star of an animated television program.

Although the number of new African American comic books continued to increase, only about a quarter of comic-book buyers are minorities. After the demise of ANIA and many other independently owned African American publishing companies, it became difficult for African Americans to produce their own publications. The two major comic-book publishers, DC Comics and Marvel Comics, both created several of their own African American comic-book characters and do not usually purchase the work of outside artists and writers unless they can own the characters outright. In addition, some of the more popular African American comic-book characters have been created by whites—for example, Spawn, Luke Cage, the Black Panther, the Falcon, and Blade (the inspiration for the movies starring Wesley Snipes). Therefore, aspiring African American comic-book artists have two options: they can find an independent publisher or self-publish. Since both approaches can be difficult, many black artists opt to work on more-established characters, like Superman, Spiderman, or Batman, to ensure their financial stability with the goal of eventually saving enough money to publish their own characters. Two notable exceptions are Alex Simmons, creator of *Blackjack,* and P. Skylar Owens, creator of *Knightmare, Team Sexecutioner,* and *CyJax.*

NEWSPAPER PUBLISHERS

The African American press is heir to a great, largely unheralded tradition. It began on March 16, 1827, with *Freedom's Journal* in New York City, the first African American newspaper. *Freedom's Journal* was edited and published by Samuel Cornish and John B. Russwurm, who declared in the first issue: "We wish to plead our own cause. Too long have others spoken for us. Too long has the publick been deceived by misrepresentations, in things which concern us dearly. " The *North Star,* the newspaper of abolitionist Frederick Douglass, first appeared on December 3, 1847. The masthead of the paper proclaimed, "Right is of no Sex—Truth is of no Color—God is the Father of us all, and we are all Brethren."

Many African American newspapers were launched in the nineteenth century but did not remain in print for long. By the 1880s, the ability of African Americans to establish a substantial cultural environment and to address the gross mistreatment of subjects relating to blacks by white-owned newspapers in many cities led to the creation of a new wave of publications, including the *Washington Bee,* the *Indianapolis World,* the *Philadelphia Tribune,* the *Cleveland Gazette,* the *Baltimore Afro-American,* and the *New York Age.* By 1900, daily African American newspapers were being published in Norfolk, Kansas City, and Washington, D.C., as well.

Prominent African American newspaper editors of the period include William Monroe Trotter, editor of the *Boston Guardian,* a self-styled "radical" paper that showed no sympathy for the conciliatory stance of Booker T. Washington; Robert S. Abbott, whose *Chicago Defender* pioneered the use of headlines; and T. Thomas Fortune of the *New York Age,* who championed free public schools in an age when many opposed the idea.

By 1940, there were more than two hundred African American newspapers around the country, mostly weeklies with local readerships, and about 120 African American magazines in circulation. The *Pittsburgh Courier,* a weekly, had a readership of about 140,000 per issue, the largest at the time.

African Americans continue to gain influence as columnists, editorial page editors, assistant managing editors, and reporters on key beats. Although progress has been made in the newsroom, annual reports by the American Society of Newspaper Editors (ASNE) indicate that the prospects of African Americans assuming positions as managers remain low. There have been exceptions, including executive editors Ken Bunting at the *Seattle Post-Intelligencer,* Robert G. McGruder at the *Detroit Free Press,* Bennie Ivory at the *Courier-Journal* in Louisville, Kentucky, and Karla Garrett Harshaw at the *Springfield News Sun* in Ohio. The *Denver Post* became the largest U.S. newspaper (highest circulation daily) with

First African American Newspaper. *Benjamin Todd Jealous, then executive director of the National Newspaper Publishers Association, points at a copy of* Freedom's Journal, *the first newspaper in the United States to be owned and operated by African Americans, in 2002. The first issue of the newspaper was published on March 16, 1827.* AP PHOTO/STEPHEN J. BOITANO

an African American executive editor with the appointment in 2002 of Gregory Moore, formerly the managing editor at the *Boston Globe*. Other papers that have had African American managing editors include the *New York Times*, the *Los Angeles Times*, the *Detroit News*, the *Philadelphia Inquirer*, the *Lansing State Journal*, the *Jackson (MS) Clarion-Ledger, the Riverside (CA) Enterprise, and the Wilmington (DE) News Journal.*

ASNE's 2002 report stated that nearly two thousand journalists left the newspaper industry in 2001. Despite the loss, there was an increase in the percentage of minority journalists working at daily newspapers. This increase was heartening after a decrease from 11.85 percent to 11.64 percent in the previous year, which was the first decline since ASNE established the annual census in 1978. As it stood in 2002, African Americans constituted approximately 5.29 percent of U.S. newsrooms staffs.

By 2006 ASNE reported that minorities accounted for 11.2 percent of all supervisors in newsrooms, up from 10.8 percent in 2005. Sixty-six percent of the 377 newspapers with no minority professionals had circulations of 10,000 or less and served small communities. The percentage of minorities at newspapers with circulations of 250,001 to 500,000 was 24, the same as the previous year; minorities at newspapers with circulations of 100,001 to 250,000 accounted for 25 percent, up from 23 percent. The number of minority interns fell from 948 in the 2005 survey to 861 in 2006, reflecting the general belt-tightening in the newspaper industry.

ASNE reported in April 2009 that American newspapers had eliminated 5,900 newsroom jobs in 2008 (an 11.3 percent reduction), 854 of which had been held by minorities. By the end of December 2008, a total of 46,700 journalists, including 6,300 minority professionals, held positions on American newspaper staffs. According to ASNE, the 2000–2009 decade saw a net increase in the number of Latino, Asian, and Native American journalists, but a net decrease in the number of African American journalists. ASNE also reported that at the end of 2008, only 8 percent of the *New York Times*'s newsroom staff was black. The *Washington Post*'s staff was 13.6 percent African American, while only 2.2 percent of the staff at the *Los Angeles Times* was black, and 8.7 percent of the *Chicago Tribune*'s staff was African American. Some smaller regional newspapers employed a larger percentage of black professionals. The staff at the *Clarion-Ledger* in Jackson, Mississippi, for example, was 27.8 percent black at the end of 2008. The *Atlanta Journal-Constitution* reported that 20.7 percent of its staffers were African American, the *Montgomery Advertiser* had a staff that was 18.6 percent black, and the staff at the *Camden News* of Arkansas was 25 percent African American.

The lack of minority representation in the newsrooms of mainstream publications has not hindered the rise of the ethnic press, which steadily built circulation and advertising revenue. Traditionally, the survival of the ethnic press depended on classified advertising and advertisements from local auto-repair stores, grocers, and travel agents. Some of the more established African American newspapers have always attracted some mainstream advertising, but publications that serve smaller and diverse communities have begun to receive many of the larger billings. Among the largest advertisers were telecommunications companies, airlines, financial services companies, and health-care corporations.

THE NATIONAL NEWSPAPER PUBLISHERS ASSOCIATION

The National Negro Newspaper Publishers Association was founded in 1940 to represent African American newspaper publishers. The organization scheduled workshops and trips abroad to acquaint editors and reporters with important news centers and news sources. These efforts led to reporting that was more progressive and interpretive. In 1956, the association changed its name to the National Newspaper Publishers Association (NNPA), but it is often also referred to as the Black Press of America. In 1999, the association represented 148 publishers. By 2007, it represented more than two hundred black newspapers across the United States, and claimed a readership

Harlem Newsroom,* Amsterdam News, *1936. *Since its founding in 1909, the* Amsterdam News *has become one of the best-known African American newspapers in the country. Among the prominent figures who have written for the paper are T. Thomas Fortune, W. E. B. Du Bois, Adam Clayton Powell, Roy Wilkins, and Malcolm X.* LUCIEN AIGNER/HISTORICAL/CORBIS

of more than fifteen million, with a buying power of more than $500 billion.

In 2000, the NNPA launched NNPA Media Services—a print and web advertising placement and press-release distribution service. The following year, the NNPA, in association with the NNPA Foundation, began building the BlackPressUSA Network—the nation's premier network of local black community news and information portals. The BlackPressUSA Network is anchored by BlackPressUSA.com, the national Web portal for the Black Press of America.

AMSTERDAM NEWS

Founded in 1909 by James H. Anderson, the *Amsterdam News* became one of the best-known African American newspapers in the nation. It was first published on December 4, 1909, in Anderson's home in New York City. At that time, it was one of only fifty African American "news sheets" in the country. The *Amsterdam News* had a staff of ten, consisted of six printed pages, and sold for two cents a copy. In 1935, the paper was sold to two African American physicians, Clilan B. Powell and Phillip M. H. Savory. In 1971, the paper was again sold to a group of investors, this time headed by Percy E. Sutton, Clarence B. Jones, and Wilbert A. Tatum.

During the mid-1970s, the *Amsterdam News* took militant positions on civil rights issues, but by the end of the decade it began to take a more moderate stand on social issues. In 1979, the paper's format was changed from standard or broadsheet size to a tabloid. Following a second labor strike in 1983, the owner-publisher's mantel was assumed by Wilbert Tatum in 1984. Under Tatum's leadership, the paper gained a reputation as an intrepid African American voice on controversial local issues.

During the twentieth century, some of the best and brightest African American personages wrote for the

Copies of the November 7, 2008, Edition of the **Amsterdam News.** *Nearly 100 years after its founding, the weekly African American newspaper* Amsterdam News *reported the election of the first African American president.* AP PHOTO/DAVID KARP

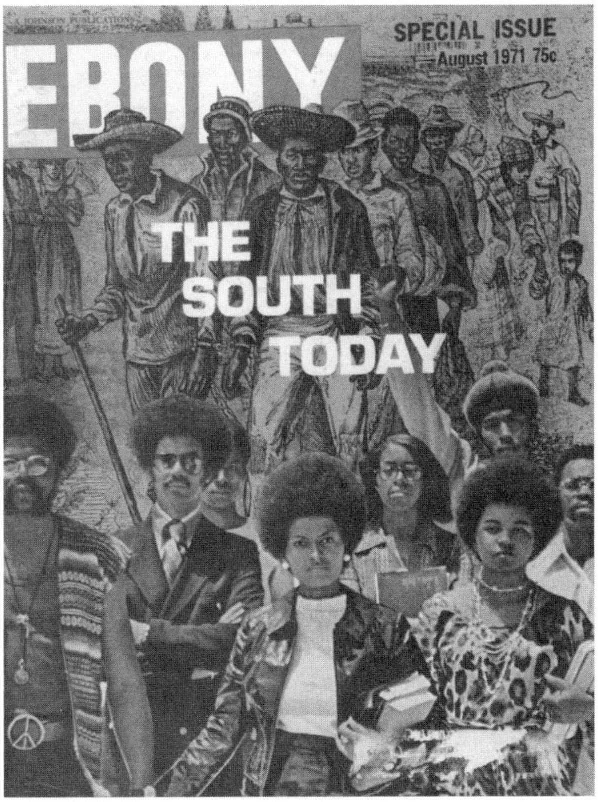

Ebony *Magazine Cover, 1971.* *Launched in 1945,* Ebony *had the largest circulation among African American–oriented magazines on the newsstands of the early twenty-first century.* IMAGE COURTESY OF THE ADVERTISING ARCHIVES

paper, including T. Thomas Fortune, W. E. B. Du Bois, Adam Clayton Powell, Roy Wilkins, and Malcolm X. In 1997, Tatums's daughter, Elinor, became publisher and editor in chief of the paper.

AFRICAN AMERICAN NEWSPAPERS IN THE TWENTY-FIRST CENTURY

A number of newspapers that began publishing in the 1960s, 1970s, and 1980s have gone out of business because of their inability to attract advertising, both locally and nationally, and because of a general economic decline. Nevertheless, in 2007, there were more than two hundred African American newspapers nationwide. The growth of the Internet has encouraged digital deals among those in the print media, often expanding readership, although in a different medium, from paper to screen.

MAGAZINE PUBLISHERS

African American magazines were being published in the United States as early as the 1830s, but the first truly successful magazines did not appear until the 1900s. In 1910, the NAACP began publishing the *Crisis*. In November 1942, John H. Johnson launched *Negro Digest*, and in 1945, he published the first issue of *Ebony*, a monthly magazine. The idea for *Ebony* came from two *Negro Digest* writers and Johnson's wife, Eunice, who suggested the magazine's name. Its first print run of 25,000 copies sold out quickly. The success of *Ebony* led to the demise of *Negro Digest*, and in 1951 the *Digest* ceased publication. In 2005, the year John H. Johnson died, Johnson Publishing Company (JPC) was the number-one African American publishing company in the world. *Ebony* magazine boasted a circulation of 1.6 million, and JPC claimed annual overall sales of $490 million.

In 1950, Johnson launched the magazine *Tan*, and in 1951 he started *Jet*, a weekly magazine. Like *Ebony*, *Jet* was an instant success, selling more than 300,000 weekly copies in its first year. *Tan*, a women's magazine, later became a now-defunct show business and personality monthly called *Black Stars*.

Since the founding of *Ebony*, several new and specialized African American magazines have appeared. *Black American Literature Review*, a journal presenting essays, interviews, poems, and book reviews, was founded in 1967. In the same year, Project Magazines Inc. began publishing *Black Careers*. Both have been discontinued. In 1969, the Black World Foundation published the first edition of the quarterly *Black Scholar*. Each issue of *Black Scholar* focuses on a selected topic. The fall 2009 issue, for example, featured essays on the politics of biracialism.

In 1970, Earl G. Graves, a young businessman, embarked on a project to publish a monthly digest of news, commentary, and informative articles for African Americans interested in business. Within a few short years, *Black Enterprise* had become an authority on African Americans in business and an important advocate for an active, socially responsive, African American middle class. By 2010, *Black Enterprise* had a readership of approximately 4.3 million. It is carried onboard most major airlines and can be found on newsstands nationwide.

Essence, published by Essence Communications Inc., is a magazine directed at black women. It has gained steadily in circulation since its inception in 1970. Featuring sections on health and beauty, fashion, entertainment, relationships, and contemporary living, *Essence* is considered one of the country's top women's magazines. As editor in chief from 1981 to 2000, Susan L. Taylor was instrumental in the magazine's success. Taylor became publications director for Essence Communications in 2001, and left the company in 2007. In 2002 the American Society of Magazine Editors inducted Taylor into the Magazine Editors' Hall of Fame. Diane Weathers succeeded Taylor as the editor in chief, and Angela Burt-Murray took over as

Oprah Winfrey and Cover of Premiere Issue of* O: The Oprah Magazine, *New York City, 2000. *TV talk-show host Winfrey ventured into publishing with the launch of her magazine, which is guided by an overall theme of leading women down a path of personal growth.* AP IMAGES. REPRODUCED BY PERMISSION.

Essence editor in chief in 2005. *Essence* boasted a monthly circulation of more than one million in 2010 and a readership of 8.5 million, about a third of which was male. Time Inc. purchased *Essence* in 2005.

Black Family, a magazine promoting positive lifestyles for African Americans, was launched in 1980. *American Visions: The Magazine of Afro-American Culture*, the official magazine of the African American Museums Association, was first published in 1986. In 1989, *Emerge*, a political magazine that covered hard news, current events, and culture from an African American perspective, was introduced. Battling low circulation, it ceased publication in 2000 when its owner, Vanguarde Media, a leading multicultural media company specializing in content aimed at the urban audience, deemed it unprofitable. *Emerge* was later replaced with *Savoy*, a lifestyle magazine, which folded in late 2003 when Vanguarde Media declared bankruptcy.

In 2000, television talk-show host and media mogul Oprah Winfrey successfully launched *O: The Oprah Magazine*. The overall aim of the magazine is to lead women down a path of personal growth. The magazine covers beauty and fashion, health and fitness, food, money matters, spirituality, and entertainment. By 2010, *O* had a won a variety of awards and had a circulation of almost 2.6 million.

By the first decade of the twenty-first century, many African American–owned magazines continued to flourish in harsh economic times because most of their revenue came from subscriptions. However, two of the landmark African American magazines, *Jet* and *Ebony*, both of which were deeply influential for black middle-class Americans following World War II, have struggled economically in light of the growing complexity and class divisions seen in the broader African American community. Securing high-end advertising has remained a problem for African American magazines. Although publishers made significant progress in attracting automotive, tobacco, and liquor advertisements, they were less successful in securing advertising from the fashion, travel, and technology industries. With the growth of the African American middle class, advertising agencies believed that they could easily reach African Americans through mainstream, rather than black, media, in particular through television.

BROADCASTING

RADIO

African American radio can be divided into three general periods of historical development: blackface radio (1920–1941), black-appeal radio (1942–1969), and black-controlled radio (beginning around 1970). White performers who imitated black humor and music for a predominantly white listening audience were the trademark of blackface radio. During this period, African Americans remained essentially outside of the commercial loop, both as radio entertainers and consumers. In the era of black-appeal radio, African Americans entered the industry as entertainers and consumers. The ownership and management of African American–oriented radio stations remained mostly in the hands of white businessmen, however. By the 1970s, this situation led to the development of independent African American radio stations. With the onset of the black-controlled radio era, African Americans began to own and operate their own radio stations, both commercial and public. Nevertheless, the percentage of African American–owned stations lagged far behind the percentage of African American radio listeners.

Although early radio shows sometimes featured African American singing groups, they featured no African American speakers. Black radio pioneer Jack L. Cooper compared this situation to "taxation without representation." On Sunday, November 3, 1929, at 5:00 p.m., Chicago's white-owned WSBC premiered *The All-Negro Hour* starring Cooper and friends, and the concept of African American radio was born. Cooper became the nation's first African American radio-station executive, the first African American newscaster, the first African American sportscaster, and the first to use radio as a service medium.

Cooper wore many hats. He played second base for a semipro baseball team. He had also been a singer, a buck-and-wing dancer, and an end man in a minstrel show, and he fought 160 amateur boxing bouts and managed theaters. Between about 1910 and 1924, he worked as a journalist, writing for a number of African American newspapers, including the *Freeman*, the *Ledger*, and the *Recorder* in Indianapolis, and the *Bluff City News* and *Western World Reporter* in Memphis. In 1924, Cooper became the assistant theatrical editor of the *Chicago Defender*.

The All-Negro Hour was similar to a vaudeville revue on the air, featuring music, comedy, and serials. When it ended its run in 1935, Cooper continued with WSBC, pioneering the African American radio format by producing several African American–oriented shows. Crucial to that format was local news and public affairs of interest to African Americans.

The first example of public-service programming aired December 9, 1938, when Cooper launched the *Search for Missing Persons* show. Aimed at reuniting people who had lost contact with friends and relatives over time, it reportedly had reunited twenty thousand people by 1950. Cooper also remodeled a van into a mobile unit to relay on-the-spot news events directly to four radio stations in the Chicago metropolitan area, including news flashes from the *Pittsburgh Courier* and interviews with famous personalities who came to town, such as boxer Joe Louis. In addition, Cooper did play-by-play for African American baseball games from the van.

Listen Chicago, a news discussion show that ran from 1946 to 1952, provided African Americans with their first opportunity to use radio as a public forum. Following Cooper's lead, the number of African American–oriented stations jumped from twenty-four to about six hundred between 1946 and 1955. News was a part of the explosion. Leonard Walk, the white owner of WHOD Pittsburgh, remarked in 1954 that "we have learned to do newscasts that answer the question, 'How is this news going to affect me as a Negro?'" Walk also noted that "church and social news deserve a unique place of importance in our daily Negro programming." By and large, these broadcasters were not trained journalists. African American stations did not begin to broadcast news in the modern style until the 1960s.

In 1972, the Mutual Black Network was formed for news and sports syndication under the auspices of the Mutual Broadcasting Network. By the end of the 1970s, the Mutual Black Network had more than one hundred affiliates and 6.2 million listeners. The Sheridan Broadcasting Corporation, an African American–owned broadcasting chain based in Pittsburgh, purchased the Mutual Black Network in the late 1970s, renaming it the Sheridan Broadcasting Network. A second African American radio network, the National Black Network, was formed in 1973. In the 1980s, it averaged close to one hundred affiliates and four million listeners. Among its regular features were commentary programs by journalist Roy Wood, whose show was titled *One Black Man's Opinion*, and Bob Law, who did *Night Talk*. In 1991, Sheridan merged with the National Black Network to form American Urban Radio Networks, which became the country's only African American–owned radio network company. By 2010, American Urban Radio Networks aired approximately two hundred weekly shows to more than three hundred radio stations around the country, reaching an estimated twenty million listeners.

The networks were a mixed blessing. They provided their affiliates with broadcast-quality programs produced from an African American perspective, but this relatively inexpensive access to news, sports, and public affairs discouraged subscribing stations from producing their own local shows. News and public affairs staffs at the African American–oriented stations remained small. There were some notable exceptions, including New York's WLIB-AM, which had an African American format that included a highly acclaimed news and public affairs department. A series of shows produced by the station on disadvantaged youth in the city won two Peabody Awards in 1970.

In Washington, D.C., the *Washington Post* donated its commercial FM radio license to Howard University in 1971. The new station, WHUR-FM, inaugurated *The Daily Drum*, an hour-long evening newscast that featured special coverage of the local African American community, as well as news from Africa and the diaspora. By 2010, it was one of the most popular stations in the Washington, D.C., area, and was the recipient of numerous awards, including a prestigious Marconi for Best Urban Station of the Year (2007) and the Crystal Radio Award for Excellence in Community Service (1999 and 2006) from the National Association of Broadcasters.

Two major formats have dominated African American–owned commercial radio since the 1970s: *talk* and *urban contemporary*. Talk-radio formats emerged on African American AM stations in the early 1970s and featured news, public affairs, and live listener call-in shows. FM stations dominated the broadcasting of recorded music because of their superior reproduction of high-fidelity and stereo signals. In 1972, Inner City Broadcasting initiated the move toward talk radio when it purchased New York's WLIB-AM, and the station became "Your Total Black News and Information Station," offering more news and public affairs programming than any other African American radio outlet in the country.

Catherine (Cathy) Liggins Hughes, a pioneer in both talk and urban contemporary formats, founded and owns Radio One, Inc., the largest African American–owned and operated broadcast company in the United States. In 2010, Radio One operated sixty-five radio stations in sixteen urban markets, including Philadelphia; Washington, D.C.; Baltimore; Atlanta; and Detroit. Radio One stations are frequently recognized for their active community involvement, which is Hughes's trademark. Hughes's son, Alfred Liggins, became president of Radio One in 1989, and CEO in 1997.

In 1971, Hughes became a lecturer at Howard University's School of Communications under the direction of Tony Brown. She was instrumental in creating a curriculum that would be accredited by academic associations around the world. In 1973, she began her transition into radio as general sales manager at WHUR-FM, eventually becoming vice president and general manager. Her skills in sales and marketing increased the station's revenue from $250,000 to $3 million in her first year, making the station the university's first profitable venture in its 100-year history. In 1975, Hughes developed the now widely imitated format known as the Quiet Storm. She purchased her first station, WOL-AM in Washington, D.C., in 1980.

The number of African Americans entering the public broadcasting arena has increased since the 1970s. In

1990, there were thirty-two public FM stations owned and operated by African American colleges around the country and another twelve owned by African American community boards of directors. The presence of radio stations based on historically black colleges and universities continued in the first decade of the twenty-first century, and public FM stations could be heard on both airwaves and cyberspace. In 2006, Howard University's WHUR-FM began broadcasting in high definition with its WHUR-WORLD. These stations are not subject to the pervasive ratings pressures of commercial radio, giving them more latitude in programming news, public affairs, talk, and unusual cultural features. As a result, the growth of African American public radio has expanded the variety and diversity of African American programming now found on the airways, while also increasing the number of African Americans working in radio.

TELEVISION

Until the late 1960s, most serious African American journalists worked in print journalism rather than broadcasting. An exception was Lionel Monagas, who started out as a traffic typist with the CBS affiliate in Washington, D.C., and by the early 1950s was working as a director for CBS-TV network programs, including *Person to Person* and *Face the Nation*. In 1956, Monagas became the first African American professional at Channel 35, a public television station in Philadelphia, later known as WHYY-TV. At WHYY, Monagas produced several children's programs, including a ten-part series on *The History of the Negro*, narrated by Ossie Davis.

Mal Goode became the first African American network television reporter in 1962 at ABC-TV. According to Goode, baseball pioneer Jackie Robinson complained to James Hagerty, an ABC vice president hired to set up a competitive news department, that the only two black people he had seen at ABC were "a lady with a white uniform in the lobby dusting and a Negro doorman." Hagerty decided to change that. Goode was a reporter for the *Pittsburgh Courier* at the time, but in 1949 Pittsburgh's KQV Radio had given the newspaper two fifteen-minute slots to fill on Tuesday and Wednesday nights. Goode read the news on the program. According to Goode, ABC chose him for the job after spending half a year interviewing thirty-eight African American male candidates. One reason he was chosen, he said, was that he was dark enough to appeal to an African American audience, but light enough so that whites would not feel threatened. Goode later worked for ABC for eleven years. He was its United Nations correspondent and covered the Cuban missile crisis, the aftermath of Martin Luther King Jr.'s assassination, and the Poor People's March on Washington.

Jobs like Goode's were hard to find. In his memoir, *Black Is the Color of My TV Tube* (1981), Emmy Award–winning African American journalist Gil Noble of New York's WABC-TV recalled being at WLIB-AM radio during this era:

> We would sit in the newsroom and fantasize about earning $300 a week, but few of our number worked at that level. Pat Connell, a former disc jockey at Newark's WNJR, known as 'Pat the Cat,' was anchoring the CBS morning newscast. Mal Goode was reporting for ABC-TV news, as well as for the local station WABC. NBC didn't have any blacks at that time, as far as I can recall, and in the mid-1960s, WNEW-TV had none, nor did WPIX-TV or WOR-TV have any.

When Noble auditioned for a major radio-station job, he would intone in the ultimate radio voice—"a Cronkite delivery that outdid the original"—only to get the familiar brush-off: "Thanks very much. You're fine, but we already have a Negro on staff."

Inside Bedford-Stuyvesant, which aired in New York City from 1968 to 1970, was the city's first program written, produced, and presented by African Americans at a time when African Americans were largely absent from television, except for news footage about protests, riots, or crime. *Inside Bedford-Stuyvesant* offered a unique look into an ignored African American neighborhood and, to a degree, African Americans. Its fifty-two half-hour programs were filmed throughout Brooklyn's Bedford-Stuyvesant neighborhood, often outdoors. Although it attracted such major celebrities as singer and actor Harry Belafonte and musician Max Roach, the show mostly revolved around the ordinary people in the neighborhood.

Film scholars and social historians consider *Inside Bedford-Stuyvesant* to be a rare video time capsule, perhaps the only one of its kind, documenting an African American community. Its creator, Charles Hobson, announced the debut of the show two months after the federal government's National Advisory Commission on Civil Disorders, also known as the Kerner Commission, issued a report on race relations, criticizing the media for failing to adequately cover African American communities.

A few African Americans made it onto the white-controlled airwaves. William C. Matney Jr., who had been managing editor of the *Michigan Chronicle*, an African American community paper, and a reporter for the *Detroit News* in 1963, became a television and radio reporter for WMAQ-TV, the NBC-owned station in Chicago. He joined NBC-TV news in 1966. Veteran newswoman Norma Quarles was hired as a trainee at NBC News in 1966, moving a year later to the NBC station in Cleveland as a reporter and anchor, and ultimately to CNN. Lem Tucker joined NBC News as a copyboy in 1965 and moved up to assistant bureau chief in Vietnam.

In 1967, a self-described "teacher moonlighting as a jazz disc jockey"—who also called play-by-play for basketball games and read the news—applied for a job at soon-to-be all-news WCBS radio in New York. Ed Bradley, who would later cohost CBS-TV's most successful news show, *60 Minutes*, impressed a news director by refusing to write copy and record it because, he explained, "You won't learn enough about me that way." Instead, he borrowed a tape recorder, went out on the street, did an update of a story about an antipoverty program, and got the job. In Portsmouth, Virginia, an audacious twenty-five-year-old newscaster named Max Robinson was terminated from a UHF station after he broke the rules by showing his face on camera. It was 1964, and only the word *news* was to appear on the screen. Many white viewers were enraged to see one of "those people" working in the studio. In 1971, Robinson became the first African American anchor in a major market when he joined WTOP-TV in Washington, D.C. Robinson later became ABC-TV's first African American regular coanchor.

It took the riots of the 1960s and a stern warning from a federal commission for the broadcast industry to undertake any concerted hiring of African Americans. When American cities began to burn, African Americans held about 3.6 percent of television news jobs, and white news directors had to scramble to find African American journalists to cover the riots. In 1968, the Kerner Commission concluded that "the world that television and newspapers offer to their black audience is almost totally white, in both appearance and attitude." "Within a year," wrote Gil Noble, "many of us found ourselves working downtown at major radio and TV stations."

In June 1969, the Federal Communications Commission (FCC) adopted rules prohibiting discrimination in broadcast industry employment, and required stations to file annual reports showing the racial makeup of their workforce by job category. African American public affairs shows, such as Noble's *Like It Is*, *Black Journal* hosted by Tony Brown, and Philadelphia's *Black Perspectives on the News*, aired in nearly every city with a substantial African American population. Still, by the time Mal Goode retired in 1973, there were only seven African American reporters at the three major networks.

By the 1990s, African Americans had begun breaking into broadcast management and ownership, yet the numbers remained small. General managers working in television included Charlotte Moore English of KSHB-TV in Kansas City; Marcellus Alexander of WJZ-TV in Baltimore; and Eugene Lothery of WCAU-TV in Philadelphia; as well as Clarence McKee, CEO and chairman of WTVT-TV in Tampa, Florida; and Dorothy Brunson, owner of a small UHF station, WGTW-TV, in Philadelphia.

Ronald Townsend, president of the Gannett Television Group, comprising ten stations, chaired the National Association of Broadcasters' television board. Jonathan Rodgers became president of the CBS Television Stations Division in August 1990, making him network television's highest-ranking African American news executive. Bryant Gumbel, cohost of NBC-TV's *Today*, CBS News correspondent Ed Bradley, and talk-show host Oprah Winfrey became three of the highest-paid and most recognized faces on television. ABC-TV's Carole Simpson became a substitute and weekend network television anchor. African Americans anchored local newscasts in markets around the country.

Another African American-owned broadcasting company that made great strides in the industry is Granite Broadcasting Corporation. Operating in geographically diverse markets that reach about 6 percent of the nation's television households, the company owns or provides services to twenty-three channels in eleven markets. Granite is also recognized as an innovator in the development of new media services that combine television broadcasting and Internet platforms.

Still, while African Americans accounted for 12 percent of the population in the 1990 census, they represented only 9.8 percent of the television news workforce and 5 percent of the radio workforce. They held 4 percent of news-director positions at commercial television stations and about 5 percent at commercial radio stations. Those heading news operations included Gary Wordlaw at WJLA-TV in Washington, D.C., and Will Wright at WWOR-TV in New York. According to a 1991 survey by the Center for Media and Public Affairs (CMPA), most of the news on nightly network television shows continued to be presented by white males. African Americans accounted for only 5 percent of all field reports and anchor stories combined. One of the most visible African American correspondents was George Strait, ABC-TV's health reporter, who tied for fifty-seventh in the number of stories filed. Carole Simpson was in sixth place, based on the number of brief news reports read.

In 2001, the diversity survey conducted by the CMPA reported that the proportion of stories covered by minorities fell from 14 percent in 1999 to 11 percent in 2000, a decline of 21 percent. In addition, minorities covered only 8 percent of ABC's stories, their lowest level of representation since 1992; only 14 percent at NBC; and a slightly better 15 percent at CBS. Furthermore, the study noted that the dominance of white males in newscasts continued, with only three minority correspondents appearing among the top ten reporters. Jim Avila (NBC) ranked sixth on the list of most-often-featured correspondents, with Bill Whitaker (CBS) and Byron Pitts (CBS) ranking seventh and tenth, respectively. Only one other minority—ABC's

Ron Claiborne, ranking forty-first—was among the top fifty correspondents. According to CMPA president S. Robert Lichter, "Despite the networks' recent commitment to diversity in prime-time entertainment, this attitude has apparently not reached their news bureaus." In 2000, newsroom diversity stood at 11 percent overall, and this percentage continued to climb, moving up to 14 percent by 2002 and 15 percent by 2007.

The number of African American television and radio owners has decreased because of the consolidation frenzy in the broadcasting industry, a situation compounded by the elimination of a federal tax credit that favored minority groups. According to a 1995 survey, of the 1,221 television stations, members of minority groups owned thirty-seven; of the 10,191 radio stations, 293 were minority owned. Although the numbers were small, they reflected a significant increase since 1978. That same year, the FCC agreed to grant tax credits to radio and television station owners who sold their properties to minority buyers. The objective of the tax-credit benefit was to broaden broadcast ownership and promote more diverse viewpoints. The result effectively lowered the acquisition costs of a television or radio station for a minority.

One benefactor of the tax credit was Ragan A. Henry, an African American lawyer and founder of U.S. Radio. He used the tax break to assemble what was the largest African American–owned radio group in the nation by 1996, with twenty-five stations. In 1996, Henry sold U.S. Radio for $140 million to Clear Channel Communications of San Antonio. His financial backers were unwilling to put up more money to buy increasingly expensive stations.

Refusing to follow the trend of selling to larger white-owned entities, Ross Love, founder of Blue Chip Broadcasting Ltd., which was established in 1995 in Cincinnati, Ohio, became a part of the Radio One family in 2001. At the time of acquisition, Blue Chip Broadcasting had fifteen radio stations in five markets—Cincinnati, Columbus, Dayton, Louisville, and Minneapolis. The radio stations owned by Blue Chip in Lexington, Kentucky, were sold separately to another party. Additionally, Radio One agreed to operate WDBZ-AM, a Blue Chip urban-talk station in Cincinnati, under a local marketing agreement. Ownership of WDBZ was supposed to transfer to a new company owned principally by Ross Love, Blue Chip's chief executive. In conjunction with this acquisition, Love was nominated to serve on Radio One's board of directors. In the press release announcing Radio One's purchase of Blue Chip Broadcasting, Love expressed his belief that the acquisition would benefit the business's employees and investors by expanding into new markets. Love added, "We share a core expertise in the Urban lifestyle formats and we share a commitment to bettering the communities which we serve."

The tax credit was eliminated in 1995 when the U.S. Congress swept aside affirmative-action policies. The program came under attack because of its use by Viacom to escape $600 million in taxes in a proposed sale of its cable television properties. Viacom had arranged to sell its cable systems to an African American entrepreneur whose company received financial backing from Tele-Communications Inc., then the nation's largest cable operator. After the elimination of the tax credit, the number of minority-owned stations declined slightly.

Although they are no longer required to adhere to the affirmative-action guidelines established by the FCC, the four major networks and several of the largest owners of radio stations agreed to continue to follow them in their outreach and recruitment efforts. The demise of the affirmative-action guidelines came about when such policies were declared unconstitutional—naysayers believed they would lead to quotas—by a federal court in the spring of 1998.

The list of companies that agreed to continue following the affirmative-action guidelines set by the FCC include ABC, CBS, NBC, the Fox network, Time Warner Inc., the Tribune Company, and Clear Channel Communications. Cox Communications, the Cablevision Systems Corporation, the TCI Group, and Comcast Corporation—all cable outlets—also agreed. According to BIA, a company that monitors revenues in broadcasting, all of these companies earned roughly one-third of the annual advertising revenue in the broadcast industry.

Cathy Hughes launched TV One, Inc., on January 19, 2004, in partnership with Comcast, the nation's largest pay-television provider. TV One caters to the adult lifestyles of African Americans. It offers quality programming and an array of original programming, including such series as *Washington Watch with Roland Martin* and specials, such as *Living the Dream: An Interview with President Barack Obama*, which aired in early 2010. Hughes, who serves on the board of TV One, is the executive producer of *Gospel of Music with Jeff Majors* and also hosts TV One's interview show, *TV One on One*.

RADIO AND TELEVISION ADVERTISING

A study conducted in the late 1990s by U.S. broadcast regulators found that advertisers discriminate against minority-owned radio and television stations or stations that target African American audiences. An FCC-sponsored report further determined that minority stations earned an estimated 63 percent less in advertising revenue per listener than similar nonminority stations. Many advertisers believed that they could reach African American listeners by sticking to mainstream radio.

The lack of advertising dollars allocated to African American–formatted stations is probably the result of the lack of minority representation at advertising firms. To remedy this situation, many advertising firms have stepped up their recruitment of minorities. In 1998, minority professionals comprised 11 percent of employees at the nation's twenty-five leading advertising agencies, up from 7.6 percent in 1995. While creative directors for leading advertising agencies continue to be white and male in the early twenty-first century, programs are in place on college campuses to promote broader diversity.

PUBLIC TELEVISION

The National Educational Television network, later known as the Public Broadcasting Service (PBS), was launched in the early 1950s. One PBS program, *Tony Brown's Black Journal*, later called simply *Tony Brown's Journal*, was well-received by African American viewers as the only national African American public affairs series on television, but it was constantly threatened with cancellation. Facing complaints about its antiadministration attitude, the show managed to stay on the air after it secured underwriting from the Pepsi-Cola Company. *Tony Brown's Journal* provided commentary, timely documentaries, and issues of special interest to the African American community until 2004.

In 1975, FCC commissioner Benjamin Hooks, an African American, joined the critics accusing public broadcasters of "arrogance" and of concentrating their efforts on cultured, white cosmopolitans. A 1975 review of public broadcasting stations showed that 108 of 184 public radio licensees (59%) and fifty-two of the 160 public television licensees (33%) had no minority staff in the top three job categories (officials, managers, and professionals).

In the early 1990s, the highest-ranking African Americans in public television were Jennifer Lawson, who joined PBS in November 1989 as its first executive vice president for national programming and promotion services; Donald L. Marbury, director of the Television Program Fund of the Corporation for Public Broadcasting; and George L. Miles Jr., executive vice president and chief operating officer of WNET-TV New York. Lawson obtained, commissioned, and promoted the programs that PBS provided to its member stations. Marbury managed the $45 million television program fund, which furnished financial support for major series in public television, such as *Frontline*.

The most visible African American journalist on public television was Charlayne Hunter-Gault, former national correspondent for *The NewsHour with Jim Lehrer*, formerly *The MacNeil/Lehrer NewsHour* and, since late 2009, *The PBS NewsHour*. A former *New York Times* reporter noted for her in-depth reporting, Hunter-Gault worked for PBS from 1977 to 1997 and for National Public Radio (NPR) from 1997 to 1999. In 1999, she became the Johannesburg, South Africa, bureau chief and correspondent for CNN. Hunter-Gault then left CNN in 2005 and went back to NPR. In the early twenty-first century, the most prominent African American journalists on PBS included Kwame Holman, a Washington correspondent for *The PBS NewsHour*; Gwen Ifill, senior correspondent for *The PBS NewsHour* and host of *Washington Week*; Michel Martin, the host of *Life 360* from 2000 to 2001, a regular panelist on *Washington Week*, and a contributor to *NOW with Bill Moyers*; and Karen Gibbs, cohost of *Wall $treet Week with FORTUNE*.

One of the most acclaimed pieces of African American journalism on PBS was *Eyes on the Prize*, a fourteen-episode documentary series on the history of the civil rights movement. The series was produced by Henry Hampton, and aired in 1987, with a sequel in 1990. *A Huey P. Newton Story*, which was based on the life of assassinated cofounder of the Black Panther Party and produced by Spike Lee, won the George Foster Peabody Award. Produced by Avon Kirkland, *Ralph Ellison: An American Journey*, which aired on PBS in 2005, explored the life and work of the influential author whose landmark novel, *Invisible Man*, won him a lifetime of awards and honors; it was nominated for a Literacy in Media Award. Other programs of note produced by African Americans on PBS included *Africans in America: America's Journey through Slavery* (1998) and *Africa: A Special Presentation of Nature* (2001), which was the first television series to explore the African continent through the eyes of Africans.

In addition, the PBS series *Great Performances* and *American Masters* have explored the lives of numerous African American artists, writers, and performers, including Duke Ellington, Aretha Franklin, James Baldwin, Sam Cooke, Marvin Gaye, and Zora Neale Hurston. PBS's *American Experience* series has covered many important chapters and figures in African American history, including Adam Clayton Powell, Marcus Garvey, and Martin Luther King Jr. Henry Louis Gates Jr. has hosted and coproduced several series on PBS, including *Wonders of the African World* (2000) and *America beyond the Color Line* (2004). Gates's *African American Lives 1* (2006) and *African American Lives 2* (2008) explored African American history through genealogy and science. In 2004, PBS began airing the awarding-winning talk show *Tavis Smiley*.

In 1980, Howard University launched WHMM-TV, becoming the first licensee of a public television station on an African American campus and the only African

American–owned public television station in the nation. In 1998 the station changed its call letters to WHUT-TV. The station has won numerous Emmys and other awards. On August 31, 1991, San Francisco's Minority Television Project went on the air with KMTP-TV, which became the nation's second African American–owned public television station. One of the principals was Adam Clayton Powell III, son of the late Harlem congressman, Adam Clayton Powell Jr.

PUBLIC RADIO

Before 1967, there were only two African American educational outlets in the country; by 1990, there were forty African American public radio stations. Many of them were community radio stations, owned and operated by nonprofit foundations, controlled by a local board of directors, and dependent on listener donations. Others could be found on college campuses. One of the most successful was WPFW-FM, a 50,000-watt outlet launched in 1977 in Washington, D.C., by the Pacifica Foundation.

Stations such as WCLK-FM at Clark Atlanta University in Atlanta, WBVA-FM in Harrodsburg, Kentucky, and WVAS-FM at Alabama State University in Montgomery tailored news and public affairs programming to their local African American audiences. WVAS was used as a broadcast journalism lab by students majoring in the field. In the 1990s and early 2000s, NPR's African American journalists Phyllis Crockett, Vertamae Grosvenor, Cheryl Duvall, Phillip Davis, and Brenda Wilson won awards for reports on South Africa and issues involving African Americans. Crockett and Duvall later left NPR. Cheryl Corley joined NPR in late 1995. Her honors include a Chicago Association of Black Journalists Award in 2000 for excellence in radio news, a Peabody Award as part of the NPR team covering the September 11 attacks, and the 2002 Distinguished Service Award from the American Psychiatric Association Alliance. The National Association of Black Journalists conferred its Award in Excellence to NPR's team coverage of the UN Conference on Racism, to which Cheryl Corley and Philip Martin—NPR's former race relations reporter—were a part.

Correspondent and news analyst Juan Williams joined NPR in 1999. After nearly a decade as a correspondent for ABC News, Michele Norris became host of the NPR's daily news program *All Things Considered* in 2002. In 2007, Michel Martin began hosting *Tell Me More*, a one-hour daily news and talk show on NPR. Newscaster and substitute host Korva Coleman joined NPR in 1990. NPR's African American reporters include Gwen Thompkins, Allison Keyes, Brenda Wilson, Audie Cornish, and Rachel Jones.

CABLE TELEVISION

The 1980s saw the explosion of cable television and the decline of television networks. Black Entertainment Television (BET), founded by former congressional aide Robert L. Johnson, made its debut in 1980 and established a news division by the end of the decade. That division produced the weekly show *BET News* and *Lead Story*, a talk show featuring African American pundits. In 2000, however, the African American community lost control of one of its largest communications companies when BET became the property of Viacom Inc., an international media giant. Johnson drew $1.6 billion out of the package, making him the first African American billionaire.

In a $3 billion deal, Viacom purchased the BET brand—the core cable channel, BET on Jazz, and BET

Media Executive Robert L. Johnson, March 2008. *As the founder, chairman, and CEO of Black Entertainment Television (BET), Johnson molded BET into the leading cable station catering to the interests of African Americans.* AP PHOTO/CRAIG RUTTLE

International. For the first time in twenty years, BET's development in these areas was not controlled by African Americans. Viacom also purchased BET.com and BET's Arabesque Books, the publishing division. The magazine arm, BET's Movies/Starz, BET's Soundstage, jazz club, and other restaurants were not part of the deal. The company turned its leading magazines, *Emerge* and *BET Weekend*, over to a new partner, Vanguarde Media Inc., owned by former VIBE publisher Keith Clinkscales, who discontinued both magazines.

The biggest development in cable journalism, however, was the spectacular growth of Ted Turner's Cable News Network (CNN), which went on the air in June 1980. By the time of the 1991 war in the Persian Gulf, CNN had established itself as the station to watch in a crisis. Transmitted across the globe, it became a medium for world leaders to communicate with one another. Until the launching of MSNBC in 1996, CNN had no competition. MSNBC, a massive joint venture between the NBC television network and Microsoft Corporation, was the only service of its kind, combining television, cable, and the Internet. This news empire claimed an immediate reach of over twenty-five million households.

Veteran journalist Bernard Shaw, CNN's principal Washington anchor, was one of three reporters who captivated audiences with their continuous coverage of the bombing of Baghdad on January 16, 1991, the first night of Operation Desert Storm. Shaw concluded his career as a full-time CNN anchor on *Inside Politics* in 2001. Other African Americans who have worked at CNN include Jay Suber, former vice president and executive producer of news features and *CNN Newsroom*; Graylian Young, southeast bureau chief; CNN anchors Andrea Arceneaux, Leon Harris, Joe Oliver, Cassandra Henderson, Lyn Vaughn, and Gordon Graham; and sports anchor Fred Hickman. Correspondent Norma Quarles joined CNN in 1988 after serving twenty-one years with NBC News and its affiliates. Roland S. Martin joined CNN in 2007 as a contributor, host, and political analyst. Other African American anchors and correspondents who joined CNN after 2000 include Tony Harris, T. J. Holmes, Don Lemon, Soledad O'Brien, Fredricka Whitfield, and Richelle Carey. Harris Faulkner joined Fox News Channel, another major cable and satellite news outlet, in 2005 as a correspondent and breaking news anchor.

AFRICAN AMERICAN MEDIA IN CYBERSPACE

By the first decade of the twenty-first century, African Americans were cruising the information superhighway—a vast electronic communications network comprised of telephones, computers, and televisions—in growing numbers. An increasing number of African Americans were using the Internet at home, work, school, and libraries.

Larry Irving, branded "the Net's Conscience," was director of the National Telecommunications and Information Administration during the administration of President Bill Clinton. Far from being the only person of color with clout on the Internet, Irving was one of many experts working in the burgeoning industry to provide access to a wide array of information for educational, business, and entertainment purposes. Other high-ranking African Americans included: Andrew C. Barrett, the only black commissioner of the FCC; Ray Winbush, director of the Bishop Joseph Johnson Black Cultural Center at Vanderbilt University—a network linking black colleges, students, and professors; Jimmy Davies, who partnered with Apple Computer to establish a national electronic bulletin board service for blacks called the African American Information Network; Eugene and Phyllis Tucker Vinson Jackson, founders of the World African Network, a twenty-four-hour pay-cable television network for blacks; and Cleo Manago, founder of the Black Men's Xchange, an Afrocentric national communications clearinghouse.

The World Wide Web comprises a major component of the "highway." An increasing number of African Americans, including Deb Sistrunk, Sokari Ekine, Wayne Bennett, Lancelot A. Smith, and Malena Amusa, maintain popular blogs. Many African American news-oriented Web sites are mentioned below. Some of the most popular African American Web sites offering information on the various subjects covered in this reference work can be found in the bibliography at the end of the volume.

SELECTED WEB SITES

http://www.aawc.com (African American Web Connection). A gateway to Afrocentric Web sources for the African American community. Topics include art and poetry, black authors, businesses, churches, entertainment, history, organizations, resources in Africa, and publications.

http://www.abouttimemag.com. An online version of *About Time* magazine. It includes selected full-text articles from recent issues, with archives planned as far back as 1994.

http://www.Afronet.com. A Web portal for information about the African and African American experience. Topics include legal services, entertainment, health, sports, trading, beauty, and business.

http://www.BET.com. An online version of the cable station Black Entertainment Television. Areas of interest include news, music, entertainment, books, food, and health. Highlights about the company and its televised programs are also featured.

http://www.BlackAmericaWeb.com. A Tom Joyner–promoted Web portal targeting African Americans. It features news and information on business, careers, books, technology, health and fitness, travel, sports, and entertainment.

http://www.black-collegian.com. An online version of the *Black Collegian*, a national career opportunities magazine. It focuses on education and career information for African American students. It also provides commentary by leading African American writers, lifestyle and entertainment features, general information on college life, and news about college campuses.

http://www.blackenterprise.com. An online version of *Black Enterprise*. It offers information about entrepreneurship, technology, personal finance, and other minority business issues.

http://www.blackfacts.com. An online searchable database for African American history facts.

http://www.blackhistorypages.com. Provides a wealth of information on a wide variety of topics about people of African descent, with links to other Web sites. Topics include black Indians, civil rights, education, entertainment, genealogy, inventors, and lynching.

http://www.blackpgs.com (Internet Black Pages). A listing of African American businesses, churches, schools, organizations, and events in black communities around the world.

http://www.BlackPlanet.com. A social-networking site that enables African Americans to cultivate meaningful personal and professional relationships, to stay informed about the world, and to gain access to goods and services that will allow them to do more in life.

http://www.BlackPressUSA.com. The only national Web site featuring news exclusively from African American journalists and community publications.

http://www.BlackVoices.com. Features a variety of topics, most of them geared toward the African American community, such as national and world news, sports, arts and entertainment, business, health, and travel, as well as an automotive section. Other features include a career center, chat rooms, and message boards.

http://www.BlackWebPortal.com. A Web portal to find black businesses, Web sites, and events. It also features discussion boards, chat rooms, weather, and e-commerce. BlackWebPortal is the only site that is 100 percent African American owned.

http://www.blackworld.com. A social-networking and search site that provides information on a myriad of topics from people of African descent around the world (Africa, the Caribbean, France, and the United Kingdom).

http://www.ebonyjet.com. An online version of *Ebony* and *Jet* magazines, with abbreviated versions of articles and features in the current issues only.

http://www.essence.com. An online version of *Essence* magazine, targeting African American women. Topics include relationships, beauty and style, wellness, food, finance, and entertainment. Although *Essence* is geared to the black female audience, it is no longer owned by African Americans.

http://www.EverythingBlack.com. An Internet directory and search engine of Web sites specifically targeting African Americans and persons of African descent worldwide.

http://www.heartandsoul.com. An online version of *Heart and Soul*, a magazine about health and wellness.

http://www.honeymag.com. An online version of *Honey* magazine, with features on entertainment, beauty, fashion, and lifestyle issues, aimed at young urban women.

http://www.MelaNet.com (The Uncut Black Experience). Dedicated to the intellectual, economic, and spiritual expression of peoples throughout the African diaspora.

http://www.netnoir.com. One of the first African American Web sites. Topics include folks and culture, news and information, entertainment, business, education, music, politics, and shopping.

http://www.niaonline.com. One of the premier Internet destinations for African American women. Topics include world news, parenting, health, money, relationships, and careers. Top African American opinion-makers and well-known columnists like Jill Nelson, Jewel Diamond Taylor, and Harriette Cole have served as contributors.

http://www.Oprah.com. An online version of *The Oprah Winfrey Show*. It also features information on *O: The Oprah Magazine*, Oprah's Angel Network, Oprah's Book Club, and other topics of interest to women.

http://www.SeeingBlack.com. A portal focusing on film, the visual and performing arts, sports, politics, media, and music.

http://www.SOHH.com (Search Online Hip-Hop). Geared toward the hip-hop music industry. It also covers entertainment, lifestyle, sports, travel, health and fitness, and technology.

http://www.soulofamerica.com. The doorway to Afrocentric treasures throughout the nation, including the arts, cultural sites, churches, historic sites, black-owned restaurants, nightclubs, radio stations, and shopping.

http://www.tavistalks.com. Features all things related to Tavis Smiley, former host of *BET Tonight with Tavis Smiley*, former political commentator for *The Tom Joyner Morning Show* on ABC Radio Networks, and host of *The Tavis Smiley Show* from Public Radio International and *Tavis Smiley* on PBS.

http://www.tjms.com. Web site of *The Tom Joyner Morning Show*, which is aired in more than one hundred U.S. radio markets. The Web site features segments from the show, as well as news, entertainment, weather, health, and education.

http://www.topblacksites.com. Provides a list of the most highly trafficked African American Web sites.

http://www.upscalemagazine.com. An online version of *Upscale* magazine, with features on style and beauty, entertainment and arts, and travel and living, as well as highlights from the current issue and a career corner.

http://www.vibe.com. An online version of the former *VIBE* magazine. It is loaded with graphics, advertisements, illustrations, and articles on popular music and culture.

RADIO AND TELEVISION PROFESSIONALS

(Some biographical profiles may appear in other chapters. To locate profiles more readily, please consult the index.)

ROBERT S. ABBOTT (1870–1940)

Newspaper Publisher. A native of St. Simons Island, Georgia, Abbott studied at Beach Institute in Savannah, and later completed his undergraduate work at Claflin College in Orangeburg, South Carolina. Migrating to Chicago, he attended Kent Law School and took a job in a printing house until he completed his law studies in 1899.

Abbott returned to Chicago and published the first edition of the *Chicago Defender* on May 5, 1905, which he initially sold door-to-door. After Abbott's death, the *Defender* was handed over to his nephew, John H. Sengstacke, who introduced a daily edition of the paper in 1956.

TYRA BANKS (1973–)

Talk-Show Host, Television Producer, Model. *The Tyra Banks Show* is an American daytime talk show hosted by Tyra Banks, a former model and the creator and host of *America's Next Top Model.* Banks's talk show premiered on September 12, 2005, and was filmed in front of a live audience at CBS Television City in Los Angeles. The show moved production to New York in 2007. Although the show covers a variety of topics, there is a significant focus on issues facing women. *The Tyra Banks Show* won an Daytime Emmy Award for Best Talk Show, Informative, in 2008. In late 2009, Banks announced that *The Tyra Banks Show* would end in 2010, after its fifth season, so she could focus on other television and movie projects. She remained involved in *America's Next Top Model,* which began its fourteenth cycle in March 2010. Banks, who began her career as a model at age seventeen, has posed for many upscale magazines and has appeared in several movies. She was born in Los Angeles.

WILLIAM BANKS (1903–1985)

Broadcasting Executive, Attorney, Minister. Born in Geneva, Kentucky, in 1903, William Banks relocated to Detroit as a young man and, after earning a law degree, he became a Baptist minister during his forties. Long active in numerous African American community organizations in the city, Banks founded the International Free and Accepted Masons and Eastern Star in 1950 and, under his guidance, the growing group soon became a financially sound and charity-driven fraternal organization. He continued to work as an attorney in private practice until well past the age of retirement.

In 1964, the Black Masons made their first venture into media ownership with a Detroit FM radio outlet that mixed rhythm-and-blues music and religious broadcasting. Banks's business savvy helped make the station a financial success in the same way that the Masons' other ventures—such as vocational schools—also helped the organization thrive. His ties to the Republican Party eventually brought him to U.S. president Richard Nixon's White House as a guest in the early 1970s, and the president helped Banks obtain the first FCC television-station license granted to an African American in the United States.

The new UHF television outlet run by Banks and the Masons took to the Detroit airwaves in 1975. It was called WGPR, for Where God's Presence Radiates. Its first years in operation were shaky, since many members of Banks's team—employees that included his wife, Ivy Bird, and his daughter, Tenicia Gregory—had little media experience. Within a few years, however, the station gained ratings and financial health. More importantly, WGPR-TV served as a training ground for a legion of African American on-air and behind-the-scenes technical personnel, a group of young people who would eventually figure prominently in Detroit media. Banks died in 1985 when he was eighty-two years old. The Black Masons organization that Banks founded owned the station until 1994, when it was purchased by CBS as a local affiliate.

DONALD H. BARDEN (1943–)

Communications Executive. Born on December 20, 1943, Don Barden struggled in a number of low-wage jobs as an adult. A savings of $500 helped him open a record store. He then launched a record label, and later a public relations firm in Lorain, Ohio. The capital Barden accumulated through these ventures was later parlayed into real-estate deals. By the early 1970s, he had become a dynamic member of Lorain's business community, owning a newspaper, holding a seat on the city council, and hosting a talk show on Cleveland's NBC affiliate.

Barden's interest in and familiarity with cutting-edge media evolved into his most lucrative undertaking. Foreseeing the rise of the cable industry—and the lack of African American representation within it—Barden invested in Lorain's new cable television provider and used his profits to begin his own cable company, Barden Cablevision. His research revealed that African American communities were considering franchise offers from giants in the industry, and Barden offered them a socially conscious alternative. One of the first cities to award Barden's company a contract was Inkster, Michigan, a suburb of Detroit. His success in wiring the city for cable service and the obvious financial soundness of his company paid off when the city of Detroit awarded Barden Cablevision a major contract.

Barden launched cable television in Detroit with the help of Canadian financing and began wiring the city in 1986. Always standing on the forefront of the communications industry, Barden's next venture was in personal communications services, a new messaging technology that would allow small devices to transmit faxes, voice messages, and computer data. In 1994, he sold his interest in Barden Cablevision for a reported $100 million, reaping a dramatic profit from the company he had started with only a few thousand dollars. In early 1995, Indiana authorities granted Barden a riverboat-casino operating license, one of two to be established in the city of Gary.

With the success of his riverboat casino in Indiana, Barden expressed an interest in obtaining a license for one of the three casinos earmarked for Detroit. When the mayor rejected his bid, Barden recruited pop star Michael Jackson to help him campaign for a contract in the hopes that Detroit voters would overturn the mayor's decision. Barden's proposed billion-dollar casino was to be called the Majestic Kingdom, and included plans for an 800-room hotel, botanical gardens, nightclubs, restaurants, and the Michael Jackson Thriller Theme Park. Despite Barden's vigorous campaigning, Detroit voters rejected his proposal in 1998.

Barden next entered into a contract with General Motors to establish automotive plants in Namibia and South Africa. He and Michael Jackson took several trips in 1998 to central and southern Africa to investigate other business opportunities there. In May 1999, Barden reached a deal to invest in Sengstacke Enterprises, owner of several African American newspapers in Chicago, Detroit, Pittsburgh, and Memphis. In 2002 Barden established the Majestic Star casino in Gary, Indiana, and he purchased three other casinos in Mississippi, Colorado, and Las Vegas. Barden is the first African American to own and operate a casino.

HALEY W. BELL (c. 1895–1973)

Broadcasting Executive. Although a dentist by profession, Haley Bell was most recognized as the cofounder of the Bell Broadcasting System, which he established with his son-in-law, Wendell Cox, in 1955. The system included WCHB-AM in Inkster (its owners' initials) and WCHD-FM in Detroit, Michigan. Bell's other interests included ownership of a finance company, a tool and die firm, a cemetery, a restaurant, an insurance company, two trade schools, and a funeral home.

Bell was the first African American to ever directly receive a license from the FCC to operate a radio station. His stations, the first black-built radio stations in the United States, served as training grounds for many local and national media personalities who broke into the airwaves through the black-owned stations. Included among those who once worked at the Bell Broadcasting System were NBC newsman William Matney; Ofield Dukes, a former assistant to Vice President Hubert Humphrey; Trudy Haynes, Detroit's first black female weather reporter; Frank Seymour of Seymour and Lundy, a public relations firm; and Martha Jean "the Queen" Steinberg, eventually an announcer on WJLB-FM, but later the owner, president, and general manager of WQBH-AM in Inkster.

Initially staffed by twenty-three experienced employees whom Bell lured away from previous jobs by offering more lucrative wages, the stations adopted the slogan "The Voice of Progress." In accordance with this slogan, the programming on both stations reflected the music, aspirations, and accomplishments of Detroit-area blacks. While most of the airtime was dedicated to news, religious programs, and music (ranging from blues to symphonies), community organizations were also granted a generous hearing.

Often referred to as the father of Detroit black radio, Bell maintained his dental office in Hamtramck, Michigan, until his retirement in 1960. Known for his generosity, Bell believed that if you kept a part of what you earned, you would always be able to give a part of what you had. His belief was further emphasized by the engraved plaque that appeared in his office with the words, "a part of all you earn is yours to keep." Organizations that benefited from Bell's benevolence included Meharry Medical College, from which he graduated in 1922, the NAACP, the United Negro College Fund, the United Foundation, the Parents Association of Jewish Residential Care, Catholic Charities, Plymouth

United Church, and numerous other groups that cut across racial lines.

Born in Brunswick, Georgia, Dr. Bell died on March 12, 1973, nine days before he was to be honored by the Detroit Cotillion Club for "his many contributions to charitable and public concerns, including personality-sponsored scholarships for students across the nation."

ED BRADLEY (1941–2006)

Television News Correspondent. Born on January 22, 1941, in Philadelphia, Edward Rudolph Bradley received a bachelor of science degree in education from Cheyney State College in 1964. From 1963 to 1967, Bradley worked as a jazz host and news reporter for WDAS radio in Philadelphia. He then spent four years at WCBS radio in New York. His first television assignment was in September 1971, when he joined CBS as a stringer in the Paris bureau. Within a few months he moved to the Saigon bureau in Vietnam, where he remained until he was assigned to the Washington bureau in June 1974. From 1974 until 1978, Bradley served as White House correspondent for CBS.

Bradley worked as an anchor for *CBS Sunday Night News* from 1976 until 1981 and as principal correspondent for *CBS Reports*. In 1981, he replaced Dan Rather as a correspondent for the weekly news program *60 Minutes*. In 1992, Bradley became host of the CBS news program *Street Stories*. An avid jazz and blues aficionado, Bradley became host of NPR's *Jazz from Lincoln Center* in 1991.

Over the course of his career, Bradley received numerous Emmy Awards, two Alfred I. du Pont–Columbia University Awards for broadcast journalism, a George Foster Peabody Broadcasting Award, a George Polk Award, and an NCAA Anniversary Award. In 1992, he won an Emmy for his *60 Minutes* segment "Made in China." The National Press

Television News Correspondent Ed Bradley. *The recipient of numerous awards, Bradley is best known for his twenty-five years of work as a correspondent for the weekly newsmagazine* 60 Minutes. CBS/LANDOV

Foundation presented Bradley with the Sol Taischoff Award in 1993.

In October 1995, Bradley filed a report called "The Other America" on *60 Minutes*. In that piece, he examined shantytown homes—known as *colonias*—in the Texas desert along the U.S.-Mexico border. The colonias were designed for low-income, mainly Hispanic families. The woman who built the shanties claimed that Bradley's report wrecked her reputation and falsely accused her and other members of her family of unethical business and political practices. She sued for defamation. However, in late 1997, a Texas jury cleared Bradley of libel in the investigation.

Bradley continued to make a name for himself in the field with his weekly reports on *60 Minutes*, as well as other news programs. In 2000, the New York chapter of the Society of Professional Journalists inducted him into the Deadline Club Hall of Fame. In 2005, he was honored with a Lifetime Achievement Award from the National Association of Black Journalists. Bradley died in 2006 from leukemia.

JAMES BROWN (1951–)

Sports Anchor. James Brown was born on February 25, 1951, in Washington, D.C. He served for more than ten seasons as cohost of *Fox NFL Sunday*, America's most watched pregame show. Brown also served as cohost of *NHL on Fox* studio segments. After joining Fox Sports in June 1994, Brown gained broad recognition as one of the most versatile and multitalented on-air personalities in television. Brown moved to CBS in 2006.

Prior to entering the communications field, Brown received a bachelor of arts degree in American government from Harvard University in 1973, and was then drafted in the fourth round by the National Basketball Association's (NBA) Atlanta Hawks. He began his broadcasting career in 1984 with WJLA-TV in Washington, D.C., and WUSA-TV (1984–1990). He also served as an analyst for the NBA's Washington Bullets local television broadcasts (1978–1983) and cohosted two weekly Washington-area sports programs. He also hosted a midday program on all-sports radio WTEM in the nation's capital.

Sportscaster James Brown, Super Bowl Pregame Show, 2005. *Brown (left), shown here with cohost Terry Bradshaw, is widely recognized as one of the most versatile and multitalented on-air personalities in television.* FRANK MICELOTTA/GETTY IMAGES ENTERTAINMENT/GETTY IMAGES

In 1984, Brown joined CBS Sports as a college basketball analyst and cohost of the National Collegiate Athletic Association (NCAA) championship (1984–1994). Other host roles for CBS included weekday program during the 1992 Winter Olympics, the Heisman Trophy Award show, the *CBS Sports Saturday/Sunday* anthology series, and the Emmy Award–winning special *Let Me Be Brave: A Special Climb of Mt. Kilimanjaro* (1991).

In addition to college basketball and National Football League (NFL) play-by-play, Brown served as a reporter for CBS coverage of the NBA Finals and the Pan-American Games. He also delved into other sports areas. He served as commentator for freestyle skiing for CBS at the 1994 Lillehammer Winter Olympics and hosted four Fox Saturday Night Fight programs, as well as several pay-per-view boxing events.

Brown was a contributor to the sports magazine program *Real Sports with Bryant Gumbel*, which premiered on HBO in April 1995, and served as a moderator for a roundtable discussion of the documentary *Hoop Dreams Reunion* (1995) on PBS. In 2002, Brown joined Sports News Radio to host *The James Brown Show*. In 2001, he received the prestigious Sportscaster of the Year Award from the Quarterback Club of Washington for his "outstanding contribution to the world of sports." Beginning with the 2006 NFL season, Brown hosted *The NFL Today* on CBS, and returned to play-by-play of CBS coverage of NCAA basketball. In 2008, Brown became one of the hosts of the weekly program *Inside the NFL* on Showtime.

LES BROWN (1945–)

Motivational Speaker, Talk-Show Host, Author. As a motivational speaker, author, and television personality, Les Brown—born Leslie Calvin Brown along with his twin brother, Wesley, on February 17, 1945—rose to national prominence by delivering a highly charged message that teaches people how to shake off mediocrity and live up to their potential.

Brown was born in low-income Liberty City, Florida. He and his brother were adopted at six weeks of age by Mamie Brown, a single woman with little education or money. As a child, Les Brown lacked the ability to concentrate, especially in reading. His restlessness and inattentiveness, coupled with his teachers' failure to recognize his real potential, resulted in him being labeled as a slow learner. Although this label damaged his self-esteem and stayed with him for many years, he overcame it through perseverance and the realization that he was responsible for his destiny. His mother's unyielding encouragement, along with support from a speech and drama teacher in high school, aided him in this journey of discovery.

Brown received no formal education past high school, but he prides himself on being self-educated. Brown's thirst for knowledge and his desire to succeed allowed him to rise from a radio announcer to a broadcast manager, from a community activist to a community leader, from a political commentator to three-term legislator, and from a banquet and nightclub emcee to a prominent motivational speaker.

In 1986, Brown formed his own company, Les Brown Unlimited, and entered the public-speaking arena full time. The company provides motivational materials, as well as workshops and personal- and professional-development programs for individuals, companies, and organizations. Brown is also the author of *Live Your Dreams* (1992) and *It's Not Over Until You Win* (1997). From 1993 to 1994, Brown hosted *The Les Brown Show*, a nationally syndicated daily television talk show that focused on solutions rather than problems.

In 1989, Brown was the recipient of the National Speakers Association's highest honor: the Council of Peers Award of Excellence. In 1990, he recorded the first in a series of speeches titled *You Deserve*, which was awarded a Chicago-area Emmy. This program eventually became a leading fund-raising program during pledges drives on PBS stations nationwide. In 1992, Brown received the Golden Gavel Award and was selected as one of the World's Top Five Speakers by Toastmasters International.

In 1997, Brown resigned from his radio show at WBLS in New York in order to devote more time to his motivational speaking. By 1998, Brown's speaking engagements and television appearances brought in about $4.5 million annually. His Detroit-based firm continued to serve high-profile clients such as Chrysler, 3M, and Xerox Corporation. In addition, Brown branched out to the training of future public speakers, concentrating on promoting the field to minorities.

TONY BROWN (1933–)

Talk-Show Host, Producer, Columnist, Author, Film Director. William Anthony Brown was born in Charleston, West Virginia, in 1933. He is best known as the producer and host of the long-running minority-affairs program *Tony Brown's Journal*. The show was selected by the *New York Daily Times* as one of the all-time top-ten television shows that presents positive African American images. In 1991, the show was also nominated for the NAACP Image Award for outstanding news, talk, or information series/special.

Brown received his bachelor of arts degree in sociology in 1959 and his master's degree in social work in 1961 from Wayne State University in Detroit. Brown then took a job with the *Detroit Courier* as a drama critic.

During this time, he began to be active in the civil rights movement, helping to organize the 1963 March to Freedom with Dr. Martin Luther King Jr. in Detroit. After leaving the paper, where Brown had been promoted to the position of city editor, he landed a job with the local PBS station, WTVS, where he became involved in television programming and production. At WTVS, he produced the station's first series aimed at a black audience, *C.P.T.* (Colored People's Time). He joined the New York staff of the PBS program *Black Journal* in 1970 as the show's executive producer and host; in 1977, the show's name was changed to *Tony Brown's Journal*.

In 1971, Brown founded and became the first dean of Howard University's School of Communications. He continued in that post until 1974. While in this position, he initiated an annual career conference because of his concern for the lack of African American representation in the communications industry.

Brown has been an advocate of community and self-help programs. In 1980, he organized a Black College Day, designed to emphasize the importance of historically African American colleges and universities. In 1985, Brown organized the Council for the Economic Development of Black Americans and launched the Buy Freedom campaign (now known as the Buy Freedom Network), which encourages African American consumers nationwide to patronize African American–owned businesses.

Brown has published three books: *Black Lies, White Lies: The Truth According to Tony Brown* (1995), *Empower the People: A 7-Step Plan to Overthrow the Conspiracy that Is Stealing Your Money and Freedom* (1998), and *What Mama Taught Me: The Seven Core Values of Life* (2003). Offering innovative plans for making America more competitive through Brown's Team America concept, the books strive to address the country's race problem through cultural diversity.

Brown wrote, produced, and directed the film *The White Girl* (1989), served as a commentator for NPR, and wrote a syndicated newspaper column. He also hosted a syndicated radio talk show, *Tony Brown*, on WLIB in New York. He is a member of the National Association of Black Television and Film Producers, the National Association of Black Media Producers, the National Communications Council, and the National Black United Fund. Brown is the recipient of a Black Emmy Award, an NAACP Image Award, the Educator of the Year Award, and the Communicator of the Year Award. He is president of Tony Brown Productions in New York.

EDWARD J. CASTLEBERRY (1928–2009)

Broadcast Journalist. Born July 28, 1928, in Birmingham, Alabama, Ed Castleberry spent two years at Miles College. His career in radio broadcasting includes many stations in the United States. He started as a disc jockey at WEDR and WJLD in Birmingham, Alabama (1950–1955), and worked in various capacities as program host, program director, and news personality at WMBM in Miami (1955–1958), WCIN in Cincinnati (1958–1961), WABQ in Cleveland (1961–1964), WVKO in Columbus (1964–1967), WHAT in Philadelphia (1967–1968), and WEBB in Baltimore. He then became an anchorman and entertainment editor at the Mutual and National Black Networks.

Castleberry was named Newsman of the Year in 1980 by both the Coalition of Black Media Women and Jack the Rapper Family Affair and received the Outstanding Citizen Award from the Alabama House of Representatives in 1983. In 1985, he was honored by the Smithsonian Institution in Washington, D.C. Later, Castleberry was awarded the World War II Victory Medal for his service in the U.S. Navy. Castleberry retired from broadcasting in the early 1990s. He died in 2009.

SPENCER CHRISTIAN (1947–)

Television Host and Weather Reporter. Spencer Christian was born in Newport News, Virginia, in 1947. He is a veteran of the U.S. Army Reserves, and received his bachelor of arts degree in English from Hampton University in 1970. After graduating, Christian taught English at the Stony Brook School in Long Island, New York, before launching his television career.

In 1971, Christian began working for WWBT-TV in Richmond as a news reporter. From 1972 to 1975, he served as the station's weatherperson. In 1975, he moved to WBAL-TV in Baltimore, where he hosted *Spencer's World*, a weekly half-hour talk show. He also produced and narrated the Emmy Award–winning five-part report on declining verbal skills, *Does Anyone Here Speak English?* In 1977, he moved to New York's WABC-TV. Christian joined the *Good Morning America* team on ABC in 1986 as weather forecaster. He left the show in 1999 to join a local television station in San Francisco. Christian is a wine enthusiast, and from 1995 to 1999, he hosted *Spencer Christian's Wine Cellar* for the Home and Garden Network.

In 1988, Christian became ABC Television's official on-air spokesperson for the Readasaurus campaign, which was part of the company's overall Project Literacy U.S., promoting interest in reading among young children. In 1993, Christian hosted the *Triple Threat* game show on Black Entertainment Television and was inducted into the Virginia Communications Hall of Fame. Later that year, he was named Virginian of the Year by the Virginia Press Association. He published *Spencer Christian's Weather*

Book (1993), *Spencer Christian's Geography Book* (1995), and *Electing Our Government* (1996), a lively refresher course on how the U.S. electoral process works. He also published a series of books for children: *Can It Really Rain Frogs?* (1997), *Shake, Rattle, and Roll* (1997), *What Makes the Grand Canyon Grand?* (1998), and *Is There a Dinosaur in Your Backyard?* (1998). In 1989, Christian cohosted an experimental late-night series on ABC called *Day's End*, which aired in twenty-seven markets across the country.

In 1996, Christian worked on a public education campaign, in conjunction with Eveready, that focused on weather emergency preparedness. In addition, he wrote a brochure with helpful weather emergency tips that was available through Energizer and endorsed by the National Weather Service. In 2000, Christian became host of the popular PBS series *Tracks Ahead*, a program about model and real trains, which began its seventh season in 2009.

Christian has worked with a variety of charities in New York and New Jersey. They include Up With People, the March of Dimes, the Huntington's Disease Society of America, the Special Olympics, Big Brothers, and the Make-a-Wish Foundation. His affiliation with the March of Dimes dates back to 1979 when he served as honorary chair of the North New Jersey chapter.

XERNONA CLAYTON (1930–)

Broadcasting Executive. Xernona Clayton was born Xernona Brewster on August 30, 1930, in Muskogee, Oklahoma. She received a bachelor of science degree from Tennessee Agricultural and Industrial State University (now Tennessee State University) in 1952 and later pursued graduate studies at the University of Chicago. She also attended the Ru-Jac School of Modeling in Chicago.

Clayton was the first African American woman to have her own television show in the South when she became host of *The Xernona Clayton Show* at WAGA-TV in Atlanta. She has also been a newspaper columnist for the *Atlanta Voice*, taught public school in Chicago and Los Angeles, and dabbled in photography and fashion modeling. In 1974, Clayton costarred in a major motion picture, *House on Skull Mountain*.

Clayton was active in the civil rights movement. Her first husband, now deceased, was the public relations director for Dr. Martin Luther King Jr. She later married Paul L. Brady, a federal administrative judge. Clayton came to the attention of Atlanta officials and was appointed to the position of community relations director of the Model Cities Program. She has also raised funds for sickle-cell anemia research and the Dr. Martin Luther King Jr. Birthplace Memorial Restoration Committee.

In 1968, Clayton won the Outstanding Leadership Award given by the National Association of Market Developers. A year later she received the Bronze Woman of the Year in Human Relations Award given by the Phi Delta Kappa sorority. She is also the recipient of the Georgia Associated Press Award for Superior Television Programming. In 1987, Clayton won an Emmy Award for a documentary on juvenile justice. She was named Media Woman of the Year in 1989. Clark Atlanta University gave her an honorary doctorate in 2000. In 2004, Spelman College honored Clayton with its Local Community Service Award. She also received a Leadership and Dedication in Civil Rights Award from the State of Georgia Commission on Equal Opportunity in 2004.

Clayton is the founder of the Atlanta chapter of the National Association of Media Women and a member of the National Academy of Television Arts and Sciences and the National Association of Press Women. She has also served as a member of the Urban League's board of directors. Her autobiography, *I've Been Marching All the Time*, written with Hal Gulliver, was published in 1991. In 1993, she became the creator and executive producer of Turner Broadcasting's long-running Trumpet Awards show, which honors the achievements of minorities around the world and is broadcast during Black History Month.

DON CORNELIUS (1936–)

Broadcasting Executive. Don Cornelius, the creative mind behind the hit African American dance show *Soul Train*, was born in Chicago on September 27, 1936, and grew up on the city's predominantly African American South Side. When he was thirty years old, he landed a part-time job as an radio announcer with WVON in Chicago. Acting as an all-around substitute became too exhausting, however, and he moved to the small UHF television station, WCIU-TV, with the seed for *Soul Train* already in mind. Although he initially had trouble convincing sponsors to take a chance on an "ethnic" show, Cornelius gained the financial backing he needed, and the first episode of *Soul Train*, hosted and produced by Cornelius, aired in Chicago on August 17, 1970. The inexpensive weekly show was essentially a dance party that featured African American performers and dancers.

The program went national about a year later, and production moved to Los Angeles. Cornelius attributed the speed of *Soul Train*'s success to the overall absence of entertainment television programs for African American audiences. The show spawned a record label, Soul Train Records, in 1975, although the label folded after three years. The Soul Train Music Awards proved to be a more

Broadcasting Executive Don Cornelius, 1994. *Pictured playing himself on an episode of* The Fresh Prince of Bel-Air, *Cornelius was the creator, executive producer, and first host of the long-running African American dance show* Soul Train. CHRIS HASTON/NBCU PHOTO BANK VIA AP IMAGES

enduring spin-off; created in 1986, the awards program was the first to be dedicated exclusively to African American musicians. By 1992, *Soul Train* had become the longest-running music program in the history of syndication. Cornelius retired in 1993 as host of the show, but he continued to stay active in the television business. In 1995, Cornelius hosted and produced *The Soul Train 25th Anniversary Hall of Fame Special.* He continued to produce *Soul Train,* as well as three annual award shows: *The Soul Train Awards, The Lady of Soul Awards,* and the *NAACP Image Awards. Soul Train* ceased production in 2006, after a thirty-six-year run, and Don Cornelius sold his interest in the show's archival footage in 2008 to MadVision Entertainment.

SAMUEL E. CORNISH (1795–1858)

Newspaper Publisher. Samuel Cornish was born in Sussex County, Delaware, in 1795. Ordained as an evangelist by the Presbyterian Church, Cornish acted as an advocate for African Americans through the mouthpiece of the newspaper he cofounded with John Russwurm, *Freedom's Journal.* The paper, which was launched in March 1827, countered racist propaganda and served as a means of communication for African Americans. Cornish changed the paper's name to *Rights of All* in May 1829, and the newspaper ceased publication later that year.

Cornish continued editing after the demise of the publication, serving as editor of the *Weekly Advocate* (later known as the *Colored American*) from 1837 to 1838. He was also involved with the African Free Schools, the Negro convention movement, the American Anti-Slavery Society, and the American Missionary Society. Cornish died on November 6, 1858, in Brooklyn, New York.

DAVID E. DRIVER (1955–)

Book Publisher, Writer, Social Activist, Investor. David E. Driver was born on October 17, 1955, and grew up on Chicago's West side. Because of his excellent grades, he attended Lindblom High School, an exceptional public trade school. From there, he earned a bachelor of arts degree from Bradley University in Peoria, Illinois, and after he passed the certified public accountant exam, he joined Arthur Young and Company as a staff accountant. In 1978, Driver took a job at the International Hospital Supply Corporation. Until 1980, Driver worked as a finance manager, specializing in foreign currency markets. He was then employed at Merrill Lynch Capital Markets, where he was promoted to vice president in 1982. While working in stock and bond futures, he received his MBA from the University of Chicago in 1984.

In 1988, with $250,000 and one book that he had written himself—*The Good Heart Book: A Guide to Volunteering*—he founded the Noble Press. Within three years, he had a staff of five, a renovated loft for office space, and books receiving critical attention. The book that earned the Noble Press its reputation was the 1993 release *Volunteer Slavery: My Authentic Negro Experience* by Janet Nelson, which sold forty thousand hardcover copies. Driver sold the paperback rights to Penguin, for whom it became a national best seller and earned an American Book Award in 1994.

By 1993, Noble's annual sales had reached the million-dollar mark, and its distribution outlets grew to six thousand. Driver founded the Black Literary Society, a book club that posted reading lists on the Internet. Driver also started Young Chicago Authors, a workshop program for aspiring teenage authors. In addition, Driver wrote *Defending the Left: An Individual's Guide to Fighting for Social Justice, Individual Rights, and the Environment*, published in 1992. He has served as secretary of the Society of Illinois Book Publishers and is a founding member of the National Association of Black Book Publishers. In the late 1990s, Driver returned to the financial services industry. He launched Visionary Forex, a Web site for investors, in 2009.

TIMOTHY THOMAS FORTUNE (1856–1928)

Newspaper Publisher. Born on October 3, 1856, in Marianna, Florida, Timothy Thomas Fortune was one of the most prominent African American journalists involved in the flourishing African American press of the post–Civil War era. The son of a Reconstruction politician, Fortune was particularly productive before his thirtieth year, completing such works as *Black and White: Land, Labor, and Politics in the South* (1884) and the pamphlet *The Negro in Politics* (1885) while in his twenties.

Fortune attended Howard University for two years, leaving to marry Carrie Smiley of Jacksonville, Florida. The couple moved to New York in 1878, with Fortune taking a job as a printer for the *New York Sun*. In time, Fortune caught the attention of *Sun* editor Charles A. Dana, who eventually promoted him to the editorial staff of the paper.

Fortune also edited the *Globe*, an African American daily, and was later chief editorial writer for the *Negro World*. In 1900, Fortune joined Booker T. Washington in helping to organize the successful National Negro Business League. His later activity with Washington gained him more notoriety than his earlier writing, although his written work is more vital in affording him an important niche in the history of African American protest.

In 1883, Fortune founded the *New York Age*, the paper with which he sought to "champion the cause" of his race. In time, the *Age* became the leading black journal of opinion in the United States. One of Fortune's early crusades was against segregation in the New York educational system.

Fortune was later responsible for coining the term *Afro-American* as a substitute for *Negro* in New York newspapers. He also set up the Afro-American Council, an organization that he regarded as the precursor of the Niagara Movement. In 1907, Fortune sold the *Age*, although he remained active in journalism as an editorial writer for several African American newspapers. He died on June 2, 1928.

MALVIN R. GOODE (1908–1995)

Television News Correspondent. Malvin Russell Goode had been with the *Pittsburgh Courier* for fourteen years when in 1962 he joined ABC to cover the United Nations. His first test was the Cuban missile crisis, during which Goode distinguished himself with incisive television and radio reports during the long hours of UN debate.

Goode was born in White Plains, Virginia, in 1908. He was educated in the public schools of Homestead, Pennsylvania, and graduated from the University of Pittsburgh in 1931. He worked for twelve years as a laborer in the steel mills while in high school and college and for five years after graduation. In 1936, he was appointed to a post in juvenile court and became boys work director of the Centre Avenue YMCA, where he led the fight to eliminate discrimination in Pittsburgh branches of the YMCA.

Goode worked for the Pittsburgh Housing Authority for six years and in 1948 joined the *Pittsburgh Courier*, a prominent African American newspaper. The following year he started a career in radio with station KQV, doing a fifteen-minute news show two nights each week. In 1950, he started a five-minute daily news program on WHOD.

Goode became news director at WHOD in 1952. He and his sister, Mary Dee, were the only brother-sister team in radio for six years. Goode was the first African American to hold membership in the Radio and Television News Directors Association and the first African American correspondent to appear on network television news.

For two months in 1963, Goode joined three colleagues to conduct courses in journalism for African students in seminars at Lagos, Nigeria; Addis Ababa, Ethiopia; and Dar es Salaam, Tanzania. On September 12, 1995, Goode died of a stroke in Pittsburgh.

ED GORDON (1960–)

Television Anchor and Host. Born Edward Lansing Gordon III in Detroit, Michigan, the future journalist was inspired to achieve by his mother, who was a schoolteacher, and his father, who was the 1932 Olympic gold medalist in the long jump. Gordon's father passed away when his son was eleven. After graduating with a degree in communications and political science from Western Michigan University in 1982, Gordon moved back to Detroit to launch his career in broadcasting.

Several years after serving an unpaid internship in 1983 with Detroit's public broadcasting affiliate, Gordon landed him a job as host of the station's *Detroit Black Journal.* During that time, he also began freelance reporting for an upstart cable network called Black Entertainment Television (BET), based in Washington, D.C. In 1988, BET hired him as an anchor and chief correspondent for their weekly news program, *BET News.* Gordon joined NBC News in 1996 as host of the Saturday edition of *Internight*, a one-hour talk and interview program on MSNBC. He also served as a daytime anchor for MSNBC and contributing correspondent for *Dateline NBC.*

Gordon was a visible presence on BET, interviewing prominent African Americans on his *Conversations with Ed Gordon* show and hosting programs of special interest, such as *Black Men Speak Out: The Aftermath*, which aired in the wake of the 1992 Los Angeles riots. During his tenure on *Conversations with Ed Gordon*, he interviewed two U.S. presidents and South African president Nelson Mandela, as well as more outspoken figures, such as Al Sharpton and Nation of Islam leader Louis Farrakhan. Gordon also hosted the BET staple *Lead Story*, anchored several *BET News* specials, and hosted the critically acclaimed interview series *Personal Diary.* Though the demands of the job at BET were arduous, Gordon derived special satisfaction from his work in journalism when young African American males pointed out to him that they never were interested in the news before his programs began airing.

In 1996, Gordon broke out of the mold of cable television news when he was selected as the first journalist to interview O. J. Simpson after Simpson was found not guilty of killing his ex-wife and a male friend. This boosted Gordon's overall image as a journalist and showed the public and executives at more prominent news organizations what he was capable of. Later in 1996, NBC hired Gordon on with a three-year $1.5 million contract. Gordon continued to work part time at BET, but left the network in 2002. He thereafter became a correspondent for National Public Radio, and in 2004 CBS hired him as a *60 Minutes* contributor. In March 2010, BET announced that Gordon would be returning to the network's news division.

EARL G. GRAVES (1935–)

Publisher and Media Executive. In the 1970s, Earl Graves emerged as one of America's leading publishers and exponents of black entrepreneurship. Within a few short years, his magazine *Black Enterprise* was accepted as the authority on African Americans in business and as an important advocate for an active, socially responsive, African American middle class. Yearly sales of the magazine exceeded $17 million in 2002. In 2010, *Black Enterprise* claimed a monthly readership of 4.3 million.

Born in Brooklyn in 1935, Graves graduated from Morgan State College in 1958 with a bachelor of arts degree in economics. In 1965, he was hired to a position on the staff of Robert Kennedy, then a senator from New York. In 1968, Graves organized Earl Graves Associates, which served as a consultant on urban affairs and African American economic development and became the publisher of *Black Enterprise.* Graves also served as president and chief executive officer of Earl G. Graves Ltd., Earl G. Graves Marketing and Research Company, and Earl G. Graves Development Company. In December 1998, he named his eldest son president of the Earl G. Graves Publishing Company.

Graves published his autobiography, *How to Succeed in Business without Being White: Straight Talk on Making It in America*, in 1997. Graves also served as president of EGG Dallas Broadcasting, which operates KNOK-AM and KNOK-FM in Fort Worth, Texas, and as chairman and president of Pepsi-Cola of Washington, D.C.

In 1998, Graves started Black Enterprise Unlimited, a service that focuses on the business, financial, and lifestyle needs of African American business professionals. In 1999, Graves was honored by the NAACP with the Spingarn Medal for his contributions to business, his commitment to education, and his support of civil and human rights. During the first decade of the twenty-first century, Graves continued his efforts to develop the African American business community. He also supported the wider community through scholarships and community service.

BRYANT GUMBEL (1948–)

Television Anchor. Bryant Gumbel, the popular newscaster who gained fame as coanchor of the *Today* show, was born in New Orleans, Louisiana, on September 29, 1948, but grew up in Chicago. He received a liberal arts degree from Bates College in Lewiston, Maine, in 1970.

Before embarking on his career in television, Gumbel was a sportswriter. After submitting his first piece to *Black Sports* magazine in 1971, he was given additional freelance assignments and was soon hired as a staff writer. Within eight months, he was elevated to editor in chief.

Gumbel began his broadcasting career in October 1972 when he became a weekend sportscaster for KNBC, the NBC station in Burbank, California. Within a year, he became weekday sportscaster and was appointed the station's sports director in 1976. He remained in that post until 1981. Gumbel made regular sports reports with NBC Sports as the host of pregame programming during coverage of the National Football League, Major League Baseball, and other sports broadcasts. Gumbel debuted as host of HBO's *Real Sports* on April 2, 1995.

In January 1982, Gumbel replaced Tom Brokaw as coanchor of the *Today* show on NBC opposite Jane Pauley. In 1997, after fifteen years and at the height of the show's popularity, he relinquished his position. During his tenure at *Today*, Gumbel distinguished himself as a steadfast anchor, gifted interviewer, and role model for minority journalists. A bidding war for his services erupted between all major networks in the months following his departure. In the end, Gumbel signed a five-year contract with CBS News that netted him $5 million a year and his own prime-time news magazine, *Public Eye with Bryant Gumbel*, which was canceled in 1998. Gumbel also agreed to do three specials each year, and was given CBS stock options and his own company for syndicated programming development. In 1999, Gumbel became anchor of *The Early Show*, CBS's daily morning show. Two and a half years later, Gumbel

Television Journalist Bryant Gumbel, 1999. *Participating here in a news conference with Andrew Heyward (left), president of CBS News, Gumbel is best known as the longtime cohost of NBC's* Today *show. Gumbel later joined CBS, where he was involved in several programs, including the prime-time newsmagazine* Public Eye with Bryant Gumbel. AP PHOTO/MARTY LEDERHANDLER

announced that he was leaving CBS when his contract expired in May 2002. He continued to host *Real Sports* for HBO. From 2005 to 2008, Gumbel was play-by-play announcer for the NFL. In December 2009, Gumbel announced that he was being treated for lung cancer.

GREG GUMBEL (1946–)

Radio and Television Sportscaster. The older brother of Bryant Gumbel, Greg Gumbel was born on May 3, 1946, in New Orleans, Louisiana. With his friendly face and affable disposition, Gumbel has graced the airways for over twenty years. He has covered local sports for WMAQ-TV in Chicago, hosted ESPN's *SportsCenter*, done play-by-play for the Madison Square Garden Network, and served as host for CBS's *The NFL Today*.

Gumbel began working as a sports announcer for CBS in 1988. He moved to NBC in 1994, but returned to CBS four years later as host and play-by-play announcer. Gumbel has worked with some of sports television's biggest names, including Terry Bradshaw, John Madden, Mike Ditka, Joe Montana, Bill Walton, and Joe Morgan. He has also worked on many large-scale sports events: the Super Bowl, the World Series, NBA and NCAA basketball championships, and the Olympics, both summer and winter. In 2006, he became a play-by-play announcer for the NFL.

Gumbel is a popular public speaker, and he has addressed students at schools across the country, as well as various chambers of commerce and town-hall gatherings, Boy Scouts organizations, the Anti-Defamation League, and March of Dimes groups. In 2007, Gumbel was honored with the Pat Summerall Award for sports broadcasting.

RAGAN A. HENRY (1934–2008)

Broadcast and Newspaper Executive. Ragan Augustus Henry was president of Broadcast Enterprises National, Inc., and former publisher of the *National Leader*, an African American national newspaper launched in May 1982, both headquartered in Philadelphia. Henry was also founder of U.S. Radio, the largest African American–owned radio group in the nation with twenty-five stations. In 1996, it was sold for $140 million to Clear Channel Communications of San Antonio, Texas.

Born in Sadiesville, Kentucky, on February 2, 1934, Henry received his bachelor of arts degree from Harvard College in 1956 and his law degree from Harvard Law School in 1961. He also attended graduate school at Temple University in 1963. From 1964 to 1977, Henry was a partner in the Philadelphia firm of Goodis, Greenfield, Henry, and Edelstein, before becoming a partner at Wolf, Black, Schorr, and Solis-Cohen, also of Philadelphia.

Henry was a lecturer at LaSalle College from 1971 to 1973, and in 1979 he became a visiting professor at Syracuse University's S.I. Newhouse School of Communications. He served on the boards of directors of Continental Bank, Abt Associates, the National Association of Black Owned Broadcasters (as president of the board), LaSalle College, and the Hospital of the University of Pennsylvania. He was also chairman of the John McKee Scholarship Committee Fellowships of the Noyes and Whitney Foundation.

In the late 1990s, Henry was honored by the Broadcasters Foundation Board of Directors with an American Broadcast Pioneer Award for his contributions to the broadcasting industry and his community. The Minority Media and Telecommunications Council gave Henry its Everett C. Parker Award in 2006. He died in 2008.

BOB HERBERT (1945–)

Journalist, Author. Born in Brooklyn, New York, in 1945, journalist Bob Herbert began his career with the *Star Ledger* of Newark, New Jersey, in 1970, and by 1973 he was the night city editor. Building upon his success in New Jersey, Herbert recrossed the Hudson River, where he joined the staff of the *Daily News* (New York) and wrote columns from 1976 until 1985. In 1988, after gaining a B.S. in journalism from Empire State College, Herbert expanded his career to television, where he was a founding panelist for *Sunday Edition* on CBS and a national correspondent for NBC from 1991 to 1993.

Since 1993, Herbert has written op-ed columns for the *New York Times*. A Manhattan resident, Herbert has chaired a jury for the Pulitzer Prize and has taught journalism at Brooklyn College and Columbia University's Graduate School of Journalism. In 2005, he published *Promises Betrayed: Waking Up from the American Dream.*

CHERYL WILLIS HUDSON (1948–)

Publishing Executive. Cheryl Willis Hudson and her husband, Wade Hudson, founded Just Us Books in 1988 to publish children's books and learning materials that focus on the African American experience. Just Us Books quickly became one of the leading publishers of African American books for young people. The company has garnered numerous awards, including the Parents' Choice Award, the Ben Franklin Award, the Multicultural Publishers' Exchange Award, and the American Booksellers Association/Blackboard Best Seller

Award. In 2006, Just Us Books was named Publisher of the Year by the African American Pavilion of Book Expo America.

Besides serving as publisher of Just Us Books, Hudson is an author of children's books. Her works include *Bright Eyes, Brown Skin* (1990), *Good Night, Baby* (1992), *Good Morning, Baby* (1992), *Hold Christmas in Your Heart: African-American Songs, Poems, and Stories for the Holidays* (1995), *The Harlem Renaissance: Profiles in Creativity* (2002), *Construction Zone* (2006), and *From Where I Stand: In the City* (2008). In 2003, she was inducted into the International Literary Hall of Fame for Writers of African Descent.

A native of Portsmouth, Virginia, Cheryl Willis Hudson graduated cum laude from Oberlin College in 1970. She also studied at Northeastern University, the Arts Students League, and Parsons School of Design. Prior to founding Just Us Books, she worked as an art editor and designer for several publishers, including Houghton Mifflin, Macmillan Publishing, Arete Publishing, and Paperwing Press/Angel Entertainment.

WADE HUDSON (1946–)

Publishing Executive. Wade Hudson is the president and chief executive officer of Just Us Books, a company that he cofounded with his wife, Cheryl Willis Hudson, in 1988 to publish children's books and learning material that focus on the African American experience. Hudson is a native of Mansfield, Louisiana. He attended Southern University in Baton Rouge and has worked with numerous civil rights organizations, including the Congress of Racial Equality (CORE), the Southern Christian Leadership Conference, and the Society for Opportunity, Unity, and Leadership, which he cofounded. Hudson also worked as a public relations specialist for Essex County and Kean colleges in New Jersey.

As publishing professionals and advocates of diversity in literature, Hudson and his wife conduct workshops and make presentations and appearances on panels across the country. They address such topics as entrepreneurship in publishing, the nuts and bolts of building a publishing company, creative packaging of Afrocentric children's books, and the publishing of multicultural books for children and young adults. Hudson has written and edited numerous books for children, including *In Praise of Our Fathers and Our Mothers: A Black Family Treasury by Outstanding Authors and Artists* (1997), *Powerful Words: More than 200 Years of Extraordinary Writing by African Americans* (2004), *The Underground Railroad* (2005), *Puddin', Jeffrey, and Leah: Best Friends* (2008), and *It's Church Going Time* (2008).

CATHERINE LIGGINS HUGHES (1947–)

Broadcasting Executive. Cathy Liggins Hughes was born Catherine Elizabeth Woods in Omaha, Nebraska, on April 22, 1947. As founder and owner of Radio One, Inc., Hughes and her son, Alfred C. Liggins III, the president and CEO, run the largest African American owned and operated broadcast company in the nation. Headquartered in Lanham, Maryland, Radio One is the first African American company in radio history to dominate in several major markets simultaneously—Atlanta, Baltimore, the District of Columbia, Detroit, and Philadelphia—and the first female-owned radio station to have ranked number one in any major market.

After taking the company public in 1999, Hughes became the first African American woman to head a firm publicly traded on a U.S. stock exchange. In 2000, *Black Enterprise* named Radio One "Company of the Year."

Broadcasting Entrepreneur Cathy Hughes, 2008. *Hughes is the founder of Radio One, Inc., the largest African American–owned radio broadcasting company in the nation.* MICHAEL TRAN/FILMMAGIC/GETTY IMAGES

Fortune rated it one of the "100 Best Companies to Work For," and it was inducted into the Maryland Business Hall of Fame.

In August 2000, Radio One purchased KBBT, "The Beat," in Los Angeles for $430 million and put actor and comedian Steve Harvey at the helm of the morning slot. The decision to hire Harvey was carefully researched. After studying the Los Angeles market, Hughes determined that he was one of the few individuals capable of turning the urban radio market around. Furthermore, she knew that advertisers had begun to realize that urban listeners were consumers with considerable spending power. Her hard work and knowledge about the urban market played a major role in the success of Harvey's show, which aired in Los Angeles until 2005.

Moving to Washington, D.C., in 1971 after a successful stint with KOWH, a black radio station in Omaha, Hughes became a lecturer in the newly established School of Communications at Howard university. She began working for the university's radio station, WHUR-FM, in 1973, as general sales manager, and is noted for increasing station revenue from $250,000 to $3 million in her first year. In 1975, she became the first female vice president and general manager of the station. During her tenure, she created the romantic evening radio format known as Quiet Storm—the most popular nighttime radio format, now heard in numerous markets nationally.

Hughes purchased her first station, WOL-AM in Washington, D.C., with her second husband, Dewey Hughes, in 1980. At WOL-AM, she pioneered yet another innovative format: twenty-four-hour talk from a black perspective. As creator of the first twenty-four-hour talk-radio station to cover news from an African American perspective, Hughes championed black causes. Outspoken, opinionated, and often controversial as host of her own program on WOL-AM for fourteen years, Hughes criticized utility companies for their shut-off policies, encouraged listeners to buy black art and to donate money to charitable causes, and led on-air protests against negative portrayals of blacks in the media. She also vehemently spoke out on such topics as the loss of black-owned farms, the adoption of black children by non-blacks, and equal pay for women.

For her dedication to minority communities, her entrepreneurial spirit, and her mentoring of women, Hughes was honored with the Lifetime Achievement Award from the Washington Area Broadcasters Association. She has also received the Seventh Congressional District Humanitarian Award, along with the Ron Brown Business of the Year Award by the Department of Commerce, the Baltimore NAACP's Parren J. Mitchell Award, the Mayor's Recognition Award, and the Everett C. Parker Award. In 2001, she received the National Association of Broadcasters's Distinguished Service Award and the Silver Medal Award from the Ad Club for "having furthered the advertising industry's standards, creative excellence and responsibility in areas of social concern." Remaining steadfast in her decision to buy black-owned radio stations that are threatened by industry consolidation, Hughes purchased the Bell Broadcasting System based in Detroit in 1997 and Blue Chip Broadcasting based in Cincinnati in 2001. With these purchases, Radio One became known as a company that could quickly turn around underperforming stations. In 2010, Radio One owned or operated fifty-three radio stations in sixteen urban markets in the United States, making it one of the largest radio broadcasting companies in the country, and the largest targeting African American and urban listeners.

Although the company has grown tremendously over the years, Hughes has said that the foundation of Radio One is based on the spirit of a family that strives to serve as the heart of the community, as well as the pulse of urban radio. In 2004, Hughes launched TV One, Inc., in partnership with Comcast, the nation's largest pay-television provider. TV One caters to adult African Americans, offering quality programming and an array of original programming. Hughes, who serves on the board of TV One, is the executive producer of *Gospel of Music with Jeff Majors*. She also hosts *TV One on One*, an interview show.

CHARLAYNE HUNTER-GAULT
(1942–)

Radio and Television Correspondent. Charlayne Hunter-Gault is a foreign correspondent for National Public Radio. Before this, she was based Johannesburg, South Africa, where she served as bureau chief for CNN from 1999 to 2005. Hunter-Gault has staked her claim as one of the leading American journalists, having won many of the top honors in her field for excellence in investigative reporting. One of the springboards into her career came when she was the subject of a journalistic investigation at the height of the civil rights era. In 1961, she became one of the first two black students at the University of Georgia, from which she received a bachelor of arts degree in 1963.

Prior to joining *The MacNeil/Lehrer Report* (later *The NewsHour with Jim Lehrer*) in 1978, Hunter-Gault held positions with the *New Yorker*, WRC-TV in Washington, D.C., and the *New York Times*. She was *The MacNeil/Lehrer Report*'s first woman anchor. Her memoir, *In My Place*, was published in 1992.

Born on February 27, 1942, in Due West, South Carolina, Hunter-Gault built a reputation as a keen investigator of social injustice, especially among African Americans. Until 1997, she was the national correspondent for *The NewsHour with Jim Lehrer*, the hour-long evening news program broadcast nightly on the Public Broadcasting Service (PBS). She also anchored *Rights and Wrongs: Human Rights Television*, a weekly half-hour newsmagazine on PBS that incorporated news, investigative reports, interviews, features, and cultural segments to examine human rights issues worldwide.

Hunter-Gault left PBS in 1997 to join her husband, Ronald Gault, a managing director of J.P. Morgan in South Africa, where she serves as a correspondent for National Public Radio. In 2000, she became the Johannesburg Bureau Chief for CNN, a post she held until 2005.

Hunter-Gault is the recipient of numerous awards, including two national news and documentary Emmy Awards and two prestigious George Foster Peabody Awards for excellence in broadcast journalism for her work on *The NewsHour's* Apartheid People series on contemporary life in South Africa, as well as her coverage on NPR of South Africa's move toward a black government. She was also honored in 2001 by the University of Georgia, which named its Holmes-Hunter Academic Building in honor of her work to end segregation at the university.

GWEN IFILL (1955–)

Journalist, Editor, Anchor. Born in New York City in 1955, Gwendolyn Ifill is the moderator and managing editor of the PBS weekly show *Washington Week*, the longest-running prime-time news program in the history of television. She is also a senior correspondent for *The PBS NewsHour.* Before PBS hired her in 1999, Ifill had worked as a correspondent for NBC News, the *New York Times*, the *Washington Post*, the *Baltimore Evening Sun*, and the *Boston Herald American*.

During her extensive and widely celebrated career as a journalist, Ifill has moderated the 2004 and 2008 vice presidential debates, covered six presidential campaigns, and in 2009 published a best-selling book, *The Breakthrough: Politics and Race in the Age of Obama*. An alumna of Simmons College in Boston, Ifill has received more than a dozen honorary doctorates and has been recognized by *Ebony* magazine as one of the 150 most influential African Americans.

EUGENE D. JACKSON (1943–)

Broadcasting Executive. Eugene D. Jackson began his entrepreneurial career in 1971 by raising $1 million to launch the Unity Broadcasting Network, parent company of the National Black Network. It was the first hourly news service distributed via satellite to African American–oriented radio stations. Jackson is also past president of Unity Broadcasting Network and four radio stations: WDAS-AM and WDAS-FM in Philadelphia and KATZ-AM and WZEN-FM in St. Louis.

Jackson was born in Waukomis, Oklahoma, on September 5, 1943. He received a bachelor of science degree in electrical engineering from the University of Missouri at Rolla in 1967 and a master of business administration from Columbia University in 1971. Jackson was an industrial engineer for Colgate-Palmolive from 1967 to 1968 and a production and project engineer for the Black Economic Union in New York City from 1968 to 1969. From 1969 to 1971, Jackson directed major industry programs for the Interracial Council for Business Opportunity in New York City.

Jackson has served on the boards of directors of the National Association of Broadcasters, the Council of Concerned Black Executives, Freedom National Bank, and TransAfrica. He was a member of the Council on Foreign Relations in 1978 and on the board of governors of the International Radio and Television Society from 1974 to 1976.

Jackson divested his interest in broadcasting to develop and invest in cable television, the cellular telephone business, and the Internet. In 1993, he formed the World African Network, and served as chairman and chief executive officer. He later became vice chairman and the largest single shareholder in the Queens Inner-Unity Cable System, a multimillion-dollar cable system serving the borough of Queens in New York as a joint venture with Time Warner, Inc.

JOHN H. JOHNSON (1918–2005)

Publisher, Media Executive. One of America's foremost businessmen, John Harold Johnson led the most prosperous and powerful African American publishing company in the United States. Beginning with *Negro Digest* in 1942 and following with *Ebony* in 1945, Johnson built a chain of journalistic successes that later included *Jet*, *EM: Ebony Man*, and *Ebony South Africa*, which marked the company's foray into international publishing.

Along with the development of these publications, Johnson bought and sold three radio stations, started a book-publishing division, and produced a syndicated television show, *Ebony/Jet Showcase*. He also created two beauty-care lines—Supreme Beauty Products and Fashion Fair Cosmetics—as well as the Ebony Fashion Fair, a traveling fashion show. In addition, he produced the annual American Black Achievement Awards for television, which first aired in 1978.

Johnson was born in Arkansas City, Arkansas, on January 19, 1918. He lost his father, a millworker, when he was six years old and was raised by his mother and stepfather. He attended local segregated schools until the family moved to Chicago, where he became a student at DuSable High School. Johnson excelled in academics and in extracurricular activities while writing for the yearbook and school paper.

In 1936, Johnson was invited to deliver a speech at a banquet given by the National Urban League to honor outstanding high school students. Harry H. Pace, president of Supreme Liberty Life Insurance, heard the speech and was so impressed that he offered Johnson a job, which enabled him to attend the University of Chicago part time on a scholarship. After two years at the University of Chicago, Johnson entered the Northwestern University School of Commerce, studying for an additional two years while continuing to work for Supreme Liberty.

While serving as editor of Supreme Liberty's company newspaper, it occurred to Johnson that a weekly or monthly digest of news of special interest to the African American community might achieve a wide readership. The idea resulted in the creation of *Negro Digest*, a periodical containing both news reprints and feature articles. In 1943, First Lady Eleanor Roosevelt contributed an essay, "If I Were a Negro," to the digest, which spurred circulation. Buoyed by success, Johnson decided to approach the market with yet another offering, a pictorial magazine patterned after *Life*. The first issue of *Ebony* sold out its press run of 25,000 copies and soon became a staple in the world of journalism as large companies began to advertise regularly in it.

In addition to serving as publisher and chief executive officer of Johnson Publishing Company, Johnson became chairman and chief executive officer of Supreme Life Insurance Company, chairman of WJPC-AM in Chicago, and president of Fashion Fair Cosmetics. He also served on the boards of directors of the Greyhound Corporation, Verex Corporation, Marina Bank, Supreme Life Insurance Company, and Zenith Radio Corporation. In addition, Johnson served as a trustee for the Art Institute of Chicago and United Negro College Fund, on the advisory council of the Harvard Graduate School of Business, as a director for the Chamber of Commerce of the United States, and on the advertising councils of Junior Achievement and the Chicago USO. Along the way, Johnson received honorary doctorates from Howard, Harvard, Morehouse, Northwestern, and numerous other colleges and universities, as well as honors and awards from many civil and professional organizations, such as the Against All Odds Award, the Making History Award, and the Trumpet Award.

Johnson published *Succeeding Against the Odds: The Autobiography of a Great American Business* in 1989. In 1996, President Bill Clinton awarded Johnson the Medal of Freedom. In 2001, Johnson became the first African American inducted into the Arkansas Business Hall of Fame. The School of Communications at Howard University was renamed the John H. Johnson School of Communications in 2003 after Johnson pledged $4 million to the university. The John H. Johnson Cultural and Educational Museum in Arkansas City opened in May 2005, shortly before Johnson's death in August 2005.

ROBERT L. JOHNSON (1946–)

Cable Television Executive, Publisher, Businessman. Born on April 8, 1946, in Hickory, Mississippi, Robert Louis Johnson graduated from the University of Illinois in 1968 and earned a master's degree in public administration in 1972 from Princeton University. He worked for the Urban League in Washington, D.C., for the Corporation for Public Broadcasting, and as a press secretary for Walter E. Fauntroy, the congressional delegate from the District of Columbia, before joining the National Cable Television Association in 1976.

While serving as vice president of government relations for the association, Johnson came up with the idea of creating a cable channel aimed at African American viewers. In 1979, he took out a $15,000 personal loan to start Black Entertainment Television (BET), a component of the parent company, BET Holdings, Inc. As the founder, chairman, and chief executive officer, Johnson molded the station into an extremely popular twenty-four-hour cable station with shows that catered to the interests of African Americans. In 2010, BET reached more than eighty-nine million households, and could be seen across the United States and in Canada and the Caribbean.

Under Johnson's leadership, BET Holdings also operated four other major cable channels: BET on Jazz: The Cable Station; BET on Jazz International, a twenty-four-hour jazz program service; BET Movies, the first twenty-four-hour all-black movie channel; and BET Action pay-per-view.

BET Holdings also ventured into businesses outside of the cable industry, including a publishing division that produced *Emerge: Black America's News Magazine*, *BET Weekend*, and *Heart & Soul*, a health, fitness, and beauty magazine. BET's Arabesque Books became the first line of original African American romance novels written by African American authors. Other businesses have included MSBET, an interactive Web site based on a joint venture with Microsoft Corporation; BET Soundstage, a music theme restaurant; BET Soundstage Club, a joint venture with Walt Disney World Resort at Disney's Pleasure Island in Orlando, Florida; and BET on Jazz Restaurant, a fine dining establishment specializing in new world cuisine.

In 1998, Johnson announced a venture to make low-budget films with African American stars, financed and produced by African Americans and largely aimed at the African American urban market. His initial plans included showcasing motion pictures and made-for-television films based on Arabesque books. Johnson also continued to diversify his investments, buying DC Airlines in 2000, making him the first African American to own a commercial airline. In 2001, Johnson served on a federal commission to change the Social Security system.

In addition to running BET, Johnson served on the boards of directors of US Airways, the Hilton Hotels Corporation, the United Negro College Fund, the National Cable Television Association's Academy of Cable Programming, the American Film Institute, and the Advertising Council. He received the Business Leader of the Year award from *Washingtonian* magazine (1998); *Broadcasting and Cable* magazine's Hall of Fame Award (1997); the Business of the Year Award from the Washington, D.C., Chamber of Commerce (1985); and the Pioneer Award from the Capitol Press Club (1984). Other awards include an NAACP Image Award (1982), a Distinguished Alumni Award from Princeton University, and the President's Award from the National Cable Television Association (1982).

In 2000, Johnson sold BET to Viacom for nearly $3 billion, making him the country's first African American billionaire. He remained with the company as CEO until January 2006, when he retired. After selling BET, Johnson founded RLJ Development, a hotel investment firm that became a division of RLJ Companies, a group of companies involved in banking, financial services, sports, real estate, film production, gaming, and the automotive industry.

CLARENCE B. JONES (1931–)

Publishing Executive. Born in Philadelphia in 1931, Clarence Benjamin Jones graduated from Columbia University and Boston University Law School and then practiced as an attorney, specializing in civil rights and copyright cases for a New York City law firm. During this period, he was counsel for Dr. Martin Luther King Jr. and the Southern Christian Leadership Conference. In 1968 and again in 1972, he served as a delegate from New York State to the Democratic Convention. Jones was also an observer at Attica Prison during the uprising there in 1971. In 1971, as head of Inner City Broadcasting, Jones led a group of investors in the purchase of the New York *Amsterdam News*, the nation's largest African American newspaper. Inner City Broadcasting also owned radio stations WLIB and WBLS-FM.

In 2005, Jones became executive adviser to Marks, Paneth and Shron (MPS), a financial services firm headquartered in New York. He also became a member of the MPS Strategy Group and a principal in MPS's Africa Strategy Group. In additional areas, he has served as senior partner of Clemensen Capital Company, an investment banking firm specializing in cross-border finance for Korea; president and CEO of CBJ Multimedia Associates, a telecommunications firm; and CEO of CBJ Associates, a company specializing in governmental, financial, and corporate banking and financial services. Jones is a scholar-in-residence at Stanford University's Martin Luther King Jr. Research and Education Institute in Palo Alto, California. His book *What Would Martin Say?* was published in 2008.

STAR JONES

See chapter 10, Law..

TOM JOYNER (1949–)

Radio Host. The jingle "Oh, Oh, Oh, It's the Tom Joyner Morning Show" can be heard in urban radio markets across the country on the four-hour syndicated program *The Tom Joyner Morning Show*. The show, hosted by Tom Joyner, debuted in January 1994. Joyner's show reaches more African Americans than any other electronic media. Known as the "Fly Jock, the hardest working man in radio" because he simultaneously hosted the morning show on KKDA in Dallas and the afternoon show for WGCI in Chicago in the 1980s, Joyner keeps audiences captivated with his educational and entertaining material.

Regular program segments include "Little Known Black History Facts," "Thursday Morning Moms," and "Real Fathers, Real Men" (segments in which people can send in a tribute to an exceptional parent and win that person $500). *The Tom Joyner Morning Show* also features live music, comedy, news, and health and relationship advice. Joyner's cohosts include Sybil Wilkes, J. Anthony Brown, Ms. Dupre, and Myra J.

Joyner was born in Tuskegee, Alabama. He graduated from Tuskegee Institute in 1970 with a degree in sociology. Entering radio by accident, Joyner received a job as a newscaster at an African American–owned station in Montgomery, Alabama, not too long after finishing college. While employed at the station and under the tutelage of Tracy Larkin, he learned that radio needs to be involved in the community. In 1996, Joyner and Tavis Smiley coordinated a voter-registration drive that attracted approximately 250,000 African Americans, helping to

Radio Personality Tom Joyner, 2009. *The first African American to be inducted into the Radio Hall of Fame, Joyner since 1994 has hosted a nationally syndicated morning radio show that is heard in more than 100 markets around the United States.* AP PHOTO/DONNA MCWILLIAM

reelect U.S. House members Cynthia McKinney of Georgia and Bennie Thompson of Mississippi after redistricting put them in political jeopardy.

As a graduate of a historically black university, Joyner teamed up with the United Negro College Fund in 1998 and established the Tom Joyner Foundation, a nonprofit organization that awards scholarships to college students in need of financial support. Each month, he announces the college or university that will be the beneficiary. In 1998, Joyner became the first African American inducted into the Radio Hall of Fame. In 2000, he married fitness guru Donna Richardson in Jamaica. Joyner continued to benefit the community when he created an album with various artists, called the *Tom Joyner All-stars*, in 2001. All of the proceeds from the album went to the Tom Joyner Foundation.

Joyner formed REACH Media in 2003 to produce his radio show and other programs of interest to African Americans. In the fall of 2005, Joyner launched a one-hour, nationally syndicated, comedy and variety television show, *The Tom Joyner Show*. The show featured Joyner as emcee and combined sketch comedy by the Tom Joyner Show Players, talent contests, and musical performances. Joyner decided to discontinue the show after one season because of the high production costs.

COLBERT KING (1939–)

Journalist, Columnist. Born in Washington, D.C., in 1939, Colbert King earned his bachelor of arts degree in government from Howard University, and distinguished himself in a military career spanning four decades. In 1990, King joined the editorial board of the *Washington Post*, earning a Pulitzer Prize for Commentary in 2004. King serves as a frequent panelist, columnist, and radio commentator, with a deep interest and expertise in urban and national affairs. His son, Rob King, is editor in chief for the Web site of the cable network ESPN.

DELANO LEWIS (1938–)

Business and Broadcasting Executive. Delano Eugene Lewis was born in Arkansas City, Kansas, on November

12, 1938, and grew up in Kansas City, Kansas. He received his bachelor of arts degree in political science and history from the University of Kansas in 1960 and a law degree from the Washburn University School of Law in 1963. Fresh out of law school, Lewis became one of only ten African American attorneys in the U.S. Department of Justice in Washington, D.C. After two years, he took a post with the Equal Employment Opportunity Commission (EEOC). In 1966, after only one year at the EEOC, he volunteered for the Peace Corps and went to Nigeria and Uganda. Returning from Africa in 1969, Lewis worked as a legislative assistant to various senators and members of Congress and donated his time to advisory boards and community service organizations.

In 1973, Lewis left government and entered the private sector, joining the Chesapeake and Potomac Telephone Company, a subsidiary of Bell Atlantic, as a public affairs manager. Subsequently, he held positions of increasing authority and responsibility, culminating in his election as president in July 1988. In January 1990, he became the chief executive officer. He then vaulted from the top of the telephone company to the role of president and chief executive officer of National Public Radio (NPR) in 1994. NPR, a membership organization of nearly six hundred public radio stations nationwide, produces and distributes the award-winning programs *All Things Considered*, *Talk of the Nation*, and *Weekend Edition*. Lewis's goal was to make NPR "the leading provider of high-quality news, information, and cultural programming worldwide." During his tenure, he focused on three areas—top-quality programming, financial strength, and customer service.

At the invitation of Vice President Al Gore, Lewis served as a cochair of the National Information Infrastructure Advisory Council from 1994 to 1996. Its members consisted of business, industry, academic, and local government leaders. The council provided recommendations to the Clinton administration on how best to develop America's communications network for full citizen participation by 2000.

After a four-year stint as the president and chief executive officer of NPR, Lewis resigned on August 1, 1998, to pursue other interests, including teaching, lecturing, and writing a book about his experiences. In 1999, Lewis was chosen by President Bill Clinton to become the U.S. ambassador to South Africa. He focused his efforts on behalf of the United States on such problems as the HIV epidemic, continued integration, and air travel. He served as ambassador until 2001, when he joined the board of directors at the Colgate-Palmolive Company in New York City. In 2006, Lewis became a senior fellow at New Mexico State University in Las Cruces, where he is founding director of the International Relations Institute.

Lewis has served on many boards of directors, including Black Entertainment Tonight, Halliburton, the Eugene and Agnes Meyer Foundation, Africare, and the Washington Performing Arts Society. He was named Man of the Year by the Greater Washington Board of Trade in 1992 and Washingtonian of the Year by *Washingtonian* magazine in 1978. He was also named to the Sovereign Military Order of Malta in 1987, and was awarded the President's Medal from Catholic University in 1978. Lewis was named 2008 Kansan of the Year by Kansas governor Kathleen Sebelius.

EDWARD T. LEWIS (1940–)

Magazine Publisher, Businessman. Edward T. Lewis was born on May 15, 1940, in the Bronx in New York City. He is the cofounder, chairman, and CEO of Essence Communications Partners (ECP), the corporation that publishes *Essence*, a major magazine for black women. In 2002, Lewis and his partner, Clarence O. Smith, ended their thirty-two-year business partnership after a 2000 merger between Essence Communications and Time Inc., the nation's largest publisher.

This historic partnership was forged to broaden the horizons of both companies. For *Essence*, the venture represented a step toward its global initiative to broaden the scope of its brand. For *Time*, the new relationship served as their entree into the burgeoning minority market, more specifically, African American women, a fast-growing but relatively uncharted area. Retaining 51 percent ownership, Lewis remarked that he saw this partnership as "a bright moment in the history of *Essence*" because it would "enable the company (Essence) to strengthen its brand in the global marketplace and open the doors to numerous media opportunities, while continuing to provide the best information and inspiration to African American women and people of African ancestry around the world."

A New York banker by profession, Lewis yearned to be on his own; he was looking for the right opportunity, which arrived in the form of a seminar for aspiring African American entrepreneurs in 1969. At this seminar, someone suggested that a black women's magazine might have potential because it was an untapped market. Knowing nothing about the publication of magazines and even less about black women, Lewis and his four partners decided to proceed with the project by creating a magazine that promised, in its May 1970 inaugural issue, to "delight and to celebrate the beauty, pride, strength, and uniqueness of all Black women."

Success did not come as quickly as the partners had assumed. The other three partners left within four years of the magazine's debut. Their departures did not deter

Lewis and Smith, who believed that advertisers could be persuaded that African Americans were viable consumers. The first issue of *Essence* contained only thirteen pages of ads out of a total of one hundred pages. The next two issues included only five pages of ads. *Essence* finally brought in enough subscription and advertisement revenue to break even in 1976.

During its first year, *Essence* had a circulation of about 50,000. By 2010, the magazine had a monthly circulation of more than one million and an estimated readership of 8.5 million. *Essence*'s readers tend to be between eighteen and fifty years old; most are women, but the magazine is also popular among African American men. *Essence* circulates primarily by subscription.

Prior to the merger with Time Inc., Lewis and Smith expanded the company into a diversified media corporation that included Essence Entertainment, the Essence Music Festival, the Essence Awards television program, Essence Travel, Essence-by-Mail, Essence Art Reproductions, Essence Books, the Essence.com Web site, and a host of other ventures.

Having served on numerous arts and educational boards throughout his career, Lewis has been recognized by *Black Enterprise* magazine, the National Association of Black Journalists, the American Advertising Federation (Diversity Achievement Role Model Award), the United Negro College Fund (Lifetime Achievement Award), the Democratic Women's Political Caucus (Good Guy Award), the Black Women's Forum (the Men Who Dare Award), Ernst and Young (Entrepreneur of the Year), and many others.

SAMUEL LOGAN JR. (1933–)

Newspaper Publisher. Samuel Logan Jr. was the publisher of the oldest African American newspaper in Michigan, the *Michigan Chronicle*. Logan was born on August 31, 1933, in Louisiana. Initially having worked in the cotton fields of Louisiana, Logan moved to Detroit, where he found employment in a factory. During the Korean War (1950–1953), he volunteered as a paratrooper with the U.S. Army, Eighty-second Airborne Division. After four years of service, he was honorably discharged in 1956. After returning to the United States, three men influenced his life: Frank Seymour, who eventually became his role model, and Tom Cleveland and Robert Leatherwood, the joint owners of Detroit's first African American advertising agency. Logan applied for a position with Cleveland and Leatherwood's agency and was hired to work as a "boy Friday" for $32 a week.

Seymour eventually sold his share of his business to Logan, whose performance had been impressive, making Logan a full partner. Later on, Logan worked as a sales representative with radio stations WCHB-AM and WCHD-FM, founded by another African American pioneer, Dr. Haley Bell. Logan's next move occurred when he joined the *Michigan Chronicle* as assistant to then-advertising manager Tremaine Shearer. Logan rose steadily through the ranks, working as advertising manager, advertising director, vice president of marketing, and general manager. On his way to the top, he took time to acquire a bachelor of arts degree in business administration from the University of Detroit, now the University of Detroit-Mercy, in 1973.

The *Michigan Chronicle* was eventually purchased by Sengstacke Enterprises of Chicago. The company also produced the daily *Chicago Defender*, the *New Pittsburgh Courier*, and the *Tri-State Defender* in Memphis, Tennessee. Logan worked closely with John Sengstacke, owner of Sengstacke Enterprises, and shortly before Sengstacke passed away in 1997, the shareholders of Sengstacke Enterprises voted Logan in as the new president of the company. However, Logan did not formally take over before Sengstacke's death, and Norman Trust, John Sengstacke's trustee, refused to acknowledge Logan's right to run the company. Trust instead gave the title to Sengstacke's children, who were left with a great deal of stock in the company. Logan was so angered that he not only stepped down from the presidency, but he left the *Michigan Chronicle* as well to pursue development of his own newspaper. In 2001, Logan began the African American–oriented paper *Front Page*. Logan returned to the *Michigan Chronicle* as publisher several years later.

During his time as general manager, the *Michigan Chronicle* was voted the best African American newspaper in the country several times by the National Newspaper Publishers Association. In addition, Logan is a member of the NAACP, the Urban League, the Michigan Historical Commission, and the Central Michigan University Scholarship Fund. He has received awards from the Metropolitan Youth Foundation, the Optimist Club of Central Detroit, Omega Psi Phi Fraternity, the State of Michigan-Minority Enterprises, and a host of other groups.

ROLAND MARTIN (1968–)

Journalist, Publisher, Columnist, Television Host. A native of Houston, Texas, Roland S. Martin is a nationally syndicated columnist and a journalist for CNN. Martin attended Texas A&M University, graduating with a bachelor's degree in journalism in 1991. He began his journalism career at the *Austin American-Statesman*, later moving on to the *Fort Worth Star-Telegram*, the *Dallas Weekly*, the *Houston Defender*, *Savory*, and the *Chicago Defender*.

A former owner and publisher of the Christian-based *Dallas–Forth Worth Heritage*, Martin joined CNN in 2007 as a member of its "Best Political Team on Television." Since 2005, he has also been the host of *Washington Watch with Roland Martin*, a Sunday morning news program on the cable network TV One. He has authored three books: *Speak, Brother! A Black Man's View of America* (2002), *Listening to the Spirit Within: 50 Perspectives on Faith* (2007), and *The First: President Barack Obama's Road to the White House* (2010). A dynamic journalist, Martin has garnered numerous awards in recognition of his excellence in journalism. He was recognized by *Ebony* magazine in 2008 and 2009 as one of the 150 Most Influential African Americans.

ROBERT C. MAYNARD (1937–1993)

Journalist, Newspaper Editor and Publisher. The youngest of six children, Robert Clyve Maynard was born on June 17, 1937, in Brooklyn, New York. Reared in a family that stressed higher education, only Maynard chose not to pursue a college career. Instead, he cut classes in high school to spend his time at the editorial offices of the *New York Age*, which published his first articles. The newspaper consumed all of Maynard's attention, and by the time he was sixteen years old, he had dropped out of school.

In 1961, Maynard's first big opportunity arose when Jim Hicks, editor of the *York Gazette and Daily* in Pennsylvania, hired him as a police and urban affairs reporter. Covering a variety of stories, he was eventually assigned to the civil rights movement in the South. Hicks also persuaded Maynard to apply for a one-year Nieman Fellowship for journalists at Harvard University. Maynard was selected for the prestigious award. His second big break occurred at the end of his fellowship. Noticing the broad range of talent that Maynard demonstrated throughout the fellowship program, Ben Bradlee, editor of the *Washington Post*, hired him in 1967. As a result, Maynard became the *Post*'s first black national correspondent.

Maynard became an immediate success at the *Post*. He had a wide range of contacts and free rein to report local and national news. He originated and wrote a powerful five-part series on the growing black militancy, which was published in September 1967. In 1972, he helped cover the Watergate scandal—the illegal break-in of Democratic Party offices by the Republican campaign committee during Richard Nixon's presidency—as well as it consequences.

Robert C. Maynard, Editor, Publisher, and Owner,* Oakland (CA) Tribune, *1991. *Maynard, in 1983, became the first African American to have a controlling interest in a major, general-circulation city daily newspaper.* **AP IMAGES. REPRODUCED BY PERMISSION.**

While at the *Post*, Maynard developed a strong interest in developing training opportunities for minority journalists. In 1972, he and Earl Caldwell, a black reporter for the *New York Times*, codirected a new summer training program in journalism at Columbia University that was funded by the Ford Foundation. When the program was discontinued two years later, Maynard took a leave of absence from the *Post* in 1977 to found a similar program known as the Institute for Journalism Education at the University of California, Berkeley.

Shortly after he founded the institute, the Gannett newspaper chain hired Maynard as an affirmative-action consultant. In 1979, Gannett also appointed him as editor of its newly acquired *Oakland Tribune*, making him the nation's first black director of editorial operations for a major daily newspaper. In spite of his ambitious efforts, the paper struggled financially. When Gannett decided to sell the newspaper, Maynard purchased the *Tribune*. The deal was made possible because of two bank loans and a long-term promissory note to Gannett. As president of the board and owner of 79 percent of the paper's stock, he became the first black person in the United States to have a controlling interest in a major general-circulation city daily.

Though Maynard failed to make the *Tribune* a financial success—primarily because of Oakland's sluggish economy and its proximity to prosperous San Francisco and the booming South Bay—his style permeated the newspaper. A symbol of racial pride under Maynard's leadership, the *Tribune* won a multitude of awards, including a Pulitzer Prize in 1990 for its photographic coverage of the 1989 Bay Area earthquake. For a short time, Maynard was able to sustain the paper with loans and assistance in erasing the original debt from Gannett. Eventually, however, matters worsened, and he became terminally ill, compelling him to sell the paper in 1992 to William Dean Singleton, owner of several newspapers in the Bay Area.

Active in many civic organizations, Maynard served on the board of trustees of the Rockefeller Foundation, the Pacific School of Religion, the Bay Area Council, and the Associated Press. He was also a member of the Pulitzer Prize Committee, the Oakland Chamber of Commerce, the Council on Foreign Relations, and the Sigma Delta Chi Society of Professional Journalists. He held honorary doctorates from York College in Pennsylvania and the California College of Arts and Crafts.

After selling the paper, Maynard kept a busy schedule during his last year of life. He became a faculty member at the Institute for Journalism Education, wrote a syndicated column, and served as a commentator on television news shows. After his death from prostate cancer on August 17, 1993, his life was celebrated in both the Bay Area and Washington, D.C.

ROBERT G. McGRUDER (1942–2002)

Journalist, Newspaper Editor. A champion of diversity, Robert Grandison McGruder, former executive editor of the *Detroit Free Press*, began his distinguished newspaper career in 1963 with the now-defunct *Dayton Journal Herald*. Three months later, he joined the *Cleveland Plain Dealer*. The only black reporter in the newsroom, McGruder once said that this was "both a high and low point" in his career. In 1964, he was drafted into the U.S. Army. After serving in the army for two years in Washington, D.C., he returned to the *Plain Dealer*, where he worked as a reporter, city editor, and managing editor.

While at the *Plain Dealer*, McGruder covered Carl Stokes, the first black mayor of a major city and a colorful political character not unlike Coleman A. Young, Detroit's first black mayor. McGruder's aggressive coverage of Stokes's leadership was the impetus for some of the legendary battles that occurred between Stokes and the Cleveland media. McGruder once traveled to the Bahamas with another reporter to investigate rumors that Stokes was involved in shady business. They found nothing. Eventually, McGruder and Stokes resolved their differences, and McGruder helped him write his 1973 autobiography, *Promises of Power*. In another fact-finding mission, McGruder and another reporter examined city financial records and wrote that Cleveland was going broke. Many residents and officials ignored their conclusion, but shortly thereafter Cleveland became the first large American city to declare bankruptcy.

Before McGruder became an editor at the *Plain Dealer*, he was a labor activist, serving as a negotiator for the Newspaper Guild in its talks with management. He was also one of the leaders of a lengthy strike. After he became city editor in 1978 and managing editor at 1981, the *Plain Dealer* won numerous local, state, and national awards, including two from the National Press Club and one from the Overseas Press Club.

McGruder arrived in Detroit in 1986. It had taken Neal Shine, the longtime managing editor and publisher at the *Detroit Free Press*, more than a decade to hire him. Initially hired as deputy managing editor, McGruder was promoted to managing editor of news in 1987, to managing editor, the second-ranking editor, in 1993, and in 1996 he became the first black executive editor at the *Free Press*. In 1995, while managing editor at the *Free Press*, McGruder became the first black president of the Associated Press Managing Editors (APME), an association of U.S. and Canadian editors whose newspapers are members of the Associated Press. Since 1931, the organization has been dedicated to the improvement, advancement, and promotion of journalism through their newspapers and relationship with the Associated Press.

In each of his positions at the *Free Press*, McGruder talked frequently about the need to diversify newspaper staffs so they could do a better job of covering their constantly evolving communities. He even led a task force for Knight-Ridder, the parent company of the *Free Press*, that resulted in major editing hires across the company. Taking his message to the national boards on which he served, McGruder once said that the best moments of his career were the opportunities to promote African Americans to jobs that had never been held by black people.

When McGruder assumed the position of executive editor, the newspaper was in the midst of a bitter strike. Having been a former labor activist, McGruder quickly learned about the concerns of those on the other side of the picket line. Maintaining his equilibrium throughout this stressful period (the strike did not end until 2000),

Robert G. McGruder, 1998. *During a distinguished career highlighted by his efforts to promote racial diversity in the newspaper industry, McGruder eventually rose to become executive editor of the* Detroit Free Press. *He was also the first African American president of the Associated Press Managing Editors.* NEWSCOM

McGruder remarked that "the strike was easily the most painful time in his life." Part of his pain was caused by the absence of many of the minorities he had worked so hard to hire over the years.

In 2001, McGruder won the John S. Knight Gold Medal, the highest honor given to an employee of Knight-Ridder. "I stand for diversity," he said when he accepted the medal. "I represent the African Americans, Latinos, Arab Americans, Asians, Native Americans ... and all the others we must see represented in our business offices, newsrooms, and newspapers if we truly want to meet the challenge of serving our communities." At the time of the award, Heath Meriwether, publisher of the *Free Press*, called McGruder "a giant in our profession" and praised his leadership at the *Free Press* and nationally as president of APME, as well as in his role as a member of the board of the American Society of Newspaper Editors. Today, many of the people that McGruder hired and nurtured hold important positions at newspapers across the country.

McGruder was a member of several nominating juries for the Pulitzer Prizes and a 1991–1992 Knight-Ridder/Duke University Fellow. He also served as director of the Michigan Press Association, as a member of the advisory board of the Institute for Minority Journalists at Wayne State University, and as a member of the Accrediting Committee of the Accrediting Council on Education in Journalism and Mass Communication.

McGruder was born on March 31, 1942, in Louisville, Kentucky. He graduated from Kent State University in 1963. After a twenty-month battle with cancer, he died on April 12, 2002. After his death, Knight-Ridder established the Robert G. McGruder Scholarship Fund in his memory. The fund supports promising journalism students enrolled at Wayne State University's Journalism Institute for Media Diversity. The company agreed to match all contributions, dollar for dollar, with a minimum grant of $50,000 to a maximum of $100,000. The *Free Press* contributed $10,000 to the fund.

RUSS MITCHELL (1960–)

Journalist, Anchor. A native of St. Louis, Missouri, Russ Mitchell earned his bachelor's degree in journalism from the University of Missouri in 1982. From 1985 until 1992, he served as a regional anchor and reporter. Mitchell joined CBS as a correspondent in 1992, and has appeared on a number of CBS news programs, including *The Early Show* and *Eye to Eye.* In 2006, he was named anchor of the *CBS Evening News, Sunday Edition*, one of the most visible positions in all of broadcast journalism. Mitchell's career is distinguished by a broad range of professional accolades; particularly noteworthy has been his coverage of the Elian Gonzalez case and the crash of TWA Flight 800, for which he was awarded an Emmy in 1997.

CARL J. MURPHY (1889–1967)

Journalist, Publisher, Civil Rights Leader, Educator. Carl James Greenburg Murphy was born in Baltimore, Maryland, on January 17, 1889, to John Henry Murphy and Martha Howard Murphy. He was educated at Howard University (1911), Harvard University (1913), and the University of Jena in Berlin (1913). Murphy served as professor of German and chairman of the German Department at Howard University between 1913 and 1918. In 1918, he joined the staff of the *Baltimore Afro-American*, a weekly newspaper run by this father. Carl Murphy became the editor and publisher of the paper following the death of his father in 1922. He developed it into one of the most widely circulated black newspapers in the nation.

Carl Murphy helped build the Maryland NAACP into one of the largest in the country. Murphy soon became a figure of national stature. As the head of an influential newspaper, he stood with publishing colleagues across black America, including Robert L. Vann at the *Pittsburgh Courier*, C. B. Powell and Phillip M. H. Savory of the *Amsterdam News*, and Robert S. Abbott of the *Chicago Defender*, as the most visible black leaders to whom white politicians and civic leaders often turned when confronted with African American concerns. Murphy's uncompromising stances on racial and social justice led the Federal Bureau of Investigation to monitor him closely in the 1940s, though no charge was ever brought against him.

Following the landmark U.S. Supreme Court decision in *Brown v. Board of Education of Topeka* (1954), Thurgood Marshall publicly acknowledged a debt of gratitude to Murphy. For his efforts on behalf of civil rights, the NAACP awarded Murphy its highest honor, the Spingarn Medal, in 1955. Morgan State University, on whose board Murphy had served as a trustee for decades, named its Fine Arts Center in his honor. Carl Murphy died on February 26, 1967.

JOHN HENRY MURPHY (1840–1922)

Publisher. John Henry Murphy was born enslaved in Baltimore, Maryland, in 1840. He became superintendent of Bethel African Methodist Episcopal Church and founded a Sunday school newspaper called the *Sunday School Helper*. In 1892, Murphy purchased the *Baltimore Afro-American* for $200. By 1922, the *Afro-American* had reached a circulation of 14,000, becoming the largest African American newspaper in the region.

At first, Murphy set the paper's type himself, having acquired this skill in his forties. Throughout, he insisted that his paper maintain political and editorial independence. With his passing on April 5, 1922, Murphy's son Carl took control of the paper.

CLARENCE PAGE (1947–)

Columnist, Author. Clarence Page began writing a column for the *Chicago Tribune* in 1984. His column, which addresses education, politics, economics, prejudice, housing, hunger, and crime, went into syndication in 1987, and now appears in about 150 papers. In 1989, Page won the Pulitzer Prize for Commentary. Based in Washington, D.C., since 1991, Page also did twice-weekly commentary on WGN-TV in Chicago.

Page was born on June 2, 1947, in Dayton, Ohio. He earned a bachelor of science degree in journalism from Ohio University in 1969. Originally joining the *Tribune* as a reporter in 1969, Page's time with the newspaper was brief because he was drafted into the military. He rejoined the *Tribune* in 1971 and resumed his journalism career in a variety of beats, including police, religion, and neighborhood news, with freelance assignments as a rock music critic for *Tempo*.

Page eventually became a foreign correspondent in Africa in 1976 and an investigative task force reporter in

1979. In 1980, he became the director of the community affairs department at WBBM-TV, a CBS-owned television station. At various times, he also assumed the role of documentary producer, reporter, and planning editor.

The highlight of those years occurred when he was assigned to the 1982 protests that evolved into the Harold Washington mayoral campaign. As that history-making story rose in prominence, locally and nationally, so did Page's career. Soon thereafter, he was recognized as a "political expert." In 1984, he returned to the *Tribune* as a columnist and a member of the editorial board.

Over the years, Page's writing has appeared in *Chicago* magazine, the *Chicago Reader*, the *Washington Monthly*, the *New Republic*, the *Wall Street Journal*, *New York Newsday*, the magazine *Emerge*, and other publications. His first book, *Showing My Color: Impolite Essays on Race and Identity*, was published in 1996 and became a best seller in Chicago. He is a regular panelist on *The McLaughlin Group* and a contributor to *The PBS NewsHour*. He has hosted several documentaries for PBS and has served as a commentator on NPR's *Weekend Edition Sunday* and other programs.

Page's awards include a 1980 Illinois UPI award for community service for an investigative series titled *The Black Tax* and the Edward Scott Beck Award for overseas reporting for a 1976 series on the changing politics of southern Africa. Page also participated in a Pulitzer Prize–winning 1972 *Chicago Tribune* task force series on vote fraud. The Illinois and Wisconsin chapters of the American Civil Liberties Union bestowed awards on him for his columns on civil liberties and constitutional rights, and in 1992 he was inducted into the Chicago Journalism Hall of Fame. Page has received honorary degrees from Columbia College in Chicago, Lake Forest College in Illinois, Chicago Theological Seminary, and other institutions of higher education, including his alma mater.

LEONARD PITTS (1957–)

Columnist, Music Critic. Leonard Pitts Jr. was born in Orange, California, and grew up in South Central Los Angeles. He received a bachelor's degree in English from the University of Southern California in 1977. As a college student, Pitts worked as a freelance writer for *SOUL* magazine, and by the age of twenty, he had became its editor. With a profound passion for writing that began in his boyhood, Pitts has followed through on those early stirrings, becoming a prolific writer and critic of popular culture.

In 1991, Pitts joined the *Miami Herald* as its music critic, and soon became a nationally syndicated columnist. As of 2010, his columns are published in more than 150 newspapers. His best-known piece is "We'll Go Forward from This Moment," written following the events of September 11, 2001. He has published two collection of essays, *Becoming Dad: Black Men and the Journey to Fatherhood* (1999) and *Forward from This Moment: Selected Columns, 1994–2008* (2009). He published his first novel, *Before I Forget*, in 2009. Pitts won the Pulitzer Prize for Commentary in 2004.

NORMA QUARLES (1936–)

Television News Correspondent. Born in New York City in 1936, Norma Quarles is an alumna of Hunter College and City College of New York. She first worked as a buyer for a New York specialty shop before moving to Chicago, where she became a licensed real-estate broker.

In 1965, she began her broadcast career in Chicago at WSDM Radio, working as a news reporter and disc jockey. She later returned to New York, where she joined NBC in 1966 for a one-year training program. After three years with WKYC-TV in Cleveland, she was transferred to WNBC-TV in 1970, anchoring the early local news broadcasts during the *Today* show. In 1978, Quarles moved to NBC News as a correspondent based in Chicago. She also began producing and reporting the *Urban Journal* series for WMAQ-TV. In 1988, Quarles left NBC after twenty-one years to join CNN's New York bureau. Quarles served as a daytime anchor at CNN until 1990, when she became a correspondent.

Quarles is a member of the National Academy of Television Arts and Sciences, the National Association of Broadcast Journalists, and Sigma Delta Chi, and a board member of the Governor's National Academy of Television Arts and Sciences. In 1990, Quarles was inducted into the National Association of Black Journalists Hall of Fame. In 1993, she earned a CINE Golden Eagle Award, as well as two New York Association of Black Journalists Awards for a one-hour CNN special on race relations called *A House Divided*, and for a feature report, "The Delany Sisters."

DUDLEY RANDALL (1914–2000)

Publisher, Poet, Librarian. Dudley Randall was born in Washington, D.C., on January 14, 1914, and was living in Detroit by the time he was nine years old. An early harbinger of Randall's poetic talent was the appearance of one of his poems in the *Detroit Free Press* when he was thirteen years old. After serving in the U.S. Army Signal Corps from 1942 to 1946, Randall worked in the foundry at the Ford Motor Company and as a postal carrier and clerk while attending Wayne State University in Detroit. He received his bachelor of arts degree in 1949 and a master of arts degree in library science from the University of Michigan in 1951. He also did graduate work at the University of Ghana.

Randall worked in progressively responsible librarian positions at Lincoln University in Jefferson City, Missouri (1951–1954), Morgan State College in Baltimore, Maryland (1954–1956), and the Wayne County Federated Library System in Wayne, Michigan (1956–1969). From 1969 to 1975, he was a reference librarian and poet-in-residence at the University of Detroit. In 1969, he also served as a visiting lecturer at the University of Michigan.

Randall's love of poetry led to his founding of the Broadside Press in 1965. He wanted to make sure that African Americans had an outlet to "speak to and for their people." His works include *Poem Counterpoem* (1966), *On Getting a Natural* (1969), and *A Litany of Friends: New and Selected Poems* (1981). He retired from Broadside Press in 1993. In 1980, he founded the Broadside Poets Theater and the Broadside Poetry Workshop.

Randall was active in many Detroit cultural organizations and institutions, including the Detroit Council for the Arts and the International Afro-American Museum in Detroit, now the Charles H. Wright Museum of African American History. In 1981, Randall received the Creative Artist Award in Literature from the Michigan Council for the Arts, and in 1986 he was named the first poet laureate of Detroit by Mayor Coleman A. Young. Randall died on August 5, 2000, in Southfield, Michigan.

AHMAD RASHAD (1949–)

Sports Commentator, Television Host. Ahmad Rashad was born Bobby Moore on November 19, 1949, in Portland, Oregon, the youngest of six siblings. He was reared in Tacoma, Washington. He changed his name after he converted to Islam in the 1970s while playing professional football for the St. Louis Cardinals.

After leaving St. Louis, Rashad played for Buffalo and Seattle before joining the Minnesota Vikings in 1976. After eleven years of playing professional football, he decided to retire in 1983. Despite his early departure, Rashad left his mark on the league. He retired with 495 catches, tenth on the all-time receiving list at the time. Unlike many athletes, prior to announcing his retirement, he had begun to prepare for the next stage in his career: broadcasting. Several times a week after practice, he would go to the CBS affiliate, WCCO-TV in Minnesota, to hone his craft.

From 1983 to 1988, Rashad worked as a pregame host for *NFL on NBC*. He also attracted attention in 1985 when he made a marriage proposal during a televised football game to Phylicia Ayers-Allen, better known as Clair Huxtable, the matriarch on the long-running sitcom *The Cosby Show*. They had one child together, a daughter, but divorced in 2001.

Rashad moved to the booth in 1989 to serve as an analyst. In 1994, he moved back to the studio after being named pregame show cohost and stayed in that position through the end of the 1997–1998 season and Super Bowl XXXII. He lent his talents to *Notre Dame Saturday*, which he hosted in 1991, and to *NBC Sports Update*, where he served as an anchor and as a commentator for various SportsWorld telecasts.

Rashad was named executive producer of *NBA Inside Stuff* and NBA Entertainment-produced specials in March 1998. As an Emmy Award–winning sportscaster, Rashad has been the host of *NBA Inside Stuff* on NBC since its inception in 1990. He also hosted the *NBA on NBC* studio show. In addition, he extended his duties to include studio hosting, feature reporting, and analysis and commentary for a variety of sports and events, especially NBC's coverage of the NBA.

In between his anchoring assignments, Rashad served as a weekend host and late-night correspondent at the 1996 Olympic Games in Atlanta, as one of the hosts of NBC's *Olympic TripleCast* from Barcelona in 1992, and as studio anchor during coverage of the Seoul Olympics in 1988. His efforts in Seoul earned him an Emmy Award for writing. Rashad has also hosted a number of game shows and reality programs on various television networks.

Rashad is a graduate of the University of Oregon, where he was a two-time All-American. In 1995, he received the university's Pioneer Award, the highest honor given to an alumnus. In addition, he served on the university's board of trustees. Rashad was a four-time Pro-Bowl selection for the Minnesota Vikings and was voted to the Vikings All-Time Twentieth Anniversary Team and the Fortieth Anniversary Team. He is also the author of the best-selling book *Rashad: Vikes, Mikes, and Something on the Backside* (1988), written with Peter Bono. Rashad was awarded an honorary doctorate from the University of Puget Sound.

WILLIAM J. RASPBERRY (1935–)

Commentator, Journalist. Born in Okolona, Mississippi, on October 12, 1935, William James Raspberry received his bachelor of science degree in history from Indiana Central College in 1958. He worked at the *Indianapolis Recorder* as a reporter, photographer, and editorial writer from 1956 through 1960. In 1960, Raspberry was drafted by the U.S. Army and served as a public information officer until his discharge in 1962. He began working for the *Washington Post* as a teletypist and soon was promoted to the positions of reporter, assistant city editor, and finally columnist in 1966. His column went into syndication in 1977, and it eventually appeared in more than two hundred newspapers around the country.

Raspberry has also appeared as a television panelist and commentator and in 1965 was named Journalist of the Year by the Capital Press Club for his coverage of the Los Angeles Watts riot. In 1967, he received a Citation of Merit in Journalism from Lincoln University in Jefferson, Missouri, for distinction in improving human relations. He is generally regarded as an independent thinker, holding to no particular orthodoxy. His book *Looking Backward at Us*, published in 1991, is similar to his other writings in that it deals with issues concerning the African American experience, social conditions, and race relations in the United States.

Raspberry has taught journalism at Howard University and the University of Maryland School of Journalism. He has served as a member of the Poynter Institute for Media Studies board of advisers, the Pulitzer Prize Board, the Grid Iron Club, the Capitol Press Club, the Washington Association of Black Journalists, and Kappa Alpha Psi. Raspberry won the Pulitzer Prize in 1994 for Distinguished Commentary, as well as the Lifetime Achievement Award from the National Association of Black Journalists. In 1997, he was named one of the fifty most influential journalists in the national press corps by the *Washingtonian* magazine. In addition, he has been awarded honorary doctorates by numerous educational institutions.

Raspberry retired from the *Washington Post* in 2005 and ended his regular column, although he continued to contribute occasional guest columns. He became the Knight Professor of the Practice of Journalism and Public Policy Studies at Duke University's Terry Sanford Institute of Public Policy, and the founder and president of Baby Steps, a training and empowerment program for low-income parents based in Raspberry's hometown of Okolona.

ROBIN ROBERTS (1960–)

Reporter, Anchor, Sportscaster. Robin Roberts is was born in Alabama and raised in Mississippi. She graduated cum laude from Southeastern Louisiana State University in 1983. Along with her stellar academic work, Roberts distinguished herself as a basketball player. She remains the university's all-time women's leader in scoring and rebounding. From 1983 until 1990, Roberts held posts as sports anchor and reporter for television stations in Mississippi, Tennessee, and Georgia. In 1990, she joined ESPN, where she gained attention with the catchphrase "Go on with your bad self!" In 1994, Roberts was inducted into the Women's Institute on Sports and Education. The next year, she joined ABC as a features reporter, while still reporting for ESPN. In 1999, she served on the advisory board for the FIFA Women's World Cup.

In 2005, Roberts was named coanchor of ABC's *Good Morning America.* She served as anchor for reports surrounding Hurricane Katrina, which destroyed her high school in Pass Christian, Mississippi. When she was diagnosed with breast cancer in 2007, she showed tremendous courage and kept viewers and fans updated on her battle; she completed her last round of chemotherapy in 2008. Her book, *From the Heart: Seven Rules to Live By*, was published in 2007. In recognition for her excellence in journalism for ESPN, Roberts has won three Emmy Awards.

MAX ROBINSON (1939–1988)

Television Correspondent, Anchor. Born in Richmond, Virginia, on May 1, 1939, Max Robinson attended Oberlin College, Virginia Union University, and Indiana University. He began his career as a newsreader at WTOV-TV in Portsmouth, Virginia. In 1965, he began working as a studio floor director at WTOP-TV (now WUSA) in Washington, D.C., before moving to WRC-TV to work as a news reporter and to WTOP-TV, where he worked as anchor.

In 1978, Robinson joined ABC's *World News Tonight*, becoming the first African American network anchor. Almost immediately, Robinson took it upon himself to fight racism at whatever cost necessary. ABC management became frustrated with Robinson and moved him to the post of weekend anchor. In 1983, Robinson left ABC for WMAQ-TV in Chicago, where he remained until 1985.

Robinson died of complications from acquired immune deficiency syndrome (AIDS) on December 20, 1988, in Washington, D.C. He was the recipient of three Emmy Awards, the Capital Press Club Journalist of the Year Award, and the Ohio State Award, as well as an award from the National Education Association. He also taught at Federal City College in Washington, D.C., and the College of William and Mary in Williamsburg, Virginia.

AL ROKER (1954–)

Weather Reporter, Features Reporter, Author, Entrepreneur. Delighting visitors from across the country on the plaza outside of New York's Studio 1-A with his humor, honesty, outgoing personality, and witty comments, Al Roker is the weatherman for NBC's *Today* show. Until 2000, he was also the weekday weathercaster for News Channel 4's *Live at Five* in New York City.

Born Albert Lincoln Roker on August 20, 1954, in New York City, Roker began his broadcasting career while still in college by landing a job as a weekend weatherman at WTVH-TV in Syracuse, New York, in 1974. After receiving a bachelor of arts degree in communications from the State University of New York at Oswego in 1976, he held a series of weathercasting jobs in Washington, D.C. (1976–1978), and Cleveland, Ohio (1978–1983), before becoming the weekend weathercaster at WNBC in New York in 1983. Roker joined NBC's *Today* show as weather and features reporter in 1996.

Besides his weathercasting duties, this six-time Emmy Award winner conducts celebrity interviews, cooking segments, and technology updates. He began hosting the annual Christmas at Rockefeller Center celebration in 1985, and has also cohosted the Macy's Thanksgiving Day Parade and the Rose Bowl Parade.

In 1994, Roker ventured into the world of entrepreneurship by creating Al Roker Productions, Inc. (now Al Roker Entertainment, Inc.). The multimedia company is involved in the development and production of network, cable, home DVD, and public television projects. Two of the company's most successful projects include a critically acclaimed PBS special, *Savage Skies*, about severe weather, and a highly rated travel series called *Going Places*. Another business venture, RokerWare, Inc., is a trademark line of merchandise designed by Roker. Inspired by the birth of his daughter, Leila, in 1998, Roker introduced the WeatherBabies line of baby clothes as part of RokerWare.

Roker has taken on a variety of roles in television. He replaced host Meredith Vieira for a week of *Who Wants to Be a Millionaire* shows in 2007. In 2000, Roker published *Don't Make Me Stop This Car! Adventures in Fatherhood*. In 2001, *Al Roker's Big, Bad Book of Barbecue: 100 Easy Recipes for Backyard Barbecue and Grilling* hit the bookshelves. His third book, *Al Roker's Hassle-Free Holiday Cookbook*, was released in 2003. Roker's other books include *Big Shoes: In Celebration of Dads and Fatherhood* (2005) and *The Morning Show Murders: A Novel* (2009), written with Dick Lochte. In 2009, Roker became cohost with Stephanie Abrams of *Wake Up with Al*, an early morning show on the Weather Channel.

Roker has been honored by many civic and charitable organizations for his professional and community-minded activities and contributions. These include the Children's Defense Fund, the National Urban League Rainforest Alliance, Read Across America, the Arthur Ashe Institute for Urban Health, the Ronald McDonald House, the Hale House, and the Harlem Boys Choir. In addition, he has served as a member of the board of directors of Family AIDS Network and as honorary chair for the Susan G. Komen Breast Cancer Foundation Race for the Cure/Three Miles of Men. In 1998, Roker's alma mater awarded him an honorary doctorate.

CARL ROWAN (1925–2000)

Commentator, Journalist, Author. Carl Thomas Rowan was born August 11, 1925, in Ravenscroft, Tennessee. He attended Tennessee A&I (now Tennessee State University) in Nashville and Washburn University in Topeka, Kansas. Rowan received his bachelor of arts degree in mathematics from Oberlin College in 1947 and a master of arts degree in journalism from the University of Minnesota in 1948.

In 1948, Rowan went to work as a copyeditor, then later as a staff writer, for the *Minneapolis Tribune*, where he worked until 1961. In 1961, he was hired by the U.S. Department of State as deputy assistant secretary for public affairs. After three years with the Department of State, Rowan was appointed U.S. ambassador to Finland by President Lyndon Johnson in 1963, and in 1964 he was appointed director of the U.S. Information Agency (USIA), which operated overseas educational and cultural programs, including the worldwide radio service Voice of America. In 1965, Rowan resigned from the USIA to work as a columnist for the *Chicago Sun-Times*. His column, which explored political, social, and economic issues, was nationally syndicated for many years.

Rowan authored numerous books, including *South of Freedom* (1952), *Wait till Next Year: The Life Story of Jackie Robinson* (1960), *Just between Us Blacks* (1974), *Dream Makers, Dream Breakers: The World of Justice Thurgood Marshall* (1993), *The Coming Race War in America: A Wake-Up Call* (1996), and a memoir titled *Breaking Barriers* (1991). He received the Alfred I. du Pont–Columbia University Silver Baton in 1987 for the television documentary *Thurgood Marshall: The Man*.

Rowan served as a political commentator for the Post-Newsweek Broadcasting Company and was a frequent panelist on the NBC program *Meet the Press* and the syndicated programs *Agronsky & Co.* and *Inside Washington*. In 1987, Rowan became the founder of Project Excellence, a scholarship program for high-achieving African American high school students.

In 1998, Rowan received the prestigious Victory Award from the National Rehabilitation Hospital in Washington, D.C., for overcoming one of the biggest obstacles in his life—learning to walk again after having his right leg amputated just below the knee because of a severe foot infection brought on by complications from diabetes. Established in 1986, the award is given to individuals who have coped with physical adversity in an exemplary manner. On September 23, 2000, Rowan died of natural causes at Washington Hospital Center in Washington, D.C. He was seventy-five.

JOHN B. RUSSWURM (1799–1851)

Newspaper Publisher. Born in Port Antonio, Jamaica, on October 1, 1799, Russwurm graduated from Bowdoin College in Brunswick, Maine, in 1826. From Brunswick, Russwurm moved to New York, where on March 16, 1827, he and Samuel E. Cornish published the first edition of *Freedom's Journal*, the nation's first African American newspaper.

In 1829, Russwurm decided to immigrate to Monrovia, Liberia, and from 1830 until 1835, he published the *Liberia Herald.* Cornish, who had left the paper in late 1827, resumed his role as editor in 1830, publishing the paper under the name *Rights of All.* Russwurm served as superintendent of education in Monrovia and later as governor of Maryland in Liberia. He died June 17, 1851.

JOHN SENGSTACKE (1912–1997)

Publishing Executive. A nephew of the great publisher Robert Abbott, John Herman Henry Sengstacke was born in Savannah, Georgia, on November 25, 1912. He received a bachelor of arts degree from Hampton Institute, now Hampton University, in 1934. After graduating, he went to work with Robert Abbott, attended school to learn printing, and wrote editorials and articles for three Abbott papers. In 1934, he became vice president and general manager of the company.

During World War II (1939–1945), Sengstacke was an adviser to the U.S. Office of War Information during a period of severe tension between the government and the African American press. He also presided over the Chicago rationing board. In 1940, after the death of his uncle, Sengstacke became president of the Robert S. Abbott Publishing Company. In 1956, Sengstacke founded the *Daily Defender*, one of only three African American dailies in the country. In 1940, he founded the Negro Newspaper Publishers Association, now known as the National Newspaper Publishers Association, comprising more than two hundred African American newspapers. He served six terms as the association's president. Sengstacke was president of Tri-State Defender, the Florida Courier Publishing Company, the New Pittsburgh Courier Publishing Company, and Amalgamated Publishers. He also served as chairman of the Michigan Chronicle Publishing Company and Sengstacke Enterprises, Inc., and as treasurer of Chicago Defender Charities.

Prior to his death on May 28, 1997, after an extended illness, Sengstacke received several academic awards and served in leadership positions with many professional, educational, and civic organizations. He was a trustee at Bethune-Cookman College and chairman of the board at Provident Hospital and the Training School Association. He was also a member of the board of directors of the American Society of Newspaper Editors, on the advisory board of the Boy Scouts of America, and a principal in Chicago United.

BERNARD SHAW (1940–)

Television News Anchor. Bernard Shaw was born on May 22, 1940, in Chicago. From 1980 to 2001, he was the principal Washington anchor for CNN. Beginning in 1992, Shaw also coanchored *Inside Politics*, the nation's only daily program devoted exclusively to political news. Shaw was on board as the Washington anchor when the cable network went on the air on June 1, 1980. He often reported firsthand on major international news stories. His reporting took him to forty-six countries spanning five continents.

Shaw was present when the Chinese government's tanks rolled into Tiananmen Square in Beijing in 1989, crushing the student-led prodemocracy movement. In January 1991, Shaw and two CNN colleagues were stranded in Baghdad when allied bombing attacks launched Operation Desert Storm. From his hotel room, Shaw provided an eyewitness account of the bombing of the city. Shaw also covered the 1995 bombing of the Alfred P. Murrah Federal Building in Oklahoma City, Oklahoma.

After his comprehensive coverage of Operation Desert Storm, Shaw received numerous national and international awards and honors. In July 1991, he received the Eduard Rhein Foundation's Cultural Journalistic Award, marking the first time that the foundation had presented this award to a non-German. In October 1992, the Italian government honored him with its President's Award, presented to those who have contributed to development, innovation, and cooperation. In December 1992, Shaw was the recipient of the David Brinkley Award for excellence in communication from Barry University.

Shaw's first job as a television journalist came in 1971 with CBS News at their Washington bureau, where he conducted an exclusive interview with Attorney General John Mitchell at the height of the Watergate scandal. In 1977, he left CBS to join ABC News as Miami bureau chief and Latin American correspondent. Shaw was one of the first reporters to film from location on the 1978 Jonestown massacre story in Guyana, and his team provided the only aerial photos of the mass suicide-murder site. ABC sent Shaw to Iran to report on the 1979

Newscaster Bernard Shaw, 2001. With fellow CNN newscaster Judy Woodruff, Shaw appears on his final broadcast after twenty years at CNN and thirty-seven years in the news business. CHRIS KLEPONIS/AFP/GETTY IMAGES

hostage crisis at the American Embassy in Tehran. He then returned to Washington as ABC's senior Capitol Hill correspondent.

Prior to joining CBS News, Shaw was a reporter for Group W, a Westinghouse Broadcasting Company, based first in Chicago and then in Washington (1966–1971). Shaw served as Group W's White House correspondent during the last year of the Johnson administration (1968). His other assignments included local and national urban affairs, the struggles of Mexican Americans and Puerto Ricans, and the plight of American Indians in Billings, Montana. In 1968, he reported on the aftermath of the assassination of Dr. Martin Luther King Jr. in Memphis and his funeral in Atlanta.

Shaw has been elected a fellow of the Society of Professional Journalists (SPJ), the highest distinction the society gives to journalists for public service. In June 1995, he was inducted into the SPJ Hall of Fame. In October 1996, he received the Paul White Award for lifetime achievement from the Radio Television Digital News Association, one of the industry's most coveted awards. One month later, he and Judy Woodruff shared the 1996 ACE for Best Newscaster of the Year for *Inside Politics*. In April 1997, Shaw was inducted into the Chicago Journalists Hall of Fame. In September 1997, he was the inaugural recipient of the Congressional Medal of Honor Society's Tex McCrary Award for journalism, which honors distinguished achievement in the field of journalism. Since his retirement in 2001, Shaw has continued to make occasional appearances on CNN.

CAROLE SIMPSON (1940–)

Television News Anchor and Correspondent. Carole Simpson was born on December 7, 1940, in Chicago. She graduated from the University of Michigan with a bachelor of arts degree in journalism and did graduate work in journalism at the University of Iowa. She first entered broadcasting in 1965 as a reporter for a local radio station, WCFL, in Morris, Illinois. In 1968, she moved to radio station WBBM in Chicago, and in 1970 she went to work as a reporter for the Chicago television station WMAQ.

Simpson made her first network appearance as a substitute anchor for *NBC Nightly News* in 1974 and as anchor on NBC's *Newsbreak* on weekends. In 1982, Simpson joined ABC in Washington as a general assignment correspondent. She anchored *World News Sunday* from 1988 to 2003, and was an Emmy Award–winning senior correspondent for ABC News. She reported frequently on family and social issues for *World News Tonight with Peter Jennings*. Her reports also appeared on *20/20*, *Nightline*, and other ABC News broadcasts and specials. She was an occasional contributor to *This Week* and substituted for Peter

Jennings on *World News Tonight*. Simpson retired from ABC News in 2006.

Simpson was suspended from reporting on air for two weeks in 2001 after she revealed the identity of an ABC News producer whose son apparently contracted anthrax while visiting the network. She also spoke about a suspicious letter received by her colleague, Cokie Roberts, contradicting earlier network statements. Simpson later said she was sorry for the remarks.

Simpson has served as president of the Radio and Television Correspondents Association, as chairperson of the ABC Women's Advisory Board, and as a member of the board of directors of the Washington chapter of the Society of Professional Journalists. She is also a member of Theta Sigma Phi, the Radio Television News Directors Association, and the National Association of Black Journalists.

Simpson has been awarded the Media Journalism Award, the Milestone Award in broadcast journalism from the National Commission of Working Women, the Turner Broadcasting "Trumpet" Award for scholastic achievement, the Leonard Zeidenberg First Amendment Award from Radio and Television News Director Foundation, and the Silver Bell Award from the Ad Council. She was inducted into the University of Iowa Communications Hall of Fame and received the University of Missouri's distinguished journalist award. In 1992, Simpson was named Journalist of the Year by the National Association of Black Journalists. She has established several college scholarships for women and minorities pursuing careers in broadcast journalism at the University of Michigan, as well as the Carole Simpson Scholarship administered by the Radio Television Digital News Association. In 1998, she established the Carole Simpson Leadership Institute in Dakar, Senegal, for African women journalists. Simpson has served on the journalism faculty at Emerson College in Boston since 2007. In 2008, she was a visiting fellow at the Pomfret School in Connecticut.

Radio and Television Host Tavis Smiley, 2010. *Smiley began hosting a late-night television talk show on PBS in 2003 and a daily radio show on Public Radio International in 2005.* FREDERICK M. BROWN/GETTY IMAGES

TAVIS SMILEY (1964–)

Radio and Television Host, Producer, Commentator, Author. Recognized for his tough interviewing tactics and strong emphasis on issues relevant to the African American community, Tavis Smiley was selected by *Time* magazine in 2009 as one of the world's most influential artists and entertainers. Earlier, *Ebony* had profiled him as one of black America's future leaders. *Newsweek* had crowned him as among "20 people changing how Americans get their news" and dubbed him one of the nation's "captains of the airwaves."

Smiley was born on September 13, 1964, in Gulfport, Mississippi. He is the author of *Hard Left: Straight Talk about the Wrongs of the Right* (1996), *How to Make Black America Better* (2001), *What I Know for Sure: My Growing Up in America* (2006), *Never Mind Success: Go for Greatness* (2006), *Accountable: Making America as Good as Its Promise* (2009), written with Stephanie Roberts, and other books.

From 1996 to 2008, Smiley offered twice-weekly political commentary on *The Tom Joyner Morning Show*, a nationally syndicated radio show. In this role, Smiley led several radio campaigns that influenced national events, such as Fox Television's decision to return the series *Living Single* to its lineup during the 1990s. Smiley's campaigns also influenced the decision of Christie's auction house to donate enslavement-era artifacts to an African American museum in 1997, the decision by

Katz Radio Group to increase its media buys on African American and Hispanic radio, and the decision to give Rosa Parks the Congressional Gold Medal in 1999. In addition to his other on-air roles, Smiley has served as a political analyst on CNN.

Smiley received a bachelor of arts degree in law and public policy from Indiana University in 1986. In 1988, he moved to Los Angeles to work for the city's first African American mayor, Tom Bradley. In 1991, Smiley started doing a short radio segment, *The Smiley Report*, which became so popular that it was nationally syndicated a year later. His popularity spread even further when he signed on as the political commentator on *The Tom Joyner Morning Show* for what was supposed to be a temporary assignment to help Joyner register voters. Smiley's appearances were such a success that Joyner invited Smiley to became a regular commentator.

In the 1990s, Smiley was perhaps best known for his television show *BET Tonight with Tavis Smiley*, which garnered Smiley three NAACP Image Awards for Best News, Talk, or Information Series. In 1999, BET chose not to renew Smiley's contract, and Smiley began working at ABC-TV as a special correspondent for *Good Morning America* and *Primetime Thursday*. In 1999, Smiley founded the nonprofit Tavis Smiley Foundation to provide leadership training for young people.

From 2002 to 2004, Smiley hosted *The Tavis Smiley Show* for National Public Radio. The half-hour *Tavis Smiley*, a late-night talk show, premiered in 2004 on PBS. Smiley's illustrious guests have included Barack Obama, Hillary Clinton, Toni Morrison, Myrlie Evers-Williams, Vicente Fox, Ted Turner, Denzel Washington, and many other performers, writers, journalists, activists, businesspeople, athletes, and politicians.

Smiley wrote, produced, and directed the documentary film *Stand*, released in 2009. The film explores the experiences of Smiley and ten male friends as they travel from Memphis to Nashville and reflect on the roles and responsibilities of black men in America.

Smiley is the recipient of numerous awards and honorary doctorates. He maintains memberships with the Kappa Alpha Psi fraternity, the National Association of Black Journalists, the NAACP, and the American Federation of Television and Radio Artists. In 2009, Smiley's alma mater, Indiana University, named the atrium of its School of Public and Environmental Affairs after him.

CLARENCE O. SMITH (1933–)

Magazine Publisher, Businessman. Clarence O'Farrell Smith was born on March 31, 1933. As cofounder of Essence Communications Partners, previously Essence Communications, Inc., Smith was once the driving force behind the success of *Essence* magazine, the company's premier publication targeted toward African American women. Smith resigned from Essence Communications in 2002. His decision to leave the company marked the end of a thirty-two-year business relationship with Edward T. Lewis, the company's other founder.

Industry experts speculate that his unexpected departure may have been a result of corporate restructuring and major staff changes that took place after Essence Communications merged with Time Inc. in 2000. The dissolution of the Lewis and Smith partnership was even more startling because both of them had been hailed in the June 2002 issue of *Black Enterprise* as "Marathon Men" in their role as managers of one of the nation's largest black-owned businesses.

Smith's ability to attract high-profile advertisers—the lifeblood of consumer publishing—to *Essence* in its early years helped to ensure its success. Securing ads in the first few years of the magazine proved to be more daunting than Smith had anticipated. Nevertheless, relying on the skills he had acquired as an insurance salesman at the Prudential Life Insurance Company in the early 1960s—when he joined the company there were only two other black agents—Smith eventually established relationships with prestigious advertisers, such as Chanel, Giorgio, and Estée Lauder, an account that took him twenty-two years to close.

Smith was also instrumental in leading the company beyond publishing into licensing, direct-mail marketing, and television production. He played a key role in the creation of *The Essence Awards*, an annual prime-time network special, and in the production of award-winning programs such as *Essence*, a weekly syndicated magazine and news-service television show. Later, he helped launch Essence-by-Mail, a mail-order catalog catering to African Americans, and Essence Art Reproductions, a company that marketed artworks by African American artists.

In the 1990s, Smith and Lewis ventured into other areas of publishing, starting with the acquisition of *Income Opportunities*, a magazine for people starting new businesses. Three years later, the company entered into a joint venture to publish *Latina*, the first bilingual lifestyle magazine that addressed the interests of Hispanic women in the United States.

Another major triumph for the company occurred in 1995 when the first Essence Music Festival was held in New Orleans. Now an annual event, the festival drew 160,000 attendees to the Superdome during each of its first three years. In 1996, Smith and Lewis nearly canceled the festival after Louisiana governor M. J. Foster Jr. announced that he was discontinuing affirmative-action programs throughout the state. Governor Foster eventually agreed to meet with Smith, Lewis, and Hugh B. Price, the president of the National Urban League, to discuss plans. After the meeting, Governor Foster issued a new executive order that offered better career opportunities for minorities in Louisiana.

A vigorous advocate for minority representation in the media, Smith has served as the chairman of the Chicago-based African American Marketing and Media Association and as a founding member of the African American Anti-Defamation Association. Like Lewis, Smith was recognized by *Black Enterprise* magazine throughout his career for his accomplishments, as well as by Ernst and Young with the Entrepreneur of the Year Award.

Although Smith is no longer with Essence Communications Partners, he will be recognized as president emeritus and cofounder of *Essence* magazine. He will also be credited with generating revenues for the company through advertising and developing the company's entertainment division. Still an active entrepreneur, Smith launched You Entertainment, a music production company, in 2005.

THOMAS SOWELL (1930–)

Economist, Professor, Author, Columnist. Since 1980, Thomas Sowell has been the Rose and Milton Friedman Senior Fellow in Public Policy at the Hoover Institution at Stanford University. He has also been associated with three other research centers during his career. From 1972 to 1974, he was project director at the Urban Institute; from 1975 to 1976, he was an adjunct scholar of the American Enterprise Institute; and from 1976 to 1977, he was a fellow at the Center for Advanced Study in the Behavioral Sciences at Stanford University.

A prolific writer—his specialties are economics, history, social policy, and ethnicity—Sowell has published numerous books, articles, and essays covering a wide range of topics, including classic economic theory, judicial activism, civil rights, immigration, and college selection. His writings have also appeared in scholarly journals in economics, law, and other fields.

In the 1990s, Sowell's research focused on cultural history from a global perspective, a subject explored in a trilogy that includes *Race and Culture* (1994), *Migrations and Cultures* (1996), and *Conquests and Cultures* (1998). In 1999, Sowell published *Barbarians inside the Gates* and *The Quest for Cosmic Justice*. Detouring from his usual style of writing, in 2000, he released his autobiography, *A Personal Odyssey*. Other titles include *Black Rednecks and White Liberals* (2004), *Basic Economics: A Common Sense Guide to the Economy* (2007), *Applied Economics: Thinking beyond Stage One* (2004, rev. ed. 2009), *Intellectuals and Society* (2009), and *The Housing Boom and Bust* (2009).

As a nationally syndicated columnist for Creators Syndicate, Sowell's column appears in major newspapers throughout the nation. He has also written columns for the Scripps-Howard News Service, the *Los Angeles Herald-Examiner*, the *New York Times*, the *Wall Street Journal*, the *Washington Post*, the *Los Angeles Times*, the *Washington Star*, *Newsweek*, *Newsday*, and the *Stanford Daily*. Typically described as a black conservative, some view his writing as groundbreaking, for it strongly favors a free-market economic policy. Others, however, strongly disagree with it because his opinions often conflict with those of the minority population.

Born on June 30, 1930, in North Carolina, Sowell grew up in Harlem. He left home without finishing high school, and the next few years were challenging, but eventually he joined the Marine Corps and became a photographer during the Korean War. After leaving the service, he entered Harvard University, where he graduated magna cum laude with a bachelor of arts degree in 1958. He received a master of arts degree from Columbia University in 1959 and a doctor of philosophy degree from the University of Chicago in 1968. His area of study for each of these degrees was economics.

In the early 1960s, Sowell held jobs as an economist with the Department of Labor and with AT&T. Yet, his real interest was in teaching and scholarship, and in 1965 he began the first of many university-level professorships. His teaching assignments include Rutgers University, Amherst University, Brandeis University, and the University of California, Los Angeles, where he taught in the early 1970s and again from 1984 to 1989.

Though Sowell had been a regular contributor to newspapers in the late 1970s and early 1980s, he did not begin his career as a newspaper columnist until 1984. Adapting to this style of writing very quickly, he was able to get to the core of issues without the abstruseness that so often accompanies academic writing.

In 1990, Sowell won the prestigious Francis Boyer Award, presented by the American Enterprise Institute. In 2002, he won the National Humanities Medal from the National Endowment for the Humanities. He received the Bradley Prize for intellectual achievement in 2003.

MARTHA JEAN STEINBERG (c. 1930–2000)

Radio Host, Broadcasting Executive. Always coy about her age, Martha Jean Steinberg, better known as "The Queen," acquired this regal title from an announcer early in her career. According to her, when she started out in the business in the 1950s, "every black disc jockey had to have a rhyming, stereotyped name." Although the name was given to her at a time when racism was prevalent in the industry, she decided to keep it after moving to Detroit in the 1960s, making it her trademark.

Before she became radio royalty and before she married and divorced a trumpet player named Luther Steinberg, she was Martha Jean Jones of Memphis, Tennessee. In 1954, she was hired to work at WDIA-AM in Memphis, a 50,000-watt powerhouse station that reached five states. As the first station in the country to air an all-black format that included black announcers and a mix of blues and gospel, WDIA-AM became a tremendous hit among both black and white listeners, including a young Elvis Presley.

While working at the station, officials noticed Steinberg doing community relations and general work. Based on her outstanding performance in both of these areas, they eventually offered her an on-air job, believing she would be a "natural" behind the microphone. Proving them correct, she spoke with supreme authority about her listeners' lives and feelings. It was a tradition she maintained throughout her forty plus years in the business. Steinberg was the only woman honored in an exhibition on legendary disc jockeys at the Rock and Roll Hall of Fame and Museum in Cleveland, Ohio. She was also recognized by the Black Radio Hall of Fame in Atlanta, Georgia, as well as the Smithsonian Institution's *Black Radio: Telling It Like It Was*, a documentary on the history of black-oriented radio. Steinberg was also featured in the Radio America series *Passing It On: Voices from Black America's Past*, a program that was broadcast on over four hundred radio stations across the country. Steinberg was selected to narrate a documentary on Berry Gordy and the early years of the Motown Sound, *The Music & the Story*, for the Henry Ford Museum in Dearborn, Michigan.

Steinberg's first radio job in Detroit was at WCHB in Inkster, Michigan. She then joined WJLB, where her show ruled from 1966 to 1982. During the 1967 riots—or rebellion, as she referred to it—she took to the airwaves for forty-eight hours straight, acting as a peacekeeper. In 1982, she left WJLB to become the vice president and general manager of WQBH. For fourteen years, she nurtured and built WQBH, establishing it as the "voice of the community." Her mission was "to bridge the gap between the power structure and the forgotten man" through her daily show, which aired from 11:00 a.m. to 2:00 p.m. on weekdays. During this time, she tripled the value of the station, and, on May 12, 1997, she purchased it for $3.9 million. Continuing to air her show after purchasing the station, Steinberg's position as a black radio scholar who helped set the guidelines and standards for black radio in America became forever etched in the industry.

While at WQBH, Steinberg experienced a religious conversion and became a self-ordained nondenominational minister. The final outcome of this transformation was the establishment of her own church, the Home of Love, a community center, a low-income housing complex on Detroit's west side, and the Queen's Community Workers, a group of individuals who aid senior citizens and youth. After her death on January 29, 2000, mourners throughout the Detroit metropolitan community commented that Steinberg's greatest gift was her ability to touch the souls of people by offering advice on a full range of human problems. It was a talent that she used on the radio and at her church.

CHUCK STONE (1924–)

Journalist, Educator. Charles Sumner Stone was born in 1924 in St. Louis to a family that lived in comfort because of his father's executive position with a hair-care company. However, alcoholism resulted in Stone's parents' divorce, and Stone's mother moved him and his three younger sisters to Connecticut. After high school, he enrolled in the famed Tuskegee training program for African American bomber pilots during World War II and became a navigator with the U.S. Air Corps. After the war, Stone earned degrees from Wesleyan University and the University of Chicago, and for a time worked with an international development agency in Africa.

In 1959, Stone was hired at the *New York Age*, a Harlem paper. Within a short time, he had become its editor, in which post he was noted for his outspoken opinions. During the early 1960s, he became the White House correspondent for the *Washington Afro-American*, for which he often wrote critically of the Kennedy administration's lack of progress on civil rights issues.

In 1965, Stone joined the staff of Adam Clayton Powell Jr., the controversial Harlem activist who was then serving as a member of the U.S. House of Representatives. When Powell's political career ended amid charges of misuse of public funds two years later, Stone channeled his feelings of anger toward the white political establishment in the fictional chronicle *King Strut* (1970). It was Stone's third book, after *Tell It Like It Is* (1968), a collection of his newspaper writings, and *Black Political Power in America* (1968).

Stone became a regular columnist for the *Philadelphia Daily News* in 1972 and spent the next several years lambasting the city's corrupt political machinery and heavy-handed police force. Stone first unleashed his critical pen on the administration of former police officer Frank Rizzo, and later at the city's first African American mayor, Wilson Goode. Stone's columns, which continued after he became senior editor in 1979, made him both a revered and feared civic personage. In an unusual development, his condemnations of police brutality in Philadelphia often prompted suspects to turn themselves in at the columnist's home or office and wait for authorities to arrest them there.

After nearly two decades, Stone resigned from the *Philadelphia Daily News* to pursue a career in academia. In 1991, he became the Walter Spearman Professor at the University of North Carolina's School of Journalism and Mass Communication in Chapel Hill. In the spring of 1996, Stone was honored with the Missouri Honor Medal for Distinguished Service in Journalism from the University of Missouri. He joined an impressive roster of past recipients that included Walter Cronkite and Charlayne Hunter-Gault. Stone was also selected to carry a torch for the Olympic flame that journeyed across the nation before the opening of the 1996 Summer Games in Atlanta, Georgia.

In 2003, Stone published a children's book, *Squizzy the Black Squirrel: A Fabulous Fable of Friendship*, with illustrations by Jeannie Jackson. In August 2004, the National Association of Black Journalists inducted him into their Hall of Fame. Stone retired as a professor at the University of North Carolina's School of Journalism and Mass Communications in 2005. In 2007, the University of North Carolina inaugurated the Chuck Stone Program for Diversity in Education and Media. Each summer, the program brings talented high school students who are interested in journalism careers to the campus for a one-week workshop in journalism and mass communications.

PIERRE MONTEAU SUTTON (1947–)

Broadcasting Executive. Pierre Sutton is president of Inner City Broadcasting Corporation in New York City and president of its radio stations in New York and California. He is the son of Percy E. Sutton, founder and chairman emeritus of the board of Inner City Broadcasting and former borough president of Manhattan. Inner City Broadcasting has several divisions, including Inner City Cable, Inner City Artists Management, and Inner City Broadcasting Corporation-Television (ICBC-TV). ICBC-TV produced *Showtime at the Apollo*, *The Apollo Comedy Hour*, and *New Music Report*.

Pierre Sutton was born in New York City on February 1, 1947. He received a bachelor of arts degree from the University of Toledo in 1968. Sutton began his career in 1971 as vice president of Inner City Research and Analysis Corporation. He was executive editor of the *New York Courier* newspaper from 1971 to 1972, and served as public affairs director for WLIB radio from 1972 to 1975. He was promoted to vice president of Inner City Broadcasting in 1975 and became president in 1977.

Sutton has served as a board member of the Minority Investment Fund, first vice president of the National Association of Black Owned Broadcasters, chairman of the Harlem Boy Scouts, member of the board and executive committee of the New York City Marathon, trustee of the Alvin Ailey Dance Foundation, board member of the Better Business Bureau of Harlem, and member of the board of the Hayden Planetarium.

SUSAN L. TAYLOR (1946–)

Editor. Susan Taylor was born in New York City on January 23, 1946, and received a bachelor of arts degree from Fordham University. From 1981 to 2000, Susan Taylor was editor in chief of *Essence*, a magazine established in 1970 for African American women. In 2010, the publication claimed a monthly circulation of more than one million and a readership of 8.5 million—many of whom were men. After Taylor stepped down as editor in chief in 2000, she became publications director for Essence Communications. She left the company in 2007.

A former actress, cosmetologist, and founder of her own cosmetics company, Nequai Cosmetics, Taylor began her relationship with *Essence* magazine as a freelance writer. In 1971, she became the magazine's beauty and fashion editor. She held this position until 1980. As editor in chief, Taylor was also executive coordinator of Essence Communications. The company was a major investor in Amistad Press, an African American–owned book publisher. The company also maintained a licensing division that included Essence Hosiery, Essence Eyewear, and the Essence Collection by Butterick; Essence Art Reproductions, a distributor of artworks by African American artists; Essence Television Productions, the producer of *The Essence Awards*, an annual salute to distinguished African Americans; and the Essence Music Festival, a three-day festival of cultural celebrations and empowerment seminars.

Taylor was the author of the *In the Spirit* column in *Essence* magazine. In 1993, she published *In the Spirit: The Inspirational Writings of Susan L. Taylor*, a collection of inspirational essays named for and taken from her monthly *Essence* column. Taylor also published *Lessons in Living* (1995) and coedited *Confirmation: The Spiritual Wisdom that Has Shaped Our Lives* (1997) and *Black Men in Their Own Words* (2002).

In 1999, Taylor became the first African American woman to receive the Henry Johnson Fisher Award for lifetime achievement in the magazine industry, given by the Magazine Publishers of America. She received an even more prestigious honor in 2002 when she was inducted into the Magazine Editor's Hall of Fame by the American Society of Magazine Editors. More recently Taylor has been focusing her attention on the Essence Cares initiative, later known as the National CARES Mentoring Movement. She launched this call to action to the African American community at the 2006 Essence Music Festival. It is a massive mentoring campaign that asks all adults—elected and appointed officials, educators, college students, and business, religious, and secular leaders—to rally their communities to guide children who need help. The goal is to create the largest mentoring campaign in the history of the nation and increase high school graduation rates among African American students by 10 percent annually. Taylor also serves on the boards of the National Underground Railroad Freedom Center and Girl Scouts of the USA.

CYNTHIA TUCKER (1955–)

Reporter, Editor, Columnist. Born in Monroeville, Alabama, in 1955, Cynthia Tucker graduated from Auburn University in 1976 as an English and journalism major. Following graduation, Tucker was hired as a reporter for the *Atlanta Journal-Constitution.* Following a stint at the *Philadelphia Inquirer* in 1980, and freelance work in Africa, Tucker returned to the *Atlanta Journal-Constitution.* She served as columnist and editorial page editor before becoming the *Journal-Constitution*'s Washington-based political columnist in 2009. Tucker's columns are syndicated in over fifty newspapers. Along with her significant contributions to print journalism, Tucker makes frequent appearances on news programs produced by PBS and CNN. Tucker was named 2006 Journalist of the Year by the National Association of Black Journalists. She won a Pulitzer Prize for Commentary in 2007.

LEMUEL TUCKER (1938–1991)

Television News Correspondent. Born in 1938 in Saginaw, Michigan, and a graduate of Central Michigan University, Lemuel Tucker worked as a Washington bureau correspondent for CBS news from 1977 until 1988. Prior to that, he was with ABC News as New York City correspondent from 1972 until 1977. From 1965 through 1972, Tucker worked for NBC News, where he served for a period as assistant bureau chief in Vietnam. He was awarded an Emmy for his reporting on hunger in the United States, a series of seven reports broadcast in 1968 and 1969. He died in March 1991 in Washington, D.C.

JUAN WILLIAMS (1954–)

Television and Radio Correspondent, Anchor, Commentator, Author. Juan Williams was born in Colón, Panama, and moved to New York with his family when he was a child. He graduated from Haverford College with a degree in philosophy in 1976. Williams joined FOX News in 1997 as a political contributor, and became a regular panelist on Fox's Sunday morning public affairs program, *FOX News Sunday* with Chris Wallace. Williams also serves as anchor of FOX News Channel's weekend daytime live coverage. He appears regularly on other FOX programs, including *The O'Reilly Factor.*

Before joining FOX, Williams spent twenty-three years at the *Washington Post,* where he served as an editorial writer, an op-ed columnist, and White House correspondent. From 2000 to 2001, Williams hosted National Public Radio's (NPR) national call-in show, *Talk of the Nation.* In that role, he traveled to cities across America for monthly radio town-hall meetings before live audiences. After leaving *Talk of the Nation,* Williams continued working for NPR as a senior correspondent and news analyst, appearing regularly on *Morning Edition* and *All Things Considered*

The recipient of an Emmy Award for television documentary writing, Williams won widespread critical acclaim for a series of documentaries, including *Politics: The New Black Power* and *A. Philip Randolph: For Jobs and Freedom.* He is the author of the nonfiction best-sellers *Eyes on the Prize: America's Civil Rights Years, 1954–1965* (1987) and *Thurgood Marshall: American Revolutionary* (1988). Williams has also written numerous columns and articles for newspapers and national magazines, including *Fortune,* the *Atlantic Monthly, Ebony, GQ,* and the *New Republic,* in addition to appearing on numerous television programs, including ABC's *Nightline,* PBS's *Washington Week in Review,* and *Oprah.* His 2006 book, *Enough! The Phony Leaders, Dead-End Movements, and Culture of Failure that Are Undermining Black America—And What We Can Do About It,* led to much spirited debate about the state of African Americans. Williams's other books include *My Soul Looks Back in Wonder: Voices of the Civil Rights Experience* (2004) and *Black Farmers in America* (2006).

MONTEL WILLIAMS (1956–)

Talk-Show Host. A former naval intelligence officer who first gained prominence delivering highly charged motivational speeches to millions of children around the country, Montel Williams became a talk-show host with a nontraditional background. Williams was born in Baltimore in 1956. He joined the U.S. Marine Corps in 1974. In 1976, Williams became the first African American to attend the prestigious Naval Academy Prep School. At Annapolis, he studied Mandarin Chinese and graduated with a degree in general engineering.

In 1988, Williams began informally counseling the spouses and families of the service personnel in his command. He was later asked to speak to a group of children in Kansas City, Missouri, about the importance of leadership and overcoming obstacles. This is how his career in motivational speaking began. His daily, hour-long talk show, *The Montel Williams Show,* premiered in 1991.

Several episodes in 1997 stressed the importance of AIDS education in communities across the country. As a result of the show's ongoing coverage of the AIDS

Montel Williams Hosting His Talk Show. *During seventeen seasons hosting* The Montel Williams Show, *which was on the air from 1991 to 2008, Williams interviewed more than 30,000 guests.* GETTY IMAGES/GETTY IMAGES ENTERTAINMENT/GETTY IMAGES

epidemic, the White House Office of National AIDS Policy invited Williams to produce public-service announcements on AIDS prevention. In addition, his After-Care Program arranged for guests to attend psychological treatment, motivational camps, drug and alcohol rehabilitation, and treatment for eating disorders.

In 1999, Williams revealed that he had been diagnosed with multiple sclerosis. He vowed to continue to host his talk show in order to be a role model for others with multiple sclerosis. He also hoped to use his show to make people aware of the disease. He started the Montel Williams MS Foundation in 1999 to raise money to combat the disease. Williams was in the news again in 2000 when he helped save a sixteen-year-old boy whose car had crashed and burst into flames in Bonners Ferry, Idaho. Williams made the teen a splint from tree branches and a belt, then carried him to safety.

A recipient of several daytime Emmy Awards, *The Montel Williams Show* was honored with a number of humanitarian awards. The Entertainment Industry Council, the National Institute on Drug Abuse, and the National Institutes of Health presented the show with a PRISM Commendation for the episode "What Parents Need to Know about Teens and Drugs." The foundation of American Women in Radio and Television gave the show an honorable mention Gracie Award in recognition for excellence in programming for the positive and realistic portrayal of women. The show also received the Nancy Susan Reynolds Award for the episode "Teenagers Living with AIDS" and the Silver Angel Award for "The Life and Times of Mother Teresa." In 2002, Williams received the first-ever Man of Courage Award at the seventh annual Race to Erase MS in Los Angeles. Williams made a quick cameo at the 2006 MTV

Video Music Awards on August 31, 2006, where he was introduced as the godfather of daytime television.

The Montel Williams Show ceased production in 2008 after seventeen years on the air, although BET and some CBS affiliates continued to air reruns of the show. From 2009 to early 2010, Williams hosted a radio show, *Montel across America*, on Air America.

OPRAH WINFREY (1954–)

Talk-Show Host, Actress, Producer, Publisher. Oprah Winfrey was born on January 29, 1954, in Kosciusko, Mississippi. Winfrey claimed in a 1991 interview with the Academy of Achievement that her birth certificate spells her name "Orpah," after a biblical figure in the book of Ruth. But people had trouble pronouncing *Orpah*, so they began to put the *p* before the *r*, and she became Oprah.

Winfrey was a precocious child who asked her kindergarten teacher to advance her to a higher grade. Her parents, who were not married, separated when she was very young and sent her to live with her grandparents. When she was six, Winfrey moved to Milwaukee to live with her mother. From the time that she was nine years old, she suffered sexual abuse at the hands of male family members and acquaintances; these events, which she did not discuss publicly until the 1980s, had a profound effect on her life.

When she was fourteen years old, Winfrey went to live with her father in Nashville, Tennessee, and it was there that she got her life back on track. Her father insisted on hard work and discipline as a means of self-improvement, and Winfrey complied, winning a college scholarship that allowed her to attend Tennessee State University. In 1971, she began working part time as a radio announcer for WVOL in Nashville. Two years later, she became a reporter at WTVF-TV in Nashville. From 1976 to 1983, she lived in Baltimore, working for the ABC affiliate WJZ-TV, progressing from news anchor to cohost of the popular show *People Are Talking*. In 1984, she moved to Chicago and took over the ailing morning show *A.M. Chicago*. Within a year, the show was so successful that it was expanded to an hour and renamed *The Oprah Winfrey Show*. Now in syndication across the nation and around the world, *The Oprah Winfrey Show* is one of the most popular television programs in history. In 1986, Oprah founded Harpo Inc., her own production company, making Winfrey the first African American woman to host a nationally syndicated weekday show, own and produce her own television show, and own a film and a television production company.

Winfrey is also a talented actress. She has appeared in a number of films, including *The Color Purple* (1985), *Native Son* (1986), and *Beloved* (1998). She also appeared in the television movies *The Women of Brewster Place* (1989), *There Are No Children Here* (1993), and *Before Women Had Wings* (1997). In addition, Winfrey has lent her voice to characters in animated films, including *Charlotte's Web* (2006), *Bee Movie* (2007), and *The Princess and the Frog* (2009). As a producer, Winfrey has contributed to several television specials and movies, notably *David and Lisa* (1998), *The Wedding* (1998), *Beloved* (1998), *Their Eyes Were Watching God* (2005), and *Precious* (2009), all based on novels. Winfrey's production company was also involved in several successful daytime television series, including *Dr. Phil*, *The Dr. Oz Show*, and *Rachael Ray*.

As a former victim of child abuse, Winfrey is a strong advocate of children's rights. When she heard the tragic story of a four-year-old Chicago girl's molestation and murder, she proposed federal child-protection legislation designed to keep nationwide records on convicted child abusers. Her efforts on behalf of abused and neglected children came to fruition on December 20, 1993, when President Bill Clinton signed the "Oprah Bill," a law designed to protect children from abuse. Winfrey also contributed $40 million to established the Oprah Winfrey Leadership Academy for Girls in South Africa. The school opened in 2007. During the 2007–2008 campaign for U.S. president, Winfrey campaigned with and raised funds for Barack Obama.

The Oprah Winfrey Show continues to be the number one talk show on the air and is broadcast to 145 countries. Reaching more than twenty million homes a day, the show continues to enlighten, educate, and entertain viewers. In 1998, the show unveiled a new set; premiered a new theme song, "Run on with Oprah," performed by Winfrey herself; and embarked on a new type of programming called "Change Your Life TV," designed to inspire viewers to make small adjustments so that they can create big results in their lives. In the spirit of her "Change Your Life TV" programming, Winfrey launched a Web site to empower viewers by enabling them to access the experts and use the information and advice offered on the show. Winfrey announced in 2008 that she would end her daily show in 2011.

Famous for her candor, forthrightness, and willingness to go the distance, Winfrey successfully won a $12 million slander suit brought against her by Texas beef producers in 1998. The beef producers took Winfrey to court over a 1996 show in which one of her guests, an antimeat activist, suggested that American beef-industry practices could cause mad cow disease. The cattlemen claimed that because of her influence with viewers, beef prices immediately slumped to a ten-year low. The jury of eight women and four men deliberated close to six hours before rejecting all claims brought by the beef producers.

In 1998, Winfrey expanded her roles to include cable network executive when she launched the Oxygen network, a cable network devoted to women and women's issues. In 2000, she also became a magazine publisher when *O: The Oprah Magazine* hit the newsstands. In 1994, Winfrey premiered a new segment on her show, Oprah's Book Club. The book club became so popular that the books Oprah chose for discussion often saw a major increase in sales. For the first eight years, Winfrey selected one book for discussion each month. After 2002, the book club was limited to only a few books per year

Winfrey continued to win awards for her work in television and film, including the Horatio Alger Award in 1993 and induction into the Television Hall of Fame in 1994. At the end of the 1995–1996 television season, she received the George Foster Peabody Individual Achievement Award, one of broadcasting's most coveted honors. She was named among "America's 25 Most Influential People of 1996" by *Time* magazine and favorite female television performer at the 1997 and 1998 People's Choice Awards. In 1999, she received the National Book Foundation's fiftieth anniversary Gold Medal, and in 2001 she was named *Newsweek* magazine's "Woman of the Century." Winfrey has also been honored with numerous Emmy Awards for Outstanding Talk Show Host and Outstanding Talk Show. In 2002, *Fortune* magazine ranked her the tenth most powerful African American executive, and *Savoy* considered her the most powerful African American in the media. By 2004, *Forbes* and *Black Enterprise* magazines listed Winfrey as the first African American female billionaire.

In 2009, Winfrey and Sirius XM Radio announced the launch of Oprah Radio, formerly Oprah and Friends, with daily and weekly radio shows hosted by Gayle King, Maya Angelou, Mehmet Oz, and others. In 2009, Winfrey announced plans to start a twenty-four-hour cable network in association with the Discovery Health Channel, with programming devoted to self-discovery. The network was to be called OWN: The Oprah Winfrey Network and was expected to premiere in January 2011.

BLACK-OWNED BROADCAST STATIONS AND NETWORKS

ALABAMA

RADIO

Booker T. Washington Broadcasting
Kirkwood Balton, President
WAGG-AM (Gospel)
WENN-FM (Urban Contemporary)
PO Box 697
Birmingham, AL 35201
(205) 741-9244

Birmingham Ebony Broadcasting
Shelley Stewart and Erskine R. Faush
WATV-AM (Urban Contemporary)
3025 Ensley Ave.
Birmingham, AL 35208
(205) 780-2014

Willis Broadcasting
Bishop L. E. Willis, President
WAYE-AM (Religious)
836 Lomb Ave. SW
Birmingham, AL 35211
(205) 786-9293

Broadcast One
Huntley Batts Sr., President
WEUP-AM (Black Contemporary)
2609 Jordan Ln. NW
Huntsville, AL 35806
(205) 837-9387

Muscle Shoals Broadcasting
Bob Carl Bailey, President
WTQX-AM (Black Contemporary)
1 Valley Creek Cir.
Selma, AL 36701
(205) 875-4487

Muscle Shoals Broadcasting
Bob Carl Bailey, President
WZZA-AM (Black Contemporary/Gospel)
1570 Woodmont Dr.
Tuscumbia, AL 35674
(205) 381-1862

All Channel TV Service and New World Communications, Inc.
George H. Clay, President
WBIL-AM/FM (Black Contemporary)
PO Box 666
Tuskegee, AL 36083-0666
(205) 727-2100

J & W Promotions, Inc.
Johnny Roland, President
WAPZ-AM (Rhythm and Blues)
2821 U.S. Hwy. 231
Wutumpka, AL 36092
(205) 567-2251

ARKANSAS

RADIO

Nameloc Broadcasting
Loretta Lever, President
KYFX-FM (Adult Contemporary)
610 Plaza West Bldg.
Little Rock, AR 72205
(501) 666-9499

Willis Broadcasting
Bishop L. E. Willis, President
KLRG-AM (Gospel)
KMZX-FM (Urban Contemporary)
200 Arch St.
Little Rock, AR 72201
(501) 376-1063

West Helena Broadcasting, Inc.
Alford Billingsley, President
KCLT-FM (Black Contemporary)
700 Martin Luther King Dr. W, Ste. 2
West Helena, AR 72390
(501) 572-9506

Simms & Simms Communications
Raymond Simms, President
KAKJ-FM (Black Contemporary)
Highway 1 N
Marianna, AR 72360
(800) 475-1053

CALIFORNIA

RADIO

Inner City Broadcasting Corp.
Pierre M. Sutton, President
KBLX-AM/FM (Adult Contemporary)
601 Ashby Ave.
Berkeley, CA 94710
(510) 848-7713

Tulare Lite Corporation
Irene Beristain, President
KOJJ-FM (Adult Contemporary)
165 N. D St., Ste. 3-4
East Porterville, CA 93257
(209) 782-1005

Goodwill Broadcasting Co.
John Pembroke, President
KJOP-AM (Hispanic Country)
15279 Hanford Armona Rd.
Lemoore, CA 93245
(209) 582-5567

Taxi Productions, Inc.
Steveland Morris (Wonder), President
KJLH-FM (Urban Contemporary)
3847 Crenshaw Blvd.
Los Angeles, CA 90008
(213) 299-5960

East-West Broadcasting
William Shearer, President
KGFJ-AM (Black Contemporary)
1100 S. LaBrea
Los Angeles, CA 90019
(213) 930-9090

1310 Incorporated
Ellihue Harris and Willie Brown
KDIA-AM (Urban Contemporary)
384 Embarcadero W., 3rd Fl.
Oakland, CA 94601
(510) 251-1400

Douglas Broadcasting
N. John Douglas, President
KMAX-FM (Religious, Ethnic)
KWIZ-FM (Christian)
3350 Electronic Dr., Ste. 130
Pasadena, CA 91107
(213) 681-2486

Douglas Broadcasting
N. John Douglas, President
KEST-AM (Asian/European International)
185 Berry St., Ste. 6500
San Francisco, CA 94107
(415) 978-5378

All Pro Broadcasting, Inc.
Willie D. Davis, President
KCKC-AM (News, Talk)
KAEV-FM (Urban Contemporary)
740 W. 4th St.
San Bernardino, CA 92410
(909) 882-2575

TELEVISION

Granite Broadcasting
W. Don Cornwell, President
KNTV-TV Channel 11

645 Park Ave.
San Jose, CA 95110
(408) 286-1111

KSEE-TV, Inc.
Marty Edelman, President
KSEE-TV Channel 24
5035 E. McKinley Ave.
Fresno, CA 93726
(209) 454-2424

COLORADO

RADIO

People's Wireless, Inc.
James Walker, President
KDKO-AM (Black Contemporary)
2559 Welton St.
Denver, CO 80205
(303) 295-1225

CONNECTICUT

RADIO

Hartcom, Inc.
John Merchant, President
WKND-AM (Black Contemporary)
PO Box 1480
Windsor, CT 06095
(203) 688-6221

DISTRICT OF COLUMBIA

RADIO

Albimar Communications
Skip Finley, President/General Manager
WKYS-FM (Urban Contemporary)
4001 Nebraska Ave. NW
Washington, DC 20016
(202) 686-9300

Almic Broadcasting Co.
Cathy Hughes, President
WOL-AM (News, Talk)
WMMJ-FM (Black Soul)
400 H St. NE
Washington, DC 20002
(202) 675-4800

Howard University Radio
James Watkins, General Manager
WHUR-FM (Black Contemporary)
529 Bryant St. NW
Washington, DC 20059
(202) 806-3500

FLORIDA

RADIO

Sunao Broadcasting Co., Inc.
Jerry Rushin, President and General Manager
WRBD-AM (Rhythm and Blues)
4431 Rock Island Rd.
Fort Lauderdale, FL 33319
(305) 731-4800

Willis Broadcasting
Bishop L.E. Willis, President
WSVE-AM (Religious)
4343 Springgrove St.
Jacksonville, FL 32209
(904) 766-1211

PSI Communications, Inc.
Charles Cherry, Chairman
WPUL-AM (Black Contemporary)
2598 S. Nova Rd.
South Daytona, FL 32121
(904) 767-1131

Rolyn Communications
Gene E. Danzey, President
WRXB-AM (Adult Contemporary)
1700 34th St. S.
St. Petersburg, FL 33711
(813) 327-9792

WTMP Radio LTD
Chris Turner, General Manager
WTMP-AM (Urban Contemporary)
5207 Washington Blvd.
Tampa, FL 33619
(813) 620-1300

TELEVISION

Black Star Communications of Florida, Inc.
John E. Oxendine, President
WBSF-TV Channel 43

4450-L Enterprise Ct.
Melbourne, FL 32934
(407) 254-4343

GEORGIA

RADIO

Keys Communications Group, Inc.
Brady Keys Jr., President
WJIZ-FM (Solid Gold)
506 W. Olgethorpe Blvd.
Albany, GA 31701
(912) 436-0012

Keys Communications Group, Inc.
Brady Keys Jr., President
WJYZ-AM (Oldies, Gospel)
2700 N. Slappey Blvd.
Albany, GA 31707
(912) 436-0112

Davis Broadcasting, Inc.
Gregory A. Davis, President
WOKS-AM (Black Contemporary)
WFXE-FM (Urban Contemporary)
PO Box 1998
Columbus, GA 31902
(706) 576-3565

Radio Cordele, Inc.
John Brooks, President
WUWU-AM (Gospel)
WKKN-FM (Country)
PO Box 4606
Cordele, GA 31015
(912) 276-0306

WHKN Radio
John Brooks, President
WHKN-FM (Country)
PO Box 346
Statesboro, GA 30458
(912) 982-5695

Willis Broadcasting
Bishop L. E. Willis, President
WTJH-AM (Inspirational)
2146 Dodson Dr.
East Point, GA 30344
(404) 344-2233

InterUrban Broadcasting Corp.
Thomas P. Lewis, President
WIZA-AM (Christian Gospel)
1601 Whitaker St.
Savannah, GA 31401
(912) 236-9926

Brown Broadcasting System Inc.
Bradford Brown, President
WBKZ-AM (Gospel/Blues)
548 Hawthorn Ave.
Athens, GA 30606
(706) 548-8800

TELEVISION

Russell Rowe Communications
Herman J. Russell, President
WGXA-TV Channel 24
PO Box 340
Macon, GA 31297
(912) 745-2424

ILLINOIS

RADIO

Midway Broadcasting Corp.
Wesley W. South, President
WVON-AM (Talk)
3350 S. Kedzie Ave.
Chicago, IL 60623
(312) 247-6200

Willis Broadcasting
Bishop L. E. Willis, President
WESL-AM (Gospel)
149 S. 8th St.
East St. Louis, IL 62201
(618) 271-7687

Mariner Broadcasters, Inc.
Charles R. Sherrell, President
WBEE-AM (Jazz)
15700 Campbell St.
Harvey, IL 60426
(708) 331-7840

LH&S Communications
Howard Q. Murphy, President
WSSQ-FM (Adult Contemporary)
WSDR-AM (News/Talk)
WZZT-FM (Urban Contemporary)
3101 Freeport Rd.

Sterling, IL 61081
(815) 625-3400

B&G Broadcasting, Inc.
Joyce Banks, President
WBGE-FM (Urban Contemporary)
516 W. Main St.
Peoria, IL 61606
(309) 637-2923

TELEVISION

Granite Broadcasting, Inc.
W. Don Cornwell, President
WEEK-TV Channel 25
2907 Springfield Rd.
E. Peoria, IL 61611
(309) 698-2525

Jovon Broadcasting, Inc.
Joseph Stroud, President
WJYS-TV Channel 62
18600 S. Oak Park
Tinley Park, IL 60477
(708) 633-0001

INDIANA

RADIO

Marshall Media Group
Pluria Marshall Jr., President
WLTH-AM (Talk)
3669 Broadway
Gary, IN 46409
(219) 884-1370

Willis Broadcasting
Bishop L. E. Willis, President
WPZZ-FM (Urban Contemporary)
645 Industrial Dr.
Franklin, IN 46205
(317) 736-4040

Focus Radio, Inc.
Abe Thompson, President
WUBU-FM (Adult Urban Contemporary)
3371 Cleveland Rd. Extension
Southbend, IN 46628
(219) 271-9333

Willis Broadcasting
Bishop L. E. Willis, President
WWCA-AM (Religious)
487 Broadway
Gary, IN 46402
(219) 883-4600

KENTUCKY

RADIO

Johnson Communications
Linda Johnson-Rice, President
WLOU-AM (Rhythm and Blues)
2549 S. 3rd St., Ste. 3244
Louisville, KY 40208
(502) 636-3535

LOUISIANA

RADIO

Citywide Broadcasting Corp.
Peter Moncrieffe, President
WXOK-AM (Rhythm and Blues)
KQXL-FM (Urban Contemporary)
7707 Waco St.
Baton Rouge, LA 70806
(504) 926-1106

Trinity Broadcasting Corp.
Gus E. Lewis, President
KBCE-FM (Urban Contemporary)
PO Box 69
Boyce, LA 71409
(318) 793-4003

R & M Broadcasting
Bishop Roy L. H. Winbush, President
KJCB-AM (Black Contemporary)
413 Jefferson St.
Lafayette, LA 70501
(318) 233-4262

Snowden Broadcasting
James Snowden, President
WYLD-AM/FM (Urban Contemporary)
2228 Gravier St.
New Orleans, LA 70119
(504) 827-6000

Willis Broadcasting
Bishop L. E. Willis, President

WBOK-AM (Gospel)
1639 Gentilly Blvd.
New Orleans, LA 70119
(504) 943-4600

Citywide Broadcasting of Lafayette, Inc.
Al J. Wallace, General Manager
KFXZ-FM (Urban Contemporary)
3225 Ambassador Caffery Parkway
Lafayette, LA 70506
(318) 898-1112

TELEVISION

Quincy Jones Broadcasting, Inc.
Quincy Jones, President
WNOL-TV Channel 38
1661 Canal St.
New Orleans, LA 70112
(504) 525-3838

MAINE

TELEVISION

Seaway Communications
James Buckner, Chairman
WVII-TV Channel 7
371 Target Industrial Cir.
Bangor, ME 04401
(207) 945-6457

MARYLAND

RADIO

Almic Broadcasting, Inc.
Cathy Hughes, President
WERQ-AM/FM (Urban Contemporary)
1111 Park Ave.
Baltimore, MD 21201
(410) 332-8200

Almic Broadcasting, Inc.
Cathy Hughes, President
WWIN-AM/FM (Urban Contemporary)
200 S. President St., Ste. 600
Baltimore, MD 21202
(410) 332-8200

MASSACHUSETTS

RADIO

Nash Communications
Bernadine Nash, President
WILD-AM (Urban Contemporary)
90 Warren St.
Boston, MA 02119
(617) 427-2222

MICHIGAN

RADIO

Bell Broadcasting Co.
Terry Arnold, President
WJZZ-FM (Contemporary Jazz)
2994 E. Grand Blvd.
Detroit, MI 48202
(313) 871-0591

WGPR, Inc.
George Matthews, President
WGPR-FM (Black Contemporary)
3146 E. Jefferson Ave.
Detroit, MI 48207
(313) 259-8862

Waters Broadcasting Corp.
Nancy Waters, President
WCXT-FM (Light Mix Contemporary)
220 Polk Rd.
Hart, MI 49420
(616) 873-7129

Bell Broadcasting Co.
Terry Arnold, President
WCHB-AM (News, Talk)
32790 Henry Ruff Rd.
Inkster, MI 48141
(313) 278-1440

Michelle Broadcasting
Richard Culpepper, President
WKWM-AM (Urban Contemporary)
PO Box 828
Kentwood, MI 49518
(616) 676-1237

Diamond Broadcasters, Inc.
Helena DeBose, President

WXLA-AM (Urban Contemporary)
101 N. Crest Rd.
Lansing, MI 48906
(517) 484-9600

Ragan Henry Communications
Don Kidwell, President
WDZR-FM (Oldies)
850 Stephenson Hwy., Ste. 405
Troy, MI 48083
(313) 589-7900

Praestantia Broadcasting
Michael Shumpert, President
WOWE-FM (Adult Contemporary)
100 S. Main St.
Vassar, MI 48768
(517) 823-3399

TELEVISION

Blackstar Communications
John E. Oxendine, President
WPXD-TV Channel 31
PO Box 2267
Ann Arbor, MI 48106
(313) 973-7900

WGPR, Inc.
George Matthews, President
WGPR-TV Channel 62
3146 E. Jefferson Ave.
Detroit, MI 48207
(313) 259-8862

Lansing 53, Inc.
Joel Ferguson, President
WLAJ-TV Channel 53
5815 S. Pennsylvania Ave.
Lansing, MI 48909
(517) 394-5300

MINNESOTA

TELEVISION

Granite Broadcasting Corp.
W. Don Cornwell, President
KBJR-TV Channel 6
230 E. Superior St.
Duluth, MN 55802
(218) 727-8484

MISSISSIPPI

RADIO

T & W Communications
Bennie Turner, President
WACR-AM/FM (Urban Contemporary)
1910 14th Ave.
Columbus, MS 39701
(601) 328-1050

Interchange Communications
William Jackson, President
WESY-AM (Gospel and Soul)
WBAD-FM (Black Contemporary)
PO Box 4426
Greenville, MS 38704
(601) 335-9265

Team Broadcasting Co., Inc.
Ruben C. Hughes, President
WGNL-FM (Urban Contemporary)
503 Ione St.
Greenwood, MS 38930
(601) 453-1646

Circuit Broadcasting Co.
Vernon C. Floyd, President
WORV-AM (Black Contemporary)
WJMG-FM (Adult Contemporary)
1204 Graveline St.
Hattiesburg, MS 39401
(601) 544-1941

TELEVISION

TV-3, Inc.
Frank E. Melton, President
WLBT-TV Channel 3
715 S. Jefferson St.
Jackson, MS 39202
(601) 948-3333

MISSOURI

RADIO

US Radio, LP
KISF-FM/KCTE-AM (Nostalgia)
10841 E. 28th St.
Independence, MO 64052
(816) 254-1073

Carter Broadcasting Group, Corp.
Michael Carter, President
KPRT-AM (Gospel, Jazz)
KPRS-FM (Urban Contemporary)
11131 Colorado Ave.
Kansas City, MO 64137
(816) 763-2040

Bronco Broadcasting Co. Inc.
Bill White, President
KIRL-AM (Jazz, Religious, Talk)
3713 Highway 94 N.
St. Charles, MO 63301
(314) 946-6600

TELEVISION

Roberts Broadcasting Co.
Michael Roberts, Chairman
WHSL-TV Channel 46
1408 N. Kingshighway
St. Louis, MO 53113
(314) 367-4600

NEW JERSEY

RADIO

WUSS-AM (Urban Contemporary)
James Cuffee, President
1507 Atlantic Ave.
Atlantic City, NJ 08401
(609) 345-7134

Vinrah of New Jersey, Inc.
WCMC-AM (Album Oriented Rock)
WZXL-FM (Album Oriented Rock)
3010 New Jersey Ave.
Wildwood, NJ 08260
(609) 522-1416

NEW YORK

RADIO

Sheridan Broadcasting Corp
Ronald R. Davenport, President
WUFO-AM (Urban Contemporary)
89 LaSalle Ave.
Buffalo, NY 14214
(716) 834-1080

Inner City Broadcasting Corp. of New York
Pierre M. Sutton, Chairman
WLIB-AM (News, Talk)
WBLS-FM (Urban Contemporary)
3 Park Ave., 40th and 41st Fls.
New York, NY 10017
(212) 661-3344

Monroe County Broadcasting Co.
Andrew A. Langston, President
WDKX-FM (Urban Contemporary)
683 E. Main St.
Rochester, NY 14605
(716) 262-2050

Unity Broadcasting Network/New York
Sydney Small, Chairman
WWRL-AM (Gospel)
41-30 58th St.
Woodside, NY 11377
(718) 335-1600

TELEVISION

WTVH, Inc.
Bill Ransom, President
WTVH-TV Channel 5
980 James St.
Syracuse, NY 13203
(315) 425-5555

NETWORK

American Urban Radio Network
Jack Bryant, President
463 7th Ave., 6th Fl.
New York, NY 10018
(212) 714-1000

NORTH CAROLINA

RADIO

Ebony Enterprises, Inc.
Willie Walls, President
WVOE-AM (Urban Contemporary)
Rte. 3, Box 39B
Chadbourn, NC 28431
(910) 654-5621

Willis Broadcasting
Bishop L. E. Willis, President
WGSP-AM (Gospel)
2730 Rozzelles Berry Rd.
Charlotte, NC 28208
(704) 399-9477

Willis Broadcasting
Bishop L. E. Willis, President
WSRC-AM (Religious)
3202 Guess Rd.
Durham, NC 27705
(919) 477-7999

Willis Broadcasting
Bishop L. E. Willis, President
WBXB-FM (Gospel)
PO Box 765
Edenton, NC 27932
(919) 482-2224

US Radio, LP
WQOK-FM (Urban Contemporary)
8601 Six Forks Rd.
Raleigh, NC 27615
(919) 848-9736

Special Markets Media, Inc.
Henry and Prentiss Monroe
WLLE-AM (Rhythm and Blues)
649 Maywood Ave.
Raleigh, NC 27603
(919) 833-3874

Northstar Broadcasting Corp.
Charles O. Johnson, President
WEED-AM (Country)
WRSV-FM (Urban Contemporary)
PO Box 2666
Rocky Mount, NC 27802
(919) 443-5976

Willis Broadcasting
Bishop L. E. Willis, President
WTNC-AM (Gospel)
PO Box 1920
726 Salem St.
Thomasville, NC 27360
(910) 472-0790

Evans Broadcasting Corp.
Mutter D. Evans, President
WAAA-AM (Black Contemporary)
PO Box 11197
4950 Indiana Ave.
Winston-Salem, NC 27116
(910) 767-0430

WSMX Radio
Bishop S.D. Johnson, President
WSMX-AM (Religious)
500 Kinnard St.
PO Box 16056
Winston-Salem, NC 27115
(910) 761-1545

Willis Broadcasting
Bishop L. E. Willis, President
WMQX-AM (Religious)
93 Salem Valley Rd.
PO Box 593
Winston-Salem, NC 27102
(919) 723-9393

OHIO

RADIO

Melodynamic Broadcasting
Leodis Harris, President
WCER-AM (Adult Mix)
4537 22nd St. NW
Canton, OH 44708
(216) 478-6666

InterUrban Broadcasting
Thomas P. Lewis, President
WIZF-FM (Urban Contemporary)
7030 Reading Rd., Ste. 316
Cincinnati, OH 45237
(513) 351-5900

Junior Broadcasting Inc.
John C. Thomas, President
WCIN-AM (Black Contemporary)
106 Glenwood Ave.
Cincinnati, OH 45217
(513) 281-7180

Ragan Henry Communications, LP
WRZR-FM (Hard Rock)
1150 Morse Rd.
Columbus, OH 43229
(614) 846-1031

Johnson Communications
Jim Johnson, General Manager/President
WDAO-AM (Rhythm and Blues)
4309 W. 3rd St.
Dayton, OH 45417
(513) 263-9326

Taylor Broadcasting Co.
James Taylor, President
WJTB-AM (Urban Contemporary)
105 Lake Ave.
Elyria, OH 44035
(216) 327-1844

OREGON

TELEVISION

Blackstar Communications
John E. Oxendine, President
KBSP-TV Channel 22
4928 Indian School Rd. NE
Salem, OR 97305
(503) 390-2202

PENNSYLVANIA

RADIO

KBT Communications, Inc.
Cody Anderson, President
WHAT-AM (Talk)
2471 N. 54th St.
Philadelphia, PA 19131
(215) 581-5161

Willis Broadcasting
Bishop L. E. Willis, President
WURD-AM (Gospel)
5301 Tacony St.
PO Box 233
Philadelphia, PA 19137
(215) 533-8900

Sheridan Broadcasting Corp.
Ronald R. Davenport, Chairman
WYJZ-AM (Oldies)
WAMO-AM/FM (Urban Contemporary)
411 7th Ave., Ste. 1500
Pittsburgh, PA 15219
(412) 471-2181

US Radio, LP
WRAW-AM (Urban Contemporary)
WRFY-FM (Urban Contemporary)
1265 Perkiomen Ave.
Reading, PA 19602
(215) 376-7173

TELEVISION

WPTT-Inc.
Eddie Edwards, President
WPTT-TV Channel 22
PO Box 2809
Pittsburgh, PA 15230
(412) 856-9010

SOUTH CAROLINA

RADIO

Vivian Broadcasting, Inc.
Vivian M. Galloway, President
WVGB-AM (Gospel)
806 Monson St.
Beaufort, SC 29902
(803) 524-4700

Midland Communications Co.
Isaac Heyward, President
WTGH-AM (Gospel)
1303 State St.
PO Box 620
Cayce, SC 29033
(803) 796-9533

Millennium Communications of Charleston
Cliff Fletcher, President
WWWZ-FM (Urban Contemporary)
1064-Gardner Rd.
Charleston, SC 29417
(803) 556-9132

WPAL, Inc.
William Saunders, President
WPAL-AM (Rhythm and Blues)
1717 Wappoo Rd.
PO Box 30999

Charleston, SC 29417
(803) 763-6330

Berkeley Broadcasting Corp.
Clary Butler, President
WMCJ-AM (Religious)
314 Rembert Dennis Blvd.
Monks Corner, SC 29461
(803) 761-6010

TENNESSEE

RADIO

Shaw Broadcasting
Johnny and Opal Shaw, Owners
WBOL-AM (Gospel)
WOJG-FM (Gospel)
PO Box 191
Bolivar, TN 38008
(901) 658-3690

Wolfe Communications
James E. Wolfe Jr., President
WFKX-FM (Urban Contemporary)
PO Box 2763
Jackson, TN 38302-2763
(901) 427-9616

Gilliam Communications
Art Gilliam, President
WLOK-AM (Gospel)
PO Box 69
Memphis, TN 38101
(901) 527-9565

Ragan Henry Communications, LP
WDIA-AM (Urban Contemporary)
WHRK-FM (Urban Contemporary)
112 Union Ave.
Memphis, TN 38103
(901) 529-4300

Babb Broadcasting Co.
Morgan Babb, President
WMDB-AM (Urban Contemporary)
3051 Stokers Ln.
Nashville, TN 37218
(615) 255-2876

Phoenix of Nashville, Inc.
Samuel Howard, President
WVOL-AM (Classic Soul)
WQQK-FM (Urban Contemporary)
1320 Brick Church Pke.
Nashville, TN 37207
(615) 227-1470

TEXAS

RADIO

Salt of the Earth Broadcasting
Darrell E. Martin, President
KWWJ-AM (Religious)
4638 Decker Dr.
Baytown, TX 77520
(713) 424-7000

Network Communications Co.
Ruth Ollison, President
KEGG-AM (Gospel)
PO Box 600
Daingerfield, TX 75638
(903) 645-3928

US Radio, LP
Don Kidwell, President
KHEY-AM/FM (Country)
2419 N. Piedras St.
El Paso, TX 79930
(915) 566-9301

Marshall Media Group
Pluria Marshall Jr., President
KHRN-FM (Urban Contemporary)
219 N. Main St., Ste. 600
Bryan, TX 77803
(409) 779-3337

KCOH, Inc.
Mike Petrizzo, General Manager
KCOH-AM (Urban Contemporary)
5011 Almeda Rd.
Houston, TX 77004
(713) 522-1001

US Radio, LP
KKZR-FM (Rock)
6161 Savoy St., Ste. 1100
Houston, TX 77036
(713) 260-3600

US Radio, LP
KJOJ-FM (Gospel)
304 Flag Lake Dr.
Lake Jackson, TX 77566
(409) 297-2103

Inner City Broadcasting
Pierre Sutton, President
KSJL-AM (Urban Contemporary)
KSAQ-FM (Urban Contemporary)
217 Alamo Plz.
San Antonio, TX 78205
(512) 271-9600

TELEVISION

TV-3, Inc.
Frank E. Melton, President
KTRE-TV Channel 9
PO Box 729
Lufkin, TX 75902
(409) 853-5873

TV-3, Inc.
Frank E. Melton, President
KLTV-TV Channel 7
PO Box 957
Tyler, TX 75710
(903) 597-5588

UTAH

RADIO

US Radio II, Inc.
KUMT-FM (Adult Contemporary)
KMXB-FM (Adult Contemporary)
KCPX-AM (Adult Contemporary)
5282 South 320 West, Ste. D-272
Salt Lake City, UT 84107
(801) 264-1075

VIRGINIA

RADIO

Broadcasting Corp. of Virginia
Eric Reynolds, President
WTJZ-AM (Gospel)
553 Michigan Dr.
Hampton, VA 23669
(804) 723-1270

US Radio, LP
WOWI-FM (Urban Contemporary)
WSVY-AM/FM (Urban Contemporary)
645 Church St., Ste. 201
Norfolk, VA 23510
(804) 627-5800

WREJ-Radio
Walton Belle and Charles Cummings, Owners
WREJ-AM (Christian)
6001 Wilkinson Rd.
Richmond, VA 23227
(804) 264-1540

Tri-City Christian Radio, Inc.
James I. Johnson Jr., President
WFTH-AM (Contemporary Gospel)
227 Eastbelt Blvd.
Richmond, VA 23224
(804) 233-0765

Willis Broadcasting Co.
Bishop L. E. Willis, President
WPCE-AM (Inspirational)
WMYK-FM (Inspirational)
645 Church St.
Norfolk, VA 23510
(804) 622-4600

TELEVISION

Tidewater Christian Communications Corp.
Samuel Corruth, Chairman
WJCB-TV Channel 49
2501 Washington Ave., 6th Fl.
Newport News, VA 23607
(804) 247-0049

WASHINGTON

RADIO

KUJ Ltd. Partnership
Patrick Prout, President/General Partner
KUJ-AM (Oldies)
KNLT-FM (Adult Contemporary)
Rte., 5 Box 513
Walla Walla, WA 99362
(509) 529-8000

WISCONSIN

RADIO

All Pro Broadcasting Co.
Willie D. Davis, President
WMCS-AM (Adult Contemporary)
WLUM-FM (Adult Contemporary)
4222 W. Capitol Dr.
Milwaukee, WI 53216
(414) 444-1290

Courier Communications
Gerald W. Jones, President
WNOV-AM (Urban Contemporary)
3815 N. Teutonia Ave.
PO Box 0638
Milwaukee, WI 53206
(414) 449-9668

UNC Media of Milwaukee
Constance Balthrop, President
WKKV-FM (Jazz)
WBJX-AM (Jazz)
2400 S. 102nd St., Ste. 230
West Allis, WI 53227
(414) 321-1007

TELEVISION

Seaway Communications
James Buckner, Chairman
WJFW-TV Channel 12
PO Box 858
S. Oneida Ave.
Rhinelander, WI 54501
(715) 369-4700

U.S. VIRGIN ISLANDS

RADIO

Family Broadcasting, Inc.
Luz A. James, President
WSTX-AM/FM (Calypso, Stardust)
PO Box 3279
Christiansted, St. Croix 00822
(809) 773-0490

Ottley Communications Corp.
Athneil Ottley, President
WSTA-AM (Adult Contemporary)
PO Box 1340
St. Thomas, VI 00804
(809) 774-1340

Trans Caribbean Broadcasting Co.
Kervin Clenace, President
WTBN-FM (Adult Contemporary)
Havensight Executive Twr., Ste. 1033, No. 19
Charlotte Amalie, VI 00802
(809) 776-2610

20

FILM AND TELEVISION

Gil L. Robertson IV

The cinema reigns supreme as the world's foremost medium for creative expression and influence in defining images that shape humanity. Although primarily seen as a form of entertainment, it plays a significant role in the manner in which society views itself and the world around it. With regard to the representation of African Americans, the medium has largely failed to provide illuminating images that reflect the complete diversity of the African American experience. Instead, it has largely focused on images that devalue African Americans by confining their representation within an ideological web of myths, stereotypes, and caricatures.

The experiences of African Americans in television have been less limiting than those realized in film. This has been due, in part, to the fact that television sought to capture an African American audience from the outset. In fact, many of the medium's earliest participants, such as Steve Allen (1921–2000), publicly stated that television would benefit from the inclusion of African American performers. Therefore, beginning with the medium's widespread use in the late 1940s and into the present day, television has provided unique avenues of expression for African Americans in acting, production, and executive roles.

AFRICAN AMERICANS IN FILM

THE SILENT FILM ERA

Beginning with the inception of the "moving camera" in the 1890s, African American images in cinema have been positioned, marginalized, and subordinated in every possible manner to glorify and relentlessly hold to America's status quo. In 1898, the first African Americans appeared in film as soldiers heading for battle in the Spanish-American War. Soon afterward though, the depiction of African Americans began to mirror the racial stereotypes of the era, and African American actors populated the screen as criminals, ministers, and, during the period in which American society grew sentimental for the Civil War era, as enslaved Africans. The most provocative example of this trend is D. W. Griffith's *The Birth of a Nation* (1915), which depicts African Americans in exaggerated portrayals of servitude.

Released at the end of the silent film era, *The Birth of a Nation* unleashed a tremendous amount of ire and controversy that is still discussed in cinematic and academic circles. Although its release represented a technical and artistic triumph for the film community, its unabashed message of racial intolerance and embellished, stereotypical images of African Americans have become symbolic of the tremendous obstacles that African Americans face in cinema. Although other early films, such as *Uncle Tom's Cabin* (1909) and *The Nigger* (1915), drew on the same anti–African American propaganda, *The Birth of a Nation*, because of its technological significance, stands out as a fundamental reference to cinema's position on African American images.

Redefining African American Images. In response to the popularity of such films, African Americans during the 1910s and 1920s launched independent film projects and formed production companies in order to create more realistic images of African American culture. Perhaps the

Movie Poster for* The Birth of a Nation *(1915). *Considered a landmark for its technical and artistic achievements, this D. W. Griffith–directed epic from the silent film era has been controversial since its release because of its message of racial intolerance and its stereotypical images of African Americans.* HULTON ARCHIVE/GETTY IMAGES

best-known African American filmmaker of this period is Oscar Micheaux (1884–1951), who managed to generate financial profits from more than thirty silent and sound features that his private studio released. Using a distribution system similar to that created by African American film producer Noble Johnson (1881–1978), Micheaux personally delivered films to movie theaters across the country, edited films on the road, and obtained money from theater owners by having actors give private performances from scenes of upcoming releases. Despite the fact that many of his films suffered from his poor technical skills, Micheaux's expert abilities as a promoter earned him a sizeable following. (Always daring, Micheaux turned the tables on Hollywood by casting light-skinned actors to play whites in several of his films.) In 1924, Micheaux's *Body and Soul* featured Paul Robeson (1898–1976) in his film debut.

After recovering from bankruptcy, Micheaux released *The Exile* in 1931—the first African American feature-length sound movie—and *God's Stepchildren* (1937), among other "talkies." As tastes began to shift from what were called "race productions," Micheaux saw his audience dwindle. His final film, released in 1948, a three-hour epic titled *The Betrayal*, was a commercial failure. While many of his films have been lost, Micheaux maintained control of his prized works, ensuring that they were protected as the legal property of his wife.

There were other African American pioneer filmmakers in this period—some of whose efforts predated Micheaux's. William "Bill" Foster began using "all-colored" casts in a number of short films in 1913. Through his Foster Photoplay Company, he released several films, the most

The Exile, *1931.* *Director Oscar Micheaux's* The Exile *was the first all-talking black independent feature film.* EVERETT COLLECTION

God's Stepchildren, ***with Alice B. Russell*** **(behind sofa),** ***and Ethel Moses and Carman Newsome*** **(on sofa),** ***1938.*** *The film was written and directed by Oscar Micheaux, one of the best-known African American filmmakers of the 1920s and 1930s.* EVERETT COLLECTION

notable of which were *The Railroad Porter*, *The Butler*, and *The Grafter and the Maid.* Although Foster genuinely believed that an African American movie company could be viable, attempting to secure technical and financial support, not to mention distribution outlets, soon brought about his company's demise.

Headed by Noble Johnson, the Lincoln Motion Picture Company, which was established in the summer of 1915, was perhaps the first company to produce significant films featuring black performers for African American audiences. The company released several films that depicted African Americans in a common, natural manner. In response to the distribution problems that often plagued African American studios, Johnson worked out a commission system that engaged African American media personnel across the United States to utilize their business relationships with movie theater owners and show his films. By doing so, Johnson was able to produce such films as *The Realization of a Negro's Ambition* (1916), *The Trooper of Company K* (1917), and *The Law of Nature* (1918). Though somewhat successful, this system could not compete with major Hollywood studios, and after Johnson's defection to Universal Films, the company soon folded.

Another early African American film pioneer was Emmett J. Scott (1873–1957). A former secretary to Tuskegee Institute founder Booker T. Washington (1856–1915), Scott believed that African American cinema could be financially supported through the sale of stock in his production company. Incorporated in July 1916, his Birth of a Race Photoplay Corporation produced *The Birth of a Race* and released the film in December 1918. Although the film did not meet original expectations, it did succeed in establishing a capital-raising method that would prove instrumental to future African American filmmakers. In addition, many other African American entrepreneurs took the gamble on producing films, with varying degrees of success. The

Frederick Douglass Film Company premiered its first film, *The Colored American Winning His Suit*, in 1916. In 1920, the Royal Gardens Film Company presented *In the Depths of Our Hearts*. In 1921, the ex-heavyweight champion Jack Johnson (1878–1946) starred in *As the World Rolls On* for Andlauer Productions. In each case, however, the African American entrepreneurs behind these ventures succumbed to the insurmountable obstacles dealt to them because of racism.

BREAKING INTO MAINSTREAM SOUND FILMS

Prior to the sound era of cinema, many film producers used white actors in "blackface," or burnt-cork makeup, to portray blacks. In order to capture the distinctive dialect and cadence of African Americans though, most producers began to employ African American actors for such limited roles during the new era of sound film.

Although short "talkies" by some white filmmakers depicted African Americans in a more authentic manner, little else changed for African American performers, who generally appeared as criminals and domestic servants, among other roles. In fact, the film widely heralded for first utilizing sound in film, *The Jazz Singer* (1927), starred ex-vaudevillian Al Jolson (1886–1950) singing in "blackface."

One favorable change for African American performers during this era was the establishment of the movie musical. From the late 1920s through the 1940s, countless movie musicals were made and featured African American performers. For the fortunate few, singing in a film was a real achievement—not only did it guarantee work on a project, but it also enabled performers to showcase broader talents. As the film community reveled in its latest trend, many multitalented African American performers, such as Lena Horne, were discovered. Already gaining impressive notoriety for her beauty and singing

Scene from the Film* Cabin in the Sky *(1943). *This musical fable about a compulsive gambler played by Eddie Anderson (*standing, center*) included among its all–African American cast Lena Horne (*seated*). Louis Armstrong and Duke Ellington contributed to the musical score.* BETTMANN/CORBIS

talent, Horne's film career actually began with the black independent film *The Duke Is Tops* (1938), as well as some short films. Lured to Hollywood in 1942 by Metro-Goldwyn-Mayer for a major role in *Panama Hattie*, Horne became the first African American performer awarded a major studio contract. Lena Horne faced unusual circumstances in Hollywood, though, because of her physical appearance. As a light-skinned African American with long flowing hair, she was viewed by many as something other than black. However, as a staunch supporter of her ethnicity, the actress refused to sacrifice pride in her heritage for greater opportunities of film stardom, and she declined to play demeaning roles, such as an enslaved person or a servant. As a result, Horne only appeared in two other major films, *Cabin in the Sky* (1943) and *Stormy Weather* (1943). Beyond these works, Horne's brief film career mostly consisted of musical numbers that could easily be edited in order to appease southern viewing audiences.

Another notable performer whose breakthrough came during this era was actor Paul Robeson. Widely respected for his work as a stage actor, Robeson eventually played important roles in nine feature films between 1929 and 1942. By sheer force of talent and charisma, Robeson succeeded where many others had failed in consistently securing roles that were central to the theme of the film. In such classic dramas as *The Emperor Jones* (1933), the musical *Show Boat* (1936), and the British film *The Proud Valley* (1940), Robeson created characters that challenged film barriers of that time. Unfortunately, the barriers of prejudice and stereotype continued to exist, and Robeson, after consistently being denied roles worthy of his talent, abandoned Hollywood to pursue a concert career.

AFRICAN AMERICAN ACTORS ENDURE RACIAL STEREOTYPES

Throughout the pantheon of early Hollywood cinema, perhaps no other African American caricature was as well entrenched as the "mammy" figure. Often the source of comic relief, these characters populated films from around 1914 through the late 1950s. No two performers better embodied that image than Louise Beavers (1902–1962) and Hattie McDaniel (1895–1952), since physically, they both met the industry's standards. Although Beavers and McDaniel both enjoyed lengthy film careers, neither was able to discard this stereotype. Beavers, who is best known for her role in the 1934 film version of *Imitation of Life*, appeared in over 120 films. McDaniel, who earned an Academy Award in 1939 for her role in *Gone with the Wind*, appeared in more than three hundred films. Despite the stereotypical roles that each performed, Beavers and McDaniel were both well respected and seen as successful members of the Hollywood film community.

Between the late 1920s and the mid-1940s, many other African American performers were successful in establishing film careers. Although virtually all had to suffer through gross indignities in pursuit of their careers, they nevertheless contributed to the growing African American presence in mainstream films. These actors and actresses included Eddie "Rochester" Anderson (1905–1977), Rex Ingram (1895–1969), Ethel Waters (1896–1977), and Nina Mae McKinney (1912–1967).

WORLD WAR II PROPAGANDA FILMS STRIVE FOR RACIAL HARMONY

With the advent of World War II (1939–1945), leaders of the civil rights movement of the early twentieth century seized the opportunity to press the U.S. government to address racial injustice, including providing equal opportunity in wartime industry and the military. At the same time, activist groups, such as the National Association for the Advancement of Colored People (NAACP), lobbied Hollywood for better film roles for African Americans.

In response, the U.S. War Department produced the groundbreaking film *The Negro Soldier* in 1944. At the same time, Hollywood produced movies that depicted a racially integrated military, years before President Harry Truman's Executive Order 9981 mandated desegregation of the armed forces. For example, in *Crash Dive* (1943), African American actor Ben Carter (1911–1946) is shown saving the life of the film's star, Tyrone Power (1914–1958). In the film *Lifeboat* (1944), African American actor Canada Lee (1907–1952) is shown among a shipwrecked group of civilians whose ship has been destroyed by enemy fire. Later in the war, the U.S. government commissioned several short civilian films that expressed the theme of racial harmony. One such effort was *The House I Live In*, which won an Academy Award for best short film in 1947. Documentaries of this period also reflected a liberal attitude toward race relations shortly after wartime. For example, documentarians Janice Loeb and Helen Levitt (1913–2009) produced *The Quiet One* in 1948. It depicted the concerted effort put forth by white social workers in dealing with disadvantaged black juveniles.

BLACKS IN POSTWAR AMERICAN FILMS

Films made in postwar America began to feature African Americans in multidimensional roles, playing characters that were more integrated into American life. In fact, a number of films that were released in the late 1940s through the mid-1960s presented African Americans with families and careers and working toward goals of a better life. As such, Hollywood films sought, if only slightly, to broaden the scope of the African American experience. One significant cause for this development was the increasing degree of political and economic influence wielded by the African American community.

Making his film debut in the 1950 drama *No Way Out,* Sidney Poitier became the cinematic model for integration. Consistently depicted as an educated, intelligent, and well-mannered black man, Hollywood was quick to capitalize on Poitier's appeal. With film credits that include *Cry, the Beloved Country* (1951), *The Defiant Ones* (1958), *A Raisin in the Sun* (1961), *Guess Who's Coming to Dinner* (1967), and *In the Heat of the Night* (1967), Poitier became Hollywood's first bona fide African American film star. In 1963, he won the Academy Award in the best actor category—the first by an African American—for his lead role in *Lilies of the Field.* Though Poitier's success symbolized the changing industry standards for African American performers during the course of the next two decades, his stardom did not come without a price. Although positioned as a leading actor, Poitier's characterizations often lacked human dimension. For instance, in all but three of the films made during this period, Poitier was never allowed to exhibit any degree of sexuality. Nonetheless, Poitier's career heralded greater acceptance of black actors as equals to their white counterparts.

In 1954, film actress Dorothy Dandridge (1922–1965) became the first African American woman to be nominated for an Academy Award in the best actress category for her role in *Carmen Jones.* With unrivaled talent and beauty, it seemed that Dandridge would become the female counterpart to Poitier's leading African American man. However, she was unable to find a subsequent role offering the same dimensions as Carmen Jones. While Dandridge repeatedly demonstrated dramatic ability and landed a respectable contract with Twentieth Century Fox, the industry mostly cast her in films as an exotic native. When the pressures of battling the film industry proved too much, Dandridge drifted from the Hollywood scene and in 1965 died of an apparent suicide.

In the case of actor Harry Belafonte, Hollywood was faced with another dilemma. A naturally romantic hero, the film industry found it difficult to contain Belafonte's sexuality. Like Dandridge, with whom he starred in *Carmen Jones* and *Island in the Sun* (1957), Belafonte's career was largely confined to playing an island native and other unflattering roles. After performing in *Odds Against Tomorrow* (1959), *The World, the Flesh, and the Devil* (1959), and *Buck and the Preacher* (1972), Belafonte began a successful career as a concert performer and prominent civil rights spokesperson, selecting future film projects only with great discretion.

Many other actors and actresses enjoyed mainstream acceptance and success in films. Among those who made a real impact during this period were Diana Sands (1934–1973), Ruby Dee, and Brock Peters (1927–2005). Along with Poitier, Dandridge, and Belafonte, their films marked the advent of the 1960s civil rights movement.

BLAXPLOITATION FILMS

During the 1960s civil rights movement and the war in Vietnam (1957–1975), American society was in the midst of a cultural revolution. As a result, films began to reflect the political and social changes brought about by the period's harsh, challenging ideology. Director Melvin Van Peebles's seminal 1971 African American action film, *Sweet Sweetback's Baadasssss Song,* seemed to define, more than any other film, this era—one marked with contempt for the white social order and its police. In the wake of the enormous success of Peebles's films, Hollywood rushed to produce similar movies that would capture this new African American audience.

Although some African American action films, notably *Shaft* (1971), *Super Fly* (1972), and *Coffy* (1973), drew a great deal of commercial success, this trend was soon dubbed *blaxploitation* by the African American media. In pursuit of increased profits, Hollywood even remade classic horror movies into blaxploitation films, including *Blacula* and *Blackenstein,* both in 1972. Along with the popularity of African American action films came the emergence of a new wave of serious African American–oriented dramas. Although most of these films failed to meet expectations, some were successful, including the 1969 releases *The Learning Tree, Slaves,* and *Putney Swope,* as well as *Sounder* (1972), to name a few.

Finally, more African Americans worked in Hollywood than ever before during this period—many behind the camera. Such screenwriters as Richard Wesley, Bill Gunn (1934–1989), and Lonne Elder (1931–1996) and directors Gordon Parks Sr. (1912–2006), Gordon Parks Jr. (1934–1979), Michael Schultz, and Stan Lathan were all called on to participate in the making of major studio films.

TRANSITIONS IN AFRICAN AMERICAN FILM

Although Motown founder Berry Gordy Jr.'s impact on the American music industry is legendary, little credit has been given to him as a film producer and director. Under his Motown Films banner, Gordy produced several films, the most successful being the 1972 release *Lady Sings the Blues,* starring Diana Ross and Billy Dee Williams. Gordy's pairing of them was the first time that African American performers were presented as romantic icons. Gordy's 1976 film *Mahogany* was also the first to feature an African American actress as glamorous, independent, and sexual.

African American comedians were enjoying enormous film success as well. Richard Pryor (1940–2005) emerged in the late 1970s as a film icon. Best known for his often provocative, iconoclastic stand-up comedy routines, Pryor rose to superstardom through supporting appearances in films. After appearing opposite Gene Wilder in the 1976 buddy film *Silver Streak*, Pryor continued to exhibit box-office clout in such films as *Greased Lightning* (1977), *Which Way Is Up* (1977), and *Bustin' Loose* (1981). He later returned to the stage and made two live concert films that permanently sealed his position in film history. Other comedians, notably Eddie Murphy in the terrifically successful *48 Hours* (1982), benefitted from Pryor's success.

THE EMERGENCE OF MODERN AFRICAN AMERICAN CINEMA

Toward the mid-1980s, African American actors and actresses appeared to be running on empty. With the roles offered by the blaxploitation era long gone, stereotypes of the past began to reemerge. The tragic mulatto, a well-used cinematic device, once again appeared as such actresses as Rae Dawn Chong (*American Flyers*), Jennifer Beals (*Flashdance*), and Lisa Bonet (*Angel Heart*) were cast in roles that made no discernable mention of their ethnicity. In addition, the African American musical made a brief resurgence in the films *Beat Street* (1984), *Krush Groove* (1985), *The Last Dragon* (1985), *The Cotton Club* (1984), and *Purple Rain* (1984).

She's Gotta Have It, *Featuring Tracy Camilla Johns and Tommy Redmond Hicks, 1986.* *Written and directed by Spike Lee, the romantic comedy is his first feature film.* ISLAND PICTURES/EVERETT COLLECTION

Another trend that enjoyed renewed popularity in cinema was "buddy movies." Although cinematic history is filled with various pairings of black and white performers, the film industry in the 1980s perfected the trend with enormous box-office success. Some notable buddy-film pairings included Carl Weathers and Sylvester Stallone in the *Rocky* films and Danny Glover and Mel Gibson in the *Lethal Weapon* series. Meanwhile, a low-budget independent film was released by a young New York University Film School graduate named Spike Lee. The 1986 release *She's Gotta Have It* resulted in the resurgence of African American cinema. Lee managed to attract large audiences for most of his commercial ventures and directed a string of successful Hollywood films, including one of the most politically charged films of the era, *Do the Right Thing* (1989).

Spike Lee's box-office successes, coupled with the achievements of University of Southern California Film School graduate John Singleton (*Boyz N the Hood*, *Poetic Justice*, and *Rosewood*) and comedian turned actor and director Robert Townsend (*Hollywood Shuffle* and *The Five Heartbeats*), seemed to guarantee a viable future for African American filmmakers.

PUSHING TOWARD A PROMISING FUTURE IN AFRICAN AMERICAN CINEMA

The beginning of the new millennium showed great promise for African American talent in film. For the first time in history, African American actors were able to establish solid careers in cinema. Among others, Angela Bassett, Halle Berry, Danny Glover, Whoopi Goldberg, Morgan Freeman, Samuel Jackson, Martin Lawrence, Eddie Murphy, Wesley Snipes, and Alfre Woodard created a lasting impact on the tapestry of film. A fresh and exciting new crop of talented actors, such as Taye Diggs and Sanaa Lathan, and directors Malcolm Lee, Rick Famuyiwa, and Gina Prince-Bythewood, also seemed well on their way to major movie careers.

The proliferation of musical artists crossing over into film has grown tremendously. Ice Cube, Queen Latifah, LL Cool J, and especially Will Smith built strongly on their pre-2000 track records. Their multimedia successes spawned opportunities for a new generation of musical talent, such as rappers DMX (*Exit Wounds*) and Eve (*Barbershop*), as well as singer Beyoncé Knowles (*Austin Powers in Goldmember*) and the late Aaliyah (*Queen of the Dammed* and *Romeo Must Die*).

Action films also broke new ground in the early 2000s, producing two major stars of African American descent. The international success of the films *The*

Mummy Returns (2001) and *Scorpion King* (2002) turned World Wrestling Entertainment champion Dwayne "The Rock" Johnson into a movie star. Meanwhile, the box-office success of films such as *The Fast and the Furious* (2001) and *XXX* (2002) catapulted Afro-Italian actor Vin Diesel into the exclusive $20 million club as an actor.

Perhaps the most surprising change took place during the 2002 Academy Awards ceremony when Denzel Washington (*Training Day*) and Halle Berry (*Monster's Ball*) each won Oscars for lead roles. Never had a black woman won for best actress, and only the great Sidney Poitier—forty years earlier—had received the best actor Oscar. As more African American performers gained responsibility for defining African American images in cinema, opportunities for black actors, filmmakers, and industry executives during the twenty-first century seemed to be very promising.

THE AFRICAN AMERICAN FILM CRITICS ASSOCIATION

In 2003, a group of African American film critics launched the African American Film Critics Association (AAFCA), the first organization of its kind in the film industry. Much like the Foreign Press Association and the New York and Los Angeles film critics associations, the AAFCA creates awareness for films produced, written, directed, and starring talent of African descent. Like the other groups, AAFCA issues an annual top-ten list comprised of films released during a calendar year. Since its inception, the nationwide body has attracted a cross section of prominent entertainment media who represent print, television, radio, and the Internet. On December 14, 2009, AAFCA reached a benchmark with its first live award show in Hollywood.

NEW MILLENNIUM OPPORTUNITIES

In the years following the historic Oscar wins of Denzel Washington and Halle Berry, opportunities continued to remain mixed for African Americans in Hollywood. Although established talent such as Will Smith, Denzel Washington, and Queen Latifah continued to enjoy robust job prospects within the film industry, the majority of African Americans were not as fortunate. With her Oscar in hand, even Halle Berry was unable to leverage the career options bestowed on her white counterparts.

In 2004, a shift took place with the release of several studio and independent films featuring African American themes and talent, the most notable of which was *Ray*. Starring Jamie Foxx and based on the life of the blind soul music icon Ray Charles, the film earned more than $75 million at the U.S. box office, and Foxx won an Oscar in the best actor category. Foxx's win was followed in 2006 by another best actor Oscar win by an African American, Forest Whitaker for *The Last King of Scotland*. The commercial viability of the black box office was further proven by veteran director Spike Lee, whose *Inside Man* (2006) earned more than $180 million at the domestic box office.

One of the most important trends to be embraced by the African American film community in the new millennium has been within the independent space of the film industry. Independent films were by definition made outside the traditional studio system, although by the beginning of the millennium more studios set up "independent divisions," which guaranteed greater visibility and stronger box office. Oscar-nominated director John Singleton was the first to make good use of the trend by producing the successful independent film *Hustle & Flow* in 2005. After earning over $25 million at the U.S. box office, and making a mainstream star out of actor Terrence Howard, the film became a model that others in black Hollywood began to follow.

THE TYLER PERRY ERA

Building on an established following among gospel-based black theater audiences, playwright and producer Tyler Perry partnered with the then fledgling independent studio Lion's Gate to release his debut film, *Diary of a Mad Black Woman* (2005). After earning more than $50 million at the U.S. box office, the film transformed Perry into a Hollywood sensation. Following up his debut with subsequent releases—*Madea's Family Reunion* (2006), *Daddy's Little Girls* (2007), *Why Did I Get Married?* (2007), *The Family that Preys* (2008), *Meet the Browns* (2008), *Tyler Perry's Madea Goes to Jail* (2009), *Tyler Perry's I Can Do Bad All by Myself* (2009), and *Why Did I Get Married Too?* (2010)—Perry has convincingly established the commercial viability of independent African American films.

In addition to the success of his films, Perry firmly cemented the new direction of twenty-first-century black independent films with the opening in 2008 of Tyler Perry Studios in Atlanta for all his future productions. In 2009, Perry and Oprah Winfrey served as executive producers of the box-office hit and Oscar contender *Precious*, directed by African American director Lee Daniels.

TWENTY-FIRST-CENTURY AFRICAN AMERICANS IN CINEMA

Not surprisingly, Tyler Perry's success has inspired a new generation of African American filmmakers to pursue their vision and dreams in Hollywood. With a successful track record of films (*Trois*, *The Gospel*, and *Stomp the Yard*, among others) that depict contemporary African American life, director Rob Hardy and producer Will Packer of Rainforest Films have established a noteworthy niche among film audiences.

Beginning with *Monster's Ball* (2001), which earned a best actress Oscar for Halle Berry, director and producer Lee Daniels has earned a reputation for hard-hitting and controversial cinema projects that focus on life's underbelly. In 2009, Daniels hit Hollywood pay dirt with the film *Precious*, which follows a young woman's inner journey to salvation. Nominated for multiple Academy Awards (including best director for Daniels), *Precious* represents one of the first films to present a transcendent view of African American life.

For the first time in its history, cinema is now the provenance of new and veteran African American filmmakers. This combination of creative talent promises to lead African American cinema into new frontiers.

THE BLACK BRITISH INVASION

Much like their Anglo counterparts, British actors of African descent have also performed well in the film industry. Sine the mid-1990s, British actors of African descent have been making inroads in American films. In 1996, British actress Marianne Jean-Baptiste earned an Oscar nomination for her role in *Secrets & Lies*. The influx of Afro-British talent to the film industry has continued into the new millennium with the arrival of such actors as Idris Elba (*The Gospel, Daddy's Little Girl*), Thandie Newton (*Mission Impossible 2, The Pursuit of Happyness*), Eamonn Walker (*Tears of the Sun*), Sophie Okonedo (*Hotel Rwanda, Skin*), and Chiwetel Ejiofor (*Amistad, Kinky Boots, Inside Man*).

TECHNOLOGY EXPANDS OPTIONS FOR FILMMAKERS

As technology has advanced with home entertainment devices such as DVDs and iPods, additional growth opportunities have come for African American filmmakers. These entertainment platforms have not only substantially increased employment options for blacks in films, but also provided a new gateway for African American–themed entertainment properties. Every studio in the film industry now has home entertainment and new technology divisions to service this growing market. Two companies, Codeblack and Image Entertainment, control the space for independent black entertainment as of 2010. That number is sure to grow as technological advances continue to expand and create new distribution opportunities for black films.

AFRICAN AMERICANS IN TELEVISION

THE EARLY YEARS OF TELEVISION

Because many early television stars were lifted from popular radio programs, African American performers began to make advances in television almost from the start. For example, entertainer and pianist Bob Howard was included in the CBS network's evening broadcast from the very beginning. Another gifted entertainer, jazz pianist Hazel Scott (1920–1981), had her own fifteen-minute broadcast three days a week. African American performers also appeared on variety and game shows, such as *Your Show of Shows*, *All Star Revue*, *Strike it Rich*, and *High Finance*, throughout the late 1940s and into the 1950s. On the ABC television network, musician Billy Daniels (1915–1988) was given his own short-lived variety show in the fall of 1952.

Although television did not make use of all the same stereotypes that cinema employed, many negative caricatures did arise. As the medium began to rebroadcast feature films and shorts that appeared in theaters, many grossly unflattering portrayals of African Americans began to appear on television. In fact, such shorts as Hal Roach's *Our Gang* (*Little Rascals*) films became television mainstays. However, the popularity of this show's "Buckwheat" character was a source of great consternation in the African American community due to the role's gender ambiguity and pickaninny imagery.

In 1950, veteran entertainer Ethel Waters appeared on the first television show in which an African American was the central figure. As the star of *Beulah* for the first two seasons, the popular show centered on the weekly trials and tribulations of a black maid or "mammy"—a supporting character on the popular *Fibber McGee and Molly* radio show. (*Beulah* ran until 1953, when protests by the NAACP and other activist groups forced its cancellation.)

Numerous other former radio performers quickly followed in Waters's wake, including Eddie "Rochester" Anderson, who played opposite Jack Benny (1894–1974) on *The Jack Benny Show*, and Willie Best (1916–1962), who was a regularly featured performer on *The Trouble with Father* and *Oh My Little Margie*. In 1953, actress Lillian Randolph (1914–1980) began to reprise the role of a maid that she played on radio for the television series *Make Room for Daddy*. Later, she appeared in the television show *Great Gildersleeve*. Perhaps no other television show, though, created as much controversy for its negative stereotyping of African Americans as *The Amos 'n' Andy Show*. This series, based on the popular 1930s and 1940s radio show *Amos 'n' Andy*, ran on television from 1951 to 1953. The show was perceived by many, both black and white, as an offensive reminder of the past, and the NAACP initiated lawsuits and boycott threats that were critical in forcing the show's cancellation. After *The Amos 'n' Andy Show* was cancelled, it continued to appear in syndication until the mid-1960s.

Throughout the early 1950s, variety shows hosted by veteran white entertainers, such as Ed Sullivan (1901–1974), Milton Berle (1908–2002), and Steve Allen, occasionally featured African American entertainers. But in 1956, NBC took the bold step of creating a slot for the variety program *The Nat King Cole Show.* Although the variety format had always been popular with television viewers, and Cole's recording success was undeniable, the network was unable to secure regular sponsors, especially after Cole touched the arm of a white female guest. The show was cancelled after its first season.

COMMERCIAL TELEVISION REACTS TO THE 1960s

Throughout the late 1950s and into the 1960s, African Americans appeared in many serious documentaries concerning rural poverty, segregation, and the civil rights movement led by the Reverend Martin Luther King Jr. (1929–1968). The powerful medium of television provided King and the other leaders the opportunity to increase the white viewing audience's awareness of their civil rights cause. Commercial television reacted to the changing political, social, and economic climate in the United States much the same way that cinema did—by including more African American performers in its programming. Ensemble television shows soon began to feature African American performers: Otis Young (1932–2001) appeared in *The Outcast*; Greg Morris (1934–1996) starred in *Mission Impossible*; and Nichelle Nichols was featured in *Star Trek.* However, the most dramatic changes in television's positioning of African American talent occurred when Sheldon Leonard (1907–1997) hired Bill Cosby in 1965 as one of two leads to star in the television show *I Spy*, and actress Diahann Carroll began starring in1968 as a widowed nurse and single mother in the drama *Julia.*

While the show only lasted three seasons, *I Spy* marked the first time that an African American television actor was so widely accepted by television viewers—primarily for his inoffensive, perfect image. Consequently, Cosby earned three Emmy Awards for his portrayal of the character Alexander Scott. Lasting from 1968 to 1971, *Julia* presented Carroll as an African American woman seemingly detached from the reality of the lives led by most African Americans. Though popular with the majority viewing audience, the show was criticized for its bland depiction of an African American. Others, however, viewed Carroll's character as an improvement over past characterizations of African Americans on television.

Blacks also began to appear on television in roles opposite whites in ways that had never before been possible. *Harlem Detective* (1953–1954) featured black and white actors cast as equals on the police force. *Eastside/Westside* (1963–1964) and *The Nurses* (1962–1965) featured African American actresses Cicely Tyson and Hilda Simms, respectively, in regularly featured roles. Although it was praised for its more balanced portrayal of African Americans, *Eastside/Westside* lasted only one season.

As the first successful African American television variety show, *The Flip Wilson Show* (1970–1974) was the first weekly program by an African American to feature "racial comedy" as a form of general audience entertainment. The show's rousing success paved the way for the development of future African American situation comedies.

THE PRESENCE OF AFRICAN AMERICANS ON TELEVISION EXPANDS

During the 1970s, television producers, such as Norman Lear with *All in the Family, Sanford and Son,* and *Good Times* and Bud Yorkin with *What's Happening* and *Carter Country,* created comedy programming to appeal to African American audiences. Though these shows flourished and made the African American presence on

Flip Wilson** (left) **and Richard Pryor, Scene from **The Flip Wilson Show, *1974.*** *The first successful African American television variety show,* The Flip Wilson Show *paved the way for the development of African American situation comedies, including* Sanford and Son *and* Good Times. **AP IMAGES. REPRODUCED BY PERMISSION.**

John Amos and Madge Sinclair in **Roots**, *1977.* Roots, *based on Alex Haley's book of the same name, became one of the most-watched television miniseries of all time.* EVERETT COLLECTION

television commonplace, critics referred to them as "new minstrelsy" and derided their perpetuation of stereotypical aspects of African American humor. One of the most significant changes occurred in children's television programming. The public television series *Sesame Street* premiered in1969 and featured a multiracial mix of children and adults interacting and learning.

In addition, animated series, such as Bill Cosby's *Fat Albert and the Cosby Kids* (1972–1985) and the *Jackson 5ive* (1971–1973), debuted, offering depictions of events relevant to the lives of young African Americans. In the category of drama, notably made-for-television movies and miniseries, two productions stood out among the rest in the 1970s: *The Autobiography of Miss Jane Pittman* (1974) and *Roots* (1977). Starring actress Cicely Tyson, *The Autobiography of Miss Jane Pittman* was set in 1962 and spanned the life of a 110-year old African American woman from the era of American enslavement to the 1960s civil rights movement. For her outstanding efforts, Tyson was awarded an Emmy Award for best lead actress in a drama-special program. *Roots*, based on the Alex Haley (1921–1992) novel, was the highest-rated miniseries ever, attracting an estimated 130 million viewers. Featuring such prominent African American actors as Louis Gossett Jr., Cicely Tyson, and Maya Angelou, the eight-part epic traced Haley's family history from Africa to its enslavement and liberation in the American South.

THE *COSBY* DECADE

Throughout the late 1970s and early 1980s, African American actors continued to appear in stereotypical comedies or made-for-television movies with few exceptions. In 1984, however, veteran entertainer Bill Cosby returned to television with a half-hour series called *The Cosby Show*. Although expected to do well, few could have predicted the level of the show's popularity. Consistently rated the top weekly television program, *The Cosby Show* ran for eight seasons and created tremendous opportunities for African American performers.

While the phenomenal success of the *Roots* miniseries had proven that all–African American television vehicles could attract a large audience, *The Cosby Show* demonstrated that an audience of similar proportions would also regularly support an entertaining, family-oriented program centered on African Americans. *The Cosby Show*'s success created a trend toward more African American–themed shows in the late 1980s. Actor Tim Reid produced and starred in the short-lived, Emmy Award–winning *Frank's Place*. Choreographer Debbie Allen produced *The Cosby Show* spin-off *A Different World*, which depicted life at a historically African American university. In addition, Quincy Jones produced *The Fresh Prince of Bel-Air* starring rap artist Will Smith. *In Living Color*, produced by comedian Keenen Ivory Wayans, featured many talented members of the Wayans family.

AFRICAN AMERICANS NAVIGATING THE CROSSROADS IN TELEVISION

Although African American programs have become an increasing rarity on the major television networks, which have begun to concentrate on offerings that deliver them the widest possible audience share, the launch of several networks brought new promise for African Americans. Clearly understanding the financial gain that could result, upstart networks like Fox, Warner Brothers (WB), and UPN (now the CW), began to vigorously court African American audiences in the 1990s. The creation of the UPN and WB networks brought new promise for African Americans in television. These networks' initial programming featured highly rated programs, such as *Roc*, *Living Single*, and *Martin*, that were major hits with both black and young white television viewers. However, in typical fashion, just as their reputations became firmly established, these networks abandoned their urban programming initiatives in favor of more "mainstream" fare. In an

Will Smith, Alfonso Ribeiro, and Tatyana Ali **(left to right)**, *in* **Fresh Prince of Bel-Air, *1996.*** Fresh Prince, *which aired from 1990 to 1996, established rap musician Smith as an actor. He went on to become the star of blockbuster movies, such as* Independence Day *(1996) and* Hancock *(2008).* NBC/EVERETT COLLECTION

attempt to counter such fallout, during the 2001 television season, network programmers introduced two new sitcoms (*My Wife and Kids* and *The Bernie Mac Show*), which enjoyed solid ratings but failed to spark another "black TV renaissance."

Although the long-term results have been mixed, a growing number of African American performers found success in the domain of daytime and late-night television. Utilizing the talk show format, African American talent like Montel Williams, Rolanda Watts, Tyra Banks, and Wendy Williams proved their ability to attract diverse and large daytime audiences. As for late-night, *The Arsenio Hall Show*, which aired from 1989 to 1994, demonstrated similar staying power, and inspired successors like *The Wanda Sykes Show* and *The Mo'Nique Show*.

THE OPRAH PHENOMENON

Since its national debut in 1986, *The Oprah Winfrey Show* has become a transformative force in pop culture that has turned its host into an international icon and one of the wealthiest women in the world. Winfrey's presence has been credited with transforming the model of daytime television, which prior to her arrival had been dominated by white men. Produced by Harpo Productions (Oprah spelled backwards), the show has consistently ranked as one of the highest-rated daytime shows and one of the most influential. From her popular book club, philanthropic outreach, and celebrity interviews, *The Oprah Winfrey Show* has demonstrated reach far beyond television. Through her production company, Winfrey is a producer of the highly rated *Rachel Ray*, *Dr. Phil*, and *Dr. Oz* talk shows, and she has produced several movies for television and the big screen that include *The Great Debaters* (2007), *Beloved* (1998), and the 2010 Oscar contender, *Precious* (2009). Winfrey's daytime show will go off the air in 2011 to give her time to focus on her newly formed cable television network OWN (the Oprah Winfrey Network).

Dee Dee Davis and Bernie Mac in* The Bernie Mac Show, *April 8, 2004. *Actor and comedian Mac began as a stand-up comic and went on to garner roles in films; in 2001 he landed a television sitcom, which ran until 2006.* WILMORE FILMS/20TH CENTURY FOX TELEVISION/THE KOBAL COLLECTION/PICTURE DESK

THE FUTURE OF AFRICAN AMERICANS IN TELEVISION

As the television industry moved into the twenty-first century, a record number of African Americans were actively involved in the industry in acting, production, and executive roles. However, while African Americans have continued to enjoy success in comedies, no dramatic primetime series focusing on African American characters has made it beyond a full television season since the 1970s. The current standard casting model is to include African American performers as part of multiethnic casts, which is a trend that may satisfy network diversity initiatives, but also somewhat dilutes a singular voice from being represented.

On the other hand, the monopolies once held by the major networks have continued to erode in the face of the growing cable market, a venue that also holds increased opportunities for black talent. Cable programming has countered traditional television fare with more provocative and engaging shows that have snatched viewership away from the major networks. The growing popularity of this new medium has created a demand for niche-market programming that introduces alternative viewing choices for African American audiences.

Black Entertainment Television (BET) Holdings, Inc., which began operations in the 1980s, became in the 1990s the first African American–controlled cable entertainment company listed on the New York Stock Exchange. Led until 2005 by industry giant Robert Johnson, BET targets subscribers internationally with a diverse slate of original and rebroadcast programming on various cable television channels that include BET Cable Network, BET J, BET Movies/Starz! and Centric. The company has diversified its holdings by expanding its programming into radio broadcasts (BET Radio), the Internet (BET.com), event production (BET Awards), and digital media (BET Gospel and Bet Hip-Hop). Although the sale of BET in November 2000 to mainstream media giant Viacom left a void in terms of black ownership within this market, the arrival of similar cable networks, such as TV One and the short-lived Black Family Channel (1999–2007), sends strong signals for solid growth opportunities for African American talent in the future.

***Cast of* Living Single.** *This television series, which was a major hit with black and young white audiences during its run from 1993 to 1998, included in its cast* (from left to right) *Queen Latifah, Kim Fields, Erika Alexander, and Kim Coles. Latifah, who had earlier conquered the music world as a rapper, went on to a successful film career, starring in such movies as* Chicago, Bringing Down the House, *and* Beauty Shop. WARNER BROTHERS TELEVISION/THE KOBAL COLLECTION

SHIFTING TRENDS IN THE TELEVISION MARKET

The most influential genre to hit the television market in the new millennium has been the advent of "reality" programming. Although originally used to describe programming that features ordinary people (nonactors) in unscripted dramatic or humorous situations, these shows have gained popularity since 2000 because of their ability to place ordinary people in extraordinary situations. Reality shows have been fruitful for African Americans. Shows like *The Apprentice* and *American Idol* have resulted in "real life" career breaks for such reality television performers as Omarosa and 2006 Oscar winner Jennifer Hudson. The reality genre helped to spawn a new career for model Tyra Banks, who debuted her reality show, *America's Next Top Model*, in 2003 and her self-titled talk show in 2005. Other notable African American entries in reality programming include BET's highly rated *College Hill* and *Keyshia Cole: The Way It Is*.

Another popular television genre experiencing a twenty-first-century comeback is ensemble television. This genre was a television mainstay through the first decades of the medium, when shows *Bonanza*, *The Waltons*, and *Hill Street Blues* ruled the airwaves. As television viewers' habits shifted in the late 1980s and 1990s, ensemble television took a backseat to comedies and other formats, before coming full circle with a vengeance at the top of the new millennium with a fresh crop of ensemble shows. This group includes several notable shows featuring African American talent and themes, such as *Oz*, *The Wire*, and *Lincoln Heights*, which remains the only African American family drama on the air in nearly thirty years.

PRIME-TIME FRANCHISE

As the creator and executive producer of *Grey's Anatomy* and its spinoff, *Private Practice*, Shonda Rhimes is the first African American to helm multiple primetime television dramas. *Grey's Anatomy* debuted on the ABC network in 2005 and *Private Practice* followed in 2007. Both shows feature multiethnic, ensemble casts set in a hospital environment.

THE FUTURE

Despite challenges from other entertainment options, television is an evolving medium that will continue to grow and expand. As new technologies emerge and market tastes shift, television will keep pace and remain at the forefront of new innovations. As for the African American presence in the medium, viewers can expect established names to continue popping up on screen and new players to step in the game who will maintain the powerful and resilient standards set by their predecessors.

FILMOGRAPHY OF SELECTED FEATURE FILMS AND DOCUMENTARIES

The following filmography includes selected feature films and documentaries that are remarkable for their depiction of themes and issues related to the experiences of African Americans throughout history. Ranging from the early silent movie era through major studio releases, documentaries, and made-for-television movies of the 1990s and first decade of the 2000s, many of these cinematic works also represent significant milestones for African Americans in the film and television industries.

Denzel Washington, Jurnee Smollett, Nate Parker, and Denzel Whitaker (*left to right*) in* The Great Debaters, *2007.
Starring and directed by Washington, the film is based on a true story of a Texas college debate team in 1935.
EVERETT COLLECTION, INC.

AFRICAN AMERICANS IN WWII: A LEGACY OF PATRIOTISM AND VALOR (2000)

In this documentary, African American war veterans from all branches of the military describe their personal experiences in World War II. Includes tributes by General Colin Powell and President Bill Clinton.

AFRICANS IN AMERICA: AMERICA'S JOURNEY THROUGH SLAVERY (1998)

A four-part television documentary that chronicles the history of African enslavement in America from the start of the Atlantic slave trade in the sixteenth century to the end of the Civil War in 1865. The series examines African enslavement from philosophical, societal, and economic viewpoints.

AKEELAH AND THE BEE (2006)

A heart-warming story about an inner-city African American girl's struggle to win the National Spelling Bee.

ALI (2001)

Boxer Muhammad Ali is depicted during a contentious decade (1964–1974), in which he converted to Islam, befriended civil rights icons, refused the draft, was stripped of his World Heavyweight Champion title, married four times, and blurred lines between sport, ethics, and society. Will Smith, who received an Oscar nomination for best actor, gives an inspired performance in and out of the ring. Jamie Foxx's performance as cornerman Drew "Bundini" Brown is also noteworthy.

AMERICAN GANGSTER (2007)

Denzel Washington and Russell Crowe starred in this crime drama directed by Ridley Scott and adapted from Mark Jacobson's story, "The Return of Superfly." Washington portrays Frank Lucas, a Harlem gangster who smuggles heroin into the United States using American service planes during the Vietnam War. Crowe appears as detective Richie Roberts, who attempts to bring Lucas down.

AMERICAN VIOLET (2009)
This film, starring Nicole Beharie as Dee Roberts, is based on the true story of Regina Kelly, who was wrongfully indicted on drug charges in Texas. The movie follows Roberts through the racially motivated drug sweep and the civil rights case that followed.

AMERICA'S DREAM (1995)
A trilogy of short stories covering African American life from 1938 to 1958: "Long Black Song," based on a short story by Richard Wright; "The Boy Who Painted Christ Black," based on a story by John Henrik Clarke; and Maya Angelou's "The Reunion."

AMISTAD (1997)
Director Steven Spielberg creates an epic about the African captives aboard the slave ship *Amistad*, led by a Mende tribesman named Cinque (Djimon Hounsou), who free themselves in 1839 and take over the ship in a bloody mutiny. Lengthy legal battles eventually reach the U.S. Supreme Court, where the Africans are found to be rightfully freed individuals in the eyes of the law.

ANTWONE FISHER (2002)
Denzel Washington's directorial debut tells the story of an abused foster child's journey into manhood.

THE AUTOBIOGRAPHY OF MISS JANE PITTMAN (1974)
The history of African Americans in the South is seen through the eyes of a 110-year-old formerly enslaved woman. Miss Pittman, played by Cicely Tyson, describes every major episode of African American history, from the Civil War through the civil rights movement, allowing the viewer to experience the injustices. The film, adapted by Tracy Keenan Wynn from the 1971 novel by Ernest J. Gaines, won nine Emmy Awards.

BABY BOY (2001)
Director John Singleton returns to the South Central Los Angeles neighborhood of his breakthrough *Boyz N the Hood* in this candid look at a culture that fosters and tolerates a lack of emotional maturity in young African American males. Jody (Tyrese Gibson) is a twenty-year-old unemployed man-child who still lives with his mother, has two children with two different women, and cheats on his current girlfriend, Yvette. Jody's life changes when his mother's boyfriend moves in. Melvin (Ving Rhames), an ex-con who's been down the road Jody is traveling on, shows no tolerance for his attitude. Jody gets a job, but his idea of earning a living is selling stolen dresses at a beauty parlor. Real trouble starts when Rodney (Snoop Dogg), a street thug and Yvette's ex, is released from prison and refuses to leave her house. Singleton toys with two endings, but finishes the story with the message that the means to fix the problems he's described are within reach.

BARBERSHOP 2: BACK IN BUSINESS (2004)
The sequel to the original 2002 comedy follows the popular barber shop as it faces greedy real-estate developers. Ice Cube and Cedric the Entertainer star.

BEAUTY SHOP (2005)
The day-to-day antics taking place at an inner-city beauty shop are vividly portrayed in this comedy spun off from the successful *Barbershop* franchise. Queen Latifah stars.

BELLY (1998)
In this film, starring rappers Nas and DMX, a pair of black gangsters experience spiritual awakenings when they realize that their lives are headed toward a dead end.

BELOVED (1998)
Oprah Winfrey's pet project (she had owned the film rights for ten years), starring Winfrey, Danny Glover, and Thandie Newton, is a faithful adaptation of Toni Morrison's Pulitzer Prize–winning novel.

BEVERLY HILLS COP (1984)
When a close friend of smooth-talking Detroit cop Axle Foley (Eddie Murphy) is murdered, he traces the murderer to the posh streets of Beverly Hills. There, he must stay on his toes to keep one step ahead of the killer and two steps ahead of the law. The first of three action comedies.

THE BINGO LONG TRAVELING ALL-STARS & MOTOR KINGS (1976)
Set in 1939, this film follows the comedic adventures of a lively group of African American baseball players (Billy Dee Williams, James Earl Jones, and Richard Pryor) who have defected from the old Negro National League. The All-Stars travel the country challenging local white teams.

BIRD (1988)
This richly textured biography follows jazz saxophone great Charlie Parker (Forest Whitaker) from his rise to stardom to his premature death via extended heroin use. The soundtrack, which features Parker's own solos remastered from original recordings, earned an Academy Award for best sound. Whitaker won the Cannes Film Festival

Black Dynamite, ***Featuring*** **(left to right)** ***Nicole Sullivan, Michael Jai White, and Salli Richardson-Whitfield, 2009.*** *Directed and cowritten by Scott Sanders,* Black Dynamite *is a parody of the blaxploitation films of the 1970s.* APPARITION/EVERETT COLLECTION

Award for best actor, while Clint Eastwood garnered the Golden Globe Award for best director.

THE BIRTH OF A RACE (1918)

Emmet J. Scott's film offers a positive depiction of African Americans during the Civil War. Although the film did not meet original expectations, it proved an inspiration to many African Americans.

BLACK DYNAMITE (2009)

A spoof of blaxploitation films, this film, starring Michael Jai White, Salli Richardson, Arsenio Hall, Kevin Chapman, and Tommy Davidson, pays homage to black movie classics from the 1970s.

BLACK GIRL (1972)

Directed by Ossie Davis, this intense drama examines the relationship between an African American woman, who feels that she is a failure, and her children.

BLACK LIKE ME (1964)

This film, featuring Roscoe Lee Browne and James Whitmore, is based on John Howard Griffin's successful 1961 book about how Griffin used a drug to turn his skin black and traveled the South to experience prejudice firsthand.

BLACK RODEO (1972)

This documentary, directed by Jeff Kanew, provides a glimpse of an all–African American rodeo held at Triborough Stadium in New York in September 1971.

BLACKBOARD JUNGLE (1955)

A popular urban drama about an idealistic teacher (Sidney Poitier) in a poor inner-city area who fights doggedly to connect with his unruly students. Bill Haley's "Rock Around the Clock" plays over the opening credits, marking the first use of rock music in a mainstream feature film.

BLACULA (1972)

In this film, the African Prince Mamuwalde (William Marshall) stalks the streets of Los Angeles trying to satisfy his insatiable desire for blood. Its mildly successful melding of blaxploitation and horror spawned a sequel, *Scream, Blacula, Scream.*

BLOOD OF JESUS (1941)

A sinful husband accidentally shoots his newly baptized wife, causing an uproar in their rural town. Director Spencer Williams Jr. later starred as Andy on the *Amos n' Andy* television series. Because of its rare treatment of African American religion, the film was named to the National Film Registry in 1991.

BLUE COLLAR (1978)

An auto assembly-line worker, tired of the poverty of his life, hatches a plan to rob his own union. Starring Richard Pryor and Yaphet Kotto, the film is a study of the working class and the robbing of the human spirit.

BODY AND SOUL (1924)

This film, made by Oscar Micheaux, features the first screen appearance of Paul Robeson, cast in a dual role as a conniving preacher and his good brother. The preacher preys on the heroine, making her life a misery. Objections by censors to the preacher's character caused him to be redeemed and become worthy of the heroine's love.

BOESMAN & LENA (2000)

This adaptation of the apartheid-era play by Athol Fugard follows the travails of a downtrodden couple, Boesman (Danny Glover) and Lena (Angela Bassett). After their shantytown home in Cape Town, South Africa, is bulldozed by the government, they take to the road with their few belongings, constantly bickering about their plight. The couple constructs a makeshift abode for the night, which attracts the attention of an old man even lower on the economic ladder, whom Lena allows to stay, to Boesman's displeasure.

BOYCOTT (2001)

This superb HBO docudrama recreates the civil rights movement's early days, from Rosa Parks's (Iris Little-Thomas) refusal to give up her seat to a white man on a segregated Montgomery bus, through the subsequent boycott of the bus system by the city's black population, to the success of the boycott and the rise to prominence of Dr. Martin Luther King Jr. (Jeffrey Wright) as the movement's most eloquent and popular leader. Through the artful use of many different visual styles, director Clark Johnson tells the story without overplaying his hand. Wright is fantastic as King, with other outstanding performances turned in by Terrence Howard as Ralph Abernathy and CCH Pounder as boycott organizer Jo Ann Robinson.

BOYZ N THE HOOD (1991)

John Singleton's debut as a writer and director is an astonishing picture of young African American men, four high school students with different backgrounds, aims, and abilities trying to survive Los Angeles gangs and bigotry. Excellent acting throughout, with special nods to Laurence Fishburne and Cuba Gooding Jr. The musical score is by Stanley Clarke. With this film, Singleton became the youngest director ever nominated for an Oscar.

THE BROTHER FROM ANOTHER PLANET (1984)

In this independently made morality fable by John Sayles, a black alien (Joe Morton) escapes from his home planet and winds up in Harlem, where he is pursued by two alien bounty hunters. The humor arises from cultural and racial misunderstandings.

BROTHER JOHN (1970)

An angel (Sidney Poitier) goes back to his hometown in Alabama to see how things are going in this early look at racial tensions and labor problems. Directed by James Goldstone with a musical score by Quincy Jones.

THE BROTHERS (2001)

A chain reaction of male introspection is set off as four successful, young African American men navigate the tricky waters of serious relationships in modern Los Angeles. All the bases are covered: the womanizing lawyer, Brian (Bill Bellamy); the one-night-stand-weary physician, Jackson (Morris Chestnut); the just-engaged Terry (Shemar Moore); and the unhappily married Derrick (D. L. Hughley). Not quite as strong as its female counterpart, the much-praised *Waiting to Exhale*, but the capable comic actors never veer too far from the exploration of modern sexual politics.

BROWN SUGAR (2002)

Described as an African American *When Harry Met Sally*, this film centers on a romance between an executive, Dre (Taye Diggs), at a hip-hop label and a magazine editor, Sidney (Sanaa Lathan), who have known each other since childhood.

BUCK AND THE PREACHER (1972)

A trail guide (Sidney Poitier) and a con man preacher (Harry Belafonte) join forces to help a wagon train of formerly enslaved men and women, including Ruth (Ruby Dee), who are seeking to homestead out West. Poitier's debut as a director.

BUFFALO SOLDIERS (1997)

This post–Civil War western concerns the all-black cavalry troops created by Congress in 1866 to patrol the American West. A formerly enslaved by-the-book army man, Sergeant Washington Wyatt (Danny Glover), leads the chase for Apache warrior Victorio (Harrison Lowe) across the New Mexico Territory while trying to deal with the common degradation suffered by his troops at the hands of white officers.

THE BUS (1964)

A documentary covering Martin Luther King Jr.'s epic 1963 March on Washington.

CABIN IN THE SKY (1943)

A musical based on a Broadway show and featuring an all–African American cast—Ethel Waters, Eddie Anderson, Lena Horne, and Rex Ingram—as well as lively dance numbers and a musical score with contributions from Louis Armstrong and Duke Ellington.

CADILLAC RECORDS (2008)

Set in the early 1940s to the late 1960s, this film chronicles the historic record company Chess Records. Adrien Brody stars as Leonard Chess, along with Cedric the Entertainer as Willie Dixon, Mos Def as Chuck Berry, Columbus Short as Little Walter, Jeffrey Wright as Muddy Waters, Eamonn Walker as Howlin' Wolf, and Beyoncé Knowles as Etta James.

CARMEN JONES (1954)

Georges Bizet's tale of femme fatale Carmen with an all–African American cast—Dorothy Dandridge, Harry Belafonte, Diahann Carroll, and Brock Peters. Dandridge's Oscar nomination for best actress was the first ever for an African American in a lead role. The film earned the 1955 Golden Globe Award for best film and was named to the National Film Registry in 1992.

CATCH A FIRE (2006)

The story of a South African oil-refinery worker who is motivated to commit acts of terrorism against the country's brutal apartheid government.

CHANGE OF MIND (1969)

Directed by Robert Stevens, this film portrays an African American male (Raymond St. Jacques) who has a white man's brain transplanted into his head. After the operation, he is accepted by the brain donor's wife as her husband. Music by Duke Ellington.

CHARLOTTE FORTEN'S MISSION: EXPERIMENT IN FREEDOM (1985)

In this fact-based story set during the Civil War, a wealthy, educated African American woman (Melba Moore), determined to prove to President Lincoln that blacks are equal to whites, journeys to a remote island off the coast of Georgia. There, she teaches recently freed men and women to read and write.

CHUCK BERRY: HAIL! HAIL! ROCK 'N' ROLL (1987)

Engaging, energetic portrait of one of rock's founding fathers, via interviews, behind-the-scenes footage, and performance clips of Chuck Berry when he was sixty years old. Featured songs include "Johnny B. Goode," "Roll Over Beethoven," and "Maybelline," with appearances by Etta James, Bo Diddley, and Robert Cray, among others.

THE CIVIL RIGHTS MOVEMENT: ORDINARY AMERICANS (2000)

A documentary film for young people that juxtaposes the contributions of Martin Luther King Jr., Malcolm X, and presidents Eisenhower, Kennedy, and Johnson with views of rank-and-file protesters. Recommended for grades seven to twelve.

CLAUDINE (1974)

Directed by John Berry, this film depicts a single mother (Diahann Carroll) who attempts to maintain her family of six children. James Earl Jones plays a trash collector and her boyfriend.

CLEOPATRA JONES (1973)

A federal government agent (Tamara Dobson) with considerable martial arts prowess takes on loathsome drug lords. Followed by *Cleopatra Jones and the Casino of Gold.*

CLOCKERS (1995)

Strike (Mekhi Phifer), the leader of a group of drug dealers (clockers), engages in a power struggle with his boss (Delroy Lindo), his do-the-right-thing brother, Victor (Isaiah Washington), and his own conscience. He is also suspected of murder by relentless narcotics cop Rocco Klein (Harvey Keitel). This poignant and compelling street drama, directed by Spike Lee, is based on the Richard Price novel, with music by Terence Blanchard.

COACH CARTER (2005)

Samuel L. Jackson stars as controversial coach Ken Carter, who becomes the basketball coach for his old high school in a poor area of Richmond, California.

COLOR ADJUSTMENT (1991)

Narrated by Ruby Dee, the film documents the modern history of race relations in the United States in the arena of television, and traces the progress of African Americans from caricatures to victims to mainstream characters as portrayed by television.

THE COLOR PURPLE (1985)

This adaptation of Alice Walker's acclaimed novel features strong lead performances from Whoopi Goldberg (in her screen debut, which earned the 1986 Golden Globe Award for best actress in a drama) and talk-show host Oprah Winfrey (also her film debut), among others. A brilliant musical score by coproducer Quincy Jones complements this strong film, directed by Steven Spielberg.

THE COOL WORLD (1963)

This tough-talking docudrama, set on the streets of Harlem, focuses on a fifteen-year-old African American boy whose one ambition in life is to own a gun and lead his gang. Named to the National Film Registry in 1994.

COOLEY HIGH (1975)

African American high school students in Chicago go through the rites of passage in their senior year during the 1960s in this funny, smart, and much acclaimed film. The soundtrack features Motown hits of the era.

CORA UNASHAMED (2000)

This adaptation of the Langston Hughes short story finds racism and tragedy in a small Iowa town in the 1930s. Cora Jenkins (Regina Taylor) and her mother (CCH Pounder) are the only blacks in the community. Cora works as a housekeeper for the Studevant family and becomes strongly attached to the family's daughter, Jessie. This bond is resented by Jessie's mother, selfish and cold Lizbeth (Cherry Jones), whose exaggerated sense of propriety brings about disaster.

CORNBREAD, EARL, AND ME (1975)

In this film, directed by Joe Manduke, a high school basketball star from the ghetto is mistaken for a murderer by cops and is shot, causing a subsequent furor of protest and racial hatred. Music by Donald Byrd.

THE CORNER (2000)

Based on a true story, this miniseries reveals how drugs infested a Baltimore neighborhood and how the residents were affected. Told in a seminarrative style by a documentary crew, the story follows the lives of drug addicts and drug dealers. *The Corner* won several Emmy Awards, including those for outstanding miniseries and outstanding directing.

COSMIC SLOP (1994)

A three-part anthology. "Space Traders," based on a story by Derrick Bell, finds a fleet of aliens offering to solve all of American society's most pressing social ills if they can have the entire black population in return (for what purpose is never explained). "The First Commandment" features a Catholic priest in a Latino parish who comes up against his parishioners' beliefs in Santeria. "Tang," based on a story by Chester Himes, finds a poor, desperately unhappy married couple dreaming about what they'll do with the rifle mysteriously delivered in a flower carton to their door.

THE COTTON CLUB (1984)

An African American musician playing at the Cotton Club falls in love with gangster Dutch Schultz's girlfriend. A black tap dancer falls in love with a member of the chorus line who can pass for white. These two love stories are told against a background of mob violence and music during the early jazz era.

COTTON COMES TO HARLEM (1970)

A successful mix of crime and comedy about a suspicious preacher's back-to-Africa scheme that detectives (Godfrey Cambridge and Raymond St. Jacques) suspect is a swindle. Based on the novel by Chester Himes, the film was the directorial debut of Ozzie Davis.

THE COURT MARTIAL OF JACKIE ROBINSON (1990)

The true story of a little-known chapter in the life of the famous athlete. During his stint in the Army, Robinson (played by Andre Braugher) refused to take a back seat on a bus and subsequently faced the possibility of court martial.

CRISIS AT CENTRAL HIGH (1981)

A dramatic television recreation of the events leading up to the 1957 integration of Central High in Little Rock, Arkansas. Based on teacher Elizabeth Huckaby's journal.

CROOKLYN (1994)

Director Spike Lee profiles an African American middle-class family growing up in 1970s Brooklyn, focusing on the only girl (Zelda Harris) as she comes of age. Music by Terence Blanchard.

DADDY DAY CARE (2003)
Eddie Murphy stars as a fired executive who decides to open a day-car center for toddlers.

DADDY'S LITTLE GIRLS (2007)
A mechanic (Idris Elba) enlists the help of a successful but lonely attorney (Gabrielle Union) while trying to wrest custody of his three daughters from his treacherous ex-wife.

DARKTOWN JUBILEE (1914)
One of the earliest feature films to star an African American, actor-comedian Bert Williams. This silent film was controversial because it portrayed African Americans in a positive manner.

DAUGHTERS OF THE DUST (1991)
Five women of a Gullah family living on the Sea Islands off the Georgia coast in 1902 contemplate moving to the mainland in this emotional tale of change. Family bonds and memories are celebrated with a quiet narrative and beautiful cinematography in Julie Dash's feature-film directorial debut. Honored by the Sundance Film Festival for best cinematography.

THE DEFIANT ONES (1958)
Thought-provoking story about racism revolves around two escaped prisoners, one black and one white (Sidney Poitier and Tony Curtis), from a chain gang in the rural South. Their societal conditioning to hate each other dissolves as they face peril together. Earned several cinematic honors, including Academy Awards for best story, screenplay, and best black-and-white cinematography, as well as the Golden Globe for best drama.

DELIVER US FROM EVA (2003)
Eva Dandridge (Gabrielle Union) is an uptight young woman who constantly meddles in the affairs of her sisters, until their husbands set her up with a local playboy (LL Cool J), who falls in love with her.

DEVIL IN A BLUE DRESS (1995)
Easy Rawlins (Denzel Washington), an unemployed aircraft worker in 1948 Los Angeles, is hired by a shady businessman to find a mystery woman, Daphne (Jennifer Beals). Realism and accuracy in period detail enhance a solid performance by Washington. Based on the Walter Mosley novel.

DIARY OF A MAD BLACK WOMAN (2005)
A woman in an abusive relationship learns to stand on her own two feet and move on with her life.

DO THE RIGHT THING (1989)
An uncompromising comedy written and directed by Spike Lee about the racial tensions surrounding a white-owned pizzeria in the Bed-Stuy section of Brooklyn on the hottest day of the summer, and the violence that eventually erupts.

DOWN IN THE DELTA (1998)
Chicago matriarch Rosa Lynn (Mary Alice) tries to prevent her jobless daughter Loretta (Alfre Woodard), a single mother, from succumbing to destructive forces by sending Loretta and her two grandchildren to live with her brother (Al Freeman Jr.) in the Mississippi Delta. Author Maya Angelou's first outing as a director skillfully demonstrates the importance of connecting to one's heritage.

A DREAM FOR CHRISTMAS (1973)
Earl Hamner Jr. (best known for writing *The Waltons*) wrote this moving made-for-television story of an African American minister whose church in Los Angeles is scheduled to be demolished.

DREAMGIRLS (2006)
Based on the hugely successful Broadway musical about a trio of inner-city singers who hit the big time during the turbulent 1960s. Starring Beyoncé Knowles, Jamie Foxx, Eddie Murphy, Danny Glover, and Jennifer Hudson.

DRIVING MISS DAISY (1989)
Tender and sincere portrayal of a twenty-five-year friendship between an aging Jewish woman (Jessica Tandy) and her African American chauffeur (Morgan Freeman). The film subtly explores the effects of prejudice in the South. Earned numerous Academy and Golden Globe awards.

DRUMLINE (2002)
A comedy about a talented street drummer from Harlem (Nick Canon) who enrolls in a southern university, expecting to lead its marching band.

THE DUKE IS TOPS (1938)
In singer Lena Horne's earliest existing film appearance, she attempts to make the "big time," while her boyfriend joins a traveling medicine show. The film helped launch the 1940s swing era.

DUTCHMAN (1967)

A film presentation of Amiri Baraka's one-act play depicting the claustrophobic reality of the African American male's situation in the late 1960s. Starring Al Freeman Jr.

8 MILE (2002)

This semiautobiographical film chronicles the early life of blue-eyed rapper Eminem.

EIGHT-TRAY GANGSTER: THE MAKING OF A CRIP (1993)

A provocative documentary that explores the experiences and social environment influencing the life decisions of an African American gang member in Los Angeles.

THE EMPEROR JONES (1933)

Loosely based on Eugene O'Neill's play, the film portrays the rise and fall of a railroad porter (Paul Robeson) whose exploits take him from a life sentence on a chain gang to the throne of Haiti.

EMPIRE (2002)

As he tries to escape the drug game, big-time dealer Victor Rosa (John Leguizamo) is hoodwinked by a Wall Street stockbroker.

EVE'S BAYOU (1997)

Set in 1962 Louisiana and told in flashback, this film presents a mesmerizing and complex story with haunting visuals about the upper middle-class Batiste family. Impressive, multilayered directorial debut from Kasi Lemmons. Music by Terence Blanchard.

EYES ON THE PRIZE: AMERICA'S CIVIL RIGHTS YEARS (1954–1965) (1987)

A comprehensive six-part series on the history of the civil rights movement. This film examines Rosa Parks and the bus boycott, the leadership of Martin Luther King Jr., and the last great march in Selma, among other moments.

EYES ON THE PRIZE II: AMERICA AT THE RACIAL CROSSROADS (1965–1985) (1990)

The civil rights movement from the mid-1960s to the mid-1980s is traced in this eight-part documentary.

A FAMILY THING (1996)

Racial issues are addressed in this character-driven story of two brothers. White southerner Earl Pilcher (Robert Duvall) learns that his biological mother was black and that he has a half brother, Ray (James Earl Jones), who is black and living in Chicago. The two brothers slowly find common ground.

FAT ALBERT (2004)

The cast of the classic cartoon comes to life to help a girl who needs friends.

FEAR OF A BLACK HAT (1994)

A good-natured comedic satire in which a rap trio known as NWH (Niggaz With Hats) are touring in support of their album and trying to convince filmmaker Nina Blackburn (Kasi Lemmons) of their street credibility. However, the more the gangsta rappers explain themselves, the less sense they make.

FEAST OF ALL SAINTS (2001)

Based on the historical novel by Anne Rice, this film depicts nineteenth-century New Orleans and the *gens de couleurs* (free people of colour). Caught between the opposing worlds of white privilege and black subjugation, the free people of colour are descended from enslaved Africans and white oppressors.

THE FIGHTING TEMPTATIONS (2003)

A New York advertising executive (Cuba Gooding Jr.) goes home to collect a big inheritance and in the process discovers his roots.

THE FIVE HEARTBEATS (1991)

Well-told story of five African American singers in the 1960s, and their successes and failures as a group and as individuals. Directed by Robert Townsend, who did research by talking to the Dells. Music by Stanley Clarke.

FOR LOVE OF IVY (1968)

Sidney Poitier is a trucking executive who has a gambling operation on the side. Ivy (Abbey Lincoln) is the black maid for a rich white family who is about to leave her job to look for romance. The two are brought together, but the road to true love does not run smoothly. Based on a story by Poitier; music by Quincy Jones.

FOR US THE LIVING: THE MEDGAR EVERS STORY (1983)

The life and assassination of civil rights activist Medgar Evers, portrayed by Howard Rollins, are dramatically presented in this adaptation of the biography by Evers's widow. The film is not just a recording of events, but provides insight into Evers's character.

48 HRS (1982)

An experienced San Francisco cop (Nick Nolte) springs a convict (Eddie Murphy in his screen debut) from jail for forty-eight hours to find an escaped con.

FRESH (1994)

An enterprising young drug dealer (Sean Nelson) draws life lessons from his chess-hustler father (Samuel L. Jackson) and heroin-dealing mentor (Giancarlo Esposito), and looks for a way out of the dead-end business. First-time director Boaz Yakin was awarded the Filmmakers Trophy and Special Jury Prize at the 1994 Sundance Film Festival.

FUNDI: THE STORY OF ELLA BAKER (1986)

Ella Baker's nickname, "Fundi," comes from the Swahili word for a person who passes skills from one generation to another. This film documents Baker's work in the civil rights movement of the 1960s and her friendship with Dr. Martin Luther King Jr.

GET ON THE BUS (1996)

Spike Lee explored the personal side of the Million Man March by following a fictional group of men who board a bus in South Central Los Angeles and head for Washington, D.C. Practically ignoring the event itself, Lee and writer Reggie Rock Bythewood focus on the men who participated, their reasons, and their interaction with each other.

GET RICH OR DIE TRYIN' (2005)

This semiautobiographical tale of rapper 50 Cent follows his life as an inner-city drug dealer to the launch of his music career.

GHOSTS OF MISSISSIPPI (1996)

Director Rob Reiner tells the story of civil rights leader Medgar Evers, murdered in 1963, and the three trials of Byron De la Beckwith (James Woods), who was finally convicted (after two hung juries) in 1994. Whoopi Goldberg plays the role of Evers's widow, Myrlie; Evers's sons, Darrell and Van, play themselves; and daughter Reena appears as a juror while her character is played by Yolanda King, the daughter of slain civil rights leader Martin Luther King Jr.

GLORY (1989)

A rich, historical spectacle chronicling the Fifty-fourth Massachusetts, the first African American volunteer infantry unit in the Union Army. Winner of Academy Awards for best cinematography and best sound, the film offers stunning performances throughout, with exceptional work from Morgan Freeman and Denzel Washington, who earned both an Academy Award and a Golden Globe Award for best supporting actor.

GLORY ROAD (2006)

The story of the first all-black basketball starting lineup (the legendary 1965–1966 Texas Western Miners), who fight to make it to the national championship.

GO, MAN, GO! (1954)

This film depicts the Harlem Globetrotters at a time when few African Americans competed in professional basketball. The traveling team works to find its place in American sports with its players' amazing skills and showmanship.

GO TELL IT ON THE MOUNTAIN (1984)

A young African American boy tries to gain the approval of his stern stepfather in this fine adaptation of James Baldwin's semiautobiographical novel set in the 1930s.

GONE ARE THE DAYS (1963)

In this adaptation of the play *Purlie Victorious*, an African American preacher (Ossie Davis) stands up to a segregationist plantation owner from whom he obtains money to establish a church.

GONE WITH THE WIND (1939)

Based on Margaret Mitchell's novel, this epic Civil War drama traces Scarlett O'Hara's survival through the tragic history of the South during the Civil War and Reconstruction period. Hattie McDaniel became the first African American to win an Academy Award for her portrayal of the loyal maid, Mammy. The award-winning film was named to the American Film Institute Top 100 list in 1998.

GOOD HAIR (2009)

A documentary comedy, produced and narrated by Chris Rock, about the culture surrounding African American women's hair. The film explores the black hairstyling industry and what society considers to be an acceptable hairstyle for an African American woman. *Good Hair* premiered at the Sundance Film Festival.

THE GOSPEL (2005)

A redemptive tale about a successful rhythm-and-blues singer (Boris Kodjoe) who returns to his gospel roots after his father dies.

GREASED LIGHTNING (1977)

The story of the first African American auto racing champion, Wendell Scott (Richard Pryor), who had to overcome racial prejudice to achieve his success. Cowritten by Melvin Van Peebles, the film also starred Pam Grier and Cleavon Little.

THE GREAT WHITE HOPE (1970)

A semifictionalized biography of boxer Jack Johnson (played by James Earl Jones), who became the first African American heavyweight world champion in 1910. Jane Alexander makes her film debut as the boxer's white lover, as both battle the racism of the times.

THE GREATEST (1977)

A biography of Cassius Clay, the boxer who would later become recognized as Muhammad Ali. Ali plays himself, and George Benson's hit "The Greatest Love of All" is introduced.

THE GREEN MILE (1999)

Paul Edgecomb (Tom Hanks) is the decent head guard at Louisiana's Cold Mountain Penitentiary in 1935. He works E block, which is death row (the title refers to the color of the floor). Among his prisoners is a hulking black man, John Coffey (Michael Clarke Duncan), whose intimidating size belies a sweet nature and something else—Coffey has the power to heal. The characters are more symbols than human beings, but Duncan's performance earned him acclaim, including Golden Globe and Screen Actor's Guild nominations for best supporting actor.

GREEN PASTURES (1936)

This film, an adaptation of Marc Connelly's Pulitzer Prize–winning play, attempts to retell biblical stories in the black English vernacular of the 1930s. Southern theater owners boycotted the controversial film, which had an all–African American cast.

GUESS WHO (2005)

Bernie Mac stars in this comedic update of the 1960s classic about interracial love.

GUESS WHO'S COMING TO DINNER (1967)

Controversial in its time, a young white woman (Katharine Houghton) brings her black fiancé (Sidney Poitier) home to meet her parents (Katharine Hepburn and Spencer Tracy). The situation tests their open-mindedness and understanding. Named to the American Film Institute Top 100 list in 1998.

HALLELUJAH! (1929)

The first all–African American feature film and the first talkie for director King Vidor was given the go-ahead by MGM production chief Irving Thalberg, though he knew the film would be both controversial and get minimal release in the Deep South. Great music included traditional spirituals and songs by Irving Berlin.

HANGIN' WITH THE HOMEBOYS (1991)

One night in the lives of four young men. Although the Bronx does not offer much for any of them, they have little interest in escaping its confines, and they are more than willing to complain. With characters insightfully written and well portrayed, the film earned honors for best screenplay at the 1991 Sundance Film Festival.

HANK AARON: CHASING THE DREAM (1995)

This docudrama combines archival footage, interviews, and reenactments to tell the story of the life and career of baseball legend Henry Aaron, with an emphasis on personal and societal issues, as well as on-the-field accomplishments.

HARLEM NIGHTS (1989)

Two Harlem nightclub owners in the 1930s battle against efforts by the mob and crooked cops to take over their territory in this high-grossing comedy directed by Eddie Murphy, who also wrote, produced, and starred in the film. Music by Herbie Hancock.

HAVING OUR SAY: THE DELANY SISTERS' FIRST 100 YEARS (1999)

A made-for-television movie based on the true story of the Delany sisters (played by Ruby Dee and Diahann Carroll), who both lived well beyond the age of one hundred after having built successful careers at a time when most women, and most African Americans, were denied opportunities. Produced by Camille Cosby.

A HERO AIN'T NOTHIN' BUT A SANDWICH (1978)

A young urban African American teenager (Larry B. Scott) gets involved in drugs and is eventually saved from ruin. Based on Alice Childress's novel.

HIGHER LEARNING (1994)

Malik (Omar Epps), Kristen (Kristy Swanson), and Remy (Michael Rapaport) are college freshmen who confront issues of racial prejudice and emerging sexuality. Laurence

Fishburne plays an instructor in this film written and directed by John Singleton.

HOLLYWOOD SHUFFLE (1987)

Robert Townsend's autobiographical comedy about a struggling African American actor in Hollywood trying to find work and getting nothing but stereotypical roles. Written, directed, and financed by Townsend, who created this clever and appealing film on a $100,000 budget.

HOME OF THE BRAVE (1949)

A black soldier is sent on a top-secret mission in the South Pacific during World War II, but finds that he must battle with his white comrades as he is subjected to subordinate treatment and constant racial slurs. Hollywood's first outstanding statement against racial prejudice.

HONEYDRIPPER (2007)

Director John Sayles's drama about the owner of a dilapidated blues club in Alabama (Danny Glover) who hires a flashy young electric guitarist (Gary Clark Jr.). The film also stars Lisa Gaye Hamilton, Vondie Curtis Hall, and Charles S. Dutton.

HOODLUM (1997)

Highly fictionalized tale of 1930s gangster "Bumpy" Johnson (Laurence Fishburne, reprising his role from *The Cotton Club*), who refuses to allow Dutch Schultz (Tim Roth) and Lucky Luciano (Andy Garcia) to muscle into the Harlem numbers rackets.

HOOP DREAMS (1994)

This exceptional documentary follows two inner-city basketball players through high school as they chase their dreams of playing in the NBA. The film offers plenty of game footage, but the more fascinating scenes deal with the young men's families and home life. Both players encounter dramatic reversals of fortune on and off the court, demonstrating the incredibly long odds they face. *Hoop Dreams* earned numerous honors, including the Audience Award at the 1994 Sundance Film Festival.

HOTEL RWANDA (2004)

Don Cheadle stars in the true story of Paul Rusesabagina, a hotel manager who protected more than a thousand Tutsi refugees during their 1994 struggle against Hutu militia in Rwanda.

HOUSE PARTY (1990)

Lighthearted, African American hip-hop version of a 1950s teen comedy, with rap duo Kid 'n' Play. Featuring real-life rappers and dynamite dance numbers, this film earned best cinematography honors at the 1990 Sundance Film Festival.

HOW STELLA GOT HER GROOVE BACK (1998)

A May-December romance based on the novel by Terry McMillan and starring Angela Bassett, Taye Diggs, and Whoopi Goldberg.

HOW U LIKE ME NOW? (1992)

Daryll Roberts's second directorial effort offers a fresh look at African Americans on film, with plenty of lively supporting characters and witty dialogue. Music by Chuck Webb.

THE HURRICANE (1999)

A moving but truncated true story about middleweight boxing champ Rubin "Hurricane" Carter (Denzel Washington), who spent twenty years in prison after being falsely accused and convicted of murder. Anchored by an Oscar-nominated performance by Washington, the film came under fire for its rearrangement of the facts behind the case.

HUSTLE & FLOW (2005)

John Singleton produced this drama about a Memphis pimp (Terrence Howard) experiencing a midlife crisis as he attempts to become a successful rapper.

I KNOW WHY THE CAGED BIRD SINGS (1979)

An African American writer's memories of growing up in the rural South during the 1930s. Strong performances from Esther Rolle and Constance Good. Based on the book by Maya Angelou.

I'LL MAKE ME A WORLD: A CENTURY OF AFRICAN AMERICAN ARTS (1999)

A PBS documentary, produced by famed documentarian Henry Hampton, that honors the achievements of twentieth-century African American writers, dancers, painters, actors, filmmakers, musicians, and other artists who changed forever who Americans are as a nation and culture.

I'M GONNA GIT YOU SUCKA (1988)

A parody of blaxploitation films popular during the 1960s and 1970s. A number of stars who made blaxploitation films, including Jim Brown, take part in the gags.

IMITATION OF LIFE (1934)

This drama, based on a Fannie Hurst novel, tells the story of a struggling widow, Beatrice Pullman (Claudette Colbert), who opens a successful pancake restaurant with her maid Delilah (Louise Beaver). Both suffer at the hands of their willful teenaged daughters.

IN THE HEAT OF THE NIGHT (1967)

An African American homicide expert (Sidney Poitier) is asked to help solve the murder of a wealthy industrialist in a small Mississippi town, despite resentment on the part of the town's chief of police (Rod Steiger). The powerful script with an underlying theme of racial prejudice is served well by Norman Jewison's taut direction and the stars' powerhouse performances. The film won several Academy and Golden Globe awards.

INSIDE MAN (2006)

Spike Lee directs this bank-heist film about a tough cop (Denzel Washington) who matches wits with a clever bank robber (Clive Owen).

INTRODUCING DOROTHY DANDRIDGE (1999)

Beautiful singer and actress Dorothy Dandridge (Halle Berry) was the first African American woman to be nominated for a best actress Oscar for her performance in 1955's *Carmen Jones.* Ten years later, at forty-two-years old, she was dead from an overdose of antidepressants after suffering a lifetime of tragedies—an abusive childhood, two failed marriages, a brain-damaged child, tumultuous affairs, limited career choices, and bad financial decisions. Berry won a Golden Globe Award for her performance.

INTRUDER IN THE DUST (1949)

A small southern community develops a lynch-mob mentality when a black man is accused of killing a white man in this powerful but largely ignored portrait of race relations in the South. Adapted from a novel by William Faulkner.

JACK JOHNSON (1971)

This documentary explores the life of the first African American heavyweight boxing champion, Jack Johnson. Brock Peters provides the voice of Johnson, and Miles Davis provides the musical score.

JACKIE BROWN (1997)

Quentin Tarantino directed this leisurely but satisfying adaptation of Elmore Leonard's *Rum Punch.* Pam Grier stars as out-of-luck flight attendant Jackie Brown, who runs money to Mexico for ruthless arms dealer Ordell (Samuel L. Jackson), until she is busted on one of her errands. Cool dialogue and chronological shifts are key ingredients, along with a heightened sense of character development. Bridget Fonda, Robert De Niro, and Robert Forster costar. The look and feel of the movie reflects the dingy world it inhabits, as well as Tarantino's love of blaxploitation films of the 1970s.

THE JACKIE ROBINSON STORY (1950)

This biographical film chronicles Robinson's rise from UCLA to his breakthrough as the first African American man to play baseball in the major leagues. Robinson plays himself. The film deals honestly with the racial issues of the time.

JASON'S LYRIC (1994)

Director Doug McHenry's intense drama focuses on the stormy relationship between two brothers (Allen Payne and Bokeem Woodbine), whose lives in an impoverished Houston neighborhood lead them along different paths.

JAY-Z: FADE TO BLACK (2004)

This documentary examines rapper Jay-Z's successful career.

JEFFERSON IN PARIS (1994)

Thomas Jefferson (Nick Nolte) confronts the personal and political issues of enslavement in America, as well as his feelings for Sally Hemings (Thandie Newton), a servant at Monticello, who traveled to Paris with Jefferson's daughter.

JO JO DANCER, YOUR LIFE IS CALLING (1986)

Richard Pryor directed and starred in this semiautobiographical price-of-fame story about a comic who must reevaluate his life after he is hospitalized for a drug-related accident. The film was a major departure from Pryor's earlier comedies. Music by Herbie Hancock.

JOEY BREAKER (1993)

This small but serious picture, filmed in New York City and St. Lucia, is dedicated to Fred Fondren, who died of AIDS in 1992.

JOHN Q (2002)

Denzel Washington portrays the title's everyman hero who is desperate and gutsy enough to bypass medical bureaucracy to get his ten-year-old son Mike (Daniel E. Smith) the heart transplant he desperately needs to live. John Quincy Archibald's plant has just cut his hours, and when his HMO gives him the runaround, he is forced to come up with $75,000 for his son's operation. Unable to find the money, John takes over the emergency room and demands that his son be placed at the top of the transplant list.

JOHNSON FAMILY VACATION (2004)

A litany of disasters awaits the Johnson Family (Cedric the Entertainer, Vanessa L. Williams, Solange Knowles, and rapper Bow Wow) while they travel from California to a family reunion down South.

THE JOSEPHINE BAKER STORY (1990)

A made-for-television biography of exotic entertainer and activist Josephine Baker (Lynn Whitfield), an African American woman from St. Louis who found stardom in prewar Europe but racism and rejection in the United States.

JUICE (1992)

This film portrays the day-to-day street life of four Harlem youths as they try to earn respect (juice) in their neighborhood. The gritty look and feel of the drama comes naturally to Ernest R. Dickerson in his directorial debut.

JUNGLE FEVER (1991)

The relationship between a married black architect (Wesley Snipes) with his white secretary (Annabella Sciorra) provides the backdrop for a cold look at interracial love. Written, produced, and directed by Spike Lee, the film focuses on the discomfort of friends and families rather than the intense world created by the lovers for themselves. Samuel L. Jackson plays the architect's drug-addicted brother.

KANSAS CITY (1995)

Director Robert Altman mixes music, politics, crime, and the movies in this bittersweet homage to his hometown, set in the jazz-driven 1930s. Styled to imitate the brilliant jazz scores played by Joshua Redman, James Carter, and others.

KING (1978)

A miniseries about the life and career of one of the greatest nonviolent civil rights leaders of all time, Martin Luther King Jr., played by Paul Winfield.

LADY SINGS THE BLUES (1972)

Jazz artist Billie Holiday's life (depicted by Diana Ross) becomes a musical drama of her struggle against racism and drug addiction in her pursuit of fame and romance. Billy Dee Williams, Richard Pryor, and Scatman Crothers head the supporting cast.

LAST HOLIDAY (2006)

Queen Latifah stars as a shy woman who decides to take a European vacation after being diagnosed with a terminal illness and being given only three weeks to live. LL Cool J costars.

THE LAST KING OF SCOTLAND (2006)

Forest Whitaker, who won an Academy Award for best actor, delivers a remarkable portrayal of Ugandan dictator Idi Amin.

LAUREL AVENUE (1993)

Looks at the life of an extended working-class African American family in St. Paul, Minnesota, over a busy weekend.

LEAN ON ME (1989)

Depicts the career of Joe Clark (Morgan Freeman), a tough New Jersey teacher who became the principal of the state's worst, crime-plagued school and, through controversial hard-line tactics, turned it around.

THE LEARNING TREE (1969)

A beautifully photographed adaptation of Gordon Park Sr.'s biographical novel about a fourteen-year-old African American boy in Kansas in the 1920s. *The Learning Tree* was the first feature film financed by a major Hollywood studio to be directed by an African American.

LETHAL WEAPON (1989)

Danny Glover and Mel Gibson work well together as a pair of cops who uncover a heroin-smuggling ring. Packed with action, violence, and humorous undertones. Followed by three sequels.

THE LIBERATION OF L. B. JONES (1970)

In this dramatic study of southern race relations, a wealthy black undertaker (Roscoe Lee Brown) wants a divorce from his wife (Lola Falana), who is having an affair with a white policeman.

LILIES OF THE FIELD (1963)

Five East German nuns enlist the aid of a free-spirited U.S. Army veteran (Sidney Poitier), whom they persuade to build their chapel and teach them English. Poitier is excellent as the itinerant laborer and became the first

African American man to win an Academy Award for best actor.

LISTEN UP! THE LIVES OF QUINCY JONES (1991)

A biography of the music legend responsible for numerous movie scores, record productions, and arrangements for the industry's top stars.

THE LONG WALK HOME (1990)

Whoopi Goldberg stars in this dramatic story about the relationship between a rich white housewife (Sissy Spacek) and her black maid, whom she drives to work during the 1956 Montgomery bus boycott.

LOOK-OUT SISTER (1948)

Louis Jordan and an all–African American cast star in this musical western, full of African American culture, slang, and music from 1940s.

LOSING ISAIAH (1994)

A controversial and emotionally moving story of a social worker (Jessica Lange) who adopts an African American baby abandoned by his drug-addicted mother (Halle Berry). Four years later, now clean and sober, the birth mother enlists the aid of a lawyer (Samuel L. Jackson) to regain custody of her child.

LOST BOUNDARIES (1949)

A respected physician, Scott Carter (Mel Ferrer in his film debut), and his family live and work in a small New Hampshire town, hiding the fact that they are black and passing for white in their segregated society. Canada Lee also stars in this film based on a true story.

LOVE JONES (1996)

A Chicago nightclub, the Sanctuary, is the gathering spot for middle-class African American urbanites looking for romance. *Love Jones* earned the Audience Award at the 1997 Sundance Film Festival.

THE MACK (1973)

The Mack is a pimp who comes out of retirement to reclaim a piece of the action in Oakland, California. This violent blaxploitation film was box-office dynamite at the time of its release.

MADEA'S FAMILY REUNION (2006)

While planning her family reunion, a pistol-packing grandmother (Tyler Perry) must contend with numerous dramas, including her love-troubled nieces and a runaway who has been placed under her care.

MALCOLM X (1992)

Marked by strong direction from Spike Lee and a number of first-rate supporting performances (especially Al Freeman Jr. as Elijah Muhammad), it is Denzel Washington's convincing performance in the title role that brings alive this tribute to the controversial African American activist. Based on *The Autobiography of Malcolm X* by Malcolm X and Alex Haley.

THE MAN (1972)

James Earl Jones plays the president pro tem of the U.S. Senate who becomes the first African American president when all the officeholders above him in the presidential line of succession become victims of accidents and illnesses.

MAN ON FIRE (2004)

Set in Mexico City, Denzel Washington stars as a former assassin who swears vengeance on those who committed an unspeakable act against the family he was hired to protect.

MENACE II SOCIETY (1993)

The lives of African American teens living in Watts during the 1990s are realistically captured by twenty-one-year-old twin directors Allen and Albert Hughes in their critically acclaimed big-screen debut.

MIRACLE AT ST. ANNA (2008)

Directed by Spike Lee, this war film follows a group of African American soldiers who are trapped behind enemy lines in war-torn Italy during World War II. Michael Ealy, Laz Alonso, Derek Luke, and Omar Benson star in the film, which was written by African American author James McBride.

MISS EVERS' BOYS (1997)

This wrenching docudrama covers a forty-year U.S. Public Health Service study in which African American men suffering from syphilis were monitored but not treated for the disease. Alfre Woodward earned an Emmy Award for outstanding lead actress in a miniseries or special for her role as nurse Eunice Evers.

MISSISSIPPI MASALA (1992)

This film portrays an interracial romance that sets off a cultural collision and escalates racial tensions in a small southern town when Mina (Sarita Choudhury), a sheltered young Indian woman, falls in love with Demetrius

(Denzel Washington), an ambitious African American man with his own carpet-cleaning business.

MO' BETTER BLUES (1990)

Bleek Gilliam (Denzel Washington) is a handsome, accomplished, self-interested jazz trumpeter who divides his limited time between two lovers (Cynda Williams and Joie Lee), bringing subtle racial issues into focus. The Branford Marsalis Quartet provides the music for Bleek's group, scored by Lee's father Bill, on whose life the script is loosely based.

MONSTER'S BALL (2001)

Georgia death-row prison guard Hank (Billy Bob Thornton) follows in his father's footsteps as a guard and a bigot. His son has also joined the family business, but does not have the heart or stomach for it. When his son gets sick during the execution of Lawrence Musgrove (Sean Combs), Hank flies into a rage that makes him reexamine his life. Soon after, he helps a waitress, Leticia (Halle Berry), from the diner he frequents after an auto accident. Leticia is Musgrove's widow, unbeknownst to Hank, who begins a relationship with her that changes both of them. Berry won the best actress Oscar for her performance.

MR. & MRS. LOVING (1996)

This fact-based movie, set in the 1960s, follows the interracial romance, marriage, and struggle of Richard Loving (Timothy Hutton) and Mildred "Bean" Jeter (Lela Rochon) and the landmark Supreme Court decision concerning miscegenation laws.

NATIVE SON (1986)

This second film adaptation of the classic Richard Wright novel tells the story of a poor African American man who accidentally kills a white woman and then hides the body.

NEW JACK CITY (1991)

Director Mario Van Peebles stars as a police detective who assigns two undercover officers (Ice-T and Judd Nelson) to capture a wealthy Harlem drug lord (Wesley Snipes). Music by Johnny Gill, 2 Live Crew, Ice-T, and others.

NO MAPS ON MY TAPS (1979)

A unique African American art form—jazz tap dancing—is shown in rare photos and Hollywood film clips from the 1930s, and in intimate portraits of three surviving dancers: Sandman Sims, Chuck Green, and Bunny Briggs.

NO WAY OUT (1950)

Sidney Poitier plays a young doctor who treats two white criminals who are wounded in an attempted robbery. After one of the men dies, the other accuses the doctor of murder.

NORMAN, IS THAT YOU? (1976)

A film adaptation of a Broadway play about the confused black parents of a homosexual son and his white lover.

NOTHING BUT A MAN (1964)

Duff Anderson (Ivan Dixon) portrays an African American laborer trying to make a life in a small Alabama town. Abbey Lincoln, Yaphet Kotto, and Gloria Foster also star in this unsentimental depiction of the times. Named to the National Film Registry in 1993.

NOTORIOUS (2009)

A biopic about the life of iconic hip-hop star Christopher Wallace, better known as Biggie Smalls or The Notorious B.I.G. The film chronicles Biggie's childhood in the early 1980s, his controversial relationship with fellow rapper Tupac Shakur, and Biggie's murder in 1997.

OBSESSED (2008)

Idris Elba stars as a happily married and successful businessman who is stalked and harassed by a fanatical coworker. Beyoncé Knowles also stars.

ONCE UPON A TIME . . . WHEN WE WERE COLORED (1995)

Actor Tim Reid makes his directorial debut with the story of an African American youngster growing up parentless in 1950s Mississippi. A nostalgic, sensitive, and heartwarming adaptation of Clifton Taulbert's autobiographical book.

ONE FALSE MOVE (1992)

Director Carl Franklin's first film is not a typical crime thriller. Franklin is more interested in a psychological character study of racism and small-town mores. He earned the 1993 Independent Spirit Award for best director.

ONE POTATO, TWO POTATO (1964)

The story of an interracial marriage between white laborer Julie Cullen (Barbara Barrie) and Frank Richards (Bernie Hamilton), an African American man whom she meets at the plant where she works.

PANTHER (1995)

A highly controversial, fictionalized account of the Black Panther movement in the late 1960s. Directed by Mario Van Peebles. Music by Stanley Clarke.

PARIS IS BURNING (1991)

Jennie Livingston's documentary about New York City's transvestite balls between 1985 and 1989. This is a compelling look at a subculture of primarily African American and Hispanic men, who come together in the one place where they can truly be themselves. Winner of the 1991 Sundance Film Festival Grand Jury Prize.

PASTIME (1991)

A bittersweet baseball elegy set in the minor leagues in 1957. A boyish forty-one-year-old pitcher cannot face his impending retirement and pals around with the team pariah, a seventeen-year-old African American rookie. Splendidly written and acted, the film won the 1991 Sundance Film Festival Audience Award.

A PATCH OF BLUE (1965)

A kind-hearted blind girl (Elizabeth Hartman) falls in love with an African American man (Sidney Poitier) without acknowledging racial differences.

PAUL ROBESON: TRIBUTE TO AN ARTIST (1980)

A documentary that examines the tremendous life of actor Paul Robeson.

PHAT GIRLZ (2006)

The comedian Mo'Nique stars in this comedy about an aspiring plus-size fashion designer who struggles to find love and acceptance.

THE PIANO LESSON (1994)

An adaptation of August Wilson's 1990 Pulitzer Prize–winning play. The film, set in 1936, concerns the prized heirloom of the Charles family—an eighty-year-old ornately carved upright piano.

PINKY (1949)

An early Hollywood treatment of the tragic choice made by some African Americans to pass as white in order to attain a better life for themselves and their families. Based on the novel *Quality* by Cid Ricketts Sumner.

POETIC JUSTICE (1993)

John Singleton's second directorial effort concerns a young hairdresser named Justice (Janet Jackson in her film debut), who copes with her boyfriend's brutal murder by writing poetry (provided by Maya Angelou). Production stopped on the South Central Los Angeles set during the 1992 riots, but the aftermath provided poignant pictures for later scenes.

PORGY AND BESS (1992)

The Glyndebourne production of Gershwin's folk opera about the denizens of Catfish Row. Simon Rattle conducts the London Philharmonic.

POSSE (1993)

Set during the Spanish-American War, this film revolves around a group of African American soldiers. Following their escape from Cuba with a fortune in gold, they travel toward Freemanville, where the group's leader (director Mario Van Peebles) avenges the death of his father.

PRECIOUS: BASED ON THE NOVEL "PUSH" BY SAPPHIRE (2009)

An adaptation of the 1996 novel *Push* by Sapphire, the film focuses on a sixteen-year-old girl from Harlem who has been repeatedly raped by her drug-addicted father and physically and mentally abused by her invalid mother. The protagonist epitomizes the lost and downtrodden youth of America. The film's mainly female cast features Gabourey Sidibe as the title character, with Mo'Nique, Paula Patton, Mariah Carey, and Lenny Kravitz in supporting roles.

PRIDE (2007)

Terrence Howard stars as real-life swim coach Jim Ellis, who starts a swim team for troubled teens at the Philadelphia Department of Recreation.

THE PRINCESS AND THE FROG (2009)

Disney's first animated film featuring African American lead characters is set in the French Quarter of New Orleans at the height of the Roaring Twenties. Naveen, a prince from the land of Maldonia, is transformed into a frog by a voodoo magician. Naveen convinces a young girl named Tiana to kiss him so as to break the spell, but the kiss instead turns Tiana into a frog as well, until the two locate the voodoo queen, Mama Odie, deep in the Bayou, and reunite as human beings. The film features voice work by Anika Noni Rose, Keith David, Terrence Howard, Oprah Winfrey, and Jenifer Lewis.

PURPLE RAIN (1984)

This quasi-autobiographical film tells the story of musician Prince's struggle for love, attention, acceptance, and artistic recognition in Minneapolis. Earned the 1984 Academy Award for best original song score and/or adaptation.

PUTNEY SWOPE (1969)

A comedy about a token African American ad man who turns a Madison Avenue agency upside down after he is mistakenly elected chairman of the board.

THE QUIET ONE (1948)

Explores the ghetto's psychological effects on a ten-year-old African American child. The film's commentary was written by James Agee.

RACE TO FREEDOM: THE STORY OF THE UNDERGROUND RAILROAD (1994)

The story of four formerly enslaved fugitives who, in 1850, struggle to get from North Carolina to the safety of Canada through a network of safe houses and people willing to risk smuggling them to asylum.

A RAGE IN HARLEM (1991)

Set in Harlem in 1956, this film tells the tale of a beautiful con woman named Imabelle (Robin Givens). Adapted from a book by Chester Himes.

RAGTIME (1981)

Based on the E. L. Doctorow novel set in 1906 America, a small unthinking act represents all the racist attacks on an African American man who, this time, refuses to back down.

A RAISIN IN THE SUN (1961)

An outstanding story of a black family trying to make a better life for themselves in an all-white neighborhood in Chicago. Based on the Broadway play by Lorraine Hansberry, who also wrote the screenplay.

RAY (2004)

Jamie Foxx delivers a tour-de-force performance in this biopic of the life of the late soul music icon, Ray Charles.

REBOUND: THE LEGEND OF EARL "THE GOAT" MANIGAULT (1996)

This film stars Don Cheadle as a 1960s Harlem playground basketball phenom who turned his life around. After dropping out of college, turning to heroin, and winding up in prison, he founded his own basketball tournament in Harlem. Music by Kevin Eubanks.

RICHARD PRYOR: LIVE ON THE SUNSET STRIP (1982)

Filmed live at the Hollywood Palladium, this film captures Richard Pryor at his funniest, including his segment "Pryor on Fire."

THE RIVER NIGER (1976)

James Earl Jones and Cicely Tyson are riveting in this adaptation of the Tony Award–winning play about African American ghetto life. Directed by Krishna Shaw, the film depicts believable characters expressing realistic emotions.

RIZE (2005)

This documentary chronicles the dance movements in South Central Los Angeles known as clowning and krumping.

ROLL BOUNCE (2005)

This coming-of-age comedy tells the story of a group of roller-skating friends who go up against a rival team.

ROOTS (1977)

The complete version of Alex Haley's made-for-television saga, which follows an African American man's search for his heritage, revealing an epic panorama of America's past. Music by Quincy Jones.

ROOTS: THE GIFT (1988)

A made-for-television movie based on the Alex Haley characters, featuring Louis Gossett and LeVar Burton, among others.

ROOTS: THE NEXT GENERATION (1979)

A sequel to the landmark television miniseries, continuing the story of author Alex Haley's ancestors from the Reconstruction era of the 1880s to 1967, culminating with Haley's visit to West Africa, where he is told the story of Kunta Kinte.

ROSEWOOD (1996)

A drama based on the true story of the prosperous African American community of Rosewood, Florida, which was destroyed by a white mob in 1923. Directed by John Singleton and starring Ving Rhames, the film accurately shows the tensions between blacks and whites of the time.

SALLY HEMINGS: AN AMERICAN SCANDAL (2000)

Soap opera-ish romance based on the relationship between Thomas Jefferson (Sam Neill) and his young, enslaved, mulatto house servant, Sally Hemings (Carmen Ejogo)—an affair that lasted for thirty-eight years. (DNA proved Jefferson to be the father of one and possibly all six of Hemings's children.) Sally remains dignified through the years, as does Jefferson. The height of the drama occurs when Sally castigates her lover about his contradictory attitudes toward black enslavement.

SAY AMEN, SOMEBODY (1982)

A documentary about gospel music and two of its greatest legends—Willie Mae Ford Smith and Thomas A. Dorsey. Aptly demonstrates the power of music sung from the heart.

SCARY MOVIE (2000)

The Wayans brothers' parody of *Scream* and its progeny. Although not as focused a satire as *I'm Gonna Git You Sucka* and more likely to offend, it was a huge hit, with teenagers especially.

SCHOOL DAZE (1988)

Director, writer, and star Spike Lee's second outing is a rambunctious comedy set at an African American college in the South.

THE SECRET LIFE OF BEES (2008)

This tale, set in 1964, concerns a fourteen-year-old girl who runs away to a South Carolina town to learn about her late mother's past. Adapted from the novel by Sue Monk Kidd, the film was directed by Gina Prince-Bythewood and produced by Will and Jada Pinkett Smith.

SEPARATE BUT EQUAL (1991)

A powerful dramatization of the 1954 *Brown v. Board of Education of Topeka* Supreme Court case that resulted in a landmark civil rights decision. Features Sidney Poitier as NAACP attorney Thurgood Marshall.

SERGEANT RUTLEDGE (1960)

The story of a court-martial, told in flashback, of an African American cavalry officer charged with rape and murder. The film is a detailed look by director John Ford at overt and covert racism. Based on the novel *Captain Buffalo* by James Warner Bellah.

Queen Latifah, Jennifer Hudson, and Alicia Keys* (left to right) *star in* The Secret Life of Bees, *2008. *Gina Prince-Bythewood, the director of this feature film, also wrote the screenplay.* TWENTIETH CENTURY FOX/EVERETT COLLECTION

SET IT OFF (1996)
In this film, four female friends in Los Angeles (Jada Pinkett, Queen Latifah, Vivica A. Fox, and Kimberly Elise) find themselves pushed over the edge and decide to take up bank robbery to escape poverty and strike a blow against "the system."

SEVEN POUNDS (2008)
Will Smith stars as a man who, after causing a car crash in which seven people died, decides to change the lives of seven other people. The film also stars Rosario Dawson, Woody Harrelson, and Michael Ealy.

SHADOWS (1960)
Director John Cassavettes's first independent feature revolves around jazz player Hugh (Hugh Hurd), his brother Ben (Ben Carruthers), and his sister Lelia (Lelia Goldoni). Light-skinned enough to pass for white, Lelia gets involved with the white Tony (Anthony Ray), who leaves when he finds out her true heritage. Music by Charles Mingus. The film was named to the National Film Registry in 1993.

SHAFT (1971)
Gordon Parks Sr. directed this sophisticated action film featuring Richard Roundtree as the African American private eye John Shaft. With an Academy Award–winning theme song by Isaac Hayes, *Shaft* earned the first Oscar for music given to an African American. Adapted from the novel by Ernest Tidyman.

SHAFT (2000)
John Singleton's update of the 1971 blaxploitation flick, with Samuel L. Jackson starring as the nephew of the coolest private eye ever (Richard Roundtree has a cameo in his original role). Jackson can more than hold his own in the cool department as he tracks down murderer Walter Wade Jr. (Christian Bale), who is after the only witness to his crime, a scared waitress (Toni Collette). Wade hires a Latino drug dealer and a couple of bad cops to find the girl and kill Shaft, setting off much gunfire and snappy dialogue.

SHE HATE ME (2004)
Harvard-educated biotech executive John Henry Jack Armstrong (Anthony Mackie) gets into the baby-making business after losing his job.

SHE'S GOTTA HAVE IT (1986)
Spike Lee wrote, directed, edited, produced, and starred in this popular romantic comedy about an independent-minded African American girl in Brooklyn and the three men and one woman who compete for her attention. Awarded the 1987 Independent Spirit Award for best first feature.

SHOW BOAT (1936)
The second of three film versions of the Jerome Kern and Oscar Hammerstein musical (based on the Edna Ferber novel) about a Mississippi showboat and the life and loves of its denizens. The film's musical numbers include Paul Robeson's immortal rendition of "Old Man River." Named to the National Film Registry in 1996.

SILVER STREAK (1976)
An energetic Hitchcock parody featuring the successful first pairing of Richard Pryor and Gene Wilder.

SKIN GAME (1971)
A fast-talking con artist (James Garner) and his African American partner (Lou Gossett Jr.) travel throughout the antebellum South setting up scams in this finely acted comedy-drama.

SLAM (1998)
After being jailed for possession and suspicion of murdering his supplier, street-smart, low-level drug dealer Ray (Saul Williams) relies on spoken-word poetry to see him through life's challenges. Awarded the Sundance Film Festival Grand Jury Prize in 1998.

SLAVES (1969)
Ossie Davis appears in this remake of *Uncle Tom's Cabin*, directed by Herbert J. Biberman.

A SOLDIER'S STORY (1984)
An African American U.S. Army attorney (Howard E. Rollins Jr.) is sent to a southern military base to investigate the murder of an unpopular sergeant. Based on the Pulitzer Prize–winning play by Charles Fuller, with most of the Broadway cast. Fine performances from Denzel Washington and Adolph Caesar. Music by Herbie Hancock.

SOMETHING NEW (2006)
Kenya McQueen (Sanaa Lathan) is a successful African American accountant who makes new discoveries about love after she accepts a blind date with a white architectural landscaper named Brian.

SOPHISTICATED GENTS (1981)
Nine boyhood friends, members of an African American athletic club, reunite after twenty-five years to honor their

old coach and discuss their lives as black men in American society. Based on the novel *The Junior Bachelor Society* by John A. Williams.

SOUL FOOD (1997)

This film depicts the lives of three sisters (Vanessa L. Williams, Vivica A. Fox, and Nia Long) who struggle to hold their family together by keeping up their mother's Sunday dinner tradition after she becomes ill. Boasts many promising debuts, including that of director and writer George Tillman Jr. Produced by Kenneth "Babyface" Edmonds.

SOUL OF THE GAME (1996)

This television movie follows the lives of three talented baseball players in the Negro League during the 1945 season as they await the potential integration of baseball: Flashy, aging pitcher Satchel Paige (Delroy Lindo); mentally unstable catcher Josh Gibson (Mykelti Williamson); and the young, college-educated Jackie Robinson (Blair Underwood).

SOUL PLANE (2004)

This urban spoof of the successful *Airplane* comedy franchise stars comedian D. L. Hughley and rappers Method Man and Snoop Dogg.

SOUNDER (1972)

This film depicts the struggles of a family of African American sharecroppers in rural Louisiana during the Great Depression. Cicely Tyson brings strength and style to her role, with fine help from Paul Winfield. Adapted from the novel by William Armstrong. Nominated for several Oscars at the 1972 Academy Awards. Music by Taj Mahal.

SOUTH CENTRAL (1992)

This low-budget urban drama set in a gang-infested Los Angeles neighborhood was the feature debut of director Steve Anderson. Based on the novel *Crips* by Donald Bakeer.

STOMP THE YARD (2006)

A troubled nineteen-year-old street dancer is courted by the top two campus fraternities, who need his fierce street-style dance moves to win the highly coveted national step show competition.

STORMY WEATHER (1943)

In this cavalcade of African American entertainment, the plot is overshadowed by the nearly nonstop array of musical numbers, showcasing the stellar cast (Lena Horne, Bill Robinson, Fats Waller, Dooley Wilson, and Cab Calloway) at their performing peak.

STRAIGHT OUT OF BROOKLYN (1991)

A bleak, nearly hopeless look at a struggling African American family in a Brooklyn housing project, revealing a segment of society seldom shown in mainstream film. Music by Harold Wheeler. Awarded the Sundance Film Festival Special Jury Prize in 1991.

SUDIE & SIMPSON (1990)

A heartwarming tale of friendship between a twelve-year-old white girl and an adult black man set in rural Georgia in the 1940s. Based on Sara Flanigan Carter's autobiographical novel.

SUGAR (2008)

A drama about a young baseball pitcher from the Dominican Republic, Miguel Santos (Algenis Perez Soto), known as Sugar, who moves to Iowa when he is nineteen years old to play in the American minor league system.

SUGAR HILL (1994)

Two brothers (Michael Wright and Wesley Snipes) are heroin dealers who have built their own crime empire in the Sugar Hill section of Harlem. Snipes is moved to reconsider his career options when he falls for an aspiring actress (Theresa Randle). Music by Terence Blanchard and Larry Joshua.

SUPER FLY (1972)

Director Gordon Parks Jr.'s controversial and pioneering blaxploitation film of the 1970s features a Harlem dope dealer (Ron O'Neal) who attempts to leave the profession after one last big score. Excellent period tunes by Curtis Mayfield.

SWEET SWEETBACK'S BAADASSSSS SONG (1971)

An African American man kills two white policemen who beat up a black militant. He uses his streetwise survival skills to elude the law and escape to Mexico. Directed by Melvin Van Peebles.

TAKE A GIANT STEP (1959)

An African American youth (Johnny Nash) struggles with society's attitude toward race and seeks the comfort of his family's maid (Ruby Dee). Directed by Philip Leacock.

THEY CALL ME SIRR (2000)

Based on the true story of Sirr Parker (Kente Scott), a talented but poverty-stricken high school football player in South Central Los Angeles. After Sirr and his younger brother are abandoned by their mother, Sirr struggles to look after his family (including an ailing grandmother) while keeping his place on the team. But the teen is finally forced to turn to his coach (Michael Clarke Duncan) for help.

A TIME TO KILL (1996)

Powerful story of revenge, racism, and the question of justice in the "new South." Based on the John Grisham novel. Samuel L. Jackson earned a Golden Globe nomination for best supporting actor.

TO KILL A MOCKINGBIRD (1962)

Faithful adaptation of Harper Lee's powerful novel. Gregory Peck's performance as a southern lawyer defending a black man (Brock Peters) accused of raping a white woman earned him the Academy and Golden Globe awards for best actor. The film was named to the National Film Registry in 1995 and the Top 100 list of the American Film Institute in 1998.

TO SIR, WITH LOVE (1967)

Skillful and warm performance by Sidney Poitier as an idealistic teacher who wins over his unruly students in London's tough East End. Based on the novel by E. R. Braithwaite.

TO SLEEP WITH ANGER (1990)

Danny Glover's best performance as a stranger from the South whose visit divides an African American middle-class family living in Los Angeles. Insightful look into the conflicting values of black America. The film earned the Sundance Film Festival Special Jury Prize in 1990.

TRAINING DAY (2001)

In this drama, Denzel Washington portrays Alonzo Harris, a veteran undercover cop who's become morally bankrupt and works on the "might makes right" theory of justice. Opposing him is rookie Jake Hoyt (Ethan Hawke), who first wants to be a part of Harris's team and then learns what it will cost him. Washington's ferocious performance won him a best actor Oscar.

TSOTSI (2005)

Six days in the life of a teenage gang leader fighting to survive amidst the poverty and violence of Johannesburg. *Tsotsi* was the winner of an Academy Award for best foreign language film.

THE TUSKEGEE AIRMEN (1995)

A made-for-television drama based on the formation and achievements of the U.S. Army Air Corps' first squadron of African American combat fighter pilots during World War II, the Fighting Ninety-ninth of the 332nd Fighter Group. Based on a story by former Tuskegee airman Robert W. Williams.

TYLER PERRY'S I CAN DO BAD ALL BY MYSELF (2009)

This film, based on a Tyler Perry play, centers around a selfish alcoholic singer who is forced to grow up when she assumes responsibility for her sister's children. The film stars Taraji P. Henson, Brian White, and Gladys Knight.

TYLER PERRY'S MADEA GOES TO JAIL (2009)

Inspired by the Tyler Perry play of the same name, this film centers on Perry's signature character, Madea Simmons, who is sent to prison as a result of her anger-management problems. The film also focuses on a developing romance between a young lawyer and a female friend from his past (whom Madea meets in jail).

TYSON (2009)

A documentary film about former heavyweight boxing champion Mike Tyson. The film starts with Tyson's World Boxing Council Heavyweight Championship win over Trevor Berbick in 1986, then explores his heroic rise to fame and epic downfall. The film revolves around Tyson's personal relationships, ranging from his father-son relationship with manager and trainer Cus D'Amato to his love-hate relationship with actress Robin Givens and disgust for boxing promoter Don King.

UNCLE TOM'S CABIN (1914)

A satisfying silent version of Harriet Beecher Stowe's tale, told from the point of view of a founder of the Underground Railroad. Sam Lucas was the first African American actor to garner a lead role in a film. Subsequent versions of this film were made in 1927 and 1987 (the first sound version).

UNDERCOVER BROTHER (2002)

poof of secret agents and blaxploitation movies. Brother (Eddie Griffin) is a secret agent from the B.R.O.T.H.E.R.H.O.O.D. sent to rescue General Warren Boutwell, a black war hero turned presidential candidate (Billy Dee Williams), who has been brainwashed in a plot by The Man to destroy African American culture. This more-hit-than-miss comedy finds many targets of all stripes to lampoon, and does so with the right amount of funk.

UPTIGHT (1968)

In a story set in Cleveland, actor Raymond St. Jacques leads a well-armed group of African American revolutionaries after the assassination of Martin Luther King Jr. Ruby Dee and Julian Mayfield costar.

UPTOWN SATURDAY NIGHT (1974)

Two working men (Sidney Poitier and Bill Cosby) attempt to recover a stolen lottery ticket from the African American underworld after being ripped off at an illegal gambling establishment. Directed by Sidney Poitier.

WAIST DEEP (2006)

A reformed gangbanger is faced with a do-or-die situation after his son is kidnapped in a carjacking.

WAITING TO EXHALE (1995)

A popular adaptation of Terry McMillan's novel about four African American women (Whitney Houston, Angela Bassett, Loretta Devine, and Lela Rochon) hoping to enter the right romantic relationship. Directed by Forest Whitaker. Music by producer Kenneth "Babyface" Edmonds.

THE WALKING DEAD (1994)

Preston A. Whitmore II's directorial debut depicts the Vietnam War from the perspectives of four black and one white Marine assigned to rescue prisoners of war from a North Vietnamese camp in 1972.

WATERMELON MAN (1970)

The tables are turned for a bigoted white man when he wakes up one morning to discover he has become a black man. Godfrey Cambridge takes on both roles. Directed by Melvin Van Peebles.

WHAT'S LOVE GOT TO DO WITH IT (1993)

Energetic biographical film of powerhouse songstress Tina Turner (Angela Bassett) and her abusive relationship with her husband, Ike (Laurence Fishburne). Based on *I, Tina* by Turner and Kurt Loder. For her performance, Bassett earned the Golden Globe Award for best actress in 1994. Music by Stanley Clarke.

WHY DID I GET MARRIED? (2007)

Tyler Perry's fourth film examines the relationships of eight married college friends who reunite in Colorado for one week. A sequel, *Why Did I Get Married Too?*, was released in 2010.

THE WIZ (1978)

A film version of the Broadway musical based on the perennial favorite *The Wizard of Oz.* The all-star cast includes Diana Ross, Michael Jackson, Lena Horne, Nipsey Russell, and Richard Pryor. Music by Quincy Jones.

THE WOMEN OF BREWSTER PLACE (1989)

A complex script gives each actress in a fine ensemble headed by executive producer Oprah Winfrey (in her dramatic television debut) time in the spotlight. This film was the pilot for the series *Brewster Place.* Based on the novel by Gloria Naylor.

THE WOOD (1999)

Based on writer-director Rick Famuyiwa's life story, this ensemble comedy flashes back between the middle and high school days of three male friends growing up in Inglewood, California, and an eventful wedding day in the late 1990s. Captures the mood and nostalgia of the 1980s through memorable rhythm-and-blues and hip-hop music.

THE WORLD, THE FLESH, AND THE DEVIL (1959)

Three survivors of a nuclear holocaust form an uneasy alliance and deal with issues of survival and racism. Features actor Harry Belafonte.

ZEBRAHEAD (1992)

Outstanding performances by the young and largely unknown cast, particularly Michael Rapaport and N'Bushe Wright, and an excellent musical score by Taj Mahal enrich the action. Awarded the Sundance Film Festival Filmmakers Trophy.

ZOOMAN (1995)

The film offers a hard-hitting message on violence and responsibility and features performances by Louis Gossett Jr. and Vondie Curtis-Hall. Based on Charles Fuller's 1978 play *Zooman and the Sign.*

ACTORS, FILMMAKERS, AND FILM AND TELEVISION EXECUTIVES

(Some biographical profiles may appear in other chapters. To locate profiles more readily, please consult the index.)

MARA BROCK AKIL (1970–)

Writer, Producer. A Los Angeles native, Mara Brock Akil was raised primarily in Kansas City. After earning a bachelor's degree in journalism from Northwestern University, she began her writing career on the critically acclaimed *South Central* series. She then joined the writing staff for *Moesha*, where she was also a producer. After a stint as supervising producer on the comedy series *The Jamie Foxx Show*, Akil created her first show, *Girlfriends*, in 2000, followed by *The Game*, which premiered in 2006.

LAZ ALONZO (1971–)

Actor. Laz Alonso, a Cuban American actor of African descent, was born in Washington, D.C. He has appeared in a number of television series and music videos, and has had supporting roles in such films as *Leprechaun: Back 2 tha Hood* (2003), *All Souls Day* (2005), *Jarhead* (2005), *This Christmas* (2007), *Stomp the Yard* (2007), *Miracle at St. Anna* (2008), *Fast & Furious* (2009), and *Avatar* (2009).

PARIS BARCLAY (1956–)

Writer, Director. Paris Barclay is an Emmy Award–winning screenwriter, director, and producer known for his work in television. The Chicago native's producing credits include the television series *City of Angels*, *Cold Case*, and *NYPD Blue*. Barclay has directed episodes for numerous popular television series, including *Glee*, *The Good Wife*, *CSI*, *In Treatment*, *House, M.D.*, *The Mentalist*, *Lost*, *The West Wing*, *ER*, and others.

ANGELA BASSETT (1958–)

Actress. Angela Bassett was born in New York City. She was one of two daughters of a single mother and grew up in public housing in St. Petersburg, Florida. Inspired to the acting craft after witnessing a stage performance by James Earl Jones when she was a teenager, Bassett earned top grades and enrolled in Yale University. After receiving a master's degree from its prestigious school of drama in the early 1980s, Bassett settled in New York City and began winning acting roles in an industry not known for its wealth of interesting, nonstereotypical roles for African American women.

Bassett eventually found work in television commercials and the CBS daytime drama *The Guiding Light*, and she debuted on Broadway in August Wilson's *Ma Rainey's Black Bottom* in 1985. In 1991, she appeared in two notable films: John Singleton's *Boyz N the Hood*, a role she secured upon the recommendation of her friend, actor Larry Fishburne; and John Sayles's *City of Hope*. Her work attracted the attention of filmmaker Spike Lee, who cast her as Betty Shabazz, wife of Malcolm X, in his 1992 film biography of the slain leader. Bassett's portrayal won praise from critics for its intensity and sensitivity.

The 1993 film *What's Love Got to Do With It*, based on Tina Turner's autobiography, catapulted Bassett into major stardom and won her rave reviews for the vivid depiction of some of the more harrowing years of the singer's life. Fishburne had agreed to play the role of Ike Turner on the condition that Bassett played the lead role. Bassett won a Golden Globe Award for her performance, as well as two NAACP Image Awards. In 1995, Bassett appeared in a lead role in the science fiction thriller *Strange Days*, opposite Ralph Fiennes, and in the Eddie Murphy comedy *Vampire in Brooklyn*. Later that year, she won further critical acclaim for her part in *Waiting to Exhale*, the box-office hit based on Terry McMillan's novel of a close-knit quartet of African American women. In 1998, Bassett starred as a woman who falls in love with a younger man in *How Stella Got Her Groove Back*, also based on a novel by McMillan. During that same year, she served as series narrator for the acclaimed PBS documentary *Africans in America: America's Journey through Slavery*.

In 1999, Bassett began work on a science fiction movie with director Walter Hill titled *Supernova*. She moved into producing in 2000 with a Showtime original movie, *Ruby's Bucket of Blood*, which she also starred in. Bassett also starred in the critically acclaimed *Boesman & Lena* in 2000. The next year, she moved back toward the mainstream with *The Score*, alongside Robert De Niro and Edward Norton. In 2002, she appeared in *Sunshine State*, an in-depth personal and political look at the state of Florida and the people who live there. Bassett's other films include *Akeelah and the Bee* (2006), *Meet the Browns* (2008), and *Notorious* (2009). She also played recurring characters on the television series *Alias* in 2005 and *ER* during the 2008–2009 season.

JENNIFER BEALS (1963–)

Actress. Jennifer Beals was born in Chicago in 1963. She graduated from Yale University with a bachelor's degree in American literature in 1987. Beals has appeared in more than fifty feature films and television shows. She is best known for her roles as Alexandra "Alex" Owens in the 1983 film *Flashdance* and as Bette Porter on the lesbian-themed dramatic series *The L Word*, which ran from 2004 to 2009 on Showtime.

HARRY BELAFONTE (1927–)

Singer, Actor. Born on March 1, 1927, in New York City, Harry Belafonte moved to the West Indies when he was eight. At thirteen, Belafonte returned to New York, where

Singer and Actor Harry Belafonte. *Pictured in a scene from the 1995 Robert Altman film* Kansas City, *Belafonte has enjoyed a distinguished career both as a singer and as an actor on stage, screen, and television. He has also received a number of honors for his work as a political activist, including the Thurgood Marshall Lifetime Achievement Award.* THE KOBAL COLLECTION. REPRODUCED BY PERMISSION.

he attended high school. He joined the U.S. Navy in 1944. After his discharge, while working as a janitor in New York, he became interested in drama. He studied acting at Stanley Kubrick's Dramatic Workshop and with Erwin Piscator at the New School for Social Research, where his classmates included Marlon Brando and Walter Matthau. A successful singing engagement at The Royal Roost, a New York jazz club, led to other engagements around the country. But Belafonte became dissatisfied with the music he was performing, and returned to New York, where he opened a restaurant in Greenwich Village and studied folk singing. His first appearances as a folk singer in the 1950s "helped give folk music a period of mass appeal," according to John S. Wilson in a 1981 *New York Times* article. During his performances at the Palace Theater in New York, Belafonte had audiences dancing in the aisles.

Belafonte produced the first integrated musical show on television, which won him two Emmy Awards. The show provoked a national furor in pre–civil rights America when white British singer Petula Clark touched Belafonte's arm during a duet. When Dr. Martin Luther King Jr. marched on Montgomery, Alabama, and Washington, D.C., Harry Belafonte joined him and brought along a large contingent of performers. Touring in the stage musical *Three for Tonight*, in which he had appeared on Broadway in 1955, Belafonte was forced to flee in the middle of a performance in Spartanburg, South Carolina, and was rushed to the airport in the mayor's car after he was warned that the Ku Klux Klan was marching on the theater.

Belafonte also appeared on Broadway in John Murray Anderson's *Almanac* (1953). Belafonte's movies include *Carmen Jones* (1954), *Island in the Sun* (1957), *The World, the Flesh, and the Devil* (1958), *Odds Against Tomorrow* (1959), *The Angel Levine* (1969), *Buck and the Preacher* (1972), *Uptown Saturday Night* (1974), and *White Man's Burden* (1995).

In the 1980s, Belafonte appeared in his first dramatic role on television in NBC's *Grambling's White Tiger*, and in 1981 Columbia Records released his first album in seven years, *Loving You Is Where I Belong*, consisting mostly of ballads. Belafonte has received numerous awards, including the 1982 Martin Luther King Jr.

Nonviolent Peace Prize and three honorary doctorates. Belafonte also received the Thurgood Marshall Lifetime Achievement Award in 1993, the National Medal of Arts in 1994, a Distinguished American Award at the John F. Kennedy Library in 2002, and a lifetime achievement award from the NAACP's Detroit chapter.

HALLE BERRY (1968–)

Actress, Model. Halle Berry was born in Cleveland, Ohio, to an interracial family. After winning the Miss Teen Ohio beauty pageant, Berry enrolled in Cleveland's Cuyahoga Community College in 1986 to study broadcast journalism. She decided to become an actor and moved to Chicago, where she studied acting and worked as a model.

Berry relocated to Manhattan in 1988 and landed her first television role on the series *Paper Dolls*. Her big break came when she was selected by director Spike Lee to appear in his 1991 film *Jungle Fever*, in which she played a crack addict.

Actress Halle Berry, 2009. *Berry was the first African American actress to win the Academy Award for best actress, for* Monster's Ball *(2001).* JIM RUYMEN/UPI/LANDOV

Berry was cast in the 1991 social satire *Strictly Business*. Some of her notable film roles during the 1990s include the 1996 action film *Executive Decision*, the 1997 comedy *B.A.P.S.*, and the 1997 made-for-television movie *Solomon & Sheba*, in which she played the queen of Sheba. Berry also starred as Dorothy Dandridge in the 1999 HBO film *Introducing Dorothy Dandridge* and in the 1998 film *Bulworth*. Her high-profile marriage to baseball star David Justice ended in divorce in 1996.

Berry's rise to true fame occurred in 2000 when she was honored for her portrayal of Dorothy Dandridge in the HBO biopic at the thirty-first NAACP Image Awards. Later that year, she won a Golden Globe and a Screen Actors Guild Award for best actress in a miniseries or television movie for her performance in *Introducing Dorothy Dandridge*. A few months later, she married singer Eric Benét in a secret ceremony at an undisclosed location. They divorced in 2005. In 2001, Berry received both a Screen Actors Guild Award for outstanding performance by a female actor in a leading role and the Academy Award for best actress for her performance in *Monster's Ball*. Since then, Berry has appeared in *Die Another Day* (2002), *Gothika* (2003), *Catwoman* (2004), *Their Eyes Were Watching God* (2005), *X-Men: The Last Stand* (2006), and *Things We Lost in the Fire* (2007), among other films.

ANDRE BRAUGHER (1962–)

Actor. A Chicago native, Andre Braugher began his film career in the highly popular *Kojak* television movies in 1989. He received a B.A. from Stanford University in 1984 and an M.F.A. from the Juilliard School in 1988. Braugher has performed in numerous Shakespeare plays for the New York Shakespeare Festival and at the Joseph Papp Public Theatre.

He gained national recognition for his starring role as Detective Frank Pembleton on the long-running dramatic series *Homicide: Life on the Street*. In 1998, Braugher earned an Emmy Award for outstanding lead actor in a drama series. Braugher's other notable television and film roles include *Glory* (1989), *Murder in Mississippi* (1990), *Simple Justice* (1993), *The Tuskegee Airmen* (1995), *Get on the Bus* (1996), *Primal Fear* (1996), *City of Angels* (1998), *Passing Glory* (1999), *All the Rage* (1999), and *Duets* (2000), with Gwyneth Paltrow. In 1999, Braugher made his directorial debut with one vignette of the Showtime trilogy *Love Songs*. He also began appearing as a regular on the television series *Gideon's Crossing*, which garnered him a nomination in 2000 for a Golden Globe award for best television actor in a drama. In 2009, Braugher joined Ray

Romano and Scott Bakula in the cast of the TNT series *Men of a Certain Age*.

JOY BRYANT (1976–)

Actress. Joy Bryant was born in the Bronx in New York City. She began her career as a model while a student at Yale University. Bryant's acting debut soon followed with a role in director Robert Townsend's *Carmen: A Hip Hopera* (2001), which led to a role in the Eddie Murphy action comedy *Showtime* (2002). Her breakthrough came when she starred in Denzel Washington's directorial debut, *Antwone Fisher* (2002). Bryant played recurring characters in the television series *ER* in 2003 and *Parenthood* in 2010. She also appeared in *Haven* (2004), *Get Rich or Die Tryin'* (2005), and *Welcome Home Roscoe Jenkins* (2008).

REGGIE BYTHEWOOD (1965–)

Writer, Director. Screenwriter, director, and playwright Reggie Bythewood was born in the Bronx in 1965. He left New York to pursue work in television and film. His list of credits includes serving as a writer on the popular television sitcom *A Different World* and on the feature films *Get on the Bus* (1996), *Dancing in September* (2000), and *Notorious* (2009). In the late 1990s, he was producer and writer for the series *New York Undercover*. He made his debut as a director with *Biker Boyz* (2003), which he also wrote.

DIAHANN CARROLL (1935–)

Actress, Singer. Diahann Carroll was born in the Bronx on July 17, 1935, the daughter of a subway conductor and a nurse. As a child, she was a member of the Abyssinian Baptist Church choir. When she was ten, Carroll won a Metropolitan Opera scholarship. Singing lessons held little appeal for her, however, so she continued her schooling at the High School of Music and Art. As a concession to her parents, Carroll enrolled at New York University, where she was to be a sociology student, but stage fever led her to an appearance on a television talent show, which netted her $1,000. A subsequent appearance at the Latin Quarter Club launched her professional career.

In 1954, Carroll appeared in *House of Flowers*, winning favorable press notices. In that year, she also appeared in a film version of *Carmen Jones*, in the role of Myrt. Movie and television appearances kept Carroll busy until 1958, the year she was slated to appear as an Asian in Richard Rodgers's *Flower Drum Song*. The part did not materialize. Three years later, Rodgers cast her in *No Strings* as a high fashion model, a role for which she earned a Tony Award in 1962.

In the late 1960s, Carroll was cast as the lead in the television series *Julia*, in which she played a nurse and war widow. She also appeared in the films *Porgy and Bess* (1959), *Goodbye Again* (1961), *Paris Blues* (1961), *Claudine* with James Earl Jones (1974), *Sister, Sister* (1982), and *The Five Heartbeats* (1991). During the 1980s and early 1990s, she had featured roles in the television series *Dynasty* and *A Different World*. She published an autobiography, *Diahann*, in 1986.

From 1996 to 1997, Carroll appeared on stage in the Broadway musical *Sunset Boulevard*. In 1998, she played a small role as a voodoo priestess in the movie *Eve's Bayou*. Carroll battled breast cancer that year and did many promotional spots for the American Cancer Society. In 1999, Carroll played Sadie Delany in the film adaptation of the play *Having Our Say: The Delany Sisters' First 100 Years* for CBS. Carroll continued to work on the small screen over the next few years, first starring in *Livin' for Love: The Natalie Cole Story*, then winning a role in 2002 as a judge on the short-lived television drama *The Court*, opposite Sally Field. Carroll appeared on several episodes of *Grey's Anatomy* in 2007 and was a recurring character on *White Collar* beginning in 2009. She published a memoir, *Legs Are the Last to Go: Aging, Acting, Marrying, and Other Things I Learned the Hard Way*, in 2008.

DON CHEADLE (1964–)

Actor. Don Cheadle, a Kansas City native, first won a part on the television series *Fame* (1982) before landing his breakout roe in *Devil in a Blue Dress* (1995). Cheadle won a Golden Globe for his portrayal of Sammy Davis Jr. in *The Rat Pack* (1999). Other notable roles include *Boogie Nights* (1997), *Out of Sight* (1998), *After the Sunset* (2004), *Crash* (2004), *Hotel Rwanda* (2004), for which he was nominated for an Academy Award, *Talk to Me* (2007), and *Traitor* (2008). He has also appeared in Steven Soderbergh's *Ocean's* series with an ensemble cast that included George Clooney, Brad Pitt, and Matt Damon. After starring in *Hotel Rwanda*, Cheadle became involved in humanitarian work in Africa. In particular, he campaigned to bring an end to ethnic violence in the Darfur region of Sudan.

JEFFREY CLANAGAN (1960–)

Film Executive. Jeff Clanagan is the president and CEO of Codeblack Entertainment, a leading film production and distribution company. His notable production credits include *Lockdown* (2000), *Civil Brand* (2002), and *Hair Show* (2004).

BILL COSBY (1937–)

Actor, Comedian. Born on July 12, 1937, Bill Cosby is one of the most successful performers and businessmen in the United States. A native of suburban Philadelphia, Cosby left high school to become a medic in the U.S. Navy. As a testament to his commitment to education, he obtained his diploma while in the service. After leaving the military, he entered Temple University, where he played football and worked evenings as a bartender.

While doing this work, Cosby began to entertain the customers with his comedy routines. Encouraged by his success, he left Temple in 1962 to pursue a career in show business. He began by playing small clubs around Philadelphia and in New York's Greenwich Village. Within two years, he was playing the top nightclubs around the country and making television appearances on shows hosted by Johnny Carson, Jack Paar, and Andy Williams. Cosby eventually won the opportunity to serve as guest host of Carson's *Tonight Show*. In the 1960s, Cosby became the first African American to star in a prime-time television series, *I Spy*, which ran from 1965 to 1968 and won Cosby three Emmy Awards.

In the 1970s, Cosby appeared regularly in nightclubs in Las Vegas, Lake Tahoe, and Reno, and did commercials for such sponsors as Jell-O, Del Monte, and Ford. From 1969 until 1972, he had his own television series, *The Bill Cosby Show*. During the early 1970s, he also developed and contributed vocals to the Saturday morning children's show *Fat Albert and the Cosby Kids*. He appeared in such films as *Uptown Saturday Night* (1974), *Let's Do It Again* (1975), *A Piece of the Action* (1977), and the award-winning television movie *To All My Friends on Shore* (1971).

In 1975, Random House published his book *Bill Cosby's Personal Guide to Tennis, or, Don't Lower the Lob, Raise the Net*. For several years, he was involved in educational television with the Children's Television Workshop. He returned to college, spending five years at the University of Massachusetts, earning a master's degree and, in 1977, a doctorate in education.

Bill Cosby, Scene from Final Episode of* The Cosby Show, *1992. *Cosby starred as Dr. Cliff Huxtable in this consistently top-rated situation comedy, which he had also created. The show was noteworthy not only for its huge popularity throughout an eight-season run but also for the tremendous opportunities it created for African American performers.* AP IMAGES

Cosby was the star and creator of the consistently top-rated *The Cosby Show* from 1984 to 1992, author of two best-selling books, *Fatherhood* (1986) and *Time Flies* (1987), and a performer at the top venues in Las Vegas, where he earned $500,000 a week. He also won top fees as a commercial spokesman for Kodak and Coca-Cola. He has recorded nearly thirty albums and has won several Grammy Awards. Cosby also hosted a new version of the old Groucho Marx game show, *You Bet Your Life*. In 1994, Cosby reunited with Robert Culp, his costar from the *I Spy* show, for a new television movie, *I Spy Returns*. He also starred in the short-lived series *The Cosby Mysteries* in 1994 to 1995. Toward the end of the decade, Cosby hosted *Kids Say the Darndest Things*, based on a show originally hosted by Art Linkletter. Cosby also starred in another sitcom titled *Cosby*, which ran from 1996 to 2000.

In 1998, Cosby was an honoree at the annual Kennedy Center Honors. During the first decade of the 2000s, Cosby continued to be active behind the scenes, with many producing credits. He also continued to make public appearances, such as giving the 2001 commencement address at Ohio State University in Columbus. Cosby appeared in rare form, dressed in a t-shirt and sweat pants—with a tassel hanging from his baseball cap.

Cosby and his wife, Camille, live in rural New England. The Cosbys made headlines when they donated $20 million to Spelman College in Atlanta. In 2002, Cosby was awarded the Presidential Medal of Freedom. In 2009, he was the recipient of the twelfth annual Mark Twain Prize for American Humor, given by the Kennedy Center. He has received honorary degrees from numerous colleges and universities, including Yale, Baylor, and Carnegie Mellon.

RUPERT CROSSE (1928–1973)

Actor. Born in Nevis in the British West Indies on November 29, 1928, Rupert Crosse moved to Harlem at an early age. Crosse returned to Nevis when he was seven, after the death of his father. Reared by his grandparents and strongly influenced by his grandfather, a schoolmaster, Crosse received a solid education before returning to New York, where he attended Benjamin Franklin High School. Crosse later worked at odd jobs before interrupting high school to spend two years in military service in Germany and Japan. Once out of the service, Crosse finished high school and entered Bloomfield College and Seminary in New Jersey. Though he intended to become a minister, it was obvious from the jobs he had held—machinist, construction worker, and recreation counselor—that his career plans were not yet definite.

Crosse subsequently studied acting and appeared in the Equity Library Theatre off-Broadway production of *Climate of Eden*. He then transferred to John Cassavetes's workshop and appeared in Cassavetes's film *Shadows* (1959), winner of a Venice Film Festival Award. Crosse later appeared in Cassavetes's *Too Late Blues* (1962). Crosse's most important film role was as Ned McCaslin in the screen adaptation of William Faulkner's Pulitzer Prize–winning novel *The Reivers* (1969), for which Crosse was nominated for an Academy Award as best supporting actor. His other film credits include *The Wild Seed* (1965) and *Ride in the Whirlwind* (1965).

Crosse's numerous stage credits include *Sweet Bird of Youth*, *The Blood Knot*, and *Hatful of Rain*. Television viewers saw Crosse in *Dr. Kildare*, *I Spy*, and *The Man from U.N.C.L.E.*, as well as several other series. Rupert Crosse died of cancer on March 5, 1973, at age forty-five at his sister's home in Nevis.

DOROTHY DANDRIDGE (1922–1965)

Actress. Dorothy Dandridge was born on November 9, 1922, in Cleveland, Ohio; her mother was the actress Ruby Dandridge. As children, Dorothy and her sister Vivian toured the United States as the Wonder Kids. In 1934, they were joined by a third performer, Etta Jones, and the trio became the Dandridge Sisters. The Dandridge Sisters were a popular act, performing at the Cotton Club in Harlem and in the motion picture *A Day at the Races* (1937). By the 1940s, Dorothy Dandridge had struck out on her own, appearing in the musical shorts *Easy Street*, *Yes, Indeed*, *Cow Cow Boogie*, *Jungle Jig*, *Paper Doll*, and *Sing for My Supper*.

Dandridge married Harold Nicholas (of the famed Nicholas Brothers dance team) in 1942, and had a daughter, Harolyn, in 1943. Harolyn was diagnosed with a severe developmental disability and was sent to an institution; shortly thereafter, Dandridge divorced Nicholas. She carried on a fairly successful career as a nightclub singer during the 1940s and 1950s. Her greatest triumph, however, came as a film actress, particularly in the all–African American musical *Carmen Jones* (1954), for which she received an Oscar nomination for best actress, becoming the first African American woman to receive this honor. Another important role was in *Island in the Sun* (1957), where she was paired romantically with a white man, John Justin—a breakthrough in screen desegregation. In 1959, Dandridge played Bess opposite Sidney Poitier's Porgy in the movie version of *Porgy and Bess*. Over her career, she appeared in more than twenty-five films.

Dandridge married the white Las Vegas restaurateur Jack Dennison in 1959, but three years later divorced and declared personal bankruptcy. She died of an overdose of a prescription antidepressant on September 8, 1965, when she was forty-two years old.

LEE DANIELS (1959–)

Writer, Director, Producer. A Philadelphia native, Lee Daniels began his career as a casting director, working on such projects as Prince's *Purple Rain* (1984) and *Under the Cherry Moon* (1986). He is best known for producing *Monster's Ball* (2001), the film that earned Halle Berry an Oscar, and for directing *Precious* (2009), which earned him a 2010 Oscar nomination for best director.

OSSIE DAVIS (1917–2005)

Actor. Ossie Davis was born Raiford Chatman Davis in Cogdell, Georgia. He grew up in Waycross, Georgia, and in 1935 entered Howard University in Washington, D.C., where Alain Locke suggested he pursue an acting career in New York. After completing service in the U.S. Army, Davis landed his first role in the 1946 play *Jeb*, where he met Ruby Dee, whom he married two years later.

After appearing in the movie *No Way Out* (1950), Davis won Broadway roles in *No Time for Sergeants*, *A Raisin in the Sun*, and *Jamaica*. In 1961, he and Dee starred in *Purlie Victorious*, a play that Davis himself had written. Two years later, they reprised their roles in the movie version, known as *Gone Are the Days*. Davis's other movie credits from this period include *The Cardinal* (1963), *Shock Treatment* (1964), *The Hill* (1965), *A Man Called Adam* (1966), and *The Scalphunter* (1968).

Actor Ossie Davis, New York City, 2001. *Davis, chairman emeritus of the landmark Apollo Theater, addresses the media regarding the upcoming musical revue* Harlem Song, *written by Tony Award–winning director George C. Wolfe.* AP PHOTO/ MATT MOYER

Davis then directed such films as *Cotton Comes to Harlem* (1970) and *Black Girl* (1972). His play, *Escape to Freedom: A Play about Young Frederick Douglass*, had its debut at Town Hall in New York and was published by Viking in 1976. Davis was also involved with television scripts and educational programming. *The Ruby Dee and Ossie Davis Story Hour*, a radio program, aired in the mid-1970s. The arts education television series *With Ossie and Ruby* ran on PBS from 1981 to 1982. Davis and Dee also founded the Institute of New Cinema Artists and the Recording Industry Training Program.

From the 1970s to the 1990s, Davis's many movie appearances included roles in *Let's Do It Again* (1975), *Hot Stuff* (1979), *Nothing Personal* (1979), *Harry and Son* (1984), and Spike Lee's *School Daze* (1988) and *Do the Right Thing* (1989). In addition, Davis appeared on such television series as *The Defenders*, *The Nurses*, *East Side, West Side*, and *Evening Shade*. In 1993, Davis starred in the television miniseries *Queen*, the sequel to the classic miniseries *Roots*. He also appeared in the 1995 television movie *The Android Affair*.

In 1996, Davis appeared in Spike Lee's *Get on the Bus*, as well as the movie *I'm Not Rappaport*. In 1997, he played a juror in a remake of the classic movie *12 Angry Men*, and in 1998 he starred in another remake, *Dr. Dolittle*, with Eddie Murphy. In 1999, Davis played small roles in television movies, such as *The Soul Collector* and *The Ghosts of Christmas Eve*. He continued to work in television in the early 2000s, popping up in miniseries, such as *Jazz* and *The Feast of All Saints*. In 2000, Davis and his wife Ruby were honored with a Life Achievement Award from the Screen Actors Guild.

Davis is also the author of *Just Like Martin* (1992), a novel for young adults. His last major role was playing the father of Jennifer Beals and Pam Grier on the hit cable show *The L Word*. He died while making a movie in Florida in 2005. A collection of Davis's speeches and writings, *Life Lit by Some Large Vision*, edited by Ruby Dee, was published posthumously in 2006.

SAMMY DAVIS JR. (1925–1990)

Actor, Comedian, Dancer, Singer. Sammy Davis Jr. was often called "the world's greatest entertainer," a title that attested to his remarkable versatility as a singer, dancer, actor, mimic, and musician. Davis was born in New York City on December 8, 1925. Four years later, he was appearing in vaudeville with his father and "uncle" in the Will Mastin Trio. In 1931, Davis made his movie debut with Ethel Waters in *Rufus Jones for President*, which was followed by an appearance in *Season's Greetings*.

Throughout the 1930s, the Will Mastin Trio continued to play vaudeville, burlesque, and cabaret. In 1943, Davis entered the U.S. Army and served for two years by writing, directing, and producing camp shows. After his discharge, he rejoined the trio, which in 1946 cracked the major club circuit with a successful Hollywood engagement.

Davis recorded a string of hits ("Hey There," "Mr. Wonderful," "Too Close for Comfort") during his steady rise to the top of show business. In November 1954, he lost an eye in an automobile accident, which fortunately did not interfere with his career. He scored a hit in his first Broadway show *Mr. Wonderful* (1956), and later repeated this success in *Golden Boy* (1964).

In 1959, Davis played Sportin' Life in the movie version of *Porgy and Bess*. Davis's other films from this period include *Ocean's 11* (1960) and *Robin and the Seven Hoods* (1964). His 1966 autobiography, *Yes, I Can*, became a best seller, and he starred in his own network television series. In addition, he spent time with a coterie of entertainers known as the Rat Pack, who were fixtures at top-dollar nightspots in Los Angeles and Las Vegas throughout the decade.

In 1968, the NAACP awarded Davis its Spingarn Medal. In the 1970s, Davis appeared in a variety of films, television, and nightclubs. In 1972, he was involved in a controversy over his support of Richard Nixon, which was publicized by a famous photograph of Nixon hugging Davis at the 1972 Republican Convention. In 1974, Davis renounced Nixon's programs. In the same year, his television commercials for Japan's Suntory Whiskey won a prize at the Cannes Film Festival, and the National Academy of Television Arts and Sciences honored him for his unique contributions to television.

In 1975, Davis became host of an evening talk and entertainment show. In 1980, he marked his fiftieth anniversary as an entertainer, and the Friars Club honored him with its Annual Life Achievement Award. Davis also embarked on a hugely successful revue tour with Frank Sinatra and Liza Minnelli. In 1989, he appeared in his final film, *Tap*, with Gregory Hines and Harold Nicholas. Later that year, he was diagnosed with throat cancer. He died on May 16, 1990. Shortly before his death, he was honored with a television special devoted to his life.

Davis married three times. His first marriage was in 1959 to singer Loray White. He married his second wife, actress May Britt, in 1961; she is the mother of his three children. In 1970, he married dancer Altovise Gore.

ROSARIO DAWSON (1979–)

Singer, Actress. Singer and actress Rosario Dawson has worked on stage, television, and film. Her notable credits include *Kids* (1995), *25th Hour* (2002), *Rent* (2005), *Sin City* (2005), *Clerks II* (2006), and *Seven Pounds* (2008).

SUZANNE DE PASSE (1948–)

Producer, Entrepreneur. Suzanne de Passe was born in 1948 in Harlem. She graduated from Manhattan High School and attended Syracuse University. She left without receiving her degree and became a booking agent for a New York theater, where she met Motown Records founder Barry Gordy, who hired her as his creative assistant. After discovering the Jackson 5 and the Commodores while working for Motown, de Passe developed a reputation for spotting talent.

In 1973, she received an Oscar nomination for co-writing the screenplay of the movie *Lady Sings the Blues*. In the early 1980s, she became the head of Motown Productions, the film and television division of Motown. Her production of *Motown 25*, an anniversary show for the company, earned several Emmy Awards. In 1989, de Passe produced the miniseries *Lonesome Dove*, which won seven Emmy Awards, a Golden Globe, and a Peabody Award. She also served as executive producer for the series' many spin-offs. In 1999, she produced *The Temptations*, a well-received docudrama based on the famous Motown singing group.

De Passe established her own production company, de Passe Entertainment, in 1992. The company produced the WB shows *Sister, Sister* and *Smart Guy*. In 1986, she was the subject of a study by the Harvard Business School. She has consistently taken less than the normal fee accorded to producers in order to get her projects funded, believing visibility is more important than profit. In 1995, de Passe was awarded the Charles W. Fries Producer of the Year Award for her outstanding contribution to the television industry.

De Passe's other executive producer credits include *Zenon, Girl of the 21st Century* (1999), which aired on the Disney Channel. She worked again with Disney as executive producer of *The Loretta Claiborne Story* for Disney/ABC Sunday Night in 2000. Also in 2000, she was executive producer of *Cheaters*, which aired on HBO. She returned to Disney in 2001 to produce *Zenon: The Zequel*. De Passe served as executive producer of the *32nd Annual NAACP Image Awards*, which aired March 2001 on the Fox Network.

RUBY DEE (1924–)

Actress. Ruby Dee was born in Cleveland on October 27, 1924, but grew up in Harlem and attended Hunter College in New York. In 1942, she appeared in *South*

Pacific with Canada Lee. Five years later, she met Ossie Davis while they were both performing in the play *Jeb.* They were married two years later.

Dee's movie roles from this period include parts in *No Way Out* (1950), *Edge of the City* (1957), *A Raisin in the Sun* (1961), Jean Genet's *The Balcony* (1963), and *Gone Are the Days* (1963), based on a play written by Davis. Dee has also appeared frequently on television since the 1960s.

In 1965, Dee became the first African American actress to appear in major roles at the American Shakespeare Festival in Stratford, Connecticut. Her film appearances included *The Incident* (1967), *Uptight* (1968), *Buck and the Preacher* (1972), *Black Girl* (directed by Davis, 1972), and *Countdown at Kusini* (1976). Her musical satire, *Take It from the Top*, in which she appeared with her husband at the Henry Street Settlement Theatre in New York, premiered in 1979.

As a team, Ruby Dee and Ossie Davis recorded several talking-story albums for Caedmon. In 1974, they produced *The Ruby Dee and Ossie Davis Story Hour*, which was sponsored by Kraft Foods and carried by more than sixty radio stations of the National Black Network. Together they founded the Institute of New Cinema Artists to train young people for jobs in film and television, and then the Recording Industry Training Program to develop jobs in the music industry for disadvantaged youths. In 1981, Alcoa funded a television series on PBS titled *With Ossie and Ruby*, an arts anthology with guest artists and performers.

Dee's later film credits include *Cat People* (1982), Spike Lee's *Do the Right Thing* (1989), *Their Eyes Were Watching God* (2005), and *American Gangster* (2007). In 1998, she narrated the PBS special *God's Gonna Trouble the Waters*. She was honored, along with husband Ossie Davis, with a Life Achievement Award from the Screen Actors Guild in 2000. In 2008, she became the oldest black actress nominated for an Academy Award (for best supporting actress) for her performance in *American Gangster*.

BILL DUKE (1943–)

Actor, Producer, Director. Bill Duke was born in Poughkeepsie, New York. He graduated with a B.A. in 1964 from Boston University and received an M.A. in 1968 from New York University. Duke began his career directing off-Broadway plays, including the New York Shakespeare Festival's production of *Unfinished Business*, for which he won the 1974 Adelco Award.

Duke made his feature film debut with *American Gigolo* in 1980. Since then, he has worked as an actor in a number of projects for film and television, including *Predator* (1987), *Commando* (1985), *Bird on a Wire* (1990), and *Action Jackson* (1988). He had small parts in the films *Get Rich or Die Tryin'* (2005) and *X-Men: The Last Stand* (2006) and appeared in the television series *Karen Sisco, Cold Case, Lost,* and *Battlestar Galactica.*

As a director, his films include *A Rage in Harlem* (1991), *Deep Cover* (1992), *The Cemetery Club* (1992), *Sister Act 2: Back in the Habit* (1993), and *Hoodlum* (1997).

In 1994, Duke completed *Black Light: The African American Hero*, a book of photo essays celebrating ninety of the greatest African American heroes of the twentieth century. He also published an inspirational book titled *The Journey* (1998).

AVA DUVERNAY (1972–)

Writer, Producer, Publicist. Ava DuVernay is an entertainment publicist who cowrote the *Epiphany* television series for the Black Family Channel. DuVernay also wrote, directed, and produced the film short *Saturday Night Life* (2006). She has worked as a publicist and promoter for numerous popular films, including *Hairspray* (2007), *The Secret Life of Bees* (2008), and *Invictus* (2009). Her film *This is the Life*, a documentary about a corner of the hip-hop culture in Los Angeles, premiered in 2008.

TRACEY EDMONDS (1967–)

Producer. As the president and CEO of Edmonds Entertainment Group, Inc., Tracey Edmonds is involved in virtually every aspect of the entertainment business. With divisions that include a record label, music publishing, film and television production, and artist management, Edmonds's power and influence is unique for an African American female in entertainment. She was formerly married to R&B superstar Kenneth "Babyface" Edmonds, with whom she ran Edmonds Entertainment.

A southern California native, Edmonds is a 1987 Stanford graduate and former real-estate executive who, in 1993, parlayed her business smarts and connections to create Yab Yum Entertainment. Originally established as a music publishing house, the company expanded into filmmaking with the 1997 release *Soul Food*, which grossed $43 million at the box office. Since then, Edmonds has produced the romantic comedy *Hav' Plenty* (1997), the teen drama *Light it Up* (1999), *Josie and the Pussycats* (2001), and the romantic comedies *Good Luck Church* (2007) and *New in Town* (2009), among other films. She also served as a producer for the Showtime series *Soul Food* (2000–2004), based on the 1997 movie, and the BET reality series *College Hill*, which premiered in 2004. Edmonds has won numerous awards for her achievements in the industry, including the Turner Broadcasting System's prestigious Tower of Power Award (2000).

CHIWETEL EJIOFOR (1974–)

Actor. Chiwetel Ejiofor is a British-born actor best known for his performance in the 2006 miniseries *Tsunami: The Aftermath.* He has also appeared in the films *Dirty Pretty Things* (2002), *Kinky Boots* (2005), *Children of Men* (2006), *Inside Man* (2006), *Talk to Me* (2007), *American Gangster* (2007), *Endgame* (2009), and *2012* (2009). Ejiofor works frequently on stage. In 2008, he won the Laurence Olivier Award for best actor for his performance in *Othello* in London. He was named an officer of the Order of the British Empire (OBE) in 2008.

IDRIS ELBA (1972–)

Actor. Idris Elba is a British television, theater, and film actor who has starred in both British and American productions. Widely known for his role as a drug dealer on the popular HBO series *The Wire,* Elba has also starred in numerous films, including *Daddy's Little Girls* (2007), *This Christmas* (2007), and *Obsessed* (2009). In 2009, he appeared in several episodes of the American version of the television series *The Office.*

STEPIN FETCHIT (1902–1985)

Actor. Stepin Fetchit's place in movie history is a controversial one. Praised by some critics as an actor who opened doors for other African Americans in Hollywood, he has been berated by others for catering to racist stereotypes and doing little to raise the status of African American actors. His characters—lazy, inarticulate, slow-witted, and always in the service of whites—have become so uncomfortable to watch that his scenes are sometimes cut when films in which he appeared are shown on television. Even at the height of his career, civil rights groups protested his roles, which they considered demeaning caricatures.

Born Lincoln Theodore Monroe Andrew Perry in Key West, Florida, on May 30, 1902, Stepin Fetchit's early career was in the Royal American Shows plantation revues. He and his partner, Ed Lee, took the names "Step 'n' Fetchit: Two Dancing Fools from Dixie." When the duo broke up, Fetchit appropriated the name "Stepin Fetchit" for himself.

Fetchit appeared in numerous motion pictures in the 1920s and 1930s, including *In Old Kentucky* (1927), *Salute* (1929), *Hearts in Dixie* (1929), *Show Boat* (1929), *Swing High* (1930), *Stand Up and Cheer* (1934), *David Harum* (1934), *One More Spring* (1936), and *Zenobia* (1939). Fetchit earned a great deal of income from these films and spent it wildly. His extravagant lifestyle ended when he filed for bankruptcy in the 1930s.

Fetchit made sporadic appearances in films later in his life, among them *Miracle in Harlem* (1949), *Bend of the River* (1952), *Amazing Grace* (1974), and *Won Ton Ton: The Dog Who Saved Hollywood* (1976).

LAURENCE FISHBURNE (1961–)

Actor. Laurence Fishburne, a native of Augusta, Georgia, made his stage debut when he was ten years old with the Negro Ensemble Theatre. Fishburne made television history as a member of daytime television's first African American family on *One Life to Live.* He made his feature film debut when he was thirteen in *Cornbread, Earl, and Me* (1975). In 1976, Fishburne moved to the Philippines for two years to costar in the Francis Ford Coppola war classic *Apocalypse Now* (1979). Other notable roles include *Rumble Fish* (1983), *The Cotton Club* (1984), *Gardens of Stone* (1987), *King of New York* (1990), *Class Action* (1991), *Deep Cover* (1992), and *Searching for Bobby Fischer* (1993).

Following his star-making performance in director John Singleton's *Boyz N the Hood* (1991), Fishburne was nominated for an Oscar for his portrayal of 1960s pop icon Ike Turner in the 1993 film *What's Love Got to Do With It.* In 1995, Fishburne played the title role in a film adaptation of the Shakespeare classic *Othello.* On stage, he starred in the Broadway production of August Wilson's *Two Trains Running* in 1992, as well as Wilson's *Fences* in 2006. In 2008, he played the title character in a Broadway production of the one-man play *Thurgood,* by George Stevens Jr. Fishburne's later film projects include *Fled* (1996), *Hoodlum* (1997), *Event Horizon* (1998), *The Matrix* (1999) and its sequels, *Akeelah and the Bee* (2006), and *The Death and Life of Bobby Z* (2007). In 2000, Fishburne expanded his filmmaking roles as he wrote, directed, starred in, and produced *Once in the Life.* He joined the cast of the hit CBS television show *CSI: Crime Scene Investigation* in 2008.

MORGAN FREEMAN (1937–)

Actor. Morgan Freeman was born in Memphis, Tennessee, on June 1, 1937, and grew up in Greenwood, Mississippi. He joined the U.S. Air Force in 1955, but left a few years later to pursue an acting career in Hollywood, taking classes at Los Angeles City College. He moved to New York City in the 1960s.

Freeman's first important role was in the short-lived off-Broadway play *The Nigger-Lovers* in 1967. Soon thereafter, he appeared in the all–African American version of the musical *Hello, Dolly!*

Morgan Freeman as Nelson Mandela in* Invictus, *2009. *Nominated for an Academy Award for best actor for this role, Freeman won an Oscar in 2005 for best supporting actor for* Million Dollar Baby. **WARNER BROS/THE KOBAL COLLECTION/PICTURE DESK**

Americans who grew up in the 1970s remember Freeman fondly as a regular on the public television program *The Electric Company*, in which he appeared from 1971 to 1976; his most notable character was the hip Easy Reader. More theater roles followed in productions of *The Mighty Gents* (1978), *Othello* (1982), *The Gospel at Colonus* (1983), and *The Taming of the Shrew* (1990).

In 1987, Freeman was cast in the Broadway play *Driving Miss Daisy*. He won an Obie Award for his portrayal of Hoke, the chauffeur for a wealthy white woman in the American South. Freeman recreated his Broadway role for the 1989 film version of the play, receiving an Academy Award nomination for best actor. In the same year, Freeman appeared in the highly successful movie *Glory*, about an all–African American Union regiment in the Civil War. His other film credits include *Clean and Sober* (1988), *Lean on Me* (1989), *Johnny Handsome* (1989), *Unforgiven* (1993), *The Shawshank Redemption* (1994), *Outbreak* (1995), and *Seven* (1995). Freeman also directed the 1993 film *Bopha!*. His later films include *Deep Impact* (1998), *Hard Rain* (2000), *Along Came a Spider* (2000), *The Sum of All Fears* (2000), *Bruce Almighty* (2003), *Batman Begins* (2005), *The Dark Knight* (2008), and *Gone Baby Gone* (2007).

In 2000, Freeman received an award from the Hollywood Film Festival for his acting career. Following several nominations, Freeman won a best supporting actor Oscar for his role in *Million Dollar Baby* (2004). He was nominated again for an Oscar in 2010 for his role as Nelson Mandela in *Invictus*. Freeman was recognized by the Kennedy Center Honors in 2008.

ANTOINE FUQUA (1966–)

Director. Antoine Fuqua, a Pittsburg native, is a former music video director (for Prince, Stevie Wonder, Usher, and others) who branched out into film, directing Jamie Foxx in *Bait* (2000). Fuqua's additional credits include *Training Day* (2001), *Tears of the Sun* (2003), *Shooter* (2007), and *Brooklyn's Finest* (2010).

DANNY GLOVER (1947–)

Actor. Born on July 22, 1947, in San Francisco, Danny Glover attended San Francisco State University and trained at the Black Actors Workshop of the American Conservatory Theatre. Glover then appeared in many stage productions, including *Island, Macbeth,* and *Sizwe Banzi is Dead.* He appeared in New York productions of *Suicide in B Flat, The Blood Knot,* and *Master Harold . . . and the Boys,* which won him a Theatre World Award.

Glover's film credits include *Escape from Alcatraz* (1979), *Chu Chu and the Philly Flash* (1984), *Iceman* (1984), *Witness* (1985), *Places in the Heart* (1985), *The Color Purple* (1985), *Lethal Weapon* (1987) and its sequels, *Bat 21* (1988); *Predator 2* (1990), *To Sleep with Anger* (1990), *Flight of the Intruder* (1991), *A Rage in Harlem* (1991), *Pure Luck* (1991), *Grand Canyon* (1991), *Bopha!* (1993), *The Saint of Fort Washington* (1993), *Angels in the Outfield* (1994), *Operation Dumbo Drop* (1995), *Beloved* (1998), *Boesman and Lena* (2000), *The Royal Tenenbaums* (2001), *Manderlay* (2005), *Honeydripper* (2007), and *2012* (2009).

On television, Glover appeared in the hit series *Hill Street Blues* (1981), the miniseries *Chiefs* (1983) and *Lonesome Dove* (1989), and other projects, including *Face of Rage* (1983), *A Place at the Table* (1987), *Mandela* (1987), and *A Raisin in the Sun* (1989).

Glover has won numerous awards, including an honorary doctorate from San Francisco State University in 1997 and several NAACP Image Awards. In 1998, Glover was appointed a goodwill ambassador for the United Nations Development Program.

RICK GONZALEZ (1979–)

Actor. A graduate of the "Fame" High School of the Performing Arts in his native New York, Rick Gonzalez made his feature film debut in *The Rookie* (2002), after several years performing in television. He has since built a growing resume of performances, with roles that include *Roll Bounce, Coach Carter,* and *War of the Worlds,* all released in 2005. He has also appeared on the television series *CSI: Crime Scene Investigation, CSI: Miami, Medium,* and *The Reaper.*

MEAGAN GOOD (1981–)

Actress. Meagan Good, a California native, began her acting career in commercials when she was four years old. When she was older, she landed numerous guest-starring parts on such television series as *The Parent Hood, Touched by an Angel,* and *Moesha.* Her work in film includes *Eve's Bayou* (1997), *Biker Boyz* (2003), and *Stomp the Yard* (2007).

LOUIS GOSSETT JR. (1936–)

Actor. Born in Brooklyn on May 27, 1936, Louis Gossett Jr. began acting when he was seventeen after a leg injury prevented him from pursuing his first love—basketball. In 1953, he won out over 445 contenders for the role of a black teenager in the Broadway play *Take a Giant Step,* for which he received a Donaldson Award as best newcomer of the year.

While performing in *The Desk Set* in 1958, Gossett was drafted by the New York Knicks, a professional basketball team, but he decided to remain in theater. Ultimately, he would appear in more than sixty stage productions, including such plays as *Lost in the Stars, A Raisin in the Sun, The Blacks,* and *Murderous Angels.*

On television, Gossett played character roles in such series as *The Nurses, The Defenders,* and *East Side, West Side.* In 1977, he won an Emmy Award for his performance in the acclaimed miniseries *Roots.* He also starred in such films as *Skin Game* (1971), *The Deep* (1977), *An Officer and a Gentleman* (1983), *Iron Eagle* (1986), *Iron Eagle II* (1988), and *Diggstown* (1993). In 1989, Gossett starred in his own television series, *Gideon Oliver.*

Gossett appeared in numerous films and television programs throughout the 1990s and early 2000s, including *Father and Son: Dangerous Relations* (1993), *Ray Alexander: A Taste for Justice* (1994), *The Inspectors* (1998), *For Love of Olivia* (2001), *Daddy's Little Girls* (2007), and *Why Did I Get Married Too?* (2010). He announced in February 2010 that he had been diagnosed with prostate cancer.

F. GARY GRAY (1969–)

Director. F. Gary Gray, a successful video and film director, was born in New York City in 1969. He made his feature film debut with the hit *Friday* (1995), starring Ice Cube. Gray's other films include *Set It Off* (1996), *The Negotiator* (1998), *The Italian Job* (2003), and *Law Abiding Citizen* (2009).

PAM GRIER (1949–)

Actress. Pamela Suzette Grier was born May 26, 1949, in Winston-Salem, North Carolina. Her father's military career kept the family moving, and Grier spent part of her childhood in Europe. When she was fourteen, her family returned to the United States, and settled in Denver, Colorado. After high school, she enrolled in Metropolitan State College with aspirations of a future career in medicine.

In 1967, Grier entered the Miss Colorado Universe contest in hopes of winning money for tuition. She placed second, but attracted the attention of an agent, who invited her to Hollywood to begin a career in acting. Grier was reluctant, but her mother encouraged her to take the agent up on his offer.

After signing with the Agency of Performing Arts, Grier attended acting classes and worked the office switchboard. She eventually landed a small part in *The Bird Cage* (1969). Throughout the 1970s, she was a box-office draw, often appearing in blaxploitation movies, such as *Coffy* (1973) and *Foxy Brown* (1974). Though she was usually cast as a strong, independent woman and enjoyed being one of the few actresses given the chance to create such portrayals, she was uncomfortable with the stereotypes these films encouraged. Although she was one of the few bankable female stars of the decade, Grier decided to retire.

Grier resumed her career in 1981 when she costarred with Paul Newman in *Fort Apache: The Bronx*, a demanding film. She felt validated by the success of the difficult role. Thereafter, Grier appeared frequently on stage, in films, and on television. She was recognized by the NAACP Image Awards as the best actress in 1986 for *Fool for Love*. In 1993, she received awards from the National Black Theatre Festival and the African American Film Society. In 1997, she appeared in Quentin Tarantino's *Jackie Brown*. Her other films include *Snow Day* (2000), *Bones* (2001), and *The Adventures of Pluto Nash* (2002). Grier appeared in the Showtime series *The L Word* from 2004 to 2009. She also appeared in several episodes of the series *Smallville* in 2010.

HENRY HAMPTON (1940–1998)

Documentary Filmmaker. As a force behind the library of documentaries that primarily seek to address the African American experience, Henry Hampton used his vast understanding of the film medium to bring cultures together. A St. Louis native and son of a prominent surgeon, Hampton received his B.A. in literature in 1961 from Washington University. He later taught at Tufts University.

In 1968, Hampton founded a production company, Blackside Inc., which initially produced industrial and documentary films. With the mission of achieving social change through entertainment, Blackside produced more than sixty films and media projects. Notable projects include the television documentary series *The Great Depression* (1993) and *America's War on Poverty* (1995), as well as "Malcolm X: Make It Plain" (1994), an episode of the PBS series *American Experience*. Hampton is best known for the critically acclaimed fourteen-hour documentary about the civil rights movement, *Eyes on the Prize*, which was broadcast on PBS in the late 1980s.

Hampton perfected the art of mixing archival news footage with contemporary interviews, which rendered the historical events more meaningful to his audience. During his career, Hampton received numerous awards, including six Emmys, an Academy Award nomination, and the duPont-Columbia University Award for excellence in journalism. At the time of his death, he was working on *I'll Make Me a World*, a six-hour documentary on African American creative artists, which was presented on PBS, in memory of Hampton, in 1999.

HILL HARPER (1966–)

Actor. Hill Harper, an accomplished film, television, and stage actor, was born in Iowa City, Iowa. Harper graduated magna cum laude from Brown University, and later earned a law degree from Harvard Law School, as well as a master's degree in public administration from the Kennedy School of Government. His notable roles include *Get on the Bus* (1996), *Loving Jezebel* (1999), *He Got Game* (1999), *The Visit* (2000), and *Constellation* (2005). Harper joined the cast of the long-running drama *CSI: NY* in 2004.

DENNIS HAYSBERT (1954–)

Actor. Dennis Haysbert was born in San Mateo, California. He made his acting debut in 1979 on the popular television series *The White Shadow*. Best known for playing a U.S. president on the series *24* from 2001 to 2006, Haysbert's other notable credits include *Love Field* (1992), *Random Hearts* (1999), *Far from Heaven* (2002), *Jarhead* (2005), *Breach* (2007), and *Goodbye Bafana* (*The Color of Freedom*) (2007). From 2006 to 2009, Haysbert played Sergeant Major Jonas Blane on the CBS series *The Unit*.

FELICIA HENDERSON (1961–)

Writer, Director, Producer. Felicia Henderson, a Los Angeles native, is a writer, director, and producer whose credits include the television series *Soul Food, Family Matters, Moesha, The Fresh Prince of Bel-Air, Gossip Girl*, and *Fringe*. She teaches screenwriting at UCLA, her alma mater.

LENA HORNE

See chapter 21, Drama, Comedy, and Dance.

DJIMON HOUNSOU (1964–)

Actor. Djimon Hounsou was born in Benin in West Africa. When he was a teenager, he moved to France, where he worked as a model. He later moved to Los Angeles, and pursued a career as an actor. He landed his first major role when he was cast in Steven Spielberg's

Amistad in 1997. In 2003, he became the first African-born actor nominated for an Academy Award for his supporting performance in *In America.* Hounsou has also appeared in *Gladiator* (2000), *The Four Features* (2002), *Beauty Shop* (2005), and *Push* (2009). He received his second Academy Award nomination for his performance in *Blood Diamond* (2006), alongside Leonardo DiCaprio.

TERRENCE HOWARD (1969–)

Actor. Known for his versatility, Terrence Howard has appeared in film and on television since the late 1980s. Since his first major role in the 1995 film *Mr. Holland's Opus,* Howard has captured leading roles in *Hustle & Flow* (2005), *Crash* (2005), and *Pride* (2007). He was nominated for a Academy Award for best actor for his performance in *Hustle & Flow.*

REGINALD HUDLIN (1961–)

Writer, Director, Producer. A Harvard University graduate, Reginald Hudlin directed the feature films *House Party* (1990), *Boomerang* (1992), *The Great White Hype* (1996), and *The Ladies Man* (2000). He has also directed episodes of numerous television series, including *The Bernie Mac Show, Everybody Hates Chris, The Office,* and *Better Off Ted.* Hudlin served as executive producer of the animated series *The Boondocks.* He was also the president of entertainment for BET Networks from 2005 to 2008. Hudlin is a fan and collector of comic books, and was a writer for the Marvel Comics series *Black Panther.*

JENNIFER HUDSON

See chapter 25, Popular Music.

HUGHES BROTHERS (1972–)

Directors, Producers, Writers. Albert and Allen Hughes are twin brothers who work together as filmmakers. They are best known for their films *Menace II Society* (1993), *Dead Presidents* (1995), *From Hell* (2001), and *The Book of Eli* (2010). They were born in Detroit.

REX INGRAM (1895–1969)

Actor. Rex Ingram, a major movie and radio personality during the 1930s and 1940s, was born on October 20, 1895, in Cairo, Illinois, aboard the *Robert E. Lee,* a Mississippi riverboat on which his father was a stoker. Ingram attended military schools, where he displayed an interest in acting. After working briefly as a cook for the Union Pacific Railroad and as head of his own small window-washing business, Ingram gravitated to Hollywood, where in 1919 he appeared in the original Tarzan film. Roles in such classics as *Beau Geste* (1926), *King Kong* (1933), *The Green Pastures* (1936), and *Huckleberry Finn* (1939) followed. During the late 1920s and early 1930s, Ingram also appeared prominently in theater in San Francisco. During the late 1930s, he starred in daytime radio soap operas and in Works Progress Administration theater projects.

Ingram's distinguished career continued on the New York stage and in film and television. In 1957, he played Pozzo in a production of Samuel Beckett's *Waiting for Godot.* Later film credits include *Elmer Gantry* (1960), *Your Cheating Heart* (1964), *Hurry Sundown* (1967), and *Journey to Shiloh* (1968). He died on September 19, 1969.

SAMUEL L. JACKSON (1948 –)

Actor. Samuel Leroy Jackson was born in Washington, D.C., and raised in Chattanooga, Tennessee. As a child, his active imagination had him recreating scenes from his favorite movies. He also acted in various school plays. His first serious involvement in acting came as a student at Morehouse College in Atlanta. After deciding on drama as a major, Jackson began to enroll in theater classes at Morehouse's sister school, Spelman College.

After receiving his dramatic arts degree, Jackson and his wife-to-be, La Tanya Richardson, moved to New York City, where Jackson performed in various shows and films between 1976 and 1981. As a cast member of Charles Burnett's *A Soldier's Play,* Jackson began to make connections. Morgan Freeman and Spike Lee both encouraged Jackson, and several years later, Jackson and Lee collaborated on the first of many films.

School Daze (1988) and *Do the Right Thing* (1989), both directed by Spike Lee, set the stage for the creation of Jackson's reputation, which was established in *Jungle Fever* (1991), also directed by Lee. This film highlighted Jackson's versatility as he portrayed a crack addict. The performance won Jackson various awards, including the Cannes Film Festival's best supporting actor award. Lead rolls in major Hollywood productions continued to propel Jackson's career forward. In the early 1990s, appearances in *Jurassic Park* (1993), *Patriot Games* (1992), and the Hughes brothers' *Menace II Society* (1993) all brought the actor praise. The height of Jackson's success came in the 1994 blockbuster *Pulp Fiction.*

Despite his success in films, Jackson wished to work on stage again, and he was cast as the male lead in the play *Distant Fires.* Movies such as *Die Hard with a Vengeance* (1995) and *The Great White Hype* (1996) kept him busy in the mid-1990s. In 1999, he starred in the much anticipated prequel to *Star Wars, Star Wars: Episode I: The Phantom Menace.*

In 2000, Jackson played a variety of roles, from the lady-loving detective in *Shaft* to the evil genius in *Unbreakable*. He continued to make movies in 2001 with roles in independent films, such as *The Caveman's Valentine* and *The 51st State*. Jackson returned to mainstream cinema in 2002 with blockbuster hits such as *Changing Lanes*, with costar Ben Affleck, and the long-awaited *Star Wars: Episode II: Attack of the Clones*. He later appeared in *Star Wars: Episode III: Revenge of the Sith* (2005), *Snakes on a Plane* (2006), *Black Snake Moan* (2006), and *Lakeview Terrace* (2008), among other films.

MARIANNE JEAN-BAPTISTE (1967–)

Actress. Trained at the Royal Academy of Dramatic Art in her native London, Marianne Jean-Baptiste made history when she became the first black British actress nominated for an Academy Award for her role in Mike Leigh's *Secrets & Lies* (1996). She joined the cast of the long-running television series *Without a Trace* in 2002.

BRODERICK JOHNSON

Producer. As the cofounder of Alcon Entertainment, Broderick Johnson has produced the box-office hits *My Dog Skip* (2000), *P.S., I Love You* (2007), and *The Blind Side* (2009).

JAMES EARL JONES (1931–)

Actor. James Earl Jones (whose father, Robert Earl Jones, was featured in the 1964 movie *One Potato, Two Potato*) was born in Tate County, Mississippi, on January 17, 1931, and raised by his grandparents on a farm near Jackson, Michigan. He turned to acting after a brief period as a premedical student at the University of Michigan (from which he graduated cum laude in 1953) and after completing military service with the U.S. Army's Cold Weather Mountain Training Command in Colorado.

After moving to New York, Jones studied at the American Theatre Wing, making his off-Broadway debut in 1957 in *Wedding in Japan*. He later appeared in numerous plays, on and off-Broadway, including *Sunrise at Campobello* (1958), *The Cool World* (1960), *The Blacks* (1961), *The Blood Knot* (1964), and *Anyone, Anyone*. Jones's career as an actor progressed slowly until he portrayed Jack Jefferson in the Broadway hit *The Great White Hope* in 1968. The play was based on the life of Jack Johnson, the first black heavyweight champion. For this performance, Jones received the 1969 Tony Award for the best dramatic actor in a Broadway play and a Drama Desk Award for one of the best performances of the 1968–1969 New York season.

By the 1970s, Jones was appearing in roles traditionally performed by white actors, including the title role in *King Lear* and an award-winning performance as Lenny in the stage adaptation of John Steinbeck's novel *Of Mice and Men*. In 1978, Jones appeared in the controversial *Paul Robeson*, a one-man show on Broadway. Many leading African Americans advocated a boycott of the show because they felt it did not measure up to the man himself. However, many critics gave the show high praise.

In 1980, Jones starred in Athol Fugard's *A Lesson from Aloes*, a top contender for a Tony Award that year. He also appeared in the Yale Repertory Theater Production of *Hedda Gabler*. In the spring of 1982, he costarred with Christopher Plummer on Broadway in *Othello*, a production acclaimed as among the best ever done. In 1987, Jones received a Tony Award for his performance in August Wilson's Pulitzer Prize–winning play *Fences*.

Jones's early film credits include *Dr. Strangelove* (1964), *River Niger* (1976), and *The Greatest* (1977). He was the screen voice of Darth Vader in *Star Wars* (1977) and its sequels, *The Empire Strikes Back* (1980) and *The Return of the Jedi* (1983). Jones also appeared in *Conan the Barbarian* (1982), *Allan Quartermain and the Lost City of Gold* (1986), *Soul Man* (1986), *Matewan* (1987), *Coming to America* (1988), *Field of Dreams* (1989), *Three Fugitives* (1989), *The Hunt for Red October* (1990), *Patriot Games* (1992), *Sommersby* (1993), *The Sandlot* (1993), *Excessive Force* (1993), *The Meteor Man* (1993), *Clean Slate* (1994), *Clear and Present Danger* (1994), *The Lion King* (1994), *Jefferson in Paris* (1995), *Cry, the Beloved Country* (1995), *A Family Thing* (1996), *Fantasia 2000*, and *Finder's Fee* (2001).

Among numerous television appearances, Jones portrayed author Alex Haley in *Roots: The Next Generation* (1979) and has narrated documentaries for PBS. During the early 1990s, Jones appeared in the television series *Gabriel's Fire* and the television movies *Percy and Thunder* and *The Vernon Johns Story*. He starred in the CBS series *Under One Roof* in 1995 and in the cable television miniseries *The Feast of All Saints* in 2001. Jones is also well known for his voice, which has been heard in numerous commercials, including those for Verizon Wireless, and in promos for the Cable News Network (CNN).

In 1976, Jones was elected to the board of governors of the Academy of Motion Picture Arts and Sciences. In 1979, New York City presented him with the Mayor's Award of Honor for Arts and Culture. He received an honorary doctorate of humane letters from the University of Michigan in 1971 and the New York Man of the Year Award in 1976. In 1985, he was inducted into the Theater Hall of Fame. He was awarded a National Medal of the Arts in 1992. In 2009, Jones was honored with a Lifetime Achievement Award from the Screen Actors Guild.

BEYONCÉ KNOWLES

See chapter 25, Popular Music.

SANAA LATHAN (1971–)

Actress. A New York native, Sanaa Latham is the daughter of Broadway actress Eleanor McCoy and television director and producer Stan Lathan. Sanaa Lathan is a graduate of the University of California, Berkeley, and the Yale School of Drama. She has built an impressive resume of leading roles in such films as *Love and Basketball* (2000), *Out of Time* (2003), *Something New* (2006), and *The Family that Preys* (2007). Lathan starred in a 2004 Broadway revival of Lorraine Hansberry's play *A Raison in the Sun*. Her performance earned her a Tony Award nomination. She also appeared in a 2008 television adaptation of the play.

MARTIN LAWRENCE (1965–)

Comedian, Actor. Martin Lawrence was born in Frankfurt, West Germany, in 1965, while his father was serving in the U.S. Air Force. He grew up in Landover, Maryland, and would entertain his mother as a child. Intent on achieving stardom, he appeared on the talent forum *Star Search*, but did not immediately meet with success. In New York City's Greenwich Village, he would tell jokes for handouts.

Lawrence moved to Los Angeles in the late 1980s and appeared in the sitcom *What's Happening Now!* before being selected for a role in Spike Lee's popular film *Do the Right Thing* (1989). In the early to mid-1990s, Lawrence appeared in the films *House Party* (1990), *Talkin' Dirty after Dark* (1991), *Boomerang* (1992), and *Bad Boys* (1995).

Lawrence's comedic style earned him his own television sitcom, *Martin*, which ran from 1992 to 1997. He played a disc jockey whose on-air confidence was at odds with his less successful personal life. In addition to playing the title character, Lawrence also played the character's mother, an outspoken young woman named Sheneneh, and other roles. Lawrence won an NAACP Image Award in 1996 for his performance in the series.

Lawrence continued to appear in movies during the late 1990s and early 2000s, including *Life* (1999), with costar Eddie Murphy, *Blue Streak* (1999), *Big Momma's House* (2000) and its sequel, *What's the Worst that Could Happen* (2001), *Black Knight* (2001), *National Security* (2003), *Wild Hogs* (2007), *Welcome Home Roscoe Jenkins* (2008), and *College Road Trip* (2008).

CANADA LEE (1907–1952)

Actor. Canada Lee was born Leonard Lionel Cornelius Canegata in New York City on May 3, 1907. After studying violin as a young boy, he ran off to Saratoga to become a jockey. Failing in this endeavor, he returned to New York and began a boxing career. In 1926, after winning ninety out of one hundred fights, including the national amateur lightweight title, he turned professional. Over the next few years, he won 175 out of some two hundred fights against such top opponents as Jack Britton and Vince Dundee. In 1933, a detached retina brought an end to his boxing career. He acquired the name Canada Lee when a ring announcer could not pronounce his real name.

In 1934, Lee successfully auditioned at the Harlem YMCA for his first acting role in a Works Progress Administration production of *Brother Moses*. In 1941, Orson Welles, who had met Lee in the Federal Theatre Project's all–African American production of *Macbeth*, chose him to play Bigger Thomas in the stage version of Richard Wright's novel *Native Son*.

In 1944, Lee served as the narrator for a radio series called *New World a-Comin'*—the first such series devoted to racial issues. That same year, he also appeared in Alfred Hitchcock's film *Lifeboat* and in the Broadway play *Anna Lucasta*. He also worked for the NBC radio network as master of ceremonies for various war-related programming.

Lee's political activism eventually ended his career. He campaigned against racism and discriminatory hiring practices, and signed a petition urging the expulsion of Mississippi racist Theodore Bilbo from the U.S. Senate. Eventually, he was blacklisted by the Hollywood establishment on the suspicion that he was a communist agent. In 1950, Lee starred in the British production of *Cry, the Beloved Country*—the first film to challenge apartheid and the wretched living conditions of blacks in South Africa. However, the emotional stress of the blacklisting affected his health, and he died of a heart attack in 1952 when he was forty-five years old.

MALCOLM LEE (1970–)

Director. Malcolm Lee began his career working as an assistant director for his cousin, director Spike Lee. Malcolm Lee made his directorial debut with *The Best Man* (1999). Other notable credits include *Undercover Brother* (2002), *Roll Bounce* (2005), *Welcome Home Roscoe Jenkins* (2008), and *Soul Men* (2008).

SPIKE LEE (1957–)

Actor, Director, Screenwriter, Producer. Shelton Jackson "Spike" Lee was born March 20, 1957, in Atlanta,

Georgia. His family moved briefly to Chicago before settling in New York in 1959. Lee received a B.A. in mass communication in 1979 from Morehouse College. After a summer internship at Columbia Pictures in Burbank, California, Lee enrolled in New York University's prestigious Institute of Film and Television. He received an M.A. in filmmaking in 1983. While at New York University, he wrote and directed *Joe's Bed-Stuy Barbershop: We Cut Heads*, for which he won the 1982 Student Academy Award given by the Academy of Motion Picture Arts and Sciences. The movie was later shown on public television's Independent Focus series.

Lee's next film, *She's Gotta Have It* (1986), led to a resurgence of African American cinema and won the Los Angeles Film Critics New Generation Award and the Prix de la jeunesse at the Cannes Film Festival. His subsequent films include *School Daze* (1988), *Do The Right Thing* (1989), *Mo' Better Blues* (1990), *Jungle Fever* (1991), *Malcolm X* (1992), *Crooklyn* (1994), *Clockers* (1995), *Girl 6* (1996), *4 Little Girls* (1997), *He Got Game* (1998), *Summer of Sam* (1999), *Bamboozled* (2000), *25th Hour* (2002), *She Hate Me* (2004), *Inside Man* (2006), and *Miracle at St. Anna* (2008). In 2001, Lee directed *A Huey P. Newton Story* for PBS. The film was created and performed by Roger Guenveur Smith, based on his play. Lee's four-hour documentary about Hurricane Katrina and its aftermath, *When the Levees Broke: A Requiem in Four Acts*, premiered on HBO in 2006.

Lee's books include *Spike Lee's Gotta Have It: Inside Guerilla Filmmaking* (1987) and *Uplift the Race* (1988). He has established a fellowship for minority filmmakers at New York University and is a trustee of Morehouse College. Lee's production company, 40 Acres & a Mule Filmworks, is located in Brooklyn in New York City.

KASI LEMMONS (1961–)

Director, Actor. Kasi Lemmons is a St. Louis native who has successfully balanced a career in directing and acting. Lemmons's notable acting roles include *School Daze* (1998), *Drop Squad* (1994), and *Waist Deep* (2006). She made her directing debut with *Eve's Bayou* (1997), which she followed with *Caveman's Valentine* (2000) and *Talk to Me* (2007).

BYRON LEWIS (1931–)

Producer. Byron Lewis was born in Newark, New Jersey, and received his B.A. in 1953 from Long Island University. He founded the UniWorld corporation in 1969. Early on, Lewis recognized the power behind ethnic markets and the buying potential of African Americans. As the marketing agency for accounts that include powerhouse corporations such as Burger King, Mars Inc., Ford, and Quaker Oats, UniWorld generated millions in revenue.

Lewis is the executive producer of the widely syndicated television show *America's Black Forum* and the founder and executive producer of the Acapulco Black Film Festival. Lewis is also a member of the National Urban League and has won many honors for his role in advertising and as a producer. Lewis spends a great deal of time talking with and teaching younger African Americans about the ways in which some companies are using African American images and music to sell their products to young people.

DEREK LUKE (1974–)

Actor. A New Jersey native, Derek made his big-screen debut in *Antwone Fisher* (2000), directed and produced by Denzel Washington. Luke's other notable credits include *Friday Night Lights* (2004), *Glory Road* (2006), *Catch a Fire* (2006), *Miracle at St. Anna* (2008), *Notorious* (2009), and *Madea Goes to Jail* (2009). He appeared in the NBC series *Trauma* from 2009 to 2010.

BERNIE MAC

See chapter 21, Drama, Comedy, and Dance.

HATTIE McDANIEL (c. 1895–1952)

Actress. Hattie McDaniel was born in Wichita, Kansas, and moved to Denver, Colorado, as a child. After a period of singing for Denver radio as an amateur, she entered vaudeville professionally, and by 1924 was a headliner on the Pantages circuit.

By 1931, McDaniel had made her way to Hollywood. After a slow start, during which she supported herself as a maid and washerwoman, she gradually began to get more movie roles. Her early film credits include *Judge Priest* (1934), *The Little Colonel* (1935), *Show Boat* (1936), *Saratoga* (1937), and *Nothing Sacred.* Her portrayal of a "mammy" figure in *Gone with the Wind*, a role for which she received an Oscar in 1939 as best supporting actress, is still regarded as a definitive interpretation. McDaniel was the first African American to receive an Academy Award.

McDaniel appeared in numerous films throughout her long career, including *The Great Lie* (1941), *In This Our Life* (1942), *Johnny Come Lately* (1943), *Since You Went Away* (1944), *Margie* (1946), *Never Say Goodbye* (1946), *Song of the South* (1946), *Mr. Blandings Builds His Dream House* (1948), *Family Honeymoon* (1948), and *The Big Wheel* (1949).

In addition to her movie roles, McDaniel enjoyed success in radio in the 1930s as Hi-Hat Hattie and in the 1940s in the title role of the successful *Beulah* series. McDaniel died on October 26, 1952, from breast cancer.

BUTTERFLY McQUEEN (1911–1995)

Actress. Butterfly McQueen's portrayal of Prissy in *Gone with the Wind* (1939) rivals Hattie McDaniel's Oscar-winning role as the "mammy," and is certainly as popular with audiences as Vivien Leigh's Scarlett O'Hara or Clark Gable's Rhett Butler.

Born Thelma McQueen on January 8, 1911, in Tampa, Florida, McQueen began her career in the 1930s performing as a radio actress in *The Goldbergs*, *The Danny Kaye Show*, *The Jack Benny Show*, and *The Beulah Show*. She also appeared on stage in *Brown Sugar* (1937), *Brother Rat* (1937), and *What a Life* (1938).

After her role in *Gone with the Wind* in 1939, McQueen was cast in other motion pictures, such as *I Dood It* (1943), *Cabin in the Sky* (1943), *Mildred Pierce* (1945), and *Duel in the Sun* (1947). She appeared as Oriole on the television series *Beulah* from 1950 to 1952.

Because of her outspokenness against racism and discrimination and her refusal to play stereotyped servant roles, McQueen's appearances after this period were sporadic. In 1968, she won accolades for her performance in the off-Broadway play *Curley McDimple*. She was cast in the television program *The Seven Wishes of Joanna Peabody* in 1978 and the film *Mosquito Coast* in 1986.

McQueen received a B.A. in Spanish from New York City College in 1975. On December 22, 1995, McQueen died after being critically burned when a kerosene heater in her cottage caught fire.

OSCAR DEVEREAUX MICHEAUX (1884–1951)

Filmmaker, Author. Oscar Micheaux was born in 1884 in Metropolis, Illinois. Little is known about his early years other than he left home at seventeen and worked briefly as a Pullman porter. In 1904, he began homesteading in Gregory County, South Dakota.

Micheaux was a hardworking farmer who loved to read and had a flair for writing. In 1913, he wrote, published, and promoted *The Conquest: Story of a Negro Pioneer*. This novel was followed by *Forged Note: Romance of the Darker Races* in 1915 and *The Homesteader* in 1917. Much of his writing was melodramatic and probably autobiographical.

In 1918, the Lincoln Picture Company, an independent African American film production company, tried to buy the film rights to *The Homesteader*. When Micheaux insisted that he direct the planned movie, the deal fell through. Micheaux went to New York, where he formed the Oscar Micheaux Corporation. Between 1919 and 1937, Micheaux made about thirty films, including *Body and Soul*, a 1924 movie in which Paul Robeson made his first cinematic appearance.

Although Micheaux was an excellent self-promoter of his books and films, his company fell into bankruptcy in 1928. By 1931, however, Micheaux was back in the film business, producing and directing *The Exile* (1931) and *Veiled Aristocrats* (1932). Between 1941 and 1943, he wrote four more books: *Wind from Nowhere*, *The Case of Mrs. Wingate*, *Masquerade*, and *The Story of Dorothy Stanfield*. In 1948, he made his last film, *The Betrayal*. While none of Micheaux's films achieved critical acclaim, they were popular with black audiences and attracted a limited white following. Although his characters broke with the African American stereotypes of the day, the themes of his movies ignored racial injustice and the day-to-day problems of African Americans.

Micheaux was known as a hard worker and a natty dresser who consumed neither alcohol nor tobacco. Although he made a great deal of money, all of it was squandered away. Micheaux died penniless in Charlotte, North Carolina in 1951.

OMAR BENSON MILLER (1978–)

Actor. Omar Benson Miller is a Los Angeles native best known for his role on the popular television show *CSI: Miami*. He also appeared in small parts in *8 Mile* (2002), *Shall We Dance* (2004), *Sex, Love, & Secrets* (2005), *Get Rich or Die Tryin'* (2005), *The Express* (2008), and *Miracle at St. Anna* (2008).

WENTWORTH MILLER (1972–)

Actor. Born in the United Kingdom and raised in Brooklyn, New York, Wentworth Miller is a graduate of Princeton University. He starred on the highly popular television show *Prison Break* from 2005 to 2009. Some of his additional acting credits include roles in *The Human Stain* (2003) and *Underworld* (2003).

MO'NIQUE (1967–)

Actress. Mo'nique Imes, known professionally as simply Mo'Nique, won a best supporting actress Oscar for her role in *Precious* (2009). Mo'Nique is best known as a popular stand-up comedian. She starred in the long-running television comedy *The Parkers* and is the host of her own late-night talk show on BET, *The Mo'Nique Show*. Mo'Nique has also appeared in the films *Baby Boy* (2001),

Actress and Comedian Mo'Nique, Hollywood, CA, 2010. *Mo'Nique won the Academy Award for best supporting actress for her role in* Precious, *directed by Lee Daniels.* DAN MACMEDAN/WIREIMAGE/GETTY IMAGES

Domino (2005), and *Phat Girlz* (2006), as well as such television shows as *Ugly Betty, Nip/Tuck, The Bernie Mac Show,* and *Moesha.* She was born in Woodlawn, Maryland.

EDDIE MURPHY (1961–)

Actor, Comedian. Eddie Murphy was born on April 3, 1961, in the Bushwick section of Brooklyn, the son of a New York City policeman and amateur comedian. As a youngster, he did imitations of cartoon characters, and, as he grew older, he began performing comic routines with impressions of Elvis Presley, Jackie Wilson, Al Green, and the Beatles.

Murphy attended Roosevelt Junior-Senior High School on Long Island and hosted a talent show at the Roosevelt Youth Center before beginning to call local talent agents to secure bookings at Long Island nightclubs. He was a little-known stand-up comedian when he made his first appearance as part of the cast of the late-night sketch-comedy show *Saturday Night Live* in 1980. Within three years he was hailed as a major new star based on his work in the hit films *48 Hours* (1982) and *Trading Places* (1983). Murphy left *Saturday Night Live* in 1984.

After his success with his first two films, Murphy starred in *Beverly Hills Cop* (1985) and its sequel *Beverly Hills Cop II* (1987), which were two of the major box-office hits of the decade. The concert film *Eddie Murphy: Raw* (1987) followed, after an effort at light-hearted fantasy, *The Golden Child* (1986). Murphy's other film appearances include *Coming to America* (1988), *Harlem Nights* (1989), which he directed, *Another 48 Hours* (1990), *Boomerang* (1992), *The Distinguished Gentleman* (1992), *Beverly Hills Cop III* (1994), *Vampire in Brooklyn* (1995), and *Bowfinger* (1999).

In the 1990s, in addition to appearing in the comedies *The Nutty Professor* (1996), *Dr. Dolittle* (1998), and *Life* (1999), Murphy also provided the voice for the main character in the television series *The PJs,* an animated sitcom that took a satirical look at life in a housing project. In 1993, Murphy married model Nicole Mitchell. They were divorced in 2006.

From 2000 to 2001, Murphy capitalized on the success of some of his former movies, starring in *The Nutty Professor II: The Klumps* and *Dr. Dolittle 2.* He also provided the voice for the Donkey in the popular animated comedy *Shrek* and its sequels, for which Murphy was honored with the People's Choice Award for best comedic performance in 2002. Murphy continued to stay active in 2002, starring in the movie *Showtime* with Robert De Niro. Murphy's later films include *The Adventures of Pluto Nash* (2002), *Daddy Day Care* (2003), *The Haunted Mansion* (2003), and *Norbit* (2007). He won a Golden Globe Award and was nominated for an Academy Award for best supporting actor for his performance in *Dreamgirls* (2006).

CLARENCE MUSE (1889–1979)

Actor, Director. Born on October 14, 1889, in Baltimore, Clarence Muse was best known for his film acting. He was, however, also successful as a director, playwright, and actor on the stage.

Muse's parents came from Virginia and North Carolina, and his grandfather from Martinique. After studying law at Dickinson University in Pennsylvania, Muse sang as part of a hotel quartet in Palm Beach, Florida. A subsequent job with a stock company took him on tour through the South with his wife and son. Coming to New York, he barely scraped a living together, mostly performing as a vaudevillian. Muse established himself as an actor and singer after performing in several plays with the Lincoln Theatre group and the Lafayette Players in Harlem. He was also involved in a Broadway production of *Dr. Jekyll and Mr. Hyde* that generated controversy when the roles of white characters were played by black actors in white face.

Muse's first movie role was in *Hearts in Dixie* (1929), produced at the William Fox Studio, in which Muse played a ninety-year-old man. When the Federal Theatre Project in Los Angeles presented Hall Johnson's *Run Little Chillun*, Muse directed the show. After its successful two-year run, Muse collaborated with the poet Langston Hughes on the screenplay for *Way Down South* (1939), which Muse also starred in.

During Muse's career, he appeared in 219 films, and was at one time one of the highest-paid African American actors, often portraying faithful servant "Uncle Tom" characters. His movie credits include *Huckleberry Finn* (1931), *Cabin in the Cotton* (1932), *Count of Monte Cristo* (1934), *So Red the Rose* (1935), *Show Boat* (1936), *The Toy Wife* (1938), *The Flame of New Orleans* (1941), *Tales of Manhattan* (1942), *Heaven Can Wait* (1943), *Night and Day* (1946), *An Act of Murder* (1948), *Porgy and Bess* (1959), *Buck and the Preacher* (1971), and *Car Wash* (1976). His last film was *Black Stallion* in 1979. He also appeared over the years in concerts, on radio, and on television.

Muse died October 13, 1979, the day before his ninetieth birthday. He had lived in Perris, California, on his Muse-a-While Ranch.

THANDIE NEWTON (1972–)

Actress. Thandie Newton, an international beauty, is the daughter of a Zimbabwean mother and a British father. Raised in Zambia, Newton moved to London to study modern dance. She made her feature film debut in *Flirting* (1991), which she followed up with parts in *Beloved* (1998), *Mission Impossible 2* (2000), *Crash* (2004), *The Pursuit of Happyness* (2006), *Norbit* (2007), *RocknRolla* (2008), and *2012* (2009). She also played a recurring character in the television series *ER*.

NATE PARKER (1979–)

Actor. Nate Parker is a former athlete who appeared in *Rome and Jewel* (2006), a hip-hop take on *Romeo and Juliet*, which he followed with lead roles in *The Great Debaters* (2007) and *The Secret Life of Bees* (2008).

TYLER PERRY (1969–)

Actor, Playwright, Screenwriter, Director, Producer. Box-office wunderkind Tyler Perry was born in New Orleans. He is best known for his gender-bending character

Director, Writer, and Actor Tyler Perry, New York, 2009. *Perry attends the premiere of* Madea Goes to Jail, *which became another financially successful film in his ouevre.* AP PHOTO/PETER KRAMER

Madea, who has appeared in several of his films. Perry's films include *Diary of a Mad Black Woman* (2005), *Madea's Family Reunion* (2006), *Daddy's Little Girls* (2007), *Why Did I Get Married?* (2007), *I Can Do Bad All By Myself* (2009), *Madea Goes to Jail* (2009), and *Why Did I Get Married Too?* (2010). Perry is one of the most successful talents in the American film and television industry. In 2008, he opened his own film studio, Tyler Perry Studios, in Atlanta. He has also created television comedy series, including *House of Payne*, which premiered in 2006, and *Meet the Browns*, which premiered in 2009.

BROCK PETERS (1927–2005)

Actor. Brock Peters is best known for his performance in the film classic *To Kill a Mockingbird* (1962). Peters also gained a following late in his career for his role as Admiral Cartwright in two *Star Trek* movies. He later appeared in a recurring role in the television series *Star Trek: Deep Space Nine*. Peters appeared in numerous other films and television programs over his long career, including the film classics *Carmen Jones* (1954) and *Porgy and Bess* (1959).

JADA PINKETT SMITH (1971–)

Actress. Jada Pinkett was born in Baltimore. She married actor Will Smith in 1997. She studied dance and choreography at the Baltimore School for the Arts before moving to Hollywood, where she landed a role on the popular sitcom *A Different World* in 1991. Pinkett made her feature film debut in *Menace II Society* (1993), and has starred in numerous films since then, including *The Nutty Professor* (1996), *The Matrix: Reloaded* (2003), *The Matrix: Revolutions* (2003), *Collateral* (2004), *Reign Over Me* (2007), and *The Women* (2008). She wrote and directed the film *The Human Contract*, released in 2009. Pinkett Smith is also the executive producer and star of the television series *Hawthorne*, a medical drama that premiered on TNT in 2009.

SIDNEY POITIER (1927–)

Actor. Sidney Poitier was born on February 20, 1927, in Miami, but moved to the Bahamas with his family at an early age. When he was fifteen, he returned to Miami. He later rode freight trains to New York City, where he found employment as a dishwasher. After the attack on

Actor Sidney Poitier, with Claudia McNeil, in Stage Production of* A Raisin in the Sun*, 1959. *In addition to his work on the stage, Poitier is perhaps best known as Hollywood's first bona fide African American film star, with his credits including* To Sir with Love, In the Heat of the Night, *and* Guess Who's Coming to Dinner. *For his lead role in the 1963 film* Lilies of the Field, *Poitier won an Academy Award, the first for an African American man.* AP IMAGES. REPRODUCED BY PERMISSION.

Pearl Harbor in 1941, he enlisted in the U.S. Army and served on active duty for four years.

Back in New York, Poitier auditioned for the American Negro Theater, but was turned down by director Frederick O'Neal. After working diligently to improve his diction, Poitier was accepted in the theater group, receiving acting lessons in exchange for doing backstage chores.

In 1950, Poitier made his Hollywood debut in *No Way Out*, followed by successful appearances in *Cry, the Beloved Country* (1952), *Red Ball Express* (1952), *Go, Man, Go* (1954), *Blackboard Jungle* (1956), *Goodbye, My Lady* (1956), *Edge of the City* (1957), *Band of Angels* (1957), *Something of Value* (1957), and *Porgy and Bess* (1959), among other films. Poitier also starred on Broadway in 1959 in Lorraine Hansberry's award-winning *A Raisin in the Sun*, and repeated this success in the movie version of the play in 1961.

In 1965, Poitier became the first African American to win an Oscar for a starring role, receiving this award for his performance in *Lilies of the Field*. Seven years earlier, Poitier had been the first African American man nominated for the award for his portrayal of an escaped convict in *The Defiant Ones* (1958).

Poitier's subsequent notable film appearances include performances in *To Sir with Love* (1967), *Heat of the Night* (1967), *Guess Who's Coming to Dinner* (1968) with Spencer Tracy and Katharine Hepburn, *Uptown Saturday Night* (1974), and *A Piece of the Action* (1977). Poitier also directed a number of films, including *Buck and the Preacher* (1972), *A Warm December* (1973), and *Uptown Saturday Night* (1974), in which he also starred. After several years of inactivity, Poitier performed in two additional films *Little Nikita* and *Shoot To Kill*, both released in 1988. His later directing ventures include *Stir Crazy* (1980) with Richard Pryor and Gene Wilder, *Hanky Panky* (1982) with Gilda Radner, the musical *Fast Forward* (1985), and *Ghost Dad* (1990), starring Bill Cosby.

Poitier spent two years writing his memoirs, *This Life*, published by Knopf in 1980. In 1981, Citadel Press published *The Films of Sidney Poitier* by Alvin H. Marill.

In 1993, Poitier won the Thurgood Marshall Lifetime Achievement Award and the Living Legend Award from the National Black Theater Festival. On December 3, 1995, he was presented with one of the Kennedy Center Honors. In 2000, Poitier received the Screen Actors Guild Lifetime Achievement Award. His second autobiography, *The Measure of a Man*, was published in 2000. The following year, Poitier was awarded a Grammy Award for Best Spoken Word Album for *The Measure of a Man* from the National Academy of Recording Arts and Sciences. In 2001, Poitier received the Hall of Fame Award from the NAACP at the organization's Image Awards ceremony. In 2002, the Academy of Motion Picture Arts and Sciences awarded Poitier a Lifetime Achievement Award for his motion picture career. Poitier's third book, *Life Beyond Measure: Letters to My Great-Granddaughter*, was published in 2008. He was awarded the Presidential Medal of Freedom, the country's highest civilian honor, in 2009.

GINA PRINCE-BYTHEWOOD (1969–)

Writer, Director, Producer. Gina Prince-Bythewood is a writer, director, and producer who has worked in television and film. Her credits include *Love & Basketball* (2000), *Biker Boyz* (2003), and *The Secret Life of Bees* (2008).

PHYLICIA RASHAD (1948–)

Actress. Known to millions as Clair Huxtable from *The Cosby Show*, Phylicia Rashad has led a distinguished acting career on television and the stage. She was born on June 19, 1948, in Houston, Texas, and until 1985 was known as Phylicia Ayers-Allen. Her sister is the actress and choreographer Debbie Allen. Both Debbie and Phylicia received early instruction in music, acting, and dance. Phylicia graduated magna cum laude from Howard University in 1970 with a B.F.A. in theater.

Early in her career, Rashad played the character Courtney Wright in the soap opera *One Life to Live*. Her big break came with *The Cosby Show*, in which she and Bill Cosby presided over the Huxtable family from 1985 to 1992. In 1997, Rashad and Cosby began a new sitcom, *Cosby*. Rashad has also appeared in Broadway, off-Broadway, and regional productions of many plays, including *The Cherry Orchard*, *The Wiz*, *Zora*, *Dreamgirls*, and *Into the Woods*. She won a Tony Award in 2004 for her performance in the Broadway revival of *A Raisin in the Sun*, a role she reprised in the 2008 television version of the play.

Rashad has received honorary doctorates from Providence College in Rhode Island and Barber-Scotia College in North Carolina. In 1995, Rashad was named spokesperson for the American Diabetes Association. In 1999, she was honored by the National Council of Negro Women with the Dorothy I. Height Dreammaker Award. In 2001, Rashad and her husband Ahmad Rashad filed for divorce after fifteen years of marriage. She later appeared in *The Old Settler*, which aired in 2001 on PBS.

ROBI REED HUMES

Casting Director, Producer. Robi Reed Humes is an Emmy Award–winning casting director and producer who has worked with many of Hollywood's brightest stars, including Vanessa Williams, Eddie Murphy, Janet Jackson, Michael Jackson, Richard Pryor, Tupac Shakur, and Denzel Washington.

SHONDA RHIMES (1970–)

Producer. Shonda Rhimes is the creator of the award-winning television shows *Grey's Anatomy* and *Private Practice.* Rhimes's other credits include *Introducing Dorothy Dandridge* (1999), *Crossroads* (2002), and *The Princess Diaries 2: Royal Engagement* (2004).

ANGELA ROBINSON (1971–)

Director. Robinson is a lesbian African American director best known for her films *D.E.B.S.* (2004) and *Herbie Fully Loaded* (2005). Robinson was also one of the executive producers and wrote and directed several episodes of the Showtime series *The L Word* (2004–2009).

CHRIS ROCK (1965–)

Comedian, Actor. Chris Rock was born in 1965 in South Carolina, but grew up in the mostly black neighborhood of Bedford-Stuyvesant in Brooklyn. Because of a busing policy, he attended school in the predominantly white neighborhood of Bensonhurst. At school, Rock had to endure daily abuse from prejudiced classmates.

Supported by his family, Rock began a stand-up career at a young age. He caught a break when one of his idols, Eddie Murphy, saw his routine and cast him in *Beverly Hills Cop II* (1987). The role led to another in *I'm Gonna Git You Sucka* (1988), a satire of blaxploitation films of the 1970s. In 1990, Rock auditioned for *Saturday Night Live* and earned a spot in the cast. On the show, Rock became known for his outspoken commentaries during the weekly send-up of the nightly news and for such characters as the talk-show host Nat X.

In 1993, Rock left *Saturday Night Live* and became a member of the cast of *In Living Color* for one season. He felt more comfortable on the set of the new show, which provided more opportunities to satirize situations involving African American characters. After appearing in *CB4* (1993), a movie about the rap industry that he cowrote, Rock's career entered a dormant period, during which his father died. During the off-time, Rock studied the work of other comedians he respected, including Bill Cosby, Eddie Murphy, Richard Pryor, Woody Allen, and Don Rickles.

In the late 1990s, Rock found an audience on cable television. He was a popular host of the *MTV Music Video Awards*, served as the 1996 presidential election correspondent for Comedy Central's *Politically Incorrect*, and earned two Emmy Awards for his comedy special *Chris Rock: Bring the Pain* (1996). From 1997 to 2000, he also hosted a variety show, *The Chris Rock Show*, on HBO, which won an Emmy Award for best writing in 1999. He also appeared as Rufus, Jesus' thirteenth apostle, in the controversial Kevin Smith film *Dogma* (1999).

Rock's other film credits include *Nurse Betty* (2000), *Down to Earth* (2001), *Pootie Tang* (2001), *Osmosis Jones* (2001), *Jay and Silent Bob Strike Back* (2001), *Bad Company* (2002), *Head of State* (2003), and the comedic documentary *Good Hair* (2009). He cowrote, directed, and starred in the romantic comedy, *I Think I Love My Wife* (2007). In 2005, Rock hosted the Academy Awards ceremony. He also produced and narrated the autobiographical television series *Everybody Hates Chris*, which ran from 2005 to 2009.

RICHARD ROUNDTREE (1942–)

Actor. Richard Roundtree is best known as John Shaft, the tough, renegade detective from the movie *Shaft* (1971). Born in New Rochelle, New York, on July 9, 1942, Roundtree graduated from New Rochelle High School, and attended Southern Illinois University on a football scholarship. After brief stints as a suit salesman and a model, he began a stage career with the Negro Ensemble Company. With *Shaft* (1971) and its sequels, *Shaft's Big Score* (1972) and *Shaft in Africa* (1973), Roundtree reached the peak of his career and became a pop icon.

Roundtree subsequently appeared in the films *Embassy* (1972), *Charley One-Eye* (1973), *Earthquake* (1974), *Diamonds* (1975), and *Man Friday* (1976). He also appeared in the television miniseries *Roots* (1977).

In 1995, Roundtree appeared in the films *Seven* and *When We Were Colored.* He also served as host of the television show *Cop Files.* In 1999, he appeared on the WB network in *Rescue 77*, a paramedic-based drama. He reprised the role of John Shaft in John Singleton's 2000 sequel, starring Samuel L. Jackson as the nephew of Roundtree's character from the 1970s. He also made appearances in the television series *Lincoln Heights*, *Heroes*, *Alias*, *The Closer*, and *Desperate Housewives*, among others.

In 2000, Roundtree announced that he had fought a seven-year bout with breast cancer. Roundtree is now an active member of the American Cancer Society and is working to make people aware of male breast cancer.

ZOE SALDANA (1978–)

Actress. Zoe Saldana, a former ballet dancer, was born in New Jersey. She first gained notice in the film *Center Stage* (2000), which she followed up with notable roles include *Drumline* (2002) and *Guess Who* (2005). Saldana reprised the role of Lieutenant Uhura in the 2009 version of *Star Trek*. She also starred in James Cameron's *Avatar* (2009), one of the highest-grossing movies of all time.

GABOUREY "GABBY" SIDIBE (1983–)

Actress. Gabby Sidibe, a New York native, made her acting debut in the 2009 film *Precious: Based on the Novel "Push" by Sapphire*, a role that garnered her a nomination for a best actress Academy Award. Her second film, *Yelling to the Sky*, premiered at the 2010 Sundance Film Festival.

JOHN SINGLETON (1968–)

Filmmaker. John Singleton was born in Los Angeles in 1968. After graduating from high school in 1986, he enrolled in the University of Southern California's prestigious Film Writing Program, which is part of the School of Cinema-Television. While there, he formed an African American Film Association and did a six-month director's internship for the *Arsenio Hall Show*. He twice won the school's Jack Nicholson Award for best feature-length screenplay. Before graduating in 1990, he signed with the well-known Creative Artists Agency.

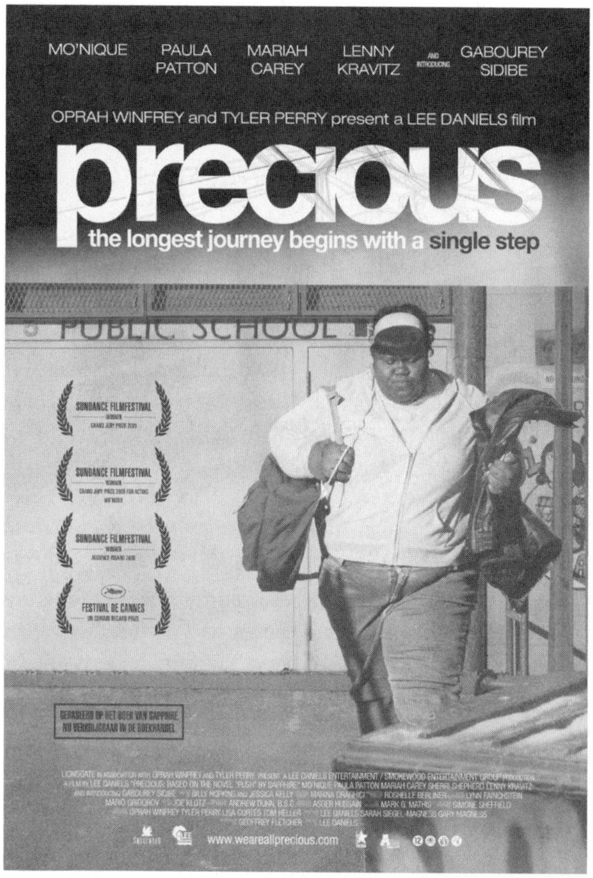

Precious, *Starring Gabourey Sidibe, 2009.* *A newcomer to the acting game, Sidibe made the world sit up and take notice—and received an Academy Award nomination for best actress for the title role in this film.* LIONS GATE/COURTESY EVERETT COLLECTION

Singleton was soon approached by Columbia Pictures to sell the film rights to *Boyz N the Hood*, his original screenplay and college thesis. Singleton agreed, but only if he would be the movie's director. The movie was released in July 1991 to mixed critical reviews. Although its first showings were marred by theater violence, it garnered Singleton an Academy Award nomination for best director. He became the first African American and the youngest person to be so honored.

After *Boyz N the Hood*, Singleton made a short cable-television film for Michael Jackson titled *Remember the Time* (1991). His second film, *Poetic Justice*, was released in the summer of 1993. His third film, *Higher Learning*, was released in 1995, followed the next year by *Rosewood*. Singleton then took a break from moviemaking as he dealt with a divorce in 1997. Shortly after, Singleton was back in the director's chair with the 2000 release of the remake of *Shaft*. He followed this up in 2001 with a return to the themes of his college thesis with the critically acclaimed *Baby Boy*. His other films include *2 Fast 2 Furious* (2003) and *Four Brothers* (2005).

WILL SMITH

See chapter 25, Popular Music.

WESLEY SNIPES (1962–)

Actor. Born in Orlando, Florida, on July 31, 1962, Wesley Snipes spent his childhood in the Bronx in New York City. He appeared in his first off-Broadway production when he was twelve years old, a minor role in the play *The Me Nobody Knows*. His interest in dance led him to enroll in New York's High School for the Performing Arts. Before completing the curriculum, however, his mother sent him back to Orlando to finish school, where he continued to study drama.

After graduating from high school, Snipes was awarded a scholarship to study theater at the State University of New York at Purchase. He subsequently appeared in productions both on and off-Broadway, including Wole Soyinka's *Death and the King's Horsemen*, Emily Mann's *Execution of Justice*, and John Pielmeier's *The Boys of Winter*. In 1987, Snipes also appeared in Michael Jackson's video "Bad" and in the HBO production *Vietnam War Story*, for which he received cable television's best actor award.

Snipes's film appearances include roles in *Wildcats* (1986), *Streets of Gold* (1986), *Major League* (1989), and *King of New York* (1990). In 1990, he appeared in Spike Lee's *Mo' Better Blues*, with Denzel Washington. This was followed by a role in Mario Van Peebles's *New Jack City* (1991) and the lead role in Spike Lee's *Jungle Fever* (1991). Snipes's other films include *White Men Can't Jump* (1992), *Passenger 57* (1992), *Rising Sun* (1993),

Sugar Hill (1993), *One Night Stand* (1997), *Blade* (1998), *The Art of War* (2000), *Disappearing Acts* (2000) for HBO, *Blade 2* (2002), and *Blade: Trinity* (2004). After a series of performances in straight-to-DVD releases, Snipes reemerged in 2010 in a major feature film, Antoine Fuqua's *Brooklyn's Finest.*

TIM STORY (1970–)

Director. Tim Story is a graduate of the University of Southern California Film School. He made his directorial debut with *Barbershop* (2002). His other directing credits include *Taxi* (2004), *Fantastic Four* (2005), and the sequel *Fantastic Four: Rise of the Silver Surfer* (2007).

ROBERT TOWNSEND (1957–)

Director, Actor. Robert Townsend began his career as an actor with bit parts in such films as *Cooley High* (1975) and *A Soldier's Story* (1984). He was born in Detroit, Michigan, and worked as a stand-up comedian before moving to Hollywood to try acting.

In 1987, Townsend responded to the paucity of film roles available to African American actors by creating and financing his own project, *Hollywood Shuffle*. The film's success launched Townsend into prominence as a director. Other notable Townsend films include the concert film *Eddie Murphy: Raw* (1987), *The Five Heart Beats* (1991), *The Meteor Man* (1993), *B.A.P.S.* (1997), the Lifetime original *Jackie's Back* (1999), and the NBC movie *Little Richard* (2000).

Townsend has won two Cable Ace Awards and multiple NAACP Image Awards. He is best known for his role as the patriarch on the long-running sitcom *The Parent Hood.* Townsend also served as host on the syndicated variety show *Motown Live*. He had a starring role in the suspense drama *Fraternity Boys* (1999). In 1999, Townsend directed the dramatic trilogy *Love Songs* and the Lifetime cable network made-for-television movie *Jackie's Back.* Since then, he has continued producing and directing, mostly for television.

CICELY TYSON (1933–)

Actress. During the early 1970s, Cicely Tyson emerged as America's leading black dramatic star. She achieved this status through two sterling performances—as Rebecca, the

Cicely Tyson* (left) *and Maya Angelou in* Madea's Family Reunion, *2006. *Tyson has garnered a host of honors during her long career as a dramatic actress.* ARCHIVES DU 7EME ART/PHOTOS 12/ALAMY

wife of a southern sharecropper in the film *Sounder* (1972), and as the lead in a television special, *The Autobiography of Miss Jane Pittman* (1974), the story of a formerly enslaved woman who, past her one-hundredth year, challenges racist authority by deliberately drinking from a "whites only" water fountain as a white deputy sheriff watches.

Cicely Tyson was born in New York City on December 19, 1933, and raised by a very religious, strict mother, who associated movies with sin and forbade Cicely to go to movie theaters. Blessed with poise and natural grace, Tyson became a model and appeared on the cover of America's two foremost fashion magazines, *Vogue* and *Harper's Bazaar*, in 1956. Interested in acting, she began to study drama, and in 1959 she appeared on a CBS culture series, *Camera Three*, with what is believed to be the first natural African hairstyle shown on television.

Tyson won a role in an off-Broadway production of Jean Genet's *The Blacks* (1961), for which she received the 1962 Vernon Rice Award. She then played a lead part in the CBS series *East Side, West Side*. Tyson subsequently moved into film parts, appearing in *The Comedians* (1967) and *The Heart Is a Lonely Hunter* (1968). Critical acclaim led to her role as Rebecca in *Sounder*, for which she was nominated for an Academy Award and named best actress by the National Society of Film Critics. She won an Emmy Award for her performance as Jane Pittman.

Tyson's other film appearances include *The Blue Bird* (1976) and *The River Niger* (1976). On television, she appeared in *Roots* (1977), *King* (1978), and *Wilma* (1978). She portrayed Harriet Tubman in *A Woman Called Moses*, and Chicago schoolteacher Marva Collins in a made-for-television movie in 1981. She also appeared in *The Women of Brewster Place* (1989) and the television series *Sweet Justice* (1995).

In 1979, Marymount College presented Tyson with an honorary doctorate in fine arts. In November 1981, she married jazz trumpeter Miles Davis, but the couple divorced in 1988. In 2001, Tyson was honored with a lifetime achievement award at the National Black Theatre Festival. Further film credits include *Diary of a Mad Black Woman* (2005), *Because of Winn Dixie* (2005), *Madea's Family Reunion* (2006), *Ildewild* (2006), and *Why Did I Get Married Too?* (2010). She also appeared with Angela Bassett in the 2002 television special *The Rosa Parks Story*. The Cicely L. Tyson Community School of Performing and Fine Arts, a magnet school in East Orange, New Jersey, was named in her honor.

GABRIELLE UNION (1972–)

Model, Actress. Gabrielle Union, a UCLA graduate, began her career as a model before landing parts in television and film. Since her breakout role in the film *Bring It On* (2000), Union has built an impressive resume of performances, with starring roles in *Two Can Play that Game* (2001), *Deliver Us from Eva* (2003), *Bad Boys II* (2003), *Daddy's Little Girls* (2007), *The Box* (2007), and *Cadillac Records* (2008). She has also appeared in the television series *Friends*, *Night Stalker*, *Ugly Betty*, and *Flash Forward*, among others.

MELVIN VAN PEEBLES (1932–)

Director, Actor, Writer. Melvin Van Peebles was born on August 21, 1932, in Chicago, Illinois. When he was a child, Van Peebles's family moved to Phoenix, Illinois, where he graduated from high school. Van Peebles received his bachelor of arts in English from Wesleyan University in 1953. After spending three and a half years as a flight navigator for the U.S. Air Force, he settled in San Francisco.

While in San Francisco, Van Peebles began to dabble in filmmaking. *Three Pickup Men for Herrick*, completed in 1958, is the best known of his early works. With success in sight, Van Peebles took his films to Hollywood. He became frustrated after several rejections, prompting him to move to the Netherlands. There, Van Peebles's luck changed. He joined the Dutch National Theater while studying astronomy at the University of Amsterdam, but troubles with his wife forced Van Peebles to move again. He found a home in Paris, where he wrote several novels in self-taught French.

Experiences in France led to Van Peebles's first international film success, *Story of a Three-Day Pass* (1968), which received generally positive criticism when it premiered at the San Francisco International Film Festival. This led to Van Peebles directing a string of films, including *Watermelon Man* (1970) and *Sweet Sweetback's Baadasssss Song* (1971), which he wrote, directed, and produced. This film, which grossed nearly $14 million dollars, used a mostly black crew and became controversial for its violence, earning an X rating. However, the money the film earned launched the "blaxploitation" film movement in Hollywood.

In 1971, Van Peebles turned his attention toward Broadway. His productions of *Ain't Supposed to Die a Natural Death* and *Don't Play Us Cheap* received mixed reviews. Despite the lack of critical enthusiasm for his work, *Ain't Supposed to Die a Natural Death* closed as the fifth-longest running show on Broadway, and *Don't Play Us Cheap* received the first prize at a Belgian festival. Throughout the 1970s, Van Peebles continued to write and direct for film, theater, and television. In 1987, his teleplay *The Day They Came to Arrest the Book* received an Emmy Award.

After a hiatus, Van Peebles returned to film directing with *Identity Crisis* (1989), featuring his son Mario, who also wrote the screenplay. In 1993, the father-son team reversed roles for *Posse,* which Mario directed and in which Melvin appeared in a supporting role. In the mid-1990s, they continued to develop a variety of projects together, including *Panther* (1995), a fictionalized film about the Black Panthers. In 1997, Melvin Van Peebles took to the small screen to portray a psychic cook in the remake of Stephen King's *The Shining.*

In 1998, Van Peebles served as honorary president for the opening of the French Black Roots cultural festival (Racines Noires '98), organized to coincide with the 150th anniversary of the abolition of African enslavement in France. He also performed a cabaret show, *Melvin Van Peebles' Roadkill Wid' Brer Soul.* In between, Van Peebles continued to work on his film *Bellyful,* which came out to rave reviews in 2000. *Bellyful* won an award at the Acapulco Black Film Festival International Films Competition, as well as the Byron E. Lewis Trailblazer Award.

DENZEL WASHINGTON (1954–)

Actor. Born on December 28, 1954, in Mt. Vernon, New York, Denzel Washington attended an upstate private high school, the Oakland Academy, and then entered Fordham University as a premed major. Washington did not originally intend to become an actor, but when he auditioned for the lead role in a student production of Eugene O'Neill's *The Emperor Jones,* he won the part over theater majors. His performance in that play, and later in a production of *Othello,* led his drama instructor to encourage Washington to pursue an acting career.

Washington's first major role was in the off-Broadway drama *A Soldier's Story.* Washington recreated his role when the play was adapted into a motion picture in 1984. He played Dr. Phillip Chandler on the television series *St. Elsewhere* from 1982 to 1988 and appeared in a string of films, including *Carbon Copy* (1980), *Cry Freedom* (1987), in which he portrayed South African activist Steven Biko, *The Mighty Quinn* (1989), *Glory* (1989), which won him an Academy Award for best supporting actor, *Mo' Better Blues* (1990), *Mississippi Masala* (1992), and *Malcolm X* (1992). Washington also starred in *Philadelphia* (1993), playing an attorney for an HIV-positive lawyer played by Oscar-winner Tom Hanks. Later, Washington starred in *Crimson Tide* (1995), *Devil in a Blue Dress* (1995), *Virtuosity* (1995), *Courage Under Fire* (1996), and *He Got Game* (1998).

In 1999, Washington played one of the most important roles of his career as incarcerated boxer Rubin Carter in the movie *The Hurricane,* based on the true story of Rubin "Hurricane" Carter. Washington was honored for his work in *The Hurricane* at the thirty-first NAACP Image Awards. He also received a Golden Globe for best actor in a drama. In 2001, Washington starred opposite Ethan Hawk in the box office hit *Training Day.* Washington was honored with the best actor award by the Los Angeles Film Critics Association for *Training Day.* Then in 2002, he was awarded the best actor Oscar for *Training Day,* becoming only the second African American to win the award.

Washington made his directorial debut in 2002 with *Antwone Fisher.* His subsequent films include *The Manchurian Candidate* (2004), *Inside Man* (2006), *American Gangster* (2007), and *The Book of Eli* (2010). His second film as a director, *The Great Debaters,* was released in 2007.

KERRY WASHINGTON (1977–)

Actor. Since graduating with a theater degree from George Washington University, Kerry Washington, a New York native, has gone on to star in several films, including *Save the Last Dance* (2001), *Ray* (2004), *Mr. & Mrs. Smith* (2005), *The Last King of Scotland* (2006), and *I Think I Love My Wife* (2007). She made her Broadway debut in the play *Race* in 2009.

ETHEL WATERS

See chapter 21, Drama, Comedy, and Dance.

DAMON WAYANS (1960–)

Comedian. Damon Wayans was born on September 4, 1960, in New York City. While growing up, Wayans wore leg braces and special shoes to correct problems caused by a foot deformity. As a result, he was often teased by fellow classmates. As an adolescent and young adult, he occasionally found himself in trouble with the law.

In the 1980s Wayans turned to stand-up comedy. His brother Keenen Ivory Wayans was already gaining a following, and Damon quickly became popular on the circuit as well. Appearances in clubs across the country eventually led to his film debut in *Beverly Hills Cop* (1984). In the mid-1980s, Wayans was a cast member on *Saturday Night Live.* He returned to stand-up after one year, and appeared in several films through the remainder of the 1980s, including *Hollywood Shuffle* (1987), *Roxanne* (1987), *Punchline* (1988), and *Earth Girls Are Easy* (1989), in which he starred as one of three aliens.

In the 1990s, Wayans joined the cast of *In Living Color.* The show, created by his brother Keenen, provided a platform for social commentary. The skits often featured characters that were members of groups that historically faced discrimination. Wayans, for example, portrayed a gay movie critic, as well as Homey, a sad-faced, black clown that refused to kowtow to "the [white] man," and Handyman, a physically challenged superhero.

After three seasons, Wayans left *In Living Color* to pursue film work. He served as the executive producer of *Mo' Money* (1992), a romantic comedy that he wrote. Wayans also played the main character, a man who tries to turn from a life of crime in order to pursue a relationship with a coworker. Wayans appeared in a number of other films in the 1990s, including *Major Payne* (1994), *Blankman* (1994), *Celtic Pride* (1996), and *The Great White Hype* (1996). In several of these films, Wayans also served in additional capacities as writer and executive producer.

Wayans returned to television in the 1990s. He created the short-lived drama *413 Hope St.*, which ran from 1997 to 1998, before returning to comedy with *Damon*, a series that reunited him with *In Living Color* costar David Alan Grier. The series only lasted a year, but Wayans came back in 2001 with the ABC hit *My Wife and Kids*, which ran until 2005. The show was a ratings success and Wayans won the People's Choice Award in 2002 for favorite male performer in a new television series. He created and starred in the Showtime sketch-comedy series *The Underground* in 2006.

KEENEN IVORY WAYANS (1958–)

Comedian. Keenen Ivory Wayans was born in New York City on June 8, 1958. He began his career as a stand-up comic at the improv clubs in New York City and Los Angeles. After appearances on such television series as *Benson*, *Cheers*, and *Chips*, and in the movies *Star 80* (1983) and *Hollywood Shuffle* (1987), Wayans struck fame with *I'm Gonna Git You Sucka* (1989)—a hilarious send up of 1970s blaxploitation films—which he wrote and produced. His greatest success was the popular television series *In Living Color* (1990–1994), an irreverent sketch-comedy show in which celebrities were often outrageously parodied. *In Living Color* won an Emmy Award in 1990.

Wayans is the oldest of a family of ten; four of his siblings—Damon, Shawn, Marlon, and Kim—were regulars on *In Living Color*. In the late 1990s, he hosted his own television talk show. Wayans wrote and directed *Scary Movie* (2000), a spoof on horror movies. He also directed the sequel, *Scary Movie 2*, released the following year. Wayans himself appeared in a small role in the first *Scary Movie*. He subsequently directed the comedies *White Chicks* (2004) and *Little Man* (2006), both starring his brothers Marlon and Shawn.

FOREST WHITAKER (1961–)

Actor. Forest Whitaker, an east Texas native, made his film debut in *Fast Times at Ridgemont High* (1982), before his portrayal of jazz icon Charlie "Bird" Parker in *Bird* (1988) made him a star. Other notable roles include *The Crying Game* (1992), *Panic Room* (2002), and *The Last King of Scotland* (2006), for which he earned an Academy Award as best actor in 2007. His directing credits include the films *Waiting to Exhale* (1995) and *First Daughter* (2004). Whitaker also appeared for two seasons (2006–2007) in the television series *The Shield.*

BILLY DEE WILLIAMS (1937–)

Actor. Billy Dee Williams, a screen, television, and stage actor, starred in some of the most commercially popular films of the 1970s and 1980s. Born William December Williams in Harlem on April 6, 1937, Williams was a withdrawn, overweight youngster who initially planned to become a fashion illustrator. While studying on scholarship at the School of Fine Arts in the National Academy of Design, a CBS casting director helped him secure bit parts in several television shows, including *Lamp Unto My Feet* and *Look Up and Live.*

Williams then began to study acting under Sidney Poitier and Paul Mann at the Actors Workshop in Harlem. He made his film debut in *The Last Angry Man* (1959), and then appeared on stage in *The Cool World* (1960), *A Taste of Honey* (1960), and *The Blacks* (1962). He later appeared briefly on Broadway in *Hallelujah Baby* (1967) and in several off-Broadway shows, including *Ceremonies in Dark Old Men* (1970).

Williams's next major role was in the acclaimed television movie *Brian's Song* (1970), a performance for which he received an Emmy nomination. Motown's Berry Gordy then signed Williams to a seven-year contract, after which he starred in *Lady Sings the Blues* (1972) and *Mahogany* (1976) with Diana Ross. His last movie for Gordy was *The Bingo Long Traveling All-Stars and Motor King* (1976).

In the early 1980s, Williams appeared in two of George Lucas's *Star Wars* adventures: *The Empire Strikes Back* (1980) and *Return of the Jedi* (1983). He has appeared in numerous television movies, including *Scott Joplin* (1977), *Christmas Lilies of the Field* (1979), and the miniseries *Chiefs* (1983). When he was cast opposite Diahann Carroll in the prime-time drama *Dynasty*, his reputation as a romantic lead was secured. During the latter half of the decade, he starred in several action films, including *Oceans of Fire* (1986) and *Number One with a Bullet* (1987).

In 1995, Williams played a detective in the television murder mystery *Falling for You.* He also hosted the Black Theatre Festival in Winston-Salem, North Carolina, and the Infiniti Sports Festival. In 1999, he took on another television series, *Code Name: Eternity*, which only lasted one season. In 2000, Williams began a movie comeback, starring in such films as *The Ladies Man* (2000), *The Last Place on Earth* (2000), *Very Heavy Love* (2001), *Good Neighbor* (2001), and *Undercover Brother* (2002). Some of Williams's paintings were featured in a computer screensaver program "Art in the Dark: Extraordinary Works by African American Artists."

VANESSA L. WILLIAMS (1963–)

Model, Singer, Actress. Vanessa Lynn Williams, a native of New York City, made history in 1983 when she became the first African American to be chosen Miss America. In 1984, she was forced to relinquish her title after *Penthouse* published nude photos of her taken years earlier.

In the wake of the pageant controversy, Williams went on to achieve success as an entertainer, signing in 1987 with Mercury/Wing Records. Her debut project, *The Right Stuff*, achieved gold record status fueled by hit singles, such as the titled track and the ballad "Dreamin." More hits followed, including "Saving the Best for Last" (1992) and "Colors of the Wind," the theme song from Disney's animated blockbuster *Pocahontas* (1995), which eventually won Academy, Golden Globe, and Grammy awards.

Williams made her film debut in *Under the Gun* (1986), and starred opposite Arnold Schwarzenegger in *Eraser* (1996). She also appeared in *Hoodlum* (1997) alongside Laurence Fishburne. Some of her other notable film roles include the family drama *Soul Food* (1997) and the romantic musical *Dance with Me* (1998). Williams made her Broadway debut in June 1994 in the musical *Kiss of the Spider Woman*. She joined the cast of the television show *Ugly Betty* in 2006. Williams's other television credits include *Stompin' at the Savoy* (1992), *The Jacksons: An American Dream* (1992), *The Odyssey* (1997), *Don Quixote* (2000), and *South Beach* (2006).

PAUL WINFIELD (1941–2004)

Actor. Born in Los Angeles on May 22, 1941, Paul Winfield grew up in a poor family. Excelling in school, he attended a number of colleges—the University of Portland, Stanford University, Los Angeles City College, and the University of California at Los Angeles. He left UCLA before graduation to pursue an acting career.

Winfield appeared on numerous television shows in the late 1960s and early 1970s—most notably as one of Diahann Carroll's boyfriends in the series *Julia*. His great success in that period was in the film *Sounder* (1972), in which he played a sharecropper father in the nineteenth-century American South. For this role, he received an Academy Award nomination for best actor.

Winfield subsequently appeared in the motion pictures *Gordon's War* (1973), *Conrack* (1974), *Huckleberry Finn* (1974), and *A Hero Ain't Nothing but a Sandwich* (1978). He received accolades for his portrayal of Dr. Martin Luther King Jr. in the NBC movie *King* (1978), for which he received an Emmy nomination. His second Emmy nomination came with his role in the television miniseries *Roots: The Next Generation* (1979).

In the 1980s, Winfield kept busy with appearances on television in *The Charmings*, *The Women of Brewster Place*, *Wiseguy*, and *227*. He appeared on film in *Star Trek II: The Wrath of Khan* (1982), *Damnation Alley* (1983), and *The Terminator* (1984), and on the stage in *A Midsummer Night's Dream*, *Othello*, and *The Seagull*. In 1990, he played the sarcastic Judge Larren Lyttle in the movie *Presumed Innocent*, and in 1992 he appeared on Broadway in the cast of *A Few Good Men*.

Winfield won several major awards, including an NAACP Image Award and election to the Black Filmmakers Hall of Fame. In 1995, Winfield won an Emmy for best guest actor on a drama series for his work in the *Picket Fences* episode "Enemy Lines." Winfield continued to be active on the large and small screens, appearing in movies such as *Mars Attacks!* (1996), *Relax . . . It's Just Sex* (1998), and *Seconds to Die* (2001), and on such television series as *Built to Last* (1997), *Teen Angel* (1997), and *Touched by an Angel*. Winfield began to speak publicly about his diabetes in 2001, and was often heard encouraging African American men to exercise and to lose weight. He died March 7, 2004.

JEFFREY WRIGHT (1965–)

Actor. Born and raised in Washington, D.C., Jeffrey Wright graduated from Amherst College in 1987. Known for his great versatility, Wright has earned Emmy, Tony, and Golden Globe awards for his work on stage, television, and film. Some of his notable roles include *Basquiat* (1996), *Angels in America* (1996), *Shaft* (2000), *Ali* (2001), *The Manchurian Candidate* (2004), *Syriana* (2005), *Casino Royale* (2006), *W* (2008), and *Quantum of Solace* (2008).

21

DRAMA, COMEDY, AND DANCE

Myla Churchill

For more than two hundred years, African American performers have appeared on the American stage. Despite the prejudices that they have faced both within the theater community and from the entertainment-seeking public, African American performers have made significant contributions to American performance art. The artistic heritage of today's African American actors, dancers, and comedians can be traced to the last decades of the eighteenth century.

THE ORIGINS OF AFRICAN AMERICAN PERFORMANCE ART

THE EARLIEST PLAYS WITH AFRICAN AMERICAN ACTORS

The first performances by African American actors on the American stage were in plays authored by white playwrights who provided blacks with narrow opportunities to portray shallow characters. Often blacks were cast as buffoons in order to appeal to the sensibilities of a bigoted public. In 1769, for example, the cast of Lewis Hallam's comedy *The Padlock* included a West Indian slave character named Mungo, who was a clown to be played by a black actor. Other white-authored plays from the period that depicted blacks in demoralizing roles were *Robinson Crusoe, Harlequin* (1792), and *The Triumph of Love* (1795) by John Randolph, which included the native black character named Sambo. As such, the earliest appearances of blacks on the American stage were as characters devoid of intellectual and moral sensibilities.

THE AFRICAN GROVE THEATRE

New York City's free African American community founded the first African American theater in 1821—the African Grove Theatre, located at Mercer and Bleecker streets "in the rear of the one-mile stone on Broadway." A group of amateur African American actors organized by Henry Brown presented *Richard III* at the theater on October 1, 1821. The African Grove Theatre subsequently produced *Othello, Hamlet,* and such lighter works as *Tom and Jerry* and *The Poor Soldier, Obi.*

One of the principal actors at the African Grove Theatre was James Hewlett, a West Indian–born black actor who distinguished himself in roles in *Othello* and *Richard III.* Hewlett later toured England and billed himself as "The New York and London Colored Comedian." Ira Aldridge, who later distinguished himself as one of the great Shakespearean tragic actors, was also a member of the permanent group that performed at the African Grove Theatre. Aldridge was cast in comic and musical roles, as well as in Shakespearean tragedies. The African Grove Theatre also featured the first play written and produced by an African American—Henry Brown's *The Drama of King Shotaway,* which was presented in June 1823.

Because of disturbances created by whites in the audience, the local police raided the African Grove Theatre on several occasions. The theater was wrecked by police and hoodlums during one of these raids, which forced its closing in late 1823. The black actors affiliated with the African Grove Theatre, determined to preserve their company, continued for several years to present plays at different rented locations throughout New York City.

MINSTRELSY

Among the earliest African American entertainers in colonial and antebellum America were enslaved laborers. On plantations throughout the South, enslaved performers using clappers, jawbones, and blacksmith rasps danced, sang, and told jokes for the entertainment of their fellow captives, as well as their masters, who often showcased their talents at local gatherings. Some plantation owners hired out their talented laborers to perform in traveling troupes.

During the late 1820s and early 1830s, white entertainers, exposed to the artistry of black performers, began to imitate them in their routines. Blackening their faces with cork, these white entertainers performed jigs, songs, and jokes with topical allusions to African Americans in their lyrics. This was how minstrelsy (sometimes known as Ethiopian minstrelsy) as a unique American theatrical form of entertainment was born.

White minstrel troupes in blackface became very popular on the American stage in the 1830s and 1840s. Among some of the more famous white minstrel performers were Thomas Dartmouth Rice, known as Daddy Rice, the original Jim Crow, Edwin Forrest, Dan Emmett, and the Christy Minstrels.

Some traveling white minstrel troupes used black performers to enhance the authenticity of their productions. One such troupe was the Ethiopian Minstrels, whose star performer was William Henry Lane, an African American dancer who used the stage name Master Juba. Lane was one of the greatest dancers of his generation. Throughout the United States and England, Master Juba was enthusiastically praised by audiences and critics alike. One anonymous British critic, quoted by dance historian Marian Hannah Winter, wrote the following critique of one of Lane's performances:

> Juba exceeded anything ever witnessed in Europe. The style as well as the execution is unlike anything seen in this country. The manner in which he beats time with feet, and the extraordinary command he possesses over them, can only be believed by those who have been present at the exhibition. ("Juba and American Minstrelsy," in *Chronicles of the American Dance* [1948], edited by Paul Magriel)

Black minstrel troupes began to appear in the 1850s, but it was not until after the Civil War (1861–1865) that they became established on the American stage. Although black minstrels inherited the negative stereotypes that white minstrels had established, the African American performer won a permanent place on the American stage, providing a training ground for the many black dancers, comedians, singers, and composers to come. Notable among these stage personalities were dancer-comedians Billy Kersands, Bert Williams, Bob Height, Dewey "Pigmeat" Markham, and Ernest Hogan; singers Gertrude "Ma" Rainey, Mamie Smith, and Bessie Smith; and composers James Bland and William Christopher Handy. To a great extent, black minstrelsy created a national appreciation for the talent of black stage entertainers, drawing audiences to black shows and other forms of black entertainment for generations to come.

RECLAIMING THE BLACK IMAGE: 1890 TO 1920

By the 1890s, African American producers, writers, and stage performers sought to reform the demeaning images of blacks that were prevalent on the American stage. *The Creole Show*, cast by African American producer Sam Jack in 1891, was the first all-black musical to depart from minstrelsy. *The Creole Show*, which was also notable for its inclusion of a chorus line, premiered in Boston in 1891 and later played at the Chicago World's Fair for the entire season. In 1895, African American producer John W. Ishaw presented *The Octoroon*, another all-black musical that avoided minstrel stereotypes. *Oriental America*, which Ishaw also produced, broke further from minstrel conventions by not closing with the traditional "walk around finale," but with an operatic medley.

Between 1898 and 1911, thirteen all-black musicals opened on Broadway, showcasing the talents of African American musicians, lyricists, directors, producers, and writers. *Trip to Coontown*, written and directed by Bob Cole in 1898, completely broke away from the minstrel tradition. The plot of this all-black performance piece was presented completely through music and dance, but was still laced with minstrel-influenced material. The first musical produced, written, and performed by African Americans on Broadway, it ushered in a new era for blacks on the American stage.

The highly popular *Clorindy: The Origin of the Cakewalk*, with music by composer Will Marion Cook and lyrics by poet Paul Laurence Dunbar, opened in 1898 at the Casino Roof Garden in New York. Cook engaged the comic-dance duo of Bert Williams and George Walker and built the show around their talents. Comedian-singer Ernest Hogan was also featured. Hogan later appeared on Broadway in both *Rufus Rastus* and *Oyster Man* (1902). Bob Cole, J. Rosamond Johnson, and James Weldon Johnson wrote and performed in *The Shoo-Fly Regiment*, another musical that opened on Broadway in 1902.

Williams and Walker premiered their first Broadway musical, *The Policy Players*, in 1899. This success was followed by the *Sons of Ham*, which played on Broadway for two seasons beginning in September 1900. Their most

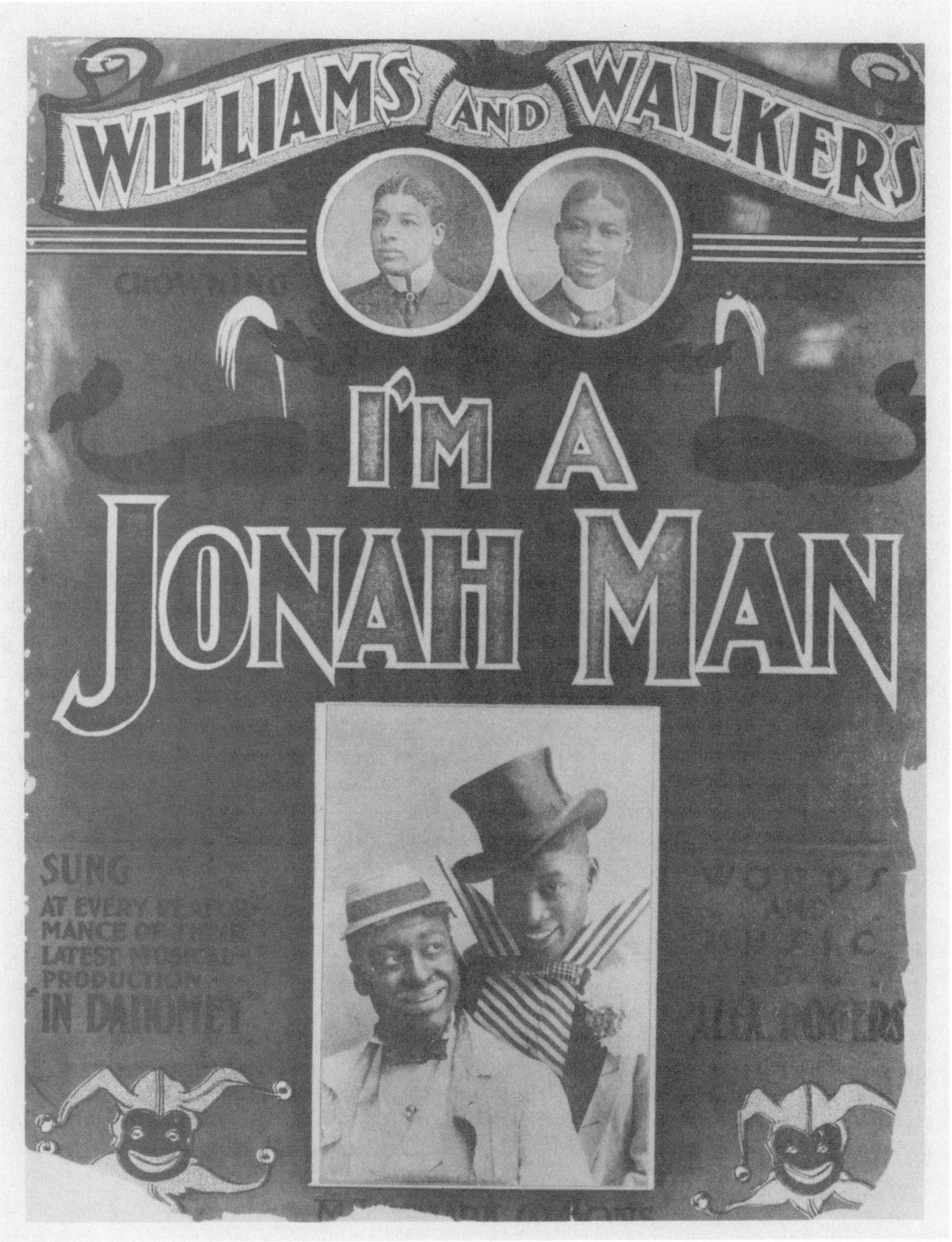

"I'm a Jonah Man" Sheet Music, 1903. *The vaudeville team of Bert Williams and George Walker was the most famous of the early black comedians, appearing in numerous black musicals between 1899 and 1909. This song was featured in their show* In Dahomey, *a success in the United States and in England.* **SCHOMBURG CENTER FOR RESEARCH IN BLACK CULTURE; THE NEW YORK PUBLIC LIBRARY; ASTOR, LENOX AND TILDEN FOUNDATIONS**

famous musical, *In Dahomey*, premiered on Broadway in 1903 and, after a long run, toured successfully in England. *The Southerners*, with music by Will Marion Cook, opened on Broadway in 1904 with an interracial cast starring Abbie Mitchell. The Williams and Walker team returned to Broadway in 1906 with a new musical, *Abyssinia*, which consistently played to a full house. Williams and Walker appeared in their last Broadway production together, *Bandanna Land*, in 1908. George Walker fell into ill health after the show closed, and he died in 1911.

Bert Williams then appeared in *Mr. Lord of Koal* on Broadway in 1909, and later he was the star comedian in the Ziegfeld Follies. The last black musical to open on Broadway before the 1920s was *His Honor the Barber* in 1911, with S. H. Dudley in the lead.

BLACK VAUDEVILLE

The unique world of black vaudeville employed dancers, comics, and pantomimes who, denied access to the American legitimate stage, developed their own revues and routines that reflected the African American popular culture. The white owners of the Theater Owners Booking Association (TOBA, known among African American performers as "Tough On Black Asses" because of the often unfavorable terms they received) hired the entertainers to play to black audiences in large and small towns across the United States from the early 1900s until the Great Depression.

Vaudeville was the stage where such dancers as Bert Williams and Bill "Bojangles" Robinson polished the craft that helped them eventually move into the mainstream white theater. Comic Dewey "Pigmeat" Markham developed his legendary "Here Come da Judge" routine on vaudeville. Tim Moore, later to be seen on *Amos 'n' Andy* as the incorrigible Kingfish, was also wildly popular.

The cakewalk, a dance that originated among the enslaved, was said to be a parody of the showy party manners of plantation owners' families, but the mimicry delighted the masters and mistresses. The cakewalk became a national and worldwide rage at the end of the nineteenth century, even though the black bourgeoisie condemned it as vulgar because women raised their legs, making it possible to see under their dresses.

Just as the cakewalk was developed to make fun of a white dancing style, ragtime was a response to European classical music. Ragtime was derived from minstrel show tunes and New Orleans street marches. Pianists Scott Joplin and Thomas Turpin made its distinctive rhythmic syncopation popular in the 1890s. One of the earliest examples of the form was Turpin's "Harlem Rag" of 1899.

Humor was used to cope with the pain and frustration of everyday life. Markham's "Here Come da Judge" routine was a critical farce on a legal system that afforded no justice or protection for African Americans. Ventriloquist Johnnie Woods, with his sidekick Little Henry, played the circuit as a dapper, prosperous gentleman berating and chiding the incorrigible dummy, dressed in a red-check suit, with bad manners and poor breeding. These comedy styles were later imitated by white performers, such as Eddie Cantor, Al Jolson, Abbott and Costello, and Laurel and Hardy, who were a success on the white stage, where blacks were not allowed.

What whites derided as demeaning and vulgar became grist for the comic and satiric black player, who took the white notion of low class and made a joke of it. The subject of race on the black stage was ground for debate, commiseration, derision, and mockery. But black performers also condemned bad manners and attitudes among themselves.

Although black performers were often able to bridge the gap from folk and vaudeville entertainment to the musical classics and drama, white audiences typically expected them to restrict themselves to the more "Negroid" comedy routines and minstrel styles. However, the privileged few of high society saw some of the best of the black players at the "colored clubs," such as the Cotton Club, Connie's Inn, and the Club Alabam' in New York. The Cotton Club boasted a chorus line of "tall, tan, and terrific" black women, as well as the hottest black entertainment.

THE BLACK PERFORMER IN EUROPE: 1900 TO 1920

Many black performers who struggled on the American circuit found great success in Europe. The "black craze" of African American art, music, and dance took Paris by storm in the 1920s. Ballroom dancers such as Fredi Washington and Al Moore, the singers Ethel Waters and Josephine Baker, and producers such as Claude Hopkins found a receptive audience among Roaring Twenties Parisians. Europe was not as color-conscious as the United States, where the elegant and refined Washington and Moore were so light-skinned that they were not totally accepted on the black circuit with their "white style" act. However, Europe welcomed their sophisticated artistry and style.

Hopkins introduced singer Josephine Baker to Paris, where she developed her flamboyant and provocative act before appreciative Europeans. Performing at the celebrated Parisian music hall, Folies Bergère, Baker pushed the boundaries of nudity and innuendo in her singing and dancing and remained an international sensation throughout her career.

The dancer and pantomime Johnny Hudgins was an enormous hit with both black and white audiences in the United States and Europe. In the 1920s, he was filmed by Jean Renoir in a short titled *Charleston*, which left behind a detailed account of his act. His characters included the "Ballroom Dancer," the "Ice Skater," and the "Pullman

The Green Pastures, ***Film, 1936.*** *Playwright Marc Connelly's* The Green Pastures *opened on Broadway on February 26, 1930, featuring an all-black cast. In 1936 it was made into the film pictured here, featuring Rex Ingram as "De Lawd."* **WARNER BROS/THE KOBAL COLLECTION/PICTURE DESK**

Porter." One of his more notable numbers involved him performing the Charleston in a lady's feather-plumed straw hat.

AFRICAN AMERICAN DRAMATIC THEATER INTO THE TWENTY-FIRST CENTURY

THE DRAMATIC THEATER: 1900 TO 1940

Black actors on the American dramatic stage, like the performers in all-black musicals, struggled to shed the demeaning image of the African American projected by most white-produced minstrelsy and drama. The presentation of three plays—*The Rider of Dreams*, *Granny Maumee*, and *Simon the Cyrenian*—by white playwright Ridgely Torrence at the Garden Theatre in Madison Square Garden on April 5, 1917, was an exceptional and highly successful effort to objectively portray African Americans on the dramatic stage.

During the Harlem Renaissance years, African American dramatic actors remained less active than black performers in musicals, and the image of blacks projected by white playwrights was generally inadequate. For example, although Charles Gilpin starred in Eugene O'Neill's *The Emperor Jones* at the Provincetown Theatre in 1920, critic Loften Mitchell noted in *Black Drama: The Story of the American Negro in the Theatre* (1967) that: "This play, while offering one of the most magnificent roles for a Negro in the American theater, is the first in a long line to deal with the Negro on this level. O'Neill obviously saw in the Negro rich subject matter, but he was either incapable or unwilling to deal directly with the matter."

Nonetheless, African American actors and actresses had to accept the roles in which they were cast by white playwrights. In 1924, the O'Neill play *All God's Chillun' Got Wings* opened at the Provincetown Theatre with Paul Robeson and Mary Blair to mixed reviews because of its interracial theme. Rose McClendon starred in Paul Green's Pulitzer Prize–winning *In Abraham's Bosom* in 1926 and was ably supported by Abbie Mitchell and Jules Bledsoe. Marc Connelly's *Green Pastures* opened on Broadway on February 26, 1930, with Richard B. Harrison playing "De Lawd." It ran for 557 performances and was taken on an extensive road tour.

In the 1930s, Langston Hughes brought the African American voice to the stage. Three of his plays were produced successfully on Broadway. *Mulatto* opened in 1935 and starred Rose McClendon and Morris McKenney. It had the longest Broadway run of any play written by an African American, with 373 consecutive performances. The other plays were *Little Ham* (1935) and *Troubled Island* (1936).

THE FEDERAL THEATRE PROJECT

In the mid-1930s, the Works Progress Administration (WPA) sponsored one of the greatest organized efforts to assist and encourage American actors, especially African American actors. The Federal Theatre Project employed a total of 851 African American actors to work in sixteen segregated units of the project in Chicago, New York, and other cities from 1935 until 1939, when Congress ended the project. While the project was in operation, African American actors appeared in seventy-five plays, including classics, vaudeville routines, contemporary comedies, children's shows, circuses, and "living newspaper" performances. Notable among the African American actors who worked in the project—and later became stars on Broadway and in film—were Butterfly McQueen, Canada Lee, Rex Ingram, Katherine Dunham, Edna Thomas, Thomas Anderson, and Arthur Dooley Wilson.

In the wake of the Federal Theatre Project, the American Negro Theater was established in Harlem by Abram Hill, Austin Briggs-Hall, Frederick O'Neal, and Hattie King-Reeves. Its objective was to authentically portray African American life and to give African American actors and playwrights a forum for their talents. Some of their productions eventually made it to Broadway. In 1944, the theater produced *Anna Lucasta* in the basement of the 135th Street Library in Harlem. It was successful enough to move to Broadway, and featured Hilda Simms, Frederick O'Neal, Alice Childress, Alvin Childress, Earle Hyman, and Herbert Henry. Abram Hill's *Walk Hard* opened in Harlem in 1946 and became a Broadway production with Maxwell Glanville in the lead. The American Negro Theater provided a training ground for many African American actors who later became stars on Broadway and in Hollywood, including Ruby Dee, Ossie Davis, Harry Belafonte, and Sidney Poitier.

DRAMATIC THEATER IN THE 1950s

The rise of television in the 1950s generally had an adverse affect on the American theater. Employment for all actors fell sharply, especially for African American actors. Ethel Waters did, however, open on Broadway in 1950 as the lead in *Member of the Wedding*, which was well received. Louis Peterson's *Take a Giant Step* opened on Broadway in September 1953 to critical praise; in the cast were Frederick O'Neal, Helen Martin, Maxwell Glanville, Pauline Myers, Estelle Evans, and Louis Gossett Jr.

One of the most successful all-black plays to appear on Broadway opened in March 1959—Lorraine Hansberry's *Raisin in the Sun*, which won the New York Drama Critics Circle Award. It was directed by the legendary African American director Lloyd Richards. Its cast included Sidney Poitier, Ruby Dee, Diana Sands, Claudia McNeil, Louis Gossett Jr., Ivan Dixon, Lonnie Elder III, and Douglas Turner Ward. Hansberry was hailed as a pioneer who paved the way for African American political and social playwrights.

THE DRAMATIC THEATER SINCE 1960

As the civil rights movement challenged the national conscience in the 1960s, every facet of African American life changed, including the performing arts. More plays about African Americans by both black and white playwrights were produced, providing increased employment for black actors. A particularly significant year was 1961.

On May 4, 1961, *The Blacks*, by French author Jean Genet, opened off-Broadway at the St. Mark's Theater. A play about black Americans written for white audiences, *The Blacks* provided employment for a host of African American actors, including Roscoe Lee Browne, James Earl Jones, Louis Gossett Jr., Helen Martin, Cicely Tyson, Godfrey Cambridge, Raymond St. Jacques, Maya Angelou, Charles Gordone, and many others who appeared in its road tours. Subsequently, African American dramatic actors appeared on and off Broadway in several major plays by white playwrights. Notable among them were *In White America* (1968) by Judith Rutherford Marechal, with Gloria Foster and Moses Gunn; *The Great White Hope* (1968) by William Sackler, starring James Earl Jones; and *So Nice, They Named It Twice* (1975) by Neil Harris, featuring Bill Jay and Veronica Redd.

Also in 1961, African American fashion designer Ellen Stewart founded La MaMa E.T.C. (Experimental

Theatre Club), the oldest remaining avant-garde theater in the United States. Known as the mother of off-off-Broadway theater, Stewart gave young American and international playwrights an incubator in which to develop their original work without the pressures or constraints of commercial theater. A venerated institution with more than fifty Obie Awards, La MaMa was the birthplace for such plays as *Hair*, *Godspell*, and *Jesus Christ Superstar*. Stewart is also credited with launching the careers of notable actors, directors, and playwrights, such as Tom Eyen (*Dreamgirls*) and Adrienne Kennedy (*Funnyhouse of the Negro*).

On May 23, 1961, when LeRoi Jones's play *The Dutchman* opened at the Cherry Lane Theatre, the black revolutionary play was introduced to theater audiences. African American actors were provided with the opportunity to perform in roles that not only affirmed blackness but portrayed black political militancy. Several subsequent black revolutionary plays afforded further opportunities for African American actors, including James Baldwin's *Blues for Mr. Charlie* (1964), with Al Freeman Jr. and Diana Sands, and *The Toilet/The Slave* (1964) by LeRoi Jones, starring James Spruill, Walter Jones, Nan Martin, and Al Freeman Jr.

That same year, Jones (who changed his name to Imamu Amiri Baraka) founded the Black Arts Repertory Theater/School to make theater more accessible by "taking it to the streets." The objective was to promote interaction between the artists and the audience. Baraka and many other playwrights, poets, and essayists believed that their primary responsibility was to create work for and about African American people. This philosophy evolved into the Black Arts movement. Artists of the Black Arts movement raged against theatrical convention and mandated that the only art of worth reflected the cultural, social, and political concerns of their communities. In addition to Baraka, some of the award-winning playwrights of the movement were Ed Bullins, *The Taking of Miss Janie* (1975); Richard Wesley, *The Black Terror* (1972); Sonia Sanchez, *Next Stop the Bronx* (1968); and Adrienne Kennedy, *The Funnyhouse of the Negro* (1964).

The dissident voices of the Black Arts movement gave rise to a wave of black regional theater companies, such as the Crossroads Theatre in New Brunswick, New Jersey; the Freedom Theatre in Philadelphia; the Penumbra Theatre in St. Paul, Minnesota; the New Federal Theatre in New York; the Inner City Cultural Center in Los Angeles; Jomandi Productions in Atlanta; and the St. Louis Repertory Theatre, to name a few. Their focus was to foster the development of playwrights, actors, managers, and technicians and to provide the African American community with plays steeped in a cultural context.

The most venerable institution of the Black Arts movement was the Negro Ensemble Company (NEC) founded in New York in 1967. This theatrical production company, initially financed by a three-year grant of $1.2 million from the Ford Foundation, was the brainchild of playwright and actor Douglas Turner Ward. Originally housed at the St. Mark's Theater, the company later moved to New York's Theater Four. Actor Robert Hooks served as executive director, Gerald Krone as administrative director, and Douglas Turner Ward as artistic director.

The Negro Ensemble staged more than one hundred productions and featured the work of many black playwrights, including Nobel laureates Wole Soyinka and Derek Wolcott. Three plays went to Broadway under Ward's direction: Joseph A. Walker's Tony Award–winning drama, *The River Niger* (1973); Leslie Lee's Obie winner, *The First Breeze of Summer* (1975); and Samm-Art Williams's Tony-nominated play, *Home* (1980). NEC also produced Charles Fuller's *A Soldier's Play* (1981), which won a Pulitzer Prize and was adapted into *A Soldier's Story* (1984), a film starring Denzel Washington. The Negro Ensemble Company provided work for a plethora of outstanding African American actors and actresses, including Louis Gossett Jr., Charles Brown, Denise Nicholas, Phylicia Rashad, Esther Rolle, Michele Shay, Rosalind Cash, Adolph Caesar, Frances and Gloria Foster, Glynn Turman, Giancarlo Esposito, Moses Gunn, and Barbara Montgomery.

Independent of the Negro Ensemble Company, several African American playwrights had plays successfully produced on Broadway. Ntozake Shange's widely acclaimed *For Colored Girls Who Have Considered Suicide/When the Rainbow Is Enuf* (1977) was produced by Woodie King Jr. of the New Federal Theatre. *For Colored Girls* had a cast of seven African American actresses, including Trazana Beverley. Beverley was the first African American actress to win a Tony Award for best featured actress in a play. Twenty-seven years later, Phylicia Rashad became the first African American woman to win a Tony Award for best actress in a play for the 2004 revival of *A Raisin in the Sun*.

In 1969, James Earl Jones became the first African American man to win a Tony Award for best actor for *The Great White Hope*. Jones won his second Tony for best actor in 1987 for *Fences* by August Wilson. Actors who have also won Tony Awards for their roles in an August Wilson play are Lawrence Fishburne (*Two Trains Running*), Ruben Santiago-Hudson (*Seven Guitars*), Mary Alice (*Fences*), L. Scott Caldwell (*Joe Turner's Come and Gone*), and Viola Davis (*King Hedley II*). Lloyd Richards also won a Tony for best direction (*Fences*).

Hailed as one the most celebrated and prolific American playwrights, August Wilson garnered countless nominations and numerous awards for his cycle of ten plays, which chronicled the experiences of African Americans in each decade of the twentieth century. Eight out of the ten plays were produced on Broadway, including *Fences*, which won the 1987 Pulitzer Prize for drama, the Tony Award for best play, and the Drama Desk Award for outstanding new play. In 1990, *The Piano Lesson* earned Wilson his second Pulitzer Prize and Drama Desk Award. He also received New York Drama Critics Awards for best play for *Ma Rainey's Black Bottom* (1984), *Fences*, *Joe Turner's Come and Gone* (1988), *The Piano Lesson*, *Two Trains Running* (1992), *Seven Guitars* (1996), and *Jitney* (2000).

Before his untimely death in 2005, Wilson completed his cycle of plays with Broadway productions of *King Hedley II* (1999), which opened on Broadway in 2001, *Gem of the Ocean* (2003), and a Yale Repertory Theatre production of his last play, *Radio Golf* (2005), which opened on Broadway in 2007. Actors turned producers Wendell Pierce and Tamara Tunie were on the production team of *Radio Golf*, which was nominated for four Tony and three Drama Desk awards.

Lincoln Center Theater's 2009 Broadway revival of *Joe Turner's Come and Gone*, directed by Bartlett Sher, sparked controversy because it was the first time one of Wilson's plays was helmed by a white director on Broadway. Despite the debate, the cast and creative team were formidable, and the production captured six Tony nominations. Dianne McIntyre choreographed the Juba dance, Taj Mahal wrote the score, and Roger Robinson won the 2009 Tony for best performance by a featured actor. August Wilson was one of the strongest voices in American theater and his influence laid the groundwork for many of the resonant voices in the twenty-first century.

Suzan-Lori Parks's *Topdog/Underdog* won the 2002 Pulitzer Prize for drama under the direction of George C. Wolfe. In November 2002, Parks committed to writing a play a day for the next 365 days, which resulted in the 365 Days/365 Plays National Festival. From November 2006 to November 2007, the festival presented the plays in more than sixty select theater companies across the country, simultaneously. This constitutes the largest collaboration in American theater history. Parks's more recent plays include her first libretto, *Ray Charles Live!* which was commissioned by the Pasadena Playhouse in 2007, and *Father Comes Home from the Wars (Parts 1,8, & 9)*, which was workshopped in 2009 by the Public LAB, a developmental collaboration between the Public Theater and the LAByrinth Theater Company in New York.

In 2009, Lynn Nottage won the Pulitzer Prize in drama for *Ruined*. Her canon of plays includes *Intimate Apparel* (2003), *Fabulation* (2004), and *Crumbs from the Table of Joy* (1995), which have been produced nationally and internationally. Some of the off-Broadway and regional theaters that have developed and produced her work are the Manhattan Theatre Club, the Goodman Theatre, the Roundabout Theatre Company, Playwrights Horizons, Center Stage, the Second Stage Theatre, the Steppenwolf Theatre Company, Freedom Theatre, the Crossroads Theatre Company, and the Repertory Theatre of St. Louis.

Other award-winning and emerging playwrights include: Regina Taylor (*Magnolia*, *Dreams of Sarah Breedlove*, *Crowns*); Keith Glover (*Dancing on Moonlight*, *Coming of the Hurricane*, *Thunder Knocking on the Door*); Charles Randolph-White (*Cuttin' Up*, *Blue*); Sarah Jones (*Bridge and Tunnel*, *A Right to Care*); Tanya Barfield (*Of Equal Measure*, *Blue Door*); Daniel Beatty (*Through the Night*, *Emergence-See!*); Marcus Gardley (*... and Jesus Moonwalks the Mississippi*, *Dance of the Holy Ghosts*; Kara Lee Corthron (*Holly Down in Heaven*, *Wild Black-Eyed Susans*, *Like a Cow or an Elephant*); Kia Corthron (*A Cool Dip in the Barren Saharan Crick*, *Life by Asphyxiation*, *Come Down Burning*); and Tarell Alvin McCraney (*The Brother/Sister Plays*).

AFRICAN AMERICAN MUSICALS INTO THE TWENTY-FIRST CENTURY

Between 1898 and 1911, thirteen all-black musicals opened on Broadway. The performances showcased the talents of Ernest Hogan and the comic-dance duo of George Walker and Bert Williams. But for nearly a decade after the close of *His Honor the Barber*, the Broadway stage did not carry *any* all-black musicals.

On May 23, 1921, *Shuffle Along* signaled the return of black musicals to the "Great White Way" and the arrival of the Harlem Renaissance on the American stage. Featuring the talented singer-dancer Florence Mills, *Shuffle Along* was written by Noble Sissle, Eubie Blake, Flournoy Miller, and Aubrey Lyles. Mills quickly became a sought-after performer, appearing in *The Plantation Revue*, which opened on Broadway on July 17, 1922, and later toured England. In 1926, Mills returned to Harlem and played the lead in *Blackbirds* at the Alhambra Theatre for a six-week run. Subsequently, Mills performed in Paris for six months.

Noble Sissle and Eubie Blake returned to Broadway on September 24, 1924, with their new musical *Chocolate Dandies*. In 1926, Flournoy Miller and Aubrey Lyles opened on Broadway in *Runnin' Wild*, which introduced the Charleston to the country. Bill "Bojangles" Robinson, starring in *Blackbirds of 1928*, dazzled Broadway audiences with his exciting tap dancing style. Miller and Lyles

Anne Brown, Singer and Actress,* Rhapsody in Blue, *1945. *Brown was the original Bess in* Porgy and Bess *on Broadway in 1935. In the film* Rhapsody in Blue *she sang Bess's song "Summertime." In 1948 she settled in Norway and became a Norwegian citizen.* **EVERETT COLLECTION**

mounted several other black musicals on Broadway during the 1920s, including *Rang Tang* (1927) and *Keep Shufflin'* (1928), with musical numbers staged by Harlem's preeminent choreographer, Leonard Harper. Harper conceived and staged *Hot Chocolates* in 1929, with music composed by Fats Waller and lyrics by Andy Razaf. *Hot Chocolates* introduced the songs "Ain't Misbehavin'" and "Black and Blue," as well as Broadway newcomers Cab Calloway and Louis Armstrong.

When *Porgy and Bess* opened on Broadway in 1935, it became the major all-black musical production of the 1930s. With music by George Gershwin, this adaptation of the novel and play by DuBose Heyward and Dorothy Heyward was an immediate success as a folk opera. Todd Duncan was cast as Porgy, with Anne Brown as Bess and comedian-dancer John W. Bubbles as the drug dealer and pimp, Sportin' Life.

In the 1940s, black musicals were once again scarce on Broadway. *Cabin in the Sky*, starring Ethel Waters, Dooley Wilson, Todd Duncan, Rex Ingram, J. Rosamond Johnson, and Katherine Dunham and her dancers, ran for 165 performances after it opened on October 25, 1940. *Carmen Jones*, perhaps the most successful all-black musical of the decade, opened in 1943 with Luther Saxon, Napoleon Reed, Carlotta Franzel, and Cozy Cove. It ran for 231 performances and was taken on tour. In 1946, *St. Louis Woman*, featuring Rex Ingram, Pearl Bailey, Juanita Hall, and June Hawkins, played a short run to mixed reviews.

The years from 1961 to the mid-1980s constituted one of the most active periods for African American performers in musical theater. Many of the black musicals produced during these years, both on and off Broadway, enjoyed substantial runs and extended road tours.

Langston Hughes's musical *Black Nativity* opened on Broadway on December 11, 1961. Directed by Vinnette Carroll, the cast was headed by gospel singers Marion Williams and the Stars of Faith and also featured Alex Bradford, Clive Thompson, Cleo Quitman, and Carl

The Wiz, *Film, 1978.* *Starring Michael Jackson, Nipsey Russell, Diana Ross, and Ted Ross (*left to right*), the film version of* The Wiz *was a commercial flop. The original Broadway production in 1977 won seven Tony Awards, including best musical. Ted Ross appeared in both the stage and film versions as the Lion.*
UNIVERSAL/THE KOBAL COLLECTION/PICTURE DESK

Ford. Although it ran for only fifty-seven performances on Broadway, it toured extensively throughout the United States and abroad.

In 1964, Sammy Davis Jr. dazzled Broadway in Clifford Odets's *Golden Boy.* Davis was supported by a brilliant cast that included Robert Guillaume, Louis Gossett Jr., Lola Falana, and Billy Daniels.

Leslie Uggams and Robert Hooks appeared in *Hallelujah Baby,* which opened at New York's Martin Beck Theatre on April 26, 1967. *Hallelujah Baby,* a musical look at five decades of black history, received five Tony Awards, including best actor and actress for Hooks and Uggams and best featured actress for Lillian Hayman.

Purlie, based on Ossie Davis's 1961 play *Purlie Victorious,* opened on May 9, 1970, with Melba Moore and Cleavon Little in lead roles. *Purlie* received good reviews. Little won the Tony Award for best actor, and Moore won for best featured actress.

Micki Grant's *Don't Bother Me, I Can't Cope,* starring Micki Grant and Alex Bradford, opened on April 19, 1972, to rave reviews. Grant received a Drama Desk Award and an Obie Award.

Virginia Capers, Joe Morton, and Helen Martin opened in *Raisin,* based on Lorraine Hansberry's play *A Raisin in the Sun,* on October 13, 1973. *Raisin* received the Tony Award for the best musical in 1974, and Capers won the best-actress Tony.

Despite initially poor reviews, *The Wiz,* a black musical version of *The Wizard of Oz,* became a highly successful show. Opening on Broadway on January 5, 1975, *The Wiz* featured an array of talented performers, including Stephanie Mills, Hinton Battle, Ted Ross, André De Shields, Dee Dee Bridgewater, and Mabel King. *The Wiz* swept the Tony Award ceremonies in 1975, winning seven awards, including best musical. The creative team was honored too. Geoffrey Holder and George Faison won best director and best choreographer, respectively. It was one of the longest-running black musicals in the history of Broadway, with 1,672 performances.

Ain't Misbehavin', another popular black musical of the 1970s, opened on May 8, 1978. Based on a cavalcade of songs composed by Thomas "Fats" Waller, *Ain't Misbehavin'* starred Nell Carter, André De Shields, Armelia McQueen, Ken Page, and Charlaine Woodard. It played to Broadway audiences for 1,604 performances, and Nell Carter received a Tony Award as best featured actress.

Three spectacular black musicals premiered on Broadway in the 1980s. *Dreamgirls,* which opened at the Imperial Theater on December 20, 1981, captivated Broadway audiences with a cast that included Obba Babatundé, Ben Harney, Cleavant Derricks, Loretta Devine, Jennifer Holiday, and Sheryl Lee Ralph. *Dreamgirls* ran for 1,522 performances on Broadway and had an extensive road tour. Ben Harney and Jennifer Holiday won Tony Awards for best actor and actress, Cleavant Derricks won for best featured actor, and Michael Peters won for best choreography. In 2006, *Dreamgirls* was adapted into a film starring Beyoncé Knowles, Jennifer Hudson, and Anika Noni Rose, who was a Tony Award winner for best featured actress in *Caroline, or Change* (2004).

In 1986, Debbie Allen opened in the lead role of *Sweet Charity.* Reviews were favorable and the show established Allen as a musical theater actress. *Black and Blue* opened in 1989 at the Minskoff Theatre. The show was reminiscent of a 1920s musical revue, spotlighting the illustrious composers of that era. *Black and Blue* won three Tony Awards, including best actress for blues singer Ruth Brown.

Bring in 'Da Noise, Bring in 'Da Funk, *c. 1995–1996. Dancers Jimmy Tate, Savion Glover, Baakari Wilder, and Vincent Bingham* (left to right) *dance in the musical that made its off-Broadway debut in 1995, moved to Broadway the next year, and ran until 1999.* EVERETT COLLECTION

A few new all-black musicals opened in the early 1990s. *Five Guys Named Moe* was a tribute to musician Louis Jordan, written by Clarke Peters and directed by Charles Augin. *Once on this Island* told a star-crossed love story set in the French Antilles. The popular musical earned eight 1991 Tony nominations and launched the career of talented newcomer LaChanze. *Jelly's Last Jam* was the brainchild of writer and director George C. Wolfe. The imaginative tribute to Jelly Roll Morton was a commercial success and received eleven Tony nominations. Tonya Pinkins won a Tony Award for best featured actress, and Gregory Hines, as Jelly Roll Morton, won the Tony for best actor in 1992.

The monumental hit *Bring in 'da Noise, Bring in 'da Funk* opened in 1995. Starring young tap wizard Savion Glover and directed by George C. Wolfe, *Noise/Funk* celebrated three hundred years of African American history in poetry, music, song, and dance. The musical won four 1996 Tony Awards, including best choreographer for Glover, best director for Wolfe, and best featured actress for Ann Duquesnay in her role as 'Da Singer.

Featured in a lavish production of *Carousel*, a young African American actress, Audra McDonald, won her first Tony Award in 1994 as best featured actress in a musical. She won her second Tony in 1996 for a featured role in *Master Class* and third in 1998 for a featured performance in the musical *Ragtime*. In 2004, Audra McDonald won not only her fourth Tony for best featured actress in the revival of *A Raisin in the Sun* but the distinction of being the first African American to do so.

In the latter half of the 1990s, African Americans began winning awards for shows that were not considered "all-black musicals." Lillias White and Chuck Cooper won Tony Awards for best featured actress and actor for their performances in *The Life*, a 1997 musical that garnered twelve Tony nominations. In 2000, two African Americans captured the Tony Awards for best actress and best actor in a musical. Heather Headley won for her title role in the musical adaptation of Verdi's opera *Aida*, and Brian Stokes Mitchell won best actor in a revival of *Kiss Me Kate*.

The twenty-first century ushered in the age of the African American producer. Whoopi Goldberg was the

Cast of* The Color Purple *Performing at the Tony Awards, New York City, June 11, 2006. *Produced by Oprah Winfrey, the stage musical version of* The Color Purple *received eleven Tony Award nominations. LaChanze* (right) *won for best actress in a musical.* AP PHOTO/JEFF CHRISTENSEN

first African American woman to receive a Tony as a producer of the best musical in 2002, *Thoroughly Modern Millie*. Her latest project, *Sister Act: A Divine Musical Comedy*, is slated for Broadway in 2010.

In 2003, Russell Simmons, Stan Lathan, and Kimora Lee Simmons won Tony Awards as producers of the best special theatrical event, *Russell Simmons' Def Poetry Jam*. In the same year, George C. Wolfe won a Tony as a producer of the best play, *Take Me Out*.

Produced and directed by George C. Wolfe, *Caroline, or Change* was nominated for six Tony Awards in 2004, including best director of a musical for Wolfe, best actress for Tonya Pinkins, and best featured actress for Anika Noni Rose.

The Color Purple, produced by Oprah Winfrey, received eleven Tony nominations in 2006, including best musical for Winfrey, best choreography for Donald Byrd, best featured actor for Brandon Victor Dixon, and best featured actress for Felicia P. Fields and Elisabeth Withers-Mendes. LaChanze won the Tony for best actress in *The Color Purple*. Sarah Jones won a 2006 Special Tony Award for her innovative one-woman show, *Bridge and Tunnel*.

Tamara Tunie was on the production team that won the best musical Tony in 2007 for *Spring Awakening*, which also earned Bill T. Jones his first Tony for best choreography.

Stew is the newest voice on the musical theater scene, breaking ground with a rock musical, *Passing Strange*, which opened on Broadway in 2008. His semiautobiographical tale was nominated for seven Tony Awards, including best musical, best score, best actor, best orchestration, and best featured actor and actress for newcomers Daniel Breaker and de'Adre Aziza. Stew won the Tony for best book of a musical. He is the first African American librettist to win in that category.

AFRICAN AMERICAN COMEDY INTO THE TWENTY-FIRST CENTURY

The earliest black comedians in America, like other early black entertainers, were enslaved Africans who in their free time entertained themselves and their masters. In the early minstrel shows, white comedians in blackface created comic caricatures of blacks, whom they referred to as "coons" (a pejorative term for African American men). When African Americans began appearing in minstrel shows shortly after the Civil War, they found themselves burdened with the "coon" comic caricatures created by white performers. The dance-comedy team of Bert Williams and George Walker were the most famous of the early black comedians, appearing in numerous black musicals between 1899 and 1909.

In the all-black musicals of the 1920s, a new comic movement emerged: the comedy of style, which emphasized such antics as rolling the eyes or shaking the hips. The venom and bite of black "folk" humor was replaced by a comedy of style that was more acceptable to the white audiences of these all-black musicals.

Real black folk humor, however, did survive and thrive in black nightclubs and black theaters, such as the Apollo in Harlem and the Regal in Chicago, in the 1930s, 1940s, and 1950s. In these settings, known as the "Chitlin' Circuit," such African American comedians as Tim Moore, Dusty Fletcher, Butterbeans and Susie, Stepin Fetchit, Jackie "Moms" Mabley, Redd Foxx, and Slappy White performed without restrictions.

African American comedians enjoyed greater exposure during the 1960s. No longer confined to the Chitlin' Circuit, comedians such as Jackie "Moms" Mabley, Redd Foxx, and Slappy White began to perform to audiences in exclusive white clubs, as well as to audiences within the black community. They used black folk humor to comment on politics, civil rights, work, sex, and a variety of other subjects. Mabley made two popular recordings: *Moms Mabley at the "UN"* and *Moms Mabley at the Geneva Conference.* In January 1972, Redd Foxx premiered on television as Fred Sanford on *Sanford and Son*, which remained popular in syndication for decades.

Several younger African American comedians came into prominence in the early 1960s. Dick Gregory used black folk humor to make political commentary. Bill Cosby specialized in amusing chronicles about boyhood in America. Godfrey Cambridge, although successful, did not rely on black folk humor. During the late 1960s and the early 1970s, Flip Wilson, who parodied historical and social experience by creating black characters who lived in a black world, became extremely popular on television. His cast of characters, which included Freddy the Playboy, Sammy the White House Janitor, and Geraldine, used black folk humor as commentary on an array of issues.

Another pivotal African American comedian who began his career in the 1960s was Richard Pryor. His sharp, well-timed, risqué folk humor quickly won him a large group of faithful fans and inspired generations of comedians to come. The late Pryor, who recorded extensively, also starred successfully in several films, including *Lady Sings the Blues* (1972), *Car Wash* (1976), and *Stir Crazy* (1980).

During the 1980s, numerous African American comedians became successful in the various entertainment media. Eddie Murphy made his first appearance on the television show *Saturday Night Live* in 1980. Murphy parlayed his television success to Hollywood and made his movie debut in the film *48 Hours* in 1982. He subsequently starred in several big-budget films, including *Trading Places* (1983), *Beverly Hills Cop* (1984), *Coming to America* (1988), *Boomerang* (1992), *The Nutty Professor* (1996), *Dr. Dolittle* (1988), and their sequels. Collectively, they have made Murphy one of the top-grossing African American actors of all time.

Murphy established his own company, Eddie Murphy Productions, to create and produce television and films, including his stand-up concerts, *Delirious* (1983) and *Raw* (1987). More recent projects include the animated television series *The PJs* (1999–2001), *Life* (1999), *The Nutty Professor II: The Klumps* (2000), and *Norbit* (2007). Murphy's vocal talents animated characters such as Mushu in Disney's *Mulan* and the donkey in Dreamworks' *Shrek*. In 2007, Murphy was nominated for an Oscar and won the Golden Globe and Screen Actor's Guild (SAG) awards for his portrayal of James "Thunder" Early in the film version of the Broadway musical *Dreamgirls*. Murphy also starred in *Meet Dave* (2008) and *Imagine That* (2009), before reprising the voice of the donkey in the *Shrek* franchise with *Shrek Forever After* in 2010.

After achieving success on the stand-up circuit, several African Americans earned opportunities on television and in films in the 1990s. Keenen Ivory Wayans and his brother Damon created and starred in the Emmy Award–winning show *In Living Color* (1990–1994). The sketch-comedy show provided a vehicle for social commentary and launched the careers of Jamie Foxx, Jim Carrey, and Jennifer Lopez. With his brothers Damon and Marlon, Keenen Ivory Wayans wrote and produced the popular slapstick comedies *Scary Movie* (2000), *White Chicks* (2004), and *Little Man* (2006). Teaming up with their nephews, Damien and Damon Jr. as director and star respectively, the Wayans team created the spoof *Dance Flick* (2009). A *White Chicks* sequel and *Super Bad James Dynomite*, a live action film of the Wayans brothers' cult comic-book series, were under development as of 2010.

Martin Lawrence appealed to audiences in a self-titled sitcom that featured him portraying himself, his mother, and his female neighbor, Sheneneh. He teamed up with Will Smith, and their comic antics made blockbuster hits of *Bad Boys* (1995) and *Bad Boys II* (2003). Lawrence produced his two successful stand-up films, *You So Crazy* (1994) and *Runteldat* (2002), as well as the immensely popular franchise *Big Momma's House* (2000, 2006). Its third sequel is scheduled for a 2012 release. Martin has also served as executive producer of *Martin Lawrence Presents: 1st Amendment Stand-up*, which premiered on the Starz Network in 2005. His most recent film appearances are in *Wild Hogs* (2007), *Welcome Home Roscoe Jenkins* (2008), *College Road Trip* (2008), and *Death at a Funeral* (2010).

Chris Rock gained popularity on *Saturday Night Live* with brash, politically informed characters that helped him earn roles in such movies as *Lethal Weapon 4* (1998), *Dogma* (1999), and *Nurse Betty* (2000). Rock also lent his distinctive vocal talent to *Osmosis Jones* (2001), *Madagascar* (2005), and *Bee Movie* (2007). A true stand-up comedian, Rock won two Emmys in 1996 for his HBO special, *Bring the Pain*, and a 2000 Grammy Award for the recording of another HBO special, *Bigger & Blacker*. His self-titled variety show on HBO (1997–2000) garnered a third Emmy for best writing, and *Everybody Hates Chris* (2005–2009), a sitcom inspired by Rock's childhood, became one of the most popular shows on the CW Network. Rock earned his fourth Emmy for outstanding writing on a Comedy Central special that spanned three continents: *Chris Rock: Kill the Messenger* (2008) chronicled his stand-up performances in London, New York, and Johannesburg.

Steve Harvey, Bernie Mac, D. L. Hughley, and Cedric the Entertainer reign as "The Original Kings of Comedy." Their two-year comedy tour was the most successful in history. It grossed $37 million for the comedians and their promoter, Walter Latham, and brought them to the attention of Spike Lee. In 2000, Lee produced a documentary of the tour that propelled the "Kings" into the forefront of mainstream media. They all joined the ranks of comedians with self-titled sitcoms.

After a five-year run on *The Steve Harvey Show* (1996–2002), Harvey began hosting the *Steve Harvey Morning Show*, a popular syndicated radio drive show. In 2006, he returned to his stand-up roots with a fifteen-city tour and a film he produced, *Don't Trip . . . He Ain't Through with Me Yet*. Harvey is an unlikely executive producer of *Mobile Home Disaster*, which premiered in 2008 on the Country Music Television Network (CMT). And, in 2010, Harvey was named as the new host for the popular game show *Family Feud*.

Bernie Mac focused on his film career, starring in the remake of *Ocean's Eleven* (2001) and its sequels, *Mr. 3000* (2004), *Charlie's Angels: Full Throttle* (2003), *Guess Who?* (2005), *Pride* (2007), and the *Transformers* (2007), before he succumbed to complications of pneumonia in 2008.

Cedric the Entertainer's vocal talents were featured in *Dr. Dolittle 2* (2001), *The Proud Family* (2001–2005), *Ice Age* (2002), *Madagascar* (2005), and *Charlotte's Web* (2006). Some of his other popular movies include *Barbershop* (2002), *Be Cool* (2005), *Talk to Me* (2007), *Street Kings* (2008), and *Cadillac Records* (2008).

D. L. Hughley returned to television during the 2006–2007 season, starring in the critically acclaimed but short-lived series *Studio 60*. He was also executive producer and star of his 2007 HBO comedy special *D. L. Hughley: Unapologetic*. Because of his candid commentary and interest in politics, Hughley was recruited in 2008 to host a self-titled CNN comedy news show, *D. L. Hughley Breaks the News*. Hughley purported that "This ain't your daddy's CNN," and his edgy take on news was often considered controversial. Shortly after he compared the Republican National Committee (RNC) to Nazi Germany, the show was cancelled, but CNN retained his services as a contributing correspondent.

Dave Chappelle developed his satirically aggressive style doing street comedy in New York City, a skill he honed in the 1990s as a regular on *Russell Simmons' Def Comedy Jam*. In 1998, he cowrote his first film, *Half-Baked* (1998), a cult classic that gave him a loyal fan base. He also appeared in such films as the *Nutty Professor* (1996), *You've Got Mail* (1998), and *Undercover Brother* (2002). A successful HBO special, *Dave Chappelle: Killin' Them Softly* (2000), increased his popularity, and in 2003 Comedy Central offered Chappelle his own sketch-comedy show.

Chappelle's Show was an instant critical and commercial success, featuring a talented ensemble cast, progressive hip-hop artists, and Chappelle's biting social commentary on matters of race and American culture. The DVD of the show's first season sold more than three million copies. At the end of the second season, it was one of the highest-rated shows on basic cable, prompting Comedy Central to offer Chappelle $50 million to continue the show for two more seasons. At the height of his popularity and in the middle of taping the third season, Chappelle abruptly left the show. He cited stress and creative differences with the show's executives as the reason. In 2005, a documentary titled *Dave Chappelle's Block Party* captured Chappelle, in rare form, hosting a star-studded free concert in Brooklyn.

Chappelle now lives an unassuming life with his wife and two kids on his farm in Ohio, but he comes out of his self-imposed hiatus for special events and impromptu performances. He and comedian Dane Cook have been jockeying for the stand-up endurance record at the famous Laugh Factory comedy club in Los Angeles. In 2007, Chappelle bested Cook and his own record with a performance time of six hours and twelve minutes. Cook recaptured the record with a seven-hour routine in 2008.

And though the audience hoped for comeback in 2009, Chappelle left Cook's record intact, taking a bow after five hours onstage. Chappelle returned to television in 2008 to host the 200th episode of *Inside the Actors Studio* and did a humorous interview with James Lipton, the show's host.

Wanda Sykes has integrated the old "boys club" of comedy. *Yeah, I Said It* (2004) is the title of her book of humorous essays and reflects the decided tone of Sykes's razor-edged wit. In 1995, she opened for Chris Rock at Caroline's Comedy Club in New York, and that fortuitous opportunity launched a fifteen-year career as a writer and performer of sketch comedy. Sykes has won Emmys for her work on *The Chris Rock Show* and *Inside the NFL*. She has been featured on the *Drew Carey Show*, *Curb Your Enthusiasm*, and *The New Adventures of Old Christine*. Although much of her career is grounded in television, Sykes remains a notable stand-up comedienne. She is ranked seventieth on the Comedy Central's 100 Greatest Stand-ups of All Time and is the only African American woman on the list. In 2009, she became the first African American woman to be featured at the White House Correspondents' Association dinner. Her controversial quips caused a stir and paved the way for another groundbreaking career development. *The Wanda Sykes Show*, which premiered in late 2009, is the first late-night talk show helmed by an African American woman.

AFRICAN AMERICAN DANCE INTO THE TWENTY-FIRST CENTURY

Black dance, like other forms of black entertainment, had its beginnings in Africa and on the plantations of early America, where the enslaved performed to entertain themselves and their owners. White minstrels in blackface incorporated many of these black dance inventions into their shows, while dancers in black minstrelsy, like "Master Juba" (William Henry Lane), thrilled audiences with their artistry.

Many performers in the early black musicals that appeared on Broadway from 1898 through 1910 were expert show dancers, such as George Walker and Bert Williams. Similarly, in the all-black musicals of the 1920s, performers such as Florence Mills and Bill "Bojangles" Robinson captivated audiences with their show dancing. The musical *Runnin' Wild* (1926) was responsible for creating the Charleston dance craze of the Roaring Twenties.

By the early 1930s, African American pioneers of modern dance were appearing on the dance stage. Four of these innovators were Hemsley Winfield, Asadata Dafora, Katherine Dunham, and Pearl Primus. Hemsley Winfield presented what was billed as "The First Negro Concert in America" in Manhattan's Chanin Building on April 31, 1931. Two suites on African themes were performed, along with solos by Edna Guy and Winfield himself. In 1933, Winfield became the first African American to dance for the Metropolitan Opera, performing the role of the Witch Doctor in *The Emperor Jones*.

Austin Asadata Dafora Horton, a native of Sierra Leone, electrified audiences in New York with his 1934 production of *Kykunkor*. Dance historian Lynne Fauley Emery concluded that *Kykunkor* "was the first performance by black dancers on the concert stage which was entirely successful. It revealed the potential of ethnic material to black dancers, and herein lay Dafora's value as a great influence on black concert dance" (*Black Dance from 1619 to Today*, 1988).

Katherine Dunham had her first lead dance role in Ruth Page's West Indian ballet *La Guiablesse* in 1933. In 1936, Dunham received a master's degree in anthropology from the University of Chicago. Her thesis, "The Dances of Haiti," was the result of her onsite study of native dances in the West Indies. For the next thirty years, Dunham and her dance company toured the United States and Europe, dazzling audiences with her choreography. During the 1963–1964 season, Dunham choreographed the Metropolitan Opera's production of *Aida*, becoming the first African American to do so.

Pearl Primus, like Katherine Dunham, was trained in anthropology. Her research in primitive African dance inspired her first professional composition, *African Ceremonial*, presented on February 14, 1943. Primus made her Broadway debut on October 4, 1944, at the Belasco Theatre. Her performance included dances of West Indian, African, and African American origin. The concert was widely acclaimed, and launched her career as a dancer. Primus traveled to Africa many times to research African dances. In 1959, she was named director of Liberia's Performing Arts Center. She later opened the Primus-Borde School of Primal Dance with her husband, dancer Percival Borde, and the Pearl Primus Dance Language Institute in New Rochelle, New York. In 1991, President George H. W. Bush honored Primus with the National Medal of Arts. She died October 29, 1994, at age seventy-three.

By the late 1950s, several African American dancers and dance companies were distinguishing themselves on the concert stage. Janet Collins was the "premiere danseuse" of the Metropolitan Opera Ballet from 1951 until 1954. Arthur Mitchell made his debut as a principal dancer with the New York City Ballet in 1955. Alvin Ailey established his company in 1958. In addition, Geoffrey Holder, who made his Broadway debut in 1954 in *House of Flowers*, became a leading choreographer.

Janet Collins, Ballet Dancer,* Out of This World, *c. 1950. *Collins, the first African American woman to dance for the Metropolitan Opera, made her debut in* Aida *in 1951. Here she dances in the Cole Porter musical on Broadway.* CONDÉ NAST ARCHIVE/CORBIS

Since the early 1960s, two of the leading dance companies in the United States have been headed by African American males and composed largely of African American dancers. They are the Alvin Ailey American Dance Theater and the Dance Theatre of Harlem. In the 1970s, several prominent African American women dancers established schools and trained young dancers in regional companies throughout the United States.

THE ALVIN AILEY AMERICAN DANCE THEATER

The Alvin Ailey American Dance Theater (AAADT), since its founding in 1958, has performed before more people throughout the world than any other American dance company. With a touring circuit that has included forty-eight states and sixty-eight countries on six continents, the AAADT has been seen by more than twenty-one million people. Today, the Alvin Ailey Dance Foundation (AADF) is the umbrella organization for the Alvin Ailey American Dance Theater, Ailey II, the Ailey School, Ailey Arts in Education & Communication Programs, and the Ailey Extension.

Between 1958 and 1988, AAADT performed 150 works by forty-five choreographers, most of whom were African American. Notable among these African American choreographers have been Tally Beatty, Donald McKayle, Louis Johnson, Eleo Romare, Billy Wilson, George Faison, Pearl Primus, Judith Jamison, Katherine Dunham, Ulysses Dove, Milton Myers, Kelvin Rotardier, Geoffrey Holder, and Gary DeLoatch. More than 250 dancers, again mostly African American, have performed with the AAADT. Among its star performers have been Judith Jamison, Clive Thompson, Dudley Williams, Donna Wood, Gary DeLoatch, George Faison, and Sara Yarborough. A prolific choreographer, Alvin Ailey created numerous works for his dance theater and other dance companies, including *Revelations* (1958), *Reflections in D* (1962), *Quintet* (1968), *Cry* (1971), *Memoria* (1974), and *Three Black Kings* (1976). Alvin Ailey choreographed *Carmen* for the Metropolitan Opera in 1973 and *Precipice* for the Paris Opera in 1983.

Alvin Ailey died in December of 1989. After his death, Judith Jamison took over as artistic director and expanded Ailey's concept of cultural community exponentially. The Ailey Arts in Education & Community Programs and the Ailey Extension provide opportunities for dance performances, training, and community programs for all people.

The Ailey School is the official school of the Ailey organization. It attracts students from across the United States and abroad and offers a certificate in dance. The center's curriculum includes training in ballet, the Dunham technique, jazz, and modern dance. It has an affiliation with Fordham University and offers a bachelor in fine arts to eligible dance students. The Ailey School graduated its first class in 2002.

Ailey II was established in 1974 as a training and performing company. Many of its graduates advance to AAADT or perform with other dance companies.

AAADT celebrated its fortieth year in December 1998 by presenting the works of many choreographers, including artistic director Judith Jamison. Long-time Ailey choreographer Geoffrey Holder redesigned and restaged his lavish 1967 production of *The Prodigal Prince*, the story of a Haitian folk artist and voodoo priest who painted with a feather, for the anniversary celebration.

Judith Jamison carried the Olympic torch prior to the 2002 Winter Olympics in Salt Lake City, and AAADT performed at the Olympic Arts Festival. In that same year, President George W. Bush awarded the National Medal of the Arts to both Jamison and the Alvin Ailey Dance Foundation. It is the first time in history that a dance organization has received such an honor.

AAADT has been a trailblazing leader among dance companies worldwide for over fifty years now. Judith

Alvin Ailey American Dance Theater,* Revelations, *Detroit Opera House, 2009. *Alvin Ailey's* Revelations, *first produced in New York in 1960, continues to be performed by the Alvin Ailey American Dance Theater and other dance companies.* **AP PHOTO/GARY MALERBA**

Jamison has been at the helm for twenty of those years, and in the 2009–2010 season the company celebrated her contributions as a dancer, choreographer, and artistic director.

THE DANCE THEATRE OF HARLEM

In 1969, Arthur Mitchell, who had established himself as one of the leading ballet dancers in the United States, and Karel Shook, a white ballet teacher, founded the Dance Theatre of Harlem (DTH). It was established after Martin Luther King Jr.'s death to provide the arts of dance and theater to young people in Harlem. DTH made its formal debut in 1971 at the Guggenheim Museum in New York City. Three of Mitchell's works were premiered at this concert: *Rhythmetron*, *Tones*, and *Fete Noire*.

Their repertory was wide-ranging. It included works in the George Balanchine tradition, such as *Serenade*, as well as culturally inspired works, such as Geoffrey Holder's *Dougla*. Among the most spectacular works performed by the theater are *Firebird*, *Creole Giselle*, *Scheherazade*, and *Swan Lake*. Some of the dancers who have had long associations with DTH are Lowell Smith, Virginia Johnson, Shelia Rohan, and Troy Game. Many of the theater's graduates have later performed with other dance companies in the United States and Europe.

In 2004, DTH celebrated its thirty-fifth anniversary with an extensive tour of the United States and the United Kingdom. Ironically, that same year, the theater ran into severe financial straits and the Repertory Company has been forced into a hiatus. The DTH School, however, remains open for training and community outreach. Their Dancing Through Barriers ensemble, comprised of students and renowned and emerging guest artists, performs for the public every second Sunday of the month in the Open House Series.

After forty years of leading the company, Arthur Mitchell became the artistic director emeritus in 2009. Virginia Johnson, one of DTH's most renowned principal dancers and the founding editor of *Pointe* magazine, became the artistic director of DTH. One of Mitchell's and Johnson's primary goals is to restore the professional company to touring status.

BLACK REGIONAL DANCE SCHOOLS

While Ailey and Mitchell built their companies in New York, African American women, such as Joan Myers Brown, Ann Williams, Cleo Parker Robinson, Lula Washington, and Jeraldyne Blunden, established young, mostly African American dance companies in other major

Firebird, *Dance Theatre of Harlem.* *The Dance Theatre of Harlem (DTH) was founded by Arthur Mitchell and Karel Shook in 1969 to provide opportunities in the arts of dance and theater to young people in Harlem. Although the ballet troupe was disbanded in 2004, the school continues its mission to train dancers.* © JACK VARTOOGIAN/FRONTROWPHOTOS

American cities. Robinson founded her Cleo Parker Robinson Dance Ensemble in 1970 in her native city, Denver. That same year, Blunden created her company in Dayton, Ohio, and Brown opened her school in Philadelphia. In 1976, Williams founded the Dallas Black Dance Theatre, and in 1980 Washington created a troupe in Los Angeles that is now known as the Lula Washington Dance Theatre.

Each institution began as a school with deep roots in African American urban communities. They all started on a shoestring with a few eager young dancers. Their focus was on the discipline of dance and the values of integrity and intelligence. Today, these troupes are nationally known for the high quality of their dancing and for repertories that include modern dance classics, some by African American choreographers. These five women have developed a cooperative network through which they exchange ideas and dancers. Collectively, they have trained thousands of dancers, some of whom have gone on to major companies. In 1997, they were honored with a daylong tribute titled "Dance Women: Living Legends," in which all five companies performed and celebrated the efforts of these tenacious women in the pursuit of dance.

Since the 1960s, many African American dancers have led distinguished careers in concert dance and show dancing. Among them have been Eleo Pomare, Debbie Allen, Rod Rogers, Fred Benjamin, Pepsi Bethel, Eleanor Hampton, Charles Moore, Carmen de Lavallade, Mary Hinkson, and Desmond Richardson. Foremost among African American choreographers have been Geoffrey Holder, Talley Beatty, Louis Johnson, Donald McKayle, Bebe Miller, George Faison, Dianne McIntyre, Michael Peters, Otis Sallid, Dwight Rhoden, Garth Fagan, Donald Byrd, and Bill T. Jones.

Debbie Allen founded the Debbie Allen Dance Academy (DADA) in 2001 in Los Angeles because she saw a lack of quality in the arts education programs available to children. Each year, DADA enrolls close to four hundred children between the ages of five and eighteen in three programs based on age and ability—the Early Bird Academy, the Pre-Academy, and the Academy. The school focuses on artistic and academic achievement. DADA students must maintain a 3.0 average while undergoing a rigorous dance curriculum. Students in the Academy are required to take a minimum of twelve classes a week in ballet, African, modern, flamenco, character, tap, jazz, hip-hop, salsa, and Dunham technique, with optional classes in aerial training, voice, and acting. DADA's mission is to train young people how to sustain professional careers in dance, musical theater, film, and television.

In 2009, Brooklyn Academy of Music's 651 Arts paid special tribute to five female luminaries of modern dance. *FLY: Five First Ladies of Dance* featured solo performances by Bebe Miller, Dianne McIntyre, Jawole Willa Jo Zollar, Germaine Acogny, and Carmen de Lavallade.

Three notable small companies that have twenty-five years or more of innovative dance history are the Bill T. Jones/Arnie Zane Dance Company, Forces of Nature Dance Theatre, and Evidence, A Dance Company.

Bill T. Jones founded his multiracial, multicultural company in 1982 with his partner Arnie Zane. The ten-member company has a distinctive repertoire that incorporates music- and text-driven work. Collaborations with artists such as Max Roach, Keith Haring, the Orion String Quartet, Cassandra Wilson, and Fado allow the Bill T. Jones/Arnie Zane Dance Company to push dance vernacular to the edge. *Last Supper at Uncle Tom's Cabin/The Promised Land*, *Still/Here*, *We Set Out Early, Visibility Was Poor*, and *Fondly Do We Hope ... Fervently Do We Pray* are some of the award-winning, evening-length works Jones is known for. As a choreographer, Jones branched out to the Broadway stage in 2006 with

Spring Awakening. As a director, he made his Broadway debut in 2009 with *FELA!*, a tribute to Nigerian activist and Afrobeat originator Fela Anikulapo Kuti.

Choreographer Abdel Salaam and executive director Dele Husbands founded Forces of Nature Dance Theatre in 1981 to synthesize the traditions of the African diaspora and American culture into dance. With the use of live and recorded music, the theater's repertoire blends mythology and ritual with modern, West African, ballet, and contemporary house dance forms, forging a new vocabulary of movement. *The Legend of Marie Laveau*, *Ancestral Earths*, *Passionfruit*, and *From the Mud Below* are some of Salaam's most celebrated creations. The 2009–2010 touring season featured two new evening-length performances, *Eclipse: Visions of the Crescent and Cross* and *Rhythm Legacy*.

Ronald K. Brown founded Evidence in 1985 to tell stories of human triumph and tragedy through dance. By melding traditional African rhythms and forms with contemporary choreography and spoken word, Brown seeks to "reinforce the importance of community in African American culture." Brown's choreography is in demand and has been featured by the Alvin Ailey American Dance Theater and the Cleo Parker Robinson Ensemble. Brown also choreographed the award-winning musical *Crowns*. His most notable creations include *Dirt Road*, *Grace*, *One Shot: Rhapsody in Black and White*, *Two-Year Old Gentleman*, and *Dancing Spirit*, a tribute to Judith Jamison. In 2010, Evidence was scheduled to tour Senegal, Nigeria, and South Africa in the inaugural DanceMotion USA project, funded by the U.S. State Department and produced by the Brooklyn Academy of Music.

Choreographers to watch in the coming decade are Gesel Mason of Mason/Rhynes Productions, Camille Brown of Camille A. Brown and Dancers, Jamel Gaines of Creative Outlet Dance Theatre, Obediah Wright of Balance Dance Theatre, and Assante Konte of the KanKouran West African Dance Company.

Prominent among the African American dancers who revived the tap dance tradition are Cholly Atkins, Buster Brown, Honi Coles, Hinton Battle, Gregory Hines, LaVaughn Robinson, Nita Feldman, Ted Levy, and Savion Glover. Glover came to prominence in the 1995 Broadway production of *Bring in 'da Noise, Bring in 'da Funk*.

STAGE ACTORS, DIRECTORS, COMEDIANS, CHOREOGRAPHERS, AND DANCERS

(Some biographical profiles may appear in other chapters. To locate profiles more readily, please consult the index.)

ALVIN AILEY (1931–1989)

Dancer, Choreographer. Alvin Ailey was born in Rogers, Texas, on January 5, 1931. He was the founder of the Alvin Ailey American Dance Theater and won international fame as both a dancer and a choreographer. Ailey studied dancing after graduating from high school, where he was a star athlete. After briefly attending college, Ailey joined the stage crew of the Lester Horton Theater in Los Angeles, for which Ailey eventually performed as a dancer. In 1953, after Horton's death, Ailey became the company choreographer. In 1954, Ailey performed on Broadway as the lead dancer in *House of Flowers*.

Ailey formed his own dance group in 1958 and began giving four performances annually. In 1962, the Ailey troupe made an official State Department tour of Australia, receiving accolades throughout the country. One critic called Ailey's work "the most stark and devastating theater ever presented in Australia." After numerous appearances as a featured dancer with Harry Belafonte and others, Ailey performed in a straight dramatic role with Claudia McNeil in Broadway's *Tiger, Tiger Burning Bright*. Other Broadway appearances included roles in *Ding Dong Bell*, *Dark of the Moon*, and *African Holiday*. Ailey also choreographed or staged several operas, including Samuel Barber's *Anthony and Cleopatra*, Leonard Bernstein's *Mass*, and Georges Bizet's *Carmen*. In addition, Ailey created works for various international ballet stars and companies.

In 1965, Ailey took his group on one of the most successful European tours ever made by an American dance company. In London, the show was held over for six weeks to accommodate the demand for tickets, and in Hamburg it received an unprecedented sixty-one curtain calls. A German critic called the performance "a triumph of sweeping, violent beauty, a furious spectacle. The stage vibrates. One has never seen anything like it." In 1970, Ailey's company became the first American modern dance group to tour the Soviet Union.

During the mid-1970s, Ailey, among his other professional commitments, devoted much time to creating special jazz dance sequences for America's bicentennial celebration. Among numerous honors, including several honorary degrees, Ailey was awarded the NAACP's Spingarn Medal in 1976. Ailey died on December 1, 1989.

IRA ALDRIDGE (1807–1867)

Actor. Born on July 24, 1807, in New York City, Ira Aldridge was one of the leading Shakespearean actors of the nineteenth century. Although he was denied the opportunity to perform before the American public in his prime, the fame that he won abroad established him as one of the prominent figures of international theater.

Aldridge's early dramatic training centered around the African Grove Theatre in New York in 1821. His first role was in *Pizarro*, and he subsequently played a variety of small roles in classical productions before accepting employment as a steward on a ship bound for England. After studying briefly at the University of Glasgow in Scotland, Aldridge went to London in 1825 and appeared in the melodrama *Surinam, or a Slave's Revenge*. In 1833, he appeared in London's Theatre Royal in the title role of *Othello*, earning wide acclaim. For the next three decades, he toured the continent with great success, often appearing before European royalty.

Aldridge died in Lodz, Poland, on August 7, 1867. He is honored by a commemorative tablet in the New Memorial Theatre in Stratford-upon-Avon in England. Howard University's main stage theater is named after him.

DEBBIE ALLEN (1950–)

Actress, Singer, Dancer, Director. Debbie Allen was born on January 16, 1950, in Houston, Texas. She began studying dance when she was three years old, and later trained with the Ballet Nacional de Mexico, the Houston Ballet, and the National Ballet School. A cum laude graduate of Howard University, she became head of the Dance Department at the Duke Ellington School of the Arts in Washington, D.C.

Allen began her career on the Broadway stage in the chorus line of the hit musical *Purlie* (1972). She then portrayed Beneatha in the Tony and Grammy award-winning musical *Raisin* (1973). Other early stage roles were in the national touring company of *Guys and Dolls* and in *Anna Lucasta*, performed for the New Federal Theatre at the Henry Street Settlement in New York.

Allen was selected in 1977 to star in an NBC pilot, *3 Girls 3*. She later appeared on other television shows, including *Good Times* and *The Love Boat*. Other roles included the television special *Ben Vereen: His Roots* (1978) and the miniseries *Roots: The Next Generation* (1979).

Allen returned to the stage in *Ain't Misbehavin'* (1979) and a revival of *West Side Story* (1980), which earned her a Tony Award nomination and a Drama Desk Award. Her talent as a choreographer garnered work on such television shows as *Midnight Special*, as well as two films, *The Fish that Saved Pittsburgh* (1979) and *Under Fire* (1981). It was the role of Lydia Grant that gave her the first real brush with *Fame* (1980), a franchise that would define much of her career. In the 2009 remake of the film, she played the school principal, Angela Simms.

The year 1982 was pivotal for Allen. She appeared in the film *Ragtime*, as well as the Joseph Papp television special *Alice at the Palace*. She also starred in a dance performance for the Academy Awards ceremonies, and her work on the television series *Fame* won her an Emmy Award for best choreography.

As each season passed on *Fame*, Allen became more involved as choreographer and was soon regularly directing episodes of the series. Her work over the five-year run of the series garnered another Emmy for choreography and a Golden Globe for acting. In 1988, she was selected by the producers to become director of the television sitcom *A Different World*.

Because of her versatility as a performer and creative talent, Allen has been afforded many opportunities to act, dance, choreograph, direct, and produce. She starred in her own television special in 1989 and choreographed the Academy Awards ceremony five times. In 1991, she won her third Emmy for outstanding choreography for *Motown 30: What's Going On*. She appeared with LL Cool J in the television show *In the House* (1995) and starred in *Michael Jordan: An American Hero* (1999). She also appeared in *The Old Settler* (2001) and *The Painting* (2002), both *PBS Hollywood Presents* productions, which she executive produced.

In 1998, Allen coproduced the historical film *Amistad*, with Steven Spielberg directing, and she also produced the musical *Brothers of the Knight* for the Kennedy Center. She published a book version of the play in 2000.

Allen has been a recurring director on popular sitcoms, such as *All of Us*, *That's So Raven*, *Girlfriends*, and *Everybody Hates Chris*. She also directed the inspirational *Life Is Not a Fairytale: The Fantasia Barrino Story*. The biographical drama, about the 2004 *American Idol* winner who triumphed over an abusive childhood, aired on Lifetime in 2007.

Allen made a move to engage community youth in 2001 when she opened the Debbie Allen Dance Academy in Los Angeles. The academy offers lessons in ballet, modern dance, jazz dance, salsa, hip-hop, flamenco, tap, Dunham technique, and African dance. The school also offers "Pre-Academy" and "Early Bird" preparatory programs. In 2006, the academy premiered *Bayou Legend*, a musical adaptation of Ibsen's *Peer Gynt*, conceived by Owen Dodson and realized by Debbie Allen, James Ingram, and Jeff Stetson.

In 2008, Allen directed a Broadway revival of Tennessee William's *Cat on a Hot Tin Roof*. The all-black cast featured James Earl Jones, Phylicia Rashad, Terrence Howard, Giancarlo Esposito, and Anika Noni Rose.

EDDIE "ROCHESTER" ANDERSON (1905–1977)

Comedian. For many years, Eddie Anderson was the only African American performing regularly on a network radio show. As the character Rochester on the Jack Benny program, he became one of the best-known African American entertainers.

Anderson was born in Oakland, California, on September 18, 1905. He was the son of "Big Ed" Anderson, a minstrel performer, and Ella Mae, a tightwire walker. During the 1920s and early 1930s, Anderson traveled throughout the country singing, dancing, and performing as a clown in small clubs. On Easter Sunday 1937, he was featured on Jack Benny's radio show in what was supposed to be a single appearance; Anderson was such a hit that he quickly became a regular on the program.

Anderson is best known for his work with Benny, in television as well as on radio, but he also appeared in a number of movies, including *What Price Hollywood?* (1932), *Cabin in the Sky* (1943), and *It's a Mad, Mad, Mad, Mad World* (1963). Anderson died on February 28, 1977, at age seventy-one.

PEARL BAILEY (1918–1990)

Singer, Actress. Born on March 29, 1918, in Newport News, Virginia, Pearl Bailey moved to Philadelphia with her family in 1933. She sang at small clubs in Scranton, Pennsylvania, and in Washington, D.C., before becoming the vocalist for the band of Cootie Williams and later for Count Basie. In the early 1940s, Bailey had her first successful New York engagements at the Village Vanguard and the Blue Angel. During World War II, she toured with the USO. Bailey made her New York stage debut in 1946 in *St. Louis Woman*, for which she won a Donaldson Award as the year's most promising

Singer and Actress Pearl Bailey,* Carmen Jones *(1954). Bailey made her film debut in* Isn't It Romantic? *(1948). In addition to film roles, she went on to a career that included working as a recording artist, nightclub headliner, and author. BETTMANN/CORBIS

new performer. She also appeared in the films *Variety Girl* (1947) and *Isn't It Romantic?* (1948).

In the 1950s, Bailey appeared in the movies *Carmen Jones, That Certain Feeling,* and *Porgy and Bess.* On Broadway, she was in *House of Flowers.* A versatile performer, Bailey worked as a recording artist, nightclub headliner, and actress. In 1967, she received a special Tony Award for her starring role on Broadway in *Hello, Dolly!* In 1969, she published an autobiography, *The Raw Pearl.* Her other books include *Talking to Myself* (1971), *Pearl's Kitchen* (1973), *Duey's Tale* (1975), and *Hurry Up, America, and Spit* (1976).

In 1975, Bailey was named a special adviser to the U.S. Mission to the United Nations. In 1976, she appeared in the film *Norman, Is That You?* with Redd Foxx, and on stage in Washington, D.C., in *Something to Do,* a musical saluting the American worker. She also received an award in 1976 from the Screen Actors Guild for outstanding achievement in fostering the finest ideals of the acting profession. Georgetown University made her an honorary doctor of humane letters in 1977.

In January 1980, Bailey gave a one-night concert at Radio City Music Hall in New York. In 1981, she performed as the voice of the cartoon character "Owl" in the Disney movie *The Fox and the Hound.*

Bailey married the jazz drummer Louis Bellson in 1952. She died on August 17, 1990, in Philadelphia.

JOSEPHINE BAKER (1906–1975)

Dancer, Singer. Born in St. Louis on June 3, 1906, Josephine Baker received little formal education. She left school at eight years old to supplement the family income by working as a kitchen helper and babysitter. While still in elementary school, she took a part-time job as a chorus girl. When she was seventeen, she performed as a chorus girl in Noble Sissle's musical comedy *Shuffle Along,* which played at Radio City Music Hall in 1923. Her next show was *Chocolate Dandies,* followed by a major dancing part in *La Revue Nègre,* an American production that introduced *le jazz hot* to Paris in 1925.

In Paris, Baker left the show to create her most sensational role, that of the "Dark Star" of the Folies Bergère. In her act, she appeared topless on a mirror, clad only in a protective waist shield of rubber bananas. The spectacular dance made her an overnight star and a public figure with a loyal following. In true "star" tradition, she catered to her fans by adopting such flamboyant eccentricities as walking pet leopards down the Champs-Élysées.

In 1930, after completing a world tour, Baker made her debut as a singing and dancing comedienne at the Casino de Paris. Critics called her a "complete artist, the perfect master of her tools." In time, she ventured into films, starring alongside French idol Jean Gabin in *Zouzou* (1934), and into light opera, performing in *La Creole* (1934), an operetta about a Jamaican girl.

During World War II, Baker served first as a Red Cross volunteer, and later did underground intelligence work through an Italian Embassy attaché. After the war, the French government decorated her with the Legion of Honor. She then returned to the entertainment world, regularly starring at the Folies Bergère, appearing on French television, and going on another extended international tour. In 1951, during a successful American tour, Baker made headlines by speaking out against discrimination and refusing to perform in segregated venues.

Beginning in 1954, Baker earned another reputation—not as a lavish and provocative entertainer, but as a progressive humanitarian. She used her fortune to begin adopting and tutoring a group of orphaned babies of all races and retired from the stage in 1956 to devote all her time to her "rainbow family." Within three years, however, her "experiment in brotherhood" had taken such a toll on her finances that she was forced to return to the stage, starring in *Paris, Mes Amours,* a musical based in part on her own fabled career.

Baker privately survived numerous financial crises. Illness hardly managed to dampen her indomitable spirit. Through her life, she retained her most noteworthy stage attributes—an intimate, subdued voice, coupled with an infectiously energetic and vivacious manner. Baker died in Paris on April 12, 1975, after opening a gala to celebrate her fiftieth year in show business.

JAMES HUBERT "EUBIE" BLAKE (1883–1983)

Musician, Composer. Eubie Blake was born in Baltimore on February 7, 1883. The son of formerly enslaved Africans, Blake was the last of ten children and the only one to survive beyond two months. His mother worked as a laundress, his father as a stevedore.

When he was six, Blake started taking piano lessons. He studied under the renowned teacher Margaret Marshall and subsequently learned musical composition from William Llewellyn Wilson, who at one time conducted an all-black symphony orchestra sponsored by the city of Baltimore. When he was seventeen, Blake was playing for a Baltimore nightclub.

In 1915, Blake collaborated with Noble Sissle. That year, Blake and Sissle sold their first song, "It's All Your Fault," to Sophie Tucker, and her introduction of the song started them on their way. Blake and Sissle moved to New York. In 1921, they teamed with Flournoy Miller and Aubrey Lyles to create one of the pioneering black musicals,

Shuffle Along. The show was produced again on Broadway in 1952. *Chocolate Dandies* and *Elsie* followed in 1924.

During the early 1930s, Blake collaborated with Andy Razaf and wrote the musical score for Lew Leslie's *Blackbirds.* Out of this association came the hit "Memories of You." During World War II, Blake was appointed musical conductor for the USO Hospital Unit. In 1946, he announced his retirement and enrolled in New York University.

For many years, Blake's most-requested song was "Charleston Rag," which he composed in 1899 and which was written down by someone else because Blake could not then read music. Among his most famous songs were "How Ya' Gonna Keep 'Em Down on the Farm," "Love Will Find a Way," and "You're Lucky to Me." Some of his other works include "I'm Just Wild About Harry," "Serenade Blues," "It's All Your Fault," and "Floradora Girls," with lyrics by Sissle.

Though known as a master of ragtime, Blake loved the music of the classical masters most. In the intimacy of his Brooklyn studio, Blake rarely played the music for which the world reveres him. In 1978, Blake's life and career were celebrated in the Broadway musical *Eubie!* Several thousand people attended concerts at the Shubert Theatre and St. Peters Lutheran Church celebrating Blake's one-hundredth birthday on February 8, 1983. Blake also received honorary doctorates from numerous colleges and universities. He died on February 12, 1983.

JOHN BUBBLES (1902–1986)

Dancer, Singer. John Bubbles was born John William Sublett on February 19, 1902, in Louisville, Kentucky. When he was seven, he teamed with a fellow bowling-alley pinboy, Ford "Buck" Washington, to form what became one of the top vaudeville acts in show business. Masters of rhythm tap dancing, Buck and Bubbles played the top theaters in the country at fees of up to $1,750 a week throughout the 1920s and 1930s. The two appeared in several films. including *Cabin in the Sky* (1943). Bubbles captured additional fame as Sportin' Life in the 1935 version of *Porgy and Bess.* After Buck's death in 1955, Bubbles virtually disappeared from show business until 1964, when he teamed up with Anna Maria Alberghetti in a successful nightclub act.

In 1979, when he was seventy-seven years old and partially crippled from an earlier stroke, Bubbles recreated his characterization of Sportin' Life for a one-night show titled *Black Broadway* at New York's Lincoln Center. The show was repeated in 1980 for a limited engagement at the Town Hall in New York. In the fall of 1980, Bubbles received a Lifetime Achievement Award from the American Guild of Variety Artists and a Certificate of Appreciation from the City of New York. Bubbles died on May 18, 1986, at age eighty-four.

ED BULLINS

See chapter 18, Literature.

ANITA BUSH (1883–1974)

Actress, Singer. Born in 1883, Anita Bush was involved with the theater from early childhood. Her father was the tailor for the Bijou, a large neighborhood theater in Brooklyn. Anita would carry the costumes to the theater for him, giving her a backstage view of performers and productions. Her singing and acting career took off in the early 1920s, when she was in the chorus of the Williams and Walker Company. With Williams and Walker, she performed in such Broadway hits as *Abyssinia* and *In Dahomey*, which also had a successful European tour. When the group split up in 1909, Bush formed the Anita Bush Stock Company, which included her own show of chorus girls and such greats as Charles Gilpin and Dooley Wilson, with whom she also founded the Lafayette Players. Bush died on February 16, 1974.

DONALD BYRD (1949–)

Choreographer. Donald Byrd, one of the most important choreographers in modern dance, has created his own unique style of dance based on the influences of several great predecessors. From the styles and movements of Alvin Ailey, the classic ballet of George Balanchine, and the innovative creations of Twyla Tharp, Byrd has established his own distinct contributions to dance.

Byrd was born on July 21, 1949, in New London, North Carolina, and raised in Clearwater, Florida. He was trained in classical flute and was active in school theatrics and the debate team. When he was sixteen, two dancers from Balanchine's New York City Ballet, Edward Villella and Patricia McBride, conducted a lecture-demonstration in Clearwater, which left a lasting impression on Byrd. An excellent student, Byrd received a scholarship for minority students to Yale University. He majored in philosophy, but his exposure to the Yale theater groups led him to consider being an actor. The racist attitudes of his classmates at Yale discouraged him, so he transferred to Tufts University in Boston.

Through his friend at Tufts, William Hurt, Byrd learned about the Alvin Ailey American Dance Theater. At a performance of Alvin Ailey's signature work *Revelations*, Byrd felt the theatrical power of dance. Inspired, he began taking dance classes at Tufts and eventually went to New York in the early 1970s to study with a variety of dance teachers, such as Tharp, and companies, including the Ailey School and the Gus Solomons Jr. company in 1976. When Solomons was named dean of the dance program at the California Institute of the Arts, he took Byrd along to teach.

While in California, Byrd began receiving acclaim for his choreography. By 1977, he was producing shows of his own work on the West Coast, as well as at the Dance Theater Workshop back in New York. Byrd founded his own company, Donald Byrd/The Group, in 1978. His style was now a unique blend of classical ballet, modern dance, and urban street dancing. Despite his company's success, Byrd struggled for several years with alcohol and drug dependency. After a scathing review by a supporter of his work in 1985, Byrd entered treatment and soon returned to his career.

In 1987, Byrd choreographed a new piece for the Ailey Repertory Company. The work, *Crumble*, was well received and from then on he continued to contribute works to the Ailey companies. Byrd staged his next piece, *Shards*, in 1988, with strong influences of Balanchine. In 1991, the Ailey Dance Theater debuted *Dance at the Gym*, a work about teen culture. Byrd's own troupe, Donald Byrd/The Group, presented *Prodigal* in 1990, a dance inspired by Balanchine's *Prodigal Son*. The next year they produced a controversial piece about racial stereotypes called *The Minstrel Show*. This show won a Bessie Award for Donald Byrd/The Group in 1992.

The 1990s were creative years for Donald Byrd. He and his company toured the United States and Europe in 1993 presenting a repertoire of works choreographed by Byrd, among them *Bristle*, a long work exploring tensions between the genders. For Christmas of 1994, Byrd developed *The Harlem Nutcracker*, an African American version of the classic *Nutcracker Suite*, using Duke Ellington–style big band arrangements of Pyotr Tchaikovsky's original music. Byrd's *The Beast* premiered in 1996 at the Brooklyn Academy of Music; the piece examines various types of domestic violence. By 1998, Byrd and his work were honored in a program of dances created by African American male choreographers called Young Choreographers Defining Dance.

In 2000, Byrd adapted another fairy tale spun to jazz music, *Sleeping Beauty*, where he played with the notions of what was beautiful and how people viewed beauty in dance. In June 2002, Byrd was forced to disband his company after twenty-four years for financial reasons; but by December of that same year, he had become the artistic director of the Spectrum Dance Theater in Seattle, where he has mounted new cutting-edge work, such as *Bhangra Fever*, *A Cruel New World*, and *Fado*.

Although Spectrum remains his home base, Byrd continues to choreograph numerous stage productions, including *The Color Purple*, for which he received a 2006 Tony nomination. In 2007, the Seattle Opera featured Byrd's choreography in their staging of Handel's baroque opera, *Julius Caesar*. In 2009, Byrd directed and choreographed *White Noise*, a musical inspired by the true-life story of Lynx and Lamb Gaede, twin lead singers of the white-separatist band Prussian Blue, at Le Petit Theatre du Vieux in New Orleans.

GODFREY CAMBRIDGE (1933–1976)

Actor, Comedian. Godfrey Cambridge was born in New York on February 26, 1933, to parents who had emigrated from British Guiana (now Guyana). He attended grammar school in Nova Scotia, while living with his grandparents. After finishing his schooling in New York at Flushing High School and Hofstra College, he studied acting.

Cambridge made his Broadway debut in *Nature's Way* (1956), and was featured in *Purlie Victorious*, both on stage in 1961 and later on screen. He also appeared off-Broadway in *Lost in the Stars* (1958), *Take a Giant Step*, and *The Detective Story* (1960). Cambridge won the Obie Award for the 1960–1961 season's most distinguished off-Broadway performance for his role in *The Blacks*. In 1965, he starred in a stock version of *A Funny Thing Happened on the Way to the Forum*.

As a comedian, Cambridge appeared on the *Tonight Show* and many other variety shows. His material, drawn from the contemporary racial situation, was often presented in the style associated with the contemporary wave of African American comedians. One of Cambridge's most memorable roles was as the star of a seriocomic Hollywood film, *The Watermelon Man* (1970), in which Cambridge played a white man who changes color overnight. Cambridge has also performed dramatic roles on many television series.

During the mid-1970s, Cambridge remained in semiretirement, making few public appearances. He died of a heart attack when he was forty-three years old in California on November 29, 1976. His death occurred on a Warner Brothers set, where he was playing the role of Ugandan dictator Idi Amin for the television film *Victory at Entebbe*.

DAVE CHAPPELLE (1973–)

Actor, Writer, Comedian. Dave Chappelle is one of the most controversial comedians of the twenty-first century, in part because of his aggressively satiric style of comedy but mostly because of his decision to leave the immensely popular *Chappelle's Show* after signing a $50 million contract with Comedy Central.

Chappelle was born on August 24, 1973, in Washington, D.C. His experiences growing up black in the capital city and the nearby suburb of Silver Springs, Maryland, became fodder for his stand-up comedy act. Chappelle's mother, a Unitarian minister, was supportive of her son's talent and accompanied him as a chaperone when he began performing stand-up comedy at age fourteen. His nerve and resilience were tested at the famous Apollo Theater in Harlem when Chappelle was booed off the stage during his stand-up comedy debut, an experience chronicled in the Apollo Theater Hall of Fame.

By the time he was a senior in high school at the Duke Ellington School of the Arts, Chappelle was periodically excused from school by the principal so that he could pursue his career "on the road." After graduation, Chappelle felt confident he could make a name for himself in the New York comedy scene, so he made a deal with his parents. Instead of college, he would go to New York and if he did not successfully launch a career in one year, he would enroll in school.

Comedian Dave Chappelle, 2006. *A controversial performer, Chappelle has an aggressively satiric style of comedy. He caused a media frenzy when he walked out on his aptly named Comedy Central program,* Chappelle's Show, *when it was filming its third season in 2005.* AP IMAGES/STEFANO PALTERA

Chappelle began building his reputation at the Boston Club in Greenwich Village. His irreverent diatribes on racism and racial division shocked the audience into laughter. Word quickly spread and within weeks he was working in clubs all around the New York City circuit. To bolster his courage and infuse his comedy with a "street-wise" edge, Chappelle also performed in the parks and sidewalks of the city.

In 1992, Chappelle won critical and popular acclaim for his television appearances on *Russell Simmons' Def Comedy Jam* on HBO. He became a regular guest on late-night television shows, such as *Politically Incorrect, The Late Show with David Letterman, The Howard Stern Show*, and *Late Night with Conan O'Brien*.

Chappelle's first film role was in *Robin Hood: Men in Tights* (1992), a comedy by Mel Brooks. He had several small character roles in other films, but it was his featured role as the nasty comic who picked on Eddie Murphy in *The Nutty Professor* (1996) that captured Hollywood's attention.

Chappelle cowrote his first film, *Half Baked* (1998), as a tribute to the drug-related slapstick comedies of Cheech Marin and Tommy Chong. Though *Half Baked* was a cult hit, Chappelle felt that the studio had weakened the film by trying to make it "more acceptable" to conservative audiences. This loss of control was an experience that would influence Chappelle's interactions with studio executives for years to come. As much as possible, he would always refuse to compromise his principles or his comedy.

After a very successful one-man show on HBO called *Dave Chappelle: Killin' Them Softly* (2000), Chappelle was offered a chance to do television on his own terms. In 2003, Comedy Central, a basic cable network, premiered *Chappelle's Show*, a half-hour program featuring Chappelle, a cast of regulars, and guest artists performing satirical sketch comedy. Even the musical guests reflected the show's hard-hitting social critique; most were hip-hop artists whose music contained pointed political messages and an appreciation of black culture.

Cable television proved to be a more suitable location for Chappelle's razor-sharp satire. The show garnered two Emmy nominations and a devoted following for Chappelle's brand of comedy. His first-season DVD sold over three million copies. At the end of the second successful season, Viacom, Comedy Central's parent company, offered Chappelle a $50 million contract for two more seasons. He accepted, but while taping the third season, Chappelle abruptly left the show for an extended stay in South Africa. In a 2006 interview with Oprah Winfrey, Chappelle deflected rumors that he was in drug or psychiatric therapy, citing an "incredibly stressful" work environment and creative content differences as the reasons for his break with Comedy Central.

Dave Chappelle's career is consistently marked by his refusal to compromise his work in order to make his comedy palatable for mainstream sensibilities. As a result, he has become especially popular with young audiences who appreciate his wry social commentary. In 2005, he produced *Dave Chappelle's Block Party*, a documentary where he hosted an outdoor party and reunion concert of the 1990s rap group the Fugees.

Barring a few impromptu comedy-club appearances, a segment on *Inside the Actor's Studio*, and a foreword in Paul Mooney's 2009 book *Black Is the New White*, Chappelle remained in a self-imposed hiatus as of 2010.

HOPE CLARKE (1943–)

Stage Director, Actress, Choreographer. From duets with Alvin Ailey to a complete revision of *Porgy and Bess*, Hope Clarke's career continues to expand the influences of African American culture in the American arts. Clarke was born in Washington, D.C., in 1943, and grew up in a segregated, close-knit African American community. Her talent and determination propelled her into a career in show business. In 1960, she won a part in the original touring company of Leonard Bernstein's *West Side Story*. From there, she became a principal dancer in two African American dance troupes: the Katherine Dunham Company and the Alvin Ailey American Dance Theater. Her duets with Ailey became legendary. Armed with talent and discipline, she left the company in the 1970s to pursue a new career in acting.

As an actress, Clarke's most notable feature film performance was in *A Piece of the Action* (1977), starring Bill Cosby and Sidney Poitier. Other film performances include *Basquiat* (1996) and *Men without Jobs* (2004). She also made television guest appearances on *The Jeffersons, Hill Street Blues, Three's Company, As the World Turns, New York Undercover*, and *Law & Order*.

Besides acting, Clarke has choreographed various stage and television shows. She worked for the New York City–based Opera Ebony, helping to produce *Porgy and Bess* in such unlikely venues as Brazil and Finland. She received a Tony nomination for best choreography for her work on the 1992 Broadway hit *Jelly's Last Jam*, written and directed by George C. Wolfe.

Clarke continued to stage projects as diverse as Dorothy Rudd Moore's *Freedom* and Mozart's *Così fan tutte*. She choreographed a production of *Frida* for the Houston Grand Opera, and in 1995 she became the first African American woman to direct and choreograph a major staging of the George Gershwin opera *Porgy and Bess*.

The Houston Grand Opera's 1995 production of *Porgy and Bess* was staged in celebration of the work's sixtieth anniversary. Clarke based the opera's setting around the Charleston-based Gullahs, an African

American group believed to be Angolan in origin. She infused the work with the cultural and linguistic integrity of this unique community. The production toured major American cities, including San Diego, Los Angeles, San Francisco, Houston, and Minneapolis. It also played engagements in Japan and at Italy's famed La Scala opera house in Milan.

In 1998, Clarke received a New York Dance and Performance Award, known as a Bessie, for her outstanding achievements as a performance professional. She later collaborated with George C. Wolfe on two more Broadway productions, the *Tempest* (1995) and the Tony-nominated musical *Caroline, or Change* (2004).

BILL COSBY

See chapter 20, Film and Television.

ANDRÉ DE SHIELDS (1946–)

Actor, Director, Choreographer. The ninth of eleven children born and reared in Baltimore, Maryland, Broadway veteran André De Shields began his professional career in a Chicago production of *Hair.* This controversial production led to a role in *The Me Nobody Knows* and membership in Chicago's Organic Theatre Company, where he created the role of Xander the Unconquerable in *Warp.*

Many doors opened for De Shields in the 1970s. He debuted on Broadway in *Warp* (1973); co-choreographed two Broadway shows for Bette Midler, the critically acclaimed *Bette Midler* (1973) and *Bette Midler's Clams on the Half Shell Revue* (1975); and starred in two Tony Award–winning musicals that made him a Broadway legend, *The Wiz* (1975), a remake of *The Wizard of Oz* with an all-black cast, and *Ain't Misbehavin'* (1978), a musical tribute to the legendary Fats Waller. In 1982, De Shields won an Emmy Award for his performance as Viper in the television special presentation of *Ain't Misbehavin'.*

De Shields's garnered his first Tony and Drama Desk Award nominations in 1997 for his featured role as Jester in *Play On!* In 2001, he received Tony, Drama Desk, and Astaire Award nominations and won an Outer Critics' Circle Award for his performance as Noah T. "Horse" Simmons in *The Full Monty,* a role he originated in London. Other Broadway credits include *Harlem Nocturne* (1984) and *Stardust* (1987).

On the concert stage, De Shields performed *Mood Ellington,* an original one-man tribute to the Duke, directed and choreographed by Mercedes Ellington. Other concert stage performances include the cabaret opera *Casino Paradise* and *Songs of Innocence & Experience* at Carnegie Hall and the Royal Festival Hall in London. He has also toured with the Chamber Music Society of Lincoln Center as the narrator for Wynton Marsalis's *A Fiddler's Tale.*

André De Shields, Actor, Director, and Choreographer, Apollo Theater, New York City, September 21, 2003. *In addition to his Broadway credits, De Shields has been a visiting professor at the City University of New York–Hunter College, New York University, University of Michigan, and Southern Methodist University.* RICHARD CORKERY/NEW YORK DAILY NEWS ARCHIVE/GETTY IMAGES

De Shields's directing credits include a restaging of *Play On!* at the Crossroads Theatre Company, featuring Leslie Uggams and Stephanie Mills. He has also directed at the Denver Center Theatre, the Cortland Repertory Theatre, the Victory Gardens Theatre, and La MaMa, E.T.C.

De Shields was featured in the films *Extreme Measures* (1996) with Hugh Grant and *Prison* (1988) directed by Renny Harlin. His television credits include guest appearances on *Sex and the City, Another World,* and *Law & Order,* as well as *I Dream of Jeannie: 15 Years Later* and two episodes of PBS's *Great Performances: Alice in Wonderland* and *Ellington: The Music Lives On.*

A dedicated educator, De Shields served as director of Carnegie Hall's Jazzed, an educational strategy for restoring the arts to the public schools. He was the Dr. Martin Luther King Jr./Rosa Parks/Cesar Chavez Visiting Professor at the University of Michigan, Ann Arbor, and in 2002 was an adjunct professor of Shakespeare at his graduate alma mater, New York University's Gallatin School of Individualized Study, where he received a Distinguished Alumni Award in 1992. The Alumni Association of his undergraduate institution, the University of Wisconsin–Madison, honored De Shields with the Distinguished Alumni and the Person of the Year awards in 2001 and an honorary doctor of fine arts in 2007.

De Shields returned to the Broadway stage in 2004 and won a Drama Desk Award playing a gorilla named Graham in the controversial play *Prymate.* He won an Obie in 2007 for sustained excellence of performance. In 2009, he had a featured role in *Impressionism,* a short-lived Broadway play starring Jeremy Irons and Joan Allen. De Shields is a resident actor with the Classical Theatre of Harlem, where he revitalized the title roles of *King Lear* in 2006 and *The Archbishop Supreme Tartuffe,* a reworking of Molière's classic, in 2009.

Katherine Dunham, Dancer and Choreographer. *Dunham, who had earned a bachelor's degree in social anthropology at the University of Chicago, used her training and her study of rituals to infuse ballet and modern dance techniques with traditional Caribbean and African rhythms, forging a vocabulary of dance known as the Dunham Technique.* GJON MILI/TIME AND LIFE PICTURES/GETTY IMAGES

KATHERINE DUNHAM (1909–2006)

Choreographer, Dancer. World-renowned as a dance pioneer, Katherine Dunham was the premier exponent of African and Caribbean dance in the world of modern choreography. Born in Chicago on June 22, 1909, Dunham attended Joliet Township Junior College and the University of Chicago, where she majored in anthropology. With funding from a Rosenwald Fellowship, she was able to conduct anthropological studies in the Caribbean and Brazil. She later attended Northwestern University, where she earned her Ph.D.

In the 1930s, she founded the Negro Dance Group, whose repertory drew on techniques Dunham learned while studying in the Caribbean. She used her training in anthropology and her study of rituals to infuse ballet and modern dance techniques with traditional Caribbean and African rhythms, forging a vocabulary of dance known as the *Dunham technique.*

In 1940, the Katherine Dunham Dance Company appeared in the stage musical *Cabin in the Sky,* which she choreographed with George Balanchine. Alone or with her company, Dunham was featured in such movies as *Carnival of Rhythm* (1939), *Star-Spangled Rhythm* (1942), *Stormy Weather* (1943), *Casbah* (1948), *Boote E Riposta* (1950), and *Mambo* (1954). Among Dunham's renowned choreographic pieces are *L'Ag'Ya* (1938), *Tropics and le Jazz Hot* (1939), *Bhahiana* (1939), *Plantation Dances* (1940), *Haitian Suite (II)* (1941), *Tropical Revue* (1943), *Havana 1910/1919* (1944), *Carib Song* (1945), *Bal Nègre* (1946), *Rhumba Trio* (1947), *Macumba* (1948), *Adeus Terras* (1949), *Spirituals* (1951), *Afrique du Nord* (1953), *Jazz Finale* (1955) *Ti Cocomaque* (1957), and *Anabacoa* (1963).

Dunham received numerous awards, including the Albert Schweitzer Music Award (1979), the Kennedy Center Honors (1983), the Samuel H. Scripps American Dance Festival Award (1987), and induction into the Hall of Fame of the National Museum of Dance (1987). In East St. Louis, Dunham founded the Katherine Dunham Center for Arts and Humanities to promote "arts-based communication techniques for people of diverse cultures" and provide "a multi-art training program to humanize and socialize individuals as well as provide them with marketable skills."

During the 1990s, it was feared that the Dunham legacy would eventually be lost because of the lack of funding and the volume of material that needed to be preserved. But in 2000, the Doris Duke Charitable

Foundation gave the Library of Congress $1 million to purchase and preserve Dunham's archives. In addition, the state of Illinois set aside a matching $1 million to ensure that Dunham's legacy would remain alive in her home state.

Over the years, Dunham influenced the careers of many dancers and choreographers, such as Syvilla Fort, Talley Beatty, Lavinia Williams, Walter Nicks, Hope Clark, Vanoye Aikens, and Carmencita Romero. The Dunham technique remains a mainstay at Alvin Ailey studios and the Debbie Allen Dance Academy. Katherine Dunham died on May 21, 2006, at age ninety-six.

GARTH FAGAN (1940–)

Choreographer. Garth Fagan was born on May 3, 1940, in Kingston, Jamaica. He discovered dance by way of gymnastics, but was discouraged from a dance career by his father, an academic. However, Fagan studied and danced with Ivy Baxter and the Jamaican National Dance Company, touring throughout Latin American while still in high school.

In 1960, Fagan left Jamaica and enrolled at Wayne State University in Detroit to study psychology. After completing his master's program, he commuted to New York to study with Martha Graham, Jose Limon, and Alvin Ailey. Fagan helped launch several Detroit-based dance companies, including Detroit's All-City Dance Company, the Detroit Contemporary Dance Company, and the Dance Theatre of Detroit. Eventually, he moved to Rochester, New York, to become a distinguished professor at the State University of New York at Brockport. There he taught young, untrained dancers who became his first company, Garth Fagan Dance.

Fagan always sought to transform dance, using the polyrhythms of Afro-Caribbean dance, modern floor techniques, the theatrics of Alvin Ailey, and the agility of ballet to create new movement. In 1986, Fagan directed and choreographed *Queenie Pie*, the Duke Ellington street opera, at the Kennedy Center.

Fagan's numerous honors include a Guggenheim Fellowship, a three-year choreography fellowship from the National Endowment for the Arts, the *Dance*

Garth Fagan Dance, National Underground Railroad Freedom Center, Cincinnati, OH, 2004. *Choreographer Garth Fagan founded his dance group in Rochester, New York, while he was a professor at the University of New York at Brockport. On August 23, 2004, the group performed at the center's opening dedication ceremonies.* AP PHOTO/DAVID KOHL

Magazine Award for "significant contributions to dance during a distinguished career," and the Bessie Award (the New York Dance and Performance Award) for sustained achievement. In 1996, he was named among twenty-five American scholars, artists, professionals, and public figures to receive the title Fulbright Fiftieth Anniversary Distinguished Fellow.

In 1998, Fagan received the Tony Award for best choreography for his critically acclaimed work in the Broadway hit *The Lion King*, which also won the Tony for best musical. Fagan himself danced in the show. He also received the Drama Desk Award, the Outer Critics Circle Award, and the Astaire Award that year.

Fagan's *Nkanyit* premiered in 1997 at the John F. Kennedy Center in Washington, D.C., and opened at the Joyce Theater in New York in November 1998. The title means "an all-encompassing respect for life, elders, and each other instilled early in childhood." This piece juxtaposes African ancestors dancing to American songs, and modern folk moving to Kenyan percussion. The heart of the work is the dynamic relationship between parent and child and the struggle to create "family." In 2001, Fagan's work was recognized when he received the Samuel H. Scripps American Dance Festival Award.

With his ability to produce entertaining, dramatic, and insightful movement, Fagan continues to push the limits, inside and out, of postmodern dance. Some of his repertory works include *Trips and Trysts* (2000), *Music of the Line/ Words in the Shape* (2001), *Translation Transition* (2002), *DANCECOLLAGEFOROMIE* (2003), *—ING* (2004), *Life: Dark/Light* (2005), *Senku* (2006), and the critically acclaimed *Mudan 175/39* (2009), for which the numbers in the title refer to the city of Rochester's 175th anniversary and the 39th anniversary season of Garth Fagan Dance.

REDD FOXX (1922–1991)

Actor, Comedian. Redd Foxx's most famous role was Fred Sanford, the junkman on the popular NBC series *Sanford and Son*, which began in 1972. Fred Sanford was the second most popular character on television after Archie Bunker in *All in the Family*. As a result, Foxx became one of the highest-paid actors in show business. In 1976, it was reported that he was earning $25,000 per half-hour episode, plus 25 percent of the producer's net profit.

Sanford is actually Foxx's family name. He was born John Elroy Sanford in St. Louis on December 9, 1922, and both his father and his brother were named Fred. As a boy, he formed a washtub band with two friends and played for tips on street corners, earning as much as $60 a night. At fourteen, Foxx and the band moved to Chicago, but the group broke up during World War II.

Foxx then moved to New York, where he worked as a rack pusher in the garment district as he sought work in nightclubs and on the black vaudeville circuit. While in New York, he played pool with a hustler named Malcolm Little, who was to change his name to Malcolm X. In the early 1950s, Foxx tried to find work in Hollywood. He had a brief stint with *The Dinah Washington Show*, but mostly survived by performing a vaudeville act and working as a sign painter. This comedy act contained adult content, which limited his bookings.

Foxx's first real success came in 1955, when he began to make party records. He ultimately made more than fifty records, which sold over twenty million copies. His television career was launched in the 1960s with guest appearances on *The Today Show*, *The Tonight Show*, and other variety programs. He also began to appear in Las Vegas nightclubs.

Throughout the long run of *Sanford and Son*, Foxx argued with his producers over money. Originally, he was not receiving a percentage of the show's profits, which led him to sit out several episodes, until the producers filed a breach-of-contract suit. There were racial undertones to these disputes, with Foxx referring to himself as a "tuxedo slave" and pointing to white stars who owned a percentage of their shows. Eventually, Foxx broke with the show and NBC.

Foxx then signed a multimillion dollar, multiyear contract with ABC, which resulted in a disastrous comedy variety hour that he quit on the air in October 1977. The ABC situation comedy *My Buddy*, which he wrote, starred in, and produced, followed. In 1978, however, ABC filed a breach-of-contract suit. In 1979, Foxx was back at NBC planning a sequel to *Sanford and Son*. He also made a deal with CBS, which sued him in 1981, allegedly to recover advances not paid back.

In 1976, Foxx appeared in the MGM movie *Norman, Is That You?* He continued his appearances in nightclubs in Las Vegas and New York. In 1979, the book *Redd Foxx, B.S.*, was published, comprised of chapters written by his friends.

In 1973, Foxx received the Entertainer of the Year Award from the NAACP. In 1974, he was named police chief of Taft, Oklahoma, an all-black village of six hundred people. He also ran a Los Angeles nightclub to showcase aspiring young comedians, both black and white. In addition, Foxx did numerous prison shows, probably more than any other famous entertainer, which he funded out of his own pocket. Foxx died on October 11, 1991.

AL FREEMAN JR. (1934–)

Actor. A veteran actor with over forty years of experience, Al Freeman Jr. has won recognition for his many roles in the theater, television, and motion pictures. His title role in the television film *My Sweet Charlie* (1970) earned him an Emmy Award nomination.

Albert Cornelius Freeman Jr. was born in San Antonio, Texas, on March 21, 1934. After attending schools in San Antonio and then Ohio, Freeman moved to the West Coast to study law at Los Angeles City College. Following a tour of duty with the U.S. Army in Germany, Freeman returned to college and decided to change his major to theater arts after being encouraged by fellow students to audition for a campus production.

Freeman did radio shows and appeared in theater productions in the Los Angeles area before performing in his first Broadway play, *The Long Dream* (1960). Other Broadway credits include *Kicks and Company* (1961), *Tiger, Tiger Burning Bright* (1962), *Blues for Mr. Charlie* (1964), *Conversations at Midnight* (1964), *The Dozens* (1969), *Look to the Lilies* (1970), and *Medea* (1973).

Off-Broadway, Freeman worked in *The Living Premise* (1963), *Trumpets of the Lord* (1963), *The Slave* (1964), and *Great MacDaddy* (1974). He also appeared in *Troilus and Cressida* (1965) and *Measure for Measure* (1966) for the New York Shakespeare Festival. He has appeared in more than a dozen feature films, including *Black Like Me* (1964), *Dutchman* (1967), *Finian's Rainbow* (1968), *Malcolm X* (1992), and *Once Upon a Time . . . When We Were Colored* (1995). In 1998, Freeman appeared in the poignant film *Down in the Delta*, with Alfre Woodard and Wesley Snipes, which was directed by poet Maya Angelou.

Throughout his career, Freeman has appeared in such television series as *The FBI*, *The Mod Squad*, *Kojak*, *Maude*, *The Cosby Show*, and *Law & Order*, with a recurring role on *Homicide*. He won an Emmy for his portrayal of Lieutenant Ed Hall in ABC's daytime drama *One Life to Live*. He also served as a director on the show, making him one of the first African Americans to direct a soap opera. Freeman teaches in the Theatre Arts Department of Howard University, where he has been a professor for more than twenty years.

CHARLES GILPIN (1878–1930)

Actor. Charles Gilpin was born in Richmond, Virginia, on November 20, 1878. After a brief period in school, he took up work as a printer's devil. In 1890, he began to travel intermittently with vaudeville troupes, a practice that continued for two decades. He worked as a printer, elevator operator, prizefight trainer, and porter during long interludes of theatrical unemployment.

From 1911 to 1914, Gilpin toured with a group called the Pan-American Octette. In 1914, he had a bit part in a New York production, *Old Ann's Boy*. Two years later he founded the Lafayette Theatre Company, one of the earliest black stock companies in New York. After Eugene O'Neill saw Gilpin in *Abraham Lincoln*, he was chosen to play the lead in *The Emperor Jones*, the role in which he starred from 1920 to 1924. In 1921, Gilpin was awarded the NAACP Spingarn Award for his theatrical accomplishments.

Gilpin lost his voice in 1926 and was forced to earn his living once again as an elevator operator. He died on May 6, 1930.

SAVION GLOVER (1974–)

Dancer, Choreographer. Tap dance wizard Savion Glover was born in Newark, New Jersey, in 1974. His mother noticed his keen sense of rhythm early on, and he began learning percussion at four years old. Three years later, ready to try something new, he began tap lessons at the Broadway Dance Center in New York City. By the time he was ten, Glover was the understudy for the lead in *The Tap Dance Kid* on Broadway, and later starred in the role

Tap Dancer and Choreographer Savion Glover, 2008. *Glover, who appeared on* Sesame Street *from 1991 to 1995, won a Tony Award for best choreography for* Bring in 'Da Noise, Bring in 'Da Funk *in 1996.* DONNA WARD/GETTY IMAGES

of the Kid. After two years in that show, he performed in *Black and Blue*, which opened first in Paris before moving to New York. His work earned him a Tony Award nomination in 1989.

Glover's talent developed quickly as he learned by imitating the techniques and sounds of tap greats such as Sandman Sims, Harold Nicholas, Jimmy Slyde, and Sammy Davis Jr., who appeared with him in the film *Tap* in 1988. He excelled in "close work" (taps without jumps or leaps) and acrobatic tap, and admits to creating moves inspired by Michael Jackson.

Glover next appeared in *Jelly's Last Jam*, which opened on Broadway in 1992, playing the young Jelly Roll Morton and costarring with Gregory Hines. From Broadway, Glover went to television to appear, from 1991 to 1995, in *Sesame Street* and in several feature shows, such as *Dance in America: Tap!* and *Black Filmmakers Hall of Fame*. He also performed at the Academy Awards ceremony in 1996 and 1999.

Glover's greatest stage success is *Bring in 'da Noise, Bring in 'da Funk*, which opened in 1995 and for which Glover was the choreographer and prime performer. The show combined poetry, tap, and such musical styles as blues, rhythm and blues, jazz, hip-hop, and street drumming in dramatic and satiric sketches that tell of the black experience in America. Glover won the Tony Award for best choreography in 1996 for *Bring in 'da Noise, Bring in 'da Funk*. That same year, he earned a *Dance Magazine* Award and a National Endowment for the Arts award, and was named Best New Theater Star by *Entertainment Weekly*. Glover moved to Hollywood to develop further shows to showcase his extraordinary talents.

In 2000, Glover appeared in the Spike Lee film *Bamboozled* as a street dancer who is recruited to play in a minstrel show in order to make fun of network executives. Glover was honored with the Flo-Bert Award from the New York Committee to Celebrate National Tap Dance Day. He appeared in the 2002 film *Bojangles*, which also starred Gregory Hines. He also appeared in *Michael Jackson: The One*, a 2004 DVD retrospective look at Michael Jackson's career.

Always an artist who stretches boundaries, Glover continues to forge innovative collaborations. In 2005, *If Trane Wuz Here*, an improvisational session inspired by the music of John Coltrane, featured spoken-word artist Reg E. Gaines and saxophonist Matana Roberts. *Classical Savion* partnered Glover with a chamber string group for a tour in 2006 to 2007. Warner Brothers' animators found it a challenge to keep up with Glover's footwork when he created the stop-motion choreography for Mumbles, the lead penguin in the Oscar-winning animated film *Happy Feet* (2007).

In another series of artistic collaborations, *Savion Glover and the OtheRz*, Glover improvised his way through several tours. Singer La Conja and musicians Tommy James, Patience Higgins, Brian Grice, and Andy McCloud provided the rhythm, while dancers Marshall Davis Jr., Maurice Chestnut, and Cartier Williams traded percussive hits with Savion. The repertory of shows included *SoLo in TiME, THE STaRz and STRiPes 4EVeR for NoW*, and *BARE SOUNDZ*.

At the Blue Note, one of the last renowned jazz clubs in Greenwich Village, Glover rekindled the connection between jazz and tap. He performed with legendary jazz improvisers McCoy Tyner, Roy Haynes, Eddie Palmieri, and Jack DeJohnette for a series of one-night-only concerts called *Jammin' with the Masters*. In his hometown of Newark, Savion opened the HooFeRzCLub School for Tap to provide a training ground for the next generation of tappers.

WHOOPI GOLDBERG (1955–)

Actress, Comedienne, Producer. Born Caryn E. Johnson in Manhattan's Chelsea district on November 13, 1955, Whoopi Goldberg began performing at eight years old with the children's program at Hudson Guild and Helen Rubinstein Children's Theatre. After trying her hand at theater, improvisation, and chorus parts on Broadway, she moved to San Diego in 1974 and appeared in repertory productions of *Mother Courage* and *Getting Out*. Goldberg joined the Blake Street Hawkeyes Theatre in Berkeley as a partner with David Schein, and then went solo to create *The Spook Show*, performing in San Francisco and later touring the United States and Europe.

In 1983, Goldberg's work caught the attention of Mike Nichols, who directed her self-titled Broadway show, *Whoopi Goldberg*, a year later. She won the 1985 Drama Desk Award for outstanding one-person show. She made her film debut in *The Color Purple* (1985), winning an NAACP Image Award, as well as the honor of being the first African American woman to win the Golden Globe Award for best actress.

Goldberg has starred in a myriad of movies, including *Jumpin' Jack Flash* (1986), *Clara's Heart* (1988), *Ghost* (1990), *Sister Act* (1992), *The Player* (1992), *Sarafina!* (1992), *Ghosts of Mississippi* (1996), *How Stella Got Her Groove Back* (1998), *Girl, Interrupted* (1999), *Rat Race* (2001), and *Star Trek: Nemesis* (2004). In addition, her voice has been cast in numerous animated projects, such as *Captain Planet and the Planeteers* (1991), *The Lion King* (1994), *The Pagemaster* (1994), *Rugrats: The Movie* (1998), *Racing Stripes* (2005), *Doogal* (2006), and *Toy Story 3* (2010).

On television, Goldberg has had recurring roles on *Star Trek: The Next Generation*, *Everybody Hates Chris*, her own short-lives series, *Whoopi*, and the A&E series

***Actress Patina Miller* (center left)*, Producer Whoopi Goldberg* (center)*, Actress Sheila Hancock* (center right)*, and the Cast of* Sister Act: The Musical** *Comedian and actress Goldberg, who starred in the film* Sister Act *(1992), serves as a producer for this musical stage version.* DAVE M. BENETT/GETTY IMAGES

The Cleaner. Goldberg brought the popular *Hollywood Squares* game show back to network television in 1998. She both produced and starred in the show until 2002.

As an executive producer, Goldberg's projects run the gamut. She began in 2000 with two cable movies, *What Makes a Family* for Lifetime Television and *Ruby's Bucket of Blood* for Showtime. She branched out to Broadway for *Thoroughly Modern Millie* in 2002, then returned to television with the Lifetime series *Strong Medicine* from 2003 to 2005 and Noggin's *Just For Kicks* in 2006. Her more recent projects include *Head Games*, a game show on the Science Channel, and *Sister Act: A Divine Musical Comedy*, which opened at the London Palladium in 2009 and is slated for Broadway in 2010.

Goldberg is a trailblazer whose career is marked by firsts. During a period in the 1990s, she was the highest-paid actress of all time. She was the first woman and the first African American to host the Academy Awards in 1994 and was invited back three more times in 1996, 1999, and 2002. Goldberg is also one of the few people to have won an Oscar (*Ghost*), a Tony (*Thoroughly Modern Millie*), an Emmy (*Beyond Tara: The Extraordinary Life of Hattie McDaniel*), and a Grammy (*Whoopi: Direct from Broadway*). In 2001, she was awarded the Mark Twain Prize for American Humor and a star on the Hollywood Walk of Fame.

In 2008, Goldberg returned to the Broadway stage in *Xanadu*. Over the years, she has starred in several revivals—*A Funny Thing Happened on the Way to the Forum* in 1996, *Ma Rainey's Black Bottom* in 2003, and *Whoopi: Back to Broadway*, to commemorate the play's twentieth anniversary, in 2005. The next year, she reunited with fellow founding members, Robin Williams and Billy Crystal, to celebrate twenty years of humanitarian efforts by Comic Relief.

Ever evolving, Goldberg's many talents include radio deejay and talk-show cohost. Her morning show, *Wake Up with Whoopi*, aired from 2006 to 2008. She replaced Rosie O'Donnell as a host on *The View* in 2007 and won a 2009 Daytime Emmy for outstanding talk host, an honor shared with her fellow hosts.

DICK GREGORY (1932–)

Comedian, Civil Rights Activist, Writer, Nutritional Advocate. Dick Gregory was born on October 12, 1932, in St. Louis. His father left the family in a state of poverty, and Gregory helped his mother by earning money through doing odd jobs. After high school, he entered Southern Illinois University on an athletic scholarship. In 1954, he was drafted into the U.S. Army. In the military, his superiors, who were not fond of Gregory's flippant attitude, challenged him to win a talent show or face court-martial charges. Gregory won the contest and continued his military stint in the Special Service's Entertainment Division.

After his discharge from the army, Gregory went to Chicago and pursued a career as a stand-up comic. He opened a club called the Apex but failed to attract enough business to make the venue successful. The venture was not a total failure: Gregory ended up marrying his financial partner, Lillian Smith. In January 1961, Gregory received the opportunity to perform at the Playboy Club for a group of southern executives. Although initially turned away by the club's booking agent, who had assumed that Gregory was white, the comedian insisted on doing his routine. Although the crowd was expectedly resistant at first, Gregory persevered and won them over. The performance resulted in a three-year contract with the club and a friendship with Hugh Hefner.

During the early 1960s, Gregory's popularity grew. His comedy relied on discussions of himself and included social commentary on such matters as racism and civil rights. Several national commentators acknowledged Gregory as the first black comedian to gain acceptance as a social satirist. In the 1960s, he published *Back of the Bus* (1962) and *Nigger: An Autobiography* (1964).

In the 1960s, Gregory became involved in the burgeoning civil rights movement. He committed himself to events that resulted in increases in political fund raising and voter registration. Not one to contribute passively to causes, Gregory was arrested on numerous occasions and risked violence from local police. His views of nonviolent participation, fostered by Martin Luther King Jr., were challenged when a sheriff kicked his wife during a protest in Missouri.

As the 1960s progressed, Gregory withdrew from the entertainment arena and participated more actively in politics. He ran for mayor of Chicago in 1967 and earned nearly 200,000 votes for president as the candidate for the Freedom and Peace Party in the 1968 national election.

Nutritional issues have been a focus for Gregory since he became a vegetarian during the 1960s. At one point in his career, he refused to perform in clubs that allowed smoking and drinking. In the 1970s, he cowrote *Dick Gregory's Natural Diet for Folks Who Eat: Cooking with Mother Nature* (1974) with Alvenia Fulton. In 1984, he founded Health Enterprises, a business focused on marketing a powdered diet drink, the popular Bahamian Diet Nutritional Drink. Gregory also participated in marathons.

In the 1990s, Gregory returned to the stage in Brooklyn to bring his comedy and social views to a new generation. His opinions on such issues as world hunger, "gangsta" rap music, drug use, and warfare come through during his performances. In 1993, he coauthored *Murder in Memphis: The FBI and the Assassination of Martin Luther King*, and seven years later he published *Callous on My Soul: The Autobiography of Dick Gregory*.

Gregory has received the Ebony-Topaz Heritage and Freedom Award, along with numerous honorary degrees from major universities. He also was honored with the Wellness of You 2001 Tree of Life Award.

On television, Gregory had a recurring role on Comedy Central's satire, *Reno 911!* (2004). He made guest appearances on MTV2's cult show *Wonder Shozen* (2005) and on the Starz Network's long-running series *Martin Lawrence Presents 1st Amendment Stand-up* (2009).

Gregory has been featured in the narrative films *Panther* (1995), *Children of the Struggle* (1999), *The Hot Chick* (2002), and *Steppin': The Movie* (2009). But most often, Gregory's uncompromising comedy, humorous recollections, and biting political opinions are sought out for documentaries. Over the years, he has appeared in over fifty documentary films, including *It's a Revolution Mother* (1968), *American Revolution 2* (1969), *In Remembrance of Martin* (1986), *The Real Malcolm X* (1992), *Muhammad Ali: The Real Story* (1996), *Mark Twain* (2001), *The N-Word: Divided We Stand* (2004), *Richard Pryor: The Funniest Man, Dead or Alive* (2005), *Joe Louis: America's Hero ... Betrayed* (2008), *Hugh Hefner: Playboy, Activist, and Rebel* (2009), *Fat, Sick, and Nearly Dead* (2009), and *Citizen Lane* (2010).

Gregory continues to stand and deliver at comedy clubs all around the country. He is eighty-first on Comedy Central's 100 Greatest Stand-ups of All Time.

MOSES GUNN (1929–1993)

Actor. Born on October 2, 1929, in St. Louis, Moses Gunn showed dramatic promise at a young age, reading monologues aloud when he was nine. Six scholarships from other schools were offered to Gunn before he chose to earn a degree in speech and drama from Tennessee State University. There he organized a student troupe called Footlights Across Tennessee, which toured the South and Midwest, staging shows written by little-known black playwrights. While completing graduate work at the University of Kansas, Gunn performed in *Othello*.

With his eye on a career on the New York stage, Gunn raised money by teaching drama at Grambling College in the early 1960s. He served as an understudy for an off-Broadway production, later joining the regular cast. Once he had gained more experience, Gunn acquired a reputation as a leading Shakespearian actor. He appeared regularly with the New York Shakespeare Festival and won off-Broadway's Obie Award for his portrayal of Aaron the Moor in a 1967 production of *Titus Andronicus*. During the same era, he became a founding member of the Negro Ensemble Company, whose production of *The First Breeze of Summer* led to the actor's second Obie in 1975.

By the 1970s, Gunn had become a favorite on the national and international scenes. As a maturing performer, he did not limit his appearances to stage. Moviegoers enjoyed his supporting performances in films ranging from *The Great White Hope* (1970) to *Shaft* (1971). As Booker T. Washington in *Ragtime* (1981), Gunn earned an Image Award from the NAACP in 1981. On television, he appeared in *Roots* (1977) and earned an Emmy nomination for his portrayal of Kintango, a seventh-century African secret-sect leader.

From a sensual Othello to a fiery Booker T. Washington, Gunn specialized in crafting strong, memorable characters in a career that spanned more than three decades. Gunn also worked tirelessly as an advocate for other African American actors during a time when the theatrical establishment seemed all too willing to limit their presence both onstage and behind the scenes. He died of asthma complications on December 17, 1993, when he was sixty-four years old.

JUANITA HALL (1902–1968)

Singer. Born on November 6, 1902, in Keyport, New Jersey, Hall studied at the Juilliard School of Music after singing in Catholic church choirs as a child. Hall devoted her life to music as a singer in stage and movie productions and choirs.

Her first major stage appearance was in Ziegfeld's *Show Boat* in 1927. She appeared as Bloody Mary in Rodgers and Hammerstein's *South Pacific* in 1949. Hall then appeared on stage in *Flower Drum Song*, and in the movie versions of both shows. She served as a soloist and assistant director of the Hall Johnson Choir (1931–1936), conducted the Works Progress Administration chorus in New York City (1936–1941), and organized the Juanita Hall Choir in 1942.

Hall performed at the Palladium in London and was a guest on the *Ed Sullivan* and *Perry Como* television shows. She was the recipient of the Donaldson Award and the Tony Award. Hall died February 29, 1968, in Bay Shore, New York.

LEONARD HARPER (1899–1943)

Dancer, Choreographer, Producer. Leonard Harper was born into show business in Birmingham, Alabama. When he was just four years old, he began dancing and picking up stage tricks from his father, vaudeville actor William Harper. When Harper's father died, leaving the family destitute, ten-year-old Leonard was thrust into show business full time as the only means of supporting his mother and little brother.

Harper took his act on the road in carnivals and small musical-comedy theaters called *jig tops*. By the time he was twelve, he had teamed up with comedian George Freeman. Together they formed a stock company and produced shows on the southern minstrel circuit. Harper longed for brighter lights, though, so he traveled to Chicago and joined an all-star minstrel show, where he met his future wife and partner, Osceola Blanks.

The couple formed the vaudeville team of Harper and Blanks, and became nationally known for their upscale attire and for introducing the dance craze "Walking the Dog." Harper and Blanks broke the theatrical color barrier when they became the first black act to tour the Shubert vaudeville circuit of white theaters. They were billed as "The Smart Set Couple" and performed their act dressed in full formal wear.

In 1922, Harper pioneered a new form of musical production, the intimate nightclub review. He staged *Plantation Days*, featuring Ethel Waters, at the Green Mill Garden, a posh club in Chicago. The show toured the United States, then traveled to London to play before the royal family at the Empire Theatre.

When Harper returned to the United States, he was immediately hired as the main floorshow producer at Connie's Inn in Harlem. His name became synonymous with the popularity of nightclub revues in New York City throughout the 1920s. Harper featured Ethel Waters and put Josephine Baker in top hat and tails for the first time in the Plantation Club's *Tan Town Tropics*. He also mounted Texas Guinan's speakeasy shows with Ruby Keeler, and integrated burlesque by being the first African American to produce and direct a whole stage show, *Hollywood Follies*, for Columbia. He also staged the debut floorshow entertainment for such famous nightspots as the Cotton Club, Smalls Paradise, and the Apollo Theater.

In 1924, Harper opened a dance studio in Times Square and personally trained the Marx Brothers, Mae West, Ruby Keeler, Jack Albert, Fred and Adele Astaire, the Busby Berkeley dancers, and other stars in what became known as the *Leonard Harper system.* On Broadway, Harper starred in Lew Leslie's *Blackbirds* with Florence Mills. He staged the musical numbers in *Keep Shufflin'* (1928), and in 1929 he conceived and staged *Hot Chocolates,* with music composed by Fats Waller and lyrics by Andy Razaf. *Hot Chocolates* featured newcomers Cab Calloway and Louis Armstrong and introduced two numbers that later became the title songs of Broadway musicals, "Ain't Misbehavin'" and "Black and Blue." Leonard Harper died while rehearsing a small nightclub show in 1943.

ROBIN HARRIS (1953–1990)

Comedian, Actor. Robin Harris was born August 30, 1953, in Chicago, Illinois. He attended Ottawa University in Kansas, where he ran a 4:18 mile on the track team. After college, he pursued a career in comedy rather than athletics, performing stand-up comedy as often as possible while working at Hughes Aircraft and Security Pacific Bank to support himself. Harris's interest in 1970s comedians, such as Redd Foxx, motivated him to create his own act in a similar style. In 1985, after years of hard work, he began to build a name for himself as the master of ceremonies at Comedy Act Theater in Los Angeles. Due primarily to Harris's influence, the Comedy Act Theater became a stopping spot for black celebrities.

Spike Lee recognized Harris's talent and cast him in his 1989 film *Do the Right Thing.* Harris also appeared in *I'm Gonna Git You Sucka* (1988), *Harlem Nights* (1989), *Mo' Better Blues* (1990), and *House Party* (1990). His movie career vaulted him into a new level of stardom, and he started playing 2,000-seat auditoriums with his comedy act, though continuing his much smaller and less-profitable gigs at the Comedy Act Theater.

By 1990, Harris's life had become hectic, with stand-up performances, an HBO special, an album, and an upcoming movie. He died on March 18, 1990, of heart failure in Chicago. The animated film version of Harris's album, *Bebe's Kids,* was released posthumously in 1992, as was his HBO comedy special.

RICHARD B. HARRISON (1864–1935)

Actor. Richard B. Harrison was one of the few actors to gain national prominence on the basis of one role, his characterization of De Lawd in *Green Pastures.* Harrison was born in Canada in 1864 and moved to Detroit as a young boy. There he worked as a waiter, porter, and handyman, saving whatever money he could to attend the theatrical offerings in town. After studying drama in Detroit, he made his professional debut in Canada in a program of readings and recitations.

For three decades, Harrison entertained black audiences with one-man performances of *Macbeth, Julius Caesar,* and *Damon and Pythias,* as well as with readings of poems by William Shakespeare, Edgar Allan Poe, Rudyard Kipling, and Paul Laurence Dunbar. In 1929, while serving on the faculty of North Carolina Agricultural and Technical College as a drama instructor, he was chosen for the part of De Lawd in *Green Pastures.* By the time of his death in 1935, Harrison had performed the role 1,656 times. His work earned him the 1930 Spingarn Medal and numerous honorary degrees.

GREGORY HINES (1946–2003)

Actor, Dancer. After a distinguished career as a tap dancer, Gregory Hines made an unusual transition to dramatic actor. Born in New York City on Valentine's Day 1946, Hines began dancing with his brother Maurice under the instruction of tap dancer Henry LeTang. When Gregory was five, the brothers began performing professionally as the Hines Kids. Appearing in nightclubs and theaters around the country, they were able to benefit from their contact with such dance legends as "Honi" Coles, Sandman Sims, the Nicholas Brothers, and Teddy Hale.

As teenagers, the two performed as the Hines Brothers. When Gregory reached age eighteen, the two were joined on drums by their father, Maurice Sr., in a trio known as Hines, Hines, and Dad. They performed internationally and appeared on *The Tonight Show.* Eventually, Gregory tired of the touring and settled in California, where he formed the jazz-rock band Severance.

Gregory Hines subsequently moved back to New York and landed a role in *The Minstrel Show* (1978). He would later appear in such Broadway musicals as *Eubie!* (1978), *Sophisticated Ladies* (1981), and *Comin' Uptown* (1990), as well as feature films, including *The Cotton Club* (1985), *White Nights* (1985), and *Running Scared* (1985). Hines starred in the 1989 Tri-Star film *Tap* with Sammy Davis Jr., not only acting and dancing, but singing as well. Hines's other notable films include *White Man's Burden* (1994), *Renaissance Man* (1995), *Waiting to Exhale* (1995), and *The Preacher's Wife* (1996).

On television, Hines appeared in the series *Amazing Stories* and the special *Motown Returns to the Apollo,* which earned him an Emmy nomination. His 1997 program, *The Gregory Hines Show,* was favorably reviewed but short-lived. He was the voice of Big Bill on the Nick Jr. animated series *Little Bill,* and he had a recurring role on *Will & Grace.* Hines also appeared as the lead character in the 2001 television movie *Bojangles.*

When not appearing in films or television, Hines toured internationally as a solo club act. His first solo album was released by CBS/Epic in 1988. The album was produced by Luther Vandross, who teamed with Hines for a single, "There's Nothing Better than Love," which reached number one on the R&B charts in 1987.

Hines received numerous awards, including the Dance Educators Award and the Theater World Award. He was nominated for several Tony Awards, and in 1992 received the award for best actor in a musical for his performance in *Jelly's Last Jam*. Hines died of liver cancer on August 9, 2003.

Holder's commanding voice was cast in the recurring role of Master Pi in *Cyberchase* (2002–2003). He was also the narrator of Tim Burton's *Charlie and the Chocolate Factory* (2005) and the animated feature *The Magistical* (2008). He also appeared in a movie called *Butterfield* (2008).

Holder has been married to dancer Carmen de Lavallade for over fifty years. The two met in 1955 while performing in *House of Flowers*, and married a year later.

GEOFFREY HOLDER (1930–)

Actor, Dancer, Choreographer, Costume Designer, Director. Geoffrey Holder has succeeded as an artist in many areas. Holder was born on August 1, 1930, in Port of Spain, Trinidad. At an early age, he left school to become the costume designer for his brother's dance troupe, which he took over in 1948. Holder led the dancers, singers, and steel-band musicians through a series of successful small revues to the Caribbean Festival in Puerto Rico, where they represented Trinidad and Tobago. His appearances with his troupe in the mid-1950s were so popular that he is credited with launching the calypso vogue.

Early in his career, Holder appeared in New York as a featured dancer in *House of Flowers* (1954). He later performed with the Metropolitan Opera and as a guest star on many television shows. His film credits include *Live and Let Die* (1973), the James Bond adventure, and *Dr. Dolittle* (1967), the children's classic starring Rex Harrison.

Holder received two Tony Awards in 1976, as director and costume designer for the Broadway show *The Wiz*, the all-black adaptation of *The Wizard of Oz*. In 1978, he directed and choreographed the successful Broadway musical *Timbuktu*. In 1982, Holder appeared in the film *Annie*, based on the hit Broadway musical, playing Punjab, a character from the original comic strip.

Holder received a Guggenheim Fellowship to pursue his painting, and his impressionist paintings have been shown in such galleries as the Corcoran in Washington, D.C. In 1995, an exhibition of Holder's paintings was held at the State University of New York in Albany. Holder has also written two books. His *Black Gods, Green Islands* is a retelling of West Indian legends, and his *Caribbean Cookbook* is a collection of recipes that Holder also illustrated.

In 1998, Holder restaged his 1967 production *The Prodigal Prince* for the fortieth anniversary celebration of the Alvin Ailey American Dance Theater. In 2000, he appeared alongside Mercedes Ellington in a cooking show called *Harmony in the Kitchen*. In 2002, Holder was honored by the International Association of Blacks in Dance for lifetime career achievement.

LENA HORNE (1917–2010)

Actress, Singer. Lena Horne has been called the most beautiful woman in the world, and her beauty has been no small factor in the success of her stage, screen, and nightclub career. Horne was born on June 30, 1917, in Brooklyn, New York. She joined the chorus line at the Cotton Club in 1933, and then left to tour as a dancer with Noble Sissle's orchestra. She was given a leading role in *Blackbirds of 1939*, but the show folded quickly, so she left to join Charlie Barnett's band as a singer. She made her first records, including the popular "Haunted Town," with Barnett. In the early 1940s, she also worked at New York's Cafe Society Downtown.

Horne then went to Hollywood, where she became the first black woman to sign a term contract with a film studio. Her films included *Panama Hattie* (1942), *Cabin in the Sky* (1943), *Stormy Weather* (1943), and *Meet Me in Las Vegas* (1956). In 1957, she took a break from her film and nightclub schedule to star in her first Broadway musical, *Jamaica*. Her popular recordings included "Stormy Weather," "Blues in the Night," "The Lady Is a Tramp," and "Mad about the Boy."

Throughout the 1960s and 1970s, Horne appeared in nightclubs and concerts. She returned to Broadway in 1981 when she opened a one-woman show called *Lena Horne: The Lady and Her Music* to critical and box-office success. Although it opened too late to qualify for the Tony Award nominations, the show was awarded a special Tony at the June ceremonies. The production ran for two years, and the soundtrack, produced by Quincy Jones, won two Grammy Awards. In December 1981, she received New York City's highest cultural award, the Handel Medallion.

Horne was married for twenty-three years to Lennie Hayton, a white composer, arranger, and conductor who died April 24, 1971. She had been married previously to Louis Jones.

In 1994, Horne released her first recording in a decade, *We'll Be Together Again*. This album was followed by *An Evening with Lena Horne* (1995), *Lena Horne at Metro-Goldwyn-Mayer* (1996), and *Being Myself* (1998). In 1999, a gala in her honor was held at New York's Avery Fisher Hall.

Horne died in New York on May 9, 2010 at the age of ninety-two. Renditions of her classic recordings can be heard on many films and television shows, including *Take the Lead, Dirty Dancing: Havana Nights, Miss Match, Six Feet Under,* and *The Family Man.* Archival footage of Horne can be seen in the documentaries *A Life in Words and Music* (2007), *Strange Frame: Love & Sax* (2009), and *Johnny Mercer: The Dream's on Me* (2009).

EDDIE HUNTER (1888–1974)

Comedian. Eddie Hunter got his start when working as an elevator operator in a building frequented by the great tenor Enrico Caruso. Hunter had been writing vaudeville comedy parts on the side, and Caruso encouraged and helped him. In 1923, Hunter's musical revue, *How Come?*, reached Broadway.

Hunter performed in his own persona in the majority of the shows he wrote. *Going to the Races*, produced at the Lafayette Theatre in Harlem, had Hunter and his partner live onstage, interacting with a movie of themselves playing on the screen. Hunter considered this show one of his best. As one of the principal performers in *Blackbirds*, he toured Europe during the late 1920s. His show *Good Gracious* also toured Europe.

Depicting himself as "the fighting comedian," Hunter developed a reputation for speaking out against racial discrimination in the performing arts. He frequently told of an experience in Phoenix, Arizona, where the male members of his show were forced to sleep in the theater where they were performing because accommodations for blacks were unavailable. Hunter characterized his European reception as being relatively free of prejudice and felt that he only received the respect and recognition due to him when abroad.

By 1923, Hunter had a full recording contract with Victor Records. His recordings included "It's Human Nature to Complain," "I Got," and "My Wife Mamie." Shortly thereafter, he suspended his recording career to travel with a new show he had developed. But when "talking" movies arrived, vaudeville fell out of favor. Eddie Hunter retired from show business and entered the real-estate business in the 1930s.

EARLE HYMAN (1926–)

Actor. Earle Hyman was born in Rocky Mount, North Carolina, on October 11, 1926. He began his acting career with the American Negro Theater in New York City. In 1963, Hyman made his foreign-language acting debut in Eugene O'Neill's *The Emperor Jones* in Oslo, Norway, becoming the first American to perform a title role in a Scandinavian language. Hyman had originally become acquainted with Norway during a European trip made in 1957. He had planned to spend only two weeks there, but found himself so enchanted with Norway that he all but forgot the rest of Europe. When Hyman returned to New York, he resolved at once to learn Norwegian, and for practice he began to study the role of Othello (which he was performing for the Great Lakes Shakespeare Festival of 1962) in that language. By sheer coincidence, the director of Den Nationale Scene of Bergen, Norway, invited him to play *Othello* there in the spring of the following year, a performance that marked Hyman's first success in the Norwegian theater.

In 1965, Hyman returned to Norway to play *The Emperor Jones* for a different theater company and received high critical acclaim for his portrayal. Hyman remained in Norway intermittently for six years and has been the subject of several Norwegian radio broadcasts and television interviews. He still spends six months each year in Scandinavia, where he performs *Othello* and other classical roles. He played Halvard Solness to Lynn Redgrave's Mrs. Alvine Solness in Henrik Ibsen's *The Master Builder* at the National Actor's Theatre in 1992. A bronze bust of Hyman as Othello has been erected in the Norwegian theater where he performed, and he has also been presented with an honorary membership in the Norwegian Society of Artists, the third foreigner and first American to be so honored. Hyman is also the first black actor to have played all four of the Shakespeare giants—*Hamlet, Othello, Macbeth,* and *King Lear.*

Hyman's many on and off-Broadway credits include: *No Time for Sergeants* (1955); *St. Joan*, with Diana Sands at Lincoln Center, (1956); *Mister Johnson* (1956); *Waiting for Godot* (1957); Lorraine Hansberry's *Les Blancs* (1970); Edward Albee's *Lady from Dubuque*, the black version of Eugene O'Neill's *Long Day's Journey into Night*, at the Public Theater (1981); and *East Texas Hot Links* (1994).

Among other film and television work, Hyman appeared on the daytime drama *Love of Life* and was nominated for an Emmy for his role as Cliff Huxtable's father in *The Cosby Show*. In more recent years, Hyman has been seen in the television movies *Hijacked: Flight 285* in 1996, *The Moving of Sophia Myles* in 2000, and the series *Twice in a Lifetime* in 2001.

In 2006, Hyman returned to the stage in the Atlantic Theater Company's double bill of Harold Pinter plays, which paired the Nobel Prize winner's most recent work, *Celebration*, with his first, *The Room*.

The cast of *The Cosby Show* celebrated their twenty-fifth reunion on the *Today Show* in May 2009, coinciding with the release of a new DVD collection of the series, which ran from 1984 to 1992.

JUDITH JAMISON (1944–)

Dancer, Choreographer. Born in Philadelphia on May 10, 1944, Judith Jamison started to study dance when she was six years old. She was discovered in her early twenties by the choreographer Agnes de Mille, who admired her spontaneous style.

From 1965 to 1980, Jamison was a principal dancer for Alvin Ailey's American Dance Theater, performing a wide gamut of roles especially choreographed for her by Ailey. She has made guest appearances with many other dance companies, including the American Ballet Theatre, and with such opera companies as the Vienna State Opera and the Munich State Opera. In the 1980s, Jamison scored a great success on Broadway in *Sophisticated Ladies,* a musical featuring the works of Duke Ellington. In 1988, she formed the Jamison Project.

Since 1989, Jamison has served as the artistic director of the Alvin Ailey American Dance Theater and has expanded the vision of her mentor in many directions, artistically and fiscally. Under the auspices of Jamison, all of the Ailey companies and schools now fall under an umbrella organization, the Alvin Ailey American Dance Foundation. The repertory company has had two groundbreaking engagements in South Africa and a tour of mainland China. The company also performed at the 1996 Olympic Games in Atlanta and the Cultural Olympiad in 2002 in St. Lake City, where Jamison carried the Olympic torch during the opening ceremonies.

Dancer and Choreographer Judith Jamison* (center)*, Linda Kent* (left)*, and Sylvia Waters,* Revelations*, 1970s. *Jamison, a principal dancer for the Alvin Ailey American Dance Theater from 1965 to 1980, became its artistic director upon Ailey's death in 1989.* **HULTON ARCHIVE/GETTY IMAGES**

Jamison developed the Women's Choreography Initiative to encourage female dancers to explore their creativity in leadership roles. A celebrated choreographer in her own right, Jamison's formidable body of work includes *Hymn* (1993) and *Riverside* (1995). *Hymn* was featured in the PBS documentary *Hymn: Remembering Alvin Ailey,* which premiered in 1999. Jamison's 1996 work, *Sweet Release,* was a collaboration with celebrated trumpeter Wynton Marsalis. Her ballet *Echo: Far From Home* opened in New York in December 1998. *Double Exposure,* another ballet, premiered at the Lincoln Center Festival in 2002.

In 1993, Jamison published the book *Dancing Spirit: An Autobiography.* She is the youngest recipient ever to receive the Dance USA Award, which was presented at the Spoleto Festival, USA, in May 1998. In 2000, President Bill Clinton paid tribute to Jamison at the Kennedy Center Honors program in Washington D.C. In 2002, Jamison was named a recipient of the National Medal of Arts. In 2003, she received the "Making a Difference" Award from the NAACP ACT-SO. More recently, Jamison received the Paul Robeson Award from the Actors' Equity Association in recognition for her outstanding contribution to the performing arts and her commitment to the right of all people to live in dignity and peace.

The 2009–2010 season of Alvin Ailey American Dance Theater celebrated Jamison's twentieth anniversary as artistic director. Among the new works featured in the season were Ronald K. Brown's tribute to Jamison in his new ballet, aptly named *Dancing Spirit. Best of 20 Years* featured highlights of the ballets that Jamison commissioned or revived in the Ailey repertory. Inspired by a series of her original artwork, Jamison choreographed a new ballet titled *Among Us (Private Spaces: Public Places).*

VIRGINIA JOHNSON (1950–)

Dancer. Virginia Johnson was the prima ballerina for the Dance Theatre of Harlem from its very beginning in 1969. Her career started early. She was born in Washington, D.C., on January 25, 1950, and began studying ballet when she was three years old at the Washington School of Ballet. She continued to study there under scholarships throughout high school and performed in productions with the American Light

Opera Company and in the annual staging of the Washington Ballet's *Nutcracker Suite.*

Although black ballerinas were rare, Johnson received a scholarship to study dance at New York University's School of the Arts. However, the emphasis on modern dance there dissatisfied her, so she joined a ballet school in Harlem being run out of a church basement by the former New York City Ballet dancer Arthur Mitchell. At nineteen, she left New York University to become part of the fledgling company. Mitchell created the Dance Theatre of Harlem (DTH) as a commitment to the Harlem community after the assassination of Martin Luther King Jr. Mitchell's aim was to establish a company of black dancers and add a new style to contemporary classical ballet. DTH and Johnson were a perfect match.

In 1974, Johnson danced her first solo role for the Dance Theatre of Harlem and became its star ballerina. Emotive, romantic, and long-limbed, Johnson was a natural for legendary choreographer George Balanchine's dances, performing them clearly and smoothly. In her tenure at DTH, she danced many traditional roles, such as the title role in *Giselle*. The DTH then reset the European tale in the bayous of Louisiana to tell the stories of a community of free Creole blacks. Critics praised Johnson's performances as "glorious and subtle, touching and authoritative."

Johnson continued to add modern roles to extend her technical facility. She danced Balanchine's *Serenade* and *Allegro Brilliante*, Glen Tetley's *Voluntaries*, and Bronislava Nijinska's *Les Biches*, and she portrayed the Accused (Lizzie Borden) in Agnes de Mille's dramatic *Fall River Legend*.

Johnson toured the world with DTH in her capacity as dance diva. During the late 1980s, Johnson was one of the first American ballerinas to visit the Soviet Union, where she performed at the Kirov State Theater of Ballet and Opera in Leningrad. In the early 1990s, Johnson traveled with the DTH to postapartheid South Africa, where she strove to be an ambassador of change through the beauty of dance.

Among her television presentations, Johnson danced in PBS's *Dance in America* series and performed *Creole Giselle* for NBC. She also danced in and choreographed the television film *Ancient Voices of Children*.

Johnson continued to receive accolades for her roles in the 1990s: as the Accused in *Fall River Legend* with the Cleveland Ballet in 1991, and as Blanche in *A Streetcar Named Desire* at the DTH's twenty-fifth anniversary season at Lincoln Center in New York City in 1994.

On September 21, 1997, Johnson retired from the stage at age forty-seven. For twenty-eight years as the DTH's prima ballerina, she brought to her dramatic performances great sensitivity, an intense ferocity, and total generosity to her company and her audiences.

In 1999, Johnson became the founding editor in chief of *Pointe* magazine. The first issue, which debuted in spring of 2000, promised to help dancers improve their technique, advance their careers, and grow in their love of the art form. During the decade that Johnson ran the magazine, she expanded circulation to the online community. In 2009, she resigned to become the new artistic director of the Dance Theatre of Harlem.

BILL T. JONES (1952–)

Dancer, Choreographer. Jones was born into a family of twelve children in Florida in the early 1950s; eventually, his migrant-worker parents moved north to New York, where Jones excelled in high school athletics. Jones enrolled in the State University of New York at Binghamton in the early 1970s with the hope of pursuing a career in theater. He was already an accomplished actor, but eventually transferred into the university's dance department. While in college, Jones developed a romantic relationship with fellow dancer Arnie Zane.

Jones and Zane left Binghamton for the wider pastures of Amsterdam for several years; when they returned to New York City, they founded the American Dance Asylum, whose early mid-1970s performances caused a stir because of the dancers' onstage nudity. Jones and Zane formed a more accessible dance company in 1982. They named the troupe after themselves, and one of their first performances that year earned critical praise at the Brooklyn Academy of Music's innovative Next Wave Festival.

The Bill T. Jones/Arnie Zane Dance Company continued to thrive until Zane fell ill with AIDS. The principal's inability to tour almost ended the troupe's existence financially, and Zane's death in 1988 added greatly to Jones's burden. However, Jones was able to channel his grief toward the creation of a dance opus paying homage to his longtime partner, and the 1989 debut of *Absence* received laudatory reviews. The death of another member of the company resulted in another work, *D-Man in the Waters* (1989), that addressed issues of loss because of AIDS within the artistic community.

Jones has also addressed issues of African American culture, especially as experienced by those of alternative sexual orientation, in such productions as *Last Supper at Uncle Tom's Cabin* (1990). He has been candid about his own status as an HIV-positive person. In 1994, he was awarded a MacArthur Foundation fellowship; the following year, saw the premier of *Still/Here* at the Brooklyn Academy of Music. Jones coauthored a book, *Last Night on Earth* (1995), and collaborated with jazz drummer

Dancer and Choreographer Bill T. Jones, Tony Awards, Radio City Music Hall, New York City, 2007. *Jones accepts the Tony for best choreography for* Spring Awakening *on June 10, 2007. He continues to serve as artistic director for the troupe he cofounded, the Bill T. Jones/Arnie Zane Dance Company.* BRYAN BEDDER/GETTY IMAGES

Max Roach and novelist Toni Morrison on a dance piece titled *Degga*, performed at Lincoln Center that same year. Later, *Still/Here* became the subject of media sniping between Jones and New Yorker writer Arlene Croce, who termed it "victim art" in early 1996. Jones asserted that the New York media is biased in favor of Jewish matters. In 1997, Jones spoke to the American Dance Therapy Association at their annual conference about the use of such works as *Still/Here* in dance therapy.

Jones has continued to create such works as *Ur-Sonata* (1996), whose name comes from a poem by Dada artist Kurt Schwitters. Another work uses poems recorded by Dylan Thomas. In January 1999, Jones staged *We Set Out Early . . . Visibility Was Poor*, a new work exposing a more ecstatic and less political side of his work. It is symbolic and lyric, mixed with a marked desire for peace after the pain of loss. Jones continues to reach into his emotional life to manifest his art. In 2000, he went on a solo tour of America and Europe called *The Breathing Show*.

In 2001, Jones received a second Isadora Duncan Dance Award for his work *Fantasy in C-Major*, with the Axis Dance Company. He won his first "Izzy" collaborating with Rhodessa Jones and Idris Ackamoor on *Perfect Courage* in 1990. Jones was also the recipient of the 2003 Dorothy and Lillian Gish Prize, and he won three major awards in 2005—the Wexner Prize, the Samuel H. Scripps American Dance Festival Award for Lifetime Achievement, and a Harlem Renaissance Award.

In 2007, Bill T. Jones celebrated a year of milestones. His company commemorated its twenty-fifth anniversary. *Spring Awakening* marked his debut as a choreographer on Broadway. And at the award ceremony, Jones danced his way down the aisle to collect his Tony for best choreography.

Jones's next project was a tribute to Nigerian activist and Afrobeat originator Fela Anikulapo Kuti. Jones co-conceived, directed, and choreographed *FELA!* This critically acclaimed musical had a successful off-Broadway run at 37 Arts Theatre.

Jones had another busy year in 2009. He was commissioned by the Ravinia Festival in Illinois to create a dance-theater project to celebrate the bicentennial of Abraham Lincoln's birth. *Fondly Do We Hope . . . Fervently Do We Pray* opened at the festival in September, before the company went out on a lengthy tour. In November 2009, *FELA!* opened on Broadway. Shaun "Jay-Z" Carter, Will Smith, and Jada Pinkett-Smith are among the producers of this groundbreaking musical. *FELA!* marks Jones's directorial debut on Broadway. On June 13, 2010, Jones won a Tony for *FELA!*'s choreography.

ADRIENNE KENNEDY

See chapter 18, Literature.

WOODIE KING JR. (1937–)

Producer, Director, Writer. Born in Mobile, Alabama, but raised in Detroit, Woodie King became interested in acting while in his teens. During his last year at Cass Technical High School, King was offered a scholarship to the Will-O-Way School of Theatre in suburban Bloomfield Hills, Michigan. There he had the opportunity to study with such luminaries as Vincent Price and Helen Hayes; however, frustrated by the lack of roles for black actors in classical plays, King was prompted to produce.

While attending Detroit's Wayne State University, King teamed up with several other black theater students to found Concept-East, a community-based black theater company. King served as director and manager from 1960 to 1963. One of the plays, *Study in Color*, received enough widespread praise that King brought a touring production of the show to New York in 1964, where it played at the American Place Theatre. Rather than return to Detroit, King chose to stay in New York, where he continued working at the American Place, staging five plays.

In 1970, King founded a new company, the New Federal Theatre (NFT), named after the Harlem-based, government-funded troupe of the 1930s. Based at the Henry Street Settlement, King envisioned the NFT as a community theater that promoted the work of writers from diverse backgrounds. Numerous playwrights gained national attention after NTF showcased their work, including J. E. Franklin, *Black Girl*; Ron Milner, *What the Winesellers Buy*; Ed Bullins, *The Taking of Miss Janie*; David Henry Hwang, *Dance and the Railroad*; Damien Leake, *Child of the Sun*; Laurence Holder, *When Chickens Came Home to Roost*; Nikos Kazantzakis, *Christopher Columbus*; Alexis De Veaux, *No*; and Endesha Ida Mae Holland, *From the Mississippi Delta*. In addition, many notable actors, including Jackee Harry, Morgan Freeman, Denzel Washington, Debbie Allen, Phylicia Rashad, Glynn Turman, Esther Rolle, Samuel L. Jackson, Laurence Fishburne, Robert Downey Jr., Debbie Morgan, and Lynn Whitfield performed in NFT productions.

King also coproduced several plays on Broadway, including Leslie Lee's *The First Breeze of Summer* (1975) and Ntozake Shange's *For Colored Girls Who Have Considered Suicide/When the Rainbow Is Enuf* (1977). In the 1980s, he was executive producer of a musical, *Reggae* (1980), and directed the Broadway cast of Ron Milner's *Checkmates* (1988).

King wrote and directed *The Black Theatre Movement: "A Raisin in the Sun" to the Present*, which aired on PBS in 1979, and he scripted teleplays for the series *Sanford and Son*. King also edited or coedited a number of important anthologies, including *Black Drama Anthology*, *Black Short Story Anthology*, and *Black Poets and Prophets: The Theory, Practice, and Esthetics of the Pan-Africanist Revolution*, all published in 1972. King's own collection of essays, *Black Theater: Present Condition*, was published in 1981.

In 1997, King received an Obie Award for sustained achievement. *American Visions* dubbed Woodie King Jr. the "king of black theater producers" in its April 2000 issue. King also won the Actors' Equity Association Paul Robeson Award in 2004.

In 2007, King produced two of the playwrights whose groundbreaking work was nurtured at NFT—a retrospective of Ntozake Shange's work and a revival of Ed Bullins's *The Taking of Miss Janie*. King produces a main stage season at NFT, as well as the Gurfein Foundation/Ntozake Shange Play Reading Series, which focuses on presenting the seminal works of new and established playwrights. The 2009 series featured Shontina Vernon's *A Lovely Malfunction*, Levy Lee Simon's *Smell the Power*, Ed Pomerantz's *A Tune Beyond Us*, Josh Kashinsky's *Heel in the Sand*, and Cori Thomas's *Pa's Hat: Liberian Liberation*. Nobel laureate Derek Walcott's new play, *Marie Laveau*, was the final reading of the season.

In an effort to bring theater to the community, King produces the National Black Touring Circuit in association with theaters and performance spaces around New York City, such as the National Black Theatre, the Dwyer Cultural Center, the Schomburg Center for Research in Black Culture, and the Castillo Theatre. King's New Federal Theatre is one of the oldest black-owned theaters in the country. In 2010, they will celebrate their fortieth anniversary.

MARTIN LAWRENCE

See chapter 20, Film and Television.

JACKIE "MOMS" MABLEY
(1894–1975)

Comedienne. Moms Mabley was born Loretta Mary Aiken in Brevard, North Carolina, on March 19, 1894, and entered show business as a teenager when the team of Buck and Bubbles gave her a bit part in a vaudeville skit called *Rich Aunt from Utah*.

With the help of comedienne Bonnie Bell Drew, Mabley developed a monologue, and was soon being booked on the black vaudeville circuit. Influenced by such acts as Butterbeans and Susie, she developed her own comic character, a world-weary old woman in a funny hat and droopy stockings, delivering her gags with a mixture of sassy folk wisdom and sly insights. Her first big success came in 1923 at Connie's Inn in New York.

Engagements at the Cotton Club in Harlem and Club Harlem in Atlantic City followed.

White audiences discovered Moms Mabley in the early 1960s. Her album *Moms Mabley at the "UN"* became a commercial success and was followed by *Moms Mabley at the Geneva Conference.* In 1962, she made her Carnegie Hall debut on a program with Cannonball Adderley and Nancy Wilson. Her subsequent Broadway, film, television, and record successes made her the favorite of a new generation. Moms Mabley died on May 23, 1975, when she was seventy-eight years old, in White Plains, New York.

BERNIE MAC (1957–2008)

Comedian, Actor. Bernard "Bernie Mac" McCullough was born in 1957, one of fifteen children, and raised on the South Side of Chicago. Almost from the start he was destined to be a comic. He was just four when he witnessed his mother laughing until she cried as she watched Bill Cosby perform on television. The power Cosby had to elicit such a reaction made an impact. By the time he graduated from high school, his comic reputation was intact. Voted class clown by his fellow students, Mac turned the title down. "I thought it was an insult," he told *Entertainment Weekly.*

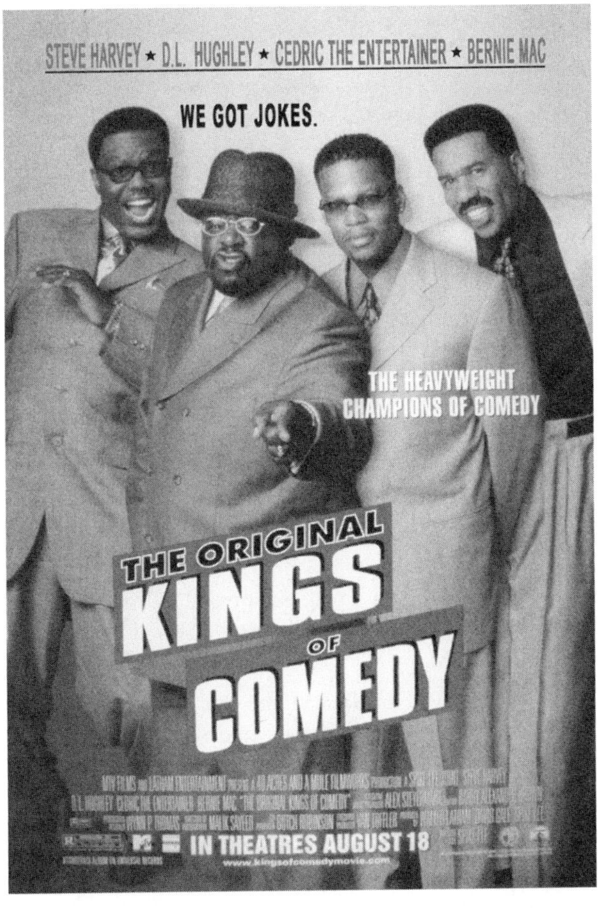

The Original Kings of Comedy, *Film, 2000.* *The stand-up comedians Bernie Mac, Cedric the Entertainer, D. L. Hughley, and Steve Harvey (*left to right*) star in the Spike Lee–directed documentary film.* PARAMOUNT/EVERETT COLLECTION

Mac's professional career started slowly. He worked a series of menial jobs to pay the rent and did impromptu stand-up in the subways, eliciting tips for laughs. Mac's first break came in Chicago in 1990 when he won the Miller Lite Comedy Search, which led to a spot on HBO's *Def Comedy Jam.* Damon Wayans was the host that night and was so impressed that he offered Mac a film debut in *Mo' Money* (1992).

Over the next few years, Mac appeared in many films. Often cast as a funny sideman, he proved himself in dramatic roles as well, most notably as Flip, a homeless ex-basketball star in *Above the Rim* (1994). Mac wrote and starred in his own HBO show, *Midnight Mac,* which was nominated for a Cable Ace Award in 1995. He developed a following because of his recurring role as Uncle Bernie on the television series *Moesha* and his featured roles in the cult films *Friday* (1995) and *Life* (1999).

Even as his small- and large-screen careers were taking off, Mac stepped up his live performance schedule. He went out on the road in 1994 with his own *Who Ya Wit* tour, which included a ten-piece band and five "Mac-A-Roni Dancers." In 1997, Mac joined four other comics, beginning the tour that would propel him into the realm of comedic royalty. Along with Steve Harvey, D. L. Hughley, and Cedric the Entertainer, Mac embarked on the *Original Kings of Comedy* tour. The show was the first comedy tour to move from headlining theaters and small arenas to selling out 11,000-seat stadiums. In fact, it became the highest-grossing comedy tour in history. The show's success drew the attention of director Spike Lee, and in February 2000 he headed to the Charlotte, North Carolina, show with twelve cameras, producing one of Hollywood's most unexpected hits, *The Original Kings of Comedy.* Mac was voted number seventy-two on Comedy Central's list of 100 Greatest Stand-ups of All Time.

Fresh off his success as a Comedy King, Mac came into national prominence in 2001 when he appeared as part of an ensemble cast of stars, including Hollywood heavy hitters Matt Damon, George Clooney, and Brad Pitt, in the remake of *Ocean's Eleven. Ocean's* was a hit, and in 2007 Mac completed the third sequel, *Ocean's Thirteen.*

In 2001, his first book, *I Ain't Scared of You: Bernie Mac on How Life Is,* was published, and FOX launched the *Bernie Mac Show,* which was an instant success and ran for five years. Among numerous other prizes and nominations, Mac's show was awarded an Emmy for outstanding writing, a Peabody Award for excellence in broadcasting, and the Humanitas Prize for television writing that promotes human dignity. *TV Guide* ranked Bernie Mac number forty-seven on their list of the "50 Greatest TV Dad's of All Time."

Besides the *Ocean's* franchise, Mac was featured in a string of popular movies, including *Charlie's Angels II* (2003), *Bad Santa* (2003), *Mr. 3000* (2004), *Guess Who?* (2005), *Pride* (2007), and *Transformers* (2007).

Bernie Mac died on August 9, 2008, as a result of complications of pneumonia. He was featured in three additional films that were released posthumously in 2008 and 2009: *Soul Men*, *Madagascar: Escape 2 Africa*, and *Old Dogs*.

AUDRA McDONALD (1970–)

Singer, Actress. Audra McDonald is one of the American theater's outstanding performers. Within a decade, she won four Tony Awards for her work in *Carousel* (1994), *The Master Class* (1996), *Ragtime* (1998), and *A Raisin in the Sun* (2004). She is the first African American to earn this distinction.

McDonald was born in Berlin, Germany, on July 3, 1970, and grew up in Fresno, California, as part of a musical family. Her parents were trained singers, and her aunts toured with a gospel-singing group. McDonald's professional career began at age nine when she performed at a dinner theater for young people. She played roles in *Hello, Dolly!*, *A Chorus Line*, *Grease*, and *The Wiz*. After graduating from the Roosevelt School of the Performing Arts in Fresno, McDonald enrolled at the prestigious Juilliard School of Music in Manhattan. However, since Broadway was always McDonald's first love, she was discontented at the classically oriented Juilliard. She took a break from her studies and landed a role in *The Secret Garden*, both on Broadway and in the touring company. She eventually went back to Juilliard and completed a bachelor's degree in 1993.

McDonald auditioned several times until she landed a role in the extravagant production of *Carousel*, staged at Lincoln Center in 1994. She won critical praise for her performance as Carrie Pipperidge, as well as the Tony, Drama Desk, Outer Critics Circle, and Theatre World awards that year. Her next star turn was as Sharon, an aspiring singer in conflict with the great opera diva Maria Callas in *Master Class*. In the show, Sharon sings a technically demanding aria from Giuseppe Verdi's *Macbeth*, a feat brilliantly carried off by McDonald. She earned a second Tony Award as best featured actress in a play.

Next, McDonald won a part in the musical *Ragtime*, based on E. L. Doctorow's best-selling 1975 novel about New York at the turn of the century. Her character, Sarah, a young black washerwoman who abandons her illegitimate child, is a small but pivotal part. McDonald won her third Tony Award for best featured actress in a musical in 1998.

Actress Audra McDonald, 2009. *Before starring in the television show* Private Practice, *McDonald made a name for herself on Broadway, winning four Tony Awards along the way. Her fourth Tony, which came in 2004, was for best featured actress for her work in* A Raisin in the Sun. **MICHAEL KOVAC/ FILMMAGIC/GETTY IMAGES**

In 1999, McDonald had the title role in a musical, *Marie Christine*, based on *Medea* and set in New Orleans and Chicago in the 1880s. That same year, McDonald appeared in ABC's remake of the musical *Annie*, as well as *Having Our Say: The Delany Sisters First 100 Years*. In 2001, the HBO movie *Wit* gained her an Emmy nomination.

McDonald made her film-acting debut with Anthony Quinn in *Seven Servants* (1996). Other films in which she was featured are *The Object of My Affection* (1998), Tim Robbin's *Cradle Will Rock* (1999), *It Runs in the Family* (2003), and *Best Thief in the World* (2004).

McDonald starred in two limited-run revivals in 2004: the Tony Award–winning *Henry IV* and Lorraine Hansberry's *A Raisin in the Sun*. Her role as Ruth Younger in the latter earned McDonald her fourth Tony for best featured actress in a play.

In 2007, McDonald starred in a Broadway revival of *110 in the Shade* and a television movie adaptation of *A Raisin in the Sun*. She won Grammys in the best classical album category and the best opera recording category for her work in *Weill: Rise and Fall of the City of Mahagonny* in 2009 and took to the stage as Countess Olivia in the Public Theater/Shakespeare in the Park's production of *Twelfth Night*.

Audra McDonald had recurring roles in three critically acclaimed but short-lived series: *Mister Sterling* (2003), *The Bedford Diaries* (2006), and *Kidnapped* (2006–2007). In 2007, she finally met with success in a *Grey's Anatomy* spinoff, *Private Practice*. McDonald plays Dr. Naomi Bennett, best friend of Dr. Addison Montgomery (Kate Walsh) and ex-wife of Dr. Sam Bennett (Taye Diggs). The series entered its third season in 2010.

DONALD McKAYLE (1930–)

Dancer, Choreographer, Company Director, Writer. Donald Cohen McKayle, born on July 6, 1930, in Harlem, New York, struggled from humble roots to become an eminent and distinguished American choreographer, performer, and director in dance, theater, film, and television. As a teenager, when McKayle saw a performance by the legendary Pearl Primus, he eagerly auditioned for the New Dance Group and, to his surprise, was awarded a scholarship. His voracious appetite for movement led him to take advantage of the multitude of dance offerings—modern, ballet, Haitian, Hindu, and tap.

There were few role models to guide his youthful aspirations, so he relied primarily on his own personal courage and persistence to pursue his dreams in the face of the social and racial restrictions. When he appeared for auditions during the late 1940s and was told no "Negroes" were wanted, he responded, "I am here, and I would like you to see me dance, maybe you'll change your mind."

In 1951, McKayle did change minds when he choreographed what would become an American classic, *Games*, based on childhood play, rhymes, and chants. Exploring

Donald McKayle, 2009. *Over his lengthy career, in addition to choreographing for dance companies, Broadway, television, and film, choreographer and dancer McKayle was a professor of dance at the University of California–Irvine, retiring in 2010 at the age of eighty.*
LYNN ISCHAY/THE PLAIN DEALER/LANDOV

the light, carefree innocence of youth and the darker social stigmas associated with racial and social divisions, *Games* brought to the concert stage over a century of inequities and prejudice. That same year, McKayle appeared on Broadway in *Bless You All*. Other Broadway performing credits include *House of Flowers* (1954), *Copper and Brass* (1957), and *West Side Story* (1957).

During the 1950s, he danced in the companies of such innovators as Jean Erdman, Mary Anthony, Merce Cunningham, Anna Sokolow, and Martha Graham. He was also artistic director and resident choreographer of Donald McKayle and Company from 1951 through 1969. His company featured artists who would eventually become prominent leaders and performers in the world dance scene, including Carmen de Lavallade, Arthur Mitchell, Alvin Ailey, Mary Hinkson, and Eliot Feld.

McKayle received five Tony nominations for his work on Broadway, including best choreographer for *Golden Boy* (1964), *Doctor Jazz* (1975), *Sophisticated Ladies* (1981), and *Raisin* (1974), which won a Tony Award for best musical plus another nomination for best director. For *Sophisticated Ladies*, he was also honored with an Outer Critics Circle Award and the NAACP Image Award. His most recent choreography for Broadway was showcased in *It Ain't Nothing' But the Blues*, which earned a Tony nomination for best musical in 1999.

McKayle's film choreography includes *The Great White Hope* (1970), *Bedknobs and Broomsticks* (1971), and *The Jazz Singer* (1980). He received Emmy nominations for *Minstrel Man* (1977) and the children's special, *Free to Be . . . You and Me* (1974).

Many international companies perform his masterworks in concert dance, including the Alvin Ailey American Dance Theater; the Batsheva Dance Company of Tel Aviv, Israel; Ballet Nuevo Mundo of Caracas, Venezuela; Ballet Contemporaneo of Buenos Aires, Argentina; and the San Francisco Ballet. In 2001, he choreographed a monumental ten-hour production of *Tantalus*, produced by the Royal Shakespeare Company for the Denver Center Theatre Company.

Appointed Claire Trevor Professor of Dance at the University of California, Irvine, McKayle received the UCI Medal, the university's highest honor, in 2000. He has also been named "One of America's Irreplaceable Dance Treasures: The First 100" by the Dance Heritage Coalition of the Library of Congress. McKayle's autobiography, *Transcending Boundaries: My Dancing Life*, was published in 2002, and *Heartbeats of a Dancemaker*, a PBS documentary about him, aired in 2003.

Rainbow Round My Shoulder, one of McKayle's most famous ballets, is featured in the 2010 season of Alvin Ailey. He remains a professor at the University of California, Irvine, and the artistic director of the UCI dance troupe.

BEBE MILLER (1950–)

Choreographer, Dancer, Artistic Director. Bebe Miller was born on September 20, 1950, to an elementary school teacher and a ship steward. Although she grew up in the housing projects of South Brooklyn, New York, her arthritic mother took the family to adult dance classes at Manhattan's Henry Street Settlement every Saturday. Soon, Miller was learning creative dance from Murray Louis and Alwin Nikolais, who taught children's dance classes there. Miller took traditional ballet classes at the Carnegie Hall School when she was thirteen. She soon stopped, unhappy with the formality of classic dance styles.

Miller resumed her study of modern dance when she was twenty and a student of fine arts at Earlham College in Richmond, Indiana. After graduating from Earlham in 1971, she moved back to New York to resume dance classes with Nikolais. She won a fellowship to study dance at Ohio State University in Columbus and earned a master's degree in 1975.

Two years later, Miller joined the modern dance company of Nina Wiener, who had studied with Alvin Ailey and Twyla Tharp. For six years, Wiener inspired Miller to infuse her technique with fun and intensity. Soon she was creating her own dances, and performing her group and solo pieces at New York City workshops devoted to developing modern dance choreographers. She left Weiner's company in 1982 and formed the Bebe Miller Company two years later.

Miller's dances have always reflected her inner and outer struggles. Her 1984 dance *Trapped in Queens* shows the difficulties of city life. *Two*, her collaborative duet with dancer Ralph Lemon, examines the changing relationships between men and women. Some of the black influences she brings to her dances show up in the accompanying music. She has used reggae (*Jammin'*, 1981), gospel (*Heart, Heart*, 1986), Duke Ellington (*Spending Time Doing Things*, mid-1980s), and Jimmie Hendrix (*The Hendrix Project*, 1991) as accompaniment. In addition to music, Miller collaborates with writers, set designers, and visual artists to create her unique performance pieces.

Miller and her company spent much of the mid-1980s touring throughout the United States and earning numerous accolades. She won four National Endowment for the Arts Choreographer's Fellowships, the New York Dance and Performance Award (the Bessie) for choreography for 1986 and 1987, and the American Choreographer Award and a John Guggenheim Memorial Fellowship in 1988.

Alvin Ailey commissioned Miller to create new works for his Alvin Ailey Repertory Ensemble in 1987. Miller produced a series of dances called *Habit of Attraction*, another look at the mysteries of relationships, the following year. Another work, *Allies*, was commissioned in 1989 by New York's Brooklyn Academy of Music and others. This was Miller's first appearance at the academy's Next Wave Festival and allowed her to work on a larger scale. *Allies* again studied human interaction and evolving relationships. Alongside *Allies*, Miller danced her signature solo, *Rain*, which describes in movement some of Miller's own social and spiritual views.

Her 1991 work, *The Hendrix Project*, tied music by Jimmie Hendrix and Bob Dylan and the vision of the 1960s to the cultural issues of the 1990s. It was danced in Los Angeles and San Francisco in a program titled *Black Choreographers Moving Towards the 21st Century*. The Bebe Miller Company then took it to New York and Europe.

In 1993, Miller conducted a residency class at the Walker Art Center in Minneapolis. She performed her works *In Mnemosyne's House* and *Again and Again*, which was a collaboration between Miller, environmental sculptor Eve Laramie, and the Minneapolis New Dance Ensemble, at the Walker. The mid-1990s saw the premieres of *Tiny Sisters*, *Yard Dance*, *Heaven and Earth*, *Blessed*, and *Rhythm Studies*.

More recently, Miller has been investigating the combination of theatrical narrative and abstract movement to express the human condition through the physical body. *Map of the Body* was developed as part of a master's class in September 1999. In 2000, Miller was named a Bill Como Fellow as part of the New York Foundation for the Arts Artists' Fellowships. Miller premiered *Verge* in 2001 at the Cultural Crossroads 651 festival. *Verge* would go on to win three New York Dance and Performance (Bessie) Awards for choreography.

In 2005, Miller's company celebrated its twentieth anniversary on the cutting edge. After two to three years of development, Miller has created a multimedia improvisational performance piece whose collaborators include dancers, dramaturges, and lighting, video, and animation artists. *Landing/Place* is an exploration of motion-capture technology as a potential choreographing tool.

Miller used the same creative team from *Landing/Place* to create another critically acclaimed, multimedia dance project. *Necessary Beauty* featured six women dancers of varying ages. It premiered in 2008 at the Wexner Center for the Arts in Columbus, Ohio, before touring the country.

In 2009, the Brooklyn Academy of Music's 651 Arts concluded its twentieth season with a tribute to five luminaries of the modern dance world. *FLY: Five First Ladies of Dance* featured solo performances by Bebe Miller, Dianne McIntyre, Jawole Willa Jo Zollar, Germaine Acogny, and Carmen de Lavallade at the Kumble Theater for the Performing Arts in Brooklyn. Miller performed *Rain*, the most popular segment of *Allies*, a thirty-five-minute piece commissioned by the Next Wave Festival twenty years earlier.

FLORENCE MILLS (1896–1927)

Singer, Dancer. Florence Mills was born in Washington, D.C., on January 25, 1896. She made her debut there when she was five years old in *Sons of Ham*. In 1903, the family moved to Harlem, and in 1910 she joined her sisters in an act called the Mills Trio. She later appeared with a group called the Panama Four, which included Ada "Bricktop" Smith.

In 1921, Mills appeared in *Shuffle Along*, a prototype for African American musicals. Her success led to a long engagement at the Plantation, a New York nightspot. After a successful appearance in London, she returned to the United States in 1924 to star in *From Dixie to Broadway*, in which she performed her trademark song, "I'm Just a Little Blackbird Lookin' for a Bluebird." Later, her own *Blackbirds* revue was a great success in London and Paris.

Mills returned to the United States in 1927. Exhausted by her work abroad, she entered the hospital on October 25 for a routine appendectomy and died suddenly on November 1.

ABBIE MITCHELL (1884–1960)

Singer, Actress. Most celebrated as a concert artist, Abbie Mitchell also performed on the stage and in light musical comedy. When she was thirteen, she returned to her native New York City from Baltimore, joining Will Marion Cook's Clorindy Company, and later achieving her first real success with the Williams and Walker Company.

By 1923, having performed in almost every European country, Mitchell returned home to give the first of her many voice concerts in the United States. Mitchell also performed with many opera companies and acted in several plays, including *Coquette* (1927), with Helen Hayes, *Stevedore* (1934), and Langston Hughes's *Mulatto* (1937). She also headed the voice department at Tuskegee Institute for three years.

ARTHUR MITCHELL (1934–)

Dancer, Choreographer. Mitchell was born in Harlem on March 27, 1934, and attended New York's famed High School of the Performing Arts. Mitchell was the first African American male to receive the high school's dance award in 1951.

After graduating in 1952, Mitchell enrolled as a scholarship student in the School of American Ballet, run by the eminent choreographer George Balanchine, who also directed the New York City Ballet. In 1955, Mitchell was invited by Balanchine to join the New York City Ballet. He integrated the company at a time when the prevailing thought was that blacks lacked "the classical line" needed for ballet. But Balanchine's only standard was talent. He sought the best dancers without regard to race. Before long, Mitchell was a principal dancer in the company, performing in such works as *Agon* and *A Midsummer Night's Dream*.

Mitchell left the New York City Ballet in 1969 to establish the Dance Theatre of Harlem (DTH), which he founded to give young African Americans an artistic outlet for their talents and to dispel the notion that blacks did not have the disposition for ballet. As the world evolved, the company adapted its mission to become a multicultural institution, employing dancers from many different ethnic groups.

Over the years, Arthur Mitchell and DTH garnered numerous awards and citations, including the Changers Award given by *Mademoiselle* magazine in 1970 and the Capezio Dance Award in 1971. In 1993, New York City mayor David Dinkins presented Mitchell with the Handel Medallion, the city's highest cultural honor. He was also one of the winners of the Kennedy Center Honors and the National Medal of Arts in 1993. The School of American Ballet presented Mitchell with a lifetime achievement award at its annual dinner on February 6, 1995. In 1999, Mitchell was inducted into the Dance Hall of Fame. In 2005, in recognition of his contributions to African American culture, Mitchell won a Fletcher Foundation Fellowship. President George W. Bush honored Mitchell and DTH at a White House dinner in 2006.

Although the DTH touring company has been on hiatus since 2004 because of financial hardship, the school remains open and viable. Dancing Through Barriers is more than an education initiative; it speaks to the heart and spirit of DTH and its cofounder, Arthur Mitchell. In 2009, Mitchell became artistic director emeritus. He has entrusted the future of the company to Virginia Johnson, one of DTH's most famous principal dancers. Mitchell and Johnson have strategic plans to reinstate the professional company to touring status.

Arthur Mitchell continues to influence the lives of dancers. The USA International Ballet Competition named Mitchell their honorary chairman in 2010. Like the Olympics, this competition takes place every four years and awards gold, silver, and bronze medals, as well as cash prizes, company contracts, and scholarships.

MO'NIQUE

See chapter 20, Film and Television.

EDDIE MURPHY

See chapter 20, Film and Television.

FAYARD NICHOLAS (1914–2006) AND HAROLD NICHOLAS (1921–2000)

Dancers. The Nicholas Brothers were one of the great tap dance teams of the first half of the twentieth century. Their acrobatics and precision were admired by the likes of Fred Astaire and George Balanchine, and their appearances in motion pictures provide a record of their astounding abilities.

Fayard Nicholas was born in 1914; Harold in 1921. Their professional debut was, ironically, on the radio program *The Horn and Hardart Kiddie Hour* in 1931. In 1932, they became a featured act at Harlem's Cotton Club. They made their first Broadway appearance in the *Ziegfeld Follies of 1936*. This was followed by *Babes in Arms* in 1937.

The Nicholas Brothers' film debut was in *Pie Pie Blackbird* in 1932, and they appeared in several other movies in the 1930s and 1940s, including *The Big Broadcast of 1936* (1936), *The Great American Broadcast* (1941), *Sun Valley Serenade* (1941), *Stormy Weather* (1943), and *The Pirate* (1948). The latter is particularly memorable for the sequence in which they are featured.

Harold Nicholas married actress Dorothy Dandridge in 1942, but the couple later divorced. The two brothers continued to be active in the world of dance into the 1980s: Harold costarred with Gregory Hines in the movie *Tap* in 1989, and Fayard won a Tony Award for best choreographer for the Broadway musical *Black and Blue* in the same year.

In 1992, the Nicholas Brothers were honored by the Kennedy Center. They received awards from *Dance Magazine* in 1995. A gala for the Nicholas Brothers, called *From Harlem to Hollywood: A Tribute to the Nicholas Brothers, Tap Legends*, was celebrated at Carnegie Hall in April 1998. It starred Gregory Hines, Lena Horne, Savion Glover, Maya Angelou, Maurice Hines, Ben Vereen, and Jimmy Slide, representing the many generations influenced and inspired by these "Tap Legends." In 2003, the Nicholas Brothers were inducted into the Hall of Fame of the National Museum of Dance.

FREDERICK O'NEAL (1905–1992)

Actor. Frederick O'Neal was the first black person to hold the position of president of Actors' Equity Association, a fitting tribute to his long years of service to the American theater as both actor and teacher. O'Neal was born on August 27, 1905, in Brookville, Mississippi. After his father's death in 1919, he moved with his family to St.

Dancers Fayard Nicholas and Harold Nicholas,* Sun Valley Serenade, *January 10, 1941. *The tap dance team of brothers performed at Harlem's Cotton Club, on Broadway, and in films. Ironically, their professional debut was on radio, in 1931.*

Louis, finishing high school there and appearing in several Urban League dramatic productions.

In 1927, with the help of some friends in St. Louis, O'Neal founded the Ira Aldridge Players, the second African American acting troupe in America. For the next ten years, he played in thirty of its productions. In 1937, he moved to New York, and three years later helped found the American Negro Theater. Its alumni include such established stars as Sidney Poitier, Earle Hyman, Harry Belafonte, Ruby Dee, Ossie Davis, and Hilda Simms.

O'Neal himself starred in *Anna Lucasta* (1944), for which he won the Clarence Derwent Award and the Drama Critics Award for the best supporting performance by an actor on Broadway. He was later featured in *Take a Giant Step*, *The Winner*, and several other stage productions. His films include *Pinky* (1949) and *The Man with the Golden Arm* (1956). He also appeared on several televised dramatic and comedy shows.

In 1964, O'Neal became the first black president of Actors' Equity. After devoting himself full-time to Actors' Equity, O'Neal was in 1970 elected international president of the Associated Actors and Artists of America, the parent union of all show business performers' unions. He later became president and chairman of the board of the Schomburg Center for Research in Black Culture, a position that included such responsibilities as raising money to conserve and preserve materials in the center, soliciting resources for the institution, and lobbying for the construction of a new building. He was a member of the New York State Council on the Arts, president of the Catholic Interracial Council, chairman of the AFL-CIO Civil Rights Committee, and vice president of the A. Philip Randolph Institute. In 1980, he received the National

Urban Coalition's Distinguished Trade Unionist Award. In 1990, he received a special tribute from the Black Filmmakers Hall of Fame. O'Neal died on April 27, 1992.

PEARL PRIMUS (1919–1994)

Dancer, Choreographer. Pearl Primus's anthropological approach to dance made her one of the most purposeful figures in that medium: for her, dance was education, not merely entertainment. Her aim was to show audiences and dancers alike the African roots of dance and to bring the African American experience alive.

Primus was born in Trinidad on November 29, 1919. Originally intending to pursue a career in medicine, she received a bachelor of arts degree in premedical sciences and biology from Hunter College in New York City, with graduate work in medical education and psychology. But 1940s America did not welcome blacks or women in medicine, and after seeking employment in vain, Primus sought assistance from the government's National Youth Administration. She was put into a youth administration dance group and by 1941 was accepted into New York City's New Dance Group. Her professional debut was at the Young Men's Hebrew Association in New York City on February 14, 1943. In April of that year, she began appearing at Cafe Society Downtown, the famed New York City nightclub. She left after ten months for an appearance on Broadway at the Belasco Theatre. By this time, she had her own dance company—Pearl Primus, Percival Borde, and Company. She toured Africa and the southern United States, and incorporated what she learned into her dance style.

Primus is best known for the dances *African Ceremonial* and *Strange Fruit*, which were incorporated into her *Solos for Performance at the Cafe Society* (c. 1944) and *Hard Times Blues* (1945). Primus died on October 29, 1994.

RICHARD PRYOR (1940–2005)

Comedian, Actor. Comedian Richard Pryor had great success as a stand-up comedian, writer, actor, and recording star. He often used elements of his unconventional upbringing and adult life as material in his comedy routines.

Born Richard Franklin Lennox Thomas Pryor III on December 1, 1940, in New York City, he was raised by his grandmother in a brothel she ran in Peoria, Illinois. His mother worked there as a prostitute. His parents married when he was three years old, but the union did not last. His grandmother was a strict disciplinarian, and young Richard was often beaten.

Pryor joined the army in 1958 and spent two years in Germany. He returned to Peoria after his military service and during the early 1960s began his work as a stand-up comic on a local circuit. In 1963, he moved to New York City's Greenwich Village, where he honed his stand-up routine. A 1964 appearance on *The Ed Sullivan Show* led to his first movie role in *The Busy Body* (1966), followed by bit parts in the 1968 films *The Green Berets* and *Wild in the Streets*. During this time, Pryor continued to play to live audiences.

Pryor played Piano Man in *Lady Sings the Blues* (1972) and earned an Academy Award nomination for his performance. Throughout the 1970s, Pryor continued his work as a stand-up comic and contributed his writing talents to *The Flip Wilson Show*, *Sanford and Son*, Mel Brooks's *Blazing Saddles* (1974), and Lily Tomlin's television special, *Lily* (1973), for which he won an Emmy Award. He won two of his five Grammy Awards for his comedy albums, *That Nigger's Crazy* (1974) and *Bicentennial Nigger* (1976). His first concert film, *Richard Pryor Live in Concert* (1979), brought his stand-up act to millions.

In 1976, Pryor wrote and starred in *The Bingo Long Traveling All-Stars & Motor Kings* and received raves for his work with Gene Wilder in *Silver Streak*. The two scored another hit with *Stir Crazy* (1980), directed by Sidney Poitier.

Pryor suffered a major heart attack in 1978, and, while freebasing cocaine in 1980, he set himself ablaze and suffered severe injuries. He addresses these incidents in his second concert movie, *Live on Sunset Strip* (1982). Pryor also cowrote, directed, and starred in *Jo Jo Dancer, Your Life Is Calling* (1985), a semiautobiographical tale of a comedian who relives his life immediately following a near fatal accident. Pryor's health continued to deteriorate. He was diagnosed with multiple sclerosis in 1986 but continued working well into the 1990s.

Pryor's other popular films include *Uptown Saturday Night* (1974), *Car Wash* (1976), *Which Way Is Up?* (1977), *Greased Lightning* (1977), *Blue Collar* (1978), *The Wiz* (1978), *California Suite* (1978), *Bustin' Loose* (1981), *The Toy* (1982), *Superman III* (1983), and *Brewster's Millions* (1985). In 1989, Pryor costarred with Eddie Murphy in *Harlem Nights*. He teamed with Gene Wilder for the last time in the 1991 film *Another You*. In 1993, Pryor was given a star on the Hollywood Walk of Fame.

In 1995, Pryor published a memoir, *Pryor Convictions and Other Life Sentences*, detailing his difficult childhood, failed marriages, and battles with cocaine addiction and multiple sclerosis. In 1998, Pryor was honored with the first Mark Twain Prize for American Humor, and in 2000 he won the MTV Lifetime Achievement Award.

Pryor successfully sued for the legal rights to the master tapes of his early comedy recordings. Rhino Records released them in 2005 as a double CD set, *Evolution/Revolution: The Early Years* (1966–1974). *Richard Pryor: I Ain't Dead Yet, #*%$#@!!*, a television documentary that aired in 2003, featured archival footage of Pryor and testimonials from fellow comedians such as Dave Chappelle on Pryor's influence on comedy. In 2004, Comedy Central voted Pryor the best stand-up comedian of all time.

Richard Pryor died of cardiac arrest on December 10, 2005, nine days after his sixty-fifth birthday. He was posthumously awarded a Grammy Lifetime Achievement Award in 2006.

PHYLICIA RASHAD

See chapter 20, Film and Television.

LLOYD RICHARDS (1923–2006)

Theatrical Director, Educator. Lloyd Richards, renowned actor, stage director, and educator, was born in Toronto, Ontario, in the early 1920s. While still young, he moved to Detroit, where he worked to support his family and eventually studied at Wayne State University, first law and then theater, receiving his degree in 1944. After serving in World War II as one of the first black pilots, he returned to Detroit and became active in radio drama and regional theater.

Soon Richards moved to New York to earn a living acting in plays and television dramas and coaching others in his own studio. In 1959, Sidney Poitier convinced him to direct an important Broadway play, Lorraine Hansberry's *Raisin in the Sun*. This play, the first by a black woman to be produced on Broadway, explores issues of segregation, thwarted ambition, and family tensions. It ran for 530 performances and made its stars and Richards famous. In the wake of that success, Richards began teaching drama at Hunter College and New York University.

In 1968, Richards was named artistic director of the prestigious National Playwrights Conference at the Eugene O'Neill Memorial Theater Center in Waterford, Connecticut. He continued to nurture such promising playwrights as August Wilson, Athol Fugard, Wendy Wasserstein, John Patrick Shanley, Charles Fuller, and David Henry Hwang, producing their plays in regional theaters. In 1979, Richards became dean of the Yale School of Drama and artistic director of the Yale Repertory Theatre.

Many famous plays debuted at the Yale Repertory Theatre under Richards's direction. These include South African playwright Athol Fugard's *Master Harold and the Boys* (1982) and two Pulitzer Prize–winning works by August Wilson, *Fences* (1987) and *The Piano Lesson* (1990). He won the Tony Award for best director for *Fences* in 1987.

Richards's most creative partnership was with August Wilson, for whom he directed not only *Fences* and *The Piano Lesson* but also *Ma Rainey's Black Bottom* (1984), *Joe Turner's Come and Gone* (1988), and *Two Trains Running* (1992), for which he was awarded the Helen Hayes Award for best director in 1992.

The Yale Repertory Theatre also attracted a number of notable actors while Richards was in residence, including James Earl Jones, Glenn Close, Jason Robards, Colleen Dewhurst, and Angela Bassett. In 1979, Richards directed Jones in a one-man show about the life and career of black actor Paul Robeson.

Lloyd Richards left the Yale Repertory Theatre in 1991, after twelve years as dean and artistic director. However, he held his post as artistic director of the Eugene O'Neill until 1999 and continued to direct, lecture, and mentor new talent in the theater. In 1995, he directed a Hallmark Hall of Fame production of *The Piano Lesson* for television, starring Charles S. Dutton and Alfre Woodard.

Among his many honors, Richards was inducted into the Theater Hall of Fame in 1990. Other distinctions include the Directors Award from the National Black Theatre Festival, a National Medal of Arts from President Bill Clinton in 1993, the Huntington Award for lifetime achievement in 1995, and a 1996 Outer Critics Award for best director of Wilson's *Seven Guitars*. Lloyd Richards died of heart failure on his eighty-seventh birthday on June 29, 2006.

BILL "BOJANGLES" ROBINSON (1878–1949)

Dancer. Bill Robinson was born in May of 1878, in Richmond, Virginia. Orphaned early, he was raised by his grandmother, who had been enslaved before Emancipation. By the time he was eight, Robinson was earning his own way by dancing in the street for pennies and working as a stable boy.

In 1887, Robinson toured the South in a show called *The South Before the War*. The following year, he moved to Washington, D.C., where he again worked as a stable boy. By 1896, he had teamed up with George Cooper. This act was successful on the circuit until the slump of 1907 caused it to fold. Robinson returned to Richmond and worked as a waiter until a year later, when he was taken up by a theatrical manager and became a cabaret and vaudeville headliner.

In 1927, Robinson starred on Broadway in *Blackbirds*, and in 1932 he had top billing in *Harlem's Heaven*, the first all-black motion picture with sound.

Child Actress Shirley Temple with Bill "Bojangles" Robinson,* The Littlest Rebel, *1935. Robinson was a cabaret and vaudeville headliner before he starred in* Blackbirds *on Broadway in 1927.* The Littlest Rebel *was one of two 1935 films he made with Shirley Temple. EVERETT COLLECTION

Later, he scored a Hollywood success by teaching his famous stair dance to Shirley Temple in *The Little Colonel* (1936). Robinson made fourteen movies, including *The Littlest Rebel* (1935), *In Old Kentucky* (1936), *Rebecca of Sunnybrook Farm* (1938), *Stormy Weather* (1943), and *One Mile from Heaven* (1938).

Throughout his long career on stage and in movies, Robinson was known as the "King of Tap Dancers." Robinson died on November 15, 1949.

CHRIS ROCK

See chapter 20, Film and Television.

NTOZAKE SHANGE

See chapter 18, Literature.

NOBLE SISSLE (1889–1975)

Lyricist, Singer. Noble Sissle was born in Indianapolis, Indiana, on July 10, 1889. He reaped his early successes teamed up with the great Eubie Blake. Sissle wrote the lyrics and sang them in performance. Blake composed and played the music. Together the two created such songs as "I'm Just Wild about Harry," "It's All Your Fault," "Serenade Blues," and "Love Will Find a Way."

In 1921, *Shuffle Along*, the first black musical with a love theme, made Sissle and Blake famous. Joining forces with the writing and comedy team of Flournoy Miller and Aubrey Lyles, Sissle and Blake wrote the words and music to more than a dozen songs for the show. *Shuffle Along* became a huge success in the United States and Europe, where it had a prolonged tour. As with most black performers in the early 1900s, Sissle and his troupe would have to travel as far as twenty or thirty miles out of their way to find a place to eat and sleep, since blacks were not welcome in the white hotels of the towns where they played.

Other Sissle and Blake shows included *Chocolate Dandies* (1924) and *Keep Shufflin'* (1928). Noble Sissle died December 17, 1975, at his home in Tampa, Florida.

WANDA SYKES (1964–)

Comedienne, Actress. Wanda Sykes was born March 7, 1964, in Portsmouth, Virginia, and grew up in the Washington, D.C., metro area with her parents and older brother. Though friends and family dubbed her a funny girl early on, Wanda's route to stand-up was circuitous. After graduating from Hampton University with a bachelor's degree in marketing in 1986, Sykes went to work for the National Security Agency (NSA). Armed with a five-minute routine she wrote at her desk, Sykes took to the stage in the Coors Light Super Talent Showcase a year later. Although she did not win, Wanda recognized comedy was her calling and spent the next few years moonlighting at local clubs to hone her skill.

In 1992, Sykes quit her day job and moved to New York to pursue comedy full time. She got her first big break opening for Chris Rock at Caroline's Comedy Club in 1995. Rock saw her potential, and in 1997 he gave her a job as a writer, performer, and coproducer on *The Chris Rock Show*. In 1999, she won her first Emmy Award for outstanding writing for a variety, music, or comedy special.

Not one to rest on her laurels, Sykes continued to explore numerous outlets for her brand of outspoken comedy. She appeared in comedic films such as *Nutty Professor II: The Klumps* (2000), *Down To Earth* (2001), and *Pootie Tang* (2001), a character sketch spin-off from *The Chris Rock Show*. Also in 2001, she made her first of many appearances on *The Tonight Show with Jay Leno*, became Drew's love interest in *The Drew Carey Show*, joined the cast of the long-running series *Curb Your Enthusiasm*, and won an American Comedy Award for outstanding female stand-up comic.

Comedienne Wanda Sykes, Century City, CA, 2010. *Stand-up comic, talk-show host, and actress Sykes accepting the Stephen F. Kolzak Award at the 21st Annual Gay & Lesbian Alliance against Defamation (GLAAD) Media Awards.* ANGELA WEISS/ GETTY IMAGES

Sykes lent her vocal talents to the irreverent Comedy Central puppet show *Crank Yankers* in 2002, but her career in voiceover animation began in earnest in 2006. In that year alone, she was cast as Sister Moon in *The Adventures of Brer Rabbit,* Stella in *Over the Hedge,* Innoko in *Brother Bear II,* and Bessy the Cow in *Barnyard,* a role she later reprised in the Emmy Award–winning children's series *Back at the Barnyard.* Other films in which Sykes has been featured include *Monster-in-Law* (2005), *Clerks II* (2006), *My Super Ex-Girlfriend* (2006), *Evan Almighty* (2007), and *License to Wed* (2007).

Wanda Sykes has written, produced, and starred in three self-titled shows, including the sitcom *Wanda at Large* (2003) on FOX and Comedy Central's *Wanda Does It* (2004). She broke both color and gender lines when she began hosting Fox's late night-talk show, *The Wanda Sykes Show,* in 2009.

An avid football fan, Wanda crashed an after party and talked her way onto the longest-running show in cable history. When an HBO executive overheard her heckling Bob Costas, she landed an ongoing gig as a correspondent on *Inside the NFL.* Her comic banter and cheeky interviews with the players earned her three shared Emmys in 2002, 2004, and 2005 for outstanding weekly studio show.

Though television has become her bread and butter, Sykes's stinging witticism was made for stand-up. Combining the two has brought her much critical acclaim. Three of her most popular televised comedy specials are *Wanda Sykes: Tongue-Tied* (2003), *Wanda Sykes: Sick & Tired* (2006), and *Wanda Sykes: I'ma Be Me* (2009), in which she makes light of her life as a recently married gay woman with children and muses about the sex life of President Barack Obama and the First Lady. It is her brazenly candid take on life that makes Wanda Sykes funny, controversial, and constantly working. In 2010, she is juggling her new family, her nightly talk show, and her fourth season on the popular CBS series *The New Adventures of Old Christine.*

LYNNE THIGPEN (1948–2003)

Actress. Lynne Thigpen spent more than twenty-five years proving that she could make a living working on stage, screen, and television as a professional actress. She grew up in Joliet, Illinois, "always a singer and always a performer." Her high school English teacher encouraged her theatrical pursuits, so, after graduation, she enrolled at the University of Illinois in Champaign-Urbana, where she majored in English and speech. Although pursuing teaching certification, she won an acting fellowship to the university and began a master's degree in theater. After one semester, she left school for New York and Broadway.

Soon after arriving in New York, Thigpen landed a two-year role in the popular musical *Godspell* on Broadway, which later led to a role in the 1973 film version. She then worked as a musical performer in various stage productions, including *Tintypes,* for which she earned a Tony nomination in 1980. Deciding that singing was not enough, Thigpen switched to acting and won recurring roles on such television shows as *All My Children, L.A. Law,* and *Law & Order.* Family programs, such as *The Cosby Show, Dear John,* and *Roseanne,* showcased her comedic talents. She also appeared in many films, among them *Tootsie* (1982), *The Paper* (1994), *Lean on Me* (1989), and *Bob Roberts* (1992).

Serious drama highlighted Thigpen's versatile talents. In 1988, she won the Los Angeles Drama Critic's Award for her role opposite James Earl Jones in August Wilson's *Fences.* She was also honored with an Obie Award for her portrayal of an itinerant South African woman in Athol Fugard's *Bozeman and Lena* in 1992.

In the 1990s, Thigpen became known for her role as the Chief on the PBS children's show *Where in the World Is Carmen Sandiego?* Over her six years in this series, she was nominated four times for Emmys as outstanding performer in a daytime children's television series. Thigpen was named associate artistic director of the Circle Repertory Company in New York City in 1995, along with Austin Pendleton, only to decline it a few months later to continue acting full-time. She played the role of a childless Jewish African American woman in Wendy Wasserstein's *An American Daughter*, winning the 1997 Tony Award for best featured actress.

Thigpen's voice alone won her recognition. She narrated numerous documentaries for PBS. She was also heard on radio on Garrison Keillor's *Prairie Home Companion.* Listeners of books on tape know her melodic voice from thoughtful narrations of works such as *The Autobiography of Miss Jane Pittman*, *Roll of Thunder, Hear My Cry*, *One Better*, and other audio productions. But few know she was the voice of the DJ in the 1979 cult film *The Warriors.*

Lynne Thigpen proved that stretching one's creative muscles in the performing arts can shape a varied and viable career. In 1999, she appeared in the movies *Random Hearts* and *Bicentennial Man.* She also starred in the off-Broadway show *Jar the Floor*, for which she won an Obie Award. In 2000, she was featured with Samuel L. Jackson in the remake of *Shaft* and became a regular on the popular television series *The District.* A year later, she appeared with Steve Martin in the comedy *Novocaine.* Her last film was *Anger Management* (2003), with Adam Sandler and Jack Nicholson.

Lynne Thigpen created such resonant and memorable characters that when she died of a cerebral hemorrhage on March 12, 2003, *The District* had a funeral for her character, and the Emmy Award–winning children's series she was featured in, *Bear in the Big Blue House*, went on hiatus for three years.

LESLIE UGGAMS (1943–)

Singer, Actress. Born in the Washington Heights section of New York City on May 25, 1943, Leslie Uggams enjoyed a comfortable childhood. She made her singing debut when she was six years old, performing with the choir of St. James Presbyterian Church in New York. Shortly thereafter, she debuted as an actress in the television series *Beulah.* A year later, Uggams began performing regularly at the famed Apollo Theater in Harlem, opening for such legends as Louis Armstrong, Ella Fitzgerald, and Dinah Washington. Uggams developed her poise and stage presence early in life, attending the Professional Children's School, where she was chosen student-body president in her senior year.

Uggams subsequently won $25,000 on the popular television quiz show *Name that Tune*, which renewed her interest in a singing career. In 1961, while studying at Juilliard, Uggams became a regular on *The Mitch Miller Show*, a variety show featuring old favorites. She was at the time the only black performer appearing regularly on network television.

Throughout the 1960s, Uggams appeared in numerous nightclubs and had several supper club and television engagements. Her big break came when she was signed as a replacement for Lena Horne in *Hallelujah Baby*, a show that presented a musical chronicle of the civil rights movement. Uggams won instant stardom and received a Tony Award for her performance.

In 1977, Uggams appeared as Kizzy in the television adaptation of Alex Haley's novel *Roots*. In May 1982, she performed in a new Broadway show, *Blues in the Night*, at the Rialto Theater in New York City. She has also appeared on television in the miniseries *Backstairs at the White House* (1979) and *The Book of Lists* (1982), in the 1972 film *Skyjacked*, and in the musicals *Jerry's Girls*, *The Great Gershwin*, and *Anything Goes*. Uggams won a Daytime Emmy for outstanding hostess of *Fantasy*, NBC's wish-fulfillment game show, in 1983.

After touring during the early 1990s in *Stringbean*, a musical based on the career of Ethel Waters, Uggams joined the cast of the hit daytime soap opera *All My Children* in 1996. Returning to the stage in 1998, Uggams appeared at Primary Stages in New York in the title role of the well-reviewed play *The Old Settler* by John Henry Redwood. In 2001, she received a Tony Award best-actress nomination for her performance in *King Hedley II*, a continuation of August Wilson's play *Seven Guitars*. A year later, Uggams helped garner critical acclaim for Keith Glover's bluesical *Thunder Knocking on the Door.*

Back on Broadway, Uggams got dazzling reviews when she joined the cast of *Thoroughly Modern Millie* in 2003. Uggams and James Earl Jones later starred in a revival of *On Golden Pond*, which was nominated for two 2005 Tony Awards but was forced to close early because Jones contracted pneumonia.

In *Stormy Weather*, a musical about Lena Horne's life, Uggams honored the diva who inadvertently gave her that first big break. The musical was originally workshopped by Amas Musical Theatre in New York in 2003. It had its world premiere at Philadelphia's Prince Music Theater in 2007, and its West Coast premiere at the Pasadena Playhouse in 2009. Uggams also starred in Stephen Sondheim's *A Little Night Music* at the Michigan Opera Theatre in 2009 and *Toe to Toe*, an indie film nominated for the Grand Jury Prize at the Sundance Film Festival.

BEN VEREEN (1946–)

Dancer, Actor, Singer. Ben Augustus Vereen was born October 10, 1946, in Miami, Florida. After his family moved to the Bedford-Stuyvesant section of Brooklyn, New York, he attended the High School of Performing Arts in Manhattan. His dancing ability was discovered almost accidentally after he was sent to dance school by his mother. Vereen has since been called America's premier song-and-dance man.

Vereen made his stage debut in 1965 in *The Prodigal Son*. He subsequently appeared in *Sweet Charity* (1966), *Golden Boy* (1968), *Hair* (1968), and *No Place to Be Somebody* (1970). Vereen is best known for his Broadway role in *Pippin* (1972), which won him a Tony Award. He was also nominated for a Tony for his costarring performance as Judas in *Jesus Christ Superstar* (1971), a role he reprised in the film. Other film appearances include roles in *Funny Lady* (1975), *All That Jazz* (1979), and *The Zoo Gang* (1985).

Vereen starred in the ABC comedy series *Tenspeed and Brown Shoe* (1980) and became known for his television specials; the highly acclaimed *Ben Vereen: His Roots* (1978) won seven Emmy Awards. He also portrayed Louis "Satchmo" Armstrong in 1976, and received wide acclaim for his performance as Chicken George in television's adaptation of Alex Haley's *Roots* (1977).

Vereen's concert tour in the late 1990s earned him the highest honors awarded by the American Guild of Variety Artists (AGVA): Entertainer of the Year, Rising Star, and Song and Dance Star. He is the first person to win three of these AGVA awards in one year. In 2002, Vereen returned to Broadway in *I'm Not Rappaport*, and in 2005 he joined the cast of *Wicked* as the Wonderful Wizard of Oz.

Ben Vereen continues to work in television and appear in movies, such as *Why Do Fools Fall in Love?* (1998), *I'll Take You There* (1999), and Anne Rice's *Feast of All Saints* (2001). He was featured with recording artists OutKast in *Idlewild* (2006) and singer/actress Vanessa Williams in *And Then Came Love* (2007).

His more recent projects include *Accidental Friendship* (2008), *21 and a Wake-Up* (2009), *Tapioca* (2009), and the film adaptation of the gospel musical *Mama, I Want to Sing* (2010), starring Ciara and Lynn Whitfield. In 2010, Vereen appeared on stage in *Fetch Clay, Make Man* at the McCarter Theatre Center. He also planned to tour his one-man show, *An Evening with Ben Vereen*, across the United States, Europe, and Abu Dhabi.

FREDI WASHINGTON (1903–1994)

Actress, Dancer, Civil Rights Activist. Born Fredericka Carolyn Washington in Savannah, Georgia, on December 23, 1903, Washington and her younger sister were sent to a convent after the death of their mother and subsequent remarriage of their father. As a teenager, she left this sheltered world to live with relatives in New York City in order to pursue a career in the performing arts.

One of Washington's first big breaks came in 1919 when she was cast as a member of the Happy Honeysuckles, the backup troupe for Josephine Baker. Two years later, she began earning a good salary in the stage production of an all-black musical called *Shuffle Along*. Washington was next discovered by Broadway impresario Lee Shubert, who urged her to audition for a play called *Black Boy*. In the 1926 production, she starred, under the stage name Edith Warren, opposite Paul Robeson, but unfortunately much media and audience attention at its debut was focused on Washington's light complexion. Indeed, she was often able to pass as white, especially when traveling in the segregated areas of the South with her first husband, a member of Duke Ellington's orchestra.

During the 1920s, Washington continued to appear in stage roles and toured Europe for a time; she also appeared in the 1930 production of *Sweet Chariot*. Moving on to film, Washington again teamed with Robeson when she appeared in the 1933 drama *The Emperor Jones*. But Hollywood censors insisted she wear makeup to darken her complexion during her love scenes with him. The following year, Washington appeared in her most acclaimed role in the film *Imitation of Life*, portraying a young woman who forsakes her heritage in order to pass as white.

Unfortunately, Washington found her acting career stymied by a lack of roles for African American women in general and especially for those with light complexions. She fought for many decades to reverse such attitudes in the film industry in Hollywood. In 1937, she founded the Negro Actors Guild of America, and she wrote extensively on the subject for the New York City–based paper *The People's Voice*, for which she served as theater critic and columnist. During the 1940s and 1950s, she worked as a cast consultant on numerous African American–themed films in Hollywood and continued to appear in stage productions. She died on June 28, 1994, in Stamford, Connecticut.

ETHEL WATERS (1896–1977)

Actress, Singer. The distinguished career of Ethel Waters spanned half a century. She showed her versatility by contributing to virtually every entertainment medium—stage, screen, television, and recordings.

Ethel Waters was born on October 31, 1896, and spent most of her childhood in her hometown of Chester, Pennsylvania. By the time she was seventeen, she was singing professionally at the Lincoln Theatre in Baltimore. During this early phase of her career, she became the first woman to perform W. C. Handy's "St. Louis Blues" on stage.

After several years in nightclubs and vaudeville, Waters made her Broadway debut in the 1927 revue *Africana*. In 1930, she appeared in *Blackbirds*, and in 1931 and 1932 she starred in *Rhapsody in Black*. The following year, she was featured with Clifton Webb and Marilyn Miller in Irving Berlin's *As Thousands Cheer*. In 1935, she costarred with Bea Lillie in *At Home Abroad*. Three years later, she played the lead in *Mamba's Daughters*.

In 1940, Waters appeared in the stage version of *Cabin in the Sky* and reprised the role in the 1943 movie version. Her other film appearances include *Rufus Jones for President* (1931), *Tales of Manhattan* (1941), *Cairo* (1942), *Stage Door Canteen* (1943), and *Pinky* (1949).

Her autobiography, *His Eye Is on the Sparrow*, was a 1951 Book-of-the-Month Club selection. The title is taken from a song that she sang in her 1950 stage success, *Member of the Wedding*. Waters died on September 1, 1977, in Chatsburg, California.

DAMON WAYANS

See chapter 20, Film and Television.

KEENEN IVORY WAYANS

See chapter 20, Film and Television.

BERT WILLIAMS (1874–1922)

Comedian, Dancer. The legendary Bert Williams is considered by many to be the greatest black vaudeville performer in the history of the American stage. Born on November 12, 1874, on New Providence Island in the Bahamas, Williams moved to New York with his family, and then to California, where he graduated from high school. After studying civil engineering for a time, he decided to try his hand at show business.

In 1895, Williams teamed with George Walker to form a successful vaudeville team. Five years later, they opened in New York in *The Sons of Ham* and were acclaimed for the characterizations that became their stock-in-trade—Walker as a dandy and Williams in blackface, complete with outlandish costumes and black dialect. The show ran for two years.

In 1902, their show *In Dahomey* was so popular that they took it to England, where it met with equal success. The partners continued to produce such shows as *The Policy Players*, *Bandanna Land*, and *Abyssinia* until Walker's death in 1909.

Thereafter, Williams worked as a featured solo performer in the Ziegfeld Follies, touring America for ten years in several versions of the show. His most famous songs were "Woodman, Spare that Tree," "O, Death, Where is Thy Sting," and "Nobody," his own composition and trademark. Williams died of pneumonia on March 4, 1922.

AUGUST WILSON

See chapter 18, Literature.

FLIP WILSON (1933–1998)

Comedian, Actor. Flip Wilson reached the pinnacle of the entertainment world with a series of original routines and ethnic characters rivaled only by those of Bill Cosby. Wilson's hilarious monologues, seen on a number of network television shows, made him the most visible black comedian of the early 1970s.

Born Clerow Wilson on December 8, 1933, Wilson was the tenth in a family of twenty-four children, eighteen of whom survived. The family was destitute, and Wilson was a troublesome youth in his hometown of Jersey City. He ran away from reform school several times and was ultimately raised in foster homes.

Wilson's comic talents first surfaced while he was serving in the U.S. Air Force. Sent overseas to the Pacific, Wilson entertained his buddies with preposterous routines. Back in civilian life, he worked as a bellhop and part-time showman. Opportunity struck in 1959 when a Miami businessman sponsored him for one year at $50 a week, which enabled Wilson to concentrate on the evolution of his routine. For the next five years or so, Wilson appeared regularly at the Apollo Theater in Harlem. In 1965, he began a series of appearances on *The Tonight Show*. Long-term contracts and several hit records followed, and Wilson became firmly established as one of the truly innovative talents in the comedy profession.

When *The Flip Wilson Show* premiered in the early 1970s, Wilson became the first African American with a self-titled, weekly prime-time television show. He became famous for his original character creations, such as Geraldine. On January 31, 1972, he appeared on the cover of *Time Magazine*. In 1976, he made his dramatic debut on television in the ABC series *The Six Million Dollar Man*.

During the early 1980s, Wilson appeared in numerous nightclubs and on television specials. He starred in the television series *People Are Funny* in 1984 and *Charlie & Co.* in 1985. He also recorded comedy albums, including *The Devil Made Me Buy this Dress*, for which he received a Grammy Award in 1970. Wilson died on December 1, 1998.

GEORGE C. WOLFE (1954–)

Playwright, Director, Producer. George Costello Wolfe was born September 23, 1954, in Frankfort, Kentucky. His father worked for the state, and his mother was an educator and later a school principal. Wolfe grew up in an insular African American community that stressed self-sufficiency and achievement. A visit to New York City as a teenager instilled in him a desire for a career in the theater, and by 1976 he had earned a bachelor's degree in theater from Pomona College.

After working for a few years in the Los Angeles theater scene, Wolfe moved to New York City in 1979. He earned two master of fine arts degrees in dramatic writing and musical theater from New York University. Minor recognition came with the 1985 off-off-Broadway production of his play *Paradise*, but Wolfe's 1986 satire on African American cultural icons, *The Colored Museum*, garnered attention and mixed reviews from critics. Eventually the play was staged at New York's Joseph Papp Public Theater. Wolfe won an Obie, and the play was broadcast on PBS.

Wolfe continued his affiliation with the Public Theater, directing several plays, including *Spunk* and *The Caucasian Chalk Circle*. With the 1992 Broadway debut of *Jelly's Last Jam*, a musical that Wolfe wrote and directed about the 1920s jazz musician Jelly Roll Morton, he rose to prominence in New York's theater community. In 1993, he directed parts one and two of the Pulitzer Prize–winning *Angels in America*, a play by Tony Kushner. For his direction of the first segment of the drama, *Millennium Approaches*, Wolfe won a Tony Award. For the second segment, *Perestroika*, he won a Tony Award for producing.

Another honor was accorded Wolfe in 1993 when he was named artistic director and producer of the Joseph Papp Public Theater and New York Shakespeare Festival. During his tenure, he was praised for giving the venerable institution a more multicultural focus. Works under his directorial aegis included a revival of *The Tempest* (1995) and the hit Broadway musical *Bring in 'da Noise, Bring in 'da Funk* (1996). *Noise/Funk* won four Tony Awards, one of them for Wolfe's direction.

Topdog/Underdog, *Ambassador Theater, New York City, April 7, 2002.* *For this work, playwright Suzan-Lori Parks became the first African American woman to win the Pulitzer Prize for Drama. At the curtain call for its Broadway debut on this day* (left to right*): actor Jeffrey Wright, director George C. Wolfe, Parks, and actor Mos Def.* GETTY IMAGES

In 1998, Wolfe revived *Macbeth*, starring Alec Baldwin and Angela Bassett. He also restaged the classic musical *On the Town*. From 1999 to 2000, Wolfe delved deeper into Shakespeare's canon with *The Taming of the Shrew* and *Julius Caesar*. He then took the theater in a new direction, mounting original work, such as Suzan Lori-Parks's *Topdog/Underdog* in 2001 and *Elaine Stritch at Liberty* in 2002.

In addition to multiple Tony Awards, Wolfe has been the recipient of Drama Desk, Outer Critics Circle, Drama-Logue, and Obie awards. He was named Person of the Year by the National Theater Conference and "a living landmark" by the New York Landmark Conservatory. His alma mater, Pomona College, gave him an honorary doctorate in 1995.

In 2004, Wolfe announced his intention to step down as the Public Theater's artistic director to pursue various creative endeavors, starting with an HBO film adaptation of Ruben Santiago-Hudson's play *Lackawanna Blues*. Wolfe continues his affiliation with the Public. He directed Tony Kushner's *Caroline, or Change* in 2004 and a New York Shakespeare Festival production of Bertolt Brecht's *Mother Courage and Her Children* in the summer of 2006. More recently in film, Wolfe appeared as an actor in *The Devil Wears Prada* (2006) and directed *Nights in Rodanthe* (2008).

In 2009, the McCarter Theatre Center gave Wolfe an incentive to return to the stage. As winner of the center's first Sallie Goodman Prize, Wolfe was awarded $20,000 and an opportunity to direct a play of his choice.

22

CLASSICAL MUSIC

Robert L. Sims

When the first Africans arrived in 1619 in Jamestown, Virginia, they brought with them a rich musical heritage. In the culture from which these continental Africans were torn, music and dance were part of nearly every activity. The songs, poems, and dances these Africans brought to the New World were integral to their very lives. These Africans were the heirs of traditions passed down orally for generations by expert musicians in their original communities.

BLACK MUSICIANS IN EARLY AMERICA

Brought as captives to the New World, the Africans were stripped of material possessions and severely restricted in expressing their cultural identity. Yet they were able to remember and pass down some of their rich cultural and musical traditions to their children. This enslaved population also absorbed much of the folk and religious music of white culture—they sang English psalms and hymns in church as they converted to Christianity, and heard folk and popular tunes in the taverns and homes in which they worked. Yet these enslaved Africans cherished their indigenous practices and adapted music from European American culture to blend with those practices. The resulting hybrid was a uniquely American style of music.

Some enslaved Africans in the South studied with itinerant music teachers, and the most talented students gained professional skills that were quickly put to use by whites. Bonded servant musicians who played such instruments as the violin, flute, and piano provided recreational music for their masters. On the self-sufficient plantations of the South, the most musically gifted domestic slaves provided evening entertainments. They also played at dance balls and dancing schools. Once public concerts became possible and popular in the New World, a few talented enslaved men and women actually gave public concerts.

EARLY AFRICAN AMERICAN COMPOSERS AND CONDUCTORS

The accomplishments of early African American musicians stretched well beyond performing instrumental music. African Americans were dance and military band leaders, composers and arrangers, singers, church choral directors, and entertainers. Free African Americans in northern cities, including Boston, Philadelphia, and New York, established remarkable careers and enjoyed wide esteem well before the Civil War (1861–1865).

Frank Johnson (c. 1792–1844) was a virtuoso bugler and flutist, a prolific composer and arranger, and a bandmaster whose organizations were in great demand for military ceremonies and public dances. Johnson was one of Philadelphia's celebrated citizens, and accomplished a number of firsts as an African American musician: he was the first to publish sheet music; the first to tour nationally and internationally (most notably in England) to wide acclaim; the first to give formal band concerts that included African American and white musicians; and the first person of any race to introduce the promenade concert to American audiences.

Sheet Music Cover for "Boone Infantry Brass Band Quick Step," 1844. *Bandmaster Francis "Frank" Johnson was a popular musician in Philadelphia. An arranger and composer, he is also known for being the first African American to publish sheet music.* THE LIBRARY OF CONGRESS

In the nineteenth century, as styles and customs changed, musicians such as Will Marion Cook (1869–1944) and James Reese Europe (1881–1919) inherited Johnson's legacy in both public acceptance of their music and their anticipation of later musical trends.

Other leading conductors of both social and military bands included James Hemmenway (1800–1849), Aaron Connor (d. 1850), Isaac Hazzard (1804–1865), and William Appo (1808–1887), all based in Philadelphia, along with Peter O'Fake (1820–1884) of Newark, and J. W. Postlewaite (1827–1889) of St. Louis.

Though there were free African American communities in Baltimore, Washington, D.C., Richmond, and Charleston, it was New Orleans that became the musical epicenter for African American musicians in the nineteenth century. Brass bands of well-trained musicians were particularly popular in New Orleans and are still part of the city's musical heritage today. As early as 1830, New Orleans was home to a 100-member Negro Philharmonic Society, which presented concerts that often featured visiting artists.

After the Civil War, African Americans found themselves in a precarious situation. The now-freed men and women had their liberty, but with no land and few worldly possessions, they were ill-equipped to advance economically. They were victimized by the sharecropping system, dehumanized by the enactment of Jim Crow laws, and terrorized by white supremacist groups, including the Ku Klux Klan. The music of newly freed African Americans reflected their experiences, the challenges of urban life, and the joy, loneliness, uncertainty, and sadness they experienced in their precious but uncertain freedom.

AFRICAN AMERICAN VIOLINISTS

The violin was popular in the southern United States during the period of enslavement. Many Africans played the instrument to entertain their owners at dances and other social events. Often the violin was the only music for these occasions. In the North, African American violinists were able to earn money as professional musicians. By the first few decades of the twentieth century, it was common to see African American violinists in quartets and pit orchestras and as soloists in silent movie theaters.

John Thomas Douglass (1847–1886) concertized extensively as a solo violinist during the 1870s. He later toured with minstrel companies and led string ensembles for society events before starting a violin studio in New York, where he taught David Mannes (1866–1959), who later founded the Mannes School of Music, among others.

Joseph Henry Douglass (1871–1935), the grandson of political leader Frederick Douglass (1817–1895), became internationally renowned as a violinist. He was featured at the World's Columbian Exposition in Chicago in 1893 and became very popular after this performance. Douglass began to make transcontinental tours, and by the 1890s he was considered the most talented violinist of his race. Douglass toured extensively for more than twenty years, performed at numerous black colleges in the South, and was the first violinist of any race to make recordings for the Victor Talking Machine Company. Douglass eventually accepted a teaching position at Howard University in Washington, D.C.

Hall Johnson (1888–1970) as a young boy was so inspired after hearing a concert played by Joseph Henry Douglass that he taught himself how to play the violin. Johnson later formed his own string quartet and played in pit orchestras before joining the illustrious orchestra of James Reese Europe. Johnson later became more interested in vocal music and formed the Hall Johnson Negro Choir. He went on to compose and arrange African American folk songs, for which he is best known today.

Irving Frederick Barnwell (1897–1990) was introduced to the violin when he was six years old by his father, who was also his first teacher. Barnwell later studied with German

Samuel Coleridge-Taylor String Quartet. *The quartet featured Irving Frederick Barnwell on viola.* USED BY PERMISSION OF DR. YSAYE BARNWELL—THE BARNWELL ARCHIVES

master teachers in New York City and became a serious student of the viola and piano, as well as the violin. During the Harlem Renaissance, Barnwell played violin and viola in the Van Houten Orchestra. He was a member of the Coleridge-Taylor String Quartet, formed his own trio, and played in Dean Dixon's Chamber Orchestra with Hall Johnson and others. Barnwell taught violin at the Martin Smith School in Harlem, at the Henry Street Settlement, and in his private studio until he was ninety years old. He introduced his only daughter, the singer and composer Ysaye Maria Barnwell, to the violin when she was two years old.

In the twenty-first century, professional African American string players perform as members of orchestras, quartets, trios, and other instrumental ensembles. This development can be attributed to the inception of orchestras and ensembles that were integrated by design, such as the first-rate Ritz Chamber Players, founded in 2002 by Terrance Patterson. African American women who play string instruments are also becoming more prominent. The all-female Marian Anderson String Quartet became the first African American ensemble to win a classical music competition when they won the International Cleveland Quartet Competition in 1991.

The Sphinx Organization, founded in 1996 by African American violinist Aaron P. Dworkin, has played a significant role in supporting young African American string players and has increased the visibility of women who play string instruments. Members of the Harlem Quartet, for example, are all past winners of the annual Sphinx Competition for young Hispanic and African American players of string instruments. Violinist Tai Murray, also a winner of the Sphinx Competition, has debuted with many major symphony orchestras in the United States and abroad and has played with the Ritz Chamber Players.

AFRICAN AMERICAN PIANISTS

African American pianists found fame in the nineteenth century, beginning with Louis Moreau Gottschalk (1829–1869) of New Orleans. Gottschalk became an international star as a touring pianist and produced a striking body of piano solos influenced by his Creole and British background (Gottschalk's father was a Jewish philanthropist from London). Thomas "Blind Tom" Bethune (1849–1908) became famous as a virtuoso with a repertoire of thousands of pieces. He was followed by the similarly gifted John "Blind" Boone (1864–1927), who achieved equal if not greater fame than Bethune as a touring recitalist. Both were child prodigies who produced descriptive showpieces that dazzled audiences.

Although other accomplished African American pianists had varying degrees of success, many of them built their primary careers as teachers in colleges and universities. Hazel Harrison (1883–1969) and Helen Hagan (1891–1964) had long teaching careers after auspicious beginnings as performers, as did Natalie Hinderas (1927–1987) and Frances Walker-Slocum. André Watts made a successful debut as a premiere pianist as a soloist with the New York Philharmonic in 1962 when he was only sixteen years old, and he became the first African American pianist to achieve international stardom. Other notable African American pianists include R. Nathaniel Dett (1882–1943), George Walker, Leon Bates, and Awadagin Pratt, whom many consider to be André Watts's successor.

AFRICAN AMERICAN FEMALE VOCALISTS

While men dominated instrumental music in the nineteenth century and beyond, women achieved varying degrees of national and international success in vocal music. In 1867, soprano Anna Madah Hyers (c. 1850s–1920s) and her sister, contralto Emma Louise Hyers (c. 1850s–1890s), premiered in a joint recital in their hometown, Sacramento, California. The Hyers sisters toured nationally from 1871 to 1876 as the critically acclaimed Hyers Sisters Concert Company. When the Hyers sisters left the concert stage in 1876, their concert company became a comic opera troupe. Elizabeth Taylor Greenfield (c. 1824–1876) was known as the "Black Swan" for her fluid and graceful phrasing, while M. Sissieretta Jones (1869–1933) was called the "Black Patti" after the famous white diva, Adelina Patti. Marie Selika Williams (c. 1849–1937), dubbed the "Queen of Staccato" by the press, gave a command performance before Queen Victoria and her royal court in 1883.

Contralto Marian Anderson (1897–1993) emerged as one of the twentieth century's highest-achieving and most-celebrated artists. In the middle of the twentieth

M. Sissieretta Jones, 1899. *Known as the Black Patti (after the Italian opera singer Adelina Patti), soprano singer Jones performed for President Benjamin Harrison at the White House in 1892.* THE LIBRARY OF CONGRESS

century, sopranos Leontyne Price, Shirley Verrett, and Jessye Norman were three of many outstanding African American singers who conquered the recital and operatic stage. Indira Mahajan, Alison Buchanan, Angela Brown, and Denyce Graves are among several successful African American divas of the early twenty-first century.

AFRICAN AMERICAN MALE VOCALISTS

African American men have not enjoyed the popularity or success of the "black prima donnas" in classical vocal music. Although classically trained African American men sang opposite the black divas in nineteenth-century comic opera troupes and minstrel shows, it was not until the twentieth century that a prominent African American male vocalist began to receive international attention. Because of his unique talent and sheer determination, tenor Roland Hayes (1887–1977) became one of the most celebrated and highest-paid concert singers of his generation. Once a member of the Fisk Jubilee Singers, Hayes eventually left the group and began more-advanced vocal study in Boston, Massachusetts. After successful concerts in Boston and New York, Hayes eventually moved to Europe, where he was summoned to give a command performance for King George V and the royal family. Hayes later mentored Marian Anderson and inspired successive generations of concert artists and opera singers.

Paul Robeson (1898–1976), noted for his natural bass-baritone voice, was a successful concert singer, as well as a stage and film actor. At the height of his career, Robeson became politically active, and his concert repertoire was delivered and interpreted as protest material. Robeson's political activism foreshadowed the role of music and musicians in the civil rights movement.

While Hayes and Robeson were the vocal giants of their generation, other African American men followed in their footsteps. Each opened the door a little wider for future generations. Charles Holland (1909–1987) was a jazz vocalist with Benny Carter's and Fletcher Henderson's jazz bands, but he was trained as an operatic tenor. When he moved to Europe, his career as a classical singer flourished. After making his debut at the Paris Opera in the role of Tamino in Mozart's *The Magic Flute*, Holland was engaged as a leading tenor with many prestigious European opera houses. He was the first African American man to debut at the Opéra-Comique in Paris, and he primarily sang in Europe until the African American impresario W. Hazaiah Williams (1930–1999) brought him to California and New York City for a series of concerts that culminated in a critically acclaimed Carnegie Hall recital and a commercial recording.

Robert Todd Duncan (1903–1998) originated the title role of Porgy in Gershwin's *Porgy and Bess* in 1935. William Warfield (1920–2002) portrayed the role of Joe in Metro-Goldwyn-Mayer's 1951 film *Show Boat*. In 1955, Robert McFerrin (1921–2006) became the first African American man to sing at the Metropolitan Opera just days after Marian Anderson's historic debut. In 1961, George Shirley became the first African American leading tenor at the Metropolitan Opera. And in 1978, Simon Estes became the first African American man to sing a leading role at the Bayreuth Festival in Germany. Not only did these singers have successful performing and recording careers, they also taught at prestigious colleges and universities, where they inspired, supported, and trained several generations of African American concert and opera singers.

Trailblazers such as Warfield, Shirley, and Estes often joined younger classical singers in an effort to inspire, teach, and continue the singing tradition of African Americans in classical vocal music. In 1999, Warfield and Benjamin Matthews (1933–2006) teamed up with baritone Robert

Three Generations Concert Trio. *In 1999, Benjamin Matthews (left) and William Warfield (center) teamed up with baritone Robert Sims for a series of concerts featuring African American spirituals. The trio was named Three Generations and toured the United States for three years until Warfield's death in 2002.* THREE GENERATIONS, COURTESY OF CANTI CLASSICS.

Sims for a series of concerts featuring African American spirituals. The trio was named Three Generations and toured the United States for three years until Warfield's death in 2002. The trio continued with George Shirley for a concert in 2003 and later with Simon Estes in 2007. In 2000, Three Mo' Tenors, a vocal trio featuring Roderick Dixon, Thomas Young, and Victor Cook, revealed to the musical world the greatness and versatility of the African American tenor. Featured on two Public Broadcasting Service television specials, Three Mo' Tenors sang opera arias, musical theater selections, jazz, spirituals, and gospel music.

AFRICAN AMERICAN OPERA COMPANIES

The Colored American Opera Company, the first opera company in Washington, D.C., was organized in 1870 by African Americans. The company presented several performances of Julius Eichberg's *Doctor of Alcantara* (1862) in Philadelphia and Washington, D.C., with much success. The opera company raised over $75,000, which was used to build a new Catholic church in a predominately black neighborhood. The church was dedicated in 1876 and was named after Saint Augustine, a bishop and African saint.

The National Negro Opera Company was founded in 1941 in Pittsburg, Pennsylvania, by Mary Cardwell Dawson (1894–1962). The company mounted productions in Washington, D.C., Chicago, Pittsburgh, and New York. Lillian Evanti (1890–1967), Robert McFerrin, Carole Brice (1918–1985), and Edward Boatner (1898–1981) were among the featured soloists. The company disbanded in 1962 after Dawson's death.

In the 1970s, two national African American opera companies were established. Opera/South was founded in Mississippi in 1970 by Sister Elise (1898–1982), a singer and white member of the Catholic order of the Sisters of the Blessed Sacrament, and by members of the Mississippi

Intercollegiate Opera Guild. The company staged productions of grand opera and of operas by African American composers, including William Grant Still's *Highway 1 USA* (1962) and *A Bayou Legend* (1941) and Ulysses Kay's *Jubilee* (1976) and *The Juggler of Our Lady* (1956). In 1973, along with three African American musicians—Margaret Harris (1943–2000), Benjamin Matthews, and Wayne Sanders—Sister Elise founded Opera Ebony in New York City. These companies were effective showcases for African American talent and often provided the first opportunities for individuals to begin careers in opera.

Three stage works were also responsible for starting many young African American performers in successful careers: Virgil Thomson and Gertrude Stein's *Four Saints in Three Acts*, which premiered in 1934; *Porgy and Bess* by George Gershwin, first produced in 1935; and *Treemonisha* by Scott Joplin, first staged in 1972 in Atlanta.

AFRICAN AMERICAN SYMPHONIC MUSIC

Since the 1930s, increasing numbers of works by African American composers have been performed by major symphony orchestras. African American symphonic music tends to fall into two major categories: (1) *black-stream* music, which is related to *third-stream* music, a genre described in the 1950s by the American composer Gunther Schuller, is serious music that is influenced by the ethnic background of the composer; and (2) traditional European styles of music created by African American composers. *Afro-American Symphony* by William Grant Still (1895–1978) falls into the former category. In 1931, *Afro-American Symphony* was the first symphonic work by an African American composer to be performed by a major symphony orchestra, the Rochester Philharmonic. Florence Price (1888–1953) was the first African American female composer to have a symphony played by a major orchestra when her *Symphony in E Minor* was performed by the Chicago Symphony Orchestra in 1933. A year later, Price conducted her *Concerto in One Movement* for piano and orchestra at the Chicago World's Fair, with her student, Margaret Bonds (1913–1972), as soloist with the Women's Symphony of Chicago.

In later years, composers such as George Walker, Howard Swanson (1907–1978), Ulysses Kay (1917–1995), Hale Smith (1925–2009), T. J. Anderson, Olly Wilson, Anthony Davis, and David Baker created a large repertoire of music based on Western European styles and forms but informed or transformed by elements from the composers' African American heritage. To varying degrees, these composers have utilized features common to sacred and secular African American music, including the basic African call-and-response pattern, along with elements drawn from spirituals, ragtime, blues, and jazz.

STUDIES IN AFRICAN AMERICAN MUSIC

BEGINNINGS OF ACADEMIC RESEARCH

African American literature, music, and art were well established as subjects of academic study by the latter half of the twentieth century. Eileen Southern's *The Music of Black Americans: A History*, published in 1971, was the first comprehensive study on the subject of African American music. The breadth and depth of information in this volume demonstrate the great variety of African American music and the creativity of its myriad creators and practitioners. Subsequent revisions of Southern's work in 1983 and 1997 show the continuing pertinence of the volume as both a textbook and reference source.

Two precursors to Southern's work were James Monroe Trotter's *Music and Some Highly Musical People* (1878), which presented the accomplishments of African American musicians and composers working in European styles, and Maud Cuney-Hare's *Negro Musicians and Their Music* (1936), which was more comprehensive in the styles covered. The ever-increasing quality and quantity of research in the field of African American music herald the development of younger scholars who can use the resources available to them at the beginning of their careers and who will increase those resources as they progress. As such, a more accurate picture of the history of American music will result.

LATER RESEARCH ON AFRICAN AMERICAN MUSIC

The Center for Black Music Research (CBMR) was founded in 1983 at Columbia College in Chicago by Samuel A. Floyd Jr., the author of *The Power of Black Music* (1995), among several other works. The center's mission is "to research and promote the music of people of African descent throughout the world ... through education, performance, publication, and scholarly discussion." The CBMR sponsors performances of contemporary and historic compositions, and disseminates research about the philosophy, history, and aesthetics of black music through *Black Music Research Journal.* The CBMR also published several newsletters, a monograph series, and, in association with the University of California Press, a book series on music of the African diaspora. In addition, the CBMR has a library and computer database of resources available to scholars all over the country. In 1999, the CBMR published the *International Dictionary of Black Composers*, which filled a large gap in study materials on African American music and musicians.

At this beginning of the second decade of the twenty-first century, the trend toward inclusion of all kinds of music—jazz, blues, classical, and sacred music—in formal study bodes well for a better understanding of African American music. Certainly, African American classical musicians of the twentieth and twenty-first centuries have worked in a wide variety of styles, from the vernacular to the avant-garde. Many of these musicians are not bound to one style or another, but move freely among them to produce work that is surprising, challenging, and unique.

CLASSICAL MUSIC COMPOSERS, CONDUCTORS, INSTRUMENTALISTS, AND SINGERS

(Some biographical profiles may appear in other chapters. To locate profiles more readily, please consult the index.)

MICHAEL ABELS (1962–)

Composer. Born in Phoenix, Arizona, in 1962, Michael Abels was raised on a small farm in South Dakota by his grandparents. He later returned to Phoenix and graduated from high school there, then studied music at the University of Southern California (USC) in Los Angeles. At USC, Abels was named Outstanding Senior among student composers for his composition Queries.

While he was a student, Abels immersed himself in the African American part of his biracial background. He studied African drumming and became a member of an African American Baptist church. Subsequently, Abels collaborated with renowned gospel artist Reverend James Cleveland on orchestral arrangements for some of the latter's gospel recordings. Abels's arrangements for gospel choir and orchestra are now performed by orchestras throughout the United States.

Among Abels's best-known works are *Global Warming*, written in 1991, and *Fredericks Fables*, composed in 1994. *Global Warming* contains elements of Irish and Arabic folk music and reflects Abels's multicultural orientation. The piece has been performed more than one hundred times and was released as a recording performed by Chicago Sinfonietta. *Dance for Martin's Dream* pays homage to Dr. Martin Luther King Jr. and was commissioned by the Nashville Symphony in 1997. In 2001, the National Symphony Orchestra premiered Abels's *Tribute*, which was inspired by the heroism displayed after the September 11, 2001, attacks on the World Trade Center in New York.

Abels is the recipient of two Meet the Composer residency grants. With his first grant, Abels held a three-year residency at the Watts Tower Arts Center in Los Angeles, where he composed music for several plays and began a mentoring program in music technology and production techniques for disadvantaged youth. During his second residency, Abels worked in Richmond, Virginia, with the Richmond Symphony and its youth orchestra as they prepared for a "side-by-side" performance of *Global Warming*.

H. LESLIE ADAMS (1932–)

Composer, Pianist, Educator. Harrison Leslie Adams was born in Cleveland, Ohio, in 1932. In high school, he studied piano with Dorothy Smith and Mina Eichenbaum and voice with John Howard Tucker. After high school, he attended Oberlin Conservatory of Music, studying composition with Herbert Elwell and Joseph Wood, voice with Robert Fountain, and piano with Emil Dannenberg. Adams received his bachelor of music degree in 1955.

Adams studied privately with Robert Starer in 1950 and Vittorio Giannini in 1960. He then earned a master of music degree in composition and choral music from California State University at Long Beach in 1967, after study with Leon Dallin and Robert Tyndall. Adams enrolled at Ohio State University in 1968, where he earned a Ph.D. in music education in 1973 under Marshall Barnes. Adams later engaged in further studies with Edward Mattila, Eugene O'Brien, and Marcel Dick.

Adams has received several grants, awards, and fellowships for composition. As a performer, he has played with or won commissions from the Prague Radio Symphony, the Detroit Symphony, the Cleveland Orchestra, and the Buffalo Philharmonic. His many works include the opera *Blake* (1986), works for orchestra, chamber orchestra, solo voice, choral music, solo piano, and piano works for ballet.

In addition to composing, Adams served as choir director at Stillman College in Alabama, associate music director for the Karamu House in Cleveland in 1964 and 1965, and Karamu artist-in-residence in 1979 and 1980. Adams also taught in the New Jersey public schools, at the New Mexico School for the Performing Arts, and at Florida Agricultural and Mechanical University.

From 1970 to 1978, Adams was choral director at the University of Kansas. He was composer-in-residence at the Cleveland Music School Settlement from 1980 to 1982. He founded Accord Associates in 1980, served as president until 1986, and as executive vice president and composer-in-residence from 1986 to 1992. In 1997, Abels became president and artist-in-residence of Creative Arts, Inc.

ADELE ADDISON (1925–)

Singer. Born July 24, 1925, in New York City, soprano Adele Addison completed her musical training at Westminster Choir College in 1946 and studied later at the University of Massachusetts. After making her recital debut at Town Hall in New York City in 1952, she performed recitals throughout the United States and Canada. In 1963, she toured the Soviet Union under a U.S. State Department cultural-exchange program.

Although she was primarily a recitalist, Addison appeared with the New England, New York City, and Washington opera companies. She gave the premiere performance of John La Montaine's *Fragments from the Song of Songs* with the New Haven Symphony in 1959 and of Francis Poulenc's *Gloria* with the Boston Symphony in 1961. She was also a soloist during the opening week of concerts at Lincoln Center in New York City in 1962. Addison began to focus on teaching rather than performing in the late 1960s, and was for many years a faculty member of the Manhattan School of Music.

BETTY ALLEN (1930–2009)

Singer, Educator. Born March 17, 1930, in Campbell, Ohio, Betty Lou Allen studied at Wilberforce University and toured with the Wilberforce Sisters, a group that included Leontyne Price. She continued her musical studies at the Hartford School of Music and at the Berkshire Music Center at Tanglewood and studied voice with Sarah Peck Moore, Paul Ulanowsky, and Zinka Milanov.

Allen made her New York debut in the Virgil Thomson and Gertrude Stein opera *Four Saints in Three Acts* with the New York City Opera in 1953. She made her debut at the Teatro Colón in Buenos Aires in 1964. She appeared as a soloist with many leading orchestras and conductors, including Leonard Bernstein, Antal Doráti, and Lorin Maazel, and she appeared as Monisha in Joplin's *Treemonisha* on Broadway. Allen held positions on the faculties of the North Carolina School of the Arts, the Curtis Institute of Music, and the Manhattan School of Music. She also served as the executive director and chair of the voice department at the Harlem School of the Arts in New York City. Allen died on June 22, 2009.

MARIAN ANDERSON (1897–1993)

Singer. Born in Philadelphia, contralto Marian Anderson was brought up in a family of church musicians and began singing publicly as a child. Her professional career began in earnest in the 1920s, but her initial New York debuts were unsuccessful. However, her success in a performance competition with the New York Philharmonic in 1925 led to further engagements, principally in Europe, where she established her reputation as a leading concert artist. After returning to the United States, a 1935 performance at Town Hall in New York City won her the acclaim that she deserved.

In 1939, Howard University wanted to present Anderson in recital at Constitution Hall in Washington, D.C., but the Daughters of the American Revolution, the owners of the facility, denied Anderson this opportunity because of her race. Public reaction to this racially motivated action was immediate and intense and, through the efforts of First Lady Eleanor Roosevelt (who resigned from the organization in protest), Anderson was invited to sing on the steps of the Lincoln Memorial. The audience was estimated at 75,000 for this unforgettable Easter Sunday concert.

In 1955, Anderson became the first African American artist to perform a solo role with the Metropolitan Opera Company in New York. She sang the role of Ulrica in Verdi's *Un ballo in maschera* for one season. Two years later, she became a goodwill ambassador for the U.S. State Department, and in 1958 she was named to the U.S. delegation to the United Nations.

As a conclusion to her lengthy career, "the world's greatest contralto" toured the nation in a series of farewell concerts that ended on Easter Sunday of 1965 at Carnegie Hall in New York City. Anderson was not only a great singer but also a humanitarian who established fellowships for young singers and toppled racial barriers for succeeding generations.

T. J. ANDERSON (1928–)

Composer, Educator. Born on August 17, 1928, in Coatesville, Pennsylvania, Thomas Jefferson Anderson began to study piano with his mother when he was five, and began performing with jazz groups in junior high school. Anderson earned a bachelor of music degree in 1950 at West Virginia State College and a master of music education degree at Pennsylvania State University the following year. He worked as a music instructor for several years before pursuing a Ph.D. at the University of Iowa, where he studied with Philip Bezanson and Richard Hervig and received his doctorate in 1958.

Anderson was composer-in-residence for the Atlanta Symphony Orchestra from 1968 to 1971. He served as orchestrator and helped stage the first complete performance of Scott Joplin's opera *Treemonisha* in 1972 in Atlanta. He also conducted the first performance of the Black Music Repertory Ensemble in 1988. Following teaching positions at West Virginia State College, Langston University, Tennessee State University, and Morehouse College, Anderson joined the faculty of Tufts University in Medford, Massachusetts, in 1972. He chaired Tuft's music department until 1980. He retired as professor emeritus in 1990, but continued to compose music.

Anderson has received numerous commissions for a variety of works. A few of his notable compositions are: *Squares: An Essay for Orchestra* (1965, West Virginia State

Singer Marian Anderson* (center)*, U.S. Department of the Interior Building, Washington, DC, 1943. *To commemorate contralto Anderson's 1939 concert on the steps of the Lincoln Memorial, a mural depicting the event was dedicated in January, 1943. Because Anderson was African American, The Daughters of the American Revolution had barred her from giving a performance at Constitution Hall in 1939.* THE LIBRARY OF CONGRESS

College); *Variations on a Theme by M.B. Tolson*, for soprano and instrumental ensemble (1969); *Transitions: A Fantasy for Ten Instruments* (1971, Berkshire Music Center at Tanglewood, and the Fromm Foundation); *Soldier Boy, Soldier*, a two-act opera (1982, Indiana University and National Endowment for the Arts); *Thomas Jefferson's Orbiting Minstrels and Contraband: A 21st Century Celebration of 19th Century Form*, for string quartet, woodwind quintet, jazz sextet, dancer, soprano, computer, visuals, and keyboard synthesizer (1984); *Walker*, a one-act opera with a libretto by Caribbean author and Nobel laureate Derek Walcott, based on the death of David Walker in 1830 in Boston (1992, Boston Athenaeum); *Spirit Songs*, commissioned by Yo-Yo Ma for cello (1993); *Slip Knot*, a two-act opera with a libretto by Yusef Komunyakaa (2000, Northwestern University School of Music); *Slavery Documents 2* (2002, Cantata Singers & Ensemble); *Boogie Woogie Concertante*, for improvised solo piano, wind instruments, and percussion (2003, Harvard University Wind Ensemble); *Gospel Ghost*, for flute and piano (2003, Brooks de Wetter-Smith at University of North Carolina–Chapel Hill); and *Tuftonia's Call and Response*, for bass quintet and percussion (2007, Tuft's University Music Department).

Anderson has received numerous awards and honors, including four MacDowell Colony fellowships, honorary doctorates, and composer residencies. He became a member of the American Academy of Arts and Letters in 2005.

Opera Stage Director David Farrar with Martina Arroyo. *Farrar, honored with the Distinguished Director Award from the National Opera Association in 1995, works with Arroyo in her summer program for young artists. Arroyo is President and Artistic Director of the Martina Arroyo Foundation.* **COURTESY OF DAVID FARRAR.**

MARTINA ARROYO (1936–)

Singer, Educator. Martina Arroyo was born to a Puerto Rican father and an African American mother in Harlem. Arroyo's mother encouraged her artistic pursuits, but expected her to enter a profession that could provide a more secure living than the arts. After attending Hunter High School, Arroyo continued her education at Hunter College, where she earned a degree in Romance languages in 1956. During her college years, she met the distinguished voice teacher Marinka Gurewich, with whom Arroyo trained almost continuously until Gurewich's death in 1990.

Like many other African American artists of her generation, Arroyo did not have an easy time breaking into American operatic performance but found success in European opera houses. In 1965, while visiting her family in New York on vacation from the Zurich Opera Company, she was called to fill in for Birgit Nilsson as Aida at the Metropolitan Opera. Her performance in this demanding Verdi role led to a contract and made her an international star virtually overnight.

Along with frequent opera appearances in the United States and abroad in the 1970s and 1980s, Arroyo had many engagements with leading orchestras, performing music ranging from Handel to Stockhausen. Arroyo officially retired from performing in 1989. Only two years later, however, she agreed to sing the leading female role, written for her, in Leslie Adams's new opera *Blake*, based on a nineteenth-century novel about an enslaved family. After retirement, Arroyo was in demand as a distinguished visiting professor. She has taught at the University of California Los Angeles, Louisiana State University, Wilberforce University, and Indiana University at Bloomington. Arroyo has also served as an honorary member of the Carnegie Hall board and as a member of the board of trustees at Hunter College. In 2000 she became a fellow of the American Academy of Arts and Sciences. In 2003 Arroyo established the Martina Arroyo

Foundation, which sponsors an international summer opera workshop.

AMADI AZIKIWE (1969–)

Violinist, Educator. Born Amadi Hummings in New York City in 1969, violinist Amadi Azikiwe began his early music lessons with his mother. Later, he was selected to attend the North Carolina School of the Arts, where his formal training began. After graduation from high school, he continued his studies at the New England Conservatory with renowned violist Marcus Thompson, also a member of the music faculty at the Massachusetts Institute of Technology. Azikiwe did further study at Indiana University, where he served as an associate instructor and received a performer's certificate. Azikiwe was awarded a master's degree from Indiana University in 1994.

As a faculty member at Old Dominion University in Norfolk, Virginia, from 1994 to 2000, Azikiwe taught violin and viola and conducted the Old Dominion University Chamber Orchestra. He has also taught at James Madison University and Indiana University. His career has included recitals in such major cities as New York, Boston, Cleveland, Chicago, Houston, Baltimore, and Washington, D.C. Azikiwe also performed at the U.S. Supreme Court. He continues to appear with symphonies around the world and at music festivals, and is a member of the Ritz Chamber Players. Azikiwe also serves as music director for the Harlem Symphony Orchestra and as the director of program development for the Gateways Music Festival, founded by his mother, Armenta Adams Hummings, in 1993.

DAVID BAKER (1931–)

Composer, Instrumentalist, Educator, Author. Born in Indianapolis, Indiana, David Nathaniel Baker was educated in the public schools and at Indianapolis's Jordan Conservatory. He earned a bachelor's degree (1953) and a master's degree (1954) in music education at Indiana University at Bloomington and later studied at the Berklee School of Music in Boston and the Lenox School of Jazz. Among his private composition teachers were George Russell, John Lewis, William Russo, and Gunther Schuller. He also studied trombone with J. J. Johnson, John Marcellus, and Bobby Brookmeyer, and cello with Jules Eskin, his Indiana colleague Janos Starker, and others.

In the late 1950s and early 1960s, Baker played in the bands of Maynard Ferguson, Quincy Jones, George Russell, Wes Montgomery, and Lionel Hampton. After joining the faculty of Indiana University in 1966 as chairman of the jazz department, Baker continued to perform with various groups. He also lectured, conducted workshops and clinics, and published a large number of books and articles in the field of jazz. In 1990, Baker became conductor and musical director of the Smithsonian Jazz Masterworks Orchestra

Baker's vast catalog of compositions includes commissioned works for solo performers and instrumental and vocal ensembles, pieces for string, chamber, and full orchestra, dramatic music, and well over 150 works for jazz ensembles. Baker has authored numerous instructional books on music improvisation and other subjects, including: *Advanced Ear Training for Jazz Musicians* (1977); *Advanced Improvisation* (1974); *Contemporary Techniques for the Trombone* (1974); *How to Play Bebop* (1985), and *How to Learn Tunes: A Jazz Musician's Survival Guide* (1997). He has also written numerous articles and liner notes.

In the course of his very active career, Baker has received many awards and honors. He served as chair of the Jazz Advisory Panel to the Kennedy Center and the Jazz/Folk/Ethnic Panel of the National Endowment for the Arts, and as president of the International Association for Jazz Education and the National Jazz Service Organization. He has also been involved with the Symphony Orchestra League, the National Jazz Foundation, and the Afro-American Music Bicentennial, and has been a member of the nominating jury for the Pulitzer Prize for music. The New England Conservatory of Music gave Baker an honorary doctorate in 2000. In 2001, he was named an Indiana Living Legend by the Indiana Historical Society. Baker received the prestigious American Jazz Masters Award from the National Endowment for the Arts in 2000, and the Living Jazz Legend Award from the Kennedy Center for the Performing Arts in 2007.

YSAYE MARIA BARNWELL (1946–)

Singer, Composer, Producer, Educator, Actor, Writer. Ysaye Maria Barnwell is an artist of many colors who wears many hats. She was born on February 28, 1946, in New York and began her musical training on violin with her father when she was two. Her studies, however, took her into the sciences. She earned her bachelor and master of science degrees in speech pathology at the State University of New York (SUNY) at Geneseo in 1967 and 1968. She also earned a Ph.D. degree in craniofacial studies from the University of Pittsburgh in 1975 and a master of science degree in public health from Howard University in Washington, D.C., in 1981. SUNY Geneseo awarded her an honorary doctor of humane letters in 1998.

Since 1979, Barnwell has been a member of Sweet Honey in the Rock, an African American women's a cappella ensemble. She composes many of the group's songs and produced their twenty-fifth anniversary album, *Twenty-Five* (1998). Barnwell's other recordings with Sweet Honey in the

Rock include *Sacred Ground* (1996), *Endings and Beginnings* (2004), the Grammy-nominated *Experience... 101* (2008), and *Go in Grace* (2008). She also edited *Continuum: The First Songbook of Sweet Honey in the Rock*, published in 2000. Barnwell has been commissioned to write music for dance, choral, film, and stage productions. She also developed the workshop Building a Vocal Community: Singing in the African American Tradition, which she conducts around the world. In 2009, she published *Singing in the African American Tradition*, a two-volume manual and set of recordings for choirs and choruses to use in conjunction with the workshop.

Barnwell is very active in the Washington, D.C., community where she makes her home. In 1976, she founded the All Souls Jubilee Singers at Washington's All Souls Unitarian Church. She spent a decade as a professor at Howard University's College of Dentistry and administered health programs at both Children's National Medical Center and Gallaudet University.

In addition to her many musical credits, Barnwell has acted on television and in film and has written children's books. She published her first book for children, *No Mirrors in My Nana's House*, in 1998. It includes illustrations by Synthia Saint James and a CD by Sweet Honey in the Rock. Her second children's book, *We Are One*, was published in 2008.

LEON BATES (1949–)

Pianist. Leon Bates, one of the country's leading pianists, was born November 3, 1949, in Philadelphia. He began studying piano and violin when he was six years old, and later studied with Irene Beck at the Settlement Music School and with Natalie Hinderas at the Esther Boyer College of Music at Temple University.

In addition to popular master classes that he gives regularly on college campuses, Bates has a varied and busy concert schedule. He has performed with many major orchestras, including the New York Philharmonic, the Cleveland Orchestra, the National Symphony, the Los Angeles Philharmonic, the San Francisco Symphony, the Detroit Symphony, the Atlanta Symphony, the Indianapolis Symphony, the Oregon Symphony, the Florida Symphony, the Dallas Symphony, the Philadelphia Orchestra, and others. In addition, Bates has played at many summer festivals, including those at Chicago's Grant Park, the Hollywood Bowl, the National Gallery of Art in Washington, D.C., Lake Tahoe, and the Philadelphia Orchestra's Mann Music Center. He has often participated in summer tours with the Boston Pops. Bates appeared with the Italian Symphony Orchestra of Bergamo on their American tour, and in Europe Bates has performed with the Orchestra of Pomeriggi Musicali di Milano in Italy and the Malmo Symphony in Sweden.

Bates has appeared frequently on both national and local radio and television programs, including NBC's *The Today Show* and CBS's *Sunday Morning*. He also hosted a radio series funded by the Pew Foundation, *Notes from Philadelphia*. His major awards include those of the National Association of Negro Musicians Competition, the National Association of Music Teachers Collegiate Artists Competition, the Symphony of the New World Competition, and the National Endowment for the Arts Solo Recitalists Fellowship Grant. Bates is also a recording artist and composer.

KATHLEEN BATTLE (1948–)

Singer. In her high school and early college years, soprano Kathleen Battle, a native of Portsmouth, Ohio, had no ambition to become a professional singer. She studied voice, piano, languages, and dance as she earned her bachelor's and master's degrees in music education from the University of Cincinnati College-Conservatory of Music. She continued her studies during two years of teaching general music in an inner-city school.

An audition with Thomas Schippers, conductor of the Cincinnati Symphony Orchestra and cofounder of the Spoleto Festival of Two Worlds, led to Battle's professional debut singing Brahms's *German Requiem* in Spoleto, Italy. In 1974, through Schippers, Battle met James Levine, who became her friend, mentor, and counselor. She sang with many orchestras as a soloist, and studied opera, song literature, and acting. In 1975, Battle was a member of the Broadway company for Scott Joplin's opera *Treemonisha*. Her New York City Opera debut followed in 1976 as Susanna in Mozart's *The Marriage of Figaro*, and her Metropolitan Opera debut took place in 1978 as the shepherd in Wagner's *Tannhäuser*. Since then, she has sung a wide range of roles in opera houses throughout the world, notably in operas by Mozart, Rossini, Massenet, and Richard Strauss.

In 1991 Battle released the award-winning *Baroque Duet* with trumpeter Wynton Marsalis. Her other recordings include *Pleasures of their Company* (1990) with the guitarist Christopher Parkening, and *Honey and Rue* (1993), a song cycle with lyrics by Toni Morrison and music by André Previn. In 1994, Battle was dismissed from the Metropolitan Opera production of Donizetti's *Daughter of the Regiment* following a much-publicized dispute with management. She nevertheless continued her concert and recording career. Many of her recordings have been very successful, and include crossovers such as *So Many Stars* (1995). In 2004, Deutsche Grammophon released *20th Century Masters: The Best of Kathleen Battle.*

Thomas "Blind Tom" Wiggins, Composer and Pianist, c. 1860s. *Also known by the last name of Bethune, Wiggins was born enslaved. After his enslavement ended, his former owner continued to manage his career. In 1999 pianist John Davis recorded a CD of Wiggins's compositions.* KEAN COLLECTION/ GETTY IMAGES

THOMAS (BLIND TOM) GREENE BETHUNE (1849–1908)

Pianist, Composer. "Blind Tom" was the stage name of pianist Thomas Greene, who was born enslaved in Columbus, Georgia. The surname Bethune was that of the family that owned Tom and his mother. His musical prowess manifested itself when he was four years old, and he received music lessons from members of the Bethune family. His remarkable skills, especially his ability to memorize pieces on first hearing, have caused speculation that he had some form of autism.

Tom began performing for money in public before the Civil War, but Colonel John Bethune kept control of Tom and his earnings. After abolition, the colonel acted, in effect, as his concert manager. Tom's renown grew rapidly after the war, and he toured throughout the United States and Europe to great acclaim.

"Blind Tom" Bethune's immense repertoire included works by standard classical composers, such as Bach, Beethoven, and Chopin. He also performed virtuoso display pieces by Gottschalk and Liszt, improvisations on current ballads and other popular tunes, and his own works, which combined elements of the virtuosic and improvisational and often described weather or military events. "The Battle of Manassas" is an example of one of his most effective works of this kind. It is a potpourri of well-known melodies with special keyboard effects, such as tone clusters and noises made on the piano. Tom retired in 1898, ten years before his death.

HAROLYN BLACKWELL (1955–)

Singer. Harolyn Blackwell was born, raised, and educated in Washington, D.C. A fourth-grade teacher introduced Blackwell to music and became her first piano and voice teacher. In high school, Blackwell began performing in musicals. When she entered Catholic University, she pursued training in classical music and musical theater. Following graduate school, Blackwell moved to New York to perform in the 1980 Broadway revival of Leonard Bernstein's *West Side Story*.

In 1981, Blackwell became an apprentice with the Chicago Lyric Opera. According to Blackwell, "that was really the beginning of my operatic career. I had already done musical theater and I knew I could come back to New York to sing on Broadway, but I had to see if I really had the wherewithal and the passion to pursue [opera]." During the apprenticeship, Blackwell represented the Chicago Midwest area in the regional auditions for the Metropolitan Opera. She was a finalist during the first year that finalists performed a full program with the Met orchestra.

The Met auditions were a turning point in Blackwell's transition to a career in opera, and paved the way for her Met debut as Pousette in *Manon* in 1989. Her later roles at the Met included Susanna in *The Marriage of Figaro*, Marie in *The Daughter of the Regiment*, Gilda in *Rigoletto*, and Adele in *Die Fledermaus*.

In 1997, Blackwell returned to Broadway as Cunégonde in Hal Prince's revival of Leonard Bernstein's *Candide*. Thereafter, Blackwell became a familiar performer at the Metropolitan Opera, the Lyric Opera of Chicago, and the San Francisco Opera. She is also an accomplished singer of the concert repertoire. In February 2006, Blackwell sang at the White House during a dinner in honor of the Dance Theatre of Harlem.

JULES BLEDSOE (1898–1943)

Singer, Actor, Composer. Jules Bledsoe was born in 1898 in Waco, Texas. He earned his undergraduate degree in 1918 at Bishop College in Dallas, and also studied at Virginia Union College. He was a medical student at Columbia University in New York City when he discovered his passion for performing. Bledsoe began voice lessons with Claude Warford, and then studied with Luigi Parisotti and Lazar Samoiloff in Europe. He made his debut at Aeolian Hall in New York City in a recital sponsored by impresario Sol Hurok in 1924. Bledsoe later appeared on Broadway in *In Abraham's Bosom* and in Frank Harling's *Deep River*, both in 1926. His most memorable role was that of Joe in Jerome Kern's *Show Boat* in 1927, a role he originated.

In 1931, Bledsoe made his Carnegie Hall recital debut, and in 1934 he appeared in the title role of Louis Gruenberg's opera *Emperor Jones* and as Amonasro in Verdi's *Aida* for the Chicago Opera at the Hippodrome Theater in New York. He also performed the role of Boris in Mussorgsky's *Boris Godunov* in the Netherlands, with the BBC Symphony in London, and with other European operas and orchestras. Bledsoe had a brief motion picture career, appearing in three musical film shorts and a series of small uncredited parts in other films.

As a composer, he wrote songs, longer pieces for voice and orchestra, and an opera, *Bondage*, based on Harriet Beecher Stowe's *Uncle Tom's Cabin*. He died in Hollywood, California, of a cerebral hemorrhage in 1943. He was buried in Waco, Texas.

MARGARET BONDS (1913–1972)

Composer, Pianist. Margaret Allison Bonds was born in Chicago and grew up in an artistic and creative family. Her first piano teacher was her mother, a church organist. Her family's friends consisted of many distinguished musicians and writers, including Florence Price and Will Marion Cook, who acted as Bonds's mentors. Bonds began to compose when she was a child. As a teenager, she worked as accompanist for nightclub acts and as a music copyist.

In the early 1930s, Bonds became one of a small number of African American students at Northwestern University in Evanston, Illinois, from which she received both a bachelor's degree (1933) and a master's degree (1934) in music. In the latter part of the decade, she founded and directed the Allied Arts Academy, which closed in 1939 because of financial difficulties. She then moved to New York City, where she resumed her studies at the Juilliard School of Music, and was active as both a solo and duo pianist and accompanist. She also gave lecture demonstrations, and was involved in many professional and community organizations.

Bonds's compositions reflect the influence of jazz, blues, and spirituals, along with a thorough mastery of the techniques of Western art music. Most of her music is vocal and choral, but there are many piano solos and dramatic works as well, including *The Ballad of the Brown King* (1954) and *Shakespeare in Harlem* (1959), based on a play by Langston Hughes.

In 1967, Bonds moved to Los Angeles, where she taught piano and worked with the Inner City Cultural Center and Repertory Theater. Her *Credo*, dedicated to the memories of Langston Hughes and the soprano Abbie Mitchell, was performed in 1972 by the Los Angeles Philharmonic conducted by Zubin Mehta shortly after Bonds's death.

JOHN WILLIAM "BLIND" BOONE (1864–1927)

Pianist, Composer. Born fifteen years after "Blind Tom" Bethune, "Blind" Boone's upbringing and education were considerably different from his predecessor's, although their careers were very similar. Both musicians had tremendous skill at the keyboard and very large repertoires at their fingertips, and they both toured extensively for many years. Boone, however, had more formal training, and received support from the citizens of Warrensburg, Missouri, who raised money for him to study at the Institute for the Education of the Blind in St. Louis (later the St. Louis School for the Blind). After less than three years of piano training at the school, Boone left in order to begin a career in music.

Several lean years passed before Boone met John Lange, a Missouri businessman and entrepreneur who set up the Blind Boone Concert Company, a partnership that provided a living for the pianist and a stipend for his mother. A typical Boone program, following the pattern used by Bethune, included classical works from Bach to Brahms, his own arrangements of popular ballads and dance tunes, descriptive and concert pieces, and, on occasion, improvisations. Unlike Bethune, Boone performed and wrote ragtime pieces as well. His familiarity with this newly popular music went back to his days as a student in St. Louis.

After Lange's death in 1916, the fortunes of the company declined, and, with the burgeoning of new entertainment media and an apparent increase in racism, so did Boone's career as a performer. Nevertheless, Boone continued to perform for African American communities and organizations, to whom he would often donate concert revenues. His "farewell concerts" began in the early 1920s, but he did not give his final concert until shortly before his death in 1927.

GWENDOLYN BRADLEY (1952–)

Singer. Soprano Gwendolyn Bradley was born in New York City, but grew up in Bishopville, South Carolina. She was a finalist in the 1977 Metropolitan Opera National Council auditions and a graduate of the North Carolina School of the Arts. She also attended the Curtis Institute of Music and the Academy of Vocal Arts in Philadelphia and studied with Margaret Harshaw and Seth McCoy.

Bradley made her professional operatic debut in 1976 with the Lake George Opera Festival in New York as Nanetta in Verdi's *Falstaff.* Other companies with which she has appeared include the Central City Opera in Colorado, Opera/South, and the Opera Company of Philadelphia. She made her Metropolitan Opera debut in 1981 in the Met's first production of Ravel's *L'enfant et les sortilèges.* She has also performed as a soloist with several orchestras, including the Philadelphia Orchestra, the Kansas City Philharmonic, the Charleston Symphony, the Los Angeles Philharmonic, and the Seattle Symphony.

CAROL BRICE (1918–1985)

Singer. Born into a musical family in Sedalia, North Carolina, Carol Brice was one of the first African American classical singers to record extensively. She was also the first African American to win the prestigious Naumburg Award in 1943 for classical musicians in North America.

Brice, a contralto, was educated at the historic Palmer Memorial Institute in Sedalia, North Carolina, and earned her bachelor of music degree from Talladega College in Alabama in 1939. She pursued further training at the Juilliard School of Music from 1939 to 1943. During her early days at Juilliard, Brice attracted much acclaim performing in *The Hot Mikado* at the New York World's Fair with Bill "Bojangles" Robinson. Brice was selected to sing at a concert for President Franklin Roosevelt's third inauguration in 1941. She had numerous stage roles to her credit, including Maria in *Porgy and Bess,* Queenie in *Show Boat,* and Maude in *Finian's Rainbow.* From 1967 to 1971, she was a member of the Vienna Volksoper.

In 1974, Brice and her husband, baritone Thomas Carey, accepted positions as professors of voice at the University of Oklahoma. Together, they founded the Cimarron Circuit Opera Company to provide Oklahoma's aspiring young singers a forum for their talents, as well as opportunities to gain solid stage experience and training beyond the classroom. Brice and Carey also hoped to enhance the social and cultural life in the state by bringing the joy of operatic and concert performances to all Oklahomans in shared community experiences.

ANGELA BROWN (1964–)

Singer. Born in Indianapolis, Brown grew up performing in local talent shows and singing gospel music at Mount Calvary Baptist Church, where her grandfather was pastor. She initially aspired to become a singing evangelist.

Brown went to vocational school and completed secretarial training, and later entered Oakwood College in Huntsville, Alabama, on a music scholarship. Oakwood professor Ginger Beazley arranged an audition for Brown at the Indiana University (IU) School of Music. She was admitted and studied in the early 1990s with distinguished professor Virginia Zeani. At IU, Brown sang with the African American Choral Ensemble and for six years served as vocal coach to the IU Soul Revue, a group that performs traditional rhythm and blues, soul, funk, and contemporary black popular music. Brown made her first recording of songs and arias while at IU and sold it from the trunk of her car.

Brown's road from her grandfather's church to center stage at the Metropolitan Opera was long and difficult. She entered the regional Metropolitan Opera national audition three times before advancing to New York and winning there on her fourth try. She was thirty-three, the competition's cutoff age for women at that time. Brown captured the attention of the opera world as "one of America's most promising Verdi sopranos," according to *Opera News,* with her stellar debut performance in the title role of *Aida* with the New York Metropolitan Opera in 2004. In 2005, Brown was called to replace soprano Jessye Norman in the world premiere of the Michigan Opera Theatre's *Margaret Garner,* with music by Richard Danielpour and a libretto by Toni Morrison.

In 2002 Brown collaborated with soprano Kishna Davis and pianist Victor Simonson to produce *Opera from a Sistah's Point of View.* The Delta Sigma Theta sorority honored Brown and Davis "for their extraordinary talent and work in broadening the musical exposure of audiences to include classical music and opera performed by African American artists." During the 2007–2008 season, Brown performed in *Aida* and as Amelia in *Un ballo in maschera* at the Metropolitan Opera, among other roles. She performed *Aida* again in 2009 for the Deutsche Oper Berlin, the Cape Town Opera in South Africa, and the Latvian National Symphony in Riga.

LAWRENCE BROWNLEE (1973–)

Singer. Lawrence Everston Brownlee Jr. has the distinction of being the only artist who was awarded both the Marian Anderson and the Richard Tucker Awards in the same year (2006). He is one of the premiere bel canto tenors of the twenty-first century.

Born in Youngstown, Ohio, in 1973, Brownlee earned a bachelor of arts degree from Anderson University and his master of music degree from Indiana University. He also participated in the young artist programs of the Wolf Trap Opera and Seattle Opera. Brownlee was a 2001 winner of the Metropolitan Opera National Council Auditions, and received a 2003 ARIA Award and a career grant from the Richard Tucker Music Foundation.

Brownlee has carved his own niche as a singer of the bel canto repertory, singing mainly Rossini, Bellini, Donizetti, Handel, and Mozart. He made his American operatic debut with the Virginia Opera and his European debut at La Scala in Milan. He has sung with major opera houses and orchestras around the world. In addition to his whirlwind schedule, he also gives master classes and is a popular recitalist. He has made several recordings, including: *Carmina Burana* with Sir Simon Rattle and the Berliner Philharmoniker, released on 2005; *Italian Songs for Tenor and Piano,* with piano accompaniment by Martin Katz, released in 2006; and *Il barbieri di Siviglia,* with Miguel Gomez Martinez leading the Munich Rundfunk Orchestra, released in 2008. In 2008, Brownlee was named Seattle Opera's Artist of the Year.

ALISON BUCHANAN (1968–)

Singer. Soprano Alison Buchanan was born in Bedford, England on September 2, 1968. She later moved to New York City. Buchanan is a graduate of the Guildhall School of Music and Drama in London and the Curtis Institute of Music in Philadelphia. She is also the winner of the Kathleen Ferrier, the Luciano Pavarotti, the Washington International, and the Maggie Teyte competitions.

After completing her degree at the Curtis Institute, Buchanan became a young artist with the San Francisco Opera in 1996. She made her debut with the company as Mimi in *La Bohème.* She made her New York City Opera debut as Bess in *Porgy and Bess* during the 2003–2004 season. Buchanan has performed with numerous other opera companies, including the Opera Company of Philadelphia, the Glyndebourne Festival Opera, the Michigan Opera, and the Wexford Opera. She has performed under the batons of many excellent conductors, including Simon Rattle, Colin Davis, Marin Alsop, Donald Runnicles, and David Agler, and with a number of orchestras, including the Royal Philharmonic, the Philippines Philharmonic, the London Symphony, the Jacksonville Symphony, the BBC Symphony Orchestra, the Baltimore and Tucson symphonies, and the Israel Kibbutz Orchestra. Buchanan made her Carnegie Hall debut during the 2006–2007 season. She is a member of the Ritz Chamber Players and makes regular appearances with the group throughout the United States.

Opera Singers Simon Estes and Grace Bumbry,* Porgy and Bess, *c. 1985. *Bass-baritone Estes and soprano/mezzo soprano Bumbry costarred in the title roles of the Metropolitan Opera's first production of the George Gershwin opera in 1985.* JACQUES M. CHENET/ DOCUMENTARY/CORBIS

GRACE ANN BUMBRY (1937–)

Singer. A native of St. Louis, Missouri, Grace Bumbry was the first African American to perform in Bayreuth, Germany, the shrine of Richard Wagner. She sang the role of Venus in *Tannhäuser* in 1961 to great acclaim. She had previously appeared in the operatic capitals of Europe, so the Bayreuth debut served as a boost to a career that was already flourishing. She made her American operatic debut in this role at the Chicago Lyric Opera in 1963.

As a teenager, Bumbry won a scholarship to the St. Louis Institute in a competition, but the segregationist policy of that school kept her out. Later, however, she attended Boston University, Northwestern University, and the Music Academy of the West in Santa Barbara, California, where her primary teacher was the renowned Lotte Lehmann. She also studied with Pierre Bernac.

Early in her career, Bumbry gradually shifted from mezzo-soprano to soprano roles, in which she achieved as much success as in the lower voice range. Among them were Lady Macbeth in Verdi's *Macbeth*, Leonora in Verdi's *Il trovatore* and *La forza del destino*, Abigaille in Verdi's *Nabucco*, Richard Strauss's *Salome*, Puccini's *Tosca*, Bellini's *Norma*, and Ponchielli'a *La Gioconda*. Bumbry has also sung the roles of both Amneris and Aida—mezzo and soprano—in Verdi's *Aida*. In 2009, Bumbry's many professional accomplishments were recognized at the prestigious Kennedy Center Honors.

HENRY (HARRY) THACKER BURLEIGH (1866–1949)

Singer, Composer, Arranger, Editor. Born in 1866, baritone Harry Thacker Burleigh did not leave his hometown of Erie, Pennsylvania, for formal music study until 1892, when he went to New York to study for four years at the National Conservatory of Music, which was then headed by composer Antonín Dvořák. Dvořák encouraged his students to use folk music and spirituals as a source for their art. This approach had a decisive influence on Burleigh's musical beliefs and practices. His vocal prowess gained him the position of soloist with a wealthy Episcopal church, where he remained for fifty years, and in the chorus of a synagogue for twenty-five years, both in New York City. He was also employed as an editor for the Ricordi Publishing Company from 1911 to 1946.

Besides his lifelong association with sacred music, Burleigh was involved with Broadway musical shows and toured widely as a recitalist, traveling to England and the European continent. He was also a private teacher of voice, music theory, and composition.

As a composer and arranger, Burleigh was the first musician to arrange spirituals in the style of art songs, blending traditional elements with chromatic embellishments and nineteenth-century romantic harmonics. He also made very popular arrangements for chorus, as well as original art songs that were widely programmed by leading singers of the day. Burleigh did not compose in large forms and he did not write dramatic music. His only instrumental works are two suites, one for piano and one for violin and piano. Burleigh was a charter member of the American Society of Composers, Authors, and Publishers. He was awarded honorary degrees by Atlanta and Howard universities.

CYNTHIA CLAREY (1949–)

Singer. Cynthia Clarey was born in Smithfield, Virginia, on April 25, 1949. When she was ten, her family moved to Rocky Mount, North Carolina, where she sang in the church and school choirs. She graduated from Booker T. Washington Senior High School in Rocky Mount in 1966, and then earned a bachelor of music degree from Howard University in Washington, D.C., in 1970. She earned a postgraduate diploma from the Juilliard School in 1972. Clarey made her operatic debut as a soprano with the American Opera Center as Pamina in Mozart's *Magic Flute*.

Clarey worked as a professional chorister in New York City, singing *Carmina Burana* and *Revelations*, the latter with the Alvin Ailey Dance Company. She later moved to Binghamton, New York, to work with the Tri-Cities Opera Company, where she sang several soprano and mezzo roles. It was there that she sang her first *Carmen*, which led to many more performances throughout the United States and the world.

Clarey's European opera debut was at the Glyndebourne Festival in *L'incoronazione di Poppea* in 1984, followed by *Porgy and Bess* in 1986. Her recording of *Porgy and Bess* with Sir Simon Rattle and the Glyndebourne cast and chorus was nominated for a Grammy Award. Clarey also has appeared at the Royal Opera at Covent Garden, the Wexford Festival Opera, the Opéra-Comique in Paris, the Aix-en-Provence Festival, the Deutsche Oper Berlin, Munich's Bayerische Stattsoper, the Bregenz Festival, the Teatro Reggio Emilia in Italy, the Teatro Real in Madrid, the Teatro Municipal in Rio de Janeiro, the Toronto Opera, the Teatro Nacional de São Carlos in Lisbon, and the CAPAB Opera in Cape Town, South Africa.

Clarey's concert performances include appearances with the New York Philharmonic, the Chicago Symphony, the Toronto Symphony, the Boston Symphony, the London BBC Orchestra, the Royal Scottish National Orchestra, the Birmingham Contemporary Music Group in England, the Berlin Philharmonic, the Vienna Philharmonic, the Los Angeles Philharmonic, the Dallas Symphony, the St. Louis Symphony, the Oakland Symphony, and the Hong Kong Philharmonic.

In 2008 Clarey joined the voice faculty of the Chicago College for the Performing Arts at Roosevelt University. She has made recordings for numerous labels.

FRANCES ELAINE COLE (1937–1983)

Violinist, Harpsichordist. Frances Cole studied violin at the Cleveland Institute of Music and at Miami University in Ohio, where she was concertmaster of the orchestra. She earned a doctorate at Teachers College of Columbia University, New York, in 1966, and during her years of study played for the National Orchestral Association. As she was finishing her doctorate, she discovered her interest in the harpsichord and began to study the instrument at the Landowska Center in Connecticut. In 1967, she became resident harpsichordist with the Gallery Players in Provincetown, Massachusetts. She appeared on several national television programs, and began touring throughout the United States and Europe.

Cole was as well known for her humor and innovation as for her elegant musical interpretations. In 1976, for example, she arrived dressed as Anna Magdalena Bach and sat in a horse-drawn carriage for an outdoor concert at Lincoln Center in New York City. She played jazz in a trio and performed as a cabaret singer under the name of Elaine Frances. She also served on the music faculties of Queens College and the Westminster Choir College and presented workshops at many colleges and universities.

WILL MARION COOK (1869–1944)

Composer, Violinist, Conductor. Will Cook's earliest musical activities focused on the violin and Western concert music. When he was fifteen, he left his hometown of Washington, D.C., to study at the Oberlin Conservatory of Music in Ohio, and after four years there he traveled to Berlin, Germany, to study with the renowned master violinist Joseph Joachim. A few years after his return to Washington, Cook left for New York, where he studied at the National Conservatory of Music with its director, Antonín Dvořák, and John White, a virtuoso violinist.

Dissatisfied with the course of his career, which he attributed partly to racial discrimination, Cook took advantage of an opportunity to conduct a newly formed orchestra in Washington. Soon thereafter, he began to work in musical theater in New York City with such collaborators as singer Bob Cole, vaudevillians George Walker and Bert Williams, and the writer Paul Laurence Dunbar. Cook was involved in a number of theatrical firsts. His *Clorindy, or, The Origin of the Cakewalk* (1898), written with Dunbar, was a ragtime operetta that introduced syncopation to Broadway and became the first all–African American musical comedy on Broadway. Cook's *Dahomey* (1903), written with Williams and Walker for the Broadway stage, became the first show written and performed by African Americans to be presented at Buckingham Palace in London.

Cook was the composer or co-composer of seventeen musical shows, in addition to songs that he wrote apart from shows. He wrote only a few piano pieces and no works for violin. Among the several younger musicians to whom he was mentor were Margaret Bonds, Duke Ellington, and Eva Jessye.

ROQUE CORDERO (1917–2008)

Composer, Educator. Roque Cordero studied clarinet and string instruments as a child growing up in Panama. He began to write popular songs before he began studying composition formally when he was seventeen. In 1943, he came to the United States to study composition with Ernst Krenek at Hamline University in St. Paul, Minnesota, and conducting with Dimitri Mitropoulos at the University of Minnesota in Minneapolis. He graduated from the latter magna cum laude with a bachelor of arts degree. Back in his native country, he joined the faculty of the National Institute of Music of Panama, serving as director from 1953 to 1964. He returned to the United States to become assistant director of the Latin American Music Center at Indiana University, Bloomington, beginning in 1966. He became a professor of music at Illinois State University in Normal in 1972, and remained there until he retired in 1987.

Cordero wrote a large number of solo and ensemble instrumental works and several for orchestra, including the prize-winning *Second Symphony* (1956) and *Violin Concerto* (1962). His style blends elements of Panamanian vernacular music with more formal Western European elements, including serialism and polytonality. A balance of these two major aesthetic components is the predominant trait of his musical language.

Among the many honors and awards that Cordero received are a Guggenheim Fellowship (1949), an honorary professorship at the University of Chile, an honorary doctorate from Hamline University (1966), and a Koussevitzky International Recording Award (1974). His commissions, numbering over twenty, came from several countries in South America and prestigious institutions in the United States, including the National Endowment for the Arts and the Kennedy Center.

ANTHONY CURTIS DAVIS (1951–)

Composer, Pianist, Educator. Anthony Davis was born in Paterson, New Jersey. His father, Charles T. Davis, was the first African American professor at Princeton University and was later chair of the Afro-American Studies Department at Yale University. The young Davis grew up in a cultural environment in which his creativity was encouraged.

Davis earned a bachelor's degree in music from Yale in 1975; he returned there to teach in the 1980s and 1990s. He has also been a visiting scholar at Harvard, Cornell, and Northwestern universities, and at the University of California, San Diego.

Davis, who studied piano in his teen years, began to play jazz with different groups while at Yale. When he moved to New York City, he quickly developed a reputation as an advanced player and highly proficient improviser. He founded his own group, Episteme (which means "knowledge"), so that he could work out his compositional ideas.

By the end of the 1990s, Davis had received more than twenty commissions from symphonies, opera and dance companies, choral groups, and other organizations. Three of his four operas are based on real characters and events: *X: The Life and Times of Malcolm X* (1986), written for the Kitchen Center; *Tania* (1992), based on the Patty Hearst kidnapping and commissioned by the American Music Theater Festival; and *Amistad* (1997), composed for the Lyric Opera of Chicago, about a slave revolt aboard a ship and its aftermath.

Critic Andrew Porter praised *X* for its "constantly impressive" score, and said "an 'ordinary' operagoer will be able to respond readily to the music." Davis himself stated, "I hope it will open a door for others to create large works and then realize that this separateness in American culture is just a byproduct of race, not a byproduct of the art. It's important for me that what I do helps the next generation of musicians." Davis's later operatic works include *Wakonda's Dream*, with a libretto by Yusef Komunyakaa, which premiered in 2007 at the Orpheum Theatre in Omaha, Nebraska, and *Lilith*, with a libretto by Allan Havis, which premiered in 2009 at the Conrad Prebys Music Center in San Diego.

In 1996, Davis was honored with an American Academy of Arts and Letters Award in Music. He was awarded a Guggenheim Fellowship in 2006, and won the Lift Every Voice Legacy Award from the National Opera Association in 2008.

MARY CARDWELL DAWSON (1894–1962)

Opera Director. Born in Madison, North Carolina, Mary Cardwell Dawson moved with her family to Pittsburgh, Pennsylvania, as a child. After graduating from the New England Conservatory of Music and Chicago Musical College, she returned to Pittsburgh to pursue a career in music in the late 1920s and 1930s. In 1927, she founded the Cardwell School of Music, at which she gave private voice lessons. She also founded the award-winning Cardwell Dawson Choir, which made appearances at Chicago's Century of Progress Exhibition and at the New York World's Fair. From 1939 to 1941, Dawson served as president of the National Association of Negro Musicians (NANM).

In 1941, after successfully presenting Verdi's *Aida* at the NANM convention, Dawson founded the National Negro Opera Company in Pittsburgh out of concern over the discrimination her talented students and other black artists faced when seeking professional opportunities in opera in the United States.

The mission of the National Negro Opera Company was to provide an outlet for aspiring opera singers, to inspire young artists to study the classics and to enter the opera profession, and to stage productions of operas that would provide employment and performance opportunities for African American singers and musicians. In the late 1940s, Dawson and the National Negro Opera Company relocated to Washington, D.C. There were also active chapters in Baltimore, Chicago, Cleveland, New York, Pittsburgh, and Red Bank, New Jersey. In 1950, the National Negro Opera Foundation was incorporated to help raise funds to sustain the company. For more than two decades, in spite of financial challenges, the National Negro Opera Company produced opera standards, including Gounod's *Faust* and Verdi's *La traviata* and *Aida*, as well as works by African American composers, such as Clarence Cameron White's *Ouanga*. R. Nathaniel Dett's oratorio, *The Ordering of Moses*, was performed by the company more frequently than any other work. The company folded soon after Dawson's death in 1962.

WILLIAM LEVI DAWSON (1899–1990)

Composer, Conductor, Educator. Born in Anniston, Alabama, William Dawson became a student at the Tuskegee Institute (now Tuskegee University) when he was fifteen years old. Dawson's studies included piano, composition, and trombone. After graduating from the institute in 1921, he moved to Kansas City, Kansas, to teach music in high school, and he excelled as a jazz trombonist during his years there. He earned a bachelor of music degree at the Horner Institute of Fine Arts in Kansas City in 1925.

In 1926, Dawson moved to Chicago, where he continued to play in jazz ensembles (including Jimmy Noone's Apex Orchestra and the Fourteen Doctors of Syncopation) and to study composition at the American Conservatory of Music and the Chicago Musical College. He received a master of music degree in 1927 from the conservatory. By this time, he was publishing arrangements of spirituals and conducting a large church choir. In addition, he worked as first trombonist in the Chicago Civic Orchestra from 1926 to 1930.

Dawson was invited to return to Tuskegee in 1931 to head the institute's School of Music, and he remained there until he retired in 1955. During his tenure, he strengthened the music curriculum and brought national recognition to the Tuskegee Choir. After his retirement, he remained active as a guest conductor in the United States and abroad.

Dawson's most famous work, *Negro Folk Symphony,* was first performed in 1934 by the Philadelphia Orchestra conducted by Leopold Stokowski. It was the first symphony by an African American composer to premiere with a major U.S. symphony orchestra. Dawson revised his symphony in 1952 after he visited West Africa and studied African rhythms and their influence on African American music. His description of *Negro Folk Symphony* expresses his goal as a "nationalist" composer: "to write a symphony in the Negro folk idiom, based on authentic folk music but in the same symphonic form used by the composers of the (European) romantic-nationalist school." Dawson's arrangements of spirituals have become staples of the choral repertoire, as have some of his original works.

JAMES ANDERSON DePREIST (1936–)

Conductor. Born in Philadelphia, James DePreist began studying piano and percussion when he was ten years old, but he did not decide on a musical career until he reached his early twenties. After finishing high school, he entered the Wharton School of the University of Pennsylvania and received a bachelor of science degree (1958) and a master of arts degree (1961). He also studied composition with Vincent Persichetti at the Philadelphia Conservatory of Music, as well as music history, theory, and orchestration.

In 1962, DePreist was engaged as an American specialist in music for a U.S. State Department cultural-exchange tour of the Near and Far East. During this tour, he was stricken with polio in Bangkok and became paralyzed in both legs. With six months of intensive therapy, he could walk with the aid of crutches and braces, and managed to win the 1963 Dmitri Mitropoulos International Music Competition for Conductors. After another overseas tour, this time as a conductor in Thailand, he returned to the United States to lead several American orchestras. He was assistant conductor of the New York Philharmonic during the 1964–1965 season, and became associate conductor of the National Symphony in Washington, D.C., in 1971. Another career highlight occurred on June 28, 1965, when he conducted the orchestra for the farewell concert of Marian Anderson, his aunt, in Philadelphia.

DePreist was music director of the Oregon Symphony for twenty-three years (1980–2003), and has been a guest conductor with symphonies throughout the United States and Europe. He has also published two volumes of poetry: *The Distant Siren* (1989) and *This Precipice Garden* (1990). In 2004, DePreist became director of conducting and orchestral studies at the Julliard School in New York City. He also served as conductor of the Tokyo Metropolitan Symphony Orchestra from 2005 to 2008. Among his many awards and honors, DePreist received the National Medal of the Arts in 2005. He is also a member of the American Academy of Arts and Sciences.

ROBERT NATHANIEL DETT (1882–1943)

Composer, Arranger, Conductor, Pianist. R. Nathaniel Dett was born in 1882 in Drummondville, Ontario, to a Canadian mother and an American father. Dett began studying the piano and played in church from an early age. In 1893, his family moved from Drummondville to Niagara Falls, New York, where he began playing in public during his teen years. In 1903, after studying for two years at a music conservatory in nearby Lockport, he transferred to the Oberlin Conservatory of Music in Ohio, where he began his career as a choral conductor. He graduated with a bachelor of music degree in 1908.

Dett held teaching positions at Lane College in Jackson, Tennessee, and Lincoln Institute in Jefferson City, Missouri, and became director of music at Hampton Institute in Virginia in 1913. He raised the performance standards of the Hampton Institute's choir, and established the spiritual as part of the basic choral repertoire. He resigned from Hampton Institute in 1931, and moved to Rochester, New York. He earned a master's degree in 1932 at the Eastman School of Music, where he studied composition under the school's director, Howard Hanson. Dett stayed on at Eastman as choir director and composer until 1937, when he joined the faculty of Bennett College in Greensboro, North Carolina. In 1943, during World War II, Dett became director of the Women's Army Corps Chorus of the United Services Organization (USO). He died a few months later after suffering a heart attack.

Dett's many choral works include collections of spirituals and large-scale dramatic compositions, notably *Chariot Jubilee* (1921) and *The Ordering of Moses,* an oratorio (1937). He also wrote works for piano. Other notable compositions include *Magnolia* (1912), *In the Bottoms* (1913), *Enchantment* (1922), and *Cinnamon Grove Suite* (1928).

Dett wrote prefaces for several of his scores, which he described as of "that class of music known as 'program music' or 'music with a poetic basis.'" Throughout his life, he supported African American folk music through his writings, arrangements, conducting, and scholarship. He received the Bowdoin Literary Prize from Harvard University in 1920 for his essay "The Emancipation of Negro Music." He was a founder of the National Association of Negro Musicians in 1919 and served as its president from 1924 to 1926. Howard University and the Oberlin Conservatory both awarded him honorary doctorates.

CARL ROSSINI DITON (1886–1962)

Pianist, Singer, Composer. Carl Diton first learned piano from his father, a professional musician. He studied at the University of Pennsylvania and received his bachelor's degree in 1909. Following graduation, he became the first African American pianist to complete a cross-country concert tour. He furthered his piano studies in Munich, Germany, with the aid of an E. Azalia Hackley scholarship. In the 1920s, he began voice study and made his concert debut in Philadelphia in 1926. He continued to study voice at the Juilliard School in New York City, where he was awarded an artist's diploma in 1930.

Thereafter, teaching began to take up more of his time, although he continued to perform. He also began to compose and received several awards, including the Harmon Award. Most of his works are art songs and arrangements of spirituals. Diton was a founding member of the National Association of Negro Musicians in 1919.

DEAN DIXON (1915–1976)

Conductor. Born in Manhattan in 1915, Dean Dixon was exposed to classical music by his parents, who often took him to Carnegie Hall. While he was still in high school, he formed his own amateur orchestra at the Harlem YMCA, which soon grew to seventy members and gave regular concerts. He was admitted to the Juilliard School of Music after a successful violin audition, and he was awarded his bachelor's degree in 1936. Three years later, he earned a master's degree from the Teachers College of Columbia University.

Dixon's Symphony Society, founded in 1932, received community support, and in 1941, Eleanor Roosevelt was instrumental in setting up a concert that eventually led to his becoming the music director of the NBC Radio Network's summer symphony. Shortly thereafter, he made his debut with the New York Philharmonic, the first African American to conduct that orchestra.

Dixon was unable to find a position as music director with an American orchestra, so he went to Europe, where he worked with several orchestras in Sweden and Germany. He later conducted the Sydney Symphony in Australia. After his return to the United States in 1970, he was a frequent guest conductor and had compiled an extensive recorded legacy by the time of his death in 1976.

MATTIWILDA DOBBS (1925–)

Singer. Soprano Mattiwilda Dobbs was born in Atlanta, Georgia, the fifth daughter of a railroad postal worker who was a leader in the local African American community. Dobbs majored in voice at Spelman College, and graduated as valedictorian in 1946. She later attended Columbia University Teachers College, where she earned a master's degree. Dobbs studied voice privately with Lotte Leonard in New York and in Paris with Pierre Bernac on a Whitney Fellowship. She won the International Music Competition held in Geneva, Switzerland, in 1951, and in 1953 became the first African American to sing a principal role at La Scala in Milan, Italy.

In 1955, Dobbs made her American operatic debut in the lead in the San Francisco Opera's *The Golden Cockerel*, becoming the first African American to play a major role in that company. This career achievement was followed in 1956 by her debut at the Metropolitan Opera in *Rigoletto*. She was only the third African American to sing on that stage and the first to sing a romantic lead. Her successful performances with American opera companies led to an even greater international fame as she toured the world, including a stop in the Soviet Union, where she was the first Met artist to appear at the Bolshoi Theatre in Moscow. At the peak of her career, her active repertoire included more than two hundred concert pieces and twenty operatic roles.

Dobbs retired from the opera stage in 1974, although she continued to perform recitals. She spent a brief period teaching at the University of Texas in Austin, then became artist-in-residence at Spelman College. Dobbs began teaching voice at Howard University in the mid-1970s. She was elected to the board of directors of the Metropolitan Opera in 1989.

ROBERT TODD DUNCAN (1903–1998)

Singer, Actor, Educator. Baritone Robert Todd Duncan was born in Danville, Kentucky, and raised in Indianapolis, Indiana. His mother, herself a musician, encouraged Duncan in his ambition to become an opera singer. He graduated in 1925 with a bachelor of music degree from Butler University. He later attended

Columbia University Teachers College in New York, where he received a master's degree in music in 1930.

After teaching briefly in a high school, Duncan joined the music faculty of Howard University in 1931. He left Howard in 1945 as the demands of his operatic and concert career increased. He became a very successful concert singer, with more than two thousand performances in fifty-six countries.

Duncan's performance in an all–African American production of Mascagni's *Cavalleria rusticana* in 1934 in New York City led to his being chosen by George Gershwin to sing the lead role of Porgy in the premiere of his opera *Porgy and Bess* in 1935. Duncan also starred in two later revivals of Gershwin's opera. During the New York City Opera's 1945–1946 season, he became the first African American member of the company with roles in *Pagliacci*, *Aida*, and *Carmen*. However, he was never invited to sing at the Metropolitan Opera.

Besides work in films, Duncan appeared in several successful Broadway shows, including *Cabin in the Sky* (1940) and Kurt Weill's *Lost in the Stars* (1949), in which he originated the role of Stephen Kumalo and for which he received the New York Drama Critics Award in 1950. Duncan retired from public performance in 1967, but continued to teach privately in Washington, D.C., for many years. Educational institutions with which he was associated during this period are Howard University and the Curtis Institute of Music. Both Valparaiso and Butler universities awarded him honorary doctorates.

LESLIE B. DUNNER (1956–)

Conductor, Clarinetist, Composer. Born in New York City on January 5, 1956, Leslie Byron Dunner graduated from Manhattan's High School of Music and Art in 1974. He earned a bachelor's degree in clarinet performance from the Eastman School of Music (1978) and continued his education at Queen's College in New York for a master's degree in music theory and musicology (1979). Dunner received a doctorate in orchestra conducting and clarinet performance from the College-Conservatory of Music of the University of Cincinnati (1982).

Dunner won third prize in 1986 at the Arturo Toscanini International Conducting Competition, making him the first American to place at this prestigious event. Dunner's other honors include the 1994 American Symphony Orchestra League Award and the NAACP's James Weldon Johnson Award in 1991.

Dunner was an assistant conductor with the New York Philharmonic from 1994 through 2001, and accompanied the philharmonic in 1995 on a major European tour. From 1987 to 1999, he was also associated in various conducting posts with the Detroit Symphony Orchestra. He was music director of the Annapolis Symphony Orchestra in Maryland from 1998 to 2003, after which he became the principal conductor of the Joffrey Ballet in Chicago. Dunner also served as music director of Symphony Nova Scotia in Halifax from 1996 to 1999.

In the late 1980s, Dunner began to work with the Dance Theatre of Harlem and had earlier served with the Pacific Northwest Ballet Company as assistant conductor. He has made appearances with many orchestras as guest conductor and has had the opportunity to work with some of the world's greatest conductors.

Dunner is also an accomplished clarinetist and composer. Several of his compositions have been recorded, including *The Motherless Child Songs* (1989). His *Whirligigs of Time: Twelfth Night Suite*, for mezzo-soprano, chorus, and orchestra, premiered in 2006.

AARON PAUL DWORKIN (1970–)

Violinist, Educator. Aaron Dworkin is a uniquely gifted violinist, charismatic music educator, and the founding president of the Detroit-based nonprofit Sphinx Organization. As a tribute to his commitment to expand access for minorities to careers in classical music, Dworkin was named a MacArthur Fellow in music education in September 2005.

Dworkin was born on September 11, 1970, in Monticello, New York, but grew up in New York City. He began playing the violin when he was five years old. When he was ten, his family moved to Hershey, Pennsylvania. Dworkin has described himself "as a biracial kid growing up as a black man in America, adopted when I was two weeks old by white parents, I am, at my spiritual, emotional, intellectual and biological core, the embodiment of diversity." Given his background and life experiences, Dworkin has experienced the power of the arts to bridge racial and cultural divides.

A graduate of the Interlochen Arts Academy in Michigan, Dworkin received his bachelor of music degree (1997) and his master of music degree (1998) in violin performance from the University of Michigan. He plays both acoustic and electric violin. In 1996, while still a college student, Dworkin founded the Sphinx Organization after noticing that he was usually the only African American in his classes and often the sole person of color in the audience at classical music performances. The Sphinx Organization's mission is "to overcome the cultural stereotype of classical music and to address the isolation and limited access that young Blacks and Latinos face in the classical music world." In 2005 Dworkin and the Sphinx Organization were awarded one of eight

National Governors' Awards for Distinguished Service to State Government in the category of artistic production.

Dworkin has made two recordings: *Ebony Rhythm* and *Bar-Talk*, released by his own label, Ethnovibe. In 2008, he served on the Arts Policy Committee for Barack Obama's presidential campaign.

RUBY ELZY (1908–1943)

Singer. Ruby Elzy is best known for her performance in the role of Serena, the second female lead in George Gershwin's opera *Porgy and Bess*. Gershwin himself cast Elzy in the part in 1934 while still writing the opera, and she performed the role hundreds of times.

Elzy was born in Pontotoc, Mississippi, on February 20, 1908. Her early life centered on her family, the local Methodist church, and getting an education, which was not easy in the segregated South. Undaunted, her mother prevailed on the officials at Rust College in Holly Springs, some sixty miles away, to admit her eleven-year-old daughter on a work scholarship. In 1926, Elzy graduated from Rust's high school and was admitted to the college's undergraduate program. Dr. Charles McCracken of Ohio State University learned of her talents, and in 1926 she entered Ohio State as a sophomore, studying voice.

Ohio provided many more opportunities and less overt discrimination than Mississippi. In 1929, Elzy and sixteen other sopranos sang with the Cleveland Orchestra in the premiere of Ernest Bloch's tone poem, *America*. In May 1929, Elzy was the first Ohio State student to perform in a solo public concert. Following her graduation in 1930 with a bachelor's degree in education and a first-place ranking from the Music Department, Elzy returned to Mississippi to teach music at Rust College.

Elzy was soon awarded a Rosenwald Fellowship, and became a student at the Juilliard School of Music in New York City. In New York, she became a member of the J. Rosamond Johnson Choir, and made her Broadway debut in 1930 in the all-black musical comedy *Brown Buddies*. In 1931, Elzy made her first network radio appearance with J. Rosamond Johnson on the NBC program *Parade of States*. She graduated from Juilliard in 1934 with a graduate diploma in voice.

Elzy traveled nationally, singing in concert halls and nightclubs. She also performed at the White House and New York's Town Hall. She appeared in supporting roles in several films, including the 1941 film *Birth of the Blues*. Elzy died in 1943 at age thirty-five during routine surgery to remove a benign tumor, cutting short a promising career. A compilation of her recordings, *Ruby Elzy in Song: Rare Recordings, 1935–1942*, was released in 2006.

SIMON ESTES (1938–)

Singer, Educator. Born in 1938, in Centerville, Iowa, the bass-baritone Simon Lamont Estes is the grandson of a slave and the son of a coal miner. An athletic scholarship to the University of Iowa provided him with the opportunity to study voice with Charles Kellis. Estes received a full scholarship to the Juilliard School of Music, where he studied with Sergius Kagen and Christopher West. In 1964, he received grants that allowed him to travel to Germany, where he was offered a contract with the Deutsche Opera in West Berlin. Estes recounted the circumstances of his debut as Ramfis in Verdi's *Aida* in April 1965: "I didn't have any rehearsal. It was the first time, literally, I had ever been on a stage. I didn't meet the conductor until the curtain parted and I saw him on the podium."

In 1966 Estes won the silver medal in the Tchaikovsky Competition in Moscow. His European career developed rapidly, and he appeared with opera companies in Vienna, Munich, Hamburg, Paris, Milan, and Florence. In 1978, Wolfgang Wagner invited him to appear at Bayreuth in the title role of *The Flying Dutchman*, and Estes became the first African American male singer to sing at the shrine of Richard Wagner.

Estes has performed with various American opera companies as well, including appearances in San Francisco, Boston, and Chicago. He also performed at the Metropolitan Opera House with the Hamburg State Opera in the lead role of Gunther Schuller's *The Visitation*. His debut with the Met company, however, did not take place until 1982, when he appeared in the role of the Landgrave in Wagner's *Tannhäuser*. Two seasons later, he played Porgy in the Met's first production of Gershwin's *Porgy and Bess*.

Estes made his concert debut in 1980 at Carnegie Hall, and has performed many recitals since then. His recordings include Beethoven's *Symphony No. 9*, Handel's *Messiah*, Fauré's *Requiem*, and Wagner's *Flying Dutchman*. He has also recorded spirituals and highlights from *Porgy and Bess*.

Estes has received numerous awards, including the Tchaikovsky Medal in 1985 and the Iowa Award of Achievement in 1996. He has taught voice at Iowa State University, the Julliard School, Wartburg College, and Boston University.

JAMES REESE EUROPE

See chapter 24, Blues and Jazz.

LILLIAN EVANS EVANTI (1890–1967)

Singer. Born in Washington, D.C., on August 12, 1890, Lillian Evans, a lyric soprano, was the first African American to receive international recognition singing opera with an organized company in Europe. Evans attended Armstrong Manual Training School and Miner Teachers College before graduating from the Howard University School of Music in 1917. After graduation, she taught in the Washington, D.C., public schools, married Roy Tibbs, an organist and professor of music at Howard, and performed as a concert artist. She left for Europe to study acting and voice in Italy and France, and to find professional opportunities that did not exist for African American opera singers in the United States at the time. In Europe, she adopted the stage name Madame Lillian Evanti, a combination of her family name, Evans, and her husband's name, Tibbs.

Evanti won the title role in Delibes's *Lakmé* at the Casino Theater in Nice, France, in 1925. She repeated her performance at the Trianon Lyrique in Paris. After five years in Europe, Evanti continued her professional operatic and concert career in the United States. In 1932, she made her Town Hall debut and gave recitals throughout the United States, Europe, and the Caribbean. In 1934, she was invited by Franklin and Eleanor Roosevelt to sing at the White House. In 1943, Evanti received wide acclaim for her performance as Violetta in Verdi's *La traviata* in a production staged by Mary Cardwell Dawson's National Negro Opera Company in Washington, D.C.

Evanti began collecting art for her Washington, D.C., residence in the 1920s. After her death in 1967, her grandson, Thurlow Tibbs Jr., founded and operated an art gallery called the Evans-Tibbs Collection, which grew to over five hundred paintings, drawings, sketches, and sculptures, as well as six thousand books. The Evans-Tibbs house was listed on the National Register of Historic Places in 1987. When Thurlow Tibbs died in 1997, he bequeathed the collection to the Corcoran Gallery of Art.

DAVID FARRAR (1944–)

Opera Stage Director. Dr. David Farrar has the distinction of being the first African American opera stage director to direct at the New York City Opera, the San Francisco Opera, the Royal Opera at Covent Garden, the Opera del Teatro Municipal in Santiago, Chile, and the Oberlin Opera Theatre in Ohio. He is also the first African American to stage a complete production of Gershwin's *Porgy and Bess*.

Farrar was born in New York City on May 27, 1944. He studied at the Music and Art High School, where he excelled as a bassoonist. He later performed as a soloist and as a member of the Santa Fe Opera Orchestra and the Santa Barbara Symphony Orchestra. He earned his doctorate from the University of Southern California in 1971.

Farrar has taught at the University of California at Santa Barbara, Lehman College of the City University of New York, the University of Washington in Seattle, and the Oberlin Conservatory of Music. As founder of the Virginia Opera in Norfolk, he served as stage director and director of productions for ten years, and helped to bring the company to national prominence. He directed the 1978 American premiere of Thea Musgrave's *Mary, Queen of Scots*, and directed subsequent productions at the New York City Opera and the San Francisco Opera. He also directed the European premiere of Musgrave's *A Christmas Carol* for the Royal Opera at Covent Garden. He has directed more than sixty productions of thirty-two operas on three continents. Farrar has been responsible for the debuts of many African American artists at the Virginia Opera and continues to mentor young singers and opera stage directors. In 1995, the National Opera Association honored him with the Distinguished Director Award for his historic role as an African American opera stage director. Farrar works with Martina Arroyo in her summer program for young artists, and funds the Dr. David Farrar Scholarship for Assistant Stage Directors.

TALMAGE FAUNTLEROY (1952–2002)

Director, Singer. Talmage Randall Fauntleroy was born in Hampton, Virginia, on September 12, 1952. He attended the Hampton public schools and graduated from Kecoughtan High in 1971. He continued his education at East Carolina University, where he received a bachelor's degree in music, and Howard University, where he received a master's degree in voice. He completed further studies at the University of Illinois.

Fauntleroy was provided a training ground by the New Theater School of Washington, with whom he organized an Opera Workshop Program. His first operatic venture as stage director was Menotti's *Amahl and the Night Visitors*, which the school produced in 1977. Later, he was hired at the Virginia Opera Association and was mentored by David Farrar.

In 1981, Fauntleroy enrolled in the language program at the University of Florence in Italy. During his time at the school, a local music association was looking for a director for their opera workshop. A friend introduced Fauntleroy to the association's president, and Fauntleroy was hired as the new director. The new workshop eventually became an international program known as Studio Lirico, based in Cortona and Anghiari in the Tuscany region.

Because of his work at Studio Lirico, Fauntleroy was invited to appear as guest clinician and guest stage director in various European and U.S. cities. This in turn led to his appointment as director of opera studies at the music conservatory in Livorno (Instituto Musicale "Pietro Mascagni"). Fauntleroy was later associated with productions of the Virginia Opera Association, the Central City Opera, the Washington Opera, and the Metropolitan Opera, among others in the United States, and in Italy with the Teatro Comunale and the Teatro alla Pergola, both in Florence.

Fauntleroy resided in Italy for more than a decade before becoming director of the University of South Carolina (USC) Opera Program in 1992. He transferred sponsorship of Studio Lirico to USC, but became ill at the conclusion of the summer 2002 session and died at age forty-nine. He was buried in Anghiari.

PAUL FREEMAN (1936–)

Conductor. Paul Freeman, founder of the Chicago Sinfonietta, was born in Richmond, Virginia, in 1936. He earned a Ph.D. at the Eastman School of Music in Rochester, New York, where he also studied clarinet and cello. He continued his studies in Berlin with the aid of a Fulbright Grant. In 1987, Freeman founded and became music director of the Chicago Sinfonietta, which promotes diversity by providing professional opportunities for minority classical musicians and composers.

Freeman has guest conducted for numerous orchestras around the world. From 1979 to 1989, he served as music director of the Victoria Symphony in Canada, guest conductor of the Helsinki Philharmonic in Finland, associate conductor of the Detroit Symphony and the Dallas Symphony, and music director of the Opera Theatre in Rochester, New York. In 1996, he became the music director and conductor for the Czech National Symphony Orchestra in Prague.

With approximately two hundred recordings, Freeman is one of America's most successful recording conductors. He has promoted the works of black composers through two series of recordings: the *Black Composers Series* and the *African Heritage Symphonic Series*.

LOUIS MOREAU GOTTSCHALK (1829–1869)

Composer, Pianist. Louis Gottschalk, a native of New Orleans, was a violin prodigy by the time he was six years old. When he reached his teens, he became an outstanding pianist and studied in Europe with leading teachers. In his mid-twenties, he made his New York City debut, having already established a brilliant reputation in Europe. He toured internationally with great success for the rest of his life.

Gottschalk's compositions for piano reflect the Creole environment of his childhood, and several of them, including the early works *Le bananier* and *Bamboula*, are based in African American and Cuban-inspired folk music. He also wrote characteristic salon pieces. His autobiographical *Notes of a Pianist*, first published in 1881, provides information about his life, methods of composing, the people he knew, and the places he visited.

DENYCE GRAVES (1965–)

Singer. Mezzo-soprano Denyce Graves is a native of Washington, D.C., where she was a student at the Duke Ellington School for the Performing Arts. In 1981, she began studying with Helen Hodam at the Oberlin College Conservatory in Ohio. She transferred to the New England Conservatory of Music in Boston in 1984. Graves received a bachelor of music degree and an

Denyce Graves, Mezzo-Soprano, Lincoln Memorial, Washington, DC, 2009. *Seventy years after Marian Anderson's Lincoln Memorial concert, Graves wears Anderson's gown during a concert to commemorate the event. Graves made her debut at the Metropolitan Opera in the title role of* Carmen *in 1995.*
AP PHOTO/ALEX BRANDON

artist's diploma in 1988 and later joined the Houston Grand Opera Studio of the University of Houston, where she worked with Elena Nikolaidi.

Early in her career, Graves won the Richard Tucker Music Foundation Award, the Eleanor Steber Award at the Opera Columbus Vocal Competition, the Marian Anderson Award, the Grand Prix Lyrique given once every three years by the Friends of the Monte Carlo Opera, and George London and Metropolitan Opera career study grants.

In the 1990s, Graves's career as opera and recital singer and orchestra soloist flourished. She has sung the title role in Bizet's *Carmen* in opera houses throughout North and South America and Europe to great acclaim. She and Plácido Domingo opened the Metropolitan Opera's 1997–1998 season in that opera. Another signature role for Graves is Dalila in *Samson et Dalila* by Saint-Saëns, which she has also sung at the Met. She has also performed solos and leading roles in Verdi's *Requiem*, and *La damnation de Faust* by Berlioz, *Shéhérazade* by Ravel, and Mahler's *Kindertotenlieder* and *Eighth Symphony*.

RERI GRIST (1932–)

Singer. Born in New York City, soprano Reri Grist received her bachelor's degree in music from Queens College in New York in 1954. Her performance of Consuela in Leonard Bernstein's *West Side Story* brought her national attention. She made an equally strong impression in Mahler's *Symphony No. 4*, which she sang with the New York Philharmonic. Since then, she has preformed at many of the world's leading opera houses, including La Scala in Milan, the Vienna State Opera, Britain's Royal Opera, and the Metropolitan Opera.

In 1960, the stage director of the Met, Herbert Graf, left that company to become director of the Zurich Opera. Grist was one of several artists to go with him. While she was in Europe, Igor Stravinsky asked Grist to sing in *Le rossignol* under his direction. Besides performing and recording, Grist has taught voice at the Hochschule für Musik in Germany and at Indiana University.

EMMA AZALIA HACKLEY (1867–1922)

Singer, Choral Director, Educator. E. Azalia Hackley did as much to promote African American musicians as she did their traditional music. Growing up in Detroit, she studied voice and piano and began to perform in public at an early age. She received a degree in music from the University of Denver in 1901 and later traveled to Paris for further voice study.

Hackley traveled extensively as a recitalist in the early years of the twentieth century, but she gradually became more occupied with furthering the careers of other young African American artists. She established scholarships, sponsored debut recitals, and helped many young performers find college-level teaching positions. Hackley founded the Normal Vocal Institute in Chicago in late 1915 and directed it until it was forced to close in 1917 because of financial difficulties. She later organized large community concerts to promote the importance of African American folk music and to raise the level of public interest and pride in the African American musical heritage. The E. Azalia Hackley Collection was established by the National Association of Negro Musicians at the Detroit Public Library in 1943 in order to preserve her papers, memorabilia, sheet music, and other materials relating to African American music and musicians.

HELEN EUGENIA HAGAN (1893–1964)

Pianist, Composer, Educator. Helen Hagan was born in Portsmouth, New Hampshire, into a musical family. Her mother played piano and her father was a baritone. After receiving her early music training from her mother and in the public school system in New Haven, Connecticut, she became the first African American pianist to earn a bachelor of music degree from Yale University in 1912. She was also the first African American to win Yale's Sanford Fellowship, which permitted her to study in Europe with Vincent d'Indy. She earned a diploma in 1914 from the Schola Cantorum and returned to the United States to earn a master's degree from Columbia University Teachers College in New York City.

Between 1914 and 1918, Hagan toured in the United States, often playing her own compositions. In 1918, she toured Europe, entertaining African American servicemen during World War I. When she gave a recital in 1921 at Aeolian Hall, she became the first African American pianist to give a solo performance in a major New York City concert hall. During the 1930s, she worked as a music teacher at Tennessee Agricultural and Industrial State College in Nashville and Bishop College in Marshall, Texas. She returned to New York in the mid-1930s and taught private classes in her own studio.

ADOLPHUS HAILSTORK (1941–)

Composer, Educator. Adolphus Cunningham Hailstork was born in Rochester, New York, on April 17, 1941. He was raised in Albany and began studying music there. He directed a boys' choral group and began to compose music while he was a student at Albany High School.

Hailstork attended Howard University, where he studied with composer Mark Fax and earned a bachelor of music degree in 1963. The summer after graduation, he traveled to France to study with Nadia Boulanger at the American Institute at Fontainebleau. When he returned to the United States, he earned a master's degree in composition at the Manhattan School of Music, studying with David Diamond, Vittorio Giannini, Ludmila Ulehla, and Nicolas Flagello. After serving in the armed forces, he earned a doctorate in composition from Michigan State University in 1971, studying with H. Owen Reed. Hailstork taught at Youngstown State University in Ohio from 1971 to 1977, Norfolk State University in Virginia from 1977 to 2000, and Old Dominion University in Virginia, where he became a professor of music in 2000.

Hailstork writes in various styles and forms, including symphonic works, piano works, solo vocal music, choral works, and band music and transcriptions. He has won many commissions and awards, including the Ernest Bloch Award for Choral Composition (1971) for *Mourn Not the Dead*; the Belwin-Mills Max Winkler Award (1977), presented by the Band Directors National Association for his *Out of the Depths*; and first prize from the University of Delaware Festival of Contemporary Music (1995) for *Consort Piece*. In 1987, he was granted a Fulbright Fellowship, and he was named a cultural laureate of the Commonwealth of Virginia in 1992. The College of William and Mary gave him an honorary doctorate in 2000.

Hailstork's works have been performed by orchestras in Philadelphia, Chicago, and New York, under conductors Lorin Maazel, Daniel Barenboim, and Kurt Masur, respectively. The Opera Theatre of St. Louis and the Kansas City Lyric Opera commissioned and premiered *Joshua's Boots*, Hailstork's second opera, in 1999. The Detroit Symphony commissioned and performed his *Symphony No. 2* that same year. Hailstork's *Symphony No. 2* and *Symphony No. 3* were recorded by David Lockington with the Grand Rapids Symphony. His choral work, *Earthrise*, premiered in 2006 at the Cincinnati May Festival. Hailstork's *Rise for Freedom: The John P. Parker Story*, an opera about the Underground Railroad, was first staged by the Cincinnati Opera in 2007.

JACQUELINE HAIRSTON (1938–)

Composer, Vocal Coach. Jacqueline Butler Hairston, born on December 18, 1938, is a multitalented pianist, composer, arranger, and vocal coach. Based in the San Francisco Bay area, her musical training was at the Juilliard School and Howard University, and she earned a master's degree in music from Columbia University. Her training is classical, but the majority of her work deals with the Negro spiritual.

Hairston's compositions and arrangements have been commissioned and performed by numerous artists and companies, including Florence Quivar, Shirley Verrett, Grace Bumbry, Benjamin Matthews, William Warfield, Robert Sims, Jubilant Sykes, New York's Opera Ebony, and the Metropolitan Orchestra of Lisbon in Portugal. Her works have been performed or recorded by the London Symphony, the Columbia Symphony, and the Oakland East Bay Symphony. Hairston's choral works have been performed by the San Francisco Women's Philharmonic, Linda Tillery and the Cultural Heritage Choir, Kathleen Battle at Carnegie Hall with the Pro Art and Collegiate Chorales, and Denyce Graves with the Orlando Opera Chorus and Orchestra, among others.

Hairston served as composer-in-residence at the Negro Spiritual Foundation of Orlando, Florida, in 1998, and was artist-in-residence at Northern Illinois University in 2001. As head of the music department at Merritt College in Oakland, she formed an award-winning choir, the New Traveling Voices. She has also taught at Oakland's New School for the Arts and the University of Creation Spirituality, and for the University of California's Young Musicians Program. Hairston often collaborated with her cousin, the late Jester Hairston, a composer, conductor, actor, and preservationist of Negro spirituals.

In 2009, Hairston released *Spiritual Roots + Classical Fruits: A Healing Harvest*, an album of her solo piano arrangements and combinations of spirituals, hymns, and classical music. Two new publications feature her arrangements: *Spirituals for Violin*, published in 2009 by Carl Fischer, and Christopher Parkening's *Duets and Concertos*, published in 2008 by Hal Leonard. Oxford University Press has contracted her to do an arrangement of spirituals for treble voices in 2010.

DOROTHY ANTOINETTE HANDY (MILLER) (1930–2002)

Flutist, Educator, Author. Flutist Dorothy Antoinette Handy was born in New Orleans in 1930. After studying violin and piano with her mother as a child, Handy decided on a career in music. Flute became her primary instrument, and she studied at Spelman College in Atlanta; the New England Conservatory of Music in Boston, where she earned a bachelor of music degree in 1952; and Northwestern University in Evanston, Illinois, where she earned a master of music degree in 1953. Later, she studied at the National Conservatory in Paris, receiving an artist's diploma in 1955.

Like so many African American musicians and vocalists in the mid-twentieth century, Handy could not secure a job as an orchestra musician in the United States because of her race. A chance audition in France yielded Handy a position as first-chair flutist with the Orchestre International, an orchestra supported by the French government that toured Germany in the interest of better foreign relations in 1954. This was the beginning of Handy's twenty-five-year career as a symphony musician with various orchestras, including the Civic Orchestra of Chicago, Musica Viva Orchestra of Geneva, Switzerland, the Symphony of the Air of the NBC Radio Network, and the Symphony of the New World.

In addition to performing, Handy devoted much of her life to teaching music history, theory, and arranging at such institutions as Florida A&M University, Tuskegee Institute, and Jackson State University. She researched African American music as a Ford Foundation Humanities Fellow in 1971, and published numerous articles for professional journals. She was also the author of *Black Women in America: Bands and Orchestras* (1981), *The International Sweethearts of Rhythm* (1983, revised 1998), *Black Conductors* (1995), and *Jazz Man's Journey* (1999).

In 1990, Handy was appointed director of the National Endowment for the Arts' Music Program. Before her retirement in 1993, Handy administered the distribution of $11–15 million in funding. This money provided backing for up-and-coming musicians and supported the creation of new music, musical performances, organizations, and training institutions.

HILDA HARRIS (1936–)

Singer, Educator. Hilda Harris was born on January 25, 1936, in Warrenton, North Carolina. She did not consider a music career until her senior year at North Carolina State University. On the advice of a teacher, she moved to New York City to study with Lola Hayes. Harris learned classical technique and repertoire while singing studio backup and Broadway chorus to support herself. She appeared in several Broadway shows, including *110 in the Shade*, *Golden Boy*, and *Mame*. During this time, she also made her Carnegie Hall recital debut. Her operatic debut was in a Martha Baird Rockefeller Foundation production of *The Marriage of Figaro* in Brevard, North Carolina, and at the Chautauqua Festival in Jamestown, New York. She then sang a four-month run of *Carmen* in Europe.

In 1972, Harris debuted with the New York City Opera. She debuted with the Metropolitan Opera in Berg's *Lulu* in 1977. She became a regular at the Met, singing many "trouser" roles, such as Cherubino in *The Marriage of Figaro*, Stephano in Gounod's *Roméo and Juliette*, Siebel in *Faust*, Sesto in *Giulio Cesare*, Hansel in *Hansel and Gretel*, and the child in *L'enfant et les sortilèges*.

Harris has appeared with numerous other opera companies around the world, singing Carmen, Rosina, Dorabella, and the title role in Rossini's *La Cenerentola* in Belgium, Brussels, Switzerland, Budapest, Holland, San Francisco, Pittsburgh, Chicago, and Seattle, and at the Spoleto Festivals in Italy and Charleston, South Carolina. She has been heard in concert with the New York Philharmonic, the Helsinki Orchestra, Sweden's Malmo Symphony, the radio orchestras of Hilversum in the Netherlands, and other orchestras in the United States, Canada, and Europe.

Harris is interested in the discovery, promotion, and performance of works of African American composers, and became a member of Chicago's Black Music Research Ensemble. She taught voice at Howard University from 1991 to 1994 and has served on the voice faculty at the Chautauqua Institute in the summer. She joined the faculty of the Manhattan School of Music in 1991, and is also a member of the music faculty at Sarah Lawrence College. She has made several recordings, including *Hilda Harris*, a solo album.

MARGARET ROSEZARIAN HARRIS (1943–2000)

Pianist, Conductor, Composer. Margaret Harris was born in Chicago in 1943. She was a child prodigy, and first performed on the piano in public when she was three. She began touring nationally when she was four, and played with the Chicago Symphony when she was ten. Harris became a student of conducting and piano at the Curtis Institute of Music in Philadelphia, and received bachelor's and master's degrees from the Juilliard School of Music in the mid-1960s.

Harris began conducting Broadway shows in 1970, starting with *Hair*. Other shows included *Two Gentlemen of Verona* (1972–1974), *Raisin* (1974–1976), *Guys and Dolls* (1980), and *Amen Corner* (1983–1984). She was a founding member of Opera Ebony and served as its music director. Among major orchestras that she conducted were the symphonies of Chicago, Minneapolis, Detroit, San Diego, St. Louis, and Los Angeles. Harris also taught at the University of West Florida (1989–2000) and Bronx Community College of the City University of New York (1991–2000).

Besides writing scores for musical productions and television shows, she composed choral and instrumental works, the scores for two ballets, and two piano concertos. Harris often served as both soloist and conductor for performances of her concertos. She died at age fifty-six in New York City on March 7, 2000, after suffering a heart attack.

HAZEL HARRISON (1883–1969)

Pianist, Teacher. Hazel Harrison was born in La Porte, Indiana, in 1883. She showed prodigious musical gifts from early childhood and may have earned a living as a dance-hall pianist if it were not for her mother's determination. Because a European debut was essential for an American concert performer, young Harrison's major teacher, Victor Heinze, arranged a German tour for her in 1904, during which she was a soloist with the Berlin Philharmonic and attracted favorable notices.

A grant allowed Harrison to return to Germany in 1911, when she became the student of the virtuoso pianist and composer Ferruccio Busoni. Busoni was the biggest influence on Harrison's musical life. With the onset of World War I, she returned to the United States and stunned critics with her impressive concerts. She debuted in New York City at Town Hall in 1930 to glowing reviews. However, segregation largely confined her talent to concerts played in African American churches, in high school gymnasiums, and on African American college campuses. This racism caused Harrison to focus on a teaching career, and she joined the faculty of Tuskegee Institute in 1931. Other academic positions followed at Howard University (1936–1955) and at Alabama State College in Montgomery (1958–1963). She gave her final public concert there in 1959. Harrison never made commercial recordings, and this is probably the reason that, in spite of glowing reviews and the devotion of generations of her students, her achievements as a performer are now little known.

ROLAND HAYES (1887–1977)

Singer. Roland Hayes was the first African American man to achieve international success as a concert singer. He was born June 3, 1887, in Curryville, Georgia, to formerly enslaved parents. In 1903, he began singing with an a cappella group called the Silver Toned Quartet, and later started private vocal studies with Arthur Calhoun in Chattanooga, Tennessee. After two years of private music lessons, Hayes attended Fisk University and toured with the Fisk Jubilee Singers. He later moved to Boston, where he began vocal studies with Arthur Hubbard. While in Boston, he managed and promoted his solo concerts, started his own record label, and sang with Harry T. Burleigh and Marian Anderson in performances of Mendelssohn's *Elijah* and Handel's *Messiah*.

In 1917 Hayes rented Boston Symphony Hall for a solo recital. The concert was sold out, and more than seven hundred concertgoers without tickets were turned away. Four years later, Hayes sang a "command" performance at Buckingham Palace for King George V and Queen Mary, and he made many successful appearances throughout Europe. In 1924, Hayes returned to the United States for a recital tour and was named the tenth recipient of the NAACP Spingarn Award. Hayes spent the next twenty years giving recitals and performing with orchestras throughout the United States and Europe. He sang for many hostile audiences at home and abroad. At the Lyric Theater in Baltimore, Hayes was spat on by a white audience member before beginning to sing. He sang Schubert's "Du bist die Ruh" to quell the situation. In 1942, MacKinley Helm published a biography about Hayes, *Angel Mo' and her Son, Roland Hayes*, and in 1948 Hayes's *My Songs: Aframerican Religious Folk Songs* was published.

In 1949, Hayes was honored by the French government for his service to French music. He received a Fellowship Award from the American Academy of Arts and Sciences in 1953. In his later years, Hayes became a faculty member at Boston University and gave a well-received farewell concert in New York's Carnegie Hall on his seventy-fifth birthday. His success in the concert field, along with that of Marian Anderson and Paul Robeson, played a large role in broadening the opportunities later available to younger African American singers.

BARBARA HENDRICKS (1948–)

Singer. Soprano Barbara Hendricks was born in Stephens, Arkansas, on November 20, 1948. She graduated from the University of Nebraska with a bachelor of science degree in chemistry and mathematics. She then attended the Juilliard School of Music in New York City and received a bachelor of music degree in voice in 1973. Hendricks made her debut in 1974 with the San Francisco Spring Opera and has since performed with major opera companies and festivals throughout the United States and Europe, including the Boston Opera, the Metropolitan Opera, the St. Paul Opera, the Santa Fe Opera, the Houston Opera, and the Deutsche Oper Berlin, and at the Aix-en-Provence and the Glyndebourne festivals. She has performed frequently as an orchestra soloist as well. Hendricks also sings jazz, and made her jazz debut in Switzerland at the 1994 Montreux Jazz Festival. She performs regularly with the Magnus Lindgren Quartet.

Hendricks's awards include a French Grammy for best performer of classical music in 1986, an honorary doctorate from Nebraska Wesleyan University in 1988, an honorary membership in the Institute of Humanitarian Law in 1990, and the Lions Club International Award in 2001. She has also served as a human rights activist and, beginning in 1987, as a goodwill ambassador for the United Nations High Commissioner for Refugees. It is in this capacity that Hendricks traveled to Rwanda, Bosnia, and Southeast Asia.

Hendricks became a citizen of Switzerland in the 1970s. She started her own record label, Arte Verum, in 2006.

ESTHER HINDS (1943–)

Singer, Educator. Born in St. Michael's, Barbados, in the West Indies on January 3, 1943, Esther Hinds developed into a soprano with great beauty of tone and exceptional acting ability. Her family moved to New York in 1952, where she attended Music and Art High School. She furthered her musical studies at Hart College of Music at the University of Hartford in Connecticut, earning a music-artist diploma in 1965.

Hinds made her professional opera debut at New York City Opera, later performing several roles there. She rose to prominence when she was chosen to sing Cleopatra in Samuel Barber's *Antony and Cleopatra* at Julliard's American Opera Center in 1982. Her collaboration with Barber and Gian Carlo Menotti in this production brought her much critical acclaim, and she performed the role again at the Spoleto Festival in Italy in 1984. The opera was recorded by New World Records and won a 1984 Grammy Award, the first for the label. Hinds sang regularly at the Spoleto festivals in Italy and in Charleston. In 1983, she was awarded the festival's prestigious Pegasus Award, the first singer to be so honored in twenty-six years of its history.

Hinds also appeared in various roles with the Houston Grand Opera, the San Diego Opera, the Cincinnati Opera, the Virginia Opera, the National Opera Ebony, the Kentucky Opera, Opera/South, and the Nevada Opera. She has been heard in concert with the Boston Symphony, the Dallas Symphony, the St. Louis Symphony, the Toronto Symphony, the Baltimore Symphony, the Brooklyn Philharmonic, the San Francisco Symphony, the Berlin Philharmonic, the Cleveland Orchestra, the Pittsburgh Symphony, the Detroit Symphony, and the Hartford Symphony. She has worked with some of the world's greatest conductors, including James Levine, Walter Susskind, Robert Shaw, Seiji Ozawa, Klaus Tennstedt, Sir Andrew Davis, Lukas Foss, Edo de Waart, Julius Rudel, Christian Badea, Christopher Keene, Yehudi Menuhin, and Michel Corboz.

Hinds is also a noted recitalist and concert artist, making her Carnegie Hall debut in Copland's *Second Hurricane* under Leonard Bernstein when she was still a student at Music and Art High School. She later appeared with Simon Estes and Everett Lee in Verdi's *Don Carlos*. She often performs with her sisters, Ruby and Grace, in the Hinds Sisters Trio. Hinds joined the faculty at Nyack College in Nyack, New York, in 2000.

ANN STEVENS HOBSON-PILOT (1943–)

Harpist. Ann Hobson-Pilot was born November 6, 1943, in Philadelphia. She became one of the first African American women to hold a permanent position in a major national symphony orchestra. Hobson-Pilot began studying piano with her mother at an early age and took up the harp in high school so that she could play an instrument on which her mother could not judge so easily what she might be doing wrong. Her first major teacher in harp was Marilyn Costello, principal harpist of the Philadelphia Orchestra and a teacher at the Philadelphia Music Academy.

After Hobson-Pilot's second year at the academy, she attended the Maine Harp Colony (her first application for admission had been rejected on racial grounds), where she met Alice Chalifoux, principal of the Cleveland Orchestra and teacher at the Cleveland Institute of Music. Hobson-Pilot decided to transfer to the Cleveland Institute.

Ann Hobson-Pilot at Carnegie Hall, New York City, 2009. *Pilot joined the Boston Symphony Orchestra in 1969, became the principal harpist in 1980, and retired in 2009, though she continues to perform on occasion.* AP PHOTO/STUART RAMSON

Chalifoux was influential in starting Hobson-Pilot on her professional orchestra career at the National Symphony Orchestra in Washington, D.C. In 1969, Hobson-Pilot joined the Boston Symphony Orchestra as the associate principal harpist. She became principal harpist in 1980.

Hobson-Pilot's other activities have included performing with the Boston Symphony Chamber Players, the New England Harp Trio, and the Ritz Chamber Players, and making solo appearances with orchestras throughout the country. She retired from the Boston Symphony Orchestra after more than forty years in 2009. Her final concert with the Boston Symphony Orchestra featured a concerto written for her on the occasion of her retirement by John Williams. The work, *On Willows and Birches*, was performed at Tanglewood and later at Carnegie Hall under the baton of James Levine. Besides conducting clinics and workshops, she has taught at the Philadelphia Musical Academy and the New England Conservatory in Boston, and was a member of the board of trustees at the Longy School of Music. Hobson-Pilot has been honored by the Professional Arts Society of Philadelphia, and received an honorary doctorate of fine arts from Bridgewater State College in 1988.

BEN HOLT (1955–1990)

Singer. Born in Washington, D.C., baritone Ben Holt attended the Oberlin College Conservatory of Music in Ohio and was a scholarship student at the Juilliard School of Music, where he worked with Sixten Ehrling, Tito Gobbi, and Manuel Rosenthal. He also took master classes with Luciano Pavarotti and worked extensively with renowned pianist and coach Martin Isepp. When he was in the Merola Program of the San Francisco Opera, taking master classes with Elisabeth Schwarzkopf, he was invited to study privately with her at her studio in Zurich, Switzerland.

Holt made his Metropolitan Opera debut in Puccini's *La Bohème* during the 1985–1986 season, and in 1986 he made his debut with the New York City Opera in the title role of *X: The Life and Times of Malcolm X*, by Anthony Davis. Leading roles in Gershwin's *Porgy and Bess* and Mozart's *The Marriage of Figaro* were also in his repertoire. Holt won many competitions, including the Joy of Singing Competition and the D'Angelo Young Artists Competition, as well as awards from the Oratorio Society of New York and Independent Black Opera Singers. Holt died from Hodgkin's disease in 1990 when he was thirty-four years old.

ISAIAH JACKSON (1945–)

Conductor. Isaiah Jackson was born in Richmond, Virginia, where he started piano lessons when he was four years old. He was sent to a private boarding school in Vermont when he was fourteen, and traveled with his high school class to the former Soviet Union.

Although Jackson had wanted to be a musician, his parents hoped that he would enter the diplomatic corps. Eventually, he enrolled at Harvard University, from which he graduated cum laude in 1966 with a degree in Russian history and literature. After graduation, he followed his first inclination and went to Stanford University for studies in music. After earning a master's degree there in 1967, he moved to the Juilliard School of Music in New York City, where he earned another master's and a doctor of musical arts degree, finishing in 1973.

Shortly thereafter, Jackson began conducting major American orchestras, including the New York and Los Angeles philharmonics and the Vienna Symphony. He was also conductor for the Dance Theatre of Harlem at the Spoleto Festival in Italy. Jackson held concurrent positions with various regional orchestras and, for fourteen years, he was associate conductor of the Rochester Philharmonic. In 1985, he was guest conductor with the orchestra of the Royal Ballet in London, and in 1987 he became the first African American to hold a leadership position—music director—with the Royal Ballet. In that year, he also became the first African American conductor of the Dayton Philharmonic Orchestra in Ohio. Jackson has served as guest conductor for orchestras around the world, and has been principal guest conductor of the Queensland Symphony Orchestra.

Jackson was the recipient of the first Governor's Award for the Arts in Virginia in 1979. He also received the Signet Society Medal for the Arts from Harvard University in 1991. Jackson is a professor at Berklee College of Music in Boston, and president and CEO of Rhythm, Rhyme, Results, an educational music and media company.

CATERINA JARBORO (1898–1986)

Singer. Soprano Caterina Jarboro became the first African American to perform with a major opera company when she sang the title role of Verdi's *Aida* in 1930 at the Puccini Opera House in Milan, Italy. She made history again on July 22, 1933, in her American debut. For the first time ever, a black woman performed the lead role with an otherwise all-white company when impresario Alfredo Salmaggi hired Jarboro to sing *Aida* with his Chicago Opera Company at the Hippodrome in New York City.

Jarboro was one of six children born in Wilmington, North Carolina, to an African American father and a Native American mother. She attended the local Catholic schools and sang Gregorian chants in Latin in her church choir while growing up. Following the deaths of her parents when she was thirteen years old, Jarboro moved to Brooklyn to live with an aunt. There she took music lessons and continued to sing at Catholic masses until she was hired for the chorus of *Shuffle Along* in 1921. In 1926, she moved to Europe, where she studied and sang in France and Italy. After Jarboro's final engagement at the New York Hippodrome in 1935, she sang in the great opera houses throughout Europe. In 1941, she returned to the United States, and performed notable recitals at Town Hall and Carnegie Hall in 1942 and 1944, respectively. She retired from the concert stage in 1955.

Jarboro died in Manhattan after a brief illness in August 1986. On December 11, 1999, Jarboro was posthumously honored by her hometown when her name was added to the Celebrate Wilmington Walk of Fame.

EVA JESSYE (1895–1992)

Choral Conductor, Composer. Eva Jessye was the first African American woman to succeed as a professional choral conductor. Because of racial discrimination, she could not attend high school in her hometown of Coffeyville, Kansas, so she went to Kansas City to study at the Quindaro State School for the Colored (now Western University). There she met the composer and conductor Will Marion Cook, who influenced her to become a musician. She also studied at Langston University in Oklahoma and, on completing her formal education, taught in public schools and at Morgan State College in Baltimore and Claflin College in Orangeburg, South Carolina.

Jessye moved to New York City in 1922 and began a career as a choral conductor. She formed her own choir, originally known as the Dixie Jubilee Singers and later as the Eva Jessye Choir. The choir performed frequently on radio shows. In 1929, Jessye was invited to train and direct the choir for the King Vidor film *Hallelujah*. She also directed the choirs for two of the operas that would be very important to the careers of many young African American singers: *Four Saints in Three Acts* (1934) by Virgil Thomson and Gertrude Stein, and George Gershwin's *Porgy and Bess* (1935), based on the book by DuBose Heyward. Jessye was involved in many later productions of this opera into the early 1960s. Her choir did not disband until 1970.

Among Jessye's compositions, based largely on spirituals, are the oratorio *Paradise Lost and Regained* (1936) and *The Chronicle of Job* (1936), a folk drama, as well as many arrangements, especially of spirituals. Her large collection of memorabilia, sheet music, scores, arrangements, and correspondence makes up the Eva Jessye Collection at the University of Michigan, Ann Arbor. Jessye lived in Ann Arbor for the last ten years of her life.

HALL JOHNSON (1888–1970)

Composer, Arranger, Director, Violinist, Filmmaker. Francis Hall Johnson was born on May 12, 1888, in Athens, Georgia. He was the son of a Methodist minister who also served as president of Allen University in Columbia, South Carolina. Johnson's mother encouraged his interest in music. After teaching himself violin as a young boy, he received an extensive education, first at Atlanta University, then at Allen University, where he earned his degree, and then at the University of Pittsburgh, the Juilliard School, and the University of Southern California.

Johnson began performing professionally as a violinist and violist in James Reese Europe's orchestra. He also played in the orchestra for the Broadway musical *Shuffle Along* in 1921. During the 1920s, he became interested in choral music, especially Negro spirituals, and he formed the Hall Johnson Negro Choir in 1925. The choir was very successful in the New York area, making its first recording for RCA Victor in 1928. In 1930, the choir sang Johnson's arrangements of spirituals for *The Green Pastures* on Broadway. Johnson's own *Run Little Chillun*, featuring his choir, was produced on Broadway in 1933. He conducted and arranged music for choir in over thirty feature-length films, several short films, and cartoons. The best-known of these are *The Green Pastures* (1936), *Lost Horizon* (1937), *Dumbo* (1941), and *Cabin in the Sky* (1943).

Johnson organized several choral groups, and his Johnson Festival Negro Chorus of New York premiered *Son of Man*, his Easter cantata, in 1946 at New York City Center. The Hall Johnson Choir toured Europe in 1951, and was sent to Berlin by the Department of State to represent the United States in the International Festival of Fine Arts.

Fluent in German and French, Johnson coached several fine singers, including Marian Anderson and Shirley Verrett. He also wrote arrangements for solo voice and piano that have been performed and recorded by many fine artists. He received numerous honors and awards, including the Urban League's Opportunity Contest Competition, the Harmon Award, the George Frideric Handel Award, and an honorary doctorate from the Philadelphia Music Academy. He was elected posthumously to the Black Filmmakers Hall of Fame in 1975. Johnson died in a fire in his apartment in New York on April 30, 1970.

JOHN ROSAMOND JOHNSON (1873–1954)

Composer, Singer. J. Rosamond Johnson was born in Jacksonville, Florida. He began piano lessons with his mother when he was four years old. At an early age, he began studying composition and voice with teachers at the New England Conservatory of Music in Boston. Around 1905, when Johnson was performing in London, he trained privately with Samuel Coleridge-Taylor.

Johnson's career as a professional performer began in 1896. In 1899, he went to New York City to work in the musical theater, first in vaudeville. He soon formed a partnership with his brother, the writer and political activist James Weldon Johnson, and Bob Cole, an established vaudevillian. They successfully produced and wrote their own works and contributed to many other musicals during the first decade of the twentieth century. After Cole's death in 1912, Johnson continued working with his brother and other partners, made several tours in the United States and England, and sang in many stage shows, including the original production of George Gershwin's *Porgy and Bess* in 1935 and in subsequent productions of that opera. He also appeared in *Cabin in the Sky* in 1941.

The Johnson brothers wrote the well-known song "Lift Ev'ry Voice and Sing," which a public school chorus in Jacksonville, Florida, first performed in 1900. The song became known as the "Negro National Anthem" and later as the "Black National Anthem." In the mid-1920s, the brothers published two collections of arrangements of spirituals for solo voice and piano. In the mid-1930s, J. Rosamond Johnson issued two more volumes of arrangements of African American folk music, the second of which is titled *Rolling Along in Song: A Chronological Survey of American Negro Music* (1937). All of these publications reflected James Weldon Johnson's concern that "a distinct African-American creative voice" be sustained in artistic works, and they attest to the brothers' interest in, knowledge of, and commitment to the preservation of the folk music of African Americans.

ELAYNE JONES (1928–)

Timpanist. Elayne Jones was born in New York City on January 30, 1928, and began to study the piano with her mother when she was six. Jones graduated from the High School of Music and Art and then attended the Juilliard School of Music on a scholarship sponsored by Duke Ellington. In 1949, she was hired by the New York City Opera and Ballet Company orchestra. She subsequently worked with many other orchestras in the New York area, including the American Symphony Orchestra from 1962, when the orchestra was founded, until 1972. In 1965, she became one of the founding members of the integrated Symphony of the New World. In 1972, she was invited by the San Francisco Symphony's music director, Seiji Ozawa, to become its timpanist. She accepted the offer and became the first African American female to hold a principal chair in a major orchestra.

After a two-year probation period, the San Francisco Symphony denied Jones tenure. She appealed the decision in 1975, and was again denied. Jones lost the fight to retain her position despite her exemplary professional record and the strong support of friends, colleagues, and the San Francisco public. She continued to perform with the San Francisco Opera and worked as a freelance timpanist in musical theater, films, and television. She also taught in many institutions in New York and San Francisco and lectured widely.

In 1993, the National Association of Negro Musicians gave her its Distinguished Service Award. Jones announced in 1994 that she would take a leave of absence from the San Francisco Opera, in order "to investigate how [to] best use [her] years of experience to benefit young African American people."

SCOTT JOPLIN (1868–1917)

Composer, Pianist. Scott Joplin was born in Texarkana in 1868 and received an early musical education in guitar and piano. Leaving home in his teens, he became a traveling musician, settling for a period of time in Sedalia and St. Louis, Missouri. He worked with minstrel companies and other musical groups and began to be recognized as an outstanding ragtime piano player. His enduringly popular "Maple Leaf Rag" was published in 1899, and was followed by many more ragtime compositions.

Joplin had ambitions to write more "substantial" works, however, and his first effort was the "ragtime opera" *A Guest of Honor*, which he took on tour in 1903. The tour was a financial failure, and all performance materials have been lost.

After Joplin's move to New York in 1907, where his compositions continued to be successfully published, he decided to return to the musical theater and in 1911 completed *Treemonisha*. He published the vocal score himself; the story was a sort of parable about education being the key to improve the lot of the African American. No performance was mounted during his lifetime. In 1972, however, *Treemonisha* premiered at the Atlanta Memorial Arts Center for the Afro-American Music Workshop of Morehouse College. T. J. Anderson orchestrated from the vocal score, and Katherine Dunham was responsible for staging and choreography. Two subsequent orchestrations were made, attesting to the work's popularity and attraction to musicians, and the opera reached Broadway for a run in 1975.

The Complete Works of Scott Joplin (piano) was issued in 1981, and there have been numerous articles, books, and dissertations on Joplin's life and works since the resurgence of interest in ragtime in the early 1970s. In 1976, he was posthumously awarded a special Bicentennial Pulitzer Prize for contributions to American music.

ROBERT JORDAN (1940–)

Pianist, Educator. Robert Jordan was born in Chattanooga, Tennessee, in 1940. He earned a bachelor of music degree in 1962 from the Eastman School of Music in Rochester, New York, where his major teacher was Cecile Genhart, and a master of music degree at the Juilliard School of Music, with Rosina Lhévinne as his major teacher, in 1965.

Jordan made a successful New York debut as a soloist with the Symphony of the New World in 1971 and as a recitalist in the next season at Alice Tully Hall at Lincoln Center. He was a Fulbright Scholar for two years, which he spent studying and performing in Germany. Jordan has performed in Africa, Asia, South America, Europe, and the United States as recitalist and orchestra soloist. In 1980, he joined the faculty of the State University of New York (SUNY) at Fredonia as a professor of piano, and he received the Chancellor's Award for Excellence in Teaching. In 1987, he served as Martin Luther King Visiting Professor at Northern Michigan University in Marquette, and in 1991 he became visiting professor at the University of Michigan, Ann Arbor. Jordan established the Mamie and Ira Jordan Minority Music Scholarship and Scholastic Achievement Award at SUNY-Fredonia in 1997. He retired from the faculty of SUNY-Fredonia in 2004 but continued to record and perform.

ULYSSES SIMPSON KAY (1917–1995)

Composer, Educator. Beginning in the mid-1940s, Ulysses Kay composed music for instrumental soloists and ensembles; string, chamber, and full orchestras; bands, vocalists, choruses, and opera; and for film and television. Many of his works were commissions. Because he was a student of Howard Hanson and Paul Hindemith, Kay's compositions are strongly based on Western European traditions, but they are also rooted in African American folk music practices.

Kay was born in Tucson, Arizona, to musical parents. His uncle was the legendary cornet player Joseph "King" Oliver, who urged his sister to give the young Ulysses piano lessons. Kay also studied violin and saxophone, sang in the school glee club, and played in the school marching band and dance orchestra. He attended the University of Arizona, where he earned a bachelor of music degree in 1938. In 1940, he received a master of music degree from the Eastman School of Music in Rochester, New York.

While serving in the U.S. Navy from 1942 to 1946, Kay wrote *Of New Horizons*, the work that first brought him critical attention. This work was performed by the New York Philharmonic in 1944. The following year, Kay's *Suite for Orchestra* received a prize from Broadcast Music, Inc., a company for which Kay acted as a consultant from 1953 until 1968. This prize was the first of many awards, fellowships, and grants that would allow Kay to concentrate on his music in both the United States and Europe.

Kay's first permanent teaching position came when he joined the faculty of Lehman College of the City University of New York in 1968. In 1988, he retired from his position as distinguished professor of composition and theory.

Kay's many works include the film score for *The Quiet One* (1948), *Six Dances for String Orchestra* (1954), *Choral Triptych* (1962), *Markings* (1966), *Southern Harmony: Four Aspects for Orchestra* (1975), and the opera *Frederick Douglass* (1991). Kay's honors and awards include a George Gershwin Memorial Award, Fulbright and Guggenheim fellowships, a National Endowment for the Arts Grant, and election to the American Academy of Arts and Letters, along with several honorary doctorates.

SYLVIA OLDEN LEE (1917–2004)

Pianist, Vocal Coach. Sylvia Olden Lee was born on June 29, 1917, in Meridian, Mississippi. She started her piano studies with her mother when she was five, and by age eight, she was accompanying her mother on French songs and her father on Schubert lieder. She then began studying voice with Frank La Forge, and she presented her first piano recital at age eleven. She attended Howard University, but left to study piano and organ at Oberlin Conservatory in Ohio on a full scholarship.

Lee began her on-the-job study by accompanying Paul Robeson on programs. She also worked as an accompanist for the studios of various music teachers, including Elisabeth Schumann, Eva Gautier, Konraad Bos, and Fritz Lehmann. By 1952, Lee was studying piano with Victor Wittgenstein, coaching opera at Tanglewood with Boris Goldovsky, and serving as technical advisor for the world premiere of Britten's *Peter Grimes*. She then studied Italian opera, oratorio, and song literature at St. Cecilia Conservatorio in Italy.

In 1954, Lee became the first African American professional musician to work at the Metropolitan

Opera when she was hired as a vocal coach. She stayed with the Met until 1956, when she began studying voice with German tenor Gerhard Huesch. Over the years, she coached and accompanied many well-known singers, such as Jessye Norman and Kathleen Battle, and was invited to perform at the White House.

Lee was married to conductor Everett Lee, and helped him prepare opera concerts with the Cosmopolitan Symphony and at Columbia University's Opera Workshop. She taught at several universities, and was professor of vocal interpretation at the Curtis Institute of Music for more than twenty years. Lee continued to coach, accompany, and give master classes until her death on April 10, 2004. She was a woman of great talent with a masterful grasp of European classical music and the Negro spiritual.

TANIA LEÓN (1943–)

Composer, Conductor, Pianist. Tania Justina León is a native of Havana, Cuba, where she earned both a bachelor's degree (1963) and a master's degree (1964) in music from the Carlos Alfredo Peyrellade Conservatory. In 1967, she emigrated to the United States and earned another bachelor's degree (1971) in music education and a master's in composition (1975) from New York University, where she studied with Ursula Mamlok and Laszlo Halasz. She also studied conducting with Seiji Ozawa and Leonard Bernstein at the Berkshire Music Festival at Tanglewood in Massachusetts.

In New York, León's first professional work in music was as an accompanist and then music director of what became Arthur Mitchell's Dance Theatre of Harlem. She went to the Festival of Two Worlds in Spoleto, Italy, with the company in 1971, and there she made her first appearance as conductor. Additionally, she wrote scores for Mitchell's choreography. She left the company in 1980. León served as music director for the Alvin Ailey Dance Company for the 1983–1984 season, and was music director for Broadway musicals from *The Wiz* in 1978 to *The Lion King* in 1996. For her contributions to music, León received the American Academy and Institute of Arts and Letters Award in 1991.

León joined the faculty of Brooklyn College in 1985 and became a professor in 1994. She was the Revson composer for the New York Philharmonic from 1993 until 1996, and its new music advisor from 1996 to 1997.

León incorporated her ethnic backgrounds—encompassing Chinese, African, South American, Cuban, and French—into the creation of works with startling juxtapositions, which are informed by her mastery of the contemporary orchestra. Her colorful works include: *Kabiosile* for piano and orchestra (1988); *Indígena* for chamber orchestra (1991); the chamber opera *Scourge of Hyacinths* for the Fourth Munich Biennale (1994); *Para viola y orquesta* (1995); *Bata* (1995); *Ancients* for two sopranos and mixed ensemble (2008); and the ballet *Inura* (2009). Her numerous honors include citations from the National Council of the Arts in Havana and the National Endowment for the Arts, a Meet the Composer Award, the Dean Dixon Achievement Award, and a Rockefeller Foundation residency. In 2000, she was named the Claire and Leonard Tow Professor in Music at Brooklyn College. She won a Guggenheim Fellowship in 2007.

HENRY JAY LEWIS (1932–1996)

Conductor, Double Bassist. Henry Lewis was born in Los Angeles and knew early on that he wanted to be a musician, in spite of his father's disapproval. He was only sixteen years old when he joined the Los Angeles Philharmonic Orchestra in 1948 as a double bassist, becoming the first African American instrumentalist to play with a major American orchestra. In 1954, he was drafted into the U.S. Army. While stationed in Germany between 1955 and 1957, he conducted the Seventh Army Symphony Orchestra. Following his discharge, he returned to the Los Angeles Philharmonic as assistant conductor. Lewis founded the String Society of Los Angeles (later known as the Los Angeles Chamber Orchestra) in 1959 and was engaged as guest conductor with virtually every major American orchestra. From 1965 to 1968, he was also the music director of the Los Angeles Opera Company.

Lewis was selected as conductor and music director of the New Jersey Symphony in 1968 and so became the first African American to serve in that position with a major American orchestra. He conducted the New York Philharmonic in 1972 and became the first African American to conduct the Metropolitan Opera Orchestra. Resigning from the New Jersey Symphony in 1976, Lewis remained active as a guest conductor in the United States and Europe, and made recordings with the Scottish Opera and the Netherlands Radio Symphony Orchestra. In 1991, he was music director of the London production of *Carmen Jones*. Lewis was founder of the Black Academy of Arts and Letters and a member of the California Arts Commission and the Young Musicians Foundation.

INDIRA MAHAJAN (1966–)

Singer. Soprano Indira Mahajan was born in August 22, 1966, in New York City of African American and South Asian heritage. She began her musical training at age five as a violinist and later studied voice with her mother, mezzo-soprano Barbara Mahajan. Indira Mahajan continued her studies at the LaGuardia High School of Music and Art and the Harlem School of the Arts in New York. She received her bachelor of arts degree from Oberlin College, her master of music degree at the Mannes College of Music, and a diploma from the Accademia Musicale Ottorino Respighi in Italy. Mahajan is also an alumna of the Glimmerglass Opera Young American Artist Program.

Mahajan made her New York operatic debut at the New York City Opera in a performance that was broadcast nationally on *Live from Lincoln Center* on PBS. This triumph was followed by performances with the New York Philharmonic and an AIDS benefit concert at Carnegie Hall. Mahajan's extensive repertoire ranges from the early music of Handel and Mozart to contemporary opera, and she has sung in major opera houses and in performances with leading orchestras around the world. Operatic highlights include: *Sémélé*, *The Marriage of Figaro*, *Don Giovanni*, *Lucia di Lammermoor*, *Madama Butterfly*, *La Bohème*, *Suor Angelica*, *La traviata*, *Rigoletto*, *Pagliacci*, *Treemonisha*, and *Porgy and Bess*.

Mahajan is the recipient of the 2008 Marian Anderson Award. She has also received the Maria Callas Award from the Dallas Opera, New York City Opera Debut Artist of the Year, and the Richard F. Gold Award from the Shoshanna Foundation, as well as prizes from the Fritz and Lavinia Jensen Foundation, the Van Lier Foundation, and the National Association of Negro Musicians.

BENJAMIN MATTHEWS (1933–2006)

Singer. Bass-baritone Benjamin Matthews was born in Mobile, Alabama, on June 20, 1933. His family moved to Chicago, where he attended high school and then enlisted in the U.S. Army. His interest in music was piqued when he won second prize in an all-army singing contest. After leaving the army, he entered the Chicago Conservatory, and later studied opera with Boris Goldovsky.

Matthews debuted at the New York City Opera in 1977 in Leon Kirchner's *Lily*. He appeared in the Metropolitan Opera's chamber production of Virgil Thomson's *Four Saints in Three Acts*, and sang with the Graz Opera, the Florentine Opera in Milwaukee, and Ebony Opera, which he cofounded with Wayne Saunders in 1973. Matthews sang in concert with the New York Philharmonic, the Chicago Symphony, and the Baltimore Symphony. He had an extensive African American music collection, from which he performed in recitals and master classes. His emphasis was on the style of singing spirituals, work songs, Creole music, and other little-known African American works.

Matthews gave a Carnegie Hall recital in 1986 and appeared often as a member of a three-baritone group, Three Generations, with William Warfield and Robert Sims. He died in a New York hospital on February 14, 2006.

DOROTHY LEIGH MAYNOR (1910–1996)

Singer, Administrator. Born in Norfolk, Virginia, Dorothy Mainor (she changed the spelling of her last name when she became a singer) grew up in an atmosphere of music and singing. She intended to become a home economics teacher, and entered the Hampton Institute College Preparatory School in 1924. However, her development as a singer in the school choir prompted her choir director, R. Nathaniel Dett, to convince her to switch her major to voice. She graduated with a bachelor's degree in 1933.

The director of the Westminster Choir heard Maynor and made it possible for her to receive a scholarship to the Westminster Choir College in Princeton, New Jersey. After receiving her bachelor's degree in music in 1935, she went to New York City and continued voice study. At the Berkshire Music Festival at Tanglewood in Massachusetts in 1939, Boston Symphony Orchestra conductor Serge Koussevitzky took an interest in furthering Maynor's career. Maynor was acclaimed by critics after her 1939 Town Hall debut in New York, launching her twenty-five-year career as recitalist, orchestra soloist, and recording artist.

Following her debut, Maynor toured the United States and the rest of the world and performed with the leading orchestras of the day. Additionally, Maynor embarked on a recording career in which she sang arias, spirituals, and operas. Her operatic work was limited to the recording studio because no opera company of the time would allow an African American to perform in their productions. Maynor was not allowed to audition for the Metropolitan Opera, but, in an ironic twist, she would become the first African American member of the Met's board of directors in 1975. In 1952, Maynor became the first African American artist to perform at Constitution Hall in Washington, D.C.

Maynor retired from singing after her husband's heart attack in 1963. She remained active in the arts through the foundation of what became the Harlem School of the Arts. By the late 1970s, the school boasted more than forty instructors and approximately one thousand students. With the school rapidly outgrowing its first home in St. James Presbyterian Church, Maynor raised

$3.5 million to erect a new building, which opened in 1979, the year she retired as the school's director.

SETH McCOY (1928–1997)

Singer. Tenor Seth McCoy is best remembered for his oratorio and concert appearances. He was born in Sanford, North Carolina, on December 17, 1928, and studied at the Agricultural and Technical College in Greensboro. He started his vocal training at the Cleveland Music School Settlement with Pauline Thesmacher and continued his training in New York City with Antonia Lavanne. McCoy served in the U.S. Army during the Korean War (1950–1953), after which he worked as a postal clerk for thirteen years.

After an audition for the Robert Shaw Chorale, McCoy was engaged as a soloist, touring the United States and South America. He moved to New York City and became a permanent soloist with the Bach Aria Group from 1973 to 1980. He toured Europe, South America, North Africa, and the Middle East as soloist with major orchestras, including the New York Philharmonic, the Boston Symphony, the Chicago Symphony, and the Los Angeles Philharmonic. He worked with many great conductors, including Erich Leinsdorf, Zubin Mehta, and Mstislav Rostropovich.

McCoy made his Metropolitan Opera debut at age fifty as Tamino in Mozart's *Magic Flute*. He also participated in the American premieres of Joplin's *Treemonisha*, Janáček's *Katya Kabanova*, and Penderecki's *Utrenja*. McCoy taught at the North Carolina School of the Arts, the University of Michigan, and the Eastman School of Music in Rochester, New York, where he died on January 22, 1997.

BOBBY McFERRIN (1950–)

Singer, Conductor, Composer. Robert McFerrin Jr., the son of opera singers Robert and Sara McFerrin, was born on March 11, 1950, in New York City. In 1958, his family moved to Los Angeles. McFerrin attended Sacramento State University and Cerritos College, but dropped out of college to play piano for several show companies. By 1977, he had decided to concentrate on a singing career, and he was discovered by Jon Hendricks. He performed at jazz festivals and began touring and recording with George Benson and Herbie Hancock, among other jazz greats. His first of many solo albums, called simply *Bobby McFerrin*, was released in 1982. He has gone on to win ten Grammy Awards. His song "Don't Worry, Be Happy" topped the popular music charts in 1989.

Bobby McFerrin attends rehearsals for Music of the Who at Carnegie Hall, New York City, 2010. *The multitalented singer-songwriter McFerrin has won ten Grammys in a number of genres, including pop, jazz, and children's. He has been recognized for his singing and for his arrangements.* BOBBY BANK/ WIREIMAGE/GETTY IMAGES

McFerrin made his conducting debut with the San Francisco Symphony in 1990, and he was appointed conductor and creative chair of the St. Paul Chamber Orchestra in 1994. In 2002, he was chosen as a recipient of the prestigious George Peabody Medal for Outstanding Contributions to Music in America. McFerrin is in demand as both vocalist and conductor for orchestras around the country and continues to present innovative programming in both capacities. His numerous recordings include *Paper Music* (1995), *Circlesongs* (1997), *Beyond Words* (2002), and *VOCAbuLarieS* (2010).

ROBERT McFERRIN (1921–2006)

Singer, Educator. Baritone Robert McFerrin, born on March 19, 1921, in Marianna, Arkansas, was brought up in St. Louis, Missouri, where he attended public schools and sang in his father's church choir. After a year at Fisk University in Nashville, McFerrin attended the Chicago Musical College, where he earned a bachelor's degree.

McFerrin began his professional singing career in Broadway shows, including *Lost in the Stars* (1949) and *The Green Pastures* (1951). He also sang with the National Negro Opera Company in William Grant Still's *Troubled Island* (1949) and in the role of Rigoletto with the New England Opera Company in 1950. After winning the 1954 Metropolitan Auditions of the Air, he became a member of the regular roster of the Metropolitan Opera for three seasons, the first African American male singer to do so.

McFerrin was a guest professor of voice at several institutions in Finland, Canada, and the United States, and performed widely in North and South America and Europe. Both Stowe Teacher's College in St. Louis and the University of Missouri awarded him honorary doctorates.

ANTHONY McGILL (1979–)

Clarinetist. Anthony McGill had the honor of performing with Itzhak Perlman, Yo-Yo Ma, and Gabriela Montero for the historic inauguration of Barack Obama, the first African American president of the United States, on January 20, 2009. McGill is the principal clarinetist of the Metropolitan Opera Orchestra and a popular soloist and chamber music artist with orchestras and chamber music groups throughout the United States.

McGill was born in Chicago, and joined the Chicago Youth Symphony when he was eleven. He graduated with a bachelor's degree from the Curtis Institute of Music in Philadelphia in 2000. He was associate principal clarinetist with the Cincinnati Symphony Orchestra from 2000 to 2004, before joining the Metropolitan Opera Orchestra. McGill has also performed with the Baltimore Symphony, the New Jersey Symphony, and the Hilton Head Symphony as a soloist. He has performed at the Marlboro Music Festival, the Sarasota Music Festival, La Musica Festival, Tanglewood, Music at Menlo, and the Grand Tetons Festival. McGill has also appeared with several string quartets, including the Guarneri Quartet, the Shanghai Quartet, the Tokyo String Quartet, the Miami String Quartet, and the Brentano String Quartet, with whom he toured Europe and Japan. He has toured many times with Musicians from Marlboro and appeared at Lincoln Center with Chamber Music Society Two.

LENA JOHNSON McLIN (1928–)

Composer, Conductor, Educator. Born September 5, 1928, in Atlanta, Lena McLin was immersed in music as a child, particularly gospel and classical. Her mother, a choir director, gave her piano lessons and exposed her to various kinds of sacred music. This foundation of religious music became even stronger during the years she lived with the family of her uncle, Thomas A. Dorsey, the "father of gospel music," in Chicago. McLin received a bachelor of music degree from Spelman College in Atlanta in 1951, and she moved to Chicago for graduate study in composition and music theory, first at the American Conservatory of Music and then at Roosevelt University, where she also studied electronic music and voice.

In 1959, McLin began a long teaching career in the Chicago public schools, which was distinguished by her development and implementation of a music curriculum for the school system. In 1977, she published a textbook for young people on music history, titled *Pulse: A History of Music.* She also conducted a variety of church and community choirs; founded an opera company, the McLin Ensemble, in 1957, and a gospel group, the McLin Singers, in 1968; and served as guest conductor and in workshops for several national organizations and educational institutions.

The varied list of McLin's compositions includes several piano solos and dozens of choral works, including the commissioned mass *Eucharist of the Soul*, the dramatic oratorio *Free at Last: A Portrait of Martin Luther King Jr.*, and *The Torch Has Been Passed*, based on President John F. Kennedy's inaugural address. Her style shows her love for and mastery of all kinds of music—gospel, rock, popular, and past and current traditions of Western concert music—which can be distinct or interwoven in her scores and always make clear and direct statements.

ABBIE MITCHELL

See chapter 21, Drama, Comedy, and Dance.

LEONA MITCHELL (1949–)

Singer. Soprano Leona Mitchell was born in Enid, Oklahoma, and graduated from Oklahoma University in 1971. She made her Metropolitan Opera debut as Micaela in Bizet's *Carmen* in 1975 and also sang the roles of Lauretta in Puccini's *Gianni Schicchi*, Pamina in Mozart's *Magic Flute*, and Mademoiselle Lidoine in Poulenc's *Dialogues of the Carmelites.*

Her outstanding vocal capabilities have caused her to be regarded as a leading American soprano, with a career that has taken her to all the major opera houses of the world. She has likewise performed with several orchestras and, in 1980, sang the role of Bess in the Cleveland Orchestra Blossom Festival production of Gershwin's *Porgy and Bess* and in the subsequent recording. In 1983, she was inducted into the Oklahoma Hall of Fame. Mitchell was one of a select group of subjects considered in Rosalyn M. Story's 1990 book, *And So I Sing: African-American Divas of Opera and Concert.*

DOROTHY RUDD MOORE (1940–)

Composer, Teacher, Singer. Born in Wilmington, Delaware, Dorothy Rudd Moore attended the Wilmington School of Music as a teenager. In 1963, she received a bachelor of music degree, magna cum laude, in theory and composition from Howard University, where her major composition teacher was Mark Fax. Later, she studied composition privately with Chou Wen Chung in New York City and with Nadia Boulanger in France at the American Conservatory in Fontainebleau. She also studied voice at Howard University and privately, and she has performed frequently as a singer.

Moore taught piano, voice, sight-singing, and ear-training at the Harlem School of the Arts, New York University, and Bronx Community College. Among her works in various media are: *Reflections* (1962), for concert band; *Dirge and Deliverance* (1971), for piano and cello, commissioned by her husband Kermit Moore; *Flowers of Darkness* (1988–1989), for tenor and piano, commissioned by William Brown; and the opera *Frederick Douglass* (1981–1985), commissioned and premiered by Opera Ebony in 1985, about which *Opera News* reported that she "displays a rare ability to wed musical and dramatic motion, graceful lyric inventiveness, [and] a full command of the orchestral palette."

KERMIT MOORE (1929–)

Cellist, Conductor, Composer. Kermit Moore was born in 1929 in Akron, Ohio. He studied the cello at the Cleveland Institute of Music and received a bachelor's degree in 1951. Moore earned a master of arts degree at New York University in 1952, and in 1956 he attended the Paris National Conservatory and was awarded an artist's diploma. He gave his New York recital debut at Town Hall in 1949 and has later performed internationally in the major capitals of Europe and Asia.

In 1964, Moore cofounded the Symphony of the New World in New York. Besides performing as cellist with the group, he also conducted occasionally. He was careful to include a wide variety of works by African American composers on his symphonic programs. One of the most unusual was the *Concerto for Violin and Orchestra*, premiered in 1867 by its composer, the Afro-Cuban Joseph White, and given its first American performance with Ruggiero Ricci as soloist in 1974. Moore has had many engagements as guest conductor in the United States.

In addition to his work with the Symphony of the New World, Moore served as conductor of the Brooklyn Philharmonic beginning in 1984. He is also one of several founders of the Society of Black Composers, as well as the Classical Heritage Ensemble. He writes instrumental solos and ensembles works, including concertos for cello and timpani, and for voice.

UNDINE SMITH MOORE (1904–1989)

Composer, Educator. A native of Jarratt, Virginia, Undine Smith Moore studied piano in Petersburg and began her college studies at Fisk University in Nashville. In 1926, she was awarded a bachelor of arts degree, cum laude, and a music school diploma, and later attended Columbia University Teachers College, where she earned a master's degree and professional diploma in 1931. She pursued further graduate studies at several schools, including the Juilliard and Eastman schools of music.

Moore taught at Virginia State College (now Virginia State University) in Petersburg from 1927 until 1972, when she became professor emerita. Her students included many illustrious contributors to the music world, such as jazz pianist Billy Taylor, opera singer Camilla Williams, conductor Leon Thompson, gospel singer Robert Fryson, music educators Michael V. W. Gordon and James Mumford, and composer Phil Medley. She cofounded the Black Music Center at Virginia State in 1969 and was codirector until 1972. After retirement, she became a visiting professor at many universities and colleges. Some of her awards include honorary doctorates from Virginia State University and Indiana University, the Seventh Annual Humanitarian Award from Fisk University, and the National Association of Negro Musicians Award. In 1982, her *Scenes from the Life of a Martyr: To the Memory of Martin Luther King Jr.*, an oratorio, was nominated for the Pulitzer Prize.

Moore's style was infused with African American influences and a tonal musical language. Choral music makes up the largest part of her output and there are many works for instrumental solos and ensembles, including *Afro-American Suite* (1969), commissioned by Antoinette Handy's Trio Pro Viva. Moore's 1987 trio *Soweto*, inspired by events in that South African town, was the last work she wrote.

MICHAEL DEVARD MORGAN (1957–)

Conductor. Michael Morgan was born in Washington, D.C., and received music training in the public schools, in addition to private piano lessons. He attended the Oberlin College Conservatory of Music from 1975 to 1979, and pursued additional studies in the Vienna master classes of Witold Rowicki and at the Berkshire Music Center at Tanglewood, where he was a conducting fellow and student of Seiji Ozawa and Gunther Schuller. Morgan was selected to work with Leonard Bernstein for one week, which culminated in Morgan's appearance with the New York Philharmonic in September 1986.

From 1980 to 1987, Morgan was Exxon/Arts Endowment assistant conductor of the Chicago Symphony Orchestra and later became affiliate artist conductor; he was also co-resident conductor of the Chicago Civic Orchestra. He became music director of the Oakland East Bay Symphony Orchestra in 1993 and has appeared as a guest conductor with many of the nation's major orchestras and abroad. Morgan also serves as artistic director of the Oakland Youth Orchestra and as conductor and music director of the Sacramento Philharmonic Orchestra.

The many awards Morgan has earned include first prize in the Hans Swarowsky International Conductors Competition (Vienna, Austria), first prize in the Gino Marinuzzi International Conductors Competition (San Remo, Italy), and first prize in the Baltimore Symphony Young Conductors Competition. In 2005, Morgan received a Concert Music Award, given by the American Society of Composers, Authors, and Publishers.

TAI MURRAY (1982–)

Violinist. Tai Murray was born in 1982 in Chicago, Illinois. She has risen rapidly in the music world to great acclaim. She began studying violin when she was five with lessons at the Sherwood Conservatory of Music in Chicago. She progressed quickly; when she was seven, her family bought her a new violin and bow that cost $1,600. This was the beginning of a major investment for her family. She made her debut with the Chicago Symphony at age nine, and was homeschooled so that she might practice as much as five hours a day. She soon began receiving invitations to perform with other orchestras, notably the Utah Symphony and the San Antonio Symphony, and returned to perform again with the Chicago Symphony.

Murray continued her studies at the University of Indiana, graduating with honors from the artist diploma program. She went to New York to study with Joel Smirnoff at the Juilliard School of Music, graduating from a three-year program in 2004. By this time, she had performed with the Oakland East Bay Symphony, and with symphonies in St. Louis, Greensboro, and Washington, D.C. She was given a spot in a two-year residency program (2004–2006) at the Chamber Music Society of Lincoln Center, and is a regular performer with chamber ensembles in New York, Jacksonville, and Philadelphia. She also finds time to play with the Ritz Chamber Players, the only black chamber orchestra in the country. Murray's awards include top honors in the Sphinx Competition, the Indiana University Concerto Competition, and the Juilliard School Concerto Competition. She was also the winner of the Avery Fisher Artist Program career grant in 2004, and was named a BBC New Generation Artist in 2008.

JESSYE NORMAN (1945–)

Singer. On September 15, 1945, soprano Jessye Norman was born into a musical family in Augusta, Georgia. Her mother, a schoolteacher, gave her children piano lessons. Jessye's musical talents were evident early, and when she was sixteen she entered the Marian Anderson Scholarship competition. She did not win, but her subsequent audition at Howard University led to a four-year scholarship.

Jessye Norman, Opera Singer, Philharmonie, Munich, Germany, 2009. *Soprano Norman has successfully expanded her repertoire beyond opera to include spirituals, popular music, blues, and jazz.* STEFAN M. PRAGER/REDFERNS

After receiving her bachelor's degree in 1967, Norman continued studying music, first at the Peabody Conservatory with Alice Dushak, and then at the University of Michigan with Pierre Bernac and Elizabeth Mannion. Norman received her master's degree in 1968. That same year, she entered the International Music Competition held in Munich, Germany, and won first place. Her operatic career in Europe was launched, and she made debuts at the Deutsche Oper Berlin, La Scala in Milan, and the Royal Opera House at Covent Garden in London. She made her American opera debut in the role of Aida at the Hollywood Bowl in Los Angeles. She debuted with the Opera Company of Philadelphia in 1982 in the double bill of Purcell's *Dido and Aeneas* and Stravinsky's *Oedipus Rex*. In 1983, she made her Metropolitan Opera debut as Cassandra in *Les Troyens* by Berlioz.

Taking a break from opera performance, Norman was a busy recitalist and orchestra soloist from 1975 to 1980, with a far-ranging repertoire. Her vocal prowess and the breadth of her musicianship are demonstrated by the variety of operas that she sings—Rameau, Mozart, Meyerbeer, Wagner, Verdi, and Bartók. Among her numerous recordings are two compact discs of spirituals (one with Kathleen Battle), many concert works and operas, and a crossover album of popular songs, *Lucky to Be Me* (1992). Norman won a Grammy Award in 1984 for her performance on *Songs of Maurice Ravel*. She has also received honorary degrees from Howard University, the Boston Conservatory, and the University of the South. In March 2009, Norman curated a month-long festival at Carnegie Hall titled *Honor! A Celebration of the African American Cultural Legacy*.

AUTRIS PAIGE (1939–)

Singer. Baritone Autris Paige was born in Houston, Texas, on August 17, 1939, and was raised in Oakland, California. He graduated from McClymonds High School and San Francisco State University before doing advanced study in musical theater at the University of Southern California.

In 1971, Paige made his debut with the Los Angeles Civic Light Opera, appearing in *Candide* at the Los Angeles Music Center and at the Curran Theatre in San Francisco. He has appeared with Ray Charles and the American Ballet Theatre and performed on Broadway in *Lost in the Stars*, *Don't Bother Me, I Can't Cope*, as Walter in *Raisin*, and in *Timbuktu* with Eartha Kitt.

Paige has sung with the New York City Opera, the Houston Grand Opera, and the Metropolitan Opera. He was featured in the PBS film and award-winning EMI recording of *Porgy and Bess*, as well as the recording of the opera *X: The Life and Times of Malcolm X*.

COLERIDGE-TAYLOR PERKINSON (1932–2004)

Composer, Conductor. A native New Yorker, Coleridge-Taylor Perkinson graduated from the High School for Music and Art. After two years at New York University, he transferred to the Manhattan School of Music, where he studied conducting with Jonel Perlea and composition with Vittorio Giannini. He also studied composition at Princeton University with Earl Kim, and conducting at the Berkshire Music Center at Tanglewood, the Mozarteum in Salzburg, Austria, and the Netherlands Radio Union.

Perkinson worked steadily as a composer and music director. Some of the groups with which he was associated are the Dessoff Choirs as assistant conductor, the Max Roach Jazz Quartet as pianist, the Symphony of the New World as founding member and associate conductor from 1965 to 1970, and the Negro Ensemble Company as composer-in-residence. He received many commissions, including commissions from three dance companies and organizations: the Arthur Mitchell Dance Company in 1971; the Dance Theatre of Harlem in 1972 and 1987; and the American Dance Theater Foundation in 1984. Perkinson was also guest conductor for orchestras in the United States and abroad. In 1998, he became artistic director of the Center for Black Music Research at Columbia College Chicago, as well as conductor and music director for the New Black Music Repertory Ensemble.

Perkinson wrote a great deal of incidental and commercial music for film and television programs, and he wrote and arranged for many different kinds of artists, including Harry Belafonte, Max Roach, Marvin Gaye, and Melvin Van Peebles. Instrumental works are predominant in his catalog, ranging from solos to mixed ensembles to string, chamber, and full orchestras. His works demonstrate his complete knowledge of twentieth-century compositional techniques and his ease in using them for highly varied expressive purposes. The folk music of African Americans was a basic part of what and how Perkinson composed.

JULIA PERRY (1924–1979)

Composer, Conductor. Julia Perry was born in Lexington, Kentucky, and raised in Akron, Ohio. As a child, she studied piano and quickly became interested in composing. In 1942, she entered the Westminster Choir College in Princeton, New Jersey, and studied composition and conducting, in addition to violin, piano, and voice. After earning a master's degree in 1948, she studied composition at the Juilliard School of Music, where her music was performed for the first time.

In the 1950s, Perry lived mostly in Europe. Having studied with Luigi Dallapiccola at the Berkshire Music Center at Tanglewood in Massachusetts, she continued studies with him in Italy on two Guggenheim Fellowships in 1954 and 1956. She also studied with Nadia Boulanger in Paris during this time and won a Boulanger Grand Prix for her *Viola Sonata* in 1952. Perry continued to study conducting as well, and she had many opportunities to conduct some of her works in Europe. She also served as a lecturer on American music under the sponsorship of the U.S. Information Service.

With her return to the United States in 1959, Perry continued to compose and was engaged to teach at several colleges. She concentrated on writing instrumental music in the 1960s, as opposed to her earlier specialty in vocal music, including choral. Her output of orchestral works included twelve symphonies. Whatever the medium, Perry was almost always availing herself of the rich resources of her African American musical heritage, while remaining firmly in command of the Western European tradition, including the latest techniques that had been developed in Europe and the United States.

Some of her most performed works are: *Stabat mater* (1951), for contralto or mezzo-soprano and string quartet or string orchestra; *A Short Piece for Orchestra* (1952), which was premiered by the Turin Symphony conducted by Dean Dixon; and *Homunculus C.F.* (1960), for eight percussionists, harp, celesta, and piano. A debilitating stroke in 1973 almost incapacitated Perry, and was a major factor in her early death.

EVELYN LA RUE PITTMAN (1910–1992)

Choral Director, Composer. While a senior at Spelman College in Atlanta studying African American history, Evelyn Pittman committed herself to teaching African American history through music. Her first work, a musical play, was produced at Spelman in 1933, the year she graduated. She taught in the public schools in Oklahoma City from 1935 to 1956, and conducted weekly broadcasts with her own professional vocal group, the Evelyn Pittman Choir, on a local radio station. Pittman also directed a 350-voice choir sponsored by the YWCA, and directed orchestras, choirs, and operettas in the schools. Songs that she composed about African American leaders were published in the collection *Rich Heritage* in 1944.

In 1948, Pittman enrolled in the Juilliard School of Music in New York City to study composition under Robert Ward. Later, she attended the University of Oklahoma at Norman and studied with Harrison Kerr, receiving a master's degree in 1954. Kerr introduced her to his former teacher, Nadia Boulanger, who became Pittman's teacher from 1956 to 1958. During that period, she completed her folk opera *Cousin Esther*, written for an African American cast. It was performed many times to favorable reviews in both France and the United States.

Pittman returned to public school teaching in 1958 in New York and continued to compose. After the assassination of Dr. Martin Luther King Jr. in 1968, she wrote the opera *Freedom Child* in his memory. After her retirement from teaching, she dedicated herself to directing a touring company of *Freedom Child* and remained committed to improving race relations through music and drama.

AWADAGIN PRATT (1966–)

Pianist, Conductor, Violinist. Awadagin Pratt was born on March 6, 1966, in Pittsburgh, and began studying piano when he was six. In 1975, his family moved to Illinois, and he entered the University of Illinois, Urbana, when he was sixteen, majoring in music. In 1986, he enrolled in the Peabody Conservatory of Music in Baltimore, where he earned performer's certificates in piano and violin in 1989 and a graduate performance diploma in conducting in 1992.

Pratt's career as a concert pianist began in 1992 when he became the first African American to win the Naumburg International Piano Competition. After several major concert successes, he was awarded the Avery Fisher Career Grant in 1994, and his full-time concert career continued at a rapid pace. He has performed with many major American orchestras, and he has given recitals throughout the United States and in Europe, Africa, and Japan.

Pratt has been interested in the education of younger musicians during his career and has given up to ten master classes a year, beginning in 1992, at such colleges as the Eastman School of Music and the universities of Washington, Missouri, Minnesota, Texas, and many others. He has served on the boards of the Pratt Music Foundation and the Next Generation Festival.

Pratt's third recording on the EMI recording label was titled *Live from South Africa* (1997), performed from the stage of the Cape Town Opera House. Asked by an interviewer from *Piano and Keyboard* magazine about how he chooses music for performance, Pratt responded that his selections "have to be works that express, that evoke something more than themselves. Music and art are about expressing some sort of joy about all states of experience—a celebration, even, of those states."

Pratt's recordings include *Play Bach* (2002), *Pratt: Transformations* (1999), *Beethoven: Piano Sonatas* (1996), and *Awadagin Pratt: A Long Way from Normal* (1994). In 2004, Pratt became associate professor of piano and artist-in-residence at the College-Conservatory of Music of the University of Cincinnati.

FLORENCE BEATRICE PRICE (1888–1953)

Composer, Pianist, Educator. Florence Price was born in Little Rock, Arkansas, in 1888. As a young child, she studied piano with her mother, and played in public for the first time when she was four. When she turned fourteen, she began studying with Frederick Converse and George Chadwick at the New England Conservatory of Music in Boston, where she earned diplomas in organ and piano in 1906. She returned to Arkansas to teach at the high school and college levels, and moved to Atlanta in 1910 to become head of the music department of Clark College.

In 1912, Florence married attorney Thomas Price in Little Rock, where they lived until moving in 1927 to Chicago—a move prompted by increasing racial tensions in the South. In Chicago, she taught privately and took advanced studies at the Chicago Musical College and the American Conservatory. Price published her first composition in 1899. After her move to Chicago, the number of her publications, especially of organ, piano, and vocal music, increased notably.

Probably the best-known of Price's orchestral works is her *Symphony in A Minor, No. 1*, which won first prize in the 1930 Wanamaker Music Contest. It was performed by the Chicago Symphony Orchestra at the Chicago World's Fair Century of Progress Exhibition in 1933. Three of her other compositions also won Wanamaker prizes: *Piano Sonata in E Minor* (first prize), *Piano Fantasie No. 4*, and the orchestral *Ethiopia's Shadow in America* (both honorable mentions). Her *Concerto in One Movement* for piano had several performances, the solo part often played by her student Margaret Bonds. Price was well-known for her songs and arrangements of spirituals, which were performed by Marian Anderson, Roland Hayes, Leontyne Price, and Blanche Thebom. Anderson championed Price's 1941 setting of Langston Hughes's *Songs to a Dark Virgin*.

Price made full use of African American folk music, both sacred and secular, and her works in standard concert form usually demonstrate this aspect of her style. Her style is often described as "neo-romantic" and "nationalistic."

LEONTYNE PRICE (1927–)

Singer. Soprano Mary Violet Leontyne Price was born on February 10, 1927, in Laurel, Mississippi, where her parents encouraged her interest in music with piano lessons and participation in their church choir. With the idea of teaching music in school, she attended Central State College in Wilberforce, Ohio. Even before her graduation in 1949 with a bachelor's degree in music education, she received a scholarship to the Juilliard School of Music in New York City. Her work there attracted the attention of critic and composer Virgil Thomson, who cast her in her first professional role as Cecilia in a revival of his and Gertrude Stein's opera *Four Saints in Three Acts*. Soon afterward, she toured Europe as Bess in a revival of George Gershwin's *Porgy and Bess* (1952–1954).

After the tour was completed, Price made her New York recital debut at Town Hall and took other operatic roles on both stage and television. She was the first African American to perform opera in television when she played Puccini's Tosca in 1955 for NBC. Her performance was so well-received that she was invited back to play Pamina and Donna Anna from Mozart's *Magic Flute* and *Don Giovanni*, respectively, and Madame Lidoine in Poulenc's *Dialogues of the Carmelites*. She made her Metropolitan Opera debut in 1961 as Leonora in Verdi's *Il trovatore*. Other Verdi roles in which she was brilliantly successful were in *Aida*, *Un ballo in maschera*, *Ernani*, and *La forza del destino*.

Soprano Leontyne Price, Farewell Performance,* Aida, *Metropolitan Opera House, New York City, 1984. *Opera singer Price began her career on Broadway in 1952. She sang in numerous venues in the 1950s and 1960s and debuted with the Metropolitan Opera in 1961.* SARA KRULWICH/NEW YORK TIMES CO./GETTY IMAGES

For the opening of the new Metropolitan Opera House in 1966, Price was Cleopatra in the specially commissioned opera by Samuel Barber, *Antony and Cleopatra.* She has sung many roles with other opera companies as well, especially the San Francisco Opera (she was awarded their medal in honor of the twentieth anniversary of her company debut) and the Lyric Opera of Chicago.

Price has received several honorary doctorates, numerous Grammy Awards, and a Kennedy Center Honor in 1980 for lifetime achievement in the arts. She ended her operatic career in 1985 in *Aida* at the Metropolitan Opera, but continued performing. Her recordings are numerous and span a wide range of repertory. There are several collections of arias (operatic and concert), art songs, Christmas and patriotic songs, and a collaboration with André Previn on twelve pop songs, *Right as the Rain* (1989). In late September 2001, Price emerged from retirement to participate in the Carnegie Hall "Concert of Remembrance," held in honor of the victims of the September 11 terrorist attacks. In 2008 she was given the National Endowment for the Arts Opera Honors Award and the Metropolitan Opera News Award.

CURTIS RAYAM (1951–)

Singer. Curtis Rayam rose to international attention in 1984 when he came to the aid of an ailing Luciano Pavarotti and sang the title role in Mozart's *Idomeneo* with much success. Rayam was born in Bellville, Florida, on February 4, 1951, and graduated from Jones High School in Orlando in 1969. He then studied at Frost School of Music at the University of Miami. His professional debut was in *Manon Lescaut* with the Miami Opera. He sprang to prominence in the role of Remus with the Houston Grand Opera's production of Scott Joplin's *Treemonisha,* which he performed on Broadway and recorded on Deutsche Grammophon.

Rayam has performed opera, concerts, and recitals in the United States, Germany, Austria, France, Israel, Vienna, and South Africa. He has made a number of recordings, including Handel's *Rodelinda* with Dame Joan Sutherland on the Decca label, Monteverdi's *Il ritorno d'Ulisse in patria* live with Sir Jeffrey Tate, and Salieri's *Axur, re d'Ormus* with the Russian Philharmonic on the Nuova Era label. He also appeared in a 1984 PBS broadcast of Berlioz's *Damnation of Faust* with the Philadelphia Opera.

Rayam joined the music faculty of Bethune-Cookman University in 1997. In addition to performing in the United States and abroad, he is active in community and church affairs. Rayam served two terms on the National Opera Association Board of Directors, and chairs its national voice competition-scholarship division. The Negro Spiritual Scholarship Foundation, which he helped found, has awarded over $100,000 in scholarships to high school students.

KAY GEORGE ROBERTS (1950–)

Conductor, Violinist. Kay Roberts was born in Nashville, Tennessee, on September 16, 1950, and began her professional musical career as a violinist when she joined the Nashville Symphony during her last year in high school. She continued to play with the orchestra until she graduated with a bachelor's degree from Fisk University in 1972. In 1971, she represented the Nashville Symphony in Arthur Fiedler's World Symphony Orchestra. She earned a master of music degree in 1975, a master of musical arts degree in 1976, and a doctor of musical arts degree in 1986 from Yale University—the first woman and second African American to do so. During her second year at Yale, Roberts's talent as a conductor first came to the attention of her instructor and, thereafter, she focused on conducting rather than the violin.

Roberts has guest conducted many orchestras, including the symphonies of Nashville, Chattanooga, Indianapolis, Des Moines, Greater Dallas, and Chicago, in addition to the Cleveland Orchestra, the Mystic Valley Chamber Orchestra, and the Bangkok Symphony in Thailand. She became the music director of the New Hampshire Philharmonic in 1982 and of the Cape Ann Symphony Orchestra in 1986.

Roberts began teaching at the College of Music at the University of Massachusetts Lowell (UML) in 1978, and was named the Nancy Donahue Professor in the Arts in 2009. She has received numerous awards throughout her career, including the 1991 Outstanding Achievement in the Performing Arts Award from the League of Black Women and the 1993 National Achievement Award from the National Black Music Caucus. She served as a fellow at Harvard University's W. E. B. Du Bois Institute for Afro-American Research from 1997 through 1999. In 2001, she founded and became director of the UML String Project, which offers training in string instruments to talented public school students. Roberts built on the success of the String Project by establishing the Lowell Youth Orchestra in 2009.

PAUL ROBESON (1898–1976)

Singer, Actor. Born in Princeton, New Jersey, bass Paul Robeson was the son of a runaway slave who worked his way through Lincoln University and became a minister. Paul Robeson entered Rutgers College (now Rutgers University) on an athletic scholarship and won a total of

Singer and Actor Paul Robeson as Othello, Theatre Guild Production, Broadway, 1943–1944. *Active in civil and human rights issues, in 1949 baritone Robeson was accused of being a Communist. As a result, eighty-five of his scheduled U.S. concerts were canceled; Robeson then made a successful concert tour in Europe.* THE LIBRARY OF CONGRESS

twelve letters in track, football, baseball, and basketball. His academic ability gained him another prize: Phi Beta Kappa honors in his junior year.

Robeson moved to New York City after graduation and began the study of law at Columbia University in 1920. He also began to act, and this profession eventually took precedence over a law career (he had been admitted to the New York State bar in 1923). He was cast in Eugene O'Neill's *The Emperor Jones* in 1923 and, two years later, in *All God's Chillun Got Wings*, gaining excellent reviews for both productions. His rich singing voice coupled with his strong interest in spirituals and international folk songs led him to perform concerts in recital, first in New York and later in Europe and England. In addition to enjoying great success on the London and Broadway stages, Robeson also acted in several films in the 1930s and early 1940s. He became one of the first African American actors to depart from stereotypical film roles.

Robeson's concern for racial justice came increasingly to the forefront in those years as well, and his travels to the Soviet Union convinced him of the honesty of that country's statements regarding the equal treatment of all people. With the Cold War settling in after World War II, Robeson's freely expressed views brought him into conflict with the U.S. Congress and federal authorities, and, despite his denials, he was accused of being a Communist. His career was effectively ended, and his passport was revoked in 1950—to be restored eight years later by a U.S. Supreme Court decision. He moved to England and traveled widely in Europe and the Soviet Union until 1963, when he returned to the United States. In 1971, his autobiography *Here I Stand*, was published. He continued to be active in civil and human rights issues until his health began to fail in the 1970s. In 1998, he was posthumously honored with a Grammy Lifetime Achievement Award.

FAYE ROBINSON (1943–)

Singer. Soprano Faye Robinson was born on February 11, 1943, in Houston, Texas. She received a bachelor of arts degree from Bennett College in Greensboro, North Carolina. Robinson has appeared in leading roles with opera companies in Paris, Vienna, Berlin, Stuttgart, Munich, Buenos Aires, San Diego, Cleveland, and New York City.

Robinson has sung and recorded with London's BBC Symphony with Andrew Davis, the Bournemouth Symphony with Richard Hickox, the Chicago Symphony with Sir Georg Solti, and the Stockholm Chamber Orchestra with Esa-Pekka Salonen. She has also performed with major orchestras, including the Los Angeles Philharmonic, the New York Philharmonic, the Philadelphia Orchestra, the National Symphony in Washington, D.C., the Cleveland Orchestra, and the Berlin Philharmonic, the Royal Concertgebouw Orchestra in Amsterdam, the Swedish Radio Symphony, and the symphonies in Boston, Houston, and Toronto. Robinson has become a specialist in interpreting the music of Sir Michael Tippett, and has made several recordings of his music on EMI and Chandos Records. Robinson is on the faculty of the University of Arizona in Tucson.

DANIEL BERNARD ROUMAIN (1971–)

Composer, Violinist, Bandleader. Haitian American Daniel Bernard Roumain, also known as DBR, wears many hats as he combines his classical training with varied forms of contemporary African American popular music. Roumain was born in Margate, Florida, and earned a bachelor's degree from Vanderbilt University's Blair School of Music in Nashville. Having earned his doctorate in composition from the University of Michigan, he writes dramatically for orchestras, chamber music groups, rock artists, and electronica.

Roumain's works have been performed and commissioned by orchestras in Dallas, Des Moines, Memphis, San Antonio, and St. Louis, as well as the Chicago Sinfonietta, the Brooklyn Philharmonic, the North Dutch Orchestra, the Stuttgart Chamber Orchestra, the American Composers Orchestra, and the Orchestra of St. Luke's. As a violinist, he has performed his arrangements of other works, while also conducting the Buffalo Philharmonic and the Seattle Symphony Orchestra at the Lincoln Center Summer Festival, the Melbourne Arts Festival, and the Other Minds Festival in San Francisco.

Roumain is also a bandleader for DBR and the Mission, a group of nine multicultural musicians. They have performed at Kennedy Center, Miami's Caleb Auditorium, New York City's Cutting Room, Northwestern University, Arizona State University, and other venues. Roumain is music director of the Bill T. Jones/Arnie Zane Dance Company and assistant composer-in-residence of the Orchestra of St. Luke's, and he has served as artist-in-residence at Arizona State University and of the Seattle Theatre Group. Roumain released his first solo album, *Pulsing*, in 2006. It was followed by *etudes4violin&electronix* in 2007 and *Woodbox Beats & Balladry* in 2010. He served as a visiting professor of composition and theory at Vanderbilt's Blair School of Music during the 2009–2010 academic year.

MARK RUCKER (1956–)

Singer. Baritone Mark Rucker has made a career singing leading roles in Verdi operas in America and around the world. Rucker was born on November 22, 1956, in Chicago. He attended Kenwood Academy High School and studied music with Lena McLin.

Rucker's operatic debut was as Renato in Verdi's *Un ballo in maschera*, with Luciano Pavarotti, for the Opera Company of Philadelphia. His Metropolitan Opera debut came in 2004 as Amonasro in Verdi's *Aida*. He then sang the title role of *Rigoletto* and Don Carlo in *La forza del destino*, as well as his signature role, Tonio in Leoncavallo's *Pagliacci*. Other North American companies with which he has performed include the New York City Opera, the San Diego Opera, the Florida Grand Opera, the Baltimore Opera, the New Orleans Opera, the Vancouver Opera, Opera Pacific, and l'Opéra de Montréal, as well as companies in Mexico City, Atlanta, Cleveland, Connecticut, Detroit, Milwaukee, North Carolina, Orlando, and Portland.

Rucker's European debut was as Alfio and Tonio with l'Opéra de Nice. He has also appeared in Amsterdam, Bologna, Graz, Dublin, Taipei, Israel, Trieste, Vienna, Berlin, and Verona. He has performed at festivals in Bregenz and Savonlinna, and in concert with the symphony orchestras of Baltimore, Detroit, Rotterdam, Israel, Columbus, San Antonio, San Francisco, and Chicago. His Carnegie Hall debut was as Don Carlo in *La forza del destino* with Maria Guleghina and Salvatore Licitra.

PHILIPPA DUKE SCHUYLER (1931–1967)

Pianist, Composer. Born in New York City to an African American father and a white mother, Philippa Schuyler embodied her parents' desire to prove to the world that the intermingling of the black and white races would result in a hybrid that would draw from the strengths of each lineage. She initially fulfilled their expectations: she could read and write by the time she was two and a half years old; by age four she was composing music; and by age five she was performing Mozart. Her IQ, tested by New York University, was 185.

Schuyler started piano lessons when she was three, and early in elementary school she began to study harmony, having already composed dozens of piano pieces (although she would not receive formal training in composition until she was fifteen). She gave her first solo piano recital when she was six. Among her teachers were Josef Hoffman, Paul Wittgenstein, and Gaston Dethier in piano, Clarence Cameron White in violin, and Dean Dixon and Antonia Brico in conducting.

With her parents pushing her career, the child prodigy wowed the critics with both the excellence of her playing and the quality of her compositions. Schuyler performed widely as a teenager and appeared as orchestra soloist and recitalist. Several of her works were performed by orchestras, including the New York Philharmonic, the Chicago Symphony, and the Detroit Symphony. She made three world tours, at first under U.S. State Department auspices, and she received numerous awards throughout her career. Among them was a 1939 World's Fair Medal as one of the "Women of Tomorrow," an Award of Merit from the Fair in 1940, a Distinguished Achievement Award from the National Negro Opera Company Foundation in 1955, gold and silver medals from Haile Selassie, the Emperor of Ethiopia, in 1955, and, after her death, the establishment of a memorial foundation in her name.

Schuyler's appeal to white America faded when she entered young adulthood. Stung by the racism she had not encountered as a child, Schuyler traveled the world and played for numerous foreign dignitaries. In spite of the acclaim she received outside of the United States, the rejection she experienced in her homeland bitterly reminded her that she was still a second-class citizen back home. Her travels became a painful search for identity, which she attempted to reconcile through her fiction and nonfiction writing. She even adopted a different identity, claiming to be Felipa Monterro, an Iberian American, in hopes of approval from white audiences in America. However, initial reviews of her concerts performed in Europe under this new identity were mediocre. In 1967, Schuyler was killed in a helicopter crash in Da Nang Bay in Vietnam, where she had gone to help in the rescue of some schoolchildren.

GEORGE SHIRLEY (1934–)

Singer. Born in Indianapolis, Indiana, on April 18, 1934, tenor George Shirley moved to Detroit with his family in 1946. There he began music lessons, sang in church choirs, and played baritone horn in a local band.

In 1955, Shirley received his bachelor's degree in music education from Wayne State University. Shortly thereafter, he was drafted and the next year became the first African American member of the U. S. Army Chorus. Following his discharge in 1959, he became the first African American appointed to teach music in a Detroit high school. He resumed his private voice lessons and eventually relocated to New York.

Though Shirley has won international acclaim for his performances with the world's leading opera houses, including the Netherlands Opera, the Metropolitan Opera, the Royal Opera at Convent Garden, the San Francisco Opera, the Chicago Lyric Opera, and the Washington Opera, his debut was with a small opera troupe at Woodstock, New York, in *Die Fledermaus.* His European debut was in Italy as Rodolfo in Puccini's *La Bohème.* In 1961, after winning the Metropolitan Opera auditions, he began eleven years of association with the Met. Shirley was the first black tenor and second African American male to sing leading roles with the Metropolitan Opera. In 1968, Shirley received a Grammy Award for singing the role of Ferrando in the prize-winning RCA recording of Mozart's *Così fan tutte.*

Over his forty-year career, Shirley performed more than eighty operatic roles and appeared frequently on the concert stage singing recitals and oratorios. Shirley is in demand as a narrator. In 1996, he narrated two poems by James Forsyth with music by the late Franz Waxman. His most recent narration was *Three Places in New England* by Charles Ives with the Chicago Symphony.

In addition to his success as a performer, lecturer, and narrator, Shirley is also an educator. From 1980 to 1987, he served as a voice professor at the University of Maryland in College Park. In 1987, he joined the faculty of the School of Music at the University of Michigan, where he was the director of the Vocal Arts Division and the Joseph Edgar Maddy Distinguished University Professor of Music until his retirement in 2007.

CALVIN E. SIMMONS (1950–1982)

Conductor. Calvin Eugene Simmons began his study of music at an early age, with piano lessons from his mother Matty. Young Simmons was quickly recognized as a prodigy in classical music. When he was eleven, he was conducting the San Francisco Boys Chorus under the tutelage of its founder, Madi Bacon.

Simmons was born on April 27, 1950, in San Francisco, California. He graduated from Balboa High School, and attended the Curtis Institute of Music in Philadelphia, where he studied piano with Rudolph Serkin and conducting with Max Rudolph. Throughout the 1970s, Simmons worked at the San Francisco Opera House as a protégé of Kurt Hebert Adler, coaching singers and playing piano for rehearsals. He worked as assistant conductor of the Los Angeles Philharmonic under Zubin Mehta, and in 1979 was named music director of the Oakland Symphony Orchestra. Simmons became the first African American conductor of a major American symphony orchestra, and was a guest conductor for many of the major orchestras in the country, including the Philadelphia Orchestra.

Simmons made his Metropolitan Opera debut in 1978 conducting Humperdinck's *Hansel and Gretel.* He also conducted at the Glyndebourne Festival Opera in England, the Opera Theatre of St. Louis, the San Francisco Opera, and the New York City Opera. He led the Oakland Symphony for four years and was loved and revered by all. His untimely death on August 21, 1982, in a canoeing accident in Lake George, New York, marked the end of his illustrious career. He is remembered in Oakland by the naming in his honor of the grand ballroom of the Oakland Marriott Hotel, the Calvin Simmons Middle School, and the Calvin Simmons Theatre at the Henry J. Kaiser Convention Center.

MARIETTA SIMPSON (1958–)

Singer. Mezzo-soprano Marietta Simpson was born in Philadelphia, Pennsylvania, on November 15, 1958, into a musical family. She earned a bachelor of music education degree from Temple University in 1981 and a master of music degree from the State University of New York at Binghamton in 1983. Simpson began her operatic training at Tri-Cities Opera in Binghamton, singing many roles with the company. She also spent several seasons with the Houston Opera Studio. She subsequently performed roles with the Minnesota Opera, the Mobile Opera, Opera Delaware, Opera North, the Augusta Opera, the New York City Opera, the Houston Grand Opera, the Chicago Lyric Opera, the Royal Opera at Covent Garden, and La Scala Milan.

Simpson is probably best known for her many performances with the conductor Robert Shaw. She is an accomplished recitalist and concert artist, and has appeared with numerous conductors, including Sir Simon Rattle, Lorin Maazel, Kurt Masur, Charles Dutoit, Wolfgang Sawallisch, Neeme Järvi, Andrew Litton, and Neville Mariner. She has performed at various festivals, including Tanglewood, Blossom, Glyndebourne in England, Bregenz in Austria, Edinburgh in Scotland, and the Lincoln Center Arts Festival.

Simpson was awarded Temple University's Certificate of Honor as a distinguished alumna, and the Philadelphia National Congress of Black Women gave her their second annual Chisholm Award. Simpson was a finalist in the Metropolitan Opera regional auditions. She has recorded on Telarc, EMI, Dorian, and Naxos Records. Her recording of *Porgy and Bess* with Rattle and the Glyndebourne festival cast was nominated for a Grammy Award. She is professor of voice at the Jacobs School of Music at Indiana University.

ROBERT SIMS (1965–)

Singer, Educator. Robert Lewis Sims, born October 10, 1965, in Chicago, Illinois, is a lyric baritone who specializes in African American folk songs and spirituals. Sims, a Gold Medal winner of the American Traditions Competition, is known for his rich tone, energetic performances, and convincing stage presence. Sims graduated from Oberlin Conservatory of Music, the State University of New York at Binghamton, Northwestern University, and the American Conservatory of Music. He also studied at the Music Academy of the West, Chautauqua Musical Institute, and the Oberlin/Urbania Vocal Institute in Urbania, Italy.

After winning the Friedrich Schorr Opera Award, Sims appeared in Massenet's *Cendrillon*, which won the National Opera America Award. His other operatic credits include roles in *Don Pasquale*, *Roméo et Juliette*, *Die Zauberflöte*, *Porgy and Bess*, *La traviata*, *Pagliacci*, *Così fan tutte*, and *Le nozze di Figaro*.

Sims is also at home with classic jazz and folk music, and has collaborated with the Georgia Guitar Quartet in repertoire ranging from Leonard Bernstein to Bob Dylan. Sims has appeared in concert with the late folk legend Odetta and has given numerous recitals and orchestral appearances throughout the United States, Europe, Africa, and Asia. He was a voice student of Lena McLin and was mentored by opera stage director David Farrar.

Career highlights for Sims include his being the first singer to give a recital exclusively of spirituals and folk songs at Carnegie Hall's Zankel Hall, in 2005. In March 2009, he was invited by Jessye Norman to participate in *Honor! A Celebration of the African American Cultural Legacy at Carnegie Hall.*

Sims toured nationally in the ensemble Three Generations, a celebration of American spirituals and folk songs with renowned African American artists George Shirley, William Warfield, and Benjamin Matthews. In 2007, he debuted with Simon Estes and Jubilant Sykes in the trio Simon, Sykes, & Sims, singing spirituals and American songs.

Sims is a founder of Canti Classics Artist Management and Production Company, and has produced four recordings: *Soul of a Singer* (1998), *Sims Sings Copland and Spirituals* (2000), *In the Spirit* (2007), and *Three Generations* (2000).

HALE SMITH (1925–2009)

Composer, Educator, Editor. Hale Smith was born on June 29, 1925, in Cleveland, Ohio. He attended Cleveland's public schools and earned bachelor (1950) and master (1952) of music degrees from the Cleveland Institute of Music. His only composition teacher, Marcel Dick, was a major influence, as were such jazz figures as Duke Ellington and Art Tatum.

In 1958, after moving to New York City, Smith began arranging for and collaborating with many different kinds of musicians, including Chico Hamilton, Dizzy Gillespie, and Oliver Nelson. Active as a music editor and consultant from 1961, he worked for several music publishing companies—Marks Music and C. F. Peters among them. He joined the faculty of the University of Connecticut at Storrs in 1970 and retired in 1984. In 1988, Hale Smith received the American Academy and Institute of Arts and Letters Award.

Smith received more than twenty commissions and many prestigious awards in the course of his career and wrote frequently on many musical subjects. A few of his outstanding compositions are: *Contours* (1961); *Ritual and Incantations* (1974); *Innerflexions* (1977); *Mirrors: Rondo-Variations for Two Pianos* (1988); and *A Ternion of Seasons for Instrumental Ensemble* (1996). Among several works for concert band, some with pedagogical aims, are: *Somersault: A Twelve Tone Adventure for Band* (1964); *Take a Chance: An Aleatoric Episode for Band* (1964); and *Expansions* (1967).

Smith used the general term *formal music* as a category for his instrumental, band, orchestra, vocal, and choral scores, and within them can be found, in varying degrees, techniques and idioms of African American music. Highly sensitive to instrumental "color" and with a strong dramatic sense, he consistently conceived of and found new ways to express a broad spectrum of musical ideas. Hale Smith died November 24, 2009.

WILLIAM GRANT STILL (1895–1978)

Composer, Conductor. William Grant Still was born in Woodville, Mississippi. Because of his father's untimely death, his mother moved to Little Rock, Arkansas, where he attended public schools. His family encouraged his interest in music, and he began to take violin lessons as a teenager. He attended Wilberforce University in Ohio, but left before receiving a premed degree to study at the Oberlin College Conservatory in Ohio.

Still began playing professionally in several bands, spent some time in the U.S. Navy, and moved to New York City to work for the Pace and Handy Music Company Band. He later became director of the classical division and then musical director for the Pace Recording Company. He had many opportunities to play in theater orchestras and to arrange for shows, radio programs, and the movies.

In the 1920s, Still studied with two very different kinds of composers: first, the traditionalist George Chadwick, who was at the New England Conservatory of Music in Boston, and then Edgard Varèse, a leading member of the avant-garde. This broad experience in Western European music expanded his compositional horizons and complemented his African American musical heritage. He was a student of and apologist for black vernacular music in both his musical and academic writings.

Still believed that folk music was the richest source for sounds needed to make American music stand apart from the European models that had dominated composed music. In his attempt to be instrumental in defining an "American sound," Still spent his life collecting, studying, and analyzing the many melodies and rhythms of the ethnic groups that make up the Western hemisphere. Although he arranged folk songs, especially African American spirituals, for various instrumental and choral combinations, he used the scales and rhythms derived from them as his primary source of inspiration in his larger forms. Still chose to compose his own melodies and to harmonize them using the richly stacked chords of jazz and blues. He wanted to elevate the blues by using its characteristic structures in symphonies, ballets, and operas.

William Grant Still. *Composer and conductor Still became the first African American to conduct a professional symphony orchestra in the United States, the Los Angeles Philharmonic in 1936.* FRANK DRIGGS COLLECTION/ARCHIVE PHOTOS/GETTY IMAGES

Still's *Afro-American Symphony* (1930, revised 1969) was the first of five symphonies that he wrote. In 1931, it was the first of Still's large orchestral works to be performed by a major orchestra, the Rochester Philharmonic, under the direction of Howard Hanson. One of his eight operas, *Troubled Island* (1941), was the first opera by an African American composer to be staged by a major U.S. company, the New York City Center's Opera Company, in 1949. Another opera, *A Bayou Legend* (1941), was the first opera by an African American composer to be telecast nationally over the Public Broadcasting Service in 1981. He was one of the most prolific composers of his generation and was active as a composer into the early 1960s.

Still was among the accomplished artists whose work will always be associated with the Harlem Renaissance of the 1920s and 1930s, and he and Duke Ellington are the leading composers of that movement. Still was often called the "dean of Afro-American composers," and his achievements as a composer testify to the validity of that title.

HOWARD SWANSON (1907–1978)

Composer. Howard Swanson was born in Atlanta to a family in which there were several educators, including his mother. He and his siblings were given music lessons and sang in church, but it was only after the family's move to Cleveland, Ohio, in 1918, that he studied the piano formally. Although Swanson began to work for the U.S. Postal Service after high school in order to help support his family, he entered the Cleveland Institute of Music, where he studied composition with Herbert Elwell and earned a bachelor of music degree in 1937.

Through a Rosenwald Fellowship that he received in 1938, Swanson was able to go to Paris to study with Nadia Boulanger at the American Academy in Fontainebleau. His study was interrupted by World War II, and he returned to the United States in 1941. After the war, he returned to Europe until 1966, when he made his permanent home in New York City. By this time, he was receiving regular commissions and his works were being performed. In 1950, for example, Marian Anderson sang his setting of Langston Hughes's *The Negro Speaks of Rivers* (1942) at Carnegie Hall, and his *Short Symphony* (1948) was premiered by the New York Philharmonic. This symphony won the New York Music Critics' Circle Award in 1952. He wrote steadily into the 1970s, and his works continued to be performed by a wide variety of ensembles and soloists.

Swanson's work is most often characterized as "neo-classic," yet his heritage of African American music and traditions is the basis of his musical language. The largest percentage of his compositional output is vocal music; he never wrote an opera or music for the theater.

KENNETH TARVER (196?–)

Singer. Considered one of the outstanding bel canto tenors of his generation, Tarver is critically acclaimed for his beautiful tone, virtuosic technique, extensive vocal range, and attractive stage presence.

Born in Detroit, Michigan, Tarver received his early musical training at the Interlochen Arts Academy and the Oberlin College Conservatory of Music. He holds a Masters of Music Performance from Yale University School of Music, where received the Dean's Award for Most Outstanding Student. He is a past winner of the Metropolitan Opera National Council Auditions, and the Metropolitan Opera's Young Artist Program.

Professionally, Tarver has appeared at the world's most prestigious opera houses, including the Royal Opera House Covent Garden, Wiener Staatsoper, Deutsche Oper Berlin, Staatsoper Unter den Linden, Bayerische Staatsoper, Dresden Semperoper, Gran Teatre del Liceu Barcelona, Opéra Comique París, Teatro Lirico di Trieste, Theatre de La Monnaie Brussels, Metropolitan Opera, Teatro San Carlos Naples, and the Festival d'Aix-en-Provence.

Tarver is a specialist in the most demanding virtuosic operatic repertoire, including the works of Handel, Rossini, Donizetti, Mozart, Haydn, Gluck, Berlioz, and Auber. He has performed live and recorded with some of the world's most celebrated conductors, including Claudio Abbado, Nikolaus Harnoncourt, Rene Jacobs, Maurizio Benini, Alberto Zedda, Ricardo Chailly, Carlo Rizzi, Frans Bruggen, Kent Nagano, James Levine, Pierre Boulez, and Sir Colin Davis. He is also featured on several recording labels, including Deutsche Grammophon, Opera Rara, Naxos, Decca, and Harmonia Mundi. Tarver is also an accomplished recitalist with many stellar orchestral and international festival appearances.

Of a recent performance as Don Ramiro in Rossini's *La Cenerentola* with Washington Concert Opera in May 2010, conducted by Antony Walker, *The Washington Post* wrote: "Her prince charming was Prince Ramiro, sung by tenor Kenneth Tarver with warmth and quiet power and with a voice that was remarkably consistent throughout its wide range.... Tarver maintained an imposing dignity and a presence in which even a raised eyebrow commanded attention." *The Baltimore Sun* wrote: "Kenneth Tarver brought a light, uncommonly sweet tenor and often exquisite phrasing to the role of the Prince." Of his Lindoro in *L'Italiana in Algeri* at Teatro Municipal in Santiago de Chile, *El Mercurio* praised his "elegant figure and style on stage with free-flowing singing and reliable top notes."

DARRYL TAYLOR (1964–)

Singer. Tenor Darryl Taylor was born July 14, 1964, in Detroit. He holds degrees from the University of Southern California and the University of Michigan.

Taylor's New York recital debut took place in 2001 at Weill Recital Hall at Carnegie Hall. He has appeared with orchestras in the United States and Europe, including the Johann Strauss Sinfonietta of Vienna, Camerata Mediterranea of Barcelona, the Aspen Music Festival Orchestra, and the W. A. Mozart Philharmonic of Cluj, Romania. Among his operatic credits is his appearance as Jimmy in the premier of the jazz opera by Nathan Davis, *Just Above My Head* (based on the novel by James Baldwin) in 2004, and lead roles in operas by Mozart,

Verdi, Handel, Britten, and Gershwin. Taylor's international itinerary includes some nineteen tours of Spain, singing to enthusiastic, capacity audiences.

In addition to his classical credits, Taylor has been associated with such notable jazz greats as Kenny Burrell, Hubert Laws, Jimmy Owens, and Nathan Davis. Taylor's recitals have regularly introduced audiences to works of such composers as William Grant Still, George Walker, Adolphus Hailstork, John Musto, Deon Nielsen Price, Edward Hart, Richard Thompson, Ted Wiprud, Leslie Adams, and Hale Smith. Many of these works were written especially for Taylor's voice. His solo recordings include *Love Rejoices: Songs of H. Leslie Adams* (2001) and *Fields of Wonder: Songs and Spirituals of Robert Owens* (2006).

Highlights of Taylor's performances include a highly successful recital at the famed Liszt Music Academy in Budapest, a recital at Merkin Concert Hall in New York, and Spanish television and radio broadcasts from Barcelona's Palau de la Música. He was a featured artist under the sponsorship of the Cultural Committee for the 1992 Olympic Games in Barcelona and was heard in *Messiah* at the Kennedy Center for the Performing Arts in Washington, D.C. Taylor serves on the faculty of the University of California, Irvine.

LOUISE TOPPIN (1961–)

Singer. Soprano Antoinette Louise Toppin was born March 26, 1961, in Akron, Ohio. She is a graduate of the University of North Carolina–Chapel Hill, the Peabody Conservatory, and the University of Michigan. Her coaches include Sylvia Olden Lee, Reri Grist, and Mattiwilda Dobbs.

Toppin has appeared in concert series at numerous venues, including Carnegie Hall, Lincoln Center, Merkin Hall, and the Kennedy Center. Her orchestral appearances include the Czech National Symphony, the Tokyo City Orchestra, and the Montevideo Philharmonic in Uruguay, as well as the North Carolina, Honolulu, Toledo, and Lafayette symphonies. She has also performed with the Bach Aria Group, the Phoenix Bach Consort, and the Washington, D.C., Bach Consort. Toppin has appeared with a number of conductors,

Shirley Verrett, Opera Singer,* Macbeth, *San Francisco Opera, 1986. *Mezzo-soprano Verrett has performed in opera houses all over the world. In 2009 she received an Opera News Award for Distinguished Achievement.* RON SCHERL/REDFERNS/GETTY IMAGES

including Paul Freeman, Richard Auldon Clark, Justin Brown, James Meena, and Guerassim Voronkov. Her opera roles include the Queen of the Night in *The Magic Flute* and Clara in *Porgy and Bess*, which she has performed with such companies as the Baltimore Opera and Opera Carolina.

Toppin performs operatic, orchestral, and oratorio repertoire in the United States, Europe, Asia, South America, and New Zealand, and is a noted champion of American and African American composers. She has premiered more than thirty works written for her by such composers as T. J. Anderson, Olly Wilson, Adolphus Hailstork, Alvin Singleton, and Roland Carter. She sang the title role in the opera *Luyala* by William Banfield, and sang Maria in the world premier of Joel Feigin's opera *Twelfth Night*. Toppin has made fifteen recordings on the Albany and Centaur labels, including an opera, songs, and spirituals by American composers. Toppin was also a finalist in the Munich International Competition, and the winner of the Metropolitan Opera regional competition.

In 1997, Toppin became the director of Videmus, a nonprofit arts organization documenting the concert music of African Americans, women, and underrepresented composers in concerts, recordings, and scholarship. She has taught at the University of North Carolina–Chapel Hill, East Carolina University, and Bowling Green State University.

SHIRLEY VERRETT (1931–2010)

Singer, Actress, Educator. Born on May 31, 1931, in New Orleans, Louisiana, soprano Shirley Verrett moved to California when she was eleven. Her father was her first voice teacher, and her earliest musical experiences were in the Seventh-Day Adventist Church. She briefly attended Oakwood College and Ventura College, where she majored in business administration.

By the mid-1950s, Verrett began taking voice lessons in Los Angeles and trained her sights on the concert stage. After winning a television talent show in 1955, she enrolled at the Juilliard School on a scholarship and earned her bachelor of music degree in 1961. She made her New York City opera debut in 1957 in a production of *Lost in the Stars*, and she returned to the city in 1964 to sing the title role in Bizet's *Carmen* at the Metropolitan Opera. By then, she had performed the role in Moscow and Spoleto, Italy, and had appeared in several concert versions of the opera. The *New York Herald Tribune*'s critic claimed her Carmen as one of the finest "seen or heard" in New York for the past generation. In 1975, Verrett opened the Teatro alla Scala season appearing as Lady Macbeth in Verdi's *Macbeth*. This was one of her greatest successes and firmly established her as one of the world's leading dramatic sopranos. Verrett's yearly recital tours brought her to major music centers throughout the world.

Between 1983 and 1986, Verrett lived in Paris and had a series of operas staged especially for her by the Paris Opera, including Rossini's *Mosè in Egitto*, Cherubini's *Médée*, and Gluck's *Iphigénie en Tauride* and *Alceste*. She made a triumphant return to the Metropolitan Opera in 1986 as Eboli in *Don Carlo* and also starred that year in a new production of *Macbeth* with the San Francisco Opera. In the 1987–1988 season, Verrett made her long-awaited Chicago Lyric Opera debut as Azucena in *Il trovatore*.

In the mid-1990s, Verrett turned to dramatic acting. She was featured in a major Broadway revival of Rodger and Hammerstein's *Carousel*. In 1996, she became the James Earl Jones Distinguished University Professor of Music at the University of Michigan in Ann Arbor. In 2003, she published a memoir, *I Never Walked Alone*, written with Christopher Brooks. In 2009 she was honored by the Metropolitan Opera Guild for her distinguished achievement in opera.

GEORGE WALKER (1922–)

Pianist, Educator. George Theophilus Walker was born into a musical family in Washington, D.C., and began studying piano when he was five. He attended public schools in Washington while also enrolled in the junior division of the Howard University School of Music. In 1941, Walker earned a bachelor of music degree at the Oberlin Conservatory of Music in Ohio. His graduate education included two artist diplomas, one in piano and one in composition, in 1945 from the Curtis Institute of Music, where he was a student of Rudolph Serkin and Rosario Scalero; a diploma in piano from the American Academy at Fontainebleau in France in 1947 (he also studied there in the 1950s with Nadia Boulanger); and a doctor of musical arts degree and artist diploma from the Eastman School of Music in 1957. He made his debut with the Philadelphia Orchestra conducted by Eugene Ormandy in 1941 in Rachmaninoff's *Piano Concerto No. 3*, and his New York recital debut at Town Hall in 1945.

Walker's promising career as a concert artist began to shift toward teaching and composition in the mid-1950s. After brief tenures at Dillard University, the Dalcroze School of Music, the New School for Social Research, Smith College, and the University of Colorado, he joined the faculty of Rutgers University in 1969, where he remained until his retirement in 1992.

Besides many works for piano, including four sonatas, Walker has written for several other instruments, chamber and full orchestra, solo voice, and chorus.

George Walker, Montclair, NJ, 1996. *Walker, a composer and retired Rutgers University professor, won the 1996 Pulitzer Prize for Music, for* Lilacs, *a composition commissioned by the Boston Symphony Orchestra to honor Roland Hayes. Hayes was the first black concert singer to appear with a U.S. orchestra.* AP PHOTO/MIKE DERER

Among his numerous honors and awards are several honorary doctorates and two Guggenheim Fellowships, along with a large number of commissions. Walker received the American Academy and Institute of Arts and Letters Award in 1982. In 1996, he won the Pulitzer Prize in Music for *Lilacs*, for soprano or tenor and orchestra, based on a text by Walt Whitman. This Pulitzer was the first for a living African American composer. Walker was inducted into the American Classical Music Hall of Fame in 2000.

A master of twentieth-century musical techniques, Walker shows a deep connection in his works with his African American musical heritage, especially spirituals and jazz. He once stated, "I believe that music is above race. I am steeped in the universal cultural tradition of my art. It is important to stress one's individuality beyond race, but I must do it as a black person who is aspiring to be a product of a civilized society." In 2007 Walker received the Lift Every Voice Legacy Award from the National Opera Association. His autobiography, *Reminiscences of an American Composer and Pianist*, was published in 2009.

WILLIAM C. WARFIELD (1920–2002)

Singer. Baritone William Caesar Warfield was born on January 22, 1920, in West Helena, Arkansas, and later moved with his family to Rochester, New York. The son of a Baptist minister, he received early training in voice, organ, and piano. In 1938, while a student at Washington Junior High School, he won the vocal competition at the National Music Educators League Convention in St. Louis, Missouri.

Warfield studied at the Eastman School of Music and received his bachelor's degree in 1942. He made his recital debut at New York's Town Hall in 1950 and, afterward, made an unprecedented tour of Australia under the auspices of the Australian Broadcasting Commission. A year later, he made his film debut in the movie version of Jerome Kern's *Show Boat* and also performed the role of Joe on the stage in several productions. He appeared on several major television shows and starred in the NBC television version of *Green Pastures.* Warfield became identified with the role of Porgy in Gershwin's *Porgy and Bess* in the 1950s and later. He married his costar, Leontyne Price, during the 1952–1954 touring revival of the opera; they were divorced in 1973.

In 1974, Warfield accepted a position as professor of music at the University of Illinois School of Music in Urbana. He retired in 1990 as chairman of the voice faculty and became a visiting professor at Eastern Illinois University and an adjunct professor of music at Northwestern University.

Warfield was active in the National Association of Negro Musicians, serving as its president in 1984. He also served as a board member of the Lyric Opera of Chicago and the New York College of Music, a trustee of the Berkshire Boys Choir, a member of the music panel of the National Association for the Arts, and a judge for the Whittaker Vocal Competition of the Music Educator's National Conference.

Warfield received honorary doctorates from the University of Arkansas, Boston University, and Milliken University. He won a 1984 Grammy Award in the spoken-word category for his recording of Aaron Copland's *A Lincoln Portrait.* He appeared frequently with orchestras as soloist and narrator and was teacher and mentor to many younger singers. Warfield died in 2002.

WILLIE ANTHONY WATERS (1951–)

Conductor. Willie Anthony Waters is one of the few African American conductors who has served as artistic director for two opera companies. He was born in Goulds, Florida, on October 11, 1951, and graduated from the Frost School of Music of the University of Miami in 1973. His first major job was as artistic administrator of the San Francisco Opera under Kurt Herbert Adler. After his tenure from 1975 to 1979 with the San Francisco Opera, where he also coached and conducted, he became artistic director and principal conductor of the Greater Miami Opera Company from 1982 to 1995. He later served as artistic director of the now defunct Connecticut Opera Association.

Waters has become a regular guest conductor of many opera companies in the United States, Canada, Europe, and Africa. He made his debut at New York City Opera in 2002, conducting Verdi's *Rigoletto.* He appeared for the first time at the Deutsche Oper Berlin in 2008, conducting the Cape Town Opera's production of Gershwin's *Porgy and Bess.* He has appeared as guest conductor with numerous other companies, including the Australian Opera, the Arizona Opera, the Boston Lyric Opera, the Chautauqua Opera, the Cincinnati Opera, the Opera Theater of Cologne, the Dayton Opera, the Edmonton Opera, the Fort Worth Opera, the San Francisco Opera, the San Diego Opera, the Vancouver Opera, the Florida Grand Opera, the Montreal Opera, and l'Opéra de Québec.

Waters is a faculty member of the University of Connecticut Department of Music and is codirector of the UConn Opera Theater. He also serves as music director for the Prelude to Performance program of the Martina Arroyo Foundation in New York City.

ANDRÉ WATTS (1946–)

Concert Pianist. One of America's most gifted pianists, André Watts was the first African American concert pianist to achieve international stardom. Born June 20, 1946, in Nuremberg, Germany, to a Hungarian mother and an African American soldier, he spent the first eight years of his life on U.S. Army posts in Europe before moving to Philadelphia. By the time he was nine years old, he was already performing with the Philadelphia Orchestra. After graduating from Lincoln Preparatory School in Philadelphia and attending the Philadelphia Academy of Music, he enrolled at Baltimore's Peabody Conservatory of Music.

In 1962, when pianist Glenn Gould was unable to appear as soloist with the New York Philharmonic, Leonard Bernstein chose Watts as a last-minute replacement. At the conclusion of his performance of Liszt's *E-flat Major Piano Concerto,* the sixteen-year-old Watts received a standing ovation, not only from the audience but also from the orchestra.

From the mid-1960s on, Watts has toured the world as a recitalist and has appeared with leading orchestras in the United States and abroad. He has also been a frequent performer of chamber music. His recordings continue to be popular and his performances of works by Liszt and other romantic composers have been especially notable.

Watts was awarded the Lincoln Center Medallion (1971), honorary doctorates from Yale University (1973) and Albright College (1975), the National Society of Arts and Letters Gold Medal (1982), and the Avery Fisher Prize (1988). In 1988, he performed a concert that was telecast nationally in honor of the twenty-fifth anniversary of his New York Philharmonic debut. Watts remains one of the world's "greatest in

André Watts, Pianist, 2005. *A child prodigy, Watts was chosen at age sixteen by Leonard Bernstein to replace an ailing Glenn Gould as the piano soloist in a 1963 concert. In 2004 Watts joined the faculty of the Indiana University School of Music.* JOHN BERRY/SYRACUSE NEWSPAPERS/THE IMAGE WORKS

demand" pianists, both as recitalist and concert soloist. In 2004, Watts become a professor of music at the Jacobs School of Music at Indiana University.

CLARENCE CAMERON WHITE (1880–1960)

Violinist, Composer, Conductor, Teacher. Clarence Cameron White, born in Clarksville, Tennessee, moved with his widowed mother to his grandparent's house in Oberlin, Ohio. They were musically inclined and encouraged their grandson in his musical interests. With his mother's remarriage, the family moved to Washington, D.C., where he studied violin with Will Marion Cook and Joseph Douglass. A period at the Oberlin College Conservatory in Ohio ended without a degree, and he began working in the Washington public schools and the Washington Conservatory of Music.

White became acquainted through correspondence with the British composer Samuel Coleridge-Taylor and performed with him in concert during one of Coleridge-Taylor's American tours. White later studied with him in London, through the aid of an E. Azalia Hackley scholarship.

After his return from London in 1911, White had a heavy schedule of touring, composing, and teaching. He was a founding member of the National Association of Negro Musicians in 1919. In 1924, he settled at West Virginia State College as head of the music department but left in 1930 to study composition with Raoul Laparra in Paris on a Rosenwald Fellowship. On his return to the United States in 1932, he chaired the music department of Hampton Institute (which was discontinued in 1935).

In 1937, White was named a music specialist for the National Recreation Association, established by President Roosevelt under the aegis of the Works Progress Administration. The association's responsibility was to offer aid in organizing community arts programs.

Through these moves and teaching positions, White's catalog of compositions was growing. He wrote, not surprisingly, many works for violin, some of which are teaching pieces. His most performed works have been *Bandanna Sketches* (1918) and *From the Cotton Fields* (1920). The most ambitious of White's compositions is *Ouanga* (1932), a three-act opera with a plot revolving around the historical figure Jean-Jacques Dessalines, who ruled Haiti and attempted to eliminate the practice of voodoo. White used the country's folk music, especially rhythmic dance patterns, with which he had become familiar through a visit to Haiti, while casting its structure in a Western European, late nineteenth-century framework. Completed in 1932, the premiere was staged in 1949 by the Burleigh Musical Association in South Bend, Indiana. White became the first African American to receive the Bispham Medal after a performance in 1932.

CAMILLA WILLIAMS (1919–)

Singer. When Camilla Williams, an operatic lyric soprano, signed with the New York City Center Opera, she became the first African American to have a contract with a major American opera company. She sang the title role of Cio-Cio San in Puccini's *Madama Butterfly* in her May 1946 debut with the New York City Center Opera. In effect, Williams opened the door for many other African American opera singers, including Marian Anderson.

Williams was born in Danville, Virginia, on October 18, 1919, and studied at Virginia State College, where she received her B.S. in 1941. After graduation, she competed and won several vocal competitions, most notably the Marian Anderson Fellowships in 1943 and 1944. These awards enabled her to study with private voice teachers in New York.

Prior to her debut with the New York City Center Opera, Williams performed on the RCA national radio network. During Williams's more than six years with the New York City Center Opera, she performed other leading roles, including Nedda in Leoncavallo's *Pagliacci*, Mimi in Puccini's *La Bohème*, and Verdi's *Aida*. In April 1954, Williams once again broke the color barrier when she became the first African American to sing a major role with the Vienna State Opera, performing her signature role of Cio-Cio San. Her distinguished career in opera was complemented by her equally accomplished work as a concert artist. She performed throughout the United States, Africa, Europe, Asia, Australia, New Zealand, and South America. In 1977, Williams became the first African American professor of voice at Indiana University's School of Music. She continued in that position until her retirement in 1997. Williams was awarded the Indiana University President's Medal for Excellence in 2009. In February 2010 she was honored with the Sagamore of the Wabash Award from the State of Indiana.

W. HAZAIAH WILLIAMS (1930–1999)

Minister, Impresario. The Reverend William Hazaiah Williams was the first major African American presenter of classical music in the United States. He was dedicated to the racial and cultural integration and expansion of the classical music audience and of the concert stage. Born on May 14, 1930, in Columbus, Ohio, Williams began his career as a presenter in 1958 with a recital by Marian Anderson at the War Memorial Opera House in San Francisco. He graduated from Wayne State University and received a master of theology degree from Boston University.

Williams started the recital series Today's Artists Concerts in 1958 and directed the program for thirty-five years. He created a roster of artists that showed a racial and ethnic diversity not seen on classical music stages. Williams gave many African American artists their debuts at Carnegie Hall and the Lincoln Center in New York City. Performances such as the American Symphony Orchestra with pianist Natalie Hinderas playing Rachmaninoff's *Concerto No. 2* and a music festival celebrating the 100-year anniversary of Franz Liszt were

Impresario W. H. Williams. *A prominent theologian and educator, Williams was the first major African American presenter of classical music in the U.S.* COURTESY OF FOUR SEASONS ART

presented both in San Francisco and in New York. Major concert and opera singers such as Grace Bumbry, Dorothy Maynor, Roland Hayes, Charles Holland, William Warfield, Sherrill Milnes, Teresa Berganza, Ewa Podleś, Gérald Sousay, and Håkan Hagegård were given San Francisco Bay Area debuts by Williams. He began the Yachats Music Festival in Oregon in 1981, and established the Four Seasons Concerts in 1993, for which he served as president and artistic director until his death.

With all his involvement with music, Williams's first love was the church. He founded an interdenominational church, the Church for Today, in Berkeley in 1956. He served there as pastor until his death. He was also a professor at the San Francisco Theological Seminary and taught at the College of San Mateo. He remained very active in the community, and founded the Alamo Black Clergy, an interfaith ministerial group. He also formed the Center for Urban Black Studies at the Graduate Theological Union in Berkeley in 1969 and served as president and professor for twenty years. Williams was on the Board of Education in Berkeley for eight years, and lectured at many colleges and universities throughout the country. He died on April 24, 1999.

OLLY WOODROW WILSON (1937–)

Composer, Educator. Olly Wilson was born in St. Louis, Missouri, on September 7, 1937, and was educated in public schools. He studied the piano and clarinet at an early age and played in his church choir and in the high school band. He graduated from Washington University in St. Louis in 1959 with a bachelor's degree, and pursued graduate studies at the University of Illinois at Urbana and the University of Iowa, where he earned a Ph.D. in 1964. In 1974, he was awarded the prestigious American Academy and Institute of Arts and Letters Award.

The diversity of Wilson's interests and the breadth of his vision are indicated by his study of electronic music in 1967 at the University of Illinois—he won the Dartmouth Arts Council Prize in the International Competition for Electronic Compositions with Cetus in 1968—and his trips to Ghana in 1971 and 1978 to study African music. Wilson taught at Florida A&M University and the Oberlin Conservatory of Music in Ohio during the 1960s. In 1970, he joined the faculty of the Department of Music at University of California, Berkeley, where he held several positions, including associate dean of the graduate division and department chair, before retiring in 2002. Not only has he been a prolific composer, but he has also written many articles on various aspects of contemporary music in general and African American music in particular.

Since the 1970s, Wilson has written mostly in the orchestral medium. His compositions include: *Akwan*, for piano/electric piano and orchestra (1972); *Spirit Song*, for soprano, double chorus, and orchestra (1972), which the composer described as "about the evolution and development of the black spiritual"; *Lumina*, for orchestra (1981); *Of Visions and Truth*, for vocal soloists and chamber orchestra (1990–1991); *Hold On*, for orchestra (1997–1998); and *Episodes*, for large orchestra (2001). His musical style is all-encompassing. He has mastered the Western European, twentieth-century tradition, as well as African American vernacular music and African rhythmic and pitch practices.

LAWRENCE WINTERS (1915–1965)

Singer. In a time when very few African Americans had careers in classical music, bass-baritone Lawrence Winters had a career that spanned about twenty years. He was born in 1915 in Salisbury, North Carolina, and began studying singing privately there, before entering Howard University in Washington, D.C. He earned a bachelor of music degree in 1944, while studying with Todd Duncan. After college, he joined the Eva Jessye Choir, and sang the leading role in a concert production of *Ouanga* by Clarence Cameron White. He then joined the U.S. Armed Forces and became the music director in the Special Services Division at Fort Huachuca in Arizona.

When World War II ended, Winters moved to New York City in 1946, and appeared on Broadway in the musical revue *Call Me Mister*. The following year, he made his Town Hall recital debut, as well as his operatic debut at New York City Opera as Amonasro in Verdi's *Aida*. He appeared in a number of roles with the company until 1955, including the four villains in Offenbach's *The Tales of Hoffmann*, Escamillo in Bizet's *Carmen*, Alfio and Tonio in a double bill of *Cavalleria rusticana* and *Pagliacci*, the title role in Verdi's *Rigoletto*, the Count in Mozart's *The Marriage of Figaro*, Joe in Kern's *Show Boat*, and Germont in Verdi's *La traviata*.

During this time, Winters was also concertizing and performing with companies in Europe, including the Royal Swedish Opera and Hamburg State Opera. In 1957, he made his New York Philharmonic debut in a performance of concert arias. He also sang at the Vienna State Opera and the San Francisco Opera, and was the principal baritone at the Deutsche Oper Berlin from 1957 to 1961. In 1960, he returned to Broadway in a non-singing role, Tyree Tucker in Ketti Frings's play *The Long Dream*, for which he earned a Tony Award nomination.

His final performance at the New York City Opera was as Porgy in a production of Gershwin's *Porgy and Bess*. His last years were spent at the Hamburg State Opera, where he was principal baritone until his death in 1965.

23

SACRED MUSIC TRADITIONS

Christopher A. Brooks

African American sacred music—whether songs of enslaved Africans, early religious songs, spirituals, or gospel music—is an expression of African American culture that is no less significant than blues and jazz. Rooted in the enslavement experiences of Africans brought to the New World, African American sacred music was later influenced by evangelical Protestant Christianity and was performed at African American churches and camp-meeting revivals. As time passed, it took on different forms and gained wider acceptance among European and white American concert audiences. Today, through live performances and commercial recordings, African American sacred music encompasses a wide range of styles and types of ensembles, and it reaches audiences worldwide. It is also recognized as a vital element in America's cultural heritage.

EARLY INFLUENCES ON AFRICAN AMERICAN SACRED MUSIC

SYNCRETIZED RELIGIONS OF THE AFRICAN DIASPORA

Of the more than twenty million Africans who were brought to the New World, the vast majority were enslaved from the sixteenth century through the middle of the nineteenth century. Despite the enslavement experience, many New World Africans maintained and practiced some variation of their traditional beliefs, culture, and musical heritage, often combining these traditions with European influences, especially in their religious practices. Many Africans in the New World—especially those in Catholic-colonized areas—may have become Christians, but they continued to practice their traditional African belief systems, which they adapted to Western religions. These syncretized religions provided fertile ground for maintaining ritualized African chanting practices and song styles, even though their worshipping practices were nominally Christian. Examples of such New World syncretized religions include Candomblé in Brazil, Santería in Cuba and Puerto Rico, Vodun in Haiti, and, to a lesser extent, Kumina in Jamaica. There is still a rich musical tradition associated with many of these religious beliefs, although local musical influences came into play as well. Many of these sacred music practices survived in one form or another well into the twentieth century.

AMERICAN COLONIAL AND ANTEBELLUM PERIODS

Most musical activity in American colonial society was vocal, although there are late eighteenth-century paintings that depict enslaved Africans playing string instruments and dancing. Since much of American colonial society (both black and white) was not literate, collective song teaching (as in a church service, for example) was accomplished using a technique known as *lining out.* This process involved a leader who sang a line or two of a song or hymn, sometimes overenunciating the words. The congregation followed by repeating the line or lines after the leader. This method remains in use in some rural African American churches.

Other indications of early African American musical activity can be gleaned from eighteenth-century newspapers from Massachusetts, New York, and Virginia. When papers in these areas reported missing or fugitive Africans, they frequently commented on their musical ability (on a particular instrument, for example), along with a physical description of the fugitive.

The period after the American Revolutionary War (1775–1783) saw the emergence of two important African American institutions: self-help benevolent societies and the African independent church movement. The benevolent societies—such as the African Union Society (Rhode Island), the Free African Society (Philadelphia), the Brown Fellowship (Charleston), the Society of Free Africans (Washington, D.C.), and the African Society of Boston—were among a number of pseudo-religious moral-aid groups that were formed to help recently freed African Americans. The Free African Society, founded in 1787 by the celebrated religious leaders Richard Allen (1760–1831) and Absalom Jones (1746–1818), was initially begun as a burial society but expanded its role by establishing African free schools among other means of assisting the race.

By the late eighteenth and early nineteenth centuries, several independent African churches began emerging in both southern and northern states. Many churches in the South, however, were either closely scrutinized or shut down as a result of uprisings that were planned or carried out by insurrectionists, such as Gabriel Prosser in Richmond, Virginia (1800), Denmark Vesey in Charleston, South Carolina (1822), and Nat Turner outside Southampton, Virginia (1831). Nat Turner had considerable knowledge of the Old and New Testaments and used this knowledge to recruit participants. While the Gabriel Prosser, Denmark Vesey, and Nat Turner campaigns were among the better-known movements, more than two hundred similar actions were staged between 1800 and 1850.

By the late eighteenth century, Methodism had attracted large numbers of African Americans because of its official antislavery stance. Richard Allen established the African Methodist Episcopal (AME) Church in 1794 after a break with the mostly white Old St. George's Methodist Church in Philadelphia (in 1816 the AME Church formally separated from the mother Methodist Church). In 1801 Allen published a volume of religious songs titled *A Collection of Spiritual Songs and Hymns from Various Authors*. It eventually became the most widely used religious songbook in African American Protestant churches around the United States and, by the end of the nineteenth century, the eleventh edition was published with notated music.

Another African American religious phenomenon of the early nineteenth century involved the camp meeting. These outdoor multiday religious services were inspired by the Second Great Awakening movement that spread across the United States in that century. Many African American participants were known to perform dances, including the *ring shout* and *shuffle step*. Such religious behavior was criticized by some purists, including Richard Allen, but gained acceptance among African American worshippers who were unschooled or had rural religious leanings.

THE EMERGENCE OF SPIRITUALS IN THE NINETEENTH CENTURY

Spirituals were perhaps the most significant musical contribution of the enslaved African population of the nineteenth century. Spirituals have attracted the most attention from collectors, scholars, and those with a casual interest in African American sacred music. They were an outgrowth of the African American enslavement experience and Protestant Christianity. A similar tradition apparently did not develop on the African continent or anywhere else within nations of the African diaspora. So to that degree, spirituals are, from all existing evidence, uniquely American.

There are few absolute features that can be pointed to when trying to distinguish one spiritual from another. An up-tempo song such as "A Great Camp Meetin'" might have been called a *jubilee*, while the equally spirited "I'm Gonna Lift Up a Standard for My King" might have been regarded as a *shout*. The terms *plantation songs*, *slave songs*, and *sorrow songs* were also used to describe spirituals. A standard feature of the spiritual, however, was its use of African American dialect. One of the earliest collections of spirituals was *Slave Songs of the United States* (1867), a collaborative work by William Allen (1830–1889), Charles Ware (1840–1921), and Lucy McKim Garrison (1842–1877), all of whom had abolitionist backgrounds. In the book's preface, they commented on the uniqueness of African American vocal styles and the inability of conventional nineteenth-century Western musical notation to accurately transcribe such vocal effects as screams, yodels, falsetto, and glissandi.

It was the apparent disregard of these performance practices, among other factors, that would lead some twentieth-century scholars, such as George Pullen Jackson (1874–1953), Newman Ivey White (1892–1948), and Donald Wilgus (1918–1989), to promote a "white" spiritual theory. They argued that because it was Europeans who gave Christianity to enslaved Africans, Europeans also gave the New World Africans music with which to worship. This argument has been soundly refuted, however, on the basis that Jackson and others compared only printed versions of spirituals (arranged in Western musical notation) to those of Western European folk songs and saw similarities in melodies and time signatures. This school of thought also neglected to

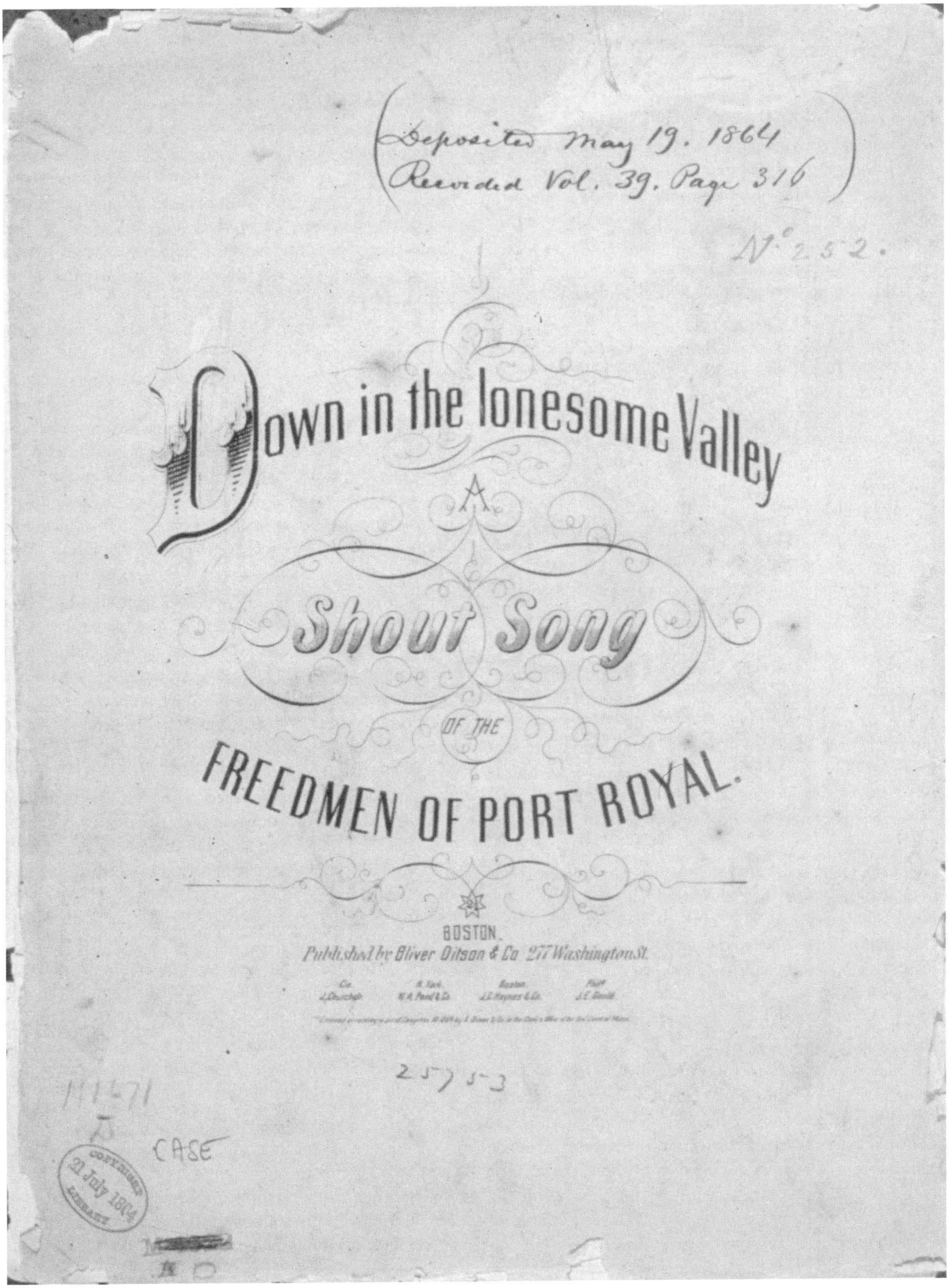

Title Page of Sheet Music for "Down in the Lonesome Valley: A Shout Song of the Freedmen of Port Royal" (1864). *Spirituals were perhaps the most significant musical contribution of the enslaved African population during the nineteenth century.* THE LIBRARY OF CONGRESS

acknowledge that the majority of spirituals employ a call-and-response performance technique, which was not a traditional feature of Western European folk songs.

ALERT SONGS AND MAP SONGS

Although they functioned in entirely different capacities, *alert songs* and *map songs* were related to spirituals. The lyrics for alert songs were ostensibly religious, but these songs expressed coded messages or signals about escape attempts or plans for secret meetings of enslaved African Americans. Examples of such songs included "Steal Away to Jesus," "Good News, the Chariot's Comin'," "Wade in the Water," and "I'm Packin' Up." Harriet Tubman (c. 1821–1913), the celebrated Underground Railroad conductor, was known to use the alert song "Wade in the Water." Wading in the water in the religious context was a reference to baptism, and the line "God's gonna trouble the water" meant God would wash away the sins of the newly baptized. In addition to the religious meaning, however, there was a functional meaning for the phrase "wade in the water." By wading in water, runaways could mask their body scent, which made it more difficult for search dogs to track them.

Another well-known alert song, "Moses," also had a strategic function:

> Moses, Moses, don't you let king pharaoh over-
> take you, (repeated)
> In some lonesome graveyard.

On the surface, this song was a call to the faithful to stay strong in the religion, but the "graveyard" was the operational word, designating a likely meeting place. Such secret meetings were sometimes used to plan undercover activities.

Map songs were designed to give directions to fugitives. In the song "Sheep, Sheep, Don't You Know the Road?" the word *road* could have encoded a message about an escape route. "Follow the Drinkin' Gourd," another map song, was a metaphoric allusion to the Big Dipper, which escapees were directed to follow north to freedom.

It was clear that by the 1870s the genre known alternately as spirituals, plantation songs, and jubilees was inextricably linked to the African American enslavement experience, and it was viewed by much of the American public as an acceptable form of religious expression. Evidence of this can be seen in the large numbers of spiritual collections that appeared throughout the balance of the nineteenth century and well into the twentieth century. Volumes and collections such as *Hampton and Its Students* (1874), *The Story of the Jubilee Singers* (1877), *The Jubilee Singers* (1883), *Jubilee and Plantation Songs* (1884), *Old Plantation Melodies* (1899), *Songs of the Confederacy and Plantation Songs* (1901), *Nine Negro Spirituals* (1918), and *Book of Negro Spirituals* (1938) illustrate this point.

SPIRITUAL CONCERTS

Attention was being drawn to spirituals not only through collections, essays, books, and articles, but through live performances as well. By the late 1880s, concerts of spirituals had become a fund-raising vehicle for several struggling African American colleges, notably Fisk University, Hampton Institute, and, to a lesser extent, Tuskegee Institute. Several of these groups made highly successful overseas tours in what Paul Fritz Laubenstein referred to as the *Ausbreitung* (spreading) of the music around the European continent.

By the 1890s, with the frequency and popularity of these overseas tours, European and American audiences were exposed to a different kind of African American music that stood in contrast to the music featured in minstrel shows. When the celebrated Bohemian composer Antonín Dvořák (1841–1904) recognized the uniqueness of this music and encouraged his students, including Harry T. Burleigh (1866–1949) and Will Marion Cook (1869–1944), to compose and arrange spirituals, the genre gained a new level of acceptance and recognition.

Other musicians, including R. Nathaniel Dett (1882–1943), also composed and arranged spirituals. Dett, an instructor at Hampton Institute, was best known for organizing a choir composed of students and community members and transforming the group into an internationally renowned touring organization that specialized in African American sacred music. Many of the songs that the choir performed were Dett's own compositions or arrangements of spirituals. Among his choristers was the celebrated soprano Dorothy Maynor (1910–1996), who became a distinguished concert singer and recitalist.

On several occasions, Dett was compelled to defend his performance of "arranged" spirituals, which were not considered to be as authentic as "folk" versions that were accompanied by claps, body swaying, and shouts. Several white observers and benefactors, such as George Foster Peabody (1852–1938), saw the Dett arrangements as imitations of white classical composers and, as such, not genuine. Nevertheless, the Hampton group conducted a highly successful tour of Europe in 1930.

The first all-spiritual solo recital seems to have been presented by Paul Robeson (1898–1976) in 1925. Robeson frequently performed spirituals in his many concerts throughout Europe, and he included them in some of his Hollywood films. Roland Hayes (1887–1977), who was born and raised in rural northeast Georgia, learned and began performing spirituals even earlier than Robeson. As a professional singer, Hayes became internationally renowned for his solo recitals, which successfully programmed Western art music with African American spirituals. He also arranged spirituals throughout his long career.

The practice of arranging spirituals continued in the skillful hands of other musical luminaries, such as Hall Johnson (1888–1970), John W. Work (1901–1967), Florence Price (1888–1953), J. Rosamond Johnson (1873–1954), W. C. Handy (1873–1958), Edward Boatner, (1898–1981), and William Dawson (1899–1990). In a later generation, Moses Hogan (1957–2003) and Jacqueline Hairston have been among those who continued the tradition.

The number of live performances and the recorded legacy of African American concert singers featuring spirituals in their recitals continued to grow throughout the twentieth century and into the twenty-first in the artistry of such singers as Marian Anderson (1897–1993), Roland Hayes, Dorothy Maynor, Todd Duncan (1903–1998), Robert McFerrin (1921–2006), Leontyne Price, Shirley Verrett, Jessye Norman, Kathleen Battle, Florence Quivar, Simon Estes, George Shirley, William Warfield (1920–2002), and Benjamin Matthews (1934–2006), who routinely devoted a section of their solo recitals to sacred songs. It has become, in fact, the expectation that African American vocalists will include them as part of their programs.

In 1999 Robert Sims, William Warfield, and Benjamin Matthews formed a group called Three Generations, which explored the African American spiritual repertoire from the three generations represented by the group's members—that is, from the group's oldest member, Warfield, to Matthews, to Sims, the youngest. The group continued after the death of Warfield in 2002. After Matthews died in 2006, Robert Sims, based in Chicago, emerged as one the country's eminent practitioners of the spiritual repertoire.

HOLY DANCING, CHURCH SONG CONCERTS, AND SHOUT PREACHERS

Although much scholarly and casual interest has been focused on spirituals, other African American sacred music traditions had emerged by the end of the nineteenth century as the African American church movement gained momentum. By the 1890s, the Holiness and Sanctified church movement had crystallized. The largest denomination within this religious development, the Church of God in Christ, was founded by the Memphis-based religious leader Charles H. Mason (1866–1961), formerly of Lexington, Mississippi. Collectively, the Holiness and Sanctified churches believed in spirit possession, speaking in tongues (a form of glossolalia), and improvisational singing. "Holy dancing" was also seen as an acceptable form of religious behavior. Certain instruments, such as drums, tambourines, triangles, guitars, and cymbals, were frequently used to accompany singing.

At the turn of the twentieth century, Reverend Charles Albert Tindley (c. 1851–1933), played a role in what would come to be called *gospel music*. Tindley was a Maryland-born Methodist camp-meeting preacher and singer who settled in Philadelphia in the 1870s. There, in 1902, he founded the East Calvary Methodist Episcopal Church, later renamed Tindley Temple. A talented musician, Tindley established a practice of sponsoring periodic concerts of church songs and had many of his compositions published in a 1916 collection titled *New Songs of Paradise*. The collection was so popular that several subsequent editions were still in print in the 1940s.

While Tindley was supported by his congregation, other religious songwriters received support from such organizations as the National Baptist Convention, which was founded in the 1890s. The convention offered groups opportunities to perform, and helped congregations and individuals become familiar with religious music. In 1921 the National Baptist Convention published *Gospel Pearls*, a collection of 165 religious songs. This work became enormously popular in African American congregations without regard for denomination.

By the 1920s, singing ministers, or so-called shout preachers, began recording three- to five-minute sermons and song performances, which might include contributions from a congregation or a small choir. Celebrated names in this tradition were F. W. McGee (1890–1971) of Memphis, J. C. Burnett of Kansas City, Theodore Frye (1899–1963) of Missouri, E. H. Hall of Chicago, and A. W. Nix and J. M. Gates (1884–1945) of Atlanta. Reverend Nix was one of the premiere singing preachers; his recorded works included "Black Diamond Express to Hell" (parts 1 and 2), "Goin' to Hell and Who Cares," and "Death May Be Your Christmas Present." He recorded close to fifty sung sermons for the Vocalion label.

As one of the best known of the shout preachers, Reverend J. M. Gates's style was captured in several recordings that were rereleased in compact-disc format in the 1990s. Mini-sermons such as "Mannish Woman," in which he challenged women who walked like men and men who walked like women, are among the many that have been preserved. "Death's Black Train Is Comin'," "Praying for the Pastor," "There's One Thing I Know," "The Need of Prayer," and "Down Here Lord, Waiting on You" are among Gates's extensive recorded religious performances. When he passed away in Atlanta in 1945, thousands of African American faithful attended his funeral.

THE RISE OF GOSPEL MUSIC IN THE TWENTIETH CENTURY

Although the term *gospel music* did not become standard in reference to a specific African American sacred musical genre until the 1930s, its predecessors were established earlier. Many scholars regard Chicago as the birthplace of gospel music because many of its churches nurtured pioneering singers and composers. The figure most closely associated with the rise of so-called blues-based gospel was Thomas A. Dorsey (1899–1993), commonly known as the father of gospel music.

THOMAS DORSEY, WILLIE MAE FORD SMITH, AND MAHALIA JACKSON

Born in rural Georgia to a minister and a local organist, Dorsey moved to Chicago in 1916, where he pursued a career as a blues musician. During this period, he continued to foster his childhood interest in religious music. He attended the National Baptist Convention in 1920, and one of his songs was later published in the convention's collection of religious songs, *Gospel Pearls*. By the 1930s, Dorsey had become devoted to composing and promoting religious music. In 1931 he formed the world's first gospel choir at Ebenezer Baptist Church in Chicago, and he opened the first publishing company devoted to the sale of gospel music. With his colleague Sallie Martin (1895–1988), he founded the National Convention of Gospel Choirs and Choruses as a vehicle for training choirs and soloists. More than any single individual, Dorsey was responsible for elevating gospel music to its current professional status.

Thomas A. Dorsey **(seated)** ***with His Female Gospel Quartet*** **(left to right)*****: Bertha Armstrong, Dettie Gay, Mattie Wilson, and Sallie Martin, Chicago, 1934.*** *In 1931, Dorsey, with Theodore Frye, organized at Ebenezer Baptist Church in Chicago what is generally recognized as the world's first gospel chorus.* **FRANK DRIGGS COLLECTION/ARCHIVE PHOTOS/GETTY IMAGES**

In addition to Martin, who also acted as Dorsey's business manager and was a celebrated figure in gospel music in her own right, Dorsey discovered a talented singer, Willie Mae Ford Smith (1904–1994). In 1936 Dorsey appointed Smith as director of the Soloists Bureau of the National Convention of Gospel Choirs and Choruses. Smith later abandoned what would have been a prominent career as a gospel singer to become an ordained evangelist in the Holiness Church of God Apostolic.

Among Dorsey's other celebrated discoveries was Mahalia Jackson (1912–1972), who became gospel music's first international star. Dorsey first met her in 1929 and became her accompanist between 1937 and 1946. Jackson began a recording career in the 1930s, but did not achieve national fame until she recorded "Move on Up a Little Higher," by the celebrated Memphis minister and composer, Reverend W. Herbert Brewster (1897–1992). The song sold over one million copies. Jackson toured extensively in Europe, gaining a wide following in several countries. While the civil rights movement was in full swing in the 1960s, gospel music became its unofficial sound track, and many gospel songs became the basis for freedom songs of the civil rights era. Mahalia Jackson was a major supporter of the Reverend Dr. Martin Luther King Jr. (1929–1968) and reached an international audience when she sang at the Lincoln Memorial during the 1963 March on Washington.

GOSPEL QUARTETS AND CHOIRS

By the end of the 1930s, gospel music had established at least two generic types of performing groups. The first was the all-male *gospel quartet*, sometimes made up of four or five singers, dressed in business suits, who sang *a cappella* in barber shop–style harmonies. The second was the *gospel chorus*, or choir, which could include seven to ten women and men (or all women) dressed in choir robes and accompanied by piano or organ. Prominent gospel quartets included the Golden Gate Jubilee Quartet, the Famous Blue Jay Singers, the Jubilaires,

Mahalia Jackson, Easter Sunday, Philharmonic Hall, Lincoln Center ***(Milton Glaser, 1967).*** *Gospel music's first international star, contralto Mahalia Jackson, sang at the historic March on Washington in 1963.* **MILTON GLASER/ART RESOURCE, NEW YORK**

the Mighty Clouds of Joy, the Fairfield Four, the Soul Stirrers, and the Five Blind Boys of Mississippi. Notable gospel choirs included the Ford Family Quartet, the Roberta Martin Singers, the Clara Ward Singers—another group that Thomas Dorsey would discover and help to promote—and later the Barrett Sisters.

THE GOLDEN AGE OF GOSPEL

Gospel music experienced a golden age from the mid-1940s to the 1950s when, in addition to the numerous recordings that were made, such women as Lucie Campbell (1885–1963), Roberta Martin (1907–1969), Queen C. Anderson (1913–1959), Ruth Davis (d. 1970), Dorothy Loves Coates (1928–2002), Edna Gallmon Cooke (1917–1967), and Bessie Griffin (1922–1989) became celebrated names in the gospel business. Their male counterparts were Julius Cheeks (1929–1981), Archie Brownlee (1925–1960), Brother Joe May (1912–1972), Alex Bradford (c. 1926–1978), James Cleveland (1932–1991), Claude Jeter (1914–2009), and Ira Tucker (1925–2008), among others. By the end of this period, gospel music had shaken itself free of its Pentecostal/Holiness roots to reach widespread acceptance in African American Protestant churches around the United States. Instrumentally, the organ became the standard accompanying instrument for most church-based gospel ensembles at this time.

By the 1960s, gospel music was undergoing other changes. Three decades earlier, religious singers such as Sister Rosetta Tharpe (1915–1973) had performed gospel music outside the church in New York's Apollo Theater.

Beamon Singers Gospel Choir, Presentation of Gospel Singer Stamps, House of Blues, Cambridge, MA, 1998. *Part of the Legends of American Music series, the Gospel Singer stamps depict four of gospel's most innovative female vocalists (*clockwise from top left*): Mahalia Jackson, Roberta Martin, Clara Ward, and Sister Rosetta Tharpe. The stamps were released on July 15, 1998.* AP PHOTO/PATRICIA MCDONNELL

However, when groups like the Clara Ward Singers performed at the Newport Jazz Festival in 1957 and, subsequently, in nightclubs in the early 1960s, gospel music blended with other popular musical genres and reached a crossover audience. Such gospel groups as the Staple Singers and the Edwin Hawkins Singers scored individual successes. Edwin Hawkins's 1969 recording of "O Happy Day" sold over a million copies, landing it on both religious and popular music charts. Large community-based gospel choirs, such as the Mississippi Mass Choir, the Abyssinian Choir led by Alex Bradford, the Greater Metropolitan Church of Christ Choir led by Isaac Whittmon, the Harold Smith Majestics, the Donal Vail Choraleers, the Charles Ford Singers, the Triboro Mass Choir led by Albert Jamison, the Chicago Community Choir led by Jessy Dixon, the Voices of Tabernacle led by James Cleveland, and the Michigan State Community Choir led by Mattie Moss Clark, made successful recordings and tours around the United States. Soloists and small groups that emerged in their own right during this era included Shirley Caesar, Albertina Walker, DeLois Barrett Campbell and the Barrett Sisters (Rhodessa Barrett Porter and Billie Barrett GreenBey), the O'Neal Twins (Edward O'Neal Jr. [1937–1990] and Edgar O'Neil [1937–2008]), and Marion Williams (1927–1994), who had been a member of the Clara Ward Singers.

CONTEMPORARY GOSPEL SOUNDS

Since the 1970s, gospel music has reached a mainstream audience and become a commercially viable tradition. In vocal harmony music, the groups Sweet Honey in the Rock and Take 6 have continued the tradition of gospel quartets and small choral groups. An *a cappella* group of female vocalists that performs an eclectic mix of political music, folk songs, spirituals, and gospel, Sweet Honey in the Rock's album *Feel Something Drawing Me On* (1989) focused on sacred music. Take 6, a male ensemble of Seventh-day Adventists, won Grammy Awards for its original song "Spread Love" (1988) and for the albums *Take 6* (1988) and *So Much 2 Say* (1991).

The tradition has also produced a number of popular musicians, such as Sam Cooke (1931–1964), Lou Rawls (1933–2006), Aretha Franklin, Ray Charles (1930–2004), Al Green, Stevie Wonder, Bobby Womack, and Johnnie Taylor (1938–2000). In fact, Sam Cooke, who had been a lead singer with the Soul Stirrers, was among the first gospel singers to have a successful crossover career and achieve equal success as a popular music performer. Other contemporary musicians who have remained more or less within the tradition while reaching large crossover audiences include Andraé Crouch, Tramaine Hawkins, Walter Hawkins, Lynette Hawkins, Jessy Dixon, the Winans Family, and Kirk Franklin.

Andraé Crouch, Sandra Crouch, and Edwin Hawkins, Gospel Singers. *In addition to their gospel music careers, Andraé Crouch (*left*) and his twin sister Sandra (*center*) are pastors of the New Christ Memorial Church in San Fernando, California. Hawkins's (*right*) 1969 recording of "O Happy Day" sold over a million copies on both religious and popular music charts.* RICK DIAMOND/WIREIMAGE FOR THE RECORDING ACADEMY/GETTY IMAGES

During the 1990s, gospel came under the influence of rap music, although gospel musicians referred to their performances as "street poetry." Large ensembles, such as Sounds of Blackness, have used rap music to reinvent sacred songs, while gospel quartets, such as the Williams Brothers, have incorporated synthesizers and percussion overdubs into their modern version of gospel. These innovations have sparked controversy among performers and listeners devoted to more traditional styles of gospel music.

While most gospel music continues to be performed at religious services and African American community events across the United States, it is now recognized as a truly significant aspect of America's cultural heritage. Its importance is reflected in the Smithsonian Institution publication *We'll Understand It Better By and By: Pioneering African American Gospel Composers* (1992) and the Smithsonian's gospel music collection *Wade in the Water* (1994).

SACRED MUSIC COMPOSERS, MUSICIANS, AND SINGERS

(Some biographical profiles may appear in other chapters. To locate profiles more readily, please consult the index.)

YOLANDA ADAMS (1961–)

Singer. Yolanda Adams was born in Houston, Texas, on August 27, 1961, the oldest of six siblings. Her family offered her a solidly religious upbringing, and as a small child she created for herself an imaginary friend she called Hallelujah. She first sang a solo in church at age three. Adams grew up with the classic gospel sounds of James Cleveland and the Edwin Hawkins Singers, but hers was a musically eclectic household. Adams's mother, a pianist who majored in music in college, introduced her daughter to jazz, classical music, and rhythm and blues. Adams joined a gospel choir, the Southeast Inspirational Choir, shortly after her father's death when she was thirteen years of age.

Adams hoped to become a fashion model even as she embarked on a career as an elementary school teacher. However, her powerful voice propelled her to the forefront of the Southeast Inspirational Choir's performances; she performed a solo on the choir's 1980 hit "My Liberty." In 1986 well-known gospel producer, composer, and pianist Thomas Whitfield (1954–1992) heard the choir and wasted no time in approaching Adams. The result was the album *Just as I Am*, released in 1987 on Sound of Gospel Records.

Adams signed with the Tribute label in 1990, and between 1990 and 1997 released four successful albums, all of which won Stellar Awards, a prestigious gospel music industry honor. The albums *Through the Storm* (1991) and *Save the World* (1993) included songs that Adams still sings in concert, such as "The Battle Is the Lord's," but it was *More Than a Melody* (1995) that really moved her style sharply in the direction of secular urban contemporary music. The album was honored with a Soul Train Lady of Soul Award and a Grammy nomination. *Yolanda ... Live in Washington* (1996) also earned the singer a Grammy nomination.

In the years following the release of *More Than a Melody*, honors and opportunities have flowed Adams's way with increasing regularity. She performed on the 1996 Soul Train Music Awards, the 1997 Essence Awards, BET's *Teen Summit*, and the *Tonight Show*. She was also honored with an invitation to perform during Christmas festivities at the White House in 1995.

During the late 1990s, Adams's reputation continued to rise. In 1997 she was featured in the fifty-city Tour of Life, organized and headed by contemporary gospel singer and composer Kirk Franklin. That same year, she married stockbroker and former New York Jets football player Tim Crawford at Houston's First Presbyterian Church (they divorced in 2004), and she enrolled in the prestigious divinity program at Howard University in Washington, D.C.

In 2001 Adams won the award for best R&B/Soul or Rap Song for "Open My Heart" at the Soul Train Lady of Soul Awards. Her albums *The Experience* (2001) and *Mountain High ... Valley Low* (2006) both won Grammy Awards for Best Contemporary Soul Gospel Album.

VANESSA BELL ARMSTRONG (1953–)

Singer. Armstrong was born Vanessa Bell on October 2, 1953, in Detroit, Michigan. During the late 1980s, her combination of gospel music with the secular stylings of influences such as Aretha Franklin laid the groundwork for successful "crossover" gospel stars like Kirk Franklin, Yolanda Adams, and CeCe Winans.

Armstrong, whose father was a minister, began singing in Detroit churches when she was only four years old. In 1966 the gospel choir leader Mattie Moss Clark (1925–1994) heard the young Armstrong perform and took her under her wing. Soon Armstrong was performing with such artists as the Reverend James Cleveland, the Mighty Clouds of Joy, and the Winans Family.

After marriage and the birth of five children, Armstrong recorded her debut album, *Peace Be Still*, in 1984. The album was an immediate success, reaching the top of the gospel charts and winning Armstrong a

Singer Yolanda Adams and President George W. Bush, White House, Washington, DC, 2007. Adams has won four Grammys, including Best Gospel Performance in 2006 for Victory. KEVIN DIETSCH-POOL/GETTY IMAGES

recording contract with the R&B label Jive Records. In 1987 she performed the theme song for the television series *Amen* and appeared in the Broadway production *Don't Get God Started.* That year she also released her second album, *Vanessa Bell Armstrong,* which blended gospel with contemporary urban music. One of the album's singles, "You Bring Out the Best in Me," became a hit on the R&B charts and proved to be a strong seller. At the same time, Armstrong received criticism from some fans of traditional gospel who accused her of "selling out" and "backsliding."

In the early 1990s, Armstrong released four albums: *Wonderful One* (1990), *The Truth about Christmas* (1990), *Chosen* (1991), and *Something on the Inside* (1993). In 1995 she chose John P. Kee as the producer of her seventh album, *The Secret Is Out.* In 1998 Armstrong released the acclaimed *Desire of My Heart: Live in Detroit,* which featured performances by her father, Elder Jesse Bell, and Marvin Winans, pastor of Detroit's Perfecting Church. The album marked a strong return to traditional gospel themes, a move that pleased many fans. Armstrong followed with *Brand New Day* in 2001. She was presented with a lifetime achievement award by the Gospel Superfest in 2004. Her album *Walking Miracle* was released in 2007.

HORACE CLARENCE BOYER (1935–2009)

Scholar, Singer, and Curator. Horace Boyer was born in Winter Park, Florida, the fourth of eight children. Coming from a very religious family, he began performing religious music as a teenager with his brother James. Known as the Boyer Brothers, they recorded "Step by Step" and other works for several labels. Boyer received

Singer Vanessa Bell Armstrong, Essence Music Festival, New Orleans, LA, 2007. *A gospel singer with crossover success, Armstrong sang the opening theme song "Shine on Me" for the 1980s television show* Amen. *She was honored with a lifetime achievement award from Gospel Superfest in 1994.* DOUGLAS MASON/GETTY IMAGES

an undergraduate degree in 1957 from Bethune-Cookman College in Daytona Beach, Florida, and earned a master's degree (1964) and a doctorate (1973) from the Eastman School of Music in Rochester, New York. He taught at several universities, but held his longest tenure (1973–1999) at the University of Massachusetts at Amherst. He also served as curator of musical instruments at the National Museum of American History, part of the Smithsonian Institution, in Washington, D.C. Boyer was a prolific scholar, but his signature work is *How Sweet the Sound: The Golden Age of Gospel*, published in 1995. Despite the demands of his scholarly and educational work, Boyer directed several music groups in the New England area, and received numerous awards. He passed away at his home in Amherst on July 21, 2009.

SHIRLEY CAESAR (1938–)

Singer. The leading gospel music singer of her generation, Shirley Caesar was born in Durham, North Carolina, in 1938. One of twelve children born to gospel great "Big Jim" Caesar, Shirley sang in church choirs as a child. At age fourteen, she went on the road as a professional gospel singer, touring the church circuit on weekends and during school vacations. Known as Baby Shirley, Caesar joined the Caravans in 1958 as an opening act. When Inez Andrews left the Caravans in 1961, Caesar became the featured artist, and provided crowds with powerful performances of such songs as "Comfort Me," "Running for Jesus," and "Sweeping through the City."

After leaving the Caravans in 1966, Caesar formed her own group, the Shirley Caesar Singers, and became one of the reigning queens of modern gospel. Her first album, *I'll Go*, remains one of her most critically acclaimed. In 1969 she released a ten-minute sermonette with the St. Louis Choir that earned her a gold record. A multiple Grammy winner, Caesar delivers sermons at the Mount Calvary Word of Faith Church in Raleigh, North Carolina, between performances and recording dates.

REVEREND JAMES CLEVELAND (1932–1991)

Singer, Pianist, Composer. Known by such titles as King James and the Crown Prince, the Reverend James Cleveland emerged as a giant of the postwar gospel music scene. Cleveland's raw bluesy growls and shouts, likened to the vocal style of Louis Armstrong (1901–1971), appeared on more recordings than any other gospel singer of his generation.

Born on December 5, 1932, in Chicago, Illinois, Cleveland first sang gospel under the direction of Thomas Dorsey at the Pilgrim Baptist Church. Inspired by the keyboard talents of gospel singer Roberta Martin, Cleveland later began to study piano. In 1951 Cleveland joined the Gospelaires, a trio that recorded several songs for the Apollo label. With the Caravans, Cleveland arranged and performed on two hits, "The Solid Rock" and an up-tempo reworking of the song "Old Time Religion." By the mid-1950s, Cleveland's original compositions had found their way into the repertoires of numerous gospel groups, and he was performing with such artists as the Thorn Gospel Singers, the Roberta Martin Singers, Mahalia Jackson, the Gospel Allstars, and the Meditation Singers. In 1960 Cleveland formed the Cleveland Singers, featuring organist and accompanist Billy Preston (1946–2006). The group's well-received "Love of God," recorded with the Detroit-based Voices of Tabernacle, won Cleveland national recognition within the gospel community. Recording for the Savoy label,

Cleveland released a long list of classic albums, including *Christ Is the Answer* and *Peace Be Still* (both 1962). As a founder of the Gospel Workshop of America in 1968, Cleveland organized annual conventions that brought together thousands of gospel singers and songwriters. A year later, he helped found the Southern California Community Choir.

In 1972 Cleveland was reunited with his former piano understudy Aretha Franklin, who featured him as a guest artist on the album *Amazing Grace.* A recipient of the NAACP Image Award, Cleveland also acquired an honorary doctorate from Temple Baptist College. Although the commercial gospel trends of the 1980s caused Cleveland's career to slump, he continued to perform the gutsy blues-based sound that brought him recognition from listeners throughout the world. Cleveland died February 9, 1991, in Los Angeles.

ANDRAÉ CROUCH (1942–)

Singer, Pianist. An exponent of a modern pop-based gospel style, Andraé Edward Crouch became one of the leading gospel singers of the 1960s and 1970s. Born on July 1, 1942, in Los Angeles, Crouch grew up singing in his father's church. Along with his brother and sister, Crouch formed the Crouch Trio, which performed at their father's services, as well as on live Sunday-night radio broadcasts. In the mid-1960s, Crouch was "discovered" by white Pentecostal evangelists and subsequently signed a contract with Light, a white religious record label. Since then, Crouch has written numerous songs, many of which have become standards in the repertoire of modern gospel groups. Among his most famous songs are "I Don't Know Why Jesus Loved Me," "Through It All," and "The Blood Will Never Lose Its Power." In recognition for this work, Crouch received an American Society of Composers, Authors, and Publishers (ASCAP) Special Songwriter Award.

During the late 1960s, Crouch, inspired by the modern charismatic revival movement, began adopting street-smart language and an informal wardrobe. After forming the Disciples in 1968, Crouch recorded extensively and toured throughout the United States and Europe. His California style of gospel music combines rock, country music, and soul with traditional gospel forms. The Disciples won Grammys in 1975 for *Take Me Back* and in 1979 for *Live in London*, which also received a Dove Award. *This Is Another Day* garnered a Dove Award in 1976, as did Crouch's 1984 solo recording *No Time to Lose.*

Since the 1970s, Crouch's backup groups have incorporated both electronic and acoustic instruments, including synthesizers. The new approach earned six Grammys for Crouch during the years from 1975 to 1984. He recorded as a solo artist and was awarded the Gospel Music Excellence Award for best male vocalist in 1982 for *More of the Best.* During this period, Crouch was also instrumental in helping the Winans Family produce their first recordings.

On September 23, 1995, Crouch became the pastor of Christ Memorial Church of God in Christ, the same pulpit that had once been under his father's guidance. Nearly one year earlier, Crouch—a two-time NAACP Image Award recipient and one-time Golden Halo awardee—released *Mercy!*, his first album since 1984. His return was well-received, and he followed it up with more recordings, including *Pray* (1997), *Gift of Christmas* (1998), and *Mighty Wind* (2006). Crouch was inducted into the Gospel Hall of Fame in 1998.

THOMAS A. DORSEY (1899–1993)

Composer, Arranger, Music Promoter. Popularly known as the father of gospel music, Thomas A. Dorsey was born on July 1, 1899, in Villa Rica, Georgia, the son of a minister. Dorsey's mother was a local organist and her son's earliest teacher. Young Dorsey sang in church choirs and occasionally traveled with his father, accompanying him on pump organ or harmonium during the elder Dorsey's evangelizing trips. When he dropped out of school at around age thirteen, he began playing in a local saloon and adopted the stage name Barrelhouse Tom, which was one of many that he used. In 1916 Dorsey went to Chicago, and that city became his home base for the rest of his life. Between 1919 and 1921, he studied at the Chicago School of Composition and Arranging. He worked with the jazz group Will Walker's Whispering Syncopators in local Chicago clubs and scored a triumph when his song "Riverside Blues" was recorded by the great cornetist Joseph "King" Oliver (1885–1938) in 1923.

Although Dorsey became a well-known blues musician as a result of his arrangements, compositions, performances, and recordings throughout much of the 1920s, his lasting contribution to the history of American music lay in his talent as a sacred music composer. As early as 1920, he experienced a religious rebirth at the National Baptist Convention, and one of his songs, "If I Don't Get There," appeared in a later edition of the convention's landmark collection, *Gospel Pearls*, first published in 1921. By 1927, he had begun promoting his religious songs in area churches, but was rejected by many ministers because of the arrangements' stylistic affinity to the blues.

In 1930 Dorsey's song "If You See My Savior" was performed at the National Baptist Convention to a tumultuous response. From that point on, he became more committed to composing, arranging, promoting, and recording gospel songs. In 1931, along with the singing

Thomas A. Dorsey, Chicago, c. 1959. *Composer and pianist Dorsey, whose father was a minister and whose mother was an organist, composed more than 400 gospel songs, including "Take My Hand, Precious Lord."* TED WILLIAMS/HISTORICAL/CORBIS

preacher Theodore Frye, he organized what is generally recognized as the world's first gospel chorus at Chicago's Ebenezer Baptist Church. During this period, Dorsey formed his own publishing company dedicated to selling gospel music and cofounded the National Convention of Gospel Choirs and Choruses, Inc., with his colleague Sallie Martin. The organization became a vehicle for training gospel choirs and coaching soloists. This booming period in Dorsey's career was not without personal tragedy, however. In 1932 his first wife, Nettie, died in childbirth. After this traumatic event, he composed his most celebrated work, "Take My Hand, Precious Lord." (The song was initially named "Take My Hand, Lord," but Frye suggested that the composer add *precious* to the title and opening of the song for emphasis.) It has been translated into more than fifty languages. Among Dorsey's most celebrated discoveries was Mahalia Jackson, who became gospel music's first international star. He served as her official accompanist between 1937 and 1946. Dorsey also promoted Clara Ward (1924–1973), along with many other singers and groups. Dorsey toured extensively in the 1930s and 1940s throughout the United States, Europe, Mexico, and North Africa, and he served as director of the National Convention of Gospel Choirs and Choruses, Inc., into the 1970s.

By the late 1970s, failing health forced Dorsey into semiretirement. He reemerged in a 1982 documentary, *Say Amen, Somebody*, in which he appeared with Mother Willie Mae Ford Smith. The documentary also featured footage of Dorsey's performances with several of his protégées, including Mahalia Jackson, the O'Neal Twins, DeLois Barrett Campbell, and the Barrett Sisters. By the late 1980s, Dorsey was suffering from the effects of Alzheimer's disease. He died in Chicago in 1993.

KIRK FRANKLIN (1970–)

Singer, Composer. Born in Fort Worth, Texas, in 1970, Kirk Franklin was reportedly abandoned by his teenage mother when he was an infant; he was adopted by his Aunt Gertrude, who was a strict Baptist. Being raised in a very religious environment, Franklin was teased by his friends, who called him "church boy." He began taking keyboard lessons at the age of four, and by the time he was eleven years old, he was leading the choir at Mount

Singer-Songwriter Kirk Franklin, Pritzker Pavilion, Chicago, 2009. *Gospel sensation Franklin has earned seven Grammys in the gospel genre and has also enjoyed success in crossing over to the R&B and pop charts as well.* RAYMOND BOYD/MICHAEL OCHS ARCHIVES/GETTY IMAGES

Rose Baptist Church near Dallas. After a troubled adolescence (which included impregnating a girl), Franklin eventually returned to his religious roots.

By the mid-1980s, Franklin was attracting the attention of religious music producers with his songs and choral works. In 1991 his compositions appeared on a recording by the Dallas–Fort Worth Mass Choir titled *I Will Let Nothing Separate Me*. By 1993 he had put together a seventeen-piece vocal group, the Family, and released his debut album, *Kirk Franklin and the Family*. Selections from this release generated crossover appeal, and Franklin's songs, while religious in text, were being played on rhythm-and-blues charts. While this caused his reputation to spread in pop music markets, it disturbed many gospel music purists who felt that the release was too pop-oriented. Franklin fueled these suspicions further by signing a record deal with B-Rite Records, which was associated with the rap label Death Row Records.

In 1995 Franklin and the Family released a Christmas recording, but his next major album, *Whatcha Lookin 4*, released in 1996, took Franklin's combination of rhythm and blues and gospel one further step—the album hit the pop charts running and scored on both the gospel and rhythm-and-blues charts. As with his first release, it won accolades among pop music followers, much to the disappointment of gospel music's conservative ranks. In 1997 Franklin was chosen as *Billboard Magazine*'s number-one gospel artist and number-one contemporary Christian artist, and he signed a multiyear recording contract with the B-Rite label. The next year, Franklin released *Nu Nation Project*, which contained biblical references and stylistically was a combination of rap music and gospel. His autobiography, *Church Boy*, was released that same year. In 2000 the Family filed a multimillion-dollar lawsuit against Franklin, claiming he had not paid them the appropriate royalties for a previous project. This led to the dissolution of the group, and Franklin began a solo career. With the release of a live album, *The Rebirth of Kirk Franklin*, in 2002, Franklin continued to receive critical and popular praise. *Rebirth* eventually went platinum. In 2007 Franklin released his tenth album, *The Fight for My Life*. Franklin is married to former rhythm-and-blues singer Tammy Renee Collins, and they have four children.

TRAMAINE HAWKINS (1957–)

Singer. Born Tramaine Davis in San Francisco, Hawkins began singing when she was only four years old in the Ephesian Church of God in Christ in Berkeley, California, where her grandfather was pastor. Though Hawkins developed her passion for gospel music during childhood, her career accelerated in 1969 when the Northern California State Choir, which she had joined, released "Oh Happy Day," which had been recorded the year before. Her first performance with the choir after the song's success was at Madison Square Garden.

As a child, Hawkins sang with the Sunshine Band and later with the Heavenly Tones. After eleven years together, the Heavenly Tones began to get offers to sing at secular events, but Hawkins felt her calling was sacred music. When the Northern California State Choir's name was changed to the Edwin Hawkins Singers and the choir started to do secular performances at venues like clubs with entertainers such as the Jackson Five and Diana Ross, Hawkins chose to leave the group.

For eleven months, she sang with Andraé Crouch's Disciples. But Hawkins missed her old group and rejoined it. In 1970, after touring Europe with the Edwin Hawkins Singers, she accepted a marriage proposal from Edwin's brother, Walter Hawkins. During their many years of marriage, she worked side by side with Walter, a singer, recording artist, composer, arranger, producer, and pastor. They later divorced, and Tramaine married Tommy Richardson, although she continued to work with Walter occasionally.

Hawkins has a controversial, contemporary style that has been criticized over the years. In 1985 she raised suspicion within the gospel community when her techno-funk hit "Fall Down," from the *Spirit of Love* album, topped the dance charts despite the religious content of its lyrics. In 1990 Hawkins gathered musicians and singers from outside the gospel field—including rock guitarist Carlos Santana (1947–), jazz organist Jimmy McGriff (1936–2008), and jazz tenor saxophonist Stanley Turrentine (1934–2000)—to participate in a live recording project. Her success in mixing traditional gospel, blues, jazz, and other singing styles helped create what is called *contemporary gospel.*

By 2009, Hawkins had recorded nine solo albums and won numerous awards, including two Grammys, two Dove Awards, and two Communications Excellence to Black Audiences Awards.

MAHALIA JACKSON (1912–1972)

Singer. Hailed as the world's greatest gospel singer during her lifetime, Mahalia Jackson's rich contralto voice became a national institution. Through her many live engagements, recordings, and television appearances, Jackson elevated gospel music to a level of popularity unprecedented in the history of African American religious music.

The third of six children, Jackson was born on October 26, 1912 (some sources indicate it was 1911), in New Orleans, Louisiana. Her given name was "Mahala," but she changed it to "Mahalia" in the early 1930s. Growing up in New Orleans, Jackson absorbed the sounds of parade music and brass bands. She later discovered the blues, a style labeled "devil's music" by regular churchgoers, and listened secretly to recordings of performers like Bessie Smith (1894–1937), whose singing was especially influential on Jackson's vocal style.

In 1927, at fifteen years old, Jackson moved to Chicago, where she joined the Greater Salem Baptist Church. Two years later, Jackson met the gospel musician and songwriter Thomas A. Dorsey, who invited her to sing at the Pilgrim Baptist Church. In 1937 Jackson recorded four sides for the Decca label, including the song "God's Gonna Separate the Wheat from the Tares."

Jackson's big break arrived in 1948 when she released gospel music's first million-selling recording, "Move On Up a Little," for the Apollo label. In 1949 her recording of the song "Let the Power of the Holy Ghost Fall on Me" won the French Academy's Grand Prix du Disque. Soon afterward, she toured Europe and recorded the gospel hit "In the Upper Room." During the 1960s, Jackson became a musical ambassador—not only did she perform at the White House and at London's Royal Albert Hall, but she sang before her largest audience at the historic 1963 March on Washington. She was asked by the Reverend Martin Luther King Jr. to sing at his funeral should she survive him. She sadly fulfilled this engagement after his assassination in 1968.

On January 27, 1972, Jackson died of a heart condition in Chicago. At her funeral at the Greater Salem Baptist Church, some 45,000 mourners gathered to pay their respects.

T. D. JAKES

See chapter 17, Religion.

BOBBY JONES (1939–)

Singer, Television Host. Bobby Jones, born in Paris, Tennessee, was a schoolteacher in Nashville for a time after earning his master's degree from Tennessee State University. He left his teaching job to become a textbook consultant specializing in elementary education. He then began teaching reading skills at Tennessee State University in the early 1970s. At about the same time, he began a second career as a singer on the gospel circuit and continued his activism in the local civil rights movement. In 1976 he helped develop Nashville's first Black Expo, which featured numerous workshops, and also attracted some of its fifty thousand attendees with a host of concerts.

Black Expo attracted the attention of local media executives and inspired Jones to suggest a local gospel show. The *Nashville Gospel Show* was a hit in the area, and in 1980 Jones was invited by Robert L. Johnson, founder of the fledgling Black Entertainment Television (BET) network, to produce an hour of gospel television for the new cable network. Similar to its counterparts in pop and soul, the show offered gospel fans live performances by well-known names in the industry, along with interviews and album reviews. Still on the air in 2010, *Bobby Jones Gospel* has become one of the longest-running programs on cable television. The show is also broadcast by the American Christian Network and the American Forces Radio and Television Service, giving Jones an audience of gospel fans around the world.

In 1989 Jones expanded his presence on BET with the half-hour show *Video Gospel,* which he hosted. 2010 marked his thirtieth year with BET. Jones has performed internationally, including engagements in Israel and Africa, and he sang at the White House for President

Jimmy Carter. Jones was also invited to perform at the Kennedy Center for the Performing Arts during the Reagan administration.

Jones also earned a doctorate in curriculum leadership from Vanderbilt University. In addition to his television responsibilities, he has brought an increased awareness to the gospel music form since 1989 with his live tours, known as Bobby Jones Gospel Explosions. His Mini-Explosions bring gospel music to audiences in smaller cities across the United States, as well as Europe and the Caribbean.

JOHN P. KEE (1962–)

Singer, Songwriter. Born into a religious family on June 4, 1962, in Charlotte, North Carolina, John Prince Kee was the fifteenth of sixteen children. By the age of thirteen, the musically gifted Kee formed his first gospel choir, and began studying voice and classical music at the North Carolina School of the Arts in Winston-Salem. Later, while attending California's Yuba College Conservatory of Music, Kee worked with such groups as Cameo and Donald Byrd & the Blackbirds. At this time, he also began using and selling cocaine, at one point going so far as to run a drug operation out of a church.

After Kee witnessed the murder of a close friend during a drug deal, he decided that his lifestyle was not only contrary to his religious upbringing, but potentially life-threatening. He decided to return to religion and gospel music, and in 1981 Kee formed the New Life Community Choir in Charlotte. The choir, which consisted of thirty inner-city recruits, was aimed at attracting the young and providing a safe place for them to flourish spiritually. Four years later, Kee received a break when he recorded "Jesus Can Do It All" and "He's My All and All" for James Cleveland's Gospel Music Workshop of America's (GMWA) annual mass choir album.

Kee and his choirs have recorded and performed prolifically since releasing *There Is Hope* in 1990. Their subsequent recordings include: *Never Shall Forget* (1991), *We Walk By Faith* (1992), *Lily in the Valley* (1993), *Colorblind* (1994), *Livin' on the Ultimate High* (1995), *Stand* (1996), *Not Guilty … The Experience* (2000), *Mighty in the Spirit* (2001), *Blessed by Association* (2002), *The Color of Music* (2004), and *The Reunion* (2005). Kee and his choirs have won two Billboard Music Awards and at least twenty GMWA Excellence Awards, and have earned several Grammy nominations.

Kee has produced albums by Shawn McClemore and New Image, Drea Randle, Vanessa Bell Armstrong, and the Victory in Praise Mass Choir. In addition to his role as a musician, choir director, and producer, Kee has run an inner-city youth program in Charlotte and served as a full-time minister. In 1995 he married Felice Sampson, and together they have nine children. He was inducted into the Christian Music Hall of Fame in 2007.

ROBERTA MARTIN (1907–1969)

Singer, Pianist. Roberta Martin, a gifted keyboardist, was born in Helena, Arkansas, on February 12, 1907. After moving to Chicago as a child, she had ambitions of becoming a concert pianist. Instead, she was hired as an accompanist for Thomas A. Dorsey and Theodore Frye's historic gospel junior choir at Ebenezer Baptist Church in the early 1930s. She cofounded, along with Frye, the Martin-Frye Quartet in 1933. The group subsequently became known as the Roberta Martin Singers. The group toured extensively in the 1940s and added new members, including a young lead soprano named DeLois Barrett. Martin also established a music publishing company and produced several of her many compositions, including "Try Jesus, He Satisfies" (1943), "Yield Not to Temptation" (1944, with Barrett as the soprano soloist), and "God Is Still on the Throne" (1959). Martin was also influential as an accompanist and promoted the careers of several other groups, including the Barrett Sisters. She died in Chicago on January 18, 1969, after a brief illness.

SALLIE MARTIN (1896–1988)

Singer. Born in Pittsfield, Georgia, on November 20, 1896 (some sources indicate 1895), Martin traveled to Chicago, Illinois, in 1919. Her church singing took on greater significance after she began a professional relationship with Thomas A. Dorsey. Martin auditioned for his choir at Ebenezer Baptist Church in the early 1930s, and they maintained an association for the next forty years. She became a song demonstrator for Dorsey, and they cofounded the National Convention of Gospel Choirs and Choruses, Inc., in 1932. Later, in 1940, Martin cofounded the Martin-Morris Music Company with musician Kenneth Morris (1917–1988). That same year, she began touring with her own group, the Sallie Martin Singers, throughout the United States and Europe. At various times, the group included Dinah Washington (1924–1963) and Brother Joe May (1912–1972).

As the civil rights movement gained momentum in the late 1950s and early 1960s, gospel music would be heavily identified with the human rights struggle. Martin was an active supporter of both the movement and its figurehead, Reverend Martin Luther King Jr. On several occasions, she represented him in his absence, such as at Nigeria's independence celebration in 1960. After retiring from live performing in the 1970s, she appeared in the *Gospel Caravan* in 1979 in France. In 1986 she was honored by the city of Chicago for her achievements as a singer, composer, and promoter of gospel music. She died two years later at the age of ninety-two.

MOTHER WILLIE MAE FORD SMITH (1904–1994)

Singer. Willie Mae Ford was born on April 21, 1904, in Rolling Forks, Mississippi. The Ford family moved to Memphis, Tennessee, when she was a young girl. Willie Mae had ambitions of becoming a concert singer, but decided to sing sacred music after hearing a performance by the singer Artelia Hutchins. In the early 1920s, Ford sang the lead in the Ford Family Quartet (made up of Willie Mae and her sisters), and they appeared at the National Baptist Convention in 1922 singing "Ezekiel Saw the Wheel" and "I'm in His Care." In 1932 she met Thomas A. Dorsey, who flattered her by saying that, had she been a blues singer, she could have outperformed Bessie Smith. In 1936 Dorsey appointed Willie Mae the director of the Soloists Bureau of the National Convention of Gospel Choirs and Choruses, Inc. In this role, she demonstrated the proper style and delivery of gospel songs to younger singers.

Because the Baptist Church did not ordain women or allow them to preach, Smith left in 1939 and joined the Holiness Church of God Apostolic. She thereafter became an ordained evangelist and limited her singing to religious services and revivals. As an evangelist, Smith frequently combined a brief sermon with a song, a form that became known as *sermonette and song*. In 1982 she was the subject of a documentary film about gospel music, *Say Amen, Somebody*, which featured footage of historic performances by Mahalia Jackson, the O'Neal Twins, and DeLois Barrett Campbell, as well as Smith's own performances. In 1988 "Mother Smith" was honored with a National Heritage Fellowship from the National Endowment for the Arts. Her last years were spent in a retirement community in Kansas City, Missouri, where she died in 1994.

SISTER ROSETTA THARPE (1915–1973)

Singer, Pianist, Guitarist. Rosetta Nubin was born on March 20, 1915, in Cotton Plant, Arkansas. Performing on the guitar and keyboard by the time she was four years old, she became known as Little Rosetta Nubin. Her mother, Katie Bell Nubin (1880–1969), was a singer in the Holiness Church of God in Christ. By the 1930s, Rosetta Tharpe began recording and making appearances in nightclubs. She appeared at New York's Cotton Club with Cab Calloway (1907–1994), accompanying herself on guitar.

In 1938 Tharpe performed gospel music as part of John Hammond's (1910–1987) *From Spirituals to Swing* show at Carnegie Hall in New York City. Tharpe subsequently performed with many well-known popular musicians, including Lucky Millinder (1900–1966), Benny Goodman (1909–1986), and eventually such blues musicians as Muddy Waters (1915–1983). However, Tharpe was principally known within religious circles for strong gospel singing and guitar playing. She later performed with the Dixie Hummingbirds and recorded with her mother. Their recording of "Daniel in the Lion's Den" became a gospel music classic. For a time, she also had a backup group known as the Rosettes. As a result of her many bus tours, Tharpe became particularly well known in rural areas of the South and Midwest. Tharpe eventually settled in Philadelphia, where she died on October 9, 1973.

CHARLES ALBERT TINDLEY (c. 1851–1933)

Composer. Believed to have been born on July 7, 1851, in Berlin, Maryland, Charles Tindley began preaching at outdoor religious gatherings, also known as camp meetings, in Maryland when he was a teenager. In the 1870s, he relocated to Philadelphia to continue his education. He furthered his religious studies by correspondence through Boston Theological Seminary and became an ordained minister in the mid-1880s. After preaching along the East Coast, Tindley returned to Philadelphia to pastor the East Calvary Methodist Episcopal Church, later renamed Tindley Temple in his honor. He held periodic religious music concerts at his church, which frequently featured songs that he had composed. His compositions include such standards as "We'll Understand It Better By and By," "What Are They Doing in Heaven Tonight," "Stand By Me," and "I'll Overcome Someday," which were published in his 1916 collection *New Songs of Paradise*. This hymnal was soon adopted by African American churches around the United States.

Frequently cited as a major influence on gospel music great Thomas A. Dorsey, Tindley helped set the stage for modern gospel music's emergence. He died on July 26, 1933, in Philadelphia.

ALBERTINA WALKER (1929–)

Singer. Affectionately known as the Queen of Gospel, Albertina Walker was born and raised on the South Side of Chicago, one of nine children in a hardworking Baptist family. Her mother was a member of the West Point Baptist Church, and Albertina and her sister Rose Marie both sang in the church's choir. When Walker was a little girl, the choir director formed a small children's gospel group called the Williams Singers. With this group, and occasionally as a duo, the Walker sisters performed in churches throughout Chicago and the Midwest.

The West Point Baptist Church hosted many gospel concerts during Walker's youth, and she was inspired by the performances of such great gospel singers as Sallie Martin, Roberta Martin, Mahalia Jackson, and Thomas A. Dorsey. When Walker entered her teens, she began singing at area Baptist and Holiness churches. The performances were broadcast on radio, which gave Walker an entry into the show business side of gospel music.

In 1952, after briefly performing with Robert Anderson's (1919–1995) ensemble, Walker formed a new group, the Caravans, with other members of Anderson's group and keyboardist James Cleveland. From the group's founding until the late 1960s, the Caravans dominated traditional gospel, performing throughout the United States and Europe and in such celebrated venues as New York's Apollo Theater, Carnegie Hall, and Madison Square Garden. After the Caravans disbanded in 1967, Walker began to perform as a soloist.

Walker was featured in the 1992 film *Leap of Faith* (with actors Steve Martin, Liam Neeson, and Debra Winger) as a member of a spirited gospel choir. In 1993 she received a Grammy Award nomination for *Albertina Walker Live*. That same year she performed a concert for Nelson Mandela during his visit to the United States. From her base in Chicago, she has been active in politics, working with the Reverend Jesse Jackson and organizing the Operation PUSH People's Choir. Her album *Songs of the Church* brought her a Grammy Award in 1995, and she received a Dove Award two years later for *Let's Go Back: Live in Chicago*. In 2006, Walker reunited with the Caravans to record the album *Paved the Way*. The album marked the first time in four decades that the group recorded new music together.

Walker is the founder of and one of the chief contributors to the Albertina Walker Scholarship Foundation, a source of educational funds for aspiring young gospel singers. She is generally recognized as one of the genre's greatest living performers.

MARION WILLIAMS (1927–1994)

Singer. Born in a poverty-stricken area of rural Miami in 1927, Marion Williams became one the last great singers of gospel music's golden age. By the time she was a teenager, she had a local reputation as a talented singer at several Miami-area African American churches. When Williams visited her sister in Philadelphia in the mid-1940s, she was invited to sing at her sister's church. In the audience was Philadelphia-based Clara Ward of the Clara Ward Singers. Ward persuaded Williams to join the group, and she eventually became a star with such works as "Packin' Up," which featured her high soprano yodels. Williams remained with the Clara Ward Singers until 1958, when she left the group after a dispute with Ward. Williams and several other members then formed the Stars of Faith, with whom Williams performed until embarking on a solo career in the mid-1960s.

One of Williams's definitive recordings from that period was "Even Me," which featured her quintessential high notes. After the death of the Reverend Martin Luther King Jr., Williams recorded a version of Thomas A. Dorsey's celebrated "Take My Hand, Precious Lord." Mahalia Jackson (who had sung the same song at King's funeral in Atlanta) described Williams's rendition as one of the finest performances she had ever heard. In 1993 Williams was awarded a MacArthur Foundation grant in recognition of her contributions to the country's musical legacy. That December, she was further recognized with the receipt of a Kennedy Center Honors award. She died the following year from a vascular condition on July 2, 1994, in Philadelphia.

THE WINANS FAMILY

Singing Group. Comprised of Benjamin "BeBe," Priscilla "CeCe," Marvin, Carvin, Michael, and Ronald (1956–2005), this Detroit-based gospel singing group has become one of gospel music's first families. The older Winans brothers, Marvin and Carvin, sang at their great-grandfather's Zion Congregational Church of Christ on Detroit's east side. The musical talents of the younger Winans children, especially BeBe and CeCe, were encouraged by their father, David "Pops" Winans Sr. (1934–2009), who was also a minister. He was the first to organize family members into a quartet, called the Testimonials. Under this name, the Winans produced two recordings *Love Covers* (1977) and *Thy Will Be Done* (1978).

The Winans family eventually came to the attention of the celebrated gospel musician Andraé Crouch, who was instrumental in helping to produce their first national release, *Introducing the Winans* (1981). The album was subsequently nominated for a Grammy Award. Two years later, another release, *Long Time Coming*, also received a Grammy nomination.

In 1987 BeBe and CeCe launched a duo career with the release *BeBe & CeCe Winans*, singing mostly jazz, rhythm and blues, and a few religious works. Their next release, *Heaven* (1988), included the songs "Heaven," "Lost Without You," and "Celebrate New Life." It reached gold-record status, rated highly on national rhythm-and-blues charts, and earned them four Grammy nominations. Their third album, *Different Lifestyles* (1991), reached number one on the national rhythm-and-blues charts. Since then, BeBe and CeCe have worked together and individually with other celebrated popular artists, including Whitney Houston, Bobby Brown, Gladys Knight, Luther Vandross (1951–2005), and Aretha Franklin. The brother-sister duo has also performed at Carnegie Hall, Culturefest in West Africa, and the 1993 inaugural celebration of President Bill Clinton. They released two additional albums, *Relationships* (1994) and *The Greatest Hits* (1996), in the 1990s.

In 2009 BeBe and CeCe released *Still*, their first album as a duo since 1996.

BeBe has recorded several solo albums, including *Love & Freedom* (2000), *Dream* (2004), and *Cherch* (2007). CeCe's numerous solo recordings include *Everlasting Love* (1998) and the self-titled *CeCe Winans* (2001), as well as *Throne Room* (2003) and *Thy Kingdom Come* (2008). *Thy Kingdom Come* was awarded a Grammy as Best Pop/Contemporary Gospel Album in 2009. The younger Winans sisters, Angie and Debbie, have recorded with the family; together, they garnered several Dove, Stellar, and Soul Train awards.

24

BLUES AND JAZZ

Christopher A. Brooks

As the world's most universal and diverse musical genre, jazz represents a long continuum of tradition coming out of the African American musical experience. This continuum began with the early arrival of enslaved Africans to America during the colonial period and developed over the next several centuries. As a synthesized genre, jazz grew out of three of its predecessors: black military-style brass bands (of the nineteenth century), ragtime (of the late nineteenth century and into the twentieth century), and most importantly, the blues.

THE BRASS BAND TRADITION

In the period following the War of 1812, all-black military-style brass bands began performing. These bands principally formed on the East Coast, but were also to be found in a few Midwestern states and in the South. They consisted of as many as ten pieces, including traditional band instruments such as trumpets, flutes, trombones, and drums. Philadelphia became a center of brass band activity because there were several well-known performers and groups there. Francis "Frank" Johnson (c. 1792–1844) became one of the most highly regarded of the musicians associated with the brass band tradition. By the time of his first published composition, *A Collection of New Cotillions* (1818), Johnson was well known in the Philadelphia area.

Throughout the 1820s, Johnson was frequently invited to perform at election day celebrations, concerts, cotillions, and other public and private engagements. He also managed to publish his works in an era when music publishing was relatively rare. Among those compositions were "Victoria Gallop," "Princeton Gallopade," "Philadelphia Gray's Quickstep," "The New Bird Waltz," and "Boone Infantry Brass Band Quickstep." He played in a variety of places around the country, including Cape May, New Jersey, Saratoga Springs, New York, and White Sulphur, Virginia.

Throughout the 1830s, Johnson continued his public performances and gathered other musicians who held tenure in his band. Among them were William Appo (c. 1808–c. 1871), Aaron J. R. Connor, Edward Roland, and Francis Seymour. In 1837, Johnson took a group of musicians to London to perform a series of concerts. Reputedly, he and his group played for the newly crowned Queen Victoria of England. The Queen supposedly presented him with a silver bugle. The music by Johnson, Connor, and others within the brass band tradition was clearly based on European art music models (or band arrangements of opera arias).

The importance of the tradition, however, was that performers and composers were all black, and the brass band tradition continued to develop throughout the nineteenth century. Bands similar to this could be found throughout the country in a variety of settings. By the end of the century, the all-black brass bands had become an American institution.

RAGTIME

There are at least two competing theories regarding the emergence of rag music as a genre. The first linked rag to the keyboard and suggested that during the period of African enslavement in America, the piano was one of few instruments that the enslaved blacks did not master (unlike string instruments). After the Civil War, blacks turned to the piano in unprecedented numbers. Even though many did not read music, they learned to play the instrument by rote (i.e., playing by ear). As a result, many black musicians began playing the keyboard.

The other theory surrounding rag music's emergence is linked to the brass band tradition. The primary characteristics of rag music were a syncopated melodic line played by the right hand, and an "oomp pah" bass pattern played by the left hand. According to the second theory, the bass line of the rag was an imitation of the low instruments in the brass bands.

First noticed in the 1890s, rag music became the most popular musical genre in the country by the turn of the century. It was also one of the first African American musical traditions to receive international recognition. Once composers such as Scott Joplin (1868–1917), Thomas Turpin (1871–1922), Louis Chauvin (1882–1908), and James Scott (1885–1938), among many others, began publishing their music and securing copyrights, their names were preserved in history and their creative genius was recognized. Western art music composers were also influenced by rag music and incorporated the syncopated melodic line and "oomp pah" bass pattern into their works. Composers such as Claude Debussy, Eric Satie, Igor Stravinsky, Paul Hindemith, and Aaron Copland were among the composers who incorporated rag components into their compositions.

BLUES

A line from Ken Burns's 2001 *Jazz* series said, "The blues became the underground aquifer that would feed all streams of American music—including jazz." That statement, while true, understates the importance of the blues as a genre. In fact, practically every popular music tradition that emerged in the twentieth century was influenced directly or indirectly by the blues. Although researchers such as Alan Lomax attempted to link the blues to African dance traditions as well as to a specific geographical location in the United States (i.e., the Mississippi Delta region), there is more persuasive information that links it, as a vocally derived musical genre, to a wide variety of singing styles, and that is where the African influence is more pronounced. There is a vastly under-explored singing continuum from Africa to the African diaspora. Stylized vocalities such as glissandi, whoops, whines, moans, shouts, falsetto, raspy voice, taut voice, ululations, and yodels, among others, are found on the African continent as well as within the African American experience. For example, these vocalities could be heard in America when men were on the streets selling their goods. (In some parts of the country such as Baltimore the singing merchants are known as "Arabers.") It could also be heard in rhythmic work songs (such as those recorded prison gangs heard throughout the South), field hollers, and sorrow songs. These vocalities were also heard in black Protestant churches, uttered by preachers delivering sermons and by church attendees. In fact, the blues has been referred to as the "profane twin" of the black Baptist church.

The blues was born in the Mississippi Delta region because of the heavy concentration of African Americans in the area. But the stylized vocalities were heard among African Americans in different parts of the country and that makes linking a genre as widespread as this one to a specific geographical location problematic. There are early twentieth century writings that paint a different picture as to where the blues was born. Perhaps the best-known citing came from William Christopher Handy (1873–1958), the great bandleader and composer who was also known as the "Father of the Blues." According to Handy, he first heard a man accompanying himself on an acoustic guitar in the small town of Tutwiler, Mississippi (in the Delta region) in 1903. There is no question that Handy was among the first to popularize the genre.

Another early mention came from the first professional blues singer, Gertrude "Ma" Rainey (1886–1939). She first heard the blues a year before Handy in 1902. According to her account, while traveling with the Rabbit Foot Minstrels in Missouri, she heard a girl singing a song about the man who had abandoned her. She imitated the girl's song and began singing it onstage. "Ma" Rainey became popularly known as the "Mother of the Blues." So there are at least two geographical locations identified at the beginning of the twentieth century that makes it difficult to pinpoint an origin. Recent scholarship has widened the area of early blues origins to include Texas and the Piedmont region (including Georgia and the Carolinas) along with the Mississippi Delta region as the forming ground of the blues.

STRUCTURE OF THE BLUES

The distinctive three-line stanza of the blues is an apparent African retention because the three-line stanza is uncommon in European folksong repertory. In the early days of the blues, there were examples of 11-, 15-, and 19-measure (or bar) blues. Between 1910 and 1920, however, the 12-bar metric structure became standard. This was another influence of W. C. Handy, who was the first to notate the tradition. The 12-bar metric structure is an example of vocal call and response between the singer and the instrumental accompaniment.

In the pattern noted above (see also figure that follows), the 12-bar structure can be divided into three lines that conform to the three-line stanza, *a a b*. Measures one and two of line one, five and six of line two, and nine and ten of line three

vocal call instrumental response

Line 1 ____ 1 ____ / ____ 2 ____ / ____ 3 ____ / ____ 4 ____

a

vocal call instrumental response

Line 2 ____ 5 ____ / ____ 6 ____ / ____ 7 ____ / ____ 8 ____

a¥

vocal call instrumental response

Line 3 ____ 9 ____ / ____ 10 ____ / ____ 11 ____ / ____ 12 ____

b

Twelve-bar Metric Structure, a Blues Standard after 1910. *Blues legend W. C. Handy was the first to notate the 12-bar structure, an example of vocal call-and-response between the singer and the instrumental accompaniment.* GALE

state or repeat the vocal call (as in "I hate to see the evening sun go down"). Measures three, four, seven, eight, and eleven and twelve represent the instrumental response to the vocal call. The call-and-response between the voice and instrument is significant because the instrumental response is acting in a vocal capacity. This principle (i.e., the instruments imitating the voice) was explored even further with the emergence of jazz.

This simple and universal pattern proved to be—and still is—highly adaptable to popular songwriting. The blues also displayed a harmonic quality that made it sound quite different from the popular music of that era. It was derived by ambiguously treating (i.e., lowering or raising) the third, sixth, or seventh scale degrees of the widely used tempered, or "classical," scale. These specially treated notes were commonly known as "blue" notes.

COUNTRY BLUES

The Country Blues was the earliest of the cohesive forms of the blues as well as the most influential. It was dominated by men who accompanied themselves on guitars or harmonicas. They played at a variety of venues including picnics, fish fries, "juke" joints (informal small clubs), and house parties, among other places. Few of these musicians were professional in the way professional musicians are currently regarded. Many of these men were migrant or seasonal workers (such as Charlie Patton), and they immortalized some of the places where they worked in songs such as "Dockery Plantation Blues" as well as the infamous prison, Parchman Farm outside of Robinsonville, Mississippi. It was common for several bluesmen to meet at some location when they were in the area and exchange playing techniques, and experiment with sounds and singing styles. Among the guitar-playing techniques they used were methods involving broken bottlenecks, animal bones, brass rings that they placed around the index finger, knife blades, and other devices to get the instrument to imitate a variety of vocal effects (e.g., drawing the knife blade along the strings could simulate the whine of the human voice).

Many of the early blues practitioners received their musical backgrounds in a religious setting, as was the case with Charlie Patton and Blind Lemon Jefferson. Although there were predecessors to these great bluesmen, the recordings of Patton and Jefferson collectively represented the height of the Country Blues tradition.

The early recordings of the Country Blues tended to be categorized in the first or second wave. The first wave generally consisted of older men in the tradition whose roots could be linked to older sources. Bluesmen within this tradition included Sylvester Weaver (1897–1960), "Papa" Charlie Jackson (d. 1938), "Sleepy" John Adam Estes (1899–1977), "Mississippi" John Hurt (c. 1893–1966), "Blind" Lemon Jefferson (born Clarence Jefferson, c. 1893–1929), and Charlie Patton (c. 1891–1934). Among those practitioners in the second wave of Country Blues recordings, which appeared in the early to mid-1930s, were Eddie James "Son" House (1902–1988), Memphis Minnie (1897–1973, one of the few women to distinguish herself in the style), Amos "Bumble Bee Slim" Easton (1905–1968), Alfonzo Lonnie Brown (1899–1970), Johnny Shines (1915–1992), and Robert Johnson (1911–1938). Johnson's twenty-nine recordings were made in November 1936 and June 1937. Of those, "Crossroad Blues," "Me and the Devil Blues," and "Hellhound on My Trail" have gained the most attention. They formed the basis of Johnson's legendary Faustian bargain with the devil. The myths surrounding Johnson's death in 1938 only added to the folklore surrounding his life.

CLASSIC BLUES

Yet another tradition of the blues emerged on February 14, 1920, when Mamie Smith (1883–1946), an ex-vaudevillian and cabaret singer, recorded "You Can't Keep a Good Man Down" and "That Thing Called Love" for Okeh Records. This was the first known recording of an African American woman performing the blues. Because of the success of that February session, Smith was invited to return to the studio later that year to record "Crazy Blues" and "It's Right Here For You." This kicked off the era of the Classic Blues and the female singers, which lasted throughout the 1920s. Unlike the Country Blues, which was dominated by men on guitars, the Classic Blues (also known as the City Blues) featured women, and they were typically accompanied by a small ensemble of five to seven instruments. It was the first time African American women dominated a style of popular music.

During the first two decades of the twentieth century, African American women singers performed in tent shows, circuses, carnivals, or in theaters which affiliated with the Theater Owner's Booking Association (TOBA). The circuit was controlled by a group of white businessmen who booked black acts. Because many performers complained about the terms of their contracts, TOBA became an acronym for "tough on black asses." Female blues singers such as "Ma" Rainey were also a part of the circuit.

There were two sub-styles within the Classic Blues that categorize many of the women performers of this era. The Vaudeville Tradition of the Classic Blues featured those women who had come from vaudeville, night club, and musical stage backgrounds as opposed to more rural traditions. In their recordings, there is a noticeable absence of those stylized vocalities such as screams, shouts, and moans referred to earlier. Within this tradition were names such as Mamie Smith, Ethel Waters (1896–1977), Edith Wilson (1896–1981), and Alberta Hunter (1895–1984). Hunter had what could only be called an amazing career as a performer (she was heard live around the world), as well as a long recording legacy. At one point in the 1950s, she retired from the stage and became a practicing nurse in the Bronx. At the age of eighty-two, she made a comeback to the stage and was introduced to a younger generation in the 1970s and 1980s.

The other sub-style of Classic Blues is known as the Southern Style. The women singers of this tradition were closer in vocal style to the men of the Country Blues. Their recordings displayed many of the vocalities mentioned above. There were many women in this tradition, but among the titans were Ma Rainey, Bessie Smith (1894–1937), and Beulah "Sippie" Wallace (1898–1986). Ma Rainey was known as "Songbird of the South," the "Gold-Neck Woman of the Blues," and the "Paramount Wildcat," a reference to the record company that signed her to an exclusive contract in 1923.

Rainey's prestige and recordings were only surpassed by those of Bessie Smith, popularly known as the "Empress of the Blues." Smith was by far the best known practitioner among all the women in the Classic Blues era and commanded the largest audiences as well. Unlike Rainey and many others, Bessie Smith was signed by a mainstream label, Columbia Records, instead of one of the "race" labels. When signing African American musicians to contracts, however, it was the practice of the record labels (whether it was a mainstream or race label) to strike through the royalty clause, which meant that regardless of how well the record sold, the musician had no further financial claim on the recording beyond what he or she was paid at the time of the recording. Bessie Smith became so famous that she was among the first African American performers to be featured in a nineteen-minute sound film, *St. Louis Blues* (1929), based on the W. C. Handy composition.

Beulah "Sippie" Wallace, often referred to as the last of the great blues queens from the 1920s era, was popularly known as the "Texas Nightingale." Although she was born in Houston, Texas, Wallace's celebrity as a blues singer developed in Chicago, where she enjoyed a long and prominent performing and recording career. After some personal tragedies (including the death of her fast-living husband Matt Wallace), she moved to Detroit and began singing religious music exclusively. In her seventies, she returned to singing the blues and did so until her death in 1986. Others in the Classic Blues tradition were Ida Cox (1896–1967), Clara Smith (1894–1935, no relation to Bessie), Bertha "Chippie" Hill (1905–1950), and Victoria Spivey (1906–1976).

MIGRATION OF THE BLUES

During the Great Depression of the 1930s, millions of African Americans left the rural South for the cities of the North, and the blues traveled with them. The majority of the bluesmen who made the trek were young. Many blues musicians were seasonal or migrant workers. Some traveled informally by rail (more commonly known as "hoboing") through various regions. These performers adapted their traditional music to their new surroundings, incorporating the concerns of urban life into their lyrics. Blues scenes began to emerge in Chicago, St. Louis, Detroit, and other Midwestern and Northern cities.

Older musicians tended to remain in the South. Nehemiah Curtis "Skip" James (1902–1969) and Mississippi John Hurt were among the many bluesmen who did not migrate until later, if ever, and whose sounds remained countrified. Even today, those geographical differences remain.

The blues players of each region tended to relocate to a particular area as they fled the South. Musicians in the Piedmont region of North Carolina drifted toward New York. Many of the Texans, meanwhile, headed westward to California. Aaron "T-Bone" Walker (a.k.a. Oak Cliff T-Bone, 1910–1975) was one of the most important representatives of this migration, which led to the development of the West Coast blues sound, including use of the electric guitar after 1940, through a lineage that included a number of important piano bluesmen as well as the internationally renowned guitarist, Riley "B. B." King.

CHICAGO BLUES

As blues artists in the Mississippi Delta and other parts of the Deep South headed to Northern cities, a fertile blues scene developed in Chicago. The evolution of Chicago blues hinged on the amplification and rearrangement for small bands of traditional solo Delta blues. Taking their cue from the work of such Mississippi legends as Robert Johnson, Southern emigrants began establishing a blues scene in Chicago even before the onset of the Depression.

Popular Chicago blues performers during the 1920s and 1930s included Memphis Minnie, Houston "Tampa Red" Woodbridge (1904–1981), William Lee Conley "Big Bill" Broonzy (c. 1898–1958), and John Lee Curtis "Sonny Boy" Williamson (1914–1948). Another, even larger wave of Southern blues musicians after World War II solidified Chicago's position as the center of the blues universe. This generation of artists included Howlin' Wolf (1910–1976), Little Walter (1930–1968), and Muddy Waters (1913–1983).

Eventually, Chicago blues began to incorporate elements of blues styles from other areas. The most obvious influence came from the Texas/West Coast guitar soloists who were working in the style of T-Bone Walker. Chicago's modern blues stars Otis Rush, Buddy Guy, and "Magic Sam" Maghett (1937–1969) were at the forefront of this new emphasis on electric lead guitar improvisation.

THE VARIED SOUNDS OF BLUES

Like jazz, the label "blues" covers an incredibly diverse body of music. It defies convenient classification systems. Nevertheless, a number of recognizable styles and movements have emerged within the blues idiom over the years. Some of them are associated with the geographical areas in which they blossomed, while others transcend the boundaries of time and location.

"Jump blues" developed during the 1940s and 1950s, primarily in California. Jump was an up-tempo, horn-driven style that relied less on guitar than many other blues forms. The predominant instruments were the alto or tenor saxophone.

Jump's proponents have included Amos Milburn (1927–1980) and Louis Jordan (1908–1975). The folk-flavored blues of the Carolina Piedmont region spawned the highly underrated Brownie McGhee (1915–1996), who influenced rock and roll, folk, and blues musicians. The term "piano blues" captures a wide variety of music spanning most of the continent and century, including the entire progression from barrelhouse to boogie-woogie to hard-rocking Chicago blues. "Big" Maceo Merriweather (1905–1953), Albert "Sunnyland Slim" Luandrew (1907–1995), Meade Anderson "Lux" Lewis (1905–1964), Albert Ammons (1907–1949), "Professor Longhair" (born Henry Roeland Byrd, 1918–1980), and Otis Spann (1930–1970) were some of the most important piano bluesmen.

Two paths that blues has taken in recent years include modern acoustic blues and modern electric blues. Modern acoustic blues is essentially a movement for the revival of the older country blues sounds. "Taj Mahal" (born Henry Saint Clair Fredericks, 1942) is one of its major proponents. Modern electric blues simply refers to the most contemporary trappings—including horns and more sophisticated studio recording techniques—placed on urban blues.

THE JAZZ TRADITION

By the end of the nineteenth century, the all-black military-style brass band tradition, which had its origins early in that century, had matured considerably. The bands were in demand in large urban areas as well as smaller rural areas. The bands had come to be called syncopated dance bands, society orchestras, or some other name. They performed in a variety of settings including funerary rituals, election day celebrations, and weekend performances in a local park.

NEW ORLEANS OR "CLASSIC" JAZZ

Although New Orleans is often cited as the birthplace of jazz, this statement must be qualified. Those traditions that jazz is a synthesis of, such as brass bands, ragtime, and the blues, were found in many parts of the country. As a major port city, New Orleans attracted visitors from other parts of the country as well as international visitors. It was also a major musical capital of the United States in the late nineteenth century, and several musical traditions were found there—such as opera performances, chamber ensembles, ballroom dances, music for street parades, picnics, funerals, and church concerts, among other traditions.

Certainly, New Orleans could be seen as a clear representation of what was taking place musically in other parts of the country, where brass bands, rag music, and blues were coalescing. In the 1890s, there were many brass bands in New Orleans and they often engaged in competitions known as "cutting," "carving," or "bucking" contests where they literally attempted to outplay each other. Among the well-known bands of the era were the Diamond Stone Brass Band, the Olympia Orchestra, the Eurekas, the Eagles, the Excelsiors, the Onwards Brass Band, and the Melrose Brass Band, among others. Prominent names of the era were John Robichaux (1866–1939) and Charles "Buddy" Bolden (1877–1931).

New Orleans also had a significant Creole (mixed race) population that, for a time, enjoyed greater access to a variety of musical experiences and privilege than their darker-skinned brothers and sisters. In 1894, when a statute lowered the Creole's social status to that of other African Americans, and they were forced to physically move into those areas where other blacks were, musical cross fertilization was inevitable.

There was also the founding of Storyville, a red light district that sanctioned activities such as gambling and prostitution, and attracted local musicians as well as those from other parts of the country because of the performing opportunities. Recent jazz studies suggest that too much emphasis has been placed on the importance of Storyville, because early jazz was played in other parts of the city and the country.

The New Orleans (also called Classic) jazz ensemble was divided into two sections. The first part, the frontline (also called the first line), had a melodic function. Instruments in the frontline were the coronet (or trumpet), clarinet, and trombone. The second part, called the rhythm section (also called the second line), had an accompanying role. Instruments in the rhythm section included the banjo (or guitar), tuba, percussion, piano, and other lower instruments. Many musicians within this tradition did not sight-read music because of the emphasis on collective improvisation. As this style of jazz spread to other parts of the country, it also came to be called "Dixieland" jazz. It was not until the late 1910s that the term "jazz" became standard when referring to the genre. In earlier periods, there were a variety of spellings including "jas," "jass," and "jasz," among others.

Prominent names associated with this style of jazz were Sidney Bechet (1897–1959), Joseph "King" Oliver (1885–1938), Edward "Kid" Ory (1886–1973), Freddie Keppard (1889–1933), Ferdinand "Jelly Roll" Morton (c. 1885–1941), and Louis Armstrong (1901–1971). After migrating to Chicago, Joe Oliver eventually sent for Armstrong, his protégé, to play second coronet and record with his band. But within a few years, Armstrong surpassed Oliver as a performer. With the encouragement of his second wife, musician Lil Hardin Armstrong (1898–1971), who was also in the Oliver band, Louis ventured out on his own. After an association with James "Fletcher" Henderson (1897–1952) in New York, he eventually became one of jazz's most celebrated names.

EARLY AFRICAN AMERICAN JAZZ RECORDINGS

As jazz grew in popularity, its spread was assisted by the growth of the recording industry. Realizing there was a growing number of African American record buyers, "race" labels emerged to record early jazz and blues practitioners. Among the better-known of these labels were Okeh, Bluebird, Phonograph, Vocalion, Paramount, and Nordskog. Black Swan, owned and operated by W. C. Handy and Harry Pace (1884–1943), was the only black-owned race label of the period. Its slogan was, "The only genuine colored record." Black Swan also boasted that it provided "the only records using exclusively Negro voices." Fletcher Henderson and Ethel Waters were among the regulars who worked for the label.

TERRITORY BANDS

By the decade of the 1920s, Chicago had taken over from New Orleans as the major African American musical capital of the United States and was attracting musicians from other parts of the country. Musicians were among those who had come from the South in what was called the "great migration." Many were in search of jobs and also attempting to escape the oppression of southern Jim Crow laws.

Throughout the 1920s and 1930s, a new type of musical ensemble known as "territory" bands appeared throughout the Midwest and the South. They were based in various cities, but traveled regionally for musical engagements. Many of them were one-night jobs to play for dances. Among some of the well-known territory bands were Walter Page's Blue Devils from Oklahoma City, the Jeter-Pillars Band from St. Louis, and the Sunset Royal Entertainers from West Palm Beach, Florida. Nat Towles, Red Perkins and the Dixie Ramblers, and the Hunter Serenaders were all from Omaha, Nebraska. Alphonse Trent was from Dallas, and Don Albert was from San Antonio. Ray Shep and his Orchestra were from Pensacola, and "Smiling" Billy Stewart and the Celery City Serenaders were from Sanford, Florida. C. S. Belton and his Florida Society Syncopators were well-known. Jesse Stone and Jay McShann were from Kansas City, Hartley Toots and "Little" George Kelly were from Miami, and Zack Whyte was from Cincinnati. Through the influence of recordings and radio broadcast (which was introduced in 1922 and eventually developed the capacity to broadcast concerts from coast to coast), several territory bands such as Andy Kirk's Clouds of Joy and Jay McShann made the transition to big name national bands.

TRANSITIONAL ERA JAZZ (1925–1934)

Classic or New Orleans refers to the frontline/rhythm section activity of the smaller jazz ensemble but, from the mid-1920s to the mid-1930s, there were several changes. The size of the ensemble increased to ten or more, and the musicians were more likely to have received formal training at a college, conservatory, or through private lessons, and were now expected to sight-read notated music. Radio broadcast played a role in dramatically increasing the number of listeners to jazz styles. New instruments such as the saxophone became more prominent in the jazz ensemble (eventually overtaking the clarinet). The electronically amplified guitar gradually

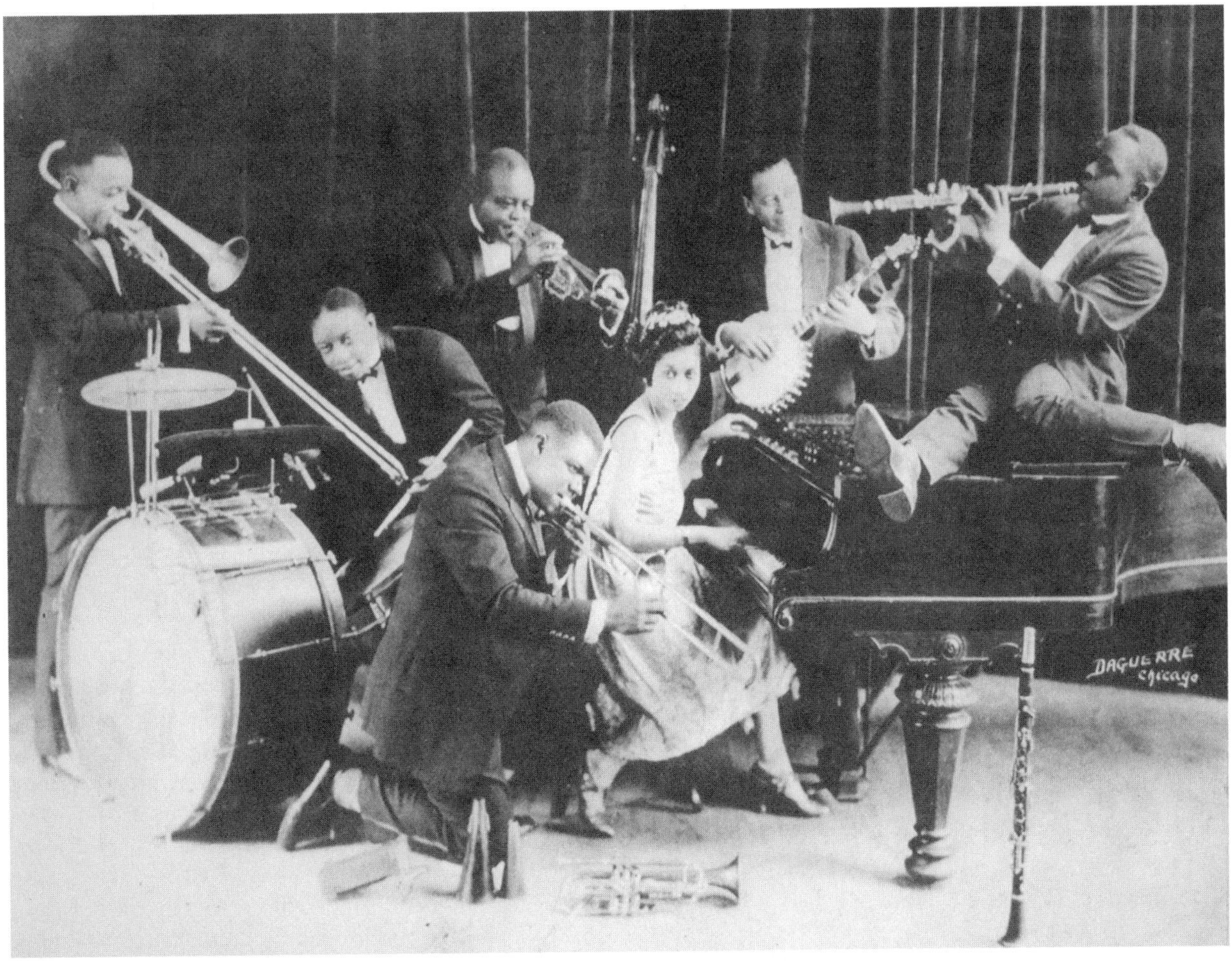

Joe "King" Oliver's Creole Jazz Band, Chicago, c. 1923. *The Creole Jazz Band in 1923 made the first important recordings by an African American jazz group. The band's members (*pictured left to right*) at the time included Louis Armstrong, slide trumpet; Baby Dodds, drums; King Oliver, coronet; Honoré Dutrey, trombone; Lil Hardin, piano; Bill Johnson, banjo; and Johnny Dodds, clarinet.*
FRANK DRIGGS COLLECTION/HULTON ARCHIVE/GETTY IMAGES

took a more prominent role in the expanded jazz ensemble. New York also became the new musical capital of the country (taking over from Chicago). Fletcher Henderson is often credited with starting the first big band. With his arranger Don Redman (1900–1964), they revolutionized jazz and helped to usher in the Swing or Big Band era.

THE SWING, OR BIG BAND, ERA

The major innovation of the new style of jazz was Don Redman's introduction initially called jazz "specialities." The melody was divided among solo instruments within the ensemble, among sections within the ensemble (e.g., the saxophones or the brass instruments), and the entire ensemble. This concept came to be known as sectionalization and became the basis of the new style. In 1932, an up-and-coming musician, Edward Kennedy "Duke" Ellington (1899–1974), introduced the song, "It Don't Mean a Thing if It Ain't Got that Swing," first performed by Ivie Anderson (1905–1949), and Swing became the name of the new jazz style.

Aside from Ellington, other great African American bandleaders of the swing era were William "Count" Basie (1904–1984), James "Jimmie" Lunceford (1902–1947), Erskine Hawkins (1914–1993), and William Henry "Chick" Webb (c. 1905–1939). Louis Armstrong was among the era's most successful jazz soloists, along with great musicians such as Lester Young (1909–1959) and Coleman Hawkins (1904–1969).

Ellington's rise to fame began when he took over an engagement at the famous Cotton Club in Harlem in 1927. He was a very fine pianist with an eye (and ear) for discovering other musical talent, but his true genius lay in his gift for composition. In fact, he remains historically one of America's most prolific composers.

Broadside Advertising "Cotton Club on Parade," Featuring Cab Calloway and His Cotton Club Orchestra, early 1930s. *During his stint as bandleader at Harlem's Cotton Club, Calloway developed his famous scat style of singing, starting with the song "Minnie the Moocher."* SCHOMBURG CENTER FOR RESEARCH IN BLACK CULTURE; THE NEW YORK PUBLIC LIBRARY; ASTOR, LENOX AND TILDEN FOUNDATIONS

It was during the swing era that the integrated band came into being, through the efforts of popular bandleader and clarinetist Benny Goodman (1909–1986). Encouraged by his brother-in-law, John Hammond Jr. (1910–1987), Goodman began the Benny Goodman Trio with drummer Gene Krupa and the African American musician Teddy Wilson (1912–1986), and the group later became a quartet when he added drummer and vibraphonist Lionel Hampton (1908–2002). Goodman also hired Fletcher Henderson as his arranger.

This era also saw the emergence of many of the greatest popular dance bands the country had ever seen. In addition to the above mentioned names, there was the McKinney Cotton Pickers, which was taken over by Don Redman. There were also major clubs that catered to dancers, such as the Savoy Ballroom in New York. Dances such as the Lindy Hop and the Jitterbug were wildly popular during that time. There were many great solo instrumentalists of the period, and at the top of most lists would be the great pianist, Art Tatum (1909–1956). Even other great pianists of the era deferred to his genius as the consummate musician.

JAZZ SINGERS

Jazz was not exclusively an instrumental genre. Singers of jazz date back to the 1920s, with Louis Armstrong's recordings of the "Heebie Jeebies" and "Hotter than Hot," where he used "scatting," which means to vocalize on nonsense syllables in place of the text. In the final recording sessions of blues singer Bessie Smith, selections like "Gimme a Pigfoot," "Do Your Duty," "Take Me for a Buggy Ride," and "Down in the Dumps" establish a clear marriage of the new swing style and traditional blues. Singers such as Billie Holiday (1915–1959), Cab Calloway (1907–1994), and Ella Fitzgerald (1917–1996) elevated the status of jazz singers.

Billie Holiday, who sang in New York clubs as a teenager, was noticed by John Hammond, who arranged for her to record with Benny Goodman. This led Holiday to more prestigious engagements with swing groups such as Count Basie and Artie Shaw. Throughout her peak performing years, Holiday battled drug and alcohol dependency issues, yet she was recognized as one of the most celebrated singers of her day. She was given the nickname "Lady Day" by tenor saxophonist Lester Young, whom she nicknamed "Prez," which was short for "president."

Although not as celebrated as Holiday, Ivie Anderson was also one of the renowned jazz singers of the period. Anderson was best known for her association with the Duke Ellington Band. Ella Fitzgerald was discovered at Harlem's Apollo Theater during the theater's popular talent night. She had a major break when she joined the Chick Webb Band and, after Webb's death, led the band as its headline singer. Cab Calloway was a highly regarded singer and bandleader whose signature song, "Minnie the Moocher," recorded in 1931, made him known as the "hi-de-ho" man. William "Billy" Eckstine (1914–1993) was a smooth-voiced singer and, in the 1940s, was also a bandleader. Joe Williams (1918–1999), another celebrated vocalist of the era, got his start in the 1930s, and worked with Count Basie in the 1950s. He was responsible for reestablishing Basie's band before the American public with "Everyday I Have the Blues."

Sarah Vaughan (1924–1990) was another winner of the Apollo's talent night who gained celebrity in her own right. Vaughan was also a gifted pianist and used her extensive vocal range in a variety of traditions, but she was primarily a jazz artist. Betty Carter (1929–1998) and Carmen McRae (1920–1994) were also distinguished jazz singers with hugely successful careers independently. In 1987, the two linked up in a live performance of the *Carmen McRae-Betty Carter Duets*, which was a commercial success.

BEBOP JAZZ

The impact of World War II brought about significant changes that affected big bands. Rationing of all sorts made large ensembles that required increased personnel impractical because of their associated costs. Many vocalists who had been featured with bands embarked on solo careers, or performed with smaller ensembles. Additionally, to protest poor wages and work conditions, the American Federation of Musicians banned its membership (i.e., union musicians) from participating in commercial recordings between 1942 and 1944.

The swing era had also produced some of the greatest instrumental soloists, with technical abilities never before heard in jazz, but many were unable to express their musical individuality in the confines of a big band. These great soloists were in many ways the impetus of the new and revolutionary style of jazz that emerged in the 1940s: "bebop."

In many ways, bebop was a musical manifestation of extra musical sentiments. The 1930s and 1940s saw a higher degree of African American antiwar sentiment. Unlike all of America's previous wars (dating from the Revolutionary War through World War I) when it could count on its men (and women) of color to stand up and participate as a show of solidarity, World War II was different. Part of this lack of enthusiasm could be linked to the emergence of the Black Muslim movement during the period. The ministers of the movement preached against African Americans signing up to fight a war in a foreign location, when their rights at home were so poorly preserved or respected.

The bebop musicians themselves were also a different breed. The musicians engaged in onstage activities that were the antithesis of performers of that period. For example, they sometimes wore sunglasses and hats on stage, smoked while performing, or often did not acknowledge applause from the audience. These musicians also wanted to be recognized as serious artists and, in many cases, were disdainful of musicians in the tradition of Louis Armstrong.

One of the central figures in the emergence of bebop was the innovative electric guitarist, Charlie Christian (1916–1942). Christian often organized informal jam sessions where instrumentalists gathered in Harlem to play at Minton's Playhouse or Monroe's Uptown House, which featured other great musicians such as trumpeter Roy Eldridge (1911–1989), tenor saxophonist Lester Young, string bass player Jimmy Blanton (1918–1942), and pianist Clyde Hart (1910–1945). Within two years of the Minton group's formation, several members had died including Charlie Christian, Clyde Hart, and Jimmy Blanton. These developments opened the door for Charlie Parker (1920–1955) and John Birks "Dizzy" Gillespie (1917–1993) to emerge as important personalities in the bebop era. The Parker/Gillespie duo made recordings after the American Federation of Musicians ban was lifted in 1944 and introduced bebop to the world. Works such as "Koko," "Billie's Bounce," and "Shaw Nuff" marked the way of the new jazz. With the exception of Ellington, Basie, Lunceford (until his death in 1947), and a few others, swing era big bands gradually phased out.

Characteristically, bebop had an unsingable melody (i.e., a melody that was not easily hummed or remembered), which frequently stopped and started. As there was no routine or steady rhythmic pulse, bebop did not lend itself well to dancing. The musicians used unexpected intervals that often created dissonance. The improvisations did not conform to a certain pattern (i.e., some intervals would be long and some short). There was an emphasis on the cymbals and the pianist no longer played a set pattern. Finally, any instrument in the ensemble could play a solo role.

As the symbol of bebopism, Charlie Parker gave the appearance of an aloof genius on the alto saxophone. He was so admired among the dance bands he played with in his early career that dancers often stopped to watch him when he was performing solos. Parker, however, was ultimately a tragic figure. Despite his phenomenal talent, substance abuse issues made him an increasingly unreliable musician and caused him several stays in treatment centers. Eventually, his substance abuse led to his death.

Dizzy Gillespie enjoyed a more stable and celebrated career. Although Charlie Parker was one of the creative geniuses of bebop, Gillespie did more to disseminate the new style. His outgoing personality and tremendous sense of humor made him a more media-friendly showman. He frequently performed outside the United States in Europe and Africa. Gillespie was also influential in the careers of other jazz musicians such as the Afro-Cuban drummer Chano Pozo (1915–1948), and after a 1970s visit to Cuba, he was a major backer of Cuban trumpeter Arturo Sandoval. Other major musicians in the bebop tradition included Thelonious Monk (1917–1982), who was the house pianist at Minton's, and Kenny Clarke (later known as Liaqat Ali Salaam, 1914–1985), a highly respected drummer. Several musicians, including Roy Eldridge and Lester Young, were involved in the new style, but did not embrace bebop once it emerged.

COOL JAZZ AND HARD BOP

As creative and revolutionary as bebop had been in the development of jazz, it lost that segment of the listening audience that wanted to dance. Inevitably, there was a reaction to the fast and frenzied style that many viewed as too esoteric. The alternative to this jazz tradition was the cool style, which began appearing at the end of the 1940s.

Many have viewed cool jazz as a reaction to bebop. It was developed mostly among white musicians. It was more tuneful, rhythmically less complex, and the improvisations were also more relaxed. Proponents within the tradition included Gerry Mulligan (1927–1996), Claude Thornhill (1909–1965), Gil Evans (1912–1988), and John Lewis (1920–2001). In 1949 and 1950, Mulligan, Thornhill, and Evans made recordings with Miles Davis (1926–1991), released as the *Birth of the Cool* by Capitol Records. One of the signature recordings from the session, "Boplicity" (i.e., the simplification of bop), marked the way for the new style of jazz. Although the group did not succeed on the East Coast, there was a more receptive audience on the West Coast, where the style was sometimes known as "West Coast Jazz." By the 1950s, however, younger audiences had gradually drifted away from jazz to the more danceable and upbeat rhythm and blues.

Nevertheless, changes in jazz's styles and audiences were still occurring. An African American reaction to cool jazz was known as hard bop. It was regarded as an East Coast reaction to the reaction that cool jazz was receiving on the West Coast. It was based on similar principals of the original bebop movement, but there were newer musicians associated with the genre such as Horace Silver, Art Blakey (1919–1990), Charlie Mingus (1922–1979), Tadd Dameron (1917–1965), Dexter Gordon (1923–1990), Julian "Cannonball" Adderley (1928–1975), Quincy Jones, and Miles Davis, who had dissociated himself from the Cool movement. Art Blakey and Charlie Mingus gave lectures on the principles of the hard bop movement.

FREE FORM JAZZ

When the decade of the 1960s arrived, teenagers and young people had long since stopped being fans of jazz. Berry Gordy's Motown sound with groups and individuals such as Marvin Gaye, Smokey Robinson and the Miracles, Stevie Wonder, the Four Tops, the Temptations, the Supremes, and the Marvellettes had young people dancing the way an earlier generation had danced to swing.

Musicians such as Sonny Rollins, Cecil Taylor, Archie Shepp, Charlie Mingus, and Miles Davis pointed the way to the new style. Free form jazz featured extreme rhythmic complexities, complicated dissonances, and harmonic progressions. It blended Western and non-Western instruments, and explored new scales and modes. At either end of the free jazz continuum were alto saxophonists John Coltrane (1926–1967) and Ornette Coleman (1930–). Coltrane was classically trained on several instruments, but his musical training was interrupted when he was drafted into the military at the end of World War II. A drug addiction during the 1950s damaged his early career, but he overcame and produced *A Love Supreme*, which marked his triumph over his substance abuse. His composition "Alabama," which first appeared in 1963, was a memorial to three black girls killed in a Birmingham church. Texas-born Ornette Coleman's principal contribution to the free jazz movement was a thirty-seven minute collective improvisation recording *Free Jazz*, made in 1960. Although the recording was denounced by other jazz musicians and purists because of its apparent abandon of harmonic and structural principles known to jazz, Coleman received noticeable attention for the style outside the United States.

AFTER FREE JAZZ MOVEMENT

Throughout the 1960s, there was continuous experimentation taking place within the jazz genre, with figures such as Thelonious Monk, Wayne Shorter, Bill Evans (1929–1980), Max Roach (1924–2007), McCoy Tyner, and Mile Davis playing key roles in its development.

John Coltrane continued to be a force in jazz development. When he left Miles Davis at the beginning of the 1960s to form his own group, he extended the use of modal harmony further. This trend was continued in the work of pianist Cecil Taylor, but by and large the audience for jazz in the United States was a fraction of what it had once been just two decades earlier. There was a brief bright light in the mid-1960s when Louis Armstrong's recording of "Hello Dolly" shot to the top of the popular charts, briefly surpassing the Beatles.

Elder jazz statesmen such as Duke Ellington, Count Basie, and to a lesser degree, Dizzy Gillespie continued playing engagements on the road, but the demand for the repertoire they played was not as great. Jazz festivals such as those in Newport, Rhode Island, continued to be an outlet for several musicians from the mid-1950s forward.

Other experimentalists such as pianist Sun Ra (c. 1914–1993) expanded the lines of jazz during the 1960s. However, with the death of John Coltrane in 1967, jazz lost one of its great names and had many (including many musicians) wondering about the viability of the genre.

Jazz received a boost when its perpetual bad boy and innovator, Miles Davis, released *Bitches Brew* in 1970. The album did quite well commercially. Davis was experimenting with what was increasingly being referred to as jazz fusion.

Within a few years, however, jazz had lost its giant and supreme entertainer, Louis Armstrong, in 1971, and by 1974, Duke Ellington, America's greatest composer, had also passed on. Perhaps it was the death of these legendary names, along with continuing decline in the genre's prestige, which prompted Miles Davis to declare in 1975, "Jazz is dead." Davis further said that jazz was the "music of the museums."

In the meantime, stalwarts such as Art Blakey continued to seek and cultivate jazz talent wherever they saw it. Through his group, the Jazz Messengers, Blakey inspired and gave a start to many generations of musicians, including alto saxophonist Jackie McLean (1931–2006), Hank Mobley (1930–1986), trumpeter Donald Byrd, pianist Bobby Timmons (1935–1974), tenor saxophonist Benny Golson, trumpeter Woody Shaw (1944–1989), trumpeter Lee Morgan (1938–1972), trumpeter Freddie Hubbard (1938–2008), pianist Keith Jarrett, saxophonist Wayne Shorter, saxophonist Branford Marsalis, and trumpeter Wynton Marsalis.

JAZZ IN THE 1980s AND BEYOND

Brothers Branford and Wynton Marsalis have become major ambassadors of jazz for a new generation. Coming from a musical New Orleans family, Wynton made news headlines in 1983 when he won Grammy Awards for the best solo classical and jazz musician. He has since been a champion of the classic, swing, and bebop traditions of jazz. His critics suggest that he has been somewhat dismissive of later jazz styles such as the free and fusion styles. His older brother, Branford, has played a greater variety of musical traditions. He has toured with rock stars Sting and Phil Collins, and was musical director of the *Tonight Show* with Jay Leno for a while. Generally regarded as jazz traditionalists, the Marsalis brothers have looked to the older masters for inspiration.

The proponents of traditionalism, the so-called "young lions" of jazz, persisted in their return to jazz roots during the 1990s. Wynton Marsalis served as a sort of godfather to this group of musicians. Tenor saxophonist Joshua Redman, son of former Ornette Coleman saxophonist Dewey Redman, is one of the most commercially successful of these "young lions." The younger Redman brought his style of hard bop to its largest audience ever—an audience that worshipped him almost as a rock star. Other successful players from this school include trumpeter Roy Hargrove, alto saxophonist Antonio Hart, trumpeter Phillip Harper, bassist Christian McBride, guitarist Mark Whitfield, pianist Marcus Roberts, and saxophonist James Carter, whose ever-expanding repertoire incorporates early

Trumpeter Wynton Marsalis with His Brothers Branford (saxophone) and Delfeayo (trombone), White House, Washington, DC, 2009. *The Marsalis brothers participate in a jazz workshop for students hosted by first lady Michelle Obama. Branford, Wynton, and Delfeayo have been major ambassadors of jazz for a new generation.* AP PHOTO/CHARLES DHARAPAK

jazz, funk, and avant-garde. These performers brought jazz to the attention of its broadest audience in decades through a reaffirmation of bop and earlier jazz. This reaffirmation led to the first-ever all-jazz music cable channel, BET Jazz, in 1996. Some older jazz artists worry that the reluctance of the younger generation to innovate or challenge the musical status quo does more harm than good to the genre. But, at the same time, many of these older musicians are seeing their careers revitalized, largely thanks to those same up-and-comers they had previously criticized.

NEOCLASSICISM

While their origins are vastly different from those of the "young lions," the many gifted players who emerged from Chicago's 1960s Association for the Advancement of Creative Music (AACM) school have also arrived at a similar approach to preserving the accomplishments of these musical traditions. In such groups as the Art Ensemble of Chicago, the World Saxophone Quartet, and Lester Bowie's Brass Fantasy, musicians from the AACM school continued to refine their take on free jazz through the 1970s and 1980s, eventually creating a style often called neoclassicism. Neoclassicism applies the freedoms gained through the free jazz movement to more structured compositions. Important neoclassicists have included David Murray, Don Pullen, Roscoe Mitchell, and Henry Threadgill. The AACM scene has remained vital, and is led by, among others, composer and saxophonist Edward Wilkerson.

RECENT JAZZ VOCALISTS

In the 1980s, Bobby McFerrin blasted onto the scene. His 1984 release *The Voice* made history as the first major label jazz album recorded entirely without accompaniment or overdubbing. A vocal improviser in the truest sense of the word, McFerrin veered away from jazz later in his career. Will Downing, Jon Lucien, and Kevin Mahogany picked up the slack in the 1990s, with Mahogany gaining recognition as the leading figure among them. The vocal sextet, Take 6, known for mixing elements of jazz, gospel, and pop, also enjoyed popular success.

Women vocalists have always left the most lasting marks on the jazz vocal tradition. A tradition begun by Billie Holiday, Ella Fitzgerald, and Sarah Vaughan was continued by Nancy Wilson and Betty Carter. Carter, with her fertile imagination and amazing technique, applied bop and post-bop styles to her vocalizing. Dee Dee Bridgewater was one of the few jazz singers to break out of obscurity in the 1970s. Since the 1980s, however, jazz vocals have made a comeback with the emergence of Diane Schuur, Diana Krall, and Dianne Reeves, all of whom draw from classic jazz vocalists: Ella Fitzgerald, Carmen McRae, Nat King Cole (1919–1965), and Ethel Waters. Indeed, to many younger jazz fans, these women represent what jazz is all about. Other popular jazz vocalists of the late twentieth century include Cassandra Wilson (a Grammy winner in 2009), Nnenna Freelon, and Shirley Horn (1934–2005).

SPOKEN WORD JAZZ AND JAZZ RAP

The roots of jazz include work songs, gospel songs, field hollers, and other vocal traditions. While most histories of jazz have focused on the music's instrumental aspects and mainstream jazz vocalists, few have paid attention to the use of spoken word in jazz.

One of the first persons to combine the more modern forms of jazz music with the spoken word was Langston Hughes (1902–1967). A leader of the African American movement in the first half of the twentieth century, Hughes wrote eloquently about both jazz and the blues. In 1958, jazz musician Charlie Mingus released *Weary Blues*, an album that featured Hughes performing his poetry. Hughes was also a songwriter, and artists such as Betty Carter, Eric Dolphy (1928–1964), Abbey Lincoln, "Taj Mahal," and Nina Simone (1933–2003, born Eunice Kathleen Waymon) have performed his songs.

Gil Scott-Heron, a poet who has had considerable success in jazz, rap, and rhythm and blues, has also released numerous albums featuring his poetry and music. Beginning with his 1970 release *Small Talk at 125th and Lennox*, which was fashioned with legendary jazz producer Bob Thiele, and through his mid-1990s albums, Scott-Heron's work has always been revealing and poignant. Ishmael Reed is similar to Scott-Heron in many ways, but he focuses on African American evolutionary prose and poetry in combination with Latin-flavored jazz.

In the 1990s, two other spoken word and jazz artists emerged on the New York scene. Sekou Sundiata (1948–2007, born Robert Franklin Feaster), a Harlem native, taught English literature at the New School for Social Research. Before his untimely death in 2007, he had combined African American consciousness poetry with soulful and jazzy music. One of the best examples of this was on his 1997 debut *The Blue Oneness of Dreams*.

The late 1980s also saw the rise of the Afro-centric/native tongue movement led by hip hop pioneer Afrika Bambaataa. The Jungle Brother's 1988 release *Straight Out the Jungle* featured several jazzy textures, and the following year the release of the group De La Soul's debut album *3 Feet High and Rising* further showcased the melding of jazz and rap influences. These two early groups were followed by A Tribe Called Quest, whose album *The Low End Theory* featured jazzy moods and textures along with samples from guitarist Grant Green and the bassist Ron Carter. By 1993, the trio known as Digable Planets released their album *Reachin' (A New*

NOTABLE HISTORICAL JAZZ VENUES

APOLLO THEATER
A celebrated entertainment club in Harlem, traditionally associated with African American performers during the artistic period known as the Harlem Renaissance. A New York City landmark, the Apollo is on the U.S. National Register of Historic Places. It remains a center of African American culture and continues to attract major performers.

BEALE STREET
A street in downtown Memphis, Tennessee, near the Mississippi River and historically home to a number of nightclubs frequented by Louis Armstrong, Muddy Waters, Memphis Minnie, B. B. King, and other celebrated blues and jazz performers. Originally Beale Avenue, the strip was renamed to capitalize on the success of W. C. Handy's "Beale Street Blues."

BIRDLAND CLUB
A New York club on Broadway near 52nd Street, named in honor of Charlie "Bird" Parker, who often served as a headliner there. The club was a popular Manhattan attraction for several well-known actors, musicians, and professional athletes.

CLEF CLUB
A society for African American musicians in Harlem during the second decade of the twentieth century, founded by African American composer and bandleader James Reese Europe. Associated musicians played at a Harlem club of the same name during this period.

CLUB DeLISA
A Southside Chicago jazz club that was popular from the mid-1930s to the late 1950s, featuring such well-known performers as Fletcher Henderson, Sun Ra, and Count Basie.

COTTON CLUB
A famous Manhattan club of the 1920s that fostered and promoted the careers of celebrated African American musicians such as Cab Calloway, Duke Ellington, Louis Armstrong, Jimmie Lunceford, and Fats Waller.

52nd STREET
A section of midtown New York between Fifth and Seventh Avenues, known historically for its abundance of jazz clubs and associated nightlife. At the height of its popularity, between the 1930s and the 1950s, 52nd Street regularly hosted such major jazz musicians as Miles Davis, Thelonious Monk, Billie Holiday, and Dizzy Gillespie.

LINCOLN THEATER
At its peak in the 1920s, Harlem's renowned Lincoln Theater hosted Bessie Smith, Ma Rainey, and Ethel Waters.

MINTON'S PLAYHOUSE
A jazz club in West Harlem that was the breeding ground for the bebop movement. Thelonious Monk, Charlie Parker, Dizzy Gillespie, and others gathered for jam sessions at Minton's during the 1940s.

MONROE'S UPTOWN HOUSE
A Harlem nightclub that, along with Minton's Playhouse, played a major role in the development of bebop jazz.

NEWPORT JAZZ FESTIVAL
A long-running jazz festival begun in the mid-1950s in Newport, Rhode Island. Major early performers included Miles Davis, Billie Holiday, Ella Fitzgerald, Muddy Waters, and Duke Ellington.

SAVOY BALLROOM
A popular dance hall on Lenox Avenue in Harlem, active between 1926 and 1958. The Lindy Hop became famous at the Savoy, where Chick Webb and Ella Fitzgerald performed in the 1930s. The jazz classic"Stompin' at the Savoy" was named in honor of this great ballroom.

SMALL'S PARADISE
A popular Harlem nightspot during the 1920s and 1930s, Small's Paradise was the most prestigious club owned by an African American during these years, and was the longest-running nightclub in Harlem before its doors were officially closed in 1986. A speakeasy during the Prohibition years, Small's offered jazz and dance entertainment to a fully integrated patronage.

STORYVILLE
A section in New Orleans where activities such as gambling and prostitution were legalized beginning in 1897. Although prostitution in the Storyville district was prohibited by a mandate of the federal government in 1917, Storyville continued to flourish for a time as an entertainment mecca, attracting jazz and blues musicians from many parts of the country.

SWING STREET
One of several jazz clubs found on New York's 52nd Street. The block of 52nd Street between Fifth and Sixth Avenues has been formally called"Swing Street" in honor of its importance to the history of jazz.

Refutation of Time and Space), which featured samples from Eddie Harris, Sonny Rollins, and Art Blakey. Following this release, the group mounted a tour that featured the pioneering use of live jazz musicians in place of the sampling.

Responding to the prevalence and popularity of hip hop artists using jazz samples in their music, Blue Note Records granted a British production duo named US3 exclusive license to use samples from its catalog in mid-1993. In early 1994, the duo had a top ten hit with "Cantaloop (Flip Fantasia)," based on samples from Herbie Hancock's *Cantaloupe Island.* The most successful fusion of live jazz and rap came in mid-1993 on an album called *Jazzmatazz.* Featuring Roy Ayers, Courtney Pine, Lonnie Liston Smith, and the support of Gang Starr's rapper Guru, the album was a true synthesis of the two styles. Other such projects followed, including *Stolen Moments: Red Hot + Cool*, Branford Marsalis's *Buckshot Lefonque*, and work by the rap band The Roots.

WOMEN IN BLUES AND JAZZ

The tradition of women singing the blues continued over the next generations with performers such as Dinah Washington (1924–1963) and Helen Humes (1913–1981), and many other women whose names were prominent in the 1920s, such as Victoria Spivey, revived their careers. Many women blues singers worked in jump blues bands, while others sang smooth, sexy ballads in trios styled after pianist Nat King Cole. Etta James, who counts Billie Holiday as one of her idols, and Koko Taylor (1928–2009), who developed her style after that of Bessie Smith, were among the prominent blues vocalists of the last few decades. As the blues sound percolated into other forms of pop music, listeners could hear its traces in the gospel-inspired voices of such soul and rock artists as Chaka Khan, Tina Turner, and, most notably, Aretha Franklin.

WOMEN IN JAZZ

Women instrumentalists in jazz during its first decades were uncommon, and women bandleaders were rare. Those women who learned to play an instrument generally played the piano and often played for church-related events. This is in accord with an African tradition that held that strings or piano were appropriate for women, but horns or drums were better suited for men. Not surprisingly, Lil Hardin Armstrong and Mary Lou Williams (1910–1981), two of the best-known women jazz instrumentalists, were pianists. All-woman bands ("girl bands") were usually regarded as a novelty, even though many of the women were excellent musicians and played technically demanding arrangements; some were superb soloists. Women occasionally were featured with male groups, for example, the trumpeter/vocalist Valaida Snow (1905–1956), or led male bands, such as Lil Hardin Armstrong. Some, such as pianist Dorothy Donegan (1922–1998), spent most of their careers as solo performers. Donegan studied with the legendary Art Tatum. In 1943, she became the first woman, as well as the first African American, to play Chicago's Orchestra Hall, sharing the bill with Vladimir Horowitz. In 1992, Donegan was honored with the NEA's American Jazz Master award following trombonist Melba Liston's (1926–1999) receipt of the award in 1987.

By the 1940s, there were more than 300 girl bands across the country, but only a fraction of them made records. The International Sweethearts of Rhythm is generally regarded as one of the best all-girl bands. Originating at the Piney Woods Country Life School in Piney Woods, Mississippi, in 1937, the band achieved considerable success, which led to a USO tour in 1945. They disbanded in the late 1940s. The Sweethearts left behind some radio broadcast acetates and also some film performances.

By the 1950s, women instrumentalists had become more common; male-female jazz combos raised few eyebrows. Detroit's Dorothy Ashby (1932–1986) brought the sounds of the harp to bebop, making her first record as a leader in 1956 and recording nine more albums as leader over the next fourteen years. Along similar lines, Alice Coltrane (1937–2007) played in her husband John Coltrane's last group and then went on to record several albums in the late 1960s and 1970s that featured her distinctive piano, harp, organ, and composing skills. During the 1980s, the all-woman band Straight Ahead was judged on its musical merits and, in the mid-1990s, Diva, an all-woman big band, offered a swinging interpretation of the genre.

There are many female jazz stars, including violinist Regina Carter, JoAnne Brackeen, and Geri Allen, saxophonist/bandleader Jane Bunnett, and Jane Ira Bloom, and drummers Cindy Blackman and Terri Lynn Carrington, to name only a few. Women playing jazz still face particular issues, but they enjoy a more level playing field than their predecessors.

Another fine instrumentalist to emerge in the early 1980s was drummer Cindy Blackman, a classically trained percussionist who has worked with Jackie McLean, Sam Rivers, and Joe Henderson, in addition to releasing four of her own albums. Having launched her recording career in 1982, pianist and composer Geri Allen has since released a dozen albums featuring such players as Oliver Lake, Ornette Coleman, Lester Bowie (1941–1999), Betty Carter, Ron Carter, and Dewey Redman (1931–2006). As an indication of her artistic excellence, Allen became the first woman to win the Danish Jazzpar Award in 1996.

Finally, violinist Regina Carter has continued to enjoy considerable success in the 1990s after her involvement with the highly respected, Detroit-based, all-female group Straight Ahead. A talented player with a beautiful tone, it has been suggested that Carter has the potential to become the most significant new violinist in jazz since Jean-Luc Ponty in the late 1960s.

JAZZ EDUCATION

In jazz's earliest years, musicians learned how to play jazz by emulating the elders they most admired, many of whom had formal musical training. In black communities, jazz and many jazz bands were often family affairs that included both immediate and extended family members. For example, both tenor saxophonist Lester Young and bassist Oscar Pettiford (1922–1960) learned to play while in their respective family bands.

Recordings were an essential means for early students to learn jazz. Students could study stylistic details of an admired musician's solo by slowing down the phonograph and learning a solo literally note by note.

The key method of learning jazz, however, was by playing in a local band. Seated alongside seasoned musicians, younger players could learn by careful listening and diligent practicing. Bands often contained established musicians who enjoyed helping youngsters; for example, bassist Milt Hinton learned how to improvise from trumpeter Dizzy Gillespie when both were members of Cab Calloway's orchestra in the late 1930s.

Jam sessions provide significant arenas for transferring information from established players to neophytes. These sessions served as forerunners of formally organized group education activity and hark back to the African traditions of oral and aural history.

Jam sessions may seem like informal affairs, but they are in fact quite structured and controlled. Established players usually determine which newcomers have access to the bandstand. They also usually specify the number of choruses a musician is allowed for his solos, as well as the length of time the neophyte can be on the bandstand.

Kansas City jam sessions of the 1930s have taken on legendary status. These often highly competitive gatherings pitted the best players against each other in "cutting contests." The story of tenor saxophone giants Coleman Hawkins and Lester Young trading solos all night long and trying hard to outplay each other by creating music more creative, beautiful, or swinging is one of the great stories in jazz lore. Determining the "winner" of a cutting contest depended on who could best sway the opinion of both the crowd and other musicians. But jam sessions today are less significant as a vehicle for teaching jazz.

Formal jazz education goes back at least eighty years to certain college campuses that offered both credit and non-credit courses. Alabama State Normal College was one of the first to offer credited courses. Some colleges had dance bands that often toured between semesters to raise money for the school. Students gained practical experience in playing and learned skills that helped them survive life "on the road."

Jazz studies on college campuses began to expand in the 1930s. Jimmie Lunceford studied popular music and received a bachelor's degree in music from Fisk in the mid-1920s. Since the 1950s, several colleges and universities have formalized jazz studies programs and they continue to thrive in the twenty-first century. Schools such as Berklee College of Music, Brigham Young University (Provo), Central State University, Florida A&M, Hofstra University, Howard University, Juilliard School of Music, Michigan State University, North Carolina Central University, Northwestern University, Ohio State University, University of Michigan, and Virginia Commonwealth University are among the more than 500 colleges and universities that offer music degrees with a concentration in jazz studies. Musicians such as Art Blakey, Betty Carter, and bassist Ray Brown used their groups as a training ground for promising younger players often recruited from colleges and universities. Jazz continues to be one of the more stable musical areas in many music curriculums in most American institutions of higher education.

THE FUTURE OF BLUES AND JAZZ

Having entered a second century, the genres of blues and jazz have evolved dramatically—this is perhaps one of the major reasons for their continued survival. Although the blues has declined in significance among young African American audiences, it has a loyal following among many Europeans and European Americans. Jazz and blues scholars must play a major role in informing new and younger listeners of the great legacy associated with these traditions. In any event, there is a thriving blues festival circuit that continues to play a part in the preservation of the genre. Jazz is the world's most universal music. There is no continent on the globe in which some style of jazz cannot be heard in the twenty-first century. When considering the range of musical practices worldwide, this is quite remarkable.

BLUES AND JAZZ COMPOSERS, MUSICIANS, AND SINGERS

(Some biographical profiles may appear in other chapters. To locate profiles more readily, please consult the index.)

MUHAL RICHARD ABRAMS (1930–)

Pianist, Composer, Bandleader. Born September 19, 1930 in Chicago, Abrams began his professional career in 1948, playing with many of the city's best musicians and bands. In 1961, he formed the Experimental Band with Roscoe Mitchell, Eddie Harris, and Donald Garrett, which soon became an informal academy for Chicago's most venturesome players. Under Abram's quiet but firm guidance and with the addition of Henry Threadgill, Joseph Jarman, Fred Anderson, and Steve McCall, the academy grew into the Association for the Advancement of Creative Music (AACM). The AACM helped young musicians perform and promote their own music, which could not be presented through established venues. Mitchell and Jarman, along with Lester Bowie, Malachi Favors, and Don Moye, later achieved worldwide prominence as the Art Ensemble of Chicago.

Though he never so appointed himself, Abrams was the recognized leader and moral and spiritual force behind the AACM. In 1976, Abrams moved to New York, where he performed with Anthony Braxton, Leroy Jenkins, and others and began a long-term relationship with the Italian Black Saint label, with whom he released sixteen albums as leader or co-leader, bringing him national and international recognition. In 1990, he was the first recipient of the prestigious Danish Jazzpar Award, and subsequent recordings include *Family Talk* (1993), *One Line, Two Views* (1995), and *The Visibility of Thought* (2001). The National Endowment for the Arts (NEA) named Abrams one of eight recipients of their 2010 Jazz Masters awards, billed as the nation's highest honor in jazz.

Trumpeter Henry "Red" Allen. *In the late 1920s and 1930s, Allen, along with Louis Armstrong, set the standard for the swing era style of trumpet playing.* GILLES PETARD/REDFERNS/GETTY IMAGES

RED ALLEN (1908–1967)

Trumpeter. Born in New Orleans January 7, 1908, Henry "Red" Allen Jr. learned to play trumpet in his father's brass band at an early age, moving on to play in such famous Crescent City bands as that of George Lewis (1923), John Handy (1925), and the riverboat bands of Fate Marable (1926). Allen joined King Oliver's band in St. Louis in 1927, traveling with Oliver to New York, before returning to Fate Marable's Band in 1928, where he was discovered by representatives of the Victor recording company looking for a performer to compete with Louis Armstrong. Through this association Allen recorded with the Luis Russell band (1929–1932) as lead trumpeter before moving to the bands of Fletcher Henderson (1933–1934) and the Mills Blue Rhythm Band (1934–1937).

After a solo career in which he, along with Louis Armstrong, set the standard for the swing era style of trumpet playing, Allen returned to Russell's band in 1937 before leaving again to record New Orleans style traditional music with Jelly Roll Morton and Sidney Bechet. In the 1940s and 1950s, Allen adapted his style to play with Coleman Hawkins, Pee Wee Russell, J. C. Higginbotham, and others.

Red's early playing, like Armstrong's, gradually developed into a fluid, light style that took advantage of the trumpet's timbral range. In early years he used trills, smears, growls, and splattered notes that later inspired free jazz players. His later playing reflected a movement away from traditional and swing styles to tight-knit combo style playing with blues influences. The hallmark of Red's playing was that he always sounded "modern" in whatever context he was playing, as aptly demonstrated on his 1957 album *World on a String.*

LIL HARDIN ARMSTRONG (1898–1971)

Pianist, Singer, Composer. Lillian Hardin Armstrong was born in Memphis, Tennessee, in 1898 but her family moved from Memphis to Chicago by 1915. Hardin was a classically trained musician who received her music education at Fisk University. One of her first jobs was

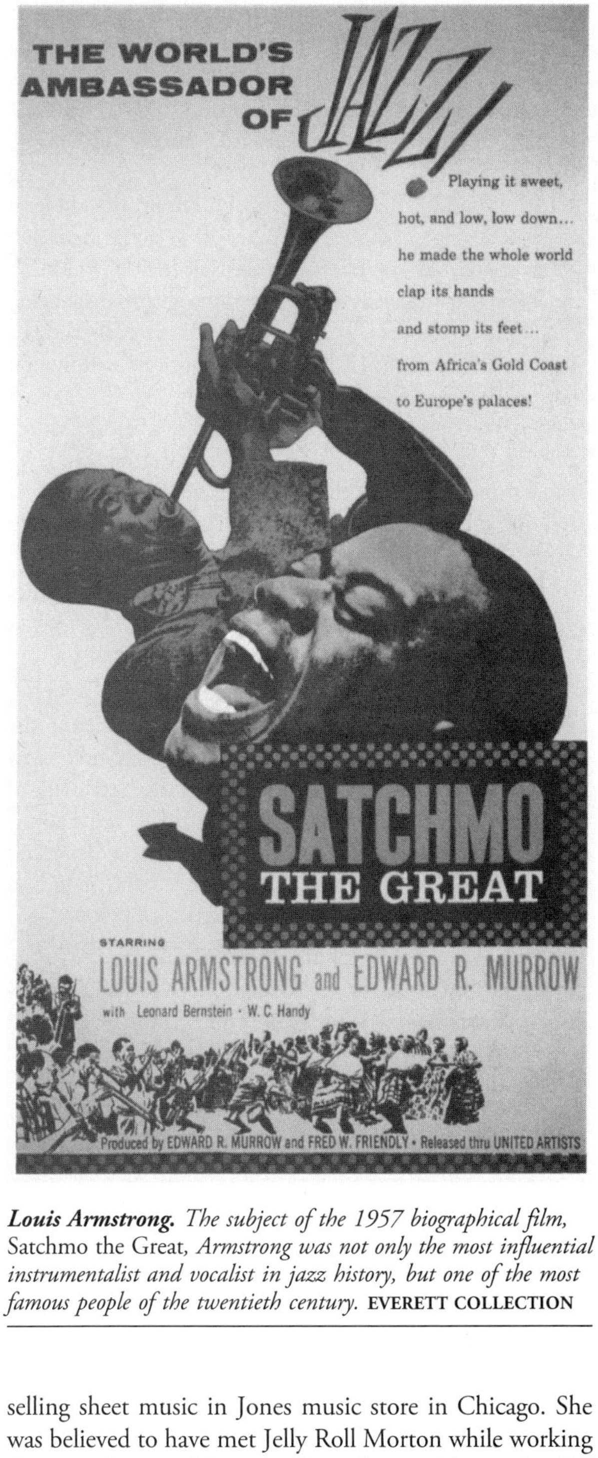

Louis Armstrong. *The subject of the 1957 biographical film,* Satchmo the Great, *Armstrong was not only the most influential instrumentalist and vocalist in jazz history, but one of the most famous people of the twentieth century.* EVERETT COLLECTION

selling sheet music in Jones music store in Chicago. She was believed to have met Jelly Roll Morton while working there, and it was Morton who influenced her style. She joined Freddy Keppard's band while still in her teens and joined King Oliver's Creole Jazz Band in 1920, where she met Louis Armstrong, who then played second trumpet. Lil and Louis were both married to other people when they met. She arranged for divorces for both of them, and Lil and Louis were married in 1924. Lil led her own band with Louis in 1925 and went on to play and write music for many of Armstrong's Hot Five and Hot Seven concerts and recordings from 1925 to 1928.

The Armstrongs divorced in 1932, but Lil and Louis remained friends for the remainder of their lives. Lil continued working as an accompanist with such players as Red Allen and Zutty Singleton until she led a series of all-star groups for Decca Records from 1937 to 1940. In 1952 she went to Europe, appearing with Sidney Bechet and as a solo artist. She returned to the United States in the early 1950s and continued playing until her death. Two of her songs, "Bad Boy" and "Just for a Thrill," became big hits in the 1960s. While playing at a tribute to Louis Armstrong at Chicago's Civic Center Plaza, Lillian Armstrong collapsed and died of a heart attack August 27, 1971, one month after Louis's death.

LOUIS ARMSTRONG (1901–1971)

Trumpeter, Singer, Bandleader. Born August 4, 1901 (although the date has often been cited as July 1, 1901), in New Orleans, Louis Armstrong was not only the most influential instrumentalist and vocalist in jazz history, but quite simply, one of the most famous people of the twentieth century.

Raised by his mother in New Orleans's Third Ward, Armstrong was arrested on December 31, 1913, for firing a pistol in the street, and was sent to the Colored Waifs Home, where he first learned to play the cornet. His skill increased with the experience that he gained from playing in the Home's band. When he was finally released from the institution, he was already proficient enough with the instrument to begin playing for money.

Befriended by his idol and mentor Joe "King" Oliver, Armstrong quickly began to develop his jazz skills. When Oliver left for Chicago in 1919, a place opened for Armstrong as a member of the Kid Ory band in New Orleans. In 1922, Oliver asked Armstrong to join him in Chicago as second cornet with his Creole Jazz Band, and it was here that Louis made his first appearance on a jazz recording in 1923.

With his skills and reputation growing, Armstrong left Chicago in 1924 to join the Fletcher Henderson band at the Roseland Ballroom in New York City. After a long tour with Henderson, he returned to Chicago in late 1925 to play with the Erskine Tate Orchestra, switching from cornet to trumpet, the instrument he played from then onward. During the next four years he made a series of recordings titled Louis Armstrong's "Hot Five" or "Hot Seven," which showcased his brilliant technique, swinging style, and improvisational ability. These recordings also featured other great players such as pianist Earl Hines, trombonist Kid Ory, and drummer Baby Dodds.

In 1929, Armstrong returned to New York and, in the revue Hot Chocolates, scored his first triumph performing a popular song with Fats Waller's "Ain't Misbehavin'." This success was a turning point in his career, leading Armstrong to begin fronting big bands and to play and sing popular songs rather than blues or original instrumentals.

With his fame growing Armstrong returned to New Orleans in 1931 and in 1932 headlined at the London Palladium, where he acquired the nickname "Satchmo" as a result of the garbling of a previous nickname in a review in London's Melody Maker magazine. From 1933 to 1935 he toured Europe, returning to the United States to film *Pennies from Heaven* with Bing Crosby. Armstrong continued to evolve from his identity as musician to that of personality-entertainer, and his singing soon became as important as his playing. In 1947, he formed a sextet that was an immediate success, and he continued to work in this context for the rest of his career, touring throughout the world.

Armstrong continued to develop his multifaceted career by appearing in numerous movies, at Newport and other major music festivals, and scoring highly in a new phenomenon, music polls. He scored a tremendous success in 1964 with his recording of "Hello, Dolly!" which bounced the Beatles from the top spot on the Top 40 list, a great feat in the age of rock. His style, melodically and harmonically simple compared to avant-garde and free jazz styles, evolved little, and his improvisations grew more infrequent. Yet his warmth and genuine appeal never faded. Though his health began to decline, he kept up his heavy schedule of international touring. When he died in his sleep at home in Corona, Queens, one month shy of his seventieth birthday, he had been preparing to resume work in spite of a serious heart attack suffered some three months prior. "The music—it's my living and my life" was his motto.

Louis Armstrong's fame as an entertainer in the later stages of his extraordinary career sometimes made people forget that he remained a great musician to the end. "You can't play a note on the horn that Louis hasn't already played," said Miles Davis. "I mean even modern." Wynton Marsalis and other contemporary musicians echo that opinion. As evidence of his lasting influence, in 1988, on the strength of its use in the film *Good Morning Vietnam*, Armstrong's recording of "What a Wonderful World" became a surprise hit, climbing to number eleven on the Billboard chart.

DAVID BAKER

See chapter 22, Classical Music.

COUNT BASIE (1904–1984)

Pianist, Bandleader. Born August 24, 1904, in Red Bank, New Jersey, William James "Count" Basie received his musical training from his mother and by picking up rudiments watching the pit bands at Harlem movie theaters. He later took informal organ lessons from Fats Waller (often crouching beside Fats in the Lincoln Theater in Harlem) before debuting in the early 1920s as an accompanist to various vaudeville acts. In 1927 Basie was stranded in Kansas City when the vaudeville act he was touring with disbanded. Remaining in Kansas City in 1928 he joined Walter Page's Blue Devils with Jimmy Rushing as the vocalist, melding his New York stride style to the hard-riffing Kansas City sound. After Page's band broke up, Basie joined the Bennie Moten band, and after Moten's death in 1935, formed his own band around the core of the Moten group. While playing at the Reno Club in Kansas City, William was soon dubbed "Count" by a local radio announcer.

At the urging of critic John Hammond, Basie brought his group to New York City in 1936, and within a year he had cut his first record and was well on his way to becoming an established presence in the jazz world. The Basie trademark was his rhythm section, which in the early years featured Basie's own clean, spare piano style, the drumming of "Papa" Jo Jones, and the bass work of Walter Paige. Outstanding soloists such as saxophonist Lester Young and trumpeter Harry "Sweets" Edison and original arrangements by Basie and other band members added to the group's distinctive sound.

Throughout the 1940s Basie maintained his big band, featuring a stream of outstanding soloists including Illinois Jacquet and J. J. Johnson. Financial constraints led Basie to a small band format with Clark Terry, Wardell Gray, and Buddy DeFranco for the years 1950 and 1951, before he returned to the big band format that he maintained for the rest of his career. In addition to maintaining a rigorous and successful international touring schedule, the Basie band scored two hits in 1955 with "April in Paris" and "Everyday I Have The Blues," featuring the vocals of Joe Williams. In 1957 his band became the first American band to play a royal command performance for the Queen of England and the first African American jazz band ever to play at the Waldorf Astoria Hotel in New York City, completing a thirteen-week engagement at the hotel. Basie and his band remained active and popular until his death on April 26, 1984.

The legacy of the Count Basie band is far reaching. His rhythm sections kept the pulse strong and propulsive yet uncluttered, providing the perfect springboard for soloists. Basie's own spare piano style laid the groundwork for modern jazz pianists, and the light, airy, and swinging sound of Lester Young's saxophone influenced virtually all jazz players to follow.

SIDNEY BECHET (1897–1959)

Saxophonist, Clarinetist. Born May 14, 1897, in New Orleans, Sidney Bechet began playing clarinet at age six and by his late teens had played with many of the early New Orleans bands including those of Freddie Keppard and "King" Oliver. After a short stay in Chicago, Bechet relocated to New York where he eventually joined Will Marion Cook's Southern Syncopated Orchestra for a tour of Europe. About this time Bechet began playing the soprano saxophone, which became his signature sound and allowed him to stand out in ensembles as only trumpet players had done previously. The group received rave reviews, and one such review by conductor Ernest Ansermet resulted in Bechet becoming the first individual jazz player to be seriously accepted as a distinguished musician.

During the early 1920s Bechet made a series of records with Clarence Williams's Blue Five, and worked briefly with Duke Ellington (one of his great admirers), Mamie Smith, and others before returning to Europe in the mid-1920s. By this time, Bechet's virtuosity and presence as a soloist was unmatched by any other reed player, with Louis Armstrong on trumpet being his only equal. From 1928 to 1938 he worked primarily with Frenchman Noble Sissle, both in Europe and the United States, but saw his popularity decline as the bands of Ellington, Basie, and Armstrong gained popular attention. After a Dixieland revival in the late 1930s, Bechet was being hailed once again by critics as a jazz luminary, and in the 1940s he made several records with Louis Armstrong, Jelly Roll Morton, and Earl Hines.

In 1949, Bechet permanently moved to France, where he enjoyed the greatest success of his career along with celebrity status. He died there of cancer on his sixty-second birthday in 1959.

JAMES HERBERT "EUBIE" BLAKE

See chapter 21, Drama, Comedy, and Dance.

ART BLAKEY (1919–1990)

(Also known as Abdullah Ibn Buhaina) Drummer, Bandleader. Born October 11, 1919, in Pittsburgh, Pennsylvania, Arthur "Art" Blakey was not only one of the greatest drummers in jazz, he was also one of the genre's foremost talent spotters and nurturers. After early experience with Fletcher Henderson in 1939 and Mary Lou Williams the following year, he joined Billy Eckstine's band in 1944, where along with Dizzy Gillespie, Charlie Parker, and Miles Davis he took part in the early stirrings of bebop. Known up to that time as a shuffle drummer, Blakey adapted his style to the complex velocities and patterns of bebop and began using triplet figures over 4/4 time. After Eckstine's band dissolved, Blakey worked as a sideman and in his own groups, further developing his style by incorporating African and Afro-Cuban tunings and techniques into his playing.

In 1954 Blakey formed the Jazz Messengers, a group that enjoyed immediate success. For the next thirty-six years, Blakey hired and helped a vast number of gifted players progress to stardom, among them Horace Silver, Lee Morgan, Freddie Hubbard, Benny Golson, Woody Shaw, Wayne Shorter, Wynton and Branford Marsalis, Keith Jarrett, Clifford Brown, and Terrence Blanchard, to name but a few. Blakey had one of the most distinctive sounds in jazz, possessed a near photographic memory for arrangements, and possessed a gift for nurturing talent that helped to produce some of the finest recordings in jazz history. Art Blakey was awarded a Grammy Lifetime Achievement Award posthumously in 2005.

JIMMY BLANTON (1918–1942)

Bassist. Born in St. Louis, Missouri, in 1918, Blanton played with Jeter Pillars and Fate Marable before joining Duke Ellington in 1939. During his short life Blanton made an incalculable contribution in transforming the use of the string bass in jazz. Until his emergence, the string bass rarely played anything but quarter notes in ensemble or solos. By playing the bass more as a horn, Blanton began sliding into eighth- and sixteenth-note runs, introducing melodic and harmonic ideas that were totally new to the instrument. His skill put him in a different class from his predecessors, making him the first true master of the bass and demonstrating the instrument's unsuspected potential as a solo vehicle. Tragically, Blanton died of tuberculosis in 1942. Had he lived, Blanton would have been a major name in the Bop movement. He was one of the original members of the Minton group that met informally at the jazz club of Harry Minton.

BUDDY BOLDEN (1877–1931)

Cornetist. Charles"Buddy" Bolden, a barber by trade, was perhaps the first jazz legend known for his drinking ability, his success with the ladies, and his flamboyant showmanship. Because his career predates the recording of jazz, the evidence of his talent as a cornet player lies in the oral tradition. By 1895 he was leading his own band, playing dances, parties, and picnics, and by the turn of the century his clear, ringing tone and his use of "blue" phrases and notes was so popular that he was often called upon to sit in with several bands on a single evening. It is unknown whether he applied improvisational techniques to his playing or simply heightened the rhythmic coloring and added melodic embellishments to the jigs, rags, and brass band tunes of the day. What is certain is that his playing and his performance style greatly influenced the players of his day and virtually all of those to follow.

In 1906, Bolden began suffering periods of mental instability, believed to be acute alcoholic psychosis, and later was diagnosed with schizophrenia (at the time known as dementia). He was committed by his family to East Louisiana State Hospital in 1907, where he remained for the last twenty-four years of his life. As he appeared before the advent of jazz recordings, Bolden's celebrated sound was never preserved. It was widely believed, however, that Joseph "King" Oliver was influenced by his playing.

WILLIAM LEE CONLEY "BIG BILL" BROONZY (1898–1958)

Guitarist, Singer. Born June 26, 1898, in Scott, Mississippi, William Lee Conley Broonzy was one of a family of seventeen. His earliest musical experience was on a homemade string instrument. Taught by his uncle, he was performing publicly by age ten in church and at social functions before working as a preacher. After serving in the Army, he moved to Chicago, switched to guitar, and began playing with Papa Charlie Jackson before beginning his recording career with Paramount in 1927. By the early 1930s he was recording hokum and blues and touring with Black Bob and Memphis Minnie as well as working sessions where the powerful new Chicago sound was being developed. He appeared at Carnegie Hall in 1938 for John Hammond's "Spirituals to Swing" series and appeared the following year with Benny Goodman and Louis Armstrong in the film *Swingin' the Dream.* He spent the 1940s barnstorming the South with Lil Green's road show and working in Chicago with Memphis Slim before touring Europe in the early 1950s and developing a worldwide following. He continued to tour and record into the mid-1950s before dying of cancer on August 15, 1958, in Chicago.

Broonzy's impressive musical skill, the size and variety of musical repertoire, and his influence on contemporaries and their followers make him one of the most important players in blues history. He wrote hundreds of songs including the classics "All by Myself" and "Key to the Highway," and his contributions to the formation of the Chicago blues sound were immense.

CLARENCE "GATEMOUTH" BROWN (1924–2005)

Guitarist, Singer. Born April 18, 1924, in Vinton, Louisiana, and raised in Orange, Texas, Clarence "Gatemouth" Brown may have earned his nickname because of his "big as a gate" voice, but it was his guitar skills that earned him a place in the blues pantheon. The son of a Cajun singer who could play accordion, banjo, fiddle, and mandolin, Brown had facility on several instruments. As a youth Brown preferred his father's lively Cajun tunes and the jazz being produced by such musicians as Count Basie and Louis Jordan over the blues. His attitude changed, though, when he was introduced to the jazz-inspired blues of guitarist T-Bone Walker.

Brown's first big break came in 1947 when he was called in as a last-minute replacement for the ailing Walker at a prominent Houston nightclub. The club's owner immediately offered Brown a long-term contract to record for his newly formed label, Peacock Records. Brown recorded more than fifty sides of music for Peacock by 1960, his blistering riffs of string-bending fury inspiring a legion of Texas players such as Albert Collins, Johnny Copeland, and Johnny "Guitar" Watson. Brown's music did not fare well on the rhythm and blues charts though, and only one of his singles,

Guitarist and Singer Clarence "Gatemouth" Brown. *A multi-instrumentalist from an early age, Brown earned a place in the blues pantheon through his guitar wizardry.* **MARC BRASZ/ CORBIS**

"Mary Is Fine"/"My Time Is Expensive" (1949), had nationwide success. But his furious instrumentals, low-down Texas blues, and horn-powered tunes became a foundation of the Texas postwar era. The early 1960s proved to be a difficult time for Brown, so in 1964 he went to Europe, where he toured and recorded widely and attained a sizable following. Rebuilding his career, he returned to the United States when blues began to show signs of resurgence. Despite winning a Grammy Award in 1981 for *Alright Again*, he never became a household name in the United States, although his releases, such as *Standing My Ground* (1989) and *Back to Bogalusa* (2001), have continued to receive acclaim. Brown was diagnosed with lung cancer in 2004. In 2005, he had to be evacuated from his home in Louisiana because of Hurricane Katrina. He died at the home of his brother in Texas within weeks of his evacuation.

CLIFFORD BROWN (1930–1956)

Trumpeter, Composer, Bandleader. Born October 30, 1930, in Wilmington, Delaware, Clifford Brown received a trumpet from his father while in high school and studied harmony, theory, trumpet, piano, vibes, and bass with a private teacher. He studied mathematics in college, graduating from Maryland State University (now known as University of Maryland Eastern Shore) in 1950. During his college years he often sat in with musicians visiting nearby Philadelphia, including Miles Davis and Fats Navarro, both of whom were significant influences on Brown. He suffered a near fatal car crash in the summer of 1950, but recovered and was soon touring with the R&B band of Chris Powell. He appeared with Tad Dameron and toured Europe with Lionel Hampton's band in 1953. In 1954 he recorded with Art Blakey and so impressed peers and audiences that he soon formed and co-led a group with drummer Max Roach, which included Sonny Rollins on tenor saxophone.

The now legendary Brown-Roach ensemble recorded and performed extensively in 1954 and 1955, during which Brown's individual style emerged. Often cited for his ability to construct intricate solos akin to those of Dizzy Gillespie, Brown also displayed a soulfulness that defined the post-bop/hard bop sound. Some of Brown's most compelling work was his masterful feel on ballads. Unfortunately, just as Brown was reaching his creative zenith, he was killed, along with Richie Powell and Powell's wife, in a car crash in the early morning of June 26, 1956.

RAYMOND MATTHEWS BROWN (1926–2002)

Bassist. Born October 13, 1926, in Pittsburgh, Ray Brown studied piano and bass while in high school before playing with Jimmy Hinsley and Snookum Russell in 1944. He moved to New York in 1945 where he played with Dizzy Gillespie, Charlie Parker, and Bud Powell, eventually joining Dizzy Gillespie's big band and making several recordings. In the late 1940s Brown was part of the great Jazz at the Philharmonic (JATP) tours playing with Lester Young and Buddy Rich, among others. In 1948 Ray married Ella Fitzgerald and led a trio for her for a short period of time (Ray and Ella divorced in 1952). In 1951 Brown recorded with Milt Jackson and John Lewis, in what would later become known as the Modern Jazz Quartet, before joining Oscar Peterson's Trio, an association that lasted fifteen years. During this time, he and Peterson produced award-winning records and were in constant demand for concerts.

Brown continued to appear on Jazz at the Philharmonic (JATP) recordings, and after leaving Peterson in 1966 he settled in California and began a successful career managing and producing other jazz acts including the Modern Jazz Quartet and Quincy Jones. Brown continued to perform and record, notably a duet with Duke Ellington in 1972, and formed the LA Four in 1974 with Bud Shank and Shelley Mann. During 1976 and 1977, Brown was the musical director of the Concord Summer Festival. He received a National Endowment for the Arts American Jazz Master Fellowship in 1995.

Brown died while on tour in Indianapolis on July 2, 2002, at the age of seventy-five. He is widely regarded as one of the finest jazz bassists in history.

RUTH BROWN (1928–2006)

Singer. Ruth Brown was born Ruth Allston Weston on January 12, 1928, in Portsmouth, Virginia. Although she came from a firm church music background, she was influenced by the singing styles of Dinah Washington and Sarah Vaughan. Her association with Atlantic Records throughout the 1950s can generally be regarded as one of the company's economic lifelines. In the mid-1940s she ran away from home with trumpeter Jimmy Brown (who was actually married at the time), whom she eventually married and later divorced. An early break for Ruth Brown came from Blanche Calloway, the sister of Cab, who also became her manager. Ruth produced a string of hits throughout the 1950s and early 1960s including "(Mama) He Treats Your Daughter Mean" (1953), "Oh What a Dream" (1954), and "Don't Deceive Me" (1960). She became known as Little Miss Rhythm and was the most popular recording artist for Atlantic Records. After a ten-year hiatus to raise a family, Ruth Brown returned to the stage in the mid-1970s. She maintained an active career with a moderate performing schedule up to the time of her death in October 2006 from complications of a stroke.

CAB CALLOWAY (1907–1994)

Singer, Dancer, Bandleader, Author. Born Cabell Calloway III, on December 25, 1907, in Rochester, New York, the second of six children born to an attorney and his teacher-wife, Calloway grew up in Baltimore, where he sometimes sang with the Baltimore Melody Boys. After moving to Chicago with his family, he enrolled in pre-law at Crane College. Calloway appeared in Plantation Days at the Loop Theatre with his sister Blanche, who along with older brother Elmer also became a bandleader, and he also worked as master of ceremonies and relief drummer at the Sunset Café. In 1928 he took over leadership of an eleven-piece band, the Alabamians, which promptly disbanded when its first New York booking at the Savoy Ballroom was a failure. Calloway stayed in New York, landing a role in the all-African American revue Connie's Hot Chocolates.

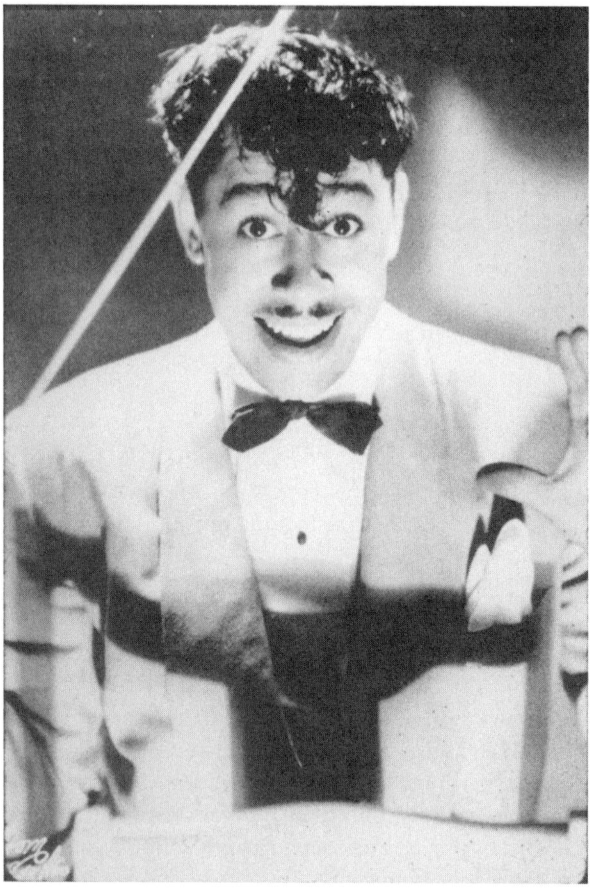

Singer and Bandleader Cab Calloway, 1936. *Honored with the National Medal of Arts in 1993, Calloway was one of the greatest entertainers of all time. His legacy is also that of a man who not only withstood the indignities of blatant racism but inspired, nurtured, and helped promote those with whom he worked.* ARCHIVE PHOTOS, INC./FRANK DRIGGS COLLECTION. REPRODUCED BY PERMISSION.

In 1929, Calloway took over as leader of another band, the Missourians, where Cab's energetic stage presence ignited the band and its audiences. This group, renamed Cab Calloway and His Orchestra, replaced Duke Ellington's band at the Cotton Club. During a radio broadcast there in 1931, Calloway swung into a recently written song called "Minnie the Moocher." According to Calloway, he realized he had forgotten the lyrics and filled in the blanks by scat-singing the first thing that came into his mind: "Hi-de-hi-de-hi-de-ho. Ho-de-ho-de-ho-de-hee." The band played along, the audience hollered back raucously, Calloway had a hit, and his band remained at the Cotton Club for nine consecutive years. Calloway created many of his other signature songs during this period, including "Reefer Man" and "Kicking the Gong Around," and he developed his famous scat style of singing. Over the years his band included many great players, such as Milt Hinton, Doc Cheatham, Dizzy Gillespie, Ben Webster, Cozy Cole, Mario Bauza, and Chu Berry, all of whom Cab helped in advancing their careers.

After his run at the Cotton Club, Calloway continued to lead his big band, and he also appeared in the 1943 film *Stormy Weather* with Lena Horne. Changing times forced Calloway to disband his orchestra in 1948, and he fronted smaller groups until 1952, when he played the breakthrough role of Sportin' Life in the Broadway revival of *Porgy and Bess.* In addition to continually appearing with jazz bands, Calloway starred with Pearl Bailey in the late 1960s all-African American production of *Hello Dolly*, published his autobiography *Of Minnie the Moocher and Me* in 1976, and appeared in the movies *Cincinnati Kid* and the *Blues Brothers.*

Calloway died on November 18, 1994. His official honors include a National Medal of Arts presented by President Clinton. However, his legacy is that of one of the greatest entertainers of all time and as a man who not only withstood the indignities of blatant racism, but inspired, nurtured, and helped promote those with whom he worked.

BENNY CARTER (1907–2003)

Saxophonist, Trumpeter, Composer, Bandleader. Bennett Lester Carter, born August 8, 1907, in New York City, was a mostly self-taught musician (i.e. he learned through imitation). He was primarily influenced by his mother. In 1925, he entered Wilberforce College in Ohio to study theology, but soon left to join Horace Henderson's territory band. In 1928, he formed his own band, which appeared at the Arcadia Ballroom in New York, before performing briefly with Fletcher Henderson, Chick Webb, and Charlie Johnson, with whom he recorded in 1929. In 1931 Carter became the musical director for McKinney's Cotton Pickers and wrote tunes for Benny Goodman before launching his own big band in 1933. Alumni of this band include Sid Catlett, Chu Berry, and Teddy Wilson. In addition to his influential work scoring for saxophone sections, Carter had few peers as a trumpeter. He appeared as a sideman with Willie Bryant in 1934 before moving to Paris and then to London in 1936, where he worked as staff arranger for BBC radio. In 1937 he played a session at a Dutch resort leading an interracial and international big band, the first successful unit of its kind in jazz history.

Returning to New York in 1938, Carter again led his own ensembles, which included working with Dizzy Gillespie. In 1944 he moved to Los Angeles, where his West Coast band included Max Roach, J. J. Johnson, and Buddy Rich. Carter was the first African American composer to break the color barrier in the Hollywood film studios. He scored many major films including *The Snows of Kilimanjaro*, as well as television shows including *Mod Squad* in the 1960s. During the 1950s and 1960s Carter also wrote and arranged for Sarah Vaughn and Abbey Lincoln while continuing to record his own projects. Carter received an honorary doctorate in music from Princeton University in 1974, and in 1988 he toured Europe, visited Japan with his own band, performed in Brazil for the first time in his career, and recorded three albums. In 1996, Carter received the Kennedy Center Honors Award for lifetime achievement. Carter's recorded legacy has documented his talents as a composer-arranger and his alto saxophone playing which, along with that of Johnny Hodges, remains as one of the most important influences of the 1930s.

BETTY CARTER (1930–1998)

Jazz Singer. Born Lillie Mae Jones in Flint, Michigan, on May 16, 1930, jazz vocalist Carter performed under the name Lorene Carter until given the nickname "Betty Bebop" by Lionel Hampton. It eventually evolved into Betty Carter. As a child, Carter studied piano at the Detroit Conservatory of Music and became fascinated by jazz while in high school. After entering talent contests and touring in small clubs in Michigan and Ohio, Carter began performing with nationally known musicians when they played in the area.

Ultimately, she attracted the attention of swing bandleader Lionel Hampton, who hired her for regular engagements with his band beginning in 1948. Carter performed with the band despite her preference for the more modern sounds of musicians such as Dizzy Gillespie. Disagreements about music eventually led to her dismissal by Hampton in 1951, but not before Carter made an auspicious appearance at Harlem's Apollo Theater.

After touring small jazz clubs on the East Coast during the early 1950s, Carter began to make a name for herself by carving out a distinctive style. She recorded the album *Meet Betty Carter and Ray Bryant* in 1955. In 1958, she recorded *Out There*, and followed it with the well-received *The Modern Sound of Betty Carter* in 1960. After recording a duet album with Ray Charles—*Ray Charles & Betty Carter* (1961)—that received national recognition, she continued to record, but like many jazz musicians in the 1960s, she saw her career suffer during the ascendancy of rock music.

Despite pressures to release more commercially viable albums, Carter continued to perform and record in the sometimes inaccessible bebop style that she had cultivated and loved. During this period, she formed her own label, Bet–Car, and gradually rebuilt her audience. She performed a New York stage show, *Don't Call Me Man*, in 1975, and appeared at the Newport Jazz Festival in 1977 and 1978. In the 1980s, Carter signed a contract with Verve Records that included the label's rerelease of several of her Bet-Car recordings. Her albums include: *At the Village Vanguard* (1970), *Now It's My Turn* (1976), *Whatever Happened to Love?* (1982), *Look What I Got* (1988), *It's Not About the Melody* (1992), and *I'm Yours, You're Mine* (1996). Widely respected for her artistic integrity and influence, Carter relished her role during the 1990s as a senior figure in jazz, and geared her focus toward jazz education. She died in Brooklyn, New York, on September 26, 1998.

CHARLIE CHRISTIAN (1916–1942)

Electric Guitarist. Born on July 29 in Bonham, Texas, and raised in Oklahoma City, Charlie Christian studied with his father, a blind itinerant musician, and played in combos around Oklahoma. Jazz critic John Hammond heard Christian in 1939 and recommended him to Benny Goodman (Hammond's brother-in-law), and Christian soon joined Goodman's sextet. Charlie Christian did for the electric guitar what Jimmy Blanton did for the bass, achieving great fame as the first electric guitarist to play single-string solos. For the first time in jazz, a guitar could be heard over the other instruments, and could function as a lead instrument rather than being relegated strictly to the rhythm section. Christian revolutionized jazz in other ways too, principally by setting up "after hours" jam sessions at clubs such as Minton's Playhouse and Monroe's in Harlem. This "Minton Group," as it would come to be known,

Electric Guitarist Charlie Christian, c. 1940. *An innovative electric guitarist, Christian was one of the central figures in the emergence of bebop. He is also credited with shifting the jazz guitar from being strictly a rhythm section instrument to a lead instrument.* JP JAZZ ARCHIVE/REDFERNS/GETTY IMAGES

included artists such as Jimmy Blanton, Roy Eldridge, Lester Young, and Clyde Hart. The new style of jazz known as bebop came to the public's attention, however, in the hands of Charlie Parker, Dizzy Gillespie, Kenny Clarke, and Thelonious Monk. Tragically, Charlie Christian did not live to enjoy the huge success of the bebop style that he helped create. In early 1941 Christian was hospitalized with tuberculosis (still known at the time as consumption) and died on March 2, 1942, at the age of twenty-five.

KENNETH SPEARMAN "KLOOK" CLARKE (1914–1985)

Drummer. Born January 9, 1914, Kenneth Spearman Clarke—later known as Liaqa Ali Salaam—was part of a musical family from Pittsburgh. Clarke studied vibraphone, piano, trombone, along with music theory and gained his early professional experience with Roy Eldridge and Edgar Hayes. He traveled to Finland and Sweden with Hayes in 1937. Between 1939 and 1940, Clarke played with Teddy Hill before the remnants of that band became the house band at Minton's in Harlem. There, working with Dizzy Gillespie, Charlie Parker, Thelonious Monk, Bud Powell, and Charlie Christian, Clarke helped develop the early sounds of bebop. During this time Clarke developed his influential style, shifting the basis of timekeeping from the bass drum to the ride cymbal, then using the bass drum and snare to interject accents against the beat, earning him the nickname of "Klook" or "Klook-mop." In addition to his work at Minton's, Clarke also toured with Louis Armstrong and Ella Fitzgerald, played with Benny Carter in 1941 and 1942, spent a year and a half in Chicago with Red Allen, and led his own band fronted by Coleman Hawkins.

After a brief service in the military beginning in 1943, Clarke returned to New York and recorded with a majority of the bebop players, notably with Dizzy Gillespie in 1946. In 1951, he toured with Billy Eckstine, and the following year he helped organize the Modern Jazz Quartet, a group he remained with for the next three years. He moved to France in 1956 where he worked with visiting American talents such as Bud Powell and Miles Davis, and worked with the Belgian pianist and arranger Frency Boland from 1961 to 1972. In addition to his influence on jazz drumming, Clarke is known for cowriting the bop classics "Salt Peanuts" with Dizzy Gillespie and "Epistrophy" with Thelonious Monk. Clarke died on January 26, 1985, in Paris, France.

NAT "KING" COLE (1919–1965)

Singer, Pianist. Nathaniel Adams Cole was born on March 17, 1919, in Montgomery, Alabama. (The family name was Coles, but Cole dropped the "s" when he formed the King Cole Trio years later.) When he was five, the family moved to Chicago, and he was soon taking piano lessons and playing organ and singing in the church where his father served as minister. While attending Phillips High School, Cole formed his own band and played with other small combos. He made his recording debut in 1936 with Eddie Cole's Solid Swingers, headed by his brother Edward playing bass and two other brothers, Fred and Isaac, accompanying.

Cole soon joined the touring revue Shuffle Along and, after the show folded, he found work in small clubs in Los Angeles. In 1939 he formed the King Cole Trio with guitarist Oscar Moore and bassist Wesley Prince. The trio played radio shows, worked nightclubs and recorded for Decca, increasing their popularity with the recording of "Sweet Lorraine" in 1940.

Moving to Capital Records in 1943, the trio recorded "Straighten Up and Fly Right," a national hit that sold more than 500,000 copies. The trio's popularity was soaring: In addition to their success with recordings they appeared in two movies and in the first Jazz at the Philharmonic (JATP) concert. Starting with the hit "The Christmas Song" in 1946, Cole begin adding string

Nat "King" Cole. *Featured in a 1955 short film about his life, Cole became an international star in the 1940s as a jazz singer. He subsequently appeared in a number of movies, toured the world, and hosted a short-lived television musical variety show.* PICTORIAL PRESS/PICTORIAL PRESS LTD/ALAMY

sections to his records, diminishing his piano playing and focusing on his singing. Between 1948 and 1949 his trio was the first African American jazz combo to have its own sponsored radio series. By the time "Mona Lisa" hit number one in 1950, Cole was an international star.

Over the next decade Cole appeared in a number of movies, toured the world, and in 1956 and 1957 hosted his own television show. The show, however, was canceled because of the lack of national sponsors. In 1958, he played the role of W. C. Handy in a film bio of the composer's life entitled *St. Louis Blues*, based on the composer's most celebrated work. Cole's career continued to soar into the early 1960s, but he received a diagnosis of lung cancer in 1964. (He had been a chain smoker for many years.) Several months after completing his final project (an appearance in the movie *Cat Ballou* with Lee Marvin and Jane Fonda), Cole died of lung cancer in 1965.

ORNETTE COLEMAN (1930–)

Saxophonist, Trumpeter, Violinist, Composer. Born on March 9, 1930, in Fort Worth, Texas, Ornette Coleman began his musical career in carnival and R&B bands. Fired by R&B guitarist-singer Pee Wee Crayton for his unconventional style of playing, Coleman eventually settled in Los Angeles, making his living as an elevator operator while studying harmony and theory textbooks on his own time. He began to compose, sat in jam sessions, and made his first album in 1958. Encouraged by John Lewis, who recommended him for a scholarship to Gunther Schuller's Lennox School of Jazz in the summer of 1959, Coleman and his quartet—Don Cherry, pocket cornet; Charlie Haden, bass; Billy Higgins, drums—opened at the Five Spot in Manhattan in the fall of 1959. In 1960, Coleman released a controversial recording entitled *Free Jazz*, which was a thirty-seven minute sustained improvisation for double quartet. To many in the music world it sounded like cacophony. Many established jazz musicians such as Miles Davis denounced Coleman, saying his performance had been disrespectful to the genre. The debate around the work was so furious that Coleman was physically threatened and, in 1962, withdrew from public appearances. During this time, he taught himself how to play the violin and trumpet.

Coleman's music, while abandoning traditional rules of harmony, tonality, and the basing solos on chord changes, was not senseless noise. In fact, the music of the first Coleman quartet, which made many recordings, was very melodic, had a strong blues feeling, and, in retrospect, sounds not so startling. Coleman continued to go his own way in music. In 1965 his "comeback" saw the unveiling of a system he called "harmolodic," which gave equal weight to harmony, melody, and "the instrumentation of the movement of forms." Eventually, Coleman was accepted by many of his peers, as evidenced by his being named a Guggenheim fellow in 1967, and some of his compositions are now considered jazz standards.

In the 1970s, Coleman composed and performed a long work for symphony orchestra and alto sax, "The Skies of America," and debuted Prime Time, a kind of jazz-fusion band with two electric guitars and two drummers. The original quartet was triumphantly reunited at the 1989 JVC Jazz Festival and also recorded again that year.

Coleman's music has influenced many players, most notably Dewey Redman, Steve Coleman, Miles Davis, and James Ulmer. Yet, his music remains a very personal means of expression; as such, it has much beauty and feeling to offer the open-minded listener. In 1993, a box set of Coleman's works entitled *Beauty Is a Rare Thing* was issued. The following year, Coleman, the father of free jazz, received a prestigious MacArthur fellowship, the so-called "genius award." In 1998, Coleman was named Jazz Artist of the Year in the Down Beat International Critics Poll, and he continues to release recordings and makes infrequent performance appearances. His album *Sound Grammar*, recorded live in Germany in 2005 and released the following year, was awarded a Pulitzer Prize for music in 2007. That same year, Coleman was honored with a Grammy Award for lifetime achievement.

JOHN COLTRANE (1926–1967)

Saxophonist, Bandleader. Born September 23, 1926, in Hamlet, North Carolina, John William Coltrane was taught to play clarinet by his father before studying alto saxophone in high school. After graduating, he moved to Philadelphia and studied music at the Ornstein School and played cocktail gigs. After playing in a Navy band in Hawaii in 1945 and 1946, he started his professional career with R&B bands, joining Dizzy Gillespie's big band on alto saxophone in 1949. When Gillespie broke up the band in 1950 and scaled down to a sextet, he had Coltrane switch to tenor sax and kept him.

After working also with groups led by two great but very different alto saxophonists, Earl Bostic and Johnny Hodges, Coltrane was hired by Miles Davis in 1955. At first, some musicians and listeners did not care for what they felt was Coltrane's "harsh" sound, but as the Davis Quintet became the most popular jazz group of its day, Coltrane was not only accepted but began to influence younger players, recording his first albums as leader. Coltrane's mounting drug problems forced Davis to release Coltrane in 1957. Returning to Philadelphia, Coltrane underwent a spiritual epiphany and kicked his drug habit. He returned to New York later that year to work with Thelonious Monk. It was during this brief period with Monk that Coltrane began being admired as an innovator as his sound became harmonically "dense." Coltrane began inserting ever more complex chord progressions every two beats as opposed to every measure or two, playing sixteenth notes in the process, and his famous "sheets of sound" style emerged.

Rejoining Miles Davis in 1958, Coltrane participated in the recording of the influential and celebrated *Kind Of Blue* studio album, and Miles's experiments with modal improvising (i.e., playing on scales rather than chord changes) set the stage for Coltrane's future work as a leader. In 1959 Coltrane composed and recorded "Giant Steps" from the album of the same name, a piece so harmonically intricate and fast that it staggered most of his fellow saxophonists and propelled Coltrane into superstardom. Coltrane left the Davis group in the spring of 1960 and formed his own group that included pianist McCoy Tyner, bassist Steve Davis, and drummer Elvin Jones (1927–2004). In 1961 this group released the album *My Favorite Things*, featuring the show tune of the same name in a performance that featured his soprano sax and lasted nearly fourteen minutes, sparking a renewed interest in the soprano sax and modality. The quartet, with rotating bassists, became one of the most tightly knit groups in jazz history; the empathy between Coltrane and Elvin Jones was astonishing, and in their live performances, the four musicians would sometimes play a single tune for more than an hour, creating music so intense that some listeners compared it to a religious experience.

Still eager to explore new and more challenging territory, Coltrane began experimenting with African and Middle Eastern song forms, unusual instrumentation, and complex arrangements by jazz musician and composer Eric Dolphy (1928–1964). Two albums from this period, *Africa/Brass* and *Live at the Village Vanguard* feature "Trane," as he was now being called, improvising over bass and drums (no piano) and incorporating braying, squawking, and split tones to convey the emotion of the tunes. Like Ornette Coleman, Coltrane was moving away from the constraints of melody, steady rhythm, and chord progressions in favor of primal drones and vamps that required his rhythm sections to rethink their roles. He continued to explore these themes, along with more traditional renderings of popular tunes, on numerous releases throughout the early 1960s.

Coltrane was himself a deeply spiritual man and in 1964 he released one of his masterpieces, the suite *A Love Supreme*, an offering of music and poetry that reflects Coltrane's inner peacefulness in the face of the storm of his other musical offerings. But by mid-1965 Coltrane was fully immersed in the avant-garde, free-jazz movement, and albums from this period such as *Ascension* feature three and four saxophonists where minimal thematic material is interspersed with long stretches of collective improvisation. Coltrane had carried his music to where the point was not the notes, but the sounds with which they were voiced. Seemingly on the cusp of breaking further musical ground, Coltrane died of liver cancer on July 17, 1967. He was awarded a posthumous Special Citation from the Pulitzer Prize Board in 2007 for his unique contributions to jazz music.

ALICE COLTRANE (1937–2007)

Pianist, Harpist, Composer, Bandleader. Born Alice McLeod on August 27, 1937 in Detroit, Michigan, Coltrane began studying classical music at age seven, learning to play both piano and harp. She expanded her skills playing organ in church and playing with R&B bands while in high school before becoming a member of local groups led by Kenny Burrell and Yusef Lateef. McLeod traveled to Paris in 1959 to study with jazz pianist Bud Powell followed by a stint recording and touring with bandleader Terry Gibbs. She met saxophonist-composer John Coltrane in 1962, and they were married in 1965. She then replaced McCoy Tyner as pianist in John Coltrane's group the following year and played with Coltrane until his death in 1967.

Alice Coltrane continued her study of composition and arrangement, and after converting to Hinduism, she began combining classical Indian instrumentation with jazz and classical musical forms. She collaborated with such jazz veterans as Pharoah Sanders, Joe Henderson, Ornette Coleman, and Rashied Ali and released several albums as leader in the late 1960s and throughout the 1970s. Her recording output and performance appearances diminished during the 1980s and 1990s. In 2004 she returned to performing for the first time in more than two decades, releasing her comeback album *Translinear Light* that same year. Coltrane gave several performances in the San Francisco area two years later, but was in frail health even then. She died January 12, 2007, of respiratory failure in Los Angeles.

MILES DAVIS (1926–1991)

Trumpeter, Composer, Bandleader. Born Miles Dewey Davis Jr. on May 25, 1926, in Alton, Illinois, Davis moved with his family to East St. Louis in 1927, where his father, a prominent dentist and substantial landowner, gave him a trumpet for his thirteenth birthday. Davis played in the high school band and studied with Elwood Buchanan, who encouraged him to develop the warm, vibrato free tone that later became Miles's trademark. In the early 1940s Davis met local star Clark Terry and sat in with his idols Charlie Parker and Dizzy Gillespie when they passed through St. Louis with the Billy Eckstine Band. In 1945, Miles's father sent him to the Juilliard School of Music in New York, but within a short time Davis was working the 52nd Street clubs with Charlie Parker and Coleman Hawkins, recording with Parker for the first time in November 1945. In 1946 Parker and Davis left for California where they split (Parker ended up in a sanitarium), and after playing with Charles Mingus, Davis joined the band of Billy Eckstine (1914–1993) which brought him back to New York.

Davis recorded again with Charlie Parker upon Parker's return to New York in 1947, but Davis and drummer Max Roach left in 1948 to pursue a new approach. The new project, a nine–piece band including Lee Konitz, Gerry Mulligan, and John Lewis, was short-lived, but its recordings had a great impact on the musicians. The primary recording that came out of that group was called *The Birth of the Cool.* Among the works included in the album was "Boplicity" (i.e., the simplification of bop). Employing such nontraditional instruments as the French horn and tuba and using arrangements of rich, complex harmonies and a "cooler" less frenetic sound, the group launched the "cool jazz" movement. The project had no commercial success and the sessions that were recorded were not released in full until years later.

In 1950 and 1951 Davis made his first recordings for the Prestige label. These were the first that were free from the restrictions of the four-minute 78 rpm disc and also featured the playing of both Sonny Rollins and Jackie McLean. Around this time, Davis's addiction to heroin began hampering his career and resulted in erratic behavior that forced his release from the Prestige label. He recorded for Blue Note and again with Prestige before kicking his habit in 1953. At that time, he asked his father if he could use one of his vacant houses, and for two weeks locked himself in a room and went "cold turkey" (i.e., without any medical assistance) to withdraw from his dependency on the drugs. He returned to New York in early 1954 and recorded two dates with Horace Silver, Percy Heath, and Art Blakey and with a slightly different group a few weeks later that introduced a new Davis style. By infusing his "cool" playing with the hard drive of the blues, these recordings signaled the beginnings of the "hard bop" style of jazz.

More success followed when in 1955 Davis formed a quintet with John Coltrane, Philly Joe Jones, Red Garland, and Paul Chambers that released a flurry of classic records for both Prestige and Columbia Records. Unfortunately drug problems resurfaced, this time with other members of the band, and the group disbanded for good in 1957. Meanwhile, Davis changed his focus again and he made his first record with arranger Gil Evans, called *Miles Ahead.* This was followed by two other collaborations with Evans, *Porgy and Bess* and *Sketches Of Spain*, both landmarks in jazz for their lush and innovative arrangements that set off Miles's haunting trumpet solos. In 1958 Davis formed a sextet with Cannonball Adderley on alto sax, Bill Evans on piano, and the return of John Coltrane on tenor. The group recorded several sessions highlighted by the album *Kind Of Blue*, which established modal improvisation in jazz and set the stage for Coltrane's later explorations on his own.

Over the ensuing six years, Davis continued to introduce new ideas and give exposure to new talent. By 1964, he had Wayne Shorter on saxophones, Herbie Hancock on piano, Ron Carter on bass, and Tony Williams (who at the time was eighteen) on drums. This group, Miles's second great quintet, introduced many new ideas, mostly in the realm of rhythmic and harmonic freedom, and over the next three years released a slate of classic albums, most notably *Miles Smiles*. However, in 1968 Davis got restless again, and attracted by the possibilities of electronic instruments, incorporated three electric pianos played by Hancock, Chick Corea, and Joe Zawinul. New bassist Dave Holland, along with John McLaughlin on electric guitar, filled out the ensemble resulting in the albums *In a Silent Way* and *Bitches Brew*, which ushered a new style—jazz fusion. Davis continued to experiment with this style through 1975, when poor health forced a six-year retirement. He returned to performing in 1981, followed shortly by experiments with hip hop and rap. Davis died on September 28, 1991.

Miles Davis changed the style of his music more often than any other jazz musician of his stature, influencing the course of jazz history and creating controversy with each change. Yet his instrumental abilities, his eye for talent, and his unique personal vision mark him as one of the greatest jazz musicians in history. His *Kind of Blue*, considered by many commentators as the greatest jazz album of all time, may also be the best selling. The Recording Industry Association of America certified *Kind of Blue* as quadruple platinum (over four million units sold) in 2008.

Blues Musician Willie Dixon, c. 1965. *One of the most important figures in blues history, Dixon inspired generations of American and European artists in both the blues and rock and roll genres.* EXPRESS/EXPRESS/GETTY IMAGES

WILLIE DIXON (1915–1992)

Musician, Singer, Songwriter. Born July 1, 1915, in Vicksburg, Mississippi, Willie Dixon was selling his songs to local bands by the time he was a teenager, singing with the Union Jubilee Singers. Afterwards he moved to Chicago, won the Illinois State Golden Gloves Championship, and recorded for Bluebird with his group, the Five Breezes, before being jailed for a year as a conscientious objector for refusing military service. By 1945 he was playing bass guitar for late night jam sessions with Muddy Waters and others and was hired as a session bassist by Chess Records in 1948.

As staff writer, arranger, and bass player, Dixon's work was primarily featured on other artists' cuts. When Muddy Waters recorded "Hoochie Coochie Man," followed by Howlin Wolf with "Evil," and Little Walter with "My Babe," Dixon's career as a songwriter was launched. Dixon became the label's tunesmith, recording manager, and bassist until the mid-1960s. Dixon also worked as musical director for a series of American folk-blues festivals in Europe, and Dixon's music caught on with British rock bands such as the Yardbirds and the Rolling Stones. After his association with Chess ended in the late 1960s, Dixon recorded *I Am the Blues*, a collection of his best-known songs, and organized the Chicago Blues All-Stars for tours of Europe, achieving fame in his own right. In the mid-1970s, realizing that he was not receiving his share of song royalties, he sued ARC Music (Chess's publishing company) and artists such as Led Zeppelin for copyright infringement and regained the rights to his songs along with financial compensation. During the 1980s Dixon helped other artists regain rights to their songs, was the first producer/songwriter honored with a boxed-set retrospective of his career, and published his autobiography. He suffered from poor health later in the decade, losing his leg to diabetes, before dying on January 29, 1992, in Burbank, California.

Willie Dixon's life and enormous body of work are a cornerstone of the blues. He is one of the first professional blues players to gain recognition and success as a songwriter, producer, and performer. His songs and style inspired generations of American and European artists in both the blues and rock and roll genres.

ERIC DOLPHY (1928–1964)

Alto Saxophonist, Clarinetist, Flutist. Born June 20, 1928, in Los Angeles, Dolphy took up alto sax in high school. After serving in the army between 1950 and1953, he gained recognition with the Chico Hamilton quintet of 1958 to 1959, playing with the band at the 1958 Newport Jazz Festival. In 1960 he moved to New York, where he collaborated with Charles Mingus and played club dates with trumpeters Booker Little and Freddie Hubbard (1938–2008). Dolphy was featured on Ornette Coleman's groundbreaking 1960 album *Free Jazz* before playing with John Coltrane, where his skills with arrangement were featured on Coltrane's Africa/ Brass release. While on tour with Mingus in 1964, Dolphy decided to stay in Europe where he recorded with Dutch, Scandinavian, and German rhythm sections. He died suddenly in Berlin on June 24, 1964, of a heart attack possibly brought on by diabetes.

Although he died at thirty-six, Dolphy's impact on jazz was substantial. He was greatly admired by fellow musicians and was honored with numerous awards including *Down Beat* magazine's New Star award for alto, flute, and miscellaneous instruments in 1961. Dolphy produced a sizable body of work because of a prolific recording schedule—from April 1960 to September 1961 he played on thirteen recording sessions—while creating a style that extended bop into new harmonic territory leading to free jazz. As well, his mastery of bass clarinet and flute helped to legitimize them as jazz instruments.

Jazz Musician Eric Dolphy, Newport, RI, 1960. *Dolphy, who played the alto saxophone, clarinet, and flute, collaborated with such jazz giants as Charles Mingus, Ornette Coleman, and John Coltrane. Despite his death at a young age, Dolphy had a substantial impact on jazz as he created a style that extended bop into new harmonic territory leading to free jazz.* ARCHIVE PHOTOS, INC. REPRODUCED BY PERMISSION.

TEDDY EDWARDS (1924–2003)

Saxophonist, Composer. Born April 26, 1924, in Jackson, Mississippi, Theodore Marcus Edwards came from a musical family—his father and grandfather were both musicians. Edwards began as an alto player, bouncing between Tampa, Florida, and Detroit, and touring with Ernie Field's orchestra before joining Roy Milton's band in Los Angeles in 1945. Shortly thereafter, he joined Howard McGhee's group and switched to tenor sax. On such classic McGhee recordings as "Up In Dodo's Room," Edwards helped to define the sound of tenor saxophone in the emerging bebop movement.

During the 1940s and early 1950s, Edwards played with many different artists including Benny Carter, Max Roach, Clifford Brown (1930–1956), Dodo Marmarosa, Dexter Gordon, and Gerald Wilson, helping fashion the West Coast bop sound. In the early 1960s he made some outstanding recordings as leader, playing with Howard McGhee and Phineas Newborn Jr. In the late 1960s and 1970s he composed and arranged for television, radio, and film before reviving his career in the 1990s through work with Tom Waits. Edwards is known for his big, warm sound that works well with bluesy ballads and on soaring solo flights.

ROY ELDRIDGE (1911–1989)

Drummer, Trumpeter, Singer. Born January 30, 1911, in Pittsburgh, David Roy Eldridge played his first "job" on the drums when he was six years old. When he was fifteen and had switched to trumpet, he ran away from home with a carnival band. After playing with some of the best bands in the Midwest, he arrived in New York in 1930, impressing the locals with his speed and range and finding jobs with good bands. By then, Eldridge had acquired the nickname "Little Jazz." He made his first record in 1935 with Teddy Hill, and by the next year he was starring in Fletcher Henderson's band. In 1937 he put together his own group and recorded as leader for the first time, introducing a trumpet style influenced by Louis Armstrong, but which assimilated the longer lines and fluid articulation of reed players such as Coleman Hawkins and Benny Carter. Eldridge's style would have a profound influence on the bop players to follow, Dizzy Gillespie in particular.

In 1941, Eldridge joined Gene Krupa's big band as trumpeter and singer, becoming the first black musician to be a featured player in a white band. (Teddy Wilson and Lionel Hampton were members of Benny Goodman's band, but not as featured players.) Eldridge's duet of "Let Me Off Uptown" with singer Anita O'Day scored a smash hit for Krupa, while his instrumental feature "Rockin' Chair" was hailed as a jazz classic. When Krupa's band dissolved in 1943, Eldridge led his own big band for a while, but joined Artie Shaw in 1944. In the late 1940s he was starring in the Jazz at the Philharmonic (JATP) tours, playing with Charlie Parker, Lester Young, and Buddy Rich. A 1950 tour with the Benny Goodman sextet brought Eldridge to Paris, where he stayed for eighteen months. During this time his career was stalled due to the advent of bebop and the trumpet innovations of his former disciple Gillespie.

In the 1950s Eldridge backed Ella Fitzgerald and toured with Jazz at the Philharmonic (JATP). He enjoyed a long association with Coleman Hawkins during this period, in addition to making a number of solid recordings throughout the 1960s. A full decade, from 1970 and onward, found Eldridge leading the house band at Jimmy Ryan's club in New York City, but a heart attack in 1980 put an end to his trumpet playing, though he still worked occasionally as a singer and gave lectures and workshops on jazz. He died on February 26, 1989. Often thought of as a stylistic bridge between Louis Armstrong and Dizzy Gillespie, Roy Eldridge's innovations and virtuosity on the trumpet qualify him as an equal.

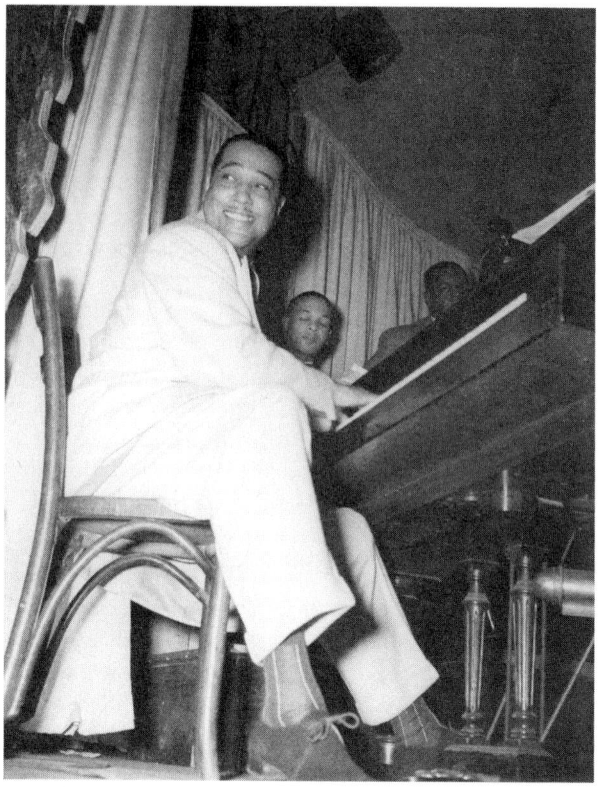

Bandleader, Composer, and Pianist Duke Ellington, 1943. *One of the leading bandleaders of jazz's swing era, Ellington was also a brilliant pianist and is considered one of the greatest composers of the twentieth century.* THE LIBRARY OF CONGRESS

DUKE ELLINGTON (1899–1974)

Bandleader, Composer, Pianist. Edward Kennedy Ellington, nicknamed Duke in his teens for his dapper dress style and courtly manners, was born into a middle-class family in Washington, D.C., on April 29, 1899. Ellington began playing piano at seven and by the time he was eighteen had formed his first band, Duke's Serenaders, and written his first composition, "The Soda Fountain Rag." Ellington was offered an art scholarship at Pratt Institute in New York, but he already had a taste of band leading and preferred to stay with music. Although he had some success in his hometown by 1923, he felt the urge to go to New York, where careers were made. Initially he did not succeed, but by 1924 he was leading his band, renamed the Washingtonians, at Club Hollywood and appearing on weekly radio broadcasts. In 1927 the young pianist-composer opened a five-year run at the Cotton Club, the most famous Harlem night spot. The job had been offered to the more celebrated Joseph "King" Oliver, but Oliver turned it down. The Cotton Club engagement led to Ellington becoming one of the most recognized names of the Swing era.

The unique Ellington style evolved at the Cotton Club, as he began composing in earnest, producing "Mood Indigo," "Tiger Rag," "The Mooche," and "Black and Tan Fantasy." The club's outrageous "Jungle Nights," arranged and overseen by Ellington, brought in huge crowds. Unlike most other groups, Ellington's band played mostly his own music and kept the same players with him. He had a great sense for their potential—almost as a great coach knows how to develop an athlete's skills—and many of Duke's bandmates who joined him during this time stayed with him for decades. (Baritone saxophonist Harry Carney [1910–1974], was in the band for nearly five decades, from 1927 until 1974. He died five months after Ellington.) Many became stars in their own right (e.g., Johnny Hodges [1906–1970], alto sax; Charles Melvin "Cootie" Williams [1911–1985], trumpet; and Barney Bigard, clarinet). Ellington knew just what to write for what he called their "tonal personalities." In 1932, the Ellington band left the Cotton Club and began touring, and in 1933 a larger version of the band completed their first European tour, where they were enthusiastically received. After they returned, the band continued to record. Ellington was one of the first musicians to understand the importance of records, and the fact that making good ones required something different than playing in public. Accordingly, he released such hits as "Solitude," "Sophisticated Lady," and "In a Sentimental Mood." In 1935, deeply touched by the death of his mother, Ellington composed "Reminiscing in Tempo." Most of his output, however, was tailored to the time limit of a little over three minutes imposed by the 78 rpm technology.

In 1939 the addition of three key players, tenor Ben Webster (1909–1973), bassist Jimmy Blanton, and associate composer-arranger Billy Strayhorn (1915–1967), who remained with Ellington until his death in 1967, propelled the band to new heights. With these additions, the Ellington band produced a string of classics, including Strayhorn's "Take the A Train" and "Chelsea Bridge," along with Ellington's "Jack the Bear" and "Bojangles." In 1943 Ellington initiated what would become an annual appearance at Carnegie Hall where he presented his first extended work,"Black, Brown and Beige." The end of the war and the close of the big band era caused the orchestra to struggle with many personnel changes, but Ellington's royalty money kept the band on the road and by the early 1950s the band was back in top form.

A second peak was reached in 1956, when Ellington's band gave a tremendous performance at the Newport Jazz Festival. The show, which was recorded, was highlighted by "Crescendo and Diminuendo In Blue," featuring twenty-seven choruses by tenor saxophonist Paul Gonsalves (1920–1974), and the 7,000 strong audience nearly rioted. Ellington once again enjoyed renewed popularity appearing on television, touring Europe in 1958 and 1959, playing all the major jazz festivals, and scoring for films once again. In the 1960s, buoyed by U.S. State Department tours, Ellington again began unveiling such compositional masterworks as *Money Jungle* (1962), *The Far East Suite* (1966), and *The Afro-Eurasian Eclipse* (1971).

Ellington and his astonishing creations have been an inspiration to generations of musicians. Most recently, Wynton Marsalis, both in his own composing and in his efforts to get Ellington's music performed live (as with the Lincoln Center Jazz Orchestra), has done much to keep the Ellington legacy in the forefront of American music. There can be no doubt that Duke Ellington, who was also a brilliant pianist, was one of the greatest composers of the twentieth century. Edward Kennedy "Duke" Ellington died of cancer on May 24, 1974, four weeks after his 75th birthday. Since his death, he has been featured on a U.S. postal stamp (1986) and commemorated in U.S. currency (the Washington, D.C., quarter, 2009). He was awarded a special citation from the Pulitzer Prize committee on the centennial anniversary of his birth in 1999.

JAMES REESE EUROPE (1881–1919)

Bandleader. James Reese Europe was born in Mobile, Alabama, on February 22, 1881, but later moved to Washington, D.C., where at ten years of age he studied violin with the U.S. Marine Band. In 1904, he moved to New York and worked as a pianist before organizing the New Amsterdam Musical Association. In 1910 James Europe formed the Clef Club, a clearinghouse for African American musicians which also had an orchestra that served as an important incubator for future jazz players. Europe had a concert at Carnegie Hall in 1914 that featured 125 musicians, twenty-five years before Duke Ellington debuted there. During World War I, Europe directed the 369th Infantry Regimental Band (popularly known as the "Hell Fighters" because of their ferocity on the battlefield), which performed throughout France and was a major force in the development of jazz in that country. Following his return to the United States, Europe toured the country with his band. In 1919 he was stabbed to death by a deranged member of his band while on tour in Boston.

JOE EVANS (1916–)

Alto Saxophone. Joseph Evans was born October 7, 1916, in Bonifay, Florida. As a teenager, he toured with the territory band, Ray Shep and His Orchestra. He left Florida for New York in 1938. Throughout the years that followed, Evans performed and recorded with many of the country's great bands, including Andy Kirk (1898–1992), Louis Armstrong, Jay McShann (1916–2006), Lionel Hampton, Johnny Hodges, and Ivory Joe Hunter (1914–1974), among others. He also performed with Billie Holiday and Charlie Parker among other soloists. In the late 1950s and early 1960s he toured with Rhythm and Blues groups. He was a studio musician with Motown before founding his own label, Carnival Records. As the CEO of the label, he recorded over thirty affiliated artists, but the label's most profitable group was the Manhattans. Evans currently resides in Richmond, Virginia. His autobiography, *Follow Your Heart*, was published by the University of Illinois Press in 2008.

ELLA FITZGERALD (1917–1997)

Singer. Born April 25, 1917, in Newport News, Virginia, Ella Fitzgerald was discovered in 1934 by drummer-band leader William "Chick" Webb (1909–1939) at an amateur contest at Harlem's Apollo Theater in New York City. She made her first recordings with Webb (who became her legal guardian) a year later. In 1936 she recorded her first efforts at "scat" singing. In 1938 she recorded "A Tisket, A Tasket," a novelty number that brought her commercial success and made her name widely known among the

Ella Fitzgerald, 1956. *Fondly known as "The First Lady of Song," Fitzgerald was the leading jazz interpreter of popular song for more than fifty years. In addition to thirteen Grammy Awards, Fitzgerald was the recipient of the National Medal of Arts and the Presidential Medal of Freedom.* GILLES PETARD/DALLE/LANDOV

general public. She soon became the first jazz vocalist to hold more popularity than the band with which she sang. When Webb died in 1939, Ella led the band for the next year. Among musicians, however, her reputation rested on her singular ability to use her voice as an instrument, improvising effortlessly in a style filled with rhythmic subtleties. Her bell-like clarity and flexibility of range were equally effective on ballads and upbeat tunes.

In the mid-1940s Ella worked with Dizzy Gillespie, witnessing the birth of bop, and recorded with Louis Jordan and Louis Armstrong. In 1948 she married bassist Ray Brown, with whom she worked and recorded "Airmail Special" (1952). In 1955, Ella began working exclusively with Norman Granz. Given more suitable material and better playing opportunities, her career soared. She appeared in several films, including *Pete Kelly's Blues* (1955) and *St. Louis Blues* (1958), presented her own concert at the Hollywood Bowl and, in celebration of the release of their four-LP collaboration, played Carnegie Hall with Duke Ellington in April 1958.

In the 1960s and the early 1970s, Ella toured the world, playing with more than forty orchestras in the United States alone, until poor eyesight forced her into semi-retirement. In 1995, Fitzgerald was inducted into the National Women's Hall of Fame. Other career highlights include fourteen Grammy Awards, Kennedy Center Honors (1979), Whitney Young Award (1984), National Medal of Arts (1987), France's Commander of Arts and Letters (1990), and the Medal of Freedom (1992), in addition to winning *Downbeat* magazine's best female jazz singer poll for eighteen consecutive years. Fitzgerald also was honored with the George and Ira Gershwin Award for Outstanding Achievement, and received honorary doctorates from Harvard, Yale, Princeton, Howard University, Dartmouth, and the University of Maryland, Eastern Shore.

In the 1970s, her health steadily declined, as she needed to be hospitalized for various ailments. In 1993, her legs were amputated below the knees as the result of complications from diabetes. Ella Fitzgerald died on June 15, 1997. No other vocalist has been so unanimously acclaimed. Fondly known as "The First Lady of Song," she was the leading jazz interpreter of popular song for more than fifty years.

TOMMY FLANAGAN (1930–2001)

Pianist. Born in Detroit on March 16, 1930, Tommy Flanagan traveled to New York in 1956 as part of the "Motor City" invasion of gifted jazz musicians and soon was playing with Charlie Parker, Dizzy Gillespie, and Ben Webster, who recognized his understated but catchy melodic talents. He was much in-demand as a sideman, recording such classic sessions as *Saxophone Colossus* with Sonny Rollins and *Giant Steps* with John Coltrane. He served as Ella Fitzgerald's accompanist and musical director on several occasions (1962–1965 and 1968–1978, a role he also filled, much more briefly, with Tony Bennett). From the mid-1970s Flanagan led his own fine trios and recorded prolifically in the United States, Europe, and Japan. His work met with critical acclaim, including his receipt of the 1993 Jazzpar Award. Flanagan was widely known as a modernist with a love of lyricism who could also play upbeat bluesy lines. He died of an aneurysm in New York City on November 16, 2001, at the age of seventy-one.

BLIND BOY FULLER (1907–1941)

Singer, Guitarist. Born Fulton Allen on July 10, 1907, in Wadesboro, North Carolina, "Blind Boy Fuller" was one of the most recorded early blues artists in the Piedmont blues tradition. Unlike his contemporaries, Big Bill and Memphis Minnie, who recorded for decades, Fuller's recordings were completed over a period of six years prior to his premature death at age thirty-three. Fuller was a fine and expressive vocalist and a masterful guitarist who could play in multiple styles including slide, ragtime, pop, and Delta blues. Although his career was spent as a street musician and house party favorite, Fuller's national steel guitar can be heard on such hits as "Rag Mama Rag," "Trucking My Blues Away," and "Step It Up and Go." Much of Fuller's repertoire remains a vital part of the Piedmont tradition.

ERROLL GARNER (1921–1977)

Pianist, Composer. Born in Pittsburgh on June 15, 1921, Garner grew up in a musical family and began picking out piano melodies before he was three years old. He started taking piano lessons at six but played all his assignments by ear instead of learning to read notes. At seven, he began playing regularly on Pittsburgh radio station KDKA. He dropped out of high school to play with a dance band and soon arrived in New York in 1944, playing the famous clubs of 52nd Street. Between 1945 and 1949 Garner freelanced recording for numerous labels. During this period he also recorded "Laura," which sold a half million copies, and his fame began to grow. By 1950 Garner had recorded with Benny Carter, Charlie Parker, Coleman Hawkins, and Teddy Edwards, among others. On March 27, 1950, he gave a solo recital at Cleveland's Music Hall, and in December of that year he performed a concert at New York's Town Hall. Garner's most famous composition, "Misty," was a big hit in 1959. During the 1960s and 1970s, Garner appeared with orchestras, composed music for film, and toured France, South America, and Asia.

A keyboard artist who played and composed by ear in the tradition of the founding fathers of jazz, Erroll Garner won the international acclaim of jazz lovers, music critics, and the general public. Strong and bouncy left-hand rhythms and beautiful melodies are the trademarks of his extremely enjoyable music. Garner was diagnosed with lung cancer, and he died at age fifty-five on January 2, 1977.

DIZZY GILLESPIE (1917–1993)

Trumpeter, Composer, Bandleader. Born October 21, 1917, John Birks "Dizzy" Gillespie received his early musical training in his native South Carolina, studying at the Laurinburg Institute from 1932–1935. After moving to Philadelphia in 1935, he joined the Frankie Fairfax Orchestra before moving to New York to work with the Teddy Hill (1909–1978) band, where he replaced his early idol, Roy Eldridge. Gillespie stayed with Hill until 1939 when he joined Cab Calloway's band, with whom he remained until 1941. Hill became manager of Minton's Playhouse, and Gillespie was soon sitting in with Kenny Clarke, Thelonious Monk, and Charlie Christian for after-hour jams where his bop experimentation was already beginning to develop and his career as an arranger began to emerge. In 1942 Gillespie recorded his first "bop" solo with Les Hite before joining Earl Hines's band in 1943. After a brief while he and Charlie Parker joined Billy Eckstine's band, with Parker as lead alto saxophone and Gillespie as musical director. After leaving Eckstine's band in 1945, Parker and Gillespie recorded Gillespie's compositions "Shaw Nuff," "Salt Peanuts," and "Hot House," sounding the first salvo of bebop. In 1946 Gillespie and Parker split as their careers took different trajectories. Gillespie formed his own big band, and among some of the musicians he hired was the talented Cuban drummer, Chano Pozo (1915–1948). Gillespie integrated Pozo's Latin clave feel into the band's rhythmic framework and virtually created Afro-Cuban jazz with notable works such as "Cubana Be, Cubana Bop," and "Manteca."

By 1948 Gillespie's trademark goatee, horn-rimmed glasses, and beret were the personifications of bebop, but Gillespie continued to move into new directions. Famed

Dizzy Gillespie, c. 1940. *In the 1940s Gillespie's trademark goatee, horn-rimmed glasses, and beret became the personifications of bebop. A true giant of jazz who is considered a genius with the trumpet, Gillespie was also a fine composer, and a number of his creations became jazz standards.* WILLIAM GOTTLIEB/REDFERNS/ GETTY IMAGES

musicians including pianist John Lewis, drummer Kenny Clarke, trombonist J. J. Johnson, and saxophonist John Coltrane all worked with Dizzy until he dissolved the big band in 1949. He then toured the world with smaller ensembles and steadily increased his reputation until by the 1970s and 1980s he was generally recognized as the elder statesman of jazz. Through it all his dazzling speed and harmonic ingenuity marked him as genius of the trumpet. His skills as composer, his use of Afro-Latin clave in swing, and his ability to improvise made him one of the true giants of the genre, with many of his compositions now jazz standards. Dizzy Gillespie died January 6, 1993, in Englewood, New Jersey.

DEXTER GORDON (1923–1990)

Saxophonist, Bandleader. Born in Los Angeles on February 27, 1923, the son of a prominent physician whose patients included famous jazz musicians, Dexter Keith Gordon began playing clarinet at seven, switching to alto and then tenor. He joined Lionel Hampton's newly formed big band in 1940. Section work with Louis Armstrong and Fletcher Henderson followed, and in 1944 Gordon made his first recording with Nat Cole. Later that year, he joined the Billy Eckstine band. After freelancing in New York, he returned home and in 1946 recorded a "tenor battle" titled "The Chase" with Wardell Gray, which became one of the biggest modern jazz hits. He sporadically continued to team up with Gray until 1952, when he was imprisoned for two years for heroin possession. His addiction plagued him for much of the next fifteen years.

Saxophonist Dexter Gordon, c. 1970. *Known for the consistently rich and robust sound of his tenor sax, Gordon was one of the prime movers behind the hard bop revolution of the 1960s.* MICHAEL OCHS ARCHIVES/GETTY IMAGES

Gordon made a major comeback in the early 1960s with a series of much-acclaimed recordings. His association with the hard bop movement at Blue Note Records, where he worked with Herbie Hancock, Bobby Hutcherson, Sonny Stitt (1924–1982), and Bud Powell, affirmed his status as the premier bop tenor stylist of the period. In 1962, he settled in Copenhagen, Denmark, where he remained for the next fourteen years, although he released two well-received records in the United States in 1969, and made brief playing visits to his homeland. In 1976, he permanently moved back to the United States, forming his own group and winning many new fans. A decade later, he starred in the French feature film *'Round Midnight*, in which his portrayal of a character based on Lester Young and Bud Powell won him an Oscar nomination as best actor.

Gordon was one of the prime movers behind the hard bop revolution of the 1960s and his rich, robust tenor sound never faltered. He never succumbed to straying into fusion or pop, choosing instead to be an expatriate to play for audiences who appreciated pure jazz. Dexter died April 25, 1990, in Philadelphia.

JOHNNY GRIFFIN (1928–2008)

Saxophonist. John Arnold Griffin III was born in Chicago in 1928 and played his first major dates with Lionel Hampton's big band (1945–1947). After a brief stay in the military, Griffin moved to New York and in 1956 recorded his first album for Blue Note Records, followed by two more recordings in 1957. These sessions established his fast and exuberant playing style. Later in 1957 he joined Art Blakey's Jazz Messengers, where he met Thelonious Monk, with whom he recorded in 1958. Griffin also engaged in collaborations with Eddie "Lockjaw" Davis (1922–1986) on "tenor battles" during this period. In December 1962, he moved to Europe and played all over the continent. He lived in Paris in the late 1960s and later moved to the Netherlands, where he owned a farm. In the late 1970s, Griffin moved back to the United States, celebrating the occasion with outstanding concerts and recordings with his friend, Dexter Gordon. He was often known as "The Little Giant" because of his stature, although he was known to produce a large sound. Griffin died of a heart attack on July 25, 2008 in Mauprévoir, France.

BUDDY GUY (1936–)

Guitarist. For the generation of 1960s British rock guitarists such as Eric Clapton, Jeff Beck, Keith Richards, and others who learned their techniques listening to blues in the early 1960s, George "Buddy" Guy was the real thing. Although it was not until the 1990s that his playing was adequately captured on tape, Guy represents a direct link between the earlier generation of Chicago blues musicians that included his mentor, Muddy Waters, and the crop of blues and rock and roll guitarists, both black and white, that presently dominate the genre.

Born on July 30, 1936, in Lettsworth, Louisiana, Guy began playing acoustic guitars as a teenager, imitating the styles of Southern blues artists Lightnin' Slim and Guitar Slim, before working his first performances in Baton Rouge in the 1950s with Big Poppa John Tilly. He left the South for Chicago in 1957, and made his mark on the local club scene. Before Guy's arrival, blues guitarists usually played sitting down. Guy not only played while standing, but would throw chairs off the stage, abuse his guitar, and wander outside with the aid of a 150-foot cord, increasing his profile immensely. Guy recorded two singles for Cobra Records in 1958, followed by a number of singles for the Chess label between 1960 and 1967, where he also backed Muddy Waters and other blues legends such as Howlin' Wolf, Sonny Boy Williamson, and Little Walter. Guy's singles from that period, including "Let Me Love You Baby" and "Stone Crazy," are some of the most popular blues of that decade.

Guy's first album for Vanguard, *A Man & the Blues* (1968), followed in the same tradition, but his later albums failed to do well. As a live act, however, Guy became a legend, both in the clubs of Chicago and at festivals around the world. In the 1970s Guy began his long and successful collaboration with harmonica player Junior Wells. Guy opened his own blues club, the Checkerboard Lounge, on Chicago's South side in 1983. He sold the Checkerboard two years later, and opened another club called Buddy Guy's Legends in 1989. In 1991, Guy issued his first domestic release in ten years, *Damn Right I've Got the Blues*, which won a Grammy Award, as did his next album, *Feels Like Rain.* He released the well-received *Sweet Tea* in 2001, and continues to record and tour. In 2006, he appeared at the Bonnaroo Music and Arts Festival in Manchester, Tennessee, and the following year at the Crossroads Guitar Festival. He was inducted into the Rock and Roll Hall of Fame in 2005.

LIONEL HAMPTON (1908–2002)

Vibraphonist, Pianist, Bandleader. Born April 20, 1908, in Louisville, Kentucky, Lionel Hampton was the first jazz musician to feature the vibraphones or "vibes," an instrument that has since maintained a vital role in jazz. Raised in Chicago, Lionel moved to California in 1928 and played drums with the Paul Howard Orchestra. His first recorded effort on vibes was for the 1930s recording "Memories of You," which featured Louis Armstrong, who was fronting the Les Hite band in California. Hampton later left Hite's band to form his own Los Angeles group. When Benny Goodman heard him in 1936, he used him on a record date, along with Teddy Wilson and Gene Krupa, and then persuaded him to join the group on a permanent basis. This decision established Goodman's band as the first to have an interracial lineup, a practice that Goodman maintained.

Hampton continued to play with the Goodman Quartet until 1940, the year he formed his own orchestra. In 1942 Hampton's band had its first big hit, "Flyin' Home," which featured a screaming brass section over a driving rhythm section and "Illinois" Jacquet's rhythm and blues solo, creating a whole new school of tenor playing. By the mid-1940s the band adopted elements of the bop sound, but Hampton's style remained essentially one of swing. His bands featured the best of jazz including Dinah Washington, Betty Carter, Dexter Gordon, Clark Terry, Art Farmer, Clifford Brown, Joe Evans, and Johnny Griffin. In addition to his long-standing big band, Hampton had his own record labels, publishing house, and other businesses. Those interests were run mostly by his wife and business manager, Gladys Hampton. In 1981, he became a professor of music at Howard University, and was honored in 1995 at the Kennedy Center Concert Hall with a tribute to his work as a United Nations music ambassador. Hampton received a host of honorary doctorates from colleges and universities across the United States, and was awarded the National Medal of Arts in 1996. Although hindered by the effects of a stroke in 1991, Hampton continued to tour the world until his death of congestive heart failure on August 31, 2002.

HERBIE HANCOCK (1940–)

Keyboardist, Composer, Bandleader. Herbie Hancock was born in Chicago on April 12, 1940, and received early training as a classical pianist. After he graduated from college in 1960, he played his first Chicago jazz dates with Coleman Hawkins and Donald Byrd. Moving to New York, he recorded two albums with Byrd before getting his own sessions in 1962 with the Blue Note label. Hancock's world class compositional skills, "soul bop" style, and excellent sidemen (i.e., Tony Williams, Ron Carter, Freddie Hubbard, and Grant Green) defined the "experimental" side of Blue Note in the mid-1960s. Concurrently Hancock became a part of Miles Davis's band (1963–1969), considered one of the top rhythm sections (again with Williams and Carter) and jazz groups of all time.

Between 1969 and 1972, Hancock formed a sextet that cut three fusion albums, recording two influential "electric jazz" albums with Davis (i.e., *Jack Johnson* and *On the Corner*) before releasing his own groundbreaking *Headhunters* (1973), where his blend of pop, funk, and jazz set the standard for fusion. In his career Hancock has released numerous albums, many of which are considered classics (e.g., *Takin' Off* and *Maiden Voyage*), and he has subsequently become one of the most commercially successful and famous jazz musicians ever. Hancock has won Grammys both for jazz composition and rhythm and blues performance, a handful of MTV Video Music Awards for the video of his 1984 hit "Rockit" and an Academy Award for best original score in 1986 for the film *'Round Midnight.* He also co-founded the record label Transparent Music in 2000.

His commercial success aside, Hancock is one of the all-time best jazz pianists. He works with integrity, creativity, and is consistently attuned to his audience.

Composer and Bandleader W. C. Handy, New York City, 1949. *Handy's work as a composer established him as the "father of the blues." His compositions included such classics as "Memphis Blues," "St. Louis Blues," and "Beale Street Blues."* **AP IMAGES. REPRODUCED BY PERMISSION.**

W. C. HANDY (1873–1958)

Trumpeter, Composer, Bandleader. Although he began his career as a cornetist and bandleader in the 1890s, William Christopher Handy's fame as the "Father of the Blues" rests almost entirely on his work as a composer. Handy was born on November 16, 1873, in Florence, Alabama. Having descended from a long line of African Methodist Episcopal ministers, Handy was expected to follow that tradition. When he indicated his interest in music, his father dismissed the idea wholeheartedly. Handy agreed to attend Oberlin College in Ohio to study for the ministry, but quickly began to follow his musical ambitions. After studying at Kentucky Musical College, he toured with an assortment of musical groups, becoming the bandmaster of the Mahara Minstrels in 1896. During his travels, Handy came into contact with many African American music traditions, and the melodies and song forms from work songs and gospel were blended into his own brass band compositions. Handy is credited with one of the early twentieth-century blues citings: When he was in a train station in Tutwiler, Mississippi, in 1903, he heard a man accompanying himself on guitar and singing three-line rhyming verses.

In 1909, during a political campaign in Memphis, Handy wrote "Mr. Crump," a campaign song for E. H. "Boss" Crump. Three years later, the song was published as "Memphis Blues," establishing the blues as an identifiable category of music. In 1914, Handy published his most famous song, "St. Louis Blues," which had been inspired by his personal hardship. He also wrote "Yellow Dog Blues" that same year. Others songs that have become perennial favorites are "Joe Turner Blues" (1915), "Beale Street Blues" (1916), "Careless Love" (1921), and "Aunt Hagar's Blues" (1922).

In the 1920s, Handy became a music publisher in New York. Despite his failing eyesight, he remained active until his death on March 29, 1958. The year that he died, a biopic entitled *St. Louis Blues* was made featuring Nat King Cole, Eartha Kitt, and Ruby Dee in starting roles. His songs extended beyond the world of jazz to find their way into the general field of popular music in many forms. Their popularity continues unabated today.

COLEMAN HAWKINS (1904–1969)

Saxophonist. Hawkins was born on November 21, 1904, in St. Louis, Missouri. When Hawkins began playing the tenor saxophone at the age of nine, he had already had four years of training on piano and cello. He continued his studies at Washburn College in Topeka, Kansas, and in 1922 toured with Mamie Smith's Jazz Hounds. In 1923, he began a ten-year association with Fletcher Henderson's band, where his style defined the sound of the saxophone until the emergence of Lester Young in the mid-1930s.

Hawkins left Henderson in 1934 to tour England and the European continent and recorded with Django Reinhardt, Benny Carter, and others. When he returned to the United States in 1939, he recorded his biggest hit, "Body and Soul," establishing himself as a national jazz name and revealing a harmonic sophistication equaled at the time only by pianist Art Tatum (1909–1956). Unlike many of his contemporaries, Hawkins was open to the experimentation of the young bop musicians, and in 1944 he formed an all-star band (including Thelonius Monk and Max Roach) for the first bop record session. During the remainder of his career, Hawkins led many of his own groups, recorded for several labels, toured regularly, and won numerous awards. He died on May 19, 1969.

In addition to being an innovator, Hawkins integrated many elements into his playing style: the "slap tongue" attack and influence of Louis Armstrong, the heavy vibrato and legato pace of cool jazz, and the reflective and introspective approach of John Coltrane. Given the position occupied by the tenor saxophone in jazz today, it is difficult to imagine that until Coleman Hawkins came along, this instrument was not seriously considered as a suitable jazz vehicle. The full, rich tone that Hawkins brought to the tenor has helped make it one of the most vital instruments in the contemporary jazz ensemble.

FLETCHER HENDERSON (1897–1952)

Bandleader, Arranger, Pianist. Born in Cuthbert, Georgia, on December 18, 1897, Fletcher Hamilton Henderson traveled to New York in 1920 to pursue a masters degree in chemistry (after receiving his undergraduate degree from Clarke University in Atlanta), but took a job to earn some extra money as house pianist and musical director for Black Swan, which was owned by W. C. Handy and Harry Pace. Black Swan was the first African American-owned and operated record company. Chemistry soon took a back seat, and in 1924 Henderson was persuaded by some of his recording studio colleagues to audition their group for a new club. The band earned the job and soon graduated to the Roseland Ballroom on Broadway, where they resided for eight years, while also touring and making hundreds of records.

The Henderson Orchestra was the first big band to achieve its reputation playing jazz, and it became the training ground for some of the greatest stars of all time, among them Louis Armstrong, Coleman Hawkins, and Benny Carter. Arranger and saxophonist Don Redman shaped the band's early style with his innovative arrangements known as "jazz specialties." When he left in 1928, Carter and others including Fletcher's younger brother Horace, also a pianist and arranger, took over. Fletcher did not begin to compose full-time for his band until 1933. However, he had such a talent for arranging that he soon became one of the architects of swing. Ironically, just as he hit his stride as a composer, his band fell on hard times, forcing him to dissolve the group in 1939. Afterwards, Henderson became a freelance arranger for, among others, Benny Goodman, for whom he wrote numerous charts and gained his widest audience. Henderson led another big band from 1941 to 1947, through which passed other great musicians such as Ben Webster, Chu Berry, and Roy Eldridge. But Henderson was unable to achieve the same level of success as his bands enjoyed during the 1920s. Late in his career, he worked as accompanist, arranged and played for *The Jazz Train* review, and led a sextet at the Café Society in New York.

Henderson's main legacy to jazz was his work as an arranger, where his simple style of pitting reed against brass sections and the use of swinging voice-blocked passages defined swing music and soon influenced all popular music. Henderson died on December 29, 1952, after a two-year paralysis brought on by a stroke.

JOE HENDERSON (1937–2001)

Saxophonist, Composer. Born April 24, 1937, Henderson studied music at Wayne State University in Detroit and played jam sessions with Sonny Stitt and other visiting musicians before forming his first group in 1960. After military service (1960–1962) he traveled to New York, where he co-led a band with trumpeter Kenny Dorham and appeared on more than thirty recordings for Blue Note Records between 1963 and 1968. He joined the groups of Horace Silver in 1964, Miles Davis in 1967, Freddie Hubbard in 1967, and Herbie Hancock in 1969. Beginning in the 1970s, he led his own groups. Henderson experimented with avant-garde structures, jazz-funk fusion, electronic effects, and at times infused his music with political awareness and social commentary. Although he was an accomplished and prolific composer, Henderson became known for his reinterpretation of standards such as his Grammy Award–winning 1992 album of Billy Strayhorn compositions entitled *Lush Life*.

Henderson was one of the foremost tenor stylists of the post-Coltrane era with an original and influential solo style that featured intense and fiery playing with a polished tone and melodic complexity. He was able to float notes with so much finesse that it made his style immediately identifiable. In 1998, Henderson suffered a stroke and stopped performing publicly. He died in San Francisco, California, on June 30, 2001.

EARL "FATHA" HINES (1903–1983)

Pianist, Bandleader. Born Earl Kenneth Hines on December 28, 1903, in Duquesne, Pennsylvania, to a musical family (his father was a trumpeter and his mother was an organist), Hines studied piano in Pittsburgh in 1914 and formed his own trio while still in high school. He began to play in local clubs with vocalist Lois Deppe before moving on to Chicago in 1923, where he worked with top Chicago bands. In 1926 Hines met Louis Armstrong, and they began recording together a brilliant series of records including their memorable performance, "Weather Bird." By 1928, Hines had become an indispensable member of Armstrong's Hot Five, and soon became known as "the trumpet-style pianist." The intricacy of his style was well beyond that of his contemporaries, and his style of right-hand single note improvisations over left-hand counter rhythms served as a touchstone for a successive generation of pianists. (His work has a brassy quality that is rhythmically intricate and makes great use of tremolos and multiple octaves.) Hines's nickname,"Fatha," as in father of modern Jazz piano, gives an indication of his influence and renown.

In 1928, Hines formed his own band at the Grand Terrace in Chicago. For the next twenty years, this band served as a proving ground for many great instrumentalists and innovators of the period—from Bud Johnson and Trummy Young in the early era to Dizzy Gillespie and Charlie Parker in the later years. After the Grand Terrace gig ended, Hines worked again with Armstrong from 1948 to 1951, before his career slumped. In 1964, a series of New York recitals revitalized his career, and he enjoyed great success in Europe, Japan, and in the United States until his death on April 22, 1983.

MILT HINTON (1910–2000)

Bassist. Considered one of the greatest bass players of jazz, Milton J. Hinton was born in Vicksburg, Mississippi, on June 23, 1910. He played with many top artists of the period, including Cab Calloway, Count Basie, Louis Armstrong, Teddy Wilson, and Benny Goodman. Hinton also appeared in concerts throughout the world and on numerous television shows, and he recorded prolifically. Known for his warm tone and rhythmic vitality, Hinton was a master of "slapping" the bass and soloing in a thoroughly modern manner. He was also an accomplished photographer and writer whose autobiography *Bass Lines* appeared in 1988. *Over Time: The Jazz Photographs of Milt Hinton* was published in 1992, and due to the diversity and longevity of Hinton's career, the work offers a valuable glimpse into jazz history. Hinton died on December 19, 2000, in Queens, New York, after an extended illness. He was ninety.

BILLIE HOLIDAY (1915–1959)

Singer. Born Eleanora Fagan in Philadelphia, Pennsylvania, on April 7, 1915, Holiday was taken to Baltimore and raised there by her teenage mother, Sadie Fagan. Her father was believed to be jazz musician Clarence Holiday, but that paternity has recently come under question. Raised as a Catholic, she was sent to New York to a Catholic reform school after reporting that she had been sexually abused at the age of ten. Released from the school two years later, Holiday remained in New York, living with her mother Sadie, and was singing in Harlem nightclubs by the time she was fifteen years old. Discovered by talent scout John Hammond, she was recommended to Benny Goodman, with whom she made her first recordings in 1933, and from 1935 to 1939 she established her reputation with a series of records made with Teddy Wilson. She also sang with her own band and those of Count Basie and Artie Shaw, and her recordings of the late 1930s with Lester Young—who dubbed her "Lady Day"—and Buck Clayton underscore how much her singing resembled the playing of an instrumentalist.

Holiday's voice was sweet, and unbelievably nuanced. Her distinctive behind-the-beat style of singing and the way she let her voice trail off for emotional impact set her apart from all other singers. Her landmark 1939 recording of "Strange Fruit," a protest against African American lynchings, was released despite the fact that her own label, Columbia Records, refused to record the tune. In her song "God Bless the Child," she departed from popular material to depict the personal alienation that she had experienced. By the time of her 1944 release of "Lover Man," she had moved from jazz to a more orchestrated pop setting, and the song is often referred to as the definitive sound of Holiday. By the late 1940s, her long-term addiction to heroin had landed her in jail. Although she returned to performing throughout the 1950s, the effect of her hopeless battle with addiction had greatly diminished her voice, if not her expressiveness.

Although she was often called a blues singer, Holiday actually sang very little blues in the tradition of Bessie Smith. Billie Holiday was, among all, a master stylist whose empathy with her fellow musicians made her a favorite among them. Despite her struggles with substance abuse, she was always generous with and respectful of her peers. Holiday died on July 17, 1959, in New York City, less than a month after her appearance at a benefit concert.

JOHN LEE HOOKER (1917–2001)

Singer, Guitarist. John Lee Hooker was born in Clarksdale, Mississippi, on August 22, 1917. He first learned to play guitar from his stepfather, Will Moore, and Moore's colleagues, James Smith and Coot Harris. Hooker traveled to Memphis, Cincinnati, and Detroit, where in 1948 he recorded a demo for Bernie Besman, owner of the Sensation label. "Boogie Chillen" and "Sally Mae" were on the first single he recorded for that label. The record became a hit on the rhythm and blues chart in 1948. Hooker followed that performance with "Crawling King Snake" in 1949 and "In the Mood for Love" in 1951, both of which were chart toppers. He then recorded for several labels under a number of pseudonyms including Delta John, Johnny Lee, and Birmingham Sam and his Magic Guitar, before landing at Vee Jay Records under his own name from 1955 to 1964. At Vee Jay, Hooker recorded with a full rhythm section that included Eddie Taylor and Jimmy Reed, and he had several successes including "Baby Lee" in 1956, "I Love You Honey" in 1958, and "Boom, Boom" in 1962. Hooker was idolized by British blues bands and was also popular on the folk coffeehouse circuit.

In the 1970s and 1980s, Hooker collaborated with such popular performers as Canned Heat, Bonnie Raitt, and Van Morrison. He also appeared in the film *The Blue Brothers*, starring John Belushi and Dan Ackroyd in 1980. Long recognized as one of the primary contributors to the blues genre, the prolific Hooker has made more than 40 albums, many of which Chess Records reissued in the 1990s. Rhino released *The Ultimate Collection (1948–1990)* in 1991. Hooker was honored with a Grammy Lifetime Achievement Award in 2000. He died at eighty-three on June 21, 2001, in San Francisco, California.

SAM "LIGHTNIN'" HOPKINS (1912–1982)

Singer, Guitarist. Born March 15, 1912, in Centerville, Texas, Sam "Lightnin'" Hopkins was one of the most prolific blues artists of all time, both in the recording studio and on stage. He claimed to have built his first guitar out of a cigar box and chicken wire at the age of eight. Inspired by famed Texas blues guitarist Blind Lemon Jefferson, Hopkins left home while still very young for a life on the road, singing and playing for money throughout Texas. During these early years, he reunited with Jefferson and served as his guide. While doing so, Hopkins learned even more from the great blues master.

During the late 1920s and much of the 1930s, Hopkins played the Houston bar circuit as a duo with his cousin, legendary Texas blues musician Texas Alexander. After working as a sharecropper near Dallas for a few years, he returned to Houston in 1946 and resumed his beer hall career with Alexander. He was soon discovered by a scout from Aladdin Records, and paired with pianist Wilson "Thunder" Smith to create the duo Thunder and Lightnin'. Hopkins and Smith recorded "Katie May" in 1946, which became a regional hit, and scored another hit with "Shotgun Blues" in 1948.

Hopkins's recordings made the rhythm and blues charts several times in the early 1950s for a variety of labels, but his popularity declined over the course of the decade as his rustic style did not compete well with rock and roll. In 1959, however, folklorist Mack McCormick rediscovered him. Introduced to a new audience consisting largely of whites, Hopkins was reinvented as a "folk-blues legend," and he quickly attained a level of acclaim that he had not previously enjoyed. Hopkins recorded and toured constantly across the United States, Canada, and Europe throughout the 1960s and 1970s, and he was featured in a number of books and film documentaries. He died of throat cancer on January 30, 1982. As one of the last great country blues musicians, Hopkins style bridged the gap between rural and urban styles.

SON HOUSE (1902–1988)

Singer, Guitarist. Born on March 21, 1902, in Riverton, Mississippi, Eddie James House Jr. ("Son" House) was preaching the gospel in Baptist churches by the time he was fifteen years old, as his family wandered between plantations looking for work. He did not pick up a guitar until he was twenty-five years old, once saying he did not even like the sound of a guitar. However, after playing a few house parties, earning some money, and discovering corn whisky, he became a blues musician. His new career was interrupted, however, when he was sentenced to a prison term for killing a man during a drunken party. Released two years later, he hit the road and soon played with Charlie Patton. Although the men were completely dissimilar in style and personalities, they shared a love for alcohol and the blues, and by the early 1930s Patton had given House entree to a recording opportunity with the Paramount label. The songs House recorded, including "My Black Mama," "Preachin' the Blues," and "Dry Spell Blues," are some of the darkest, most gut-wrenching, and rawest blues ever laid down on disk. The recordings hardly sold at the time but those who heard them were enthralled, and in 1941 Library of Congress folklorist Alan Lomax visited House to once again record his music. These recordings were mostly solo performances, but some which were backed by string band provided a glimpse into the future of blues as well as rock and roll.

House moved to Rochester, New York, and did not record again until 1964, when guitarist Alan Wilson (later of the blues-rock group Canned Heat) "rediscovered" him. House began touring again, recorded his work, appeared at Carnegie Hall in 1965, and was the subject of a documentary. House fell ill from Parkinson's and Alzheimer's diseases in the mid-1970s, and retired from performing in 1975. Eddie James House Jr. died on October 19, 1988, in Detroit, Michigan.

Son House was a major innovator in the Delta blues tradition. Along with his former partner Charlie Patton, he stands at the top of the blues hierarchy. He was a primary inspiration to both Muddy Waters and Robert Johnson, and was one of the most powerful performers in the blues tradition.

HOWLIN' WOLF (1910–1976)

Singer, Harmonica Player. Blues singer and harmonica player Howlin' Wolf was born Chester Arthur Burnett in West Point, Mississippi, on June 10, 1910. When he was eighteen years old, he met guitarist Charlie Patton and, although he never matched Patton's prowess on guitar, the elder musician's influence was obvious in Burnett's later growl of a voice and entertaining ability. He learned to play the harmonica from blues musician Aleck "Rice" Miller (Sonny Boy Williamson II) who married his half-sister Mary. By the end of the 1930s he was playing local juke joints. After a four-year stay in the Army he first settled down as a farmer, but by 1948 was a radio personality in West Memphis, where he and guitarist Willie Johnson debuted their electric band. He made his first recording in 1951 for Sam Phillips (Sun Records), where his baying style of singing won him the name Howlin' Wolf, and by 1953 he was picked up by the Chess label in Chicago.

At Chess, Howlin' Wolf was paired with guitarist Hubert Sumlin, and the two cut several hits including "Evil" and "Smokestack and Lightning" in 1956. The two were then paired with Willie Dixon, who was Chess's staff writer, and over the next several years the trio had major hits with "I Ain't Superstitious," "The Red Rooster," "Back Door Man," and "Wang Dang Doodle." Most of these songs became blues classics but were also picked up by such British bands as the Rolling Stones. Wolf and Dixon parted ways in 1964, and Wolf recorded his own songs, including "Killing Floor." By the end of the decade, rock and roll idols such as the Doors, Cream, and Jeff Beck were recording Wolf's material. Throughout the 1970s, Wolf was increasingly ill and suffered several heart attacks. He died from complications of an operation on January 10, 1976.

ALBERTA HUNTER (1895–1984)

Singer. Born April 1, 1895, in Memphis, Tennessee, Alberta Hunter debuted as a club singer in Chicago about 1912, making her first recording in 1921. She wrote "Down Hearted Blues," which became Bessie Smith's first hit in 1923. In Hunter's early 1920s recordings she used prominent sidemen such as Fletcher Henderson, Eubie Blake (1887–1983), Fats Waller (1904–1943), Louis Armstrong, and Sidney Bechet. She starred in the stage show *Showboat* with Paul Robeson in London from 1928 to 1929 and worked in Paris for many years. After returning to the United States, she worked for the USO during World War II and the Korean War before retiring in 1956 to become a nurse. She was forced to retire from nursing in 1977 when it was discovered that she was eighty-two years old. At about that time, she made a comeback as a jazz singer, appearing regularly at the Cookery in New York City, until her death in 1984.

ILLINOIS JACQUET (1922–2004)

Saxophonist, Bandleader. Jean-Baptiste"Illinois" Jacquet was born in Broussard, Louisiana, on October 31, 1922, and raised in Texas. He began playing drums as a teenager before learning the soprano and alto saxophones. Jacquet began his career as an alto saxophonist, but when he joined Lionel Hampton's band in 1942 he switched to tenor. Soon thereafter, Jacquet recorded his famous sixty-four-bar honking solo on Hampton's "Flyin' Home," making a name for himself and gaining favorable attention for the band.

After performing with Cab Calloway beginning in 1943, Jacquet initiated a long association with the Jazz at the Philharmonic (JATP) touring group the following year, starring in tenor "battles" with Flip Phillips and others. He took over Lester Young's chair in the Count Basie Orchestra in 1945, and soon after formed his own big band (along with a small jazz combo), becoming a mainstay in the international jazz circuit. Decades later, as the first jazz artist in residence at Harvard University, Jacquet formed the big band Jazz Legends in 1984, a group with which he continued to tour and record.

Jacquet was one of the first to "overblow" the tenor sax, reaching high harmonics that were dismissed by some as a circus stunt but really got to audiences; eventually, of course, such over blowing became part and parcel of the instrument's vocabulary, as in the later work of John Coltrane and in the style of David Murray. But Jacquet was also a warm ballad player. He died of a heart attack in 2004.

ELMORE JAMES (1918–1963)

Singer, Guitarist. Born on January 27, 1918, in Richland, Mississippi, James adapted to music at an early age. He learned to play bottleneck on a homemade instrument made from a broom-handle and a lard can. By the age of

Singer and Guitarist Elmore James. *The most influential slide guitarist of the postwar period, James recorded a number of songs that became blues classics, including his signature tune from 1951, "Dust My Broom."* **MICHAEL OCHS ARCHIVES/GETTY IMAGES**

fourteen, he was a weekend musician working diners and juke joints under the names "Cleanhead" or Joe Willie James. He also worked with visiting players such as Robert Johnson, Howlin' Wolf, and Sonny Boy Williamson before forming his first band in the late 1930s. James served for three years with the U.S. Navy in Guam during World War II, and after his discharge he moved to Memphis, where he became one of the first "guest stars" on the "King Biscuit Time" blues radio show (broadcast from Helena, Arkansas). James's first recording came in 1951 with "Dust My Broom," which was a surprise top ten rhythm and blues hit and subsequently became James's signature tune. He then moved to Chicago where over the course of the 1950s he assembled his famous band, the Broomdusters, and recorded numerous songs that made the charts and became blues classics. A regular performer in Chicago's blues clubs and on the radio, James began to suffer from poor health in the late 1950s. After a return to Mississippi, he traveled back to Chicago to record "The Sky is Crying" before legal troubles with record labels and the musicians' union forced him back to Mississippi. He returned again to Chicago in 1963 where he suffered a fatal heart attack on May 24th.

Elmore James was the most influential slide guitarist of the postwar period. His attitude and tone on the guitar updated the sound of Robert Johnson, and his signature guitar licks are a foundation in blues guitar. A radio repairman by trade, James reworked his guitar amplifiers to produce raw, distorted sounds that helped inspire the rock and roll music of the 1960s. His voice was loud, forceful, and prone to crack in the high registers, conveying a sense of hysteria. His bands were as loud and powerful as any blues band in Chicago, helping to launch the Electric Chicago Blues movement.

SKIP JAMES (1902–1969)

Singer, Guitarist, Songwriter. Nehemiah Curtis "Skip" James was born on June 9, 1902, in Bentonia, Mississippi, home to a thriving Delta blues tradition. His father, a Baptist minister, was competent on both organ and guitar. When James became interested in blues—an interest sparked primarily by local player Henry Stuckey—at about age seven, his father was happy to become his first guitar teacher.

In his teens, James moved to Memphis to play dance hall and barrelhouse music. He returned to Mississippi in the 1920s, settling in Jackson. There his unique falsetto and his from-the-heart presentation earned him regional fame. In 1931 James traveled north to record twenty-six songs for Paramount Records. Only a handful of the songs were ever released, and James gradually withdrew from public performing.

By the 1940s, James was out of the music business. In addition to becoming an ordained minister, he worked at a variety of jobs during the next couple of decades. He was "rediscovered" by blues revivalists John Fahey and Bill Barth in 1964, and by the following year he was earning standing ovations at blues festivals from audiences larger than any he had played for during his prime. James's highly personal style had an air of authenticity, completely devoid of commercial awareness, that was well accepted by the folk purists who made up his new generation of fans. James died on October 3, 1969, in Philadelphia, Pennsylvania.

BLIND LEMON JEFFERSON (1893–1929)

Guitarist, Singer. "Blind" Lemon Henry Jefferson (some sources reported his first name as "Clarence") was one of the pioneers of Texas blues. Born poor and blind on September 24, 1893, in Couchman, Texas, music was one of the few career options open to Lemon—which was his given name, not a nickname. Jefferson's performing career began when he was fourteen years old. He made daily treks on foot into the nearest town, Wortham, where he would sit in front of some store and begin to play for money. He eventually acquired a sizable local following and was invited to play at country picnics and other such events. When he was twenty years old, Jefferson moved to Dallas, where he made money playing in brothels and taverns. Among the local adolescents that he hired as guides during this period were the young Lightnin' Hopkins and T-Bone Walker.

In 1925 and 1926, Jefferson made a series of recording trips to Chicago, home of the Paramount record label. His first recordings, however, were not blues songs, but religious ones. His records sold well coast to coast, and he became possibly the very first country blues recording star. He made about eighty records over the next couple of years. Information surrounding his death in 1929 has now become urban legend. One story reported that after drinking heavily, Jefferson got lost in a blizzard after leaving a party in Chicago and froze to death. Yet another legend indicated that he was poisoned, or that he was killed in a botched robbery attempt in Chicago. Still another suggested that he died of a cardiac episode.

Jefferson was a serious showman who balanced a driving guitar style with a booming two-octave voice. A brilliant improviser, he often halted at the end of vocal lines to play guitar solos and could play in unusual meters. Many blues musicians were influenced by Jefferson and his recordings. His songs, favorites of American folk fans, have since been covered by countless folksingers and rock and roll artists over the years, and he was honored in the naming of the rock group Jefferson Airplane in the 1960s. An annual blues festival is staged in Wortham, Texas, not far from where Lemon Jefferson was born.

Trombonist J. J. Johnson. *Widely considered the greatest jazz trombonist of all time, Johnson in the 1940s and early 1950s collaborated with such jazz legends as Benny Carter, Count Basie, Dizzy Gillespie, Bud Powell, Miles Davis, and Charlie Parker. During this period, his trombone playing was as widely imitated as the trumpet and alto saxophone playing of Gillespie and Parker.* AP IMAGES. REPRODUCED BY PERMISSION.

JAMES LOUIS "J. J." JOHNSON (1924–2001)

Trombonist, Bandleader, Composer. Born January 22, 1924, in Indianapolis, Indiana, James Louis Johnson was the unchallenged master of the modern jazz trombone. He was the first musician to have adapted this instrument to the demanding techniques called for by the advent of Bop. Early in his career, Johnson displayed such skill in performing high speed and intricate solos that those who knew him only from records found it hard to believe that he was actually using a slide—and not a valve—trombone.

Johnson started playing the trombone in 1938 and within three years was playing with "Snookum" Russell. Shortly afterward, he met Fats Navarro, who was an early musical influence. By 1942, Johnson joined Benny Carter and began arranging music for him before joining the Count Basie Orchestra in 1945. After relocating to New York, Johnson played with Dizzy Gillespie, Bud Powell, Miles Davis, and Charlie Parker, all of whom were important in the bop movement. During those years, his trombone solos were as widely imitated as the trumpet and alto saxophone solos of Gillespie and Parker. In 1952, Johnson retired for a time, only to return in 1954 as partner of fellow trombonist Kai Winding in the popular Jay and Kai Quintet. They released several well-received recordings.

By the late 1960s, Johnson's ability as a composer took priority over his public performing and he concentrated his efforts on writing music for films and television. Despite his absence from the stage, in 1995 *Down Beat* readers and critics both voted him into the magazine's hall of fame. The man widely considered one of the greatest jazz trombonists of all time died on February 4, 2001, in his hometown, Indianapolis.

JAMES PRICE JOHNSON (1894–1955)

Pianist, Composer. James P. Johnson was born on February 1, 1894, in New Brunswick, New Jersey, and studied with his mother and other private teachers as a child. The family moved to New York in 1908, and Johnson was soon working professionally during his school breaks. He began leading a band at the Clef Club, working vaudeville and cabaret shows, and he also made piano rolls before releasing his first recordings in 1917. He was musical director for road shows and scored several black musical revues, touring England and Europe with the revue *Plantation Days*, before moving to Hollywood to write the classical score for Bessie Smith's nineteen-minute short film, *St. Louis Blues* (1929). In 1928 he appeared at a Carnegie Hall concert before retiring to Jamaica, New York, in the 1930s to concentrate on writing concert music based on traditional African American themes. He completed a tone poem in 1930, the "Symphony Harlem" in 1932, and a symphonic jazz treatment of "St. Louis Blues" in 1936. Johnson was partially paralyzed by a stroke in 1940 and was semi-active until 1951 when another stroke left him bedridden until his death in New York on November 17, 1955.

Johnson's more serious works were neglected because African American composers in art music were not afforded proper consideration at the time. He is more famously known now as the master of the "stride piano," an instrumental style which derives its name from the strong, striding, left hand of the player playing bass notes and chords while the right hand plays melody. "Stride piano" came into its own during the 1920s in conjunction with the phenomenon known as the "rent party," where an apartment building's residents might hire musicians to perform at a party and thus help to raise rent money for a month. Johnson, along with Fats Waller and Willie "the Lion" Smith, were among the many who sharpened their skills in the rent party training ground.

LONNIE JOHNSON (1899–1970)

Guitarist, Singer. Johnson was born February 8, 1899, in New Orleans. By 1912 he was playing on the streets with his father who was a violinist. Johnson began developing

Guitarist and Singer Lonnie Johnson, c. 1970. *Although he never achieved major stardom, Johnson is considered the single most influential guitar player in the history of the blues and is credited as the inventor of the guitar solo.* MICHAEL OCHS ARCHIVES/GETTY IMAGES

his unique style very early. During World War I, he played with a theater troupe that entertained Allied soldiers. He moved to St. Louis to play on riverboats in 1920 after losing thirteen family members to the deadly influenza epidemic (popularly known as the "Spanish flu"). Johnson signed a recording contract with Okeh Records in 1925 after winning a blues contest, and he quickly gained a sizable following among African American buyers of the race label's recordings.

In addition to his work as a blues musician, Johnson made recordings with a number of top jazz artists in the 1920s, including Louis Armstrong, Duke Ellington, and Eddie Lang. He also served as accompanist for several classic blues singers during this period. Altogether, Johnson made about 130 recordings between 1925 and 1932. He moved around quite a bit, eventually settling in Chicago, where he began working the nightclub scene around 1937. He recorded for the Bluebird label for five years beginning in 1939 before joining King Records in 1947. There he recorded hits such as "Tomorrow Night," "So Tired," and "Confused." In the early 1950s, Johnson toured in the United States and internationally.

In spite of his tremendous activity, however, Johnson never achieved major stardom. By the middle 1950s, his career was in decline and he took a job as a janitor at a Philadelphia hotel. He was rediscovered in 1959 by jazz and blues scholar Chris Albertson, who arranged a new recording contract with the Prestige label. Although Johnson became quite popular with young white audiences in the United States and Europe during the blues revival of the 1960s, these listeners preferred the raw country blues of Skip James, Son House, and others. In 1969, Johnson was accidently struck by a car in Toronto, Canada, and he died on June 16, 1970, of complications resulting from his injuries.

ROBERT JOHNSON (1911–1938)

Singer, Guitarist. Robert Johnson was born on May 8, 1911, in Hazelhurst, Mississippi, to Julia Dodd and Noah Johnson. Although Julia was married to Charles Dodd at the time of Robert's birth, Dodd was not the birth father of Johnson. Robert Johnson's formal education was sparse. It was believed that he learned to play the harmonica as a youth, but had ambitions to play the guitar. He married young, but his wife and child died during childbirth. Johnson then wandered the Delta looking for work, committing himself to being a full-time musician. After approximately one year of studying with Ike Zinneman, an unrecorded blues musician, Johnson emerged with the astounding ability to play guitar in a variety of styles and to write carefully constructed songs with original lyrics. His skills were further honed by his constant work as a street musician and party circuit player, activities that required him to play blues, pop, and hillbilly songs. His seemingly quick rise to virtuosity were the source of much of the legend and myth surrounding Johnson's supposed Faustian bargain with the devil (i.e., trading his soul for his incredible guitar-playing ability). The Robert Johnson devil myth was perpetuated in popular culture by the feature film *Crossroads* (1986), loosely based on the concept of a blues artist selling his soul to the devil.

Johnson did not record as much as his contemporaries Charlie Patton, Lonnie Johnson, or Blind Lemon Jefferson, but he traveled more than all of them. After his first recordings were released and "Terraplane Blues" became his signature work, he toured the Delta, Chicago, Detroit, and St. Louis. However, in August 1938, at a juke joint outside Greenville, Mississippi, he was reportedly poisoned by a jealous husband who had given him a jug of tainted liquor, and he died several days later. Johnson's music remained popular only among devotees and British rock and roll stars that covered his songs. However, a retrospective of his work was released by Columbia in the mid-1960s. Later, a complete boxed set including the only two known pictures of Johnson (which only added to his mystique and the devil-bargain legend) was released in 1990, and the set became the first blues recordings to sell more than a million units, evidence of Johnson's rising stature as a blues pioneer.

Johnson's most enduring contribution to blues style was his ability to accompany himself by playing a boogie bass line on the bottom strings, while playing melody on the top strings. His use of rundowns, turnbacks, and repeats were all new in his day, and his playing inspired many other great blues musicians to follow in his path, including Jimmy Reed, Elmore James, and Lightnin' Slim. His recordings of "Love in Vain," "Crossroads," and "Sweet Home Chicago" are blues standards that place Johnson at the top of the genre. In 2003, *Rolling Stone* magazine released their list of the one hundred top guitarists of all time. Robert Johnson appeared at number five on the list. He has received a host of other posthumous honors as well, including a Grammy (Best Historical Album) for his *Complete Recordings* in 1990, and a 2006 Grammy for Lifetime Achievement.

ELVIN RAY JONES (1927–2004)

Drummer, Bandleader. The youngest of the remarkable Jones Brothers (Hank, Thad, and Elvin), Elvin Ray was born September 9, 1927, in Pontiac, Michigan. He developed his musical skill in the vibrant jazz scene of Detroit, where he made his first records (displaying an already remarkable style) in 1953. Jones arrived in New York

Drummer Elvin Jones, c. 2000. *One of jazz's master drummers, Jones was a member of John Coltrane's quartet in the early 1960s before becoming the leader of his own groups.* ANDREW LEPLEY/REDFERNS/GETTY IMAGES

two years later, and worked with highly regarded musicians such as J. J. Johnson, Sonny Rollins, and Donald Byrd before joining John Coltrane's quartet in 1960.

With this group—the most influential of its time—Elvin Jones astonished musicians and listeners with his awesome independence of limbs (keeping four rhythms going at once), amazing drive, and ability to respond within mini-seconds to Coltrane's furious flow of ideas. Elvin Jones left Coltrane in 1965 and soon led his own groups which featured such fine saxophonists as Frank Foster, George Coleman, and Coltrane's son, Ravi.

One of jazz's master drummers, Elvin Jones integrated the drums with the frontline (melody) players to a farther extent than anyone had done before, always maintaining the pulse while featuring complex cross-rhythms and atypical resolutions to phrases. He died of heart failure in Englewood, New Jersey, in 2004.

HANK JONES (1918–)

Pianist. The eldest of the three extraordinary Jones brothers (Hank, Thad, and Elvin), Henry "Hank" Jones was born in Vicksburg, Mississippi, on July 31, 1918, and raised near Detroit, where he began his professional career as a jazz musician. He traveled to New York City in 1944 and recorded with the great trumpeter and singer Hot Lips Page. His brilliant keyboard technique and skill as both soloist and accompanist soon found him in the company of such giants as Coleman Hawkins and Charlie Parker. He toured with Jazz at the Philharmonic (JATP) beginning in 1947, and became Ella Fitzgerald's accompanist the following year.

Settling into studio work in New York, Hank Jones became one of the most recorded jazz musicians—he is to piano what Milt Hinton and George Duvivier were to the bass—in all sorts of contexts. Jones joined the CBS

Orchestra in 1959 and remained until the ensemble disbanded in 1974. From the 1970s onward, he began to do more work in clubs and on tour and to record more as a soloist and trio leader with various star bassists and drummers (his trios involved ensembles billed as "The Great Jazz Trio"). At more than ninety years old, Jones remains at the head of the pack when it comes to great jazz pianists. He currently resides in upstate New York.

THAD JONES (1923–1986)

Trumpeter, Composer, Arranger, Bandleader. Born March 28, 1923, the middle brother of the gifted Jones family (Hank, Thad, and Elvin), Thaddeus Joseph Jones played in a band led by brother Hank during his teen years before working with Sonny Stitt and briefly serving in the Army (1943–1946). Thad played with Billy Mitchell in Detroit and made his first records there in 1953. Traveling to New York in 1954, he was quickly discovered by Charles Mingus, who recorded him for his Debut label, and then joined Count Basie's band that same year, remaining with Basie for almost a decade. During this time Jones honed his writing skills, contributing numerous arrangements and original tunes for the band and providing the solo on Basie's biggest instrumental hit "April In Paris."

In 1963, Thad Jones joined forces with the great drummer Mel Lewis to colead what began as a rehearsal band but soon became the most talked about new big band in jazz. As the Thad Jones-Mel Lewis Jazz Orchestra, the group gave new life to the language of big band jazz. Thad Jones blossomed into a composer and arranger of music that was swinging but fresh. Perhaps his best-known composition, however, is the beautiful ballad "A Child Is Born." The band held together until 1979, when Thad Jones moved to Denmark and Mel took over, keeping much of Thad's "book" alive. Thad led his own bands in Scandinavia, traveling back to the United States briefly in 1984 to take on leadership of the Count Basie Band. He returned to Denmark in ill health six months before his death on August 20, 1986.

Thad Jones possessed great skills as both a trumpeter and a composer-arranger, making him one of the few "complete" jazz musicians. A player of great agility and melodic invention, Jones's playing displayed a tart and razor sharp sound.

Singer and Guitarist B. B. King. *King's passionate guitar playing and his expressive singing have made him one of the most successful artists in the history of the blues. In addition to winning multiple Grammy Awards, King was honored with the National Medal of Arts and was inducted into the Rock and Roll Hall of Fame.* **RUNE HELLESTAD/CORBIS**

B. B. KING (1925–)

Singer, Guitarist, Bandleader. Riley B. "B. B." King is one of the most successful artists in the history of the blues. King was born on September 16, 1925, in Itta Bena, Mississippi, not far from Indianola. He was first exposed to the blues through an aunt who owned a phonograph. When he was a teenager, King purchased his first guitar for eight dollars, which he had earned working in the cotton fields. At nineteen he hitchhiked to Memphis where his cousin, country blues guitarist Bukka White, taught him the basics of blues guitar. In 1948, King played at the 16th Street Grill for $12 per night. He then found a spot on a newly opened radio station, WDIA, where he played for ten minutes each afternoon. King later became a disc jockey at the station. He was named "The Boy from Beale Street" and, thereafter, he was known as B. B. King.

King made his first record in 1949 for the Bullet label: a single titled "Miss Martha King," named after the wife he had left in Mississippi. He then signed with RPM Records and made several sides for them in Memphis under the supervision of Sam Phillips. Soon King had his first rhythm and blues chart topper in 1951 with "Three O'Clock Blues." King hit the road to promote the song, and during this period he named his guitar Lucille, after a woman who had inspired a barroom brawl and fire that almost cost King his life. Throughout the 1950s, King had a string of rhythm and blues hits, with more than twenty of his songs scoring on the charts. In 1969, he recorded and released "The Thrill Is Gone," for which he received the first of many Grammy Awards. Soon King won international acclaim, influencing such artists as the Rolling Stones.

In addition to hundreds of performances around the world each year, King has opened two jazz clubs—one in Memphis and the other in Universal City, California—and cofounded the Foundation for the Advancement of Inmate Recreation and Rehabilitation with lawyer F. Lee Bailey. King's many prestigious honors include an honorary doctorate from Yale University (1977), induction into the Rock and Roll Hall of Fame (1987), the Lifetime Achievement Award from the National Academy of Recording Arts and Sciences (1987), and the Presidential Medal of the Arts (1990). In 1995 King was one of the recipients of the Kennedy Center Honors, and he was awarded the Presidential Medal of Freedom in 2006. A year earlier, he announced a farewell tour, citing his age and health issues. Although he has cut back dramatically on performing, he continues to make appearances throughout the United States and Europe. And the accolades continue to mount: In 2009, *Time* magazine listed B. B. King as number three on its shortlist of the ten best electric guitarists of all time.

JOHN AARON LEWIS (1920–2001)

Pianist, Composer, Bandleader. Born May 3, 1920, in La Grange, Illinois, Lewis was raised in a middle-class environment in Albuquerque, New Mexico. He began studying classical piano with his mother when he was a child. Lewis later studied music and anthropology at the University of New Mexico. Just months before his graduation, he was drafted into the U.S. Army during World War II. He began serving in 1942, and was eventually stationed in France. After three years in the Army, Lewis went to New York City, where he became pianist and arranger with Dizzy Gillespie's band. Two years later at Carnegie Hall, Gillespie's band performed Lewis's first major work, "Toccata for Trumpet and Orchestra."

After a European tour with Gillespie, Lewis returned to the United States to play with Lester Young and Charlie Parker and to arrange for Miles Davis. In 1952, after having finished his studies at the Manhattan School of Music, Lewis founded The Modern Jazz Quartet (MJQ) along with drummer Kenny Clarke, vibraphonist Milt Jackson, and bassist Percy Heath. After Clarke was replaced by Connie Kay in 1956, the group stayed together until 1974, with occasional reunions thereafter. With the MJQ, Lewis developed his trademark spare, cool sound with a strong classical presence, and wrote many compositions including his classic "Django." Lewis also composed film scores, collaborated with other "Third Stream" jazz proponents including Gunther Schuller (Third Stream suggesting a new, third musical form, blending jazz with classical styles), taught jazz studies, and cofounded the American Jazz Orchestra. Lewis released a well-received solo album entitled *Evolution* in 1999, and followed it up with *Evolution II*, a live recording issued in 2001. His economical piano style recalled that of Count Basie in its perfection of note selection and retention of the blues form. He died in 2001 of prostate cancer.

ABBEY LINCOLN (1930–2010)

Singer. Born Anna Marie Wooldridge on August 6, 1930, in Chicago, Lincoln graduated from Kalamazoo Central High School in Kalamazoo, Michigan, and later studied music for a number of years in Hollywood under several prominent vocal and dramatic coaches. She began her professional career in Jackson, Michigan, in 1950, after winning an amateur singing contest. Initially performing in California nightclubs as Gaby Lee, she began recording in 1956, changing her name to Abbey Lincoln before the release of her album *Affair … A Story of a Girl in Love.* During this period, Lincoln also began singing in a group led by drummer Max Roach, whom she married in 1962 (the couple divorced in 1970). The group's recording, *We Insist! Max Roach's Freedom Now Suite*, mingled social and

Abbey Lincoln, c. 1956. *Throughout her long career as a jazz singer, Lincoln was known for the emotional depth and versatility of her vocal stylings.* **GILLES PETARD/REDFERNS/GETTY IMAGES**

political theory with jazz and became a popular anthem for the civil rights movement.

Lincoln made several film appearances during the 1950s and 1960s as well, including *The Girl Can't Help It* (1956), *Nothing But a Man* (1964), and *For the Love of Ivy* (1968). She earned critical acclaim for her work, and merited induction into the Black Filmmakers Hall of Fame in 1975. That same year, she produced her own play, *A Pig in a Poke*.

As a soloist, Lincoln toured in Africa, Asia, Europe, and the Far East before becoming an assistant professor of African American theater and Pan-African studies at California State University in 1974. She was hailed by many outstanding African American jazz performers, including Coleman Hawkins, Benny Carter, and Charles Mingus, as a singer with nuance who could shift accents and rhythmic delivery, while maintaining a conversational feel to her performance. Fairly inactive in the 1980s, Lincoln regained her prominence in 1993 via a television documentary entitled *You Gotta Pay the Band: The Words, the Music, and the Life of Abbey Lincoln*, which aired on PBS. Throughout the 1990s, Lincoln contributed to and produced numerous well-received albums, including her 1999 release *Painted Lady*. In March 2002, Lincoln performed in a three-concert retrospective of her career, entitled *Over the Years: An Anthology of Her Songs*, sponsored by Jazz at Lincoln Center. She was honored with a Jazz Masters Award from the National Endowment for the Arts in 2003.

In the years that followed, Lincoln suffered from deteriorating health. In 2007, she underwent heart surgery. Abbey Lincoln died in a Manhattan nursing home on August 14, 2010.

MELBA LISTON (1926–1999)

Arranger, Trombonist. Melba Liston, who has played with the greatest names in jazz, was one of the very few jazz female trombonists to rise to such a status. Liston was born in Kansas City, Missouri, on January 13, 1926, but her family later moved to California. Her musical history began in 1937, in a youth band under the tutelage of Alma Hightower. Liston continued her trombone studies, in addition to music composition, throughout high school, and found work with the Los Angeles Lincoln Theater upon graduation. She met band leader Gerald Wilson on the night club circuit, and he introduced her to Dizzy Gillespie, Count Basie, Duke Ellington, Charlie Parker, and Dexter Gordon, all of whom she worked or recorded with in the mid-1940s. By the late 1940s, Liston was playing with John Coltrane and John Lewis in Gillespie's band, and she later toured with Billie Holiday as her assistant musical director and arranger. When the big band era waned, Liston left the music circuit and returned to California, where she took a job with the Los Angeles board of education.

During the late 1950s, Liston was coaxed back to the stage by Dizzy Gillespie for his great State Department band (1956–1957) and then toured with Quincy Jones from 1959 to 1961. During the next twenty years she led an all-female jazz group and performed freelance arrangements for Ellington, Basie, Gillespie, and Diana Ross. In 1974, Liston traveled to Jamaica to explore reggae. When she returned to the United States in 1979, she formed Melba Liston and Company, in which she revived various swing, bebop, and contemporary compositions, many of which were her own, until a stroke forced her to give up performing in 1985. Liston subsequently began composing with the aid of a computer and, beginning in the early 1990s, worked with Randy Weston, Abbey Lincoln, and T. S. Monk. She was regarded as a brilliant and creative arranger and an exceptional trombonist who possessed a beautiful, polished tone. Liston died on April 23, 1999, in Inglewood, California.

JIMMIE LUNCEFORD (1902–1947)

Bandleader. Born on June 6, 1902, in Fulton, Missouri, James Melvin Lunceford grew up in Denver, where he studied several instruments in school with instructor Wilberforce Whiteman (the father of bandleader Paul Whiteman). Lunceford later played alto sax with George Morrison and received his B.A. from Fisk University in Nashville, where he met Willie Smith, Eddie Wilcox, and Henry Wells. He eventually worked with all of them in the Lunceford Orchestra for many years. Lunceford also studied at City College in New York. After having become proficient on all reed instruments, clarinet, flute, guitar, and trombone, Lunceford began teaching music and sports at a high school in Memphis in 1926. He soon formed a musical ensemble, composed of talented high school students and enhanced by a few professional musicians. By 1934, Lunceford's band was playing at the Cotton Club in Harlem, hosting nightly radio broadcasts, and recording for Decca Records. During the next decade, the Lunceford band was as well known as those of Basie and Ellington. His powerhouse swing/dance band featured flashy costume uniforms, choreographed dance moves by the musicians, and a host of brilliant instrumentalists playing original charts of high-energy jazz. The "Lunceford style" was based on very tight ensemble playing with very creative arrangements. He was also among the few celebrated African American conductors of the swing era who did not conduct from an instrument (in the manner of Count Basie or Duke Ellington). Lunceford died of a heart attack on July 13, 1947, while the band was on tour in Seaside, Oregon.

BRANFORD MARSALIS (1960–)

Saxophonist, Bandleader. Branford Marsalis was born on August 26, 1960, in Breaux Bridge, Louisiana. A very gifted saxophone player, he got his start as a member of Art Blakey's Jazz Messengers in 1980 while he was still a student at Berklee College of Music in Boston. From 1982 to 1985, Marsalis played in his brother Wynton's quartet. He has since performed with a multitude of artists, from Miles Davis and Dizzy Gillespie to Tina Turner and the group Public Enemy. Only fourteen months older than his brother Wynton, Branford has gained equal fame, as a result of his wide exposure as band leader for the *Tonight Show* from 1992 to 1995. An inventive soloist and an imaginative leader-organizer, Marsalis won a Grammy in 1993, formed the group Buckshot LeFonque, a hip hop and jazz ensemble, in 1994, and has hosted "JazzSet" on National Public Radio. Marsalis won another Grammy in 2001, this time for his album *Contemporary Jazz*.

Branford Marsalis's activities beyond jazz include mid-1980s tours with pop/rock acts Sting, Bruce Hornsby, and the Grateful Dead. Marsalis's forays into acting have included parts in several feature films including *Throw Momma From the Train* (1987) and director Spike Lee's motion picture *School Daze* (1988). Marsalis's quartet provided the music for Lee's *Mo' Better Blues* in 1990. More outgoing than his brother Wynton, Branford is an open-minded neo-traditionalist who is willing to nurture rather than preserve jazz. He is currently artist-in-residence at North Carolina Central University.

WYNTON MARSALIS (1961–)

Trumpeter, Bandleader. Wynton Marsalis was born on October 18, 1961, into a musical family in New Orleans—his father, Ellis, is a prominent pianist and teacher, and his brothers, Branford and Delfeayo, are both musicians in their own right. Marsalis was trained in both the jazz and classical traditions. At seventeen years old, he won an award at the prestigious Berkshire Music Center for his classical prowess. Marsalis traveled to New York to attend the Juilliard School of Music in 1978. Two years later, he left Juilliard to join the Jazz Messengers, studying under drummer and bandleader Art Blakey.

After touring and recording in Japan and the United States with the Herbie Hancock quartet in 1981, Marsalis made his first LP, formed his own group, and toured solo extensively. Soon he made a classical album, and in 1984 became the first instrumentalist to win simultaneous Grammy awards as best jazz and classical soloist. He received the Pulitzer Prize in 1997 for his oratorio *Blood on the Fields*—the first jazz-based work to win the coveted prize. *Standard Time, Vol. 5: The Midnight Blues* followed a year later. In 1999, Wynton Marsalis released *Marsalis Plays Monk: Standard Time, Vol. 4* to coincide with the popular PBS special of the same name. Beyond recordings, he has composed music for films and ballet and cofounded the Lincoln Center Jazz Orchestra. Wynton Marsalis faced criticism for the position he took in the 2001 Ken Burns series *Jazz*. Many jazz specialists felt that he played down the impact of more recent jazz musicians in favor of greats such as Louis Armstrong and Duke Ellington.

A brilliant virtuoso of the trumpet with total command of any musical situation in which he chooses to place himself, Wynton Marsalis has also made himself a potent spokesman for the highest musical standards in jazz, to which he is firmly and proudly committed. He has urged young musicians to acquaint themselves with the rich tradition of jazz and to avoid the pitfalls of "crossing over" to pop, fusion, and rock. In 1994, the same year his septet disbanded, Marsalis published *Sweet Swing Blues on the Road*, a collection of essays about the jazz life. Marsalis has received honorary doctoral degrees from a host of major colleges and universities. He was awarded the U.S. National Medal of Arts in 2005.

HOWARD "MAGGIE" McGHEE (1918–1987)

Trumpeter. Born on March 6, 1918, in Tulsa, Oklahoma, McGhee was raised in Detroit, where he played clarinet in high school before switching to trumpet. His early band engagements were at the Club Congo in Detroit followed by work with Lionel Hampton and Andy Kirk in New York, with whom he made his first recording,"McGhee Special," in 1942. During this time, McGhee occasionally participated in the historic after-hour jam sessions at Minton's Playhouse in Harlem (these sessions ultimately gave birth to the be-bop movement of the 1940s). In 1945 McGhee toured with Coleman Hawkins, which took him to California, where he recorded several tracks with Charlie Parker for Dial Records. After returning to New York, McGhee recorded with both Milt Jackson and Fats Navarro, becoming one of the most acclaimed jazz trumpeters by the end of the 1940s. In the 1950s, however, McGhee suffered from a long bout with drug addiction. He returned in the early 1960s to produce some very good recordings, and again in the late 1970s, after another long period of inactivity. Perhaps as a result of the uneven pattern of his career (short bursts of creativity and recordings, followed by long periods of obscurity), McGhee remained relatively unknown to successive generations of jazz enthusiasts. Howard McGhee died on July 17, 1987, in New York City.

CARMEN McRAE (1920–1994)

Singer, Pianist. Born in New York City on April 8, 1920, Carmen McRae developed a talent on the piano that won her numerous music scholarships. During her teen years, she was greatly influenced by the vocal style of Billie Holiday. An early highlight for McRae came when Holiday recorded "Dream of Life," one of McRae's compositions. After finishing her education, McRae moved to Washington, D.C., working as a government clerk by day and a nightclub pianist/singer by night. In the 1940s, she returned to New York, working with Benny Carter and then with Mercer Ellington and Count Basie. She recorded her first solo albums, *Easy to Love* and *Carmen McRae* in 1954, and was dubbed "best new female singer" by *Down Beat* magazine that same year, leading to a recording contract with Decca in 1955. McRae released several acclaimed albums with Decca and then with Columbia Records between 1955 and 1965.

In 1967, McRae's appearance in the film *Hotel*, marked the beginning of a string of periodic television and film appearances that extended into the 1980s. She also had a part in the 1978 television series *Roots* and in the 1986 film *Jo Jo Dancer, Your Life Is Calling*. McRae engaged in a flurry of activity (performing, traveling, and recording) through the early 1990s, recording six albums between 1990 and 1991 alone. *Carmen Sings Monk* was nominated for a Grammy Award in 1990—McRae's seventh Grammy nomination. In 1994 McRae was honored with a National Endowment for the Arts American Jazz Masters Award. Later that year she suffered a stroke that eventually led to her death on November 10, 1994. McRae was best known for her evocative interpretations of songs, smoky voice, and her behind-the-beat phrasing that reflected the influence of Billie Holiday.

MEMPHIS MINNIE (1897–1973)

Guitarist, Singer. Born Lizzie Douglas on June 3, 1897, in Algiers, Louisiana, and raised in Walls, Mississippi, Memphis Minnie learned to play banjo and guitar as a child. She ran away from home at thirteen, traveling alone to Memphis in 1910. Minnie played on the streets, toured the South with medicine shows and circuses, and lived with blues guitarist Casey Bill Weldon, who tutored her and whom she subsequently married. In 1929, she

Singer and Guitarist Memphis Minnie, 1941. *Credited with more than 250 blues recordings over a lengthy career spanning four decades, Minnie was the most popular and prolific female blues artist outside the vaudeville tradition.* FRANK DRIGGS COLLECTION/GETTY IMAGES

began her second marriage, to guitarist "Kansas" Joe McCoy, with whom she formed a marvelous, inventive duo with a rural flavor. With McCoy, Minnie recorded some masterpieces of guitar playing, such as "Hoodoo Lady," and her style became more urbanized. Her style continued to evolve, and in 1938 she formed a duo with her third husband, guitarist Ernest "Little Son Joe" Lawlers, whose compositions "Digging My Potatoes," "Me and My Chauffeur," and "I'm So Glad," and delicate accompaniment combined with stunning guitar interplay helped to increase Minnie's popularity and success.

With her health beginning to fail in the 1950s, and with public interest in her music declining, Minnie retired to Memphis in 1957. Lawlers died in 1961, and Minnie eventually moved into a nursing home. She died on August 6, 1973, in Memphis.

Memphis Minnie earned the respect of her peers throughout her long career with solid musicianship and more than 250 blues recordings over four decades, some of which are still widely performed by contemporary artists. Undoubtedly, she was the most popular and prolific female blues artist outside the vaudeville tradition.

CHARLES MINGUS (1922–1979)

Bassist, Composer, Bandleader. Born on April 22, 1922, in Nogales, Arizona, Mingus grew up in the Watts area of Los Angeles. He began lessons on trombone and cello, but eventually settled on the bass and studied composition during his school years with trumpeter Lloyd Reese. Mingus also later studied with Red Callender (1916–1992), a noted jazz player, and Herman Rheinschagen, a classical musician. Early in his professional career, Mingus moved to San Francisco and worked with Barney Bigard (1906–1980) in a band that included the veteran New Orleans trombonist Kid Ory, and he toured briefly in Louis Armstrong's big band. He also led his own groups and recorded with them locally. After a brief stay with Lionel Hampton's band, which recorded his composition "Mingus Fingers," Mingus joined Red Norvo's trio and traveled with that ensemble to New York in 1951.

Settling in New York, Mingus worked with many leading performers, including Dizzy Gillespie and Charlie Parker, and founded the record label Debut with Max Roach. He also formed his first of many jazz workshops in which new music, mostly written by himself, was rehearsed and performed by four to eleven musicians taking verbal cues from Mingus. Believing in spontaneity as well as discipline, Mingus often interrupted public performances by his band if the playing did not meet his standards, sometimes firing players on the spot. Although controversial because of these tactics, Mingus inspired the loyalty of drummer Dannie Richmond (1935–1988), who played with Mingus from 1956 to 1970 and again between 1974 and 1977. Other long-time associates included trombonist Kimmy Knepper, pianist Jaki Byard, saxophonists Eric Dolphy, Booker Ervin, John Handy, and Bobby Jones, and trumpeter Jack Walrath.

Mingus's music was as volatile as his temper. His compositions were filled with ever-changing melodic ideas and textures, as well as shifting, often accelerating, rhythmic patterns. Mingus was influenced by Duke Ellington, Art Tatum, and Charlie Parker, and his music often reflected psychological states and social issues—Mingus was a staunch fighter for civil rights and wrote such protest pieces as "Fables of Faubus," "Meditations On Integration," and "Eat That Chicken." He was also steeped in the music of the Holiness Church ("Better Git It In Your Soul" and "Wednesday Night Prayer Meeting") and in the whole range of the jazz tradition ("My Jelly Roll Soul," "Theme For Lester Young," "Gunslinging Bird," and "Open Letter To Duke"). He composed for films and ballet and experimented with larger forms as well. His most ambitious work, an orchestral suite called "Epitaph," was more than two hours long and was not performed in full during his lifetime. Charles Mingus died in 1979 from amyotrophic lateral sclerosis (or Lou Gehrig's disease), with which he struggled valiantly, composing and directing from a wheelchair almost until the end of his life.

At its best, Mingus's music—angry, humorous, always passionate—ranks with the greatest in jazz. He also wrote a strange but interesting autobiography *Beneath the Underdog*, which was published in 1971. That same year, Mingus received a Guggenheim fellowship in composition, and he was honored by President Carter at a White House jazz event in 1978. Mingus was posthumously awarded a Lifetime Achievement Grammy in 1997. A jazz ensemble, Mingus Dynasty, formed after the composer's death in 1979, continues to perform his music.

KEB' MO' (1952–)

Guitarist, Banjo Player, Singer, Songwriter. Born Kevin Moore on October 3, 1951, in Los Angeles, Keb' Mo' was exposed to gospel and blues at an early age. By the time he was thirteen, he was an accomplished guitarist. At twenty-one, he joined a rhythm and blues band that was later hired for a tour by Papa John Creach—the band played on three of Creach's albums. Keb' Mo' later opened for such jazz and rock and roll artists as the Mahavishnu Orchestra, Jefferson Starship, and Loggins

Keb' Mo', Hollywood Bowl, 2008. *A blues artist heavily influenced by the old-fashioned country blues style of Robert Johnson, Keb' Mo' is a three-time Grammy Award–winner for best contemporary blues album.* MICHAEL BEZJIAN/WIREIMAGE/ GETTY IMAGES

and Messina. These experiences helped broaden Keb' Mo's musical horizons and abilities. In 1980 he recorded a rhythm and blues–based solo album *Rainmaker* for Casablanca. In 1983, he joined Monk Higgins's band as a guitarist and met a number of blues musicians who helped to increase his understanding of the genre. He subsequently joined a vocal group called The Rose Brothers and worked around the Los Angeles area.

In 1990, Moore portrayed a Delta blues musician in a local play titled *Rabbit Foot* and later played the role of Robert Johnson in a docudrama called *Can't You Hear the Wind Howl?* He released his self-titled debut album as *Keb' Mo'* in 1994, featuring two Robert Johnson covers, "Kind Hearted Woman," and "Come On in My Kitchen." The other songs on the album were written or cowritten by Moore, and featured his guitar and banjo work. Keb' Mo' performed a well-received set at the 1995 Newport Folk Festival. Keb' Mo's second release on Okeh Records, *Just Like You,* won a Grammy Award and was one of the best-selling blues albums in 1996. He followed up with the albums *Slow Down* (1998), *The Door* (2000), and *Big Wide Grin* (2001). In 2003, Keb' Mo' collaborated with celebrated director Martin Scorsese in the miniseries *The Blues* with several other well-known musicians. In 2006, Keb' Mo' released the album *Suitcase,* and in 2009 released a live album, *Live & Mo'.*

Keb' Mo' has drawn heavily on the Country Blues style of Robert Johnson (a major musical influence on him), but writes much of his own material, keeping his sound contemporary with touches of soul and folksy storytelling.

THELONIOUS MONK (1917–1982)

Pianist, Composer. Born on October 10, 1917, in Rocky Mount, North Carolina, Thelonious Sphere Monk moved with his family to New York when he was a child. By his early teens, he was providing piano accompaniment for his mother in church. He later toured with an evangelist before studying briefly at the Julliard School of Music and then working with the Lucky Millender Band (1942), Coleman Hawkins (1943–1945), and Cootie Williams (1945), who first recorded Monk's "Round Midnight." In addition to these bands and Dizzy Gillespie's big band, Monk was the house pianist at Minton's Playhouse in Harlem, the primary breeding ground for the bop movement. From 1947 to 1952, Monk recorded several important tracks for Blue Note Records, including "'Round Midnight," "Ruby, My Dear," "Straight, No Chaser," and "Epistrophy," all of which are now considered classics. Monk's career was seriously harmed when he was arrested on drug charges in 1951 and lost his cabaret card (an antiquated and sometimes discriminatory system which allowed musicians to play in New York clubs where alcoholic beverages were served) for a six year period, forcing him to survive on session and out-of-town work. After he regained his right to work in New York in 1957, he had a long run at the Five Spot club headlining a quartet that included John Coltrane, and his recordings from this period are often considered to be his best. Monk's fame began to grow as he appeared at numerous festivals, on television, and by the mid-1960s was featured on the cover of *Time* magazine. By the end of that decade, health problems cut into his activities, and his last major tour was from 1971 to 1972. When he died on February 17, 1982, he had not played in public for six years.

Although associated with the bop movement and that genre's harmonic advancements, Monk stood apart from bop in his approach to structure, rhythm, and style of improvisation. His lightning fast right-hand figures and compositions that featured unusual and challenging tempo changes made him thoroughly modern. He insisted that improvisations should be derived from the melody rather than the chord changes as practiced in bop. Monk has been called the first jazz post-modernist and most important jazz composer since Duke Ellington. Many of his compositions, including "Round About Midnight," "Ruby My Dear," "Off Minor," and "Epistrophy," have become jazz standards.

JELLY ROLL MORTON (1885?–1941)

Composer, Pianist, Bandleader. Born about 1885 (the precise date and year is currently contended) in New Orleans, Ferdinand Joseph "Jelly Roll" LeMonthe (later he took the surname of his stepfather, Mouton, and changed it to "Morton") was playing piano in the Storyville brothels of New Orleans by 1902. Restless and ambitious, he worked in vaudeville and minstrel shows, was a pool hustler, a pimp, he ran gambling halls, and traveled as far as Alaska and Mexico. He finally settled in Chicago in 1923, where he was contracted to make recordings for Victor. Morton was backed by a group of jazz players from New Orleans that came to be called the Red Hot Peppers. Jelly Roll Morton & His Red Hot Peppers recorded a number of tracks between 1926 and 1928, many of which are now considered jazz classics. These recordings featured Morton's own compositions and arrangements, and they showed that he was a major talent, quite possibly the first real composer of jazz. (Morton often claimed that he invented the genre.) The recordings also occurred historically just as Louis Armstrong was changing the shape of jazz, and Morton's style, which emphasized collective improvisation and polyphony, clashed with Armstrong's virtuoso performances and big band–ensemble playing. The result was that Morton was consistently overlooked.

In 1928 Morton moved to New York and made some very good recordings, but he was considered out-of-date when big band and swing began to emerge. Nevertheless, "King Porter Stomp," one of Morton's signature compositions, became a swing anthem. In 1938 Morton was discovered living in Washington, D.C., and managing an obscure night club by Library of Congress musical folklorist Alan Lomax, who recorded a series of solo performances and reminiscences that revived Morton's career and resulted in a few more sessions. Failing health and restlessness led Morton to drive to California, where he had a lady friend. But the trip made him ill, and he died, just before the revival of interest in traditional jazz, which would have given him the break he needed.

Few musicians in jazz were as colorful or talented as Jelly Roll Morton. He may not have invented jazz, but he certainly was an important bridge between ragtime and jazz as one of the early musical notators of the genre. A pool hustler, pimp, and tireless self-promoter, Morton's ego and attitude alienated many people. But his compositions, which were often constructed in three distinct sections and displayed unison melody lines, time choruses, instrumental breaks, and group improvisations, are undeniably brilliant. His piano playing influenced many players after him, including Earl "Fatha" Hines.

FATS NAVARRO (1923–1950)

Trumpeter. Theodore "Fats" Navarro was born in Key West, Florida, in 1923. He started playing trumpet at age thirteen, and also played tenor sax (his first paid gigs, in fact, were for saxophone performances with the Walter Johnson band in Miami). Navarro was first heard nationally in 1943–1944 as a trumpeter with Andy Kirk's band. Dizzy Gillespie recommended Navarro to Billy Eckstine, with whom Navarro subsequently played for eighteen months, capably filling the vacancy created by the departing Gillespie, who left Eckstine to form his own band. By 1946 Fats Navarro had established himself as a top soloist, and he left Eckstine to work with Illinois Jacquet, Lionel Hampton, and Coleman Hawkins. He also recorded with smaller and less constraining groups, first as a leader between 1946 and 1947, and then in a supporting capacity with Tadd Dameron, Bud Powell, and Howard McGhee in 1948 and 1949. These sessions set the course for jazz trumpeting, as Navarro's full, rich, and melodious solos later influenced the styles of Clifford Brown and Lee Morgan. Inactive for the last year of his life, Navarro died on July 7, 1950, from the effects of drug addiction and tuberculosis.

KING OLIVER (1885–1938)

Cornetist, Trumpeter. Born May 11, 1885, in Abend, Louisiana, Joseph "King" Oliver started on trombone but switched to cornet and began playing with the Melrose Brass Band in 1907. Oliver first earned the nickname "King" in 1917 in Kid Ory's band, after establishing himself as the best cornet performer of his day. During the Storyville era (from the late nineteenth century through the 1910s), Oliver met and befriended young Louis Armstrong, becoming Armstrong's mentor. With the close of Storyville, Oliver left for Chicago in 1919, and Armstrong replaced him in Ory's band. By 1922, Oliver had a steady employment at Lincoln Gardens and invited Armstrong to Chicago to play in his Creole Jazz Band as second cornetist. In 1923, the Creole Jazz Band made the first important recordings by an African American jazz group. Other sidemen in Oliver's band included Baby Dodds, Johnny Dodds, Barney Bigard, and Lil Hardin (later Lil Hardin Armstrong). Between 1925 and 1927 Oliver led the Dixie

Syncopators at the Plantation Café, and constructed a new type of jazz that combined the skills of well-trained musicians with more spontaneous players associated with the earlier New Orleans styles. These innovations gave Chicago a leading role in the burgeoning jazz movement.

Changing tastes, a disastrous tour, and business errors caused Oliver's career to decline, however, and failing health added to the performer's woes. Dental problems forced him to give up playing, after touring mainly in the South during the early 1930s. Oliver worked in a poolroom beginning in 1936 until his death in Savannah, Georgia, on April 8, 1938.

Oliver is remembered as one of the major innovators of early jazz who used mutes and buckets to alter the sound of his horn and often imitated vocal sounds with his cornet. His distinctive phrasing formed the early vocabulary of the great trumpeters who followed him.

KID ORY (1886–1973)

Trombonist, Bandleader. Edward "Kid" Ory was born on December 25, 1886, on a plantation near La Place, Louisiana. He was the best known of the so-called tailgate trombonists—trombone players who employed a style that featured rhythmic effects and the imitation of vocal effects such as glissandi, falsetto, moans, and other stylizations. Ory led his own bands in New Orleans and Los Angeles, where in 1922 he led Spike's Seven Pods of Pepper as the first African American band to record on the West Coast in the New Orleans style. In 1925 Ory moved to Chicago to play with Joseph "King" Oliver, Jelly Roll Morton, and with Louis Armstrong's Hot Fives and Hot Sevens, with whom he recorded his famous composition "Muskrat Ramble" in 1926.

Ory returned to the West Coast in 1929. After playing for a time with local bands, he retired to run a successful chicken ranch from 1930 to 1939. In the 1940s, he gradually returned to music with Barney Bigard, Bunk Johnson, and other New Orleans notables. Ory toured Europe successfully in 1956 and again in 1959, and he spent his final years living comfortably in Hawaii before his death on January 23, 1973.

CHARLIE PARKER (1920–1955)

Saxophonist. Charles Christopher Parker Jr. was born in Kansas City, Kansas, on August 29, 1920, and raised in Kansas City, Missouri. He was the only child of Charles and Addie Parker. He began to play alto saxophone after being presented with the instrument as a gift from his mother in 1931. Parker left school at sixteen (without any objections from his mother) to become a professional musician in Kansas City, Missouri. After an initial lack of success, which was attributed to his early drug use, Parker found work with pianist Jay McShann and others in the late 1930s. He first visited New York in 1939, and on his return in 1941 he recorded his first works with McShann. He also met Dizzy Gillespie, who was developing parallel ideas that would emerge in the bop movement some four years later.

Alto Saxophonist Charlie Parker, c. 1954. *One of the most influential jazz musicians of all time, Parker was a seminal figure of the bebop era.* ELIOT ELISOFON/TIME LIFE PICTURES/GETTY IMAGES

In the early 1940s, Parker played with the bands of Earl Hines, Cootie Williams, and Andy Kirk, as well as the original Billy Eckstine band—the first big band formed expressly to feature the new jazz style in both solos and arrangements. In 1945, Parker made a series of remarkable recordings under Gillespie's name that became some of the definitive examples of the bebop style. Although Parker was revered by a host of younger musicians, his innovations, at first, were met with a great deal of opposition from traditionalist jazz musicians and critics. However, once they began connecting to his innovative genius, many younger musicians attempted to transcribe his improvisations note for note.

Traveling to California with Gillespie and his band in 1945, Parker, still battling his addiction to heroin, suffered a breakdown and was confined to a state hospital there the following year. He eventually recovered and returned to the East Coast, where he recorded two sessions with Erroll Garner for Dial Records that stand as pinnacles of his career—as influential in Parker's day as Armstrong's "Hot Fives" sides were in the 1920s. From that point, Parker confined most of his activity to working with quintets, at times featuring Miles Davis, Kenny Dorham, Al Haig, Max Roach, and Roy Haynes. Parker also recorded and toured with a string section and visited Europe in 1949 and 1950. The late 1940s and early 1950s were the most fertile period of Parker's life as a performer and recording artist. Later, Parker went through cycles of illness brought on by his addictions. He made his final appearance in 1955 at Birdland (the club that had been named in his honor), one week before he died at the Manhattan apartment of his friend, the Baroness Pannonica de Koenigswater (a member of the wealthy Rothschild family and a bebop enthusiast).

Parker's influence on the development of jazz has been felt not only in the realm of the alto saxophone, which he dominated, but on the whole spectrum of jazz ideas. The astounding innovations that he introduced melodically, harmonically, tonally, and rhythmically made it impossible for any jazz musician from the mid-1940s forward to develop artistically without reflecting some of Parker's influence.

CHARLIE PATTON (c. 1891–1934)

Singer, Guitarist. Charlie Patton was one of the very earliest documented practitioners of the Delta country blues style. As such, he profoundly influenced succeeding generations of blues artist, as the Delta sound evolved into the genre's modern recognizable form. His raspy and impassioned singing along with his fluid guitar style made him one of the early kings of the Delta blues. Born around 1891 (although some sources place his birth as early as 1881) in Edwards, Mississippi, Patton received his musical training from a man whom he identified as Henry Sloan (an African American musician of the period, about whom little is known today).

Around 1900, when Patton was still young (depending on his actual birth date), his family moved to the Will Dockery Plantation, where music was a constant part of the sharecropper lifestyle. Patton learned from Sloan, and gradually became one of the earliest composers of songs in the twelve-bar metric pattern that came to be recognized as the standard blues form.

For the next thirty years or so, Patton played wherever he could—at picnics, on the street, or at other plantations. He gradually developed a sophisticated guitar style that helped lay the groundwork for what eventually coalesced into the Delta style. Although his musical skills were polished, his performance style was not. On the stage, Patton was a clown, performing guitar tricks, singing or speaking unintelligibly at times, and improvising at will. He was almost as well-known for his hard-drinking ways and constant womanizing (he had several common law wives, including Bertha Patton and Minnie Toy, with whom he recorded) as he was for his baritone singing voice. Nonetheless, his singing inspired a young Howlin' Wolf, and his propulsive guitar beat and keen rhythmic sense planted the seeds for John Lee Hooker's boogie style.

In 1929 Patton was brought North to record for the Paramount label. He recorded approximately sixty works for both Paramount and Vocalion over the next few years, but the quality of the surviving recordings makes it difficult to know how Patton really sounded. He is regarded as one of the first artists to tie the blues to a strong, syncopated rhythm and to utilize the slide for vocal-like effects. In addition, he is thought to have pioneered the popping of his bass strings and the technique of using the guitar like a drum to reinforce beats or make counter rhythms. Patton died in Indianola, Mississippi, on April 28, 1934, of heart disease. *Screamin' and Hollerin' the Blues: The Worlds of Charley Patton* (2001), a boxed collection of Patton's recorded works, received three Grammy Awards, including a Grammy for Best Historical Album.

OSCAR PETTIFORD (1922–1960)

Bassist. Pettiford was born September 30, 1922, on a reservation for Native Americans in Okmulgee, Oklahoma. He was raised in Minneapolis. Pettiford's mother was Choctaw and his father was half Cherokee and African American. Until Pettiford was nineteen years old, he toured with the family band (father and eleven children), and was well known in the Midwest. In 1943, Charlie Barnet heard him in Minneapolis and hired him to team up with bassist Chubby Jackson. Pettiford left Barnet in New York later that year, frequenting Minton's Playhouse and playing with Roy Eldridge, before Pettiford and Dizzy Gillespie led the first bebop group to perform on 52nd Street. Pettiford also cut his first sides in 1943 and played with Coleman Hawkins and Duke Ellington, with whom he recorded "Swamp Fire," a fine example of Pettiford's power and attack.

Pettiford's fame grew during the 1950s through his recordings and his tours of Europe and Asia, and he continued to lead his own sextet. In 1958, he settled permanently in Europe, where he worked until his death in Copenhagen in 1960. During his peak in the 1940s, Pettiford was a unique bassist who was melodically inventive and technically agile on both bass and cello. Building on the concepts first explored by Jimmy Blanton, Pettiford extended the range and complexity of jazz bass. Pettiford was also a fine composer who wrote "Bohemia After Dark" and "Blues in the Closet."

BUD POWELL (1924–1966)

Pianist, Composer. Earl Rudolph "Bud" Powell was born September 27, 1924, into a family of musicians in New York City. A piano prodigy, he had his first big-time job with trumpeter Cootie Williams's big band in 1943 and became involved in the "birth of bebop" at Minton's Playhouse in Harlem and on 52nd Street.

Powell suffered from mental illness for most of his life. In 1945 he was severely beaten about the head by Philadelphia police in a racially motivated incident, and suffered the first of several nervous breakdowns that plagued him for the rest of his life. In 1947 he was formally committed to a sanitarium and underwent electric shock treatments for more than a year. The treatment resulted in memory difficulties thereafter. Powell worked with Dizzy Gillespie and took part in bop combo sessions for Savoy Records in the late 1940s, although he was often in the care of a mental hospital. He lived in Paris from 1959 to 1964 and frequently worked with his old friend Kenny Clarke. Bud Powell died in New York on July 31, 1966, and reportedly more than 5,000 people attended his funeral in Harlem.

Powell is considered to be the first to transfer the melodic, harmonic, and rhythmic innovations of bop to the piano keyboard, setting the style for modern jazz piano. Although he was greatly influenced by Art Tatum and Teddy Wilson, his rapid right-handed melody lines played to match the horns combined with his random and dissonant left-hand chords were completely his own style.

CHANO POZO (1915–1948)

Drummer, Singer, Dancer. Born in Havana, Cuba, on January 7, 1915, Luciano "Chano" Pozo y Gonzales was hailed by Dizzy Gillespie as one of the greatest drummers he had ever heard. While a boy, Pozo was a juvenile delinquent who frequently got into fights and engaged in other petty crimes. As a result, he was sent to a reformatory. During his incarceration, he developed an interest in a West African secret society. (Some sources indicate that it was Abkwa and others indicate it was the better known Santeria.) A result of his membership in that society, he mastered Yoruba chanting and drumming traditions. He eventually became well known as a talented conguero (conga player) on the island of Cuba. Pozo migrated to New York in 1947. That same year, he met Dizzy Gillespie. Pozo and Gillespie recorded "Cubana Be," "Cubana Bop," and "Manteca." Chano Pozo's meteoric rise to celebrity was apparently too much for him to absorb because he lapsed back into some of his reckless ways. In addition to dressing very lavishly, he bought and wrecked a series of new cars without sustaining any injuries (he quipped that the gods were protecting him). Tragically, however, Pozo was murdered in New York City on December 2, 1948.

SUN RA (1914–1993)

Pianist, Composer, Bandleader. Born Herman "Sonny" Poole Blount on May 22, 1914, in Birmingham, Alabama, Sun Ra spent the early part of his career in Chicago, where he played rhythm and blues, jazz, and blues with a number of groups—including Fletcher Henderson's band at the Club DeLisa in 1947. During the 1950s, while Ornette Coleman, Cecil Taylor, and Miles Davis were crafting their personal styles, Blount changed his name to Sun Ra and assembled a band to play his unorthodox and challenging music.

Sun Ra's "Arkestra" (his own new spelling for orchestra) had three distinct stylistic periods: The group performed big band/hard bop music in the 1950s; free jazz in the 1960s; and swing from the mid-1970s onward. The Arkestra also fused African-style polyrhythms, unusual harmonies, and audacious stage performances to create an often spectacular event. Ra's group, which counted more than 100 members over its history, lived communally, first in Chicago and later in Philadelphia, and released records on Ra's own Saturn label.

Ra's music pushed into mystical abstraction and theater, and audiences often participated in the experience. An admirer of American popular music, Ra often incorporated compositions by Ellington, Gershwin, and others into his performance. His interpretations—arrangements, tempos, and unique instrumentation—gave these works a different sound. A recipient of the American Jazz Masters Award from the National Endowment for the Arts in 1982, Sun Ra died on May 30, 1993, following a series of strokes.

MA RAINEY (1886–1939)

Singer. Gertrude "Ma" Rainey, known popularly as the mother of the blues, was one of the earliest professional singers in the genre and one of the most influential of the so-called "Southern style." Born Gertrude Malissa Nix Pridgett in Columbus, Georgia, on April 26, 1886, she gave her first public performance in a local talent show and subsequently appeared in a local musical, *A Bunch of Blackberries,* at the age of fourteen. In 1904 she married singer/dancer William "Pa" Rainey (who was several years her senior), and the duo embarked on a long entertainment career, touring around the South with minstrel shows, circuses, and tent shows with the billing, "Assassinators of the Blues." Ma Rainey eventually split from her husband and toured very successfully on her own.

Around 1912, Rainey introduced Bessie Smith (then a teenager) into her act, a move that was later seen as having a major impact on blues singing styles. Rainey made her first recording in 1923 for Paramount Records and was soon recording with Fletcher Henderson, Louis Armstrong, and Coleman Hawkins. Between 1923 and 1928, when she stopped recording, she had released over 100 songs, including the blues classics "C. C. Rider" and "Bo Weavil Blues." Though Rainey continued to tour the South for a few more years, blues singing by females had become less popular than blues singing by their male counterparts. Rainey retired in 1933 and, until her death on December 22, 1939, managed the two theaters that she owned in Columbus, Georgia: "The Airdrome" and "The Lyric." Similar to other classic blues singers of her time, Rainey sang minstrel songs, and blues tunes, but she delivered them with a heavier, tougher, and earthier delivery than the cabaret blues singers that followed her.

DEWEY REDMAN (1931– 2006)

Saxophonist. Born Walter Dewey Redman in Fort Worth, Texas, on May 17, 1931, Dewey Redman started playing the clarinet when he was twelve, taking private lessons briefly for six months before he turned to self-instruction. At fifteen, he earned a job with an eight-piece band that performed in church as the minister passed the collection plate. Later, at Prairie View A&M College, Redman teamed up with a piano and bass player to work in local clubs, found a spot in the Prairie View "swing" band, and graduated in 1953 with a degree in industrial arts and a grasp on a new instrument with which he had experimented—the saxophone. After a stay in the Army, Redman obtained a master's degree in education at North Texas State University and taught school and directed school bands in western and southern Texas.

In 1959, Redman traveled to California, eventually settling in San Francisco, where he remained for seven years, studying music and working on his own theories of chord progressions, improvisation, and technique. In 1967, he moved to New York City and joined Ornette Coleman, who brought him into his group with Dave Izenson on bass and Denardo Coleman on drums.

By 1973, Dewey Redman was dividing his playing time between solo efforts, gigs with Ornette Coleman and Keith Jarrett, and the composition of "Peace Suite" dedicated to the late Ralph Bunche. Later he cofounded the group Old and New Dreams. Dewey Redman spent most of his life in a creative search for greater understanding of the tenor saxophone—and in constantly reevaluating his relationship to his music. His son, Joshua, emerged in the 1990s as one of the finest young tenor saxophonists of his day.

DON REDMAN (1900–1964)

Saxophonist, Composer. Born in Piedmont, West Virginia, on July 29, 1900, Donald Matthew Redman was a child prodigy who played trumpet at the age of three, joined a band at six, and later studied harmony, theory, and composition at Boston and Detroit conservatories. In 1924, he joined Fletcher Henderson's band in New York, as lead saxophonist and staff arranger, and he also recorded as accompanist during this period for such leading blues singers as Bessie Smith, Ma Rainey, and Alberta Hunter. When Louis Armstrong joined the Henderson band, Redman adopted Armstrong's sense of swing, and in 1928 he became leader of McKinney's Cotton Pickers, thereby helping to build both McKinney's and Henderson's bands into two of the best in jazz history.

During most of the 1930s, Don Redman (the uncle of saxophonist Dewey Redman) led his own band, which was regarded as one of the leading African American orchestras of its time and was the first to play a sponsored radio series. Redman also wrote for many other prominent bands, black and white. In 1951, he became musical director for Pearl Bailey. From 1954 to 1955, he appeared in a small acting role in the musical *House of Flowers* on Broadway. He continued to arrange and record until his death on November 30, 1964. Redman was the chief architect of the integration of popular orchestral dance music and jazz, using both written and improvised parts to create the feel of swing.

JIMMY REED (1925–1976)

Singer, Guitarist. Born September 6, 1925, on a plantation near Dunleith, Mississippi, Reed learned the basics of guitar and harmonica from Eddie Taylor, a semi-professional musician. In 1943 Reed moved to Chicago, but was soon drafted into the Navy. After two years of service during World War II, he moved back to Mississippi to marry before relocating to Gary, Indiana, where he found work in a meat packing plant. In the early 1950s Reed was working as a harmonica player with John Brim's band Gary Kings before the drummer in the band, future guitar legend Albert King, introduced him to Vee-Jay Records, where he made his first recordings. At Vee-Jay, Reed was reunited with Taylor. Their partnership lasted the rest of Reed's life, and resulted in Reed's first hit single, "You Don't Have to Go," which reached number five on

Singer and Guitarist Jimmy Reed, c. 1960. *Reed's best-known songs—"Big Boss Man," "Bright Lights, Big City," and "Baby, What You Want Me to Do"—are part of the standard blues repertoire and have been covered numerous times.* CHRIS MORPHET/REDFERNS/GETTY IMAGES

the rhythm and blues charts. Unfortunately, Reed's severe drinking problem became legendary, and he struggled to perform or record. With the help of his wife and Taylor, Reed managed to function, even in spite of being diagnosed with epilepsy in 1957, and he placed eleven songs on the Hot 100 chart and fourteen on the rhythm and blues charts in the 1950s and 1960s. Reed worked sporadically during the 1970s before becoming a recluse and obtaining treatment for his illnesses. He died in Oakland, California, on August 29, 1976.

Reed's best-known songs, including "Big Boss Man," "Bright Lights, Big City," and "Baby, What You Want Me to Do," are part of the standard blues repertoire and have been played by everyone from garage bands to Elvis Presley. His bottom-string boogie rhythm guitar patterns, two-string turnarounds, country harmonica, and mush mouth vocals served as the first introduction to the blues for many people. While lacking the technical proficiency of Son House and Elmore James, and also lacking a voice as powerful as Muddy Waters and Howlin' Wolf, Jimmy Reed managed to form a popular contrast with simple tunes and a laid back feel, making aspiring players worldwide feel that they could participate in the blues.

MAX ROACH (1924–2007)

Percussionist, Composer. Born Maxwell Lemuel Roach on January 10, 1924, in Newland, North Carolina, and raised in Brooklyn, New York, Roach was one of the key figures in the development of modern jazz. He made his record debut in 1943 with Coleman Hawkins and was part of the first group led by Dizzy Gillespie to play bebop on 52nd Street in New York (1943–1944). He later worked with Charlie Parker's finest group (1947–1948). In 1954, Roach joined the brilliant young trumpeter Clifford Brown as coleader of the Clifford Brown-Max Roach Quintet, an ensemble that defined the hard bop sound. After Brown's untimely death in a car crash, Roach began to lead his own groups of various sizes and instrumentation, including interesting work with solo and choral voices, an all-percussion band, and a jazz quartet combined with a string quartet. His many compositions include "We Insist—Freedom Now," a suite with a strong and direct social and political message, written with his wife at the time, singer Abbey Lincoln.

A phenomenally gifted musician with a matchless percussion technique, Roach developed the drum solo into new heights of structural refinement; he has been an influence on every drummer to come along since the 1940s. Along with Kenny Clarke and Art Blakey, Roach is considered to be one of the founding fathers of bop drumming. Over his career Roach has played with Bud Powell, Miles Davis, Thelonious Monk, and Sonny Rollins. Roach taught as a professor of music at the University of Massachusetts from the early 1970s to the mid-1990s. He also became the first jazz artist to receive a MacArthur Fellowship in 1988, the most prestigious and lucrative award in the world of arts and letters. After retiring his professorship, he moved to New York, where he died peacefully on August 16, 2007.

SONNY ROLLINS (1930–)

Saxophonist, Bandleader. Born on September 7, 1930, in New York City, Theodore Walter "Sonny" Rollins took piano lessons when he was nine but lost interest in music until learning to play the alto saxophone in 1944. He soon had paying jobs on tenor saxophone, and made his recording debut at the age of nineteen with Babs Gonzalas for Capitol Records. Shortly thereafter, he joined in recording sessions with trombonist J. J. Johnson, who recorded Rollins's first composition "Audubon," and pianist Bud Powell. Distinctively personal from the outset, Rollins's style developed as he worked with pianist Thelonious Monk, Powell, drummer Art Blakey, and trumpeter Miles Davis. In 1956 he voluntarily entered the federal penitentiary at Lexington, Kentucky, to kick his drug habit. After his release he joined the Clifford Brown-Max Roach Quintet, where he came into his own style. Later that year he recorded *Saxophone Colossus*, marking a major breakthrough with songs such as "St. Thomas" and "Blue 7" that featured his thematic improvisations. Employing a piano-less trio, a form he pioneered, Rollins followed with two more records: *Way Out West*, which showcased his love for off-beat pop and show tunes, and *Freedom Suite*, which was built around meditations on segregation and civil rights in American society. Also during this period, he cut several albums for Blue Note Records that featured his own compositions, along with oddball cover tunes made fresh and unique by his quality sidemen (i.e., Philly Joe Jones, Max Roach, J. J. Johnson, Horace Silver, and Thelonious Monk) and Rollins's early hard bop stylings.

Saxophonist and Bandleader Sonny Rollins, early 1960s. *One of the towering figures of the post-bebop era of jazz, Rollins is best known as an instrumentalist and improviser.* GILLES PETARD/REDFERNS/GETTY IMAGES

In 1959, Rollins took two years off from active playing, studying, and practicing. When he reappeared at the helm of his own quartet in 1961, he surprised even those who already knew the quality of his work with the power and conviction of his performance on *The Bridge* (1962). A string of excellent albums on several labels followed until another "retirement" at the end of the 1960s. Rollins was named a Guggenheim fellow in 1972 and continued to release acclaimed recordings throughout the 1970s and 1980s. Rollins maintained an active schedule into the 1990s, and in 2001 won a Grammy for his album *This Is What I Do*. Known for his impressive endurance and stamina, Rollins has often been called a force of nature akin to a volcano. On September 11, 2001, during the"9/11" terrorist attacks, Rollins was forced to flee New York City with only his instrument. He traveled to Boston for a benefit concert for the Berklee School of Music five days later. A recording of that concert, entitled *Without a Song: The 9/11 Concert*, was released in 2005, and won a Grammy the following year for best jazz instrumental solo for Rollins's performance of "Why Was I Born?"

Rollins has written many fine tunes in his career, but it is as an instrumentalist and improviser that he is best known. His robust, almost hard tone, use of grace notes, and ability to create harmonically imaginative but melodic statements, even at amazingly fast tempos, is unmatched. He is recognized as the first jazz soloist to improvise in terms of a complete pattern of a solo, or as Thelonious Monk once said, "play the melody, not the changes." Rollins stands as one of the most commanding musical voices in jazz history.

OTIS RUSH (1935–)

Guitarist, Singer. Otis Rush has been a mainstay of the Chicago blues scene for more than fifty years. A pioneer of the "West side" style of blues guitar work, Rush's sound combines the best elements of the South side, Delta-influenced approach with the smoother, modern, urban stylings that B. B. King and T-Bone Walker brought to the blues.

One of seven children, Rush was born on April 29, 1935, in Philadelphia, Mississippi. Although he was attracted to the country blues guitar of Lightnin' Hopkins and others, Rush started out as a harmonica player. In 1948 he moved to Chicago, where he continued to develop his harmonica skills while working a day job in the stockyards. Rush did not begin studying guitar until 1953. Initially, his guitar role model was Muddy Waters, but he gradually began to infuse more modern phrasing in the tradition of Walker and King into the deep Mississippi foundation that he had inherited from Waters.

Rush was noticed playing in the clubs by bassist Willie Dixon, who got him a contract with the newly established Cobra label. His first single for Cobra, "I Can't Quit You Baby," became a hit in 1956, and his work over the next few years was generally well-received. In 1959, Rush signed with Chess Records and recorded the successful single "So Many Roads, So Many Trains." He was unable to sell consistently for Chess, however, and his career slumped badly in the first half of the 1960s. He signed with Houston-based Duke Records in 1962, but saw only one single released by that company. Meanwhile, he continued to perform regularly on the Chicago club circuit and occasionally in other cities.

Rush's appearance on the 1966 compilation album *Chicago: The Blues Today* revived his flagging career, gaining him a new generation of fans (including a number of white rock musicians). Nevertheless, large-scale stardom continued to elude Rush, with the exception of a wildly enthusiastic reception in Japan in 1975. Discouraged, Rush stopped performing for a short time in the early 1980s. By the middle of the decade, however, blues was enjoying another revival, and a revitalized Rush managed to establish himself as a true giant of the modern blues scene. His 1994 album *Ain't Enough Comin' In* and the 1998 Grammy Award–winning *Any Place I'm Going* helped to cement that reputation. In 2004, Otis Rush suffered a stroke which has kept him from performing.

JIMMY RUSHING (1903–1972)

Singer. Born on August 26, 1903 (some sources say 1901), in Oklahoma City, Oklahoma, into a musical family (his father played trumpet and brother and mother were singers), James Andrew Rushing played piano and violin as a youth, but entered music professionally as a singer in the Californian after-hours world in 1925. After that, Rushing was linked with leading bands and musicians: Walter Page (from 1927 to 1928); Bennie Moten (in 1929); and as a mainstay of the famed Count Basie Band (from 1936 to 1949), where his intense, high-pitched style of blues singing propelled the band to new heights.

Rushing formed his own small group when he left Basie, and in the ensuing years worked most often solo. Following the upsurge in popularity of the blues in the mid-1950s, Rushing appeared at all the major jazz festivals and made several successful European tours with his own and Benny Goodman's bands. These performances earned him critical acclaim and commercial success. His style endured for more than four decades of jazz, largely due to its great warmth, Rushing's sure, firm melodic line, and his swinging use of rhythm. Rushing died of leukemia on June 8, 1972, in New York City. The song "Mister Five by Five," written in tribute to him, is an apt physical description of Jimmy Rushing, who was one of the greatest male jazz and blues singers.

NOBLE SISSLE

See chapter 21, Drama, Comedy, and Dance.

BESSIE SMITH (1894–1937)

Singer. Bessie Smith was born on April 15, 1894, in Chattanooga, Tennessee. Called "The Empress of the Blues," she had no peers. Her magnificent voice, sense of the dramatic, clarity of diction, and incomparable time and phrasing set her apart from the competition and made her appeal as much to jazz lovers as to lovers of the blues. Her first recording, Alberta Hunter's "Down Hearted Blues," sold approximately 750,000 copies in 1923—figures that only Caruso and Paul Whiteman were achieving at that time.

By the early 1920s, Bessie Smith had been singing professionally for some fifteen years. However, recordings by African American women singing the blues had only begun in 1920, and only by much less earthy voices. Smith auditioned for several race labels and was rejected because they found her voice "too rough." However, she already had a sizeable following and had appeared in large shows, so Columbia Records (a mainstream label) signed her as an exclusive artist. It was the company's good fortune to have signed her because the sale of her records helped the label out of financial difficulty. (A common practice for record labels at the time was to strike through the royalty clause for African American artists, so that the artists could make no further claim on their material after recording it—regardless of how well it sold. Columbia exercised this practice with Bessie Smith.) Smith's first recording, "Downhearted Blues," proved her value to the label. Within a short time, Bessie Smith was backed by the best of jazz players, including Louis Armstrong, and by 1925 she starred in her own touring show—a show that traveled in its own private Pullman car. By 1927, Smith was the highest paid African American artist in the world. In 1929 she made a short film, *St. Louis Blues,* that captured some of her magnetism as a stage performer.

But tastes in music were changing rapidly, and though Bessie Smith remained with the times by adding popular songs to her repertoire, the Depression nearly ended the jazz and blues record business altogether. In 1931, Columbia dropped Smith, and she soon began touring as a "single." John Hammond, however, arranged for her return to the studio in 1933. Her recordings, including "Down In the Dumps," "Do Your Duty," "Give Me a Pigfoot," and "Take Me For a Buggy Ride," reflected the shift to swing jazz, but they apparently did not sell well at the time. The last two songs of this series are Smith's most popular. These recordings, however, turned out to be her last. She still found plenty of work on the traveling circuit, but it proved to be less financially rewarding. Early one morning on a road in Mississippi, she was fatally injured in a car collision. She died on September 26, 1937. Smith was given a funeral service back in her adopted hometown, Philadelphia. Thousands of mourners paid their respects to this great artist, whose recordings still sell well nearly ninety years after she first entered the studio.

BILLY STRAYHORN (1915–1967)

Composer, Arranger, Pianist. Born in Dayton, Ohio, on November 29, 1915, and raised in Pittsburgh, William Thomas Strayhorn showed an unusually sophisticated gift for songwriting when he was quite young. Initially, he wanted to have a career as a classical pianist. While still in his teens, he wrote "Lush Life," a song he demonstrated to Duke Ellington in 1938. A short time later Ellington recorded the Strayhorn tune "Something to Live For" and by 1939 Strayhorn joined the Ellington entourage in New York. Duke first thought of Strayhorn as a lyricist, but soon found out that Strayhorn had a talent for arranging and was an accomplished pianist as well.

Before long the two musicians had established a working relationship that remains unique in the history of music. Between 1940 and1942, Strayhorn contributed many standout tunes to the Ellington repertoire, such as "Take the A Train," "Passion Flower," "Chelsea Bridge," and "Rain Check." After the mid-1940s, Ellington and Strayhorn began sharing credit for their compositions, and Strayhorn led small group sessions drawn from Ellington's larger band. Strayhorn also co-composed and arranged hundreds of tunes and extended works including "The Deep South Suite," "A Drum is a Woman," "Such Sweet Thunder," and "The Perfume Suite." Strayhorn rarely recorded on his own, and his death from cancer on May 31, 1967, inspired Ellington's great album *And His Mother Called Him Bill.* Strayhorn is still remembered for his great harmonic sophistication and beautiful touch that perfectly complemented Ellington's more percussive and expansive vision.

ART TATUM (1909–1956)

Pianist. Born on October 13, 1909, in Toledo, Ohio, Arthur Tatum was arguably the greatest pianist the jazz genre has ever produced. Blind in one eye and partially sighted in the other, Tatum could read some music with the assistance of braille, but he learned primarily by ear. He made his professional debut on radio in Toledo before going to New York City in 1932 as accompanist for singer Adelaide Hall (1901–1993), with whom he made his first recordings. Tatum was soon making his own records and appearing in the popular clubs on New York's 52nd Street. He eventually settled in Chicago, and by the mid-1930s his reputation was international. Known primarily as a soloist, Tatum began working in a 1943 trio patterned after Nat King Cole's group, with Slam Stewart on bass and either Tiny Grimes or Everett Barksdale on guitar. While he maintained this format for most of the balance of his career, in 1953 he began working with Norman Granz, with whom he recorded a monumental 121 unaccompanied solos, and engaged in a series of small group sessions with Benny Carter, Buddy DeFranco, and Ben Webster. It is the recordings with Granz on which his reputation was built among both critics and musicians. Though he enjoyed a full career and recorded quite prolifically, Tatum lived too soon to benefit from the acceptance that came to jazz as concert hall music, which would have been an ideal medium for him. He died from uremia on November 5, 1956, in Los Angeles, California.

For sheer technical mastery, Tatum had few peers—perhaps only Earl Hines and Cecil Taylor have come close to matching Tatum's skill. A child prodigy, Tatum seemed to have all the elements of his style in place by early adulthood. His harmonic and linear invention, unusual phrase lengths, radical leaps in logic, and relaxed execution were his trademarks. Tatum exerted a strong influence on the bop movement and all who followed. His left-hand figures were reminiscent of such early stride players as Fats Waller, while his intricate right-hand lines and habit of varying the tempo suggest the technique of Earl Hines. In addition, Tatum's ability to never abandon the melody line but to change, obscure, and reharmonize it at will remain legendary.

BILLY TAYLOR (1921–)

Pianist, Composer, Educator. Born in Greenville, North Carolina, on July 24, 1921, William Taylor Jr. began his career shortly after graduating from Virginia State College (now Virginia State University) in 1942 with a B.A. in music. He played with Ben Webster's Quartet on New York's 52nd Street in 1944, and soon established himself as a pianist on the New York scene, becoming a regular on "Swing Street." He played with Billie Holiday, Ella Fitzgerald, Coleman Hawkins, Roy Eldridge, and others. A protégé of Art Tatum and Teddy Wilson (both master pianists), Taylor played with the celebrated Afro-Cuban musician Machito (1909–1984, born Francisco Raúl Gutiérrez Grillo). He also toured Europe with Don Redman, and replaced Errol Garner in the Slam Stewart trio. Between 1949 and 1951, he was the house pianist for the famed Birdland club where he backed visiting stars. Taylor then played a year-long engagement at Club Le Downbeat with a trio that included Charles Mingus.

Taylor made recordings with a variety of jazz artists for numerous labels during the 1950s and started his own record company before embarking on a campaign to educate the public in the arts through print, radio, and television. In 1958, he hosted "The Subject Is Jazz" on the Educational Television Network. He also hosted radio programs on two New York City stations and garnered a Peabody Award for his work. In the late 1960s, Taylor served as musical director for Tony Brown's *Black Journal Tonight*, and in 1965 he founded Jazzmobile as part of the Harlem Cultural Council's summer programs. Starting out as an idea for a parade float, Jazzmobile eventually developed into a service that seasonally brought major jazz artists out to poor urban areas for free performances.

From 1968 to 1972, Taylor led an eleven-piece band for television's *David Frost Show*. He returned to school, earning a doctorate in music education from the University of Massachusetts in 1975. His dissertation was later published as *Jazz Piano: History and Development* and became the text for a course offered on National Public Radio (NPR). Taylor directed *Jazz Alive!* for NPR from the late 1970s to early 1980s. He also became a regular on *CBS Sunday Morning* and for years served as the program's jazz correspondent. In 1983, he earned an Emmy Award for a segment on Quincy Jones. Taylor has served on numerous boards and panels including a position with the prestigious National Council on the Arts. In 1994, he was named Artistic Advisor for Jazz at the John F. Kennedy Center for the Performing Arts, and he continues in that position today.

Taylor has received several honors in his career. Among them have been recognition for lifetime achievement (1984) from *Down Beat* and induction into the magazine's Hall of Fame; a Jazz Masters Fellowship from the National Endowment for the Arts (1988); induction into the International Association of Jazz Educators Hall of Fame (1991); a Tiffany Award from the International Society of Performing Arts Administrators (1991); a National Medal of Arts (1992); and Man of the Year from the National Association of Jazz Educators. Few musicians have done more for the cause of jazz than Dr. Billy Taylor, who has been credited with obtaining proper respect and recognition for African American music since the 1950s.

CECIL PERCIVAL TAYLOR (1929–)

Pianist, Composer. Born about March 15, 1929, in New York, New York, Cecil Percival Taylor attended the New England Conservatory, but said that he learned more from listening to Duke Ellington. Another early influence on Taylor was Bud Powell. Taylor's early jobs included work with Hot Lips Page and Johnny Hodges before he made his first recording with soprano saxophonist Steve Lacy in 1956. The following year Taylor appeared at the Newport Jazz Festival and was also recorded there. Settling in New York City, Taylor often struggled with lack of work and acceptance, but he continued to go his own musical way. He worked mostly in live settings with drummer Sonny Murray and alto saxophonist Jimmy Lyons in the early 1960s before releasing a breakthrough album, *Unit Structures*, in 1966 on Blue Note Records. In the late 1960s, he experimented with larger frameworks for his playing, recording with the Jazz Composers Orchestra. In the early 1970s, Taylor taught at several universities. Meanwhile, he had gained a following in Europe and Japan, and in the 1980s completed a series of excellent recordings including some brilliant solo efforts. He also teamed up for concerts with Mary Lou Williams and Max Roach. In 1988, Taylor was featured in a month-long festival of concerts and workshops in Berlin, and some of the results were issued in a lavish eleven-CD boxed set. Always fascinated by dance, Taylor was also inspired to team up with the famous ballet star Mikhail Baryshnikov in concert during the 1980s. Despite lacking the acceptance of the mainstream, Taylor received a MacArthur Fellowship in 1992. His live recordings over the last two decades, including *Qu'a: Live at the Irridium, Vol. 1* and *Qu'a Yuba: Live at the Irridium, Vol. 2* (1998), along with *The Willisau Concert* (2002), have garnered stellar reviews.

Taylor has set his own path in music, combining post-bop, contemporary classical music, and experimental noise into a unique and powerfully personal statement. As one of the leaders of creative-improvised music, Taylor's place in jazz is somewhat similar to John Cage's place in modern classical music. Influenced by Bud Powell, Thelonious Monk, and Duke Ellington, Taylor creates fierce and elegant soundscapes of shifting textures and accents. He once said "I approach the keyboard as if it were 88 tuned drums." Taylor continues to stand as a unique force in jazz.

KOKO TAYLOR (1928–2009)

Singer, Songwriter. As the undisputed "Queen of the Chicago Blues," Koko Taylor was one of the few women to achieve legendary status in a genre dominated by men wielding electric guitars. Taylor's raspy vocal style was a throwback to the early Delta blues tradition, and she credited her success to her refusal to dilute her singing to conform to modern fads.

Taylor was born Cora Walton on September 28, 1928, on a farm near Memphis. After her mother died in 1939, her sharecropper father raised her, along with her five older siblings. Working in the cotton fields, the entire family sang in the evening as a means of entertaining themselves. They also listened to the Classic Blues songs played by B. B. King on his Memphis radio show. When she was eighteen, Cora married Robert "Pops" Taylor and moved with him to Chicago, where he landed a job in a slaughterhouse.

In Chicago, Taylor worked as a domestic during the day and frequented South side blues clubs by night. She frequently sang with legendary Chicago blues musicians such as Howlin' Wolf, Buddy Guy, and Junior Wells. Taylor was soon "discovered" by blues star Willie Dixon, who introduced her to Chess Records. Taylor recorded Dixon's "Wang Dang Doodle" for Chess in 1965, and the single became a huge hit, reaching number four on the rhythm and blues charts the following year.

Taylor quickly became a prominent member of the Chicago blues community. After Chess folded, she signed with Alligator Records in 1975. She played a large role in that label's transformation into a major blues outfit, and eight of the nine albums she recorded for the label were Grammy-nominated. In 1994 she opened a blues restaurant, which closed in 1999. Koko Taylor died on June 3, 2009, from complications of a recent surgery, less than a month after her final performance for the Blues Music Awards.

McCOY TYNER (1938–)

Pianist, Composer, Bandleader. Born on December 11, 1938, in Philadelphia, pianist McCoy Tyner attended the Granoff School of Music and then joined the Art Farmer-Benny Golson Jazztet. After six months with the Jazztet, Tyner joined John Coltrane's quartet in 1960. During his five years with Coltrane, Tyner developed a unique two-handed, densely harmonic style that matched Coltrane's model approach and could also stand up to Elvin Jones's polyrhythmic drumming. While with Coltrane, he participated in the recordings of such milestone albums as *My Favorite Things*, *Crescent*, *A Love Supreme*, and *Ascension*.

After leaving Coltrane, Tyner made a number of albums as leader of his own groups of various sizes—from trios to a unique big band—for Blue Note, Milestone (1972–1980), and Columbia Records, before signing with Impulse Records in 1995. Enjoying a resurgence of popularity in the 1990s, Tyner's band was named Jazz Big Band of the Year by *Down Beat* readers in 1994. The group's recording "Journey" featured vocalist Dianne Reeves and trombonist Slide Hampton. With the 1999

Pianist and Composer McCoy Tyner, 1997. *Best known for his work with John Coltrane, Tyner is one of the most distinctive and influential pianists in jazz. In his role as a bandleader, he has also proven himself to be a superb composer and arranger.* © JACK VARTOOGIAN. REPRODUCED BY PERMISSION.

release of *McCoy Tyner and the Latin All-Stars,* Tyner demonstrated his ability to mix his unique style with a Latin rhythm. In 2000, *Jazz Roots: McCoy Tyner Honors Jazz Piano Legends of the 20th Century* was released on the TelArc label.

Tyner is one of the most distinctive and influential pianists in jazz as well as a superb composer and arranger whose own work is often unfairly overshadowed by his work with Coltrane.

SARAH VAUGHAN (1924–1990)

Singer. Sarah Lois Vaughan was born on March 27, 1924, in Newark, New Jersey. She sang in church, accompanied the choir on the piano, and tried a few pop songs at high school parties. As part of a dare, she entered the Wednesday night amateur contest at Harlem's famed Apollo Theater. Billy Eckstine happened to be backstage, ran out front as soon as he heard her voice, and recommended the young woman to his boss, band leader Earl Hines, who promptly hired her. In the Hines band at that time were Charlie "Bird" Parker and Dizzy Gillespie. They and Vaughan left Hines when Eckstine decided to start his own big band, the first to feature the new sounds of bop. By 1945, Vaughan made her first recordings under her own name, including the classic "Lover Man" with Bird and Dizzy—Vaughan being the only singer to record with the two together.

A year later Vaughan started her solo career, gained wide recognition as part of the Jazz at the Philharmonic (JATP) tour, and signed with Columbia in 1949. The move to Columbia launched Vaughan to international fame. Though she had some big pop hits during her long and rich career, she never strayed from jazz for long, and her 1950 jazz session with Miles Davis became a classic. Between 1954 and 1967, she made an array of pop and jazz recordings with Clifford Brown, Count Basie, Roy Haynes, Benny Carter, and Gerald Wilson. In the 1970s and 1980s, she continued to record prolifically, exploring Brazilian songs and the Duke Ellington songbook, but rarely working in the jazz format.

Remarkably, as Vaughan grew older, she got better, losing none of her amazing top range and adding to the bottom, while her mastery of interpretation also increased. Vaughn was a virtuoso who had complete control of pitch, timbre, and dynamics. Able to use her contralto voice as a horn, she embellished melodies with the leaps of a polished reed instrumentalist, leading her fans to call her "the Divine One," or "Sassy." Sarah died on April 3, 1990, in Los Angeles, California, six months after her last performance.

T-BONE WALKER (1910–1975)

Guitarist, Songwriter. The electric guitar is now the predominant solo instrument in American pop music, primarily because of Aaron Thibeaux Walker. He was the first blues artist to use amplification as a music-making tool, and his playing represents a bridge between early jazz and modern, guitar-driven rock. He is cited as an important influence by countless guitarists, blues, and rock and roll musicians alike.

Guitarist and Composer T-Bone Walker, 1940s. *The recordings of electric guitar pioneer Walker included "Call It Stormy Monday," which became a blues standard of the highest order.* **FRANK DRIGGS/ARCHIVE PHOTOS, INC. REPRODUCED BY PERMISSION.**

Walker was born on May 28, 1910, in Linden, Texas, and grew up in Dallas. Both of his parents were working musicians, and Walker was exposed to many different instruments as a youth. Walker also worked for a time as Blind Lemon Jefferson's guide, escorting the legendary guitarist around town. By the time he was sixteen years old, T-Bone (a corruption of his middle name) was himself a working professional guitarist.

'Recording as Oak Cliff T-Bone, Walker released two singles for Columbia Records in 1929. In 1934 he relocated to Los Angeles, where he played in small combos at jazz clubs before joining Les Hite's Cotton Club Orchestra as a singer, guitarist, and composer in 1939. With Hite, Walker established himself as one of the pioneers of the electric guitar, which he used to successfully compete on equal terms with the band's horn section.

Having established his own reputation, Walker went solo in 1940. He recorded (for Capital Records) such tunes as "Mean Old World" (1942) and "I Got a Break Baby," which featured his fluid, elegant riffs and mellow vocals. Walker signed with Black & White Records in 1946. A year later, he recorded his most famous hit, "Call It Stormy Monday," which quickly became a blues standard. His blues single "T-Bone Jumps Again," from the same session, is an up-tempo instrumental that displays his dexterity playing at faster speeds.

Walker continued to record impressive work for a number of labels for most of the 1950s. He toured tirelessly during the 1960s, living the rugged, hard-drinking lifestyle that often went with touring. However, as so many other of his peers from the postwar rhythm and blues ranks, Walker had difficulty competing with the advent of rock and roll. His 1970 release *Good Feelin'* won a Grammy Award, but stomach ailments and a stroke in 1974 slowed him down. He died of pneumonia on March 16, 1975, in Los Angeles.

An incurable showman, Walker dazzled audiences with an arsenal of tricks, such as behind-the-back guitar playing while doing the splits, that may have influenced rock and roll performer Jimi Hendrix. Modern day electric blues guitar can be traced directly back to Walker, who was its first innovator.

"Fats" Waller, c. 1940. *One of the greatest showmen of jazz and a terrific organist, fine singer, and talented songwriter, Waller cut more than 500 sides between 1934 and his untimely death at thirty-nine in 1943. Among the hit songs he wrote were "Ain't Misbehavin'" and "Honeysuckle Rose."* ARCHIVE PHOTOS, INC. REPRODUCED BY PERMISSION.

FATS WALLER (1904–1943)

Composer, Pianist, Singer, Bandleader. Born in Greenwich Village in New York City on May 21, 1904, Thomas Wright Waller's father wanted him to follow in his footsteps as a preacher. However, the younger Waller liked the good times that came with playing the piano, which he did almost from the age of six. By the age of fifteen, Waller turned professional, accompanying singers in Harlem clubs and playing piano for silent movies at the Lincoln Theater. In the early 1920s he became a protégé of stride pianist James P. Johnson, who helped him get jobs cutting piano rolls. Waller also accompanied a number of classic blues singers such as Bessie Smith and Alberta Hunter, and began writing songs. By the end of the 1920s Waller was a force in New York, performing on a regular radio broadcast, recording with Fletcher Henderson and Sidney Bechet, and advising talented musicians (such as Duke Ellington). He developed a clear talent for songwriting. His first and biggest hit was "Ain't Misbehavin" from 1929, which remains his most popular song. Others included "Honeysuckle Rose," "Blue Turning Gray Over You," and "The Jitterbug Waltz." He also wrote "London Suite" for solo piano.

With his own small group and occasional big band, Waller made more than 500 recordings between 1934 and his untimely death at the age of thirty-nine in 1943. Waller's style really came across on records—no matter how trite the tune, he transformed it into a jazz gem. He also appeared in films, including *Stormy Weather* with Lena Horne, and toured Europe. Waller also enjoyed playing Bach, especially on the organ, which he was the first to use as a jazz instrument. In 1932, the world-famous composer and musician Marcel Dupré invited Fats to play the organ at the Notre Dame Cathedral in Paris. On a return train trip from Hollywood, where he had played the Zanzibar Room, to New York City, Waller died of pneumonia on December 15, 1943.

Weighing more than 300 pounds and standing more than six feet tall, Waller came by his nickname "Fats" naturally. He was one of the greatest and most popular showmen of jazz, a terrific organist, fine singer, and talented songwriter.

DINAH WASHINGTON (1924–1963)

Singer. Washington was born Ruth Lee Jones on August 29, 1924, in Tuscaloosa, Alabama, and got her start singing gospel music at St. Luke's Baptist Church on Chicago's South side. She toured churches with her mother, playing the piano and singing solo, until another opportunity beckoned—an amateur talent contest at Chicago's Regal Theater. Her triumphant performance during that event led to performances at local nightclubs, and in 1943 the nineteen-year-old singer successfully auditioned for a slot in Lionel Hampton's band. She was soon discovered by composer and critic Leonard Feather, and Washington and Feather together created several outstanding songs, including "Baby Get Lost," "Salty Papa Blues," "Evil Gal Blues," and "Homeward Bound." Washington then worked with Milt Jackson and Charles Mingus in 1945. Over time, Washington moved from singing blues to performing more jazz-oriented material. By the 1950s she was a successful crossover artist, gaining legendary status with "What a Difference a Day Makes" and "Unforgettable." Washington died of an overdose of alcohol and diet pills on December 14, 1963, in Detroit.

Washington's popularity as a blues singer in the tradition of Bessie Smith and her ability to cross over into jazz and pop genres have won her many fans in the decades since her death. Able to sound seductive and tough at the same time, Washington was an immensely talented vocalist.

MUDDY WATERS (1913?–1983)

Guitarist, Harmonica Player, Singer. Waters was born McKinley Morganfield near Rolling Fork, Mississippi, on April 4, 1913 (some sources say 1915), and grew up in nearby Clarksdale on Stovall's plantation. He began playing guitar at seventeen, performing mostly at house parties and fish fries. Waters, who idolized Son House, was first captured on tape in field recordings by Alan Lomax in 1941. After running a juke joint in the early 1940s, Waters moved to Chicago in 1943, where he

Muddy Waters, Capital Radio Jazz Festival, 1979. *A guitarist, harmonica player, and singer known as the "Father of Electric Blues," Waters was inducted into both the Blues Foundation Hall of Fame and the Rock and Roll Hall of Fame and was also the recipient of the Grammy Lifetime Achievement Award.* DAVID REDFERN/REDFERNS/GETTY IMAGES

played in clubs during the evening and worked as a laborer during the day.

In 1946 Waters made recordings for Columbia Records, but his urban sound was not well-received, and the records were not released. Appearing as a sideman in 1947 with Sunnyland Slim, Waters also made another two recordings for Chess Records before hitting his stride with "I Feel Like Going Home" in 1948, which became his first national rhythm and blues hit. On the single, he fronted his own band that included Little Walter on harmonica. In the 1950s, Waters produced such masterpieces as "I'm Your Hoochie Coochie Man" (written by Willie Dixon), "Got My Mojo Working," "Tiger in Your Tank," and "Mannish Boy." His music popularized by white British youth, Muddy Waters eventually played on stage with many of these performers, including Eric Clapton and Mike Bloomfield, both of whom considered Waters a guitar master and a living legend.

In the late 1960s and into the 1970s, Waters began receiving the kind of widespread recognition he deserved, winning three Grammy Awards and a Trendsetter Award and being inducted into the Ebony Readers' Poll Black Hall of Fame. The postwar Chicago blues scene would have been incomplete without Muddy Waters. His aggressive, swaggering, Delta-rooted vocal sound and piercing slide guitar instrumentals made him the "Father of Electric Blues." Waters died on April 30, 1983.

BEN WEBSTER (1909–1973)

Saxophonist. Born in Kansas City, Missouri, on March 27, 1909, Benjamin Francis Love Webster was initially a pianist, but switched to saxophone in his late teens. He worked with the family band led by Lester Young's father and with many other Midwestern bands. Ben joined Bennie Moten's band in 1932, and was a featured performer on the landmark recording of "Moten Swing." After gaining a name among musicians as one of the most gifted disciples of Coleman Hawkins, he made many records and toured with many prominent bands, including those of Fletcher Henderson, Cab Calloway, Benny Carter, and Teddy Wilson.

When Webster joined Duke Ellington in 1940, along with Jimmy Blanton and Billy Strayhorn, he blossomed as a tenor soloist and soon became an influence in his own right. When he left Ellington in 1943, he generally led his own small groups, recorded prolifically, and became one of the first African American musicians to join a network (CBS) radio's musical staff in 1944. By the 1950s Webster moved to the West Coast and recorded with Art Tatum, Coleman Hawkins, and Billie Holiday. In 1965, he left on what had been planned as his first brief visit to Europe, but he never returned home. Webster settled in Copenhagen, Denmark, where he spent the final decade of his life as a revered and beloved elder statesman of jazz. During this period, his always masterful ballad playing ripened to full maturity, and his sound, ranging from a whisper to a gruff roar, became one of the unsurpassed landmarks of classic jazz. He died on September 20, 1973, in Amsterdam, Netherlands. One of the big three tenor saxophone players of the 1930s and 1940s, along with Coleman Hawkins and Lester Young, Webster is remembered for the full-bodied tone, warm vibrato, and bluesy melodies that made him an icon.

MARY LOU WILLIAMS (1910–1981)

Pianist, Composer, Arranger. Most women who have achieved fame in jazz have been singers, from Bessie Smith to Betty Carter. An exception to this rule was Mary Lou Williams, dubbed the "First Lady of Jazz." Born in Atlanta on May 8, 1910, and raised in Pittsburgh, Mary Elfrieda Scruggs had already performed in public at the age of six and was a professional by thirteen. Three years later she married saxophonist John Williams, with whom she made her recording debut. When John joined Andy Kirk's band, Mary Lou took over his old group. Soon, however, she was writing arrangements for Kirk, and in 1931 she became the band's pianist and musical director.

Although she also wrote for Benny Goodman, Earl Hines, and Tommy Dorsey, Williams stayed with Kirk until 1942, helping to make the band one of the swing era's best. After a return home to Pittsburgh in 1942, she formed her own band that included a young Art Blakey, and settled in New York. A champion of modern jazz, she gave advice and counsel to such rising stars as Dizzy Gillespie and Thelonious Monk and contributed scores for Gillespie's big band. Williams joined Duke Ellington's band and served as staff arranger, contributing more than 15 works during 1946. She led her own groups (sometimes all female) and began to compose longer works including the "Zodiac Suite," performed at Town Hall in 1946 by the New York Philharmonic Orchestra.

Williams lived in England and France from 1952 to 1954. After returning to the United States, she retired from active performing for approximately three years, and formed a charitable organization to assist musicians with substance abuse issues and other health problems. After resuming her career, she toured widely, including a 1957 appearance at the Newport Jazz Festival with Gillespie, and wrote several religious works including a jazz mass performed at St. Patrick's Cathedral. In 1977, she became artist-in-residence and teacher of jazz history and performance at Duke University, a position that she held until her death on May 28, 1981, in Durham, North Carolina.

Williams was a highly regarded instrumentalist, primarily in the swing idiom, and a gifted composer. Most importantly, she was the only major jazz artist who lived and adapted her playing style throughout all of the jazz eras including spirituals, ragtime, blues, Kansas City swing, boogie woogie, bop, and avant-garde.

"SONNY BOY" WILLIAMSON (?–1965)

Singer, Harmonica Player. Very little is known of Williamson's childhood and his young adult years. His real name was believed to have been Aleck Ford "Rice" Miller, but that cannot be verified. What is known is that by the mid-1930s, Williamson was traveling the Delta working under the alias of Little Boy Blue with such blues legends as Robert Johnson, Robert Nighthawk, and Elmore James. By the early 1940s he was appearing on "King Biscuit Time," the first live blues radio show. (The sponsor of the show had Williamson pose as John Lee "Sonny Boy" Williamson, an established Chicago blues star, in order to increase sales of their product. Apparently the ruse succeeded and when John Lee was murdered, Williamson became "the original Sonny Boy.") The show was an immediate hit, but Williamson did not record his work until the 1950s when his first single, "Eyesight to the Blind" became a hit. Williamson also participated in Elmore James's "Dust My Broom" session before recording his first session for Chess Records in August 1955, releasing "Don't Start Me to Talkin'." In 1963 he headed to Europe and enjoyed tremendous success, recording with British blues-rock groups the Yardbirds and the Animals before releasing the hit "Help Me." Two years

Sonny Boy Williamson, c. 1964. *A legendary blues singer and harmonica player who enjoyed tremendous popularity among blues purists and rock and roll fans, Williamson wrote and played what are considered some of the best blues songs of all time.* DAVID REDFERN/REDFERNS/GETTY IMAGES

later, he returned to the United States, where he died of a heart attack in Helena, Arkansas, on May 25.

Sonny Boy Williamson was one of the great blues legends who enjoyed tremendous popularity among blues purists and rock and roll fans. He wrote and played some of the best blues songs ever. His distinctive vocal delivery, combined with his powerful harmonica playing, made his sound unique.

Tenor Saxophonist Lester Young, Village Vanguard, New York City, 1940. *"Prez" Young is remembered for his style, which formed a bridge from hot and swing jazz to bebop and cool jazz.* CHARLES PETERSON/HULTON ARCHIVE/GETTY IMAGES

TEDDY WILSON (1912–1986)

Pianist, Bandleader. Born on November 24, 1912, in Austin, Texas, Theodore Wilson studied music theory at Talladega College before moving to Detroit in 1929, where he played in local bands, and Chicago the following year. From 1931 to 1933, Wilson played in Louis Armstrong's big band and with others, before he was brought to New York by Benny Carter in 1933.

In 1935, Wilson began to make a series of records with Billie Holiday, Ben Webster, and Johnny Hodges. Meanwhile, he became famous as the first black jazz musician to be featured with a white band when he was hired that same year to play with the Benny Goodman Trio (with Gene Krupa), with whom he stayed until 1939. (The group also included Lionel Hampton for a time, and performed as the Benny Goodman Quartet.) Wilson's marvelously clear, harmonically impeccable piano style was a big influence on the pianists of the swing era. He formed his own big band in 1939, but it was not a commercial success. From that point forward, Wilson mostly led small groups or appeared as a soloist, touring worldwide and making hundreds of records. Though seriously ill, he continued to perform until a week before his death on July 31, 1986, in New Britain, Connecticut. Two of his three sons are professional musicians.

Wilson's style evolved from the early influence of Earl Hines, Art Tatum (who befriended him early in his career), and Fats Waller, but became a neat and quietly swinging style that featured single note lines that were revolutionary at the time. Wilson was also a fine but little known arranger and writer.

LESTER "PREZ" YOUNG (1909–1959)

Saxophonist. Born August 27, 1909, in Woodville, Mississippi, Lester Willis Young was instructed on trumpet, violin, alto sax, and drums by his father, a trained musician who studied at Tuskegee. Young's family moved to New Orleans during Lester's infancy, and by age ten Lester was playing drums in the family band. He spent his youth on the carnival circuit in the Midwest, choosing to concentrate on the saxophone at age thirteen (i.e., the C melody saxophone after his idol Frankie Trumbauer). Young's first major job was playing baritone saxophone with the Bostonians in 1929 and 1930, before touring all over the Midwest with the bands of Joseph King Oliver and Walter Page.

After a brief stay with Count Basie, Young was offered Coleman Hawkins's chair in Fletcher Henderson's orchestra, but he was criticized for not having the same style as his predecessor and he soon left. He returned to Kansas City to play with Andy Kirk, and then with Count Basie from 1936 to 1940. During the Basie years, Young surpassed Hawkins as the most vital influence on the tenor. Hardly a tenor man from the mid-1940s through the 1950s achieved prominence without building upon the foundations laid by Lester Young. After leaving Basie's band, Young worked in several small combos in the early 1940s before entering the Army in 1944. During his fifteen-month service, Young suffered what many characterized as traumatic racial prejudice that affected him for the rest of his life. After his return to civilian life, he worked in numerous small combos and toured with the Jazz at the Philharmonic (JATP) units. He suffered a complete emotional breakdown in 1955, but made a comeback the following year. He died from a combination of mental problems, alcoholism, and malnutrition on March 15, 1959, within hours of returning from a long engagement in Paris.

It was Lester Young who gave Billie Holiday the name "Lady Day" when both were with Count Basie, and it was Holiday, in turn, who christened Lester Young "President" (later shortened to "Prez"). Young is remembered for his style, which formed the bridge from hot and swing jazz to bebop and cool jazz. Young transformed the big, full-tone, and dotted eighth- and sixteenth-note phrasing to a moodier, laconic sound utilizing a series of evenly placed eighth notes played legato.

25

POPULAR MUSIC

Debra Newman Ham
Guthrie P. Ramsey Jr.
Delano Greenidge-Copprue
William Hobbs III

THE RISE OF RHYTHM AND BLUES

The emergence of rhythm and blues or "R&B" marks one of the most important developments in American popular music. Before rhythm and blues, the swing style of jazz was considered the most popular music of the day. Although artists such as Benny Goodman (1909–1986), Duke Ellington (1899–1974), and Count Basie (1904–1984) reigned in America's popular imagination and on the record sales charts, musical expression made a significant shift in the mid-1940s.

The term *rhythm and blues* describes a number of historically specific styles that have grown out of the African American vernacular music tradition since the mid-twentieth century. Rhythm and blues laid the foundation for numerous subsequent styles, including rock and roll, soul, disco, funk, jazz fusion, rap, and, most recently, "smooth" (contemporary) jazz. R&B artists combined the conventions of several popular music styles: swing jazz, boogie-woogie, gospel blues, blues, and, in some cases, novelty pop. From the swing tradition, rhythm-and-blues musicians adopted the riff-based horn arrangements and driving rhythms of groups such as Count Basie and His Orchestra. Gospel and blues music provided a system of dramatic vocal techniques, which were crafted by artists into highly stylized personal mannerisms. Gospel, jazz, and blues also provided musical forms, such as thirty-two-bar songs and twelve-bar blues patterns, to the new style. Unlike the swing-era big bands, "jump-blues" groups featured fewer horns and a heavy rhythmic approach marked by a walking boogie bass line, honking saxophone solos, and a two-four drum pattern. Among the greatest exponents of postwar jump blues were guitarist T-Bone Walker (1910–1975), saxophonist Eddie "Cleanhead" Vinson (1917–1988), and blues shouter Big Joe Turner (1911–1985).

Singer and saxophonist Louis Jordan (1908–1975) fronted a supremely popular jump-blues ensemble that featured his singing, which was a smooth gospel-influenced vocal style. In 1949, the popularity of the style championed by Jordan and others led producer Jerry Wexler (1917–2008), who was working at *Billboard* magazine, to change its African American pop-chart title to rhythm and blues, coining the name of this new music. The new sound, originally dubbed *jump blues* and later *rhythm and blues*, proved extremely popular beyond the African American community, marking one of many important "crossover" moments in American popular music history.

The melding of musical techniques that distinguished rhythm and blues is related to the specific sociohistorical context of midcentury America. Because of the ample supply of jobs caused by World War II (1939–1945), black and white southerners flooded the North seeking new opportunities and life chances. This migration created a dramatic shift in the demographics of major cities in the North, Midwest, and West. The burgeoning U.S. economy during the war provided these migrants with the resources to seek different kinds of entertainment in their new locales.

The lyrics of rhythm-and-blues songs reflected ways in which some migrants negotiated these changes. Many rhythm-and-blues lyrics speak of life in the South through a nostalgic lens; others use metaphors that reference country living; and others speak of hardships associated with life in the urban North. As African Americans pressured the U.S. government to end Jim Crow and the laws of the land that denied them equal rights, the color line between the races became less rigid, and as a result, both white and black Americans gained greater access to each other's cultures, especially music. Like jazz music, rhythm and blues was an important source of cultural exchange. In fact, the popularity of rhythm and blues paved the way for rock and roll's replacing jazz as America's quintessential popular music in the 1950s. But the music remained rooted in the sound of the African American church, though not exclusively. Some of the early recordings exemplifying the gospel influence on rhythm and blues were Cecil Grant's 1945 hit "I Wonder," Roy Brown's 1947 classic "Good Rocking Tonight," and Wynonie Harris's 1949 disc "All She Wants to Do Is Rock."

Dinah Washington (1924–1963) was one of the earliest female rhythm-and-blues singers to make a mark on the entertainment industry during the 1940s. Her song stylings combined jazz, blues, gospel, and pop ballads. During her childhood, Washington honed her musical skills in the Baptist churches in Chicago, although she, like many others, was born in the South. After scoring hits with "Evil Gal Blues" and "Salty Papa Blues" early in her career, she recorded a string of hits for the Mercury label, with which she began an association in 1948. Washington's recorded work sprawls over several categories, including rhythm and blues, pop, jazz, and country.

Louis Jordan, however, is considered the most important jump-blues or rhythm-and-blues performer of the 1940s. He formed his group Louis Jordan and His Tympani Five in 1938 with an eye toward entertaining and capturing some of the white market. His repertoire was eclectic: jump blues, ballads, and novelty songs. With titles such as "Beans and Cornbread," "Saturday Night Fish Fry," and "Ain't Nobody Here but Us Chickens," the group's chart-busting songs, as writer Nelson George has noted, "suggest country life, yet the subject of each is really a city scene."

It was not long before this kind of raw-edged rhythm and blues emerged from hundreds of independent recording labels that appeared across the country in the postwar era. With the increased availability of rhythm-and-blues recordings, a handful of African American radio disc jockeys became locally famous as the first promoters and salesmen of this music. Bringing their colorful street language to the airwaves, pioneer African American DJs such as Al Benson and Vernon Winslow not only helped to popularize rhythm and blues, but set the trend for modern pop and African American radio programming.

RHYTHM AND BLUES AND THE AFRICAN AMERICAN CHURCH

In the early 1950s, numerous gospel quartets and street-corner singing groups set out to establish careers in the African American popular music scene. Influenced by gospel groups, such as the Golden Gate Quartet and the Harmonizing Four, and the secular singing of such groups as the Inkspots, vocal groups appeared that performed complex harmonies in a cappella style. As they would for rap artists in decades to come, street corners in urban neighborhoods became training grounds for thousands of young aspiring African American artists. This music, known as *doo-wop*, first arrived on the scene with the formation of the Ravens in 1945. Not long afterward, there followed a great succession of doo-wop "bird groups," including the Orioles who, in 1953, scored a

Singer-Songwriter Sam Cooke, c. 1958. *Here pictured with Gertrude Hall, Cooke recorded a string of hit songs starting in 1957 with "You Send Me," a song that achieved popularity among both black and white audiences.* MICHAEL OCHS ARCHIVES/GETTY IMAGES

nationwide hit with "Crying in the Chapel"—a song that, for the first time in African American popular music, walked an almost indistinguishable line between gospel and mainstream pop music. In the same year, Billy Ward (1921–2002) formed the Dominoes, featuring lead singer Clyde McPhatter (1933–1972), the son of a Baptist minister.

In the wake of the success of these vocal groups, numerous gospel singers left the church to become pop music stars. In 1952, for example, the Royal Sons became the pop group Five Royales. They later changed their name to the Gospel Starlighters (with James Brown), and finally the Blue Flames. Five years later, a young gospel singer named Sam Cooke (1935–1964) landed a number-one pop hit with "You Send Me," a song that achieved popularity among both black and white audiences.

The strong relationship between gospel and rhythm and blues was evident in the music of more hard-edged rhythm-and-blues groups, such as Hank Ballard (1936–2003) and the Midnighters. Maintaining a driving blues-based sound, Ballard's music, while featuring gospel-based harmonies, retained secular themes, as evidenced in his 1954 hit "Work with Me Annie." However, the capstone of gospel rhythm and blues appeared in the talents of Georgia-born pianist and singer Ray Charles (1930–2004), who in 1954 hit the charts with "I Got a Woman," which was based on the gospel song "My Jesus Is All the World to Me." Charles's 1958 recording "What I'd Say" is famed for its call-and-response pattern, which directly resembled the music sung in Holiness churches.

ROCK AND ROLL

The rise of white rock and roll around 1955 served to open the floodgates for thousands of black rhythm-and-blues artists longing for a nationwide audience. A term applied to black rhythm and blues and its white equivalents during the mid-1950s, *rock and roll* represented a label given to a musical form by the white media and marketplace in order to attract a mass multiracial audience. Alan Freed (1922–1965), a white DJ from Ohio, is credited with being the first to air radio programming dubbed "rock 'n' roll," and is therefore remembered in some circles as the "Father of Rock and Roll." While the term itself had been used in black vernacular language for years, it was used by white promoters of rock and roll to distinguish it from rhythm and blues, which was, of course, closely associated with black music culture.

Many southern whites expressed outrage at the growing interest in rhythm and blues and rock and roll among white teenagers, and various authorities mounted "Don't Buy Negro Records" campaigns. As African American music writer Nelson George explained, naming this music *rock and roll* "dulled down the racial identification and made young white consumers of Cold War America feel more comfortable." Taken from a term common among the Delta and electric blues cultures, rock and roll was actually rhythm and blues rechristened with a more "socially acceptable" title. Of course, the term *rock and roll* had sexual connotations as well; this, along with its roots in black culture, allowed white cultural conservatives of the time to demonize the form.

The majority of rhythm-and-blues performers never made the distinction between rhythm and blues and rock and roll. Ike Turner (1931–2007), a talent scout for the pioneering Sun Studios record label, was a formidable bandleader and guitarist; his 1951 cut "Rocket 88" has been considered by some to be the very first rock-and-roll record. The song's distorted guitar tone was achieved by accident—coming from a broken amplifier speaker—but would influence the gritty sound of many subsequent rock and blues guitarists. Turner achieved mainstream success in collaboration with his wife, singer Tina Turner, whose fame would later eclipse him.

Singer and Pianist Fats Domino. *A rhythm and blues artist who established a prosperous career in rock and roll, Domino first hit the charts in 1955 with "Ain't That a Shame" and then proceeded with such classics as "Blueberry Hill," "I'm Walkin," and "Whole Lotta Loving."* PICTORIAL PRESS LTD/ALAMY

One rhythm-and-blues artist who established a prosperous career in rock and roll was New Orleans–born pianist Antoine "Fats" Domino. Although he had produced a great amount of strong rhythm-and-blues material before his career in rock and roll, Domino did not hit the charts until 1955 with "Ain't That a Shame," followed by the classics "Blueberry Hill," "I'm Walkin," and "Whole Lotta Loving."

Another rhythm-and-blues pianist and singer to enter the rock-and-roll field was Little Richard Penniman, a former Pentecostal gospel singer whose career in pop music began in 1956 with the hit "Tutti Frutti." Little Richard's fiery vocalizations, featuring screams, hollers, and falsetto whoops were only matched for intensity by his explosive and rhythmic piano playing, which drew on blues and gospel traditions. Before entering a Seventh-Day Adventist seminary in 1959, Little Richard produced a string of hits: "Long Tall Sally," "Rip It Up," "The Girl Can't Help It," and "Good Golly Miss Molly."

In 1955, as Fats Domino's New Orleans–style rhythm-and-blues tunes climbed the charts, a young guitarist from St. Louis named Chuck Berry achieved nationwide fame when his country-influenced song "Maybelline" reached number five on the charts. Backed by the rhythm section of bluesman Muddy Waters (1913–1983), "Maybelline" offered a unique form of rhythm and blues, combining white hillbilly, or rockabilly, with jump blues. Berry revolutionized rhythm and blues by featuring the guitar as a lead rather than a rhythm instrument. Modeled after his blues guitar mentor T-Bone Walker, Berry's double-string guitar bends and syncopated upstroke rhythm created a driving backdrop for his colorfully poetic tales of teenage life. A very eclectic and creative musician, Berry incorporated the sounds of urban blues, country, calypso, Latin, and even Hawaiian music into his unique brand of rhythm and blues. His classic "Johnny B. Goode," recorded in 1958, became a standard in almost every rock-and-roll band's repertoire, including 1960s rock guitar hero Jimi Hendrix (1942–1970). According to music scholar Timothy D. Taylor, many early African American rockers, such as Berry, made a concerted effort to court an integrated audience, a notion that is evident in changes he made to a later recording of the song "Johnny B. Goode."

"CROSSOVERS" INTO COUNTRY MUSIC

African American musicians did not remain consigned to styles closely associated with African American culture. Dinah Washington, for example, recorded several pop tunes, beginning with the mainstream "What a Difference a Day Makes" in 1959, her first major hit. She also recorded what were known as "reverse crossovers," songs that originally appeared in the country or pop category but which Washington performed in her patented jazz-blues-gospel manner. In addition, Chuck Berry was not the only African American to take an interest in country music. Ray Charles's crossover into country music in the early 1960s caused controversy in many circles. In 1959, Charles recorded "I'm Moving On," a country tune by Hank Snow. Despite opposition, Charles recorded a fine collection of songs in 1962 titled *Modern Sounds in Country Music.* Filled with soulful ballads and backed by colorful string sections, the session produced two classic numbers, "You Don't Know Me" and "I Can't Stop Loving You." Its popularity spawned a 1963 sequel, *Modern Sounds in Country Music, Volume 2,* producing several more hits, including Hank Williams's "Your Cheating Heart" and "Take These Chains from My Heart."

Unlike other mainstream African American country artists, Charles's renditions remained immersed in his unique gospel-blues sound. Before Charles's entrance into the country music field, there had been many African American country artists, such as DeFord Bailey (1899–1982), a partially disabled harmonica player who became a regularly featured performer on the Grand Ole Opry from 1925 to 1941. However, it was not until 1965, when Charley Pride arrived on the country music scene with his RCA recordings "Snakes Crawl at Night" and "Atlantic Coastal Line" that an African American artist emerged as a superstar in the country tradition. Pride's songs were so steeped in the country tradition that many radio listeners were astounded when they found out his racial identity. With the arrival of Pride, there appeared other African American country artists, such as Linda Martell from South Carolina, O. B. McClinton (1940–1987) from Mississippi, and Oklahoma-born Big Al Downing (1940–2005) and Stoney Edwards (1929–1997). Edwards, the most noted of these artists, recorded two nationwide hits in 1968 with Jesse Winchester's "You're on My Mind" and Leonard Cohen's "Bird on a Wire."

SWEET SOUL MUSIC AND SOCIAL REVOLUTION

The tremendous social upheavals of the 1960s—including but not limited to the civil rights, Black Power, and women's movements and the coalescence of a youth-based subculture—were paralleled by numerous new musical forms. Perhaps no single genre of popular song encapsulated the highs and lows of this period more than soul music. Soul music drew on several idioms of African

Sly and the Family Stone. *Featuring a psychedelic rock tinge and communal good vibes over a bedrock funk groove, Sly and the Family Stone in the late 1960s and early 1970s released a string of hits that included "Dance to the Music," "Everyday People," and "You Can Make It If You Try."* PICTORIAL PRESS LTD/ALAMY

American music, including gospel, jazz, and blues. According to music scholar David Brackett, gospel vocal techniques that signified spiritual ecstasy in the religious context were transplanted by soul singers into the secular context with important results. The most prominent of these is a sense of raw passion that identified the singers with the songs and the songs with the African American community. Being born in the African American church, where testifying preachers and harmonizing choirs shepherded their congregations to weekly ecstasy, the form was escorted into the secular world by a handful of artists schooled simultaneously in gospel, jazz, country blues, rhythm and blues, and rock and roll.

Although he had precursors, such as vocalist Clyde McPhatter, who recorded with the Dominoes and the Drifters, singer-keyboardist Ray Charles has been credited as one of the founders of the soul genre. His earliest hits—notably, "What'd I Say" and "I Got a Woman"—brought the emotional testifying and call-and-response arrangements associated with gospel music into a nonreligious context. He added the earthy pull of the blues and a jazz-influenced harmonic complexity to his distinctive musical blend. This hybrid of blues groove and spirit was the secular gospel known as soul music. Such innovations were controversial, but the sounds of soul sweetened and enriched rhythm-and-blues music from then on. Blind "Brother Ray" became a cultural icon in the ensuing decades.

While rhythm and blues had functioned for some time as gospel's sinful, worldly counterpart—focusing largely on the concerns of the body while church music addressed the spirit—soul refused to deny either side of human experience. Even so, the young genre's exuberance and ambition made it ideal for reflecting the growing aspirations of America's black population. Inspired by the teachings and nonviolent organizing of Dr. Martin Luther King Jr. and other civil rights leaders, African Americans also responded to songs that trumpeted change. "People Get Ready" and "We're a Winner" by Curtis Mayfield and the Impressions were early anthems as soul grew and drew many more listeners.

Singer-bandleader James Brown (1933–2006), meanwhile, combined uplift and hard groove, gradually moving from heady soul and rhythm and blues into a new territory called *funk* with hits such as "I Got You (I Feel Good)" and "Cold Sweat." Brown ran one of the tightest ships around, alternately inspiring and browbeating his musicians; turnover was high, but the ensemble was always a well-oiled machine. Though he would refine the funk style—with driving rhythms emphasizing the "one" or first beat of each measure; repetitive vocal phrases and improvised, "churchy" shouts; and minimal, almost dissonant, instrumental figures—during the early 1960s, its content remained largely sexual for some time. Brown's mid-1960s work began laying the musical foundation for funk, and his music primarily celebrated the dynamic tradition of African American social dancing in songs such as "There Was a Time" and "Licking Stick," often naming popular dances, such as the "boogaloo" and the "funky chicken," in songs. Brown's political message did not fully materialize until the end of the decade. By then, his funky sermons championed African American economic independence and freedom from addiction. Brown had a seismic affect on pop; not only funk artists but also scores of rock and rap musicians took his work as a point of departure.

Following Brown's lead, Sly and the Family Stone—led by Sylvester "Sly Stone" Stewart, a northern California DJ and producer—added a psychedelic rock tinge and communal good vibe to the bedrock funk groove. Featuring musicians that were both black and white, male and female, the group offered one of the most inclusive visions in pop history. While "Dance to the Music" mapped out their utopia in musical terms, they trumpeted tolerance and equality in happy hits, such as "Everyday People," "Everybody Is a Star," and "You Can Make It if You Try." Stone's vision would darken substantially later on, however.

The syncopated rhythms of New Orleans were also fundamental to the development of modern funk. The Meters began as an instrumental foursome and eventually backed up acts as diverse as singer Lee Dorsey (1924–1986), the vocal group the Pointer Sisters, and British popster Robert Palmer (1949–2003). During the 1960s, they scored some instrumental hits, notably "Cissy Strut," before adding vocals in the 1970s. Though they eventually disbanded and were partly subsumed by soul survivors the Neville Brothers, the Meters were profoundly influential.

SOUL NORTH AND SOUTH: STAX/VOLT, ATLANTIC, AND MOTOWN

Soul music's increasing hold on the public imagination during the 1960s had a great deal to do with two record companies, the Atlantic Records subsidiary Stax/Volt in the South and Motown in the North. Stax/Volt was a Memphis-based label that introduced the world to the rough-hewn "funky" sound of southern soul and rhythm and blues. The company's greatest successes came during the 1960s, thanks to a roster of powerful artists, gifted songwriters, and one of the best "house bands" in music history. The band in question, led by keyboardist Booker T. Jones, was a formidable mixed-race groove machine that not only backed the whole Stax roster and numerous acts on its parent label, Atlantic, but also achieved success as an instrumental recording act, Booker T. and the MG's. Their smoldering workouts "Green Onions" and "Hip Hug-Her" became signature themes of the era.

Stax's roster included vocal duo Sam and Dave (Sam Moore and Dave Prater [1937–1988]), Rufus Thomas (1917–2001) and Carla Thomas, Eddie Floyd, and Otis Redding (1941–1967). House songwriters Isaac Hayes (1942–2008) and David Porter wrote hits such as "Soul Man" and "Hold on, I'm Coming" for Sam and Dave. Hayes himself would later become a pop/soul superstar. Redding was both an extraordinary singer and a gifted tunesmith; he penned the luminous "Dock of the Bay" and the righteous "Respect." The latter song was transformed into an anthem of nascent feminism and African American dignity thanks to the alchemy of Atlantic Records and Aretha Franklin. Franklin, a gospel-bred singer turned pop maven, would become the "Queen of Soul" and one of the most enduring figures in popular music. While Franklin made "Respect" and other celebrated recording tracks, such as "Chain of Fools," the incandescent "(You Make Me Feel Like a) Natural Woman," and "I Never Loved a Man," at the Fame studios in Muscle Shoals, Alabama, other Atlantic soul stars traveled to Memphis to make their hit records. The Stax crew collaborated with Wilson Pickett (1941–2006) on hugely successful singles, such as "In the Midnight Hour" and "Land of 1,000 Dances." Ultimately, however, Stax lost its commercial momentum and by the 1970s was struggling to compete with a panoply of rivals.

As soul music gained a mass following in the African American community, an African American–owned, family-run Detroit record company emerged as one of the largest and most successful African American business enterprises in the United States. In 1959, Berry Gordy Jr., a Detroit entrepreneur, songwriter, and modern jazz enthusiast, established the Motown Record Corporation.

With its headquarters located in a modest two-story home, the company proudly displayed a sign on its exterior reading Hitsville USA. Taking advantage of the diversity of local talent, Gordy employed Detroit-based contract teams, writers, producers, and engineers. Motown's studio became a great laboratory for technological innovations, advancing the use of echo, multitracking, and overdubbing. In the studio, Gordy employed the city's finest jazz and classical musicians to accompany the young singing talent signed to the company.

Unlike the soul music emerging in studios such as Stax and Muscle Shoals, Motown's music was also marketed at the white middle class. Gordy called his music "the Sound of Young America" and sought to produce glamorous and well-groomed acts. "Blues and R&B always had a funky look to it back in those days," explained Motown producer Mickey Stevenson. "We felt that we should have a look that the mothers and fathers would want their children to follow." Indeed, a meticulously controlled and glamorous image was an extremely important component in Berry Gordy's Motown ideology. He required artists signed to the label to attend classes on etiquette, stage presence, and choreography. In fact, the strict division of labor that Gordy established in this company might be compared to the automobile assembly lines for which Detroit is well known.

Accordingly, Motown set out to produce a sound that it considered more refined and less "off-key" than the music played by mainstream soul and blues artists. In its early years of operation, Motown retained a rhythm-and-blues influence as evidenced in such songs as the Marvelettes' "Please Mister Postman" (1961), Mary Wells's "You Beat Me to the Punch" (1962), and Marvin Gaye's "Pride and Joy" (1963).

The Marvelettes, c. 1961. *One of Motown Record's key acts in the 1960s, the female singing group the Marvelettes scored their first success in 1961 with "Please Mister Postman," which reached number one on both the U.S. pop and R&B charts.* **GILLES PETARD/REDFERNS**

One of the main forces responsible for the emergence of a unique "Motown sound" appeared in the production team of Brian Holland, Eddie Holland, and Lamont Dozier, or H-D-H, as they came to be known. Utilizing the recording techniques of Phil Spector's "wall of sound," the H-D-H team brought fame to many of Motown's "girl groups," such as Martha and the Vandellas and the Supremes, featuring Diana Ross. In 1966 and 1967, H-D-H began to use more complex string arrangements based upon minor chord structures. This gave rise to what has been referred to as their "classical period." As a result, many Motown songs reflected the darker side of lost love and the conditions of ghetto life. This mood was captured in such songs by the Four Tops as "Reach Out, I'll Be There," "Bernadette," and "Seven Rooms of Gloom."

After the Holland-Dozier-Holland team left Motown in 1968, the company, faced with numerous artistic and economic problems, fell into a state of decline. A year later, Gordy signed the Jackson Five, the last major act to join the label before its demise. The Jacksons landed thirteen consecutive hit singles, including "ABC" and "I'll Be There," championing a style that might be called "bubblegum soul"—African American music directed at a preteen and young adolescent audience, a legacy that was seen in such 1980s and 1990s groups as New Edition and Boyz II Men. In 1971, Gordy moved the Motown Record Corporation to Los Angeles, where the company directed its efforts toward filmmaking. Through the late 1970s and early 1980s, Motown continued to sign such acts as the Commodores, Lionel Richie, and DeBarge. But in 1984, Gordy entered into a distribution agreement with MCA records and eventually sold Motown to an entertainment conglomerate.

PSYCHEDELIC SOUL TO DISCO

Disillusionment after the deaths of Black Power advocate Malcolm X in 1965 and civil rights champion Dr. Martin Luther King Jr. in 1968, along with the lingering trauma of the Vietnam War (1957–1975) and the worsening plight of America's inner cities, had a marked influence on soul's direction. Curtis Mayfield (1942–1999) projected a vision of wary hope in his early 1970s work. His landmark soundtrack for the 1972 "blaxploitation" film *Super Fly* reflected the new soul paradigm: at once gritty and symphonic, encompassing soul's far-reaching ambition and funk's uncompromising, earthy realism.

The Supremes, 1965. *At their peak as Motown hit-makers in the mid-1960s, the female singing group the Supremes included (*left to right*) Florence Ballard, Mary Wilson, and Diana Ross. Their first smash hit, "Where Did Our Love Go," was followed by such chart-toppers as "Baby Love" and "Stop! In the Name of Love."* FRANK DRIGGS COLLECTION/HULTON ARCHIVE/GETTY IMAGES

Isaac Hayes's theme from *Shaft* (1971), another urban action film, earned an Academy Award. Much of the funk and soul of this period drew not only on the percolating rhythms developed by Brown but also on the trailblazing guitar work of Jimi Hendrix.

Hailed by many as the greatest electric guitarist of all time, Hendrix had toiled as a sideman for numerous rhythm-and-blues acts but emerged as a rocker of the first order during the mid-1960s. By the time of his death in 1970, he had revolutionized lead guitar playing forever; his use of the wah-wah pedal, an effect that lent a powerful percussive dimension to the instrument, became a staple of funk. His melding of psychedelic rock, hard blues, and soul tropes, meanwhile, influenced the "psychedelic soul" that emerged in his wake.

Commercial soul addressed the tenor of the times. Trailblazers Sly and the Family Stone, the first interracial American rock band, formed in San Francisco and focused less on the rainbow-colored sentiments of the preceding era and more on urban turmoil with their landmark album *There's a Riot Going On*, as did Marvin Gaye (1939–1984) with hits such as "Trouble Man" and "What's Goin' On." The O'Jays enjoyed chart success with such anxious singles as "Backstabbers" and "For the Love of Money," and the Temptations wrapped their prodigious vocal chops around inner-city woes on "Papa Was a Rolling Stone," among other smashes.

These commercial laments were outstripped in daring—though not in sales—by the work of Detroit's Funkadelic. Fronted by singer and hairstylist George Clinton, who led a doo-wop group called The Parliaments in the 1950s, Funkadelic mixed acid rock's cosmic guitar excursions with funk's relentless grooves; a danger existed in their work that limited its commercial appeal but profoundly influenced rock and rap.

Eventually, Clinton established another group, Parliament, which focused on horn-driven funk and elaborate, fantasy-oriented concept albums. Funkadelic and Parliament, though manifestly different at first, gradually moved into similar territory as P. Funk, the "P" meaning

***The Temptations, c. 1966.** One of the most successful groups on the Motown label, and the first to earn a Grammy Award, the Temptations used their unique vocal and artistic talents to create such hits as "My Girl," "I Can't Get Next to You," and "Papa Was a Rollin' Stone."* BETTMANN/CORBIS. REPRODUCED BY PERMISSION.

"pure." Soon P. Funk was the umbrella term for a family of bands that included Bootsy's Rubber Band and the Brides of Funkenstein. Clinton scored in the 1980s as a solo artist, most notably with the megahit "Atomic Dog." P. Funk was so influential that for a time Parliament found itself competing with acts that appropriated its sound and themes, including such hit-makers as the Ohio Players, Rick James (1948–2004), George Duke, and Earth,

Wind, and Fire. Though funk declined during the 1980s, artists such as Prince took it in a new, eclectic direction.

The decade did not lack for more traditionally romantic performers, however. Apart from Marvin Gaye, the period's most seductive male vocalists were arguably Al Green and Barry White (1944–2003). Green's rich falsetto and intimate phrasing on hits such as "Let's Stay Together" and "Love and Happiness" quickly established him as a visionary in the genre. Though he left pop music to sing gospel music and preach, he remained a beloved figure in the soul world and returned to the fold for a 1995 album. White's bedroom soundtracks, meanwhile, kept lovers in thrall with an intoxicating blend of his baritone vocals and symphonic arrangements. Another funk direction coalesced in the work of jazz-based artists such as Herbie Hancock and Patrice Rushen, both of whom scored hits in the 1970s and 1980s that coincided with the appearance of the so-called "Quiet Storm" format in rhythm-and-blues radio programming. Each drew on jazz, rhythm and blues, and funk in their recordings, some of them featuring piano solos that extended them beyond the length of typical rhythm-and-blues recordings.

During the mid-1970s, club dance floors were increasingly dominated by the pulsating sounds of disco. With its thumping beat and lush arrangements, the music was viewed by many as a saccharine and escapist form that betrayed the mission of funk and soul. While a number of powerful performers emerged from the disco scene, few could approach the star power of diva Donna Summer, who enjoyed a wave of hits before a religious conversion moved her into gospel. Though disco's "crossover" success meant that a number of artists who scored in that format were white, several all–African American acts, notably Chic, Kool and the Gang, and LaBelle, flourished during this period.

RAP: FROM SUBCULTURE TO MASS APPEAL

While funk sold millions of records and received extensive radio airplay in the mid-1970s, rap music emerged within a small circle of New York artists and entertainers in neighborhoods in Upper Manhattan and the South Bronx. Rap music belongs to a larger cultural system known as hip-hop, which comprises graffiti writing and break dancing (and its derivatives), together with rapping itself. Disc jockeys at private parties discovered how to use "little raps" between songs to keep dancers on their feet. From behind the microphone, DJs created a call-and-response pattern with the audience.

Rapping consists of a vocalist performing non- to semi-melodic oral declamations over a rhythmic background, which can be as sparse as a single drum track or an elaborate, multitextured, multiple instrumental track. Taking advantage of their master-of-ceremonies status, rappers often boasted of their intellectual or sexual prowess. "Soon a division of labor emerged," explained Jefferson Morley. "DJs concentrated on perfecting the techniques of manipulating the turntables, while master of ceremonies (MCs or rappers) concentrated on rapping in rhymes." Through the use of a special stylus, rappers moved records back and forth on the turntable in order to create a unique rhythmic sound, known within the rap culture as *needle rocking* and later as *scratching*.

In its short history, both the MC and DJ aspects of rap music have undergone significant changes, and the genre has exploded in many artistic directions and satellite idioms, such as hip-hop soul, New Jack swing, and gangsta rap, among other approaches. The subject matter addressed in rap music has been equally eclectic, covering many topics, including male and female braggadocio, highly sexualized content, gender relationships, race politics, partying, and youthful leisure.

Long before the modern rap, or hip-hop, culture emerged, however, there were African American artists who performed in a rap-style idiom. In 1929, for instance, New York singer-comedian Pigmeat Markham (1904–1981) gave performances representative of an early rap style. The rhyming style of boxing legend Muhammad Ali's prefight boasts is also of note.

Rap music is also rooted in the talking jazz style of a group of ex-convicts called the Last Poets. During the 1960s, this ensemble of African American intellectuals rapped in complex rhythms over music played by jazz accompanists. Last Poet member Jalal Nuriddin, recording under the name Lightning Rod, released an album titled *Hustler's Convention* (1973). Backed by the funk band Kool and the Gang, Nuriddin's recording became very influential to the early New York rappers.

Among one of the first New York rap artists of the early 1970s was Jamaican-born Clive Campbell, also known as Kool Herc. A street DJ, Herc developed the art of sampling, the method of playing a section of a recording over and over in order to create a unique dance mix. Others performers who joined the New York scene were black nationalist DJ Afrika Bambaataa from the southeast Bronx and Joseph Saddler, known as Grandmaster Flash, from the central Bronx. Saddler formed the group Grandmaster Flash and the Three MCs (Cowboy, Kid Creole, and Melle Mel). Later he added Kurtis Blow and Duke Bootee, who founded the Furious Five.

However, rap music did not reach a broad audience until 1980 when the Sugar Hill Gang's song "Rapper's Delight" received widespread radio airplay. Small record companies began to affect the development of pop for the first time in years. Def Jam spearheaded the rise of influential rappers LL Cool J, Run-DMC, and Public Enemy, while Tommy Boy Records contributed to the rise of electro-funk.

As rap groups assembled during the decade, they began to use their art to describe the harsh realities of inner-city life. Unlike early rap music, which was generally upbeat and exuberant in tone, the rap style of the 1980s exhibited a strong sense of racial and political consciousness. Grandmaster Flash's "The Message" (1982) was the first blatantly political rap hit; its yearning and desperation recalled the angst-ridden soul records of the preceding decade and hinted at rap's potential. Toward the end of the decade, rap came to express an increasing sense of racial militancy. Inspired by the Nation of Islam and the teachings of martyred race leader Malcolm X, rap groups such as Public Enemy turned their music into a voice supporting Black Power. Public Enemy's second LP, *It Takes a Nation of Millions to Hold Us Back* (1988), sold more than one million copies. Their song "Fight the Power" appeared in director Spike Lee's 1989 film *Do the Right Thing*. The group's third album, *Fear of a Black Planet*, was released in 1990. While it is a statement against "western cultural supremacy," according to group member Chuck D., it is also "about the coming together of all races" in a "racial rebirth." Rapper KRS-One of Boogie Down Productions provided eloquent, barbed political commentary as well.

Women have also played a role in the shaping of rap music. Rap artists such as Queen Latifah, MC Lyte, and the group Salt-N-Pepa represented a growing number of female rappers who spoke for the advancement of black women in American society. Queen Latifah emerged as a critic of male dominance in the music.

The late 1980s also saw the birth of the "native tongues" school of rap, the graduates of which employed an eclectic array of samples and more heavily relied on humor and baroque rhymes than did their hardcore and political counterparts. The best-known groups of this school were De La Soul, A Tribe Called Quest, and the Pharcyde. Digital Underground, meanwhile, openly aspired to be "Sons of the P" and wove elaborate Parliament-esque concepts. Artists with a more bohemian bent began to rely heavily on jazz; some, such as Digable Planets and US3, sold briskly. A few, such as Arrested Development and Spearhead, stayed close to their soul and funk roots.

The biggest story in rap during the 1990s was the rise of "gangsta" rap, which utilized old-school funk beats and dwelt on hustling and violence, usually without soul's veneer of guarded optimism. The group N.W.A. (Niggaz With Attitude) upset social conservatives with their 1988 megahit "F___ Tha Police," and its alumni Dr. Dre, Ice Cube, and Eazy-E would all become major solo artists. Ice-T put a slightly more deliberative spin on his gangster tales, but it was Dre's Snoop Doggy Dogg and former Digital Underground member Tupac Shakur (1971–1996) who would become the biggest crossover acts of all. Snoop's laid-back style in particular earned him pop status with cuts such as "Gin and Juice," "Murder Was the Case," and "Doggy Dogg World."

The crossover success of these recordings was so worrisome to the aforementioned conservatives that gangsta rap lyrics became a staple in political speeches, and politicians and activist groups threatened to take action against record companies that released such material. Shakur, Notorious B.I.G. (Biggie Smalls, 1972–1997), and Lil' Kim all made impacts on hip-hop culture with powerfully explicit lyrics. The murders of Shakur and Notorious B.I.G. sent shock waves throughout the entertainment industry and inspired passionate pleas from insiders to tone down some of the more violent lyrics in some artists' work.

Some pop rappers, such as MC Hammer (who eventually dropped the "MC") and DJ Jazzy Jeff and the Fresh Prince, enjoyed periodic success and then faded from the charts. Those who retained a bit more street-level credibility, on the other hand, such as Naughty by Nature, who had a mega-smash in 1991 with "O.P.P.," and Coolio, who ruled the charts and scored a Grammy Award for his 1995 hit "Gangsta's Paradise," enjoyed a longer reign. Beginning in the mid-1980s and into the 1990s, rap artists such as Will Smith (the Fresh Prince), Ice Cube, Ice-T, Tupac Shakur, and Queen Latifah crossed over successfully into film and television projects (some of them with hip-hop themes), confirming the widespread acceptance of these artists throughout American culture. Some of these films, such as Spike Lee's *Do the Right Thing* and John Singleton's 1991 drama *Boyz N the Hood*, enjoyed critical acclaim and popularity.

In the mid-1990s, creative rhyme style and techniques were perpetuated by Das EFX, Fu-Schnickens, Mystikal, Bone Thugs-n-Harmony, Busta Rhymes, and the Fugees, among others. With its array of styles and points of view, rap has emerged as a primary cultural form for young African Americans. Similar to the music of its predecessors, rap is filled with artistic energy and descriptions of the human experience. As a 1999 *Time* magazine cover story exclaimed, rap music and hip-hop rose in twenty short years from a subcultural expression to one that changed the course of American popular culture in profound ways.

As hip-hop realized commercial success, its most widely recognized form came to be known for its focus on reckless materialism. Although civic-minded artists such as Common, Lupe Fiasco, and André 3000 fare well in popularity, Jay-Z, Gucci Mane, Diddy, and others dominate the airwaves and magazine covers with lyrics that focus on luxury cars, jewelry, and money. Instead of addressing the struggle of urban life as discussed in what rapper and former Jay-Z nemesis Nas calls the "dungeon of rap," heavily promoted hip-hop merely celebrates the penthouse lifestyle of conspicuous consumption. Nonetheless, the evolution of the music itself is innovative, with such styles as Dirty South, crunk, and chopped and screwed, as well as T-Pain's sing-song use of the Auto-Tune with vocals. As the effects of downloaded and pirated music continue to impact the industry, a mixtape movement has taken place, where up-and-coming rappers present their music and remixes outside of the industry's traditional channels in order to connect with their audience and remain relevant. Notable artists such as Lil' Wayne, J. Cole, and Drake have firmly established themselves through mixtapes. Their examples offer up-and-coming artists a means to express themselves beyond the materialistic/gangsta format and be heard in ways unavailable through corporate-driven radio.

A SMOOTH SOUND EN ROUTE TO HIP-HOP SOUL

Perhaps in part to counter the increasing dominance of hardcore hip-hop in the marketplace, rhythm and blues and soul moved in a softer direction during the 1980s. As bands were replaced by sequenced keyboards and drum machines, recordings in this genre were increasingly dominated by producers and vocalists. Even longtime soul legends such as Aretha Franklin and Chaka Khan moved in a glossier direction. This period saw the rise of a handful of phenomenally successful singers, notably Whitney Houston, whose mother Cissy had sung with Franklin and others. Following a highly successful debut, Houston collected a string of hits and awards; her apotheosis came with the gargantuan sales of the soundtrack to the 1992 film *The Bodyguard*, in which she also had a starring role.

Houston's athletic vocal chops paved the way for a number of other new soul divas, including Toni Braxton and Mariah Carey. Producers L. A. Reid and Babyface were among the preeminent hit-makers of this era. Like Babyface, R. Kelley was successful both as producer and recording artist. Producer Teddy Riley's New Jack swing, which combined soul singing, hip-hop grooves, and intermittent rap performances, captured dance audiences in the late 1980s and early 1990s. The Minneapolis-based producing team of Jimmy Jam and Terry Lewis, also important innovators in the New Jack swing idiom, helped to define the sound of pop hip-hop in the early 1990s. The duo is credited with crafting pop entertainer Janet Jackson's extremely popular sound as her career matured.

While the soft-edged trend continued through the 1990s, some artists within the fold, such as the smash groups Boyz II Men and En Vogue, flirted with old-school soul. As contemporary R&B evolved, hip-hop came closer to being the world's most ubiquitous musical art form. Perhaps the most successful producer and performer in regard to this phenomenon has been producer and mogul Sean Combs (also known as Puff Daddy, Puffy, P. Diddy, and Diddy), who almost single-handedly defined the sound of mainstream hip-hop in the mid to late 1990s. In addition to hardcore popular hip-hop act Biggie Smalls, Combs is responsible for introducing Mary J. Blige, the "Queen of Hip-Hop Soul," in 1992 with *What's the 411?* Blige quickly reached multiplatinum success and commanded the respect of both the hip-hop and contemporary R&B communities. Combs continued to marry the smooth soul of the times with hip-hop's edge. Combs worked with such artists as Jodeci, Faith Evans, and Carl Thomas, who came out with their own style of hip-hop soul.

NEW DIRECTIONS WITH THE OLD AND THE NEW: NEO-SOUL

Meanwhile, a movement called *neo-soul* emerged at the margins, thanks to artists such as bassist and singer-songwriter Meshell Ndegeocello and her 1993 debut, *Plantation Lullabies*. Dionne Farris's hit "Hopeless" became the signature song for the neo-soul sensibilities of the 1997 underground movie *Love Jones*. A seminal influence is D'Angelo, who is credited with bringing unabashed soul and the vintage sound of live instrumentation back to the consciousness of hip-hop and contemporary R&B audiences with his 1995 debut *Brown Sugar*.

Artists such as Erykah Badu expanded neo-soul's palette with her 1997 debut, adding mystical Afrocentric leanings and an eclectic fashion sense to the movement's spectrum. Badu soon exemplified this loose network of artists with her hairstyles and clothing. This collective of artists embraced the cultural aesthetics of the Black Power movement, combining poetry, social consciousness, and cultural critique with a sound that developed an affinity for the production values of hip-hop and acid jazz à la forerunners Roy Ayers and Gil-Scott Heron.

By 2000, neo-soul's artistic range continued to expand, inspiring many to refer it as *nu soul, new classic soul*, or *underground soul*. This is personified best by Philadelphia's gifted vocalist and poet Jill Scott. Her 2000 debut, *Who Is Jill Scott? Words and Sounds Vol. 1*, garnered such praise that she and Badu are seen as the premier female singers of their generation. Thanks to Scott, Badu, and more recent artists, such as Maxwell and Van Hunt, the genre reinvents itself while adding new connections to musical traditions of the past.

POPULAR MUSIC COMPOSERS, MUSICIANS, PRODUCERS, AND SINGERS

(Some biographical profiles may appear in other chapters. To locate profiles more readily, please consult the index.)

YOLANDA ADAMS

See chapter 23, Sacred Music Traditions.

NICHOLAS ASHFORD (1942–)
VALERIE SIMPSON (1946–)

Singers, Songwriters. One of the most enduring songwriting teams to emerge from Motown is the duo of Nicholas Ashford and Valerie Simpson. For nearly five decades, the team has written hit songs for artists from Ray Charles to Diana Ross.

Nick Ashford was born in Fairfield, South Carolina, on May 4, 1942; Valerie Simpson was born in the Bronx section of New York City on August 26, 1946. The two met in the early 1960s while singing in the same choir at Harlem's White Rock Baptist Church. With Ashford's gift for lyrics and Simpson's exceptional gospel piano and compositional skills, the two began to write for the staff of Scepter Records in 1964. Two years later, their song "Let's Go Get Stoned" became a hit for Ray Charles.

In 1962, Ashford and Simpson joined Motown's Jobete Music, where they wrote and produced hit songs for Marvin Gaye and Tammi Terrell, including "Ain't Nothing Like the Real Thing," "Good Loving Ain't Easy to Come By," and the "Onion Song." Next, they worked with Diana Ross, who had just set out to establish a solo career, producing such hits as "Remember Me," "Reach Out (and Touch Somebody's Hand)," and an updated version of "Ain't No Mountain High Enough."

Ashford and Simpson's success as songwriters led them to release their own solo recording, *Exposed*, in 1971. After signing with Warner Bros. in 1973, they recorded a number of hit LPs: *Is It Still Good to Ya* (1978); *Stay Free* (1979); *A Musical Affair* (1980); and their biggest seller, *Solid* (1985). The duo temporarily retired from recording in the late 1980s, but they returned to the recording scene in 1996 when they launched their own label, Hopsack and Silk. Their first release was a collaboration with renowned poet Maya Angelou titled *Been Found*. In 1999, the couple celebrated their twenty-fifth wedding anniversary with a gala in New York.

On August 16, 2006, *Playbill Online* reported that Ashford and Simpson were writing a score for a musical based on E. Lynn Harris's novel *Invisible Life*. In January 2007, they, along with Tina Turner, Mary J. Blige, Mariah Carey, Sidney Poitier, director Spike Lee, and comedian Chris Tucker, accompanied Oprah Winfrey when she opened a school for disadvantaged girls in South Africa.

ERYKAH BADU (1971–)

Singer, Songwriter, Poet, Actress. Erykah Badu was born in South Dallas, Texas, on February 26, 1971, as Erica Abi Wright. Her mother, Kolleen Maria Gipson (Wright), raised Badu and her two siblings alone after their father abandoned the family. Badu's mother performed as an actress in theatrical productions. By age four, young Badu began singing and dancing with her mother on stage.

As a teen, she decided to change the spelling of her name from Erica to Erykah. The syllable *kah* connotes the inner self. The name Badu is also of African origin, signifying the tenth-born child by way of the Akan people in Ghana. Badu graduated from Booker T. Washington High School for the Performing and Visual Arts and studied theater at Grambling State University. She left the university in 1993 before graduating to concentrate solely on music. She collaborated with her cousin, Robert "Free" Bradford, to record a nineteen-song demo. The demo attracted the attention of neo-soul impresario Kedar Massenburg. The result was a duet with Badu and D'Angelo, "Your Precious Love." Badu soon signed a record deal with Universal Records.

Badu's debut album, *Baduizm*, reached number two in 1997 on the *Billboard* charts. Her reflective lyrics and sparse, jazzy sound drew comparisons to jazz legend Billie Holiday. *Baduizm* eventually went triple platinum. It's debut single, "On & On," won several Grammy Awards. During this period, Badu became romantically involved with singer André 3000 of OutKast.

Badu recorded her first live album, *Live*, in 1998. *Live* reached double-platinum sales thanks to the hit single "Tyrone." Badu then collaborated with the Roots on their breakthrough 1999 album, *Things Fall Apart*. She was featured on the album's Grammy-winning song, "You Got Me," cowritten by Jill Scott. Badu's relationship with André 3000 ended in the late 1990s after she gave birth to their son Seven.

Recording Artist Erykah Badu Visits BET Studios in New York City, 2010. *Badu's debut album,* Baduism, *went triple platinum in 1997, with its single "On and On" winning several Grammy Awards.* BRYAN BEDDER/GETTY IMAGES

In 2000, Badu's second studio album, *Mama's Gun*, was more organic in sound than her previous studio album. Its hit single, "Bag Lady," was nominated for a Grammy. Badu became romantically linked with rapper Common at this time. They collaborated on the Grammy-winning "Love of My Life (An Ode to Hip-Hop)," which was featured on the soundtrack of the film *Brown Sugar* (2002).

Badu toured extensively before returning to the studio to record the album *Worldwide Underground* (2003). The free-flowing album was another bold departure in song structure and format and received four Grammy nominations. Badu began an intense creative period between 2007 and 2008. Her next album, titled *New Amerykah, Part One (4th World War)*, was to be the first installment of a trilogy. It was released with excitement generated by "Honey," a new single that was leaked online, but the recording failed to receive the commercial and critical success of her prior albums.

Badu is the mother of three children, her eldest being her son Seven Sirius with ex-partner André 3000. In 2004, Badu gave birth to a daughter, Puma Sabti, whose father is West Coast rapper The D.O.C. Badu gave birth in 2009 to a girl named Mars Merkaba, whose father is rapper Jay Electronica.

In 2010, Erykah Badu released her fifth studio album, *New Amerykah, Part Two (Return of the Ankh)*. The video for the single "Window Seat" caused controversy when Badu removed her clothes near the site of the John F. Kennedy assassination in Dallas. Ever the maverick, Badu stated on *The Wanda Sykes Show* on April 3, 2010, that her point was "grossly misunderstood all over America. JFK is one of my heroes, one of the nation's heroes. John F. Kennedy was a revolutionary; he was not afraid to butt heads with America, and I was not afraid to show America my butt-naked truth."

ANITA BAKER (1958–)

Singer. One of the most sophisticated soul divas to emerge in the 1980s, Baker considers herself "a balladeer" dedicated to singing music rooted in the tradition of gospel music and jazz. Inspired by her idols Mahalia Jackson, Sarah Vaughan, and Nancy Wilson, Baker brings audiences a sincere vocal style that defies commercial trends and electronic overproduction.

Born on January 26, 1958, in Toledo, Ohio, Baker was raised in a single-parent middle-class family in Detroit. She first sang in storefront churches, where it was common for the congregation to improvise on various gospel themes. After graduating from Central High School, Baker sang in the Detroit soul-funk group Chapter 8. Although Chapter 8 recorded the album *I Just Want to Be Your Girl* for the Ariola label, the group's lack of commercial success caused it to disband, and for the next three years, Baker worked as a receptionist in a law firm.

In 1982, after signing a contract with Beverly Glen, Baker moved to Los Angeles, where she recorded the critically acclaimed solo album *Songstress* (1983). Following a legal battle with Glen, Baker signed with Elektra and recorded her hit album *Rapture* in 1986. As the album's executive producer, Baker sought "a minimalist approach," featuring simple recording techniques that captured the natural sounds of her voice. The LP's single, "Sweet Love," brought Baker immediate crossover success. Baker's follow-up effort, the multiplatinum-selling *Giving You the Best I Got*, is considered one of the finest pop music albums of the 1990s. Her third effort, *Compositions*, recorded in 1990, featured a number of backup musicians, including Detroit jazz guitarist Earl Klugh.

After a nearly four-year hiatus, Baker released the double-platinum *Rhythm of Love* in 1994. In 1996, Baker filed lawsuits against Elektra, her management, and her legal staff. She subsequently joined the Atlantic label. In 2002, Rhino released a compilation album of Baker's recordings, *The Best of Anita Baker.* Winner of five Grammys, two NAACP Image Awards, two American Music Awards, two Soul Train Awards, and a star on Hollywood's Walk of Fame, Baker has brought her audience music of eloquence and integrity that sets her apart from most of her contemporaries.

HARRY BELAFONTE

See chapter 20, Film and Television.

CHUCK BERRY (1926–)

Singer, Songwriter, Guitarist. Chuck Berry was the first guitar hero of rock and roll. His jukebox hits of the 1950s remain some of the most imaginative poetic tales in the history of popular music. Influenced by such bluesmen as Aaron T-Bone Walker and the picking styles of rockabilly and country musicians, Berry's solo guitar work brought the guitar to the forefront of rhythm and blues. His driving ensemble sound paved the way for the emergence of bands from the Beach Boys to the Rolling Stones.

Born on October 18, 1926, in San Jose, California, Charles Edward Anderson Berry grew up in a middle-class neighborhood on the outskirts of St. Louis. Berry first sang gospel music at home and at the Antioch Baptist Church. Although Berry was drawn to the sounds of bluesmen, such as Tampa Red, Arthur Crudup, and Muddy Waters, he did not become serious about music until he was given a guitar by local rhythm-and-blues musician Joe Sherman. Taken by the sounds of rhythm and blues, Berry formed a trio with Johnny Jones on piano and Ebby Harding on drums. Hired to play backyard barbecues, clubs, and house parties, the trio expanded their repertoire to include Nat "King" Cole ballads and country songs by Hank Williams.

By 1955, the twenty-eight-year-old Berry had become a formidable rhythm-and-blues guitarist and singer. While in Chicago, Berry visited a club to hear his idol, Muddy Waters, perform. At the suggestion of Waters, Berry visited Chess Studios, and eventually signed with the label. Berry's first hit for Chess was "Maybelline," a country song formerly entitled "Ida May." In 1956, Berry continued on a path toward superstardom with the hits "Roll Over Beethoven," "Oh Baby Doll," "Rock and Roll Music," and the guitar anthem "Johnny B. Goode."

Released from the Indiana Federal Prison in 1964 after serving a sentence for violating the Mann Act, Berry resumed his musical career, recording "Nadine" and "No Particular Place to Go." Berry's 1972 release of the novelty tune "My-Ding-a-Ling" became his best-selling single. In 1987, Taylor Hackford paid tribute to the guitar legend in his film *Hail! Hail! Rock 'n' Roll.* Berry was also a featured performer at the opening of Cleveland's Rock and Roll Hall of Fame and Museum in 1995. In 2000, Berry was honored at the Kennedy Center Honors gala as one of the twentieth-century's most influential musicians. In 2004, *Rolling Stone* magazine ranked Berry number five on their list of "The Immortals: 100 Greatest Artists of All Time."

Singer-Songwriter and Guitarist Chuck Berry, 1959. *Berry revolutionized rhythm and blues by featuring the guitar as a lead, rather than a rhythm, instrument. The driving sound of his many hit songs—including "Maybelline," "Roll Over Beethoven," and "Johnny B. Goode"—paved the way for the emergence of the major rock and roll groups of the 1960s.* THE LIBRARY OF CONGRESS

MARY J. BLIGE (1971–)

Singer. Born in 1971 in the Bronx in New York City, Mary Jane Blige was raised in the Schlobohm housing projects in Yonkers. In her youth, Blige was influenced by the rhythm-and-blues, soul, and funk albums that her mother played, as well as the early lessons that her father, a professional jazz musician, gave her. She landed a record deal when André Harrell of Uptown Records heard a karaoke tape that she had recorded at age sixteen.

Called the inventor of "New Jill swing" by *Stereo Review*, Blige's debut album, *What's the 411?* (1992), sold more than three million copies, and her second album, *My Life* (1994), went multiplatinum, establishing her as an international recording star. She won a Grammy Award in 1996 for "You're All I Need," a duet with the rapper Method Man. Her third album, *Share My World* (1997), also reached multiplatinum status. Blige has been dubbed the "Queen of Hip-Hop Soul," a designation that reflects the hallmarks of her style, which features soulful melodies over hip-hop rhythm tracks.

In 1999, Blige's album *Mary* hit the charts, with such singles as "All That I Can Say" and "Sexy." In 2001, she released her fifth album, *No More Drama*, a deeply personal recording that was a collective effort musically yet reflected more of Blige's songwriting than any of her previous efforts. In 2006, Blige released an album of duets, *Mary J. Blige & Friends*, with an accompanying DVD. All of the proceeds from the album through February 2007 went to the Boys & Girls Clubs of America.

Blige received eight Grammy Award nominations in 2006 for her 2005 album *The Breakthrough*, the most nominations for any artist that year. "Be Without You" was nominated for both record of the year and song of the year. She won in three categories: best female R&B vocal performance, best R&B song, and best R&B album.

On December 12, 2006, *Reflections: A Retrospective* was released. The album featured some of Blige's top songs, as well as four new songs, including the singles "We Ride (I See the Future)" and "Reflections (I Remember)." Both songs were written and produced with the help of Bryan Michael Cox and Johnta Austin, the team that made "Be Without You." The first single from the album in the United Kingdom was "MJB Da MVP," which was only included on the international version of the album.

In 2007, Blige released *Growing Pains*, her eighth studio album. She followed it in 2009 with *Stronger with Each Tear*. She also contributed to the soundtrack for the award-winning 2009 film *Precious*.

BOW WOW (1987–)

Singer, Actor. Bow Wow, who was born Shad Gregory Moss in Columbus, Ohio, started his career in rap when he was five years old using the name Kid Gangsta. One year later, in 1993, he performed at a Chronic tour in Columbus with rappers Snoop Dogg and Dr. Dre, who subsequently gave him the stage name Lil' Bow Wow. Dr. Dre later hired him as an opening act, officially gaining him a spot on the Death Row Records roster. Lil' Bow Wow appeared in a skit on Snoop's 1993 debut, *Doggystyle*. By 1998, Bow Wow was introduced to record producer Jermaine Dupri, who helped shape his career.

In 2000, after Lil Bow Wow released his first album, *Beware of Dog*, and the single "Bounce With Me," he became a successful recording artist under Dupri's mentorship. Two years after the success of his debut album, he released *Doggy Bag*, which contained the songs "Thank You" and "Take You Home," among others. During this time, he dropped the "Lil" from his professional name. He eventually broke out on his own in 2003 with the album *Unleashed*, which was his first without Dupri's writing assistance; the album's sales were lower than those of his earlier releases. In addition to his albums, Bow Wow has appeared as a guest on several televisions shows.

Bow Wow made his acting debut in the 2002 film *Like Mike*, in which he starred as a young orphan who gets a shot at the NBA. Two years later, he costarred with Cedric the Entertainer, Vanessa Williams, and Solange Knowles in *Johnson Family Vacation*. His subsequent film projects include *Roll Bounce* (2005) and *The Fast and the Furious: Tokyo Drift* (2006). Bow Wow also appeared on the television series *Smallville* in November 2006 in the episode "Fallout." He appeared in a recurring role on the HBO series *Entourage* beginning in the 2008–2009 season.

In 2005, Bow Wow released his fourth album, *Wanted*, on which he once again worked with Jermaine Dupri. The album featured two singles that reached number one on the R&B charts, "Let Me Hold You," featuring Omarion, and "Like You," featuring Ciara. In July 2006, he received a Hollywood Life Award for being the " most exciting crossover artist." Bow Wow's fifth album, *The Price of Fame*, was released on December 19, 2006. He and Omarion collaborated on the 2007 album *Face Off*. Bow Wow released his sixth solo studio album, *New Jack City II*, in 2009. Bow Wow has also developed a clothing line known as Shago.

BRANDY (1979–)

Singer, Actress. Brandy became one of the biggest pop stars of the 1990s while she was still a teenager. Her talent came through not only in her singing career, but also in her success as a television and film actress. Born Brandy Rayana Norwood on February 11, 1979, in McComb, Mississippi, Brandy's family moved to Los Angeles when she was four. The daughter of a choir director, Brandy's vocal training began in her church's youth choir. Early on, she and her younger brother, Ray-J, displayed enough talent to be featured in choir performances. By age eleven, Brandy had begun singing at local events, and even placed second in an all-ages talent show. Just a year later, she landed a spot as a backup singer for the R&B group Immature.

In 1993, when she was fourteen, Brandy signed a recording contract with Atlantic Records. That year, she also earned a role on the short-lived ABC sitcom, *Thea*. Brandy released her self-titled debut album in 1994, becoming a sensation with the singles "I Wanna Be Down," "Baby," and "Brokenhearted." She also experienced success as a contributor to the soundtracks for the films *Waiting to Exhale* (1995, "Sittin' Up in My Room"), *Batman Forever* (1995, "Where Are You Now?"), and *Set It Off* (1996, "Missing You").

Brandy returned to acting in 1996, landing the starring role on the successful UPN sitcom *Moesha*. The show ran until 2001, earning Brandy an even larger following. In 1997, she appeared in the starring role of Disney's television version of *Cinderella*. In 1999, she appeared alongside Diana Ross in the television movie *Double Platinum*. Brandy also made her feature film debut that year in *I Still Know What You Did Last Summer*.

Brandy's second solo album, *Never S-A-Y Never* (1998), proved even more successful than her first. "The Boy Is Mine," a duet with fellow teen sensation Monica, topped both the pop and R&B charts for weeks and earned the Grammy Award for best R&B performance by a duo or group. *Never S-A-Y Never* eventually sold more than five million copies. In 2002, Brandy released her third album, *Full Moon*, and caused a stir by announcing that she had been secretly married for months to producer and songwriter Robert Smith. Her fourth album, *Afrodisiac*, was released in 2004. A compilation of her singles, *The Best of Brandy*, came out in 2006. In 2008, she released her fifth album, *Human*.

BOBBY BROWN (1969–)

Singer. Singer Bobby Brown possessed a charismatic charm that earned him numerous million-selling records. Born on February 5, 1969, in Boston, he was a founding member of the successful group New Edition. Brown remained with the group from 1984 to 1987. His solo debut album, *King of Stage* (1986), featured the single "Girlfriend." Brown's second release, *Don't Be Cruel* (1988), produced the single "Don't Be Cruel" and the video hits "My Prerogative" and "Every Little Step."

In 1990, Brown embarked on a worldwide tour after releasing a successful single from the soundtrack to the hit movie *Ghostbusters II*. In July 1992, Brown married singer and actress Whitney Houston in a star-studded ceremony. Two years later, the two performed together for the first time on the televised 1994 *Soul Train Music Awards* program.

Brown's violent temper and brushes with the law were the subject of much publicity, even eclipsing the release of his 1993 recording, *Remixes in the Key of B*, and his 1997 album, *Forever*. In early 1998, he was convicted of drunk driving. Later that year, he was arrested for misdemeanor sexual battery, but the charges were eventually dropped. In July 2000, Brown served sixty-five days in jail for violating his probation. He attempted to get his career back on track in 2001 by appearing in the movie *Two Can Play at That Game*. In June 2005, Brown launched his own reality series, *Being Bobby Brown*, on the Bravo television network. The show ran for one season.

In the fall of 2005, New Edition performed some of their hits on BET's twenty-fifth anniversary celebration and brought Brown onstage to perform "Mr. Telephone Man." Brown then brought the house down with his big solo hit, "My Prerogative." It was announced later that Brown had rejoined New Edition. In 2006 and 2007, magazines, newspapers, and gossip columns covered Houston's separation and divorce from Brown, as well as Brown's child-support issues. In 2008, Brown and two other former members of New Edition, Ralph Tresvant and Johnny Gill, formed the group Heads of State.

CHRIS BROWN (1989–)

Singer, Actor. Chris Brown was born on May 4, 1989, and raised in the small town of Tappahannock, Virginia. As a youth, he performed in local talent shows. When he was thirteen, Brown was discovered by a local production team who visited his father's gas station searching for new talent. Brown began his recording career and moved to New York, staying there for two years. His first album, *Chris Brown*, was released in 2005. It was followed by *Exclusive* (2007) and *Graffiti* (2009).

Brown branched out into acting, making short appearances on UPN's *One on One* and The-N's *The Brandon T. Jackson Show*. In addition, Brown appeared as a band geek in the fourth season of FOX's *The O.C.* in January 2007. He made his big-screen debut in *Stomp the Yard* in 2007.

In 2006, Brown won the Soul Train Music Award for the best new R&B/soul artist, the NAACP Image Award for outstanding new artist, BET awards for best new artist and viewers choice, and the *Billboard* Award for male artist of the year.

JAMES BROWN (1933–2006)

Singer, Bandleader. James Brown's impact on American and African popular music has been seismic. His explosive onstage energy and his gospel- and rhythm-and-blues-based sound earned him numerous titles, including the "Godfather of Soul," "Mr. Dynamite," and the "Hardest Working Man in Show Business." During the 1960s and early 1970s, Brown and his backup group, known

Singer James Brown,* The Ed Sullivan Show, *May 1966. *During the 1960s and 1970s, Brown—known as "The Godfather of Soul"—regularly topped the R&B charts. The funky rhythms of his songs formed the basis for hip-hop and had a wide influence on later pop music as well.* **CBS PHOTO ARCHIVE/GETTY IMAGES**

variously as the Flames, the Famous Flames, and the JBs, emerged as one of the greatest soul bands in the history of modern music, one that served as a major force in the development of funk and fusion jazz.

Born in Barnell, South Carolina, on May 3, 1933, Brown moved to Augusta, Georgia, when he was four years old. Although he was raised by various relatives in conditions of economic deprivation, Brown possessed an undaunted determination to succeed at an early age. When not picking cotton, washing cars, or shining shoes, he earned extra money by dancing on the streets and at amateur contests. In the evening, Brown watched shows by such bandleaders as Louis Jordan and Lucky Millinder.

When he was fifteen years old, Brown quit school and took up music full time. He sang in churches with the Swanee Quartet and the Gospel Starlighters, which soon became the rhythm-and-blues group the Flames. During this period, he also sang and played drums with other rhythm-and-blues bands. Brown toured extensively with the Flames, performing a wide range of popular material, including the Five Royales' "Baby Don't Do It," the Clovers' "One Mint Julep," and Hank Ballard and the Midnighters' "Annie Had a Baby."

In 1956, Brown's talents caught the attention of Syd Nathan, founder of King Records. In the same year, after signing with the Federal label, a subsidiary of King, Brown recorded "Please, Please, Please." After the Flames disbanded in 1957, Brown formed a new Flames ensemble, featuring former members of Little Richard's band. Back in the studio the following year, Brown recorded "Try Me," which became a top-fifty pop hit. On the road, Brown polished his stage act and singing ability, producing what became known as the "James Brown sound." His 1965 hit, "Papa's Got a Brand New Bag," earned him a Grammy for best rhythm-and-blues recording, a feat he repeated in 1986 with "Living in America," a song that appeared on the soundtrack of the 1985 film *Rocky IV.*

After the release of *Out of Sight* in 1964, Brown's music exhibited a more polyrhythmic sound as evidenced in staccato horn bursts and contrapuntal bass lines. Each successive release explored new avenues of popular music. Brown's 1967 hit *Cold Sweat* and the 1968 release *I Got the Feeling* not only sent shock waves through the music industry, they served as textbooks of rhythm for thousands of aspiring musicians. In 1970, Brown disbanded the Flames and formed the JBs, featuring Bootsy Collins. The group produced a string of hits, such as "Super Bad" (1971) and "Sex Machine" (1970). *Universal James* (1993) was Brown's seventy-ninth album.

Despite some negative publicity, Brown's career remained effervescent in the late 1980s to 1990s. Inducted into the Rock and Roll Hall of Fame in 1986, Brown received the Ray Charles Lifetime Achievement Award from the Rhythm and Blues Foundation as part of the organization's Pioneer Awards program in 1993. Later that year, he was honored for lifetime achievement at the Black Radio Exclusive Awards banquet in Washington, D.C. Many of his recordings were reissued in the 1990s, and hundreds of his records have been sampled by rap and hip-hop performers, illustrating Brown's continuing musical influence. In October 2001, Brown performed at RFK Stadium in Washington, D.C., in United We Stand: What More Can I Give, a benefit concert for victims of the September 11, 2001, terrorist attacks.

On November 14, 2006, Brown was inducted into the UK Music Hall of Fame. Brown was a recipient of the Kennedy Center Honors on December 7, 2003. In 2004, *Rolling Stone* magazine ranked Brown number seven on its list of the "100 Greatest Artists of All Time." Brown was also honored in his hometown of Augusta for his philanthropy and civic activities. On November 20, 1993, Mayor Charles DeVaney of Augusta dedicated a section of Ninth Street between Broad and Twiggs streets to Brown, renaming the street James Brown Boulevard. On May 6, 2005, as a seventy-second birthday present, the city of Augusta unveiled a life-sized bronze statue of the singer on Broad Street.

In January 2004, Brown was arrested in South Carolina on a domestic violence charge after Tomi Rae Hynie accused him of pushing her to the floor during an argument at their home in which she suffered scratches and bruises. Later that year, Brown pleaded no contest to the domestic-violence incident, but he served no jail time. Instead, Brown was required to forfeit a $1,087 bond as punishment.

Brown continued to perform regularly, even when he was ill. He died on December 25, 2006, in Atlanta. After Brown's death, his relatives and friends and thousands of fans attended public memorial services at the Apollo Theater in New York on December 28, 2006, and at the James Brown Arena in Augusta on December 30, 2006. A private memorial service was held in North Augusta, South Carolina, on December 29 for Brown's family and close friends. Numerous celebrities attended the memorial services, including Joe Frazier, Dick Gregory, MC Hammer, Jesse Jackson, Michael Jackson, and Don King.

RUTH BROWN (1928–2006)

Singer. Born Ruth Weston on January 30, 1928, in Portsmouth, Virginia, Brown was initially influenced by jazz greats Sarah Vaughan, Dinah Washington, and Billie Holiday. She ran away from home in 1945 with trumpeter Jimmy Brown, whom she soon married. Initial career frustrations, including a serious car accident that hospitalized her for nine months in 1948 and 1949, delayed her debut. However, her first recording for Atlantic in 1949, the torch ballad "So Long," was a hit. In the early 1950s, her seductive vocal delivery placed her on the rhythm-and-blues charts with such tunes as "Teardrops in My Eyes," "I Know," "5-10-15 Hours," and "He Treats Your Daughter Mean." By 1960, she had a dozen rhythm-and-blues hits before her career declined.

Brown raised two sons and worked a nine-to-five job before reviving her career in the mid-1970s with television, movie, and stage appearances, including a 1989 Broadway show, *Black and Blue*, for which she won a Tony Award. Ruth issued several fine recordings in the 1990s, including: *Fine and Mellow* (1991); *Songs of My Life* (1993); *Live in London* (1996); *R+B=Ruth Brown* (1997); and *Good Day for the Blues* (1999). She also hosted radio shows on National Public Radio, and formed the nonprofit Rhythm and Blues Foundation, an organization that helps musicians recoup their share of royalties (Ruth personally endured a nine-year fight with Atlantic to win back her royalties). In 1996, Brown published *Miss Rhythm: The Autobiography of Ruth Brown, Rhythm and Blues Legend*, chronicling her career and the rise of blues music.

Brown's hit-making reign during the 1950s helped establish the blues as a market force. She died at age seventy-eight in Las Vegas on November 17, 2006.

MARIAH CAREY (1970–)

Singer, Songwriter, Actress. Mariah Carey was born on Long Island in New York in 1970 to an Irish mother and a black Hispanic father. A day after her high school graduation, Mariah moved to New York City to pursue a singing career. Her first album, *Mariah Carey*, released in 1990, made it to number one on the charts. Her second album, *Emotions*, released in 1991, was also successful. Her third album, *Music Box*, released in 1993, included the number-one singles "Dreamlover" and

Singer Mariah Carey,* The Oprah Winfrey Show, *2009. *One of the top pop artists of the 1990s, Carey returned to prominence with her 2005 multiplatinum album,* The Emancipation of Mimi, *for which she earned three Grammy Awards.* GEORGE NAPOLITANO/FILMMAGIC/GETTY IMAGES

"Hero." In 1994, Carey released a holiday album, *Merry Christmas*, followed by the albums *Daydream* in 1995 and *Butterfly* in 1997. Carey released a compilation of her thirteen hit singles, *#1s*, in 1998. The following year, she released *Rainbow*.

After signing with Island/Def Jam, she set up her own label, MonarC Music, and released *Charmbracelet* in 2002 and *The Emancipation of Mimi* in 2005, a multi-platinum hit. *The Emancipation of Mimi*, featuring the hit single "We Belong Together," earned eight Grammy nominations. She won three, including one for best contemporary R&B album. Her subsequent albums include *E = MC²* (2008) and *Memoirs of an Imperfect Angel* (2009).

Carey is also an actress and has made a variety of television and movie appearances. She received enthusiastic reviews and several awards for her supporting performance as a social worker in the 2009 film *Precious*.

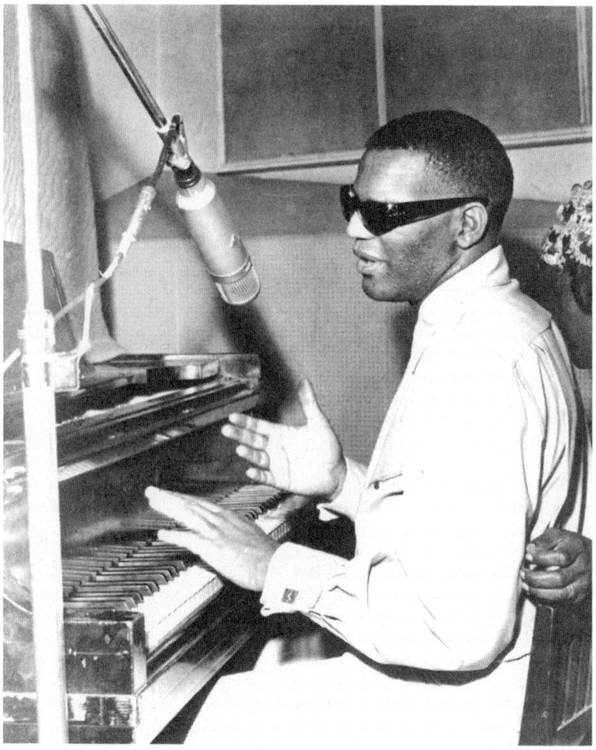

Ray Charles, c. 1960. *Credited as one of the founders of soul music, Charles garnered numerous honors during his career, including more than a dozen Grammy Awards, a Grammy for Lifetime Achievement, and the Presidential Medal for the Arts. He was also one of the first inductees into the Rock and Roll Hall of Fame.* MICHAEL OCHS ARCHIVES/GETTY IMAGES

RAY CHARLES (1930–2004)

Singer, Pianist, Bandleader. Ray Charles Robinson was born on September 23, 1930, in Albany, Georgia. Blinded by glaucoma when he was six, Charles received his first musical training at a school for the blind in St. Augustine, Florida. His parents died while he was in his teens, and after playing with local bands, Charles moved to Seattle in 1947, where he formed a trio. Influenced by the smooth pop rhythm-and-blues style of Charles Brown and Nat "King" Cole, Charles scored a top-ten rhythm-and-blues hit with "Baby Let Me Hold Your Hand." In the early 1950s, he teamed with Guitar Slim and Ruth Brown before scoring a number-two rhythm-and-blues hit with "I Got a Woman" in 1955. This recording was the first to capture Charles's gospel moan and horn-driven arrangements, which became his trademarks.

Throughout the 1950s, Charles released a string of hits that combined sophisticated arrangements with the emotional grit of rhythm and blues, a style that would become known as "soul" music. Charles also scored his first top-ten pop hit with "What'd I Say," which highlighted his pleading church vocals with a rock-and-roll piano line. His singing and piano playing drew on many sources, including jazz, and he cut pure jazz sides with David "Fathead" Newman and Milt Jackson, helping to imbibe a sense of "soul" and instrumental "funkiness" to the jazz idiom.

By the end of the 1950s, Charles had switched to ABC Records and gained artistic control of his work. His pop success was assured with "Hit the Road Jack," followed in 1962 by "I Can't Stop Loving You," a country-and-western song that topped the charts. Charles was immensely popular through the mid-1960s, before his career was halted in 1965 by his involvement with drugs. He emerged with more hits in the late 1960s, although he had begun to focus almost entirely on pop music.

Charles received a National Medal of Arts in 1993 and took part in the 1995 JVC Newport Jazz Festival. The recipient of more than ten Grammy Awards, Charles was also honorary life chairman of the Rhythm and Blues Hall of Fame and an inductee into the Pop Hall of Fame, the Rock and Roll Hall of Fame, and the Songwriters Hall of Fame. He received an honorary doctorate in 1999 from Wilberforce University. In 2001, Charles teamed up with Bally's Entertainment to create the first slot machine for the blind. Charles continued to perform and make music, releasing *Thanks for Bringing Love Around Again* in 2002, marking his sixth decade in the music business.

Charles was involved in the early stages of production for the biopic *Ray*, a 2004 film that portrays Charles's life and career between 1930 and 1966, starring Jamie Foxx as Charles. Foxx won the 2005 Academy Award for best actor for his performance. Before shooting began, Foxx met Charles, and they sat down at two pianos and played together. For two hours, Charles challenged Foxx, who revealed the depth of his talent, and finally, Charles stood up, hugged Foxx, and gave his blessing. Ray Charles died on June 10, 2004, after a long battle with cancer. His last studio album, *Genius Loves Company*, was released posthumously in 2004.

CIARA (1985–)

Singer. Ciara Princess Harris, born on October 25, 1985, in Austin, Texas, grew up on army bases in the United States and Germany because her parents were in the military. When she was a teenager, Ciara, impressed when she watched performances of Destiny's Child, decided that she wanted to pursue a career in music. She joined a girl group called Hearsay and tried to perfect her songwriting skills, but left after a short time. Ciara later met producer Jazze Pha, who assister her in signing with LaFace Records after she graduated from high school in 2003.

Ciara made her debut in the summer of 2004 with the *Billboard* number-one single "Goodies," which appeared on an album of the same name. The album became a commercial success in the United States, selling more than two and a half million copies and reaching number one in both the United States and the United Kingdom. The second and third single "1, 2 Step," featuring Missy Elliott, and "Oh," featuring Ludacris, became top-five singles in both countries. In 2006, Ciara won her first Grammy Award for Missy Elliott's "Lose Control" in the best short-form music video category. In April 2006, Ciara was featured on Field Mob's top-ten single "So What." The following month, she made her acting debut in the MTV Films production *All You've Got*. Ciara completed her second album, *Ciara: The Evolution*, in 2006. Her third album, *Fantasy Ride*, was released in 2009.

GEORGE CLINTON (1941–)

Singer, Songwriter, Bandleader, Producer. George Clinton, the father of P. Funk (the P stands for "pure"), spun the funk formula refined by James Brown into an institution. His groups Parliament and Funkadelic and a panoply of offshoots left the rest of the rhythm-and-blues world straining to keep up during the 1970s. By the 1990s, the prodigious body of work recorded under the P. Funk moniker exercised a huge influence on rap, soul, and rock. Though he relied heavily on a group of talented musicians to bring his music to life, Clinton was the visionary behind the legendary "Parliafunkadelicment Thang."

Born in North Carolina, Clinton moved with his family to New Jersey during his adolescence. There he helped form a doo-wop group called the Parliaments. After years of struggling and a move to Detroit, the group managed to sell some songs to other artists, but never achieved success on its own. With the advent of psychedelic rock in the mid-1960s, The Parliaments began to change in form. They morphed into Funkadelic by 1968, adding hard-rock guitar and spacey grooves. The early Funkadelic albums, notably *Maggot Brain* (1971), became classics of untamed funk rock.

Clinton deployed Parliament as a slightly more conventional funk vehicle in the early 1970s, emphasizing horns and more dance-oriented arrangements. By the middle of the decade, Parliament had become a major hit maker with its fantasy-themed concept albums and its circuslike performances. Songs such as "Flash Light," "Bop Gun (Endangered Species)," "Mothership Connection," and "Aqua Boogie" became funk staples.

Funkadelic began to take a more commercial turn, particularly after signing with Warner Bros. Records. Its biggest hits came with the albums *One Nation Under a Groove* (1978) and *Uncle Jam Wants You* (1979). Clinton helped his bassist, Bootsy Collins, become a funk legend in his own right, and oversaw albums by such P. Funk enterprises as the Brides of Funkenstein, Parlet, and the P. Funk All-Stars, among many others. He also released a slew of solo recordings; his biggest hit in this capacity was the boisterous "Atomic Dog" (1982).

Though business declined for these acts during the 1980s, Clinton's influence was constant in African American pop. By the 1990s, P. Funk recordings were among the most sampled in hip-hop. Clinton went so far as to set up an easy licensing system for rap artists who wanted to lift from his work. Thanks to the adoration of everyone from Dr. Dre to rockers such as the Red Hot Chili Peppers, Clinton became a ubiquitous figure on the pop culture scene. He fronted the P. Funk All-Stars at the Lollapalooza festival and appeared in numerous films and television commercials.

In 1999, Clinton filed a lawsuit against his record company for the rights to his songs from the 1960s and 1970s. Clinton lost his lawsuit in 2001 because of a contract that he signed in 1983. Clinton continues to tour with the P. Funk All-Stars and can often be seen on college campuses and smaller venues and at festivals. He has also continued to record, releasing *How Late Do U Have 2BB4UR Absent* (2005) and *George Clinton and His Gangsters of Love* (2008), among other titles.

NATALIE COLE (1950–)

Singer. With five gold records and a star on Hollywood Boulevard, Natalie Cole has emerged since the 1980s as a major pop music star. Born on February 6, 1950, in Los Angeles, Natalie was the second daughter of jazz pianist and pop music legend Nat "King" Cole. During the early

1970s, Natalie Cole performed in nightclubs while pursuing a degree in child psychology at the University of Massachusetts. In 1975, she recorded her first album, *Inseparable*, at Curtis Mayfield's Custom Studios. Her other albums include: *Thankful* (1978); *I'm Ready* (1983); *Good to Be Back* (1989); *Take a Look* (1993); and *Holly and Ivy* (1994), which coincided with her PBS special, *Natalie Cole's Untraditional Traditional Christmas*.

In 1991, Cole released a twenty-two-song collection of her father's hits. The album, which contains a remixed version of the original title track, "Unforgettable," features a duet between Cole and her father and earned her Grammy Awards for record of the year and album of the year, complementing the Grammys she won in 1976 for best new artist and in 1976 and 1977 for best rhythm-and-blues female vocal performance. Cole also won two NAACP Image Awards in the mid-1970s and an American Music Award in 1978.

In 1996, Cole released her next album, *Stardust*. She delayed touring with the album so that she could join the cast of the animated movie *Cats Don't Dance*, which arrived in theaters in 1997. In 1998, Cole published an autobiography, *Angel on My Shoulder*, which described her triumph over drug use and bad marriages. In late 2000, NBC aired *Livin' for Love: The Natalie Cole Story*. In 2002, Cole wed Bishop Kenneth H. Dupree and also signed a contract with Verve Records to produce her next few albums. In September 2006, she released *Leavin'*, a cover album of tracks made popular by Shelby Lynne, Kate Bush, Sting, and Fiona Apple, among others; the album is a hybrid of rock, pop music, and R&B. In 2008, Cole released *Still Unforgettable*, a collection of standards from her father's era, as well as a Christmas album, *Caroling, Caroling: Christmas with Natalie Cole*.

SEAN COMBS (1969–)

Music Company Executive, Rapper, Entrepreneur, Actor. Sean Combs, also known as Puff Daddy, Puffy, P. Diddy, and Diddy, was born in New York City in 1969. He began to attract notice in New York's hip-hop scene by the time he was nineteen. As an intern at Uptown Records, Combs's talents earned him a permanent position. He headed Uptown's Artist and Repertoire Department, where his primary responsibilities were signing and developing new talent.

In 1991, Combs's luck took a turn for the worse when anxious fans for a charity basketball game and concert he had organized rushed the entrance to the City College gym, killing nine people. Media attacks and a mayoral investigation pushed Combs into a depression. Within a year, Uptown had fired him. His talent had earned him a reputation, however, prompting Arista Records to hire him to direct Bad Boy Entertainment. Success soon followed as Bad Boy released hits by rappers Craig Mack and the Notorious B.I.G., both of whom Combs is credited with discovering.

The ability to find talent sets Combs apart from many other hip-hop producers, and the success of Bad Boy led to the development of numerous new artists. Various projects, including the 1996 release of singer Faith Evans's debut, kept Combs busy. After the shooting death of his friend, Notorious B.I.G., in 1997, Combs rewrote some of the lyrics on his own debut album, *No Way Out*. The album produced three hit singles, including "I'll Be Missing You," a tribute to Notorious B.I.G. In the late 1990s, Combs also opened a soul food restaurant in Manhattan and launched a clothing label.

Early in the first decade of the 2000s, Combs was indicted on two counts of criminal possession of a weapon. Later that year, he pleaded not guilty to bribery charges related to a December 1999 shooting at a New York nightclub. Combs's former driver, Wardel Fenderson, sued Combs for $3 million, claiming he suffered personal injuries while helping Combs flee the shootout. Combs was acquitted of all four counts of criminal gun possession and one count of bribing a witness in 2001. Combs's 2001 album, *The Saga Continues*, with the Bad Boy Family, peaked at number two on the pop charts. In 2002, Combs was back in court settling a paternity lawsuit brought by his ex-girlfriend, the mother of his son. Combs was also back in the studio recording *We Invented the Remix*, which debuted in 2002 at number one on the album charts.

Combs presides over a media empire that includes the record label Bad Boy, the clothing lines Sean John and Sean by Sean Combs, a movie production company, and two restaurants. He has served as recording executive, performer, and producer of MTV's *Making the Band*. He also hosted the 2005 MTV Video Music Awards, and was named one of the "100 Most Influential People of 2005" by *Time* magazine. Combs released the album *Press Play* on October 17, 2006. It was his first album in four years. The album featured a variety of guest appearances from popular musical stars, including Christina Aguilera, Keyshia Cole, Mario Winans (signed to Bad Boy Records), Nas, will.i.am (Black Eyed Peas), Mary J. Blige, Nicole Scherzinger (Pussycat Dolls), Jamie Foxx, Big Boi (OutKast), Ciara, and Brandy. The album reached number one in its first week on the charts.

Combs is also an actor and film producer. He appeared in supporting parts in *Monster's Ball* (2001) and *Carlito's Way: Rise to Power* (2005), among other film and television projects. In 2004, he appeared in the Broadway revival of Lorraine Hansberry's *A Raisin in the Sun*. He reprised the role in the 2008 television version of the production.

COMMON (1972–)

Rapper, Actor. Common (previously known as Common Sense) was born Lonnie Rashied Lynn Jr. on March 13, 1972. The South Side Chicago native is the son of a former ABA basketball player turned youth counselor, Lonnie Lynn, and an educator, Dr. Mahila Ann Hines.

While attending Luther High School South in Chicago, Lynn's rap trio C.D.R. opened for established acts, including Big Daddy Kane and N.W.A. After graduating from high school, he attended Florida A&M University to study business administration on a scholarship. His career in rap gained momentum when he was featured in *The Source* magazine's *Unsigned Hype* column. In 1992, he debuted under the name Common Sense with the single "Take It EZ," which was followed by the album *Can I Borrow a Dollar?* The album helped him attain a sizable underground following.

Common Sense's audience expanded with the 1994 release of *Resurrection*, which included the song "I Used to Love H.E.R.," considered a hip-hop classic. However, the song provoked controversy because the lyrics lamented the path hip-hop music was taking and were interpreted by some as critical of West Coast gangsta rap. Westside Connection, a West Coast rap group, responded with the 1995 song "Westside Slaughterhouse" and other tracks voicing their issues with the East Coast rap community. Hostilities escalated until both sides met with Louis Farrakhan and settled their differences. A lawsuit by an Orange County–based reggae band with the same name of Common Sense followed, forcing the rapper to shorten his stage name to Common.

Rapper Common performs at Farragut Career Academy in Chicago, June 2010. *The Grammy-winning singer is also a noted actor and activist.* RAYMOND BOYD/MICHAEL OCHS ARCHIVES/GETTY IMAGES

Common continued to experience mainstream success. The album *One Day It'll All Make Sense*, which included collaborations with such artists as De La Soul, Q Tip, Lauryn Hill, and Black Thought, was released in 1997 to acclaim for taking a stand against the mentality underlying gangsta rap. Its success resulted in a major-label contract with MCA Records. Common's first child, his daughter Omoye, was born shortly after the album's release. Her birth was significant in Common's growth as an artist.

Common's first major-label album, *Like Water for Chocolate* (2000), earned tremendous commercial success and critical acclaim. In it, Common explored political themes that, except for Mos Def, were unheard for a rap artist. "The Light," by far the album's most recognized song, was nominated for a Grammy Award. Common followed up with the highly eclectic *Electric Circus* in 2002. It featured contributions from Prince and other performers that purposely went beyond the traditional rap format. Common won his first Grammy for "Love of My life (An Ode to Hip-Hop)," which guest-starred Erykah Badu. The song was the theme for the 2002 movie *Brown Sugar*.

The majority of Common's 2005 album, *Be*, was produced by fellow Chicagoan Kanye West and the late J Dilla. Although only reaching gold status, *Be* was lauded by critics and nominated for four Grammy Awards. Common's seventh LP picked up where *Be* left off. *Finding Forever*, released in 2007, featured not only West and J Dilla at the helm, but will.i.am. West predicted that *Finding Forever* would bring home a Grammy Award for best rap album. The album's "Southside," featuring West, won a Grammy for best rap performance by a duo or group. A best-of album titled *Thisisme* was released in late 2007.

"Universal Mind Control," a single from Common's eighth album of the same title, was released to favorable response in 2008. Always politically active, Common supports animal rights, PETA, and the "Knowing Is Beautiful" movement, a campaign promoting HIV/AIDS awareness. He made an appearance in the video for "Yes We Can" in support Barack Obama's presidential campaign. Common has also enjoyed an impressive acting career, with supporting roles in such films as *Smokin' Aces* (2006), *American Gangster* (2007), *Street Kings* (2008), *Wanted* (2008), *Terminator Salvation* (2009), and *Date Night* (2010).

SAM COOKE (1931–1964)

Singer, Songwriter. Sam Cooke's sophisticated vocal style and refined image made him one of the greatest pop music idols of the early 1960s. One of the first gospel music artists to cross over into popular music, Cooke produced songs of timeless quality, filled with human emotion and spiritual optimism.

Born in Clarksdale, Mississippi, on January 2, 1931, Sam Cooke grew up the son of a Baptist minister in Chicago, Illinois. When he was nine years old, Cooke, along with two sisters and a brother, formed a gospel group called the Singing Children. While a teenager, he joined the gospel group the Highway QCs, which performed on the same bill with nationally famous gospel acts.

By 1950, Cooke had replaced tenor Rupert H. Harris as lead singer for the renowned gospel group the Soul Stirrers. Cooke's first recording with the Soul Stirrers, "Jesus Gave Me Water," was released by Art Rupe's Specialty label. Although the song revealed the inexperience of the twenty-year-old Cooke, it exhibited a quality of immense passion and heightened feeling. Under the pseudonym Dale Cooke, Sam recorded the pop song "Loveable" in 1957. That same year, in a session for producer Bumps Blackwell on the Keen label, Cooke recorded "You Send Me," which climbed to number one on the rhythm-and-blues charts. Cooke recorded eight more consecutive hits for Keen, including "Everyone Likes to Cha Cha Cha," "Only Sixteen," and "Wonderful World," all of which were written or cowritten by Cooke.

After his contract with the Keen label expired in 1960, Cooke signed with RCA, and was assigned to staff producers Hugo Peretti and Luigi Creatore. In August, Cooke's recording of "Chain Gang" reached the number-two spot on the pop charts. Under the lavish production of Hugo and Luigi, Cooke produced a string of hits, such as "Cupid" in 1961, "Twistin' the Night Away" in 1962, and "Another Saturday Night" in 1963. Early in 1964, Cooke appeared on the *Tonight Show*, debuting two songs from his upcoming LP, which included the gospel-influenced composition "A Change Is Gonna Come." On December 11, 1964, Cooke checked into a three-dollar-a-night motel, where he demanded entrance into the night-manager's room. After a brief physical struggle, the manager fired three pistol shots, which mortally wounded Cooke. Despite his tragic death, Cooke left behind a catalog of classic recordings and more than one hundred original compositions, including the hit "Shake," which was released posthumously in 1965.

D'ANGELO (1974–)

Singer, Songwriter, Producer. Michael Eugene Archer, known in the music world by his stage name, D'Angelo, was born on February 11, 1974, in Richmond, Virginia. Archer was raised in a strict Pentecostal household by a preacher father and a strong-willed mother. Archer proved to be a prodigy at piano and began to perform for his church under the watchful eye of his parents.

D'Angelo experienced early success in his late teens by writing the hit song "U Will Know" for the soundtrack to the 1994 film *Jason's Lyric*. The song was performed by a group of accomplished R&B and gospel artists calling

D'Angelo at MTV Movie Awards, 2000. *D'Angelo was credited with bringing unabashed soul and the vintage sound of live instrumentation back to the consciousness of hip-hop and contemporary R&B audiences with his 1995 debut* Brown Sugar. FRANK MICELOTTA/GETTY IMAGES.

themselves Black Men United. Soon thereafter, D'Angelo began recording his debut album, *Brown Sugar*, for EMI Records. The album was released in 1995 and caught on with the public thanks to its chart-topping hit, "Lady." *Brown Sugar* enjoyed platinum status and was invaluable in establishing the industry's recognition of the neo-soul movement.

D'Angelo spent the next five years contributing to soundtracks and other artists' albums. He was featured on a duet with Lauryn Hill in "Nothing Even Matters," a touching ballad from Hill's groundbreaking *The Miseducation of Lauryn Hill* (1998). He contributed songs to a number of soundtracks, including covers of "Girl You Need a Change of Mind" by Eddie Kendricks for Spike Lee's 1996 film *Get on the Bus*, "She's Always in My Hair" by Prince for Wes Craven's 1997 film *Scream 2*, and "Heaven Must Be Like This" by the Ohio Players for Maya Angelou's 1998 film *Down in the Delta*, as well as the original song "Devil's Pie" for the 1998 film *Belly*.

D'Angelo's Grammy-winning follow-up to *Brown Sugar*, *Voodoo*, was released in 2000. The album's second single, "Untitled (How Does It Feel)" was a tribute to Prince. The song's popularity was heightened by the famous video, in which D'Angelo appeared to be nude, though only revealing himself from his face to his hips. After *Voodoo*'s release, D'Angelo's supporting international tour became the stuff of legend. He was backed by an incomparable band and put on a live show that regaled concertgoers with its song list and conceptual staging.

Since 2000, D'Angelo has run into legal troubles stemming from drunk driving and his solicitation of a female police officer for sex. Outside of inconsistent demos and minor collaborations with other artists, he has not performed or released any new material or granted interviews. Speculation continues as to when a follow up to *Voodoo* will be released.

FATS DOMINO (1928–)

Singer. Antoine Domino was born on February 26, 1928, in New Orleans. As a teenager, Domino received piano lessons from Harrison Verret. In between nightclub gigs, Domino worked at a factory and mowed lawns around New Orleans. At age twenty, he took a job as a pianist with bassist Billy Diamond's combo at the Hideaway Club. At some point in his early career, Domino's five-foot, five-inch, 200-pound frame led to the nickname "Fats."

In 1949, while playing with Diamond's group, Domino was discovered by David Bartholomew, a talent scout, musician, arranger, and producer for the Imperial label. During the following year, Domino hit the charts with the autobiographical tune "Fat Man." After the release of "Fat Man," he played on tour, backed by Bartholomew's band.

Although Domino released a number of sides during the early 1950s, it was not until 1955 that he gained national prominence with the hit "Ain't That a Shame." In the next six years, Domino scored thirty-five top hits with such songs as "Blueberry Hill" (1956), "Blue Monday" (1957), "Whole Lotta Loving" (1958), and "I'm Walkin'" (1959). Domino's recording success led to his appearance in several films in the 1950s, including *The Girl Can't Help It*, *Shake Rattle and Roll*, *Disc Jockey Jamboree*, and *The Big Beat*.

After Domino's contract with Imperial expired in 1963, he signed with ABC, for whom he made a number of commercial recordings. Domino moved to Mercury in 1965, and then to Reprise in 1968. In the early 1970s, he began to tour with greater regularity than he had during the peak of his career. In 1995, while on tour in England, Domino was hospitalized for infection and exhaustion. Despite suggestions that his health was in decline, Domino continued to work on new material, and honors flew his way, including a Rhythm and Blues Foundation Pioneer Award in 1995 and a National Medal of Arts in 1998. Domino made special appearances at such venues as Harrah's Jazz Casino, where he put on shows in 1999, 2000, 2001, and 2002. In 2005 his childhood home was damaged by Hurricane Katrina, but efforts were soon made to rebuild it. A biography, *Blue Monday: Fats Domino and the Lost Dawn of Rock 'n' Roll*, written by Rick Coleman, was released by Da Capo Press in 2006.

DR. DRE (1965–)

Rapper, Producer. Dr. Dre was born Andre Ramelle Young in Compton, California, in 1965. From the time he was four years old, he was serving as a DJ at his mother's parties. In 1981, he heard a song by Grandmaster Flash that inspired him to become a professional DJ and to change his name in honor of basketball star Julius "Dr. J." Erving. Dr. Dre began spinning records at a Los Angeles nightclub, producing the dance tapes in the club's four-track studio. In addition to using the rap trademarks of sampling, scratching, and drum machines, he added keyboards and vocals.

In 1982, when Dre was seventeen years old, he formed the World Class Wreckin' Cru with another DJ. Their first independently released single sold fifty thousand copies. The following year, Dre graduated from Compton's Centennial High School. He was offered a mechanical-drafting position with an aircraft firm, but he turned it down to devote himself to music. In 1985, Dr. Dre joined the newly formed group N.W.A. (Niggaz With Attitude), along with Ice Cube, Eazy-E, Yella,

M. C. Ren, and Arabian Prince. That year, he also produced Eazy-E's first platinum album, *Eazy-Duz-It*.

N.W.A's successful yet controversial body of work included the multiplatinum *Straight Outta Compton*, released in 1988 on Eazy-E and Dr. Dre's Ruthless Records label. Dr. Dre also produced an album for The D.O.C., a rapper he had discovered in Texas. The resulting album, *No One Can Do It Better* (1989), reached number one on *Billboard*'s R&B album chart. Dre also produced a platinum album for Michel'le, another number-one recording.

In January 1990, Ice Cube left N.W.A. over a financial dispute, and N.W.A. recorded the last of their four recordings without him in 1991. Later that year, Dre left Ruthless to cofound Death Row Records with Suge Knight. Dre's first solo effort, *The Chronic*, was released in 1993. The album, which featured such budding rap artists as Snoop Doggy Dogg, sold three million copies. Dre subsequently produced Snoop's debut, *Doggystyle* (1993).

In 1994, Dre received a Grammy Award for best rap solo performance. At the *Source* Awards, he was named best producer and solo artist, and *The Chronic* was named best album. The following year, he was named "One of the Top 10 Artists that Mattered Most, 1985–1995" by *Spin*. In 1996, Dre stunned the hip-hop community by announcing that he was leaving Death Row. He had hoped that the label would spread into other genres, such as jazz and reggae, but rap continued to bring in the money, and others did not share his vision. Instead, Dre started his own label, Aftermath Entertainment. He continued to edit videos, in addition to penning his biography. In addition, he appeared in a small part in the 1996 film *Set It Off*.

In 2000, Dre joined the rock group Metallica in a legal fight against Napster Inc., a company that produces software allowing Internet users to share music from their computer hard drives. They and other artists succeeded in protecting their copyrighted material from being downloaded on Napster. Later that year, Dr. Dre received a Lifetime Achievement Award at the *Source* Hip-Hop Music Awards. It was the first awards show dedicated to hip-hop music. In 2001, Dre won Grammys for producer of the year (nonclassical) and for best rap performance by a duo or group for "Forgot about Dre," his duet with Eminem. He also was honored with an American Music Award in the favorite rap/hip-hop artist category. As the founder and current CEO of Aftermath Entertainment, he has produced many albums with a variety of artists. By 2007, Dre's personal wealth was estimated to exceed $150 million.

KENNETH "BABYFACE" EDMONDS (1958–)

Singer, Songwriter, Producer. Kenneth Edmonds was born in 1958 in Indianapolis, Indiana, and spent his high school years finagling interviews with pop star idols, such as the Jackson 5 and Stevie Wonder. After performing in a number of rhythm-and-blues bands, Edmonds began a collaboration with Antonio "L.A." Reid in 1981. They were then members of an act called the Deele, but soon gained acclaim writing and producing songs for other artists, such as Shalamar and Bobby Brown.

In 1989, Edmonds and Reid formed their own company, LaFace Records, backed by the Arista label. They continued their success in writing and producing pop, soul, and rhythm-and-blues hits for such artists as Paula Abdul and Whitney Houston. Edmonds and Reid are also credited with supporting the early careers of TLC and Toni Braxton. The duo has won numerous Grammy Awards, including one for producer of the year for the soundtrack to the 1992 Eddie Murphy film *Boomerang*. They have also shared several songwriter-of-the-year honors from Broadcast Music Inc. (BMI).

Edmonds is also a popular solo artist and performer in his own right, with several well-received releases to his name, including *For the Cool in You* (1993), a platinum seller whose hit "When Can I See You" brought him the 1993 Grammy for best male rhythm-and-blues vocalist. For several months between 1994 and 1995, Edmonds was on the road, performing as an opening act for Boyz II Men, yet another of the enormously successful groups for whom he has written and produced. He gained further accolades for producing the soundtrack for the 1995 film *Waiting to Exhale*. In 1997, Edmonds released the recording *Babyface: MTV Unplugged* and followed it up with a Christmas album in 1998. In 2001, Edmonds's *Face2Face* was released. His subsequent solo albums include *Grown & Sexy* (2005) and *Playlist* (2007). Edmonds continues to flourish as a record mogul, performer, songwriter, and producer.

MISSY ELLIOTT (1971–)

Rapper, Singer, Songwriter. Melissa Arnette Elliott, born July 1, 1971, in Portsmouth, Virginia, was first known as "Misdemeanor" Elliott, though she later used the name "Missy" Elliott. By 2007, Elliott had sold over twenty-four million records worldwide, which made her one of the highest-selling female rappers. She was the fourth female rapper to ever go platinum, behind Lil' Kim, Foxy Brown, and Da Brat. Elliott is the only female rapper with six platinum albums. Missy Elliott is also a critics' favorite, with two of her singles ranked in the top ten of the "Top 200 Songs from the 2000s" on the Web site Acclaimed Music.

Elliott is known for a series of hits, including "The Rain (Supa Dupa Fly)," "Hit 'Em Wit Da Hee," "Get Ur Freak On," "One Minute Man," "Work It," and "Lose

Control." Her albums include *Supa Dupa Fly* (1997), *Da Real World* (1999), *Miss E . . . So Addictive* (2001), *Under Construction* (2002), *This Is Not a Test!* (2003), *The Cookbook* (2005), and *Respect M.E.*, a greatest-hits compilation released in 2006. In addition, she has received recognition as one of the most successful songwriters of the modern music era, having written many hit records for such artists as Melanie B, Fantasia, Aaliyah, 702, Total, Nelly Furtado, Ciara, Nicole Wray, and Tweet, often with her childhood friend Timbaland. Elliott has won a number of Grammy Awards as a performer and some as a producer. She has also performed in film and television.

LUPE FIASCO (1982–)

Rapper, Producer. Hip-hop rapper Lupe Fiasco was born Wasalu Muhammad Jaco on February 16, 1982, in Chicago. As one of nine children from parents of West African descent, he studied martial arts as a child, attaining his first black belt at age ten. He grew up as a Muslim and was disgusted by hip-hop music because of its vulgarity. He had a change of heart in the eighth grade after hearing Nas's 1996 album, *It Was Written.* Impressed with the possibilities of rap, he followed Nas's career and began rapping himself. The name *Fiasco* was adopted from a song called "Firm Fiasco" on a 1996 album by the Firm, a group to which Nas belonged. Lupe Fiasco has claimed that he "just liked the way it looked on paper."

Rap Artist Lupe Fiasco, Coachella Music Festival, Indio, CA, 2009. *Fiasco rose to fame following the 2006 release of his critically acclaimed debut album,* Lupe Fiasco's Food & Liquor. *The album garnered three Grammy Award nominations.*
C FLANIGAN/FILMMAGIC/GETTY IMAGES

When he was nineteen years old, Lupe Fiasco joined a group called Da Pak, which signed with Epic Records and released one single before breaking up. Fiasco suffered more setbacks when he signed as a solo artist with Arista Records, only to be dropped when its president, L. A. Reid, was fired. Fiasco remained active with guest appearances on Tha' Rayne's "Didn't You Know" and "Kiss Me," as well as K Foxx's "This Life" in 2004. He also released a song called "Coulda Been" for the MTV compilation *Advance Warning.*

Fiasco gained greater visibility in 2005 after guest-starring on Kanye West's single "Touch the Sky." The single, along with his politically charged "Conflict Diamonds" mixtape over Kanye West's "Diamonds from Sierra Leone" track, piqued mainstream interest. Fiasco inked a marketing deal with Reebok in 2006: Lupe, Mike Jones, and Lil Wayne were to design their own personal take on the Reebok "O.G" shoe. The rapper also started a fashion label named Trilly & Truly. He collaborated with several other partners for another line called Japanese Cartoon.

More mainstream success came Lupe Fiasco's way when rapper and mogul Jay-Z heard Fiasco. Impressed with his talent, Jay-Z assisted him in producing his debut album, *Lupe Fiasco's Food & Liquor*, released in late 2006. While in production, Lupe released a featured single, "Kick, Push." The song was unique in that it focused on his passion for skateboarding and was a highlight in the videogame *NBA Live 2007.* Unlike many conscious rappers, the album's production roster was stocked with major artists, such as the Neptunes, Kanye West, and Jay-Z. Other singles from the album include "I Gotcha" and "Daydreamin'," which features Jill Scott. Critics gushed over the album, and it scored three Grammy nominations, including best rap album. *GQ* magazine voted Fiasco as the "Breakout Man of the Year."

While he was recording his next album, *The Cool* (2007), his father died. In addition, his business partner, Charles "Chilly" Patton, began a four-year sentence for attempting to supply heroin. Even though the album had a darker tone than its predecessor, its first single, "Superstar," was received enthusiastically. HBO's *Hard Knocks* program featured it. The movie *Street Kings* (2008) featured the songs "Put You on Game" and "Little Weapon" on its soundtrack.

Lupe and his band, 1500 or Nothin, joined the line-up on Kanye West's Glow in the Dark Tour. In 2008, Fiasco was named the "Seventh Hottest MC in the Game" by MTV. His "Superstar" was added to the soundtrack of the video game *Lips*. In late 2009, Fiasco hit the mixtape circuit with *Enemy of the State: A Love Story*. Standout tracks include the freestyles "Say Something" and "Turnt Up."

In 2009, Lupe contributed to *The People Speak*, a documentary film that explores the diaries, letters, and speeches of everyday Americans. On January 7, 2010, Lupe joined an expedition to the top of Mount Kilimanjaro to raise awareness of the billions of people worldwide who lack sanitary drinking water. Later that month, he and the musician Kenna released the song "Resurrection" in response to the 2010 earthquake in Haiti. "Resurrection" is part of a compilation to raise funds for Haitians coping with the disaster.

50 CENT (1975–)

Rapper, Actor, Entrepreneur. Curtis James Jackson III was born on July 6, 1975, in the borough of Queens in New York City. He later became known to the world as 50 Cent. His father was never a part of his life, and his mother Sabrina was murdered in a drug war for territory. After his mother's death, the young boy went to live with his grandparents. When he was twelve years old, Jackson took to boxing and selling drugs in the midst of the 1980s crack epidemic. After arrests and a stint in a boot camp, he decided to walk away from it and pursue a career in rapping. He embraced the nickname "50 Cent" to represent the change in his life. Jackson's then-girlfriend, Shaniqua Tompkins, gave birth to his son Marquise in 1997.

In 2000, as 50 Cent worked toward a debut album and tried to cut his ties to the street life, he was shot nine times by drug-dealing rivals. His label, Columbia Records, panicked because of the violence surrounding his attempted murder. They dropped him from the label and did not release *Power of the Dollar*, which was slated to be his debut album.

50 Cent released his album *Guess Who's Back?* on an independent label, Full Clip Records, in 2002. The album, powered by a bold mixtape campaign, caught the attention of rapper Eminem and resulted in 50 being signed to Interscope Records. With production wizard Dr. Dre at the controls, 50 recorded and released his next album, *Get Rich or Die Tryin'*, on Interscope in 2003. It was easily one of the most-hyped albums in rap history because 50 Cent had survived a shooting and because of his mixtape reputation. It entered the *Billboard* 200 at number one and sold an astonishing 872,000 copies in four days. The album ultimately sold fifteen million copies. "In da Club," its first single, holds the record in the *Billboard* archives as the most listened-to song in radio history within the span of a week.

Rap Artist 50 Cent (Curtis Jackson), Madison Square Garden, New York City, 2009. *50 Cent gained fame through the release of two multiplatinum albums,* Get Rich or Die Tryin' *(2003) and* The Massacre *(2005).* JIM SPELLMAN/WIREIMAGE

50 Cent has proven himself to be a man of exceptional business acumen. He and Reebok secured a five-year relationship wherein Reebok distributed the G-Unit Sneakers line for 50 Cent's G-Unit Clothing Company. In 2003, 50 Cent formed his own label, G-Unit Records. Young Buck, Tony Yayo, and Lloyd Banks joined G-Unit's roster. West Coast rapper The Game joined by way of a joint venture with Dr. Dre's Aftermath Entertainment. As the G-Unit team went to work on their individual albums, 50 released *The Massacre* in 2005. It went platinum and held the number-one position on the *Billboard* 200 for six weeks. Singles from *The Massacre* include "Disco Inferno," "Candy Shop," and "How We Do."

When Coca-Cola purchased Glacéau in 2007, *Forbes* estimated that 50 Cent, who owned a stake in the company, was worth $100 million. He inked a deal with

Right Guard to promote Pure 50 RGX Body Spray. He also agreed to a multiyear deal with Steiner Sports, allowing the company to sell his memorabilia. 50 Cent's relationship with The Game grew strained. When The Game left, rap group Mobb Deep and singer Olivia signed with G-Unit Records. While other members of his G-Unit group produced moderately successful albums, 50 released *Curtis*, his third album, in 2007. Sales for *Curtis* were sluggish, which made 50's proclaimed competition in sales with Kanye West's *Graduation* (released at the same time) an unwise marketing ploy.

In 2009, 50 Cent released *Before I Self Destruct*, which was to be his final record for Interscope. The album fared even worse than *Curtis*, and failed to reach gold-record-level sales. Interscope blamed release delays and songs leaked over the Internet for the lackluster sales.

A respectable career in acting has been in the rapper's sights for years. 50 Cent starred in the semiautobiographical film *Get Rich or Die Tryin'* in 2005. He also appeared in the Iraq War films *Home of the Brave* (2006) and *Righteous Kill* (2008). Determined to prove his serious intent as an actor, 50 Cent lost fifty-four pounds in 2010 for the film *Things Fall Apart*, in which he plays a college football player struggling with cancer.

ROBERTA FLACK (1939–)

Singer, Pianist. Born in Black Mountain, North Carolina, on February 10, 1939, Roberta Flack moved to Washington, D.C., with her parents when she was nine years old. Three years later, she began studying classical piano with prominent African American concert musician Hazel Harrison. After winning several talent contests, Flack won a scholarship to Howard University, where she graduated with a bachelor's degree in music education. During the early 1960s, Flack taught music in the Washington, D.C., public school system.

Singer Roberta Flack, 2010. *Flack earned Grammy Awards for Record of the Year two years in a row for her songs "The First Time Ever I Saw Your Face" (1972) and "Killing Me Softly with His Song" (1973).* JORDAN STRAUSS/WIREIMAGE/GETTY IMAGES

While playing a club date in 1968, Flack was discovered by Les McCann, whose connections resulted in a contract with Atlantic Records. Flack's first album, *First Take*, appeared in 1970 and included the hit song "The First Time Ever I Saw Your Face." During the 1970s, Flack landed several hits, such as "Killing Me Softly with His Song" and "The Closer I Get to You," a duet with Donny Hathaway; both songs earned Grammys. In the early 1980s, Flack collaborated with Peabo Bryson to record the hit "Tonight I Celebrate My Love for You." In 1991, Flack enjoyed another top-ten hit, "Set the Night to Music," a duet with Maxi Priest. In 1994, she released the album *Roberta*, a Grammy-nominated recording of jazz, blues, and pop classics.

Flack's music was brought to a new generation in 1996 when the Fugees remade her hit "Killing Me Softly with His Song." She even played the Fugees' cover on *Brunch with Roberta Flack*, a weekly syndicated radio program that aired from 1995 to 1998. In 1997, she put out an album of holiday songs simply titled *Christmas Album*. In 1999, Flack started an international tour and was allowed the honor of singing to Nelson Mandela during her stop in South Africa. In 2003, Flack released another Christmas album, *Holiday*, which includes a collection of seasonal songs and a few of her classics. She also participated in the album *Songs from the Neighborhood*, an all-star tribute to the late Fred "Mister" Rogers, released in 2005. In 2006, Flack released a retrospective album called *The Very Best of Roberta Flack*.

ARETHA FRANKLIN (1942–)

Singer, Songwriter. Aretha Franklin, the daughter of the famous Reverend Charles L. Franklin, was born on March 25, 1942, in Memphis, Tennessee. Raised on Detroit's east side, Franklin sang at her father's New Bethel Baptist Church. Although she began to study piano at age eight, Franklin refused to learn what she considered juvenile and simple tunes. Instead, she learned piano by ear, occasionally receiving instruction from such individuals as the Reverend James Cleveland. Franklin's singing skills were modeled after gospel music singers and family friends, including Clara Ward, and rhythm-and-blues artists such as Ruth Brown and Sam Cooke.

When she was fourteen years old, Franklin quit school to go on the road with her father's Franklin Gospel Caravan. After four years on the road, Aretha moved to New York City to establish her own career as a pop artist. In 1960, she signed with Columbia Records talent scout John Hammond. Her six years at Columbia

Singer Aretha Franklin,* The Andy Williams Show, *1969. A gospel-bred singer turned pop maven who became known as "The Queen of Soul," Franklin is one of the most enduring figures in popular music. Her hit songs include "Respect," "Chain of Fools," and "(You Make Me Feel Like a) Natural Woman." **FRED A. SABINE/NBCU PHOTO BANK/AP IMAGES**

produced only a few hits and little material that suited Franklin's unique talents.

In 1966, Franklin signed with Atlantic Records, and the following year she recorded a session for Wexler that resulted in the breakthrough hit "I Never Loved a Man (The Way That I Loved You)." That same year, Franklin's career received another boost when her reworking of Otis Redding's song "Respect" hit the charts. This achievement was followed by a succession of artistically and commercially successful albums, including *Aretha Arrives* (1967), *Lady Soul* (1968), *Aretha Now!* (1968), and *This Girl's in Love with You* (1970). Her prominence grew so great that Franklin appeared on the cover of *Time* magazine in 1968. That year, she performed at Martin Luther King Jr.'s funeral and at the Democratic National Convention.

During the 1970s, Franklin continued to tour and record. In 1971, she released the LP *Aretha Live at the Fillmore West*, backed by the horn and rhythm section of Tower of Power. Her next release, *Amazing Grace* (1972), featured Reverend James Cleveland and the Southern California Community Choir. In 1977, she performed at President Jimmy Carter's inauguration, later doing the same for President Bill Clinton in 1993 and President Barack Obama in 2009.

In 1980, Franklin appeared in the film *The Blues Brothers*. She also appeared in a number of television specials, including *Aretha* (1986), *Aretha Franklin: The Queen of Soul* (1988), and *Duets* (1993). The 1980s also saw Franklin score her first big commercial success in more than a decade with the album *Who's Zooming Who?*, featuring the single "Freeway of Love." In 1988, she released a double live LP, *One Lord, One Faith, One Baptism*, an effort dedicated to her father, who had passed away the previous year.

Franklin has won numerous Grammy Awards, including a Lifetime Achievement Award, bestowed in 1995. Other honors include an American Music Award and an *Ebony* magazine American Black Achievement Award, both in 1984, declaration as a "natural resource" of the state of Michigan in 1985, induction into the Rock and Roll Hall of Fame in 1987, an *Essence* Award in 1993, and a Kennedy Center Honor in 1994. Only Janet Jackson has matched Franklin's record of fourteen gold singles, the most by a female solo artist.

Franklin stayed active in the 1990s, a decade in which many of her classic recordings were reissued. She was a headliner at the 1994 New Orleans Jazz and Heritage Festival and lent a track to the soundtrack for the 1995 film *Waiting to Exhale*. In 1995, Franklin launched her own label, World Class Records. She also performed on the 1998 VH-1 concert special "Divas Live," along with Gloria Estefan, Celine Dion, Mariah Carey, Shania Twain, and others. The concert raised money to fund music education in elementary schools. Franklin performed the national anthem during a celebrated July 17, 1999, concert of the Three Tenors (Luciano Pavarotti, Jose Carreras, and Placido Domingo) in Detroit. She received the National Medal of Arts in 1999 from President Bill Clinton.

Franklin published her autobiography *Aretha: From These Roots*, written with Davis Ritz, in 2000. In 2001, she was saluted in VH1's *Divas Live: The One and Only Aretha Franklin*. The event featured Franklin singing with various groups and soloists, including Mary J. Blige, Jill Scott, Celia Cruz, Marc Anthony, Kid Rock, Nelly Furtado, and the Backstreet Boys.

Numerous compilations of Franklin's recordings have been issued, including an album with her and the late Otis

Redding. Her album *So Damn Happy* was released in 2003. *Rolling Stone* magazine ranked her ninth on their 2004 list of the "100 Greatest Artists of All Time." She was awarded the Presidential Medal of Freedom in 2005 by President George W. Bush. Her citation read:

> The Queen of Soul, Aretha Franklin has recorded more than 20 number-one singles and revolutionized American music. Her instantly recognizable voice has captivated listeners ever since she toured with her father's gospel revue in the 1950s. She is among our Nation's greatest musical artists and has captured the hearts of millions of Americans. The United States honors Aretha Franklin for her lifetime of achievement and for helping to shape our Nation's artistic and cultural heritage.

In 2006, Franklin became the second woman to be inducted into the UK Music Hall of Fame. She was also presented an honorary doctor of music degree by the Berklee College of Music in Boston. In 2006, Franklin received a Grammy for best traditional R&B vocal for "A House Is Not a Home," a track from the Luther Vandross tribute, *So Amazing*.

KIRK FRANKLIN (1970–)

Singer. Kirk Franklin was born in Fort Worth, Texas, in 1970 and was raised by an elderly aunt who was a regular church attendee. He began playing the piano when he was only four years old. At eleven, he was appointed music minister of his church. When he was nineteen years old, Kirk made his first home recording. In 1992, he selected seventeen singers and formed the Family. The group released its first gospel album, *Kirk Franklin & the Family*, in 1993. The album blasted to the top of the *Billboard* gospel charts. Franklin has since won many Grammys and has produced numerous platinum-selling albums. Besides Kirk Franklin and the Family, Franklin has led several other contemporary gospel choirs, including Kirk Franklin's Nu Nation, God's Property, and 1NC. His music blends gospel, hip-hop, and R&B.

On October 2005, Franklin's album *Hero* was released, with the singles "Looking For You" and "Imagine Me." Franklin's songs are published by Zomba Music Publishing, a division of BMG Music. Franklin won two Grammy Awards for *Hero*. Franklin's *Songs for the Storm, Vol. 1* was released in 2006, followed by *The Fight of My Life* in 2007. He was also featured on the song "Lose My Soul" on tobyMac's 2007 album *Portable Sounds*. Almost all of Franklin's albums were gold or platinum. He has collaborated with the biggest names in gospel music, including Mary Mary, Tonex, Donnie McClurkin, Richard Smallwood, Crystal Lewis, Pastor Shirley Caesar, tobyMac, Jaci Velasquez, and Willie Neal Johnson.

THE FUGEES

Hip-Hop Singing Group. With a sound most often described as "eclectic," the Fugees landed on the hip-hop charts in 1994 with their Ruffhouse debut, *Blunted on Reality*. Initially known as the Tranzlator Crew, Lauryn Hill, Prakazrel "Pras" Michel, and Wyclef Jean had been working together since they were teenagers in northern New Jersey. They were forced to change their name when a 1980s new-wave band called Translator filed a legal protest. Released under the name Fugees, their first album received rave reviews. Sales for the album were moderate, however, while critics announced that Hill should pursue a solo career.

With sales of seventeen million, the trio's second release, *The Score* (1996), made them the biggest-selling rap act in history. Produced by Jean and Hill, the album included covers of Roberta Flack's "Killing Me Softly with His Song" and Bob Marley's "No Woman, No Cry." The band made great strides in bringing hip-hop with a positive attitude to a new generation.

The members of the Fugees have begun to focus on individual projects, leaving the group's future in doubt. In 1997, Jean released his multiplatinum solo debut, *The Carnival*, which was well-received in the United States and in his native Haiti. He followed it up with *The Ecleftic: 2 Sides II a Book* (2000). Michel's solo efforts produced *Ghetto Superstar* (1998) and *Win Lose or Draw* (2005). Hill released her debut solo album, *The Miseducation of Lauryn Hill*, in 1998. It won an unprecedented five Grammy Awards. Her *MTV Unplugged* appearance was released as *MTV Unplugged No. 2.0* in 2002. The group reunited for some performances in 2005 and 2006, but has not made another album.

MARVIN GAYE (1939–1984)

Singer, Songwriter. The son of a Pentecostal minister, Marvin Gay was born on April 29, 1939, in Washington, D.C. (the final "e" on his surname was not added until the early 1960s). Raised in a segregated slum-ridden section of Washington D.C., Gaye experienced a strict religious upbringing. As Gaye later recalled: "Living with my father was like living with a king, a very peculiar, changeable, cruel, and all-powerful king." Gaye found a release in music. Around the age of three, he began singing in church. While attending Cardozo High School, Gaye studied drums, piano, and guitar. Uninspired by his formal studies, Gaye often cut classes to watch James Brown and Jackie Wilson perform at the Howard Theatre.

Soon afterward, Gaye served a short time in the U.S. Air Force. After his discharge in 1957, Gaye returned to Washington, D.C., and joined the doo-wop group the

Singer-Songwriter Marvin Gaye. *During the 1960s, Gaye enjoyed a long succession of Motown hits, culminating with 1968's "I Heard It through the Grapevine," which was a number one single in both the United States and the United Kingdom.* NBCU PHOTO BANK VIA AP IMAGES

Marquees. After recording for Columbia Record's subsidiary label, Okeh, the Marquees moved to the Chess/ Checker label, for whom they recorded with Bo Diddley. Although the Marquees performed their own compositions and toured regularly, they failed to gain popularity. It was not until they were introduced to Harvey Fuqua, who was in the process of reforming the Moonglows, that the Marquees attracted notice in the pop music world. Impressed by their sound, Fuqua hired the Marquees to form a group under the new name Harvey and the Moonglows. Still under contract at Chess, Fuqua brought the Moonglows to the company's studio in Chicago to record the 1959 hit "Ten Commandments of Love."

In 1960, Fuqua and Gaye traveled to Detroit, where Fuqua set up his own label and signed with Motown's subsidiary, Anna. After a stint as a backup singer, studio musician, and drummer in Smokey Robinson's touring band, Gaye signed a contract with Motown as a solo artist. Gaye's first album, released in 1962, was a jazz-oriented effort titled *The Soulful Moods of Marvin Gaye.* With his sights on a career modeled after the ballad singer Frank Sinatra, Gaye was not enthusiastic when Motown suggested he record a dance record of rhythm-and-blues material. Nevertheless, Gaye recorded the song "Stubborn Kind of Fellow" in 1962; it entered the top-ten R&B charts. This song was followed by a long succession of Motown hits, including "Hitch Hike," "Pride and Joy," "Can I Get a Witness," and "Wonderful One."

Motown's next projects for Gaye included a number of vocal duets, the first of which was a 1964 album with Mary Wells, *Together.* In collaboration with singer Kim Weston, Gaye recorded the 1967 hit LP *It Takes Two.* His most successful partnership, however, was with Tammi Terrell. In their two-year association, Gaye and Terrell recorded, under the writing and production team of Ashford and Simpson, such hits as "Ain't No Mountain High Enough," "Your Precious Love," and "Ain't Nothing Like the Real Thing."

Back in the studio as a solo act, Gaye recorded the hit "Heard It through the Grapevine." With his growing success, Gaye achieved greater creative independence at Motown, which led him to coproduce the 1971 album *What's Going On,* a session producing the best-selling singles "What's Going On," "Mercy Mercy (the Ecology)," and "Inner City Blues (Make Me Wanna Holler)."

After his last LP for Motown, *In Our Lifetime* (1981), Gaye signed with CBS Records in April 1981, and within the next year released the album *Midnight Lover,* featuring the Grammy Award–winning hit "Sexual Healing." On Sunday, April 1, 1984, after a heated argument, Gaye was fatally shot by his father in Los Angeles. Despite his public image, Gaye had suffered from years of inner conflict and drug abuse. After his death, his longtime friend Smokey Robinson commented that "this tragic ending can only be softened by the memory of a beautiful human being," adding "he could be full of joy sometimes, but at others, full of woe, but in the end how compassionate, how wonderful, how exciting was Marvin Gaye and his music."

BERRY GORDY JR. (1929–)

Music Company Executive. From assembly-line worker to impresario of the Motown Record Corporation, Berry Gordy Jr. emerged as the owner of one of the largest African American–owned businesses in American history. A professional boxer, songwriter, producer, and businessman, Gordy helped create one of the most celebrated sounds of modern music.

The seventh of eight children, Gordy was born on November 28, 1929, in Detroit. Berry Gordy Sr., the owner of a grocery store, a plastering company, and a printing shop, taught his children the value of hard work and family unity. After quitting high school to become a professional boxer, Gordy won several contests before leaving the profession in 1950. A year later, Gordy was drafted into the U.S. Army, where he earned a high school equivalency diploma.

Berry Gordy Jr., at Motown 50 Golden Gala, Detroit, MI, 2009. *Berry Gordy, the founder of Motown Records, was among the attendees at this event marking the fiftieth anniversary of the company's founding. Proceeds benefited the Motown Museum in Detroit.* PAUL WARNER/WIREIMAGE

Upon returning from a military tour of Korea in 1953, Berry opened the 3-D Record Mart, a jazz-oriented retail store. Forced into bankruptcy, Berry closed the store in 1955, and subsequently took a job as an assembly-line worker at the Ford Motor Company. His nightly visits to Detroit's thriving jazz and rhythm-and-blues scene inspired Gordy to take up songwriting. In 1957, one of Gordy's former boxing colleagues, Jackie Wilson, recorded the hit "Reet Petite," a song written by Berry, his sister Gwen, and Billy Davis. Over the next four years, the writing team provided Wilson with four more hits: "To Be Loved," "Lonely Teardrops," "That's Why (I Love You So), and "I'll Be Satisfied."

By 1959, Billy Davis and Gwen Gordy founded the Anna label, which distributed material through Chess Records in Chicago. Barret Strong's 1959 recording of "Money (That's What I Want)," written by Berry Gordy and Janie Bradford, became the label's biggest-selling single. With a background as a writer and producer with the Anna label, Gordy decided to start his own company. In 1959, he formed Jobete Music Publishing, Berry Gordy Jr. Enterprises, Hitsville USA, and the Motown Record Corporation. Employing a staff of local studio musicians, writers, and producers, Berry's label scored its first hit in 1961 with Smokey Robinson's "Shop Around." By the mid-1960s, Gordy had assembled a wealth of talent, including the Supremes, the Four Tops, the Marvelettes, Marvin Gaye, and Stevie Wonder.

In 1971, Gordy relocated the Motown Recording Corporation to Los Angeles. Although most of the original acts and staff members did not join the company's migration to the West Coast, Gordy's company became one of the country's top African American–owned businesses. Throughout the 1970s and 1980s, Motown continued to produce such artists as the Jackson Five, the Commodores, Lionel Richie, Rick James, and DeBarge. Gordy also tried his hand at producing feature films. *Lady Sings the Blues* (1972), *Mahogany* (1975), and *The Last Dragon* (1985) were not critical successes, but they attracted the participation of such celebrities as Diana Ross, Billy Dee Williams, Richard Pryor, and Vanity. Faced with financial problems, Gordy signed a distribution agreement with MCA in 1984 and sold the label in entirety to MCA six years later.

Gordy's induction into the Rock and Roll Hall of Fame in 1988 brought recognition to a giant of the recording industry who helped transform the sound of popular music. He was honored with a lifetime achievement award at the 1993 Black Radio Exclusive Awards banquet ceremony. Among *Forbes*'s 400 richest Americans in the mid-1980s,

Gordy published his autobiography, *To Be Loved: The Music, the Magic, the Memories of Motown*, in 1994. In 1997, Berry gained co-composing credits on the songs "I'll Be There" and "You've Made Me So Very Happy." Gordy was honored in 1998 with the *Essence* Image Maker Award. In 2001, he was inducted into the Independent Music Hall of Fame. A renewed conversation about Gordy and Motown was generated in 2006 by the release of *Dreamgirls*, a movie loosely based on the rise of the Supremes to stardom.

AL GREEN (1946–)

Singer, Songwriter, Preacher. Possessing one of the supplest voices in popular music, Al Green recorded a series of soul hits during the early 1970s, but turned his back on pop later in the decade to sing gospel and preach in a Memphis church. Alfred Green was born in Forrest City, Arkansas, and spent his early years singing gospel in the South, but switched to pop and scored a hit, "Back Up Train," in 1967. It was not until he hooked up with producer Willie Mitchell, however, that he found his niche. Recording for Mitchell's Hi Records in Memphis with an ace band, Green managed a remarkable synthesis of intimate, romantic pop and gritty soul. The fruits of this union included "Tired of Being Alone," "Love and Happiness," "Let's Stay Together," and "I'm Still in Love with You." His smoldering "Take Me to the River" was covered by numerous other artists.

Though he was "born again" into Christianity in 1973, Green continued to record largely secular music, albeit with a religious tinge, for several years. After founding his own church, the Full Gospel Tabernacle in Memphis, he returned to gospel music. His recordings won regular honors in gospel circles and even a Grammy Award, but his presence continued to be felt in the soul and rhythm-and-blues world. Apart from the occasional duet, however, he steered clear of pop until his return in 1995 with "Your Heart's in Good Hands."

In 2000, Green published his autobiography, *Take Me to the River*, written with Davin Seay. In 2001, Green was honored at the Rhythm and Blues Foundation Annual Awards Gala with a Lifetime Achievement Award. Green continues to record music, both secular and sacred, and released *I Can't Stop* in 2003, followed by *Everything's OK* (2005) and *Lay it Down* (2008). He has also released a number of compilation albums, including *The Definitive Greatest Hits* (2007).

M. C. HAMMER (1963–)

Rapper. Born Stanley Kirk Burrell in 1963 in East Oakland, California, M. C. Hammer began his career with a group called the Holy Ghost Boys, with whom he performed religious raps during the mid-1980s in Oakland clubs. Hammer recorded his first song, "Ring 'Em," in his basement and sold copies out of his car trunk. The song rose to number one in the San Francisco Bay Area.

In 1988, Capitol Records rereleased his first album, *Let's Get It Started*, which produced three top-ten singles and went double platinum. Hammer's second album, *Please Hammer, Don't Hurt 'Em*, released in 1990, remained on *Billboard*'s pop chart for twenty-one weeks. Hammer became internationally known for his "crossover" rap, colorful costumes, and showy style of dance. His "Can't Touch This" single produced a hit video that was hailed for its innovative production and Hammer's energetic dancing. Hammer's 1991 *Too Legit to Quit*, which went multiplatinum, leveled a critique at the use of samples in hip-hop music by using live musicians and vocalists. Hammer's star rose quickly, and he became a veritable cottage industry in the early 1990s.

Hammer turned to the production end of the business and launched the careers of 3.5.7., Angie B., and Special Generation. He also managed Heavy D & the Boyz, Troop, Ralph Tresvant, and boxer Evander Holyfield for a short time. He won many honors, including three Grammy Awards, seven American Music Awards, three Soul Train Awards, and two MTV Awards. After a slump in popularity, mounting criticism from the hip-hop critics about his blatant commercialism, and ensuing financial problems, Hammer returned to Christian music in 1997, proclaiming a new music ministry of evangelism with the project *Family Affair*. In 2001, Hammer continued his message of hope and religion with his new album, *Active Duty*. Hammer filmed a music video by the U.S. Capitol's reflecting pool for the album's first single, "No Stoppin' Us-USA." All of the proceeds from the video and the single went to those affected by the September 11, 2001, terrorist attacks.

HERBIE HANCOCK

See chapter 24, Blues and Jazz.

ANDRE HARRELL (1960–)

Music Company Executive, Producer, Musician. Andre O'Neal Harrell was born in the Bronx in New York City on September 26, 1960. While growing up in the housing projects there, young Harrell teamed up with Alonzo Brown to form the playful rap duo Dr. Jekyll (Harrell) and Mr. Hyde (Brown). Before long, they had three top-twenty hits under their belts and were carving a niche for themselves in rap.

Despite his early rap success, Harrell enrolled in classes at the Bronx's Lehman College. After three years of study in communications and business management, Harrell met Russell Simmons in 1983. Simmons lured Harrell to Rush Management, a company that helped define the hip-hop of the day. Within two years, Harrell had worked his way to vice president and general manager and was instrumental in building the careers of such rap icons as LL Cool J, Run-DMC, and Whodini.

Harrell left Rush Management to begin his own record company, Uptown Records. In 1988, the achievements of Uptown Records prompted a $75,000 record deal from MCA. Artists such as Al B. Sure!, Guy, and Heavy D all prospered under Harrell's direction. By 1992, Uptown and its artists had blazed a trail of gold and platinum albums and landed an unprecedented $50 million multimedia agreement with MCA. Soon major projects, such as the television show *In Living Color* and a showcase of Uptown recording artists, including Mary J. Blige and Jodeci on MTV's *Unplugged*, were in the works.

In 1995, Harrell left Uptown to become president and CEO of Motown Records. After two years at Motown, Harrell resigned, admitting that he was unable to return Motown to its former glory. After his tenure at Motown, Harrell formed Harrell Entertainment and returned to working and consulting with new artists. In the fall of 1998, Sean Combs, founder and CEO of Bad Boy Entertainment, hired Harrell as a consultant. While talking about Harrell with writer Anita M. Samuels from *Billboard*, Combs said, "He's one of the wisest men in the business, he taught me almost everything I know." In 2005 and 2006, Harrell developed two television programs.

ISAAC HAYES (1942–2008)

Singer, Pianist, Producer. Born on August 20, 1942, in Covington, Tennessee, Isaac Hayes moved to Memphis when he was seven years old. In Memphis, he was introduced to the sounds of blues, country western, and the music of idol Sam Cooke. Through the connections of saxophonist Floyd Newman, Hayes began a career as a studio musician for Stax Records in 1964. After playing piano on a session for Otis Redding, Hayes formed a partnership with songwriter Dave Porter. Together they were responsible for supplying a number of hits to Carla Thomas, William Bell, and Eddie Floyd.

The first real break for the Hayes-Porter team came when they were recruited to produce the Miami-based soul duo Sam and Dave. In the span of four years, Hayes and Porter succeeded in making Sam and Dave Stax's hottest-selling act, producing such hits as "Hold On I'm Coming," "Soul Man," and "I Thank You!" During this period, Hayes and Porter continued to perform in a group that established them as an underground legend in the Memphis music scene.

In the late 1960s, Hayes's solo career emerged in an impromptu fashion when a late-night session with drummer Al Jackson and bassist Duck Dunn prompted Stax to release his next effort. *Hot Buttered Soul* went double platinum in 1969. Featuring a soul version of the country song "By the Time I Get to Phoenix," Hayes's rendition set a trend for the disco/soul sound of the 1970s. Following the release of the albums *To Be Continued* (1970) and *The Isaac Hayes Movement* (1970), Hayes recorded the soundtrack for the "blaxploitation" film *Shaft* (1971) and the album *Black Moses* (1971). In 1971, "Theme from Shaft" won an Academy Award for best song in a motion picture and Grammy Awards for best instrumental and best original score for a motion picture. *Black Moses* earned a Grammy for best pop instrumental performance.

Hayes left the Stax label to join ABC in 1974. He recorded a series of disco albums. In 1977, the commercial downturn in Hayes's career forced him to file for bankruptcy. Though he composed Dionne Warwick's "Déjà Vu," which won a Grammy in 1978, his last gold record, *Don't Let Go*, was released on the Polydor label in 1979. During the 1980s and 1990s, Hayes appeared on television shows and in such films as the futuristic thriller *Escape from New York* (1981) and the comedy *Robin Hood: Men in Tights* (1993).

Winner of a 1994 Georgy Award from the Georgia Music Hall of Fame, Hayes heavily influenced the music of the late 1980s and early 1990s. Together with James Brown, Hayes has been one of the most frequently sampled artists by purveyors of rap. Choosing not to jump ship, however, Hayes stuck to his own brand of "hot buttered soul." In 1995, he issued his first new recordings in seven years, *Branded* and *Raw and Refined*, and contributed a track to the Hughes brothers' 1995 film *Dead Presidents*. Hayes also lent his voice to the role of Chef on the Cable Ace Award–winning animated show *South Park*, a role that introduced him to a new generation of fans.

In 2002, Hayes was inducted into to the Rock and Roll Hall of Fame. In 2004, he appeared as Jaffa Tolok on the television series *Stargate SG-1*. The following year, he appeared in the independent film *Hustle & Flow*. Hayes was inducted into the Songwriters' Hall of Fame in 2006.

JIMI HENDRIX (1942–1970)

Guitarist, Singer, Songwriter. When Jimi Hendrix arrived on the international rock-music scene in 1967, he redefined the sound of the electric guitar. His extraordinary approach to the instrument shaped the course of music from jazz fusion to heavy metal. Johnny Allen Hendrix was born on November 27, 1942, in Seattle, Washington, to an enlisted soldier in the U.S. Army and a teenage mother. Four years later, Johnny Allen was renamed James Marshall Hendrix. Because of his mother's fondness for nightclub life and his father's frequent absences, Hendrix was a lonely yet creative child. At school, he won several contests for his science fiction poetry and visual art. When he was eight years old, Hendrix, unable to afford a guitar, strummed out rhythms on a broom. Eventually, he graduated to a fabricated substitute made from a cigar box, followed by a ukulele, and finally an acoustic guitar that was purchased by his father.

By the late 1950s, Hendrix had begun playing with local bands in Seattle. While a teenager, he played along with recordings by blues artists such as Elmore James and John Lee Hooker. After a twenty-six-month stint in 1961 and 1962 with the 101st Airborne Division, Hendrix entered the Nashville rhythm-and-blues scene with bassist Billy Cox. For the next three years, Hendrix performed under the name Jimi James, backing up such acts as Little Richard, Jackie Wilson, Ike and Tina Turner, and the Isley Brothers.

In 1964, Hendrix moved to New York City, where he performed in various Greenwich Village clubs. While in New York, he formed the group Jimi James and the Blue Flames. After being discovered by producer and manager Chas Chandler, the former bassist with the Animals, Hendrix was urged to leave for England. Arriving in England in 1966, Hendrix, along with bassist Noel Redding and drummer Mitch Mitchell, formed the Jimi Hendrix Experience. In 1967, after touring Europe, the trio hit the charts with a cover version of the Leaves song "Hey Joe." In the same year, the group released the groundbreaking album *Are You Experienced?*

In 1968, the Experience recorded *Axis Bold as Love*, which led to extensive touring in the United States and Europe. On the Experience's next LP, *Electric Ladyland*, Hendrix sought to expand the group's trio-based sound. A double record, *Electric Ladyland* featured numerous guest artists, such as keyboardists Steve Winwood and Al Kooper, saxophonist Freddie Smith, and conga player Larry Faucette. The record also contained "All Along the Watchtower," a song written by Hendrix's musical and poetic idol, Bob Dylan.

After the Experience broke up in 1969, Hendrix played the Woodstock Music and Arts Festival with the Gypsy Sons and Rainbows, featuring bassist Billy Cox. Along with drummer Buddy Miles, Hendrix and Cox formed the Band of Gypsys, and in 1970 the group released an album under the same title. Months later, Mitchell replaced Miles on drums. In August 1970, the Mitchell-Cox lineup played behind Hendrix at his last major performance at the Isle of Wight Festival in England. On September 18, 1970, Hendrix died of an overdose of sleeping pills in a hotel room in England. Despite his short career, Hendrix established himself as a major figure in pop music history. In 1992, Hendrix was inducted into the Rock and Roll Hall of Fame.

WHITNEY HOUSTON (1963–)

Singer, Actress. A multiple Grammy Award winner whose face has graced the covers of magazines from *Glamour* to *Cosmopolitan*, Whitney Houston emerged as one of the most vibrant popular music talents during the 1980s. A talented singer, model, and actress, Houston dominated the pop charts into the 1990s. Her biggest successes were associated with two motion pictures in which she had major roles.

Born on August 9, 1963, Houston grew up in East Orange, New Jersey. As a member of the New Hope Baptist Choir, she made her singing debut at age eleven. Later, Houston appeared as a backup singer on numerous recordings featuring her mother, Cissy Houston, and her cousin, Dionne Warwick. Despite her success as a fashion model, Houston found the profession "degrading," and quit in order to pursue a career in music. She subsequently served as a backup singer for such performers as Chaka Khan, Lou Rawls, and the Neville Brothers.

By the time she was nineteen, Houston had received several recording contract offers. In 1985, she released her debut album on the Arista label, *Whitney Houston*, which produced four hits: "Saving All My Love for You," which won the Grammy for best female pop performance; "You Give Good Love"; "How Will I Know," which earned an MTV Video Music Award for best female video; and "The Greatest Love of All." The album won seven American Music Awards, a feat she would duplicate in 1994. Houston's second LP, *Whitney*, appeared in 1987 and also led to a number of hits, including "I Wanna Dance with Somebody," "Didn't We Almost Have It All," "So Emotional," "Where Do Broken Hearts Go?" and "Love Will Save the Day." The album received four American Music Awards. Following the success of her second record, Houston released *One Moment in Time* (1988) and the slickly produced *I'm Your Baby Tonight* (1990).

In 1992, Houston married singer Bobby Brown and made her acting debut in the film *The Bodyguard*, costarring Kevin Costner. The first single from the soundtrack, a cover of Dolly Parton's "I Will Always Love You," spent fourteen straight weeks on top of the pop singles chart. According to statistics from *Billboard* magazine, Houston set a record for the most time spent at the top of the charts, edging out Boyz II Men's "End of the Road" (thirteen weeks) and Elvis Presley's "Don't Be Cruel"

Singer Whitney Houston, Backstage, American Music Awards, Los Angeles, 1994. *For the soundtrack to* The Bodyguard, *a movie in which she also had a leading role, Houston won seven American Music Awards and three Grammy Awards. More than 44 million copies of the soundtrack have been sold, making it the best-selling soundtrack of all time.* AP PHOTO/DOUGLAS PIZAC

(eleven weeks). Her vocal performance on the soundtrack won her seven American Music Awards, including the 1994 Award of Merit; four Grammy Awards, including record of the year, album of the year, and best female pop performance; two Soul Train Music Awards, including the Sammy Davis Jr. Entertainer of the Year Award and the Female Rhythm and Blues Single Award for "I Will Always Love You;" four NAACP Image Awards; and the National Association of Black-owned Broadcasters' Lifetime Achievement Award. Later in the year, AT&T signed Houston as the spokesperson for the corporation's "True Voice" campaign; Houston sang in two of the company's commercials.

Houston costarred with Angela Bassett, Lela Rochon, and Loretta Devine in the 1995 film adaption of Terry McMillan's novel *Waiting to Exhale*. A box-office winner, the movie's soundtrack was written by producer Babyface and featured, in addition to Houston, such performers as Aretha Franklin and Toni Braxton. Houston sang the very successful first single, "Exhale (Shoop Shoop)." Her next film, *The Preacher's Wife* (1996), allowed Houston to return to her gospel roots. Her next album, *My Love is Your Love*, was released in the fall of 1999.

In 2000, Houston released *Whitney: The Greatest Hits*. A few weeks later, she was charged with marijuana possession stemming from an incident earlier in the year. In March 2001, the charges against her were dropped. In August 2001, Houston signed a multimillion-dollar contract with Arista Records. Her first album for Arista, *Love, Whitney*, came out a few months later. Houston filed for divorce from Bobby Brown in 2006.

In 2003, Houston released a Christmas album, *One Wish: The Holiday Album*. Her next album, *I Look to You*, was released in 2009. Sales for Houston's 2009 album were weak, and her subsequent tour was marred by poor performances, leading many to believe that her years of hard living had claimed her career.

JENNIFER HUDSON (1981–)

Singer, Actress. Jennifer Hudson was born in Chicago on September 12, 1981. She performed as a youth in her

Jennifer Hudson, performing with Smokey Robinson at the White House, February 2010. *A number of celebrated entertainers were invited to the White House during Black History month in 2010 for "In Performance at the White House: A Celebration of Music from the Civil Rights Movement." Award-winning singer and actress Jennifer Hudson was among the honored participants.* BROOKS KRAFT/CORBIS

local church with the support and encouragement of her grandmother, Julia Hudson. After graduating from high school, Hudson worked in a fast-food restaurant while performing in a professional production of the musical *Big River* in Chicago. In 2002, she was hired as an entertainer on the *Disney Wonder* cruise ship.

In 2004, Hudson decided to try out for the *American Idol* program and made it to the top twelve. Although she finished in seventh place, her performances on the show brought her to the attention of fans and producers in the United States and Europe, which led to many opportunities. In 2005, she was cast as Effie White in the film *Dreamgirls*, which appeared in theaters in 2006. Her electrifying dramatic and musical performances, especially her rendition of the song, "And I'm Telling You I'm Not Going," led to a string of awards, including the Golden Globe Award in 2006 and an Oscar in 2007, both for best supporting actress. She also received a 2007 Image Award from the NAACP.

In 2008, Hudson appeared in supporting roles in the popular films *Sex and the City* and *The Secret Life of Bees.* That year, she also released her first album, *Jennifer Hudson.* The shocking 2008 murders of Hudson's mother, brother, and nephew stunned the country and drew millions to her in support. Hudson remained admirably composed through the ordeal and continues to record and plan for future projects.

PHYLLIS HYMAN (1949–1995)

Singer. Phyllis Hyman was a singer of the heart, appreciated by connoisseurs of both romantic jazz and rhythm and blues. She was born in Philadelphia on July 6, 1949, and raised in Pittsburgh. An elementary school teacher noticed and nurtured her vocal talents, but she grew up poor and prepared for a career as a legal secretary.

Nevertheless, Hyman reached New York in her early twenties and soon began working as a vocalist. By 1974, she formed her own band, Phyllis Hyman and the PH Factor, and became a regular at the tony Upper West Side clubs Rust Brown's and Mikell's. In 1976, she was discovered by percussionist and producer Norman Connors and became a featured performer on his album *You Are My Starship*, singing the ballad "Betcha by Golly Wow." One of the song's writers, Linda Creed, became Hyman's longtime friend.

Hyman signed with the record label Arista in 1977. One of her first releases, *Somewhere in My Lifetime* (1978), was produced by vocal star Barry Manilow and rose high in the rhythm-and-blues charts. Her signature hit was the ballad "You Know How to Love Me." Her marriage to manager Larry Alexander in the late 1970s ended in divorce.

Hyman's career took an upswing in the late 1970s when she joined the Broadway cast of *Sophisticated Ladies*, a revue of Duke Ellington's music. She sang in the show for three years and earned a Tony nomination for her performance in 1981. Her rendition of "In a Sentimental Mood" is on the original cast album. In 1986, Hyman moved to the Philadelphia International label and made some of her best recordings. *Living All Alone* (1986) featured her signature lush, sad romantic ballads, including a new song written by Creed. Hyman began writing songs that reflected her life story, which is why her songs were so emotionally true and compelling. The 1991 album *Prime of My Life* included songs with such titles as "It's Not about You (It's about Me)," "It Takes Two," and "Why Not Me?"

In 1988, she appeared in the Spike Lee film *School Daze*. She also toured the United States, Europe, and Japan in the late 1980s with a successful show that played the Harlem Apollo, Oakland's Paramount, and the Fox Theatre in St. Louis. She was a stunning performer, tall, and dressed in African-style clothing.

On talk shows, Hyman was open about her lifelong search for love and admitted to being lonely. When Creed died in 1986 from breast cancer, it was rumored that Hyman was struggling with alcohol and drugs. On June 30, 1995, shortly before a performance at the Apollo, she died from an overdose of pills. Five albums were released after her death, including *We Love You Phyllis: A Tribute to Phyllis Hyman* (1998), featuring Norman Connors and Jean Carne.

ICE CUBE (1969–)

Rapper, Actor. Behind his often misogynistic and racist gangster image, rapper and actor Ice Cube is a serious artist and a staunch spokesperson for black nationalism.

Ice Cube looks upon his music as a means of launching a "mental revolution" in order to awaken African American youth to the value of education and the creation of private African American economic enterprises.

Born Oshea Jackson in 1969, Ice Cube grew up in South Central Los Angeles. While in the ninth grade, Jackson wrote his first rhyme in typing class. Prompted by his parents to pursue an education after high school, he attended a one-year drafting course at the Phoenix Institute in 1988. The following year, Ice Cube achieved great commercial success as a member of N.W.A. (Niggaz With Attitude). As one of the group's founding members, along with Dr. Dre and Eazy-E, Ice Cube wrote or co-wrote most of the material for N.W.A.'s first two albums. Ice Cube's authoritative baritone won him a legion of fans for his N.W.A. rap anthem "Gangsta Gangsta." He also scripted much of Eazy-E's first solo work, *Eazy-Duz-It*, followed by N.W.A.'s platinum *Straight Outta Compton*, which included the controversial single "F___tha Police."

Though he still worked sporadically with Dr. Dre after leaving N.W.A., Ice Cube's 1990 solo album, *AmeriKKKa's Most Wanted*, was produced with Public Enemy's Chuck D. and the Bomb Squad. The recording went gold within three months. He then formed Street Knowledge, a record production company, and produced female rapper Yo Yo's *Make Way for the Motherlode*, released in 1991.

Ice Cube made his acting debut in John Singleton's 1991 film *Boyz N the Hood*. He later starred in a number of films, including *Trespass* (1992) with Ice-T; Singleton's *Higher Learning* (1994); the comedy *Friday* (1995), which he helped write and produce; Charles Burnett's 1995 film *The Glass Shield*; *Anaconda* (1997); *I Got the Hook Up* (1997); *The Players Club* (1998); *Three Kings* (1999); and *Ghost of Mars* (2001). Ice Cube returned to comedy in 2000 with a sequel to his 1995 hit *Friday*, titled *Next Friday*, and another movie in the series, *Friday after Next*, in 2002.

Having recorded his own *Kill at Will* and *Death Certificate* in 1991, Ice Cube remained active in Yo Yo's career, serving as executive producer of her *Black Pearl* in 1992. He also worked with other artists, directing videos for blues-rock performer Ian Moore in 1993. Ice Cube focused on his own music as well, releasing *The Predator* in 1992; the recording debuted at number one on *Billboard*'s pop and rhythm-and-blues charts, the first recording to do so since Stevie Wonder's *Songs in the Key of Life* in 1976. In 1992, Ice Cube joined the lineup of Lollapalooza II, an annual traveling rock festival. His 1993 album, *Lethal Injection*, featured the smash single "It Was a Good Day." Ice Cube also issued *Bootlegs & B-Sides* (1994), and in 1995 he contributed to the soundtrack for the film *Street Fighter*.

In 1998, Ice Cube released volume one of his hard-hitting best seller *War and Peace*, which featured collaborations with such artists as a Mr. Short Khop, Mack Ten, and Korn. The second volume of *War and Peace* hit the stands in 2000. That same year, Ice Cube received a Lifetime Achievement Award at the *Source* Hip-Hop Music Awards. In 2006, he released his eighth solo album, *Laugh Now, Cry Later*, on his Da Lench Mob Records label. The album featured the creative work of Lil Jon and Scott Storch, who produced the lead single "Why We Thugs."

Ice Cube has also continued to work in film and television. He has appeared in the movies *Barbershop* (2002), *Barbershop 2: Back to Business* (2004), *Are We There Yet?* (2005), *First Sunday* (2008), and *The Longshots* (2008), among other projects. He has also continued to record music, releasing *Raw Footage* in 2008.

ICE-T (1958–)

Rapper, Singer, Actor. With his image as a streetwise hustler, Ice-T became one of the West Coast's first major rap artists, laying down a style that would later be adopted by "gangsta" rappers such as Dr. Dre and Snoop Doggy Dogg. Ice-T, who became one of the first rappers to have warning labels placed on his albums, also set the tone for much of the controversy that would follow rap music during the 1990s and into the new millennium.

Born Tracey Morrow in Newark, New Jersey, on February 14, 1958, Ice -T moved to Los Angeles following the deaths of both his parents when he was a child. He attended Crenshaw High School, and took the name Ice-T after reading the books of Iceberg Slim, a former pimp. During the 1980s, Ice-T made several recordings and had minor roles in the films *Breakin'* (1984), *Breakin' 2: Electric Boogaloo* (1984), and *Rappin'* (1985).

In 1987, Ice-T signed a major-label recording contract with Sire Records. He released *Rhyme Pays* the same year. Along with the title track to the movie *Colors* (1988), the album's portrayal of ghetto life, violence, and criminal activity brought Ice-T national attention. He followed with *Power* (1988) and *The Iceberg/Freedom of Speech . . . Just Watch What You Say* (1989). Ice-T's 1991 release, *O.G. Original Gangster*, proved to be a seminal record in the history of gangsta rap. The album included "New Jack Hustler," which became the title track of the film *New Jack City* (1991), in which Ice-T starred with Wesley Snipes.

O.G. Original Gangster also featured the debut of Ice-T's rap/metal band Body Count, which released a full-length album, *Body Count*, in 1992. The album included the notorious song "Cop Killer," which sparked protests from police and politicians, and earned Ice-T a place on the FBI's national threat list. Finally, in response to threats of boycotts of stores selling the album, Sire pulled the record and reissued it without the controversial song.

The controversy surrounding Ice-T gradually began to fade. He continued to record solo rap albums, including *Home Invasion* (1993), *The Last Temptation of Ice* (1995), *Cold as Ever* (1996), *VI: Return of the Real* (1996), *Seventh Deadly Sin* (1999), and *Gangsta Rap* (2006). He also found further success in acting.

Ice-T has made numerous television appearances. In addition to a starring role on the series *Law & Order: Special Victims Unit*, he has also appeared as the host of *Being Tough*. Ice-T's film and television credits include *Trespass* (1992), *Surviving the Game* (1994), *Johnny Mnemonic* (1995), *Rhyme and Reason* (1997), *Mean Guns* (1997), *Body Count* (1997), *Crazy Six* (1998), *Urban Menace* (1999), *The Wrecking Crew* (1999), *Leprechaun in the Hood* (1999), *Judgment Day* (1999), *Sonic Impact* (2000), *Ablaze* (2000), *Kept* (2001), *Gangland* (2001), and *Ice-T's Rap School* (2006), among other projects.

JANET JACKSON (1966–)

Singer, Actress. Janet Jackson is a tremendously energetic performer, whose singing and dance styles have reached immense popularity around the world. She is the youngest and one of the most successful of a family of highly talented performers that included her brother Michael, the King of Pop. In the 1990s, Janet emerged from his shadow and became a full-fledged sex symbol and role model.

Born on May 16, 1966, in Gary, Indiana, Janet Jackson began performing with her brothers at age six, doing impressions of famous stars, such as Mae West and Cher. She made her professional singing debut at one of the Jackson Five's shows at the MGM Grand Hotel in Las Vegas. Before she was ten years old, Jackson was spotted by television producer Norman Lear, resulting in her appearances on such television shows as *Good Times*, *Different Strokes*, and *Fame*.

In 1982, Jackson's debut album for the AM label, *Janet Jackson*, produced only a few minor hits. Teamed with producers Jimmy Jam and Terry Lewis, Jackson released a more commercially successful LP, *Dream Street*, in 1984. Her 1986 release, *Control*, scored six hit singles: "What Have You Done for Me Lately," "Nasty," "When I Think of You," "Control," "Let's Wait Awhile," and "Pleasure Principle." Under the direction of Jam and Lewis, Jackson released the quadruple-platinum, dance-oriented album *Janet Jackson's Rhythm Nation 1814* in 1989. Among the record's numerous singles were "Miss You Much," "Come Back to Me," and "Black Cat."

After an extensive world tour in 1990, Jackson left the AM label for Virgin Records in 1991. Her four-album contract was worth an estimated $80 million, with $50 million guaranteed up front. Two years later, she starred alongside Tupac Shakur in John Singleton's *Poetic Justice*. Jackson played a soul-searching hairdresser who also wrote poetry; Maya Angelou, who was featured in the film, provided the poems Jackson's character read.

In 1994, Jackson released *janet*, which was a critical and commercial success. The song "Any Time, Any Place" earned Jackson her fourteenth gold single, the most by any female solo artist other than Aretha Franklin. The following year, Jackson collaborated with her brother Michael on the song "Scream." The visually stunning video associated with the single was one of the most expensive ever made. Later in 1995, her *Design of a Decade: 1986/1996*, a greatest-hits album, made a splashy debut. She also contributed a song to the soundtrack for the 1994 film *Ready to Wear*. Her follow-up album to *janet*, *The Velvet Rope* (1997), debuted at the number-one position on the *Billboard* 200 chart, a testament to her star power.

In 2000, Jackson's "secret husband" of nine years, René Elizondo, made their marriage public by filing for divorce. In April 2001, Jackson's seventh album, *All for You*, was released to critical success. The album won her an American Music Award in the favorite pop/rock female artist category, as well as a Grammy for best dance recording for "All for You."

Between 1986 and 1992, Jackson garnered four *Billboard* Awards, seven American Music Awards, two MTV Video Music Awards, one Grammy Award, three Soul Train Awards, a BMI Pop Award, and the 1992 Sammy Davis Jr. Award for entertainer of the year. In 1990, she acquired a star on Hollywood Walk of Fame. In 1992, the NAACP gave her its Chairman's Award. Three years later, she received an *Essence* Award. Jackson is also the recipient of the Lena Horne Award for outstanding career achievements (1997). In 2001, Jackson received a special award at the American Music Awards for her outstanding musical contribution. She also received a *Billboard* Artist Achievement Award that year for her perseverance in the music industry. Jackson released another album in 2004, *Damita Jo*, followed by *20 Y.O.* in 2006 and *Discipline* in 2008.

Jackson continues to perform live around the world, as well as in television, film, and videos. She appeared opposite Eddie Murphy in *Nutty Professor II: The Klumps* in 2000. She also starred in Tyler Perry's 2007 film *Why Did I Get Married?*, as well as the 2010 sequel, *Why Did I Get Married Too?*

MICHAEL JACKSON (1958–2009)

Singer, Composer, Dancer. From child singing star with the Jackson Five to his success as a solo performer in the

1980s, Michael Jackson amassed the largest following of any African American singer in the history of popular music. Jackson's audience transcended the boundaries of nations and bridged the gaps brought about by generational differences.

The fifth of nine children, Michael Jackson was born on August 29, 1958, in Gary, Indiana. As a child, Michael, along with his brothers Tito, Jermaine, Jackie, and Marlon, comprised the Jackson Five. Under the tutelage of their father, Joe, the five boys learned to sing and dance. On weekends the family group traveled hundreds of miles to perform at amateur contests and benefit concerts.

After two years on the road, the group landed an audition with Motown Records. After signing with the label in 1969, the Jackson Five hit the charts with the number-one hit "I Want You Back," a song arranged and produced by Berry Gordy Jr. On recordings and television shows, Michael's wholesome image and lead vocals attracted fans from every racial and age group. During the group's six-year stay at Motown, the Jackson Five scored thirteen consecutive top-twenty singles, including "ABC," "The Love You Save," and "I'll Be There."

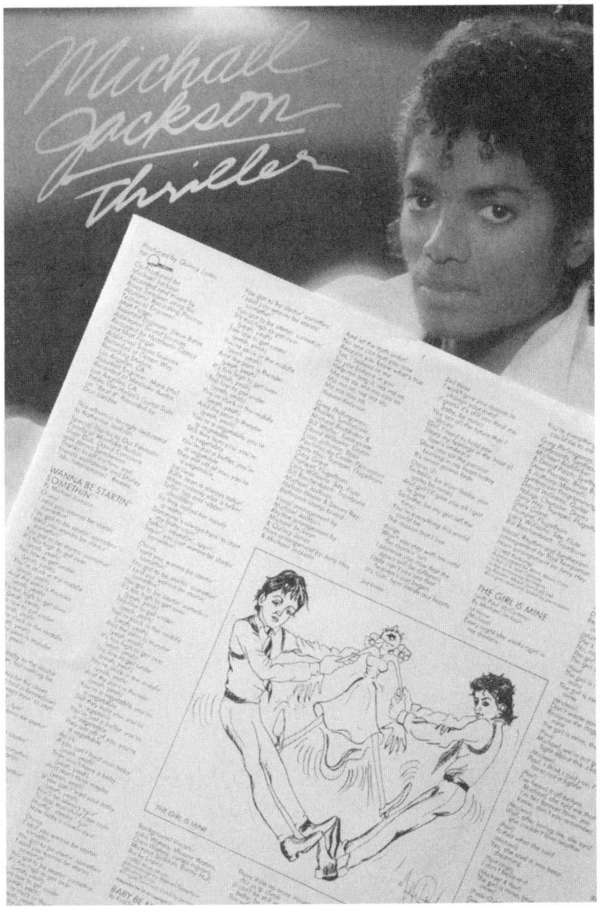

Michael Jackson,* Thriller *Album Cover and Lyrics Insert. *Released in 1982, Jackson's* Thriller *eventually became the top-selling album of all time. Seven of the album's nine tracks became hit singles in the United States.* CAROLYN JENKINS/ALAMY

In 1971, while still the lead vocalist for the Jackson Five, Michael signed a separate contract with Motown, formalizing a solo career that produced the hits "Got to Be There" in 1971, "Ben" in 1972, and "Just a Little Bit of You" in 1975. When cast in the role of the scarecrow in the 1975 Motown film *The Wiz*, Jackson met producer Quincy Jones, who later collaborated with him to record the 1979 hit *Off the Wall* on the Epic label. Two years later, guided by the production skills of Jones, Jackson recorded the biggest-selling album of all time, *Thriller*. The seven hit singles included "Beat It," "Billie Jean," "Wanna Be Startin' Something," and the title track, which featured a voiceover by cult horror figure Vincent Price. The landmark video for the song was a fourteen-minute film directed by John Landis and starring Jackson as a dancing werewolf, with special effects that rivaled any full-length feature film.

In 1985, Jackson cowrote the song "We Are the World" for the USA for Africa famine-relief fund. After joining Jones to produce *Bad* in 1987, Jackson led the most commercially successful tour in history. Four years later, Jackson released *Dangerous*, which included the hit single "Black or White."

In 1993, Jackson announced that the progressive lightening of his skin was the result of a skin disorder known as vitiligo and not intentional bleaching. The public declaration was one of many Jackson would find himself making about various topics in the ensuing years. Scandal-ridden, Jackson hit a backslide in his career following allegations of child molestation, charges that were later dropped, and the revelation of an addiction to pain medication brought about by poor health.

Coming on the heels of such devastating disclosures, the double album *HIStory: Past, Present, and Future, Book I* (1995) featured hits from the past, as well as new works. Compared to his previous recordings, sales were disappointing, and the recording was not considered a commercial success. Fan loyalty to the gifted musician, however, drove some of the new songs into chart contention, including "The Earth Song," the controversial "They Don't Care About Us," and the lilting ballad "You Are Not Alone." The compilation also gave Jackson a chance to work with his sister Janet when the two collaborated on the duet "Scream," the first single to be released. The ensuing video for "Scream" cost seven million dollars, making it one of the most expensive and eye-catching videos ever produced. Jackson's follow-up to *HIStory*, *Blood on the Dance Floor*, was released in 1997. It included both new material and remixed recordings.

In 2001, Jackson released *Invincible*, his first completely original album since 1992's *Dangerous*. The Jackson Five reunited in 2001 for a thirtieth-anniversary tribute to Michael Jackson. Also appearing on the show to honor Jackson were music greats Ray Charles, guitarist Slash, and Quincy Jones.

Jackson made headlines in 1994 when he married Lisa Marie Presley, daughter of the late rock legend Elvis Presley. The marriage of Jackson and Presley was considered highly unusual, and many critics dismissed it as a publicity stunt. On June 14, 1995, Jackson and Presley were interviewed by Diane Sawyer on ABC's *Prime Time Live*. During the interview, the two insisted they were deeply in love and planned to eventually have children. However, in January 1996, Presley announced that she and Jackson were divorcing. Later that year, Jackson married his longtime friend Debbie Rowe. A son was born to them in early 1997, followed by a daughter in the spring of 1998.

Jackson's business ventures had more staying power. An astute businessman, he entered into a $600 million joint-publishing deal with Sony in 1995. The deal combined Sony's music-publishing division with Jackson's ATV music catalog, which owned the rights to the Beatles' entire collection of work.

More importantly, Jackson continued to garner acclaim, despite his setbacks. In 1993, he received three American Music Awards, including the first-ever International Artist Award, and was recognized at the World Music Awards ceremony in Monte Carlo. In addition, he received special Grammy honors that year. Two years later, he won three MTV Video Awards. Jackson released the album *Invincible* in 2001. The following year, he was honored with an Artist of the Century Award at the American Music Awards.

While many argue that his work was uneven, his contributions to modern pop have been enormous. Indeed, Jackson redefined stardom for the video era. In the fall of 2006, Raymone Bain, Jackson's press agent, announced that Jackson had sold over 750 million albums and singles worldwide, making Jackson one of the best-selling music artists of all time. Along with the adulation came allegations of child molestation. The resulting trial in 2005 took a toll on Jackson's popularity and drew more scrutiny to his unconventional parenting of his two children.

On June 25, 2009, Jackson was pronounced dead at the UCLA Medical Center as a result of cardiac arrest. True to the life he led, Jackson, even in death, was surrounded by cameras and speculation over the possibility of a wrongful death when his personal physician, Dr. Conrad Robert Murray, was accused of administering opiate drugs to Jackson the day he died.

ETTA JAMES (1938–)

Singer. Born Jamesetta Hawkins on January 25, 1938, Etta James was a child prodigy, singing gospel music on the radio in Los Angeles by the time she was five years old. As a teenager in 1950, she formed a singing group called the Creolettes with two friends. The trio was discovered by rhythm-and-blues star Johnny Otis in 1954. Otis changed the group's name to the Peaches and took the girls on the road with him. The Peaches recorded their first song, "Roll with Me, Henry," which topped the charts in 1955, along with "Good Rocking Daddy." The success of that record led to a tour with rock-and-roll star Little Richard and studio backup-vocal jobs with Marvin Gaye, Minnie Riperton, and Chuck Berry. James signed with Chess and released ten chart-making hits between 1960 and 1963, including "At Last," "Trust in Me," and "Something's Got a Hold on Me." In 1967, she traveled to the famous studio at Muscle Shoals, Alabama, where she recorded many of her biggest hits, including "I'd Rather Go Blind" and "Tell Mama."

Although successful on the rhythm-and-blues charts, James did not manage to catch on with wider audiences in the 1960s. She continued to record with moderate success for Chess through 1975 in the gray zone between blues, soul, rhythm and blues, and rock. After a recording lapse lasting for much of the 1980s, she released *The Seven Year Itch* for Island Records in 1988. Despite her inability to establish herself as a mainstream star, James was a major influence on many singers who did attain that status, including Diana Ross and Janis Joplin.

In 1993, James was inducted into the Rock and Roll Hall of Fame. In 1995, she published her autobiography, *Rage to Survive: The Etta James Story*, written with David Ritz. She continued to put out albums throughout the 1990s and early 2000s, including *Stickin' to My Guns* (1990), *The Right Time* (1992), *Respect Yourself* (1997), *The Heart of a Woman* (1999), *Blue Gardenia* (2001), *Let's Roll* (2003), *Blues to the Bone* (2004), *The Definitive Collection* (2006), and *All the Way* (2006).

JAY-Z (1969–)

Rapper, Producer, Entrepreneur. Jay-Z was born Shawn Corey Carter on December 4, 1969, in Brooklyn, New York. He is a hip-hop recording artist and a former president and CEO of Def Jam and Roc-A-Fella Records. In addition, he is part owner of the 40/40 Club and the NBA's New Jersey Nets. Jay-Z has proven to been one of the most savvy financial managers and entrepreneurs among hip-hop artists. Jay-Z was one of the founders of Roc-A-Fella Records, a hip-hop record label that also launched the careers of artists such as Beanie

Sigel, Kanye West, Memphis Bleek, Young Gunz, Freeway, and Rihanna.

From the beginning of his commercial recording career, when no major label gave him a record deal, Jay-Z created Roc-A-Fella Records as his own label. After making a deal with Priority to distribute his material, Jay-Z released his 1996 debut album, *Reasonable Doubt*. In 1997, Def Jam released Jay-Z's follow-up, *In My Lifetime, Vol. 1*, with the aid of executive producer Sean Combs. His *Vol. 2 . . . Hard Knock Life* (1998) proved to be the biggest hit of his career at the time. It was multi-platinum in the United States and sold over eight million copies worldwide. In 1999, Jay-Z released *Vol. 3 . . . Life and Times of S. Carter*. The album was successful and sold more than 5.6 million records worldwide.

Around 2000, Jay-Z decided to begin developing other artists. He and Damon Dash signed various performers, including Beanie Sigel and Freeway, and began introducing them to the public. Jay-Z next appeared on *The Dynasty: Roc La Familia*, which was intended as a compilation album to introduce these new artists, though the album had Jay-Z's name on it to strengthen market recognition. *The Blueprint*, released on September 11, 2001, is considered a hip-hop classic. The album debuted at number one, selling more than 450,000 copies in its first week. The success of the album was overshadowed by the terrorist attacks that occurred the same day of its release. Eminem was the only guest artist on the album, producing and rapping on the single "Renegade." Four of the thirteen tracks on the album were produced by Kanye West.

Jay-Z's next solo album was 2002's *The Blueprint 2: The Gift & the Curse*, a double album. It was reissued in a single-disc version, *The Blueprint 2.1*, in 2003, with half of the tracks from the original. Two hit singles emerged from the album, "Excuse Me Miss" and "Bonnie and Clyde," featuring Jay-Z's girlfriend of four years, Beyoncé Knowles, whom he married in 2008. In 2003, Jay-Z released *The Black Album*, which was multiplatinum. His subsequent albums include *Kingdom Come* (2006), *American Gangster* (2007), and *The Blueprint 3* (2009).

WYCLEF JEAN (1972–)

Singer, Producer, Activist. Neluset Wyclef Jean, whose Haitian Creole name is pronounced *wigh-clef*, was born in Haiti on October 17, 1972. Jean, the son of a Nazarene pastor, was brought up in a deeply religious family. The family moved from Haiti to Brooklyn, New York, while Jean was a young child. They moved again not long afterward to northern New Jersey.

Jean grew attracted to hip-hop as a teenager and considered the possibilities of blending the genre with his Caribbean influences. He formed a three-member group known as the Fugees (The Refugee Camp), which consisted of his cousin Prakazrel "Pras" Michel and Lauryn Hill. The Fugees signed with Ruffhouse Records and released *Blunted on Reality*, their debut, in 1994. The double-platinum album showcased their unique approach to sampling, singing, and production. It also gave them an underground presence with the "Vocab" and "Nappy Heads (Mona Lisa)." Jean married fashion designer Marie Claudinette in 2004.

Musician Wyclef Jean, Nobel Peace Prize Concert, Oslo, Norway, 2009. *Haitian American recording artist and producer Wyclef Jean performs at a concert honoring Nobel Peace Prize winner Barack Obama.* PATRICK VAN KATWIJK/PICTURE ALLIANCE/DPA/PHOTOSHOT

Honing in on their apparent strengths, the Fugees returned in 1996 with *The Score*, which sold over eighteen million copies and became one of the best-selling hip-hop albums in history. Instead of merely sampling a section of a song, the trio performed their renditions of classics in a way that was unmistakably theirs. Songs such as the Delfonics' "Ready or Not Here I Come (Can't Hide from Love)" got an atmospheric, brooding update in the Fugees' version, "Ready or Not." Bob Marley and the Wailers' "No Woman, No Cry" was also retooled, as was the album's biggest hit, "Killing Me Softly with His Song," by Roberta Flack. The album won two 1997

Grammy Awards for best R&B vocal performance by a duo or group and best rap album.

Jean embarked on a solo career in 1997 with *Wyclef Jean Presents the Carnival, Featuring Refugee Allstars*, also known as *The Carnival*. Although a solo venture, the album featured guest appearances by Jean's siblings Melky Sedeck and Farel Sedeck Guerschom Jean, as well as Pras and Lauryn Hill. Other notables included Celia Cruz and the Neville Brothers. Jean scored two hits with the album, "Gone Till November" (recorded with the New York Philharmonic Orchestra) and "We Trying to Stay Alive" (adapted from the Bee Gees' "Stayin' Alive").

In 2000, Jean expanded his diverse artistic scope through collaborations in *The Ecleftic: 2 Sides II a Book*, his second solo album. Its guests included Kenny Rogers, the Rock, Mary J. Blige, Youssou N'Dour, and Earth, Wind, and Fire. The album sold well and produced the hit "911," featuring Blige. Jean's ties to his homeland of Haiti always kept philanthropy at the forefront of his consciousness. He contributed his rendition of Bob Marley's "Redemption Song" to the 9/11 benefit concert, *America: A Tribute to Heroes*.

Jean's third album, *Masquerade*, was released in 2002 and featured the singles "Masquerade" and "Two Wrongs." Now respected for his musicianship as a guitarist and producing talent, as well as for his rapping and singing, he released his fourth album, *The Preacher's Son*, in 2003. Though not as successful in sales as previous albums, it boasted the same array of big names for collaborations. Rah Digga, Patti LaBelle, and Redman made guests appearances, along with guitar hero Carlos Santana. A standout on the album was the hit "Party to Damascus." Wyclef produced most of the album, which solidified his signature technique of mixing live instrumentation with sampling.

Jean created the nongovernmental organization Yéle Haiti in 2004 to provide humanitarian aid and other assistance to the Haitian diaspora. Jean continued to delve deeper into his Caribbean roots with each album after *The Preacher's Son*, a trend that became more apparent with his fifth album, *Sak Pasé Presents Wyclef Jean: Welcome to Haiti, Creole 101*, released in 2004.

Jean lent his talents to soundtracks as well. He covered Credence Clearwater Revival's "Fortunate Son" for the 2004 remake of *The Manchurian Candidate*. Jean also penned "Million Voices" for the 2004 film *Hotel Rwanda*. Mindful of projects that shed light on conditions in his homeland, as well as other third-world countries, Jean contributed songs for *The Agronomist*, a 2003 documentary about Haitian activist and radio personality Jean Dominique. With longtime collaborator and producer Jerry "Wonder" Duplessis, Jean also composed the score for the 2006 documentary *Ghosts of Cité Soleil*.

After the Fugees reunited for a performance in "*Dave Chappelle's Block Party* (2006), fans hoped for a new Fugees album. Those hopes were dashed when Pras and Wyclef indicated that Lauryn Hill remained opposed to the group collective. In 2007, Wyclef released *Carnival Vol. II: Memoirs of an Immigrant* as a sequel to his first solo album, *The Carnival*. Having the same multicultural concept as the earlier album, the second included a song called "Sweetest Girl (Dollar Bill)," featuring Akon and Lil Wayne. Paul Simon was also featured in a song called "Fast Car." Makers of the video game *Burnout Paradise* collaborated on the song's accompanying video.

Jean delved into the use of alter egos when he released *From the Hut, to the Projects, to the Mansion* in 2009. It tells the story of Jean's alter ego, Toussaint St. Jean, a character based on the Haitian revolutionary Toussaint Louverture. Although the album boasts seventeen tracks, it is considered an EP. Guests include Timbaland, Eve, Cyndi Lauper, and Lil' Kim.

When an earthquake rocked Haiti in 2010, Raymond Alcide Joseph, Jean's uncle and Haitian ambassador to the United States, came to prominence as a spokesman for the country. After the earthquake, Jean called on the public to donate to his foundation's Yéle Haiti Earthquake Fund. Although ABC News discovered e-mail spammers posing as Jean to siphon money from potential donors, Jean continues to work for the betterment and rehabilitation of Haiti, bringing a worldwide audience to his cause.

QUINCY JONES (1933–)

Trumpeter, Composer, Arranger, Producer. Composer, arranger, and producer Quincy Jones was born on March 14, 1933, in Chicago. At age ten, he moved to Bremerton, Washington. As a member of Bump Blackwell's Junior Orchestra, Jones performed at local Seattle social functions. In 1949, Jones played third trumpet in Lionel Hampton's band in Seattle nightclubs. After befriending jazz bassist Oscar Pettiford, Jones established himself as an able musician and arranger.

From 1950 to 1953, Jones became a regular member of Hampton's band, and he subsequently toured the United States and Europe with Hampton. During the mid-1950s, Jones began to record jazz records under his own name. In 1956, he toured the Middle East and South America with the U.S. State Department Band headed by Dizzy Gillespie.

In 1961, Jones was appointed musical director at Mercury Records, where he began producing popular music, including Leslie Gore's 1963 hit "It's My Party." Jones's growing prestige at Mercury led to his promotion to vice president of the company, marking the first time an African American had been placed in an executive position at a major label. During this time, Jones also began to write and record film scores. He composed the score for the 1967 movie *In the Heat of the Night*. He also wrote the score for the television miniseries *Roots* (1977), based on the book by Alex Haley. Jones later coproduced the film adaptation of Alice Walker's *The Color Purple* (1985) with director Steven Spielberg.

After his production of the 1978 Motown-backed film *The Wiz*, Jones produced the film's star, Michael Jackson, on such recordings as *Off the Wall* (1979) and the record-breaking hit *Thriller* (1985). Jones's 1989 release, *Back on the Block*, a Grammy winner, was praised by critics and signaled Jones's continuing role in the future development of African American popular music. Two years later, Jones sat down with his old buddy Miles Davis. The musical encounter was recorded and released in 1993 as *Miles & Quincy Live at Montreux*, along with a video documentary of the same name. In 1995, Jones released his album *Q's Jook Joint*, featuring updated versions of tunes popularized in roadhouses of the post-enslavement period.

Jones is also influential in the media industry and served as chairman of Quest Broadcasting. In 1994, the group partnered with Chicago's Tribune Company to buy television stations in Atlanta and New Orleans. His joint venture with Time Warner, *VIBE* magazine, which Jones founded, was very successful. The publication covered urban music and culture and had a high readership among African Americans and Latinos. In 1990, Jones became head of Quincy Jones Entertainment, which produced the television series *The Fresh Prince of Bel-Air*.

In 1997, Jones received the WGCI-AM/FM Granville White Lifetime Achievement Award for excellence in the music industry. In 1999, he was honored with the James D. Patterson Award, which recognizes individuals who have helped to ensure the continued existence of historically black colleges and universities and the education of black students. Early in 2001, Jones sold Qwest Records to Warner Music and began concentrating full time on his television and movie production company. He also published *Q: The Autobiography of Quincy Jones* that year, the recorded version of which won a Grammy Award in 2001 for best spoken-word album. In December 2001, Jones's contributions were celebrated at the Kennedy Center Honors.

Jones's music remains popular with younger performers, as was demonstrated when rapper Ludacris sampled Jones's "Soul Bossa Nova" for his 2005 single "Number One Spot." Jones was also featured in the video. Earlier, he had performed a cameo in the 2002 comedy *Austin Powers in Goldmember*, which used "Soul Bossa Nova" on its soundtrack.

LOUIS JORDAN (1908–1975)

Singer, Alto Saxophonist, Bandleader. Louis Jordan led one of the most popular and influential bands of the 1940s. The shuffle-boogie rhythm of his jump-blues ensemble, the Tympany Five, had a profound impact on the emergence of rhythm and blues. As guitarist Chuck Berry acknowledged, "I identify myself with Louis Jordan more than any other artist." It was Jordan's swinging rhythms, theatrical stage presence, and songs about everyday life that made him a favorite among musicians and listeners throughout the 1940s.

Born in Brinkley, Arkansas, July 8, 1908, Jordan was the son of a bandleader and music teacher. He received his music education in the Brinkley public schools and the Baptist College in Little Rock. Jordan's early music career as a clarinetist included stints with the Rabbit Foot Minstrels and Ruby Williams's orchestra. Soon after moving to Philadelphia in 1932, Jordan joined Charlie Gaines's group. Sometime around 1936, he joined drummer Chick Webb's band.

After Webb's death in 1938, Jordan started his own group. Because Jordan performed for both white and black audiences, he, to use his own words, learned to "straddle the fence" by playing music ranging from blues to formal dance music. Signing with Decca Records in 1938, Jordan began a recording career which, by the early 1940s, produced a string of million-selling recordings, such as "Is You Is or Is You Ain't (My Baby)," "Choo Choo Ch'Boogie," "Saturday Night Fish Fry," and "Caledonia." Aside from working with artists such as Louis Armstrong, Bing Crosby, and Ella Fitzgerald, Jordan appeared in several films, including *Shout Sister Shout* (1949).

In the early 1950s, although failing to achieve the success he had experienced during the 1940s, Jordan fronted a big band. During the 1960s and 1970s, he continued to tour the United States, Europe, and Asia. His career came to an end in 1975 when he suffered a fatal heart attack in Los Angeles. Jordan was inducted into the Rock and Roll Hall of Fame in 1987. He was further celebrated in 1990 in the hit stage production *Five Guys Named Moe*.

R. KELLY (1967–)

Singer, Songwriter, Producer. Born on the South Side of Chicago on January 8, 1967, Robert Sylvester Kelly would come to be known as R. Kelly to the music world. As a youngster, Kelly sang in the church and attended the Kenwood Academy in Chicago's Hyde Park neighborhood. Kelly made a name for himself while still in his teens by performing under the Chicago "L" trains. The young man formed a group called MGM (Musically Gifted Men) in 1989. The group competed on the

Los Angeles *A prolific songwriter, R. Kelly has contributed hit singles for a variety of movie soundtracks, including "I Believe I Can Fly" for* Space Jam, *for which he garnered three Grammy Awards.* DR. BILLY INGRAM/WIREIMAGE/GETTY IMAGES

television talent show *Big Break* and won the $100,000 grand prize.

Kelly took his career to the next level by joining the group Public Announcement. Their debut album, *Born into the 90's*, was released in 1992. The group achieved moderate success. The ambitious Kelly embarked on a solo career the following year. His first album, *12 Play*, was released in 1993 and was a runaway success. "Bump n' Grind," the first single, was number one for a record-breaking twelve weeks on the Hot R&B singles and *Billboard* R&B singles charts. Other hits from the album, including "Sex Me" and "Your Body's Callin'," made the album go multiplatinum six times over.

Kelly achieved considerable success as a producer, starting with then-fifteen-year-old Aaliyah's 1994 debut album, *Age Ain't Nothing but a Number.* Kelly wrote the song "You Are Not Alone" for Michael Jackson's album *HIStory* during that same year. Kelly was also rumored to have married Aaliyah. The *Chicago Sun-Times* printed the marriage certificate, emphasizing that Aaliyah stated she was eighteen at the time. The marriage was quickly annulled in 1995. He released his next album, the quadruple platinum *R. Kelly*, in 1995. Its singles include "You Remind Me of Something" and his famous duet with Ronald Isley, "Down Low." Kelly married dancer Andrea Lee in 1996. Although the union produced two daughters and a son and appeared to give Kelly the stability he needed, they eventually divorced in 2009.

"I Believe I Can Fly," an inspirational song Kelly penned for the *Space Jam* movie soundtrack, won three Grammy Awards in 1997. The indefatigable Kelly released a double album called *R.* in 1998. It featured the singles "When a Woman's Fed Up" and "Half on a Baby." The album went eight times platinum. During that same year, Kelly masterminded the debut album of his new female protégé, Sparkle. The album went platinum largely from the strength of the hit "Be Careful," a Kelly and Sparkle duet. He made major contributions to soundtracks for the updated version of the film *Shaft* (2000), as well as the movies *Ali* (2001) and *Batman and Robin* (1997). Kelly and Wyclef Jean produced and wrote the soundtrack to the Eddie Murphy and Martin Lawrence movie *Life* (1999).

Kelly's *TP-2.com* was released in 2000, featuring such hits as the remix to "Fiesta" and "I Wish." Kelly and Jay-Z came out with a joint album in 2002 called *The Best of Both Worlds*. When a video surfaced in 2002 of a man rumored to be Kelly having sex with an allegedly underage girl, Kelly found himself indicted on several counts of child pornography. Because he was embroiled in legal troubles, promotion for *The Best of Both Worlds* was sluggish, and the album sold below expectations. Kelly followed in 2003 with the heavily bootlegged *Chocolate Factory*. In spite of leaks over the Internet, the album went triple platinum from the popularity of such hits as "Step in the Name of Love." The prolific Kelly celebrated his career with a greatest-hits collection titled *The R. in R&B Collection, Volume 1* later that year.

In 2004, Kelly's two-disc *Happy People/U Saved Me* featured a first disc of jovial stepping-inspired tracks. The second disc featured more gospel-oriented material. Later in 2004, Kelly teamed with Jay-Z for a highly anticipated follow-up to their *Best of Both Worlds* album, called *Unfinished Business*. The supporting tour was hobbled by a rivalry between the two.

Kelly came into 2008 with *Double Up*, his eighth studio album. The album was disappointing, but did include "I'm a Flirt (Remix)" and "Same Girl," for which Kelly collaborated with Usher. After several delays, Kelly's child-pornography case finally went to trial in 2008. The jury found Kelly not guilty on all counts. In 2009, fresh from his legal woes, Kelly decided to offer a different approach to his music by releasing his first mixtape, *The "Demo" Tape (Gangsta Grillz)*, presented by DJ Skee and DJ Drama. Another album, called *Untitled*, was released in late 2009 to lukewarm reviews. Kelly's uplifting "Sign of a Victory" was selected as the World Cup 2010 anthem. He performed it at the opening ceremony in Johannesburg, South Africa, in June 2010.

EDDIE KENDRICKS (1939–1992)

Singer. As a member of the Temptations in the 1960s, Eddie Kendricks's articulate soulful falsetto provided Motown with a number of pop music classics. Kendricks's gospel music background "enabled him to bring an unusual earnestness to the singing of love lyrics," wrote music historian David Morse. "He can be compared only with Ray Charles in his ability to take the most threadbare ballad and turn it into a dramatic and completely convincing statement."

Born on December 17, 1939, in Birmingham, Alabama, Kendricks grew up with Paul Williams, who also became a member of the Temptations. In 1956, Kendricks and Williams quit school and traveled north to become singing stars in the tradition of their idols, Clyde McPhatter and Little Willie John. In Detroit, Kendricks and Williams formed the doo-wop singing group the Primes, which performed at talent contests and house parties. In 1961, the Primes recorded the song "Mother of Mine" and the dance tune "Check Yourself" for Berry Gordy's short-lived Miracle label.

Upon the suggestion of Gordy, the Primes changed their name to the Temptations, and, after adding David Ruffin as lead vocalist, they set out to become one of the most successful groups on the Motown label. During the decade, Kendricks sang lead on several songs, including the classics "My Girl" in 1965, "Get Ready" in 1966, and "Just My Imagination (Running Away with Me)" in 1972.

In 1971, Kendricks began his pursuit of a solo career and eventually recorded two disco-influenced hits, "Keep on Truckin'" in 1973 and "Boogie Down" in 1974. Kendricks's career soon fell into decline. Unable to find material to suit his unique artistic sensibility, Kendricks switched record labels several times before reuniting with the Temptations in 1982. After the reunion, Kendricks performed with the Temptations on the Live Aid broadcast and with Ruffin on the album *Hall & Oates Live at the Apollo with David Ruffin and Eddie Kendricks* (1985). In 1987, Ruffin and Kendricks signed a contract with RCA and recorded the aptly titled LP *Ruffin and Kendricks*. Stricken by lung cancer, Kendricks died in October 1992.

ALICIA KEYS (1981–)

Singer, Songwriter, Musician. Alicia Augello-Cook was born on January 25, 1980, in Harlem to an Irish-Italian mother, Terri Augello, and a Jamaican father, Craig Cook. In 1985, Keys and a group of other girls won parts as Rudy Huxtable's sleepover guests in an episode of *The Cosby Show*. She began playing piano when she was seven, learning classical music by composers such as Beethoven, Mozart, and Chopin. She wrote her first song, "Butterflyz," when she was fourteen; the song was later recorded for her debut album.

Keys graduated from the Professional Performing Arts School, a high school in Manhattan, at sixteen. Although she was accepted to Columbia University, she decided instead to pursue a musical career. Keys signed a deal with Jermaine Dupri and his So So Def label, then distributed by Columbia Records. She wrote and recorded a song titled "Dah Dee Dah (Sexy Thing)," which appeared on the soundtrack to the 1997 blockbuster, *Men in Black*. The song was Keys's first professional recording; it was never released as a single, and her record contract with Columbia Records was ended quickly. Keys later met Clive Davis, who signed her to Arista Records, and, later, the J Records label. She recorded the songs "Rock wit U" and "Rear View Mirror," which were

Alicia Keys, World AIDS Day Charity Concert, New York City, 2009. *Keys is one of the best-selling musical artists of the early twenty-first century, with her second album,* The Diary of Alicia Keys *(2003), selling more than eight million copies worldwide. By 2010 she had won thirteen Grammy Awards along with a host of other honors.* AP PHOTO/STEPHEN CHERNIN

featured on the soundtracks to the films *Shaft* (2000) and *Dr. Dolittle 2* (2001), respectively. Keys released her debut album, *Songs in A Minor*, in 2001.

Keys performed Donny Hathaway's "Someday We'll All Be Free" at the *America: A Tribute to Heroes* televised benefit concert following the September 11, 2001, attacks. Another single from *Songs in A Minor*, "A Woman's Worth," made the top ten in the United States as well. Keys and the album won five Grammy Awards in 2002, including those for best new artist and song of the year for "Fallin'." Later in 2002, Keys released *Remixed & Unplugged in A Minor*, a reissue of *Songs in A Minor*, which includes eight remixes and versions of some of the songs on her debut album. Critical reviews of the album were mostly positive.

Keys followed up her debut in 2003 with *The Diary of Alicia Keys*, which sold eight million copies worldwide. The singles "You Don't Know My Name" and "If I Ain't Got You" both reached the top five of the *Billboard* Hot 100 chart, and another single, "Diary," entered the top ten. "If I Ain't Got You" became the first single by a female artist to remain on the sixty-three-year-old *Billboard* Hot R&B/Hip-Hop Songs chart for more than one year, surpassing Mary J. Blige's "Your Child" (forty-nine weeks). Keys became the best-selling female R&B artist of 2004.

At the 2004 MTV Video Music Awards, Keys won an award for best R&B video for "If I Ain't Got You." In 2005, she won the best R&B video award in her second year in a row for "Karma." She also won four Grammy Awards that year: best R&B album for *The Diary of Alicia Keys*, best female R&B vocal performance for "If I Ain't Got You," best R&B song for "You Don't Know My Name," and best R&B performance by a duo or group with vocals for "My Boo" with Usher.

Keys performed and taped her installment of the *MTV Unplugged* series on July 14, 2005, at the Brooklyn Academy of Music. During this live session, Keys added new arrangements to her original songs, such as "A Woman's Worth" and "Heartburn," and performed a few choice covers. Part of Keys's audience also included her guest performers; she collaborated with rappers Common and Mos Def on "Love It or Leave It Alone," reggae artist Damian Marley on "Welcome to Jamrock," and Maroon 5 lead singer Adam Levine on a cover of the Rolling Stones' 1971 "Wild Horses." In addition to a cover of "Every Little Bit Hurts," previously performed by such singers as Aretha Franklin and Brenda Holloway, Keys also premiered two new songs: "Stolen Moments," which she cowrote with producer Lamont Green, and "Unbreakable."

Known simply as *Unplugged*, the album peaked at number one on the U.S. *Billboard* 200 chart. Keys's *Unplugged* ranked as the highest debut for an *MTV Unplugged* album since Nirvana's 1994 *MTV Unplugged in New York* and became the first *Unplugged* by a female artist to debut at number one. It was nominated for four Grammy Awards and won three NAACP Image Awards.

Keys released her third studio album, *As I Am*, in 2007. It was followed by *The Element of Freedom*, in 2009. She is also pursuing an acting career, and has appeared in supporting roles in *The Nanny Diaries* (2007) and *The Secret Life of Bees* (2008).

CHAKA KHAN (1953–)

Singer. Born Yvette Marie Stevens at the Great Lakes Naval Training Station in Illinois in 1953, Chaka Khan changed her name after becoming involved with the Affro Arts Theater in Chicago. Early in her career, she sang with a number of groups, including Lyfe, Lock and Chains, Baby Huey and the Babysitters, and Ask Rufus, which shortened its name to Rufus and signed with ABC in 1973. After a modest-selling debut album, Rufus's sophomore project, *Rags to Rufus* (1974), featured Stevie

Wonders's composition "Tell Me Something Good." Soon, Khan earned the billing "featuring Chaka Khan," and the group produced a string of successful projects, including *Rufusized* (1974), *Rufus Featuring Chaka Khan* (1975), and *Ask Rufus* (1977).

Khan embarked on a solo career in 1978. During this time, she collaborated with industry giants Quincy Jones ("Stuff Like That"), Joni Mitchell ("Don Juan's Reckless Daughter"), George Benson, the Average White Band, the Brecker Brothers, and Phil Upchurch. During the 1980s, Khan expanded her reputation with eclectic recordings of jazz standards, rock, and hard-hitting soul. She collaborated with a dizzying mix of musicians, such as Prince, Freddie Hubbard, Chick Corea, and Grandmaster Melle Mel.

In the 1990s, the songs of her earlier career remained staples in both the rhythm-and-blues and smooth jazz radio formats. Her 1998 release, *Come 2 My House*, is a collaborative project with "the artist formerly known as Prince" and features Khan's signature vocal style: a wide range, intense musicality, clarion tone, and sensual feeling. That same year, Chaka Khan received ASCAP's first Rhythm and Soul Heritage Award. In 2000, she was honored with the Granville White Lifetime Achievement Award.

In October 2004, Khan released her cover album, *ClassiKhan*, on her own label, Earth Song Records and Sanctuary Records. This album featured the London Symphony Orchestra and was recorded primarily at Abbey Road Studios in London. In early 2006, she signed with Sony BMG's new label, Burgundy Records, to release her studio cover album set, *I-Khan Divas* (2007). In addition, Khan, who had embraced Christianity, participated in a live all-star gospel concert recording for Christian recording artist Richard Smallwood's 2007 album *Journey: Live in New York*. Khan is featured on the song "Holy Is Your Name." On February 11, 2007, Khan headlined and performed at the National Academy of Recording Arts and Sciences Grammy Award official post-party, held immediately after the award ceremony at the Los Angeles convention center. She released the album *Funk This* later that year.

GLADYS KNIGHT (1944–)

Singer. Born May 28, 1944, in Atlanta, Georgia, Gladys Knight was raised in a family that valued education and the sounds of gospel music. At age four, Knight began singing gospel music at the Mount Moriah Baptist Church. When she was eight, Knight won first prize on the television program *Ted Mack's Amateur Hour* for a rendition of the song "Too Young." Between 1950 and 1953, Knight toured with the Morris Brown Choir of Atlanta. Around this time, Knight joined her sister Brenda, brother Merald, and cousins William and Eleanor Guest to form a local church singing group. In 1957, the group took the name the Pips upon the suggestion of cousin and manager James "Pips" Woods.

Two years later, Langston George and Edward Patten replaced Brenda Knight and Eleanor Guest. Though Gladys periodically left the group, she rejoined in 1964. After recording for several record labels, the Pips finally signed with Motown's subsidiary, Soul. Despite their lack of commercial success, the group released a number of fine recordings under the supervision of Motown's talented production staff, including Norman Whitfield and Ashford and Simpson. In 1967, the Pips released the single "I Heard It through the Grapevine," which reached number two on the *Billboard* charts. Following a long string of hits on Motown, the Pips signed with the Buddah label in 1973, releasing the album *Imagination*, which provided the group with two gold singles, "Midnight Train to Georgia" and "I've Got to Use My Imagination."

By the late 1970s, the Pips, facing legal battles and contract disputes, began to fall out of popularity. For three years, the group was barred from recording or performing together. As a result of an out-of-court settlement in 1980, the Pips signed a new contract with CBS, where they remained until 1985. Joined by Dionne Warwick and Elton John, Knight recorded the Grammy Award–winning gold single "That's What Friends Are For" in 1986. Released in 1988, the title cut of the Pip's *Love Overboard* album became their biggest-selling single in decades. That same year, Knight recorded the theme for the James Bond film *License to Kill.* Released on the MCA label, Knight's 1991 album, *Good Women*, featured guest stars Patti LaBelle and Dionne Warwick. Knight released another album, *Just for You*, in 1994. In 1995, Gladys Knight and the Pips were inducted into the Rock and Roll Hall of Fame.

In 1998, Knight released *Many Different Roads*, her first album to fully focus on the spiritual side of music. In 2001, Knight returned to more contemporary music with her album *At Last.* She also married business consultant William McDowell that year. It was her fourth marriage and his second. In 2002, Knight was back in the limelight when she won a Grammy Award for best traditional R&B vocal album for *At Last.*

In 2005, Knight received a Grammy for best gospel performance for "Heaven Help Us All," her duet with Ray Charles from his album, *Genius Loves Company.* Oprah Winfrey honored Knight as one of twenty-five accomplished and influential African American women at her Oprah Legends ball. Knight was honored in 2005 with a Lifetime Achievement Award from the BET cable network. In 2006, Knight received a Legendary Award by the Las Vegas Music Awards. She won another Grammy Award in 2007 in the category of best gospel choir or gospel chorus for *One Voice*, made with the Saints Unified Voices.

BEYONCÉ KNOWLES (1981–)

Singer, Actress. Born in Houston, Texas, on September 4, 1981, Beyoncé Giselle Knowles started performing at age seven. From dance classes to singing in the church choir, Beyoncé excelled. After she and her cousin, Kelly Rowland, met LaTavia Roberson, they formed a group with LeToya Luckett. Mathew Knowles, Beyoncé's father and Rowland's legal guardian, became the girls' manager. Their group, Destiny's Child, debuted in 1990 and became one of the most popular female R&B groups of all time. By 2002, Destiny's Child had sold more than thirty-three million albums and had won Grammys and other awards. Their songs "Jumpin' Jumpin'," "Bills, Bills, Bills," "Say My Name," and "Survivor" became top hits.

In 2001, the members of the group launched solo careers. In 2001, Knowles became the first African American female artist and second woman ever to win the annual ASCAP Pop Songwriter of the Year Award. An appearance on the MTV drama *Carmen: A Hip Hopera* (2001) quickly followed, but it was her role as Foxxy Cleopatra in *Austin Powers in Goldmember* in 2002 that moved Knowles from the stage to the screen.

Singer-Songwriter Beyoncé, 2010. *Beyoncé has enjoyed success both as a member of the popular female R&B group Destiny's Child and as an award-winning and top-selling solo artist.* JASON KEMPIN/GETTY IMAGES

Knowles's first single, "Work It Out," coincided with the release of the Mike Myers comedy and cemented her celebrity status. A guest spot on Jay-Z's 2003 "Bonnie & Clyde" was equally popular when it was released in October. In 2003, she rejoined Jay-Z for her proper debut single, "Crazy in Love." Knowles's debut album, *Dangerously in Love* (2003), featured collaborations with Sean Paul, Missy Elliott, and OutKast's Big Boi. At the 2004 Grammy Awards ceremony, Knowles won a record-tying five Grammys for her solo effort, including best female R&B vocal performance for "Dangerously in Love 2," best R&B song for "Crazy in Love," and best contemporary R&B album. Three other female artists held this record: Lauryn Hill (1999), Alicia Keys (2002), and Norah Jones (2003). Knowles also won a 2004 Brit Award for best international female solo artist.

In December 2005, Knowles released "Check on It," featuring rappers Slim Thug and (on the official remix) Bun B. The song was from the Destiny's Child's greatest-hits compilation, *#1's* and the soundtrack to the 2006 film *The Pink Panther*. It was Knowles's sixth top-five hit and third number-one in the United States. Nearly two years after the release of another Destiny's Child album (*Destiny Fulfilled*), Knowles released her second solo album, *B'Day* (2006).

In 2005, Knowles won a Grammy Award in the category of best R&B performance by a duo or group with vocals for the song "So Amazing," a duet with Stevie Wonder from the Luther Vandross tribute album, *So Amazing: An All-Star Tribute to Luther Vandross*. Knowles received five Grammy nominations and won best contemporary R&B album for *B'Day* in 2006.

Knowles's third studio album, *I Am... Sasha Fierce*, was released in 2008. It included the hit single "Single Ladies (Put a Ring on It)," which won a Grammy for song of the year in 2010, among other awards. Knowles won a record-breaking six Grammy Awards in 2010. In January 2009, she performed the Etta James classic "At Last" in Washington, D.C., during the festivities following the inauguration of President Barack Obama.

KRS-ONE (1965–)

Rapper, Producer. A self-described teacher whose Boogie Down Productions (BDP) was an important influence on hardcore rap, KRS-One survived street life, prison, homelessness, the murder of a close friend, and negative criticism to emerge as one of rap's most powerful figures. Born Lawrence Parker around 1965 in Brooklyn, New York, KRS-One (initially representative of "Kris, Number One," later an acronym for "Knowledge Reigns Supreme Over Nearly Everyone"), also went by Krishna Parker or Kris Parker. Leaving home at thirteen, he lived on the streets, taking odd jobs when available and hanging out in public libraries. Self-educated, he served a short stint in jail for selling marijuana. Upon his release, the nineteen-year-old met Scott Sterling, a social worker and DJ who worked under the name Scott LaRock. Together, the two formed BDP.

BDP recorded one album, *Criminal Minded*, before LaRock was killed while trying to break up a fight. Persevering, KRS-One kept their music alive, recording several critically acclaimed works with the various musicians who comprised the BDP crew. In 1990, he created H.E.A.L., or Human Education Against Lies, an Afrocentric, pro-educational organization. KRS-One also founded Edutainer Records that year. In 1991, KRS-One recorded *Live Hardcore Worldwide*, one of the first live rap albums, and produced such artists as Queen Latifah and the Neville Brothers. His 1992 album, *Sex and Violence*, returned to the earlier hardcore sound of BDP, while his 1997 recording, *I Got Next*, produced raw funk on tracks such as "The MC."

KRS-One took a four-year sabbatical from the music industry, but returned strongly with his 2001 release, *The Sneak Attack*. He then surprised many fans and critics with his 2002 album, *Spiritual Minded*, a gospel record that preaches the ways of a religious lifestyle in rap format. In 2003, he founded the Temple of Hip Hop and released a new album, *Kristyles*, which was preceded by *KRS-One: The Mixtape*. In the summer of 2004, KRS-One released *Keep Right*, followed by *Life* in 2006. His subsequent recordings include *Hip-Hop Lives* (2007), *Adventures in Emceeing* (2008), *Maximum Strength* (2008), and *Survival Skills* (2009), a collaboration with the rapper Buckshot. He also released a greatest-hits album, *Playlist: The Very Best of KRS-One*, in 2010. KRS-One is also an author; his works include *Ruminations* (2003) and *The Gospel of Hip Hop: The First Instrument* (2009).

Hip-Hop Artist Talib Kweli, South by Southwest Music Festival, Austin, TX, 2008. *Kweli has gained widespread acclaim as a rapper in the early twenty-first century, raising social awareness through his music.* TIM MOSENFELDER/GETTY IMAGES

TALIB KWELI (1974–)

Rapper, Philanthropist. Rapper Talib Kweli Greene, known in the music world as Talib Kweli, was born on October 3, 1974, in Brooklyn, New York. His name reflects the trajectory of his career: Talib is Arabic for "student" or "seeker," and Kweli is Swahili for "truth." The son of professors of English and sociology, Greene took to rapping at an early age. He was attracted to the Afrocentric rap scene, where acts such as De La Soul and other members of the Native Tongues Posse held court. Kweli struck out professionally in 1997 to work with a Cincinnati, Ohio, group called Mood. While there, he met DJ Hi-Tek and formed a group called Reflection Eternal. Their recordings circulated throughout the underground scene.

Kweli returned to New York and formed the group Black Star with Brooklyn rapper Mos Def. Hi-Tek came on board to produce their only album, *Mos Def and Talib Kweli Are Black Star*. The critically acclaimed album came out in 1998 during a resurgence of conscious-raising hip-hop and made a decent showing in sales. Black Star disbanded soon afterward. Kweli and Hi-Tek carried on with Reflection Eternal's *Train of Thought* (2000). This too was praised by the critics, but saw only modest sales.

After 2000, Kweli embarked on a solo career with the intent of capturing a more mainstream sound. His solo debut, *Quality* (2002), boasted a roster of production talent in order to accomplish this goal. The song "Get By," produced by Kanye West, proved instrumental in drawing mainstream exposure, along with the praise of critics. Kweli continued to find innovative ways to increase his visibility by opening for the Beastie Boys on their Challah at Your Boy World Tour. Kweli was featured on a live remix of a Dilated Peoples song that was used as a soundtrack for the video game *NBA Street Vol. 2*. He also contributed to the song "Yelling Away" on Zap Mama's 2004 album *Ancestry in Progress*.

Television appearances became part of Kweli's strategy as well. He appeared on MTV's *Wild 'N Out*, and enjoyed several performances on *Chappelle's Show*, rapping with Black Star cohort Mos Def. Chappelle added his star power to Kweli's cause by impersonating several people in skits dispersed throughout Kweli's albums *Train of Thought* and *Quality*. Kanye West also helped by featuring Kweli on "Get 'Em High," a song from his hugely successful debut album, *College Dropout* (2004). Kweli's profile as a conscious rapper was substantial enough for him to be featured in an NCAA's Big Ten Conference commercial, where he raps about the league's teams. Kweli also lent his voice to the 2006 graffiti-themed video game *Marc Eckō's Getting Up: Contents under Pressure*.

Always community-minded, Kweli teamed up with Mos Def to buy Nkiru, Brooklyn's oldest black-owned bookstore. They converted the store into the Nkiru Center for Education and Culture. The hip-hop community continued to show its appreciation for Kweli. This was most evident in Jay-Z's "Moment of Clarity," a song from his 2003 release, *The Black Album*: "If skills sold, truth be told/I'd probably be, lyrically, Talib Kweli." Kweli returned the compliment on his track "Ghetto Show" from *The Beautiful Struggle* (2004): "If lyrics sold then truth be told/I'd probably be just as rich and famous as Jay-Z." Critics panned the album, claiming it was too mainstream and that Kweli was taking on a tougher, street-oriented pose. Kweli fired back by forming his own Blacksmith Records and releasing *Mixtape-CD* (2005). The complete title, *Right about Now: The Official Sucka Free Mix CD*, is believed to be his answer to the critical backlash from *The Beautiful Struggle*. One of the most touching songs in Kweli's career is featured on this album, a tribute to Lauryn Hill called "Ms. Hill."

Kweli made a bold move in 2006, releasing nine songs he recorded in his home with well-respected underground producer Madlib. Kweli worked in conjunction with Madlib's label, Stones Throw Records, to make the album, *Liberation*, available for free download. The album received rave reviews from critics and further solidified Kweli's status in the underground scene. Kweli continued to expand his empire by signing rapper Jean Grae and the group Strong Arm Steady to his label. Kweli secured a new distribution deal with Warner Bros. Records for Blacksmith.

Kweli then released *Eardrum*, which became his highest-charting solo album to date thanks to "Listen," a single featured on the soundtrack for the 2006 movie *Freedom Writers*. Ever mindful of using his music to raise people's social consciousness, Kweli performed the song "Broken Glass" for the "rockumentary" *Call+Response*, a project protesting modern-day enslavement and human trafficking. Kweli reunited with DJ Hi-Tek for the 2010 release of the second Reflection Eternal album, *Revolutions per Minute*.

PATTI LaBELLE (1944–)

Singer. Born Patricia Holte in Philadelphia, Pennsylvania, in 1944, Patti LaBelle has remained one of the most respected divas of the pop-soul tradition. Known for her dramatic vocalizations and stage presentations, LaBelle has managed to maintain a successful career for several decades by keeping up with popular trends without sacrificing her signature vocal gymnastics.

While still a teenager, LaBelle formed the Bluebelles with Cindy Birdsong, Sarah Dash, and Nonah Henderson. They scored hits with "I Sold My Heart to the Junkman" (1962) and "Down the Aisle" (1963) during the height of the girl-group fad in popular music. Shortly thereafter, the group adopted the name Patti LaBelle and the Bluebelles, which was later shortened to LaBelle, and they turned to a harder rock style in the early 1970s. The group scored a million-seller hit with the energetic "Lady Marmalade." They disbanded in 1976, and LaBelle embarked on a solo career.

In the mid-1980s, she recorded the hits "New Attitude" (1985) and "Oh People" (1986), as well as "On My Own" (1986), a song written by Carole Bayer-Sayer and Burt Bacharach, which LaBelle sang with Michael McDonald of the Doobie Brothers. LaBelle is the recipient of numerous Grammy and Emmy Award nominations. In 1992, she received a Grammy for best R&B vocal performance. She produced numerous albums throughout the 1990s, including *Burnin'* (1991), *Gems* (1994), and *Flame* (1997). While her recordings from the 1980s and 1990s met with mixed commercial success, she has established herself as a sentimental favorite among pop-soul audiences. In 2000, LaBelle put out the studio album, *When a Woman Loves*. In 2001, she received the Lena Horne Award for outstanding career achievement at the Soul Train's Lady of Soul Awards. LaBelle continues to perform, and in 2006 she released another album, *The Gospel According to Patti LaBelle*.

LIL WAYNE (1982–)

Singer, Songwriter. Dwayne Michael Carter, a hip-hop artist known as Lil Wayne, was born in the Hollygrove neighborhood of New Orleans, Louisiana, on September 27, 1982. Carter wrote his first rap when he was eight, and within three years he was featured spinning freestyle rhymes on the answering machines of Bryan Williams, rapper and founder of Cash Money Records. When he was thirteen, Lil Wayne dropped out of school after accidentally shooting himself with a .44 caliber gun and began his career as a hip-hop artist in earnest, becoming the youngest member of Cash Money Records.

Lil Wayne has proven himself to be a true game-changer in the hip-hop arena. Combining musical idioms of the Dirty South, he has emerged as one of the most commercially successful and musically innovative artists ever to enter the recording studio. With signature compositions such as "Swagga Like Us," "Lollipop," and "Can't Believe It," he has established himself as a revolutionary artist with an excellent capacity for collaboration, creating opportunities for a wide range of emerging artists.

Lil Wayne became president of Cash Money Records in 2005, the same year he founded Young Money Entertainment. He turned over the management reigns of both ventures in 2007. On November 11, 2008, fulfilling a dream to play guitar, Lil Wayne became the first hip-hop artist ever to perform at the Country Music Awards. In a stellar career that has already witnessed the production of seven studio albums in the span of a decade, along with musical collaborations, mixtapes, film and television appearances, and his distinctive vocal work in Gatorade's "G" campaign, Lil Wayne has faced legal battles over possession of drugs and weapons. In March 2010, he began serving a one-year sentence at Rikers Island, part of the New York City Department of Corrections.

Little Richard, 1956. *Known for his flamboyant showmanship, singer and pianist Little Richard was a key figure in the transition from rhythm and blues to rock and roll in the 1950s. He enjoyed a string of hits in the latter years of that decade, including "Tutti Frutti," "Long Tall Sally," and "Good Golly Miss Molly."* **MICHAEL OCHS ARCHIVES/HISTORICAL/CORBIS**

LITTLE RICHARD (1932–)

Singer, Pianist. Flamboyantly dressed, with his hair piled high in a pompadour, Little Richard is a musical phenomenon, an entertainer hailed by pop superstar Paul McCartney as "one of the greatest kings of rock and roll." Richard's image, mannerisms, and musical talent set the trend for the emergence of modern popular music performers from Jimi Hendrix to Prince.

One of twelve children, Richard Wayne Penniman was born on December 5, 1932, in Macon, Georgia. As a child in Macon, Richard heard the sounds of gospel music groups, street musicians, and spiritual-based songs emanating from homes throughout his neighborhood. Nicknamed the "War Hawk" for his unrestrained hollers and shouts, Richard's voice projected with such intensity that he was once asked to stop singing in church. Richard's first performance before an audience was with the Tiny Tots, a gospel group featuring his brothers Marquette and Walter. Later Richard sang with his family in a group called the Penniman Singers; they appeared at churches, camp meetings, and talent contests.

In high school, Richard played alto saxophone in the marching band. After school he took a part-time job at the Macon City Auditorium, where he watched the bands of Cab Calloway, Hot Lips Page, Lucky Millinder, and Sister Rosetta Thorpe. At age fourteen, Richard left home to become a performer in Doctor Hudson's Medicine Show. While on the road, he joined B. Brown's Orchestra as a ballad singer, performing such compositions as "Good Night Irene" and "Mona Lisa." Not long afterward, he became a member of the traveling minstrel show of Sugarfoot Sam from Alabama.

Richard's first break came in 1951, when the RCA label recorded him live on the radio, producing the local hit "Every Hour." Traveling to New Orleans with his band, the Tempo Toppers, Richard's group eventually played the Houston rhythm-and-blues scene, where he attracted the attention of Don Robey, president of Peacock Records. After cutting some sides for the Peacock label, Richard sent a demo tape to Art Rupe's Los Angeles–based Specialty label. Under the direction of Specialty's producer Bumps Blackwell, Richard recorded the 1956 hit "Tutti Frutti" at JM Studios in New Orleans. Richard's subsequent sessions for Specialty yielded a long list of classic hits, such as "Long Tall Sally," "Lucille," "Jenny, Jenny," and "Keep a Knockin'." In 1956, Richard appeared in the films *Don't Knock the Rock* with Bill Haley and *The Girl Can't Help It*, starring Jane Mansfield.

The following year, Richard quit his rock-and-roll career and later entered the Oakland Theological College in Huntsville, Alabama. Between 1957 to 1959, Richard released several gospel recordings and toured with such artists as Mahalia Jackson. In 1962, Richard embarked on a tour of Europe with Sam Cooke. One year later, Richard hired a then unknown guitarist, Jimi Hendrix, who worked under the pseudonym of Maurice James. In Europe, Richard played on the same bills as the Beatles and Rolling Stones.

By the 1970s, Richard pursued a career as a full-fledged evangelist and performer. In 1979, he set out on a nationwide evangelist tour. In the following decade, he appeared in the film *Down and Out in Beverly Hills* (1986) and recorded "Rock Island Line" on the tribute LP to Leadbelly and Woody Guthrie titled *Folkways: A Vision Shared* (1988).

Richard's continuing activity in show business represents the inexhaustible energy of a singer who had a profound impact on the careers of artists such as Otis Redding, Eddie Cochran, Ritchie Valens, Paul McCartney, and Mitch Ryder. Having earned special Grammy honors in 1993, Richard was honored with a lifetime achievement award by the Rhythm and Blues Foundation the following year. He headlined the 1994 New Orleans Jazz and Heritage Festival, and he is a charter member of the Rock and Roll Hall of Fame and Museum. The House of Blues Foundation called upon him to assist in the organization's Blues School House program in 1995.

Little Richard continued to tour throughout the 1990s and has appeared in numerous television shows and movies, usually as himself. In 2000, NBC produced a television special about his life titled *Little Richard*, directed by Robert Townsend. Also in 2000, Richard was named a goodwill ambassador to his hometown of Macon, Georgia. Richard was among the 2002 inductees into the NAACP Hall of Fame, and the next year he was inducted into the Songwriters Hall of Fame. In 2004, *Rolling Stone* magazine ranked Little Richard as number eight on their list of the "100 Greatest Artists of All Time."

LL COOL J (1968–)

Rapper, Actor. In the mid-1980s, LL Cool J became one of rap music's first major stars. Along with a handful of other musicians, he played a key role in rap's entry and acceptance into the mainstream of American pop music. Even with the enormous shifts and changes in the industry since then, LL Cool J has remained a successful rap musician. In addition to his long-lived prominence as a rapper, LL Cool J has also cultivated a successful television and film acting career.

Born James Todd Smith on January 14, 1968, LL Cool J (short for "Ladies Love Cool James") grew up in Queens, New York. When he was sixteen years old, he released "I Need a Beat," the first record issued on Russell Simmons's and Rick Rubin's Def Jam label. The single proved to be very popular, and he released his debut album, *Radio* (1985), the following year. With the success of the album, LL Cool J was invited to perform a version of his single "I Can't Live without My Radio" in the film *Krush Groove* (1985). He also appeared as a rapper in the film *Wildcats* (1986).

His second album, *Bigger and Deffer* (1987), proved to be an even bigger hit than *Radio*. The album's single, "I Need Love," became the first rap song to top *Billboard* magazine's R&B chart, expanding the appeal of rap music to a broader audience. That year, "Going Back to Cali," a single from the soundtrack for the film *Less than Zero*, proved to be another major hit. LL Cool J followed with the albums *Walking with a Panther* (1989), *Mama Said Knock You Out* (1990), *14 Shots to the Dome* (1993), *Mr. Smith* (1995), *Phenomenon* (1997), *G.O.A.T. Featuring James T. Smith* (2001), *The DEFinition* (2004), *Todd Smith* (2006), and *Exit 13* (2008).

The onset of the 1990s saw LL Cool J explore film and television, both as a musician and an actor. In 1991, he became the first rap artist to appear on MTV's *Unplugged*, and he turned in an impressive performance as an undercover policeman in the film *The Hard Way* (1991). A year later, he appeared in the film *Toys* (1992). In 1995, LL Cool J was given his own television series, *In the House*. The sitcom, which premiered on NBC before moving to the UPN network, ran until 1999. LL Cool J's acting credits include roles in the following films: *Out-of-Sync* (1995), *B.A.P.S* (1997), *Caught Up* (1998), *Woo* (1998), *Halloween: H20* (1998), *Deep Blue Sea* (1999), *In Too Deep* (1999), *Any Given Sunday* (1999), *Charlie's Angels* (2000), *Kingdom Come* (2001), *Rollerball* (2002), *S.W.A.T.* (2003), *Mindhunters* (2004), and *Last Holiday* (2006). By 2007, he was also marketing several lines of clothing and had authored or coauthored a number of books, including an autobiography. He joined the cast of the CBS series *NCIS: Los Angeles* in 2009.

MASTER P (c. 1970–)

Music and Film Company Executive, Rapper, Actor. Born Percy Miller, Master P grew up in a housing project in New Orleans's Third Ward, an area with a reputation for a high crime rate and violence. His parents divorced when he was eleven years old, and his mother moved to California. Though he traveled between New Orleans and California, the teenaged Percy settled in the Crescent City, attended Booker T. Washington and Warren Eason high schools, and played basketball at both schools. After graduation, he reportedly earned a basketball scholarship to the University of Houston. However, he was sidelined by a leg injury and headed home rather than sit out the season. With some junior college business courses to his credit, Master P moved to Richmond and opened a small record store, No Limits Records, financing the store with $10,000 that he received as part of a medical malpractice settlement related to the death of his grandfather.

Master P was soon able to turn his successful store into a powerhouse producer of southern-influenced gangsta rap albums. He self-produced his first album, *The Ghetto's Tryin' to Kill Me*, in 1994, selling 200,000 copies out of the trunk of his car. Master P then took the profits from this album and produced two collections of rap music: *Down South Hustlers, Vol. 1* and *West Coast Bad Boys, Vol. 1*. By 1997, the four-year-old label had a cluster of artists who, while not household names, were well known to rap fans.

Master P next targeted the film industry. In 1997, he produced, directed, and acted in a low-budget semiautobiographical film titled *I'm 'Bout It* without any outside backing. The success of this direct-to-video film led to *I Got the Hook Up* the following year. This time, he had no problem signing Dimension Records as a distributor for the film. A third film, *MP Da Last Don*, soon followed.

No Limits then moved to Baton Rouge and undertook a number of new enterprises. A sports-management company, No Limit Sports Management, was launched in 1997 and began representing such professional players as Ron Mercer of the Boston Celtics and Derek Anderson of the Cleveland Cavaliers. By 1998, No Limits Records had incorporated twelve businesses in Baton Rouge, including a complex called the Ice Cream Shop, which had five recording studios, a dorm, a gym, a pool, an aquarium, a sundeck, a movie theater, a domed basketball court, and fifteen Hummers for transportation. The Master P Foundation was also a supporter of the schools and community of Baton Rouge.

In 1998, Master P tried out for the Continental Basketball Association's Fort Wayne Furies and was signed as a free agent in October. His performance with the Furies brought an invitation to try out with the NBA's Charlotte Hornets, but he did not make the cut. His basketball career behind him, Master P continued to make music. In 1999, he came out with *Only God Can Judge Me*, followed by *Ghetto Postage* (2000), *Game Face* (2002), *Good Side, Bad Side* (2004), *Ghetto Bill* (2005), and *America's Most Luved Bad Guy* (2006).

Master P, a multimillionaire, has made a number of good investments and has continued to increase his net worth. He also manages the career of his son, rap star Lil' Romeo, later known as simply Romeo. Romeo, born Percy Romeo Miller Jr. in 1989, has performed on film and television and has his own clothing line. Romeo's albums include *Lil' Romeo* (2001), *Game Time* (2002), *Romeoland* (2004), *Young Ballers: The Hood Been Good to Us*, with Rich Boyz (2005), *Lottery* (2006), *God's Gift* (2006), and *Get Low* (2009).

MAXWELL (1973–)

Singer, Songwriter. Gerald Maxwell Rivera was born on May 23, 1973, in Brooklyn, New York, to a Puerto Rican father and Haitian mother. His father was killed in a plane crash when he was three years old. The experience invoked a deep sense of spirituality in young Gerald, leading him to begin singing in his Baptist church. He began to write his own R&B-influenced songs when he was seventeen years old. After adopting his middle name as a stage moniker, Maxwell began working the New York club scene in 1991. Within three years, he had secured a recording contract with Columbia.

Columbia lacked confidence in the final product that was to be Maxwell's debut, *Maxwell's Urban Hang Suite*. The album, with its classic soul music sound, was shelved for two years and released in 1996. As Columbia feared, *Urban Hang Suite* did not catch on with audiences initially. It took the release of its second single, "Ascension (Don't Ever Wonder)," to draw the attention the album needed to make it double platinum and earn a Grammy nomination.

Maxwell taped an episode of the concert series *MTV Unplugged* in New York City in 1997. Standout performances included a cover of the Kate Bush song "This Woman's Work" and a soulful rendition of the Nine Inch Nails song "Closer."

Maxwell released his ambitious, moderately successful second studio album, *Embrya*, in 1998. The following year, he performed an R. Kelly–penned tune called "Fortunate," which was featured on the soundtrack for the 1999 film *Life*. The chart-topping single would become Maxwell's most successful song to date.

Maxwell's third studio album, *Now*, fared better on the charts than the second. *Now* was released in 2001, and became his first number-one album on both the *Billboard* R&B album and the *Billboard* 200 album charts. Gems from the album included a studio version of "This Woman's Work" and the hit single "Lifetime."

Singer/Songwriter Maxwell Performing on the Jay Leno Show, December 2009. *Maxwell won two Grammy awards, best R&B album and best male R&B vocal performance, in 2010 for his work on* BLACKsummer'snight. AP IMAGES/NBCU/ STACIE MCCHESNEY

Maxwell took several years off before coming out with *BLACKsummers'night* in the summer of 2009. The artistically daring album debuted at number one on the *Billboard* albums Top 200 chart thanks to the hit single "Pretty Wings." Accolades for the album continued to grow as the singer toured to support it. The album received six Grammy nominations in 2009, including best R&B album and best male R&B vocal performance.

CURTIS MAYFIELD (1942–1999)

Singer, Songwriter, Producer. Born on June 3, 1942, in Chicago, Curtis Mayfield learned to sing harmony as a member of the Northern Jubilee Singers and the Traveling Souls Spiritualist Church. In 1957, Mayfield joined the Roosters, a five-man doo-wop singing group led by his close friend Jerry Butler. Renamed the Impressions, the group released the 1958 hit "Your Precious Love," featuring Butler's resonant baritone and Mayfield's wispy tenor. But in the following year, Butler left the group to pursue a solo career. In search of material, Butler collaborated with Mayfield to write the hit songs "He Will Break Your Heart" and "I'm a-Telling You."

In 1960, Mayfield recruited Fred Cash to take Butler's place in the newly reformed Impressions. In the next year, the Impressions hit the charts with the sensual soul tune "Gypsy Women." In collaboration with Butler, Mayfield also established the Curtom Publishing Company. With the loss of original members Richard Brooks and Arthur Brooks, the three remaining members of the Impressions, Mayfield, Cash, and Sam Goodman, continued to perform as a trio. Under the direction of jazz musician and arranger Johnny Pate, the Impressions recorded "Sad Sad Girl" and the rhythmic gospel-based song "It's All Right," released in 1963.

During this time, Mayfield also wrote a number of songs for his Chicago contemporaries, including "Monkey Time" for Major Lance, "Just Be True" for Gene Chandler, and "It's All Over Now" for Walter Jackson. Writing for the Impressions, however, Mayfield turned to more socially conscious themes reflecting the current of the civil rights era. Mayfield's finest "sermon songs" were "People Get Ready" (1965), "We're a Winner" (1968), and "Choice of Colors" (1969).

After leaving the Impressions in 1970, Mayfield released his debut album, *Curtis*. On his 1971 LP, *Curtis Live!*, Mayfield was accompanied by a tight four-piece backup group, which included guitar, bass, drums, and percussion. Mayfield composed the score for the 1972 hit film *Super Fly*. The soundtrack became Mayfield's biggest commercial success, providing him two hits with the junkie epitaph "Freddie's Dead" and the wah-wah guitar funk classic "Super Fly." Despite his commercial success, Mayfield spent the remainder of the decade in collaboration with other artists, working on such projects as the soundtrack for the 1974 film *Claudine*, featuring Gladys Knight and the Pips, and the production of Aretha Franklin's 1978 album *Sparkle*.

During the 1980s, Mayfield recorded such albums as *Love Is the Place* (1981) and *Honesty* (1982). Joined by Jerry Butler and newcomers Nate Evans and Vandy Hampton, the Impressions reunited in 1983, for a thirty-city anniversary tour. In 1983, Mayfield released the LP *Come in Peace with a Message of Love*. In August 1990, while performing at an outdoor concert in Brooklyn, New York, he sustained an injury that left him paralyzed from the neck down. In the following year, Mayfield's contributions to popular music were recognized when the Impressions were inducted into the Rock and Roll Hall of Fame. In 1994, Mayfield was presented with the Grammy Legend Award. Earlier that year, a number of his peers, including Aretha Franklin, got together to record *All Men Are Brothers: A Tribute to Curtis Mayfield.* Despite his injuries, Mayfield triumphed by producing the Grammy-nominated album *New World Order* in late 1996. Mayfield was inducted into the Rock and Roll Hall of Fame on April 5, 1999. He died December 26, 1999, in Roswell, Georgia, at age fifty-seven.

BOBBY McFERRIN

See chapter 22, Classical Music.

PRAS MICHEL

See The Fugees.

MOS DEF (1973–)

Actor, Activist, Rapper, Entrepreneur. Dante Terrell Smith-Bey, known as Mos Def, was born on December 11, 1973, in the Bedford-Stuyvesant neighborhood of Brooklyn in New York City to Sheron and Abdul Rahman. Dante developed a love for rapping and acting when he was six years old. He later graduated from Philippa Schuyler Middle School in Bushwick and New York University's Gallatin School of Individualized Study.

Mos Def's hip-hop career began in a group called Urban Thermo Dynamics. While a part of the group, he made guest appearances on albums by Da Bush Babees and De La Soul. Mos Def became a fixture in the underground hip-hop scene of the late 1990s. In 1998, he formed the duo Black Star with Talib Kweli. They released their debut, *Mos Def and Talib Kweli Are Black Star,* in that same year. The album featured the stellar hit single "Definition."

Mos Def kept his profile as an individual artist, releasing the album *Black on Both Sides* in 1999, the highly experimental *The New Danger* in 2004, the endearing *True Magic* in 2006, and the chart-topping *The Ecstatic* in 2009. In addition to his solid career in music, Mos Def has become a respected film and theater actor.

***Mos Def as Chuck Berry in the 2008 Film* Cadillac Records.** *Mos Def's 2009 album* The Ecstatic *earned him a Grammy nomination for best rap album.* MOVIESTORE COLLECTION LTD/ALAMY

He has appeared in Spike Lee's *Bamboozled* (2000) and the Oscar-winning *Monster's Ball* (2001), among other projects. Mos won many hearts in *Brown Sugar* (2002) as an underground rapper reluctant to sign to a major label. In 2002, Mos ventured into theater for an impressive portrayal of the character Booth in Suzan-Lori Parks's Tony-nominated and Pulitzer-winning Broadway play *Topdog/Underdog*. In 2005, Mos Def appeared as Ford Prefect in *The Hitchhiker's Guide to the Galaxy*. He played the role of Chuck Berry in the 2008 film *Cadillac Records*. In addition, Mos Def walks the political talk of his lyrics by weighing in on social and political issues like the plight of New Orleans residents after Hurricane Katrina.

A constant collaborator, Mos Def has worked with Kanye West, Stephen Marley, Somali rapper K'naan, and the Roots, among others. A lover of jazz, Mos Def traveled to South Africa in 2009, where he performed a rendition of the John Coltrane classic "A Love Supreme" at the Cape Town International Jazz Festival.

R&B Artist Musiq, Heineken Red Star Soul Concert, Philadelphia, PA, 2008. *Since his debut in 2000, Musiq has had two platinum albums, two gold albums, and seven hit singles, and has been nominated for eleven Grammy Awards.* LISA LAKE/ WIREIMAGE FOR MANNING SELVAGE & LEE/GETTY IMAGES

MUSIQ SOULCHILD (1977–)

Singer, Songwriter. Taalib Johnson, better known by his stage name Musiq Soulchild or Musiq, was born on September 16, 1977, in Philadelphia, the eldest of nine children. To the chagrin of his parents, Musiq dropped out of high school. He became known for his freestyling and beat-boxing skills throughout Philadelphia. This led him to develop his own style of scat for jazz clubs and the open-mic circuit. He took on the name "Musiq" and added "Soulchild" later as a tribute to such soul icons as James Brown, Patti LaBelle, Stevie Wonder, Sly and the Family Stone, and Billie Holiday. Musiq Soulchild has maintained a penchant for titling his albums and songs in ways that eschew rules of punctuation, capitalization, and spelling.

Musiq Soulchild released his debut album, *Aijuswanaseing*, in 2000. Its two singles, "Just Friends (Sunny)" and "Love," established Musiq's presence in the neo-soul movement. His 2002 follow-up, *Juslisen*, entered the *Billboard* charts at number one and went platinum on the strength of the singles "Dontchange" and "Halfcrazy."

In 2003, Musiq released *Soulstar*, his third album. Notable singles include "Whoknows" and "Forthenight." Musiq changed his management and label during a four-year break. He returned in 2007 with *Luvanmusiq*, his fourth album. Standout singles are "Teachme," "B.U.D.D.Y.," and "Makeyouhappy."

Musiq's fifth album, *OnMyRadio*, was released on December 2, 2008. One of the most remarkable songs in Musiq's career, and the most well-received song on the album, was the ballad "SoBeautiful." The singer has also kept active with collaborations. He was featured on the soundtrack to Tyler Perry's movie *Daddy's Little Girls* (2007) and Carlos Santana's album *Shaman* (2002), as well as projects by Talib Kweli and the Roots. In addition, he contributed to the Earth, Wind, and Fire tribute album, *Interpretations: Celebrating the Music of Earth, Wind, and Fire* (2007). Musiq has been honored with American Music Awards and numerous Grammy nominations. As of 2010, he had two platinum albums, two gold albums, and seven hit singles to his credit.

NOTORIOUS B.I.G. (1972–1997)

Rapper. Notorious B.I.G., also known as Biggie Smalls and B.I.G., was born Christopher Wallace in the Bedford-Stuyvesant section of Brooklyn in 1972. A self-described former "100 percent hustler" and high school dropout, Notorious B.I.G. became within his short career one of most influential and respected talents in hip-hop history.

Noted for his massive six-foot, three-inch, 300-plus-pound frame, a husky-voiced yet fluid and rhythmically inventive delivery style, and explicit lyrics, he began his career making amateur tapes for fun with the OGB (Old Gold Brothers). His talents caught the attention of rapper Big Daddy Kane's DJ, and he was soon featured in the rap trade magazine *The Source* in its *Unsigned Hype* column, a showcase for new rappers. A record deal with Uptown Records followed shortly thereafter, and he created the song "Party and Bullshit" for the 1993 film *Who's the Man?* After he signed with his business associate and friend Sean Combs's Bad Boy label, Notorious B.I.G. recorded *Ready to Die* in 1994, and the project went platinum. He was named rap artist of year in 1995 at the *Billboard* Awards.

Notorious B.I.G.'s star rose quickly within hip-hop culture's inner circle, and he became a much sought-after guest rapper on numerous recordings. His collaborators included Junior M.A.F.I.A., Mary J. Blige, and Total, among others. In March 1997, Notorious B.I.G. died a violent death after being shot in a Los Angeles parking lot. No one has ever been charged with the murder, and there remains widespread speculation that it was a result of East Coast/West Coast animosities that involved West Coast gang members as possible henchmen. Another recording project, ironically titled *Life after Death...'Til Death Do Us Part,* was released posthumously in late 1997. A film about his short life, *Notorious,* directed by George Tillman Jr. and starring Jamal Woolard as Wallace, was released in 2009.

OMARION (1984–)

Singer. In 1998, Omarion became the leading man of the hip-hop/R&B boy band B2K. The four-member band was made up of Omarion, Jarell "J-Boog" Houston, DeMario "Raz-B" Thornton, and Dreux "Lil' Fizz" Frederic. B2K released its debut album, *B2K,* in 2002. Their second album, *Pandemonium,* released later in the same year, was more successful, reaching the top ten on the *Billboard* 200, giving them their first number-one single with "Bump, Bump, Bump." Following their third album, a soundtrack to the 2004 movie *You Got Served,* B2K broke up.

Almost a year after B2K's split, Omarion released his debut album, *O.* It debuted at number one on the *Billboard* 200, eventually going platinum. The album included the relatively successful song, "O." In 2006, Omarion was featured on Bow Wow's hit song "Let Me Hold You." The song reached number four on the *Billboard* 100, making it Omarion's first top-ten single as a solo artist. In December 2006, Omarion released his sophomore album, *21.* "Entourage," the first single, rose to only fifty-eight on the Hot 100. The second single, "Ice Box," produced by Timbaland, gained significant radio airplay and became his biggest single to date. Omarion released his third solo album, *Ollusion,* in 2010.

TEDDY PENDERGRASS (1950–2010)

Singer. Theodore Pendergrass was born in 1950 in Philadelphia. He learned how to sing from his mother, who performed in nightclubs, and during a childhood apprenticeship in church. Although he became known as one of the most prominent soul balladeers of the late 1970s and 1980s, he began his professional career as a drummer for the group the Cadillacs.

In 1970, Pendergrass moved from his duties as drummer and began singing with Harold Melvin and the Blue Notes, which had started as a doo-wop group in the 1950s and had signed with the producers Gamble and Huff's label, Philadelphia International, in 1972. Pendergrass's powerful and passionate baritone ultimately earned him the lead spot in the Blue Notes, and for six years his vocals became the group's signature sound. During this period, the Blue Notes recorded such hits as "I Miss You" and "If You Don't Know Me by Now," among others, establishing themselves as one of the premiere soul groups of the decade.

In 1976, Pendergrass left the group to pursue a successful solo career, remaining with Gamble and Huff and producing a string of hits, such as "I Don't Love You Anymore" (1976) and the number-one rhythm-and-blues single, "Close the Door" (1978). Pendergrass became a heartthrob among female fans, mounting successful tours with his Teddy Bear Orchestra and recording albums that were commercially profitable.

Pendergrass's life changed in 1982 when he was involved in a near-fatal car crash in Philadelphia that paralyzed him from the waist down. He maintained a recording career despite these challenges, releasing the album *You and I* in 1997, and some of his later recordings did well on the charts. In 1999, Pendergrass published an autobiography, *Truly Blessed,* written with Patricia Romanowski. In 2002, he released *From Teddy with Love.* Pendergrass continued to tour the country, performing musically and speaking about the rights of the disabled. He announced in 2006 that he had retired from show business. He died in early 2010 following surgery for colon cancer.

CHARLEY PRIDE (1938–)

Singer. The first African American superstar of country music, Charley Pride is a multiple Grammy Award winner whose supple baritone voice has won him international fame. In 1967, he became the first African American to perform with the Grand Ole Opry in more than fifty years. A prolific artist, Pride has recorded more than thirty

Singer Charley Pride, 2005. *A three-time Grammy Award winner, Pride emerged as the first African American superstar of country music. In 2000 he became the first African American to be inducted into the Country Music Hall of Fame.* MARIO ANZUONI/REUTERS/LANDOV

albums, including *Comfort of Her Wings* (2003) and *Pride & Joy: A Gospel Music Collection* (2006).

Born on March 18, 1938, in Sledge, Mississippi, Charley Pride grew up listening to late-night radio broadcasts of the Grand Ole Opry, country music's most famous showcase. Although he taught himself to play the guitar at age fourteen, Pride soon turned his attention to a professional baseball career. At age sixteen, he left the cotton fields of Sledge for a stint in the Negro American League. During his baseball career, Pride sang on public address systems and in taverns. In 1963, country singer Red Sovine heard Pride and arranged for him to attend an audition in Nashville one year later. This led to a recording contract with the RCA label and produced the 1965 hit "Snakes Crawl at Night."

Throughout the 1960s, Pride toured continuously, appearing at concert dates and state fairs, as well as on radio and television. In 1967, he debuted at the Grand Ole Opry, and within the year hit the charts with the singles "Does My Ring Hurt Your Finger?" and "I Know One." With the release of *The Sensational Charley Pride* in 1969 and the subsequent year's *Just Plain Charley*, Pride found himself entering the decade of his greatest recognition. By the time he received the Country Music Award for entertainer of the year in 1970, Pride had achieved tremendous success as a major figure in the popular cultural scene of the United States. Other honors included *Billboard*'s Trendsetter Award and the Music Operators of America's Entertainer of the Year Award.

In the 1980s, Pride not only continued to find success as a music star, he became a successful entrepreneur. Making his home on a 240-acre estate in North Dallas, Texas, Pride emerged as a majority stockholder in the First Texas Bank and part owner of Cecca Productions. Pride made more history in 1993 when he became the first African American to join the cast of the Grand Ole Opry since DeFord Bailey. The following year, he published his autobiography, *Pride: The Charley Pride Story*. In 1999, Pride was honored with a star on the Hollywood Walk of Fame. A year later, he became the first African American inducted into the Country Music Hall of Fame.

PRINCE (1958–)

Singer, Songwriter, Producer. The son of a jazz pianist, Prince Rogers Nelson was born on June 7, 1958, in Minneapolis, Minnesota. By the time he was fourteen years old, Prince had taught himself to play piano, guitar, and drums. Drawn to many forms of rock and soul, Prince explained that he never grew up in one particular culture: "I'm not a punk, but I'm not a rhythm-and-blues artist either because I'm a middle-class kid from Minnesota."

It was his eclectic taste that led Prince to create what came to be known as the Minneapolis sound. After forming the band Grand Central in high school in 1973, Prince renamed the group Champagne and eventually recruited Morris Day. In 1978, Prince signed with Warner Bros. and recorded his debut album, *For You*. His follow-up album, *Prince* (1979), featured the hit "I Wanna Be Your Lover." Prince's third LP, *Dirty Mind*, released in 1980, was rooted in the music of Sly and the Family Stone and Jimi Hendrix.

Two years later, Prince achieved superstardom with his album *1999*, an effort that was followed by a spectacular tour comprised of Prince and the Revolution, the Time, and the bawdy girl trio Vanity 6. The 1984 film *Purple Rain*, along with its soundtrack, received rave reviews for Prince's portrayal of a struggling young musician. The film grossed $60 million at the box office in the first two months of its release. Near the end of 1985, Prince established his own record label, Paisley Park, with a warehouse and studio located in the wooded terrain of Chanhassen,

Prince, performing with Beyoncé, Grammy Awards, Staples Center, Los Angeles, 2004. *As the opening act at the 2004 Grammy Awards, Prince and Beyoncé perform a medley of Prince's classic songs "Purple Rain," "Let's Go Crazy," and "Baby I'm a Star" and Beyoncé's "Crazy in Love."* TIMOTHY A. CLARY/STAFF/GETTY IMAGES

Minnesota. That same year, Prince released the album *Around the World in Day*, featuring the hit singles "Raspberry Beret," "Paisley Park," and "Pop Life."

Prince's next film project, *Under the Cherry Moon* (1986), filmed in France, was completed under his direction. The soundtrack, *Parade Music from Under the Cherry Moon*, produced a number of hit singles, including "Kiss" and "Mountains." After reforming the Revolution, Prince released *Sign O the Times* (1987), which included a duet with Sheena Easton titled "I Could Never Take the Place of Your Man." Following the 1988 LP *Lovesexy*, Prince recorded several songs that appeared on the soundtrack for the 1989 film *Batman*. This was followed by another film and accompanying soundtrack, *Graffiti Bridge*, in 1990.

In September 1992, Prince signed a six-album contract with Warner Bros. Backed by a first-rate new ensemble, the New Power Generation, Prince embarked in April 1993 on a nationwide tour that proved the most impressive since his commercial breakthrough in the early 1980s. Prince also contributed a set of original music to the Joffrey Ballet for a production of *Billboards*, which opened in January 1993 to rave reviews.

In 1993, Prince changed his name to an unpronounceable symbol and announced the retirement of "Prince" from recording. He made this move in protest of his contract with Warner Bros., which he felt was too restrictive concerning the amount of product he could put into the market. He recorded under the symbol until 2000, when his contract with Warner Bros. ended. During this period, people began to refer to him as "the artist formerly known as Prince." In 1994, he debuted interactive CD-ROM software and New Power Generation retail establishments. Two years later, the longtime bachelor married on Valentine's Day and commissioned a symphony from his band to commemorate the occasion.

Recording under the title "the artist formerly known as Prince," he produced the albums *Gold Experience* (1995), *Chaos and Disorder* (1996), the three-disc *Emancipation* (1996), the multidisc outtake album *Crystal Ball* (1998), *New Power Soul* (1998), *Rave Un2 the Joy Fantastic* (1999), and *The Rainbow Children* (2001). Prince also received a great deal of radio and television airplay in the year before the millennium, when his 1982 single "1999" became the theme song for almost all New Year's Eve celebrations. He released *One Nite Alone ... Live!* in 2002 and the all-instrumental *N.E.W.S.* in 2003, receiving a Grammy nomination for best pop instrumental album. Another album of jazz, *Xpectation*, was released via download to members of the NPG Music Club in 2003.

On February 8, 2004, Prince made an appearance at the Grammy Awards with Beyoncé Knowles. In a performance that opened the show, Prince and Beyoncé performed a medley of his classics "Purple Rain," "Let's Go Crazy," and "Baby I'm a Star," as well as Beyoncé's "Crazy in Love," to rave reviews. The following month, Prince was inducted into the Rock and Roll Hall of Fame. The award was presented to him by Alicia Keys, along with Big Boi and André 3000 of OutKast.

In April 2004, Prince released *Musicology* through a one-album agreement with Columbia Records. That same year, *Pollstar* named Prince the top concert draw among American musicians. Grossing an estimated $87.4 million, Prince's *Musicology* tour, with ninety-six concerts, was the most profitable tour in the industry in 2004. *Musicology* received two Grammy wins, for best male R&B vocal performance for "Call My Name" and best traditional R&B vocal performance for the title track.

In 2004, *Rolling Stone* magazine ranked Prince number twenty-eight on their list of the "100 Greatest Artists of All Time." In December 2004, *Rolling Stone*'s readers named him the best male performer and most welcome comeback. During that same month, Prince was named number five on the "Top Pop Artists of the Past 25 Years" chart. In late 2005, Prince struck a deal with Universal Records to release his next album, *3121*. Prince achieved his first career number-one debut on the *Billboard* 200 with *3121* on February 4, 2006. He released a compilation album, *Ultimate*, in 2006.

On June 12, 2006, Prince was honored with a Webby Lifetime Achievement Award in recognition of his "visionary" use of the Internet, which included becoming the first major artist to release an entire album—*Crystal Ball* (1997)—exclusively on the Web. On June 27, 2006, Prince appeared at the BET Awards, where he was named best male R&B artist. On November 14, 2006, Prince was inducted into the UK Music Hall of Fame, appearing to collect his award but not performing. In November 2006, Prince opened a nightclub named 3121 in Las Vegas at the Rio All-Suite Hotel and Casino, where he performed weekly on Friday and Saturday nights. He has since issued several more recordings, including the albums *Planet Earth* (2007) and the three-disc *Lotusflow3r* (2009).

PUBLIC ENEMY

Rap Group. As spokesmen of racial pride and proponents of militant public activism, Public Enemy, formed in 1982, has refined the political sound and the message of rap music. The formation of Public Enemy centered around Adelphi University in Long Island, New York, where the group's founder, Carlton Ridenhour (also known as Chuck D.), a graphic design major, joined fellow students Hank Shocklee and Bill Stephney at radio station WBAU. First appearing on Stephney's radio show, Ridenhour soon hosted his own three-hour program. Ridenhour's powerful rap voice attracted a number of loyal followers. Ridenhour soon recruited the talents of William Drayton (Flavor Flav), Norman Rodgers (Terminator X), and Richard Griffin (Professor Griff) to form Public Enemy. Shocklee and his production-oriented peers in the group came to be known as the Bomb Squad, and their talents were often sought by other artists.

In 1987, Public Enemy released the debut album *Yo! Bum Rush the Show*, which sold more than 400,000 copies. Two years later, Professor Griff, the group's "minister of information," was fired by Chuck D. for making anti-Semitic comments. Under the leadership of Chuck D., the group recorded the song "Fight the Power" for director Spike Lee's 1989 film *Do the Right Thing*. The group's second album, *It Takes a Nation of Millions to Hold Us Back*, became a million seller.

Rap Group Public Enemy, Bonnaroo Music and Arts Festival, Manchester, TN, 2009. *Formed in 1982, Public Enemy has released several albums featuring politically charged lyrics, including 1988's* It Takes a Nation of Millions to Hold Us Back, *which sold more than one million copies.* TIM MOSENFELDER/GETTY IMAGES ENTERTAINMENT/GETTY IMAGES

Public Enemy's 1990 release, *Fear of a Black Planet*, featured themes regarding a world struggle for the advancement of the black race. The controversial song "911 Is a Joke" led to widespread discourse over the song's allegations that emergency personnel respond more slowly, if at all, to calls originating from inner-city or predominantly African American areas. The follow-up album, *Apocalypse '91: The Enemy Strikes Black* (1991), was a startling statement of social and racial consciousness and featured a collaboration with the heavy-metal band Anthrax on "Bring the Noise," a track that had originally appeared on *It Takes a Nation*. Another single, "By the Time I Get to Arizona," sparked a nationwide debate over the refusal of Arizona state officials to recognize Martin Luther King Jr.'s birthday as a legal holiday.

Greatest Misses, a hits compilation released in 1992, seemed to signal the end of an era for the Public Enemy camp. In a departure from their earlier work, *Muse Sick-n-Hour Mess Age* (1994) traded the sonic dissonances of the Bomb Squad for samples from classic soul recordings. Meanwhile, most of the members had established themselves as solo artists or developed other career directions in the early 1990s, but overall the group's popularity seemed to wane as gangsta rap commandeered the airwaves. The group proved that they could incorporate the more modern sounds of hip-hop into their music with the critically innovative album *He Got Game* (1998), the soundtrack for the Spike Lee movie of the same name. However, like many of their later 1990s offerings, the rap-buying audiences passed over this album.

Public Enemy returned to their hardcore rap roots with their 1999 offering *There's a Poison Goin' On...*, but critics paid more attention to the album than fans did. Public Enemy continued to tour and released their eighth studio album, *Revolverlution*, in 2002. In 2005, they released *New Whirl Odor*, followed by *Rebirth of a Nation* (2006) and *How You Sell Soul to a Soulless People Who Sold Their Soul???* (2007).

QUEEN LATIFAH (1970–)

Singer, Actress. Born Dana Owens, singer and actress Queen Latifah grew up in East Orange, New Jersey, and began performing in high school as the human beat box for the rap group Ladies Fresh. In 1989, she launched her solo recording career with the album *All Hail the Queen*, an Afrocentric, pro-woman work. Her other recordings include: *Nature of a Sista'* (1991), featuring the single "Latifah Had It Up 2 Here"; *Black Reign* (1993), which led to the feminist anthem "U.N.I.T.Y."; *Order in the Court* (1998), which *Entertainment Weekly* called "fun and funky"; *She's the Queen: A Collection of Hits* (2002); *The Dana Owens Album* (2004); *Trav'lin' Light* (2007); and *Persona* (2009).

Queen Latifah managed the careers of other rap artists through her New Jersey–based Flavor Unit Records and Management Company. In addition, she was a regular on the Fox network's *Living Single*, along with costars Kim Fields, Erika Alexander, and Kim Coles. She also made appearances on *The Fresh Prince of Bel-Air* and in such films as the Hudlin brothers' *House Party II* (1991), Spike Lee's *Jungle Fever* (1991), and Ernest Dickerson's *Juice* (1992). She had a lead role in *Set It Off* (1996). In 1998, Queen Latifah gave a performance as a jazz singer in the movie *Living Out Loud*. The following year, she was named one of *People* magazine's "50 Most Beautiful People." She also released an autobiography, *Ladies First: Revelations of a Strong Woman* (1999), and briefly hosted her own television talk show.

Queen Latifah was nominated for an Academy Award, a BAFTA Award, and a Golden Globe Award, among other nominations, for her supporting performance in the 2002 musical *Chicago*. She won a Gold Globe Award and a Screen Actors Guild Award, along with other awards and nominations, for her lead performance as an HIV-positive woman in *Life Support*, which aired in 2007 on HBO. Her other film performances include *Bringing Down the House* (2003), *Barbershop 2: Back in Business* (2004), *Beauty Shop* (2005), *Ice Age: The Meltdown* (2006) and its 2009 sequel, *Last Holiday* (2007), *Hairspray* (2007), *The Secret Life of Bees* (2008), and *Just Wright* (2010).

OTIS REDDING (1941–1967)

Singer, Songwriter. Born on September 9, 1941, in Dawson, Georgia, Otis Redding moved with his parents at age three to the Tindall Heights housing project in Macon. In grade school, Redding played drums and sang in a church gospel group. A few years later, he learned the vocals and piano style of his idol, Little Richard. Quitting school in the tenth grade, Redding went on the road with Little Richard's former band, the Upsetters. Redding's first professional break came when he joined Johnny Jenkins and the Pinetoppers. Redding's debut single was a Little Richard imitation tune, "Shout Bamalama." Accompanying Jenkins to a Stax studio session in Memphis, Redding was afforded some remaining recording time. Backed by Jenkins on guitar, Steve Cropper on piano, Lewie Steinberg on bass, and Al Jackson on drums, Redding cut "Hey Hey Baby" and the hit "These Arms of Mine."

Signed to the Stax label, Redding released the 1963 album *Pain in My Heart*. Backed by members of Booker T. and the MGs, Redding's follow-up LP, *Otis Blue (Otis*

Redding Sings Soul), featured the 1965 hit "Respect." In the next year, Redding broke attendance records at shows in Harlem and Watts. After releasing a cover version of the Rolling Stones' song "Satisfaction" in 1966, Redding embarked on a European tour that included his appearance on the British television show *Ready Steady Go!*

In August 1966, Redding established his own record company, Jotis, which distributed recordings through the Stax label. Following a few commercially unsuccessful ventures, Redding recorded singer Arthur Conley, who provided the label with the million-selling single "Sweet Soul Music." Redding's "Try a Little Tenderness" and the vocal duet "Tramp," featuring Carla Thomas, hit the charts in 1967. On June 16, Redding, backed by the MGs, performed a stunning high-paced set at the Monterey Pop Festival. On December 10, Redding's career came to a tragic end when the twin-engine plane carrying him to a concert date in Wisconsin crashed in Lake Monona near Madison. As if in tribute, Redding's song "Sitting on the Dock of the Bay," released a few weeks after his death, became his first gold record.

LIONEL RICHIE (1949–)

Singer, Songwriter, Pianist. Lionel Brockman Richie was born on June 20, 1949, in Tuskegee, Alabama. His grandmother, Adelaide Foster, a classical pianist, became his music instructor, introducing him to the works of Bach and Beethoven. While a freshman at the Tuskegee Institute, Richie formed the Mighty Mystics, who, along with members of the Jays, became the Commodores. Combining gospel, classical, and country-western music, the Commodores emerged as a formidable live act throughout the 1960s and 1970s. After signing with the Motown label, the group landed its first hit in 1974 with the song "Machine Gun." In 1981, Richie and Diana Ross recorded the hit theme song for Franco Zeffirelli's film *Endless Love*.

A year later, Richie released his first solo album, *Lionel Richie*, which featured the hits "Truly," "You Are," and "My Love." His follow-up release, *Can't Slow Down* (1983), produced five more hits: "All Night Long (All Night)," "Running with the Night," "Hello," "Stuck on You," and "Penny Lover." In collaboration with Michael Jackson, Richie wrote "We Are the World" for USA for Africa, the famine-relief project organized and produced by Quincy Jones. In 1985, Richie won an Academy Award for best original song for his composition "Say You, Say Me," which appeared on the *White Nights* soundtrack. A year later, Richie's third album, *Dancing on the Ceiling*, provided him with the hits "Dancing on the Ceiling," "Love Will Conquer All," "Ballerina Girl," and "Se La."

Richie was inducted into the Songwriters Hall of Fame in 1994. After taking a hiatus from recording, Richie released *Back to Front* in 1992, which yielded the hit "Do It to Me." This album was followed by *Time* (1998), *Renaissance* (2001), *Encore* (2002), *Just for You* (2004), *Coming Home* (2006), and *Just Go* (2009).

TEDDY RILEY (1967–)

Producer, Songwriter, Musician. Born on October 8, 1967, Teddy Riley grew up in Harlem, New York. By age ten, he could play guitar, bass, several horns, and keyboards. In his early twenties, Riley merged aspects of hip-hop, pop, and soul to create a new kind of music called *New Jack swing*. In the mid-1980s, Riley formed his first band, Wreckx-N-Effect, with brothers Markell and Brandon Mitchell, which produced the hit single "New Jack Swing" (1984).

In 1987, Riley formed the group Guy with Aaron Hall and Timmy Gatling. Their first effort on the Uptown/MCA label, *Guy* (1988), topped *Billboard*'s rhythm-and-blues chart and sold over two million copies. The group toured, selling out many venues. Their second album, *The Future* (1990), had a more pop sound. *The Future* went platinum and received strongly positive reviews.

Success was followed by difficult times. After his younger brother, Brandon Mitchell, was killed by gunfire, Riley decided to move to Virginia Beach. Riley and his longtime manager, Gene Griffen, then split over a money dispute, and Guy disbanded.

In 1991, Riley formed Blackstreet with Chauncey "Black" Hannibal, Dave Hollister, and Levi Little. After the release of their first album, *BLACKstreet* (1994), Hollister and Little left the group and were replaced by Eric Williams and Mark Middleton. The members of Blackstreet see themselves as role models and keep their music and image clean. The single "No Diggity" (1997) went platinum and topped the charts. Blackstreet won a Grammy Award for the best rhythm-and-blues performance in 1998. In 1999, Riley and Blackstreet put out their third album, *Finally*, which included the single "I Got What You On." Riley released a solo album, *Black Rock*, in 2001, and another album with Blackstreet in 2003, *Level II*.

Riley has written and produced numerous platinum and gold albums and singles for a variety of artists, including Michael Jackson, Keith Sweat, Wreckx-N-Effect, Bobby Brown, and Kool Moe Dee. In 1990, Riley founded Future Records Recording Studio, LOR Records Management, and Future Entertainment Group Ltd. in Virginia Beach. In early 2006, Riley launched the New Jack swing revival with the New Jack

Reunion Tour, featuring Blackstreet, After 7, SWV, and Tony Toni Toné.

SMOKEY ROBINSON (1940–)

Singer, Songwriter, Producer. Proclaimed by Bob Dylan to be one of America's greatest poets, Smokey Robinson is a pop music legend. He has risen to fame as a brilliant songwriter, producer, and singer. His instantly recognizable falsetto voice continues to bring Robinson gold records and a legion of loyal fans.

William Robinson Jr. was born in Detroit, on February 19, 1940. After his mother died when he was ten years old, Robinson was raised by his sister. Nicknamed "Smokey" by his uncle, Robinson was a bright student who enjoyed reading books and poetry. A reluctant saxophone student, Robinson turned his creative energy to composing songs that he collected in a dime-store writing tablet. While attending Detroit's Northern High School in 1954, Robinson formed the vocal group the Matadors, which performed at battle-of-the-band contests and at recreation centers.

Smokey Robinson and the Miracles. *The Miracles, an R&B vocal group led by Robinson (*second from right*), enjoyed a string of hits starting with 1961's "Shop Around," which was the first smash hit for Motown Records.* PICTORIAL PRESS LTD/ALAMY

Robinson's introduction to Berry Gordy in 1957 resulted in the Matadors' first record contract with George Goldner's End label. Upon joining the newly formed Motown label in 1960, the group changed their name, at Gordy's suggestion, to the Miracles. Although the Miracles' debut album failed to attract notice, they provided Motown with its first smash hit, "Shop Around," in 1961, a song written and coproduced by Robinson.

In close collaboration with Gordy, Robinson spent the following decade as one of Motown's most integral singers and producers. With the Miracles, he recorded such hits as "You Really Got a Hold on Me" (1963), "Tracks of My Tears" (1965), "I Second That Emotion" (1967), and "Tears of a Clown" (1970). As a writer, he provided the label with such hits as "My Guy" for Mary Wells, "I'll Be Doggone" for Marvin Gaye, and "My Girl" for the Temptations.

In 1972, Robinson left the Miracles to launch a solo career. Despite the moderate success of his records during the disco craze of the 1970s, Robinson continued to perform and record. In 1979, Robinson experienced a comeback with the critically acclaimed hit "Cruisin." Three years later, Robinson appeared on the NBC-TV special *Motown 25: Yesterday, Today, and Tomorrow.* Between 1986 and 1991, Robinson released five more albums, including *Smoke Signals* (1986), *One Heartbeat* (1987), and *Love, Smokey* (1990). He was inducted into both the Rock and Roll Hall of Fame and the Songwriters Hall of Fame in 1986. In 1987, he won a Grammy Award for his vocal performance on "Just to See Her." Robinson continued to make music through the 1990s with such albums as *Double Good Everything* (1991) and *Intimate* (1999). In 1995, Robinson was signed by Music by Design, a British company that solicits artists to create original music for television and radio commercials.

Robinson has continued to periodically perform and tour. In 2003, he served as a guest judge for *American Idol.* He issued a gospel LP, *Food for the Spirit,* in 2004 as a testimony to his Christian faith. A new album of pop standards, *Timeless Love,* was released in June 2006. In May 2006, at its 138th commencement convocation, Howard University conferred on Robinson an honorary doctor of music degree. In December 2006, Robinson was one of five Kennedy Center honorees. During the ceremony, his music was said to have created "the soundtrack for the lives of a generation of Americans." In February 2007, Robinson sang "Tracks of My Tears" at the forty-ninth annual Grammy Awards ceremony as part of an R&B trio that included Lionel Richie performing "Hello" and Chris Brown performing a hip-hop version of his single "Run It." In 2009, Robinson released a new album, *Time Flies When You're Having Fun.*

DIANA ROSS (1944–)

Singer, Actress. Diane Ross, one of six children, was born in Detroit on March 26, 1944. An extremely active child, Ross swam, ran track, and sang in church. In 1959, she joined the Primettes, a group comprised of Mary Wilson, Florence Ballard, and Barbara Martin. After failing to attract the attention of the Lupine label, the group auditioned for Berry Gordy Jr., who signed them to Motown. Upon the suggestion of Berry, the group changed its name to the Supremes. Their song "I Want a Guy," featuring Ross on lead vocals, was released in 1961, but failed to reach the charts. Not long afterward, following Martin's departure, the trio began recording with Ross on lead vocal.

The Supremes did not find commercial success on the Motown label until 1964, when they were placed under the guidance of the Holland-Dozier-Holland production team. In 1964, H-D-H turned out the Supreme's first smash hit, "Where Did Our Love Go?" followed by numerous hits, such as "Baby Love" in 1964, "I Hear a Symphony" in 1965, "You Can't Hurry Love" in 1966, and "Reflections" in 1967. With preferential treatment by Gordy, Ross became the dominant figure of the group. By the mid-1960s, Ross's emerging talent prompted Gordy to bill the group as Diana Ross and the Supremes.

In 1970, Ross left the Supremes to launch her solo career. Her debut album, *Diana Ross,* featured the writing and production talents of Ashford and Simpson, an effort that included the hit "Reach Out and Touch (Somebody's Hand)." One year later, she made her film debut in the Motown-sponsored movie *Lady Sings the Blues,* for which she won an Oscar nomination for her biographical portrayal of jazz singer Billie Holiday. Her role in the 1975 Motown-backed film *Mahogany* brought her not only a second Oscar nomination, but the number-one selling single, "Do You Know Where You're Going To." In 1978, Ross starred in the film version of *The Wiz,* the last full-scale motion picture to be backed by Motown.

Singer Diana Ross, Nobel Peace Prize Concert, Oslo, Norway, 2008. *During a concert honoring Nobel Peace Prize winner Martti Ahtisaari, Ross performed two of her number one hit singles—"Do You Know Where You're Going To" and "Ain't No Mountain High Enough."* INTS KALNINS/REUTERS/LANDOV

After leaving Motown in 1981, Ross signed a $20 million contract with the RCA label. Her first RCA album, *Why Do Fools Fall in Love?* went platinum. This was followed by four more LPs for RCA, including *Silk Electric* (1982), *Swept Away* (1984), and *Eaten Alive* (1985). Two years later, Ross left RCA for the London-based EMI label, which produced the albums *Red Hot Rhythm 'n' Blues* (1987), *Working Overtime* (1987), and *Greatest Hits, Live* (1990). Meanwhile, Ross had returned to Motown Records as a recording artist and partial owner in 1989, one year after being inducted into the Rock and Roll Hall of Fame.

In the 1990s, Ross continued to enjoy popularity around the world. She achieved tremendous success as the owner of her own multimillion-dollar corporation, Diana Ross Enterprises. Her autobiography, *Secrets of a Sparrow: Memoirs,* was published in 1993, and a compilation called *Diana Extended/The Remixes* hit the stores in 1994. Ross also continued to act occasionally, appearing as a schizophrenic in the television movie *Out of the Darkness* (1994) and alongside the young star Brandy in *Double Platinum* (1999). In 2000, VH1 honored Ross with *Divas 2000: A Tribute to Diana Ross.* The show included performances by Mariah Carey, Faith Hill, Donna Summer, RuPaul, Destiny's Child, and Ross herself with the Supremes.

In 2005, Ross returned to the charts with "I Got a Crush on You," a duet recorded with Rod Stewart for his album *The Great American Songbook.* She also recorded a duet with Westlife, a remake of Ross's 1991 single, "When You Tell Me You Love Me." In 2006, Motown released an archived album titled *Blue,* which was a collection of jazz standards recorded after Ross filmed *Lady Sings the Blues.* Released in June to stellar reviews, *Blue* peaked at number-two on the jazz albums chart. The album *I Love You* (2006) gave Ross her first top-forty album since *Swept Away* more than two decades earlier. In 2007, Ross appeared on a number of television shows across the United States to promote her new album. She also appeared on *American Idol* as a mentor to the contestants.

SALT-N-PEPA

Rap Group. The hip-hop group Salt-N-Pepa was formed in 1985 in Queens, New York. The group included Salt (Cheryl James), Pepa (Sandy Denton), and Spinderella (Deidre "Dee Dee" Roper). They were the first female rap group to go platinum and are widely recognized as paving the way for later female rap stars. Originally known as Super Nature, they changed their name to Salt-N-Pepa in 1987. Roper replaced Latoya Hanson, the first Spinderella.

Salt-N-Pepa's debut project, *Hot, Cool, and Vicious* (1986), went platinum, setting the stage for a decade of megahits for the group, including "Push It" (1987); the album *A Salt with a Deadly Pepa* (1988), which was nominated for a Grammy; the single "Expressions" (1989); and their third album, *Blacks' Magic* (1990). Their single "Let's Talk about Sex" was used in a public-service video to educate youth about the dangers of AIDS. Their fourth album, *Very Necessary* (1993), produced the hits "Whatta Man" and "Shoop." The same year, James and Denton appeared in the comedy film *Who's the Man?* They released their fifth album *Brand New* in 1997. Following the release of the album, James and Denton began to focus more on their acting careers. Salt-N-Pepa's greatest-hits album, *Salt-N-Pepa: The Best Of* was released in 2000. The group officially disbanded in 2002 but has occasionally reunited to perform.

Jill Scott Performs during the BET Honors Show in Washington, DC, 2008. *Scott's 2000 debut,* Who Is Jill Scott? Words and Sounds Vol. 1, *garnered such praise that she is seen as one of the premier female singers of her generation.* **AP IMAGES/ JACQUELYN MARTIN**

JILL SCOTT (1972–)

Singer, Songwriter, Poet, Actress. Born in 1972, Scott grew up in North Philadelphia as an only child with her mother, Joyce Scott, and her grandmother. Raised as a Jehovah's Witness, Scott attended the Philadelphia High School for Girls. After graduating, she attended Temple University. Scott majored in secondary education and had planned on becoming a high school English teacher. After a stint as a teacher's aide, Scott grew disillusioned with teaching and left the profession.

Scott began her creative journey as a spoken-word artist, performing her work at poetry readings. Roots drummer ?uestlove took notice, and a collaboration resulted with the song, "You Got Me." In 2000, the song earned Erykah Badu and the Roots a Grammy for best rap performance by a duo or group. Scott signed on to the Hidden Beach Recordings label in 2000, and her debut album, *Who Is Jill Scott? Words and Sounds Vol. 1*, was released that same year.

Though Scott experienced moderate success and a Grammy nomination with the album, the diehard following she garnered among black women was noteworthy. She released a live album, *Experience: Jill Scott 826+*, in November 2001. Her second studio album, *Beautifully Human: Words and Sounds Vol. 2*, was released 2004. Scott won a Grammy Award in 2005 for "Cross My Mind."

Scott remains a poet at heart. In 2005, St. Martin's Press published a volume of her poems titled *The Moments, the Minutes, the Hours.* Scott added a new dimension to hip-hop artist Lupe Fiasco's 2006 single "Daydreaming," which won a Grammy and was featured in a new collection of songs by Scott. The collection, aptly titled *Collaborations*, was released in 2007. A third studio album, *The Real Thing: Words and Sounds Vol. 3*, was released to a solid reception within that same year. Scott collaborated with George Benson and Al Jarreau for their 2007 version of "God Bless the Child." The song earned her yet another Grammy Award for best traditional R&B vocal performance. Scott released her second live album, *Live In Paris+*, in 2008. The album documents a stellar performance and features a bonus DVD of the concert.

Interspersed between Scott's musical projects is a burgeoning flair for acting that she has pursued as far back as 2000. In 2004, she appeared in several episodes of the UPN sitcom *Girlfriends* as Donna, love interest to the main character, William Dent. In 2007, Scott's portrayal as Sheila in Tyler Perry's *Why Did I Get Married?* earned rave reviews. Scott expanded her acting resume in 2008 by taking on the role of Precious Ramotswe in the television adaptation of Alexander McCall Smith's series of books *The No. 1 Ladies' Detective Agency*. In 2010, she returned to her role as Sheila in *Why Did I Get Married Too?* and guest-starred in an episode of *Law & Order: Special Victims Unit*.

TUPAC SHAKUR (1971–1996)

Rapper, Actor. Born Tupac Amaru Shakur in the Bronx in 1971, Shakur was a multitalented rap artist and actor who became a powerhouse in hip-hop culture. He made his acting debut in an Apollo Theater production of *A Raisin in the Sun* in 1984 as a benefit for Jesse Jackson's presidential campaign. After his family moved to Baltimore, Shakur attended the High School of the Performing Arts and wrote his first rap song following the violent death of a friend. He dropped out of high school, moved to California, and began circulating tapes of his music until he landed a job as a roadie with the group Digital Underground, eventually working his way to a guest spot as a rapper in their stage show.

In 1991, Shakur signed with Interscope Records and released his debut project, *2Pacalypse Now*. A string of commercially successful and critically acclaimed projects followed, including *Strictly 4 My N.I.G.G.A.Z.* (1993), *Me Against the World* (1995), and *All Eyez on Me* (1996). Shakur's rap style was celebrated for its versatile vocal inflection, rhythmically subtle delivery, and the range of lyrical topics, although the latter was also the source of much criticism because of its frequently explicit content.

Shakur also received accolades for his performances in films, among them *Juice* (1992), *Poetic Justice* (1993), *Above the Rim* (1994), and *Gang Related* (1997). Shakur's career was marred by controversies, which included intermittent trouble with the law, for which he spent time incarcerated. Like his contemporary, Notorious B.I.G., Shakur died in a drive-by shooting in Las Vegas in 1996. Although the alleged shooter, a Crips gang member, was killed before he could be charged, insiders speculate that the murder was gang-related in that Shakur appeared to be affiliated with Suge Knight's Bloods gang, sworn enemies of the Crips.

RUSSELL SIMMONS

See chapter 14, Entrepreneurship.

WILL SMITH (1968–)

Rapper, Actor. Born on September 25, 1968, in Wynnefield, Pennsylvania, Will Smith became a successful rap musician in the late 1980s and had a hit television show during the early 1990s. By the turn of the century, he personified the media megastar, racking up both multiplatinum-selling albums and movie box-office hits.

When he was eighteen, Smith and Jeff Townes formed the rap duo DJ Jazzy Jeff and the Fresh Prince. They were successful on the local scene, and after landing a record deal with Jive Records, released *Rock the House* in 1987. Their second album, *He's the DJ, I'm the Rapper*, was released a year later. It became one of the biggest-selling rap albums up to that point, due mainly to the success of the single, "Parents Just Don't Understand." That year, the single also brought the duo a Grammy Award for best rap performance. DJ Jazzy Jeff and the Fresh Prince subsequently released three more albums: *And in This Corner . . .* (1989), *Homebase* (1991), and *Code Red* (1993).

Smith's popularity as a rap musician led to a starring role in the NBC sitcom *The Fresh Prince of Bel-Air*. The show proved successful and ran from 1991 to 1996, earning Smith a Golden Globe nomination for best actor in a television program in 1992. Smith also began to appear in feature films, landing roles in *Where the Day Takes You* (1992), *Six Degrees of Separation* (1993), *Made in America* (1993), and *Bad Boys* (1995).

The box-office success of *Independence Day* (1996) established Smith as a major film star capable of handling both action and comedy roles. It was followed by *Men in Black* (1997), *Enemy of the State* (1998), and *Wild Wild West* (1999). His abilities as a dramatic actor were showcased in *The Legend of Bagger Vance* (2000) and *Ali* (2001). In addition to critical praise, Smith received an Oscar nomination for his portrayal of the former heavyweight champion. Smith followed the performance with *Men in Black II* (2002). He later starred or appeared in a number of other films, including *Bad Boys II* (2003), the documentary *A Closer Walk* (2004, narrator), *Jersey Girl* (2004), *American Chopper* (2004), *I, Robot* (2004) *Shark Tale* (2004, voice), the documentary *There's a God on the Mic* (2005), *Hitch* (2005, as producer and star), *The Pursuit of Happyness* (2006, as producer and star; his son Jaden also appeared in the film), *I Am Legend* (2007), and *Hancock* (2008).

In addition to his work as an actor, Smith continued to make well-received rap albums. He released *Big Willie Style* in 1997. The album contained the hit singles "Gettin' Jiggy Wit It," "Miami," and "Just the Two of Us." Smith followed with two more solo albums, *Willenium* (1999) and *Born to Reign* (2002). His collaborative retrospective albums include *Platinum & Gold Collection* (2003) and *The Very Best of D. J. Jazzy Jeff & the Fresh Prince* (2006). He released another solo album, *Lost and Found*, in 2005.

DONNA SUMMER (1948–)

Singer. One of the biggest stars of the disco era, Donna Summer first won notice with a pulsating Euro-hit, then gained mainstream popularity. She ruled the charts through the late 1970s, though the fading of disco left her with little choice but to streamline her style. Although her popularity declined in the ensuing years, she became one of the few stars of the era to transcend the kitsch that surrounded it.

Born LaDonna Gaines in Boston, the singer got her first break when she was cast in a traveling production of a rock musical. While in Germany, she met Helmut Sommer, whom she married. She later made the acquaintance of Italian producer Giorgio Moroder, who produced her first hit, "Love to Love You Baby." Summer's moans and groans were her initial route to stardom. Through the late 1970s, however, she continually expanded her range. Her hits included a cover version of the pop standard "MacArthur Park," as well as "On the Radio," "Bad Girls," "Hot Stuff," and "Last Dance."

Singer Donna Summer, Los Angeles, 1979. *One of the biggest stars of the disco era, Summer took home three American Music Awards in 1979 for favorite disco female artist, album, and single. Over the course of her career, she has also been honored with five Grammy Awards.* AP IMAGES. REPRODUCED BY PERMISSION.

Summer became a born-again Christian in the early 1980s, and gradually turned toward inspirational music. She earned Grammy Awards for best inspirational performance in 1984 and 1985, but she surfaced less and less frequently in the pop world. Summer continues to produce, and she has put out more albums, including a recording of her VH1 concert called *VH1 Presents: Live More Encore!* in 1999 and *Greatest Hits 2001* in 2001. In 2003, Summer released a greatest-hits compilation called *The Journey*, which reached the UK top ten the following year. On September 20, 2004, Summer was among the first artists to be inducted into the newly formed Dance Music Hall of Fame in New York City. In July 2006, Summer joined forces with Pure Tone Music, an A&R consulting and full-service independent music company, located just outside of New York City. She released the album *Crayons* in 2008.

TINA TURNER (1939–)

Singer. With a music career spanning more than thirty years, Tina Turner has come to be known as the "hardest working woman in show business." From soul-music star to rock goddess, Turner's vocal style and energetic stage act remain a showstopping phenomenon.

Born Annie Mae Bullock on November 25, 1939, in Brownsville, Tennessee, Turner moved to Knoxville with her parents at age three. She first sang in church choirs and at local talent contests. After moving with her mother to St. Louis at age sixteen, she met pianist Ike Turner, leader of the R&B group the Kings of Rhythm. Hired by the band to sing at weekend engagements, Annie Bullock married Ike Turner in 1958 and took the stage name Tina Turner. When the band's scheduled session singer failed to appear at a recording session in 1960, Tina stepped in to record the R&B song "A Fool in Love," which became a million seller.

With a major hit behind them, the Turners formed the Ike and Tina Turner Revue, complete with the Ikettes. Major international success came for the Turners in 1966 when producer Phil Spector combined his "wall of sound" approach with an R&B sound to record the hit "River Deep, Mountain High." Subjected to years of physical abuse by her husband, Turner divorced Ike in 1976 and set out on a solo career. That same year, she costarred in the Who's rock opera film *Tommy* as the Acid Queen.

In 1984, Turner's career skyrocketed with the commercial success of the album *Private Dancer*, which featured the hit singles "What's Love Got to Do with It" and "Better Be Good." Turner's sensuously vibrant image soon appeared on high-budget videos and magazine covers and in films, such as the 1985 release *Mad Max*

Beyond Thunderdome, in which she played the tyrannical Aunty Entity. With the immense commercial success of her 1989 album *Foreign Affair*, Turner closed out the decade as one of the most popular singers on the international music scene.

In 1991, Tina and Ike Turner were inducted into the Rock and Roll Hall of Fame. That same year, Turner released the album *Simply the Best*. In 1993, a movie based on her life, *What's Love Got to Do with It*, was released, starring Angela Bassett as Turner. In 1996, Turner returned to recording with *Wildest Dreams*. Because of the album's popularity, Turner returned to touring in 1997. She continued to tour through 2001 and also found time to put out the album *Twenty Four Seven* (1999). In 2004, Turner released a greatest-hits album, *All the Best*, which made the highest *Billboard* 200 debut of her career, entering at number two. In 2005, she was a Kennedy Center honoree.

USHER (1978–)

Singer, Actor. Usher Raymond IV, better known to the world by his mononym Usher, was born on October 14, 1978, in Dallas, Texas. His father, Usher Raymond III, left the family, and Usher moved to Chattanooga, Tennessee, with his mother, Jonetta Patton. He spent most of his childhood there with his mother, stepfather, and half-brother. His family played a powerful role in his future career. When he was nine years old, Usher joined a local church youth choir that his mother directed. While there, his grandmother took notice of his singing talents. The family moved to Atlanta, Georgia, confident that the big city would offer more opportunities for a singer on the rise.

A brief stint in an R&B group called the NuBeginnings produced an album called *NuBeginning*. Usher left the group because his mother felt it was not a favorable arrangement. He competed on *Star Search* and wound up auditioning for LaFace Records cofounder L. A. Reid. Usher signed with LaFace, and his mother began focusing full-time on her role as manager of his career. Usher was featured on the song "Call Me a Mack" for the soundtrack to the 1993 film *Poetic Justice*. His self-titled debut album was released the following year. It made a respectable showing at number twenty-five on the *Billboard* top R&B/hip-hop albums chart. Three of its standout singles were "Think of You," "Can U Get Wit It," and "The Many Ways."

After graduating from high school, Usher began to focus on his sophomore album. LaFace also helped him by pairing him up with fellow Atlantan and teen singing sensation Monica for their 1995 rendition of "Let's Straighten It Out." Usher also performed on "Dreamin'" for *Rhythm of the Games*, LaFace's 1996 Olympic Games benefit album.

Hip-Hop Vocalist Usher Performing at Nokia Theatre L.A. Live in Los Angeles, 2010. *Usher enjoyed the rare distinction of winning Grammy Awards for best male R&B vocal performance in back to back years, 2002 and 2003.* C FLANIGAN/FILMMAGIC/GETTY IMAGES

Usher's celebrity truly started to take off after the release of his third album, *My Way*, in 1997. His acting debut on the UPN television series *Moesha* gave him more visibility. He earned a recurring role on the series, as well as his first film role in *The Faculty* (1998). He took on a minor role in the soap opera *The Bold and the Beautiful* and starred in the films *She's All That* (1999) and *Light It Up* (1999). Meanwhile, *My Way* went multiplatinum, as did his next album, *8701* (2001). Its two singles, "U Remind Me" and "U Got It Bad," were mainstays on the charts for several weeks. Usher won a Grammy Award the following year for best male R&B vocal performance for "U Remind Me." He won another in the same category in 2003 for "U Don't Have to Call," a feat only achieved earlier by Luther Vandross and Stevie Wonder.

Usher's fourth album, *Confessions* (2004), eclipsed the previous two by selling more than ten million copies in the United States alone. The album holds the record for the highest first-week sales for an R&B artist in history and remained on the *Billboard* 200 chart for a total of ninety-five weeks. "Burn," "Yeah!' and "Confessions II" are the best-known singles. A lot of excitement over the album came from the controversy behind Usher's breakup with TLC member Rozonda "Chilli" Thomas. Fans inferred the reasons for the breakup through the lyrics of the album.

His 2008 album *Here I Stand* has been certified platinum. The momentum of that album was largely the result of the title track. *Raymond v. Raymond* followed in 2010. Many assumed that the album would become as popular as Usher's *Confessions*, since it was released only months after his divorce from Tameka Foster. "Papers," one of its singles, was believed to be inspired by their relationship. "There Goes My Baby" has become the album's best-known single.

Usher has become a successful businessman as well. The singer is part owner of the Cleveland Cavaliers franchise, has opened several restaurants, and signs acts to his own record label, US Records. His sense of philanthropy is also well documented. Usher founded New Look, a nonprofit charity organization that provides "young people with a new look on life through education and real-world experience." In 2006, New Look launched an initiative called Our Block, which works to helped rebuild and revitalize city blocks in New Orleans.

LUTHER VANDROSS (1951–2005)

Singer, Composer, Producer. One of the premier pop artists of the 1980s, Luther Vandross was responsible for the emergence of a new school of modern soul singers. Born in New York City on April 20, 1951, Vandross was the son of a gospel singer and a big band vocalist. Vandross received his musical education by listening to recordings of Aretha Franklin and the Supremes. In high school, he formed numerous singing groups. Throughout the 1970s, he was a backup singer, performing with such artists as David Bowie, Carly Simon, and Ringo Starr. He also sang advertising jingles, such as ATT's theme "Reach Out and Touch."

Following the release of his first album, *Never Too Much*, in 1981, Vandross was called upon to sing duets with a number of pop artists, including Aretha Franklin and Dionne Warwick. As a successful writer and producer, he released five albums in the 1990s, including *Power of Love* (1991), *Never Let Me Go* (1993), *Songs* (1994) *Your Secret Love* (1996), and *I Know* (1998). Vandross continued to tour and record in the early 2000s, producing albums such as *Smooth Love* (2000) and *Luther Vandross* (2001). He released three albums in 2003: *Dance with My Father*, *The Essential Luther Vandross*, and *Live from Radio City Music Hall*. Vandross suffered a stroke in 2003 and died in 2005 at age fifty-four. Several previously unreleased tracks and compilations of Vandross's music have been released since his death.

MARY WELLS (1943–1992)

Singer. Born in 1943 and raised in Detroit, Michigan, Mary Wells started her music career as a featured soloist in her high school choir. When she was seventeen years old, Wells signed a contract with Motown. With Smokey Robinson as her main producer and writer, Wells scored a number of hits, such as "I Don't Want to Take a Chance" in 1961, "You Beat Me to the Punch" in 1962, and "My Guy" in 1964. In the same year, she recorded the album *Together* with Marvin Gaye and toured England with the Beatles.

At the peak of her career, Wells left the Motown label to become an actress, although she continued to work as a singer. After relocating in Los Angeles, she signed a contract with Twentieth Century Fox Records. Unfortunately, Wells could never find a producer who equaled Robinson's ability to record her material. Her 1965 single "Use Your Head" achieved only modest commercial success. In the 1970s, Wells left music to raise her children. For a brief period, she was married to Cecil Womack, brother of the rhythm-and-blues great Bobby Womack.

During the 1980s, Wells returned to music, performing on the oldies circuit. In 1985, she appeared in *Motown's 25th Anniversary* television special. Diagnosed as having cancer of the larynx in August 1990, Wells, without medical insurance to pay for treatment, lost her home. Not long afterward, the Rhythm and Blues Foundation raised over $50,000 for Wells's hospital costs. Funds were also sent by such artists as Bruce Springsteen, Rod Stewart, and Diana Ross. Despite chemotherapy treatments, Wells died on July 26, 1992, and was buried at Forest Lawn Memorial Park in Los Angeles.

KANYE WEST (1977–)

Rapper, Singer, Producer. Kanye Omari West was born on June 8, 1977, in Atlanta, Georgia, to parents who were divorced by the time he was three. West moved with his mother, an English professor, to Chicago's South Side and spent summers with his father, an award-winning photographer.

West developed a love for music while attending Polaris High School. He completed one year of art school at Chicago State University before pursuing a career in rap and local music production. In 2001, West moved to New York, where rapper Jay-Z hired him to produce songs for his 2001 album *The Blueprint*, which came to be revered as a hip-hop classic. West's success as a producer threatened to overshadow his dreams of becoming a rapper in his own right.

While continuing to produce others, West cut his own demo and scored a deal with Jay-Z's Roc-A-Fella Records in 2002. While driving home from a session in Los Angeles in October 2002, West fell asleep at the wheel, resulting in a head-on collision. With his jaw wired shut as a result of his injuries, West completed his debut,

Rapper Kanye West during Concert Performance. *West's 2004 debut album,* The College Dropout, *went double platinum and earned him a Grammy Award for best rap album.* STEVE BLACK / ALAMY.

The College Dropout. The album was released in 2004, went double platinum, and earned him a Grammy Award for best rap album. West proved his worth as an artist by matching that feat with *Late Registration* (2005) and *Graduation* (2007).

West continued to win accolades for his work when tragedy struck in 2007. His mother, Dr. Donda West, died from surgery-related complications. This loss, along with the breakup of his engagement to designer Alexis Phifer, emanated throughout his next album, *808s & Heartbreak* (2008). The recording was a resounding success and an artistic departure from his previous three albums. The following year, West released two compilation albums on the same day—*Good Morning, Good Night: Dusk* and *Good Morning, Good Night: Dawn.* Both featured songs from other artists, ranging from the well-known Alicia Keys to the more underground Malik Yusef.

WILL.I.AM (1975–)

Rapper, Songwriter, Singer, Actor, Producer, Activist. William James Adams Jr., better known as will.i.am (pronounced will-eye-AM), was born on March 15, 1975. He was raised in the projects of East Los Angeles by his mother Debra. William was urged by his mother to be his own person and to resist the negative influence of other young people in his neighborhood. He was given a chance to hone his musical talents by attending school in Pacific Palisades.

While there, William rapped under the name Will-1X and befriended Allan Lindo (also known as apl.de.ap). The two formed a conscious group called Atban Klann and performed in East Los Angeles clubs. After several other members joined, the group caught the attention of N.W.A. rapper Eazy-E, who signed them to his Ruthless Records label in 1992. Will.i.am contributed production

Musician will.i.am, We Are One: Inaugural Celebration, Lincoln Memorial, Washington, DC, 2009. *After supporting the candidacy of Barack Obama for U.S. president in part by writing the song "Yes We Can," will.i.am performed for the inaugural celebration at the Lincoln Memorial. The musician is best known as the front man and cofounder of the hip-hop and pop group the Black Eyed Peas.* JASON REED/REUTERS /LANDOV

work for Eazy-E's 1992 EP *5150: Home 4 tha Sick.* Eazy-E died of AIDS-related complications in 1995.

Will.i.am left Ruthless soon afterward to form a group that would become known as the Black Eyed Peas. The group released its first album, *Behind the Front,* in 1998. The song "Joints & Jam" was featured on the soundtrack for the 1998 film *Bulworth.* "Be Free" made its way into the 1999 film *She's All That.* The group's second album, *Bridging the Gap* (2000), included the Macy Gray–assisted song "Request + Line." The album's poor performance on the charts was attributed to the new phenomenon of illegally downloaded music over the Internet.

Will.i.am's first solo album, *Lost Change* (2001), received a quiet reception, a far cry from the response to *Elephunk,* the Black Eyed Peas 2003 follow-up, which truly put the group on the map. *Elephunk* also eclipsed will.i.am's second solo release, *Must B 21* (2003), by selling 8.5 million copies worldwide. Will.i.am produced most of *Elephunk,* which was the first to feature the group's new vocalist, Stacy "Fergie" Ferguson. The *Elephunk* single "Where Is the Love?" featured Justin Timberlake and dominated the singles charts in more than ten countries.

Monkey Business (2005), the fourth Black Eyed Peas album, solidified their move from hip-hop and soul to more dance-oriented music. The album sold over ten million copies worldwide and won a Grammy Award for best rap performance by a duo or group for "Don't Phunk with My Heart."

Will.i.am's third solo release, *Songs about Girls* (2007), performed better on the charts than his two previous albums. His work as a producer grew primarily from his production credits with the Black Eyed Peas. In 2008, Michael Jackson enlisted will.i.am to produce and remix songs for Jackson's *Thriller* rerelease, *Thriller 25.* Also showing his more philanthropic side, he donated his song "One People" to *Songs for Survival* (2008), the Survival International charity album. An ardent supporter of Barack Obama, will.i.am wrote "Yes We Can" for Obama's 2008 presidential campaign. Jesse Dylan directed a video for the song, which won an award for new approaches in daytime entertainment at the Thirty-fifth Annual Creative Arts and Entertainment Daytime Emmy Awards.

In 2009, will.i.am returned to his hip-hop roots through production of rapper Flo Rida's new album, *R.O.O.T.S.* Will.i.am also worked on Rihanna's fourth album, *Rated R* (2009). *The E.N.D.* (short for The Energy Never Dies), released in 2009, was the fifth album by the Black Eyed Peas and proved to be their most successful. The infectious singles "Imma Be," "Alive," and "Meet Me Halfway" topped the charts.

JACKIE WILSON (1934–1984)

Singer. Between 1958 and 1963, Jackie Wilson reigned as one of the most popular rhythm-and-blues singers in the United States. Dressed in sharkskin suits and sporting a process hairstyle, Wilson exhibited a dynamic stage presence and a singing range that equaled his contemporaries James Brown and Sam Cooke.

Jack Leroy Wilson was born on June 9, 1934, in Detroit, Michigan. Wilson's mother sang spirituals and gospel songs at Mother Bradley's church. As a youngster, he listened to the recordings of the Mills Brothers, the Ink

Spots, and Louis Jordan. In high school, he became a boxer, and, at age sixteen, he won the American Amateur Golden Gloves welterweight title. But upon the insistence of his mother, Wilson quit boxing and pursued a career in music. While a teenager, Wilson sang with the Falcons in local clubs and at talent contests held at the Paradise Theater. He also worked in a spiritual group with later members of Hank Ballard's Midnighters.

In 1953, Wilson replaced Clyde McPhatter as the lead singer of the Dominoes. Wilson's only hit with the Dominoes was the reworking of the religious standard "St. Theresa of the Roses." Upon the success of the recording, Wilson signed a contract as a solo artist with the Brunswick label. Wilson's 1957 debut album, *Reet Petite,* featured a hit title track written by Berry Gordy Jr. and Billy Taylor. Gordy and Taylor also provided Wilson with the subsequent hits, "To Be Loved" in 1957, "Lonely Teardrops" in 1958, and "That's Why I Love You So" and "I'll Be Satisfied" in 1959.

During the early 1960s, Wilson performed and recorded numerous adaptations of classic music compositions in a crooning ballad style. This material, however, failed to bring out the powerful talent of Wilson's R&B vocal style. Although Wilson's repertoire contained mostly supper-club standards, he did manage to produce the powerful pop classics "Dogging Around" in 1960 and "Baby Workout" in 1963. Teamed with writer and producer Carl Davis, Wilson also recorded the hit "Whispers" and the rhythm-and-blues masterpiece "Higher and Higher" in 1967.

Following Wilson's last major hit, "I Get the Sweetest Feeling," in 1968, he performed on the oldies circuit and on Dick Clark's *Good Ol' Rock 'n' Roll Revue.* In 1975, Wilson suffered a serious heart attack on stage at the Latin Casino in Cherry Hill, New Jersey. Forced into retirement, he spent his last eight years in a nursing home, until his death on January 21, 1984.

MARY WILSON (1944–)

Singer. As a member of the Motown supergroup the Supremes, Mary Wilson's musical career represents an American success story. Born on March 6, 1944, in Greenville, Mississippi, Wilson moved to Detroit at age eleven. Raised in the Brewster-Douglas housing project on the city's east side, Wilson learned to sing by imitating the falsetto voice of Frank Lyman. Along with Barbara Martin and Betty Travis, Wilson formed the Primettes. Upon the departure of Travis, another neighborhood girl named Diana Ross joined the group. Appearing at talent shows and sock hops, the Primettes won first prize at the 1960 Detroit/Windsor Freedom Festival talent contest. Although the Primettes cut two singles on the Lupine label featuring Wilson on lead vocal, they failed to achieve commercial success.

On January 15, 1961, the sixteen-year-old Wilson and fellow Primettes Diana Ross, Florence Ballard, and Barbara Martin signed with the Motown label as the Supremes. Wilson's effort to win the lead vocal spot, however, soon gave way to the dominance of Diana Ross. Released in 1964, the group's first gold single, "Where Did Our Love Go?" made Wilson and the Supremes overnight celebrities. Between 1964 and 1968, Wilson sang background vocals on a number of hits, including "Baby Love," "You Can't Hurry Love," and "Reflections." Before leaving the group in 1976, Wilson also sang such recordings as "Love Child," "I'm Living in Shame," and "Someday We'll Be Together."

In 1983, Wilson was briefly reunited with the Supremes on the *Motown's 25th Anniversary* television special. In 1994, Wilson was thrust into the media spotlight when a car she was driving overturned and killed her son. The accident ended her longstanding feud with Diana Ross. In 2000, Wilson considered going on tour again with Ross and the Supremes, but negotiations did not work out. Instead, Wilson decided to go back to school, and in 2001 she earned an associate's degree in arts from New York University. Making her home in Los Angeles, Wilson occasionally appears on the oldies circuit and at small Supremes revival shows. She also occasionally records and makes television and film appearances.

NANCY WILSON (1937–)

Singer. Nancy Wilson was born in Chillicothe, Ohio, in 1937. Her musical talents were first noticed when, as a child, she performed for her family at various gatherings. The performances continued as Wilson became a member of her church choir. Influence from artists such as Billy Eckstine and Nat "King" Cole helped Wilson determine that singing would be her career. As a teen, Wilson and her family moved to Columbus, Ohio. Wilson soon became the host of her own radio show, *Skyline Melody,* during which she performed phoned-in requests.

In 1955, Wilson enrolled in classes at Ohio's Central State College to pursue teaching credentials. Her stint in school was short-lived, however, as Wilson dropped out to pursue her singing career. She spent the next three years touring the country as a member of Rusty Byrant's Carolyn Club Band. The experience Wilson gained while touring gave her the courage to go solo. New York City became Wilson's new home as her career skyrocketed.

Shortly after her arrival in the Big Apple, Wilson obtained permanent work at a local nightclub. Word of her masterful performances soon spread all over the city, prompting a recording session with Capitol Records. Her debut album, *Like in Love*, and her first major hit, "Save Your Love for Me," were released in 1960. The song "How Glad I Am" won a Grammy in 1964, beginning a thirty-year streak of acclaim.

Wilson's blend of rhythm and blues, jazz, and pop styles captivated thousands of fans around the world. Television executives began to take advantage of Wilson's talents, giving her a weekly variety show. The Emmy Award–winning *Nancy Wilson Show* was merely the beginning of Wilson's television appearances. Guest spots on *The Tonight Show*, *The Merv Griffin Show*, and *The Today Show* soon followed.

During the late 1970s and early 1980s, technology began to influence the fashion in which studio recordings were made. Wilson continued to record and tour despite differences with various recording companies over issues of sound. She was named Global Entertainer of the Year in 1986 by the World Conference of Mayors, and the NAACP gave her an Image Award that year as well.

In 2001, Wilson released her first Christmas album, *A Nancy Wilson Christmas*. With a star on the Hollywood Walk of Fame, an *Essence* Award, and a Martin Luther King Center for Social Change Award to her name, Wilson's bevy of honors is a symbol of her timelessness and a testimony to the loyalty of her fans. She was named a National Endowment for the Arts Jazz Master in 2004. That year, Wilson released *R.S.V.P. (Rare Songs, Very Personal)*. It won a 2005 Grammy Award for best jazz vocal album and brought her the 2005 NAACP Image Award for best jazz artist. Other honors Wilson has received include a UNCF Trumpet Award celebrating African American achievement, a Lifetime Achievement Award from the NAACP in Chicago, and Oprah Winfrey's Legends Award. Wilson has retired from touring, but she continues to record and to perform select engagements. Her third album with MCG Jazz, *Turned to Blue*, won a Grammy in 2006.

Musician Stevie Wonder, Warner Theater, Washington, DC, 2010. *During his lengthy career, pop music giant Stevie Wonder has recorded more than thirty U.S. top ten hits and has earned twenty-five Grammy Awards. He has also been inducted into both the Songwriters Hall of Fame and the Rock and Roll Hall of Fame.* FRANK MICELOTTA/GETTY IMAGES ENTERTAINMENT/GETTY IMAGES

STEVIE WONDER (1950–)

Singer, Songwriter, Pianist. Popular music's genius composer and singer Stevie Wonder has remained at the forefront of musical change. His colorful harmonic arrangements have drawn upon jazz, soul, pop, reggae, and rap-derived New Jack rhythms. Wonder's gift to pop music is his ability to create serious music dealing with social and political issues, while at the same time revealing the soulful and deeply mysterious nature of the human experience.

Steveland Morris Judkins was born on May 13, 1950, in Saginaw, Michigan. Raised in Detroit, Wonder first sang in the church choir. He was most attracted to the sounds of Johnny Ace and B. B. King, which he heard on late-night radio programs. By age eight, Wonder had learned to play piano, harmonica, and bongos. Through the connections of Ronnie White of the Miracles, Wonder auditioned for Berry Gordy Jr., who immediately signed the thirteen-year-old prodigy, giving him the stage name Little Stevie Wonder. After releasing his first singles, "Thank You (for Loving Me All the Way)" and "Contract of Love" in 1963, Wonder's "Fingertips, Pt. 2" became the first live performance of a song to reach the top of the pop charts. That year, Wonder also became the first recording artist to hold number-one spots on the *Billboard* Hot 100 R&B singles and album charts simultaneously. In the following year, Wonder hit the charts with "Hey Harmonica Man."

With the success of his recording career, Wonder began touring more frequently. Motown assigned Wonder a tutor from the Michigan School for the Blind, allowing him to continue his education while on the road. In 1964, he performed in London with the *Motown Revue*, a package featuring Martha and the Vandellas, the Supremes, and the Temptations. Wonder's subsequent recording of the punchy rhythm-and-blues single "Uptight (Everything's Alright)" became a smash hit in 1966. Wonder's growing commercial success at Motown brought him greater artistic freedom in the studio. In collaboration with Clarence Paul, Wonder produced a long succession of hits, including Bob Dylan's "Blowing in the Wind" in 1966, "I Was Made to Love Her" in 1967, and "For Once in My Life" in 1968. In 1969, President Richard Nixon gave Wonder a Distinguished Service Award from the President's Committee on Employment of Handicapped People. That year, the album *My Cherie Amour* generated a single of the same name.

After recording the 1970 album *Signed, Sealed, & Delivered*, featuring the title track, Wonder moved to New York City, where he founded Taurus Production Company and Black Bull Publishing Company, both of which were licensed under Motown. With complete control over his musical career, Wonder began to write lyrics addressing social and political issues. Through the technique of overdubbing, he played most of the instruments on his recordings, including the guitar, bass, horns, percussion, and brilliant chromatic harmonica solos. *Music of My Mind* (1972), *Talking Book* (1972), *Innervisions* (1973), and *Fulfillingness' First Finale* (1974) all feature Wonder's distinctive synthesizer accompaniment.

Released in 1979, Wonder's *Journey through the Secret Life of Plants* was an exploratory musical soundtrack for a film documentary. In 1984, Wonder's soundtrack for the film *Woman in Red* won him an Academy Award for best song with "I Just Called to Say I Love You." One year later, Wonder participated in the recording of "We Are the World" for USA for Africa, a famine-relief project. He also teamed up with Paul McCartney for the hit single "Ebony and Ivory." Wonder's 1985 Grammy-winning album *In Square Circle* produced the hit singles "Part-Time Lover" and "Overjoyed."

After Wonder was inducted into the Rock and Roll Hall of Fame in 1989, he composed material for the soundtrack to Spike Lee's film *Jungle Fever*. Eight years in the making, Wonder's 1995 album *Conversation Peace* was released the same year as his double-live recording *Natural Wonder*. He also contributed to the tribute recording *Inner City Blues: The Music of Marvin Gaye* and to Quincy Jones's *Q's Jook Joint*. He also won an *Essence* Award that year.

Wonder founded the SAP/Stevie Wonder Vision Awards, which honor research and the development of products that enable visually impaired people to enter the workforce. In 2000, President Bill Clinton paid tribute to Wonder at the Kennedy Center Honors ceremony in Washington, D.C. In 2002, Wonder received a lifetime achievement award from the Songwriters Hall of Fame in New York.

In 2004, *Rolling Stone* magazine ranked Wonder number fifteen on their list of the "100 Greatest Rock and Roll Artists of All Time." Wonder's first new album in ten years, *A Time to Love*, released in 2005, features Prince on guitar and background vocals from En Vogue. The single "From the Bottom of My Heart" was a hit on adult-contemporary R&B radio. The album also features a duet with India.Arie on the title track, "A Time to Love." Wonder has received numerous Grammy Awards, including one in 2007 with Tony Bennett for best pop collaboration with vocals for the song "For Once in My Life." In 2007, an episode of *American Idol* featured the finalists singing Stevie Wonder hits and a guest appearance by Wonder himself. In 2009, Wonder was awarded the Library of Congress Gershwin Prize for Popular Song.

26

VISUAL AND APPLIED ARTS

Phyllis J. Jackson

Continental Africans and their resilient descendants channeled their creative energies toward beautifying objects and making visual arts since their 1619 arrival on the North American continent. From these first indentured Africans in a remote British colony, through the resourceful survivors of the Middle Passage, to the Ivy league–trained artists emerging in the era of Barack Obama's astounding rise to the U.S. presidency, men and women of the African diaspora have developed a distinctive aesthetic voice and inventive visual vocabulary, shaping and reshaping the American imagination and visual culture.

Some African American artists are well-known figures, such as Henry Ossawa Tanner, Jacob Lawrence, Elizabeth Catlett, Romare Bearden, Martin Puryear, and Lorna Simpson. Legends in their own times for an array of individual expressive firsts heralded by mainstream arts institutions, the milestones of their prolific careers meld into a multigenerational cultural narrative of Africans in the Americas. In contrast, many other talented artists, including Scipio Moorhead, Dave Drake, Mary Edmonia Lewis, James Presley Ball, Robert Duncanson, and Meta Warrick Fuller, were trailblazing visionaries with long productive careers, but they are familiar to a relatively small group of collectors and historians specializing in African American arts.

Art produced by African American artists over the centuries includes innumerable drawings, designs, paintings, sculptures, carvings, ceramics, architecture, photographs, prints, cartoons, computer graphics, Web pages, furniture, clothing, jewelry, utensils, site-specific installations, performance pieces, and independent cinema. Across media and genres, African American art appeals to pro-black sensibilities, inspires confidence, raises awareness, and challenges the long-standing assumptions and representational conventions of mainstream culture. This history of collective creativity positions African American art as one of the most important bodies of creative works shaping aesthetic, intellectual, and visual culture throughout the world.

THE AFRICAN ROOTS OF AFRICAN AMERICAN ART

Millions of Africans were captured and transported to the Americas, and the majority came from regions in West and Central Africa. Shipped in the cargo holds of British, French, Dutch, Spanish, and Portuguese traders of human flesh, Africans in the Americas originated from cultures and ethnic groups as disparate as the Akan, Bambara, Chokwe, Edo, Fante, Igbo, Kongo, Mandinka, Mende, Wolof, and Yoruba.

Within each of these ethnic groups, there was a common language (an estimated two thousand languages were spoken on the continent), cosmology, spiritual tradition, and political-economic history that shaped the related art-making practices. Consequently, a diverse artistic legacy emerged across the African continent, with each society developing its own unique arts traditions (i.e., subjects, forms, styles, iconography, materials, and usage). For example, the stylized abstract copper reliquary figures from Gabon differ sharply from the naturalistic Ile Ife terra-cotta and bronze sculptures.

Africans transported an appreciation for their culture's language, cosmology, spiritual beliefs, ceremonies, rituals, ancestry, and political history. In addition, they brought knowledge of the aesthetic values, artistic practices, and visual customs of their individual cultures. Many Africans carried skills and talents from prior work as artists and artisans in one of the many gender-segregated workshops and guilds. African art guilds produced objects as varied as sculpture, jewelry, textiles, and pottery, made from materials as diverse as gold, bronze, wood, ivory, cotton, silk, fur, raffia, clay, beads, and shells. For example, the Edo artists that cast the world-renowned "Benin bronzes" for the Edo royal courts of the fourteenth to eighteenth centuries worked within a very different artistic and political tradition than the ivory carvers of saltcellars that were imported from the Kongo during the European Renaissance. Some art forms, styles, and techniques survived, while others were retained in modified versions and adapted to the American cultural milieu.

THE FORMATION OF AN ARTS TRADITION

Synthesis and resistance, driven by a belief in the value of black life and the virtue of black creativity, are the cultural and creative hallmarks of African American art. Culturally, African American art is a hybrid tradition of the aesthetic values and artistic practices of Africa, the African diaspora, western Europe, and Euro-America. Each of these cultural groups, within their historical era, has its own set of prevailing social values, economic conditions, and political relations, as well as individual and collective artistic interests. Changing social and historical factors combine to affect the changing proportion of African or European influences on the underlying aesthetics and visual styles of black artists' work. The most formative influence arises from the fusion of so many African ethnic heritages into the revitalized amalgam now known as African American culture.

African and African diasporic visual-arts traditions are dramatically different from European traditions in both form (medium/material, style/technique) and content (subject/themes, motifs/meaning). African visual traditions assume the humanity, beauty, intelligence, and worth of African and African-descended people. Conversely, Eurocentric traditions have exploited and manipulated the authority of Western philosophy, aesthetics, social theory, and science to associate full human potential with people of European descent only, with the heterosexual male atop an imagined hierarchy, and African women at the very bottom. The ultimate tension is that white European traditions are based on principles that radically conflict in their regard for African life, art, and culture.

Necessarily, black art is a resilient representational practice, thriving despite cultural imperialism and European and Euro-American hegemony. From the colonial period of enslavement to the present day, black artists worked within and against a mainstream visual culture that customarily demonizes blackness and devalues all things African. As a result, black artists' work, self-consciously and by its mere existence, undermines European racial mythologies, along with the social, political, and economic hierarchies that those European-derived myths justify. Black art, therefore, is an artistic and aesthetic heritage that values blackness and black people as worthy artistic subject matter, while simultaneously redeeming the diverse cultural heritages of Africa in the imaginations of Europeans, and decolonizing the hearts and minds of African descended peoples.

THE AFRICAN LEGACY IN COLONIAL AMERICA

Art and artifacts created by Africans in colonial America reveal an indebtedness to Africa's myriad cultural traditions. The majority of African artists during the seventeenth and eighteenth centuries were enslaved, and art created under these adverse conditions falls into two broad categories. First, Africans with technical skills were forced to use their time and creative talents making items for the use and benefit of their captors. For example, enslaved Africans built or assisted in the construction of many of the plantation manors and crafted the interior woodwork and furniture. The names of five men (Tom, Peter, Ben, Harry, and Daniel) appear on the 1795 government payroll for carpenters at the White House; three were enslaved by the building's architect.

Africans' metal-crafting skills helped produce beautiful decorative arts, as well as the shackles used for their bondage. Women made myriad household items and the fashionable dresses worn by slaveholders' wives. Second, since slaveholders forced Africans to work from the proverbial "sunup to sundown," Africans only had "from dusk to dawn" to apply their creative energies to benefit themselves, their families, or their friends, and only if they could secure the material resources. The earliest known pieces of art believed to have been made by the enslaved for their own use are a decorated wooden drum made in the style of the Akan that was acquired in Virginia by a British physician in 1645 and transported to London, and a late eighteenth-century wrought-iron standing figure that was excavated from a blacksmithing site in the African quarters of a Virginia plantation.

Generally, black artists in the colonies did not have the liberty to practice the arts of painting and sculpture, nor did they have the resources to work with such precious materials as canvas oil, marble, or gold. And they were denied access to institutions of training well into the twentieth century. Rather, they adapted skills and techniques once employed to make objects for daily use, sacred ceremonies, or African royal courts. Artistic and aesthetic Africanisms, whether carried over or retained from one generation to the next, can be found embedded in the details of architectural ornaments, building designs, handcrafted furniture, quilts, clothing, and tools.

African carpenters designed and built their one-room quarters using styles and techniques originating in Africa. These techniques and motifs testify to the cultural and historical difficulties that surface when trying to draw concrete boundaries between what are black arts and what are Euro-American arts. Some arts and architecture that have been preserved and celebrated as Euro-American were actually produced by enslaved and free black people.

SECURING COMPENSATION FOR EARLY BLACK ARTISTS

African women and men were often marketed and purchased based on their skills. Some were "hired out" by their enslavers and occasionally permitted to keep a small portion of the earned income. In this way, some enslaved Africans were able to save enough money to buy their own and their family members' freedom. They often worked as anonymous apprentices and journeyman in occupations as varied as pottery, silversmithing, cabinetmaking, and tailoring.

The proportion of emancipated or even freeborn black people and artists was higher in the North than in the South. Yet, northerners also lived and labored within the legal and cultural oppression of white supremacist culture. To secure monetary or material compensation for their work, free black artisans made objects that appealed to the aesthetic sensibilities of the patron class—primarily whites with discretionary funds.

Portrait of Phillis Wheatley ***(Scipio Moorhead, 1773).*** *Moorhead, the first black artist with an attributed work, created an ink drawing that served as the frontispiece of Wheatley's celebrated publication* Poems on Various Subjects, Religious and Moral. **STOCK MONTAGE/STOCK MONTAGE/GETTY IMAGES**

BLACK ARTISTS AND THE FOUNDATION OF EARLY AMERICA

Scipio Moorhead (born c. 1750) is the first African visual artist to enter colonial historical records with his creation in 1773 of an ink drawing of another African—the youthful lyrical poet Phillis Wheatley (c. 1753–1784). Moorhead also wrote verse and made paintings, yet this remarkable portrait is his only remaining artistic work. Moorhead's portrait is the only known rendering of Wheatley by a contemporary artist of any race or gender.

In Moorhead's representation of the Senegambian-born poet, the writer actively engages in the creative process. And her journey to international acclaim was arduously productive. The child initially entered the world and was reared in a West African region where a synthesis of Islamic and indigenous cultures had been evolving since the eleventh century. Captured at the tender age of five or six, she survived the horrors of the Middle Passage on a slave-trading vessel named *Phillis.* She was sold as property in 1761 to a Presbyterian minister named Wheatley immediately after her arrival in a Boston slave market. She was then accepted as "a gift" from the reverend by his slaveholding wife. Phillis Wheatley converted to Puritanism, learned English within sixteen months, flourished to publish her first elegy in 1761, and cemented a position as a legendary abolitionist by becoming the first African woman in the British colonies to secure financial patronage for the publication of a book of poetry. She also commissioned an artist to envision an artistic representation suitably expressive of her humble religious character, intellectual accomplishments, physical likeness, and African people's human potential.

While historical records capture the child prodigy's accomplishments, Puritan cultural imperialism ensured the complete erasure of her birth name, amputating any linkage to the originating culture that nourished her initial genius and inspired her determined search for expression. Fortunately, Moorhead's portrait stands as an enduring physical image—a visual reminder of the legendary African poet. In Moorhead's line-drawn portrayal, the African poet sits on a wood-trimmed upholstered desk chair, facing a small oval writing table. Posed as if contemplating a new line of verse, Moorhead renders her torso in three-quarter turn toward the viewer, and casts her head in profile, eye humbly gazing toward the heavens.

In the visual conventions of European Enlightenment portraiture, facial profiles were supposed to reveal a subject's essential character, with a prominent forehead suggesting an attendant large cranial cavity containing a large brain.

European and Euro-American philosophers, scientists, statesmen, and artists declared that brain weight and size were self-evident proof of an individual's inherent intellectual capacities. The bigger the better. In this logic system, each degree of a forehead's backward slant signified a smaller cranial cavity and a God-given decrease in natural intellectual capabilities. Prominent elite patrons adopted the assertion that the possession of rational intelligence served as the marker distinguishing humans from animals (more accurately described as human primates and nonhuman primates) in a God-given, and therefore natural, hierarchy called the *great chain of being*.

This ranking system assigned every element of the material world to its station on the great chain of being, starting with rocks and minerals at the bottom, through plants and nonhuman animals, with humans at the top and thereby closer to God. They also imagined three subdivisions of humans, and called the groupings "the races of Caucasoid, Mongoloid, and Negroid," more recently replaced with the terms European, Asian, and African. They placed all European males and females at the top, and all African men and women at the bottom of the human category, just above simians. Necessarily, the more prominent the forehead the closer a person was to God, with any hint of recession suggesting closer links to simians.

White artists and patrons accepted these pronouncements as objective and fixed truths, and they expected art to simply reflect them, resulting in the production of visual codes, styles, and genres of art that have been passed off as "realism" in the arts. For example, a class of professional character readers actually emerged, claiming they could read a person's character from a simple black-paper silhouette. Consciously or inadvertently, Moorhead rejects these racist conventions by depicting Wheatley with a prominent forehead—the key signifier of intelligence according to the visual conventions of the Age of Reason or Enlightenment. Moorhead does what every subsequent great African and African diasporan artist has had to do—harness their creative drive and produce art that challenges the politics of (re)presentation, unsettles naturalized aesthetic values, and inspires alternative visions of a just world for all its peoples.

To enclose his composition and create emphasis on the rectilinear page, Moorhead also drew a faux oval frame and inscribed the following words around this elliptical border: "Phillis Wheatley Negro Servant to Mr. John Wheatley of Boston." This has become the portrait's title. No records indicate that the artists or their individual Bostonian, slaveholding, Protestant ministers ever met, although published accounts at the time described the drawing as a fine likeness.

Since no colonial printer would publish the volume, Wheatley traveled to London with her enslaver's son to seek financial patronage and a willing printer. An engraving of Moorhead's portrait served as the frontispiece of Wheatley's celebrated 1773 publication, *Poems on Various Subjects, Religious and Moral.* The engraving was probably made in Boston and shipped to England.

The elbow of Wheatley's bent left arm is perched near the table's edge, stabilizing the gently raised hand resting on her chin. She was sketched wearing a ruffled bonnet and a modestly collared and cuffed frock—staple Puritan attire in the Massachusetts Bay Colony. The tools of Wheatley's craft neatly grace the table surface. A slightly curled sheet of paper, an ink well, and a small, untitled, leather-bound book signal Wheatley's literacy and post-enslavement training based on a blend of stern Puritanism with a liberal fascination with ancient Greek and Latin classics. The quill pen in her right hand hovers over the partially filled sheet of paper, anticipating the transformation of thought into written word.

One poem in Wheatley's precedent-setting collection, "To S. M., A Young African Painter, On Seeing His Work," is an homage to Moorhead's artistic skills and an articulation of a shared call to arms—an unveiled oath to direct eternal creative human energies toward the truthful expression of visual and poetic rewards beyond those of mortal experience.

> .... On deathless glories fix thine ardent view:
> Still may the painter's and the poet's fire
> To aid thy pencil, and thy verité conspire!

It is a heroic clarion call announcing a new chapter in the always unfolding narrative on African American art.

Dave Drake (c. 1780s–1864) was one of the most prolific ceramicists in the Edgefield district of South Carolina. "Dave the Potter" stands as the most celebrated enslaved African-descended artisan in the records of American art history. Sold and purchased five times, Drake worked in the pottery factories of four separate enslavers, creating a distinctive style of large, glazed stoneware jars, jugs, pitchers, and churns. He left an enduring legacy by signing his name across dozens of these vessels. He also enhanced his renown by inscribing, into the exterior surface of over twenty pots, short prophetic verses, such as "this noble jar will hold 20 / fill it with silver then you'll have plenty" (March 31, 1858). It is unclear how Drake learned to read and write, but he did so even though it was a violation of South Carolina law.

Needle, thread, and design skills were important crafts for many African Americans in the antebellum and postbellum periods. For Elizabeth Keckley (1818–1907), they were the tools of liberation. She was born on a plantation in Dinwiddie County, Virginia. Keckley's mother, Agnes, was held in bondage by Colonel Armistead Burwell, while her stepfather, George Hobbs, who called Elizabeth "my Little Lizzie," was enslaved on a neighboring plantation. Keckley learned to sew as a young child by helping her mother meet the demanding role of primary household seamstress on a plantation where whippings and beating were so frequent that Lizzie's uncle hung himself rather than accept another flogging. It was a plantation where women were punished if they revealed a "sorrowful" rather than "sunshine" face when a child was sold along with the hogs. Wheatley's own parents were given two hours notice that her stepfather would accompany his enslaver on a permanent move to Tennessee. The trio's tearful separation was lifelong, the pain eased only by the exchange of letters over the years.

Resisting and surviving repeated beatings and sexual assaults, Keckley perfected her dressmaking skills and mustered entrepreneurial gumption. She created dresses and gowns for affluent and influential clients in Virginia, North Carolina, and Missouri—locations determined by her various slaveholders' rise and fall in fortune. In St. Louis, Keckley's enslaver planned to "rent" her aged mother. Distraught at the mere thought, Keckley begged for a chance to prove her ability to earn sufficient money. Reporting, "with my needle I kept bread in the mouths of seventeen persons for two years and five months," Keckley eventually earned an additional $1,200 to pay off a loan that purchased her freedom, along with that of her only son, George, in 1855. When Keckley moved to Baltimore in 1860 and Washington, D.C., the following year, she continued to attract influential patrons, including Mrs. Jefferson Davis, who encouraged her to move south as war was on the horizon.

Inaugural Ball Gown of Mary Todd Lincoln (1861). *After successfully completing a last-minute order for Lincoln's inaugural ball gown, dressmaker Elizabeth Keckley secured a position as the first lady's tailor and confidante.* MATHEW B. BRADY/BETTMANN/CORBIS

Keckley stayed in Washington. After successfully completing a last-minute order from a new client—Mary Todd Lincoln, for her inaugural ball gown, Keckley secured a permanent position as Mrs. Lincoln's sole tailor and eventual confidante. The inaugural dress is now in the collection of the Smithsonian National Museum of American History. During the Civil War (1861–1865), Keckley served as founder and president of the Contraband Relief Association. Passing for white, her son joined the Union Army. His death in battle was heartbreaking. From scraps of exquisite fabric gleaned from projects for Mary Todd Lincoln, Keckley created a piece-quilt with a flag-shaped patch bearing the word *Liberty*. It is now held by the costume department of the Kent State University Museum in Ohio.

In 1868, Keckley published *Behind the Scenes, or, Thirty Years a Slave and Four Years in the White House, by Elizabeth Keckley, Formerly a Slave, But Recently Modiste and Friend to Mrs. Lincoln.* The book's revelation of private details created a social firestorm and infuriated the insolvent widow and her son. Reportedly, Keckley penned the book to help rehabilitate the publically scorned Mrs. Lincoln's image, yet tensions in their personal relationship were never overcome. As a result, Keckley suffered a devastating loss of patrons and spiraled into financial ruin.

Keckley moved to Ohio in 1892 when Wilberforce University offered her a faculty position as head of the Department of Sewing and Domestic Science Arts. From that position, she organized a dress exhibit for the "Negro Hall" of the 1893 World's Columbian Exposition, also known as the Chicago World's Fair. In May 1907, Keckley died as a resident of the National Home for Destitute Colored Women and Children in Washington, D.C.—ironically, an institution she helped found. The 2008 election of Barack Obama, accompanied by Michelle Obama's ascension as an international fashion icon, opened a new chapter in the historical evolution of the interrelated narratives of U.S. presidents, the White House, first ladies, the creative accomplishments of black women, and the world of women's fashion.

THE RISE OF PROFESSIONAL ARTISTS

In the late eighteenth and nineteenth centuries, many black people wanted to express themselves creatively in the "fine arts" of painting and sculpture. Among these early black artists, some were born free and others were emancipated, but all accepted work when and where they could find it. Generally, these artists worked independently, absent the support of artists' collectives or the encouragement of black arts movements. More often than not, only Euro-Americans possessed the financial resources to purchase or commission hand-painted portraits, still-life studies, history pictures, landscapes, mythological or genre scenes, monumental public sculpture, private garden sculpture, elaborate cemetery markers, or delicate decorative arts. As a result, black artists' financial success and artistic expression catered to the tastes of elite patrons. Artistic opportunities rested on a repression of African-derived forms or aesthetics and the complete avoidance of subject matter celebrating or respecting the humanity of African people or their ancestral heritage.

Historical records indicate that Joshua Johnston (c. 1763–1830) was the first artist of African descent to work as a professional portrait painter. After being freed in 1796, Johnston earned worked as a "limner" or self-taught artist. He advertised his services in the newspapers and painted modest portraits of prosperous merchants and their families in the Baltimore area. There are now eighty paintings signed by or attributed to Johnston. This relatively large body of work suggests that Johnston's seemingly naive style met with the conservative and puritanical aesthetic tastes of affluent whites in the early American republic. Only two of Johnston's portraits are of men of African descent, and both wear cleric's collars. Art, thereby, links Johnston to a class of free black anti-enslavement activists in his home city. Historians suggest that one painting, *Portrait of a Cleric*, is of Daniel Coker (1780–1846), a black abolitionist and forefather of the African Methodist Episcopal (AME) Church. As a founding father of black art, Johnston created works that met the needs of patrons in conflicting classes—a paradoxical legacy that continues today.

Portrait of Susan Ball ***(James Presley Ball, early to mid-1870s).*** *In addition to using his photography to raise awareness of the horrors of African enslavement, the photographer and abolitionist James Presley Ball also turned the camera on his own family, capturing polished images of free black people with access to middle-class comforts before and after the Civil War.* JAMES PRESLEY BALL/CINCINNATI MUSEUM CENTER/GETTY IMAGES

PROFESSIONAL AFRICAN AMERICAN ARTISTS DEPICT THEIR CULTURE

In terms of subject and style, it is often difficult to distinguish the work of nineteenth-century black painters, sculptors, or photographers from that of their white counterparts. The Hudson River School–style landscape paintings of Robert Duncanson (1821–1872), capturing the grandeur of the American wilderness, provide no indication that the artist is of African ancestry. Similarly, Jules Lion (1810–1866) was a pioneering artist and one of fifty documented black daguerreotypists who operated successful portrait studios or traveling businesses in the decades immediately following the invention of the art of permanently fixing a human image in daguerreotypes and photographs in 1839. Most of their clients were Euro-Americans looking to capture their portraits with the new medium. The most important distinction in the art of black artists in comparison to white artists occurs in the small percentage of professional African American artists' work that portrays black people.

Black artists infused their representations of black historical figures, as well as fictional characters, with a dignity and strength of character foreign to white artists' works. James Presley Ball (1825–c. 1904/5) and Augustus Washington (1820–1875) were ardent abolitionists, and they used their work to challenge the horrors of African enslavement. Ball also turned the camera on his own family, capturing polished images of free black people with access to middle-class comforts before and after the Civil War. Although these family photos make up a small percentage of Ball's pictures, they stand in sharp contrast to the tattered and unkempt look customarily used to represent nineteenth-century black people by white artists.

Patrick Henry Reason (1817–1898) was born in New York City to parents born in the Caribbean. As a child, he attended the African Free School, founded by white abolitionists for the training of black children. He revealed his artistic talents while young, by drawing a picture of the school building when he was only thirteen years old. An engraving of his *New York African Free School #2* was used as the frontispiece to *The History of the New York African Free-Schools: From Their Establishment in 1787 to the Present Time* (1830), which was commissioned by the founders. Distinguished as the youngest African American artist with a published work, Reason was apprenticed to a white engraver in 1833 and quickly developed a love of portraiture. His 1837 lecture before the Phoenixonian Literary Society in New York on the philosophy of fine arts received complimentary reviews in the press. Reason's portraits appeared in dozens of publications, especially the narratives of the formerly enslaved. Although employed by Harper's, other New York publishers, and the government, Reason battled racism. He opened his own engraving firm at 148 Church Street in New York because employers refused to hire him after white guild members refused to work with a black man. In 1866, he moved his family to Cleveland, Ohio, where he entered the retail jewelry business.

Reason's portrait engraving of Henry Bibb (1815–1854) is a dignified portrayal of the antislavery lecturer and celebrated author of the 1849 *Narrative of the Life and Adventures of Henry Bibb, an American Slave, Written by Himself.* Book in hand, Henry Bibb stares boldly out at the viewer. The pose refers to his command of the art of writing and his courage to resist the institution of African enslavement. Reason's carefully rendered representation undermines the proslavery myth that black people were docile creatures who happily accepted positions of servitude and lacked the capacity to reason.

Newspaper Boy (1869) by Edward Mitchell Bannister (1828–1901) is an engaging portrait of an industrious black lad and a reminder of the importance of nineteenth-century black newspapers. This seemingly uncomplicated portrait is exceptional because white artists represented black youth either as ingratiating servants or as lazy, mischievous, and troublesome thieves. In this and other works, black artists rejected the demeaning facial caricatures and stereotypical scenes favored by Euro-American artists and collectors.

In the aftermath of the Civil War and Reconstruction, white Americans developed so many representations of grinning, deferential black male banjo players that the pictorial theme became a defaming and humiliating staple in the visual vocabulary of American culture. In 1893, however, Henry Ossawa Tanner (1859–1937) took up the banjo subject in *The Banjo Lesson,* one of his three "genre" paintings portraying African Americans. Tanner's painting of an aged man passing on a cherished skill to a young boy turned a convention of gross caricature into a sensitive representation that respects rather than ridicules black musical talent and familial relations. Under risky circumstances, nineteenth-century artists therefore used the visual arts as an arena to exercise their creativity, while simultaneously struggling to undermine and rebuke hostile cultural imagery that perpetuated African American oppression.

AFRICAN AMERICAN ARTISTS IN EUROPE

The most ambitious African American artists throughout the nineteenth century and the first half of the twentieth century sought critical acclaim, patronage, and financial success working as formally trained fine artists. To work in the academic or avant-garde styles of their day, African American artists (like their white counterparts) with the necessary financial resources or social connections traveled to France, England, Germany, and Italy to train in the academies and studios of prominent European painters and sculptors. In many cases, black artists such as the neoclassical sculptor Mary Edmonia Lewis (c. 1845–1911) and Henry Ossawa Tanner preferred to live and work in Europe. Many black expatriates found more opportunities and greater acceptance in Europe than in segregated America.

During the twentieth century, more and more creative African Americans swelled the ranks of formally trained and professional artists. They built on the scattered personal efforts of their predecessors, fashioning a modern art tradition as individuals, art collectives, and participants of broad cultural movements. Disparate intellectual trends, political ideologies, and aesthetic values emerged during the century, each informing the form, content, and cultural significance of African American art. Influences as varied as the New Negro and Harlem Renaissance, pan-Africanism, modernism, Black Power, feminism, Afrocentrism, and postmodernism shaped the diverse artistic styles of artists as dissimilar as Augusta Savage, Palmer Hayden, Elizabeth Catlett, Norman Lewis, Faith Ringgold, Charles Searles, John Biggers, Renee Stout, Lorna Simpson, and David Hammons.

Twentieth-century creative visionaries expanded the form of African American art by working in styles, techniques, and materials considered experimental, innovative, and avant-garde, as well as those deemed conservative and derivative. By broadening the parameters for acceptable subject matter to include representations of black people and black life, these artists dramatically transformed the power of American visual culture. In addition, African American artists and their supporters have engaged in century-long dialogues regarding the role of black artists, the purpose of their work, their relationship to black communities, and their responsibility to try to improve the conditions under which black people live.

The Banjo Lesson ***(Henry Ossawa Tanner, 1893).*** *Responding to the caricature of a grinning, deferential black banjo player prevalent in the late 19th century, Tanner's painting of an aged man passing on a cherished skill to a young boy respected, rather than ridiculed, black musical talent and familial relations.*

THE "NEW NEGRO" ERA

African American artists who came of age at the beginning of the twentieth century emerged during an era that supported artistic sensibilities and creative concerns focusing on the cultivation and uplift of the "New Negro." As a concept or term, the "New Negro" came to designate an ideology of resistance and a form of progressive social activism that stood against all forms of oppression. This new attitude prompted nearly two million African Americans to migrate from the rural agrarian South to the urban industrial North to escape dire economic circumstances, the horrors of Jim Crow segregation, forced sharecropping, white supremacist night riders, and lynch-mob culture. The Great Migration (1910–1930) promoted a surge in political organizing, social mobilization, and cultural renewal usually referred to as the New Negro movement, the Negro Renaissance, or the Harlem Renaissance.

New Negro intellectuals and political leaders embraced a form of race consciousness that allowed them to value black culture and arts, actually celebrating them as integral to America's contemporary richness and future greatness. Their activism gave birth to a generation of modern African American artists with twentieth-century, rather than nineteenth-century, artistic concerns. These artists worked in diverse media and styles, yet their aesthetic convictions rested on the assumption that black people and culture were worthy and significant subjects for modern art.

W. E. B. Du Bois (1868–1963) routinely urged such African American artists as Henry Ossawa Tanner and Meta Warrick Fuller (1877–1968) to develop visual imagery that would rehabilitate the image of black people in the public imagination. He urged artists to produce paintings and sculptures that challenged the European and Euro-American tradition of representing black people in a litany of fine arts servants and gross advertising caricature. Some accepted the call to create art in service of social uplift, while others only wanted to make art as an individual form of expression. Whatever their creative inspiration, the works of New Negro–era artists are revered icons that serve as the collective cornerstone of twentieth-century and twenty-first-century African American art and aesthetics.

Meta Warrick Fuller's 1914 bronze sculpture *Ethiopia Awakening* is a landmark artistic statement. It is the earliest example of African American art to overtly validate African arts and cultures. The nearly life-size sculpture is a personification of Africa as a human female wearing the headdress of an ancient Kemetic (*Egyptian* is a term of Greek origins) queen. She appears to be emerging from her mummy-like wrapping, though the lower portion of her body remains bound. *Ethiopia Awakening* directly challenged a favored Western figurative theme called the *Four Continents*—a visual theme comprised of four female figures personifying Europe, Asia, America, and Africa. By convention, white artists portrayed the African continent as asleep or contributing only captive labor to the development of human civilizations. Throughout the twentieth century, however, many artists became more knowledgeable about Africa and its cultures, allowing them to completely abandon Western-derived assertions that the continent of Africa lay dormant.

The photographs of James VanDerZee (1886–1983) represent the vitality of Harlem in its heyday as the mecca of black life and culture. For example, his portraits of Marcus Garvey (1887–1940) and photographs of the Universal Negro Improvement Association parades are meaningful historical documents and creative aesthetic statements. VanDerZee also permanently fixed the image of thousands of Harlemites whose names have been lost, although their upwardly mobile images continue to testify to the cultural energy of urban life. In addition, such painters as Edward Harleston, Malvin Gray Johnson, William Edouard Scott, and Laura Wheeler Warring captured the vibrancy of black culture in their portraits and pictorial scenes.

THE HARLEM RENAISSANCE AND THE WORKS PROGRESS ADMINISTRATION

At the dawn of the twentieth century, agitation for social, political, and economic justice gave rise to the New Negro movement, sparking an associated flowering of artistic creativity among African American writers, musicians, singers, theater performers, and fine artists. The movement generated an unprecedented level of patronage from private individuals and organizations. For example, the National Association for the Advancement of Colored People (NAACP) and the National Urban League, founded in 1909 and 1910 respectively, instituted important art awards. Their respective publications, *Crisis* and *Opportunity*, became venues for artists and for critical reviews of New Negro art exhibitions. When World War I ended in 1918, Harlem, an uptown section of Manhattan, was home to the largest black population in urban America and became the cultural heart of this artistic activity. Frequently referred to as the Harlem Renaissance, it was a national and international movement in black arts and culture encompassing other urban centers, such as Chicago, Cleveland, and Washington, D.C., as well as the Caribbean and Europe.

Alain Locke (1885–1954), a Howard University philosophy professor and Rhodes scholar, was a prominent architect of the Harlem-based arts revival. He believed that if black artists demonstrated their creative and intellectual mastery of literature and the fine arts to the American public, they would garner respect for the black race and thereby change white attitudes and improve race relations. To stimulate critical and financial support for black artists, Locke served as guest editor in 1925 for *Harlem: Mecca of the New Negro*, a special issue of the journal *Survey Graphic*. Contributing essayists theorized and celebrated the aesthetics of African art and the achievements of African American arts and culture.

Locke's essay, "The Legacy of the Ancestral Arts," urged black artists to draw on the artistic and cultural legacies of Africa in the creation of their art. Locke maintained that if the stylized abstraction of West African sculpture could inspire avant-garde artists (e.g., Pablo Picasso, Georges Braque, or Emil Nolde) to create important modern styles such as cubism or German expressionism, it could also lead New Negro artists to develop a unique visual vocabulary. The ideas of Locke and his contributors were culturally progressive at the time. Yet, they rested on two concepts refuted today: the existence of biologically determined racial essences and a form of romantic primitivism. The latter not only cast Africa and Africans as "primitive," but as the polar opposite of "civilized" Europe and Europeans.

Nonetheless, artists as diverse as Aaron Douglas, Palmer Hayden, Sargent Claude Johnson, Archibald Motley Jr., James Lesesne Wells, and Augusta Savage temporarily or permanently abandoned the conventions of their European training to experiment with African-inspired styles or subjects. Aaron Douglas (1899–1979) is most frequently highlighted as the quintessential Harlem Renaissance artist. A trained portrait painter, Douglas abandoned his realist style, developing instead a stylized Kemetic form of figurative painting that graced numerous Harlem Renaissance publications, including illustrations and designs in Alain Locke's book *The New Negro* (1925) and James Weldon Johnson's *God's Trombones: Seven Negro Sermons in Verse* (1927).

The principal sponsorship of Harlem Renaissance art came from the Harmon Foundation, which was established by the white real-estate investor William E. Harmon (1862–1928) in 1922 to promote African American art. The foundation awarded prizes and sponsored juried exhibitions and shows that traveled around the United States. The foundation exercised creative control over the type of art produced or promoted. As a result, the foundation, the exhibits, the awards, and even the artists were subject to social and critical controversy.

Occurring during the high point of the Harlem Renaissance, the stock market crash of 1929 cast the United States into the Great Depression. The Federal Arts Project (1935–1943) was one of the New Deal relief programs sponsored by Franklin D. Roosevelt's Works Progress Administration (WPA). The Federal Arts Project paid artists to produce works celebrating America and American art styles for the public. The Federal Arts Project promoted an environment where figuration and social realism were valued over abstraction and allegory. In many ways, Federal Arts Project funding contributed to black artists' turning away from the stylistic Africanisms encouraged by Locke and the Harmon Foundation, focusing instead on African American folk culture and regionalized realist style.

The Migration of the Negro *(Jacob Lawrence, c. 1940).* *Lawrence traced the migration of the African American population from the South to the North in a series of sixty paintings. The artist completed other series of paintings of such individuals as Harriet Tubman and the abolitionist John Brown.* THE JACOB AND GWENDOLYN LAWRENCE FOUNDATION/ART RESOURCE, NEW YORK

The Federal Arts Project employed a young Jacob Lawrence (1917–2000) and provided him early support in his career. He subsequently became one of America's most celebrated black artists. Lawrence titled a series of sixty paintings *The Migration of the Negro* (1940–1941). The series secured him critical acclaim, a feature in *Fortune* magazine, a one-man show at the prestigious Downtown Gallery in New York, and the acquisition of several paintings by the Museum of Modern Art. In Chicago, the Southside Community Art Center provided early career opportunities for such artists as Archibald Motley Jr., Charles Sebree, and Gordon Roger Parks. In addition, Hughie Lee-Smith and Charles Sallee found teaching opportunities and support at Karamu House Artist Association in Cleveland (established in 1935). Although hundreds of centers opened under the auspices of the WPA and the Federal Arts Project, the Southside Community Art Center and the Karamu House are the only two still operating in 2010.

Clearly, the Federal Arts Project and the WPA were important for the development of African American art. Yet, black artists complained that the program administrators routinely discriminated against them. The Harlem Artists Guild (1935–1941), a collective founded by Augusta Savage, Elba Lightfoot, Charles Alston, and Arthur Schomburg, made the redressing of the problems an important organizational goal.

AFRICAN AMERICAN ARTISTS AND MODERNISTIC ART FORMS

By the late 1930s and early 1940s, such artists as William H. Johnson, Charles Alston, Hale A. Woodruff, and Norman Lewis were less inspired by social realism and more interested in the formalist concerns of European modernism, especially expressionism and abstraction. Eldzier Cortor and Hughie Lee-Smith (1915–1999), for instance, explored the visual power of surrealism in paintings. They preferred the challenge of working in styles that most Americans considered foreign, and they experimented with such a range of approaches that in some abstract paintings the subject is recognizable, while in other paintings the subjects are completely nonrepresentational. Romare Bearden (1911–1988) was an African American artist who began working with representational abstraction. During the 1940s, however, he became an early practitioner of abstract expressionism, a modern art movement that catapulted New York onto the world art scene, effectively displacing Paris as the leading center of the Western art world.

The modernist disdain for realism took hold among American avant-garde artists, as well as their critics and patrons. The latter two groups cultivated an arts environment in which Euro-American collectors could "discover" and champion the art of such self-trained African American artists as the painter Horace Pippin (1888–1946) and the sculptor William Edmondson (c. 1870s–1951) because they did not employ the conventions of representation realism. White collectors believed these self-taught artisans found modernist expression without the struggle of rejecting formal training or attempting to surpass tradition. White collectors and curators commonly referred to these self-taught artists as "folk artists," "native artists," and "Negro-primitives," frequently preferring and promoting them over professionally trained African American artists. Although many professionally trained African American artists and segments of their various communities rigorously critiqued the underlying racial ideology and adamantly challenged these affluent white mainstream collecting and exhibiting practices, self-taught artists have continued to be important contributors to African American art.

FROM BLACK ART TO AFROCENTRISM

The Black Arts movement, also known as the artistic branch of the Black Liberation movement, emerged during the tumultuous 1960s. The slogan "Black Power" captured the movement's defiant opposition to the normalization of the Western or Eurocentric aesthetic, which regulated the appreciation and production of art and culture in the United States. The founders and proponents of the Black Arts movement challenged themselves and other members of black creative communities across the United States and the African world to redefine the roles of artists and their art in light of an increasingly radicalized black political agenda. Black aestheticism championed the belief that the first step toward black liberation required black people to construct a new worldview. It insisted that black people must develop a black consciousness or perspective that is Africa-centered rather than Europe-centered as a form of intellectual growth and personal empowerment.

The Black Arts debates were heated and polemical. Definitions and interpretations of black aestheticism were conflicting. Addison Gayle's anthology *The Black Aesthetic* (1971) captured the theoretic diversity among literary and visual artists. Yet, proponents universally embraced some qualities. First and foremost, they rejected the notion that art and politics were separate domains of human activity. The critic and poet Larry Neal (1937–1981), one of the movement's most influential theorists, proclaimed "the artist and the political activist are one." He maintained that the difference between the Black Arts and Black Power concepts is that "one is concerned with the relationship between art and politics; the other with the art of politics."

Under this theoretic formation, art was not a luxury, but a basic and necessary weapon in black people's struggle against the social and political order of racial apartheid in the United States. In theory and practice, those embracing black aestheticism rejected the idea that art was destined for the pedestals and walls of private galleries, public museums, or homes of the affluent. They attacked the modernist doctrine of "art for art's sake" as bourgeois and ethnocentric and as merely reproducing white supremacist navel-gazing, asserting that art must inspire an individual and collective consciousness raising and promote a black political revolution.

Black visual artists across the United States heeded the call, creating a body of paintings, sculptures, prints, assemblages, and public murals that sought to inform and inspire black people to aggressively resist domination. Political awareness was recentered on African histories, African ancestral legacies, and African cultural traditions. One stream of black aesthetic artists created works that were inspired by the revolutionary idealism of African liberation struggles against European colonialism. Another stream of Black Arts visionaries deemphasized the political tensions and focused on

The Wall of Respect ***(1967).*** *Painted by a group of African American artists, this mural was located on Forty-third and Langley in Chicago's South Side. It included portraits of historical black figures, including Frederick Douglass, Marcus Garvey, and Malcolm X.* ROBERT ABBOTT SENGSTACKE/ARCHIVE PHOTOS/GETTY IMAGES

celebrating the glory of ancient and contemporary African cultures.

A landmark example of the evolution of community-centered art practice and its artistic accessibility was represented by the emergence of a group called COBRA, or the Coalition of Black Revolutionary Artists. Members of the group collaborated on a community mural project in Chicago, the *Wall of Respect*, in 1967, featuring portraits of historical black figures, including Frederick Douglass, Marcus Garvey, and Malcolm X. Their celebration of black history as heritage rather than shame became a beacon for similar black-consciousness murals in Chicago, Detroit, Boston, Los Angeles, and across urban America. COBRA later reorganized and transformed its name to AFRICOBRA, or the African Commune of Bad Relevant Artists.

Prior to this period, affluent Euro-Americans were the main collectors, patrons, and consumers of the work of black artists. Therefore, solicitation by black artists of a black audience marked a critical turning point in the development of the African American artistic tradition. Conceptually, these artists rejected the label "protest art," which had been embraced during the civil rights era, because according to black aesthetic definitions, protest art played to the moral conscience of a liberal white audience. Theoretically, the Black Arts movement spoke to those who actually lived the black social, cultural, political, and economic experience.

In 1967, Faith Ringgold's painting *US Postage Stamp Commemorating the Advent of Black Power* indicated her embrace of the more militant tendencies of the organized struggle for black human rights over those of the civil rights movement. Elizabeth Catlett aligned herself with specific political activists and a particular political organization in her 1969 prints *Malcolm Speaks for Us* and *Homage to the Panthers*. Dana Chandler's paintings *(4)00 More Years* and *Molotov Cocktail* are representative of a trend in artworks that launched a pictorial assault against American cultural symbols, such as the U.S. flag.

Other works, such as Betye Saar's mixed-media construction *The Liberation of Aunt Jemima* (1972), were visual attacks on demeaning pictorial caricatures that had assaulted the hearts, minds, and souls of black men, women, and children since the late nineteenth century. Working solely with found objects, Saar appropriated and redressed a commercially mass-produced notepad holder. Fabricated as a ceramic figurine supposedly representing a mythological "Mammy" (a heavy-set woman wearing a floor-length shirtwaist, apron, and red head rag, with pitch black paint for the skin). This kitchen knickknack was just one of a myriad of decorative designs for a wide variety of "decorative arts" marketed to enhance constructions of whiteness and avidly consumed by white consumers. In Saar's assemblage, the figurine assumed a new position as a guerilla warrior armed with a miniature rifle and tiny pistol instead of the original broom and pencil,

The Liberation of Aunt Jemima ***(Betye Saar, 1972).*** *In Saar's mixed-media assemblage, the figurine assumed a new position as a guerilla warrior armed with a miniature rifle and tiny pistol instead of the original broom and pencil, signifying the mammy of legend's mythic rejection of her role as caretaker to the world.* COLLECTION OF UNIVERSITY OF CALIFORNIA, BERKELEY ART MUSEUM; PURCHASED WITH THE AID OF FUNDS FROM THE NATIONAL ENDOWMENT FOR THE ARTS (SELECTED BY THE COMMITTEE FOR THE ACQUISTION OF AFRO-AMERICAN ART). COURTESY OF MICHAEL ROSENFELD GALLERY, LLC, NEW YORK, NY.

signifying the mammy of legend's mythic rejection of her role as caretaker to the world. Artists such as Saar, Murry DePillars, Jeff Donaldson, and Joe Overstreet created pieces that robbed established advertising clichés, such as Aunt Jemima and Uncle Ben, of their widespread cultural currency, undermining their social acceptability.

The second stream of artists focused on cultural reclamation rather than political activism, which paved the way for their celebrations of African religions, social and spiritual traditions, ceremonial rituals, and artistic aesthetics. As more and more African countries gained independence, beginning with Ghana in 1957, black artists began traveling to the African continent. Earlier artists had learned of Africa from books and the written records of colonial agents, including missionaries, merchants, military officials, travelers, anthropologists, and art collectors. These younger artists, however, learned about African art and culture from first-hand experience rather than books written by Europeans or Euro-Americans.

The cultural nationalist stream created art honoring legendary African kings and queens, as well as colorful scenes of African villages and busy marketplaces. They produced works such as Thomas Feelings's *Senegalese Woman* (1960) and John Biggers's *Jubilee: Ghana Harvest Festival* (completed 1959–1963), which capture the strength and beauty of African women while emphasizing the vibrancy of their traditional dress. In contrast to this documentary quality, such artists as Charles Searles and Faith Ringgold created colorful, African-inspired paintings and sculptures, borrowing African formal elements and materials and reworking them into generic stylized visions. In this visual tradition, representations drawing on African civilizations, empires, and kingdoms function as the healing antidote to centuries of internalized European historical narratives that by law and custom devalued all things African in an attempt to destroy Africans' appreciation of their African heritage.

Since the streams never settled on definitive boundaries, numerous artists drew on both concepts, self-consciously attempting to balance the formal and the political. The civil rights and Black Power movements generated tremendous debate and activity among creative artists, and some white critics dismissed the art as angry, romantic, or merely propagandistic. As organized activism waned in the mid to late 1970s, the Black Arts movement lost much of it collective momentum. Nonetheless, many of the artists who emerged during the era became artistic elders and continued to create, exhibit, and teach. Their artistic theories, artistic strategies, and aesthetic concerns laid another foundation stone for the African American contemporary arts.

CONTEMPORARY ARTS

Since the 1980s and 1990s, there has been a virtual explosion in the number of self-taught and formally trained African Americans who have created, exhibited, and marketed their art. Contemporary artists have opportunities to work with a diverse array of materials, media, new technologies, and critical concepts. They are able to employ styles, techniques, and approaches unimagined by their creative predecessors.

During this period, individual African American artists received critical recognition, saw an increase in gallery representation, experienced greater inclusion in group and solo museum shows, and became the subject of academic scholarship. The visually engaging work by artists such as Emma Amos, Jean-Michel Basquiat, Robert Colescott, Houston Conwill, Lyle Ashton Harris, Glenn Ligon, Renee Green, Lorraine O'Grady, Howardena Pindell, Alison Saar, and Fred Wilson has been the focus of breathtaking exhibits. In addition, African American visual artists have been the recipients of prestigious prizes and awards. In 1987, Romare Bearden was awarded the Presidential Medal of Honor. MacArthur Fellowships have been awarded to Robert Blackburn, David Hammons, Kerry James Marshall, Martin Puryear, John T. Scott, Kara Walker, Deborah Willis, and Fred Wilson.

Contemporary African American art manifests as multiple aesthetic and artistic trends, not as a single consciously constructed art movement. Afrocentricity, feminism, and postmodernism are a few of the influential intellectual and cultural currents shaping the work of painters, sculptors, photographers, and video, mixed-media installation, and performance artists. Additionally, individual artists have the insight and liberty to hold a multiplicity of interests. They explore issues of race, gender, sexuality, sexual orientation, and class as intersecting rather than mutually exclusive constructs. This stands in contrast to the Harlem Renaissance or Black Arts movement, which primarily challenged racism, with the latter movement frequently dismissing feminists' calls to end sexism as hampering racial unity. Today, works by artists such as Lorna Simpson, Carrie Mae Weems, and Adrian Piper build on the groundbreaking feminist work of such artists as Elizabeth Catlett and Faith Ringgold, who themselves continued to produce.

Carrie Mae Weems and Lorna Simpson combine written text with photographic or figurative imagery. This contemporary practice allows them to create art that can challenge the viewer, pose questions, and offer devastating cultural critiques that focus on dismantling racial and sexual mythologies. Simpson was the first African American woman to have a solo exhibition at New York's Museum of Modern Art, while Weems became the first African American woman to have a major exhibition at the National Museum for Women in the Arts in Washington, D.C.

Other contemporary artists, such as Dawoud Bey, Renee Cox, Anthony (Tony) Gleaton, Fern Logan, and Coreen Simpson, use the medium of photography in innovative and profoundly illuminating ways. Following the lead of Roy DeCarava (1919–2009) and Gordon Parks (1912–2006), this new generation of artists turns their cameras on people, scenes, and cityscapes, transforming documentary photography into aesthetically stimulating art.

Additionally, there is an important contingent of contemporary African American painters and sculptors who consider abstraction and the skillful manipulation of materials far more rewarding than figuration or overt cultural criticism. Barbara Chase-Riboud, Melvin Edwards, Sam Gilliam, Richard Hunt, Maren Hassinger, Alvin D. Loving Jr., Martin Puryear, Raymond Saunders, and William T. Williams continue to follow the abstractionist path paved by such artists as Alma Thomas (1891–1978), Hale Woodruff (1900–1980), and Norman Lewis (1909–1979).

Charles Bibbs, Varnette Honeywood, and Synthia Saint James are representative of a group of artists who celebrate African American culture in their work. They create symbolic images about love, strength, fortitude, survival, spirituality, and vitality. Their colorful, figurative works pay tribute to historical figures, as well as the daily activities that are the heart and soul of African American life and culture. They create heartwarming, esteem-building scenes that recall church and family gatherings, along with children playing, men laboring, women quilting or braiding hair, people dancing, and lovers embracing. Artists working in this trend self-consciously cultivate an appreciation for African-inspired aesthetics, design principles, forms, concerns, and subject matter. The annual National Black Arts Festival, founded in 1988, is a citywide event held in Atlanta, Georgia, that showcases art of this type.

In many instances, these artists specifically create for popular culture rather than the so-called fine art market, where collectors pay high prices for the unique art object. The celebratory images easily translate into accessibly priced reproductions, such as prints, posters, cards, mugs, T-shirts, book illustrations, and even Internet pages catering to an African American buying public. It was virtually impossible to find reproductions of African American art in the mid-1980s. A decade into the twenty-first century, however, art containing black subjects and aesthetics can be purchased from galleries, frame shops, mail-order catalogs, and Internet vendors.

With the information revolution, computer technology, public media, and visual images have emerged as important forms of expression. Such artists as Leah Gilliam, Glenn Ligon, and Betye Saar began creating and appropriating visual images to make computer-generated art for distribution on CDs or for display in the early days of the Internet. Many artists, such as Renee Cox, Hank Willis Thomas, and Alonzo Adams, maintain their own Internet sites, allowing them to take African American art directly to a global audience.

ARTS-RELATED SUPPORT PROFESSIONS

Historically, black artists have expressed their creativity even though they did not receive equal and unrestricted access to institutions that support the making, exhibiting, and collecting of art. Despite the modernist myth that art and aesthetics are separate and distinct from the political arena, the making and consuming of art are deeply enmeshed in social politics. Many art schools, museums, and galleries, as well as private and public patrons, followed the Jim Crow and gender segregation dictated by U.S. laws or social customs. Therefore, black men and women were denied equal access to training, severely limiting the number of people who could become artists. Moreover, in the arena of creative expression, white males have had and continue to receive privileges not extended to women of all races or to men of color. Fortunately, opportunities increased dramatically during the post–civil rights era, and this exponentially increased the number of black people who chose to train and define themselves as artists and independent craftspeople. Consequently, there was an unprecedented flowering of African American arts and culture during the last three decades of the twentieth century and the first years of the twenty-first century, as countless black women and men embraced the visual arts as a form of expression.

There remains a need to increase the intelligently informed support for black artists and their work. The majority of African American artists still struggle to find support and encouragement from teachers, curators, dealers, collectors, critics, and historians. Black artists must depend on support from arts-related professionals to promote awareness and appreciation of their work. These arts-related professionals include art critics who evaluate the merit of art and art shows; curators who acquire, preserve, and exhibit art for public museums and private collectors; commercial art dealers who promote interest in specific artists, sell their original art, and market more accessibly priced reproductions; and art historians who study the types of art that creative people make. Necessarily, art historians are interested in providing insight about the beliefs and philosophies underpinning aesthetic preferences, criticism, patronage, collection, use, and exhibition patterns. They also chronicle the emergence of forms, subjects, styles, conventions, and techniques, and try to account for their transformation and change over time.

These arts-related professionals are necessary forces in the development of scholarly and critical literature (i.e., books, catalogs, and journal articles) and exhibitions that showcase black art. Black artists and their work will begin to gain more scholarly and critical attention, exhibitions, gallery space, and sales as the number of art-related professionals with formal training in African American art expands.

Books and exhibition catalogs are an important source for stimulating interest in African American art. Four illustrated surveys published in the 1990s provide comprehensive accounts of African American visual arts. Samella Lewis's *African American Art and Artists* (1990) offers brief historical overviews and artists' biographies. Crystal A. Britton's *African American Art: The Long Struggle* (1996) is a narrative of a collective visual tradition. Richard J. Powell's *Black Art and Culture in the 20th Century* (1997) is a more theoretical analysis of themes, trends, and high moments uniting black cultural production. Originally written as a new addition to the multivolume series *World of Art* published by Thames and Hudson, Powell's book was the first in the collection to focus on African American art and culture.

In 1998, Oxford University Press released Sharon F. Patton's *African-American Art* as a historic addition to its series *Oxford History of Art.* Patton's work is a textbook that includes glossaries, timelines, and penetrating analyses. As the first African American art surveys by major mainstream publishing houses, Powell's and Patton's landmark books were trendsetting scholarly publications.

Lisa Gail Collins's *The Art of History: African American Women Artists Engage the Past* (2002) and Lisa E. Farrington's *Creating Their Own Image: The History of African-American Women Artists* (2005) broke new ground as books framed by key interconnected issues of gender, feminism, and race. Artist and author Earthlyn Marselean Manuel's *Black Angel Cards: A Soul Revival Guide for Black Women* (1999) used the arts to provide spiritual and mental healing. In addition, Hampton University Museum publishes a quarterly periodical, *The International Review of African American Art.*

EXHIBITING AFRICAN AMERICAN ART

The decades of the 1970s through the 1990s gave birth to a group of influential exhibitions dedicated to resurrecting, presenting, and discussing African American art and artists. Curators organized these special exhibitions to fill the void left by the institutionalized exclusion of black artists and their art from mainstream shows in public museums and private galleries. Initially, these shows possessed a strong archaeological quality. Curators mined the collections of a wide variety of public and private patrons, excavating and assembling images by artists working in diverse media from many historical eras and stylistic periods.

The first wave of shows and catalogs had a documentary character, focusing on demonstrating the existence of black professional fine artists. Art that had languished in storerooms for generations was made available for public viewing in such shows and catalogs as: *Forever Free: Art by African-American Women, 1862–1980,* an exhibition organized by Arna Bontemps and Jacqueline Fonvielle-Bontemps; Lynda R. Hartigan's *Sharing Traditions: Five Black Artists in Nineteenth-Century America* (1985); Keith Morrision's *Art in Washington and Its Afro-American Presence: 1940–1970* (1985); Bucknell University's *Since the Harlem Renaissance: 50 Years of Afro-American Art* (1984); David Driskell's *Hidden Heritage: Afro-American Art, 1800–1950* (1985); Edmund Barry Gaither's *Massachusetts Masters: Afro-American Artists* (1988); and *African-American Artists, 1880–1987: Selections from the Evans-Tibbs Collection* (1989), by Guy C. McElroy, Richard J. Powell, and Sharon F. Patton. These catalogs broke new ground simply in the quality of their richly illustrated color pages. Since exhibitions are temporary, making the reproductions available to a relatively wide audience allowed students and scholars the opportunity to continue to study works that had been hidden from both the contemporary and historical view. The majority of artists featured are male, but the works of a few women, such as Edmonia Lewis, Lois Mailou Jones, and Alma Thomas, also appear.

Another group of exhibits focused on the crafts art made by enslaved Africans, as well as those forms of creative expressions made by self-taught artists after the abolition of black enslavement. John Michael Vlach organized *The Afro-American Tradition in Decorative Arts* (1978), and the catalog is a foundational text on art produced by enslaved people. The exhibited objects and collection of essays edited by Edward Campbell Jr. and Kym S. Rice in *Before Freedom Came: African-American Life in the Antebellum South* (1991) are extremely valuable for understanding the material production, as well as its archaeological and ideological contexts. In addition, Jane Livingston and John Beardsley's *Black Folk Art in America, 1930–1980* (1982), William Ferris's *Afro-American Folk Arts and Crafts* (1983), and *Baking in the Sun: Visionary Images from the South, Selections from the Collection of Sylvia and Warren Lowe* (1987) discuss folk arts practices through the first half of the twentieth century.

The years leading up to the 1976 U.S. bicentennial gave birth to a recovery movement championing American art and culture. Although it primarily celebrated white artists, the recovery movement brought legitimacy to American folk arts, especially women's quilting traditions. In the following decade, the folk arts revival converged with the growing interest in African American arts, paving the way for such exhibitions and catalogs as Gladys-Marie Fry's *Stitched from the Soul: Slave Quilts from the Ante-Bellum South* (1990), Cuesta Benberry's brilliant *Always There: The African American Presence in American Quilts* (1992), Maude Wahlman's *Signs and Symbols: African Images in African-American Quilts* (1993), and Moira Roth's *Faith Ringgold: Change: Painted Story Quilts* (1987), which showcased quilts made by women of African descent from the period of enslavement to the present. These shows placed an important body of art before the public for appreciation and scholarly study. It is worth noting that nonblack museums, galleries, and curators supported these quilt shows at a higher rate than they did shows by formally trained, professional black women artists. Furthermore, the curators who created the most conceptually challenging study of African American art organized exhibitions that explored themes, movements, or styles.

A series of exhibitions mounted in the late 1970s and the 1980s advanced the scholarship on African American artists. The Studio Museum in Harlem, while under the directorship of Mary Schmidt Campbell, took the lead in the development of such creative, thought-provoking, and historically based shows as *New York/Chicago: WPA and the Black Artists* (1978); *Ritual and Myth: A Survey of African American Art* (1982); *An Ocean Apart: American Artists Abroad* (1983); *Tradition and Conflict: Images of a Turbulent Decade, 1963–1973* (1985); and the richly illustrated *Harlem Renaissance: Art of Black America* (1987). The catalogs are collaborative efforts, containing sets of essays from a wide range of contributors. Essayists do not explore issues impacting women artists or contrast any of the formal or thematic concerns of women with those of men. The strength of these publications is that the writers discuss the art critically and historically, moving beyond the formula of recounting biographical information and describing the art's formal qualities.

In 1989, a large number of well-financed exhibitions and catalogs appeared after decades of little activity. Gary A. Reynolds and Beryl J. Wright organized *Against the Odds: African-American Artists and the Harmon Foundation* at the Newark Museum. Richard Powell organized *The Blues Aesthetic: Black Culture and Modernism* at the Washington Project for the Arts. Alvia Wardlow curated *Black Art Ancestral Legacy: The African Impulse in African-American Art* at the Dallas Museum of Art. The California Afro-American Museum opened *Introspectives: Contemporary Art by Americans and Brazilians of African Descent* and *The 1960s: A Cultural Awakening Re-evaluated, 1965–1975.* Deborah Willis and Howard Dodson curated *Black Photographers Bear Witness: 100 Years of Social Protest* at the Williams College Museum of Art. Leslie King-Hammond curated *Black Printmakers and the WPA* for the Lehman College Art Gallery in the Bronx. The catalogs accompanying these shows also reveal tremendous depth in the archival research, the resurrection of buried histories, and the production of historical analyses.

In connection with the 1990 National Black Arts Festival in Atlanta, the Nexus Contemporary Art Center mounted *AFRICOBRA: The First Twenty Years.* Regina A. Perry published her long-awaited *Free within Ourselves: African-American Artists in the Collection of the National Museum of American Art* in 1992. *Dream Singers, Story Tellers: An African-American Presence* (1992), with essays and text in both English and Japanese, provided a refreshingly new approach for an international audience. Bomani Gallery's *Paris Connections: African American Artists in Paris* (1992) examined production from an international perspective. Curator Thelma Golden organized *Black Male: Representations of Masculinity in Contemporary American Art* (1994) for the Whitney Museum of American Art. The art selected for the show examined notions of race and gender in the minds of artists of different races and the public at large. Beryl Wright's catalogs for *African-American Art: Twentieth Century Masterworks* (1993) and Richard J. Powell's *Exultations: African-American Art: Twentieth Century Masterworks, II* (1995) were unapologetically focused on canon building. Deborah Willis's *Reflections in Black: A History of Black Photographers, 1840 to the Present* (2000), and the Brooklyn Museum's *Committed to the Image: Contemporary Black Photographers* (2001) are landmark exhibitions with lushly illustrated catalogs of historical figures and their work, as well as cutting-edge, contemporary photographic movements.

Likewise, the Studio Museum in Harlem's co-sponsorship of *To Conserve a Legacy: American Art from Historically Black Colleges and Universities* (1999) and organization of the provocative exhibition *Freestyle* (2001) reveal the historical diversity of African American artistic legends. The latter show focused on a new generation who came of age in the post–civil rights era, in the hip-hop heyday of the 1980s. According to curator Thelma Golden, these artists create from a *postblack* aesthetic—a conceptual approach and label that sparked heated debate among artists, critics, and audiences nearly a decade before Barack Obama's presidential campaign made the term *postracial* part of popular discourse.

These exhibits and catalogs demonstrate that African American artists have been and continue to be important agents in the struggle for social, political, and economic justice in the United States. African American artists stand among the legions of incredibly resilient, courageous, and visionary black people who acted on their beliefs that the life that they wanted for themselves and others must be free of racial, economic, cultural, political, and visual barriers. The core of what artists have to say on canvas, in stone, or on video parallels what artists in literature, music, or theater have been thinking and verbalizing for centuries. In spirit, however, African American visual artists add another dimension to the chorus of voices that celebrate the ways that people of African descent thrive in the United States.

Duke University Chapel, Durham, NC, April 2007. *Completed in 1935, this chapel was designed by Julian F. Abele, the first major African American architect.* JIM R. BOUNDS/ BLOOMBERG VIA GETTY IMAGES

ARCHITECTURE AND DESIGN PROFESSIONALS

Since the early twentieth century, African Americans have carved out careers in the elite fields of architecture and professional design. In 1904, Julian F. Abele (1881–1950) became the first African American to graduate from the Pennsylvania School of Fine Arts and Architecture. He stands as the first major African American architect. As chief designer of the Philadelphia-based firm Horace Trumbauer and Associates, Abele contributed to designs for Philadelphia's Free Library and Museum of Art and Harvard University's Widener Library, as well as the chapel and many other buildings of Trinity College in Durham, North Carolina (now Duke University) and the James B. Duke mansion on Fifth Avenue and Seventy-eighth Street in New York City (now New York University's Graduate Institute of Fine Arts). In 1926, Paul Revere Williams (1894–1980) became the first black member of the American Institute of Architects. He is the most well-known African American architect, celebrated for designing part of the Los Angeles International Airport and the homes of entertainers such as William Holden, Lucille Ball, Frank Sinatra, Bill "Bojangles" Robinson, and Betty Grable. Williams and Howard H. Mackey organized the first juried exhibit of the work of "Negro architects" at Howard University in 1931.

These early architects also worked on projects for affluent African Americans and middle-income to low-income communities. For example, Wallace A. Rayfield (1874–1941) designed the Sixteenth Street Baptist Church in Birmingham, Alabama (1911), site of the 1963 bombing that killed four girls. John A. Lankford (1874–1946) of Washington, D.C., designed churches and taught at the architecture school at Howard University. George Washington Foster (1866–1923) teamed with Vertner Woodson Tandy (1885–1949)—the first black person to graduate from Cornell University's architecture school—to found the firm that built St. Philip's Episcopal Church in New York in 1911 and the Harlem townhome of hair-care millionaire Madame C .J. Walker.

Clarence W. ("Cap") Wigington (1883–1967) was the first registered African American architect in Minnesota and the first African American municipal architect in the nation. Between 1915 and 1947, in the Office of the City Architect of St. Paul, he designed an array of schools, fire stations, park structures, and municipal buildings that helped define the city's landscape. Wigington's nearly sixty St. Paul buildings comprise one of the most significant collections of works by an early African American architect.

Although they make up less than 2 percent of the nation's fifty thousand registered architects, contemporary designers continue to work in tradition styles and break racial and cultural design barriers. They build on the legacy of early black architects who mastered conventional Western design formulas. With increasing frequency, contemporary architects, such as Jack Travis, incorporate African-inspired design aesthetics. Melvin L. Mitchell's *The Crisis of the African-American Architect: Conflicting Cultures of Architecture and (Black) Power* (2001) examines the many concerns they faced. African American professionals in the fields of graphic design, visual communications, interior design, fashion design, and industrial design encounter many of the same obstacles.

In 1990, David H. Rice founded the Organization of Black Designers (OBD) to address the concerns and promote the work of black architectural, graphic, advertising, product, interior, fashion, and industrial and transportation designers. While under the directorship of Shauna Stallworth, the organization had a membership of over six thousand. In 1995, Rice penned the essay that serves as the OBD manifesto, *What Color Is Design?* It boldly states that "Lack of Diversity = Design Sterility." Rice asserts that:

> In such a highly competitive new world order, we as Americans cannot afford to deny, in any way, the development of the potential of any segment of our citizenry. The creativity of Black Americans has contributed much to the cultural richness of our society even under stringent restrictions. That same creativity lives in the hearts and minds of countless Black youngsters and Black professionals who only need the opportunity to allow its full expression. America can no longer afford to waste human resources. It is no longer a matter of "divide and conquer," but "unite and prosper." Our future depends upon it.

VISUAL AND APPLIED ARTISTS

(Some biographical profiles may appear in other chapters. To locate profiles more readily, please consult the index.)

CHARLES ALSTON (1907–1977)

Painter, Sculptor, Muralist. Born in Charlotte, North Carolina, in 1907, Charles Henry Alston received his B.A. and M.A. from Columbia University in New York. He was later awarded several fellowships and grants to launch his painting career.

Alston's paintings and sculpture are in the collections of IBM and the Detroit Institute of Arts, among others. He was a member of the National Society of Mural Painters, and his murals depicting the history of medicine adorn the facade of Harlem Hospital in New York. His other notable works include *Exploration and Colonization* (1949), *Blues with Guitar and Bass* (1957), *Blues Song* (1958), *School Girl* (1958), *Nobody Knows* (1966), *Sons and Daughters* (1966), and *Frederick Douglass* (1968).

BENNY ANDREWS (1930–2006)

Painter. Born in Madison, Georgia, on November 13, 1930, Benny Andrews studied at Fort Valley State College in Georgia and later at the University of Chicago. He was awarded a B.F.A. from the Art Institute of Chicago in 1958. During his career, he taught at the New York School of Social Research, New York City University, and Queens College in New York. His works have appeared at museums and galleries around the country, including the Boston Museum of Fine Arts, the Martha Jackson Gallery in New York City, and others.

Andrews directed the Visual Arts Program for the National Endowment for the Arts (NEA) from 1982 to1984. He became director of the National Arts Program in 1985, offering children and adults an opportunity to exhibit and compete for prizes in many cities across the United States. Other honors include an honorary doctorate from the Atlanta School of Art (1984), a John Hay Whitney Fellowship (1965–1967), a New York Council on the Arts Grant (1971), an NEA Fellowship (1974), a Bellagio Fellowship from the Rockefeller Foundation (1987), and an NEA Painting Fellowship (1986). His notable works include *The Family*, *The Boxer*, *The Invisible Man*, *Womanhood*, *Flora*, and *Did the Bear*.

EDWARD MITCHELL BANNISTER (1828–1901)

Painter. Born in Nova Scotia in 1828, Edward Mitchell Bannister was the son of a West Indian father and African American mother. Both parents died when he was very young. Bannister moved to Boston in the early 1850s, where he learned to make solar plates and worked as a photographer.

Bannister was influenced by the Barbizon style popular at the time. His paintings convey his love of the quiet beauty of nature and his pleasure in picturesque scenes with cottages, cattle, dawns, sunsets, and small bodies of water.

In 1871, Bannister moved from Boston to Providence, Rhode Island, where he lived until his death in 1901. Unlike many other nineteenth-century African American artists, Bannister did not travel to Europe to study art, believing that he was an American and wished to paint as an American. Bannister became one of the leading artists in Providence in the 1870s and 1880s. In 1880, he became one of seven founders of the Providence Art Club, which later became known as the Rhode Island School of Design. His notable works include *After the Storm, Driving Home the Cows, Newspaper Boy,* and *Narragansett Bay.*

ERNIE BARNES (1938–2009)

Painter. Ernest Barnes Jr. was born on July 15, 1938, in Durham, North Carolina. From 1957 to 1960, Barnes attended North Carolina Central College (now North Carolina Central University), where he majored in art and played on the football team. He left school without graduating when the Washington Redskins drafted him. After playing for other National Football League teams and a Canadian football league, Barnes retired because of an injury.

Barnes had continued to paint throughout his football career, and his teammates dubbed him "Big Rembrandt." With his experience as a player and his painterly talents, Barnes became a sports artist. He secured a contract to paint for the American Football League and New York Jets owner Sonny Werblin. Barnes was the official artist for the 1984 Olympic Games in Los Angeles.

Barnes painted in a colorful and expressive style, and he exaggerated the muscularity and physical attributes of his figures. He received national attention when his paintings, including *Sugar Shack,* appeared on the 1970s television show *Good Times* and the Marvin Gay album *I Want You.* In 1997, Barnes completed a commission for the Naismith Memorial Basketball Hall of Fame in Springfield, Massachusetts. In 2004, the American Sport Art Museum and Archives in Daphne, Alabama, named him America's Best Painter of Sports.

RICHMOND BARTHÉ (1901–1989)

Sculptor. James Richmond Barthé was born on January 28, 1901, in Bay St. Louis, Mississippi. Barthé was educated at the Art Institute of Chicago (1924–1928), where he studied under Charles Schroeder and Albin Polasek. Barthé's first love was painting, but after he exhibited two busts in the 1927 *Negro in Art Week Exhibition* and the Chicago Art League's annual exhibition in 1928, his experiments with figurative sculpture brought him to the attention of art critics. Barthé's pioneering naturalism focused on the physicality, muscularity, and sensuality of the black body. The acclaim resulting from these early sculptures led to a one-man show in Chicago at the Women's City Club. He also won a Julius Rosenwald Fund Fellowship for study in New York City, where he set up a studio and ran in the same creative circles as such Harlem legends as Wallace Thurman, Countee Cullen, and Langston Hughes. Ralph Ellison became Barthé's first sculptural student. Barthé later lived in Jamaica, Switzerland, Spain, and Italy, before settling in Pasadena, California, late in life.

Barthé's early commissions included a bust of Henry Ossawa Tanner; monumental public sculptures of revolutionary leaders Toussaint-Louverture and Jean-Jacques Dessalines for the Haitian capital in Port-au-Prince; and a sculpture of black actress Rose McClendon for Frank Lloyd Wright's Fallingwater house in Mill Run, Pennsylvania. Barthé's work has been exhibited at several major American museums. The Metropolitan Museum of Art in New York City purchased *The Boxer* in 1943. In 1946, he received the first commission given to an African American artist, for a bust of Booker T. Washington for New York University's Hall of Fame. A year later, he was named one of a committee of fifteen artists chosen to help modernize sculpture in Catholic churches of the United States. Barthé held membership in the National Academy of Arts and Letters, and his art can be found in the collections of the Whitney Museum of American Art in New York and the Art Institute of Chicago.

Barthé last sculpture was a bust of actor James Garner, who provided financial support in the last years of the artist's life. Barthé died on March 6, 1989, at his home in Pasadena. He was the first African American gay male sculptor to produce a noteworthy body of work, which includes *Feral Benga, Singing Slave, Maurice Ens, Lot's Wife,* and *Henry O. Tanner.*

JEAN-MICHEL BASQUIAT (1960–1988)

Painter. Jean-Michel Basquiat was born on December 20, 1960, in Brooklyn, New York. His mother, the daughter of Puerto Rican immigrants, was also born in Brooklyn, and his father immigrated from Port-au-Prince, Haiti. Basquiat began his career spray-painting images, often described as graffiti, on buildings throughout New York. SAMO (slang for "same old shit") was his signature and trademark. In a brief, tragic career, Basquiat gained attention from wealthy collectors as a young street artist "discovered" by Andy Warhol and promoted by other art consultants. He attracted the attention of the New York art world with his tangled dreadlocks and trendy personal appearance as a musician and artist by the time he was eighteen.

A 1981 *Artforum* article titled "The Radiant Child" brought wider attention and helped Basquiat secure a 1982 solo exhibition at the Annina Nosei Gallery, which catapulted him to the center of the New York art scene. The Nosei exhibition was followed by a wider series of exhibiting opportunities. Basquiat's rapid ascendancy stirred resentments among some formally trained black artists and critics, who dismissed the artist and his art as pandering to white ethnographic fascinations. After shifting from street art to established galleries featuring neo-expressionists, he often used his SAMO tag in his painted composition to preserve his edgy reputation.

Basquiat's works are autobiographical, and his style blends the raw coding of graffiti and the formal interests of modernism. In February 1985, he was a featured artist on the cover of the *New York Times Magazine*. He was shown shoeless, in a suit, shirt, and tie.

Basquiat produced more than six hundred works, reportedly valued in the tens of millions of dollars. His works are held in the collections of the Museum of Modern Art and the Whitney Museum of American Art in New York City, the Guggenheim Bilbao in Spain, the Fukuoka Art Museum in Japan, the Museum of Fine Arts in Houston, the Museum of Contemporary Art in Los Angeles, and the Musée d'Art Contemporain in Marseille, France. He died in 1988, reportedly from a drug overdose, when he was twenty-seven years old. His notable works include *Self Portrait as a Heel #3*, *Untitled (History of Black People)*, *Hollywood Africans*, and *CPRKR (in Honor of Charlie Parker)*.

ROMARE BEARDEN (1911–1988)

Painter, Collagist. Romare Bearden was born on September 2, 1911, in Charlotte, North Carolina. His family moved to Pittsburgh and later to Harlem. Bearden started college at Lincoln University, but transferred to Boston University and then New York University, where he studied art, including cartooning, and earned a degree in education. Bearden then studied with George Grosz at the Art Students League of New York. Later, on the G.I. Bill, Bearden went to Paris, where he met Henri Matisse, Joan Miró, and Carl Holty.

Bearden was the product of a new generation of African Americans who had migrated from the rural South to the cities of the North. His work reflected the era of industrialization, and his images depict urban life, jazz, and city people. Bearden's early works belonged to the school of social realism, but after his return from Europe, his images became more abstract.

In the 1960s, Bearden changed his approach and began to make collages, soon becoming one of the best-known collagists in the world. His images are montages of his memories of past experiences and of stories told to him by other people. For Bearden, the collages were "an attempt to redefine the image of man in terms of the black experience."

Bearden's paintings and collages are in collections as varied as the Museum of Modern Art in New York, the Pennsylvania Academy of the Fine Arts, the Albright-Knox Art Gallery in Buffalo, the St. Louis Art Museum, the Studio Museum in Harlem, the National Gallery of Art in Washington, D.C., and the Library of Congress. Bearden's achievements included election to the American Academy of Arts and Letters (1966) and the National Institute of Arts and Letters (1972), and receipt of the National Medal of Arts (1987). In addition, numerous institutions awarded him honorary doctorates, including Atlanta University, Carnegie Mellon University, Davidson College, and Pratt Institute. His notable works include *Street Corner*, *He Is Arisen*, *The Burial*, *Sheba*, and *The Prevalence of Ritual*.

JOHN BIGGERS (1924–2001)

Painter, Muralist. Born in Gastonia, North Carolina, on April 13, 1924, John Biggers derived much of his subject matter from the contributions made by African Americans to the development of the United States. Classes at Hampton University with Austrian immigrant Viktor Lowenfeld sparked Biggers's lifelong dedication to the arts. He received his B.A. and M.A. from Pennsylvania State University in 1948. In 1949, Biggers moved to Houston to become the founding chairman of the art department at Texas State University for Negroes (now Texas Southern University). He retired in 1983 to focus on his art, which always expressively featured the resiliency and richness of black southern culture and African culture. Biggers had a significant influence on young African American painters.

Some of his most powerful pieces were created as a result of his travels in Africa, which began with a 1957 UNESCO-sponsored fellowship trip to the new nation of Ghana, as well as to Benin, Nigeria, and Togo. His works of this period include *The Time of Ede, Nigeria*, a series done in the 1960s. In 1962, Biggers donated a fifty-foot mural, *The Web of Life*, to Texas Southern University. It graced the walls of the University Museum when it opened in 2002. His other notable works include *Cradle*, *Mother and Child*, *The Contributions of Negro Women to American Life and Education*, and *Shotgun, Third Ward #1*.

CAMILLE BILLOPS (1933–)

Sculptor, Photographer, Filmmaker. Sculptor Camille Billops was born in California in 1933. She graduated from California State College in 1960, and then studied sculpture under a grant from the Huntington Hartford Foundation. In 1960, Billops had her first solo exhibition at the African Art Exhibition in Los Angeles, followed in 1963 by an exhibition at the Valley Cities Jewish Community Center in Los Angeles. In 1966, she participated in a group exhibition in Moscow. Since then, her artistic talents, which include poetry, book illustration, and jewelry making, have earned the praise of critics throughout the world, particularly in Sri Lanka and Egypt, where she has also lived and worked.

Billops has taught extensively. In the 1970s, she served on the faculties of the City University of New York and Rutgers University in New Jersey. In addition, she has conducted special art courses in the Tombs, a New York City jail. She lectured in India for the U.S. Information Agency in 1972, and participated in an exhibit at the New York Cultural Center in 1973.

Billops is a also printmaker, filmmaker, and photographer. She has been active in the mail-art movement, which has made art more accessible to the public. She has also written articles for the *New York Times*, the *Amsterdam News*, and *Newsweek*. She has received grants for film from the New York State Council on the Arts (1987–1988), the New York Foundation for the Arts (1989), the Rockefeller Foundation (1991), and the National Endowment for the Arts (1994).

In 1992, Billops won the prestigious Sundance Film Festival's Grand Jury Prize for best documentary with her movie *Finding Christa*, an edited combination of interviews, home movies, still images, and dramatic acting. Her other notable works include: three ceramic sculptures titled *Tenure*, *Black American*, and *Portrait of an American Indian*; *Year after Year*, a painting; and the films *Suzanne, Suzanne* (1982), *Older Women and Love* (1987), *A String of Pearls* (2002), and *The K.K.K. Boutique Ain't Just Rednecks* (1995). Billops is also the coauthor of *The Harlem Book of the Dead* (1978), written with James VanDerZee and Owen Dodson.

ROBERT BLACKBURN (1920–2003)

Printmaker. Robert Hamilton Blackburn was born of Jamaican parents in Summit, New Jersey, in 1920. He studied at the WPA-sponsored Harlem Community Art Center, the Art Students League, and the Wallace Harrison School of Art. His exhibitions include *Art of the American Negro* (1940) at the Downtown Gallery in New York and the Albany Museum of Art, *Contemporary Art of the American Negro* (1966), and numerous print shows in the United States and Europe. His work is owned by the Library of Congress, the Brooklyn Museum, the Baltimore Museum of Art, and the Clark Atlanta University Collections of African American Art.

Blackburn was a member of the art faculty of Cooper Union. Along with his other accomplishments, he founded the Creative Graphics Workshop as an artist-run cooperative in 1948. In 1971, the workshop was renamed the Printmaking Workshop and was incorporated as a nonprofit printmaking studio for work in lithography, etching, relief, and photo-processes. The workshop, which became a magnet for third-world and minority artists, is Blackburn's living legacy. It remains a haven for artists "to turn out prints for the love of it" and to do anything from experimental hodgepodge to polished pieces. In 1988, Blackburn and the Printmaking Workshop were given the Governor's Art Award for making "a significant contribution to the cultural life of New York State." In 1992, he received the MacArthur Award. His notable works include *Boy with Green Head* and *Negro Mother*.

SELMA BURKE (1900–1995)

Sculptor, Educator. Selma Burke was an artist whose career spanned more than sixty years. She was born in Mooresville, North Carolina, on December 31, 1900. She attended Slater Industrial and State Normal School (now Winston-Salem State University) and earned a nursing degree from St. Augustine College in 1924. She later earned an M.F.A from Columbia University in 1941 and a Ph.D. from Livingston College in 1970. Burke received her training as a sculptor at Columbia University. She also studied with Aristide Maillol in Paris and with Michael Powolny in Vienna.

Burke worked as an instructor in art and sculpture at the Friends School, St. George's School, and Forrest House in New York City from 1930 until 1949. From 1963 to 1976, she served as an instructor in art and sculpture at the Sidwell School, Haverford College, Livingston College, and Swarthmore College. The A. W. Mellon Foundation employed Burke as a consultant from 1967 to 1976. She founded the Selma Burke School of Sculpture in New York City in 1940 and the Selma Burke Art Center in Pittsburgh in 1968, where she taught and supported many young artists.

Burke received honorary degrees from Livingston College, the University of North Carolina, and Moore College of Art. The Pearl S. Buck Foundation Woman's Award was given to her in 1987 for her professional distinction and devotion to family and humanity. Burke's best-known work is the sculptural relief portrait of Franklin Delano Roosevelt that was minted on the American dime. Her other notable works include *Falling Angel*, *Peace*, and *Jim*.

STEPHEN BURROWS (1943–)

Fashion Designer. Stephen Burrows was born on September 15, 1943, in Newark, New Jersey. He helped his grandmother complete sewing projects as a boy and started making clothes at a young age. He later studied at the Philadelphia Museum College of Art and the Fashion Institute of Technology in New York City.

With a partner, Burrows opened "O" boutique in 1968. He worked for Henri Bendel as in-house designer from 1969 to 1973, from 1977 to 1982, and in 1993. Among his other accomplishments, Burrows was the founding director of Burrows Inc. in New York City, a Seventh Avenue firm that he and a partner ran until 1982.

Known for his unique color combinations, Burrows used patches of cloth for decorative motifs in the 1960s. His top-stitching of seams in contrasting threads and his top-stitched hems, known as "lettuce hems" because of their fluted effect, were widely copied. He preferred soft, clinging, easy-moving fabrics, such as chiffon and matte jersey. He also liked asymmetry. Disco dancers readily adopted his nonconstricting designs in natural, flowing fabrics. He won a Coty American Fashion Critics Award in 1974 and a special Coty Award in 1977, a Council of American Fashion Critics Award in 1975, and the Knitted Textile Association Crystal Ball Award in 1975. He was also honored with a bronze plaque along the "Fashion Walk of Fame" on Seventh Avenue in New York City.

ELIZABETH CATLETT (c. 1919–)

Sculptor, Painter. Elizabeth Catlett was the granddaughter of enslaved Africans living in North Carolina. She was raised in the northwest district of Washington, D.C. As a young woman, Catlett attempted to gain admission into an all-white art school, the Carnegie Institute of Technology in Pittsburgh, Pennsylvania. She was refused entry and instead went to Howard University, from which she graduated with honors in 1935. In 1940, she entered the University of Iowa, where she became the first sculptor to receive an M.F.A.

Catlett's exhibition history dates to 1937 and includes group and solo presentations at all the major American art museums, as well as institutions in Mexico City, Moscow, Paris, Prague, Tokyo, Beijing, Berlin, and Havana. Catlett's public sculpture can be found in Mexico City, New Orleans, Washington, D.C., New York, and Jackson, Mississippi. Her work can be found in the permanent collections of over twenty museums throughout the world.

Catlett accepted teaching positions at various African American colleges in order to earn a living, but by 1946 she had moved to Mexico, where she eventually settled after marrying Mexican artist Francisco Mora. Always a promoter of human struggle—and visually concerned with the recording of economic, social, and political themes—Catlett became deeply involved with the civil rights movement, which contributed greatly to her philosophy of life and art.

Catlett has won numerous prizes and honors, both in Mexico and the United States. Her notable works include *Black Unity* and *Homage to My Young Black Sisters* (1968), *Target Practice* (1970), *Mother and Child* (1972), and *Woman Resting* (1981). Catlett provided the illustrations for James Weldon Johnson's book *Lift Every Voice and Sing* (1993). She received honorary doctorates from Morgan State University (1993), the New School for Social Research (1995), and Carnegie Mellon University (2008).

DANA CHANDLER (1941–)

Painter. Dana Chandler is one of the country's most visible African American painters. Chandler's huge, colorful Black Power murals can be spotted throughout the ghetto area of Boston, a constant reminder of the resolve and determination displayed by the new breed of young African American urban dwellers.

Chandler's easel works are bold and simple. One piece, *The Golden Prison*, shows an African American man with a yellow and red striped flag, "because America has been yellow and cowardly in dealing with the black man." *Fred Hampton's Door* shows a bullet-splintered door bearing a stamp of U.S. government approval.

Born in Lynn, Massachusetts, in 1941, Chandler received his B.S. from the Massachusetts College of Art in 1967. Chandler has worked as a critic of African American art for the *Bay State Banner*, an assistant professor of art and art history at Simmons College in Boston, and an artist-in-residence at Northeastern University. Chandler has been a member of the National Conference of Black Artists, the Boston Black Artists Association, the National Conference of Artists, the Boston Union of Visual Artists, and the American Association of University Professors. His notable works include: *Martin Luther King, Jr. Assassinated*; *Death of Uncle Tom*; *Rebellion '68*; *Dynamite*; and *Death of a Bigot*.

BARBARA CHASE-RIBOUD (1939–)

Sculptor, Novelist, Poet. Barbara Chase-Riboud was born in Philadelphia, Pennsylvania, in 1936. She received a B.F.A. from Temple University in 1957 and an M.F.A. from Yale University in 1960. As a child, Chase-Riboud was encouraged to express herself artistically by her mother, a jazz musician, and her father, whom she describes as a "frustrated painter." She enrolled in the Fletcher Art School when she was seven years old, and she studied piano and ballet as a child. Building on this early training, she majored in art at Temple University in Philadelphia. She then used a fellowship from the John Hay Whitney Foundation to study at the American Academy in Rome for one year. She also exhibited her work at the Spoleto Festival in Italy in 1957. Chase-Riboud later returned to the United States and attended the Yale School of Art and Architecture.

After moving to Paris, Barbara Chase married the French photojournalist Marc Riboud. She has lived and worked in Europe as a sculptor and writer since 1961, marrying her second husband, art expert Sergio Tosi, in 1981. Chase-Riboud's mixed-media sculptures combine "soft" and "hard" materials, such as silk cords juxtaposed to metals, usually bronze, cast in the lost-wax technique. She uses contrasting materials to explore formal concerns, and metaphorically comments on issues regarding race and society. Chase-Riboud's work has been exhibited in numerous solo and group shows, including *Three Generations of African-American Women Sculptors: A Study in Paradox* (1997) and *Explorations in the City of Light: African-American Artists in Paris, 1945–1965* (1996). Her notable works include *Malcolm X* (1970), *Confession for Myself* (1973), *Cleopatra's Cape* (1973), and *Africa Rising* (1998), a large public installation at the Ted Weiss Federal Building in New York City.

In addition to making visual arts, Chase-Riboud writes historical novels and poetry. Her publications include: *Sally Hemings: A Novel* (1979); *Valide: A Novel of the Harem* (1986); *Echo of Lions* (1989); *The President's Daughter* (1994); and *Hottentot Venus: A Novel* (2004).

ROBERT COLESCOTT (1925–2009)

Painter. Robert Colescott was born in California in 1925. A World War II veteran, Colescott received his B.A. from the University of California in 1949 and his M.A. in 1952. In 1953, Colescott studied in Paris with Fernand Léger. His works have been exhibited at such major institutions as the Whitney Museum of American Art in New York, the Hirshhorn Museum and Sculpture Garden in Washington, D.C., and the Institute of Contemporary Art at the University of Pennsylvania. His works are held in the collections of the Museum of Modern Art, the Corcoran Gallery of Art, the Portland Art Museum, the Delaware Museum of Art, the Baltimore Museum of Art, and the Museum of Fine Arts in Boston.

Colescott began his teaching career at Portland State University in 1966, followed by a position at the American Research Center in Cairo, Egypt. He later taught at California State University, Stanislaus; the University of California, Berkeley; and the San Francisco Art Institute. He retired from the University of Arizona, Tucson, in 1998 as professor emeritus.

Colescott was a controversial artist who was criticized by both African American groups and traditionalists. His work questions the "heroic" and pushes the standards of taste. Colescott explores the tension created by notions of race and sex, along with other taboos and stereotypes. He has substituted black figures in place of white figures in famous European paintings. His notable works include: *George Washington Carver Crossing the Delaware: Page from an American History Textbook*; *Homage to Delacroix: Liberty Leading the People*; *Eat Dem Taters*; *Shirley Temple Black and Bill Robinson White*; and *The Power of Desire, the Desire for Power*.

HOUSTON CONWILL (1947–)

Sculptor, Performance Artist, Environmental Artist. Born in Kentucky in 1947, Houston Conwill spent three years studying for the priesthood. His strong Catholic upbringing and Catholic ritual play a part in his art, which draws from both American and African myths and religions. He mostly uses nontraditional materials, such as latex in place of canvas. The environments that he builds, paints, and fills with real chalices, candlesticks, carpets, or sand are works to which he adds his own personal iconography, along with ancient symbols.

Conwill has collaborated with his sister, the poet Estella Conwill Majozo, and the architect Joseph DePace on numerous site-specific projects in key cities across the United States. He is spiritually driven to honor the sacredness of space and place in black history. His projects include *Revelation: Martin Luther King Jr. Peace Memorial* for the Yerba Buena Performing Arts Center in San Francisco. His 1988 terrazzo and brass floor mosaic and threshold, *Rivers: Langston Hughes Memorial*, at the Schomburg Center for Research in Black Culture in Harlem, celebrates Hughes's poem "The Negro Speaks of Rivers" and the bibliophile Arthur Schomburg. Conwill and his collaborators design their exquisite works to encourage viewers' physical experience of art and location.

Conwill's awards include the Prix de Rome Fellowship (1984), the Louis Comfort Tiffany Foundation Award (1987), and the Art Commission Award for Excellence in Design (1990). His other notable works include *The Cakewalk Manifesto*, *Passion of St. Matthew*, *East Shout*, and *JuJu Funk*.

EMILIO ANTONIO CRUZ JR. (1938–2004)

Painter, Poet. Emilio Cruz was born in the Bronx on March 15, 1938. His studied at the Art Students' League under Edwin Dickinson, George Grosz, and Frank J. Reilly; the New School for Social Research in New York; the University of Louisville in Kentucky; and the Seong Moy School of Painting and Graphics in Provincetown, Massachusetts.

Cruz exhibited widely beginning in 1959, earning his first solo exhibition at Zabriskie Gallery in New York City in 1963. Other exhibitions were held at the Anita Shapolsky Gallery (1986, 1991), the Studio Museum in Harlem (1987), the Portland Museum of Art (1987), the Rhode Island School of Design (1987), the Gwenda Jay Gallery in Chicago (1991), and the G.R. N'Namdi Gallery in Birmingham, Michigan (1991). His last exhibition before his death from pancreatic cancer in 2004 was *I Am Food I Eat the Eater of Food* at Alitash Kebede Gallery in Los Angeles. Cruz's works are narrative and formalistic, emphasizing color and forms as the dominant elements. He often combined these two theoretical approaches with figurative subjects.

Cruz's awards include the Cintas Foundation Fellowship (1965–1966), the John Hay Whitney Fellowship (1964–1965), and the Walter Gutman Foundation Award (1962).

His notable works include *Silver Umbrella, Figure Composition 6,* and *Striated Voodoo.* In the 1970s, Cruz lived in Chicago and taught at the School of the Art Institute of Chicago. He returned to New York in 1982 and resumed teaching in the late 1980s. At the time of his death, Cruz held assistant professorships at both Pratt Institute and New York University.

ROY DECARAVA (1919–2009)

Photographer. Roy DeCarava was born in 1919 in Harlem. He began his career as a commercial artist in 1938 after studying painting at Cooper Union. In 1930 to 1942, he studied at the Harlem Art Center, where he concentrated on painting and printmaking. By the mid-1940s, he began to use photography as a convenient method of recording ideas for his paintings. In 1958, DeCarava gave up his commercial work and became a full-time freelance photographer. Edward Steichen suggested that he apply for a Guggenheim Fellowship. This award allowed DeCarava the financial freedom to take pictures and tell his story. One of DeCarava's photographs from this period appeared in Steichen's 1955 exhibition *Family of Man* at the Museum of Modern Art in New York. Later, Langston Hughes worked with DeCarava on the book *Sweet Flypaper of Life* (1955).

DeCarava worked as a photographer for *Sports Illustrated* and became a professor of photography at Hunter College in New York in 1975. His work can be found in many important collections throughout the United States, including the Art Institute of Chicago, the Corcoran Gallery of Art in Washington, D.C., and the Museum of Modern Art in New York. DeCarava received a Distinguished Career in Photography Award in 1991 from the Friends of Photography. That same year, the American Society of Magazine Photographers presented him with a special citation for photographic journalism. He was awarded the National Medal of the Arts in 2006. DeCarava also received honorary doctorates from the Maryland Institute College of Art, the Rhode Island School of Design, and Wesleyan University.

BEAUFORD DELANEY (1901–1979)

Painter. Born in Knoxville, Tennessee, in 1901, Beauford Delaney was described by his elder brother Samuel as a "remarkably dutiful child." For Beauford Delaney, recognition came by way of an elderly white Knoxville artist named

Beauford Delaney's Self-Portrait (1962). *This oil on canvas painting shows the yellow color that was central to Delaney's work. To Delaney, yellow signified light and healing.* **AP PHOTO/SEVANS**

Lloyd Branson. Branson gave Delaney lessons and, after a time, urged him to go to a city where he might study and come into contact with the art world. In 1924, Delaney moved to Boston to study at the Massachusetts Normal School, later studying at the Copley Society, where he took evening courses while working full-time at the South Boston School of Art. From Boston, Delaney moved to New York.

It was in New York that Delaney took on the life of a bohemian, living in the village in coldwater flats. Much of his time was spent painting the portraits of the personalities of the day, such as Louis Armstrong, Ethel Waters, and Duke Ellington. In 1938, Delaney gained national attention when *Life Magazine*, in an article on "negroes," featured a photograph of him surrounded by a group of his paintings at the annual outdoor exhibition in Washington Square in New York. In 1945, Henry Miller wrote the essay "The Amazing and Invariable Beauford Delaney," which was later reprinted in *Remember to Remember*.

In the 1950s, Delaney left New York with the intention of studying in Rome. He sailed to Paris on the *Ile de France*, later visiting Greece, Turkey, and northern Italy, but he never got to Rome. Returning to Paris for one more visit, Delaney began to paint, make new friends, and create a new social life. Paris was to become Delaney's permanent home.

By 1961, Delaney was producing paintings at such an intense rate that the pressure began to wear on his strength, and he suffered his first mental collapse. He was confined to a clinic in Vincennes, and his dealer and close friends began to organize his life, hoping to help relieve some of the pressure. For the rest of his life, Delaney was to suffer repeated breakdowns, and by 1971 he was back in a sanitarium, where he remained until his death in 1979.

Delaney's numerous exhibitions took place in such venues as the Artists Gallery in New York (1948), the Roko Gallery in New York (1950–1953), the Musée d'Art Moderne in Paris (1963), the American Negro Exposition in Chicago (1940), and the Newark Museum in New Jersey (1971). His work can be found in the collections of the Whitney Museum of American Art in New York, the Newark Museum, and Morgan State College in Baltimore. His notable works include *Greene Street*, *Yaddo*, *Head of a Poet*, and *Snow Scene*.

MURRY N. DePILLARS (1938–2008)

Draughtsman, Painter, Illustrator, Educator, Historian. Murry N. DePillars was born and raised amid the rich cultural milieu of Chicago's West Side. Inspired by the gospel, blues, and jazz infused cultural rhythms of his all-black community, DePillars began his formal study of the arts at Chicago-based institutions, earning his first degree, an A.A. in fine arts, from Kennedy-King Community College. After returning from a tour of duty with the U.S. military in Vietnam, DePillars resumed his pursuit of higher education at Chicago's Roosevelt University, receiving his B.A. in art education (1968) and his M.A. in urban studies (1970). In 1971, DePillars left the urban north and traveled south to serve as assistant dean of the School of the Arts at Virginia Commonwealth University (VCU). By 1976, DePillars had earned a Ph.D. in art education from Pennsylvania State University and became dean of VCU's School of the Arts—an institution-shaping leadership position that he held until his retirement in 1995.

DePillars came of age as an artist during the height of the Black Arts movement, and reproductions of his early pen-and-ink drawings, as well as his paintings, appear in *Black Artists on Art*, Volume 2, which fellow artist and art historian Samella Lewis coauthored with artist Ruth G. Waddy in 1969 (rev. ed. 1976). The publication includes a one-line artist's statement summing up DePillars's creative motivation: "The decisive factor in my work is the political and social plight of Blacks throughout the world." Moreover, in a book where most artists are represented by only one or two artworks, DePillars was given four reproductions, inscribing him into the founding historical text on visual artists of the Black Arts movement.

Of the three drawings by DePillars—*Children at Play and Fifi*; *Muh Deah (Tribute to Adillsha)*; and *Aunt Jemima (Section 22 for Ron Smith and John Carlos)*—the latter is the most frequently discussed early work. In *Aunt Jemima* (1968), the trademark pancake chef's black-gloved and raised fist wields a huge spatula as a weapon rather than a kitchen tool. Her pose echoes the Black Power salute of the 1968 Mexico City Olympic track stars who were stripped of their gold and bronze medals. The oil painting, *And There Was a Call From the East*... (1970), foreshadows DePillars's later turn toward African-inspired subjects and aesthetics.

Over his artistic career, DePillars received many honors and awards, and early recognition frequently came from other creative artists. The legendary saxophonist Anthony Braxton titled a 1968 jazz recording "To Artist Murray DePillars" and included it as track number three on his groundbreaking album *For Alto* (1969). Braxton was an early member of the Association for the Advancement of Creative Musicians (AACM), founded by Chicago-based jazz musicians in 1965. Their motto, "Great Black Music, Ancient to the Future," reveals the interrelated beliefs and goals of the visual artists, writers, musicians, and performers of the Black Arts movement.

In 1980, DePillars joined AFRICOBRA, founded in Chicago in the late 1969s, embracing the group's African-informed aesthetics and vibrantly colored and rhythmically expressive figurative painting style. He claimed that his "approach to painting has been influenced by the six aesthetic priorities of early African American quilt makers, and their concept of 'building' rather than sewing a quilt." *Queen Candace-Diamond Quilt (Quilt Series)*, an acrylic on canvas, is representative of this period. DePillars participated in numerous solo and group shows, as well as retrospectives. In building their collections, the Whitney Museum of American Art in New York, the Museum of Contemporary Art in Chicago, the Studio Museum in Harlem, the Mississippi Museum of Art, and the Orlando Museum of Art all acquired work by DePillars.

DePillars, affectionately known as "Richmond's Jazz Man," was the illustrator for the 1989 children's book *The Story of Kwanzaa*, by Safisha Madhubuti. He transitioned to ancestor on May 31, 2008, in Richmond, Virginia.

AARON DOUGLAS (1899–1979)

Painter, Illustrator. Born in Topeka, Kansas, on May 26, 1899, Aaron Douglas achieved considerable eminence as a muralist, illustrator, and academician. Douglas graduated from the University of Nebraska in 1922, as well as Columbia University Teachers College and l'Académie Scandinave in Paris. He had one-person exhibitions at the universities of Kansas and Nebraska and also exhibited in New York at the Gallery of Modern Art. In 1939, Douglas was named to the faculty of Fisk University and later became head of its Department of Art.

Douglas was one of the most important painters and illustrators of the Negro Renaissance, now known as the Harlem Renaissance. He developed a distinct modernist style: a blend of Kemetic (Egyptian) conventions and iconography, using a subtle palette and an overlay of concentric circles to explore the triumphs and trials of the African and African diasporic peoples. His notable works include murals at Fisk University and in the Countee Cullen branch of the New York Public Library, as well as illustrations in the NAACP's *The Crisis*, Alain Locke's *The New Negro*, and books by Countee Cullen, James Weldon Johnson, and Langston Hughes. Alexander Dumas, Marion Anderson, and Mary McLeod Bethune are among the many African Americans whose portraits he painted or rendered in charcoal. Douglas died on February 2, 1979. In 1992, Fisk University opened a new gallery in his memory.

DAVID CLYDE DRISKELL (1931–)

Painter, Art Historian, Curator. Born in Eatonton, Georgia, in 1931, David Driskell studied at Howard University and earned his M.F.A. from the Catholic University of America in 1962. He also studied at the Skowhegan School of Painting and Sculpture and the Netherlands Institute for History of Art. Driskell later taught at Talladega College, Fisk University, and the Institute for African Studies at the University of Ife in Nigeria. He joined the faculty of the University of Maryland's Department of Art in 1977 and has been a professor emeritus since 1997.

Immediately after the death of Alonzo Aden, Driskell was invited to become the director of the Barnett-Aden Collection of African American Art. He organized and mounted a number of important exhibitions of African American art, including the groundbreaking *Two Centuries of Black American Art, 1950–1950* (1976), which traveled to major museums across the United States. The show revealed a long-repressed history of African American creative practice and opened doors for black artists, black art, and historians and curators of African American arts. In 2001, the David C. Driskell Center for the Study of the Visual Arts and Culture of African Americans and the African Diaspora opened at the University of Maryland to continue Driskell's pioneering work.

Driskell has been the recipient of many awards, including the John Hope Award, as well as prizes from the Danforth Foundation, the American Federation of Arts, and the Harmon Foundation. President Bill Clinton awarded him the National Humanities Medal in 2002. Driskell's work has been exhibited at the Corcoran Gallery of Art and the National Gallery of Art in Washington, D.C., the High Museum of Art in Atlanta, the Yale University Art Gallery, and the Rhodes National Gallery in Salisbury, Rhodesia. His notable works include *Movement*, *The Mountain*, *Still Life with Gateleg Table*, and *Shango Gone*.

ROBERT DUNCANSON (1821–1872)

Painter. Robert Duncanson was the son of an African American mother and a Scottish Canadian father. Born in upstate New York in 1821, he spent much of his childhood in Canada. During his youth, he and his mother moved to Mt. Healthy, Ohio, where in 1840 the Western Freedom's Aid Society, an antislavery group, raised funds to send him to Glasgow, Scotland, to study art. Returning to Cincinnati three years later, Duncanson advertised in the local newspaper as the proprietor of a daguerreotype studio. He continued to work at his studio until 1855, when he began to devote all of his time to painting. Like many landscape artists of the period, Duncanson traveled around the United States, drawing his compositions from the images of nature before him. In 1853, he made his second trip to Europe—this time to visit Italy, France, and England.

Although Duncanson was active during and after the Civil War, with the exception of his painting *Uncle Tom and Eva* (1853), he rarely represented the social or political turmoil within the United States or the racial discrimination he experienced. Once, in a letter to his son, he commented, "I have no color on the brain; I have color on the brain."

Duncanson's landscapes were included in the 1842 and 1843 Annual Exhibition of Paintings and Statuary at the Western Art Union in Cincinnati, Ohio; the 1864 Art Association of Montreal's Dublin Exhibition and their Canadian show in 1865; and the 1871 Western Art Gallery exhibition in Detroit, Michigan. His paintings are in the collections of the Smithsonian American Art Museum, the Detroit Institute of Arts, the Museum of Fine Arts in Boston, the Los Angeles County Museum of Art, the California African American Museum in Los Angeles, the Cincinnati Art Museum, the Cleveland Museum of American Art, and the Maier Museum of Art at Randolph College. His notable works include *The Belmont Murals* (1850–1852) at the Taft Museum of Art in Cincinnati, *The Rainbow* (1859), and *Land of Lotus Eaters* (1861).

WILLIAM EDMONDSON (c. 1870s–1951)

Sculptor. William Edmondson was a stonecutter and self-taught sculptor. Born in Nashville, Tennessee, around 1870, he supported himself working as a hospital orderly and manual laborer. Edmondson created his hand-hewn, limestone sculptures of animals, birds, and biblical characters for the local community. He often worked on tombstones. An art patron and collector brought Edmondson to the attention of the Museum of Modern Art in New York, which gave him a solo show in 1937. His work was also received extremely well in an exhibition of self-taught artists. Thereafter, private collectors and museums began to purchase his sculptures.

Edmondson created his sculptures at the home he shared with his mother and sister. After they died, Edmondson continued to live alone and work at his home until his own death in 1951. Notable works include *Choir Girls*, *Lion*, and *Crucifixion*.

ELTON CLAY FAX (1909–1993)

Illustrator, Writer. Elton Clay Fax was born on October 9, 1909, in Baltimore. He graduated from Syracuse University with a B.F.A. in 1931. Fax taught art at Claflin University from 1935 to 1936 and was an instructor at the Harlem Community Art Center from 1938 to 1939. His work was exhibited at the Baltimore Art Museum (1939) and the American Negro Exposition (1940), and later at the Metropolitan Museum of Art and the New York Visual Arts Gallery (1970). Examples of his work are included in several American university collections, including those of Texas Southern University, the University of Minnesota, and Virginia State University.

Fax wrote a number of books, including *Seventeen Black Artists* (1971), *Garvey: The Story of a Black Nationalist* (1972), *West Africa Vignettes* (1973), and *Black Artists of the New Generation* (1977). He traveled widely, and wrote about and illustrated what he experienced. His book *Hashar* (1980), for example, describes the life of the peoples of Soviet Central Asia and Kazakhstan. Fax also illustrated numerous books by other authors. His notable works include *Steelworker*, *Ethiopia Old and New*, *Contemporary Black Leaders*, and *Through Black Eyes*. Elton Fax died in Queens, New York, in May 1993.

TOM FEELINGS (1933–2003)

Illustrator. Born in Brooklyn, New York, on May 19, 1933, Thomas Feelings grew up in the Bedford-Stuyvesant neighborhood. He began to draw cartoons when he was four years old, and his artwork flourished under the guidance of an African American artist named Thipadeux, who encouraged Feelings to draw the people in his neighborhood. After high school, Feelings attended the Cartoonists and Illustrators' School in New York City on a three-year scholarship. His art studies were interrupted by four years of service for the U.S. Air Force in England, but after completing his military service, he continued his studies at the New York School of the Visual Arts.

While in art school, Feelings produced *Tommy Traveler in the World of Negro History*, a comic strip published in *New York Age*, a Harlem newspaper. Completing art school in 1961, Feelings marketed his portfolio to earn freelance assignments and began to get work with magazines of primarily African American readership. In 1964, Feelings traveled to Tema, a city in Ghana, with other African Americans enlisted by Kwame Nkrumah, then head of the Ghanaian government, to help guide the newly independent country. The experience changed Feelings's art on a spiritual and stylistic level. In 1966, he was forced to leave Ghana when the Nkrumah government fell in a coup.

Feelings returned to the United States hungry for work. At the time, there was a huge demand for works by and depicting African Americans, especially children's books. In this new climate, Feelings illustrated such books as *To Be a Slave* (1968) and *Moja Means One: Swahili Counting Book* (1971), which won a Caldecott Honor Award in 1972. From 1971 to 1974, Feelings administered the Guyanese Ministry of Education's children's book project while living in Guyana. There he wrote his autobiography, *Black Pilgrimage*, published in 1972. After returning to the United States, Feelings illustrated more books over the next ten years, including a 1987 collaboration with the writer Maya Angelou titled *Now Sheba Sings the Song*.

While serving as an artist-in-residence at the University of South Carolina, Feelings completed illustrations for two books. In 1993, he finished illustrations for *Soul Looks Back in Wonder*, a compilation of poems by African American authors. Two years later, he completed *The Middle Passage: White Ships/Black Cargo*, which portrays the passage of slave ships from Africa to the Western Hemisphere. Both books received Coretta Scott King Awards from the American Library Association.

Feelings earned many awards for his illustrations, including two Outstanding Achievement Awards from the New

York School of Visual Arts. He also earned a Visual Artists Fellowship and National Endowment for the Arts grants, as well as the 1991 Distinguished Service to Children through Art Award from the University of South Carolina.

Ethiopia Awakening ***(Meta Warrick Fuller, c. 1910).*** *A near life-size personification of Africa, Fuller's bronze sculpture is the earliest example of African American art overtly validating African arts and cultures.* ART RESOURCE, NY

META VAUX WARRICK FULLER (1877–1968)

Sculptor. Meta Vaux Warrick Fuller lived and worked during the transitional period between the nineteenth-century artists who chose to simulate Euro-American subjects and styles and the later artistic periods. Born in 1877 in Philadelphia and educated at the School of Industrial Art and the Pennsylvania Academy, Fuller's interest in sculpture led her to study with Charles Grafly and at the Académie Colarossi in Paris with Auguste Rodin. She was the first African American woman to become a professional artist. Her African American–themed sculpture *The Wretched* was exhibited at the Paris Salon in 1903 and 1904.

Fuller married and settled in the Boston area, where in 1910 most of her works were destroyed by a fire. The Boston Art Club and the Harmon Foundation later exhibited many of her surviving and later works, and representative pieces of her sculpture can be found in the collections of the Cleveland Museum of Art and other museums. Her notable works include *Ethiopia Awakening* and *Mary Turner: A Silent Protest Against Mob Violence.*

SAM GILLIAM (1933–)

Painter. Born in Mississippi in 1933, Sam Gilliam produces canvases that feature pure color pigments rather than shades or tones. The artist bunches these pigments in different configurations on drooping, drapelike canvases, giving the effect, in the words of *Time* magazine, of "clothes drying on a line." His canvases are said to be "like nobody else's, black or white."

Gilliam received his M.A. from the University of Louisville and was later awarded grants from the National Endowment for the Humanities. He has had one-man and group shows at the Washington Gallery of Modern Art, the Jefferson Place Gallery, the Adams-Morgan Gallery, the Phillips Collection, and the Corcoran Gallery of Art in Washington, D.C.; the Art Gallery of Washington University in St. Louis; the Speed Museum in Louisville, Kentucky; the Philadelphia Museum of Art; the Museum of Modern Art and the Whitney Museum of American Art in New York; the San Francisco Museum of Modern Art; and the Walker Art Center in Minneapolis. Gilliam is represented in the permanent collections of more than forty-five American museums. Important group exhibitions in which Gilliam's work was shown include the *First World Festival of Negro Arts* in Dakar, Senegal (1966), *The Negro in American Art* at the University of California, Los Angeles (1967), and the Whitney Museum's American Art Annual (1969).

In 1980, Gilliam was commissioned, with thirteen other artists, to design work for installation in the Atlanta International Airport, one of the largest airports in the world and the first to install contemporary artwork for public viewing. Gilliam's notable works include *Watercolor 4* (1969), *Herald*

(1965), *Carousel Change* (1970), *Mazda* (1970), *Plantagenets Golden* (1984), and *Golden Element Inside Gold* (1994).

TYREE GUYTON (1955–)

Multimedia Artist. Born in Detroit on August 24, 1955, Tyree Guyton has transformed the blighted urban pocket in which he has spent much of his life into an enormous ongoing art project that utilizes the debris of the abandoned cityscape. Guyton was interested in the arts from a young age. After high school, he served in the U.S. Army and then worked at Ford Motor Company for several years and as a firefighter. He also began a family and in his spare time took art classes.

In 1984, Guyton left his firefighting job to become a full-time artist. He started transforming the small city block in which he and his family lived. His grandfather, a former housepainter, was both a source of early inspiration and an integral contributor to Guyton's artistic project. Using ordinary house paint, old toys, bicycles, and other found objects they salvaged from the junk piles that plague the city, Guyton transformed Detroit's Heidelberg Street into a dynamic and unique art installation. A crack house, one of the many abandoned residences on the street, was painted in bright colors, discouraging the drug sales that even narcotics squad raids had not been able to stop. A tree was nailed several yards high with vintage bicycles. Polka dots decorated the street, Guyton's own home, and nearly every other available surface. The combination of dots, stripes, and lively patterning and the reinvention of discarded objects had been inspired by the style in which Guyton's mother had decorated their home on a tight budget when he was growing up.

Long heralded by the international artistic community, Guyton's art has periodically come under criticism, however. Other residents of the eastside Detroit neighborhood, who desire a return to the days of neatly manicured lawns, dismiss the out-of-town visitors and laudatory praise heaped on the Heidelberg Project. In the fall of 1991, city bulldozers demolished several of the houses that Guyton had transformed, one of which had been slated for inclusion on a tour of local artistic sites. Ironically, that year he was named the Michiganian of the Year, and the following year, he earned the Governor's Arts Award. Guyton sued the city—with the support of prominent members of Detroit's artistic community—but dropped the suit when a more sympathetic mayoral administration came into power in 1994. However, action by the Detroit City Council led to the partial dismantling of the project by 1999. The award-winning HBO Films documentary *Come Unto Me: The Faces of Tyree Guyton* (1999) brought more support and attention, including coverage in the television documentary *Urban Shrines* (2005) and the French documentary *Detroit: The Cycles of the Mental Machine* (2007).

RICHARD HUNT (1935–)

Painter, Sculptor. Richard Hunt was born in Chicago in 1935 and began his formal career after studying at the School of the Art Institute of Chicago, where he received a number of awards. After graduating in 1957, Hunt was awarded the James Nelson Raymond Traveling Fellowship. He later taught at the School of the Art Institute of Chicago and at the University of Illinois. From 1962 to 1963, he pursued his craft under a Guggenheim Fellowship.

Hunt's work has been exhibited at the Cleveland Museum of Art, the Milwaukee Art Museum, the Museum of Modern Art in New York, the Art Institute of Chicago, the Springfield Art Museum in Massachusetts, and the Indianapolis Museum of Art. His work also traveled throughout Africa with a U.S. government–sponsored show that was organized by the Los Angeles Museum of African American Art. Hunt sits on the board of governors at the School of the Art Institute of Chicago and the Skowhegan School of Painting and Sculpture in Maine. He is also a commissioner at the Smithsonian American Art Museum in Washington, D.C., and he serves on the advisory committee at the Getty Center for Education in the Arts in Malibu.

Hunt's works are held in the collections of many major museums in the United States and abroad, including the Museum of Modern Art, the Cleveland Museum of Art, the Art Institute of Chicago, the Milwaukee Art Museum, the Baltimore Museum of Art, the Hirshhorn Museum in Washington, D.C., and the Israel Museum in Jerusalem. His notable works include *Man on a Vehicular Construct* (1956), *Linear Spatial Theme* (1962), *The Chase* (1965), and *Arching* (1986).

JOSHUA JOHNSTON (c. 1763–1830)

Painter. Joshua Johnston (also written as Johnson), who was active between 1789 and 1824, was the first known African American portrait painter. At least two dozen paintings have been attributed to Johnston, who was listed as a "free householder of colour, portrait painter." He lived in the Baltimore area, and his name appears in Baltimore directories in various studio locations.

Johnston may have been enslaved by Charles Wilson Peale, an artist who opened a drawing school in Maryland in 1795. Johnston may have simply known Peale and been familiar with his work, however. In either case, Johnston was most likely self-taught. As a portraitist working in the style of the period, his paintings now seem quaint. Only one black subject has been attributed to him, *Portrait of a Cleric.* His notable works include *Portrait of Adelia*

The Westwood Children ***(Joshua Johnston, c. 1807).*** *This portrait of the children of a prominent family from Baltimore, Maryland, is one of about eighty portraits that have been attributed to Johnston, who is thought to be the earliest artist of African descent to work as a professional portrait painter in the United States.* THE ART ARCHIVE/NATIONAL GALLERY OF ART WASHINGTON/SUPERSTOCK/PICTURE DESK

Ellender, Portrait of Mrs. Barbara Baker Murphy, and *Portrait of Sea Captain John Murphy.*

LARRY JOHNSON (1949–)

Painter, Illustrator, Editorial Cartoonist. Born in Boston, Massachusetts, in 1949, Larry Johnson attended the School of the Boston Museum of Fine Arts. In 1968, he became a staff illustrator at the *Boston Globe,* for which he produced courtroom sketches, editorial sports cartoons, illustrations of sports and entertainment events, and pictures for other features. Johnson's work is nationally syndicated through Universal Press Syndicate.

Barry Gaither, director of the National Center of African American Artists in Boston, observed that "Johnson's works can be divided horizontally between commercial illustration and fine art, and vertically between drawings and paintings in acrylics and watercolor." In addition to working for the *Boston Globe,* Johnson drew pictures for the now defunct *National Sports Daily,* designed book jackets for Little Brown, and completed commissions for the Pepsi-Cola Company, the *Old Farmer's Almanac,* the National Football League, and *Fortune,* among others. He left the *Globe* to freelance and run his own company, Johnson Editions, a producer of fine arts prints, greeting cards, and other products. Johnson was awarded the Associated Press Editorial Cartoon Award in 1985. His notable works include *Island Chisel, Rainbow,* and *Promises.*

In 1995, several of Johnson's photographs were included in a six-artist exhibition titled *New Testament,* which was hosted by the Marc Foxx Gallery in Santa Monica, California. The Margo Leavin Gallery in Los Angeles also hosted an exhibition of Johnson's artwork in 1995.

LESTER L. JOHNSON (1937–)

Painter, Educator. Born in Detroit, Michigan, in 1937, Lester Larue Johnson Jr. attended the University of Michigan, where he received a B.F.A. in 1973 and an M.F.A. in 1974. He teaches at the College for Creative Studies in Detroit, Michigan.

Johnson's works are held in many collections, including those of the Detroit Institute of Arts, Osaka University Arts in Japan, Johnson Publishers and the Masonite Corp. in Chicago, Sonnenblick-Goldman Corp. in New York, Taubman Company in Bloomfield Hills, Michigan, and the St. Paul Company in St. Paul, Minnesota. His Detroit-area commissions include Urban Wall Murals (1974) and the New Detroit Receiving Hospital (1980). Johnson's work has been exhibited at numerous major institutions, including the Whitney Museum of American Art (1973), the Carnegie Institute in Pittsburgh, the National Academy of Design in New York (1977), and the Edward Thorp Gallery in New York (1994). Among his awards are the Andrew W. Mellon Foundation Grant (1982, 1984) and a Recognition Award from the African American Music Art Association.

SARGENT JOHNSON (1888–1967)

Sculptor. Sargent Claude Johnson, who won the Harmon Foundation's medal as the nation's outstanding African American artist on three occasions, worked in stylized idioms heavily influenced by the art forms of Africa in sculpture, mural bas-reliefs, metal sculpture, and ceramics.

Born in Boston in 1888, Johnson studied at the Worcester Art School and moved to the San Francisco Bay area in 1915, where his teachers were Beniamino Bufano and Ralph Stackpole. Johnson's work was exhibited at the San Francisco Artists Annual (1925–1931), the Harmon Foundation (1928–1931, 1933), the Art Institute of Chicago (1930), the Baltimore Museum (1939), and the American Negro Exposition in Chicago (1940). He was the recipient of numerous awards and prizes.

From the beginning of his career, Johnson spoke of his sculpture as an attempt to show the "natural beauty and dignity of the pure American Negro." He claimed that he wished to present "that beauty not so much to the white man as to the Negro himself. Unless I can interest my race, I am sunk." His notable works include *Sammy, Esther, Forever Free,* and murals at the Golden Gate Exposition Aquatic Park.

WILLIAM HENRY JOHNSON (1901–1970)

Painter. William H. Johnson was a pioneer African American modernist whose style varied from abstract expressionist landscape and flower studies influenced by Vincent van Gogh, to studies of black life in America, and finally to abstract figure studies in the manner of Georges Rouault.

Born in Florence, South Carolina, on March 18, 1901, Johnson studied at the National Academy of Design in New York and the Cape Cod School of Art under Charles Hawthorne. He also studied in southern France from 1926 to1929, and in Denmark and Norway from 1930 to 1938. His work was exhibited at the Harmon Foundation, where he won a gold medal in 1929; the Baltimore Museum in 1939; and the American Negro Exposition in Chicago in 1940. He produced one-person shows in Copenhagen in 1935 and at the Artists Gallery in New York in 1938. His notable works include *Booker T. Washington*, *Young Man in Vest*, *Descent from the Cross*, and *On a John Brown Flight*. He died on April 13, 1970.

BEN JONES (1942–)

Painter, Sculptor. Ben Franklin Jones was born in Patterson, New Jersey, in 1942. He earned a B.F.A. from Paterson University in Wayne, New Jersey; an M.A. from New York University; and an M.F.A. from Pratt Institute in New York.

Jones is a professor of fine arts at New Jersey City University. During the height of the Black Arts movement of the 1970s, Jones worked as a sculptor. He cast his sculptures in plaster from living models and painted them in brightly colored patterns resembling traditional African symbols. His works include masks, arms, and legs arranged in multiples or singly, which seem to have roots in African ceremony ritual and magic.

Jones's pieces can be found in such collections as the Newark Museum in New Jersey, the Studio Museum in Harlem, Howard University, and Johnson Publications in Chicago. His work has been exhibited at the Museum of Modern Art in New York, the Studio Museum in Harlem, the Newark Museum, Fisk University in Nashville, and the Black World Arts Festival in Lagos, Nigeria.

Jones's awards have included grants from the National Endowment for the Arts (1974–1975, 2007), the New Jersey Arts Council, the Delta Sigma Theta Sorority, the Puffin Foundation (2005), and the Joan Mitchell Foundation (2002). His notable works include *Black Face and Arm Unit* and *High Priestess of Soul*.

KARL KANI (1968–)

Fashion Designer. Karl Kani was born Carl Williams in 1968 in New York. He was preoccupied with style as a youth, and his fashion sense was first noticed on the streets of Brooklyn's Flatbush neighborhood. While his peers were buying the latest clothes, Williams was busy purchasing material he would later bring to various tailors, instructing them to make garments exactly how he wanted for a relatively low price. As time passed, people who had seen Williams in one of his "originals" wanted their own made-to-order clothes. Williams began taking orders and supplying the demand.

While working at Seasons Sportswear in South Central Los Angeles, Williams developed the name Kani, based on the question "Can I?" as in "Can I do it?" In 1989, Kani met Carl Jones, cofounder of Threads 4 Life. Jones, who had already proven his ability to sell clothes with his Cross Colours line, agreed to help Kani get his designs to the public. By 1992, the Kani line of clothing had added roughly $35 million to the Threads 4 Life profit margin. Disagreements with Threads 4 Life eventually led Kani to venture off on his own.

Kani began Karl Kani Infinity in 1994. Although competition in the hip-hop clothing market had become fierce, Kani saw potential in the previously ignored market. Rap stars such as Dr. Dre, Snoop Dogg, Puff Daddy (Diddy), and Tupac Shakur began wearing his designs and lending their image to ad campaigns, spreading the Kani name. In 1995, his designs were sold in more than three hundred stores nationwide. By 1996, Kani became the first fashion designer to have his sneakers worn by NBA players. *Black Enterprise* magazine recognized his firm as Company of the Year, and *Sportswear International Magazine* listed Kani among the Fifty Most Influential People in Fashion. He launched his European campaign in 1999, earning an estimated $84 million in 2000. Kani's 2010 spring apparel and footwear collections are sold online and in stores across America and Europe, pushing his pioneering urban fashion to new international commercial popularity.

JACOB LAWRENCE (1917–2000)

Painter. Born on September 7, 1917, in Atlantic City, New Jersey, Jacob Lawrence received his early training at the Harlem Art School and the American Artist School. He worked under the guidance of such artists as Charles Alston, Henry Bannarn, Anton Refregier, Sol Wilson, Philip Reisman, and Eugene Morley. Lawrence's rise to prominence was ushered in by his painting of several series of biographical panels commemorating important episodes in African American history. A narrative painter, Lawrence evoked the "philosophy of Impressionism" within his work. Capturing the meaning and personality behind the natural

Painter Jacob Lawrence, 1993. *With the help of early support from a Federal Art Project assignment, Lawrence subsequently became one of the most celebrated black artists in the United States. Among his honors were the Spingarn Medal from the NAACP and the National Medal of Arts.* AP IMAGES. REPRODUCED BY PERMISSION.

appearance of a historical moment, Lawrence created series of small paintings that depict important episodes in American history, such as *The Migration Series ("...and the Migrants Keep Coming")*, which traces the migration of African Americans from the South to the North, or in the course of an individual's life (e.g., Toussaint- L'Ouverture and John Brown).

Lawrence was a visual American historian. His paintings record African Americans in trade, theater, mental hospitals, neighborhoods, and sports. His works can be found in the Metropolitan Museum of Art, the Museum of Modern Art, the Whitney Museum of American Art, the Smithsonian American Art Museum, and the Wadsworth Atheneum in Hartford, Connecticut.

Lawrence lived in Seattle, Washington. His notable works include *The Life of Toussaint L'Ouverture* (forty-one panels, 1937), *The Life of Harriet Tubman* (forty panels, 1939), and *The Negro Migration Northward in World War* (sixty panels, 1942). He also produced commissioned book and magazine illustrations, murals, posters, drawings, and prints. Among these are a 1976 print for the U.S. bicentennial, illustrations for a 1983 special edition of John Hersey's *Hiroshima*, and a 1984 poster for the National Urban League. Lawrence also wrote and illustrated the book *The Great Migration: An American Story* (1993).

In 1970, Lawrence was awarded the NAACP's Spingarn Medal. He also received an invitation to paint a picture of the 1977 presidential inauguration of Jimmy Carter. President George H. W. Bush bestowed on Lawrence the National Medal of Arts in 1990. Lawrence was also the recipient of numerous honorary degrees.

HUGHIE LEE-SMITH (1915–1999)

Painter. Hughie Lee-Smith was born on September 20, 1915, in Eustis, Florida. He moved to Atlanta and then Cleveland as a child. Lee-Smith studied at the Cleveland Institute of Art and Wayne State University, where he received his B.S. in art education in 1953.

From childhood, Lee-Smith was encouraged to pursue his art, and he enjoyed a long career. He worked for the Ohio

Works Progress Administration and the Ford Factory at River Rouge during the 1930s and 1940s. He did a series of lithographic prints and painted murals at the Great Lakes Naval Station in Illinois. He taught art at Karamu House in Cleveland, the Grosse Pointe War Memorial in Michigan, Princeton Country Day School, Howard University, the Art Students League, and other institutions.

Lee-Smith's works can be seen in museums, schools, galleries, and collections across the United States, including the Southside Community Art Center in Chicago; the Detroit Artists Market; the Cleveland Museum of Art; the Whitney Museum of American Art, the Museum of Modern Art, and the June Kelly Gallery in New York City; and the Evans-Tibbs Collection in Washington, D.C. His paintings often depict decaying or ghetto environments in a state of revitalization, peopled by a single or sometimes double-figured occupant. His subjects suggest desolation or alienation, but they often wave banners or balloons in the scene, suggesting hope and gaiety.

Lee-Smith's one-person shows and exhibitions were numerous. He received more than a dozen important prizes, including the Founders Prize of the Detroit Institute of Arts (1953), the Emily Lowe Award (1957, 1985), the Binny and Smith Award (1983), and the Ralph Fabri Award (1982) and Len Everette Memorial Prize (1986) from Audubon Artists. He was a member of Allied Artists of America, the Artists Equity Association, and the Michigan Academy of the Arts, Sciences, and Letters. His notable works include *Portrait of a Sailor, Old Man and Youth, Waste Land, Little Diana*, and *Aftermath*.

EDMONIA LEWIS (c. 1845–1911)

Sculptor. Mary Edmonia Lewis was America's first black female artist and also the first of her race and sex to be recognized as a sculptor in the United States. Born on July 4, 1845, in Albany, New York, she was the daughter of a Chippewa Indian woman and a free African American man. From 1859 to 1863, under the patronage of a number of abolitionists, she was educated at Oberlin College in Ohio.

After completing her schooling, Lewis moved to Boston, where she studied with Edmund Brackett and completed a bust of Colonel Robert Gould Shaw, the commander of the first black regiment organized in the state of Massachusetts during the Civil War. In 1865, she moved to Rome, where she soon became a prominent artist. Returning to the United States in 1874, she fulfilled many commissions, including a bust of Henry Wadsworth Longfellow that was executed for the Harvard College Library.

Lewis's works are fine examples of the neoclassical sculpture that was fashionable during her lifetime. It is believed that she died in Rome sometime after 1911. Her notable works include *Hagar in the Wilderness, Forever Free*, and *Hiawatha*.

NORMAN LEWIS (1909–1979)

Painter. Norman Lewis was born in New York City in 1909. He studied at Columbia University, and later under Augusta Savage, Raphael Soyer, Vaclav Vytlacil, and Angela Streater. During the Great Depression, Lewis taught art through the Federal Art Project from 1936 to 1939 at the Harlem Art Center. He received a Carnegie International Award in Painting in 1956 and had several one-person shows at the Willard Gallery in New York.

As one of the artists to develop the abstract movement in the United States, Lewis participated in many group shows in such institutions as the Whitney Museum of American Art, the Metropolitan Museum of Art, and the Art Institute of Chicago. His notable works include *Arrival and Departure* and *Heroic Evening*.

IONIS BRACY MARTIN (1936–)

Painter, Printmaker, Educator. Born on August 27, 1936, in Chicago, Ionis Bracy Martin attended the Junior School of the Art Institute of Chicago before going to Fisk University, where she studied with Aaron Douglas and earned her B.S. in 1957. Martin also received an M.Ed. degree from the University of Hartford in Connecticut (1969) and an M.F.A. from Pratt Institute in New York (1987).

Martin began her forty-year teaching career in 1961 in the Hartford and Bloomfield school districts. She became a lecturer in African American art at Central Connecticut State University in 1985. Martin also lectures on and demonstrates serigraphy. She was a member of the advisory board of the CRT Craftery Gallery in Hartford (1973) and a cofounder of the Artists Collective (with Jackie McLean, Dollie McLean, Paul Brown, and Cheryl Smith) in 1972. She began serving as a trustee for the Wadsworth Atheneum in 1977, and became a trustee and chairperson of the Ella Burr McManus Trust for the Alfred E. Burr Sculpture Mall in 1985.

Martin's work has been exhibited in the Hartford area and in New York, as well as in Boston, Springfield, and Northampton in Massachusetts, Fisk University in Nashville, and the University of Vermont in Burlington. Among her many prizes and honors are a grant from the Connecticut Commission on the Arts (1969), a graduate fellowship in printmaking from Pratt Institute (1981), a Summer-Six Fellowship from Skidmore College (1987), and a fellowship with the W.E.B. Du Bois Institute at Harvard University (1994). Her notable works include

Mother and Child, Allyn's Garden, Gran' Daddy's Garden, and the series *Little Women of the Amistad*.

GERALDINE McCULLOUGH (1917–2008)

Sculptor. Geraldine McCullough was a renowned sculptor and painter. She was born Geraldine Hamilton on December 1, 1917, in Kingston, Arkansas, and raised in Chicago from the time she was three years old. McCullough attended the School of the Art Institute of Chicago, receiving a B.A. in 1948 and an M.A. in art education in 1955. As a student, she earned a John D. Standecker Scholarship, a Memorial Scholarship, and a Figure Painting Citation.

McCullough taught at Wendell Phillips High School in Chicago from 1950 to 1964 and at Rosary College (later Dominican University) in River Forest, Illinois. During this period, she began exhibiting her paintings at various galleries, receiving first prize in 1961 at an art exhibition at Atlanta University. With help from her husband, Lester McCullough, she took up welded sculpture and made her sculpting debut in 1963 at the Century of Negro Progress Exposition in Chicago.

McCullough's steel and copper abstraction *Phoenix* won the George D. Widener Gold Medal at the 1964 exhibition of the Pennsylvania Academy of Fine Arts. In earning this award, she added her name to a roster of artists who had already won the same honor, including Jacques Lipchitz and Theodore Roszak.

In 1967, McCullough became the chairperson of the Art Department at Rosary College. After retiring from the school in 1989, she was given an honorary doctorate. McCullough's works are informed by African ritual art, as well as European and American art. She was a distinguished guest artist of the Russian government and her work was exhibited at such respected venues as the Smithsonian Institution and the National Museum of Women in the Arts in Washington, D.C.

McCullough received many awards and commissions, and her works are represented in collections around the country. Her notable works include *Bessie Smith, View from the Moon, Todd Hall Front, Atomic Rose, Phoenix*, and *Martin Luther King*.

EVANGELINE J. MONTGOMERY (1933–)

Jeweler, Photographer, Sculptor. Evangeline Juliet Montgomery was born in New York City on May 2, 1933. She received an associate's degree from Los Angeles City College in 1958 and her B.F.A. from the California College of Arts and Crafts in 1969. She also studied at the University of California, Berkeley, and California State University, Los Angeles.

Montgomery has worked as a freelance artist, as program director for Arts America, and as an art consultant to museums, community organizations, and colleges for EJ Associates. Known primarily for her metal boxes, incense burners, and jewelry, Montgomery has also been awarded prizes for her photography. Her works are in the collections of the Oakland Museum of California and the University of Southern Illinois.

Montgomery has been active with many organizations. She has served on the San Francisco Art Commission, the advisory board of Parting Ways Museum of Afro-American Ethno-History in Massachusetts, and the boards of directors of the District of Columbia Arts Center, the Museum of the National Center of Afro-American Artists in Boston, the Michigan chapter of the National Conference of Artists, the College Art Association, the American Museums Association, and the Women's Art Caucus. Her awards have included a Smithsonian Fellowship and a museum grant from the National Endowment for the Arts. In 1989, Montgomery was presented with a Special Achievement Award from Arts America. Her notable works include *Ancestor Box 1* and *Justice for Angela Davis*.

ARCHIBALD MOTLEY (1891–1981)

Painter. Born on January 15, 1891, in New Orleans, Archibald John Motley's artistic talent was apparent by the time he attended high school. His father wanted him to become a doctor, but Archibald insisted on art and began formal training at the Art Institute of Chicago. During this time, he worked as a laborer, coming into contact with the drifters, scavengers, and hustlers who are now immortalized in his street scenes. His genre scenes are highly stylized and colorful and are often associated with the Ash Can school of art, a popular style in the 1920s. Although he never lived in Harlem, Motley was a vital part of the cultural flowering that was centered in Harlem but took place in African American artists' studios across the Unites States and in Paris.

In 1928, Motley had a one-person show in downtown New York and became the first artist, black or white, to make the front page of the *New York Times*. He was awarded a Guggenheim Fellowship in 1929 and studied in France. He was also the recipient of a Harmon Foundation Award for an earlier portrait. His notable works include *The Jockey Club, The Plotters, Parisian Scene, Black Belt*, and *Old Snuff Dipper*. Motley died in 1981.

JOHN WILFRED OUTTERBRIDGE (1933–)

Sculptor. John Wilfred Outterbridge was born in Greenville, North Carolina, on March 12, 1933. He studied at North Carolina A&T University in Greensboro, the Chicago Art Academy, the American Academy of Art in Chicago, and the

Art Center School of Design in Los Angeles. From 1964 until 1968, Outterbridge worked as an artist/designer for the Triad Corporation. He became a cofounder of the Communicative Arts Academy in 1969, and served as director until 1975. He also taught at California State University and the Pasadena Art Museum. Outterbridge was director of the Watts Towers Art Center in Los Angeles from 1976 until 1992.

Outterbridge was featured in *Black Artists on Art*, Volume 1 (1969, rev. ed. 1976), edited by Samella Lewis and Ruth Waddy. His sculptures are assemblages constructed from discarded materials. Some of his works are tributes to African ancestors and their descendants in Los Angeles and in other communities. Outterbridge is known for making and helping create "street art," a combination of painting, relief sculpture, and construction that incorporates words and symbols expressing community goals and social ideas. His has participated in numerous exhibitions in California, and won commissions to create public murals for the Los Angeles Metrorail and the Armory Center for the Arts in Pasadena. His notable works include *Shoeshine Box*, *Mood Ghetto*, and *Ethnic Heritage Group*.

In 1990, Outterbridge received the Malcolm X Freedom Award from the New Afrikan People's Organization and the Lifetime Achievement Award from the First Annual King Boulevard Memorial Project. In 1994, the National Endowment for the Arts awarded Outterbridge a Visual Arts Fellowship. He also won a J. Paul Getty Visual Arts Fellowship and received an honorary doctorate of fine arts from Otis College of Arts and Design.

GORDON PARKS SR. (1912–2006)

Photographer, Composer, Writer, Director. Gordon Parks Sr. was born on November 30, 1912, in Fort Scott, Kansas. After the death of his mother, Parks moved to St. Paul, Minnesota, to live with relatives. Despite having fond childhood memories of his father on the family farm, Parks had a dysfunctional upbringing. He attended Central and Mechanical Arts High Schools, and later worked at a variety of jobs, including janitor, busboy, and semipro basketball player. Parks was always interested in the arts, and tried sculpting, writing, and touring with a band, but these artistic endeavors were largely without focus.

In 1933, Parks joined the Civilian Conservation Corps and in the late 1930s, while working as a railroad porter, he became interested in photography as a medium on which he could finally concentrate his artistic interests. After purchasing a used camera, Parks worked as a freelance photographer

***American Photographer and Film Director Gordon Parks with his 1942 portrait* American Gothic.** *One of Parks's most famous works, which depicts a cleaning woman holding a mop and broom beneath a large American flag, is a parody of Grant Woods's painting of the same name.* JOHN PINEDA/HULTON ARCHIVE/GETTY IMAGES

and as a photojournalist. In 1942, he became a correspondent for the Farm Security Administration, and from 1943 to 1945 he was a correspondent for the Office of War Information. After the war, he worked for Standard Oil Company of New Jersey, and in 1948 he became a staff photographer for *Life* magazine. He soon achieved national acclaim for his photographs, and in the mid-1950s he began doing consulting work on Hollywood productions. In the 1960s, Parks began directing television documentaries. He published his biography, *A Choice of Weapons*, in 1966.

Parks is the author of the following works: *Flash Photography* (1947); *Camera Portraits: The Techniques and Principals of Documentary Portraiture* (1948); *The Learning Tree* (1963); *Gordon Parks: A Poet and His Camera* (1968); *Born Black* (1971); *Gordon Parks: Whispers of Intimate Things* (1971); *Moments without Proper Names* (1975); *Flavio* (1977); *To Smile in Autumn: A Memoir* (1979); *Shannon* (1981); *Voices in the Mirror: An Autobiography* (1990); *Arias in Silence* (1994); and *Eyes with Winged Thoughts* (2005). In 1968, Parks produced, directed, and wrote the script and music for the film version of his book *The Learning Tree*. Parks also directed and scored the following movies: *Shaft* (1971), *Shaft's Big Score* (1972), *The Super Cops* (1974), *Leadbelly* (1976), *Solomon Northrup's Odyssey* (1984), and *Moments without Proper Names* (1986).

Parks was a recipient of the NAACP's Spingarn Medal (1972), the Rhode Island School of Design's President's Fellow Award (1984), and Kansan of the Year (1986). In 1988, President Ronald Reagan presented him with the National Medal for the Arts. That same year, Parks won the World Press Photo Award. In 1989, the Library of Congress National Film Preservation Board added *The Learning Tree* to the National Film Registry. Parks was also presented with the New York Mayor's Award and the Artist of Merit Josef Sudek Medal in 1989.

Parks was a member of the NAACP, the Urban League, the Newspaper Guild, the Association of Composers and Directors, the Writer's Guild, the American Federation of Television and Radio Artists, the International Mark Twain Society, the American Film Institute, the Academy of Motion Pictures Arts and Sciences, the American Society of Magazine Photographers, and the American Society of Composers, Authors, and Publishers. On July 7, 1995, the Library of Congress announced that it had acquired Parks's archives. The archives include roughly fifteen thousand manuscript pages of Parks's poems, novels, and screenplays, as well as several thousand photographs and negatives.

MARION PERKINS (1908–1961)

Sculptor. Born in Marche, Arkansas, in 1908, Marion Perkins was a self-taught artist. His early works were composed while he tended a newspaper stand on Chicago's South Side. He later studied privately with Simon Gordon after the two men became close friends.

Perkins's work has been exhibited at the Art Institute of Chicago, the American Negro Exposition (1940), Xavier University, and Rockford College in Illinois (1965). As artist-in-residence at Jackson State College in Mississippi, where much of his sculpture is housed, Perkins founded a scholarship fund for art students. Perkins died in 1961.

HOWARDENA PINDELL (1943–)

Painter. Born in Philadelphia on April 14, 1943, Howardena Pindell received a B.F.A. from Boston University in 1965 and an M.F.A. from Yale University in 1967. She first gained national recognition in the *American Drawing Biennial XXIII* (1969) at the Norfolk Museum of Arts and Sciences in Virginia. By the mid-1970s, Pindell's work began appearing in such exhibitions as *Eleven Americans in Paris* at the Gerald Piltzer Gallery in Paris (1975), *Recent Acquisitions: Drawings* at the Museum of Modern Art in New York (1976), and *Pindell: Video Drawings* at the Sonja Henie Onstad Foundation in Oslo, Norway (1976).

Pindell has traveled around the world as a guest speaker. Her lectures have included "Current American and Black American Art: A Historical Survey" at Madras College of Arts and Crafts in Madras, India (1975), and "Black Artists, U.S.A." at the Academy of Art in Oslo (1976). She joined the faculty at State University of New York at Stony Brook in 1979.

Pindell's work is part of the permanent collections of more than thirty museums, including the High Museum in Atlanta, the Newark Museum in New Jersey, the Fogg Museum in Cambridge, Massachusetts, and the Brooklyn Museum, the Whitney Museum of American Art, the Museum of Modern Art, and the Metropolitan Museum of Art in New York. Pindell has received two National Endowment for the Arts Fellowships and a Guggenheim Fellowship.

Pindell has received numerous awards throughout her career. In 1990, she won the College Art Association Award for Best Exhibitor. She received the Studio Museum in Harlem Award and Joan Mitchell Fellowship in 1994. In 1996, the Women's Caucus for Art presented Pindell with its Distinguished Contribution to the Profession Award.

JERRY PINKNEY (1939–)

Illustrator. Born in Philadelphia on December 22, 1939, Jerry Pinkney studied at the Philadelphia Museum College of Art. Pinkney has exhibited in illustrator shows throughout the country and is best known for his illustrations for children's books and textbooks. From his studio in his home in Croton-on-Hudson, New York, Pinkney has been a major contributor to the U.S. Postal Service's Black Heritage series of stamps. He contributed the designs for stamps depicting

Self-Portrait ***(Horace Pippin, 1941).*** *Pippin, a self-taught artist, is known for the vivid battle scenes in his artworks, which were based on his experiences in World War I. As a result of a wartime injury, he had to guide his right arm with his left hand in order to produce oil paintings.* ALBRIGHT-KNOX ART GALLERY/ CORBIS

Benjamin Banneker, Martin Luther King Jr., Scott Joplin, Jackie Robinson, Sojourner Truth, Carter G. Woodson, Whitney Moore Young, Mary McLeod Bethune, and Harriet Tubman.

Pinkney has illustrated numerous children's books, including *The Talking Eggs: A Folktale from the American South* (1989) by Robert San Souci, which earned Pinkney a Caldecott Honor. *The Talking Eggs* also received a Coretta Scott King Honor Book Award, was named an American Library Association Notable Book, and won the Irma Simonton Black Award from the Bank Street College of Education. In 1994, Pinkney won the Caldecott Medal for his illustrations in the book *John Henry* by Julius Lester. That same year, he won two Parent's Choice Awards for his illustrations in *John Henry* and *The Sunday Outing*, written by his wife, Gloria Jean Pinkney.

Pinkney is one of the founders of Kaleidoscope Studio in Boston, where he also worked for the National Center of Afro-American Art. He was a visiting critic for the Rhode Island School of Design, and has taught at Pratt Institute, the University of Delaware, and the State University of New York at Buffalo. His illustrations have appeared in many books, including *The Tales of Uncle Remus* (1987) by Julius Lester, an edition of Armstrong Sperry's *Call It Courage* published by Aladdin Books, and *Back Home* (1992) by Gloria Jean Pinkney.

HORACE PIPPIN (1888–1946)

Painter. Horace Pippin has been ranked in the company of the French painter Henri Rousseau because of his accomplishments as a self-taught artist. Born on February 22, 1888, in West Chester, Pennsylvania, Pippin began painting in 1920, and continued until his death on July 6, 1946. Among his most vivid works are battle scenes that he remembered from his own experience in World War I.

Pippin's earliest works are designs burned into wood with a hot poker. He created his first oil painting in 1930. This task was complicated by a wartime injury that required him to guide his right arm with his left hand in order to paint. Pippin painted family reunions, Bible stories, and historical events. His notable works include *John Brown Goes to a Hanging, Flowers with Red Chair, The Den, The Milk Man of Goshen,* and *Dog Fight Over the Trenches.*

JAMES A. PORTER (1905–1970)

Art Historian, Painter. James Amos Porter was a painter who also earned acclaim as a writer and educator. Born in Baltimore in 1905, he studied at Howard University, receiving a B.S. in 1927. He later trained at the Art Students League in New York and the Sorbonne in Paris. He received an M.A. from New York University in 1937. Porter was awarded numerous travel grants that enabled him to study African and European art firsthand. Among his ten one-person shows are exhibits at Port-au-Prince, Haiti (1946), the Dupont Gallery in Washington, D.C. (1949), and Howard University (1965). His works are in the collections of Howard University, Lincoln University in Missouri, the Harmon Foundation, IBM, and other organizations.

Porter was the first African American art historian. He published *Modern Negro Art* (1943), as well as numerous articles. In 1953, he became chairman of the Department of Art and director of the Gallery of Art at Howard University, a position he held until his death. He was a delegate to the UNESCO Conference on Africa held in Boston in 1961, and to the International Congress of African Art and Culture held in Salisbury in Southern Rhodesia in 1962. In 1965, at the twenty-fifth anniversary of the founding of the National Gallery of Art, Porter was named "one of America's most outstanding men of the arts." His notable works include *On a Cuban Bus, Portrait of F.A. as Harlequin, Dorothy Porter,* and *Nude.*

MARTIN PURYEAR (1941–)

Sculptor. Martin Puryear was born in Washington, D.C., in 1941. He attended Catholic University of America and received an M.F.A. from Yale University in 1971. Puryear also studied in Sweden and worked in Sierra Leone with the Peace Corps from 1964 to 1966.

Representing the United States in the 1989 São Paulo Biennial in Brazil, Puryear received first prize. His work has been described as postminimalist, but it really defies categorization. He executes his own large pieces in wood and metal. Puryear was the only African American artist in the contemporary section of *Primitivism in Twentieth-century Art: Affinity of the Tribal and Modern*, an exhibition held at the Museum of Modern Art in New York in 1984. His work has also been exhibited at the Brooklyn Museum (1988–1989), the Whitney Biennial (1989), and various other museums and galleries. The Museum of Modern Art organized a major retrospective of his work in 2007.

Puryear studied in Japan in 1987 on a Guggenheim Fellowship. He was elected to the American Academy and Institute of Arts and Letters in 1992 and received an honorary doctorate from Yale University in 1994. Other honors include a MacArthur Foundation Award, a Louis Comfort Tiffany Grant, and the Skowhegan Medal for Sculpture. His notable works include *For Beckwith, Maroon Desire*, and *Sentinel*. His works since 1985 have been untitled.

FAITH RINGGOLD (1930–)

Painter, Fiber Artist, Book Illustrator, Activist. Born in Harlem on October 8, 1934, Faith Ringgold was raised by parents who made sure she would enjoy the benefits of a good education. She received her B.S. in 1955 and her M.F.A. in 1959 from the City College of New York. Ringgold has received two National Endowment for the Arts awards, an award from the National Museum of Women in the Arts, and seventeen honorary doctorates. Since 2007, a Hayward, California elementary/middle school bears her name. She is a professor emeritus at the University of California, San Diego, Department of Visual Arts.

Committed to the revolutionary perspectives of the 1960s in politics and in aesthetics, Ringgold created twenty paintings that became *The American People Series* between 1963 and 1967, and then worked on twelve more for *The Black Light Series* from 1968 to 1969. Ringgold worked in a symbolic expressionist style, and her figurative paintings focused on being black in America during the turbulent transition from the civil rights movement to the black liberation struggle. *The Flag Is Bleeding, Flag for the Moon: Die Nigger, Mommy & Daddy*, and *Soul Sister: Woman on a Bridge* are representative pieces from her early series.

Ringgold's boldly political work has been exhibited in major museums in the United States and around the world. Her paintings are included in the collections of the Metropolitan Museum of Art, the Museum of Modern Art, the Bank Street College of Education, and the Solomon R. Guggenheim Museum in New York City.

In 1972, Ringgold became one of the founders of Women Students and Artists for Black Liberation, an organization whose principal goal was to make sure that all exhibitions of African American artists gave equal space to paintings by men and women. In line with her interest in gender parity, Ringgold donated a large mural depicting the roles of women in American society to the Women's House of Detention in Manhattan.

Ringgold is also known for her distinctive story quilts featuring paintings on canvas bordered with quilted textiles and handwritten fabric panels containing autobiographical and fanciful stories. They blur the lines between craft, high art, and storytelling. Her first quilt, *Echoes of Harlem: Tar Beach*, was completed in 1980. Other quilts produced by Ringgold include *The Sunflower Quilting Bee at Arles* and *Who's Afraid of Aunt Jemima.*

In 1991, Ringgold illustrated and wrote a children's book, *Tar Beach*, followed in 1992 with *Aunt Harriet's Underground Railroad in the Sky*. She has since published several more children's books, including *Cassie's Colorful Day* (1999) and *Cassie Word Quilt* (2002). She has also illustrated books by other authors. Ringgold published her memoirs, *We Flew Over the Bridge*, in 2005.

BETYE SAAR (1926–)

Painter, Sculptor. Betye Saar was born in Los Angeles on July 30, 1926. She studied at the University of California, Los Angeles, where she received a B.A. in 1949, as well as the University of Southern California and California State University, Long Beach. After college, she married and raised her children, while creating artwork from discarded pieces of postcards, photographs, flowers, buttons, fans, and ticket stubs.

Saar earned fellowships and grants from the J. Paul Getty Fund for the Visual Arts (1990), the National Endowment for the Arts (1974, 1984), and the Guggenheim Memorial Foundation (1991). She also received the Twenty-second Annual Artist Award from the Studio Museum in Harlem (1990), the James VanDerZee Award from the Brandywine Workshop (1992), the Distinguished Artist Award from the Fresno Art Museum (1993), and the Visual Artists Award from the Flintridge Foundation (1997). Five colleges have presented Saar with honorary doctorates.

Saar's art ranges from spiritual altars and memorial boxes honoring her aunts to surrealist-inspired assemblages critiquing the beliefs and social-political structures that oppress black women, men, and children. *The Liberation of Aunt Jemima* (1972), her most frequently reproduced work, was featured in the 2007 international retrospective *WACK! Art and the Feminist Revolution*, organized by the Museum of Contemporary Art in Los Angeles. In 1978, Saar's life and work was explored in the documentary film *Spirit Catcher: The Art of Betye Saar*, produced by WNET-13 in New York as part of *The Originals: Women in Art* series.

Saar has exhibited throughout the United States and internationally, including shows in Australia, New Zealand, and Taiwan. In 1994, Saar's works were displayed with those of more than two hundred artists from some seventy countries at Brazil's Biennial exhibition. Her notable works include *The Vision of El Cremo*, *Africa*, *The View from the Sorcerer's Window*, and *House of Gris Gris*, a mixed-media installation created with her daughter, the sculptor Alison Saar.

Saar's work can be found in permanent collections across the nation, including the Smithsonian American Art Museum and the Hirshhorn Museum and Sculpture Garden in Washington, D.C., the Los Angeles County Museum of Art, the Museum of Fine Arts in Boston, the Metropolitan Museum of Art and the Whitney Museum of American Art in New York City, the Philadelphia Museum of Art, and the San Francisco Museum of Modern Art.

SYNTHIA SAINT JAMES (1949–)

Illustrator, Author, Architectural Designer. Synthia Saint James was born in 1949 in Los Angeles, California. She is a self-taught illustrator and author whose work has been exhibited in Los Angeles, New York City, Salt Lake City, and Washington, D.C., as well as internationally in Stockholm, Paris, Seoul, and Quebec.

Saint James's colorful figurative images celebrate the daily life and culture of African Americans. The stylized silhouettes take shape through the use of broad sweeps of contrasting color. Her pictures grace the covers of numerous books, including those by Terry McMillan, Iyanla Vanzant, and Alice Walker. Dozens of corporations, organizations, and individuals have commissioned Saint James to design work for their licensed products, events, and commemorative posters. The U.S. Postal Service commissioned her to create the first Kwanzaa stamp, released on October 22, 1997.

Saint James is an award-winning author and illustrator of several children's books, including *The Gifts of Kwanzaa* (1994), *Sunday* (1996), and *Girlfriends* (1997). She has also illustrated children's books by other authors, and received a 1997 Coretta Scott King Honor for her illustrations in Karen English's *Neeny Coming, Neeny Going*. Saint James also provided the illustrations for *No Mirrors in My Nana's House* (1998), written by singer Ysaye Barnwell, and *Girls Together* (1999) by Sherley Anne Williams. In addition, Saint James has published poetry, children's activity books, a cookbook, and a book of postcards. In 2003, her illustrations appeared in *Enduring Wisdom: Sayings from Native Americans*, edited by Virginia Driving Hawk Sneve.

AUGUSTA SAVAGE (1892–1962)

Sculptor. A leading sculptor who emerged during the Harlem Renaissance, Augusta Savage was one of the artists represented in the first all-black exhibition in the United States, sponsored by the Harmon Foundation at International House in New York City. In 1939, her symbolic group piece, *Lift Every Voice and Sing*, was shown at the New York World's Fair Community Arts Building.

Savage was born in Green Cove Springs, Florida, on February 29, 1892. She studied at Tallahassee State Normal School and Cooper Union in New York City. She also studied in France after receiving fellowships from the Carnegie and Rosenwald foundations. She was the first African American to

Augusta Savage Viewing Two of Her Sculptures, December 1937. *A leading sculptor who emerged during the Harlem Renaissance, Savage was the first African American to be elected into the National Association of Women Painters and Sculptors.* **BETTMANN/CORBIS**

win acceptance into the National Association of Women Painters and Sculptors.

In the 1930s, Savage taught in her own School of Arts and Crafts in Harlem. She helped many of her students take advantage of Works Progress Administration projects for artists during the Great Depression. Her other notable works include *Gamin*, *The Chase*, *Black Women*, *Lenore*, *Marcus Garvey*, and *W.E.B. Du Bois*.

CHARLES SEARLES (1937–)

Painter, Educator. Charles Searles was born in Philadelphia in 1937. He studied at Fleisher Art Memorial in Philadelphia and at the Pennsylvania Academy of Fine Arts (1968–1972). Searles has taught at the Philadelphia Museum of Art Studio, the University of the Arts in Philadelphia, the Brooklyn Museum Art School, New Jersey City University, and Bloomfield College in New Jersey.

Searles won commissions to execute several murals, including one for the U.S. General Services Administration interior. He also completed a mural called *Celebration* (1976) for Philadelphia's William J. Green Federal Building, as well as wall sculptures for the Amtrak Station (1985) and the Dempsey Service Center (1989) in Newark, New Jersey.

Searles's works have been exhibited in galleries and museums around the country, and can be found in the collections of the Smithsonian Institution in Washington, D.C., the New York State Office Building, the Philadelphia Museum of Art, the Federal Railroad Administration, Ciba-Gigy Inc., the Dallas Museum of Art, the Montclair Art Museum in New Jersey, Phillip Morris Inc., and Howard University. The human figure, color, and rhythmic patterns dominate Searles's paintings. His other notable works include *Cultural Mix*, *Rhythmic Forms*, *Play Time*, and *Celebration*.

LORNA SIMPSON (1960–)

Photographer, Conceptual Artist. Simpson was born in Brooklyn, New York, on August 13, 1960, and attended the School of Visual Arts in Manhattan, where she earned her B.F.A. in 1982. She received her M.F.A. from the University of California, San Diego, in 1985.

Simpson was among the young photographers of the late 1980s and early 1990s who broke through the race and gender barriers of traditional arts-world values. She received mainstream recognition as a conceptual artist by juxtaposing enigmatic text on adjacent walls or across photographs. Her large-scale photos are populated with African American women, always dressed in nondescript shifts and posed to deny the viewer a direct view of the models' eyes, described since the Italian Renaissance as the "window to the soul." Early works, such as her 1989 *Guarded Conditions*, made up of twenty-one photos composing a wall mural, simultaneously question presumptions of the gaze, practices of looking, and the power of language and words. Simpson also challenges the self-conscious and subconscious production of multiple and contradictory meanings, while prompting viewers to question the visual and cultural clichés that surround intersecting notions of gender, race, identity, culture, history, and memory.

In 1990, Simpson became the first African American woman to have her work featured in the Venice Biennale, an international art exhibition. Her work has also been exhibited at the Museum of Modern Art in New York, the Museum of Contemporary Art in Chicago, the Miami Art Museum, the Walker Art Center in Minneapolis, the Irish Museum of Modern Art in Dublin, and the Galerie Nathalie Obadia in Paris. Simpson has served on the advisory boards of the New Museum and Artists Space in New York. She was the 2010 recipient of the International Center of Photography's Infinity Award in Art.

In the mid-1990s, Simpson began printing her large multipanel photographs on felt, with images suggestive of secret, yet public, sexual encounters. Later in the 1990s, she shifted to the mediums of film and video, producing works such as *Call Waiting*, which presents individuals engaged in fragmented conversations about identity and desire. Her additional notable works include *Outline*, *Guarded Conditions*, *Easy for Who to Say*, *Flipside*, *Bio*, *Untitled ("prefer/refuse/decide")*, and the interactive multimedia composition *Five Rooms*.

NORMA MERRICK SKLAREK (1928–)

Architect. Norma Merrick Sklarek was born on April 15, 1928, in New York City. She received a B.A. in architecture from Barnard College of Columbia University in 1950. In 1954, she became the first African American woman to be licensed as an architect in the United States. In 1966, Sklarek became the first African American woman to be named a fellow of the American Institute of Architects.

Sklarek's career began at Skidmore, Owens, Merrill, where she worked as an architect from 1955 until 1960. She also served on the faculty of New York City College from 1957 until 1960. In 1960, she took a position with Gruen and Associates in Los Angeles, where she worked for the next twenty years. She also served as a faculty member at UCLA from 1972 until 1978. Sklarek became vice president of Welton Becket Associates in 1980 and worked there until 1985. From 1985 until 1989, Sklarek was a partner in the firm Siegel, Sklarek, and Diamond, the largest female-owned architectural firm in the United States. In 1989, she began working as a principal for the Jerde Partnership, before retiring in 1992.

Among the notable structures designed by Sklarek are the U.S. Embassy in Tokyo; Courthouse Center in Columbus,

Indiana; City Hall in San Bernardino, California; and Terminal One at the Los Angeles International Airport.

MONETA SLEET JR. (1926–1996)

Photographer. Moneta Sleet Jr. was born on February 14, 1926, in Owensboro, Kentucky. He studied at Kentucky State College under Dr. John Williams, a family friend, dean of the college, and an accomplished photographer. In 1947, Sleet received his B.A. from Kentucky State. He earned a master's degree from New York University in 1950.

Sleet taught photography at Maryland State College from 1948 until 1949. He moved to New York City in 1950 to work as a sportswriter for *Amsterdam News*. He also worked as a photographer for *Our World* from 1951 until 1955. Sleet then moved to Chicago and took a job with the Johnson Publishing Company, where he became staff photographer for *Ebony* and *Jet* magazines.

In 1969, Moneta Sleet became the first African American to win a Pulitzer Prize in photography. Although employed by *Ebony*, he was eligible for the award because his photograph of Coretta Scott King at her husband's funeral was picked up by a wire service and published in daily newspapers throughout the country. He also received awards from the Overseas Press Club of America, the National Urban League, and the National Association of Black Journalists. In 1989, the University of Kentucky inducted Sleet into its Kentucky Journalism Hall of Fame. Sleet was a member of the NAACP and the Black Academy of Arts and Letters.

Sleet's work appeared in several group exhibitions at museums, including the Studio Museum in Harlem and the Metropolitan Museum of Art in New York. In 1970, solo exhibitions were held at the City Art Museum of St. Louis and at the Detroit Public Library. Other solo exhibitions of Sleet's work were held at the New York Public Library, the Newark Public Library, the Chicago Public Library Cultural Center, the Milwaukee Public Library, the Martin Luther King Jr. Memorial Library, the Albany Museum of Art, the New York State Museum, and the Schomburg Center for Research in Black Culture.

WILLI SMITH (1948–1987)

Fashion Designer. Willi Smith was born on February 29, 1948, in Philadelphia. He studied at the Parsons School of Design in New York on a scholarship. Smith was known for designing cross-seasonal, affordable clothes made of natural fibers. He designed sportswear pieces that mixed readily with "Williwear" from previous years and with other clothes. Smith was innovative in mixing and matching plaids, stripes, and vivid colors. He designed practical and functional clothes for both men and women. His clothes were manufactured in India, and Smith traveled there several times a year to supervise the making of his collections. In 1983, Smith received the Coty American Fashion Critics Award for Women's Fashion. Smith died in 1987 when he was thirty-nine years old from pneumonia and shigella, contracted while he was in India.

NELSON STEVENS (1938–)

Muralist, Painter, Graphic Artist. Born in Brooklyn, New York, in 1938, Nelson Stevens received a B.F.A. from Ohio University in 1962 and an M.F.A. from Kent State University in 1969. Stevens is an active member of AFRICOBRA, a group exploring the aesthetics of African American art, which includes the use of the human figure, bright colors, and African-inspired patterns, text, letters, and other symbols relating to the African American experience. He is also a member of the National Conference of Artists.

From 1977 to 2003, Stevens was a professor of art at the University of Massachusetts in Amherst. His work has been exhibited at the National Center of Afro-American Artists in Boston, the Studio Museum in Harlem, Howard University, and Kent State University. Notable works include *Madonna and Child* for a 1993 calendar, *Art in the Service of the Lord*, *Malcolm—King of Jihad*, and *A Different Kind of Man*.

HENRY OSSAWA TANNER (1859–1937)

Painter. Alain Locke called Henry Ossawa Tanner the leading talent of the "journeyman period" of African American art. He was the first African American artist to receive international acclaim. Born in Pittsburgh on June 21, 1859, Tanner chose painting rather than the ministry as a career, overcoming the objections of his father, an African Methodist Episcopal bishop. After attending the Pennsylvania Academy of Fine Arts, he taught at Clark University in Atlanta while working as a photographer. Some of Tanner's most compelling work, such as *The Banjo Lesson* (1893), was produced during this period, in which he emerged as the most promising African American artist of his day.

In the mid-1890s, Tanner abandoned black subject matter and left the United States for the Académie Julian in Paris, where he joined the American Art Students Club of Paris. In France, he focused on painting Bible-themed canvases, which he pursued for the duration of his time abroad. In an article written in 1909 for the magazine *World's Work*, "The Story of an Artist's Life," Tanner recounts his encounters with the racism in American art circles that drove him to seek training, professional opportunities, and life in Europe. He also traveled to the Middle East to study the terrain and culture.

Tanner's 1896 painting *Daniel in the Lion's Den*, a mixture of realism and mystical symbolism, won honorable mention at the Paris Salon. The following year, the French government purchased his *Resurrection of Lazarus*. In 1900, Tanner received the Medal of Honor at the Paris Exposition, as well as the Lippincott Prize.

Tanner died in 1937. His other notable works include *Flight into Egypt*, *The Annunciation*, *The Thankful Poor*, and *The Sabot Makers*.

ALMA W. THOMAS (1891–1978)

Painter. Alma Woodsey Thomas was born in Columbus, Georgia, in 1891. She moved to Washington, D.C., as a teenager. Thomas enrolled at Howard University and was the first graduate of its art department in 1924. In 1934, she received her M.A. from Columbia University and later studied at American University.

After a thirty-eight-year career teaching in public schools, Thomas began to concentrate solely on painting. She is best known for her nonobjective, mosaic-like works that emphasize color, pattern, and space. The optical relationships of her colors in flat shapes create three-dimensional forms, enlivening the painted surfaces with movement and pulsating rhythms. It is this later work that brought her many prizes and awards. In 1972, the Whitney Museum of American Art in New York held a solo exhibition of Thomas's works.

Thomas's works are in the collections of the Smithsonian American Art Museum, the Columbus Museum in Georgia, Howard University, the National Museum of Women in the Arts, the Corcoran Gallery of Art, and others. Her notable works include *The Eclipse*, *Arboretum Presents White Dogwood*, *Elysian Fields*, *Red Sunset*, and *Old Pond Concerto*.

BOB THOMPSON (1937–1966)

Painter. Born in Louisville, Kentucky, in 1937, Robert Thompson studied at the Boston Museum School in 1955 and later spent three years at the University of Louisville. In 1960, Thompson participated in a two-person show at Zabriskie Gallery in New York, and two years later he received a John Hay Whitney Fellowship. Over the next few years, Thompson had several one-person exhibitions in New York and Chicago. His work was also seen in Spain. He died in Rome when he was twenty-nine years old.

Thompson's work is in several permanent collections around the country, including the Chrysler Museum in Provincetown, Massachusetts. In 1970, Thompson's work was featured in an exhibition of African American artists at the Boston Museum of Fine Arts. His notable works include *Ascension to the Heavens*, *Untitled Diptych*, *The Dentist*, and *Expulsion and Nativity*.

JAMES VANDERZEE (1886–1983)

Photographer. James VanDerZee was born on June 29, 1886, in Lenox, Massachusetts. His parents had moved there from New York in the early 1880s after serving as maid and butler to Ulysses S. Grant. The second of six children, James grew up in a family filled with creative people. Everybody painted, drew, or played an instrument, so it was not considered out of the ordinary when, after receiving a camera in 1900, VanDerZee became interested in photography.

By 1906, VanDerZee had married and moved to New York, where he took odd jobs to support his growing family. In 1907, he moved to Virginia, where he worked in the dining room of the Hotel Chamberlin in Old Point Comfort. During this time, he also worked as a photographer on a part-time basis. In 1909, he returned to New York.

By 1915, VanDerZee had secured his first photography job as an assistant in the Gertz Department Store in Newark, New Jersey. With the money he saved from this job, he was able to open his own studio in 1916. Over the course of a half century, VanDerZee would record the visual history of Harlem. His subjects included Marcus Garvey, Sweet Daddy Grace, Father Divine, Joe Louis, Madame Walker, and many other famous African Americans.

In 1969, the exhibition Harlem On My Mind, produced by Thomas Hoving, then director of the Metropolitan Museum of Art, brought James VanDerZee international recognition. He died in 1983.

LAURA WHEELER WARING (1887–1948)

Painter. Born in 1887 in Hartford, Connecticut, Laura Wheeler Waring received her first training at the Pennsylvania Academy of Fine Arts, where she studied for six years. In 1914, she won the Cresson Memorial Scholarship, which enabled her to continue her studies at the Académie de la Grande Chaumière in Paris.

Waring returned to the United States to work as an art instructor at Cheney State Teachers College in Pennsylvania. Eventually, she became head of the art department. Her work, particularly portraiture, has been exhibited at several leading American art galleries. In 1927, she received the Harmon Award for achievement in fine art. In the 1940s, with Betsy Graves Reyneau, Waring completed a set of twenty-four re-paintings of a variety of works, titled *Portraits of Outstanding Americans of Negro Origin*, for the Harmon Foundation.

Waring was also the director in charge of African American art exhibits at the Philadelphia Exposition in 1926 and was a member of the national advisory board of Art Movements, Inc. She died in 1948. Her notable portraits include *Alonzo Aden*, *W.E.B. Du Bois*, *James Weldon Johnson*, and *Mother and Daughter*.

CARRIE MAE WEEMS (1953–)

Photographer, Conceptual Artist. Carrie Mae Weems was born in Portland, Oregon, in 1953. She received her B.F.A. from the California Institute of the Arts in 1981 and an M.F.A. from the University of California, San Diego, in 1984. She also received an M.A. in African American folklore from the University of California, Berkeley.

Weems explores stereotypes, especially those of African American women. Formerly a photo documentarian, Weems also taught filmmaking and photography at Hampshire College in Amherst, Massachusetts. Her new works are "about race, gender, class, and kinship." Weems has exhibited at the Rhode Island School of Design, the Wadsworth Atheneum in Hartford, Connecticut, and other galleries and museums. Her notable works include *Black Woman with Chicken, High Yella Girl, Colored People, Family Pictures and Stories, Ain't Jokin'*, and *Mirror, Mirror.*

EDWARD T. WELBURN (1950–)

Automobile Designer. Edward Thomas Welburn was born in Philadelphia and graduated from Howard University in 1972. Welburn began his career with the General Motors (GM) Design Staff as a creative designer in 1972, advancing to the positions of senior creative designer and assistant chief designer of automobiles for GM's Oldsmobile Studio. In 1992, his design for the Olds Achieva was honored as one of the outstanding designs of the model year. While a member of the GM Design Staff, he also designed the Cutlass Supreme, the Cutlass Ciera, and the Oldsmobile Calais.

Welburn was on the design team for the 1985 Indianapolis 500 pace car. He was named 1989 Alumni of the Year by the Howard University Student Association. Welburn also won the Industrial Designers Society of America Award for Design Excellence for his part in the design for the Oldsmobile Aerotech in 1992.

Welburn has served on numerous boards and is a member of the Cabinet and the Founders Society of the Detroit Institute of Arts. In 2003, he became vice president of design for GM North America. He was appointed vice president of global design at General Motors in 2005.

JAMES LESESNE WELLS (1902–1993)

Artist. Born on November 2, 1902, in Atlanta, James Lesesne Wells was a pioneer of modern American printmaking. After graduating from high school, Wells lived with relatives in New York City and worked for two years to earn money for college. He studied drawing at the National Academy of Design for one term (1918–1919). Wells spent one year at Lincoln University before transferring in 1923 to Teachers College at Columbia University, where he earned a B.S. in 1927 and an M.S. in 1938.

After earning his undergraduate degree, Wells focused on creating African American print illustrations for magazines. He also made connections with art dealer and gallery owner J. D. Neumann, who included Wells's work in a 1929 exhibition of international modernists. These projects captured the attention of Howard University's James V. Herring, who invited Wells to join the prestigious school's art faculty that year. Thus began a thirty-nine-year career at the university, during which Wells established a graphics arts department and taught several soon to be well-known artists, including Charles Alston and Jacob Lawrence. Wells taught clay modeling, ceramics, sculpture, metals, and block printing.

During the Great Depression, Wells devoted himself to making prints with themes from African American history and industry. Despite a lack of critical recognition, Wells's work won numerous art competitions throughout the 1930s, including the George E. Haynes Prize in 1933. At this time, he also served as the director of a summer art workshop that preceded the Harlem Community Art Center.

After World War II, Wells spent a sabbatical year working at Stanley Hayter's famous Atelier 17 in New York, then the most innovative center of etching and printmaking in the United States. Wells continued to teach and win awards for his artwork in the 1950s and 1960s. After he moved Washington, D.C., he joined his brother-in-law, Eugene Davidson, president of the local NAACP, in segregation protests. The harassment Wells suffered as a result of his outspokenness—a cross was burned in his yard in 1957—may have inspired the religious themes of much of his work from the era. He took first prize in a religious art exhibition sponsored by the Smithsonian in 1958.

After retiring from Howard in 1968, Wells continued to paint and make prints into the 1980s. In 1980, Jimmy Carter presented Wells with a presidential citation for lifelong contributions to American art. Four years later, Washington, D.C., held a James L. Wells Day. Designated a "living legend" by the National Black Arts Festival in 1991, Wells's work was featured in a retrospective exhibition organized by the Harmon Foundation, which had recognized him for his artwork as early as 1916, when he took first prize in painting and second prize in woodworking. He died of congestive heart failure when he was ninety years old.

CHARLES WHITE (1918–1979)

Painter, Lithographer. Charles White was born on April 2, 1918, in Chicago. He was influenced as a young boy by Alain Locke's 1925 book *The New Negro,* which opened his eyes to African and African American culture, history, and creativity. White studied at the Chicago Art Institute and the Art Students League. When he was twenty-three,

Theme Building, Los Angeles International Airport (1961). *Paul Revere Williams, the first black member of the American Institute of Architects, helped design this futuristic Los Angeles landmark.* ANDREA PISTOLESI/TIPS ITALIA/PHOTOLIBRARY

he won a Rosenwald Fellowship, which enabled him to work in the South for two years. While in the South, he painted a celebrated mural depicting the black people's contribution to American democracy. It is now the property of the Hampton Institute in Virginia.

The bulk of White's work is done in sepia and white, a symbolic motif favored for its expressive impact. White taught at Otis Art School in Los Angeles from 1965 until his death in 1979. His other notable works include *Let's Walk Together*, *Frederick Douglass Lives Again*, *Women*, and *Gospel Singer*.

PAUL REVERE WILLIAMS (1894–1980)

Architect. Paul Revere Williams was born in Los Angeles on February 18, 1894. He graduated from the University of California, Los Angeles, and later attended the Beaux Arts Institute of Design in Paris. He received honorary degrees from Howard, Lincoln, and Atlanta universities, as well as Hampton Institute.

Williams became a certified architect in 1915. After working for Reginald Johnson and John Austin, he opened his own firm in 1923 in Los Angeles. Williams designed some four hundred homes and a total of three thousand buildings, including homes for Cary Grant, Barbara Stanwyck, William Holden, Frank Sinatra, Betty Grable, Bill "Bojangles" Robinson, and Bert Lahr.

In 1926, Williams became the first African American to join the American Institute of Architects. He served on the National Monument Commission as an appointee of President Calvin Coolidge. His notable works include the Los Angeles County Airport, the Palm Springs Tennis Club, and Saks Fifth Avenue in Beverly Hills. He died on January 23, 1980.

WILLIAM T. WILLIAMS (1942–)

Painter. William Thomas Williams was born in Cross Creek, North Carolina, on July 17, 1942. He received his B.F.A. from Pratt Institute in 1966 and his M.F.A. from Yale University in 1968. In 1970, Williams taught painting classes at Pratt Institute and at the School of Fine Arts. In 1971, he became a professor of art at City University of New York, Brooklyn College. He also served as a visiting professor of art at Virginia Commonwealth University.

Williams has been the recipient of several awards. In 1992, the Studio Museum in Harlem presented him with its Annual Award for Lifetime Achievement. He was also awarded the Mid-Atlantic Foundation Fellowship in 1994. In addition, Williams received a John Simon Guggenheim Fellowship (1987), two National Endowment for the Arts awards (1965, 1970), and a Joan Mitchell Foundation Award (1996). In 2005, he won the James VanDerZee Award from the Brandywine Workshop for lifetime achievement.

Exhibitions of Williams's work have been presented at, among others, the Studio Museum in Harlem, the Wadsworth Atheneum, the Art Institute of Chicago, and the Whitney Museum of American Art. His notable works include *Elbert Jackson L.A.M.F. Port II*, *Big Red for N.C.*, and *Buttermilk*.

JOHN WILSON (1922–)

Painter, Printmaker. John Wilson was born in Boston on April 14, 1922. He studied at the Boston Museum of Fine Arts, the Fernand Léger School in Paris, and the Instituto Politécnico Nacional and Escuela de las Artes del Libro in Mexico City. In 1947, Wilson received a B.A. from Tufts University. He has been a teacher at Boston Museum, Pratt Institute, and Boston University.

Exhibitions of Wilson's work have been held at the Albany Institute, the Library of Congress, Smith College, the Carnegie Institute, and the American International College in Springfield, Massachusetts. His work is represented in the collections of the Museum of Modern Art and the Schomburg Center in New York, the Department of Fine Arts of the French government, Atlanta University, and the Bezalel Museum in Jerusalem. His notable works include *Roxbury Landscape*, *Trabajador*, and *Child with Father*.

Wilson designed the Dr. Martin Luther King Jr. Monument in Buffalo, New York, in 1983, as well as the Dr. Martin Luther King Jr. commemorative statue at the U.S. Capitol in Washington, D.C. In 1987, he completed the monument *Eternal Presence*, which resides at the Museum of the National Center of Afro-American Artists in Boston, Massachusetts.

HALE WOODRUFF (1900–1980)

Painter, Muralist. Hale Woodruff's paintings were largely modernist landscapes and formal abstractions, but he also painted rural Georgia scenes evocative of the "red clay" country. Born in Cairo, Illinois, in 1900, he graduated from the John Herron Art Institute in Indianapolis. Encouraged by an award that he won in the 1926 Harmon Foundation competition, Woodruff went to Paris to study at both the Académie Scandinave and the Académie Moderne, as well as with Henry Ossawa Tanner.

In 1931, Woodruff became art instructor at Atlanta University, and he later accepted a similar post at New York University. In 1939, he received a commission from Talladega College for the *Amistad Murals*, an episodic depiction of a revolt led by enslaved Africans.

In 1948, Woodruff teamed with Charles Alston to work on the Golden State Mutual Life Insurance Company Murals in California, which presented the contributions of African Americans to the development of California. Woodruff's last mural assignment came in 1950, when he developed a series of mural panels for Atlanta University titled *The Art of the Negro*. His other notable works include *Ancestral Remedies* and *The Little Boy*.

RICHARD YARDE (1939–)

Painter. Richard Yarde was born in Boston on October 29, 1939. He studied at the School of the Museum of Fine Arts and at Boston University, where he received a B.F.A. in 1962 and an M.F.A. in 1964. Yarde has taught at Boston University, Wellesley College, Amherst College, Massachusetts College of Art, Mount Holyoke College, and the University of Massachusetts.

Yarde has received numerous awards for his art, including Yaddo fellowships in 1964, 1966, and 1970. He also won McDowell Colony awards in 1968 and 1970 and the Blanche E. Colman Award in 1970. The Boston Museum of Fine Arts, the Wadsworth Atheneum, the Rose Art Museum, the National Museum of African-American Artists, and the Studio Museum in Harlem have all exhibited his works. He has held one-person shows at numerous galleries and universities, and his works are in many collections. Yarde's notable works include *The Stoop*, *Passage Edgar and I*, *The Corner*, *Paul Robeson as Emperor Jones*, *Head and Hands I*, *Josephine's Baffle Triptych*, and *Richard's Cards*.

MUSEUMS AND GALLERIES EXHIBITING AFRICAN AMERICAN ART

Association of African American Museums
PO Box 427
1350 Brush Row Rd.
Wilberforce, OH 45384
(937) 376-4944, ext. 123
http://www.blackmuseums.org

The Association of African American Museums supports museums focused on African and African American issues, in addition to professionals involved in African and African American art, history, and culture. Many of the museums listed below are members of this organization.

ALABAMA

Birmingham Civil Rights Institute
520 16th St. N
Birmingham, AL 35203
(205) 328-9696
http://www.bcri.org

George Washington Carver Museum
305 N Foster St.
Dothan, AL 36303
(334) 712-0933
http://www.gwcarvermuseum.org/

Central Carver Foundation, Inc.
1030 Tuscaloosa Ave., PO Box 8563
Gadsden, AL 35902
(256) 549-4742

CALIFORNIA

African American Museum and Library at Oakland
659 14th St.
Oakland, CA 94612
(510) 637-0200
http://www.oaklandlibrary.org/AAMLO/

California African American Museum
Exposition Park
600 State Dr.
Los Angeles, CA 90037
(213) 744-7432
Fax: (213)744-2050
http://www.caamuseum.org/

Mayme A. Clayton Library and Museum
4130 Overland Ave.
Culver City, CA 90230-3734
(310) 202-1647
http://www.wsbrec.org/

de Young Museum
50 Hagiwara Tea Garden Dr., Golden Gate Park
San Francisco, CA 94118
(415) 750-3600
http://www.famsf.org/deyoung/

Museum of African American Art
4005 S. Crenshaw Blvd., 3rd Fl.
Los Angeles, CA 90008
(323) 294-7071
http://www.maaala.org

Museum of San Diego African American History and Black Historical Society of San Diego
740 Market St.
San Diego, CA 92101-6423
(619) 232-1480
http://www.blackhistoricalsociety.org/contact_us.htm

San Francisco African American Historical and Cultural Society
762 Fulton St., 2nd Fl.
San Francisco, CA 94102
(415) 292-6172
http://www.sfaahcs.org

COLORADO

Black American West Museum
3091 California St.
Denver, CO 80205
(303) 482-2242
http://www.blackamericanwestmuseum.com/

CONNECTICUT

Artists Collective, Inc.
1200 Albany Ave.
Hartford, CT 06112
(860) 527-3205
http://artistscollective.org/

Connecticut Afro-American Historical Society Collection
Southern Connecticut State University, Ethnic Heritage Center
501 Crescent St.
New Haven, CT 06515
(888) 500-7278
http://www.southernct.edu/ethnic_heritage_center/ehc/research/

John E. Rogers African American Cultural Center
PO Box 1931
Hartford, CT 06105
(860) 232-2887

DISTRICT OF COLUMBIA

Anacostia Community Museum, Smithsonian Institution
1901 Fort Pl. SE
Washington, DC 20020

(202) 633-4820
http://anacostia.si.edu/

Mary McLeod Bethune Council House National Historic Site
National Archives for Black Women's History
1318 Vermont Ave. NW
Washington, DC 20005
(202) 673-2402
Fax: (202) 332-6319
http://www.nps.gov/mamc/index.htm

Frederick Douglass National Historic Site
1411 W St. SE
Washington, DC 20020
(202) 426-5961
http://www.nps.gov/frdo/

Howard University Gallery of Art
2455 6th St. NW
Washington, DC 20059
(202) 806-7070
Fax: (202) 806-6503
http://www.howard.edu/CollegeFineArts/gallery_final/GalleryofArt.html

National Museum of African Art, Smithsonian Institution
950 Independence Ave. SW
Washington, DC 20560
(202) 357-4600
Fax: (202) 357-4879
http://www.nmafa.si.edu/

Sign of the Times Cultural Workshop and Gallery
605 56th St. NE
Washington, DC 20019
(202) 399-3400
http://www.signofthetimes.org/

FLORIDA

Appleton Museum of Art of Central Florida Community College
4333 E Silver Springs Blvd.
Ocala, FL 34470-5001
(352) 291-4455
http://www.appletonmuseum.org/

Black Heritage Museum
PO Box 570327
Miami, FL 33257-0327
(305) 252-3535

Gallery Antiqua
5138 Biscayne Blvd.
Miami, FL 33137
(305) 759-5355

Southeastern Regional Black Archives Research Center and Museum, Florida A&M University
Historic Carnegie Library, Florida A&M University
PO Box 809
Tallahassee, FL 32307
(850) 599-3020
http://www.cis.famu.edu/BlackArchives/

GEORGIA

Apex Museum
135 Auburn Ave. NE
Atlanta, GA 30303
(404) 521-2739
www.apexmuseum.org

Clark Atlanta University Art Galleries
223 James P. Brawley Dr. SW
Trevor Arnett Hall, 2nd Level
Atlanta, GA 30314
(404) 880-6102
www.cau.edu/Academics_Art_Galleries.aspx

Hammonds House Museum
503 Peeples St. SW
Atlanta, GA 30310
(404) 612-0500
http://www.hammondshouse.org/

Herndon Home
587 University Pl. NW
Atlanta, GA 30314
(404) 581-9813

High Museum of Art
1280 Peachtree St.
Atlanta, GA 30309
(404) 733-4422
http://www.high.org

The King Center, Cultural Affairs Program
449 Auburn Ave. NE
Atlanta, GA 30312
(404) 524-1956
http://www.thekingcenter.org/

Martin Luther King Jr. National Historic Site and Preservation District
522 Auburn Ave. NE
Atlanta, GA 30312
(404) 331-5190
http://www.nps.gov/malu/index.htm

King-Tisdell Cottage Foundation
Beach Institute
502 E Harris St.
Savannah, GA 31401
(912) 234-8000
http://kingtisdell.org/

National Black Arts Festival
Promenade II
1230 Peachtree St NE, Ste. 500
Atlanta, GA 30309
(404) 730-7315
http://www.nbaf.org/

Uncle Remus Museum
214 S Oak St.
Eatonton, GA 31024
(706) 485-6856
http://www.uncleremus.com/museum.html

ILLINOIS

Art Institute of Chicago
111 S. Michigan Ave.
Chicago, IL 60603
(312) 357-1052
http://www.artic.edu/aic/

Bronzeville Children's Museum
9301 S. Stony Island Ave.
Chicago, IL 60617
(773) 721-9301
http://www.bronzevillechildrensmuseum.com/

Du Sable Museum of African American History, Afro-American Genealogical and Historical Society
740 E 56th Pl.
Chicago, IL 60637
(773) 947-0600
http://www.dusablemuseum.org/

Springfield, Illinois, African American History Foundation
823 S. 15th St.
Springfield, IL 62703
(217) 698-6339
http://www.spiaahf.org/

INDIANA

Evansville African American Museum
579 Garvin St.
Evansville, IN 47713
(812) 423-5188
http://evansvilleaamuseum.wordpress.com/

Indiana University Art Museum
1133 E. 7th St.
Bloomington, IN 47405-7309
(812) 855-5445
Fax:(812) 855-1023
http://www.indiana.edu/iuam/iuam_intro.htm

KANSAS

Muhammad Ali Center
144 N. 6th St.
Louisville, KY 40202
(502) 584-9254
http://www.alicenter.org

Brown v. Board of Education National Historic Site
1515 SE Monroe
Topeka, KS 66612
(785) 354-4273
http://www.nps.gov/brvb

Kansas African American Museum
601 N. Water St.
Wichita, KS 67203
(316) 262-7651

LOUISIANA

Arna Bontemps African American Museum
1327 3rd St.
Alexandria, LA 71302
(318) 473-4692
http://www.arnabontempsmuseum.com

Louisiana Association of Museums
PO Box 4434
100 North Blvd.
Baton Rouge, LA 80801
(225) 383-6800
http://www.louisianamuseums.org

Louisiana Museum of African American History
PO Box 850906
New Orleans, LA 70178
(504) 432-9901

Louisiana State Museum
751 Chartres St.
New Orleans, LA 70116
(504) 568-6969
http://lsm.crt.state.la.us

River Road African American Museum
406 Charles St.
Donaldsonville, LA 70346
(225) 474-5553
http://www.africanamericanmuseum.org

MARYLAND

African Art of Maryland Museum
5430 Vantage Point Rd.
Columbia, MD 21044-0105
(410) 730-7106
Fax: (410) 730-7105
http://www.africanartmuseum.org/

Baltimore's Black American Museum
1765 Carswell St.
Baltimore, MD 21218
(410) 243-9600

Banneker-Douglass Museum
84 Franklin St.
Annapolis, MD 21401
(410) 216-6180
http://www.bdmuseum.com/

Mabel Jones Moore Museum
1630 Burnwood Rd.
Baltimore, MD 21239
(410) 323-5928
http://www.mabeljmooremuseum.org/

Reginald F. Lewis Museum of Maryland African American History and Culture
830 E. Pratt St.
Baltimore, MD 21202
(443) 263-1800
Fax: (410) 333-1138
http://www.africanamericanculture.org/

James E. Lewis Museum of Art
Morgan State University
Carl J. Murphy Fine Arts Center
2100 Argonne Dr.
Baltimore, MD 21251
(410) 885-3030
http://www.murphyfineartscenter.org/jelma.htm

National Great Blacks in Wax Museum
1601-03 E. North Ave.
Baltimore, MD 21213
(410) 563-3404
Fax: (410) 675-5040
http://www.ngbiwm.com/

MASSACHUSETTS

Institute of Black Invention and Technology
PO Box 2034
Amherst, MA, 01004
(413) 256-6407
http://www.tibit.biz

Museum of African American History
14 Beacon St., Ste 719
Boston, MA 02108
(617) 725-0022
http://www.maah.org/

National Center of Afro-American Artists
300 Walnut Ave.
Boston, MA 02119
(617) 442-8614
http://www.ncaaa.org/

Wendell Street Gallery
17 Wendel St.
Cambridge, MA 02138
(617) 864-9294

MICHIGAN

Black Folk Arts
425 W. Margaret
Detroit, MI 48203
(313) 865-4546

Detroit Institute of Arts
5200 Woodward Ave.
Detroit, MI 48202
(313) 833-7900
www.dia.org

Muskegon County Museum of African American History
7 E. Center St.
Muskegon Heights, MI 49444
(231) 739-9500

G.R. N'Namdi Gallery
52 E Forest
Detroit, MI 48201
(313) 831-8700
http://www.grnnamdi.com/

University of Michigan Museum of Art
525 S. State St.
Ann Arbor, MI 48109
(734) 764-0395
http://www.umma.umich.edu/

Charles H. Wright Museum of African American History
315 E. Warren Ave.
Detroit, MI 48201-1443
(313) 494-5800
www.maah-detroit.org

MINNESOTA

Pillsbury House
3501 Chicago Ave. S
Minneapolis, MN 55407
(612) 824-0708

MISSISSIPPI

African American Military History Museum
Historic USO Club
305 E 6th St.
Hattiesburg, MS, 39401
(601) 450-1942
http://www.hattiesburguso.com/

Smith Robertson Museum and Cultural Center
PO Box 3259
Jackson, MS 39207
(601) 960-1457

MISSOURI

Black Archives of Mid-America
2033 Vine St.
Kansas City, MO 64108
(816) 701-3590
Fax: (816) 483-1341
www.blackarchives.org

Scott Joplin House State Historic Site
2658 Delmar
St. Louis, MO 63103
(314) 340-5790
http://www.mostateparks.com/scottjoplin.htm

Missouri History Museum
5700 Lindell Blvd.
PO Box 11940
St. Louis, MO 63112
(314) 746-4599
http://www.mohistory.org

Vaughn Cultural Center
3701 Grandel Sq.
St. Louis, MO 63108
(314) 615-3624
http://www.ulstl.org/vaughn_cultural_center.aspx

NEBRASKA

Loves Jazz and Art Center
2510 N. 24th St.
Omaha, NE 68110
(402) 502-5291
http://www.lovesjazzartcenter.org/

NEW JERSEY

African American Heritage Museum of Southern New Jersey
661 Jackson Rd.
Newtonville, NJ 08346
(609) 704-5495
http://www.aahmsnj.org/

African Art Museum of the SMA Fathers
23 Bliss Ave.
Tenafly, NJ 07670
(201) 894-8611
www.smafathers.org/mus_web/Ten_museum.htm

"Lest We Forget" Black Holocaust Museum of Slavery
1064 Swallow Dr.
Cherry Hill, NJ 08003
856-427-4262
http://www.lestweforgetmuseumofslavery.com
Viewings by appointment only

Newark Museum
49 Washington St.
Newark, NJ 07102-3176
(973) 596-6550
Fax: (201) 642-0459
http://www.newarkmuseum.org/

NEW YORK

Africa-America Institute
420 Lexington Ave., Ste. 1706
New York, NY 10170-0002

(212) 949-5666
Fax: (212) 682-6174
http://www.aaionline.org/

African-American Cultural Center, Inc.
350 Masten Ave.
Buffalo, NY 14209
(716) 884-2013
http://www.africancultural.org/

African American Museum of Nassau County
110 Franklin St.
Hempstead, NY 11550
(516) 572-0730
http://aamoflongisland.org/home.htm

Louis Armstrong House Museum
34-56 107th St.
Corona, NY 11368
(718) 478-8274
http://www.louisarmstronghouse.org/

Bedford-Stuyvesant Restoration Center for Arts and Culture
1368 Fulton., Ste. 4G
Brooklyn, NY 11216
(718) 636-6995
http://www.restorationplaza.org/arts-and-culture

Black Filmmaker Foundation
670 Broadway, Ste. 305
New York, NY 10012
(212) 253-1690
Fax: (212) 253-1689
http://www.dvrepublic.com/about.php

Black Spectrum Theatre Company
Roy Wilkens Pk.
119-07 Merrick Blvd
Jamaica, NY 11434
(718) 723-1800
www.blackspectrum.com

Brooklyn Museum
200 Eastern Pky.
Brooklyn, NY 11238-6052
(718) 638-5000
Fax: (718) 638-3731
www.brooklynmuseum.org/

Community Folk Art Center
African American Studies, Syracuse University
805 E Genesee St.
Syracuse, NY 13210
(315) 442-2230
Fax: (315) 442-2972
http://communityfolkartcenter.org/AboutUs.htm

Grinnell Gallery
800 Riverside Dr., Apt GRI
New York, NY 10032
http://www.audubonparkny.com/AudubonParkGrinnell800RiversideDrive-1016.html

Harlem School of the Arts
645 St. Nicholas Ave.
New York, NY 10030
(212) 926-4100
http://www.harlemschoolofthearts.org/

Hatch-Billops Collection, Inc.
491 Broadway, 7th Fl.
New York, NY 10012
(212) 966-3231
www.hatch-billopsarchive.org/

International Agency for Minority Artists Affairs, Inc.
163 W. 125th St.
New York, NY 10027
(212) 749-5298

June Kelly Gallery
166 Mercer St.
New York, NY 10012
(212) 226-1660
http://www.junekellygallery.com

Kenkeleba Gallery (House)
214 E. 2nd St.
New York, NY 10009-8031
(212) 674-3939

Museum of Contemporary African Diasporan Arts
80 Hanson Pl.
Brooklyn, NY 11217-1506
(718) 230-0492
Fax: 718-230-0246
http://www.mocada.org

Jackie Robinson Museum and Education Center
Jackie Robinson Foundation
75 Varick St., 2nd Fl.
New York, NY 10013-1917

(212) 290-8600
http://www.jackierobinson.org

Schomburg Center for Research in Black Culture
515 Malcolm X Blvd.
New York, NY 10037-1801
(212) 491-2200
http://www.nypl.org/research/sc/

Studio Museum in Harlem
144 W. 125th St.
New York, NY 10027
(212) 864-4500
Fax: (212) 666-5753
http://www.studiomuseum.org

Underground Railroad History Project of the Capital Region, Inc.
PO Box 10851
Albany, NY 12201
(518) 432-4432
http://www.ugrworkshop.com/

NORTH CAROLINA

African American Atelier, Greensboro Cultural Center
200 N. Davie St., Box 14
Greensboro, NC 27401
(336) 333-6885
http://www.africanamericanatelier.org/

African American Cultural Complex
119 Sunnybrook Rd.
Raleigh, NC 27610
(919) 250-9336
http://www.aaccmuseum.org

Diggs Art Gallery
Winston-Salem State University
601 Martin Luther King Jr. Dr.
Winston-Salem, NC 27110
(336) 750-2458
http://www.wssu.edu/WSSU/UndergraduateStudies/College+of+Arts+and+Sciences/Diggs+Gallery/

Harvey B. Gantt African-American Arts+Cultural
551 S Tryon St.
Charlotte, NC 28202
(704) 547-3700
http://www.ganttcenter.org/

Huff Art Studio
2846 Patterson Ave.
Winston-Salem, NC 27105
(336) 724-7581
http://www.huffartstudio.com/

Nasher Museum of Art at Duke University
2100 Campus Dr.
Durham, NC 27705
(919) 684-5135
http://nasher.duke.edu/

NCCU Art Museum
PO Box 19555
Durham, NC 27703
(919) 530-6211
http://web.nccu.edu/artmuseum/

St. Augustine's College Art Gallery
Department of Art, Saint Augustine's College
1315 Oakwood Ave
Raleigh, NC 27610
(919) 516-4027

Shaw University Art Center
Shaw University Department of Art
Raleigh, NC 27602
(919) 546-8420

Weatherspoon Art Gallery
North Carolina A&T State University
PO Box 26170
Greensboro, NC 27402-6170
(336) 334-5770
Fax: (336) 334-5907
http://weatherspoon.uncg.edu/

YMI Cultural Center
39 S. Market St.
Asheville, NC 28801
(828) 252-4614
http://www.ymicc.org/

OHIO

Allen Memorial Art Museum
Oberlin College
87 North Main St.
Oberlin, OH 44074
(440) 775-8665
http://www.oberlin.edu/amam/

Cincinnati Art Museum
953 Eden Park Dr.
Cincinnati, OH 45202-1596
(513) 639-2995

Fax: (513) 721-0129
http://www.cincinnatiartmuseum.org

Karamu House
2355 E 89th St.
Cleveland, OH 44106
(216) 795-7070
http://www.karamu.com

Malcolm Brown Gallery
20100 Chagrin Blvd.
Shaker Heights, OH 44122
(216) 751-2955
http://www.malcolmbrowngallery.com

Howard Mims African American Cultural Center
Cleveland State University
Black Studies Program
2121 Euclid Ave., UC 103
Cleveland, OH 44115
(216) 687-3656
http://www.csuohio.edu/class/blackstudies/mims/

National Afro-American Museum and Cultural Center
Ohio Historical Society
1350 Brush Row Rd.
Wilberforce, OH 45384
(937) 376-4944 or (800) 752-2603
http://ohsweb.ohiohistory.org/places/sw13/

OKLAHOMA

Greenwood Cultural Center
322 N. Greenwood Ave.
Tulsa, OK 74120
(918) 506-1020
http://www.greenwoodculturalcenter.com/

Oklahoma Historical Society
800 Nazih Zuhdi Dr.
Oklahoma City, OK 73105
405-521-2491
http://www.okhistory.org/

NTU Art Association of Oklahoma
PO Box 36205
Oklahoma City, OK 73136
(405) 424-1655
http://www.ntuartokc.org

PENNSYLVANIA

African Cultural Art Forum
221 S. 52nd St.
Philadelphia, PA 19139
(215) 476-0680

African American Museum in Philadelphia
701 Arch St.
Philadelphia, PA 19106
(215) 574-0380
http://www.aampmuseum.org

Senator John Heinz History Center
1212 Smallman St.
Pittsburgh, PA 15222
(412) 454-6373
http://www.heinzhistorycenter.org/

Minority Arts Resource Council
1421 W. Girard Ave.
Philadelphia, PA 19130
(215) 236-2688

Philadelphia Doll Museum
2253 N. Broad St.
Philadelphia, PA 19132
(215) 787-0220
http://www.philadollmuseum.com/

August Wilson Center for African American Culture
980 Liberty Ave.
Pittsburgh, PA, 15222
(412) 258-2700
http://www.augustwilsoncenter.org/

RHODE ISLAND

Rhode Island Black Heritage Society
65 Weybosset St., Ste 29
Providence, RI 02903
(401) 751-3490
Fax: (401) 751-0040
http://www.providenceri.com/RI_BlackHeritage/
index.html

SOUTH CAROLINA

Avery Research Center for Afro-American History and Culture
University of Charleston
125 Bull St.
College of Charleston
Charleston, SC 29401
(843) 953-7609
http://avery.cofc.edu/

York W. Bailey Museum at Penn Center National Historic Landmark District
Martin Luther King Jr. Dr., Box 126
St. Helena Island, SC 29920

(843) 838-2432
http://www.penncenter.com/

Mann-Simons Cottage: Museum of African-American Culture
Historic Columbia Foundation
1403 Richland St.
Columbia, SC 29201
(803) 252-1770
http://historiccolumbia.org/

Old Slave Mart Museum
6 Chalmers St.
Charleston, SC 29401
(843) 958-6467

Rice Museum
633 Front St.
Georgetown, SC 29442
(843) 546-7423
Fax: (843) 545-9093

I.P. Stanback Museum and Planetarium
South Carolina State University
300 College St. NE
Orangeburg, SC 29117
(803) 536-7174
http://www.scsu.edu/researchoutreach/ipstanbackmuseumampplanetarium.aspx

TENNESSEE

Black Cultural Exchange Center
1927 Dandridge Ave.
Knoxville, TN 37915
(865) 524-8461
Fax: (865) 524-8462
http://www.beckcenter.net/

Blues City Cultural Center
39 Carnes Ave.
Memphis, TN 38114
http://www.bcccmemphis.org/

Chattanooga African American Museum
200 E. Martin Luther King Blvd.
Chattanooga, TN 37403
(423) 266-8658
Fax: (423) 267-1076
http://www.caamhistory.org/

Memphis Black Arts Alliance
985 S. Bellevue Blvd.
Memphis, TN 38106
(901) 948-9522
Fax: (901) 948-993
http://www.memphisblackartsalliance.org/home.htm

Carl Van Vechten Gallery
Fisk University
Dr. D. B. Todd Blvd & Jackson St. N
Nashville, TN 37203
(615) 329-8720
http://www.fisk.edu/CampusLife/FiskUniversityGalleries/CarlVanVechtenGallery.aspx

TEXAS

African American Museum
3536 Grand Ave., Fair Park
Dallas, TX 75210-1005
(214) 565-9026
Fax: (214) 421-8204
http://www.aamdallas.org/

Black Heritage Gallery
5408 Almeda Rd.
Houston, TX 77004
(713) 529-7900

Calaboose African American History Museum
200 W. Martin Luther King Dr.
San Marcos, TX 78667-0481
(512) 393-8421

George Washington Carver Museum and Cultural Center
1165 Angelina St.
Austin, TX 78702
(512) 974-4926
http://www.ci.austin.tx.us/carver/

National Multicultural Western Heritage Museum
3400 Mt. Vernon Ave.
Fort Worth, TX 76103
(817) 534-8801
http://www.cowboysofcolor.org

UTAH

Utah Museum of Fine Arts
University of Utah, Marcia and John Price Museum Building
410 Campus Center Dr.
Salt Lake City, UT 84122-0350
(801) 581-7332
Fax: (801) 585-5198
http://www.utah.edu/umfa

VIRGINIA

Alexandria Black History Museum
902 Wythe St.
Alexandria, VA 22314
(703) 746-4356
Fax: (703) 706-3999
http://oha.alexandriava.gov/bhrc/

Black History Museum and Cultural Center of Virginia
00 Clay St.
Richmond, VA 23219
(804) 780-9093
Fax: (804) 780-9107
http://www.blackhistorymuseum.org/

Hampton University Museum and Archives
11 Frissell Ave.
Hampton, VA 23669
(757) 727-5308
http://museum.hamptonu.edu/

Harrison Museum of African American Culture
523 Harrison Ave. NW
Roanoke, VA 24016
(540) 345-4818
http://www.harrisonmuseum.com/

Newsome House Museum and Cultural Center
2803 Oak Ave.
Newport News, VA 23607
(757) 247-2360
http://www.newsomehouse.org/

27

SCIENCE AND TECHNOLOGY

Genevieve Slomski
Ticora V. Jones

EARLY AFRICAN AMERICAN INVENTORS

Perhaps in science more than in other areas, African Americans have been afforded few sanctioned opportunities to offer contributions. However, will and intelligence helped individuals bring their ideas and dreams into the light. The Industrial Revolution swept African Americans along just as dramatically as it did the rest of the world. Though not all of them became household names, African Americans have made their mark in science and technology. For example, when Alexander Graham Bell invented the telephone in 1876, he chose Lewis H. Latimer to draft the plans. Later, Latimer became a member of the Edison Pioneers, a group of inventors who worked for Thomas Edison through 1885.

One of the earliest African American stars of science was Benjamin Banneker, a free African American who lived in the 1700s. Considered the first African American scientist, Banneker was an expert in mathematics and astronomy, both of which he studied during his friendship with an influential white Quaker neighbor. In 1753, Banneker constructed one of the first striking clocks made in the United States. Later, Banneker and the Quaker's son were reportedly selected to lay the plans for the city of Washington, D.C., making Banneker one of the first African American civil engineers. In the early 1790s, his almanac—a yearlong calendar with weather and astronomical information that was especially useful to farmers—was published with much success. New editions were issued for several years.

In 1790, the U.S. government passed the U.S. Patent Act, which extended patent rights to inventors, including free blacks. Enslaved Africans would not have this right until the passage of the Fourteenth Amendment in 1868. In one of history's most absurd bureaucratic fiats, not only could enslaved blacks not be granted patents, they also could not assign patents to their masters. The underlying theory was that because the enslaved population did not have citizenship, they could not enter into contracts with their owners or the government. As a result, the efforts of enslaved Africans were dismissed or credited to their masters. Historians can only speculate on the extent to which slaves were active in invention. For example, Joe Anderson, who was enslaved, was believed to have played a major role in the creation of a grain harvester, or reaper, that his master Cyrus McCormick was credited with inventing, but available records are insufficient to determine the degree to which Anderson was involved. Similarly, Benjamin Montgomery, also enslaved, belonging to Confederate president Jefferson Davis, is thought to have designed an improved boat propeller. Because the race of patent seekers was rarely noted and many African American inventions were simply never patented, historians cannot be sure how many inventions were made by free blacks either.

The first free blacks to have their inventions recorded were Thomas L. Jennings, whose dry-cleaning methodology received patent protection in 1821, and Henry Blair, who invented a seed planter in 1834. Free black Norbert Rillieux patented his sugar-refining evaporator in 1843, thus revolutionizing the industry. The son of a French planter and a black enslaved woman, Rillieux left his home in New Orleans to study engineering in Paris. After teaching mathematics there and experimenting with steam evaporation, he created his vacuum pan evaporator.

With his invention, a single person could do work that once required several people working at once. He returned to the United States and became wealthy as the device was implemented in sugar refineries in his home state and abroad in Cuba and Mexico. Racial tensions in the United States wore on him, however, and in 1854 he moved to France, where he spent the remainder of his life.

In 1848, free black Lewis Temple invented the toggle harpoon for killing whales, a major industry at the time. Temple's invention, which greatly diminished a whale's ability to escape after being hooked, almost completely replaced the type of harpoon formerly used. Prior to the Civil War, Henry Boyd created an improved bed frame, and James Forten, one of the few African Americans from that era to gain extreme wealth from an invention, produced a device that helped guide the large sails of ships. He used the money he earned to expand his sail factory.

The Reconstruction era opened the door to creativity that had been suppressed in African Americans. Between 1870 and 1900, a time when nearly 80 percent of African American adults in the United States were illiterate, African Americans were awarded several hundred patents. Elijah McCoy worked as a locomotive fireman on a Michigan line, lubricating the hot steam engines during scheduled train stops. In 1872, after years of work, McCoy perfected and patented an automatic lubricator that regularly supplied oil to the engine as the train was in motion. The effect on the increasingly important railway system was profound in that conductors were no longer forced to make oiling stops. McCoy adapted his invention for use on ships and in factories.

In 1884, Granville T. Woods invented an improved steam boiler furnace in his Cincinnati electrical engineering shop. Three years later, Woods patented an induction telegraph or "synchronous multiplex railway telegraph," which allowed train personnel to communicate with workers on other trains while in motion. He was also responsible for what later became known as the trolley when he produced an overhead electrical power supply system for streetcars and trains. A prolific inventor, Woods, known as the "black Edison," patented more than sixty valuable inventions, including an air brake that he eventually sold to George Westinghouse.

Jan Matzeliger came to the United States from South America and eventually settled in Lynn, Massachusetts, in 1877, obtaining work in a shoe factory. There he witnessed the tedious process by which shoe soles were attached to shoe uppers by workers known as hand lasters. For six months, he secretly labored at inventing a machine to automate the work. Unsatisfied with his original design, he spent several more years tweaking and perfecting his creation so that by the time he was granted a patent in 1883, the equipment was so successful that manufacturers the world over clamored for it.

Progress has been a gift from women as well as men. Sarah Goode is credited with creating a folding cabinet bed in 1885, while Sarah Boone patented an improvement to the ironing board in 1892. Madame C. J. Walker, often regarded only as an entrepreneur, was one of the most successful woman inventors. She developed an entire line of hair-care products and cosmetics for African Americans, claiming that her first idea had come to her in a dream.

In the early twentieth century, Garrett A. Morgan patented a succession of products, including a hair-straightening solution that remained on the market for many decades; a gas mask, or breathing device, for firefighters; and an improved traffic signal. Morgan tried to pass himself off as Native American. Once his identity as an African American was discovered, several of his purchase orders were canceled.

Nonetheless, the early inventors paved the way for future African American inventors. These men and women, as well as the countless unknown individuals, were forced to endure the by-products of racism. Whites were often hesitant to buy African American inventions unless the reality of eventual monetary gains was too strong to ignore. McCoy, Woods, and several others died poor, although their creations sold extremely well.

EARLY AFRICAN AMERICAN SCIENTISTS

The contributions of African American scientists are better known than those of African American inventors, partly because of the recognition awarded to George Washington Carver, an agriculturalist who refused to patent most of his inventions. Born enslaved around 1864, Carver was the first African American to graduate from Iowa State Agricultural College (now Iowa State University), where he studied botany and agriculture. One year after earning a master's degree, Carver joined Tuskegee Institute's Agriculture Department. In his role as department head, he engineered a number of experimental farming techniques that had practical applications for farmers in the area. Through his ideas, from crop rotation to replenishment of nutrient-starved soil to his advocacy of peanuts as a cash crop, Carver left an indelible mark in his field. An inventor at heart, he was behind the genesis of innumerable botanical products, by-products, and even recipes. Recognition of his efforts came in several forms, including induction into England's Royal Society for the Encouragement of the Arts, Manufactures, and Commerce in 1916. In 1923, he received a Spingarn Medal from the National Association for the Advancement of Colored People (NAACP). In 1948, five years after his death, Carver was pictured on a U.S. postage stamp. He was commemorated on another U.S. postage stamp in 1998.

Ernest Everett Just, who was born approximately ten years before Carver earned his bachelor's degree, was a pioneering marine biologist who graduated magna cum laude from Dartmouth College in 1907. In 1915, Just became the first-ever recipient of a Spingarn Medal. His first paper, "The Relation of the First Cleavage Plane to the Entrance Point of the Sperm," was published in 1912. The work showed how the location of cell division in the marine worm *nereis* is determined by the sperm's entry point on an egg. Just did the majority of his research at the Marine Biological Laboratory in Woods Hole, Massachusetts, where he spent many summers. Teaching at Howard University for many years, he had a tenuous relationship with the school, paving the way for him to accept an offer to conduct research at the Kaiser Wilhelm Institute for Biology in Berlin, Germany. The first American to be invited to this internationally respected institution, Just remained there from 1930 to 1933, at which point the Nazi regime was surging to power. Because he preferred working abroad to being shut out of the best laboratories in the United States on the basis of race, Just spent the next several years in France, Italy, Spain, and Portugal. He died in 1941, shortly after returning to the United States.

African Americans have had successes in engineering and mathematics as well. In 1876, Edward Bouchet became the first African American to earn a doctorate from a university in the United States, when he acquired a Ph.D. in physics from Yale University. In 1918, Elmer Samuel Imes, the husband of Harlem Renaissance writer Nella Larsen, received a Ph.D. in physics from the University of Michigan. In his dissertation, Imes took the work of white scientists Albert Einstein, Ernest Rutherford, and Niels Bohr one step further, definitively establishing that quantum theory applied to the rotational states of molecules. His efforts would later play a role in space science.

Chemist Percy Julian carved a brilliant career for himself after obtaining a doctorate from Switzerland's University of Vienna in 1931. His specialty was creating synthetic versions of expensive drugs. Much of his work was conducted at his Julian Research Institute in Franklin Park, Illinois. In the 1940s, another scientist, Benjamin Peery, switched his focus from aeronautical engineering to physics while still an undergraduate at the University of Minnesota. After garnering a Ph.D. from the University of Michigan, Peery had a lengthy career teaching astronomy at Indiana University, the University of Illinois, and Howard University.

Between 1875 and 1943, only eight African Americans were awarded doctorates in pure mathematics. David Blackwell became the first tenured African American professor at the University of California, Berkeley, in 1955. An expert in statistics and probability, he was a trailblazer despite a racially motivated setback he incurred soon after completing his doctoral work at the University of Illinois. After receiving a Rosenwald Fellowship from the Institute for Advanced Study at Princeton University, Blackwell was rejected because of his race. Undaunted, he eventually became the first African American mathematician to be elected into the National Academy of Sciences.

AFRICAN AMERICANS IN MEDICINE

The medical profession has yielded a number of African Americans of high stature. As early as the 1860s, African Americans had entered medical schools in the North and had gone on to practice as full-fledged physicians. In fact, during the Civil War, Dr. Alexander T. Augusta was named head of a Union Army hospital and Rebecca Lee Crumpler became the first woman African American doctor by graduating from the New England Female Medical College in Boston. She was able to attend on a scholarship that she received from Benjamin Wade, an abolitionist senator from Ohio. Crumpler used her schooling to provide health care to formerly enslaved Africans in the former confederate capital of Richmond, Virginia. Her *Book of Medical Discourses* (1883) taught women how to address their own health issues, as well as those of their children.

Rebecca J. Cole was the second African American woman to become a physician and the first African American graduate of the Women's Medical College of Pennsylvania. For over fifty years, she devoted her life to improving the lot of the poor. Her positions included performing a residency at the New York Infirmary for Women and Children and running Washington, D.C.'s Government House for Children and Old Women and Philadelphia's Woman's Directory, a medical-aid center.

In 1867, Susan McKinney Steward began studying at the New York Medical College for Women. Three years later, she earned the distinction of being the third African American woman physician in the United States and the first in the state of New York. She specialized in homeopathic treatments and had black and white patients of both genders as clients. After opening a second office in New York City, she cofounded the Brooklyn Women's Hospital and Dispensary. She also served at the Brooklyn Home for Aged Colored People. Steward vigorously supported the women's suffrage movement and conducted missionary work with her second husband, a chaplain for the buffalo soldier regiment. She ended her career by taking on the role of school doctor at Wilberforce University.

In 1868, Howard University opened its College of Medicine, becoming the first African American medical school in the country. The school nearly failed five years later when financial problems arose and salaries for faculty were unavailable. Thanks to the efforts of Dr. Charles Purvis, who persuaded the school to let him and his peers continue teaching on a nonpaid basis, the school survived the crisis. Purvis was later appointed chief surgeon of Washington, D.C.'s Freedmen's Hospital (later Howard University Hospital). Purvis was thus the first African American to run a civilian hospital. He did so until 1894, when he began a private practice.

Meanwhile, in 1876, Nashville's Meharry Medical College was founded. Despite the decidedly low number of jobs for African American physicians, who were routinely turned away from nearly every facility other than Freedmen's Hospital, the school was another sign of the slowly developing progress by African American physicians. This progress included the appointment of Dr. Daniel Hale Williams as Purvis's successor at Freedmen's. Williams advanced Freedmen's through internships, better nurses' training, and the addition of horse-drawn ambulances.

Williams had graduated from the Chicago Medical College in 1883 and then entered into private practice almost immediately. Business was slow until 1890, when he met Emma Reynolds, an aspiring African American nurse, whose skin color had kept her from gaining admission to any of the nursing schools in Chicago. Inspired by her unfortunate dilemma, Williams decided to operate his own hospital in hopes of initiating a program for nurses. With twelve beds, Provident Hospital became the first African American–operated facility in the United States, and Reynolds was the first to enroll in Williams's classes. Near the end of his career, Williams was appointed the first African American associate surgeon at Chicago's St. Luke's Hospital and later was the only African American charter member of the American College of Surgeons. During his career, Williams helped persuade forty hospitals to treat African American patients.

African Americans in the South also received improved care in the late 1890s, thanks to Alice Woodby McKane and her spouse, who was also a doctor. In 1893, they founded the first training school for African American nurses—in Savannah, Georgia. McKane had obtained her medical degree one year earlier from the Women's Medical College of Pennsylvania. In 1895, the couple set up their first hospital in Monrovia, Liberia, before establishing the McKane Hospital for Women and Children in Georgia the following year.

Progress moved westward as another African American woman used her training to benefit the region's African American population, though her patients transcended all racial barriers. Beginning in 1901, Denver's "Baby Doctor," Justina Ford, proudly served her community as the only African American physician in Colorado for over fifty years. An obstetrician, she delivered more than seven thousand babies, conducting most of her business by house calls.

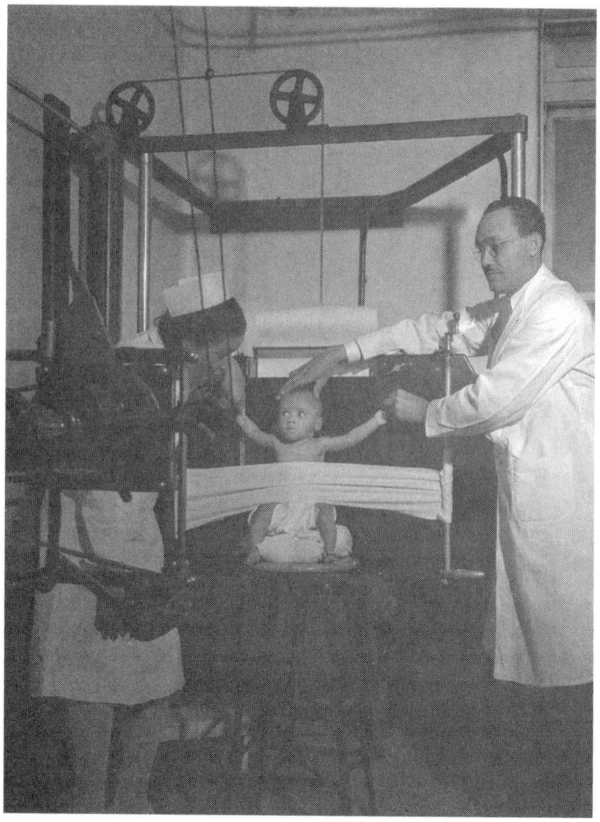

Baby Being X-Rayed, Provident Hospital, Chicago. *Provident was the first African American–operated hospital in the United States. It was founded in 1891 by Dr. Daniel Hale Williams, a pioneer in open-heart surgery.* **THE LIBRARY OF CONGRESS**

Back in the East, Freedmen's Hospital was the training ground for future head-trauma authority, Dr. Louis T. Wright, a Harvard Medical School graduate whose high academic standing meant nothing to Boston-area hospitals that refused to hire African Americans. When World War I erupted, Wright enlisted and found himself in charge of his unit's surgical ward. After the war, Wright, who had received a Purple Heart, became the first African American physician to work in a New York City hospital when he was appointed to Harlem Hospital in 1919. Later, he became director of surgery and president of the medical board and was admitted to the American College of Surgeons. In 1948, four years before his death in 1952, he founded the Cancer Research

Foundation at Harlem Hospital. The son of two physicians, his father and his stepfather, the latter of whom was the first African American graduate of Yale Medical School, Wright had two daughters who continued the family legacy by becoming doctors.

An almost legendary legacy was created by Dr. Charles R. Drew, a star high school athlete whose interest lay in medicine. His experiments in blood preservation and blood transfusions helped him earn a doctorate in medical science in 1940. During World War II, Drew helped Great Britain develop a national blood-collection program, and he was later asked to do the same for the U.S. Armed Forces. Unfortunately, African American donors were first completely excluded from the program and later were allowed to donate only to other African American servicemen. Drew withdrew from the program, briefly resuming his teaching career at Howard University before joining the staff of Freedmen's Hospital as medical director.

Howard University continued developing new talents. Dr. Roland B. Scott, a longtime physician at the university's College of Medicine, became a pioneer in the study and treatment of sickle-cell anemia. His research was pivotal in drawing public attention to the disorder and prompting the U.S. government to devote money to more extensive study. Under the Sickle Cell Anemia Control Act passed in 1972, Congress forced the National Institutes of Health to set up treatment centers for patients. Scott was named director of the program, which involved screening as well as treatment for those already afflicted.

In more recent years, African Americans have made great strides in the field of medicine. Alexa Canady became the first female African American neurosurgeon in 1976. She was a leader and innovator in the areas of craniofacial abnormalities, epilepsy, hydrocephalus, pediatric neurosurgery, and tumors of the spinal cord and brain. She also contributed to special research areas, such as head injury, hydrocephalus and shunts, complications of shunts during pregnancy, neuroendoscopy and the development of neuroendoscopic equipment, and the evaluation of programmable pressure-change valves in hydrocephalus. Another African American neurosurgeon who advanced the field to new heights was Dr. Benjamin S. Carson. In 1987, Carson led a seventy-member surgical team at Johns Hopkins Hospital to separate Siamese twins who were joined at the cranium. This type of surgery had never been attempted before, but Carson was able not only to perform the surgery but also to save both twins with minimal brain damage.

Canady and Carson changed the way the medical profession handled injuries and complications to the brain. Ten years after Carson's groundbreaking surgery, a pair of doctors changed the way that the medical community dealt with multiple births. Drs. Paula Mahone and Karen Drake led a team of forty specialists involved in the delivery of the McCaughey septuplets at Iowa Methodist Medical Center, the first set of septuplets to be born and survive in the United States. Mahone, Drake, Canady, and Carter provide but a few examples of the major new discoveries and achievements that African Americans have made in the medical field.

African Americans have also begun to break into positions of power and prestige in the medical community. In 1989, Renee Rosalind Jenkins became the first African American president of the Society of Adolescent Medicine. Roselyn Epps took over as the first African American president of the American Medical Women's Association in 1990 and as the first woman president of the Medical Society of the District of Columbia a year later. In 1993, Dr. Barbara Ross-Lee was named the dean of Ohio University's College of Osteopathic Medicine, making her the first African American woman to lead a U.S. medical school.

These rises in positions in the medical community for African Americans were also seen in government In 1993, Dr. Joycelyn Elders became the first African American to be appointed U.S. surgeon general. Five years later, Dr. David Satcher was sworn in as both U.S. surgeon general and assistant secretary of the Department of Health and Human Services. In 2009, President Barack Obama appointed Dr. Regina M. Benjamin as the eighteenth surgeon general of the United States.

AFRICAN AMERICANS IN AIR AND SPACE

In 1920, Texan Bessie Coleman was accepted into the French flying school École d'Aviation des Freres, following a string of rejections from aviation schools in the United States. Having completed seven months of instruction and a rigorous qualifying exam, she earned her international aviator's license from the Fédération Aéronautique Internationale and studied further with the American aircraft designer Anthony H. G. Fokker. Known to an admiring public as "Queen Bess," Coleman was the first African American woman ever to fly an airplane, the first American to earn an international pilot's license, and the first African American woman stunt pilot. During her brief yet distinguished career as a performance flier, she appeared at air shows and exhibitions across the country, earning wide recognition for her aerial skill, dramatic flair, and tenacity. The tragic demise of the professional aviatrix occurred in 1926, when she was scheduled to parachute jump from a speeding plane at 2,500 feet. Ten minutes after takeoff, the plane careened wildly out of control, flipping over and dropping

Coleman, who plunged 500 feet to her death. The pilot was killed instantly when the plane crashed to the ground. A service wrench that had been mistakenly left behind in the engine was later found to have been the cause of the accident.

Six years later, in 1932, pilot James Herman Banning and mechanic Thomas C. Allen flew from Los Angeles to New York City in forty-one hours and twenty-seven minutes. The transcontinental flight was followed by the first round-trip transcontinental flight the next year. That feat was accomplished by Albert Ernest Forsythe and Charles Alfred Anderson, who flew from Atlantic City to Los Angeles and back in eleven days, foreshadowing the advent of commercial flight.

Willa B. Brown became the first African American woman to hold a commercial pilot's license in the United States in 1937. She was also the first African American woman to ascend to the rank of lieutenant in a Civil Air Patrol squadron. With her husband, Cornelius R. Coffey, Brown founded the National Airmen's Association of America, the first aviators group for African Americans. Brown and Coffey also established the first African American–owned flying school, the Coffey School of Aeronautics, which became the first African American–owned school to receive certification from the Civil Aviation Authority. Brown became the first African American member of the Federal Aviation Administration's Women's Advisory Committee on Aviation in 1972.

The second African American woman to earn a full commercial pilot's license was Janet Harmon Bragg, a Georgia nurse who took an interest in flying when she began dating Johnny Robinson, one of the first African American aviation instructors. The first woman of any race to be admitted to Chicago's Curtiss Wright School of Aeronautics, she was initially denied her commercial license despite having successfully fulfilled all the preliminary requirements including the airborne portion of the test. Her white instructor from the Federal Aviation Administration made it quite clear that he would not grant a license to an African American woman. Rather than give up, Bragg merely tested again with another instructor the same year and was granted her license in 1942. Along with a small group of African American aviation devotees, she formed the Challenger Air Pilots Association (CAPA). Together, members of CAPA opened an airport in Robbins, Illinois, the first owned and operated by African Americans.

Other African American notables in the field of aviation include Perry H. Young, who in 1957 became the first African American pilot for a scheduled passenger commercial airline, New York Airways; Otis B. Young Jr., who in 1970 became the first African American pilot of a jumbo jet; and former naval pilot Jill Brown, who in 1978 became the first African American woman to pilot for a major airline.

Military men were the first African Americans to enter into the line of space exploration. In 1961, U.S. Air Force Captain Edward Dwight was invited by President John F. Kennedy to apply to test-pilot school. Two years later, Dwight was in the midst of spaceflight training when Kennedy was assassinated. Without the president's support, Dwight was largely ignored by the National Aeronautics and Space Administration (NASA). Air Force Major Robert H. Lawrence thus became the first African American astronaut a few years later. A doctor of physical chemistry, Lawrence was killed in a plane crash in December 1967, just six months after his selection by NASA. African Americans would not make inroads in space until the genesis of the Space Shuttle Program.

African American scientists were, however, prevalent. For example, Katherine Johnson joined the National Advisory Committee on Aeronautics, the precursor to NASA, in 1953. Initially, all she was asked to do was basic number crunching, but she spent a short period filling in at the Flight Mechanics Branch. There her valued interpretation of data helped in the making of prototype spacecraft, and she soon developed into an aerospace technologist. She developed trajectories for the Apollo moon-landing project and devised emergency navigational methods for astronauts. She retired in 1986.

Emergencies of another sort have been tackled by Air Force flight surgeon Vance Marchbanks, whose research showed that adrenaline levels could affect the exhaustion level of flight crews. His work brought him to the attention of NASA, and he became a medical observer for NASA's Project Mercury. Along with several other personnel scattered about the globe, Marchbanks, stationed in Nigeria, was responsible for monitoring pioneering astronaut John Glenn's vital signs as he orbited earth in 1962. Later, Marchbanks received the civilian post of chief of environmental health services for United Aircraft Corporation, where he had a hand in designing the space suit and medical monitoring systems used in Project Apollo.

Also specializing in design, aeronautical test engineer Robert E. Shurney spent nearly his entire career, from the late 1960s to 1990, at the Marshall Space Flight Center, specializing in design utility. His products included refuse disposal units that stored solids in the bottom and liquid in tubes to prevent any materials from floating openly and contaminating an entire cabin. The units were used in the Apollo program, Skylab, and on the first space shuttle missions. He also crafted strong yet lightweight aluminum tires for the lunar rover. Much of his experimentation was conducted on KC-135 test planes in order to achieve the condition of weightlessness.

Assertiveness enabled O. S. Williams to bring forth his own achievements. In 1942, Williams talked his way into employment at Republic Aviation Corporation as part of the technical staff. Better known as Ozzie, he took the experience he earned there to NASA contractor Grumman Aircraft Engineering Corporation. The small rocket engines that he codeveloped saved the lives of the *Apollo 13* astronauts when the ship's main rocket exploded during flight in 1970.

Three missions later, George R. Carruthers, a Naval Research Laboratory astrophysicist, designed the far-ultraviolet camera/spectrograph for use on *Apollo 16.* This semiautomatic device was able to photograph deep space—regions too far to be captured by regular cameras—once it had been set up on the surface of the moon. Carruthers earned a Ph.D. in aeronautical and astronautical engineering from the University of Illinois in 1964 and was granted his first patent in 1969 for an electromagnetic radiation image converter.

With a 1967 Ph.D. in atomic and molecular physics from Howard University, George E. Alcorn, a contemporary of Carruthers, was one of the most prominent people working with semiconductors and spectrometers. Working for private industry, including IBM, and NASA, Alcorn holds a number of patents, including secret projects concerning missile systems.

In a less clandestine fashion, aerospace engineer Christine M. Darden has been a leading NASA researcher in supersonic and hypersonic aircraft. Her main goal has been the reduction of sonic boom, a phenomenon that creates an explosive burst of sound that can traumatize those on the ground. Darden works at manipulating an aircraft's wing or the shape of its nose to try to control the feedback produced by air waves resulting from a plane's flight.

Dealing with people rather than machinery as the director of psychophysiology at NASA's Ames Research Center, Patricia S. Cowings has touched on such fields as aerospace medicine and bioastronautics in her postdoctoral work. Since the late 1970s, she has assisted astronauts by teaching them biofeedback techniques—how to impose mind over matter when zero gravity wreaks havoc with one's system. By studying physical and emotional problems that arise in such a setting, she can seek the cause and prescribe a therapy to alleviate stress. She was also the first woman of any race in the United States to receive astronaut training.

These individuals are joined by numerous others in the field of aviation and space flight, including chemical engineer Henry Allen Jr., a liquid and solid rocket-fuel specialist; missile expert and inventor Otis Boykin; health services officer Julian M. Earls; astrodynamicist Robert A. Gordon; and operations officer Isaac T. Gillam IV, to name a few. Once the Space Shuttle Program began in earnest, however, African Americans also took to the skies.

In the field of astrophysics, Neil deGrasse Tyson, who is the author of several books on astronomy and was named one of the "50 Most Important Blacks in Research Science" in 2004, is the Frederick P. Rose director of the Hayden Planetarium at the American Museum of Natural History in New York City—the youngest director in the planetarium's history. His research interests include star formation, exploding stars, dwarf galaxies, and the structure of the Milky Way.

Traveling in the space shuttle *Challenger*, U.S. Air Force Colonel Guion "Guy" Bluford became the first African American in space. After his first mission in 1983, during which he coordinated experiments and was in charge of deploying satellites, Bluford participated in three more. Astronaut Ronald E. McNair was aboard the tragic *Challenger* flight of 1986, his second trip on the shuttle. The vehicle exploded seventy-three seconds after liftoff, killing all seven crew members. Charles F. Bolden Jr.'s first mission was aboard the 1986 flight of space shuttle *Columbia.* He has also flown on *Discovery.* In July 2009 President Barack Obama appointed Bolden to the post of NASA administrator, making him the first African American to head the agency on a permanent basis. The first African American to pilot a space shuttle was Frederick D. Gregory, who did so in 1985, on his first journey to outer space. A veteran pilot of both helicopters and airplanes, Gregory became an astronaut in 1978. Gregory also made history on his fourth flight, when he commanded the first mission comprised of Russians and Americans. Later, in 2005, he served as acting administrator of NASA. Mae C. Jemison served as a science specialist in 1992 on the joint U.S.–Japanese project on the shuttle *Endeavour*, thereby becoming the first African American woman in space. The following year, Bernard A. Harris Jr. took off in the space shuttle *Columbia.* He served as a mission specialist in Spacelab D2, alongside Germans and other Americans, and also became the first African American to walk in space.

MODERN CONTRIBUTIONS TO SCIENCE AND TECHNOLOGY

The achievements of African American inventors and scientists of the mid-twentieth to early twenty-first centuries have been obscured by reasons more complex than racial prejudice. The main reasons include the advent of government and corporate research-and-development teams. Such work, whether contracted or direct, often precludes individual recognition, regardless of a person's race. Nonetheless, in the corporate world, as well as in academia, African American scientists and engineers have played a substantial role in the development of solid-state devices, high-powered and ultrafast lasers, hypersonic flight—2,000 to 3,000 miles per hour—and elementary particle science. African American engineers employed by NASA in managerial and research positions have made, and continue to make, considerable contributions.

African American manufacturing and servicing firms in various computer and engineering areas have been established. For example, African American entrepreneur Marc R. Hannah made a niche for himself in the field of computer graphics as a cofounder of Silicon Graphics, Inc. As chief scientist and vice president of the company, Hannah adapted his electrical engineering and computer science know-how to a variety of applications, including military flight simulators and CAT scan devices. In addition, his computer-generated, 3-D special effects were featured in such major films as *Terminator 2* (1991), *Aladdin* (1992), and *Jurassic Park* (1993).

Academia has more African American science and technology faculty members, college presidents, and school of engineering deans than in the past. Many of these academics are serving in the country's most prestigious institutions. This progress has not continued, however, and there is cause for concern in the future. The 1970s was a decade of tremendous growth for minorities in science and engineering. In the 1980s, though, there was a progressive decline in the production of African American scientists, even though the numbers of Asian American and women scientists were still growing. In 1977, for example, people of color earned 13 percent of science and engineering doctorates, with Asian Americans earning 3 percent of these doctorates. By 1993, 16 percent of the degrees went to people of color, and Asian Americans earned 7 percent of them. In addition, women earned 40 percent of science and engineering doctorates in 1993, up from 25 percent in 1977. The numbers of African Americans entering scientific fields has slowly increased since the late 1980s, although they continue to be grossly underrepresented.

Another area in which African Americans have been faltering is medicine. In the mid to late 1990s, the number of African American applicants to medical school was declining at a high rate. The search for potential African American physicians neared crisis-level status. This shortage made it difficult for the poor and elderly to find African American attendants if they so desired. Primary-care specialists—including internists, pediatricians, obstetricians, and gynecologists—were particularly in demand.

The health-care profession began responding to this problem in 1991, when the Association of American Medical Colleges initiated Project 3000 by 2000—the primary aim being to graduate three thousand minorities by the year 2000. Xavier University was the top school in the country for African American placement into medical school, gaining a reputation for placing an average of 70 percent of its premed seniors into medical schools each year. Meanwhile, African American doctors already in practice were forming cooperatives to serve African American patients who were discriminated against by health-maintenance organizations (HMOs) that considered them too poor or sick to be participants.

The situation is not as dire in engineering, perhaps in part because of a mentoring program established in 1975 by the National Action Council for Minorities in Engineering. With industry backing, the council has focused on youngsters as early as the fourth-grade level. More than 4,700 of their students have acquired engineering degrees, and their graduates make up 10 percent of all engineers from minority groups. There is some indication, however, that fewer African Americans have been entering engineering fields since 1980. As of 1996, about 29 percent of the college-age population was made up of African Americans, Hispanic Americans, and Native Americans. This same group, though, accounted for less than 3 percent of engineering doctoral recipients.

Still, the importance of role models cannot be overlooked, and some African American scientists have entered into the public consciousness. For example, in 1973, Shirley Ann Jackson became the first African American woman in the United States to earn a Ph.D. in theoretical particle physics, as well as the first woman African American to earn a Ph.D. from the prestigious Massachusetts Institute of Technology. Jackson has had a distinguished career, including her 1995 appointment as chair of the Nuclear Regulatory Commission by President Bill Clinton. In 2009, President Barack Obama appointed her to the President's Council of Advisors on Science and Technology, along with another prominent African American physicist, S. James Gates Jr., a professor of physics and the director of the Center for String and Particle Theory at the University of Maryland, College Park.

Other noted African Americans in the science policy realm include Walter E. Massey and Shirley M. Malcom. Massey, who rose to the position of National Science Foundation (NSF) director, the highest science-related administrative post in the United States, ultimately was able to create a number of programs to provide science-oriented training to young African Americans. During his two-year stint at the NSF, from 1991 to 1993, Massey repeated the kind of success he had when he began the Inner City Teachers of Science program while teaching at Brown University. Malcom, as director of the Education and Human Resources division at the American

Association for the Advancement of Science since the 1990s, has worked to expand educational opportunities for underrepresented groups and promote public understanding of science and technology.

In the field of medical research, Charles F. Whitten in 1971 founded the National Association for Sickle Cell Disease, later renamed the Sickle Cell Disease Association of America. His work has been complemented more recently by Griffin Rodgers, who began serving as head of the Molecular and Clinical Hematology Branch of the National Institute of Diabetes and Digestive and Kidney Diseases (NIDDK) in 1998. Rodgers was instrumental in the development of the first effective therapy for the sickle-cell anemia. Later, in 2007, Rodgers was named director of the NIDDK.

Patients with prostate cancer have been encouraged by the work of Detroit-based urologist and oncologist Isaac J. Powell. In 1995, the Centers for Disease Control and Prevention named his screening program the outstanding community-health project of the year. Powell's program centered on advanced diagnostic testing for African American men. Through a partnership with the Karmanos Cancer Center and area churches, nurses, and hospitals, Powell worked to educate the public about the importance of undergoing prostate cancer screening. Benefiting from a prostate-specific antigen test, a number of patients had their cancer caught early enough to undergo successful surgery. Powell's program was later exported to other cities in the United States.

The cancer research of a young African American biologist, Jill Bargonetti, has garnered much attention. She discovered a correlation between a specific gene's ability to bind with the genetic matter known as DNA and its ability to suppress tumors. In 1996, she received a $300,000, three-year grant from the American Cancer Society and a $200,000, four-year award from the Department of Defense to pursue her study of breast cancer.

Outside of medical research, Olympic track-and-field medalist and engineering physicist Meredith Gourdine earned a Ph.D. from the California Institute of Technology in 1960. He then formed Gourdine Systems, a research-and-development firm geared toward patenting inventions using state-of-the-art power sources developed from advanced research in physics. Though blinded by diabetes in 1973, Gourdine launched Energy Innovations that same year. An inventor at heart, Gourdine was issued around seventy patents during his lifetime, and he was inducted into the Engineering and Science Hall of Fame in 1994.

The energy of earthquakes was the central concern of geophysicist Waverly J. Person. His interest in seismology paid off when he was named director of the U.S. Geological Survey's National Earthquake Information Center in 1977. One of the first African American earthquake scientists, Person was also the first African American in more than thirty years to hold such a prominent position within the U.S. Department of the Interior.

Similarly, meteorologist Warren M. Washington has been concerned with earth's climate. Since 1987, he has been director of the Climate Change Research Section of the National Center for Atmospheric Research's Climate and Global Dynamics Division. In 1994, he was elected to a one-year term as the first African American president of the American Meteorological Society. Washington also cofounded the Black Environmental Science Trust, a nonprofit foundation dedicated to increasing African American participation in environmental research and policymaking.

Majora Carter and Van Jones have been fighting for environmental justice in New York and California, respectively. Carter has been focused on city planning and urban renewal through an environmental lens, while Jones, who briefly worked for the Obama administration as "green jobs czar," has been advocating for green jobs through vocational education to support energy efficiency. Also new to the national stage is Lisa P. Jackson. President Obama appointed Jackson the administrator of the Environmental Protection Agency (EPA) in early 2009, handing her responsibility for leading the agency's efforts to protect human health and the environment for all Americans. Jackson is the first African American to serve as EPA administrator. She has made it a priority to focus on vulnerable groups that are particularly susceptible to environmental and health threats, including children, the elderly, and low-income communities.

In the 1990s and into the early twenty-first century, personal computers and the World Wide Web have been one of the largest areas of scientific and industrial invention. In 1989, Philip Emeagwali, one of the "fathers" of the Internet, created a formula that used 65,000 separate computer processors to perform 3.1 billion calculations per second. This feat allowed computer scientists to comprehend the capabilities of computers to communicate with one another. Another innovator is Omar Wasow, the cofounder of BlackPlanet.com who created the "community" strategy of running Web domains that almost all Internet sites use to maximize efficiency. African Americans have also used the computer to create programs to aid everyday life and government. One such example is Athan Gibbs, who in 2002 introduced the TruVote validation system, a computer touch-screen system that allows voters to touch the picture of the candidate they chose to vote for, eliminating confusion among voters and possible corruption of ballots.

Along with hundreds of other notable African Americans, scientists have been working toward restoring scientific education at all levels. Their presence, whether inside or outside of the public eye, is felt. Younger African Americans who learn of their endeavors are encouraged to free their creative science minds. Organizations that support the careers of African American scientists, engineers, and health practitioners include the National Action Council for Minorities in Engineering, the National Organization for the Professional Advancement of Black Chemists and Chemical Engineers, the National Society of Black Engineers, the National Society of Black Physicists, the National Technical Association, the National Black Nurses Association, the National Dental Association, and the National Medical Association.

ENGINEERS, MATHEMATICIANS, INVENTORS, PHYSICIANS, AND SCIENTISTS

(Some biographical profiles may appear in other chapters. To locate profiles more readily, please consult the index.)

Physicist George E. Alcorn. *One of the most prominent people working with semiconductors and spectrometers in the late twentieth and early twenty-first centuries, Alcorn holds a number of patents and has served in a variety of roles in private industry and at NASA.* **IMAGE PROVIDED BY GEORGE E. ALCORN.**

GEORGE E. ALCORN (1940–)

Physicist. George Edward Alcorn was born on March 22, 1940, in Miami, Florida. He graduated with a B.S. in physics from Occidental College in 1962 and then earned an M.S. in nuclear physics from Howard University in 1963. In 1967, he earned his Ph.D. from Howard University in atomic and molecular physics. After earning his Ph.D., Alcorn spent eleven years working in industry at Perkin-Elmer, Philco-Ford, and IBM.

Alcorn left IBM, where he had worked as a second plateau inventor, to join NASA in 1978. While at NASA, Alcorn invented an imaging X-ray spectrometer using thermomigration of aluminum, for which he earned a patent in 1984, and two years later he devised an improved method of fabrication using laser drilling. His work on imaging X-ray spectrometers earned him the 1984 NASA/Goddard Space Flight Center (GSFC) Inventor of the Year Award. During this period, he also served as deputy project manager for advanced development and was responsible for developing new technologies required for the space station Freedom. He also managed the GSFC Evolution Program, concerned with ensuring that over its thirty-year mission the space station develops properly while incorporating new capabilities.

From 1992 to 2004, Alcorn served as chief of Goddard's Office of Commercial Programs, supervising programs for technology transfer, small business innovation research, and the commercial use of space programs. He managed a shuttle flight experiment that involved the Robot Operated Material Processing System in 1994. In 2005, he became assistant director for standards/excellence in the Applied Engineering and Technology Directorate at Goddard.

In 1999, Alcorn received the *Government Executive Magazine*'s Government Technology Leadership Award for developing and commercializing a mapping system called the Airborne LIDAR Topographic Mapping System. In 2001, he was awarded special congressional recognition for his efforts in assisting Virgin Islands businesses use NASA technology and programs.

Alcorn holds a number of patents. He is a recognized pioneer in the fabrication of plasma semiconductor devices, and his patent "Process for Controlling the Slope of a Via Hole" was an important contribution to the process of plasma etching. This procedure is now used by many semiconductor manufacturing companies. Alcorn was one of the first scientists to present a computer-modeling solution of wet-etched and plasma-etched structures, and he has received several cash prizes for his inventions of plasma-processing techniques.

ARCHIE ALEXANDER (1888–1958)

Civil Engineer. Born on May 14, 1888, in Ottumwa, Iowa, Archie Alphonso Alexander graduated from the University of Iowa with a B.S. in civil engineering in 1912. During his collegiate years, he was a star football player who earned the nickname Alexander the Great on the playing field.

His first job was as a design engineer for the Marsh Engineering Company, a company that specialized in building bridges. Two years later, in 1914, Alexander formed his own company, A.A. Alexander, Inc. Most of the firm's contracts were for bridges and sewer systems. So successful was he that the NAACP awarded him its Spingarn Medal in 1928. The following year, he formed Alexander and Repass with a former classmate. Alexander's new company was also responsible for building tunnels, railroad trestles, viaducts, and power plants. Some of Alexander's biggest accomplishments include the Tidal Basin Bridge and K Street Freeway in Washington, D.C.; a heating plant for his alma mater, the University of Iowa; a civilian airfield in Tuskegee, Alabama; and a sewage disposal plant in Grand Rapids, Michigan.

A member of Kappa Alpha Psi, Alexander was awarded their "Laurel Wreath" for great accomplishment in 1925. Alexander received honorary civil engineering degrees from the University of Iowa in 1925 and Howard University in 1946. In 1947, he was named one of the University of Iowa's outstanding alumni and "one of the first hundred citizens of merit." Politically active, Alexander was appointed governor of the Virgin Islands in 1954 by President Dwight Eisenhower, though he was forced to resign one year later because of health problems. He died at his home in Des Moines, Iowa, on January 4, 1958.

BENJAMIN BANNEKER (1731–1806)

Mathematician, Statistician, Astronomer, Surveyor, Explorer, Publisher. Benjamin Banneker was born on November 9, 1731, on a tobacco farm near Baltimore, Maryland. His mother was a free woman, and his father had been enslaved to her. She purchased his freedom and they married. When he was twenty-one, Banneker became interested in watches and later constructed a clock based on a pocket watch he had seen, calculating the ratio of the gears and wheels and carving them from wood. The clock operated for more than forty years.

Benjamin Banneker Commemorative Stamp, 1980. *Banneker was honored with a 15-cent stamp as part of the Black Heritage series. Considered the first African American scientist, Banneker in the late eighteenth century published an almanac that was the first scientific book by an African American. He served on the surveying team that helped lay out the base lines and initial boundaries for Washington, D.C.* **UPI/CORBIS-BETTMANN. REPRODUCED BY PERMISSION.**

Banneker's aptitude for mathematics and knowledge of astronomy enabled him to accurately predict the solar eclipse of 1789. Two years later, he began publishing an almanac that contained tide tables, weather information, data on future eclipses, and a listing of useful medicinal products and formulas. The almanac, which was the first scientific book published by an African American, appeared annually for more than a decade. Banneker sent a copy to Thomas Jefferson, and the two corresponded, debating the subject of African enslavement.

In the early 1790s, Banneker served as a surveyor on the six-person team that helped lay out the base lines and initial boundaries for Washington, D.C. He died in 1806 on October 25 (some sources say October 9).

REGINA M. BENJAMIN (1956–)

Doctor, Entrepreneur, Surgeon General. Vice Admiral Regina M. Benjamin is the eighteenth surgeon general of the U.S. Public Health Service. Born on October 26, 1956, in Mobile, Alabama, Benjamin has a B.S. in chemistry from Xavier University in New Orleans, an M.D. from the University of Alabama, Birmingham, and an M.B.A. from Tulane University. She attended Morehouse School of Medicine and completed her family medicine residency in Macon, Georgia.

Prior to her appointment as surgeon general in 2009, Benjamin was founder and CEO of the Bayou La Batre Rural Health Clinic in Alabama, associate dean for rural health at the University of South Alabama College of Medicine in Mobile, and chair of the Federation of State Medical Boards. In 1995, she became the first physician under age forty and the first African American woman to be elected to the Board of Trustees of the American Medical Association (AMA). She served as president of the AMA Education and Research Foundation and chair of the AMA Council on Ethical and Judicial Affairs. In 2002, she became president of the Medical Association of the State of Alabama, making her the first African American woman president of a state medical society in the United States.

Benjamin is a member of the National Academy of Science's Institute of Medicine and a fellow of the American Academy of Family Physicians. She was a Kellogg National Fellow and a Rockefeller Next Generation Leader. Her numerous board memberships include the Robert Wood Johnson Foundation, the Kaiser Commission on Medicaid and the Uninsured, the Catholic Health Association, and Morehouse School of Medicine. In addition to being awarded a MacArthur Fellowship (often called the "genius grant"), Benjamin has been the recipient of a number of other honors, including the Nelson Mandela Award for Health and Human Rights and the National Caring Award, an award inspired by the life of Mother Teresa.

DAVID BLACKWELL (1919–)

Mathematician, Professor. Considered by some to be the greatest African American mathematician of all time, David Blackwell, the eldest of four children, was born on April 24, 1919, in Centralia, Illinois. As a schoolboy, Blackwell gravitated toward the study of geometry and then, after taking a course in introductory analysis, fell in love with mathematics.

Following high school graduation, Blackwell began mathematics study at the University of Illinois in 1935, when he was sixteen years old. He earned an A.B. in 1938 and an A.M. a year later, before earning a Ph.D. in 1941 at age twenty-two. After graduation, he received an appointment to a prestigious postdoctoral fellowship—the Rosenwald Fellowship—at Princeton University's Institute for Advanced Study. Although his colleagues wished to renew his one-year appointment, the president of the university organized a protest and admonished the institute for offering the fellowship to an African American. However, during this period—the 1950s and 1960s—Martin Luther King Jr. and other civil rights leaders brought the issue of racial equality to the forefront of the American consciousness, and Blackwell was able to rise in the ranks of academia at other institutions.

Blackwell obtained instructorships at Southern University and Clark College before being named to the faculty of Howard University in 1944. In three years, Blackwell advanced from his instructor position to full professor, then to chairman of the department. He also spent time at RAND Corporation and was a visiting professor of statistics at Stanford University from 1950 to 1951.

While at Stanford, Blackwell met M. A. Girshick, a faculty member in the agriculture department. The two men began a collaboration that lasted about a decade and resulted in many articles and a book, *Theory of Games and Statistical Decisions* (1954), which became a classic in the field.

Blackwell returned to Howard University, where he remained until 1954. He then was appointed professor of statistics and chairman of the statistics department at the University of California, Berkeley, where he remained until his retirement in 1989. He was that university's first tenured African American professor. In his career, Blackwell published over eighty papers in topics that included Bayesian statistics, probability, game theory, set theory, dynamic programming, and information theory.

Blackwell served as president of the Institute of Mathematical Sciences in 1955; vice president of the American Statistical Association, the International Statistical Institute, and the American Mathematical Society; and president of the Bernoulli Society. In 1965, he became the first African American to be named to the National Academy of Sciences. In addition, he was named honorary fellow of the Royal Statistical Society and a member of the American Academy of Arts and Sciences.

Among his numerous honorary degrees and prizes, Blackwell in 1979 was awarded the John von Neumann Theory Prize by the Operations Research Society of America. In 2002, the Mathematical Sciences Research Institute at Berkeley and Cornell University established the Blackwell-Tapia Award to honor Blackwell and fellow mathematician Richard A. Tapia for inspiring generations of African American and Hispanic American students and professionals in the mathematical sciences. The University of California, Berkeley, Department of Statistics, where Blackwell is a professor emeritus, has also established the David Blackwell Fund to support high-achieving graduate students within the department.

GUION S. BLUFORD JR. (1942–)

Space/Atmospheric Scientist, Aerospace Engineer, Air Force Officer, Airplane Pilot. Guion S. "Guy" Bluford Jr. was born on November 22, 1942, in Philadelphia. In 1964, he graduated with a B.S. in aerospace engineering from Pennsylvania State University. He then enlisted in the U.S. Air Force and was assigned to pilot training at Williams Air Force Base in Arizona. Bluford served as a fighter pilot in Vietnam and flew 144 combat missions, 65 of them over North Vietnam. Attaining the rank of lieutenant colonel, Bluford received both an M.S. (1974) and a Ph.D. (1978), both in aerospace engineering, from the Air Force Institute of Technology.

In 1979, Bluford was accepted into NASA's astronaut program as a mission specialist. On August 30, 1983, with the liftoff of the space shuttle *Challenger*, Bluford became the first African American in space. He flew three other space shuttle missions—aboard *Challenger* in 1985 and aboard *Discovery* in 1991 and 1992—for a total of 688 hours in space.

Bluford left NASA in July 1993 and retired from the Air Force to take a post of vice president and general manager of the Engineering Services Division of NYMA, Inc., based in Greenbelt, Maryland. In May 1997, he became vice president of the Aerospace Sector of Federal Data Corporation and then in October 2000 became vice president of Microgravity R&D and Operations for Northrop Grumman Corporation. He retired from Northrop Grumman in September 2002 to become president of the Aerospace Technology Group, an engineering consulting organization in Cleveland, Ohio.

Bluford has won numerous awards, including the Distinguished National Scientist Award given by the National Society of Black Engineers (1979), the NASA Group Achievement Award (1980, 1981, 1989, and 2003), the NAACP Image Award (1983), and the Air Force Institute of Technology Distinguished Alumni Award (2002). His military honors include the National Defense Service Medal (1965), the Vietnam Campaign Medal (1967), Air Force Commendation Medal (1972), Air Force Meritorious Service Award (1978), and the

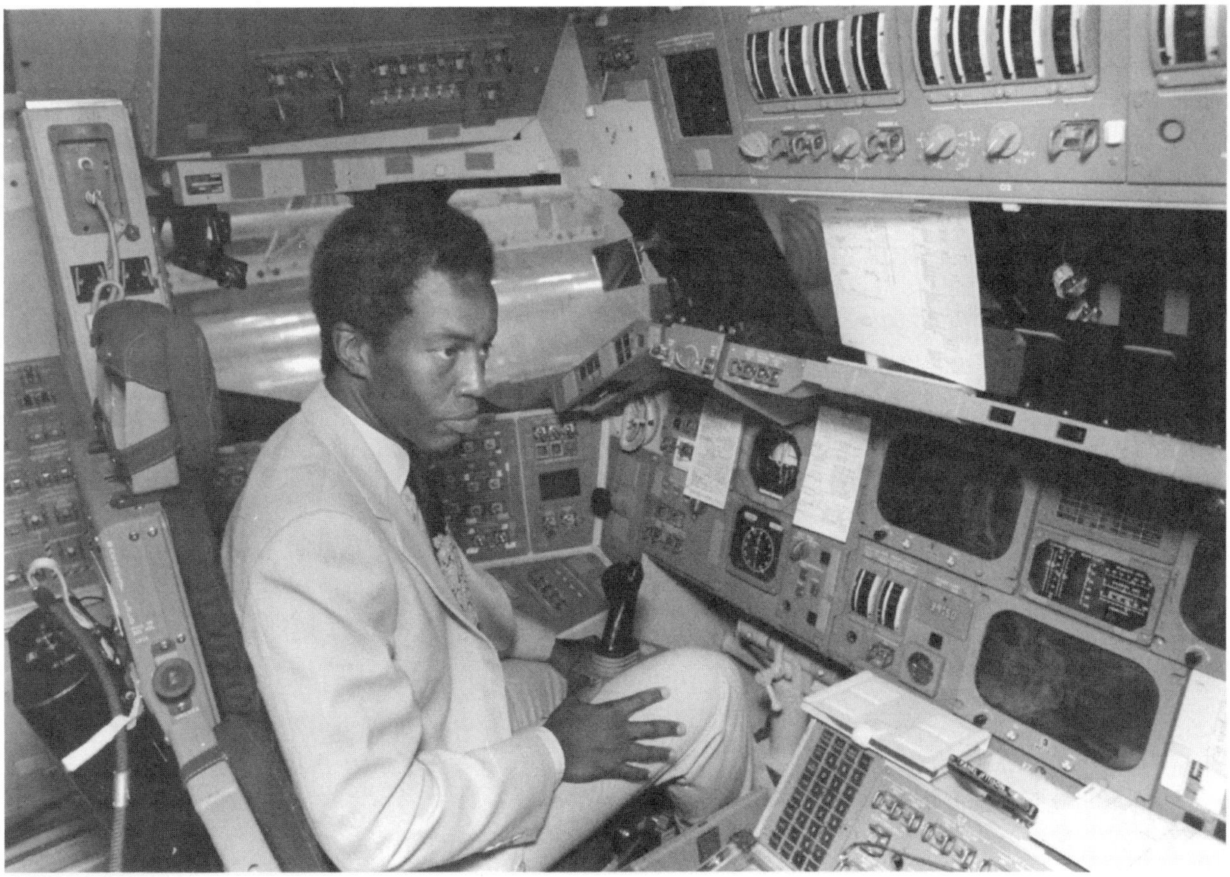

Guion S. Bluford Jr. *A U.S. Air Force pilot and officer and an aerospace engineer, Bluford became the first African American in space during a 1983 mission of the space shuttle* Challenger. *He later participated in three more shuttle missions, all as a mission specialist.* **AP IMAGES**

USAF Command Pilot Astronaut Wings (1983). In 1997, Bluford was inducted into the International Space Hall of Fame.

CHARLES F. BOLDEN JR. (1946–)

NASA Administrator, Airplane Pilot, Space/Atmospheric Scientist, Marine Officer, Operations and Systems Researcher and Analyst. Nominated by President Barack Obama and confirmed by the U.S. Senate, Charles Frank Bolden Jr., a retired Marine Corps major general, began his duties as the twelfth administrator of the National Aeronautics and Space Administration on July 17, 2009. As administrator, he leads the NASA team and manages its resources to advance the agency's missions and goals.

Bolden's confirmation marked the beginning of his second stint with the nation's space agency. His thirty-four-year career with the Marine Corps included fourteen years as a member of NASA's Astronaut Office. After joining the office in 1980, he traveled to orbit four times aboard the space shuttle between 1986 and 1994, commanding two of the missions. His flights included the deployment of the Hubble Space Telescope and the first joint U.S.–Russian shuttle mission, which featured a cosmonaut as a member of his crew.

Born in Columbia, South Carolina, on August 19, 1946, Bolden earned a B.S. in electrical science from the U.S. Naval Academy in 1968 and an M.S. in systems management from the University of Southern California in 1977. He began his career as a second lieutenant in the Marine Corps, becoming a naval aviator by 1970. In 1972 and 1973, he flew more than 100 combat missions while stationed in Thailand. Upon his return to the United States, Bolden began a tour as a Marine Corps selection and recruiting officer. In 1979, he graduated from the U.S. Naval Test Pilot School.

Bolden has been awarded the Defense Superior Service Medal, the Defense Meritorious Service Medal, the Air Medal, the Legion of Merit, and the Strike/Flight Medal. He was appointed assistant deputy administrator of NASA headquarters in 1992 and was promoted to the rank of major general in 1998. He served as commanding general of the Third Marine Aircraft Wing from 2000 to 2002. After retiring from NASA in 2003, Bolden served as senior vice president at TechTrans International, Inc., until 2005. Prior to his appointment and confirmation as NASA administrator, Bolden was CEO of JackandPanther LLC, a privately held military and aerospace consulting firm.

MARJORIE L. BROWNE (1914–1979)

Mathematician, Statistician, Educator. Marjorie Lee Browne was born on September 9, 1914, in Memphis, Tennessee. She received a B.S. in mathematics from Howard University in 1935, an M.S. from the University of Michigan in 1939, and a Ph.D. in mathematics, again from the University of Michigan, in 1949. Browne was one of the first two African American women to earn a Ph.D. in mathematics. She taught at the University of Michigan in 1947 and 1948. She accepted the post of professor of mathematics at North Carolina College (later North Carolina Central University) in 1949 and became department chairperson in 1951. In 1960, she received a grant from IBM to establish one of the first computer centers at a minority university.

Browne's doctoral dissertation dealt with topological and matrix groups, and she was published in the *American Mathematical Monthly*. She was a fellow of the National Science Foundation from 1958 to 1959 and again from 1965 to 1966. Browne was a member of the American Mathematical Society, the Mathematical Association of America, and the Society for Industrial and Applied Mathematics. She died on October 19, 1979.

ALEXA I. CANADY (1950–)

Neurosurgeon. Alexa Irene Canady, the first African American woman to become a neurosurgeon in the United States, was born to Elizabeth Hortense (Golden) Canady and Clinton Canady Jr., a dentist, on November 7, 1950, in Lansing, Michigan. Canady was recognized as a National Achievement Scholar while in high school, and she attended the University of Michigan, where she received a B.S. in 1971 and an M.D. in 1975. As a medical student, she was elected to the Alpha Omega Alpha honorary medical society and received the American Medical Women's Association citation.

Canady's internship was spent at the Yale–New Haven Hospital from 1975 to 1976. She gained her landmark residency in neurosurgery at the University of Minnesota from 1976 to 1981. She was the first woman and first African American to be granted a residency in neurosurgery at the hospital. Following her residency, Children's Hospital in Philadelphia awarded Canady a fellowship in pediatric neurosurgery in 1981–1982. In addition to treating patients directly, Canady served as an instructor in neurosurgery at the University of Pennsylvania College of Medicine.

In 1982 she accepted a position at Henry Ford Hospital in Detroit. The following year, Canady transferred to pediatric neurosurgery at Children's Hospital of Michigan, where she became the assistant director of neurosurgery at Children's Hospital three years later and director in 1987.

She began teaching at Wayne State University's School of Medicine as a clinical instructor in 1985 and assumed a clinical associate professorship at the same institution in 1987. Canady retired in 2001, at which point she was the chief of neurosurgery at Children's Hospital of Michigan. Among her numerous honors and awards, Canady was inducted into the Michigan Women's Hall of Fame and was named Woman of the Year in 1993 by the American Women's Medical Association. Throughout her career, Canady worked to change the perception of African Americans as patients and as physicians. Having been lured out of retirement Canady continues to work as a pediatric neurosurgeon at Sacred Heart Medical Group's Institute for Neurology and Neurosurgery in Pensacola, Florida.

GEORGE R. CARRUTHERS (1939–)

Astrophysicist. George Robert Carruthers was one of the two Naval Research Laboratory people responsible for the *Apollo 16* far-ultraviolet camera/spectrograph, which was placed on the lunar surface in April 1972. It was Carruthers who designed the instrument, while William Conway adapted the camera for the lunar mission. The spectrographs, obtained from eleven targets, include the first photographs of the ultraviolet equatorial bands of atomic oxygen that girdle earth. The camera was also used on Skylab in 1974.

Carruthers, who was born on October 1, 1939, in Cincinnati, Ohio, grew up on Chicago's South Side. He built his first telescope when he was ten years old. He received his Ph.D. in aeronautical and astronautical engineering from the University of Illinois in 1964.

In 1966, Carruthers became a research assistant at the Naval Research Laboratory's E. O. Hulburt Center for Space Research, where he began work on the lunar surface far-ultraviolet camera/spectrograph. The images received from the moon gave researchers invaluable information about earth's atmosphere, including possible new ways to control air pollution. The images also aided in the detection of hydrogen in deep space—evidence that plants are not the only source of earth's oxygen.

Carruthers has continued his research and became a senior astrophysicist in the Space Science Division of the Naval Research Laboratory in 1982. He is the recipient of the NASA Exceptional Scientific Achievement Medal for his work on the far-ultraviolet camera/spectrograph. Carruthers also won the Arthur S. Fleming Award in 1971 and the 2000 Outstanding Scientist Award presented by the National Institute of Science. In 2003 he was inducted into the National Inventors Hall of Fame in Akron, Ohio. In 2004 he was chosen as one of "50 Most Important Blacks in Research Science," and in 2009 Carruthers was honored as a Distinguished Lecturer at the Office of Naval Research for his achievements in the field of space science.

BENJAMIN S. CARSON (1951–)

Neurosurgeon. Born Benjamin Solomon Carson on September 18, 1951, in Detroit, Michigan, Carson has been recognized throughout the international medical community for his prowess in performing complex neurosurgical procedures, particularly on children with pediatric brain tumors.

Among his accomplishments are a number of successful hemispherectomies, a process in which a portion of the brain of a critically ill seizure victim or other neurologically diseased patient is removed to radically reduce the incidence of seizures. Carson's most famous operation took place in 1987, earning him international acclaim. That year, he successfully separated a pair of West German Siamese, or conjoined, twins who had been attached at the backs of their heads. The landmark operation took twenty-two hours; Carson led a surgical team of seventy doctors, nurses, and technicians.

Carson was raised in Detroit. His mother, Sonya Carson, had dropped out of school in the third grade and married at age thirteen. She divorced when Carson was eight years old and raised her two sons as a single mother, working several jobs. Known for his quick temper, Carson was a problem student—he almost killed a peer during a knife fight when he was fourteen years old. He was also a failing student, and although she could barely read herself, his mother imposed a reading program on him and limited his television viewing until his grades improved.

In high school, he continued to excel and was accepted at Yale University in 1969 with a scholarship. With a B.A. in psychology from Yale, Carson entered the University of Michigan, where his interest shifted to neurosurgery and where he obtained his M.D. in 1977. For one year, he served as a surgical intern at the Johns Hopkins Hospital, later doing his residency there. From 1983 to 1984, Carson practiced at the Sir Charles Gairdner Hospital in Perth, Australia. In 1984, at thirty-three years of age, he became the youngest chief of pediatric neurosurgery in the United States. Then, in 1985, Johns Hopkins named him director of the division of pediatric neurosurgery. Carson is a professor of neurosurgery, oncology, plastic surgery, and pediatrics at Johns Hopkins. He is also the codirector of the Johns Hopkins Craniofacial Center.

In 2002, Carson, a devout Seventh-day Adventist, was diagnosed with a high-grade prostate cancer that was treated successfully with surgery. He later stated that his experience as a patient made him a more empathetic physician and more devoted to disease prevention.

Carson has written four best-selling books: *Gifted Hands* (1990), *Think Big* (1992), *The Big Picture* (1999), and *Take the Risk* (2008). He has also established a scholarship fund, called the Carson Scholars Fund, with the aid of his wife, Candy Carson, and cofounded the Benevolent Endowment Network Fund to assist underinsured and uninsured patients requiring brain surgery.

Carson has been awarded more than three dozen honorary degrees and numerous awards for his work, including the Spingarn Medal, which the NAACP presented to him in 2006. Carson was inducted into Indiana Wesleyan University's Society of World Changers in 2007, and a year later President George W. Bush presented him with a Presidential Medal of Freedom.

GEORGE WASHINGTON CARVER
(c. 1864–1943)

Educator, Agricultural/Food Scientist, Farmer. George Washington Carver devoted his life to research projects connected primarily with southern agriculture. The products he derived from the peanut and the soybean revolutionized the economy of the South by liberating it from an excessive dependence on cotton.

Born enslaved in Diamond Grove, Missouri, sometime between 1861 and 1865, Carver was only an infant when his mother was abducted from his owner's plantation by a band of raiders. His mother was sold and shipped away, and Carver was raised by his mother's owners, Moses and Susan Carver. Carver was a frail and sickly child, and he was assigned lighter chores around the house. Later, he was allowed to attend high school in a neighboring town.

Carver worked odd jobs while he pursued his education. He was the second African American student admitted at Simpson College in Indianola, Iowa. He then

George Washington Carver, Tuskegee Institute, Alabama, c. 1920. *Long associated with Tuskegee, Carver left an indelible mark on Southern agriculture through his ideas ranging from crop rotation to replenishment of nutrient-starved soil and his advocacy of peanuts as a cash crop.* **SCHOMBURG CENTER FOR RESEARCH IN BLACK CULTURE; THE NEW YORK PUBLIC LIBRARY; ASTOR, LENOX AND TILDEN FOUNDATIONS**

attended Iowa State Agricultural College (now Iowa State University), where, while working as the school janitor, he received a degree in agricultural science in 1894. Two years later, he received a master's degree from the same school and became the first African American to serve on its faculty. Within a short time, his fame spread, and Booker T. Washington offered him a post at Tuskegee Institute (later Tuskegee University). It was at Tuskegee's Agricultural Experimental Station that Carver did most of his work.

Carver revolutionized the southern agricultural economy by showing that three hundred products could be derived from the peanut. By 1938, peanuts had become a $200 million industry and a chief product of Alabama. Carver also demonstrated that one hundred different products could be derived from the sweet potato.

Although he did hold three patents, Carver never patented most of the discoveries he made while at Tuskegee, saying, "God gave them to me, how can I sell them to someone else?" In 1940 he established the George Washington Carver Foundation and willed the rest of his estate to the organization, so his work might be carried on after his death. He died in Tuskegee on January 5, 1943.

JEWEL PLUMMER COBB (1924–)

Cell Biologist. Born in Chicago on January 17, 1924, Jewel Plummer Cobb grew up exposed to a variety of African American professionals through her parents. Her father, Frank Plummer, was a physician, and her mother, Carriebel (Cole) Plummer, was an interpretive dancer. By 1950, she had completed her M.S. and Ph.D. in biology, both earned from New York University. As a cell biologist, her focus was the action and interaction of living cells. She was particularly interested in tissue culture, in which cells are grown outside the body and studied under microscopes.

Among her most important work was her study—with Dorothy Walker Jones—of how new cancer-fighting drugs affect human cancer cells. Cobb also conducted research into skin pigment. She was particularly interested in melanoma, a form of skin cancer, and melanin's ability to protect skin from damage caused by ultraviolet light.

Cobb noted the scarcity of women in scientific fields, and she wrote about the difficulties women face in a 1979 paper, "Filters for Women in Science." In this piece, Cobb argued that various pressures, particularly in the educational system, act as filters that prevent many women from choosing science careers. The socialization of girls has tended to discourage them from pursuing math and the sciences from a very early age, and even those women who got past such obstacles have struggled to get university tenure and the same jobs (at equal pay) as men.

From 1969 to 1976, Cobb served as dean of Connecticut College, where she was also a professor of zoology. She then moved on to Rutgers University's Douglass College for a five-year stint as dean and professor of biological sciences. After serving as president of California State University in Fullerton from 1981 to 1990, Cobb was named president emerita. Throughout her career, she was active in her community, recruiting women and minorities to the sciences, and she also founded a privately funded gerontology center in Orange County, California.

Among her numerous honors and awards, Cobb in 1993 was awarded the Lifetime Achievement Award from the National Science Foundation for her contributions to the advancement of women and underrepresented minorities. On October 30, 2008, she was inducted into the Connecticut Women's Hall of Fame, where she was recognized for her distinguished career in cell biology and for her efforts to encourage women and minorities to enter scientific careers.

W. MONTAGUE COBB (1904–1990)

Anthropologist, Organization Executive and Founder, Medical Researcher, Educator, Editor. William Montague Cobb was born on October 12, 1904, in Washington, D.C. For more than forty years, he was a member of the Howard University Medical School faculty; thousands of medical and dental students studied under his direction. At Howard, he built a collection of more than six hundred documented skeletons and a comparative anatomy museum in the gross anatomy laboratory. In addition to a B.A. from Amherst College (1925), an M.D. from Howard University (1929), and a Ph.D. from Western Reserve University (1932, later Case Western), he received many honorary degrees. Cobb died on November 20, 1990, in Washington, D.C.

As editor of the *Journal of the National Medical Association* for twenty-eight years, Cobb developed a wide range of scholarly interests manifested by the nearly seven hundred published works under his name in the fields of medical education, anatomy, physical anthropology, public health, and medical history. He was the first African American elected to the presidency of the American Association of Physical Anthropologists and served as the chairman of the anthropology section of the American Association for the Advancement of Science. Among his many scientific awards is the highest award given by the American Association of Anatomists. For thirty-one years, he was a member of the board of directors of the NAACP and served as the president of the board from 1976 to 1982.

PRICE M. COBBS (1928–)

Psychiatrist, Author, Management Consultant. Cobbs was born Price Mashaw Cobbs in Los Angeles on November 2, 1928, and followed in his father's path when he enrolled in medical school after earning a B.A. from the University of California, Berkeley, in 1954. He graduated from Meharry Medical College with an M.D. in psychiatric medicine in 1958 and, within a few years, had established his own San Francisco practice in psychiatry.

With his academic colleague at the University of California, William H. Grier, Cobbs cowrote the groundbreaking 1968 study, *Black Rage*. In it, the authors argued that a pervasive social and economic racism had resulted in an endemic anger that stretched across all strata of African American society, from rich to poor; this anger was both apparent and magnified by the social unrest of the 1960s. Cobbs and Grier also cowrote a second book, *The Jesus Bag* (1971), which discussed the role of organized religion in the African American community. In 2003, Cobbs cowrote *Cracking the Corporate Code: The Revealing Success Stories of 32 African-American Executives* with Judith L. Turnock. Cobbs's autobiography, *My American Life: From Rage to Entitlement*, was published in 2005.

A seminar Cobbs held in the mid-1970s with other mental health-care professionals eventually led him to found his own diversity training company, Pacific Management Systems (PMS). The company has been instrumental in providing sensitivity training for *Fortune* 500 companies, community groups, law enforcement bodies, and social service agencies.

Cobbs belongs to numerous African American professional and community organizations, and has served as an assistant clinical professor at the University of California at San Francisco. He continues to guide PMS well into its fourth decade. The firm has pioneered the concept of ethnotherapy, which uses the principles of group therapy to help seminar participants rethink their attitudes toward members of other ethnic groups, persons with disabilities, and those of alternative sexual orientations.

PATRICIA S. COWINGS (1948–)

Psychophysiologist. Patricia Suzanne Cowings, the first woman scientist trained as an astronaut—although she never was sent into space—was born in New York City on December 15, 1948. She was fascinated by astronomy as a young girl, and this interest continued through high school, at New York City's High School of Music and Arts, and in college.

Cowings received her B.A. in psychology from the State University of New York, Stony Brook, in 1970 and her M.A. and Ph.D. in psychology from the University of California, Davis, in 1973. She received a research scholarship at NASA and then taught for some time before returning to NASA in 1977.

Cowings spent more than thirty years at the NASA Ames Research Center in Moffett Field, California, where she was director of the Gravitational Research Branch and the science director of the Psychophysiological Research Laboratory. In addition to working with Russian cosmonauts for several years, Cowings spent fifteen years as the principal investigator for space shuttle experiments on autogenic feedback training, a method she developed for preventing zero-gravity sickness, which is comparable with motion sickness on earth. Her program, which combines training and biofeedback, offers an effective method for controlling such processes as heart rate, blood pressure, and body temperature during space flight. She believes in the ability of the mind to control the body's responses in adapting to an unfamiliar environment.

Cowings has received numerous honors and awards, including the Research Leadership Award at the Eleventh Annual National Women of Color Technology Awards Conference in 2006. Cowings was inducted into the Women in Technology International (WITI) Hall of Fame in 2009 for her "contributions to science and technology [that] help shape the next generation of scientists and technologists and make the world a better place."

ELBERT F. COX (1895–1969)

Educator, Mathematician, Statistician. Elbert Frank Cox was born in Evansville, Indiana, on December 5, 1895. He received his B.A. from Indiana University in 1917 and his Ph.D. from Cornell University in 1925. His dissertation dealt with polynomial solutions and made Cox the first African American to be awarded a Ph.D. in pure mathematics.

Cox was an instructor at Shaw University from 1921 to 1923, a professor in physics and mathematics at West Virginia State College from 1925 to 1929, and an associate professor of mathematics at Howard University from 1929 to 1947. He was made full professor in 1947 and retired in 1966.

During his career, Cox specialized in interpolation theory and differential equations. Among his professional accolades were memberships in such educational societies as Beta Kappa Chi, Pi Mu Epsilon, and Sigma Pi Sigma. He was also active in the American Mathematical Society, the American Physical Society, and the American Physics Institute. Cox died on November 28, 1969.

ULYSSES G. DAILEY (1885–1961)

Editor, Health Administrator, Surgeon, Diplomat. From 1908 to 1912, Ulysses Grant Dailey served as surgical assistant to Dr. Daniel Hale Williams, founder of Provident Hospital and noted heart surgeon. Born in Donaldsonville, Louisiana, in 1885, Dailey graduated in 1906 from Northwestern University Medical School, where he was appointed a demonstrator in anatomy. He later studied in London, Paris, and Vienna, and in 1926 he set up his own hospital and sanitarium in Chicago. Dailey was associated with Provident Hospital after his own hospital closed in 1932, and he retained a position there until his death.

A member of the editorial board of the *Journal of the National Medical Association* for many years, Dailey traveled around the world in 1933 under the sponsorship of the International College of Surgeons, of which he was a founding member. In the 1950s, he traveled to Pakistan, India, Ceylon, and Africa for the U.S. State Department. In 1954, he was named honorary consul to Haiti, moving there in 1956 when he retired.

CHRISTINE M. DARDEN (1942–)

Aerospace Engineer. Christine Mann Darden was born on September 10, 1942, in Monroe, North Carolina. Valedictorian of her class at Allen High School in Asheville, North Carolina, she attended the Hampton Institute in Hampton, Virginia, and graduated with a B.S. in mathematics in 1962.

Darden joined NASA as a mathematician in 1967, but her interests began to shift to engineering. After teaching high school mathematics for a time, Darden began taking engineering classes at Virginia State College in Petersburg, Virginia. She received her M.S. in applied mathematics from Virginia State in 1978. In 1983, Darden earned a Ph.D. in mechanical engineering, specializing in fluid mechanics (the flow of gases and liquids), from George Washington University in Washington, D.C.

Darden returned to NASA and was given her first independent research project, which led to her study of sonic boom—an explosive sound caused by the shock wave that occurs when an airplane flies faster than the speed of sound. She later headed a team in the Supersonic Transport Research Project. Darden attempted to replicate the computer model in a real system to test her theory that the sonic boom of a supersonic flight could be minimized. She succeeded in her attempt when she was serving as a consultant to the joint Defense Advanced Research Projects Agency.

Darden served as a senior project engineer in the Advanced Vehicles Division at the NASA Langley Research Center in Hampton, Virginia, where she was the head of the Sonic Boom Group. Her team worked on aircraft that fly faster than the speed of sound (supersonic aircraft). By using wind tunnels and modifying the design of aircraft, her group's simulations of supersonic flight identified aircraft shapes that could reduce the effects of sonic boom. Reducing sonic boom, combined with new technology, enables significant reductions in air-flight times. In 2007, Darden retired from her position as the director of the Strategic Communications and Education program at NASA Langley.

CHARLES R. DREW (1904–1950)

Educator, Medical Researcher, Health Administrator, Surgeon, Physician. Using techniques already developed for separating and preserving blood, Charles Richard Drew pioneered further into the field of blood preservation and organized procedures from research to a clinical level, leading to the founding of the world's two largest blood banks just prior to World War II. Born on June 3, 1904, in Washington, D.C., Drew graduated from Amherst College in Massachusetts in 1926. He was not only an outstanding scholar but also the captain of the track team and a star halfback on the football team.

After receiving his medical degree from McGill University in 1933, Drew returned to Washington, D.C., to teach pathology at Howard University. In 1940, while working on his doctorate in medical science at Columbia University, he wrote a dissertation on "banked blood" and soon became such an expert in this field that the British government asked him to help set up the first blood bank in England. He also initiated the use of bloodmobiles, trucks equipped with refrigerators to transport blood and plasma to remote locations.

During World War II, Drew was appointed director of the American Red Cross blood donor project. Later, he served as chief surgeon at Freedmen's Hospital in Washington, D.C., as well as professor of surgery at Howard University's College of Medicine from 1941 to 1950. A recipient of the 1944 Spingarn Medal from the NAACP, Drew was killed in an automobile accident on April 1, 1950.

JOYCELYN ELDERS (1933–)

Physician, Endocrinologist, U.S. Surgeon General. Dr. Joycelyn Elders was born Minnie Lee Jones on August 13, 1933, in Schaal, Arkansas. The first of eight children, she grew up working in cotton fields. An avid reader, Jones earned a scholarship to Philander Smith College in Little Rock. Jones studied biology and chemistry in hopes of becoming a lab technician. She was inspired toward greater ambitions after meeting Edith Irby Jones (no relation), the first African American woman to study at the University of Arkansas School of Medicine. In college, Jones changed her name to Minnie Jocelyn Lee, but later dropped the name Minnie.

After obtaining her B.A., Jones served as a physical therapist in the U.S. Army in order to fund her postgraduate education. She was able to enroll in the University of Arkansas School of Medicine in 1956. However, as the only African American woman, and one of only three African American students, she and the other African Americans were forced to use a separate university dining facility—the one provided for the cleaning staff.

After a brief first marriage following college, Jones married Oliver B. Elders in 1960. The newly dubbed Joycelyn Elders fulfilled a pediatric internship at the University of Minnesota and then returned to Little Rock in 1961 for a residency at the University of Arkansas Medical Center. Her success in the position led her to be appointed chief pediatric resident, in charge of the all-white, all-male battery of residents and interns.

During the next twenty years, Elders forged a successful clinical practice, specializing in pediatric endocrinology (the study of glands). She published more than one hundred papers in that period and rose to professor of pediatrics, a position she held from 1976 until 1987, when she was named director of the Arkansas Department of Health.

Over the course of her career, Elders's focus shifted from diabetes in children to sexual behavior. At the Department of Health, Elders was able to pursue her public advocacy in regard to teenage pregnancy and sexually transmitted diseases. In 1993, President Bill Clinton nominated Elders for the U.S. surgeon general post, making her the first African American and the second woman to hold this position. Though her nomination was not unchallenged—many decried her liberal stance—the Senate confirmed her appointment on September 7, 1993.

Dr. Joycelyn Elders, Capitol Hill, Washington, DC, 1993. *Elders in 1993 became the first African American to hold the post of U.S. surgeon general.* AP PHOTO/DOUG MILLS

During her tenure, Elders attacked Medicaid for failing to help poverty-stricken women prevent unwanted pregnancies and faulted pharmaceutical companies for overpricing contraceptives. Between 1993 and December 1994, she spoke out in support of the medicinal use of marijuana, studying drug legalization, and family planning, and against toy guns for children. An uproar was raised when Elders was reported to have recommended that masturbation be discussed in schools as part of human sexuality. When she refused to resign over this controversy, Clinton fired her in December 1994.

Elders returned to the University of Arkansas Medical School and resumed teaching, though the state's General Assembly budget committee tried to block her return. In 1995, she joined the board of the American Civil Liberties Union. In 1996, her autobiography, titled *Joycelyn Elders M.D.: From Sharecropper's Daughter to Surgeon General of the United States of America*, was published. Although Elders retired from medicine in 1999, she continues to lecture throughout the United States on health-related and civic issues.

PHILIP EMEAGWALI (1954–)

Mathematician, Engineer, Computer Scientist. Philip Chukwurah Emeagwali, considered a "father" of the Internet, was born on August 23, 1954, in Akure, Nigeria. Emeagwali was a young math prodigy, but his high school studies were interrupted when he and his family—like most Igbos—were forced to flee to eastern Nigeria during the country's civil war. After living in refugee camps and serving as a cook in the Biafran army, Emeagwali entered Christ the King College in Onitsha and later, in 1973, earned a general certificate of education from the University of London.

Emeagwali ventured to the United States the following year to pursue further studies. He earned a B.S. in mathematics from Oregon State University in 1977; an M.S. in civil engineering from George Washington University in 1981; a post-master's degree in ocean, coastal, and marine engineering from George Washington in 1986; an M.A. in applied mathematics from the University of Maryland in 1986; and a Ph.D. in scientific computing from the University of Michigan in 1993. Emeagwali became a U.S. citizen in 1981 when he married Dale Brown, a renowned scientist and cancer researcher.

In the mid-1970s, Emeagwali began working with computers, eventually becoming a supercomputer programmer. By 1989, he had set the world record for the fastest computation, using 65,000 separate computer processors to perform 3.1 billion calculations per second. This work was important in that it enabled scientists to grasp the capacities of supercomputers, as well as the theoretical uses of linking numerous computers to communicate—an idea that eventually led to the creation of the Internet. For his work, Emeagwali earned the 1989 Gordon Bell Prize, a highly coveted award in the computing world. Later, Emeagwali's background in engineering combined with his knowledge of computers also led to an important breakthrough in the field of petroleum engineering.

Emeagwali, who works as an independent consultant and dubs himself a "public intellectual," has performed engineering duties for the Maryland State Highway Administration and the U.S. Bureau of Reclamation. In addition to work as a researcher at the National Weather Service and the University of Michigan during the 1980s, he was a research fellow at the University of Minnesota's Army High Performance Computing Research Center from 1991 to 1993. He is the recipient of more than one hundred awards, including Computer Scientist of the Year from the National Technical Association (1993), Eminent Engineer from Tau Beta Pi National Engineering Honor Society (1994), International Man of the Year from the Minority Technology Council of Michigan (1994), and Best Scientist in Africa Award of the Pan African Broadcasting, Heritage, and Achievement Awards (2001). Emeagwali was inducted in to the United Nations' Gallery of Prominent Refugees in 2001.

SOLOMON C. FULLER (1872–1953)

Neurologist, Psychiatrist. Born on August 11, 1872, in Monrovia, Liberia, Solomon Carter Fuller Jr. was the son of a coffee planter and government official whose father had been enslaved in Virginia. The younger Fuller sailed to the United States in 1889, and he earned his M.D. from the Boston University School of Medicine in 1897.

By 1900, he had started his own study of mental patients, and he traveled to Germany four years later to study with the influential neuropsychiatrist Emil Kraepelin and with Alois Alzheimer, the discoverer of the disease that bears his name. During his stay in Germany, Fuller had an opportunity to spend an afternoon with Paul Ehrlich, who in 1908 would win the Nobel Prize for his research in immunology.

Fuller's most significant contribution was in the study of Alzheimer's disease. By the early twenty-first century, scientists still had not reached full agreement as to its cause. At the time of Fuller's work, the prevailing belief was that arteriosclerosis, or hardening of the arteries, caused Alzheimer's. Fuller disagreed and put forth this opinion in the course of diagnosing the ninth documented case of Alzheimer's. Proof of his ideas came in 1953, the year he died, when other medical researchers confirmed the lack of any linkage between arteriosclerosis and Alzheimer's.

HELENE D. GAYLE (1955–)

Epidemiologist, AIDS Researcher, Nonprofit CEO. An expert on health, global development, and humanitarian issues, Helene Doris Gayle spent nearly twenty years with the Centers for Disease Control and Prevention, working primarily on HIV/AIDS. Gayle then worked at the Bill and Melinda Gates Foundation, directing programs on HIV/AIDS and other global health issues. In 2006, she was named president and CEO of CARE USA.

Gayle was born on August 16, 1955, in Buffalo, New York, the third of five children of an entrepreneur father and social worker mother. After graduating from Barnard College in 1976, she then won acceptance to the University of Pennsylvania's medical school.

Hearing a speech on the cure of smallpox inspired Gayle to pursue public health medicine, and her direction would prove a significant one in the years to come as the plague of AIDS came to decimate communities across the globe. She received her M.D. from the University of Pennsylvania as well as a master's degree in public health from Johns Hopkins University, both in 1981. After a residency in pediatrics, she was selected in 1984 to enter the epidemiology training program at the Centers for Disease Control and Prevention (CDC) in Atlanta, the nation's top research center for infectious diseases.

For much of the 1980s, Gayle was intensely involved in the CDC's research into AIDS and HIV infection, first through her work in the center's Epidemic Intelligence Service and later as a chief of international AIDS research, a capacity in which she oversaw the scientific investigations of over 300 CDC researchers. Gayle has been instrumental in raising public awareness about the disease and is especially driven to point out how devastating AIDS has been to the African American community. Sex education, better health care for the poor, and substance-abuse prevention are some of the proposals Gayle has championed that she believes will help reduce deaths from AIDS.

In 1992, Gayle was hired as a medical epidemiologist and researcher for the AIDS Division of the U.S. Agency for International Development, cementing her reputation as one of the international community's top AIDS

Epidemiologist Helene D. Gayle. *After working on HIV/AIDS and other global health issues for the Centers for Disease Control and Prevention and the Bill and Melinda Gates Foundation for more than two decades, Gayle became president and CEO of the poverty-fighting organization CARE USA in 2006.* DOMINIC BRACCO II/UPI/LANDOV

scientists. Gayle has served as director of CDC's National Center for HIV, STD, and TB Prevention and in 2001 was named program director for HIV/AIDS and TB for the Bill and Melinda Gates Foundation. She was also named assistant surgeon general and rear admiral in the U.S. Public Health Service. In 2006, Gayle was named president and CEO of CARE USA, a humanitarian organization dedicated to fighting poverty and disease.

The author of numerous scientific articles, Gayle has been the recipient of a number of awards and honors, including the Medical Leadership in Industry Award, one of the Women of Color Health, Science, and Technology Awards given in 2002. In 2009, the administration of President Barack Obama appointed her the chair of the Presidential Advisory Council on HIV/AIDS, as well as to a position on the President's Commission on White House Fellowships.

EVELYN BOYD GRANVILLE (1924–)

Author, Educator, Lecturer. Born in Washington, D.C., on May 1, 1924, Evelyn Boyd Granville earned an A.B. in mathematics from Smith College in 1945 and then an M.A. in mathematics from Yale University just a year later. She received a Ph.D. from Yale in 1949, making her one of the first two African American women to be awarded a Ph.D. in pure mathematics.

Granville's first teaching position was as an instructor at New York University (1949–1950). She then moved to Fisk University, where she was an assistant professor (1950–1952). From 1956 to 1960, Granville worked for IBM on the Project Vanguard and Project Mercury space programs, analyzing orbits and developing computer procedures. Over the next seven years, Granville held positions at the Computation and Data Reduction Center of the U.S. Space Technology Laboratories; the North American Aviation Company's Space and Information Systems Division; and IBM, where she was a senior mathematician.

Granville returned to teaching in 1967, taking a position at California State University in Los Angeles and teaching there until her retirement in 1984. In addition to her role as a college-level instructor, Granville worked to improve mathematics skills at all levels. From 1985 to 1988, Granville emerged from retirement to teach mathematics and computer science at Texas College in Tyler, Texas. In 1990, she accepted an appointment to the Sam A. Lindsey Chair at the University of Texas at Tyler, and in subsequent years she taught there as a visiting professor. Granville is the coauthor of *Theory and Applications of Mathematics for Teachers* (1975). She received an honorary doctorate from Smith College in 1989 and another from Spelman College in 2006.

FREDERICK D. GREGORY (1941–)

Airplane Pilot, Astronaut. Frederick Drew Gregory was born on January 7, 1941, in Washington, D.C. He is the nephew of Dr. Charles R. Drew, the noted blood plasma specialist. Under the sponsorship of U.S. Representative Adam Clayton Powell, Gregory attended the U.S. Air Force Academy and graduated with a B.S. in 1964. In 1977, he received a master's degree in information systems from George Washington University.

Gregory was a helicopter and fighter pilot for the Air Force from 1965 to 1970 and served as a research and test pilot for the Air Force and the National Aeronautics and Space Administration in 1971. In 1978, he was accepted into NASA's astronaut program, making him the second African American astronaut in NASA's history. In 1985, he went into space aboard the space shuttle *Challenger* as a pilot, a first for an African American. He was a member of two more shuttle missions, in 1989 and 1991. Gregory served with NASA's Office of Safety and Mission Assurance until 2001, when he was named acting associate administrator for the Office of Space Flight. He remained in that position until 2002, when he was appointed deputy administrator. Gregory briefly served as acting administrator of NASA in 2005. After retiring from NASA, Gregory took a position with Lohfeld Consulting Group, Inc., as managing director of aerospace and defense strategy.

Gregory, who retired from the Air Force with the rank of colonel, belongs to the Society of Experimental Test Pilots, the Tuskegee Airmen, the American Helicopter Society, and the National Technical Association. He has been awarded a number of honorary doctorates, as well as civic and community honors. He has also won numerous medals and awards, including the Meritorious Service Medal, the Air Force Commendation Medal, and three NASA Space Flight Medals. He has twice received the Distinguished Flying Cross. He is also the recipient of George Washington University's Distinguished Alumni Award, NASA's Outstanding Leadership Award, and the National Society of Black Engineers' Distinguished National Scientist Award. In 2003, he received the Presidential Rank Award for Distinguished Executives. Gregory was inducted into the U.S. Astronaut Hall of Fame on May 1, 2004.

LLOYD A. HALL (1894–1971)

Research Director, Chemist. Grandson of the first pastor of Quinn Chapel A.M.E. Church, the first African American church in Chicago, Lloyd Augustus Hall was born in Elgin, Illinois, on June 20, 1894. A top student and athlete at East High School in Aurora, Illinois, he graduated in the top ten of his class and was offered scholarships to four different colleges in Illinois. In 1916, Hall graduated from Northwestern University with a B.S. in chemistry. He continued his studies at the University of Chicago and the University of Illinois.

During World War I, Hall served as a lieutenant, inspecting explosives at a Wisconsin plant. After the war, Hall joined the Chicago Department of Health Laboratories, where he quickly rose to senior chemist. In 1921, he took employment at Boyer Chemical Laboratory. He became president and chemical director of the Chemical Products Corporation the following year. In 1924, he was offered a position with Griffith Laboratories. Within one year, he was chief chemist and director of research.

While there, Hall discovered curing salts for the preserving and processing of meats, which helped revolutionize the meatpacking industry. He also discovered how to sterilize spices and researched the effects of antioxidants on fats. Along the way, he registered more than one hundred patents for processes used in the manufacturing and packing of food, especially meat and bakery products.

In 1954, Hall became chairman of the Chicago chapter of the American Institute of Chemists. The following year, he was elected a member of the national board of directors, becoming the first African American man to hold that position in the institute's thirty-two-year history. After his retirement from Griffith in 1959, Hall continued to serve as a consultant to various state and federal organizations. In 1961, he spent six months in Indonesia, advising the Food and Agricultural Organization of the United Nations. From 1962 to 1964, he was a member of the Food for Peace Council, an appointment made by President John F. Kennedy.

MARC R. HANNAH (1956–)

Computer Scientist. Marc Regis Hannah, a native Chicagoan, was born on October 13, 1956. In high school, he took a computer science course that kindled his interest in this relatively new field. Also inspired by the example of an older brother, he earned high grades that qualified him for a Bell Laboratories–sponsored scholarship to engineering school. He eventually earned a Ph.D. from Stanford University in 1985.

While at Stanford, he met James Clark, an engineering professor who was a pioneer in computer graphics, having invented a special computer chip that was the heart of an imaging process. Hannah redesigned the chip to operate five times faster, an advance that impressed Clark enough to invite Hannah to join him in founding a computer graphics company called Silicon Graphics, Inc. Founded in 1981, the company became an international market leader in 3-D computer graphics. Silicon Graphics' technology was used to enhance many devices, such as military flight simulators and medical computerized axial tomography (CAT) scans. Among the most lucrative areas for this technology, and certainly the best known, is that of video and film animation. The special effects made possible by three-dimensional imaging appeared in such films as *Star Wars*, *Terminator II*, and *Jurassic Park*. Hannah is currently vice president of technology development at Omniverse Digital Solutions.

MATTHEW A. HENSON (1866–1955)

Seaman, Explorer, Surveyor, Author. Matthew Alexander Henson was born on August 6, 1866, in Charles County, Maryland, near Washington, D.C. He attended school in Washington, D.C., for six years, but when he was thirteen, he signed on as a cabin boy on a ship headed for China. Henson worked his way up to seaman while he sailed over many of the world's oceans. After several odd jobs in different cities, Henson met U.S. Navy surveyor Robert Edwin Peary in Washington, D.C. Peary, who was planning a trip to Nicaragua, hired Henson on the spot as his valet. Henson was not pleased at being a personal servant, but he nonetheless felt his new position held future opportunities.

Peary eventually made seven trips to the Arctic, starting in 1893. He became convinced that he could be the first man to stand at the North Pole. Henson accompanied Peary on these trips to Greenland and became an integral part of Peary's plans. The pair made four trips looking for a passageway to the North Pole. In 1909, Peary and Henson made their final attempt at reaching the pole. Although Peary was undoubtedly the driving force of these expeditions, he was increasingly reliant on Henson. Henson's greatest assets were his knowledge of the Inuit language and his ability to readily adapt to their culture. He was also an excellent dog driver and possessed a physical stamina that Peary lacked because he was suffering from leukemia. Henson felt that he was serving the African American race by his example of loyalty, fortitude, and trustworthiness.

By the end of March 1909, they were within 150 miles of their goal. Most accounts indicate that Henson, because of his strength, would break trail and set up camp for the night, while Peary followed. On April 6, Henson thought he had reached the pole; Peary arrived later to affirm the belief. Henson then had the honor of planting the U.S. flag.

In 1912, Henson published *A Negro Explorer at the North Pole*, but the book aroused little interest until it was reissued decades later. By the 1930s, Henson began receiving recognition for his contributions to arctic exploration. In 1937, he was the first African American elected to the Explorers Club in New York. In 1944, he and other surviving members of the expedition received congressional medals. In 1954, Henson received public recognition for his deeds from President Dwight D. Eisenhower. Henson died on March 9, 1955, and was buried in New York. In 1988, his remains were exhumed and buried with full military honors at Arlington National Cemetery, next to the grave of Peary.

WILLIAM A. HINTON (1883–1959)

Lecturer, Medical Researcher, Educator. Long one of the world's authorities on venereal disease, Dr. William Augustus Hinton was responsible for the development of the Hinton test, a reliable method for detecting syphilis. He also collaborated with Dr. J. A. V. Davies on what is now called the Davies-Hinton test for the detection of this same disease.

Born in Chicago on December 15, 1883, Hinton graduated from Harvard University in 1905. In 1912, he finished his medical studies in three years at Harvard Medical School. After graduation, he was a voluntary assistant in the pathological laboratory at Massachusetts General Hospital. This was followed by eight years of laboratory practice at the Boston Dispensary and at the Massachusetts State Department of Public Health. In 1923, Hinton was appointed lecturer in preventive medicine and hygiene at Harvard Medical School, where he served for twenty-seven years. In 1949, he became the first African American to be granted a professorship there.

In 1931, at the Boston Dispensary, Hinton started a training school for poor girls so that they could become medical technicians. From these classes of volunteers grew one of the country's leading institutions for the training of technicians. Though he lost a leg in an automobile accident, Hinton remained active in teaching and at the Boston Dispensary's laboratory, which he directed from 1916 to 1953. He died in Canton, Massachusetts, on August 8, 1959.

LISA P. JACKSON (1962–)

Government Official, Engineer. Born on February 8, 1962, in Philadelphia, Lisa Perez Jackson was adopted weeks after her birth and raised in Pontchartrain Park, a predominantly African American middle-class neighborhood of New Orleans. She graduated in 1979 as valedictorian from Saint Mary's Dominican High School in New Orleans and proceeded to Tulane University, where she earned a B.S. in chemical engineering in 1983. Three years later, Jackson earned a master's degree in chemical engineering from Princeton University.

Appointed by President Barack Obama and confirmed by the Senate on January 22, 2009, to be administrator of the Environmental Protection Agency (EPA), Jackson leads EPA's efforts to protect human health and the environment for all Americans. Jackson has pledged to focus on core issues of protecting air and water quality, preventing community exposure to toxic contamination, and reducing greenhouse gases. She has promised that all of EPA's efforts will follow the best science, adhere to the rule of law, and be implemented with unparalleled transparency. Jackson is the first African American to serve as EPA administrator. She has made it a priority to focus on vulnerable groups that are particularly susceptible to environmental and health threats, including children, the elderly, and low-income communities.

Prior to becoming EPA administrator, Jackson spent sixteen years as an employee of the EPA before joining New Jersey's Department of Environmental Protection (DEP) in 2002. At DEP, she headed numerous programs, including land-use regulation, water supply, geological surveying, water monitoring and standards, and watershed management. She focused on developing a system of incentives for stimulating what was in her opinion the right growth in the right places. Under her leadership, DEP developed regulatory standards for implementing the landmark Highlands Water Protection and Planning Act. Jackson was commissioner of DEP from February 2006 to November 2008 and then very briefly served as chief of staff to Jon S. Corzine, then governor of New Jersey.

SHIRLEY ANN JACKSON (1946–)

University President, Physicist, Government Official. Born in Washington, D.C., on August 5, 1946, Shirley Ann Jackson graduated as valedictorian of her class from Roosevelt High School in 1964. In 1968, she received a B.S. degree from Massachusetts Institute of Technology (MIT), where she was one of only two African American women in her undergraduate class. In 1973, she became the first African American woman in the United States to earn a Ph.D. in physics, which she also earned from MIT. She was later named a life member of MIT Corporation, the institute's board of trustees.

Jackson's first position—as a research associate at the Fermi National Accelerator Laboratory in Batavia, Illinois—reflected her interest in the study of subatomic particles. Jackson later worked as a member of the technical staff on theoretical physics at AT&T Bell Laboratories, as a visiting scientist at the European Organization for Nuclear Research in Geneva, and as a visiting lecturer at the NATO International Advanced Study Institute in Belgium. From 1991 to 1995, Jackson was a professor of physics at Rutgers University.

In 1995, President Bill Clinton named Jackson chair of the Nuclear Regulatory Commission (NRC). Under Jackson's direction, the NRC became more aggressive about inspections and forced some top officials out of office because of their lax enforcement of safety regulations. In 2001, she was elected to the board of the Public Service Enterprise Group, just one day after being appointed a director of AT&T Corporation. Jackson has also been named to the boards of several other publicly traded companies since July 1999, when she became the eighteenth president of Rensselaer Polytechnic Institute. Throughout her career, Jackson has been active in many organizations, including the National Academy of Sciences, the American Association for the Advancement of Science, and the National Science Foundation.

In April 2009, President Barack Obama appointed Jackson to serve on the President's Council of Advisors on Science and Technology. This group of leading scientists and engineers advises the president and vice president and formulates policy in the many areas where understanding of science, technology, and innovation is key to strengthening the economy and forming policy that works for the American people.

Jackson has been awarded more than forty honorary doctoral degrees and was inducted into the National Women's Hall of Fame in 1998 for her work as a scientist and an advocate for education, science, and public policy. Jackson was named one of seven fellows for the year 2004 by the Association for Women in Science, an organization dedicated to achieving equity and full participation of women in all areas of science and technology. In 2007, Jackson was awarded the Vannevar Bush Award for "a lifetime of achievements in scientific research, education, and senior statesman–like contributions to public policy." Her senior leadership positions in government, industry, research, and academia led *Time* magazine in 2005 to call Jackson "perhaps the ultimate role model for women in science."

Mae C. Jemison, 1987. *Jemison, a physician and surgeon, served as a science specialist on a 1992 flight of the space shuttle* Endeavour, *thereby becoming the first African American woman in space.* AP IMAGES

MAE C. JEMISON (1956–)

Physician, Surgeon. Mae Carol Jemison was born on October 17, 1956, in Decatur, Alabama, but her family moved to Chicago when she was three years old. She attended Stanford University on a National Achievement Scholarship and received a B.S. in chemical engineering and a B.A. in Afro-American studies in 1977. She then enrolled in Cornell University's medical school and graduated in 1981. Her medical internship was at the Los Angeles County/University of Southern California Medical Center in 1982. She was a general practitioner with the INA/Ross Loos Medical Group in Los Angeles until the end of 1982, followed by more than two years as a Peace Corps medical officer in Sierra Leone and Liberia. Returning to the United States in 1985, she began working for CIGNA Health Plans of California, a health-maintenance organization based in Los Angeles, and applied for admission into NASA's astronaut program.

In 1987, Jemison was accepted into the astronaut program. Her first assignment was representing the astronaut office at the Kennedy Space Center in Cape Canaveral, Florida. On September 12, 1992, Jemison became the first African American woman in space on the shuttle *Endeavour*, serving as a science specialist. As a physician, she studied the effect of weightlessness on herself and other crew members. Jemison resigned from NASA in 1993 to pursue personal goals related to science education and health care in West Africa. In 1993, she was appointed to a Montgomery Fellowship at Dartmouth College, where she established the Jemison Institute for Advancing Technology in Developing Countries. That same year, she founded the Jemison

Group, an advanced technologies research and consulting firm. In 1994, Jemison founded the International Science Camp in Chicago to help young people become enthusiastic about science. In 1999, Jemison founded BioSentient Corporation, a medical technology devices and services company focused on improving health and human performance through physiologic awareness and self-regulation.

In 1988, Jemison won the Science and Technology Award given by *Essence* magazine, and in 1990 she was Gamma Sigma Gamma's Woman of the Year. In 1991, she received an honorary doctorate from Lincoln University. She also served on the board of directors of the World Sickle Cell Foundation from 1990 to 1992. In 2001, she published a memoir for children called *Find Where the Wind Goes*. Jemison was awarded the 2003 Intrepid Award by the National Organization for Women and was inducted into the International Space Hall of Fame in 2004.

FREDERICK M. JONES (1893–1961)

Mechanic, Inventor. Around 1935, Frederick McKinley Jones built the first automatic refrigeration system for long-haul trucks. Later, the system was adapted to various other carriers, including railway cars, ships, and trucks. Previously, foods were packed in ice, so slight delays led to spoilage. Jones's new method instigated a change in the eating habits of the entire nation and allowed for the development of food-production facilities in almost any geographic location. Refrigerated trucks were also used to preserve and ship blood products during World War II.

Jones was born in Covington, Kentucky, on May 17, 1893. His mother left the family when he was a baby, and his father left him at age five to be raised by a priest at a rectory until he was sixteen years of age. There, Jones received a sixth-grade education. When he left the rectory, he worked as a pin boy, as a mechanic's assistant, and finally as chief mechanic on a Minnesota farm. After serving in World War I, his mechanical fame spread in the late 1920s when he developed a series of devices to adapt silent movie projectors into sound projectors.

Jones also developed an air-conditioning unit for military field hospitals, a portable X-ray machine, and a refrigerator for military field kitchens. During his lifetime, a total of sixty-one patents were issued in his name. He died in Minneapolis, Minnesota, on February 21, 1961.

PERCY L. JULIAN (1899–1975)

Educator, Medical Researcher, Research Director. Born on April 11, 1899, in Montgomery, Alabama, Percy Lavon Julian attended DePauw University in Greencastle, Indiana. He graduated Phi Beta Kappa from DePauw and was valedictorian of his class after having lived during his college days in the attic of a fraternity house where he worked as a waiter. For several years, Julian taught at Fisk University, West Virginia State College, and Howard University, where he was associate professor and head of the chemistry department. He left to attend Harvard University and the University of Vienna, where he earned a Ph.D. in 1931. Julian then continued his research and teaching duties at Howard.

In 1935, Julian synthesized the drug physostigmine, which is used today in the treatment of glaucoma. He later became director of research and chief chemist and did soybean research at the Glidden Company, where he specialized in the production of sterols, which he extracted from the oil of the soybean. The method perfected by Julian eventually lowered the cost of sterols to less than twenty cents a gram and, ultimately, enabled millions of people suffering from arthritis to obtain relief through the use of cortisone, a sterol derivative. Later, Julian developed methods for manufacturing sex hormones from soybean sterols, with progesterone used to prevent miscarriages and testosterone used to treat diminishing sex drive in older men. Both hormones were important in the treatment of cancer.

In 1953, he left Glidden to found his own company, Julian Laboratories, in Chicago and Mexico. Years later, the company was sold to Smith, Kline & French. In 1947, the NAACP awarded Julian the Spingarn Medal, and in 1964 he founded Julian Research Institute and Julian Associates, Inc., both based in Franklin Park, Illinois. He was awarded the Chemical Pioneer Award by the American Institute of Chemists in 1968. Julian died on April 19, 1975, in Waukegan, Illinois.

ERNEST EVERETT JUST (1883–1941)

Editor, Zoologist, Marine Biologist. Born in Charleston, South Carolina, on August 14, 1883, Ernest Everett Just received his B.A. with high honors from Dartmouth College in 1907 and his Ph.D. in 1916 from the University of Chicago. His groundbreaking work on the embryology of marine invertebrates included research on fertilization—a process known as parthenogenesis—but his most important achievement was his discovery of the role protoplasm plays in the development of a cell.

Just began teaching at Howard University in 1907 and started graduate training at the Marine Biological Laboratory in Woods Hole, Massachusetts, in 1909. He performed most of his research at this site over the next twenty summers. Between 1912 and 1937, he published more than fifty papers on fertilization, parthenogenesis, cell division, and mutation. He also published a textbook in 1939 that was the result of his research in cell functioning and the structure and role of protoplasm within a cell.

A member of Phi Beta Kappa, Just received the Spingarn Medal in 1915 from the NAACP and served as associate editor of *Physiological Zoology*, the *Biological Bulletin*, and the *Journal of Morphology*. In 1930, Just was one of twelve zoologists to address the International Congress of Zoologists, and he was elected vice president of the American Society of Zoologists. Just left the United States in 1929 because of racist attitudes that prevented his career from advancing. He died on October 27, 1941, in Washington, D.C., shortly after returning to the country.

SAMUEL L. KOUNTZ (1930–1981)

Physician, Surgeon, Medical Researcher. Born on October 20, 1930, in Lexa, Arkansas, Samuel Lee Kountz graduated third in his class at the Agricultural, Mechanical and Normal College of Arkansas in 1952, having initially failed his entrance exams. He pursued graduate studies at the University of Arkansas, earning an M.S. in chemistry in 1956. Senator J. William Fulbright, whom Kountz met when he was a graduate student, advised Kountz to apply for a scholarship to medical school. Kountz won the scholarship on a competitive basis and was the first African American to enroll at the University of Arkansas Medical School in Little Rock, graduating with his M.D. in 1958. Kountz was responsible for finding out that large doses of the drug methylprednisolone could help reverse the acute rejection of a transplanted kidney. The drug was used for a number of years in the standard management of kidney transplant patients.

While he was still an intern, Kountz assisted in the first West Coast kidney transplant. In 1964, working with Dr. Roy Cohn, one of the pioneers in the field of transplantation, Kountz again made medical history by transplanting a kidney from a mother to a daughter—the first transplant between humans who were not identical twins. At the University of California in 1967, Kountz worked with other researchers to develop the prototype of a machine capable of preserving kidneys for up to fifty hours after removal from the body of a donor. The machine, called the Belzer Kidney Perfusion Machine, was named for Dr. Folkert O. Belzer, who was Kountz's partner. Kountz eventually built one of the largest kidney transplant training and research centers in the nation. He died on December 23, 1981, in Great Neck, New York, after a long illness contracted on a trip to South Africa in 1977.

LEWIS H. LATIMER (1848–1928)

Draftsperson, Electrical Engineer. Lewis Howard Latimer, a pioneer in the development of the electric light bulb, was employed by Alexander Graham Bell to make the patent drawings for the first telephone. He later became chief draftsman for both the General Electric and Westinghouse companies.

Born in Chelsea, Massachusetts, on September 4, 1848, and raised in Boston, Latimer enlisted in the Union Navy when he was fifteen and began studying drafting upon completion of his military service. In 1881, he invented a method of making carbon filaments for the Maxim electric incandescent lamp and later patented this method. He also supervised the installation of electric light in New York, Philadelphia, Montreal, and London for the Maxim-Weston Electric Company. In 1884, he joined the Edison Electric Light Company. Latimer died on December 11, 1928, in New York City.

THEODORE K. LAWLESS (1892–1971)

Physician, Philanthropist. Theodore Kenneth Lawless was born on December 6, 1892, in Thibodeaux, Louisiana. He received his B.S. from Talladega College in 1914 and continued to further his education at the University of Kansas and Northwestern University, where he received his M.D. in 1919. He then pursued a master's in dermatology, which he finished at Columbia University in 1920. From there he furthered his studies at Harvard University, the University of Paris, the University of Freiburg, and the University of Vienna.

Upon his return to the United States in 1924, Lawless started his own practice in Chicago's predominantly African American South Side, which he continued until his death in 1971. He soon became one of the premiere dermatologists in the country and earned great praise for researching treatments and cures for a variety of skin diseases, including syphilis and leprosy. During the early years of his career, he taught dermatology at Northwestern University Medical School, where his research was instrumental in devising electropyrexia, a treatment for those suffering cases of syphilis in its early stages. Before he left Northwestern in 1941, he aided in building the university's first medical laboratories.

After leaving Northwestern, Lawless entered the business world beginning as president of 4213 South Michigan Corporation, which sold low-cost real estate, and later as president of the Service Federal Savings and Loan Association. By the 1960s, he was well-known as one of the thirty-five richest African American men in the United States.

During his lifetime, Lawless served on dozens of boards of directors and belonged to countless organizations. He served on the Chicago Board of Health, as senior attending physician at Provident Hospital, as associate examiner in dermatology for the National Board of Medical Examiners, as chairman of the Division of Higher Education of the American Missionary Association, and as consultant to the Geneva Community Hospital in Switzerland. He was also recognized with many awards for his exemplary breakthroughs in medicine, public service, and philanthropy, including the Harmon Award in Medicine in 1929, the Churchman of the Year in 1952, the Spingarn Medal from the NAACP in 1954, and the Daniel H. Burnham Award from Roosevelt University in 1963. He died in Chicago on May 1, 1971.

ROBERT H. LAWRENCE JR. (1935–1967)

Astronaut, Airplane Pilot. Air Force officer Robert Henry Lawrence Jr. was the first African American astronaut to be appointed to the Manned Orbiting Laboratory. Lawrence was born in Chicago on October 2, 1935. While still in elementary school, he became a model-airplane hobbyist and a chess enthusiast. Lawrence became interested in biology during his time at Englewood High School in Chicago. As a student at Englewood, Lawrence excelled in chemistry and track. When he graduated, he placed in the top 10 percent of his class.

Lawrence entered Bradley University, joining the Air Force Reserve Officers' Training Corps and attaining the rank of lieutenant colonel, making him the second-highest-ranking cadet at Bradley. Lawrence was commissioned a second lieutenant in the U.S. Air Force in 1956 and soon after received his bachelor's degree in chemistry. Following a stint at an air base in Germany, Lawrence entered Ohio State University through the Air Force Institute of Technology as a doctoral candidate, earning his Ph.D. in 1965. Lawrence's career came to an end on December 8, 1967, when his F-104D Starfighter jet crashed on a runway in the California desert, killing him instantly.

WALTER E. MASSEY (1938–)

Physicist, Educator, Administrator. Walter Eugene Massey was born in Hattiesburg, Mississippi, on April 5, 1938. At the end of the tenth grade, he accepted a scholarship to Morehouse College. He almost quit after a few weeks but graduated four years later with a B.S. in physics. He completed his Ph.D. in physics at Washington University in St. Louis in 1966.

Massey's research interests have included solid-state theory (the study of properties of solid material) and theories of quantum liquids and solids. While still a graduate student, he studied the behavior of both solid and liquid helium-3 and helium-4, publishing a series of papers on this work in the early 1970s. He became a full professor at Brown University in 1975 and was named dean of the college that same year. Massey's best-known accomplishment at Brown was his development of Inner City Teachers of Science, a program aimed at improving science instruction in inner-city schools. He was awarded the American Association of Physics Teachers' Distinguished Service Citation for his development of this program.

In 1979, the University of Chicago invited Massey to become professor of physics and director of the Argonne National Laboratory, which the university operates for the U.S. Department of Energy. The facility was beset by financial troubles at the time, and Massey has been credited with its successful recovery. In the fall of 1990, Massey was chosen by President George H. W. Bush to head the National Science Foundation, a position he held until 1993. He was only the second African American to hold that post. Massey was president of Morehouse College from 1995 to 2007. He has also served on the boards of several major corporations and was the chairman of Bank of America Corporation from April 2009 to April 2010.

JAN MATZELIGER (1852–1889)

Inventor, Shoemaker, Leather Worker. Born on September 15, 1852, in Paramaribo, Dutch Guiana (now Suriname), Jan Matzeliger found employment in the government machine works when he was only ten years old. Nine years later, he left home and eventually immigrated to the United States, settling in Philadelphia, where he worked in a shoe factory. He later moved to New England, settling permanently in Lynn, Massachusetts, in 1877. The Industrial Revolution had by this time resulted in the invention of machines to cut, sew, and tack shoes, but none had been perfected to "last" a shoe, which involved stretching the leather over a model foot. Observing this, Matzeliger designed and patented a device, one that he refined over the years to a point where it could last the leather, arrange the leather over the sole, drive in the nails, and deliver the finished product—all within one minute.

Matzeliger's patent was subsequently bought by Sidney W. Winslow, who established the United Shoe Machinery Company. The continued success of this business brought about a 50 percent reduction in the price of shoes across the nation, doubled wages for unskilled workers, and improved working conditions for millions of people dependent on the shoe industry for their livelihood. Between 1883 and 1891, Matzeliger received five patents on his inventions, all of which contributed to the shoemaking revolution. His last patent was issued in September 1891, two years after his death.

Matzeliger died of tuberculosis on August 24, 1889, at age thirty-seven, long before he had the chance to realize a share of the enormous profit derived from his invention. He never received any money. Instead, he was issued company stock that did not become valuable until after his death.

ELIJAH McCOY (c. 1843–1929)

Inventor, Machinist. Born in 1843 or 1844 in Canada, Elijah McCoy traveled to Scotland at the age of sixteen. There he was apprenticed to a master mechanic and engineer. After the Civil War, he moved to Ypsilanti, Michigan, where he sought work as an engineer. However, he was able to obtain employment only as a fireman and oiler for the Michigan Central Railroad.

McCoy's first invention was a lubricating cup that used steam pressure to drive oil into channels that brought it to a steam engine's moving parts. It was patented in 1872. The automatic device kept the engine better lubricated than was possible with older methods. Variations of this cup came to be used on many types of heavy machinery. Although McCoy received at least seventy-two patents in his lifetime, little money would reach his pockets as a result of his ideas. Because he lacked the capital to invest in manufacturing, he sold most of his patents for modest sums of money, while the manufacturers made millions. Later in his life, he helped found the Elijah McCoy Manufacturing Company, but he died just a few years later, on October 10, 1929.

RONALD E. McNAIR (1950–1986)

Astronaut. Ronald Ervin McNair was born on October 21, 1950, in Lake City, South Carolina. He graduated from North Carolina A&T State University in 1971 with a B.S. degree in physics. He also received a Ph.D. in physics from the Massachusetts Institute of Technology in 1976. He was presented an honorary doctorate of laws from North Carolina A&T in 1978.

McNair was working on the use of lasers in satellite communications when he was selected by NASA in 1978 to train as an astronaut. In August 1979, he completed a one-year training and evaluation period that made him eligible for assignment as a mission specialist on space shuttle flight crews. In 1984, he became the second African American to orbit earth on a NASA mission. During his career as a physicist, he presented papers in the areas of lasers and molecular spectroscopy and gave many presentations in the United States and Europe.

Despite the rigorous training in the NASA program, he taught karate at a church, played the saxophone, and found time to interact with young people. McNair was aboard the shuttle *Challenger* that exploded shortly after liftoff from Cape Kennedy and plunged into the waters off the Florida coast on January 28, 1986. The shuttle had a crew of seven persons, including two women—one a mission specialist, the other a teacher-in-space participant.

GARRETT A. MORGAN (1877–1963)

Inventor. Born in Paris, Kentucky, on March 4, 1877, Garrett A. Morgan moved to Cleveland at an early age. Although he was most famous for his invention of the gas inhalator, an early gas mask, he also invented an improvement on the sewing machine that he sold for $150, as well as a hair-refining cream that straightened human hair. The cream remained in use for many decades. In 1923, having established his reputation with the gas inhalator, he sold an improved traffic signal to the General Electric Company.

In 1912, Morgan developed his safety hood, a gas inhalator that was a precursor to the gas mask. The value of his invention was first acknowledged during a successful rescue operation of several men trapped by a tunnel explosion in the Cleveland Waterworks, some 200 feet below the surface of Lake Erie. During the emergency, Morgan, his brother, and two other volunteers were the only men able to descend into the smoky, gas-filled tunnel and save several workers from asphyxiation.

Orders for the Morgan inhalator soon began to pour into Cleveland from fire companies all over the nation, but as soon as Morgan's racial identity became known, many of them were canceled. In the South, it was necessary for Morgan to use the services of a white man to demonstrate his invention. During World War I, Morgan's inhalator technology was used in gas masks for combat troops. Morgan died on July 27, 1963, in Cleveland—the city that had awarded him a gold medal for his devotion to public safety.

WAVERLY J. PERSON (1927–)

Geophysicist, Seismologist. Waverly J. Person, born in Blackridge, Virginia, on May 1, 1927, is best known as the first African American to hold the prominent position of director of the U.S. Geological Survey's National Earthquake Information Center. A respected geophysicist and seismologist, he was also one of the first African

Americans in his field. He also worked to encourage minority students to consider the earth sciences as a career.

While working as a technician at the U.S. Department of Commerce's earthquake services department from 1962 to 1973, Person completed graduate work at American University and George Washington University. His supervisors increasingly assigned him more challenging tasks that he performed well, gaining notice among his peers. Soon, he was qualified as a geophysicist and transferred to the U.S. Geological Survey's National Earthquake Information Center in Colorado. In 1977, Person was named director of the center.

Person was honored with many distinguished awards throughout his professional life. These include: an honorary doctorate in science from St. Paul's College in 1988; an Outstanding Government Communicator Award from the National Association of Government Communicators in 1988; the Meritorious Service Award from the U.S. Department of the Interior in 1989; and a Multicultural Award from Boulder County's Community Services Department in 1990. During his long stint as head of the National Earthquake Information Center, Person was often called on as an earthquake expert by national and international media. After fifty-one years of educating audiences around the globe about earthquakes, Person, who had come to be known as "Mr. Earthquake" because of the comfort and clarity by which he related information on earthquakes, retired from the U.S. Geological Survey in 2006.

NORBERT RILLIEUX (1806–1894)

Inventor, Mechanical Engineer. Norbert Rillieux's inventions were of great value to the sugar-refining industry. The method formerly used called for gangs of enslaved laborers to ladle boiling sugarcane juice from one kettle to another—a primitive process known as the "Jamaica Train." Rillieux invented a vacuum evaporating pan (a series of condensing coils in vacuum chambers) that reduced the industry's dependence on gang labor and helped manufacturers create a superior product at a greatly reduced cost. He received a patent on this invention in 1843, and the first Rillieux evaporator was installed two years later at Myrtle Grove Plantation in Louisiana. In the following years, factories in Louisiana, Cuba, and Mexico converted to the Rillieux system.

A native of New Orleans born on March 17, 1806, Rillieux was the son of Vincent Rillieux, a wealthy engineer, and Constance Vivant, who was enslaved on his plantation. Young Rillieux's higher education was obtained in Paris, where his extraordinary aptitude for engineering led to his appointment as an instructor of applied mechanics at L'École Centrale when he was twenty-four years old. Rillieux returned to Paris permanently in 1854, securing a scholarship and working on the deciphering of hieroglyphics.

When his evaporator process was finally adopted in Europe, he returned to inventing with renewed interest—applying his process to the sugar beet. In so doing, he cut production and refining costs in half.

Rillieux died in Paris on October 8, 1894, leaving behind a system that is in universal use throughout the sugar industry, as well as in the manufacture of soap, gelatin, glue, and many other products.

MABEL K. STAUPERS (1890–1988)

Association Executive, Nurse, Civil Rights Advocate. As president of the National Association of Colored Graduate Nurses, Mabel Keaton Staupers led a successful drive to integrate the mainstream nursing profession and to end segregation in the nurse corps of the U.S. Army and Navy during World War II.

Staupers was born in Barbados, West Indies, on February 27, 1890, and migrated to the United States in 1903, settling in Harlem. She began her nursing education in 1914 at Freedmen's Hospital School of Nursing (later known as Howard University College of Nursing) in Washington, D.C., and in 1917 graduated with class honors. After graduation, she began private-duty nursing until, with the assistance of physicians Louis T. Wright and James Wilson, she helped found the Booker T. Washington Sanitarium in Harlem in 1920. This served as Harlem's first inpatient center for African American patients with tuberculosis.

With a working fellowship, Staupers spent time at Jefferson Hospital Medical College in Philadelphia. She then conducted a survey of health needs in Harlem for the New York Tuberculosis and Health Association. She identified the health-care problems of minorities, leading to the establishment of the Harlem Committee of the New York Tuberculosis and Health Association. Ultimately, she served twelve years as the committee's executive secretary.

In 1934, Staupers became executive secretary of the National Association of Colored Graduate Nurses (NACGN). Over the next decade, Staupers worked closely with NACGN president Estelle Massey Riddle Osborne in a fight to integrate African American nurses into the mainstream of nursing. On January 20, 1945, the surgeon general of the U.S. Army announced that race would no longer be a factor in accepting nurses into the Army Nurse Corps. The U.S. Navy followed five days later by integrating the Navy Nurse Corps.

Later, Staupers fought to end the racial barriers of the American Nurses Association (ANA); in 1948, its House of Delegates opened the organization to African American members. In 1949, Staupers was named president of the NACGN, but that same year she persuaded the organization's members that the organization had realized its goals and had become obsolete. The organization's convention that year voted to dissolve the organization, and Staupers presided over the formal dissolution, which occurred in 1950.

In recognition of her leadership and efforts to remove racial barriers for African American women in the military and the ANA, Staupers was widely honored. Among her honors was the Spingarn Medal, which she received from the NAACP in 1951. She recorded the plight of African American nurses in her 1961 book, *No Time for Prejudice: A Story of the Integration of Negroes in Nursing in the United States.* Staupers died in Washington, D.C., on November 29, 1989.

LEWIS TEMPLE (1800–1854)

Inventor. The toggle iron harpoon—the standard harpoon used in American whaling from the mid-nineteenth through the early twentieth centuries—was invented by Lewis Temple. This harpoon, which had a movable head that prevented a whale from slipping loose, was an improvement over the barbed-head harpoon and led to a doubling of the annual catch.

Little is known of Temple's early life, except that he was born enslaved in Richmond, Virginia, in 1800 and had no formal education. He obtained his freedom and as a young man moved to New Bedford, Massachusetts, then a major New England whaling port. Finding work as a metalsmith, Temple modified the design of the whaler's harpoon and, in 1848, manufactured a new version of the harpoon with a barbed and pivoting head, making it much harder for a harpooned whale to escape. Using the toggle harpoon, the whaling industry soon entered a period of unprecedented prosperity. Temple, who never patented his harpoon, accidentally fell and never completely recovered from his injuries. He died in May 1854, destitute.

VIVIEN THOMAS (1910–1985)

Surgical Research Technician. Born in Nashville, Tennessee, on August 29, 1910, Vivien Theodore Thomas had dreamed of a career as a physician since childhood. As a teenager, he worked as a carpenter and as an orderly to earn money for college, and he then enrolled in Tennessee Agricultural and Industrial State College in 1929. The stock market crash later that year eradicated Thomas's savings, and he was forced to quit school.

The following year, he was hired for a research assistant post at Vanderbilt University Medical School. He went on to become a trauma researcher and an assistant to surgeon Alfred Blalock. For the next decade, Thomas worked long hours in the lab, conducting medical experiments for Blalock that eventually led to lifesaving advances in medicine during World War II, especially in the use of blood transfusions.

When Blalock was hired by the prestigious medical school at Johns Hopkins University in 1941, he would accept the post only if they hired Thomas as well. One of their most significant achievements together was a surgical procedure that restructured the blood vessels around an infant's heart if the child was in danger of death because of poor circulation of blood into the lungs.

Thomas became a well-known and well-regarded figure on the campus of Johns Hopkins. He remained at the institution even after his mentor passed away in 1964, and in 1971 he was honored by graduates of its medical school for his achievements. He became a medical school faculty member in 1977 and received an honorary degree in 1976. He retired in 1979. Thomas died on November 26, 1985, just days before the publication of his autobiography, titled *Pioneering Research in Surgical Shock and Cardiovascular Surgery: Vivien Thomas and His Work with Alfred Blalock.*

MARGARET E. M. TOLBERT (1943–)

Analytical Chemist. Margaret Ellen Mayo Tolbert was born on November 24, 1943, in Suffolk, Virginia. The third of six children, Tolbert was still young when her parents separated, and, shortly thereafter, her mother died. The six children were cared for by various neighbors and friends until they moved in with their paternal grandmother. Tolbert earned her undergraduate degree in 1967 from Tuskegee Institute (later Tuskegee University), and she then obtained an M.S. in analytical chemistry in one year of study at Wayne State University. In 1970, she was recruited to join the doctoral program in biochemistry at Brown University, earning her Ph.D. in 1974. Her research on biochemical reactions in liver cells was partially funded by a scholarship from the Southern Fellowship Fund.

In 1979, Tolbert spent five months at the International Institute of Cellular and Molecular Pathology in Brussels, Belgium, studying how different drugs are metabolized in rat liver cells. After her return to the United States, she was appointed director of the Carver Research Foundation, which George Washington Carver had established at Tuskegee in 1940. She was the foundation's first woman director. During her tenure,

Tolbert was able to bring several large scientific research contracts to Tuskegee from the federal government—contracts that expanded the research capabilities of the entire school.

From 1988 to 1990, Tolbert served as a director of the Birmingham Branch of the Federal Reserve System Board. From 1988 to 1990, she was the highest-ranking African American woman employed at the BP America Research Center in Warrensville Heights, Ohio, working as a senior planner and senior budgets and control analyst. In academia, she has served as visiting associate professor of medical sciences at Brown University in Providence, Rhode Island; professor of chemistry and associate provost for research and development at Tuskegee University; instructor in mathematics and science at the Opportunities Industrialization Center in Providence, Rhode Island; and associate dean of the School of Pharmacy and professor of pharmaceutical science at Florida A&M University in Tallahassee. From 1990 to 1993, Tolbert directed the National Science Foundation's Research Improvement in Minority Institutions program, which worked to strengthen the infrastructure of research programs at minority colleges and universities.

In 1996, Tolbert became the first African American woman director of the New Brunswick Laboratory at Argonne National Laboratories. She served in that position until 2002. As only the third director in the laboratory's almost fifty-year history, Tolbert was able to help the entire country by enhancing nuclear security and supporting international nonproliferation efforts. Involved in educational outreach throughout her career, Tolbert in 2002 accepted a position as senior adviser for the National Science Foundation's Office of Integrative Activities. In this position, she worked to promote the foundation's efforts to increase the participation in science of women, underrepresented minorities, and persons with disabilities.

Tolbert was elected a fellow of the American Association for the Advancement of Science in 1998. She is a member of Sigma Xi, the American Chemical Society, and the American Association of University Women, among other organizations. She has been the recipient of numerous awards and honors, including a 2001 Women of Color in Government and Defense Technology Award in managerial leadership.

OMAR WASOW (1970–)

Computer Programmer, Entrepreneur. Omar Wasow was born on December 22, 1970, in Nairobi, Kenya, but spent his formative adolescent years in New York City. He received a B.A. in race and ethnic relations from Stanford University in 1992. Wasow has become a leading commentator on the challenges and opportunities of new media and the new economy. His reports appear on various newscasts and Web sites. He also serves as the Internet analyst for MSNBC and National Public Radio. In addition, Wasow cofounded and is a strategic adviser to BlackPlanet.com, a social networking Web site providing an African American–oriented online community.

In 1994, a year after predicting a shift in online demographics from hackers and academics to mainstream users, Wasow produced a widely admired local online community, New York Online. As his reputation grew, corporate clients retained his company to assist them in launching successful Internet ventures of their own. These clients have included United Artists, Samsung, and several magazines, such as *Vibe*, *Essence*, *Consumer Reports*, *Latina*, and the *New Yorker*. His rising profile led the *New York Times* to tag him as a "pioneer in Silicon Alley" and *Newsweek* magazine to name him one of the "50 most influential people to watch in cyberspace."

During his career, Wasow was a member of the board of contributors of *USA Today* and wrote an Internet business column for FeedMag.com. Active in a number of social issues, particularly school reform, Wasow served as cochair of the Coalition for Independent Public Charter Schools. In that capacity, he helped push passage of the New York State Charter Schools Act of 1998. Wasow also helped found Brooklyn Excelsior Charter School, an elementary and middle school that opened in 2003.

Wasow has been a member of several nonprofit boards, including the New York Software Industry Association, WorldStudio, and the Refugee Project. As a result of his longstanding commitment to civic participation, Wasow was selected to be a fellow in the Rockefeller Foundation's Next Generation Leadership program in the late 1990s and was later selected by the Aspen Institute for the Henry Crown Fellowship, which recognizes emerging leaders. In 2005, Wasow began graduate studies at Harvard University, working toward a doctorate in African American studies and political science.

LEVI WATKINS JR. (1945–)

Surgeon, Educator. Levi Watkins Jr. was born in Parsons, Kansas, on June 13, 1945, but his father moved the family to Alabama for a job with Alabama State University. Watkins grew up in Montgomery, Alabama, where, through his involvement in local churches, he became acquainted with civil rights leaders Ralph David Abernathy and the Reverend Martin Luther King Jr. Both were prominent members of the Montgomery community, as was Watkins's own father, a college professor. The teenager's participation in civil rights issues did not stop him from excelling academically. He graduated as valedictorian of his high school class and then earned an honors degree from Tennessee State University in 1966.

Watkins's awareness of issues of racial inequality led him to apply to Vanderbilt University School of Medicine. He learned of his acceptance as its first African American student by reading the newspaper headline announcing the breakthrough. He graduated in 1970 and began his internship and surgical training at the prestigious medical school at Johns Hopkins University. Watkins also studied at Harvard Medical School and conducted research that led to the lifesaving practice of prescribing angiotensin blockers for patients susceptible to heart failure.

In 1978, Watkins became Johns Hopkins' first African American chief resident in cardiac surgery, and he became a faculty member that year as well. Two years later, he made medical history with the first successful surgical implantation of an automatic implantable defibrillator, a device that has been credited with saving countless lives through its ability to restore a normal heartbeat during an attack of arrhythmia. In 1991, he became a full professor of cardiac surgery at Johns Hopkins, another first for the institution, and was named dean for postdoctoral programs and faculty development. For several years, however, Watkins had been working to increase the minority presence at this elite medical school, and he instituted a special minority recruiting drive when he was appointed to the medical school's admissions committee in 1979.

Watkins has been the recipient of numerous honors and awards, and in 2000 he received national recognition from the Guidant Corporation for his pioneering work on the automatic defibrillator. Watkins continues to serve as a professor of surgery and associate dean of the School of Medicine at Johns Hopkins University.

DANIEL HALE WILLIAMS (1856–1931)

Surgeon, Physician. A pioneer in open-heart surgery, Daniel Hale Williams was born in Hollidaysburg, Pennsylvania, on January 18, 1856. In 1878, he apprenticed to a prominent physician, which gave him the training to enter the Chicago Medical College in 1880.

Williams opened his office on Chicago's South Side at a time when Chicago hospitals did not allow African American doctors to use their facilities. In 1891, Williams founded Provident Hospital, which was open to patients of all races. At Provident Hospital on July 10, 1893, Williams performed the operation on which his later fame rests. A patient was admitted to the emergency ward with a knife wound in the pericardium, or the membrane enclosing the heart. With the aid of six staff surgeons, Williams made an incision in the patient's chest and successfully repaired the tear. The patient fully recovered and was soon able to leave the hospital.

In 1894, President Grover Cleveland appointed Williams surgeon-in-chief of Freedmen's Hospital in Washington, D.C. He completely reorganized and updated procedures at the hospital, adding specialty departments, organizing a system of horse-drawn ambulances, and initiating more sanitary medical practices. After some political infighting at Freedmen's, he resigned his post in 1898 to return to Provident.

Williams was instrumental in the forming of the Medico-Chirurgical Society and the National Medical Association. In 1913, he was inducted into the American College of Surgeons at its first convention. Over the course of his career, Williams helped establish over forty hospitals in twenty states to serve African American communities. He died in Idlewild, Michigan, on August 4, 1931, after a lifetime devoted to his two main interests—the NAACP and the construction of hospitals and training schools for African American doctors and nurses.

O. S. WILLIAMS (1921–)

Aeronautical Engineer. Oswald S. "Ozzie" Williams was born on September 2, 1921, in Washington, D.C., but he was raised in New York City, graduating from Boys High School in Brooklyn in 1938. He became interested in engineering as a teenager. He attended New York University and in 1943 became the second African American to receive a degree in aeronautical engineering. He earned his master's in the field in 1947.

Around 1950, Williams took an engineering position at Greer Hydraulics, Inc. There he was responsible for the development of the first experimental airborne radio beacon, which was used to locate crashed airplanes. This device, however, was never produced commercially. At Grumman Aircraft Engineering Corporation, where he was hired as a propulsion engineer in 1961, Williams managed the development of the Apollo Lunar Module reaction-control subsystem. He was fully responsible for the $42 million effort for eight years. He managed the three engineering groups that developed the small rocket motors that guided the Lunar Module, the part of the Apollo spacecraft that actually landed on the moon. Williams had a stellar career in marketing at Grumman, culminating in his election as a company vice president in 1974.

After leaving Grumman, Williams taught marketing at St. John's University in Queens, New York, where he completed an M.B.A. in 1981. Williams was a member of the American Institute of Aeronautics and Astronautics and an associate fellow and chair of the institute's Liquid Rockets Technical Committee.

GRANVILLE T. WOODS (1856–1910)

Electrical Engineer, Inventor. Sometimes referred to as the "black Edison" because of his important electrical inventions, Granville T. Woods was born in Columbus, Ohio, on April 23, 1856. He attended school in Columbus until he was ten years old, but he was forced to leave school. Woods then began learning on the job as a machine-shop apprentice and later became a machinist and blacksmith. As a young man, Woods attended night school and studied privately; he understood the importance of education and training in achieving his goals. Later, in his free time, he studied electronics.

From 1872 to 1874, Woods worked first as a fireman and then as an engineer on the Iron Mountain Railroad in Missouri. In 1874, he moved to Springfield, Illinois, where he worked in a mill in which iron and steel were rolled into plates and bars. He took a job aboard a British steamer in 1878 and was promoted to chief engineer of the steamer within two years. From 1880 to 1884, Woods ran a steam locomotive on the Danville and Southern Railroad in Missouri.

Woods eventually settled in Cincinnati, Ohio. His interest in thermal power and steam-driven engines led Woods to file his first patent, for an improved steam boiler furnace, in 1884. In 1887, he patented a railway telegraph system that allowed moving trains to communicate with the station and with other trains in the area. In this way, it was possible to pinpoint the locations of trains between stations and avoid accidents and collisions. Thomas Edison later sued Woods, claiming that he was the first inventor of this "multiplex telegraph" system. After Woods won the suit, Edison offered Woods a prominent position in the engineering department at the Edison Electric Light Company in New York, but Woods rejected his offer. Alexander Graham Bell's company purchased the rights to Woods's telegraph system, which allowed Woods the means to pursue inventing full-time.

In 1888, Woods developed an overhead system of electrical railway lines. This invention led to the overhead

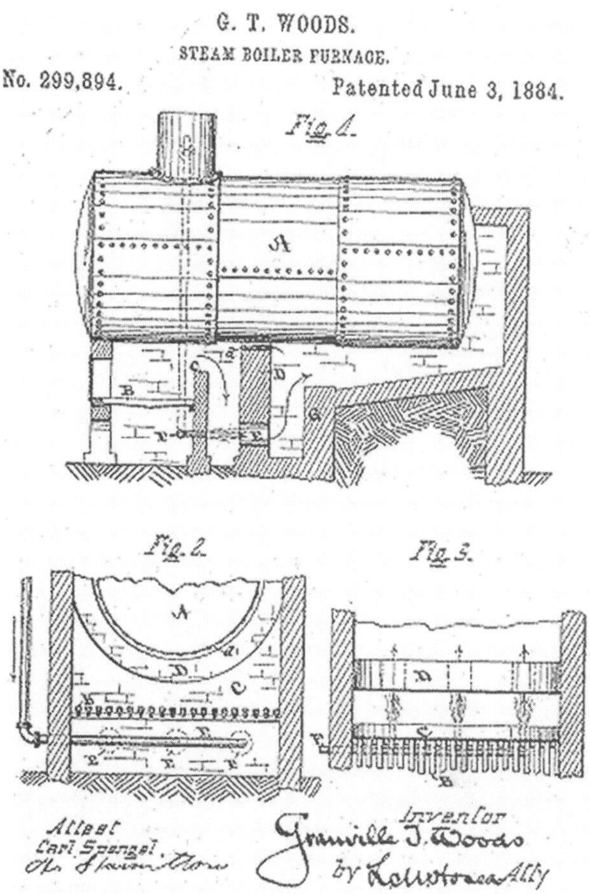

First Patent of Granville T. Woods, Issued on June 3, 1884. *Sometimes referred to as "the Black Edison," Woods received his first patent for an improved steam boiler furnace.* U.S. PATENT OFFICE

railroad system found in major cities such as Chicago, St. Louis, and New York City.

During his illustrious career, Woods patented over thirty-five electrical inventions, which, in addition to Bell Telephone, were sold to major companies such as General Electric and Westinghouse. His automatic air brake, used to slow or stop trains, cut down on train accidents and was just one of the inventions that made the railways safer.

Woods spent the last years of his life in court battles, attempting to gain control over his own inventions. On January 30, 1910, he died in New York City, in near poverty.

28

SPORTS

Delano Greenidge-Copprue

Despite various racial barriers of the nineteenth and twentieth centuries, African Americans have excelled in practically every sport that was developed in or introduced into the United States. In addition to accomplishing a number of athletic feats, African American athletes have helped push societal changes forward. The integration of baseball in 1947 by Jackie Robinson and the legacy of heavyweight boxing champion Joe Louis helped launch the civil rights movement. Additionally, the rise in black nationalism of the 1960s and 1970s was projected by the words and deeds of African American athletes such as Muhammad Ali, Wilt Chamberlain, and Curt Flood.

Professional and some amateur sports have also given African Americans the opportunity for instant fame and wealth not often afforded by other areas. For some, success on the athletic field has carried over into the private sector, as many African American athletes have used their wealth and prestige to start businesses and give their time to a variety of community efforts. Now that the twenty-first century is well under way, new barriers have presented themselves. Most notably, few African Americans have been given employment in front-office positions or been granted ownership of professional sports teams.

BASEBALL

Professional baseball began in Hoboken, New Jersey, in 1846. The game was dominated by amateurs and roving semiprofessionals until the National League was formed in 1876. Initially, there was no prohibition against African Americans playing in the National League or its rivals—the American Association, the Union League, and the Players League. Moses Fleetwood Walker, the first prominent African American professional baseball player, played for the Toledo Blue Stockings of the American Association (then a major-league baseball association) during the 1880s. However, in an exhibition game with a National League team, the Chicago White Stockings, the "color line" was drawn in baseball for the first time, when White Stockings player/manager Adrian "Cap" Anson refused to play on the same field with Walker. Later, Anson used his influence to initiate a "gentlemen's agreement" among major league teams not to sign any African American players. This agreement became the standard in organized baseball.

Efforts to sneak African Americans into the major leagues under the guise of being Cuban or American Indian also failed. Until the 1920s, the only way for African Americans to play baseball was as semiprofessionals touring and playing wherever they got the chance. In 1920 Rube Foster and others established an organized, professional Negro National League to give African Americans the chance to play big-league baseball. The Negro National League featured teams such as the Detroit Stars, Homestead Grays, Baltimore Elite Giants, and others that played wherever they could find a stadium and funding. They frequently filled Major League Baseball stadiums when given the chance, and the quality of their product was evidenced by such Hall of Fame players as Satchel Paige, Josh Gibson, Ray Dandridge, "Cool Papa" Bell, Oscar Charleston, Buck Leonard, and Judy Johnson, several of whom later played together on the Pittsburgh Crawfords, an independent club that became a charter member of a second Negro National League in 1933.

The Negro National League was never financially stable, however, and teams frequently folded. Many chose—or

The 1935 Pittsburgh Crawfords. *The Crawfords, a Negro Leagues baseball team that is considered among the greatest in the history of the sport, featured five (future) Hall of Fame members: Oscar Charleston, Judy Johnson, James "Cool Papa" Bell, Josh Gibson, and Leroy "Satchel" Paige.* **SCHOMBURG CENTER FOR RESEARCH IN BLACK CULTURE; THE NEW YORK PUBLIC LIBRARY; ASTOR, LENOX AND TILDEN FOUNDATIONS**

felt their best option was—to play for pay in Cuba or the Dominican Republic. Despite efforts by Kenesaw Mountain Landis, the Major League Baseball commissioner, to stop them, many exhibition games were arranged between Negro League and Major League all-star teams. The exhibitions were competitive, and the Negro League players demonstrated their skill by winning many of the contests. As long as Landis was commissioner of Major League Baseball, however, integration was impossible.

In 1945, following the death of Landis and the appointment of Happy Chandler as commissioner, Brooklyn Dodger general manager and part-owner Branch Rickey began a search for an African American to integrate Major League Baseball. He settled on UCLA alumnus Jackie Robinson. In 1946 Robinson played for the Dodgers' top minor league team in Montreal. In 1947 he integrated baseball despite virulent opposition from teammates, opposing players, and all of the other Major League Baseball owners. Robinson was named the National League's Rookie of the Year in 1947 and won the Most Valuable Player (MVP) award in 1949. The Cleveland Indians integrated the American League in 1947 with Larry Doby.

By 1958 all Major League Baseball teams had integrated their rosters, and African American players became stars in both leagues. In 1975 Frank Robinson became the first African American manager of a Major League Baseball team with the Cleveland Indians. Nevertheless, baseball's front-office positions remained generally closed to African Americans, as few became managers or general

Baseball Player Curt Flood, 1970. *Flood* (right) *challenged his trade from the St. Louis Cardinals to the Philadelphia Phillies on the grounds that baseball's reserve clause—binding players to their existing teams—violated federal antitrust laws. Although he lost his court battle, Flood's challenge played a key role in the subsequent ending of the reserve system and the establishment of free agency.* BETTMANN/CORBIS

managers in the decade following Robinson's hiring. The power structure changed slightly in 1988 when former player Bill White became the first African American president of the National League. White was succeeded in 1994 by another African American, Leonard Coleman.

In addition, many of baseball's top stars have been African American. In 2007 Barry Bonds became Major League Baseball's all-time home run leader. Hank Aaron drove in more runs than anyone in history. Rickey Henderson holds the record for most steals and for most runs scored. Additionally, African American players have been the recipients of the MVP award in the American or National League over 35 percent of the time during the last half century.

Curt Flood also changed the face of baseball. In 1969 Flood decided to challenge his trade from the St. Louis Cardinals to the Philadelphia Phillies on the grounds that baseball's reserve clause—binding players to their existing teams—violated federal antitrust laws. A lawsuit brought by Flood was eventually heard by the U.S. Supreme Court, which ruled against Flood and decided that baseball could retain its position as the only professional sport exempted from federal antitrust legislation. In 1975, however, an agreement between the players and management ended the reserve system and established free agency.

The percentage of African American players in Major League Baseball has declined since its peak in the 1970s, to a low of 8.2 percent in 2007 (this percentage increased slightly to 9 percent in 2009). One factor responsible for this change is the streamlining of inner-city baseball programs and urban little leagues because of financial problems. The economic situation has become so bad in some U.S. cities that even scholastic athletic programs are threatened with cutbacks or dissolution. Nevertheless, many of the game's top players are African American, including Carl Crawford, Prince Fielder, Ryan Howard, Torii Hunter, Derek Jeter, and Jimmy Rollins.

In 1997—the fiftieth anniversary of the game being racially integrated—Major League Baseball honored Jackie Robinson's pioneering feat. Commissioner Bud Selig retired

Baseball Player Derek Jeter. *One of the top players in baseball in the late twentieth and early twenty-first centuries, Jeter has played his entire career with the New York Yankees, helping the team capture five World Series championships. The shortstop has been an eleven-time All-Star selection, was named MVP of the 2000 World Series, and has served as captain of the Yankees since 2003.* PHOTOGRAPH BY SCOTT MARTIN. AP IMAGES. REPRODUCED BY PERMISSION.

his number, 42, from use by *any* baseball team; the only current exception is closer Mariano Rivera of the New York Yankees, who was wearing number 42 at the time of Selig's mandate. President Bill Clinton offered remarks on Robinson's legacy at a ceremony in New York's Shea Stadium. Also that summer, Robinson's widow, Rachel, took part in a ceremony at the National Baseball Hall of Fame dedicating a wing to African Americans.

NATIONAL BASEBALL HALL OF FAME

1962: Jackie Robinson

1969: Roy Campanella

1971: Leroy R. "Satchel" Paige

1972: Josh Gibson; Walter F. "Buck" Leonard

1973: Roberto W. Clemente; Monte Irvin

1974: James T. "Cool Papa" Bell

1975: William J. "Judy" Johnson

1976: Oscar M. Charleston

1977: Ernest Banks; Martin Dihigo; John H. Lloyd

1979: Willie Mays

1981: Andrew "Rube" Foster; Robert T. "Bob" Gibson

1982: Hank Aaron; Frank Robinson

1983: Juan A. Marichal

1985: Lou Brock

1986: Willie L. "Stretch" McCovey

1987: Ray Dandridge; Billy Williams

1988: Willie Stargell

1990: Joe Morgan

1991: Rod Carew; Ferguson Jenkins

1993: Reggie Jackson

1995: Leon Day

1996: Willie Foster

1997: Willie Wells

1998: Larry Doby

1999: Orlando Cepeda; Joe Williams

2000: Tony Pérez; Norman "Turkey" Stearnes

2001: Kirby Puckett; Hilton Smith; Dave Winfield

2002: Ozzie Smith

2003: Eddie Murray

2006: Negro League Players: Ray Brown, Willard Brown, Andy Cooper, Biz Mackey, Mule Suttles, Cristóbal Torriente, Jud Wilson; Pre–Negro League Players: Frank Grant; Pete Hill; José Méndez, Louis Santop, Ben Taylor; Negro League Executives: Effa Manley (first woman), Alex Pompez, Cum Posey, J. L. Wilkinson (white owner); Pre–Negro League Executive: Sol White.

2007: Tony Gwynn

2009: Rickey Henderson; Jim Rice

2010: Andre Dawson

FOOTBALL

Unlike the other major American sports, professional football was integrated from its inception. Beginning in 1919 with Fritz Pollard of the Akron Indians of the American Professional Football League (later renamed the National Football League [NFL]), African Americans participated in professional football. At the peak of hard

Barry Sanders, 1996. *One of the greatest running backs in football, winner of the 1988 Heisman Trophy while at Oklahoma State University, Sanders spent his entire ten-year professional career with the Detroit Lions until retiring abruptly in 1999 while within striking distance of the all-time career rushing record.* PHOTOGRAPH BY TIM SHAEFER. AP IMAGES. REPRODUCED BY PERMISSION.

times brought on by the Great Depression, however, white players complained that African Americans reduced the number of jobs available to them. Team owners then joined in an unwritten pact that African Americans would no longer be allowed to play the game professionally.

The NFL was bereft of African American players until the Los Angeles Rams signed Kenny Washington and Woody Strode in 1946. Later that year, Cleveland Browns fullback Marion Motley became the first black player in a rival league, the All-American Football Conference (AAFC), and he went on to become the earliest African American pro football star. Motley led the AAFC in rushing, was instrumental in the Browns' multiple AAFC championships, and continued to do the same when the team was absorbed by the NFL. Syracuse University's Jim Brown began his career with the Browns shortly after the retirement of Motley and became the top running back in the league. Brown led the league in rushing for eight of his nine years and held the career yardage mark for nineteen years after his retirement.

By the end of Brown's career in the mid-1960s, other African American stars had emerged. New York Giants safety Emlen Tunnell—the first black player for the Giants since reintegration—retired in 1961 with 79 career interceptions, a record that was not eclipsed until 1979. With 14 touchdowns in 1965, rookie Chicago Bears running back Gale Sayers immediately gained fame as one of the most exciting running backs of the era. In 1966 and 1969 Sayers led the league in rushing, and in 1977 he became the youngest man ever inducted into the Professional Football Hall of Fame. African Americans excelled at every position except quarterback, which for a time in the history of the game remained unofficially reserved for white players.

African American stars continued to proliferate in the 1960s and 1970s. Charley Taylor was the first African American to lead the league in receptions twice. Willie Wood was the first to lead the NFL in interceptions. In 1973 the Buffalo Bills' O. J. Simpson became the first player to rush for more than 2,000 yards in a single season. Only four players have managed that feat since, and all of them happened to be African American. It took Eric Dickerson (2,105 yards in 1984), Barry Sanders (2,053 in 1997), Terrell Davis (2,008 in 1998), and Jamal Lewis (2,066 in 2003) sixteen games to achieve what Simpson accomplished in fourteen. The visibility of African Americans in the NFL was demonstrated by the popularity of certain teams' defensive lines and their familiar nicknames. The Minnesota Vikings offered the "Purple People Eaters," including Carl Eller, future state supreme court justice Alan Page, and Jim Marshall. David "Deacon" Jones and Rosey Grier were mainstays on the Los Angeles Rams' "Fearsome Foursome." The great Pittsburgh Steelers defenses of the 1970s were known as the "Steel Curtain" and included "Mean" Joe Greene.

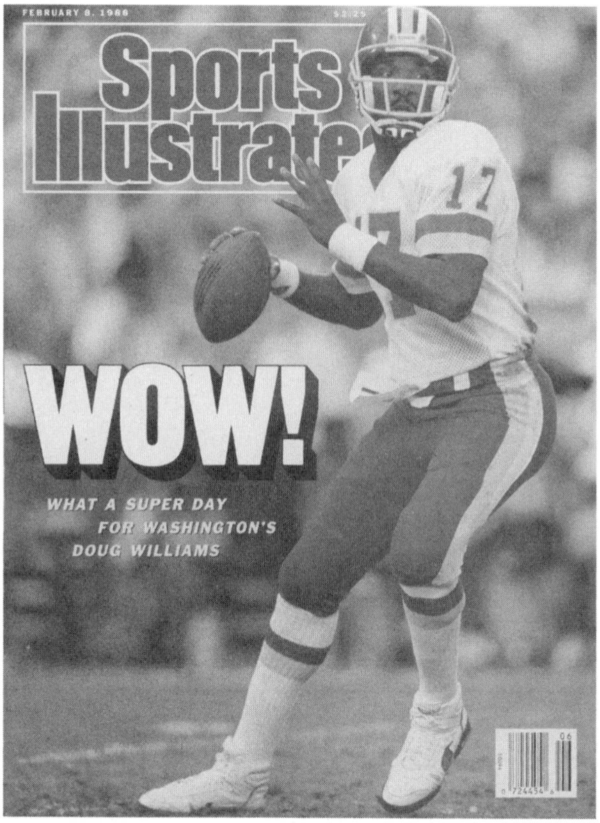

Doug Williams,* Sports Illustrated *Cover, February 8, 1988. *As a member of the Washington Redskins, Williams in 1988 became the first African American to quarterback his team to a Super Bowl victory.* **JOHN BIEVER/SPORTS ILLUSTRATED/GETTY IMAGES**

During the 1980s, the New York Giants' Lawrence Taylor revolutionized the position of outside linebacker. In 1984 Walter Payton of the Bears eclipsed Jim Brown's record for career rushing yards and concluded his brilliant career in 1987 with 16,726 yards, a record that stood for fifteen years. In 1988 the Washington Redskins' Doug Williams became the first African American to quarterback his team to a Super Bowl victory. The 1990s were dominated by three running backs who won MVP awards in the NFL: the Detroit Lions' Barry Sanders, the Dallas Cowboys' Emmitt Smith (who broke Payton's record for career rushing yards in 2002), and the Denver Broncos' Terrell Davis. The San Francisco 49ers' wide receiver Jerry Rice holds the NFL record for most touchdowns scored in a career. Cornerback Deion "Prime Time" Sanders became one of the game's most visible and dominant defensive players. He was also notably dangerous as a kick and punt returner.

In the late 1990s African Americans represented approximately 70 percent of those playing in the NFL. The proportion of African Americans in the coaching ranks and team front offices, however, has not grown at the same pace. African Americans made up less than 20 percent of the head coaches in the league and held none of the upper-level management positions. In 2002, pro football Hall of Famer Ozzie Newsome became the first black general manager in the NFL. By 2010, the thirty-two-team NFL had three black general managers and six black head coaches.

There is a similar problem in college football, as most coaching jobs are still held by whites. The major avenue for African Americans in coaching—and at one time in playing—was through historically African American colleges. Eddie Robinson, the longtime head coach at Grambling State University, produced several NFL stars as did other predominantly African American colleges. The integration of major southern universities, however, has weakened the influence of African American colleges.

PRO FOOTBALL HALL OF FAME

1967: Emlen Tunnell

1968: Marion Motley

1969: Fletcher "Joe" Perry

1971: Jim Brown

1972: Ollie Matson

1973: Jim Parker

1974: Richard "Night Train" Lane

1975: Roosevelt Brown; Leonard "Lenny" Moore

1976: Leonard "Len" Ford

1977: Gale Sayers; Bill Willis

1980: Herb Adderley; David "Deacon" Jones

1981: Willie Davis

1983: Bobby Bell; Bobby Mitchell; Paul Warfield

1984: Willie Brown; Charley Taylor

1985: O. J. Simpson

1986: Ken Houston; Willie Lanier

1987: Joe Greene; John Henry Johnson; Gene Upshaw

1988: Alan Page

1989: Mel Blount; Art Shell; Willie Wood

1990: Junious "Buck" Buchanan; Franco Harris

1991: Earl Campbell

1992: Lem Barney; John Mackey

1993: Larry Little; Walter Payton

1994: Tony Dorsett; Leroy Kelly

1995: Lee Roy Selmon; Kellen Winslow

1996: Charlie Joiner; Mel Renfro

1997: Mike Haynes

1998: Mike Singletary; Dwight Stephenson

1999: Eric Dickerson; Ozzie Newsome; Lawrence Taylor

2000: Ronnie Lott

2001: Jackie Slater; Lynn Swann

2002: John Stallworth

2003: Marcus Allen; Elvin Bethea; James Lofton

2004: Bob "Boomer" Brown; Carl Eller; Barry Sanders

2005: Fritz Pollard

2006: Harry Carson; Warren Moon; Reggie White; Rayfield Wright

2007: Michael Irvin; Charlie Sanders; Thurman Thomas

2008: Fred Dean; Darrell Green; Art Monk; Emmitt Thomas; Andre Tippett

2009: Bob Hayes; Randall McDaniel; Bruce Smith; Derrick Thomas; Rod Woodson

2010: Rickey Jackson; Floyd Little; John Randle; Jerry Rice; Emmitt Smith

BOXING

African American athletes have been boxing professionally since colonial times and have dominated the sport—especially in the heavyweight division—since the 1930s. In 1890 George "Little Chocolate" Dixon became the first African American to win a world boxing title. In 1908 Jack Johnson became the first to win the heavyweight title. Joe Walcott (not to be confused with "Jersey" Joe Walcott, a heavyweight contemporary of Joe Louis) lost his only shot at the world lightweight championship in 1897. In 1901, however, he captured the welterweight title. Throughout Walcott's tumultuous career, he fought in handicap events where he was required to weigh much less than his opponent—and much less than his normal body weight. Walcott also fought light heavyweights and heavyweights with unbelievable success. Because of this, many boxing experts called him the greatest welterweight and greatest "pound-for-pound" fighter of all time. Middleweight champion "Sugar" Ray Robinson and light-heavyweight Roy Jones Jr. are also mentioned in such discussions. Joe Louis held the world heavyweight title for a record eleven years and eight months in the 1930s and 1940s. Henry Armstrong held three world titles at once—featherweight, lightweight, and welterweight—during the Great Depression.

Boxer Joe Louis. *Louis held the world heavyweight title for a record eleven years and eight months in the 1930s and 1940s.* POPPERFOTO/GETTY IMAGES

Louis, Robinson, and Armstrong were stars in what is considered the first golden age of African Americans in boxing. A new golden age was ushered in on March 8, 1971, when Muhammad Ali and Joe Frazier drew the sport's first multimillion-dollar gate. Ali, a national figure since winning an Olympic gold medal in 1960, was also one of the first athletes to comment on U.S. political and social events despite the danger that such a stance could pose to his career.

Other boxing divisions have also featured African American stars. During the 1970s and 1980s attention shifted to talented fighters in the middleweight and welterweight divisions including "Sugar" Ray Leonard, "Marvelous" Marvin Hagler, and Thomas "Hit Man" Hearns. When Ali was no longer able to defend his heavyweight crown, new challengers such as his former sparring partner Larry Holmes and Michael Spinks ascended to the championship ranks.

As purses for major boxing events reached the $100 million mark in the mid-1980s, a new generation of fighters arose. "Iron" Mike Tyson became the best-known heavyweight champion since Ali and the wealthiest boxer of all time. He also became the youngest heavyweight champion of all time, capturing his first belt when he was twenty years old. His tumultuous reign ended in Japan in 1990 with a knockout by James "Buster" Douglas, who in turn lost the title to Evander Holyfield. Even without a title to his name, Tyson continued to be the most visible figure in boxing. In 1992 he was convicted of sexual assault and sentenced to jail. While incarcerated he made headlines for his conversion to Islam and his admissions of youthful indiscretions. After his release, he quickly regained his title until Holyfield won it from him in 1996. In a 1997 rematch, Tyson bit Holyfield twice during the early rounds, prompting Tyson's disqualification and suspension from boxing. Despite the lifting of that suspension, legal troubles and prison time have clouded the career of the sport's most infamous figure.

Other stars, including Pernell Whitaker and Roy Jones Jr., have since shone brightly, but none have held the attention of the public as Tyson had. While many experts see the lack of a popular heavyweight champion as a sign of the death of the sport of boxing, this may not entirely be the case. While the heavyweight ranks, once the prize of the boxing world and of masculinity, have garnered less attention, middleweights such as Bernard Hopkins, with a record twenty title defenses, and welterweights such as Floyd Mayweather Jr. and "Sugar" Shane Moseley continue to demonstrate technical excellence and superior skill within the sport of boxing.

Top boxers can conceivably earn as much as $100 million for less than a dozen major ring events. The advent of pay-per-view television and cable network sponsorship has led to soaring profits for the sport and its practitioners, although declining ratings and public interest threaten this trend. Colorful entrepreneur Don King is the most famous, wealthy, and controversial boxing promoter of the modern era. His powerful position within the sport and his hold on Tyson allowed him to control championship boxing, despite frequent troubles with the Internal Revenue Service and complaints from former fighters who worked under King.

BASKETBALL

African Americans' presence in basketball dates to the early days of the sport. College basketball dominated the first half of the twentieth century as no major professional league existed until the late 1940s. In 1916, educators, coaches, and faculty members from Hampton Institute, Shaw, Lincoln, Virginia Union, and Howard University formed the Central Intercollegiate Athletic Association, the first African American collegiate conference. Others soon followed, including the Southeastern Conference, Southwestern Athletic Conference, and Southern Intercollegiate Athletic Conference.

Much of the legacy of African American basketball history lies in its pioneers. Bob Douglas, who founded the Harlem Renaissance (also known as the New York Renaissance) in the 1920s, is considered the "Father of Black Professional Basketball." His innovations included monthly player contracts, a custom-designed team bus, and tours in the South. John McLendon, a coach during the 1950s and 1960s, is recognized as the strategic architect of the fast break, was the first African American to publish a book detailing his coaching philosophy, and was the first to coach a professional team. Additionally, McLendon was a prominent advocate of the desegregation of intercollegiate athletics.

For years, most top college African American players signed with the Harlem Globetrotters, an internationally known barnstorming team. From their inception in 1926, the Globetrotters have delighted basketball fans worldwide with their unique combination of skill and humor. Famous Globetrotters include "Meadowlark" Lemon, "Curly" Neal, "Goose" Tatum, and Marques Haynes. The Globetrotters brought an improvisational, jazzlike cadence to basketball that continues in the early twenty-first century with the mix tapes and tours sponsored by the athletic shoe company AND1.

Professional basketball organized in the late 1940s as the National Basketball Association (NBA) and was integrated in 1950. In the same year Chuck Cooper of Duquesne University was the first African American to be drafted into the league. Nat "Sweetwater" Clifton was the first to sign a professional contract. However, on October 31, 1950, when Earl Lloyd of the then Washington Capitols took the court, he became the first African American to actually participate in an NBA game.

Basketball grew in the 1950s and 1960s as African American players such as Bill Russell, Wilt Chamberlain, Elgin Baylor, and Oscar Robertson enjoyed success in both college and then as professionals. In 1966 Texas Western University became the first college team to win the NCAA national championship with an all–African American starting five. They beat the favored and all-white University of Kentucky, a milestone that began the end of segregated basketball teams.

The late 1960s and 1970s featured the rise of two of the great stars of the game—Kareem Abdul-Jabbar and Julius Erving. Abdul-Jabbar starred at UCLA and led the Bruins to three straight NCAA crowns. He then became a professional star with the Milwaukee Bucks and Los Angeles Lakers. Along with Earl Monroe, Willis Reed, Elvin Hayes, and others, African American players began to dominate the league. The rival American Basketball Association (ABA) began the slam dunk competitions that dominate the NBA All-Star Weekend. Erving, widely known as "Dr. J," became the most popular player in the ABA because of his dunks and acrobatics.

The 1980s and 1990s featured the growth of basketball into one of the most popular sports in the United States and around the world. The huge success of the NCAA Final Four led to large financial revenues for colleges. In 1982 John Thompson of Georgetown University became the first African American to coach in the Final Four. Two years later his team won the tournament. The talents of Magic Johnson, Isiah Thomas, Charles Barkley, Karl Malone, Alonzo Mourning, Carmelo Anthony, and others led to large growth of the college game and the NBA. These players became celebrities as well as athletes.

The most famous player of both decades, however, was Michael Jordan. Considered the greatest basketball player of all time, Jordan's success and personality made him one of the most famous people in the world. He led the University of North Carolina to an NCAA title in 1982 and led the Chicago Bulls to six NBA titles. His

COLLEGE BASKETBALL PREVIEW: GEORGETOWN IS No.1
Sports Illustrated
THERE THEY GO AGAIN
John Thompson
President Reagan
Patrick Ewing

Basketball Coach John Thompson, 1984. *With the help of such star players as Patrick Ewing, Thompson coached Georgetown University to an NCAA national championship in 1984.* LANE STEWART/SPORTS ILLUSTRATED/GETTY IMAGES

endorsements established athletic shoe maker Nike as one of the largest apparel companies in the world.

African Americans now occupy more than 80 percent of the spots on NBA rosters, including such stars as Shaquille O'Neal, Kobe Bryant, Kevin Garnett, Dwayne Wade, Allen Iverson, Tim Duncan, and LeBron James. Other areas, especially coaching and management positions, have less representation. Lenny Wilkens holds the career record for most NBA wins by an African American coach, with 1,332 victories, and Glenn "Doc" Rivers coached the Boston Celtics to their seventeenth world championship in 2008. Approximately 15 percent of top management and administrative positions are held by African Americans. In 1989 Bertram M. Lee and Peter C. B. Bynoe became the first African American owners of a professional sports franchise with the purchase of the Denver Nuggets. Robert Johnson became the majority owner of the Charlotte Bobcats in 2002, and Michael Jordan became the majority owner of the same franchise in 2010.

Incidents from the late 1990s and early twenty-first century involving high-profile players have dented the popularity and rapid growth of professional basketball. In 1997 Latrell Sprewell, an NBA All-Star player, attempted to strangle his coach, P. J. Carlesimo, at a practice. Following a league suspension, Sprewell returned to the NBA as a player for the New York Knicks. Sprewell's return was delayed along with the NBA season by a labor dispute that resulted in a lockout by NBA owners that did not end until early January 1999, resulting in a shortened season. In February 2002 retired NBA star Jayson Williams was charged with manslaughter in the shooting death of a limousine driver. Months later, Allen Iverson, a league MVP, as well as one of its most visible and talented players, was arraigned on charges that he had threatened two men while armed with a gun.

NAISMITH MEMORIAL BASKETBALL HALL OF FAME

1963: New York Renaissance (team)

1972: Robert L. "Bob" Douglas (contributor)

1975: Bill Russell

1977: Elgin Baylor; Charles Cooper

1979: Wilt Chamberlain

1980: Oscar Robertson

1982: Clarence Gaines; Willis Reed

1984: Sam Jones

1985: Nate Thurmond

1987: Walt "Clyde" Frazier

1988: Wes Unseld

1989: William "Pop" Gates; K. C. Jones; Lenny Wilkens (player)

1990: Dave Bing; Elvin Hayes; Earl "The Pearl" Monroe

1991: Nate "Tiny" Archibald

1992: Lusia Harris-Stewart (first woman, along with Nera White); Connie Hawkins; Bob Lanier

1993: Walt Bellamy; Julius "Dr. J" Erving; Calvin Murphy

1995: Kareem Abdul-Jabbar; Cheryl Miller

1996: George Gervin; David Thompson

1997: Alex English

1998: Marques Haynes; Lenny Wilkens (rehonored as a coach)

1999: Wayne Embry (contributor); John Thompson (coach)

2000: Bob McAdoo; Isiah Thomas

2001: John Chaney (coach); Moses Malone

2002: Harlem Globetrotters (team); Earvin "Magic" Johnson

2003: Meadowlark Lemon; Earl Lloyd; Robert Parish; James Worthy

2004: Clyde Drexler; Maurice Stokes; Lynette Woodard

2006: Charles Barkley; Joe Dumars; Dominique Wilkins

2007: Texas Western (team)

2008: Adrian Dantley; Patrick Ewing; Hakeem Olajuwon

2009: Michael Jordan; David Robinson; C. Vivian Stringer (coach)

2010: Dennis Johnson, Gus Johnson, Karl Malone, Scottie Pippen

OTHER SPORTS

African American athletes have excelled in track and field, winning medals at various Olympiads and other competitions. This tradition began at the 1908 London Olympics, when John Baxter Taylor became the first African American to capture a gold medal as part of the 1,600-meter relay team.

Jesse Owens was the star of the first half of the twentieth century. Owens is best known for his four gold medals won at the 1936 Olympics in Berlin, Germany, overturning racist notions of African American inferiority. However, it was on May 25, 1935, in Ann Arbor, Michigan, that Jesse Owens provided the greatest performance in track and field history at the Big Ten Championships as a member of Ohio State University's team. Owens began the day by equaling the world record in the 100-yard dash. He then proceeded to set world records in the long jump, 220-yard dash, and 220-yard low hurdles.

Owens began a string of medal-winning performances by African Americans in track and field. At the 1960 Olympics, Ralph Boston broke Owens's long jump record to win the gold medal. In so doing, he also became one of only two track stars to break a world record on six separate occasions. Rafer Johnson won the decathlon in the same Olympics. Bob Beamon, at the 1968 Mexico City Games, leaped 29′ 2 1/2″ in the long jump competition to win the gold medal and extend the world record by almost two feet. Beamon's record sat unbeaten and presumed out of reach for a quarter of a century, until Mike Powell surpassed it by two inches at the 1991 World Track and Field Championships in Tokyo. In 1984, in Los Angeles, Carl Lewis became the first athlete since Owens in 1936 to win four gold medals in the same games. Edwin Moses became the greatest 400-meter hurdler in history, winning gold medals in 1976 and 1984 as well as winning 122 straight races. At the 1996 Olympics in Atlanta, Michael Johnson emerged as the next African American star, becoming the first man to win the 200-meter and 400-meter races in the same games. Later, sprinters such as Tyson Gay continued to build upon the legacy established by such pioneers as Taylor and Owens.

One of the most controversial events in Olympic history occurred in 1968 during an awards ceremony. After finishing first and third, respectively, in the 200-meter dash, Tommie Smith and John Carlos, while on the victory stand, without shoes, in recognition of global poverty, raised their arms in unison with black gloves on their clenched fists. This became known as the "Black power salute." Their protest led to their suspension from the U.S. team and removal from the Olympic Village.

Historically, African American Olympic athletes have not fared well at the Winter Games. Debi Thomas became the first to win a medal of any kind when she earned a bronze in figure skating in 1988. Not until the 2002 Olympiad did another African American ascend the podium for a medal. That year, Jarome Iginla won a gold medal with the Canadian men's ice hockey team. More notably, however, Vonetta Flowers won gold at the same games with her white teammate for their two-woman bobsled performance. Similarly, half of the U.S. four-man bobsled team that year was African American: Garrett Hines and Randy Jones captured silver medals to become the first African American men to place at a Winter Olympiad. In 2002, Shani Davis became the first black speed skater to earn a spot on the U.S. national team, and he is a current world record holder and Olympic medalist.

The professional tennis community was largely devoid of African Americans through World War II, as they were not welcomed by the United States Lawn Tennis Association (USLTA). In a sport primarily associated with the upper class, the only avenues of competition open for African Americans were universities and colleges, clubs, and various minor tournaments. Shortly after the war, the USLTA loosened its discriminatory policies. In 1948 Oscar Johnson became the first African American player to win a USLTA-sanctioned event.

Arthur Ashe, a classy and congenial champion, won three Grand Slam events—the U.S. Open in 1968, the Australian Open in 1970, and Wimbledon in 1975—along with several less-celebrated tournaments during his career. He represented the United States as a member of the Davis Cup team ten times and was its captain from 1981 to 1984. Ashe also made contributions off the court. He made significant contributions as a human rights activist and retained a dignity and grace during his battle with AIDS. In 1996 MaliVai Washington became the first African American since Ashe to reach the Wimbledon finals. Later, Venus and Serena Williams excelled on the tennis court and beyond.

African Americans' attempts to break into golf prior to World War II paralleled those of their tennis counterparts. The Professional Golfers Association (PGA), however, did not rescind its white-only policy until 1959, when Charlie Sifford became the first African American to be issued a PGA card as an "approved player." In 1967 Renee Powell became the first African American female to be issued a card from the Ladies Professional Golf Association (LPGA). Sifford was the best known of the initial participants on the tour. He was the first to win a predominantly white event with his victory at the 1957 Long Beach Open. In 1975 Lee Elder became the first African American to compete at the Masters tournament. In the 1980s Calvin Peete enjoyed success on the tour, and he was a member of the 1983 and 1985 U.S. Ryder Cup teams.

Not until the arrival of Tiger Woods in the mid-1990s, however, did an African American golfer become a superstar. Woods was a child prodigy, winning several junior tournaments before he was a teenager. In 1994 Woods became the first African American to win the U.S. Amateur title. He repeated this feat the next two years, becoming the first man to win the amateur title three years in a row. In 1997, after becoming a professional, Woods won the Masters tournament with a record score. He also rose to the ranking of the world's top player. These accomplishments indicate the level of fame Woods

Tiger Woods, Masters Tournament, Augusta National Golf Club, Augusta, GA, 2010. *The first African American to win a Grand Slam golf tournament, Woods returned from his self-imposed break from competition in late 2009 and early 2010 to finish tied for fourth at the 2010 Masters Tournament.* SHAUN BEST/REUTERS/LANDOV

quickly achieved. Following the retirement of basketball superstar Michael Jordan, Woods became the preeminent African American athlete. A number of endorsement deals made him one of sport's only billionaires.

African American luminaries exist in other sports. By winning the Brunswick Memorial World Open in 1986, George Branham III became the first African American bowler to win a Professional Bowlers Association (PBA) title. Branham went on to win four other titles, including the prestigious Firestone Tournament of Champions in 1993, which was the first time an African American had won bowling's most prestigious event. During a career spanning three decades, weightlifter John Davis was a two-time Olympic champion (1948 and 1952) and set sixteen world records. Superlative bodybuilder Lee Haney reached the top of his field by winning eight consecutive Mr. Olympia titles from 1984 to 1991. Picking up where Haney left off, Lenda Murray captured every Ms. Olympia title from 1990 through 1995 and later won two more titles in 2002 and 2003. Following in their footsteps, and matching Haney's accomplishment, Ronnie Coleman won the Mr. Olympia title eight straight times between 1998 and 2005.

At the dawn of the twentieth century, cyclist Marshall Taylor was among the three most celebrated African American athletes in the world. During the same era, jockey Isaac Murphy, viewed as the greatest in the world at his craft, was part of a triumphant half century of African American jockeys. In 1875 Oliver Lewis won the inaugural Kentucky Derby riding the horse Aristides. Yet, until Marlon St. Julien rode to a seventh-place finish in the 2000 derby, no African American had ridden in the prestigious race since 1921.

One sport in which African Americans have had a negligible influence is auto racing. Willy T. Ribbs is the only African American to drive at the Indianapolis 500, participating in the 1991 and 1993 races, although he later failed in his efforts to put together a successful NASCAR team. In the late 1990s Julius Erving and former football star Joe Washington became the first African American owners of a NASCAR team, although they raced with a white driver. Wendell Scott is the only African American to win a NASCAR race, doing so in 1963.

Along with Erving, Earvin "Magic" Johnson and LeBron James have made their presence known on the stock car racing circuit. Racing legend Willy T. Ribbs cites as a source of early inspiration Leonard W. Miller, a black racing pioneer and race team owner. In 2005, Miller's team became the first African American group to win a NASCAR event.

WOMEN IN SPORTS

Although not provided with the same opportunities that have been traditionally afforded to men, African American women have still made a significant contribution to the sports world. African American women are on the vanguard of the new opportunities, achieving success in a variety of sports, ranging from tennis to basketball.

In 1948 Alice Coachman became the first African American woman to capture an Olympic gold medal, with her first place finish in the high jump. Coachman was the first of many African American women to excel at track and field. At the 1952 Summer Games, fifteen-year-old Barbara Jones became the youngest woman to win an Olympic gold medal in track and field. Wilma Rudolph overcame debilitating childhood illnesses to win three gold medals at the 1960 Olympiad in Rome. In the 1968 games, Wyomia Tyus became the second African American to win more than one gold medal in a single Olympiad as well as the first to set world records in two events. Track and field stars of the late twentieth century included Florence Griffith

Joyner, winner of four medals during the 1988 Olympiad, including three gold medals; Jackie Joyner-Kersee, winner of three Olympic gold medals; and Gail Devers, who overcame the effects of Graves' disease to win a gold medal at the 1992 Olympic Games and two more gold medals four years later. More recent stars include Dawn Harper, Sanya Richards, and Allyson Felix, all of whom earned medals during the 2008 Summer games held in Beijing. On the Winter Olympic side, Debi Thomas in 1988 became the first African American woman to win an Olympic medal in figure skating. African American sprinter Marion Jones won five medals in the 2000 Summer Olympiad, but was later stripped of those medals after confessing to the use of performance-enhancing substances.

The first African American woman athlete to dominate her sport was tennis's Althea Gibson. A superb athlete, Gibson was named 1957's Female Athlete of the Year during which she captured the prestigious Wimbledon singles title and the U.S. National Championship (later the U.S. Open). She won both titles again in 1958 and was the undisputed number one women's player in the world during those years. Earlier, she had become the first African American, man or woman, to capture a Grand Slam event with her singles and doubles championships at the 1956 French Open. Zina Garrison-Jackson was the next prominent African American tennis player, eventually reaching a top-ten ranking and becoming a 1990 Wimbledon finalist.

In the mid-1990s the Williams sisters, Venus and Serena, entered the international tennis scene, bringing new attention to the sport among African Americans. Serena, the younger sister, became the first of the two to win a Grand Slam title, taking the U.S. Open in 1999. Venus followed with back-to-back victories at the U.S. Open and Wimbledon in 2000 and 2001. The sisters have gone on to dominate the sport, winning a number of additional Grand Slam titles.

Basketball has been a major outlet for African American women athletes. Cheryl Miller is one of the most famous women basketball players. She was named an All-American at the conclusion of each of her four years at the University of Southern California, was national player of the year three times, and was inducted into the Basketball Hall of Fame in 1994. The decade of the 1970s featured the great center Lusia Harris, the first woman (along with Nera White) to be inducted into the Basketball Hall of Fame. Others who have left their marks in basketball annals include University of Kansas star Lynette Woodard, perhaps best known for becoming the first female member of the Harlem Globetrotters, in 1985.

Two professional basketball leagues for women were established in 1996: the Women's National Basketball Association (WNBA), supported by the men's NBA, and the American Basketball League (ABL). Both leagues allowed stars such as Cynthia Cooper, Lisa Leslie, Sheryl Swoopes, and Chamique Holdsclaw the chance to exhibit their skills beyond the college level. The ABL folded before it could launch its third season, but the WNBA continued on with much success. The league, which was originally comprised of eight teams, had expanded to sixteen by 2000 before contracting to twelve teams over the next ten years.

Other notables in sports include volleyball player Flo Hyman; bodybuilder Lenda Murray, who won the Ms. Olympia title eight times; Toni Stone, who in 1953 became the first African American woman to play professional baseball, playing that season with the Indianapolis Clowns of the Negro American League; and Olympic gymnast Dominique Dawes. In 1978 Wendy Hilliard became the first African American member of the U.S. National Rhythmic Gymnastics Team.

Unfortunately, very few of the above-mentioned women ever had the opportunity to display their talents on a professional level. Women's athletics has long been hamstrung by the lack of non-amateur forums in which African American women athletes could participate. For many, the Olympic Games or intercollegiate athletics have been the final step of their careers.

Women's athletics received a boost with the enactment of Title IX of the Education Amendments of 1972, which stipulated that any university receiving federal funds was obligated to provide an equal or proportionate number of scholarships for women. While the law provides opportunities to women, it has been criticized in its implementation as many universities have cut men's programs to fund scholarships for women.

ATHLETES, COACHES, AND SPORTS EXECUTIVES

(Some biographical profiles may appear in other chapters. To locate profiles more readily, please consult the index.)

HANK AARON (1934–)

Baseball Player, Sports Executive. Henry Louis Aaron was born in Mobile, Alabama, on February 5, 1934. He played sandlot ball as a teenager and later played for a local team named the Black Bears. He first played professional baseball with the Indianapolis Clowns of the Negro American League.

In June 1952 Aaron's contract was purchased by the Boston Braves. The following season, playing for their minor league team in Jacksonville, his .362 average led the South Atlantic League. In 1954 he was promoted to the Braves, then based in Milwaukee.

Baseball Hall of Famer Hank Aaron, 2010. *Aaron became Major League Baseball's all-time home run leader in 1974 when he surpassed the mark set by Babe Ruth. Aaron's record stood for thirty-three years, until it was bested by Barry Bonds in 2007.* AP PHOTO/ BEBETO MATTHEWS

Aaron enjoyed perhaps his finest season in 1957, when he was named National League MVP and led his team to a world championship. He batted .322, with 44 homers, 132 RBIs, and 118 runs scored.

In 1974 Aaron became the all-time home run leader when he hit his 715th, breaking Babe Ruth's mark of 714 home runs. He played his final two seasons in the American League with the Milwaukee Brewers, completing his career with a total of 755 home runs.

During his career, Aaron won a pair of batting titles and hit over .300 in fourteen seasons. He won the home run and RBI crowns four times apiece, hit 40 or more homers eight times, and hit at least 20 home runs for twenty consecutive years, a National League record. In addition, he was named to twenty consecutive All-Star teams.

Aaron was inducted into the Baseball Hall of Fame in 1982. His autobiography *I Had a Hammer* was published in 1991, and statues of Aaron grace the entrances of both Turner Field and Miller Park where, respectively, the Braves and Brewers play. The Braves have also honored Aaron by changing the address of the stadium to Hank Aaron Drive. In 2002 Aaron was awarded the Presidential Medal of Freedom, the nation's highest civilian honor.

One of the first African Americans to play in Major League Baseball, Aaron after his playing days served as vice president of player development for the Braves. In 1989 the Braves named him senior vice president and assistant to the president.

KAREEM ABDUL-JABBAR (1947–)

Basketball Player. Kareem Abdul-Jabbar was born Ferdinand Lewis Alcindor Jr. on April 16, 1947, in New York City. In high school, at 7' 1/2" tall, he established a New York City career record of 2,067 points and 2,002 rebounds, leading Power Memorial High School to three straight championships. Power won ninety-five and lost only six games during his years with the team.

Abdul-Jabbar combined great height with catlike moves and a deft shooting touch to lead UCLA to three consecutive NCAA championships. Twice, as a sophomore and a senior, he was chosen as the top collegiate player in the country. He finished his career at UCLA as the ninth all-time collegiate scorer, accumulating 2,325 points in eighty-eight games. After leading UCLA to its third consecutive national title, Abdul-Jabbar signed a contract with the Milwaukee Bucks for $1.4 million.

In his rookie season, 1969–1970, he led the Bucks, a recently established expansion club, to a second place finish in the NBA's Eastern Division. After being voted Rookie of the Year, he went on to win the scoring championships in 1971 and 1972. He led Milwaukee to a world championship in 1971. In 1973 he finished second in scoring with a 30.2 point average, but he eventually became dissatisfied with life in Milwaukee. At the end of the 1974–1975 season he was traded to the Los Angeles Lakers. Abdul-Jabbar enjoyed a very successful career with the Lakers, leading the team to NBA championships in 1980, 1982, 1985, 1987, and 1988.

Abdul-Jabbar converted to the Hanafi sect of Islam while in college, though he did not change his name until 1971. Greatly influenced by the life and struggles of Malcolm X, he believed that the Islamic religion is distinct from the nationalistic Black Muslims.

Abdul-Jabbar announced his retirement after the 1988–1989 season, one year after the Lakers had won back-to-back NBA championships. He was inducted into the Basketball Hall of Fame in 1995.

Abdul-Jabbar has applied his experience and knowledge of the game to the areas of coaching and scouting. In 2000 he served as an assistant coach for the Los Angeles Clippers, and in 2001 he took a position as scout, consultant, and assistant coach for the Indianapolis Pacers. In 2005 Abdul-Jabbar returned to the Lakers as a special assistant to Phil Jackson, the team's head coach.

MUHAMMAD ALI (1942–)

Boxer. Born Cassius Marcellus Clay, in Louisville, Kentucky, on January 17, 1942, Muhammad Ali started boxing as a youth. After winning the 1960 Olympic gold

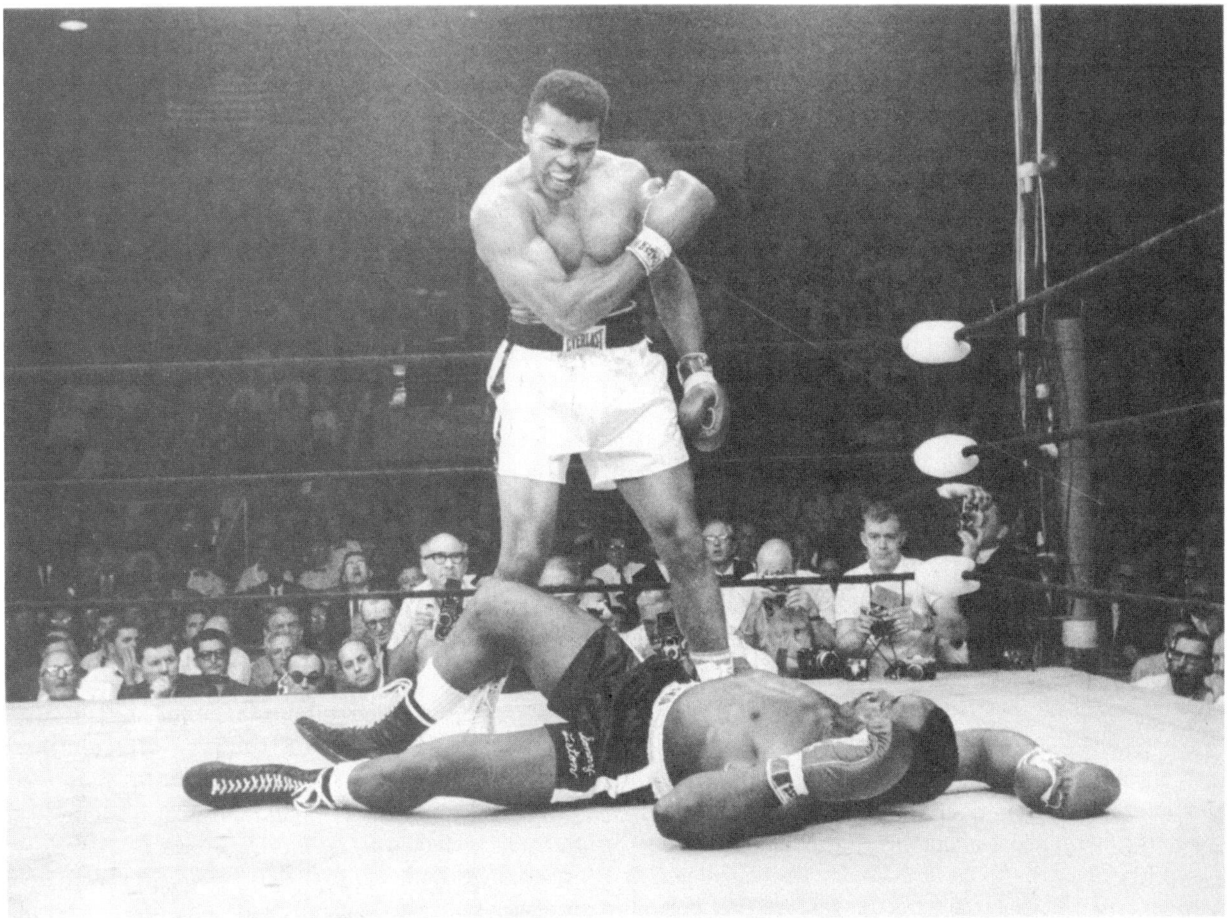

Boxer Muhammad Ali, St. Dominick's Arena, Lewiston, ME, May 25, 1965. *In a rematch of their championship bout from a year earlier, Ali knocks out Sonny Liston to retain the heavyweight title.* AP IMAGES. REPRODUCED BY PERMISSION.

medal as a light heavyweight, Clay turned pro. In 1963 he converted to Islam and changed his name to Muhammad Ali. A year later, Ali won the world heavyweight championship by knocking out Sonny Liston.

After nine successful title defenses, Ali refused to serve in the armed forces during the Vietnam War. He maintained that it was contrary to his Muslim beliefs. Although he was stripped of his title and banned from boxing in the United States, Ali refused to back down and was finally cleared on a technicality by the U.S. Supreme Court in 1970.

Coming back to the ring after a layoff of three and a half years, he was defeated by heavyweight champion Joe Frazier in March 1971. In 1974, when neither held a title, Ali defeated Frazier to earn a shot at regaining the title.

Few fans gave Ali a chance against heavyweight champion George Foreman when they met in Zaire on October 30, 1974. A four to one underdog at ring time, Ali amazed the boxing world and knocked out his stronger, younger opponent. After regaining the crown, Ali defeated Frazier in their third and decisive fight in Manila. Ali then lost his title to Leon Spinks in 1978, briefly regained it, and then retired.

In 1980 Ali came out of retirement to fight his former sparring partner, heavyweight champion Larry Holmes. He was defeated. After a 1981 loss to Trevor Berbick, he retired again.

Forced to fight when he was past his prime, Ali took tremendous beatings late in his career. In the early 1980s the former champion was diagnosed with Parkinson's disease. Despite the disease, Ali maintained a public presence. This was most notably demonstrated in his being chosen to light the Olympic torch at the 1996 Summer Olympics in Atlanta.

Ali continued to work for various causes including international hunger and poverty relief. In 2001 the National Association of Broadcasters Education Foundation awarded Ali with a Service to America Leadership Award, in part for his founding of the nonprofit Muhammad Ali Center. That year a biographical film of Ali's life was released. Titled *Ali*, the film starred Will Smith, and both he and supporting actor Jon Voight (portraying broadcaster Howard Cosell) earned Academy Award nominations for their performances.

Ali, a devout Muslim, continues to travel the world promoting humanitarian endeavors. On November 19, 2005, the $60 million, nonprofit Muhammad Ali Center officially opened in Louisville. The facility serves as an international education center focusing on issues of peace, social responsibility, respect, and personal growth, while also providing space to display Ali's boxing memorabilia. In honor of his work in the civil rights movement and with the United Nations, Ali was awarded the Presidential Medal of Freedom and the prestigious Otto Hahn Peace Medal in Gold from the United Nations.

HENRY ARMSTRONG (1912–1988)

Boxer. The only boxer ever to hold three titles at the same time is Henry Armstrong, who accomplished this feat on August 17, 1938, when he added the lightweight championship to his featherweight and welterweight titles.

Armstrong was born on December 12, 1912, in Columbus, Mississippi. In 1931, while fighting under the name of Honey Mellody, he was knocked out in his professional debut in Pittsburgh. Two weeks later he won his first fight. For the next eight years he traveled from coast to coast, fighting until he was finally given a shot at the featherweight title on October 29, 1937. He won the title when he defeated Petey Sarron.

Less than a year later, on May 31, 1938, Armstrong picked up his second title with a decision over welterweight champion Barney Ross. Within three months he added the lightweight crown, winning a decision over Lou Ambers.

Armstrong was inducted into the Black Athletes Hall of Fame in 1975 and died in 1988.

ARTHUR ASHE (1943–1993)

Tennis Player, Television Commentator. Born in Richmond, Virginia, on July 10, 1943, Arthur Ashe learned the game of tennis at the Richmond Racket Club, which had been formed by local African American enthusiasts. Dr. R. W. Johnson, who had also served as an adviser and benefactor to Althea Gibson, sponsored Ashe's tennis.

By 1958 Ashe had reached the semifinals in the under-fifteen division of the National Junior Championships. After winning two junior indoors singles titles in 1960 and 1961, Ashe entered UCLA on a tennis scholarship.

While still an amateur, Ashe won both the U.S. Amateur and U.S. Open tennis championships and became the first African American ever named to a Davis Cup team. After turning professional, Ashe won the Australian Open in 1970 and then five years later defeated Jimmy Connors to win Wimbledon.

In 1979, at the age of thirty-five, Ashe suffered a heart attack. Following quadruple bypass heart surgery, Ashe retired from active tennis. He began writing a nationally syndicated column and contributed monthly articles to *Tennis Magazine*. He wrote a tennis diary *Portrait in Motion*, his autobiography *Off the Court*, and the book *Advantage Ashe*. In addition, he compiled the historical work *A Hard Road to Glory: A History of the African-American Athlete.*

Ashe was named captain of the U.S. Davis Cup team in 1981. He served as president and a member of the board of directors of the Association of Tennis Professionals and was a cofounder of the National Junior Tennis League. Late in his career, he also served as a television sports commentator.

In April 1992 Ashe announced that he had contracted AIDS as the result of a tainted blood transfusion received during the heart bypass surgery. He died on February 6, 1993.

ERNIE BANKS (1931–)

Baseball Player. Born on January 31, 1931, in Dallas, Ernie Banks was slightly built at six feet one, 180 pounds, but his powerful wrists helped him produce a career total of 512 home runs. His 44 homers and 5 grand slams in 1955 were single-season records for shortstops. His best season was 1958, during which he led the National League in at bats (617), home runs (47), runs batted in (129), and slugging percentage (.614). He was named the league's MVP after the 1958 and 1959 seasons.

Banks, who was moved to first base during the 1961 season and played in 717 consecutive games, may have the somewhat dubious distinction of being the greatest player to never play in a World Series, as his Chicago Cubs rarely produced winning ball clubs during his tenure.

Banks, along with second baseman Gene Baker, formed the majors' first all–African American double-play combination. He was the second African American to play for the Cubs, after Baker. Banks was inducted into the Baseball Hall of Fame in 1977 and is also a member of the Texas Sports Hall of Fame.

After his playing career, Banks became a bank executive with Seaway National Bank. He remained visible in the community, becoming a board member of the Chicago Transit Authority, the Chicago Metropolitan YMCA, and the Los Angeles Urban League. Nicknamed "Mr. Cub," Banks is known for his exuberant love for the game, which is captured in his famous saying, "Let's play two!"

ELGIN BAYLOR (1934–)

Basketball Player, Basketball Coach, Sports Executive. Born on September 16, 1934, in Washington, D.C., Elgin Baylor first attracted attention while attending Spingarn High School. He became an All-American at Seattle University, leading the Chieftains to the Final Four in 1958. In 1959 Baylor made his professional debut with the Minneapolis Lakers, becoming the first rookie to be named MVP in the All-Star Game. He also was named to the All-League team and set a scoring record of 64 points in a single game.

After five years as a superstar, Baylor injured his knee during a 1965 playoff game and never played at the same level again. He totaled 23,149 points in his career, and his scoring average of 27.4 is the fourth highest in NBA history. His best year was 1961–1962, when he averaged 38.2 points a game. When he retired in 1968, Baylor had been an All-NBA selection nine times and had played in eight consecutive All-Star games.

Baylor was inducted into the Black Athletes Hall of Fame in 1975 and the Basketball Hall of Fame in 1977. He was head coach of the New Orleans Jazz in 1978–1979. Between 1986 and 2008, Baylor served as executive vice president of basketball operations for the Los Angeles Clippers. In 2006 Baylor was selected the NBA Executive of the Year.

DAVE BING

See chapter 14, Entrepreneurship.

BARRY BONDS (1964–)

Baseball Player. Barry Bonds was born on July 24, 1964, in Riverside, California. He was exposed to baseball heavily during childhood. Bonds's father, Bobby, and his godfather, Hall of Famer Willie Mays, were Major League outfielders. Bonds played three sports in high school—baseball, basketball, and football. Although he was offered a contract to play with the San Francisco Giants after graduating, he opted to attend college at Arizona State University.

After success at the collegiate level, Bonds was selected by the Pittsburgh Pirates as the sixth selection in the 1985 baseball draft. He spent a brief time in the minor leagues before being called up at age twenty-one by the National League club. During his rookie season, he led all of the first-year players in home runs, runs batted in, stolen bases, and walks.

In 1990 Bonds earned league MVP honors. He hit 33 home runs, stole 52 bases, batted in 114 runs, scored 104 runs, and earned his first of four consecutive Gold Gloves for defensive play. With Bonds's support the Pirates won the Eastern Division of the National League but ended up losing to the Cincinnati Reds in a postseason series.

The Pirates entered the playoffs during the next two seasons but met with postseason frustration both years. The 1992 campaign was notable because Bonds earned his second MVP award. Regardless of his success during

Barry Bonds, San Francisco Giants, August 7, 2007. *Bonds hits his 756th career home run during a game at AT&T Park in San Francisco, thus becoming Major League Baseball's all-time home run leader.* JED JACOBSOHN/GETTY IMAGES

the regular season, however, Bonds was unable to contribute in the same fashion during the playoffs.

Following the 1992 season, Bonds signed a lucrative deal with the San Francisco Giants. The contract provided him with $43.75 million over the course of six years, making him the highest-paid player at the time. Although some critics doubted that any player was worth such a salary, Bonds quieted them by earning another MVP award on the strength of a season featuring 46 home runs and 123 RBIs. The Giants failed to make the playoffs, though, losing to the Atlanta Braves on the last day of the season.

Although Bonds continued to post strong numbers over the next several years, his team made the playoffs only twice, in 1997 and 2000. Bonds's continued success during the regular season was remarkable given that opposing pitchers rarely offered him decent pitches. They preferred walking Bonds to risking giving up an extra-base hit.

In 1998 Bonds became the first player with more than 400 home runs and 400 stolen bases in a career; within five years he became the first to reach the 500 mark in these two categories. In the 2001 season Bonds amassed an amazing 73 home runs, 3 more than the previous record. Not only did many consider the record of 70 homers in a season unmatchable, but Bonds hit his 73 with limited at bats as most managers instructed their pitchers to intentionally walk him rather than letting him swing away. Also at the end of the 2001 season, he won his fourth National League MVP award, becoming the first player in Major League Baseball history to win the award more than three times. On August 12, 2002, he hit his 600th home run, making him only the fourth player in Major League history to do so.

Bonds broke two home run records in 2004. On April 12 Bonds hit his 660th home run, tying Willie Mays, and on September 17 he hit his 700th home run, becoming only the third person to achieve this level. On September 23, 2006, Bonds hit his 734th home run, capturing the National League record previously held by Hank Aaron. In 2007 Bonds hit his 756th career home run on August 7, passing Aaron to attain the top spot on the all-time Major League home run list. He finished the 2007 season, his last, with 762 career home runs.

LOU BROCK (1939–)

Baseball Player, Baseball Coach, Business Executive. Born in El Dorado, Arkansas, on June 18, 1939, Lou Brock is the second-highest base stealer in baseball history. He stole 938 bases during his nineteen-year career with the Chicago Cubs and St. Louis Cardinals. In 1977 Brock collected his 893rd steal, eclipsing the mark that had been held by Ty Cobb for forty-nine years. In 1974, at thirty-five years of age, Brock stole 118 bases, breaking Maury Wills's single-season record. Brock registered at least 50 steals in twelve consecutive seasons and at the time of his retirement was the only player to hold both the Major League single-season and career records in any major statistical category.

In 1967 Brock led the league in at bats, runs scored, and steals. The following season he set the pace in doubles, triples, and steals, leading the Cardinals to pennants both seasons. With Brock, St. Louis also won world championships in 1964 and 1967.

Brock went on to become a coach and business executive and was presented with the Jackie Robinson Award by *Ebony* magazine. He won the Roberto Clemente Award in 1975. He was also the recipient of the B'nai B'rith Brotherhood Award and was voted Man of the Year by the St. Louis Jaycees. Brock was inducted into the Baseball Hall of Fame in 1985.

JIM BROWN (1936–)

Football Player, Actor, Community Activist. James Nathaniel Brown was born on February 17, 1936, on St. Simons Island, Georgia, but moved to Manhasset, Long Island, New York, when he was seven. While at Manhasset High School he became an outstanding competitor in baseball, football, track and field, basketball, and lacrosse and following graduation had a choice of forty-two college scholarships, as well as professional offers from the New York Yankees and Boston Braves. Brown chose to attend Syracuse University. An All-American performer in both football and lacrosse, he turned down the opportunity to compete in the decathlon at the 1956 Olympic Games because it would have conflicted with his football schedule. He also spurned a three-year, $150,000 offer to become a professional fighter.

Hall of Fame Running Back Jim Brown. *During his nine-year career with the Cleveland Browns in the late 1950s and early 1960s, Brown led the NFL in rushing in eight of those years. He set the career yardage mark for the league, a record that stood for nineteen years after his retirement.* WALTER IOOSS JR./SPORTS ILLUSTRATED/GETTY IMAGES

In 1957 Brown began his professional football career with the Cleveland Browns. In his rookie season, he led the league in rushing, helped Cleveland to a division championship, and was unanimously named Rookie of the Year. Brown broke the single-season and lifetime rushing and scoring records and was named to the Pro Bowl team every season of his career. His records included most yards gained, lifetime (12,312), and most touchdowns, lifetime (106). He was voted Football Back of the Decade for the 1960s.

Brown announced his retirement in the summer of 1966, deciding to devote his attention to his movie and business careers. He made several films including *Rio Conchos*, *The Dirty Dozen*, and *100 Rifles*. In addition to his film activities, he is president and founder of Amer-I-Can and an outspoken activist in issues relating to African Americans and sports.

In 2002 film director Spike Lee produced the film *Jim Brown: All American*, which was a retrospective on Brown's professional and personal lives.

KOBE BRYANT (1978–)

Basketball Player. Born in Philadelphia on August 23, 1978, Kobe Bryant ranks among the legends of professional basketball. The son of Joe "Jellybean" and Pamela Bryant, Kobe moved with his family to Rieti, Italy, in 1984, where he learned basketball under the tutelage of his father, who, after a career as a collegiate and professional player in the United States, was playing in the Italian Basketball League. While attending school in Italy with his two older sisters, Kobe gained fluency in both Italian and Spanish and also studied tapes of Magic Johnson and other NBA stars.

Bryant returned to the United States as an eighth grader, and his legend as a basketball player began at Lower Merion High School in Philadelphia. He led the school to a state title and became the all-time leading scorer in southeastern Pennsylvania, surpassing the career points of Wilt Chamberlain and Carlin Warley. He concluded his high school playing career with local, statewide, and national accolades.

In the 1996 NBA draft, Bryant, at age seventeen, became the youngest player ever drafted. Selecting Bryant as the thirteenth overall pick, the Charlotte Hornets traded him to the Los Angeles Lakers in the summer of 1996 for Vlade Divac. Bryant has played guard for the Lakers ever since.

Celebrity and stellar play on the hardwood has not been without its difficulties for Bryant. In July 2003 he was arrested and charged with sexual assault in Eagle, Colorado. Although the charges against him were eventually dropped, Bryant's image suffered in the court of public opinion. While Bryant formed a formidable duo with legendary center Shaquille O'Neal, the two separated following the 2003–2004 season when O'Neal was traded to the Miami Heat. The Lakers–Heat game played on Christmas Day in 2004 scored impressive television ratings.

Over his long career with the Lakers, Bryant became one of the all-time leading scorers in the history of the NBA, and his four world championship titles established him as one of the game's most celebrated stars. Often called the "next Michael Jordan," Bryant elevated his game above the shadow of Jordan to establish his own unique style of play.

ROY CAMPANELLA (1921–1993)

Baseball Player. Roy Campanella was born on November 19, 1921, in Philadelphia, and at age fifteen began playing semiprofessional baseball with the Bacharach Giants. In 1946 Campanella was signed by the Brooklyn Dodgers. Over the next eight years, the Dodger catcher played with five National League pennant winners and one world championship team. He played on eight consecutive National League All-Star teams (1949 to 1956) and won three league MVP awards (1951, 1953, and 1955).

In January 1958 Campanella's career was ended by an automobile accident that left him paralyzed and confined to a wheelchair. He was inducted into the Baseball Hall of Fame in 1969 and into the Black Athletes Hall of Fame in 1975. Campanella died on June 26, 1993.

WILT CHAMBERLAIN (1936–1999)

Basketball Player. Wilton Norman Chamberlain was born in Philadelphia on August 21, 1936. By the time he entered high school, he was already six feet eleven. When he graduated from high school, he had his choice of seventy-seven major colleges and 125 smaller schools. He chose the University of Kansas but left following his junior year after being a two-time All-American and playing in the 1957 Final Four.

Before entering the NBA in 1959, Chamberlain played with the Harlem Globetrotters. Although dominating the sport statistically from his rookie season, Chamberlain was a member of only two championship teams, the 1967 Philadelphia 76ers and the 1972 Los Angeles Lakers. For his efforts in defeating the New York Knicks in the 1972 series, including playing the final game with both hands painfully injured, he was voted MVP. At the start of the 1973–1974 season, he left the Lakers to become player-coach of the ABA's San Diego Conquistadors for a reported $500,000 contract.

Wilt Chamberlain still holds most major records for a single game, including most points (100), field goals made (36), free throws (28), and rebounds (55). His season records include: highest scoring average (50.4), highest field goal percentage (.727), and most rebounds per game (27.2). Chamberlain is also the all-time leading rebounder in NBA history, with 23,924.

Chamberlain was inducted into the Basketball Hall of Fame in 1979 and owned various businesses after leaving professional basketball. He was involved with a number of charitable groups and appeared in several motion pictures. In 1991 Chamberlain published his autobiography, *View from Above.* The book caused quite a controversy because of revelations about his sexual relations. Chamberlain died of a heart attack on October 12, 1999, in Los Angeles.

ALICE COACHMAN (1923–)

Track and Field Athlete. Born in Albany, Georgia, on November 9, 1923, Alice Coachman made a name for herself when, as a seventh grader, she high jumped 5 feet 4 1/2 inches, less than an inch from the world record. On August 7, 1948, Alice Coachman became the first African American woman to win an Olympic gold medal. She did it by setting a world record in the high jump. In college, she attended both the Tuskegee Institute (now University) and Albany State College (now University) where she won a number of Amateur Athletic Union (AAU) outdoor titles, including four 50-meter dash titles, three 100-meter dash titles, and ten high jump titles. During AAU indoor meets, Coachman won the 50-meter dash twice and the high jump three times. She was also an outstanding basketball player, earning All-American honors as a guard at Tuskegee.

Coachman's ten consecutive high jump victories, between 1939 and 1948, remains an AAU record. She is a member of eight different halls of fame including the National Track and Field Hall of Fame, the Black Athletes Hall of Fame, the Tuskegee Athletic Hall of Fame, and the Georgia Sports Hall of Fame. In a 2002 issue of *Ebony* magazine, she was named one of the ten greatest women athletes of all time, and at the 1996 Summer Games held in Atlanta she received recognition as one of the 100 greatest U.S. Olympic athletes of all time.

LEONARD S. COLEMAN JR. (1949–)

Major League Baseball Executive, State Government Official, Business Executive. Leonard Coleman Jr. was born on February 17, 1949, in Newark, but he grew up in Montclair, New Jersey. At Montclair High School, Coleman played baseball and football. He was named all-state and All-American during his senior year. He continued playing baseball and football as an undergraduate at Princeton University, becoming the first African American to score a touchdown for that prestigious Ivy League school. As a sophomore, he joined two other African American players in a protest, charging the Princeton football program with violations of the university's policy of equal opportunity for minorities. When the complaints drew national attention, Coleman and his two friends were dismissed from the team, but a panel charged with investigating the incident urged greater sensitivity toward minority students in the athletic program. Coleman attributes that experience to helping him develop a keen social consciousness.

After earning his bachelor's degree from Princeton in 1971, Coleman moved on to Harvard University, where he pursued dual master's degrees in public administration and education. In 1976 he accepted a position as a missionary to Africa for the Protestant Episcopal Church. All told he spent four years in Africa, serving in seventeen different countries and cultivating a close friendship with South African Archbishop Desmond Tutu.

Returning to the United States in 1980, Coleman first served as president of the Greater Newark Urban Coalition. In 1982 he was appointed commissioner of the New Jersey Department of Energy. In 1986 Coleman was named commissioner of the New Jersey Department of Community Affairs. He left the public sector two years later for a job as an investment banker with Kidder, Peabody & Co. Eventually, he was named vice president of municipal finance.

In 1991 Coleman accepted his first position with Major League Baseball, as director of marketing development. In that position, he was credited with further encouraging the Reviving Baseball in Inner Cities (RBI) initiative, aimed at keeping city teenagers active in the sport after they leave Little League Baseball. In 1994 Coleman was unanimously chosen to succeed Bill White as president of the National League.

During his tenure, he carried out his vision for professional baseball—less drug abuse among players, including the discouragement of chewing tobacco; less fighting during games; and promotion of baseball as entertainment for the whole family. Coleman also acted as a crusader for the rights of African American baseball players, especially former Negro League participants and their spouses. In 1996 Coleman was named chairman of the Jackie Robinson Foundation.

Coleman's career as a Major League Baseball executive ended in 1999 when the league presidential offices were eliminated. He then took over as president of Newark Sports & Entertainment, Inc. and in November 2001 was named director of Churchill Downs Incorporated.

CYNTHIA COOPER (1963–)

Basketball Player, Basketball Coach. Cynthia Cooper was born in Chicago on April 14, 1963. She played college basketball at the University of Southern California (USC). Her team at USC is considered one of the greatest in the history of women's college basketball. It included Hall of Famer Cheryl Miller and won NCAA titles in 1983 and 1984.

Following college, Cooper spent many years playing professional basketball in Europe. In 1988 she was on the U.S. Olympic team that captured a gold medal at the Seoul Olympiad. She was also a member of the bronze medal team in 1992 at the Barcelona Olympiad.

With the formation of the WNBA in 1997, Cooper had the chance to compete professionally in the United States. The 5′10″ guard was a member of the Houston Comets. Cooper became one of the most prominent players in the league, winning the WNBA's first two MVP awards. In addition, she led the Comets to four straight league titles and was named the MVP of the four championship series in which she played.

Cooper retired as a player following the 2000 season. In January 2001 she was named head coach of the WNBA's Phoenix Mercury, a post she held for less than two seasons, as she resigned in June 2002.

Cooper returned to the game for the 2003 season, but announced her final retirement in 2004. In May 2005 Cooper was named head coach of the women's basketball team at Prairie View A & M University.

DOMINIQUE DAWES (1976–)

Gymnast, Actress. Born in Silver Spring, Maryland, on November 20, 1976, Dominique Dawes became the first African American to excel in gymnastics, and only the second African American to qualify for the U.S. Olympic gymnastics team. She also holds a record for winning the most national championships (15) since 1963 of any athlete, male or female.

Dawes began competing in gymnastics at age five. In 1992 at the Barcelona Olympiad she was a member of the U.S. team awarded the bronze medal. At the U.S. National Championships in 1994, Dawes became the first African American to win the all-around title as best gymnast. In 1996 at the Atlanta Olympiad she won two individual bronze medals as well as being a member of the U.S. team awarded the gold medal. Dawes was also a member of the U.S. team at the 2000 Sydney Olympiad.

While attending the University of Maryland, from which she graduated with a bachelor's degree in 2002, Dawes also appeared as an analyst for televised gymnastic events, including coverage of the 2001 Goodwill Games for TNT. Her acting credits include a 1996 role in the

Broadway musical *Grease* and an appearance on *The Jersey*, a Disney television series. In addition to her involvement in a number of charitable activities, Dawes served as president of the Women's Sports Federation from 2004 to 2006.

TONY DUNGY (1955–)

Football Coach. Born in Jackson, Michigan, on October 6, 1955, Anthony Kevin Dungy distinguished himself early on as a scholar of the game of American football. As a six-year-old, Dungy would tell his father details from the televised games of the Detroit Lions. Upon entering high school, Dungy was the star quarterback of Jackson High School, and his exploits on the field led him to the University of Minnesota, where he became the starting quarterback for the Golden Gophers. From 1973 to 1976, Dungy was a prolific collegiate player, finishing fourth in total offense in the entire history of the Big Ten Conference.

Despite his exceptional collegiate career, Dungy went undrafted in the professional football draft, but was signed as a free agent by Chuck Knoll of the Pittsburgh Steelers—as a defensive back, not a quarterback. While Knoll cited Dungy's size as the reason for the position change, others cited racism—at the time, only one African American, James Harris of the Los Angeles Rams, started at quarterback in professional football. The Steelers, however, did have an African American, Joe Gilliam, serve as the backup quarterback to Terry Bradshaw. Nonetheless, Dungy excelled as a defensive back for the vaunted Steel Curtain defense of the Steelers, recording a team-leading six interceptions during the 1978 season and helping the Steelers win that season's Super Bowl. The following year, Dungy was traded, and within two seasons he had retired as a player.

Always a cerebral player, Dungy was a natural fit as a coach. He assisted with the Golden Gophers program before beginning his professional coaching career in 1981, first with the Steelers. He was twenty-five years old. Within two years, he had become the first African American to serve as a defensive coordinator in the NFL. Throughout his time coaching players on the defensive side of the football, Dungy established his unique coaching style, one that enabled a player to bring forth his qualities to the game of football.

In 1996 Dungy became head coach of the Tampa Bay Buccaneers, transforming a beleaguered team into one of the league's premier squads. He led the Bucs through the 2001 season, and he then was hired the following year as head coach of the Indianapolis Colts, leading the team to a Super Bowl victory on February 4, 2007. The game itself was historic because, for the first time in the history of professional football, two black coaches faced each another to compete for the Lombardi Trophy. With his victory over the Chicago Bears, Dungy became the first African American head coach to win a Super Bowl.

After retiring from coaching in 2009, Dungy became a football analyst for NBC Sports.

LEE ELDER (1934–)

Golfer, Entrepreneur. Lee Elder was born in Dallas, Texas, on July 14, 1934. He first was involved with golf as a caddie at the age of fifteen. After his father's death during World War II, Elder and his mother moved to Los Angeles, where he met the famed African American golfer Ted Rhodes. He was later drafted by the U.S. Army, where he sharpened his skills as captain of the golf team.

Following his discharge from the army, he began to teach golf. In 1962 he debuted as a professional, winning the national title of the United Golf Association (an African American organization). Elder played seventeen years with the United Golf Association before making his debut with the PGA in November 1967. Elder was the first African American professional golfer to reach $1 million in earnings and, in 1975, was the first to play at the Masters. Elder won eight tournaments on the Senior PGA Tour and was inducted into the NCAA Hall of Fame for his work with predominantly black colleges.

In 1997, when Tiger Woods became the first African American to win the Masters, Elder was present and was thanked by Woods for his pioneering efforts in the integration of the PGA Tour and the Masters.

JULIUS ERVING (1950–)

Basketball Player, Television Analyst, Sports Executive. Julius Winfield Erving, known to fans as "Dr. J," was born in Roosevelt, Long Island, on February 22, 1950. As a player at Roosevelt High School, Erving made the all-county and all–Long Island teams. He was awarded an athletic scholarship to the University of Massachusetts, and after completing his junior year he signed a $500,000, four-year contract with the Virginia Squires of the ABA. Voted Rookie of the Year in 1972, Erving eventually signed with the New Jersey Nets for $2.8 million over four years.

In his first season with the Nets, Erving led the league in scoring for the second consecutive year and led his team to the ABA championship. After being traded to the Philadelphia 76ers, Erving became a favorite with fans, leading the team to the NBA championship in 1983. He retired following the 1986–1987 season, having become the third player in professional basketball history

Basketball Player Julius Erving, 1982. *The most popular player in the American Basketball Association because of his dunks and acrobatics, Erving (pictured wearing number six) later led the Philadelphia 76ers to the 1993 National Basketball Association championship.* AP IMAGES. REPRODUCED BY PERMISSION.

to score 30,000 points. He is credited with popularizing the slam dunk. Erving, who was inducted into the Basketball Hall of Fame in 1993, served as a broadcaster for NBC and in 1997 was named executive vice president of the Orlando Magic. He continues to serve on boards of directors for various organizations, and is the president of a managing and marketing firm.

GEORGE FOREMAN (1948–)

Boxer, Minister. Born in Marshall, Texas, on January 10, 1948, George Foreman emerged as one of boxing's most endearing figures. During his childhood in Houston, Foreman was a truant, snatching purses and participating in petty larcenies. His early success in boxing included a gold medal performance at the 1968 Summer Olympics. After turning pro, he quickly became a top contender, recording 42 knockouts in his first 47 bouts.

Foreman captured the heavyweight title with his victory over Joe Frazier in Kingston, Jamaica, on January 22, 1973. Having twice defended his belt successfully, he prepared to face Muhammad Ali on October 30, 1974, in Kinshasa, Zaire. The fight became known as the "Rumble in the Jungle." Despite being a four to one favorite, Foreman was outfought by Ali, who used his "rope-a-dope" tactic to tire Foreman and knock him out in the eighth round.

Foreman soon retired to become a minister and transformed his image into that of a congenial and very popular ex-champion. He initiated a comeback and recaptured the heavyweight crown when he defeated Michael Moorer on November 5, 1994. Foreman, thereby, became the oldest man in history to win the heavyweight championship of the world. He retired shortly thereafter to his gym in Houston.

Foreman became a born-again Christian and was ordained as a minister. In the mid-1990s, Foreman entered the arena of entrepreneurship promoting his Lean and Mean Grilling Machine. He used the slogan "knock out the fat" and has gained both revenue and notoriety. By the early twenty-first century, Foreman was involved with multiple business and charitable activities.

ALTHEA GIBSON (1927–2003)

Tennis Player. Althea Gibson was born on August 25, 1927, in Silver, South Carolina, but was raised in Harlem. She began her tennis career when she entered and won the Department of Parks Manhattan Girls' Tennis Championship. In 1942 she began to receive professional coaching at the Cosmopolitan Tennis Club, and a year later she won the New York State Negro Girls Singles Title. She was victorious in the National Negro girls singles championship in 1945 and 1946 and won the title in the women's division in 1948.

A year later Gibson entered Florida A&M, where she played tennis and basketball. In 1950 she was runner-up for the National Indoor Championship and became the first African American to play at the U.S. Open at the Forest Hills Country Club. The following year she became the first African American to play at Wimbledon.

In 1957 at Wimbledon, Gibson won the singles crown and teamed with Darlene Hard to earn the doubles championship. In 1957 and 1958 Gibson won the U.S. Open women's singles title. In 1963, just five years after she retired from tennis, Gibson became the first African American to join the LPGA Tour.

Gibson served as a recreation manager, as a member of the New Jersey State Athletic Control Board, on the Governor's Council on Physical Fitness, and as a sports consultant. She was also the author of the book *I Always Wanted to Be Somebody.* In 1997 her seventieth birthday was celebrated and her groundbreaking career was honored by the U.S. Tennis Association during the dedication of Arthur Ashe Stadium, where the U.S. Open tournament is

Tennis Player Althea Gibson, 1956. *Gibson became the first African American to capture a Grand Slam event when she won singles and doubles championships at the 1956 French Open.* **THOMAS D. MCAVOY/TIME LIFE PICTURES/GETTY IMAGES**

held. In a 2002 issue of *Ebony* magazine, she was named one of the ten greatest women athletes of all time.

On September 28, 2003, Gibson died of respiratory failure in East Orange, New Jersey. She was seventy-six years old.

BOB GIBSON (1935–)

Baseball Player, Baseball Coach, Radio Announcer. Pack Robert Gibson was born on November 9, 1935, in Omaha, Nebraska, into poverty. Fatherless, he was one of seven children who lived in a four-room wooden shack. Denied a spot on Omaha Technical High School's baseball team because he was African American, he was permitted to join the track and field and basketball teams. He attended Creighton University in Omaha and became the first African American athlete to play both basketball and baseball.

Gibson's skill at basketball allowed him to play with the Harlem Globetrotters. While with them, he accepted an offer to join the St. Louis Cardinals' minor league team in Omaha for a salary of $3,000 and a $1,000 bonus. Gibson debuted with the Cardinals in 1959, beginning a Hall of Fame career that lasted seventeen seasons and included five 20-victory seasons and thirteen consecutive winning seasons. His highlights include a 1968 campaign in which he recorded a remarkable 13 shutouts, 22 victories, 268 strikeouts, and an earned run average of 1.12, still a modern-era Major League record.

During his career, Gibson recorded 3,117 strikeouts and finished with an ERA of 2.91. He won seven and lost two games in three World Series appearances, with an ERA of 1.89. In game one of the 1968 series he struck out 17 Detroit Tigers. Gibson pitched the Cardinals to world championships in 1964 and 1967. He was inducted into the Baseball Hall of Fame in 1981. In 2004 *The Sports List*, a Fox Sports Net television series, named Gibson the most intimidating pitcher of all time.

In addition to stints as a coach with the New York Mets and Atlanta Braves, Gibson has been a special pitching consultant to many teams. He has also served as a broadcaster for the St. Louis Cardinals.

JOSH GIBSON (1911–1947)

Baseball Player. Joshua Gibson was born in Buena Vista, Georgia, on December 21, 1911, and moved to Pittsburgh, where he left school at age fourteen to work for Gimbels department store. Gimbels had a baseball team, which is where Gibson first attracted attention.

Gibson was a catcher whose entire sixteen-year career was spent in the Negro Leagues. His career began in 1929. With the exception of a stint with the Pittsburgh Crawfords between 1932 and 1936, and two seasons in Mexico in 1940 and 1941, Gibson played with the Homestead Grays. His first game with Homestead took place on July 25, 1929, when, as a spectator, he was called out of the stands to replace an injured starter in a game against the Kansas City Monarchs.

Baseball Hall of Famer Josh Gibson. **BETTMANN/CORBIS**

Gibson was known for his legendary power. Playing at Yankee Stadium, he once hit a home run over the left field bullpen and out of the stadium. Gibson also hit a 580-foot home run over the top of the bleachers. Though accurate records are unavailable, Gibson is credited with hitting as many as 800 home runs in his career, including one season (1936) in which he hit 84.

Plagued by debilitating headaches, believed to have been the result of a cancerous brain tumor, Gibson eventually died in 1947, from a stroke. An apparent contributing factor was his alcoholism. He was inducted into the Baseball Hall of Fame in 1972.

KEN GRIFFEY JR. (1969–)

Baseball Player. Ken Griffey Jr. was one of the most famous professional athletes in the United States in the 1990s and early twenty-first century. Griffey's talent and flair made him one of the most popular baseball players of his era, as evidenced by his thirteen All-Star Game appearances.

Born on November 21, 1969, in Donora, Pennsylvania, Griffey was drafted first overall in 1987 by the Seattle Mariners while still in high school in Cincinnati. He broke into Major League Baseball in 1989 when he was nineteen years old. He subsequently won ten Gold Gloves for his play in centerfield and drove in more than 100 runs eight times. In 1997 Griffey was unanimously selected as the MVP of American League, and in 1997 and 1998 he accomplished the rare feat of hitting 50 home runs in back-to-back years. His chase of the single-season home run record with Mark McGwire and Sammy Sosa in the summer of 1998 caught the attention of the entire nation. A vote of fellow major league players gave Griffey the title of Player of the Decade for the 1990s.

In 2000 Griffey signed what was, at the time, the richest contract in the history of Major League Baseball, a nine-year, $112.5 million deal with the Cincinnati Reds. The trade brought Griffey back to his hometown.

Griffey was plagued with injuries during the 2001 to 2004 seasons. In 2004 he hit his 500th home run, placing him among only twenty-four other players who have achieved that mark. In 2005 Griffey played more than he had over the previous few seasons, earning him the award for National League Comeback Player of the Year. One of the game's greatest sluggers and outfielders, Griffey in 2009 returned to the Seattle Mariners, where he had started his professional career, and proved himself capable of remaining a productive player.

LUSIA HARRIS (1955–)

Basketball Player, Basketball Coach, Motivational Speaker. Born on February 10, 1955, in Minter City, Mississippi, Lusia Harris participated on the silver medal–winning Olympic basketball team in 1976. She was high scorer at the Olympics and at the 1975 World University and Pan American Games. In college, she led Delta State University to three Association for Intercollegiate Athletics for Women championships from 1975 to 1977. She was named Mississippi's first amateur athlete of the year in 1976. Harris was also selected as Delta State's homecoming queen, the first African American so honored.

Harris, the dominant female player of her era, broke hundreds of records and won countless U.S. and international awards. As a graduate student, she became an assistant basketball coach and admissions counselor at Delta State. She played briefly with the Houston Angels of the Women's Professional Basketball League in 1980.

In the 1990s Harris coached basketball and taught physical education in Mississippi. In 1992, along with Nera White, Harris became the first woman inducted into the Basketball Hall of Fame. She is also a motivational speaker.

CHAMIQUE HOLDSCLAW (1977–)

Basketball Player. Chamique Holdsclaw was born on August 9, 1977, in Queens, New York. Holdsclaw left New York to attend the University of Tennessee and play for coach Pat Summitt.

At Tennessee, Holdsclaw became the most honored female basketball player since Cheryl Miller. Holdsclaw was a three-time All-American, two-time collegiate player of the year, and winner of three NCAA titles. In 1998 Holdsclaw became the first African American female basketball player to win the Sullivan Award, given to the top amateur athlete in the United States.

A 6' 2" forward who drew comparisons to both Cheryl Miller and Michael Jordan, Holdsclaw was the first pick in the 1999 WNBA draft by the Washington Mystics. Coming out of college, she was viewed as a commercial and athletic star counted on to increase the visibility of the WNBA. She delivered by earning Rookie of the Year honors her first season and being selected as a starter in the WNBA All-Star Game for three consecutive years. In the 2000 Summer Olympics, Holdsclaw led the U.S. women's basketball team to the gold medal. After a March 2005 trade, Holdsclaw played for the Los Angeles Sparks for a little more than two seasons. She retired briefly before returning to the WNBA to play for the Atlanta Dream in 2009. Through the 2009 season, Holdsclaw had career averages of 17.3 points and 7.9 rebounds per game.

LARRY HOLMES (1949–)

Boxer. Larry Holmes was born on November 3, 1949, in Cuthbert, Georgia, and turned professional at age twenty-four after serving as a sparring partner for Muhammad Ali. On June 9, 1978, he won the World Boxing Council heavyweight title from Ken Norton. On October 2, 1980, in Las Vegas, he defeated Ali by a technical knockout.

Holmes defended his title twelve times until losing to Michael Spinks on September 21, 1985, and again on April 19, 1986, in fifteen-round decisions. In all, Holmes held the heavyweight title for seven years, three months, and thirteen days. A brief comeback attempt ended in a knockout by Mike Tyson on January 22, 1988. During a second comeback, Holmes fought and lost title bids against Evander Holyfield in 1992 and Oliver McCall in 1995. Holmes continued to fight because of monetary difficulties stemming from his relationship with his former promoter Don King. He retired for the final time in 2002, having amassed a career record of 69 wins and 6 losses. Holmes was inducted into the International Boxing Hall of Fame in 2008.

Boxer Evander Holyfield, 2006. *A popular champion because of his talent and humility, Holyfield has won a world heavyweight title four separate times.* AP PHOTO/MATT SLOCUM

EVANDER HOLYFIELD (1962–)

Boxer. Evander Holyfield is known for his championship boxing ability, his devout religious faith, and his humble demeanor. In boxing, a sport dominated by braggadocio and large egos, Holyfield became a popular champion because of his talent and humility.

Holyfield was born on October 19, 1962, in Atmore, Alabama. In the 1984 Olympics, he won the bronze medal in the light heavyweight division. He immediately turned professional and in 1986 won the cruiserweight title from Dwight Muhammad Qawi. By 1989 he was the undisputed cruiserweight champion.

Holyfield entered the heavyweight division that same year and in 1990 defeated James "Buster" Douglas to win the heavyweight title. After several defenses of his title, Holyfield was defeated by Riddick Bowe in 1992 and retired as a result of health-related issues.

Holyfield, a light heavyweight, underwent strenuous training to be able to fight against the bigger fighters in the heavyweight division. In 1993 he came out of retirement to defeat Bowe and regain his title. After losing his title to Michael Moorer, Holyfield finally fought heavyweight champion Mike Tyson in 1996. Holyfield upset Tyson to regain the heavyweight title and then defeated Tyson the next year when Tyson bit Holyfield twice and was disqualified.

With the World Boxing Association (WBA) heavyweight title his, Holyfield next faced Moorer for a second time in Las Vegas on November 8, 1997. An eighth-round TKO gave Holyfield the victory and unified the WBA and International Boxing Federation (IBF) heavyweight championships. After successful defenses of the titles, Holyfield lost both in a 1999 rematch against Lennox Lewis.

Holyfield managed to regain the WBA title in his next fight, as he defeated John Ruiz in August 2000. The two later fought twice more, with the second fight resulting in a loss for Holyfield and the third being ruled a draw. Holyfield continued to successfully pursue the heavyweight title, defeating another former heavyweight champion, Hasim Rahman, on June 1, 2002. Although banned from boxing in New York in August 2005 for "diminishing skills," Holyfield continued to fight elsewhere. In his attempt to gain a fifth heavyweight championship belt, Holyfield has fought valiantly in losses against Sultan Ibragimov in 2007 and Nikolai Valeuv in 2008. After a brief period of inactivity, Holyfield contended for the crown once again in April 2010. He defeated Francis Botha in Las Vegas, scoring an eighth round knockout to become the first five-time heavyweight champion. By early 2010, Holyfield had compiled a

Baseball Player Reggie Jackson, October 1977. *Because of his prowess in postseason play, including hitting this home run in the 1977 World Series, Jackson became known as "Mr. October." He helped the Oakland Athletics capture three straight World Series championships, from 1972 to 1974, and then was instrumental in the New York Yankees' championships in 1977 and 1978.* WALTER IOOSS JR./SPORTS ILLUSTRATED/GETTY IMAGES

record of 43 wins, 10 losses, and 2 draws, with 28 wins by knockout.

MARK INGRAM (1989–)

Football Player. Born on December 21, 1989, in Hackensack, New Jersey, Mark Ingram Jr., son of former NFL receiver Mark Ingram, received fame as a running back at the University of Alabama. Ingram was a standout athlete in Michigan, garnering accolades on the local, state, and national levels for his performances in track and football. As a freshman at Alabama during the 2008 season, Ingram led the Crimson Tide in rushing touchdowns, even though Glen Coffee, a future NFL running back, was the feature back in the Tide offense that year. In 2009 Ingram asserted his importance to the Crimson Tide's success, setting a single-season school record for rushing yards (1,658) and becoming the first Heisman Trophy winner in the storied history of Alabama football.

REGGIE JACKSON (1946–)

Baseball Player. Because of his outstanding performance in postseason play, Reggie Jackson became known as "Mr. October." During his years with the Oakland Athletics and New York Yankees, Jackson captured or tied thirteen World Series records to become baseball's top record holder in series play.

Born in Wyncote, Pennsylvania, on May 18, 1946, Jackson followed his father's encouragement to become an all-around athlete while at Cheltenham High School. He ran track, played halfback in football, and was a star hitter on the school baseball team. An outstanding football and baseball player at Arizona State University, he left after his sophomore year to join the Athletics (then located in Kansas City).

In 1968, his first full season with the Athletics, Jackson hit 29 homers and batted in 74 runs, but made 18 errors and struck out 171 times, which at the time ranked as the worst seasonal total by a left-handed hitter in baseball history. After playing a season of winter ball under Frank Robinson's direction, his performance continued to improve, and in 1973 he batted .293; led the league with 32 home runs, 117 RBIs, and a slugging percentage of .531; and was selected the American League's MVP.

While with Oakland, Jackson helped the Athletics to three straight World Series championships, from 1972 to 1974. Later in 1977 and 1978 the New York Yankees, with Jackson, won the World Series. The Yankees also won the American League pennant in 1981. In 1977, he was named World Series MVP, after hitting five home runs in the series—including three on three consecutive pitches in the sixth and deciding game.

The first of the big-money free agents, Jackson hit 144 homers, drove in 461 runs, and boosted his career home total to 425 while with the Yankees. He subsequently played five years for the California Angels and one return year with the Athletics. After retiring in 1987 having hit a total of 563 home runs, Jackson occasionally served as a commentator during baseball broadcasts. His tumultuous relationship with Yankees owner George Steinbrenner continued through various jobs Jackson held with the organization. Jackson was inducted into the Baseball Hall of Fame in 1993.

LEBRON JAMES (1984–)

Basketball Player. Born on December 30, 1984, in Akron, Ohio, LeBron Raymone James is one of the great ambassadors for the game of basketball. He attended high school at St. Vincent-St. Mary in Akron, where he was an all-state wide receiver in football and a three-time "Mr. Basketball" award winner. As a fifteen-year-old, James's talent as a basketball player was recognized by his head coach who said, "This guy is going to be the best guy I've ever seen." James was instrumental in leading St. Vincent-St. Mary to a state championship and undefeated season in his freshman year, and success continued in his sophomore season, when he brought the school to national prominence with a second consecutive state championship. The Fighting Irish lost only one game in James's first two seasons, a 79–78 defeat to Oak Hill.

By his junior year, James was in the media spotlight, featured on the covers of *SLAM*, *ESPN The Magazine*, and *Sports Illustrated* and gaining the nickname "King

James." His high school games were televised on ESPN2 and regional pay-per-view. NBA stars such as Shaquille O'Neal could often be found in attendance at his games, and practices for the Fighting Irish were moved to a larger venue. The Irish did not repeat as state champions, however, because increased enrollment pitted the team against tougher competition. James's attempt to enter the NBA draft following his junior year was unsuccessful.

During his senior year, James once again led St. Vincent-St. Mary to a state championship, and he garnered local, state, and national accolades along the way. He also garnered some unwanted media attention when his mother, Gloria James, purchased for her son's eighteenth birthday a Hummer valued at $80,000. It was determined, however, that no rules had been violated. Yet, at the end of January 2003, a state rule preventing amateur athletes from receiving gifts larger than $100 in value was violated when James received two throwback jerseys valued at over $800 for making an appearance at a Cleveland-area clothing store. While the rule stipulates that the athlete should be suspended for the remainder of the year, it was determined that James made an innocent mistake, for which the penalty was his team forfeiting one game, their only loss of his senior year.

Before he was drafted to play professional basketball, James signed a seven-year, $90 million contract with Nike. With the first pick in the 2003 NBA draft, the Cleveland Cavaliers selected James, ushering in a new era for the beleaguered franchise. James's stellar play on the court, along with his commercial successes off the court made him one of the sport's most sought-after athletes. Within his first six years as a professional basketball player, he won NBA Rookie of the Year and MVP awards and was voted to the All-Star team five times. An Olympic gold medalist as well, James has become one of the most recognizable basketball stars on the planet.

EARVIN "MAGIC" JOHNSON (1959–)

Basketball Player, Basketball Coach, Sports Executive, Talk Show Host, Entrepreneur. Earvin Johnson Jr. was born August 14, 1959, in Lansing, Michigan, and attended Everett High School. While playing for Everett he picked up the nickname "Magic" because of his ball-handling abilities. While in high school, Johnson made the all-state team and for three years was named the Prep Player of the Year in Michigan by United Press International.

After enrolling at Michigan State University in 1977, Johnson led the Spartans to the national championship in 1979. He then turned professional and was selected by the Los Angeles Lakers in the NBA draft. He led the Lakers to five NBA titles in the 1980s. Johnson played with the Lakers until his retirement in 1991 after he tested positive for the HIV virus.

Johnson was the recipient of many awards and was chosen to play on a number of all-star teams. In college, he was a consensus All-American selection his sophomore season and named the Most Outstanding Player of the 1979 NCAA Tournament. During his professional career, he was a three-time league MVP (1987, 1989, 1990) and was named to the NBA All-Rookie team (1980) and the All-NBA team (1982–1989, 1991). He was also recognized as the NBA Finals MVP (1987) and the NBA All-Star Game MVP (1990, 1992).

During his retirement, Johnson played on the U.S. Olympic basketball team in 1992 and in the 1992 NBA All-Star Game, where he won another MVP award. He also coached the Lakers briefly at the end of the 1993–1994 season, became team vice president, and had an ownership stake in the Lakers, which he was forced to surrender upon his short-lived return in 1996 as a player. Johnson hosted a late-night talk show in 1998 that was canceled a few months after its debut. In 2001 he was honored with a star on the Hollywood Walk of Fame. Johnson returned briefly to the game in 2006 as part of the NBA All-Star Weekend Skills Challenge. He remains a prominent entrepreneur investing in urban renewal and working to extend economic opportunities to others.

JACK JOHNSON (1878–1946)

Boxer. Jack Johnson became the first African American heavyweight champion by winning the crown from Tommy Burns in Sydney, Australia, on December 26, 1908.

John Arthur Johnson was born in Galveston, Texas, on March 31, 1878. He was so small as a child that he was nicknamed "Lil' Arthur," a name that stuck with him throughout his career. As a young man, he drifted around the country, making his way through Chicago, Boston, and New York. He learned to box by working out with veteran professionals whenever he could. When he finally got his chance at the title, he had already been fighting for nine years and had lost only 3 of 100 bouts.

With his victory over Burns, Johnson became the center of a bitter racial controversy, as his flamboyant lifestyle and outspokenness aroused white resentment. Public pressure forced former champion Jim Jeffries to come out of retirement and challenge Johnson for the title. When the two fought on July 4, 1910, in Reno, Nevada, Johnson knocked out Jeffries in the fifteenth round.

In 1913 Johnson left the United States because of legal difficulties. Two years later he defended his title against Jess Willard in Havana, Cuba, and was knocked out in the twenty-sixth round. His career record was 77 wins and 13 losses.

Basketball Player Earvin "Magic" Johnson, 1983. *During his Hall of Fame career, Johnson led the Los Angeles Lakers to five NBA titles and was named league MVP three times.* ANDREW D. BERNSTEIN/NBAE/GETTY IMAGES

Johnson died on June 10, 1946, in an automobile crash in North Carolina. He was inducted into the International Boxing Hall of Fame in 1990.

CULLEN JONES (1984–)

Swimmer. Born on February 29, 1984 in the Bronx, New York, Cullen Jones is an Olympic swimmer who earned a gold medal in the 2008 Olympiad in Beijing as a member of the U.S. 400-meter freestyle relay team. Along with striking gold in Beijing, Jones has earned medals at the World Championships and the Pan Pacific Championships, where he and his teammates, Michael Phelps, Jason Lezak and Neil Walker, in 2006 set the world record in the 400-meter freestyle relay. The first African American to hold a world record in long-course swimming, Jones set the U.S. record for the 50-meter freestyle in July 2009.

MARION JONES (1975–)

Track and Field Athlete. Marion Lois Jones was born in Los Angeles on October 12, 1975. As a child living in Thousand Oaks, California, Jones participated in many sports, but she was first attracted to running and jumping while watching track superstars Evelyn Ashford, Carl Lewis, and Jackie Joyner-Kersee on television as they competed in the 1984 Olympics. By the time she had finished high school she had received two High School Athlete of the Year awards for her performance in the 100-meter and 200-meter dashes as well as being named California Division I Player of the Year for basketball during her senior year.

Jones played basketball for the University of North Carolina and took the team to three Atlantic Coast Conference championships and a national title. Her love, however, was still track and field, as she had dreams of running in the Olympics. She decided to forgo playing basketball during her junior year of college to focus purely on her running in preparation for the 1996 Summer Olympics. A foot injury in late 1995, however, ended those aspirations. After the 1996 Olympics, Jones rededicated herself to the goal of running in the Olympics by training with Jamaican track star Trevor Graham.

Jones trained during 1996, and in 1997 she won both the 100-meter title and the long jump title at the USA Outdoor Championships. She became the first woman in nine years to win both events. Jones also won a gold medal in the 100-meter dash and was on the gold-winning 400-meter relay team at the Outdoor World Championships later that same year. Jones continued to dominate the world of women's track by setting a U.S. record in the 60-meter dash in the Gunma International competition in Japan in 1998. She also anchored the Nike International team to a new U.S. record in the 800-meter relay at the Penn Relays in Philadelphia that same year. Shortly after, she became the second-fastest woman in the world behind Florence Griffith Joyner when she ran 10.71 seconds in the 100-meter dash at a meet in Chengdu, China. By the end of 1999, Jones had won thirty-seven consecutive races at international and national track and field competitions, including the World Cup and the USA Outdoor Championships. In addition, *Track and Field News* named her the top woman athlete of the year for three consecutive years.

In Sydney, Australia, host to the 2000 Summer Games, Jones took home three gold medals and two bronze medals fulfilling her dream of not only running in but winning at the Olympics. Her victories were momentarily overshadowed by the publicity surrounding her then husband, a shot-putter who tested positive for steroid use in pre-Olympics testing. Still, Jones was honored with numerous awards after her Olympic victories, including being named female World Athlete of the Year by the International Association of Athletic Federations. Jones continued to compete in track and field, winning a gold medal in the 100-meter race in the 2001 Goodwill Games.

In December 2004 Jones was openly accused of using performance-enhancing drugs during her career as a runner. The charges could not be substantiated because Jones had never failed a drug test. In June 2006 at the USA Track and Field Championship in Indianapolis, Jones failed a drug test. She was later cleared of these charges as a second sample showed negative.

After missing the 2004 Olympics because of the birth of her son, Tim Jr., Jones had set her sights on the 2008 Olympic Games. Such visions were interrupted, however, by her admission that she had lied under oath about her use of steroids and her role in a check-fraud scheme. She appeared on *The Oprah Winfrey Show* in 2008 after serving six months in a Texas prison and acknowledged that prior to the 2000 Olympics she had used the performance-enhancing drug tetrahydrogestrinone (THG), also known as "the clear." The International Olympic Committee stripped Jones of her five Olympic medals. In March 2010 Jones embarked on a return to athletic competition by signing a contract to play basketball for the Tulsa Shock of the WNBA.

MICHAEL JORDAN (1963–)

Basketball Player, Sports Executive. Michael Jordan was born in Brooklyn, New York, on February 17, 1963, and attended the University of North Carolina. He won the NCAA championship as a freshman with the Tar Heels. As a rookie with the Chicago Bulls in 1985, Jordan was named to the All-Star team. A skilled ball handler and a slam dunk artist, he became the second NBA player in history to score more than 3,000 points in a single season (1986–1987).

Jordan was the NBA's individual scoring champ from 1987 through 1993. He was also named the NBA's MVP at the end of the 1987–1988 season. In 1991 Jordan led the Chicago Bulls to their first NBA championship and was again named the league's MVP. Under Jordan's leadership, the Bulls repeated as champions in 1992 and 1993. In 1992 Jordan played for the U.S. Olympic basketball "Dream Team," which captured the gold medal in Barcelona.

In October 1993, following the brutal murder of his father, Jordan announced his retirement from basketball to pursue another lifelong dream—to become a professional baseball player. Jordan began his professional baseball career in 1994 with the Chicago White Sox's Class AA team, the Birmingham Barons. Despite having only a .202 batting average for the year, Jordan was voted the most popular man in baseball in a national poll and remained at the top of *Forbes* magazine's list of the world's top-paid athletes for the third consecutive year, mostly because of endorsements.

Basketball Player Michael Jordan, New York City, 1998. *During a peak period for the popularity of basketball in the 1980s and 1990s, Jordan was the sport's best-known player—and eventually came to be considered the greatest basketball player of all time. He led the University of North Carolina to an NCAA title in 1982, and the Chicago Bulls to six NBA titles.* **PHOTOGRAPH BY RAY STUBBLEBINE. ARCHIVE PHOTOS, INC. REPRODUCED BY PERMISSION.**

In March 1995 Jordan returned to the NBA with the Bulls. He was named the 1996 All-Star Game MVP. Jordan led the Bulls to three straight titles from 1996 to 1998. During the 1995–1996 season, the team set an NBA record for most wins (72) in a season. After hitting the shot that won the 1998 NBA championship, Jordan retired again.

In 2000 Jordan took on yet another role, as it was announced that he would serve as part owner of and president of basketball operations for the NBA's Washington Wizards, a position that Jordan would hold for only so long, as he decided in September 2001 to come out of retirement once again, this time as a player for the Wizards. Jordan's return was met with much enthusiasm by fans and media. On January 4, 2002, facing his former team, the Chicago Bulls, Jordan became only the fourth NBA player to reach 30,000 career points. Just a few months later, Jordan was placed on the injured list with a painful knee injury that shortened his season. Despite the setback, Jordon played successfully through the 2002–2003 season. That year he was selected for his fourteenth and final All-Star Game, becoming that event's all-time leading scorer. During Jordan's final season, tributes to him were presented in arenas all over the country. Jordan retired from the game of basketball, having scored 32,292 points, the third-highest total in professional basketball history, behind only Kareem Abdul-Jabbar and Karl Malone. He was inducted into the Basketball Hall of Fame in 2009, and became majority owner of the Charlotte Bobcats in March 2010.

FLORENCE GRIFFITH JOYNER (1959–1998)

Track and Field Athlete. Born in Los Angeles on December 21, 1959, Florence Griffith started in track at an early age. She first attended California State University–Northridge but later transferred with her coach Bob Kersee when he moved to UCLA. In 1987 she married 1984 Olympic gold medalist Al Joyner.

At the 1984 Olympic Games she won a silver medal. She returned to the Olympic Games in 1988, winning gold medals in the 100-meter, 200-meter, and 400-meter relay races, along with a silver in the 1,600-meter relay. She set world records in the 100-meter and 200-meter races that year.

Nicknamed "Flo-Jo," she was inducted into the National Track and Field Hall of Fame in 1995. In 1998 she died suddenly in her sleep of an apparent heart seizure.

JACKIE JOYNER-KERSEE (1962–)

Track and Field Athlete, Community Activist, Sports Agent. Often touted as the greatest female athlete of her day, Jackie Joyner-Kersee won six Olympic medals during her career, including two gold medals in 1988 and another gold in 1992.

Joyner-Kersee was born on March 3, 1962, in East St. Louis, Illinois. Prior to winning her 1988 gold medals, she participated in the 1984 Olympics and won the silver medal for the heptathlon despite a torn hamstring muscle.

The only woman to gain more than 7,000 points in the heptathlon four times, she set a world record with 7,291 points at the 1988 Olympics. Joyner-Kersee also earned another gold medal in the heptathlon and a bronze medal in the long jump at the 1992 Olympics in Barcelona, Spain. In 1996 at the Atlanta Olympics she won a bronze medal in the long jump, her sixth medal, the most in the history of U.S. women's track and field.

Joyner-Kersee briefly played professional basketball in the American Basketball League, before retiring from sports to devote time to charitable causes. In addition, Joyner-Kersee is one of the few female sports agents in the United States.

"SUGAR" RAY LEONARD (1956–)

Boxer, Television Analyst. One of the flashiest and most popular fighters of the modern era, Sugar Ray Leonard brought fame to the lighter divisions of boxing, which traditionally have not garnered the same amount of attention as the heavyweight division. Ray Charles Leonard was born in Wilmington, North Carolina, on May 17, 1956, and won the gold medal in the light welterweight division at the 1976 Montreal Olympics.

Leonard rose through the professional ranks, winning the welterweight title from Wilfred Benitez in 1979. His fights with Roberto Duran and Tommy Hearns established his fame. After losing his first fight and his title to Duran, Leonard used a taunting style and flamboyant ring persona to force Duran to quit in the middle of their second fight. In 1981 he defeated Hearns in the fourteenth round by technical knockout, rallying from a point deficit. He retired shortly thereafter because of a detached retina.

In 1984 Leonard made a comeback by upsetting middleweight champion Marvelous" Marvin Hagler in a twelve-round decision. He retired following his defeat to Terry Norris in 1991, concluding a career that was also highlighted by "Fighter of the Year" recognition from *Ring* magazine in 1979, 1981, and 1987.

Leonard's public persona has led to many sponsorship deals. In addition, he has served as a boxing analyst for HBO and ESPN Classic Sports. Inducted into the U.S. Olympic Hall of Fame and the International Boxing Hall of Fame, Leonard is one of the great ambassadors of boxing, as suggested by his involvement as host and boxing mentor in the reality television show *The Contender.*

CARL LEWIS (1961–)

Track and Field Athlete. Carl Lewis was born on July 1, 1961, in Birmingham, Alabama. At the 1984 Olympics in Los Angeles, Lewis became the first athlete since Jesse Owens in 1936 to win four gold medals in the same Olympic competition.

An often controversial track and field performer, the New Jersey native went into the 1984 competition with the burden of tremendous expectations as the result of intense pre-Olympic publicity. He did not set any Olympic records and, despite his four gold medals, found himself criticized in the media.

Lewis went to the 1988 Olympics in Seoul, South Korea, hoping to duplicate his four gold medal wins. He was the focus of interest as he faced off against his Canadian archrival Ben Johnson. Lewis won gold medals in the long jump and the 100-meter dash (after Johnson was disqualified for steroid use) and a silver medal in the 200-meter dash. At the 1992 Olympics in Barcelona, Lewis won gold medals in the long jump and the 400-meter relay. He won his final gold medal at the 1996 Atlanta Olympiad in the long jump.

Lewis was inducted into the National Track and Field Hall of Fame in 2001.

JOE LOUIS (1914–1981)

Boxer. Joe Louis held the heavyweight championship for the longest stretch in history—more than eleven years, and he defended the title more often than any other heavyweight champion. His twenty-five title fights were more than the combined total of the eight champions who preceded him.

Born on May 13, 1914, in a sharecropper's shack in Lafayette, Alabama, Joseph Louis Barrow moved to Detroit as a small boy. Taking up boxing as an amateur, he won 50 of 59 bouts (43 of which were by knockout), before turning professional in 1934.

In 1935 Lewis fought Primo Carnera, a former boxing champion. Louis knocked out Carnera in six rounds, earning his nickname, "The Brown Bomber." After knocking out ex-champion Max Baer, Louis suffered his lone pre-championship defeat at the hands of Max Schmeling, who knocked him out in the twelfth round. Less than a month later, Louis knocked out another former champion, Jack Sharkey, in three rounds. He later won a rematch with Schmeling in a racially charged fight that earned him national attention. After defeating a number of other challengers, he was given a title fight with Jim Braddock on June 22, 1937. He stopped Braddock in the eighth round to gain the title.

After winning a disputed decision over Joe Walcott in 1947, Louis knocked out Walcott six months later, and then went into retirement. Monetary problems forced Louis into several comebacks that resulted in losses to new heavyweight champions Ezzard Charles and Rocky Marciano. These monetary difficulties were a problem for Louis for the rest of his life. He died April 12, 1981, at the age of sixty-six.

WILLIE MAYS (1931–)

Baseball Player. During his twenty-two seasons in Major League Baseball, Willie Mays hit more than 600 home runs. Besides being a solid hitter, Mays also was one of the game's finest defensive outfielders and base runners.

Born in Westfield, Alabama, on May 6, 1931, William Howard Mays made his professional debut on July 4, 1948, with the Birmingham Black Barons. He was signed by the New York Giants in 1950 and reached the major leagues in 1951. He was named the National League's Rookie of the Year for his 20 home runs and 68 RBIs, as well as his fielding, all of which contributed to the Giants' pennant victory.

After two years in the U.S. Army, Mays returned to lead the Giants to the World Championship in 1954, gaining recognition as the league's MVP for his 41 homers, 110 RBIs, and .345 batting average.

After the Giants moved to San Francisco in 1958, Mays continued his home run hitting, and he led his team to a 1962 pennant. A year later, *Sport* magazine named him "the greatest player of the decade." He won the MVP award again in 1965, after hitting 52 home runs and batting .317.

Traded to the New York Mets during the 1972 season, he continued to play outfield and first base. At the end of the 1973 season—his last—his statistics included 2,992 games, 3,283 hits, and 660 home runs. At the time, his home run total ranked third all-time. Willie Mays is one of only fourteen ballplayers to hit four home runs in a single game. After acting as a coach for the Mets, Mays left baseball to pursue a business career. He was inducted into the Baseball Hall of Fame in 1979. In 2000 the San Francisco Giants dedicated a plaza and statue to him outside their new stadium.

CHERYL MILLER (1964–)

Basketball Player, Television Analyst, Basketball Coach. Cheryl "Silk" Miller was born and raised in Riverside, California. As a basketball player, she was occasionally overshadowed by her brother Reggie, a guard who played for the Indiana Pacers for eighteen seasons. Another brother, Darrell, played baseball professionally with the California Angels in the late 1980s.

The 6'3" Miller began attracting notice in high school, having once scored 105 points in a game at Riverside Polytechnic High School. Miller was offered nearly 250 scholarships before deciding to enroll at the University of Southern California (USC). There she led the Trojans to two national titles, was All-American four times, and was named National Player of the Year three times.

Miller was a member of numerous national teams including the U.S. Junior National Team in 1981 and the National Team the following year. She participated in the World Championships and the Pan American Games in 1983. In 1984 she was a member of the U.S. team that earned the Olympic gold medal.

Following her playing career, Miller worked as a television basketball commentator. In 1993 she became the women's head basketball coach at her alma mater, USC, but announced her retirement in 1995. That same year, she was inducted into the Basketball Hall of Fame. Miller held the post of head coach of the WNBA's Phoenix Mercury from 1997 to 2000 and also served as the team's general manager.

In 1999 she became an inaugural member of the Women's Basketball Hall of Fame.

EDWIN MOSES (1955–)

Track and Field Athlete, Olympic Committee Chairperson. Born in Dayton, Ohio, on August 31, 1955, Edwin Moses became an internationally known track star in hurdles. Having attended Morehouse College, he was the top ranked intermediate hurdler in the world by 1976. That same year he earned a gold medal at the Olympic Games, a feat to be duplicated eight years later. Moses also won a bronze medal at the 1988 Games. A world record holder in the 400-meter hurdles, he recorded 122 consecutive victories in competition. *Sports Illustrated* presented Moses with its Athlete of the Year award in 1984, one year after he won the Sullivan Award, given annually to America's best amateur athlete. He was inducted into the National Track and Field Hall of Fame in 1994.

Moses received an MBA from Pepperdine University in 1994 and worked as a financial consultant. He has served as the chairperson of the U.S. Olympic Committee's Substance Abuse Center as well on the International Olympic Committee's Ethics Commission.

SHAQUILLE O'NEAL (1972–)

Basketball Player. Born in Newark, New Jersey, on March 6, 1972, to a military family, Shaquille O'Neal has become one of the most famous athletes in the United States. O'Neal has also appeared in movies and has released his own rap albums.

O'Neal's size and talent attracted attention while he was in high school. While attending Louisiana State University, he was named a collegiate All-American in 1992 and left school to pursue a professional career. He was the first pick of the 1992 NBA draft by the Orlando Magic and starred for them until 1996. He led the Magic to the 1995 NBA finals. In 1996 he signed a free agent contract with the Los Angeles Lakers.

O'Neal has enjoyed great success with the Lakers, leading them to three straight NBA championship titles in 2000, 2001, and 2002. He was selected MVP of the finals in each of the three championship series and was named the league's MVP for the 1999–2000 season. A fifteen-time NBA All-Star selection, O'Neal led the league in scoring twice (the 1994–1995 and 1999–2000 seasons).

In 2004 O'Neal welcomed a trade to the Miami Heat and promised to bring the team a championship. In 2006 the Heat, led by O'Neal and Dwayne Wade, won their first NBA championship. It was O'Neal's fourth title in seven seasons. With his powerful low-post game and affable media persona, resulting in commercials, movies, and rap recordings, O'Neal is one of the most influential centers in the history of basketball.

JESSE OWENS (1913–1980)

Track and Field Athlete. The track and field records Jesse Owens set have all been eclipsed, but his reputation as one of the first great athletes with the combined talents of a sprinter, low hurdler, and long jumper has not diminished.

Born James Cleveland Owens in Oakville, Alabama, on September 12, 1913, Owens and his family moved to Ohio when he was still young. In 1932, while attending East Technical High School in Cleveland, Owens was clocked at 10.3 seconds in the 100-meter dash. Two years later, Owens entered Ohio State University and became known as "The Ebony Antelope." While competing in the Big Ten Championships in Ann Arbor, Michigan, on May 25, 1935, Owens had what has been called "the greatest single day in the history of man's athletic achievements." In the space of about seventy minutes, he tied the world record for the 100-yard dash and surpassed the world record for three other events: the long jump, the 220-yard low hurdles, and the 220-yard dash.

In 1936, at the Berlin Olympics, Owens won four gold medals, at the time the most universally acclaimed feat in the history of the Olympic Games. He still faced discrimination in the United States, however, after his victories. He never graduated from Ohio State but did eventually found his own public relations firm.

SATCHEL PAIGE (1906–1982)

Baseball Player, Baseball Coach. Long before Jackie Robinson broke the color barrier of "organized baseball," Leroy Robert "Satchel" Paige was the most famous African American baseball player. As an outstanding performer in the Negro Leagues, Paige became a legendary

Jesse Owens Commemorative Stamp, 1998. *Owens's performance at the 1936 Berlin Olympics, during which he won four gold medals in track events, shocked Adolf Hitler, who espoused the superiority of the Aryan race.* **AP PHOTO/U.S. POSTAL SERVICE**

figure whose encounters with Major League Baseball players added considerably to his athletic reputation.

Paige was born in Mobile, Alabama, on July 7, 1906. He began playing semiprofessional ball while working as an iceman and porter, acquiring the sobriquet "Satchel" while playing for Chattanooga. In the mid-1920s he became a professional player with the Birmingham Black Barons.

For the next two decades, Paige was the dominant pitcher in Negro League baseball. In 1933, he won 31 games and lost 4. Paige also dominated winter ball in Latin America during the 1930s. In 1942 Paige led the Kansas City Monarchs to victory in the Negro World Series, and four years later he helped them to the pennant by allowing only 2 runs in 93 innings, a performance which included a string of 64 straight scoreless innings.

In 1948 he was recruited into the major leagues. Despite being well past his prime, he still was able to contribute 6 victories in Cleveland's pennant drive and pitched in the World Series. Four years later, while pitching for the St. Louis Browns, he was named to the American League All-Star squad.

Until the 1969 baseball season, Paige was active on the barnstorming circuit with the Harlem Globetrotters and a host of other exhibition teams. In 1969 the Atlanta Braves, in an attempt to make Paige eligible for baseball's pension plan, signed him to a one-year contract as coach. Paige died in June 1982.

WALTER PAYTON (1954–1999)

Football Player, Entrepreneur. Walter Payton was born on July 25, 1954, in Columbia, Mississippi. When he retired as a running back for the Chicago Bears after the 1987 season, he was the NFL's all-time leading rusher, breaking a record held for many years by Jim Brown.

A graduate of Jackson State University, Payton played his entire career in Chicago, receiving numerous awards and helping to lead the Bears to a victory in Super Bowl XX. He broke O. J. Simpson's single-game rushing record after gaining 275 yards during a 1977 contest with the Minnesota Vikings. Seven years later, during a game against the New Orleans Saints, he surpassed Brown's career rushing record. Payton concluded his career with a total of 16,726 rushing yards.

Payton funded several auto racing teams and fronted a group of businesspeople in an attempt to bring a professional football team to the city of St. Louis. He was inducted into the Professional Football Hall of Fame in 1993. In 1998 Payton was diagnosed with a fatal liver disease. He died on November 1, 1999.

CALVIN PEETE (1943–)

Golfer. Calvin Peete was born in Detroit, on July 18, 1943. During World War II, Peete moved with his family to Pahokee, Florida. One of nineteen children, as a youth he was a farm laborer and itinerant peddler, selling wares to farmers along the East Coast.

He began golfing at the age of twenty-three and soon realized he possessed some aptitude for the sport. Unlike other African American golfers of his era, who were forced into caddying as a means of gaining entrance into the sport, Peete was able to move directly toward a professional career. Peete did, however, face the handicap of a left arm that he was unable to completely straighten, leading experts to tell him that he would never be successful.

After turning pro in 1971, Peete struggled. In 1978 he placed 108th in total money winnings on the PGA Tour. Peete's first tour victory came at the 1979 Greater Milwaukee Open, which he won again in 1982, along with the Anheuser-Busch Classic, BC Open, and the Pensacola Open. In 1981 and 1982 he finished first on the tour in the categories of driving accuracy and greens reached in regulation.

Despite his success, Peete was not considered fully accredited because the PGA does not recognize a golfer unless he has obtained a high school diploma. This was a requirement toward obtaining a spot on the prestigious Ryder Cup team. In 1982, with the assistance of his wife, Peete passed the Michigan general equivalency examination twenty-four years after leaving high school. *Ebony* magazine

Golfer Calvin Peete and the U.S. Ryder Cup Team, 1985. *Prior to the emergence of Tiger Woods, Peete (*back row, third from left*) was the most successful African American on the PGA Tour. In addition to his twelve PGA Tour wins, Peete was a two-time member of the U.S. Ryder Cup team, participating in 1983 and 1985.* BOB THOMAS/GETTY IMAGES

rewarded him with its Black Achievement Award, and, in 1983 Peete was presented with the Jackie Robinson Award.

Peete captured two more PGA titles in 1983—the Georgia-Pacific Atlanta Classic and the Anheuser-Busch Classic. He was also asked to represent the United States as a member of the Ryder Cup team. That same year, he won the Ben Hogan Award. The following year, Peete had the best scoring average on the PGA Tour. He joined the PGA's senior tour in 1993.

JERRY RICE (1962–)

Football Player. Jerry Rice was born in Starkville, Mississippi, on October 13, 1962. As a collegiate wide receiver at Mississippi Valley State, Rice set eighteen Division II records. Drafted in the first round by the San Francisco 49ers in 1985, Rice combined with quarterbacks Joe Montana and Steve Young to form the most elite pass-catching combination in pro football history. He traces the development of his superb hands to his childhood, during which his father would toss him bricks during construction work.

During his twenty-year NFL career, Rice set the career record for touchdowns at 208. His eleven straight seasons with more than 1,000 receiving yards was another league record. His best season was the strike-shortened 1987 campaign, during which he scored 22 touchdowns in only twelve regular season games. In that same year, Rice scored touchdowns in thirteen straight games. In a 1990 contest with the Atlanta Falcons, Rice scored five touchdowns. He was named to the Pro Bowl every season until slowed by an injury in 1997. He was named the NFL's Player of the Year by the *Sporting News* in 1987 and 1990. Rice was MVP in the 49ers' Super Bowl XXIII victory over the Cincinnati Bengals.

Rice helped lead the 49ers to additional Super Bowl victories after the 1988, 1989, and 1994 seasons. After playing wide receiver for the 49ers for sixteen seasons, Rice in 2001 signed a multiyear contract with the Oakland Raiders.

Rice excelled in 2001 with the Raiders and was instrumental in the Raiders' appearance in Super Bowl XXXVII. In 2004, with a slowing of his performance, Rice moved to the Seattle Seahawks and later to the

Denver Broncos. In 2005 he decided to retire. In order to retire with the 49ers, the team he began his career with, Rice was given a one-day contract. On August 24, 2005, Rice officially retired from the game.

Along with his authorship of two books, Rice has remained a presence in popular culture with his appearances in such shows as *Dancing with the Stars* and *Pros vs. Joes.*

OSCAR ROBERTSON (1938–)

Basketball Player, Business Executive, Community Activist. Oscar Robertson was born in Charlotte, Tennessee, on November 24, 1938, before moving to Indiana and attending Indianapolis' Crispus Attucks High School. He led his team to the prestigious Indiana state basketball title on two occasions and shortly thereafter became the first African American to play at the University of Cincinnati. He helped Cincinnati reach the Final Four in 1959 and 1960, was twice named the U.S. Basketball Writers Association's College Player of the Year, and set fourteen major collegiate records. He also became the first to lead the NCAA in scoring for three consecutive seasons.

In 1960, after participating on the U.S. gold-medal-winning Olympic basketball team as cocaptain, Robertson signed a $100,000 contract with the Cincinnati Royals, earning Rookie of the Year honors during his initial season in the NBA. At six feet five, 210 pounds, he would become the NBA's first true "big guard." The multidimensional Robertson, known as the "Big O," was a textbook fundamental player and unyieldingly physical. During the 1961–1962 season he led the NBA in assists, at 11.4 per game. His best season was the 1963–1964 campaign in which he averaged 31.4 points per game and was named the league's MVP.

Over the course of five separate seasons, Robertson averaged more than 30 points and 10 assists per game, something no other player in NBA history has accomplished. He was named the MVP of the 1961, 1964, and 1969 All-Star games. Late in his career, Robertson joined the Milwaukee Bucks and led Milwaukee to its only NBA championship in 1971.

Between 1964 and 1974, Robertson served as president of the NBA Players Association (NBAPA). Under his leadership, the NBAPA established collective bargaining with the league's owners. He was inducted into the Basketball Hall of Fame in 1979 and was named a year later to the NBA's 35th anniversary all-time team. Robertson was also inducted into the Olympic Hall of Fame in 1984.

Robertson has remained visible off the court, founding Orchem, Inc. (later Orchem Corporation), a successful chemical company, in 1981, and starting Oscar Robertson and Associates in 1983. He is a member of the NAACP Sports Board, a trustee of the Indiana High School and Basketball Halls of Fame, has served as national director of the Pepsi-Cola Hot Shot Program, and was president of the NBA Retired Players Association from 1993 to 1999. Robertson was also the developer of affordable housing units in Cincinnati and Indianapolis. He served in the U.S. Army for eight years.

EDDIE G. ROBINSON (1919–2007)

College Football Coach. Eddie Gay Robinson was born on February 13, 1919, in Jackson, Louisiana. As a gifted athlete in high school, Robinson earned a scholarship to Leland College in Louisiana. A star quarterback, Robinson got involved in his first coaching clinic there. After obtaining his bachelor's degree, Robinson took his first college coaching job in 1941. Though he was only twenty-two years old at the time, Grambling State gave him the opportunity to coach.

The early success of Grambling State's football team established Robinson as a fixture at the college. He coached numerous NFL stars and successful teams during his tenure as coach. In 1985 Robinson surpassed Bear Bryant as the career leader in victories by a head coach. He retired following the 1997 season with 408 victories, making him the first college football coach ever to win over 400 games. Two years later his autobiography, *Never Before, Never Again*, was published. Robinson was inducted into the College Football Hall of Fame in 1997. In all, Robinson, or Coach Rob as he is fondly remembered, coached for fifty-six seasons at one school, a record-breaking tenure, and his mark on the game of college football is evident by the Eddie Robinson Award, given annually to the college football coach of the year. Robinson died in 2007 at the age of eighty-eight.

FRANK ROBINSON (1935–)

Baseball Player, Baseball Manager, Sports Executive. Although born in Beaumont, Texas, on August 31, 1935, Frank Robinson grew up from the age of five in Oakland, California. During his teens, he was a football and baseball star at McClymonds High School. After graduation in 1953, he signed with the Cincinnati Reds.

In 1956 Robinson debuted in Major League Baseball, hitting 38 homers and winning Rookie of the Year honors. During the next eight years, he hit 253 homers and had more than 800 RBIs. In 1961 Robinson was named MVP for leading Cincinnati to the National League pennant. Five years later, after being traded to the Baltimore Orioles, Robinson won the American League's Triple Crown and became the first player to win the MVP in both leagues. He retired as an active player after the 1976 season with a lifetime batting average of .294 in 2,808 games along with 586 home runs, 2,943 hits, 1,829 runs, and 1,812 RBIs. Robinson was inducted into the Baseball Hall of Fame in 1982.

Robinson was Major League Baseball's first African American manager. He was named to the head post of the Cleveland Indians in 1975. After being fired by the Indians in 1977, Robinson a year later became the manager of the Rochester Red Wings, a minor league team. In 1981 Robinson was hired by the San Francisco Giants, where he managed the team until 1984. He also managed the Baltimore Orioles from 1988 to 1991. He later became the assistant general manager of that team. After serving three years as vice president of on-field operations for Major League Baseball, Robinson became manager for the Montreal Expos/Washington Nationals. Operating from his gut instincts, Robinson's techniques as a manager were considered controversial and were highly criticized. After serving as manager from 2002 to 2006, Robinson's contract was not renewed. In 2005 Robinson received the Presidential Medal of Freedom.

JACKIE ROBINSON (1919–1972)

Baseball Player, Business Executive, Community Activist. Born in Cairo, Georgia, on January 31, 1919, Jack Roosevelt Robinson was raised in Pasadena, California. At UCLA he gained All-American honorable mention as a halfback, but he left college in his junior year to play professional football for the Los Angeles Bulldogs. After serving as a U.S. Army lieutenant during World War II, Robinson returned to civilian life with the hope of becoming a physical education coach. He began to play Negro League baseball to establish himself.

In 1945 while Robinson was playing with the Kansas City Monarchs, Branch Rickey of the Brooklyn Dodgers signed him to a contract. In 1946 Robinson played for the Dodgers' top minor league club in Montreal. Just prior to the start of the 1947 season, the Dodgers announced they had purchased Robinson's contract, and on April 15, 1947, he began his Major League Baseball career. During a ten-year career, he hit .311 in 1,382 games with 1,518 hits, 947 runs, 273 doubles, and 734 RBIs. He won the National League's MVP award in 1949 and played on six National League pennant winners, as well as one world championship team. Robinson was inducted into the Baseball Hall of Fame in 1962.

After his retirement from baseball, Robinson became a bank official, president of a land development firm, and a director of programs to combat drug addiction. He died on October 24, 1972, in Stamford, Connecticut.

Baseball Player Jackie Robinson, Hall of Fame Induction Ceremony, Cooperstown, NY, 1962. *Robinson, who integrated Major League Baseball in 1947, was the first African American to be enshrined in baseball's Hall of Fame.* BETTMANN/CORBIS

"SUGAR RAY" ROBINSON (1921–1989)

Boxer. Born Walker Smith Jr. in Detroit on May 3, 1921, he took the name Robinson from the certificate of an amateur boxer whose identity enabled him to meet the age requirements for getting a match in Michigan.

As a youth, Robinson had watched a Detroit neighbor, Joe Louis, train for an amateur boxing career. When Robinson moved to New York two years later, he began to spend most of his time at local gyms in preparation for his own amateur career. After winning all eighty-nine of his amateur bouts and the 1939 Golden Gloves featherweight championship, he turned professional in 1940 at Madison Square Garden.

Robinson beat Tommy Bell in an elimination title bout in December 1946 to win the welterweight title. He successfully defended the title for five years, and on February 14, 1951, took the middleweight crown from Jake LaMotta.

In July 1951 he lost the title to Randy Turpin, only to win it back two months later. Retiring for a time, Robinson subsequently fought a series of exciting battles with Carl "Bobo" Olson, Carmen Basilio, and Gene Fullmer before retiring permanently on December 10, 1965, having won six titles.

Suffering from diabetes, hypertension, and Alzheimer's disease, Robinson died of natural causes at the Brotman Medical Center in Culver City, California, on April 12, 1989. Over his career, he won 175 of 202 professional bouts and titles in three weight classes.

WILMA RUDOLPH (1940–1994)

Track and Field Athlete, Track and Field Coach, Community Activist, Lecturer. Wilma Rudolph was born on June 23, 1940, in Clarksville, Tennessee, the seventeenth of nineteen children. At an early age, she survived polio and scarlet fever. Through daily leg massages administered in turn by different members of her family, she progressed to the point where she was able to walk with the aid of a special shoe. Three years later, however, she discarded the shoe and began joining her brother in backyard basketball games. At Burt High School in Clarksville, Rudolph broke the state basketball record for girls. As a sprinter, she was undefeated at high school track meets.

In 1957 Rudolph enrolled at Tennessee State University and began training for the Olympic Games in Rome. She gained national recognition in college meets, setting the world record for 200-meters in July 1960. At the Olympics, she earned the title of the "world's fastest woman" by winning gold medals for the 100-meter dash, for the 200-meter dash (setting an Olympic record), and for anchoring the 400-meter relay (setting a world record). She was named by the Associated Press as the U.S. Female Athlete of the Year for 1960 and also won United Press Athlete of the Year honors.

Rudolph served as a track coach, an athletic consultant, and the assistant director of athletics for the Mayor's Youth Foundation in Chicago. She was also the founder of the Wilma Rudolph Foundation. In addition, Rudolph was a talk show host and active on the lecture circuit. On November 12, 1994, Rudolph died at her home in Brentwood, Tennessee, of a brain tumor.

BILL RUSSELL (1934–)

Basketball Player, Basketball Coach, Sports Executive, Television Commentator. Bill Russell, who led the Boston Celtics to eleven NBA titles, including eight in a row, is regarded as the finest defensive basketball player in the game's history. The 6'10" star is also the first African American to coach an NBA team.

William Felton Russell was born on February 12, 1934, in Monroe, Louisiana. The family settled in Oakland, California, when Russell was a youth. At McClymonds High School, Russell proved to be an awkward but determined basketball player who eventually received a scholarship to nearby University of San Francisco.

In his sophomore year he became the most publicized athlete on the West Coast. Over the next two years, his fame spread across the nation as he led his team to a record 60 consecutive victories and two straight NCAA titles.

The Celtics had never won an NBA championship before Russell's arrival in 1956. With the help of Russell's defensive abilities, the Celtics became the most successful team in the history of professional sports, winning the world championship eight years in a row. Russell himself was named MVP on five separate occasions (1958, 1961–1963, and 1965). In 1966 Russell became the Celtics player/coach.

After the 1968–1969 season, having led the Celtics to their eleventh NBA crown, Russell retired as both coach and player. He left the game as its all-time leader in minutes played (40,726). He was inducted into the Basketball Hall of Fame in 1975. In 1980 the Professional Basketball Writers Association of America selected Russell as the greatest player in NBA history.

After retirement, Russell was a color commentator on NBC-TV's NBA Game of the Week. In 1974 he accepted a lucrative contract to become head coach and general manager of the Seattle Supersonics. He remained at Seattle's helm through 1977 and returned to the coaching ranks ten years later for a one-year stint with the Sacramento Kings. He also served as the team's director of player personnel in 1988.

DEION SANDERS (1967–)

Football Player, Baseball Player. Deion Sanders was born in Fort Myers, Florida, on August 9, 1967, and first achieved fame as an All-American defensive back at Florida State University. Also a baseball star at the school, Sanders left college in 1989 to pursue professional careers in both sports.

Sanders was drafted by the football Atlanta Falcons and later played for the San Francisco 49ers, Dallas Cowboys, Washington Redskins, and Baltimore Ravens. He was selected an All-Pro eight times and was named the top defensive player in the league in 1994. Sanders won Super Bowls with San Francisco in 1994 and Dallas in 1995. He announced his retirement from football in July 2001 but returned to the sport for a two-year stint with the Ravens in 2004 and 2005.

Sanders's baseball career was also successful. He was drafted and played with the New York Yankees until traded to the Atlanta Braves in 1991. He played in one World Series with the Braves and later played with the San Francisco Giants and Cincinnati Reds. Sanders's baseball career was cut short by injuries suffered while playing football.

Sanders is known for his fun-loving image, evidenced by his nickname, "Prime Time." Known for flashy clothing and on-field theatrics, Sanders became one of the most visible athletes in the United States, and is the only athlete to have played in both the Super Bowl and the World Series. A brush with depression, however, caused him to change his image and rediscover his Christian faith in 1998. He joined the NFL network as an analyst in the summer of 2006.

GALE SAYERS (1943–)

Football Player, Athletic Director, Community Activist, Entrepreneur. Gale Eugene Sayers was born in Wichita, Kansas, on May 30, 1943. He participated in football and track while in high school and enrolled at the University of Kansas. He signed with the Chicago Bears before graduating but returned after his professional football career was over to finish his bachelor's degree and also earn a master's degree.

Sayers garnered All-Pro honors in his rookie season of 1965 and the next four seasons as well. Sayers led the league in rushing in 1966 and 1969. In a 1965 game against the San Francisco 49ers, he tied an NFL record by scoring six touchdowns.

Sayers's career was ended after the 1971 season because of a knee injury. His final totals included 56 touchdowns—39 rushing, 9 receiving, 6 on kickoff returns (including a 103-yarder in 1967), and 2 on punt returns. He was named to the "AFL-NFL 1960–1984 All-Star Team" as a kick returner. Despite his brief career, he was inducted into the Professional Football Hall of Fame in 1977.

Following his playing career, Sayers was named assistant to the athletic director at the University of Kansas, and between 1976 and 1981 he served as the athletic director at Southern Illinois University. Active in the community, Sayers has been the commissioner of the Chicago Park District; the cochairperson of the Legal Defense Fund for Sports, NAACP Coordinator; and an honorary chairman of the American Cancer Society in addition to his involvement in the Reach Out Program. Sayers founded his own computer supplies firm in 1982. In 2000 the School of Education at the University of Kansas dedicated the Gale Sayers Microcomputer Center.

Gale Sayers, Book Signing Appearance, Chicago, 2007. *Highlights of Sayers's Hall of Fame career as a running back for the Chicago Bears include leading the NFL in rushing in 1966 and 1969, garnering All-Pro honors five times, and scoring six touchdowns in a single game in 1965.* RAYMOND BOYD/MICHAEL OCHS ARCHIVES/GETTY IMAGES

CHARLIE SIFFORD (1922–)

Golfer. Born in Charlotte, North Carolina, on June 2, 1922, Charles Sifford was the first African American to participate in a predominately white golf event, the 1957 Long Beach Open. Sifford's entry into golf began as a caddie at the age of nine. At thirteen, he won a caddie tournament shooting a 70. After moving to Philadelphia, Sifford worked as a teaching professional and chauffeur.

Sifford became the first African American to be awarded a PGA card as an approved player in 1959 when the tour lifted its "Caucasian only" clause. He was also the first to win a major PGA event, the 1967 Greater Hartford Open. On the PGA's senior tour, Sifford triumphed at the PGA Seniors' Championship (1975) and the Suntree Classic (1980). He also won the National Negro Open six times, including five consecutively from 1952 to 1956. Sifford's autobiography, *Just Let Me Play: The Story of Charlie Sifford, The First Black PGA Golfer*, published in 1992, exposed the racism that remained after he joined the PGA Tour.

O. J. SIMPSON (1947–)

Football Player, Television Commentator, Actor. Born in San Francisco on July 9, 1947, Orenthal James Simpson starred at the University of Southern California (USC), winning the Heisman Trophy in 1968. One year prior to that, he was a member of the USC relay team that set a world record of 38.6 seconds in the 440-yard run. ABC Sports voted him College Player of the Decade. He signed with the Buffalo Bills in 1969 and three years later won his first rushing title.

Simpson enjoyed his finest season in 1973. On opening day, he rushed for 250 yards against the New England Patriots, breaking the record of 247 yards held by Willie Ellison. His yardage total of 2,003 for the entire season surpassed the previous mark of 1,863 held by Jim Brown. In addition, he scored 12 touchdowns, averaged 6 yards per carry, and had more rushing yardage than fifteen other NFL clubs. He was named Player of the Year and won the Jim Thorpe Trophy.

Simpson retired from football in 1979. He has appeared in several feature films and worked as a sports commentator for ABC-TV and NBC-TV. In 1995 a jury found Simpson not guilty of charges that he had brutally slain his ex-wife and a male friend. The decision was rejected by many Americans, and Simpson has since been forced to live a reclusive lifestyle. In 2007, however, Simpson made headlines again following a Las Vegas run-in with sports memorabilia dealers. A jury in 2008 found him guilty of twelve charges, including kidnapping and theft, and he was sentenced to a minimum of nine years in prison.

LOVIE SMITH (1958–)

Football Coach. Born in Gladewater, Texas, on May 8, 1958, Lovie Lee Smith is the first African American coach to lead an NFL team to the Super Bowl. Raised in Big Sandy, Texas, Smith expressed a desire to coach football beginning in sixth grade. He attended Big Sandy High School, where, as a linebacker and defensive end, he led the Wildcats to three state championships, earning all-state accolades each year in the process. Smith went on to play defensive back at the University of Tulsa, where he was a two-time All-American and graduated in 1979.

Rather than becoming a professional football player, Smith next turned to coaching, beginning at his high school in 1980. From there, Smith honed his coaching craft at a range of institutions, including Arizona State University, the University of Tennessee, and Ohio State University, along with some coaching positions in professional football, notably the Tampa Bay Buccaneers, where he worked under Tony Dungy.

On January 15, 2004, Smith began his tenure as the thirteenth head coach of the Chicago Bears. After winning the Coach of the Year award in 2005, Smith led the Bears to a 13-3 record during the 2006 regular season. The postseason, too, proved productive as the Bears won the NFC Championship Game, ensuring their berth in Super Bowl XLI. With the conclusion of the AFC Championship Game a few hours later, Dungy became the second African American head coach to lead his team to the Super Bowl. Dungy went on to guide the Colts to a 29–17 victory over Smith, his former linebackers coach, and the Bears.

Only a few years into his tenure as Chicago's head coach, Smith had proven himself to be a capable leader, returning the Bears to NFC North dominance. Through the 2009 season, he ranked third all-time in coaching victories for the Bears, trailing only George Halas and Mike Ditka, both of whom are enshrined in the Professional Football Hall of Fame.

LAWRENCE TAYLOR (1959–)

Football Player. Born in Williamsburg, Virginia, on February 4, 1959, Lawrence Taylor revolutionized the linebacker position in the NFL by virtue of his strength and speed.

After an outstanding career at the University of North Carolina where he was named Atlantic Coast Conference Player of the Year in 1980, Taylor was selected by the New York Giants with the second pick of the 1981 draft. Taylor amassed 132.5 career sacks and was an integral part of two Giants Super Bowl championships, following the 1986 and 1990 seasons. He was named to the NFL's all-decade team for the 1980s.

Problems with substance abuse and taxes have marked his post-football career, at one point leading him to attempt a professional wrestling career in order to earn money. Despite these troubles, Taylor is still acknowledged as one of the finest linebackers in the history of the NFL. He was inducted into the Professional Football Hall of Fame in 1999.

MARSHALL W. "MAJOR" TAYLOR (1878–1932)

Cyclist. Marshall W. "Major" Taylor became the first African American world cycling champion in 1899.

Born in Indianapolis on November 26, 1878, the son of a coachman, he worked at a bicycle store part-time as a teen. After attending his first race, his boss suggested that Major enter a couple of races. He won a 10-mile race and proceeded to compete as an amateur.

By the time he was sixteen years old, he went to work in a factory owned by a former champion and, with his new boss's encouragement, competed in races in Canada, Europe, Australia, and New Zealand. During nearly sixteen years of competition, he won numerous championships and set several world records. Taylor was inducted into the U.S. Bicycling Hall of Fame in 1989. He died in 1932.

DEBI THOMAS (1967–)

Figure Skater. Born in Poughkeepsie, New York, on March 25, 1967, Debra Janine Thomas was the first African American figure skater to win a major championship. Thomas was the winner at the 1985 National Sports Festival in Baton Rouge, Louisiana. The following year she captured the U.S. and world figure skating titles, becoming the first African American to capture an international singles meet.

Thomas won a bronze medal at the 1988 Olympic Games in Calgary, becoming the first African American to win an Olympic medal in a winter sport. Dividing her time between collegiate studies and a professional skating career as a member of "Stars on Ice," Thomas earned her bachelor's degree from Stanford University in 1991. She retired from the sport the following year to pursue a career in medicine. In 1997 Thomas completed her medical studies at Northwestern University and eventually became a practicing orthopedic surgeon.

JOHN THOMPSON (1941–)

College Basketball Coach. John Thompson was born in Washington, D.C., on September 2, 1941. He played college basketball at Providence College and graduated in 1964. Thompson played with the Boston Celtics of the NBA from 1964 to 1966. The Celtics won NBA titles both seasons, with Thompson backing up Hall of Fame center Bill Russell.

In 1966 Thompson began coaching St. Anthony's High School in Washington, D.C. In 1972 he was offered the head coaching job at Georgetown University. Thompson subsequently turned Georgetown into a national powerhouse. In 1982 he led the Hoyas to the national championship game, becoming the first African American to coach in the Final Four. The Hoyas won the championship in 1984 and were runner-up the next season. Thompson's Hoyas won six Big East titles and he developed a number of star players, including Patrick Ewing, Alonzo Mourning, Dikembe Mutombo, and Allen Iverson.

In 1988 Thompson coached the U.S. Olympic basketball team to a bronze medal at the Seoul Olympiad. He frequently criticized the NCAA for tighter academic standards, which he felt discriminated against African Americans. Several times he walked off the court before games to protest increasing test scores for freshman students. Thompson resigned in early 1999 because of personal problems. He was inducted into the Basketball Hall of Fame later that year.

GENE UPSHAW (1945–2008)

Football Player, NFL Union Executive, Community Activist. Born in Robstown, Texas, on August 15, 1945, Eugene Thurman Upshaw attended Texas College of Arts and Industries. He was named All-Pro eight times and inducted into the Professional Football Hall of Fame in 1987.

Upshaw served for twenty-five years as the executive director of the National Football League Players Association. Under his leadership, the organization expended considerable resources on substance abuse education and rehabilitation. Upshaw was also the president of the Federation of Professional Athletes AFL-CIO, as well as a member on the California Governor's Council on Wellness and Physical Fitness. He was the coordinator for voter registration and fund-raising in Alameda County (California) and served as a planning commissioner for that same county.

Upshaw was the recipient of the Byron "Whizzer" White Humanitarian Award as voted by the NFL players in 1980. In 1982 he was presented with the A. Philip Randolph Award. Following his death in 2008, NFL players wore a "GU" sticker on their helmets during the first game of that year's season in honor of Upshaw's life and work.

MICHAEL VICK (1980–)

Football Player. Michael Dwayne Vick was born on June 26, 1980, in Newport News, Virginia, and graduated from Warwick High School in 1998, where he starred as a quarterback. Following a redshirt first year at Virginia Tech, Vick burst onto the national stage in 1999, garnering first-team All-American honors as well as finishing third in that year's Heisman Trophy vote. He was a true hybrid quarterback, one who was a legitimate passing and running threat.

During his sophomore season, Vick led the Hokies to a 10-1 record during the regular season, along with a top-ten finish in the national rankings. In the college football postseason, the Hokies, led by Vick, won the Gator Bowl over Clemson. Vick then left Virginia Tech and declared himself eligible for the NFL draft.

In 2001 the Atlanta Falcons drafted Vick, making him the first African American quarterback to be selected as the number one overall pick in the NFL draft. From 2001 until 2006, Vick took snaps from center for the Falcons, compiling over 11,000 passing yards and 71 passing touchdowns. And, true to his dual-threat status, Vick rushed for nearly 4,000 yards and scored 21 rushing touchdowns. A truly electrifying player, Vick had become an NFL icon.

Vick's career path changed suddenly in April 2007 when investigations began into alleged dogfighting on his property in Virginia. Vick, a registered dog breeder, at first denied knowledge of any illegal activity. Yet with increased media exposure and scrutiny by local, state, and federal authorities, it was discovered, by late July 2007, that Vick was indeed connected to Bad Newz Kennels, a dogfighting ring. The fallout was shattering. Vick was suspended from the NFL, lost a significant portion of his multimillion-dollar signing bonus, lost lucrative endorsements, and was sentenced to twenty-three months in prison.

Following his release from prison in 2009, Vick signed a contract to play quarterback for the Philadelphia Eagles. He spent the 2009 season as a backup to starter Donovan McNabb.

BILL WHITE (1934–)

Baseball Player, Baseball Announcer, Baseball Executive. William DeKova White was born in Lakewood, Florida, on January 28, 1934. He began his Major League Baseball career with the New York Giants in 1956 and spent thirteen years as a player, including stints with the San Francisco Giants, St. Louis Cardinals, and Philadelphia Phillies. During his career, White was named to the National League All-Star team five times and won seven Gold Gloves. He retired from baseball in 1969 and two years later joined Phil Rizzuto as a television announcer for the New York Yankees.

On April 1, 1989, Bill White became the first African American president of the National League. He held the post until he was succeeded in 1994 by another African American, Leonard Coleman.

LENNY WILKENS (1937–)

Basketball Player, Basketball Coach. Leonard Randolph Wilkens was born on October 28, 1937, in New York City. He developed his game on the city's streets and then starred at Providence College. Wilkens was drafted by the St. Louis Hawks of the NBA in 1960. He was named to nine All-Star teams over the course of his fifteen-year playing career and was MVP of the 1971 game while a member of the Seattle SuperSonics. Wilkens was Seattle's player-coach from 1969 to 1972 and also took on these dual responsibilities for the Portland Trail Blazers during the 1974–1975 season, his final as a player. He then served as Portland's coach for an additional year.

Wilkens returned to Seattle as coach in 1978 and led the Sonics to the NBA championship in 1979. He coached with the Sonics until 1985, when he left to coach the Cleveland Cavaliers. In 1993 Wilkens was named coach of the Atlanta Hawks, and on January 6, 1995, he won his 939th game, breaking Red Auerbach's record for most victories by an NBA head coach. Wilkens coached the Hawks for seven seasons before taking the head coaching position with the Toronto Raptors in 2000. Later, he had a brief stint as head coach of the New York Knicks in 2004 and 2005.

In 1996 Wilkens coached the men's basketball team that won the gold medal at the Atlanta Olympiad. He was twice inducted into the Basketball Hall of Fame—in 1989 as a player and in 1998 as a coach.

SERENA WILLIAMS (1981–)

Tennis Player. Serena Williams was born in Saginaw, Michigan, on September 26, 1981. She and her sister Venus became tennis prodigies in the mid-1990s under the coaching of their father, Richard. Although the Williams sisters were featured in various articles and televisions shows, Richard Williams refused to let his daughters join the professional tennis tour until he thought they were ready. In 1997, in just her fifth professional tournament, the 304th-ranked Serena showed the tennis world a glimpse of what was to come as she defeated two of the world's top-ten players.

Serena's success on the circuit continued, and by June 1998 she had entered the Women's Tennis Association (WTA) top twenty. Early in 1999 Serena won her first WTA tour title at the Open Gaz de France. She went on to take three more titles that year, including her first Grand Slam singles title at the U.S. Open.

A victory over her sister in the finals of the 2002 French Open brought Serena her second Grand Slam singles title. With the victory, which was her fifteenth professional tournament title overall, Serena became the second-ranked player in the world, one spot behind her older sister. When she defeated her again at Wimbledon that same year, the sisters swapped rankings.

Serena has enjoyed success in doubles competition, as well. She teamed with Venus to win Grand Slam titles in the Australian Open (2001, 2003, 2009, and 2010), French Open (1999), U.S. Open (1999 and 2009), and Wimbledon (2000, 2002, 2008, and 2009). In addition to their growing number of accomplishments on the

Venus and Serena Williams, 2009. *Through mid-2010, Venus Williams (*left*) had won nine Grand Slam singles titles, while her sister Serena (*right*) had earned thirteen. Partnering in doubles, the sisters have won an additional twelve Grand Slam titles.* KARIM JAAFAR/AFP/GETTY IMAGES

professional tour, the sisters won the Olympic gold medal for women's doubles at both the 2000 Sydney Games and the 2008 Beijing Games. In 1998 Serena paired with Max Mirnyi to win the mixed doubles competition at both Wimbledon and the U.S. Open. By early 2010, Serena Williams had amassed twelve Grand Slam singles titles and had earned more prize money than any other woman in the history of sports.

VENUS WILLIAMS (1980–)

Tennis Player. Born in Lynwood, California, on June 17, 1980, Venus Williams made her professional debut in 1994. In her first tournament, the fourteen-year-old Williams nearly beat Arantxa Sanchez Vicario, who was ranked number two in the world at the time. The showing stunned both fans and media but came as no surprise to Richard Williams, her father and coach, who had predicted that his oldest daughter would one day become the world's greatest tennis player.

In her first few years on the professional circuit, Venus was guided along slowly, playing only a small number of tournaments. Despite her limited schedule, Venus by 1997 had reached number 64 in the world rankings. She won her first singles title on March 1, 1998, at the IGA Tennis Classic in Oklahoma City, and she quickly followed it up with a victory at the Lipton Championships in Miami, Florida.

Since then, Venus has won more than forty additional singles titles, including back-to-back Wimbledon and U.S. Open championships in 2000 and 2001. She later won three singles titles at Wimbledon, in 2005, 2007, and 2008. She also won the gold medal at the 2000 Sydney Olympics in the women's singles event. On February 25, 2002, Venus became the top-ranked player in the world.

Venus has combined with her sister, Serena, to claim doubles titles at each of the four Grand Slam titles: the Australian Open (2001, 2003, 2009, and 2010), French Open (1999), U.S. Open (1999 and 2009), and Wimbledon (2000, 2002, 2008, and 2009). The team also won Olympic gold medals for women's doubles at the 2000 and 2008 games. In addition, Venus teamed with Justin Gimelstob to capture mixed doubles titles at both the Australian Open and the French Open in 1998.

Celebrated for the grace and power she brings to tennis, Venus Williams by early 2010 had won nine Grand Slam singles titles.

TIGER WOODS (1975–)

Golfer. Tiger Woods is one of the most successful athletes in history. Born Eldrick Tont Woods in Cypress, California, on December 30, 1975, Woods was a child prodigy in golf. He became the first player to win the U.S. Amateur title three straight years, from 1994 to 1996, while a student at Stanford University.

In 1996 Woods turned professional. In the spring of the following year, Woods won the Masters Tournament, becoming the first African American to win a Grand Slam event. He went on to dominate the PGA Tour, winning over ninety tournaments through the 2009 season. Woods became the youngest player, and only the fifth in history, to complete the career Grand Slam of professional major championships when he won the 2000 British Open. His fourteen triumphs in golf's majors rank second behind only Jack Nicklaus and include the Masters in 1997, 2001, 2002, and 2005; the PGA Championship in 1999, 2000, 2006, and 2007; the U.S. Open in 2000, 2002, and 2008; and the British Open in 2000, 2005, and 2006. He is already the all-time career money leader on the PGA Tour, becoming the first athlete to top one billion dollars in earnings.

In 2004 Woods married Swedish model Elin Nordegren. Two years later, in May 2006, he lost his father and mentor, Earl Woods, who died after a lengthy battle with prostrate cancer. The loss was devastating to Woods. He continues to be a major force in the game of golf, although his image was tarnished by allegations of marital infidelity that led him to take a break from golf in late 2009 and early 2010. In February 2010 Woods admitted that he had been unfaithful to his wife and publicly apologized for his actions. He returned to golf in time for the 2010 Masters tournament at Augusta, finishing five strokes behind winner Phil Mickelson.

29

MILITARY

Lean'tin L. Bracks
Kevin C. Kretschmer
Christopher A. Brooks

In their effort to prove their worthiness for full citizenship, America's sons and daughters of African ancestry rallied to fight the country's battles, from the Revolutionary War to the wars in Iraq and Afghanistan. For a good part of its history, however, the U.S. government did not officially recognize or reward the sacrifices made by its African American countrymen and countrywomen. Whether it was the fight for independence from a European power, the preservation of the union internally, the right of self-determination, or the promotion of democracy in Southeast Asia, the country could always count on this segment of the population to stand up and fight in its behalf.

THE COLONIAL PERIOD

Prior to the formal outbreak of the Revolutionary War in 1775, both enslaved and free Africans were involved in British colonial expansionist activities vis-à-vis Native Americans. The Massachusetts Bay government required African men, both free and enslaved, to undergo militia training. In contrast, Virginia, less concerned with the threat of Native American attacks than African insurrectionary activity, forbade the arming of its enslaved population. In several instances prior to the Revolutionary War, such fears were justified. In a daring display of African militarism, for example, a group of enslaved Africans staged an insurrection outside of Charleston, South Carolina, near the Stono River in 1739. Eventually called the Stono Rebellion (also known as Cato's Revolt after the movement's African leader), the military undertaking involved more than eighty armed Africans who marched on Charleston. The inevitable conflict with a local white militia resulted in the deaths of more than twenty whites and nearly half of the eighty assembled Africans.

As tensions mounted between Great Britain and the American colonies, confrontation led to bloodshed in the Boston Massacre of March 5, 1770. On that day, a crowd of angry Bostonians confronted a group of British soldiers in protest against the manner of British taxation and authority. One of the soldiers fired on the crowd, and a formerly enslaved African and a sailor at the time of the conflict, Crispus Attucks (who was also of Native American ancestry), was struck dead at the feet of the British soldiers. Four white fellow protesters also died, but Attucks is often cited as the first martyr in the cause of American independence.

THE REVOLUTIONARY WAR (1775–1783)

By 1775, isolated skirmishes were taking place throughout the British colonies, and enslaved and free blacks were participants. Blacks were combatants in the well-known battles of Lexington, Concord, and Bunker Hill, but within a few years, the British shifted their focus to the southern theater, where they were able to factor in the enormous and untapped enslaved population.

As early as November 1775, the deposed royal governor of Virginia, John Murray, Earl of Dunmore, issued an emancipation proclamation offering freedom to any enslaved African who fought for the Loyalist cause. Within a week, the governor's Ethiopian Regiment had formed with more than three hundred participants, half of whom were runaway Africans. They had no particular loyalty to the British, and the promise of freedom was the principal motivating factor. The Dunmore emancipation proclamation forced the council of Continental generals led by George Washington to reverse its decision (taken just months before the Dunmore edict) to bar Africans from participating in the conflict. Although the Continental forces authorized the recruitment of enslaved and free Africans, they mostly served in support roles, such as musicians, and scouts, and pioneers (i.e., spies). They were generally not armed.

The original Declaration of Independence drafted by Thomas Jefferson in 1776 recognized the cruelty and barbarism of African enslavement. It condemned the British ruler, King George III, by declaring that he had "waged cruel war against human nature itself" by enslaving Africans in a distant land, or allowing them to die during their transportation there. This clause was, however, stricken from the final draft.

As the active fighting of the Revolutionary War began to wind down in the early 1780s, the British reneged on several promises of emancipation made to their African soldiers. As part of the peace settlement, George Washington and his British counterpart, General Guy Carleton, agreed that formerly enslaved Africans who had joined the Loyalist forces prior to November 30, 1782, would be covered under a general amnesty and evacuated out of the country. Escapees who joined after that date could be re-enslaved. The British would then be required to compensate plantation owners who had lost men as a result of escape and evacuation. Most of the black evacuees were relocated to Nova Scotia, Canada, while some were relocated to Jamaica, and others were repatriated back to the African continent.

Formerly enslaved Africans who fought for the Continental forces fared slightly better. Many changed their names to reflect their new status. Surnames like Liberty, Freeman, and Freedom, as well as first names such as Fredena and Fredonia, began appearing during the war and its aftermath. All-black units were mostly formed in northern colonies, such as Rhode Island and Massachusetts. Ultimately, some five thousand enslaved and free Africans served in the Continental Army and naval forces in a variety of capacities in the young country's war for independence. (About four times that number fought for the British Loyalist forces because they were promised their freedom.) Some won their freedom, while others gained respect in their communities and a measure of economic security.

The Revolutionary War presented the idea that, through military service, African Americans could secure freedom and

Salem Poor Stamp, 1975. *Revolutionary War hero Poor was honored with a 10-cent stamp issued in 1975. Poor served with distinction at the Battle of Bunker Hill and later with George Washington at Valley Forge.*

liberty. These ideas were reinforced as several of the northern and mid-Atlantic colonies formally prohibited the practice of African enslavement. The Revolutionary War also established a historical trend that in time of military need, the government made promises to this segment of its population that were soon forgotten once the crisis ended. It was only when African enslavement was abolished during another war in the nineteenth century that one of the promises was fulfilled.

THE WAR OF 1812 (1812–1815)

Following the Revolutionary War, the exclusion of African Americans from military service was reinstated. In 1792, Congress restricted military service to "free able-bodied white males." Six years later, the secretary of war sent an order to the commandant of the Marine Corps directing that "no Negro, mulatto or Indian is to be enlisted." The Navy, however, did not place the same restrictions on its recruitment of black sailors because the Navy traditionally needed to bolster its numbers. In fact, African American sailors comprised nearly 20 percent of the Navy's personnel during the War of 1812. Commodore Oliver Hazard Perry welcomed the African American sailors who served in his armada, which defeated the British on Lake Erie in September 1813.

Although the U.S. Army and Marine Corps continued to exclude African Americans, the Louisiana legislature authorized the enlistment of free African American landowners. The combat bravery of these troops was a key factor in the U.S. victory at the Battle of New Orleans in January 1815. Because African Americans were not authorized to serve, their contributions went unrecognized by the U.S. Army.

THE CIVIL WAR (1861–1865)

Even though the Civil War did not properly commence until the beginning of the 1860s, the issue of African enslavement and differences surrounding it in the northern and southern states had polarized the regions and caused tensions to simmer for decades before the first shot of the conflict was fired in 1861. Several developments incited both sides. The formation of abolitionist organizations throughout the country, along with the publication of David Walker's 1829 antislavery pamphlet, *An Appeal to the Colored People of the World*, infuriated plantation owners of the South. In addition, the celebrated *Amistad* incident of 1839, which made its way to the U.S. Supreme Court, tested the question of who could be enslaved. But one of the immediate forerunners to the war was the raid on the Harpers Ferry armory in West Virginia in 1859 by the arch abolitionist John Brown.

Within weeks of the Confederate assault on Fort Sumter in 1861, African Americans from Ohio's Wilberforce College responded to Abraham Lincoln's call for volunteers to help subdue the uprising. Similar offers came from Washington, D.C., and New York, where Governor Edwin Morgan offered three African American regiments to serve for the duration of the war. Their weapons, clothing, equipment, pay, and provisions were all to be provided by the African American citizens of the state. These and similar offers of service were rejected because the war was expected to be short. More importantly, however, Lincoln feared that by enlisting and arming African American soldiers, border states such as Maryland were more likely to join the Confederate cause. As far as the president was concerned, the conflict was to preserve the Union and not to free enslaved Africans.

On the other side, however, the Confederacy not only enjoyed the fruits of slave labor in the construction of fortifications and related combat service-support roles, that government relied on it. By 1864, several southern states, including Alabama, Florida, Louisiana, Mississippi, and South Carolina, were conscripting free African Americans for military service.

The issue of arming enslaved and free blacks had been an ongoing debate among the Confederate hierarchy throughout the years of conflict, but the notion had always been rejected as fundamentally antithetical to its ideology by President Jefferson Davis. By 1862, however, the all-black First Louisiana Native Guard, primarily a militia group, had formed. It lasted only a few months, although other all-black militias had been formed earlier in Louisiana at the beginning of the war.

Two years after the failed First Louisiana Native Guard experiment, however, the Confederate general Patrick Cleburne, along with several other high-ranking officers, again urged the arming of enslaved blacks, but the idea was rejected at the top. It was not until January 1865, when the Confederate cause was all but lost, that the supreme military commander, General Robert E. Lee, wrote the Confederate Congress requesting that it authorize enslaved blacks to fight for the Confederacy in exchange for their freedom. When the order was finally executed two months later, it required the consent of the owner of such a recruit.

After the conflict had ended, several southern states, including Tennessee, paid pensions to hundreds of African Americans for their service to the Confederacy. Free blacks (and presumably those who had been enslaved) were also found among the Confederate naval forces. Estimates of the precise numbers of those who served are not very reliable.

Although the initial offers for African Americans to fight for the preservation of the Union were rebuffed, prominent individuals such as Frederick Douglass, among many other abolitionists, passionately appealed at every level of the government for their inclusion. In essence, he was arguing for the right of African Americans to die for their country in order to prove their loyalty.

Though prohibited from enlisting African Americans for military duty as troops, some Union generals began using African American fugitives from so-called "slave states" as teamsters, cooks, and laborers. Only after important military setbacks, as well as considerable debate in the press and Congress, did the legislature authorize the employment of African American soldiers with the Militia Act of July 17, 1862. The War Department had not yet given permission to recruit African American soldiers when General Jim Lane organized and trained the First Kansas Colored Volunteers and sent them into action against Confederate troops near Butler, Missouri, in late October 1862. The success of African American troops in their first engagements as part of the Union Army helped to reduce opposition to their recruitment.

U.S. COLORED TROOPS (USCT)

Following the announcement in September 1862 of the Emancipation Proclamation (which did not take effect until January 1, 1863, and targeted emancipation only for enslaved persons in those states that were still in rebellion), systematic recruitment of African Americans began throughout the country. Massachusetts organized the Fifty-fourth and Fifty-fifth Massachusetts Infantry Regiments. Raised by Colonel Robert Gould Shaw, the Fifty-fourth led the Union attack on Fort Wagner in South Carolina on July 18, 1863. This strategically located Confederate position on Morris Island dominated the shipping channel leading into the harbor at Charleston. The Fifty-fourth Massachusetts fought gallantly, but was ultimately unsuccessful in taking Fort Wagner. Yet the bravery and heroism that these soldiers displayed became legendary and boosted the government's effort to recruit other African Americans to fight on behalf of the Union.

Despite repeated demonstrations of their ability and courage, skepticism regarding the usefulness of African American soldiers remained. General Benjamin Butler was determined to prove that the African American troops under his command were fit to bear arms. On the dawn of September 29, 1864, Butler ordered his troops of the Seventeenth Corps to storm a fortified Confederate position at New Market Heights, Virginia. The bayonet attack drove the Confederates from their position on the high ground at great cost. Butler recorded in his memoirs that "the capacity of the Negro race for soldiers had then and there been fully settled forever."

With the exception of the Fifty-fourth and Fifty-fifth Massachusetts, the majority of the African American Union soldiers were designated as U.S. Colored Troops (USCT). There were more than thirty such regiments in place by the mid-1860s. Following the establishment of USCT regiments, African Americans fought and died in every major Civil War action. For a period, they did so with substantially less pay than their white counterparts. While white privates received $13 per month plus a $3.50 clothing allowance, African American troops of any rank were paid only $10 per month with an optional $3.00 clothing deduction (i.e., making their pay approximately half that of the white soldiers). In some units, African American soldiers would not accept the lesser pay. Several men from an African American Rhode Island artillery unit on duty in Texas were sentenced to hard labor for refusing the inferior pay. When Sergeant William Walker persuaded the men of his South Carolina regiment to refuse to perform any duty unless they received pay equal to that of white troops, he was brought up on charges of mutiny and executed by firing squad. After vigorous protests by newspaper editors, legislators, and prominent officers of African American units, the 1864 Army Appropriation Act was enacted to provide identical pay scales for all soldiers.

The passions of the Civil War caused both Union and Confederate leaders to ignore the then-emerging doctrines of land warfare concerning such issues as treatment of noncombatants and prisoners of war. The most serious documented breaches of land warfare standards were committed by the Confederacy. African American Union soldiers who fell into Confederate hands were enslaved, re-enslaved, or summarily executed. An especially brutal event was the Confederate massacre at Fort Pillow in Tennessee on April 12, 1864. Congressional Report No. 65, titled "Fort Pillow Massacre" (April 24, 1864), identified the Confederate leader responsible as General Nathan Bedford Forrest, who became a principal founder of the Ku Klux Klan after the war. According to the report:

> The rebels commenced an indiscriminate slaughter, sparing neither age nor sex, white or black, soldier or civilian. The officers and men seemed to vie with each other in the devilish work; men, women, and even children, wherever found, were deliberately shot down, beaten, and hacked with sabers; some of the children not more than ten years old were forced to stand up and face their murderers while being shot; the sick and wounded were butchered without mercy, the rebels even entering the hospital building and

dragging them out to be shot or killing them as they lay there unable to offer the least resistance.

Although the report exaggerated in the interest of propaganda, it clearly established that African American troops were slaughtered while attempting to surrender. The murders at Fort Pillow and the subsequent killing of captured and wounded African American troops at the Battle of Poison Spring in Arkansas on April 18, 1864, would not go unanswered. African American troops assaulted their Confederate adversaries with ferocious intensity as they shouted their battle cries, "Remember Fort Pillow!" and "Remember Poison Spring!"

An especially daring naval act of bravery took place when Robert Smalls stole the Confederate ship to which he had been assigned while he was enslaved. With several other enslaved sailors, Smalls commandeered the 300-ton side-wheel steamer *Planter* in the early morning of May 13, 1862, and sailed it out of Charleston Harbor. He delivered it to the U.S. Navy's blockade offshore. Fitted with two guns and carrying four others as cargo, the *Planter* was a welcomed addition to the Union fleet. In recognition of his bravery, Smalls received an officer's commission in the Union Navy and for a time served as pilot of the *Planter*. He was subsequently assigned to pilot the gunboat *Keokuk*. During Reconstruction, Smalls was elected to the U.S. Congress as a representative from the state of South Carolina and became a major general in the state's militia.

Although they were not accepted into the Union forces, African American women also played an important role during the Civil War. Many endured great hardships in their efforts to keep their families together as their husbands, fathers, and sons marched off to war. While some African American women served as volunteer nurses, others took a more activist role in support of the Union cause. Both Sojourner Truth (born Isabella Baumfree) and Harriet Tubman used their knowledge of Underground Railroad routes to guide federal forces operating in hostile territory. In one such instance, Tubman led three hundred Union cavalrymen on a raid in South Carolina that freed eight hundred enslaved persons and destroyed crops valuable to the Confederacy.

THE MEDAL OF HONOR

America's highest decoration for valor was established during the Civil War when Congress authorized issuance of a Medal of Honor on December 21, 1861. Eligibility was initially limited to enlisted men of the Navy and the Marine Corps, but was expanded to include the Army on July 12, 1862. On March 3, 1863, commissioned officers also became eligible for the Medal of Honor. During the Civil War, 1,523 Medals of Honor were awarded, twenty-three to African American servicemen. The first African American recipient was Sergeant William H. Carney of the Fifty-fourth Massachusetts Infantry for combat valor on July 18, 1863, at Fort Wagner, South Carolina. Thirteen of the medals were awarded to African American soldiers who fought in the Battle of New Market Heights, Virginia, on September 29 to 30, 1864.

Although the Union did not actively recruit African Americans until 1863, their numbers proved significant during the Civil War. U.S. Colored Troops constituted 13 percent of the Army, while African American sailors accounted for about 8 percent of the Union Navy. By the end of the war, more than 37,000 African American servicemen had died, constituting nearly 35 percent of all African Americans who served in combat. According to official government records, 186,097 African Americans served in the Civil War in more than 160 units. Of that number, more than seven thousand were officers.

THE INDIAN CAMPAIGNS (1866–1890)

In the post–Civil War period, the country established its first African American regular Army regiments: the Ninth and Tenth Cavalry, and the Twenty-fourth and Twenty-fifth Infantry. They would become known as *buffalo soldiers*. This nickname was given to the soldiers by Plains Indians who saw a resemblance between their hair and that of the buffalo (or American bison), an animal the Indians considered sacred. Although the term buffalo soldiers initially denoted the four post-Civil War regiments mentioned above, it was later proudly adopted by veterans of all racially segregated African American Army ground units of the 1866–1950 era.

The general perception today of the makeup of the U.S. Army during the post–Civil War westward expansion does not reflect its true composition. Approximately 20 percent of Army soldiers on duty in the West were African American. The mythology of the cavalry riding to the rescue of endangered settlers does not acknowledge that many of these armed horsemen were African American. Despite often working with rejected horses, inadequate rations, and deteriorating equipment—compounded by the disdain often shown to them by many white settlers, as well as some of their own officers—the African American regiments enjoyed the lowest desertion rates of all Army units.

The heroism of African American soldiers is attested to by the eighteen Medals of Honor they earned during what historians term both the Indian Campaigns and the Plains War. Nevertheless, 370 Medals of Honor were awarded during that era of American military history, so the eighteen given to African American soldiers does not reflect their percentage among soldiers serving during the Plains War. The first Medal of Honor awarded to an

African American soldier during the period was presented to First Sergeant Emanuel Stance of Company F, Ninth Cavalry, for actions occurring on May 20, 1870, in the Battle of Kickapoo Springs, Texas.

African American participation in the war against Native Americans was embedded in historical ironies, both in terms of fighting another race that was also subjugated by Anglo-Americans, and in terms of anti–African American sentiment within the U.S. military itself. One of many painful episodes for the original buffalo soldiers was the case of Second Lieutenant Henry Ossian Flipper. Born in Thomasville, Georgia, on March 21, 1856, Flipper was the first African American to graduate from the U.S. Military Academy at West Point, New York. He ranked fiftieth among the seventy-six members of the class of 1877 and became the only African American commissioned officer in the regular Army. Assigned initially to Fort Sill in Oklahoma Territory, Lieutenant Flipper was eventually sent to Fort Davis in Texas. He also acquired combat experience fighting the Apache, who were led by Chief Victoria.

In August 1881, Lieutenant Flipper was arrested and charged with failing to mail checks in excess of $2,000 to the Army chief of commissary. The young lieutenant was tried for embezzlement and conduct unbecoming an officer and a gentleman. He was acquitted of the first charge (the checks were found in his quarters), but convicted of the second. On June 30, 1882, after his sentence was confirmed by President Chester Arthur, Flipper was dismissed from the service. Returning to civilian life, Flipper used his West Point education as a surveyor and engineer and worked for several mining companies. He also published his memoirs, as well as technical books dealing with both Mexican and Venezuelan law. Additionally, Flipper served as a translator for the Senate Committee on Foreign Relations, and became a special assistant to the secretary of the interior.

Nearly a century after Flipper left West Point, a review of his record indicated that he had been framed by his fellow officers. In 1977, the Army reversed Flipper's conviction, and his record was corrected. Additionally, he was granted an honorable discharge from the Army and formally pardoned by President Bill Clinton in 1999, nearly sixty years after his death in 1940. On the one hundredth anniversary of his graduation from West Point, a memorial bust and alcove in the cadet library at the U.S. Military Academy were dedicated in his honor.

There were only two other nineteenth-century African American graduates of West Point: John H. Alexander (1864–1894), in the class of 1887, and Charles A. Young (1864–1922), in the class of 1889. It would be forty-seven years before another African American cadet graduated from the U.S. Military Academy.

THE SPANISH-AMERICAN WAR (1898)

America's four-month war with Spain in 1898 marked the nation's emergence as a global colonial power. Although the United States had just completed its own Indian Campaigns, the tension between the two nations arose from Spain's treatment of Cuba's indigenous population. In 1885, open rebellion by the Cuban people resulted in brutal suppression by the Spanish. The American battleship USS *Maine* was sent to Cuba to protect U.S. interests there and to remind the Spanish of America's intention to enforce the Monroe Doctrine. On the evening of February 15, 1898, a gigantic internal explosion rocked the ship, causing it to sink rapidly into Havana Harbor, killing 266 U.S. sailors—thirty-three of them African American. Even though the cause of the explosion was undetermined at the time, the incident inflamed American passions against Spain. The American press promoted popular protest slogans to reflect anger over the lost ship: "Remember the Maine, to hell with Spain!" was widely printed and became a call to war against the Spanish Empire, which was accused of having sunk the *Maine*.

On March 29, the United States issued an ultimatum to Spain, demanding the release of Cubans from brutal detention camps, the declaration of an armistice, and preparations for peace negotiations to be mediated by President William McKinley. The Spanish government did not comply and, on April 19, the U.S. Congress proclaimed Cuba free and independent. In its proclamation, Congress authorized the president to use U.S. troops to remove Spanish forces from Cuba.

The Spanish-American War was of special significance for the African American enlistees in the regular Army, as well as African American officers. Among the volunteer units involved were the Seventh, Eighth, Ninth, Tenth, and Eleventh U.S. Volunteer Infantry (Colored Troops), as well as National Guard Infantry units from Alabama, Indiana, Virginia, Kansas, North Carolina, and Ohio.

The war with Spain was also an expeditionary campaign requiring maritime deployment to foreign lands. Instead of a mobilize-and-defend situation, the United States had to mobilize and transport before deploying. It was the nation's first large-scale exposure to the complex logistics of overseas operations, an experience that would evolve into occupation duty and related counterinsurgency warfare.

Although the war was with Spain, most of the fighting took place in Cuba. On June 24, 1898, one squadron of the Tenth Cavalry, one squadron from the regular Army's First Cavalry, and two squadrons of Rough

Riders, which were a regiment of U.S. cavalry volunteers recruited by Theodore Roosevelt, attacked and defeated twice their number of Spanish soldiers. When the Rough Riders were pinned down by Spanish fire while crossing open ground near Las Guasimas, troops from the First and Tenth Cavalries arrived and relieved the pressure. John J. "Black Jack" Pershing, the Tenth Cavalry's regimental quartermaster, credited his men with "relieving the Rough Riders from the volleys that were being poured into them from that portion of the Spanish line."

The Twenty-fifth Infantry also took part, storming the village of El Caney on the morning of July 1. Armed with a battery of Hotchkiss automatic guns, the Tenth Cavalry figured prominently in the taking of Kettle Hill, while the Twenty-fourth Infantry, along with the Seventy-first New York Volunteers, stormed San Juan Hill. African American soldiers also manned trenches around Santiago de Cuba, which capitulated in mid-July, ending the war in Cuba. The end of the war, however, did not end the danger to the occupying troops. The celebrated charge on San Juan and Kettle Hills represented America's most integrated battle up to that time. Rough Rider and future secretary of the Navy, Frank Knox, later noted of the African American troops participating in the charge, "I must say that I never saw braver men anywhere."

Even after hostilities between the United States and Spain officially ended in August 1898, U.S. troops in Cuba faced a challenge more deadly than the Spanish forces. More than three of every four deaths among U.S. troops were attributed to disease, particularly typhoid and yellow fever. In the mistaken belief that peoples of African descent had a natural immunity to tropical diseases, troops of the Twenty-fourth Infantry were assigned to work details at hospitals treating victims of typhoid and yellow fever. Roughly half of the African American troops assigned to the hospitals contracted the illnesses. Many of the African American female volunteer nurses who cared for the sick and dying also became victims.

African Americans also served in the U.S. Volunteer Infantry (USVI), a manpower augmentation of 175,000 troops from the federalized national guard reserves. The USVI was to include the nation's oldest African American national guard unit, which had its organizational roots in Chicago, Illinois. Formed in the wake of the 1871 Chicago fire, the unit was originally known as the Hannibal Guards. It became an Illinois militia unit on May 5, 1890, as the Ninth Battalion, commanded by Major Benjamin G. Johnson, an African American. When the Spanish-American War erupted, other African American militia regiments were organized: the Third Alabama, the Twenty-third Kansas, the Third North Carolina, the Ninth Ohio, and the Sixth Virginia.

Until it was converted into several artillery battalions during World War II, the Eighth Illinois USVI was always commanded by an African American officer. Colonel John R. Marshall was the highest-ranking African American officer of the Spanish-American War and commanded the Eighth Illinois until 1914. Marshall was born on March 15, 1859, in Alexandria, Virginia. After attending public schools in Alexandria and Washington, D.C., he eventually moved to Chicago, where he was appointed deputy clerk of Cook County. Marshall joined the Illinois National Guard, organized a battalion, and served in it as a lieutenant and major. In June 1892, he was commissioned a colonel and assumed command of the Eighth Illinois USVI Regiment. He led the regiment to Cuba, where it joined with the Twenty-third Kansas and the Third North Carolina in occupation duty.

The Spanish-American War led to a small increase in the number of African American regular Army officers. Benjamin O. Davis Sr. served as a lieutenant in the Eighth Illinois USVI. After his discharge, he enlisted in the regular Army on June 14, 1899, as a private in the Ninth Cavalry. He was promoted to corporal and then to sergeant major. Davis was commissioned a U.S. Army second lieutenant of cavalry on February 2, 1901. Also commissioned as regular Army officers at that time were John R. Lynch and John E. Green. As the twentieth century began, the U.S. Army had four African American commissioned officers (excluding chaplains): Captain Charles Young, and Lieutenants Davis, Green, and Lynch. In 1940, Davis became the nation's first African American general.

Although the conflict only lasted four months, the Spanish-American War produced fifty-two Medal of Honor recipients, among them six African Americans. Five were from the Tenth Cavalry, which fought as infantry in Cuba, while the sixth was an African American sailor stationed aboard the USS *Iowa*, which saw action in the waters off Santiago.

WORLD WAR I (1914–1918)

The United States entered World War I in April 1917. During that year, events occurred that undermined the African American presence within the U.S. military and sidetracked the uneven progress of the country's African American fighting forces. In August 1917, Private Alonzo Edwards of the Third Battalion, Twenty-fourth Infantry, saw a local police officer in Houston, Texas, beating an African American woman. Although he was unarmed, Edwards attempted to stop the assault, but was himself beaten and arrested. When Charles Baltimore, the African

American corporal charged with maintaining peaceful relations between the black soldiers and the townspeople, went to check on the detained Edwards, the same police officer beat and arrested him as well. It took the intervention of the battalion's white officers to secure the release of Edwards and Baltimore and ensure that disciplinary actions were taken against the white policeman. Once word of the incident reached the battalion, however, a group of about one hundred African American soldiers commandeered some weapons and marched on the police station. Within a few hours, the soldiers had killed five policemen and ten townspeople, and more than a dozen others were wounded. The battalion lost four of its men.

The War Department court-martialed more than sixty of the soldiers. Thirteen were given death sentences (all but three were later commuted by President Woodrow Wilson). The others received varying degrees of hard labor or lesser sentences. In light of the Houston incident, the United States engaged in World War I with African Americans pushed to the sidelines. It was the only conflict involving the United States in which there was not a single African American Medal of Honor recipient since the recognition was established in 1862.

The nation's entry into World War I raised the question of how to utilize African American troops, especially in the aftermath of the Houston incident. The Army's existing African American units were kept on patrol in the Southwest or sent for duty in the Philippines. The majority of African American draftees or enlistees were assigned to stevedore units at ports or to labor units as quartermaster troops. Of the more than 400,000 African American soldiers who served during the war, only about 10 percent saw combat duty. Those who did see action came from either the Ninety-second or the Ninety-third Infantry Division (Provisional). The Ninety-second was mostly draftees, while the Ninety-third had three regiments made up of National Guard units from Connecticut, Illinois, Maryland, Massachusetts, New York, Ohio, Tennessee, and the District of Columbia, with a fourth regiment of draftees. Neither infantry division trained as a unit in the United States. Because many white Americans feared arming a substantial number of African Americans in a single location, the Army stationed the individual regiments of each division in widely separated areas of the country. The regiments did not link up as divisions until they reached France.

The most difficult problem for the War Department was the demand that African Americans be trained as commissioned officers. Among the more prominent national figures making such a demand was Tuskegee's celebrated administrator Emmett Scott. Initially, the idea was dismissed as ludicrous, for it was said to be "common knowledge" that African Americans inherently lacked leadership qualities. African American organizations such as the NAACP and the Urban League, along with African American newspapers such as the *Chicago Defender*, took up the cause and persisted until the War Department changed its policy. An African American Officer Training School was established at Fort Des Moines in Iowa, and on October 14, 1917, the school graduated and commissioned the first class of 639 African American officers. By the close of the war, 1,200 African American officer candidates had earned commissions from the school. Although that number was far greater than had been commissioned in prior wars, it still represented only seven-tenths of one percent of the officer corps. By comparison, African American troops accounted for 13 percent of the total active duty force. In addition, the War Department had an ironclad rule that no African American officer could command white officers or enlisted men.

To comply with this rule, the War Department needed to find a way of skirting the problem posed by Lieutenant Colonel Charles Young, the Army's highest-ranking African American officer and a West Point graduate. Young had trained African American troops for combat and led them in action, causing some white officers to fear that he would assume command of the Tenth Cavalry, which was otherwise commanded by whites. Pressured by these officers, the U.S. senators who represented them in Congress, President Wilson, and the War Department developed a strategy to eliminate Young from command consideration. By the time he was fifty-three, Young had developed a kidney infection (formerly known as Bright's disease), but his overall physical health was excellent. Based on a medical examination in July 1917, a report was forwarded to the War Department's retiring board, which recommended that Young be removed from active duty because of health concerns.

To prove his fitness for active duty, Colonel Young rode on horseback (walking a quarter of the distance for good measure) from Xenia, Ohio, to Washington, D.C. Starting on June 6, 1918, he covered the 497-mile distance in sixteen days, taking just one day off to rest. Young received support from the African American press and many powerful friends, but the War Department relented only five days before the end of World War I. He was promoted to full colonel in retirement, and was called to active service to command a company of trainees at Camp Grant in Illinois, an assignment usually given to officers at the rank of captain. Young was never given the opportunity to command troops in Europe, which likely would have resulted in his promotion to brigadier general. Though he remained on active duty until his death in West Africa on January 8, 1922, as a military attaché, Young never received another promotion.

One of the more legendary African American infantry forces of World War I was the celebrated 369th Infantry

Regiment, Fifteenth New York, which established the best record of any Army infantry regiment throughout the entire war. Attached to the French Fourth Army, the 369th served for 191 consecutive days in the trenches, longer than any other U.S. unit. During that time, they never lost a foot of ground to the enemy, nor had a single soldier taken prisoner by the Germans. The 369th gathered many nicknames. They called themselves the "Black Rattlers," while the French dubbed them the "Men of Bronze." But it was the name given to the regiment by their German opponents that would became famous—the "Harlem Hell Fighters." The most celebrated person associated with the 369th was the African American bandleader James Reese Europe. He had a well-established reputation as a bandleader in the United States by the time World War I began. After volunteering to serve in the Army, he was asked by his commander, Colonel William Hayward, to form a band that would boost the morale of the fighting men in Europe and help recruit other soldiers. Lieutenant Europe willingly did so, and introduced what would come to be called "jazz" to France. The genre eventually spread throughout the European continent.

In 1919 Columbia University president Nicholas Murray Butler gave *Harper's Weekly* his assessment of the 369th Infantry Regiment: "No American soldier saw harder or more constant fighting and none gave better accounts of themselves. When fighting was to be done, this regiment was there."

Unlike the Ninety-third Infantry Division, which only came together as a unit in France before being parceled out to various French commands, the Ninety-second Infantry Division remained intact. Unfortunately, the Ninety-second did not fare nearly as well as the Ninety-third. The commander, Major General Charles C. Ballou, shared the prejudices of many white officers and rarely stood up for his African American troops. Ballou seldom ensured that the soldiers of the Ninety-second were provided with proper training, equipment, and support services. After they arrived in France, the ill-prepared African American soldiers under his command were immediately sent into the fray. Led by white senior officers and unseasoned African American junior officers, the disorganized regiments suffered heavy casualties during several key offenses late in the war.

Ballou's response to the failings of the Ninety-second was to blame his junior officers, and he brought thirty of them up for court-martial on charges of cowardice. Several officers were convicted by an all-white court-martial board and given harsh sentences before the trials were suspended with the transfer of the Ninety-second to the command of Lieutenant General Robert L. Bullard. Under Bullard, the morale and training of the Ninety-second improved, as did its fighting effectiveness. Nevertheless, the damage was done. Bullard was unhappy with the general performance of the division and worried about its reflection on him as a leader. As soon as the war ended, he recommended the immediate transfer of the division back to the United States. The result of the Ninety-second Infantry's substandard performance was to bolster the already negative opinions of critics of African American units.

Despite the Jim Crow atmosphere, African American soldiers earned an impressive number of awards for combat bravery in defeating German troops. Sergeant Henry Johnson and Private Needham Roberts of New York's 369th Infantry Regiment were the first Americans, black or white, to receive the French Croix de Guerre. France awarded this medal to thirty-four African American officers and eighty-nine African American enlisted men during the war. Fourteen African American officers and forty-three African American enlisted men in the Ninety-second Infantry earned the U.S. Army's Distinguished Service Cross (DSC). About ten officers and thirty-four enlisted men of the Ninety-third Infantry were DSC recipients.

The African American presence in the U.S. Navy during World War I was negligible. Because they were restricted to ratings in the messmen branch, where they served as cooks, stewards, and mess attendants, few African Americans enlisted in the Navy. Of a total naval strength of 435,398, only 5,328 were African American by June 30, 1918. Continuing its policy of preventing African Americans from earning commissions, the naval officer corps remained completely white. In addition, some naval captains refused to transport African American Army troops home after the war.

Although they were not permitted to serve in the Armed Forces, African American women contributed to the U.S. effort in World War I. They made bandages, worked in hospitals and troop centers, and promoted the purchase of Liberty Bonds to finance the war effort. They also served in the Red Cross, YWCA, and other relief organizations.

African American women who served as "Y-secretaries" were in a unique position to witness the indignities suffered by African American soldiers during World War I. Typically serving as tutors to assist troops with reading and writing, a number of African American women worked throughout the United States and in France. After the war, Addie Hunton and Kathryn Johnson wrote a book, *Two Colored Women with the American Expeditionary Forces* (1920), which detailed the routine humiliations imposed on African American troops.

POSTHUMOUS MEDAL OF HONOR AWARDED

No Medal of Honor was awarded to an African American serviceman during World War I. In 1988, the

Department of the Army researched the National Archives to determine whether racial barriers had prevented the awarding of the nation's highest decoration for valor to an African American. The search produced evidence that Corporal Freddie Stowers of Anderson County, South Carolina, had been recommended for the award. For "unknown reasons," the recommendation had not been processed. Stowers was a squad leader in Company C, 371st Infantry Regiment, Ninety-third Infantry Division. On September 28, 1918, he led his squad through heavy machine-gun fire and destroyed the gun position on Hill 188 in the Champagne Marne sector in France. Mortally wounded, Stowers led his men through a second trench line. Unable to proceed any further, Stowers continued to yell encouragement to his comrades until dying on the field of battle. On April 24, 1991, President George Bush belatedly presented the Medal of Honor to Stowers's surviving sisters in a White House ceremony.

THE INTERWAR YEARS (1919–1940)

With the end of the war, the nation generally returned to applying the separate-but-equal doctrine established in 1896 by *Plessy v. Ferguson*. Some senior white Army officers advocated barring enlistment or reenlistment of African Americans all together. Such an action would have eventually eliminated the four African American regular Army regiments by attrition.

African American commissioned officers became a focal point of the Army's discriminatory sentiment. Despite countless well-documented cases of superb combat leadership, most African American officers were eliminated from active duty following World War I. An effective argument against retaining African American officers was their alleged poor performance, which was "supported" by critics from the African American Officer Training School (OTS) in Des Moines, Iowa. One of the severest critics was Major General Ballou, commander of the Ninety-second Infantry Division during World War I. Ballou emphasized that while white candidates were required to be college graduates, "only high school educations were required for ... the colored ... and in many cases these high school educations would have been a disgrace to any grammar school. For the parts of a machine requiring the finest steel, pot metal was provided."

Nevertheless, there were combat-experienced white officers who held a decidedly different view of African American officer training. These included Major Thomas A. Roberts, who wrote in April 1920: "As I understand the question, what the progressive Negro desires today is the removal of discrimination against him; that this can be accomplished in a military sense I believe to be largely possible, but not if men of the two races are segregated." Noting his appreciation of the "tremendous force of the prejudice against association between Negroes and whites," Roberts declared, "my experience has made me believe that the better element among the Negroes desires the removal of the restriction rather than the association itself."

The exclusionary campaign was also evident in the Army's civilian components, the National Guard and Officers Reserve. New York's 369th Infantry Regiment was maintained at full strength, though the Eighth Illinois lost one battalion.

As for commissioned officers, the Reserve Officers Training Corps (ROTC) detachments at Howard and Wilberforce universities provided the majority of new African American second lieutenants. With no allocations for African American officers to attend service schools, the lack of opportunity to maintain proficiency caused considerable attrition in the number of African American reserve officers. To retain their commissions, other officers took advantage of correspondence and specially organized seminar courses.

WORLD WAR II (1939–1945)

Less than two months after World War II began in Europe in 1939, the nation's preeminent African American organizations, the NAACP and the National Urban League, mobilized in an effort to defeat U.S. racial segregation, as well as Axis fascism. African American leaders foresaw that the United States would eventually ally itself with Britain and France in war against Germany, Italy, and Japan.

Military mobilization began on August 27, 1940, with the federalizing of the National Guard and activation of the Organized Reserve. When Japan attacked Pearl Harbor on December 7, 1941, there were 120,000 officers and 1,523,000 enlisted men on active duty in the Army and its air corps. On September 16, 1940, the nation began its first peacetime draft. By the end of World War II, the Selective Service System had inducted 10,110,104 men, of which 1,082,539 (10.7%) were African American. In addition, America's war effort required rapid expansion of both military and industrial power. Victory depended on the constant provision of ammunition, guns, planes, tanks, naval vessels, and merchant ships.

Unlike America's other wars, where the nation could count on African Americans to stand up and fight, World War II presented a different scenario. There was a higher incidence of African American draft dodgers than in any previous conflict. This occurred, in part, because of the position taken by the Nation of Islam's founder, Elijah Muhammad, who discouraged African Americans from becoming a part of the war and encouraged them to ignore the Selective Service. He was briefly imprisoned in 1942 for failing to register for the draft, and then served a four-year prison term after advocating for a Japanese victory.

The traditional civil rights organizations, such as the NAACP and Urban League, joined forces with several black newspapers, including the *Chicago Defender* and the *Pittsburgh Courier*, to report on the segregation practices of the U.S. military by sending war correspondence to the battle theaters. They found blatant discrimination against African American soldiers. Civil rights organizations also challenged governmental structures for the inadequate share of civilian-defense employment opportunities open to African Americans.

Soon, the NAACP and the Urban League were joined by African American activists in the March on Washington movement, led by A. Philip Randolph of the Brotherhood of Sleeping Car Porters. (Randolph had been briefly jailed during World War I for urging African Americans not to join that war effort.) Randolph predicted that upwards of 100,000 African Americans would march on Washington demanding equal employment opportunities in defense-plant employment. On June 25, 1941, a week before the scheduled march, President Franklin D. Roosevelt preempted the event by issuing Executive Order 8802. The president's order established a Committee on Fair Employment Practice "to provide for the full and equitable participation of all workers in defense industries, without discrimination." The executive order did not apply to the armed services.

The necessity of winning the war opened the economy to millions of African American men and women who surged into defense plants and earned the same wages as their white counterparts. The war years brought unprecedented upward economic mobility to African American civilians. The postwar benefits of the G.I. Bill of Rights

Boxer Joe Louis Receives the Legion of Merit for His Contribution to the Armed Forces during World War II. *The heavyweight champion served in the U.S. Army's Special Services Division, entertaining about two million of his fellow soldiers by participating in ninety-six exhibition bouts in the United States and overseas.* HULTON-GETTY/LIAISON AGENCY. REPRODUCED BY PERMISSION.

also played a major role in dramatically increasing the numbers of African American college graduates and homeowners.

The U.S. Army took its first steps toward racial integration early in World War II. The obvious waste resulting from duplicated facilities caused the Army to operate all of its twenty-four officer candidate schools as racially integrated institutions, because the primary goal was to cultivate leadership. The "ninety-day wonders" who survived the standard three-month course were commissioned as second lieutenants from each of the twenty-four Army branches, ranging from the Army Air Forces Administrative School (Miami, Florida) to the Tank Destroyer School (Camp Hood, Texas). After graduating, African American officers were only assigned to African American units.

THE ARMY AIR FORCES (AAF)

The Army Air Forces Aviation Cadet program, which trained pilots, bombardiers, and navigators, represented an exception to the racially integrated system of Army officer procurement during World War II. Ironically, African American nonflying officers graduated from the integrated AAF Officer Candidate School at Miami Beach. A total of 926 African American pilots earned their commissions and wings at the segregated Tuskegee Army Air Field (TAAF) near Chehaw, Alabama. The 673 single-engine TAAF pilot graduates would eventually form the four squadrons of the 332nd Fighter Group.

Led by Lieutenant Colonel Benjamin O. Davis Jr., a 1936 West Point graduate, the Ninety-ninth Fighter Squadron was assigned to the Thirty-third Fighter Group commanded by Colonel William Momyer. The Ninety-ninth's first operational mission was a June 2, 1943, strafing attack on the Italian island of Pantelleria. On that date, Captain Charles B. Hall scored the squadron's first air victory by shooting down an FW-190 and damaging an ME-109. The Ninety-ninth then settled into normal operations.

The squadron did have its detractors, who, among other things, accused the Tuskegee pilots of not displaying sufficient daring to make them effective fighters. In October 1943, Davis appeared before a War Department committee governing the "Tuskegee Experiment." He later recalled that the racial vitriol that he experienced in that meeting was beyond belief. In response, he quietly presented the facts of the successful missions flown by his Tuskegee pilots. After an official investigation, it was determined that the Tuskegee airmen actually had a higher success rate than their white counterparts.

By October 13, 1942, the Army had activated the 100th, 301st, and 302nd Fighter Squadrons. Combined with the Ninety-ninth, the four squadrons became the 332nd Fighter Group. Colonel Robert R. Selway Jr., a white pilot, was its initial commanding officer. With the Ninety-ninth's official vindication, Davis assumed command of the Fighter Group at Selfridge Army Air Field in Michigan. The three squadrons of the 332nd, previously based in the United States, departed for Italy on January 3, 1944, absorbing the Ninety-ninth after its arrival.

During the period that the Ninety-ninth was deployed and the 332nd was organizing, the TAAF program was expanded to train two-engine B-25 pilots. Whereas fighter pilots fought alone, the B-25 "Mitchell" medium bomber required a five- to six-man crew that included two pilots, a bombardier, and a navigator. The 253 medium-bomber pilots who were trained at TAAF joined 393 African American navigators and bombardiers from Hondo and Midland Fields in Texas to form the nation's second African American flying organization when the AAF activated the four-squadron 477th Bombardment Group (Medium) in June 1943.

The 477th was plagued from the start by a shortage of enlisted aircrew members, ground technicians, and even airplanes. Fifteen months after activation, the 477th was still short twenty-six pilots, forty-three co-pilots, two bombardier-navigators, and all of its authorized 288 gunners. Moving from base to base for "operational training," the 477th logged 17,875 flying hours in one year without a major accident. Although finally earmarked for duty in the Pacific, the war ended before the 477th was deployed overseas.

As for the 332nd Fighter Group, it became a famous flying escort for heavy bombers. It was the only AAF fighter group that never lost an escorted bomber to enemy planes. The wartime record of the 332nd Fighter Group was 103 enemy aircraft destroyed during 1,578 combat missions. In addition to more than one hundred Distinguished Flying Crosses, the 332nd also earned three Distinguished Unit Citations. In sum, the Tuskegee Experiment proved that African Americans could fly advanced aircraft and could also conduct highly successful combat operations meeting AAF standards.

THE GROUND WAR

During World War II, the U.S. Army fielded two major African American combat organizations: the Ninety-second Infantry Division in Europe and the Ninety-third Infantry Division in the Pacific.

As in World War I, the Ninety-third Infantry Division suffered from fragmentation. Major General Raymond G. Lehman's headquarters sailed from San Francisco on January 11, 1944, while the artillery and infantry battalions and division headquarters assembled on Guadalcanal at the end of February. This would be the last time all of the components of the division would be in the same place. The division would spend the rest of the war island-hopping, relieving units that had defeated Japanese troops. By the war's end, the Ninety-third had suffered twelve killed in action, along with 121 wounded and five who died of their wounds.

The Ninety-second Infantry Division, by contrast, gained a reputation as a chaotic outfit. During its preparation for deployment overseas, portions of the Ninety-second were sprinkled across the United States. While the division headquarters were at Fort Huachuca, Arizona, subordinate units were stationed at Fort McClellan, Alabama; Camp Robinson, Arkansas; Camp Breckinridge, Kentucky; and Camp Atterbury, Indiana. The division's World War II casualty figures were vastly different from those of the Ninety-third: 548 were killed in action, 2,187 were wounded in action, and 68 died of wounds sustained in battle. From its training in the United States through combat in Europe, the division's main problem seemed to be its commander, Major General Edward M. Almond. Many veterans of the Ninety-second blamed General Almond for the division's reputation and casualties.

"Ned" Almond was apparently racist. In a 1984 interview, retired Lieutenant General William P. Ennis Jr. gave a "warts and all" description of Almond. As a World War II brigadier general, Ennis had commanded the corps artillery that supported the Ninety-second Infantry Division. According to Ennis, Almond and many white southern officers in the division were selected because "in theory, they knew more about handling Negroes than anybody else, though I can't imagine why because [Almond] just despised the ground they walked on." One African American officer, Captain Hondon B. Hargrove, was a 1938 Wilberforce University ROTC graduate. After his wartime service in the division's 597th Field Artillery Battalion, he commented that Almond did not believe "any black, no matter what his file showed, or how much training he had, was able in an officer's position.... He firmly believed only white officers could get the best out of [Negro troops] ... [and] just could not countenance black officers leading them."

While Almond denigrated the competence of African American officers, Officer Candidate School (OCS) commandants generally held the opposite view. For example, Brigadier General H. T. Mayberry, who commanded the Tank Destroyer OCS, observed in a 1945 interview that "a considerable number of young, potentially outstanding Negro officers were graduated. It was surprising—to me, at least—how high the Negroes (those who graduated) stood in the classes." Lieutenant Colonel Robert C. Ross, a field artillery battalion commander in the Ninety-second Infantry Division, reported to Almond on five African American officers who completed the basic artillery course: three were made course instructors, while two were selected "as outstanding students from the entire forty-eight officers, both white and colored, from the first Officers Basic School."

General Almond established his headquarters at Viareggio, Italy, on October 5, 1944. Two days later, the division's 370th Infantry Regiment began its assault on Massa. In *The Employment of Negro Troops* (1966), Ulysses Lee described the Ninety-second Infantry Division's major weakness: "It was a problem in faith and lack of it—the wavering faith of commanders in the ability and determination of subordinates and enlisted men, and the continuation in the minds of enlisted men of training period convictions that they could not trust their leaders" (p. 549). As a consequence, the Massa attack degenerated into chaos. In what was to be a major charge against the division, the men began to "melt away" from the fighting. After Massa, there were increasing cases of mutinous behavior toward both black and white officers.

In February 1945, the Ninety-second became the focus of serious Pentagon scrutiny. Truman K. Gibson Jr., an African American insurance lawyer from Chicago and a civilian aide to secretary of war Henry L. Stimson, examined the situation. In his assessment, Gibson refused to generalize about the capabilities of African American soldiers based on the performance of General Almond's division. In a March 14 news conference in Rome, Gibson maintained, "If the division proves anything, it does not prove that Negroes can't fight. There is no question in my mind about the courage of Negro officers or soldiers and any generalization on the basis of race is entirely unfounded."

On May 14, 1945, a week after Germany surrendered, Lieutenant Colonel Marcus H. Ray wrote a letter to Gibson. A Chicagoan, as was Gibson, Colonel Ray was a National Guard officer of the Eighth Illinois when it mobilized in 1940, and ended the war as commanding officer of the 600th Field Artillery Battalion of the Ninety-second Infantry Division. Colonel Ray closed his letter to Gibson by observing that "those who died in the proper performance of their assigned duties are our men of the decade and all honor should be paid them. They were Americans before all else. Racially, we have been the victims of an unfortunate chain of circumstances backgrounded by the unchanged American attitude as regards the proper 'place' of the Negro.... I do not believe the 92nd a complete failure as a combat unit, but when I think of what it might have been, I am heartsick."

THE 761ST TANK BATTALION

The most highly acclaimed African American ground-combat unit of World War II was the 761st Tank Battalion. As an organization, it enjoyed substantially better circumstances than the Ninety-second Infantry Division. Before the United States entered World War II, some white U.S. Army officers favored opening opportunities for black soldiers. They rejected the dogma of their colleagues who declared that modern weaponry was "too technical" for African Americans. One such officer, Lieutenant General Lesley James McNair, became the commanding general of Army ground forces. In that post, he spent most of his time visiting the nationwide array of ground forces training camps. When he visited the 761st at Camp Claiborne in Louisiana, he openly praised and encouraged the Army's first African American tankers. When the 761st went ashore in France on October 10, 1944, the men believed, rightly, that their outfit's existence was the result of McNair's effort and his belief in their abilities. (General McNair was killed by U.S. friendly fire on July 25, 1944, in France. The Joint Chiefs of Staff National Defense University in Washington, D.C., is located at Fort Lesley J. McNair, named in the general's honor.)

The 761st joined the Twenty-sixth Division on October 31 and was welcomed by the division commander, Major General Willard S. Paul (1894–1966) with these words: "I am damned glad to have you with us. We have been expecting you for a long time, and I am sure you are going to give a good account of yourselves." Two days later, Lieutenant General George S. Patton visited and welcomed the 761st. Equipped with Sherman Tanks, the 761st saw its earliest combat on November 8, 1944, at Athaniville, France; it was the first of 183 continuous days of combat for the battalion. The battalion is credited with killing 6,266 enemy soldiers and capturing 15,818. Despite its outstanding combat record, the 761st did not receive a Presidential Unit Citation until January 24, 1978.

One veteran of the 761st Tank Battalion, Company A, was posthumously awarded the Medal of Honor in January 1997. Staff Sergeant Ruben Rivers of Tecumseh, Oklahoma, was severely wounded on November 16, 1944, when his tank hit a German mine at a railroad crossing outside of Guébling, France. With his lower thigh sliced to the bone, Rivers declined a morphine injection and refused evacuation. Instead, he took command of another tank at the head of the column and led the advance toward their next objective, Bourgaltroff. Three days later, fierce fighting ensued when Company A was met at Bourgaltroff by enemy tanks and antitank weapons. Under heavy fire, Rivers's company commander ordered his tanks to pull back below the crest of a hill. Rivers had spotted the enemy positions, however, and he radioed his commander that he would press the fight. Rivers continued firing until the tank was hit in the turret by an armor-piercing round, killing him and wounding the other members of the crew.

Because of a policy of racial segregation and discrimination, most of the one million African Americans in uniform during World War II were not assigned to combat duty. Instead, they were assigned duty in the Service of Supply (SOS). In this capacity, they proved instrumental in the outcome of the war by operating bulldozers and cranes, setting up communications systems, and transporting essential supplies to the front. More than 70 percent of the truck companies in the Army's Motor Transport Service were African American. Their role was critical in Europe because the railroads in France were destroyed by retreating German forces, and Allied forces had to be supplied by truck. The Red Ball Express was established to meet this need in August 1944, with an original route between Saint-Lô and Paris. On a normal day, nearly nine hundred vehicles traveled the Red Ball Express on a trip that took an average of fifty-four hours.

The White Ball Route replaced the Red Ball Express in November 1944. Four of the nine truck companies transporting supplies from Le Havre and Rouen to forward areas were African American. They also saw duty on the Antwerp-Brussels-Charleroi Route in Belgium and the Green Diamond Route between Normandy and the Brest Peninsula in France. The 3917th Gasoline Supply Company supplied the Third Army with up to 165,000 gallons of gas a day. African American truckers were also well represented among the twelve amphibious truck companies. Although they were assigned transport duty, African American truckers were subject to hostile fire and were called on to fight in emergencies. A number received military honors from both the United States and France for courage and meritorious service in combat.

THE WOMEN'S AUXILIARY ARMY CORPS

With the creation of the Women's Auxiliary Army Corps on May 14, 1942, African American women could serve in the U.S. military in greater numbers than ever before. Many of the four thousand black volunteers, however, were assigned duties that were different from those assigned to their white counterparts. While white women typically worked as typists in offices, most African American women were assigned to cleanup details, laundry, and mess duty. There were notable exceptions in the branch that would soon be renamed the Women's Army Corps. Overseas, the 6888th Central Postal Battalion was commanded by Major Charity Adams, an African American who arrived in England in 1945. The unit was later sent to the European mainland, where it improved the mail delivery system, which was invaluable to troop morale.

African American women also served in the Army Nurse Corps. Initially, African American nurses were only permitted to care for black patients, but that policy proved impractical. The resentment generated when African American women were assigned to care for German prisoners of war ultimately led to a change in policy that enabled African American nurses to care for all wounded Americans, regardless of race.

THE SEA SERVICES

Following a decade of African American exclusion from enlistment, the U.S. Navy decided to form a separate African American branch in 1932. The branch was known as the Stewards' Service, though members were referred to in the African American community as the "seagoing bellhops." In 1940 the Navy consisted of 170,000 men, of whom 4,007 (or 2.3%) were African Americans in the Stewards' Service. In addition to African Americans, Navy stewards were also recruited from among Filipinos and other Asian American populations.

World War II transformed the situation. President Roosevelt had served as assistant secretary of the Navy during World War I and considered it "his branch" of the armed services. Therefore, his January 9, 1942, memo to the Navy had tremendous impact. The president noted to Secretary of the Navy Frank Knox: "I think that with all the Navy activities, Bureau of Navy might invent something that colored enlistees could do in addition to the rating of messman." The Navy relented on April 7, 1942, by announcing it would accept 14,000 African American enlistees in all ratings and branches. The initial training of African American sailors was conducted at the Great Lakes Naval Training Station north of Chicago, Illinois.

It was at that station that the Navy finally made a breakthrough in regard to African American personnel. In January 1944, sixteen African American petty officers began a special and intensive course of instruction that was conducted without public announcement. Three months later, the Navy announced the commissions of twelve African American ensigns and one warrant officer. They came to be known as the Navy's "Golden Thirteen." Collectively, the group recorded some of the highest scores in the history of the reserve officers training program.

Shortly after the Golden Thirteen were commissioned, the Navy opened the V-12 officer training programs to African Americans. Among the V-12 graduates who became Navy officers in World War II were Samuel L. Gravely Jr. and Carl T. Rowan. Gravely became the Navy's first African American admiral, while Rowan became an awarding-winning syndicated columnist and commentator.

By the end of World War II, 165,000 African Americans had served with distinction in the Navy, along with 17,000 in the Marine Corps; 5,000 in the Coast Guard; 12,000 in Navy Construction Battalions (Seabees); and 24,000 in the Merchant Marines. Notable among them was mess steward Doris "Dorie" Miller, who on December 7, 1941, manned a machine gun aboard the USS *West Virginia* as Japanese aircraft attacked Pearl Harbor. Miller was credited with destroying four planes before being ordered to abandon the sinking ship, making him one of World War II's first American heroes. Initially, the Navy attempted to conceal Miller's heroic feat, but eventually he was awarded the Navy Cross by Admiral Chester W. Nimitz. Miller was also promoted to mess attendant first class. Miller died when the escort aircraft carrier USS *Liscome Bay* was sunk on November 24, 1943. Three other African American mess attendants received the Navy Cross during World War II: Eli Benjamin (USS *Intrepid*), Leonard Harmon (USS *San Francisco*), and William Pinkney (USS *Enterprise*). Doris Miller is memorialized by one of a small number of Navy warships named for African Americans: the frigate USS *Miller*, which was in service from 1973 to 1991.

BELATED RECOGNITION FOR AFRICAN AMERICAN HEROES

Despite their many accomplishments, African American soldiers were not sufficiently honored for their heroics during World War II. Even though 1.2 million African Americans served in the U.S. Armed Forces during the war, not one received the nation's highest military award at the time, the Medal of Honor. Additionally, only nine were awarded the military's second highest honor, the Distinguished Service Cross. This was scant recognition, considering that more than 142,000 African Americans died in the war.

In 1992 the U.S. Army contracted with Shaw University for a group of professional military historians to comb the nation's archives and the memories of its veterans, both black and white, to discover why no African Americans had received a Medal of Honor during World War II and to determine whether some deserved the honor. After a fifteen-month study, the historians cited the racially biased climate of the Army for the lack of African American recognition and identified ten soldiers who might be deserving of that ultimate military honor. They passed the list of names on to a special Army Senior Officer Awards Board, which narrowed the list to nine, then sent it to the Joint Chiefs of Staff, who reduced it to seven. The Pentagon then sent those seven names to the U.S. Congress and the White House. Because the time limit for awarding the medal had expired in

1952, Congress included a waiver for the seven in the 1997 defense authorization bill. Congress approved a resolution to honor the nominees, and sent it to the president.

At a White House ceremony on January 13, 1997, President Bill Clinton presented Medals of Honor to the families of Staff Sergeant Edward A. Carter Jr., First Lieutenant John R. Fox, Private First Class Willy F. James Jr., Staff Sergeant Ruben Rivers, First Lieutenant Charles L. Thomas, Private George Watson, and to the lone survivor, First Lieutenant Vernon J. Baker. The seventy-six-year-old Baker, a twenty-eight-year Army veteran, was most gracious in accepting the honor, stating that he had long ago come to terms with any bitterness that he had felt toward the Army for its past racial discrimination.

World War II Veteran Vernon Baker and President Bill Clinton, White House, Washington, DC, 1997. *On this date, President Clinton presents First Lieutenant Baker (left) with the Medal of Honor for his heroic actions in April 1945. Baker, who was the only recipient still living, and six other World War II veterans became the first black soldiers of that war to receive the medal.* AP PHOTO/RUTH FREMSON

THE DESEGREGATION OF THE MILITARY (1946–1949)

As the Allied victory approached in World War II, the highest levels of the U.S. government recognized that a new era of domestic racial relations had emerged. The war to defeat fascism had, indeed, involved the entire U.S. population.

One impetus for a change in military policy regarding African Americans was an August 5, 1945, letter from Colonel Noel F. Parrish, commander of Tuskegee Army Air Field, to Brigadier General William E. Hall at Headquarters Army Air Forces. Colonel Parrish recommended "that future policy, instead of retreating defensibly further and further, with more and more group concessions, openly progress by slow and reasonable but definite steps toward the employment and treatment of Negroes as individuals which law requires and military efficiency demands."

Although Secretary of War Henry Stimson often revealed clear racial biases, his assistant, John R. McCloy, was considerably more progressive. When Robert P. Patterson succeeded Stimson, he adopted McCloy's suggestion for a study on the future use of African Americans in the military. A board of three Army generals conducted the study: Lieutenant General Alvan C. Gillem Jr., a former corps commander; Major General Lewis A. Pick, who built the Ledo Road in Burma; and Brigadier General Winslow C. Morse of the Army Air Forces. During a six-week period, the "Gillem Board" took testimony concerning the Army's postwar racial policy from more than fifty witnesses. Two key individuals who worked with the Gillem Board were African American Chicagoans who had served as civilian aides to the secretary of war: Truman K. Gibson Jr. and the recently discharged Lieutenant Colonel Marcus H. Ray.

The Gillem Board's findings leaned toward more efficient use of African American manpower, but did not advocate actual desegregation. That ambiguity reactivated the prewar coalition of the NAACP, the National Urban League, and the grassroots labor forces led by A. Philip Randolph.

The advent of the Cold War led to the National Security Act of 1947. The new law provided for the establishment of the Department of Defense (DOD), with the subordinate departments of the Army, Navy, and Air Force. The act also created the Central Intelligence Agency (CIA).

In the continuing movement toward desegregation of the Armed Forces, 1947 brought two important African American personnel shifts within the Department of Defense: Lieutenant Colonel Marcus H. Ray returned to active duty as senior advisor on racial matters in Europe, and in the Pentagon, Dr. James C. Evans, a Howard University professor and Department of Army official, moved to the new post of special assistant to the secretary of defense. As the highest-ranking African American civilian in the Department of Defense, Dr. Evans served under ten secretaries of defense until his retirement in 1970.

The demand for desegregation of the military became a key political issue in black America. As preparations for the 1948 presidential election intensified, President Harry Truman faced a campaign against Republican Thomas E. Dewey (who had also courted the African American vote by calling for the Armed Forces to be integrated), states' rights segregationist Strom Thurmond, and the Progressive Party of former Vice President Henry A. Wallace. In such a fragmented situation, the African American vote became crucial. By May 1948, President Truman had decided to desegregate the Armed Forces by executive order. Nevertheless, the decision required two political concessions. First, no deadlines would be imposed. Second, the order would not denounce racial segregation. On July 26, President Truman issued Executive Order 9981, which signaled an end to segregation in the military.

In June 1949, Wesley A. Brown became the first African American ever to graduate from the U.S. Naval Academy in Annapolis, Maryland. Brown, who had excelled as a student at Washington, D.C.'s Dunbar High School, was appointed to the academy by New York congressman Adam Clayton Powell Jr. in 1945. Since Annapolis had opened in 1850, only five African Americans had been admitted to the school. All had either resigned or been dismissed for alleged academic or disciplinary reasons. Despite harassment by classmates and hostility from instructors, Brown became the 20,699th midshipman to earn a commission from the Naval Academy.

Ensign Wesley A. Brown, U.S. Navy, Annapolis, MD, June 4, 1949. *The first African American graduate of the U.S. Naval Academy, Brown shows his girlfriend Sylvia Johnson Hicks his commission. Brown had been harassed by some of his classmates but had also received support from others, such as the future U.S. president Jimmy Carter.* FRED MORGAN/NEW YORK DAILY NEWS ARCHIVE VIA GETTY IMAGES

THE KOREAN WAR (1950–1953)

On June 25, 1950, North Korean forces surged across the Thirty-eighth Parallel and invaded South Korea. They routed U.S. ground forces in Korea and drove them south. At the start of the Korean War, the Air Force was the only completely desegregated branch of the military.

The first victory by U.S. troops in the Korean War occurred on July 20, 1950, at Yechon, thanks to the African American soldiers of the Twenty-fourth Infantry Regiment. Group commander Captain Charles M. Bussey, a World War II Tuskegee Airman, earned a Silver Star for his role in the battle. Two African American soldiers received posthumous Medals of Honor during the Korean War: Private First Class William Thompson and Sergeant Cornelius H. Charlton, both of the Twenty-fourth Infantry Regiment.

Thompson distinguished himself by bravery and determination above and beyond the call of duty in action on August 6, 1950, near Haman, Korea. While his platoon was reorganizing under cover of darkness, enemy forces overwhelmed the unit with a surprise attack. Thompson set up his machine gun in the path of the onslaught and swept the enemy with fire, momentarily halting their advance. His quick actions permitted the remainder of his platoon to withdraw to a more secure position. Although hit repeatedly by grenade fragments and small-arms fire, he resisted his comrades' efforts to induce him to withdraw. Steadfast at his machine gun, he continued to deliver fire until he was mortally wounded by an enemy grenade.

Charlton, a member of Company C, distinguished himself in action on June 2, 1951, near Chipo-ri, Korea. During an attack on heavily defended positions on an enemy-held ridge line, his platoon leader was wounded and evacuated. Charlton assumed command, rallied the men, and spearheaded the assault up the hill. Personally eliminating two hostile positions and killing six of the enemy with rifle fire and grenades, he continued up the slope until the unit stalled with heavy casualties. Regrouping the men, he led them forward, only to be forced back again by a shower of grenades. Despite a severe chest wound, Charlton refused medical attention and led a third charge that advanced to the crest of the ridge. He then charged a remaining enemy position on a nearby slope alone and, though hit by a grenade, raked the position with fire that routed the defenders. He died of wounds received during his daring exploits.

The first African American naval officer to lose his life in combat during the Korean War was Ensign Jesse L. Brown, who was also the first African American to earn naval aviator's wings. Brown, a Navy pilot, was shot down shortly after takeoff from the aircraft carrier USS *Leyte* on December 4, 1950. He crash-landed his plane on a snow-covered mountain near North Korea's Chosin Reservoir, but was unable to remove himself from the wreckage. A white pilot landed his aircraft near Brown's, but failed to pull him free. Other flyers radioed for help and, though a rescue helicopter made it to the location, the tangled metal could not be cut away quickly enough to save the life of the injured airman. Brown, who had previously flown twenty air combat missions, was posthumously awarded a Distinguished Flying Cross and a Purple Heart. On March 18, 1972, the U.S. Navy launched the destroyer escort USS *Jesse L. Brown*, marking the first time a Navy ship was ever named in honor of an African American naval officer.

THE KOREAN WAR EVOLUTION

The early defeats that U.S. forces experienced in Korea prompted President Truman to replace his close friend, Secretary of Defense Louis A. Johnson, with retired general of the Army George C. Marshall, who had been Truman's secretary of state from 1947 to 1949. One of Marshall's first acts as secretary of defense was the creation of a new entity: the Office of Assistant Secretary of Defense for Manpower and Reserves (OASD [MPR]). Marshall appointed Anna M. Rosenberg, a forty-eight-year-old New York City labor and public relations consultant, as head of the office. In 1944, she had persuaded President Roosevelt to have Congress enact the education provisions of the World War II GI Bill of Rights. James Evans's Office of Special Assistant became a part of the OASD (MPR), which brought together two individuals knowledgeable in the rigors of discrimination—a Hungarian Jewish immigrant and an African American college professor. Known affectionately in the Pentagon as "Aunt Anna," Rosenberg's OASD (MPR) was responsible for industrial and military manpower, including Selective Service System policies. Secretary Rosenberg viewed military desegregation as an impetus for societal reform, observing that, "In the long run, I don't think a man can live and fight next to one of another race and share experiences where life is at stake, and not have a strong feeling of understanding when he comes home."

The effective implementation of Executive Order 9981 turned on how well African American military personnel could use their opportunities. Many African American generals and admirals owe their stars to the wise counsel of James Evans, who often mentored young African American officers by suggesting advantageous career paths in the military. By the close of the Korean War, racial segregation had been totally removed from the U.S. Armed Forces. In the years preceding the Vietnam War, African Americans entered the military and opted for full careers in increasing numbers. Between 1953 and 1961, there was a slow increase in the number of African American career officers in each branch of the service.

THE VIETNAM WAR (1964–1973)

During the brief cease-fire period between the end of the Korean War and the heightening of conflict in Vietnam, the John F. Kennedy administration—prompted by Congressman Adam Clayton Powell Jr. and others—sought to end any remaining discrimination in the U.S. Armed Forces. Through Secretary of Defense Robert McNamara, Kennedy stressed to military leaders the need to foster equal opportunities for African American service members, both on and off base.

Extensive U.S. involvement in Vietnam began during the summer of 1964 following an attack on the USS *Maddox* by North Vietnamese naval vessels in the Gulf of Tonkin. Within four months, the United States had 23,000 soldiers fighting in Vietnam. Soon, the Army, Navy, and Marine Corps were all engaged in the action in ever-increasing numbers. While the U.S. fighting force in Vietnam comprised all of the nation's racial and ethnic groups, African Americans were disproportionately represented. Furthermore, they were more likely to be placed in combat units. Although African Americans constituted about 10.5 percent of the Army, they accounted for nearly 13 percent of those killed or wounded. By 1965, the conflict in Vietnam had escalated into a full-scale war, mounted to support the democracy of the South Vietnamese and to protect U.S. interests in Southeast Asia. The Vietnam War proved deadlier than the Korean War and lasted longer than any other war in U.S. history.

The uncertain objectives, the high casualty rates, and the disproportionate number of African American soldiers in Vietnam caused tremendous controversy in the African

American community. In 1965, Malcolm X claimed that the U.S. government was "causing American soldiers to be murdered every day, for no reason at all." Martin Luther King Jr. criticized African American involvement in Vietnam, remarking that "we are taking young black men who have been crippled by our society and sending them 8,000 miles away to guarantee liberties in Southeast Asia which they have not found in southwest Georgia or East Harlem."

With the assassinations of Dr. King and Senator Robert Kennedy in 1968, some African American soldiers became increasingly demoralized and disenchanted. Their anger intensified as racial prejudice remained common in Vietnam, on stateside military bases, and aboard the aircraft carriers USS *Kitty Hawk*, USS *Constellation*, and USS *Franklin D. Roosevelt*. One of the most famous African American protesters of the Vietnam War was heavyweight champion Muhammad Ali. A Muslim, Ali declared himself a conscientious objector in 1968 on religious grounds. He was convicted of violating the Selective Service Act, stripped of his heavyweight boxing championship, and threatened with an extensive jail term. In 1970, the U.S. Supreme Court overturned his conviction.

By the early 1970s, when the United States withdrew all of its troops from Vietnam (which resulted in South Vietnam's collapse within a matter of a few years), close to sixty thousand American lives had been lost. Unlike World Wars I and II, twenty African Americans received the Medal of Honor for their heroism in the conflict. Several of those were awarded posthumously.

MILITARY PARTICIPATION IN THE 1970s AND 1980s

In 1971, two years before the withdrawal of U.S. troops from Vietnam, the NAACP issued the report, *The Search for Military Justice*, which identified residual discrimination in the military long after Truman had taken steps to outlaw it. In particular, it found that a disproportionate number of disciplinary incidents involved African Americans and Hispanics, who were often punished more severely than whites. In the 1970s, African Americans represented about 13 percent of discharged servicemen, but received 33 percent of dishonorable discharges, 21 percent of bad-conduct discharges, 16 percent of undesirable discharges, and 20 percent of general discharges. A less-than-honorable discharge can negatively affect a veteran for life, threatening his or her civilian career, earning ability, and level of veterans' benefits.

High-ranking government and military officials moved to eliminate racial prejudices and barriers. Unquestionably, this became easier as African Americans, despite their relatively low numbers in the officer ranks, rose to the highest levels of the military. In 1975, Daniel "Chappie" James became the first African American to be promoted to full general in the U.S. Air Force. Two years later, President Jimmy Carter appointed lawyer and politician Clifford L. Alexander Jr. to be secretary of the Army, making him the first African American to hold that post. Alexander had previously served in the administrations of John F. Kennedy, Lyndon B. Johnson, and Richard Nixon. As Army secretary, Alexander was responsible for 1.9 million soldiers and a budget of $34 billion. He served in the post until 1980.

By the 1980s, the military was demonstrably less discriminatory than the civilian world. The decade also saw increasing numbers of women joining the military, working side by side with men in many jobs. These advancements facilitated the breakdown of gender, as well as racial, obstacles to success in the military. By the end of the decade, African Americans represented 28 percent of the total enlisted Army force, while African American women accounted for nearly 45 percent of enlisted women in the U.S. Armed Forces' largest branch. Beginning in the 1990s, however, military recruiters have faced more difficulty attracting and retaining talented African American officers as a result of competition from industry and private-sector employers who can typically offer higher salaries.

In August 1989, President George H. W. Bush appointed General Colin L. Powell of the U.S. Army to be chairman of the Joint Chiefs of Staff, the nation's highest military post. General Powell's emergence was a result of Army secretary Clifford Alexander's refusal to sign off on a list of potential promotions that did not include any African American candidates. Powell became the first African American and the youngest person in U.S. Armed Forces history to hold that title.

THE PERSIAN GULF WAR (1991)

African Americans were divided over U.S. involvement in the 1991 Gulf War, with almost 50 percent of those polled at the time opposed to it. Several African American leaders, including Representative Charles Rangel of New York, were especially concerned about the high number of African Americans fighting to liberate Kuwait from Iraq. General Colin Powell initially favored economic sanctions (embargoes) over military action, until war became the stated policy of President Bush. From then on, Powell drafted and put into action a brilliant military campaign—beginning with a large-scale air attack—that minimized the loss of U.S. lives. U.S. military objectives were met in just a few weeks.

About 104,000 of the 400,000 troops serving in the Persian Gulf War were African American. According to the Department of Defense, African Americans accounted for 30 percent of Army, 21 percent of Navy, 17 percent of

Marine Corps, and 14% of Air Force personnel stationed in the Persian Gulf (in 1991, African Americans comprised 12.4% of the U.S. population). Powell interpreted the high participation rate of African Americans in the Gulf War as a positive, rather than a negative. According to him, it was merely a reflection of the opportunities that the military provided for African Americans who might not have had such choices otherwise.

AN EVOLVING INSTITUTION

During the 1990s, African Americans continued to make strides in rising to the highest military ranks. The percentage of African American officers in the U.S. Armed Forces remained on an upward trend, rising above 7 percent by 1994. In 1993, Togo D. West Jr. became the second African American to hold the presidential appointment of secretary of the Army. West served in that position until late 1997, when President Bill Clinton tapped him to replace Jesse Brown as secretary of veterans affairs. Brown, who had vacated the post in July 1997, was the first African American to serve as the department's secretary. A decorated Marine who served in Vietnam, Brown held the post for more than four years. With more than 215,000 employees and an annual budget exceeding $40 billion in the late 1990s, the Department of Veterans Affairs was the second-largest department in the president's cabinet.

Another important African American first was the selection of Command Sergeant Major Gene C. McKinney to become the sergeant major of the Army in 1995. That singular post represents the highest-ranking noncommissioned officer in the U.S. Army. McKinney, the former command sergeant major of the U.S. Army Europe, became the tenth enlisted man to hold the title. The sergeant major of the Army's job is to advise the Army chief of staff on issues concerning the organization's 420,000 enlisted personnel.

Since the end of the Persian Gulf War, African American military men and women have been well represented in peacekeeping missions in Somalia, Haiti, and the republics of the former Yugoslavia. Polls of African American service personnel indicate that the vast majority regarded the U.S. Armed Forces as mostly free of racism and discrimination. It was also the feeling of many that it offered the greatest opportunity for career advancement.

Nevertheless, a pair of scandals chiefly involving African American enlisted men rocked the Army during the latter half of the 1990s, causing some to question the fairness of military justice. The first of the two scandals took place at Maryland's Aberdeen Proving Ground and involved eleven African American enlisted men and one African American officer accused of sexual misconduct in multiple incidents with white female recruits. All of the enlisted men were drill sergeants, who allegedly took advantage of the recruits under their direct supervision during basic training. The charges included both consensual sex and rape; in the military, consensual sex between soldiers of unequal rank in cases involving direct subordinates is a crime for both parties. The first charges came out in September 1996, though a number of the recruits were slow to point fingers and admitted willing participation in the acts. Army investigators later faced allegations that they had themselves tried to influence recruits to make the more serious charge of rape. Though some of the rape charges were dropped, several of the men were convicted and sentenced, while others had their military careers effectively ended.

The second scandal involved Sergeant Major of the Army Gene C. McKinney. The scandal became public in February 1997 when McKinney's former public relations aide, retired Sergeant Major Brenda Hoster, charged him with sexual harassment. Eventually, five other women—four subordinates and one officer—came forward to accuse McKinney of additional sexual abuse charges. All of the women were white. On March 13, 1998, a military jury of four Army officers (including two women) and four enlisted men acquitted McKinney of eighteen of the nineteen charges, including all of the sexual misconduct charges. McKinney was only found guilty of a related obstruction of justice charge. McKinney was demoted one rank, though he was not given prison time. Many in the media concluded that the Pentagon had allowed a "show trial" in an effort to declare to the country its policy of "zero tolerance" of sexual harassment. Others conjectured that McKinney had been singled out, as white defendants in other Army sexual abuse cases occurring concurrently had been quietly slapped on the wrist.

In 1997 the Defense Manpower Data Center (DMDC) released the Armed Forces Equal Opportunity Survey (EOS), which was the first of its kind for the military. The EOS was conducted by the DMDC from September 1996 through February 1997. The survey covered a wide range of items measuring members' perceptions and actions relating to race relations. In general, the survey detected major differences in the perceptions of service members of different racial/ethnic groups in respect to equal opportunity. Significantly, whites, who comprise the majority population in the U.S. Armed Forces, were more positive than minority members regarding racial/ethnic issues in the military. For the most part, race relations on military installations and ships were perceived to be better than those in local civilian communities. Those perceptions, however, were not expressed in equally strong measure by whites and African Americans. Although more members said that race relations both in the military and in the nation were better at that time than in the previous five years, African Americans were less likely than other racial/ethnic groups to make those same claims. Despite the survey's conclusions among African Americans when compared to those of other racial/ethnic groups, the relative levels of satisfaction among African Americans in the U.S. Armed Forces appeared to indicate an overall favorable impression of the military by the group. Still, the EOS indicated areas of concern that could be addressed by military leadership. The impact of President Barack Obama's 2008 election on the attitudes and perceptions of African American military personnel has yet to be determined.

The U.S. Armed Forces has continued to provide a primary avenue of upward mobility for African Americans who are ambitious, willing to apply themselves, and might not have other opportunities available to them. The overall percentage of African Americans in the military indicates that many are attempting to take that road to success.

The table below provides Department of Defense figures for the total number of African Americans serving in the U.S. Armed Forces. Collectively, in 2010 African Americans represented approximately 20 percent of the 1,596,400-strong U.S. military.

Active	*African Americans*	*Percentage of Total*
Army	105,200	21.0%
Navy	64,845	19.0%
Air Force	50,211	14.7%
Marine Corps	18,925	10.6%
Coast Guard	2,500	6.2%
Reserve/Guard	*African Americans*	*Percentage of Total*
Army National Guard	46,898	13.5%
Army Reserve	43,895	23.3%
Navy Reserve	10,860	15.6%
Marine Corps Reserve	3,100	7.9%
Air National Guard	9,009	8.5%
Air Force Reserve	11,484	15.7%
Coast Guard Reserve	374	4.6%

Source: Department of Defense.

THE WAR ON TERRORISM

Americans were caught off-guard by the September 11, 2001, terrorist attacks on the World Trade Center in New York City, the Pentagon in Arlington, Virginia, and the downed flight near Shanksville, Pennsylvania (whose intended target was the White House). President George W. Bush immediately declared a "war on terrorism," stating that the United States would use whatever force was necessary to ensure internal security and dismantle the external terrorist threat. That threat was quickly identified as directed by Osama bin Laden and his Afghanistan-based al-Qaeda terrorist network. In spite of early success by coalition-backed U.S. forces against the so-called Islamic jihad, the terrorist threat remained real as top-level al-Qaeda leaders were rumored to have escaped to other Islamic nations. African American support for the war has been strong, even among Muslims, who feel that bin Laden does not represent the spirit and truth of Islam.

WAR IN IRAQ

After the September 11 attack on the United States, the Bush administration acted on longstanding plans regarding Iraq. Iraq's alleged "weapons of mass destruction" became the pretext for war, although no such weapons were found. To expose the level of the threat posed by Iraq, the United States called on the UN Security Council to once again send weapons inspectors to that country. Although the Iraqi regime allowed the UN inspectors access to weapons sites, where they found nothing but evidence supporting defectors' claims that the weapons had been destroyed years ago, the U.S. government charged Iraq with evasion and obstruction.

After failing to secure support for an invasion of Iraq from France, China, and Russia, the U.S. government acted against the judgment of most world opinion. Backed by the United Kingdom and a number of smaller countries in a "coalition of the willing," the United States invaded Iraq on March 20, 2003. With President Bush declaring "mission accomplished," the war was deemed a victory on May 1, 2003. However, the insurgency, resistance, and civil war continued, as American soldiers attempted to secure a deteriorating situation. As of early 2010, more than 4,200 American soldiers had lost their lives in the war, with more than 30,000 wounded. The number of Iraqi dead has been estimated by researchers to be in excess of 100,000. In 2009 President Obama increased the U.S. presence in Afghanistan to include the Taliban in the war on terrorism. In August 2010, he withdrew the last of the U.S. combat troops from Iraq, formally ending the War in Iraq. Although 50,000 U.S. troops remained in Iraq at that point to help train its police force and military, full U.S. withdrawal is scheduled for the end of 2011.

OUTSTANDING MILITARY FIGURES

(Some biographical profiles may appear in other chapters. To locate profiles more readily, please consult the index.)

CLARA L. ADAMS-ENDER (1939–)

Brigadier General, Army Nurse Corps. Clara Mae Leach was born July 11, 1939, near Willow Springs in Wake County, North Carolina. She was the fourth child of ten born to sharecroppers Otha Leach and Caretha Bell (Sapp) Leach. Although her parents did not complete their education, they placed a high value on the education of their children. Clara attended Fuquay Springs Consolidated High School, which comprised primary grades through high school. From age five until entering college, Leach worked on the farm while going to school. In 1956, she graduated from high school at sixteen years old and entered the School of Nursing at North Carolina Agricultural and Technical State University, located in Greensboro. During her college years, she joined an Army program that financed her junior and senior years. As an Army reservist in college, she started as a private, later gaining a commission as a second lieutenant in March 1961, three months before graduating. After completing her degree, she entered the active U.S. Army Nurse Corps.

Leach began her active Army career as a general duty nurse at Walson Army Hospital in Fort Dix, New Jersey, where she was assigned from 1961 to 1963. She spent the next thirteen months overseas in Ascom, Korea, with the 121st Evacuation Hospital. During that assignment, she learned a great deal about nursing administration, as well as how to lead nursing assistants and manage nursing practice. She also discovered that she had an affinity for teaching. Leach was able to develop her teaching skills when she was assigned to the U.S. Army Medical Training Center at Fort Sam Houston, Texas, as a nursing instructor between 1965 and 1967. In 1967, she became the first female in the Army to earn the Expert Field Medical Badge. She also began graduate studies at the University of Minnesota, majoring in medical surgical nursing. After graduating with a master's degree in nursing in 1969, she was assigned to the Walter Reed Army Institute of Nursing in Washington, D.C., where she was originally a nursing instructor, then an assistant professor.

In 1974 Leach became assistant chief of the department of nursing at Kimbrough Army Hospital in Fort Meade, Maryland. She then entered the U.S. Army Command and General Staff College at Fort Leavenworth, Kansas, and completed a master of military arts and sciences degree in 1976. Subsequently, she was assigned to Headquarters, Health Services Command, at Fort Sam Houston as inspector general.

She began her second overseas assignment at the Army Regional Medical Center in Frankfurt, West Germany, in 1978. She began as the assistant chief of the department of nursing, then, after a year, became chief. When she was thirty-nine, she was promoted to full colonel. In Germany, she took part in a collaborative working relationship with German nurses at a nearby trauma hospital, while learning the German language, local customs, and culture. She also met her husband, a German doctor, Heinz Ender, whom she married in 1981, three months after returning to the United States.

In 1981 Adams-Ender was assigned to the U.S. Army Recruiting Command in Fort Sheridan, Illinois, as chief of the Army Nurse Corps division. Despite heavy job responsibilities, she continued to seek educational opportunities whenever possible. When she graduated from the U.S. Army War College in 1982, she became the first black Army Nurse Corps officer to do so. In 1984, she was appointed chief of the department of nursing at Walter Reed Army Medical Center, where she engaged in clinical practice, teaching, nursing administration, and nursing research. Her experiences and education provided a broad base for her next assignment.

In 1987 Adams-Ender was appointed to the Office of the Surgeon General as the eighteenth chief of the U.S. Army Nurse Corps; with it came a promotion to brigadier general. As the surgeon general's director for medical personnel during the 1991 Gulf War, Adams-Ender was responsible for more than 25,000 military health-care professionals who served in the region of conflict. Ordinarily, the holder of that prestigious title retires after her assignment ends, but Adam-Ender added another highlight to her distinguished military career before retiring. In 1991, she became the commanding general at Fort Belvoir, Virginia, while simultaneously serving as deputy commanding officer of the Military District of Washington. Such high-profile appointments were a rarity for both black females and nursing corps officers. She held those posts until her retirement in August 1993.

Following her retirement from the military, Adams-Ender founded her own management consulting agency, Caring About People with Enthusiasm (CAPE) Associates, Inc. As president and CEO of CAPE, she specializes in personnel and organizational management issues and is a frequent speaker and lecturer. Adams-Ender chronicled her life story in *My Rise to the Stars: How a Sharecropper's Daughter Became an Army General*, which she wrote with Blair S. Walker. The autobiography was self-published in 2001.

Adams-Ender is involved with numerous professional organizations. She is a member of the American Nurses Association, the American Red Cross Nursing Service, Chi Eta Phi Nursing Sorority, the National Association for Female Executives, and the National League for Nursing, to name a few. She is also involved with many charitable organizations, including the NAACP and the National Council of Negro Women.

During her military career, Adams-Ender was awarded a Distinguished Service Medal with oak leaf cluster, a Legion of Merit, a Meritorious Service Medal with three oak leaf clusters, and an Army Commendation Medal. She has been honored with many civilian awards, including the Roy Wilkins Meritorious Service Award by the NAACP, the Gertrude E. Rush Award for Leadership from the National Bar Association, and the Regents' Distinguished Graduate Award from the University of Minnesota. In 1993, she was recognized for career achievement when she was selected to be in Dominion's Strong Men and Women: Excellence in Leadership series.

CRISPUS ATTUCKS

See chapter 6, Africans in America

GUION S. BLUFORD JR.

See chapter 27, Science and Technology

CHARLES F. BOLDEN JR.

See chapter 27, Science and Technology

JESSE L. BROWN (1926–1950)

Ensign, Naval Aviator. Jesse Leroy Brown was born on October 13, 1926, in Hattiesburg, Mississippi. He graduated from Eureka High School in 1944 and studied engineering at Ohio State University from 1944 to 1947. In 1946, he joined the U.S. Naval Reserve and became an aviation cadet the following year.

Brown's flight training occurred at Pensacola, Florida, and in 1948 he became the first African American to fly for the Navy. In 1949, Brown worked aboard the aircraft carrier USS *Leyte*, earning an Air Medal and a Korean Service Medal for his twenty air-combat missions. On December 4, 1950, while flying air support for Marines at the Battle of the Chosin Reservoir, his plane was hit by enemy fire. He crash-landed his aircraft, but was trapped inside and died before rescuers could cut through the wreckage to extract him. He was posthumously awarded a Purple Heart and a Distinguished Flying Cross for exceptional courage, airmanship, and devotion to duty. Brown was the first African American naval officer to lose his life in combat during the Korean War. In March 1972, a destroyer escort, the USS *Jesse L. Brown*, was named in his honor and launched at the Avondale Shipyards near Westwego, Louisiana. It marked the first time that a ship was named for an African American naval officer.

SHERIAN G. CADORIA (1940–)

Brigadier General, U.S. Army. Born to a poor rural family on January 26, 1940, in Marksville, Louisiana, Sherian Grace Cadoria credits her mother with instilling within her the qualities of discipline, honesty, and perseverance. When she was a child, she helped supplement the family income by picking cotton and carrying 100-pound bags through the fields. To attend school, she and her two siblings walked five miles each way, passed daily by a "whites only" school bus that traveled the same route. After high school, Cadoria attended Southern University in Baton Rouge. During her junior year, she was recruited for a four-week Women's Army Corps (WAC) training program. Though she was actually more interested in joining the Navy, she attended the WAC program, which was conducted at Fort McClellan, Alabama, during the summer of 1960. After graduating with a B.S. in business education in 1961, she decided to make the Army her career.

It was not long before Cadoria realized that, to many in the Army, she had two strikes against her: she was both African American and female. At Fort McClellan in the early 1960s, she suffered numerous indignities and was

Sherian G. Cadoria, U.S. Army Officer, 1980s. *Cadoria attained the rank of brigadier general in 1985, the first female African American in the regular U.S. Army to do so. She retired from the army in 1990.* U.S. ARMY PHOTOGRAPH

denied several opportunities as a result of her race. As she advanced through the ranks, however, she faced greater resistance because of her gender than because of her race. Cadoria was not content to take either of the typical paths open for female advancement, such as administration and nursing. Instead, she rose through the ranks of the military police.

From 1967 to 1969, while U.S. involvement in Vietnam was at its peak, Cadoria spent thirty-three months in the Southeast Asian country. The severity of the experience almost caused her to give up her military career, and she seriously considered joining a convent on her return. The turning point came in December 1969 when she was selected to attend the Command and General Staff College, becoming the first African American woman to be chosen for the school.

Even the dissolution of the WAC in 1978 and the integration of its members into the regular Army did not slow her ascent. Among her marks of distinction, Cadoria was the first woman to command a male battalion; the first African American director of manpower and personnel for the Joint Chiefs of Staff (a position that required her to fill openings in all branches of the armed services, both active and reserve); and the first woman to achieve the rank of general apart from the nursing corps. She is also a graduate of the U.S. Army War College and the National Defense University. Cadoria even managed to find enough time outside her busy career to attend the University of Oklahoma, where she earned an M.A. in social work in 1974. In 1985, Cadoria was promoted to brigadier general, becoming only the second African American female, and the first in the regular U.S. Army, to attain the rank. Cadoria retired from the military on November 30, 1990.

Following her retirement from the military, Cadoria returned to Louisiana. She headed her own company, Cadoria Speaker and Consultancy Service, before retiring in 2004. She also became a much-in-demand keynote, inspirational, and motivational speaker. During the late-1990s, Cadoria put her business on hold for two years to serve as volunteer principal of Holy Ghost Catholic School in her native Marksville. She was also appointed to the Louisiana Gaming Control Board and became the senior Army representative on the Advisory Board of Vietnam Women Veterans. Cadoria was named Woman of the Year by the national organization of Business and Professional Women in 1995, was a National Athena Award winner in 1998, and was among the honorees of Dominion's Strong Men and Women: Excellence in Leadership series in 1999.

During nearly three decades of military service, Cadoria was awarded an Air Medal, an Army Commendation Medal with three oak leaf clusters, a Bronze Star with two oak leaf clusters, a Defense Superior Service Medal, a Distinguished Service Medal, a Meritorious Service Medal with oak leaf cluster, and a Joint Chiefs of Staff Identification Badge.

WILLIAM H. CARNEY (1840–1908)

Sergeant, First African American Medal of Honor Recipient. William H. Carney was born in Norfolk, Virginia, in 1840. When he was fourteen, he attended a secret school run by a local minister. In 1856, his father moved the family to New Bedford, Massachusetts. Carney, a man of growing religious conviction, considered becoming a minister, but the Civil War disrupted his plans. Instead, he enlisted in the Fifty-fourth Massachusetts Colored Infantry Regiment on February 17, 1863.

As a member of Company C of the Fifty-fourth, Sergeant Carney was part of the force assigned to lead the advance on Fort Wagner in South Carolina on July 18, 1863. Fort Wagner, a vital Confederate position in the defense of Charleston, was heavily fortified. Led by Colonel Robert Gould Shaw, a white commander, the African American troops attempted a valiant, but ultimately disastrous, assault in the late afternoon. During the attack, the flag bearer was wounded, but before the stars and stripes fell to the ground, Carney grabbed the staff and continued onward. With most of his comrades falling around him, Carney led the charge. He wound up at the fort's entrance—alone. Hiding in the shadows of the fort, Carney avoided rounds and shells falling around him, while clutching the flag. Eventually, a Confederate squad stumbled on his position and he was forced to flee. Shot twice, he still managed to escape, later joining up with a white soldier who bandaged his wounds. Together, they retreated to the safety of the Union lines, but not before another shot grazed Carney's head. After further medical treatment, Carney returned to his regiment, where his fellow troops cheered his return, flag in hand. "Boys, the old flag never touched the ground," he proclaimed proudly. Unfortunately, approximately half of Carney's comrades, as well as Colonel Shaw, met their end in the unsuccessful undertaking.

For his actions, Carney was awarded the Medal of Honor. Among African American soldiers or sailors who were awarded a Medal of Honor for actions during the Civil War, Carney's occurred earliest, though he was not issued his medal until May 23, 1900.

On June 30, 1864, Sergeant Carney was discharged from the infantry at Black Island, South Carolina. He was granted disability for lingering medical problems resulting from the wounds he received in the famed battle. After a short sojourn to California, Carney returned to New

U.S. Army Brigadier General Benjamin O. Davis Sr. and Colonel Benjamin O. Davis Jr. of the 332nd Fighter Group, Italy, 1944. *Davis Sr. (*right*), who in 1940 became the first African American brigadier general in the U.S. Army, pins the Distinguished Flying Cross on his son, Davis Jr., who in 1954 became the first African American general in the U.S. Air Force.* **ARCHIVE PHOTOS/ STRINGER/GETTY IMAGES**

Bedford, where he served as a mail carrier for thirty-two years. After retirement, he moved to Boston to accept a job as a messenger in the State House. He was injured in an elevator accident on November 23, 1908, and died on December 9. Carney was buried in New Bedford.

BENJAMIN O. DAVIS SR. (1877–1970)

First African American Brigadier General in the U.S. Armed Forces. Born in Washington, D.C., on June 1, 1877, Benjamin Oliver Davis Sr. came from a middle-class family. Davis wanted to become a soldier, and in high school he joined the Cadet Corps, an extracurricular organization that introduced him to military training and procedure. Following high school, Davis attended classes at Howard University, but despite his parents' objections, he left college in 1898 for an opportunity to fight in the Spanish-American War.

Hoping to see action in Cuba, Davis left the District of Columbia National Guard, where he was a second lieutenant in Company D, for the Eighth U.S. Volunteer Infantry, with whom he accepted a temporary commission as a first lieutenant in Company G. Neither unit, however, made it out of the states. After the conclusion of the war, Davis sought an Army commission through other avenues.

On June 14, 1899, he enlisted as a private in Troop I, Ninth U.S. Cavalry, an African American regular Army unit. In August of the following year, he submitted an application to take the officer candidate examination. A few months later he completed the battery of tests and finished among the top candidates. On February 2, 1901, he was commissioned a second lieutenant in the regular Army. His first assignment was with Troop F, Tenth U.S. Cavalry, then stationed in the Philippines.

Over the next three decades, Davis received a number of assignments meant to keep him from being in a position to command white soldiers. He served as a military attaché to Liberia from 1909 to 1911, commanding officer of a supply troop in the Philippines from 1917 to 1920, and instructor of the 372nd Infantry of the Ohio National Guard from 1924 to 1929. Between these service assignments, he taught military science and tactics at Wilberforce University and Tuskegee Institute. Promotions for African American officers were rare in those years, but Davis rose through the ranks until he became a full colonel on February 18, 1930. In 1938, Davis took command of the African American 369th Cavalry of the New York National Guard.

Davis's promotion to brigadier general on October 25, 1940, made him the first African American general in the history of the U.S. Armed Forces. The promotion was seen by many detractors as a political ploy by President Franklin D. Roosevelt to garner African American votes in an election year. Davis had spent a forty-year military career, however, in assignments that offered him few opportunities to shine. The promotion capped a difficult career marred by continuing discrimination. Davis retired just a few months later, having reached the official retirement age of sixty-four.

Within months of this retirement, Davis was called back to active service to supervise the introduction of 100,000 African American soldiers into the Army, an institution rampant with policies of segregation. During World War II, Davis inspected African American units, heard complaints about discrimination, and handled public relations duties throughout the European military theater as a member of the Washington-based inspector general's staff. Davis's strenuous efforts on behalf of African American servicemen brought him prominence in the African American press.

After the war, Davis served as assistant to the inspector general of the Army from 1945 to 1947, then as special assistant to the secretary of the Army from 1947 to 1948. His focus throughout that period was the orderly integration of units in the military's largest branch. On July 20, 1948, Davis retired from the Army a second and final time at a special White House ceremony, during which his career was lauded by President Harry S. Truman. The president's Executive Order 9981, the historic order that led to the integration of the entire military, was issued six days after Davis's retirement.

Later in life, Davis became a member of the American Battle Monuments Commission. Deteriorating eyesight and health problems brought his public life to an end in 1960. He died of leukemia on November 26, 1970, in Chicago, Illinois, and was buried in Arlington National Cemetery. Davis's military honors included a Bronze Star and a Distinguished Service Medal, as well as such foreign decorations as the Croix de Guerre with Palm (from France) and the Grade of Commander of the Order of the Star of Africa (from Liberia).

BENJAMIN O. DAVIS JR. (1912–2002)

First African American Brigadier General in the U.S. Air Force. Born in Washington, D.C., on December 18, 1912, Benjamin Oliver Davis Jr., the son of Brigadier General Benjamin O. Davis Sr., moved often in his early years. The family lived for a time in Alabama, where his father taught military science at Tuskegee Institute, and Cleveland, where Benjamin Jr. graduated as president of his high school class. Davis attended both Western Reserve University and the University of Chicago before accepting an appointment to the U.S. Military Academy in 1932, having been nominated by longtime Chicago congressman Oscar De Priest.

When Davis entered West Point, no African American had graduated from the academy in forty-three years. In an attempt to get Davis to resign, his fellow cadets forced him to endure four years of "silencing." That behavior, encouraged by superiors who also wanted Davis to fail, meant that few would speak to him (except to issue an order), and his classmates would not room with him (though he lived in a two-man room) or eat with him for his entire stay at the academy. Nevertheless, Davis excelled, graduating thirty-fifth in a class of 276 in 1936. Although the Army generally allowed West Point graduates with high class rank to choose their branch of service, Davis was denied his selection of the U.S. Army Air Corps. Instead, he was assigned to Fort Benning in Georgia as an infantry officer, where he experienced further institutional and de facto racism.

After five years in the infantry, and following a stint at Fort Riley in Kansas, Davis was allowed to transfer to the Army Air Corps just months before the United States entered World War II in 1941. The transfer was part of a daring military experiment championed by President Roosevelt: the creation of an African American flying unit. The Sixty-sixth Air Force Training Detachment was based at the Army Air Field in Tuskegee, Alabama, and Davis was in the first training class. On September 2, 1941, he became the first African American to officially fly solo as an Army Air Corps officer. Shortly after graduation in 1942, Davis—as the only previously commissioned officer in the class—became commander of the African American Ninety-ninth Pursuit Squadron (later renamed the Ninety-ninth Fighter Squadron). Davis quickly earned promotions, rising to the rank of lieutenant colonel by the time the Ninety-ninth arrived in French Morocco for combat duty on April 24, 1943.

In late August 1943, Davis returned to the United States to command the African American 332nd Fighter Group, made up of three squadrons and later the Ninety-ninth. In April 1944, the 332nd arrived in Italy, where it flew missions deep into France and Germany. The sterling record of the 332nd contributed to Davis's promotion to full colonel just a few months later. In two hundred escort missions, the unit never lost a bomber to Nazi aircraft fire. During World War II, Davis flew sixty missions and logged 224 combat hours. For individual heroism, he was honored with several decorations, including a Silver Star (pinned to his uniform by his father) and a Distinguished Flying Cross, the Corps' highest award.

Davis's post–World War II career was no less significant. He played a leading role in the integration of the military in 1949. During the Korean War, he commanded the Fifty-first Fighter Interceptor Wing, later serving as director of operations and training for the Far East Air Forces. His promotion to brigadier general in 1954 made him the first African American general in U.S. Air Force history, as well as the highest-ranking African American in the U.S. military at the time. Other notable assignments included service as deputy chief of staff of the U.S. Air Force in Europe beginning in 1957; director of manpower and organization for the U.S. Air Force headquarters beginning in 1961; and chief of staff of the United Nations Command and U.S. Forces in Korea beginning in 1965. Davis was named a major general in 1957 and a lieutenant general in 1965, becoming the first African American to hold either rank in the U.S. Armed Forces. Named to command the Philippines-based Thirteenth Air Force in August 1967, Davis was responsible for all Air Force units in Southeast Asia, including those serving in Vietnam. Davis retired from active duty in 1970.

After retiring from the military, Davis served under President Richard M. Nixon as assistant secretary of transportation for environment, safety, and consumer affairs. In 1991, the Smithsonian Institution Press published his memoirs, *Benjamin O. Davis Jr., American: An Autobiography*. On December 9, 1998, in order to right a perceived wrong, President Bill Clinton bestowed upon Davis a fourth star, bringing his rank to full general.

Among Davis's many military decorations are a Distinguished Service Medal with two oak leaf clusters, an Army and an Air Force Silver Star, a Distinguished Flying Cross, a Legion of Merit with two oak leaf clusters, and an Air Medal with five oak leaf clusters.

Davis resided in Arlington, Virginia, during his retirement. On July 4, 2002, General Davis Jr. died at the Walter Reed Army Medical Center from the affects of Alzheimer's disease.

CHARITY ADAMS EARLEY
(1918–2002)

Lieutenant Colonel, First African American Woman Commissioned in the Women's Auxiliary Army Corps. Charity Edna Adams was born in Columbia, South Carolina, in 1918. She was the valedictorian of her high school class and continued her studies at Ohio's Wilberforce University, where she was awarded a B.A. in 1938. After graduating, she returned to Columbia and taught high school math while studying for a master's degree in psychology.

In the fall of 1941, the War Department began considering ways in which women could be used in support roles so that soldiers in noncombat specialties could be freed up for combat. The result was the creation of the Women's Auxiliary Army Corps (WAAC), which began recruiting by early 1942. One method used to recruit officer candidates was to ask colleges to compile lists of names for consideration. Wilberforce University submitted a list that included Charity Adams. At the time, Adams was enrolled at Ohio State University, working on a master's degree in vocational psychology. In June 1942, Adams submitted a WAAC application.

Within a month, Adams was sent to Fort Des Moines in Iowa as a member of the first WAAC officer candidate school class. Though Adams and the thirty-eight other African Americans trained alongside white officer candidates, they were surprised to find all non-training facilities, such as housing and seating in the mess hall, rigidly segregated. Adams graduated from basic training on August 30, 1942, and became the first African American woman to be commissioned in the WAAC. She was then appointed commander of the basic training company for enlisted females. Her administrative abilities quickly impressed the post's commanding officer.

Adams was soon promoted to captain and was assigned to the Fort Des Moines Plans and Training Section. Her new responsibilities included supervising and training recruits in such skills as office administration, photography, and radio operation. As part of her job, she made frequent trips to duty stations in other states, including Massachusetts, New Jersey, and North Carolina. She even had occasion to visit the newly completed Pentagon, located just outside Washington, D.C. By mid-1943, the WAAC was renamed the Women's Army Corps (WAC), and Adams had received a promotion to major.

Despite Adams's stellar record, neither she nor any other African American WACs were being posted overseas. Finally, in December 1944, Adams became the first African American WAC to be selected for overseas duty. She flew to Birmingham, England, to command the newly formed 6888th Central Postal Battalion. The all-black 850-woman unit was responsible for directing all incoming and outgoing mail for seven million U.S. Armed Forces personnel, Seabees, and American Red Cross workers serving in the European theater of operations. Several months of backed-up mail awaited the new arrivals. Adams quickly organized her command into five companies, then set the women into eight-hour, round-the-clock shifts. She also created lists to track units, sought means to differentiate between persons with similar names, and traced persons whose whereabouts were unknown. In May 1945, as the war in Europe ended, the 6888th was moved to Rouen, France, later relocating to Paris, where it continued its duties with reduced personnel.

Adams was relieved of command in December 1945 and sent back to the United States for discharge. At the separation center, Adams was promoted to lieutenant colonel just days before leaving the service. Such promotions were a courtesy to service personnel who were deemed deserving of elevated rank but had not been promoted on active duty. At separation, Adams was the highest-ranking African American officer in the WAC.

Within weeks of her discharge, Adams was back at Ohio State University, where she completed her master's program in 1946. She married Stanley A. Earley, a medical doctor, in 1949. Her postwar positions included registration officer at the Cleveland office of the Veterans Administration, personnel officer at both Tennessee A&I University in Nashville and Georgia State College in Savannah, and employment and personnel counselor for the YWCA in New York City. Earley recalled her wartime experiences in the 1989 book *One Woman's Army: A Black Officer Remembers the WAC.* In 1991 she received honorary doctorates from Wilberforce University and the University of Dayton. Earley died January 13, 2002, in Dayton, Ohio, her longtime home. She was eighty-three.

HENRY O. FLIPPER (1856–1940)

Lieutenant, First African American Graduate of the U.S. Military Academy. Henry Ossian Flipper was born enslaved in Thomasville, Georgia, on March 21, 1856. After the Civil War, his father moved the family to Atlanta. Flipper's father was a skilled shoemaker who created a successful business that allowed him to educate his two sons. In 1866, Flipper began attending schools established by the American Missionary Association and, in 1869, he started taking classes at Atlanta University. In 1873, he received an appointment to the U.S. Military Academy at West Point, New York. Though Flipper was the fifth African American to enter the academy, he was the first to withstand the intensely discriminatory practices of the institution, graduating fiftieth in a class of seventy-six in June 1877. He also has the distinction of being the first African American graduate of an engineering school in the United States. A year after graduation, his surprisingly restrained memoir of the experience was published as *The Colored Cadet at West Point.*

Flipper was commissioned a second lieutenant and received his assignment of choice: the African American Tenth U.S. Cavalry. The regiment was one of two units that Native Americans had nicknamed "buffalo soldiers." Flipper served at various frontier installations in the Southwest during the next several years, including Fort Sill in Oklahoma and Fort Concho in Texas. An incident that occurred at Fort Concho may have played a role in ending Flipper's military career a short time later: He was seen in the company of an attractive white woman. Racist white officers thereafter sought ways to remove him from the Army. In 1882, while serving as commissary officer at Fort Davis in Texas, Flipper was brought up on charges

Second Lieutenant Henry Ossian Flipper, c. 1870s. *Flipper in 1877 became the first African American to be graduated from the U.S. Military Academy at West Point, New York.* NATIONAL ARCHIVES AND RECORDS ADMINISTRATION

by his commander, who accused him of embezzling funds and of conduct unbecoming an officer and a gentleman. At the court-martial, Flipper was acquitted of the former charge, but was found guilty of the latter and was dismissed from the Army, as was required by the conviction.

Up until his death, Flipper protested his innocence, and he never stopped trying to clear his name. His battle went all the way to the halls of Congress, where he hoped a bill introduced by Wisconsin congressman Michael Griffin in 1898 would restore him to the duty, grade, rank, pay, and station in the Army he would have attained had he not been unjustifiably discharged. But Flipper's efforts to clear his name met with failure.

Flipper's dismissal from the Army did not cause him to fail in civilian life. He became a notable figure in the American Southwest and in Mexico, working as a civil and military engineer. He became much sought after by both private and governmental bodies as a surveyor, engineer, and consultant. He later became a translator of Spanish land grants. His *Spanish and Mexican Land Laws: New Spain and Mexico* was published by the Department of Justice in 1895. As his reputation spread, job opportunities increased. He served as consulting engineer to the builders of one of the earliest railroads in the Alaska Territory. He also worked for an oil company in Venezuela, and was an aide to the U.S. Senate Committee on Foreign Relations. In the course of his career, he befriended such prominent Washington officials as Senator A. B. Fall of New Mexico. When Fall became secretary of the interior, Flipper became his assistant until the infamous Teapot Dome scandal severed their relationship in the mid-1920s. Flipper returned to Atlanta at the close of his career, living with his brother until his death on May 3, 1940.

In 1978 Flipper's body was disinterred and moved from Atlanta to Thomasville, where he was given a full military funeral attended by nearly five hundred people. In 1997, the Texas Christian University Press published *Black Frontiersman: The Memoirs of Henry O. Flipper, First Black Graduate of West Point*, which was compiled and edited from Flipper's papers by Theodore D. Harris.

Though Flipper died before he could be absolved, others took up his fight. In 1976, descendants and supporters approached the Army Board for the Correction of Military Records on his behalf. Although the board stated that it did not have the authority to overturn Flipper's conviction, it found that the penalty had been "unduly harsh and unjust" and recommended that Flipper's dismissal be commuted to a good conduct discharge. Subsequently, with other appropriate approvals, the Department of the Army issued an honorable discharge in Flipper's name, dated June 30, 1882, the date he had been dismissed from the Army. On October 21, 1997, a private law firm filed an application of pardon with the secretary of the Army. After several months of review by U.S. Army and Department of Justice personnel, President Bill Clinton pardoned Flipper on February 19, 1999.

SAMUEL L. GRAVELY JR. (1922–2004)

First African American Admiral in the U.S. Navy. Samuel Lee Gravely Jr. was born in Richmond, Virginia, on June 4, 1922. He enrolled at Virginia Union University when the United States entered World War II, but quit school to enlist in the U.S. Naval Reserve on September 15, 1942. He received recruit training at the Great Lakes Naval Training Center in Illinois and further training at the Service School at Hampton Institute in Virginia. He then attended the Officer Training Camp at the University of California, Los Angeles, as well as the Pre-Midshipmen School in Asbury Park, New Jersey, and the Midshipmen School at Columbia University in New York City, where he trained from August to December 1944. The first African American graduate of a midshipman school, Gravely was commissioned an ensign in the U.S. Naval Reserve on December 14, 1944.

Gravely's initial assignment was as the assistant battalion commander at the Great Lakes Naval Training Center. Later, he became the first African American officer to be assigned shipboard duty when he held such titles as communications officer, electronics officer, executive officer, and personnel officer aboard the submarine chaser USS *PC-1264*. After a brief stint as communications watch officer with the Fleet Training Group in Norfolk, Virginia, Gravely was released from active duty on April 16, 1946. He then returned to college and received a B.A. in history from Virginia Union University in 1948. Though he had plans of becoming a teacher and coach, he took a job in Richmond as a railway postal clerk following graduation.

In 1948 Harry Truman's historic Executive Order 9981 forced the U.S. Armed Forces to integrate, and the military intensified its recruitment of African Americans. On August 30, 1949, Gravely returned to duty as assistant to the officer in charge of recruiting at the Naval Recruiting Station in Washington, D.C. After attending the Communications Officers Short Course, Gravely saw active duty aboard a pair of ships that engaged the enemy during the Korean War: first as radio operator on the battleship USS *Iowa* and later as communications officer on the cruiser USS *Toledo*. His reputation as a communications expert played a vital role in subsequent assignments. After more than a decade in the military, Gravely finally decided to make the Navy his career, and he formally transferred from the Naval Reserve to the regular Navy on August 16, 1955. From that point on, Gravely frequently shifted between land-based administrative positions and shipboard assignments, with occasional periods spent in training.

Steadily promoted through the ranks, Gravely was the touchstone for African American achievement in the Navy. He became the first African American officer to command a U.S. Navy ship on January 15, 1961, when he assumed temporary command of the destroyer USS *Theodore E. Chandler*. When he accepted command of the destroyer escort USS *Falgout* on January 31, 1962, he became the first African American to command a fighting ship. From August 1963 to June 1964, Gravely attended the senior course in naval warfare at the Naval War College in Newport, Rhode Island. He then became program manager for the National Command Center and the National Emergency Airborne Command Post at the Defense Communications Agency in Arlington, Virginia. In 1966, when Gravely guided the USS *Taussig* into direct offensive action during the Vietnam War, he became the first African American naval officer to command a U.S. warship under combat conditions since the Civil War.

On June 2, 1971, the day he was relieved of command of the guided-missile frigate USS *Jouett*, Gravely became the first African American to be promoted to the rank of rear admiral. In mid-July of that year, he was made commander of the Naval Communications Command and director of the Naval Communications Divisions under the chief of naval operations, dual posts he held for two years. In August 1975, Admiral Gravely assumed duties as commander of the Eleventh Naval District. On August 28, 1976, he was promoted to vice admiral, another first for an African American naval officer. The next month, he was placed in command of the U.S. Navy's Third Fleet, making him the first African American to command a U.S. Navy fleet. As commander of the Third Fleet, Gravely was in charge of one hundred ships and sixty thousand officers overseeing fifty million miles of ocean (approximately a quarter of the earth's surface). His final naval assignment was as director of the Defense Communications Agency, a post he held from September 15, 1978, until his retirement on August 1, 1980.

After retiring from the U.S. Navy, Gravely worked for several private-sector companies. He was senior corporate advisor for Potomac Systems Engineering, director of the Command Support Division for Automated Business Systems and Services, Inc., vice president for Navy programs at CTEC, and chairman of the Tredegar National Civil War Center Foundation Board. He also served on the Board of Directors for Draper Laboratory. In 1991, he was named an aide-de-camp to then-Virginia governor L. Douglas Wilder. In 2002, Gravely was among those honored for Dominion's Strong Men and Women: Excellence in Leadership series. He received an honorary doctor of law degree from his alma mater, Virginia Union University, in 1979. Shortly after suffering a massive stroke, Gravely died on October 22, 2004, at Bethesda Naval Hospital.

MARCELITE HARRIS (1943–)

Two-star General, U.S. Air Force. Marcelite Jordan was born on January 16, 1943, in Houston, Texas. She attended Houston public schools, graduating from Kashmere Gardens Junior-Senior High School in 1960. At Spelman College in Atlanta, Jordan studied speech and drama in hopes of becoming an actress. While she was in college, she took part in a USO tour of Germany and France. The experience gave her an opportunity to learn about the military, but it did not spark any career interest within her at the time. After earning a B.A. in 1964, she struggled to find stage work. She took a job with a Head Start program at a Houston YMCA, while studying law at night. Finding it difficult to maintain that pace, Jordan decided to look into other career options and chose the U.S. Air Force.

Jordan began at the Officer Training School at Lackland Air Force Base in Texas in September 1965 and was commissioned a second lieutenant on December 21 of that year. Her first assignment was as assistant director for administration with the Sixtieth Airlift Wing at California's Travis Air Force Base. In January 1967, she received her first promotion and transferred to Bitburg Air Base in West Germany. At Bitburg, Jordan served as administrative officer of the Seventy-first Tactical Missile Squadron for two years. Then, in May 1969, at the suggestion of a superior, she changed career tracks to maintenance. She was reassigned as maintenance analysis officer of the Thirty-sixth Tactical Fighter Wing, also based at Bitburg. As the first female Air Force officer in a "man's field," Jordan faced hostility from many of the men under her command. In order to gain credibility with the maintenance crews that she supervised, Jordan decided to learn more about aircraft engineering. She applied for the Aircraft Maintenance Officer Course, but was turned down at first. Jordan persisted and was later accepted to the eight-month course, graduating in May 1971.

Jordan's next assignment took her to Thailand's Korat Royal Thai Air Force Base, where she was maintenance supervisor of the Forty-ninth Tactical Fighter Squadron from August 1971 to May 1972. Despite initial resistance from the maintenance crews under her command, Jordan forged a cooperative relationship with her personnel. The result was a superb performance record for the aircraft piloted by a tactical fighter squadron flying sorties over Vietnam.

Jordan returned to the United States for a three-year stint at Travis Air Force Base in California before accepting a very visible assignment in Washington, D.C., in September 1975. For more than two and a half years, Jordan served as personnel staff officer and White House social aide during the Ford and Carter administrations. During the late 1970s, she was assigned to the U.S. Air Force Academy in Colorado Springs, Colorado, then to McConnell Air Force Base in Kansas. On November 29, 1980, while at McConnell, she married Maurice Anthony Harris. Harris's last assignment on foreign soil was a three-and-a half-year stretch as director of maintenance at the Pacific Air Forces Logistic Support Center at Kadena Air Base in Japan, starting in November 1982. While in Japan, Harris earned a B.S. in business management from the University of Maryland University College's Asian Division in 1986.

Returning to the United States in March 1986, Harris became deputy commander of maintenance at Keesler Air Force Base in Mississippi. She was promoted to full colonel on September 1, 1986. In December 1988 she was named commander of the 3300th Technical Training Wing at Keesler, becoming the third female to attain that level in the history of the U.S. Air Force. On May 1, 1991, while stationed at Tinker Air Force Base in Oklahoma, Harris became the first African American woman to attain the rank of brigadier general in the Air Force. Following a short stint at Randolph Air Force Base in Texas, she became director of maintenance at U.S. Air Force Headquarters, Washington, D.C., in September 1994.

On May 25, 1995, Harris became the first African American female to be promoted to the rank of major general. Her promotion not only made her the highest-ranking African American woman in the Air Force, but in the Department of Defense as a whole. As director of maintenance and deputy chief of staff for logistics, she was accountable for the maintenance operations of every Air Force installation, commanding a workforce of more than 125,000 and maintaining an aerospace weapons system inventory worth more than $260 billion. Harris retired from the U.S. Air Force on February 22, 1997.

After retiring, Harris settled in Merritt Island, Florida, and joined United Space Alliance, an aerospace industry firm, as Florida site director. She also served on the Advisory Committee on Women Veterans, a special fourteen-member panel that advised the secretary of veterans affairs.

Among the decorations awarded to Harris during her thirty-one-year career were a Legion of Merit with oak leaf cluster, a Bronze Star, a Meritorious Service Medal with three oak leaf clusters, an Air Force Commendation Medal with oak leaf cluster, a Presidential Unit Citation, an Air Force Outstanding Unit Award with "V" device and eight oak leaf clusters, a National Defense Service Medal with oak leaf cluster, and a Vietnam Service Medal with three oak leaf clusters. Among her many civilian honors are *Dollars and Sense* magazine's Most Prestigious Individual (1991), Journal Recording Publishing Company's Woman of Enterprise (1992), the National Federation of Black Women Business Owners' Black Woman of Courage (1995), the Ellis Island Medal of Honor (1996), the Women's International Center's Living Legacy Patriot Award (1998), and the University of Maryland University College's Distinguished Alumna Award (2000).

MICHELLE J. HOWARD (1960–)

Rear Admiral, U.S. Navy. Michelle Janine Howard grew up and attended school in Aurora, Colorado. After graduating from high school in 1978, she attended the Naval Academy in Annapolis, Maryland, graduating with a degree in math in 1982. She also received a master's degree in military science from the U.S. Army's Command and General Staff College in 1998.

Howard had tours of duty on the USS *Hunley* (1982–1985) and USS *Lexington* (1986–1987). While serving on the *Lexington*, she was awarded the Navy League Captain Winifred Collins Award. During Operation Desert Storm/Desert Shield in the early 1990s, Howard served as a chief engineer on the USS *Mount Hood.* She subsequently served on the USS *Flint*, and became the executive officer on the USS *Tortuga* in 1996. In 1999, Howard was appointed as commanding officer of the USS *Rushmore.* This was the first time that an African American woman had taken command of a ship in the U.S. Navy. In the early 2000s, Howard held several positions, including executive assistant to the Joint Staff director of operations in Washington and senior military assistant to the secretary of the Navy.

In April 2009, as a rear admiral, Howard emerged on the international stage. She had recently assumed command of the Expeditionary Strike Group and Combined Task Force 151 aboard the amphibious assault ship USS *Boxer.* The task force was charged with preventing and deterring piracy off of the horn of Africa. In early April, four Somali pirates hijacked the U.S.-flagged ship *Maersk Alabama* and took its captain hostage. After several days of negotiation, three of the pirates were killed by a Navy assault team, and the fourth was taken into custody to stand trial in the United States.

DANIEL JAMES JR. (1920–1978)

First African American Four-star General, U.S. Air Force. Daniel James Jr. was born on February 11, 1920, in Pensacola, Florida. The youngest boy in a large family, he grew up in a home with strict parents who stressed education, hard work, and honesty as means to success. At an early age, James borrowed the nickname "Chappie" from an older brother, a star athlete whom he idolized. James was educated in the private school run by his mother until secondary school age, when he attended Washington High. At Tuskegee Institute in Alabama, James worked for the college in exchange for credit hours. In 1941, two months before graduating, Daniel was expelled for fighting.

During his senior year of college, James enrolled in the Civilian Pilot Training Program. Indirectly sponsored by the War Department, the program operated at six African American colleges to train pilots under segregated conditions. James quickly earned his pilot's license and proved himself among the more capable flyers. After his expulsion from college, he was hired to train the first class of cadets selected for the "Tuskegee Experiment." Among the first student flyers was Benjamin O. Davis Jr., who would become the first African American Air Force general. Captivated by flying, James turned his attention away from academics to focus on becoming an Air Force officer. He applied for the Aviation Cadet Program and was accepted in January 1943. Graduating in July of that year, James was commissioned a second lieutenant in the U.S. Air Force. He was then assigned to the 617th Bombardment Squadron, 477th Bombardment Group at Selfridge Field, Michigan, for combat training on B-25 bombers. During World War II, however, racially motivated bureaucratic waffling kept most African American pilots from being assigned overseas, and James never left the United States.

In the fall of 1949, James received his first overseas assignment. He became flight leader of the Twelfth Fighter Bomber Squadron, Eighteenth Fighter Wing at Clark Air Base in the Philippines. During the Korean War, the Twelfth was based in Japan and Korea. Usually in F-51 Mustangs, James flew 101 combat missions during the war, most during the early days of the conflict. One such mission, in support of United Nations ground forces, resulted in James being awarded a Distinguished Flying Cross. Leading four bom

General Daniel "Chappie" James Jr., McGuire Air Force Base, NJ, 1975. *About to receive his fourth star, James indicates where it will be placed, as he becomes the first African American four-star general in any branch of the U.S. military.* AP PHOTO/JACK KANTHAL

bers through heavy enemy fire and low visibility on October 15, 1950, James was credited with personally killing more than one hundred enemy troops.

Following the Korea War, James was assigned to a base near Rome, New York, where a racist commanding officer boasted he would rid the unit of the African American flyer. Despite the forced integration of the military, which had begun several years earlier, racism still played a major role in duty assignments at the time. Subsequently, James was reassigned to Otis Air Force Base on Cape Cod, Massachusetts. Among his assignments at Otis, James was given command of the all-white 437th Fighter Interceptor Squadron in the Air Defense Command in April 1953. His loyal and supportive leadership style, as well as his insistence on excellence, earned his men's allegiance and his superiors' respect. In 1957, he graduated from the Air Command and Staff College at Maxwell Air Force Base in Alabama. His next assignment was at the Pentagon in the Air Defense Division, a job he admitted not particularly enjoying, though he understood the importance of it.

James spent the early 1960s at the Royal Air Force base at Bentwaters, England, where he held three assignments with the Eighty-first Fighter Wing. He returned to the United States in the fall of 1964 and held several command positions at Davis-Monthan Air Force Base in Arizona, during which time he was promoted to colonel. In 1966, during the early stages of the Vietnam War, James was assigned to the Eighth Tactical Fighter Wing at Thailand's Ubon Royal Thai Air Force Base. He flew seventy-eight missions over Vietnam in F-4C Phantom jets as deputy commander for operations, then vice commander, of the unit, popularly known as the "Wolf Pack."

James's next assignment brought him just fifty miles from his hometown to Florida's Eglin Air Force Base. After Eglin, he was sent out of the country once again, assuming command of the 7272nd Fighter Training Wing at Wheelus Air Base in Libya. His stay there was shortened, however, when Colonel Muammar Gadhafi deposed King Idris in 1969 and pushed for the closing of the base. Despite James's objections, the U.S. Embassy in Libya decided to shut Wheelus down. James then distinguished himself by overseeing an orderly removal of U.S. personnel and equipment from the base.

After returning to the United States, James was quickly promoted through the upper echelons of the U.S. Air Force. On March 31, 1970, he was sworn in as a deputy assistant of defense for public affairs by Secretary of Defense Melvin R. Laird. James quickly became a much-in-demand speaker, and the Pentagon eagerly used his talents by sending him around the country to make speeches in support of military policies. James was rewarded for his willingness to appear before the public, especially since his audiences sometimes used his appearances as a venue to demonstrate against the Vietnam War. He was promoted to brigadier general that summer, and his subsequent rise through the ranks proved exceedingly swift. He was made a major general on August 1, 1972, and less than a year later, on June 1, 1973, he was elevated to lieutenant general.

James left the Pentagon in August 1974 and became vice commander of Military Airlift Command the next month. He earned his final promotion on August 29, 1975, when he became the first African American to become a four-star general. The next day he took command of the North American Air Defense Command (NORAD), the binational defense force of 65,000 service personnel assigned the task of protecting the United States and Canada from surprise nuclear attack, and NORAD's American subunit, the U.S. Air Force Aerospace Defense Command, both of which are headquartered at Colorado Springs, Colorado. In September 1977, James suffered a heart attack. After thirty-five years of service, he retired from the U.S. Air Force on January 26, 1978. One month later, on February 25, 1978, he suffered a second, fatal heart attack. James was buried with highest military honors at Arlington National Cemetery in Virginia.

One of the most highly decorated servicemen in Air Force history, among the awards James received were a Distinguished Service Medal with oak leaf cluster, a Legion of Merit with oak leaf cluster, a Distinguished Flying Cross with two oak leaf clusters, a Meritorious Service Medal, an Air Medal with thirteen oak leaf clusters, an American Defense Service Medal, an American Campaign Medal, a World War II Victory Medal, a Korean Service Medal with four service stars, and a Vietnam Service Medal with four service stars. James also received awards from an astounding number of civilian organizations, including the Arnold Air Society, the Phoenix Urban League, Kappa Alpha Psi Fraternity, the American Legion, the Veterans of Foreign Wars, the Capital Press Club, and the United Negro College Fund, to name a few. He also received honorary degrees from the University of West Florida, the University of Akron, Virginia State College, Delaware State College, and St. Louis University.

HENRY JOHNSON (c. 1897–1929)

Sergeant, 369th Infantry Regiment, Ninety-third Division, U.S. Army. Henry Johnson was born around 1897 in Winston-Salem, North Carolina, and grew up in Albany, New York. He enlisted in the Army on June 5, 1917, shortly after the United States entered World War I. He was mustered into Company C, Fifteenth National

Guard of New York (later renamed the 369th Infantry Regiment), as a private on July 25. The unit received its training at Camp Wadsworth in Spartanburg, South Carolina.

The 369th landed in Brest, France, on January 1, 1918. In March, the 369th was attached to the Sixteenth Division of the French Army, making it the first African American unit to reach the war zone. According to his muster roll, Johnson was promoted to the rank of sergeant on May 1. Several days later, U.S. troops captured a German-held bridge near the Aisne River, and Johnson's unit was assigned to guard it. In the early morning hours of May 14, a force of about thirty-two Germans tried to retake the bridge. Johnson and fellow soldier Needham Roberts were on sentry duty at the time, armed with pistols and a few hand grenades. The two groups exchanged fire, and Johnson was wounded three times, while Roberts was injured twice. After the pair ran out of ammunition, the Germans rushed them, capturing Roberts. Johnson pulled a bolo knife and, along with the butt of his pistol, fought hand-to-hand, rescuing his badly wounded compatriot. The startled Germans retreated, preventing them from launching a surprise attack that would likely have inflicted heavy casualties on the regiment. When the skirmish was over, Johnson was credited with killing at least four Germans and wounding some ten others.

Johnson was hospitalized for several weeks with serious wounds to his back, left arm, face, and feet, most of which were inflicted by knives or bayonets. For their heroism, the French government awarded him and Roberts the Croix de Guerre with gold leaf. In the process, they became the first Americans to receive the French medal for individual heroism in combat. Johnson was cited by the French as a "magnificent example of courage and energy." The U.S. Army did not award Johnson any decoration for his part in the incident—not even a Purple Heart.

Despite his injuries, Johnson received no disability allowance when he was discharged from the Army on February 14, 1919. On his return to Albany, he received a hero's welcome. New York governor Alfred E. Smith and other state officials greeted Johnson's arrival at the Albany train station with a homecoming reception. For a while after the war, Johnson's celebrity allowed him to tour the country promoting the sale of Liberty Bonds. Afterward, however, his injuries proved too disabling for him to return to regular work. Johnson died in poverty at Walter Reed Army Hospital in Washington, D.C., on July 2, 1929. He was buried with full military honors in Arlington National Cemetery in Virginia.

HAZEL W. JOHNSON-BROWN (1927–)

First Female African American Brigadier General, U.S. Army. Hazel Winifred Johnson was born on October 10, 1927, in West Chester, Pennsylvania. She grew up on a farm near Malvern in Chester County and attended high school in nearby Berwyn. She received her registered nurse diploma in New York City at Harlem Hospital's School of Nursing in 1950 and enlisted in the U.S. Army Nurse Corps in 1955. Johnson took advantage of civilian educational opportunities to rapidly advance through the ranks of the nurse corps. She earned a bachelor's degree in nursing from Villanova University in 1959, and was commissioned as a second lieutenant by direct appointment on May 11, 1960. Three years later, she earned a master's degree in nursing education from Teachers College, Columbia University, in New York City.

Johnson was a staff member of the U.S. Medical Research and Development Command in Washington, D.C., from 1967 to 1973, and dean of the Walter Reed Army Institute of Nursing at the famed Walter Reed Army Medical Center, also in Washington, D.C., from 1976 to 1978. She earned a Ph.D. in educational administration from Catholic University of America in 1978 before beginning a brief assignment as chief nurse with the U.S. Army Medical Command in Korea. On September 1, 1979, Johnson became the first African American woman in U.S. military history to advance to the rank of brigadier general. At that time, she was also made chief of the Army Nurse Corps, Office of the Surgeon General in Washington, D.C. She held that post until August 31, 1983, when she retired from the U.S. Army. She married David Brown shortly before her retirement.

Johnson-Brown served as director of the government affairs division of the American Nursing Association from 1983 until 1986, when she joined the faculty of Virginia's George Mason University as a professor of nursing. She is now professor emerita of nursing at that institution, where she once chaired the college's Board of Advisors and advised doctoral candidates. She also served as a member of the Villanova University Board of Trustees. Among her military decorations are a Distinguished Service Medal, a Legion of Merit, a Meritorious Service Medal, and an Army Commendation Medal with oak leaf cluster. In 1997, Johnson-Brown received an honorary degree from Long Island University's Brooklyn Campus.

DORIS (DORIE) MILLER (1919–1943)

Mess Attendant First Class, U.S. Navy. The son of sharecroppers, Doris Miller was born on a farm near Waco, Texas, on October 12, 1919. Working in the fields with his parents, Miller grew into a solidly built young man.

He became a star fullback on the football team at Waco's Moore High School. At nineteen years old, Miller enlisted in the U.S. Navy as a messman, the only job open to African American naval recruits at the time.

Miller was assigned to the battleship USS *West Virginia* as a mess attendant second class. He was nearing the end of his first hitch when, on December 7, 1941, he was thrust into one of the most important events in U.S. history: Japan's surprise attack on the U.S. naval base at Pearl Harbor on Oahu Island in Hawaii. At 7:55 a.m. on that typically quiet Sunday morning, Miller was below deck collecting laundry. Suddenly, the crew heard a mid-ship explosion. The blast knocked Miller down. Sirens soon called the crew to their battle stations. Miller arrived on deck to witness Japanese planes in full attack on the U.S. Pacific Fleet. Bombing runs were supplemented by machine-gun fire as Japanese aircraft swooped down on virtually undefended ships. In the confusion, sailors ran in all directions, many of them jumping overboard to avoid strafing runs by the enemy flyers. Amid walls of smoke and flame, Miller made his way to his assigned post on the signal bridge. When he arrived, Miller found the ship's commander lying on deck, bleeding from his stomach and chest. He dragged the mortally wounded officer out of direct fire to a place where a medic and other sailors attempted to treat him. Miller returned to the bridge, where he spotted an unmanned machine gun. Without any prior weaponry training, Miller started firing the antiaircraft gun. He brought down four Japanese planes before exhausting the gun's ammunition and being ordered to abandon the sinking ship.

"above and beyond the call of duty"
DORIE MILLER
Received the Navy Cross
at Pearl Harbor, May 27, 1942

Doris "Dorie" Miller, U.S. Navy Mess Attendant Third Class, c. 1942. *During the attack on Pearl Harbor, Miller—with no weaponry training—shot down four Japanese planes. In light of his heroism, he received the Navy Cross and his photo appeared in this recruiting poster.* **HULTON ARCHIVE/GETTY IMAGES**

For his heroism, Miller was awarded the Navy Cross, which was conferred on him by the commander in chief of the Pacific Fleet, Admiral Chester W. Nimitz. Miller was commended for "distinguished devotion to duty, extreme courage, and disregard of his personal safety during attack." He also received a Purple Heart and was subsequently promoted to mess attendant first class.

Miller became the first African American hero of the war and traveled around the nation to promote the sale of war bonds. After that tour of duty ended, he was sent to Bremerton, Washington, to qualify as a cook. Though he had shown enormous ability as a gunner, Navy policy still restricted African Americans to the Stewards Branch. Miller later served as a mess attendant on the light aircraft carrier USS *Liscome Bay.* A Japanese submarine torpedoed the vessel on November 24, 1943. The resulting explosion killed most of the crew, including Miller, before the vessel sank in the South Pacific.

After the war, legislation was introduced on two occasions to posthumously award Miller the Congressional Medal of Honor for his Pearl Harbor heroics, but it was defeated both times. Nevertheless, the Navy honored Miller in succeeding years by naming several things after him, most notably, the destroyer escort USS *Miller,* which was christened in 1973.

FRANK E. PETERSEN (1932–)

First African American General in the U.S. Marine Corps. Frank Emmanuel Petersen Jr. was born March 2, 1932, in Topeka, Kansas, where he attended public schools and graduated from Topeka High School in 1949. He attended Topeka's Washburn University for a year before dropping out to enlist in the U.S. Navy Reserve in June 1950 as an apprentice seaman. He also served as an electronics technician. While attending the Navy's electronics school, he applied for admission to the Naval Aviation Cadet Program. He was accepted, and, during flight training at the U.S. Naval Air Station in Pensacola, Florida, he applied for a commission in the U.S. Marine

Corps. Petersen earned his wings and accepted a second lieutenant's commission in the Corps on October 22, 1952, becoming the branch's first African American aviator.

Petersen received further training at the Marine Corps Air Station El Toro in Santa Ana, California, before being sent to Korea in 1953. He flew a total of sixty-four combat missions during the latter stages of the Korean War and built a reputation as a superb fighter pilot. In July 1954, he returned to the Marine Corps' Santa Ana facility, where he remained until January 1960. During the 1960s and 1970s, Petersen took advantage of many civilian and military educational opportunities. He twice attended George Washington University, where he earned a B.S. in 1967 and an M.S. in 1973. He also attended several service schools, including the Marine Corps Amphibious Assault School, the Aviation Safety Officers' Course, and the National War College. Petersen has the distinction of being the first African American corpsman to attend the latter school.

At the height of the Vietnam War, Petersen became the first African American officer to command a squadron in the U.S. Navy or Marine Corps. In June 1968, he took command of VMF-314, Marine Aircraft Group 13, Republic of Vietnam. The unit, popularly known as the "Black Knights," excelled with Petersen as commander, being named the most outstanding fighter squadron in the entire Marine Corps during the year he was in charge. Petersen was also a fighter pilot and flew more than two hundred missions in F-4 Phantom jets.

Petersen became the first African American to reach the rank of brigadier general in the U.S. Marine Corps in February 1979. While assigned to Marine Corps headquarters in Washington, D.C., during the early to mid-1980s, he was promoted to major general and then lieutenant general. Starting in 1985, Petersen served as senior ranking pilot in the U.S. Navy and U.S. Marine Corps, and was the senior pilot of the entire U.S. Armed Forces from 1986 until his retirement on August 1, 1988. In all, he flew more than 350 combat missions covering 4,000 hours in the air.

In 1989 Petersen became vice president of Corporate Aviation at DuPont de Nemours, Inc., where he remained for a decade before becoming an independent corporate consultant. Petersen's affiliations with boards and organizations are numerous. Among them are the Tuskegee Airmen, the National Marrow Donor Foundation (for which he served as board chair from 1998 to 2000), the National Aviation Research and Education Foundation, the Higher Education Assistance Foundation, Opportunity Skyway, the Institute for the Study of American Wars, the Montford Point Marines Association, the Educational Credit Management

Frank E. Petersen, U.S. Marine Corps, c. 1968. *Petersen, who retired in 1988 with the rank of lieutenant general, became, in 1979, the first African American general in the Marines.* PICTORIAL PARADE/ARCHIVE PHOTOS/GETTY IMAGES

Corporation, and Business Executives for National Security. Petersen is also a frequent public speaker and lecturer. In 1998, *Into the Tiger's Jaw: America's First Black Marine Aviator*, Petersen's autobiography (written with assistance from J. Alfred Phelps), was published.

Petersen is a recipient of more than twenty individual medals for combat valor, including a Distinguished Flying Cross, an Air Medal with silver star, a Meritorious Service Medal, a Legion of Merit with Combat V, a Navy Commendation Medal with Combat V, a National Defense Service Medal with bronze star, an Air Force Commendation Medal, and a Purple Heart.

COLIN L. POWELL (1937–)

General, First African American Chairman of the Joint Chiefs of Staff. Colin Luther Powell was born in New York City on April 5, 1937, and graduated from Morris

High School in the South Bronx in 1954. In 1958, he received a B.S. in geology from City College of New York.

On June 9, 1958, Powell was commissioned a second lieutenant in the U.S. Army. He attended infantry officers basic training, as well as the airborne and ranger schools at Fort Benning in Georgia, before receiving his first regular duty assignment. In 1959, he was sent to West Germany, where he became a platoon leader, executive officer, and rifle company commander during his three-year stay. In 1962, he was assigned as a military advisor to a South Vietnamese infantry battalion. In the second year of that tour, he was wounded by a Vietcong booby trap and was awarded a Purple Heart. Powell returned to Vietnam in 1968 as an infantry officer, serving in such capacities as battalion executive officer and division operations officer. That tour ended prematurely when he was injured in a helicopter crash in which he rescued two fellow soldiers from the burning wreckage.

After returning to the United States, Powell enrolled in the M.B.A. program at George Washington University and graduated in 1971. In 1972, he was named a White House fellow and served as assistant to the deputy director of the Office of Management and Budget. From 1973 to 1975, he commanded the First Battalion, Thirty-second Infantry in South Korea. Powell was already receiving relatively high-profile assignments before graduating from the National War College in June 1976, but from that point on his career accelerated. He next commanded the Second Brigade, 101st Airborne Division (Air Assault) at Fort Campbell, Kentucky, from 1976 to 1977. Several appointments in Washington, D.C., followed. He was executive to the special assistant to the secretary and deputy secretary of defense starting in 1977, executive assistant to the secretary of energy for several months in 1979, and senior military assistant to the deputy secretary of defense later that year. Powell was promoted to brigadier general on June 1, 1979.

In April 1989, he was promoted to four-star general. In August of that year, Powell was named chairman of the Joint Chiefs of Staff, the highest military post in the United States. Powell not only became the first African American in U.S. Armed Forces history to hold that title, but also the youngest. From that position, Powell received international recognition as one of the chief architects of the successful 1989 assault on Panamanian dictator Manuel Noriega and of the 1991 Persian Gulf War against Iraq. Both military actions achieved swift and thorough victories with minimal U.S. casualties. Powell retired from the U.S. Army on September 30, 1993.

The public acclaim Powell received for those one-sided military victories opened to him the possibility of a future in nationally elected political office. Powell wrote his memoir, *My American Journey*, and embarked on a nationwide tour to promote the book in 1995. During the tour, there was widespread speculation that he would seek the nomination for president the next year. On November 9, 1995, however, Powell held a press conference to announce that he would not enter the presidential race. The decision not to seek the office surprised many who considered Powell a strong potential candidate.

Shying away from the political arena, Powell turned his attention to public-service activities. In 1996, he was named to the Board of Trustees of Howard University. Then, in April 1997, Powell helped found America's Promise Alliance, and became its first chairman. The nonprofit organization, based in Arlington, Virginia, works to improve the lives of at-risk youths by increasing their employability. After some initial difficulties, Powell was able to get the organization running smoothly. Powell's wife Alma became chair of the organization's Board of Directors in 2004.

Powell stepped back into the national spotlight on July 31, 2000, when he delivered a keynote address at the Republican National Convention in Philadelphia. In what was considered a highlight of the convention, Powell endorsed Republican presidential candidate George W. Bush, saying that he believed the candidate "can help bridge our racial divides." Later that year, on December 16, 2000, President-elect Bush nominated Powell to become the sixty-fifth secretary of state. Following a unanimous confirmation by the U.S. Senate, Powell was sworn in on January 20, 2001. He is the first African American to hold that post. As secretary of state, he was highly visible, especially in relation to the continuing war on terrorism that began in September 2001.

Powell was successful in rallying other nations to the war on terrorism and enforcing the United Nations' resolutions for the disarming of Iraq. With the reelection of President Bush, Powell announced his resignation on November 15, 2004. Even though his tenure was marked by disagreements with administrators over policy, Powell was considered an effective and eloquent spokesman. He was well respected and admired all over the world, which made many encourage him to run for office. So far, he has not pursued that path.

Once leaving his post, Powell returned to the private sector. In July 2005 he became a limited partner with Kleiner Perkins Culfield & Byers, a venture capital firm, and in May 2006 he succeeded Henry Kissinger and became the eighth chairman of the Eisenhower Fellowship Program. He has also been active with the Colin Powell Center for Policy Studies, established in his honor in 1997 at his alma mater, the City College of New York. He also served as a member of the Board of Directors of the United Negro College Fund, the Board of Directors of the Boys and Girls Clubs of America, and the Advisory Board of the Children's Health Fund, among others.

General Colin L. Powell, Chairman of the Joint Chiefs of Staff, Press Briefing on the Persian Gulf War, 1991. *In 1989 President George H. W. Bush appointed Powell chairman of the Joint Chiefs of Staff, making him the first African American to hold this post, the highest in the U.S. military. Powell was one of the chief architects of the Persian Gulf War against Iraq, a swift and thorough victory with minimal U.S. casualties.* TERRY ASHE/TIME LIFE PICTURES/GETTY IMAGES

During his tenure in the military, Powell was the recipient of numerous decorations, including a Purple Heart, a Bronze Star, a Legion of Merit with oak leaf cluster, a Soldier's Medal, an Air Medal, a Distinguished Service Medal, a Defense Superior Service Medal, a Joint Service Commendation Medal, and an Army Commendation Medal. He has received many civilian honors as well, including two Presidential Medals of Freedom, the President's Citizens Medal, the Congressional Gold Medal, the Secretary of State Distinguished Service Medal, the Secretary of Energy Distinguished Service Medal, and the Ronald Reagan Freedom Award. Powell has also received honorary degrees from universities and colleges across the nation, and several schools and other institutions have been named in his honor.

J. PAUL REASON (1943–)

First African American Four-star Admiral, U.S. Navy. Joseph Paul Reason was born on March 22, 1943, in Washington, D.C., where he attended primary and secondary school. After high school, he attended Howard University for three years before receiving a nomination to the U.S. Naval Academy from Michigan congressman Charles Diggs.

While at the Naval Academy, Reason applied to the Navy's nuclear propulsion program, run by Vice Admiral Hyman G. Rickover, "father" of the nuclear submarine. Rickover interviewed Reason and accepted him into the program. Rickover, the first Jewish admiral, took a special interest in Reason as an officer, monitoring Reason's progress from behind the scenes and ensuring that he received fair treatment during his career. Reason's initial assignment was on the destroyer escort USS *J.D. Blackwood*, but after completing the nuclear propulsion program in 1968, he transferred to the nuclear-powered missile cruiser USS *Truxtun*. In 1970, he earned a master's degree in computer systems management.

In 1971, Reason began a four-year stint on the nuclear-powered aircraft carrier USS *Enterprise*, during which he was twice deployed to the Southeast Asia and

Indian Ocean region during the Vietnam War. He rejoined the USS *Truxtun* in 1975 as the combat systems officer. From there, he became an assignment officer at the Bureau of Naval Personnel. In late 1976, Reason was named naval aide to the White House for the Gerald Ford administration, a position he kept after Jimmy Carter assumed the presidency in January 1977. In 1979, Reason was assigned to the USS *Mississippi* as the ship's executive officer. After a six-year stay aboard that ship, Reason was given command of his own ship, the USS *Coontz*, in 1985. Shortly afterward, he became commander of a nuclear-powered guided-missile cruiser, the USS *Bainbridge*.

Between 1986 and 1988, Reason served as commander of Naval Base Seattle, where he was responsible for all naval activities in Oregon, Washington, and Alaska. His next assignment put him in command of Cruiser-Destroyer Group One, which he led from 1988 to 1994. During that time, he also commanded Battle Group Romeo through operations in the Pacific and Indian Oceans, as well as in the Persian Gulf. Reason was promoted to vice admiral in early 1994 and put in charge of the Naval Surface Force of the U.S. Atlantic Fleet. In August of that year, he was made deputy chief of naval operations for plans, policy, and operations, a post he held for two years.

In May 1996, President Bill Clinton nominated Reason for a promotion and assignment as commander in chief of the U.S. Atlantic Fleet, based in Norfolk, Virginia. His promotion in December 1996 made him the U.S. Navy's first African American four-star admiral. As chief of the Atlantic Fleet, Reason commanded roughly half of the U.S. Navy, or more than 124,000 service personnel. He oversaw an annual budget of $19.5 billion and the operations of 195 warships and 1,357 aircraft based at eighteen major shore facilities. Reason retired from active duty in November 1999.

Following his retirement from the military, Reason became president and chief operating officer of Metro Machine Corporation of Norfolk, Virginia. In January 2000, he joined NASA's Aerospace Safety Advisory Panel as a consultant. Reason has also served on the boards of Norfolk Southern, Amgen, and Walmart.

Among Reason's many military decorations are a Distinguished Service Medal, a Legion of Merit, a Navy Commendation Medal, a Venezuelan Almirante Luis Brion Medal, a National Defense Service Medal, an Armed Forces Expeditionary Medal, a Republic of Vietnam Honor Medal, a Vietnam Service Medal, a Sea Service Deployment Ribbon, and a Republic of Vietnam Campaign Medal. In 1998, Reason was among those honored for Dominion's Strong Men and Women: Excellence in Leadership series.

ROSCOE ROBINSON JR. (1928–1993)

First African American Four-star General in the U.S. Army. Roscoe Robinson Jr. was born on October 28, 1928, in St. Louis, Missouri, where he graduated from Charles Sumner High School. He received an appointment to the U.S. Military Academy at West Point, New York, and graduated with a B.S. in military engineering in 1951.

On June 1, 1951, Robinson was commissioned a second lieutenant in the U.S. Army. He attended the Associate Infantry Officer Course and the Basic Airborne Course at Fort Benning, Georgia, before joining the Eleventh Airborne Division at Fort Campbell, Kentucky. In October 1952, he was assigned to the Thirty-first Infantry Regiment, Seventh Infantry Division in Korea. During the Korean War, his unit saw combat action and Robinson received a bronze star for bravery as commander of a rifle company. Among his assignments in the late 1950s was a tour with the U.S. military mission to Liberia.

From 1965 to 1967, Robinson was the personnel management officer of the Infantry Branch of the Officer Personnel Management Directorate in the Office of Personnel Operations for the U.S. Army in Washington, D.C. Starting in 1968, Robinson commanded the Second Battalion, Seventh Cavalry, the historic African American unit that was part of the regular Army in 1866 as Company B, Seventh Cavalry. The unit, part of the First Cavalry Division (Airmobile), U.S. Army Pacific, Vietnam, engaged in fighting during the war, with Robinson being awarded a silver star for valor. In the early 1970s, Robinson served with the U.S. Pacific Command in Hawaii, including a period of service as executive to the chief of staff.

In addition to battlefield heroics, Robinson helped his career by expanding his education. He earned a master's degree in international affairs from the University of Pittsburgh and received further military training at the U.S. Army Command and General Staff College at Fort Leavenworth, Kansas, and at the National War College in Washington, D.C.

In 1972 Robinson became commanding officer of the Second Brigade, Eighty-second Airborne Division at Fort Bragg in North Carolina. He was promoted to the rank of brigadier general on July 1, 1973, and was made deputy commander of the U.S. Army Garrison, Okinawa Base Command, in Japan. Robinson became a two-star general on July 1, 1976, and, in November of that year, he returned to Fort Bragg to become commanding general of the Eighty-second Airborne Division. In 1978, he was made deputy chief of staff for operations, U.S. Army Europe and the Seventh Army. On June 1, 1980, he was promoted to lieutenant general and became commanding general of the U.S. Army, Japan IX Corps. Robinson became the first African American four-star general in the history of the U.S. Army and the second in the U.S. Armed Forces on August 30, 1982. From 1982 to 1985, he served as the U.S. representative to the North Atlantic Treaty Organization (NATO), becoming the nation's first African American to serve in that capacity. Robinson retired from active military service in 1985.

After his retirement from the Army, Robinson served on the boards of several companies, including Comsat, Giant Food, Metropolitan Life, and the parent company of Northwest Airlines. In 1987, he was asked to oversee the work of a panel tasked with reviewing the Korean War performance records of certain African American Army units that had been criticized at the time. On July 22, 1993, Robinson died of leukemia at the Walter Reed Army Medical Center in Washington, D.C. He is buried in Arlington National Cemetery in Arlington, Virginia.

During his thirty-four-year career, Robinson was the recipient of numerous military awards, including a Silver Star with oak leaf cluster, a Legion of Merit with two oak leaf clusters, a Distinguished Flying Cross, a Bronze Star, ten Air Medals, a Defense Distinguished Service Medal, and an Army Commendation Medal.

RODERICK K. von LIPSEY (1959–)

Fighter Pilot, U.S. Marine Corps. Roderick K. von Lipsey was born on January 13, 1959, in Philadelphia, Pennsylvania. Beginning in third grade, he was educated in private schools, first at Norwood Academy, then at La Salle College High School, where he graduated in 1976. He attended the U.S. Naval Academy in Annapolis, Maryland, majoring in English literature. After graduating, von Lipsey joined the U.S. Marine Corps and was commissioned a second lieutenant in May 1980.

In January 1981, after completing basic Marine Corps training, von Lipsey went to Pensacola, Florida, and Kingsville, Texas, to learn to fly aircraft that would earn him the "naval aviator" designation. Then, starting in September 1982, he spent an additional six months at the Marine Corps base at Yuma, Arizona, to become combat ready on the F-4 Phantom fighter jet.

In 1983 von Lipsey was assigned to Fort Beaufort, South Carolina, to gain experience in aircraft maintenance and maintenance quality assurance. The following year, he became the officer in charge of aircraft maintenance for F-4 Phantoms at the base. Von Lipsey began training on the F/A-18 Hornet fighter jet in 1985. In 1986, he was deployed to NATO exercises in Europe and the Mediterranean, for which he was awarded a Navy Commendation Medal for his performance of logistics responsibilities. In January 1987, von Lipsey was sent to the prestigious Navy Fighter Weapons School at Naval Station Miramar in California. Informally known as TOPGUN, the grueling six-week training program hones the technique of experienced fighter pilots and teaches them how to use newly developed skills to instruct others. In 1989, von Lipsey was stationed at the Marine Fighter Attack Squadron at Kaneohe Bay, Hawaii. Also in 1989, he completed work on a master of arts degree in international affairs from the Catholic University of America.

When Iraq invaded Kuwait on August 2, 1990, von Lipsey was sent to Saudi Arabia to take part in Operation Desert Shield. While in the Middle East, von Lipsey joined Marine Fighter/Attack Squadron 235. On January 20, 1991, at the start of Operation Desert Storm, von Lipsey led an attack of thirty-five aircraft from the Third Marine Aircraft Wing. The daring 600-mile journey to a secret air base in eastern Iraq resulted in the demolition of the base's maintenance and repair hangars, as well as the network of railroad tracks that were its supply lines. All of the planes under von Lipsey's command returned safely. For his meritorious service in the execution of this highly successful mission, he was awarded the Distinguished Flying Cross. That attack was just one of more than forty sorties flown by von Lipsey during the Gulf War.

Following his return from the Middle East in 1991, von Lipsey was chosen as one of two aides-de-camp to the chairman of the Joint Chiefs of Staff, General Colin L. Powell. Initially the junior aide, and later the senior, von Lipsey helped orchestrate the general's busy travel schedule, which included trips to such countries as Belgium, Czechoslovakia, Hungary, Jamaica, Poland, and Somalia. He remained in that assignment until 1993, when he was awarded a White House fellowship, serving as a special assistant in the areas of foreign and security policy to White House chief of staff Thomas F. McLarty III. Often traveling on Air Force One as a member of President Clinton's entourage, von Lipsey provided national security updates and background information for McLarty at high-level meetings with foreign political leaders. Von Lipsey was awarded a second fellowship in 1994 with the Council on Foreign Relations. In December of that year, von Lipsey was honored by *Time* magazine as one of America's most promising leaders under forty years old in a special report titled "Fifty for the Future."

When the fellowship ended in mid-1995, von Lipsey was assigned to Marine Corps Air Squadron El Toro, based in Santa Ana, California. He received a promotion to lieutenant colonel shortly afterward. During this period, he also edited and contributed to the book *Breaking the Cycle: A Framework for Conflict Intervention* (1997), which presented new ways of dealing with countries plagued by violent intergroup disputes. In 1997 von Lipsey was selected by the Rockefeller Foundation for its first cohort of Next Generation Leadership Fellows. Also in 1997, he became planning officer at Marine Corps Headquarters, then in 1998 he was assigned to the National Security Council as director for defense policy and arms control. He remained in that post through 1999, when he retired from the U.S. Marine Corps after twenty years of service.

In 2000 von Lipsey was named vice president and chief operating officer for Investment Management Services at Goldman Sachs Private Wealth Management in Washington, D.C. He has served on the boards of the Atlantic Council of the United States, the Aspen Institute Berlin, the leadership organization Public Allies, and the New York City Outward Bound Center. He has also been a member of the Council on Foreign Relations, the International Institute for Strategic Studies, and the Distinguished Flying Cross Society.

In addition to the Distinguished Flying Cross with Combat V, von Lipsey has received a Defense Meritorious Service Medal, a Single Mission Air Medal with Combat V, a Strike/Flight Air Medal with Numeral 4, a Joint Service Commendation Medal, and two Navy Commendation Medals.

Awards and Honors

This appendix lists selected awards and honors presented to African Americans artists, scholars, educators, journalists, public servants, civil rights activists, soldiers, athletes, and other achievers. The list is divided into the following primary sections: Public Service and Military Awards; Arts and Letters Awards and Honors; African American Olympic Medalists; Other Sports Awards, and Miscellaneous Awards and Honors.

PUBLIC SERVICE AND MILITARY AWARDS

PRESIDENTIAL MEDAL OF FREEDOM

1963: Marian Anderson; Ralph J. Bunche

1964: Leontyne Price; A. Philip Randolph

1969: Duke Ellington; Ralph Ellison; Roy Wilkins; Whitney M. Young Jr.

1976: Jesse Owens

1977: Martin Luther King Jr. (posthumous)

1980: Clarence M. Mitchell Jr.

1981: James Hubert "Eubie" Blake; Andrew Young

1983: James Cheek; Mabel Mercer

1984: Jackie Robinson (posthumous)

1985: Count Basie (posthumous); Jerome "Brud" Holland (posthumous)

1987: Frederick D. Patterson

1988: Pearl Bailey

1991: Colin L. Powell

1992: Ella Fitzgerald

1993: Arthur Ashe (posthumous); Thurgood Marshall (posthumous); Colin L. Powell

1994: Dorothy I. Height; Barbara Jordan

1995: William T. Coleman Jr.; John Hope Franklin; A. Leon Higginbotham Jr.

1996: John H. Johnson; Rosa Parks

1998: James L. Farmer Jr.

2000: Marian Wright Edelman; Jesse Jackson Sr.; Gardner Taylor

2002: Hank Aaron; Bill Cosby

2003: Roberto Clemente (posthumous)

2004: Edward W. Brooke

2005: Muhammad Ali; Aretha Franklin; Frank Robinson

2006: B. B. King; Norman C. Francis; John "Buck" O'Neil (posthumous)

2007: Benjamin L. Hooks

2008: Benjamin S. Carson

2009: Joseph E. Lowery; Sidney Poitier

CONGRESSIONAL GOLD MEDAL

1977: Marian Anderson

1982: Joe Louis

1984: Roy Wilkins

1988: Jesse Owens

1991: Colin L. Powell

1998: "Little Rock Nine": Jean Brown Trickey, Carlotta Walls LaNier, Melba Patillo Beals, Terrence Roberts, Gloria Ray Karlmark, Thelma Mothershed Wair, Ernest Green, Elizabeth Eckford, and Jefferson Thomas

1999: Rosa Parks

2003: Dorothy I. Height

2004: Martin Luther King Jr. and Coretta Scott King

2005: Jackie Robinson

2006: Tuskegee Airmen

2007: Edward W. Brooke

CONGRESSIONAL MEDAL OF HONOR: CIVIL WAR (1861–1865)

U.S. Army

William H. Barnes, Private, Company C, Thirty-eighth U.S. Colored Troops

Powhatan Beaty, First Sergeant, Company G, Fifth U.S. Colored Troops

James H. Bronson, First Sergeant, Company D, Fifth U.S. Colored Troops

William H. Carney, Sergeant, Company C, Fifty-fourth Massachusetts Infantry, U.S. Colored Troops

Decatur Dorsey, Sergeant, Company B, Thirty-ninth U.S. Colored Troops

Christian A. Fleetwood, Sergeant Major, Fourth U.S. Colored Troops

James Gardiner, Private, Company 1, Thirty-sixth U.S. Colored Troops

James H. Harris, Sergeant, Company B, Thirty-eighth U.S. Colored Troops

Thomas R. Hawkins, Sergeant Major, Sixth U.S. Colored Troops

Alfred B. Hilton, Sergeant, Company H, Fourth U.S. Colored Troops

Milton M. Holland, Sergeant, Fifth U.S. Colored Troops

Alexander Kelly, First Sergeant, Company F, Sixth U.S. Colored Troops

Robert Pinn, First Sergeant, Company I, Fifth U.S. Colored Troops

Edward Radcliff, First Sergeant, Company C, Thirty-eighth U.S. Colored Troops

Charles Veal, Private, Company D, Fourth U.S. Colored Troops

U.S. Navy

Aaron Anderson, Landsman, USS *Wyandank*

Robert Blake, Powder Boy, USS *Marblehead*

William H. Brown, Landsman, USS *Brooklyn*

Wilson Brown, USS *Hartford*

John Lawson, Landsman, USS *Hartford*

James Mifflin, Engineer's Cook, USS *Brooklyn*

Joachim Pease, Seaman, USS *Kearsarge*

CONGRESSIONAL MEDAL OF HONOR: INTERIM PERIOD

U.S. Navy

Daniel Atkins, Ship's Cook First Class, USS *Cushing*

John Davis, Seaman, USS *Trenton*

Alphonse Girandy, Seaman, USS *Petrel*

John Johnson, Seaman, USS *Kansas*

William Johnson, Cooper, USS *Adams*

Joseph B. Noil, Seaman, USS *Powhatan*

John Smith, Seaman, USS *Shenandoah*

Robert Sweeney, Seaman, USS *Kearsarge*, USS *Jamestown*

CONGRESSIONAL MEDAL OF HONOR: WESTERN CAMPAIGNS (INDIAN CAMPAIGNS OR PLAINS WAR)

U.S. Army

Thomas Boyne, Sergeant, Troop C, Ninth U.S. Cavalry

Benjamin Brown, Sergeant, Company C, Twenty-fourth U.S. Infantry

John Denny, Sergeant, Troop C, Ninth U.S. Cavalry

Pompey Factor, Seminole Negro Indian Scouts

Clinton Greaves, Corporal, Troop C, Ninth U.S. Cavalry

Henry Johnson, Sergeant, Troop D, Ninth U.S. Cavalry

George Jordan, Sergeant, Troop K, Ninth U.S. Cavalry

Isaiah Mays, Corporal, Company B, Twenty-fourth U.S. Infantry

William McBreyar, Sergeant, Troop K, Tenth U.S. Cavalry

Adam Paine, Private, Seminole Negro Indian Scouts

Isaac Payne, Private (Trumpeter), Seminole Negro Indian Scouts

Thomas Shaw, Sergeant, Troop K, Ninth U.S. Cavalry

Emanuel Stance, Sergeant, Troop F, Ninth U.S. Cavalry

Augustus Walley, Private, Troop 1, Ninth U.S. Cavalry

John Ward, Sergeant, Seminole Negro Indian Scouts

Moses Williams, First Sergeant, Troop 1, Ninth U.S. Cavalry

William O. Wilson, Corporal, Troop 1, Ninth U.S. Cavalry

Brent Woods, Sergeant, Troop B, Ninth U.S. Cavalry

CONGRESSIONAL MEDAL OF HONOR: SPANISH-AMERICAN WAR (1898)

U.S. Army

Edward L. Baker Jr., Sergeant Major, Tenth U.S. Cavalry

Dennis Bell, Private, Troop H, Tenth U.S. Cavalry

Fitz Lee, Private, Troop M, Tenth U.S. Cavalry

William H. Thompkins, Private, Troop G, Tenth U.S. Cavalry

George H. Wanton, Sergeant, Troop M, Tenth U.S. Cavalry

U.S. Navy

Robert Penn, Fireman First Class, USS *Iowa*

CONGRESSIONAL MEDAL OF HONOR: WORLD WAR I (1914–1918)

U.S. Army

Freddie Stowers, Corporal, Company C, 371st Infantry Regiment, Ninety-third Infantry Division

CONGRESSIONAL MEDAL OF HONOR: WORLD WAR II (1939–1945)

U.S. Army

Vernon Baker, First Lieutenant

Edward A. Carter Jr., Staff Sergeant

John R. Fox, First Lieutenant

Willy F. James Jr., Private First Class

Ruben Rivers, Staff Sergeant

Charles L. Thomas, First Lieutenant

George Watson, Private

CONGRESSIONAL MEDAL OF HONOR: KOREAN WAR (1950–1953)

U.S. Army

Cornelius H. Charlton, Sergeant, Twenty-fourth Infantry Regiment, Twenty-fifth Division

William Thompson, Private, Twenty-fourth Infantry Regiment, Twenty-fifth Division

CONGRESSIONAL MEDAL OF HONOR: VIETNAM WAR (1957–1975)

U.S. Army

Webster Anderson, Sergeant, Battery A, Second Battalion, 320th Artillery, 101st Airborne Division

Eugene Ashley Jr., Sergeant, Company C, Fifth Special Forces Group (Airborne), First Special Forces

William M. Bryant, Sergeant First Class, Company A, Fifth Special Forces Group, First Special Forces

Lawrence Joel, Specialist Sixth Class, Headquarters and Headquarters Company, First Battalion, 173rd Airborne Brigade

Dwight H. Johnson, Specialist Fifth Class, Company B, First Battalion, Sixty-ninth Armor, Fourth Infantry Division

Garfield M. Langhorn, Private First Class, Troop C, Seventh Squadron, Seventeenth Cavalry, First Aviation Brigade

Matthew Leonard, Platoon Sergeant, Company B, First Battalion, Sixteenth Infantry, First Infantry Division

Donald R. Long, Sergeant, Troop C, First Squadron, Fourth Cavalry, First Infantry Division

Milton L. Olive III, Private First Class, Company B, Second Battalion 503rd Infantry, 173rd Airborne Brigade

Riley L. Pitts, Captain, Company C, Second Battalion, Twenty-seventh Infantry, Twenty-fifth Infantry Division

Charles C. Rogers, Lieutenant Colonel, First Battalion, Fifth Infantry, First Infantry Division

Rupert L. Sergeant, First Lieutenant, Company B, Fourth Battalion, Ninth Infantry, Twenty-fifth Infantry Division

Clarence E. Sasser, Specialist Fifth Class, Headquarters Company, Third Battalion, Sixtieth Infantry, Ninetieth Infantry Division

Clifford C. Sims, Staff Sergeant, Company D, Second Battalion, 501st Infantry, 101st Airborne Division

John E. Warren Jr., First Lieutenant, Company C, Second Battalion, Twenty-second Infantry, Twenty-fifth Infantry Division

U.S. Marines

James A. Anderson Jr., Private First Class, Second Platoon, Company F, Second Battalion, Third Marine Division

Oscar P. Austin, Private First Class, Company E, Seventh Marines, First Marine Division

Rodney M. Davis, Company B, First Battalion, Fifth Marines, First Marine Division

Robert H. Jenkins Jr., Private First Class, Third Reconnaissance Battalion, Third Marine Division

Ralph H. Johnson, Private First Class, Company A, First Reconnaissance Battalion, First Marine Division

MARTIN LUTHER KING JR. NONVIOLENT PEACE PRIZE

1973: Andrew Young

1975: John Lewis

1976: Randolph Blackwell

1977: Benjamin E. Mays

1978: Kenneth D. Kaunda

1980: Rosa Parks

1982: Harry Belafonte

1983: Martin Luther King Sr.

1990: Joseph E. Lowery

1993: Jesse Jackson Sr.

SPINGARN MEDAL

1915: Ernest Everett Just (head of the department of physiology at Howard University Medical School)

1916: Charles Young (major in the U.S. Army)

1917: Henry (Harry) Thacker Burleigh (composer, pianist, singer)

1918: William Stanley Braithwaite (poet, literary critic, editor)

1919: Archibald H. Grimké (author, U.S. consul in Santo Domingo, president of the American Negro Academy, president of the District of Columbia branch of the NAACP)

1920: W. E. B. Du Bois (author, editor, organizer of the first Pan-African Congress)

1921: Charles S. Gilpin (actor)

1922: Mary B. Talbert (president of the National Association of Colored Women)

1923: George Washington Carver (head of research and director of the experiment station at Tuskegee Institute)

1924: Roland Hayes (singer)

1925: James Weldon Johnson (author, editor, U.S. consul in Venezuela and Nicaragua, secretary of the NAACP)

1926: Carter G. Woodson (editor, historian, founder of the Association for the Study of Negro Life and History)

1927: Anthony Overton (businessman, president of the Victory Life Insurance Company (the first African American organization permitted to do business under the rigid requirements of the state of New York)

1928: Charles W. Chesnutt (author)

1929: Mordecai Wyatt Johnson (the first African American president of Howard University)

1930: Henry A. Hunt (principal of Fort Valley High and Industrial School, Fort Valley, Georgia)

1931: Richard Berry Harrison (actor)

1932: Robert Russa Moton (principal of Tuskegee Institute)

1933: Max Yergan (secretary of the YMCA in South Africa)

1934: William Taylor Burwell Williams (dean of Tuskegee Institute)

1935: Mary McLeod Bethune (founder and president of Bethune-Cookman College)

1936: John Hope (president of Atlanta University)

1937: Walter White (executive secretary of the NAACP)

1939: Marian Anderson (singer)

1940: Louis T. Wright (surgeon)

1941: Richard Wright (author)

1942: A. Philip Randolph (labor leader, international president of the Brotherhood of Sleeping Car Porters)

1943: William H. Hastie (jurist, educator)

1944: Charles R. Drew (scientist)

1945: Paul Robeson (singer, actor)

1946: Thurgood Marshall (NAACP special counsel)

1947: Percy L. Julian (research chemist)

1948: Channing H. Tobias (minister, educator)

1949: Ralph J. Bunche (international civil servant, acting United Nations mediator in Palestine)

1950: Charles Hamilton Houston (chairman of the NAACP Legal Committee)

1951: Mabel K. Staupers (leader of the National Association of Colored Graduate Nurses)

1952: Harry T. Moore (state leader of the Florida NAACP)

1953: Paul R. Williams (architect)

1954: Theodore K. Lawless (physician, educator, philanthropist)

1955: Carl Murphy (editor, publisher, civic leader)

1956: Jackie Robinson (athlete)

1957: Martin Luther King Jr. (minister, civil rights leader)

1958: Daisy Bates and the Little Rock Nine (for their pioneer role in upholding the basic ideals of American democracy in the face of continuing harassment and constant threats of bodily injury)

1959: Duke Ellington (composer, musician, orchestra leader)

1960: Langston Hughes (poet, author, playwright)

1961: Kenneth B. Clark (professor of psychology at the City College of the City University of New York, founder and director of the Northside Center for Child Development, prime mobilizer of the resources of modern psychology in the attack upon racial segregation)

1962: Robert C. Weaver (administrator of the Housing and Home Finance Agency)

1963: Medgar Evers (NAACP field secretary for Mississippi, World War II veteran)

1964: Roy Wilkins (executive director of the NAACP)

1965: Leontyne Price (singer)

1966: John H. Johnson (founder and president of the Johnson Publishing Company)

1967: Edward W. Brooke (the first African American to win popular election to the U.S. Senate)

1968: Sammy Davis Jr. (performer, civil rights activist)

1969: Clarence M. Mitchell Jr. (director of the Washington Bureau of the NAACP, civil rights activist)

1970: Jacob Lawrence (artist, teacher, humanitarian)

1971: Leon H. Sullivan (minister)

1972: Gordon Parks (writer, photographer, filmmaker)

1973: Wilson C. Riles (educator)

1974: Damon Keith (jurist)

1975: Hank Aaron (athlete)

1976: Alvin Ailey (dancer, choreographer, artistic director)

1977: Alex Haley (author, biographer, lecturer)

1978: Andrew Young (U.S. ambassador to the United Nations, diplomat, cabinet member, civil rights activist, minister)

1979: Rosa Parks (community activist)

1980: Rayford W. Logan (educator, historian, author)

1981: Coleman A. Young (mayor of Detroit, public servant, labor leader, civil rights activist)

1982: Benjamin E. Mays (educator, theologian, humanitarian)

1983: Lena Horne (performer, humanitarian)

1984: Tom Bradley (government executive, public servant, humanitarian)

1985: Bill Cosby (comedian, actor, educator, humanitarian)

1986: Benjamin L. Hooks (executive director of the NAACP)

1987: Percy E. Sutton (public servant, businessman, community leader)

1988: Frederick D. Patterson (doctor of veterinary medicine, educator, humanitarian, founder of the United Negro College Fund)

1989: Jesse Jackson Sr. (minister, political leader, civil rights activist)

1990: L. Douglas Wilder (governor of Virginia)

1991: Colin L. Powell (general in the U.S. Army, chairman of the Joint Chiefs of Staff)

1992: Barbara C. Jordan (educator, congresswoman)

1993: Dorothy I. Height (president of the National Council of Negro Women)

1994: Maya Angelou (poet, author, performing artist)

1995: John Hope Franklin (historian)

1996: A. Leon Higginbotham Jr. (jurist, judge)

1997: Carl T. Rowan (journalist)

1998: Myrlie Evers-Williams (chair of the NAACP board of directors)

1999: Earl G. Graves (publisher and media executive)

2000: Oprah Winfrey (television personality and executive)

2001: Vernon E. Jordan (head of National Urban League and the United Negro College Fund)

2002: John Lewis (chairman of the Student Nonviolent Coordinating Committee, U.S. congressman from Georgia)

2003: Constance Baker Motley (civil rights leader, judge)

2004: Robert L. Carter (litigator, federal court judge)

2005: Oliver W. Hill (civil rights lawyer, civic leader)

2006: Benjamin S. Carson (neurosurgeon)

2007: John Conyers (congressman)

2008: Ruby Dee (actress)

2009: Julian Bond (activist)

NOBEL PEACE PRIZE

1950: Ralph J. Bunche

1964: Martin Luther King Jr.

2009: Barack Obama

ARTS AND LETTERS AWARDS AND HONORS

KENNEDY CENTER HONORS

1978: Marian Anderson

1979: Ella Fitzgerald

1980: Leontyne Price

1981: Count Basie

1983: Katherine Dunham

1984: Lena Horne

1986: Ray Charles

1987: Sammy Davis Jr.

1988: Alvin Ailey

1989: Harry Belafonte

1990: Dizzy Gillespie

1991: Fayard and Harold Nicholas

1992: Lionel Hampton

1993: Arthur Mitchell; Marion Williams

1994: Aretha Franklin

1995: B. B. King; Sidney Poitier

1996: Benny Carter

1997: Jessye Norman

1998: Bill Cosby

1999: Judith Jamison; Stevie Wonder

2000: Chuck Berry

2001: Quincy Jones

2002: James Earl Jones

2003: James Brown

2004: Ossie Davis and Ruby Dee

2005: Tina Turner

2006: Smokey Robinson

2007: Diana Ross

2008: Morgan Freeman

2009: Grace Bumbry

MACARTHUR FELLOWSHIPS ("GENIUS" GRANTS)

1981: Henry Louis Gates Jr. (literary studies)

1981: Elma Lewis (education)

1981: James Alan McPherson (fiction)

1981: Derek Walcott (poetry)

1982: Robert Parrish Moses (education)

1984: Sara Lawrence-Lightfoot (education)

1984: Billie Jean Young (public affairs)

1985: Ellen Stewart (performing arts)

1985: Marian Wright Edelman (public affairs)

1986: Jay Wright (poetry)

1987: Muriel Sutherland Snowden (public affairs)

1987: William Julius Wilson (sociology)

1988: Charles Burnett (filmmaking)

1988: Max Roach (music)

1989: Byllye Y. Avery (public affairs)

1989: Martin Puryear (visual arts)

1989: Bernice Johnson Reagon (music)

1989: George Russell (music)

1990: Lisa Delpit (education)

1990: Thomas Cleveland Holt (history)

1990: Calvin R. King (public affairs)

1990: Otis Pitts Jr. (public affairs)

1990: Robert L. Woodson (public affairs)

1991: David Hammons (visual arts)

1991: Sophia Bracy Harris (public affairs)

1991: Arnold Rampersad (nonfiction)

1991: Cecil Taylor (music)

1992: Robert H. Blackburn (visual arts)

1992: Unita Blackwell (public affairs)

1992: Barbara Fields (history)

1992: Paule B. Marshall (fiction)

1992: John T. Scott (visual arts)

1993: Stanley Couch (criticism)

1993: Ernest J. Gaines (fiction)

1993: Aaron Shirley (medicine)

1993: John Edgar Wideman (fiction)

1993: Marion Williams (performing arts)

1994: Jeraldyne K. Blunden (choreography)

1994: Anthony Braxton (music)

1994: Ornette Coleman (music)

1994: Bill T. Jones (dance and choreography)

1994: Joseph E. Marshall Jr. (public affairs)

1994: Arthur Mitchell (dance and choreography)

1995: Octavia Butler (fiction)

1995: Virginia Hamilton (fiction)

1995: Donald Hopkins (medicine)

1995: Bryan Stevenson (public affairs)

1996: Louis Massiah (filmmaking)

1996: Vonnie C. McLoyd (psychology)

1996: Thylias Moss (poetry)

1996: Anna Deavere Smith (performing arts)

1996: William Strickland (public affairs)

1997: Kerry James Marshall (visual arts)

1997: Kara Elizabeth Walker (visual arts)

1997: Brackette F. Williams (anthropology)

1998: Charles R. Johnson (fiction)

1998: Ishmael Scott Reed (fiction)

1998: Eddie Williams (public affairs)

1999: David Levering Lewis (history)

1999: Gay J. McDougall (public affairs)

1999: Fred Wilson (visual arts)

2000: Deborah Willis (visual arts)

2001: Danielle Allen (classicism and political science)

2001: Suzan-Lori Parks (drama)

2002: George Lewis (music)

2002: Stanley Nelson (filmmaking)

2002: Colson Whitehead (fiction)

2003: Angela Johnson (fiction)

2003: Eve Troutt Powell (history)

2003: Lateefah Simon (public affairs)

2004: Edward P. Jones (fiction)

2004: Tommie Lindsey (education)

2004: Aminah Robinson (visual arts)

2004: Reginald R. Robinson (music)

2005: Marjora Carter (public affairs)

2005: Aaron Dworkin (music)

2006: Regina Carter (music)

2006: John A. Rich (medicine)

2006: Jennifer Richeson (psychology)

2007: Lisa Cooper (medicine)

2007: Corey Harris (music)

2007: Whitfield Lovell (visual arts)

2007: Lynn Nottage (performing arts)

2008: Chimamanda Adichie (fiction)

2008: Will Allen (urban farming)

2008: Mary Jackson (fiber arts)

2009: Mark Bradford (mixed-media arts)

2009: Edwidge Danticat (fiction)

NATIONAL MEDAL OF ARTS

1985: Ralph Ellison (writer); Leontyne Price (singer)

1986: Marian Anderson (singer)

1987: Romare Bearden (artist); Ella Fitzgerald (singer)

1988: Gordon Parks (photographer and filmmaker)

1989: Katherine Dunham (choreographer and dancer); Dizzy Gillespie (musician)

1990: B. B. King (musician)

1991: James Earl Jones (actor); Billy Taylor (musician)

1994: Harry Belafonte (singer)

1995: Gwendolyn Brooks (poet); Ossie Davis (actor); Ruby Dee (actress)

1996: Harlem Boys Choir (chorale); Lionel Hampton (musician)

1997: Betty Carter (singer)

1998: Fats Domino (singer)

1999: Aretha Franklin (singer); Odetta (singer); Rosetta LeNoire (actress)

2000: Maya Angelou (poet); Benny Carter (musician)

2001: Judith Jamison (choreographer and dancer)

2002: Smokey Robinson (singer and songwriter)

2003: Buddy Guy (musician)

2004: Wynton Marsalis (musician and conductor)

2005: James DePreist (symphonic conductor)

2006: Roy DeCarava (photographer)

2007: Lionel Hampton Jazz Festival

2008: Hank Jones (musician and composer); Fisk Jubilee Singers (chorale)

2009: Jessye Norman (singer)

ACADEMY AWARD OF THE AMERICAN ACADEMY AND INSTITUTE OF ARTS AND LETTERS

1946: Gwendolyn Brooks; Langston Hughes

1956: James Baldwin

1962: John A. Williams

1970: James Alan McPherson

1971: Charles Gordone

1972: Michael S. Harper

1974: Henry Van Dyke

1978: Lerone Bennett Jr.; Toni Morrison

1985: John Williams

1987: Ernest J. Gaines

1992: August Wilson

1994: Adrienne Kennedy

2001: Carl Phillips

2002: Charles Johnson

2004: Faith Ringgold

CLARENCE L. HOLTE LITERARY PRIZE

1979: Chancellor Williams, *The Destruction of Black Civilization: Great Issues of a Race from 4500 B.C. to 2000 A.D.*

1981: Ivan Van Sertima, *They Came before Columbus: The African Presence in Ancient America*

1983: Vincent Harding, *There Is a River: The Black Struggle for Freedom in America*

1986: John Hope Franklin, *George Washington Williams: A Biography*

1988: Arnold Rampersad, *The Life of Langston Hughes*, Vol. 1: *1902–1941: I, Too, Sing America*

NATIONAL BOOK AWARD

1953: Ralph Ellison, *Invisible Man*, Fiction

1969: Winthrop D. Jordan, *White over Black: American Attitudes toward the Negro, 1550–1812*, History and Biography

1975: Virginia Hamilton, *M. C. Higgins, the Great*, Children's Book

1983: Gloria Naylor, *The Women of Brewster Place*, First Novel; Joyce Carol Thomas, *Marked by Fire*, Children's Fiction (paperback); Alice Walker, *The Color Purple*, Fiction (hardcover)

1990: Charles Johnson, *Middle Passage*, Fiction

1999: Ai, *Vice: New and Selected Poems*, Poetry

2000: Lucille Clifton, *Blessing the Boats: New and Selected Poems, 1988–2000*, Poetry

2006: Nathaniel Mackey, *Splay Anthem*, Poetry

2008: Annette Gordon-Reed, *The Hemingses of Monticello: An American Family*, Nonfiction

NOBEL PRIZE IN LITERATURE

1993: Toni Morrison

PEN/FAULKNER AWARD FOR FICTION

1982: David Bradley, *The Chaneysville Incident*

1984: John Edgar Wideman, *Sent for You Yesterday*

1991: John Edgar Wideman, *Philadelphia Fire*

PULITZER PRIZES

Letters: Biography or Autobiography

1994: *W. E. B. Du Bois: Biography of a Race, 1868–1919*, David Levering Lewis

2001: *W. E. B. Du Bois: The Fight for Equality and the American Century, 1919–1963*, David Levering Lewis

Letters: History

2009: *The Hemingses of Monticello: An American Family*, Annette Gordon-Reed

Letters: Fiction

1978: *Elbow Room*, James Alan McPherson

1983: *The Color Purple*, Alice Walker

1988: *Beloved*, Toni Morrison

Letters: Poetry

1950: *Annie Allen*, Gwendolyn Brooks

1987: *Thomas and Beulah*, Rita Dove

1994: *Neon Vernacular*, Yusef Komunyakaa

Letters: Drama

1970: *No Place to Be Somebody*, Charles Gordone

1982: *A Soldier's Play*, Charles Fuller

1987: *Fences*, August Wilson

1990: *The Piano Lesson*, August Wilson

2002: *Topdog/Underdog*, Suzan-Lori Parks

2009: *Ruined*, Lynn Nottage

Letters: Music

1996: George Walker, *Lilacs, for Voice and Orchestra*

1997: Wynton Marsalis, *Blood on the Fields*

2007: Ornette Coleman, *Sound Grammar*

Letters: Special Awards and Citations

1976: Scott Joplin

1977: Alex Haley

1999: Duke Ellington (special posthumous award)

2006: Thelonious Monk (special posthumous award)

2007: John Coltrane (special posthumous award)

Journalism: Commentary

1989: Clarence Page

1994: William Raspberry

1996: E. R. Shipp

2003: Colbert I. King

2004: Leonard Pitts

2007: Cynthia Tucker

2009: Eugene Robinson

Journalism: Criticism

1995: Margo Jefferson

2006: Robin Givhan

Journalism: Feature Writing

1994: Isabel Wilkerson

1999: Angelo B. Henderson

ACADEMY AWARDS (OSCARS)

Best Performance by an Actor in a Leading Role

1963: Sidney Poitier, in *Lilies of the Field*

2002: Denzel Washington, in *Training Day*

2004: Jamie Foxx, in *Ray*

2006: Forest Whitaker, in *Last King of Scotland*

Best Performance by an Actress in a Leading Role

2002: Halle Berry, in *Monster's Ball*

Best Performance by an Actor in a Supporting Role

1982: Louis Gossett Jr., in *An Officer and a Gentleman*

1989: Denzel Washington, in *Glory*

1996: Cuba Gooding Jr., in *Jerry Maguire*

2004: Morgan Freeman, in *Million Dollar Baby*

Best Performance by an Actress in a Supporting Role

1939: Hattie McDaniel, in *Gone with the Wind*

1990: Whoopi Goldberg, in *Ghost*

2010: Mo'Nique, in *Precious*

Best Original Score

1984: Prince, for *Purple Rain*

1986: Herbie Hancock, for *'Round Midnight*

Best Sound Mixing

1990: Russell L. Williams, for *Glory*

1991: Russell L. Williams, for *Dances with Wolves*

EMMY AWARDS—PRIMETIME

Outstanding Lead Actor in a Drama Series

1966–1968: Bill Cosby, in *I Spy*

1991: James Earl Jones, in *Gabriel's Fire*

1998: Andre Braugher, in *Homicide: Life on the Street*

Outstanding Performance in a Variety or Musical Program

1960: Harry Belafonte, in *The Revlon Revue*

Outstanding Lead Actor in a Comedy, Variety, or Music Series

1985: Robert Guillaume, in *Benson*

Outstanding Lead Actress in a Comedy, Variety, or Music Series

1981: Isabel Sanford, in *The Jeffersons*

Outstanding Lead Actress in a Comedy or Drama Special

1974: Cicely Tyson, in *The Autobiography of Miss Jane Pittman*

Outstanding Lead Actress in a Miniseries or Special

1991: Lynn Whitfield, in *The Josephine Baker Story*

1997: Alfre Woodard, in *Miss Evers' Boys*

2000: Halle Berry, in *Introducing Dorothy Dandridge*

2005: S. Epatha Merkerson, in *Lackawanna Blues*

Outstanding Lead Actor in a Miniseries or Special

2006: Andre Braugher, in *Thief*

Outstanding Supporting Actor in a Comedy, Variety, or Music Series

1979: Robert Guillaume, in *Soap*

Outstanding Supporting Actor in a Miniseries or Special

1991: James Earl Jones, in *Heatwave*

2004: Jeffrey Wright, in *Angels in America*

Outstanding Supporting Actress in a Drama Series

1984: Alfre Woodard, in "Doris in Wonderland" episode of *Hill Street Blues*

1991: Madge Sinclair, in *Gabriel's Fire*

1993: Mary Alice, in *I'll Fly Away*

Outstanding Supporting Actress in a Comedy, Variety, or Music Series

1987: Jackée Harry, in *227*

Outstanding Supporting Actress in a Miniseries or Special

1991: Ruby Dee, in "Decoration Day," *Hallmark Hall of Fame*

Outstanding Directing in a Drama Series

1986: Georg Stanford Brown, in "Parting Shots" episode of *Cagney & Lacey*

1990: Thomas Carter, in "Promises to Keep" episode of *Equal Justice*

1991: Thomas Carter, in "In Confidence" episode of *Equal Justice*

1992: Eric Laneuville, in "All God's Children" episode of *I'll Fly Away*

1998: Paris Barclay, in "Lost Israel" episode of *N.Y.P.D. Blue*

1999: Paris Barclay, in "Hearts and souls" episode of *N.Y.P.D. Blue*

Outstanding Producing in a Variety, Music, or Comedy Special

1983: Suzanne de Passe, in *Motown 25: Yesterday, Today, and Forever*

1985: Suzanne de Passe, in *Motown Returns to the Apollo*

Outstanding Variety, Music, or Comedy Special

1997: *Chris Rock: Bring the Pain*

Outstanding Achievement in Music Composition

1971: Ray Charles, in *The First Nine Months Are the Hardest*

1972: Ray Charles, in *The Funny Side of Marriage*

Outstanding Achievement in Music Composition for a Series

1977: Quincy Jones and Gerald Fried, in *Roots*

Outstanding Choreography

1982: Debbie Allen, for "Come One, Come All" episode of *Fame*

1983: Debbie Allen, for "Class Act" episode of *Fame*

1991: Debbie Allen, for *Motown 30: What's Goin' On!*

1999: Judith Jamison, for *Dance in America: A Hymn for Alvin Ailey (Great Performances)*

EMMY AWARDS—DAYTIME

Outstanding Talk Show

1987–1989, 1991–1992, 1994–1997: *The Oprah Winfrey Show*

2003: *The Wayne Brady Show*

2008–2009 (informative): *The Tyra Banks Show*

Outstanding Talk Show Host

1987: Oprah Winfrey, *The Oprah Winfrey Show*

1991–1995: Oprah Winfrey, *The Oprah Winfrey Show*

1996: Montel Williams, *The Montel Williams Show*

1998: Oprah Winfrey, *The Oprah Winfrey Show*

2003–2004: Wayne Brady, *The Wayne Brady Show*

2009: Whoopi Goldberg (cohost), *The View*

Outstanding Lead Actor

1979: Al Freeman Jr., in *One Life to Live*

1985: Darnell Williams, in *All My Children*

Outstanding Supporting Actor

1983: Darnell Williams, in *All My Children*

2000: Shemar Moore, in *The Young and the Restless*

2008: Kristoff St. John, in *The Young and the Restless*

Outstanding Supporting Actress

1989: Debbi Morgan, in *All My Children*

Outstanding Younger Actor

1992: Kristoff St. John, in *The Young and the Restless*

1996–1997: Kevin Mambo, in *The Guiding Light*

2007: Bryton McClure, in *The Young and the Restless*

EMMY AWARDS—SPORTS

Outstanding Sports Personality/ Studio Host

1998–1999: James Brown

2007: James Brown

Outstanding Sports Event Analyst

1997: Joe Morgan

2004: Joe Morgan

2008: Tom Jackson

Outstanding Sports Journalism

1995: "Broken Promises" and "Pros and Cons" episodes of *Real Sports with Bryant Gumbel*

1998: "Diamond Buck$" and "Winning at All Costs" episodes of *Real Sports with Bryant Gumbel*

TELEVISION HALL OF FAME INDUCTEES

1992: Bill Cosby

1994: Oprah Winfrey

NEW YORK DRAMA CRITICS' CIRCLE AWARD

Best American Play

1959: Lorraine Hansberry, *A Raisin in the Sun*

1975: Ed Bullins, *The Taking of Miss Janie*

1982: Charles Fuller, *A Soldier's Play*

1992: August Wilson, *Two Trains Running*

2007: August Wilson, *Radio Golf*

Best Play

1985: August Wilson, *Ma Rainey's Black Bottom*

1987: August Wilson, *Fences*

1988: August Wilson, *Joe Turner's Come and Gone*

1990: August Wilson, *The Piano Lesson*

1996: August Wilson, *Seven Guitars*

2000: August Wilson, *Jitney*

2004: Lynn Nottage, *Intimate Apparel*

2009: Lynn Nottage, *Ruined*

Best Musical

1978: Fats Waller and Richard Maltby Jr., *Ain't Misbehavin'*

2008: Stew and Heidi Rodewald, *Passing Strange*

Special Citation

1981: Lena Horne, *Lena Horne: The Lady and Her Music*

1994: Anna Deavere Smith, *Twilight—Los Angeles*

TONY AWARDS

Best Actor (Dramatic)

1969: James Earl Jones, *The Great White Hope*

1975: John Kani, *Sizwe Banzi*; Winston Ntshona, *The Island*

1987: James Earl Jones, *Fences*

2010: Denzel Washington, *Fences*

Best Supporting or Featured Actor (Dramatic)

1982: Zakes Mokae, *Master Harold and the Boys*

1992: Laurence Fishburne, *Two Trains Running*

1994: Jeffrey Wright, *Angels in America: Perestroika*

1996: Ruben Santiago-Hudson, *Seven Guitars*

2009: Roger Robinson, *Joe Turner's Come and Gone*

Best Actor (Musical)

1970: Cleavon Little, *Purlie*

1973: Ben Vereen, *Pippin*

1982: Ben Harney, *Dreamgirls*

1992: Gregory Hines, *Jelly's Last Jam*

2000: Brian Stokes Mitchell, *Kiss Me Kate*

Best Supporting or Featured Actor (Musical)

1954: Harry Belafonte, *John Murray Anderson's Almanac*

1975: Ted Rose, *The Wiz*

1981: Hinton Battle, *Sophisticated Ladies*

1982: Cleavant Derricks, *Dreamgirls*

1983: Charles "Honi" Coles, *My One and Only*

1984: Hinton Battle, *The Tap Dance Kid*

1991: Hinton Battle, *Miss Saigon*

1997: Chuck Cooper, *The Life*

Best Actress (Dramatic)

2004: Phylicia Rashad, *A Raisin in the Sun*

2010: Viola Davis, *Fences*

Best Supporting or Featured Actress (Dramatic)

1977: Trazana Beverley, *For Colored Girls Who Have Considered Suicide/When the Rainbow Is Enuf*

1987: Mary Alice, *Fences*

1988: L. Scott Caldwell, *Joe Turner's Come and Gone*

1996: Audra McDonald, *Master Class*

1997: Lynne Thigpen, *An American Daughter*

2001: Viola Davis, *King Hedley II*

2004: Audra McDonald, *A Raisin in the Sun*

2005: Adriane Lenox, *Doubt*

Best Actress (Musical)

1962: Diahann Carroll, *No Strings*

1968: Leslie Uggams, *Hallelujah, Baby*

1974: Virginia Capers, *Raisin*

1982: Jennifer Holliday, *Dreamgirls*

1989: Ruth Brown, *Black and Blue*

2000: Heather Headley, *Aida*

2006: La Chanze, *The Color Purple*

Best Supporting or Featured Actress (Musical)

1950: Juanita Hall, *South Pacific*

1968: Lillian Hayman, *Hallelujah, Baby*

1970: Melba Moore, *Purlie*

1972: Linda Hopkins, *Inner City*

1975: Dee Dee Bridgewater, *The Wiz*

1977: Delores Hall, *Your Arms Too Short to Box with God*

1978: Nell Carter, *Ain't Misbehavin'*

1985: Leilani Jones, *Grind*

1992: Tonya Pinkins, *Jelly's Last Jam*

1994: Audra McDonald, *Carousel*

1996: Ann Duquesnay, *Bring in 'da Noise, Bring in 'da Funk*

1997: Lillias White, *The Life*

1998: Audra McDonald, *Ragtime*

2004: Anika Noni Rose, *Caroline, or Change*

Best Director (Dramatic)

1987: Lloyd Richards, *Fences*

1993: George C. Wolfe, *Angels in America: Millennium Approaches*

Best Play (Dramatic-Playwright)

1974: Joseph A. Walker, *The River Niger*

1987: August Wilson, *Fences*

Best Play (Dramatic-Producer)

1994: George C. Wolfe, the Public Theater, and the New York Shakespeare Festival, *Angels in America: Perestroika*

2003: George C. Wolfe, the Public Theater, and the New York Shakespeare Festival, *Take Me Out*

Best Director (Musical)

1975: Geoffrey Holder, *The Wiz*

1996: George C. Wolfe, *Bring in 'da Noise, Bring in 'da Funk*

Best Musical (Producer)

2002: Whoopi Goldberg, *Thoroughly Modern Millie*

2007: Tamara Tunie and StyleFour Productions, *Spring Awakening*

Best Book of a Musical

2008: Stew, *Passing Strange*

Best Score (Music and Lyrics)

1975: Charlie Smalls, *The Wiz*

Best Choreographer

1975: George Faison, *The Wiz*

1982: Michael Peters, *Dreamgirls*

1989: Cholly Atkins, Henry LeTang, Frankie Manning, and Fayard Nicholas, *Black and Blue*

1996: Savion Glover, *Bring in 'da Noise, Bring in 'da Funk*

1998: Garth Fagan, *The Lion King*

2007: Bill T. Jones, *Spring Awakening*

2010: Bill T. Jones, *Fela!*

Best Costume Designer

1975: Geoffrey Holder, *The Wiz*

Special Tony Award

1981: Lena Horne, *Lena Horne: The Lady and Her Music*

2006: Sarah Jones, *Bridge and Tunnel*

Special Theatrical Event (Producer)

2002: George C. Wolfe, the Public Theater, and the New York Shakespeare Festival, *Elaine Stritch at Liberty*

2003: Russell Simmons, Stan Lathan, and Kimora Lee Simmons, *Russell Simmons' Def Poetry Jam on Broadway*

GRAMMY AWARDS

Record of the Year

1963: "I Can't Stop Loving You," Count Basie

1967: "Up, Up, and Away," 5th Dimension

1969: "Aquarius/Let the Sun Shine In," 5th Dimension

1972: "The First Time Ever I Saw Your Face," Roberta Flack

1973: "Killing Me Softly with His Song," Roberta Flack

1976: "This Masquerade," George Benson

1983: "Beat It," Michael Jackson

1984: "What's Love Got to Do with It," Tina Turner

1985: "We Are the World," USA for Africa; produced by Quincy Jones

1988: "Don't Worry, Be Happy," Bobby McFerrin

1991: "Unforgettable," Natalie Cole with Nat "King" Cole

1993: "I Will Always Love You," Whitney Houston

2004: "Here We Go Again," Ray Charles and Norah Jones

Album of the Year

1973: *Innervisions*, Stevie Wonder; produced by Stevie Wonder

1974: *Fulfillingness' First Finale*, Stevie Wonder; produced by Stevie Wonder

1976: *Songs in the Key of Life*, Stevie Wonder; produced by Stevie Wonder

1983: *Thriller*, Michael Jackson; produced by Quincy Jones

1984: *Can't Slow Down*, Lionel Richie; produced by Lionel Richie and James Anthony Carmichael

1990: *Back on the Block*, Quincy Jones; produced by Quincy Jones

1991: *Unforgettable*, Natalie Cole; produced by David Foster, Andre Fischer, and Tommy LiPuma

1999: *The Miseducation of Lauryn Hill*, Lauryn Hill; produced by Lauryn Hill

2003: *Speakerboxxx/The Love Below*, OutKast, produced by Carl Mo

2004: *Genius Loves Company*, Ray Charles and various artists, produced by John Burk, Don Mizell, Phil Ramone, and Herbert Wall

2007: *River: The Joni Letters*, Herbie Hancock and various artists

ROCK AND ROLL HALL OF FAME AND MUSEUM INDUCTEES

1986: Chuck Berry; James Brown; Ray Charles; Sam Cooke; Fats Domino; Little Richard; Robert Johnson; Jimmy Yancey

1987: The Coasters; Bo Diddley; Aretha Franklin; Marvin Gaye; Louis Jordan; B. B. King; Clyde McPhatter; Smokey Robinson; Big Joe Turner; T-Bone Walker; Muddy Waters; Jackie Wilson

1988: The Drifters; Berry Gordy Jr.; The Supremes

1989: The Ink Spots; Otis Redding; Bessie Smith; The Soul Stirrers; The Temptations; Stevie Wonder

1990: Louis Armstrong; Hank Ballard; Charlie Christian; The Four Tops; Holland, Dozier, and Holland; The Platters; Ma Rainey

1991: La Vern Baker; John Lee Hooker; Howlin' Wolf; The Impressions; Wilson Pickett; Jimmy Reed; Ike and Tina Turner

1992: Bobby "Blue" Bland; Booker T. and the M.G.'s; Jimi Hendrix; Isley Brothers; Elmore James; Professor Longhair; Sam and Dave

1993: Ruth Brown; Etta James; Frankie Lymon and the Teenagers; Sly and the Family Stone; Dinah Washington

1994: Willie Dixon; Bob Marley; Johnny Otis

1995: Al Green; Martha and the Vandellas; The Orioles

1996: Little Willie John; Gladys Knight and the Pips; The Shirelles

1997: Mahalia Jackson; The Jackson Five; Parliament

1998: Jelly Roll Morton; Lloyd Price

1999: Charles Brown; Curtis Mayfield; The Staple Singers

2000: Nat "King" Cole; King Curtis; Earth, Wind, and Fire; Billie Holiday; James Jamerson; The Moonglows; Earl Palmer

2001: Solomon Burke; The Flamingos; Michael Jackson; Johnnie Johnson

2002: Isaac Hayes

2004: Prince; The Dells

2005: Percy Sledge; The O'Jays

2006: Miles Davis

2007: Grandmaster Flash and the Furious Five

2009: Run-D.M.C.

2010: Otis Blackwell; Jesse Stone

AFRICAN AMERICAN OLYMPIC MEDALISTS

1904: ST. LOUIS, MISSOURI

Men's 200-meter Hurdles

George Poage, Bronze

Men's 400-meter Hurdles

George Poage, Bronze

1908: LONDON

Men's 1,600-meter Relay

J. B. Taylor, Gold (3:29.4)

1924: PARIS

Men's Long Jump

Dehart Hubbard, Gold (24' 5.125")

Edward Gourdin, Silver (23' 10")

1932: LOS ANGELES

Men's 100-meter Dash

Eddie Tolan, Gold (10.3)

Ralph Metcalfe, Silver (10.3)

Men's 200-meter Dash
Eddie Tolan, Gold (21.2)
Ralph Metcalfe, Bronze (21.5)

Men's Long Jump
Edward Gordon, Gold (25' .75")

1936: BERLIN

Men's 100-meter Dash
Jesse Owens, Gold (10.3)
Ralph Metcalfe, Silver (10.4)

Men's 200-meter Dash
Jesse Owens, Gold (20.7)
Matthew Robinson, Silver (21.1)

Men's 400-meter Dash
Archie Williams, Gold (46.5)
James DuValle, Silver (46.8)

Men's 800-meter Run
John Woodruff, Gold (1:52.9)

Men's 110-meter Hurdles
Fritz Pollard Jr., Bronze (14.4)

Men's 400-meter Relay
Jesse Owens, Gold (39.8)
Ralph Metcalfe, Gold (39.8)

Men's High Jump
Cornelius Johnson, Gold (6'8")

Men's Long Jump
Jesse Owens, Gold (26' 5.75")

1948: LONDON

Men's 100-meter Dash
Harrison Dillard, Gold (10.3)
Norwood Ewell, Silver (10.4)

Men's 200-meter Dash
Norwood Ewell, Gold (21.1)

Women's 200-meter Dash
Audrey Patterson, Bronze (25.2)

Men's 400-meter Dash
Malvin Whitfield, Bronze (46.9)

Men's 400-meter Relay
Lorenzo Wright, Gold (40.6)

Men's 1,600-meter Relay
Harrison Dillard, Gold (3:10.4)
Norwood Ewell, Gold (3:10.4)
Mal Whitfield, Gold (3:10.4)

Women's High Jump
Alice Coachman, Gold (5' 6.125")

Men's Long Jump
Willie Steele, Gold (25' 8")
Herbert Douglass, Bronze (25' 3")

1952: HELSINKI

Men's 200-meter Dash
Andrew Stanfield, Gold (20.7)

Men's 400-meter Dash
Ollie Matson, Bronze (46.8)

Men's 800-meter Run
Mal Whitfield, Gold (1:49.2)

Men's 110-meter Hurdles
Harrison Dillard, Gold (13.7)

Men's 400-meter Relay
Harrison Dillard, Gold (40.1)
Andrew Stanfield, Gold (40.1)
Ollie Matson, Gold (40.1)

Women's 400-meter Relay
Barbara Jones, Gold (45.9)

Men's Long Jump
Jerome Biffle, Gold (24' 10")
Meredith Gourdine, Silver (24' 8.125")

Decathlon
Milton Campbell, Silver (6,975 pts.)

Javelin
Bill Miller, Silver

Boxing: Flyweight
Nathan Brooks, Gold

Boxing: Light Welterweight
Charles Adkins, Gold

Boxing: Middleweight
Floyd Patterson, Gold

Boxing: Light Heavyweight
Norvel Lee, Gold

1956: MELBOURNE

Men's 200-meter Dash
Andrew Stanfield, Silver (20.7)

Men's 400-meter Dash
Charles Jenkins, Gold (46.7)

Men's 110-meter Hurdles
Lee Calhoun, Gold (13.5)

Men's 400-meter Relay
Ira Murchison, Gold (39.5)
Leamon King, Gold (39.5)
Charles Jenkins, Gold (39.5)

Women's 400-meter Relay
Margaret Matthews, Bronze (44.9)
Isabelle Daniels, Bronze (44.9)
Mae Faggs, Bronze (44.9)
Wilma Rudolph, Bronze (44.9)

Men's 1,600-meter Relay
Lou Jones, Gold (3:04.8)

Men's High Jump
Charles Dumas, Gold (6' 11.25")

Women's High Jump
Mildred McDaniel, Gold (5' 9.25")

Men's Long Jump
Gregory Bell, Gold (25' 8.25")

Women's Long Jump
Willye White, Silver (19' 11.75")

Decathlon
Milton Campbell, Gold (7,937 pts.)
Rafer Johnson, Silver (7,587 pts.)

Men's Basketball, Gold
K. C. Jones
Bill Russell

Boxing: Light Heavyweight
James Boyd, Gold

1960: ROME

Women's 100-meter Dash
Wilma Rudolph, Gold (11.0)

Men's 200-meter Dash
Les Carney, Silver (20.6)

Women's 200-meter Dash
Wilma Rudolph, Gold (24.0)

Men's 400-meter Dash
Otis Davis, Gold (44.9)

Men's 110-meter Hurdles
Lee Calhoun, Gold (13.8)
Willie May, Silver (13.8)
Hayes Jones, Bronze (14.0)

Women's 400-meter Relay
Martha Judson, Bronze (44.5)
Lucinda Williams, Bronze (44.5)
Barbara Jones, Bronze (44.5)
Wilma Rudolph, Bronze (44.5)

Men's 1,600-meter Relay
Otis Davis, Gold (3:02.2)

Men's High Jump
John Thomas, Bronze (7' .25")

Men's Long Jump
Ralph Boston, Gold (26' 7.75")
Irvin Robertson, Silver (26' 7.25")

Decathlon
Rafer Johnson, Gold (8,392 pts.)

Women's Shot Put
Earlene Brown, Bronze (53' 10.25")

Men's Basketball, Gold
Oscar Robertson
Walt Bellamy
Bob Boozer

Boxing: Light Welterweight
Quincelon Daniels, Bronze

Boxing: Light Middleweight
Wilbert McClure, Gold

Boxing: Middleweight
Edward Crook, Gold

Boxing: Light Heavyweight
Cassius Clay (Muhammad Ali), Gold

1964: TOKYO

Men's 100-meter Dash
Robert Hayes, Gold (9.9)

Women's 100-meter Dash
Wyomia Tyus, Gold (11.4)
Edith McGuire, Silver (11.6)

Men's 200-meter Dash
Henry Carr, Gold (20.3)
Paul Drayton, Silver (20.5)

Women's 200-meter Dash
Edith McGuire, Gold (23.0)

Men's 110-meter Hurdles
Hayes Jones, Gold (13.6)

Men's 400-meter Relay
Robert Hayes, Gold (39.0)
Paul Drayton, Gold (39.0)
Richard Stebbins, Gold (39.0)

Women's 400-meter Relay
Wyomia Tyus, Silver (43.9)
Edith McGuire, Silver (43.9)
Willye White, Silver (43.9)
Marilyn White, Silver (43.9)

Men's High Jump
John Thomas, Silver (7' 1.75")
John Rambo, Bronze (7' 1")

Men's Long Jump
Ralph Boston, Silver (26' 4")

Men's Basketball, Gold
Walt Hazzard
Lucius Jackson

Boxing: Flyweight
Robert Carmody, Bronze

Boxing: Featherweight
Charles Brown, Bronze

Boxing: Lightweight
Ronald Harris, Bronze

Boxing: Heavyweight
Joe Frazier, Gold

1968: MEXICO CITY

Men's 100-meter Dash
Jim Hines, Gold (9.9)
Charles Greene, Bronze (10.0)

Women's 100-meter Dash
Wyomia Tyus, Gold (11.0)
Barbara Ferrell, Silver (11.1)

Men's 200-meter Dash
Tommie Smith, Gold (19.8)
John Carlos, Bronze (20.0)

Men's 400-meter Dash
Lee Evans, Gold (43.8)
Larry James, Silver (43.9)
Ron Freeman, Bronze (44.4)

Women's 800-meter Run
Madeline Manning, Gold (2:00.9)

Men's 110-meter Hurdles
Willie Davenport, Gold (13.3)
Ervin Hall, Silver (13.4)

Men's 400-meter Relay
Jim Hines, Gold (38.2)
Charles Greene, Gold (38.2)
Mel Pender, Gold (38.2)
Ronnie Ray Smith, Gold (38.2)

Women's 400-meter Relay
Wyomia Tyus, Gold (42.8)
Barbara Ferrell, Gold (42.8)
Margaret Bailes, Gold (42.8)
Mildrette Netter, Gold (42.8)

Men's 1,600-meter Relay
Lee Evans, Gold (2:56.1)
Vince Matthews, Gold (2:56.1)
Ron Freeman, Gold (2:56.1)
Larry James, Gold (2:56.1)

Men's High Jump
Edward Caruthers, Silver (7' 3.5")

Men's Long Jump
Bob Beamon, Gold (29' 2.5")
Ralph Boston, Bronze (26' 9.25")

Men's Basketball, Gold
Spencer Haywood
Charlie Scott
Michael Barrett
James King
Calvin Fowler

Boxing: Featherweight
Albert Robinson, Silver

Boxing: Lightweight
Ronald Harris, Gold

Boxing: Light Welterweight
James Wallington, Bronze

Boxing: Light Middleweight
John Baldwin, Bronze

Boxing: Middleweight
Alfred Jones, Bronze

Boxing: Heavyweight
George Foreman, Gold

1972: MUNICH

Men's 100-meter Dash

Robert Taylor, Silver (10.24)

Men's 200-meter Dash

Larry Black, Silver (20.19)

Men's 400-meter Dash

Vince Matthews, Gold (44.66)

Wayne Collett, Silver (44.80)

Men's 110-meter Hurdles

Rod Milburn, Gold (13.24)

Men's 400-meter Relay

Eddie Hart, Gold (38.19)

Robert Taylor, Gold (38.19)

Larry Black, Gold (38.19)

Gerald Tinker, Gold (38.19)

Women's 1,600-meter Relay

Cheryl Toussain, Silver (3:25.2)

Mable Fergerson, Silver (3:25.2)

Madeline Manning, Silver (3:25.2)

Men's Long Jump

Randy Williams, Gold (27' .25")

Arnie Robinson, Bronze (26' 4")

Decathlon

Jeff Bennett, Bronze (7,974 pts.)

Boxing: Light Welterweight

Ray Seales, Gold

Boxing: Middleweight

Marvin Johnson, Bronze

1976: MONTREAL

Men's 200-meter Dash

Millard Hampton, Silver (20.29)

Dwayne Evans, Bronze (20.43)

Men's 400-meter Dash

Fred Newhouse, Silver (44.40)

Herman Frazier, Bronze (44.95)

Men's 110-meter Hurdles

Willie Davenport, Bronze (13.38)

Men's 400-meter Hurdles

Edwin Moses, Gold (47.64)

Men's 400-meter Relay

Millard Hampton, Gold (38.83)

Steve Riddick, Gold (38.83)

Harvey Glance, Gold (38.83)

John Jones, Gold (38.83)

Men's 1,600-meter Relay

Herman Frazier, Gold (2:58.7)

Benny Brown, Gold (2:58.7)

Maxie Parks, Gold (2:58.7)

Fred Newhouse, Gold (2:58.7)

Women's 1,600-meter Relay

Rosalyn Bryant, Silver (3:22.8)

Sheila Ingram, Silver (3:22.8)

Pamela Jiles, Silver (3:22.8)

Debra Sapenter, Silver (3:22.8)

Men's Long Jump

Arnie Robinson, Gold (27' 4.75")

Randy Williams, Silver (26' 7.25")

Men's Triple Jump

James Butts, Silver (56' 8.5")

Men's Basketball, Gold

Phil Ford

Adrian Dantley

Walter Davis

Quinn Buckner

Kenneth Carr

Scott May

Philip Hubbard

Women's Basketball, Silver

Lusia Harris

Charlotte Lewis

Boxing: Flyweight

Leo Randolph, Gold

Boxing: Lightweight

Howard David, Gold

Boxing: Light Welterweight

Sugar Ray Leonard, Gold

Boxing: Middleweight

Michael Spinks, Gold

Boxing: Light Heavyweight

Leon Spinks, Gold

Boxing: Heavyweight

Johnny Tate, Bronze

1984: LOS ANGELES

Men's 100-meter Dash

Carl Lewis, Gold (9.9)

Sam Graddy, Silver (10.19)

Women's 100-meter Dash

Evelyn Ashford, Gold (10.97)

Alice Brown, Silver (11.14)

Men's 200-meter Dash

Carl Lewis, Gold (19.80)

Kirk Baptiste, Silver (19.96)

Women's 200-meter Dash

Valerie Brisco-Hooks, Gold (21.81)

Florence Griffith, Silver (22.04)

Men's 400-meter Dash

Alonzo Babers, Gold (44.27)

Antonio McKay, Bronze (44.71)

Women's 400-meter Dash

Valerie Brisco-Hooks, Gold (48.83)

Chandra Cheeseborough, Silver (49.05)

Men's 800-meter Run

Earl Jones, Bronze (1:43.83)

Women's 800-meter Run

Kim Gallagher, Silver (1:58.63)

Women's 100-meter Hurdles

Benita Fitzgerald-Brown, Gold (12.84)

Kim Turner, Silver (12.88)

Men's 110-meter Hurdles

Roger Kingdom, Gold (13.20)

Greg Foster, Silver (13.23)

Men's 400-meter Hurdle

Edwin Moses, Gold (47.75)

Danny Harris, Silver (48.13)

Women's 400-meter Hurdles

Judi Brown, Silver (55.20)

Men's 400-meter Relay

Sam Graddy, Gold (37.83)

Ron Brown, Gold (37.83)

Calvin Smith, Gold (37.83)

Carl Lewis, Gold (37.83)

Men's 1,600-meter Relay

Sunder Nix, Gold (2:57.91)

Roy Armstead, Gold (2:57.91)

Alonzo Babers, Gold (2:57.91)

Antonio McKay, Gold (2:57.91)

Women's 1,600-meter Relay

Valerie Brisco-Hooks, Gold (3:18.29)

Chandra Cheeseborough, Gold (3:18.29)

Lillie Leatherwood, Gold (3:18.29)

Sherri Howard, Gold (3:18.29)

Men's Long Jump

Carl Lewis, Gold (28' .25")

Men's Triple Jump

Al Joyner, Gold (56' 7.5")

Mike Conley, Silver (56' 4.5")

Heptathlon

Jackie Joyner (-Kersee), Silver (6,386 pts.)

Men's Shot Put

Michael Carter, Gold (69' 2.5")

Men's Basketball, Gold

Patrick Ewing

Vern Fleming

Michael Jordan

Sam Perkins

Alvin Robertson

Wayman Tisdale

Leon Wood

Women's Basketball, Gold

Cathy Boswell

Teresa Edwards

Janice Lawrence

Pamela McGee

Cheryl Miller

Lynette Woodard

Boxing: Flyweight

Steven McCrory, Gold

Boxing: Featherweight

Meldrick Taylor, Gold

Boxing: Lightweight

Pernell Whitaker, Gold

Boxing: Light Welterweight

Jerry Page, Gold

Boxing: Welterweight

Mark Breland, Gold

Boxing: Light Middleweight

Frank Tate, Gold

Boxing: Middleweight

Virgil Hill, Silver

Boxing: Light Heavyweight

Evander Holyfield, Bronze

Boxing: Heavyweight

Henry Tillman, Gold

Boxing: Super Heavyweight

Tyrell Biggs, Gold

1988: SEOUL

Men's 100-meter Dash

Carl Lewis, Gold (9.92)

Calvin Smith, Silver (9.99)

Women's 100-meter Dash

Florence Griffith-Joyner, Gold (10.54)

Evelyn Ashford, Silver (10.83)

Men's 200-meter Dash

Joe DeLoach, Gold (19.75)

Carl Lewis, Silver (19.79)

Women's 200-meter Dash

Florence Griffith-Joyner, Gold (21.34)

Men's 400-meter Dash

Steve Lewis, Gold (43.87)

Butch Reynolds, Silver (43.93)

Danny Everett, Bronze (44.09)

Women's 800-meter Run

Kim Gallagher, Bronze (1:56.91)

Men's 110-meter Hurdles

Roger Kingdom, Gold (12.98)

Tonie Campbell, Bronze (13.38)

Men's 400-meter Hurdles

Andre Phillips, Gold (47.19)

Edwin Moses, Bronze (47.56)

Women's 400-meter Relay

Sheila Echols, Gold (41.98)

Florence Griffith-Joyner, Gold (41.98)

Evelyn Ashford, Gold (41.98)

Alice Brown, Gold (41.98)

Men's 1,600-meter Relay

Butch Reynolds, Gold (2:56.16)

Steve Lewis, Gold (2:56.16)

Antonio McKay, Gold (2:56.16)

Danny Everett, Gold (2:56.16)

Women's 1,600-meter Relay

Denean Howard-Hill, Silver (3:15.51)

Valerie Brisco, Silver (3:15.51)

Diane Dixon, Silver (3:15.51)

Florence Griffith-Joyner, Silver (3:15.51)

Men's Long Jump

Carl Lewis, Gold (28' 7.25")

Mike Powell, Silver (27' 10.25")

Larry Myricks, Bronze (27' 1.75")

Women's Long Jump

Jackie Joyner-Kersee, Gold (24' 3.5")

Heptathlon

Jackie Joyner-Kersee, Gold (7,291 pts.)

Baseball, Gold

Tom Goodwin

Ty Griffin

Men's Basketball, Bronze

Willie Anderson

Stacey Augmon

Bimbo Coles

Jeff Grayer

Hersey Hawkins

Danny Manning

J. R. Reid

Mitch Richmond

David Robinson

Charles E. Smith

Women's Basketball, Gold

Cindy Brown

Vicky Bullett

Cynthia Cooper

Teresa Edwards

Jennifer Gillom

Bridgette Gordon

Katrina McClain

Teresa Weatherspoon

Boxing: Bantamweight

Kennedy McKinney, Gold

Boxing: Middleweight

Roy Jones, Silver

Boxing: Light Heavyweight

Andrew Maynard, Gold

Boxing: Heavyweight

Ray Mercer, Gold

Boxing: Super Heavyweight

Riddick Bowe, Silver

Tennis: Women's Singles

Zina Garrison, Bronze

Tennis: Women's Doubles

Zina Garrison (with Pam Shriver), Gold

Wrestling: Lightweight (Freestyle)

Nate Carr, Bronze

Wrestling: Welterweight (Freestyle)

Kenny Monday, Gold

1992: BARCELONA

Men's 100-meter Dash

Dennis Mitchell, Bronze (10.04)

Women's 100-meter Dash

Gail Devers, Gold (10.82)

Men's 200-meter Dash

Mike Marsh, Gold (20.01)

Michael Bates, Bronze (20.38)

Women's 200-meter Dash

Gwen Torrence, Gold (21.81)

Men's 400-meter Dash

Quincy Watts, Gold (43.50)

Steve Lewis, Silver (44.21)

Men's 800-meter Run

Johnny Gray, Bronze (1:43.97)

Men's 110-meter Hurdles

Tony Dees, Silver (13.24)

Men's 400-meter Hurdles

Kevin Young, Gold (46.78)

Women's 400-meter Hurdles

Sandra Farmer, Silver (53.69)

Janeene Vickers, Bronze (54.31)

Men's 400-meter Relay

Mike Marsh, Gold (37.40)

Leroy Burrell, Gold (37.40)

Dennis Mitchell, Gold (37.40)

Carl Lewis, Gold (37.40)

Women's 400-meter Relay

Evelyn Ashford, Gold (42.11)

Esther Jones, Gold (42.11)

Carlette Guidry-White, Gold (42.11)

Gwen Torrence, Gold (42.11)

Men's 800-meter Relay

Andrew Valmon, Gold (2:55.74)

Quincy Watts, Gold (2:55.74)

Michael Johnson, Gold (2:55.74)

Steve Lewis, Gold (2:55.74)

Women's 800-meter Relay

Natasha Kaiser, Silver (3:20.92)

Gwen Torrence, Silver (3:20.92)

Jearl Miles, Silver (3:20.92)

Rochelle Stevens, Silver (3:20.92)

Men's High Jump

Hollis Conway, Bronze (7' 8")

Men's Long Jump

Carl Lewis, Gold (28' 5.5")

Mike Powell, Silver (28' 4.25")

Joe Greene, Bronze (27' 4.5")

Women's Long Jump

Jackie Joyner-Kersee, Bronze (23' 2.5")

Men's Triple Jump

Mike Conley, Gold (59' 7.5")

Charlie Simpkins, Silver (57' 9")

Heptathlon

Jackie Joyner-Kersee, Gold (7,044 pts.)

Men's Basketball, Gold

Charles Barkley

Clyde Drexler

Patrick Ewing

Magic Johnson

Michael Jordan

Karl Malone

Scottie Pippen

David Robinson

Women's Basketball, Bronze

Vicky Bullett

Daedra Charles

Cynthia Cooper

Teresa Edwards

Carolyn Jones

Katrina McClain

Vickie Orr

Teresa Weatherspoon

Boxing: Flyweight

Tim Austin, Bronze

Boxing: Middleweight

Chris Byrd, Silver

Wrestling: Middleweight (Freestyle)

Kevin Jackson, Gold

Wrestling: Welterweight (Freestyle)

Kenny Monday, Silver

1996: ATLANTA

Women's 100-meter Dash

Gail Devers, Gold (10.94)

Gwen Torrence, Bronze (10.96)

Men's 200-meter Dash

Michael Johnson, Gold (19.32)

Men's 400-meter Dash

Michael Johnson, Gold (43.49)

Men's 110-meter Hurdles

Allen Johnson Gold (12.95)

Mark Crear, Silver (13.09)

Men's 400-meter Hurdles

Derrick Adkins, Gold (47.54)

Calvin Davis, Bronze (47.96)

Women's 400-meter Hurdles

Kim Batten, Silver (53.08)

Tonja Buford-Bailey, Bronze (53.22)

Men's 400-meter Relay

Tim Harden, Silver (38.05)

Jon Drummond, Silver (38.05)

Michael Marsh, Silver (38.05)

Dennis Mitchell, Silver (38.05)

Women's 400-meter Relay
Gail Devers, Gold (41.95)

Chryste Gaines, Gold (41.95)

Gwen Torrence, Gold (41.95)

Inger Miller, Gold (41.95)

Men's 1,600-meter Relay
LaMont Smith, Gold (2:55.99)

Alvin Harrison, Gold (2:55.99)

Derek Mills, Gold (2:55.99)

Anthuan Maybank, Gold (2:55.99)

Women's 1,600-meter Relay
Rochelle Stevens, Gold (3:20.91)

Maicel Malone, Gold (3:20.91)

Kim Graham, Gold (3:20.91)

Jearl Miles, Gold (3:20.91)

Men's High Jump
Charles Austin, Gold (7' 10")

Men's Long Jump
Carl Lewis, Gold (27' 10.75")

Joe Greene, Bronze (27' .50")

Women's Long Jump
Jackie Joyner-Kersee, Bronze (22' 11")

Men's Triple Jump
Kenny Harrison, Gold (59' 4")

Decathlon
Dan O'Brien, Gold (8,824 pts.)

Baseball, Bronze
Jacque Jones

Men's Basketball, Gold
Mitch Richmond

Scottie Pippen

Gary Payton

Charles Barkley

Hakeem Olajuwon

David Robinson

Penny Hardaway

Grant Hill

Karl Malone

Reggie Miller

Women's Basketball, Gold
Teresa Edwards

Ruth Bolton

Lisa Leslie

Katrina McClain

Sheryl Swoopes

Nikki McCray

Dawn Staley

Venus Lacey

Carla McGhee

Women's Gymnastics: Floor Exercise
Dominique Dawes, Bronze

Women's Gymnastics: Team
Dominique Dawes, Gold

Boxing: Featherweight
Floyd Mayweather, Bronze

Boxing: Lightweight
Terrance Cauthen, Bronze

Boxing: Light Middleweight
David Reid, Gold

Boxing: Middleweight
Rhoshii Wells, Bronze

Boxing: Light Heavyweight
Antonio Tarver, Bronze

Boxing: Heavyweight
Nate Jones, Bronze

2000: SYDNEY

Men's 100-meter Dash
Maurice Green, Gold (9.87)

Women's 100-meter Dash
Marion Jones, Gold (10.75) (forfeited in 2007)

Women's 200-meter Dash
Marion Jones, Gold (21.84) (forfeited in 2007)

Men's 400-meter Dash
Michael Johnson, Gold (43.83)

Alvin Harrison, Silver (44.40)

Women's 100-meter Hurdles
Melissa Morrison, Bronze (12.65)

Men's 110-meter Hurdles
Terrence Trammell, Silver (13.16)

Mark Crear, Bronze (13.22)

Men's 400-meter Hurdles
Angelo Taylor, Gold (47.50)

Men's 400-meter Relay
Maurice Green, Gold (37.61)

Jonathan Drummond, Gold (37.61)

Brian Lewis, Gold (37.61)

Bernard Williams, Gold (37.61)

Women's 400-meter Relay
Marion Jones, Bronze (42.20) (forfeited in 2007)

Torri Edwards, Bronze (42.20)

Chryste Gaines, Bronze (42.20)

Nanceen Perry, Bronze (42.20)

Men's 1,600-meter Relay
Michael Johnson, Gold (2:56.35)

Alvin Harrison, Gold (2:56.35)

Antonio Pettigrew, Gold (2:56.35)

Calvin Harrison, Gold (2:56.35)

Women's 1,600-meter Relay
Marion Jones, Gold (3:22.62) (forfeited in 2007)

La Tasha Colander-Richardson, Gold (3:22.62)

Monique Hennagan, Gold (3:22.62)

Jearl Miles(-Clark), Gold (3:22.62)

Women's Long Jump
Marion Jones, Bronze (22' 8.25") (forfeited in 2007)

Decathlon
Chris Huffins, Bronze (8,595 pts.)

Men's Pole Vault
Lawrence Johnson, Silver (19' 4.25")

Baseball, Gold
Travis Dawkins

Anthony Sanders

Ernie Young

Men's Basketball, Gold
Shareef Abdur-Rahim

Ray Allen

Vin Baker

Vince Carter

Kevin Garnett

Tim Hardaway

Allan Houston

Jason Kidd

Antonio McDyess

Alonzo Mourning

Gary Payton

Steve Smith

Women's Basketball, Gold

Ruth Bolton-Holifield

Teresa Edwards

Yolanda Griffith

Chamique Holdsclaw

Lisa Leslie

Nikki McCray

DeLisha Milton

Dawn Staley

Natalie Williams

Boxing: Bantamweight

Clarence Vinson, Bronze

Boxing: Light Middleweight

Jermain Taylor, Bronze

Boxing: Light Welterweight

Ricardo Williams Jr., Silver

Tennis: Women's Singles

Venus Williams, Gold

Tennis: Women's Doubles

Serena Williams, Gold

Venus Williams, Gold

Men's Beach Volleyball

Dain Blanton, Gold

2002: SALT LAKE CITY (WINTER)

Bobsled: Two-woman

Vonetta Flowers (with Jill Bakken), Gold

Bobsled: Four-man

Garrett Hines, Silver

Randy Jones, Silver

Bill Schuffenhauer, Silver

2004: ATHENS

Men's 100-meter Dash

Justin Gatlin, Gold (9.85)

Maurice Greene, Bronze (9.87)

Women's 100-meter Dash

Lauryn Williams, Silver (10.96)

Men's 200-meter Dash

Shawn Crawford, Gold (19.79)

Bernard Williams, Silver (20.01)

Justin Gatlin, Bronze (20.03)

Women's 200-meter Dash

Allyson Felix, Silver (22.18)

Men's 400-meter Dash

Otis Harris, Silver (44.16)

Derrick Brew, Bronze (44.42)

Women's 100-meter Hurdles

Melissa Morrison-Howard, Bronze (12.53)

Men's 110-meter Hurdles

Terrence Trammell, Silver (13.18)

Men's 4X100-meter Relay

Shawn Crawford, Silver (38.08)

Justin Gatlin, Silver (38.08)

Maurice Greene, Silver (38.08)

Men's 4X400-meter Relay

Otis Harris, Gold (2.55.91)

Derrick Best, Gold (2.55.91)

Darold Williams, Gold (2.55.91)

Women's 4x400-meter Relay

DeeDee Trotter, Gold

Monique Henderson, Gold

Sanya Richards, Gold

Monique Hennagan, Gold

Men's Long Jump

Dwight Phillips, Gold (8.60)

Men's Basketball, Bronze

Carmelo Anthony

Carlos Boozer

Tim Duncan

Allen Iverson

LeBron James

Richard Jefferson

Stephon Marbury

Shawn Marion

Lamarr Odom

Emeka Okafor

Amare Stoudmere

Dwyane Wade

Women's Basketball, Gold

Swintayla "Swin" Cash

Tamika Catchings

Yolanda Griffith

Shannon "Pee Wee" Johnson

Lisa Leslie

Sheryl Swoopes

Tina Thompson

Women's Football (Soccer), Gold

Briana Scurry

Angela Hucles

Boxing: Middleweight

Andre Durell, Bronze

Boxing: Light Heavyweight

Andre Ward, Gold

2006: TORINO (WINTER)

Speedskating: Men's Individual 1,000-meter Race

Shani Davis, Silver (1:08.9)

Speedskating: Men's Individual 1,500-meter Race

Shani Davis, Gold (1:46.9)

2008: BEIJING, CHINA

Men's 100-meter Dash

Walter Dix, Bronze (22:30)

Men's 200-meter Dash

Shawn Crawford, Silver (22.20)

Walter Dix, Bronze (22:20)

Women's 200-meter Dash

Allyson Felix, Silver (19:30)

Men's 400-meter Dash

LaShawn Merritt, Gold (21:20)

David Neville, Bronze (21:20)

Women's 100-meter Hurdles

Dawn Harper, Gold (12:54)

Men's 110-meter Hurdles

David Oliver, Bronze (13:02)

David Payne, Silver (13.17)

Men's 400-meter Hurdles

Kerron Clement, Silver (47.98)

Bershawn Johnson, Bronze (48.06)

Women's 400-meter Hurdles

Sheena Tosta, Silver (53.70)

Men's 4X400-meter Relay

LaShawn Merritt, Gold (21:05)

David Neville, Gold (21:05)

Women's 4X400-meter Relay

Allyson Felix, Gold (20:40)

Monique Henderson, Gold (20:40)

Sanya Richards, Gold (20:40)

Men's Baseball, Gold

Dexter Fowler

Men's Basketball, Gold

Carlos Boozer

Chris Bosh

Kobe Bryant

Anthony Carmello

Dwight Howard

LeBron James

Jason Kidd

Chris Paul

Tayshaun Prince

Michael Redd

Dwyane Wade

Deron Williams

Women's Basketball, Gold

Seimone Augustus

Sue Bird

Tamika Catchings

Sylvia Fowles

Kara Lawson

Lisa Leslie

DeLisha Milton(-Jones)

Candace Parker

Cappie Pondexter

Katie Smith

Diana Taurasi

Tina Thompson

Boxing: Heavyweight

Deontay Wilder, Bronze

Men's Swimming, 4X100-meter Freestyle Relay

Cullen Jones, Gold

Women's Softball, Silver

Natasha Watley

Tennis: Women's Doubles

Venus and Serena Williams, Gold

2010: VANCOUVER (WINTER)

Speedskating: Men's Individual 1,000-meter Race

Shani Davis, Gold (1:08.94)

Speedskating: Men's Individual 1,500-meter Race

Shani Davis, Silver (1:46.10)

Bobsled: Two-woman

Elana Meyers (with Erin Pac), Bronze

OTHER SPORTS AWARDS

ASSOCIATED PRESS ATHLETE OF THE YEAR

Male

1935: Joe Louis (boxing)

1936: Jesse Owens (track and field)

1954: Willie Mays (baseball)

1960: Rafer Johnson (track and field)

1962: Maury Wills (baseball)

1966: Frank Robinson (baseball)

1973: O. J. Simpson (football)

1974: Muhammad Ali (boxing)

1979: Willie Stargell (baseball)

1983–1984: Carl Lewis (track and field)

1985: Dwight Gooden (baseball)

1991–1993: Michael Jordan (basketball)

1994: George Foreman (boxing)

1996: Michael Johnson (track and field)

1997: Tiger Woods (golf)

1999–2000: Tiger Woods (golf)

2001: Barry Bonds (baseball)

2006: Tiger Woods (golf)

Female

1957–1958: Althea Gibson (tennis)

1960–1961: Wilma Rudolph (track and field)

1987: Jackie Joyner-Kersee (track and field)

1988: Florence Griffith Joyner (track and field)

1993: Sheryl Swoopes (college basketball)

2000: Marion Jones (track and field)

2002: Serena Williams (tennis)

2008: Candace Parker (basketball)

2009: Serena Williams (tennis)

BILL RUSSELL NBA FINALS MOST VALUABLE PLAYER AWARD (BASKETBALL)

1970: Willis Reed, New York Knicks, center/forward

1971: Kareem Abdul-Jabbar (né Lew Alcindor), Milwaukee Bucks, center

1972: Wilt Chamberlain, Los Angeles Lakers, center

1973: Willis Reed, New York Knicks, center/forward

1976: Jo Jo White, Boston Celtics, guard

1978: Wes Unseld, Washington Bullets, center/forward

1979: Dennis Johnson, Seattle SuperSonics, guard

1980: Magic Johnson, Los Angeles Lakers, guard

1981: Cedric Maxwell, Boston Celtics, forward

1982: Magic Johnson, Los Angeles Lakers, guard

1983: Moses Malone, Philadelphia 76ers, center/forward

1985: Kareem Abdul-Jabbar, Los Angeles Lakers, center

1987: Magic Johnson, Los Angeles Lakers, guard

1988: James Worthy, Los Angeles Lakers, forward

1989: Joe Dumars, Detroit Pistons, guard

1990: Isiah Thomas, Detroit Pistons, guard

1991–1993: Michael Jordan, Chicago Bulls, guard

1994–1995: Hakeem Olajuwon, Houston Rockets, center

1996–1998: Michael Jordan, Chicago Bulls, guard

1999: Tim Duncan, San Antonio Spurs, forward/center

2000–2002: Shaquille O'Neal, Los Angeles Lakers, center

2003: Tim Duncan, San Antonio Spurs, forward/center

2004: Chauncey Billups, Detroit Pistons, guard

2005: Tim Duncan, San Antonio Spurs, forward/center

2006: Dwyane Wade, Miami Heat, guard

2007: Tony Parker, San Antonio Spurs, guard

2008: Paul Pierce, Boston Celtics, forward/guard

2009–2010: Kobe Bryant, Los Angeles Lakers, guard

HEISMAN MEMORIAL TROPHY

1961: Ernie Davis, Syracuse University, running back

1965: Mike Garrett, University of Southern California, running back

1968: O. J. Simpson, University of Southern California, running back

1972: Johnny Rodgers, University of Nebraska, running back

1974: Archie Griffin, Ohio State University, running back

1975: Archie Griffin, Ohio State University, running back

1976: Tony Dorsett, University of Pittsburgh, running back

1977: Earl Campbell, University of Texas, running back

1978: Billy Sims, University of Oklahoma, running back

1979: Charles White, University of Southern California, running back

1980: George Rogers, University of South Carolina, running back

1981: Marcus Allen, University of Southern California, running back

1982: Herschel Walker, University of Georgia, running back

1983: Mike Rozier, University of Nebraska, running back

1985: Bo Jackson, Auburn University, running back

1987: Tim Brown, University of Notre Dame, wide receiver

1988: Barry Sanders, Oklahoma State University, running back

1989: Andre Ware, University of Houston, quarterback

1991: Desmond Howard, University of Michigan, wide receiver

1993: Charlie Ward, Florida State University, quarterback

1994: Rashaan Salaam, University of Colorado, running back

1995: Eddie George, Ohio State University, running back

1997: Charles Woodson, University of Michigan, cornerback/wide receiver

1998: Ricky Williams, University of Texas, running back

1999: Ron Dayne, University of Wisconsin, running back

2005: Reggie Bush, University of Southern California, running back (forfeited in 2010)

2006: Troy Smith, Ohio State University, quarterback

2009: Mark Ingram, University of Alabama, running back

INTERNATIONAL FEDERATION OF BODYBUILDING AND FITNESS, BODYBUILDING CHAMPIONS

Mr. Olympia

1967–1969: Sergio Oliva

1982: Chris Dickerson

1984–1991: Lee Haney

1998–2005: Ronnie Coleman

2008: Dexter Jackson

Ms. Olympia

1983: Carla Dunlap

1990–1995: Lenda Murray

2002–2003: Lenda Murray

2004: Iris Kyle

2006–2009: Iris Kyle

MAJOR LEAGUE BASEBALL (MLB) MOST VALUABLE PLAYER AWARD

American League

1963: Elston Howard, New York Yankees, C

1966: Frank Robinson, Baltimore Orioles, OF

1971: Vida Blue, Oakland Athletics, LHP

1972: Dick Allen, Chicago White Sox, 1B

1973: Reggie Jackson, Oakland Athletics, OF

1977: Rod Carew, Minnesota Twins, 1B

1978: Jim Rice, Boston Red Sox, OF

1979: Don Baylor, California Angels, DH

1987: George Bell, Toronto Blue Jays, OF

1990: Rickey Henderson, Oakland Athletics, OF

1993–1994: Frank Thomas, Chicago White Sox, 1B

1995: Mo Vaughn, Boston Red Sox, 1B

1996: Juan González, Texas Rangers, OF

1997: Ken Griffey Jr., Seattle Mariners, OF

1998: Juan González, Texas Rangers, OF

2002: Miguel Tejada, Oakland Athletics, SS

2004: Vladimir Guerrero, Anaheim Angels, OF

2005: Alex Rodriguez, New York Yankees, 3B

2007: Alex Rodriguez, New York Yankees, 3B

National League

1949: Jackie Robinson, Brooklyn Dodgers, 2B

1951: Roy Campanella, Brooklyn Dodgers, C

1953: Roy Campanella, Brooklyn Dodgers, C

1954: Willie Mays, New York Giants, OF

1955: Roy Campanella, Brooklyn Dodgers, C

1956: Don Newcombe, Brooklyn Dodgers, RHP

1957: Hank Aaron, Milwaukee Braves, OF

1958–1959: Ernie Banks, Chicago Cubs, SS

1961: Frank Robinson, Cincinnati Reds, OF

1962: Maury Wills, Los Angeles Dodgers, SS

1965: Willie Mays, San Francisco Giants, OF

1966: Roberto Clemente, Pittsburgh Pirates, OF

1967: Orlando Cepeda, St. Louis Cardinals, 1B

1968: Bob Gibson, St. Louis Cardinals, RHP

1969: Willie McCovey, San Francisco Giants, 1B

1975–1976: Joe Morgan, Cincinnati Reds, 2B

1977: George Foster, Cincinnati Reds, OF

1978: Dave Parker, Pittsburgh Pirates, OF

1979: Willie Stargell, Pittsburgh Pirates, 1B

1985: Willie McGee, St. Louis Cardinals, OF

1987: Andre Dawson, Chicago Cubs, OF

1989: Kevin Mitchell, San Francisco Giants, OF

1990: Barry Bonds, Pittsburgh Pirates, OF

1991: Terry Pendleton, Atlanta Braves, 3B

1992: Barry Bonds, Pittsburgh Pirates, OF

1993: Barry Bonds, San Francisco Giants, OF

1995: Barry Larkin, Cincinnati Reds, SS

1998: Sammy Sosa, Chicago Cubs, OF

2001–2004: Barry Bonds, San Francisco Giants, OF

2005: Albert Pujols, St. Louis Cardinals, 1B

2006: Ryan Howard, Philadelphia Phillies, 1B

2007: Jimmy Rollins, Philadelphia Phillies, SS

2008–2009: Albert Pujols, St. Louis Cardinals, 1B

NATIONAL BASKETBALL ASSOCIATION (NBA) MOST VALUABLE PLAYER AWARD

1957–58: Bill Russell, Boston Celtics, center

1959–60: Wilt Chamberlain, Philadelphia Warriors, center

1960–63: Bill Russell, Boston Celtics, center

1963–64: Oscar Robertson, Cincinnati Royals, guard

1964–65: Bill Russell, Boston Celtics, center

1965–68: Wilt Chamberlain, Philadelphia 76ers, center

1968–69: Wes Unseld, Baltimore Bullets, center/forward

1969–70: Willis Reed, New York Knicks, center/forward

1970–72: Kareem Abdul-Jabbar (né Lew Alcindor), Milwaukee Bucks, center

1972–73: Dave Cowens, Boston Celtics, center

1973–74: Kareem Abdul-Jabbar (né Lew Alcindor), Milwaukee Bucks, center

1974–75: Bob McAdoo, Buffalo Braves, forward/center

1975–77: Kareem Abdul-Jabbar, Los Angeles Lakers, center

1978–79: Moses Malone, Houston Rockets, center/forward

1979–80: Kareem Abdul-Jabbar, Los Angeles Lakers, center

1980–81: Julius Erving, Philadelphia 76ers, forward

1981–83: Moses Malone, Houston Rockets, center/forward

1986–87: Magic Johnson, Los Angeles Lakers, guard

1987–88: Michael Jordan, Chicago Bulls, guard

1988–90: Magic Johnson, Los Angeles Lakers, guard

1990–92: Michael Jordan, Chicago Bulls, guard

1992–93: Charles Barkley, Phoenix Suns, forward

1993–94: Hakeem Olajuwon, Houston Rockets, center

1994–95: David Robinson, San Antonio Spurs, center

1995–96: Michael Jordan, Chicago Bulls, guard

1996–97: Karl Malone, Utah Jazz, forward

1997–98: Michael Jordan, Chicago Bulls, guard

1998–99: Karl Malone, Utah Jazz, forward

1999–2000: Shaquille O'Neal, Los Angeles Lakers, center

2000–01: Allen Iverson, Philadelphia 76ers, guard

2001–03: Tim Duncan, San Antonio Spurs, forward/center

2003–04: Kevin Garnett, Minnesota Timberwolves, forward

2007–08: Kobe Bryant, Los Angeles Lakers, guard

2008–10: LeBron James, Cleveland Cavaliers, forward

NATIONAL FOOTBALL LEAGUE MOST VALUABLE PLAYER AWARD (ASSOCIATED PRESS)

1957–1958: Jim Brown, Cleveland Browns, running back

1965: Jim Brown, Cleveland Browns, running back

1971: Alan Page, Minnesota Vikings, defensive tackle

1972: Larry Brown, Washington Redskins, running back

1973: O. J. Simpson, Buffalo Bills, running back

1977: Walter Payton, Chicago Bears, running back

1979: Earl Campbell, Houston Oilers, running back

1985: Marcus Allen, Los Angeles Raiders, running back

1986: Lawrence Taylor, New York Giants, linebacker

1991: Thurman Thomas, Buffalo Bills, running back

1993: Emmitt Smith, Dallas Cowboys, running back

1997: Barry Sanders, Detroit Lions, running back

1998: Terrell Davis, Denver Broncos, running back

2000: Marshall Faulk, St. Louis Rams, running back

2003: Steve McNair, Tennessee Titans, quarterback

2005: Shaun Alexander, Seattle Seahawks, running back

2006: LaDainian Tomlinson, San Diego Chargers, running back

NATIONAL TRACK AND FIELD HALL OF FAME INDUCTEES

1974: Ralph Boston; Lee Calhoun; Harrison Dillard; Rafer Johnson; Jesse Owens; Wilma Rudolph; Malvin Whitfield

1975: Alice Coachman; Ralph Metcalfe

1976: Mae Faggs; Robert Hayes; Hayes Jones

1977: Robert Beamon; Andrew Stanfield

1978: Tommie Smith; John Woodruff

1979: Jim Hines; William DeHart Hubbard; Edith McGuire

1980: Dave Albritton; Wyomia Tyus

1981: Willye White

1982: Willie Davenport; Eddie Tolan

1983: Lee Evans; LeRoy Walker

1984: Madeline Manning Mims; Joe Yancey

1986: Norwood Barney Ewell

1987: Eulace Peacock; Martha Watson

1988: Gregory Bell; Barbara Ferrell

1989: Milt Campbell; Nell Jackson; Edward Temple

1990: Charles Dumas

1992: Charlie Jenkins; Archie Williams

1993: Stan Wright

1994: Cornelius Johnson; Edwin Moses

1995: Valerie Brisco; Florence Griffith Joyner

1997: Evelyn Ashford; Henry Carr; Renaldo Nehemiah

1998: Greg Foster

1999: Willie Banks; Larry Ellis

2000: Chandra Cheeseborough

2001: Carl Lewis; Larry Myricks

2002: Gwen Torrence

2003: John Carlos

2004: Mike Conley; Michael Johnson; Jackie Joyner-Kersee

2005: Earlene Brown; Mike Powell

2006: Dan O'Brien; Kevin Young

2007: Calvin Smith

2008: Johnny Gray

2009: Joetta Clark Diggs; Andre Phillips; Willie Steele; Randy Williams

PGA PLAYER OF THE YEAR

1997: Tiger Woods

1999–2003: Tiger Woods

2005–2007: Tiger Woods

2009: Tiger Woods

SPORTS ILLUSTRATED SPORTSMAN/SPORTSWOMAN OF THE YEAR

1958: Rafer Johnson (track and field)

1968: Bill Russell (basketball)

1974: Muhammad Ali (boxing)

1979: Willie Stargell (baseball)

1981: Sugar Ray Leonard (boxing)

1984: Edwin Moses (track and field)

1985: Kareem Abdul-Jabbar (basketball)

1987: Judi Brown King (track and field); Rory Sparrow (basketball); Reggie Williams (football)

1991: Michael Jordan (basketball)

1992: Arthur Ashe (tennis)

2000: Tiger Woods (golf)

2003: David Robinson (basketball); Tim Duncan (basketball)

2006: Dwyane Wade (basketball)

2009: Derek Jeter (baseball)

SULLIVAN AWARD, AMATEUR ATHLETIC UNION

1955: Harrison Dillard (track and field)

1960: Rafer Johnson (track and field)

1961: Wilma Rudolph (track and field)

1981: Carl Lewis (track and field)

1983: Edwin Moses (track and field)

1986: Jackie Joyner-Kersee (track and field)

1988: Florence Griffith Joyner (track and field)

1991: Mike Powell (track and field)

1993: Charlie Ward (football)

1996: Michael Johnson (track and field)

1998: Chamique Holdsclaw (basketball)

SUPER BOWL MOST VALUABLE PLAYER AWARD

1975: Franco Harris, Pittsburgh Steelers, running back

1976: Lynn Swann, Pittsburgh Steelers, wide receiver

1978: Harvey Martin, Dallas Cowboys, defensive end

1984: Marcus Allen, Los Angeles Raiders, running back

1986: Richard Dent, Chicago Bears, defensive end

1988: Doug Williams, Washington Redskins, quarterback

1989: Jerry Rice, San Francisco 49ers, wide receiver

1991: Ottis Anderson, New York Giants, running back

1994: Emmitt Smith, Dallas Cowboys, running back

1996: Larry Brown, Dallas Cowboys, cornerback

1997: Desmond Howard, Green Bay Packers, kick returner/punt returner

1998: Terrell Davis, Denver Broncos, running back

2001: Ray Lewis, Baltimore Ravens, linebacker

2003: Dexter Jackson, Tampa Bay Buccaneers, safety

2005: Deion Branch, New England Patriots, wide receiver

2006: Hines Ward, Pittsburgh Steelers, wide receiver

2009: Santonio Holmes, Pittsburgh Steelers, wide receiver

U.S. OPEN (TENNIS)

Men's Singles

1968: Arthur Ashe

Women's Singles

1957: Althea Gibson

1958: Althea Gibson

1999: Serena Williams

2000: Venus Williams

2001: Venus Williams

2002: Serena Williams

2008: Serena Williams

Women's Doubles

1999: Serena Williams and Venus Williams

2009: Serena Williams and Venus Williams

Mixed Doubles

1957: Althea Gibson (with Kurt Nielsen)

1998: Serena Williams (with Max Mirnyi)

WIMBLEDON (TENNIS)

Men's Singles

1975: Arthur Ashe

Women's Singles

1957: Althea Gibson

1958: Althea Gibson

2000: Venus Williams

2001: Venus Williams

2002: Serena Williams

2003: Serena Williams

2005: Venus Williams

2007: Venus Williams

2008: Venus Williams

2009: Serena Williams

Women's Doubles

1956: Althea Gibson (with Angela Buxton)

1957: Althea Gibson (with Darlene Hard)

1958: Althea Gibson (with Maria Bueno)

2000: Venus Williams and Serena Williams

2002: Venus Williams and Serena Williams

2008: Venus Williams and Serena Williams

2009: Venus Williams and Serena Williams

Mixed Doubles

1988: Zina Garrison (with Sherwood Stewart)

1990: Zina Garrison (with Rick Leach)

1998: Serena Williams (with Max Mirnyi)

AUSTRALIAN OPEN (TENNIS)

Men's Singles

1970: Arthur Ashe

Men's Doubles

1977: Arthur Ashe (with Tony Roche)

Women's Singles

2003: Serena Williams

2005: Serena Williams

2007: Serena Williams

2009: Serena Williams

2010: Serena Williams

Women's Doubles

1957: Althea Gibson (with Shirley Fry)

2001: Serena Williams and Venus Williams

2003: Serena Williams and Venus Williams

2009: Serena Williams and Venus Williams

2010: Serena Williams and Venus Williams

Mixed Doubles

1987: Zina Garrison (with Sherwood Stewart)

1998: Venus Williams (with Justin Gimelstob)

FRENCH OPEN (TENNIS)

Men's Doubles

1971: Arthur Ashe (with Marty Riessen)

Women's Singles

1956: Althea Gibson

2002: Serena Williams

Women's Doubles

1956: Althea Gibson (with Angela Buxton)

1999: Venus Williams and Serena Williams

Mixed Doubles

1998: Venus Williams (with Justin Gimelstob)

WOMEN'S NATIONAL BASKETBALL ASSOCIATION (WNBA) MOST VALUABLE PLAYER AWARD

1997–1998: Cynthia Cooper, Houston Comets, guard

1999: Yolanda Griffith, Sacramento Monarchs, center

2000: Sheryl Swoopes, Houston Comets, guard

2001: Lisa Leslie, Los Angeles Sparks, center

2002: Sheryl Swoopes, Houston Comets, guard

2004: Lisa Leslie, Los Angeles Sparks, center

2005: Sheryl Swoopes, Houston Comets, guard

2006: Lisa Leslie, Los Angeles Sparks, center

2008: Candace Parker, Los Angeles Sparks, forward

WORLD SERIES MOST VALUABLE PLAYER AWARD

1967: Bob Gibson, St. Louis Cardinals, RHP

1969: Donn Clendenon, New York Mets, 1B

1971: Roberto Clemente, Pittsburgh Pirates, OF

1973: Reggie Jackson, Oakland Athletics, OF

1977: Reggie Jackson, New York Yankees, OF

1979: Willie Stargell, Pittsburgh Pirates, 1B

1981: Pedro Guerrero, Los Angeles Dodgers, OF

1989: Dave Stewart, Oakland Athletics, RHP

1990: José Rijo, Cincinnati Reds, RHP

1997: Liván Hernández, Florida Marlins, RHP

1999: Mariano Rivera, New York Yankees, RHP

2000: Derek Jeter, New York Yankees, SS

2004: Manny Ramirez, Boston Red Sox, OF

2005: Jermaine Dye, Chicago White Sox, OF

MISCELLANEOUS AWARDS AND HONORS

BEAUTY PAGEANTS

Miss America

1984: Vanessa L. Williams (New York); Suzette Charles (New Jersey)

1990: Debbye Turner (Missouri)

1991: Marjorie Vincent (Illinois)

1994: Kimberly Clarice Aiken (South Carolina)

2003: Erika Harold (Illinois)

2004: Ericka Dunlap (Florida)

2010: Caressa Cameron (Virginia)

Miss Black America

1968: Sandy Williams (Pennsylvania)

1969: G. O. Smith (New York)

1970: Stephanie Clark (District of Columbia)

1971: Joyce Warner (Florida)

1972: Linda Barney (New Jersey)

1973: Arnice Russell (New York)

1974: Von Gretchen Sheppard (California)

1975: Helen Ford (Mississippi)

1976: Twanna Kilgore (District of Columbia)

1977: Claire Ford (Tennessee)

1978: Lydia Jackson (New Jersey)

1979: Veretta Shankle (Mississippi)

1980: Sharon Wright (Illinois)

1981: Pamela Jenks (Massachusetts)

1982: Phyllis Tucker (Florida)

1983: Sonia Robinson (Wisconsin)

1984: Lydia Garrett (South Carolina)

1985: Amina Fakir (Michigan)

1986: Rachel Oliver (Massachusetts)

1987: Leila McBride (Colorado)

1989: Paula Swynn (District of Columbia)

1990: Rosie Jones (Connecticut)

1991: Sharmelle Sullivan (Indiana)

1992: Marilyn DeShields

1993: Pilar Ginger Fort

1994: Karen Wallace

1995: Asheera Ahmad

Miss USA

1990: Carole Gist (Michigan)

1992: Shannon Marketic (California)

1993: Kenya Moore (Michigan)

1994: Frances Louise "Lu" Parker (South Carolina)

1995: Chelsi Smith (Texas)

1996: Ali Landry (Louisiana)

2000: Lynnette Cole (Tennessee)

2002: Shauntay Hinton (District of Columbia)

2007: Rachel Smith (Tennessee)

2008: Crystle Stewart (Texas)

U.S. POSTAL SERVICE STAMPS DEPICTING AFRICAN AMERICAN HISTORY

Alvin Ailey

Marian Anderson

Louis Armstrong

Arthur Ashe

James Baldwin

Benjamin Banneker

Count Basie

Jim Beckwourth
Mary McLeod Bethune
James Hubert "Eubie" Blake
Ralph J. Bunche
George Washington Carver
Charles W. Chesnutt
Roberto Clemente
Nat "King" Cole
Bessie Coleman
John Coltrane
Anna Julia Cooper
Allison Davis
Benjamin O. Davis Sr.
Desegregation of Public Schools
Frederick Douglass
Charles R. Drew
W. E. B. Du Bois
Jean Baptiste Point du Sable
Paul Laurence Dunbar
Duke Ellington
Emancipation Proclamation
Ella Fitzgerald
Erroll Garner
Josh Gibson
W. C. Handy
Patricia Roberts Harris
Coleman Hawkins
Matthew A. Henson
Billie Holiday
Howlin' Wolf
Langston Hughes
Zora Neale Hurston
Mahalia Jackson
James Price Johnson
James Weldon Johnson
Robert Johnson
Scott Joplin
Percy L. Julian
Ernest Everett Just
Martin Luther King Jr.
Leadbelly (Hudson William Ledbetter)
Joe Louis
Malcolm X
Thurgood Marshall
Roberta Martin
Jan E. Matzeliger
Hattie McDaniel
Clyde McPhatter
Charles Mingus
Thelonious Monk
Jelly Roll Morton
Jesse Owens
Satchel Paige
Charlie "Bird" Parker
Ethel L. Payne
Bill Pickett
Salem Poor
Ma Rainey
A. Philip Randolph
Otis Redding
Paul Robeson
Jackie Robinson
Sugar Ray Robinson
Wilma Rudolph
Jimmy Rushing
Bessie Smith
Henry Ossawa Tanner
Sonny Terry
Sister Rosetta Tharpe
Thirteenth Amendment
Sojourner Truth
Harriet Tubman
Madame C. J. Walker
Clara Ward
Booker T. Washington
Dinah Washington
Ethel Waters
Muddy Waters
Ida B. Wells-Barnett
Josh White
Roy Wilkins
Carter G. Woodson
Whitney M. Young Jr.

Bibliography

Helen Houston

This bibliography is arranged according to the topics covered in the African American Almanac. *It contains recommended books as well as noteworthy magazine and journal articles published through early 2010. All of these sources should be easily accessible in undergraduate libraries or through public library networks. Also included are Internet sites related to this volume's topics.*

CHRONOLOGY

"The African-American Mosaic: A Library of Congress Resource Guide for the Study of Black History & Culture." Available online at http://lcweb.loc.gov/exhibits/african/intro.html (cited June 9, 2010).

"African American World Timeline." Available online at http://www.pbs.org/aaworld/timeline.html (cited June 9, 2010).

Anacostia Museum and Center for African American History and Culture. *The Black Washingtonians: The Anacostia Museum Illustrated Chronology*. Hoboken, NJ: John Wiley, 2005.

Blackfacts.com. Available online at http://www.blackfacts.com (cited June 9, 2010).

Charles H. Wright Museum of African American History. Available online at http://www.maah-detroit.org (cited June 9, 2010).

Christian, Charles M., with Sari J. Bennett. *Black Saga: The African American Experience*. Boston: Houghton Mifflin, 1985.

Cowan, Tom, and Jack Maguire. *Timelines of African-American History: 500 Years of Black Achievement*. New York: Roundtable Press/Perigee Books, 1994.

Hauser, Christopher. *The Negro Leagues Chronology: Events in Organized Black Baseball, 1920–1948*. Jefferson, NC: McFarland, 2006.

Hornsby, Alton, Jr. *Chronology of African-American History: Significant Events and People from 1619 to Present*. Detroit: Gale, 1991.

Hornsby, Alton, Jr. *Milestones in 20th-Century African American History*. Detroit: Visible Ink Press, 1993.

Kinshasa, Kwando M. *African American Chronology: Chronologies of the American Mosaic*. Westport, CT: Greenwood Press, 2006.

Kullen, Allan S. *The Peopling of America: A Timeline of Events That Helped Shape Our Nation*. Beltsville, MD: Portfolio Project, 1998.

The New York Public Library African American Desk Reference. New York: John Wiley, 1999.

Talbert, Marilyn Magee. *The Past Matters: A Chronology of African Americans in the United Methodist Church*. Nashville, TN: Discipleship Resources, 2005.

Taylor, Quintard. *America I AM Black Facts: The Timelines of African American History, 1601–2008*. New York: SmileyBooks, 2009.

AFRICAN AMERICAN FIRSTS

Goodwin, Robert. *Crossing the Continent, 1527–1540: The Story of the First African-American Explorer of the American South*. New York: Harper, 2008.

"The Internet African American History Challenge." Available online at http://www.brightmoments.com/blackhistory (cited June 9, 2010).

The New York Public Library African American Desk Reference. New York: John Wiley, 1999.

Potter, Joan. *African American Firsts: Famous, Little-Known, and Unsung Triumphs of Blacks in America*. Rev. ed. New York: Kensington, 2009.

Smith, Jessie Carney, ed. *Black Firsts: 4,000 Ground-Breaking and Pioneering Historical Events*. 2nd ed. Detroit: Visible Ink Press, 2003.

Webster, Raymond B. *African American Firsts in Science and Technology*. Detroit: Gale, 1999.

SIGNIFICANT DOCUMENTS IN AFRICAN AMERICAN HISTORY

Boyd, Herb, ed. *Autobiography of a People: Three Centuries of African American History Told by Those Who Lived It*. New York: Doubleday, 2000.

"Documents from the Black Arts Movement." Available online at http://www.english.illinois.edu/maps/blackarts/documents.htm (cited June 9, 2010).

Douglass, Frederick. *Frederick Douglass: Selected Speeches and Writings*. Edited by Philip S. Foner. Chicago: Lawrence Hill Books, 1999.

Dunbar, Alice Moore, ed. *Masterpieces of Negro Eloquence: The Best Speeches Delivered by the Negro from the Days of Slavery to the Present Time*. New York: Bookery, 1912.

Dunbar, Alice Moore, ed. *Masterpieces of Negro Eloquence, 1818–1913*. Mineola, NY: Dover, 2000.

"Exhibit Hall: The Emancipation Proclamation." Available online at http://www.archives.gov/exhibit/featured_documents/emancipation_proclamation/ (cited June 9, 2010).

Fishel, Leslie H., Jr., and Benjamin Quarles. *The Black American: A Documentary History*. 3rd ed. Glenview, IL: Scott, Foresman, 1976.

Frazier, Thomas R., ed. *Readings in African-American History*. 3rd ed. Belmont, CA: Wadsworth/Thomson Learning, 2001.

"Freedmen's Bureau Online: Records of the Bureau of Refugees, Freedmen and Abandoned Lands." Available online at http://www.freedmensbureau.com (cited June 9, 2010).

Green, Robert P., Jr., ed. *Equal Protection and the African American Constitutional Experience: A Documentary History*. Westport, CT: Greenwood Press, 2000.

Halliburton, Warren J., ed. *Historic Speeches of African Americans*. New York: Franklin Watts, 1993.

Marable, Manning, ed. *Freedom on My Mind: The Columbia Documentary History of the African American Experience*. New York: Columbia University Press, 2003.

Meier, August; Elliott Rudwick; and Francis L. Broderick, eds. *Black Protest Thought in the Twentieth Century*. 2nd ed. New York: Macmillan, 1971.

Mintz, Steven, ed. *African American Voices: A Documentary Reader, 1619–1877*. 4th ed. Malden, MA: Wiley-Blackwell, 2009.

Nalty, Bernard C., and Morris J. MacGregor. *Blacks in the Military: Essential Documents*. Wilmington, DE: Scholarly Resources, 1981.

Sigler, Jay A., ed. *Civil Rights in America: 1500 to the Present*. Detroit: Gale, 1998.

Sterling, Dorothy, ed. *We Are Your Sisters: Black Women in the Nineteenth Century*. New York: W. W. Norton, 1984.

Woodson, Carter G. *Negro Orators and Their Orations*. Washington, DC: Associated Press, 1925.

AFRICAN AMERICAN LANDMARKS

African American Civil War Memorial and Museum. Available online at http://www.afroamcivilwar.org/ (cited June 9, 2010).

"Black Heritage Hideaways," *Ebony*, February 1998.

Cantor, George. *Historic Landmarks of Black America*. Detroit: Gale, 1994.

Chase, Henry, ed. *In Their Footsteps: The American Visions Guide to African-American Heritage Sites*. New York: Henry Holt, 1994.

Edison-Swift, Anne. "On the Trail: Discovering African American History in Virginia," *Humanities*, November–December 2001.

Eskridge, Ann E. "Discovering the Power of History," *American Visions*, October–November 1998.

Fitzpatrick, Sandra, and Maria R. Goodwin. *The Guide to Black Washington: Places and Events of Historical and Cultural Significance in the Nation's Capital*. Rev. ed. New York: Hippocrene Books, 2001.

Horton, James Oliver. *Landmarks of African American History*. New York: Oxford University Press, 2004.

Lee, Deborah A. *Honoring Their Paths: African American Contributions along the Journey Through Hallowed Grounds*. Waterford, VA: Journey through Hallowed Ground Partnership, 2009.

National Underground Railroad Freedom Center. Available online at http://www.freedomcenter.org/ (cited June 9, 2010).

"Our Shared History: African American Heritage; National Park Service." Available online at http://www.cr.nps.gov/aahistory/parks/parks.htm (cited June 9, 2010).

Robinson, Wayne C. *The African-American Travel Guide*. Edison, NJ: Hunter Publishing, 1998.

Savage, Beth L., ed. *African American Historic Places*. New York: John Wiley, 1994.

AFRICA AND THE AFRICAN DIASPORA

Africa Online. Available online at http://www.africaonline.com (cited June 9, 2010).

Appiah, Kwame Anthony, and Henry Louis Gates Jr., eds. *Africana: The Encyclopedia of the African and African*

American Experience. 2nd ed. New York: Oxford University Press, 2005.

Asante, Molefi K. *The African-American Atlas: Black History and Culture*. New York: Macmillan, 1998.

BBC World Service/Network Africa. Available online at http://www.bbc.co.uk/worldservice/networkafrica/ (cited June 9, 2010).

Bracks, Lean'tin L. *Writings on Black Women of the Diaspora: History, Language, and Identity*. New York: Garland, 1998.

Brooks, Christopher. "Post-Colonial Africa." In *Berkshire Encyclopedia of World History*, edited by William H. McNeill. Great Barrington, MA: Berkshire, 2005, pp. 25–31.

Brooks, Christopher, and Laura Moriarty. "Central African Republic." In *World Police Encyclopedia*, edited by Dilip K. Das. New York: Routledge, 2006, pp. 168–171.

Conniff, Michael L., and Thomas J. Davis. *Africans in the Americas: A History of the Black Diaspora*. Caldwell, NJ: Blackburn Press, 2002.

Gates, Henry Louis, Jr. *Wonders of the African World*. New York: Knopf, 1999.

Hall, Gwendolyn Midlo. *Slavery and African Ethnicities in the Americas: Restoring the Links*. Chapel Hill: University of North Carolina Press, 2005.

Hine, Darlene Clark; Trica Danielle Keaton; and Stephen Small, eds. *Black Europe and the African Diaspora*. Urbana: University of Illinois Press, 2009.

Hine, Darlene Clark, and Jacqueline McLeod, eds. *Crossing Boundaries: Comparative History of Black People in Diaspora*. Bloomington: Indiana University Press, 1999.

Hine, Darlene Clark, and Kathleen Thompson, eds. *The Facts on File Encyclopedia of Black Women in America: Four Centuries of Achievements and More Than 1,000 Profiles*. 11 vols. New York: Facts on File, 1997.

Kasule, Samuel. *The History Atlas of Africa*. New York: Macmillan, 1998.

Okpewho, Isidore; Carole Boyce Davies; and Ali A. Mazrui, eds. *The African Diaspora: African Origins and New World Identities*. Bloomington: Indiana University Press, 1999.

Palmer, Colin A., ed. *Encyclopedia of African-American Culture and History: The Black Experience in the Americas*. 2nd ed. 6 vols. Detroit: Macmillan Reference USA, 2006.

Price, Sally, and Richard Price. *Maroon Arts: Cultural Vitality in the African Diaspora*. Boston: Beacon Press, 1999.

Scott, William R., and William G. Shade, eds. *Upon These Shores: Themes in the African-American Experience, 1600 to the Present*. New York: Routledge, 2000.

Universal Black Pages. Available online at http://www.ubp.com (cited June 9, 2010).

AFRICANS IN AMERICA: 1600 TO 1900

"African-American Pioneers." Available online at http://afgen.com/pioneer.html (cited June 9, 2010).

"Africans in America." Available online at http://www.pbs.org/wgbh/aia/ (cited June 9, 2010).

"American Slave Narratives: An Online Anthology." Available online at http://xroads.virginia.edu/HYPER/wpa/wpahome.html (cited June 9, 2010).

Amistad Research Center. Available online at http://www.tulane.edu/~amistad (cited June 9, 2010).

Appiah, Kwame Anthony, and Henry Louis Gates Jr., eds. *Africana: The Encyclopedia of the African and African American Experience*. 2nd ed. New York: Oxford University Press, 2005.

Boyd, Herb, ed. *Autobiography of a People: Three Centuries of African American History Told by Those Who Lived It*. New York: Doubleday, 2000.

Franklin, John Hope, and Alfred A. Moss Jr. *From Slavery to Freedom: A History of African Americans*. 8th ed. New York: Knopf, 2000.

Govenar, Alan B. *African American Frontiers: Slave Narratives and Oral Histories*. Santa Barbara, CA: ABC-CLIO, 2000.

Hinks, Peter, and John McKivigan, eds. *Encyclopedia of Antislavery and Abolition*. 2 vols. Westport, CT: Greenwood Press, 2007.

Horton, James Oliver, and Lois E. Horton. *Hard Road to Freedom: The Story of African America*. New Brunswick, NJ: Rutgers University Press, 2001.

"Images of African Americans from the 19th Century." Available online at http://digital.nypl.org/schomburg/images_aa19 (cited June 9, 2010).

Johnson, Charles, and Patricia Smith. *Africans in America: America's Journey through Slavery*. New York: Harcourt Brace, 1998.

Kelley, Robin D. G., and Earl Lewis, eds. *To Make Our World Anew: A History of African Americans*. New York: Oxford University Press, 2000.

Painter, Nell Irvin. *Creating Black Americans: African-American History and Its Meanings, 1619 to the Present*. New York: Oxford University Press, 2006.

Robertson, Natalie S. *The Slave Ship* Clotilda *and the Making of AfricaTown, USA*. Westport, CT: Praeger, 2008.

Rodriguez, Junius P., ed. *Encyclopedia of Slave Resistance and Rebellion*. 2 vols. Westport, CT: Greenwood Press, 2007.

Schwartz, Marie Jenkins. *Born in Bondage: Growing Up Enslaved in the Antebellum South*. Cambridge, MA: Harvard University Press, 2000.

Scott, William R., and William G. Shade, eds. *Upon These Shores: Themes in the African-American Experience, 1600 to the Present.* New York: Routledge, 2000.

Thompson, Kathleen, and Hilary Mac Austin, eds. *The Face of Our Past: Images of Black Women from Colonial America to the Present.* Bloomington: Indiana University Press, 1999.

Wilkins, Roger. *Jefferson's Pillow: The Founding Fathers and the Dilemma of Black Patriotism.* Boston: Beacon Press, 2002.

Zuczek, Richard, ed. *Encyclopedia of the Reconstruction Era.* 2 vols. Westport, CT: Greenwood Press, 2006.

CIVIL RIGHTS

"African American Odyssey: The Civil Rights Era (Part 1)." Available online at http://memory.loc.gov/ammem/aaohtml/exhibit/aopart9.html (cited June 9, 2010).

"African-American Pioneers." Available online at http://afgen.com/pioneer.html (cited June 9, 2010).

Allison, Robert J., ed. *History in Dispute: American Social and Political Movements, 1945–2000: Pursuit of Liberty.* Detroit: St. James Press, 2000.

Ball, Howard. *A Defiant Life: Thurgood Marshall and the Persistence of Racism in America.* New York: Crown, 1999.

"Black History." Available online at http://www.nyise.org/blackhistory/index.html (cited June 9, 2010).

Branch, Taylor. *Parting the Waters: America in the King Years, 1954–63.* New York: Simon and Schuster, 1988.

Branch, Taylor. *Pillar of Fire: America in the King Years, 1963–65.* New York: Simon and Schuster, 1998.

Branch, Taylor. *At Canaan's Edge: America in the King Years, 1965–68.* New York: Simon and Schuster, 2006.

Clar, D. *The Eyes on the Prize: Civil Rights Reader: Documents, Speeches, and Firsthand Accounts from the Black Freedom Struggle.* Edited by David J. Garrow, Gerald Gill, Vincent Harding, and Clayborne Carson. New York: Penguin, 1991.

Collier-Thomas, Bettye, and V. P. Franklin, eds. *Sisters in the Struggle: African American Women in the Civil Rights–Black Power Movement.* New York: New York University Press, 2001.

Davis, Townsend. *Weary Feet, Rested Souls: A Guided History of the Civil Rights Movement.* New York: W. W. Norton, 1998.

Fairclough, Adam. *Better Day Coming: Blacks and Equality, 1890–2000.* New York: Viking, 2001.

Gottheimer, Josh, ed. *Ripples of Hope: Great American Civil Rights Speeches.* New York: Basic Civitas, 2003.

Green, Robert P., Jr., ed. *Equal Protection and the African American Constitutional Experience: A Documentary History.* Westport, CT: Greenwood Press, 2000.

Halberstam, David. *The Children.* New York: Random House, 1998.

Honey, Michael Keith. *Black Workers Remember: An Oral History of Segregation, Unionism, and the Freedom Struggle.* Berkeley: University of California Press, 1999.

Knight, Gladys L., ed. *Icons of African American Protest: Trailblazing Activists of the Civil Rights Movement.* Westport, CT: Greenwood Press, 2009.

Lewis, David L. *W. E. B. Du Bois: Biography of a Race, 1868–1919.* New York: Henry Holt, 1994.

Lewis, David L. *W. E. B. Du Bois: The Fight for Equality and the American Century, 1919–1963.* New York: Henry Holt, 2000.

Litwack, Leon F. *Trouble in Mind: Black Southerners in the Age of Jim Crow.* New York: Knopf, 1998.

Lovett, Bobby. *The Civil Rights Movement in Tennessee: A Narrative History.* Knoxville: University of Tennessee Press, 2005.

Lowery, Charles D., and John F. Marszalek, eds. *Greenwood Encyclopedia of African American Civil Rights.* 2 vols. Westport, CT: Greenwood Press, 2003.

Martin, Waldo E., Jr., and Patricia Sullivan, eds. *Civil Rights in the United States.* New York: Macmillan Reference USA, 2000.

McWhorter, Diane. *Carry Me Home: Birmingham, Alabama, the Climactic Battle of the Civil Rights Revolution.* New York: Simon and Schuster, 2002.

Meacham, Jon, ed. *Voices in Our Blood: America's Best on the Civil Rights Movement.* New York: Random House, 2001.

National Civil Rights Museum. Available online at http://www.civilrightsmuseum.org (cited June 9, 2010).

Patterson, James T. *Brown v. Board of Education: A Civil Rights Milestone and Its Troubled Legacy.* New York: Oxford University Press, 2001.

Pinkney, Andrea Davis. *Let It Shine: Stories of Black Women Freedom Fighters.* New York: Harcourt Brace, 2000.

Sigler, Jay A., ed. *Civil Rights in America: 1500 to the Present.* Detroit: Gale, 1998.

Terborg-Penn, Rosalyn. *African American Women in the Struggle for the Vote, 1850–1920.* Bloomington: Indiana University Press, 1998.

Wexler, Sanford. *An Eyewitness History of the Civil Rights Movement.* New York: Checkmark Books, 1999.

Winters, Paul A., ed. *The Civil Rights Movement.* San Diego, CA: Greenhaven Press, 2000.

BLACK NATIONALISM

Adeleke, Tunde. *UnAfrican Americans: Nineteenth-Century Black Nationalists and the Civilizing Mission.* Lexington: University Press of Kentucky, 1998.

Alexander, Amy, ed. *The Farrakhan Factor: African-American Writers on Leadership, Nationhood, and Minister Louis Farrakhan.* New York: Grove Press, 1998.

Black Panther Party. Available online at http://www.blackpanther.org (cited June 9, 2010).

Brooks, Christopher. "Garveyism." In *The Greenwood Encyclopedia of African American Folklore,* edited by Anand Prahlad. Westport, CT: Greenwood Press, 2006, pp. 502–505.

Collier-Thomas, Bettye, and V. P. Franklin, eds. *Sisters in the Struggle: African American Women in the Civil Rights–Black Power Movement.* New York: New York University Press, 2001.

Cone, James H. *Black Theology and Black Power.* Maryknoll, NY: Orbis Books, 1997.

Dixon, Chris. *African America and Haiti: Emigration and Black Nationalism in the Nineteenth Century.* Westport, CT: Greenwood Press, 2000.

Evanzz, Karl. *The Messenger: The Rise and Fall of Elijah Muhammad.* New York: Pantheon Books, 1999.

Foner, Philip S., ed. *The Black Panthers Speak.* 2nd ed. New York: Da Capo Press, 2002.

Gates, Henry Louis, Jr., and Cornel West. *The African-American Century: How Black Americans Have Shaped Our Country.* New York: Free Press, 2000.

Jones, Charles E., ed. *The Black Panther Party (Reconsidered).* Baltimore, MD: Black Classic Press, 1998.

Nation of Islam Online. Available online at http://www.noi.org (cited June 9, 2010).

Stancliff, Michael. *Frances Ellen Watkins Harper: African American Reform Rhetoric and the Rise of a Modern Nation State.* New York: Routledge, 2010.

Winbush, Raymond A., ed. *Should America Pay? Slavery and the Raging Debate on Reparations.* New York: Amistad, 2003.

Woodard, Komozi. *A Nation within a Nation: Amiri Baraka (Leroi Jones) and Black Power Politics.* Chapel Hill: University of North Carolina Press, 1999.

NATIONAL ORGANIZATIONS

Bell, Janet Cheatham, ed. *Till Victory Is Won: Famous Black Quotations from the NAACP.* New York: Pocket Books, 2002.

College Language Association. Available online at http://www.clascholars.org/ (cited June 9, 2010).

Dickerson, Dennis C. *Militant Mediator: Whitney M. Young, Jr.* Lexington: University Press of Kentucky, 1998.

Fairclough, Adam. *Better Day Coming: Blacks and Equality, 1890–2000.* New York: Viking, 2001.

Garrow, David J. *Bearing the Cross: Martin Luther King, Jr., and the Southern Christian Leadership Conference.* Repr. New York: Quill, 1999.

Jordan, Vernon E., Jr., with Annette Gordon-Reed. *Vernon Can Read! A Memoir.* New York: Public Affairs, 2001.

National Association for the Advancement of Colored People. Available online at http://www.naacp.org (cited June 9, 2010).

National Society of Black Engineers. Available online at http://national.nsbe.org/ (cited June 9, 2010).

National Urban League. Available online at http://www.nul.org (cited June 9, 2010).

"100+ Organization Leaders," *Ebony,* May 2000.

Parks, Gregory, ed. *Black Greek-Letter Organizations in the Twenty-first Century: Our Fight Has Just Begun.* Lexington: University Press of Kentucky, 2008.

Wedin, Carolyn. *Inheritors of the Spirit: Mary White Ovington and the Founding of the NAACP.* New York: John Wiley, 1998.

LAW

Allison, Robert J., ed. *History in Dispute: American Social and Political Movements, 1945–2000: Pursuit of Liberty.* Detroit: St. James Press, 2000.

Asim, Jabari, ed. *Not Guilty: Twelve Black Men Speak Out on Law, Justice, and Life.* New York: Amistad, 2001.

Ball, Howard. *A Defiant Life: Thurgood Marshall and the Persistence of Racism in America.* New York: Crown, 1999.

Bell, Derrick. *Race, Racism and American Law.* 6th ed. New York: Aspen, 2008.

Browne-Marshall, Gloria J. *Race, Law, and American Society: 1607 to Present.* New York: Routledge, 2007.

Green, Robert P., Jr., ed. *Equal Protection and the African American Constitutional Experience: A Documentary History.* Westport, CT: Greenwood Press, 2000.

Horowitz, David. *Uncivil Wars: The Controversy over Reparations for Slavery.* San Francisco: Encounter Books, 2002.

King, Lovalerie, and Richard Schur, eds. *African American Culture and Legal Discourse.* New York: Palgrave Macmillan, 2009.

Markowitz, Michael W., and Delores D. Jones-Brown, eds. *The System in Black and White: Exploring the Connections between Race, Crime, and Justice.* Westport, CT: Praeger, 2000.

Motley, Constance Baker. *Equal Justice under Law: An Autobiography.* New York: Farrar, Straus and Giroux, 1998.

NAACP Legal Defense and Educational Fund. Available online at http://www.naacpldf.org (cited June 9, 2010).

National Bar Association. Available online at http://www.nationalbar.org (cited June 9, 2010).

O'Brien, Gail Williams. *The Color of the Law: Race, Violence, and Justice in the Post–World War II South.* Chapel Hill: University of North Carolina Press, 1999.

Patterson, James T. *Brown v. Board of Education: A Civil Rights Milestone and Its Troubled Legacy.* New York: Oxford University Press, 2001.

Richardson, Henry J., III. *The Origins of African-American Interests in International Law.* Durham, NC: Carolina Academic Press, 2008.

Sollors, Werner, ed. *Interracialism: Black-White Intermarriage in American History, Literature, and Law.* New York: Oxford University Press, 2000.

Spann, Girardeau A. *The Law of Affirmative Action: Twenty-five Years of Supreme Court Decisions on Race and Remedies.* New York: New York University Press, 2000.

Williams, Juan. *Thurgood Marshall: American Revolutionary.* New York: Times Books, 1998.

POLITICS

Alexander, Amy, ed. *The Farrakhan Factor: African-American Writers on Leadership, Nationhood, and Minister Louis Farrakhan.* New York: Grove Press, 1998.

"Black History." Available online at http://www.nyise.org/blackhistory/index.html (cited June 9, 2010).

Brandt, Eric, ed. *Dangerous Liaisons: Blacks and Gays and the Struggle for Equality.* New York: New Press, 1999.

Colburn, David R., and Jeffrey S. Adler, eds. *African-American Mayors: Race, Politics, and the American City.* Urbana: University of Illinois Press, 2001.

Collier-Thomas, Bettye, and V. P. Franklin, eds. *Sisters in the Struggle: African American Women in the Civil Rights–Black Power Movement.* New York: New York University Press, 2001.

Congressional Black Caucus Foundation. Available online at http://www.cbcfinc.org/ (cited June 9, 2010).

Dailey, Jane; Glenda Elizabeth Gilmore; and Bryant Simon, eds. *Jumpin' Jim Crow: Southern Politics from Civil War to Civil Rights.* Princeton, NJ: Princeton University Press, 2000.

Dupuis, Martin, and Keith Boeckelman. *Barack Obama, the New Face of American Politics.* Westport, CT: Praeger, 2008.

Haskins, James. *Distinguished African American Political and Governmental Leaders.* Phoenix, AZ: Oryx Press, 1999.

Marable, Manning. *Black Leadership.* New York: Columbia University Press, 1998.

Marable, Manning, and Kristen Clarke, eds. *Barack Obama and African American Empowerment: The Rise of Black America's New Leadership.* New York: Palgrave Macmillan, 2009.

Minority On-Line Information Service. Available online at http://www.molis.org/ (cited June 9, 2010).

National Organization of Blacks in Government. Available online at http://www.bignet.org (cited June 9, 2010).

Obama, Barack. *Dreams from My Father: A Story of Race and Inheritance.* New York: Three Rivers Press, 2004.

Obama, Barack. *The Audacity of Hope: Thoughts on Reclaiming the American Dream.* New York: Crown, 2006.

Reed, Adolph, Jr. *Stirrings in the Jug: Black Politics in the Post-Segregation Era.* Minneapolis: University of Minnesota Press, 1999.

Reed, Adolph, Jr., and Kenneth W. Warren, eds. *Renewing Black Intellectual History: The Ideological and Material Foundations of African American Thought.* Boulder, CO: Paradigm, 2010.

West, Cornel. *The Cornel West Reader.* New York: Basic Civitas Books, 1999.

POPULATION

"Black Population Surged during '90s: U.S. Census," *Jet,* August 27, 2001.

Cohn, D'Vera. "Reversing a Long Pattern, Blacks Are Heading South," *Washington Post,* May 5, 2001.

Frey, William H. "Minority Majorities," *American Demographics,* October 1998.

Hornor, Louise L., ed. *Black Americans: A Statistical Sourcebook.* Palo Alto, CA: Information Publications, 2000.

Sigelman, Lee, and Richard G. Niemi. "Innumeracy about Minority Populations; African Americans and Whites Compared," *Public Opinion Quarterly,* Spring 2001.

"U.S. Black Population Is Younger, Growing Faster, Census Bureau Reports," *Jet,* February 28, 2000.

"U.S. Census Bureau: The Black Population in the United States." Available online at http://www.census.gov/population/www/socdemo/race/black.html (cited June 9, 2010).

EMPLOYMENT AND INCOME

Arnesen, Eric. *Brotherhoods of Color: Black Railroad Workers and the Struggle for Equality.* Cambridge, MA: Harvard University Press, 2001.

Browne, Irene, ed. *Latinas and African American Women at Work: Race, Gender, and Economic Inequality.* New York: Russell Sage Foundation, 1999.

Honey, Michael Keith. *Black Workers Remember: An Oral History of Segregation, Unionism, and the Freedom Struggle.* Berkeley: University of California Press, 1999.

Hornor, Louise L., ed. *Black Americans: A Statistical Sourcebook*. Palo Alto, CA: Information Publications, 2000.

Jones, Jacqueline. *American Work: Four Centuries of Black and White Labor*. New York: W. W. Norton, 1998.

Nelson, Bruce. *Divided We Stand: American Workers and the Struggle for Black Equality*. Princeton, NJ: Princeton University Press, 2001.

Sigler, Jay A., ed. *Civil Rights in America: 1500 to the Present*. Detroit: Gale, 1998.

Venkatesh, Sudhir Alladi. *American Project: The Rise and Fall of a Modern Ghetto*. Cambridge, MA: Harvard University Press, 2000.

ENTREPRENEURSHIP

Barber, John T., and Alice A. Tait, eds. *The Information Society and the Black Community*. Westport, CT: Praeger, 2001.

Broussard, Cheryl D. *Sister CEO: The Black Woman's Guide to Starting Her Own Business*. New York: Viking, 1997.

Bundles, A'Lelia Perry. *On Her Own Ground: The Life and Times of Madam C. J. Walker*. New York: Scribner, 2001.

Clarke, Caroline V. *Take a Lesson: Today's Black Achievers on How They Made It and What They Learned along the Way*. New York: John Wiley, 2001.

Dingle, Derek T. *Black Enterprise Titans of the B.E. 100s: Black CEOs Who Redefined and Conquered American Business*. New York: John Wiley, 1999.

Fairlie, Robert W., and Alicia M. Robb. *Race and Entrepreneurial Success: Black-, Asian-, and White-Owned Businesses in the United States*. Cambridge, MA: MIT Press, 2008.

Fraser, George C. *Race for Success: The Ten Best Business Opportunities for Blacks in America*. New York: William Morrow, 1998.

Hunt, Martin K., and Jacqueline E. Hunt. *History of Black Business: The Coming of America's Largest Black-Owned Businesses*. Chicago: Knowledge Express, 1998.

Mitchell, Niki Butler. *The New Color of Success: Twenty Young Black Millionaires Tell You How They're Making It*. Rocklin, CA: Prima, 1999.

Network Journal: Black Professional and Small Business Magazine. Available online at http://www.tnj.com (cited June 9, 2010).

Rogers, W. Sherman. *The African American Entrepreneur: Then and Now*. Santa Barbara, CA: Praeger, 2010.

Smith, Cheryl A. *Market Women: Black Women Entrepreneurs—Past, Present, and Future*. Westport, CT: Praeger, 2005.

Smith, Jessie Carney, ed. *Encyclopedia of African American Business*. 2 vols. Westport, CT: Greenwood Press, 2006.

Walker, Juliet E. K., ed. *The History of Black Business in America: Capitalism, Race, Entrepreneurship*. New York: Macmillan, 1998.

Walker, Juliet E. K., ed. *Encyclopedia of African American Business History*. Westport, CT: Greenwood Press, 1999.

FAMILY AND HEALTH

African American Web Connection. Available online at http://www.aawc.com (cited June 9, 2010).

Alexander, Adele Logan. *Homelands and Waterways: The American Journey of the Bond Family, 1846–1926*. New York: Pantheon Books, 1999.

Ball, Edward. *Slaves in the Family*. New York: Farrar, Straus and Giroux, 1998.

Black Family Network. Available online at http://www.blackfamilynet.net (cited June 9, 2010).

Burroughs, Tony. *Black Roots: A Beginner's Guide to Tracing the African American Family Tree*. New York: Fireside Books, 2001.

Coleman, Christopher Lance, and Christopher A. Brooks. *Dangerous Intimacy: Ten African American Men with HIV*. Deer Park, NY: Linus Publications, 2009.

Gay, Kathlyn. *African-American Holidays, Festivals, and Celebrations: The History, Customs, and Symbols Associated with Both Traditional and Contemporary Religious and Secular Events Observed by Americans of African Descent*. Detroit: Omnigraphics, 2007.

Harris, Phyllis Y. *From the Soul: Stories of Great Black Parents and the Lives They Gave Us*. New York: G. P. Putnam's Sons, 2001.

Henry, Neil. *Pearl's Secret: A Black Man's Search for His White Family*. Berkeley: University of California Press, 2001.

Kwanzaa Information Center. Available online at http://www.melanet.com/kwanzaa/whatis.html (cited June 9, 2010).

Lanier, Shannon, and Jane Feldman, eds. *Jefferson's Children: The Story of One American Family*. New York: Random House, 2000.

Lee, Essie E. *Nurturing Success: Successful Women of Color and Their Daughters*. Westport, CT: Praeger, 2000.

Reverby, Susan M. *Examining Tuskegee: The Infamous Syphilis Study and Its Legacy*. Chapel Hill: University of North Carolina Press, 2009.

Rushdy, Ashraf H. A. *Remembering Generations: Race and Family in Contemporary African American Fiction*. Chapel Hill: University of North Carolina Press, 2001.

Scruggs, Afi-Odelia E. *Claiming Kin: Confronting the History of an African American Family*. New York: St. Martin's Press, 2002.

Sollors, Werner, ed. *Interracialism: Black-White Intermarriage in American History, Literature, and Law.* New York: Oxford University Press, 2000.

Wamba, Philippe E. *Kinship: A Family's Journey in Africa and America.* New York: Dutton, 1999.

Wiencek, Henry. *The Hairstons: An American Family in Black and White.* New York: St. Martin's Press, 1999.

Young, Yolanda. *On Our Way to Beautiful: A Family Memoir.* New York: Villard, 2002.

EDUCATION

Anderson, James D. *The Education of Blacks in the South, 1860–1935.* Chapel Hill: University of North Carolina Press, 1988.

Anderson, Noel S., and Haroon Kharem, eds. *Education as Freedom: African American Educational Thought and Activism.* Lanham, MD: Lexington Books, 2009.

Baumann, Roland M. *Constructing Black Education at Oberlin College: A Documentary History.* Athens: Ohio University Press, 2010.

Bennett College. Available online at http://www.bennett.edu/ (cited June 9, 2010).

Bower, Beverly L., and Mimi Wolverton. *Answering the Call: African American Women in Higher Education Leadership.* Sterling, VA: Stylus, 2009.

Carter G. Woodson Institute for African-American and African Studies. Available online at http://minerva.acc.virginia.edu/~woodson (cited June 9, 2010).

Espenshade, Thomas J., and Alexandria Walton Radford. *No Longer Separate, Not Yet Equal: Race and Class in Elite College Admission and Campus Life.* Princeton, NJ: Princeton University Press, 2009.

Fairclough, Adam. *Teaching Equality: Black Schools in the Age of Jim Crow.* Athens: University of Georgia Press, 2001.

Fisk University. Available online at http://www.fisk.edu/ (cited June 9, 2010).

Fraser, James W. *Between Church and State: Religion and Public Education in a Multicultural America.* New York: St. Martin's Press, 1999.

Hale, Janice E. *Learning While Black: Creating Educational Excellence for African American Children.* Baltimore, MD: Johns Hopkins University Press, 2001.

Hampton University. Available online at http://www.hamptonu.edu (cited June 9, 2010).

Hoffschwelle, Mary S. *The Rosenwald Schools of the American South.* Gainesville: University Press of Florida, 2006.

Howard University. Available online at http://www.howard.edu (cited June 9, 2010).

Hrabowski, Freeman A., III, Kenneth I. Maton, and Geoffrey L. Greif. *Beating the Odds: Raising Academically Successful African American Males.* New York: Oxford University Press, 1998.

Hrabowski, Freeman A., III, Kenneth I. Maton, Monica L. Greene, and Geoffrey L. Greif. *Overcoming the Odds: Raising Academically Successful African American Young Women.* New York: Oxford University Press, 2002.

Jackson, Cynthia L. *African American Education: A Reference Handbook.* Santa Barbara, CA: ABC-CLIO, 2001.

Lomotey, Kofi, ed. *Encyclopedia of African American Education.* Los Angeles: SAGE, 2010.

Marable, Manning, ed. *The New Black Renaissance: The Souls Anthology of Critical African-American Studies.* Boulder, CO: Paradigm, 2005.

McWhorter, John H. *Losing the Race: Self-Sabotage in Black America.* New York: Free Press, 2000.

Morehouse College. Available online at http://www.morehouse.edu (cited June 9, 2010).

Paige, Rod, and Elaine Witty. *The Black-White Achievement Gap: Why Closing It Is the Greatest Civil Rights Issue of Our Times.* New York: AMACOM, 2010.

Patterson, James T. *Brown v. Board of Education: A Civil Rights Milestone and Its Troubled Legacy.* New York: Oxford University Press, 2001.

Perry, Theresa, and Lisa Delpit, eds. *The Real Ebonics Debate: Power, Language, and the Education of African-American Children.* Boston: Beacon Press, 1998.

Ross, E. Wayne, and Valerie Ooka Pang, eds. *Race, Ethnicity, and Education.* 4 vols. Westport, CT: Praeger, 2006.

Smrekar, Claire E., and Ellen B. Goldring, eds. *From the Courtroom to the Classroom: The Shifting Landscape of School Desegregation.* Cambridge, MA: Harvard Education Press, 2009.

Spelman College. Available at http://spelman.edu/ (cited June 9, 2010).

Williams, Heather Andrea. *Self-Taught: African American Education in Slavery and Freedom.* Chapel Hill: University of North Carolina Press, 2007.

Wilson, Erlene B. *The 100 Best Colleges for African-American Students.* Rev. ed. New York: Plume, 1998.

Zamani-Gallaher, Eboni M., Denise O'Neil Green, M. Christopher Brown II, and David O. Stovall. *The Case for Affirmative Action on Campus: Concepts of Equity, Considerations for Practice.* Sterling, VA: Stylus Publishing, 2009.

RELIGION

Anderson, Victor. *Creative Exchange: A Constructive Theology of African American Religious Experience.* Minneapolis, MN: Fortress Press, 2008.

Best, Felton O., ed. *Black Religious Leadership from the Slave Community to the Million Man March: Flames of Fire*. Lewiston, NY: Edwin Mellen Press, 1998.

Billingsley, Andrew. *Mighty Like a River: The Black Church and Social Reform*. New York: Oxford University Press, 1999.

Bolden, Tonya. *Rock of Ages: A Tribute to the Black Church*. New York: Knopf, 2001.

Bridges, Flora Wilson. *Resurrection Song: African-American Spirituality*. Maryknoll, NY: Orbis Books, 2001.

Cone, James H., and Gayraud S. Wilmore, eds. *Black Theology: A Documentary History*. 2nd ed. Maryknoll, NY: Orbis Books, 1993.

Evanzz, Karl. *The Messenger: The Rise and Fall of Elijah Muhammad*. New York: Pantheon Books, 1999.

Floyd-Thomas, Stacey M. *Deeper Shades of Purple: Womanism in Religion and Society*. New York: New York University Press, 2006.

Fraser, James W. *Between Church and State: Religion and Public Education in a Multicultural America*. New York: St. Martin's Press, 1999.

Glazier, Stephen D., ed. *Encyclopedia of African and African-American Religions*. New York: Routledge, 2001.

Grant, Jacquelyn. *White Women's Christ and Black Women's Jesus: Feminist Christology and Womanist Response*. Atlanta, GA: Scholars Press, 1989.

National Baptist Convention, U.S.A. Available online at http://www.nationalbaptist.com/ (cited June 9, 2010).

Olupona, Jacob K., ed. *African Spirituality: Forms, Meanings, and Expressions*. New York: Crossroad, 2000.

Raboteau, Albert J. *Canaan Land: A Religious History of African Americans*. New York: Oxford University Press, 2001.

Riggs, Marcia Y., and Barbara Holmes, eds. *Can I Get a Witness? Prophetic Religious Voices of African American Women: An Anthology*. Maryknoll, NY: Orbis Books, 1997.

LITERATURE

African American Literature Book Club. Available online at http://aalbc.com (cited June 9, 2010).

Andrews, William L; Frances Smith Foster; and Trudier Harris, eds. *The Concise Oxford Companion to African American Literature*. New York: Oxford University Press, 2001.

Bascom, Lionel C., ed. *A Renaissance in Harlem: Lost Voices of an American Community*. New York: Bard, 1999.

Berry, Faith, ed. *From Bondage to Liberation: Writings By and About Afro-Americans from 1700 to 1918*. New York: Continuum, 2001.

Cataliotti, Robert H. *The Songs Became the Stories: The Music in African-American Fiction, 1970–2005*. New York: Peter Lang, 2007.

Chapman, Abraham, ed. *Black Voices: An Anthology of African-American Literature*. Rev. ed. New York: Signet Classic, 2001.

Dance, Daryl Cumber, ed. *From My People: 400 Years of African American Folklore*. New York: W. W. Norton, 2002.

Dawahare, Anthony. *Nationalism, Marxism, and African American Literature between the Wars: A New Pandora's Box*. Jackson: University Press of Mississippi, 2007.

Gabbin, Joanne V., ed. *The Furious Flowering of African American Poetry*. Charlottesville: University Press of Virginia, 1999.

Gates, Henry Louis Jr., et al. *The Norton Anthology of African American Literature*. New York: W. W. Norton, 1997.

Glasrud, Bruce A., and Laurie Champion, eds. *The African American West: A Century of Short Stories*. Boulder, CO: University Press of Colorado, 2000.

Harper, Michael S., and Anthony Walton, eds. *The Vintage Book of African American Poetry*. New York: Vintage Books, 2000.

Harris, Trudier. *Saints, Sinners, Saviors: Strong Black Women in African American Literature*. New York: Palgrave, 2001.

Harris, Trudier. *The Scary Mason-Dixon Line: African American Writers and the South*. Baton Rouge: Louisiana State University Press, 2009.

Hatch, Shari Dorantes, and Michael R. Strickland, eds. *African-American Writers: A Dictionary*. Santa Barbara, CA: ABC-CLIO, 2000.

Helbling, Mark. *The Harlem Renaissance: The One and the Many*. Westport, CT: Greenwood Press, 1999.

Howes, Kelly King, and Christine Slovey, eds. *Harlem Renaissance*. Detroit: UXL, 2001.

Hurston, Zora Neale. *Zora Neale Hurston: A Life in Letters*. Edited by Carla Kaplan. New York: Doubleday, 2001.

Mullane, Deirdre, ed. *Crossing the Danger Water: Three Hundred Years of African-American Writing*. New York: Anchor Books, 1993.

Nelson, Emmanuel S., ed. *African American Authors, 1745–1945: Bio-bibliographical Critical Sourcebook*. Westport, CT: Greenwood Press, 2000.

Porter, Dorothy, ed. *Early Negro Writing 1760–1837*. Boston: Beacon Press, 1971.

Powell, Kevin, ed. *Step into a World: A Global Anthology of the New Black Literature*. New York: John Wiley, 2000.

Prince, Valerie Sweeney. *Burnin' Down the House: Home in African American Literature*. New York: Columbia University Press, 2004.

Ramey, Lauri. *Slave Songs and the Birth of African American Poetry*. New York: Palgrave Macmillan, 2010.

Richards, Phillip M., and Neil Schlager, eds. *Best Literature By and About Blacks*. Detroit: Gale, 2000.

Rodgers, Marie E. *The Harlem Renaissance: An Annotated Reference Guide for Student Research*. Englewood, CO: Libraries Unlimited, 1998.

Rodriguez, Max; Angeli R. Rasbury; and Carol Taylor, eds. *Sacred Fire: The QBR 100 Essential Black Books*. New York: John Wiley, 1999.

Rushdy, Ashraf H. A. *Remembering Generations: Race and Family in Contemporary African American Fiction*. Chapel Hill: University of North Carolina Press, 2001.

Singh, Amritjit, and Daniel M. Scott III, eds. *The Collected Writings of Wallace Thurman*. New Brunswick, NJ: Rutgers University Press, 2003.

Smith, Valerie, ed. *African American Writers*. 2nd ed. New York: Scribner, 2001.

Sollors, Werner, ed. *Interracialism: Black-White Intermarriage in American History, Literature, and Law*. New York: Oxford University Press, 2000.

Stepto, Robert B. *A Home Elsewhere: Reading African-American Classics in the Age of Obama*. Cambridge, MA: Harvard University Press, 2010.

"Voices from the Gaps: Women Writers of Color." Available online at http://voices.cla.umn.edu (cited June 9, 2010).

Wideman, John Edgar, ed. *My Soul Has Grown Deep: Classics of Early African-American Literature*. Philadelphia: Running Press, 2001.

Wilkinson, Brenda, ed. *African American Women Writers*. New York: John Wiley, 2000.

Wilson, Sondra Kathryn, ed. *The Messenger Reader: Stories, Poetry, and Essays from the Messenger Magazine*. New York: Modern Library, 2000.

Young, Kevin, ed. *Giant Steps: The New Generation of African American Writers*. New York: Perennial, 2000.

MEDIA

Barber, John T., and Alice A. Tait, eds. *The Information Society and the Black Community*. Westport, CT: Praeger, 2001.

Barlow, William. *Voice Over: The Making of Black Radio*. Philadelphia: Temple University Press, 1999.

Black Entertainment Network. Available online at http://bet.com (cited June 9, 2010).

Black Voices. Available online at http://www.blackvoices.com (cited June 9, 2010).

Chambers, Jason. *Madison Avenue and the Color Line: African Americans in the Advertising Industry*. Philadelphia: University of Pennsylvania Press, 2008.

Coleman, Robin R. Means, ed. *Say It Loud! African-American Audiences, Media, and Identity*. New York: Routledge, 2002.

Covington, Jeanette. *Crime and Racial Constructions: Cultural Misinformation about African Americans in Media and Academia*. Lanham, MD: Lexington Books, 2010.

Dates, Jannette L., and William Barlow, eds. *Split Image: African Americans in the Mass Media*. 2nd ed. Washington, DC: Howard University Press, 1993.

Entman, Robert M., and Andrew Rojecki. *The Black Image in the White Mind: Media and Race in America*. Chicago: University of Chicago Press, 2000.

Essence.com. Available online at http://www.essence.com (cited June 9, 2010).

Jacobs, Ronald N. *Race, Media, and the Crisis of Civil Society: From Watts to Rodney King*. New York: Cambridge University Press, 2000.

Kamalipour, Yahya R., and Theresa Carilli, eds. *Cultural Diversity and the U.S. Media*. Albany: State University of New York Press, 1998.

Newkirk, Pamela. *Within the Veil: Black Journalists, White Media*. New York: New York University Press, 2000.

Riley, Sam G., ed. *African Americans in the Media Today: An Encyclopedia*. 2 vols. Westport, CT: Greenwood Press, 2007.

Soul in Motion Players, Inc. Available online at http://www.soulinmotionplayers.org/cast.htm (cited on June 9, 2010).

Squires, Catherine R. *African Americans and the Media*. Malden, MA: Polity, 2009.

Ward, Brian, ed. *Media, Culture, and the Modern African American Freedom Struggle*. Gainesville: University Press of Florida, 2001.

Washburn, Patrick S. *The African American Newspaper: Voice of Freedom*. Evanston, IL: Northwestern University Press, 2006.

FILM AND TELEVISION

African American Film Critics Association. Available online at http://www.aafca.com (cited June 9, 2010).

Bernardi, Daniel, ed. *Classic Hollywood, Classic Whiteness*. Minneapolis: University of Minnesota Press, 2001.

Berry, S. Torriano, and Venise T. Berry. *The 50 Most Influential Black Films: A Celebration of African-American Talent, Determination, and Creativity*. New York: Citadel Press, 2001.

Berry, S. Torriano, and Venise T. Berry. *Historical Dictionary of African American Cinema*. Lanham, MD: Scarecrow Press, 2007.

Black Entertainment Network. Available online at http://bet.com (cited June 9, 2010).

Black Film Center/Archive. Available online at http://www.indiana.edu/~bfca (cited June 9, 2010).

Bobo, Jacqueline, ed. *Black Women Film and Video Artists.* New York: Routledge, 1998.

Bogle, Donald. *Primetime Blues: African Americans on Network Television.* New York: Farrar, Straus and Giroux, 2001.

Bogle, Donald. *Toms, Coons, Mulattoes, Mammies, and Bucks: An Interpretive History of Blacks in American Films.* 4th ed. New York: Continuum, 2001.

Bowser, Pearl; Jane Gaines; and Charles Musser, eds. *Oscar Micheaux and His Circle: African-American Filmmaking and Race Cinema of the Silent Era.* Bloomington: Indiana University Press, 2001.

Chadwick, Bruce. *The Reel Civil War: Mythmaking in American Film.* New York: Knopf, 2001.

Everett, Anna. *Returning the Gaze: A Genealogy of Black Film Criticism, 1909–1949.* Durham, NC: Duke University Press, 2001.

Lawrence, Novotny. *Blaxploitation Films of the 1970s: Blackness and Genre.* New York: Routledge, 2008.

Sampson, Henry T. *That's Enough, Folks: Black Images in Animated Cartoons, 1900–1960.* Lanham, MD: Scarecrow Press, 1998.

Torres, Sasha, ed. *Living Color: Race and Television in the United States.* Durham, NC: Duke University Press, 1998.

Ward, Brian, ed. *Media, Culture, and the Modern African American Freedom Struggle.* Gainesville: University Press of Florida, 2001.

Zook, Kristal Brent. *Color by Fox: The Fox Network and the Revolution in Black Television.* New York: Oxford University Press, 1999.

Zook, Kristal Brent. *I See Black People: The Rise and Fall of African American–Owned Television and Radio.* New York: Nation Books, 2008.

DRAMA, COMEDY, AND DANCE

Ailey, Alvin, with A. Peter Bailey. *Revelations: The Autobiography of Alvin Ailey.* Secaucus, NJ: Replica Books, 2000.

Curtis, Susan. *The First Black Actors on the Great White Way.* Columbia: University of Missouri Press, 1998.

DeFrantz, Thomas F., ed. *Dancing Many Drums: Excavations in African American Dance.* Madison: University of Wisconsin Press, 2001.

Dunning, Jennifer. *Alvin Ailey: A Life in Dance.* New York: Da Capo Press, 1998.

Elam, Harry J., and David Krasner, eds. *African-American Performance and Theater History: A Critical Reader.* New York: Oxford University Press, 2001.

Gavin, Christy, ed. *African American Women Playwrights: A Research Guide.* New York: Garland, 1999.

Gill, Glenda E. *No Surrender! No Retreat! African-American Pioneer Performers of Twentieth-Century American Theater.* New York: St. Martin's Press, 2000.

Gottschild, Brenda Dixon. *Waltzing in the Dark: African American Vaudeville and Race Politics in the Swing Era.* New York: Palgrave Macmillan, 2000.

Gottschild, Brenda Dixon. *Digging the Africanist Presence in American Performance: Dance and Other Contexts.* Westport, CT: Praeger, 2001.

Johnson, Anne E. *Jazz Tap: From African Drums to American Feet.* New York: Rosen, 1999.

Jomandi Productions. Available online at http://www.jomandi.com (cited June 9, 2010).

Nelson, Emmanuel S. *African American Dramatists: An A to Z Guide.* Westport, CT: Greenwood Press, 2004.

Peterson, Bernard L., Jr. *Profiles of African American Stage Performers and Theatre People, 1816–1960.* Westport, CT: Greenwood Press, 2001.

Reed, Bill. *Hot from Harlem: Twelve African American Entertainers, 1890–1960.* Rev. ed. Jefferson, NC: McFarland, 2010.

Soul in Motion Players, Inc. Available online at http://www.soulinmotionplayers.org (cited June 9, 2010).

Swanson, Meg, ed. *Playwrights of Color.* Yarmouth, ME: Intercultural Press, 1999.

Watkins, Mel. *On the Real Side: Laughing, Lying, and Signifying—The Underground Tradition of African-American Humor.* New York: Simon and Schuster, 1994.

Watkins, Mel. *On the Real Side: A History of African American Comedy.* Chicago: Lawrence Hill, 1999.

Wilson, James F. *Bulldaggers, Pansies, and Chocolate Babies: Performance, Race, and Sexuality in the Harlem Renaissance.* Ann Arbor: University of Michigan Press, 2010.

CLASSICAL MUSIC

Boyle, Sheila Tully, and Andrew Bunie. *Paul Robeson: The Years of Promise and Achievement.* Amherst: University of Massachusetts Press, 2001.

Floyd, Samuel A., Jr., ed. *International Dictionary of Black Composers.* Chicago: Fitzroy Dearborn, 1999.

Keiler, Allan. *Marian Anderson: A Singer's Journey.* New York: Scribner, 2000.

Nicholls, David, ed. *The Cambridge History of American Music.* New York: Cambridge University Press, 1998.

Robeson, Paul, Jr. *The Undiscovered Paul Robeson: An Artist's Journey, 1898–1939.* New York: John Wiley, 2001.

Slonimsky, Nicolas. *Baker's Biographical Dictionary of Twentieth-Century Classical Musicians.* New York: Schirmer Books, 1997.

Verrett, Shirley, with Christopher Brooks. *I Never Walked Alone: The Autobiography of an American Singer.* Hoboken, NJ: John Wiley, 2003.

SACRED MUSIC TRADITIONS

Black Gospel Music Clef Network. Available online at http://www.blackgospel.com (cited June 9, 2010).

Brooks, Christopher. "Black Hymnody." In *Encyclopedia of African and African-American Religions*, edited by Stephen D. Glazier. New York: Routledge, 2001, pp. 199–205.

Carpenter, Delores, and Nolan E. Williams, eds. *African American Heritage Hymnal.* Chicago: GIA Publications, 2001.

Crawford, Richard. *America's Musical Life: A History.* New York: W. W. Norton, 2001.

Newman, Richard. *Go Down Moses: A Celebration of the African-American Spiritual.* New York: Clarkson Potter, 1998.

Nicholls, David, ed. *The Cambridge History of American Music.* New York: Cambridge University Press, 1998.

Reagon, Bernice Johnson. *If You Don't Go, Don't Hinder Me: The African American Sacred Song Tradition.* Lincoln: University of Nebraska Press, 2001.

Santelli, Robert; Holly George-Warren; and Jim Brown, eds. *American Roots Music.* New York: H. N. Abrams, 2001.

Southern, Eileen. *Biographical Dictionary of Afro-American and African Musicians.* Westport, CT: Greenwood Press, 1982.

Warren, Gwendolin Sims, ed. *Ev'ry Time I Feel the Spirit: 101 Best-Loved Psalms, Gospel Hymns, and Spiritual Songs of the African-American Church.* New York: Henry Holt, 1999.

BLUES AND JAZZ

Bjorn, Lars, with Jim Gallert. *Before Motown: A History of Jazz in Detroit, 1920–60.* Ann Arbor: University of Michigan Press, 2001.

Blue Highway. Available online at http://www.thebluehighway.com (cited June 9, 2010).

Blue Note Records. Available online at http://www.bluenote.com (cited June 9, 2010).

Blues Foundation. Available online at http://www.blues.org (cited June 9, 2010).

Conyers, James L., Jr., ed. *African American Jazz and Rap.* Jefferson, NC: McFarland, 2001.

Crawford, Richard. *America's Musical Life: A History.* New York: W. W. Norton, 2001.

Dalton, David. *Been Here and Gone: A Memoir of the Blues.* New York: William Morrow, 2000.

Davis, Angela Y. *Blues Legacies and Black Feminism: Gertrude "Ma" Rainey, Bessie Smith, and Billie Holiday.* New York: Pantheon Books, 1998.

Dicaire, David. *Blues Singers: Biographies of 50 Legendary Artists of the Early 20th Century.* Jefferson, NC: McFarland, 1999.

Evans, Joe, with Christopher Brooks. *Follow Your Heart: Moving with the Giants of Jazz, Swing, and Rhythm and Blues.* Urbana: University of Illinois Press, 2008.

Gerard, Charley. *Jazz in Black and White: Race, Culture, and Identity in the Jazz Community.* Westport, CT: Greenwood Press, 1998.

Hasse, John Edward, ed. *Jazz: The First Century.* New York: William Morrow, 2000.

Jasen, David A., and Gene Jones. *That American Rag: The Story of Ragtime from Coast to Coast.* New York: Schirmer Books, 2000.

Jasen, David A., and Gene Jones. *Black Bottom Stomp: Eight Masters of Ragtime and Early Jazz.* New York: Routledge, 2002.

Kirchner, Bill, ed. *The Oxford Companion to Jazz.* New York: Oxford University Press, 2000.

Nicholls, David, ed. *The Cambridge History of American Music.* New York: Cambridge University Press, 1998.

Ward, Geoffrey C. *Jazz: A History of America's Music.* New York: Knopf, 2000.

POPULAR MUSIC

Abbott, Lynn, and Doug Seroff. *Out of Sight: The Rise of African American Popular Music, 1889–1895.* Jackson: University Press of Mississippi, 2002.

Bond, Julian, and Sondra Kathryn Wilson, eds. *Lift Every Voice and Sing: A Celebration of the Negro National Anthem.* New York: Random House, 2000.

Conyers, James L., Jr., ed. *African American Jazz and Rap.* Jefferson, NC: McFarland, 2001.

Crawford, Richard. *America's Musical Life: A History.* New York: W. W. Norton, 2001.

Forman, Murray. *The 'Hood Comes First: Race, Space, and Place in Rap and Hip-Hop.* Middletown, CT: Wesleyan University Press, 2002.

George, Nelson. *Hip Hop America.* New York: Viking, 1998.

Lee Bailey's Electronic Urban Report (EURweb). Available online at http://www.eurweb.com (cited June 9, 2010).

Malaco Music Group. Available online at http://www.malaco.com/ (cited June 9, 2010).

Nicholls, David, ed. *The Cambridge History of American Music*. New York: Cambridge University Press, 1998.

Ogg, Alex, and David Upshal. *The Hip Hop Years: A History of Rap*. New York: Fromm International, 2001.

Richardson, C. Perry, ed. *"What'd I Say?" The Atlantic Story: 50 Years of Music*. New York: Welcome Rain Publishers, 2001.

Roberts, John Storm. *Black Music of Two Worlds: African, Caribbean, Latin, and African-American Traditions*. 2nd ed. New York: Schirmer Books, 1998.

Smith, Suzanne E. *Dancing in the Street: Motown and the Cultural Politics of Detroit*. Cambridge, MA: Harvard University Press, 1999.

Stewart, Earl L. *African American Music: An Introduction*. New York: Schirmer Books, 1998.

VIBE Lifestyle Network. Available online at http://www.vibe.com (cited June 9, 2010).

Winfield, Betty Houchin, and Sandra Davidson, eds. *Bleep! Censoring Rock and Rap Music*. Westport, CT: Greenwood Press, 1999.

VISUAL AND APPLIED ARTS

California African American Museum. Available online at http://www.caam.ca.gov (cited June 9, 2010).

Canvas Paper and Stone: African American, Latin American and Native American Art and Online Framing. Available online at http://www.canvaspaperandstone.com (cited June 9, 2010).

Collins, Lisa Gail. *The Art of History: African American Women Artists Engage the Past*. New Brunswick, NJ: Rutgers University Press, 2002.

Duffy, Damian, Keith Knight, and John Jennings. *Black Comix: African American Independent Comics, Art, and Culture*. New York: Mark Batty, 2010.

National Museum of African Art. Available online at http://www.si.edu/nmafa (cited June 9, 2010).

The New York Public Library African American Desk Reference. New York: John Wiley, 1999.

Patton, Sharon F. *African-American Art*. New York: Oxford University Press, 1998.

Visoná, Monica Blackmun, et al., eds. *A History of Art in Africa*. New York: H.N. Abrams, 2001.

Willis, Deborah. *Reflections in Black: A History of Black Photographers, 1840 to the Present*. New York: W. W. Norton, 2000.

SCIENCE AND TECHNOLOGY

Barber, John T., and Alice A. Tait, eds. *The Information Society and the Black Community*. Westport, CT: Praeger, 2001.

Bedini, Silvio A. *The Life of Benjamin Banneker: The First African-American Man of Science*. 2nd ed. Baltimore: Maryland Historical Society, 1999.

"The Faces of Science: African Americans in the Sciences." Available online at https://webfiles.uci.edu/mcbrown/display/faces.html (cited June 9, 2010).

Jordan, Diann. *Sisters in Science: Conversations with Black Women Scientists about Race, Gender, and Their Passion for Science*. West Lafayette, IN: Purdue University Press, 2006.

Krapp, Kristine, ed. *Notable Black American Scientists*. Detroit: Gale, 1999.

Warren, Wini. *Black Women Scientists in the United States*. Bloomington: Indiana University Press, 1999.

Webster, Raymond B., ed. *African American Firsts in Science and Technology*. Detroit: Gale, 1999.

SPORTS

Aaseng, Nathan. *African-American Athletes*. Rev. ed. New York: Facts on File, 2010.

Ackmann, Martha. *Curveball: The Remarkable Story of Toni Stone, the First Woman to Play Professional Baseball in the Negro League*. Chicago: Lawrence Hill Books, 2010.

Adelson, Bruce. *Brushing Back Jim Crow: The Integration of Minor-League Baseball in the American South*. Charlottesville: University Press of Virginia, 1999.

Ashe, Arthur R., Jr. *A Hard Road to Glory: A History of the African-American Athlete, 1919–1945*. Vol. 2. New York: John Wiley, 2005.

Ashe, Arthur R., Jr. *A Hard Road to Glory: A History of the African-American Athlete, 1946–1969*. Vol. 3. New York: John Wiley, 2005.

Ashe, Arthur R., Jr. *A Hard Road to Glory: A History of the African-American Athlete, 1970–Present*. Vol. 4. New York: John Wiley, 2005.

Collins, Ace, and John Hillman. *Blackball Superstars: Legendary Players of the Negro Baseball Leagues*. Greensboro, NC: Avisson Press, 1999.

Goldman, Robert M. *One Man Out: Curt Flood versus Baseball*. Lawrence: University Press of Kansas, 2008.

Halberstam, David. *Playing for Keeps: Michael Jordan and the World He Made*. New York: Random House, 1999.

Harlem Globetrotters. Available online at http://www.harlemglobetrotters.com (cited June 9, 2010).

Holway, John B. *The Complete Book of Baseball's Negro Leagues: The Other Half of Baseball's History*. New York: Hastings House, 2001.

Hotaling, Edward. *The Great Black Jockeys: The Lives and Times of the Men Who Dominated America's First National Sport*. Rocklin, CA: Forum, 1999.

National Association of Black Scuba Divers. Available online at http://www.nabsdivers.org (cited June 9, 2010).

National Brotherhood of Skiers. Available online at http:// www. nbs.org (cited June 9, 2010).

"Negro Baseball Leagues." Available online at http://www .blackbaseball.com (cited June 9, 2010).

Negro League Baseball. Available online at http://www .negroleaguebaseball.com/ (cited June 9, 2010).

Remnick, David. *King of the World: Muhammad Ali and the Rise of an American Hero.* New York: Random House, 1998.

Ross, Charles Kenyatta. *Outside the Lines: African Americans and the Integration of the National Football League.* New York: New York University Press, 1999.

Sailes, Gary A., ed. *African Americans in Sport: Contemporary Themes.* New Brunswick, NJ: Transaction Publishers, 1998.

Saunders, James Robert. *Black Winning Jockeys in the Kentucky Derby.* Jefferson, NC: McFarland, 2003.

Sinnette, Calvin H. *Forbidden Fairways: African Americans and the Game of Golf.* Chelsea, MI: Sleeping Bear Press, 1998.

Wigginton, Russell T. *The Strange Career of the Black Athlete: African Americans and Sports.* Westport, CT: Praeger, 2006.

MILITARY

African American Civil War Memorial and Museum. Available online at http://www.afroamcivilwar.org/ (cited June 9, 2010).

Astor, Gerald. *The Right to Fight: A History of African Americans in the Military.* Novato, CA: Presidio, 1998.

Broadnax, Samuel L. *Blue Skies, Black Wings: African American Pioneers of Aviation.* Westport, CT: Praeger, 2007.

Buckley, Gail Lumet. *American Patriots: The Story of Blacks in the Military from the Revolution to Desert Storm.* New York: Random House, 2001.

Clinton, Catherine. *The Black Soldier: 1492 to the Present.* Boston: Houghton Mifflin, 2000.

Davis, Lenwood G., and George Hill, eds. *Blacks in the American Armed Forces, 1776–1983: A Bibliography.* Westport, CT: Greenwood Press, 1985.

Edgerton, Robert B. *Hidden Heroism: Black Soldiers in America's Wars.* Boulder, CO: Westview Press, 2001.

Field, Ron, and Alexander Bielakowski. *Buffalo Soldiers: African American Troops in the US Forces, 1866–1945.* New York: Osprey, 2008.

Hanna, Charles W. *African American Recipients of the Medal of Honor: A Biographical Dictionary, Civil War through Vietnam War.* Jefferson, NC: McFarland, 2002.

Hardesty, Von. *Black Wings: Courageous Stories of African Americans in Aviation and Space History.* New York: HarperCollins, 2008.

Harris, Stephen L. *Harlem's Hell Fighters: The African-American 369th Infantry in World War I.* Washington, DC: Brassey's, 2003.

Haskins, James. *African American Military Heroes.* New York: John Wiley, 1998.

Hawkins, Walter L. *Black American Military Leaders: A Biographical Dictionary.* Jefferson, NC: McFarland, 2007.

Knoblock, Glenn A. *African American World War II Casualties and Decorations in the Navy, Coast Guard, and Merchant Marine: A Comprehensive Record.* Jefferson, NC: McFarland, 2009.

Latty, Yvonne, ed. *We Were There: Voices of African American Veterans, from World War II to the War in Iraq.* New York: Amistad, 2004.

Leckie, William H. *The Buffalo Soldiers: A Narrative of the Negro Cavalry in the West.* Norman: University of Oklahoma Press, 1967.

Lentz-Smith, Adriane. *Freedom Struggles: African Americans and World War I.* Cambridge, MA: Harvard University Press, 2009.

Leonard, Elizabeth D. *Men of Color to Arms!: Black Soldiers, Indian Wars, and the Quest for Equality.* New York: W. W. Norton, 2010.

Steward, T. G. *Buffalo Soldiers: The Colored Regulars in the United States Army.* Amherst, NY: Humanity Books, 2003.

366th Infantry Regiment Veterans Association HomePage. Available online at http://www.wiz-worx.com/366th (cited June 9, 2010).

Trudeau, Noah Andre. *Like Men of War: Black Troops in the Civil War, 1862–1865.* Boston: Little, Brown, 1998.

Wright, Kai. *Soldiers of Freedom: An Illustrated History of African Americans in the Armed Forces.* New York: Black Dog and Leventhal, 2002.

Index

Page numbers in **boldface** indicate the primary article about the subject. Page numbers in *italic* indicate illustrative material, and *italic* page numbers followed by an italicized letter *t* indicate that the subject can be found within tabular material on the page. This index is sorted alphabetically word by word.

C

D

F

K

N

O

P

V

W

X

Y